PENGUIN HANDBOOKS

The Penguin Guide to Compact Discs and Cassettes New Edition

EDWARD GREENFIELD has been Record Critic of the *Guardian* since 1954, and from 1964 its Music Critic too. At the end of 1960 he joined the reviewing panel of *Gramophone*, specializing in operatic and orchestral issues. He is a regular broadcaster on music and records for the BBC not just on Radios 3 and 4 but also on the BBC World Service. In 1958 he published a monograph on the operas of Puccini. More recently he has written studies on the recorded work of Joan Sutherland and André Previn. He has been a regular juror on International Record awards and has appeared with such artists as Dame Elisabeth Schwarzkopf, Dame Joan Sutherland and Sir Georg Solti in public interviews.

ROBERT LAYTON studied at Oxford with Edmund Rubbra for composition and with Egon Wellesz for the history of music. He spent two years in Sweden at the universities of Uppsala and Stockholm. He joined the BBC Music Division in 1959 and has been responsible for such programmes as *Interpretations on Record*. He has contributed a 'Quarterly Retrospect' to *Gramophone* for a number of years, and he has written books on Berwald and Sibelius and has specialized in Scandinavian music. His recent publications include a monograph on the Dvořák symphonies and concertos for the BBC Music Guides, of which he is General Editor, and the first two volumes of his translation of Erik Tawastsjerna's definitive study of Sibelius. In 1987 he was awarded the Sibelius Medal and in the following year was made a Knight of the Order of the White Rose of Finland for his services to Finnish music.

IVAN MARCH is a former professional musician. He studied at Trinity College of Music, London, and at the Royal Manchester College. After service in the RAF Central Band, he played the horn professionally for the BBC and travelled with the Carl Rosa and D'Oyly Carte opera companies. Now director of the Long Playing Record Library, the largest commercial lending library for classical music on compact discs in the British Isles, he is a well-known lecturer, journalist and personality in the world of recorded music. As a journalist, he contributes to a number of record-reviewing magazines, including *Gramophone* and *Classics*.

The Penguin Guide to Compact Discs and Cassettes New Edition

Ivan March, Edward Greenfield, Robert Layton

Edited by Ivan March

Penguin Books

PENGUIN BOOKS

Published by the Penguin Group
Penguin Books Ltd, 27 Wrights Lane, London W8 5TZ, England
Penguin Books USA Inc., 375 Hudson Street, New York, New York 10014, USA
Penguin Books Australia Ltd, Ringwood, Victoria, Australia
Penguin Books Canada Ltd, 10 Alcorn Avenue, Toronto, Ontario, Canada M4V 3B2
Penguin Books (NZ) Ltd, 182 – 190 Wairau Road, Auckland 10, New Zealand

Penguin Books Ltd, Registered Offices: Harmondsworth, Middlesex, England

First published 1992
10 9 8 7 6 5 4 3 2 1

Typeset by Barbers Ltd, Wrotham, Kent

Made and printed in Great Britain by
Clays Ltd, St Ives plc

Contents

Preface

Although our new *Guide* remains comprehensive, it is no longer possible to include every CD currently available within its 1,350 or so pages, which is the reasonable limitation of a single volume. In choosing what to include, among both older and newer recordings, our guideline has been excellence of performance and quality of recording, although reasonable allowances have to be made for the actual sound of historical records, where the inspiration and intensity, warmth and spontaneity of the music-making can sometimes override almost any technical considerations.

It is extraordinary that in the middle of a recession the expansion of the recorded repertoire continues with undiminished enthusiasm, from small and large record companies alike. Another astonishing statistic is that the number of CD players in the Western world, although growing steadily, is still remarkably small (especially when compared with similar figures for tape playback/recording machines). So the huge current output of CDs is being mopped up by a relatively small number of music-lovers, all of whom seem to want to duplicate (or continually to replace) their records of standard repertoire, along with a seemingly insatiable appetite for first recordings of hitherto unavailable music.

A remarkably large number of new names make their début in the composer index of the present volume, including Antheil, Atterberg, Bacewicz, Boulanger, Buller, Certon, Cesti, Czerny, David, Delalande, Dering, Diamond, Maurice Emmanuel (a real discovery), Englund, Forqueray, Gaubert, Goldschmidt, Gorecki, Headington, Isaac (the remarkable German contemporary of Josquin des Prés), Lajtha, Michel Lambert (who lived almost exactly 300 years before Constant!), MacMillan, Pizzetti, Rautavaara, Luigi Rossi and Ruders; and much of the music discussed under their entries is very stimulating indeed. Such is the ability of the gramophone to widen our musical knowlege and experience; and this applies equally to more familiar composers.

Considerable extension of the available repertory brings a new awareness of the scope and achievement of, for instance, Alkan, Alwyn, Barber, Bloch, Kokkonen, Liszt (where Leslie Howard has already reached Volume 18 in a Hyperion complete survey of Liszt's solo piano works), Respighi and Rodrigo. A two-disc set of the latter's piano music undertaken by Gregory Allen on the enterprising Bridge label suggests that there is far more to this famous Spanish composer than just the *Concierto de Aranjuez*.

An expansion of the available Rossini operas on CD, several on the Philips label, has been matched by the current mid-priced reissue by EMI of Sargent's distinguished recordings of the major Gilbert and Sullivan operas. Perhaps Decca will now follow suit by adding works like *Princess Ida* to their existing D'Oyly Carte CD repertoire. Popular musicals have also received their due, and the achievements of Gershwin and Cole Porter in this field have been worthily celebrated. With Vivaldi's ubiquitous *Four Seasons* now the most popular and familiar piece of classical music ever written, we have chosen some twenty versions from the multitude available, and we are content that our description of their various merits and idiosyncrasies will provide a recording for almost every conceivable taste.

The last two or three years have seen a major expansion in the general public's awareness of the potential pleasures such readily accessible classical music provides. The sight of Pavarotti singing in the park, in a torrential downpour of English rain, was a heartening reminder of the stoicism of the British spirit, unquenchable in the face of their hero's winning smile – which not all were close enough to see. His superbly eloquent singing, courtesy of Decca engineering, was amplified accurately enough to delight everyone. This recognition of the joys of opera will undoubtedly bring many more people into the record shops and ensure, at the very least, that the essential renewal of the standard repertoire continues.

But there are also many signs of interest in new music, provided it is not 'barbed wire' intellectualism and that it communicates directly. No better example exists than the appearance on record of John Tavener's *Protecting Veil* (a major new work for cello and orchestra) which ascended immediately into the Top Ten of the classical charts and even reached Number One.

The expansion of the bargain and mid-priced repertoire continues apace, to rebut grumbles that 'records are too expensive'. In real terms they are cheaper than they ever were, especially if one makes a direct cost comparison with the war years when a Beethoven symphony, offered on five 78-

r.p.m. shellac discs, cost more than £2. Those who complain about the pricing policies of the major companies should remember that they are finally determined by the marketplace and that it is always possible to extract gems from the bargains (of which Naxos and Harmonia Mundi's Musique d'Abord label, offering rarer repertoire, are two excellent examples). Before making financial judgements, however, it should also be remembered that the recent highly distinguished new Domingo/Solti Decca recording of Richard Strauss's opera, *Die Frau ohne Schatten*, which earned the great Hungarian conductor yet another Rosette, also generated recording costs of approximately £1 million!

Two criticisms must be restated concerning major problems that refuse to go away: the continuing lack of consistency in the digital remastering of analogue recordings, and the too-frequent inadequacy of CD back-up documentation. Too many CD transfers are still being offered in which there is an obvious loss of quality when comparison is made with the originals, whether LP or 78s. Technology of this kind should always be questioned, and there is much evidence that too often an 'automatic pilot' process is applied to the remastering of analogue LPs, which sometimes works favourably, sometimes less so. Added clarity and presence are unacceptable if this means that the upper range of the sound becomes unpleasantly edgy.

The inadequate documentation, not only of reissues but also sometimes of premium-priced CDs, is another factor that record companies should take more seriously. Philips, which should know better, has recently been publishing records with documentation devoted solely to an – often embarrassing – eulogy of the performers. When all that is provided concerning the music is a list of titles, the collector has every cause to be dissatisfied (the more so if the record contains vocal material sung in a foreign language).

Fortunately, however, the current CD catalogue offers a profusion of alternatives, and our current survey will surely help the collector in making his or her choice.

Edward Greenfield, Robert Layton and Ivan March

Introduction

The object of *The Penguin Guide to Compact Discs and Cassettes New Edition* is to give the serious collector a comprehensive survey of the finest recordings of permanent music on CD. As most records are issued almost simultaneously on both sides of the Atlantic and use identical international catalogue numbers, this *Guide* should be found to be equally useful in Great Britain and the USA. The internationalization of repertoire and numbers is increasingly applying to CDs issued by the major international companies and by many smaller ones too, while most of the smaller European labels are imported in their original formats into both Britain and the USA.

The sheer number of records of artistic merit now available causes considerable problems in any assessment of overall and individual excellence. While in the case of a single popular repertoire work it might be ideal for the discussion to be conducted by a single reviewer, it has not always been possible for one person to have access to every version, and division of reviewing responsibility becomes inevitable. Also there are certain works and certain recorded performances for which one or another of our team has a special affinity. Such a personal identification can often carry with it a special perception too. We feel that it is a strength of our basic style to let such conveyed pleasure or admiration for the merits of an individual recording come over directly to the reader, even if this produces a certain ambivalence in the matter of choice between competing recordings. Where disagreement is more positive (and this has rarely happened), then readers will find an indication of this difference in the text. In the present edition, the Balakirev Symphonies are an obvious example of such divergence of views.

We have considered and rejected the use of initials against individual reviews, since this is essentially a team project. The occasions for disagreement generally concern matters of aesthetics, for instance in the manner of recording balance, where a contrived effect may trouble some ears more than others, or in the matter of style, where the difference between robustness and refinement of approach appeals differently to listening sensibilities, rather than involving a question of artistic integrity. But over the years our views seem to grow closer together, rather than to diverge; perhaps we are getting mellower, but we are seldom ready to offer strong disagreement following the enthusiastic reception by one of the team of a controversial recording, if the results are creatively stimulating. Our perceptions of the advantages and disadvantages of performances of early music on original (as against modern) instruments seem fairly evenly balanced; again, any strong feelings are indicated in the text.

EVALUATION

Most recordings issued today by the major companies are of a high technical standard and offer performances of a quality at least as high as is experienced in the concert hall. In adopting a starring system for the evaluation of records, we have decided to make use of from one to three stars. Brackets round one or more of the stars indicate some reservations about its inclusion, and readers are advised to refer to the text. Brackets round all the stars usually indicate a basic qualification: for instance, a mono recording of a performance of artistic interest, where considerable allowances have to be made for the sound-quality, even though the recording may have been digitally remastered.

Our evaluation system may be summarized as follows:

*** An outstanding performance and recording in every way.
** A good performance and recording of today's normal high standard.
* A fair performance, reasonably well or well recorded.

Our evaluation is normally applied to the record as a whole, unless there are two main works or groups of works, and by different composers. In this case, each is dealt with separately in its appropriate place. In the case of a collection of shorter works, we feel that there is little point in giving a separate starring to each item, even if their merits are uneven, since the record has to be purchased as a complete programme.

ROSETTES

To a few records we have awarded a rosette: ❀.

Unlike our general evaluations, in which we have tried to be consistent, a rosette is a quite arbitrary compliment by a member of the reviewing team to a recorded performance which, he finds, shows special illumination, magic, or a spiritual quality, or even outstanding production values, that places it in a very special class. The choice is essentially a personal one (although often it represents a shared view), and in some cases it is applied to an issue where certain reservations must also be mentioned in the text of the review. The rosette symbol is placed before the usual evaluation and the record number. It is quite small – we do not mean to imply an 'Academy Award' but a personal token of appreciation for something uniquely valuable. We hope that, once the reader has discovered and perhaps acquired a 'rosetted' CD, its special qualities will soon become apparent.

DIGITAL RECORDINGS

Nearly all new compact discs are recorded digitally, but an increasingly large number of digitally remastered, reissued analogue recordings are now appearing, and we think it important to include a clear indication of the difference:

Dig. This indicates that the master recording was digitally encoded.

BARGAIN AND SUPER-BARGAIN ISSUES

Since the publication of our last main volume we have seen a huge expansion of the mid- and bargain-price labels from all the major companies. These are usually standard-repertoire works in excellent analogue recordings, digitally remastered. Often these reissue CDs are generous in playing time, increasing their value to the collector. There are now also even cheaper classical CDs at super-bargain price, usually featuring performances by artists whose names are not internationally familiar, notably on the now rightly famous Naxos label. Many of these recordings derive from Eastern Europe, where recording costs have been currently much lower than in the West. Most of them are digitally encoded and some offer outstanding value, both technically and musically. Thus the collector has plenty of scope in deciding how much to pay for a recorded performance, with a CD range from about £5 up to nearly three times that amount.

Our listing of each recording first indicates if it is not in fact in the premium-price category, as follows:

(M) Medium-priced label

(B) Bargain-priced label

(BB) Super-bargain label

See below for price structures for CDs and cassettes in the UK and the USA.

LAYOUT OF TEXT

We have aimed to make our style as simple as possible, even though the catalogue numbers of recordings are no longer as straightforward as they once were. So, immediately after the evaluation and before the catalogue number, the record make is given, often in abbreviated form (a key to the abbreviations is provided on pages xvii – xviii). In the case of a set of two or more CDs, the number of units involved is given in brackets after the catalogue number.

AMERICAN CATALOGUE NUMBERS

The numbers which follow in square brackets are US catalogue numbers, while the abbreviation [id.] indicates that the American number is identical to the European, which is increasingly the case.

There are certain small differences to be remembered by American readers. For instance, a CBS/Sony number could have a completely different catalogue number on either side of the Atlantic, or use the same digits with different alphabetical prefixes. Both will be clearly indicated. EMI/Angel use extra digits for their British compact discs; thus the US number CDC 47001 becomes CDC7 47001-2 in Britain (the -2 is the European indication that this is a compact disc). We have taken care to check catalogue information as far as is possible, but as all the editorial work has been done in England there is always the possibility of error; American readers are therefore invited, when ordering records locally, to take the precaution of giving their dealer the fullest information about the music and recordings they want.

The indications (M), (B) and (BB) immediately before the starring of a disc refer only to the British record, as pricing systems are not always identical on both sides of the Atlantic.

Where no American catalogue number is given, this does not necessarily mean that a record is not available in the USA; the transatlantic issue may not have been made at the time of the publication of this *Guide*. Readers are advised to check the current *Schwann* catalogue and to consult their local record store.

ABBREVIATIONS

To save space we have adopted a number of standard abbreviations in listing orchestras and performing groups (a list is provided below), and the titles of works are often shortened, especially where they are listed several times. Artists' forenames are sometimes omitted if they are not absolutely necessary for identification purposes. Also we have not usually listed the contents of operatic highlights and collections; these can sometimes be found in *The Classical Catalogue*, published by *Gramophone* magazine (177 – 179, Kenton Road, Kenton, Harrow, Middlesex, England, HA3 0HA).

We have followed common practice in the use of the original language for titles where it seems sensible. In most cases, English is used for orchestral and instrumental music and the original language for vocal music and opera. There are exceptions, however; for instance, the Johann Strauss discography uses the German language in the interests of consistency.

ORDER OF MUSIC

The order of music under each composer's name broadly follows that adopted by *The Classical Catalogue*: orchestral music, including concertos and symphonies; chamber music; solo instrumental music (in some cases with keyboard and organ music separated); vocal and choral music; opera; vocal collections; miscellaneous collections.

The Classical Catalogue now usually includes stage works alongside opera; in the main we have not followed this practice, preferring to list, say, ballet music and incidental music (where no vocal items are involved) in the general orchestral group. Within each group our listing follows an alphabetical sequence, and couplings within a single composer's output are *usually* discussed together instead of separately with cross-references. Occasionally and inevitably because of this alphabetical approach, different recordings of a given work can become separated when a record is listed and discussed under the first work of its alphabetical sequence. The editor feels that alphabetical consistency is essential if the reader is to learn to find his or her way about.

CONCERTS AND RECITALS

Most collections of music intended to be regarded as concerts or recitals involve many composers, and it is quite impractical to deal with them within the alphabetical composer index. They are grouped separately, at the end of the book, in three sections. In each section, recordings are usually arranged in alphabetical order of the performers' names: concerts of orchestral and concertante music under the name of the orchestra, ensemble or, if more important, conductor or soloist; instrumental recitals under the name of the instrumentalist; operatic and vocal recitals under the principal singer or vocal group, as seems appropriate.

In certain cases where the compilation features many different performers, it is listed alphabetically under its collective title, or the key word in that title (thus *Favourite operatic duets* is listed under 'Operatic duets'). Sometimes, for complicated collections, and especially compilations of favourite operatic arias, only brief details of contents and performers are given; fuller information can often be found in *The Classical Catalogue*.

CATALOGUE NUMBERS

Enormous care has gone into the checking of CD catalogue numbers and contents to ensure that all details are correct, but the editor and publishers cannot be held responsible for any mistakes that may have crept in despite all our zealous checking. When ordering CDs, readers are urged to provide their record-dealer with full details of the music and performers, as well as the catalogue number.

DELETIONS

Compact discs, especially earlier, full-priced issues not too generous in musical content, are now steadily succumbing to the deletions axe, and more are likely to disappear during the lifetime of this book. Sometimes copies may still be found in specialist shops, and there remains the compensatory fact that most really important and desirable recordings are eventually reissued, usually costing less!

COVERAGE

As the output of major and minor labels continues to expand, it will obviously be impossible for us to mention every CD and cassette that is available, within the covers of a single book; this is recognized as a practical limitation if we are to update our survey regularly. We have to be carefully selective in choosing the discs to be included (although on rare occasions a recording has been omitted simply because a review copy was not available); anything which eludes us can always be included next time. However, we do welcome suggestions from readers about such omissions if they seem to be of special interest, and particularly if they are inexpensive. But borderline music on specialist labels that are not readily and reliably obtainable on both sides of the Atlantic cannot be given any kind of priority.

ACKNOWLEDGEMENTS

Our thanks, as ever, are due to Roger Wells, our Copy Editor, who has worked closely alongside us throughout the preparation of this book and, as a keen CD collector himself, also frequently made valuable creative suggestions. Kathleen March once again zealously checked the proofs for errors and reminded us when the text proved ambiguous, clumsily repetitive in its descriptive terminology, or just plain contradictory. Barbara Menard contributed to the titling – never an easy task, and especially complicated in the many boxed anthologies involving a bouquet of different performers. Our team of Penguin proof readers are also indispensable. Grateful thanks also go to all those readers who write to us to point out factual errors and remind us of important recordings which have escaped our notice.

Finally, we again welcome back to our cover the whimsical portrait of Nipper, the most famous dog in the world. He is associated with a deservedly world-famous trademark and reminds us that fine records have been available from this source for almost exactly one hundred years!

PRICE RANGES — UK and USA

Compact discs and cassettes in all price-ranges are more expensive in Britain and Europe than they are in the USA but, fortunately, in nearly all cases the various premium-price, mid-price, bargain and superbargain categories are fairly consistent on both sides of the Atlantic. However, where records are imported in either direction, this can affect their domestic cost. For instance, (British) EMI's Classics for Pleasure and Eminence labels are both in the mid-price range in the USA, whereas CfP is a bargain series in the UK. Similarly Naxos, a super-bargain digital label in the UK, is a bargain label in the USA. LaserLight, however, is a super- bargain series in both markets.

Vox Boxes are exceptionally good value at super-budget price in America, while in Britain they are comparable with EMI's 'two for the price of one' series. Of course retail prices are not fixed in either country, and various stores may offer even better deals at times, so our price structure must be taken as a guideline only. One major difference in the USA is that almost all companies make a dollar surcharge (per disc) for mid-priced opera sets (to cover the cost of librettos) and Angel applies this levy to all their boxed sets. The Pickwick RPO and MCD compact disc series is an upper-mid-price label in the UK (costing just under our upper mid-price limit of £10) and – like the ASV bargain label – appears to be available only as a special import in the USA. The Vanguard CD label (except for the 8000 Series, which retails at around $15) is upper-mid-price in the USA but lower-mid-price in the UK. In *listing* records we have not used the major record companies' additional label subdivisions (like Decca/London's Headline and Ovation, DG's Privilege, EMI's Studio, Philips's Concert Classics, and so on) in order to avoid further confusion, although these designations are sometimes referred to in the text of reviews.

(M) MID-PRICED SERIES (sets are multiples of these prices)

Includes: BMG/RCA; Chandos; Collins; Decca/London; DG; EMI/Angel (Studio and Références; Eminence); Erato/Warner (UK), Erato/WEA (USA); HM/BMG (UK), DHM/BMG (USA); Mercury; Philips; Saga; Sony (including Portrait and Essential Classics); Teldec/Warner (UK), Teldec/WEA (USA); Tuxedo (UK only); Unicorn (UK only).

UK

CDs: under £10; more usually £8 – £9
Cassettes: under £5

USA

CDs: under $11
Cassettes: $5 – 6.50

(B) BARGAIN-PRICED SERIES (sets are multiples of these prices)

Includes: BMG/RCA; Decca/London; CfP (UK only); DG; EMI Laser; Hungaroton White Label; MCA Double-decker (USA only); Philips; Pickwick; Sony.

UK

CDs: £5 – 6
Cassettes: under £4

USA

CDs: under $7
Cassettes: under $4

SPECIAL SETS: Vox Boxes cost only $5 per disc in the USA, but (alongside the Turnabout Doubles) are UK imports and are priced at around £5 per disc in Britain where available. MCA Doubles are $6 per disc in the USA and, with one or two exceptions, have no British equivalent.

(BB) SUPER-BARGAIN SERIES – CDs

Includes: ASV (UK only); BMG/Victrola; LaserLight; Naxos; Pickwick (PWK); Virgin (Virgo).

UK

CDs: under £5

USA

CDs: under $7 (LaserLight under $4)

(In some cases equivalent cassettes are available, usually costing slightly less than bargain cassettes.)

An International Mail-Order Source for Recordings

Readers are urged to support a local dealer if he is prepared and able to give a proper service, and to remember that obtaining many CDs involves perseverance. If, however, difficulty is experienced locally, we suggest the following mail-order alternative, which operates world-wide:

PG Dept
Squires Gate Music Centre
Squires Gate Station Approach
Blackpool
Lancashire FY8 2SP
England
Tel: 0253 44360
Fax: 0253 406686

This organization (which is operated under the direction of the Editor of the *Penguin Guide to Compact Discs and Cassettes New Edition*) patiently extends compact disc orders until they finally come to hand. A full guarantee of safe delivery is made on any order undertaken. Please write for further details, enclosing a stamped and self-addressed envelope if within the UK.

American readers seeking a domestic mail-order source may write to the following address where a comparable supply service is in operation (for both American and imported European labels). Please write for further details (enclosing a stamped, self-addressed envelope if within the USA) or send your order to:

PG Dept
Serenade Records
1713 G St, N.W.
Washington DC 20006
USA
Tel: (202) 638-6648
Fax: (202) 783-0372
Tel: (for US orders only) 1-800-237-2930

Editor's Note

The logistics of producing this book on schedule have been almost, but not quite, insurmountable. Everything came together finally but, as the Duke of Wellington said after the Battle of Waterloo, 'It was a damned close-run thing!' Indeed our alphabetical layout by title is less scrupulous than usual.

The New Edition of our *Guide* is essentially a distillation of the principal contents of our 1990 *Penguin Guide to Compact Discs* and the following (1991) *Yearbook*, to which a survey of newer issues (in all price-ranges) has been added. Our *Bargain Guide* is intended to be used as a companion volume to the present book since it contains reviews of hundreds of attractive but inexpensive CDs and tapes for which there is simply no longer room in our overall survey. The present *Guide* is concerned with *excellence*, irrespective of cost – the yardstick of any true collector. This has led to a record number of Rosettes.

Of course such a limitation certainly includes the *crème de la crème* of lower-priced issues; these are listed and discussed briefly in relation to their more expensive competitors. All earlier reviews have been made more succinct and many have been rewritten in the light of newer recordings and remastered CD reissues, which take up a high proportion of the current volume.

So far as is humanly possible, listings of deleted records have been removed. In order to do this, almost every catalogue number has had to be checked against the manufacturers' lists, for often recordings are arbitrarily withdrawn and restored to circulation without any kind of notification being given, while company computers are notorious for reporting wrongly as to the availability of a given item. In the process of our researches we discovered that at least one of the major manufacturers had no printed inventory of actual records current, even for in-house use by their promotional department!

One addition to the current volume – made in response to an outcry from our readers – is the inclusion of cassette numbers (where such tape versions exist), and again their availability has been zealously checked against existing documentation. But here we must issue a warning that cassettes usually disappear long before the equivalent CDs are withdrawn, and almost always without any kind of notice, although tape equivalents for bargain and mid-priced reissues usually stay around longer than those for premium-price repertory. At the time of going to press, which – by the extraordinary provisions of modern technology – is within only a few weeks of publication, we are as certain as we can be that the documentation included in this book is accurate.

Ivan March (Editor)

Abbreviations

Ac.	Academy, Academic
AAM	Academy of Ancient Music
Amb. S.	Ambrosian Singers
Ang.	Angel
Ara.	Arabesque
arr.	arranged
ASMF	Academy of St Martin-in-the-Fields
Bar.	Baroque
Bav.	Bavarian
BPO	Berlin Philharmonic Orchestra
Cal.	Calliope
Cap.	Caprice
CBSO	City of Birmingham Symphony Orchestra
CfP	Classics for Pleasure
Ch.	Choir; Chorale; Chorus
Chan.	Chandos
CO	Chamber Orchestra
COE	Chamber Orchestra of Europe
Col. Mus. Ant.	Musica Antiqua, Cologne
Coll.	Collegium
Coll. Aur.	Collegium Aureum
Coll. Mus.	Collegium Musicum
Concg. O	Royal Concertgebouw Orchestra of Amsterdam
cond.	conductor, conducted
Cons.	Consort
DG	Deutsche Grammophon
Dig.	digital recording
E.	England, English
ECCO	European Community Chamber Orchestra
ECO	English Chamber Orchestra
Ens.	Ensemble
Fr.	French
GO	Gewandhaus Orchestra
HM	Harmonia Mundi France
HM/RCA	Deutsche Harmonia Mundi
Hung.	Hungaroton
L.	London
LAPO	Los Angeles Philharmonic Orchestra
LCO	London Chamber Orchestra
LMP	London Mozart Players
LOP	Lamoureux Orchestra of Paris
LPO	London Philharmonic Orchestra
LSO	London Symphony Orchestra
Mer.	Meridian
Met.	Metropolitan
movt	movement
N.	North
nar.	narrated
Nat.	National
NY	New York

O	Orchestra, Orchestre
OAE	Orchestra of the Age of Enlightenment
O-L	Oiseau-Lyre
Op.	Opera (in performance listings); opus (in music titles)
orch.	orchestrated
ORTF	L'Orchestre de la radio et télévision française
Ph.	Philips
Phd.	Philadelphia
Philh.	Philharmonia
PO	Philharmonic Orchestra
Qt	Quartet
R.	Radio
RLPO	Royal Liverpool Philharmonic Orchestra
ROHCG	Royal Opera House, Covent Garden
RPO	Royal Philharmonic Orchestra
RSO	Radio Symphony Orchestra
S.	South
SCO	Scottish Chamber Orchestra
Sinf.	Sinfonietta
SNO	Royal Scottish Orchestra
SO	Symphony Orchestra
Soc.	Society
Sol. Ven.	I Solisti Veneti
SRO	Suisse Romande Orchestra
Sup.	Supraphon
trans.	transcription, transcribed
V.	Vienna
Van.	Vanguard
VCM	Vienna Concentus Musicus
VPO	Vienna Philharmonic Orchestra
VSO	Vienna Symphony Orchestra
W.	West

Abel, Carl Friedrich (1723–87)

6 Symphonies, Op. 7.
**(*) Chan. Dig. CHAN 8648; ABTD 1334 [id.]. Cantilena, Shepherd.

The six *Symphonies* of Op. 7 were composed in 1764. The symphonies speak much the same language as J. C. Bach or early Mozart, but they are often quite characterful and well worth hearing. The performances are not the last word in elegance, but they are both lively and enjoyable as well as being well recorded. An eminently serviceable issue that fills a gap in the catalogue.

Adam, Adolphe (1803–56)

Giselle (ballet): complete.
(M) *** Decca Dig. 433 007-2 (2) [id.]. ROHCG O, Richard Bonynge.

Giselle (1841) is the first of the great classical ballets. Bonynge's performance offers the complete original score, exactly as Adam scored it, with all repeats. Also included are the *Peasants' Pas de deux* in Act I with music by Frédéric Bürgmuller, and two other insertions, possibly by Minkus. The recording, on two CDs, provides for well over two hours of musical pleasure and this costs not too much more than Tilson Thomas's new Sony CD listed below.

Giselle (ballet); abridged version.
*** Sony Dig. SK 42450 [id.]; *40-42450*. LSO, Michael Tilson Thomas.
(M) **(*) Decca 417 738-2; *417 738-4* [id.]. VPO, Karajan.

Sony offer an outstanding, modern (1986), digital recording, made – like the Bonynge set – in London's Henry Wood Hall. Michael Tilson Thomas's CD doesn't include the Bürgmuller interpolations but, apart from that, nothing of consequence is omitted. The LSO playing is beautifully polished, warm, graceful and elegant; the element of melodrama is present but never overdone, and Giselle's own tune is wistfully alluring as it should be. There are many individual, affectionate touches – as there are, of course, with Karajan – and with over 76 minutes of music offered, this may be regarded as first choice for those not insisting on having everything heard in the theatre. The documentation is good, including a track-by-track analysis of the stage action linked to the 33 separate cues, although for some reason this falters when the Wilis intercept Albrecht after his *pas de deux* with Giselle's spectre in Act II. From then to the end of the story, one has to rely on the synopsis.

Karajan's performance offers sixty minutes of music: he effectively combines drama with an affectionate warmth, and the phrasing of the lyrical passages produces much lovely – if sometimes suave – playing from the Vienna strings. However, this now needs to be reissued at bargain price.

Adams, John (born 1947)

Fearful symmetries; (i) *The wound dresser.*
*** Nonesuch/Warner Dig. 7559 79218-2; *7559 79218-4* [id.]. (i) Sanford Sylvan; St Luke's O, composer.

In *The wound dresser* Adams rises well above the limitations of minimalism in one of his most moving works. It is an extended setting of a Walt Whitman poem, inspired by the American Civil War, telling of the poet's experiences with the wounded and dying. The piece also reflects the composer's emotions over his dying father. Sanford Sylvan is an ideal soloist, bringing out the work's intensity with natural expressiveness, helped by the composer's own unforced but understanding direction. *Fearful symmetries* is the totally contrasted work for orchestra alone that Adams wrote almost simultaneously with the cantata as a kind of counterblast. It is a characteristically strong, energetic piece, more varied in its tonal contrasts than many examples of minimalism. Excellent, well-balanced sound.

Shaker loops.
❀ *** Virgin VC7 91168-2; *VC7 91168-4* [id.]. LCO, Warren-Green – GLASS: *Company* etc.; REICH: *8 Lines;* HEATH: *Frontier.* ***
*** Ph. 412 214-2 [id.]. San Francisco SO, De Waart – REICH: *Variations for winds.* ***

The inspired performance by Christopher Warren-Green and his London Concert Orchestra is full of imaginative intensity, and understandably it received the composer's imprimatur. It is part of a well-conceived programme of minimalist music, almost all of which is worth returning to. Adams's four-part *Shaker loops* works within its minimalist 'straitjacket' with the utmost imagination and emotional resource. The title refers both to the weird practices of the religious group of that persuasion and to the musical devices of trills and shakes; the loops are its melodic basis. The outer movements are highly animated and strong in dynamic graduation; the inner movements are haunting, from the 'slow languid glissandi' of the *Hymning slews* to the more tangible *Loops and verses.* Outstandingly vivid recording.

The alternative Philips version is also first rate and very well recorded, but the coupling is less generous.

Harmonium (for large orchestra and chorus).
*** ECM 821 465-2 [id.]. San Francisco SO & Ch., Edo de Waart.

Harmonium is a setting of three poems. John Donne's curiously oblique 'Negative love' opens the piece, with the orchestra lapping gently round the chorus. The other two poems are by Emily Dickinson. 'Because I could not stop for death' is a dream-like sequence musing on the arrest of time. Then, after a sombre, ominous preparation in the lower reaches of the orchestra, the third poem, 'Wild nights', breaks into the reverie, engulfing the listener in its violent erotic passion. The work was commissioned by the San Francisco Symphony Orchestra and dedicated to Edo de Waart, who gives it the performance of a lifetime: the disembodied continuum of the opening and closing evocation is as hypnotically compelling as the wild fury of the choral response at the beginning of the third poem. The magnificent, resonantly expansive 1984 analogue recording is certainly worthy of the performance; one might complain that this CD plays for only just over 32 minutes, yet for some ears it may seem longer.

Addinsell, Richard (1904–77)

Warsaw concerto.
(M) *** Decca Dig. 430 726-2; *430 726-4* [id.]. Ortiz, RPO, Atzmon – GERSHWIN: *Rhapsody* **(*); GOTTSCHALK: *Grand fantasia* ***; LITOLFF: *Scherzo* ***; LISZT: *Hungarian fantasia.* ***

Warsaw concerto.
*** Ph. Dig. 411 123-2 [id.]. Dichter, Philh. O, Marriner (with Concert of concertante music ***).

Richard Addinsell's pastiche miniature concerto, written for the film *Dangerous Moonlight* in 1942, is perfectly crafted and its atmosphere combines all the elements of the Romantic concerto to great effect; moreover it has a truly memorable main theme.

Cristina Ortiz offers a warmly romantic account, spacious in conception, with the resonant ambience of Walthamstow Assembly Hall providing beguilingly rich string-timbres.

It is also beautifully played in the Marriner recording, which reveals the most engaging orchestral detail. The sound is first rate.

Aguado, Dionisio (1784–1849)

Adagio, Op. 2/1; Polonaise, Op. 2/2; Introduction and Rondo, Op. 2/3.
**(*) BMG/RCA Dig. RD 84549 [RCD1 4549]. Julian Bream (guitar) – SOR: *Fantaisies* etc. **(*)

Aguado was a contemporary of Sor, with whom his music is coupled – the two composers played duets together in Paris. The *Adagio* is the most striking piece, serene and introspective; it might have been even more effective had Bream been slightly less deliberate and reflective and chosen to move the music on a little more. However, the other pieces have plenty of life, and all are played with Bream's characteristic feeling for colour. The New York recording is truthful and realistic.

Aho, Kalevi (born 1949)

(i) *Violin concerto; Hiljaisuus (Silence); Symphony No. 1.*
*** BIS Dig. CD 396 [id.]. (i) Manfred Gräsbeck; Lahti SO, Vänskä.

The Finnish composer Kalevi Aho is now in his early forties. He was a pupil of Rautavaara, under whose guidance he composed his *First Symphony* in 1969. Its serious tone betokens an impressive musical personality at work: the first movement has something of the gravity of Nielsen, Bartók or Shostakovich. The second has the latter's macabre sense of humour, perhaps with a touch of Britten. The least successful of the four movements is probably the baroque-like third; the finale, however, has an impressive eloquence. Those who like Robert Simpson's music will feel at home here. *Silence* (1982) is an imaginative piece whose stillness and glowing colours recall the luminous wind chords of the Prelude to Sibelius's *Tempest* incidental music, as well as the tone-clusters of the avant-garde. It is related to (and was conceived as an introduction to) the post-expressionist and more 'radical' and trendy *Violin concerto* (1981). All the same, it is a work of considerable resource and imaginative intensity. Good performances and recording.

Albéniz, Isaac (1860–1909)

Iberia (suite; orch. Arbós).
*** Chan. Dig. CHAN 8904; *ABTD 1513* [id.]. Philh. O, Yan Pascal Tortelier – FALLA: *Three-cornered hat.* ***

The transcriptions of five of the twelve piano pieces which make up *Iberia* were made by Albéniz's contemporary and friend, Enrique Arbós. The music itself glows and flickers with the nuances of Spanish dance-rhythms, and Yan Pascal Tortelier brings out all the sultry languor of its atmospheric pictorialism. The gaudy spectacle of the climaxes of *Fête-Dieu à Séville* is dramatically handled, yet the closing section of this piece brings a haunting, sustained pianissimo, while the kaleidoscopic changes of mood and colour of the closing *El Albaicín* – much admired by Debussy – are handled with considerable subtlety. The Philharmonia's response brings glowing woodwind colours and seductive string phrasing, well projected by the warmly resonant recording which blurs only a little at the height of the Corpus Christi festivities.

Suite española (arr. Frühbeck de Burgos).
(M) *** Decca 417 786-2; *417 786-4*. New Philh. O, Frühbeck de Burgos – FALLA: *El amor brujo* *** (with GRANADOS: *Goyescas: Intermezzo* ***).

Albéniz's early *Suite española* offers light music of the best kind, colourful, tuneful, exotically scored and providing orchestra and recording engineers alike with a chance to show their paces, the sound bright and glittering.

GUITAR MUSIC

Cantos de España: Córdoba, Op. 232/4; Mallorca (Barcarola), Op. 202; Piezás caracteristicás: Zambra Granadina; Torre Bermaja, Op. 92/7, 12; Suite española: Granada; Sevilla; Cádiz; Asturias, Op. 47/1, 3–5.
*** Sony Dig. MK 36679 [id.]. John Williams (guitar).

Some of Albéniz's more colourful miniatures are here, and John Williams plays them most evocatively. His mood is slightly introvert, and the underlying technical skill is hidden in his concern for atmosphere. A most engaging recital, recorded with great faithfulness and not over-projected.

Cantos de España: Córdoba, Op. 234/4; Mallorca, Op. 202. Suite española, Op. 47: Cádiz; Granada; Sevilla.
❀ *** BMG/RCA Dig. RCD 14378 [id.]. Julian Bream (guitar) – GRANADOS: *Collection.* *** ❀

Julian Bream is in superb form in this splendid recital, his own favourite record, vividly recorded in the pleasingly warm acoustic of Wardour Chapel, near his home in Wiltshire. The CD is electrifying, giving an uncanny impression of the great guitarist sitting and making music just beyond the loudspeakers. The playing itself has wonderfully communicative rhythmic feeling, great subtlety of colour, and its spontaneity increases the impression that one is experiencing a 'live' recital. The performance of the haunting *Córdoba*, which ends the group, is unforgettable.

PIANO MUSIC

Cantos de España; Suite española.
(M) *** Decca Analogue/Dig. 433 923-2 (2). Alicia de Larrocha – GRANADOS: *12 Danzas españolas* etc. ***

Alicia de Larrocha's *Suite española* was recorded in 1987 and offers Decca's finest digital recording, but the earlier set of three *Cantos de España*, made in 1973, also sounds very realistic. This is most rewarding repertoire – the eight pieces which make up the *Suite española* are remarkably diverse in character and mood – and de Larrocha's playing is imbued with many subtle changes of colour and has refreshing vitality.

Iberia (complete); *España (6 Hojas de album), Op. 165: Malagueña; Tango. Pavana-capricho, Op. 12. Recuerdos de viaje: Puerta de Tierra; Rumores de la caleta.*
(M) *** Decca 433 926-2 (2) [id.]. Alicia de Larocha – FALLA: *Fantasía bética* etc. ***

Iberia; Navarra; Suite española.
❀ *** Decca Dig. 417 887-2 [id.]. Alicia de Larrocha.

Iberia (complete); *Suite española* (excerpts): *Granada; Cataluna; Sevilla; Cadiz; Aragon; Navarra. Pavana-Capricho, Op. 12; Espana (6 Hojas de album): Tango* (only); *Recuerdos de vieje: Rumores de la caleta; Puerta de Tierra.*
(M) *** EMI CMS7 64504-2 (2). Alicia de Larrocha.

Iberia comprises four books of impressions which Albéniz composed during the last few years (1906–9) of his all-too-short life. On her digital Decca version, Alicia de Larrocha brings an altogether beguiling charm and character to these rewarding miniature tone-poems and makes light of their sometimes fiendish technical difficulties. There is plenty of atmosphere, lyricism and warmth, a masterly command of keyboard and colour, crisp, light articulation and beautifully judged rubato. Miss Larrocha completes the set with the early *Suite española*, begun in the 1880s, and *Navarra*, with which Albéniz had originally intended to end *Iberia*. The recording is among the most successful of piano sounds Decca has achieved.

The EMI set offers de Larrocha's earliest stereo recording of Albéniz's great piano suite, *Iberia*, made for Hispavox in 1962, 25 years before she recorded her masterly digital version for Decca. The recording has a high tape-hiss, but the piano-sound is satisfyingly full and forward, adding to the impact of dazzling performances. The younger de Larrocha is far tougher, more daring, more fiery and if anything even more warmly expressive than she became later. Her speeds are consistently on the fast side, but never rushed, always idiomatic. Where the Decca digital set has all eight movements of the *Suite española* as fill-up, the EMI discs offer the five most popular plus four shorter pieces, including the haunting *Tango*, deliciously done, the most celebrated of all Albéniz's music, making this a more popular collection than the alternative Decca analogue set made a decade after the Hispavox recordings .

Alicia de Larrocha's second analogue set of *Ibéria* dates from 1973 and shows her special authority in this repertoire just as readily as the later digital recording. Her fingerwork invites admiration for the clarity of her articulation and rhythmic attack. As in the earlier Hispavox version, she plays with rather more full-blooded temperament and fire than in her most recent digital set, both here and in the other colourful genre pieces included in the recital and though there are occasional touches of wilful rubato, her natural overriding spontaneity carries the day. The piano recording is excellent in its realism and range, more natural than on the EMI set, and has been vividly transferred to CD. Although the later digital set of *Iberia* is even finer, on both artistic and technical grounds, this mid-priced reissue is uncommonly rewarding. Besides the generous Albéniz package, these records also include music by Falla.

Sonata in D.
(M) *** Decca 433 920-2 (2) [id.]. Alicia de Larrocha – GRANADOS: *Goyescas* etc. *** ❀; SOLER: *Sonatas.* ***

Albéniz's delectably cool *Sonata*, with its obvious homage to Domenico Scarlatti, has enormous character; even though it is only three minutes long, it stands out when heard following a collection of eight Sonatas by his compatriot, Padre Soler. It is beautifully played and recorded.

Albinoni, Tommaso (1671–1750)

Adagio in G min. for organ and strings (arr. Giazotto).
*** Ph. Dig. 410 606-2 [id.]. I Musici (with Baroque Concert. ***)
*** Virgin Dig. VCy 791081-2; *VCy 791081-4* [id.]. LCO, Warren-Green – VIVALDI: *4 seasons;* PACHELBEL: *Canon.* ***
(B) *** Pickwick Dig. PCD 802; *CIMPC 802.* Scottish CO, Laredo (with String masterpieces. ***)
(M) *** Decca 417 712-2; *417 712-4* [id.]. Stuttgart CO, Münchinger – PACHELBEL: *Canon* ***; VIVALDI: *4 Seasons.* **(*)

I Musici gave the *Adagio* its CD début; collectors who have a soft spot for the piece will find this performance thoroughly recommendable, with nicely judged expressive feeling giving the melodic line a restrained nobility. The sound is excellent too, and the rest of the programme is equally successful.

Christopher Warren-Green's version is as impressive as any in the catalogue, opening with an attractively volatile violin solo and leading to a richly upholstered climax, with the strings matching the organ in sonority. Splendid sound.

No less telling is the bargain-priced, digitally recorded Pickwick account, strongly contoured and most responsively played by the Scottish Chamber Orchestra under Jaime Laredo. Other versions are listed in the Concerts section.

Münchinger's sumptuous yet stylish version is also available within a mid-priced concert of baroque lollipops (Decca 417 781-2; *417 781-4*).

12 Concerti a cinque, Op. 5.
(M) *** Ph. Dig. 422 251-2; *422 251-4* [id.]. Pina Carmirelli, I Musici.

This fine body of concertos has variety and resource to commend it. I Musici, with Pina Carmirelli as the solo player, are every bit as fresh as the music, and they are accorded altogether first-rate sound.

Concerti a cinque, Op. 7/2, 3, 5, 6, 8, 9, 11 & 12.
(M) *** DG 427 111-2; *427 111-4* [id.]. Holliger, Elhorst, Bern Camerata.

This splendid DG reissue contains eight of the twelve concertos comprising Albinoni's Op. 7. The playing of Heinz Holliger, Hans Elhorst and the Bern Camerata is refined, persuasive and vital, and the CD could hardly be more truthful or better detailed.

Oboe concertos, Op. 7/3, 6, 9 & 12; Op. 9/2, 5, 8 & 11.
*** Unicorn Dig. DKPCD 9088; *DKPC 9088* [id.]. Sarah Francis, L. Harpsichord Ens.

Those looking for a selection of *Oboe concertos* from both Opp. 7 and 9 could hardly better this generous digital collection (over 73 minutes) from Unicorn-Kanchana. Sarah Francis is an immensely stylish and gifted soloist: her decoration is nicely judged, her legato playing is as appealing as her light, clean articulation of allegros. She is accompanied with warmth and grace, and the recording is first class, transparent yet full and naturally balanced.

Concerti a cinque, Op. 9/1, 4, 6–7, 10 & 12.
(M) *** Ph. 426 080-2; *426 080-4.* Ayo, Holliger, Bourgue, Garatti, I Musici.

This excellent mid-priced CD includes all the Opus 9 concertos with violin, plus two of the four double oboe concertos. The recording, excellent for its period, sounds fresh and vivid, if a little dry.

Concerti a cinque, Op. 9/2, 3, 5, 8, 9 & 11.
(M) *** Ph. 434 157-2; *434 157-4* [id.]. Holliger, Bourgue, I Musici.

The second CD completes the I Musici set of Op. 9, with Holliger and Maurice Bourgue by including all the solo oboe concertos, plus the remaining two double concertos. As on the companion disc they are played with much finesse and style and the 1966 recording is brightly remastered.

Alfvén, Hugo (1872–1960)

Symphony No. 1 in F min., Op. 7; Andante religioso; Drapa (Ballad for large orchestra); Uppsala rhapsody, Op. 24.
*** BIS Dig. CD 395 [id.]. Stockholm PO, Neeme Järvi.

Järvi's version of the *First Symphony* supersedes the earlier Westerberg version; it is superior both artistically and technically and leaves the listener more persuaded as to its merits. Though the symphony has a certain warmth and freshness, it remains amiable rather than memorable, likeable rather than lovable. The *Uppsala rhapsody* is based on student songs, but it is pretty thin stuff compared with its predecessor, the justly celebrated *Midsummer vigil.* The *Andante religioso* is rather let down by its sugary closing pages. Drapa opens with some fanfares, full of sequential clichés and with a certain naïve pomp and splendour that verges on bombast.

Symphony No. 2 in D, Op. 11; Swedish rhapsody No. 1 (Midsummer vigil).
*** BIS Dig. CD 385 [id.]. Stockholm PO, Neeme Järvi.

Like those of its predecessor, the ideas of the *Second Symphony* are pleasing though they do not possess a particularly individual stamp. If you expect anything as characteristically Swedish or as fresh as the *Midsummer vigil* (1903), you will surely be disappointed, but there is still much to enjoy. On the whole, Järvi is very persuasive in the symphony and gives a delightful performance of the popular *Midsummer vigil.*

(i) *Symphony No. 4 (Havsbandet – From the outermost skerries), Op. 29; A Legend of the Skerries, Op. 20.*
*** BIS Dig. CD 505 [id.]. Stockholm PO, Järvi, (i) with Christina Högman, Claes-Håkan Ahnsjö.

Alfvén's *Fourth Symphony* is perhaps his most ambitious work. It occupied him on and off for the best part of a decade: the first ideas came to him as early as 1908, and he put the final touches on the score in 1918–19 after spending some months in the sparsely inhabited outer archipelago of Stockholm, whose magical atmosphere it evokes. The work lasts almost fifty minutes without a break and is scored for large forces (quadruple wind, eight horns, two harps, celeste and piano) and, like Nielsen's *Sinfonia espansiva*, calls for two solo singers. There is a romantic programme relating to the emotions of two young lovers, whose wordless melisma is heard to excellent effect in this very fine recording. However, the results are conventionally voluptuous rather than ethereal as in the Nielsen. The nearest analogy that springs to mind is the *Alpine Symphony* of Strauss, both in its pictorial ambition and in its opulence. The symphony often sounds very Straussian just as the somewhat earlier *Legend of the Skerries* owes much to Wagner. There are some highly imaginative moments in the symphony and others of less than impeccable taste. All the same, Alfvén's scoring is eminently resourceful, and no one with an interest in this composer will be disappointed either by the performance, which is sensitive and persuasive, or by the superbly balanced recording with its natural perspective and admirable detail.

Aliabiev, Alexander (1787–1851)

(i; ii) *Introduction and theme with variations in D min.;* (iii; ii) *Souvenir de Moscou, Op. 6;* (iv) *Piano trio in A min.;* (v) *12 Romances.*
*** Olympia OCD 181 [id.]. (i) Venyavsky; (ii) USSR Ac. SO, Verbitsky; (iii) Grauch; (iv) Voskresensky, Ambarpumyan, Knyasev; (v) Pluzhnikov, Mishuk.

Aliabiev's (or Alyabiev's) *Trio in A minor* is a delightful piece with something of the fluency of Weber and Mendelssohn, and it is heard to good advantage here. (Mikhail Voskresensky is a refined and brilliant pianist.) The *Introduction and theme with variations in D minor* is sandwiched between two groups of songs, nearly all of which have great charm and appeal. The *Trio* and the songs are well recorded, though the piano is placed rather backwardly in relation to the violin, to which the engineers give a slight hardness. The recording of the two insubstantial pieces for violin and orchestra comes off less well, though the *Souvenir de Moscou variations* bring splendid playing from Eduard Grauch. This disc almost gives the lie to the impression that Russian music begins with Glinka.

Piano trio in A min.
*(*) Chan. Dig. CHAN 8975 [id.]. Borodin Trio – TCHAIKOVSKY: *Piano trio.* *(*)

Though this new Chandos version is better recorded and has a more present aural image, the performance has less charm than the Olympia issue. The usually impeccable Rostislav Dubinsky makes one or two unappealing sounds (and even some odd sour notes), and Luba Edlina is not on best form either.

Alkan, Charles (1813–88)

Grand duo concertante in F sharp min. for piano and violin, Op. 21; Piano trio in G min., Op. 30; Sonate de concert in E for piano and cello, Op. 47.
** Marco Polo Dig. 8.223383. Trio Alkan.

This is a welcome introduction to Alkan's instrumental and chamber music. All three works have plenty of character, although the most striking is the emotionally ambitious *Grand duo concertante* with its ecstatic secondary theme of the first movement repeated three times, the third 'avec exaltation'. The darkly enigmatic slow movement, *L'enfer* then leads to a brilliant release of tension in the finale, marked: *Aussi vite que possible.* The *Cello sonata* also has a virtuoso finale *alla saltarello*, but it is the central movements, the engaging 6/8 *Siciliano* and the *Adagio* that are the most memorable sections. The *Piano trio*, the first work to be written, is the most conventional-sounding piece here but it, too, demands scintillating bravura from the pianist in the closing *Vite*. These artists find the necessary bravura and flair – the violin sonata comes off best, as the cellist does not produce a very expansive tone. But he is not flattered by the Heidelberg Studio acoustic and, while the recording is fully acceptable and certainly vivid, the ear craves a little more opulence in such music. But the interest of the repertoire triumphs over the sonic limitations.

Barcarolle; Gigue, Op. 24; Marche, Op. 37/1; Nocturne No. 2, Op. 57/1; Saltarelle, Op. 23; Scherzo diabolico, Op. 39/3; Sonatine, Op. 61.
(B) *** HM HMA 190 927 [id.]. Bernard Ringeissen.

Bernard Ringeissen could be more flamboyant but he is fully equal to the cruel technical demands of this music. The *Sonatine*, an extended, big-boned piece, is particularly successful, but all this music is of interest. The recording, from the beginning of the 1970s, is first class; it has splendid presence and body in its remastered format.

Grande sonate (Les quatre ages), Op. 33; Prelude: La chanson de la folle au bord de la mer, Op. 31/8. 12 Studies in all minor keys, Op. 39 (excerpts): *Comme le vent; En rythme molossique; Scherzo diabolique; Le festin d'Ésope. 12 Studies in all major keys, Op. 35: Allegro barbaro* (only).
(M) *** EMI CDM7 64280-2 [id.]. Ronald Smith.

The *Grande sonate* dates from 1847, some six years before the Liszt *Sonata*, and is a quite extraordinary piece. Its four movements describe four decades of a man's life: his twenties, thirties, forties and fifties, each getting progressively slower. The first movement is a whirlwind of a scherzo whose difficulties Ronald Smith bestrides almost nonchalantly; the second, *Quasi-Faust*, is the most Lisztian perhaps, while the last two are the most searching and individual. The *Twelve Studies in all minor keys* include the *Symphony for piano* (Studies 4–7) and the *Concerto for piano* (Studies 8–10). These are not included here, although Ronald Smith has recorded them. Of what we are offered in this remarkable 77-minute recital, only the very first, *Comme le vent* ('Like the wind . . .'), could reasonably be described as a study in the normal sense of the word. *Le festin d'Ésope* (No. 12) is a highly individual and colourful set of 25 variations. Some of the other music is quite astonishing, and it goes without saying that Ronald Smith's virtuosity is remarkable and his understanding of this repertoire beyond question. The piano-sound is realistic and clean. It could perhaps have done with a shade more resonance and sounds slightly drier on CD than on LP, but it is by no means confined, and the playing is so compelling that this is of little consequence. Inadequate back-up notes.

25 Preludes, Op. 31.
*** Decca Dig. 433 055-2 [id.]. Olli Mustonen – SHOSTAKOVICH: *24 Preludes.* ***

Lauren Marin's earlier Marco Polo set is completely superseded by this newcomer on Decca. The *Preludes* are more poetic than barnstorming and date from 1847. They go through all the major and minor keys, returning to C major in No. 25, and are designed for piano or organ or the pedalier (a piano with pedal-board), the instrument for which Alkan had a special affection. Some of the pieces are affecting in their simplicity and the young Finnish pianist Olli Mustonen – whose début this is on the Decca label – plays them supremely well. And whereas Laurent Martin gave us only the Alkan, Mustonen gives us a very well-filled disc with the Shostakovich Op. 34 *Preludes* as a coupling. The recording is absolutely first class, though the pedal-stamping in the *Tenth Prelude, Dans le style fugué*, should have been curbed. Strongly recommended.

Allegri, Gregorio (1582–1652)

Miserere.

*** Gimell CDGIM 339; *1585-T-39* [id.]. Tallis Scholars, Phillips – MUNDY: *Vox patris caelestis;* PALESTRINA: *Missa Papae Marcelli.* ***

(M) *** Decca 421 147-2; *421 147-4* [id.]. King's College Ch., Willcocks – PALESTRINA: *Collection.* ***

(M) **(*) EMI Dig. CD-EMX 2180; *TC-EMX 2180.* St John's College, Cambridge, Ch., Guest – LASSUS: *Missa super bella* **(*); PALESTRINA: *Veni sponsa Christi.* ***

Mozart was so impressed with Allegri's *Miserere* when he heard it in the Sistine Chapel (which originally claimed exclusive rights to its performance) that he wrote the music out from memory so that it could be performed elsewhere. On the much-praised Gimell version, the soaring treble solo is taken by a girl, Alison Stamp, and her memorable contribution is enhanced by the recording itself. The Tallis Scholars are ideally balanced in Merton College Chapel, Oxford, and Peter Phillips, their conductor, emphasizes his use of a double choir by placing the solo group in the echoing distance and the main choir directly in front of the listener. The contrasts are dramatic and hugely effective.

The famous King's performance of Allegri's *Miserere*, with its arresting treble solo so beautifully and securely sung by Roy Goodman, is now coupled with Palestrina at mid-price.

The new digital recording from St John's is finely sung, and the three-dimensional balance is very realistic, but the unnamed treble soloist sings less ethereally than Roy Goodman, with a strong upward leap in his famous repeated phrase.

Alwyn, William (1905–85)

(i) *Autumn legend* (for cor anglais and string orchestra); (ii) *Lyra Angelica* (concerto for harp and string orchestra); (iii) *Pastoral fantasia* (for viola and string orchestra); *Tragic interlude.*

*** Chan. Dig. CHAN 9065 [id.]. (i) Nicholas Daniel; (ii) Rachel Masters; (iii) Stephen Tees; City of L. Sinfonia, Richard Hickox.

Autumn legend (1954) is a highly atmospheric tone-poem, very Sibelian in influence, a bit like an extended *Swan of Tuonela*, only more romantically animated. It is beautifully played – Nicholas Daniel's timbre is darkly sonorous – and its simple poetry comes over admirably. The *Pastoral fantasia,* written much earlier in 1939, also contains a curious Sibelius quotation – perhaps unconscious – near the beginning, but its influences are mainly drawn from Delius and Vaughan Williams (who loved to feature a viola solo in his orchestral works). Yet the piece has its own developing individuality. Again a fine performance, with Stephen Tees highly sympathetic to the music's fluid poetic line. The *Tragic interlude* is a powerful lament for the dead of wars past, written on the eve of World War II. Passionately agitated at first, the music dissolves into a closing elegiac threnody. But the highlight of the disc is the *Lyra Angelica*, the composer's own favourite among his works: the first movement was played at his funeral. It is a radiantly beautiful, extended piece (just over half an hour in length), inspired by the metaphysical poet, Giles Fletcher's '*Christ's victorie and triumph*', and the memorable tune which dominates the work almost fits the words of the line quoted to capture the mood of the expansive opening adagio, 'I looke for angel's songs and here Him crie'. There are four movements, the first three richly lyrical and expansive and the closing *Allegro jubiloso* ('How can such joy as this want words to speake?') brimming over with exultation in life itself. The performance here is very moving, and the recording has great richness of string-tone and a delicately balanced harp texture. Rachael Masters's contribution is distinguished. This is the record to start with for those beginning to explore the music of this highly rewarding composer.

Concerti grossi Nos. 1 in B flat for chamber orchestra; 2 in G for string orchestra; 3 for woodwind, brass and strings; (i) *Oboe concerto.*
*** Chan. Dig. CHAN 8866 [id.]. (i) Daniel; City of L. Sinfonia, Hickox.

The fine two-movement *Oboe concerto* was written after dark during the war years, and reflects the restless nights of the London Blitz, when the composer was an Air-raid Warden and experiencing deep nostalgia for the countryside of peacetime England. Its pastoralism has a haunting ambivalence of feeling, expressed immediately at the restless opening, while the equally engaging finale contrasts a Pan-like piping and busy violins with a natural lyricism, returning finally to the atmosphere of the beginning and finding peace. Its improvisatory feeling and changing moods are beautifully caught by Nicholas Daniel, with Hickox and the Sinfonia players providing admirable support. They then turn to the more extrovert and strongly contrasted *Concerti grossi*. The first is a miniature concerto for orchestra with a haunting *alla siciliano Adagio*; the second is perhaps the finest of the three. In the ripest tradition of English string writing it offers spaciously energetic outer movements, bustling with vitality, framing a most beautiful and tender *Adagio* where the solo quartet is ethereally contrasted with the main body of strings. The third is a fine *in memoriam* for Sir Henry Wood, opening with a strongly confident maestoso and ending with what is almost a funeral march, with the sense of passionate loss – powerfully expressed in the brass – dominating the closing pages. Excellent Chandos sound, gaining from the warm ambience of St Jude's in north-west London, yet with textures unclouded.

Symphonies Nos. 1; 4.
*** Lyrita SRCD 227 [id.]. LPO, composer.

The first of Alwyn's symphonies dates from 1950 and is a work of considerable power and maturity. Its gestures are occasionally overblown, particularly in the finale, and offer obvious echoes of the film-scores of which Alwyn is so consummate a master. But the work is not only expertly wrought and marvellously scored but is also genuinely imaginative and involving. The three-movement *Fourth* is even more impressive. Those not attuned to the English symphonic tradition may not respond to its rhetoric, but its power is undeniable and one cannot but warm to the composer's lyricism and his ability to tackle a large symphonic canvas with such confidence. The LPO responds splendidly to the composer's direction and the Lyrita analogue recording – in the demonstration class in its day – has been naturally remastered for CD: the sound has fine presence, body and clarity.

Symphonies Nos. 2–3; 5 (Hydriotaphia).
*** Lyrita SRCD 228 [id.]. LPO, composer.

The *Second Symphony* dates from 1953 and is a powerfully inventive work that shows an original cast of mind. Its language is not exploratory either in terms of new harmonies or of sonorities, but it is coherent and personal. Structured in two movements (lasting together for just short of half an hour) it is magnificently scored and moves towards a powerful Sibelian denouement. The *Third Symphony* was the result of a BBC commission and was first performed by the BBC Symphony Orchestra under Sir Thomas Beecham. It is a well argued and imaginative score, richly coloured and at times even reminiscent of Bax. The scoring is opulent and masterly, and the germinal four-note figure (D, E, F, A flat) evolves like the *Second Symphony*, and exhibits a genuine organic coherence. The *Fifth* dates from 1973, and its title derives from Sir Thomas Browne, whose 'Urn Burial' or *Hydriotaphia* is its source of inspiration. However, it was Browne's magnificently flowery prose that captured the composer's imagination and is quoted to express the feeling of each of the work's four sections, within a compressed (15-minute), one-movement structure. Again the music is impressively wrought and emotionally eloquent. All three works reward the listener, and the composer's performances could hardly be more authoritative. The LPO responds splendidly and the analogue recording (from the early to mid-1970s) was in the demonstration bracket in its day and had been transferred to CD very successfully indeed. The sound is full and naturally balanced, with fine presence and clarity,

Symphony No. 4; Elizabethan dances; Festival march.
*** Chan. Dig. CHAN 8902 [id.]. LSO, Richard Hickox.

Richard Hickox's conception of the *Fourth* is marginally more spacious than the composer's own – as the timings of the outer movements demonstrate. Yet he has a masterly grip on the score and the forward momentum is strong and positive: the work's opening paragraphs are particularly well sustained, with some notably fine horn-playing. There are moments elsewhere when the effect produced by Lyrita is marginally the more vehement, but that is partly owing to the extra bite of the sound of woodwind and brass on the earlier recording. Under Hickox, the moving eloquence of the climax of the *Meno mosso* central section of the scherzo is no less passionately projected by the LSO players, and the mysterious, calm serenity of the opening of the *Passacaglia* finale has deep underlying expressive feeling, with the work's resolution powerfully conveyed. The Chandos digital recording, made in St Jude's, in London NW 11, is superbly rich and spacious and yet brings clear outlines without ecclesiastical blurring: the violins have a fine sweep, and the brass admirably combines rich sonority with bite. The couplings are relatively slight. The *Elizabethan suite* doesn't bridge the opposing styles of the times of the queens, Elizabeth I and II, too convincingly, but there is a graceful waltz, an engaging mock-morris dance and a pleasing pavane, with hints of Constant Lambert in the rousing finale. The *Festival march*, commissioned for the 1951 Festival of Britain, is agreeable enough, but its grand tune lacks the memorability of those by Elgar and Walton.

(i) *Rhapsody for piano quartet. String quartet No. 3; String trio.*
*** Chan. Dig. CHAN 8440; *ABTD 1153* [id.]. (i) David Willison; Qt of London.

Alwyn's serialism is skin deep and never strays far from a fundamentally tonal language. Although the other two works are impressive, the *Third Quartet* is the most important work on this record; like its two predecessors, it is a concentrated and thoughtful piece of very considerable substance, elegiac in feeling. The playing of the Quartet of London throughout (and of David Willison in the *Rhapsody*) is both committed and persuasive. As a recording, this is in the very first flight and the recording brings the musicians vividly into one's living-room.

Fantasy-Waltzes; 12 Preludes.
**(*) Chan. Dig. CHAN 8399; *ABTD 1125* [id.]. John Ogdon (piano).

The *Fantasy-Waltzes* are highly attractive and are excellently played by John Ogdon, who is also responsible for a perceptive insert-note. The *Twelve Preludes* are equally fluent and inventive pieces that ought to be better known and well repay investigation. The recording, made at The Maltings, Snape, is first rate and carries the imprimatur of the composer in whose presence it was made. Recommended.

Anderson, Leroy (1908–75)

Orchestral music (almost complete).
(B) *** MCA Double Decker stereo/mono (2) [MCAD2-9815-A/B]. O, cond. composer.

Belle of the ball; Blue tango; Chicken reel; China doll; Fiddle-faddle; The first day of spring; The girl in satin; Horse and buggy; Jazz legato; Jazz pizzicato; The phantom regiment; Plink, plank, plunk!; Promenade; Saraband; Scottish suite: The bluebells of Scotland. Serenata; Sleigh ride; Song of the bells; Summer skies; The syncopated clock; The typewriter; The waltzing cat. Arr. of HANDEL: *Song of Jupiter.*
(M) *** Mercury 432 013-2 [id.]. Eastman-Rochester Pops O, or O, Frederick Fennell.

Belle of the ball; Bugler's holiday; Fiddle-faddle; Forgotten dreams; Jazz pizzicato; Plink, plank, plunk!; Sandpaper ballet; Sarabande; Serenata; Sleigh ride; Song of the bells; The syncopated clock; Trumpeter's lullaby; The typewriter.
(M) **(*) Van. 08.6008.71 [OVC 6008]. Utah SO, Maurice Abravanel.

Leroy Anderson, who studied under both Walter Piston and George Enesco, was in his varied musical career bandmaster, church organist, choirmaster, double-bass player and orchestral conductor. At the beginning of the 1950s he was asked by Arthur Fiedler to provide a series of specially written 'lollipops' for use as encores at the Boston Pops concerts. In response he produced a series of instantly memorable vignettes, wittily scored and usually melodically indelible. Over two decades he wrote two dozen such pieces in the best tradition of American popular music, and the finest of them sound as freshly attractive as the day they were written. The composer was a naturally spontaneous exponent of his own music and he recorded a great deal of it for the American Decca label between 1950 and 1962. This MCA Double CD pack includes nearly all of it. The sound is bright and vivid, with a nicely judged hall ambience. The strings have slightly less body here than on the Vanguard collection. However the rhythmic lift and warmth of the composer's performances is special. Unfortunately this set, which is discussed more fully in our *Bargain Guide*, is currently available only in the USA.

The reissue of Fennell's Mercury performances is therefore most welcome; although certain key numbers such as *Bugler's holiday, Forgotten dreams, Sleigh ride* and *A Trumpeter's lullaby* are missing; they will no doubt, arrive on a later issue, together with Fennell's outstanding version of the *Irish suite*. Fennell does offer the infectious *Chicken reel*, and the arrangement of Handel's *Where'er you walk* from *Semele*, both omitted from the MCA set. His performances have a witty precision which is most attractive. Most of the recordings date from the late 1950s and were made in the slightly studioish acoustics of the Eastman Theatre in Rochester, but a smaller group were recorded in Watford Town Hall (presumably with members of the LSO) in 1964. Of these *The Phantom regiment* in particular, gains from the greater ambient effect. But the sound throughout is truthful, if not opulent.

The collection by the Utah Symphony Orchestra under Maurice Abravanel is also very enjoyable, affectionate and polished, if not as racy as Anderson's own recordings. Numbers like *Bugler's holiday* and *Fiddle-faddle* are about half a minute longer than the composer's versions. Some might also feel that the Utah acoustic is a bit resonant for this lightly orchestrated writing, but it does not blunt the music's wit (the special effects in the *Sandpaper ballet* flit enthusiastically from speaker to speaker) and the glowing sound, richer in colour, gives an added warmth to the charming *Forgotten dreams* and the winsome *Trumpeter's lullaby*.

Antheil, George (1900–1959)

Symphony No. 4.

** Bay Cities BCD 1016 [id.]. LSO, Goossens – GOULD: *Formations* etc. ***

George Antheil is probably better known nowadays for his autobiography, *Bad Boy of Music*, than for any of his compositions, though his *Ballet Mécanique* for aeroplane propeller, siren, electric bell, four xylophones, eight pianos, one player-piano and percussion enjoyed some notoriety in the mid-1920s. He was something of a polymath, earning a living as a writer, and he even won honorary life membership of the Paris police force for his study of glandular disturbances in criminals. His *Fourth Symphony* (1942) is resolutely tonal and has a directness of expression that is not unappealing. There is a lot of Shostakovich in the piece too. The transfer greatly improves (particularly in bass definition) on the 1958 Everest recording, which originally appeared on LP with Ginastera's *Estancia* as a coupling. The Antheil *Symphony* is a curiosity rather than a wholly satisfying musical experience, but it is well worth hearing all the same.

Arensky, Anton (1861–1906)

(i) *Piano concerto No. 2 in F min., Op. 2;* (ii) *Egyptian nights, Op. 50a.*

** Olympia OCD 107 [id.]. (i) Cherkassov; USSR RSO, (i) Alexeev; (ii) Demchenko – IPPOLITOV-IVANOV: *Caucasian sketches.* **

Arensky's *F minor Concerto* is something of a rarity; the work is worth investigating, for the performance is a good one; Alexei Cherkassov brings sensibility and a convincing sense of rubato to the lyrical writing. The recording is somewhat two-dimensional and the piano timbre is not ideally rich but remains fully acceptable. The *Egyptian nights suite* is not the most potent of cheap music – it has something in common with Luigini's *Ballet Égyptien*, even if thematically much less indelible. The bright brash playing here projects the music quite effectively, though the recording has a degree of coarseness; the interest of the repertoire (including the coupling) earns the disc its place in the catalogue.

Violin concerto in A min., Op. 54.

*** Olympia Dig. OCD 106 [id.]. Stadler, Leningrad PO, Chernushenko – TCHAIKOVSKY: *Suite No. 3.* ***

This concerto is a much later work than the *Piano concerto* and is a winning piece with a particularly endearing second-subject group theme. The work is most persuasively played by Sergei Stadler, who has a firm rich line and a full understanding of the work's nostalgic feeling; the accompaniment is quite admirable. If the soloist is balanced a shade closely, in all other respects the clear recording, which has excellent presence and detail, is worthy of the performance and should make many new friends for this engaging work.

Silhouettes (Suite No. 2), Op. 23.
*** Chan. Dig. CHAN 8898; *ABTD 1509* [id.]. Danish Nat. RSO, Järvi – SCRIABIN: *Symphony No. 3.* ***

Arensky's *Silhouettes* have a lot of period charm – particularly *Le rêveur*, which is almost the Russian equivalent of Elgar's *Dream children.* They derive from a set of pieces for two pianos dating from 1892 and are scored with great skill and, in the case of *La coquette* and *Polichinelle*, great delicacy. The Danish Radio Orchestra play for Neeme Järvi with great freshness and elegance, as if they are enjoying making the acquaintance of this rarely heard music – as we did!

Symphonies Nos. 1 in B min., Op. 4; 2 in A, Op. 22; Dream on the Volga overture.
** Olympia OCD 167 [Mobile Fidelity MFCD 878 (without Overture)]. USSR Ac. SO, Svetlanov.

Arensky's *First Symphony*, composed shortly after his graduation in 1882, is a work of great fluency and charm. It is beautifully put together and has considerable melodic freshness. The *Second* is the more individual of the two and is full of highly attractive ideas: its four movements are linked together, the finale returning to the material of the opening movement; however, there is little serious attempt at organic cohesion. The *Overture* to the opera, *Dream on the Volga* (1888), opens bombastically but also has its attractive moments, though its inspiration is less consistent than either of the symphonies. The analogue recordings date from 1983; the performances are spirited though the brass are at times raw in climaxes.

Variations on a theme of Tchaikovsky, Op. 35a.
*** ROH ROH 304/5; *ROHMC 304/5* [id.]. ROHCG O, Ermler – TCHAIKOVSKY: *Nutcracker ballet.* **(*)
** Opus Dig. OPS 57-9203 [id.]. Byelorussian CO, Valery Poliansky – TCHAIKOVSKY: *String serenade; Legend.* *(*)

Warm and easy on the ear, particularly in this ripely recorded performance, Arensky's unpretentious string work – new to the CD catalogue – makes an attractive fill-up for Mark Ermler's Covent Garden recording of Tchaikovsky's *Nutcracker.*

It was a happy idea to pair Arensky's attractively affectionate set of variations with the original *a cappella* choral version of the Tchaikovsky *Legend* on which it is based. However, the performance of the *Variations* is acceptable rather than memorable and the Tchaikovsky *String serenade*, which is the main coupling, is curiously lifeless.

Piano trio No. 1 in D min., Op. 32.
*** Chan. Dig. CHAN 8477; *ABTD 1188* [id.]. Borodin Trio – GLINKA: *Trio.* ***
*** CRD CRD 3409; *CRDC 3409* [id.]. Ian Brown, Nash Ens. – RIMSKY-KORSAKOV: *Quintet.* ***
*** Delos Dig. DE 3056 [id.]. Cardenes, Solow, Golabek – TCHAIKOVSKY: *Trio.* **(*)

The shades of Mendelssohn, Borodin and Tchaikovsky can clearly be discerned in the *Piano trio*, while the invention is fertile and has an endearing period charm; at the same time the ideas have undoubted freshness. The Borodins give a lively and full-blooded account of the *Trio.* The Scherzo comes off well, and the whole does justice to the Borodins' genial playing.

The account by members of the Nash Ensemble is first class in every way. These fine players capture the Slav melancholy of the *Elegia*, and in the delightful *Scherzo* Ian Brown is both delicate and nimble-fingered. The warm, resonant 1982 analogue recording has transferred naturally to CD and, although inner detail is not sharp, the effect is very pleasing. There is an excellent cassette.

The Cardenes group on Delos also give an admirable account of this attractive work, catching the full measure of its charm. It is not an assertive performance, yet it is full of affection. In the scherzo there is a scintillating contribution from the pianist, Mona Golabek, and all the playing is polished and nicely blended. The recording is realistically balanced, not too forward, and a highly appropriate and generous coupling makes this well worth considering.

Piano trio No. 2 in F min., Op. 73.
*(*) Chan. Dig. CHAN 8924; *ABTD 1522* [id.]. Borodin Trio – PROKOFIEV: *Overture on Hebrew themes* **; SHOSTAKOVICH: *7 Romances* *(*).

The *F minor Trio* is a bigger piece than its better-known predecessor in D minor, and a work of considerable eloquence and charm – as well as dignity. As is often the case with this distinguished Trio, the Borodins rarely permit the music to speak for itself. They tend to overproject and oversweeten the piece, particularly in the *Romance* and the trio section of the exuberant scherzo. Here the violinist is not quite impeccable and, although the scherzo itself comes off beautifully, the playing here is horribly sugary. However, there is no current alternative, and the group is very vividly recorded.

String quartet No. 2 in A min., Op. 35.
*** Mer. Dig. CDE 84211; *KE 77211* [id.]. Arienski Ens. – BORODIN: *Sextet movements;* TCHAIKOVSKY: *Souvenir de Florence.* **

Arensky composed his *A minor Quartet* for the unusual combination of one violin, one viola and two cellos, which lends its textures a dark quality (there is also a later version for the usual combination). A charming three-movement work whose middle movement, the variations on a theme of Tchaikovsky, is best known in its transcription for full strings, it has, like so much of this composer's music, real quality. The sleeve gives the key as A major and transliterates the composer as Arienski but has an excellent note by the cellist Moray Welsh. The playing is very committed indeed.

Arne, Thomas (1710–78)

Organ concertos Nos. 1 in C; 2 in G; 3 in A; 4 in B flat; 5 in G min.; 6 in B flat.
*** Chan. Dig. CHAN 8604/5; *DBTD 2013* (2) [id.]. Roger Bevan Williams, Cantilena, Shepherd.

Though Arne's concertos are simpler in style and construction than those of Handel, their invention is consistently fresh; their galant tunefulness and vigour give lasting pleasure. While their basic structural layout looks forward classically, the baroque influence remains strong, and the orchestral ritornellos recall both Vivaldi and the orchestral suites of Bach. The performances here have admirable style and spirit, and the recording (made in the Henry Wood Hall, Glasgow) is wonderfully fresh and ideally balanced – the organ seems perfectly chosen for this consistently engaging music. A highly recommendable set in every respect.

Cymon and Iphigenia; Frolic and free (cantatas); Jenny; The Lover's recantation; The Morning (cantata); Sigh no more, ladies; Thou soft flowing Avon; What tho' his guilt.
*** Hyp. Dig. CDA 66237; *KA 66237* (id.]. Emma Kirkby, Richard Morton, Parley of Instruments, Goodman.

The present collection admirably shows the ingenuous simplicity of Arne's vocal writing, very much in the mid-eighteenth-century English pastoral school with its 'Hey down derrys'. Emma Kirkby has the perfect timbre and all the vocal freshness to bring this music charmingly to life. Richard Morton sings well too; though his style has not always quite the easy manner of Kirkby, he is always responsive. Excellent, warm recording, with the voices naturally projected. A most entertaining concert.

Arnold, Malcolm (born 1921)

(i) *Clarinet concerto No. 1, Op. 20;* (ii) *Flute concerto No. 1, Op. 45;* (iii) *Horn concerto No. 2, Op. 58;* (iv) *Double violin concerto, Op. 77.*
*** Conifer Dig. CDCF 172 [id.]. (i) Collins; (ii) Jones; (iii) Watkins; (iv) Sillito and Fletcher; L. Musici, Mark Stephenson.

These works provide outstanding examples of a genre which Arnold has cultivated with conspicuous success and which might be described as 'the quarter-hour concerto'. Within this frame, neo-classical in scale and aim, he has consistently shown his brilliance in compressing his arguments, writing with jewelled concision for particular performers. Often he adopts neo-classical stylistic patterns, but that rarely gets in the way of his lyrical gift, which regularly blossoms in amiable, often catchy tunes.

On Conifer in the *Double concerto* Kenneth Sillito and Lyn Fletcher are sweetly matched in writing which presents the most severe demands on purity of intonation, while both Michael Collins and Karen Jones give urgent, exhilarating readings of works which aim for brilliance above all, with the solo writing in the *Flute concerto* concentrating on spiky lines, and with the low chalumeau register of the clarinet surprisingly avoided. The horn soloist, Richard Watkins, may not quite match the wonderfully wide tonal range that the late Alan Civil achieved on the earlier recording, but he is weightier in the slow movement and even brisker in the finale. Mark Stephenson, who founded the London Musici string ensemble, draws out a sound from his players that would do credit to a much larger ensemble, set against the helpful acoustic of The Maltings at Snape.

(i) *Flute concerto No. 1, Op. 45;* (ii) *Oboe concerto, Op. 39; Sinfoniettas Nos. 1–3, Opp. 48, 65 & 81.*
*** Hyp. Dig. CDA 66332; *KA 66332* [id.]. (i) Beckett, (ii) Messiter; L. Festival O, Ross Pople.

It makes a delightful programme having Arnold's three *Sinfoniettas* framing two wind concertos that come from the same early period, the 1950s. Though, particularly in his later works, Arnold's music has grown much darker, these all reveal him at his most accessible. Crisp allegros and freely lyrical slow movements never outstay their welcome for a moment, with five minutes seemingly set as an outside limit for each. The *Third Sinfonietta*, written slightly later than the rest in 1964 on a commission from the Philharmonia Orchestra, maintains that pattern in its four brief movements. The performances here are all excellent, with warm, well-balanced sound. Anyone hesitating between this version of the *Flute concerto No. 1* and the rival accounts on Conifer and EMI can safely make the choice on preference of coupling.

Guitar concerto.
*** Decca Dig. 430 233-2; *430 233-4* [id.]. Eduardo Fernández, ECO, Barry Wordsworth – BROUWER: *Retrats Catalans;* CHAPPELL: *Guitar concerto No. 1.* ***

There are few guitar concertos to match the effectiveness of this jazz-inflected piece, written in 1959 for Julian Bream. This brilliant version by Eduardo Fernández, superbly recorded, brings glowing sound from the ECO in a fizzing performance, spikily incisive in bringing out the jazz overtones. Fernández makes the haunting melody of the second subject warm and not sentimental, and the full depth of the blues-inspired slow movement is movingly conveyed. With the unusual Brouwer pieces and Chappell's colourful concerto for couplings, this can be warmly recommended.

(i) *Double violin concerto. Serenade for small orchestra, Op. 26; Sinfoniettas Nos 1–2.*
**(*) Koch Dig. 37134-2 [id.]. (i) Igor and Vesna Gruppman; San Diego CO, Barra.

These are warm-hearted performances, very well recorded, of four of Malcolm Arnold's most attractive earlier works, each in his favourite form of three compact movements. The *Serenade for small orchestra*, the first of the four, with the most ambitious orchestration, is particularly valuable, when otherwise it is unavailable on CD. The San Diego Chamber Orchestra gives a winning account, full of high spirits, of what Hugo Cole rightly describes in his excellent study of Arnold's music as 'one of the most delightful of Arnold's lighter works'. The recording has a fullness and warmth to bring out the brilliance and refinement of the orchestration. The exuberantly brassy finale is very winning. In the first two of the three Arnold *Sinfoniettas* the Americans are more relaxed, more openly expressive than Ross Pople on the rival Hyperion disc containing all three *Sinfoniettas*. In No. 2 the balance is in favour of the San Diego performance, with its lightness and charm and an extra hushed beauty in the slow movement. Consistently the American players rise to the dashing challenge which Arnold makes in the finales of all these works, but they are less successful in evoking the Bachian overtones of the *Double Violin concerto*, with the central *Andantino* too romantic in style, and the soloists consistently adopting too heavy a vibrato, with the occasional portamento.

Divertimento for flute, oboe and clarinet, Op. 37; Duo for flute and viola, Op. 10; Flute sonata, Op. 121; Oboe quartet, Op. 61; Quintet for flute, violin, viola, horn and piano, Op. 7; 3 Shanties for wind quintet, Op. 4.
*** Hyp. Dig. CDA 66173; *KA 66173* [id.]. Nash Ens.

Duo for 2 cellos, Op. 85; Piano trio, Op. 54; Viola sonata No. 1, Op. 17; Violin sonatas Nos. 1, Op. 15; 2, Op. 43; Pieces for violin and piano, Op. 54.
*** Hyp. Dig. CDA 66171; *KA 66171* [id.]. Nash Ens.

Clarinet sonatina, Op. 29; Fantasies for wind, Opp. 86–90; Flute sonatina, Op. 19; Oboe sonatina, Op. 28; Recorder sonatina, Op. 41; Trio for flute, bassoon and piano, Op. 6.
*** Hyp. Dig. CDA 66172; *KA 66172* [id.]. Nash Ens.

There is much here that belies Malcolm Arnold's image as just an entertaining and genial tunesmith. All the pieces on the first disc show conspicuous resource in the handling of the instruments, whether in the *Duo for flute and viola* or in the *Oboe quartet*, composed for Leon Goossens, a fine piece let down by an empty finale. The *Flute sonata* is the most recent work, written in 1977, and has a vaguely Satie-like Andantino movement, with a touch of Poulenc in the finale. The second disc includes two *Violin sonatas*, which exhibit some Gallic traits: they are cool, civilized and intelligent. The *Piano trio* of 1956 has a powerful sense of direction; it is vital and ingenious, and for the most part the music on this disc is worth getting to know. As a glance at the third listing shows, this collection concentrates on the wind music. This is perhaps more for admirers of Arnold's music than for the generality of collectors. The playing is brilliant and sympathetic throughout all three discs and the recording first rate.

8 English dances.
(M) (***) Decca mono 425 661-2 [id.]. LPO, Boult – WALTON: *Façade* etc. *** ❀

Arnold's first essay in writing colourful regional pieces receives a vividly sympathetic performance under Boult, with the mono recording still sounding remarkably well.

Cornish dances, Op. 91; English dances, Set 1, Op. 27; Set 2, Op. 33; Irish dances, Op. 126; Scottish dances, Op. 59; Solitaire (ballet): *Sarabande; Polka.*
*** Lyrita SRCD 201 [id.]. LPO, composer.
*** Chan. Dig. CHAN 8867; *ABTD 1482* [id.]. Philh. O, Bryden Thomson.

Arnold's four sets of British national dances not only make a wonderfully varied and colourful musical entertainment but, when listened to in sequence, admirably survey the stylistic changes of his composing career, from the exuberant and immensely successful *English dances*, which firmly established his reputation in 1950–51, through to the much darker, even valedictory *Irish dances* of 1986. In between come the *Scottish dances* of 1957 and the relatively sombre *Cornish dances* of a decade later. The Scottish set, besides evoking bagpipes and the snapping rhythms of strathspeys and reels, includes a wonderful slow movement, picturing the glorious Highland countryside; while the central movements of the *Cornish dances*, for all their brevity, have remarkable musical substance and powerful atmosphere. (Thomson is less dramatic and more genial here.) The two numbers specially written for *Solitaire* in 1956 augmented the eight *English dances*, to form the ballet of this name. The *Sarabande* has a wistful charm and the *Polka* brings chararacteristically witty orchestral colouring.

Bryden Thomson has the advantage of the extra definition superb digital sound brings, with no loss of ambient feeling. The strings are brightly lit, but the rich brass sonorities and horn whoops are vividly and excitingly defined. The composer's tempi are usually fractionally slower than Thomson's, underlining contrasts, yet Arnold's strong rhythmic pointing, as in the *Giubiloso* final *English dance* and the *Pesante* opening *Scottish dance*, brings even greater bite and thrust. Both these sets of performances are admirable in different ways, and those who choose the Chandos disc for its digital spectacle will not be disappointed.

(i) *Symphony No. 1;* (ii) *Concerto for 2 pianos (3 hands), Op. 104;* (iii) *English dances Nos. 3 & 5;* (i) *Solitaire: Sarabande; Polka;* (iii) *Tam O'Shanter: overture, Op. 51.*
(M) *** EMI CDM7 64044-2; *EG 764044-4.* (i) Bournemouth SO; (ii) Phyllis Sellick and Cyril Smith, CBSO; (iii) Philh. O; composer.

This is a strong performance of the *First Symphony* under the composer, while the concerto is a delightful, undemanding work, superbly played by the dedicatees, which makes a good foil alongside the rumbustious overture, *Tam O'Shanter*. Finally come the two pieces Arnold added to his *English dances* for the ballet *Solitaire*, and two of the most attractive of the *Dances*.

(i) *Symphony No. 2, Op. 40;* (ii) *Symphony No. 5, Op. 74;* (i) *Peterloo: overture.*
(M) *** EMI CDM7 63368-2 [id.]. (i) Bournemouth SO, Groves; (ii) CBSO, composer.

The recoupling of two of Arnold's most impressive symphonies can be warmly welcomed. Both recordings date from the 1970s. The composer secures an excellent response from the Birmingham orchestra, as Groves, in Bournemouth, is equally dedicated. The CD transfer is outstandingly successful, and the Overture makes a highly effective encore. Splendid value at mid-price.

Symphony No. 4, Op. 71.
*** Lyrita Dig. SRCD 200 [id.]. LPO, composer.

Arnold's *Fourth Symphony* was commissioned by the BBC and, after its broadcast first performance in 1960, Andrew Porter described it as 'a symphony for fun . . . exuberant, melodious, unabashed, likeable'. It is certainly that – and more than that, too. The scoring liberally includes Latin-American percussion instruments to create original and exotic orchestral effects, and the first movement is dominated by one of those entirely winning Arnoldian lyrical tunes, which overcomes the jagged dissonance of the central episode. The slow movement brings a long-breathed, almost Mahlerian melodic flow, and the relatively gentle scherzo is catchily rhythmic and ingeniously constructed. The finale, complete with fugue, has its bizarre moments, yet in the end almost resolves the work's contradictions. Arnold's performance brings a vital and spontaneous response from his old orchestra, the LPO, and much superb playing. The recording has the remarkable naturalness of balance and feeling of realism which has always distinguished issues on the Lyrita label, but now with the subtle extra definition of digital techniques.

Symphonies Nos. 7, Op. 113; 8, Op. 124.
*** Conifer CDCF 177; *MCFC 177* [id.]. RPO, Vernon Handley.

The bitterness in the *Seventh* is inescapable. Dedicated to the composer's three children, the writing is most strongly influenced by his son Edward, tragically autistic. Even the characteristic Arnoldian whooping horn figures of the first movement are robbed of any sense of joy, and the Andante, dominated by a darkly sombre trombone cantilena, becomes an obsessive soliloquy of despair. In the finale there is a bizarre, even unnerving, change of mood, when the composer introduces a piping, folksy Irish theme which appears and disappears like a fleeting spectre, and the work ends without the clouds lifting. The *Eighth* is emotionally hardly less pungent, even if some of the pessimism seems to have lifted when the first movement brings another whimsically piquant Irish marching tune. Bleakness dominates the *Andante*, but the finale brings, at last, a return of the irrepressible vitality which we associate with Arnold's music; and the work closes in exuberance. Handley's performances of both symphonies generate great power and depth of feeling, with the most eloquent response from the RPO players, and the recording is outstandingly real and vivid. However, neither work offers an easy listening experience.

Arriaga, Juan (1806–26)

String quartets Nos. 1 in D min.; 2 in A; 3 in E flat.
*** CRD CRD 33123 (2) [id.]. Chilingirian Qt – WIKMANSON: *String quartet No. 2.* ***

These CRD recordings come from the mid-1970s and still sound good. The Chilingirians play with both conviction and feeling. There are times perhaps when they could have more lightness of touch (the minuet and finale of the *D minor* are a case in point). However, these are generally very satisfying performances, and their reappearance on CD must be warmly welcomed. These three *Quartets* are marvellous works of great warmth and spontaneity that can hold their own in the most exalted company. It is barely credible that a boy still in his teens could have produced them.

Atterberg, Kurt (1887–1974)

Symphony No. 6 in C, Op. 31; Ballad without words, Op. 56; A Värmland rhapsody, Op. 36.
** BIS Dig. CD 553 [id.]. Norrköping SO, Jun'ichi Hirokami.

In 1928 Atterberg won the $10,000 prize offered by the Columbia Graphophone [*sic.*] Company on the occasion of the Schubert Centenary with his *Sixth Symphony*; the runner-up was the *Third Symphony* of Franz Schmidt! It was immediately recorded by Sir Thomas Beecham, and Toscanini played it in 1943, since when it has unaccountably languished in neglect. It is a colourful and inventive score which deserves wide popularity. *A Värmland rhapsody* (1933) was commissioned by the Swedish Radio to mark the 75th birthday of the writer Selma Lagerlöf and it is, appropriately enough, strongly folkloric. The *Ballad without words* is much later (1958) and has many imaginative touches. The Norrköping orchestra has boasted several conductors of repute, including Herbert Blomstedt and Franz Welser-Möst, and obviously includes many sensitive players, but the string-tone lacks weight and opulence and the recording, though very clean, calls for richness.

Auber, Daniel (1782–1871)

Overtures: The Bronze horse; Fra Diavolo; Masaniello.
❀ (M) *** Mercury 434 309-2 [id.]. Detroit SO, Paray – SUPPÉ: *Overtures.* ***

Dazzling performances, full of verve and style, which will surely never be surpassed. The graceful, finely etched violin-playing in the delectable *Fra Diavolo Overture* is alone worth the Rosette, and the music-making has tremendous spirit, especially in the jaunty secondary tune of *Masaniello*. This opera, incidentally, started a Flemish uprising when it was first performed in Belgium, which led to a happy ending – a declaration of independence was signed within the year! The present recordings, made in the suitably resonant acoustic of Detroit's Old Orchestra Hall, shows Mercury engineering (1959 vintage) at its very finest.

Auric, Georges (1899–1983)

L'Éventail de Jeanne (complete ballet, including music by Delannoy, Ferroud, Ibert, Milhaud, Poulenc, Ravel, Roland-Manuel, Roussel, Florent Schmitt). *Les Mariés de la Tour Eiffel:* (complete ballet, including music by Honegger, Milhaud, Poulenc, Tailleferre).
❀ *** Chan. Dig. CHAN 8356 [id.]. Philh. O, Simon.

A carefree spirit and captivating wit run through both these composite works. The Ravel *Fanfare* is among the shortest and most original of the contributions to *L'Éventail de Jeanne*, and there are many other charming things apart from the best-known number, Poulenc's *Pastourelle*. In fact these pieces are full of imagination and fun – even the Ibert *Valse* quotes the Ravel *Valses nobles*. Geoffrey Simon and the Philharmonia Orchestra give a very good account of themselves and the Chandos recording is little short of spectacular. Its detail is quite marvellously sharp on CD.

Bacarisse, Salvator (1898–1963)

Concertino in A min. for guitar and orchestra, Op. 72.
(B) **(*) DG Compact Classics 413 156-2 (2) [id.]. Yepes, Spanish R. & TV O, Alonso – CASTELNUOVO-TEDESCO: *Guitar concerto* ***; FALLA: *Nights in the gardens of Spain* ***; RODRIGO: *Concertos.* **

This is the least distinctive component in DG's two-CD bargain compilation of concertante works for guitar, harp and piano. In Yepes's hands the slow movement has plenty of atmosphere and the variations of the finale are pleasing enough. The 1973 recording is clear and fresh.

Bacewicz, Grazyna (1909–69)

(iii; v) *Concerto for orchestra;* (i; iii; vi) *Double piano concerto;* (ii; iii; vi) *Viola concerto;* (iv) *Divertimento for strings;* (iii; v) *Pensieri Notturni.*
**(*) Olympia OCD 311 [id.]. (i) Maksymiuk, Witkowski; (ii) Kamasa; (iii) Warsaw Nat. PO; (iv) Warsaw Nat. Philharmonic CO, Teutsch; (v) Rowicki; (vi) Wislocki.

Grazyna Bacewicz was born in Lodz and studied composition with Nadia Boulanger and the violin with Carl Flesch and for a time read philosophy at Warsaw University. Before the war she pursued a career as a soloist playing under such conductors as Herman Abendroth, Kletzki and Silvestri. The present compilation of recordings, made between 1965 and 1972, serves as an admirable visiting card and reveals a composer of integrity and imagination. All the music recorded here dates from the last decade of Bacewicz's life; the *Pensieri Notturni* (1961) is evidently a key work in which she turned her back on the neo-classicism that marked her earlier pieces, and the *Concerto for orchestra* (1962) makes use of a fertile range of colouristic devices that call to mind Lutoslawski and, in the *Vivo* movement, even the scherzo of Prokofiev's *Third Symphony*. *Divertimento for strings* (1965) shows a strong sense of atmosphere, rather similar to Bartók or Blomdahl. Bacewicz shows a cultured and resourceful creative mind rather than a strongly individual profile: there is just a touch of general-purpose modernity about her music, but all the same it is well worth hearing and has far more substance to it than, say, Penderecki. Dedicated performances, particularly of the *Viola concerto* (1968) which is splendidly played by the dedicatee, Stefan Kamasa. Decent and eminently serviceable analogue recordings.

(i) *String quartets Nos. 4, 7;* (ii) *Piano quintet No. 1.*
**(*) Olympia OCD 310 [id.]. (i) Grazyna Bacewicz Warsaw String Qt; (ii) Warsaw Piano Quintet.

Grazyna Bacewicz composed seven string quartets in all, the first in 1938 and the last four years before her death. The three chamber works assembled here show much expertise in writing for the strings (she was an accomplished violinist herself). The *Fourth Quartet* (1951) and the *Piano Quintet No. 1* (1952) are rather Gallic in feeling, the *Seventh Quartet* (1965) is in a more general-purpose, post-serial style. Good performances, though the *Piano Quintet* recorded in 1969 is rather too closely balanced for comfort.

Bach, Carl Philipp Emanuel (1714–88)

Cello concertos: in A min., Wq.170; in B flat, Wq.171; in A, Wq.172.
*** Virgin Dig. VC7 90800-2; *VC7 90800-4* [id.]. Anner Bylsma, O of Age of Enlightenment, Leonhardt.

These concertos also have alternative versions for both keyboard and flute, but they suit the cello admirably. The allegros are full of life, and slow movements are impressive, particularly the hauntingly volatile *Largo con sordini, mesto* of H.439. It is difficult to imagine a better partnership to provide authentic versions of these three fine works. Outer allegros are engagingly lighthearted and alert, and in slow movements Bylsma's expressive intensity communicates strongly, without ever taking the music outside its boundaries of sensibility. These artists convey their commitment to this music persuasively and Bylsma underlines his sure understanding of its style in his excellent cadenzas.

Cello concertos: in B flat, Wq.171; in A, Wq.172.
(B) **(*) Hung. White Label HRC 117 [id.]. Csába Onczay, Liszt CO, Rolla (with CHERUBINI: *13 Contredanses* **).

Onczay, who has a warm, well-focused tone, plays very sympathetically. The accompaniments for him are polished, elegant and alert, and the recording has a pleasing ambience.

Cello concerto in A, Wq.172.
(BB) *** Virgin/Virgo Dig. VJ7 91453-2; *VJ7 91453-4* [id.]. Caroline Dale, Scottish Ens., Jonathan Rees – J. S. BACH: *Violin concertos.* ***

Caroline Dale at a spacious *Largo* plays the slow movement of the splendid *A major Cello concerto* with full expressiveness. With vigorous outer movements, this is a valuable work to have as makeweight for three of J. S. B.'s most popular violin concertos.

Flute concertos: in D min., Wq.22; in A min., Wq.166; in B flat, Wq.167; in A, Wq.168; in G, Wq.169.
*** Capriccio Dig. 10 104 (Wq.22, 166, 168); 10 105 (Wq.167, 169) [id.]. Eckart Haupf, C. P. E. Bach CO, Haenchen.

Eckart Haupf gives lively, cleanly articulated performances of these concertos, written for the court of Frederick the Great, well supported by the strong, full-bodied and vigorous accompaniments of the C. P. E. Bach Chamber Orchestra under Hartmut Haenchen. Full, atmospheric recording from East German VEB engineers.

Flute concerto in D min., Wq.22.
(BB) **(*) ASV CDQS 6012; *ZCQS 6012.* Dingfelder, ECO, Mackerras – HOFFMEISTER: *Concertos Nos. 6 & 9.* **(*)

Flute concertos: in A min.; in B flat, Wq.166/7.
(M) **(*) DG 427 132-2; *427 132-4* [id.]. Stephen Preston, E. Concert, Pinnock.

Stephen Preston plays a period instrument and gives performances of considerable accomplishment and virtuosity. He receives excellent support from Pinnock, and the recording quality has fine presence and detail.

Those who are interested in the Hoffmeister coupling rather than a C. P. E. Bach collection will find Ingrid Dingfelder's playing both spirited and stylish.

Flute concertos: in A, Wq.169; in G, Wq.169; in D min. (from *Harpsichord concerto*).
*** BMG/RCA Dig. RD 60244; *RK 60244* [60244-2-RC]. James Galway, Württemberg CO, Joerg Faerber.

James Galways plays these three works with his customary musicianship, virtuosity and polish; any stylistic doubts about his vibrato and the the warm espressivo of slow movements – from soloist and orchestra alike – are silenced by the beauty of the line and the elegance of the phrasing. Decoration is nicely judged. Galway is very nimble in finales and finds great dash for the closing *Allegro di molto* of the *D minor Concerto.* Faerber and his Württemberg orchestra accompany persuasively, with no attempt made to create 'authentic' textures. Excellent recording. Recommended, except to authenticists.

Harpsichord concerto in G min., Wq.6.
*** Capriccio Dig. 10 283 [id.]. Gerald Hambitzer, Concerto Köln – J. C. BACH: *Sinfonia;* J. C. F. BACH: *Sinfonias;* W. F. BACH: *Sinfonia* etc. ***

The *G minor Concerto,* Wq.6 (1740), is one of the most remarkable of C. P. E. Bach's early works. It moves away from the baroque concerto principles of Vivaldi and Handel to a more clearly defined dialogue between soloist and ensemble. Gerald Hambitzer is an expert and persuasive soloist, and the performance has abundant vitality and imagination. The recording is very naturally balanced.

(i) *Harpsichord concerto in D min., Wq.23;* (i–ii) *Double harpsichord concerto in F, Wq.46;* (iii) *Oboe concerto in E flat, Wq.165.*
(M) **(*) HM/BMG GD77061 [77061-RG-2]. (i) Leonhardt, (ii) Curtis, (iii) Hucke; Coll. Aur., Maier.

The better-known *D minor concerto,* Wq.23, receives a dashing and fiery performance from Gustav Leonhardt and the Collegium Aureum. The *Oboe concerto* is much later (1765) and is notable for its forward-looking and expressive slow movement. All these performances have a spirit and expressive vitality that are sometimes missing from more modern ensembles.

Double concerto in E flat for harpsichord and fortepiano; Double concerto in F for 2 harpsichords, Wq.46.
*** Erato/Warner Dig. 2292 45306-2 [id.]. Koopman, Mathot, Amsterdam Baroque O.

(i) *Double concerto in E flat for harpsichord and fortepiano; Organ concerto in G, Wq.34;* (ii) *Double harpsichord sonatina No. 2 in D, Wq.109.*
**(*) ASV Novalis Dig. 150 025-2 [id.]. Haselböck, (i) Fuller; (ii) Rainer; V. Academy.

This spirited and delightful *E flat Concerto for harpsichord and fortepiano,* which comes from Bach's last year, is recorded in this Erato version with period instruments and the inevitably lower pitch, but this does not seem to have dampened its spirits, and the textures are lucid and transparent. The *F major Concerto for two harpsichords* comes from a different world: it was composed almost half a century earlier for Frederick II's court. The Erato recording is as good as the playing. The only grumble: at 43 minutes this is short measure – but what it wants in quantity it certainly makes up for in quality.

An alternative version of the *E flat Concerto for harpsichord and fortepiano* comes from Martin Haselböck, Richard Fuller and a Viennese ensemble. The *Organ concerto* finds Carl Philipp Emanuel at his most inventive and, in its slow movement, most poetic. The *Sonatina* is another highly interesting piece. The Vienna Academy is a period-instrument group who play with much spirit though their violins are disagreeably nasal at times. The Erato issue is to be preferred.

Oboe concertos: in B flat, Wq.164; in E flat, Wq.165; Sonata for oboe and continuo in G min., Wq.135.
(M) *** Erato/Warner Dig. 2292 45430-2 [id.]. Ku Ebbinge, Amsterdam Bar. O, Koopman.

C. P. E. Bach's pair of *Oboe concertos* are very appealing in their wide range of mood, and the *Largo e mesto* of Wq.164 is plaintively haunting in Ku Ebbinge's hands. Koopman provides gracefully alert accompaniments and the recording balance is fresh and realistic, with textures transparent.

Organ concertos: in G; in E flat, Wq.34–5; Fantasia and fugue in C min., Wq.119/7; Prelude in D, Wq.70/7.
*** Capriccio Dig. 10 135 [id.]. Roland Munch, C. P. E. Bach CO, Haenchen.

With much of the writing involving simple alternation of orchestra and soloist, Hartmut Haenchen and his admirable C. P. E. Bach Chamber Orchestra reinforce the lively expressiveness of the music, alongside the soloist, Roland Munch, on a Berlin baroque organ of the 1750s. The two solo pieces are impressive too, though here the scale is much less ambitious. Full, atmospheric recording.

Berlin sinfonias: in C; in F, Wq.174/5; in E min.; in E flat, Wq.178/9; in F, Wq.181.
*** Capriccio Dig. 10 103 [id.]. C. P. E. Bach CO, Haenchen.

The *Berlin sinfonias* are most welcome as they have not previously been recorded. The playing of Haenchen's excellent C. P. E. Bach group is alert and vigorous, with airy textures and attractively sprung rhythms. Modern instruments are used in the best possible way. Slow movements have expressive commitment without any suggestion of romanticism, and there is a fine sense of balance so that the boldness of Bach's inspiration is well projected. Excellent sound.

6 Hamburg sinfonias, Wq.182/1–6.
*** DG 415 300-2 [id.]. E. Concert, Pinnock.
*** Capriccio Dig. 10 106 [id.]. C. P. E. Bach CO, Haenchen.

The six *Hamburg string sinfonias* are magnificent examples of Bach's later style when, after the years at the Berlin court, he had greater freedom in Hamburg. They are particularly striking in their unexpected twists of imagination, with wild, head-reeling modulations and sudden pauses which suggest the twentieth century rather than the eighteenth. The English Concert under Pinnock offers a performing style which, while lacking the abrasiveness of some competitors in the field of authenticity, retains great concern for eighteenth-century poise and elegance. The 1960 analogue recording sounds splendidly fresh and clear in its remastered format.

Hartmut Haenchen and the strings of the C. P. E. Bach Chamber Orchestra give attractively warm, red-blooded performances. Though ensemble is not always ideally refined, allegros are strong and vigorous, and the extra sweetness of the lovely *Adagios* is most welcome. Vivid, full recording to match.

4 Hamburg Sinfonias, Wq.183/1–4.
*** Erato/Warner Dig. 2292 45430-2 [id.]. Amsterdam Bar. O, Koopman.

Unlike the six *Hamburg sinfonias* which C. P. E. Bach wrote earlier for Baron von Swieten, these four later works involve wind as well as strings, pairs of horns, flutes and oboes, as well as a bassoon. The writing is just as refreshing in its unexpectedness and originality, product of Bach's years of relative freedom in Hamburg, after his long stint at the Prussian court in Berlin. Unlike the rival Capriccio version from the C. P. E. Bach Chamber Orchestra, this one from Koopman and his talented Amsterdam players is on period instruments, and the performances gain from that, not only in transparency of texture and natural balance but in their easy-sounding spontaneity, for Koopman tends to favour relatively relaxed speeds. Excellent Erato recording.

4 Hamburg sinfonias, Wq.183/1–4; Sinfonias: in E min., Wq.177; in C, Wq.182/3.
(M) *** Ph. 426 081-2 [id.]. ECO, Leppard.

Like their predecessors, the four *Sinfonias*, Wq.183, are not merely interesting historically but are often characterized by an emotional insistence that is disturbing and by a capacity to surprise that is quite remarkable. Leppard's performances are full of drive and have an alert intensity appropriate to this astonishing composer.

CHAMBER AND INSTRUMENTAL MUSIC

Fantasia (Fantasy-sonata) in F sharp min. (Empfindungen), Wq.80; Sonatas for piano and violin in B min., Wq.76; C min., Wq.78.
*** Denon Dig. CO 72434 [id.]. Huguette Dreyfus, Eduard Melkus.

These little-known pieces are primarily keyboard sonatas with violin obbligato, not violin sonatas in the same sense as those of Mozart or Beethoven. The subtitle of the *Fantasy-sonata*, *Empfindungen* (*The Sentiments*), gives some idea of its introspective character, which emerges immediately in the first of its twelve sections; it finds Bach at his most individual. Its two companions are less striking – though in their different way they are rewarding. They are excellently played, though the recording places Melkus marginally more forward than is ideal. In the earlier *Sonatas* Huguette Dreyfus uses a harpsichord (a Hemsch of 1754) and for the *Fantasy* a Neupert fortepiano. Strongly recommended.

Flute sonatas: in D, Wq.83; in E, Wq.84; in G, Wq.85; in G, Wq.86; in C, Wq.87.
(BB) **(*) Naxos Dig. 8.550513 [id.]. Béla Drahos, Zsuzsa Pertis (harpsichord).

These sonatas are less exploratory in idiom and less unpredictable than is often the case with this composer. They are pleasing and just avoid blandness in these simply stated and highly musical performances by Drahos and Pertis. They are recorded in an ecclesiastical acoustic; the flute is forward and seems to float in mid-air, while the harpsichord is more backward although clearly etched against the resonance. Better this than jangle and, although the acoustic could with advantage gave been drier, the effect is natural, and this replaces the previous, full-priced Delos disc by Adorján and Dreyfus which offered one sonata fewer and 22 minutes less playing time.

Flute sonatas: in E min., Wq.124; in G; in A min.; in D, Wq.127–9; in G, Wq.133; in G, Wq.134.
*** Capriccio Dig. 10 101 [id.]. Eckart Haupf, Siegfried Pank, Armin Thalheim.

This issue in the C. P. E. Bach series collects six of the composer's eleven flute sonatas in fresh, lively performances, well recorded. The six pieces last, in all, less than 50 minutes, ending with one written in Bach's Hamburg period, two years before he died, altogether lighter and more conventionally classical, presenting an interesting perspective on the rest.

Trio sonatas: in B min., Wq.76 (H.512); in A, Wq.146 (H.570); in D, H.585.
*** HM/BMG Dig. RD 77250 [77050-2-RC]. Les Adieux – J. C. BACH: *Quintets;* J. C. F. BACH: *Quartet.* ***

These three sonatas span three decades: between them, they give a good idea of the composer's artistic development. They are played with admirable style and no mean virtuosity by Les Adieux; their members include Mary Utiger, who makes a consistently beautiful sound, as does the flautist Wilbert Hazelzet in the *A major sonata*. Excellent recording.

Quartets (Trios) for flute, viola, fortepiano: in A min., D & G, Wq.93/95.
(M) *** HM/BMG GD 77052 [77052-2-RG]. Les Adieux.

Quartets for flute, viola, fortepiano (& optional) *cello: in A min., D & G, Wq.93/5;* (Keyboard) *Fantasy in C.*
*** O-L 433 189-2 [id.]. McGegan, Mackintosh, Pleeth, Hogwood.

The three quartets come from the last year of Bach's life and are all beautifully fashioned, civilized pieces with many of the expressive devices familiar from this composer. There is a highly chromatic slow movement for the D major work and some of the outer movements are characteristically unpredictable. Although the works were designated by Bach as *Quartets*, no bass part survives. Piano, flute and viola are musically handled so equally, and everything is so minutely written out, that an added cello would always remain 'the fifth wheel on the wagon'. The playing of Les Adieux matches the music in its finish, lightness of touch and spontaneity.

In the Oiseau-Lyre performances the cello line is added judiciously where it seems useful to reinforce the texture, and the result has that bit more weight and gravitas without losing any of the charm of the writing. Christopher Hogwood uses a fortepiano rather than harpsichord and makes a good case for doing so (with documentary support in the notes). He secures a wide dynamic range and clean, intelligent articulation. The playing overall is absolutely first rate; the recording is most naturally balanced and could hardly be bettered. Moreover the keyboard *Fantasia in C* is a most remarkable work – it is roughly contemporary with Mozart's *C minor Fantasy* and is more than just a bonus. It is splendidly played. This costs more than the Harmonia Mundi CD but is well worth it.

Sinfonia a tre voci in D; 12 Variations on La Folia, Wq.118/9; Trio sonatas: in B flat, Wq.158; in C min. (Sanguineus & Melancholicus), Wq.161/1; Viola da gamba sonata in D, Wq.137.
*** Hyp. Dig. CDA 66239 [id.]. Purcell Qt.

The *Variations on La Folia* are fresh and inventive, particularly in Robert Woolley's hands, but the remaining pieces are hardly less rewarding. The *C minor Trio sonata* of 1749 presents a most imaginative dialogue between two players, depicting two of the four temperaments. It is as individual – indeed, quirky – as much of his later music. The Purcell Quartet play with sensitivity and seem well attuned to the particularly individual sensibility of this composer, and in the *Gamba sonata* Richard Boothby is most persuasive. The Hyperion recording is well balanced, faithful and present.

VOCAL MUSIC

Anbetung dem Erbamer (Easter cantata) Wq.243; Auf, shicke dich trecht feierlich (Christmas cantata), Wq.249; Heilig, Wq.217; Klopstocks Morgengesang am Schöpfungfeste, Wq.239.
*** Capriccio Dig. 10 208 [id.]. Schlick, Lins, Pregardien, Elliott, Varcoe, Schwarz, Rheinische Kantorei, Kleine Konzert, Hermann Max.

Carl Philipp Emanuel Bach was a friend of the poet, Klopstock, who was to write his epitaph; and *Klopstocks Morgengesang am Schöpfungfeste* (*Klopstock's morning song on the celebration of Creation*) bears eloquent witness to their friendship, for it is a work of many beauties and is well performed by these artists. *Anbetung dem Erbamer* (*Worship of the merciful*) is another late work, written for the Easter celebrations of 1784, and full of modulatory surprises. *Auf, shicke dich trecht feierlich* (*Up, be reconciled*) was written for Christmas 1775, though the subject-matter is only tenuously seasonal. *Heilig* (*Holy*) (1779) was also part of a Christmas work. A record of unusual interest, very well performed and naturally recorded.

(i) *Die Auferstehung und Himmelfahrt Jesu (The Resurrection and Ascension of Jesus), Wq.240;* (ii) *Gott hat den Herrn auferweckt (Easter cantata), Wq.244.*
*** Capriccio Dig. 10 206/7 (2) [id.]. (i) Schlick, Lins, Pregardien; (ii) Elliott, Varcoe, Schwarz; Rheinische Kantorei, Kleine Konzert, Hermann Max.

Carl Philipp Emanuel numbered *Die Auferstehung und Himmelfahrt Jesu* among his finest works. It was composed in the late 1770s and was highly regarded by Mozart, who conducted three performances of it in 1788. This two-CD set offers good solo singing and generally very good playing; the choral singing for the most part is respectable without being distinguished. The oratorio lasts about 75 minutes and the second CD offers an earlier *Easter cantata* from 1756. Impressive music which no one with an interest in this composer should pass over.

Die letzten Leiden des Erlösers (The Last Sufferings of the Saviour), Wq.233.
(M) *** HM/BMG GD 77042 [77042-2-RG]. Schlick, Reyghere, Patriasz, Prégardien, Egmond, Ghent Coll. Vocale, La Petite Bande, Kuijken.

Die letzten Leiden has good claims to be considered one of Carl Philipp Emanuel's masterpieces, and it is given a first-class performance by the excellent team of soloists assembled here. The singing of the Collegium Vocale of Ghent is eloquent, and the playing of La Petite Bande under Sigiswald Kuijken is predictably vivid and alive. Fine, well-balanced recording.

Magnificat, Wq.215.
(M) *** Decca 421 148-2. Palmer, Watts, Tear, Roberts, King's College Ch., ASMF, Ledger – J. S. BACH: *Magnificat.* ***

With vividly atmospheric recording, the performance under Philip Ledger comes electrically to life, with choir, soloists and orchestra all in splendid form. Aptly coupled with Johann Sebastian's earlier setting, this CD can be strongly recommended. It sounds extremely vivid.

Bach, Johann Christian (1735–82)

Bassoon concertos: in B flat; in E flat.
(B) ** Hung. White Label HRC 041 [id.]. Gábor Janota, Liszt CO, Rolla; or József Vajda, Budapest SO, Lehel – HUMMEL: *Bassoon concerto.* ***

Good playing from both soloists (especially from Janota in the latter) and warm, polished accompaniments.

Sinfonia in G min. Op. 6/6.
*** Capriccio Dig. 10 283 [id.]. Concerto Köln – C. P. E. BACH: *Harpsichord concerto;* J. C. F. BACH: *Sinfonias;* W. F. BACH: *Sinfonia* etc. ***

This remarkable symphony, written in 1770 when Johann Christian was at the height of his fame, is altogether darker than is usual with this most gracious and genial of composers, and the

Concerto Köln discover greater dramatic intensity in it than do most ensembles. It is recorded as excellently as it is played.

Sinfonia concertante in A for violin, cello and orchestra; Grand Overture in E flat.
(*) Sony MK 39964 [id.]. Yo-Yo Ma, Zukerman, St Paul CO – BOCCHERINI: *Cello concerto* (arr. Grützmacher). *

Generally this is an enjoyable pairing and the playing of the soloists in the *Sinfonia concertante* establishes a fine musical interplay, although the cadenza is over-elaborated. Good sound, with excellent stereo effects.

Sinfonias concertantes in A for violin, cello and orchestra, SC 3; E flat for 2 violins, 2 violas, cello and orchestra (MSC E flat 1); E flat for 2 clarinets, bassoon and orchestra (MSC E flat 4); G for 2 violins, cello and orchestra, SC 1.
*** ASV CDDCA 651 [id.]. London Festival O, Ross Pople.

There are some 18 *Sinfonias concertantes*, and the four recorded here are delightfully fresh and inventive. The performances are eminently vital and enthusiastic – this band is obviously composed of excellent players, and the recording is very bright and present. This is an invigorating disc which can be recommended strongly. (The numbering above is based on Ernest Warburton's system, SC indicating works published in the eighteenth century, and MSC those printed only recently.)

Oboe quartet in B flat, Op. 8/6.
*** Denon Dig. C37 7119 [id.]. Holliger, Salvatore Qt – M. HAYDN: *Divertimenti;* MOZART: *Adagio.* ***

The unpretentious elegance of J. C. Bach's *Oboe quartet* is beautifully caught by the incomparable Holliger and his stylish partners. An excellent coupling for even more compelling works, all vividly recorded.

Quintets: in C, Op. 11/1; in D, Op. 11/6; in D, Op. 22/1. Sextet in C.
*** DG Dig. 423 385-2 [id.]. English Concert.

This is a self-recommending collection. The music, delectably scored for unexpected combinations of instruments, is wonderfully fresh and inventive in these spirited performances, with the sounds of the original instruments adding bite and colour and readily finding the music's charm. The sound has splendid realism and presence.

Quintets (for flute, oboe, violin, viola & continuo) in G & F, Op. 11/2–3.
*** HM/BMG Dig. RD 77250 [77050-2-RC]. Les Adieux – C. P. E. BACH: *Trio sonatas;* J. C. F. BACH: *Quartet.* ***

The *Quintets* both come from 1774, when the composer was spending some time at the Mannheim court, and find Johann Christian at his most delightful. Their charm has a freshness and innocence that it is difficult to resist; there are moments of considerable expressive poignancy, which these imaginative and elegant players make the most of. This is one of the best records devoted to the sons of Bach and the sound-quality is first class.

The Bach family before Johann Sebastian

Bach, Johann Christoph (1642–1703) **Bach, Johann Michael** (1648–94)

Bach, Georg Christoph (1642–97) **Bach, Heinrich** (1615–92)

J. C. BACH: Cantatas: *Ach, dass ich Wassers g'nug hätte; Er erhub sich Streit; Die Furcht des Herren; Herr wende dich und sei mir gnädig; Meine Freundin; Wir bist du denn.* J. M. BACH: Cantatas: *Ach bleib uns, Herr Jesu Christ; Ach, wie sehnlich wart' ich der Zeit; Auf lasst uns den Herren loben; Es ist ein grosser Gewinn; Liebster Jesu, hör mein Flehen.* G. C. BACH: Cantata: *Siehe, wie fein und lieblich.* H. BACH: *Ich danke dir, Gott.*
*** DG 419 253-2 (2) [id.]. Soloists, Rheinische Kantorei, Col. Mus. Ant., Goebel.

These two CDs include all the cantatas and vocal concertos by Bach's forefathers that he preserved, with, in addition, a vocal concerto, *Herr, wende dich*, by Johann Christoph Bach. This set breaks new ground for the gramophone and does so with great distinction, for the performances and recording are of the very highest quality. An invaluable issue and indispensable for collectors with an interest in Johann Sebastian.

Bach, Johann Christoph Friedrich (1732–95)

Sinfonias: in D min.; E flat, Wfv 1/3 & 10.
*** Capriccio Dig. 10 283 [id.]. Concerto Köln – C. P. E. BACH: *Harpsichord concerto;* J. C. BACH: *Sinfonia;* W. F. BACH: *Sinfonia* etc. ***

Johann Christoph Friedrich spent the greater part of his life in relative isolation at the court of Bückenburg. Much of his work was lost during the Second World War. The rather Italianate *D minor Symphony* recorded here turned up recently in the Archives of the Moravian Church in North Carolina. The other and later symphony (*c.* 1770), which came to light in the collection of a Belgian antiquarian dealer in the mid-1960s, is far more indebted to Carl Philipp Emanuel. Both works recorded here are elegantly written and are well worth investigating, even if Johann Christoph Friedrich does not have the strong musical personality of his brothers. The playing of the Concerto Köln is enthusiastic, sprightly and sensitive, and they are excellently recorded.

Flute quartet No. 3 in C.
*** HM/BMG Dig. RD 77250 [77050-2-RC]. Les Adieux – C. P. E. BACH: *Trio sonatas;* J. C. BACH: *Quintets.* ***

There are six *Flute quartets* from 1768 and this is the first recording of the delightful *C major*. Johann Christoph Friedrich's music is untroubled by any depths but has a genuine charm that is beautifully communicated by these accomplished players. Excellent recording.

Musikalisches Vielerley: Cello sonata in A.
*** Sony Dig. SK 45945 [id.]. Anner Bylsma, Bob van Asperen – J. S. BACH: *Viola da gamba sonatas Nos 1–3.* ***

This *Sonata* first appeared in 1770, when it was published in a music periodical, *Musikalisches Vielerley*, edited by Carl Philipp Emanuel Bach. It is a work of slight but not negligible musical interest, and it is here played imaginatively by Anner Bylsma, using a piccolo cello, and by Bob van Asperen on a 'trunk' or chamber organ. Excellently recorded.

Bach, Johann Sebastian (1685–1750)

Brandenburg concertos Nos. 1–6, BWV 1046/51; Orchestral Suites Nos. 1–4, BWV 1066/9.
❀ (M) (**(*)) EMI mono CHS7 640472 (3) [id.]. Adolf Busch Chamber Players, Busch.
**(*) EMI Dig. CDS7 47881-8 (3). ASMF, Marriner.
(M) **(*) DG 423 492-2 (3). E. Concert, Pinnock.

It is fascinating to hear performances from the mid-1930s, which then marked a breakthrough in Bach playing. At that time it was still common to hear these works on a full orchestra. By contrast Adolf Busch assembled a small chamber force much closer to what Bach would have expected, though even *Brandenburg No. 3* has multiple strings, not one per part, and when continuo is used, it is played on the piano, not the harpsichord. Nevertheless this version of the *Brandenburgs* must take a special place. For some older collectors it may even be the preferred choice, but it is not solely a matter of nostalgia; even younger collectors coming to these performances afresh will find them rather rather special. Although modern instruments are used, there is a greater 'authenticity' of spirit than in many rigid modern performances. Rudolf Serkin, Busch's son-in-law, plays the piano, and the other soloists are all artists of comparable calibre, including Evelyn Rothwell on the oboe, Aubrey Brain (father of Dennis) on the horn, George Eskdale on the Bach trumpet and Marcel Moyse on the flute. Serkin was at the height of his form at this period, and his playing is distinguished by the greatest delicacy: indeed his contribution to No. 5 is quite exceptional. The most memorable single movement is the *Adagio* of No. 1 with its eloquent dialogue between Adolf Busch and Evelyn Rothwell which has a poignant tenderness and poetry that is unforgettable. Though slow movements are not sentimentalized, the phrasing has full expressive warmth, and speeds are almost always slower than we would expect today. That is also true of many of the fast movements, as in the outer movements of Nos 1 and 6, but with such bouncy, resilient rhythms the results never drag. The

Suites also stand up well; there is none of the mass-produced music-making that afflicts so many modern Bach performances. But there the interpretation is rather more controversial, when the slow speeds for the introductions do become very heavy without double-dotting. The celebrated *Air* of No. 3 is lovingly affectionate at a broad speed, with the piano continuo prominent. The sound is naturally not as fresh or vivid as a modern recording but it is more than acceptable.The transfers have plenty of body and a sense of presence, but the treble emphasis often puts an acid edge on violins and the surface-noise is consistently prominent. The result is watercolour rather than a freshly cleaned oil painting, but the actual performances could hardly be more richly hued.

Marriner's latest, EMI digital recordings of the *Brandenburgs* and *Suites* are linked together on three CDs. This is his third recording, with fine teamwork, superb ensemble and well-judged speeds, never too hectic. However, although the playing is freshly conceived, it also has a certain urbane quality (although this does not apply to George Malcolm's harpsichord contribution, notably in the special link provided in No. 3). Many will like performances with a little more eccentricity, not quite so safe, and they will turn to Marriner's earlier Philips set (see below) or, if original instruments are required, to Gardiner, or to Pinnock. Marriner's new recording of the *Suites* is a worthy successor to his earliest, Argo set, and the vividness of the playing is enhanced by the excellent sound, full in texture yet transparent, too.

The merits of Pinnock's *Brandenburg concertos* are considerable, but the *Suites* are somewhat more controversial, bringing a distinct loss of breadth and grandeur.

Brandenburg concertos Nos. 1–6; Orchestral Suites Nos. 2–3, BWV 1067/8.
(M) *(*) Teldec/Warner Dig. 9031 75858-2; *9031 75858-4* (*Concertos Nos. 1, 2 & 4; Suite No. 2*); 9031 75859-2; *9031 75859-4* [id.]. (*Concertos Nos. 3, 5 & 6; Suite No. 3*). VCM, Harnoncourt.

Admirers of Harnoncourt may be tempted by his authentic approach to the *Brandenburgs*, recorded in the early 1980s, particularly as the two favourite *Suites* are also included. However, the playing in the latter works is disappointingly lacking in finesse and the otherwise vivid recording is not always convincingly balanced. There is some expert playing, both solo and ensemble, in the *Brandenburgs* but Harnoncourt's speeds are slow, rhythms heavy and the effect too often sounds laboured. Moreover the artificially bright and clinically clear recording gives an aggressive projection to the music-making.

Brandenburg concertos Nos. 1–6, BWV 1046/51.
(M) *** DG Dig. 435 081-2; *435 081-4* (*Nos. 1, 3 & 5*); 435 082-2; *435 082-4* (*Nos. 2, 4 & 6*) [id.]. E. Concert, Trevor Pinnock.
*** Ph. 400 076/7-2 (2) [id.]. ASMF, Marriner.
(B) *** Pickwick Dig. PCD 830; *CIMPC 830* (1–3); PCD 845; *CIMPC 845* (4–6) [id.]. ECO, Ledger.
(M) *** Ph. 420 345/6-2 [id.]; *420 345/6-4*. ECO Leppard.
(M) **(*) Collins Dig. 3054-2 (*Nos. 1–3*); 3055-2 (*Nos. 4–6*). Consort of London, Robert Haydon Clark.
**(*) Virgin Dig. VCD7 90747-2; *VCD7 90747-4* (2) [id.]. O. of Age of Enlightenment.
**(*) DG Dig. 431 660-2 (2) [id.]. COE.

The reissue of Pinnock's set of *Brandenburgs* at mid-price could be a clear first recommendation for those favouring these works played on original instruments, were it not for the Linde EMI compilation – see below – which includes in addition the *Musical offering*. Undoubtedly Pinnock's DG versions represent the peak of his achievement as an advocate of authentic performance, with sounds that are clear and refreshing but not too abrasive.

For those who still cannot quite attune their ears to the style of string playing favoured by the authentic school, there are several excellent alternatives. Marriner's analogue Philips set has been remastered since it was first issued and the sound is both natural and lively. Above all, these performances communicate warmth and enjoyment; and they are strong in personality, with star soloists adding individuality to the concertos without breaking the consistency of beautifully sprung performances. George Malcolm is the ideal continuo player, as he is in the later EMI recording. However, this set has to face strong competition in the mid-priced range.

On Pickwick, Ledger has the advantage of fresh and detailed digital recording. He directs resilient, well-paced readings of all six concertos, lively yet never over-forced. The slow movements in particular are most beautifully done, persuasively and without mannerism. Flutes rather than recorders are used in No. 4.

Leppard's Philips set, in the mid-priced range, is higher-powered than Ledger's, whose gentler manner will for many be easier to live with. But the exhilaration of the Leppard set is undeniable; there is much to enjoy here. The remastered analogue sound is full and ample.

Robert Haydon Clark draws on the scholarship of the late Thurston Dart for his new set of *Brandenburgs* (as Sir Neville Marriner once did before him), which aims at recreating the first edition of these works, long before Bach thought of sending them to the Margrave of Brandenburg. However Haydon Clark has revised Dart's scholarship by making judgements of his own. Thus, although he uses a horn instead of a trumpet in No. 2, he abandons the squeaky sopranino recorders favoured in the old Philips/Marriner set, replacing them with specially constructed treble recorders in G (instead of the usual F), and very effective they prove. The substitution of the horn is another matter; to most ears the trumpet sounds more convincing. In the *Third concerto* the simple cadence separating the two outer movements has been extended by the interpolation of the *Adagio* from the *Trio Sonata in G*, BWV 1038, which one welcomes, for the beautifully warm, serene playing in slow movements is one of the most enjoyable features of this music-making. Allegros are sprightly, lively but not raced, and solo playing is consistently polished, with Virginia Black making a fine keyboard contribution to the *Fifth concerto*. In the *Sixth*, cellos are chosen, rather than a pair of viole da gamba, and the sonority is appealingly full even if there is some loss of transparency; indeed the sounds of the modern instruments used here combine warmth with freshness, as the recording is first class. So for those looking for an alternative view of these many-faceted masterpieces, this could prove highly rewarding.

With the direction shared among four violinists, Monica Huggett (Nos. 2, 4 and 6), Catherine Mackintosh (No. 1), Alison Bury (No. 3) and Elizabeth Wallfisch (No. 5), the Orchestra of the Age of the Enlightenment presents an amiable set of *Brandenburgs* on period instruments. These performances bring all the advantages of light, clear textures and no sense of haste, even when a movement is taken faster than has become traditional. With generally excellent recording, this makes a good alternative to the outstanding version by Trevor Pinnock on DG Archiv; but the OAE ensemble cannot quite match that of the English Concert in crispness.

A spirit of fun infects the COE version. Using modern instruments, these are among the happiest performances ever, marked by easily bouncing rhythms and warmly affectionate – but never sentimental – slow movements. Some may want more severity but the joyful exuberance of Bach's inspiration is inescapable. Unfortunately, the first movement of No. 1 – the movement which many will sample first – takes relaxation too far, becoming almost ragged; conversely, the first movement of No. 6 is uncharacteristically rigid. Otherwise these performances, well recorded, give pure joy.

Brandenburg concertos Nos. 1–6; A Musical offering.
(M) *** EMI Dig./Analogue CMS7 63434-2 (2). Linde Cons.

With sprung rhythms and generally well-chosen tempi, the Linde Consort deserve to rank alongside Pinnock's set. But, quite apart from the considerable bonus of the *Musical offering*, many will prefer their version of the *Brandenburgs*, for the 1981 EMI recording is rather fuller than the DG Archiv sound, with the strings very slightly less immediate. Linde is as stylish and accomplished as any of his rivals, and he and his six colleagues offer the preferred version of this work using original instruments. They are again warmly as well as clearly recorded.

Flute concertos: in C (from *BWV 1055*); *in E min.* (from movements of *Cantata No. 35*); *in G min.* (from *BWV 1056*); *Sinfonia* from *Cantata No. 209*.
(M) **(*) Sony Dig. MDK 46510 [id.]. Rampal, Ars Redivivia, Munclinger.

If you enjoy transcriptions of Bach for the flute – and they are easy to enjoy here – it is difficult to imagine them being played better than by Jean-Pierre Rampal. Munclinger, who made the arrangements, provides sympathetic accompaniments, although rhythmically he does not quite display Rampal's lightness of touch. However, those who count minutes will note that there are only 42½ of them here.

(i) *Flute concerto in E min. (from BWV 1059 and BWV 35; ed. Radeke); Suite No. 2 in B min., BWV 1067;* (ii) *Trio sonata No. 4 in G, BWV 1039; The Musical offering: Trio sonata in C min., BWV 1079.*
(M) ** BMG/RCA GD 86517. James Galway; (i) Zagreb Soloists, Ninic; (ii) Kyung-Wha Chung, Moll, Welsh.

The eminently musical James Galway plays freshly in the concertante works (though the accompaniment in the *B minor Suite* is heavier, less chimerical than its soloist). He seems equally at home in the *Trio sonatas*, although here he dominates in the sound balance, and the playing of his excellent partners is made to sound thin and understated. The digital remastering has brightened everything up, and removed some of the glamour from the string textures; even the flute sounds slightly less rounded than on the original LPs

Harpsichord concertos Nos. 1 in D min.; 2 in E; 3 in D, 4 in A; 5 in F; 6 in F; 7 in G min., BWV 1052/8.
*** DG Dig. 415 991-2 (1–3); 415 992-2 (4–7) [id.]. Pinnock, E. Concert.

Trevor Pinnock plays with real panache, his scholarship tempered by excellent musicianship. There are occasions when one feels his tempi are a little too fast and unrelenting, but for the most part there is little cause for complaint. On the contrary, the performances give much pleasure and the period instruments are better played than on most issues of this kind. Both CDs have the advantage of great clarity of texture. Apart from the very quick tempi, which may strike an unsympathetic note, this set is thoroughly recommendable.

Harpsichord concertos Nos. 1 in D min., BWV 1052; 5 in F min., BWV 1056; Double harpsichord concerto No. 1 in C min., BWV 1060; Triple harpsichord concerto No. 2 in C, BWV 1064; Quadruple harpsichord concerto in A min., BWV 1065.
(M) *** Ph. 422 497-2 [id.]. Leppard, Andrew Davis, Ledger, Verlet, ECO, Leppard.

Harpsichord concertos Nos. 2 in E, BWV 1053; 4 in A, BWV 1055; Double harpsichord concerto No. 2 in C, BWV 1061; Triple harpsichord concerto No. 1 in D min., BWV 1063.
(M) *** Ph. 426 084-2 [id.]. Leppard, Andrew Davis, Ledger, ECO, Leppard.

Harpsichord concerto Nos. 3 in D, BWV 1054; 6 in F, BWV 1057; 7 in G min., BWV 1058; (i) *Double harpsichord concerto No. 3 in C min., BWV 1062.*
(M) *** Ph. 426 448-2 [id.]. Leppard; (i) Ledger, ECO, Leppard.

For those happy with modern instruments, Leppard and Davis play with skill and flair, as do their colleagues in the multiple concertos; the ECO shows plenty of life and the performances communicate such joy in the music that criticism is disarmed. The Philips sound is very realistic.

Clavier concertos Nos. 1–7, BWV 1052/8.
*** Decca Dig. 425 676-2 (2) [id.]. András Schiff (piano), COE.

Clavier concertos Nos. 1 in D min., BWV 1052; 2 in E, BWV 1053; 3 in D, BWV 1054.
(BB) *** Naxos Dig. 8.550422 [id.]. Hae-won Chang (piano), Camerata Cassovia, Robert Stankovsky.

Clavier concertos Nos. 4 in A, BWV 1055; 5 in F min., BWV 1056; 6 in F, BWV 1057; 7 in G min., BWV 1058.
(BB) *** Naxos Dig. 8. 550423 [id.]. Hae-won Chang (piano), Camerata Cassovia, Robert Stankovsky.

András Schiff has already given us three concertos, BWV 1052 and 1055–6 on Denon C37 7236, but they are now superseded by this complete set for Decca, most naturally recorded, with a well-nigh perfect balance and greater transparency and realism in the orchestral sound. As in his solo Bach records, Schiff's control of colour and articulation never seeks to present merely a harpsichord imitation, and his shaping of Bach's lovely slow movements brings fine sustained lines and a subtle variey of touch, notably the *Siciliana* of BWV 1053 and the famous *Largo* of BWV 1056 which have a pleasing simplicity and natural eloquence. He directs the Chamber Orchestra of Europe from the keyboard and chooses spirited, uncontroversial tempi for allegros, at the same time providing decoration that always adds to the joy and sparkle of the music-making. This makes a clear first choice for those who, like us, enjoy Bach on the piano and is altogether preferable to Gavrilov's competing EMI set, although Gavrilov has his own insights to offer.

The splendid Naxos set marks the début both of the highly gifted young Korean pianist, Hae-won Chang, and of the excellent chamber ensemble drawn from members of the CSSR State Philharmonic Orchestra, based in Košice. Miss Chang is a highly sympathetic Bach exponent, playing flexibly yet with strong rhythmic feeling, decorating nimbly and not fussily. Robert Stankovsky directs freshly resilient accompaniments; and both artists understand the need for a subtle gradation of light and shade. The digital recording, made in the House of Arts, Košice, is first class, with the piano balanced not too far forward.

Clavier concertos Nos. 1 in D min., BWV 1052; 2 in E, BWV 1053; 4 in A, BWV 1055; 5 in F min., BWV 1056.

(M) **(*) EMI Dig. CDD7 64055-2 [id.]. Andrei Gavrilov (piano), ASMF, Marriner.

(i) *Clavier concertos Nos. 3 in D, BWV 1054; 6 in F, BWV 1057; 7 in G min., BWV 1058. French suite No. 5 in G, BWV 816.*
(M) **(*) EMI Dig. CDD7 64293-2 [id.]; *ET 764293-4.* Andrei Gavrilov (piano); (i) ASMF, Marriner.

In terms of dexterity and clarity of articulation Andrei Gavrilov cannot be faulted and he produces some beautiful sound when his playing is lyrical and relaxed. If at times one feels he is pushing on relentlessly and that his incisive touch can be a bit unremitting in some movements, there are a lot of memorable things, too. The 1986 Abbey Road recordings are excellently balanced. The second reissued disc includes also the most popular of the Bach *French suites.* Here again Gavrilov's playing has plenty of life and character and the part-writing is always clear. The piano recording is most believable.

Clavier concerto No. 1 in D min., BWV 1052.
(B) **(*) Pickwick Dig. PCD 964; *IMPC 964* [id.]. Orazio Maione, ECCO, Aadland – HAYDN: *Piano concerto in D;* MOZART: *Piano concerto No. 8.* **(*)

This disc is a showcase for three talented young Italian pianists. The thirty-year-old Orazio Maione shows himself no mean Bach player, articulating cleanly and buoyantly in the allegros and finding a cool, expressive line for the *Adagio.* Eivind Aadland directs spirited accompaniments with the ECCO and the recording is well balanced and truthful.

Clavier concertos Nos. 1 in D min., BWV 1052; 3 in D, BWV 1054; 5 in F min., BWV 1056; 6 in F, BWV 1057.
(M) *** Teldec/Warner Dig. 9031 74779-2 [id.]. Cyprien Katsaris (piano), Liszt CO, Rolla.

Cyprien Katsaris possesses the most remarkable technique and feeling for colour, which are to be heard to excellent advantage in this vividly recorded and well-filled disc. The playing of the Liszt Chamber Orchestra, surely one of the very finest chamber ensembles in the world, is splendidly supportive. Exhilarating and imaginative performances all round.

Double harpsichord concertos: Nos. 1 in C min.; 2 in C; 3 in C min., BWV 1060/2.
**(*) DG Dig. 415 131-2 [id.]. Pinnock, Gilbert, E. Concert.

The character of the Pinnock performances is robust, with the balance forward and the performances very strongly projected. The combination of period instruments and playing of determined vigour certainly makes a bold impression, but the relatively unrelaxed approach to the slow movements will not appeal to all ears. The lively recording has very striking presence on CD.

Double clavier concertos Nos. 1 in C min., BWV 1060; 2 in C, BWV 1061; Triple clavier concerto in D min., BWV 1063; Quadruple clavier concerto in A min., BWV 1065.
*** DG Dig. 415 655-2 [id.]. Eschenbach, Frantz, Oppitz, Schmidt (pianos), Hamburg PO, Eschenbach.

Helmut Schmidt, the German ex-Chancellor, joins his friends, Eschenbach and Frantz, alongside Gerhard Oppitz in the *Quadruple concerto* – and very enjoyable it is. The other concertos are presented with comparable vigour, with slow movements correspondingly thoughtful and responsive. The recording is rather resonant, but the spirit of this record is very communicative. In spite of the resonance the overall sound-picture is very believable.

Double harpsichord concertos Nos. 1 & 3, BWV 1060 & 1062; Double concerto for violin & oboe, BWV 1060; Double violin concerto in D min., BWV 1043.
*** O-L Dig. 421 500-2 [id.]. Schröder, Hirons, Rousset, Hogwood, Mackintosh, Hammer, AAM, Hogwood.

Jaap Schröder's and Christopher Hirons' account of the *D minor concerto for two violins* comes from the early 1980s. Oiseau Lyre have added new recordings of the transcription for violin and oboe and for two harpsichords (a Hemsch of 1761 and a Ruckers of 1646 modified by Taskin in 1785) imaginatively played by Christopher Hogwood and Christophe Rousset. This may be didactic in purpose but the results are pleasing particularly in view of the clean and truthful recording.

Triple harpsichord concertos Nos. 1 in D min.; 2 in C, BWV 1063/4; Quadruple harpsichord concerto in A min., BWV 1065.

**(*) DG Dig. 400 041-2 [id.]. Pinnock, Gilbert, Mortensen, Kraemer, E. Concert.

Fine playing here but the slightly aggressive style of the music-making – everything alert, vigorously paced and forwardly projected – emphasizes the bravura of Bach's conceptions.

Oboe concertos: in A (from *BWV 1055*); *in D min.* (from *BWV 1059*); *in F* (from *BWV 1053*).
*** DG Dig. 429 225-2; *429 225-4* [id.]. Douglas Boyd, COE.
*** Ph. Dig. 415 851-2 [id.]. Heinz Holliger, ASMF, Iona Brown.

Douglas Boyd, the brilliant principal oboe of COE from its foundation, as soloist directs his colleagues in delectable performances of concertos reconstructed from keyboard concertos and cantata movements. Boyd's resilient and imaginative playing goes with well-sprung rhythms, bringing an infectious sense of fun. On the whole this may be preferred to Holliger, who at times leans towards Romantic expressiveness in slow movements. First-rate sound.

Organ concertos (reconstructed and ed. Schureck): *Nos. 1 in D min.* (from *BWV 146 & BWV 1052*); *2 in D* (from *BWV 49, BWV 169 & BWV 1053*); *3 in D min.* (from *BWV 35* and *BWV 1059*); *Sinfonia in D, BWV 1045; Canatata No. 29: Sinfonia.*
*** Argo Dig. 425 479-2; *425 479-4* [id.]. Peter Hurford (organ of Lyons Concert Hall, York University), N. Sinfonia, Richard Hickox.

These works have nothing to do with Bach's solo organ concertos but are reconstructions from cantata sinfonias, scored for organ, wind and strings. Bach also used these allegros for the outer movements of his harpsichord concertos, and the remaining music is taken from this same source. R. J. Schureck argues that the originals may have been conceived with the organ in mind, as recent research suggests that the cantatas predate the works for harpsichord. Whatever the truth of the matter, these arrangements are highly effective and, given Peter Hurford's bright registrations on this eminently suitable York organ and the light, clean orchestral textures, this lively music-making is very enjoyable. Two extra sinfonias are thrown in for good measure: the *Sinfonia in D* is Bach's spectacular transcription of the *Prelude* from the *Unaccompanied Violin partita No. 3 in E*, BWV 1006.

Violin concertos Nos. (i) *1, BWV 1041;* (ii) *2, BWV 1042;* (iii) *Double violin concerto, BWV 1043;* (iv) *Double concerto for violin & oboe in D min., BWV 1060.*
❀ (M) *** Ph. 420 700-2. Grumiaux; (iii) Krebbers, (iv) Holliger; (i–iii) Les Solistes Romandes, Arpad Gerecz; (iv) New Philh. O, Edo de Waart.
(M) *(*) Ph. Dig. 432 036-2; *432 036-4* [id.]. Kremer; (iv) Holliger; ASMF.

Arthur Grumiaux is joined in the *Double concerto* by Hermann Krebbers. The result is an outstanding success. The way Grumiaux responds to the challenge of working with another great artist comes over equally clearly in the concerto with oboe, reconstructed from the *Double harpsichord concerto in C minor.* Grumiaux's performances of the two solo concertos are equally satisfying. Les Solistes Romandes under Gerecz provide crisply rhythmic allegros and are sensitively supportive in the expressive music. The digital remastering produces transparently fresh yet warm sound and gives the soloists great presence.

Kremer adopts (by electronic means) both solo roles in the *Double concerto* and thus the interplay of human personality is lost in this most human of works. Kremer also directs the accompanying ensemble, so these interpretations cannot be accused of any kind of artistic inconsistency – indeed they have the forward thrust of a determined advocate, in slow movements as well as allegros which are extremely vigorous. The end effect is relentless and, despite excellent recording – the CD is exceptionally vivid – this collection offers only limited musical rewards. Holliger is at his distinguished best in BWV 1060 and Kremer makes a good partner in a fresh performance with a serene central *Adagio*, but this hardly compensates for the lack of appeal of the other three concertos.

Violin concertos Nos. 1 in A min.; 2 in E; (i) *Double concerto, BWV 1041/3.*
(M) *** HM/BMG GD 77006; *GK 77006* [77006-2-RG; *77006-4-RG*]. Sigiswald Kuijken; (i) Lucy van Dael; La Petite Bande.
(M) *** DG 427 114-2 [id.]. Melkus, (i) Rantos; Vienna Capella Academica (with VIVALDI: *Concerto for viola d'amore and lute, RV 540* ***).

Kuijken is a fine Bach player, and these performances of the *Violin concertos* go to the top of the list for those wanting period performances on original instruments. The slight edge on the solo timbre is painless and La Petite Bande provide lively, resilient allegros, the playing both polished and alert. Excellent, well-balanced, 1981 digital recording.

Melkus has the advantage of well-balanced DG recording from the early 1970s. Throughout, one has the impression of a happy balance between scholarship and musical freshness. His coupling is Vivaldi's *Concerto for viola d'amore and lute*, RV 540, in which he is ably partnered by Konrad Ragossnig. This is most memorably played and beautifully recorded.

Violin concertos Nos. 2 in E, BWV 1042; in G min. (from *BWV 1056);* (i) *Double violin concerto in D min., BWV 1043.*
(BB) *** Virgin/Virgo Dig. VJ7 91453-2; *VJ7 91453-4* [id.]. Jonathan Rees, (i) with Jane Murdoch; Scottish Ens., Jonathan Rees – C. P. E. BACH: *Cello concerto.* ***

With forward and bright sound, well detailed, Jonathan Rees directs the Scottish Ensemble in warm, buoyant readings of three of Bach's violin concertos. Allegros are infectiously sprung, while slow movements are allowed full expressiveness without sentimentality. A bargain.

Double concerto for violin and oboe in D min., BWV 1060.
*** Ph. Dig. 411 466-2 [id.] (with *Easter oratorio: Sinfonia*). Holliger, Kremer – VIVALDI: *Oboe; Violin concertos.* **(*)
**(*) ASV Dig. CDCOE 803 [id.]. Blankenstein, Boyd, COE, Schneider – MOZART: *Sinfonia concertante;* VIVALDI: *Concerto, RV 556.* **(*)

Double concerto for violin and oboe; Triple concerto for flute, violin and harpsichord in A min., BWV 1044.
**(*) Denon Dig. C37 7064 [id.]. Kantorow, Bourgue, Adorján, Dreyfus, Netherlands CO, Bakels.

Holliger is at his distinguished best in the *Double concerto*, and Kremer makes a good partner in a fresh performance with a serene central *Adagio*. But what makes this coupling memorable is the improvisatory quality which Holliger brings to his beautiful account of the solo in the *Sinfonia* from the *Easter oratorio* which sounds just like the slow movement of a concerto. The recording is first class, the ambience nicely judged, and the oboe is especially tangible in the CD format.

In the Denon version the *Double concerto* is dominated by Maurice Bourgue, with phrasing and tonal nuances that consistently ensnare the ear. Jean-Jacques Kantorow makes another fine contribution, not quite so individual but producing immaculate playing. The *Triple concerto* is less compellingly done, and there one is more aware of the often inappropriately beefy style of the Netherlands Chamber Orchestra, as recorded here. Huguette Dreyfus's harpsichord is rather aggressively recorded, but otherwise the sound is very good.

Recorded live, with stage and audience noises audible, the ASV version from the Chamber Orchestra of Europe is not immaculate, with the opening allegro rather sluggish of rhythm, but the solo playing from the oboist Douglas Boyd and the violinist Marieka Blankenstein is outstanding. Atmospheric recording, not ideally balanced.

The Musical offering, BWV 1079.
*** Ph. 412 800-2 [id.]. ASMF, Marriner.

Sir Neville Marriner uses his own edition and instrumentation: strings with three solo violins, solo viola and a solo cello; flute, organ and harpsichord. He places the three-part *Ricercar* (scored for organ) at the beginning and the six-part *Ricercar* at the very end, scored for strings. As the centrepiece comes the *Trio sonata* (flute, violin and continuo), and on either side the *Canons*. The performance here is of high quality, though some of the playing is a trifle bland. It is, however, excellently recorded and overall must be numbered among the most successful accounts of the work.

The Musical offering, BWV 1079; (i) *Suite No. 2 in B min, BWV 1067.*
(M) **(*) Decca 430 266-2; *430 266-4*. Stuttgart CO, Münchinger, (i) with Rampal.

Münchinger's 1976 version of the *Musical offering* is strikingly well recorded: it has fullness, presence and good detail. Moreover it offers playing of genuine breadth and eloquence, particularly in the *Trio sonata*. For the reissue, the 1962 recording of the *B minor Suite* for flute and strings has been added, the best of the set.

Orchestral Suites Nos. 1–4, BWV 1066/9.
(M) *** Decca 430 378-2; *430 378-4* [id.]. ASMF, Marriner.
*** O-L Dig. 417 834-2 (2) [id.]. AAM, Hogwood.
*** Hung. Dig. HCD 31018 [id.]. Liszt CO, Janos Rolla.

(M) **(*) HM/BMG Dig. GD 77008 (2) [77008-2-RG]. La Petite Bande, Kuijken.
**(*) HM/BMG Dig. RD 77864; *RK 77864* (2) [7864-2-RC; *7864-4-RC*]. Amsterdam Bar. O, Koopman.

Orchestral Suites Nos. 1 in C; 3 in D; 4 in D, BWV 1066, 1068 & 1069.
(M) *** Ph. 420 888-2. ECO, Leppard.

Orchestral Suite No. 2 in B min., BWV 1067; (i) *Violin concertos Nos. 1 in A min.; 2 in E, BWV 1041/2;* (ii) *Triple concerto for flute, violin and harpsichord in A min., BWV 1044.*
(M) *** Ph. 420 889-2. (i) Grumiaux; (ii) Garcia, Adeney, Leppard; ECO, Leppard.

Marriner's 1970 recording of the Bach *Suites* with the ASMF comes on a single CD (77 minutes 48 seconds) and the remastering of the fine (originally Argo) recording is fresh and vivid. The playing throughout is expressive without being romantic, and always buoyant and vigorous. Perhaps the CD transfer loses a little of the weight of the originals but not their musical strength. A fine bargain for those not insisting on original instruments; there is nothing remotely unstylish here.

For Philips's Silverline mid-price reissue of the four Bach *Orchestral Suites*, Grumiaux's 1964 performances of the two solo *Violin concertos* have been added (with their purity of line and matching vitality) plus an attractive version of the *Triple concerto*, its slow movement striking for the colourful interchanges of timbre. The *Suites* come from the pre-authentic era, but they are sparklingly played by excellent soloists; overall, Leppard's conception balances gravitas and elegance with baroque ebullience.

Hogwood's set of the Bach orchestral *Suites* illustrates how the Academy of Ancient Music has developed in refinement and purity of sound, modifying earlier abrasiveness without losing period-instrument freshness. That comes out in the famous *Air* from the *Suite No. 3* where, with multiple violins and an avoidance of the old squeezed style, the tone is sweet even with little or no vibrato – a movement which in the Pinnock version on DG Archiv, for example, sounds very sour. *Allegros* tend to be on the fast side, but are well sprung, not breathless. The refinement of the ensemble is enhanced by the slight distancing of the recording, giving sharper, leaner ensembles than in most rival versions, but with less-defined contrasts between solo and ripieno passages. Hogwood aficionados need not hesitate.

Like Marriner, Rolla offers all four *Orchestral Suites* on a single CD (at less than premium price) playing for 74 minutes. Rolla's tempi are brisk, with rhythms consistently resilient, but not always swifter than those of others; he misses the repeats of the second parts of the overture, a practice most listeners will accept. The performances are alive, straightforward and stylish. Even if they are not 'authentic' (in the sense that modern instruments are used), the woodwind colours and incisive trumpets have a true baroque sound. Most important, the music-making is spontaneous; other versions may have more individuality (especially in the matter of embellishment), but these are direct in the best possible way, and the recording is excellent.

Kuijken with La Petite Bande shows that authentic performance need not be acidly over-abrasive. Set against a warm acoustic – more comfortable for the trumpet-sound, if not always helpful to clarity – these are brightly attractive performances with their just speeds and resilient rhythms. But they cost twice as much as the Marriner set.

Winner of one of the *Gramophone* Awards in 1990, Koopman's set of the Bach *Suites* brings warmly recorded performances with little of the abrasiveness that marked many earlier versions on period instruments. Slow introductions at relatively broad speeds have traditional grandeur, helped by the reverberant recording, and such a movement as the celebrated *Air* from the *Suite No. 3* is also allowed expressive breadth. Allegros are well sprung, both strong and elegant, and the *Suite No. 2* is crowned by the superb playing of the flautist, Wilbert Hazelzet, delectably light and clean at high speed in the final *Badinerie*. The snag is the extravagant layout: two full-price discs, with less than 80 minutes of music altogether, are very poor value.

Orchestral suites Nos. 1–4; The Musical offering, BWV 1079.
(B) *** EMI CZS 767350-2 (2) [id.]; (*Suites* only) *EG 764266-4*. Bath Festival O (members), Sir Yehudi Menuhin.

Menuhin's set of the *Orchestral suites* was recorded at the beginning of the 1960s. The sound was first class in its day, clear and well balanced, and it does not seem dated now, with excellent CD transfers. Those who respond to Bach from the 'pre-authentic era' will find Menuhin's humanity shows an admirable balance between freshness and warmth, conveying the music's spirit and breadth without inflation. The famous *Air* from the *Third suite* is particularly beautifully played. For this economically priced reissue the *Musical offering*, recorded at the same time by distinguished soloists from the orchestra, has been added. They use a new edition by Neville Boyling intelligently scored for a small group. The Trio sonata is played stylishly by Menuhin, Elaine Schaeffer and Kinloch Anderson, whose chamber-music approach helps the score yield up its secrets. There is nothing cerebral or introspective about the playing here or in the canon in augmentation and contrary motion, and the feeling of the interpretations shows how the music has affected the performances. The recording balance is rather forward, but the sound is otherwise excellent. The cassette omits *The Musical offering*.

CHAMBER MUSIC

The Art of fugue, BWV 1080.
*** Sony Dig. S2K 45937 (2) [id.]. Juilliard Qt.

The very first records of *The Art of fugue* were made by the Roth String Quartet with Sir Donald Tovey playing his conjectural completion of the unfinished quadruple fugue. Even Schweitzer spoke of it as 'a purely theoretical work' and it only entered the repertoire in 1927 in Wolfgang Graeser's edition. Hermann Diener recorded it with the strings of the Collegium Musicum, and Scherchen also recorded his transcription but it was not until the LP era that the idea of recording it on keyboard instruments finally gained ground. Of course there are versions for early instruments, for a mixture of wind and strings, and even for brass. To hear it now on a stringed instrument ensemble is the exception rather than the rule, and to have it on a modern string quartet very rare indeed. The Juilliard Quartet's new version has the field virtually to itself in this respect, and hearing it again in this medium gives undoubted pleasure. After all, as Gerhard Herz reminds us in his excellent notes, no less a figure than Mozart arranged five of the *48* for string quartet! The Juilliard play with far less vibrato than usual (at times one is tempted to feel that they are aspiring to the condition of a consort of viols) and they convey a feeling of intimacy and a clarity of the part-writing that is very satisfying. Moreover, so as to avoid transposing those fugues with passages which lie outside the normal range of his instrument, Samuel Rhodes, the violist of the Juilliard, commissioned the luthier Marten Cornellisten to make an instrument large enough so that it could extend the normal viola range downwards by a fourth. This is a very worthwhile alternative to the relatively abundant keyboard versions, and musically very satisfying.

(Unaccompanied) *Cello suites Nos. 1–6, BWV 1007/12.*
*** EMI Dig. CDS7 47471-8 (2). Heinrich Schiff.
*** BMG/RCA Dig. RD 70950 (2). Anner Bylsma.
(M) *** DG 419 359-2 (2) [id.]. Pierre Fournier.
(M) (***) EMI mono CHS7 61027-2 (2) [Ang. CDH 61028/9]. Pablo Casals.
(M) *** Ph. 422 494-2; *422 494-4* (*Nos. 1, 4 & 6*); 422 495-2; *422 495-4* (*Nos. 2, 3 & 5*). Maurice Gendron.
*** EMI Dig. CDC7 47035-2 (*Nos. 1, 4 & 5*); 47036-2 (*Nos. 2, 3 & 6*). Paul Tortelier.
**(*) Decca Dig. 414 163-2 (2) [id.]. Lynn Harrell.
**(*) Sony Dig. M2K 37867 (2) [id.]. Yo-Yo Ma.
(B) **(*) EMI CMS7 69431-2 (2). Paul Tortelier.

(Unaccompanied) Cello suites Nos. 1–6, BWV 1007/12; (i) *Viola da gamba sonatas Nos. 1–2, BWV 1027/8.*
(M) **(*) Mercury 432 756-2 (2) [id.]. Janos Starker, (i) with György Sebök.

Schiff blows any cobwebs away from these dark and taxing works, not with consciously authentic performances that risk desiccation but with sharply direct ones, tough in manner and at speeds generally far faster than usual. For once one is constantly reminded that these are suites of dance movements, with Schiff's rhythmic pointing a delight. So even the *Sarabandes* emerge as stately dances, not unfeeling but freed of the heavy romanticism which is often plastered on them. Equally, the fast movements are given a lightness and resilience which make them sound fresh and new. Strong and positive, producing a consistent flow of beautiful tone at whatever dynamic level, Schiff here establishes his individual artistry very clearly. He is treated to an excellent recording, with the cello given fine bloom against a warm but intimate acoustic. The CDs have striking presence and realism.

Anner Bylsma's set of the *Cello suites* on a baroque cello appeared on three LPs in 1981 and was held in the highest esteem among both early-music specialists and cellists. Making its acquaintance on CD, one can see why. Bylsma brings a vivid musical imagination and an ardent intensity to each movement. Mind you, his intensity is not of the kind that squeezes all the expressive potential out of each phrase, leaving the listener emotionally exhausted. Rather he articulates each phrase in a way that makes the most of its character so that dance movements are light and have a spring in their gait and the preludes possess an eloquence that seems quite new. He is rhythmically flexible and always thoughtful, and he brings the music alive in an unforced, seemingly natural way. Even if you have such artists as Tortelier, Yo-Yo Ma, Gendron and Maisky, all admirable in their different ways, this is worth acquiring as it offers new insights.

Fournier's richly phrased and warm-toned performances were recorded in 1961 and dominated the catalogue during the 1960s. They carry an impressive musical conviction. Fournier can be profound and he can lift rhythms infectiously in dance movements, but above all he conveys the feeling that this is music to be enjoyed. The recording, made in a resonant but not overblown ambience, does not sound in the least dated.

It was Casals who restored these pieces to the repertory after long decades of neglect. Some of the playing is far from flawless; passage-work is rushed or articulation uneven, and he is often wayward. But he brought to the *Cello suites* insights that remain unrivalled. Casals brings one closer to this music than do most (one is tempted to say, any) of his rivals. The sound is inevitably dated but still comes over well in this transfer.

Maurice Gendron's phrasing is unfailingly musical and, although these readings have a certain sobriety (save perhaps for No. 6, which has distinct flair), their restraint and fine judgement command admiration.

Recorded in the reverberant acoustic of the Temple Church in London, Tortelier's 1983 performances of the *Suites* present clear contrasts with his version of twenty years earlier. His approach remains broadly romantic by today's purist standards, but this time the rhythms are steadier, the command greater, with the preludes of each suite strongly characterized to capture the attention even in simple chattering passage-work. Some will prefer a drier acoustic than this, but the digital sound is first rate, with striking presence on CD.

The spareness and restraint of Harrell's performances contrast strongly with the more extrovert manner of most virtuosi, but rarely if ever is he guilty of understatement. The simple dedication of the playing, combined with cleanness of attack and purity of tone, bring natural unforced intensity. One might disagree with the occasional tempo, but the overall command is unassailable. Excellent, aptly intimate recorded quality.

Yo-Yo Ma gives deeply satisfying performances. He commands the highest artistry, and his playing invariably offers both technical mastery and elevation of spirit. Moreover, the CBS engineers have given him truthful and well-balanced sound. However, his intonation is not always absolutely impeccable: his present set cannot be counted a first recommendation.

Janos Starker's performances come from 1963 and 1965 and are of great integrity and dedication, without having quite the same electric communication of his earlier mono recording. The two *Viola da gamba sonatas* are not ideally balanced and favour György Sebök's piano; though there is no question of his artistry.

In his earlier set, Tortelier's rhythmic grip is strong, his technique masterly and his intonation true. At the same time, however, there are touches of reticence: it is as if he is consciously resisting the temptation to give full rein to his musical and lyrical instinct. Nevertheless the faster movements are splendidly played, and the *Prelude* to the *E flat major Suite* finds him at his most imposing. The recording, though made in the first half of the 1960s, sounds most realistic.

Flute sonatas Nos. 1–6, BWV 1030/35; in G min., BWV 1020; Partita in A min. (for solo flute), *BWV 1013.*
*** CRD CRD 3314/5 (2) [id.]. Stephen Preston, Trevor Pinnock, Dordi Savall.
(M) **(*) Ph. 422 943-2 (2) [id.]. Maxence Larrieu, Rafael Puyana, Wieland Kuijken.

Two of these *Sonatas*, BWV 1031 and 1033, are unauthenticated, but still contain attractive music. Using an authentic one-key instrument, Stephen Preston plays all six with a rare delicacy. By its nature, the baroque instrument he uses can cope with only a limited dynamic range; but Preston is finely expressive, not least in the splendid *Partita* for solo flute. Unfortunately, its inclusion in the set has contributed to an uneconomic layout on a pair of CDs. Of the works with continuo, the two minor-key sonatas, BWV 1030 and BWV 1034, are particularly fine. A reconstruction of the first movement of the *A major*, where bars are missing, is featured here. Throughout, the continuo playing, led by Trevor Pinnock, is of the highest standard; for those willing to stretch to the expense of two premium-priced records, this is a clear first choice for this repertoire.

Maxence Larrieu plays a modern flute, Rafael Puyana an instrument modelled on a large German harpsichord of the eighteenth century, and Wieland Kuijken a seven-stringed viola da gamba from the Tyrol and probably dating from the second half of the eighteenth century. The performances are highly accomplished and often persuasive. The set, which is economically priced, makes very agreeable listening.

Lute music transcribed for guitar

Lute suites (arr. for guitar): *Nos. 1–4, BWV 995/7 and 1006a.*
*** Sony MK 42204 [id.]. John Williams (guitar).

With all four *Suites* conveniently fitted on to a single compact disc, this CBS issue offers a clear first choice in this repertoire. John Williams shows a natural feeling for Bach; the flair of his playing with its rhythmic vitality and sense of colour is always telling. His is a first-class set in every way: the linear control and ornamentation are equally impressive. The CD transfer is made at the highest level; but with the volume control turned down a bit, the close balance does not affect the fullness of timbre.

Lute suites Nos. 1–2, BWV 996/7; Fugue in G min., BWV 1000.
*** DG Dig. 410 643-2 [id.]. Göran Söllscher (guitar).

Lute suites Nos. 3, BWV 995; 4, BWV 1006a; Prelude in C min., BWV 999; Prelude, fugue and allegro in E flat, BWV 998.
*** DG Dig. 413 719-2 [id.]. Göran Söllscher (guitar).

Göran Söllscher is a highly musical player. He is well attuned to Bach, his style is fluent and there is a judicious use of light and shade. The playing is technically impeccable – as is the recorded sound, which is suitably intimate, though not to be reproduced at too high a volume level.

Other guitar transcriptions

Arrangements: (Unaccompanied) *Cello suites Nos. 1 in G, BWV 1007* (trans. *in E flat*); *2 in D min., BWV 1008* (trans. *in G min.*); *6 in D, BWV 1012* (trans. *in E flat*): *Saraband & Gavotte* (only). (Unaccompanied) *Violin sonata No. 3 in C, BWV 1005* (trans. *in B flat*).
**(*) DG Dig. 435 471-2 [id.]. Göran Söllscher (guitar).

There is no reason in principle why Bach's works for solo string instruments should not be transcribed for guitar, even if this necessitates changes of pitch. Göran Söllscher plays this music in a convincingly improvisational manner and he is thoroughly musical and sympathetic. However, the music just fails to lift off in this format, although here the soloist is at his very best in the *Sarabandes*, played very freely. Realistic sound, though the balance is close.

Trio sonatas Nos. 1 in D min., 2 in C, 3 & 4 in G, BWV 1036/9.
*** HM Dig. HMC 901173; *HMC 401173* [id.]. L. Bar.

This disc contains two sonatas of established authenticity, the *G major*, BWV 1039, and (perhaps less certain) its companion in the same key, BWV 1038, which exists in a set of parts in Bach's own hand. The other two are of less certain authorship. The playing of the London Baroque has great freshness and spirit, and readers wanting this repertoire need not hesitate. The recording is eminently satisfactory, too.

Viola da gamba sonatas Nos. 1–3, BWV 1027/9.
*** Sony Dig. MK 37794 [id.]. Yo-Yo Ma (cello), Kenneth Cooper.
*** DG Dig. 415 471-2 [id.]. Mischa Maisky (cello), Martha Argerich (piano).
(M) *** HM/BMG GD 77044 [77044-2-RG]. Wieland Kuijken, Gustav Leonhardt.
*** Sony Dig. SK 45945 [id.]. Anner Bylsma, Bob van Asperen – J. C. F. BACH: *Cello sonata in A.* ***

Yo-Yo Ma plays with great eloquence and natural feeling. His tone is warm and refined and his technical command remains, as ever, irreproachable. Kenneth Cooper is a splendid partner. The CD has wonderful clarity and presence, and admirers of this cellist will undoubtedly want to acquire this issue.

Mischa Maisky is also a highly expressive cellist and, unlike Yo-Yo Ma, he opts for the piano – successfully, for Martha Argerich is a Bach player of the first order. In fact the sonority of the cello and the modern piano seems a happier marriage than the compromise Ma and Cooper adopt. The recording is extremely well balanced too, and the acoustic pleasingly warm. A most enjoyable account for collectors who do not care for period instruments.

Kuijken and Leonhardt are both sensitive and scholarly musicians, their tempi well judged and their artistry in good evidence. Their phrasing is finely shaped and natural, and there is no sense of the relentless flow that can so often impair the faster movements. This is the most authentic account to have appeared on the market in recent years and is among the most rewarding.

On Sony/Vivarte, Anner Bylsma uses a piccolo cello and Bob van Asperen plays a 'trunk' organ, a small chamber organ. Bylsma argues the case for using these instruments in a persuasive (if not totally convincing) sleeve-note, and readers who wish to hear these marvellous pieces on a gamba and harpsichord should look elsewhere. The cello piccolo produces an almost viola-like tone-quality in the upper register, and aurally the two instruments match beautifully. The sound is much less austere than Kuijken and Leonhardt, and the brighter sonorities are undoubtedly appealing. The recording is extremely clean and well balanced.

(Unaccompanied) *Violin sonatas Nos. 1–3, BWV 1001, 1003 & 1005; Violin partitas Nos. 1–3, BWV 1002, 1004 & 1006.*
❀ *** EMI Dig. CDS7 49483-2 (2) [id.]. Itzhak Perlman.
*** ASV CDDCD 454 (2) [id.]. Oscar Shumsky.
*** Orfeo C 130853H (2) [id.]. Dmitry Sitkovetsky.
(M) *** DG 423 294-2 (2) [id.]. Milstein.
(M) *** HM/BMG GD 77043 (2) [77043-2-RG]. Sigiswald Kuijken.
(M) (**(*)) BMG/RCA mono GD 87708 (2) [7708-2-RC]. Jascha Heifetz.
(M) ** Teldec/Warner 9031 761338-2 (2). Thomas Zehetmair.
(B) * Naxos Dig. 8.550569 (*Partita No. 1; Sonatas Nos. 1–2*); 8.550570 (*Partitas Nos. 2–3; Sonata No. 3*). Christiane Edinger.

The range of tone in Perlman's playing adds to the power of these performances, infectiously rhythmic in dance movements but conveying the intensity of live performance in the great slow movements in hushed playing of great refinement. Some may still seek a greater sense of struggle conveyed in order to bring out the full depth of the writing, but the sense of spontaneity, of the player's own enjoyment in the music, makes this set a unique, revelatory experience. Perlman's finest achievement comes in the supreme test of the great *Chaconne* which concludes the *D minor Partita*, the Everest of violin music. Here the scale of the playing is all-embracing. The climax which Perlman builds at the end of the first big group of minor-key variations is almost orchestral in its power, and the tempo allows him to give the complete illusion, ventriloquial, of voices answering one another – as also in the fugues. Then the sudden dramatic moment of hush, as the first major-key variation begins, has rarely been caught on record with such intensity. Perlman here triumphantly demonstrates his insight in bringing out the deepest qualities of these six searching masterpieces.

Shumsky's clean attack and tight vibrato, coupled with virtuosity of the highest order, make for strong and refreshing readings, full of flair and imagination. If you want big-scale playing of Bach, this supplies the need splendidly, though the dry, close acoustic reduces the scale and undermines tenderness.

Dmitry Sitkovetsky is not only a player of exceptional virtuosity but a real stylist. He conveys no sense of haste and he has a splendidly fluid sense of line and firm rhythms. The excellence and naturalness of the recording make the claims of this set very strong indeed.

Milstein's set from the mid-1970s makes a first-class mid-price recommendation. Every phrase is beautifully shaped and there is a highly developed feeling for line. Intonation is not always absolutely impeccable, but there is no want of virtuosity and it is always put at the service of the music. These performances have an aristocratic poise and a classical finesse which are very refreshing.

Those who tire of the sweetness and beauty of even the finest modern performances will find the sharper sounds of Kuijken very refreshing. With wonderfully true intonation and G-string tone of gutty firmness, these accounts are as little painful or scratchy as you are ever likely to get in the authentic field.

The dry and limited mono sound of Heifetz's classic set, dating from the 1950s, does not prevent one being thrilled by the astonishing bravura of his playing. Speeds are often extremely fast – phenomenally so in the fugues – yet rhythms are superbly controlled. Heifetz's creative imagination in his phrasing has one consistently registering the music afresh.

Thomas Zehetmair's style is curiously restless; his line tends to have subtle dynamic surges, a feeling almost of rocking between phrases, and the effect is at times emotionally jagged; even the famous *Chaconne* of BWV 1004 could be more positive. Yet the pieces which depend on running passage-work (the *Courant* of the *Partita in B minor*, the *Gigue* of the *D minor* or the brilliant *Presto* of the *G minor Sonata*) are played with a wonderful, lightly articulated bravura which has much imaginative light and shade, while the *Fuga* of the *A minor Sonata* has its simple polyphony well under control without being tense. But in a piece like the *Siciliana* which precedes that *Presto* of BWV 1001 the improvisational restlessness disturbs Bach's underlying serenity, and elsewhere the feeling that the music runs like a mountain stream, over pebbles certainly but essentially flowing onward, is often disturbed in these readings. The recording is close but faithful and gives a very realistic impression against a acoustic which is not too dry.

Christiane Edinger made her début at the 1962 Berlin Festival, yet hers is not a familiar recording name. She makes a beautiful sound on her 1632 Amati fiddle, and the resonant Naxos recording flatters her tone, which is beautiful, and her playing, which is technically impressive. But she needs much more self-discipline in Bach. Her waywardly romantic espousal of the opening *Adagio* of the *G minor Sonata* takes 5 minutes 31 seconds as against Milstein's 3 minutes 54 seconds and – making a similar comparison – she also adds nearly three minutes to the famous *Chaconne* of the *Partita in D minor*, which needs much more grip to be convincing.

(Unaccompanied) *Violin partita No. 1 in B min., BWV 1002.*
*** Ph. Dig. 420 948-2 [id.]. Viktoria Mullova – BARTÓK: *Sonata* *** (also with PAGANINI: *Introduction and variations on Nel cor più non misento* ***).

There is no doubt that Viktoria Mullova is an artist of remarkable intelligence as well as enormous technical accomplishment. Her account of the *B minor Partita* is undeniably impressive and is in every way compelling. Apart from the tonal finesse which she commands, there is a strong sense of line and pure intonation. Good if forward recording.

Transcriptions of works for unaccompanied violin: *Sonatas in G min.* (from *BWV 1001*); *in D* (from *BWV 1005*); *Suite in D* (from *Suite for viola pomposa, BWV 1012*).
(M) *** HM/BMG GD 77014 [77014-2-RG]. Gustav Leonhardt (harpsichord).

What need is there of an arrangement when the original is so readily accessible? There is no lack of precedents both in the nineteenth century (Raff, Busoni, etc.) and in Bach's own time. The *Suite in D* (transposed up a tone from the C major original) fares particularly well from being fleshed out. Gustav Leonhardt plays a 1755 instrument of Nicholas Lefebvre of Rouen, restored by the Bremen maker, Martin Skowroneck, and the recording has excellent presence and bloom.

Violin sonatas (for violin and harpsichord) *Nos. 1–6, BWV 1014/9.*
(M) *** HM/BMG GD 77170 (2) [77170-2-RG]. Sigiswald Kuijken, Gustav Leonhardt.
*** Ph. Dig. 410 401-2 (2) [id.]. Monica Huggett, Ton Koopman.

Violin sonatas Nos. 1–6, BWV 1014/9; 1019a; Sonatas for violin and continuo, BWV 1020/4.
❀ (M) *** Ph. 426 452-2; *426 452-4* (2). Arthur Grumiaux, Christiane Jaccottet, Philippe Mermoud (in *BWV 1021* & *1023*).

Violin sonatas (for violin and harpsichord) *Nos. 1–6, BWV 1014/9; Sonatas for violin and continuo, BWV 1021 & 1023.*
**(*) Virgin Dig. VCD7 90741-2; *VCD7 90741-4* (2) [id.]. John Holloway, Davitt Moroney, Susan Sheppard.

The Bach *Sonatas for violin and harpsichord* and *violin and continuo* are much less well known than the works for unaccompanied violin or cello, but they contain music of great character and beauty. They are marvellously played, with all the beauty of tone and line for which Grumiaux is renowned; they have great vitality too. His admirable partner is Christiane Jaccottet, and in BWV 1021 and 1023 Philippe Mermoud (cello) joins the continuo. There is endless treasure to be discovered here, particularly when the music-making is so serenely communicative.

Sigiswald Kuijken uses a baroque violin, and both he and Gustav Leonhardt give us playing of rare eloquence. This reissue is an admirable example of the claims of authenticity and musical feeling pulling together rather than apart. This is a wholly delightful set and the transparency of the sound is especially appealing.

Monica Huggett, one of the outstanding exponents of authentic performance, plays with refined expressiveness in a beautifully unified conception of these six endlessly inventive works. Other versions may be more vigorous but, with excellent recording, detailed and well balanced, period instruments are projected most persuasively. Two alternative versions are given of the slow movement of BWV 1019.

In addition to the six *Sonatas for violin and harpsichord*, the Virgin set presents the two surviving *Sonatas for violin and continuo* (in the latter, Davitt Moroney uses a chamber organ) known to be authentic. John Holloway has long experience in the early-music field, but violin tone is as much a matter of personal taste as is the human voice. Some will find the actual sound he makes unpleasing: it is vinegary and at times downright ugly. Yet those who take a different view will find him not wanting in artistry. Both Davitt Moroney and Susan Sheppard give excellent support, and the recording cannot be faulted in its clarity and presence; for those who must have original-instrument performances, first choice remains with Monica Huggett and Ton Koopman who, although they omit BWV 1021 and 1023, are no less authentic.

KEYBOARD MUSIC

'Bach and Tureck at home' (A birthday offering): (i) *Adagio in G, BWV 968; Aria and 10 variations in the Italian style, BWV 989; Capriccio on the departure of a beloved brother, BWV 992; Chromatic fantasia and fugue, BWV 903; Fantasia, adagio and fugue in D, BWV 912; The Well-tempered clavier, Book 1: Prelude & fugue in B flat, BWV 866.* (ii) *English suite No. 3 in G min., BWV 808; Italian concerto, BWV 971; Sonata in D min., BWV 964* (trans. from Unaccompanied *Violin sonata No. 2 in A min., BWV 1003*); *Well-tempered clavier, Book 1: Preludes & fugues: in C min; in C, BWV 847/8; Book 2: Preludes & fugues in C sharp, BWV 872; in G, BWV 884.* (iii) *Goldberg variations, BWV 988;* (iv) *Partitas Nos. 1 in B flat, BWV 825; 2 in C min., BWV 826; 6 in E min., BWV 830.*

❀ *** (i) Troy 010; (ii) Troy 009; (iii) Troy 007; (iv) Troy 008 (available separately). Rosalyn Tureck (piano).

These recordings originated in the home of William F. Buckley at Wallach's Point, Stamford, Connecticut. They were planned as an inspired birthday present by his wife, but the initial event expanded to five evenings, the first on 24 November 1979 and the last in May 1984. The acoustic of the large sitting-room at Wallach's Point was ideal for home music-making, and the admirable analogue recording gives an intimate impression without being too dry; the piano has a vivid presence. Such was the balancing skill of the recording engineer, Ed Sidlawski, however, that the effect is very real without being too close for comfort. The audience makes its presence felt only by discreet applause at the end of each work. The result is a series of Bach programmes that have all the advantages of live music-making – notably a wonderfully spontaneous feeling of music taking wing as one listens – and none of the disadvantages.

Rosalyn Tureck's Bach playing is legendary, and the performances here show that her keyboard command and fluent sense of Bach style are as remarkable as ever. The variety of articulation and colour in the *Variations in the Italian style* offer endless stimulation, while the *Chromatic fantasia* is dazzling and its companion fugue opens very gently and builds to a superb climax. Later in this first CD recital, the *Adagio in D major* (which Mr Buckley tells us was the opening work of his first concert) is wonderfully dark in colouring, and the closing fugue of BWV 912 is unforgettably buoyant and life-enhancing. The second programme is hardly less successful, including as it does excerpts from *The Well-tempered clavier*, the work for which Miss Tureck is justly famous; while the *Andante* of the *Sonata in D minor*, BWV 964, is sustained at a very relaxed tempo with raptly intense concentration. Her thoughtful presentation of the *Aria* on which the *Goldberg variations* is based is also (like its final reprise) quite magical. What comes in between provides very great musical variety and satisfaction. The *Partitas*, too, show Miss Tureck at her most imaginative, with an infinite variety of touch: the opening *Sinfonia* of *No. 2 in C minor* is made to seem almost orchestral, while the *Toccata* which begins *No. 6 in E minor* is hardly less commanding. Miss Tureck uses a wide dynamic and expressive range with consummate artistry, her decoration always adds to the musical effect, and she makes us feel that Bach's keyboard music could be played in no other way than this – the hallmark of a great artist. All but one of these four discs plays for over 70 minutes (and the odd one for 66) and we must express gratitude to Mrs Buckley for her forethought in planning such bounty.

The Art of fugue, BWV 1080 (see also string quartet and orchestral versions).
*** HM HMC 901169/70; *HMC 401169/70* [id.]. Davitt Moroney (harpsichord).
**(*) DG Dig. 427 673-2 [id.]. Kenneth Gilbert (harpsichord).

Davitt Moroney's account commands not only the intellectual side of the work but also the aesthetic, and his musicianship is second to none. Moroney makes some alterations in the order of the various contrapuncti but he argues his case persuasively – and he is eminently well served by the engineers. Davitt Moroney has imagination as well as scholarship.

Kenneth Gilbert's is a version of special interest. He turns to the earlier autograph version, edited by Christoph Wolff and published by Peters Edition in 1987. It differs from the 1751 edition primarily in omitting four of the movements familiar from 1751 and fits conveniently on to a single CD. Kenneth Gilbert plays a fine 1671 harpsichord by Jan Couchet of Antwerp, enlarged by the Parisian makers, Blanchet (*c.* 1759) and Taskin (1778). He is splendidly recorded, though some may be troubled by the rather literal, almost Teutonic approach he adopts. A valuable supplementary issue, but not a first recommendation for obvious reasons.

The Art of fugue, BWV 1080; Italian concerto, BWV 971; Partita in B min., BWV 831; Prelude, fugue and allegro in E flat, BWV 998.
(M) *** HM/BMG GD 77013 (2) [77013-2-RG]. Gustav Leonhardt (harpsichord).

Under the fingers of Leonhardt every strand in the texture emerges with clarity and every phrase is allowed to speak for itself. In the 12th and 18th fugues Leonhardt is joined by Bob van Asperen. Leonhardt does not include the unfinished fugue, but that will be the only reservation to cross the minds of most listeners. This is a very impressive and rewarding set, well recorded and produced.

Capriccio in B flat, BWV 992; Fantasia and fugue in A min., BWV 904; Prelude, fugue and allegro in E flat, BWV 998; Suite in E min., BWV 996 (originally for lute); *Toccata in E min., BWV 914.*
*** Ph. Dig. 416 141-2 [id.]. Gustav Leonhardt (harpsichord).

Gustav Leonhardt plays a William Dowd harpsichord, modelled on an instrument by Mietke of Berlin dating from 1715. The sonorities are rich and the great Dutch player exploits them with characteristic resourcefulness. His well-planned recital has vitality, freshness and imagination, and everything comes vividly to life, thanks perhaps to a splendidly articulate recording.

Chromatic fantasia and fugue in D min., BWV 903; Chorale Preludes: Ich ruf zu dir, BWV 639; Nun komm' der Heiden Heiland, BWV 659 (both arr. Busoni); *Fantasia in A min., BWV 922; Fantasia and fugue in A min., BWV 904; Italian concerto in F, BWV 971.*
*** Ph. 412 252-2 [id.]. Alfred Brendel (piano).

Brendel's fine Bach recital originally appeared in 1978. The performances are of the old school with no attempt to strive after harpsichord effects, and with every piece creating a sound-world of its own. The *Italian concerto* is particularly imposing, with a finely sustained sense of line and beautifully articulated rhythms. The recording is in every way truthful and present, bringing the grand piano very much into the living-room before one's very eyes. Masterly.

Chromatic fantasia and fugue in D min., BWV 903; 4 Duets, BWV 802/5; Italian concerto in F, BWV 971; Partita in B min., BWV 831.
❀ *** O-L Dig. 433 054-2 [id.]. Christophe Rousset (harpsichord).

Christophe Rousset's Oiseau-Lyre disc is one of the best Bach harpsichord recitals of recent years. His playing has been collecting golden opinions and we have also been much taken with his set of two Rameau CDs. The playing combines the selfless authority and scholarly dedication of such artists as Leonhardt and Gilbert with the flair and imagination of younger players like Scott Ross and Skip Sempé. Rousset plays a fine instrument from 1751 by Henri Hemsch, and all the performances here have a taste and musical vitality that reward the listener. Strongly recommended.

Chromatic fantasia & fugue in D min., BWV 903; Fantasias: in C min., BWV 906; G min., BWV 917; C min., BWV 919; Fantasia & fugue in A min., BWV 904; Preludes: in C min., BWV 921; A min., BWV 922; Preludes & fugues: in A min., BWV 894; F, BWV 901; G, BWV 902.
*** HM/BMG RD 77039 [RCA 77039-2-RC]. Andreas Staier (harpsichord).

Andreas Staier will be familiar to most collectors as a member of the Cologne Musica Antiqua, but in recent years he has pursued a solo career both on harpsichord and fortepiano. On this CD he plays a copy of an instrument from 1702–4 by the Berlin maker, Michael Mietke, and alongside the familiar *Chromatic fantasia and fugue*, he offers less-often-recorded repertoire, always with imagination and flair. What is good about his playing is its air of freedom, for although he keeps a firm grip on rhythm he is never rigid or inflexible, and his approach and registration are varied enough for his programme to be heard at one sitting. The recording has impressive clarity and presence and is made in a pleasingly warm acoustic. Strongly recommended.

Chromatic fantasia and fugue in D min., BWV 903; Fantasy, BWV 906; Toccatas, BWV 912/4, 916.
*** DG Dig. 431 659-2 [id.]. Kenneth Gilbert (harpsichord).

Kenneth Gilbert plays a harpsichord of 1671 by the Flemish maker, Jan Couchet, enlarged by Taskin in 1778 and restored by Hubert Bédard ten years ago, and it sounds admirably rich and full-bodied. The playing is scholarly and yet by no means didactic; only in the fugue of the *Chromatic fantasia and fugue* does one feel that Gilbert is a touch heavy-handed. The four *Toccatas* are played with great spirit, though with perhaps less spontaneity than Bob van Asperen achieves on EMI (see below).

Chromatic fantasia and fugue, BWV 903; Italian concerto in F, BWV 971; Partita No. 1 in B flat, BWV 825; Prelude, fugue and allegro, BWV 998; Toccata, adagio and fugue, BWV 916.
*** Virgin Dig. VC7 90712-2; *VC7 90712-4* [id.]. Maggie Cole.

This is Maggie Cole's first solo recital, and very good it is too. She uses a Ruckers harpsichord of 1612 from the Royal Collection, tuned in unequal temperament. Her playing is splendidly unfussy, free from interpretative mannerisms and not bound by rigid rhythms; her virtuosity in the *Chromatic fantasia and fugue* seems effortless and unforced, and there is an agreeable naturalness about the whole recital. The recording is thoroughly faithful and the acoustic lively, if small.

4 Duets, BWV 802–5; English suite No. 6 in D min., BWV 811; Italian concerto, BWV 971; Toccata in C minor, BWV 911.
(M) *** DG Dig. 429 975-2; *429 975-4*. Angela Hewitt (piano).

In both the *Italian concerto* and the *English suite* Angela Hewitt's playing is enormously alive and stimulating. She plays with vital imaginative resource, totally free from idiosyncrasy and affectation. The piano is beautifully captured on this recording, which must be numbered as one of the most successful DG have given us.

English suites Nos. 1–6, BWV 806/11.
*** Decca Dig. 421 640-2 (2) [id.]. András Schiff (piano).
(M) **(*) DG 427 146-2 (2) [id.]. Huguette Dreyfus (harpsichord).

Schiff is straightforward, finely articulated, rhythmically supple and vital. Ornamentation is stylishly and sensibly observed. Everything is very alive, without being in the least over-projected or exaggerated in any way. The Decca recording is altogether natural and present and places the odd- and even-numbered *Suites* together. Readers looking for the complete set played on the piano are unlikely to be disappointed.

Huguette Dreyfus recorded the *English suites* in 1972 but the recording does not sound dated. She plays very musically on an unnamed modern harpsichord and has plenty of rhythmic spirit.

English suites Nos. 2 in A min.; 3 in G min., BWV 807/8.
*** DG Dig. 415 480-2 [id.]. Ivo Pogorelich (piano).

The young Yugoslav pianist plays both *Suites* with a welcome absence of affectation. He observes all repeats and, although some of the *Sarabandes* are really rather slow, which may strain the allegiance of some listeners, there is generally speaking an impressive feeling of movement. It is all beautifully articulate and fresh. The recording is one of DG's best, with natural piano sound and an excellent sense of presence.

English suite No. 2 in A min., BWV 807; Partita No. 2 in C min., BWV 826; Toccata in C min., BWV 911.
(M) *** DG 423 880-2 [id.]. Martha Argerich (piano).

Martha Argerich does not disappoint: her playing is alive and keenly rhythmic but also wonderfully flexible and rich in colour. There is an intellectual and musical vitality here that is refreshing. Moreover Miss Argerich is very well recorded.

French suites Nos. 1–6, BWV 812/17. Capriccio, BWV 992.
(M) *** DG 427 149-2 (2) [id.]. Huguette Dreyfus (harpsichord).
**(*) HM HMC 90437/8 [id.]. Kenneth Gilbert (harpsichord).

French suites Nos. 1–6; Suites: in A min., BWV 818a; in E flat, BWV 819; Allemande, BWV 819a.
*** O-L Dig. 411811-2 (2) [id.]. Christopher Hogwood (harpsichord).

Huguette Dreyfus's playing is admirably straightforward, authoritative and vital; she commands splendid articulation in handling ornaments and, though she shows a strong rhythmic grip, there is no sense of metronomic rigidity. An enjoyable and recommendable set.

Christopher Hogwood uses two harpsichords, a Ruckers of 1646 enlarged and modified by Taskin in 1780, and a 1749 instrument, basically the work of Jean-Jacques Goujon and slightly modified by Jacques Joachim Swanen in 1784. They are magnificent creatures and Hogwood coaxes superb sounds from them: his playing is expressive, and the relentless sense of onward momentum that disfigures so many harpsichordists is pleasingly absent. These performances have both style and character and can be recommended with some enthusiasm. To the *French suites* themselves he adds the two others that Bach had obviously intended to include as Nos. 5 and 6. The useful notes describe the tuning which was adopted for each suite.

Kenneth Gilbert's recording dates from the mid-1970s. He uses a 1636 Ruckers, rebuilt by Hemsch, which is made to sound full and robust by the forward balance. One needs to set the volume control cautiously and perhaps make further adjustments at times. As in his set of the *English suites*, the playing has a natural flow; there is an obvious feeling for the strongly rhythmic French style, yet his flexibility prevents any sense of rigidity. Tempi are well judged and ornamentation is discreet. This is fine playing, but Hogwood has the advantage of digital recording and offers more music. Gilbert's set is played a semitone lower than normal present-day pitch.

Goldberg variations, BWV 988.
*** EMI Dig. CDC7 54209-2 [id.]. Bob van Asperen (harpsichord).
*** DG 415 130-2 [id.]. Trevor Pinnock (harpsichord).
*** Decca Dig. 417 116-2 [id.]. András Schiff (piano).
(M) *** Sony SBK 48173 [id.]. Charles Rosen (piano).
*** HM Dig. HMC 901240; *HMC 401240* [id.]. Kenneth Gilbert (harpsichord).
(M) *** HM/BMG GD 77149 [77149-2-RG]. Gustav Leonhardt (harpsichord).
*** Denon Dig. CO 73677 [id.]. Huguette Dreyfus (harpsichord).
**(*) ECM Dig. 839 622-2 [id.]. Keith Jarrett (harpsichord).

Goldberg variations, BWV 988. Adagio in G, BWV 968; Chromatic fantasia and fugue, BWV 903; Fantasia in C min., BWV906/1; Prelude in G, BWV 902/1.
*** Collins 7003-2 (2) [id.]. Virginia Black (harpsichord).

The excellence of Bob van Asperen's Bach has been amply demonstrated in recent years and his CD has one special claim on our attention – namely, the harpsichord he uses, which is by Michael Mietke. It is said to be the only surviving example by this maker, from whom Bach himself ordered an instrument. Of course that is not its only claim, for van Asperen is an artist of keen musical intelligence and sensitivity, whose thoughtful playing is well captured by the engineers. He does not observe every repeat but his CD accommodates 80 minutes music.

Trevor Pinnock uses a Ruckers dating from 1646, modified over a century later by Taskin and restored most recently in 1968 by Hubert Bédard. He retains repeats in more than half the variations – which seems a good compromise, in that variety is maintained yet there is no necessity for an additional disc. The playing is eminently vital and intelligent, with alert, finely articulated rhythm. The recording is very truthful and vivid.

For those who enjoy Bach on the piano, András Schiff's set can receive the most enthusiastic advocacy. The part-writing emerges with splendid definition and subtlety: Schiff does not play as if he is performing a holy ritual but with a keen sense of enjoyment of the piano's colour and sonority. The Decca recording is excellent in every way, clean and realistic.

To get Virginia Black's account on Collins you have to run to a second CD. She takes absolutely every repeat as did Tureck (on her earlier recording on a pair of HMV LPs) and Richter (Karl, not Sviatoslav) before her, which means making a change of disc, which breaks the spell. Hers is undoubtedly a performance of strong character and refined musicianship and she fills out the rest of the second disc admirably. No quarrels with her spirited account of these pieces or the quality of the Collins recording. It is not really possible to opt for one or the other as a first choice. You can't go far wrong with any of them. Turek's newer recording (TROY 007

– see above), made live in Stamford, Connecticut, is also pretty special, though not for authenticists.

Utterly different from Rosalyn Tureck's approach, Charles Rosen's set is bold, clear and direct. His intellectual grasp is impressive, his articulation strikingly clear and positive, yet there is no suggestion of rhythmic inflexibility. If you like your Bach straight, this has a great deal going for it. With 76 minutes playing time, Rosen had been able to be generous with repeats and there is a total absence of fussy ornamentation. At a concert this would be very well received; the balance is close and the 1967 studio sound is a little dry but not airless. Perhaps not a first choice, but very impressive.

Kenneth Gilbert gives a refreshingly natural performance of the *Goldberg*. He uses a recent copy of a Ruckers–Taskin, and it makes a very pleasing sound. His is an aristocratic reading; he avoids excessive display and there is a quiet, cultured quality about his playing that is very persuasive. An essentially introspective account, recorded in a rather less lively acoustic than is Pinnock on Archiv, and he is a thoughtful and thought-provoking player.

Gustav Leonhardt's third (1978) version of the *Goldberg* is most beautifully recorded. This is an introvert and searching performance, at times rhythmically very free and with the *Black Pearl* variation a case in point; but the reading is so thoughtful that no one can fail to draw illumination from it: this account is altogether fresher and more personal than his earlier one on Teldec. The CD transfer is wholly convincing.

Huguette Dreyfus plays a fine instrument, a Hemsch of 1754, and plays with her customary intelligence and musicianship. She observes all repeats (excepting the *Aria da capo*) though her account is only a minute shorter than Bob van Asperen's. Hers is a thoroughly recommendable account though the recording needs to be played (as is common throughout the discography not only of the *Goldberg* but practically all harpsichord music these days) at a lower than usual level setting.

There is a thoughtful integrity about Keith Jarrett's account of the *Goldberg variations* that is consistently impressive and, if at times (the *Adagio* of Variation 25, for instance) his approach seems a little introverted and literal, at other moments he can bring a keen concentration or produce an attractively spontaneous burst of vitality. He plays a Takahashi double-manual harpsichord, and he is naturally recorded within an intimate but not airless acoustic: the effect is realistic and pleasing. However, no notes are included about the music.

15 2-part Inventions, BWV 772/786; 15 3-part Inventions, BWV 787/801.
*** Capriccio Dig. 10 210 [id.] (with *6 Little preludes, BWV 933/8*). Ton Koopman (harpsichord).
*** Denon Dig. C37 7566 [id.]. Huguette Dreyfus (harpsichord).
*** DG Dig. 415 112-2 [id.]. Kenneth Gilbert (harpsichord).
**(*) Decca Dig. 411 974-2 [id.]. András Schiff (piano).

Begun in 1720 for his eldest son, ten-year-old Wilhelm Friedemann, these pieces were originally placed in order of difficulty, but Bach subsequently arranged them in ascending key order. Ton Koopman scores over such rivals as Kenneth Gilbert and Huguette Dreyfus in offering the *Six Little preludes* in addition to the two sets of *Inventions*. The disc does not identify Koopman's instrument, but it is obviously a fine one and Koopman plays with somewhat greater spontaneity and sparkle than does Gilbert. As usual, the recording places us too close to the instrument and one has to listen at a rather low-level setting to achieve a truthful and realistic result.

Dreyfus is very impressive, her playing relaxed though rhythmically vital. Her instrument is a Hemsch and her recording was made at Notre Dame in 1978. Mme Dreyfus is a shade warmer and freer than Gilbert and some will prefer her record.

Kenneth Gilbert plays a magnificent 1671 harpsichord by the Antwerp maker, Jan Couchet, which was restored in 1980 by Bédard. It has a rich, almost pearl-like sound, which is enhanced by the acoustic of Chartres Museum, where it was recorded. Gilbert's playing has exemplary taste and sense of musical purpose.

Readers who prefer their Bach on the piano will welcome András Schiff's excellent recording on Decca. His playing is (for this repertoire) rather generous with rubato and other expressive touches, but elegant in the articulation of part-writing. This is at times a bit overdone; such is his musicianship and pianistic sensitivity, however, that the overall results are likely to persuade most listeners. There is a lot of life and colour in the playing and much to enjoy. The recording is excellent; the instrument sounds extraordinarily lifelike, as if in one's very room.

Partitas Nos. 1–6, BWV 825/30.
*** DG Dig. 415 493-2 (2) [id.]. Trevor Pinnock (harpsichord).
*** Erato/Warner Dig. 2292 45345-2 (2) [id.]. Scott Ross (harpsichord).
*** Decca Dig. 411 732-2 (2) [id.]. András Schiff (piano).
**(*) EMI Dig. CDS7 47996-8 (2) [Ang. CDCB 47996]. Gustav Leonhardt (harpsichord).

Trevor Pinnock uses a copy of a Hemsch (*c.* 1760) by David Jacques Way, tuned to unequal temperament and sounding marvellously present in this recording. Tempi are generally well judged, rhythms vital yet free, and there is little to justify the criticism that he rushes some movements. He also conveys a certain sense of pleasure that is infectious and he has great spirit.

Scott Ross uses an unidentified instrument and is recorded with both warmth and clarity. He plays with style and panache and, despite one or two minor points (in the *B flat Gigue* not every note speaks evenly and at times elsewhere greater rhythmic freedom would be welcome), his readings make an eminently competitive alternative recommendation.

Schiff is a most persuasive advocate of Bach on the piano, consistently exploiting the modern instrument's potential in range of colour and light and shade, not to mention its sustaining power. Though few will cavil at his treatment of fast movements, some may find him a degree wayward in slow movements, though the freshness of his rubato and the sparkle of his ornamentation are always winning. The sound is outstandingly fine.

Gustav Leonhardt's EMI set was recorded on a Dowd (modelled on an eighteenth-century German instrument by Michael Mietke) in the excellent acoustic of the Doopsgezinde Gemeente Kerk in Haarlem. In terms of sheer sound it is among the most satisfactory available versions, and in terms of style it combines elegance, spontaneity and authority. There is nothing didactic about this playing, but it is never less than thought-provoking. In many respects it is musically the most satisfying of current sets, save for the fact that Leonhardt observes no repeats. This will undoubtedly diminish its appeal, which is a great pity since both illumination and pleasure are to be had from this set.

8 Preludes for W. F. Bach, BWV 924/32; 6 Little preludes, BWV 933/8; 5 Preludes, BWV 939/43; Prelude, BWV 999; Prelude, fugue and allegro in E flat, BWV 998; Preludes and fughettas: in F and G, BWV 901/2; Fantasia and fugue in A min., BWV 904.
**(*) DG Dig. 419 426-2 [id.]. Kenneth Gilbert (harpsichord).

Splendid artistry from this scholar-player; he is predictably stylish and authoritative. He uses a harpsichord by a Flemish maker, Jan Couchet, enlarged by Blanchet in 1759 and by Taskin in 1778, overhauled by Hubert Bédard. Even played at the lowest setting, the sound seems a bit unrelieved and overbright. This really has 'presence' with a vengeance. The excellence of the playing however is not in question.

Toccatas: in F sharp min.; C min.; D; D min.; E min.; G min.; G; BWV 910/16.
*** EMI Dig. CDC7 54081-2 [id.]. Bob van Asperen (harpsichord).

Bob van Asperen plays an instrument of 1728 by the Hamburg maker, Christian Zell, and, as is all too often the case with the harpsichord, is recorded at a high level. However, a lower than usual volume-setting will produce eminently satisfactory results. The *Toccatas* are very varied and this distinguished Dutch player conveys their improvisatory character with great flair. This is one of the most enjoyable Bach keyboard issues of recent years and can be recommended with confidence; where they overlap (in BWV 912–14 and 916), they score very slightly in terms of spontaneity over Kenneth Gilbert's excellent disc on DG Archiv (see above).

The Well-tempered Clavier (48 Preludes & fugues), BWV 846/893.
*** DG Dig. 413 439-2 (4) [id.]. Kenneth Gilbert (harpsichord).
**(*) HM Dig. HMC 901285/8; *HMC 401285/8* [id.]. Davitt Moroney (harpsichord).
(M) (**(*)) EMI mono CHS7 63188-2 (3) [Ang. CDH 63188]. Edwin Fischer.

The Well-tempered Clavier, Book I, Preludes and fugues Nos. 1–24, BWV 846/69.
❀ *** Decca Dig. 414 388-2 (2) [id.]. András Schiff (piano).
(M) (***) BMG/RCA mono GD 86217 (2) [6217-2-RC]. Wanda Landowska (harpsichord).

The Well-tempered Clavier, Book II, Preludes and fugues Nos. 25–48, BWV 870/93.
❀ *** Decca Dig. 417 236-2 (2) [id.]. András Schiff (piano).
(M) (***) BMG/RCA mono GD 87825 (3) [7825-2-RC]. Wanda Landowska (harpsichord).

Gilbert has made some superb harpsichord records, but his set of the 'Forty-eight' crowns them all. By a substantial margin it now supplants all existing harpsichord versions, with readings that are resilient and individual, yet totally unmannered. Though Gilbert deliberately refuses to use the sort of wide changes of registration which are now thought unauthentic, the range of his expression and the beauty of his instrument, made originally in Antwerp in 1671 and later enlarged in France, give all the variety needed. There is a concentration and purposefulness about each performance over the widest range of moods and expression, and the quality of recording, immediate without being too aggressive, adds to that, although some might feel that the acoustic is just a shade too resonant.

There are no advocates of Bach on the piano more imaginative or persuasive than András Schiff. His set of the 'Forty-eight', conveniently divided into two boxes of two discs, one for each book, is a delight throughout. Schiff – who at an early age found a mentor in Bach with the harpsichordist, George Malcolm – often takes a very individual view of particular preludes and fugues but, as with a pianist like Wilhelm Kempff, his unexpected readings regularly win one over long before the end. Consistently he translates this music into pianistic terms, rarely if ever imitating the harpsichord, and though his very choice of the piano will rule him out with those seeking authenticity, his voyage of discovery through this supreme keyboard collection is the more riveting, when the piano is an easier instrument to listen to over long periods. First-rate sound.

Davitt Moroney uses a modern harpsichord (built in 1980), which has a full-bodied yet cleanly focused image, but is rather too closely balanced. Yet the effect is certainly tangible and realistic, the perspective more convincing than with Leonhardt. His thoughtful, considered approach is satisfying in its way, stylistically impeccable, although the playing is less concentrated than with Gilbert, the result less exuberantly spontaneous than with András Schiff. But it will suit those who like a thoughtful, unostentatious approach to Bach, yet one that does not lack rhythmic resilience.

It is good that RCA have restored Landowska's celebrated records of the 'Forty-eight' to circulation, together with her original notes. They were recorded between 1949 and 1954 and are now accommodated on five well-filled CDs. They still sound marvellous and have a colour, vitality, authority and grandeur that make it difficult to stop listening to them.

Edwin Fischer's was the first ever 'Forty-eight' to be put on shellac, being recorded in 1933–6. After more than half a century the sound is inevitably dated and the piano tone papery and shallow but there is nothing shallow about these interpretations. Fischer produces a beauty of sound and a sense of line that is an unfailing source of musical wisdom and nourishment. The performance is economically laid out on three mid-price CDs, each accommodating close on 80 minutes.

The Well-tempered Clavier, Book II, Preludes and fugues Nos. 25–48, BWV 870/93.
*** ECM Dig. 847936-2 [id.]. Keith Jarrett (harpsichord).

Keith Jarrett recorded Book I on a modern piano, which we liked very much for its dedication and integrity. There was no attempt at any excessive indulgence in keyboard colour and, although on the face of it it is rather an odd idea to revert to the harpsichord in Book II and if his reasoning does not completely persuade us, his qualities of musicianship do. He is a highly intelligent and musical player, whose readings can hold their own against the current opposition.

ORGAN MUSIC

Complete organ music

Volume 1: *Fantasias, BWV 562, 570, 572; Fantasias & fugues, BWV 537, 542, 561; Fugues, BWV 575/577, 579, 581, 946; Kleines harmonisches Labyrinth, BWV 591; Passacaglia & fugue, BWV 582; Pedal-Exercitium, BWV 598; Preludes & fugues, BWV 531/533, 535, 548/551; Toccata, adagio & fugue, BWV 564; Toccatas & fugues, BWV 538, 540, 565; Trios, BWV 583, 585.*
(M) *** Decca 421 337-2 (3) [id.]. Peter Hurford (organs of Ratzeburg Cathedral, Germany, Church of Our Lady of Sorrows, Toronto).

Volume 2: *Chorale preludes, BWV 672/675, 677, 681, 683, 685, 687, 689; 24 Kirnberger Chorale preludes, BWV 690/713; Clavier-Übung, Part 3: German organ Mass (Prelude & fugue in E flat, BWV 552 & Chorale preludes, BWV 669/671, 676, 678, 680, 682, 684, 686, 688); 6 Trio sonatas, BWV 525/530.*
(M) *** Decca 421 341-2 (3) [id.]. Peter Hurford (organs of Chapels at New College, Oxford, &

Knox Grammar School, Sydney; Church of Our Lady of Sorrows, Toronto; Ratzeburg Cathedral).

Volume 3: *Canonic variations: Vom Himmel hoch, BWV 769; Chorale partitas: Christ, der du bist; O Gott, du frommer Gott; Sei gegrüsset, Jesu gütig, BWV 766/768; Chorale preludes, BWV 726/740; Schübler chorale preludes, BWV 645/650; Chorale variations: Ach, was soll ich sünder machen; Allein Gott in der Höh' sei Ehr, BWV 770/771. Concertos Nos. 1–6, BWV 592/597.*
❀ (M) *** Decca 421 617-2 (3) [id.]. Peter Hurford (organs as above, & Melk Abbey, Austria, and Eton College, Windsor).

Volume 4: *35 Arnstedt chorale preludes, BWV 714, 719, 742, 957 & 1090/1120* (from Yale manuscript, copied Neumeister); *18 Leipzig chorale preludes, BWV 651/58. Chorale preludes, BWV 663/668 & BWV 714/725.*
(M) *** Decca Dig./Analogue 421 621-2 (3) [id.]. Peter Hurford (Vienna Bach organ, Augustinerkirche, Vienna, & organs of All Souls' Unitarian Church, Washington, DC, St Catharine's College Chapel, Cambridge, Ratzeburg Cathedral, Knox Grammar School, Sydney, and Eton College, Windsor).

Volume 5: *Allabreve in D, BWV 589; Aria in F, BWV 587; Canzona in D min., BWV 588; Fantasias, BWV 563 & BWV 571; Fugues, BWV 574, BWV 578 & BWV 580; Musical offering, BWV 1079: Ricercar. Pastorale, BWV 590; Preludes, BWV 567/569; Preludes & fugues, BWV 534, 535a* (incomplete), *BWV 536, BWV 539, BWV 541, BWV 543/547; 8 Short Preludes & fugues, BWV 553/560; Prelude, trio & fugue, BWV 545b; Toccata & fugue in E, BWV 566; Trios, BWV 584, BWV 586 & BWV 1027a.*
(M) *** Decca 425 631-2 (3). Peter Hurford (organs of the Church of Our Lady of Sorrows, Toronto; Ratzeburg Cathedral; Eton College, Windsor; St Catharine's College Chapel, Cambridge; New College, Oxford; Domkirche, St Pölten, Austria; Stiftskirche, Melk, Austria; Knox Grammar School, Sydney).

Volume 6: *Chorale preludes Nos. 1–46 (Orgelbüchlein), BWV 599/644. Chorale preludes, BWV 620a, BWV 741/748, BWV 751/2, BWV 754/5, BWV 757/763, BWV 765, BWV Anh. 55; Fugue in G min., BWV 131a.*
(M) *** Decca 425 635-2 (2) [id.]. Peter Hurford (organs of the Church of Our Lady of Sorrows, Toronto; St Catharine's College Chapel, Cambridge; Eton College, Windsor).

With the exception of the *Arnstedt chorale preludes*, which were added in 1986 (and are digital), Peter Hurford recorded his unique survey of Bach's organ music for Decca's Argo label over a period of eight years, 1974–1982. Performances are consistently fresh and engrossing in their spontaneity; there is no slackening of tension and the registration features a range of baroque colour that is almost orchestral in its diversity. Hurford plays a number of different organs, moving, say, from Sydney to Toronto, then on to Washington, DC, back to Ratzeburg Cathedral in Germany, and thence home again to Oxford and Windsor. The digital recording of the Vienna Bach organ, used for the recently discovered *Arnstedt chorale preludes*, is particularly beautiful. Hurford here omits the three pieces which were already familiar (BWV 601, 639 and 737) but includes BWV 714 (which in the Neumeister manuscript is 27 bars longer than previously known versions), BWV 719 and 742 (hitherto not thought to be authentic Bach), and BWV 957 (until now not regarded as an organ work). This brings about a duplication of BWV 714 and 719, which were also recorded in Sydney in 1977.

Anyone wishing to explore the huge range of this repertoire could hardly do better than begin with one of these boxes, and perhaps a good jumping-off point would be Volume 3, to which we award a token Rosette: this includes many of the *Chorale preludes* and *Chorale variations*, in particular the splendid half-dozen chorales which were published at the very end of Bach's life and which commemorate the name of an otherwise unknown music-engraver called Schübler. The only real drawback to these otherwise admirable reissues is their sparse documentation. The organ specifications are included, but too little about the music itself. Volume 1, which includes many of the fantasias and fugues, preludes and fugues, and toccatas and fugues, is disgracefully inadequate in this respect, although Volumes 3 and 4 are much better. But with generous measure of music in each of the boxes, this remains overall the most rewarding assessment of Bach's organ music ever committed to record. These records are discussed more fully in our companion *Bargain Guide*.

Allabreve in D, BWV 589; Canzona in D min. BWV 589; Chorales: Wo soll ich fliehen hin, BWV 694; Wir Christenleut habn jetzund Freud, BWV 710; Fugues in C min., BWV 575; G, BWV 577;

Fugue sopra Magnificat: Meine Seele erhebet den Herren, BWV 733; Kleines Harmonisches Labyrinth, BWV 591. Partita sopra O Gott, du frommer Gott; Preludes & fugues in A min., BWV 551; C, BWV 545; D min., BWV 539.
** Erato/Warner Dig. 2292 45702-2 [id.]. Marie-Claire Alain (Silberman organ, Freiberg).

Orgelbüchlein: excerpts: *Chorales, BWV 618–624; 626; 627* (3 versions); *628–632. Prelude and fugue in G min., BWV 535; Toccata and fugue in D min. (Dorian), BWV 538.*
** Erato/Warner Dig. 2292 45701-2 [id.]. Marie-Claire Alain (Silberman organ, Freiberg).

It would appear that Marie-Claire Alain, using the splendid and highly suitable organ at Freiburg, is beginning a new, digitally recorded, Bach survey, favouring balanced miscellaneous recitals rather than putting the music in genre groups. She registers very pleasingly, but, as the *Alla breve* readily illustrates – which is very 'breve' indeed – these performances perpetuate the scholarly German tradition, which lays everything out in front of the listener soberly and finds no excuse whatsover for high spirits. The most animated of the *Preludes and fugues* is the *G minor*, BWV 535, and even here the fugue, though nicely registered, could use more momentum. The jolly *G major Fugue à la gigue*, BWV 577, is incredibly measured. The *Chorale preludes* come off best, though clearly in her interpretations of the briefer examples from the *Orgelbüchlein* (which centre on Easter and Whitsun) she has not taken the hyperbole of her own programme notes very much to heart, with their descriptions of 'tortured rhythms and brutal harmonies' (BWV 620) or the 'suffering and cruel destiny' of BWV 624. The recording of this entirely authentic organ is very realistic, but without the inner clarity that is sometimes achieved with baroque instruments; however, that may be partly to do with the organist's style of articulation.

Adagio in C (from *BWV 565); Chorales: Herzlich tut mich verlangen, BWV 727; Liebster Jesu, BWV 730; Wachet auf, BWV 645; Fantasia and fugue in G min., BWV 542; Fugue in E flat (St Anne), BWV 552; Passacaglia and fugue in C min., BWV 582; Toccata and fugue in D min., BWV 565.*
(M) *** Decca 417 711-2 [id.]. Peter Hurford (various organs).

An admirable popular recital. Performances are consistently alive and the vivid recording projects them strongly. A self-recommending issue.

(i) *Allabreve, BWV 589; Canzona, BWV 588; Fantasia in G, BWV 572; Prelude in A min., BWV 569;* (ii) *Trio sonatas: Nos. 1 in E flat, BWV 525; 2 in C min., BWV 526; 5 in C, BWV 529.*
(M) *** DG Dig. 431 705-2; *431 705-4.* Ton Koopman (organs of (i) Grote Kerk, Maassluis; (ii) Waalse Kerk, Amsterdam).

An excellent recital, with both organs beautifully recorded, with the single proviso that it was a pity to place the *Canzona* immediately after the *Allebreve*, as they are both slow pieces in rather similar style.

Allabreve in D, BWV 589; Chorale prelude: Ach Gott und Herr, BWV 714; Preludes and fugues, BWV 532 and BWV 553/560; Toccata and fugue in D min., BWV 565.
*** Mer. ECD 84081 [id.]. David Sanger (organ of St Catherine's College, Cambridge).

The organ at St Catherine's College, Cambridge, was completely rebuilt in 1978/9. The result is a great success, and its reedy clarity and brightness of timbre are especially suitable for Bach, as is immediately shown in the famous opening *D minor Toccata and fugue* which David Sanger presents with fluent vigour. His playing throughout is thoughtful and well structured; registration shows an excellent sense of colour without being flamboyant. The *Preludes and fugues* are laid out simply before the listener and, although Sanger's style is essentially relaxed, the forward momentum is maintained convincingly and Bach's music is allowed to speak for itself. The *Preludes and fugues in B flat*, BWV 560, and *in D*, BWV 532 (which ends the recital) are particularly convincing, and the latter makes a fine demonstration item alongside BWV 565 for its delightful registration in the fugue as well as for the light clarity of Sanger's touch.

35 Arnstadt chorale preludes, BWV 714, 719, 742, 957 & 1090/1120. Chorale prelude, BWV 639; Preludes and fugues: in C, BWV 531; in D min., BWV 549a; in G min., BWV 535; in E, BWV 566.
*** ASV Gaudeamus Dig. CD GAU 120/121; *ZC GAU 120/121* (available separately). Graham Barber (organ of St Peter Mancroft, Norwich).

33 Arnstadt chorale preludes (from Yale manuscript).
(B) *** HM Dig. HMA 905158 [id.]. Josph Paye (organ of St Paul's, Brookline, Mass).

This recording of the early, so-called *Neumeister chorales*, only recently discovered in the Music Library of Yale University, introduces a brilliant young organist, Graham Barber, and a fine new (1984) organ at Norwich, built with an ear to simulating the North German organs of the seventeenth century by Arp Schnitger and his contemporaries. In Graham Barber's hands it seems ideally suited for this early Bach repertoire, with the *Preludes and fugues* used to frame two separate recitals of the *Chorales*. Barber plays these opening and closing pieces with splendid vitality and structural grip, and presents the chorale variants simply and effectively, constantly changing colours and sound-weighting. The recording is very much in the demonstration class.

Joseph Payne uses the 1983 Bozeman-Gibson organ at St Paul's Church, Brookline, near Boston, which makes very suitable noises. The sound has a splendid definition and, though the acoustic is not particularly warm, this record collects the complete set together on a single CD and is very economically priced. Now reissued on Harmonia Mundi's budget Musique d'Abord label, this is even more attractive.

Chorale partita on Sei gegrüsset, Jesu gutig, BWV 768; Prelude and fugue in D, BWV 532; Prelude in G, BWV 568; Sonata No. 4 in E min., BWV 528.
*** Denon Dig. C37 7376 [id.]. Jacques Van Oortmerssen (organ of Waalse Kerk, Amsterdam).

The organ of the Waalse Kerk is a magnificent instrument. The opening *Prelude in G* massively demonstrates the power and variety of timbre it commands and Jacques Van Oortmerssen, although not an international virtuoso, is fully its master in the buoyant performance of the *Prelude and fugue in D*. His registration in the *Andante* of the *E minor Sonata* is a delight; in the extended variations of the *Sei gegrüsset partita* he is consistently imaginative in his choice of colouring. The playing, always alive, is traditional in the best sense, and the CD recording is superbly realistic. A most rewarding recital.

Chorale preludes Nos. 1–45 (Orgelbüchlein), BWV 599–644 (complete).
*** DG Dig. 431 816-2 [id.]. Simon Preston (organ of Sorø Abbey, Denmark).

Simon Preston conveniently gathers all 45 chorales of the *Orgelbüchlein* on to a single (74-minute) CD and plays them with persuasive musicianship on a fine Danish organ, reconstructed in 1942. It sounds well in this clear but sonorous recording, yet Preston does not quite find the range of colour that makes Hurford's recordings so aurally stimulating, and the effect is more monochrome and essentially more sober. Even so, this is a thoroughly recommendable survey and now replaces Jørgen Hansen's set on Denon, which is on two discs.

Chorale preludes for Christmas: BWV 600–2, 607–10, 611, 614, 659, 701, 710, 703. Canonic variations on Vom himmel hoch, BWV 769. Pastorale in F, BWV 590; Trio: Herr Jesu Christ, dich zu uns wend, BWV 655.
(B) ** HM HMA 90717 [id.]. Lionel Rogg (Silbermann organ, Arlesheim).

A selection of chorales associated with the theme of Christmas is a happy idea, and the Arlesheim organ is the right instrument. Its flute stop is appealingly piquant, as we hear in the *Fugue* on *Von Himmel Hoch*, the chorale, *In dulci jubilo*, and the *Pastorale*, BWV 590. Lionel Rogg plays the music immaculately; his style, however, is rather sober and reserved, and at times one feels the need of a bolder use of colour and a sense of joy in Bach's invention. The recording is very faithful.

Chorale preludes: Ach bleib' bei uns, BWV 649; Liebster Jesu, BWV 731; O Mensch, bewein, BWV 662; Wachet auf, BWV 645; Fantasia in G, BWV 572; Fugue in E flat (St Anne), BWV 552; Prelude and fugue in C, BWV 545; Toccata and fugue in D min., BWV 565.
(B) **(*) CfP CD-CFP 4479; *TC-CFP 4479*. Noel Rawsthorne (organ of Liverpool Cathedral).

Those who like their Bach on a really big, modern organ, rather than seeking the reedier quality of a baroque instrument, will find that Noel Rawsthorne's performances have plenty of vigour and they are effectively registered too, especially the chorale preludes, where the colouring is always apt. Certainly the flute stop at the opening of the *Fantasia in G* is highly effective, though its chimera emphasizes the weightiness of the majestic central section and the more florid close. The two larger works have the right balance of momentum and controlled tension and, although the sound has a sense of spectacle, this is a (1979) Brian Culverhouse recording and inner detail is only slightly blurred by the resonance. The CD transfer is most impressive, firming up the sound and adding to its tangibility. Excellent notes about the music, but none about the organ specification.

Chorale preludes: Ich ruf' zu dir, Herr Jesu Christ, BWV 639; Nun komm der Heiden Heiland, BWV 659; Schübler chorale: Wachet auf, BWV 645; Fantasia and fugue in G min., BWV 542; Partita: O Gott, du frommer Gott, BWV 767; Prelude and fugue in E flat (St Anne), BWV 552; Toccata and fugue in D min., BWV 565.
*** Novalis Dig. 150 005-2 [id.]. Ton Koopman (Christian Müller organ, Waalse Kerk, Amsterdam).

Ton Koopman opens with three of Bach's most powerfully structured works for this instrument. The *Prelude and fugue*, BWV 552, were designed separately to frame the third part of the *Clavierübung* (the so-called *German organ Mass*) and, heard together, they extend to just over 14 minutes. The *Partita* based on *O Gott, du frommer Gott* has eight diverse variations but is by no means lightweight. Then follows the *Fantasia and fugue in G minor*: the *Fantasia* bold and improvisatory, the *Fugue* swiftly moving and here buoyantly paced. The three chorales make a contrasting centrepiece with *Nun komm der Heiden Heiland* poignantly serene and the famous Schübler chorale, *Wachet auf*, infectiously jaunty. For the most popular of all Bach's organ pieces Ton Koopman then changes to a more flamboyant style. The organ is itself a 'co-star' of the programme, producing magnificent, unclouded sonorities in the spacious tapestry of BWV 552 and a wide palette of colour, which Koopman uses so effectively in the *Partita* and *Chorale preludes*. The recording is in the demonstration bracket, the microphones in exactly the right place for a proper illusion of reality.

Chorale preludes: Liebster Jesu, BWV 633; Wachet auf, BWV 645; Wir gläuben all, BWV 680; Chorale preludes from Cantatas: Jesu, joy of man's desiring, BWV 147; Awake thou wintry earth, BWV 129. Fugue in G min., BWV 578; Prelude and fugue in A min., BWV 543; Toccata, adagio and fugue in C, BWV 564; Toccata and fugue in D min., BWV. 565. Other arrangements: *Cantata No. 29: Sinfonia. Keyboard concerto No. 5: Arioso. Suite No. 3, BWV 1068: Air.*
(M) **(*) Decca 430 746-2; *430 746-4* [id.]. Carlo Curley (organ of Girard College Chapel, Philadelphia).

Carlo Curley finds it impossible to be dull in Bach, but not everyone will respond to his unbridled flamboyance. Yet the magnificent Philadelphia organ (described in detail in our Recitals section under its player) brings some superb sounds in the *Toccata and fugue in D minor* (and some individual flourishes too) and is equally magnificent in the other fugal set-pieces (although elsewhere Curley's fugal style is rather steady and positive). In a piece like *Awake thou wintry earth*, even the dead surely could not remain asleep, such is Curley's persuasive vigour, but the slower chorales are played slowly, with respectfully warm sentiment, as is the famous orchestral *Air*.

Chorale preludes: Nun komm der Heiden Heiland, BWV 659; Wachet auf, BWV 645; Concerto in A min. (after Vivaldi), *BWV 593; Fantasia and fugue in G min., BWV 542; Passacaglia in C min., BWV 582; Toccata, adagio and fugue in C, BWV 564; Toccata and fugue in D min., BWV 565.*
(M) ** EMI CD-EMX 2189; *TC-EMX 2189*. Lionel Rogg (Metzler organs of St Peter's Cathedral, Geneva, & Klosterkirche, Muri, Switzerland; Anderson organ of Sorø Abbey, Denmark).

Lionel Rogg has made three surveys of Bach's organ music in stereo, the first an integral set on the BACH label for Oryx in the 1960s, then again for Harmonia Mundi a decade later. These recordings come from his further HMV series, mostly from 1975–6, but with the two chorales recorded as recently as 1985. His style is relaxed and somewhat didactic, though he takes a brisk view of the famous *Toccata and fugue in D minor* which opens the programme. He is at his best in the works which gain from a measured pulse and a clear grasp of the architecture, like the *Passacaglia in C minor* and BWV 564, although the lighter *Concerto* after Vivaldi is also quite successful. The sound is very clear, but the digital remastering has brought just a touch of harshness to the reeds; although the ambient effect is still telling, the originals had more warmth of sonority.

Chorale preludes: Vater unser im Himmelreich, BWV 682; Jesu Christus, unser Heiland, BWV 688; Fantasia in G, BWV 572; Partita: Sei gegrüsset, Jesu gütig, BWV 768; Prelude and fugue in A min., BWV 543; Toccata and fugue in D min. (Dorian), BWV 538; Trio sonata in G, BWV 530.
*** Novalis Dig. 150 036-2 [id.]. Ton Koopman (organ of Grote Keerk, Leeuwarden).

Another outstanding recital, extremely well played and splendidly recorded, using an organ admirably suited to Bach's music. The effect has resonance and power yet never really clouds detail, so that the engagingly light bravura of the playing of the brilliant *Fantasia in G* is as effective as the colourful variants of the famous *Partita, Sei gegrüsset, Jesu gütig*. Ton Koopman is strikingly fluent in the fugues; that of the *A minor* work, BWV 543, has an exhilarating momentum, while the *Trio sonata* is given apt contrasts of registration. The programme runs for over 70 minutes and is very well laid out for continuous listening.

Concertos (for solo organ) *Nos. 1 in G* (after ERNST: *Concerto*); *2 in A min.* (after VIVALDI: *Concerto, Op. 3/8*); *3 in C* (after VIVALDI: *Concerto, Op. 7/11*); *4 in C* (after ERNST: *Concerto*); *5 in D min.* (after VIVALDI: *Concerto, Op. 3/11*), *BWV 592/6*.
*** DG Dig. 423 087-2 [id.]. Simon Preston (organ of Lübeck Cathedral).

It was Prince Johann Ernst who introduced Bach to the Italian string concertos; these are Bach's arrangements, with the music for the most part left with little alteration or embellishment. The two Ernst works show a lively and inventive if not original musicianship. The performances are first class and the recording admirably lucid and clear, yet with an attractively resonant ambience.

Fantasia in G, BWV 572; Preludes and fugues: in C, BWV 545; in C min.; in G, BWV 549/50; in G min., BWV 535; Pastorale, BWV 590; Toccata and fugue in D min., BWV 565.
(M) *** Ph. 420 860-2. Wolfgang Rübsam (organ of Frauenfeld, Switzerland).

A splendid collection of early works, nearly all dating from Bach's Arnstadt and Weimar periods and full of exuberance of spirit. The quality of the recorded sound is splendid. Highly recommended.

Fantasia and fugue in G min., BWV 542; Pastorale in F, BWV 590; Passacaglia and fugue in C min., BWV 582; Preludes and fugues in A min., BWV 543; in B min., BWV 544; in C, BWV 545.
(M) **(*) Sony SBK 46551 [id.]. E. Power Biggs (Flenthrop organ in the Busch-Reisinger Museum, Harvard University).

As we know from Carlo Curley's records, Europe does not have a monopoly of fine organs, and the Dutch-built Harvard instrument, installed in 1958, has the fullest reserves of power yet also a commendable clarity. Moreover the reeds have an attractively bright, fluid quality that is suited to music of most sources and periods. E. Power Biggs conveys his enjoyment in an easily produced flowing line and inner clarity, but he makes the mistake of relaxing too much. It is all very well to enjoy the colours of the registration (and that one certainly does – in the *Pastorale* the organ's flute-tones having a charming colouring all their own) but Bach implies inner tension too and that is not always fully sustained. The famous *D minor Toccata and fugue* is certainly stimulating, and in its middle section the bright piping noises are most attractive. But the final pages, which culminate in one of Bach's most impressive cadences, appear and pass with a surprising degree of nonchalance. The *Passacaglia and fugue in C minor* is a little stoic but well structured, and the *Fantasia and fugue in G minor* and closing *B minor* and *C major Preludes and fugues* show Biggs at his best, presenting the music in a clear, unforced manner with vivid registration, letting the splendid organ and Bach's musical argument combine in the most positive way. These three pieces were recorded in 1971, the rest of the programme in 1960 or 1964. But the transfers to CD are of the highest quality and this programme is technically most impressive. The organ-sound is thrilling yet natural: the listener's experience is of actually being in the Romanesque Hall at Harvard University.

Fantasia and fugue in G min., BWV 542; Passacaglia and fugue in C min., BWV 582; 6 Schübler chorales, BWV 645/50; Toccata, adagio and fugue in C, BWV 564; Toccata and fugue in F, BWV 540.
❀ *** DG Dig. 435 381-2 [id.]. Simon Preston (Sauer organ in St Peter's, Waltrop, near Dortmund).

Simon Preston's recital at St Peter's, Waltrop, is a magnificent demonstration of the splendour and power of Bach's more ambitious organ statements, admirably contrasted with music which is inherently less weighty, if not less inspired. Preston is in his element in the flamboyant *Toccata in C*, which opens with a skittish flourish then produces an irrepressible cascade of florid writing that is consistently exhilarating, given such improvisational bravura and crisp, clean articulation. When, after the more solemn *Adagio*, the fugue arrives, it has a playfully rhythmic main theme which here persists in its light-hearted buoyancy to the very end of the work. The *Fantasia in G minor* is hardly less rhetorical in spirit, but massive in its complex texture and close-knit weave of colour; in Simon Preston's hands, the fugue which follows opens with genial high spirits, then moves with increasing tension to a hugely impressive final cadence with an overwhelming sense of apotheosis. The majestic *Toccata in F* has a quite remarkable forward drive, which Preston sustains throughout its 8-minute span, and it is followed by a fugue of comparable contrapuntal intensity. The famous *Passacaglia and fugue in C* brings an sense of absolute inevitability; in controlling its overall span, Preston is able to let the tension fall back a little at the opening of the fugue, before moving on to the remorseless dénouement. The engaging *Schübler chorales* are used to provide contrast at the centre of the 71-minute recital, and Preston chooses a lighter, more pointed style than usual. He begins jauntily with *Wachet auf* and registers to provide complete transparency of texture so that the *cantus firmus* does not need forceful enunciation. His style is particularly effective in the piquant fantasia of the closing *Kommst du nun*. The Sauer organ in Waltrop is a modern instrument (1984) of splendid range, with a diversity of colour that is ideal for baroque repertoire and Bach in particular. There is an enormous reserve of power in the pedals, and the richer sonorities elsewhere bring no attendant clouding. This is one of the very finest Bach collections of the digital CD era.

Fugue à la gigue in F, BWV 577; Prelude and fugue in E flat (St Annes), BWV 552; Trio sonata No. 5 in C, BWV 529; 6 Schübler chorale preludes, BWV 645/50.
(M) *(**) EMI CDM7 64192-2 [id.]; *EG 764192-4*. Ralph Downes (organ of Royal Festival Hall) – WIDOR: *Toccata*. ***

The *Fugue à la gigue* – a delightfully spirited reading – and the spectacular coupled Widor *Toccata* date from the very earliest days of stereo, and the Pye disc which included these performances was among the first stereo pressings available in the UK. The other recordings date from a decade later. Ralph Downes helped to design the Festival Hall organ which (because of its wide spatial layout) is ideal for stereo. The point source of the different pipes means that in the *Schübler chorales* (splendidly played) the cantus firmus can appear from one side of the audio spectrum and the supple counter-melodic flow from the other; and Downes makes the very most of this in his registration. This is aurally intriguing as well as musically effective. Unfortunately the master tapes appear to have become degraded and there is some insecurity of pitch towards the end of the *Schübler chorales*; and the *Fugue à la gigue* brings further pitch differential at the opening. No matter, this is still a fascinating disc, and the playing is first class.

8 Little Preludes and fugues, BWV 553/560; Prelude and fugue in D, BWV 532; Toccata, adagio & fugue in C, BWV 564; Trio sonata No. 1 in E flat, BWV 525.
*** ASV Novalis Dig. 150 066-2; *150 066-4* [id.]. Ton Koopman (organ of Grote Kerk, Maassluis).

Ton Koopman's continuing series never fails to stimulate, and this is one of the very finest of his recitals, demonstrating a magnificent instrument, highly suitable for Bach, of which he is completely the master. He brings the eight *Little Preludes and fugues* splendidly to life and is even more commanding in the excitingly intricate *Prelude and fugue in D minor* and the superb *Toccata, adagio and fugue*, which demands comparable bravura. Both works come from the composer's early Weimar period. The *Trio sonata* makes an effective contrast after the latter work. The digital recording is first rate: Bach organ records don't come any better than this.

6 Schübler chorales, BWV 645/650; Pastorale in F, BWV 590; Passacaglia in C min., BWV 582; Toccata, adagio & fugue in C, BWV 564; Toccata & fugue in D min., BWV 565.
(M) *** DG Dig. 427 801-2; *427 801-4*. Ton Koopman (organs of Grote Kerk, Maassluis, & Waalse Kerk, Amsterdam).

In these earlier, DG recordings, Ton Koopman uses two different organs, principally the Grote Kerk, Maassluis; but the *Schübler chorales* are recorded on the Waalse Kerk, Amsterdam, whose reeds are livelier almost to the point of stridency, underscored by the emphatically rhythmic style of the playing. The effect is certainly full of character. The programme includes the famous *D minor Toccata and fugue*, BWV 565, and this performance has an engaging eccentricity in that Koopman introduces decoration into the opening flourishes. Excellent contrast is provided by the *Pastorale*. The other performances are well structured and alive, if sometimes rather considered in feeling.

VOCAL MUSIC

Volume 1: *Cantatas Nos. 1: Wie schön leuchtet uns der Morgenstern; 2: Ach Gott, vom Himmel; 3: Ach Gott, wie manches Herzeleid; 4: Christ lag in Todesbanden.*
(M) *** Teldec/Warner 2292 42497-2 (2) [id.]. Treble soloists from V. Boys' Ch., Esswood, Equiluz, Van Egmond, V. Boys' Ch., Ch. Viennensis, VCM, Harnoncourt.

Volume 2: (i) *Cantatas Nos. 5: Wo soll ich fliehen; 6: Bleib bei uns;* (ii) *7: Christ unser Herr zum Jordan kam; 8: Liebster Gott.*
(M) *** Teldec/Warner 2292 42498-2 (2) [id.]. Esswood, Equiluz, Van Egmond, (i) Treble soloists from V. Boys' Ch., Ch. Viennensis, V. Boys' Ch., VCM, Harnoncourt; (ii) Regensburg treble soloists, King's College Ch., Leonhardt Cons., Leonhardt.

Volume 3: (i) *Cantatas Nos. 9: Es ist das Heil; 10: Meine Seele erhebt den Herrn;* (ii) *11: Lobet Gott in seinen Reichen.*
(M) *** Teldec/Warner 2292 42499-2 (2) [id.]. Esswood, Equiluz, Van Egmond; (i) Regensburg treble soloists, King's College Ch., Leonhardt Cons., Leonhardt; (ii) Treble soloists from V. Boys' Ch., Ch. Viennensis, V. Boys' Ch., VCM, Harnoncourt.

The remarkable Teldec project, a complete recording of all Bach's cantatas, began in the early 1970s and has now reached completion. The digital remastering has proved consistently successful. The CDs retain the English translations of the texts and excellent notes by Alfred Dürr. The authentic character of the performances means that boys replace women, not only in the choruses but also as soloists, and the size of the forces is confined to what we know Bach himself would have expected. The simplicity of the approach brings its own merits, for the imperfect yet other-worldly quality of some of the treble soloists refreshingly focuses the listener's attention on the music itself. Less appealing is the quality of the violins, which eschew vibrato – and, it would sometimes seem, any kind of timbre! Generally speaking, there is a certain want of rhythmic freedom and some expressive caution. Rhythmic accents are underlined with some regularity and the grandeur of Bach's inspiration is at times lost to view. These cantatas are discussed in greater detail in our *Bargain Guide*.

Cantata No. 10: Meine Seele erhebt den Herrn.
(M) *** Decca 425 650-2 [id.]. Ameling, Watts, Krenn, Rintzler, V. Ac. Ch., Stuttgart CO, Münchinger – *Easter oratorio.* ***

An excellent coupling for a first-rate account of the surprisingly little-recorded *Easter oratorio*. This fine cantata is very well sung and played, with all the performers at their best. The recording too is freshly vivid.

Volume 4: *Cantatas Nos. 12: Weinen, klagen, sorgen, zagen; 13: Meine Seufzer, meine Tränen; 14: Wär Gott nicht mit uns diese Zeit; 16: Herr Gott, dich loben wir.*
(M) *** Teldec/Warner 2292 42500-2 (2) [id.]. Gampert, Hinterreiter, Esswood, Equiluz, Van Altena, Van Egmond, Tölz Boys' Ch., King's Coll. Ch., Leonhardt Cons., Leonhardt.

Volume 5: *Cantatas Nos. 17: Wer Dank opfert, der preiset mich; 18: Gleichwie der Regen und Schnee vom Himmel; 19: Es erhub sich ein Streit; 20: O Ewigkeit, du Donnerwort.*
(M) *** Teldec/Warner 2292 42501-2 (2) [id.]. Treble soloists from V. Boys' Ch., Esswood, Equiluz, Van Egmond, V. Boys' Ch., Ch. Viennensis, VCM, Harnoncourt.

Volume 6: *Cantatas Nos.* (i) *21: Ich hatte viel Bekümmernis;* (ii) *22: Jesus nahm zu sich die Zwölfe; 23: Du wahrer Gott und Davids Sohn.*
(M) **(*) Teldec/Warner 2292 42502-2 (2) [id.]. Esswood, Equiluz; (i) Walker, Wyatt, V. Boys' Ch., Ch. Viennensis, VCM, Harnoncourt; (ii) Gampert, Van Altena, Van Egmond, King's College Ch., Leonhardt Cons., Leonhardt.

Volume 7: *Cantatas Nos. 24: Ein ungefärbt Gemüte; 25: Es ist nicht Gesundes an meinem Leibe; 26: Ach wie flüchtig, ach wie nichtig; 27: Wer weiss, wie nahe mir mein Ende!.*
(M) *** Teldec/Warner 2292 42503-2 (2). Esswood, Equiluz, Van Egmond, Nimsgern, V. Boys' Ch., Ch. Viennensis, VCM, Harnoncourt.

Volume 8: *Cantatas Nos. 28: Gottlob! nun geht das Jahr zu Ende; 29: Wir danken dir, Gott; 30: Freue dich, erlöste Schar.*
(M) *** Teldec/Warner 2292 42504-2 (2). Esswood, Equiluz, Van Egmond, Nimsgern, V. Boys' Ch., Ch. Viennensis, VCM, Harnoncourt.

Volume 9: *Cantatas Nos.* (i) *31: Der Himmel lacht! die Erde jubilieret;* (ii) *32: Liebster Jesu, mein Verlangen; 33: Allein zu dir, Herr Jesu Christ;* (i) *34: O ewiges Feuer, O Ursprung der Liebe.*
(M) *** Teldec/Warner 2292 42505-2 (2). (i) Esswood, Equiluz, Nimsgern, V. Boys' Ch., Ch. Viennensis, VCM, Harnoncourt; (ii) Gampert, Jacobs, Van Altena, Van Egmond, Hanover Boys' Ch., Leonhardt Cons., Leonhardt.

Volume 10: *Cantatas Nos. 35: Geist und Seele wird verwirret; 36: Schwingt freudig euch empor; 37: Wer da gläubet und getauft wird; 38: Aus tiefer Not schrei ich zu dir.*
(M) *** Teldec/Warner 2292 42506-2 (2). Esswood, Equiluz, Van der Meer, V. Boys' Ch., Ch. Viennensis, VCM, Harnoncourt.

Cantatas Nos. 35: Geist und Seele wird verwirret; 53: Schlage doch, gewunschte Stunde; 82: Ich habe genug.
**(*) HM Dig. HMC 901273; *HMC 401273* [id.]. René Jacobs, Ens. 413, Banchini.

This CD offers three solo vocal cantatas, sung by the Belgian counter-tenor, René Jacobs. No. 82, *Ich habe genug*, was originally written for bass, but subsequently Bach arranged it for soprano, and in 1735 for alto, replacing the oboe with a flute. Jacobs elects to retain the oboe and sings it with great intelligence, though his tone at the top end of his tessitura is not always pleasing. The instrumental contribution is expert (incidentally, the Ensemble 413 takes its name from one of the tuning pitches used in the baroque period) and the recording is first class.

Volume 11: *Cantatas Nos.* (i) *39: Brich dem Hungrigen dein Brot;* (i; ii) *40: Dazu ist erschienen der Sohn Gottes;* (iii) *41: Jesu, nun sei gepreiset; 42: Am Abend aber desselbigen Sabbats.*
(M) ** Teldec/Warner 2292 42556-2 (2). (i) Jacobs, Van Egmond, Hanover Boys' Ch., Leonhardt Cons., Leonhardt; (ii) Van Altena; (iii) Esswood, Equiluz, Van der Meer, V. Boys' Ch., Ch. Viennensis, VCM, Harnoncourt.

Volume 12: *Cantatas Nos.* (i) *43: Gott fähret auf mit Jauchzen; 44: Sie werden euch in die Bann tun;* (ii) *45: Es ist dir gesagt, Mensch, was gut ist; 46: Schauet doch und sehet.*
(M) *** Teldec/Warner 2292 42559-2 (2) [id.]. (i) Jelosits, Esswood, Equiluz, Van der Meer, V. Boys' Ch., Ch. Viennensis, VCM, Harnoncourt; (ii) Jacobs, Equiluz, Kunz, Hanover Boys' Ch., Leonhardt Cons., Leonhardt.

Volume 13: *Cantatas Nos. 47: Wer sich selbst erhöhet; 48: Ich elender Mensch, wer wird mich erlösen; 49: Ich geh' und suche mit Verlangen; 50: Nun ist das Heil und die Kraft.*
(M) *** Teldec/Warner 2292 42560-2 (2) [id.]. Jelosits, Esswood, Equiluz, Van der Meer, V. Boys' Ch., Ch. Viennensis, VCM, Harnoncourt.

Cantata No. 51: Jauchzet Gott in allen Landen.
*** Ph. Dig. 411 458-2 [id.]. Emma Kirkby, E. Bar. Soloists, Gardiner – *Magnificat.* ***

Jauchzet Gott is one of Bach's most joyful cantatas; Emma Kirkby follows the example of the opening trumpeting (Crispian Steele-Perkins – in excellent form) when she begins. It is a brilliantly responsive performance, admirably accompanied and very well recorded.

Volume 14: *Cantatas Nos. 51: Jauchzet Gott im allen Landen; 52: Falsche Welt, dir trau ihr nicht; 54: Widerstehe doch der Sünde; 55: Ich armer Mensch, ich Sündenknecht; 56: Ich will den Kreuzstab gerne tragen.*
(M) *** Teldec/Warner 2292 42422-2 (2) [id.]. Kweksilber, Kronwitter, Esswood, Equiluz, Schopper, Hanover Boys' Ch., Leonhardt Cons., Leonhardt.

Cantatas Nos. 54: Widerstehe doch der Sünde; 169: Got soll allein; 170: Vergnügte Ruh'.
*** Hyp. Dig. CDA 66326; *KA 66326* [id.]. James Bowman, King's Consort, King.

James Bowman is on impressive form and his admirers need not hesitate here. In No. 54 he comes into competition only with Paul Esswood in the complete Teldec series, and this particular volume is one of the best in the Teldec series. In any case, their different musical insights and vocal quality are not mutually exclusive. The present disc is very desirable and the King's Consort under Robert King give excellent support. Good recorded sound.

Cantatas Nos. 56: Ich will den Kreuzstab gerne tragen; 82: Ich habe genug; (i) *158: Der Friede sei mit dir.*
*** O-L Dig. 425 822-2. Opalach, (i) Monahan, Stevens, Hite; Bach Ens., Rifkin.

Joshua Rifkin's series has so far been very uneven, but this newcomer challenges territory conquered in the past by Fischer-Dieskau, Haefliger, Souzay and Hans Hotter among others. In the two solo cantatas, Jan Opalach is magnificent and is excellently supported by Rifkin and his group. Perhaps the marvellous opening ritornello to *Ich habe genug* could have been handled more imaginatively and held together better, though the individual instrumentalists are sensitive. *Der Friede sei mit dir* is much more of a rarity but hardly less rewarding; the other soloists listed take the one-to-a-part voices in the chorales. A refreshingly successful issue.

Volume 15: *Cantatas Nos. 57: Selig ist der Mann; 58: Ach Gott, wie manches Herzeleid; 59: Wer mich liebet, der wird mein Wort halten; 60: O Ewigkeit, du Donnerwort.*
(M) **(*) Teldec/Warner 2292 42423-2 [id.]. Jelosits, Kronwitter, Esswood, Equiluz, Van der Meer, Tölz Boys' Ch., VCM, Harnoncourt.

Cantatas Nos. 57: Selig ist der Mann; 58: Ach Gott, wie manches; 59: Wer mich lieber; 152: Tritt auf die Glaubensahn.
*** Hung. Dig. HCD 12897 [id.]. Zádori, Polgár, Savaria Vocal Ens., Capella Savaria, Pál Németh.

These dialogue cantatas are well served by the Capella Savaria, a Hungarian period-instrument ensemble of considerable quality, and the two soloists. Mária Zádori and László Polgár are obviously singers of no mean accomplishment (the soprano sings with great spirit) and have a good sense of style. A rewarding, well-recorded issue and good value at slightly less than full price.

Volume 16: *Cantatas Nos. 61: Nun komm, der Heiden Heiland; 62: Nun komm, der Heiden Heiland; 63: Christen, ätzet diesen Tag; 64: Sehet, welch eine Liebe.*
(M) **(*) Teldec/Warner 2292 42565-2 (2) [id.]. Jelosits, Kronwitter, Esswood, Equiluz, Van der Meer, Tölz Boys' Ch., VCM, Harnoncourt.

Volume 17: *Cantatas Nos.* (i) *65: Sie werden aus Saba alle kommen*; (ii) *66: Erfreut euch, ihr Herzen; 67: Halt' im Gedächtnis Jesum Christ;* (i) *68: Also hat Gott die Welt geliebt.*
(M) ** Teldec/Warner 2292 42571-2 (2) [id.]. (i) Jelosits, Equiluz, Van der Meer, Tölz Boys' Ch., VCM, Harnoncourt; (ii) Esswood, Equiluz, Van Egmond, Hanover Boys' Ch., Ghent Coll. Vocale, Leonhardt Cons., Leonhardt.

Cantatas Nos. 67: Halt' im Gedächtnis Jesum Christ; 130: Herr Gott, dich loben alle wir.
(M) **(*) Decca 433 175-2. Ameling, Watts, Krenn, Krause, Lausanne Pro Arte Ch., SRO, Ansermet – *Magnificat.* ***

A good and very enjoyable Bach cantata pairing. No. 130 is a particularly fine piece which, apart from the excellent choir and soloists, offers distinguished obbligato flute playing from André Pepin. The sound is good and the *Magnificat* coupling well worth while.

Volume 18: *Cantatas Nos. 69 & 69a: Lobe den Herrn, meine Seeele; 70: Wachet! betet! betet! wachet!; 71: Gott ist mein König; 72: Alles nur nach Gottes Willen.*
(M) *** Teldec/Warner 2292 42572-2 (2) [id.]. Esswood, Equiluz, Van der Meer, Visser, Tölz Boys' Ch., VCM, Harnoncourt.

Volume 19: *Cantatas Nos. 73: Herr, wie du willt, so schicks mit mir; 74: Wer mich liebet, der wird mein Wort halten; 75: Die Elenden sollen essen.*
(M) ** Teldec/Warner 2292 42573-2 [id.]. Erler, Klein, Esswood, Equiluz, Kraus, Van Egmond, Hanover Boys' Ch., Ghent Coll. Vocale, Leonhardt Cons., Leonhardt.

Volume 20: *Cantatas Nos.* (i) *76: Die Himmel erzählen die Ehre Gottes;* (ii) *77: Du sollt Gott, deinen Herren, lieben; 78: Jesu, der du meine Seele;* (ii) *79: Gott der Herr ist Sonn' und Schild.*
(M) **(*) Teldec/Warner 2292 42576-2 (2) [id.]. Esswood, (i) Wiedl, Equiluz, Van der Meer, Tölz Boys' Ch., VCM, Harnoncourt; (ii) Bratschke, Kraus, Van Egmond, Hanover Boys' Ch., Ghent Coll. Vocale, Leonhardt Cons., Leonhardt.

Cantatas Nos. 78: Jesu, der du meine Seele; 198: Lass, Furstin nich einen Strahl (Trauerode).
**(*) HM Dig. HMC 901270; *HMC 401270* [id.]. Schmithüsen, Brett, Crook, Kooy, Paris Chapelle Royale Ch. & O, Herreweghe.

The *Trauerode* is a huge piece in ten numbers, divided into two parts which were separated by the funeral oration. This recording has been well received and, indeed, there are many felicitous touches, some good solo singing and beautifully transparent orchestral textures. At the same time, Herreweghe takes the opening chorus far too briskly: the effect is jaunty (one is almost tempted to say bouncy) and there is a resultant loss of both dignity and breadth. However, it is only fair to say that much else here is well judged. This also has the advantage of offering another masterpiece, *Jesu, der du meine Seele*, which offers some excellent solo contributions from Ingrid Schmithüsen and Charles Brett. The balance of the recording is exemplary, with cleanly focused and well-defined detail.

Volume 21: *Cantatas Nos. 80: Ein' feste Burg; 81: Jesus schläft, was soll ich hoffen?; 82: Ich habe genug; 83: Erfreute Zeit im neuen Bunde.*
(M) *(*) Teldec/Warner 2292 42577-2 (2) [id.]. Esswood, Equiluz, Van der Meer, Huttenlocher, Van Egmond, Tölz Boys' Ch., V. Boys' Ch., Ch. Viennensis, VCM, Harnoncourt.

Cantatas Nos. 80: Ein' feste Burg ist unser Gott; 140: Wachet auf, ruft uns die Stimme.
**(*) Decca Dig. 414 045-2 [id.]. Fontana, Hamari, Winbergh, Krause, Hymnus Boys' Ch., SCO, Münchinger.

Münchinger, who uses the trumpets and timpani added by Bach's eldest son, Wilhelm Friedemann, has the advantage of excellently transparent and well-detailed Decca digital recording and a fine team of soloists. Karl Münchinger does not bring quite the warmth or musicality that distinguishes the finest performances of Bach, but there is little of the pedantry that has at times afflicted his music-making. Extra pleasure is afforded by the attractive ambience – the concert-hall balance is expertly managed – and by the tangibility of the chorus, whose vigorous contribution is given striking body and presence.

Cantata No. 82: Ich habe genug.
❀ (M) (***) EMI CDH7 63198-2 [id.]. Hans Hotter, Philh. O, Bernard – BRAHMS: *4 ernste Gesänge; Lieder.* (***) ❀

One of the greatest cantata performances ever. Glorious singing from Hans Hotter and wonderfully stylish accompanying from Anthony Bernard and the Philharmonia. This 1950 mono recording was never reissued on LP, and it sounds eminently present in this fine transfer.

Cantatas Nos. (i; ii) *82: Ich habe genug;* (i; iii; iv) *159: Sehet, wir gehn hinauf gen Jerusalem;* (iii) *170: Vergnügte Ruh', beliebte Seelenlust.*
❀ (M) *** Decca 430 260-2; *430 260-4.* (i) Shirley-Quirk; (ii) Lord; (iii) J. Baker; (iv) Tear, St Anthony Singers; ASMF, Marriner.

John Shirley-Quirk's performance of *Ich habe genug* is much to be admired, not only for the sensitive solo singing but also for the lovely oboe obbligato of Roger Lord. The mid-1960s sound is also remarkably fresh and present. But this reissue is to be prized even more for the other two cantatas. Both Dame Janet Baker and Shirley-Quirk are in marvellous voice, and *Vergnügte Ruh'* makes a worthy companion. These are also from the mid-1960s and both are performed superbly and recorded very naturally. This is among the half-dozen or so cantata records that ought to be in every collection.

Volume 22: *Cantatas Nos.* (i) *84: Ich bin vergnügt mit meinem Glücke; 85: Ich bin ein guter Hirt; 86: Wahrlich, wahrlich, ich sage euch; 87: Bisher habt ihr nichts gebeten;* (ii) *88: Siehe, ich will viel Fischer aussenden; 89: Was soll ich aus dir machen, Ephraim?; 90: Es reisset euch ein schrecklich Ende.*
(M) ** Teldec/Warner 2292 42578-2 (2) [id.]. Esswood, Equiluz, (i) Wiedl, Van der Meer, Tölz Boys' Ch., VCM, Harnoncourt; (ii) Klein, Van Egmond, Hanover Boys' Ch., Ghent Coll. Vocale, Leonhardt Cons., Leonhardt.

Volume 23: *Cantatas Nos.* (i) *91: Gelobet seist du, Jesus Christ; 92: Ich hab' in Gottes Herz und Sinn;* (ii) *93: Wer nur den lieben Gott lässt walten; 94: Was frag' ich nach der Welt.*
(M) *** Teldec/Warner 2292 42582-2 (2) [id.]. Esswood, Equiluz, (i) Bratschke, Van Egmond, Hanover Boys' Ch., Ghent Coll. Vocale, Leonhardt Cons. Leonhardt; (ii) Wiedl, Van der Meer, Huttenlocher, Tölz Boys' Ch., VCM, Harnoncourt.

Volume 24: *Cantatas Nos.* (i) *95: Christus, der ist mein Leben; 96: Herr Christ, der ein'ge Gottesohn; 97: In allen meinen Taten;* (ii) *98: Was Gott tut, das ist wohlgetan.*
(M) **(*) Teldec/Warner 2292 42583-2 [id.]. Esswood, Equiluz, (i) Wiedl, Huttenlocher, Van der Meer, Tölz Boys' Ch., VCM, Harnoncourt; (ii) Lengert, Van Egmond, Hanover Boys' Ch., Ghent Coll. Vocale, Leonhardt Cons., Leonhardt.

Volume 25: *Cantatas Nos.* (i) *99: Was Gott tut, das ist wohlgetan;* (ii) *100: Was Gott tut, das ist wohlgetan;* (i) *101: Nimm von uns, Herr, du treuer Gott; 102: Herr, deine Augen sehen nach dem Glauben.*
(M) **(*) Teldec/Warner 2292 42584-2 (2) [id.]. Esswood, Equiluz, (i) Wiedl, Huttenlocher, Tölz Boys' Ch., VCM, Harnoncourt; (ii) Bratschke, Van Egmond, Hanover Boys' Ch., Ghent Coll. Vocale, Leonhardt Cons., Leonhardt.

Volume 26: *Cantatas Nos.* (i; ii) *103: Ihr werdet weinen und heulen;* (iii; iv) *104: Du Hirte Israel, höre;* (v; iv) *105: Herr, gehe nicht ins Gericht;* (vi; ii) *106: Gottes Zeit ist die allerbeste Zeit (Actus tragicus).*
(M) *** Teldec/Warner 2292 42602-2 [id.]. (i) Esswood, Equiluz, Van Egmond; (ii) Hanover Boys' Ch., Ghent Coll. Vocale, Leonhardt Cons., Leonhardt; (iii) Esswood, Huttenlocher; (iv) Tölz Boys' Ch., VCM, Harnoncourt; (v) Wiedl, Equiluz, Van der Meer; (vi) Klein, Harten, Van Altena, Van Egmond.

Cantatas Nos. 106: Gottes Zeit ist die allerbeste Zeit; 118: O Jesu Christ, mein Lebens Licht (2nd version); *198: Lass, Fürstin, lass noch einen Strahl.*
*** DG Dig. 429 782-2 [id.]. Argenta, Chance, Rolfe Johnson, Varcoe, Monteverdi Ch., E. Bar. Soloists, Eliot Gardiner.

Gardiner directs dedicated, intense performances of three of Bach's finest cantatas, all valedictory works. A youthful inspiration, written when Bach was only 22, the *Actus tragicus*, BWV 106, comes with the much later and more elaborate mourning ode, BWV 198. The third item – which Gardiner also recorded earlier for Erato along with his set of the motets – is the magnificent chorale-based motet, *O Jesu Christ, mein Lebens Licht*. The new account of that motet is more intimate than the 1980 version, less grandly dramatic, more devotional; the whole record suggests a scale of performance apt for a small chapel. That allows the elaborate instrumentation to come out clearly, with the two longer works giving the lie to the idea of mourning music necessarily sounding sombre. Well-balanced sound.

Cantatas Nos. 106: Gottes Zeit ist die allerbeste Zeit; 131: Aus der Tiefen.
*** O-L Dig. 417 323-2 [id.]. Monoyios, Rickards, Brownlees, Opalach, Bach Ens., Rifkin.

Rifkin's one-voice-to-a-part principle is applied here, and readers who do not respond to it will doubtless take avoiding action. In doing so, however, they will miss a performance of considerable merit: the opening of *Gottes Zeit* is one of the most beautiful moments in all Bach and is beautifully done. *Aus der Tiefen* is hardly less fine, and the singers are all first class. One feels the need for greater weight and a more full-blooded approach at times, but this is outweighed by the sensitivity and intelligence that inform these excellently balanced recordings.

Volume 27: *Cantatas Nos.* (i) *107: Wass willst du dich betrüben;* (ii) *108: Es ist euch gut, dass ich hingehe; 109: Ich glaube, lieber Herr, hilf meinem Unglauben!; 110: Unser Mund sei voll Lachens.*
(M) *** Teldec/Warner 2292 42603-2 (2) [id.]. Equiluz, (i) Klein, Van Egmond, Hanover Boys' Ch., Ghent Coll. Vocale, Leonhardt Cons., Leonhardt; (ii) Wiedl, Frangoulis, Stumpf, Lorenz, Esswood, Van der Meer, Tölz Boys' Ch., VCM, Harnoncourt.

Volume 28: *Cantatas Nos.* (i) *111: Was mein Gott will, das gescheh' allzeit; 112: Der Herr ist mein getreuer Hirt;* (ii) *113: Herr Jesu Christ, du höchstes Gut; 114: Ach, lieben Christen, seid getrost.*
(M) *** Teldec/Warner 2292 42606-2 (2) [id.]. Equiluz, (i) Huber, Esswood, Van der Meer, Tölz Boys' Ch., VCM, Harnoncourt; (ii) Hennig, Jacobs, Van Egmond, Hanover Boys' Ch., Ghent Coll. Vocale, Leonhardt Cons., Leonhardt.

Volume 29: *Cantatas Nos.* (i; iii; iv) *115: Mache dich, mein Geist, bereit; 116: Du Friedefürst, Herr Jesu Christ;* (ii; v; vi) *117: Sei Lob und Erh dem höchsten Gut;* (i; iii; vii) *119: Preise, Jerusalem, den Herrn.*
(M) *** Teldec/Warner 2292 42608-2 (2) [id.]. (i) Tölz Boys' Ch., VCM, Harnoncourt; (ii) Equiluz, Hanover Boys' Ch., Ghent Coll. Vocale, Leonhardt Cons., Leonhardt; with (iii) Huber, Esswood; (iv) Huttenlocher; (v) Jacobs; (vi) Van Egmond; (vii) Holl.

Volume 30: *Cantatas Nos. 120: Gott, mann lobet dich in der Stille; 121: Christum wir sollen loben; 122: Das neugebor'ne Kindelein; 123: Liebster Immanuel, Herzog der Frommen.*
(M) *** Teldec/Warner 2292 42609-2 (2) [id.]. Treble soloists from Tölz Ch., Esswood, Equiluz, Huttenlocher or Holl, Tölz Ch., VCM, Harnoncourt.

Volume 31: *Cantatas Nos.* (i) *124: Meinen Jesum lass ich nicht; 125: Mit Fried und Freud ich fahr dahin; 126: Erhalt uns, Herr, bei deinem Wort;* (ii) *127: Herr Jesu Christ wahr' Mensch und Gott.*
(M) *** Teldec/Warner 2292 42615-2 [id.]. (i) Bergius, Rampf, Esswood, Equiluz, Thomaschke, Tölz Boys' Ch., VCM, Harnoncourt; (ii) Hennig, Van Egmond, Hanover Boys' Ch., Ghent Coll. Vocale, Leonhardt Cons., Leonhardt.

Volume 32: *Cantatas Nos.* (i) *128: Auf Christi Himmelfahrt allein; 129: Gelobet sei der Herr, mein Gott;* (ii) *130: Herr Gott, dich loben alle wir; 131: Aus der Tiefen rufe ich, Herr, zu dir.*
(M) **(*) Teldec/Warner 2292 42617-2 (2) [id.]. Hennig, Bergius, Jacobs, Rampf, Equiluz, Van Egmond, Heldwein, Holl; (i) Hanover Boys' Ch., Ghent Coll. Vocale, Leonhardt Consort, Leonhardt; (ii) Tölz Boys' Ch., VCM, Harnoncourt.

Cantatas Nos. (i) *128: Auf Christi Himmelfahrt allein; 129: Gelobet sei der Herr, mein Gott;* (ii) *130: Herr Gott, dich loben alle wir.*
(M) **(*) Teldec/Warner 2292 43055-2 [id.]. (recordings as above).

Volume 33: *Cantatas Nos. 132: Bereitet die Wege, bereitet die Bahn; 133: Ich freue mich in dir; 134: Ein Herz, das seinen Jesum lebend weiss; 135: Ach Herr, mich armen Sünder.*
(M) **(*) Teldec/Warner 2292 42618-2 (2) [id.]. Hennig, Jacobs, Van Altena, Van Egmond, Hanover Boys' Ch., Ghent Coll. Vocale, Leonhardt Cons., Leonhardt.

Volume 34: *Cantatas Nos. 136: Erforsche mich, Gott, und erfahre mein Herz; 137: Lobe den Herren, den mächtigen König der Ehren; 138: Warum betrübst du dich, mein Herz?; 139: Wohl dem, der sich auf seinen Gott.*
(M) ** Teldec/Warner 2292 42619-2 [id.]. Bergius, Rampf, Esswood, Equiluz, Holl, Heldwein, Hartinger, Tölz Boys' Ch., VCM, Harnoncourt.

Volume 35: *Cantatas Nos.* (i) *140: Wachet auf, ruft uns die Stimme;* (ii) *143: Lobe den Herrn, meine Seele; 144: Nimm, was dein ist, und gehe hin;* (i) *145: Ich lebe, mein Herze, zu deinem Ergötzen; 146: Wir müssen durch viel Trübsal.*
(M) *** Teldec/Warner Dig. 2292 42630-2 (2) [id.]. Esswood, Equiluz, (i) Bergius, Hampson, Tölz Boys' Ch., VCM, Harnoncourt; (ii) Cericius, Pfeiffer, Van Egmond, Hanover Boys' Ch., Ghent Coll. Vocale, Leonhardt Cons., Leonhardt.

Cantatas Nos. 140: Wachet auf, ruft uns die Stimme; 147: Herz und Mond und Tat und Leben.
*** DG Dig. 431 809-2; *431 809-4* [id.]. Holton, Chance, Johnson, Varcoe, Monteverdi Ch., E. Bar. Soloists, Gardiner.

Two popular Bach cantatas are coupled in highly accomplished performances under John Eliot Gardiner. The level of instrumental playing is generally more polished than in the celebrated Teldec series and Ruth Holton manages to combine the purity of a boy's voice with the security of a mature singer. Anthony Rolfe Johnson gives ample evidence of his sensitivity and intelligence in, for example, the recitative *Gebenedeiter Mund* in *Herz und Mond und Tat und Leben*, and Michael Chance and Stephen Varcoe make equally satisfying contributions. The recordings are immediate and well balanced. A strong recommendation.

Volume 36: *Cantatas Nos.* (i) *147: Herz und Mund und Tat und Leben; 148: Bringet dem Herrn Ehre seines Namens;* (ii) *149: Man singet mit Freuden vom Sieg; 150: Nach dir, Herr, verlanget mich; 151: Süsser Trost, mein Jesus kömmt.*
(M) *** Teldec/Warner Dig. 2292 42631-2 (2) [id.]. Bergius, Hennig, Esswood, Equiluz, Hampson, Ván Egmond; (i) Tölz Boys' Ch., VCM, Harnoncourt; (ii) Ghent Coll. Vocale, Leonhardt Cons., Leonhardt.

Volume 37: *Cantatas Nos. 152: Tritt auf die Glaubensbahn; 153: Schau, lieber Gott, wie meine Feind; 154: Mein liebster Jesus ist verloren; 155: Mein Gott, wie lang, ach lange; 156: Ich steh' mit einem Fuss im Grabe.*
(M) **(*) Teldec/Warner Dig. 2292 42632-2 (2) [id.]. Wegmann, Bergius, Rampf, Esswood, Equiluz, Hampson, Tölz Boys' Ch., VCM, Harnoncourt.

Volume 38: *Cantatas Nos.* (i) *157: Ich lasse dich nicht, du segnest mich denn; 158: Der Friede sei mit dir; 159: Sehet, wir geh'n hinauf gen Jerusalem;* (ii) *161: Komm, du süsse Todesstunde; 162: Ach! ich sehe, jetzt, da ich zur Hochzeit gehe; 163: Nur jedem das Seine.*
(M) ** Teldec/Warner Dig. 2292 42633-2 (2) [id.]. Eiwanger, Esswood, Equiluz, Van Egmond,

Tölz Boys' Ch., (i) Wegmann, Ghent Coll. Vocale, Leonhardt; (ii) Iconomou, Holl, VCM, Harnoncourt.

Volume 39: *Cantatas Nos.* (i) *164: Ihr, die ihr euch von Christo nennet; 165: O heil'ges Geist und Wasserbad; 166: Wo gehest du hin?;* (ii) *167: Ihr Menschen, rühmet Gottes Liebe; 168: Tue, Rechnung! Donnerwort; 169: Gott soll allein mein Herze haben.*
(M) ** Teldec/Warner Dig. 2292 42634-2 (2) [id.]. Esswood, Equiluz, Tölz Boys' Ch.; (i) Wegmann, Eiwanger, Van Egmond, Ghent Coll. Vocale, Leonhardt Cons., Leonhardt; (ii) Iconomou, Immler, Holl, VCM, Harnoncourt.

Volume 40: *Cantatas Nos.* (i) *170: Vergnügte Ruh', beliebte Seelenlust;* (ii) *171: Gott, wie dein Name, so ist auch dein Ruhm;* (i) *172: Erschallet, ihr Lieder;* (ii) *173: Erhöhtes Fleisch und Blut; 174: Ich liebe den Höchsten von ganzem Gemüte.*
(M) **(*) Teldec/Warner Dig. 2292 42635-2 (2) [id.]. (i) Esswood, Van Altena, Van Egmond, Hanover Boys' Ch., Ghent Coll. Vocale, Leonhardt Cons., Leonhardt; (ii) Equiluz, Holl, Tölz Boys' Ch., VCM, Harnoncourt.

Volume 41: *Cantatas Nos.* (i) *175: Er rufet seinen Schafen mit Namen; 176: Es ist ein trotzig und verzagt Ding;* (ii) *177: Ich ruf zu dir, Herr Jesu Christ; 178: Wo Gott der Herr nicht bei uns hält; 179: Siehe zu, dass deine Gottesfurcht.*
(M) ** Teldec/Warner Dig. 2292 42428-2 (2) [id.]. (i) Echternach, Esswood, Van Altena, Van Egmond, Hanover Boys' Ch., Coll. Vocale, Leonhardt Cons., Leonhardt; (ii) Wittek, Iconomou, Equiluz, Holl, Tölz Boys' Ch., VCM, Harnoncourt.

Volume 42: *Cantatas Nos* (i) *180: Schmücke dich, o liebe Seele; 181: Leichtgesinnte Flattergeister;* (ii) *182: Himmelskönig, sei wilkommen; 183: Sie werden euch in den Bann tun;* (i) *184: Erwunschtes Freudenlicht.*
(M) *** Teldec/Warner Dig. 2292 42738-2 (2) [id.]. (i) O'Farrell, Esswood, Equiluz, Van Egmond, Hanover Boys' Ch., Coll. Vocale, Leonhardt Cons., Leonhardt; (ii) Wittek, Holl, Hampson, Tölz Boys' Ch., VCM, Harnoncourt.

Volume 43: *Cantatas Nos.* (i) *185: Barmherziges Herze der ewigen Liebes; 186: Ärgre dich, o Seele, nicht;* (ii) *187: Es wartet alles auf dich;* (i) *188: Ich habe meine Zuversicht.*
(M) **(*) Teldec/Warner Dig. 2292 44179-2 (2). (i) Wittek, Equiluz, Hampson, Holl, Tölz Boys' Ch., VCM, Harnoncourt; (ii) Emmermann, Esswood, Van Egmond, Hanover Boys' Ch., Ghent Coll. Vocale, Leonhardt Cons., Leonhardt.

Volume 44: *Cantatas Nos.* (i) *192: Nun danket alle Gott;* (ii) *194: Höchsterwünschtes Freudenfest;* (iii) *195: Dem Gerechten muss das Licht immer wieder aufgehen.*
(M) **(*) Teldec/Warner Dig. 2292 44193-2 [id.]. (i) Wittek, (i; ii) Hampson, (ii) Stricker, Gienger, Equiluz, (iii) O'Farrell, Jacobs, Elwes, Van der Kamp; (i & ii) Tölz Boys' Ch., VCM, Harnoncourt; (iii) Hanover Boys' Ch., Ghent Coll. Vocale, Leonhardt Consort, Leonhardt.

Volume 45: *Cantatas Nos.* (i) *196: Der Herr denket an uns;* (ii) *197: Gott ist unsrer Zuversicht;* (iii) *198: Lass, Fürstin, lass noch einen Strahl;* (iv) *199: Mein Herze schwimmt im Blut.*
(M) ** Teldec/Warner Dig. 2292 44194-2 (2) [id.]. (i) Wittek, Equiluz, Hampson, (ii; iii) O'Farrell, Jacobs, Van der Kamp, (iii) Elwes, (iv) Bonney; (i) Tölz Boys' Ch., (ii; iii) Hanover Boys' Ch., Ghent Coll. Vocale; (i; iv) VCM, Harnoncourt; (ii; iii) Leonhardt Consort, Leonhardt.

Cantata No. 205: Der zufriedengestellte Äolus.
(M) *** Teldec/Warner Dig. 2292 42957-2 [id.]. Kenny, Lipovšek, Equiluz, Holl, Arnold-Schönberg Ch., VCM, Harnoncourt.

Bach describes this cantata as '*Dramma per musica*'. The performance is very good indeed, though the heavy accents in the opening chorus of the winds and the wooden orchestral tutti in the second number must be noted. Alice Harnoncourt's obbligato in *Angenehmer Zephyrus* ('Delightful Zephyr') is a model of good style and is beautifully articulated. The singers, particularly Yvonne Kenny's Pallas and Kurt Equiluz's Zephyrus, are good; the recording has a decently spacious acoustic and no lack of detail. Recommended.

Cantata No. 208: Was mir behagt, ist nur die muntre Jagd (Hunt cantata).
*** Hyp. Dig. CDA 66169; *KA 66169* [id.]. Jennifer Smith, Emma Kirkby, Simon Davis, Michael George, Parley of Instruments, Goodman.

This delightful piece comes from 1713, when Bach was in his twenties, and celebrates the birthday of the Duke of Sachsen-Weissenfels, whose passion was hunting. It is a cantata rich in melodic invention of the highest quality. On this record the cantata is framed by movements from the *Sinfonia*, BWV 1046a, the original version of the *First Brandenburg concerto*. The performance has the benefit of excellent soloists and first-class instrumental playing.

Cantatas Nos. 211: Schweigt stille, plaudert nicht (Coffee cantata); 212: Mer hahn en neue Oberkeet (Peasant cantata).
*** O-L Dig. 417 621-2 [id.]. Kirkby, Rogers, Covey-Crump, Thomas, AAM, Hogwood.

Emma Kirkby is particularly appealing in the *Coffee cantata* and her father is admirably portrayed by David Thomas. Hogwood opts for single strings, and those accustomed to hearing these pieces with more substantial forces may find they sound thin. However, there is a corresponding gain in lightness and intimacy. The recording is altogether first class and strikes an excellent balance between voices and instruments.

Christmas oratorio, BWV 248.
*** DG Dig. 423 232-2 (2) [id.]. Rolfe-Johnson, Argenta, Von Otter, Blochwitz, Bär, Monteverdi Ch., E. Bar. Soloists, Gardiner.
(***) Ph. Dig. 420 204-2 (3) [id.]. Donath, Ihle, Lipovsek, Schreier, Buchner, Holl, Leipzig R. Ch., Dresden State O, Schreier.
(M) **(*) Teldec/Warner 2292 42495-2 (3) [id.]. Treble soloists from V. Boys' Ch., Esswood, Equiluz, Nimsgern, V. Boys' Ch., Ch. Viennensis, VCM, Harnoncourt.

Christmas oratorio; Magnificat, BWV 243.
(M) *** Decca 425 441-2 (3) [id.]. Ameling, Watts, Pears, Krause, Ch., Stuttgart CO, Münchinger.

The freshness of the singing and playing in the DG set is a constant pleasure, with Gardiner's often brisk speeds sounding bright and eager, not breathless. Far more than usual, one registers the joyfulness of the work, from the trumpets and timpani at the start onwards. The haunting shepherds' music of the second cantata is lightly sprung and the celebrations of the third, with trumpets again prominent, are typical. Solo voices are light and clear. Anthony Rolfe-Johnson makes a pointful and expressive Evangelist, and also outstanding is Anne Sofie von Otter with her natural gravity and exceptionally beautiful mezzo. Beauty of tone consistently marks the singing of Nancy Argenta and Hans-Peter Blochwitz; though Olaf Bär is a baritone rather than a bass, his detailed expressiveness, lieder-like, makes up for any lack of weight. The whole oratorio is neatly contained on only two discs, with three cantatas on each instead of two. The sound is full and atmospheric without clouding detail, a fine addition to an excellent series.

Münchinger directs an admirably fresh performance of the *Christmas oratorio*, sharp in tone and bright in recording (which dates from 1967). With an excellent team of soloists and with Lübeck trebles adding to the freshness, this is a good middle-of-the-road version, representative of modern scholarship as determined in the immediate pre-authentic era. Münchinger's recording of the *Magnificat* dates from 1969 and was another of his finest Bach performances.

Peter Schreier contributes a fine, fresh version of the *Christmas oratorio*, similarly taking on the double duties of conducting and singing the central part of the Evangelist. As in the *St Matthew*, the Leipzig Radio Choir sings responsively; though modern instruments are used, Schreier consistently shows how he has been influenced by new ideas of authentic performance on period instruments. Though the scale is larger than in a period performance, the speeds are regularly very fast, sprightly rather than breathless, with string articulation crisp and light. None of the other soloists quite matches Schreier, but they make a strong, consistent team. Full, bright and atmospheric recording, but the layout on three CDs makes this issue uncompetitive alongside Gardiner.

Harnoncourt has rarely been more successful than here. It will not be to everyone's taste to have a boy treble and male counter-tenor instead of women soloists, but the purity of sound of these singers is most affecting. Above all Harnoncourt in this instance never allows his pursuit of authentic sound to weigh the performance down; it has a lightness of touch which should please everyone. The sound, as usual from this source, is excellent, but the use of three discs, even at mid-price, is disadvantageous.

Christmas oratorio: Arias and choruses.
(M) *** DG Dig. 435 088-2; *435 088-4* [id.]. Argenta, Von Otter, Bär, Blochwitz, Monteverdi Ch., E. Bar. Soloists, Gardiner.

(M) *** Teldec/Warner 9031 74893-2 [id.] (from above recording with VCM; cond. Harnoncourt).

This 70-minute selection on DG offers choruses and arias from all six cantatas and includes the *Sinfonia* to introduce the four items from Part Two.

With the complete set uneconomically laid out on three discs, the highlights from Harnoncourt's outstandingly spontaneous performance of the *Christmas oratorio* are doubly attractive, particularly as the CD plays for nearly 78 minutes. The opening chorus with its explosive accents and authentic brass has a unique impact and the soloists sing very beautifully, not only Paul Esswood and Kurt Equiluz (whose *Frohe Hirten* with recorder obbligato is ravishing) but also the unnamed treble soloist from the Vienna Boys' Choir who sings *Flösst mein Heiland* so beautifully, with its echo effects evocatively managed. The recording from 1973, immaculately transferred to CD, sounds as fresh as the day it was made.

Easter oratorio.

(M) *** Decca 425 650-2 [id.]. Ameling, Watts, Krenn, Krause, Stuttgart CO, Münchinger – *Cantata No. 10.* ***

Münchinger is at his finest in the *Easter oratorio*, giving a spacious and impressive reading. He is well supported by his splendid team of soloists, and the Decca recording is well up to the lively standard of his Stuttgart series.

Magnificat in D, BWV 243.

*** Ph. Dig. 411 458-2 [id.]. Argenta, Kwella, Kirkby, Brett, Rolfe-Johnson, David Thomas, E. Bar. Soloists, Gardiner – *Cantata No. 51.* ***

(M) *** Decca 421 148-2. Palmer, Watts, Tear, Roberts, King's College Ch., ASMF, Ledger – C. P. E. BACH: *Magnificat.* ***

(M) *** Decca 433 175-2. Ameling, Van Borkh, Watts, Krenn, Krause, V. Ac. Ch., Stuttgart CO, Münchinger – *Cantatas Nos. 67 & 130.* **(*)

The better-known D major version of the *Magnificat* receives an exhilarating performance from John Eliot Gardiner. Tempi are consistently brisk, but the vigour and precision of the chorus are such that one never has the feeling that the pacing is hurried; when there is need to relax, Gardiner does so convincingly. A splendid team of soloists, and the accompaniment is no less impressive. This is first class in every way, and the recorded sound is well balanced, fresh and vivid.

Philip Ledger's account, recorded by Argo in the late 1970s, is most attractive, highly recommendable if boys' voices are preferred in the chorus.

Münchinger tends to stress the breadth and spaciousness of the *Magnificat*, and the Decca engineers have captured the detail with admirable clarity and naturalness – and plenty of weight, too. However, most will prefer Ledger's coupling.

Magnificat in E flat (original version), BWV 243a.

*** O-L 414 678-2 [id.]. Nelson, Kirkby, Watkinson, Elliot, D. Thomas, Christ Church Ch., AAM, Preston – VIVALDI: *Gloria.* ***

The original version of the *Magnificat* is textually different in detail (quite apart from being a semitone higher) and has four interpolations for the celebration of Christmas. Preston and the Academy of Ancient Music present a characteristically alert and fresh performance, and the Christ Church Choir is in excellent form. One might quibble at the use of women soloists instead of boys, but these three specialist singers have just the right incisive timbre and provide the insight of experience.

Mass in B min., BWV 232.

*** DG Dig. 415 514-2 [id.]. Argenta, Dawson, Fairfield, Knibbs, Kwella, Hall, Nichols, Chance, Collin, Stafford, Evans, Milner, Murgatroyd, Lloyd-Morgan, Varcoe, Monteverdi Ch., E. Bar. Soloists, Gardiner.

*** EMI Dig. CDS7 47293-8 [Ang. CDCB 47292] (2). Kirkby, Van Evera, Iconomou, Immler, Kilian, Covey-Crump, David Thomas, Taverner Cons. and Players, Parrott.

**(*) Ph. 416 415-2 (2) [id.]. Marshall, Baker, Tear, Ramey, Ch. and ASMF, Marriner.

**(*) None. Dig. CD 79036-2 (2) [id.]. Nelson, Baird, Dooley, Minter, Hoffmeister, Brownlees, Opalach, Schultze, Bach Ens., Rifkin.

John Eliot Gardiner gives a magnificent account of the *B minor Mass*, one which attempts to keep within an authentic scale but which also triumphantly encompasses the work's grandeur.

Where latterly in 'authentic' performances we have come to expect the grand six-part setting of the *Sanctus* to trip along like a dance movement, Gardiner masterfully conveys the majesty (with bells and censer-swinging evoked) simultaneously with a crisply resilient rhythmic pulse. The choral tone is luminous and powerfully projected. In the earlier parts of the *Mass*, Gardiner generally has four voices per part, but key passages – such as the opening of the first *Kyrie* fugue – are treated as concertinos for soloists alone. The later, more elaborate sections, such as the *Sanctus*, have five voices per part, so that the final *Dona nobis pacem* is subtly grander than when it appears earlier as *Gratias agimus tibi*. The regular solo numbers are taken by choir members making a cohesive whole. The alto, Michael Chance, deserves special mention for his distinctively warm and even singing in both *Qui sedes* and *Agnus Dei*. The recording is warmly atmospheric but not cloudy.

Parrott, hoping to re-create even more closely the conditions Bach would have expected in Leipzig, adds to the soloists a ripieno group of five singers from the Taverner Consort for the choruses. The instrumental group is similarly augmented with the keenest discretion. Parrott's success lies in retaining the freshness and bite of the Rifkin approach – see below – while creating a more vivid atmosphere. Speeds are generally fast, with rhythms sprung to reflect the inspiration of dance; however, the inner darkness of the *Crucifixus*, for example, is conveyed intensely in its hushed tones, while the *Et resurrexit* promptly erupts with a power to compensate for any lack of traditional weight. Soloists are excellent, with reduction of vibrato still allowing sweetness as well as purity. If you want a performance on a reduced scale, Parrott scores palpably over Rifkin in the keener, more dramatic sense of contrast, clearly distinguishing choruses and solos. The recording, made in St John's, Smith Square, is both realistic and atmospheric.

Predictably, many of Marriner's tempi are daringly fast; *Et resurrexit*, for example, has the Academy chorus on its toes, but the rhythms are so resiliently sprung that the result is exhilarating, never hectic. An even more remarkable achievement is that in the great moments of contemplation such as *Et incarnatus* and *Crucifixus* Marriner finds a degree of inner intensity to match the gravity of Bach's inspiration, with tempi often slower than usual. That dedication is matched by the soloists, the superb soprano Margaret Marshall as much as the longer-established singers. This is a performance which finds the balance between small-scale authenticity and recognition of massive inspiration, neither too small nor too large, and with good atmospheric recording, not quite as defined as it might be on inner detail; this is fully recommendable.

Whether or not you subscribe to the controversial theories behind the performance under Joshua Rifkin, the result is undeniably refreshing and often exhilarating. Rifkin here presents Bach's masterpiece in the improbable form of one voice to a part in the choruses and one gets a totally new perspective when, at generally brisk speeds, the complex counterpoint is so crisp and clean, with original (relatively gentle) instruments in the orchestra adding to the freshness and intimacy. The soloists also sing with comparable brightness, freshness and precision, even if lack of choral weight means that dramatic contrasts are less sharp than usual. An exciting pioneering set, crisply and vividly recorded, which rightly won *Gramophone*'s choral award in 1983.

(Short) *Masses:* (i) *in F, BWV 233; in A, BWV 234;* (ii) *in G min., BWV 235; in G, BWV 236.*
(M) ** Ph. 432 494-2 (2) [id.]. (i) Giebel, Litz, Prey, Lausanne Pro Arte Ch., Munich Pro Arte O, Redel; (ii) Ameling, Finnilä, Altmeyer, Reimer, Westphalian Singers, German Bach Soloists, Winschermann.

It is not clear what prompted the composition of Bach's four Lutheran *Missae breves*, but they appear to date from the late 1730s, a decade after the cantatas were written – on which they draw for much of their musical material. They are 'parody' works in that new texts are fitted to old music, but the result is consistently refreshing. Even though all four works here have the same structural layout, with an opening *Kyrie* and *Gloria in excelsis* and closing *Cum Sancto Spiritus* framing three central arias, the latter often decorated with oboe or violin obbligati, the character of each is quite different. The *F major*, for instance, features exuberant horn-parts in the opening and closing choruses, and the *Kyrie* of the *A major*, with its charmingly intertwining flutes, sets a pastoral atmosphere, while the serenely sober opening of the *G major* leads to a lilting *Gloria* and this work closes with a sprightly fugue. The solo parts are demanding and, while both sopranos here are impressive and Hermann Prey's contribution does not disappoint, on the whole Winschermann's solo team is preferable to Redel's, while the choral singing in Westphalia is stronger and rather better focused by the 1969 recording. Winschermann not only directs freshly but he plays the oboe obbligati with distinction. Redel's 1965 performances have rather less vitality but are still enjoyable. The CD transfers are well managed, but the earlier recording shows its age in the less sharp imagery. But musically there is much to relish here.

Motets: *Singet dem Herrn ein Neues Lied, BWV 225; Der Geist hilft unser Schwachheit, BWV 226; Jesu meine Freude, BWV 227; Der Gerechte Kommt um Fürchte dich nicht, BWV 228; Komm, Jesu, Komm, BWV 229; Lobet den Herrn, BWV 230; Sei Lob und Preis mit Ehren, BWV 231.*
*** Conifer Dig. CDCF 158; *MCFC 158* [id.] (without *BWV 231*). Trinity College, Cambridge, Ch., Marlow, G. Jackson and R. Pearce.
(M) *** DG 435 087-2; *435 087-4* [id.] (without *BWV 229*). Regensburger Domspätzen, Hamburg Bläserkreis, V. Capella Academica, Schneidt.
**(*) HM HMC 901231; *HMC 401231* [id.] (without *BWV 231*). Soloists, Ghent Coll. Vocale, Chapelle Royale Ch. & O, Herreweghe.

Motets: *Lobet den Herrn, alle Heiden, BWV 230; Sei Lob und Preis mit Ehren, BWV 231. Ich lasse dich nicht, du segnest mich denn, BWV Anh./App.159* (attrib. – probably by J. C. Bach).
(M) *** DG 427 142-2. Regensburg Domspätzen, V. Capella Academica, Schneidt – VIVALDI: *Gloria; Kyrie.* ***

The Conifer issue of Bach's great motets by Richard Marlow and the Trinity College Choir brings delightfully crisp and resilient performances of the six regular motets, marked by refined ensemble and transparent textures. With discreet organ accompaniment, this is a fine version for those who prefer traditional performances using sopranos instead of boy trebles, consistently stylish, set against a helpful acoustic, with plenty of presence.

Hans-Martin Schneidt's set of six motets (*Komm, Jesu, komm* is omitted) brings highly enjoyable performances which have a lusty freshness, enhanced by the brightness of boy trebles. The accompaniments on period instruments at lower pitch add to the bluffness.

Under Philippe Herreweghe the *Motets* are presented in fresh, meticulously clean performances, with instruments doubling vocal lines. One oddity is that the extended five-part motet, *Jesu meine Freude,* is sung by soloists and not the choir. Any gain in intimacy must be measured against an obvious loss of dramatic contrast in Bach's vivid setting of the words. Excellent sound.

St John Passion, BWV 245.
*** DG Dig. 419 324-2 (2) [id.]. Rolfe Johnson, Varcoe, Hauptmann, Argenta & soloists, Monteverdi Ch., E. Bar. Sol., Gardiner.
**(*) Chan. Dig. CHAN 0507-8 (2) [id.]. Partridge, Wilson-Johnson, Kwella, James, Kendall, The Sixteen Ch. & O, Christophers.
**(*) Ph. Dig. 422 088-2 (2) [id.]. Schreier, Holl, Scheibner, Alexander, Lipovsek, Bär, Leipzig R. Ch., Dresden State O, Schreier.
(M) **(*) Teldec/Warner 2292 42492-2 (2) [id.]. Equiluz, Van t'Hoff, Van Egmond, Villisech, Schneeweis, treble soloists from V. Boys' Ch., Ch. Viennensis, VCM, Harnoncourt.

Gardiner conducts an exhilarating performance, so dramatic in its approach and so wide-ranging in the emotions conveyed it might be a religious opera. Speeds are regularly on the fast side but, characteristically, Gardiner consistently keeps a spring in the rhythm and urgently intensifies such points as the violence of the *Kreuzige* (Crucify) choruses and the section involving the casting of lots. The very opening chorus is made the more agonizing when the wind writing itself seems to suggest howls of pain. Yet Gardiner's refusal to dawdle even at the moment of the Crucifixion does not prevent the whole performance from conveying necessary dedication. Chorales are treated in contrasted ways, which may not please the more severe authenticists but, as with so much of Gardiner's work, here is a performance using authentic scale and period instruments which speaks in the most vivid way to anyone prepared to listen, not just to the specialist. Soloists – regular contributors to Gardiner's team – are all first rate, with Anthony Rolfe Johnson light and resilient as the Evangelist, and Nancy Argenta exceptionally sweet-toned. The alto solos are beautifully taken by the counter-tenor Michael Chance, bringing necessary gravity to *Es ist vollbracht*. Warm and atmospheric, yet clear and detailed recording. A selection of arias and choruses is available on DG 427 319-2.

Recorded (like The Sixteen's previous Hyperion sets of Handel's *Messiah* and the Monteverdi *Vespers*) at a series of live performances at St John's, Smith Square, in London, Harry Christophers' version brings a period performance that has warmth as well as freshness. It is chiefly remarkable for the uniquely mellifluous singing of Ian Partridge as the Evangelist, deeply expressive as well as sweet to the ear, and he is well matched by David Wilson-Johnson as Jesus in the dramatic exchanges of extended recitative. What mars the set is the backward balance of the chorus, and at times of the other soloists as well. The great opening and closing choruses are beautifully sung but lack inner clarity and bite. Happily, the chorales and brief turba (crowd) choruses fare much better, being simpler, for Christophers' direction has plenty of vigour. With first-rate performances from all the soloists to back up Partridge's glowing contribution, there is much to enjoy.

Schreier's telling of the Crucifixion story is riveting in its variety of tone, expression and pace. With his dry, piercing sound, he is even better suited to the biting drama of the *St John* than to the visionary expansiveness of the *St Matthew*. The arias too find him in his freshest voice, not least two extra ones, formidably difficult and never recorded before, which Bach wrote for performance in 1725, the year following the first accredited performance. In also directing the performance, Schreier – still using modern instruments – applies the lessons taught by the Authentic Movement. Two reservations have to be made. Schreier has taken the idea of detached phrasing to such an extreme that in places – notably in the great choruses at the beginning and end – the flow is impaired and the music becomes choppy. Schreier's treatment of the chorales is also controversial, when he so markedly uses rubato to give the words of these hymns extra expressiveness; the singers of the superb Leipzig Radio Choir, thirty-five strong, respond with ensemble of the highest polish, but the result is fussy. The three other principal soloists are first rate too – notably Olaf Bär, who sings the first and most original of the extra (1725) arias, in which briskly angular writing for the soloist is set against a chorale. Particularly for that supplement, this is an essential set for Bach devotees and comes on two generously filled discs, very well recorded.

Harnoncourt's version is a fresh, brisk tour through Bach's most dramatic choral work, helped by the light, distinctive narration of Kurt Equiluz and the bright singing of the Viennese choristers, men and boys. Soloists from the Vienna Boys' Choir sing the soprano and alto arias, and within its chosen approach this remains a positive and characterful reading.

St Matthew Passion, BWV 244.
*** DG Dig. 427 648-2 (3) [id.]. Rolfe Johnson, Schmidt, Bonney, Monoyios, Von Otter, Chance, Crook, Bär, Hauptmann, Monteverdi Ch., E. Bar. Soloists, Gardiner.
*** Ph. Dig. 412 527-2 (3) [id.]. Schreier, Adam, Popp, Lipovsek, Holl, Dresden Children's Ch., Leipzig R. Ch., Dresden State O, Schreier.
(M) *** EMI CMS7 63058-2 (3). Pears, Fischer-Dieskau, Schwarzkopf, Ludwig, Gedda, Berry, Hampstead Parish Church Ch., Philh. Ch. & O, Klemperer.
*** Decca Dig. 421 177-2 (3) [id.]. Te Kanawa, Von Otter, Rolfe Johnson, Krause, Blochwitz, Bär, Chicago Ch., Children's Ch. & SO, Solti.
(M) **(*) Decca 414 057-2 (3) [id.]. Pears, Prey, Ameling, Höffgen, Wunderlich, Krause, Stuttgart Hymnus Boys' Ch., Stuttgart CO, Münchinger.
**(*) HM/BMG Dig. RD 77848 (3) [7848-2-RC]. Prégardien, Van Egmond, Fliegner, Kiener, Jacobs, Cordier, Schäfer, Elwes, Mertens, Lika, Tölz Boys' Ch., La Petite Bande (male) Ch. & O, Leonhardt.
**(*) HM HMC 901155/7 [id.]. Crook, Cold, Schluck, Jacobs, Blochwitz, Kooy, Chapelle Royale Ch., Ghent Coll. Mus., Herreweghe.

Gardiner's version of the *St Matthew Passion*, the culminating issue in his Bach choral series for DG Archiv, brings an intense, dramatic reading which now makes a clear first choice, not just for period-performance devotees but for anyone not firmly set against the new authenticity. As Gardiner sees it, Bach's plan was to divide both parts of the Passion into scenes, 12 in the first part, 15 in the second, each rounded off with a commentary, either collective in the form of a chorale, or individual in the form of an aria. As he says, 'The cumulative effect is similar to that of the 14 stations of the Cross in Catholic tradition, with the same arbitrary but carefully considered division of the Passion story.' The result is an invigorating, intense telling of the story, with Gardiner favouring high dynamic contrasts and generally fast speeds which are still geared to the weighty purpose of the whole work. He and his performers were recorded in what proved an ideal venue, The Maltings at Snape, where the warm acoustic gives body and allows clarity to period textures. Anthony Rolfe Johnson excels himself as the Evangelist, sweeter-toned than he has sometimes been on record, underlining the dramatic tensions in his narration. Andreas Schmidt makes an aptly young-sounding, virile Jesus, while no current recording of this work has a finer line-up of other soloists, singers with young, clear voices like the tenor, Howard Crook, and the baritone, Olaf Bär. Crowning the team are two singers in the alto parts – not just the vividly characterful Anne Sofie von Otter (delectable in *Buss und Reu*) but also the countertenor, Michael Chance, whose performance of the longest aria of all, *Erbarme dich*, brings a high point in the performance. It is good too that the chorales bring no gimmicks; they are expressive and pointed without mannerism. The substantial but not over-ample chorus – with boy trebles and teen-age girls for the chorale descant of the great opening number – sings with all the freshness and bite that is characteristic of Gardiner's work, not least in the dramatic crowd (turba) choruses which favour relatively relaxed speeds.

Schreier's aim in Bach interpretation is to bring new lightness without following the full dictates of authentic performance, and in this he succeeds superbly. Such meditative arias as the contralto's *Erbarme dich* or the soprano's *Aus liebe* bring a natural gravity and depth of expression, though Marjana Lipovsek has a tendency to sit on the flat side of the note, and Lucia Popp's silvery soprano is not always caught at its sweetest. The end result is a refreshing and cohesive performance, ideal for records, when there is no tendency for the piece to drag. The recording is first rate, with the choral forces well separated.

While it certainly will not appeal to the authentic lobby, Klemperer's 1962 Philharmonia recording of the *St Matthew Passion* represents one of his greatest achievements on record, an act of devotion of such intensity that points of style and interpretation seem insignificant. The whole cast clearly shared Klemperer's own intense feelings, and one can only sit back and share them too, whatever one's preconceptions.

Solti uses a reduced-size Chicago Symphony Orchestra and himself hand-picked the choir. With him the *Passion* is less devotional than celebratory. With speeds on the fast side, resilient rhythms and bright choral tone, he brings it closer than usual to the *St John Passion*, with its message of heavenly joy. Clean, fresh solo singing, too, with Hans-Peter Blochwitz the sweetest-toned Evangelist on record. Olaf Bär as Jesus is youthfully virile, Anne Sofie von Otter makes a radiant alto soloist, giving natural gravity to *Erbarme dich*. Brilliant, full, Decca recording with fine presence and clarity.

Münchinger's direction does not attain the spiritual heights of an interpretation such as Klemperer's, but his version is consistently fresh and alert, and it has the degree of authenticity of its period (1965) – although much has happened to Bach performances since then. All the soloists are excellent and the recording is first class.

Leonhardt directs a spacious reading of the *St Matthew Passion* using period instruments, an all-male choir and a fine team of soloists. Christoph Prégardien makes an outstanding Evangelist and, with slow speeds and restrained manner, Leonhardt brings out the work's devotional qualities rather than the dramatic. On a satisfying scale, the performance has the necessary weight while keeping textures clean, with period instruments sounding sweet rather than abrasive. What mars the result is Leonhardt's tendency to underline rhythms too heavily, with first-beats-in-bars emphasized and with chorales becoming heavy. Well-balanced recording.

Herreweghe's version presents a good choice for anyone wanting a performance on period instruments at lower pitch. Howard Crook is an excellent, fresh-toned Evangelist, and the other tenor, Hans-Peter Blochwitz, is first rate too. The alto part is taken by the celebrated countertenor, René Jacobs, rather hooty in *Erbarme dich*; but Barbara Schluck, with her bright, clear soprano voice, sings radiantly. The instrumental group plays in authentic style but not abrasively so; Herreweghe's control of rhythm, however, tends to be too heavy. Chorales are often slow and over-accented, and heavy stressing mars the big numbers too.

St Matthew Passion: Arias and choruses.
(M) *** DG Dig. 435 089-2; *435 089-4* [id.]. Bonney, Monoyios, Von Otter, Chance, Crook, Hauptmann, Monteverdi Ch., L. Oratory Junior Ch., E. Bar. Soloists, Gardiner.

This 66-minute sampler readily demonstrates the dramatic intensity of Gardiner's music-making and the excellence of the recording.

St Matthew Passion: Arias and choruses (sung in English).
(B) ** Decca 436 147-2; *436 147-4*. Tear, Shirley-Quirk, Lott, Hodgson, Jenkins, Roberts, Bach Ch., Boys from St Paul's Cathedral Ch., Thames CO, Willcocks.
(M) (**) Decca mono 433 469-2. Ferrier, Suddaby, Greene, Parsons, Bach Ch., Jacques O, Jacques.

It is a comment on current taste (of record companies and perhaps now of the public) that the 1978 Decca set conducted by Sir David Willcocks is the only complete recording to have been made in English for some four decades. Now Decca have decided to put out just the highlights (admittedly some 75 minutes of music) on CD. The pity is that the performance fails to lift quite as it ought, remaining earthbound and conscientious, where it should have the qualities of a spiritual experience. Willcocks, most experienced of choirmasters, draws light and rhythmic singing from the choirs in the choruses, and the chorales avoid heaviness. There is a good team of soloists, headed by Robert Tear, but Peter's denial – usually a supremely moving moment – is here prosaic. The recording, made in the Kingsway Hall, sounds splendid, warm and full, with the words of the soloists clear; but this disc can be recommended only to those for whom the English text is essential.

Recorded in 1947/8, the alternative collection, part of the Kathleen Ferrier Edition, is of interest only for her personal contribution, and it might have been better to extract the individual items in which she participates, as Decca once did for a mono Ace of Clubs LP (ACL 308). These arias, sung in English with radiant vocal freshness (*Master and my Lord . . . Grief for sin*; *Have mercy, Lord on me*; and *O gracious God . . . If my tears be unavailing*) show that from the start there was a projection of forceful personality and natural musicianship that was uniquely powerful. The soprano/alto duet with Elsie Suddaby (*Behold, my Saviour now is taken*) is interrupted by the mushy chorus, and the arias, *Ah! now my Saviour is gone . . . Have mercy, Lord on me* and *Ah, Golgotha! . . . See ye! See the Saviour's outstretched hands*, again bring the ill-focused choral sound, although here Ferrier's contribution rides over everything. Whatever the flaws in these transfers, the singer's commanding presence lights up the record, and it is fascinating to play these excerpts alongside the inspired performances recorded only five years later with Boult in order to see the development.

Vocal collections

Arias: *Bist du bei mir; Cantata 202: Weichet nur, Betrubte Schatten. Cantata 209: Ricetti gramezza. St Matthew Passion: Blute nur; Ich will dir mein Herze schenken.*
**(*) Delos Dig. D/CD 3026 [id.]. Arleen Augér, Mostly Mozart O, Schwarz – HANDEL: *Arias.* **(*)

Arleen Augér's pure, sweet soprano, effortlessly controlled, makes for bright performances of these Bach arias and songs, ideally suited to *Bist du bei mir*, less so to such a dark aria as *Blute nur* from the *St Matthew Passion*, not helped by relatively coarse accompaniment, over-recorded. Still very recommendable for admirers of this delightful singer, well coupled with Handel arias.

Arias: *Mass in B min.: Agnus dei; Qui sedes. St John Passion: All is fulfilled. St Matthew Passion: Grief for sin.*
(M) (***) Decca mono 433 474-2; *433 474-4*. Kathleen Ferrier, LPO, Boult – HANDEL: *Arias.* (***) ❀

On 7th and 8th October 1952, Kathleen Ferrier made her last and perhaps greatest record in London's Kingsway Hall, coupling four arias each by Bach and Handel. The combined skill of John Culshaw and Kenneth Wilkinson ensured a recording of the utmost fidelity by the standards of that time; with the advent of stereo, Sir Adrian Boult and the LPO, who provided the original accompaniments, were persuaded by Culshaw to return and record a new orchestral backing, over the old, and the result was something of a musical and technological miracle. It might seem perverse, therefore, that for the CD issue Decca have returned to the original mono master tape, yet the results fully justify that decision. Close comparison between mono CD and stereo LP shows that in masking the earlier recording the voice became very slightly clouded, particularly in its upper range. Now it re-emerges with extraordinary naturalness and presence. The mono accompaniments were beautifully balanced and orchestral detail is clarified further, with the harpsichord continuo coming through the more transparent texture in *Grief for sin* and Ambrose Gauntlett's viola da gamba obbligato for *All is fulfilled* more tangible. Of course the upper strings sound thinner, but that adds an 'authentic' touch, and they are given a far more dramatic bite in the climax at the words: *The Lion of Judah fought the fight.* The pre-Dolby background noise is still apparent but is in no way distracting. This is now reissued at mid-price as part of the Kathleen Ferrier Edition.

Transcriptions

Transcriptions: arr. BUSONI: *Chaconne* (from *Violin Partita No. 2*); *Chorales: Ich ruf zu dir; Nun freut euch, lieben Christen; Nun komm der Heiden Heiland; Wachet auf; Toccata & fugue in D min.* arr. LISZT: *Prelude & fugue in A min.* arr. LORD BERNERS: *In dolci jubilo.* arr. MYRA HESS:

Jesu, joy of man's desiring. arr. KEMPFF: *Siciliano.* arr. LE FLEMING: *Sheep may safely graze.* arr. RACHMANINOV: *Suite from Partita No. 3 in E.*
*** ASV Dig. CDDCA 759; *ZCDCA 759* [id.]. Gordon Fergus-Thompson (piano).

A highly entertaining collection, played with much flair and, in the case of the lyrical pieces at the centre of the recital (notably Wilhelm Kempff's delightful *Siciliano* and Dame Myra Hess's famous arrangement of *Jesu, joy of man's desiring*), stylish charm. Busoni arranged Bach flamboyantly but with authority, Liszt was unashamedly romantic and Lord Berners engagingly eccentric. (His boisterously prolix piece, with its mis-spelt title, is more composed than arranged.) But the most enjoyably characterful of all is Rachmaninov's triptych (*Preludio, Gavotte* and *Gigue*) from the *Violin partita in E major* which, pianistically, he makes very much his own. Gordon Fergus-Thompson plays this *Suite* with obvious relish and fine rhythmic sparkle. He is equally commanding in the famous opening *Chaconne* and turns the closing *Toccata and fugue in D minor*, BWV 565, into an exciting *tour de force* of bravura.

Arrangements: Bach – Stokowski

Chorales: Jesu, joy of man's desiring; Sheep may safely graze; We all believe in one God (Fugue on *Wir glauben all an einen Gott), BWV 680; English suite No. 2, BWV 807: Bourrée. Komm süsser Tod, BWV 478); Chaconne* (from *Partita No. 2 in B min.* for unaccompanied violin), *BWV 1004; Well-tempered Clavier*, Book 1: *Prelude in B min., BWV 869. Easter oratorio: Chorale. Toccata and fugue in D minor, BWV 565.*
❀ (M) *** BMG/RCA mono GD 60922; *GK 60922* [id.]. SO, Leopold Stokowski.

The *Toccata and fugue in D minor* is a mono recording made in 1947, and absolutely no technical apologies need be made for it. The sound is clear and full and has an impressively resonant bass. The violins sound more real than many stereo recordings made in America over the next two decades. The rest of the programme dates from three years later. The sobriquet, 'Symphony Orchestra', in this case describes a pick-up group of musicians drawn from the New York Philharmonic and NBC Symphony. They play marvellously in Stokowski's great Bach showpiece: the ensemble is quite remarkable, when the old magician's extremely brilliant performance of the fugue is consistently and wilfully flexible in the matter of rubato. Stokowski – obviously revelling in the orchestral bravura – never bettered this account (nor has anyone else since): it has thrilling power and absolute spontaneity. The chorales are enjoyable too (this is Stokowski's only recording of *Jesu, joy of man's desiring*) although the calculated dynamic bulges in the line will not appeal to all tastes. The 'little' *G minor Fugue* is treated buoyantly and lightly – the woodwind-sounds are a joy, and the lively *Bourrée* from the *English suite* has an agreeable elegant warmth. The brass voicing in the *Easter Oratorio Chorale* is unashamedly flamboyant. But the collector's item here is the incredibly wayward account of Bach's famous *Chaconne*, with its funereal opening tempo. Milstein's account takes 14 minutes; Stokowski stretches it out to 17 minutes 22 seconds and his indulgent *espressivo* alters its character entirely. I.M.'s Rosette is partly for the conductor's endearingly outrageous perversity in this piece, but principally for his unforgettably thrilling account of the *D minor Toccata and fugue* which at every point recalls Disney's inspired *Fantasia* imagery.

Bach, Wilhelm Friedemann (1710–84)

Sinfonia in D, F64; Adagio & fugue in D min., F65.
*** Capriccio Dig. 10 283 [id.]. Concerto Köln – J. C. F. BACH: *Sinfonia;* C. P. E. BACH: *Harpsichord concerto;* J. C. BACH: *Sinfonia.* ***

Wilhelm Friedemann's three-movement *Sinfonia in D major*, composed in the mid-1740s, was intended for use as an introduction to the Whitsun cantata, *Dies ist der Tag*, though it was also played in its own right as an independent piece. The better-known *Adagio and fugue in D minor* is possibly the last two movements of a symphony, though for some time it was thought to have been an introduction to a birthday cantata for Frederick the Great, written in 1758. It is a very extraordinary and expressive piece and makes one wonder whether Wilhelm Friedemann did not possess the most powerful imagination of all the sons. It is played by this period group with great expressive vitality and is well recorded.

Keyboard fantasias: Nos. 1–8 & 10, F.14–21 & F.23.
*** Denon Dig. CO 72588 [id.]. Huguette Dreyfus (harpsichord).

The *E minor Fantasia* (Falck 21), which opens the disc, comes from Wilhelm Friedemann's period in Dresden (1733–46) and is highly dramatic (at times almost operatic). These works are engagingly unpredictable, all bringing quite bold and daring harmonic sleights of hand, and this holds as good of the earlier ones – such as the *A minor* (F.23) – as of the later. The *E minor* (F.20) is from 1770, and two others come from the last year of his life. They are full of flair. So, too, is the excellent playing of Huguette Dreyfus, who has the advantage of an outstanding recording.

Baermann, Heinrich (1784–1847)

Adagio for clarinet and orchestra.
*** ASV Dig. CDDCA 559; *ZCDCA 559* [id.]. Emma Johnson, ECO, Groves – CRUSELL: *Concerto No. 2* *** ❀; ROSSINI: *Introduction, theme and variations****; WEBER: *Concertino.* ***

Heinrich Baermann's rather beautiful *Adagio*, once attributed to Wagner, is offered by a young clarinettist who plays the work warmly and sympathetically; Emma Johnson provides a very fresh performance.

Balakirev, Mily (1837–1910)

In Czechia.
** Olympia OCD 237 [id.]. USSR Ac. SO, Svetlanov – RACHMANINOV: *Symphony No. 2.* **

The sleeve omits the colon and bills the piece in Satiesque fashion as *M. Balakirev in Czechia.* It is otherwise known as *In Bohemia* and is included in a Marco Polo anthology under that title. It dates from 1867, when it was first called *Overture on Czech themes*, but Balakirev subsequently revised it in 1905, giving it its new title, *In Czechia.* This Russian performance under Yevgeni Svetlanov is in every way superior, and has plenty of atmosphere. While the Rachmaninov symphony with which it is coupled is digital, this is an analogue recording dating from 1978. It has some of the defects we associate with recordings from this period (shrill upper strings and a rather crude balance), but they are not serious enough to inhibit a recommendation.

Islamey (orch. Lyapunov).
** Olympia OCD 129 [id.]. USSR Ac. SO, Svetlanov – LYAPUNOV: *Hashish* etc. **(*)

An effective performance here of Lyapunov's effective (and once much-played) orchestration of *Islamey.* It makes a logical coupling for an interesting disc of Lyapunov's very Balakirevian orchestral music. Rough-and-ready but acceptable recording.

Symphony No. 1; Russia (symphonic poem).
**(*) Hyp. Dig. CDA 66493; *KA 66493* [id.]. Philh. O, Svetlanov.

Symphony No. 1 in C; Tamara (symphonic poem).
(M) **(*) EMI CDM7 63375-2 [id.]. RPO, Beecham.

Balakirev's sumptuously lyrical *First Symphony* had long and extended birthpangs: the first ideas came to him in the mid-1860s, but it was not until the late 1890s that it was finished. It took a further half-century to reach the gramophone in a performance of memorable artistry by this same orchestra under Karajan. Its representation in the catalogue has always been meagre and the present version makes a welcome modern alternative to the Beecham, coupled at mid-price with *Tamara.* That has many felicities and the early (1955) stereo has responded quite well to the CD face-lift, although the lack of amplitude in the string-tone is disadvantageous. *Tamara*, played with characteristic Beecham panache and subtlety of colour, was recorded a year earlier and the mono sound-balance compares favourably with the stereo in the *Symphony.*

Svetlanov's last account of the *Symphony* on Chant du Monde was with the USSR Academic Symphony Orchestra whose strings gave much pleasure despite a somewhat resonant recording. His approach remains largely unchanged, and there is some beautiful playing from the Philharmonia Orchestra in both works. The soaring clarinet solo at the beginning of the slow movement is ravishingly done (presumably by Michael Collins). However, there is some disagreement among us concerning Svetlanov's grip on the first three movements. R.L. finds the performance well paced and free from overheated romanticism; for E.G., the playing lacks bite and tension. Both are agreed that in the finale the emotional thrust of this music is powerfully caught, and the Hyperion recording, warm and full, deserves the highest grading. The coupling is both apt and successful in all respects.

Symphony No. 2 in D min.; Overture on Russian themes; Tamara.
**(*) Hyp. Dig. CDA 66586 *KA 66493* [id.]. Philh. O, Svetlanov.

The *Second Symphony* is the product of Balakirev's last years (1900–1908) though, as Professor Edward Garden observes in his excellent note, its *Scherzo alla cossacca* is earlier and was originally intended for the *First Symphony*. The first movement is tautly constructed and is an impressive testimony to Balakirev's mastery of the sonata process. The work's hold on the catalogue is even more tenuous than that of the *First* and, though both Rozhdestvensky (1977) and Svetlanov (1985) have recorded it previously, this is its finest version to date. The Philharmonia playing is cultured and the sound pleasingly natural and well balanced. It comes with the attractive *Overture on three Russian themes* and *Tamara*, arguably Balakirev's masterpiece, based on the gruesome tale recounted in Lermontov, of which Svetlanov made a vivid and evocative recording in the late 1970s. For R.L. this new version is powerfully atmospheric, not perhaps as savage and biting as the earlier Russian one, with the Philharmonia strings leaner and more cultivated than their Russian counterparts. Yet once again there is lack of consensus over Svetlanov's reading of the *Second Symphony*. R.L. enjoys its spacious breadth; however, while agreeing that it is tauter than that of the *First*, E.G. suggests that it does little to promote a symphony which inevitably runs the risk of seeming a repetition of the earlier work. Despite some beautiful playing, particularly from the strings, he feels that the performance is too relaxed, too easy-going, even in the second-movement *Scherzo alla cossacca*. Though the ensemble in the finale is crisp enough, the warm but rather distant balance takes some of the bite away. *Tamara* too – almost as extended as a one-movement symphony – needs to be stronger and more purposeful, as Beecham's version demonstrates.

Berceuse; Islamey.
**(*) Nuova Era Dig. 6826 [id.]. Michele Campanella – MUSSORGSKY: *Pictures* etc. **(*)

Michele Campanella is an Italian pianist of real distinction who made a great impression in his UK concert appearances and broadcasts during the mid-1980s. The *Berceuse* is played with taste and style. Campanella's fine account of *Islamey* is impressive even if in terms of sheer excitement it does not eclipse memories of Simon Barere's celebrated performance (see Recitals).

Islamey (oriental fantasy).
(M) *** EMI CDM7 64329-2; *EG 764329-4*. Andrei Gavrilov – PROKOFIEV: *Concerto No. 1;* TCHAIKOVSKY: *Piano concerto No. 1* etc. ***

Gavrilov's dazzling account of Balakirev's fantasy is outstandingly charismatic; it is well recorded, too. It comes in harness with an equally dazzling version of Prokofiev's *First Piano concerto* and a performance of the Tchaikovsky *B flat minor Concerto* which is rather less convincing, but this remains an outstanding showcase for the soloist.

Piano sonata in B flat min.
**(*) Olympia OCD 354 [id.]; Archduke *MARC 2*. Donna Amato – DUTILLEUX: *Sonata*. **(*)
**(*) Kingdom Dig. KCLCD 2001; *CKCL 2001* [id.]. Gordon Fergus-Thompson – SCRIABIN: *Sonata No. 3* etc. **(*)

The Balakirev is arguably the greatest Russian piano sonata of the pre-1914 era. Donna Amato gives a musicianly account of it, well paced and authoritative – not surprisingly, since she studied with Louis Kentner, who made the very first recording of it after the war. The recording is very lifelike, and this is a most desirable issue, even if the playing time at 47 minutes is not particularly generous.

Gordon Fergus-Thompson, too, is fully equal to the considerable demands of the Balakirev *Sonata* and offers excellent playing, though the recording is reverberant and the piano not always dead in tune. Fergus-Thompson also includes Balakirev's arrangement of Glinka's *The Lark* as an encore.

Bantock, Granville (1868–1946)

Celtic Symphony; Hebridean Symphony; The Sea reivers; The Witch of Atlas.
*** Hyp. Dig. CDA 66450; *KA 66450* [id.]. RPO, Handley.

Vernon Handley conducts warmly atmospheric performances of four of Bantock's Hebridean inspirations. Most ambitious is the *Hebridean Symphony* of 1913, with nature music echoing Wagner and Delius as well as Sibelius, whose music Bantock introduced into Britain. The two tone-poems are attractive too, but best of all is the *Celtic Symphony*, a late work written in 1940, which uses strings and six harps. This is in the grand string tradition of Vaughan Williams's *Tallis fantasia* and Elgar's *Introduction and allegro*, a beautiful, colourful work that deserves to be far better known. With warm, atmospheric recording to match, Handley draws committed performances from the RPO.

Fifine at the fair (tone poem No. 3).
(M) (***) EMI mono CDM7 63405-2 [id.]. RPO, Sir Thomas Beecham – BAX: *Garden of Fand;* BERNERS: *Triumph of Neptune.* (***)

Beecham always had a soft spot for *Fifine at the fair* and his advocacy is so persuasive that one could wish for the piece to be restored to the repertoire. The early (1949) sound is a bit confined and opaque, but it is full and not edgy, and one is readily seduced by the Beecham magic. The CD transfer makes the very most of the 78-r.p.m. master.

The Pierrot of the Minute: overture.
*** Chan. CHAN 8373 [id.]. Bournemouth Sinf., Del Mar – BRIDGE: *Summer*, etc.; BUTTERWORTH: *Banks of green willow.* ***

Bantock's overture is concerned with Pierrot's dream in which he falls in love with a Moon Maiden who tells him their love must die at dawn, but he will not listen. He wakes to realize that his dream of love lasted a mere minute. The writing is often delicate and at times Elgarian, and the piece is well worth investigating. The recording sounds remarkably fresh.

Barber, Samuel (1910–81)

Adagio for strings, Op. 11.
*** Argo 417 818-2 [id.]. ASMF, Marriner – COPLAND: *Quiet city;* COWELL: *Hymn;* CRESTON: *Rumor;* IVES: *Symphony No. 3.* ***
(M) *** DG Dig. 427 806-2; *427 806-4*. LAPO, Bernstein – BERNSTEIN: *Overture Candide; West Side Story; On the Town* ***; GERSHWIN: *Rhapsody in blue.* **(*)
(M) *** DG Dig. 431 048-2; *431 048-4* [id.]. LAPO, Bernstein – COPLAND: *Appalachian spring* ***; GERSHWIN: *Rhapsody in blue.* **(*)
(M) *** EMI Dig. CDM7 64306-2 [id.]. St Louis SO, Slatkin – COPLAND: *Fanfare* etc.; THOMSON: *Autumn* etc. ***

Marriner's 1976 performance of Barber's justly famous *Adagio* is arguably the most satisfying version we have had since the war, although Bernstein's alternative has the advantage of digital recording. The quality of sound on the remastered Argo CD retains most of the richness and body of the analogue LP, but at the climax the brighter lighting brings a slightly sparer violin texture than on the original LP.

Bernstein's powerfully expressive and deeply felt reading of Barber's *Adagio* has an expansively restrained, elegiac feeling, but his control of the climax – in what is substantially a live recording – is unerring.

Slatkin's performance is gently elegiac, not as passionate as some, yet undoubtedly affecting, with a slow burst of tension on the last chord of the climax. The couplings are worthwhile too, and the sound is first rate.

(i) *Adagio for strings;* (i; ii) *Cello concerto, Op. 22;* (ii; iii) *Cello sonata, Op. 6.*
*** Virgin Dig. VC7 91083-2; *VC 791083-4* [id.]. (i) SCO; Saraste; (ii) Ralph Kirshbaum; (iii) Roger Vignoles.

Kirshbaum's view of the Barber *Cello concerto*, with splendid support from Saraste and the Scottish Chamber Orchestra, is darker and spikier than those of his direct rivals, and rather more urgent in the outer movements, yet it is just as beautifully played. He is equally convincing in Barber's other, much rarer cello work, the *Cello sonata* of 1932. Roger Vignoles copes well with piano-writing unhelpful to a degree surprising from a pianist-composer. The celebrated *Adagio*, coolly done, makes a worthwhile fill-up. Spacious, well-focused recording.

Adagio for strings; (i) *Piano concerto, Op. 38; Medea's meditation and Dance of vengeance, Op. 23a.*
*** ASV Dig. CDDCA 534 [id.]. (i) Joselson; LSO, Schenck.

In Barber's *Concerto* Tedd Joselson is marvellously and dazzlingly brilliant, as well as being highly sensitive and poetic. What also shows this score to better advantage than before is the greater richness and detail of the ASV recording and the unforced and poetic orchestral contribution from the LSO under Andrew Schenck. The LSO also give a singularly fine account of the *Medea* excerpt (not to be confused with the Suite) and a restrained and noble one of the celebrated *Adagio.*

(i) *Adagio for strings;* (ii) *Essay No. 2 for orchestra; Music for a scene from Shelley; Serenade for strings, Op. 1;* (ii; iii) *A Stopwatch and an ordnance map, Op. 15;* (iv) Chorus: *Let down the bars, O Death!* (ii; v) *A Hand of bridge* (chamber opera), *Op. 35.*
(M) *** Van. 08.4016.71 [OVC 4016]. (i) I Solisti di Zagreb, Antonio Janigro; (ii) Symphony of the Air, Golschmann; (iii) with Robert De Cormier Chorale; (v) with Neway, Alberts, Lewis, Maero; (iv) Washington Cathedral Ch., Callaway.

An admirable and highly rewarding anthology of works by a composer whose *Adagio for strings* has wrongly overshadowed his achievement elsewhere. Excellent singing and playing throughout, and a balance of warmth and vitality from Golschmann makes this collection stand out from other Barber records; the 1960 recording, vivid and with plenty of ambience, has been transferred very effectively to CD.

Cave of the heart (original version of *Medea*).
*** Koch Dig. 3-7019-2; *2-7019-4* [id.]. Atlantic Sinf., Schenck – COPLAND: *Appalachian spring.* ***

This disc makes a logical coupling and brings together two scores written for Martha Graham. The original version of *Medea* was called *Serpent heart* when it first appeared in 1946 and was retitled *Cave of the heart* the following year. Although it shares much of the same material as the concert suite Barber fashioned from the ballet, in places it sounds very different. It was first described as brilliant, bitter and full of amazing energy; in this original form it sounds much darker in feeling and harder-edged, and it has stronger Stravinskian overtones. The scoring is for a small group of fifteen players, yet the effect in this full-blooded, vividly present recording is, if anything, brawnier than the more sumptuous revision. A most interesting and stimulating score.

Cello concerto, Op. 22.
*** Sony Dig. MK 44900 [id.]. Yo-Yo Ma, Baltimore SO, Zinman – BRITTEN: *Cello symphony.* ***
*** Chan. Dig. CHAN 8322; *ABTD 1085* [id.]. Wallfisch, ECO, Simon – SHOSTAKOVICH: *Cello concerto No. 1.* ***

With his masterly sense of line, Yo-Yo Ma gives a richly lyrical reading of Barber's beautiful *Cello concerto.* The subtleties in the reading are enhanced by having the soloist naturally placed, not spotlit, in relation to the well-balanced orchestra. This work of 1945 makes an unusual but apt and attractive coupling for Ma's superb account of the Britten *Cello symphony.*

Wallfisch also gives an impressive and eloquent reading, and the elegiac slow movement is especially fine. Wallfisch is forwardly balanced, but otherwise the recording is truthful; the orchestra is vividly detailed. Indeed the sound is outstandingly realistic; given the excellence of the coupling, this must also receive the strongest recommendation.

(i; ii) *Piano concerto, Op. 38;* (ii) *Symphony No. 1, Op.9;* (i; iii) *Souvenirs, Op. 28* (arr. piano, 4 hands); *Canzone.*
*** BMG/RCA Dig. RD 60732 [60732-2-RC]. (i) John Browning; (ii) St Louis SO, Leonard Slatkin; (iii) Slatkin (piano).

Following closely on Neeme Järvi's Chandos version of Samuel Barber's *Symphony No. 1,* this rival RCA version of a work which in its time marked a breakthrough in American music, helps to rectify its long-term neglect. The symphony by Mrs Beach may make a more unusual coupling on Chandos, but with his all-Barber collection Slatkin has an obvious advantage. At the very start, the tautness of attack by the St Louis players immediately commands attention, while Järvi builds tension more gradually. Generally Slatkin favours allegros taken slightly faster than Järvi's, but the slow section is broader. In the lovely oboe melody of that *Andante tranquillo* the St Louis principal is allowed a more generous espressivo, playing very beautifully, but the simpler folk-like treatment that Järvi's oboist gives at the more flowing speed is more rarefied in its beauty, a very valid alternative. Though Järvi's sense of spontaneity gives extra warmth at times, Slatkin secures ensemble a degree crisper. One incidental advantage is that the RCA disc provides separate tracks for each of the four distinct sections in this one-movement work, where the Chandos has it on a single track. The coupling will be the decisive point for many, and on RCA it is good to have a new recording of the *Piano concerto* by John Browning, the pianist for whom Barber originally wrote this formidable half-hour work. Browning recorded it for CBS not long after the first performance, with George Szell and the vintage Cleveland Orchestra, and that classic account, not yet issued here on CD, still stands supreme for its passionate thrust and power. At rather broader speeds, with the piano balanced more forwardly, this new version is not so high-powered, but in the slow movement it is more sensuous, with figuration magically delicate. As an exceptionally generous makeweight Slatkin joins Browning in a piano duo playing Barber's two-piano piece, *Souvenirs*, as Browning points out a work of 'pure nostalgia', played here with winning lightness. The piano sound is on the fruity side, but the St Louis recording of the works with orchestra is clean and full, if not so rich as Järvi's Chandos alternative.

Violin concerto, Op. 14.
(M) *** EMI Dig. CDM7 64305-2 [id.]. Elmar Oliveira, St Louis SO, Slatkin – COPLAND: *Clarinet concerto* ***; GERSHWIN: *Concerto in F.* **
*** ASV Dig. CDRPO 8013; *ZCRPO 8013* [id.]. Anne Meyers, RPO, Seaman – BRUCH: *Concerto No. 1.* **(*)

(i) *Violin concerto; Essay for orchestra No. 2; The School for scandal: Overture. Vannesa: Prelude and Intermezzo.*
*** Pro Arte Dig. CCD 241 [id.]. (i) Silverstein; Utah SO.

Anyone who enjoys Barber's *Adagio for strings* must respond to the *Violin concerto.* It is genuinely beautiful and has consistent warmth, freshness and humanity. Elmar Oliveira's version responds to the nostalgia of the *Andante* with a vein of bitter-sweet yearning that is most affecting. It is a fine performance overall, with a brilliantly played finale, and is warmly and realistically recorded, with Slatkin directing an entirely sympathetic accompaniment. Rich, atmospheric sound.

The merit of Anne Meyers' performance lies in its unforced naturalness. The sleeve material tells us nothing about the soloist, who is an artist of quality. Her playing has an effortless lyrical flow and she captures its world of feeling and sense of youthful rapture marvellously. This is not high-powered, jet-setting playing, though there is no want of virtuosity or, in the slow movement, tenderness. She is well supported by the RPO under Christopher Seaman, and the recording is as musically balanced and as lifelike as the playing. An altogether first-class performance; it is a pity the coupling was not more imaginatively chosen.

The alternative version from Joseph Silverstein is in some ways an even stronger performance than Oliviera's, with the Utah orchestra providing a fervently passionate accompaniment. Both soloist and orchestra are forwardly projected by the extremely vivid Pro Arte recording, at the expense of some fierceness on the fortissimo massed violins, but in consequence Silverstein's image is bigger than Oliviera's, which suits the style of the playing. Silverstein also directs the other works, which are well worth having.

Essays Nos. 1, Op. 12; 2, Op. 17; 3, Op. 47.
*** Chan. Dig. CHAN 9053; *ABTD 1589* [id.]. Detroit SO, Järvi – IVES: *Symphony No. 1.* ***

When he was once asked to explain his use of the word *Essay* in a musical context, Barber referred his questioner to the O.E.D.: 'a composition of moderate length on a particular subject . . . more or less elaborate in style though limited in range', which one might adapt to read symphonic in style but not scale. The *First Essay* with its strongly Sibelian overtones dates from 1937 and a successor followed some years later; the *Third Essay* (1978) was his very last work. All three have a mixture of youthful innocence and neo-romantic lushness that should ensure their future in the repertoire. Both in terms of sonority and approach, Neeme Järvi's account of these appealing works differ from their American predecessors. The strings have a lightness and subtlety and are highly responsive. The recording is very natural and present, beautifully balanced without any trace of woodwind highlighting or other distortions of a concert hall perspective.

Essay for orchestra No. 3, Op. 47; Fadograph of a Yestern Scene, Op. 44; Medea: suite, Op. 23.
*** Koch Dig. 3-7010-2; *2-7010-4* [id.]. New Zealand SO, Andrew Schenck.

A welcome recording of two Barber rarities from the 1970s in sympathetic performances by the New Zealand orchestra under Andrew Schenck. The *Fadograph of a Yestern Scene* was inspired by a passage in James Joyce's *Finnegan's Wake* and is not otherwise available in Europe. It is a lyrical piece, reflective in mood and full of warmth; the *Third Essay* is a rarity in the concert hall – though there are two rival recordings – and is powerfully argued and concentrated in atmosphere. The more familiar *Medea suite*, dating from the period of the *Second Symphony* and composed for Martha Graham, is well played. The recording has outstanding clarity and definition, but the acoustic has the very slightly dry quality of a studio rather than the expansiveness of a concert hall.

Medea (ballet): suite.
(M) *** Mercury 462 016-2 [id.]. Eastman-Rochester O, Howard Hanson – GOULD: *Fall River legend* etc. ***

This pungent score contains some of Barber's most intensely serious music, as well as some of the most expressive. As with all good ballets, however, the rhythmic element is vital. Hanson's performance is both polished and dramatic, and the brilliant 1959 Mercury recording has astonishing clarity and vivid presence.

Souvenirs.
*** Koch Dig. 3-7005-2; *2-7005-4* [id.]. New Zealand SO, Schenck – MENOTTI: *Amahl* etc. ***

Souvenirs dates from the early 1950s and began life as a series of piano duets. It is an absolutely enchanting score which was first recorded by Efrem Kurtz (on a 10-inch mono LP) and was then consigned to oblivion. It has bags of charm and, unlike the delightful Menotti with which it is coupled, every idea is so memorable that it instantly replaces the one that came before. It is puzzling that such good music with all its wit, elegance and charm has languished, unloved, for so long. It is very well played here by the New Zealand Symphony Orchestra under Andrew Schenck and is eminently well recorded too. Strongly recommended.

Symphony No. 1 (in one movement), *Op. 9; Essays for Orchestra Nos. 1, Op. 12; 2, Op. 17; Night flight, Op. 19a.*
(M) *** Unicorn UKCD 2046 [id.]. LSO, David Measham.

Symphony No. 1; The School for scandal: Overture, Op. 5.
*** Chan. Dig. CHAN 8958; *ABTD 1550* [id.]. Detroit SO, Järvi – BEACH: *Symphony in E min.* ***

Neeme Järvi's account of Barber's *First Symphony* is broader than usual and gains enormously in symphonic coherence. He manages its rapid shifts of mood and tempi far more convincingly than most other versions. Barber's youthful *Overture* to *The School for scandal* with its marvellously fresh and lyrical second theme is equally well served. The *Second Symphony* would no doubt have made a more logical coupling, but the *Symphony* of Mrs Beach is well worth having instead. Good playing from the Detroit orchestra and very good recorded sound.

David Measham, principal second violin of the LSO before he launched into conducting, also proves a splendid advocate of Barber's *First Symphony*, securing a passionately committed performance and bringing out its (at times) somewhat Waltonian manner. Those looking for a mid-priced version should be well pleased, for the first two *Essays for orchestra*, written in 1938 and 1942 respectively, are very well played, as is the hauntingly evocative movement, *Night flight*, all that the composer allowed to survive from his *Symphony No. 2*.

Summer music.
*** Crystal CD 750 [id.]. Westwood Wind Quintet – CARLSSON: *Nightwings;* LIGETI: *Bagatelles;* MATHIAS: *Quintet.* ***
(M) **(*) Sony SMK 46250 [id.]. Members of the Marlboro Festival – NIELSEN: *Woodwind quintet;* HINDEMITH: *Octet.* **

Samuel Barber's *Summer music* is an evocative mood-picture of summer, a gloriously warm and lyrical piece whose neglect on record is difficult to understand. The Crystal CD offers superbly committed and sensitive playing and vivid, warm recording.

Barber's delightful *Summer music* is also sensitively played by the artists at the Marlboro

Festival, who capture its air of tenderness and melancholy very well. The 1981 sound-quality is very acceptable and the coupling valuable.

PIANO MUSIC

Ballade, Op. 46; 4 Excursions, Op. 20; Nocturne (Homage to John Field), Op. 33; Sonata, Op. 26.
**(*) Hyp. CDH 88016 [id.]. Angela Brownridge.

This CD performs a useful function in the catalogue: it accommodates Barber's entire output for the piano, offering the only available version of the *Ballade* (1972) and the endearing *Four Excursions*. These are not quite so crisp or characterful as in the old Andor Foldes mono record from the 1950s but in some details are more sensitive. Angela Brownridge gives a good account of herself in the dazzling *Sonata*. Though she may not perhaps possess the transcendental virtuosity of a Horowitz (or of Van Cliburn, whose recording is currently available on RCA); nevertheless she is fully equal to its demands. The recording is not first class; the resonant acoustic makes the piano sound slightly unfocussed, though it is firmer on CD than it was on LP and the ear soon adjusts.

Piano sonata, Op. 26.
(M) **(*) BMG/RCA GD 60415; *GK 60415* [60415-2-RG; *60415-4-RG*]. Van Cliburn – DEBUSSY: *Estampes* etc. **; MOZART: *Piano sonata No. 10.* **

Van Cliburn's recording is pretty masterly and, although the sound could be more ingratiating and have a warmer ambience, it is still acceptable.

VOCAL MUSIC

Agnus Dei.
*** Hyp. Dig. CDA 66129; *KA 66129* [id.]. Corydon Singers, Matthew Best – BERNSTEIN: *Chichester Psalms;* COPLAND: *In the beginning* etc. ***

Barber's *Agnus Dei* is none other than our old friend the *Adagio*, arranged for voices by the composer in 1967. Matthew Best's fine performance moves spaciously and expansively to an impressive climax. The sound is very fine, with the acoustics of St Jude-on-the-Hill, Hampstead, admirably suited to the music.

(i) *Andromache's farewell;* (ii) *Dover Beach;* (iii) *Hermit songs;* (iv) *Knoxville: summer of 1915.*
(M) (***) Sony mono/stereo MPK 46727 [id.]. (i) Arroyo, NYPO, Schippers; (ii) Fischer-Dieskau, Juilliard Qt; (iii) Leontyne Price, composer; (iv) Eleanor Steber, Dumbarton Oaks O, William Strickland.

This collection of vintage recordings makes a splendid mid-priced Barber compendium, representing four of his finest vocal works, all in superb performances. Excellent CD transfers. No texts are provided but words are exceptionally clear.

The Lovers, Op. 43. Prayers of Kierkegaard, Op. 30.
*** Koch Dig. 3-7125-2. Dale Duesing, Sarah Reese, Chicago Ch. & SO, Andrew Schenck.

The Lovers, written in 1971, was Barber's last major work, a substantial choral cantata setting nine erotic poems by the Chilean, Pablo Neruda. It is music of heartwarming richness, here given a splendid first recording, taken from live performances given in Chicago in October 1991. After the débâcle of his big Shakespearean opera, *Antony and Cleopatra*, commissioned for the opening of the new Metropolitan opera-house in New York, Barber at first lacked the confidence to continue composing. But then in *The Lovers* he found a more relaxed style, letting his melodic gift flower in free-flowing tunefulness, set against crisply rhythmic writing. The nine songs, varied in mood and length, follow the development of a love affair from first passion past various states of ecstasy through to the sadness and disillusion of lost love. The sensuousness of some of the songs even gives a reminder of Canteloube's *Songs of the Auvergne*, though the writing here is deeper and subtler. It makes a moving sequence, with the soloist, Dale Duesing, matching the responsivness of the outstanding Chicago Symphony Chorus. *The Prayers of Kierkegaard*, written in 1952, is a tougher, more uncompromising work, but approachable too, again with magnificent writing for chorus. With minimal audience noise Schenck's colourful performances bring a timely memorial for a fine conductor who died early in 1992. It was he who earlier revived Barber's *Symphony No. 2*, misguidedly withdrawn by the composer.

Vanessa (opera): complete.
(M) *** BMG/RCA GD 87899 (2) [7899-2-RG]. Steber, Elias, Resnik, Gedda, Tossi, Met. Op. Ch. & O, Mitropoulos.

Vanessa inhabits much the same civilized world as Strauss or Henry James. Although it has not held the stage, its melodic freshness and warmth will ensure a reversal of its fortunes some day. This, its only recording so far, was made at the time of its first performance in 1958, but no apologies are needed for its quality; it stands the test of time as well as does the opera itself.

Bargiel, Woldemar (1828–97)

Octet in C min. for strings, Op. 15a.
*** Hyp. Dig. CDA 66356; *KA 66356* [id.]. Divertimenti – MENDELSSOHN: *Octet.* ***

Wilhelm Altmann speaks of Bargiel in the 1928 *Cobbett's Encyclopaedia* as 'an adherent of Schumann'; but what strikes one about this music is its independence of outlook and dignity. It is far more individual than, say, Gade and throughout is well schooled, cultivated and inventive, the extended first movement of over 18 minutes being well sustained and well shaped. Indeed it is something of a discovery; the delightful scherzo-like section embedded in the slow movement is particularly felicitous. Divertimenti play it with real feeling and conviction and are excellently recorded.

Barrios, Augustin (1885–1944)

Aconquija; Aire de Zamba; Le catedral; Cueca; Estudio; Una limosna por el amor de Dios; Madrigal (Gavota); Maxixa; Mazurka appassionata; Minuet; Preludio; Un sueño en la floresta; Valse No. 3; Vallancico de Navidad.
(M) *** Sony SBK 47669 [id.]. John Williams – PONCE: *Folia de España.* ***

In the expert hands of John Williams this collection provides a very entertaining recital, ideal for late-evening listening. The recording is excellent. The remarkable extended set of Ponce *Variations* added for the CD reissue brings the total playing time up to 77 minutes.

Bartók, Béla (1881–1945)

Concerto for orchestra.
(M) *** Decca 417 754-2 [id.]. Chicago SO, Solti – MUSSORGSKY: *Pictures.* ***
(*) Decca Dig. 425 694-2 [id.]. Cleveland O, Dohnányi – LUTOSLAWSKI: *Concerto for orchestra.* *

Concerto for orchestra; Music for strings, percussion and celesta.
*** EMI Dig. CDC7 54070-2; *EL 754070-4* [id.]. Oslo PO, Jansons.
*** Decca Dig. 421 443-2; *421 443-4* [id.]. Montreal SO, Dutoit.
(M) **(*) Sony SMK 47510 [id.]. NYPO, Bernstein.
(M) **(*) BMG/RCA GD 60175 [60175-2-RG]. Chicago SO, Fritz Reiner.

Jansons and the Oslo Philharmonic give outstanding performances of both works, making this by a small margin a first recommendation in this now-favourite coupling of two Bartók masterpieces. Reflecting his Russian training, Jansons points rhythms with flair and resilience, setting the fun in the second and fourth movements against the power and intensity of the rest. The Oslo orchestra plays with unfailingly crisp ensemble, and the sound is excellent too, full and open, with the EMI engineers mastering the difficult Oslo Konzerthus acoustic.

Solti gave Bartók's *Concerto for orchestra* its compact disc début. The upper range is very brightly lit indeed, which brings an aggressive feeling to the upper strings. This undoubtedly suits the reading, fierce and biting on the one hand, exuberant on the other. Superlative playing from Solti's own Chicago orchestra, and given vivid sound.

Decca has made a speciality of brilliant recordings of this showpiece work, and Dohnányi's brings an even fuller, richer sound than Solti's with the Chicago orchestra or Dutoit's with the Montreal Symphony. Dohnányi's reading is relatively straight – the night music of the third movement lacks mystery, and the humour of the fourth-movement trio is a little stiff – but, with ensemble even crisper than on either rival disc, the bite and power of much of the playing is sharply contrasted with the extreme refinement and delicacy of the string articulation, as in the scurrying main theme of the finale.

Helped by warm and atmospheric recording, Dutoit conducts performances of both these masterpieces which convey the message that Bartók is a composer of warmth and refinement rather than of barbarism. Dutoit is particularly successful in bringing out the vein of humour, too, not only in the *Concerto* but also in the *Music for strings, percussion and celesta*. There have been more electrifying performances of both works than these, but none more beautiful; some listeners might seek a greater degree of bite, and they can turn to Solti.

Bernstein's coupling of Bartók's two most popular pieces bring fizzing performances, typical of his work in New York at end of the 1950s and beginning of the 1960s (the recording dates are 1959 and 1961 respectively). The remastering has made the very most of the sound, which does not lack atmosphere, but the violins are brightly lit and a bit thin above the stave. The performances are full of excitement and vitality (the finale of the *Concerto* is breathtaking) but the recording is fairly forward, which prevents any hushed pianissimo effects from registering, although because of the drama of the playing there is still plenty of dynamic contrast. Yet for the animal energy which Bernstein finds in Bartók this is still a record worth hearing.

Reiner's version of the *Concerto for orchestra* was recorded in 1955, but the sound is unbelievably good, spacious and vivid. The performance is most satisfying, surprisingly straightforward from one brought up in Central Europe but with plenty of cutting edge. The *Music for strings, percussion and celesta*, recorded three years later, suffers from a forward balance which prevents any true pianissimo quality, even in the first movement.

Concerto for orchestra; Dance suite; The Miraculous Mandarin: suite.
(M) *** Decca 425 039-2; *425 039-4* [id.]. LSO, Solti.

Concerto for orchestra; (i) *The Miraculous Mandarin* (complete ballet).
**(*) Virgin Dig. VC7 91106-2; *VC7 91106-4* [id.]. (i) Dumont Singers; Melbourne SO, Iwaki.

There will be many who prefer Solti's earlier (1965) LSO version of the *Concerto for orchestra*, for the 1960s' recording – outstanding in its day – shows its age only very marginally in the string-tone; in all other respects it is of high quality. The performance has all the fire and passion one could wish for, but also a touch more of wit and idiosyncrasy than the later, digital, Chicago version (see above). The inclusion of two fill-ups is most welcome. The streak of ruthlessness in Solti's make-up that sometimes mars performances of less barbaric music is then given full rein in *The Miraculous Mandarin suite*, recorded with comparable vividness and colour two years earlier, and again benefiting from the Kingsway Hall ambience.

Iwaki and the Melbourne orchestra have an obvious advantage over their direct rivals in presenting the complete *Miraculous Mandarin* ballet, not just the suite, as coupling for the *Concerto for orchestra*. The recording is excellent, spacious and full, though transferred at a rather low level. The playing is finely pointed but is often too well-mannered for Bartók, lacking something in fierceness and excitement. The ballet is generously indexed with tracks.

(i) *Concerto for orchestra;* (ii) *Dance suite; 2 Portraits, Op. 5; Mikrokosmos* (orch. Serly): *Bourrée; From the diary of a fly.*
(M) *** Mercury 432 017-2 [id.]. (i) LSO; (ii) Philharmonia Hungarica, Dorati.

Dorati's electrifying version of the *Concerto for orchestra* dates from 1962 and many collectors still regard it as the account by which all later versions are to be judged. Dorati secures outstandingly brilliant and committed playing from the LSO. The recording, made in Wembley Town Hall, shows characteristic expertise of balance. The rest of the programme was recorded in 1958 in the Grosse Saal of the Vienna Konzerthaus, which affords Dorati's fine orchestra of Hungarian émigrés plenty of body without blurring outlines. They play these highly attractive genre pieces with striking tonal vigour, and the luminous intensity of the strings and brass in particular is enhanced by the hall acoustics.

Piano concertos Nos. 1–3.
(M) *** Ph. 426 660-2. Stephen Kovacevich, LSO or BBC SO, C. Davis.

Piano concertos Nos. 1–3; Music for strings, percussion & celesta; Rhapsody for piano and orchestra; Scherzo for piano and orchestra.
*** Ph. Dig. 416 831-2 (3) [id.]. Kocsis, Budapest Festival O, Fischer.

(i) *Piano concertos Nos. 1–3; Rhapsody for piano and orchestra; Concerto for orchestra.*
(M) *** DG 427 410-2 (2) [id.]. (i) Géza Anda, Berlin RSO, Fricsay.

(i) *Piano concertos Nos. 1–3;* (ii) *Sonata for 2 pianos and percussion.*
(M) *** Decca Dig./Analogue 425 573-2 (2) [id.]. Vladimir Ashkenazy; (i) LPO, Solti; (ii) Vovka Ashkenazy, D. Corkhill, Andrew Smith.

This outstanding Philips set dominates the catalogue in this repertoire. Kocsis recorded the *First* and *Second Piano concertos* in the early 1970s for Hungaroton; but these new versions are even more vibrant, and the *Third* is superbly done, to make it perhaps the finest on record. The inclusion of the *Music for strings, percussion and celesta* may be counted a disadvantage by some, particularly as the resonant acoustic and rather forward balance prevent an absolute pianissimo and detract from the feeling of mystery; but this is still an exciting and involving performance. We have had the *Rhapsody* before, and the account here is as fine as the *Concertos*; what is especially welcome is the *Scherzo*. Its style is fascinatingly eclectic, but the writing is extremely spontaneous and the work springs to life when the performers are so obviously enjoying themselves. The full-bodied recording with a rich, tangible piano-image is very satisfying.

Kovacevich's direct, concentrated readings of the three *Piano concertos* come at mid-price in this generous coupling on a Philips Silver Line reissue. Sir Colin Davis accompanies sensitively and vigorously. Kovacevich seems intent on countering the idea that No. 3 is a facile work, with the central *Adagio religioso* played with hushed dedication between spiky outer movements, giving concentrated intensity to compare with late Beethoven.

Ashkenazy's versions of both the *First Concerto* and the *Sonata* (with his son, Vovka) are tough, even aggressive performances, biting, never relaxing, spectacularly caught in (1984) digital sound with the widest range of dynamics. The *Second* and *Third Concertos*, recorded four years earlier, are analogue, but the recording, although reverberant, is comparably vivid and present. With the Slavonic bite of the soloist aptly matching the Hungarian fire of the conductor, the readings of both works are urgently involving and incisive. Tempi tend to be fast, while slow movements bring hushed inner concentration, beautifully captured in Decca's atmospheric recording. If anything, the *Third Concerto* is even more gripping than the *Second*.

Anda's recordings of the Bartók *Concertos* and the *Rhapsody*, which is attractively volatile, have acquired classic status. Anda seems ideally cast as soloist and Fricsay is a natural Bartókian. The performances are refined yet urgent, incisive but red-blooded too. Fricsay's *Concerto for orchestra* was recorded in 1957 and is a first-class example of DG's expertise in the pre-stereo era. A most enjoyable performance and no apologies for the sound.

Piano concertos Nos. 1 in A; 2 in G.
*** DG 415 371-2 [id.]. Pollini, Chicago SO, Abbado.

The DG issue forms an exuberant partnership between two of the most distinguished Italian musicians of the day. Virtuosity goes with a sense of spontaneity. Rhythms in fast movements are freely and infectiously sprung to bring out bluff Bartókian high spirits. The Chicago orchestra, vividly recorded, is in superb form and the CD gives a new lease of life to the 1979 analogue recording.

Concerto for 2 pianos, percussion and celesta.
*** Ph. Dig. 416 378-2 [id.]. Freire, Argerich, L. and J. Pustjens, Concg. O, Zinman – KODÁLY: *Dances of Galánta.* ***

Martha Argerich with Stephen Kovacevich recorded a fierily vibrant performance of the *Sonata*, and there is much of the same high-voltage electricity in her recording of the orchestral version with Nelson Freire. The recording with pianos placed relatively close is well detailed but lacks something in mystery.

Viola concerto; Violin concerto No. 1; (i) *Rhapsodies Nos. 1–2.*
(M) *** EMI CDM7 63985-2 [id.]. Sir Yehudi Menuhin, New Philh. O, Dorati; (i) BBC SO, Boulez.

Menuhin plays the earlier concerto that Bartók wrote for Stefi Geyer. The *Viola concerto* is a less finished example of Bartók's inspiration, although it comes from the very end of his career. The sketches alone were what existed at the time of the composer's death; however, Tibor Serly, who had worked closely with Bartók, fitted them together and constructed the outline as Bartók undoubtedly intended. The drawing-together process is helped enormously by an interpreter such as Menuhin with his strongly creative imagination: he plays the *Adagio religioso* central movement with characteristic nobility of feeling, and he and Dorati make much of the Hungarian dance rhythms of the finale. There is a comparably earthy, peasant manner in Menuhin's playing of the two *Rhapsodies*, and it is matched by Boulez's approach, warm and passionate rather than clinical. The soloist is rather close. However, the balance responds to the controls, and this remains one of Menuhin's most worthwhile reissues.

Viola concerto; Violin concerto No. 2.
*** BMG/RCA Dig. RD 60749 [60749-2-RC]. Zukerman, St Louis SO, Slatkin.

Pinchas Zukerman gives an attractively lively account of the Bartók *Violin concerto No. 2*, aptly coupled with the *Viola concerto*, with Zukerman once again demonstrating his supreme mastery on the bigger string instrument. It is a work which Bartók would no doubt have tidied up had he lived, but which in such a performance as this is a warmly sympathetic example of his last-period style. Fine orchestral playing and excellent sound.

Viola concerto (arr. cello)
*** BMG/RCA Dig. RD 60717 [60717-2-RC]. Starker, St Louis SO, Slatkin – DVOŘÁK: *Cello concerto.* *(*)

Though Bartók never fully completed his *Viola concerto* before he died, he did sanction a cello version, which his friend, Tibor Serly, proceeded to publish soon after the viola version appeared. Long buried, it was taken up by the veteran, Janos Starker, who made this first recording. In some ways, with its richer tone and lower register, it is more effective than the original, and Slatkin and the St Louis Orchestra – who recorded the viola version with Pinchas Zukerman at the same period – give warm support. Unfortunately, it is coupled with a disappointing version of the Dvořák concerto.

Violin concertos Nos. 1 and 2.
(M) *** Decca Dig./Analogue 425 015-2; *425 015-4* [id.]. Kyung Wha Chung, Chicago SO or LPO, Solti.

Decca's mid-price issue in the Ovation series brings a generous and apt coupling of two earlier recordings, No. 1 in digital sound done in Chicago in 1983, No. 2 done in London in 1976 with first-rate analogue sound, well transferred. Though the soloist is rather forwardly balanced, the hushed intensity of the writing, as well as bitingly Hungarian flavours, is caught superbly, thanks to the conductor as well as to the soloist. Though the expressive warmth behind Bartók's writing is fully brought out, there is no sentimental lingering. This leads the field in both works.

Violin concerto No. 2.
* DG Dig. 431 626-2 [id.]. Anne-Sophie Mutter, Boston SO, Seiji Ozawa – MORET: *En rêve.* **

(i) *Violin concerto No. 2 in B min.;* (Solo) *Violin sonata.*
**(*) Virgin VC7 91483-2 [id.]. Christian Tetzlaff, LPO, Michael Gielen.

Christian Tetzlaff gives a serious and likeable account of the *Violin concerto* with the LPO under Michael Gielen on Virgin Classics. He does not press it into service as a mere vehicle for his own display but, on the contrary, is completely at *its* service. He gets very good support from Gielen and copes well with the formidable difficulties of the solo *Sonata*. Good recording and, if not a first choice, this is a musically satisfying disc.

Anne-Sophie Mutter plays with stunning virtuosity and brilliance. It is all very high-powered, slick and smooth, and technically breathtaking and, if that is what you are primarily looking for, you are unlikely to find anything better in the current catalogue. It is the kind of playing which is determined to astonish the listener, even at the expense of the music. She exaggerates dynamic or tempo markings, and in the *scherzando* section of the second movement (at about 7 minutes in) she is very much faster than the metronome marking (Bartók's scrupulousness in these matters is well-known) and the result is to sensationalize and ultimately cheapen the passage. It may seem odd to give this accomplished playing only one star but, whereas the early Menuhin recordings and later ones by Szeryng, Chung or Perlman brought one close to this music, Mutter does not.

Divertimento for strings; Music for strings, percussion and celesta.
*** Hung. Dig. HCD 12531 [id.]. Liszt CO, Rolla.

Divertimento for strings; Romanian folkdances.
**(*) DG 415 668-2 [id.]. Orpheus CO – JANÁČEK: *Mládi.* **(*)

On Hungaroton both performances are expert and distil a powerful atmosphere in the slow movements of each piece. They command beautifully rapt *pianissimo* tone and keen intensity. The sound is less reverberant than some rivals, but there is no lack of ambience.

The American Orpheus Chamber Orchestra also give an eminently well-prepared account of the *Divertimento*. Good though their performance is, it is not quite as idiomatic in its sense of mystery or intensity of feeling as the Hungaroton, even if it possesses both in good measure. The recording, though very clean and well balanced, is not so atmospheric. The popular *Romanian folkdances* are also attractively done.

Hungarian sketches; Romanian folkdances.
(M) *** Mercury 432 005-2 [id.]. Minneapolis SO, Dorati – KODÁLY: *Dances; Háry János.* ***

Dorati, himself a Hungarian, provided the pioneer stereo recording of these works, yet the 1956 sound is vivid and full and wears its years very lightly indeed. The Minneapolis orchestra, on top form, provides plenty of ethnic feeling and colour. This is Bartók at his most winningly approachable, and the style of the music-making has an agreeable air of authenticity.

The Miraculous Mandarin (complete ballet), *Op. 19.*
(*) Delos Dig. DE 3083 [id.]. Seattle SO, Gerard Schwarz – KODÁLY: *Háry Janos; Galánta dances.* *

(i) *The Miraculous Mandarin* (complete ballet), *Op. 19;* (ii) *2 Portraits, Op. 5.*
*** DG Dig. 410 598-2 [id.]. (i) Amb. S.; LSO, Abbado; (ii) with Minz – PROKOFIEV: *Scythian suite.* ***

Abbado directs a fiercely powerful performance of Bartók's barbarically furious ballet – including the wordless chorus in the finale – but one which, thanks to the refinement of the recording, makes the aggressiveness of the writing more acceptable while losing nothing in power. The Prokofiev coupling is highly appropriate and equally successful; before that, however, the ear is sweetened by Minz's warmth in the *Portraits.*

Gerard Schwarz directs the Seattle orchestra in a powerfully atmospheric account of Bartók's malignant ballet score, not as idiomatically aggressive as some, but with plenty of grip and excitement at the climax. The expansive acoustics of Seattle Opera House bring an unexpected richness of colour to the scoring. The entry of the wordless chorus is particularly telling, beautifully balanced within a recording that is at once highly spectacular while giving a spacious concert-hall effect. Aptly and generously coupled with Kodály, this can be strongly recommended as a genuine alternative to Abbado's more pungent approach.

4 Orchestral pieces, Op. 12; (i) *The Miraculous Mandarin* (complete ballet), *Op. 19;* (ii) *3 Village scenes.*
(M) *** Sony SMK 45837 [id.]. (i) Schola Cantorum; (ii) Camerata Singers; NYPO, Pierre Boulez.

The *Four Orchestral pieces* was the nearest Bartók came to writing a symphony. The *Three Village scenes – Wedding, Lullaby* (with two soloists) and *Men's dance* – have a Stravinskian flavour as well as pungent folk influences: they are colourful and exciting. Boulez proves a strong and sympathetic advocate in all this music, and his approach is surprisingly warm. This is even more striking in *The Miraculous Mandarin.* The New York orchestra responds with deeply expressive playing and, with spacious recording, many will prefer it on that account.

The Wooden prince (ballet), *Op. 13* (complete); *Hungarian pictures.*
*** Chan. Dig. CHAN 8895; *ABTD 1506* [id.]. Philh. O, Järvi.

By contrast with Bartók's other two dramatic works, also one-Acters – the ballet *The Miraculous Mandarin* and the opera *Bluebeard's Castle* – this other ballet, first performed in 1917, presents the composer at his most euphonious and least barbaric. Unlike the other two, it was an instant success in Budapest, but latterly has often seemed lacking in flavour, even to Bartók devotees. Järvi's red-blooded performance relates the work to romantic sources, even to Wagner's *Rheingold* at the very start. The drama of the fairy story is told in glowing colours and, unlike most rivals, Järvi ignores the many little cuts that the composer sanctioned, reluctantly or not, over the years. The opulent playing of the Philharmonia is greatly enhanced by the full, vivid Chandos recording. The suite, *Hungarian pictures*, drawn from various folk-based piano pieces, provides a colourful if trivial makeweight.

CHAMBER AND INSTRUMENTAL MUSIC

Contrasts for clarinet, violin and piano.
*** Delos Dig. D/CD 3043 [id.]. Shifrin, Bae, Lash – MESSIAEN: *Quatuor.* ***

David Shifrin and his colleagues from Chamber Music Northwest admirably capture the diverse moods of Bartók's triptych, including the mordant wit and vitality of the outer sections and the dark colouring of the centrepiece. They are very well recorded in an agreeable acoustic.

(i) *Contrasts. Mikrokosmos*: excerpts.
(M) (***) Sony mono MPK 47676 [id.]. Composer; (i) with Joseph Szigeti, Benny Goodman.

Contrasts was commissioned by Benny Goodman, at the suggestion of Szigeti; when it arrived in 1938, however, it was in two movements. In 1940 Bartók added a further movement, and it was in this form that the three artists made their recording. That same year Bartók recorded 31 pieces from *Mikrokosmos* and these performances are indicative of the wide range and delicacy of keyboard colour that Bartók commanded. The sound is surprisingly good, given that it is over half a century old! An indispensable issue.

Sonata for 2 pianos and percussion.
*** Sony Dig. MK 42625 [id.]. Perahia, Solti, Corkhill, Glennie – BRAHMS: *Variations on a theme by Haydn.* ***

An unexpected and highly creative partnership produces a vivid and strongly characterized performance. The combination of star conductor, taking time off from the rostrum, and his distinguished associate, each striking sparks off the other, with Solti bringing Hungarian flair to the proceedings, makes for great eloquence in this powerful work. The recording is vivid to match, giving the players great presence.

(i) *Sonata for 2 pianos and percussion;* (ii) (Solo) *Violin sonata.*
*** Accord Dig. 149047. (i) Janka and Jurg Wyttenbach, Schmid, Huber; (ii) Schneeberger.

The Accord recordings were made in Basle in the wake of the Bartók centenary celebrations. Hans-Heinz Schneeberger is obviously an accomplished artist and his account can withstand comparison with most if not all rivals. The *Sonata for 2 pianos and percussion* receives an exhilarating performance, and the CD recording is astonishingly good and also very natural. There is impressive range and the percussion players sound as if they are there in one's living-room.

String quartets Nos. 1–6.
*** DG Dig. 423 657-2 (2) [id.]. Emerson Qt.
**(*) EMI Dig. CDS7 47720-8 (3) [Ang. CDCC 47720]. Alban Berg Qt.
(**(*)) ASV Dig. CDDCS 301 (3) [id.]. Lindsay Qt.

The Emerson Quartet's set comes on only two CDs (the odd-numbered quartets on one and the even-numbered on the other) so that, in economy alone, it scores over past rivals. They project very powerfully and, in terms of virtuosity, finesse and accuracy, outstrip most of their rivals. At times their projection and expressive vehemence are a bit too much of a good thing. The *pesante* idea that opens the main section of the first movement of the *Sixth Quartet* is one such moment; the Tokyo Quartet on a now-deleted DG recording kept some sonority in reserve and had a more natural expressive eloquence. All the same, these are concentrated and brilliant performances that are very well recorded.

The Alban Berg Quartet is one of the great ensembles of the day; in terms of sheer virtuosity and attack, as well as great beauty of sound, they are unsurpassed. These are very impressive performances indeed, technically almost in a class of their own. They are very well recorded too, but the presentation, on three full-priced CDs, now seems uneconomic. At times the Alban Berg appear to treat this music as a vehicle for their own supreme virtuosity.

The Lindsay performances, searching, powerful and expressive, are now reissued together. The digital recording, though first class, occupies three discs which, like the Alban Berg set, places it at a distinct disadvantage to the DG Emerson version.

String quartets Nos. 1, Op. 7; 2, Op. 17.
**(*) Chan. Dig. CHAN 8588; *ABTD 1280* [id.]. Chilingirian Qt.

String quartets Nos. 3, 4 & 5.
*** Chan. Dig. CHAN 8634; *ABTD 1323* [id.]. Chilingirian Qt.

String quartet No. 6; (i) *Piano quintet.*
*** Chan. Dig. CHAN 8660; *ABTD 1346* [id.]. (i) Steven De Groote; Chilingirian Qt.

The Chilingirian performances have a warm, gutsy quality, based on boundless rhythmic energy and orchestrally rich textures, rather than on knife-edged precision of ensemble. There is the consistent feeling of live communication and, in the slow movements of Nos. 4 and 5 especially, the concentration and intensity of the playing are magnetic. These red-blooded performances receive warm and immediate recording to match. Chandos have then coupled No. 6 with the *Piano quintet* but, for those wanting the six *Quartets*, the Emersons have an added economy of layout and remain first choice.

Violin sonatas Nos. 1 and 2.
**(*) Hung. HCD 11655-2. Kremer, Smirnov.

Both *Sonatas* come from the early 1920s and are among Bartók's most original compositions. Kremer and Smirnov play with total commitment and their performances can only be described as masterly. The recording (from the early 1970s) is rather closely balanced and the acoustic somewhat drier than is ideal, otherwise this would receive a full three-star recommendation, for the performances merit it.

Violin sonata No. 1.
*** DG Dig. 427 351-2 [id.]. Gidon Kremer, Martha Argerich – JANÁČEK: *Sonata* **(*); MESSIAEN: *Theme and variations.* ***

The *First Violin sonata* (1921) is one of Bartók's most uncompromising pieces and a work of enormous originality; there are moments when one is reminded of the world of the Szymanowski *Mythes.* It is played with great expressive intensity, enormous range of colour and effortless virtuosity by Gidon Kremer and Martha Argerich; indeed it would be difficult to improve on their performance or the excellent DG recording.

(Solo) *Violin sonata.*
*** Ph. Dig. 420 948-2 [id.]. Viktoria Mullova – BACH: *Partita No. 1 in B min.* *** (with PAGANINI: *Introduction and variations on Nel cor più non misento* ***).
*** EMI Dig. CDC7 47621-2; *EL 747621-4* [id.]. Nigel Kennedy – ELLINGTON: *Mainly black.* ***

Viktoria Mullova's account of the Bartók *Sonata* is undoubtedly the best now before the public. She brings keener musical insights and more finesse to this remarkable score than Kennedy on EMI. She is much closer to Bartók's own timing, too, and has the benefit of excellent recording.

Nigel Kennedy also gives a deeply felt reading. With vivid recording, full of presence, Kennedy draws beautiful sounds from his instrument and the immediacy of his response communicates strongly.

PIANO MUSIC

Allegro barbaro; Andante; 3 Burlesques; 10 Easy pieces; 3 Rondos on folk tunes; Rumanian folk dances; 2 Rumanian dances.
*(**) ASV Dig. CDDCA 687; *ZCDA 687* [id.]. Peter Frankl.

Peter Frankl plays with splendid fire and spirit, and with no lack of sensitivity. He is totally inside this music and is wholly persuasive, but he is let down by a rather unflattering and not fully focused recording balance. The piano itself sounds as if it is in less than first-class condition and the acoustic is reverberant. This disc has much in its favour artistically, but its sonic deficiences make a recommendation difficult.

Dance suite; Hungarian peasant songs; 3 Rondos on folk tunes; Rumanian dances.
*** Denon Dig. C37 7092 [id.]. András Schiff (piano).

András Schiff, whose reputation rests on his keenly imaginative readings in the classical repertory, here demonstrates his red-blooded Hungarian fervour. His range of mood, tone and expression brings vivid colouring and these *Rumanian dances* have rarely been played with such infectious rhythms. The piano sound is first rate, with plenty of bite, and losing inner clarity only with the heaviest textures of the *Dance suite.*

For Children (Books 1–4) complete; *Mikrokosmos (Books 1–6)* complete.
(M) *** Teldec/Warner 9031 76139-2 (3). Dezsö Ránki.

Bartók's pieces *For Children* is a collection of Hungarian (Book 1) and Slovak (Book 2) folksongs which possess a beguiling simplicity and (when taken in small doses) unfailing musical interest. The Hungarian pianist, Dezsö Ránki (still young when these recordings were made, in 1976/7), has made a name for himself as a brilliant virtuoso, but here he shows his musicianship and plays all 85 pieces with the utmost persuasion and with the art that conceals art, for the simplicity of some of these pieces is deceptive; darker currents lurk beneath their surface. He gives us the composer's original edition of 1908–9. Ránki also plays the *Mikrokosmos* with an effortless eloquence and a welcome straightforwardness. He resists the temptation to make expressive points where none are required and plays with total dedication and command. He is very clearly if forwardly recorded, yet the well-defined sound is not too dry for comfort, and he is given a realistic presence.

Mikrokosmos (complete).
(B) **(*) HM HMA 90968/9 [id.]. Claude Helffer (with Haakon Austbö).

Claude Helffer gives an intelligent account of all six Books of Bartók's *Mikrokosmos*, though at times he tends to invest detail with rather more expressive emphasis than this most simple of music can bear. The first Books are more for the delectation of the younger player – uncomplicated teaching pieces that are scarcely intended to be listened to – but the later pieces are richly inventive and make for rewarding listening. Here greater simplicity would have yielded even stronger artistic results, although Helffer's way is preferable to a bald presentation of the notes, and there is undoubtedly some fine playing during the course of the two discs. In the pieces requiring a second pianist Helffer is well partnered by Haakon Austbö. The piano recording is realistic and naturally remastered. Even though the cueing is ungenerous (there are only twelve bands to cover 153 pieces), this is good value in the bargain range.

OPERA

Bluebeard's Castle (sung in Hungarian).
*** Sony Dig. MK 44523 [id.]. Eva Marton, Samuel Ramey, Hungarian State O, Adám Fischer.
(M) *** Decca 433 082-2 [id.]. Kovats, Sass, Sztankay (speaker), LPO, Solti.
**(*) Decca 414 167-2 [id.]. Ludwig, Berry, LSO, Kertész.

The glory of the CBS version is the magnificent singing of Samuel Ramey in the title-role. With his dark bass, firm and true, beautiful up to a high F, he carries the necessary threat but equally brings nobility to the part. With him, Bluebeard is virile and even heroic, the master of his fate; and that goes with a tellingly rugged account of the score from Hungarian forces under a Hungarian conductor, all of whom understand this music from the inside. Eva Marton, also Hungarian-born, may lack the vulnerability as well as the darker tone-colours of the ideal Judith but, with more than a touch of abrasiveness in the voice, she still gives a powerful reading. The recording brings full and brilliant sound, well balanced and clear. The single CD comes with libretto in a separate box.

Solti directs a richly atmospheric reading of Bartók's ritualistic opera, not as searingly dramatic as one might have expected but with analogue recording of spectacular range. The performance is introduced by the Hungarian verses which are printed in the score. The Hungarian soloists are tangily authentic, though their voices are not always perfectly steady, but Sylvia Sass with her exquisite pianissimo singing is more appealing than Eva Marton on CBS. The Kingsway Hall recording, produced by Christopher Raeburn and engineered by Kenneth Wilkinson – less analytical than is normal from Decca – produces a rich carpet of sound to which the CD transfer adds an extra degree of brilliance. The resulting effect is more romantic than usual, even revealing an affinity with Richard Strauss. With full libretto included, this makes a fine mid-priced alternative to the CBS/Sony version, dominated by Samuel Ramey.

Kertész's outstanding Decca version is admirably vivid and present, with voices and orchestra beautifully balanced. The serious snag – astonishing in a reissue at full price – is that, unlike the rival versions, it provides no libretto, very important in a work that consists entirely of spoken exchanges and with the sparest of plots.

Bax, Arnold (1883–1953)

(i) *Cello concerto; Cortège; Mediterranean; Northern Ballad No. 3; Overture to a picaresque comedy.*

*** Chan. Dig. CHAN 8494; *ABTD 1204* [id.]. (i) Wallfisch; LPO, Bryden Thomson.

The *Cello concerto* (1934) was Bax's first major work after the *Fifth Symphony*. It is rhapsodic in feeling and Raphael Wallfisch plays it with marvellous sensitivity and finesse, given splendid support by the LPO under Bryden Thomson. The other pieces are of mixed quality: the *Third Northern Ballad* is a dark, brooding score, while the *Overture to a picaresque comedy* is first-rate Bax, high-spirited and inventive. Here Bryden Thomson sets rather too measured a pace for it to sparkle as it should. The recording maintains the high standards of the Bax Chandos series.

(i) *Violin concerto. Golden Eagle* (incidental music): *suite; A Legend; Romantic overture.*
*** Chan. Dig. CHAN 9003 [id.]. (i) Lydia Mordkovitch; LPO, Bryden Thomson.

Bax composed his *Violin concerto* for Heifetz in 1937–8, immediately before embarking on his last full-scale orchestral work, the *Seventh Symphony*. Heifetz did not take to the concerto and Bax himself withheld it until a commission came along in 1943. It is full of good, easily-remembered tunes, yet, apart from a broadcast by the late-lamented Ralph Holmes, it languished unplayed and unrecorded until this present issue. There is a plangent bitter-sweet quality about many of its ideas and an easygoing Mediterranean-like warmth that is very appealing. One passage derives from a piano sonata composed in 1905. Lydia Mordkovitch plays it with commitment and conviction. The *Romantic overture* comes from 1926, and was written for Delius after Bax and Warlock had spent some time at Grez-sur-Loing. Unusually for Bax, it is for chamber orchestra and has a prominent role for the piano. There is an amusing allusion to the Franck symphony. *A Legend* was his last tone poem (1944) and the incidental music for the *Golden Eagle*, a play by his brother Clifford about Mary Queen of Scots composed two years later, is less interesting. All this music is new to the catalogue and the concerto deserves to be popular.

The Garden of Fand (symphonic poem).
(M) (***) EMI mono CDM7 63405-2 [id.]. RPO, Sir Thomas Beecham – BANTOCK: *Fifine at the fair;* BERNERS: *Triumph of Neptune.* (***)

The Garden of Fand found a ready advocate in Sir Thomas Beecham, who related its atmospheric feeling to the music of Delius. It is played superbly here, although the 1947 recording is a bit confined and two-dimensional; it is very well transferred to CD, however.

The Garden of Fand; The happy forest; November woods; Summer music.
*** Chan. Dig. CHAN 8307; *ABTD 1036* [id.]. Ulster O, Bryden Thomson.

The Celtic twilight in Bax's music is ripely and sympathetically caught in the first three items, while *Summer music*, dedicated to Sir Thomas Beecham and here given its first ever recording, brings an intriguing kinship with the music of Delius. The Chandos recording is superb.

Malta G.C. (complete); *Oliver Twist: suite* (film-scores).
(M) *** ASV Dig. CDWHL 2058; *ZCWHL 2058*. RPO, Kenneth Alwyn – ARNOLD: *The Sound Barrier.* ***

Both these film-scores are in the form of a series of miniatures; on the whole, *Oliver Twist* stands up more effectively without the visual imagery. In *Malta G.C.* much of the score is concerned with wartime action: it is the gentler music, the *Intermezzo* and *Reconstruction* and again the final apotheosis, that brings the most memorable writing. Kenneth Alwyn conducts the RPO with fine flair and commitment.

In the faery hills; Into the twilight; Rosc-Catha; The tale the pine-trees knew.
*** Chan. Dig. CHAN 8367; *ABTD 1133* [id.]. Ulster O, Bryden Thomson.

The tale the pine-trees knew is one of the better-known as well as one of the most evocative of Bax's tone-poems, here done with total sympathy. The other three tone-poems form an Irish trilogy. The first two are filled with typically Baxian Celtic twilight, but the last (*Rosc-Catha* meaning 'battle hymn') presents the composer in vigorous, extrovert mood, making an excellent contrast. The performances and recording are well up to the high standard of this series.

On the sea-shore.
*** Chan. Dig. CHAN 8473; *ABTD 1184* [id.]. Ulster O, Handley – BRIDGE: *The Sea;* BRITTEN: *Sea interludes.* ***

Bax's Prelude, *On the sea-shore*, sensitively orchestrated by Graham Parlett from the composer's short-score, makes a colourful and atmospheric companion to the masterly Bridge and Britten pieces on the disc, played and recorded with similar warmth and brilliance.

Phantasy for viola and orchestra.
**(*) Conifer Dig. CDCF 171; *MCFC 171* [id.]. Golani, RPO, Handley – ELGAR: *Concerto* etc. **

Bax's *Phantasy* is in effect a three-movement viola concerto, drawing heavily on his Irish vein in its use of folk-material. The first movement tends to meander in Bax's semi-improvisatory style, an amiable example of Celtic twilight in music. For all Vernon Handley's devoted advocacy, the piece sounds flabby next to the Elgar with which it is coupled. Excellent recorded sound.

Spring fire; Northern Ballad No. 2; Symphonic scherzo.
*** Chan. Dig. CHAN 8464; *ABTD 1180* [id.]. RPO, Vernon Handley.

Spring fire is an early work, but Bax's command of the orchestra is already richly in evidence. The second *Northern Ballad* is dark and bleak, strongly tied to the landscape of the rugged northern coasts. The *Symphonic scherzo* is of less moment than its companions. Highly idiomatic playing from Vernon Handley and the RPO, and a thoroughly lifelike and characteristically well-detailed recording from Chandos.

Symphonic variations for piano and orchestra; Morning Song (Maytime in Sussex).
*** Chan. Dig. CHAN 8516; *ABTD 1226* [id.]. Margaret Fingerhut, LPO, Bryden Thomson.

The *Symphonic variations* is an ambitious score, almost 50 minutes in duration. Margaret Fingerhut reveals it as a work of considerable substance with some sinewy, powerful writing in the more combative variations, thoughtful and purposeful elsewhere. The balance between piano and orchestra could hardly be better judged and more natural; and the orchestral playing under Bryden Thomson is first class. The amiable but discursive *Morning song* makes an agreeable bonus. This CD is in the demonstration class.

Symphonies 1–7.
(M) *** Chan. Dig. CHAN 8906/10 [id.]. LPO or Ulster O, Bryden Thomson.

Chandos have repackaged the cycle of seven symphonies on five CDs. Nos. 3 and 7 have discs to themselves, while Nos. 1 and 6 share a disc. Only the *Fourth* is split between two discs: the first two movements are placed after the *Fifth Symphony* and the finale precedes the *Second Symphony*. Inevitably, the fill-ups that accompanied the symphonies first time around are sacrificed. But, of course, it makes better sense for those primarily interested in these richly imaginative symphonies to pay for five rather than seven CDs, and the recordings continue to make a strong impression.

For those who prefer to have the symphonies separately and with their original couplings, and for tape collectors, we list below full details.

Symphony No. 1 in E flat; Christmas Eve.
*** Chan. Dig. CHAN 8480; *ABTD 1192* [id.]. LPO, Bryden Thomson.

Symphony No. 2; Nympholept.
*** Chan. Dig. CHAN 8493; *ABTD 1203* [id.]. LPO, Bryden Thomson.

Symphony No. 3; Paean; The Dance of Wild Irravel.
*** Chan. Dig. CHAN 8454; *ABTD 1165* [id.]. LPO, Bryden Thomson.

Symphony No. 4; Tintagel.
*** Chan. Dig. CHAN 8312; *ABTD 1091* [id.]. Ulster O, Bryden Thomson.

Symphony No. 5; Russian suite.
*** Chan. Dig. CHAN 8669; *ABTD 1356* [id.]. LPO, Bryden Thomson.

Symphony No. 6; Festival overture.
*** Chan. Dig. CHAN 8586; *ABTD 1278* [id.]. LPO, Bryden Thomson.

Symphony No. 7 in A flat; (i) *4 Songs: Eternity; Glamour; Lyke-wake; Slumber song.*
*** Chan. Dig. CHAN 8628; *ABTD 1317* [id.]. (i) Martyn Hill; LPO, Bryden Thomson.

Symphony No. 3.
(M) (***) EMI mono CDH7 63910-2. Hallé O, Barbirolli – IRELAND: *Forgotten rite* etc. (***)

Barbirolli's account of the *Third* was the first Bax symphony ever to be recorded and, though the 1944 sound is obviously limited in frequency range, remarkably few allowances need be made for this transfer. Recorded under wartime conditions the orchestral playing is not as refined as Bryden Thomson's version for Chandos but there is an authentic feel to Barbirolli's performance which successfully captures the epic quality of this symphony and does justice to the composer's imaginative vision. For many collectors it was the gateway to Bax's symphonic landscape and its reappearance in this excellent transfer is a cause for celebration.

The Truth about the Russian dancers (incidental music); *From dusk till dawn* (ballet).
*** Chan. Dig. CHAN 8863; *ABTD 1478* [id.]. LPO, Bryden Thomson.

Bax was a frequent visitor to Diaghilev's 1911 season at Covent Garden and, inspired by its brilliance, worked throughout the year on a ballet called *Tamara*, only to find in the following season that Balakirev's tone-poem of the same name was being danced. Its main theme is quoted in the second movement of *The Truth about the Russian dancers*. Bax abandoned the ballet, but some of its music found its way into the later ballet, *From dusk till dawn* (1917), and into the music to J. M. Barrie's whimsical play, *The Truth about the Russian dancers* (1920), in which Karsavina danced. The latter is vintage Bax, full of characteristic writing decked out in attractive orchestral colours. *From dusk till dawn* has many evocative ideas with some impressionistic orchestral touches, but each of its twenty movements is very short, the whole work lasting as many minutes. Not top-drawer Bax but often delightful, and very well played by the London Philharmonic under Bryden Thomson, and splendidly recorded.

Winter Legends; Saga fragment.
*** Chan. Dig. CHAN 8484; *ABTD 1195* [id.]. Margaret Fingerhut, LPO, Bryden Thomson.

The *Winter Legends*, for piano and orchestra, comes from much the same time as the *Third Symphony*, to which at times its world seems spiritually related. The keyboard writing is ambitious; this is in some ways a sinfonia concertante for piano and orchestra rather than a concerto proper. The soloist proves an impressive and totally convincing advocate for the score and it would be difficult to imagine the balance between soloist and orchestra being more realistically judged. The companion piece is a transcription of his one-movement *Piano quartet* of 1922. A quite outstanding disc.

CHAMBER AND INSTRUMENTAL MUSIC

Clarinet sonata.
(*) Chan. CHAN 8683; *ABTD 1078* [id.]. Janet Hilton, Keith Swallow – BLISS: *Clarinet quintet;* VAUGHAN WILLIAMS: *6 Studies.* *

Bax's *Clarinet sonata* opens most beguilingly, and Janet Hilton's phrasing is quite melting. Perhaps the second-movement *Vivace* is less individual, but the playing is very persuasive and on CD the sound is realistically focused within its resonant acoustic. Moreover the Bliss coupling is indispensable.

(i) *Harp quintet;* (ii) *Piano quartet; String quartet No. 1.*
*** Chan. Dig. CHAN 8391; *ABTD 1113* [id.]. (i) Skaila Kanga, (ii) John McCabe; English Qt.

The *First String quartet* has a strong folk element in the finale and the first movement comes close to the sound-world of the Dvořák quartets. Perhaps the finest of the three movements is its elegiac centrepiece. But it is all music with a strong and immediate appeal. The *Harp quintet* is more fully characteristic and has some evocative writing to commend it. The *Piano quartet*, with its winning lyricism, was reworked in the early 1930s for piano and small orchestra as was the *Saga fragment* (see above). These may not be Bax's most important scores, but they are rewarding; and the performances are thoroughly idiomatic and eminently well recorded.

Oboe quintet.
*** Chan. Dig. CHAN 8392; *ABTD 1114* [id.]. Sarah Francis, English Qt – HOLST: *Air & variations*, etc.; MOERAN: *Fantasy quartet;* JACOB: *Quartet.* ***

Bax's *Oboe quintet*, written for Leon Goossens, is a confident, inventive piece with a hauntingly inspired *Lento* and a gay Irish jig for its finale, though even this movement has a reflective inner core. Sarah Francis proves a most responsive soloist – though she is balanced too close; in all other respects the recording is up to Chandos's usual high standards, and the playing of the English Quartet is admirable.

(i) *Piano quintet in G min.; String quartet No. 2.*
**(*) Chan. Dig. CHAN 8795 [id.]. Mistry Qt; (i) with David Owen Norris.

The *Piano quintet* is symphonic in scale. Its first movement alone lasts for twenty minutes and is marked 'passionate and rebellious'. At times its expansive gestures and ambitious proportions cry out for the orchestra; the only real disappointment is the rather folksy and discursive finale, though this has imaginative moments too. The playing of the Mistry Quartet is dedicated and David Owen Norris is the excellent and sensitive pianist. The *Second Quartet* is tauter and more powerful, though its chromatic part-writing poses occasional problems for the players, who do not seem quite as comfortable here as they are in the *Quintet*. However, the performance has plenty of feeling and gives little cause for real complaint; the recording is excellent, and mention should be made of the useful and informative notes that Lewis Foreman has contributed throughout the Chandos Bax cycle.

Piano trio in B flat.
**(*) Chan. Dig. CHAN 8495; *ABTD 1205* [id.]. Borodin Trio – BRIDGE: *Trio No. 2.* **(*)

The *Piano trio* was Bax's last chamber work, dating from 1946 when his creative fires burned less fiercely. The playing of the Borodin Trio is very distinguished indeed and they seem completely attuned to the idiom. Even if it is not Bax at his best, this is most welcome, particularly in view of the excellence of both performance and recording.

Rhapsodic Ballad (for solo cello).
*** Chan. Dig. CHAN 8499; *ABTD 1209* [id.]. Raphael Wallfisch – BRIDGE: *Cello sonata;* DELIUS: *Cello sonata;* WALTON: *Passacaglia.* ***

The *Rhapsodic Ballad* for cello alone comes from 1939 and is a freely expressive piece, played with authority and dedication by Raphael Wallfisch. The recording has plenty of warmth and range.

Violin sonatas Nos. 1 in E; 2 in D.
*** Chan. Dig. CHAN 8845; *ABTD 1462* [id.]. Erich Gruenberg, John McCabe.

Both *Sonatas* are early and pre-date the symphonies. The *Second* is the finer of the two and is thematically linked with *November woods*. Rhapsodic and impassioned, this is music full of temperament. Erich Gruenberg is a selfless and musicianly advocate, though some may find his tone not always uniformly beautiful; John McCabe makes an expert partner.

PIANO MUSIC

Apple-blossom time; Burlesque; The maiden with the daffodil; Nereid; O dame get up and bake your pies (Variations on a north country Christmas carol); On a May evening; The princess's rose-garden (Nocturne); Romance; 2 Russian tone pictures: Nocturne (May night in the Ukraine; Gopak); Sleepy-head.
**(*) Chan. Dig. CHAN 8732; *ABTD 1372* [id.]. Eric Parkin.

The smaller pieces have considerable charm, and often substance too, as with the *Russian Nocturne* and the comparable *Princess's rose-garden*. They are not among Bax's most important works but in Eric Parkin's hands they certainly sound pleasingly spontaneous.

Piano sonatas Nos. 1 & 2; Country Tune; Lullaby (Berceuse); Winter waters.
**(*) Chan. Dig. CHAN 8496; *ABTD 1206* [id.]. Eric Parkin (piano).

Piano sonatas Nos. 3 in G sharp min.; 4 in G; A Hill tune; In a vodka shop; Water music.
**(*) Chan. Dig. CHAN 8497; *ABTD 1207* [id.]. Eric Parkin.

These *Sonatas* are grievously neglected in the concert hall and even on the gramophone; they are far from negligible, even if they do not show the fires of Bax's inspiration burning at white heat. Eric Parkin proves a sympathetic guide in this repertoire. The recording is on the resonant side and on the second disc the piano is not absolutely perfectly tuned in some of the shorter pieces, but the playing is outstandingly responsive.

Beach, Amy (1867–1944)

Symphony in E min. (Gaelic).
*** Chan. Dig. CHAN 8958; *ABTD 1550* [id.]. Detroit SO, Järvi – BARBER: *Symphony No. 1* etc. ***

Amy Beach is a rather more remarkable figure than she is given credit for outside (or even in) the United States. She did not study in Europe and, apart from lessons with Junius Hill and Karl Baermann in Boston, she was largely self-taught. Her orchestration she learnt from Berlioz's treatise which she translated. Her *Symphony in E minor*, her only essay in the form, was performed with great success in Boston in 1896. It begins with a slightly Lisztian flourish, and Dvořák was obviously a major influence, but it was the 'simple, rugged and unpretentious beauty' of a collection of old Irish melodies she came across that provided its main inspiration. There is nothing 'new' or profoundly original in this music, but it operates at a high level of accomplishment and has a winning charm, particularly its delightful and inventive second movement. Once heard, this haunting movement is difficult to exorcize from one's memory. A very persuasive performance by the Detroit orchestra under Neeme Järvi, and good recorded sound.

Becker, John (1886–1961)

Symphonia brevis.
** Albany TROY 027-2 [id.]. Louisville O, Mester – HARRIS: *Epilogue to profiles in courage* etc.; SCHUMAN: *Symphony No. 4* etc. **

John Becker is little known outside the United States but he is associated with Ives, Carl Ruggles, Henry Cowell and Wallingford Riegger – though this short symphony, his *Third*, composed in 1933, does not make quite as individual an impression as do they. Written as a 'protest against a world civilization that starves its millions in peacetime and murders those same millions in wartime', it remains anonymous, particularly in comparison with such strong musical personalities as Roy Harris and William Schuman. The recording dates from the early 1970s.

Beethoven, Ludwig van (1770–1827)

Piano concertos Nos. 1–5.
(M) *** Sony M3K 44575 (3) [id.]. Perahia, Concg. O, Haitink.

(i) *Piano concertos Nos. 1–5;* (ii) *Triple concerto for violin, cello and piano, Op. 56.*
(M) *** Sony SB3K 48397 (3) [id.]. (i) Fleisher, Cleveland O, Szell; (ii) Stern, Rose, Isomin, Phd. O, Ormandy.

Piano concertos Nos. 1–5; Rondos, Op. 51/1–2.
(M) (***) DG mono 435 744-2 (3) [id.]. Wilhelm Kempff, BPO, Van Kempen.

Piano concertos Nos. 1–5; (i) *Choral Fantasia, Op. 80.*
*** EMI Dig. CDC7 54063-2 (3) [Ang. CDCC 54063]. Melvyn Tan, L. Classical Players, Norrington.
(M) *** EMI CMS7 63360-2 (3) [Ang. CDMC 63360]. Daniel Barenboim, New Philh. O, Klemperer, (i) with John Alldis Ch.
(B) **(*) Ph. 422 937-2 (3). Alfred Brendel, LPO, Haitink, (i) with LPO Ch.

Piano concertos Nos. 1–5; Andante favori; Polonaise in C, Op. 89.
(**) Arabesque mono Z 6549 (*Nos. 1–2*); Z 6550 (*Nos. 3–4*); Z 6551 (*No. 5, Andante* and *Polonaise*) [id.]. Artur Schnabel, LSO or LPO, Sargent.

(i) *Piano concertos Nos. 1–5; Piano sonata No. 32 in C min., Op. 111.*
(B) *** DG 427 237-2 (3) [id.]. Kempff; (i) BPO, Leitner.

Perahia brings us as close to the heart of this music as any. These are masterly performances, and it is good that their more competitive price will bring them within the reach of an even wider audience. The sound is full and well balanced.

There is a mood of carefree delight running through the earlier of Kempff's two cycles of the Beethoven *Piano concertos*. Even more than his stereo cycle, this one, recorded in mono in 1953, finds Kempff at his most individual, turning phrases and pointing ornamentation with a sparkle and sense of fun to have you smiling in response. The articulation is uniquely crisp and clear – the main theme of the finale in No. 1 has rarely been so cleanly defined, bringing out the wit. The lightness of touch is so extraordinary that he barely seems to brush the keys in such passages as the opening of the finale in No. 4. The slow movements, flowing easily and lyrically, yet convey a depth of meditation rarely equalled, and Kempff's bright, muscular attack in the opening movement of the *Emperor* gives it formidable power combined with clarity. Kempff is often idiosyncratic, as in his decision in the first four concertos to play his own cadenzas, making them sound like spontaneous improvisations. This is a classic recording guaranteed to give delight, which has been transferred to CD in full, immediate, well-detailed sound, with low tape-hiss unlikely to disturb anyone. (What a pity it is that all mono-to-CD transfers cannot sound as natural and believable as this!). Even if you already have an integral set of Beethoven's piano concertos – and even if it is Kempff's later stereo version – these records will give enormous additional refreshment.

Apart from No. 4, which was recorded first in 1959 (and is the finest performance of the set), Fleisher made his series with Szell during 1961. Throughout their musical partnership was at its peak, and these performances are uncommonly rewarding. Nos. 2 and 4 and the *Emperor* (together with its fine Philadephia coupling of the *Triple concerto*) are available separately, and are discussed in detail below. In the *First concerto* the tempo for the opening movement is unusually fast and Fleisher uses the longest of Beethoven's three cadenzas; the middle movement is unusually slow and nicely expressive in a Bellinian way. Where Fleisher falls slightly short is in the finale, where he fails to give much of a spring to the rhythm. This same vigorous manner informs the first movement of the C minor work, but in the finale the brilliance is much more effective, though again it is on the tense side. But there is fine expressive playing from the soloists in the slow movement, if not always quite matched by the orchestra. The remastering has greatly improved the recording, flattering the piano more than it did on LP, while the orchestra gains from the Severance Hall ambience.

Kempff's stereo accounts offer an additional price advantage since, although the individual issues are all at mid-price, the set is offered at bargain price; the magisterial account of Op. 111 remains coupled with the *Emperor*. The performances all come from the early 1960s and still sound remarkably good for their age, and the wisdom Kempff dispensed is as fresh as ever.

Those wanting a complete set of the Beethoven *Concertos* on period instruments need look no further than this fine EMI three-CD set. The Tan–Norrington partnership has great spontaneity and Melvyn Tan has a flair and poetic feeling that is rather special.

The earlier combination of Barenboim and Klemperer, recording together in 1967/8, is nothing if not stimulating and, for every wilfulness of a measured Klemperer, there is a youthful spark from the spontaneously combusting Barenboim. The recordings were made much more quickly than usual, with long takes allowing a sense of continuity rare on record. The spontaneity easily compensates for any minor shortcomings, but the concentration is formidable and especially compelling in the slow movements. The *Choral Fantasia* too is given an inspired performance. The remastered sound is vivid and clear and quite full, but orchestral tuttis are less refined than in the Kovacevich/Davis Philips recordings.

Given an artist of Brendel's distinction, it would be surprising if his analogue set with Haitink were not artistically rewarding, even if there are moments (for instance in the *Emperor*) when one's mind returns to his earlier Vox Turnabout recordings, which sounded less studied. Generally, however, there is no lack of spontaneity and the recordings are full and well balanced in the best Philips tradition.

Schnabel's performances fall into a special category. The concertos were recorded in 1932–3, save for the *B flat*, which dates from 1935; the solo pieces come from 1938 and some were unpublished. His playing has such enormous character that it transcends the limitations of sound that are inevitable at this period. The orchestral playing is occasionally lacking in the finesse that we take for granted nowadays, but Schnabel's impulsive, searching and poetic playing offers special rewards. Not everything is equally successful: there is some roughness in the first movement of No. 3, but there are also some marvellously spirited touches. The CD transfers are crystal clear and very little of the 78 r.p.m. hiss is apparent. However, for modern ears some adjustment is necessary to the dry orchestral texture, especially for the listener beginning with No. 1, where there is no bloom on the strings; the *Emperor*, however, sounds surprisingly well. Such is the electricity of the playing that one soon forgets the primitive recording and succumbs to Schnabel's spell. The three CDs are available separately.

Piano concerto No. 1 in C min., Op. 15.
(M) **(*) Sony SMK 47519 [id.]. Leonard Bernstein, NYPO – MOZART: *Concerto No. 25.* **

Bernstein directs the orchestra from the keyboard and takes the first movement at a fairly measured tempo (he is much more deliberate than Brendel). He plays with excellent vitality and brilliance, yet there is no playing to the gallery or idle showmanship; the performance is finely shaped and is only let down by a recording, which though now sounding better than it did on LP. is still less than ideal in terms of beauty of sound. The Mozart coupling, too, is not one of his more memorable recordings.

Piano concertos Nos. 1 in C, Op. 15; 2 in B flat, Op. 19.
*** Sony Dig. MK 42177 [id.]. Perahia, Concg. O, Haitink.
*** DG Dig. 415 682-4 [id.]. Argerich, Philh. O, Sinopoli.
*** EMI Dig. CDC7 49509-2 [id.]. Tan (fortepiano), L. Classical Players, Norrington.
(B) *** Ph. 422 968-2; *422 968-4* [id.]. Kovacevich, BBC SO, Sir Colin Davis.
(M) *** DG 419 856-2 [id.]. Kempff, BPO, Leitner.
(M) *** Ph. 420 882-2. Brendel, LPO, Haitink.
** Decca 433 320-2; *433 320-4* [id.]. Ashkenazy, Cleveland O.

Murray Perahia's coupling of Nos. 1 and 2 brings strong and thoughtful performances very characteristic of this pianist, which yet draw a sharp distinction between the two works. No. 2, the earlier, brings a near-Mozartian manner in the first movement, but then rightly a deep and measured account of the slow movement takes Beethoven into another world, hushed and intense, looking directly forward to the slow movement of the *Fourth Concerto*. The *First Concerto* finds Perahia taking a fully Beethovenian view from the start, bringing a weight to it which leads naturally to his choice of cadenza, the longest that Beethoven wrote, here given with dash and fantasy. In the finale, too, the cadenza brings special point, when Perahia records for the first time an extended version discovered only recently among the composer's sketches. Bernard Haitink proves a lively and sympathetic partner, with the Concertgebouw playing superbly. The recording sets the orchestra in a pleasingly warm acoustic, with the piano sound agreeable if a little dull. There is separate cueing for the cadenzas.

The conjunction of Martha Argerich and Giuseppe Sinopoli in Beethoven produces performances which give off electric sparks, daring and volatile. Argerich's contribution in phrase after phrase brings highly individual pointing. She is jaunty in allegros rather than lightweight – one might even ask for more *pianissimo* – and slow movements are songful, not solemn. Very distinctive and stimulating performances, given full, vivid – albeit not ideally balanced – sound in a rather reverberant acoustic.

Melvyn Tan's coupling of the first two concertos (using a Derek Adlam reproduction of an 1814 fortepiano) brings performances of natural, unselfconscious expressiveness which will delight those looking for versions on period instruments. Norrington with his London Classical Players observes the fast metronome markings in the score, in this instance put there by Czerny who, as his pupil, should have known Beethoven's mind. Even when Tan's speeds for slow movements are very fast indeed, his ease of expression makes them very persuasive, avoiding breathlessness while simultaneously conveying more gravity than you might expect. It is good too to have the very fast *Allegros* so clean and clear in warm, well-balanced recording.

These first two works, ideally coupled, bring characteristically crisp and refreshing readings from Stephen Kovacevich with Sir Colin Davis, which convey their conviction with no intrusive idiosyncrasies. That these model performances and recordings come on the cheapest Philips label is something to marvel at.

Kempff's coupling is second to none, and the digitally remastered recording sounds remarkably fresh and vivid. Leitner's contribution, too, is strong and sympathetic, and the orchestral response is memorable throughout. The balance between piano and orchestra is particularly natural.

There is a spontaneity in Brendel's 1979 studio recordings with Haitink which eluded his later partnership with Levine in the concert hall. With very good recording, admirers of Brendel need not hesitate.

Ashkenazy's newest Cleveland readings are broad and positive, but the bright, forward recording gives the piano a clangy sound, so that the subtlety of Ashkenazy in Beethoven is undermined. No. 2 is rhythmically heavy-handed too.

Piano concertos Nos. (i) *1 in C, Op. 15;* (ii) *4 in G, Op. 58.*
(M) (**(*)) BMG/RCA mono GD 60268. (i) Dorfman; (ii) Serkin; NBC SO, Toscanini.

Though the opening orchestral tutti of No. 4 brings some of the worst ensemble ever heard from Toscanini on disc, this live recording with Serkin, made in 1944, brings an inspired partnership. Serkin was one of the few pianists not overawed by the maestro, and the dialogue between the soloist and orchestra in the slow movement is presented with telling dramatic contrasts. The recording is very dry and clear, as it is in the better-known recording of No. 1 with the Russian-born pianist, Ania Dorfman, lively and robust, if hardly subtle.

Piano concertos Nos. 2–3.
(M) ** EMI Dig. CD-EMX 2190; *TC-EMX 2190*. Kovacevich, Australian CO.

With the Australian Chamber Orchestra giving well-pointed support, Kovacevich presents both concertos on a convincing chamber scale, playing with imagination and a sense of fantasy. The *Adagio* of No. 2 becomes a spacious, hushed meditation; but in other places he hardly matches his earlier Philips versions with Sir Colin Davis, rushing the finale of No. 2 and missing the inner intensity of the Largo of No. 3. The recording captures the scale well but lacks a little in inner clarity. A disappointment.

Piano concertos Nos. 2; 4.
(M) *** Sony SBK 48165 [id.]. Fleisher, Cleveland O, Szell.

Leon Fleisher was George Szell's favourite concerto pianist over his last years in Cleveland, and this disc brings masterly examples of their inspired artistry. No. 2 receives a powerful, intense, spontaneous-sounding performance, giving weight to early Beethoven; but the brisk speeds for the outer movements also bring elegance and refined rhythmic pointing. In No. 4 Fleisher and Szell are even more searching, with the soloist's refreshingly imaginative playing matched by glorious sounds from the Cleveland Orchestra, then at its very peak under Szell. The bright, forward recordings, both made in Severance Hall and dating from 1959 (No. 4) and 1961, have been transferred with satisfying fullness and body.

Piano concertos Nos. 2; 5 (Emperor), Op. 73.
(M) **(*) Decca 417 703-2 [id.]. Ashkenazy, Chicago SO, Solti.

In both concertos the partnership of Ashkenazy and Solti works well, with the vivid orchestral articulation matched by the responsive solo playing. The *Emperor* is an excitingly dramatic performance on the largest possible scale, yet one which is consistently imbued with poetry. The remastered recording is brilliantly vivid, and some will want a more ample sound in the *Emperor*.

Piano concertos Nos. 3 in C min., Op. 37; 4 in G, Op. 58.
*** Sony Dig. MK 39814 [id.]. Murray Perahia, Concg. O, Haitink.
*** EMI Dig. CDC7 49815-2 [id.]. Melvyn Tan (fortepiano), L. Classical Players, Norrington.
(B) *** Ph. 426 062-2 [id.]. Kovacevich, BBC SO, Sir Colin Davis.
(M) *** DG 419 467-2 [id.]. Kempff, BPO, Leitner.
**(*) Decca Dig. 433 321-2; *433 321-4* [id.]. Ashkenazy, Cleveland O.
(M) **(*) Ph. 420 861-2. Brendel, LPO, Haitink.

Perahia gives readings that are at once intensely poetic and individual, but also strong. In many ways he gives reminders of Wilhelm Kempff, a supreme Beethovenian of his time, with pointing and shading of passage-work that consistently convey the magic of the moment caught on the wing. As with Kempff, the diamond clarity and the touches of poetry may suggest for some an approach not rugged enough for Beethoven; but with Haitink and the Concertgebouw giving firmly sympathetic support, power is conveyed through sharpness of contrast, helped by fine, spacious and open recorded sound.

With the fortepiano balanced naturally against the orchestra of period instruments, not at all spotlit, Melvyn Tan gives fresh and individual performances of both concertos that will delight those who want to hear Beethoven in period style. Though Norrington – relying on the composer's metronome markings – has tended to surprise listeners by his fast speeds in the Beethoven symphonies, that is not a problem here; these accounts of the concertos, using Czerny's metronome marks, bring speeds that would be apt enough for performances with modern instruments. Tan's individual expressiveness comes over naturally and unforcedly, to make these readings characterful without unwanted wilfulness. Naturally balanced, undistracting sound-quality.

The Philips versions of Nos. 3 and 4 from Kovacevich and Sir Colin Davis would be top recommendations even if they cost far more. In both works the playing of the soloist has a depth and thoughtful intensity that have rarely been matched. The refined Philips recording has transferred admirably to CD: the balance is altogether excellent.

Kempff's delicacy of fingerwork and his shading of tone-colour are as effervescent as ever, and the fine control of the conductor ensures the unity of the reading. In both concertos the recording of the orchestra is bright and resonant, the piano tone warm as well as clear.

Among his new recordings made in Cleveland, Ashkenazy is at his very finest in No. 3, always a favourite concerto with him. His account of No. 4 is sensitive but lacks meditative depth, and the bright, forward recording makes the piano clangy.

On Philips, Brendel in No. 3 provides an easy, relaxed account of the first movement. If the other two movements are less tense, with the finale thrown off in a mercurial manner, this adds up to a very persuasive performance. No. 4 brings a contrastingly strong, even tough reading, which suggests the immediacy of live music-making, rather than the extra care of the studio. The remastered sound is impressively firm and realistic.

Piano concertos Nos. 3 in C min.; 5 in E flat (Emperor).
(M) *(*) Sony SMK 47520 [id.]. Rudolf Serkin, NYPO, Bernstein.

Serkin and Bernstein between them give a super-brilliant performance of the *C minor concerto*'s outer movements which almost brutalizes the music. The pace for the first movement is unbelievably hard-driven and the repose of the *Largo* is little compensation. In the *Emperor* the results are much more commanding and the partnership works productively. But it is not just the coarse recording quality which prevents this from being among the more recommendable versions; both soloist and orchestra fall short on occasion. Those wanting Serkin in the *Emperor* should turn to his later, Telarc recording.

Piano concerto No. 4 in G, Op. 58.
(M) *** Sony MYK 44832 [MYK 37762]. Leon Fleisher, Cleveland O, Szell – MOZART: *Piano concerto No. 25.* ***

Fleisher's is a magical performance, memorable in every bar, to rival even Kempff's version, although the 1959 CBS recording is rather less agreeable than the DG balance. It has, however, been skilfully remastered for CD and can be made to sound well.

Piano concerto No. 5 in E flat (Emperor), Op. 73.
*** Ph. Dig. 416 215-2; *416 215-4* [id.]. Arrau, Dresden State O, Sir Colin Davis.
*** Sony Dig. MK 42330 [id.]. Perahia, Concg. O, Haitink.
**(*) Telarc Dig. CD 80065 [id.]. Serkin, Boston SO, Ozawa.
(M) (***) BMG/RCA mono GD 87992 [7992-2-RG]. Horowitz, RCA Victor SO, Reiner – TCHAIKOVSKY: *Piano concerto No. 1.* (***) ❀

Piano concerto No. 5 in E flat (Emperor); Grosse Fuge in B flat, Op. 133.
❀ (M) *** EMI Dig. CD-EMX 2184; *TC-EMX 2184.* Stephen Kovacevich, Australian CO.

(i) *Piano concerto No. 5 in E flat (Emperor); Piano sonata No. 30 in E, Op. 109.*
(B) *** Ph. 422 482-2; *422 482-4.* Kovacevich; (i) LSO, C. Davis.

Piano concerto No. 5 in E flat (Emperor); Piano sonata No. 32 in C min., Op. 111.
(M) *** DG 419 468-2; *419 468-4* [id.]. Kempff, BPO, Leitner.

Piano concerto No. 5 (Emperor); (i) *Choral Fantasia, Op. 80.*
❀ *** EMI Dig. CDC7 49965-2; *EL 749965-4.* Melvyn Tan, (i) Schütz Ch.; L. Classical Players, Roger Norrington.
(M) **(*) Ph. 434 148-2; *434 148-4* [id.]. Brendel, LPO, Haitink; (i) with LPO Ch.
** Decca Dig. 433 322-2 [id.]. Ashkenazy, Cleveland O; (i) with Cleveland Ch.

Kovacevich is unsurpassed today as an interpreter of this most magnificent of concertos. His superb account for Philips, now on Concert Classics, has set a model for everyone and, with its sonata coupling, remains highly recommendable. This new Eminence version, recorded at the Sydney Opera House in 1989 with the soloist directing from the keyboard, is recognizably from the same inspired artist, though speeds are consistently faster and the manner is sharper and tauter. So the first movement is now more thrillingly urgent, while the central *Adagio* is rapt and pure, but the faster speed allows the soloist's melodic line to flow more easily, while the tension in the finale is even greater than before. The piano sound on the digital recording is aptly brighter and more faithful than on the Philips, making this a first choice for this much-recorded work, even with no allowance for price. For fill-up, Kovacevich conducts a comparably electrifying account of the *Grosse Fuge.*

Melvyn Tan plays with real flair and musical imagination. He has a poetic fire and brilliance all his own. The disc conveys the feeling of a live performance rather than an academic exercise, and the artists follow Czerny's brisk (and authoritative) tempo markings. The inspiriting account of the *Choral fantasia* possesses a mercurial quality and a panache that show this sometimes underrated work in a most positive light. Norrington and the chorus and orchestra are no less persuasive. In the *Concerto* Tan plays a copy of an 1814 Nanette Streicher, a maker much admired by Beethoven (and with which Tan is associated on record), and in the *Choral Fantasia* a copy by Neupert of an instrument from 1815 by Louis Dulcken. A splendidly natural recording completes the attractiveness of this fine disc. The physical effect of the original instruments makes an obvious contrast with Kovacevich's new EMI version (to which we have also given a Rosette), yet the insights here are every bit as stimulating.

The wonder is that Arrau, for long an inhibited artist in the studio, should in his *Emperor* recording, made when he was over eighty, sound so carefree. There are technical flaws, and the digital recording is rather resonant in bass, but with Sir Colin Davis and the Dresden State Orchestra as electrifying partners, the voltage is even higher than in his earlier versions of the mid-1960s. One would expect Arrau in his eighties to become more reflective, but the opposite is the case. The slow movement flows more freely, less hushed and poised than before, while the finale at a relaxed speed is joyful in its jaunty rhythms. Intensely individual, the very opposite of routine, this is from first to last a performance which reflects new searching by a deeply thinking musician. This is a thrillingly expansive *Emperor* which will give much satisfaction.

Perahia's account of the *Emperor*, strong and thoughtful yet with characteristic touches of poetry, rounds off an outstanding cycle of the Beethoven concertos. The approach is spacious, and with Bernard Haitink and the Concertgebouw Orchestra firm, responsive partners, each movement immediately takes wing, though a touch of bass-heaviness in the recording needs correcting, even on CD.

On Philips, with alert, sharp-edged accompaniment from Sir Colin Davis, Kovacevich gives a clean, dynamic performance of the outer movements, then in the central slow movement finds a depth of intensity that completely explodes any idea of this as a lighter central resting-point. The 1969 sound begins to show its age, with the bass a little boomy and the piano rather clattery on fortissimos, though well defined. For coupling there is one of the most deeply perceptive performances of a late Beethoven sonata on record.

Kempff's version remains very desirable. Although it is not on an epic scale, it has power in plenty and excitement, too. As ever, Kempff's range of tone-colour is extraordinarily wide. Leitner's orchestral contribution is of high quality and the Berlin orchestral playing has vigour and warmth. Some reservations need to be made about the sound, though it does not seriously detract from the music-making. Opus 111 is undoubtedly a great performance and makes a generous coupling.

Horowitz's fine record was made in Carnegie Hall in 1952 and few apologies need be made for the sound, which is full and resonant; here Reiner is at the helm and the two great artists form a splendid partnership. For all the excitement of the outer movements, it is the *Adagio* that stays in the mind, classical in line, tender in poetic feeling.

With extraordinarily vivid recording, Serkin's Telarc *Emperor* is very satisfying. The great pianist is almost as commanding as ever, with fire and brilliance in plenty in the outer movements; yet there is also a degree of relaxation, of conscious enjoyment, that increases the degree of communication. The hushed expressive pianism that provides the lyrical contrast in the first movement is matched by the poised refinement of the *Adagio*; the finale is vigorously joyful. Ozawa's accompaniment is first class.

Brendel's earlier (1976) account with Haitink is beautifully balanced, with a wide range and warmth, and the piano timbre is outstandingly natural. It goes without saying that from the artistic point of view there is also much to admire. The reading is spaciously conceived and the phrasing is eloquent. Yet there is also a studied quality about the music-making, particularly in the first movement, which prevents this attaining the top of the list. One has only to turn to the coupling, a splendid (1977) performance of the *Choral Fantasia*, to have the difference highlighted by the electrifying solo playing at the very opening, where Brendel has a long solo cadenza. At mid-price this issue remains very good value, with the recording projecting well on CD. However, in the present reissue on the Insignia label the accompanying notes concentrate on Brendel and have nothing to say about the music.

Completing his Cleveland cycle, Ashkenazy gives a muscular reading of the *Emperor*, forwardly recorded with the piano clangy on top and rather boomy below. The coupling with the *Choral Fantasia* is an attractive one, but the mid-price Philips issue offering the same two works with Brendel and Haitink brings even more individual and more compelling performances.

(i) *Piano concerto No. 5 (Emperor);* (ii) *Violin concerto, Op. 61;* (iii) *Fidelio: overture, Op. 72b* (CD only: (iv) *Leonora overture No. 2, Op. 72a;* (iii) *Leonora overture No. 3, Op. 72b*).
(B) *** DG Compact Classics 413 145-2 (2); *413 145-4* [id.]. (i) Eschenbach, Boston SO, Ozawa; (ii) Schneiderhan, BPO, Jochum; (iii) Dresden State O, Boehm. (CD only: (iv) BPO, Jochum).

Eschenbach gives a deeply satisfying interpretation of the *Emperor*, helped by the equally youthful urgency of his accompanist, Ozawa. With thoughtfulness, power and bravura nicely balanced, this interpretation is very impressive. Schneiderhan's stereo version of the *Violin concerto* is among the greatest recordings of this work: the serene spiritual beauty of the slow movement, and the playing of the second subject in particular, have never been surpassed on record; the orchestra under Jochum provides a background tapestry of breadth and dignity. As an added point of interest, Schneiderhan uses cadenzas that were provided for the transcription of the work for piano and orchestra. The pair of CDs offer the extra pair of overtures which are well worth having, particularly Jochum's *Leonora No. 2*. In either format this is an outstanding coupling.

(i) *Piano concerto No. 5 in E flat (Emperor);* (ii) *Triple concerto for violin, cello and piano in C, Op. 56.*
(M) *** Sony SBK 46549 [id.]. (i) Leon Fleisher, Cleveland O, Szell; (ii) Stern, Rose, Istomin, Phd. O, Ormandy.

Leon Fleisher is a pianist who worked with special understanding in the Szell regime at Cleveland, and by any count his reading of the *Emperor* is impressive for its youthful dramatic vigour, so the advantages of youth and experience are combined with exceptional intensity. The 1961 recording is very bright, but the Severance Hall ambience ensures fullness too. For the coupling, Stern, Rose and Istomin – three friends who invariably reveal their personal joy in making music together – make a wonderful trio of soloists. Ormandy, too, proves to be a marvellous accompanist. Unfortunately the CBS balance, as usual, favours the soloists so that the contrast of their soft playing is endangered; but the performance as a whole is so compelling that it would take a much more serious recording fault to undermine the concentration.

Violin concerto in D, Op. 61.
*** EMI Dig. CDC7 54072-2 [id.]; *EL 754072-4*. Kyung-Wha Chung, Concg O, Tennstedt – BRUCH: *Violin concerto No. 1.* ***
*** Chesky CD 52 [id.]. Erich Gruenberg, New Philh. O, Horenstein – SCHUMANN: *Piano concerto.* **(*)
*** Denon Dig. C37 7508 [id.]. Kantorow, Netherlands CO, Ros-Marba.
*** DG 413 818-2 [id.]. Mutter, BPO, Karajan.
(*) BMG/RCA RD 85402 (RCD1 4502). Heifetz, Boston SO, Munch – BRAHMS: *Concerto.* *
(M) *** EMI CD-EMX 2069; *TC-EMX 2069*. Yehudi Menuhin, VPO, Silvestri.
(M) (***) EMI mono CDH7 69799-2 [id.]. Yehudi Menuhin, Philh. O, Furtwängler – MENDELSSOHN: *Concerto.* (***)
(M) **(*) BMG/RCA Dig. GD 86536 [RCA 6536-2-RG]. Ughi, LSO, Sawallisch – MENDELSSOHN: *Concerto.* **(*)

(i) *Violin concerto in D, Op. 61;* (ii) *Romances Nos. 1 in G, Op. 40; 2 in F, Op. 50.*
*** EMI Dig. CDC7 49567-2 [id.]. Perlman, BPO, Barenboim.
❀ (B) *** DG 427 197-2; *427 197-4* [id.]. (i) Schneiderhan, BPO, Jochum; (ii) D. Oistrakh, RPO, Goossens.
(B) *** Ph. 426 064-2; *426 064-4* [id.]. Grumiaux; (i) New Philh. O, Galliera; (ii) Concg. O, Haitink.
(M) *** Ph. 420 348-2; *420 348-4* [id.]. Grumiaux, (i) Concg. O, C. Davis; (ii) New Philh. O, De Waart.
*** BMG/RCA Dig. RD 87777 [7777-2-RC]. Joseph Swensen, RPO, Previn.
(M) *** DG 435 099-2; *435 099-4* [id.]. Zukerman; (i) Chicago SO; (ii) LPO; Barenboim.
(BB) *** Naxos Dig. 8.550149; *4550149* [id.]. Takako Nishizaki, Slovak PO (Bratislava), Kenneth Jean.
(B) **(*) Pickwick Dig. PCD 977; *CIMPC 977* [id.]. Laredo, Scottish CO.

Violin concerto in D; Romance No. 2 in F, Op. 50.
(BB) *** ASV Dig. CDQS 6080; ZCQS 6080 [id.]. Shumsky, Philh. O, Andrew Davis.

(i) *Violin concerto in D; Overtures: The Consecration of the House; Leonora No. 3.*
(M) **(*) Sony SMK 47451 [id.]. (i) Isaac Stern; NYPO, Bernstein.

Violin concerto in D; Overture Egmont, Op. 84.
(B) *** Ph. 422 971-2; *422 971-4*. Hermann Krebbers, Concg. O, Haitink.

Perlman's Berlin recording was made at a live performance in the Philharmonie in Berlin in 1986. The live occasion prompts the soloist to play with extra flair and individuality, spontaneous in imagination, with depth of insight married to total technical command. The power and purposefulness of Perlman's playing are established on his very first entry after the opening tutti; from then on he plays with a persuasiveness even beyond the similarly spacious reading he recorded in the studio just a little over five years earlier, with Giulini conducting (EMI CDC7 47002-2, which is still available). Like most latterday recordings, this one has the Kreisler cadenzas, and in playing them Perlman caps all rivals in sheer excitement and bravura. Though (as always with Perlman) the solo violin is balanced well forward, the sound is not overbearing. Anyone wanting a modern digital version cannot do better than opt for this. The two *Romances*, recorded by the same performers in the studio, are just as persuasive, with Perlman particularly sweet and tender in his expansive account of No. 2.

Kyung-Wha Chung has recorded the Beethoven concerto before; but in a generous and attractive coupling, this EMI performance, recorded live in the Concertgebouw, is far more spontaneous in its expressive warmth. The collaboration with Tennstedt is searching and intense. If Chung's studio recording with Kondrashin on Decca tended to lack impetus – the fault of the conductor rather than of the soloist – this one sustains spacious speeds very persuasively indeed. Next to Perlman on another live recording from EMI, Chung is lighter and more mercurial. She is more freely flexible in her approach to Beethoven, as Tennstedt is too, but magnetically she still keeps an overall command. The element of vulnerability in Chung's reading adds to the emotional weight, above all in the slow movement, which in its wistful tenderness is among the most beautiful on record, while the outer movements are full of flair. The recording, with the soloist not balanced too close, is remarkably full and atmospheric for one made live. The coupling with the Bruch concerto is apt, generous and unusual.

Schneiderhan's outstanding version of the Beethoven *Concerto* is here available without the Compact Classics coupling of the *Emperor* (see above). David Oistrakh's accounts of the *Romances* are of high quality too, and the remastering is well managed.

Erich Gruenberg, a distinguished orchestral leader as well as an inspired soloist, proves an excellent partner for the veteran, Jascha Horenstein, in one of his late recordings. The power of the *Concerto* is brought out effortlessly from the opening tutti onwards; and Horenstein's positive direction never gets in the way of the poetry and imagination of Gruenberg's performance, which is expressive without ever lapsing into waywardness. His tone is consistently fresh and clear and, with first-rate, well-balanced 1967 sound, this is an excellent recommendation for anyone wanting this unusual and generous coupling.

One of the joys of Shumsky's super-bargain version of the *Violin concerto* with the Philharmonia is its sense of naturalness and style. His playing is distinguished by a total lack of affectation and by great purity of line, and there seems to be good rapport between soloist and orchestra. The performance is unhurried and refreshingly unanxious to impress: he is agreeably old-fashioned without being overtly romantic (he pulls back for the G minor episode in the first movement, as did Kreisler, whose cadenzas he plays). The only reservation of note is that Shumsky is placed slightly too much to the fore in the aural picture, though this emphasis is in no sense excessive (indeed, there are many worse offenders: EMI for Perlman, DG for Mutter, Philips for Szeryng, and so on), and orchestral detail is never obscured. He has sympathetic support from the Philharmonia and Andrew Davis.

Kantorow, who has also recorded a very successful set of the Mozart concertos for Denon, follows a performing tradition in the Beethoven *Violin concerto* whose most distinguished recent advocate was Wolfgang Schneiderhan. Kantorow's playing has a comparable incandescent classical lyricism and unforced naturalness of line and phrasing, and his reading takes its place alongside the very finest recorded versions. The slow movement is very moving in its gentle sustained intensity, while the finale is nimble in articulation, yet with lyrical feeling still very much to the fore. The use of a chamber-sized accompanying group enhances the classical scale of the performance, with Ros-Marba providing an understanding if relaxed supporting role. The recording is first class, very well balanced in a spacious acoustic framework which never clouds detail.

The slow basic tempi of Anne-Sophie Mutter's beautiful reading on DG were her own choice, she claims, and certainly not forced on her by her superstar conductor. The first two movements have rarely, if ever, been more expansively presented on record, but the purity of the solo playing and the concentration of the whole performance make the result intensely convincing. The finale is relaxed too, but is well pointed, at a fair tempo, and presents the necessary contrast. Good atmospheric recording against the warm acoustic of the Philharmonie Hall in Berlin.

Grumiaux recorded the Beethoven *Violin concerto* twice for Philips in stereo, the first occasion in the late 1960s with Galliera in London, and again in the mid-1970s with Sir Colin Davis in Amsterdam. The balance of advantage between the two versions – both among the finest ever committed to disc – is very difficult to resolve, although the earlier version has a price advantage. The Concertgebouw recording is fuller and richer, even if there is not absolute clarity, and there is less background noise. Grumiaux imbues both performances with a spirit of classical serenity. But in the slow movement there is not quite the same sense of repose or of spontaneous magic in the later account. Both discs include the *Romances*, appealingly played, and in each instance the recording is of a slightly different vintage, brighter and clearer.

Joseph Swensen is an American player, born in 1960, with a mixture of Norwegian and Japanese ancestry. His account of the *Concerto* is one of the most thoughtful to have appeared in recent years. He gives an unemphatic, reflective account of the solo part in which overstatement plays no part and, as one would expect, is immaculate in matters of intonation and technique. He uses the four cadenzas which Beethoven wrote for the transcription of the work as a piano concerto (commissioned by Clementi). The RPO under André Previn are supportive and the recording produces a very natural balance. The two *Romances* are well played too. Not the most powerful version, but a most satisfying one.

Menuhin's first stereo recording with Silvestri is a noble performance, very comparable with his mono record with Furtwängler, but of course the sound is greatly improved. Menuhin's warmth and humanity show in his instinctive shaping of phrases, and his slightly slower tempi add breadth and boldness to a design that can easily be spoiled by ill-judged emphasis. The remastering is vividly successful, with the orchestra reasonably full-bodied.

Another highly recommendable version comes from Zukerman and Barenboim. If warmth and tonal richness are the qualities most wanted, then this is the ideal version, with the immaculate playing of the Chicago Symphony Orchestra ripely recorded in 1977. Zukerman also offers fine accounts of the two *Romances*, recorded in London three years earlier.

Those looking for a super-bargain, digital version will find that Nishizaki's highly spontaneous performance can measure up to many accounts by more famous names. Helped by a strongly sympathetic backing from the excellent Slovak Philharmonic under Kenneth Jean, her playing is individual yet unselfconscious and has a fresh simplicity of approach which is consistently appealing. The *Larghetto* is poised and serene, and the finale is nicely buoyant. The two *Romances* are also very well played. The digital recording, made in the Reduta Concert Hall in Bratislava, is first class, the violin well forward but with the resonantly full orchestral tapestry spaciously caught.

Hermann Krebbers plays with an appealing naturalness and a totally unforced spontaneity. In his hands the slow movement has a tender simplicity which is irresistible, and it is followed by a delightfully relaxed and playful reading of the finale. Haitink and his soloist form a partnership which brings out the symphonic strength and, if the balance of the soloist is a shade too close, the recording is otherwise excellent.

Heifetz's unique coupling of the Beethoven and Brahms *Concertos* on a single disc is only possible because of his consistent refusal to linger. RCA's digital transfer of a recording originally made in the very earliest days of stereo has a fine sense of realism and presence, with the soloist only a little closer than is natural. The extra immediacy of CD reinforces the supreme mastery of a performance which may adopt fast speeds but never sounds rushed, finding time for individuality and imagination in every phrase. For some listeners, the comparative lack of serenity in the first movement (though not in the *Larghetto*) will be a drawback, but the drama of the reading is unforgettable. Heifetz's unique timbre is marvellously captured; the assured aristocracy of the playing confounds criticism.

Laredo, directing the outstanding players of the Scottish Chamber Orchestra, gives a clean-cut, satisfying reading of the *Concerto*, presented on a convincing chamber scale. Speeds are a degree faster than usual in all three movements and some of the dramatic contrasts are reduced, with the closeness of sound in the slow movement not allowing a really gentle pianissimo, but that is apt for the scale. At bargain price, there are even more inspired readings, but with the *Romances* as coupling, well recorded in full digital sound, this is certainly worth considering.

Recorded only months before the conductor's death, Menuhin's version with Furtwängler is a classic which emerges with extraordinary freshness. Rarely if ever has the Beethoven *Violin concerto* been recorded with such sweetness and tenderness, yet with firm underlying strength. With its generous coupling, it is a compact disc which defies the years. One hardly registers that this is mono recording.

The reissue of Isaac Stern's 1959 performance on Sony shows the intense creative relationship established between Stern and Bernstein. Stern's reading has a tremendous onward flow, his personality projected strongly, yet Bernstein keeps the orchestra well in the picture. The opening tutti is particularly vibrant – seldom have the timpani strokes sounded more tellingly – and the energy of the music-making is compulsive. Even though the remastering has greatly improved the sound, the close CBS recording means that a real pianissimo in the slow movement is not possible, but the intensity is in no doubt, and the finale is comparably vigorous. Both Overtures are similarly vital, *Leonora No. 3* and very exciting at the end.

Ughi's version has first-class digital recording, realistic and very well balanced. The performance of the Beethoven is first rate, fresh and unaffected, marked by consistent purity of tone in every register.

(i) *Piano concerto in D* (arr. from *Violin concerto*), *Op. 61;* (ii) *Romances Nos. 1–2, Opp. 40 & 50.*
(M) **(*) DG 429 179-2; *429 179-4* [id.]. (i) Barenboim, ECO; (ii) Zukerman, LPO, Barenboim.

Beethoven's transcription of his *Violin concerto* alters the character of the music, bringing down the emotional scale and substituting charm where in the original there is great spiritual depth. The work could not receive a more dedicated or affectionate performance than it does here. Zukerman's performances of the *Romances* are a welcome makeweight.

Konzertsatz (Concerto movement) in C, WoO 5; Romance No. 1 in G, Op.40.
(M) *** DG 431 168-2; *431 168-4* [id.]. Kremer, LSO, Tchakarov – SCHUBERT: *Konzertstück* etc. ***

The early *Concerto movement in C* is performed in a completion by Wilfried Fischer that is effective enough; and the mixed bag of Schubert which acts as coupling is certainly apt. All the music is beautifully played by Kremer; the 1978 recording, made in the London Sir Henry Wood Hall, has transferred splendidly to CD.

Triple concerto for violin, cello and piano in C, Op. 56.
(B) *** Pickwick Dig. PCD 917; *IMPC 917.* Trio Zingara, ECO, Heath – BOCCHERINI: *Concerto No. 7.* ***
*** Capriccio Dig. 10 150 [id.]. Funke, Timm, Rösel, Dresden PO, Kegel – *Choral fantasia.* ***
(B) **(*) EMI CDZ7 62854-2; *LZ 762854-4.* David Oistrakh, Knushevitzky, Oborin, Philh. O, Sargent – BRAHMS: *Double concerto.* ***

(i) *Triple concerto, Op. 56;* (ii) *Symphony No. 10: First movement* (realized & completed by Barry Cooper).
(M) *** Chan. Dig. CHAN 6501; *MBTD 6501* [id.]. (i) Kalichstein–Laredo–Robinson Trio, ECO, Gibson; (ii) CBSO, Weller.

(i) *Triple concerto, Op. 56; Piano sonata No. 17 in D min. (Tempest), Op. 31/2.*
(M) **(*) EMI CDM7 69032-2 [id.]; *EG 769032-4.* Sviatoslav Richter, (i) with D. Oistrakh, Rostropovich, BPO, Karajan.

The 1984 Chandos version of the *Triple concerto* with three young American soloists is exceptionally well recorded. Sharon Robinson, the cellist, takes the lead with pure tone and fine intonation, though both her partners are by nature more forceful artists. A clean-cut, often refreshing view of the work, it is now reissued coupled with Weller's strong version of Barry Cooper's completion of the first movement of Beethoven's projected *Tenth Symphony*, also very well recorded.

On Pickwick, Felix Schmidt, who is also the cello soloist in the Boccherini, plays with consistently beautiful, firm and clean tone, well matched by his two partners, creating the illusion of live performance, full of bounce and vigour. Also at mid-price, in full and vivid digital sound, it makes an excellent recommendation.

In the East German performance the three soloists, Christian Funke, Jürnjacob Timm and Peter Rösel, play rather as a team in the outer movements, but in the slow movement their personalities blossom, particularly that of the fine cellist, while in the finale there is a striking lightness of articulation and a lively rhythmic emphasis from the conductor, Herbert Kegel. The recording is realistically balanced. While other versions may offer stronger projection up front, this performance has plenty of energy and momentum and also an outstanding coupling, a most successful version of the *Choral Fantasia*.

The star-studded cast on the EMI recording make a breathtaking line-up. The results are predictably arresting, with Beethoven's priorities among the soloists well preserved in the extra dominance of Rostropovich over his colleagues. This is warm, expansive music-making that confirms even more clearly than before the strength of the piece. The resonant recording suffers from loss of focus in some climaxes, but this is not too serious. Richter's powerful reading of Beethoven's *D minor Sonata* makes a good coupling.

On the alternative EMI bargain version Sargent is authoritative and musical, and his soloists make a good team, as well as displaying plenty of individual personality. The slow movement is strikingly eloquent.

12 Contredanses, WoO 14; 12 German dances, WoO 8; 12 Minuets, WoO 17; 11 Mödlinger dances, WoO 17.
(BB) *** Naxos 8.550433 [id.]. Capella Istropolitana, Oliver Dohnányi.

It is always a delight to catch Beethoven relaxing and showing how warmly he felt towards the Viennese background in which he lived. The excellent Capella Istopolitana group used for the recording seems to be of exactly the right size, and they play the music with light rhythmic feeling, yet with plenty of spirit. Dipped into, this will give pleasure.

The Creatures of Prometheus: Overture and ballet music, Op. 43 (complete).
*** DG Dig. 419 608-2 [id.]. Orpheus CO.

As this splendid recording demonstrates, there is much to admire in this lesser-known Beethoven score, often anticipating later, greater works in sudden flashes, with moods varying widely from tragedy to country-dance felicity. The very talented conductorless orchestra plays most stylishly, helped by bright, clean recording.

OVERTURES

Overtures: The Consecration of the house, Op. 124; Coriolan, Op. 62; The Creatures of Prometheus, Op. 43; Egmont, Op. 84; Fidelio, Op. 72c; King Stephen, Op. 117; Leonora Nos. 1–3, Opp. 138; 72a; 72b; The Ruins of Athens, Op. 113; Zur Namensfeier, Op. 115.
(M) *** DG 427 256-2 (2) [id.]. BPO, Karajan.

Karajan's set of overtures was recorded in the mid- and late 1960s. They are impressive performances that have stood the test of time. They show an imposing command of structure and detail as well as the customary virtuosity one expects from this conductor and the Berlin Philharmonic. The sound is fresh and bright.

Overtures: The Consecration of the house, Op. 124; Coriolan, Op. 62; The Creatures of Prometheus, Op. 43; Egmont, Op. 84; Fidelio, Op. 72c; King Stephen, Op. 117; Leonora No. 2, Op. 72a; The Ruins of Athens, Op. 113.
**(*) Nimbus NI 5205 [id.]. Hanover Band, Roy Goodman or Monica Huggett.

Recorded at various periods in conjunction with the Hanover Band's other Beethoven recordings for Nimbus, this compilation makes a generous and attractive collection, an admirable supplement to this orchestra's Beethoven symphony cycle. Anyone who wants the principal Beethoven overtures played on period instruments will be well pleased.

Overtures: The Consecration of the house, Op. 124; Coriolan, Op. 62; The Creatures of Prometheus, Op. 43; Egmont, Op. 84; Fidelio, Op. 72c; King Stephen, Op. 117; Leonora No. 3, Op. 72b; The Ruins of Athens, Op. 113; Zur Namensfeier, Op. 115.
(B) *** Ph. 426 630-2; *426 630-4*. Leipzig GO, Kurt Masur.

These performances are more direct than those of Karajan and are wholly satisfying in their strong motivation and lack of mannerism. The Philips recording, from the early 1970s, is of high quality, and the remastering has enhanced its vividness and impact.

Overtures: *Consecration of the House, Op. 124; Coriolan, Op. 62; Creatures of Prometheus, Op. 43; Egmont, Op. 84; Leonora No. 2, Op. 72b; Leonora No. 3, Op. 72a;* arr. of *String quartet in F, Op. 135.*
(M) (**(*)) BMG/RCA mono GD 60296 [id.]. NBC SO, Toscanini.

The sound-quality varies greatly in this collection of overtures, recorded between 1938 and

1947 in the days of short-playing 78-r.p.m. discs. Yet these performances are all naturally expressive, with freer and less metrical rhythms than his later NBC versions, with the electrical intensity coming over at an even higher voltage.

Overtures: Coriolan, Op. 62; The Creatures of Prometheus, Op. 43; Egmont, Op. 84; Leonora No. 1, Op. 138; Leonora No. 3, Op. 72b; The Ruins of Athens, Op. 113.
(M) *** Sony Dig. MDK 44790 [id.]. Bav. RSO, C. Davis.

This Sony/CBS CD is very well recorded and Sir Colin Davis secures playing of distinction from the Bavarian orchestra and, while it was a pity that *Leonora No. 2* was omitted, this remains a distinguished collection.

Romances for violin and orchestra Nos. 1 in G, Op. 40; 2 in F, Op. 50.
*** Ph. Dig. 420 168-2 [id.]. Zukerman, St Paul CO – DVOŘÁK: *Romance;* SCHUBERT: *Konzertstücke* etc. ***

Beethoven's two *Romances* could hardly be played more winningly than they are within this attractively chosen collection of short concert pieces for violin and orchestra. A disc which is more than the sum of its parts.

SYMPHONIES

Symphonies Nos. 1–9.
*** Teldec/Warner Dig. 2292 46452-2 (5) [id.]. Margiono, Remmert, Schasching, Holl, Arnold Schoenberg Ch. (in No. 9); COE, Harnoncourt.
(B) *** DG 429 036-2 (5) [id.]. Janowitz, Rössel-Majdan, Kmentt, Berry & V. Singverein (in No. 9), BPO, Karajan.
**(*) Nimbus Dig. NI 5144/8 (5). Soloists, Ch., Hanover Band, Monica Huggett (*Nos. 1, 2 & 5*), Roy Goodman (*Nos. 3, 4, 6, 7–9*).
(M) (**(*)) EMI mono CHS7 63606-2 (5). VPO or Stockholm PO, Furtwängler, (with soloists & Ch. in No. 9).

Symphonies Nos. 1 in C, Op. 21; 3 (Eroica).
(M) (*(*)) Arkadia mono CDGI 755.1. Philh. O, Klemperer.

Symphonies Nos. 2 in D, Op. 36; 7 in A, Op. 92.
(M) (*(*)) Arkadia mono CDGI 756.1. Philh. O, Klemperer.

Symphonies Nos. 4 in B flat, Op. 60; 8 in F, Op. 93; Egmont: Overture.
(M) (*) Arkadia mono CDGI 757.1. Philh. O, Klemperer.

Symphonies Nos. 5 in C min., Op. 67; 6 in F (Pastoral).
(M) (*) Arkadia mono CDGI 758.1. Philh. O, Klemperer.

Symphony No. 9 (Choral); Overture Coriolan.
(M) (*) Arkadia mono CDGI 759.1. Soloists, Ch., Philh. O, Klemperer.

Symphonies Nos. 1–9; Overtures: Coriolan; Creatures of Prometheus; Egmont.
**(*) EMI Dig. CDS7 49852-2 (6). Kenny, Walker, Power, Salomaa, Schütz Ch. (in No. 9), L. Classical Players, Norrington.

Symphonies Nos. 1–9; Overtures: Coriolan; The Creatures of Prometheus; Egmont; Fidelio; Leonora No. 3; The Ruins of Athens.
(M) *** DG 429 089-2 (6). Tomowa-Sintow, Baltsa, Schreier, Van Dam, V. Singverein, BPO, Karajan.

Symphonies Nos. 1–9; Overtures: Coriolan; Egmont.
**(*) O-L Dig. 425 696-2 (6) [id.]. Augér, Robbin, Rolfe Johnson, Reinhard, LSO Ch. (in No. 9); AAM, Hogwood.

Symphonies Nos. 1–9; Overtures: Coriolan; Egmont; Fidelio; Leonora No. 3.
** DG Dig. 415 066-2 (6) [id.]. Soloists, V. Singverein, BPO, Karajan.

Symphonies Nos. 1–9; Overtures: Egmont; Fidelio; King Stephen.
(M) **(*) Sony SB5K 48396 (5). Cleveland O, George Szell (with Addison, Hobson, Lewis, Bell & Cleveland Ch. in No. 9).

Symphonies Nos. 1–9; Overture Leonora No. 3.
(M) (***) BMG/RCA mono GD 60324 (5) [60324-2-RG]. Farrell, Merriman, Peerce, Scott, Shaw Chorale (in No. 9), NBC SO, Toscanini.

Symphonies Nos. 1–9; 10 (realized Cooper): *1st movt; Overtures: Coriolan; The Creatures of Prometheus* (with rehearsals of *Symphonies Nos. 6 & 10*).
*** Chan. CHAN 8712/7; *DBTD 6001* (6) [id.]. Barstow, Finnie, Rendall, Tomlinson, CBSO Ch., CBSO, Weller.

Harnoncourt's cycle with the Chamber Orchestra of Europe, presented convincingly on a biggish chamber scale, is among the most refreshing of any and deservedly won the *Gramophone* Orchestral Award for 1992. Reflecting his work as a period-performance pioneer, Harnoncourt makes rhythms light and textures clean and with sparing vibrato. Periodically, as in the opening movement of the *Eroica*, he adopts a hectically fast tempo, but that is the exception. More usually, his choice of speeds is regularly geared to bringing out the rhythmic and expressive finesse characteristic of this brilliant young orchestra. That the performances so consistently display the joy in Beethoven, his natural exuberance, reflects the way they were made, done live over an intensive period in Graz in the summer of 1990. The live conditions also heighten the impact of Harnoncourt's austere view of the great *Funeral march* in the *Eroica*, made chillingly intense, as well as the high contrasts in the slow movement of No. 4, with soaring lyricism over nagging rhythmic figures below. The *Ninth* was recorded almost a year after the rest and equally refreshingly reflects the lessons of period performance, though the dry manner in the great *Adagio*, taken at a flowing speed, underplays the emotional depth. Excellent sound. Admirers of Harnoncourt need not hesitate. The records comprising this set are also available separately, with the symphonies coupled as follows: Nos. 1 and 3 (9031 75708-2), Nos. 2 and 5 (9031 75712-2), Nos. 4 and 7 (9031 75714-2), Nos. 6 and 8 (9031 75709-2), No. 9 (9031 75713-2).

Of Karajan's four recorded cycles, this 1961–2 set is the most consistent and in many ways the most compelling, combining high polish with a biting sense of urgency and spontaneity. There is one major disappointment, in the over-taut reading of the *Pastoral*, which in addition omits the vital repeat in the scherzo. Otherwise these are incandescent performances, superbly played. Designedly, Karajan left the *Eroica* and the *Ninth* till last in the intensive recording sessions, and that helped to give extra power of communication to those supreme masterpieces. On CD the sound is still excellent, the best-balanced in any of his Beethoven series and on five CDs at bargain price, this makes outstanding value for money.

Karajan's 1977 cycle is offered on six CDs at mid-price, including the major overtures. Interpretatively his view on Beethoven had changed relatively little, but some differences are significant. The *Eroica* presents the one major disappointment of this cycle, at least in the outer movements, which are faster and slightly rushed, though the *Funeral march* remains measured and direct. As against this, the first movement of the *Pastoral*, angular and tense in the 1962 cycle, has more elegance and joyfulness at tempi barely any slower. The cycle is capped by a version of the *Choral Symphony* that is among the finest ever committed to disc. However, in terms of sound the later cycle does not necessarily show an improvement, and for most collectors the earlier set will prove the more rewarding purchase.

Walter Weller's Beethoven cycle for Chandos is by far his finest achievement on record. Although this is the City of Birmingham Symphony Orchestra, there is a warm, refined, Viennese quality in the playing and interpretation, to remind you that this conductor started his career as concertmaster of the Vienna Philharmonic. The Chandos sound is full and glowing to match, by far the finest to date given to any conductor in a collected Beethoven cycle. The sixth (supplementary) disc brings Dr Barry Cooper's re-creation of the first movement of No. 10, plus substantial extracts of rehearsal and two overtures. Broadly speaking, one might categorize Weller as a Beethovenian whose sympathies centre on the even-numbered symphonies, rather than on the odd-numbered works with their cataclysmic symphonic statements. Not that the great odd-numbered symphonies lose freshness or bite under Weller; but these are all friendly performances which, in their continuing alertness and the feeling of live communication, give consistent pleasure. There is an exuberance and a sense of joyful adventure running through all of them, so that even the first movement of the *Eroica* (with exposition repeat observed) is presented in happy optimism rather than in epic grandeur. The *Seventh* and the *Pastoral*, incidentally, are the only two symphonies in which Weller omits exposition repeats. These are not the most monumental readings you will find, but they are the most companionable; and that applies too to the final culmination, the *Ninth*.

Of the Beethoven cycles on period instruments Hogwood's with the Academy of Ancient Music in many ways makes the safest recommendation. It is the most vividly recorded, with the keenest sense of presence and, above all, the sound adds appropriate weight to the *Ninth*, with the LSO Chorus fuller and more vivid than rival choirs for Norrington and Goodman. Hogwood also has the finest quartet of soloists, though in the first movement he is too rigid. Like his rivals, Hogwood has taken note of Beethoven's metronome markings, but he applies them rather less consistently. His pointing of rhythms is not always as alert or imaginative as that of his direct rivals; as a whole, the cycle may lack something in individual moments of insight but, with clean and generally well-disciplined playing, it is consistently satisfying.

Norrington's set is most strongly characterized. It is also most controversial, when he makes it a point of principle to observe Beethoven's often questionable metronome markings, generally very fast, and at times with breathless results. Yet with the tang of authentic brass and timpani steadfastly brought out, and with imaginative detail that regularly magnetizes the ear, they make a consistent and satisfying series. Even more than his rivals, Norrington makes you listen afresh. The recording is not always as clean or well focused as it might be, but the only major blot is the disappointing singing of the male soloists in the finale of the *Ninth*.

Squeezed on to only five discs and presented in chronological order, two symphonies per disc with No. 9 taking up the last, the Hanover Band's set makes a very attractive package. Though the performances are variable, the big challenges are splendidly taken: these readings convey the fire and exuberance of live performance. In characteristic Nimbus manner, the recordings are set in a reverberant acoustic, which means that the woodwind sometimes appear a little disembodied; but the sound is warm and undistracting. In Nos. 1 and 2, the string-playing is scrawnier than it later became, and the sound has less body. No. 5, also recorded early, is different: a strong and biting performance, full of energy and imagination. In the later recordings Goodman draws consistently fresh, individual readings from his team, with rhythms well sprung in exhilarating *allegros*. Even more remarkable is the way he can convey hushed intensity in slow movements, even when, following Beethoven's metronome markings, his speeds are much faster than we are used to. That is true also of the slow movement of the *Ninth*, in contrast to Norrington's exploratory version; but so too even more strikingly of the *Eroica* Funeral march. In the *Allegretto* of No. 7 too, the wistful melancholy of the main theme has rarely been so touchingly conveyed. Consistently the feeling of spontaneity is most winning.

Szell's set comes on five discs at mid-price, with three overtures thrown in for good measure. His compellingly strong, direct view of Beethoven brings much to stimulate, and the performances throughout the cycle are remarkably consistent, refreshing as well as intense. The marvellously polished and always responsive Cleveland playing never brings a suspicion of routine, but reservations must be made about the close CBS sound-balance which prevents a real pianissino from registering, even though the ear readily senses when the orchestra is playing gently. Because of the Cleveland ambience, there is no lack of body and atmosphere in these excellently remastered new transfers, which – apart from the limited range of dynamic – are far more faithful than the earlier LPs.

In Karajan's last, digital set, the recording seems to have been affected by the need to have a video version recorded at the same sessions. The gain is that these performances have keener spontaneity, the loss that they often lack the brilliant, knife-edged precision of ensemble one has come to regard as normal with Karajan. Though there is relatively little homing-in of microphones to spotlight individual detail, the sound too often grows thick and congested in big fortissimo tuttis. However, with the earlier recordings now issued at mid-price or less, the attractions of this digital box are much reduced even if, with speeds generally a little less extreme, there are a number of movements which sound more persuasive than before.

The NBC Toscanini versions are faster and more tense than the earlier Beethoven readings that he committed to records, but they are far from rigid or unloving, and they are crowned by performances of breathtaking power in the *Eroica* and the *Ninth*. Toscanini drew out melodic lines with Italianate affection, even while he was presenting the whole at a high voltage, rarely matched. Listening to this Beethoven is never a relaxing experience, but it is a uniquely involving one. In the *Ninth*, treble emphasis needs taming, and the *Fourth* and *Fifth* are given in live (as opposed to studio) recordings, with more variable results. The recordings sound at their best at a high volume, but the intrusive hum which marred the first CD transfers has been virtually eliminated. *Leonora No. 3* was recorded much earlier, from a 1939 broadcast.

By unearthing a live recording of No. 2, made in the Royal Albert Hall in 1948, and borrowing a radio recording of No. 8 made in Stockholm, EMI managed to put together a complete Furtwängler cycle, and very impressive it is interpretatively. The sound of those two ad hoc recordings may be very rough indeed, with heavy background noise, but the performances – with one or two oddities – are electrifying. No. 9 comes in the dedicated performance given at Bayreuth in 1951, uniquely historic, but the others are EMI's studio versions, not always as inspired as Furtwängler's live performances but still magnetic and, with generally well-balanced mono sound, very well transferred.

Klemperer's live recordings on Arkadia, presumably taken from broadcasts, were made at the Wiener Festwochen in Vienna in June 1960. Though the mono sound is dry and limited, with violins generally thin and unalluring and with the balance often favouring the woodwind, the tension of Klemperer's conducting is well caught. Speeds are generally faster than in the Beethoven cycle that Klemperer was just completing in the studio with far fuller stereo sound for EMI at the same time, but the approach is broadly the same. In the *Pastoral* Klemperer's controversially slow speed for the *Peasants' merrymaking* remains as in the studio, but in this symphony the scrawny violin sound is particularly worrisome. In Nos. 3, 5 and 7 Klemperer is closer in these live performances to his more spontaneous (1955) mono recordings for EMI, but there too the EMI sound is fuller than in the Vienna recordings. The first-movement Allegro of No. 7 flows here more persuasively, as also do a few other movements. What is disappointing is that the limited dynamic range of the recording undermines the dramatic impact, as at the start of the finale in the *Ninth Symphony*, and the opening of that culminating work is surprisingly lacking in tension. Characteristically, after the expansive account of the Scherzo (with all the repeats taken as in the studio) he takes the *Adagio* at flowing speeds, refusing to linger. One gain here is that the soprano soloist, Wilma Lipp, is sweeter and purer than on the EMI version; and the tenor soloist is the young Fritz Wunderlich. A brief burst of applause is given at the end of each symphony.

Symphonies Nos. 1–9 (arr. Liszt).
**(*) Teldec/Warner Dig. 9031 71619-2 (6) [id.]. Cyprien Katsaris (piano).

We have greeted most (though not all) of the individual issues in Cyprien Katsaris's cycle of the Liszt/Beethoven transcriptions. He uses a Bechstein in Nos. 1–3, a Steinway in No. 5 and an instrument by Mark Allen in the rest. The sound generally speaking is a bit synthetic; but in the *Eroica*, the *Eighth* and the *Choral*, the playing is really quite astonishing, not only in purely pianistic terms and in a feeling for texture but also for architecture. The *Fifth* is the only real let-down.

Symphonies Nos. 1 in C, Op. 21; 2 in D, Op. 36.
(M) *** Ph. 432 274-2; *432 274-4* [id.]. ASMF, Sir Neville Marriner.

Marriner presents the first two symphonies on modern instruments but on an authentic scale with a Mozart-sized orchestra, and the result is fresh and lithe, with plenty of character but with few, if any, quirks and mannerisms.

Symphonies Nos. 1 and 2 (trans. Liszt).
*** Teldec/Warner Dig. 2292 43661-2 [id.]. Cyprien Katsaris (piano).

Transcendental technique and a fine musical intelligence are the distinguishing features of these performances, which remain without peer in the Beethoven–Liszt discography. The recordings are finer than in earlier issues in the cycle.

Symphonies Nos. 1 in C, Op. 21; 3 in E flat (Eroica), Op. 55.
(M) **(*) Sony SMK 47514 [id.]. NYPO, Bernstein.
(M) (***) BMG/RCA mono GD 60252 [60252-2-RG]. NBC O, Toscanini.

Bernstein's 1960s cycle of the Beethoven symphonies has not been available in the UK since the late 1970s. Now it reappears as part of the Sony Royal Edition with the quality impressively remastered by a process called 'high definition sound'. The scrawny violin timbre of those earlier LPs has been cleaned up and refocused and, although a degree of fierceness remains, the ambience of the Manhattan Center provides plenty of underlying warmth. No. 1 receives a well-shaped reading, with no lack of momentum and pace (first-movement exposition repeat included). The warmly elegant *Andante* contrasts with a scherzo which fizzes vibrantly and, like the finale, clearly looks forward to the coupled, electrically intense *Eroica*, also dating from 1964. Here Bernstein takes the first movement almost as fast as Toscanini, and he maintains the tension over the fullest span by again including the exposition repeat. The *Funeral march* is darkly tragic, and the reading as a whole has great power. The bright yet full sound offers dramatic projection.

It is welcome to have the individual issues in Toscanini's Beethoven cycle also available separately. These are performances which convey breathtaking power, notably the magnificent account of the *Eroica*, never comfortable but far from rigid or unloving.

Symphonies Nos. 1 in C, Op. 21; 4 in B flat, Op. 60; Egmont overture.
(M) *** DG 419 048-2; *419 048-4* [id.]. BPO, Karajan.

Karajan's 1977 version of No. 1 is exciting, polished and elegant; in No. 4 the balance is closer, exposing every flicker of tremolando. Yet the body and ambience of the recording combine to give a realistic presence, and overall this is very impressive.

Symphonies Nos. 1 in C, Op. 21; 6 in F (Pastoral), Op. 68.
(M) *** BMG/RCA GD 60002 [60002-2-RG]. Chicago SO, Reiner.
(M) **(*) Sony SMK 45891 [id.]. Marlboro Festival O, Pablo Casals.

Symphonies Nos. 1 in C, Op. 21; 6 in F (Pastoral), Op. 68; Overture Egmont, Op. 84.
(M) **(*) Sony SBK 46532 [id.]. Cleveland O, Szell.

In its newly remastered form, Reiner's 1961 *Pastoral* sounds wonderfully warm and full, once again demonstrating the beauty of the acoustics of the Chicago Orchestral Hall at that time. The performance too is among the finest ever recorded, outstandingly fresh and enjoyable. The exposition repeat is observed in the first movement, to add to the architectural strength. The *First Symphony*, recorded in the same year, is weighty and direct, less incandescent but still a considerable account.

Casals's Marlboro *Pastoral* radiates integrity and warmth. It is totally free from any expressive exaggeration and tempi are well judged. These are performances of a vital sensitivity and, paradoxically, although everything is kept on a pretty tight rein it all seems relaxed and unhurried. The recording quality is dryish but eminently acceptable.

In the *First Symphony*, the clarity, the polish, the dynamism, the unfailing alertness of Szell's performance make up for any absence of charm. In the *Pastoral* (recorded in 1962), where the quality is smoother and warmer, Szell is subtle in his control of phrasing, for all the firmness of his style. However, it is a pity that the close-up sound robs the slow movement of much of its gentleness and delicacy of atmosphere. The finale, by contrast, is attractively relaxed.

Symphonies Nos. 1; 7 in A, Op. 92.
(BB) **(*) ASV CDQS 6066; *ZCQS 6066*. N. Sinfonia of England, Richard Hickox.
(M) **(*) EMI CDM7 63354-2 [id.]; *EG 763354-4*. Philh. O, Klemperer.

From Hickox comes a generous coupling in the super-bargain range for those wanting chamber-scale performances, though the warm acoustic of Trinity Hall, Newcastle, where the recordings were made, gives a result hardly smaller-sounding than from a full-scale symphony orchestra. Hickox's view of both works is unaffected and direct and so gets the best of both worlds: finely detailed yet substantial; and the very lack of idiosyncrasy makes for easy listening. The CD transfer is full and agreeable but provides a rather resonant bass.

With Klemperer the slow speeds and heavyweight manner in both works – in principle not apt for No. 1, while undermining the dance-like element in No. 7 – will for many get in the way of enjoyment. That said, the compulsion of Klemperer in Beethoven remains strong, with rhythmic pointing consistently preventing stagnation.

Symphonies Nos. 2 in D; 4 in B flat, Op. 60.
(M) *** EMI CDM7 63355-2 [id.]. Philh. O, Klemperer.

The coupling for CD emphasizes the consistency of Klemperer's approach to Beethoven, with both the *Second* and *Fourth* symphonies sounding the more powerful through weighty treatment. Only in the finale is the result rather too gruff. The *Fourth* brings one of the most compelling performances of all, with Klemperer's measured but consistently sprung pulse allowing for persuasive lyricism alongside power. Exposition repeats are observed in the first movements of both symphonies. The sound is fresh yet full.

Symphonies Nos. 2 in D; 5 in C min., Op. 67.
(M) **(*) Sony SBK 47651 [id.]. Cleveland O, George Szell.
**(*) Chan. Dig. CHAN 8752 [id.]. CBSO, Weller.

There is some marvellously clean articulation from the strings in the first movement of Szell's No. 2 and the adrenalin runs free; yet here, as in the similarly brilliant account of No. 5, Szell understands the need to give full scope to the lyrical elements. The recording is respectably transferred: because of the forward balance it cannot convey a real pianissimo but, as usual, the Severance Hall ambience ensures an acceptable degree of amplitude.

Consistent with his approach in the rest of the cycle, Weller makes the first movement of the *Fifth* optimistic rather than bitingly tragic. For some, the first three movements at least will be too comfortable, at broad speeds lacking something in dramatic tension. But in the finale the performance conveys the sort of eager enjoyment that marks the rest of the cycle. With an unusual coupling in Weller's beautifully sprung version of the *Second Symphony*, the disc has its place. Full, warm sound.

Symphonies Nos. 2 in D; 7 in A, Op. 92.
(M) *** DG 419 050-2; *419 050-4* [id.]. BPO, Karajan.
(M) **(*) Sony SMK 47515 [id.]. NYPO, Bernstein.

As with Karajan's coupling of Nos. 1 and 4, the digitally remastered versions of the 1977 recordings of the *D* and *A major Symphonies* are remarkably successful, the sound vivid and clear, yet with plenty of body. In No. 2 the firm lines give the necessary strength. The *Seventh* is tense and exciting, with the conductor emphasizing the work's dramatic rather than its dance-like qualities.

In Bernstein's No. 2 the NYPO play as if their very lives depended on it. Bernstein observes the exposition repeat and the movement is wholly free of any mannerisms. The slow movement is sensitively shaped, and the tempo relationships between first and second movements are well judged. Both the other movements are very fast and have a Toscanini-like sense of drive. The *Seventh* is hardly less vital, with the *Allegretto* bringing an intense climax and the finale very exciting without being overdriven. In both symphonies the 1964 sound is a bit fierce on top but has plenty of underlying body.

Symphonies Nos. 2; 8 in F, Op. 93.
*** EMI Dig. CDC7 47698-2 [id.]. L. Classical Players, Norrington.
(BB) **(*) ASV Quicksilva CDQS 5067; *ZCQS 5067.* N. Sinfonia, Hickox.

The coupling of Nos. 2 and 8 was the first of Norrington's Beethoven series and showed the London Classical Players as an authentic group with a distinctive sound, sweeter and truer in the string section than most, generally easier on non-specialist ears. Though the recording is warmly reverberant, Norrington secures admirably transparent textures, with the braying of the natural, valveless horns adding an apt tang and with the authentic small-size timpani adding military bite. In following Beethoven's own metronome markings for both symphonies the results are exhilarating, never merely breathless, bringing far more than proof of an academic theory. Formidable as the scholarship is, the important point is the freshness and imagination of the communication.

Richard Hickox directs his chamber-scale orchestra in fresh, warm and relaxed readings of these two even-numbered symphonies. Playing is refined and rhythms resilient, with the slow movement of No. 2 warmly moulded at a spacious speed, and with the scherzo bouncy at an easy, unforced tempo. The scale is well established by the slightly backward balance of the modest string section, with the focus rather sharper in No. 8 than in No. 2. Otherwise there is little to disconcert the listener used to full orchestral performances, and this makes an enjoyable recommendation in the lowest price range.

Symphony No. 3 in E flat (Eroica), Op. 55.
*** Ph. Dig. 410 044-2 [id.]. ASMF, Marriner.
*** Decca 417 235-2 [id.]. AAM, Hogwood.
(M) (***) BMG/RCA mono GD 60271; *GK 60271* [60271-2-RG; *60271-4-RG*]. NBC SO, Toscanini – MOZART: *Symphony No. 40.* (**)
(BB) ** ASV CDQS 6068; *ZCQS 6068.* N. Sinf., Richard Hickox.

Symphony No. 3 (Eroica); Grosse Fuge, Op. 133.
(M) *** EMI CDM7 63356-2 [id.]. Philh. O, Klemperer.

(i) *Symphony No. 3 (Eroica);* (ii) *Overture, Coriolan.*
(B) *** Pickwick Dig. PCD 900; *CIMPC 900* [id.]. LSO, Wyn Morris.
(B) **(*) Sony MBK 42599 [id.]. Columbia SO, Walter.

Symphony No. 3 (Eroica); Creatures of Prometheus: Overture.
*** EMI Dig. CDC7 49101-2. L. Classical Players, Norrington.

Symphony No. 3 (Eroica); Egmont overture.
**(*) DG Dig. 415 506-2 [id.]. BPO, Karajan.

Symphony No. 3 (Eroica); Overtures: Leonora Nos. 2 & 3.
(M) (***) EMI mono CDM7 63855-2 [id.]. Philh. O, Klemperer.

Symphony No. 3 (Eroica); Overture: Leonora No. 3.
(M) **(*) DG 419 049-2; *419 049-4* [id.]. BPO, Karajan.

(i) *Symphony No. 3 (Eroica);* (ii) *Serenade in D, for string trio, Op. 8.*
(BB) *** Virgo Dig. VJ7 91567-2 [id.]. (i) Scottish CO, Saraste; (ii) Sitkovetsky, Caussé, Geringas.

The digital remastering of Klemperer's spacious 1961 version of the *Eroica* reinforces its magnificence, keenly concentrated to sustain speeds slower than in his earlier, mono account. The reissue includes the stereo version of the *Grosse Fuge* and the sound is first rate, vivid and well balanced.

The alternative, mono version by Klemperer was among the very first records he made with the Philharmonia for EMI, but the success of these first Beethoven works revealed his full strength. Even now they have an electricity that he did not quite match in his re-recordings in stereo, with the *Eroica* one of his supreme achievements. The overtures were originally done in 1954, the symphony in 1955.

Saraste directs the Scottish Chamber Orchestra in one of the most compelling of modern *Eroicas*, the first one fully to present the work satisfyingly on a chamber scale, thanks to the relatively intimate recording. Far from diminishing the work, the scale gives it greater immediacy. The playing is beautifully refined, yet the whole performance conveys concentrated power, with a brisk opening allegro (exposition repeat observed) and a spacious *Funeral march*. The coupling is generous and unusual: a well-characterized and stylish account of the Opus 8 *Serenade for string trio* which, by contrast with the *Symphony*, is set in rather too reverberant an acoustic. At super-bargain price, this is an outstanding issue in every way.

For those seeking a modern, digital recording, Sir Neville Marriner's version is in every way outstanding, for although the Academy may use fewer strings, the impression is of weight and strength, coupled with a rare transparency of texture and extraordinary resilience of rhythm. The dance-rhythms of the fast movements are brought out captivatingly with sforzandos made clean and sharp. The *Funeral march* may emerge as less grave and dark than it can be, but Marriner's unforced directness is most compelling. The recorded sound is among the best ever in a Beethoven symphony.

Norrington's account of the *Eroica* is among the most enjoyable of his Beethoven symphony series with the London Classical Players, well coupled with the *Prometheus overture*. He is consistently even faster than his two closest period-performance rivals – Hogwood on Oiseau-Lyre and Goodman on Nimbus – yet one quickly forgets any feeling of haste when rhythms are so crisp and supple in their spring, and the great *Funeral march* has natural gravity. The recording has more presence than most of the others, with clearer perspectives.

Wyn Morris on the Pickwick label conducts a taut reading of the *Eroica*, dark and intense, with allegros consistently urgent, and the LSO responds with both bite and refinement. At budget price and with a coupling, it makes an excellent bargain, matching and even outshining most full-price rivals.

Walter's interpretation has all the ripeness of the best of his work with the Vienna Philharmonic Orchestra between the wars. The disc opens with a superb account of the *Coriolan overture*, spacious, warm and dramatic, and the sound-balance is especially telling.

The gain in Karajan's digital version of the *Eroica* over his previous recordings lies most of all in the *Funeral march*, very spacious and intense, with dynamic contrasts intensified. Here, and even more noticeably in the allegros, the playing is marginally less polished than before, lacking something of the knife-edged bite associated with Karajan. As with others in the series, the oddly balanced recording grows congested in big tuttis. Nevertheless, the power and concentration make it an epic reading.

Recorded live at Carnegie Hall, New York, in December 1953, Toscanini's version has a far keener emotional intensity than the studio recording which appeared earlier as part of his Beethoven cycle in the BMG Toscanini series. The great *Funeral march* particularly gains, though the ensemble does not always have quite such pinpoint precision. Toscanini had a special insight into this of all Beethoven's symphonies, making this disc a valuable addition to his discography.

Not everyone will identify readily with the fiery intensity of fast tempi in the outer movements of Karajan's 1977 performance, even if this version includes a more intense account of the *Funeral march* than in earlier recordings. An exciting performance of *Leonora No. 3* makes a very generous bonus.

With broad speeds Hickox directs a spacious, refined account of the *Eroica*, lacking a little in dramatic tension. The recording is warmly reverberant, allowing fair clarity but preventing the chamber scale from being fully appreciated.

Symphonies Nos. 3 in E flat (Eroica); 8 in F, Op. 93.
(M) (***) BMG/RCA mono GD 60269. NBC SO, Toscanini.
(M) **(*) Sony SBK 46328 [id.]. Cleveland O, Szell.

Toscanini's 1939 recording of the *Eroica*, made live, brings one of the most compelling recordings he ever made, one which confounds the idea that his conducting of Beethoven was inevitably too rigid. Not only does he conduct at white heat, he is far more flexible in his musical manners than he became later, both moulding melodic lines with Italianate warmth and allowing himself far freer rubato. The grinding dissonances at the climax of the first movement have never been thrust home with quite such elemental power as here, and the *Funeral march* is the more moving for being taken at an exceptionally broad speed, markedly slower than in his later recordings of 1949 and 1953. As for the sound, long regarded as intolerably harsh, the CD transfer gives it a sense of presence, with a satisfying immediacy and body in the string-tone, and with only a subdued crackle of surface noise to indicate a 78-r.p.m. source. The *Eighth* comes in another long-neglected recording, also made in 1939, but in the studio. The sound is even drier, but again the harshness is assuaged by the body given to the sound in the CD transfer. Defying the idea of this as Beethoven's 'little one', the reading is hard-driven and on the biggest scale (Toscanini, exceptionally for the days of 78s, observes the exposition repeat in the first movement). Yet this is a performance which sustains a satisfying power, far more persuasive in rhythm and phrasing than Toscanini's later NBC version.

Szell's is a fine performance in the Toscanini tradition, hard-driven and dramatic. The slow movement is most impressive; the prominence of the trumpet in the great climax may strike some listeners as vulgar, but it cannot be denied that this is an exciting performance, and the final subdued disintegration of the theme is most deeply felt. The digital remastering is very successful: the sound is firm, full and brilliant. The performance of the *Eighth* is also a compelling one. The first-movement repeat is taken and the performance is not over-driven; indeed, the finale is slower than usual, with plenty of consideration for the players' comfort.

Symphony No. 4 in B flat, Op. 60.
(M) ** Sony SMK 46246 [id.]. Marlboro Festival O, Casals – SCHUBERT: *Symphony No. 5.* **(*) ❀

Like his magisterial account of the *Seventh*, Casals's recording of the *Fourth Symphony* comes from the 1969 season at Marlboro. There is a real sense of mystery at the opening and Casals keeps a firm grip on proceedings, with good choice of tempi and finely judged phrasing. As is the case with other Marlboro recordings, the acoustic is dryish and the balance far from perfect, but this is dedicated music-making which has a sense of musical purpose that puts you completely under its spell.

Symphonies Nos. 4 in B flat, Op. 60; 5 in C min., Op. 67.
*** EMI Dig. CDC7 49656-2 [id.]. L. Classical Players, Norrington.
*** O-L Dig. 417 615-2 [id.]. AAM, Hogwood.
(B) *** Pickwick Dig. PCD 869; *CIMPC 869* [id.]. LSO, Wyn Morris.
(M) **(*) Sony MK 42011. Columbia SO, Bruno Walter.
(BB) **(*) ASV Dig. CDQS 6054; *ZCQS 6054*. N. Sinfonia, Richard Hickox.

Symphonies Nos. 4 in B flat, Op. 40; 5 in C min., Op. 67; Egmont: Overture.
(M) **(*) Sony SMK 47516 [id.]. NYPO, Bernstein.

Though the knocking of Fate at the start of the *Fifth* may initially seem perfunctory as Norrington briskly presents it, it is surprising how one adjusts, even by the time the exposition repeat returns, barely a minute later. This coupling of Nos. 4 and 5 – the same as Oiseau-Lyre offers in the rival Hogwood series – shows Norrington at his most refreshing and inspired, relishing his fast speeds, showing how even a fast *Adagio* in the slow movement of No. 4 can flow easefully and lyrically, always finding new detail to bring out, thanks to imaginative use of period instruments. So the woodwind copes with fine clarity in the rapid passage-work of No. 4, and the finale of No. 5 has infectious swagger even at a very fast speed. The sound is up to the high standard of the series, though in the blazing of brass it cannot match the exceptionally vivid Decca recording for Hogwood which, in its extra weight, provides far less of a contrast with traditional performance than the Norrington.

Hogwood's generous coupling of Nos. 4 and 5 brings fresh, lively readings which, with generally fast speeds, present excellent alternative versions for anyone wanting performances on period instruments. Dramatic contrasts are strongly marked, with no feeling of miniaturization, and the clarity of textures is admirable, with natural horns in particular braying out superbly. Vivid sound, set in a believable acoustic.

Wyn Morris's coupling of Nos. 4 and 5 makes a first-rate budget recommendation. He generally adopts speeds close to those of Karajan and, though he cannot match that master in sharpness of focus or pointed intensity, his urgency goes with fine, biting strength, helped by some first-rate playing from the LSO. The sound is bright and slightly abrasive, but with enough body to sustain that. The weight of the readings is enhanced by the observance of all repeats. A bargain.

Bernstein's performance of the *Fourth* has genuine stature. There is a certain loss of mystery at the opening; instead, there is a warmth of anticipation, and the playing soon pulsates with highly disciplined energy. Overall this reading has splendid grip. The *Fifth* is a strong, dramatic reading, not quite as memorable as the *Eroica* but concentrated and vital, with a balancing warmth in the slow movement. The 1961 recording has more ambient depth than usual, which well supports Bernstein's relatively expansive approach to the first movement.

Walter's 1959 reading of the *Fourth* is splendid, the finest achievement of his whole cycle. There is intensity and a feeling of natural vigour which makes itself felt in every bar. All aspects of this symphony are welded together here and show what depths it really contains. Walter's reading of the *Fifth* lacks the kind of nervous tension that distinguishes the finest versions. The finale, taken at a spacious, natural pace, is joyous and sympathetic but fails to convey the ultimate in tension. The digital remastering for CD has left behind a residue of pre-Dolby background hiss, but it is not too distracting.

Richard Hickox's versions of Nos. 4 and 5 receive strong, direct readings, well scaled, with the reverberant recording giving a chamber-sized string-band plenty of body. No. 4 is the more successful, a buoyant performance which has the sharper impact through its full analogue recording. The *Fifth*, in which the digital recording distances the sound, lacks a degree of bite as well as of mystery, but the finale brings a powerful, flamboyant conclusion.

Symphonies Nos. 4 in B flat, Op. 60; 6 in F (Pastoral), Op. 68.
(M) (***) BMG/RCA mono GD 60254 [60254-2-RG]. NBC SO, Toscanini.

Toscanini's reading of the *Pastoral* contradicts one's preconceptions. This was one of his favourite Beethoven symphonies and the first movement in this 1952 performance has a natural, unforced freshness which allows the most delicate shading and persuasive moulding between sections. The second movement flows beautifully, with elegant phrasing and, though the scherzo and *Storm* are fast and intense, the finale brings a fresh, simple manner, not as tender as it might be but still persuasive. No. 4 is more characteristic of the later Toscanini, though the fast, fierce manner in the first movement conveys joyful exuberance, and the slow movement brings fine moulding. The recording is coarser than in the *Pastoral*, with a heavier tape-hiss.

Symphonies Nos. 4 in B flat; 7 in A, Op. 92.
*** Chan. Dig. CHAN 8753 [id.]. CBSO, Weller.

Symphonies Nos. 4 in B flat; 7 in A; King Stephen overture, Op. 117.
(M) *** Sony SBK 48158 [id.]. Cleveland O, Szell.

Szell is at his finest in both symphonies. The 1960s sound is transferred with satisfying weight and immediacy, even if – characteristic of Szell's Severance Hall recordings – pianissimos are not ideally hushed. Along with powerful outer movements, tense and spontaneous-sounding, go exceptional accounts of the slow movements in both symphonies. The radiant violins of the Cleveland Orchestra in the great melody of the *Adagio* in No. 4 are compellingly contrasted with the briefly intrusive tuttis; and in No. 7 Szell makes the second movement a genuine *Allegretto*, taking it almost as fast as a period specialist like Roger Norrington, and with magnetic concentration. Exposition repeats are omitted in both symphonies, but this remains a fine memorial to Szell's work with an orchestra which under him was often counted the finest in the world.

It is surprising that Nos. 4 and 7 are not coupled together more often, when structurally they are so closely related. Each begins with a massive slow introduction, and exceptionally brings a scherzo in A-B-A-B-A form. Weller and the CBSO are at their finest in both works, warm and companionable, giving the impression of live communication. Warm, full recording.

Symphonies Nos. 4 in B flat; 8 in F; Overtures: King Stephen, Op. 117; The Ruins of Athens, Op. 113.
**(*) Nimbus NI 5130 [id.]. Hanover Band, Roy Goodman.

Taken from the Hanover Band's fresh and alert Beethoven cycle on period instruments, this Nimbus coupling brings the substantial bonus of the two rare overtures, equally well done. The sound is reverberant in the characteristic Nimbus manner.

Symphonies Nos. 4; 8 in F (trans. Liszt).
*** Teldec/Warner Dig. 2292 43259-2 [id.]. Cyprien Katsaris (piano).

Simply astonishing! The opening of the finale of the *Eighth Symphony* is an extraordinary feat of articulation. Apart from his dazzling technique, Katsaris has enormous musicianship, a great range of colour and a real sense of scale. It is as if one is encountering this music for the first time.

Symphony No. 5 in C min., Op. 67.
(***) DG Dig. 410 028-2 [id.]. LAPO, Giulini.
(***) DG 415 861-2 [id.]. LAPO, Carlos Kleiber.
**(*) Decca Dig. 430 505-2; *430 505-4* [id.]. VPO, Solti – SHOSTAKOVICH: *Symphony No. 9.* **(*)

Symphony No. 5; Overtures: The Creatures of Prometheus; Egmont.
**(*) Nimbus Dig. NI 5007 [id.]. Hanover Band, Monica Huggett.

Those issues which offer the *Fifth Symphony* either alone or with just an overture as fill-up on premium-priced CD now seem uneconomic. Giulini certainly has the advantage of excellent digital sound, and his performance possesses majesty in abundance and conveys the power and vision of this inexhaustible work, but DG need to withdraw this, add some more music and perhaps bring the price down, too. Carlos Kleiber's electrifying *Fifth* similarly needs coupling, perhaps to his version of the *Seventh* if the combined playing time allows this. It remains an exceptional performance: the gradation of dynamics from the hushed pianissimo at the close of the scherzo to the weight of the great opening statement of the finale has not been heard on disc with such overwhelming effect since Toscanini.

Solti's live recording, taken from a performance given in the Vienna Musikverein in May 1990, provides an illuminating contrast with his earlier studio recordings in Chicago. The first movement is fast and fierce, rather in the manner of the young Solti, while the *Andante* is warm and expansive, and the last two movements bring big-scale, emphatic performances. The Viennese horns sound glorious in the finale. With its unexpected Shostakovich coupling it makes a good supplement to Solti's main recorded oeuvre.

Recorded while Monica Huggett was still directing, the Hanover Band's version of the *Fifth Symphony* is strong and lithe, with the doctrine of period performance imaginatively rather than ruthlessly applied. The Nimbus recording helps in that, full and natural enough to convey the dramatic impact of the outer movements, yet mellow in a church acoustic, although the balance is not entirely convincing.

Symphony No. 5 in C min.; Talk: *'How a great symphony was written'.*
(B) **(*) Sony SXK 47645 [id.]. NYPO, Bernstein.

Before giving his fine 1961 New York performance of the *Fifth*, which if lacking something in intensity is also admirably free of hard-driving neurosis and has unexpectedly full-bodied recording, Bernstein talks (in four languages – separately banded, two to each channel!) a little about the *Andante*, but mostly about the first movement. Using pages from Beethoven's sketchbooks, which he had scored himself, as examples of passages which were rejected by the composer for his final scheme, Bernstein convincingly explains why, most fascinatingly concerning the first movement's coda, which Beethoven thought was too short and then, after he had extended it, finally decided that the initial draft was too long.

Symphonies Nos. 5 in C min.; 6 in F (Pastoral).
(M) **(*) Ph. 434 156-2; *434 156-4* [id.]. Leipzig GO, Kurt Masur.

Symphonies Nos. 5; 7 in A, Op. 92.
(M) *** Decca Dig. 430 701-2; *430 701-4* [id.]. Philh. O, Ashkenazy.
(M) (***) EMI mono CDM7 63868-2 [id.]. Philh. O, Klemperer.
(M) **(*) DG Dig. 435 093-2; *435 093-4* [id.]. VPO, Claudio Abbado.

Symphonies Nos. 5; 8 in F, Op. 93.
(B) *** Ph. 422 474-2. Concg. O, Jochum.
(M) **(*) EMI CDM7 63357-2 [id.]. Philh. O, Klemperer.

Symphonies Nos. 5; 8; Fidelio: overture.
(M) *** DG 419 051-2; *419 051-4* [id.]. BPO, Karajan.

Symphonies Nos. 5; 8; Overture: Leonora No. 3.
(M) (**(*)) BMG/RCA mono GD 60255; [60255-2-RG]. NBC O, Toscanini.

Karajan's 1977 version of the *Fifth* is magnificent in every way, tough and urgently incisive, with fast tempi bringing weight as well as excitement. The recording has satisfying body and a wide dynamic range. The coupling is an electrically intense performance of the *Eighth* plus the *Fidelio overture*.

Ashkenazy's reading of the *Fifth* is urgent and vivid and is notable for its rich, Kingsway Hall recording. Well-adjusted speeds here, with joyful exuberance a fair substitute for grandeur. The reading of the *Seventh* is equally spontaneous, a generally direct performance taken steadily at unexaggerated speeds; the result is glowingly convincing, thanks to fine playing and recording that set new standards in this work, full and spacious yet warmly co-ordinated. This mid-priced digital CD ranks high among records of these two symphonies, especially for those for whom outstanding recording quality is a priority.

Klemperer never surpassed these first EMI interpretations of either symphony. Though the recording is in mono only, both works have a clarity, immediacy and fidelity of balance that enhance electrifying readings, revealing Klemperer at his peak. These are among the finest versions of either symphony ever put on disc, and a generous coupling, too.

Jochum launches into a vigorous reading of the *Fifth*, unmarred by any romantic exaggeration but gripping in a totally natural and unforced way. The *Eighth*, too, is attractively unmannered, satisfyingly paced and superbly played. The sound is extremely good.

Masur's Beethoven has much to recommend it; it is naturally expressive and dramatic without being over forceful. The response of the Leipzig Orchestra is warm and immaculately disciplined and the early 1979s recording fresh and full. Yet neither Masur's *Fifth* nor his *Pastoral* quite matches the finest in the catalogue. The *Fifth* does not have the blazing intensity of Carlos Kleiber, and the latter, although beautifully played, does not eclipse Boehm. However, coupled together they are easy to enjoy, particularly No. 6.

As with the others in his mid-priced series on EMI, Klemperer's stereo renditions of Nos. 5 and 8 bring a clean and natural sound on top, notably in violin tone. The *Fifth* is plainly less electric than his earlier, mono version but, with exposition repeats observed in both outer movements, this retains its epic quality.

Abbado offers a weighty and spacious account of the *Fifth*, with powerful outer movements, but in which the speed for the *Andante* is dangerously slow. It is paired with an electrifying, incandescent performance of the *Seventh*, fresh and rhythmic, and, though the 1987 live recording is not ideally clear on inner detail, the sound is full and atmospheric, whereas in the *Fifth* it is thicker.

Symphony No. 6 in F (Pastoral), Op. 68.
(M) *** DG 413 721-2 (2) [id.]. VPO, Boehm – *Symphony No. 9.* ***
(B) *(*) Decca 433 622-2; *433 622-4*. VPO, Schmidt-Isserstedt.

Symphony No. 6 (Pastoral); Overture: The Consecration of the house.
**(*) Ph. Dig. 416 385-2 [id]. ASMF, Marriner.

Symphonies No. 6 (Pastoral); Overtures: Coriolan; Creatures of Prometheus.
(BB) *** ASV CDQS 6053; *ZCQS 6053*. N. Sinfonia, Richard Hickox.

Symphony No. 6 (Pastoral); Overtures: Coriolan; Egmont.
*** O-L Dig. 421 416-2 [id.]. AAM, Hogwood.

Symphony No. 6 (Pastoral); Overture: The Creatures of Prometheus; (i) *Egmont: Overture; Die Trommel geruhet; Freudvoll und leidvoll; Klarchens Tod, Op. 84.*
(M) *** EMI CDM7 63358-2 [id.]. Philh. O, Klemperer; (i) with Birgit Nilsson.

Symphony No. 6 (Pastoral); Overtures: Egmont; Leonora No. 3.
(M) *** Decca Dig. 430 721-2; *430 721-4* [id.]. Philh. O, Vladimir Ashkenazy.

Symphonies Nos. 6 (Pastoral); 8 in F; King Stephen: Overture.
(M) **(*) Sony SMK 47517 [id.]. NYPO, Bernstein.

Symphony No. 6 (Pastoral); Overture: Leonora No. 2, Op. 72a.
(B) *** Sony MYK 42536 [(d.) MYK 36720]. Columbia SO, Walter.
(B) *** Ph. 426 061-2; *426 061-4* [id.]. Concg. O, Jochum.

Ashkenazy's performance has a beguiling warmth and it communicates readily. With generally spacious tempi, the feeling of lyrical ease and repose is most captivating, thanks to the response of the Philharmonia players and the richness of the recording, made in the Kingsway Hall. After a *Storm* that is civilized rather than frightening, the performance is crowned by a radiant account of the *Shepherds' thanksgiving*. The sound, with its fairly reverberant acoustic, is particularly impressive. The two overtures make a thoroughly satisfactory makeweight.

Boehm's reading of the *Pastoral* has a natural, unforced beauty and is very well played (with strings, woodwind and horns beautifully integrated). It is here coupled with a fine digital version of the *Choral Symphony* on a pair of mid-priced discs.

Bruno Walter's recording dates from the beginning of the 1960s. It is an affectionate and completely integrated performance from a master who thought and lived the work all his life. The sound is beautifully balanced, with sweet strings and clear, glowing woodwind, and the bass response is firm and full. The quality is very slightly shallower in the *Overture Leonora No. 2* which opens the disc.

Hickox directs a persuasively paced reading, with a small orchestra used to give a performance of high contrasts, intimate in the lighter textures, as at the start, and elegant in the slow movement, but expanding dramatically in the tuttis, as in the *Storm*, while the finale, fresh and pure, brings a glowing climax. With warm, analogue recording giving a fine sense of presence, this is one of the best of the Hickox Beethoven series. The two *Overtures* come in vigorously dramatic readings.

Klemperer's account of the *Pastoral* is one of the very finest of all his records. The scherzo may be eccentrically slow but, with superbly dancing rhythms, it could not be more bucolic, and it falls naturally into place within the reading as a whole. The exquisitely phrased slow movement and the final *Shepherds' hymn* bring peaks of beauty, made the more intense by the fine digital transfer, reinforcing the clarity and balance of the original sound, with violin tone amazingly fresh and clean for 1958, although thinner than we would expect today. The *Egmont* music follows the *Symphony*, an unusual but valuable coupling with Nilsson in her prime, unexpectedly but effectively cast in the two simple songs, the first made to sound almost Mahlerian. The CD also offers the *Creatures of Prometheus overture*.

Although he chooses a joyfully buoyant tempo for the opening movement, Bernstein (as usual in Beethoven) is admirably free of undue expressive vehemence in his 1963 *Pastoral* and he finds a balancing element of repose in the slow movement, which flows most warmly. At the same time there is not the subtlety or richness of detail that one finds in, say, the Boehm reading. The recording is fuller than usual in this series. By contrast, the brightly lit *Eighth* is given tremendous sweep and power; indeed Bernstein has something of the breadth and urgency that inform Carlos Kleiber's Beethoven. Tempi are admittedly on the brisk side, and the work gains in tautness and concentration as a result. The overture was recorded later, in 1966.

Jochum's Philips recording of the *Pastoral* is primarily a leisurely reading, the countryside relaxing in the sunshine. With beautiful playing from the Concertgebouw Orchestra, the reading is sustained without a hint of lethargy.

The clarity and vivid sense of presence in Hogwood's period performance of the *Pastoral* go with fresh, resilient playing from the Academy of Ancient Music. As in this conductor's earlier Beethoven recordings, the extra detail is presented without fussiness, and the sense of live rather than canned performance reflects Hogwood's ever-increasing assurance in this repertory. The *Storm* comes over with particular excitement, thanks to the clarity of texture, with piccolo and dry-toned timpani cutting through superbly. Altogether this is far preferable to Norrington's version, coupled with No. 1 (EMI CDC7 49746-2). The *Overtures* too – not a generous coupling by today's standards, but more than many old LPs provided – bring similarly invigorating performances.

Marriner's view of the *Pastoral* is genial, with a relaxed account of the first movement leading to an unusually spacious reading of the *Scene by the brook*, and with the *Shepherds' thanksgiving* mingling joy and elegance. There are more powerful and individual performances but, beautifully played and recorded, it is a happy reading, well coupled – if not generously – with the still under-appreciated *Consecration of the house overture*.

The *Pastoral* was the one disappointment in Schmidt-Isserstedt's late-1960s cycle with the VPO. There is a lack of atmosphere and warmth, evident in the approach rather than the playing, and certainly an absence of charm, while the somewhat overbright violin sheen in the remastered recording does not help. The *Eighth* is a much stronger performance which also sounds fuller. The first-movement exposition repeat is included and the tempo, slightly slower than normal, emphasizes the symphonic argument. There is a crisp, light *Allegretto* and a Minuet more heavily pointed than usual, with a Brahmsian touch in the Trio. But one wishes Decca had retained the original coupling with the very successful *Fifth Symphony*.

Symphonies Nos. 6 in F (Pastoral), Op. 68; 8 in F, Op. 93.
(M) *** EMI Dig. CDD7 63891-2 [id.]. LPO, Tennstedt.
***Chan. Dig. CHAN 8754 [id.]. CBSO, Walter Weller.

Tennstedt's fresh, alert and imaginative performance of the *Pastoral* comes in a generous coupling with the *Eighth*, given an equally enjoyable reading in which the second-movement *Allegretto* at a fast speed is made into a scherzo while the Minuet is spaciously lyrical. In the *Pastoral*, the slow movement brings a finely moulded performance from Tennstedt, a dramatic account of the *Storm* and a radiant reading of the finale. Well-balanced recording, bright and fresh. If the coupling is suitable, this is strongly recommendable.

Weller directs a glowing, amiable account of the *Pastoral*, one of the most treasurable performances in his cycle. The first three movements are very relaxed; the *Storm*, even more than usual, then provides an electrifying contrast, with the finale bringing the most joyous apotheosis, with the violins of the CBSO playing with heady sweetness. The *Eighth* is relatively weighty, with broad speeds underlining the symphonic strength in the outer movements, contrasted with easy-going accounts of the *Allegretto* and Minuet. Warmly atmospheric recording.

Symphony No. 7 in A, Op. 92.
(**(*)) DG 415 862-2 [id.]. VPO, Carlos Kleiber.
(**) Decca mono 425 987-2 [id.]. Concg. O, Erich Kleiber – MOZART: *Symphony No. 40* (*).

Symphony No. 7; Overtures: Coriolan; Creatures of Prometheus; Egmont.
(B) *** DG 429 509-2; *429 509-4* [id.]. VPO, Boehm.

Symphony No. 7; Overture: The Creatures of Prometheus.
(M) *** EMI CDM7 69183-2 [id.]; *EG 769183-4*. Philh. O, Klemperer.

Symphony No. 7; (i) *The Ruins of Athens (Overture and incidental music), Op. 113.*
(M) *** EMI CDM7 69871-2. RPO, Beecham; (i) with Beecham Choral Soc.

Symphony No. 7; Wellington's victory (Battle Symphony), Op. 92.
**(*) Ph. Dig. 426 239-2 [id.]. ASMF, Marriner.

Symphonies Nos. 7; 8 in F, Op. 93.
*** DG Dig. 423 364-2 [id.]. VPO, Abbado.
**(*) O-L Dig. 425 695-2 [id.]. AAM, Hogwood.
(B) **(*) Pickwick Dig. PCD 917; *CIMPC 917* [id.]. LSO, Wyn Morris.

Symphonies Nos. 7 in A, Op. 92; 8 in F, Op. 93; The Creatures of Prometheus: Overture.
(**(*)) Music Memoria/Scott Butler mono 30269 [id.]. VPO, Weingartner.

Klemperer's 1955 recording of the *Seventh* is among his very finest Beethoven interpretations on disc, and it sounds all the more vivid and full of presence in the stereo version, issued for the first time. Speeds are consistently faster, the tension more electric, with phrasing moulded more subtly, than in the later Philharmonia version. Though the later recording carries extra weight with its wider range, the 1955 sound is very acceptable, with good inner detail. The 1959 *Prometheus* is not a generous makeweight.

The *Seventh* has always been a favourite symphony with Abbado, and the main allegro of the first movement is beautifully judged at a fastish speed, which is yet made resilient. Similarly, the finale blazes fearlessly but never becomes a gabble and, though the live recording is not ideally clear on inner detail, the sound is full and atmospheric, as it also is in the *Eighth* which, with such weight, is instantly established as more than a little symphony. As in the *Seventh*, speeds are beautifully judged, and the tensions of a live occasion are vividly conveyed, as they were not in the first issues of the series. A splendid coupling.

With sforzandos sharply accented and rhythms lightly sprung, Norrington is at his finest in the *Seventh*. Even when he adopts characteristically fast speeds in obedience to Beethoven's metronome markings – as in the second-movement *Allegretto* – he finds time for detail and fine moulding of phrase. The recording is warm, but not ideally clear on inner detail. The *Overtures* are given performances of comparable point.

Once again strong reservations have to be expressed about the CDs offering only a single symphony, without coupling, which have become uncompetitive at premium price in the current marketplace. Carlos Kleiber's DG version dates back to 1976, but the digital remastering has improved the sound and this is an incisively dramatic reading, marked with sharp dynamic contrasts and thrustful rhythms. Like his father, Kleiber maintains the pizzicato for the strings on the final brief phrase of the *Allegretto*, a curious effect.

Hogwood gives clean performances of both *Symphonies*, well played and recorded, but rhythmically a degree less resilient than those of his direct period-performance rivals. In the *Seventh* in particular, that brings moments of stodginess; but they are hardly serious enough to undermine a recommendation for those who want this particular coupling on period instruments.

Boehm's 1972 recording with the VPO is excellent, full and fresh, and the whole performance has lift and spontaneity. Boehm's direct style is most satisfying: full of impetus, yet with plenty of weight. The overtures go well too, especially *Egmont*.

Beecham's 1959 *Seventh* is one of the briskest accounts of the symphony ever, yet the result is exhilarating. Only the slow movement reverts to old-fashioned slow manners in what is in effect an *Andante* rather than an *Allegretto*, but Beecham's rhythmic sense and care for phrasing still avoid heaviness. The fill-up of incidental music makes a valuable and enjoyable rarity. However, the recording of the *Symphony* is also available in EMI's 'Armchair concert' series (CDM7 64446-2), more generously coupled with Brahms's *Academic festival overture* and Mozart's *Clarinet concerto* (Jack Brymer) – see our Concerts section, below.

Weingartner's 1936 record of the *Seventh* is of a less high voltage than his earlier, RPO account but has a wonderfully natural feel about it. While listening to these performances one soon comes to believe that this is the voice of Beethoven in much the same way as one does about Schnabel's late sonatas. There are sonic limitations, and side-joins are not always expert: a couple of beats are added in the middle of the first movement of No. 8. However, the insights Weingartner brought to this music were special and his selfless classical view of both symphonies still retains its allure.

Marriner's crisp and well-sprung reading of No. 7 – though with a slow, rather dull *Allegretto* – comes in coupling with a delightful squib, an inspired recording of the *Battle Symphony*. This starts, not with music, but with the sounds of nature (recorded not on the battlefield of Vittoria in Spain but at Waterloo in Belgium), and then you hear the respective armies arriving, together with their anthems. Sonically, it is a *tour de force* – which is a help with a work not among Beethoven's most inspired. Marriner and the ASMF give an exemplary account of music which presents surprising difficulties in performance. Vivid sound.

Wyn Morris directs strong, spontaneous-sounding readings of both *Symphonies*, not always as refined in execution as the finest, but superbly recorded. Though there are some distracting fluctuations of speed, Morris draws consistently resilient playing from the LSO, a vital quality in these two works written in parallel, with No. 8 becoming, like No. 7, an apotheosis of the dance.

Erich Kleiber's eminently taut recording of the *Seventh Symphony* with the Concertgebouw Orchestra was made in 1950. It is a performance of some stature, very classical and with a strong sense of line, even if it is not of the calibre of his *Eroica* or *Pastoral*. In the 1950s *The Record Guide* spoke well of the performance but did not give the recording its highest rating, and it must be conceded that it sounds even thinner and edgier in the CD transfer.

Symphony No. 7 (trans. Liszt).
**(*) Teldec/Warner Dig. 2292 43065-2 [id.]. Cyprien Katsaris (with SCHUMANN: *Exercises on Beethoven's Seventh Symphony* **).
(*) Nimbus NI 5013 [id.]. Ronald Smith (with BACH/BUSONI: *Chaconne* *).

Cyprien Katsaris does wonders in translating Liszt's transcription into orchestral terms. His is very clean, precise playing, often powerful, with textures commendably clear and with generally steady, unexceptionable tempi. The *Schumann Exercises* make an apt if hardly inspiring fill-up, based on the main theme of the symphony's *Allegretto*. But the symphony is another matter, providing an unexpectedly illuminating listening experience. The sound is excellent.

Ronald Smith, much more than Katsaris, turns the Liszt transcription into a pianistic essay, treating the music with more expressive freedom, often more seductively. He is daring in the *Presto scherzo*, then unexpectedly light and easy in the finale, with an attractive spring in the rhythm. The performance is not technically flawless but here, and even more in the superb Bach–Busoni transcription, he consistently plays with virtuosic flair. The reverberant recording is pleasantly atmospheric, but not every note is clear.

Symphony No. 8 in F, Op. 93.
(M) (***) EMI mono CDM7 63398-2 [id.]. RPO, Beecham – MENDELSSOHN: *Symphony No. 4;* SCHUBERT: *Symphony No. 8.* (***)

Symphony No. 8; Overtures: Coriolan; Fidelio; Leonora No. 3.
**(*) DG Dig. 415 507-2 [id.]. BPO, Karajan.

Beecham loved the *Eighth*, as this characteristic reading makes plain. Speeds tend to be on the relaxed side, but Beecham's rhythmic spring never lets them drag. Such moments as the entry of the recapitulation in the first movement at the very culmination of the development have the thrill of first discovery, and the delicate pointing of that movement's gentle pay-off is very Beechamesque. The mono recording does not help the strings to sound very sweet, but this EMI transfer is far clearer than ever the original LPs were.

Karajan's more relaxed view of the *Eighth* (compared with his 1977 Berlin version) is almost always pure gain. Nevertheless, Karajan's is a massive view of what has often been dubbed Beethoven's 'little symphony', taking it well into the powerful world of the nineteenth century, with fierceness part of the mixture in the outer movements. The three overtures are made massively Olympian too, with *Coriolan* especially impressive. The recording is marginally brighter and clearer than in most of the series, though there is still some congestion in fortissimos.

Symphony No. 9 in D min. (Choral), Op. 125.
(M) *** EMI Dig. CD-EMX 2186; *TC-EMX 2186*. Joan Rodgers, Della Jones, Peter Bronder, Bryn Terfel, RLPO Ch. & O, Sir Charles Mackerras.
(M) *** DG 415 832-2; *415 832-4* [id.]. Tomowa-Sintow, Baltsa, Schreier, Van Dam, V. Singverein, BPO, Karajan.
*** DG 429 861-2 [id.]. Anderson, Walker, König, Rootering, various Chs., Bav. RSO, Dresden State O, etc., Bernstein.
(BB) *** ASV CDQS 6069; *ZCQS 6069* [id.]. Harper, Hodgson, Tear, Howell, Sinfonia Ch., LSO Ch. (members), N. Sinfonia, Hickox.
(M) *** Decca 430 438-2; *430 438-4* [id.]. Lorengar, Minton, Burrows, Talvela, Chicago Ch. & SO, Solti.
(B) *** Ph. 422 464-2; *422 464-4* [id.]. Rebmann, Reynolds, de Ridder, Feldhoff, Netherlands R. Ch., Concg. O, Jochum.
(B) *** EMI CDZ7 67256-2; *LZ 767256-4*. Armstrong, Reynolds, Tear, Shirley-Quirk, LSO Ch., LSO, Giulini.
*** O-L Dig. 425 517-2 [id.]. Augér, Robbin, Rolfe Johnson, Reinhart, LSO Ch., AAM, Hogwood.
(M) *** DG 431 026-2; *431 026-4* [id.]. Gwyneth Jones, Schwarz, Kollo, Moll, V. State Op. Ch., VPO, Bernstein.
*** Chan. Dig. CHAN 8750 [id.]. Barstow, Finnie, Rendall, Tomlinson, CBSO Ch., CBSO, Weller.
(M) *** DG Dig. 427 802-2; *427 802-4* [id.]. Norman, Fassbaender, Domingo, Berry, Concert Singers of V. State Op., VPO, Boehm.
(M) *** DG Dig. 413 721-2 (2) [id.]. Norman, Fassbaender, Domingo, Berry, Concert Singers of V. State Op., VPO, Boehm – *Symphony No. 6.* ***
(B) *** Decca 433 617-2; *433 617-4* [id.]. Sutherland, Horne, King, Talvela, V. State Op. Ch., VPO, Schmidt-Isserstedt.

(BB) *** Pickwick (Decca) PWK 1150. Sutherland, Procter, Dermota, Arnold van Mill, Brassus Ch., Ch. Vaudoise, SRO, Ansermet.
**(*) Decca Dig. 417 800-2 [id.]. Norman, Runkel, Schunk, Sotin, Chicago Ch. & SO, Solti.
**(*) DG Dig. 410 987-2 [id.]. Perry, Baltsa, Cole, Van Dam, V. Singverein, BPO, Karajan.
**(*) EMI Dig. CDC7 49221-2 [id.]. Kenny, Walker, Power, Salomaa, L. Schutz Ch., L. Classical Players, Norrington.
**(*) Nimbus Dig. NI 5134 [id.]. Harrhy, Bailey, Murgatroyd, George, Oslo Cathedral Ch., Hanover Band, Goodman.
(M) (***) EMI mono CDH7 69801-2 [id.]. Schwarzkopf, Höngen, Hopf, Edelmann, Bayreuth Festival Ch. & O, Furtwängler.
(M) (**(*)) BMG/RCA mono GD 60256; [60256-2-RG]. Farrell, Merriman, Peerce, Scott, Shaw Ch., NBC O, Toscanini.

Symphony No. 9 (Choral); Overture: Coriolan.
(M) *** DG 435 095-2; *435 095-2* [id.]. Janowitz, Rössel-Majdan, Kmentt, Berry, V. Singverein, BPO, Karajan.

Symphony No. 9 (Choral); Overture Fidelio, Op. 72b.
(M) **(*) Sony SMK 47518 [id.]. Arroyo, Sarfaty, Di Virgilio, Scott, Juilliard Ch., NYPO, Bernstein.
(M) **(*) Sony SBK 46533 [id.]; *40-46533*. Addison, Hobson, Lewis, Bell, Cleveland O Ch. & O, Szell.

Sir Charles Mackerras conducts the Royal Liverpool Philharmonic in an exceptional, inspired account of the *Ninth*, one which – more than any other with a traditional symphony orchestra – has learnt from the lessons of period performance. Articulation is light and clean, vibrato is used sparingly, making textures unusually clear; and, like Roger Norrington, Sir Charles has taken careful note of Beethoven's controversial metronome markings. However, he does not apply them quite so strictly, so that, though the great *Adagio* slow movement flows relatively quickly, the speed still allows tenderly expressive lyricism, while the drum-and-fife episode of the finale becomes a swinging march and does not sag, as Norrington's very slow (full-price) account does. The recording is among the very finest ever given to this symphony, warm yet transparent and with plenty of body; and the singing in the finale is splendid, even if the tenor, Peter Bronder, is on the strenuous side. The other soloists are outstanding, not least the bass, Bryn Terfel, who delivers a gloriously resonant account of his first entry, *O Freunde, nicht diese Töne*. Anyone wanting a refreshingly different version of the *Ninth*, which yet brings all the dramatic power and intensity of a more conventional reading, need not hesitate.

Of the three stereo recordings Karajan has made of the *Ninth*, his 1977 account (415 832-2/*4*) is the most inspired in its insight, above all in the *Adagio*, where he conveys spiritual intensity at a slower tempo than in his earlier, 1962 version (435 095-2/*4*) and more searchingly than in the later, digital recording, where the effect is more lyrical in its beauty. In the finale, the concluding eruption has an animal excitement rarely heard from this highly controlled conductor. The soloists make an excellent team, with contralto, tenor and bass all finer than their predecessors and the soprano markedly more secure than her successor in 1985. The sound has tingling projection and drama. Though Karajan's 1962 version is less hushed and serene in the slow movement, the finale blazes even more intensely, with Janowitz's contribution radiant in its purity. The disc opens with the fine 1965 recording of *Coriolan*, rather fuller in sound than the symphony.

Recorded live on the morning of Christmas Day 1989, Bernstein's Berlin version may have been issued to commemorate a particular occasion of celebration, but it is far more than just a memento of a historic event, the destruction of the Berlin Wall. It brings a performance that has something special to say, even after all the many recordings of this work, and not only because Bernstein substitutes the word '*Freiheit*', 'Freedom', for '*Freude*' in the choral finale, something of which Beethoven himself might well have approved. The ensemble may have the odd blemish, and noises from the audience and other sources – not least from the conductor in his more balletic movements – intrude at times; but, at speeds far more spacious than in his previous recordings, and notably in a dedicated account of the slow movement, the tensions of a live occasion are thrillingly conveyed. The orchestra, drawn mainly from Germany, both East and West, the Bavarian RSO and Dresden Staatskapelle, also included members of the Kirov Theatre Orchestra in Leningrad, the New York Philharmonic, the Orchestre de Paris and the LSO. The choirs similarly came from East and West Germany, while the soloists represented four countries: America (June Anderson), Britain (Sarah Walker), Germany (Klaus König) and Holland (Jan-Hendrik Rootering). Rootering above all makes a splendid impact in his '*Freiheit*' solo, helped by amazingly vivid sound, with the chorus full-bodied to achieve a thrilling culmination. For many, the uniqueness of this version and the emotions it conveys will make it a first choice, despite obvious flaws.

Hickox's performance, using an orchestra of the size Beethoven originally had, brings some of the advantages of period performance: clarity of articulation and texture; otherwise one might not realize that the string band is any smaller than one on a regular recording of the *Ninth*. In his pacing throughout the work, Hickox is unerring and conveys from first to last the tension of a genuine performance, in a way that some of his rivals among international stars do not manage. This is the most successful issue in his Beethoven series for ASV. The performance culminates in a glowing account of the choral finale with four excellent soloists. The sole reservation one has is that, in a reverberant acoustic, the slight distancing of the players and chorus gets in the way of full expansion on crescendos. In the performance there is no lack of power at all. At super-bargain price this is very competitive indeed.

If you regard the sublime slow movement as the key to this epic work, then Solti is clearly with you in his earlier, analogue version. With spacious, measured tempi he leads the ear on, not only with his phrasing but also with his subtle shading of dynamic down to whispered pianissimo. Here is *Innigkeit* of a concentration rarely heard on record, even in the *Ninth*. Solti in the first movement is searing in his dynamic contrasts – maybe too brutally so – while the precision of the finale, with superb choral work and solo singing, confirms this as one of the finest *Ninths* on CD.

Jochum's 1969 version makes an excellent recommendation, powerfully conducted and intense, beautifully played with exceptionally crisp wind articulation and with the glory of the Concertgebouw string-tone well caught by the recording despite obvious signs of age. There is a demonic quality in Jochum's reading. That quality is strongly set against a rapt and spacious account of the slow movement and a reading of the finale which underlines the joy of the writing. Soloists are a clear and fresh team and the chorus is powerful and responsive. The sound has good presence and clarity, though lacking a little in body.

Giulini's reading is positively affected by the recording acoustic, close, immediate and rich. His tempo in the first movement is unusually slow – like Solti (see below) he insists on precise sextuplets for the opening tremolendo, with no mistiness – and he builds the architecture relentlessly, finding his resolution only in the concluding coda. The scherzo is lithe and powerful with shattering timpani. The slow movement is warm and Elysian rather than hushed, while the finale, not always quite perfect in ensemble is dedicatedly intense, with fine contributions from the soloists. The remastering for CD is very successful indeed, giving a full-bodied presence to the choir and this is among the very finest of the bargain versions.

Hogwood with his period forces is very well recorded. The ensemble is clear and well balanced both in the instrumental movements and in the choral finale, where an apt scale is achieved, neither too large nor too small. Like his direct rivals among period performers, Hogwood has taken close note of Beethoven's controversial metronome markings; so it is that the first and third movements are faster than usual, the second and fourth generally slower. But Hogwood's manner is not too rigorous and he scores significantly over his direct rivals, not just in the sound-quality but in the quality of solo and choral singing. Though rhythms are not always ideally resilient, this is the most recommendable period performance of the *Ninth* currently available.

Bernstein, as in the rest of his live Vienna cycle, directs a powerful and distinctive reading of the *Ninth*. The very start conveys immediate electricity, the scherzo is resilient, the *Adagio* deeply convincing in its distinctive contrasting of inner meditation with lighter, more carefree interludes. Though in the choral finale Gwyneth Jones has her raw moments, overall it is a superb account, sung and played with dedication. The recording is among the finest in the series, given extra space and presence in the CD transfer.

For his New York *Choral Symphony*, recorded in 1964, Bernstein moved to the Avery Fisher Hall – with generally impressive results. The recording here shows a remarkable improvement over its last LP incarnation, with a notably clean choral focus. Bernstein's first movement is finely shaped and has genuine breadth and eloquence. Then comes a scherzo where the Trio must be the fastest on record – at least until Benjamin Zander's fascinating account, which uses what he believes to be Beethoven's true tempi indications. Obviously Bernstein instinctively agreed with him, and the result sparkles refreshingly. The slow movement has considerable warmth but not quite enough inwardness and repose; the finale is often intense and dramatic, with some fine contributions from the soloists and chorus. Not a first choice, but not an account to be ignored.

In Weller's reading, the choral finale explodes in joy, with John Tomlinson firm and commanding in his opening solo. The tenor, David Rendall, is a shade tremulous and the soprano, Josephine Barstow, cannot sing gently in her highest register; but all the soloists are responsive and intelligent. The Birmingham Chorus, trained by another talented conductor, Simon Halsey, is superb, and the balance between voices and orchestra is among the most natural yet. Weller gives positive, well-sprung readings of the first three movements. The first and third may lack something in mystery, the one full and strong rather than cataclysmic, the other sweet and easily lyrical; but, helped by rich recording quality with an impressively wide range, this is one of the most satisfying of the modern digital versions.

As bitingly dramatic as Toscanini in the first movement and electrically intense all through, Szell directs a magnetic, seemingly inevitable account of the *Ninth* which demonstrates the glories of the Cleveland Orchestra. With speeds never as extreme as Toscanini's, he yet captures a comparable fire. The chorus sings with similarly knife-edged ensemble, set behind the orchestra but not too distantly. At mid-price a first-rate recommendation for those wanting a commanding reminder of a great conductor's work. The performance of the *Fidelio* overture is electrifying.

Karl Boehm's reading is spacious and powerful, and in its broad concept it has much in common with Klemperer's version. Yet overall there is a transcendent sense of a great occasion; the concentration is unfailing, reaching its peak in the glorious finale, where ruggedness and strength well over into inspiration. With a fine, characterful team of soloists and a freshly incisive chorus formed from singers of the Vienna State Opera, this is strongly recommendable. It is available separately at mid-price, and also coupled to another outstanding Boehm recording – of the *Pastoral Symphony*.

Schmidt-Isserstedt, with no exaggeration and few if any high-flown purple patches, gives a most satisfying reading of the *Ninth* to act as a suitable culmination for his impressive cycle from the late 1960s. It is the fine singing of soloists and chorus in the finale that above all makes this one of the keenest recommendations in the bargain range. All four soloists are on peak form and few rival versions match the beauty and balance of ensemble. The recording quality is outstanding for its period (1965).

Ansermet's 1965 recording of the *Choral Symphony* was one of the first successful stereo versions to appear on a single LP. Ansermet was inspired beyond his usual achievement by the greatest challenge of all in Beethoven, helped by a fine group of soloists and incisive choral singing. In the first two movements he is clear-cut and rhythmically precise (though by no means inflexible), and the slow movement, if not wearing its heart on its sleeve, certainly does not lack expressive feeling. The finale is strong and exciting, with the quality of the recording telling, even if, like the first movement, it lacks some weight (as did the original LP).

The spaciousness of Solti's reading, with unusually slow basic speeds in the first and third movements, has remained constant in his digital version, with basic tempi even a fraction slower than before. The biting drama of the first movement and the resonant lyricism of the third are as intense as ever, though lines are now sculpted a shade more carefully. The choral finale is exuberant, with fine solo singing led by the dominant Jessye Norman. It is a pity that with rather backward balance the glowing contribution of the Chicago Symphony Chorus is not more sharply focused; otherwise, the sound is of excellent Chicago vintage, bright and full.

The high point of Karajan's digital version of the *Ninth* is the sublime slow movement, here exceptionally sweet and true, with the lyricism all the more persuasive in a performance recorded in a complete take. The power and dynamism of the first two movements are striking too, but the choral finale is flawed above all by the singing of the soprano, Janet Perry, far too thin of tone and unreliable. The sound of the choir has plenty of body but is rather ill-defined.

Much of the sharp intensity and exhilaration of Norrington's reading of the *Ninth* comes over on his record, with many of his contentions over observing Beethoven's fast metronome markings validated in the success of the performance. What has to remain controversial is the slow movement which, at tempi far swifter than we are used to, becomes a sweet interlude rather than a meditation, far shorter than the other movements. A more serious snag is the contribution of the male soloists. Petteri Salomaa's tremulous, aspirated singing on the command '*Nicht diese Töne*' is painful, while Patrick Power's plaintive tenor timbre goes with a very slow pace for the drum-and-fife march passage. Nevertheless, the impact of the whole performance is considerable, with reverberant recording still allowing the bite of timpani and valveless horns to cut through the texture. In no sense, except in the number of performers involved, is this a small-scale performance, rather an intensely refreshing view of a supreme masterpiece.

Goodman's reading of the *Ninth* is just as refreshing and even more sympathetic than Roger Norrington's mould-breaking rival version on period instruments. Like the rest of the set, the performances convey a sense of spontaneity. Though – like Norrington on EMI – Goodman broadly follows Beethoven's controversial metronome markings – very fast in the slow movement, with some of the *allegros* in the finale unusually slow – he applies the doctrine less ruthlessly. Though the slow movement flows along very briskly, he introduces a degree of easing which conveys necessary gravity, a sense of repose. His springing of rhythm in the 6/4 section of the finale is then rather more winning than in Norrington's version, and the soloists have fewer flaws. With characteristically reverberant Nimbus recording, generally undistracting, it makes an attractive recommendation overall, quite apart from its authenticity of approach.

It is thrilling to have a CD transfer of the historic recording made at the re-opening of the Festspielhaus in Bayreuth in 1951. The chorus may sound washy in the distance, almost as though placed at the bottom of the Rhine, and the lack of perspective in the mono sound is brought out the more on CD (along with audience noises), but the extra clarity and freshness impressively enhance a reading without parallel. The spacious, lovingly moulded account of the slow movement is among Furtwängler's finest achievements on record and, with an excellent quartet of soloists, the finale crowns a great performance.

Toscanini's electrifying account of the *Ninth* is marred somewhat by the excessive treble emphasis, more noticeable than on the earlier, full-priced reissue.

Symphony No. 9 in D min. (Choral) (new version, conjecturally using Beethoven's intended metronome markings).
(M) **(*) Pickwick Dig. MCD 40; *MCC 40* [id.]. Labelle, Fortunato, Cresswell, Arnold, Pro Musica Ch., Boston PO, Benjamin Zander.

Benjamin Zander is deeply concerned with authenticity, but, unlike Norrington, Hogwood and Harnoncourt, the sound of original instruments does not stir his passions; his concern is with correct tempi. He has already given us a revelatory recording of Stravinsky's *Rite of spring*, where he made a convincing case for a much faster tempo for the final, sacrificial dance. Now he turns his attention to the *Choral Symphony*. His extensive research, over a period of years, on Beethoven's metronome markings has already been acknowledged by Roger Norrington in his version of this work, but Zander believes that Norrington does not go far enough. The question all hinges on Beethoven's communication of the critical tempi indications to his publisher, which were not conveyed directly but through the composer's nephew, Karl. Zander argues that in certain instances Karl misunderstood his uncle's intentions, and the result has perpetuated a tradition of performance that is wholly incorrect. Zander argues his case convincingly and in depth in the booklet which accompanies this extraordinarily 'different' recorded performance. It is sufficient therefore to indicate the most controversial changes. The very quick pacing for the Trio of the Scherzo had been suggested earlier by Stravinsky, acting intuitively rather than because of any documentary research, and it has already been approximated by Bernstein in his New York recording. But the other two principal differences are even more revolutionary. Taken at Zander's much faster tempo, the character of the slow movement is totally altered, becoming altogether lighter in emotional feeling and much nearer that of the *Pastoral Symphony*. The other change concerns the piquant *Alla marcia* section of the finale. The composer's marking is *Allegro assai vivace*, which conflicts in spirit with the pacing adopted by almost every traditional performance. Zander virtually doubles that tempo, arguing that the exultant words of the tenor solo, 'As joyously his suns fly across the glorious landscape of the heavens', fit this exuberant pacing. Moreover, when it is adopted there is no need for any accelerando either during this part of the work or in the fugato that follows. When the chorus re-enters overwhelmingly with '*Freude, schöner Götterfunken*', the theme is now only slightly faster than when it was first heard.

Zander provides a vibrant account of the *Symphony* to illustrate his ideas, and the very well-rehearsed Boston Philharmonic Orchestra (a dedicated ensemble, part professional, part amateur) make a strong impression in a reading that is nothing if not full of conviction. In the finale the soloists are very good (there are many groups of starrier names on record that do not sing so well) and the chorus is resplendent in its fervour. The recording could be cleaner in its focus but is fully acceptable and rises to the occasion in the last movement. There is no record of the *Choral Symphony* more generously cued, and each cue is linked both to Zander's accompanying essay and to the Breikopf score. You may not like everything in this performance

– the first hearing of the *Adagio* is a distinct culture-shock – and you may not agree with Zander's conclusions, but you cannot ignore either. For ears not too overwhelmed by tradition, once one adjusts, the slow movement sounds uncommonly fresh presented this way, although perhaps the playing might have been just a little more flexible in pacing the movement's closing section.

Symphony No. 9 (trans. Liszt).
**(*) Teldec/Warner Dig. 2292 42985-2 [id.]. Cyprien Katsaris (piano).

Liszt made no attempt to create pianistically 'effective' arrangements, yet in his transcription of the *Ninth Symphony* he conveys so much of the character of an orchestra storming the heavens. Cyprien Katsaris's performance is nothing short of a *tour de force*: his virtuosity is altogether remarkable and there is a demonic Beethovenian vehemence and drive. He must have as many hands as an octopus has tentacles, for his ability to convey the teeming activity of the finale, to bring various strands to the foreground and then disappear into the mêlée, is astonishing. The piano is closely observed in a reverberant acoustic ambience and listeners may at times be disturbed by its somewhat jangly quality.

Symphony No. 10 in E flat: 1st movement (realized and completed by Dr Barry Cooper – includes lecture by Dr Cooper).
(B) *** Pickwick Dig. PCD 911; *CIMPC 911* [id.]. LSO, Wyn Morris.

As re-created from Beethoven's sketches by Dr Barry Cooper, this movement from what was planned as the *Tenth Symphony* is, as Dr Cooper says, no more than an 'artist's impression'. What he has put together from those and other sketch sources makes a fascinating and satisfying symphonic concept: a noble slow movement in E flat with obvious echoes of the *Ninth Symphony*, in the centre of which is a compressed *Allegro* sonata-form movement in C minor, the whole lasting almost 20 minutes. The broad *Andante* sections with their *Ninth*-like descants to the *Pathétique*-like main theme are plausibly Beethovenian. What is far less convincing is the *Allegro*, based as it is on relatively feeble material, with conventional working-out but with one or two surprising strokes culled from the sketches which, for all their oddity, must be counted Beethovenian. The master would have moulded this into something far greater, but it is well worth hearing music that so dwells in the mind.

Wyn Morris in this first recording directs a broad, strong reading, very well played and recorded. Dr Cooper's half-hour lecture fascinatingly amplifies and illustrates his detailed notes, making clear his scholarly credentials as well as his devotion to Beethoven's plan.

Wellington's victory (Battle symphony), Op. 91.
** Telarc Dig. CD 80079 [id.]. Cincinnati SO, Kunzel – LISZT: *Hunnenschlacht.* **

With a characteristically natural overall sound-balance, Kunzel's Telarc recording is technically the most sophisticated presentation of Beethoven's 'Battle' Symphony on record, though the real musketry and cannon featured in the recording sound curiously like a fireworks display. The performance is musically conceived and well played, but has no special individuality. By far the most successful recording of *Wellington's victory* is Marriner's version, coupled with *Symphony No. 7* (see above).

CHAMBER MUSIC

Allegro and minuet in G for 2 flutes; Serenade (arr. for flute and piano), *Op. 41; Sonata in B flat* (for flute & piano); *6 Themes and variations for flute and piano, Op. 105; 10 Themes and variations for flute and piano, Op. 107; Trio in G for 3 flutes; Trio concertante in G, for flute, bassoon and piano.*
(B) *** VoxBox (2) [CDX 5000]. Rampal, Larde, Veyron-Lacroix.

The VoxBox sensibly gathers together all Beethoven's music featuring the solo flute, and, if the *Sonata in B flat* is almost certainly spurious, it is pleasing enough. The *Serenade* is offered in a transcription by other hands (perhaps those of Franz Xaver Kleinheinz), which Beethoven himself revised. With Rampal showing polish and finesse as well as vivacity, well partnered by Robert Veyron-Lacroix, it is very enjoyable here. The *Themes and variations* are an offshoot of Beethoven's arrangements of British folksongs, inspired and commissioned by the Scottish publisher, Thomson, and engagingly feature Tyrolean, Irish (including *St Patrick's Day*), Welsh, Scottish and Russian airs. Good sound and a programme well worth dipping into. This is not yet available in the UK.

Cello sonatas Nos. 1–5, Op. 5/1–2; Op. 69; Op. 102/1–2.
*** Decca Dig. 417 628-2 [id.]. Lynn Harrell, Vladimir Ashkenazy.
**(*) Ph. 412 256-2 [id.]. Mstislav Rostropovich, Sviatoslav Richter.
**(*) Sony Dig. M2K 42446 (2) [id.]. Yo-Yo Ma, Emanuel Ax.

Cello sonatas Nos. 3 in A, Op. 69; 5 in D, Op. 102/2.
*** Sony Dig. MK 39024 [id.]. Yo-Yo Ma, Emanuel Ax.

Lynn Harrell and Vladimir Ashkenazy have the advantage of superb recording: they are sensibly balanced, neither instrument being too prominent or too reticent. Artistically, too, these performances are in the first league – they are unfailingly sensitive and alert, well thought-out and yet seemingly spontaneous. They will be a first recommendation for many collectors, especially those interested in first-class sound.

Made in the early 1960s, the classic Philips performances by Mstislav Rostropovich and Sviatoslav Richter, two of the instrumental giants of the day, have withstood the test of time astonishingly well and sound remarkably fresh in this compact disc transfer. Apart from the usual gains in continuity and freedom from background, there is so much greater presence and realism. But this should now be reissued at mid-price.

With the CBS set by Yo-Yo Ma and Emanuel Ax there are balance problems in the coupling of the two Op. 5 *Sonatas*, where the piano often masks the refined lines that Yo-Yo Ma draws. In Opp. 69 and 102, the internal balance is much better judged. Emanuel Ax often produces a big, wide-ranging tone which must have posed problems, when related to the more introvert style of the cellist. Yo-Yo Ma plays with extraordinary sensitivity and imagination, even if there are times when one might think his pianissimo a bit overdone. The sound-quality is well focused and truthful.

Cello sonatas Nos. 1–5; 7 Variations on Bei Männern (from Mozart's *Die Zauberflöte), WoO 45; 12 Variations on 'See the conqu'ring hero comes'* (from Handel's *Judas Maccabaeus), WoO 46; 12 Variations on Ein Mädchen, Op. 66.*
(M) *** EMI CMS7 63015-2 (2). Jacqueline Du Pré, Daniel Barenboim.
(M) *** DG 423 297-2 (2) [id.]. Pierre Fournier, Wilhelm Kempff.
**(*) Hyp. Dig. CDA 66281/2; *KA 66281/2* (available separately). Anthony Pleeth, Melvyn Tan (fortepiano).

The set of performances by Jacqueline Du Pré with Daniel Barenboim was recorded live for the BBC during the Edinburgh Festival of 1970. The playing may not have the final polish that studio performances would no doubt have achieved, but the concentration and intensity of the playing are wonderfully caught; and though the Scottish audience was often maddeningly bronchial, the performances remain totally compelling, with Barenboim bringing discipline, his wife drawing out lyrical intensity. The recording emerges with good presence on CD, not as full as it might be.

By a strange coincidence, Fournier and Kempff also recorded their cycle of the *Sonatas* at live festival performances. However, the Paris audience is considerably less intrusive than the Edinburgh ones on EMI and, like their younger colleagues, these artists were inspired by the occasion to produce intensely expressive playing, performances which are marked by light, clear textures and rippling scale-work, even in the slow introductions which are taken relatively fast. Some of the weight is missing; but such a stylish spontaneity is irresistible, and admirers of both artists can be warmly recommended to the set. The balances are not ideal, but there is no lack of CD presence.

Though the cello is rather forwardly balanced in relation to the fortepiano, the Hyperion collection of Beethoven's cello and piano music – not just the five *Sonatas* but the three sets of variations too – makes an attractive issue for anyone wanting period performances. Tan recorded these performances with Pleeth in 1987, not long before he began his Beethoven series for EMI, and his imagination is comparably keen here. The two discs, both generously filled, are available separately.

Cello sonatas Nos. 1 in F; 2 in G min., Op. 5/1–2; 7 Variations on 'Bei Männern, welche Liebe fühlen'; 12 Variations of 'Ein Mädchen oder Weibchen' (Die Zauberflöte).
*** DG Dig. 431 801-2 [id.]. Mischa Maisky, Martha Argerich.

Vital and imaginative playing from Mischa Maisky and Martha Argerich in the Op. 5 *Sonatas*; they have the edge over Harrell and Ashkenazy in including the two sets of variations on themes from *Die Zauberflöte*. Those who have found Maisky somewhat prone to emote heavily, as he does in his solo Bach, can be reassured that this partnership works and that the balance between head and heart is well maintained. The DG balance tends to favour the cellist but the sound throughout is very truthful.

Cello sonata No. 3 in A, Op. 69; 7 Variations on 'Bei Männern'; Serenade in D for string trio, Op. 8.
(M) (**) EMI mono CDH7 64250-2 [id.]. Emanuel Feuermann, Hess, Goldberg, Hindemith – SCHUBERT: *Arpeggione sonata.* (**(*))

Anyone who possesses his electrifying 78s of Bloch's *Schelomo* with Stokowski and the Philadelphia Orchestra will know just what a glorious and sumptuous sound Feuermann made. His 1937 account of the Beethoven *A major Cello sonata* with Myra Hess is a further reminder of his artistry though neither here nor in the *Variations* on *'Bei Männern, welche Liebe fühlen'* is the partnership quite as memorable. Feuermann is a touch remote and unyielding in matters of phrasing though in the 1935 *Serenade in D*, Op. 8, with Szymon Goldberg leading and with Hindemith as violist, there is greater sense of spontaneity and give-and-take. The transfers are excellent.

Cello sonatas Nos. 3 in A, Op. 69; 5 in D, Op. 102/2.
(M) *** EMI CDM7 69179-2; *EG 769179-4*. Jacqueline du Pré, Kovacevich.

The Du Pré/Bishop-Kovacevich recordings of Nos. 3 and 5 come from 1966, the year after Jacqueline had made her definitive record of the Elgar *Concerto*. The very opening of the *D major Sonata* underlines an unbuttoned quality in Beethoven's writing and when, after the hushed intensity of the slow introduction of Op. 69, the music launches into the allegro, both artists soar away fearlessly. More remarkable still is the range of expressiveness in the slow movement of Op. 102/2. Du Pré's tone ranges from full-blooded fortissimo to the mere whisper of a half-tone, and these artists allow the most free range of expressive rubato. With excellent recording, these performances are most welcome on CD, sounding crisp and present in their new format.

Clarinet trio in B flat, Op. 11.
(B) **(*) Pickwick PCD 959; *IMPC 959*. David Campbell, Iwan Llewelyn-Jones, Lionel Handy – BRAHMS: *Clarinet trio.* **(*)

No quarrels with the Musicfest Trio, who play with evident spirit and vitality. They show sound musicianship and no mean sensitivity, and the only ground for reservation is the over-reverberant acoustic. A pity, as this is a very promising début.

Piano quartet in E flat; Op. 16; Serenade in D for string trio, Op. 16.
** Mer. CDE 84154; *KE 77154* [id.]. Nelly Ben-Or, Jerusalem String Trio.

The *Piano quartet* is Beethoven's own arrangement of the *Piano and wind quintet*; it sounds more homogeneous using strings but inevitably loses some of its colour. It is well played here, the *Andante* taken rather slowly, to good effect. The *Serenade* is pleasingly done too, although at times the mood seems rather too serious. Good, smooth recording.

Piano trios Nos 1–9; 10 (Variations on an original theme in E flat), Op. 44; 11 (Variations on 'Ich bin der Schneider Kakadu'), Op. 121a; Allegretto in E flat, Hess 48.
*** EMI Dig. CDS7 47455-8 [Ang. CDCD 47455] (4). Ashkenazy, Perlman, Harrell.

Piano trios Nos. 1–9; 10 (Variations on an original theme in E flat), Op. 44; 11 (Variations on 'Ich bin der Schneider Kakadu'), Op. 121a.
(M) **(*) Sony SM4K 46738 (4) [id.]. Eugene Istomin, Isaac Stern, Leonard Rose.

Piano trios Nos. 1–11; Trio in E flat (from Septet), Op. 38; Trio in D (from *Symphony No. 2*); *Trio movement in E flat.*
(M) **(*) Ph. Analogue/Dig. 432 381-2 (5) [id.]. Beaux Arts Trio.

Piano trios Nos. 1–3; 5–7; 9–10 (Variations on an original theme in E flat); 11 (Variations on 'Ich bin der Schneider Kakadu'); Allegretto in E flat, Hess 48.
(M) **(*) EMI CMS7 63124-2 (3) [Ang. CDMC 63124]. Daniel Barenboim, Pinchas Zukerman, Jacqueline du Pré.

Piano trios Nos. 1 in E flat; 2 in G, Op. 1/1–2.
*** Hyp. Dig. CDA 66197; *KA 66197* [id.]. L. Fortepiano Trio.

Piano trios Nos. 1 – 3; 5 – 7.
(M) **(*) DG 415 879-2 (3) [id.]. Kempff, Szeryng, Fournier.

Piano trio No. 5 in D (Ghost), Op. 70/1.
(M) *** Ph. 434 146-2; *434 146-4* [id.]. Beaux Arts Trio – SCHUBERT: *Trout quintet.* **
(B) *** DG Compact Classics 413 845-2 (2); *413 845-4* [id.]. Kempff, Szeryng, Fournier – MOZART: *Hunt quartet* ***; SCHUBERT: *Trout quintet* ** (CD only: HAYDN: *Lark quartet* **(*)).

Piano trios Nos. 5 in D (Ghost), Op. 70/1; 7 in B flat (Archduke), Op. 97.
(M) **(*) DG 429 712-2; *429 712-4* [id.]. Kempff, Szeryng, Fournier.

Piano trio Nos. 7 (Archduke); 9 in B flat, WoO 39.
*** EMI Dig. CDC7 47010-2 [id.]. Ashkenazy, Perlman, Harrell.

Piano trios Nos. 7 (Archduke); 11 (Variations on 'Ich bin der Schneider Kakadu').
(B) *** Pickwick Dig. PCD 874; *CIMPC 874* [id.]. Kalichstein, Laredo, Robinson.

Ashkenazy, Perlman and Harrell lead the field in this repertoire. Their four CDs comprise all of Beethoven's output for the piano trio. They also include the various additional works for the medium, the *Kakadu variations*, the isolated movements with WoO suffixes (works without opus numbers) and the early *Allegretto in E flat*, which most ensembles omit from their complete surveys. The recordings have been made over a period of five years and at various locations, but the sound is consistently fresher, warmer, more richly detailed and more present than with most other rivals. The playing is unfailingly perceptive and full of those musical insights that make one want to return to the set. The *Archduke*, coupled with *No. 9 in B flat*, is available separately on CD.

At present the London Fortepiano Trio have the field to themselves in the realm of 'authentic' performances. Monica Huggett and her partner, Linda Nicholson, play with considerable virtuosity, particularly in the finales, which are taken at high speed and to considerable effect. The use of a fortepiano serves to enhance clarity of texture in this particular repertoire, and readers should make an effort to sample what one assumes will be a complete cycle.

Unlike their earlier set, made in the late 1960s, the present Beaux Arts box offers absolutely everything Beethoven composed (or arranged) for this grouping. Four of the recordings are digital, and everything has been economically fitted on five CDs, four of which have playing times of over 70 minutes. The transfers are well up to the usual high Philips standard and the performances are as accomplished and musical as one would expect from this celebrated team. However, it has to be said that the earlier, analogue set had a freshness and sparkle that these new accounts do not wholly match. They couple the *Ghost trio* with an enjoyable version of Schubert's *Trout quintet*. The *Ghost* comes off marvellously and sounds very fresh, and the 1979 recording has responded well to digital remastering; the sound is firm, clear and truthfully balanced. The *Trout*, however, is rather less successful; the timbre of Isidore Cohen's violin is made to sound thinner and edgier than it actually is. This Insignia reissue has notes about the players but not about the music.

The DG alternative is one of the more recommendable Compact Classics couplings, even if the playing-time on the two CDs (100 minutes) could be more generous. The performance of the *Ghost trio* is comparatively restrained, sweet and lyrical rather than overtly dramatic, but with plenty of life and impetus. The transfer is very successful in both formats and the cassette (lacking the Haydn) is excellent value.

The Barenboim/Zukerman/du Pré set (by omitting Nos. 4 and 8) is fitted economically on to three mid-priced CDs. Even more than usual, the individual takes involved long spans of music, often complete movements, sometimes even a complete work. The result is music-making of rare concentration, spontaneity and warmth. Any tendency to self-indulgence – and this aspect of the playing may seem intrusive to some ears – plus a certain leaning towards romantic expressiveness, is counterbalanced by the urgency and intensity. Speeds tend to be extreme in both directions, and the *Innigkeit* of some of the slow movements, especially in the *Ghost trio*, Op. 70, No. 1, has the depth of really mature artistry, extraordinary in the work of musicians so young at the time of the recordings. The excellent recording has been freshened on CD, and the players are given a natural presence; although at times the definition is not absolutely clean and there is a touch of dryness on fortissimo tuttis, overall the effect is pleasingly natural.

The Kempff/Szeryng/Fournier team recorded their survey of the Beethoven *Trios* in the early 1970s. Wilhelm Kempff is an unfailingly interesting artist, and both Henryk Szeryng and that aristocrat of cellists, Pierre Fournier, are in impressive form throughout. On their separate coupling of the two most famous works, Kempff and his colleagues give a crystalline reading of the *Archduke*, and the performance of the *Ghost trio* is again relatively restrained. These are essentially lyrical readings and it is the clarity and imagination of Kempff's playing which grip the listener's attention with his many individual touches so that, by comparison, Szeryng and Fournier sound less inspired. The CD transfers are fresh and clear and the 1970 recording has plenty of fullness as well as a natural presence.

The Sony set includes everything but the early *Allegretto in E flat*; it is therefore more complete than its two mid-priced competitors – but in doing so it runs to four discs and is thus considerably more expensive. In New York the music-making is strong, polished and alive, and Istomin is always thoughtful and imaginative in slow movements, while Rose, although a less extovert artist than Stern, holds his own by the warmth and finesse of his lyrical phrasing. One of the highlights of the Sony set is the *Archduke*, bold and immediate, less controversial than the more wayward EMI account; the *Ghost trio* also shows these artists at their most communicative, while they do not miss the charm of the early Op. 1 works. The recording is characteristically forward in the CBS manner of the late 1960s: piano tone is comparatively shallow and Stern's upper range is given a degree of fierceness, and the effect is not entirely natural.

The Kalichstein/Laredo/Robinson Trio's interpretations of both the *Archduke* and the *Variations* are unaffected, supremely musicianly and thoughtful. A marvellous performance and a very good, splendidly clean recording, even if it is bright and forward.

Piano trios Nos. 8 in E flat, Op. 38 (after *Septet, Op. 20*); *11 (Variations on 'Ich bin der Schneider Kakdu'); Allegretto in B flat, WoO 39.*
** Unicorn Dig. DKPCD 9118[id.]. Raphael Piano Trio.

Beethoven himself made the transcription of his ever popular *Septet* in 1802–3 for his doctor friend, Johannes Schmidt, and his pianist daughter. The Raphael Piano Trio of New York give an eminently well-prepared and thoughtful account of the Op. 38 arrangement, but both here and in the *'Ich bin der Schneider Kakdu' Variations*, more sparkle and spontaneity would have been welcome.

Piano and wind quintet in E flat, Op. 16.
*** Sony Dig. MK 42099 [id.]. Perahia, members of ECO – MOZART: *Quintet.* ***
(M) *** Decca 421 151-2; *421 151-4*. Ashkenazy, L. Wind Soloists – MOZART: *Quintet.* ***
(B) *** Hung. White Label HRC 169 [id.]. Sándor Fálvai, Hungarian Wind Qt – MOZART: *Quintet.* ***
*** Ph. Dig. 420 182-2 [id.]. Brendel, Holliger, Brunner, Baumann, Thunemann – MOZART: *Quintet.* ***
(M) * DG 435 593-2. Gulda, Wind Ens. of VPO (members) – MOZART: *Piano and wind quintet.* *(*)

The view that Beethoven's *Piano and wind quintet* is less interesting than its Mozartian predecessor (which plainly inspired it) is almost confounded by Perahia's CBS version, recorded at The Maltings. The first movement is given more weight than usual, with a satisfying culmination. In the *Andante*, Perahia's playing is wonderfully poetic and serene and the wind soloists are admirably responsive. The pacing of the finale is ideally judged; and with the recording most realistically balanced, this issue can be recommended with all enthusiasm.

Ashkenazy's recording from 1966 is also in every way recommendable. The *Andante cantabile* of the Beethoven is given a particularly appealing tranquillity, and the *Rondo* is both gracious and sprightly. The sound is first class in every way, the balance rather forward but very vivid and real.

The excellent, bargain-priced Hungaroton coupling stands up well to the distinguished competition. Sándor Fálvai dominates with fresh, rhythmic articulation and shapely phrasing. The Hungaroton recording is clear and natural, and the acoustic and balance are equally felicitous. Altogether most enjoyable.

Brendel and his colleagues are hardly less impressive in the Beethoven than they are in the Mozart coupling. The quality of the recording is remarkably clean and fresh and, generally speaking, the sound is well in the demonstration bracket. This will rightly delight admirers of these artists.

The Gulda recording, which dates from 1960 and has long been out of the catalogue, proves disappointing. The performance lacks real verve and the slow movement is suave and lifeless. The recording, too, has not been flattered by its remastering.

Septet in E flat, Op. 20.
(M) *** Decca 421 093-2; *421 093-4* [id.]. V. Octet (members) – MENDELSSOHN: *Octet.* **(*)

Septet in E flat, Op. 20; Sextet in E flat, Op. 81b.
*** Hyp. Dig. CDA 66513 [id.]. Gaudier Ens.

(i) *Septet in E flat, Op. 20;* (ii) *Duo for clarinet and bassoon in B flat, WoO 27/3.*
*** Novalis Dig. 150 021-2 [id.]. (i) Schweizer Soloists; (ii) Kurt Weber, Tomas Sosnowski.

The young members of the Gaudier Ensemble give an exuberant performance of the *Septet*, bringing it home as one of the young Beethoven's most joyfully carefree inspirations. The rhythmic bounce of the playing in the fast movements and the warmth of phrasing in the slow are consistently winning. The only tempo out of the ordinary is that for the finale, faster than usual. That is a fair reflection of the marking *Presto*, when the playing remains delightfully bouncy with brilliant articulation. The rarer *Sextet* for two horns and string quartet makes a generous coupling. Much earlier than its opus number might indicate, it is a delightful work too. There is virtuoso writing for the two horns in all three of the compact movements, not least the jig-like finale with its hunting-calls. Excellent sound, with the wind well forward.

The splendid new digital CD, made by a young Swiss group, in almost all respects supersedes the distinguished older version on Decca. At the very outset one is struck by the freshness of their playing, by the excellent internal blending, helped by a naturally balanced recording, and by the spirit and warmth of their music-making. Tempi are consistently apt and the ear revels in the interplay between these artists. The finale is particularly fluent and infectious, as indeed is the whole performance. With such realistic recording one has the sense of live music-making taking place in one's very room. The *Duo* which follows is also played with much charm and confirms the natural partnership between clarinet and bassoon that had already blossomed in the *Septet*.

The Decca recording was made by the older generation of the Vienna Octet – which consists of the first desks of the VPO. Their performance has elegance but also conveys a sparkle and a sense of enjoyment that are thoroughly exhilarating. The CD transfer is very successful.

Serenade in D for flute, violin and viola, Op. 25.
❀ (BB) *** Pickwick/CDI Dig. PWK 1139. Israel Flute Trio (with Recital: '*Flute Serenade*' ***).

The light and charming combination of flute, violin and viola inspired the youthful Beethoven to write in an unexpectedly carefree and undemanding way. The sequence of tuneful, unpretentious movements reminds one of Mozart's occasional music, and this delectable Israel performance brings out all its charm. Er'ella Talmi is a superb flautist and she receives admirable support from her colleagues. The recording is wonderfully natural in sound and balance: it is as if the players were making music in one's own room.

Serenade in D for flute, violin and viola, Op. 25; Serenade in D for string trio, Op. 8.
** Virgin Dig. VC7 90755-2 [id.]. Sitkovetsky, Adorján, Caussé, Gerigas.

The recording of the longer work here, the Opus 8 *Serenade for string trio*, is also available in coupling with Saraste's outstanding version of the *Eroica* on the bargain Virgo label. Here at full price the ungenerous if logical coupling is the jauntily unpretentious little *Serenade* which Beethoven wrote at the same period for flute, violin and viola. It too is delightfully played, but the reverberant recording seems inappropriate for such intimate music.

Serenade in D, Op. 8 (arr. Matiegka).
*** Mer. Dig. CDE 84199; *KE 77199* [id.]. Clive Conway, Paul Silverthorne, Gerald Garcia – KREUTZER; MOLINO: *Trios.* ***
(M) ** BMG/RCA GD 87870; *GK 87870* [7870-2-RG; *7870-4-RG*]. Heifetz, Primrose, Piatigorsky – SPOHR: *Violin concerto No. 8* etc. (***)

Beethoven's early *Serenade* for string trio was arranged for violin, viola and guitar as early as 1807 by the Bohemian composer and guitarist, Wenceslaus Matiegka. Gerald Garcia has here rearranged it for the present unusual and delightful combination, offering the violin part to the flute, and giving the guitar a more taxing contribution. As a companion-piece for the rare Kreutzer and Molino items, it makes a charming oddity in its seven brief movements, very well played and warmly recorded.

The Heifetz–Primrose–Piatigorsky record was made in 1960 at the same time as the *D major Trio*, Op. 9, No. 2. The sound is dry but not unacceptably so, and the playing is immaculate.

String quartets

String quartets Nos. 1–16; Grosse Fuge, Op. 133.
(M) *** Valois V 4400 (8) [id.]. Végh Qt.
*** Valois V 4401 (*Nos. 1 & 5*); V 4402 (*Nos. 2–4*); V 4403 (*Nos. 6–7*); V 4404 (*Nos. 8–9*); V 4405 (*Nos. 10 & 12*); V 4406 (*Nos. 11 & 15*); V 4407 (*Nos. 13 & Grosse Fugue*); V 4408 (*Nos. 14 & 16*) [id.]. Végh Qt.
(M) (***) EMI mono CZS7 67236-2 (7). Hungarian Qt.
(M) **(*) DG 423 473-2 (7) [id.]. Amadeus Qt.

The Végh performances were recorded in the mid-1970s; they have been rightly hailed for their simplicity and depth. Intonation may not always be absolutely immaculate, but flaws are few and trivial when one considers the wisdom and experience the Végh communicate. In short they are in a different league from most of their rivals: there is no cultivation of surface polish though there is both elegance and finesse. They observe all the first-movement exposition repeats, which is why they don't fit the Op. 18 set on two records. The Végh bring very special insights to this music; their playing is deep and searching, and when listening to them you are conscious only of Beethoven's voice. The CD transfers are successful in producing an altogether cleaner image and a slightly firmer focus than the original analogue LPs, although the imbalance towards the cello remains. The eight discs are now available together at mid-price.

Recorded in 1953 before the age of stereo, the Hungarian Quartet's first recorded cycle of the Beethoven *Quartets* has long been overshadowed by their later, stereo set of 1966. Yet this very welcome reissue, with the mono sound firm and full and with fine presence, brings out the palpable advantages of the earlier performances. The Hungarians' matching is superb, with tonal beauty never an end in itself. The *senza vibrato* playing of the chorale in the great *Heilige Dankgesang* of Opus 132 has never been more perfectly achieved. Polished ensemble goes with a sense of spontaneity in readings fresher and more direct than those of 1966. The spacious, unhurried playing of the great slow movements here has rarely been matched. Those primarily concerned with the music as opposed to sound-quality will find little difficulty in adjusting to the recording; indeed, on first hearing, so vivid and full is the sound that it would be easy to believe one was listening to a very early stereo recording, while the layout on only seven discs makes it a bargain too. Unlike the Amadeus's seven-disc cycle on DG, this one has exposition repeats observed.

The Amadeus are at their best in the Op. 18 quartets, where their mastery and polish are heard to good advantage. In the middle-period and late quartets, their sumptuous tone and refinement of balance are always in evidence, but they do not always penetrate very far beneath the surface, particularly in the late quartets. The recording, from the beginning of the 1960s, is fresh and lifelike and the set is economically priced on seven CDs.

String quartets Nos. 1–6, Op. 18/1–6.
*** EMI Dig. CDS7 47127-8 [Ang. CDC 47126] (3). Alban Berg Qt.
(M) **(*) Ph. 426 046-2 (3) [id.]. Italian Qt.
**(*) Cal. CAL 9633/4 [id.]. Talich Qt.
** Teldec/Warner Dig. 2292 46337-2 (3) [id.]. Vermeer Qt.

String quartets Nos. 1 in F; 2 in G, Op. 18/1–2.
**(*) HM HMC 901222; *HMC 401222* [id.]. Brandis Qt.

String quartets Nos. 1–3, Op. 18/1–3.
*** Nimbus Dig. NI 5173 [id.]. Medici Qt.

The Alban Berg undoubtedly offer a polish and tonal finesse that put them in a class of their own. The playing is immaculate and the sound has all the usual advantages of the medium: excellent definition, presence and body. The CDs are also available separately (CDC7 47127/8/9-2).

The Italian performances are in superb style. The only reservations concern Nos. 2 and 4: the latter is perhaps a little wanting in forward movement, while the conventional exchanges at the opening of No. 2 seem a shade too deliberate. The balance is truthful but the digital remastering does draw the ear to a certain thinness in the treble, slightly more noticeable in the earliest recordings.

The Medici offer all but a few seconds short of 80 minutes of playing time, and without sacrificing first-movement exposition repeats. They are not a jet-set ensemble; their playing is refreshingly unglamorous and yet thoroughly polished; nor do they fail to penetrate the depths – their account of the slow movement of the *F major* is far from superficial. They are given a very natural and well-balanced recording, and these performances will give considerable satisfaction.

The Talich offer all six Op. 18 *Quartets* on two CDs. Their performances have the merit of directness and simplicity of utterance; as music-making there is a refreshing naturalness about this approach. Sometimes they are inclined to be a little measured and wanting in urgency, but if there is some prose in this set there is no want of poetry either. First-movement exposition repeats are preserved except in Nos. 1 and 6. The Calliope recording is very clean and present, if a trifle dry.

The Brandis Quartet can more than hold their own with their current rivals. Tempi are well chosen, there is an enviable unanimity of ensemble and no lack of polish. The slow movement of the *F major* does not obliterate memories of the greatest performances of the past but, generally speaking, no one investing in these well-recorded performances need fear disappointment.

The Vermeer Quartet bring to the Op. 18 set the same qualities of intelligence and musicianship that distinguish the remainder of their cycle. They are performances of integrity, free from any expressive idiosyncrasy and very well executed in every respect. However, for all their merits of dedication, they are somewhat lacking in warmth and spontaneity.

String quartets Nos. 1–6, Op. 18/1–6; 10 in E flat (Harp), Op. 74; 11 in F min., Op. 95.
*** ASV CDDCS 305 (3) [id.]. Lindsay Qt.

The great merit of the Lindsay Quartet in Beethoven lies in the natural expressiveness of their playing, most strikingly of all in slow movements where, even in these early works, such movements as the D minor *Adagio affetuoso* of No. 1 has a hushed inner quality too rarely caught on record. The sense of spontaneity necessarily brings the obverse quality: these performances are not as precise as those in the finest rival sets; but there are few Beethoven quartet recordings that so convincingly bring out the humanity of the writing, its power to communicate. The recording of Op. 18, set against a fairly reverberant acoustic, is warm and realistic, and the CD transfer is very successful: the 1979 sound is fuller in the treble than the quality Philips have achieved in their remastering of the Quartetto Italiano. The Lindsays are equally penetrating and unhurried in the slow movements of Op. 74 and Op. 95; elsewhere there are one or two rough edges, tonally speaking, but again the transfers reflect the fact that the recordings are more modern and rather fuller than the remastered Philips quality for the Italian group.

String quartets Nos. 3, 4 & 6; Op. 18/3, 4 & 6.
**(*) Hyp. Dig. CDA 66402; *KA 66402* [id.]. New Budapest Qt.

This is a great improvement over the first release in the Hyperion/New Budapest series. There is more fire and a greater sense of involvement and the players are far more attentive to dynamic nuance – though, even so, contrasts between *forte* and *piano* could with advantage be stronger. Although there are better versions of each quartet, these can still hold their own in the catalogue, and they are very well recorded.

String quartets Nos. 5 in A, Op. 18/5; 7 in F (Rasumovsky), Op. 59/1.
**(*) Hyp. Dig. CDA 66403; *KA 66403* [id.]. New Budapest Qt.

The New Budapest players produce consistent refinement of sound and have impeccable intonation. Their account of the *A major Quartet* has no want of vitality in its outer movements, though the middle two movements suffer a little from gentility. All the more surprising, then, to find them so impressive in the first *Rasumovsky quartet*. The slow movement may not match the finest rival accounts in depth of feeling but the performance holds together remarkably well and the meticulous care taken over detail pays strong musical dividends. Very good recording.

String quartets Nos. 7–9 (Rasumovsky Nos. 1–3), Op. 59/1–3; 10 in E flat (Harp), Op. 74; 11 in F min., Op. 95.
(M) *** Ph. 420 797-2 (3) [id.]. Italian Qt.
*** BMG/RCA Dig. RD 60462 (3) [60462-2-RC]. Tokyo Qt.
**(*) EMI Dig. CDS7 47131-8 [Ang. CDC 47130] (3). Alban Berg Qt.

String quartets Nos. 7–9 (Rasumovsky Nos. 1–3), Op. 59/1–3.
*** ASV Dig. CDDCS 207 (2) [id.]. Lindsay Qt.

String quartet No. 7 in F (Rasumovsky No. 1), Op. 59/1.
*** ASV Dig. CDDCA 553 [id.]. Lindsay Qt.

String quartets Nos. 8 in E min.; 9 in C (Rasumovsky Nos. 2–3), Op. 59/2–3.
*** ASV Dig. CDDCA 554 [id.]. Lindsay Qt.

String quartets Nos. 7, Op. 59/1; 10 (Harp), Op. 74.
*** Cal. CAL 9636 [id.]. Talich Qt.

String quartets Nos. 8, Op. 59/2; 13 in B flat, Op. 130.
*** Cal. CAL 9637 [id.]. Talich Qt.

String quartets Nos. 9, Op. 59/3; 14 in C sharp min., Op. 131.
*** Cal. CAL 9638 [id.]. Talich Qt.

The Lindsay set contains performances of real stature; and though they are not unrivalled in some of their insights, among modern recordings they are not often surpassed. The *F major*, Op. 59/1, available separately on CD, is very impressive indeed. This is the most masterly account to have appeared for many decades. In each movement of the *E minor*, Op. 59/2, the Lindsays find the *tempo giusto* and all that they do as a result has the ring of complete conviction. The opening of Op. 59/3 has real mystery and awe, and how splendidly they convey the pent-up torrent of energy released in the fugal onrush of the *Allegro molto*. The two remaining quartets, Opp. 74 and 95, are also highly competitive. As a recording, this set is comparable with most of its competitors and superior to many; artistically, it can hold its own with the best. They are now placed together in a box, with some saving in cost.

The Tokyo Quartet's account of the *F major*, by general consent the greatest of the three *Rasumovsky quartets*, is one of the very finest in the catalogue. The opening movement is superbly paced and shaped, and there is no want of depth in the slow movement. Those who find the Végh Quartet strong on conception but vulnerable on execution should find satisfaction here. The tempi throughout are splendidly judged and the peformance as a whole is beautifully proportioned. There is, however, some minor cause for reservation in Op. 59, No. 3. The fugal finale is rather too headlong in pace and there are some traces of slickness elsewhere. No grumbles in the *Harp* quartet until the third movement where the virtuosity and brilliance of the Tokyo players get the better of them, and the thrust of the jet engine rather than gentler pace of a horse-drawn vehicle is the order of the day. But for the most part this is a powerful set and its strengths far outweigh its weaknesses. The account of the *F minor*, Op. 95, is appropriately taut and concentrated. The recording is excellent, rich in sonority yet completely truthful and unglamorized. All in all, this is a set worth considering alongside the very best now available.

The Talich have an impressive technical address, no less formidable than any of their current rivals, and they win our confidence by the essentially private character of their performances. One feels a privileged eavesdropper on an intimate discourse rather than a concert-hall listener waiting for another jet-setting, over-projecting ensemble. There is a real understanding of what this music is about. The recordings, which seemed a bit bottom-heavy when they first appeared, are more firmly defined and better focused than on LP and, while the sound is not in the demonstration class, the instruments are well placed and the timbre truthful – in fact, one quickly forgets about it and loses oneself in the music. Each of these three CDs offers exceptionally good value, containing over 70 minutes of music.

The remastered Italian set still sounds well: there is now only a slight thinness on top to betray their age, with no lack of body and warmth in the middle range. Their superiority in terms of sheer quartet playing is still striking: purity of intonation, perfectly blended tone and superb ensemble and attack. Their tempi are perfectly judged and every phrase is sensitively shaped. Yet there is no attempt to 'beautify' Beethoven, and these performances remain very recommendable at mid-price.

The Alban Berg recordings favour rather brisk tempi in first movements, which they dispatch with exemplary polish and accuracy of intonation. There is much perceptive music-making but there is also a distinct tendency to exaggerate dynamic extremes. The introduction to Op. 59/3 suffers in this respect and the results sound self-conscious. In the first movements of Op. 59/2 and Op. 95 the brilliance of the attack almost draws attention to itself and perhaps the recording quality, which is closely balanced, gives it a slightly more aggressive quality than it really has.

String quartets Nos. 7 in F; 8 in E min. (Rasumovsky), Op. 59/1–2.
(M) **(*) Sony SBK 46545 [id.]. Budapest Qt (Joseph Roisman; Alexander Schneider, Boris Kroyt, Mischa Schneider).

The Budapest Quartet on CBS are closely balanced, which does not help in the provision of pianissimos, yet there is no real lack of light and shade. At times the leader's intonation is less than ideal; but this is powerfully felt playing of a kind we do not often encounter today – the *Adagio* of the *E minor*, Op. 59/2, shows this readily. Moreover the music-making is strongly communicative – the rough edges are caused by commitment to Beethoven, not by lack of rehearsal, and the ensemble playing generally has the most powerful unanimity.

String quartets Nos. 8–9 (Rasumovsky Nos. 2–3), Op. 59/2–3.
*** Hyp. Dig. CDA 66404; *KA 66404* [id.]. New Budapest Qt.

The New Budapest accounts of the *E minor* and *C major Rasumovskys* come into direct competition with the Lindsay Quartet on ASV. In the slow movement of the *F major*, they did not quite match the Lindsay's expressive depth, but in both of its companions they more than hold their own. They play with excellent intonation and tonal finesse and their judgement in matters of phrasing and tempo cannot easily be faulted. (There is a sudden spurt forward at the trio section of the *Grazioso* movement of the *C major* but that is the only reservation of any note.) They are very well recorded, with clarity, body and presence.

String quartets Nos. 8, Op. 59/2; 10 (Harp), Op. 74.
(B) *** Hung. White Label HRC 063. Bartók Qt.

The Bartók Quartet give strong, well-paced readings of Op. 59/2 and the *Harp quartet*, with slow movements to match any rival versions at whatever price. With excellent Hungaroton recording, this is an outstanding bargain in the White Label series.

String quartet No. 11 in F min., Op. 95, arr. Mahler.
*** BMG/RCA Dig. RD 60988 [60988-2]. Moscow Soloists, Bashmet – SCHUBERT: *String quartet No. 14.* ***

String quartet Nos. 11 in F min., Op. 95 (arr. Mahler); *Grosse Fuge.*
*** EMI Dig. CDC7 49931-2 [id.]. ECO, Tate (with MOZART: *Adagio & Fugue* ***).

The *Grosse Fuge* is frequently heard on full strings and in recent times, fired by the example of Mitropoulos, Bernstein took to playing the *C sharp minor*, Op. 131, in this way. In 1889 Mahler arranged the *F minor*, Op. 95, though it was greeted with some hostility at its first Vienna performance. It is understandable that at a time when the Beethoven quartets were accessible mainly to those who could play them or were musically literate enough to read them in score, there was some justification for performing them in this way. As in the case of the *Grosse Fuge* (or Weingartner's celebrated transcription of the *Hammerklavier sonata*), fuller forces remove something essential: the sense of struggle between the musical ideas and the medium. Of the two available versions, the BMG/RCA Moscow performance is probably a more brilliant and sensitive account than its EMI rival. Some may find dynamic and other expressive nuances a little overdone but there is much beauty of tone and an excellent recording. The coupling with Mahler's transcription of *Death and the Maiden quartet* is also both more logical and better value in terms of playing time. However, there are no quarrels with either the well-balanced and full-blooded recording or the performances by the ECO under Jeffrey Tate, though at 48 minutes it is short measure. It is difficult to imagine collectors replaying this very often, but there is no reason to withhold three stars. The Mozart is also impressive.

String quartets Nos. 11 in F min., Op. 95; 12 in E flat, Op. 127; Grosse Fuge, Op. 133.
*** Cal. CAL 9635 (id.]. Talich Qt.

String quartets Nos. 15 in A min., Op. 132; 16 in F, Op. 135.
*** Cal. CAL 9639 [id.]. Talich Qt.

Having Opp. 132 and 135 on one disc is quite a bargain, especially so, given the quality of the performances. These penetrating accounts can hold their own with the very finest, and the quality of the recorded sound – though not spectacular in any way – is more than acceptable. Indeed in the new format it is eminently clean and well focused though not as warm or as alive as in some of the most recent rivals.

String quartets Nos. 12 in E flat, Op. 127; 13 in B flat, Op. 130; 14 in C sharp min., Op. 131; 15 in A min., Op. 132; 16 in F, Op. 135; Grosse Fuge in B flat, Op. 133.
*** ASV DCS 403 (4) [id.]. Lindsay Qt.
(M) **(*) Ph. 426 050-2 (4) [id.]. Italian Qt.
**(*) DG Dig. 415 676-2 (3) [id.]. Melos Qt.
**(*) EMI Dig. CDS7 47135-8 (4) [Ang. CDC 47134]. Alban Berg Qt.

The Lindsays get far closer to the essence of this great music than most of their rivals. They have the benefit of very well-balanced recording (better than the Végh and the Talich, which are both a little bottom-heavy – see above); the sound of the ASV set is more present. They seem to find tempi that somehow strike the listener as completely right and which enable them to convey so much of both the letter and the spirit of the music. They bring much rich musical characterization and musical strength. Taken overall, these are among the very finest versions to have been made in recent years.

The merits of the Italian Quartet's performances are considerable. The sonority that they produce is beautifully blended and splendidly focused. They do not sound as sumptuous as some modern quartet recordings and their reissue on four medium-price CDs is less competitive than it might be, when their Melos competitors are available on three. However, for many the Italians' searching and thoughtful interpretations will ultimately prove most satisfying.

The Melos Quartet seem more naturally attuned to the late quartets than to the early or middle-period works. Overall these are warmly satisfying readings, and the players are particularly impressive in their powerful reading of the *Grosse Fuge*. Though speeds are not excessively fast, all six works are fitted on to three CDs with vividly immediate sound. A small but important final point: the pauses between movements are often too short (only three seconds between the second movement of Op. 132 and the *Heiliger Dankegesang*).

Some listeners may find the sheer polish of the Alban Berg Quartet gets in the way. Others dig deeper into the soul of this music – the Lindsays do – and this tells in movements like the *Heiliger Dankegesang* of Op. 132 or the *Cavatina* of Op. 130. The CDs have great clarity of focus, particularly at the bottom end of the spectrum, and a distinct presence, yet it is difficult to suppress the feeling that others convey even more of the stature and depth of these great and profound works.

String quartets Nos. 12 in E flat, Op. 127; 14 in C sharp min., Op. 131.
(B) *** Hung. White Label HRC 125. Bartók Qt.

On the Bartók Quartet's very generous coupling of Opp. 127 and 131 the sweetness and purity of the string-playing matches that of any rival versions; but the sureness of control over the span of the sublime slow movements still makes this an outstanding version, even taking no account of price.

String quartets Nos. 12 in E flat, Op. 127; 16 in F, Op. 135.
(M) *** Ph. 422 840-2. Italian Qt.
**(*) EMI CDC7 47135-2 [id.]. Alban Berg Qt.

The Italians give a most searching account of the first movement of Op. 127, and their account of the whole work goes far deeper than that of many full-priced rivals. Some may quarrel with their tempi in the inner movements of Op. 135; but on the whole this too is a magnificent account, sounding very fresh and immediate.

String quartet No. 13 in B flat, Op. 130; Grosse Fuge in B flat, Op. 133.
*** ASV CDDCA 602 [id.]. Lindsay Qt.
**(*) EMI CDC7 47136-2 [id.]. Alban Berg Qt.
** Nuova Era Dig. 6861 [id.]. Prazak Qt.

The Lindsay's account of Op. 130 includes both the *Grosse Fuge* as an ending and also the finale Beethoven substituted, so that listeners can choose for themselves. The merits of their performance are well known, and in its CD format their interpretation ranks very high indeed – along with the Végh and the Talich. They also have the advantage of better recording than either.

The Prazak Quartet gives us the Op. 130 with the *Grosse Fuge* as the finale, omitting Beethoven's alternative finale. Most rivals offer both though the absence of the one or the other would not matter if the players offered exceptional insights. As it is, the performance, while far from negligible (they are fine players), is not in any way exceptional. It opens well but many readers may find the sudden bulges in the *Alla danza tedesca* and the leader's occasional throb a little disturbing. The *Grosse Fuge* itself is very impressive in their hands but, given the abundance of choice with which the collector is now confronted, the CD as a whole is uncompetitive.

String quartet No. 14 in C sharp min., Op. 131.
*** ASV CDDCA 603 [id.]. Lindsay Qt.
**(*) EMI CDC7 47137-2 [id.]. Alban Berg Qt.

The Lindsay's account of Op. 131 is as fine as any in the catalogue. It must be remembered that the competing Talich disc (Cal. CAL 9638) offers also Op. 59/3 and, with fine performances of both works, represents even better value; but the ASV recording is somewhat clearer in focus, with the digital remastering very successful.

String quartet No. 14 in C sharp min., Op. 131; Grosse Fuge, Op. 133 (orchestral versions).
**(*) Capriccio Dig. 10 356 [id.]. International Musical Seminar Soloists, Végh.

The practice of performing this repertory for full strings dates back to the beginning of the century. (Mahler even played Schubert's *Death and the Maiden quartet* in that form.) If you are going to do it at all, these serious and dedicated performances by a group of accomplished musicians working with an artist of Végh's insights show how it should be done. There are four players to a part, and their numbers include some distinguished soloists who appear in these pages in their own right. Moreover they play with great responsiveness and understanding in both works. The sound is varied – there is none of the opulence of the Vienna Philharmonic strings who recorded this with Bernstein for DG, but the sonority is much more varied. The *Grosse Fuge* is more frequently encountered on full strings (from Furtwängler and Klemperer, among others), but this performance is as fine as any. The recording is also good, though there is a less than pleasing coldness about the upper strings that may be the product of the acoustic or the recording.

String quartet No. 15 in A min., Op. 132.
*(*) Nuova Era Dig. 6862 [id.]. Prazak Qt.

The Prazak are accomplished players and begin promisingly. However their performance is not untouched by expressive exaggeration (dynamic bulges in some phrases are just a little too much) and there is little depth or insight in the *Heiliger Dankgesang*. They are well enough recorded but in so competitive a field and at full price, this is not a strong contender.

String quartet No. 16 in F, Op. 135.
(*) DG Dig. 431 814-2 [id.]. Hagen Qt – SCHUBERT: *String quartet No. 14.* *

The Hagens' account of the *F major Quartet* is a bit self-aware, pianissimos are somewhat intrusively whispered, and they could do with more sinew in the first movement, which at times comes a little too close to gentility. But the *Quartet* is beautifully played throughout – if not as searchingly or selflessly as the Végh, Talich, Lindsay or the Italians – and equally beautifully recorded.

(i) *String quintet in C, Op. 29; String quartet No. 7 in F (Rasumovsky), Op. 59/1.*
** Nimbus Dig. NI 5207 [id.]. Medici Qt; (i) with S. Rowland-Jones.

The neglect of the *String quintet* is unaccountable. Dating from the year before the *First Symphony*, it is full of memorable ideas. Its opening (and much of the invention in the finale) foreshadows Schubert, and readers who enjoy the Op. 18 *Quartets* will find this more than their equal; yet the Medici account on Nimbus remains its only current representation on CD. This performance does it justice: tempi are well judged and there is no glamorization or any kind of egocentric mannerism. The interpretation is sensible and straightforward, and the recording, made at The Maltings, Snape, is truthful. The *Rasumovsky*, however, is another matter. The first movement is very fast (though not faster than the Alban Berg on EMI) and not unacceptable. The third movement is the disappointment for, though the playing is beautiful, the Medici players do not penetrate its depths as do the Végh, Lindsay and Talich versions.

String trios Nos. 1 in E flat, Op. 3; 2 in G; 3 in D; 4 in C min., Op. 9/1–3; Serenade in D (for string trio), Op. 8.
**(*) DG Dig. 427 687-2 (2) [id.]. Mutter, Giuranna, Rostropovich.

String trio No. 1 in E flat, Op. 3; Serenade in D, Op. 8.
*** Unicorn Dig. DKPCD 9059 [id.]. Cummings Trio.

String trios Nos. 2 in G; 3 in D; 4 in C min., Op. 9/1–3.
*** Unicorn Dig. DKPCD 9042 [id.]. Cummings Trio.

The playing of the Cummings Trio is cultured but not overcivilized; there is an unforced naturalness about it all, nothing glamorous at all and nothing which ever takes one's attention away from Beethoven. The *G major* is of particular interest, as its scherzo includes a newly discovered second trio. The *Serenade* is, of course, entertainment music. These players let

Beethoven speak for himself and in quieter moments there is a winning sense of repose: in short, this is real chamber-music-making, with excellent recording; indeed it is in the demonstration class.

The *String trios* come in a two-CD package from Anne-Sophie Mutter, Bruno Giuranna and Mstislav Rostropovich, and they are splendidly played; however, the less glamorous but highly accomplished Cummings Trio is to be preferred. The sound in the DG is rather forward and dry.

Violin sonatas Nos. 1–10.
(M) *** Decca 421 453-2 (4). Itzhak Perlman, Vladimir Ashkenazy.
(M) *** DG 415 874-2 (3) [id.]. Yehudi Menuhin, Wilhelm Kempff.
(M) (***) Ph. mono 422 140-2 (3). Arthur Grumiaux, Clara Haskil.
(M) ** BMG/RCA RD 60991 (4) [id.]. Zukerman, Neikrug.

Perlman and Ashkenazy's set of the *Violin sonatas*, now reissued on four mid-priced CDs, will be difficult to surpass. These performances offer a blend of classical purity and spontaneous vitality that it is hard to resist; moreover the realism and presence of the recording in its CD format are very striking.

Menuhin and Kempff met together in London in June 1970 to record their cycle. Though these are not always the most immaculate performances on disc, they consistently reflect the joy and sense of wonder of pianist and violinist alike, often relaxed in tempo but magnetic from first to last, brightly transferred to CD, with the rippling articulation of Kempff a constant delight.

Arthur Grumiaux and Clara Haskil made their celebrated recordings in 1956–7 and they sound remarkably well for their age. The performances are wonderfully civilized and aristocratic, and no one investing in them will regret it. They accommodate all ten *Sonatas* on three CDs at mid-price, as opposed to the four of Perlman and Ashkenazy.

RCA offer the Pinchas Zukerman–Marc Neikrug set of the sonatas at a discount rather than at mid-price (the CDs are sold four the price of three). The playing is highly polished and very professional and there are often illuminating touches – and some ugly ones, too (the heavy accents in the third movement of Op. 30, No. 3). Zukerman, who can often sound merely slick as if he is on automatic pilot, plays with some degree of freshness and spontaneity. At a normal volume-level the piano is rather overpowering and Zukerman, too, is somewhat forwardly balanced but with use of the controls the sound can be tamed. Whatever the merits of this recording, it must be admitted that there are more enjoyable performances around.

Violin sonatas Nos. 1 in D; 2 in A; 3 in E flat, Op. 12/1–3.
*** DG Dig. 415 138-2 [id.]. Gidon Kremer, Martha Argerich.

The partnership of Kremer and Argerich, two inspirational artists, works superbly in the first three sonatas. Each sparks the other into individual, but never wilful, expression, with the to-and-fro exchanges typical of early Beethoven consistently delightful. The CD gives a keen sense of presence.

Violin sonatas Nos. 4 in A min., Op. 23; 6 in A; 8 in G, Op. 30/1 & 3.
*** Decca 417 574-2 [id.]. Itzhak Perlman, Vladimir Ashkenazy.

A further outstanding recoupling from the Perlman/Ashkenazy series, well up to the standard of the rest. The digital remastering is highly successful: the sound gives both violin and piano admirable presence and reality.

Violin sonatas Nos. 5 in F (Spring), Op. 24; 7 in C min., Op. 30/2.
(M) (***) EMI CDH7 63494-2. Adolf Busch, Rudolf Serkin (with BACH: *Violin partita No. 2* (***)).

Music-making from another age, unhurried, humane and of supreme integrity. The *Sonatas* were recorded in the early 1930s and the *Partita* in 1929, though the latter sounds more vivid, since the violin is placed more forwardly. Playing of such naturalness and artistry transcends the inevitable sonic limitations.

Violin sonatas Nos. 5 in F (Spring), Op. 24; 9 in A (Kreutzer), Op. 47.
(M) *** EMI CDM7 69021-2 [id.]; *EG 769021-4*. Pinchas Zukerman, Daniel Barenboim.
*** Decca 410 554-2 [id.]. Itzhak Perlman, Vladimir Ashkenazy.
(M) *** DG 435 101-2; *435 101-4* [id.]. Sir Yehudi Menuhin, Wilhelm Kempff.
(BB) *** Naxos Dig. 8.550283; *4550283* [id.]. Takako Nishizaki, Jenö Jandó.
(M) **(*) Teldec/Warner Dig. 9031 75856-2; *9031 75856-4* [id.]. Thomas Zehetmair, Malcolm Frager (fortepiano).

Violin sonatas Nos. 5 in F (Spring); 9 in A (Kreutzer); 10 in G, Op. 96.
(M) **(*) Sony SBK 46342; *40-46342* [id.]. Zino Francescatti, Robert Casadesus.

Zukerman and Barenboim's coupling of the two favourites among Beethoven's *Violin sonatas* brings disarmingly spontaneous-sounding performances. The CD transfer scarcely betrays its age.

On Decca an obvious recoupling from the Perlman/Ashkenazy series. The dynamism is there but never becomes too extrovert, and the music unfolds naturally and spontaneously. The recording quality is excellent and has transferred smoothly to CD, though the EMI transfer of the Zukerman/Barenboim recordings is even more impressive.

There is no doubt that Menuhin and Kempff give inspirational accounts of both works, and the recording has striking presence and naturalness on CD.

Takako Nishizaki does not produce a large sound but the balance with Jandó is expertly managed, and the result is very natural and real. The performances are delightful in their fresh spontaneity. This is a bargain.

Casadesus's playing is always illuminating; Francescatti is warm-timbred, though not all ears will take to the slightly febrile quality of his vibrato. No one could fail to respond to the joyous vigour of the finale of the *Kreutzer*, following after a fine set of variations. Op. 96 is a more intimate performance and an appealing asset to the disc. Very good remastering with good presence for both artists.

On Teldec it is good to have spontaneous performances of these two favourite sonatas featuring the sound of an 1805 Broadway fortepiano that the composer would have recognized. The *Kreutzer* is vibrant (especially the dancing finale) and the *Spring* full of life and feeling, if less strong on charm. The balance is not ideal. The violin is given a most realistic presence but the fortepiano, which Malcolm Frager plays very convincingly, is a little backward. But this music-making is full of life.

Violin sonatas Nos. 6 in A; 7 in C min.; 8 in G, Op. 30/1–3.
(BB) **(*) Naxos Dig. 8.550286 [id.]. Takako Nishizaki, Jenö Jandó.

All three of the Op. 30 *Sonatas* on one CD represents very good value for money, particularly as the playing is of considerable quality. The recording, made in a Bratislava Radio studio, tends to favour the piano a little too much to warrant an unreserved three-star recommendation. However, these performances give much pleasure.

Violin sonatas Nos. 7 in C min., Op. 30/2; 10 in G, Op. 96.
*** Decca 411 948-2 [id.]. Itzhak Perlman, Vladimir Ashkenazy.

These Decca performances emanate from the 1977 set and the sound is improved, firmer and fresher than ever. No phrase is unimaginatively handled, and the playing of Perlman and Ashkenazy is masterly.

Violin sonatas Nos. 8 in G, Op. 30/3; 9 in A (Kreutzer), Op. 47.
**(*) Amon Ra CDSAR 16 [id.]. Ralph Holmes, Richard Burnett.

Ralph Holmes recorded these two Beethoven sonatas not long before he died. They reveal his art at its freshest and most alert in a period performance, accompanied by Richard Burnett on a sweet-toned Graf fortepiano of around 1820. Inevitably Holmes's Stradivarius overtops the fortepiano but, with recording realistically set in a helpful but intimate acoustic, the textures are admirably clear. The twanginess of the instrument is distracting only in sustained melodic passages, and Burnett's clean articulation is as much a delight as Holmes's strong and imaginative phrasing.

(Wind) *Octet in E flat, Op. 103; Quintet in E flat for oboe, 3 horns & bassoon; Rondino in E flat for wind octet, WoO 25; Sextet in E flat, Op. 71.*
*** ASV Dig. CDCOE 807; *ZCCOE 807* [id.]. Wind Soloists of COE.

(Wind) Octet in E flat, Op. 103; Rondino in E flat, WoO 25; Sextet in E flat, Op. 71.
**(*) Amon Ra Dig. CDSAR 26 [id.]. Classical Winds.

The wind soloists of the Chamber Orchestra of Europe give strong and stylish performances of this collection of Beethoven's wind music, marked by some outstanding solo work, notably from the first oboe, Douglas Boyd. With the little *Rondino* included alongside Opus 103, as well as the three-movement *Quintet*, it makes a generous collection, recorded in warm but clear sound with good presence.

Using period instruments, Classical Winds give bright, sometimes abrasive performances of Beethoven's two major wind works, including the *Rondino* not as a separate work but as the fourth movement of Opus 103 immediately before the finale, citing interesting evidence for that incorporation. Generally these are fresh, lively performances very well recorded, not as stylish or persuasive as those from the COE soloists using modern instruments, but recommendable to anyone who prefers period style at a lower pitch.

SOLO PIANO MUSIC

Piano sonatas Nos. 1–32 (complete).
❀ (M) (***) EMI mono CHS7 63765-2 (8) [Ang. CDHH 63765]. Artur Schnabel.
(B) *** DG 429 306-2 (9) [id.]. Wilhelm Kempff.
(M) *** EMI CZS7 62863-2 (10). Daniel Barenboim.
(M) **(*) Decca 425 590-2 (10). Vladimir Ashkenazy.
**(*) Nimbus Dig. NI 5050 (*Nos. 1, 22 & 23* (*Appassionata*)); NI 5051 (*Nos. 2, 24 & 28*); NI 5052 (*Nos. 3, 19 & 21* (Waldstein)); NI 5053 (*Nos. 4, 10 & 26* (Les Adieux)); NI 5054 (*Nos. 5–7*); NI 5055 (*Nos. 11, 15 (Pastoral) & 20*); NI 5056 (*Nos. 17* (*Tempest*), *18 & 25*); NI 5057 (*Nos. 13 & 29* (*Hammerklavier*)); NI 5058 (*Nos. 9, 16 & 30*); NI 5059 (*Nos. 12, 14* (*Moonlight*) *& 31*); NI 5060 (*Nos. 8* (*Pathétique*), *27 & 32*) [id.]. Bernard Roberts.

Piano sonatas Nos. 1–32; Andante favori in F, G.170.
**(*) Ph. 412 575-2 (11) [id.]. Alfred Brendel.

Piano sonatas Nos. 1–32; 6 Variations in F, Op. 43; Variations and fugue in E flat on a theme from Prometheus (Eroica), Op. 35; 32 Variations in C min., WoO 80.
(M) *** Ph. 432 301-2 (11) [id.]. Claudio Arrau.

Piano sonatas Nos. 1–15.
**(*) DG Dig. 413 759-2 (6) [id.]. Daniel Barenboim.

Piano sonatas Nos. 16–32.
**(*) DG Dig. 413 766-2 (6) [id.]. Daniel Barenboim.

For many music-lovers and record collectors of an older generation, Schnabel was the voice of Beethoven; returning to this pioneering set again, one realizes that his insights were deeper than those of almost anyone who followed him, though his pianism has been surpassed. It was Schnabel who said that this music is better than it can ever be played, but his profound understanding of it shines through almost every bar. This is one of the towering classics of the gramophone and, whatever other individual Beethoven sonatas you may have, this is an indispensable reference point.

Kempff's recordings, all dating from 1964/5, are to the 1960s what Schnabel's were to the pre-war years – performances that represent a yardstick by which all others are judged. The original LPs lacked the warmth of sonority and bloom of the very finest piano records of the analogue era, but the CD transfers bring a distinct improvement: the sound is fuller and firmer now, and the sense of presence is very striking. Some slight background hiss remains, but Kempff's shading of pianistic colour is so imaginative that the ear readily accommodates any slight dryness in the upper range. The interpretations have a commanding stature, yet Kempff brings his own individuality to every bar and a clarity and sparkle that make you want to go on listening. Of the boxed sets of Beethoven's sonatas now before the public, this would be a first choice for many collectors, and rightly so.

Barenboim's earlier set of the Beethoven *Sonatas*, recorded for EMI when he was in his late twenties, remains one of his very finest achievements on record. The readings are sometimes idiosyncratic, with unexpected tempi both fast and slow, but the spontaneous style is unfailingly compelling. At times Barenboim's way is mercurial, with an element of fantasy. But overall this is a keenly thoughtful musician living through Beethoven's great piano cycle with an individuality that puts him in the line of master pianists.

Ashkenazy's comparable set occupied him over a decade or longer. These are eminently sound, well-recorded performances that deserve to rank among the best. Crisply articulated, intelligently shaped, not always inspired, they are never less than musically satisfying, but the CDs are not always as full and natural as the EMI transfers of the Barenboim cycle.

With eleven hours of music on eleven CDs, the Brendel CD transfers bring out the discrepancies between different recordings made between 1970 and 1977. As to the performances, though they lack some of the fighting spontaneity of the young Brendel many years ago on Turnabout, they have a dark, thoughtful, deeply satisfying quality that consistently gives pleasure.

Spontaneity and electricity, extremes of expression in dynamic, tempo and phrasing as well as mood, mark Barenboim's DG cycle, as they did his much earlier one for EMI. Some of his more extreme readings – such as the sleep-walking tempo for the finale of the *Waldstein* – have been modified to fall short of provocation or eccentricity. This time he has a tendency to rush his fences, particularly in the early sonatas, giving a hint of breathlessness to already fast speeds. That is exceptional, and so is the hint of technical stress. The sound is warm and spacious, much more consistent than before. The CDs – taking the sonatas in consecutive order but on one more disc than his previous recording – come in two separate boxes. However, the earlier set, now available on EMI at bargain price, remains preferable on almost all counts.

Bernard Roberts's series for Nimbus has an inspired directness, with few if any distracting idiosyncrasies but with fine concentration and comparable intensity. The sound on CD is vivid, a full-bodied recording well focused in a helpful but fairly intimate setting. These readings consistently reflect Roberts's dedication as a chamber-music pianist intent on presenting the composer's argument as clearly as possible, not drawing attention to himself. The layout allows one to appreciate the pianist's consistency, when his treatment has an element of toughness even in the early sonatas, and the mature sonatas are marked by rugged power. The eleven discs are available separately, not in a box. In sound, this is the finest Beethoven sonata-cycle yet on CD.

Arrau's Beethoven cycle, recorded during the 1960s, is a survey of extreme distinction. The great Chilean pianist possessed a quite distinctive keyboard sonority, rich and aristocratic in its finesse. Even if one could part company with some of the expressive hesitations that occasionally disrupt the line, there is no doubt that they arise from deeply held musical conviction. The late sonatas show his artistry at its most consummate: one of the very finest of these performances (and one of the very finest records he ever made) is his *Hammerklavier*, which represents his art at its most fully realized. No apologies need be made for the recordings, which belie their age.

Piano sonatas Nos. 1 in F min.; 2 in A; 3 in C, Op. 2/1–3.
(BB) **(*) Naxos Dig. 8.550150; *4550150* [id.]. Jenö Jandó.

Jenö Jandó's complete recording of the Beethoven *Piano sonatas* offers a consistently high standard of musicianship and excellent digital recording. The piano sound is real, full and bold, and well placed within the highly suitable acoustics of the Italian Institute of Budapest, which are neither dry nor too resonant. Apart from the ten separate issues discussed here, the records are also available in two flimsy slip-cases, each comprising five CDs (8.505002 and 8.505003). This first CD (actually Volume 3) establishes Jandó's credentials as a strong, unidiosyncratic Beethovenian. If there is not the individuality of a Kempff or a Barenboim, the playing is always direct and satisfying.

Piano sonatas Nos. 1 in F min., Op. 2/3; 5 in C min.; 6 in F, Op. 10/1–2; 9 in E; 10 in G, Op. 14/1–2; 13 in E flat; 14 in C sharp min. (Moonlight), Op. 27/1–2; 15 in D (Pastoral), Op. 28.
(B) **(*) VoxBox (2) [CDX 5056]. Alfred Brendel.

Though fantasy in a strict sense is not one of his strongest suits, Brendel consistently holds the attention with his unforced and straightforward manner but by his very reticence misses some of the charm which a pianist like Barenboim in his more idiosyncratic way uses to heighten the music's effect. The recordings, made between 1962 and 1964, have been excellently remastered: the piano image is bright, bold and resonant with fine presence, the somewhat clattery quality of the original LPs now better controlled within the ambience, and no lack of sonority. Good notes. These first two Brendel Vox Boxes are not yet issued in the UK.

Piano sonatas Nos. 2 in A, Op. 2/2; 4 in E flat, Op. 7.
*** DG Dig. 415 481-2 [id.]. Emil Gilels.

Gilels's magisterial Beethoven sonatas are one of the glories of the catalogue, and his leonine strength was tempered by a delicacy and poetry that few matched and none have surpassed. His accounts of the *A major Sonata* and the *E flat*, Op. 7, are as masterly as one expects and silence criticism. The recording is clear and well lit in the DG fashion, and does not perhaps do the fullest justice to the sound he produced in the concert hall; but, given such playing, there is no need to withhold the strongest recommendation.

Piano sonatas Nos. 4 in E flat, Op. 7; 13 in E flat, Op. 27/1; 19 in G min., 20 in G, Op. 49/1–2; 22 in F, Op. 54.

(BB) **(*) Naxos Dig. 8.550167; *4550167* [id.]. Jenö Jandó.

The performances of both the *E flat Sonata*, Op. 7, with its memorable slow movement, and the *Sonata quasi una fantasia*, Op. 27/1, in which Jandó is comparably responsive to Beethoven's wide expressive range, show the continuing excellence of this series, and the three shorter works are also freshly presented.

Piano sonatas Nos. 5 in C min.; 6 in F; 7 in D, Op. 10/1–3; 25 in G, Op. 79.
*** EMI Dig. CDC7 54207-2 [id.]. Melvyn Tan (fortepiano).
(BB) *** Naxos Dig. 8.550161 [id.]. Jenö Jandó.

The young Singapore-born Melvyn Tan gives performances of the three Op. 10 *Sonatas* that have both brilliance and sensitivity in equal measure. As in his other recordings in this series, he uses an instrument by Derek Adlam based on a Nanette Streicher of 1815, and even collectors whose taste inclines to the modern piano rather than the fortepiano will surely find both the sounds and the musical sense well conveyed here. Tan's survey of the Beethoven *Sonatas* is proving as illuminating and as satisfying as his set of the *Concertos*. Recommended with enthusiasm.

The three splendid Op. 10 *Sonatas* show Jandó at his most perceptive and unselfconscious. The performances are spontaneous and admirably paced, and the musical characterization is strong.

Piano sonatas Nos. 5 in C min.; 10 in G, Op. 14/2; 19 in G min.; 20 in G, Op. 49/1–2.
**(*) DG Dig. 419 172-2 [id.]. Emil Gilels.

Gilels manages to make one believe that his is exactly the *tempo giusto* even when one feels tempted to question the very deliberate speed he adopts in the slow movement of the *C minor*, Op. 10, No. 1. He can even almost convince one in what at first seems (and is) an eccentricity: the explosive opening to the second group of the first movement, a staccato sforzando sustained on the middle pedal. This really disturbs the balance of the phrase. However, such is his magic that, while under his spell, doubts are silenced. He is well recorded, too.

Piano sonatas Nos. 7 in D, Op. 10/3; 18 in E flat, Op. 31/3; 15 Variations and fugue on a theme from Prometheus (Eroica variations), Op. 35.
*** DG 423 136-2 [id.]. Emil Gilels.

Gilels's account of the *Eroica variations* is masterly. In the *D major Sonata* he is hardly less impressive, though there are odd mannerisms. Op. 31, No. 3 is distinguished, too, though the recording acoustic is somewhat drier than that of its companions.

Piano sonatas Nos. 7 in D; 23 in F min. (Appassionata), Op. 57.
*** Sony Dig. MK 39344 [id.]. Murray Perahia.

Intense, vibrant playing from Perahia in the *D major Sonata*, with great range of colour and depth of thought. The slow movement is a model of sensitivity and keyboard colour, and the *Appassionata* is a performance of comparable stature. These are among the few interpretations to have appeared in recent years that can be recommended alongside Gilels. The recorded sound is truthful.

Piano sonatas Nos. 8 (Pathétique), Op. 13; 13; 14 (Moonlight), Op. 27/1–2.
**(*) DG Dig. 400 036-2 [id.]. Emil Gilels.

Gilels's compact disc, coupling the two Op. 27 sonatas and the *Pathétique*, does not quite rank among his very best (such as the *Waldstein* and Op. 101). The opening movement of the *Moonlight* is wonderfully serene, and there are many felicities. But the first movement of the *E flat Sonata* is strangely reserved, as if Gilels feared the charge of self-indulgence or out-of-period sentiment. However, such are the strengths of this playing that few will quarrel with the magnificence of his conceptions of all three pieces. The digital recording is lifelike, although the balance is very close.

Piano sonatas Nos. 8 in C min. (Pathétique), Op. 13; 14 in C sharp min. (Moonlight), Op. 27/2; 15 in D (Pastoral), Op. 28; 23 in F min. (Appassionata), Op. 57; 26 in E flat (Les Adieux), Op. 81a (CD only: *17 in D min. (Tempest), Op. 31/2*).
(B) *** DG Compact Classics 413 435-2 (2); *413 435-4* [id.]. Wilhelm Kempff.

Piano sonatas Nos. 8 in C min. (Pathétique), Op. 13; 14 in C sharp min. (Moonlight), Op. 27/2; 15 in D (Pastoral), Op. 28; 24 in F sharp, Op. 78.

(M) *** DG 415 834-2; *415 834-4* [id.]. Wilhelm Kempff.

Kempff's masterly recordings show so well his ability to rethink Beethoven's music within the recording studio. Everything he does has his individual stamp, and above all he never fails to convey the deep intensity of a master in communion with Beethoven.

Piano sonatas Nos. 8 in C min. (Pathétique), Op. 13; 14 in C sharp min. (Moonlight), Op. 27/2; 23 in F min. (Appassionata), Op. 57.
*** Decca 410 260-2; *410 260-4* [id.]. Vladimir Ashkenazy.
**(*) Ph. 411 470-2 [id.]. Alfred Brendel.
(M) **(*) Sony MYK 42539 [id.]. Rudolf Serkin.
(BB) **(*) Naxos Dig. 8.550045; *4550045* [id.]. Jenö Jandó.

Ashkenazy's *Pathétique* is perhaps slightly understated for so ebulliently youthful a work, with the finale unusually gentle; nevertheless the performance conveys the underlying power. The *Moonlight* is generally successful, and the *Appassionata* is admirable. He is well served by the engineers and the analogue recordings are very well transferred to CD. However, the *Moonlight* and the *Appassionata* are also available at mid-price – see below.

Brendel's performances, too, are undoubtedly impressive, the *Moonlight* beautifully played, the others strong and thoughtful, yet not lacking power. The sound is full-bodied and clear, although plainly from an analogue source.

Serkin's aristocratic approach is immediately apparent at the opening of the *Moonlight Sonata*, and in the allegros he is as incisive and dramatic as ever. As with all master pianists, one finds many points of insight emerging as well as one or two points of personal mannerism. The piano recording, from the early 1960s, is firmer and more real than in its previous LP incarnation.

Jandó's grouping of the three most famous named sonatas immediately establishes the lifelike nature of the Naxos recording. Jandó's clean, direct style and natural spontaneity are particularly admirable in the slow movements of the *Pathétique* and *Appassionata*, warmly lyrical in feeling, yet not a whit sentimental. Only in the coda of the finale of the *Appassionata* does one feel a loss of poise, when the closing *presto* becomes *prestissimo* and the exuberance of the music-making nearly gets out of control.

Piano sonatas Nos. 8 in C min., (Pathétique); 29 in B flat, (Hammerklavier); Fantasy in G min., Op. 77.
(M) ** Sony SBK 42766. Rudolf Serkin.

Serkin's account of the *Hammerklavier* has great renown and music lovers speak with awe of his concert performances in the 1970s. This version comes from 1970 and can be recommended to his admirers rather than the uninitiated. There is plenty of obtrusive (very obtrusive) pedal stamping and some ugly tone in fortissimos; he pulls some phrases out of shape too and then suddenly takes one by surprise by some particularly thoughtful insight. The performance as a whole has an intimidating reputation but seems more to be admired for being admired than for its real musical merits. The recording is somewhat two dimensional and shallow. Readers who are not Serkin fanatics are directed to the impressive accounts on the market by Gilels, Kempff, Arrau and Brendel. The *Pathétique* is of earlier provenance and though it is more closely balanced sounds curiously fresher.

Piano sonatas Nos. 9 in E; 10 in G, Op. 14/1–2; 24 in F sharp, Op. 78; 27 in E min., Op. 90; 28 in A, Op. 101.
(BB) *** Naxos Dig. 8.550162; *4550162* [id.]. Jenö Jandó.

These readings are freshly immediate and communicative, very like being at a live recital. Opp. 90 and 101 show this artist at full stretch. These are demanding works and Jandó does not fall short, particularly in the slow movements, which are very eloquent indeed. The piano sound is most believable.

Piano sonatas Nos. 11 in B flat, Op. 22; 12 in A flat (Funeral march), Op. 26; 15 in D (Pastoral).
(BB) **(*) ASV CDQS 6059; *ZCQS 6059*. John Lill.

No. 11 is strongly characterized here, but charm plays no part at all in John Lill's Beethoven; that is clear, not just in the rugged account of the *Funeral march* of Op. 26, but also in the first two movements, the lyrical variations and the sparkling scherzo. Lill adopts very deliberate tempi in the *Pastoral*, where one feels some want of flow, yet the playing has a strong profile throughout. The sound on CD is undeniably impressive, bold and with good presence and a fuller sonority than in Jandó's Naxos series.

Piano sonatas Nos. 11 in B flat, Op. 22; 18 in B flat, Op. 31/3.
**(*) Dell'Arte DBS 7004. Earl Wild.

These are distinguished performances. The interrelationships of mood and pacing of the *B flat Sonata* are particularly finely judged. Its good-tempered character is caught well, and the *Adagio*'s songful *con molto expressione* is a highlight of the reading. Op. 31/2 is equally successful, with Wild's technical command at its most impressive in the strongly articulated Scherzo and the brilliant closing *Presto con fuoco*. These performances have the excitement of live music-making, and the clear, bold, 1984 recording brings out the special colour and sonority of Wild's chosen Bösendorfer. But it is a pity that a third sonata was not included – there was plenty of room for one.

Piano sonatas Nos. 11 in B flat, Op. 22; 29 in B flat (Hammerklavier), Op. 106.
(BB) **(*) Naxos Dig. 8.550234; *4550234* [id.]. Jenö Jandó.

Jandó's articulation in the first movement of this *B flat Sonata*, Op. 22, (as in the *Waldstein*) is almost too clear and clean in its precision; the *Adagio*, however, is played most expressively. From its very opening bars the *Hammerklavier* is commanding; there is rapt concentration in the slow movement, and the closing fugue runs its course with a powerful inevitability. Again, most realistic recording.

Piano sonatas Nos. 12 in A flat, Op. 26; 16 in G; 18 in E flat, Op. 31/1 & 3.
(BB) **(*) Naxos Dig. 8.550166 [id.]. Jenö Jandó.

Volume 7 with its trio of middle-period sonatas can be recommended with few reservations. No. 18 is a considerable success, and there is much to stimulate the listener's interest here. Excellent sound.

Piano sonatas Nos. 13 in E flat, Op. 27/1; 15 (Pastoral), Op. 28; 21 (Waldstein), Op. 53.
*** DG Dig. 423 577-2 [id.]. Daniel Barenboim.

This triptych shows Barenboim at his best, with the lyrical flow in both the *Waldstein* and the *Pastoral* as evident as the undoubted spontaneity of the music-making. Good recording.

Piano sonatas Nos. 14 in C sharp min. (Moonlight), Op. 27/2; 17 in D min. (Tempest), Op. 31; 26 in E flat (Les Adieux), Op. 81a.
(M) **(*) DG Dig. 427 803-2; *427 803-4* [id.]. Daniel Barenboim.

A good example of Barenboim's spontaneous studio style in his second set of Beethoven sonatas, recorded digitally for DG in 1984. Perhaps the opening of the *Moonlight* could be less withdrawn, but the rest of the work springs readily to life. Realistic recording, with a natural presence.

Piano sonatas Nos. 14 in C sharp min. (Moonlight), Op. 27/2; 21 in C (Waldstein), Op. 53; 23 in F min. (Appassionata), Op. 57.
*** Virgin Dig. VC 790737-2 [id.]. Mikhail Pletnev.
(M) *** Decca 417 732-2. Vladimir Ashkenazy.
(M) **(*) BMG/RCA GD 60375 [60375-2-RG]. Vladimir Horowitz.
(M) **(*) DG Dig. 435 100-2; *435 100-4* [id.]. Daniel Barenboim.
(BB) **(*) Naxos Dig. 8.550294 [id.]. Jenö Jandó.

Pletnev is an artist of stature, strong in personality and with a commanding sense of keyboard colour. Some will find the *Moonlight* a bit mannered (the second movement is undoubtedly quirky), but he has the capacity to make you listen intently – as every great pianist does. The clarity of articulation is altogether remarkable in the finale, and in the *Waldstein*; he also finds the right depths in its slow movement and finale. The account of the *Appassionata* is masterly: it has a sense of scale and grand design, and a feeling for both line and refinement of detail. The engineering is immaculate and does justice to Pletnev's individual sound-world.

An excellent mid-priced grouping of three popular sonatas from Ashkenazy. The *Waldstein* (1975) is splendidly structured and the *Appassionata* (1973) superb, although those who feel strongly about matters of tempo may well find Ashkenazy a little too free in the first movement.

Horowitz was not thought of primarily as a Beethoven pianist, but these recordings, made in 1956 (the *Moonlight* and *Waldstein*) and 1959, show how powerful he could be in the music of this composer. His delicacy, too, is equally impressive. There is prodigious bravura, too, as in the finale of the *Appassionata*, where he matches – and perhaps even surpasses – Richter in exuberance. The sound has been improved in the remastering process; there is some hardness on top but little shallowness, and the bass sonority is telling.

Barenboim plays the *Appassionata* with real panache, and his straightforwardly lyrical account of the *Waldstein* is more persuasive than was his earlier version for EMI, with its controversial tempi in the outer movements (and especially in the finale); this time all three movements are convincing in their lyricism.

This is a separate, alternative grouping of the named sonatas in Jandó's highly musical and well-recorded performances, not included in the boxed sets.

Piano sonatas Nos. 15 in D (Pastoral), Op. 28; 17 in D min. (Tempest), Op. 31/2.
** DG Dig. 419 161-2 [id.]. Emil Gilels.

Gilels's *Pastoral* is a strange performance – a laboured, almost hectoring first movement, very deliberate in tempo and character, with little sense of flow and only occasional glimpses of the wisdom and humanity one associates with this great artist. The *Tempest sonata*, Op. 31, No. 2, is another matter; this performance has excited universal acclaim, and rightly so. The balance of the recording is excessively close.

Piano sonatas: No. 15 in D (Pastoral), Op. 28; (Kurfürstensonaten) in E flat, F min., D, WoO 47/1–3; in C (incomplete), *WoO 51; Sonatinas: in G, F, Anh. 5/1–2.*
(BB) ** Naxos Dig. 8.550255 [id.]. Jenö Jandó.

Jandó's playing is fresh, clean and intelligent and, if the two *Sonatinas* are not authentic, they make agreeable listening here. The *Pastoral sonata* is admirably done.

Piano sonatas Nos. 16 in G; 17 in D min. (Tempest); 18 in E flat, Op. 31/1–3.
*** Decca 417 663-2 [id.]. Vladimir Ashkenazy (piano).

The CD grouping of the Op. 31 sonatas is highly successful. The performances are among the best of Ashkenazy's Beethoven cycle: he brings concentration of mind, together with spontaneity of feeling. The command of keyboard colour is, as always, impressive and in terms of both dramatic tension and the sense of architecture these are thoroughly satisfying performances. The recordings date from 1976/7.

Piano sonatas Nos. 16 in G; 17 in D min. (Tempest); 18 in E flat, Op. 31/1–3; 19 in G min., Op. 49/1; 21 in C (Waldstein), Op. 53; 22 in F, Op. 54; 23 in F min. (Appassionata), Op. 57; 26 in E flat (Les Adieux), Op. 81a.
(B) **(*) VoxBox (2) [CDX 5052]. Alfred Brendel.

This box contains two of Brendel's very finest Beethoven performances. Op. 31/2 with its romantic echoes of Beethoven's improvisational style, produces electrically sharp playing and spontaneity; in the *Waldstein* too, Brendel's fresh and straightforward concentration produces a cleanly satisfying version, spontaneous-sounding but controlled. The *Appassionata*, however, is one of the less imaginative readings in Brendel's Vox cycle. The slow movement of *Les Adieux* lacks a hushed quality; the finale is strong and direct. The other sonatas here are well up to the standard of the series and there is more in this box to admire than to cavil at. Again the 1962–4 recordings have been remastered effectively and the piano recording has plenty of body and presence.

Piano sonatas Nos. 17 in D min., Op. 31/2; 18 in E flat, Op. 31/3; 26 in E flat (Les Adieux), Op. 81a.
*** Sony Dig. MK 42319 [id.]. Murray Perahia.

Wonderfully concentrated performances. The *D minor*, Op. 31, No. 2, is magisterial in its control and command of poetic feeling: the finest since Solomon. All these readings have the blend of authority, finesse and poetry that distinguishes this great artist at his best. The recording is acceptable.

Piano sonatas Nos. 17 in D min. (Tempest), Op. 31/2; 21 in C (Waldstein), Op. 53; 25 in G, Op. 79; 26 in E flat (Les Adieux), Op. 81a.
**(*) DG 427 642-2 [id.]. Maurizio Pollini.

Pollini's impeccable keyboard mastery is always evident, though the recital as a whole is a little problematic: the opening of the 'little' *G major*, Op. 79, is tossed off rather uncaringly, and there is little of the lightness of touch it calls for. The *Waldstein* has a fine sense of pace and *Les Adieux* is impressive, if a little lacking in poetic intensity. Op. 31, No. 2, brings a perfectly proportioned account, but one that seems to draw us into its world only sporadically. The engineers do not allow too much of the ambience of the acoustic to help him and, though the piano sound is not dry, it is somewhat close and clinical.

Piano sonatas Nos. 17 in D min. (Tempest), Op. 31/2; 21 in C (Waldstein), Op. 53; 26 in E flat (Les Adieux), Op. 81a.
(BB) **(*) Naxos Dig. 8.550054 [id.]. Jenö Jandó.

Jandó offers here the other three famous named sonatas, and very enjoyable they are in their direct manner, if lacking that little extra imaginative touch that Kempff, for one, can bring to the *Waldstein*. But *Les Adieux* has a simplicity that is disarming, and Op. 31/2 has strength and fine control of the work's emotional ebb and flow.

Piano sonatas Nos. 17 in D min. (Tempest), Op. 31/2; 29 in B flat (Hammerklavier), Op. 106.
(M) *** DG 419 857-2 [id.]. Wilhelm Kempff.

Kempff's *Hammerklavier* performance represents his interpretative approach to Beethoven at its most extreme and therefore controversial. Here his preference for measured allegros and fastish andantes gives a different weighting to movements from the usual, but there is a thoughtfulness of utterance which brings profundity. The coupling also has its own special insights, and the sound is clean and clear.

Piano sonatas Nos. 21 in C (Waldstein), Op. 53; 23 in F min. (Appassionata), Op. 57; 26 in E flat (Les Adieux), Op. 81a.
❀ *** DG 419 162-2 [id.]. Emil Gilels.
*** EMI Dig. CDC7 49330-2 [id.]. Melvyn Tan (fortepiano).
(M) *** DG 419 053-2 [id.]. Wilhelm Kempff.

This recoupling offers three of Gilels's finest analogue recordings dating from 1972–5. The piano is believably present, but much less closely observed than in his later digital recordings, to great advantage. The account of the *Appassionata* has previously been hailed by us as among the finest ever made, and much the same must be said of the *Waldstein*. It has a technical perfection denied even to Schnabel, and Gilels is hardly less searching and profound. Moreover, Gilels's fastidiously sensitive yet commanding *Les Adieux* is also one of the most impressive ever committed to disc. These are all performances to relish, to study and to keep for special occasions.

Melvyn Tan offers a CD for those who are unconverted to the fortepiano and find its exponents tame. Tan has a strong musical personality and attacks his instrument with tremendous spirit and flair; every phrase lives and he is not afraid to present the widest dynamic spectrum and expressive range. In all three sonatas he exhibits consummate artistry and real temperament and fire. Nor is there any want of poetic feeling. He plays on a copy by Derek Adlam of a Streicher (1814), an instrument for which Beethoven himself expressed a strong preference. The EMI recording is excellent: in short, an outstanding issue.

Kempff's *Appassionata* is characteristically clear, classically straight in the same way that the *Waldstein* is cooler and fresher than usual, with a wonderful purity in the rippling quavers. *Les Adieux*, like the *Appassionata*, may be less weightily dramatic than in other readings, but the concentration is irresistible.

Piano sonata No. 23 in F min. (Appassionata), Op. 57.
(M) *** BMG/RCA 7863 56518 [RCA 6518-2-RG]. Sviatoslav Richter – BRAHMS: *Piano concerto No. 2.* ***

Richter's thrilling 1960 *Appassionata* is a superb example of a studio recording sounding like a live performance, with the wide dynamic range bringing out both the drama and passion of this boldly contrasted sonata. Some might feel that Richter goes over the top in the coda of the finale but the fervour is unmistakable.

Piano sonatas Nos. 24 in F sharp, Op. 78; 25 in G, Op. 79; 26 in E flat (Les Adieux), Op. 81a; 28 in A, Op. 101.
(BB) **(*) ASV CDQS 6062; *ZCQS 6062*. John Lill.

The poised opening of No. 24, Op. 78, shows Lill at his most appealingly direct, and this CD offers some of the most characteristic performances in his cycle. There is no compromise in Op. 79 and the first movement is played brutally fast, emphasizing the contrast with the *Andante*; the finale, however, flows pleasingly. *Les Adieux* is a distinct success, the *Vivacissimante* finale strong and positive, while the *Adagio* of No. 28 again shows the keen grip and intelligence of

Lill's approach. The piano is recorded close, but the sound is well balanced and the presence is convincingly real. Excellent value.

Piano sonatas Nos. 24 in F sharp, Op. 78; 29 in B flat (Hammerklavier), Op. 106.
**(*) Ph. 412 723-2 [id.]. Alfred Brendel.

The CD coupling of the *Hammerklavier* and Opus 78 comes not from Brendel's complete sonata cycle but from a live recording made at the Queen Elizabeth Hall in London a decade later. Though there is greater urgency and dramatic tension in the allegro movements, the great *Adagio* of the *Hammerklavier*, intense as it is, lacks the spacious sublimity of his earlier (1972) version, taken even more slowly.

Piano sonatas Nos. 28 in A, Op. 101; 29 (Hammerklavier), Op. 106; 30 in E, Op. 109; 31 in A flat, Op. 110; 32 in C min., Op. 111.
**(*) DG 429 569-2 (*28 & 29*); 429 570-2 (*30–32*) [id.]. Pollini.

Pollini's recordings of the late *Sonatas* (which on LP originally included No. 27) won the 1977 *Gramophone* Critics' award for instrumental music and they contain playing of the highest order of mastery. Joan Chissell spoke of the 'noble purity' of these performances, and that telling phrase aptly sums them up, if also hinting perhaps at a missing dimension, which the CD transfer seems to emphasize. The sound has great presence but on the first disc there is hardness to the timbre in Opus 101 which becomes almost brittle in the fortissimos of the *Hammerklavier* with an adverse effect on the music-making. Pollini's *Hammerklavier* is undoubtedly eloquent, and so is Op. 111, which has a peerless authority and power. However, the slow movement of Op. 110 may be a trifle fast for some tastes, and in the A major work Gilels has greater poetry and humanity. The second disc brings a close balance to Opp. 109 and 110 but the recordings seem fractionally mellower, although a touch of hardness comes back in Op. 111. The two discs are now reissued separately, with no price reduction.

Piano sonatas Nos. 28 in A, Op. 101; 29 in B flat (Hammerklavier), Op. 106.
(M) *** DG Dig. 429 485-2; *429 485-4* [id.]. Daniel Barenboim.

In his second digital cycle for DG, Barenboim was at his finest in the late *Sonatas*, and the sustained concentration of the slow movement of the *Hammerklavier* is, like the brief Adagio before the *attaca* into the finale, another passage of Barenboim magic. Excellent recording, with real presence.

Piano sonata No. 29 (Hammerklavier), Op. 106.
*** DG Dig. 410 527-2 [id.]. Emil Gilels.

Gilels's *Hammerklavier* is a performance of supreme integrity, Olympian, titanic, subtle, imperious, one of the finest accounts ever recorded. Speeds for the outer movements are surprisingly spacious and relaxed, with clarity of texture and refinement of detail brought out. Yet the concentration brings the most powerful impact – not just in those movements but in all four. The recording is close and bright and harder than ideal.

Piano sonatas Nos. 30 in E, Op. 109; 31 in A flat, Op. 110.
*** DG Dig. 419 174-2 [id.]. Emil Gilels.
❀ (M) (***) EMI mono CDH7 63787-2 [id.]. Myra Hess (with BACH: *Jesu, joy of man's desiring* and music by BEETHOVEN, BRAHMS, GRANADOS, MENDELSSOHN and D. SCARLATTI (***)).

On DG the opening movement of Op. 110 is enormously spacious and its breadth of vision (and tempo) can only be called Olympian. Both sonatas are given performances of stature that seek out their profoundest truths. Even when Gilels storms the greatest heights in the closing fugue of Op. 110, no fortissimo ever sounds percussive or strained. DG seem to have found a more truthful sound-balance here than they did for his *Moonlight* and *Pathétique*.

These celebrated performances by Dame Myra Hess were recorded in mono in 1953, and to say that the sound is greatly improved is something of an understatement: it is much firmer at both ends of the register and is altogether more cleanly focused. Myra Hess was in her mid-sixties at this time and her playing is every bit as masterly and seraphic as one had remembered; Desmond Shawe-Taylor and Edward Sackville-West in *The Record Guide* said that her Beethoven performances could 'safely be held up as models of style'. At times, some might feel the need for a more firmly etched line (in the final movement of Op. 110, for instance), but most collectors will wonder at her great plasticity of touch and sheer tonal beauty. The record comes with a generous recital of encore pieces, ranging from her famous arrangement of Bach's *Jesu, joy of man's desiring*, Brahms, Beethoven (*Für Elise*), two Scarlatti sonatas, Granados (*The*

Maiden and the nightingale) and a Mendelssohn *Song without words*, all recorded in the late 1950s. But it is for the Beethoven collector that these thoughtful and deeply musical performances will be essential.

Piano sonatas Nos. 30 in E, Op. 109; 31 in A flat, Op. 110; 32 in C min., Op. 111.
(BB) *** Naxos Dig. 8.550151 [id.]. Jenö Jandó.
*** Calliope CAL 9648 [id.]. Inger Södergren.

The last three sonatas of Beethoven, offered in Volume 4, are very imposing indeed in Jandó's hands. Moreover they are given very realistic recording, with great presence. There is serenity and gravitas in these readings and a powerful control of structure.

Inger Södergren is a Swedish pianist, little known in her native country, who lives in France where she enjoys a considerable reputation; indeed her performances and recordings are regarded there with as much respect as those of Brendel. Her analogue accounts of Opp. 110 and 111 come from 1979, when they earned golden opinions. They are musically most impressive. She is obviously a pianist of keen musical insights. Her recording of Op. 109 is new: it is brighter and more forward; while Op. 110 reminds one a little of Myra Hess's old mono LP, but this reading is even stronger. These performances are fit to keep exalted company even if the recordings of Opp. 110 and 111 are not quite three-star.

Piano sonatas Nos. 31 in A flat, Op. 110; 32 in C min., Op. 111.
**(*) DG Dig. 423 371-2 [id.]. Daniel Barenboim.

Though Barenboim's readings of the last two sonatas – taken from his DG cycle of all 32 – are not as spaciously spontaneous-sounding as they were in his earlier series for EMI, they make a splendid coupling, deeply thoughtful and strongly expressed.

Miscellaneous piano music

Allegretto in C min., WoO 53; Andante favori, WoO 57; Für Elise, WoO 59; 6 Variations in F, Op. 34.
*** EMI CDC7 49793-2 [id.]. Melvyn Tan (fortepiano) – SCHUBERT: *Moments musicaux* etc. ***

Melvyn Tan plays a copy by Richard Adlam of an 1814 fortepiano by Nanette Streicher, and brings to these pieces his customary flair and panache. He is a spirited artist and an enormously persuasive exponent of the fortepiano. The *F major Variations* come off splendidly: there is plenty of colour and imagination throughout. Despite his rather brisk *Andante favori*, this is a thoroughly enjoyable recital and is recorded with great realism and presence in The Maltings at Snape.

7 Bagatelles, Op. 33; 11 Bagatelles, Op. 119; 6 Bagatelles, Op. 126.
(B) *** Ph. 426 976-2; *426 976-4*. Stephen Kovacevich.
(BB) **(*) Naxos Dig. 8.550474 [id.]. Jenö Jandó.

Beethoven's *Bagatelles*, particularly those from Opp. 119 and 126, have often been described as chips from the master's workbench; but rarely if ever has that description seemed so apt as in these searchingly simple and completely spontaneous readings by Kovacevich.

Jandó plays the early set of *Bagatelles*, which date from 1802, with a crisply rhythmic style, almost at times as if he was thinking of a fortepiano. He is also attractively impulsive in manner. Then in the later works he finds more depth of tone and is thoughtful as well as flamboyant. He certainly characterizes strongly in Op. 126. He has an excellent, modern, digital recording (made in the Budapest Unitarian Church), and his playing is both stimulating and enjoyable, if not quite as distinctive as with Kovacevich.

6 Bagatelles, Op. 126; 6 Écossaises, WoO 83; Für Elise, WoO 59; 15 Variations and fugue on a theme from Prometheus (Eroica variations), Op. 35.
*** Ph. 412 227-2 [id.]. Alfred Brendel.

Brendel may lack some of the sheer bravura of his own early playing in this collection of shorter pieces, but his consistent thoughtfulness and imagination bring out the truly Beethovenian qualities of even the most trivial pieces. The *Eroica variations*, not as flamboyant as with some, plainly point to the magnificence of their culminating development in the *Eroica* finale. Excellent recording: the CD is outstandingly realistic.

Bagatelles, Op. 126; Polonaise in C, Op. 89; Variations and fugue on a theme from Prometheus (Eroica variations), Op. 35.
*** Nimbus Dig. NIM 5017 [id.]. Bernard Roberts.

Bernard Roberts gives a characteristically fresh and forthright reading of the *Eroica variations*, recorded in exceptionally vivid sound. He may not have quite the dash of Brendel, but the crispness and clarity of his playing are most refreshing. The shorter pieces bring performances even more intense, with the *Bagatelles* for all their brevity given last-period intensity.

6 Variations in F, Op. 34; 15 Variations and fugue on a theme from Prometheus in E flat (Eroica variations), Op. 35; 2 Rondos, Op. 51; Bagatelle: Für Elise, WoO 59.
*** Chan. Dig. CHAN 8616; *ABTD 1305* [id.]. Louis Lortie.

The Canadian pianist Louis Lortie is an artist of distinction, and his performances of both the *Eroica* and the *F major variations*, Op. 34, deserve the highest accolade. His readings have both grandeur and authority, and his pianism has an elegance and sensitivity that are always put to musical ends. The Chandos recording, made at The Maltings, Snape, does full justice to the wide range of colour and dynamic nuance he commands. This account of the *Eroica variations* belongs in exalted company and can be recommended alongside such magisterial accounts as that of Gilels.

6 Variations in F, Op. 34; 6 Variations in G on 'Nel cor più non mi sento', WoO 70; 5 Variations in D on Rule Britannia, WoO 79.
*** Ph. Dig. 432 093-2; *432 093-4* [id.]. Alfred Brendel – SCHUMANN: *Symphonic études.* ***

Brendel's Philips accounts of the *F major variations*, Op. 34, and the *G major* set on *'Nel cor più non mi sento'* from Paisiello's *La mollinara* come as a pendant to his magisterial account of the Schumann *Études symphoniques.* This is among the best records he has given us in recent years, full of intelligence and, in the *Rule Britannia* variations, wit. Exemplary recordings made in The Maltings, Snape, fuller and more natural than his early records of this repertoire for Vox.

33 Variations on a Waltz by Diabelli, Op. 120.
(B) *** Ph. 422 969-2; *422 969-4*. Stephen Kovacevich.
*** Ph. Dig. 426 232-2 [id.]. Alfred Brendel.
**(*) Unicorn Kanchana Dig. DKPCD 9084; *DKPC 9084* [id.]. Peter Hill.
**(*) Ph. 416 295-2 [id.]. Claudio Arrau.
**(*) Sony Dig. SK 48060 [id.]. Stefan Vladar.
(B) ** HM HMA 905127. Friedrich Gulda.
* DG Dig. 435 615-2 [id.]. Anatol Ugorski.

33 Variations on a waltz by Diabelli, Op. 120; 32 Variations in C min.
*** ASV Dig. CDDCA 715; *ZCDCA 715* [id.]. Benjamin Frith.

Benjamin Frith's is the finest of all the new generation of digital recordings of the *Diabelli variations.* Frith, who won the Artur Rubinstein International Piano Competition in Tel-Aviv in 1989, brings out both rhythmic urgency and power, playing with a consistent sense of spontaneity, persuasively leading on from one variation to the next. It is remarkable that a young pianist should not only play this virtuoso work with such fire and flair, but should bring such intensity to the great meditative variations. Not that his speeds are slow, but in the great *Adagio* variations he has the gift of conveying magnetic intensity in the way he controls the flow of the music. He then takes the great fugue just before the end at a sensible speed that allows him to spring the rhythms and shape it effectively, rounding the work off with a crisply pointed account of the final *Minuet*, which keeps in mind its dance origin. On a generously filled disc Frith also offers a masterfully dramatic account of the *32 Variations in C minor*, in which flamboyant virtuosity and poetry are well contrasted. Good, bright piano sound set in a helpfully warm acoustic.

Kovacevich gives one of the most deeply satisfying performances ever recorded. Avoiding the idiosyncrasies of most other interpreters, he may at times seem austere, but his concentration is magnetic from first to last, and the variety of expression within his unmannered approach has one thinking direct to Beethoven, with fearless dynamic contrasts enhanced in the CD transfer.

Unlike his previous CD version, taken from a live performance given at the Queen Elizabeth Hall in London in 1977, Brendel's later recording was done in digital sound in the studio. The glory of the earlier performance was its daring, with the mercurial side of Brendel given full rein; to an amazing degree Brendel, here working in the studio, recaptures that earthshaking dynamism, the sense of an irresistible force building up this immense structure, section by section. It would be hard to imagine a more dramatic reading, sparked off by the cheeky wit of Brendel's treatment of the Diabelli theme itself. The keynotes are power and urgency, and it follows that Brendel is reluctant to treat the great slow variations, Nos. 14, 29, 30 and 31, as deeply meditative, even avoiding half-tones. But the whirlwind power of the whole performance is irresistible, and the piano sound is full and immediate.

Peter Hill gives a thoughtful reading of the *Diabelli variations*, relatively intimate in manner. Though the more taxing virtuoso variations seem a degree too cautious, giving them too small a scale, his performance rises to a telling climax in the big meditative variations, notably those near the end of the great sequence. At generally spacious speeds, well recorded, this has its distinctive place.

Arrau in his eighties demonstrates formidable virtuosity in tackling this Everest of the keyboard, even if at times the strain shows. What matters is the concentration of his playing, his ability to hold the whole massive structure together, whatever the problems of detail, full of new insights. The sound is very immediate, perhaps too much so for such a work.

Stefan Vladar is a formidable young Austrian pianist who gives a flamboyant reading of Beethoven's monumental set of variations, relishing the technical difficulties, often adopting daringly fast speeds, and falling short only in the deeper, more meditative variations, where the underlining of expressiveness conveys a hint of self-consciousness. Good recording.

Gulda in his vintage performance adopts speeds so fast that at times they are scarcely credible. His overall timing of under 45 minutes (as against a full hour from many pianists) may give an idea of that haste. Yet his eccentricities go with a fine rhythmic control, so that the sheer exuberance of his playing carries one along. Unfortunately, the 1970 sound is disconcertingly boxy and close.

The Russian pianist, Anatol Ugorski, would take a prize for wilful eccentricity, even against such previous DG-nominated stars of the keyboard as Lazar Berman and Ivo Pogorelich. Like them he plays with charismatic intensity, but the unsteady speeds and distorted rhythms, often at totally impossible speeds make his recording of the *Diabelli* a curiosity and little more.

VOCAL MUSIC

Lieder: *Adelaide; Ich liebe Dich; Der Kuss; Resignation.*
(M) **(*) DG 429 933-2 [id.]. Fritz Wunderlich, Hubert Giesen – SCHUBERT: *Lieder;* SCHUMANN: *Dichterliebe.* ***

Wunderlich was thirty-five when he recorded these songs and the unique bloom of the lovely voice is beautifully caught. Though the accompanist is too metrical at times, the freshness of Wunderlich's singing makes one grieve again over his untimely death.

Ah! perfido (concert aria), *Op. 65.*
(M) ** EMI CMS7 63625-2 (2) [Ang. CDMB 63625]. Callas, Paris Conservatoire O, Rescigno – CHERUBINI: *Medea.* **

Recorded in 1964 at what proved to be the very end of her recording career, this Beethoven scena exposes the flaws that sadly emerged in the great Callas voice, but her fire-eating manner is irresistible. A welcome fill-up for the Cherubini opera.

An die ferne Geliebte, Op. 98. Lieder: *Adelaide; L'amant impaziente; Es war einmal ein König; In questa tomba oscura; Maigesang; Zartliche Liebe.*
**(*) DG 415 189-2 [id.]. Dietrich Fischer-Dieskau, Joerg Demus – BRAHMS: *Lieder.* **(*)

Recorded in 1966, Fischer-Dieskau's DG Beethoven selection finds him at his vocal peak, and though Demus's accompaniment is not as imaginative as the singer received in other versions of these songs, Fischer-Dieskau's individuality is as positive as ever, with detail touched in as with no one else.

An die ferne Geliebte, Op. 98. Lieder: *Adelaide; Andenken; An die Hoffnung; Aus Goethes Faust (Song of the flea); Busslied; Ich liebe dich; Der Kuss; Mailied; Neue Liebe; Resignation; Der Wachtelschlag; Der Zufriedene.*
**(*) Amon Ra CDSAR 15. Ian Partridge, Richard Burnett.

Partridge, accompanied on an 1800 fortepiano, gives delightful performances of a wide-ranging and generous collection of Beethoven songs. The honeyed tones of Partridge's tenor and his finely detailed feeling for words come over well – particularly suited not only to the song-cycle but also to such soaring lyrical songs as *Adelaide* and *An die Hoffnung*. The twangy fortepiano is recorded much more dully.

Bundeslied, Op. 122; Eligischer Gesang, Op. 118; King Stephen (incidental music), *Op. 117; Meeresstille und glückliche Fahrt (Calm sea and a prosperous voyage), Op. 112; Opferlied, Op. 121b.*
*** Sony Dig. CD 76404 [MK 33509]. Amb. S., LSO, Tilson Thomas.

With the 1975 CBS sound fresher and more atmospheric than ever on CD, Tilson Thomas's collection of Beethoven choral rarities plus the *King Stephen* incidental music makes an attractive out-of-the-way disc for Beethovenians. Except for *Meeresstille* (*Calm sea and a prosperous voyage*) with its deeply meditative, highly original first half, these are no more than random chips from the master's workbench; but with excellent singing and playing they are all enjoyable.

Choral fantasia in C, Op. 80.
*** Capriccio Dig. 10 150 [id.]. Rösel, Leipzig R Ch., Dresden PO, Kegel – *Triple concerto*. ***

With four excellent vocal soloists from the chorus and a splendid contribution from the pianist, Peter Rösel, Hubert Kegel shapes a highly convincing account of Beethoven's *Choral fantasia*, clearly looking ahead to the *Choral symphony* in the closing pages, with the chorus making a thrilling climax. The recording is first rate, very well balanced and vivid.

The famous Brendel/Haitink version from the late 1970s is available on CD, coupled with the *Emperor concerto* (see above).

(i) *Choral Fantasia* (for piano, chorus & orchestra), *Op. 80;* (ii) *Missa solemnis in D, Op. 123.*
(M) *** Sony SM2K 47522 (2) [id.]. (i) Rudolf Serkin, (i; ii) Westminter Ch.; (ii) Farrell, Carol Smith, Lewis, Borg; NYPO, Bernstein – HAYDN: *Mass No. 12*. ***

Bernstein is at his most intense in this fine, dedicated account of Beethoven's supreme choral masterpiece. If anyone had thought that this conductor might dramatize the music too crudely, that is something that simply did not happen and, more than Klemperer or Karajan, he succeeds in creating a unity in this work. It is an inspirational performance; though he does not quite match Jochum in spiritual intensity, the drama and power of the reading make full compensation. The 1960 recording is not as refined as Karajan's earlier, DG set, but it has come up surprisingly well on CD, fresh and clear rather than rich and weighty, to suit the interpretation. It is a drawback that, like the Jochum set, it overlaps on to a second disc when, with an overall playing time of about 77 minutes, it could easily have been accommodated on a single CD. However, the couplings are recommendable and worth having, especially the Haydn (digital) *Theresia Mass*. Serkin's *Choral Fantasia* opens with a solo cadenza almost to rival Brendel's (though the CBS piano recording is less natural). It is a forceful performance, but its drama is certainly compulsive, even if Brendel's mellower approach is in the last resort more persuasive.

Christus am Ölberge, Op. 85.
(M) **(*) Sony MPK 45878 [id.]. Raskin, Lewis, Herbert Beattie, Temple University Choirs, Phd. O, Ormandy.
**(*) HM HMC 905181; *HMC 405181* [id.]. Pick-Hieronimi, Anderson, Von Halem, Ch. & O Nat. de Lyon, Baudo.

Though the Ormandy version dates from the mid-1960s, the CBS sound as transferred on the Sony disc is full and forward, with satisfyingly resonant strings. Ormandy is at his most purposeful and warmly understanding, and the soloists are outstandingly fine, with the pure-toned Judith Raskin very aptly cast as the Seraph and with Richard Lewis at his freshest and most expressive as Jesus.

With Beethoven depicting Christ as another Florestan, it is appropriate that Monica Pick-Hieronimi, a singer of some power, should bring Leonore-like qualities to her role as Seraph. Baudo directs an energetic and lively account of it which, if lacking the utmost refinement of detail, generates urgency and breadth in the fine closing section. The chorus sings vividly and the Lyon orchestra is committed too in a recording which projects well and is convincingly balanced.

Egmont: Overture and incidental music: (2 Entr'actes, Die Trommel gerühret, Freudvoll und Leidvoll, Victory Symphony), Op. 84.
(M) *** Decca 425 972-2. Lorengar, VPO, Szell – TCHAIKOVSKY: *Symphony No. 4*. ***

Szell's splendid 1970 version of the *Egmont Overture and incidental music* comes as an odd but attractive fill-up to his searingly intense account of Tchaikovsky's *Fourth Symphony*.

(i) *King Stephen* (incidental music), *Op. 117: Overture and excerpts. The Ruins of Athens* (incidental music), *Op. 113: Overture and excerpts.* (ii) *The Creatures of Prometheus overture.*
(B) *** Hung. White Label HRC 118 [id.]. (i) Hungarian R. & TV Ch., Budapest PO, Oberfrank; (ii) Hungarian State O, Kórodi.

Beethoven's incidental music, though not always characteristic, is full of imagination and vitality. The fervour of the singing of the Hungarian Radio Chorus adds much to the sparkle of the performances, admirably conducted by Géza Oberfrank; as an apt encore, András Kórodi directs a lively account of *The Creatures of Prometheus overture*.

Mass in C, Op. 86.
(M) *** Decca 430 361-2; *430 361-4* [id.]. Palmer, Watts, Tear, Keyte, St John's College, Cambridge, Ch., ASMF, Guest – BRUCKNER: *Motets.* ***

(i) *Mass in C, Op. 86; Meeresstille und glückliche Fahrt (Calm sea and a prosperous voyage), Op. 112.*
**(*) Decca Dig. 417 563-2 [id.]. (i) Dunn, Zimmermann, Beccaria, Krause; Berlin RIAS Chamber Ch. & RSO, Chailly.

(i) *Mass in C, Op. 86. The Ruins of Athens (Overture and incidental music), Op. 113.*
(M) *** EMI CDM7 64385-2 [id.]. (i) Vyvyan, Sinclair, Lewis, Nowakowski, Beecham Ch. Soc.; RPO, Beecham.

Beecham's is a vintage performance of the *C major Mass*, passionately committed, and it makes one appreciate how this strong and dramatic work followed directly on from the late and great Haydn Masses, a commission from Prince Esterhazy. With a first rate team of soloists and excellent choral singing, Beecham leads the field. The fill-up of incidental music – also available coupled with the *Seventh Symphony* – is equally vibrant, with Beecham roaring through the *Chorus of Dervishes* (finely sung by the Beecham Choral Society), whiskers obviously bristling. In both works the 1958 stereo is very good for its period and the transfer is vivid and lively with clear choral sound.

George Guest's reading is designedly intimate. Naturally, with boys' voices in the choir and a smaller band of singers, the results are less dramatic; but, with splendid recording, the scale works admirably and the result is refreshing.

The Chailly performance is on the right expansive scale; the singing of the Berlin RIAS Chorus has vigour and exuberance, yet conveys the full range of emotions expressed in the *Kyrie* and *Sanctus*. The solo team is also very good although the tenor, Bruno Beccaria, is too histrionically operatic in style. The recording has the widest dynamic range, and this adds drama to the fine performance of the rare cantata which is used as an encore (it is comparatively short, just over 8 minutes). The balance favours the singers, but the recording overall is admirably vivid.

Missa solemnis in D, Op. 123.
❀ *** DG Dig. 429 779-2; *429 779-4* [id.]. Margiono, Robbin, Kendall, Miles, Monteverdi Ch., E. Bar. Soloists, Eliot Gardiner.
*** EMI Dig. CDC7 49950-2 [id.]. Vaness, Meier, Blochwitz, Tschammer, Tallis Chamber Ch., ECO, Tate.
(M) *** DG 423 913-2 (2) [id.]. Janowitz, Ludwig, Wunderlich, Berry, V. Singverein, BPO, Karajan – MOZART: *Mass No. 16.* **(*)
(M) *** Ph. 426 648-2 (2). Giebel, Höffgen, Haefliger, Ridderbusch, Netherlands R. Ch., Concg. O, Jochum.
*** DG 413 780-2 (2) [id.]. Moser, Schwarz, Kollo, Moll, Netherlands Ch., Concg. O, Bernstein.
**(*) DG Dig. 419 166-2 (2) [id.]. Cuberli, Schmidt, Cole, Van Dam, V. Singverein, BPO, Karajan.
**(*) Nimbus Dig. NI 5109 [id.]. Hirsti, Watkinson, Murgatroyd, George, Oslo Cathedral Ch., Hanover Band, Kvam.
(M) (**(*)) BMG/RCA mono GD 60272; *GK 60272* (2) [60272-RG-2; *60272-RG-4*]. Marshall, Merriman, Conley, Hines, Robert Shaw Ch., NBC SO, Toscanini – CHERUBINI: *Requiem.* (**(*))

(i) *Missa solemnis in D;* (ii) *Choral Fantasia in C, Op. 80.*
(M) **(*) EMI CMS7 69538-2 (2) [Ang. CDMB 69538-2]. (i) Söderström, Höffgen, Kmentt, Talvela, New Philh. Ch.; (ii) Barenboim, Alldis Ch.; New Philh. O, Klemperer.

This superb issue from DG marks a breakthrough in period performance of Beethoven. Gardiner's inspired reading matches even the greatest of traditional performances on record in dramatic weight and spiritual depth, while bringing out the white heat of Beethoven's inspiration with new intensity. The sense of a superman creator wrestling with the deepest meaning of the liturgy comes over more acutely than ever. Speeds tend to be on the fast side, but they quickly come to seem right, establishing a symphonic tautness. Even in the hushed dedication of the *Sanctus* Gardiner rivals such masters as Karajan and Jochum in their much slower readings; while the rhythmic swing of the compound time in the *Dona nobis pacem* has a joy in it that no traditional performance can quite match. Though the performers are fewer in number than in traditional accounts, the gain in sharpness of focus makes the results even more dramatic, with the period instrument players stretched to the limit. The Monteverdi Choir sings with bright, luminous tone, and the four soloists are excellent – two strong, sensitive and clear-toned newcomers, the soprano Charlotte Margiono and the bass Alastair Miles, joined by the mezzo Catherine Robbin and the tenor William Kendall. The recording is vivid too, and it comes on a single disc instead of the more usual two. Even those who normally resist period performance will find this very compelling.

Tate's EMI version also presents the whole work on a single disc. Tate, with chorus and orchestra on a modest chamber scale, gains in incisiveness and loses hardly at all in weight, with bright, fresh singing from the Tallis Chamber Choir, challenged at times by Tate's fast speeds for some of the big fugatos. For the controversial case of *Pleni sunt coeli* he opts to use the soloists – as the score says – rather than chorus, as has become customary. The soloists make an outstanding quartet, with Hans Tschammer adding to Tate's deeply devotional treatment of the *Agnus Dei*. Both there and at a number of other points, Tate is marginally slower than Klemperer, and nowhere is there a feeling of excessive haste, just one of dramatic urgency. The well-balanced recording is at rather a low level, but sounds well at full volume.

On Karajan's earlier DG version of the *Missa solemnis* both the chorus and, even more strikingly, the superbly matched quartet of soloists, never surpassed as a team in this work, convey the intensity and cohesion of Beethoven's deeply personal response to the liturgy. Gundula Janowitz is even more meltingly beautiful here than in her later EMI recording for Karajan. Christa Ludwig, as there, is a firm and characterful mezzo, while Walter Berry is a warmly expressive bass. Best of all is the ill-fated Fritz Wunderlich, whose lovely, heroic but unstrained tenor adds supremely to the radiance of the performance, one of his great recordings. The balance between soloists, chorus and orchestra is far clearer and more precise than in most recent recordings, and the clarity of detail is exemplary.

Jochum's soloists not only make a splendid team, they are individually finer than we had remembered. The CD transfer is excellent too, more vivid than the LPs were, heightening the incandescence of a performance which comes over with the sort of glow one experiences only rarely, even in the concert hall. Maddeningly, Philips have reissued it on two mid-priced discs (instead of choosing a bargain format).

Bernstein's DG version with the Concertgebouw was edited together from tapes of two live performances, and the result has a spiritual intensity matched by very few rivals. Edda Moser is not an ideal soprano soloist, but the others are outstanding, and the *Benedictus* is made angelically beautiful by the radiant playing of the Concertgebouw concertmaster, Hermann Krebbers. The recording is a little light in bass, but outstandingly clear as well as atmospheric. The CD clarifies the sound still further.

The later, digital set for DG was one of Karajan's recordings made in conjunction with a video film, and that brings both gains and losses. The sense of spontaneity, of a massive structure built dramatically with contrasts underlined, makes for extra magnetism, but there are flaws of ensemble and at least one serious flaw of intonation in the singing of Lella Cuberli, otherwise a full, sweet-toned soprano.

On Nimbus, a brisk, refreshing performance on period instruments which has the incidental advantage of being on a single disc. The conductor, Terje Kvam, is chorus-master of the Oslo Cathedral Choir; not surprisingly, he is no match for such high-powered conductors as Klemperer and Bernstein in weight or gravity, but the simple intensity of the performance, with period instruments giving extra clarity and bite, brings a scale and manner to make it seem more liturgical than usual, partly because of the reverberant acoustic.

The glory of Klemperer's set is the superb choral singing of the New Philharmonia Chorus; it is not just their purity of tone and their fine discipline but the real fervour with which they sing that makes the choral passages so moving. The soloists are less happily chosen: Waldemar Kmentt seems unpleasantly hard and Elisabeth Söderström does not sound as firm as she can be. It was, however, a happy idea to include the *Choral Fantasia* as a bonus.

Toscanini's tensely dramatic account of the *Missa solemnis* leaves you in no doubt as to the work's magisterial power, even if the absence of a true pianissimo makes it less meditative than usual. The supreme revelation comes at the end of the *Dona nobis pacem*, in which – after the menacing sounds of war – the final coda brings a sense of culmination such as few other conductors have achieved. Fine singing from choir and soloists alike, though the typical harshness of the recording is unappealing.

OPERA

Fidelio (complete).
❀ (M) *** EMI CMS7 69324-2 (2) [Ang. CDMB 69324]. Ludwig, Vickers, Frick, Berry, Crass, Philh. Ch. & O, Klemperer.
(M) *** EMI CMS7 69290-2 (2) [Ang. CDMB 69290]. Dernesch, Vickers, Ridderbusch, Van Dam, Kelemen, German Op. Ch., BPO, Karajan.
*** Ph. Dig. 426 308-2 (2) [id.]. Jessye Norman, Goldberg, Moll, Wlaschiha, Coburn, Blochwitz, Dresden State Op. Ch. & O, Haitink.
*** DG 419 436-2 (2) [id.]. Janowitz, Kollo, Sotin, Jungwirth, Fischer-Dieskau, Popp, V. State Op. Ch., VPO, Bernstein.

Klemperer's great set of *Fidelio* arrives on CD, sounding admirably fresh, to sweep the board in its new format. Its incandescence and spiritual strength are unique, with wonderful performances from all concerned and with a final scene in which, more than in any other recording, the parallel with the finale of the *Choral Symphony* is underlined.

Comparison between Klemperer's version and Karajan's strong and heroic reading is fascinating. Both have very similar merits, underlining the symphonic character of the work with their weight of utterance. Both may miss some of the sparkle of the opening scene, but it is better that seriousness should enter too early than too late. Since seriousness is the keynote, it is rather surprising to find Karajan using bass and baritone soloists lighter than usual. But Jon Vickers as Florestan is if anything even finer than he was for Klemperer; and though Helga Dernesch as Leonore does not have quite the clear-focused mastery of Christa Ludwig in the Klemperer set, this is still a glorious, thrilling performance, outshining lesser rivals than Ludwig.

The unsurpassed nobility of Jessye Norman's voice is perfectly matched to this noblest of operas. In detail of characterization she may not outshine Christa Ludwig, Klemperer's firm and incisive Leonore, or Helga Dernesch, Karajan's warmly emotional heroine, but her reading is consistently rich and beautiful, like those rivals bringing a new revelation. That is so, not just in her singing but in her speaking of the dialogue, with the personality beaming out in individuality even before she starts singing. The Canon quartet of Act I is then taken dangerously slowly, but it is superbly sustained by Haitink at a steady tempo, with Pamela Coburn and Hans Peter Blochwitz well matched as Marzelline and Jaquino, and the resonant Kurt Moll as the jailer, Rocco. The great test of the *Abscheulicher* then finds Norman at her peak, not as animated as Dernesch but rich and varied. Reiner Goldberg, strained at times and no match for Jon Vickers on both the Klemperer and Karajan sets, is still an impressive Florestan by latterday standards, and Ekkehard Wlaschiha, best known for his portrayal of Alberich in various *Ring* cycles, is a superb Pizarro, strong and sinister. With excellent digital sound and with strong, forthright conducting from Haitink, this is the finest of modern versions, even if it does not replace Klemperer or Karajan.

Bernstein, as one would expect, directs a reading of *Fidelio* full of dramatic flair. The recording was made in conjunction with live performances by the same cast at the Vienna State Opera. Lucia Popp as Marzelline is particularly enchanting, and though Bernstein later rises splendidly to the high drama of Act II, it remains a drama on a human scale. Gundula Janowitz sings most beautifully as Leonore. Kollo as Florestan is intelligent and musicianly but indulges in too many intrusive aitches, and the rest of the cast make strong contributions.

Fidelio: highlights.
(M) *** EMI CDM7 63077-2; *EG 763077-4* (from above set; cond. Karajan).

Those who acquire Klemperer's classic set will welcome just under an hour of well-chosen highlights from the fine alternative Karajan recording, made in 1970.

Bellini, Vincenzo (1801–35)

Norma (complete).
(M) *** Decca 425 488-2 (3) [id.]. Sutherland, Horne, Alexander, Cross, Minton, Ward, LSO Ch., LSO, Bonynge.
**(*) Decca Dig. 414 476-2 (3) [id.]. Sutherland, Pavarotti, Caballé, Ramey, Welsh Nat. Op. Ch. & O, Bonynge.
(M) **(*) EMI CMS7 63000-2 (3) [Ang. CDMC 63000]. Callas, Corelli, Ludwig, Zaccharia, Ch. & O of La Scala, Milan, Serafin.

In her first, mid-1960s recording of *Norma*, Sutherland was joined by an Adalgisa in Marilyn Horne whose control of florid singing is just as remarkable as Sutherland's own, and who sometimes even outshines the heroine in musical imagination. The other soloists are very good indeed, John Alexander and Richard Cross both young, clear-voiced singers. Sutherland's own contribution is dramatically very much after the school of Callas, while at the same time ensuring that something as near as possible to musical perfection is achieved, even if occasionally at the expense of masked diction. But overall this is a most compelling performance, helped by the conducting of Richard Bonynge, who keeps musical interest alive in the many conventional accompaniment figures with sprung rhythm and with the most subtle attention to the vocal line. The Walthamstow recording is vivid but also atmospheric in its CD format.

Dame Joan Sutherland was fifty-eight when her second *Norma* recording was made. The coloratura is still remarkably flexible, but the conjunction of Sutherland with Pavarotti and Caballé does not always work easily. Though Pavarotti is in some ways the set's greatest strength, easily expressive yet powerful as Pollione, Caballé as Adalgisa seems determined to outdo Sutherland in mooning manner, cooing self-indulgently. However, in the big Act II Trio the three principals effectively and excitingly sink their stylistic differences. Bonynge, as in the earlier, mid-priced Sutherland recording (still a first choice on CD), paces Bellini well, and the Welsh National Opera Orchestra and Chorus respond most sympathetically. Full, brilliant, well-balanced recording of the complete score.

By the time Callas came to record her 1960 stereo version, the tendency to hardness and unsteadiness in the voice above the stave, always apparent, had grown more serious, but the interpretation was as sharply illuminating as ever, a unique assumption, helped – as her earlier mono performance was not – by a strong cast. Christa Ludwig as Adalgisa brings not just rich, firm tone but a real feeling for Italian style and, despite moments of coarseness, Corelli sings heroically. Serafin as ever is the most persuasive of Bellini conductors, and the recording is very good for its period – not surprisingly, as Walter Legge masterminded the original production.

Norma: highlights.
(M) *** Decca 421 886-2; *421 886-4* [id.] (from above complete recording with Sutherland, Horne; cond. Pritchard).
(M) **(*) EMI CDM7 63091-2 (from above complete set with Callas, Corelli; cond. Serafin).

Those who have the alternative Sutherland version of *Norma* with Pavarotti will certainly want a reminder of the earlier set in which her partnership with Marilyn Horne produced such a dramatic symbiosis. This highlights CD (65 minutes) includes their classic collaboration in the famous duets from both Acts. *Mira O Norma* is taken rather slowly, with a degree more mannerism than the singers might later have allowed themselves. An excellent, vivid transfer of the full-blooded 1964 Walthamstow recording.

Those who already have Maria Callas's mono set will surely want the later (63 minutes) stereo highlights disc which includes, of course, *Casta diva* and the three principal Norma/Adalgisa duets.

I Puritani (complete).
*** Decca 417 588-2 (3). Sutherland, Pavarotti, Ghiaurov, Luccardi, Caminada, Cappuccilli, ROHCG Ch. & O, Bonynge.

Whereas her earlier set was recorded when Sutherland had adopted a soft-grained style, with consonants largely eliminated and a tendency to lag behind the beat, this time her singing is fresher and brighter. The lovely aria *Qui la voce* is no longer a wordless melisma, and though the great showpiece *Son vergin vezzosa* is now taken dangerously fast, the extra bite and tautness are exhilarating. Pavarotti shows himself a remarkable Bellini stylist, rarely if ever coarsening a legato line, unlike so many of his Italian colleagues. Ghiaurov and Cappuccilli make up an impressive cast, and the only disappointing contributor is Anita Caminada in the small role of Enrichetta – Queen Henrietta Maria in disguise. Vivid, atmospheric recording, enhanced and given added presence by the digital remastering.

La Sonnambula (complete).
*** Decca Dig. 417 424-2 (2) [id.]. Sutherland, Pavarotti, Della Jones, Ghiaurov, L. Op. Ch., Nat. PO, Bonynge.
(***) EMI mono CDS7 47378-8 (2) [CDCB 47377]. Callas, Monti, Cossotto, Zaccaria, Ratti, La Scala, Milan, Ch. and O, Votto.

Sutherland's singing here is even more affecting and more stylish than her earlier version, generally purer and more forthright, if with diction still clouded at times. The challenge of singing opposite Pavarotti adds to the bite of the performance, crisply and resiliently controlled by Bonynge. The star tenor may be stylistically coarser than Nicola Monti on Sutherland's earlier set, but the beauty and size of the voice help to focus the whole performance more positively, not least in such ensembles as the finale of Act I. The rest of the cast is vocally strong too, and the early digital recording comes up very vividly.

Substantially cut, the Callas version was recorded in mono in 1957, yet it gives a vivid picture of the diva at the peak of her powers. By temperament she may not have related closely to Bellini's heroine, but the village girl's simple devotion through all trials is touchingly caught, most of all in the recitatives. The recording has transferred remarkably well to CD. Nicola Monti makes a strong rather than a subtle contribution but blends well with Callas in the duets; and Fiorenza Cossotto is a good Teresa. Callas admirers will find this enjoyable as an overall performance.

Ben-Haim, Paul (1897–1984)

Sweet Psalmist of Israel.
(M) **(*) Sony SM2K 47533 (2). Marlowe, Stavrache, NYPO, Bernstein – BLOCH: *Sacred service;* FOSS: *Song of songs.* ***

As the biblical King David was a versatile musician, Ben-Haim represents him here by the use of both concertante harp and (more dubiously) harpsichord in his vividly scored triptych. The first movement pictures David refreshing Samuel with his harp with neo-classical interludes, and the slow central *Invocation* shows the King in meditative mood. The third is a rather garrulous hymn of praise, made the less effective by the very forward balance of the recording, made in Carnegie Hall (in 1959), with the microphones too close, especially to the solo instruments. However, the early movements have a certain textural charm.

Benjamin, George (born 1960)

(i) *Ringed by the flat horizon.* (ii) *At first light. A Mind of winter.*
*** Nimbus Dig. NI 5075 [id.]. (i) BBC SO, Elder; (ii) Penelope Walmsley-Clark, L. Sinf., composer.

Ringed by the flat horizon is a 20-minute orchestral piece that conceals the detailed complexity of its argument in warmly expressive, evocative use of the orchestra, with the big climax masterfully built. *A Mind of winter* is a 9-minute setting of *The Snowman* by Wallace Stevens, beautifully sung by the soprano Penelope Walmsley-Clark, with Benjamin himself conducting the London Sinfonietta. It has been aptly described as a winter equivalent of Debussy's *L'après-midi d'un faune.* Sound of great warmth and refinement to match the music make this a collection well worth exploring.

Bennett, Robert Russell (1894–1981)

Symphonic songs for band.
(M) *** Mercury 432 009-2 [id.]. Eastman Wind Ens., Fennell – HOLST: *Hammersmith* ***; JACOB: *William Byrd suite* ***; WALTON: *Crown Imperial.* *** ❀

Bennett's triptych, not surprisingly, relies more on colouristic manipulation and sonority than on content, although the opening *Serenade* is catchily rhythmic and the final *Celebration* is certainly rumbustious (if empty). Marvellous playing and Mercury's best recording. The disc also includes a *Fanfare and allegro* by Clifton Williams, which is self-descriptive and equally well presented.

Berg, Alban (1885–1935)

Chamber concerto for piano, violin & 13 wind.
*** Teldec/Warner Dig. 2292 46019-2; *2292 46019-4* [id.]. Maisenberg, COE, Holliger – SCHOENBERG: *Chamber symphony.* ***

(i) *Chamber concerto;* (ii) *Violin concerto.*
(M) *** Decca Analogue/Dig. 430 349-2 [id.]. (i) Pauk, Crossley, L. Sinf., Atherton; (ii) Kyung Wha Chung, Chicago SO, Solti.

Atherton rightly takes the view that, for all its complexity, the *Chamber concerto* is romantic at heart so that one hears it as a melodic work, full of humour, and the waltz rhythms are given a genuine Viennese flavour. György Pauk and Paul Crossley are outstanding soloists, the Sinfonietta plays with precision as well as commitment, and the 1980 analogue recording is excellent, cleanly detailed yet not too dry. The appropriate coupling is Kyung Wha Chung's fine 1983 version of the *Violin concerto.* Chung may not be as powerful as Perlman (at full price), but her tenderness and poetry bring an added dimension to the music.

Despite rather reticent soloists, the Teldec version of the *Chamber concerto* also brings out all the necessary warmth, with superb playing from the COE. Those wanting a modern digital recording, and for whom the coupling with Schoenberg is suitable, will find this gives every satisfaction. Unlike Atherton on Decca and the rival analogue Boulez issue (which is coupled with the *Clarinet pieces* and *Piano sonata*), this one observes the long repeat in the finale, which radically affects the balance of movements. Excellent recording.

(i) *Chamber concerto;* (ii) *4 Pieces for clarinet and piano, Op. 5; Piano sonata, Op. 1.*
(M) *** DG 423 237-2 [id.]. Barenboim with (i) Zukerman & Ens. InterContemporain, Boulez; (ii) Antony Pay.

Boulez sets brisk tempi in the *Chamber concerto,* seeking to give the work classical incisiveness; but the strong and expressive personalities of the pianist and violinist tend towards a more romantic view. The result is characterful and convincing. The apt coupling combines the high-romantic *Piano sonata* in one movement with the *Clarinet pieces*; here Antony Pay is an outstanding soloist.

Violin concerto.
*** DG 413 725-2 [id.]. Itzhak Perlman, Boston SO, Ozawa – STRAVINSKY: *Concerto.* ***
(M) *** EMI CDM7 63989-2 [id.]. Sir Yehudi Menuhin, BBC SO, Boulez – BLOCH: *Violin concerto.* ***
(M) *** DG 431 740-2. Szeryng, Bav. RSO, Kubelik – SCHOENBERG: *Concertos.* **(*)

Perlman's performance is totally commanding. The effortless precision of the playing goes with great warmth of expression, so that the usual impression of 'wrong-note Romanticism' gives way to total purposefulness. The Boston orchestra accompanies superbly and, though the balance favours the soloist, the recording is excellent. It has been convincingly remastered for CD, although the detail is less sharp than in either the Decca or EMI alternative.

Menuhin's is a warm and vibrant performance, one that shows him at his finest and that is manifestly on the largest scale and most expressive wavelength; one has no sense whatsoever of an intellectual serialist at work. Boulez's insistence on orchestral precision gives Menuhin extra confidence and, though technically this is not as dashing or immaculate a performance as several others on record, it is one that compels admiration on its own terms of greatness. The basically warm (1968) Abbey Road recording has been brightened in the remastering but retains its ambience and body.

An outstanding version of Berg's *Violin concerto* also comes from Henryk Szeryng, who gives a persuasive, perceptive and sympathetic account of this fine work, and is well accompanied by the Bavarian orchestra under Kubelik. Given such superb playing, and a recording that has transferred well to CD, this makes an attractive supplement to the two Schoenberg concertos with which it is coupled.

Lyric suite: 3 Pieces; 3 Pieces for orchestra, Op. 6.
(M) *** DG 427 424-2 (3) [id.]. BPO, Karajan – SCHOENBERG; WEBERN: *Orchestral pieces.* ***

Karajan's justly famous collection of music by the Second Viennese School is here available as a set of three mid-priced CDs. No more persuasive view could be taken – though, next to Schoenberg and Webern, Berg appears here as the figure who overloaded his music, rather than as the most approachable of the three composers. Beautiful, refined recording, admirably transferred to CD.

3 Pieces for orchestra, Op. 6.
*** DG Dig. 419 781-2 [id.]. BPO, Levine – SCHOENBERG; WEBERN: *Pieces.* ***

Levine gives a powerful, warmly emotional reading of Berg's Opus 6. He is particularly impressive in the big build-up of the third and last piece, the *March*, though there as elsewhere odd emphasis of individual lines is intrusive in an otherwise full and vivid recording.

3 Pieces for orchestra, Op. 6; (i) *Lulu: symphonic suite.*
(M) *** Mercury 432 006-2 [id.]. (i) Helga Pilarczyk; LSO, Dorati – SCHOENBERG; WEBERN: *Orchestral pieces.* ***

In his pioneering 1962 Mercury coupling Dorati set the pattern for later recordings of this twentieth-century orchestral triptych, none recorded more clearly or vividly. The LSO plays fluently and warmly. For the CD reissue, the recording of the *Lulu suite*, recorded a year earlier, has generously been added. Helen Pilarczyk, in her first recording, is most impressive: the murder produces the most blood-curdling scream.

3 Pieces for orchestra, Op. 6; 5 Orchestral songs, Op. 4; (i) *Lulu: symphonic suite.*
(M) *** DG 423 238-2 [id.]. (i) M. Price; LSO, Abbado.

Abbado makes it clear above all how beautiful Berg's writing is, not just in the *Lulu* excerpts but in the early Opus 4 *Songs* and the Opus 6 *Orchestral pieces*, among which even the formidable march movement has sumptuousness as well as power. The recording from the early 1970s is still outstanding.

Lulu (with orchestration of Act III completed by Friedrich Cerha).
*** DG 415 489-2 (3) [id.]. Stratas, Minton, Schwarz, Mazura, Blankenheim, Riegel, Tear, Paris Op. O, Boulez.

The full three-Act structure of Berg's *Lulu*, first unveiled by Boulez in his Paris Opéra production and here treated to studio recording, was a revelation with few parallels. The very end of the opera, with Yvonne Minton singing the Countess Geschwitz's lament, is most moving, though Lulu remains to the last a repulsive heroine. Teresa Stratas's bright, clear soprano is well recorded, and there is hardly a weak link in the cast. Altogether this is an historic issue, presenting an intensely involving performance of a work which in some ways is more lyrically approachable than *Wozzeck*.

(i) *Lulu;* (ii) *Wozzeck.*
(M) ** DG 435 705-2 (3) [id.]. Lear, Fischer-Dieskau; (i) Johnson, Grobe; (ii) Melchert, Stolze, Wunderlich, Kohn, Schönberger Sängerknaben German Op. Ch.; German Opera O, Berlin, Boehm.

With Evelyn Lear and Fischer-Dieskau common to both operas, it was a good idea to pair Boehm's recordings of *Lulu* and *Wozzeck* for CD reissue. In both scores Boehm reveals more beauties in the writing than one would have thought possible. Berg himself is quoted as saying that Lulu must be regarded as a female counterpart of Don Juan; if that is so, Boehm's leaning away from harshness is justified. Evelyn Lear – not a singer one would have expected to be cast in the role – matches Boehm in his approach, and the keen intelligence of Fischer-Dieskau as Dr

Schön confirms this as a performance without hysteria. If it fails to convey Berg's full message, it is in every way a worthy counterpart to Boehm's companion reading of *Wozzeck*.

Thanks largely to the timbre of Fischer-Dieskau's voice and to the intensity of projection in his words, one can hardly picture Wozzeck here as in any way moronic. His situation is much closer to conventional tragedy than one imagines Berg (or, for that matter, Büchner, original creator of the character) ever conceived. The result may be unconventional, inauthentic even, but it certainly makes one listen to the opera afresh, and on record there is a case for a performance which brings out clarity, precision and beauty, even in a work like this. Evelyn Lear makes a fairly convincing Marie, though hardly ideal, and generally the supporting cast is vocally assured. But the lack of any feeling of vibrant drama means that a dimension is missing, in spite of the atmospheric DG sound.

Lulu: symphonic suite.
*** EMI Dig. CDC7 49857-2 [id.]. Arleen Augér, CBSO, Rattle – SCHOENBERG: *5 Pieces;* WEBERN: *6 Pieces.* ***

Rattle steers a perfect course between traditional austerity and overtly romantic warmth in this music. Augér's pure, true soprano in the vocal passages of the *Lulu suite* is presented as an adjunct to the orchestra, rather than as a salient solo. The sound is of demonstration quality, one of the very finest recordings that Rattle and the CBSO have received, adding enormously to the attractiveness of the disc, and the couplings are equally positive and red-blooded.

Wozzeck (complete).
*** Decca Dig. 417 348-2 (2) [id.]. Waechter, Silja, Winkler, Laubenthal, Jahn, Malta, Sramek, VPO, Dohnányi – SCHOENBERG: *Erwartung.* ***
**(*) DG 423 587-2 (2) [id.]. Grundheber, Behrens, Haugland, Langridge, Zednik, V. State Op. Ch., VPO, Abbado.

Dohnányi, with refined textures and superb playing from the Vienna Philharmonic, presents an account of *Wozzeck* that not only is more accurate than any other on record but also is more beautiful. It may lack some of the bite of Claudio Abbado's DG version, but with superb digital sound the Decca set stands as first choice. Unfortunately the beauty of the performance does not extend to Eberhard Waechter's vocal quality in the name-part, but he gives a thoughtful, sensitive performance. The edge of Anja Silja's voice and her natural vibrancy of character make her a memorable Marie, first cousin to Lulu. An excellent supporting cast too, and the recording has a spectacular sense of presence and clarity; it also comes with a substantial coupling in Schoenberg's monodrama, *Erwartung*, also with Silja.

The Abbado version, recorded live in the opera house, is very compelling in its presentation of the drama, given extra thrust through the tensions of live performance. However, there are drawbacks, too. Not only do you get the stage noises; the voices are also set behind the orchestra, with the instrumental sound putting a gauze between listener and singers. The cast is a good one, headed by a clear-toned if lightweight Wozzeck in Franz Grundheber. Hildegard Behrens sings affectingly as Marie, but the microphones exaggerate the flutter in her voice and she produces unpleasantly curdled tones, even in the scene where she sings a lullaby to her child. The Decca Dohnányi set is clearly preferable.

Bergman, Erik (born 1911)

Bim bam bum; Fåglarna; Hathor Suite; Nox.
*** Chan. Dig. CHAN 8478 [id.]. Walmsley-Clark, Varcoe, Potter, New London Chamber Ch., Endymion Ens., James Wood.

The Finnish composer, Erik Bergman, is at his best and most characteristic in writing for voices. *Nox* (1970) is a setting of four poems on the theme of Night, while for *Bim bam bum* (1976) he turns to Morgenstern, whose gallows-songs inspired earlier works. *Fåglarna* (*The Birds*) is earlier (1962) but is no less resourceful in its use of choral colour; and the *Hathor Suite* is based on ancient Egyptian cult texts dedicated to the goddess Hathor. All four are well performed and recorded, and the record forms an invaluable introduction to a highly imaginative and sensitive artistic personality.

Berio, Luciano (born 1925)

Différences; 2 Pieces; (i) *Sequenza III;* (ii) *Sequenza VII;* (i) *Chamber music.*
(M) *** Ph. 426 662-2. (i) Cathy Berberian; (ii) Heinz Holliger; Juilliard Ens. (members), composer.

The biggest work here is *Différences* for five instruments and tape; but the two virtuoso solos – *Sequenza III* for voice (Cathy Berberian) and *Sequenza VII* for oboe (Heinz Holliger) – are if anything even more striking in their extensions of technique and expressive range. The *Two Pieces* and *Chamber music* are both collections of brief inspirations, the latter with voice as well as instrumental trio. First-rate sound, well transferred.

Eindrucke; Sinfonia.
*** Erato/Warner Dig. 2292 45228-2 [id.]. Pasquier, New Swingle Singers, O Nat. de France, Boulez.

It was in 1969 that Berio's *Sinfonia*, written for the New York Philharmonic, made a far wider impact on the music world than is common with an avant-garde composer. The colour and energy of his writing, his wit (not least in the vocal commentary for the Swingle – now the New Swingle – Singers) make for a piece that is both memorable and attractive. His own CBS recording, made in New York at the time, enjoyed a deserved success, but it omitted the fifth movement, which he had added within months to the original four. Boulez records the complete work for the first time in this fine Erato version, and that substantial finale proves essential to an appreciation of the whole piece when, with its reminiscences, it sums up what has gone before. *Eindrucke*, written between 1973 and 1974, is another powerful work, much more compressed, bare and uncompromising in its layering of strings and wind. Boulez draws vivid performances of both from his French players, and the recording is colourful to match, though vocal balances sometimes sound contrived.

Coro (revised version).
(M) *** DG 423 902-2 [id.]. Cologne R. Ch. and SO, composer.

Coro is one of the most ambitious of Berio's works, with each of forty singers paired with an instrumentalist and with folk verse on basic themes contrasted with poems of Pablo Neruda. The composer directs a committed performance here, helped by the impact of the forward sound.

A-Ronne; The Cries of London.
(M) *** Decca 425 620-2. Swingle II, composer.

A-Ronne, literally 'A–Z', is an extraordinary setting of a multilingual poem by Edoardo Sanguinetti. From time to time the eight voices briefly break into singing, but for the most part the characteristic musical collage consists of shouts, snarls and organized crowd-noises, with the fragmentary word-sequence run through some twenty times. *The Cries of London* is almost equally surrealistic, an updating of the cries used by Elizabethan madrigal composers but with musical references to medieval patterns. The performances by Swingle II are nothing less than brilliant and they are recorded with stunning immediacy.

Berkeley, Lennox (1903–89)

Improvisation on a theme of Falla, Op. 55/2; Mazurka, Op. 101/2; 3 Mazurkas (Hommage à Chopin), Op. 32; Paysage; 3 Pieces; Polka, Op. 5a; 6 Preludes, Op. 23; 5 Short pieces, Op. 4; Sonata, Op. 20.
**(*) Kingdom KCLCD 2012; *CKCL 2012* [id.]. Christopher Headington.

With the exception of the *Sonata*, all these pieces are miniatures, some of considerable elegance. Christopher Headington is a sympathetic exponent. Sometimes (as in the third of the *Six Preludes*) his playing is wanting the last ounce of finish, but it is not lacking in charm, and he is completely attuned to the idiom. The recording is eminently serviceable and truthful, but not in the demonstration class.

Berkeley, Michael (born 1948)

Or shall we die? (oratorio).
(M) *** EMI Dig. CDM7 69810-2. Harper, Wilson-Johnson, LSO Ch., LSO, Hickox.

Michael Berkeley's oratorio on the pain and problems of a nuclear world confidently uses an openly eclectic style that communicates immediately to any listener. Despite flaws, it is a strong, confident and colourful work which it is good to have on record. The recording is first rate.

Berlin, Irving (1888–1989)

Annie get your gun (musical).
❀ *** EMI Dig. CDC7 54206-2 [id.]; *EL 754206-4*. Criswell, Hampson, Luker, Amb. Ch., L. Sinf., John McGlinn.

This is one of the most delectable of all show records. John McGlinn follows up the pattern of his best-selling set of Jerome Kern's *Show Boat* with another performance that is at once scholarly and pulsing with life. Not only is the singing strong, characterful and idiomatic, the whole performance – not least from the players of the London Sinfonietta – is full of fun, conveying the exuberance of a score that contains more 'standards' among its numbers than almost any other Broadway show. *Doin' what comes natur'lly*, *The girl that I marry*, *You can't get a man with a gun*, *There's no business like show business* and *They say it's wonderful* are five that appear consecutively early in Act I, with such unforgettable numbers as *Anything you can do* – hilariously done by Kim Criswell and Thomas Hampson – still to come. Though the full complement of numbers is included on the single disc, McGlinn also manages to include in an appendix the brilliant duet – added to the score at the 1966 revival, 20 years after the original show – *An old-fashioned wedding*, with its G & S-style superimposition of lyrical ballad and point number. Kim Criswell as Annie with her electric personality and bitingly bright voice here confirms herself as the natural successor to Ethel Merman, the original Annie Oakley, characterizing strongly while pitching precisely. Equally remarkably, Thomas Hampson makes an ideal hero, an opera-singer with an exceptionally rich and firm baritone who naturally gets inside the idiom. First-rate, full-bodied sound. The disc comes with a booklet containing copious documentation and the full lyrics.

Berlioz, Hector (1803–69)

(i) *Harold in Italy, Op. 16; Overture: Le Carnaval romain, Op. 9.*
*** DG Dig. 415 109-2 [id.]. (i) Christ; BPO, Maazel.

(i) *Harold in Italy, Op. 16. Overtures: Le Carnaval romain, Op. 9; Le Roi Lear, Op. 4.*
(M) (*(**)) Sony mono MPK 47679 [id.]. (i) William Primrose; RPO, Beecham.

(i) *Harold in Italy, Op. 16; Overtures: Le Corsaire, Op. 21; Rob Roy.*
**(*) Decca Dig. 421 193-2 [id.]. (i) Zukerman; Montreal SO, Dutoit.

(i) *Harold in Italy;* (ii) *Tristia: (Méditation religieuse; La mort d'Ophélie; Marche funèbre pour la dernière scène de Hamlet), Op. 18; Les Troyens à Carthage: Prelude to Act II.*
*** Ph. 416 431-2 [id.]. (i) Imai; (ii) Alldis Ch.; LSO, C. Davis.

(i) *Harold in Italy, Op. 15. Roméo et Juliette, Op. 17* (excerpts).
(M) (***) BMG/RCA mono GD 60275 [60275-2-RG]. (i) Carlton Cooley; NBC SO, Toscanini.

The Philips account offers splendid value. In addition to a noble account of *Harold* in which Nobuko Imai is on top form, this CD offers the *Tristia*, which includes the haunting *Funeral march for the last scene of Hamlet* given with chorus, as well as the *Prelude* to the second Act of *Les Troyens*. The sound is completely natural and realistic, and has impressive transparency and detail. The recordings emanate from the 1970s but still lead the field. A first recommendation.

Maazel's *Harold* is undoubtedly very fine; the structure is held together well, with a vivid sense of forward movement and no lack of poetic feeling; there is some imaginative phrasing, and he invariably finds the *tempo giusto*. Wolfram Christ is an eloquent and dignified protagonist. Moreover, the overture, *Le Carnaval romain*, combines exhilaration with an infectious sparkle. The DG recording is marvellously clean and vivid.

Dutoit's version of *Harold in Italy* is very richly recorded. With as characterful a soloist as Zukerman, highly individual and warmly expressive, if not always at his purest, the centre of gravity of the work is shifted. Though the beauty of the writing is very satisfying, the work seems to lose some of its purpose when the soloist comes to be phased out. With the viola's contribution all but eliminated, the *Orgy* seems just a little tame, and speeds throughout tend to be on the broad side. *Rob Roy* and *Le Corsaire* make appropriate Byronic couplings.

Toscanini's famous 1953 recording of *Harold in Italy* is of very high voltage, with Carlton Cooley an excellent soloist. The demonic fires glow with great intensity in the *Orgy of the Brigands*; perhaps the *Pilgrims' march* is just a shade hard driven. In spite of the sonic limitations, the excitement of the performance still comes across the decades. It seems likely that this new transfer is drawn not only from the NBC broadcast but also the Carnegie Hall rehearsal the previous day. It is made at a somewhat lower level than the earlier full-priced CD, and sounds fractionally cleaner this time round, but most listeners will find few significant differences. The *Romeo and Juliet* excerpts were recorded in 1947 (and omit the *Queen Mab scherzo*). Harris Goldsmith's authoritative notes are helpful.

When Beecham made his recording of *Harold in Italy* in 1951, William Primrose was incontestably the greatest viola-player in the world. His imagination here matches that of Beecham, but he is not helped by the close balance of the solo instrument. Beecham finds an extra fire and intensity in the concluding movement, the *Brigands' orgy*, when the soloist's role is virtually eliminated. The transfer of the mono recordings is clear but limited, with some harshness at the top. As in the EMI version of the *Symphonie fantastique*, you have both *Roman carnival* and *King Lear* for fill-up, but in 1954 recordings, both in sound similar to that of the symphony.

Overtures: *Béatrice et Bénédict; Le Carnaval romain, Op. 9; Le Corsaire, Op. 21; Rob Roy; Le Roi Lear, Op. 4.*
**(*) Chan. Dig. CHAN 8316; *ABTD 1067* [id.]. SNO, Gibson.

Rob Roy is the rarity of Sir Alexander Gibson's Berlioz collection. It adds an aptly Scottish tinge to the record, even when traditional melodies – *Scots wha hae* at the opening – are given distinctly Berliozian twists, and finds Gibson and the SNO at their most dashingly committed. *King Lear*, another rarity, also comes out most dramatically, and though *Béatrice et Bénédict* is not quite so polished, the playing is generally excellent. With first-rate digital recording, this can be generally recommended.

Overtures: *Le Carnaval romain, Op. 9; Le Corsaire, Op. 21; Les Francs Juges, Op. 3; Le Roi Lear, Op. 4; Waverley, Op. 26.*
**(*) Ph. 416 430-2. LSO, C. Davis.

Sir Colin Davis's collection of overtures dates from the mid-1960s and, while the CD transfer has freshened the recording, the original balance was not ideal, although the woodwind detail remains well integrated. This is music which ideally calls for modern digital sound; in spite of this, Sir Colin's collection can hold its own, even though it should now be in the mid-price bracket. The playing undoubtedly has fire and brilliance, *Les Francs Juges* is exhilarating and the performance of *King Lear* is outstanding, challenging comparison with Beecham.

Roméo et Juliette: Queen Mab scherzo.
(M) (**) BMG/RCA mono GD 60314 [60314-2-RG]. Phd. O, Toscanini – MENDELSSOHN: *Midsummer Night's Dream.* (***)

Toscanini's quicksilver reading of this fairy scherzo has much in common with his fine Philadelphia recording of Mendelssohn's fairy music. The 1941 recording is clear but lacking in dynamic subtlety.

Symphonie fantastique, Op. 14.
*** Ph. 411 425-2 [id.]. Concg. O, C. Davis.
*** Denon Dig. CO 73208 [id.]. Frankfurt RSO, Inbal.
*** Denon Dig. DC 8097 [id.]. Tokyo Metropolitan SO, Jean Fournet – SAINT-SAËNS: *Danse macabre.* ***
**(*) EMI Dig. CDC7 49541-2 [id.]. L. Classical Players, Norrington.
**(*) DG 415 325-2 [id.]. BPO, Karajan.
**(*) Ph. Dig. 432 151-2; *432 151-4* [id.]. VPO, Sir Colin Davis.

**(*) EMI Dig. CDC7 54479-2 [id.]. Concg. O, Jansons.
**(*) Decca Dig. 414 203-2 [id.]. Montreal SO, Dutoit.
(M) **(*) EMI CMD7 64143-2 [id.]; *EG 764143-4*. Philh. O, Klemperer (with BEETHOVEN: *Leonora overture No. 1* ***; GLUCK: *Overture: Iphigénie en Aulide* *).
(BB) **(*) Pickwick PWK 1147. Paris Conservatoire O, Argenta.
(M) **(*) Sony SBK 46329; *40-46329* [id.]. Phd. O, Ormandy – DUKAS: *L'apprenti sorcier;* MUSSORGSKY: *Night.* ***
** Collins Dig. EC 1001-2 [id.]. LSO, Frémaux.

Symphonie fantastique; La damnation de Faust, Op. 21: Danse des sylphes; Marche hongroise; Menuet des follets; Overture: Le Carnaval romain, Op. 9.
(M) **(*) EMI CDM7 63762-2 [id.]; *EG 763762-4*. Hallé O, Barbirolli.

Symphonie fantastique; Overtures: Benvenuto Cellini; Le carnaval romain. Damnation of Faust: Hungarian march.
(M) *(**) Sony SMK 47525 [id.]. NYPO, Bernstein.

(i) *Symphonie fantastique;* (ii) *Overtures: Le Carnaval romain, Op. 9; Le Corsaire, Op. 31.*
*** EMI Dig. CDC7 54010-2 [id.]. Capitole de Toulouse O, Plasson.
(BB) **(*) BMG/RCA VD 60478; *VK 60478* [60478-2-RV; *60478-4-RV*]. Boston SO, (i) Prêtre; (ii) Munch.

(i) *Symphonie fantastique; Overtures:* (ii) *Le Carnaval romain;* (iii) *Le Roi Lear.*
(M) (***) EMI mono CDM7 64032-2 [id.]; *EG 764032-4*. (i) O. Nat. de l'ORTF; (ii) LPO; (iii) RPO, Sir Thomas Beecham.

Symphonie fantastique, Op. 14; Overture: Le Corsaire, Op. 21.
(M) *** Pickwick/RPO Dig. CDRPO 7016; *ZCRPO 7016* [id.]. RPO, Previn.

Symphonie fantastique, Op. 14; Les Troyens: Royal hunt and storm.
*** DG Dig. 431 624-2 [id.]. BPO, Levine.

Sir Colin Davis's 1974 Concertgebouw recording – his first with that orchestra – remains a primary recommendation, although Martinon coupled with *Lélio* (see below) should not be forgotten. The Philips recording was always a fine one, but the digital remastering for CD has been outstandingly successful and there is a very striking improvement in the firmness of focus, detail is clearer, while in brilliance and definition the overall balance is very satisfying. The Concertgebouw performance has superb life and colour. The slow movement, most beautifully played, is wonderfully atmospheric and the final two movements are very exciting indeed, with a fine rhythmic spring given to the *March to the scaffold* and the finale gripping to the last bar.

With full-ranging digital sound, well balanced with fine presence and atmosphere, André Previn conducts the RPO in a keenly dramatic reading marked by characteristically well-lifted rhythms, with dynamic contrasts powerfully underlined. The rhythmic pointing at central speeds as shrewdly judged as Davis's, helps to bring out the element of jollity which heightens the sinister side of the composer's nightmare vision. This is one of Previn's RPO recordings which matches his achievements in his vintage days with the LSO, and at a price less than the full premium rate, complete with a brilliant performance of the overture as coupling, it makes an excellent recommendation.

Eliahu Inbal with the Frankfurt Radio Symphony Orchestra brings to his recording of the *Symphonie fantastique* the same clear-headed perception that marks his fine series of Mahler recordings, also for Denon; moreover the digital sound is exceptionally full and atmospheric. Inbal's freshness and directness have a similar impact to that of Sir Colin Davis but, for all the brilliance of the Frankfurt performance, Inbal cannot quite match Davis in his electricity, not helped in the first two movements by speeds that are marginally slower. Nevertheless this stands out among recent versions and, for anyone insisting on a spectacular modern digital recording, this is a first-rate recommendation.

Levine's is one of the highest-powered readings of any, marked by brilliantly polished playing and forward, larger-than-life sound. It makes a fine addition to his impressive Berlioz series, and brings the benefit of an exceptionally attractive fill-up in the *Royal hunt and storm*, recorded complete with chorus. The sense of purpose is irresistible, but some of the subtler elements in the score are underplayed in such an approach, as for example the wry playfulness. The result may be too heavy for some, with less sparkle than usual, but in sheer power few versions can match this.

Even in a competitive market, Michel Plasson's recording deserves to rank among the best. He finds new things to say about this familiar score and brings to it a keen and vital sensitivity. The Toulouse orchestra respond with both enthusiasm and discipline and the recording, though reverberant, is eminently detailed. The first movement has fire and a notable sense of purpose. Sir Colin Davis remains first choice for this work, but Plasson's is a performance of character, and it has the advantage of fine digital sound.

Jean Fournet draws thoroughly idiomatic playing and an appropriately Gallic sonority from his fine Tokyo orchestra. There is no point-making in this completely unaffected and well-recorded interpretation, and nowhere does this much underrated conductor interpose himself between us and Berlioz. Although the *Marche au supplice* could perhaps have higher voltage, this 1983 recording has much to commend it. Among the many recommendable versions of the *Symphonie fantastique*, this has a place of honour, though it does not necessarily displace Martinon, which comes in harness with *Lélio* at mid-price on two discs (see below).

Though Berlioz was writing so soon after the death of Beethoven, he represented a leap forward in the art of orchestration. The gains from using period instruments are less striking here than in Beethoven, but the rasp of heavy brass and the bite of authentic timpani stand out more vividly. As in his Beethoven, Norrington does his utmost to observe the composer's metronome markings; but where his Beethoven is consistently fast, some of these speeds are more relaxed than we are used to – as in the *March to the scaffold* and the *Ronde du sabbat*. As usual, his lifting of rhythms prevents the music from dragging, at the same time giving new transparency; and his revelations here certainly give his version a key place. The sound is warm and well balanced, more firmly focused than some recordings by the London Classical Players at the EMI studio.

Karajan's reading is highly individual in its control of tempo in the first movement, but the Berlin Philharmonic are fully equal to his quixotic pacing, and the effect is certainly compelling. In the slow movement, the intensity of pianissimo playing is enhanced by the beautiful orchestral sound; the *Waltz* has characteristic panache and the spacious yet immensely dramatic finale sends the adrenalin racing. Unlike Sir Colin Davis, Karajan does not observe the first-movement repeat, and there is no doubt that Davis's structural control and overall pacing are more convincing. Karajan's 1965 performance, now on DG's bargain Privilege label, with two dances from *La damnation de Faust* as a bonus (429 511-2), is altogether too erratic to be entirely convincing.

Barbirolli provides a reading of the *Symphonie fantastique* which is not only impulsively exciting but also possesses a breadth of imagination that is missing in many other performances. A lyrical spaciousness is felt in the slow movement, which is played most beautifully; and in the finale there is a demonic impulse, with the detailed realization of Berlioz's orchestration vividly projected, not least the plangent bell-toll. The overture is full of adrenalin too, but most striking of all are the three pieces from *La damnation de Faust*, with the *Danse des sylphes* given a gossamer delicacy. Unfortunately the (originally Pye) recording, dating from 1959, has been remastered fiercely and, although the original ambience remains to give fullness and atmosphere, the upper range needs a great deal of control to sound comfortable at fortissimo levels.

The Beecham Edition version of the *Symphonie fantastique* with the Orchestre National is a mono recording, made only a short time before his stereo account. What is surprising is to discover how different the two performances are. The mono version is faster in all five movements, with an astonishing difference in overall timing of six minutes in a three-quarter-hour work. More important is the difference of tension, with the final *March to the scaffold* and *Witches' sabbath* much more exciting in the faster, mono version. Beecham's incisive control of rhythm goes with the most persuasive feeling for overall line, not just in the symphony but in the two overtures that come as fill-up, *King Lear* and *Roman carnival*. Transfers are clean, but with some edge on top.

No conductor has a more acute feeling for pacing and line in the *Symphonie fantastique* than Sir Colin Davis. With the Vienna Philharmonic in the third of his recordings of it for Philips he maintains the freshness and natural idiomatic feel which has characterized all his readings. It has a digital recording, and that helps to bring out the ripe resonance of the Vienna orchestra, the strings in particular. But once that is said, this is a marginally less taut, less dramatic performance, less crisp in the ensemble, than either of his previous ones, the first with the LSO, the second, even finer with the Royal Concertgebouw. The latter is the one which fully conveys the magic which Davis can bring to this work, and one hopes that it will continue to be available, when the sound is exceptionally fine for its period (1974).

Mariss Jansons and the Royal Concertgebouw give a ripely resonant reading which instantly demonstrates the warmth of expressiveness in a finely moulded account of the slow introduction to the first movement, *Rêveries*. Jansons presents this very much as a full-blooded romantic symphony, which no doubt influences him towards not observing the formal exposition repeat in the first movement, a perfectly valid view. Though the playing in the first, fourth and fifth movements is too finely controlled to convey quite as much excitement as some rivals, the warmth and purposefulness are very convincing. The digital recording is full and rounded to match, with the Concertgebouw strings in particular sounding glorious.

The spectacular, wide-ranging recorded sound is the first point to note with the Dutoit version. But he tends to prefer slower speeds than usual, and that sometimes makes him seem less exciting than his finest rivals. Yet by keeping the pulse steady, he adds to structural strength while never limiting expressive warmth in lyrical passages or the crisp lifting of rhythm in allegros, and the power is most impressive.

Weight is the keynote of Klemperer's highly individual reading. Yet the effect is always spontaneous and no one could be in any doubt that this was the work of a great conductor. From the first movement onwards – not without its impetuous feeling but far more clearly symphonic than usual – Klemperer conveys a rugged strength which, in the massiveness of the *Witches' sabbath* for example, brings you close to Satan himself. There is certainly no lack of adrenalin and the *March to the scaffold*, its rhythms clipped, is also given commanding power, while the close is made the more impressive by a recording that is outstanding for its period, sounding superbly expansive on CD with rich, resonant strings and full, sonorous brass. The Beethoven *Leonora No. 1* is an exciting and fresh performance from Klemperer's first Beethoven series in 1954, but an all-pervading heaviness of style quite ruins *Iphigénie en Aulide*.

Ataulfo Argenta's (originally Decca) recording from the earliest days of stereo was considered to be of demonstration standard in its day, and the overall balance is still very impressive, with the French brass full of character yet not sounding too blatant. The reading is individual and distinguished. The balance between reflection and neurosis is admirable. Argenta observed the repeat in the *March to the scaffold* – for the first time on disc – and the finale is strong on atmosphere as well as drive.

Prêtre's excitingly chimerical Boston account was recorded at about the same time as Argenta's, but the upper range is less full. However, the Boston ambience brings weight and the sound is otherwise resonantly spacious, with exciting projection for the brass. It is a highly volatile performance but Prêtre's sense of neurosis is convincing, and the finale combines an element of the grotesque with high adrenalin flow. An individual and involving account. Munch's famous accounts of the two *Overtures* make a thrilling bonus, but here the sound tends to shrillness.

Bernstein's recording was made in the Avery Fisher Hall in 1968 and the sound is very bright, with the violins lacking richness above the stave. There is plenty of atmosphere and the tolling bell and deep brass of the final have a demonic resonance. However although there is fine playing in the *Adagio*, the first movement is distractingly wilful and the reading overall has a tendency to go over the top. Bernstein's later EMI recording is far preferable. The two overtures and *Rákóczy march* offered as a bonus have comparable free-flowing adrenalin.

Ormandy's 1961 account, with the Philadelphia Orchestra playing brilliantly, is certainly gripping. There are one or two mannered touches in the first movement, but the *Waltz* has panache and the last two movements have plenty of pungency and spectacle; there is no doubting the Satanic feeling in the finale. The very brilliantly lit recording does not lack fullness, but tends to emphasize the hyperbole of the reading. The outstanding Dukas coupling brings a very real bonus to this version.

Frémaux's reading with the LSO is disappointing, brightly recorded but not polished enough in ensemble to be competitive, though his natural feeling for the Berlioz idiom helps him to whip up excitement in the extrovert moments of the later movements.

Symphonie fantastique, Op. 14; (i) *Lélio (Le retour à la vie), Op. 14b.*
(B) *** EMI CZS7 62739-2 (2). (i) Gedda, Burles, Van Gorp, Sendrez, Topart, Ch. of R. France; ORTF Nat. O, Martinon.

Berlioz intended *Lélio* as a sequel to the *Symphonie fantastique*, and Martinon conveniently offers the works paired at bargain price. His account of the *Symphonie* shows a unique seductiveness. Martinon gives the first-movement exposition repeat and provides the often omitted extra brass parts; though the result is brilliant, he never presses on too frenetically. The *March to the scaffold* is aptly menacing. But most of all this reading is outstanding for its warm shaping of phrase, even if the finale, with its tolling bells of doom, has a flamboyance and power to match any available. The 1973 sound remains remarkably vivid.

Lélio quotes the *idée fixe* from the *Symphonie*, which helps the listener to feel at home. It is difficult to imagine this performance being bettered, and the 1974 sound is suitably atmospheric.

VOCAL MUSIC

La damnation de Faust, Op. 24.
*** Ph. 416 395-2 (2) [id.]. Veasey, Gedda, Bastin, Amb. S., Wandsworth School Boys' Ch., LSO Ch., LSO, C. Davis.
*** Decca Dig. 414 680-2 (2) [id.]. Riegel, Von Stade, Van Dam, King, Chicago Ch. & SO, Solti.
**(*) Ph. Dig. 416 199-2 (2) [id.]. Myers, Lafont, Von Otter, Schirrer, Edinburgh Festival Ch., Lyon Opera O, Gardiner.

La damnation de Faust: highlights.
**(*) Decca Dig. 410 181-2 [id.] (from above recording; cond. Solti).

Both Gedda as Faust and Bastin as Mephistopheles are impressive in the 1974 Philips set. The response of the chorus and orchestra is never less than intelligent and, in the quieter passages, highly sensitive and the recording perspective is outstandingly natural and realistic. The subtlety and fantasy of Davis's reading are finely matched. The only snag is the tape-hiss, but that is easily ignored.

Solti's performance, searingly dramatic, is given stunning digital sound to make the *Ride to Hell* supremely exciting. But with Von Stade singing tenderly, this is a warmly expressive performance too; and the *Hungarian march* has rarely had such sparkle and swagger. The extra brightness matches the extrovert quality of the performance, less subtle than Davis's.

Gardiner's version was recorded live by Radio France at the Berlioz Festival in Lyon in September 1987; though this means that sound-balances are not always ideal, there is a natural sense of presence to bring out the vitality and dramatic thrust of the performance. Gardiner persuasively draws on the spark of humour in this work, lifting rhythms, finding the sparkle in Berlioz's inspiration more readily than his current rivals. His solo team is a strong one: Michael Myers as Faust gives a warm, relaxed performance, producing beautiful tenor tone, a believable, vulnerable hero; Anne Sofie von Otter makes an appealingly tender Marguerite, but Jean-Philippe Lafont is a lightweight – if lively – Mephistopheles, not firm or dark enough. The singing of the Edinburgh Festival Chorus adds to the bite of the drama, even though they are balanced a little too distantly.

L'enfance du Christ, Op. 25.
*** Erato/Warner Dig. 2292 45275-2 (2) [id.]. Von Otter, Rolfe Johnson, Van Dam, Cachemaille, Bastin, Monteverdi Ch., Lyons Op. O, Gardiner.
**(*) Ph. 416 949-2 (2) [id.]. Baker, Tappy, Langridge, Allen, Herincx, Rouleau, Bastin, Alldis Ch., LSO, C. Davis.
**(*) EMI Dig. CDS7 49935-2 (2); *EX 749935-4*. Ann Murray, Thomas Allen, Wilson Johnson, Finley, King's College Ch., RPO, Cleobury.

John Eliot Gardiner has the advantage of fine modern recording, made in the Church of Sainte-Madeleine, Pérouges, very well balanced but with the resonance bringing warm atmosphere rather than great clarity. He has some fine soloists, too; some will prefer Anthony Rolfe-Johnson's mellow narration to Eric Tappy's rather more characterful but less melliflous contribution on the Davis set. Anne Sofie von Otter's Mary is outstanding, by far the best currently on record, sung with rapt simplicity; Van Dam's Herod is also debatably the best we have at present. The others are more mixed in appeal, although Giles Cachemaille is a very impressive Joseph. Gardiner often – though not always – adopts brisker tempi than Davis, and his vibrancy brings a new dimension to some of the music. This is a very vivid reading, marred only by two questionable speeds. Generally, however, Davis's choice of pacing is even more apt – he has a special feeling for this work, born of long experience, notably so in the *Shepherds' chorus*, where he moves the music on more firmly than Gardiner.

In Sir Colin Davis's second recording for Philips the beautifully balanced recording intensifies the colour and atmosphere of the writing, so that for example the *Nocturnal march* in the first part is wonderfully mysterious. There is a fine complement of soloists, and though Eric Tappy's tone as narrator is not always sweet, his sense of style is immaculate. Others are not always quite so idiomatic, but Dame Janet Baker and Thomas Allen, as ever, both sing beautifully.

Stephen Cleobury directs a brisk, dramatically taut reading, atmospherically recorded against the reverberant acoustic of King's College Chapel. The freshness is enhanced by the singing of King's College Choir with its trebles, and the soloists are a characterful team, if not as sweet-toned as some. David Wilson Johnson is a powerful Herod, though the voice as recorded has a rather rough edge. Ann Murray as Mary sings movingly, but ideally one would look for a firmer tone. Thomas Allen as Joseph is warmer than he was in Colin Davis's Philips version and Robert Tear is at his most expressive, helped by the acoustic. Cleobury, though occasionally fussy with detail, as in the *Shepherds' farewell*, has a fine feeling for dramatic timing and tension.

(i) *Herminie; La mort de Cléopâtre;* (ii) *La belle voyageuse;* (iii) *La captive;* (iv) *Le chasseur danois;* (v) *Le jeune pâtre breton;* (ii) *Zaïde.*
*** Ph. 416 960-2 [id.]. (i) Dame Janet Baker; (ii) Sheila Armstrong; (iii) Josephine Veasey; (iv) John Shirley-Quirk; (v) Frank Patterson; LSO, C. Davis.

These two dramatic scenes, *Herminie* and *La mort de Cléopâtre*, make an apt coupling, early works which yet give many hints of the mature Berlioz. Dame Janet Baker sings with passionate intensity while Sir Colin Davis draws committed playing from the LSO. Sheila Armstrong is very successful in her two songs provided as the fill-up; Josephine Veasey's contribution is also an individual one; but Frank Patterson, the weakest of the soloists, lacks the necessary charm. Nevertheless this compilation is a major addition to the Berlioz CD discography.

(i) *Lélio, Op. 14b* (without narration); (ii) *Les nuits d'été. Op. 7.*
**(*) Ph. 416 961-2 [id.]. (i) Carreras, Allen, Alldis Ch.; (ii) Armstrong, Veasey, Patterson, Shirley-Quirk; LSO, C. Davis.

By not using the spoken dialogue, Sir Colin Davis is able to include on his record not only the music of *Lélio* but also his interesting version of Berlioz's deeply expressive song-cycle, with different voices singing different songs. (The tessitura here ranges so wide that it is hard for any one singer to encompass them all.) Yet the success of this apparently logical venture is limited. Davis's insight is not in doubt, but the unity of the work is undermined and the contribution of the four singers involved is uneven. Sheila Armstrong is at her finest in her two songs (including the final exhilarating *L'île inconnue*), but Frank Patterson's opening *Villanelle* is less appealing. *Lélio* is altogether more convincing within its structural limitations.

Mélodies: *Aubade; La belle voyageuse; La captive; Le chasseur danois; Le jeune pâtre breton; La mort d'Ophélie; Les nuits d'été; Zaïde.*
*** Erato/Warner Dig. 2292 045517-2 [id.]. Montague, Robbin, Fournier, Crook, Cachemaille, Lyon Op. O, Gardiner.

Mélodies: *La belle voyageuse; La captive; Les nuits d'été, Op. 7; Zaïde.*
*** Virgin Dig. VC7 91164-2; *VC7 91164-4* [id.]. Dame Janet Baker, City of L. Sinf., Hickox – RESPIGHI: *La sensitiva.* ***

John Eliot Gardiner here divides the six keenly atmospheric songs of *Les nuits d'été* between four singers, in some ways an ideal solution when each song demands such different timbre and different tessitura. His choice of singers is inspired. Catherine Robbin, with clear echoes of Dame Janet Baker, gives a rich and moving account of *La spectre de la rose* (as she does also of the final item from among the miscellaneous orchestral songs, *La mort d'Ophélie*), and Diana Montague is full and bright in her two songs, coping splendidly with Gardiner's very fast speed for the final *L'île inconnue*, which brings a delightful pay-off. Pierre Cachemaille gives a thrilling bite to *Sur les lagunes*, and Howard Crook, with his rather thin, reedy tenor, is well suited to *Au cimetière* but is even more striking in the extraordinary *Aubade*, the rarest of the miscellaneous songs, with its accompaniment for two cornets and four horns. Above all, the presiding genius of the conductor makes this a memorable Berlioz disc and the Lyon Opera Orchestra is helpfully recorded, not in the dry acoustic of the opera house, but atmospherically in a Lyon church.

Like Gardiner's Erato issue, Dame Janet's new recording of *Les nuits d'été* also includes extra orchestral songs. Helped by full, rich recording and a warmly sympathetic accompaniment from Hickox, the interpretation, if anything, glows even more warmly than in Dame Janet's classic EMI reading with Barbirolli, and the voice shows next to no sign of the passing years. Respighi's sensitive setting of Shelley in Italian translation, *La sensitiva*, makes a generous fill-up, equally well recorded.

(i) *La Mort de Cléopâtre;* (ii) *Les nuits d'été, Op. 7* (see also below).
*** DG Dig. 410 966-2 [id.]. (i) Jessye Norman; (ii) Kiri Te Kanawa, O de Paris, Barenboim.

The coupling of Jessye Norman in the scena and Dame Kiri Te Kanawa in the song-cycle makes for one of the most ravishing of Berlioz records, with each singer at her very finest. Norman has natural nobility and command as the Egyptian queen in this dramatic scena, while Te Kanawa encompasses the challenge of different moods and register in *Les nuits d'été* more completely and affectingly than any singer on record in recent years.

Les nuits d'été (song-cycle), *Op. 7.*
*** Decca 417 813-2 [id.]. Régine Crespin, SRO, Ansermet (with *Recital of French songs* ***).
(M) (***) Decca mono 425 988-2 [id.]. Suzanne Danco, Cincinnati SO, Thor Johnson – RAVEL: *2 Mélodies hébraïques* etc. (***)

(i) *Les nuits d'été* (song-cycle), *Op. 7;* (ii) *La mort de Cléopâtre* (lyric scena); (ii; iii) *Les Troyens, Act V, Scenes ii & iii.*
❀ (M) *** EMI CDM7 69544-2. Dame Janet Baker, (i) New Philh. O, Barbirolli; (ii) LSO, Gibson; (iii) with Greevy, Erwen, Howell & Amb. Op. Ch.

The collaboration of Dame Janet Baker at the peak of her powers and Sir John Barbirolli in what is probably the most beautiful of all orchestral song-cycles produces ravishing results. Berlioz's early scena on the death of a famous classical heroine is also beautifully performed. But even more desirable is Dame Janet's deeply moving rendering of the concluding scenes of Berlioz's epic opera. This makes an essential supplement to the complete recording for any dedicated Berliozian. Fine remastered sound.

Crespin's richness of tone and a style which has an operatic basis do not prevent her from bringing out the subtlety of detail. *Le spectre de la rose* (a wonderful song) has a breadth of line and colouring and an immediate sense of drama that conjure up the opera house at once and, with Ansermet accompanying brilliantly, this glowing performance is a *tour de force.* The remastered sound (from the 1960s) retains the atmosphere of the original most successfully, while adding presence.

Suzanne Danco's record, made in 1951, was the first complete version of Berlioz's magical song-cycle. The purity of her tone and diction, her poise and sense of style shine through. She evokes not only the heady atmosphere of these songs but also their essentially classical feeling. Thor Johnson draws playing of much sensitivity from the Cincinnati orchestra. This is one of the classics of the gramophone and should not be missed. The ethereal sound Danco produces long resonates in the memory, and the Ravel coupling is no less magical.

(i) *Requiem mass (Grande messe des morts). Overtures: Benvenuto Cellini; Le carnaval romain; Le Corsaire.*
**(*) DG Dig. 429 724-2 (2) [id.]. (i) Pavarotti, Ernst-Senff Ch.; BPO, Levine.

(i) *Requiem Mass (Grande messe des morts), Op. 5;* (ii; iii) *La Mort de Cléopâtre;* (iii) *Roméo et Juliette, Op. 17* (orchestral music only).
(M) **(*) Sony SM2K 47526 (2) [id.]. (i) Stuart Burrows, Ch. of R. France, O Nat. de France, O Philharmonique; (ii) Jennie Tourel; (iii) NYPO; Bernstein.

(i) *Requiem mass;* (ii) *Symphonie funèbre et triomphale, Op. 15.*
**(*) Ph. 416 283-2 (2) [id.]. (i) Dowd, Wandsworth School Boys' Ch., LSO Ch.; (ii) John Alldis Ch.; LSO, Sir Colin Davis.

(i) *Requiem mass;* (ii) *Te Deum, Op. 22.*
(M) **(*) Sony M2YK 46461 (2) [id.]. (i) Stuart Burrows, Ch. of R. France, O Nat. de France, O Philharmonique, Bernstein; (ii) Jean Dupory, Jean Guillov, Ch. d'Enfants de Paris, Maîtrise de la Resurrection, Paris Ch. & O, Barenboim.

For Sir Colin Davis's recording of the *Requiem* Philips went to Westminster Cathedral, which should have been atmospheric enough; but then the engineers managed to negate the massiveness of the forces in anything but the loudest fortissimos, thanks to the closeness of the microphones: in many passages one can hear individual voices in the choir. However, the large-scale brass sound is formidably caught and the choral fortissimos are glorious, helped by the fresh cutting edge of the Wandsworth School Boys' Choir. It was Davis's idea, not Berlioz's, to have boys included, but it is entirely in character. The LSO provides finely incisive accompaniment, and there is no doubt that the CD remastering has added to the overall impact and tangibility. The *Symphonie funèbre et triomphale* is a fascinating product of Berlioz's eccentric genius, designed as it was to be performed not just in the open air but on the march. The *Funeral march* itself provides the most haunting music, but it needs more persuasive handling than Sir Colin's if it is not to outstay its welcome.

Levine's account of the *Requiem*, one of his Berlioz series with the Berlin Philharmonic, is the most recommendable of the modern, digitally recorded versions, though in dramatic bite it cannot quite match the vintage Colin Davis reading on Philips. Levine's speeds generally flow a little faster, but tension is lower, and the Ernst-Senff Choir falls short of its usual high standards in the raggedness of some of the choral entries. Levine's reading, far from being too highly coloured, runs the risk of being too restrained, as in the *Rex tremendae*, yet the richness and weight of the sound, as recorded, is consistently satisfying, with a far wider dynamic range than on the Davis analogue recording of 1969. Having Pavarotti as a characterful, imaginatively expressive soloist in the *Sanctus* is an advantage, but Ronald Dowd for Davis is no less mellifluous and he is recorded with a more natural, less spotlit balance. Levine's coupling of three of Berlioz's most popular overtures is not as unusual as Davis's *Symphonie funèbre* but works very well in these excellent performances.

In a characteristically powerful and vibrant reading, Bernstein adopts a moulded, consciously persuasive style, and the result is atmospheric and dramatic. In *Rex tremendae*, for example, his expansiveness is well in scale with the music. In the *Lacrymosa* he is faster and more urgent, with an irresistible, wave-like rhythm; and he is notable for warmth and expressiveness. The acoustic is reasonably ample, and this allows the chorus to sound larger than some. The remastering improves the effect enormously – indeed the impact of drums and brass in the *Dies irae* is almost overwhelming. At lower dynamic levels textures are fresh and appealing, the flutes especially radiant. Stuart Burrows's headily ardent solo in the *Sanctus* is tellingly projected, and altogether the 1975 performance communicates vividly. The new couplings which come in this reissue as part of Sony's 'Royal' Bernstein Edition (graced with one of the Prince of Wales's paintings) are more logical and indeed the 1961 performance of *Le Mort de Cléopâtre*, with Jennie Tourel the vibrant soloist, is histrionically compulsive in a way that is so characteristic of a conductor/composer with a theatrical feeling in his very being. The closing *Recitativo misurato* with its stabbing orchestral comments and dark finality is memorable. Bernstein's temperament is equally well suited to Berlioz's dramatic symphony, *Romeo and Juliet*, and it is a pity that his 1959 recording (offering remarkably good sound for its period) includes only the orchestral sections of the score, presented with smouldering passion and much ardour for the *Scène d'amour*. Fine orchestral playing, especially in the glittering *Queen Mab scherzo*. The earlier coupling of the *Requiem* plus Barenboim's exciting (1977) French recording of the *Te Deum* (M2YK 46461) is presumably to be withdrawn, although it remains equally recommendable, and some collectors may prefer it.

Roméo et Juliette, Op. 17.
**(*) Ph. 416 962-2 (2) [id.]. Kern, Tear, Shirley-Quirk, Alldis Ch., LSO Ch. & O, C. Davis.

(i) *Roméo et Juliette, Op. 17. Symphonie funèbre et triomphale, Op. 15.*
*** Decca 417 302-2 (2) [id.]. (i) Quivar, Cupido, Krause, Tudor Singers, Montreal Ch. & SO, Dutoit.

Roméo et Juliette, Op. 17; Les nuits d'été.
**(*) DG Dig. 427 665-2 (2) [id.]. Von Otter, Langridge, Morris, Berlin RIAS Chamber Ch., Ernest Senff Ch., BPO, Levine.

Dutoit's is a masterly, heart-warming reading of Berlioz's curious mixture of symphony, cantata and opera, superbly recorded in richly atmospheric sound, with a triumphantly successful account of the *Symphonie funèbre et triomphale* as a generous coupling. Dutoit consistently brings out the romantic lyrical warmth of the work, not least in the great orchestral love-scene. When that is coupled with brilliant choral singing, incisive and atmospheric, it is an unassailable mixture. Though the mezzo, Florence Quivar, is less steady than she should be, the other soloists are first rate, Alberto Cupido witty in his scherzetto, Tom Krause aptly firm and resonant. In the *Symphonie funèbre*, Dutoit is at his most uninhibited, brilliantly skirting the very edge of vulgarity in this outgoing ceremonial piece.

Levine gives a powerful performance of Berlioz's great dramatic symphony, marked by playing of exceptional polish and precision from the Berlin Philharmonic, and with Anne Sofie von Otter outstanding alongside two other very positive soloists. Von Otter adds to the attractions of the set in the generous fill-up, *Les nuits d'été*, again fresh and radiant, underlining the dramatic contrasts between the songs. Levine is nevertheless rather heavy-handed in his treatment of Berlioz. Compare him in the music for the Capulets' party with such an outstanding rival as Dutoit on Decca and, for all the precision and power, he has less feeling of jollity. There is also less sparkle in the *Queen Mab scherzo*, for all the high brilliance of the playing, while the night music of the love scene emerges in the full brightness of day. Yet the very weight of Levine's reading, his electricity, still puts this version high on the list. The recording, made in the Jesus Christus Kirche in Berlin, is very full and weighty to match, while catching pianissimo strings most delicately, even if it falls short of the Decca in transparency.

Sir Colin Davis – it hardly needs saying – has a rare sympathy with this score and secures playing of great vitality and atmosphere from the LSO. His soloists are excellent too, and so is the chorus. The 1968 recording still sounds excellent; it is natural in tone and balance, and the CDs bring added presence. But with no coupling and at full price, this is not very competitive, especially compared with Dutoit.

Te Deum, Op. 22.
*** DG Dig. 410 696-2 [id.]. Araiza, LSO Ch., LPO Ch., Woburn Singers, Boys' Ch., European Community Youth O, Abbado.
**(*) Ph. 416 660-2 [id.]. Tagliavini, Wandsworth School Boys' Ch. LSO Ch. & O, N. Kynaston (organ), C. Davis.

The newest DG recording from Abbado is very impressive. The sound is wide-ranging, with striking dynamic contrasts and a much greater sense of presence than its predecessors. Artistically, too, it is of considerable merit: Abbado brings great tonal refinement and dignity to this performance, and the spacious sound helps. Francisco Araiza is altogether first class. The choirs are responsive, as are the young players Abbado has assembled.

Davis's 1969 Philips recording has been successfully remastered. He conveys massiveness without pomposity, drama without unwanted excesses of emotion, and his massed forces with the LSO respond superbly. The expansive choral climaxes and Nicolas Kynaston's fine organ contribution are impressively contained; but this reissue should have been offered at mid-price.

OPERA

Béatrice et Bénédict (complete).
*** Ph. 416 952-2 (2) [id.]. Baker, Tear, Eda-Pierre, Allen, Lloyd, Van Allan, Watts, Alldis Ch., LSO, C. Davis.
*** Erato/Warner Dig. 2292 45773-2 (2) [id.]. Graham, Viala, McNair, Robbin, Bacquier, Cachemaille, Le Texier, Lyon Opera Ch. & O, John Nelson.

Béatrice et Bénédict here reveals itself as less an opera than a dramatic symphony, one of the important Berlioz works which refuse to fit in a conventional category. The score presents not just witty and brilliant music for the heroine and hero (Dame Janet Baker and Robert Tear at their most pointed) but sensuously beautiful passages such as the duet for Hero and Ursula at the end of Act I and the trio they later share with Beatrice, both incidental to the drama but very important for the musical structure. First-rate solo and choral singing, brilliant playing and sound refined and clear in texture, bright and fresh, even if minimal hiss betrays an analogue source.

The Lyon Opera version conducted by John Nelson makes an excellent alternative to the vintage Colin Davis recording. In spacious, modern, digital sound it offers substantially more of the French dialogue, well spoken by actors but more dryly recorded than the musical numbers. Nelson's reading is light and crisp but, at generally faster speeds, sparkles rather less than Davis's. The radiant ensembles for women's voices – the *Duo Nocturne* for Hero and Ursule which ends Act I and the Act II Trio with Béatrice in addition – are taken more flowingly here but, with well-matched voices, are comparably beautiful. Susan Graham is a characterful Béatrice, lighter in the big aria than Janet Baker for Davis but aptly younger-sounding. Jean-Luc Viala is a comparably light Bénédict, pointing the fun in his big aria, and Sylvia McNair and Catherine Robbin are superb as Hero and Ursule.

Les Troyens, Parts 1 & 2 (complete).
❀ *** Ph. 416 432-2 (4) [id.]. Veasey, Vickers, Lindholm, Glossop, Soyer, Partridge, Wandsworth School Boys' Ch., ROHCG Ch. & O, C. Davis.

Throughout this long and apparently disjointed score Davis compels the listener to concentrate, to appreciate its epic logic. His tempi are generally faster than in the theatre, and the result is exhilarating but with no hint of rush. Only in the great love scene of *O nuit d'ivresse* would one have welcomed the more expansive hand of a Beecham. It is interesting too to find Davis pursuing his direct, dramatic line even in Dido's death scene at the end. Veasey on any count, even next to Dame Janet Baker, makes a splendid Dido, single-minded rather than seductive, singing always with fine heroic strength. Of the rest, Berit Lindholm as Cassandra, in the first half of the opera, is the only soloist who falls short – the voice is not quite steady – otherwise one cannot imagine a more effective cast, with Vickers a ringing Aeneas. The Covent Garden Chorus and Orchestra excel themselves in virtuoso singing and playing, while CD brings out the superb quality of sound all the more vividly, and the Acts are arranged on the four discs with no break within any Act.

Berners, Lord (1883–1950)

The Triumph of Neptune (ballet suite): excerpts.
(M) (***) EMI mono CDM7 63405-2 [id.]. LPO, Sir Thomas Beecham – BANTOCK: *Fifine at the fair;* BAX: *Garden of Fand.* (***)

The Triumph of Neptune was a rare example of music by an English composer being commissioned and performed by Diaghilev's Ballets Russes (at the London Coliseum in 1926). Beecham recorded excerpts from it twice. This is the first set, taken from 78s. What is offered (the *Schottische, Hornpipe, Polka: the sailor's return, Harlequinade, Dance of the fairy princess, Intermezzo: Sunday morning* and *Apotheosis of Neptune*) is irresistible. The LPO playing has all the whimsical flair one would expect, and the CD transfer by Michael Dutton and John Holland admirably retains the fullness and atmosphere of those old shellac discs. The sound may be confined but it is never thinned out or made edgy.

Bernstein, Leonard (1918–90)

(i) *Candide: overture; Facsimile* (choreographic essay); *Fancy Free* (ballet); *On the Town* (3 dance episodes); (ii) *On the Town* (musical); (i) *On the Waterfront* (symphonic suite); (iii) *Trouble in Tahiti (opera in 7 scenes);* (i) *West Side story: Symphonic dances* (orch. Sid Ramin & Irwin Kostal).
(M) *** Sony SM3K 47154 (3) [id.]. (i) NYPO; (ii) Betty Comden, Adolph Green, Nancy Walker, John Reardon, Cris Alexander, George Gaynes, Ch. & O; (iii) Nancy Williams, Julian Patrick & Vocal Trio, Columbia Wind Ens.; all cond. composer.

Candide overture – placed at the beginning of Disc 2 – provides the perfect curtain-raiser for this indispensable box of Bernstein's vibrant, early recordings of his theatrical and film music. The New York Philharmonic, in cracking form, play the overture with exhilarating zest in just over four minutes. The New Yorkers display similar virtuosity and tremendous spirit in the ballet music and comparable gusto in the noisily pungent film score, plus a natural command of the jazz rhythms, while the tender moments in the *West Side story* dances have great poignancy. But Bernstein comes completely into his own in the music for the musical theatre. *On the Town* is very much a traditional musical with Hollywood associations, but the style of *Trouble in Tahiti* (for which Bernstein wrote both words and music) lies somewhere between the musical and the opera house. In 1983 Bernstein incorporated his early score as a flashback sequence into a sequel, *A Quiet Place*, but there is no doubt that the earlier music has greater vitality, besides having a very strong lyrical element, and the performances under the composer have great flair and theatrical adrenalin. The recordings are remarkably vivid and have been impressively remastered to sound more atmospheric than in their earlier, LP incarnations.

Candide: overture; West Side story: symphonic dances.
(M) *** Sony SMK 47529 [id.]. NYPO, composer – GERSHWIN: *American in Paris* etc. ***

Fancy free (ballet); *On the Town* (3 Dance episodes); *On the Waterfront* (symphonic suite).
(M) **(*) Sony SMK 47530 [id.]. NYPO, composer.

Bernstein's exhilarating and definitive New York performances of his theatre music are now reissued separately as part of the Sony 'Royal Edition'. Here they are in two separate groupings, admirably remastered. The first disc is especially desirable as it includes the breathtaking 1960 version of the *Overture Candide* and is coupled with Bernstein's unsurpassed Gershwin performances, made at the end of the 1950s. The second CD, playing for just over 52 minutes, could have been more generous. However, perhaps some listeners will feel compensated by having Prince Charles's watercolour paintings fronting each box.

(i) *Candide: overture;* (ii) *On the Town: 3 Dance episodes;* (i) *West Side story: Symphonic dances;* (iii) *America.*

(M) *** DG Dig. 427 806-2; *427 806-4.* (i) LAPO; (ii) Israel PO; (iii) Troyanos with O; composer – BARBER: *Adagio* ***; GERSHWIN: *Rhapsody in blue.* **(*)

In his later DG account of the *Overture* to *Candide* the composer still directs with tremendous flair, his speed a fraction slower than in his New York studio recording for CBS. The colourful and vigorous dances from *On the Town* are joined by a highly idiomatic account of the orchestral confection devised from his most successful musical, *West Side story*, with the players contributing the necessary shouts in the *Mambo* representing a street fight. Vivid if close-up digital sound, obviously more modern than in the CBS/Sony versions.

Divertimento for orchestra; (i) *Halil (Nocturne);* (ii) *3 Meditations from Mass; On the Town (3 Dance episodes).*

**(*) DG 415 966-2 [id.]. (i) Rampal; (ii) Rostropovich; Israel PO, composer.

Early Bernstein is well represented in the colourful and vigorous dances from *On the Town* while the other three works show the later Bernstein sharply sparked off by specific commissions. The *Divertimento*, easily and cheekily moving from one idiom to another, is often jokey, but amiably so. The two concertante pieces, *Halil* for flute and strings and the *Meditations* for cello and orchestra, both beautifully reflect the individual poetry of the two artists for whom they were written and who perform masterfully here. The aggressive digital sound of the original recording bites even more on CD, with a brilliant top and spectacular bass leaving the middle light. With Bernstein, such sound does little harm.

Fancy Free (ballet); (i) *Serenade after Plato's Symposium* (for solo violin, string orchestra, harp and percussion).

*** DG 423 583-2 [id.]. Israel PO, composer, (i) with Kremer.

The *Serenade* must rank among Bernstein's most resourceful and inspired creations, full of ideas, often thrilling and exciting, and equally often moving. Gidon Kremer has all the nervous intensity and vibrant energy to do justice to this powerful and inventive score. The ballet, *Fancy Free*, is an attractive example of Bernstein's freely eclectic style, raiding Stravinsky, Copland or Gershwin and putting the result together effectively, thanks to his exuberant sense of colour and rhythm. The Israel Philharmonic Orchestra plays with tremendous spirit and also enjoys the benefit of outstanding recording quality.

(i) *3 Meditations* (for cello and orchestra) from *Mass; On the Waterfront* (symphonic suite); (ii) *Symphony No. 1 (Jeremiah).*

(M) *** DG Dig./Analogue 431 028-2; *431 028-4* [id.]. (i) Rostropovich; (ii) Christa Ludwig; Israel PO, composer.

Three Meditations, a concertante piece for cello and orchestra, beautifully reflects the individual poetry of the artist for whom it was written and who performs masterfully here. The *Jeremiah Symphony* dates from Bernstein's early twenties and ends with a moving passage from Lamentations for the mezzo soloist. This performance with the Israel Philharmonic is not always quite as polished or as forceful as Bernstein's earlier recording in New York but it never fails to reflect the warmth of Bernstein's writing. The aggressive digital sound, with a brilliant top and spectacular bass, leaves the middle light. With Bernstein, such sound does little harm.

(i) *On the Town: suite;* (ii) *7 Anniversaries.*

(M) (***) BMG/RCA mono GD 60915 [60915-2]. (i) On the Town O, Bernstein; (ii) Bernstein (piano) – COPLAND: *Billy the Kid* etc. (***)

There is always something special about first recordings, and particularly so in this case when Bernstein (in 1945) conducted the original theatre band in, not the usual three, but five dance numbers from the show, *On the Town*, with the brass and reeds having a genuine 1940s swing band character. There is great vitality and swagger here and no apologies need be made for the mono recording, which though slightly shrill has great vividness. The stage music is followed by *Seven anniversaries*, a set of vignettes composed in 1943, dedicated to family and musical friends, opening with Aaron Copland and closing with William Schumann. This is the chrysalis of Bernstein's personal 'Enigma variations' (he added further movements later in his life), for here the thematic material grows out of the very first piece. Brilliant playing, too, with the young composer's feelings strongly projected.

Prelude, fugue and riffs.
(***) Sony MK 42227. Goodman, Columbia Jazz Combo, composer – COPLAND: *Clarinet concerto;* STRAVINSKY: *Ebony concerto;* BARTÓK: *Contrasts;* GOULD: *Derivations.* (***)
*** BMG/RCA Dig. RD 87762 [7762-2-RC]. Stolzman, LSO, Leighton Smith – COPLAND; CORIGLIANO: *Concertos.* ***

Bernstein's exuberant, sometimes wild, yet structured *Prelude, fugue and riffs* fits well within this CBS collection of jazz-inspired pieces in a vintage performance, directed by the composer. It sounds exceptionally vivid on CD.

Like Benny Goodman before him, Richard Stolzman couples Bernstein's *Prelude, fugue and riffs* with Copland's masterly concerto and makes the most of its unbuttoned jazziness. He is better recorded than Goodman, and his record can be recommended strongly on all counts.

Symphonies Nos. (i) *1 (Jeremiah);* (ii) *2 (The age of anxiety) for piano and orchestra;* (i; iii) *3 (Kaddish): To the beloved memory of President Kennedy* (original version); (vi) *Prelude, fugue and riffs;* (iv) *Serenade after Plato's Symposium* (for solo violin, string orchestra, harp & percussion); (v) *Chichester Psalms.*
(M) *** Sony SM3K 47162 (3) [id.]. (i) Tourel; (ii) Entremont; (iii) F. Montealegre (speaker), Camerata Singers; Columbus Boychoir; (iv) Francescatti; (v) J. Bogart, Camerata Singers; (i–iv) NYPO; (vi) Benny Goodman, Columbia Jazz Combo; all cond. composer.

Bernstein's three symphonies have been undervalued because of his theatre music and his willingness to draw on popular influences, but their surface facility is deceptive: the writing has eloquence and depth and they will eventually find their way into the pantheon of memorable twentieth-century symphonies. All three recordings were made in the Manhattan Center, New York, in the early 1960s; the acoustic is agreeably spacious, the bass resonantly full and the strings have plenty of body, so that no apologies need be made for the sound-quality. The *Chichester Psalms,* also impressively transferred to CD, was written in response to a commission from the Dean of Chichester, but Bernstein chose to use the original Hebrew for the actual setting of the Psalm texts. The *Serenade* is based on Plato's account of an Ancient Greek banquet in which those present take turns to soliloquize on the nature of love. Full of ideas, often thrilling and exciting, often moving, it must rank among Bernstein's most resourceful and inspired creations. Francescatti responds naturally to the Hebrew flavour of the lyrical writing but he is very closely balanced, as is the orchestra, and Bernstein's passionate climaxes are given an aggressive fierceness. Finally comes the *Prelude, fugue and riffs,* which Benny Goodman commissioned; so his performance is definitive. With any reservations noted, this is a most stimulating box.

Symphonies Nos. 1 (Jeremiah); (i) *2 (The age of anxiety) for piano and orchestra.*
*** DG 415 964-2 [id.]. Israel PO, composer; (i) with Lukas Foss.

The *Jeremiah symphony* dates from Bernstein's early twenties and ends with a moving passage from Lamentations for the mezzo soloist. As its title suggests, the *Second Symphony* was inspired by the poem of W. H. Auden. These performances with the Israel Philharmonic are not always quite as polished or as forceful as those Bernstein recorded earlier in New York, but with excellent recording they never fail to reflect the warmth of Bernstein's writing. In No. 2 the concertante piano part is admirably played by Lukas Foss.

(i) *Symphony No. 2 (Age of anxiety); Overture Candide; Fancy Free* (ballet).
*** Virgin Dig. VC7 91433-2 [id.]. (i) Kahane; Bournemouth SO, Andrew Litton.

Unsurprisingly, Andrew Litton is less forceful than Bernstein himself in either of his recordings of this Auden-inspired Symphony, a point underlined by the more recessed, more refined recording. Bernstein holds nothing back, but Litton in his less thrusting way is just as compelling and often more subtly expressive, helped by a more poetic, less muscular pianist, Jeffrey Kahane. Above all Litton demonstrates what an original piece this is in its six scenes broadly encapsulating the Auden poem. Anyone fancying Litton's popular coupling need not hesitate.

(i) *Symphony No. 3 (Kaddish),* rev. 1977; (ii) *Dybbuk* (ballet): *Suite No. 2.*
*** DG 423 582-2 [id.]. (i) Caballé, Wagner, V. Jeunesse Ch., Berlin Boys' Ch., Israel PO; (ii) NYPO; composer.

The impressive *Third Symphony,* written in memory of President Kennedy, is recorded here in its revised version (with a male speaker), which concentrates the original concept of a dialogue between man and God, a challenge from earth to heaven. With excellent sound, the performance with the Israel Philharmonic is extremely vivid. The shorter, more contemplative *Second Suite* from his powerful ballet score, *Dybbuk* (on the sinister subject of a lost spirit), makes a splendid foil for the symphony – a strong and colourful performance, cleanly recorded.

West Side story: Symphonic dances.
(B) **(*) DG Compact Classics 413 851-2 (2); *** *413 851-4* [id.]. San Francisco SO, Ozawa – GERSHWIN: *American in Paris* etc. **(*) (CD only: RUSSO: *3 Pieces for Blues band & orchestra, Op. 50* – with the Siegel-Schwall Band).

Ozawa's performance is highly seductive, with an approach that is both vivid and warm, yet concealing any sentimentality. The 1973 recording sounds equally brilliant in its tape and CD formats. However, the additional item on the pair of CDs by William Russo is no great asset, not very convincingly inhabiting that curiously indeterminate middle ground between popular and concert-hall music.

VOCAL MUSIC

Arias and Barcarolles. On the Town: Some other time; Lonely town; Carried away; I can cook. Peter Pan: Dream with me. Songfest: Storyette, H. M.; To what you said. Wonderful Town: A little bit in love.
*** Koch International Classics Dig. 37000-2 [id.]. Judy Kaye, William Sharp; Michael Barrett, Steven Blier.

Arias and Barcarolles for two soloists and piano duet is a family charade of a work that, thanks to Bernstein's genius in simultaneously writing with complex ingenuity and immediate attractiveness, skirts all the potential embarrassments of baby talk, nursery stories and numbers telling of Jewish weddings and insubordinate children. Completed in 1988, it draws on some earlier material, as in a touching celebration of fatherhood, *Greeting*, and in the final, wordless number, *Nachspiel*, with the two soloists humming a slow nostalgic waltz. It is a charming piece, here given – with the composer himself approving the performance – in the original version with piano and excellent, characterful soloists. The bizarre title relates to a comment made by President Eisenhower, after he had heard Bernstein play a Mozart concerto: 'I like music with a theme, not all them arias and barcarolles.' It became a Bernstein family joke. That half-hour work, very well recorded, is coupled with an equivalent collection of eight of Bernstein's most haunting songs and duets, including three from *On the Town* of 1944 and two from *Songfest* of 1977.

Chichester Psalms.
(M) *** Pickwick/RPO Dig. CDRPO 7007; *ZCRPO 7007* [id.]. Aled Jones, LSO Ch., RPO, Hickox – FAURÉ: *Requiem.* ***

Chichester Psalms (reduced score).
*** Hyp. Dig. CDA 66219 [id.]. Martelli, Corydon Singers, Masters, Kettel, Trotter; Best – BARBER: *Agnus Dei;* COPLAND: *In the beginning* etc. ***

Bernstein's *Chichester Psalms* make an instant communication and respond to familiarity too, especially in Richard Hickox's fresh and colourful reading, with Aled Jones bringing an ethereal contribution to the setting of the 23rd Psalm. The recorded sound is firm and well focused.

Martin Best uses the composer's alternative reduced orchestration, which omits the three trumpets and three trombones specified in the original commission and settles for a single harp (instead of a pair), organ and percussion, spectacularly played here by Gary Kettel. The treble soloist, Dominic Martelli, cannot match Aled Jones, but his chaste contribution is persuasive and the choir scales down its pianissimos to accommodate him, with elegiac effect. Indeed the singing of the Corydon Singers is first rate, rising well to the catchy 7/4 rhythms in Psalm 100. Excellent sound, with the acoustic of St Jude-on-the-Hill, Hampstead, creating the right atmosphere.

(i) *Dybbuk* (ballet): complete; (ii) *Mass (for the death of President Kennedy).*
(M) *** Sony SM3K 47158 (3) [id.]. (i) David Johnson, John Ostendorf, NY City Ballet O; (ii) Alan Titus (celebrant), Scribner Ch., Berkshire Boys' Ch., Rock Band & O; composer.

Outrageously eclectic in its borrowings from pop and the avant garde, Bernstein's *Mass* presents an extraordinary example of the composer's irresistible creative energy. With a scenario that boldly defies all sense of good taste, the celebrant smashing the holy vessel before the altar, its impact is even more remarkable in the CD format, which loses nothing in atmosphere but increases the sense of spectacle. The recording now assumes a historical as well as a musical significance.

Bernstein wrote his ghoulish ballet on lost spirits for Jerome Robbins and the New York City Ballet in 1974, when this splendidly atmospheric recording was made. The score presents much the same happy and colourful amalgam of influences as you find in other Bernstein ballets, a touch of the *Rite of spring* here and a whiff of *West Side story* there – although, at 48 minutes, it is less concentrated than the shorter works. The vocal parts, although fairly substantial (and very well done here), are merely incidental.

(i) *Songfest* (cycle of American poems); (ii) *Chichester Psalms.*
*** DG 415 965-2 [id.]. (i) Dale, Elias, Williams, Rosenshein, Reardon, Gramm, Nat. SO of Washington; (ii) Soloist from V. Boys' Ch., V. Jeunesse Ch., Israel PO; composer.

Songfest, one of Bernstein's most richly varied works, is a sequence of poems which ingeniously uses all six singers solo and in various combinations. Characteristically, Bernstein often chooses controversial words to set, and by his personal fervour welds a very disparate group of pieces together into a warmly satisfying whole. The *Chichester Psalms* were recorded live in 1977. One might have slight reservations over the treble soloist from the Vienna Boys' Choir, but otherwise the performance is first class, with the music's warmth and vigour compellingly projected.

Songs: *La bonne cuisine* (French and English versions); *I hate music* (cycle); *2 Love songs; Piccola serenata; Silhouette; So pretty; Mass: A simple song; I go on. Candide: It must be so; Candide's lament. 1600 Pennsylvania Ave: Take care of this house. Peter Pan: My house; Peter Pan; Who am I; Never-Never Land.*
*** Etcetera Dig. KTC 1037 [id.]. Roberta Alexander, Tan Crone.

A delightful collection, consistently bearing witness to Bernstein's flair for a snappy idea as well as his tunefulness. There is a charming artlessness about the four songs he wrote for a 1950 production of *Peter Pan* with Jean Arthur and Boris Karloff; even earlier is the cycle of five *Kid songs, I hate music*; while it is good to have the haunting number from the unsuccessful bicentennial musical, *1600 Pennsylvania Avenue.* Roberta Alexander's rich, warm voice and winning personality are well supported by Tan Crone at the piano. The recording is lifelike and undistracting.

Stage works

Candide (musical: original Broadway production): *Overture and excerpts.*
(M) *** Sony SK 48017 [id.]. Adrian, Cook, Rounseville and original New York cast, Krachmalnick.

This exhilarating CBS record encapsulates the original 1956 Broadway production and has all the freshness of discovery inherent in a first recording, plus all the zing of the American musical theatre. The lyrics, by Richard Wilbur, give pleasure in themselves. Brilliantly lively sound.

Candide (final, revised version).
❀ *** DG Dig. 429 734-2; *429 734-4* (2) [id.]. Hadley, Anderson, Green, Ludwig, Gedda, Della Jones, Ollmann, LSO Ch., LSO, composer.

John Mauceri, dissatisfied with the results of his 1982 score of *Candide*, undertook yet a further revision in the mid-1980s, this time with Bernstein's collaboration. The original order of the music was restored, as were several musical numbers not heard since the first production. Perhaps most importantly, the spirit of the original was recaptured, and two of the finest songs are placed where the composer wanted them and *Candide's lament* (so movingly sung by Jerry Hadley) is again heard near the beginning of the show. This version was first performed by Scottish Opera in 1988, and it forms the basis for the new recording. Bernstein saw his work – written in the wake of McCarthyism during the chilliest days of the Cold War, when the American government even withdrew the composer's own passport – as essentially serious. Its humour, satirically reflecting Voltaire's rubbishing of enforced establishment values, at one point draws a ready parallel between the Spanish Inquisition and Bernstein's own experience during America's darkest political era.

The result is a triumph, both in the studio recording which Bernstein made immediately after the concert performances and in the video recording of the actual concert at the Barbican. It confirms *Candide* as a classic, bringing out not just the vigour, the wit and the tunefulness of the piece more than ever before, but also an extra emotional intensity, something beyond the cynical Voltaire original. Bernstein was a great devotee of Gilbert and Sullivan, and here he not only revels in a comparable topsy-turvy world, as in such hilarious ensembles as *What a day, what a day for an auto da fe!*, but draws out an underlying depth of feeling, just as Sullivan did. So the expansion of the title-role gives Candide himself a series of meditations that strike a deeper note, matching the tender fulfilment of the final ensemble when Candide and Cunegonde are united, *Make our garden grow*. There Bernstein grabs our hearts as he always loved to do, but with a finesse he did not always achieve.

There is no weak link in the cast. Jerry Hadley is touchingly characterful as Candide, producing heady tone, and June Anderson as Cunegonde is not only brilliant in coloratura but warmly dramatic too, making *Glitter and be gay* into much more than a tinkly showpiece. The character roles are brilliantly cast too. It was an inspired choice to have Christa Ludwig as the Old Woman, stopping the show with *I am easily assimilated*, and equally original to choose Adolph Green, lyric writer for Broadway musicals as well as cabaret performer, for the dual role of Dr Pangloss and Martin, the equivalent of the Grossmith roles in G & S. Green is helped out on his falsetto top notes for the very Sullivan-like *Dear boy*, first by his baritone colleague, Kurt Ollman, singing Maximilian, and finally by the chorus, a delicious *tour de force*. Nicolai Gedda also proves a winner in his series of cameo roles, and the full, incisive singing of the London Symphony Chorus adds to the weight of the performance without inflation.

What is missing in the CD set is the witty narration, prepared by John Wells and spoken by Adolph Green and Kurt Ollman in the Barbican performance. As included on the video of the live concert (laser disc DG 072 423-1; VHS DG 072 423-3), those links leaven the entertainment delightfully, whereas reading them from the booklet is not the same, particularly when the plot lurches so improbably from one situation to the next, often with characters dying and then being resurrected. Even those with the CDs should investigate the video version, which also includes Bernstein's own moving speeches of introduction before each Act. And seeing Christa Ludwig as the Old Lady provocatively clicking her castanets as she sings *I am easily assimilated* adds yet further delight.

Candide: highlights.
*** DG Dig. 435 487-2; *435 487-4* [id.] (from above set cond. composer).

Those who don't wish to purchase the complete set (perhaps because they already have the video of the Barbican live performance) may be glad to have this 64-minute CD of highlights, offering most of the key numbers including the *Overture*, *Candide's Meditation* and *Lament*, *Auto-da-fé*, *Glitter and be gay*, *I am easily assimilated*, and the finale, *Make our garden grow*.

A Quiet place (complete).
*** DG Dig. 419 761-2 (2) [id.]. Wendy White, Chester Ludgin, Beverly Morgan, John Brandstetter, Peter Kazaras, Vocal Ens., Austrian RSO, composer.

In flashbacks in Act II of *A Quiet place*, Bernstein incorporates his 1951 score, *Trouble in Tahiti*, with its popular style set in relief against the more serious idiom adopted for the main body of the opera. The opening Act is sharply conceived, set in a funeral parlour. The wife from *Trouble in Tahiti* has just died in a car crash, and for the first time in years the family is reunited, along with an assortment of relatives and friends, all sharply characterized. Sadly, those characters never reappear; the central figures of the family quickly seem to have come not from a grand opera but from a soap opera. Bernstein's score is full of thoughtful and warmly expressive music, but nothing quite matches the sharp, tongue-in-cheek jazz-influenced invention of *Trouble in Tahiti*. The recording was made in Vienna, with an excellent cast of American singers, and with the Austrian Radio orchestra responding splendidly on its first visit to the Vienna State Opera. Considering the problems of live recording of opera, the sound is excellent, remarkably well balanced.

West Side story: complete recording; *On the Waterfront (Symphonic suite)*.
❀ *** DG Dig. 415 253-2 (2) [id.]. Te Kanawa, Carreras, Troyanos, Horne, Ollman, Ch. and O, composer.

Bernstein's recording of the complete score of his most popular work – the first time he had ever conducted the complete musical himself – takes a frankly operatic approach in its casting, but the result is highly successful, for the great vocal melodies are worthy of voices of the highest calibre. Dame Kiri Te Kanawa may not be a soprano who would ever be cast as Maria on stage, and José Carreras may be apparently miscast, but the beauty of such songs as *Maria* or *Tonight*, or even a sharp number like *Something's coming*, with floated pianissimos and subtly graded crescendos, has one admiring the score the more. Tatiana Troyanos, herself brought up on the West Side, spans the stylistic dichotomy to perfection in a superb portrayal of Anita, switching readily from full operatic beauty to a New York snarl and back, and Kurt Ollman as Riff equally finds a nice balance between the styles of opera and the musical. The clever production makes the best of both musical worlds, with Bernstein's son and daughter speaking the dialogue most affectingly. Bernstein conducts a superb instrumental group of musicians 'from on and off Broadway', and they are recorded with a bite and immediacy that is captivating, whether in the warm, sentimental songs or, above all, in the fizzing syncopated numbers, sounding even more original when precisely played and balanced as here. The power of the music is greatly enhanced by the spectacularly wide dynamic range of the recording, with a relatively dry acoustic keeping the sound-picture within an apt scale but without losing bloom. The two-disc set includes, besides the musical, the vivid *Symphonic suite*, which was arranged from Bernstein's film music for the Marlon Brando film, *On the Waterfront*, written about the same period.

West Side story: highlights.
(M) **(*) DG Dig. 431 027-2; *431 027-4* (from complete recording, with Te Kanawa, Carreras, Troyanos, Horne, Ollman; cond. composer).

By cutting the dialogue, all the main numbers are included here, presented as vividly as on the complete (full-price) set; but with only just over 53 minutes of music included this is not especially good value, even though the highlights disc is now offered at mid-price. The moving *Tonight* sequence, for example, loses much without the spoken interchanges between the lovers, and clearly there was room for this on the disc. In the USA this selection is issued at full price.

Bertrand, Anthoine de (1540–81)

Amours de Ronsard, Book 1; *Amours de Cassandre:* excerpts.
(B) *** HM Dig. HMA 431147 [id.]. Clément Janequin Ens.

Anthoine de Bertrand's chansons as recorded here by the Clément Janequin Ensemble show him to be, if not a great master, at least a composer of feeling and considerable resource. (*Mon Dieu, mon Dieu que ma maistresse est belle*, for instance, is both touching and memorable.) They are interspersed with four short, rather anonymous pieces by the French lutenist and composer, Guillaume de Morlaye, active in the 1550s. The performances are excellent throughout, and admirably recorded. At bargain price this is well worth trying.

Berwald, Franz (1797–1868)

Symphonies Nos. 1 in G min. (Sérieuse); 2 in D (Capricieuse); 3 in C (Singulière); 4 in E flat.
*** DG Dig. 415 502-2 [id.]. Gothenburg SO, Järvi.

Franz Berwald's first four symphonies receive a distinguished and auspicious CD début. The present set of recordings outclasses the previous Björlin versions on EMI and almost all previous rivals. First, the orchestral playing has abundant spirit and energy: this is music that is wholly in the life-stream of the Gothenburg orchestra; and secondly, the excellent acoustic of the Gothenburg Hall shows the scores to great advantage. Neeme Järvi sets generally brisk tempi, yet the pacing feels right. The sound is altogether superb, with every detail coming through with great clarity, and this can be strongly recommended.

Symphonies Nos. 3 in C (Sinfonie singulière); No. 4 in E flat.
*** Bluebell ABD 037 [id.]. LSO, Sixten Ehrling.

Sixten Ehrling's records of Berwald's masterpiece, the *Sinfonie singulière*, and its sunny and high-spirited companion, the *Symphony No. 4 in E flat*, written only a month later, were made in 1967 for Decca and still sound as fresh and satisfying as ever. It is amazing that both symphonies should have had to wait so long for their first performance: neither was performed in Berwald's lifetime and the *Singulière* had to wait until the present century for its première. In our 1972 volume we spoke of Ehrling's reading of the *Singulière* as 'the best yet committed to disc'; twenty years on, despite the admirable recording by Neeme Järvi and the Gothenburg

Orchestra, there is no real reason to modify that verdict. Much the same must be said of the *E flat Symphony*, which is given a crisp and vital performance. Although the sound is not digital, there is no reason to withhold a third star, particularly in view of the paucity of representation of these works on CD.

Grand septet in B flat.
*** CRD CRD 3344 [id.]. Nash Ens. – HUMMEL: *Septet.* ***

Berwald's only *Septet* is a work of genuine quality and deserves a secure place in the repertory instead of on its periphery. It dates from 1828 and is for the same forces as the Beethoven and Kreutzer *Septets*; the invention is lively and the ideas have charm. It is eminently well played by the Nash Ensemble, and finely recorded.

(i) *Piano quintet No. 1 in C min.;* (ii) *Piano trios Nos. 1 in E flat; 3 in D min.*
**(*) MS Dig. MSCD 521 [id.]. (i) Stefan Lindgren, Berwald Qt; (ii) Bernt Lysell, Ola Karlsson, Lucia Negro.

The performances of the *Trios* are very good indeed, though not necessarily superior to those of the Prunyi–Kiss–Onczay team on Marco Polo. One minor quibble: a little more space round and distance from the instruments would have shown these fine players to even greater advantage. They are too closely observed, as for that matter are Stefan Lindgren and the eponymous Berwald Quartet in the *C minor Quintet*, though this is not a fatal handicap. Their performance is every bit a match for the Vienna Philharmonia Quintet and vastly superior to the old Benthien. The sleeve notes by Hans Epstein are a model of their kind, thorough and scholarly. Recommended.

Piano trios Nos. 1 in E flat; 2 in F min., 3 in D min.
*** Marco Polo Dig. 8.223170 [id.]. Prunyi, Kiss, Onczay.

Although he is best known for the four symphonies, written in the 1840s, Berwald composed a considerable amount of chamber music, most notably in the 1850s when he was again living in Sweden. There are several piano trios – there is a *C major Trio* from 1845 and a fragmentary work in the same key from about the same time – before the *First Trio* (1849) included on this CD. Berwald started another trio in the same key (E flat) that same year, but it remained incomplete. The *F minor* and *D minor Trios* both come from 1851 (and there is an even later *Trio in C major* which was published in Copenhagen in 1896). These Hungarian players give spirited accounts of all three recorded here and make out a persuasive case for this music which has so often been idly dismissed as Mendelssohnian. The string players (András Kiss and Czaba Onczay) are both highly accomplished; perhaps the most demanding writing is for the piano and it is a pity that Ilona Prunyi proves at times to be a little less imaginative than her companions. The recording, made at the Italian Institute in Budapest, is very good indeed, fresh and present. A valuable issue, which conveniently fills a gap in the catalogue.

Biber, Heinrich (1644–1704)

Rosenkranz sonatas Nos. 1–16.
(M) **(*) HM/BMG Dig. GD 77102 (2) [77102-RG]. Franzjosef Maier, Franz Lehrndorfer, Max Engel, Konrad Junghänel.

Biber's *Sonatas* for violin and basso continuo, based on the Mysteries of the rosary, include music of great poetic feeling and sensibility; each is prefaced by a small copperplate depicting one of the Mysteries, and these are reproduced in the accompanying booklet. Franzjosef Maier and his colleagues made their Harmonia Mundi set in 1981. The playing is of high quality and, although the recording could provide better internal definition, it is full and pleasing.

Birtwistle, Harrison (born 1934)

Carmen Arcadiae mechanicae perpetuum; Secret theatre; Silbury air.
*** Etcetera Dig. KTC 1052 [id.]. L. Sinf., Elgar Howarth.

Silbury air, named after an archaeological site in south-west England, is one of Birtwistle's 'musical landscapes', bringing ever-changing views and perspectives on the musical material and an increasing drawing-out of melody. With melody discarded, *Carmen Arcadiae mechanicae perpetuum* (*The perpetual song of Mechanical Arcady*) superimposes different musical mechanisms to bring a rhythmic kaleidoscope of textures and patterns. The title of *Secret theatre* is taken from a poem by Robert Graves which refers to 'an unforeseen and fiery entertainment', and there is no doubting the distinctive originality of the writing, utterly typical of the composer. Howarth and the Sinfonietta could hardly be more convincing advocates, recorded in vivid, immediate sound.

Earth dances.
*** Collins Dig. Single 2001-2. BBC SO, Eötvös.

This generously filled (37 minutes) CD single in Collins Classics' 20th-century Plus series offers a characteristically rugged and characterful piece by Birtwistle, recorded live at the Proms in 1991 in spectacular sound. It is a generally slow-moving ritual, brilliantly written for the orchestra, with musical landmarks that increasingly catch in the mind on repetition. Unfortunately, there are no separate tracks for the individual sections.

Bizet, Georges (1838–75)

L'Arlésienne suites Nos. 1–2; Carmen: extended suite; Jeux d'enfants.
** DG Dig. 431 778-2 [id.]. O de la Bastille, Myung-Whun Chung.

Myung-Whun Chung's record is a disappointment The orchestral playing is polished but in no way distinctive and the players are not helped by being set back in a very resonant acoustic (the Paris Opéra Bastille), which clouds detail and almost blunts Bizet's vivid scoring.

L'Arlésienne: suites Nos. 1–2; Carmen: suite No. 1.
(B) *** DG 431 160-2; *431 160-4* [id.]. BPO, Karajan (with OFFENBACH: *Contes d'Hoffmann: Barcarolle; Orpheus in the Underworld: overture* **(*)).
(M) *** DG 423 472-2 [id.]. LSO, Abbado.

L'Arlésienne: suites Nos. 1–2; Carmen: suite No. 1; suite No. 2: excerpts.
(B) *** DG Compact Classics 413 422-2 (2); *413 422-4* [id.]. LSO, Abbado (with CHABRIER: *España;* DUKAS: *L'apprenti sorcier;* RIMSKY-KORSAKOV: *Capriccio espagnol* **(*) and on CD only: FALLA: *Three-cornered hat*: dances).

Among analogue couplings of *L'Arlésienne* and *Carmen suites*, Abbado's 1981 DG recording stands out, available either at medium price on CD only or, on Compact Classics at bargain price, on a pair of CDs or a double-length cassette. The orchestral playing is characteristically refined, the wind solos cultured and eloquent, especially in *L'Arlésienne*, where the pacing of the music is nicely judged. A vibrant accelerando at the end of the *Farandole* only serves to emphasize the obvious spontaneity of the music-making. On the Compact Classics compilation Abbado's selection from the *Carmen* suite is supplemented with two extra items, well played by the Hague Philharmonic Orchestra under Willem van Otterloo. The other highlight of this collection is Lorin Maazel's famous (1959) recording of Rimsky-Korsakov's *Capriccio espagnol*, lustrously played by the Berlin Philharmonic Orchestra in sparkling form. This remains the most electrifying account of Rimsky's famous orchestral showpiece in the current catalogue, and the remastering is extraordinarily vivid. There are also lively accounts of *L'apprenti sorcier* (Fiedler and the Boston Pops) and Chabrier's *España*, in a spirited performance by the Warsaw Philharmonic Orchestra under Jerzy Semkow. On the pair of CDs, four dances from Falla's *Three-cornered hat*, brilliantly – if not distinctively – done by Maazel and the Berlin Radio Symphony Orchestra make a lively if none too generous bonus.

The metallic clash of the cymbals for the opening *Carmen Prélude* on Karajan's 1971 disc sets the seal on the brilliance of both the orchestral playing and the recording. Yet the acoustic is attractively resonant, allowing plenty of orchestral bloom. There is some marvellously crisp and stylish woodwind playing, and the characterization of the music is dramatic and vivid. This version is undoubtedly fresher than Karajan's later, digital recording with the same forces, in which the conductor sounds at times too languid. The two Offenbach encores, polished and vivacious, are welcome, although in the *Overture* the 1981 digital recording sounds rather dry.

L'Arlésienne (incidental music): *suites Nos. 1–2.*
*** EMI CDC7 47794-2 [id.]. RPO, Beecham – *Symphony.* ***

L'Arlésienne: suites Nos. 1–2; Carmen: suite No. 1.
**(*) DG Dig. 415 106-2 [id.]. BPO, Karajan.

L'Arlésienne (incidental music): *suites Nos. 1 & 2; Carmen* (opera): *suites Nos. 1 & 2.*
*** Decca Dig. 417 839-2 [id.]. Montreal SO, Dutoit.

With playing that is both elegant and vivid, and with superb, demonstration-worthy sound, Dutoit's polished yet affectionate coupling of the *L'Arlésienne* and *Carmen* suites makes a clear first choice. The inclusion of 73 minutes of music means that a good deal of *Carmen* involves orchestral instruments standing in for voices, but the various wind and string soloists are always persuasive; the overall stylishness, particularly of the string phrasing, is a constant pleasure. All the colour of Bizet's palette is glowingly caught by the Decca engineers and the percussion component is never overdone.

Most performances of Bizet's enchanting incidental music for *L'Arlésienne* are overshadowed by Beecham's magical set, dating from 1957 but still sounding remarkably well. Besides the beauty and unique character of the wind solos, Beecham's deliciously sprightly *Minuet* and his affectingly gentle sense of nostalgia in the *Adagietto* (both from the first suite) are as irresistibly persuasive as the swaggering brilliance of the closing *Farandole* of the second.

Karajan, too, secures marvellous playing from the Berlin Philharmonic Orchestra, but he is less naturally at home in this repertoire, and tempi are not always ideally apt. The modern digital recording has the widest possible range of dynamic, but the effect sometimes seems rather inflated in tuttis. The *Carmen* suite, taken from his complete opera recording of 1983, is vividly played throughout – Karajan is at his best here.

L'Arlésienne (incidental music): *suite No. 2; Jeux d'enfants.*
(M) **(*) Sony MDK 46508 [id.]. Toronto SO, Andrew Davis – ROSSINI/RESPIGHI: *La boutique fantasque.* *** ❀

Davis's *Second suite* is well played and recorded, and the charming *Jeux d'enfants* has both sparkle and affection. This latter is more than acceptable as a bonus for the outstanding Rossini/Respighi coupling.

Jeux d'enfants (Children's games), Op. 22.
(B) *** CfP CD-CFP 4086; *TC-CFP 4086.* SNO, Gibson – RAVEL: *Ma Mère l'Oye;* SAINT-SAËNS: *Carnival.* ***

From Classics for Pleasure a fresh approach, lively orchestral playing and excellent mid-1970s sound. The lyrical movements, shaped by Gibson with gentle affection, give much pleasure and, with excellent couplings, this is highly recommendable.

Symphony in C.
*** DG Dig. 423 624-2 [id.]. Orpheus CO – BRITTEN: *Simple symphony;* PROKOFIEV: *Symphony No. 1.* ***
*** EMI CDC7 47794-2 [id.]. French Nat. R. O, Beecham – *L'Arlésienne.* ***
(M) *** Decca 417 734-2 [id.]. ASMF, Marriner – PROKOFIEV: *Symphony No. 1;* STRAVINSKY: *Pulcinella.* ***
(BB) **(*) Virgin/Virgo Dig. VJ7 91469-2; *VJ7 91469-4* [id.]. SCO, Saraste – RAVEL: *Ma Mère l'Oye* etc. ***
(M) **(*) Sony SMK 47532 [id.]. NYPO, Bernstein – OFFENBACH: *Gaîté parisienne* etc. **

Symphony in C; Jeux d'enfants: suite.
*** Ph. 416 437-2 [id.]. Concg. O, Haitink – DEBUSSY: *Danses sacrée et profane.* ***

The freshness of the seventeen-year-old Bizet's *Symphony* is well caught by the Orpheus group who present it with all the flair and polished ensemble for which they are famous. They offer the first-movement exposition repeat and make an excellent case for including it, while in the *Adagio* the oboe solo is wistful and tender. After a characterful minuet, the sparkling *moto perpetuo* finale is joyfully exhilarating, helped by the bouncing rhythms and crisp articulation. First-rate sound, most realistic in effect.

Beecham's version from the beginning of the 1960s above all brings out its spring-like qualities. The playing of the French orchestra is not quite as polished as that of Marriner's group or the Concertgebouw, but Beecham's panache more than compensates and the slow movement is delightfully songful, even if there is a moment of suspect intonation at its opening and close. The remastered sound is bright on top, without glare.

Marriner's performance is played with all the polish and elegance characteristic of the vintage ASMF records of the early 1970s; the slow movement has a delectable oboe solo and the finale is irrepressibly gay and high-spirited. The recording, originally rather reverberant, is now drier, the bass less expansive; but at mid-price and with highly desirable couplings, this remains excellent value.

The warmest, most pleasing sound comes from Haitink's sunny 1979 Concertgebouw performance. His reading obviously takes into account the Amsterdam acoustics for it is essentially spacious, although the finale does not lack vivacity. The serene slow movement is particularly eloquent, with a beautiful oboe solo. *Jeux d'enfants* is also delectably played; here, the recording is demonstration-worthy in its sparkling detail. However, this, like Beecham's CD, is still at full price.

With allegros brisk and well sprung, the first movement rhythmically bold and with the haunting slow movement taken spaciously, Saraste offers a refreshing, modern account of Bizet's youthful *Symphony*. The interpretation does not have the individuality of the Marriner Academy version, but this makes an unusual but apt coupling for Ravel's complete *Mother Goose*. Reverberant yet refined recording.

Bernstein's version is played with ebullient brilliance, especially the last two movements. The *Adagio* is affectionately done with a fine, slightly plangent oboe from Harold Gomberg, and the contrast in the middle section heightened by the precision of the playing. The 1963 Manhattan Center recording is very lively indeed; the glassiness in the violins has been mitigated, yet they were closely balanced and remain very brightly lit and slightly spiky. But there is an underlying ambience, and if this CBS sound picture is acceptable the performance has genuine charisma and lots of energy.

Jeux d'enfants, Op. 22.
*** Ph. Dig. 420 159-2 [id.]. Katia and Marielle Labèque – FAURÉ: *Dolly;* RAVEL: *Ma Mère l'Oye.* ***

Even were other versions to appear, it would not be easy to surpass the Labèque sisters. They characterize Bizet's wonderfully inventive cycle of twelve pieces with vitality, great wit and delicacy of feeling and touch. Superb recording in the best Philips tradition.

OPERA

Carmen (opera; complete).
*** DG Dig. 410 088-2 (3) [id.]. Baltsa, Carreras, Van Dam, Ricciarelli, Barbaux, Paris Op. Ch., Schoenberg Boys' Ch., BPO, Karajan.
(M) *** DG 427 440-2 (3) [id.]. Horne, McCracken, Krause, Maliponte, Manhattan Op. Ch., Met. Op. O, Bernstein.
(M) *** BMG/RCA GD 86199 (3) [6199-2-RG]. Leontyne Price, Corelli, Merrill, Freni, Linval, V. State Op. Ch., VPO, Karajan.
**(*) Decca 414 489-2 (2) [id.]. Troyanos, Domingo, Van Dam, Te Kanawa, John Alldis Ch., LPO, Solti.
**(*) DG 419 636-2 (3) [id.]. Berganza, Domingo, Cotrubas, Milnes, Amb. S., LSO, Abbado.
**(*) EMI CDC7 49240-2 (3) [Ang. CDCB 49240]. De los Angeles, Gedda, Blanc, Micheau, Fr. R. Ch. and O, Petits Chanteurs de Versailles, Beecham.

Karajan's newest DG set of *Carmen* makes a clear first choice among currently available versions, with the performance combining affection with high tension and high polish, using the Oeser edition with its extra passages and spoken dialogue. In Carreras he has a Don José, lyrical and generally sweet-toned, who is far from a conventional hero-figure, more the anti-hero, an ordinary man caught up in tragic love. The Micaela of Katia Ricciarelli is similarly scaled down, with the big dramatic voice kept in check. José van Dam – also the Escamillo for Solti – is incisive and virile, the public hero-figure; which leaves Agnes Baltsa as a vividly compelling Carmen, tough and vibrant yet musically precise and commanding, larger than life but still a believable figure, with tenderness under the surface.

Bernstein's 1973 *Carmen* was recorded at the New York Metropolitan Opera, the first recording undertaken there for many years. It was based on the Met.'s spectacular production with the same cast and conductor as on record, and the sessions plainly gained from being interleaved with live performances: Bernstein adopted the original version of 1875, with spoken dialogue but with variations designed to suit a stage production. Some of his slow tempi will be questioned, too; but what really matters is the authentic tingle of dramatic tension which permeates the whole entertainment. The full theatrical flavour of Bizet's score is strongly conveyed, and Marilyn Horne – occasionally coarse in expression – gives a most fully satisfying reading of the heroine's role, a great vivid characterization, warts and all. The rest of the cast similarly works to Bernstein's consistent overall plan. The singing is not all perfect, but it is always vigorous and colourful, and so (despite often questionable French accents) is the spoken dialogue. It is very well transferred and comes on three bargain CDs.

With Karajan's RCA version, made in Vienna in 1964, much depends on the listener's reaction to the conductor's tempi and to Leontyne Price's smoky-toned Carmen. Corelli has moments of coarseness, but his is still a heroic performance. Robert Merrill sings with gloriously firm tone, while Mirella Freni is, as ever, enchanting as Micaela. With often spectacular recording, this three-disc set, now offered at mid-price, remains a keen competitor.

Solti's Decca performance is remarkable for its new illumination of characters whom everyone thinks they know inside out. Tatiana Troyanos is quite simply the subtlest Carmen on record. Escamillo too is more readily sympathetic, not just the flashy matador who steals the hero's girl, whereas Don José is revealed as weak rather than just a victim. Troyanos's singing is delicately seductive too, with no hint of vulgarity, while the others make up a most consistent singing cast. Solti, like Karajan, uses spoken dialogue and a modification of the Oeser edition, deciding in each individual instance whether to accept amendments to Bizet's first thoughts. Though the CD transfer brings out the generally excellent balances of the original analogue recording, it exaggerates the bass to make the orchestra sound boomy, although the voices retain their fine realism and bloom.

Through the four Acts of the Abbado set there are examples of idiosyncratic tempi, but the whole entertainment hangs together with keen compulsion, and the discipline is superb. Conductor and orchestra can take a large share of credit for the performance's success, for though the singing is never less than enjoyable, it is on the whole less characterful than on some rival sets. Teresa Berganza is a seductive Carmen – not without sensuality, and producing consistently beautiful tone, but lacking some of the flair which makes for a three-dimensional portrait. Ileana Cotrubas as Micaela is not always as sweetly steady as she can be; Sherrill Milnes makes a heroic matador. The spoken dialogue is excellently produced, and the sound is vivid and immediate.

Beecham's approach to Bizet's well-worn score is no less fresh and revealing. His speeds are not always conventional but they always *sound* right. It seems he specially chose De los Angeles to be his Carmen, although she had never sung the part on the stage before making the recording. He conceived the *femme fatale* as someone winning her admirers not so much by direct assault and high voltage as by genuine charm and real femininity. De los Angeles's characterization of Carmen is absolutely bewitching. Gedda is pleasantly light-voiced as ever, Janine Micheau is a sweet Micaela, and Ernest Blanc makes an attractive Escamillo. There seems to have been little attempt at stage production, but in the CD transfer the recording does not show its age too greatly.

Carmen: highlights.
*** DG Dig. 413 322-2 [id.] (from above recording with Baltsa, Carreras; cond. Karajan).
(M) *** Decca 421 300-2 (from above recording with Troyanos; cond. Solti).
(M) *** DG 435 401-2; *435 401-4* [id.] (from above recording, with Berganza, Domingo; cond. Abbado).
(M) ** EMI CDM7 63075-2. Callas, Gedda, Massard, René Duclos Ch., Children's Ch., Paris Nat. Op. O, Prêtre.

Karajan's DG set offers a good representative selection with recording to match. However, his CD remains at full price.

The reissued compilation of 'scenes and arias' from Solti's sharply characterful set is generous and offered at medium price, and the remastered recording sounds better than the complete set.

Although issued as part of the 'Domingo Edition', the 69-minute selection from the Abbado recording is well balanced and does not just concentrate on Domingo's contribution. It is vividly and atmospherically transferred and thus fairly reflects the qualities of the complete set. There is no libretto, but the cued synopsis is perfectly adequate with this opera.

The selection from the Callas set is very generous with a playing time of 71 minutes 35 seconds but is not designed so much to highlight the heroine as to provide as many 'pops' as possible from the opera.

Carmen: highlights (sung in English).
(B) **(*) CfP CD-CFP 4596; *TC-CFP 4596*. Johnson, Smith, Herincx, Robson, Hunter, Greene, Stoddart, Moyle, Sadler's Wells Ch. & O, Sir Colin Davis.

Those who enjoy opera in English will find this a highly successful example, thanks both to the strongly animated conducting of Sir Colin Davis and to the rich-voiced, reliable singing of Patricia Johnson as Carmen. Nor is Johnson reliable and nothing more: time and again her phrasing is most imaginative and memorable. It is good that the microphone catches her voice so well. Donald Smith, the Don José, provides a wonderfully attractive, ringing tone. The selection is well made, if not especially generous (52 minutes) and the ensemble has the authentic enthusiasm of a live performance. The CD transfer is extremely natural, and it is easy to be beguiled by this attractive singing, even if Johnson's portrayal of Carmen is less plangent than usual.

Carmen (ballet): suite (arr. and scored for strings & percussion by Rodion Shchedrin).
**(*) Olympia Dig. OCD 108 [id.]. Moscow Virtuosi CO, Armenian State Ch. Ens. & Percussion Ens., Spivakov – SHCHEDRIN: *Frescoes of Dionysius.* **

Rodion Shchedrin's free adaptation of Bizet's *Carmen* music uses Bizet's tunes, complete with harmony, and reworks them into a new tapestry using only strings and percussion (including vibraphone). The playing of the Moscow Virtuoso group justifies its name; Vladimir Spivakov maintains the electricity throughout an exciting performance. He is helped by the concert-hall acoustics of the brilliant digital recording; however, the brightness of the upper strings does bring a degree of harshness in the vivid climax of the *Flower song*.

(i) *Les pêcheurs de perles* (complete). (ii) *Ivan IV: highlights.*
** EMI Dig. CDS7 49837-2 (2) [Ang. CDCB 49837]. Hendricks, Aler, Quilico, Capitole, Toulouse, Ch. & O, Plasson.

EMI's new version of *Pearlfishers*, well recorded, should have provided an ideal recommendation for this lovely opera, but, for all its qualities, it falls well short of that. Michel Plasson with the choir and orchestra of the Capitole, though sympathetic, fails to draw out as warmly committed a performance as he usually does in his French opera recordings. John Aler and Gino Quilico as the two fishermen sing cleanly and with lyrical freshness, but often their phrasing could be more affectionate. Barbara Hendricks is aptly alluring as Leila, beloved of both of them, but too often she attacks notes from below, coming near to crooning her lovely Act II solo, *Comme autrefois*, as well as the following love-duet. The original text has been used but, rightly, this new set (unlike EMI's last) gives the listener the choice of versions of the great *Pearlfishers duet.* The original version, given as an appendix, is maddening when it fails to bring a reprise for the big tune and instead launches into a trivial *Polonaise-cabaletta.*

Blake, Howard (born 1938)

Clarinet concerto.
*** Hyp. Dig. CDA 66215; *KA 66215* [id.]. Thea King, ECO, composer – LUTOSLAWSKI: *Dance preludes;* SEIBER: *Concertino.* ***

Howard Blake provides a comparatively slight but endearing *Clarinet concerto*, which is played here with great sympathy by Thea King, who commissioned the work. With its neo-classical feeling, it is improvisatory and reflective in its basic style, but produces plenty of energy in the finale with its whiff of Walton. Both couplings are extremely attractive; admirers of the clarinet and of Thea King will find this a most rewarding collection. It is extremely vividly recorded on CD – there is almost a sense of over-presence.

Bliss, Arthur (1891–1975)

Checkmate (ballet): *5 dances.*
(M) *** Chan. CHAN 6576 [id.]. West Australian SO, Schönzeler – RUBBRA: *Symphony No. 5* ***; TIPPETT: *Little music.* **(*)

Checkmate was Arthur Bliss's first ballet score and was composed for the Royal Ballet's first visit to Paris in 1937. The idea of a ballet based on chess with all its opportunities for symbolism and heraldic splendour appealed to Bliss, and the score he produced remains one of his most inventive creations. The five dances on the Chandos issue are well played under Hans-Hubert Schönzeler and, with its valuable Rubbra coupling, this is welcome back in the catalogue at mid-price. The 1978 recording was made in the ABC studios but has a concert-hall ambience and is of high quality.

(i) *Piano concerto; March of homage.*
(M) **(*) Unicorn Dig. UKCD 2029; *UKC 2029.* (i) Philip Fowke; RLPO, David Atherton.

From the dashing double octaves at the start, the pianistic style of Bliss's concerto has much of Rachmaninov and Liszt in it, though the idiom is very much Bliss's own, with some of his most memorable material. It is a work which needs a passionately committed soloist, and that is what it finds in Philip Fowke, urgent and expressive, well matched by David Atherton and the Liverpool orchestra. The occasional piece is also given a lively performance. The digital recording is full and vivid, with the piano naturally balanced, less forward than is common.

A Colour symphony; Checkmate (ballet): *suite.*
*** Chan. Dig. CHAN 8503; *ABTD 1213* [id.]. Ulster O, Handley.

Bliss's *Colour symphony* comes from the early 1920s. Each of its movements evokes the heraldic symbolism of four colours – purple, red, blue and green – and the quality of his invention and imagination is fresh. Vernon Handley directs with complete authority and evident enthusiasm; the *Checkmate* ballet is less of a rarity on record and is given with equal success. Chandos has an enviable reputation for the quality of its engineering, and this issue is one of its very best.

A Colour Symphony; Metamorphic variations.
*** Nimbus Dig. NI 5294; *NC 5294* [id.]. BBC Welsh SO, Wordsworth.

On Wordsworth's excellent Nimbus disc the first major orchestral work of Bliss is very well coupled with the premiere recording of his last, completed two years before his death. The title, *Metamorphic variations*, may be unattractive, but this is one of the most cogent of Bliss's mature works, offering over the 14 variations lasting 35 minutes the widest range of mood and expression. When Bliss's strong suit was his ability to attract the ear instantly with a striking idea, setting a mood precisely, variation form suited him well, and it is a pity he did not use it more. *A Colour Symphony* dates from 50 years earlier, and also represents Bliss at his most immediately appealing. Wordsworth is a degree broader in his approach than Vernon Handley on the rival Chandos version, yet his control of rhythm and line makes his reading just as warm and sympathetic. This is one of the finest Nimbus orchestral recordings yet, made in Brangwyn Hall, Swansea, with more inner detail than many, though the woodwind balance is backward. In the third movement of the symphony that brings an advantage when the fluttering solo flute at the beginning is the more evocative and full of fantasy when set at a distance. As recorded, the Welsh string-tone is not quite so full and warm as that of Handley's Ulster Orchestra, but anyone who wants this exceptionally generous and apt coupling is unlikely to be disappointed.

Conversations; Madam Noy; (i; ii) *Rhapsody;* (ii) *Rout; The Women of Yueh; Oboe quintet.*
*** Hyp. CDA 66137; *KA 66137* [id.]. Nash Ens., (i) Anthony Rolfe Johnson; (ii) Elizabeth Gale.

The predominant influence in *Rout*, for soprano and chamber orchestra, and in the *Rhapsody*, with its two wordless vocal parts, is Ravel – one readily forgets how strong it was in that period, even in the light-hearted and diverting *Conversations* for flute and oboe (and their relatives, the bass flute and cor anglais) and string trio. *Madam Noy* sets a poem of F. W. H. Meyerstein that is close to *Old Mother Hubbard*. The longest piece on the disc is the *Oboe quintet*, also a work of considerable quality. The music assembled here represents Bliss at his very best. A lovely disc, which can be warmly recommended, and eminently well engineered, too.

Clarinet quintet.
*** Chan. Dig. CHAN 8683; *ABTD 1078* [id.]. Hilton, Lindsay Qt – BAX: *Sonata;* VAUGHAN WILLIAMS: *Studies.* ***

The *Clarinet quintet*, composed in the early 1930s, is arguably Bliss's masterpiece; the present performance is a worthy successor to the 1963 recording by Gervase de Peyer and members of the Melos Ensemble. These artists have the measure of its autumnal melancholy; the recording is natural and well focused, and the music-making is of the highest quality.

String quartets Nos. 1 in B flat; 2 in F min.
*** Hyp. CDA 66178 [id.]. Delmé Qt.

These performances by the Delmé Quartet are not only thoroughly committed but enormously persuasive and can be recommended even to readers not normally sympathetic to this composer. Both quartets are fine pieces: the *First* is a work of strong character, finely proportioned and not dissimilar in quality of inspiration to the *Music for strings*, written a few years earlier. Bliss regarded the *Second* as his finest chamber work, and the Delmé certainly do it justice. Strongly recommended.

(i) *Viola sonata;* Piano works: *2 Interludes; Masks; Toccata; Triptych.*
*** Chan. Dig. CHAN 8770; *ABTD 1408* [id.]. Kathron Sturrock, (i) with Emanuel Vardi.

Bliss once called the viola 'the most romantic of instruments, a veritable Byron in the orchestra . . . the dark, sombre quality – now harsh, now warm – of its lowest string, the passionate rhetoric of the highest and its whole rather restless and tragic personality make it an ideal vehicle for romantic and oratorical expression'. His feeling for it is clearly evident in his *Sonata*, written in 1933, two years after the *Clarinet quintet* at the peak of his maturity, a powerful piece intended for Lionel Tertis. The first movement has heroic thrust, masterfully interpreted by the American viola-player, Emanuel Vardi, who with his rich, firm tone makes light of the formidable virtuoso writing. The broad lyricism of the slow movement and the dashing energy of the tarantella finale find him equally sympathetic, with Kathron Sturrock a powerful partner, both of them helped by the warm, forward recording. The solo piano pieces which complete the disc mostly date from the 1920s, when Bliss was much influenced by a prolonged stay in America. Many of these pieces with their jazzy syncopations are like Gershwin with an English flavour. From much later comes the *Triptych* – written for Louis Kentner in 1970, right at the end of his career – two measured pieces in a relatively gritty style, followed by a dashing *Toccata* that reverts to his earlier manner. Sturrock is a warm and understanding interpreter.

Piano sonata; Pieces: *Bliss (One-step); Miniature scherzo; Rout trot; Study. Suite; Triptych.* Arr. of BACH: *Das alte Jahr vergangen ist (The old year had ended).*
*** Chan. Dig. CHAN 8979 [id.]. Philip Fowke.

Apart from Solomon's magisterial recording of the *Piano concerto*, Bliss's output for the piano has found few advocates; indeed most of this repertoire is not otherwise available. He composed relatively little for the instrument which is surprising considering that Bliss himself was a capable pianist and even considered a concert career. The biggest work on the disc is the *Sonata* (1952), written for Noel Mewton-Wood who made the first LP recording of the concerto. Its neo-romantic rhetoric is less convincing than some of the earlier pieces he composed, in particular the *Suite* (1925) which reaches the gramophone for the first time. One of its movements is an dignified and affecting *Elegy* (Track 3), an outpouring of grief at the loss of his brother, which was to find further expression in *Morning heroes*. There are some other lighter pieces like the *The Rout trot* and *Bliss (A One-step)*, written in the 1920s when his inspiration was at its freshest. These show him at his best. *Das alte Jahr vergangen ist* is a Bach transcription (Bliss long used to play Bach each morning on the piano) written for Harriet Cohen. Good performances and excellent recording made in The Maltings, Snape.

VOCAL MUSIC

Lie strewn the white flocks.
*** Hyp. CDA 66175; *KA 66175* [id.]. Shirley Minty, Judith Pierce (flute), Holst Singers & O, Hilary Davan Wetton – BRITTEN: *Gloriana: Choral dances;* HOLST: *Choral hymns from Rig Veda.* ***

Bliss's *Pastoral* may be severely classical in its inspiration, from Pan and the world of shepherds and shepherdesses, but its warm and natural expressiveness makes it one of Bliss's most immediately appealing works. It is given a winning performance by the Holst Singers and Orchestra, with the choral sections (the greater part of the work) aptly modest in scale but powerful in impact. With glowing sound and very attractive works for coupling, this is an outstanding issue.

Morning heroes.
(M) **(*) EMI CDM7 63906-2. Westbrook (nar.), RLPO Ch. & O, Groves.

Morning heroes is an elegiac work, written as a tribute to the composer's brother and to all who fell in the First World War, and it is good that one of Bliss's most ambitious works should be available in so strong a performance, even if the music itself has a curious element of complacency. Fine recording and an excellent transfer.

Bloch, Ernest (1880–1959)

Concerti grossi Nos. 1 & 2; (i) *Schelomo.*
(M) *** Mercury 432 718-2 [id.]. Eastman-Rochester O, Hanson, (i) with Miquelle.

Bloch's two *Concerti grossi* were written in 1925 and 1952 respectively. Although separated by more than a quarter of a uniquely fast-moving century, they are surprisingly similar in style. The neo-classical style brings a piano continuo in the Baroque manner in No. 1; the second, for strings alone, is more intense in feeling. The performances here are admirable, lively and sympathetic; the slightly spiky tinge to the otherwise full Mercury sound is like an attractive condiment, although the violin-timbre is distinctly astringent. *Schelomo*, with Georges Miquelle its soloist, makes a useful bonus for this mid-priced reissue.

Violin concerto.
(M) *** EMI CDM7 63989-2 [id.]. Menuhin, Philh. O, Kletzki – BERG: *Violin concerto.* ***

(i) *Violin concerto. Baal Shem.*
*** ASV Dig. CDDCA 785; *ZCDCA 785.* (i) Michael Guttman; RPO, Serebrier (with SEREBRIER: *Momento; Poema* **).

(i) *Violin concerto;* (ii) *3 Poèmes juifs.*
(M) ** Vanguard 08.4046.71 [OVC 4046]. (i) Roman Totenberg, V. State Op. O, Golshmann; (ii) Hartford SO, Fritz Mahler (with BARTÓK: *Rhapsody No. 1* **).

Menuhin's version of Bloch's powerful and intensely atmospheric *Violin concerto* was only the second recording of this powerful work. This deeply felt and finely recorded 1963 account is passionate and committed from the very first note, and any weaknesses in the score are quite lost when the playing is so compelling. Paul Kletzki accompanies with equal distinction and a real sense of atmosphere, and the Philharmonia playing is first rate. The 1964 Kingsway Hall recording sounds very well indeed, brighter than on LP but with plenty of ambient glow.

The newcomer from Michael Guttman has plenty going for it: it has both fire and colour, and no attempt is made to rein in the freely rhapsodic flow of the piece. It also has well balanced modern digital recording. Menuhin's record with Kletzki is paired with the Berg and many may prefer this to the present coupling, two well-written but not strongly individual pieces by the conductor José Serebrier.

Roman Totenberg plays the *Violin concerto* well enough but without quite the ardour and subtlety of Menuhin. The principal interest here lies in the *Trois poèmes juifs* (*Danse*; *Rite*; *Cortège funèbre*), written at Satigny, near Geneva, in 1913 and dedicated to the memory of the composer's father. This is music with plenty of interest and, although characteristically rhapsodical in feeling and interpolating free, cadenza-like passages free from metrical accents, Bloch's ideas are far better integrated here than in *America*. Bartók's attractive *Rhapsody* makes a thoroughly welcome bonus for a CD which is generously full (75 minutes).

(i) *Israel Symphony;* (ii) *Schelomo.*
(M) **(*) Vanguard 08 4047.71 [OVC 4047]. (i) Christensen, Basinger, Fraenkel, Politis, Heder, Watts; (ii) Nelsova; Utah SO, Abravanel.

Bloch's *Israel Symphony* was begun in 1912 and was written over a span of about four years. It is a large-scale work, but its way of anticipating the style of Hollywood film composers (one thinks especially of Dmitri Tiomkin, over whom Bloch had considerable influence) means that the music has something in common with the soundtracks of Hollywood's biblical epics. Bloch's writing has more refinement of course, but it is better to regard the work on the level of highly coloured programme music, of which it is an attractive example. The performance here has the vigour and spontaneity that are characteristic of Abravanel's Utah performances, and the only snag is that the soloists, who are introduced at the end of the work, are wobbly and not especially distinguished. *Schelomo* is an appropriate coupling, for not only is it roughly contemporary with the *Symphony* in Bloch's output but it also has a musical affinity, although its conciseness of form gives it greater concentration. Nelsova has recorded it twice before; here she is stimulated by the warmth of Abravanel's accompaniment and, although the reading is drier than Rostropovich's or Fournier's, one remembers that she was the composer's choice of soloist when he recorded the work on 78s. The recordings were made in 1967 and are transferred to CD with great success.

Schelomo: Hebrew rhapsody (for cello and orchestra).
*** BMG/RCA Dig. RD 60757 [60757-2-RC]. Ofra Harnoy, LPO, Mackerras – BRUCH: *Adagio on Celtic themes* etc. ***
*** Virgin Dig. VC7 90735-2; *VC 790735-4* [id.]. Isserlis, LSO, Hickox – ELGAR: *Cello concerto.* **(*)
(B) **(*) DG 429 155-2; *429 155-4* [id.]. Fournier, BPO, Wallenstein – DVOŘÁK: *Cello concerto* **(*); BRUCH: *Kol Nidrei.* **

Part of a well-planned anthology of shorter works for cello and orchestra, Ofra Harnoy's account of *Schelomo* is as fine as almost any. She catches the passionate, Hebraic feeling of the melodic line and in this is matched by Mackerras, whose central climax is riveting. Fine, well-balanced and expansive sound, recorded in Watford Town Hall.

The dark intensity of Isserlis's solo playing and the sharp, dramatic focus of Hickox in the big climactic orchestral tuttis are here magnetic, preventing Bloch's youthful outpouring on Solomon and the Song of Songs from sounding self-indulgent. Warm, refined recording.

Fournier's fervent advocacy of Bloch's *Hebrew rhapsody* is given sympathetic support by Alfred Wallenstein. Fournier is closely balanced, but the 1976 recording is warmly atmospheric and, if orchestral detail is not always fully revealed, the CD sound is otherwise impressive.

Piano quintets Nos. 1–2.
** Koch Dig. 3-7041-2 [id.]. American Chamber Players.

No less a critic than Ernest Newman hailed Bloch's *Second Quartet* as one of the masterpieces of our time in the post-war years when the Grillers recorded it. The sleeve note reminds us that he hailed the *First Piano quintet* in no less extravagant terms. Yet neither features in concert programmes or record catalogues nowadays and the present issue is the only current version of either of the *Piano quintets.* Over three decades separate them; the *First* was composed in 1921–3 and the *Second* (and less interesting) in 1957, two years before the composer's death. It would be good to give this release an unqualified welcome but, though the performances have no lack of commitment, the recordings are serviceable rather than distinguished, claustrophobic rather than spacious. There is not really enough air round the instruments in the *First Quintet* and even less in the *Second*, which is really rather coarse and shallow. The string players remain the same; Lambert Orkis is the pianist in No. 1, Ann Schein (whom the engineers do not flatter) takes over for No. 2.

America (Epic rhapsody).
(M) ** Vanguard 08.8014.71. American Concert Ch., Symphony of the Air, Stokowski.

Ernest Bloch's musical tribute to his adopted country is a real oddity with regrettably little musical value. Each of the three movements represents a different period of American history, ending with a section that naturally brings in some jazz influences. In the second part, Bloch quotes *Way down upon the Swanee River* and he is constantly introducing the first phrase of *America.* At the end, the choir joins in a full version of this national hymn. It is all endearingly ingenuous but, for a non-American – and perhaps for some Americans too – it is all rather embarrassing, for Bloch's confection of unlikely material is not even constructed with the customary craftsmanship that holds his music firmly together. As one would expect, Stokowski is just the man to do what he can in a forlorn cause, and the recording (from the beginning of the 1960s) is remarkably vivid and spacious. There is a brief comment from the composer at the end of the performance.

Sacred service (Avodath Hakodesh).
(M) *** Sony SM2K 47533 (2) [id.]. Robert Merrill, Rabbi Juhah Cahn, Choirs of Metropolitan Synagogue & NY Community Church, NYPO, Bernstein – FOSS: *Song of songs* ***; BEN-HAIM: *Psalmist of Israel.* **(*)

Bernstein pioneered this work on record as early as 1958, but the age of the recording, made in the St George Hotel, Brooklyn, is disguised by the remastering which preserves the spaciousness and enhances the vividness of this persuasively committed performance, which has far more ardour and intensity than the more recent version on Chandos. Robert Merrill is the excellent soloist and the only possible drawback for repeated listening by the non-Jewish listener is the inclusion in the Epilogue of the spoken Kaddish Prayer and, of course, the Benediction. The documentation helpfully includes the picturesque original Hebrew, and a line-by-line translation of romanised Hebrew text. The irritating thing about this reissue in the Royal Bernstein Edition, is that the Bloch and the stimulating Foss coupling could both have been fitted onto a single CD, as their total playing time is just over 78 minutes.

Blow, John (1649–1708)

(i) *Ode on the death of Mr Henry Purcell;* (ii) *Amphion Angelicus* (song collection): *Ah, heaven! What is't I hear?; Cloe found Amintas lying all in tears; Loving above himself; Shepherds deck your crooks; Why weeps Asteria?; Epilogue: Sing, sing, ye muses.*
(M) **(*) HM/BMG GD 71962. (i) René Jacobs, James Bowman; (ii) Yamamoto, Van der Speek, Jacobs, Van Altena, Van Egmond, Ens., Leonhardt.

John Blow's *Ode on the death of Purcell*, a highly eloquent setting of an allegorical poem by John Dryden, makes a worthy memorial to the great English composer. The other items in the programme are taken from a collection of 50 songs, published in 1700, and admirably demonstrate the range and variety of Blow's art. They are effectively presented, especially the closing *Epilogue* for vocal quartet. Gustav Leonhardt and his chamber ensemble (two recorders are used in the main work) accompany authentically, and the 1973 recording has a good ambience and no lack of presence.

Ode on the death of Mr Henry Purcell: Mark how the lark and linnet sing. Ah, heav'n! What is't I hear?.
*** Hyp. Dig. CDA 66253; *KA 66253* [id.]. James Bowman, Michael Chance, King's Consort, King – PURCELL: *Collection.* ***

James Bowman's re-recording of Blow's fine Purcellian *Ode for Hyperion* not only comes within an entirely different context – a collection of counter-tenor duets and solos, concentrating mainly on Purcell – but is also different in character. Where Leonhardt on RCA is spacious in his concept and more detailed in his concern for word-meanings, the result also more polished, Robert King's spontaneous style is infectious with the orchestral comments engagingly animated. Bowman's voice blends more readily with that of Michael Chance so that their interchanges are smoother, but that is not necessarily an advantage, for the stronger vocal contrast with René Jacobs is attractively characterful. Both performances are highly rewarding, and in the last resort couplings will dictate choice. The Hyperion disc is more expensive but includes a quarter of an hour more music.

Venus and Adonis.
(M) *** HM/BMG GD 77117 (2). Kirkby, Tubb, King, Wistreich, Bonner, Holden, Cass, Nichols, Cornwell, Müller, Consort of Musicke, Rooley – GIBBONS: *Cupid and Death.* ***
(B) *** HM Dig. HMA 90 1276; *HMA 431276* [id.]. Argenta, Dawson, Varcoe, Covey-Crump, L. Bar. & Ch., Medlam.

Venus and Adonis is like a Lully opera in miniature. Its length makes it more likely to suit twentieth-century taste, with the Prologue and three brief Acts presenting a fast-moving sequence of choruses, dances and 'act-tunes' as well as arias, often with chorus. Rooley directs an elegant, lightly sprung performance, very well sung, recorded in good analogue sound (1984) in a warm acoustic. It takes up only part of the first disc of the two-disc set, now reissued by BMG at mid-price.

Charles Medlam with London Baroque gives a sprightly account of John Blow's delightful masque, one of the few that have survived today as a living entertainment. Though this is a period performance, the ensemble is substantial, and Medlam takes care that the early instruments are well blended rather than edgy and the choral sound is full, bright and clean. The *Huntsmen's chorus* in Act I has splendid bite and panache. The soloists too are all remarkable for sweetness and freshness of tone, with the bright, clear tones of Nancy Argenta as Cupid and Lynne Dawson as Venus nicely counterpointed, and with Stephen Varcoe a clear, youthful-sounding Adonis. This record is now offered at bargain price in the Musique d'Abord series.

Boccherini, Luigi (1743–1805)

Cello concerto No. 2 in D, G.479.
(M) *** DG 429 098-2; *429 098-4.* Rostropovich, Zurich Coll. Mus., Sacher – TARTINI; VIVALDI: *Concertos.* ***

Rostropovich in Boccherini offers a highly individual musical experience. Although essentially a performance in the grand manner (with Rostropovich providing his own cadenzas), the music-making has tremendous vitality, with extremely lively outer movements to balance the eloquence of the *Adagio*. Rostropovich is so compelling that reservations are swept aside. He is given an alert accompaniment by Sacher, and the recording has fine body and presence.

Cello concerto No. 7 in G, G.480.
(B) *** Ph. 422 481-2. Gendron, LSO, Leppard – HAYDN: *Cello concerto in C.* ***
(B) *** Pickwick Dig. PCD 917; *IMPC 917.* Felix Schmidt, ECO, Heath – BEETHOVEN: *Triple concerto.* ***

This is the concerto from which Grützmacher extracted the slow movement in his phoney, cobbled-together 'Boccherini Concerto', the movement everyone remembers. It was Maurice Gendron who originally unearthed the work and made its first recording. It is admirably played and usefully coupled with Haydn's lesser-known *C major Concerto.*

The Boccherini *Concerto* also makes an unusual but apt and attractive coupling for the Trio Zingara's excellent version of the Beethoven *Triple concerto*. The recording, as in the Beethoven, is full and vivid.

Cello concerto in B flat (arr Grützmacher).
*** Sony MK 39964 [id.]. Yo-Yo Ma, St Paul CO, Zukerman – J. C. BACH: *Sinfonia concertante* etc. **(*)
(BB) *** Naxos Dig. 8.550059; *4550059* [id.]. Ludovít Kanta, Capella Istropolitana, Peter Breiner – HAYDN: *Cello concertos Nos. 1 & 2.* ***
(*) EMI CDC7 47840-2 [id.]. Jacqueline du Pré, ECO, Barenboim – HAYDN: *Concerto in D.* *

Like Jacqueline du Pré before him, Yo-Yo Ma chooses the Grützmacher version of the Boccherini *Concerto*, romantically derived from three different Boccherini works, but highly effective in its own right. He plays it with taste and finesse, not wearing his heart on his sleeve as obviously as du Pré, but with his warm, if refined, timbre and style not missing the romanticism. The recording is first class.

Ludovít Kanta is a very fine player and gives an eloquent account of the Boccherini *Cello concerto* in the Grützmacher version. Although he does not possess the commanding personality of Fournier or Rostropovich, there is nothing second-class about this performance. His playing is distinguished by imaginative and musicianly phrasing and a warm tone. The Slovak players under Peter Breiner give a good account of themselves and the (perhaps slightly forward) recording is made in a bright, warm acoustic. This can hold its own against versions costing twice or three times as much.

Working for the first time in the recording studio with Daniel Barenboim, du Pré was inspired to some really heart-warming playing, broadly romantic in style – but then that is what Grützmacher plainly asks for. The 1967 recording has retained much of its fullness and atmosphere, and the solo cello has good presence, but the orchestral sound is rather less well focused than the Haydn coupling. An endearing performance none the less.

Symphony in C min.
(M) ** Decca 433 169-2; *433 169-4* [id.]. Orchestra Rossini di Napoli, Franco Caracciolo – VIVALDI: *Concertos.* ***

This is a very conventional piece of writing. The performance here is quite nicely turned, but the actual orchestral playing is better in the string departments than in the wind. The recording is clear and fresh, and this makes an agreeable enough bonus for a desirable collection of Vivaldi concertos.

Symphonies: in D; in C, Op. 12/3; in D min., Op. 12/4; in B flat, Op. 35/6; in D min., Op. 37/3; in A, Op. 37/4.
**(*) Chan. Dig. CHAN 8414/5; *DBTD 3005* (3) [id.]. Cantilena, Adrian Shepherd.

In all, Boccherini composed twenty symphonies, seven of which are included in this set. The *D minor*, Op. 12, No. 4, is the celebrated *La casa del diavolo*, whose finale is based on the chaconne of Gluck's *Don Juan* ballet. Adrian Shepherd and his Cantilena have the measure of this music's grace and gentleness, and are scrupulous in observing repeats. These are sympathetic rather than high-powered performances and will give considerable pleasure, though lacking the last ounce of finish. But there is no want of feeling for this unjustly neglected repertoire, and the symphonies are well recorded.

Symphonies: in D min. (La casa del diavolo), Op. 12/4; in A, Op. 12/6; in A, Op. 21/6.
*** Hyp. Dig. CDA 66236 [id.]. L. Festival O, Ross Pople.

Ross Pople's record duplicates only one work included in the more ambitious Chandos collection, *La casa del diavolo*, Op. 12/4; in his account the demons are certainly let loose in the finale, with the most frantically energetic playing from the strings. Elsewhere the performances are the soul of elegance; in the sunny *A major*, Op. 12/6, where the flutes add a helping of cream to the strawberries, the finesse of the playing gives much pleasure in itself; altogether this well-played and well-recorded collection can be given the warmest welcome.

CHAMBER MUSIC

Cello quintet, Op. 37/7 (Pleyel).
(B) **(*) Decca 421 637-2; *421 637-4*. ASMF – MENDELSSOHN: *Octet*. **(*)

This is an inspired piece: it would be worth getting for its own sake – and the coupled performance of the Mendelssohn *Octet* is a particularly fine one. The recording shows its age just a little in the upper range.

Guitar quintets Nos. 3 in B flat, G.447; 9 in C (La ritirata di Madrid), G.453.
(M) **(*) Ph. 426 092-2. Pepe Romero, ASMF Chamber Ens.

The picturesque evocation of Spanish life (*La ritirata di Madrid*) is created with a set of twelve short variations set in a long, slow crescendo, followed by a similarly graduated decrescendo, a kind of Spanish patrol with the 'night watch' disappearing into the distance at the close. Both works here are melodically engaging in Boccherini's elegant rococo style, and they are beautifully played. The guitar is well balanced within the string group, yet is able to dominate when required. On CD, detail is cleaner but the string timbre is slightly more astringent than it was on the original LP, not entirely to Boccherini's advantage.

Guitar quintets Nos. (i) *4 in D (Fandango); 7 in E min., G.451; 9 in C (La ritirata di Madrid).*
(B) *** DG 429 512-2; *429 512-4* [id.]. Yepes, Melos Qt; (i) with Lucero Tena.

The DG bargain compilation (from 1971) offers a cleaner sound-picture than its Philips competitor: indeed the sound is very good, full yet lively and well projected. The playing is expert and, in the boisterous *Fandango* finale of No. 4, Lucero Tena makes a glittering contribution with his castanets.

6 Oboe quintets, Op. 45.
(M) *** Decca 433 173-2 [id.]. Sarah Francis, Allegri Qt.

An attractive collection, very persuasively played and recorded. These *Quintets*, written in 1797, were published as Op. 45, though Boccherini's own catalogue lists them as 55. They have a sunny grace that is altogether beguiling, and a gentle, wistful lyricism that is unfailing in its appeal.

Piano quintets: in A min., Op. 56/2, G.412; in E flat, Op. 56/3, G.410; in E min., Op. 57/3, G.415; in C, Op. 57/6, G.418.
(M) *** BMG/RCA Dig. GD 77053 [77053-2-RG]. Les Adieux.

The most haunting of the four quintets included here are the lovely *E minor* (Op. 57/3), which starts the disc, and the *A minor* (Op. 56/2); both have those hints of beguiling, almost sultry melancholy that makes this composer's musical language so distinctive. This accomplished period-instrument group turn in performances of great finesse and charm, though the recording balance places the listener very much in the front row of the salon. But this music has much more to it than it is given credit for.

String quintets: in E, Op. 11/5, G 275; in D min., Op. 13/4, G 280; in D, Op. 39/3, G 339; in C min., Op. 51/2, G 377.
**(*) Denon Dig. CO 2199 [id.]. Berlin Philh. Ens.

Boccherini composed more than 100 string quintets, of which the first recorded here, containing the famous *Minuet*, is the best known. The whole disc offers music-making of great elegance and charm (perhaps too much at times, as the first movement of Op. 11, No. 5, is just a little undervitalized). There is depth and pathos in some of these *Quintets* (the *Andante* of the *D minor* or the *Andantino con innocenza* of the *C minor*, for example) as well as the customary finish. There is some beguiling music in the *D major* (the *Pastorale*) as well. These fine musicians play with dedication, though at times there is a degree of caution as if they are a little inhibited by courtly manners. Good if rather forward recording.

Boieldieu, François (1775–1834)

Harp concerto in 3 tempi in C.

❀ (M) *** Decca 425 723-2; *425 723-4*. Marisa Robles, ASMF, Iona Brown – DITTERSDORF; HANDEL: *Harp concertos* etc. *** ❀

Boieldieu's *Harp concerto* has been recorded elsewhere but never more attractively. Much play is made with the possibilities of light and shade, the harp bringing gentle echo effects in repeated phrases. The slow movement is delightful and the lilt of the finale irresistible. The (originally Argo) recording is still in the demonstration class and very sweet on the ear. To make the reissue even more attractive, three beguiling sets of *Variations* have been added, derived from a separate solo LP, including music by Handel, Beethoven's *Six Variations on a Swiss song* and a *Theme, variations and Rondo pastorale* attributed to Mozart.

Boito, Arrigo (1842–1918)

Mefistofele (opera, complete).

**(*) Decca Dig. 410 175-2 [id.]. Ghiaurov, Pavarotti, Freni, Caballé, L. Op. Ch., Trinity Boys' Ch., Nat. PO, Fabritiis.

Boito's *Mefistofele* is a strange episodic work to come from the hand of the master-librettist of Verdi's *Otello* and *Falstaff*, but it has many fine moments. The modern digital recording given to the Fabritiis set brings obvious benefits in the extra weight of brass and percussion – most importantly in the heavenly prologue. With the principal soloists all at their best – Pavarotti most seductive in *Dai campi, dai prati*, Freni finely imaginative on detail, Caballé consistently sweet and mellifluous as Elena, Ghiaurov strongly characterful if showing some signs of strain – this is a highly recommendable set, though Fabritiis in his last recording lacks a little in energy, and the chorus is placed rather distantly.

Mefistofele: Prologue.

(M) (***) BMG/RCA mono GD 60276; *GK 60276* [60276-2-RG; *60276-4-RG*]. Moscona, Robert Shaw Ch., Columbus Boychoir, NBC SO, Toscanini – VERDI: *I Lombardi; Rigoletto*: excerpts. (**)

(M) **(*) DG 431 171-2 [id.]. Ghiaurov, V. State Op. Ch., VPO, Bernstein – R. STRAUSS: *Salome* etc. **(*)

Whatever the limitations of the broadcast sound, the hair-raising intensity of Toscanini's performance gives Boito's multi-layered *Prologue* a cogency never matched since on record. The dryness of sound even seems to help, when offstage choruses are accurately focused, and the singing of the Robert Shaw Chorale has thrillingly dramatic bite.

The DG recording was made in Vienna in 1977 and finds Ghiaurov in excellent form. Bernstein, too, conducts this highly imaginative piece vividly and atmospherically. The CD transfer has greatly improved the focus and now the offstage choruses register impressively. This does not quite have the electricity of Toscanini but, for those wanting a modern version, it will serve admirably.

Nerone (complete).

**(*) Hung. Dig. HCD 12487/9-2 [id.]. Nagy, Tokody, Dene, Miller, Takács, Gregor, Hungarian R. and TV Ch., Hungarian State Op. O, Queler.

Eve Queler conducts a powerful and atmospheric performance of Boito's massive, uncompleted opera. There are plenty of marvellous ideas here, starting with the strikingly original opening, sliding in like *Aida* updated. Later too the piece is full of prayers and ceremonial music, all of it richly colourful and superbly performed by the company of the Hungarian State Opera, whose soloists are far less afflicted with Slavonic wobbles than is common in Eastern Europe. Notable in the cast are Ilona Tokody as the heroine, Klara Takács, Lajos Miller as the Christian leader, and Janos Nagy as a disconcertingly engaging Nero, a tenor role. The recording is of outstanding quality, with the atmospheric perspectives demanded by the score most realistically conveyed.

Borodin, Alexander (1833–87)

Petite suite (arr. Glazunov).
*** Olympia OCD 114 A/B (2) [id.]. USSR RSO, Cherkassov – MUSSORGSKY: *Sorochinsky Fair.* ***

Not long before Borodin died, he compiled a suite of piano pieces for the Belgian countess who had been his patroness in France, and these became the *Petite suite* which Glazunov orchestrated after Borodin's death. It is a colourful, undemanding work, very well played and recorded.

Symphonies Nos. 1 in E flat; 2 in B min.; 3 in A min. (completed Glazunov); *In the Steppes of Central Asia; Nocturne* (orchestrated Nicolai Tcherepnin); *Petite suite* (arr. Glazunov); *Prince Igor: Overture;* (i) *Polovtsian dances.*
*** DG Dig. 435 757-2 (2) [id.]. Gothenburg SO, Neeme Järvi; (i) with Gothenburg Ch.

At last come highly recommendable performances of the three Borodin *Symphonies*, from Järvi and the Gothenburg Orchestra in first class digital recordings. The *First* (which can too easily sound like a trial run for the *Second*) has plenty of individuality here. The Scherzo is beautifully sprung and vivaciously coloured, its charming middle section most engagingly presented, the slow movement is radiant, and the finale made to anticipate the *Prince Igor Overture* in its bright rhythmic pointing. The *Third* (which Glazunov completed from the composer's sketches – relying on his memory of Borodin's performances on the piano) is also highly attractive, particularly the opening with its delicate scoring for woodwind. The *Second Symphony* is a strong, spacious reading, at its finest in the *Andante*, when the key melody, so beautifully introduced by the solo horn, returns on the full strings in a flood of romanticism. However, alongside Tjeknavorian, the first movement is a little lacking in rhythmic bite and thrust, although the return of the dominating idea on the brass in the coda is very powerful. The other works, which include even the little known *Petite suite* (notable for its opening evocation of convent bells and appealing finale), are equally well played and Järvi combines the two themes of *In the Steppes of Central Asia* most winningly, the one spirited, the other languorous. There are some reservations about Tcherepnin's very exotic orchestration of the famous *Nocturne*, from the *D major String quartet*: it certainly sounds vivid, but the music's warm romantic feeling comes over better on strings alone. The *Prince Igor Overture* is splendidly done, but – like the *Second Symphony's* first movement – Järvi does't quite pull out all the stops in his account of the *Polovtsian dances.* This includes the percussion-led opening number, but while the choral singing is impressive, and there is even a brief solo contribution representing the Khan, these Swedish singers lack the unbuttoned exuberance of the John Alldis Choir under Tjeknavorian. Nevertheless, as a set, this pair of DG CDs upstages the current competition, notably Svetlanov's readings on two Chant du Monde discs, but also the fine performances from Andrew Davis and the Toronto Symphony Orchestra on Sony, which are let down by close-miked CBS recording, lacking in natural ambience and bloom – the very qualities these works need to blossom fully. ASV and Naxos have both managed to fit all three symphonies on a single CD. Serebrier's accounts with the Rome Symphony Orchestra (on ASV CDDCA 706) are sensibly paced and direct, but not very Russian in feeling. The symphonies fare better in Bratislava. One ideally needs more opulent sound than the Slovak Radio Orchestra provide, but Gunzenhauser's readings are fresh and lively, if not distinctive, and this 76 minute CD is undoubtedly good value in the lowest price-range (Naxos 8.550238). But the Järvi set will prove a much more satisfying investment and is well worth its extra cost.

Symphony No. 2 in B min.; In the Steppes of Central Asia; Prince Igor: Overture; (i) *Polovtsian march; Polovtsian dances.*

(B) *** BMG/RCA VD 60535; *VK 60535* [60535-2-RV; 60535-4-RV]. Nat. PO, (i) with John Alldis Ch.; Tjeknavorian.

For those collectors content with only the *Second Symphony* – Borodin's masterpiece – BMG/RCA have come to the rescue with a super-bargain reissue, recorded in London by the National Philharmonic Orchestra in 1977 under Loris Tjeknavorian. This is far preferable to the comparably priced bargain alternative from Bátiz, whose performance with the Mexico State Symphony Orchestra is spirited and vivid but lacks the finesse of real orchestral virtuosity which this work undoubtedly demands (ASV CDQS 6018; *ZCQS 6018*). Tjeknavorian is an Armenian by birth and he knows what this music is about. His pacing, swift and vital, of the first movement of this most Russian of symphonies is admirably judged: the reading has a powerful rhythmic thrust, the orchestral playing is polished and full of colour. The vibrant scherzo bursts upwards like rockets exploding in the sky, and the ardour of the slow movement brings a climax of great passion. The finale, too, has plenty of gusto. Don't look for the last degree of refinement here but, with full and spacious recording, if not as sumptuous as with Järvi on DG, this is very involving. So too is the fine performance of Borodin's evocative *In the Steppes of Central Asia*, which comes comes as a rich-hued interlude before vibrant accounts of the *Overture*, *Polovtsian march* and *Polovtsian dances* from *Prince Igor*, including the percussion-led *Dance of the Polovtsian Maidens*. The choral dances are Beechamesque in exuberance and bring a dynamic contribution from the John Alldis Choir, with a burst of energy in the closing pages.

Sextet (2 movements).
** Mer. Dig. CDE 84211 [id.]. Arienski Ens. – ARENSKY: *Quartet* ***; TCHAIKOVSKY: *Souvenir de Florence*. **

Borodin composed his *Sextet* on a visit to Heidelberg in 1860 but, unfortunately, only two of its movements survive. The composer himself described it as Mendelssohnian – which it most certainly is. No one listening to it blindfold would guess who wrote it. The sleeve transposes the timings of the two movements. The Arienski Ensemble play with enthusiasm and conviction and are decently recorded.

String quartets Nos. 1 in A; 2 in D.
*** EMI CDC7 47795-2 [id.]. Borodin Qt.

String quartet No. 2 in D.
*** Olympia Dig. OCD 138 [id.]. Borodin Qt – TANEYEV: *Quintet*. ***
(M) **(*) Decca 425 541-2; *425 541-4* [id.]. Borodin Qt – SHOSTAKOVICH; TCHAIKOVSKY: *Quartets*. **(*)

The EMI performances from the eponymous Borodin Quartet are admirable in all respects. They are completely effortless and idiomatic; indeed, so total is their sense of identification with these scores that one is scarcely conscious of the intervention of the interpreter. The quality achieved by the Melodiya engineers has fine clarity; on CD the focus of the first violin line is firmer than before. The ambient warmth remains, although the sound is perhaps just a shade harder than on the original (1980) analogue LP.

On Olympia, the alternative version of No. 2 from the Borodin Quartet is equally masterly. The performance is virtually indistinguishable in quality from their EMI version and they are beautifully recorded. The Olympia CD has a slight price advantage, and the Taneyev *Quintet* is certainly well worth investigating.

The Borodins' first version on Decca was recorded in 1962; this performance is hardly less fine than the later (full-price) versions and it is very generously coupled. However, the forward recording, though rich-textured, is given a boldly outlined treble, approaching fierceness in the CD transfer, and some will prefer a softer-grained effect.

Songs: *Arabian melody; Arrogance; The beauty no longer loves me; The false note; The fisher-maiden; From my tears; From the shores of thy far native land; Listen to my song little friend; The magic garden; The queen of the sea; The sea; The sleeping princess; Song of the dark forest; There is poison in my songs; Those people; Why art thou so early, dawn?*
(M) *** EMI CMS7 63386-2 (3) [Ang. CDMC 63386]. Christoff, Tcherepnin, Reiss, Lamoureux O, Tzipine – *Prince Igor*. **(*)

Accompanied at the piano in all but three of the songs by the composer, Alexander Tcherepnin, Christoff gives glorious performances of these rare items. They were recorded in the

1960s, when the voice was at its richest and most expressive, providing an invaluable makeweight for Semkow's cut version of *Prince Igor*.

Prince Igor (opera) complete.
*** Sony Dig. S3K 44878 (3) [id.]. Martinovich, Evstatieva, Kaludov, Ghiuselev, Ghiaurov, Miltcheva, Sofia Nat. Op. Ch. & Festival O, Tchakarov.
(M) **(*) EMI CMS7 63386-2 (3) [Ang. CDMC 63386]. Chekerliiski, Christoff, Todorov, Sofia Nat. Theatre Op. Ch. & O, Jerzy Semkow – *Songs*. ***

Issued as one of the first offerings on the new Sony Classical label, Tchakarov's complete recording of *Prince Igor* fills one of the most important gaps in the catalogue. It may give an idea of the quality of the singing that the soloist over whom there are most reservations, Nicola Ghiuselev as Galitsky, powerful but rather unsteady, is one of the two most celebrated international stars in the Sofia cast. The other, Nicolai Ghiaurov, makes a splendid Konchak, if not quite as characterful as Christoff on the EMI set. Boris Martinovich makes a firm, very virile Igor, and both the principal women have vibrantly Slavonic voices which still never distract in wobbling: Stefka Evstatieva very moving and young-sounding as Igor's wife, Yaroslavna, and Alexandrina Miltcheva as Konchak's daughter. Kaludi Kaludov sings with Slavonic tightness at times, but that too is apt. Tchakarov takes a generally brisk view of the score. The dramatic tension in this long work is held very well and its richness of invention over its very episodic span comes across vividly, notably in all its memorable melody and high colour. The performance is particularly moving in Act III, where – thanks to the 'creative editing' of Rimsky-Korsakov and Glazunov – the score is enhanced by the ideas they also used in the *Overture*, culminating in the glorious final trio between Igor, his son and Konchak's daughter. Full, brilliant recording to match the orchestration.

Recorded in Paris in 1966, the colourful EMI recording of *Prince Igor* has one great flaw in that Act III is completely omitted, on the grounds that it was almost entirely the work of Rimsky-Korsakov and Glazunov. The great glory of the performance is the singing of Boris Christoff as both Galitszky and Konchak, easily outshining all rivals. Jerzy Semkow with his Sofia Opera forces is most sympathetic, but the other soloists are almost all disappointing, with the women sour-toned and the men often strained and unsteady. There is no libretto; but EMI is very generous with cueing points, and you can follow the story easily by checking them against the very detailed synopsis. The sound is limited but agreeably atmospheric.

Prince Igor: Overture and Polovtsian dances.
*** EMI CDC7 47717-2 [id.]. Beecham Choral Soc., RPO, Beecham – RIMSKY-KORSAKOV: *Scheherazade*.***
(B) *** Decca 417 689-2; *417 689-4*. LSO Ch., LSO, Solti – MUSSORGSKY: *Khovanshchina prelude; Night;* GLINKA: *Russlan overture*. ***
*** Telarc Dig. CD 80039. Atlanta Ch. and SO, Shaw – STRAVINSKY: *Firebird suite*. **(*)

Prince Igor: Polovtsian dances.
(M) *** DG 419 063-2; *419 063-4* [id.]. BPO, Karajan – RIMSKY-KORSAKOV: *Scheherazade*. ***
(M) **(*) Mercury 434 308-2 [id.]. LSO Ch., LSO, Dorati – RIMSKY-KORSAKOV: *Capriccio espagnol* etc. ***

Beecham's 1957 recording of the *Polovtsian dances*, made in EMI's Abbey Road studios, sweeps the board, even though it omits the percussion-led opening *Dance of the Polovtsi Maidens*. Beecham draws an almost Russian fervour from his choristers, who sing with enormous enthusiasm, and the orchestral playing creates a comparable excitement, building to a tremendous climax. The recorded sound is little short of astonishing in its fullness, vividness and clarity.

Solti's performance is also among the finest ever recorded, with good choral singing – even if the chorus takes a little while to warm up. The *Overture* too has fine dash, with the LSO players consistently on their toes.

On Telarc the choral singing is less clearly focused in the lyrical sections of the score than at climaxes, but the singers undoubtedly rise to the occasion. The entry of the bass drum is riveting and the closing section very exciting. The vivid sound-balance is equally impressive in the *Overture*, and if the Atlanta orchestra does not possess the body of string timbre to make the very most of the sweeping second subject, the playing has vitality and spontaneity in its favour.

Karajan's Berlin Philharmonic version has great flair and excitement, though it lacks a chorus.

Dorati's Mercury recording is early in provenance (1956) and neither the singing of the LSO

Chorus nor the recording itself is among the most refined from this source. But no one could say that effect lacks vividness or boisterous vitality, and the climax is exhilarating.

Bottesini, Giovanni (1821–89)

Gran duo concertante for violin, double-bass and orchestra; Gran concerto in F sharp min. for double-bass; Andante sostenuto for strings; Duetto for clarinet and double-bass.
**(*) ASV Dig. CDDCA 563; *ZCDCA 563* [id.]. Garcia, Martin, Emma Johnson, ECO, Andrew Litton.

The ASV recording combines the *Gran duo concertante* with another *Duo for clarinet and double-bass* which Emma Johnson ensures has plenty of personality. The *Andante sostenuto for strings* is pleasant enough, but the *Double-bass concerto* fails to convince. To be frank, none of this amiable music is very distinctive. The recording is excellent, well balanced and truthful.

Capriccio di bravura; Elegia in Re; Fantasia on Beatrice di Tenda; Fantasia on Lucia di Lammermoor; Grand allegro di concerto; Introduzione e Bolero; Romanza drammatica; (i) *Romanza: Une bouche aimée.*
** ASV Dig. CDDCA 626; *ZCDCA 626* [id.]. Thomas Martin, Anthony Halstead; (i) with J. Fugelle.

The mechanical limitations of the double-bass mean that harmonics performed with scientific accuracy are out of tune. Thomas Martin is a superb virtuoso of the instrument, and he obviously relishes these display pieces, but some of the high tessitura is inevitably uncomfortable. In *Une bouche aimée* he is joined by the charmingly eloquent voice of Jacquelyn Fugelle and the double-bass provides the obbligato, which makes a welcome central interlude. There are excellent accompaniments from Anthony Halstead, better known as a fine horn player. The recording is most realistic.

Boughton, Rutland (1878–1960)

(i) *Oboe concerto; Symphony No. 3 in B min.*
*** Hyp. Dig. CDA 66343; *KA 66343* [id.]. (i) Sarah Francis; RPO, Vernon Handley.

Rutland Boughton's *Third Symphony* comes from 1937 and proves something of a surprise. It is old-fashioned in idiom; some of it would not be out of place in Dvořák or Borodin, and its debt to Elgar above all is overwhelming. However, it is expertly fashioned, often imaginative and (save in the rumbustious scherzo, where the closing pages are clumsily scored) hardly puts a foot wrong. The *Oboe concerto* of 1936, which Boyd Neel took to Salzburg in the same year as he presented Britten's *Variations on a theme of Frank Bridge*, is hardly less rewarding. The recording is in the demonstration class and the performances are totally committed, even if the strings of the RPO are not quite on top form.

The Immortal hour (opera): complete.
*** Hyp. Dig. CDA 66101/2 [id.]. Kennedy, Dawson, Wilson-Johnson, Davies, Geoffrey Mitchell Ch., ECO, Melville.

There is far more to *The Immortal hour* than the still-celebrated *Faery song*, which hauntingly is heard first at the end of Act I, sung by a chorus in the distance. Analysed closely, much of it may seem like Vaughan Williams and water; but this fine performance, conducted by a lifelong Boughton devotee, brings out the hypnotic quality which had 1920s music-lovers attending performances many times over, entranced by its lyrical evocation of Celtic twilight. The simple tunefulness goes with a fine feeling for atmosphere. The excellent cast of young singers includes Anne Dawson as the heroine, Princess Etain, and Maldwyn Davies headily beautiful in the main tenor rendering of the *Faery song*. Warm, reverberant recording, undoubtedly enhanced in its CD format.

Boulanger, Lili (1893–1918)

(i) *Cortège; D'un matin de printemps; Nocturne* (3 pieces for violin & piano); (ii) *Du fond de l'abîme;* (iii) *Pié Jesu;* (iv) *Psaume 24;* (v) *Psaume 129;* (vi) *Vieille prière bouddhique.*
(M) (*(**) EMI mono/stereo CDM7 64281-2 [id.]. (i) Menuhin, Curzon; (ii) Dominguez, Amade; (iii) Fauqueur; (iii; iv) Grunenwald; (iv) Sénéchal; (v) Mollet; (ii; iv–vi) Chorale Elizabeth Brasseur; (ii–vi) LOP, Markevitch.

This record reveals Lili Boulanger to have possessed a creative talent of real quality. She was six years younger than her sister, Nadia who conducted many performances of her work. Like the somewhat older Lekeu (1870–94), she died in her twenties but had already established a voice of her own. The most substantial and quite individual piece here is *Du fond de l'abîme*, eloquently argued and powerfully atmospheric. It is a haunting piece that quite transcends its very dated, dryish 1958 mono recording by Oralia Dominguez and the Lamoureux Orchestra of Paris under Igor Markevitch. Anyone listening to it will be amazed that it is not a repertoire piece. The opening of the *Psaume 24* almost looks forward to the Honegger of *Le roi David*, and the *Vieille prière bouddhique* to Holst. The three pieces for violin and piano, *Cortège; D'un matin de printemps; Nocturne* are more Ravel-like, and are beautifully played by Yehudi Menuhin and Clifford Curzon, and were recorded in stereo in 1973. An altogether fascinating disc: the music deserves three stars, the recordings only one. Amazingly, the liner-notes provided not only do not give the text of *Du fond de l'abîme* but don't even mention it! Dominique Jameux in *Grove* calls it 'a vast piece of striking solemnity and grandeur, densely but subtly written', and gives its date as 1914–17. In places it almost anticipates Honegger.

Boulez, Pierre (born 1926)

Rituel: In memoriam Bruno Maderna; Éclat-Multiples.
(M) *** Sony SK 45839 [id.]. BBC SO, Ens. InterContemporain, composer.

Éclat-Multiples started (in 1964) simply as *Éclat*, a brilliant showpiece, an exuberant mosaic of sounds; but then, in 1970, it started developing from there in the pendant work, *Multiples.* On this recording the two sections are played without a break. *Rituel* is even more remarkable, the most moving music that Boulez has ever written, inspired by the premature death of his friend and colleague, Bruno Maderna. It brings what even an uninitiated listener will recognize as a great funeral procession, darkly intense, building up with an emotional intensity hardly less involving than a Mahler funeral march. This record, very well played and recorded, provides both a challenge and a reward.

Le soleil des eaux.
(M) *** EMI CDM7 63948-2 [id.]. Nendick, McDaniel, Devos, BBC Ch. & SO, composer – KOECKLIN: *Les Bandar-Log;* MESSIAEN: *Chronochromie* etc. ***

Boulez's cantata is best thought of initially in its atmospheric context, for it served originally as incidental music to a poetic radio drama about the poisoning of a river. As ever with Boulez, the concentration is formidable, but Josephine Nendick, the principal soloist, is breathtakingly precise and the result is far more enjoyable as a result. Both performance and recording are of a high standard and the CD transfer gives striking presence.

Boyce, William (1710–79)

Concerti grossi: in B flat; in B min.; in E min. Overtures Nos. 10–12.
(M) *** Chan. CHAN 6541 [id.]. Cantilena, Adrian Shepherd.

This reissue completes Cantilena's set of the Boyce *Overtures* and includes the three *Concerti grossi.* Though these works do not quite have the consistent originality which makes the Boyce *Symphonies* so refreshing, the energy of the writing – splendidly conveyed in these performances – is recognizably the same, with fugal passages that turn in unexpected directions. Excellent sound, fresh, vivid and with plenty of character to the string textures but without edge.

Overtures Nos. 1–9.
(M) *** Chan. CHAN 6531; *MBTD 6531* [id.]. Cantilena, Adrian Shepherd.

The eight Boyce *Symphonies* have been recorded many times, but the composer's collection of a dozen *Overtures*, put together in 1770 – although including at least one work from as early as 1745 – has much of comparable vigour. As it happens, the first overture is not one of the best; but each has its attractions and those which bring out the brass are most exciting. This 73-minute disc includes nine of the set, and Cantilena's performances readily convey the freshness of Boyce's inspiration. The recording is oddly balanced but is both atmospheric and vivid and provides a refreshing musical experience.

Symphonies Nos. 1–8.
*** DG Dig. 419 631-2 [id.]. E. Concert, Pinnock.
*** CRD CRD 3356 [id.]. Bournemouth Sinf., Ronald Thomas.

Pinnock's disc of the Boyce *Symphonies* is a delight, the first recording to use period instruments. It wears its scholarship very easily and in so doing brings not only lively, resilient playing but fresh revelation in the treatment of the *vivace* movements, which are normally taken faster than is authentic, when that marking in eighteenth-century England did not have its modern connotation of speed. Nicely scaled recording, bright but atmospheric.

Thomas's tempi are often brisk, and certainly swifter-paced than Pinnock's 'new look'. But even against such strong competition as this, the buoyant playing of the Bournemouth Sinfonietta still gives much pleasure by its sheer vitality. Bright, clear sound.

Organ voluntaries Nos. 1, 2, 4 & 10. (i) Anthems: *By the waters of Babylon; I have surely built Thee a house; O where shall wisdom be found; Turn unto me, O Lord.*
(M) *** Saga SCD 9006. Arthur Wills, (i) Ely Cathedral Ch., Gerald Clifford.

It is a salutary contrast to hear formal eighteenth-century settings of words which have been set dramatically in our own century by Sir William Walton; but the music of Boyce is most compelling, especially when sung with such warmth. The organ voluntaries are placed as interludes between the anthems and are very well played on an organ that gives them plenty of character. This makes a most stimulating introduction to valuable and rare repertoire, and the CD transfer catches the cathedral ambience to perfection.

Solomon (serenata).
*** Hyp. Dig. CDA 66378; *KA 66378* [id.]. Bronwen Mills, Howard Crook, Parley of Instruments, Goodman.

William Boyce's *Solomon* could hardly provide a stronger contrast with the magnificent oratorio of the same name that Handel wrote in 1748, six years after Boyce's gentle *Serenata* had been completed. It is a totally secular piece, a dialogue between She and He, with the verses freely based on the *Song of Solomon*. The only actual reference to the King is in the opening chorus; the rest of this gentle entertainment is a sequence of recitatives and airs, plus two duets, with the chorus making only brief contributions. By the nineteenth century it had fallen out of the repertory, when the erotic overtones of the text had become less acceptable and choral societies did not want to perform a work almost entirely devoted to two soloists. But, as this stylish and alert period performance using young, fresh-voiced soloists makes clear, it has some delightful inspirations, less influenced by Italian models than by popular English song. First-rate sound.

Brade, William (1560–1630)

Hamburger Ratsmusik: Allemandes, Canzonas, Courantes, Galliards, Intradas (1609, 1614 & 1617 collections).
(M) *** HM/BMG Dig. GD 77168 (2) [77168-2-RG]. Hespèrion XX, Jordi Savall.

This collection of dances is based on the three main prints which appeared in 1609, 1614 and 1617 in Hamburg and Lübeck, and embraces all the contemporary forms, Allemand, Paduana, Galliard and a variety of descriptive pieces. Their realization is absolutely delightful, varied in both content and instrumental colour, and excellently played by Hespèrion XX under Jordi Savall, while the recording, from 1981, is very good indeed.

Brahms, Johannes (1833–97)

(i) *Piano concertos Nos. 1;* (ii) *2;* (Piano) *Rhapsody No. 2 in G min., Op. 79/2; Variations and fugue on a theme of Handel, Op. 24; 16 Waltzes, Op. 39.*
(B) ** EMI CZS7 62883-2 (2) [id.]. Bruno-Leonardo Gelber, (i) Munich PO, Franz-Paul Decker; (ii) RPO, Kempe.

Bruno-Leonardo Gelber made his recording début for EMI with an inspired and imaginative account of Beethoven's *Emperor Concerto*. After this, his Brahms proves slightly disappointing. In the *First Concerto* (recorded in 1965, some years before the *Second*) his playing is cleanly confident to match Brahms's youthful inspiration; but the *Second*, with a leisurely first movement, brings less than its full weight of utterance, the more surprisingly as Kempe is at the helm. The orchestral support is warm and polished (in both works) but the *B flat Concerto* refuses to spring fully to life, in spite of a full Brahmsian sound-picture. The solo recordings were made in the mid-1970s in the Salle Wagram, which brings the usual close balance but a fully acceptable piano image. Both the *Variations* and the *Waltzes* bring flexibility and imaginative detail and the *Rhapsody* is strong; but in the last resort these performances are not really distinctive either.

Piano concerto No. 1 in D min., Op. 15.
*** Ph. Dig. 420 071-2 [id.]. Brendel, BPO, Abbado.
(M) **(*) Sony SBK 48166 [id.]. Rudolf Serkin, Cleveland O, Szell – MENDELSSOHN: *Capriccio brillant* **; SCHUMANN: *Intro. and allegro appassionata.* **(*)
**(*) Decca Dig. 410 009-2 [id.]. Ashkenazy, Concg. O, Haitink.
**(*) BMG/RCA RD 85668 [RCA 5668-2-RC]. Rubinstein, Chicago SO, Reiner.
(M) **(*) Ph. 420 702-2 [id.]. Arrau, Concg. O, Haitink.

(i) *Piano concerto No. 1;* (ii) *Variations on a theme of Haydn, Op. 56a.*
(M) *** EMI CDM7 63536-2 [id.]. (i) Barenboim, Philh. O; (ii) VPO; Barbirolli.

(i) *Piano concerto No. 1. 4 Ballades, Op. 10.*
(M) *** DG 431 595-2; *431 595-4* [id.]. Gilels, (i) BPO, Jochum.

(i) *Piano concerto No. 1 in D min. Rhapsody in B min., Op. 79/1.*
(B) (*(**)) Pickwick IMPX 9039. Kovacevich; (i) LSO, Sir Colin Davis.

(i) *Piano concerto No. 1. Variations and fugue on a theme of Handel, Op. 24.*
(M) **(*) BMG/RCA GD 60357 [60357-2-RG]. Van Cliburn, (i) Boston SO, Leinsdorf.

(i) *Piano concerto No. 1;* (ii) *Variations on a theme by Schumann, Op. 23.*
*** Decca Dig. 425 110-2 [id.]. (i) Schiff, VPO, Solti; (ii) Schiff, Solti.

Gilels's reading of the *D minor Concerto* has a magisterial strength blended with a warmth, humanity and depth that are altogether inspiring. Jochum is a superb accompanist and the remastered 1972 recording has a better focus on CD, if slightly less glowing warmth than the original LP. The *Ballades*, recorded three years later, make a considerable bonus. They have never been played so marvellously on record, and the recording is very believable.

Brendel produces a consistently beautiful sound and balances the combative and lyrical elements of the work with well-nigh perfect judgement. With Claudio Abbado and the Berlin Philharmonic as understanding partners, the result is both strong and spontaneous. His control of Brahmsian rubato is masterly, when it is easily flexible but totally unexaggerated, and the basic tempi are well and steadily set. The balance is not too forward and the effect is warmly satisfying.

Barenboim recorded the two Brahms *Piano concertos* with Barbirolli in 1968. Their performance of the *First Concerto* is among the most inspired ever committed to disc. If at first the opening tempo seems disconcertingly measured, it falls into place on a second hearing. The playing is heroic and marvellously spacious, and the performance is sustained by the intensity of concentration, especially in the pianissimo passages of the slow movement; the joyous finale uplifts the spirit and communicates a life-enhancing confidence. The *Variations*, laid out for the listener in affectionate detail, again show the conductor at his finest; the late-1960s recordings have transferred splendidly to CD, with plenty of body and the upper range brighter but without edginess.

Serkin's 1968 account with Szell, his third on LP, brought tremendous command and grandeur. This is undoubtedly a memorable performance and the support from Szell and the Cleveland Orchestra has great power. The Schumann coupling is very fine too. The CBS/Sony recording has been considerably improved in the current remastering and is fuller than before, but the balance still lacks a natural perspective and the sound ideally needs more opulence and depth. However the hall's ambience prevents brashness and admirers of Serkin will still want this CD.

Ashkenazy gives a commanding and magisterial account of the solo part that is full of poetic imagination. The performance is very impressive indeed and there is superlative playing from the Concertgebouw Orchestra. The recording is enormously vivid, though the balance may worry some collectors. The forward placing of the soloist gives the lower and middle registers of the piano a disproportionate amount of aural space.

Schiff's performance has an imposing sense of line and is powerful and rich in sonority. It presents a very truthful and realistic balance between piano and orchestra, with the soloist not given undue prominence. The playing of the Vienna orchestra under Solti is glorious. It is worth considering not only for its own sake but in particular for the *Schumann duet Variations* in which, once again, Solti reminds us that he is a pianist of finesse.

With its rugged opening, Van Cliburn's account of the *D minor Concerto* soon develops a full head of steam. Leinsdorf is hardly less sympathetic than he is for Richter in No. 2, and this is a compelling reading, full of spontaneous vigour. The slow movement has eloquence and atmosphere, and the finale plenty of fire. What makes the disc especially attractive is the splendid account of the *Handel variations*, which acts as an exhilarating (26-minute) encore. Van Cliburn plays with splendid dash and often with great bravura. The 1964 sound in the *Concerto* is good if not always ideally expansive, in spite of the Boston acoustics, but the solo work, recorded a decade later, gives little if any cause for complaint. This is one of Van Cliburn's best records.

Rubinstein's is a poetic and essentially lyrical reading, impulsive and avoiding Brahmsian stodginess – though it is by no means without power, for Reiner's control of the orchestra, volatile and imaginative, has a spacious strength. The only snag is the forward balance of the piano, which means that a real pianissimo fails to register, although the 1954 recording attractively brings out the brightness of Rubinstein's tone against the warm Chicago backcloth. However, this is surely due for a mid-price reissue.

Arrau's reading has vision and power and, though there are some characteristic agogic distortions that will not convince all listeners, he is majestic and eloquent. There is never an ugly sonority even in the moments of the greatest vehemence. By the side of Gilels he seems idiosyncratic but, given the excellence of the digitally remastered recording and the warmth of Haitink's support, this is well worth considering in the medium-price range.

If recording quality was very much a secondary consideration, Stephen Kovacevich's account of the concerto should figure high on the lists. He plays with great tenderness and lyrical feeling. In the hushed slow movement he achieves great inwardness of feeling and poetry, and in the first movement he makes no attempt either to exaggerate or to understate the combative, leonine side of the solo part. He is sympathetically supported by Sir Colin Davis and the LSO, and though woodwind intonation is not above reproach, there is no lack of orchestral power. Unfortunately, the Philips sound (unbelievably, from 1980) is unfocused and bottom-heavy, with moments of roughness, which the AAD transfer does nothing to clean up.

Piano concerto No. 2 in B flat, Op. 83.
*** Ph. Dig. 432 975-2; *432 975-4* [id.]. Brendel, BPO, Abbado.
(M) *** BMG/RCA 7863 56518 [RCA 6518-2-RG]. Sviatoslav Richter, Chicago SO, Leinsdorf – BEETHOVEN: *Piano sonata No. 23.* ***
(M) *** DG 419 471-2 [id.]. Pollini, VPO, Abbado.
(M) **(*) Ph. 420 885-2 [id.]. Arrau, Concg. O, Haitink.
** Teldec/Warner Dig. 2292 44936-2 [id.]. Katsaris, Philh. O, Inbal.

(i) *Piano concerto No. 2;* (ii) *Academic festival overture; Tragic overture.*
(M) *** EMI CDM7 63537-2 [id.]. (i) Barenboim, Philh. O; (ii) VPO; Barbirolli.

(i) *Piano concerto No. 2 in B flat. Variations on a theme of Haydn, Op. 56a.*
(M) *** Sony SMK 47359 [id.]. (i) André Watts; NYPO, Bernstein.

(i) *Piano concerto No. 2 in B flat. Fantasias, Op. 116.*
(M) *** DG 435 588-2 [id.]. Gilels; (i) BPO, Jochum.

(i) *Piano concerto No. 2; Intermezzi: in E min., Op. 116/5; in B flat min., Op. 117/2; Rhapsody in G min., Op. 79/2.*
*** BMG/RCA RD 85671. Rubinstein; (i) RCA SO, Josef Krips.

(i) *Piano concerto No. 2;* (ii) *6 Piano pieces, Op. 118.*
(B) **(*) DG 431 162-2; *431 162-4*. (i) Géza Anda, BPO, Karajan; (ii) Wilhelm Kempff.

(i) *Piano concerto No. 2 in B flat, Op. 83. Rhapsody in G min., Op. 79/2.*
(B) **(*) IMPX 9040. Kovacevich; (i) LSO, Sir Colin Davis.

The partnership of Gilels and Jochum produces music-making of rare magic and the digital remastering has improved definition: the sound is full in an appropriately Brahmsian way. In the *Fantasias*, Op. 116, Gilels displays artistry of an order that silences criticism, and the CD transfer is again very believable in terms of piano timbre. With nearly 74 minutes of music offered, this DG reissue will be hard to beat.

Brendel's new account of the concerto is massive and concentrated, and has greater depth than his earlier account with Haitink. It has the advantage of impressive and weighty recorded sound, and the Berlin Philharmonic under Abbado produce an equally splendid warmth. It is a worthy successor to their *D minor*, though in terms of humanity and wisdom it does not displace the celebrated Gilels-Jochum version, now reissued at mid-price on DG.

Richter's 1960 RCA performance has all the intensity of a live occasion and finds him in splendid form. It is wayward, mannered in places, but the basic structure is always kept in sight; there is impressive weight and authority as well as a warm, Brahmsian lyrical feeling. The Chicago acoustics ensure that the orchestral texture is full-bodied and atmospheric and the piano timbre sounds fuller than before. With an exciting account of Beethoven's *Appassionata Sonata* as coupling, this is highly recommendable.

Pollini's 1977 recording makes a good alternative choice, also at mid-price. His account is powerful, in many ways more classical in feeling than Richter's. He has the measure of the work's scale and breadth and is given first-rate support by the Vienna Philharmonic under Abbado. The remastered sound has a Brahmsian body and warmth and it sounds more modern than the RCA CD.

While Barenboim's reading with Barbirolli remains an individual view, the tendency to slow tempi brings the advantage that the lyrical passages merge spontaneously into the whole. The first two movements remain grandly heroic and the slow movement has something of the awed intensity you find in the middle movement of the *First Concerto*, while the finale erupts gracefully into rib-tickling humour. Barenboim's touch here reminds one of Rubinstein's famous version. This is a performance to love in its glowing spontaneity; the first-rate 1968 recording has splendid Brahmsian body and breadth, and no lack of brilliance. Of the fill-ups, the *Tragic overture* is a performance of considerable distinction; but many will feel that the measured account of the *Academic festival overture* could do with more sparkle.

Kovacevich is better served by the Philips engineers in this Pickwick account of the *Second concerto* than he was in the *First*, recorded at the same time (the early 1980s). The AAD quality is somewhat middle and bottom-heavy, but its warmth is highly suitable for Brahms and it seems likely that a future ADD remastering could firm up the focus and sharpen inner detail; there are plentiful reserves of ambience and bloom, and the balance between the piano and orchestra is natural. The performance combines poetic feeling and intellectual strength and reflects an unforced natural eloquence that compels admiration. The first movement unfolds simply without any false urgency; the second is sparkling and fresh (if made to seem heavier than it is by the resonance), and in the *Adagio* there is a rapt, poetic quality which becomes magnetically hushed at the close; Douglas Cummings, the cello soloist plays with tenderness and nobility. The finale has wit and delicacy and brings a spontaneous surge of adrenalin at the close. Sir Colin Davis provides wholly sympathetic support throughout. This is the finest recorded performance we have had since the Gilels/Jochum, and except for those who demand a bright, cleanly focused sound picture, can be recommended alongside it.

André Watts also gives a powerful and compelling performance that stands as one of the finest on record. At every point he shows deep feeling and intelligence. His Brahms style is boldly lyrical. Tempi are less idiosyncratic than those of Barenboim and Barbirolli, and after a beautifully sustained *Andante* the finale is very successful in not subduing the chimerical element with the warm lyrical feeling and weight. Bernstein accompanies very positively and the only surprising element is the variably exact ensemble that he secures from the orchestra. Even so this is a very rewarding and spontaneous account and the *Haydn variations* are also characteristically alive and by no means predictable. The 1968 Avery Fisher Hall recording of the concerto is impressively remastered, remarkably full and spacious; the *Variations* date from 1971; they have slightly less body to the sound, but this suits Bernstein's reading. This is one of the most rewarding reissues made in Sony's prestigious Royal Bernstein Edition.

Rubinstein was at his peak (in 1958) and his technical mastery brings a scintillating response to the changing moods of the first movement, while the finale is a delight with its deftness of articulation and rippling lyricism. Krips brings a Viennese touch to the orchestra and matches Rubinstein's spontaneity. This is a reading which emphasizes the bright and luminous aspects of the work and is all the more refreshing for that, even if the piano, for all its vivid realism, is almost in one's lap, and the close balance means that a true pianissimo is never registered. The three substantial encores are well chosen to make a miniature (15-minute) solo recital after the concerto; once again, the sound is realistic and the playing distinguished. We hope this is due for a mid-priced reissue.

Arrau's account of the concerto brings one or two idiosyncratic touches, but the playing has a splendid combination of aristocratic finesse and warmth of feeling. Haitink and the Concertgebouw Orchestra give excellent support and the engineers strike the right balance between the piano and orchestra.

The 1968 partnership of Anda with the BPO provides much fine playing from soloist and orchestra alike. Anda is wayward at times, although he is always commanding. But there is poetry here, and undoubted power. There is much to enjoy, not least the glorious orchestral response. The recording is appropriately bold and full, and the balance is good. In the six *Klavierstücke*, Op. 118, Kempff shines in exactly those pieces where many modern pianists fall short, emphasizing poetry rather than brilliance, subtle timbres rather than virtuosity.

Cyprien Katsaris made a strong impression in the Liszt transcriptions of the Beethoven symphonies on the Teldec label but his Brahms *B flat Concerto*, for all its many felicities, is neither as big-boned and spacious as such artists as Gilels, Kovacevich, Richter and Rubinstein nor as characterful. There are good things, of course, but the reading does not resonate in the mind afterwards as great performances do. Good sound and a natural balance from the engineers, but not a front-runner all the same.

Violin concerto in D, Op. 77.
*** ASV CDDCA 748; *ZCDCA 748* [id.]. Xue-Wei, LPO, Ivor Bolton – MENDELSSOHN: *Violin concerto.* ***
*** Chan. Dig. CHAN 8974; *ABTD 1563* [id.]. Hideko Udagawa, LSO, Mackerras – BRUCH: *Concerto No. 1.* ***
(M) *** Ph. 420 703-2. Grumiaux, New Philh. O, C. Davis – BRUCH: *Concerto No. 1.* **(*)
(B) *** Decca Dig. 433 604-2; *433 604-4* [id.]. Belkin, LSO, Fischer (with MASSENET: *Thaïs: Méditation:* Nigel Kennedy, National PO, Bonynge ***).
*** BMG/RCA RD 85402 [RCD1 5402]. Heifetz, Chicago SO, Reiner – BEETHOVEN: *Concerto.* **(*)
(M) (***) EMI mono CDH7 61011-2. Ginette Neveu, Philh. O, Issay Debrowen – SIBELIUS: *Concerto.* (***)
(M) **(*) Sony SMK 47540 [id.]. Francescatti, NYPO, Bernstein – SIBELIUS: *Concerto.* **(*)
(BB) **(*) BMG/RCA VD 60479; *VK 60479* [60479-2-RV; *60479-4-RV*]. Ughi, Philh. O, Sawallisch – BRUCH: *Concerto No. 1.* **(*)
(M) **(*) EMI CDM7 69034-2 [id.]. David Oistrakh, French Nat. R. O, Klemperer.
**(*) DG Dig. 400 064-2 [id.]. Mutter, BPO, Karajan.
**(*) EMI CDC7 47166-2 [id.]. Perlman, Chicago SO, Giulini.
**(*) EMI Dig. CDC7 54187-2; *EL 754187-4* [id.]. Nigel Kennedy, LPO, Klaus Tennstedt.

(i) *Violin concerto in D;* (ii) *Hungarian dances Nos. 1, 3, 5, 6, 17–21.*
(B) *** EMI CDZ7 62608-2; *LZ 762608-4*. (i) Menuhin, BPO, Kempe; (ii) RPO, Kubelik.

(i) *Violin concerto in D. Academic festival overture, Op. 80.*
**(*) DG Dig. 423 617-2 [id.]. (i) Mintz; BPO, Abbado.

(i) *Violin concerto in D. Tragic overture, Op. 81.*
(B) *** Ph. 422 972-2; *422 972-4*. (i) Hermann Krebbers; Concg. O, Haitink.

(i) *Violin concerto in D;* (ii) *Violin sonata No. 1 in G, Op. 78.*
(B) **(*) DG 429 513-2; *429 513-4* [id.]. Ferras, (i) BPO, Karajan; (ii) Pierre Barbizet.

(i) *Violin concerto in D;* (ii) *Violin sonata No. 2 in A, Op. 100.*
(M) **(*) DG 415 838-2 [id.]. Zukerman, (i) O de Paris, Barenboim; (ii) Barenboim (piano).

Hermann Krebbers, concertmaster of the Concertgebouw Orchestra, here gives one of the most deeply satisfying readings of the Brahms *Violin concerto* ever recorded: strong and urgent yet tenderly poetic too, and always full of spontaneous imagination. The total commitment behind the performance is not just the achievement of the soloist but also that of his colleagues and their conductor, who perform as at a live concert. The vintage, 1973 recording has been successfully remastered: the effect, with the violin slightly forward but not too obtrusively so, is full and immediate. The *Tragic overture* makes a suitable encore after the *Concerto*.

Xue-Wei's version of the Brahms, fresh and well-mannered, is particularly attractive when it is so generously coupled with the Mendelssohn *Concerto*, equally well done. There is a degree of emotional reticence here compared with more flamboyant performers but, with Ivor Bolton drawing first-rate playing from the LPO, it is a performance to live with and can be warmly recommended. The sound is first rate too.

Hideko Udagawa gives a powerful, persuasively spontaneous-sounding reading. Her daring in virtuosity, her biting attack on the most taxing passages, is often thrilling, even if her violin sound is not always the sweetest. The personality of the player and her magnetic temperament submerge reservations on detail, particularly when Mackerras draws comparably powerful playing from the LSO, with the opening tutti building tension strongly. Warm, full and well-balanced recording.

Reissued in EMI's bargain Laser series, with Kubelik's group of *Hungarian dances* offered as an engaging additional incentive, Menuhin's recording from the end of the 1950s can be given the strongest recommendation. He was in superb form, producing tone of great beauty, while the reading is memorable for its warmth and nobility. He was splendidly accompanied by Kempe, and the Berlin Philharmonic was inspired to outstanding playing – the oboe solo in the slow movement is particularly fine. The sound remains satisfyingly well balanced, and now compares very favourably indeed with any of the top recommendations for this work.

Grumiaux's performance, it goes without saying, is full of insight and lyrical eloquence, and Sir Colin Davis lends his soloist the most sympathetic support; at mid-price, coupled with the Max Bruch *G minor Concerto*, this excellent CD could well be first choice for many readers, particularly in view of the excellence of the remastered Philips sound.

Those looking for a bargain digital recording should be well pleased with Boris Belkin's 1983 Decca issue. The performance is deeply felt, direct and spontaneous and makes a strong impression. The tempo of the first movement is measured and spacious, though not as slow as Nigel Kennedy's full-priced version; and it is Kennedy who plays very appealingly in the Massenet lollipop which acts as an encore. With excellent sound and as good balance, this reissue is very competitive.

Like the Beethoven with which it is coupled, the CD transfer of Heifetz's dazzling performance makes vivid and fresh what on LP was originally a rather harsh Chicago recording, more aggressive than the Boston sound in the Beethoven. With the CD, the excellent qualities of RCA's Chicago balance for Reiner come out in full, giving a fine three-dimensional focus. The speeds for all three movements may be fast, but Heifetz's ease and detailed imagination make them more than just dazzling, while the central *Andante*, at a flowing speed, is delectably songful.

Ginette Neveu's is a magnificent performance, urgently electric, remarkable not just for the sweetness of tone and her pinpoint intonation but for the precision and clarity of even the most formidable passages of double-stopping. Though dynamic contrasts are limited, the transfer from the original 78s brings satisfyingly full-bodied sound, surprisingly good on detail.

The Francescatti/Bernstein performance (reissued generously coupled with Sibelius in Sony's Royal Bernstein Edition) show strongly those characteristics for which both artists are famous. Francescatti's tone is a very individual one, but this is passionate, warm-blooded playing, which Bernstein supports brilliantly. However the 1961 recording, made in the Manhattan Center, is artificially balanced and very brightly lit indeed: the orchestral violins are shrill and there is a strong forward placing for the soloist.

Ughi's account has the advantage of a strong and passionate orchestral backing from Sawallisch and first-rate (1983) digital sound, with a good balance. As with the Bruch coupling, this is a fresh, direct reading, not as charismatic as some, but with moments of considerable lyrical intensity and by no means unimaginative in the control of light and shade.

The conjunction of two such positive artists as Oistrakh and Klemperer makes for a reading characterful to the point of idiosyncrasy, monumental and strong rather than sweetly lyrical. Oistrakh sounds superbly poised and confident and in the finale, if the tempo is a shade deliberate, the total effect is one of clear gain. The 1961 recording is quite full, but the bright CD transfer has brought an element of steeliness to the solo violin timbre.

Zukerman's is a well-conceived reading that has finish and facility and is sweet-toned, but his general approach can often seem a little bland by comparison with some other versions. For the reissue the *A major Violin sonata* has been added, but this is also available, more appropriately coupled, with the other two sonatas – see below.

In many ways the playing of Anne-Sophie Mutter combines the unforced lyrical feeling of Krebbers with the flair and individuality of Perlman. There is a lightness of touch, a gentleness in the slow movement that is highly appealing, while in the finale the incisiveness of the solo playing is well displayed by the clear (yet not clinical) digital recording. Needless to say, Karajan's accompaniment is strong in personality and the Berlin Philharmonic play beautifully; the performance represents a genuine musical partnership between youthful inspiration and eager experience. The recording is given vivid presence, although its clarity emphasizes the close balance of the soloist, and there is a touch of fierceness in the orchestral upper range in tuttis. The lack of any coupling must also reduce the claims of this version.

Shlomo Mintz and Claudio Abbado give a beautifully cultured reading that is both relaxed and lyrical. Mintz is less than generously coupled, but he does have the advantage of a superbly balanced recording and predictably fine orchestral playing. Only in the rather heavy-handed finale does it fall short of real excellence; it belongs among the best without actually being a first choice – not that there can be any in these days of such duplication – but no one investing in it will be greatly disappointed. The *Academic festival overture*, well played though it is, hardly affects choice.

A distinguished account of the solo part from Perlman, finely supported by Giulini and the Chicago Symphony Orchestra, a reading of darker hue than is customary, with a thoughtful, searching slow movement rather than the autumnal rhapsody which it so often becomes; granted a certain want of impetus in the first movement, this is an impressive and convincing performance. However, with no coupling this seems too highly priced.

Kennedy's much-advertised version of the Brahms is by a fair margin the slowest ever put on disc. Not only are the basic speeds slow – notably in the first two movements – he allows himself extra slowings and tenutos at the least excuse. In principle the result may be intolerably self-indulgent, but Kennedy's musical personality (as opposed to his media image) and his devotion to the work (as he claims, his desert-island concerto) give an intensity to sustain all the eccentricities. The finale, less eccentric, is relatively small-scale and wild at times but conveys a winning sense of fun. This is a version to hear as a one-off experience rather than to live with; if through being a best-seller it brings new listeners to a supreme violin masterpiece, then it will have served its purpose. Tennstedt draws concentrated playing from the LPO, the whole richly recorded.

Violin concerto (with cadenzas by Busoni, Joachim, Singer, Hermann, Auer, Ysaÿe, Ondricek, Kneisel, Marteau, Kreisler, Tovey, Kubelik, Busch, Heifetz, Milstein, Ricci).
*** Biddulph Dig. LAW 002 [id.]. Ruggiero Ricci, Sinf. of London, Del Mar.

The Biddulph label, which has concentrated on resurrecting great recordings of string players of the past, here presents a tribute to the cadenza. The veteran, Ruggero Ricci, not only gives a strong, assured performance of the concerto, he adds no fewer than 16 cadenzas as well, any of which can be programmed into the main performance on CD. It is fascinating to find that the pianist, Busoni, wrote one of the most imaginative cadenzas, including the most dramatic timpani part. It may well have given Elgar the idea for the accompanied cadenza of his *Violin concerto*. Donald Tovey, another pianist-composer, provides one of the longest, most cogently argued cadenzas, but mainly they are by the great violinists of the past, not just Joachim, Auer, Ysaÿe and Kreisler, but Heifetz, Milstein and Ricci himself. Though Ricci is no longer as fiery or incisive as he once was, his is an attractive performance of the concerto, well recorded.

(i) *Violin concerto in D, Op. 77;* (ii) *Double concerto for violin, cello and orchestra, Op. 102.*
(M) **(*) Sony SBK 46335 [id.]. Stern, (ii) with Rose; Phd. O, Ormandy.

Stern's splendid 1959 account of the *Violin concerto* with Ormandy now returns to the catalogue satisfactorily remastered and, although the balance still spotlights the solo violin, the overall impression is of a better integration than in previous CD incarnations. For the first time we are also offered a coupling that is both generous and suitable, the mid-1960s' collaboration with Leonard Rose in the *Double concerto*. The two soloists unfailingly match each other's playing. Each has a creative ear in pointing a comment so that the response is made to sound like an unfolding conversation, with Ormandy always an understanding accompanist. The forward balance of the soloists brings glorious tone, even if this means that there are no pianissimos (although one can tell when they are playing quietly from the tone-colour). The CD transfer is well managed; though light in bass, the sound overall is full and clear.

Double concerto for violin, cello and orchestra in A min., Op. 102.
*** Sony Dig. MK 42387 [id.]. Isaac Stern, Yo-Yo Ma, Chicago SO, Abbado – *Piano quartet No. 3.* **
(B) *** EMI CDZ7 62854-2; *LZ 762854-4.* D. Oistrakh, Fournier, Philh. O, Galliera – BEETHOVEN: *Triple concerto.* **(*)
(B) **(*) Sony MYK 44771 [id.]. Francescatti, Fournier, Columbia SO, Bruno Walter – SCHUMANN: *Piano concerto.* **(*)

Double concerto; Tragic overture, Op. 81.
**(*) DG Dig. 410 603-2 [id.]. Mutter, Meneses, BPO, Karajan.

The CBS version with Isaac Stern, Yo-Yo Ma and the Chicago Symphony Orchestra under Claudio Abbado is one of the more successful of recent years and deserves a full recommendation. The balance is well judged, not too up-front as is the case with some rivals. There are occasional moments when Yo-Yo Ma reduces his tone to the barest whisper rather than a pianissimo, but for the most part expressive exaggeration is minimal and the playing of both soloists and orchestra alike is glorious. The *Piano quartet* coupling, however, is rather less successful.

With two young soloists, Karajan conducts an outstandingly spacious and strong performance. Anne-Sophie Mutter conveys a natural authority comparable to Karajan's own, and the precision and clarity of Meneses' cello as recorded make an excellent match. The central slow movement in its spacious way has a wonderful Brahmsian glow, and all these qualities come out the more vividly on CD, though the relatively close balance of the soloists – particularly the cellist – is evident, too. However, the coupling is not remarkably generous.

David Oistrakh's recording with Fournier dates from 1959, but it was balanced by Walter Legge and the sound remains remarkably satisfying. The performance is distinguished, strong and lyrical – the slow movement particularly fine – with Galliera and the Philharmonia providing excellent support.

Bruno Walter's recording with Francescatti and Fournier dates from 1959, and the CD represents another example of successful digital remastering which enhances the original balance within an attractively warm ambience. Fournier is magnificent and, if one can adjust to Francescatti's rather intense vibrato, this can stand among the most satisfying of available versions. Walter draws playing of great warmth from the Columbia orchestra.

Hungarian dances Nos. 1–21 (complete).
❀ (BB) *** Naxos Dig. 8.550110; *4550110* (Nos. 1–2; 4–21) Budapest SO, István Bogár.

(i) *Hungarian dances Nos. 1–21;* (ii) *Variations on a theme of Haydn, Op. 56a.*
(M) *** DG Dig./Analogue 431 594-2; *431 594-4* [id.]. (i) VPO; (ii) Dresden State O; Abbado.

Hungarian dances Nos. 1–21 (complete).
*** Ph. Dig. 411 426-2 [id.]. Leipzig GO, Masur.

The Budapest recording of the Brahms *Hungarian dances* is sheer delight from beginning to end. The playing has warmth and sparkle, and the natural way the music unfolds brings a refreshing feeling of rhythmic freedom. Yet there are also many delightful individual touches from the conductor, with the woodwind joyfully producing some most engaging colours. Bogár's rubato is wholly spontaneous; the strings bring plenty of temperament to their phrasing of the more sultry tunes, while their lighter articulation is infectious. The recording is warm and full, yet transparent, with just the right brilliance on top. This is an outright winner among the available versions, but there is a small snag with the layout and documentation. The *Third dance* (a charming *Allegretto* in F major, led by the woodwind) has inadvertently been added to track 2 and follows on immediately after the *Second dance*. The listing on the CD anticipates the presence of all 21 dances, separately banded and, from No. 3 (actually No. 4) onwards, gives the wrong timings, with each applying to the previous number. Even with this minor problem, which is primarily one of access, one would far rather have this set of dances (particularly on such an inexpensive disc) than any of the other alternative versions.

Abbado's fine complete digital set of the *Hungarian dances* now reappears at mid-price, coupled with his excellent 1972 Dresden account of the *Haydn variations*, a work he always did well.

In Nos. 5 and 6 Masur uses Parlow's scoring instead of Martin Schmelling (as preferred by Abbado) and in Nos. 7 and 8 he opts for Schollum rather than Hans Gál. Masur is just a shade more relaxed and smiling and the timbre of the strings is generally richer and warmer than that achieved by the DG engineers in Vienna. Abbado has great sparkle and lightness, but the Leipzig orchestra is hardly less dazzling than the Viennese. The Philips issue has the finer sound but costs much more and has no coupling.

Piano quartet in G min. (orch. Schoenberg).
*** Collins Dig. 1175-2; *1175-4* [id.]. LPO, Rozhdestvensky – RACHMANINOV: *Études-tableaux.* ***

Piano quartet in G min. (orch. Schoenberg); *Variations and fugue on a theme by Handel, Op. 24* (orch. Rubbra).
*** Chan. Dig. CHAN 8825; *ABTD 1450* [id.]. LSO, Järvi.

The current craze for Schoenberg's transcription of the Brahms *Piano quartet in G minor* is puzzling, and even more so is Schoenberg's recourse to glockenspiel and xylophone, which could be compared – if it hasn't been already – to painting a moustache on the Mona Lisa. When one recalls the relative neglect of the marvellous orchestral *Serenades*, it seems a pity that Schoenberg's essay should be so often duplicated. Brahms knew a thing or two about the orchestra and, had he wanted to score this quartet, he would doubtless have done so. If you want to hear it in this form, however, Neeme Järvi's new version with the LSO is as good as any. It is performed with some enthusiasm and well recorded.

So too, for that matter is Gennady Rozhdestvensky's account with the London Philharmonic, which makes out every bit as good a case for Schoenberg's often masterly scoring. Choice will probably depend on the coupling. Edmund Rubbra's transcription of the *Variations and fugue on a theme by Handel* is the more logical, though not all of it comes off equally well. Respighi was a greater man of the orchestra – though not perhaps so deep a composer – and his celebrated version of Rachmaninov's *Études-tableaux* sounds splendidly idiomatic.

Serenades Nos. 1 in D, Op. 11; 2 in A, Op. 16.
(B) **(*) Decca 421 628-2. LSO, Kertész.
(M) **(*) Ph. 432 510-2; *432 510-4* [id.]. Concg. O, Haitink.
**(*) Orfeo C 008101A [id.]. VSO, Gary Bertini.

The Kertész performances of the two *Serenades* are beautifully relaxed but at the same time alert, and the 1968 Decca recording emerges more clearly in detail, with a drier effect at the bass end, yet with the hall ambience retaining most of the bloom. But in some ways the original LPs sounded sweeter.

Haitink's account of the *D major Serenade* is finely proportioned, relaxed yet vital. The Concertgebouw wind-playing is particularly distinguished. However, the resonant Concertgebouw acoustics, while giving agreeably full textures, do not afford the same degree of freshness and transparency to the sound-picture as on the competing Decca version: the effect is more symphonic, less light-hearted. The *A major Serenade* has lighter scoring (the string section does without violins altogether) and, while the recording is warm, it is yet more lucid in detail. Haitink's performance is similarly sound in conception and well shaped, and the conductor's warmth is obvious. The Kertész performances have a slightly more vivid characterization and the Decca sound-quality is undoubtedly fresher and, if with less body to the strings, produces brighter wind colouring.

Bertini's account of the opening movement of the *D Major Serenade*, with its rollicking horns, has a boisterous geniality which is engaging, and throughout both works he draws much fine playing from the Vienna Symphony Orchestra; the woodwind provide appealing colour. Bertini maintains a fairly strong momentum for the *Adagio* slow movements, which is sensible enough, but he captures the relaxed atmosphere better in Op. 16 than in Op. 11. The resonant recording sounds really lovely at lower dynamic levels, but in fortissimos the opulence also brings a suggestion of heaviness. However, there is much agreeable Brahmsian warmth here; in general the greater amplitude of the sound is an advantage, and this is marginally preferable to the Kertész coupling.

Serenade No. 1 in D, Op. 11 (arr. Boustead for 9 players).
*** Ph. Dig. 426 298-2 [id.]. ASMF Chamber Ens. (with WAGNER: *Siegfried idyll* ***).

The Academy's version of the *D major Serenade* is one with a difference. The piece was originally designed for a chamber ensemble and owes its familiar orchestral form to Joachim, who persuaded Brahms to score it. The original score was subsequently destroyed and the present disc is a *conjectural* arrangement for a nonet of wind and string instruments reconstructed with no mean skill by Alan Boustead, whose notes give ample details of his reasoning. The result is both transparent and pleasing, though it is unlikely that this would ever displace the original from our affections. Wagner's *Siegfried idyll*, also in its original chamber scoring, makes a very suitable coupling and is beautifully played.

Serenade No. 1 in D, Op. 11; Academic festival overture; Tragic overture.
*** Sony Dig. SK 45932 [id.]. LSO, Michael Tilson Thomas.

This Sony version of the glorious *D major Serenade* has a sunny geniality and a youthful radiance that are most persuasive. Tilson Thomas's reading has both vitality and sensitivity in its favour, and the recording is very natural and well detailed. If the *Serenade* is your priority, the new Sony version must take precedence.

Serenade No. 2 in A, Op. 16; Academic festival overture; Variations on a theme by Haydn.
**(*) BMG/RCA Dig. RD 87920; *RK 87920* [7920-2-RC; *7920-4-RC*]. St Louis SO, Slatkin.

Leonard Slatkin gets very musical results from the excellent St Louis orchestra in the *Serenade No. 2*, and there is nothing slick about this sensitive, unforced performance. The recording is just a little two-dimensional and wanting in bloom. There was sufficient room to have given us the *D major Serenade* instead of yet another account of the *Academic festival overture* and the *St Anthony chorale variations*, which Michael Tilson Thomas also chooses for his Sony disc.

Serenade No. 2 in A, Op. 16; Hungarian dances Nos. 1, 3, 10, 17–21; Variations on a theme of Haydn (St Anthony chorale), Op. 56a.
*** Sony Dig. SK 47195 [id.]. LSO, Michael Tilson Thomas.

Sony missed a trick in not coupling Michael Tilson Thomas's musicianly accounts of the *Serenades* together. The *Second* comes with the *St Anthony chorale variations* and some *Hungarian dances*. Most collectors will hesitate before buying two full-price discs in order to get these lovely works, when there are very acceptable one-disc pairings at mid-price from Kertész and Haitink coupling both. All the same, those drawn towards this particular coupling need not hesitate. Tilson Thomas gets admirable results from the LSO and the Sony engineers serve them both well.

Symphonies Nos. 1–4.
(M) **(*) DG 429 644-2 (3) [id.]. BPO, Karajan.
(M) **(*) HM/BMG Dig. GD 60085; *GK 60085* (3) [60085-2-RG; *60085-4-RG*]. N. German RSO, Wand.

Symphonies Nos. 1–4; Academic festival overture.
(M) (**) EMI mono CHS7 64256-2 (2) [id.]. LSO, or LPO, Felix Weingartner.

Symphonies Nos. 1–4; Academic festival overture; Tragic overture; Variations on a theme of Haydn; (i) *Hungarian dances Nos. 17–21.*
(M) **(*) Sony SB3K 48398 (3). Cleveland O, George Szell; (i) Phd. O, Ormandy.

Symphonies Nos. 1–4; Tragic overture; Variations on a theme of Haydn.
**(*) DG Dig. 427 602-2 (3) [id.]. BPO, Karajan.

Broadly, Karajan's 1978 analogue cycle shows that his readings of the *Symphonies*, with lyrical and dramatic elements finely balanced, changed little over the years. It is worth noting that his approach to No. 3 is stronger and more direct, with less mannered phrasing in the third movement, but that he continues to omit the first-movement exposition repeat. The playing of the Berlin Philharmonic remains uniquely cultivated: the ensemble is finely polished, yet can produce tremendous bravura at times, as in the finales to the *First* and *Second Symphonies*. The remastering has freshened the sound: textures are clear and clean, but the effect is slightly polarized, with a bright, clean treble and a strong, firmly focused bass. There is less emphasis in the middle frequencies so that the Brahmsian richness is conveyed less readily.

Szell's powerful view of Brahms is consistently revealed in this masterful series of performances, recorded in the 1960s when he had made the Cleveland Orchestra America's finest. His approach is generally plain and direct, crisp and detached rather than smooth and moulded. Speeds are broad, but only in the first movement of No. 4 does that undermine the electric tension of conductor and orchestra. In the manner of the time, no exposition repeats are observed, not even in No. 3. Though the sound, as transferred, is not as full as on the original LPs, it is clear and bright, with superb detail. The woodwind have bloom and the acoustics of Severance Hall provide an attractive ambience and weight. The overtures are comparably vibrant; the *Variations* are particularly successful, rather more mellow. However, the five *Hungarian dances* tacked on to the end of the first disc are less impressively transferred. Ormandy and his splendid orchestra play them with fine panache, but the 1957 recording produces comparatively emaciated violin-tone. The woodwind have bloom and the acoustics of Severance Hall provide an attractive ambience and weight. The overtures are comparably vibrant; the *Variations* are particularly successful, rather more mellow. However, the five *Hungarian dances* tacked on to the end of the first disc are less impressively transferred. Ormandy and his splendid orchestra play them with fine panache, but the 1957 recording produces comparatively emaciated violin-tone.

Wand's complete cycle, originally on EMI and now reissued on three mid-priced Deutsche Harmonia Mundi discs, has the advantage of digital recording, although the sound brings a degree of fierceness on violin tone in all but No. 2. Wand's is a consistently direct view of Brahms, yet the reading of each symphony has its own individuality. In the opening movement of the *First*, he brings great intensity to the slow introduction by choosing an unusually fast speed, then leading naturally by modular pacing into the main allegro. The extra unity is clear. Even though he does not observe the exposition repeat, Wand's reading of the *Second* is the pick of his Brahms series, a characteristically glowing but steady reading, recorded with a fullness and bloom that are missing in his companion issues. In the *Third Symphony* Wand does observe the exposition repeat and his wise way with Brahms, strong and easy and steadily paced, works beautifully here, bringing out the autumnal moods, ending with a sober view of the finale. By contrast, the reading of No. 4 initially seems understated. At a fastish speed, the first movement is melancholy rather than tragic, while the slow movement, similarly steady and flowing, makes no great expansion for the big melody of the counter-subject. It is quite a strong reading, but marred by recording that is less than ideally clear, with edgy violins as in Nos. 1 and 3.

With variably focused sound, Karajan's last cycle of the Brahms *Symphonies* is not his finest; but he remained a natural Brahmsian to the last, and this compilation, with Nos. 2 and 3 on the second disc, and No. 4 coupled with the *Variations*, makes a better investment than the original issues, for those who must have digital sound. However, this set is at full price.

Weingartner's 'lean-beef' Beethoven (to use Peter Stadlen's memorable phrase) is long overdue for reissue, and should perhaps have taken priority over his Brahms symphonies with the London orchestras. All the same these are a joy to listen to as a reminder of a music-making now almost lost to view. Weingartner gives straightforward, no nonsense readings, totally classical in conception without perhaps the tautness, or intensity of Toscanini or the richness of Furtwängler. Cultured and unfussy music-making though there are moments of less than absolutely true intonation. The sound calls for some tolerance (one is conscious of the limited frequency range) and the transfers are not the most distinguished of recent months.

Symphonies Nos. 1–4; Academic festival overture; (i) *Double concerto in A min., Op. 102. Hungarian dances Nos. 1, 17, 20 & 21; Tragic overture; Variations on a theme of Haydn;* (ii) *Liebeslieder-Walzer, Op. 52;* (iii) *Song of the Fates (Gesang der Parzen). Op. 89.*
(M) (***) BMG/RCA mono GD 60325; *GK 60325* (4) [60325-2-RG; *60325-4-RG*]. NBC SO, Toscanini, with (i) Mischakoff, Miller; (ii) Ch., Artur Balsam, Joseph Kahn; (iii) (without O) Robert Shaw Ch.

The *First Symphony* starts very fast and intensely; but often speeds are surprisingly broad, and the *Fourth Symphony*, Toscanini's favourite, brings a magnificent performance. The soloists in the *Double concerto* were principals in the NBC orchestra, Mischa Mischakoff and Frank Miller, both very fine artists, even though Toscanini allowed them less expressive freedom than they really needed. The CD transfers do everything possible for the dry and limited original sound. The extra items date mainly from 1948, recorded several years earlier than the symphonies.

Symphony No. 1 in C min., Op. 68.
(B) *** DG 431 161-2; *431 161-4* [id.]. BPO, Karajan – SCHUMANN: *Overture, Scherzo and Finale.* ***
(B) **(*) Sony MYK 44827 [id.]. Columbia SO, Bruno Walter.
**(*) DG Dig. 423 141-2 [id.]. BPO, Karajan.
(*) Chesky CD 19. LSO, Jascha Horenstein (with WAGNER: *Tannhäuser: Venusburg Bacchanale* *).

Symphony No. 1; Academic festival overture, Op. 80.
(B) *** Pickwick Dig. PCD 882; *CIMPC 882* [id.]. Hallé O, Skrowaczewski.

Symphony No. 1; Academic festival overture; Tragic overture.
(M) *** EMI CDM7 69651-2 [id.]. Philh. O, Klemperer.
(M) *** Ph. 432 275-2; *432 275-4.* Concg. O, Haitink.

Symphony No. 1; Serenade No. 2 in A, Op. 16.
(M) *(**) Sony SMK 47536 [id.]. NYPO, Leonard Bernstein.
(M) (**) BMG/RCA mono GD 60277 [60277-2-RG]. NBC SO, Toscanini.

Symphony No. 1; Variations on a theme of Haydn, Op. 56a.
(M) *** DG 427 253-2; *427 253-4* [id.]. BPO, Karajan.

(i) *Symphony No. 1; Variations on a theme of Haydn;* (ii) *Hungarian dances Nos. 17–21.*
(M) **(*) Sony SBK 46534 [id.]. (i) Cleveland O, Szell; (ii) Phd. O, Ormandy.

Symphony No. 1; (i) *Alto rhapsody, Op. 53.*
(B) *** CfP CD-CFP 4594; *TC-CFP 4594* [id.]. Hallé O, James Loughran; (i) with Bernadette Greevy and Hallé Ch.

Klemperer's spacious opening with its thundering, relentless timpani strokes is as compelling as ever and the close of the work has a comparable majesty. Elsewhere, other versions may find greater incandescence, but the reading remains unique for its feeling of authority and power, supported by consistently fine Philharmonia playing. The remastered sound has gained in clarity while retaining its fullness. The *Tragic overture* suits Klemperer particularly well, but the *Academic festival overture* is made to sound grand rather than high-spirited.

Karajan's 1978 analogue recording – his fourth – is also highly recommendable (especially at bargain price and now with its present Schumann coupling), and the sound is still remarkably good.

Haitink's 1972 version of the *First Symphony* emerges splendidly in its remastered CD format. It is a strong, well-argued reading of considerable power, and superbly played. Haitink does not observe the first-movement exposition repeat but, that apart, it remains among the very finest versions, with recording that is full and spacious and well balanced. The *Tragic overture* is also a particularly arresting account, and the *Academic festival overture* has plenty of vitality.

With the return of a justly famous Classics for Pleasure Brahms series, James Loughran provides a fully recommendable bargain version which, on its original issue (1974), was the first to observe the exposition repeat in the opening movement. The reading is refreshingly spontaneous from first to last. The second and third movements both have a spring-like quality, and the slow movement is less sweet than usual, while the 6/8 trio of the third movement is for once taken at a speed which allows the climax not to sound breathless. The introduction to the finale, with fine horn and trombone playing, is weighty and concentrated, while the great string melody is richly presented, yet not smoothed over at all. The entry of the chorale at the end finds Loughran charateristically refusing to slow down to half-speed. The whole orchestra – during a peak period – shows a natural feeling for Brahms's style. The recording is sucessfully remastered and retains its body and freshness. The reissue offers an almost equally fine performance of the *Alto rhapsody* with Bernadette Greevy in glorious voice. She gives a forthright account of the solo part, not subtle but warmly enjoyable.

Szell's account of No. 1 is one of the most impressive of his set. His bold, direct thrust gives the outer movements plenty of power and impetus, and the inner movements bring relaxation and a fair degree of warmth. The *Variations* are strongly characterized, too, and have plenty of finesse in the matter of light and shade. But, as in the symphony, Szell does not seek to charm. The sound is remarkably good. For an encore Ormandy chooses the last five *Hungarian dances,* as orchestrated by Dvořák, and plays them with characteristic flair. However, the recording is much thinner here.

Bernstein's Sony recording of Brahms's *First* is highly idiosyncratic, but not as wilfully inconsistent in the finale as in his later Vienna version. In New York the great string tune, presented slowly and warmly, is at least played at the same tempo each time it appears, and Bernstein waits until after its reprise before setting off to provide an exhilarating burst of free-flowing adrenalin for the closing section, which nearly goes over the top. The whole performance, with its constant ebb and flow of tension and rubato, has all the hallmarks of his live music-making; both the outer movements commence with a powerful display of histrionics, yet the *Andante*, has an appealing simplicity and warmth, for all its freedom of manner. The 1960 sound is surprisingly full, with the acoustics of the Manhattan Center giving plenty of space, even though the microphones are fairly close to the orchestra. The *Serenade*, however, is a non-starter. Bernstein gives an uncharacteristically dull performance. There are glimmerings of charm at the beginning of the first and last movements, but the *Adagio* drags. The 1966 sound is warm and glowing.

Walter's first two movements have a white-hot intensity that shows this conductor at his very finest. The third movement begins with a less than ravishing clarinet solo and, though the 6/8 section is lively enough, the playing is not as crisp as in the first two movements. In the finale the performance reasserts itself, although some might find the big string tune too slow. The remastered recording makes the strings sound richly beautiful here; and later the brass is comparably sonorous.

Skrowaczewski conducts the Hallé in a powerful performance of No. 1, both warmly sympathetic and refined, with sound which is fresh, bright and clear and with a good, open atmosphere. The first movement is ideally paced, purposeful without undue rush – and also without the exposition repeat. His view of the finale is big and bold, but with a rather old-fashioned slowing for the final appearance of the chorale theme in the coda. With an account of the *Academic festival overture* textured with similar refinement, it makes an excellent bargain-price digital choice.

Karajan in his 1987 digital recording draws a typically powerful and dramatic performance from the Berlin Philharmonic. The sound is full and weighty to match on CD, but tends to be thick and generalized in tuttis. It is comfortable enough overall but could be better defined. Characteristically Karajan does not observe the first-movement exposition repeat; with any reservations about that and the relative lack of inner clarity, this still takes its place among the list of recommendations.

The refinement of Horenstein's reading comes out incomparably at the start of the *Andante*, wonderfully delicate in lyricism at a really hushed pianissimo. Horenstein is a Brahmsian who, with a broadly expressive style from phrase to phrase, yet prefers to keep a basically steady pulse through a movement. The LSO was at its peak when this record was made, at Walthamstow Town Hall, for Reader's Digest magazine in the 1960s (the horn playing is magnificent) and, with well-balanced recording, this can be strongly recommended to Horenstein admirers, although the fact that it is a premium-price reissue will make it less attractive for the general collector. The curious coupling of the *Venusberg* sequence from *Tannhäuser* makes an attractive bonus, with spacious direction and fine singing from the Beecham Choral Society.

The *First Symphony* is the performance Toscanini recorded in Carnegie Hall during 1941, and which subsequently appeared on a 78-r.p.m. set containing an announcement of his resignation from the NBC. It differs from the version he made ten years later with the same orchestra in the greater breadth of the first movement allegro, and in the tenderness he shows in the *Andante*, which at the same time remains completely unsentimental. The sound is not at all bad for the period though more critical equipment will tame the acidulated top. There is however little one can do with the 1942 broadcast – made in Studio 8-H – of the *Serenade*. The performance, too, is held together on a tight rein and sounds somewhat unrelaxed. The scherzo movement is particularly unbeguiling.

(i) *Symphonies Nos. 1;* (ii) *4 in E min., Op. 98* (CD only: (iii) *Tragic overture;* (iv) *Variations on a theme of Haydn*).
(B) *** DG Compact Classics 413 424-2 (2); *413 424-4* [id.]. (i) BPO; (ii) VPO, Boehm (CD only: (iii) BPO, Maazel; (iv) LSO, Jochum).

Anyone learning their Brahms from Boehm's performances cannot go far wrong, and these very satisfying readings comprise one of the very finest issues in DG's Compact Classics series. His Berlin Philharmonic version of the *First* is a centrally recommendable version, with tempi that are steady rather than volatile; but, with polished playing from the Berliners, the performance is undoubtedly very compelling and the well-balanced recording emerges here to excellent effect. Boehm's account of the *Fourth* was the most successful performance in his Vienna cycle, with a spacious and noble reading of the first movement and a finely contrasted view of the final *Passacaglia*, lyrical and dramatic elements sharply defined. It remains among the very finest performances of this work ever committed to disc. The remastered sound is full-blooded and has plenty of life and warmth on CD and tape alike, with the bass rather more resonant on cassette. For the pair of digitally remastered CDs, Maazel's self-consciously brilliant account of the *Tragic overture* has been added, plus Jochum's fresh LSO version of the *St Anthony Variations.*

Symphony No. 2 in D, Op. 73.
(M) *** DG 435 067-2; *435 067-4* [id.]. BPO, Karajan – SCHUMANN: *Symphony No. 2.* ***
(M) **(*) Unicorn UKCD 2036 [id.]. Danish RSO, Horenstein (with recorded interview between Jascha Horenstein and Alan Blyth).
*** Decca Dig. 430 324-2; *430 324-4* [id.]. Concg. O, Chailly – WEBERN: *Im Sommerwind.* ***

Symphony No. 2; Academic festival overture, Op. 80.
(B) *** Sony MYK 44870. Columbia SO, Bruno Walter.

Symphony No. 2; Academic festival overture; Tragic overture.
(B) *** CfP CD-CFP 4595; *TC-CFP 4595.* Hallé O, James Loughran.
(M) **(*) DG Dig. 431 592-2; *431 592-4* [id.]. VPO, Bernstein.

Symphony No. 2; Academic festival overture; (i) *Song of destiny.*
(M) **(*) EMI CDM7 63221-2; *EG 763221-4.* (i) Beecham Ch. Soc.; RPO, Beecham.

Symphony No. 2; Tragic overture, Op. 81.
(B) **(*) Pickwick Dig. PCD 857; *CIMPC 857* [id.]. Hallé O, Skrowaczewski.

Symphony No. 2; Variations on a theme of Haydn, Op. 56a.
*** DG Dig. 423 142-2; *423 142-4* [id.]. BPO, Karajan.

Symphony No. 2; (i) *Alto rhapsody, Op. 53.*
*** DG Dig. 427 643-2 [id.]. (i) Lipovšek, Senff Ch.; BPO, Abbado.
(M) *** EMI CDM7 69650-2 [id.]; *EG 769650-4.* (i) Ludwig, Philh. Ch.; Philh. O, Klemperer.

This was the first recording to be issued from Abbado with the Berlin Philharmonic after his appointment was announced as chief conductor of the orchestra. Though the recording was made before the decision was taken, its glowing intensity from first to last reflects a special relationship, one of his very finest discs in years, bringing DG sound of exceptional fullness, vividness and reality. Among modern versions this now stands as an easy first choice, particularly when, with Marjana Lipovšek a radiant soloist, it also contains a gravely beautiful account of the *Alto rhapsody*. Abbado's approach to Brahms is generally direct, but his control of rhythm and phrase makes the performance instantly compelling. He observes the exposition repeat in the first movement; and there, as well as in the slow movement, the nobility of Brahms's inspiration is fully brought out, while in the finale, through his rhythmic control, Abbado makes a relatively measured speed sound much more exciting than it does with any of the speed-merchants. This is an outstanding version in every way.

Karajan's 1978 recording of the Brahms *Second* is helped by superb playing from the Berlin Philharmonic on peak form. Overall the reading is more direct, less mellow than the earlier (1964) account – see below – and this is most striking in the third movement. The finale has even more impetus than before, its brilliant pacing challenging the Berliners to exciting virtuosity. Some will prefer the earlier version, but the sound here is obviously more modern; it is balanced relatively close, but with lively atmosphere, and the coupling with Schumann is very generous.

In his 1987 digital Brahms series, Karajan's reading of the *Second Symphony* suffers less than the *First* from the thick, undifferentiated recording, when textures in this later work tend to be lighter. It is a magnificent reading, even warmer and more glowing than his previous versions, with consistently fine playing from the Berlin Philharmonic, who approach with striking freshness a symphony which they must have played countless times. As in the *First Symphony*, Karajan omits the first-movement exposition repeat, but compensates with an appealing performance of the *Haydn variations.* However, his splendid mid-1960s version is now available, coupled with No. 3 and offered at bargain price – see below.

Walter's performance of Brahms's *Second Symphony* is wonderfully sympathetic, with an inevitability, a rightness which makes it hard to concentrate on the interpretation as such, so cogent is the musical argument. It is a masterly conception overall and one very easy to live with. The CD opens with a vigorous and yet expansive account of the *Academic festival overture*, sumptuously recorded; in the remastering of the *Symphony* there is some loss in the lower-middle and bass, which is less richly resonant than in the *First Symphony*. But the bloom remains, and at bargain price this remains highly recommendable.

Klemperer's is also a great performance, the product of a strong and vital intelligence. He may seem a trifle severe and uncompromising, but he was at his peak in his Brahms cycle and he underlines the power of the *Symphony* without diminishing its eloquence in any way. The *Alto rhapsody*, with Klemperer at his most masterful and Ludwig on fine form, is a beautifully expressive performance that brings out the work's strength as well as its lyricism. Ludwig sings gloriously in the opening section, and later her voice blends naturally with the male chorus.

Anyone who fancies a nature tone-poem as lusciously evocative as any Delius to accompany their Brahms will find the Chailly version the perfect answer. The Webern makes the perfect 'Guess what?' item, and the Brahms performance is attractively fresh and direct, superbly played and recorded in full, bright, Decca sound, with plenty of detail. Chailly prefers a relatively plain and detached Brahms style with generally steady tempi, but there is no lack of warmth either. Only in an account of the third movement that is rather short on charm does the directness obtrude at all.

The Beecham magic makes his volatile reading consistently compelling. The horns at the opening may be disappointing but the first movement is then urgently riveting at speeds faster than usual. Beecham is also on the fast side in the second-movement *Adagio*, but his fine detailing there and in the third movement is totally distinctive, and the finale, rough at times, predictably brings an exhilarating close. The fill-ups are equally desirable, particularly the rare *Song of destiny*, sung in Denis Vaughan's English translation.

As a Brahmsian James Loughran is a master of tradition, and his account of No. 2 has a natural, warm flow, carrying the listener on, even while the basic approach is direct and unfussy. On interpretation his reading – exposition repeat included – matches and even outshines any in the catalogue, at whatever price, and the recording is warm and naturally balanced, though there are one or two noticeable tape joins. The Hallé ensemble and string-tone are not always quite as polished as in the versions from metropolitan orchestras, but the sense of spontaneity is ample compensation. The *Academic festival overture* is also a fine performance, after a rather limp start. The CD transfers are first rate, freshening the sound without loss of body and bloom to the strings.

With beautifully open and transparent sound, Skrowaczewski and the Hallé Orchestra give a measured and restrained reading, unsensational, fresh and thoughtful. The opening may seem sleepy, but Skrowaczewski's broad speeds and patient manner build up increasingly as the work progresses. With exposition repeat observed and a generous fill-up, plus excellent digital recording, luminous to match the performance, it is a good bargain-priced recommendation.

Bernstein's live 1982 recording is a warm, expansive account, notably less free and idiosyncratic than the others in his Vienna cycle, yet comparably rhythmic and equally spontaneous-sounding. With good recording, considering the limitations of a live concert, this is worth considering at mid-price.

Horenstein's highly characterful account of the *Second Symphony* was recorded live in Copenhagen in March 1972. The reading – which includes the first-movement exposition repeat – is marked by spaciousness and lyricism, and only in the finale, which avoids any suspicion of whipping up excitement, will some listeners feel that the result is a shade reserved, though the performance does not lack spontaneous feeling. Well-balanced radio recording, which has transferred well to CD. The recording includes a 20-minute BBC interview, with the conductor talking to Alan Blyth. This will be of interest to admirers of the conductor, although it has no connection with the present record.

Symphonies Nos. 2–3.
(B) *** DG 429 153-2; *429 153-4* [id.]. BPO, Karajan.
(M) **(*) Ph. 426 632-2; *426 632-4*. Concg. O, Haitink.
(M) **(*) Sony SMK 47537 [id.]. NYPO, Leonard Bernstein.

(i) *Symphonies Nos. 2–3;* (ii) *Academic festival overture.*
(B) **(*) DG Compact Classics *415 334-4*. (i) VPO, Boehm; (ii) BPO, Abbado.

Karajan's 1964 reading of the *Second* is among the sunniest and most lyrical accounts, and its sound is fully competitive even now. The companion performance of the *Third* is marginally less compelling, but still very fine. He takes the opening expansively – which makes it surprising that he omits the exposition repeat. But clearly he sees the work as a whole: the third movement is also slow and perhaps slightly indulgent, but the closing pages of the finale have a memorable autumnal serenity. A bargain.

Haitink's account of No. 2 opens soberly. The sunshine quickly breaks through, however, so that the gentle high entry of the violins is magically sweet. This is a thoughtful reading, marked by beautifully refined string playing, but in a way it is too controlled. The *Third* is much more impressive. The playing of the Concertgebouw Orchestra here is distinguished by unanimity of attack and chording, wonderfully true intonation and homogeneity of tone; and Haitink's firmness of grip and lyrical eloquence make this a very satisfying account. The sound is fresh yet full in the Philips manner.

Bernstein's record of the *Second* was made in 'tuning week' at the Lincoln Center's Avery Fisher Hall in May 1962 and the original LP was dim and muddy. But the transfer engineers have worked wonders with the sound balance, and the results (if more like a European than an American recording), have more body and weight in the bass than the other symphonies in his Brahms cycle. The performance – exposition repeat omitted – is enjoyable, if not outstanding, although in the finale the high running adrenalin brings a thrilling close to the work. The *Third*, made in the Mantattan Center in 1964 sounds brighter, with a brilliant sheen on the violins not quite balanced by the degree of weight in the bass. But here Bernstein brings real warmth to Brahms, not surface emotion but feeling from the heart. The first movement – exposition repeat included – is particularly successful; although not hard driven it yet has an urgency that makes most rivals seem reticent. The finale, too, is particularly satisfying. It is a pity that the close balance prevents a real pianissimo from being conveyed, an important point in Brahms. This disc may not quite rival the best current versions, but any Bernstein admirer should certainly hear it.

Boehm's readings of the two middle symphonies will seem to most Brahmsians more idiosyncratic than those of Nos. 1 and 4. His approach to the *Second Symphony* is certainly volatile in the first movement, with the *Adagio* very expansive indeed. But here the conductor's moulded style rivets the attention and one quickly accepts the extra spaciousness. After a gracefully phrased *Allegretto*, the finale is strong. The *Third Symphony* is very broadly conceived, the reins held comparatively slackly throughout until the finale, where the increased momentum creates a sense of apotheosis. The recordings date from 1976 and sound well. The excellent account of the *Academic festival overture* by Abbado makes a good bonus for a chrome cassette already offered at bargain price. This has not yet been issued on CD.

Symphony No. 3 in F; Tragic overture.
(B) *** CfP CD-CFP 4599; *TC-CFP 4599*. Hallé O, James Loughran.

Symphony No. 3 in F; Tragic overture; (i) *Song of Destiny (Schicksalslied), Op. 54.*
*** DG Dig. 429 765-2; *429 765-4* [id.]. BPO, Abbado; (i) with Ernest-Senff Ch.

Symphony No. 3; Variations on a theme of Haydn, Op. 56a.
(B) *** Sony CD 42022 [id.]. Columbia SO, Bruno Walter.
(B) *** Pickwick Dig. PCD 906; *CIMPC 906* [id.]. Hallé O, Skrowaczewski.

As in his earlier recording of No. 2 with the Berlin Philharmonic, Abbado directs a glowing, affectionate performance of No. 3, adopting generally spacious speeds and finely moulded phrasing but never sounding self-conscious, thanks to the natural tension which gives the illusion of live, spontaneous music-making. The rich, well-balanced, clean-textured recording underlines the big dramatic contrasts, and the playing matches the finest achieved by this great orchestra in the Karajan period, smooth still but with more emphasis on clarity. This now heads the list of modern digital recordings of this symphony. The *Tragic overture* brings a brisk, keenly dramatic performance, and the rare cantata makes a very welcome extra, given a warm, intense performance, beautifully sung.

Bruno Walter's *Third* is no less highly recommendable, both as a performance and as a recording. His pacing is admirable and the vigour and sense of joy which imbues the opening of the first movement (exposition repeat included) dominate throughout, with the second subject eased in with wonderful naturalness. The central movements provide contrast, though with an intense middle section in II. There is beautifully phrased string and horn playing in the *Poco*

Allegretto. The finale goes splendidly, the secondary theme given characteristic breadth and dignity and the softening of mood for the coda sounding structurally inevitable. The CD transfer brings soaring upper strings, excellent detail with glowing woodwind, and a supporting weight. The account of the *Variations* is relaxed and smiling, with deft and affectionate detail, moving forward to a majestic restatement of the chorale.

Skrowaczewski chooses consistently slow tempi for the central movements, yet with refined playing there is no hint of dragging. In the third movement he underlines the tender wistfulness, with a gorgeous horn solo in the reprise, full and spacious. The hush at the start of the finale then leads to a powerfully rhythmic performance, ending with a most refined account of the gentle coda. An excellent digital bargain-price version, well coupled with a fresh reading of the *Haydn variations*.

Loughran, so urgently spontaneous in the first two Brahms symphonies, takes an unexpectedly measured view of No. 3. Though initally his slow tempi for all four movements may seem to undermine tension, on repetition this emerges as an unusually satisfying reading, presenting the symphony as an autumnal work, with lighter scoring than in its companions. The total impression is of toughness and restraint, set alongside flowing lyricism. As is habitual with Loughran, the exposition repeat is observed in the first movement, an important point in this of all Brahms symphonies. Full atmospheric recording: a welcome bargain recommendation, even if the coupling is ungenerous.

Symphonies Nos. (i) *3 in F, Op. 90;* (ii) *4 in E min., Op. 98.*
(M) *** EMI CDM7 69649-2 [id.]. Philh. O, Klemperer.
(M) *** DG 431 593-2; *431 593-4* [id.]. BPO, Karajan.
(*(**)) Koch Legacy mono 3-7120-2 [id.]. (i) VPO; (ii) BBC SO, Bruno Walter.

For all his expansiveness, Klemperer does not make No. 3 sound opulent. There is a severity about his approach which may at first seem unappealing but which comes to underline the strength of the architecture. Similarly in No. 4, Klemperer's granite strength and his feeling for Brahmsian lyricism make his version one of the most satisfying ever recorded. The finale may lack something in sheer excitement, but the gravity of Klemperer's tone of voice, natural and unforced in this movement as in the others, makes for a compelling result. The remastering, like the others in the Klemperer/Brahms series, brings brightly lit violin timbre, with woodwind fairly forward, and there is no lack of body in the middle, while the bass is firmer.

In his 1978 recording Karajan gives superb grandeur to the opening of the *Third Symphony* but then characteristically refuses to observe the exposition repeat. Comparing this reading with Karajan's earlier, 1964 version (coupled with No. 2), one finds him more direct, noticeably less mannered in his treatment of the third movement and strikingly more dynamic and compelling. Though one may criticize the recording balance, the result is powerful and immediate. In the *Fourth Symphony* Karajan refuses to overstate the first movement, starting with deceptive reticence. His easy, lyrical style, less moulded in this 1978 reading than in his 1964 account, is fresh and unaffected and highly persuasive. The scherzo, fierce and strong, leads to a clean, weighty account of the finale. The overall performance is very satisfying. The recording is vivid but, as with the *F major Symphony*, balances are not quite natural.

The Koch Legacy reissue is a splendid reminder of the humane values of music-making under Bruno Walter in the 1930s. His account of the *Third Symphony* was recorded with the Vienna Philharmonic in 1936 and remains (along with Koussevitzky's 1947 Boston account) one of the very greatest to appear on 78s. It has the tautness and lyricism of his Columbia account but paradoxically has a sunnier, more relaxed quality, full of humanity and warmth. Although it was not perhaps as impressive as Karl Boehm's account of the *Fourth Symphony* with the Saxon State Orchestra, of which we badly need a really fine CD transfer, Walter's BBC account is well worth having as a reminder of how well the then newly-founded BBC Symphony Orchestra could stand up to the Vienna Orchestra. One suspects that these recordings could sound even better if transferred by the technicians who managed the recent 'Elgar Edition'; here the upper strings sound a bit raw and wanting in bloom, but one soon forgets sonic limitations so compelling are these performances.

Symphony No. 4 in E min., Op. 98.
**(*) DG Dig. 400 037-2 [id.]. VPO, Carlos Kleiber.
**(*) Chesky CD 6 [id.]. RPO, Fritz Reiner (with BEETHOVEN: *Egmont overture*, cond. René Leibowitz).

Symphony No. 4; Academic festival overture; Tragic overture.
(M) ** Sony SMK 47538-2 [id.]. NYPO, Bernstein.

Symphony No. 4; Hungarian dances Nos. 1, 3 & 10.
(B) *** Pickwick Dig. PCD 897; *CIMPC 897* [id.]. Hallé O, Skrowaczewski.

Symphony No 4; Tragic overture, Op. 81.
*** DG Dig. 429 403-2; *429 403-4* [id.]. VPO, Giulini.
(B) *** Sony MYK 44776 [id.]. Columbia SO, Bruno Walter.
*** DG Dig. 410 084-2 [id.]. VPO, Bernstein.

Symphony No. 4; Variations on a theme of Haydn (St Anthony chorale), Op. 56a.
(M) **(*) Decca 430 440-2; *430 440-4* [id.]. Chicago SO, Solti.

In considering recordings of the *Fourth Symphony*, Karl Boehm's outstanding VPO version should not be forgotten, coupled with No. 1 on DG's Compact Classics – see above.

Very characteristically, Giulini takes the most spacious view in his live recording with the Vienna Philharmonic, and though in principle the speeds are too slow, the result has a radiance and luminosity that magnetically set it apart. As the delicate opening demonstrates, Giulini's affectionate control of line completely disguises any slowness, and in the development the big, dramatic fortissimo contrasts bring a rugged manner, equally compelling. The great melody of the slow movement is rapt and refined as well as warm, and the last two movements bring satisfyingly extreme contrasts of tension and dynamic, helped by the rich and refined recording. The *Tragic overture* is given a similarly spacious and affectionate reading, with slow speeds again masterfully sustained. There is no applause at the end of either work, suggesting that there was an editing session after the live concert.

Walter's opening is simple, even gentle, and the pervading lyricism is immediately apparent; yet power and authority are underlying. The conductor's refusal to linger by a wayside always painted in gently glowing colours adds strength, building a cumulative effect. The slow movement, essentially serene yet intense at its central climax, is balanced by a vivacious, exhilarating scherzo. The finale has an underlying impetus so that Walter creates a feeling of inevitability throughout. The *Tragic overture* opens the record powerfully, so that the mellow opening of the *Symphony* is the more striking. The CD brings full, well-balanced sound in an attractively spacious ambience.

Bernstein's Vienna version of Brahms's *Fourth*, recorded live, is exhilaratingly dramatic in fast music, while the slow movement brings richly resonant playing from the Vienna strings, not least in the great cello melody at bar 41, which with its moulded rubato comes to sound surprisingly like Elgar.

The refinement of the very opening in Skrowaczewski's Pickwick version leads to an exceptionally satisfying reading, outstanding in the bargain-price range and finer than many full-price versions. The phrasing is affectionate without ever sounding self-conscious, and the alertness as well as the refinement of the Hallé playing confirms the excellence; if the coupling of only three *Hungarian dances* is hardly generous, they are certainly attractively presented.

Solti's *Fourth*, the finest of his cycle, returns to the catalogue at mid-price with a comparably fine account of the *Variations* as coupling. The reading shows him at his most vibrantly individual when, after a very direct, strongly motivated first movement, his view of the *Andante moderato* second movement is more an *Adagio*, unfailingly pure and eloquent. The scherzo has ebullience and the finale undoubted power. The playing of the Chicago orchestra is magnificent and the recording, full and precise, has been remastered and the bass made firm.

Any record from Carlos Kleiber is an event, and his is a performance of real stature. Everything is shaped with the attention to detail one would expect from this great conductor. A gripping and compelling performance. However, the limitations of the early digital recording are exposed here. The strings above the stave sound a little shrill and glassy, while there is a want of opulence in the bass.

Reiner's *Fourth*, one of his rare recordings with the RPO, was made for *Reader's Digest* in the early 1960s. It is one of the tautest readings available, without any loss of warmth. The RPO made this record with Beecham personnel still present, and the incisive playing brings strength as well as warmth and polish. The first movement may strike some readers as too fast and its opening not sufficiently spacious, but few would question its sense of flow and urgency. The excellent recording was made in Walthamstow Town Hall. Leibowitz provides a vibrant filler in a strong account of the *Egmont overture*. However, the attractions of this reissue are diminished by its no longer being in the mid-price range, as it once was on LP.

The *Fourth*, which was the most successful of Bernstein's later DG Vienna set of the symphonies, is here the least charismatic of the series of recordings made for CBS in the early 1960s. The reading, rather plain and direct, while always lyrical in phrasing, fails to catch fire, not even in the slow movement, which was to be so full of ardour in Vienna two decades later. Here Bernstein is not helped by the close balance, which prevents any kind of hushed quality in the *Andante*. Otherwise the sound is good for its period, but in the lively accounts of the two overtures which follow, one immediately feels an increase of tension.

CHAMBER MUSIC

Cello sonatas Nos. 1 in E min., Op. 38; 2 in F, Op. 99.
*** DG Dig. 410 510-2 [id.]. Mstislav Rostropovich, Rudolf Serkin.
*** Decca 414 558-2. Lynn Harrell, Vladimir Ashkenazy.
*** Hyp. Dig. CDA 66159; *KA 66159* [id.]. Steven Isserlis, Peter Evans.

The partnership of the wild, inspirational Russian cellist and the veteran Brahmsian pianist is a challenging one. It proves an outstanding success, with inspiration mutually enhanced, whether in the lyricism of Op. 38 or the heroic energy of Op. 99. Good if close recording.

Harrell and Ashkenazy give almost ideal performances of the two Brahms *Cello sonatas*, strong and passionate as well as poetic. However, although they are naturally recorded and well balanced, the acoustic is resonant and the imagery lacks the last degree of sharpness of focus.

Using gut strings, Isserlis produces an exceptionally warm tone, here nicely balanced in the recording against the strong and sensitive playing of his regular piano partner. In every way these perceptive and well-detailed readings stand in competition with the finest. The heroic power of the opening of the *F major* is presented with all the projection – if at less sheer volume – that Brahms himself would have expected. Warm, unaggressive Hyperion sound.

Clarinet quintet in B min., Op. 115.
(M) *** EMI CDM7 63116-2 [id.]. Gervase de Peyer, Melos Ens. – MOZART: *Quintet.* ***
(B) *** Pickwick Dig. PCD 883; *CIMPC 883* [id.]. Keith Puddy, Delmé Qt – DVOŘÁK: *Quartet No. 12.* ***

(i) *Clarinet quintet in B min., Op. 115;* (ii) *Clarinet sonata No. 2 in E flat, Op. 120/2.*
(M) *** Chan. CHAN 6522; *MBTD 6522* [id.]. Janet Hilton, (i) Lindsay Qt; (ii) Peter Frankl.

(i) *Clarinet quintet in B min., Op. 115;* (ii) *Clarinet trio in A min., Op. 114.*
*** Hyp. CDA 66107; *KA 66107* [id.]. King, (i) Gabrieli Qt; (ii) Georgian, Benson (piano).

(i) *Clarinet trio in A min., Op. 114;* (ii) *Horn trio in E flat, Op. 40.*
**(*) Decca Dig. 410 114-2 [id.]. (i) Schmidl, (ii) Hogner; András Schiff, New Vienna Octet (members).

Thea King and the Gabrieli Quartet give a radiantly beautiful performance of the *Clarinet quintet*, as fine as any put on record, expressive and spontaneous-sounding, with natural ebb and flow of tension as in a live performance. Not only does Thea King produce heavenly pianissimos, above all in the slow movement, she plays with exceptional bite and point in such a passage as the central Hungarian section in that movement. The *Trio*, a gentler work, brings a less positive performance – but still a most sensitive one. The recording of the strings is on the bright side, very vivid and real.

Gervase de Peyer's vintage performance of the *Clarinet quintet* with the Melos Ensemble, recorded in 1964, returns to the catalogue at mid-price in an apt and generous coupling with Mozart. It is a warmly lyrical reading, dominated by the clarinettist, who brings out wistfully autumnal overtones. The sound is full and immediate, set in a relatively dry acoustic.

Keith Puddy's warm tone is well suited to Brahms and, with spacious speeds in all four movements, this is a consistently sympathetic reading; the digital recording is equally fine, vivid and full. Excellent value.

Janet Hilton's essentially mellow performance of the *Clarinet quintet*, with the Lindsay Quartet playing with pleasing warmth and refinement, has a distinct individuality. Her lilting syncopations in the third movement are delightful and the theme and variations of the finale are full of character. The 1980 analogue recording has a natural presence without being obtrusively close. Hilton's partnership with Peter Frankl in the *E flat Clarinet sonata* is rather less idiosyncratic and individual; nevertheless this performance offers considerable artistic rewards, even if the resonance means that the aural focus is a little diffuse.

With members of the New Vienna Octet joining András Schiff on Decca, the *Clarinet trio* is given a delightful performance, relaxed and warm. The *Horn trio* has less urgency, though dramatic contrasts of dynamic are strongly brought out. Schiff's incisive playing is brightly caught on the full and realistic digital recording.

(i) *Clarinet quintet, Op. 115;* (ii) *Piano quintet, Op. 34. String quintets Nos. 1–2, Opp. 88 & 111; String sextets Nos. 1–2, Opp. 18 & 36.*
(M) **(*) DG 419 875-2 (3) [id.]. (i) Leister; (ii) Eschenbach; augmented Amadeus Qt.

(i) *Clarinet quintet in B min., Op. 115. String quintet No. 2 in G, Op. 111.*
**(*) Delos Dig. DE 3066 [id.]. (i) David Shifrin; Chamber Music NorthWest.

These Amadeus performances were first issued in 1969. The playing is consistently polished and tempi are well chosen. Karl Leister plays with considerable sensitivity in the *Clarinet quintet*, while in the *Piano quintet* Christoph Eschenbach gives a powerful account of the piano part. Perhaps it is at times over-projected, but the performance has no want of life. Elsewhere the element of suavity which at times enters the Amadeus contribution seems minimized by the immediacy of the sound, and there is much to enjoy here.

David Shifrin plays most beautifully in the *Clarinet quintet* and fully catches its serenity and autumnal nostalgia. He receives highly sympathetic support from Chamber Music NorthWest who find a parallel in the atmosphere of the *Adagio* of the *String quintet*, which is also played with a natural Brahmsian feeling. The recording projects Shifrin's rich, yet never too opulent timbre beautifully in a warm acoustic, but the microphones are a shade too near the strings and there is a hint of wiriness in the violins, especially in the *String quintet*.

Clarinet sonatas Nos. 1 in F min.; 2 in E flat, Op. 120/1–2.
*** Chan. Dig. CHAN 8563; *ABTD 1265* [id.]. Gervase de Peyer, Gwenneth Prior.
*** Virgin Dig. VC7 91076-2; *VC 791076-4*. Collins, Pletnev – WEBER: *Grand Duo concertante in E flat, Op. 48*. ***
(M) **(*) BMG/RCA GD 60036 [60036-2-RG]. Richard Stoltzman, Richard Goode.
**(*) Hyp. Dig. CDA 66202; *KA 66202* [id.]. Thea King, Clifford Benson.

Superb performances from Gervase de Peyer and Gwenneth Prior, commanding, aristocratic, warm and full of subtleties of colour and detail. The recording too is outstandingly realistic.

Another fine version of the *Clarinet sonatas* comes from Michael Collins and Mikhail Pletnev, and this has an impressive range of feeling and colour to commend it. These are commanding, strongly masculine performances without being in the least overpowering: they embrace the greatest delicacy of feeling and sensitivity of phrasing. The artists are excellently recorded and this makes a strong alternative recommendation to the Chandos disc.

Stoltzman's readings of both works have a relaxed, improvisatory style. Richard Goode makes a sensitive partner, but his piano timbre as recorded is a little dry, although the sound overall is balanced truthfully.

Thea King and Clifford Benson give finely paced, warm and musicianly accounts of both works. Even if it is possible to imagine readings of greater intensity, the performances will give pleasure on all counts, and the recording is well balanced and truthful.

Clarinet trio in A min., Op. 114.
(B) **(*) Pickwick PCD 959. David Campbell, Iwan Llewelyn-Jones, Lionel Handy – BEETHOVEN: *Clarinet trio*. **(*)

The Musicfest Trio give a good account of the Brahms *Clarinet trio* and they have no lack of spirit or sensitivity; as with the Beethoven coupling, however, the over-reverberant acoustic considerably diminishes its appeal.

Clarinet trio in A min., Op. 114; Piano quintet in F min., Op. 34.
*** Decca Dig. 425 839-2; *425 839-4* [id.]. Ashkenazy, Cleveland O Qt.

Vladimir Ashkenazy and musicians from the Cleveland Orchestra give impressive accounts of both the *A minor Clarinet trio*, which Brahms wrote towards the end of his life for Richard Mühlfeld, and the *F minor Piano quintet*, which had given him so many problems 30 years earlier. In the *Quintet* the playing has fire and authority, and there is plenty of warmth. The Decca recording is excellent and in the best traditions of the house. This issue more than holds its own with the best of the current opposition.

Horn trio in E flat, Op. 40 (see also above).
(M) *** Decca 433 695-2 [id.]. Tuckwell, Perlman, Ashkenazy – FRANCK: *Violin sonata;* SAINT-SAËNS: *Romance;* SCHUMANN: *Adagio & allegro.* ***

(i) *Horn trio in E flat;* (ii) *String sextet No. 2 in G, Op. 36.*
❀ (M) **(*) Sony SMK 46249 [id.]. (i) Myron Bloom, Michael Tree, Rudolph Serkin; (ii) Pina Carmirelli, Toth, Naegele, Caroline Levine, Arico, Reichenberger.

The performance of the *Horn trio*, recorded at the Marlboro Festival in 1960, is quite splendid, the warmly romantic feeling of the first movement matched by subtlety of colour in the *Adagio* and the wonderful bite and rhythmic exhilaration of the scherzo and finale. Myron Bloom's horn playing is superb, and Michael Tree matches his lyrical feeling, while Serkin holds the performance together so that, when the fervour of the music-making brings a few slips in rhythmic precision, the listener is carried along by the exhilaration of the moment. The *Trio* comes paired with another Marlboro performance, of the *G major String sextet*, by a string group led by Pina Carmirelli. Recorded in 1967, this is at an altogether lower voltage. But even if the playing is not in any way memorable, its direct response to one of Brahms's most lyrical string works is not unappealing.

A superb performance of Brahms's marvellous *Horn trio* from Tuckwell, Perlman and Ashkenazy. They realize to the full the music's passionate impulse, and the performance moves forward from the gentle opening, through the sparkling scherzo and the more introspective but still outgiving *Adagio*, to the gay and spirited finale. The recording is worthy of the playing although, in their care not to out-balance the violin with the horn, the engineers have placed the horn rather backwardly. The new ADD transfer of the 1968 recording seeks to provide a more sharply defined sound-picture than before, but the original analogue recording was resonantly atmospheric and the attempt to clarify its imagery brings moments when the refinement of texture slips at climaxes. The effect verges on roughness but fortunately is not serious enough to impair enjoyment.

Piano quartets Nos. 1 in G min., Op. 25; 2 in A, Op. 26; 3 in C min., Op. 60.
*** Sony Dig.S2K 45846 (2) [id.]. Jaime Laredo, Isaac Stern, Yo Yo Ma, Emanuel Ax.
(B) *** VoxBox (2) [CDX 5052]. Eastman Qt.
** Chan. Dig. CHAN 8809/10 [id.]. Borodin Trio with Rivka Golani.

Piano quartet No. 1 in G min., Op. 25.
*** Sony Dig. MK 42361 [id.]. Murray Perahia, Amadeus Qt (members).

Piano quartets Nos. 1 in G min.; 3 in C min., Op. 60.
*** Virgin Dig. VC7 90709-2; *VC 790709-4* [id.]. Domus.
(M) **(*) BMG/RCA GD 85677 [5677-2-RG]. Rubinstein, Guarneri Qt.

The Stern–Laredo–Ma–Ax partnership produce some pretty high-voltage playing and a real sense of give-and-take. There is little sense of four stars just coming together for a recording session but more of a genuine musical rapport. The listener is placed rather closer to the artists than some readers might like, and some may prefer the more relaxed, less high-powered Domus accounts on Hyperion or at bargain price the marvellously unforced and musical playing of the Eastman Quartet on Vox. All the same no one investing in the Sony set is likely to be in the least disappointed.

The Eastman Quartet were recorded in 1968 but the sound, though more forward than ideal, is acceptably warm. The set is distinguished by some very fine playing, in particular from the pianist Frank Glazer, whose sensitivity and imagination are always in evidence. The musical insights that he brings and the fine musicianship and teamwork shown by his colleagues make this a particularly rewarding set. There is nothing sensational or jet-setting about this playing; it is relaxed, unforced and musical through and through. It is a pity that three CDs were not used (perhaps for the price of two) as the *A major* is split between the two discs; so compelling are these readings that one regrets the distraction of having to change discs. This Vox Box still awaits issue in the UK.

This Perahia version of the *G minor Piano quartet* has an expressive power and eloquence that silence criticism. The sound has both warmth and presence in its CD format and this is arguably the finest account of the work since Gilels recorded it with the same string group.

However, Domus offer not only the *G minor Quartet* but also the *C minor*, and they give marvellously spontaneous accounts of both works, urgent and full of warmth, yet with no lack of subtlety. The full, vivid recording can be recommended strongly.

Rubinstein can be a persuasive Brahms advocate and here he is at his most commanding, clearly inspiring the Guarneri players to match his power and emotional warmth. The performances have tremendous spontaneity and conviction; however, the remastered recording, although well blended and properly balanced and clear, lacks something in warmth in the middle frequencies, although the upper range is not shrill.

The Borodin Trio and Rivka Golani on Chandos are also very impressive but they do tend towards a higher emotional temperature than some other partnerships on record (Domus) and tend to emote heavily from time to time. All the same it would be unfair to suggest that they wear their hearts on their sleeve; these are undoubtedly felt readings and well recorded, too but not a first choice.

Piano quartet No. 2 in A, Op. 26.
*** Virgin Dig. VC7 90739-2; *VC 790739-4* [id.]. Domus – MAHLER: *Quartet movement.* ***

With this CD, Domus complete their set of the Brahms *Piano quartets*, and one need hardly say more than that this record is fully worthy of its companion. This is real chamber-music-making that conveys a sense of pleasure; although the recording acoustic seems less than ideal, the ear soon adjusts and it is only in tutti passages that one becomes conscious of excessive reverberation.

Piano quartet No. 3 in C min., Op. 60.
** Sony Dig. MK 42387 [id.]. Stern, Ma, Laredo, Ax – *Double concerto.* ***

Excellent playing from all concerned on the CBS disc, even if Emanuel Ax delivers too thick a fortissimo tone at times – though he can produce beautiful pianissimo tone as well. There are pianists more sensitive in this respect on rival recordings.

Piano quintet in F min., Op. 34.
(BB) *** Naxos Dig. 8.550406; *4550406* [id.]. Jenö Jandó, Kodály Qt – SCHUMANN: *Piano quintet.* ***
**(*) DG 419 673-2 [id.]. Pollini, Italian Qt.

There is some electrifying and commanding playing from Pollini, and the Italian Quartet is eloquent too. The balance, however, is very much in the pianist's favour and occasionally masks the lower strings. The CD has opened up the sound somewhat, but at fortissimo levels the piano and strings could ideally be better separated.

Although not quite as refined as some of its full-price competitors, this fine Naxos account has a great deal going for it, even though it does not include the first-movement exposition repeat. The playing is boldly spontaneous and has plenty of fire and expressive feeling. The opening of the finale has mystery too, and overall, with full-bodied recording and plenty of presence, this makes a strong impression. It is certainly a bargain.

Piano trios Nos. 1 in B, Op. 8; 2 in C, Op. 87; 3 in C min., Op. 101; 4 in A, Op. posth.
*** Teldec/Warner Dig. 9031 76036-2 (2) [id.]. Trio Fontenay.

We have already praised the separate issues of the Teldec recordings of the first two *Trios* – see below. Now they come in a box with Nos. 3 and 4, which are hardly less impressive. Powerful, spontaneous playing with a real Brahmsian spirit, given excellent, modern recording, puts these admirable performances by the Trio Fontenay at the top of the list.

Piano trio No. 1 in B, Op. 8.
*** Teldec/Warner Dig. 2292 44924-2 [id.]. Trio Fontenay – IVES: *Trio.* ***

The Trio Fontenay are excellent in Op. 8 and hardly put a foot wrong throughout. They are also given an excellently clear but not oppressively close recording.

Piano trio No. 2 in C, Op. 87.
*** Teldec/Warner Dig. 2292 44177-2 [id.]. Trio Fontenay – DVOŘÁK: *Piano trio No. 1.* ***

A very good performance from the Trio Fontenay which has sparkle and drama without being over-projected. The recording is first class too.

Piano trios Nos. 1 in B, Op. 8; 2 in C, Op. 87.
(M) *** Decca 421 152-2; *421 152-4.* Julius Katchen, Josef Suk, Janos Starker.

Piano trios Nos. 1 in B, Op. 8; 2 in C, Op. 87; 3 in C min., Op. 101; 4 in A, Op. posth.
*** Ph. Dig. 416 838-2 (2) [id.]. Beaux Arts Trio.

Piano trios Nos. 1–3.
**(*) Chan. Dig. CHAN 8334/5; *DBTD 2005* (2) [id.]. Borodin Trio.

Piano trios Nos. 1 in B, Op. 8; 3 in C min., Op. 101.
**(*) CRD CRD 3432 [id.]. Israel Piano Trio.

Piano trio No. 2 in C, Op. 87.
**(*) CRD CRD 3433 [id.]. Israel Piano Trio – SCHUMANN: *Piano trio No. 1.* **(*)

The new digital recordings by the Beaux Arts Trio were made in La Chaux-de-Fonds, Switzerland, and they bring one close to the artists, the bottom end of the piano being larger than life, at times strikingly so. The playing, however, is always highly vital and sensitive. There is a splendid, finely projected sense of line and the delicate, sensitive playing of Menahem Pressler is always a delight.

The Katchen/Suk/Starker recordings were made in The Maltings in July 1968, representing Katchen's last sessions before his untimely death. The performances are warm, strong and characterful. The richness of the acoustics at The Maltings adds to the Brahmsian glow; and if the sound of the remastered disc is a little limited in the upper range, it provides a real Brahmsian amplitude which is very satisfying.

The Borodin Trio give most musical and sensitive accounts of the three *Trios* that convey the sense of music-making in the home. Theirs are not high-powered performances and they are accorded strikingly natural recording. There is strength when it is called for, lightness of touch and a sense of repose. They are not always perfectly in tune, and this might well prove tiresome on repetition. However, the odd imperfections should not stand in the way of a recommendation.

The Israel Piano Trio give powerful accounts of all three *Trios*. In the first movements they tend towards 'public' rather than chamber performances, the pianist at times sounding as if he is tackling a concerto, but they have no lack of eloquence or feeling. Throughout, however, the intensity is such that they always hold one's attention. Their intonation is very accurate and their playing shows a Brahmsian feel and is commanding and spontaneous. The CDs offer fine presence and tangibility.

String quartets Nos. 1–3.
*** DG Dig. 423 670-2 (3) [id.]. Melos Qt – SCHUMANN: *Quartets Nos. 1–3.* **(*)

String quartets Nos. 1 in C min.; 2 in A min., Op. 51/1–2.
*** Chan. Dig. CHAN 8562; *ABTD 1264* [id.]. Gabrieli Qt.
*** Decca Dig. 425 526-2; *425 526-4* [id.]. Takács Qt.
*** DG Dig. 427 641-2 [id.]. Melos Qt.

Richly recorded in an agreeably expansive ambience, the Gabrielis give warm, eloquent performances of both the Op. 51 *Quartets*, deeply felt and full-textured without being heavy; the *Romanze* of Op. 51, No. 1, is delightfully songful. There are both tenderness and subtlety here, and the sound is first class.

The Takács Quartet coupling of the *C minor* and *A minor Quartets* has vitality and sensitivity, and their accounts of both works are eminently well shaped. The recording is not as reverberant as their Haydn Op. 76 of some years ago and in most respects they are to be preferred to the Melos on DG and may be recommended alongside the Gabrielis on Chandos.

These Melos performances are generally well-shaped accounts with no want of fire and free from exaggeration, though they are at times short on charm – as, for example, in the *B flat Quartet*. The recordings are well (some may find them too well) lit and a bit forward, but on the whole this makes a firm recommendation for the Op. 51 *Quartets*.

String quintets Nos. 1 in F, Op. 88; 2 in G, Op. 111.
(M) **(*) Ph. 426 094-2; *426 094-4*. BPO Octet (members).

These splendid works are quite well served by the 1970 Philips reissue. Although the remastering has brought a thinner, more astringent treble response than the original LP, the underlying sound is full and well balanced. The performances by the Berlin Philharmonic group are searching and artistically satisfying, combining freshness with polish, warmth with well-integrated detail.

String sextets Nos. 1 in B flat, Op. 18; 2 in G, Op. 36.
*** Hyp. Dig. CDA 66276; *KA 66276* [id.]. Raphael Ens.

The *Sextets* are among Brahms's most immediately appealing chamber works; they have a breadth of scale and texture that relates them closely to the orchestral music, yet they have the added freshness and transparency of writing in which there is one player to each part. The Raphael Ensemble are fully responsive to all their subtleties as well as to their vitality and warmth. In short, these are superb performances; the recording is very vivid and immediate, although some ears might find it a shade too present.

Violin sonatas Nos. 1 in G, Op. 78; 2 in A, Op. 100; 3 in D min., Op. 108.
*** Hyp. Dig. CDA 66465; *KA 66465* (without *Scherzo*) [id.]. Krysia Osostowicz, Susan Tomes.
*** Sony Dig. SK 45819 [id.]. Itzhak Perlman, Daniel Barenboim.
(M) *** DG 431 599-2; *431 599-4* [id.]. Pinchas Zukerman, Daniel Barenboim.
*** EMI Dig. CDC7 47403-2 [id.]. Itzhak Perlman, Vladimir Ashkenazy.
(M) **(*) Decca 421 092-2; *421 092-4* [id.]. Josef Suk, Julius Katchen.

Violin sonatas Nos. 1 in G, Op. 78; 2 in A, Op. 100; 3 in D min., Op. 108; Scherzo in C min.
*** Decca Dig. 430 555-2 [id.]. Pierre Amoyal, Pascal Rogé.

Krysia Osostowicz and Susan Tomes on an excellent recorded Hyperion CD bring fresh insights to bear on these familiar classics. Their performances are wholly untouched by routine; they combine both finesse and vitality in their approach; no detail of phrasing is overstated, nothing is italicized and the music is left to speak for itself. Theirs makes a welcome change from the slick overprojected virtuoso approach of so many star players.

Pierre Amoyal and Pascal Rogé are hardly less fine; they are unfailingly musical in their responses and they do have the advantage of offering the *C minor scherzo* movement into the bargain. One does not associate Rogé with this repertoire (though he made a fine LP of the *Handel variations* for Decca some years ago), and at times his approach may strike some listeners as too soft-grained. However this may be, these are lovely performances that can be recommended alongside the finest in the catalogue.

Both Perlman and Barenboim have versions of the three Brahms *Violin sonatas* in the CD catalogue, but with different partners. This Sony recording, made at a live recital in Chicago, finds Perlman in far more volatile form, more urgently persuasive with naturally flowing speeds and more spontaneous rubato than he adopts in his spacious readings with Ashkenazy on EMI. Barenboim too is less aggressive and more fanciful than he was with Zukerman on DG. The sound is more limited in dynamic range than the earlier, studio recordings but is still very acceptable, and this makes a very enjoyable concert.

Zukerman and Barenboim are inspired to take a more expansive view of Brahms to produce songful, spontaneous-sounding performances that catch the inspiration of the moment. Compared with Perlman and Ashkenazy, the manner is warmer, less self-conscious – if at times less refined. Recorded in 1975, the sound is ripe and warm to match. But either of these two CDs will give much pleasure.

Perlman and Ashkenazy bring out the trouble-free happiness of these lyrical inspirations, fully involved yet avoiding underlying tensions. In their sureness and flawless confidence at generally spacious speeds, they are performances which carry you along, cocooned in rich sound.

Suk's personal blend of romanticism and the classical tradition is warmly attractive but small in scale. These are intimate performances and, in their way, very enjoyable, since the remastered 1967 recording remains smoothly realistic, with only a hint of rawness on top.

Viola sonatas Nos. 1 in F min.; 2 in E flat, Op. 120/1 & 2.
**(*) Chan. Dig. CHAN 8550; *ABTD 1256* [id.]. Imai, Vignoles – SCHUMANN: *Märchenbilder.* **(*)

Nobuko Imai is an almost peerless violist and it is difficult to find a flaw in her accounts of the two Op. 120 *Sonatas* with Roger Vignoles. She brings great warmth and a splendid feeling for line to these fine works, and has altogether excellent support from her partner. The reverberant acoustic does not show the piano to good advantage but, apart from that, this is an impressive issue.

PIANO MUSIC

4 Ballades, Op. 10.
*** Ph. Dig. 426 439-2 [id.]. Alfred Brendel – WEBER: *Piano sonata No. 2.* ***

A thoughtful (and at times self-aware) account of the Op. 10 *Ballades* in a wonderfully clear, digital recording. There is some highlighting of subsidiary part-writing that may strike some as just a little self-conscious but much else that will delight the listener. This is playing of stature that should be heard by all the great pianist's admirers. The Gilels set, now available with his Brahms *D minor Concerto* (see above), or the Kovacevich are no less masterly and authoritative, yet are a shade more spontaneous in feeling.

4 Ballades, Op. 10; 7 Fantasias, Op. 116; Hungarian dances Nos. 1–10; (i) *Nos. 11–21. 3 Intermezzi, Op. 117; 8 Piano pieces, Op. 76; 6 Piano pieces, Op. 118; 4 Piano pieces, Op. 119; Piano sonata Nos.1 in C, Op. 1; 2 in F sharp min., Op. 2; 3 in F min., Op. 5; 2 Rhapsodies, Op. 79; Variations on a Hungarian song, Op. 21/2; Variations on a theme by Paganini, Op. 35; Variations and fugue on a theme by Handel, Op. 24; Variations on a theme by Schumann, Op. 9; Variations on an original theme, Op. 21/1; Waltzes, Op. 39.*
(M) **(*) Decca mono/stereo 430 053-2 (6). Julius Katchen, (i) with Marty.

Brahms often brought out the best in Katchen, and he is particularly good in the impulsive early music. If at times one could make small criticisms, the spontaneity and understanding are always there, and of course the excitement that comes when bravura is controlled by a sensitive and musical mind. Katchen's style in Brahms is distinctive: there is a boldness about it that suits some works more than others. In general the bigger, tougher pieces come off better than the gentle *Intermezzi* of Opp. 116 and 117, which lack the sort of inner tension that Kovacevich can convey. Even so, there is much beautiful playing here. Such pieces as the two *Rhapsodies*, Op. 79, are splendidly done, and so are the *Ballades*. The *Waltzes* come somewhere in between. Katchen's playing in the first two *Sonatas* hardly achieves the compelling intensity of some of his rivals, but the result is always exciting. The playing is extremely brilliant and assured, and a certain lack of resilience in the style scarcely mars the performances, rather giving them a tough individuality; and his account of Op. 5 is similarly commanding. The lesser-known *Variations on a Hungarian song* and *On an original theme*, plus those *On a theme by Schumann*, are particularly successful. They are played with the utmost persuasiveness and artistry. On the other hand, the *Handel* and *Paganini* sets, Opp. 24 and 35, are very extrovert in style. Katchen plays Book One of the *Hungarian dances* in Brahms's later arrangement for piano solo; the remaining dances are offered in the more traditional form with Jean-Pierre Marty as Katchen's partner. On CD the recordings, made between 1962 and 1966, are remarkably realistic, full in timbre and with good presence. The four *Ballades* are mono. A fine set which will give much satisfaction. But it is a pity that the cueing is so ungenerous in the *Variations* and (especially) the *Waltzes*.

4 Ballades, Op. 10 (see also below).
*** DG Dig. 400 043-2 [id.]. Michelangeli – SCHUBERT: *Sonata No. 4*. **

4 Ballades, Op. 10; Variations and fugue on a theme of Handel, Op. 24; Variations on a theme of Schumann, Op. 9.
*** ASV Dig. CDDCA 616 [id.]. Jorge-Federico Osorio.

Michelangeli gives the *Ballades* a performance of the greatest distinction and without the slightly aloof quality that at times disturbs his readings. He is superbly recorded and this compact disc approaches demonstration standard.

Jorge-Federico Osorio's account of the *Variations and fugue on a theme of Handel* is tremendously impressive. There is no want of clarity, but the texture has plenty of warmth and colour and he balances the sonorities in a most musical way. He possesses an unfailing sense of the Brahms style, and this is undoubtedly his best record to date, for the Schumann set and the four *Ballades* are also played with fine sensitivity and character. ASV provide excellent, well-focused sound with plenty of depth.

7 Fantasias, Op. 116; 3 Intermezzi, Op. 117; 4 Pieces, Op. 119.
*** Ph. 411 137-2 [id.]. Stephen Kovacevich.

3 Intermezzi, Op. 117; 6 Pieces, Op. 118; 4 Pieces, Op. 119; 2 Rhapsodies, Op. 79.
*** Decca 417 599-2 [id.]. Radu Lupu.

6 Pieces, Op. 118; 2 Rhapsodies, Op. 79; 12 Waltzes, Op. 39.
*** Ph. Dig. 420 750-2 [id.]. Stephen Kovacevich.

The pair of well-recorded discs from Stephen Kovacevich can receive the strongest recommendation. He finds the fullest range of emotional contrast in the Op. 116 *Fantasias*, but he is at his finest in the Op. 117 *Intermezzi* and four *Klavierstücke*, Op. 119, which contain some of Brahms's most beautiful lyrical inspirations for the keyboard. The companion disc offers playing of comparable distinction. The playing is not only thoughtful but full of the sharpest contrasts. The result is most compelling, both in the much-loved *Waltzes* and in the later, more demanding pieces.

Radu Lupu's late Brahms is quite outstanding in every way. The analogue recordings date from 1971 and 1978, and the CD transfer has brought greater emphasis on the middle and lower sonorities in the earlier recordings (Op. 79/1 and Op. 117). The quality of the recorded sound is otherwise wide in range and Lupu's warmth and delicacy of colouring are most truthfully conveyed. There is great intensity and inwardness when these qualities are required and a keyboard mastery that is second to none. This is undoubtedly one of the most rewarding Brahms recitals currently before the public.

Intermezzi, Op. 117; 6 Pieces, Op. 118; Variations on a theme by Paganini, Op. 35.
*** DG Dig. 431 123-2 [id.]. Lilya Zilberstein.

Lilya Zilberstein made an impressive début with a Rachmaninov/Shostakovich disc and her Brahms is hardly less striking, even if it would not necessarily be a first choice. She has flawless technique and keen musical instincts. The instrument is in perfect condition and sounds excellent, and the recording is marvellously present and clear (one can almost see one's own reflection in the high black polish of the grand piano). In Opp. 116 and 118 Lupu and Kovacevich have the greater maturity and wisdom and, in the former, Gilels is also to be preferred. In the *Paganini variations* she can hold her own in the present catalogue.

Variations and fugue on a theme by Handel, Op. 24.
(M) *** Decca 417 791-2. Jorge Bolet – REGER: *Variations.* ***

This was Jorge Bolet's début record for Decca, and very impressive it is. His playing in Brahms's best-loved set of piano variations is incisive and brightly revealing, intensely refreshing and concentrated. With excellently remastered analogue sound, this makes a first-class coupling with music by Reger which is much less familiar.

Piano sonatas Nos. 1 in C, Op. 1; 2 in F sharp min., Op. 2; 3 in F min., Op. 5; 4 Ballades, Op. 10; Scherzo in E flat, Op 4.
**(*) DG 423 401-2 (2) [id.]. Krystian Zimerman.

Krystian Zimerman's account of the lesser-known *C major Sonata* is powerful and concentrated. The work emerges with altogether fresh urgency and expressive power. His version of the *F minor*, Op. 5, is also particularly commanding and is worthy to stand alongside the great performances of the past. There is leonine power, tempered with poetic feeling. There is no want of tenderness as well as strength in the Op. 10 *Ballades*, while the recording sound is very good, although in adding presence the digital remastering has brought a degree of hardness to the upper range at higher dynamic levels.

Piano sonata No. 1 in C, Op. 1.
**(*) BMG/RCA Dig. RD 60859; *RK 60859*. Sviatoslav Richter – LISZT: *Consolation* etc. **(*)

Richter's recording of the *C major Sonata* was made at the 1988 Schleswig-Holstein Festival and is a performance of intense concentration and finesse. Even if this Op. 1 is a long way from being Brahms at his most compelling, Richter's is the kind of playing that grips one from start to finish. The recording is not altogether ideal: it inclines towards tonal shallowness – though the bass is strong – and that may be in some measure due to the instrument itself he is using. Collectors who have the (recently deleted) Zimerman set on DG need not feel unhappy, but for others wanting just this sonata need not be too worried about these reservations, for this is a performance of some stature and better than anything else that is currently around.

Piano sonata No. 3 in F min., Op. 5.
**(*) Hung. Dig. HCD 12601 [id.]. Zoltán Kocsis.

Piano sonata No.3 in F min., Op. 5; Capriccio in B min., Op. 76/2; Intermezzo in E flat min., Op. 118/6; Rhapsodies: in B min., Op. 79/1; E flat, Op. 119/4.
*** Sony Dig. SK 47181 [id.]; *40-47181*. Murray Perahia.

Piano sonata No. 3 in F min., Op. 5; 2 Rhapsodies, Op. 79; Theme and variations in D min. (from *String sextet, Op. 18*).

*** Teldec/Warner Dig. 2292 44186-2 [id.]. Cyprien Katsaris.

Piano sonata No. 3; Theme and variations in D min. (from *String sextet, Op. 18*).
*** Decca Dig. 417 122-2. Radu Lupu.

Murray Perahia's account of the Brahms *Sonata in F minor* belongs in exalted company, along with the Curzon, Lupu (both Decca) as well as the magisterial early stereo LP from Kempff (DG). We are not short of fine versions in the current catalogues but this is undoubtedly the most eloquent and thoughtful (as well as beautiful) among recent recordings. And whereas some pianists' rubato (among them Emanuel Ax on the same label) fails wholly to convince, such is Perahia's artistry that all the subtle agogic shifts that arise in the course of these pieces seem completely natural and convincing. Sony particularly deserve praise for the excellence of the recorded sound they have achieved (the Royce Hall in Los Angeles for the *Sonata* and Hamburg for the shorter pieces), which has naturalness and refinement, though the pianist has not a little to do with the latter! The smaller pieces are equally successful.

Noble, dignified and spacious are the adjectives that spring to mind when listening to Lupu's Op. 5; he does not, perhaps, have the youthful ardour of Kocsis or the communicative qualities of Krystian Zimerman's account; Lupu's view is inward, ruminative and always beautifully rounded. The recording is most realistic, the piano set slightly back, the timbre fully coloured, and the focus natural.

Cyprien Katsaris possesses a pretty breathtaking technique and his Brahms *F minor Sonata* is second to none. While it does not displace Lupu or Zimerman, it can certainly be recommended alongside them. Katsaris takes few of the agogic liberties that have sometimes distinguished him in the romantic repertoire and, although he does not have quite the same grasp of structure as Zimerman or the same classical purity, this is strong, exciting playing, and the recording is excellent.

Kocsis gives an ardent account of the *F minor Sonata*. His performance is spacious and expansive, and there is no lack of warmth. The slow tempo (an adagio rather than andante) he adopts in the second and fourth movements is not quite as disturbing as the small agogic exaggerations in which he indulges. Yet what wonderful points he makes elsewhere. For all one's reservations, this is playing of great imagination and artistry, and the recording is eminently truthful.

Variations on a theme of Haydn, Op. 56a (arr. for piano duet).
*** Sony Dig. MK 42625 [id.]. Murray Perahia, Sir Georg Solti – BARTÓK: *Sonata for 2 pianos and percussion.* ***

It seems likely that Brahms wrote out his *Variations* in piano score (for two pianos, four hands) before completing the orchestration. Murray Perahia and Solti bring out the fullest possible colouring in their performance, so that one hardly misses the orchestra. Highly spontaneous music-making which gives great pleasure, and very well recorded too.

ORGAN MUSIC

11 Chorale preludes, Op. 22; Chorale preludes and fugue on 'O Trauerigkeit, O Herzeleid'; Fugue in A flat min.; Preludes and fugues: in A min.; G min.
*** CRD Dig. CRD 3404; *CRDC 4104* [id.]. Nicholas Danby (organ).

Nicholas Danby playing the organ of the Church of the Immaculate Conception in London, which seems ideally suited to this repertoire, gives restrained, clean-cut readings (which yet have a strong profile) of Brahms's complete organ works. He is refreshingly at home both in the early and amiable *Preludes and fugues* – piano style not completely translated – and in the very late *Eleven Chorale preludes* from the period of the *Four Serious Songs*. The sound of the Farm Street organ is beautifully caught by the recording – there is not a hint of turgidity, the effect incisive rather than over-ample. The CD brings added firmness and presence, but the chrome tape, too, is impressively faithful.

VOCAL MUSIC

Lieder: *Ach, wende diesen Blick; Die Mainacht; Heimweh; Mädchenlied; Meine Liebe ist grün; O kühler Wald; Ständchen; Unbewegte laue Luft; Von ewiger Liebe; Wie rafft' ich mich auf; Wiegenlied.* (i) *2 Songs with viola: (Gestille Sehnsucht & Geistliches Wiegenlied), Op. 91. 3 Volkslieder: Dort in den Weiden; Sonntag; Vergebliches Ständchen. 8 Zigeunerlieder Op. 103/1–7 & 11.*
*** DG Dig. 429 727-2 [id.]. Anne Sofie von Otter, Bengt Forsberg, (i) with Nils-Erik Sparf.

Anne Sofie von Otter gives these Brahms Lieder the natural freshness of folksong, which so often they resemble, or even quote, as in the radiant melody of *Sonntag*. Aptly, the collection begins with eight of the often rumbustious *Gypsy songs* of Opus 103 and embraces songs from the early *Wie rafft' ich mich auf*, written when Brahms was thirty, through the Daumer settings, Op. 57, to the later songs of Opp. 106 and 107. Von Otter's open, easy style conceals high art in the poise and control of her exceptionally beautiful and even mezzo voice. She phrases unerringly, holding and changing tension and mood as in a live recital. Compared with some, there is still a degree of expressive restraint – as in *Von ewiger Liebe* – but there are few Brahms song-recital discs to match this one, and her accompanist is the strongly supportive Bengt Forsberg, who plays with intelligence and sensitivity. In the Op. 91 settings they are joined by Nils-Erik Sparf, who plays with admirable taste. A varied, well-chosen and beautifully recorded programme that will give pleasure to this artist's admirers.

Lieder: *Dein blaues Auge hält; Dort in den Weiden; Immer leiser wird mein Schlummer; Klage I & II; Liebestreu; Des Liebsten Schwur; Das Mädchen; Das Mädchen spricht; Regenlied; Romanzen und Lieder, Op. 84; Salome; Sapphische Ode, Op. 94/4; Der Schmied;* (i) *2 Songs with viola, Op. 91; Therese; Vom Strande; Wie Melodien zieht es; Zigeunerlieder, Op. 103.*
(M) *** DG Dig. 431 600-2; *431 600-4* [id.]. Jessye Norman, Daniel Barenboim; (i) Wolfram Christ.

Jessye Norman's glorious Lieder recital with Barenboim, recorded in 1981/2, is one of her finest records, while Wolfram Christ makes a distinguished contribution to Op. 91. The heroic scale of *Der Schmied* is superb, as is the open simplicity of the *Zigeunerlieder*, while the gentler songs find Norman's gloriously ample voice scaled down exquisitely. The recording is wonderfully vivid, giving the artists a tangible presence.

Vier ernste Gesänge, Op. 121; Lieder: *Auf dem Kirchhofe; Botschaft; Feldeinsamkeit; Im Waldeseinsamkeit; Minnelied III; Mondenschein; O wüsst ich doch den Weg züruck; Sapphische Ode; Sommerabend; Ständchen.*
❀ (M) (***) EMI CDH7 63198-2 [id.]. Hotter, Moore – BACH: *Cantata No. 82: Ich habe genug.* (***) ❀

Glorious singing from Hans Hotter, wonderfully accompanied by Gerald Moore. Those who have treasured the old LP will know how eloquent this is; others should not pass over singing and artistry of this eloquence. An excellent transfer.

Lieder: *Abendregen; Alte Liebe; Feldensamkeit; Immer leiser wird mein Schlummer; Der Jäger; Liebestreu; Mädchenfluch; Mädchenlied; Das Mädchen spricht; Meine Liebe is grün; Regenlied; Salome; Der Schmied; Sommerabend; Therese; Der Tod, das ist die kühle Nachte; Von ewiger Liebe; Vor dem Fenster; Wir wandelten.*
*** Orfeo C 058831A [id.]. Margaret Price, James Lockhart.

Margaret Price gives a delightful Brahms recital; sensitively supported by James Lockhart, she sings radiantly, with the voice ideally suited to the soaring lines of many of these songs, finely coloured over the changes of mood in a song such as *Alte Liebe*. Clean, bright recording.

Lieder: *Alte Liebe; Auf dem Kirchhofe; Feldeinsamkeit; Nachklang; O wusst' ich doch; Verzagen. Vier ernste Gesänge (4 Serious Songs), Op. 121.*
**(*) DG 415 189-2 [id.]. Dietrich Fischer-Dieskau, Joerg Demus – BEETHOVEN: *Lieder.* **(*)

Recorded in the late 1960s, Fischer-Dieskau's Brahms selection on CD brings consistently imaginative singing. His darkness and intensity in the *Four Serious Songs* are hardly matched in the relatively lightweight accompaniments from Demus – placed at a disadvantage by the recording balance; but, with excellent transfers, the disc can be recommended.

Lieder: *An Die Nachtigall; Bottschaft; Dein blaues Auge hält so still; Feldeinsamkeit; Der Gang zum Liebchen; Geheimnis; Im Waldeseinsamkeit; Komm bald; Die Kränze; Die Mainacht; Meine Liebe ist grün; Minnelied; Nachtigall; O wüsst ich doch den Weg zurück; Sah dem edlen Bildnis; Salamander; Die Schale der Vergessenheit; Serenade; Sonntag; Ständchen; Von ewiger Liebe; Von waldbekränzter Höhe; Wie bist du, Meine Königin; Wiegenlied; Wir Wandelten.*
*** Virgin Dig. VC7 91130-2; *VC 791130-4* [id.]. Thomas Allen, Geoffrey Parsons.

Thomas Allen, in one of his most successful Lieder records yet, gives fresh, virile performances of a particularly attractive collection of Brahms songs. There is less underlining of words than in Brahms sung by Fischer-Dieskau or Bär but still a keen and detailed feeling for meaning as well as mood. If one generally associates the great song *Von ewiger Liebe* with a woman's voice, Allen triumphantly shows what benefits there are from having a baritone, hushed and intimately confidential at the start and bitingly powerful at the climax in heightened contrast. There are many such felicities here, with Geoffrey Parsons an ever-sympathetic accompanist and with sound more cleanly focused than in earlier Lieder issues from this source.

(i) *Alto rhapsody, Op. 53. 4 Gesänge, Op. 17.*
*** Virgin Dig. VC7 91123-2; *VC7 91123-4* [id.]. (i) J. Baker; LSO Ch., L. Sinf., Hickox – MENDELSSOHN: *Infelice* etc. ***

Though the Virgin recording of the *Alto rhapsody* was recorded after Dame Janet's retirement from the concert platform, the voice is in glorious condition, superbly controlled. This is a more openly expressive and spacious reading than her earlier, EMI one with Boult, matching her performances in the two Mendelssohn items. The four early Brahms songs, Opus 17, for women's chorus with two horns and harp accompaniment, are delightfully done.

(i) *Alto rhapsody, Op. 53; Funeral ode, Op. 13; Nänie, Op. 82; Song of the Fates, Op. 89.*
**(*) HM Orfeo C 025821A [id.]. (i) Alfreda Hodgson; Bav. R. Ch. and SO, Haitink.

(i) *Alto rhapsody, Op. 53;* (ii) *Vier ernste Gesange (4 Serious Songs), Op. 121;* (iii) *2 Songs with viola, Op. 91.*
(M) (***) Decca 433 477-2. Kathleen Ferrier, (i) LPO Ch., LPO, Krauss; (ii) John Newmark; (iii) Gilbert, Spurr – MAHLER: *Rückert Lieder.* (***)

Alfreda Hodgson and Bernard Haitink make a good partnership in the *Alto rhapsody*. The other works combine refinement and moments of fervour in much the same way, and there is some splendid singing from the Bavarian choir, especially in the *Funeral ode*. The 1981 analogue recording was made in a concert-hall setting. Not everything is crystal clear, but the overall impression suits the music admirably and gives a convincing sense of realism.

This vintage Ferrier record – reissued as part of the Kathleen Ferrier Edition – brings together a group of the great contralto's early recordings for Decca. The earliest of all here, first issued in 1948, is of the *Alto rhapsody*, a glowing performance which culminates in a heart-warming final section. The *Four Serious Songs*, issued three years later, are even more intense, with the voice more suited to these dark, weighty songs than to most Lieder. The digital transfers capture the voice fairly enough, but present the accompaniments less agreeably.

German requiem, Op. 45.
❀ *** Ph. Dig. 432 140-2; *432 140-4* [id.]. Margiono, Gilfry, Monteverdi Ch., O Révolutionaire et Romantique, Eliot Gardiner.
(M) *** Teldec/Warner Dig. 9031 75862-2; *9031 75862-4* [id.]. M. Price, Ramey, Amb. S., RPO, Previn.
(M) *** Ph. Dig. 432 038-2; *432 038-4* [id.]. Janowitz, Krause, V. State Op. Ch., VPO, Haitink.
(M) *** DG Dig. 429 486-2; *429 486-4*. Lucia Popp, Wolfgang Brendel, Prague Philharmonic Ch., Czech PO, Sinopoli.
(M) *** DG Dig. 431 598-2; *431 598-4* [id.] (as above, cond. Sinopoli).
*** EMI CDC7 47238-2 [id.]. Schwarzkopf, Fischer-Dieskau, Philh. Ch. & O, Klemperer.
(M) **(*) EMI CDM7 69229-2 [id.]; *EG 769229-4*. Tomowa-Sintow, Van Dam, V. Singverein, BPO, Karajan.
**(*) DG Dig. 431 651-2 [id.]. Hendricks, Van Dam, V. Singverein, VPO, Karajan.

Gardiner's 'revolutionary' account of the *German requiem* was recorded in the studio immediately after the orchestra's very first public appearances at Queen Elizabeth Hall, and the range of choral sound is even more thrilling than in the concert hall. With period instruments and following Viennese practice of the time, speeds tend to be faster than usual, but not rigid and not by much, and the result is tough, muscular and very dramatic. With relatively thin violins set against warm choral sound, the contrasts of dynamic and timbre are heightened, making this anything but small-scale. *Denn alles Fleisch* ('Then all flesh is grass') has rarely sounded so thrilling and the sixth movement ('Death is swallowed up in victory') rarely so taut, though the speed for the big fugue is surprisingly relaxed. Charlotte Margiono makes an ethereal soprano soloist, while the American baritone, Rodney Gilfry, despite a rapid vibrato, is aptly fresh and young-sounding. One could not ask for a more complete renovation of a masterpiece often made to sound stodgy and square.

It is the seeming simplicity of Previn's dedicated approach, with radiant singing from the chorus and measured speeds held steadily, that so movingly conveys an innocence in the often square writing, both in the powerful opening choruses and in the simple, songful *Wie lieblich*. The great fugatos are then powerfully presented. Both soloists are outstanding, Margaret Price golden-toned, Samuel Ramey incisively dark. The recording is warmly set against a helpful church acoustic with the chorus slightly distanced.

Haitink chooses very slow tempi in the *German requiem*. There is a rapt quality in this glowing performance that creates an atmosphere of simple dedication; at slow speed *Denn alles Fleisch (All flesh is grass)* is made the more relentless when, with total concentration, textures are so sharply clarified. The digital recording offers beautiful sound and, with outstanding soloists – Gundula Janowitz notably pure and poised – this is very persuasive. This makes a fine digital alternative to Previn at mid-price.

Sinopoli's DG version of the *Deutsches Requiem* brings a performance of extremes: generally measured but consistently positive and often dramatically thrilling, helped by the wide-ranging recording, excellent soloists and an incisive contribution from the Prague Philharmonic Chorus. The 1983 digital recording is full, clear and realistically balanced.

Measured and monumental, Klemperer's performance defies preconceived doubts. The speeds are consistently slow – too slow in the vivace of the sixth movement, where Death has little sting – but, with dynamic contrasts underlined, the result is uniquely powerful. The solo singing is superb, and the Philharmonia singers were at the peak of their form. The CD transfer is excellent, with voices and instruments placed in a realistic sound-spectrum.

The reissue of Karajan's 1977 EMI set on a mid-priced CD offers considerable competition to his later, digital version at full price. The chorus here is both full and clearly focused, and soloists and orchestral detail are vividly projected. Indeed the most striking difference between this and the digital DG set lies in the choral sound, here bigger and closer, with sharp dramatic contrasts. The soloists are both excellent. The remastering is certainly a success, and this is generally also preferable to the alternative mid-priced Karajan reissue from DG.

The last of Karajan's four recordings of the *German requiem*, originally issued on two discs with fill-up, is here reissued on a single CD. The chorus sounds disappointingly opaque, but otherwise it is a warmly persuasive reading, not quite as polished as his previous versions but with a keener sense of spontaneity. For all her sweetness of tone, however, Barbara Hendricks does not sound innocent enough for *Ich habt nun Traurigkeit*, thanks to her rapid vibrato.

Gesänge, (i) *Op. 17; Opp. 42 & 104;* (ii) *Liebeslieder waltzes, Op. 52;* (iii) *Quartet, Op. 92*.
** Ph. Dig. 432 152-2; *432 152-4* [id.]. Shaw, Salmon, Monteverdi Ch.; (i) Wynne (harp), Halstead, Rutherford (horns); (ii–iii) Levin (piano); (ii) Perry (piano); John Eliot Gardiner.

Under Gardiner the members of the Monteverdi Choir give beautifully moulded, finely sprung performances of this varied selection of Brahms's smaller choral pieces. Unfortunately the reverberant acoustic of St Giles', Cripplegate, combined with rather backward placing of the singers, is totally unsuited to the intimate charms of the first book of *Liebeslieder waltzes*. It does not help that, both here and in the Opus 92 *Quartets*, an 1860 Riedl fortepiano is used. The music loses its smiling quality, the sense of domestic music-making that Brahms had in mind. The other pieces work much better in such a setting, with the accompaniment for women's voices of two horns and harp for Opus 17 sounding magical. It is fascinating to deduce the influence of polyphonic and baroque composers on Brahms, a great scholar, in the superb six-part *a cappella* pieces of Opus 42.

Liebeslieder waltzes, Op. 52; New Liebeslieder waltzes, Op. 65; 3 Quartets, Op. 64.
*** DG Dig. 423 133-2 [id.]. Mathis, Fassbaender, Schreier, Fischer-Dieskau; Engel and Sawallisch (pianos).

For its Brahms edition, DG assembled these characterful yet well-matched voices. The result brought one of the most successful recordings yet of the two seductive but surprisingly difficult sets of *Liebeslieder waltzes*. The CD has fine realism and presence.

Motets: *Ave Maria, Op. 12; 3 Fest- und Gedensprüche, Op. 109; Geistliche Chöre, Op. 37; Geistliches Lied, Op. 30; 2 Motets, Op. 29; 2 Motets, Op. 74; 3 Motets, Op. 110; Psalm 13, Op. 27*.
*** Conifer Dig. CDCF 178; *MCFC 178* [id.]. Trinity College, Cambridge, Ch., Richard Marlow.

Richard Marlow and his excellent Cambridge choir add to their distinguished list of records with this invaluable collection, bringing together all sixteen of the motets – mostly unaccompanied but some with organ – which Brahms wrote over the course of his long career. Early in life he was choirmaster at both Detmold and Hamburg, and that experience brought him the gift of writing with a warm understanding of singers and voices. What is surprising here is to discover how close Brahms regularly comes to the example of Bach, whether in the chorales or in such a delightful motet as the lively setting for women's voices of *Regina coeli*, with its brightly rhythmic contrapuntal entries. Most ambitious is the first of the two Opus 74 motets, *Warum ist das Licht gegeben*, with linked sections setting carefully chosen texts from the Book of Job, the Epistle of St James and Martin Luther, a fine work with something of the solemnity of the German requiem. With superb singing recorded vividly, this is an outstanding issue.

Brian, Havergal (1876–1972)

Symphony No. 1 (Gothic).
*** Marco Polo Dig. 8.223280/1; *4.223280/1* [id.]. Jenisová, Pecková, Dolezal, Mikulás, Slovak Philharmonic Ch., Slovak Nat. Theatre Op. Ch., Slovak Folk Ens. Ch., Lucnica Ch., Bratislava Chamber Ch. & Children's Ch., Youth Echo Ch., Czech RSO (Bratislava), Slovak PO, Ondrej Lenárd.

Was Havergal Brian, composer of 32 symphonies, 20 of them written after he was eighty, a genius or just an obsessed megalomaniac? Whatever the answer, this first of the symphonies, 1 hour 50 minutes long and involving performers by the hundred, here receives a passionately committed performance from Slovak forces. Despite a few incidental flaws, it conveys surging excitement from first to last, helped by a rich recording which gives a thrilling impression of massed forces. On one level this is music for wallowing in; yet on repetition it is a work which firmly establishes its landmarks in the memory, starting with such simple, direct effects as the timpani outbursts at the very start and the still horn-chords that keep echoing Wagner's *Rheingold*. The final *Te Deum*, alone lasting 72 minutes, brings fervent choral writing of formidable complexity, with the challenge superbly taken up by the Czech musicians.

Symphony No. 3 in C sharp min.
**(*) Hyp. Dig. CDA 66334; *KA 66334*. Ball, Jacobson, BBC SO, Friend.

A welcome addition to the growing representation of Havergal Brian in the catalogue. The *Third Symphony* began life as a concerto for piano; this perhaps explains the prominent role given to two pianos in the score, splendidly played here by Andrew Ball and Julian Jacobson. The work is full of extraordinarily imaginative and original touches, but the overall lack of rhythmic variety is a handicap. The playing of the BBC Symphony Orchestra under Lionel Friend is well prepared and dedicated, but the recording does not open out sufficiently in climaxes. However, this is an important and interesting record of a challenging and thought-provoking work.

Symphonies Nos. 10 in C min.; 21 in E flat.
(M) **(*) Unicorn UKCD 2027. Leicestershire Schools SO, Loughran or Pinkett.

Both these *Symphonies* are works of old age; No. 10, a powerfully wrought and original one-movement piece, is the more appealing of the two; No. 21 dates from the composer's late eighties. There need be no serious reservations about the recordings, and the performances are astonishingly accomplished.

Bridge, Frank (1879–1941)

Enter spring (rhapsody); (i) *Oration (Concerto elegiaco).*
*** Pearl SHECD 9601 [id.]. (i) Baillie; Cologne RSO, Carewe.

Oration (Concerto elegiaco) for cello and orchestra.
(M) *** EMI Dig. CDM7 63909-2. Isserlis, City of L. Sinfonia, Hickox – BRITTEN: *Symphony for cello and orchestra.* ***

Completed in 1930, *Oration* is in effect a massive cello concerto in nine linked sections, lasting a full half-hour, which reflects the composer's continuing desolation over the deaths of so many of his friends in the First World War. Bridge's idea of writing an elegiac work made for the opposite of comfortable consolation. In its often gritty textures and dark concentration it is fundamentally angry music, stylistically amazing – like other late Bridge – for a British composer to have been writing at the time. Though Isserlis is not always as passionate as Julian Lloyd Webber was on the earlier, Lyrita version, his focus is sharper, and with Hickox he brings out the originality of the writing all the more cleanly. It is fascinating to find some passages anticipating the more abrasive side of Britten, and specifically the *Cello symphony* with which this is coupled.

Alexander Baillie is certainly an eloquent advocate, at times wearing his heart unashamedly on his sleeve, at others more thoughtfully reticent. John Carewe matches his rhapsodic approach and secures wholly idiomatic playing from the fine Cologne orchestra, both here and in a splendidly fluid account of the expansive tone-poem, *Enter spring*, which is wholly spontaneous and generates considerable power. The studio recording is vivid and wide-ranging.

2 Entr'actes: Rosemary; Canzonetta. Heart's ease. 3 Lyrics for piano: No. 1, Heart's ease (orch. Cornford). *Norse legend;* (i) *Suite for cello and orchestra (Morning song; Elegie; Scherzo),* arr. & orch. Cornford. *Threads* (incidental music); *2 Intermezzi. 3 Vignettes de danse. The turtle's retort (one-step),* orch. Wetherell.
*** Pearl SHECD 9600 [id.]. (i) Lowri Blake; Chelsea Op. Group O, Howard Williams.

Those who enjoy Elgar's lighter music will surely find much to delight them in this diverse and very tuneful collection, even if a number of the items are arrangements by other hands. The *Norse legend* is quite brief; then comes the Elgarian *Rosemary*; but the *Suite for cello and orchestra* is by no means insubstantial and it has a sympathetic, rich-toned soloist in Lowri Blake. The incidental music for *Threads* brings more nostalgia; *Heart's ease* has a delicious oriental delicacy and the *Three Vignettes* recall three lady friends, obviously of very contrasting dispositions. *The turtle's retort* ends the programme in good rhythmic spirits, and Eric Wetherell's scoring is nicely judged. Altogether this is a most entertaining concert that is more than the sum of its constituents. The Chelsea orchestra are a semi-professional group, but no apologies need be made for their response or their ensemble, and Howard Williams directs with spontaneous warmth and an apt sense of pacing. The recording is first rate, with plenty of colour and ambient warmth.

Phantasm for piano and orchestra.
*** Conifer Dig. CDFC 175; *MCFC 175* [id.]. Kathryn Stott, RPO, Handley – IRELAND: *Piano concerto;* WALTON: *Sinfonia concertante.* ***

Bridge's curiously titled *Phantasm* is a large-scale piano concerto, some 26 minutes long, in a single, massive movement. It makes a generous and very welcome coupling for two of the most colourful of concertante piano works written by English composers. Completed in 1931, *Phantasm* is one of Bridge's later works and seriously disconcerted his admirers with its tough, uncompromising idiom, very different from his easier, more lyrical early style. Starting with an extended slow introduction, the sections are clearly defined – though, sadly, Conifer fail to provide any CD tracks for them – with an energetic main allegro relaxing into a waltz-like second subject. That in turn subsides into a central Andante, before the allegro material is recapitulated, building to a formidable climax which finally dies away in a mood of disillusion. Kathryn Stott, most sympathetically accompanied by Vernon Handley and the RPO, proves a persuasive, committed interpreter, matching her achievement in the other two works on the disc. Warm, generally well-balanced recording.

The Sea (suite).
*** Chan. Dig. CHAN 8473; *ABTD 1184* [id.]. Ulster O, Handley – BAX: *On the sea-shore;* BRITTEN: *Sea interludes.* ***

The Sea was a work which Benjamin Britten heard as a boy at the Norwich Festival in 1924. It impressed him so deeply that, before long, it led to his taking composition lessons with the older composer. It receives a brilliant and deeply sympathetic performance from Handley and the Ulster Orchestra, recorded with a fullness and vividness to make this a demonstration disc.

Suite for strings.
*** Chan. Dig. CHAN 8390; *ABTD 1112* [id.]. ECO, Garforth – IRELAND: *Downland suite; Holy Boy; Elegiac meditations.* ***
*** Nimbus Dig. NI 5068 [id.]. E. String O, Boughton – BUTTERWORTH: *Banks of green willow; Idylls; Shropshire lad;* PARRY: *Lady Radnor's suite.* ***

Suite for strings; Summer; There is a willow grows aslant a brook.
*** Chan. CHAN 8373 [id.]. Bournemouth Sinf., Del Mar – BANTOCK: *Pierrot of the minute;* BUTTERWORTH: *Banks of green willow.* ***

Summer is beautifully played by the Bournemouth Sinfonietta under Norman Del Mar. The same images of nature permeate the miniature tone-poem, *There is a willow grows aslant a brook*, an inspired piece, very sensitively managed. The *Suite for strings* is equally individual. Its third movement, a *Nocturne*, is lovely. The CD transfer is excellent and one can relish its fine definition and presence.

The ECO also play well for David Garforth in the *Suite for strings*. This performance, though not scrupulous in observing the composer's metronome markings, is extremely committed; it is certainly excellently recorded, with great clarity and presence. The slow movement in particular is played with great eloquence. The disc does not score high marks on playing time – it runs for under 50 minutes – but it scores on every other point.

The Nimbus collection is more generous and is certainly well chosen. Here Bridge's *Suite* again receives a lively and responsive performance, from William Boughton and his excellent Birmingham-based orchestra, treated to ample, sumptuously atmospheric recording, more resonant than its competitors.

CHAMBER MUSIC

Cello sonata.
*** Chan. Dig. CHAN 8499; *ABTD 1209* [id.]. Raphael and Peter Wallfisch – BAX: *Rhapsodic ballad;* DELIUS: *Sonata;* WALTON: *Passacaglia.* ***

Cello sonata; 2 Pieces: Meditation; Spring song.
**(*) ASV Dig. CDDCA 796; *ZCDCA 796* [id.]. Bernard Gregor-Smith, Yolande Wrigley – DEBUSSY; DOHNÁNYI: *Sonatas.* **(*)

At first sight the *Cello sonata* seems to bear all the imprints of the English pastoral school with its pastel colourings and gentle, discursive lines, but there is no lack of fibre here and a pervasive sense that the pre-war Edwardian world was gone beyond recall. It is a distinctive world that Bridge evokes and one to which Raphael Wallfisch and his father, Peter, are completely attuned. There is a sense of scale about their reading which is impressive, and they are beautifully recorded.

The *Cello sonata* of Frank Bridge long languished in neglect and reached the gramophone only when Mstislav Rostropovich and Benjamin Britten recorded it in the 1960s. This version will doubtless return to circulation in due course, but among the present recordings of the work the ASV account by Bernard Gregor-Smith and Yolande Wrigley can hold its head high. It is played with intensity and sensitivity. The recording is a bit close – certainly not as beautifully balanced as the old Decca – but those wanting the coupling (and the Dohnányi is an excellent piece) need not hesitate.

3 Idylls for string quartet.
*** Conifer Dig. CDCF 196; *MCFC 196.* Brindisi Qt – BRITTEN: *String quartet No. 2;* Imogen HOLST: *String quartet No. 1.* ***

The *Three Idylls* are an early work, dating from 1906 and following close on the heels of the *First Quartet*. It was on the *Second Idyll* that Benjamin Britten based his celebrated *Variations*. They are currently unrepresented in the catalogue except by this CD, and are well served by the Brindisi Quartet.

(i) *Phantasie (quartet) in F sharp min. Phantasie trio in C min.; Piano trio No. 2.*
*** Hyp. Dig. CDA 66279; *KA 66279* [id.]. Dartington Trio; (i) with P. Ireland.

Piano trio No. 2.
(*) Chan. Dig. CHAN 8495; *ABTD 1205* [id.]. Borodin Trio – BAX: *Piano trio.* *

The playing of the *Phantasie trio* by the Dartington Trio is of exceptional eloquence and sensitivity. They are no less persuasive in the *F sharp minor Phantasy*. Their account of the visionary post-war *Piano trio No. 2* of 1929 is more completely inside this score than is the Borodins' very well-recorded version on Chandos. The Hyperion recording is altogether superb, in the demonstration bracket, perfectly natural and beautifully proportioned.

The playing of the Borodin Trio is also very distinguished, if not quite as compelling as that by the Dartington group on Hyperion; but, given such advocacy and the excellence of the Chandos recording, let us hope that this will win more new friends for this music.

Phantasie trio in C min.
*** Gamut Dig. GAMCD 518 [id.]. Hartley Trio – CLARKE: *Piano trio;* IRELAND: *Phantasie.* ***

Bridge was the most successful of the composers who took up the challenge of W. W. Cobbett to develop the idea of one-movement chamber works, incorporating various sections like the Elizabethan *Fantasies*. Bridge's *Phantasie trio*, just over 15 minutes long, is an urgent and passionate piece which richly deserves this revival, along with trios by other pupils of Stanford. Warmly persuasive playing, well recorded.

String quartet No. 3.
*** Virgin Dig. VC7 91196-2 [id.]. Endellion Qt – WALTON: *String quartet*. ***

Bridge's keenly imaginative string quartets have, surprisingly, been neglected on CD, but this superb performance of what is arguably the finest of the four helps to fill a serious gap. Like the *Piano sonata*, this was a work profoundly influenced by the composer's response to the First World War and the deaths of many friends, bringing a rejection of his earlier English-based idiom. Often bald in expression, bitter and abrasive, the three large-scale movements no longer seem disturbing in their idiom, though they are still disturbing in their emotions. This is the deeply felt and original expression of a composer whose achievement lay in his own music, not just in discovering and drawing out the talents of Benjamin Britten. The Endellion Quartet, one of our very finest, plays with polish, purpose and passion, and is very well recorded.

PIANO MUSIC

Arabesque; Capriccios Nos. 1–2; Dedication; Fairy tale suite; Gargoyle; Hidden fires; In autumn; 3 Miniatures; Pastorals, Sets 1–2; Sea idyll; 3 Improvisations for the left hand; Winter pastoral.
*** Continuum Dig. CCD 1016 [id.]. Peter Jacobs.

Berceuse; Canzonetta; 4 Characteristic pieces; Dramatic fantasia; Étude rhapsodic; Lament; Pensées fugitives; 3 Pieces; 4 Pieces; 3 Poems; Scherzettino.
*** Continuum Dig. CCD 1018 [id.]. Peter Jacobs.

Piano sonata; Graziella; The Hour-glass; 3 Lyrics; Miniature pastorals, Set 3; Miniature suite (ed. Hindmarsh); *3 Sketches*. arr. of BACH: *Chorale: Komm, süsser Tod, BWV 478.*
*** Continuum Dig. CCD 1019 [id.]. Peter Jacobs.

Peter Jacobs has been a consistent champion of neglected piano music, including the sonatas of Harold Truscott. Here he provides a complete survey of the piano music of Frank Bridge, and it proves an invaluable enterprise. What an intelligent and sensitive player this artist is, and how pleasing to hear an instrument in such good condition! The recorded sound is very good indeed: clean, well defined and present, and the acoustic lively. Bridge has a much larger body of keyboard music to his credit than is generally supposed, and the present set covers almost three decades of creative activity, from the *Capriccio No. 1 in A minor*, written in 1903 and entered for a competition sponsored by Mark Hambourg, through to the *Gargoyle* (1928). The *Sonata*, written in memory of his friend and fellow composer, Ernest Farrar, who was a casualty of the war in 1917, is outstanding by any standards; but many of the shorter pieces are highly imaginative, and almost everything is very rewarding. Calum MacDonald's excellent notes tracing his development over these years are worth a mention too.

Piano sonata; Capriccios Nos. 1 & 2; Ecstasy; The Hour-glass; Sea Idyll; Vignettes de Marseille.
*** Conifer Dig. CDCF 186; *MCFC 186* [id.]. Kathryn Stott.

Kathryn Stott provides a formidable and illuminating single-disc and -tape selection from the piano music of Frank Bridge, for those who are unable or unwilling to stretch to Peter Jacobs's indispensable complete survey. Kathryn Stott's recital culminates in the masterly large-scale *Sonata* that Bridge wrote in disillusion in the years after the First World War, and she gives it a powerfully concentrated account. That darkly elegiac piece marked a breakthrough in Bridge's work, when he cast aside conventional English attitudes and produced a piece which took note of the then avant garde in Europe. It is arguably the greatest piano sonata ever written by a British composer. The short early pieces, brilliantly and imaginatively written, give little inkling of such a development. The *Vignettes de Marseille* were inspired by a holiday that the Bridges spent with his patron, Elizabeth Sprague Coolidge, in 1925 and are highly colourful and atmospheric display pieces which owe more to Ravel than to Schoenberg; but the three thoughtful little vignettes which make up *The Hour-glass* have a depth and originality that belie their scale, while *The Dusk* in *The Hour-glass* almost calls to mind the Debussy of the *Études*. Kathryn Stott is responsive to every changing mood, and these are outstanding performances, very well recorded.

Britten, Benjamin (1913–76)

An American overture, Op. 27; Occasional overture, Op. 38; Sinfonia da Requiem. Op. 20; Suite on English folk tunes: A time there was, Op. 90.
*** EMI Dig. CDC7 47343-2 [id.]. CBSO, Rattle.

While the most ambitious piece here is the *Sinfonia da Requiem*, written after the death of Britten's parents, the *Folk tunes suite* is a good deal more diverse in mood than one might expect, and the early *American overture*, with its attractive whiff of Copland, is matched by the much later Occasional overture in its brilliant orchestral command. The whole programme is splendidly played by the City of Birmingham orchestra under Rattle, whose passionate view of the *Sinfonia da Requiem* is unashamedly extrovert, yet finding subtle detail too. The recording is admirably vivid and clear.

(i) *Piano concerto in D, Op. 13. Paul Bunyan overture.*
*** Collins Dig. 1102-2; *1102-4* [id.]. (i) Joanna MacGregor; ECO, Bedford – SAXTON: *Music to celebrate the resurrection of Christ.* ***

When still only 26, Britten wrote his formidable *Piano concerto* for a Prom in 1938. He later rejected the slow movement, a quirky *Recitative and aria* with tongue-in-cheek hints of blues, a polka and even Rachmaninov. He replaced it in 1945 with an *Impromptu*, simpler and more obviously apt. The sparkiness of the young Britten makes the original well worth hearing too; the characterful young Joanna MacGregor gets the best of both worlds by recording both slow movements, so that you can take your pick. She may not quite match the command of Sviatoslav Richter in his classic recording of the later version with the composer conducting but, with Steuart Bedford a deeply understanding conductor, this is a ripe and refreshing performance, well recorded. The brassy *Paul Bunyan overture*, never used with the operetta, has been orchestrated by Colin Matthews.

(i) *Piano concerto, Op. 13;* (ii) *Violin concerto, Op. 15.*
(M) *** Decca 417 308-2. (i) Sviatoslav Richter; (ii) Lubotsky; ECO, composer.
*** Collins Dig. 1301-2 [id.]. (i) Joanna MacGregor; (ii) Lorraine McAslan; ECO, Bedford.

Richter is incomparable in interpreting the *Piano concerto*, not only the thoughtful, introspective moments but the Liszt-like bravura passages (many of them surprising from this composer). With its highly original sonorities the *Violin concerto* makes a splendid vehicle for another Soviet artist, Mark Lubotsky. Recorded in The Maltings, the playing of the ECO under the composer's direction matches the inspiration of the soloists. The 1971 recording sounds splendid on this reissued CD.

This apt recoupling of Britten's two concertos in these outstanding Collins recordings makes an attractive disc, though the original slow movement of the *Piano concerto* – in the earlier issue included as a fascinating supplement to Joanna MacGregor's performance – has here been omitted.

(i) *Violin concerto, Op. 15. Canadian carnival overture, Op. 19; Mont Juic* (written with Lennox Berkeley).
❀ *** Collins Dig. 1123-2; *1123-4* [id.]. (i) Lorraine McAslan, ECO, Steuart Bedford.

Lorraine McAslan studied with the celebrated Dorothy Delay, whose pupils included Itzhak Perlman and Cho-Liang Lin, and hers is a performance of consummate and commanding artistry. The virtuosity is effortless and always subservient to musical ends; her artistic insights are unusually keen and she brings to the *Concerto* a subtle imagination and great emotional intensity. There is a demonic fire to the scherzo which is even more effective than the composer's own version with Mark Lubotsky. Steuart Bedford gets first-class playing from the English Chamber Orchestra and underlines the pain and poignancy underlying much of this music. The recording is remarkably well balanced: those who dislike the upfront, larger-than-life aural image found in so many concerto recordings (Perlman's for example) will welcome this truthful and exceptionally wide-ranging and vivid recording. *Mont Juic* and the *Canadian carnival overture* are eminently well served by these splendid musicians and the engineers.

(i) *Lachrymae (Reflections on a song by John Dowland), Op. 48a; Prelude and fugue for 18-part string orchestra, Op. 29; Simple symphony, Op. 4.* PURCELL, arr. Britten: *Chacony in G min.*

**(*) Virgin Dig. VCy7 91080-2; *VCy 791080-4* [id.]. (i) Roger Chase; LCO, Christopher Warren-Green.

Though Christopher Warren-Green's Britten programme is not quite as successful as his Elgar/Vaughan Williams coupling, the playing here has comparable commitment and ardour. The sheer energy of the opening movement of the *Simple symphony* is breathtaking; this is surely too fast, even for a *Boisterous bourrée*, but with bold articulation the effect is certainly exhilarating. The *Sentimental saraband*, by contrast, is very relaxed and winningly nostalgic; the incandescent energy returns in the finale. The players of the LCO obviously enjoy themselves in Britten's arrangement of the great Purcell *Chaconne*, expanded from its sparer original version into a grand – even sumptuous – affair for a full string orchestra.

(i) *Matinées musicales; Soirées musicales;* (ii; iv) *Young person's guide to the orchestra;* (iii; iv) *Peter Grimes: 4 Sea interludes and Passacaglia.*
(M) *** Decca 425 659-2; *425 659-4* [id.]. (i) Nat. PO, Bonynge; (ii) LSO; (iii) ROHCG O; (iv) composer.

Britten wrote his *Soirées musicales* for a GPO film-score in the 1930s; the *Matinées* followed in 1941 and were intended as straight ballet music. Both are wittily if rather sparsely scored, deriving their musical content directly from Rossini. Bonynge's versions are brightly played and extremely vividly recorded in the best Decca manner. They are now reissued at mid-price, coupled with Britten's brilliant account of the *Young person's guide to the orchestra* and the *Sea interludes and Passacaglia* from *Peter Grimes*. The latter are taken from the complete recording, and this means that odd extracts from the vocal parts are included so that the general effect is not as tidy as the concert version. That proviso apart, these are wonderfully vital accounts of some superbly atmospheric music.

Prelude and fugue for 18 solo strings, Op. 29; Simple symphony, Op. 4; Variations on a theme of Frank Bridge, Op. 10.
*** ASV Dig. CDDCA 591; *ZCDCA 591* [id.]. N. Sinfonia, Hickox.

Among available collections of Britten's string music, the ASV issue is notable for an outstandingly fine account of the *Frank Bridge variations*, which stands up well alongside the composer's own version. Throughout, the string playing is committedly responsive, combining polish with eloquence, the rich sonorities resonating powerfully in the glowing ambience of All Saints' Quayside Church, Newcastle. The reverberation also recalls Britten's own famous account of the *Simple symphony*, made in The Maltings, even if Hickox does not quite match the composer's rhythmic bounce in the *Playful pizzicato*. The *Prelude and fugue* is comparably eloquent, although here the playing is marginally less assured. The recording is first class, with the bright upper range well supported by the firm bass.

The Prince of the Pagodas (complete).
❀ *** Virgin Dig. VCD7 91103-2; *VCD 791103-4* (2) [id.]. L. Sinf., Knussen.

(i) *The Prince of the Pagodas (ballet), Op. 57* (complete); (ii) *Diversions for piano (left hand) and orchestra, Op. 21.*
**(*) Decca 421 855-2 (2) [id.]. (i) ROHCG O; (ii) Julius Katchen, LSO, composer.

The multicoloured instrumentation – much influenced by Britten's visit to Bali – is caught with glorious richness in Oliver Knussen's really complete version for Virgin of the full-length ballet. Knussen confesses to having loved Britten's own recording from childhood, and his own performance is no less dramatic and persuasive. But in addition he scores significantly in opening out more than 40 cuts, most of them small, which Britten only sanctioned to fit the three Acts on to four LP sides. So Knussen includes four whole numbers omitted before, as well as important transitions and 'middle-eights' which, as Knussen explains, are integral to the musical argument. The tracking on the CD is very generous and is complemented by a detailed synopsis of the plot, which cues in the track-numbers.

The composer's own recording was originally made after the first performances at Covent Garden, early in 1957, with Britten drawing playing of electric intensity and knife-edged precision from the orchestra. The stereo has come up with astonishing vividness on CD, with some thinness only on violin tone to betray the age. Britten's many offbeat fanfares ring out superbly, and his re-creation of oriental textures is caught magically. With Julius Katchen as soloist in the distinctive left-hand piano part, Britten conducts the LSO in an equally inspired account of the *Diversions*, the most neglected of his full-scale concertante works. The 1954 sound is amazingly vivid too, though (without acknowledgement on the CD box) this is in mono only, and the quality is inevitably flatter than in the complete ballet.

(i) *Sinfonia da requiem, Op. 20;* (ii) *Symphony for cello and orchestra, Op. 68;* (iii) *Cantata misericordium, Op. 69.*
(M) *** Decca 425 100-2 [id.]. (i) New Philh. O; (ii) Rostropovich, ECO; (iii) Pears, Fischer-Dieskau, LSO Ch., LSO; composer.

Britten's own 1964 recordings of the *Sinfonia da requiem* and the *Cello symphony* appear on CD with the *Cantata misericordium* added for good measure. All the performances are definitive, and Rostropovich's account of the *Cello symphony* in particular is everything one could ask for. It is a marvellous piece. The CD transfers are admirably managed.

Simple symphony (for strings), Op. 4.
*** DG Dig. 423 624-2 [id.]. Orpheus CO – BIZET: *Symphony;* PROKOFIEV: *Symphony No. 1.* ***

(i) *Simple symphony, Op. 4; Variations on a theme of Frank Bridge, Op. 10;* (ii) *The Young person's guide to the orchestra (Variations and fugue on a theme of Purcell), Op. 34.*
**(*) Decca 417 509-2. (i) ECO, (ii) LSO; composer.

These Decca recordings arrive on CD with very tangible strings and great clarity and presence overall; some ears, however, might decide that the violins are too brightly lit. Britten takes a very brisk view of his *Young person's guide*, so brisk that even the LSO players cannot always quite match him. But every bar has a vigour which makes the music sound more youthful than usual, and the headlong, uninhibited account of the final fugue (trombones as vulgar as you like) is an absolute joy. In the *Frank Bridge variations* Britten goes more for half-tones and he achieves an almost circumspect coolness in the waltz-parody of the *Romance*; in the *Viennese waltz* section later, he is again subtly atmospheric; and in the *Funeral march* he is relatively solemn. The *Simple symphony* makes a splendid foil, with its charm and high spirits; no one else has found quite the infectious bounce in the *Playful pizzicato* that the composer does, aided by the glowing resonance of The Maltings where the recording was made.

The *Simple symphony* goes nicely alongside the Bizet and Prokofiev works, especially when played as freshly and characterfully as here by the Orpheus group. They are especially gentle and touching in the *Sentimental saraband*, and the *Boisterous bourrée* is contrastingly robust. Britten himself found more fun in the *Playful pizzicato*, and perhaps the Orpheus account of the *Frolicsome finale* could be more inconsequential in spirit; but the reading is all-of-a-piece and enjoyably spontaneous. Excellent, realistic sound.

(i) *Spring Symphony, Op. 44;* (ii) *Welcome ode, Op. 95;* (iii) *Psalm 150, Op. 67.*
**(*) Chan. Dig. CHAN 8855; *ABTD 1472* [id.]. (i) Gale, Hodgson, Hill, Southend Boys' Ch., LSO; (ii) City of London Schools' Ch., LSO; (iii) City of London Schools' Ch. and O; Richard Hickox.

Richard Hickox's version brings the advantage not only of warm and refined digital sound but also of a first recording of Britten's last completed work, the *Welcome ode*, an unpretentious little suite of five movements, three of them choral, written for children only three months before he died. It makes an apt fill-up when its mood of optimism so closely reflects the exhilarating close of the *Spring Symphony*, with its descant of *Sumer is icumen in*. The third work, equally apt, is the boisterous setting of *Psalm 150*, which Britten wrote for the preparatory school he had attended as a boy in Lowestoft. With more variable soloists – the tenor Martyn Hill outstandingly fine, the soprano Elizabeth Gale often too edgy – Hickox's version of the *Spring Symphony* does not quite match the composer's own in gutsy urgency, even in the final ensemble, but there is compensation in the refinement of detail and of sound.

Suite on English folk-songs (A time there was); Young person's guide to the orchestra, Op. 34; Peter Grimes: 4 Sea interludes and Passacaglia.
(M) **(*) Sony SMK 47541. NYPO, Leonard Bernstein.

Bernstein's charismatic account of the *Young person's guide to the orchestra* brings much exhilarating bravura from the New York soloists, notably the flutes, clarinets and trumpets. The violins sound a bit glassy in their brilliance, but Purcell's tune, both at the opening and at the culmination of the fugue, is treated grandly and made to sound dignified. The 1961 recording, made in the New York Manhattan Center, is fuller than usual from this source and provides plenty of sonority for the brass while underscoring the percussion with a weighty bass drum. The other pieces are studio recordings from the mid-1970s and the sound is vivid but less expansive. The performance of *A time there was* (its title quoting from Hardy) reveals a darkness and weight of expression behind the seemingly trivial plan. The third movement, *Hankin Booby*, is an angular piece in which woodwind squeals in imitation of medieval manners. The other movements are less abrasive. For violins alone, *Hunt the squirrel* is brief, brilliant and witty; the final movement, *Lord Melbourne*, with its extended cor anglais solo, is plainly written in the shadow of death. Bernstein misses a little of the wit but is warmly sympathetic, and the dramatic account of the *Grimes interludes*, with a powerful *Passacaglia*, makes a good coupling.

Symphony for cello and orchestra, Op. 68.
*** Sony Dig. MK 44900 [id.]. Yo-Yo Ma, Baltimore SO, Zinman – BARBER: *Cello concerto.* ***
(M) *** EMI Dig. CDM7 63909-2. Stephen Isserlis, City of L. Sinfonia, Hickox – BRIDGE: *Oration.* ***

(i) *Symphony for cello and orchestra, Op. 68. Death in Venice: suite, Op. 88* (arr. Bedford).
*** Chan. Dig. CHAN 8363; *ABTD 1126* [id.]. (i) Wallfisch; ECO, Bedford.

With a comparison ready to hand, it is the more remarkable how closely Wallfisch manages to match Rostropovich's earlier version (see above). If Wallfisch's tone is not as resonant as that of the Russian cellist, the slight help from the recording balance gives it all the power needed. Sounding less improvisatory than Rostropovich, he and Bedford give a more consistent sense of purpose, and the weight and range of the brilliant and full Chandos recording quality add to the impact, with Bedford's direction even more spacious than the composer's, the effect emphasized by the Chandos ambience, spacious and warm. Steuart Bedford's encapsulation of Britten's last opera into this rich and colourful suite makes a splendid coupling, but it is a pity that the CD does not have bands between the separate sections.

Yo-Yo Ma, in partnership with David Zinman, gives a superb performance of the Britten *Cello symphony*. The wayward mystery in the first movement, rather than its more aggressive qualities, is what predominates, and in the scherzo Ma is masterly in bringing out the lightness and fantasy. The third-movement *Adagio* is softer-grained than usual, with the soloist placed naturally, leading on to an account of the finale, a shade faster than usual, compellingly purposeful, which brings out the Copland-like swagger of the main passacaglia theme. The orchestra plays with brilliance and commitment in a full and well-balanced recording.

Stephen Isserlis provides a valuable mid-priced alternative to Wallfisch and Ma. With speeds generally a little slower, Isserlis is not quite as taut and electric as his rival, partly because the recording does not present the solo instrument so cleanly. It remains a powerful, dramatic performance and makes excellent value, if the Bridge coupling is suitable.

Sinfonia da requiem, Op. 20; The Young person's guide to the orchestra, Op. 34; Peter Grimes: 4 Sea interludes & Passacaglia, Op. 34.
**(*) Virgin Dig. VC7 90834-2; *VC 790834-2* [id.]. RLPO, Libor Pešek.

Though Pešek fails to convey the full ominous weight of the first movement of the *Sinfonia da requiem*, he then directs a dazzling account of the central *Dies Irae scherzo*, taken breathtakingly fast, and finds an intense repose in the calm of the final *Requiem aeternam*. The *Sea interludes* – given here complete with the fine *Passacaglia* – are also well played, though they sound very literal, not ideally atmospheric. The *Young person's guide* lacks a degree of tension, with the fugue not dashing enough. The recording is comfortably reverberant and full, but takes some of the bite from the playing.

Variations on a theme of Frank Bridge, Op. 10.
(M) *** Decca 421 391-2; *421 391-4* [id.]. ASMF, Marriner – BUTTERWORTH: *Banks of green willow* etc.; WARLOCK: *Capriol suite.* ***

Although not even Marriner quite matches the natural warmth of expression of the composer himself in this music, his is a superb performance, if anything even more polished, and recorded with remarkable vividness, the CD giving the impression of great presence and immediacy.

The Young person's guide to the orchestra (Variations and fugue on a theme of Purcell), Op. 34.
(M) *** EMI Dig. CD-EMX 2165; *TC-EMX 2165* (without narration). LPO, Sian Edwards – PROKOFIEV: *Peter and the wolf* **(*); RAVEL: *Ma Mère l'Oye.* **
(M) ** EMI Dig. CDD7 64300-2; *ET 764300-4*. Minnesota O, Marriner – HOLST: *The Planets.* **

Sian Edwards, always impressive in the recording studio, provides an excellent mid-priced digital version of Britten's orchestral showpiece. She does not press the earlier variations too hard, revelling in the colour of her wind soloists, yet the violins enter zestfully and the violas make a touching contrast. The brass bring fine bite and sonority. The fugue has plenty of vitality and the climax is spectacularly expansive in the resonant acoustics of Watford Town Hall.

Marriner's Minnesota account of the *Young person's guide* is well played but a little stiff. It has the advantage of being introduced by an authentic performance of Purcell's tune (from *Abdelazer*) on which the variations are based, from Andrew Parrott and his Taverner Players.

The Young person's guide to the orchestra; Gloriana: Courtly dances (suite).
(*) Telarc Dig. CD 80126 [id.] (without narration). RPO, Previn – PROKOFIEV: *Peter.* *

Unlike Previn's earlier, EMI version, in which he gave a spoken narration, the Telarc disc brings a straight performance, rather relaxed compared with the composer's own – see above – too well-behaved at times (as in the percussion section) but ending with a fizzing account of the finale. The *Gloriana dances*, done with great flair, make a welcome filler. The CD has only four tracks but plentiful index points for the different variations and movements.

CHAMBER MUSIC

Cello sonata, Op. 65.
**(*) Sony Dig. MK 44980 [id.]. Yo-Yo Ma, Emanuel Ax – R. STRAUSS: *Sonata.* **(*)

Yo-Yo Ma and Emanuel Ax give an account of the *Cello sonata* which is very carefully thought out – perhaps too carefully, for one is left with the impression that these artists are striving too hard to shed new light on the piece. It is at times just too self-aware, with exaggerated pianissimi and self-conscious phrasing. The recording is very truthful, though the sound Decca provide for Rostropovich and the composer is more present. However, this is still very good and worth considering.

(i) *Cello sonata in C, Op. 65;* (Unaccompanied) *Cello suites Nos. 1, Op. 72; 2, Op. 80.*
(M) *** Decca 421 859-2 [id.]. Rostropovich; (i) with composer.

This strange five-movement *Cello sonata* was written specially for Rostropovich's appearance at the Aldeburgh Festival of 1961, and the recording was made soon after the first performance. Here it is coupled with two of the *Suites for unaccompanied cello.* This is rough, gritty music in Britten's latterday manner, but Rostropovich gives such inspired accounts that the music reveals more and more with repetition. The CD transfers serve to add presence to recordings which are already very impressive.

Cello suites (Suites for unaccompanied cello) Nos. 1, Op. 72; 2, Op. 80; 3, Op. 87.
*** BIS Dig. CD 446 [id.]. Torleif Thedéen.

Torleif Thedéen is a young Swedish cellist, still in his twenties, who came to international prominence in the mid-1980s. He has magnificent tonal warmth and eloquence, and he proves a masterly advocate of these *Suites*, which were composed for Rostropovich but which sound no less convincing in his hands.

Cello suite No. 3.
*** Virgin Dig. VC7 91474-2 [id.]. Steven Isserlis – TAVENER: *The Protecting Veil.* ***

Steven Isserlis, in his dedicated performance of the third of the suites that Britten wrote for Rostropovich, brings out the spiritual element in a work which draws on traditional Russian themes, including Orthodox church music. In its sequence of short movements it is the most approachable of Britten's cello works, and in such a performance relates well to the Tavener works with which it is coupled. Excellent sound.

Lachrymae, Op. 48.
*** EMI Dig. CDC7 54394-2 [id.]. Tabea Zimmermann, Hartmut Höll – SHOSTAKOVICH: *Viola sonata;* STRAVINSKY: *Élégie.* ***

Britten composed his moving *Lachrymae* ('Reflections on a song of John Dowland') in 1950 for William Primrose. Tabea Zimmermann gives them with an altogether exemplary eloquence and is recorded with great naturalness and presence.

(i) *Sinfonietta, Op. 1;* (ii) *String quartets Nos. 2, Op. 36; 3, Op. 94.*
(M) *** Decca 425 715-2. (i) Vienna Octet; (ii) Amadeus Qt.

Britten's Opus 1 was written when he was in his teens. It has some characteristic fingerprints but points atypically towards Central Europe – reflection no doubt of his desire at the time to study with Berg in Vienna. Its mixture of seriousness and assurance is not unappealing and its astringency is brought out well in this appropriately Viennese chamber performance. The *Third Quartet*, a late work, was written for the Amadeus, who play it convincingly. It is spare, seemingly wayward, but with an underlying depth of feeling which comes to the surface in its brooding *Passacaglia*. The *Second* ends with a forceful *Chaconne*. The contrasts of style and mood are developed well here, in performances that could be regarded as definitive. On CD the recording is full, vivid and realistic.

String quartet No. 1 in D, Op. 25a.
*** CRD CRD 3351 [id.]. Alberni Qt – SHOSTAKOVICH: *Piano quintet.* **(*)

String quartets Nos. 2 in C, Op. 36; 3, Op. 94.
*** CRD CRD 3395 [id.]. Alberni Qt.

The Alberni Quartet have good ensemble and intonation, and they play with considerable feeling; moreover the CDs are available separately. The recording is vivid and clear in its remastered format.

String quartet No. 2 in C.
*** Conifer Dig. CDCF 196; *MCFC 196*. Brindisi Qt – BRIDGE: *3 Idylls;* I. HOLST: *String quartet No. 1.* ***

The Brindisi on Conifer give an excellent account of the *Second Quartet* which can hold its own with the best and comes with interesting couplings. They are an accomplished body and are well (if a shade too forwardly) recorded.

String quartet No. 3, Op. 94.
*** ASV Dig. CDDCA 608; *ZCDCA 608* [id.]. Lindsay Qt – TIPPETT: *Quartet No. 4.* ***

The Lindsay performance brings the most expansive and deeply expressive reading on record. The commitment of the performers makes the final slow movement all the more affecting, baring the inner heart of Britten's rarefied inspiration. The ASV recording is vivid, with fine presence; but extraneous sounds are intrusive at times: heavy breathing, snapping of strings on finger-board, etc.

(i) *Suite for harp, Op. 83;* (ii) *2 Insect pieces, for oboe & piano; 6 Metamorphoses after Ovid (for oboe solo), Op. 49.*
*** Mer. CDE 84119 [id.]. (i) Osian Ellis; (ii) Sarah Watkins; Ledger – *Tit for Tat* etc. ***.

It was for Osian Ellis that Britten wrote the *Harp suite*, which sounds surprisingly unlike any other harp music at all. Ellis remains the ideal performer. A younger artist, the oboist Sarah Watkins, gives biting and intense performances of the unaccompanied *Metamorphoses*, as well as the two early *Insect pieces*, with Philip Ledger – a long-time Aldeburgh associate – at the piano. The sound is full and immediate, set convincingly in a small but helpful hall. This is part of a cleverly planned recital which includes *Tit for Tat* and six folksong arrangements with their original harp accompaniments (see below).

PIANO MUSIC

Music for 2 pianos: (i) *2 Lullabies; Mazurca elegiaca; Introduction and Rondo alla burlesca.* (Piano): *3 Character Pieces; Holiday Diary; Notturno; Sonatina romantica; 12 Variations; Five Walztes.*
*** Virgin Dig. VC7 91203-2; *VC 791203-4* [id.]. Stephen Hough, (i) with Ronan O'Hora.

Though he was a brilliant pianist himself, Britten wrote relatively little piano music. This superb disc, with Stephen Hough an inspired interpreter, generously collects it all, including early pieces revived since the composer's death. The earliest music is the charming set of *Walztes* (his original boyhood mis-spelling) that he wrote between the ages of ten and twelve, published in 1970 with only minor modification. In the *Notturno*, written for the first Leeds Piano Competition, Hough's love of keyboard sonorities masterfully overcomes the awkwardness of the writing. Hough is joined by a most sympathetic partner for the items for two pianos, the early *Lullabies* and the larger-scale wartime pieces, the *Mazurka* and the *Rondo*, both grittily demanding. Excellent sound.

VOCAL MUSIC

(i) *A Boy was born, Op. 3;* (ii) *The Little Sweep (Let's make an opera).*
(M) (***) Decca stereo/mono 430 367-2; *430 367-4* [id.]. (i) Hartnett, Purcell Singers, English

Op. Group Boys' Ch.; Choristers of All Saints', Margaret St; (ii) Vyvyan, Cantelo, Marilyn Baker, Soskin, Hemmings, Ingram, Fairhurst, Lyn Vaughan, Nancy Thomas, Pears, Anthony, Alleyn's School Ch., E. Op. Group O; composer.

Though Britten's own recording of *The Little Sweep* is in mono only, it sounds amazingly vivid still in the CD transfer, with voices in particular full and immediate. As a performance it has never been surpassed in its vigour and freshness, with the film-star-to-be, David Hemmings, here as impressive in the title-role for treble, as he also was in *The Turn of the Screw*. Others in the cast, like Jennifer Vyvyan and April Cantelo, represent the accomplished group of singers that Britten gathered for his Aldeburgh Festival performances. The choruses, usually sung by the audience, are here done by the school choir. The unaccompanied Christmas cantata, *A Boy was born*, is the product of Britten's early maturity. Again, it has never been more convincingly recorded than here in the composer's own reading, which uses the revised text he prepared in 1955, in places simplifying the complex part-writing.

A.M.D.G.; (i) *A Boy was born; Hymn to St Cecilia; A Shepherd's carol.*
*** Virgin Dig. VC7 90728-2; *VC 790728-4* [id.]. London Sinf. Voices, (i) St Paul's Cathedral Choristers, Terry Edwards.

A.M.D.G. (*Ad majorem Dei gloriam*, 'To the greater glory of God', the motto of the Jesuit order) is a collection of choral settings of poems by Gerard Manley Hopkins. As is plain from this beautiful and brilliant first recording of what is in effect a choral suite, they contain some masterly inspirations, ending with the loveliest song of all, a Prayer. The Sinfonietta Voices sing with the same sensitive virtuosity in the equally taxing set of choral variations on a Christmas theme, *A Boy was born*, firmer and more dramatic than the rival one from the Corydon Singers on Hyperion. Using solo voices, with Edwards himself singing the bass part, the record also has a fresh and incisive account of *A Hymn to St Cecilia*, made the sharper and cleaner in its gently jazzy rhythms by the slimmer texture. As a charming supplement comes another rarity, the *Shepherd's carol*, written in 1944 for a BBC radio play. Fine recording, both atmospheric and clear.

A boy was born, Op. 3; Festival Te Deum, Op. 32; Rejoice in the Lamb, Op. 30; A Wedding anthem, Op. 46.
*** Hyp. CDA 66126; *KA 66126* [id.]. Corydon Singers, Westminster Cathedral Ch., Best; Trotter (organ).

All the works included here are sharply inspired, usually to match the requirements of particular occasions. *Rejoice in the Lamb* is the most masterly of the pieces, poignantly matching the pain as well as the innocence of the words of the mad poet, Christopher Smart. The refinement and tonal range of the choirs could hardly be more impressive, and the recording is refined and atmospheric to match.

The Burning fiery furnace (2nd Parable), Op. 77.
(M) *** Decca 414 663-2. Pears, Tear, Drake, Shirley-Quirk, Ch. & O of E. Op. Group, composer and Viola Tunnard.

The story of *Burning fiery furnace* is obviously dramatic in the operatic sense, with vivid scenes like the *Entrance of Nebuchadnezzar*, the *Raising of the Idol*, and the putting of the three Israelites into the furnace. Britten is as imaginative as ever in his settings, and one must mention also the marvellous central interlude where the instrumentalists process round the church, which is stunningly well conveyed by the recording. The performers, both singers and players, are the same hand-picked cast that participated in the first performance at Orford Parish Church, where this record was made. The recording now emerges on CD with even greater vividness and presence.

Canticles Nos. 1, My beloved is mine, Op. 40; 2, Abraham and Isaac, Opp. 51; 3, Still falls the rain, Op. 55; 4, Journey of the Magi, Op. 86; 5, Death of St. Narcissus, Op. 89. A birthday hansel. Arr. of PURCELL: *Sweeter than roses.*
(M) *** Decca 425 716-2. Peter Pears, Hahessy, Bowman, Shirley-Quirk, Tuckwell, Ellis, composer.

This CD brings together on a single record all five of the miniature cantatas to which Britten gave the title 'Canticle', most of them performed by their original performers. To the new collection, the *Birthday hansel,* written in honour of the seventy-fifth birthday of Queen Elizabeth the Queen Mother, and a Purcell song-arrangement are added for good measure. The

Canticles all share the spiritual intensity which stemmed from the composer's religious faith. A beautiful collection as well as a historical document, with recording that still sounds well.

A Ceremony of carols, Op. 28; Festival Te Deum; Hymn to St Colomba; Hymn to St Peter; Hymn to the Virgin; Jubilate Deo; Missa brevis; Rejoice in the Lamb, Op. 30.
(M) *** Decca 430 097-2; *430 097-4*. Tear, Forbes Robinson, St John's College Ch., Guest; Robles; Runnett.

An exceptionally attractive and generous compilation of St John's recordings, derived from the old Argo catalogue. Guest's account of the delightful *Ceremony of carols* has tingling vitality, spacious sound and a superb contribution from Marisa Robles who plays with masterly sensitivity, especially in her solo *Interlude*. The performance of *Rejoice in the Lamb* is very similar to Britten's own, but much better recorded, and the Missa brevis has the same striking excellence of style. Of the other items added for the CD reissue, the *Hymn to the Virgin* is an engaging early work written in 1930. All these shorter pieces show the choir in superb form and the Argo analogue engineering at its most impressive.

A Ceremony of carols; Deus in adjutorium meum; Hymn of St Columba; Hymn to the Virgin; Jubilate Deo in E flat; Missa brevis, Op. 63.
*** Hyp. Dig. CDA 66220; *KA 66220* [id.]. Westminster Cathedral Ch., David Hill; (i) with S. Williams; J. O'Donnell (organ).

It was for the trebles of Westminster Cathedral Choir – when directed by George Malcolm – that Britten wrote his *Missa brevis*. Under David Hill, the present choir shows brilliantly how well standards have been kept up, not least in the treble section. Particularly impressive is the boys' singing in the *Ceremony of carols*, where the ensemble is superb, the solo work amazingly mature, and the range of tonal colouring a delight. Along with the other, rarer pieces, this is an outstanding collection, beautifully and atmospherically recorded.

(i) *A Ceremony of carols, Op. 28; Hymn to St Cecilia, Op. 17;* (ii) *Jubilate Deo;* (i) *Missa brevis, Op. 63;* (ii; iii) *Rejoice in the Lamb, Op. 30; Te Deum in C.*
*** EMI CDC7 47709. King's College, Cambridge, Ch., (i) Willcocks with Ellis; (ii) Ledger with James Bowman, D. Corkhill, J. Lancelot.

The King's trebles under Willcocks may have less edge in the *Ceremony of carols* than some of their rivals, while the *Missa brevis* can certainly benefit from throatier sound. Yet these Willcocks performances, made towards the end of his stay at Cambridge, are dramatic as well as beautiful, and well recorded, too. To make a particularly generous concert, EMI have added Philip Ledger's new version of the cantata, *Rejoice in the Lamb*, with timpani and percussion added to the original organ part. The biting climaxes are sung with passionate incisiveness, while James Bowman is in his element in the delightful passage which tells you that 'the mouse is a creature of great personal valour'. The *Te Deum* setting and the *Jubilate* make an additional bonus and are no less well sung and recorded.

4 Chansons françaises; Les illuminations; Serenade for tenor, horn and strings.
**(*) Chan. Dig. CHAN 8657; *ABTD 1343* [id.]. Felicity Lott, Anthony Rolfe Johnson, Michael Thompson, SNO, Bryden Thomson.

The *Four French songs* were written when Britten was only fourteen. These are colourful and evocative settings of Victor Hugo and Verlaine, scored with astonishing finesse, if with occasional echoes of Debussy and Ravel. The boy composer's response to the words has remarkable maturity and emotional depth, with flashes of genius worthy of Britten at his finest. Felicity Lott gives a strong and sensitive performance, as she does of the other early French cycle on the disc, *Les illuminations*, bringing out the tough and biting element rather than the sensuousness. Anthony Rolfe Johnson, soloist in the *Serenade*, gives a finely controlled performance, but is not always helped by the slight distancing of the voice in the recording balance. Nor is Michael Thompson as evocative in the horn solo as his most distinguished predecessors have been. Bryden Thomson draws crisp, responsive playing from the SNO, and the recording is warm and spacious, with plenty of presence.

The Company of Heaven. Paul Bunyan: Overture; Inkslinger's aria; Lullaby of dream shadows.
*** Virgin Dig. VC 791107-2 [id.]. Allen, Barkworth (narrators), Pope, Dressen, LPO Ch., ECO, Brunelle.

Britten wrote this big cantata, *The Company of Heaven*, for radio in 1937 as an offering for the Feast of St Michael and All Angels, but the score was lost for many years. The music, some half-hour of it, links extensive readings from texts on the theme of angels, and there is much that echoes such works of the time as the *Frank Bridge variations* and *Les illuminations*, with Britten's use of a congregational hymn in the last item anticipating both *Noye's Fludde* and *St Nicholas*. It was here too that Britten wrote, with the voice of Peter Pears in mind, a jaunty setting of Emily Brontë. Also very striking is the movement, *War in heaven*, with the men in the chorus delivering the words in sing-speech. Philip Brunelle made this recording soon after the first concert performance at The Maltings in 1989, using the same excellent forces, with the spoken contributions more effective on record than in concert. The brief excerpts from *Paul Bunyan* include an infectious 'Overture' (completed from sketches, by Colin Matthews) and a rather engaging *Lullaby*, here performed most persuasively. The recording throughout is excellent, spacious and with fine balance and presence.

Curlew River (1st parable for church performance).
(M) *** Decca 421 858-2 [id.]. Pears, Shirley-Quirk, Blackburn, soloists, Instrumental Ens., composer and Viola Tunnard.

Curlew River was initially inspired by Britten's recollection of a Noh-play which he saw in Japan. There are overtones too of Eastern music (Balinese rather than Japanese) in the highly original instrumentation and often free approach to rhythm, but mainly the work's ultimate success stems from the vividness of atmosphere within a monastery setting. Harold Blackburn plays the Abbot of the monastery who introduces the drama, while John Shirley-Quirk plays the ferryman who takes people over the Curlew River and Peter Pears sings the part of the madwoman who, distracted, searches fruitlessly for her abducted child. The recording is outstanding even by Decca standards, as the vivid CD transfer readily demonstrates.

Folk-song arrangements: *The ash grove; Avenging and bright; La belle est au jardin d'amour; The bonny Earl o' Moray; The brisk young widow; Ca' the yowes; Come you not from Newcastle; Early one morning; The foggy, foggy dew; How sweet the answer; The last rose of summer; The Lincolnshire poacher; The miller of Dee; The minstrel boy; Oft in the stilly night; O Waly, Waly; The plough boy; Le roi s'en va-t'en chasse; Sally in our alley; Sweet Polly Oliver; Tom Bowling.*
(M) *** Decca 430 063-2; *430 063-4* [id.]. Peter Pears, Benjamin Britten.

It is good to have the definitive Pears/Britten collaboration in the folksong arrangements back in the catalogue on CD. To the main LP recital, made in the Kingsway Hall in 1961, Decca have added four earlier recordings from 1959, including the most famous, *The foggy, foggy dew* and *The Lincolnshire poacher*, with its witty obbligato to match the whistle of *The plough boy*. Excellent, faithful recording, well transferred to CD.

Folksong arrangements: *The ash grove; La belle est au jardin d'amour; The bonny Earl o' Moray; The brisk young widow; Ca' the yowes; Come you not from Newcastle?; The foggy, foggy dew; The Lincolnshire poacher; Little Sir William; The minstrel boy; O can ye sew cushions; Oliver Cromwell; O Waly, Waly; The plough boy; Quand j'étais chez mon père; Le roi s'en va-t'en chasse; The Sally Gardens; Sweet Polly Oliver; The trees they grow so high.*
(M) *** EMI CDM7 69423-2. Robert Tear, Philip Ledger.

Close as Robert Tear's interpretations are to those of Peter Pears, he does have a sparkle of his own, helped by resilient accompaniment from Philip Ledger. In any case, some of these songs are unavailable in the Pears versions, and the record is a delight on its own account. *Oliver Cromwell* is among the most delectable of pay-off songs ever written. Fine recording.

(i) *The Golden Vanity;* (ii) *Noye's Fludde.*
(M) *** Decca 425 161-2. (i) Wandsworth School Boys' Ch., Burgess, composer (piano); (ii) Brannigan, Rex, Anthony, East Suffolk Children's Ch. & O, E. Op. Group O, Del Mar.

The Golden Vanity is a 'vaudeville' written for the Vienna Boys' Choir. The Wandsworth Boys are completely at home in the music and sing with pleasing freshness. The coupling, Britten's infectious children's oratorio, setting words from the Chester Miracle Play, was recorded during the 1961 Aldeburgh Festival, and not only the professional choristers but the children too have the time of their lives to the greater glory of God. All the effects have been captured miraculously here, most strikingly the entry into the Ark, while a bugle band blares out fanfares which finally turn into a rollicking march. Altogether this coupling makes a wonderful record, with the stereo readily catching the sense of occasion and particularly the sound of *Eternal Father* rising above the storm at the climax of *Noye's Fludde*.

(i; iii) *The Holy sonnets of John Donne, Op. 35;* (ii; iii) *Songs and proverbs of William Blake, Op. 74.*
*** Decca 417 428-2 (3) [id.]. (i) Peter Pears; (ii) Dietrich Fischer-Dieskau; (iii) composer – Billy Budd. ***

This performance of the John Donne cycle sets a definitive standard, with Pears's voice still amazingly even, coping beautifully with both the dramatic outbursts and the lyrical soaring which in fine contrast put this among the richest of modern song-cycles. The Blake cycle makes an excellent coupling. It is just as tough and intense a setting of equally visionary words but it presents fewer moments of sweetness or relaxation. Ideal performances, with the composer re-creating his inspiration.

(i) *Les Illuminations (song-cycle), Op. 18;* (ii) *Nocturne;* (iii) *Serenade for tenor, horn and strings, Op. 31.*
*** Decca 417 153-2 [id.]. Peter Pears, (i; iii) ECO; (iii) with Barry Tuckwell; (ii) wind soloists, LSO strings; composer.
**(*) Virgin Dig. VC 790792-2 [id.]. Martyn Hill, (iii) with Frank Lloyd; City of L. Sinfonia, Hickox.

With dedicated accompaniments under the composer's direction, these Pears versions of *Les Illuminations* and the *Serenade* (with its horn obbligato superbly played by Barry Tuckwell) make a perfect coupling. For the CD release Decca have added the recording of the *Nocturne* from 1960. It is a work full – as so much of Britten's output is – of memorable moments. Each song has a different obbligato instrument (with the ensemble unified for the final Shakespeare song), and each instrument gives the song it is associated with its own individual character. Pears as always is the ideal interpreter, the composer a most efficient conductor, and the fiendishly difficult obbligato parts are played superbly. The recording is brilliant and clear, with just the right degree of atmosphere.

From his student days onwards, Martyn Hill has been an outstanding interpreter of Britten's song-cycles, and here he gives heartfelt performances of three great orchestral cycles, to provide rewarding alternatives to the classic recordings by their inspirer, Peter Pears. With Richard Hickox a warmly sympathetic interpreter, relishing delicate textures, Hill produces ravishing half-tones in such delicate songs as the opening Cotton item in the *Serenade.* He is able to give heroic weight when necessary, though the recording balance does not help him; placed among the orchestra rather than in front of it, he is not always able to bite through heavy textures, though it is very satisfying to have such a weighty orchestral climax in the deeply moving final Shakespeare setting of the *Nocturne.* Most remarkable of all in some ways is the dashingly fast account of *Queen and huntress* in the *Serenade,* with the horn soloist, Frank Lloyd, extraordinarily agile in playing the fast triplets. It is a pity that he is barely audible in his offstage solo at the end, yet the atmospheric beauty of the digital recording presents a powerful case for this Virgin issue, even next to the Pears.

The Prodigal Son (3rd parable), Op. 81.
(M) *** Decca 425 713-2. Pears, Tear, Shirley-Quirk, Drake, E. Op. Group Ch. & O, composer and Viola Tunnard.

The last of the parables is the sunniest and most heart-warming. Britten cleverly avoids the charge of oversweetness by introducing the Abbot, even before the play starts, in the role of Tempter, confessing he represents evil and aims to destroy contentment in the family he describes: 'See how I break it up' – a marvellous line for Peter Pears. An ideal performance is given here with a characteristically real and atmospheric Decca recording.

St Nicholas; Hymn to St Cecilia.
*** Hyp. Dig. CDA 66333; *KA 66333* [id.]. Rolfe Johnson, Corydon Singers, St George's Chapel, Windsor, Ch., Girls of Warwick University Chamber Ch., Ch. of Christ Church, Southgate, Sevenoaks School, Tonbridge School, Penshurst Ch. Soc., Occasional Ch., Edwards, Alley, Scott, ECO, Best.

For the first time in a recording, the congregational hymns are included in Matthew Best's fresh and atmospheric account of *St Nicholas.* That adds enormously to the emotional impact of the whole cantata, for they have an effect which is similar to the hymns Britten was to incorporate into his later children's piece, *Noye's Fludde.* Though the chorus is distanced slightly, the contrasts of timbre are caught well, with the waltz-setting of *The birth of Nicholas* and its bath-tub sequence delightfully sung by boy-trebles alone. The unaccompanied *Hymn to St Cecilia* makes an apt and generous coupling, also beautifully sung, with gentle pointing of the jazzy syncopations in crisp, agile ensemble and with sweet matching among the voices.

(i) *St Nicholas, Op. 42;* (ii) *Rejoice in the Lamb, Op. 30.*
(M) (***) Decca mono 425 714-2. (i) Hemmings, Pears, St John Leman School, Beccles, Girls' Ch., Ipswich School Boys' Ch., Aldeburgh Festival Ch. & O; R. Downes; (ii) Hartnett, Steele, Todd, Francke, Purcell Singers, G. Malcolm; composer.

With rare exceptions, Britten's own first recordings of his own works have a freshness and vigour unsurpassed since. Here are two fine examples which vividly draw on the brightness of boys' voices – not least that of David Hemmings as the youthful St Nicholas. The expression may be direct but the emotions behind both these works are more complex than one might at first appreciate. Britten's performances capture the element of vulnerability, not least in the touching setting of words by the deranged poet, Christopher Smart, *Rejoice in the Lamb.*

Serenade for tenor, horn and strings.
*** ASV Dig. CDRPO 8023; *ZCRPO 8023* [id.]. Martyn Hill, Bryant, RPO, Ashkenazy – KNUSSEN: *Symphony No. 3;* WALTON: *Symphony No. 2.* ***

If it seems strange that Martyn Hill has made a second recording of this masterpiece so soon after the Virgin Classics one with Hickox, the choice of Jeffrey Bryant for the horn part brings ample justification, quite apart from Ashkenazy's red-blooded direction. For many years Bryant has been an outstanding principal in the orchestra, and here at last he gets his due recognition on record in a superb performance, ripe-toned and expressive. Though, unlike the two symphonies with which it is coupled, this was recorded in the studio, Ashkenazy's reading has the expansiveness and warmth of a live performance. The oddly balanced recording – with tenor and horn set behind the strings – hardly interferes with the compulsion of the performance.

Songs and proverbs of William Blake, Op. 74; Tit for Tat; 3 Early songs: Beware that I'd ne'er been married; Epitaph; The clerk. Folksong arrangements: Bonny at morn; I was lonely; Lemady; Lord! I married me a wife!; O Waly, Waly; The Sally Gardens; She's like the swallow; Sweet Polly Oliver.
**(*) Chan. Dig. CHAN 8514; *ABTD 1224* [id.]. Benjamin Luxon, David Williamson.

Benjamin Luxon's lusty baritone gives an abrasive edge whether to early songs, folksong settings or the Blake cycle originally written for Dietrich Fischer-Dieskau. Only rarely does he become too emphatic. The Blake cycle is commandingly done, despite some signs of strain, and the most valuable items of all are the five very late folksong settings, originally with harp accompaniment, ending with the most touching, the hauntingly melancholy *She's like the swallow.* Excellent, sensitive accompaniment and first-rate recording.

(i) *Tit for Tat;* (ii) Folksong arrangements: *Bird scarer's song; Bonny at morn; David of the White Rock; Lemady; Lord! I married me a wife!; She's like the swallow.*
*** Mer. CDE 84119; *KE 77119* [id.]. Shirley-Quirk; (i) Ledger; (ii) Ellis – *Suite for harp* etc. ***

This Meridian collection celebrates a nicely varied group of works which Britten wrote for friends to perform at the Aldeburgh Festival. John Shirley-Quirk was the baritone who first sang the cycle, *Tit for Tat*, with the composer at the piano, and he is still unrivalled in the sharp yet subtle way he brings out the irony in these boyhood settings of De la Mare poems. It is also good to have him singing the six late folk-settings with harp accompaniment, here played by Osian Ellis for whom (with Peter Pears) they were originally written – much more distinctive in these original versions than with piano accompaniment. The recording is naturally balanced and immediate.

War Requiem, Op. 66.
*** Decca 414 383-2 [id.]. Vishnevskaya, Pears, Fischer-Dieskau, Bach Ch., LSO Ch., Highgate School Ch., Melos Ens., LSO, composer.
*** EMI Dig. CDS7 47034-8 [id.]. Söderström, Tear, Allen, Trebles of Christ Church Cathedral Ch., Oxford, CBSO Ch., CBSO, Rattle.

(i) *War Requiem;* (ii) *Ballad of heroes, Op. 14; Sinfonia da requiem, Op. 20.*
*** Chan. Dig. CHAN 8983/4; *DBTD 2032* [id.]. (i) Harper, Langridge, Shirley-Quirk, (ii) Hill; St Paul's Cathedral Choristers, LSO Ch., LSO & CO, Richard Hickox.

Richard Hickox's Chandos version rivals even the composer's own definitive account in its passion and perception, and must be now regarded at a first choice. With none of the tape-hiss which marred Britten's old Decca recording, it offers the richest sound yet in a work which makes so many dramatic points through the contrast of full orchestra set against chamber forces. Hickox thrusts home the big dramatic moments with unrivalled force, helped by the weight of the Chandos sound. The crescendo is shattering at the end of the *Recordare*, when it spills over into the angry Owen poem about the field-gun, *Be slowly lifted up, thou long black arm*. The boys' chorus from St Paul's Cathedral is exceptionally fresh, and most atmospherically recorded. Heather Harper is as golden-toned as she was at the very first Coventry performance, fearless in attack. Philip Langridge has never sung more sensitively on disc, and both he and John Shirley-Quirk bring many subtleties to their interpretations of the Owen-inspired poems beyond even the original interpreters, who contributed to the composer's recording. Adding to the attractions of the set come two substantial choral works, also in outstanding performances. That coupling is the more relevant, when the two works relate so illuminatingly to the main one.

The vivid realism of Britten's own 1963 recording of the *War Requiem*, one of the outstanding achievements of the whole analogue stereo era, comes over the more strikingly in the CD transfer, with uncannily precise placing and balancing of the many different voices and instruments; and John Culshaw's contribution as producer is all the more apparent. The recorded performance comes near to the ideal, but it is a pity that Britten insisted on Vishnevskaya for the soprano solos. Having a Russian singer was emotionally right, but musically Heather Harper would have been better still. The digital remastering, as with Peter Grimes, brings added textural refinement and makes the recording sound newly minted; it also reveals a degree of background hiss.

The most striking difference between Rattle's interpretation and that of Britten himself lies in the relationship between the settings of Owen's poems and the setting of the liturgy in Latin. With Söderström a far more warmly expressive soloist than the oracular Vishnevskaya, the human emotions behind the Latin text come out strongly with less distancing than from the composer. If Tear does not always match the subtlety of Pears on the original recording, Allen sounds more idiomatic than Fischer-Dieskau. Rattle's approach is warm, dedicated and dramatic, with fine choral singing (not least from the Christ Church Cathedral trebles). The dramatic orchestral contrasts are superbly brought out, as in the blaze of trumpets on *Hosanna*. The various layers of perspective are impressively managed by the superb digital recording. Yet in its combination of imaginative flair with technical expertise, the Culshaw recording of two decades earlier is by no means surpassed by this new EMI venture, although the EMI set has the considerable digital advantage of a silent background.

OPERA

Albert Herring (complete).

**(*) Decca 421 849-2 (2) [id.]. Pears, Fisher, Noble, Brannigan, Cantelo, ECO, Ward, composer.

The CD transfer of Britten's own 1964 recording of the comic opera, *Albert Herring*, is a delight. The comedy comes over with an immediacy and sense of presence which have you involved straight away in the improbable tale of the May King, chosen when no local girl is counted suitable. Peter Pears's portrait of the innocent Albert was caught only just before he grew too old for the role, but it is full of unique touches. Sylvia Fisher is a magnificent Lady Billows, and it is good to have so wide a range of British singers of the 1960s so characterfully presented – as, for example, Sheila Rex, whose tiny portrait of Albert's mother is a gem. The recording, made in Jubilee Hall, remains astonishingly vivid.

Billy Budd (complete).

*** Decca 417 428-2 (3) [id.]. Glossop, Pears, Langdon, Shirley-Quirk, Wandsworth School Boys' Ch., Amb. Op. Ch., LSO, composer – *Holy sonnets of John Donne* etc. ***

The libretto of *Billy Budd*, by E. M. Forster and Eric Crozier, with its all-male cast is more skilled than those Britten usually set, and the range of characterization – so apparently limited in a tale of good and evil directly confronting one another – is masterly, with Peter Pears's role of Captain Vere presenting the moral issue at its most moving. Britten's master-stroke of representing the confrontation of Vere and the condemned Billy in a sequence of 34 bare common chords is irresistible, and the many richly imaginative strokes – atmospheric as well as dramatic – are superbly managed. An ideal cast, with Glossop a bluff, heroic Billy, and Langdon a sharply dark-toned Claggart, making these symbol-figures believable. Magnificent sound. The layout on three CDs begins with the *John Donne Holy sonnets* and *Songs and proverbs of William Blake*, with the Prologue and Act I of the opera beginning thereafter.

Death in Venice (complete).
*** Decca 425 669-2 (2) [id.]. Pears, Shirley-Quirk, Bowman, Bowen, Leeming, E. Op. Group Ch., ECO, Bedford.

Thomas Mann's novella, which made an expansively atmospheric film, far removed from the world of Mann, here makes a surprisingly successful opera, totally original in its alternation of monologue for the central character (on two levels, inner and external) and colourful set-pieces showing off the world of Venice and the arrival of the plague. Britten's inspiration, drawing together threads from all his earlier operas from *Peter Grimes* to the *Church parables*, is nothing less than exuberant, with the chamber orchestra producing the richest possible sounds. Pears's searching performance in the central role of Aschenbach is set against the darkly sardonic singing of John Shirley-Quirk in a sequence of roles as the Dionysiac figure who draws Aschenbach to his destruction. The recording is extremely vivid in its CD format and, though Steuart Bedford's assured conducting lacks some of the punch that Britten would have brought, the whole presentation makes this a set to establish the work outside the opera house as the very culmination of Britten's cycle of operas.

Gloriana: Choral dances.
*** Hyp. CDA 66175; *KA 66175* [id.]. Martyn Hill, Thelma Owen, Holst Singers & O, Hilary Davan Wetton – BLISS: *Lie strewn the white flocks;* HOLST: *Choral hymns from the Rig Veda.* ***

It is little short of a scandal that so great an opera as *Gloriana* still remains to be recorded complete. The composer's own choral suite, made up of unaccompanied choral dances linked by passages for solo tenor and harp, makes a valuable if tantalizing sample, an excellent coupling for the equally attractive Bliss and Holst items. Excellent, atmospheric recording.

A Midsummer Night's Dream (complete).
*** Decca 425 663-2 (2) [id.]. Deller, Harwood, Harper, Veasey, Watts, Shirley-Quirk, Brannigan, Downside and Emmanuel School Ch., LSO, composer.

Britten and Pears together prepared the libretto for this opera by careful compression of the Shakespeare words. What this recording confirms – with the aid of the score – more than any live performance, is how compressed the music is, as well as the words. At first one may regret the absence of rich and memorable tunes, but there is no thinness of argument, and the atmosphere of every scene is brilliantly re-created in the most evocative orchestral sounds. The beauty of instrumental writing comes out in this recording even more than in the opera house, for John Culshaw, the recording manager, put an extra halo round the fairy music to act as a substitute for visual atmosphere. The problem of conveying the humour of the play-scene at the end with the 'rude mechanicals' cavorting about the stage proved more intractable. Humour is there all right, but the laughter of the stage audience is too ready for comfort. Britten again proves himself an ideal interpreter of his own music and draws virtuoso playing from the LSO (marvellous trumpet sounds for Puck's music). Among the singers Peter Pears has shifted from his original role as Flute (the one who has the Donizetti mad-scene parody to sing) to the straight role of Lysander. The mechanicals are admirably led by Owen Brannigan as Bottom; and among the lovers Josephine Veasey (Hermia) is outstanding. Deller, with his magical male alto singing, is the eerily effective Oberon.

(i) *Noye's fludde* (children's opera); (ii) *Serenade for tenor, horn & strings, Op. 31.*
**(*) Virgin Dig. VC7 91129-2; *VC7 91129-4* [id.]. (i) Maxwell, Ormiston, Pasco, Salisbury & Chester Schools Ch. & O, Coull Qt, Alley, Watson, Harwood, Endymion Ens. (members); (ii) Martyn Hill, Frank Lloyd, City of L. Sinf., Hickox.

A modern digital recording of Britten's vividly atmospheric setting of the Chester Miracle Play is timely, when the Decca version, with the original team of performers conducted by Norman Del Mar, is 30 years old. The sound for this fine Hickox performance is clearer, fuller and richer, and the performance generally has cleaner attack and discipline, yet in one important way it does not match its predecessor. On the Virgin disc the instrumental forces, including a schools' orchestra as well as professional soloists, are relatively recessed. Compare the storm sequence here with the Decca account (425 161-2, coupled with *The Golden Vanity*), and the distancing undermines any feeling of threat so that the entry of the hymn, *Eternal Father*, instantly submerges the orchestral sound, instead of battling against it. There the Del Mar performance remains far more exciting, and not even Donald Maxwell as Noah, strong and virile, can efface memories of the incomparable Owen Brannigan. The entry of the animals and birds is also caught less dramatically, though it is much more precise on detail. Taken on its own, this is a splendid issue, made the more attractive by the inclusion of Martyn Hill's account of the *Serenade*. This is alternatively available in coupling with the *Nocturne* and *Les illuminations* (VC7 90792-2; *VC 790792-4*).

Paul Bunyan (complete).
❀ *** Virgin Dig. VCD 790710-2 (2) [id.]. James Lawless, Dan Dressen, Elisabeth Comeaux Nelson, soloists, Ch. & O of Plymouth Music Series, Minnesota, Philip Brunelle.

Aptly, this first recording of Britten's choral operetta comes from the state, Minnesota, where the story of this legendary giant is set. The Plymouth Music Series under Philip Brunelle fields a team not of international singers but of enthusiasts. That they are American brings an immediate advantage not just in the spoken and sung accents but in the idiomatic feeling for the syncopated rhythms in this bold but initially unsuccessful attempt of the poet, W. H. Auden, and Britten to invade Broadway. When the principal character is a giant who can appear only as a disembodied voice, the piece works rather better on record or radio than on stage. Musically, Britten's conscious assumption of popular American mannerisms does not prevent his invention from showing characteristic originality. It is not just the jazzy, ballad-like songs and ensembles that stick in the memory but such charming numbers as *Tiny's song* (sung very freshly and sweetly by Elisabeth Comeaux Nelson). Also most memorable is the choral section of the Prologue, with its lines by Auden which moved Britten particularly: *But once in a while the odd thing happens, / Once in a while the dream comes true.* He confessed many years later that he was thinking how he met Peter Pears. Recorded in clean, vivid sound, with Philip Brunelle a vigorous conductor, this excellent first recording richly deserves the prizes it won for the Virgin Classics label.

Peter Grimes (complete).
❀ *** Decca 414 577-2 [id.]. Pears, Claire Watson, Pease, Jean Watson, Nilsson, Brannigan, Evans, Ch. and O of ROHCG, composer.
(M) *** Ph. 432 578-2 (2) [id.]. Vickers, Harper, Summers, Bainbridge, Cahill, Robinson, Allen, ROHCG Ch. & O, C. Davis.

The Decca recording of *Peter Grimes* was one of the first great achievements of the stereo era. Few opera recordings can claim to be so definitive, with Peter Pears, for whom it was written, in the name-part, Owen Brannigan (another member of the original team) and a first-rate cast with Claire Watson a highly sympathetic Ellen Orford. James Pease, as the understanding Captain Balstrode, is brilliantly incisive musically and dramatically; but beyond that it becomes increasingly unfair to single out individual performances. Britten conducts superbly and secures splendidly incisive playing, with the whole orchestra on its toes throughout. The recording, superbly atmospheric, has so many felicities that it would be hard to enumerate them, and the Decca engineers have done wonders in making up aurally for the lack of visual effects. Moreover, the digital remastering for CD miraculously has improved the sound still further. The striking overall bloom remains, yet solo voices and chorus are vividly clear and fully projected. Some background noise remains, of course, but it is not really intrusive and, that apart, one might believe this to be a modern digital set.

Sir Colin Davis takes a fundamentally darker, tougher view of *Peter Grimes* than the composer himself. In some ways the result on Davis's set is even more powerful, if less varied and atmospheric, with the Borough turned into a dark place, full of Strindbergian tensions, and Grimes himself, physically powerful (not a misplaced intellectual), turned into a Hardy-like figure. Jon Vickers's heroic interpretation sheds keen new illumination on what arguably remains the greatest of Britten's operas, even if it cannot be said to supplant the composer's own version. Plainly close in frame and spirit to Crabbe's rough fisherman, Vickers, slow-spoken and weighty, is frighteningly intense. Heather Harper as Ellen Orford is very moving, and there are fine contributions from Jonathan Summers as Captain Balstrode and Thomas Allen as Ned Keene. The lack of atmospheric effects in this set reinforces Davis's contention that the actual notes need no outside aid. The recording is full and vivid, with fine balancing.

Peter Grimes: 4 Sea interludes and Passacaglia.
*** Chan. Dig. CHAN 8473; *ABTD 1184* [id.]. Ulster O, Handley – BAX: *On the Sea-shore;* BRIDGE: *The Sea.* ***

Britten's suite is made up of four *Interludes*, taken from an opera consistently rich in evocation, that with the *Passacaglia* make a finely balanced concert piece. Handley draws brilliant and responsive playing from the Ulster Orchestra in readings that fully capture the atmospheric beauty of the writing, helped by vivid recording of demonstration quality.

(i) *The Rape of Lucretia* (complete); (ii) *Phaedra, Op. 93*.
*** Decca 425 666-2 (2) [id.]. (i) Pears, Harper, Shirley-Quirk, J. Baker, Luxon, ECO, composer; (ii) J. Baker, ECO, Bedford.

In combining on CD *The Rape of Lucretia* with *Phaedra*, Decca celebrates two outstanding performances by Dame Janet Baker, recorded at the peak of her career. In particular her performance as Lucretia underlines the depth of feeling behind a work which, in its formal classical frame, may superficially seem to hide emotion. The logical problems of the story remain – why should Lucretia feel so guilty? – but with Baker the heart-rending tragedy of the heroine is conveyed with passionate conviction, her range of tone-colours, her natural feeling for words and musical phrase used with supreme artistry. Similarly *Phaedra* – written at the very end of Britten's life – provides vocal writing which brings out every glorious facet of her voice. Setting words from Robert Lowell's fine translation of Racine's play, the composer encapsulated the character of the tragic heroine. The use of harpsichord in the recitatives linking the sections of this scena is no mere neo-classical device but a sharply dramatic and atmospheric stroke. Among other distinguished vocal contributions to the opera, Peter Pears and Heather Harper stand out, while Benjamin Luxon makes the selfish Tarquinius into a living character. The stylization of the drama with its frame of Christian comment comes over even more effectively when imagined rather than seen. The seductive beauty of the writing – Britten then at his early peak – is splendidly caught, the melodies and tone-colours as ravishing as any that he ever conceived.

The Turn of the screw.
(M) (***) Decca mono 425 672-2 (2) [id.]. Pears, Vyvyan, Hemmings, Dyer, Cross, Mandikian, E. Op. Group O, composer.

Though the recording is in mono only, the very dryness and the sharpness of focus give an extra intensity to the composer's own incomparable reading of his most compressed opera. With such sound, the claustrophobic quality of this weird ghost story is intensified, along with the musical cogency of this sequence of fifteen closely knit scenes. Peter Pears as Peter Quint is superbly matched by Jennifer Vyvyan as the governess and by Joan Cross as the housekeeper, Mrs Grose. It is also fascinating to hear David Hemmings as a boy treble, already a confident actor. Excellent CD transfer.

Brouwer, Leo (born 1939)

Retrats Catalans.
*** Decca Dig. 430 233-2; *430 233-4* [id.]. Eduardo Fernández, ECO, Barry Wordsworth – ARNOLD: *Guitar concerto;* CHAPPELL: *Guitar concerto No. 1.* ***

An unusual coupling for two superb guitar concertos, Chappell's as well as Arnold's. With the solo instrument well integrated in Brouwer's pieces, textures go in search of a theme in the first, and turn into a dance in the second. Both were inspired by great Catalonian figures, the composer Mompou and the architect Gaudi.

Bruch, Max (1838–1920)

Adagio on Celtic themes, Op. 56; Ave Maria, Op. 61; Canzone, Op. 55; Kol Nidrei, Op. 55.
*** BMG/RCA Dig. RD 60757 [60757-2-RC]. Ofra Harnoy, LPO, Mackerras – BLOCH: *Schelomo* etc. ***

Ofra Harnoy undoubtedly has the full measure of Bruch's sombre, Hebraic lyricism in the best-known piece here, *Kol Nidrei*, and she receives warm support from Mackerras. The rest of the programme creates a lighter mood, with the engaging *Adagio on Celtic themes* recalling the *Scottish fantasia. Ave Maria* has the melodic line nicely embroidered before its simple reprise.

An excellent recording, made in Watford Town Hall, creates an expansive orchestral tapestry against which the soloist is convincingly projected.

Violin concertos Nos. 1 in G min.; 2 in D min., Op. 44; 3 in D min., Op. 58; Adagio appassionato, Op. 57; In Memoriam, Op. 65; Konzertstücke, Op. 84; Romanze, Op. 42; Serenade, Op. 75.
(M) *** Ph. 432 282-2 (3) [id.]. Salvatore Accardo, Leipzig GO, Kurt Masur.

This valuable set gathers together all Bruch's major works for violin and orchestra. Although no other piece quite matches the famous *G minor Concerto* in inventive concentration, the delightful *Scottish fantasia*, with its profusion of good tunes, comes near to doing so, and the first movement of the *Second Concerto* has two themes of soaring lyrical ardour. The *Third Concerto* brings another striking lyrical idea in the first movement and has an endearing *Adagio* and a jolly finale. The engagingly insubstantial *Serenade* was originally intended to be a fourth violin concerto. The two-movement *Konzertstück* dates from 1911 and is one of Bruch's last works. As in the case of the *Serenade*, Bruch had toyed with the idea of calling it a violin concerto, but he finally decided on *Konzertstück* since the piece has only two movements; the second, an *Adagio*, is really very touching. *In Memoriam* is finer still (Bruch himself thought highly of it); it has genuine depth and nobility. The *Adagio appassionato* and *Romanze* are strongly characterized pieces and their eloquence is striking in performances of this calibre. Throughout the set Accardo's playing is so persuasive in its restrained passion that even the less inspired moments bring pleasure, and there are many pages of music that show the composer nearing his finest form. Because of the resonant Leipzig acoustics, the Philips engineers put their microphones rather too close to the soloist and his image is balanced very forwardly, almost out of the hall acoustic, and there is at times a degree of shrillness on his upper range. This is most noticeable on the first disc, containing the *G minor Concerto*, but the ear adjusts; throughout the rest of the collection one's pleasure is hardly diminished, for the orchestral recording is full and spacious.

Violin concerto No. 1 in G min., Op. 26.
(M) *** Sony/CBS Dig. MDK 44902; *40-44902* [id.]. Cho-Liang Lin, Chicago SO, Slatkin – MENDELSSOHN: *Concerto* *** (with Sandra Rivers (piano): SARASATE: *Introduction and Tarantella* ***; KREISLER: *Liebesfreud* ***).
*** EMI Dig. CDC7 54072-2 [id.]; *EL 754072-4*. Kyung-Wha Chung, LPO, Tennstedt – BEETHOVEN: *Concerto.* ***
*** ASV Dig. CDDCA 680; *ZCDCA 680.* Xue Wei, Philh. O, Bakels – SAINT-SAËNS: *Concerto No. 3.* ***
(B) *** CfP Dig. CD-CFP 4566; *TC-CFP 4566* [Ang. CDB 62920]. Tasmin Little, RLPO, Handley – DVOŘÁK: *Concerto.* ***
(M) *** Decca 417 707-2 [id.]. Kyung Wha Chung, RPO, Kempe – SAINT-SAËNS: *Havanaise;* TCHAIKOVSKY: *Concerto.* ***
(B) *** Pickwick Dig. PCD 829; *CIMPC 829* [id.]. Jaime Laredo, SCO – MENDELSSOHN: *Concerto.* ***
(M) *** EMI CDM7 69003-2 [id.]; *EG 769003-4.* Menuhin, Philh. O, Susskind – MENDELSSOHN: *Concerto.* ***
*** DG 419 629-2. Shlomo Mintz, Chicago SO, Abbado (also with KREISLER: *Caprice viennoise; Liebeslied; Liebesfreud*) – MENDELSSOHN: *Concerto.* **(*)
*** DG Dig. 400 031-2 [id.]. Mutter, BPO, Karajan – MENDELSSOHN: *Concerto.* ***
*** EMI Dig. CDC7 49663-2; *EL 749663-4* [id.]. Nigel Kennedy, ECO, Tate – MENDELSSOHN: *Concerto;* SCHUBERT: *Rondo.* ***
*** Chan. Dig. CHAN 8974; *ABTD 1563* [id.]. Hideko Udagawa, LSO, Mackerras – BRAHMS: *Concerto.* ***
(M) **(*) Sony/CBS CD 45555 [MYK 37811]; *40-45555.* Stern, Phd. O, Ormandy – LALO: *Symphonie espagnole.* **(*)
(BB) **(*) BMG/RCA VD 60479; *VK 60479* [60479-2-RV; *60479-4-RV*]. Ughi, LSO, Prêtre – BRAHMS: *Concerto.* **(*)
(*) ASV Dig. CDRPO 8013; *ZCRPO 8013* [id.]. Anne Meyers, RPO, Seaman – BARBER: *Violin concerto.* *
(B) **(*) EMI CDZ7 62519-2; *LZ 762519-4.* Menuhin, LSO, Boult – MENDELSSOHN: *Violin concerto.* **(*)
(M) **(*) Ph. 420 703-2. Grumiaux, New Philh. O, Wallberg – BRAHMS: *Concerto.* **(*)
(B) **(*) Sony MBK 44717 [id.]. Zukerman, LAPO, Mehta – LALO: *Symphonie espagnole.* **(*)

(B) ** CfP CD-CFP 4374; *TC-CFP 4374*. Milstein, Philh. O, Leon Barzin – MENDELSSOHN: *Concerto*. **

Sony, taking note of the competition, have now issued Cho-Liang Lin's radiantly beautiful 1986 account of the *G minor Concerto*, recoupled with the Mendelssohn, to make an outstanding mid-priced digital recommendation. There have been few accounts on record of Bruch's slow movement that begin to match the raptness of Lin. He is accompanied most sensitively by Slatkin and the Chicago orchestra, and this reading is totally compelling in its combination of passion and purity, strength and dark, hushed intensity. The Kreisler and Sarasate bonuses, recorded three years earlier, are also presented with great flair. The recording is excellent.

Unlike the Beethoven with which it is coupled, Chung's EMI version of the Bruch was recorded in the studio with the LPO. Compared with her earlier Decca recording, it reflects her growing ease in recording. Her expressive rubato is more marked, so that in the first movement the opening theme is more impulsive, and her freedom in the second subject vividly conveys the sort of magic you find in her live performances. The slow movement brings extreme contrasts of dynamic and expression from orchestra as well as soloist, and the finale is again impulsive in its bravura. The only rival disc offering this excellent coupling is EMI's own mid-price issue of David Oistrakh's vintage recordings. That makes this an exceptionally attractive issue and an essential one for this much-loved violinist's admirers.

Xue Wei is a Chinese soloist of very considerable calibre. His approach to the concerto is at once passionately committed and refined in its delicacy of detail. Fortunately he is accompanied superbly by Kees Bakels, who provides exciting orchestral tuttis to lead the ear on from the ardour of the solo playing, while Wei can equally seduce the listener with a most magical pianissimo. The slow movement is ravishing in its poetic flair, and the finale is full of fire. The recording balance is a shade artificial, with a bold presence for the soloist and bright orchestral violins against an essentially resonant acoustic, but it is fully acceptable. An outstanding début.

The first recording by a highly talented young violinist, Tasmin Little, is a generous and unique coupling of Bruch and Dvořák. The movement in the Bruch where Little's individuality comes out most clearly is the central *Adagio*, raptly done with a deceptive simplicity of phrasing, totally unselfconscious, that matches the purity of her sound. Her speeds in the outer movements are broader than those of such rivals as Lin. The finale may not have quite the thrusting excitement of Lin's in particular, but the clarity and precision of her playing are fair compensation, along with the fuller, more faithful sound. At full price this would be a first-rate recommendation: on CfP it is an outstanding bargain.

The magic of Kyung Wha Chung, a spontaneously inspired violinist if ever there was one, comes over very beguilingly in her mid-priced Decca interpretation, while Kempe and the Royal Philharmonic give a sympathetic, if not always perfectly polished accompaniment, well caught in a glowing recording from the early 1970s which has responded well to its remastering.

Jaime Laredo with consistently fresh and sweet tone gives a delightfully direct reading, warmly expressive but never for a moment self-indulgent. His is a beautiful, reflective account of the slow movement. The orchestral ensemble is particularly impressive, when no conductor is involved. With first-rate modern digital recording, this is a highlight of the Pickwick budget-price catalogue.

Menuhin's performance with Susskind has a fine spontaneity, the work's improvisatory quality very much part of the interpretation, and there is no doubting the poetry Menuhin finds in the slow movement or the sparkle in the finale. The bright, forward sound of the 1960 recording has transferred vividly to CD.

Shlomo Mintz certainly makes the listener hang on to every phrase and his playing is undoubtedly compelling. The vibrato is wide but his approach is so distinctive and interesting that few listeners will not be fired. The Chicago Symphony Orchestra plays with great brilliance and enthusiasm, and Abbado's direction is most sympathetic. The vivid recording has transferred splendidly to CD. As an encore Mintz plays the three Kreisler lollipops with great flair.

In Anne-Sophie Mutter's hands the *Concerto* has an air of chaste sweetness, shedding much of its ripe, sensuous quality but retaining its romantic feeling. There is a delicacy and tenderness here which are very appealing and, although the tuttis have plenty of fire, Karajan sensitively scales down his accompaniment in the lyrical passages to match his soloist. The digital recording provides a natural balance and a vivid orchestral texture.

Kennedy's is a warm, positive performance, consistently sympathetic, with the English

Chamber Orchestra anything but lightweight. Kennedy's masculine strength goes with a totally unsentimental view of Bruch's lyricism, as in the central slow movement. This may not have quite the individual poetry of the very finest versions; but, coupled with an outstanding account of the Mendelssohn and a bonus to that usual coupling in the rare Schubert *Rondo*, it makes an excellent recommendation. The recording is full, warm and well balanced.

Full of temperament, Hideko Udegawa gives a persuasively passionate performance of the Bruch, very well recorded, and with strong, colourful playing from the orchestra too. Her violin sound is not always of the sweetest, but it is always true and clear, and the hushed opening of the slow movement is caught beautifully. A generous coupling for her strong, daring performance of the Brahms.

It is good to welcome back to the catalogue Stern's 1967-vintage recording with Ormandy. Although the balance is totally unrealistic, this is one of the great classic recordings of the work, gloriously warm-hearted and with a very involving account of the slow movement, which sustains the greatest possible intensity. The finale, too, has wonderful fire and spirit. Ormandy's accompaniment is first class and triumphs over the unrealistic balance and a less than refined orchestral image.

Those looking for a bargain coupling with the Brahms *Concerto* and very good (1982) digital recording might well choose Uto Ughi on RCA. His is a fresh, direct reading. It may not have the individuality of Lin or the extrovert ardour of Stern, but it is still a fine performance, and good value too.

Anne Meyers' performance with the RPO under Christopher Seaman is keenly musical, though competition is stiffer here than in the Barber coupling. Her performance is both refined and lyrical, though she is perhaps slightly lacking in dramatic scale; but it is still a satisfying account, if the fine Barber coupling is wanted.

Menuhin's second stereo recording of the Bruch *Concerto* was made in the early 1970s. While he is obviously on familiar ground, there is no sign of over-familiarity and the lovely slow movement is given a performance of great warmth and humanity. Boult accompanies admirably and the recording is obviously fuller and more modern than the earlier version with Susskind, even if the solo playing is technically less immaculate.

Grumiaux's version with Wallberg would not be counted a first choice; but as a coupling for an outstanding performance of the Brahms *Concerto* it offers a refreshingly different view, civilized, classical in its refinement, if slightly cool. Yet Grumiaux brings all his beauty of tone and expressive technique to this music-making, and he is well accompanied and recorded.

Zukerman's account of the *G minor Concerto* is splendidly eloquent, and the slow movement is played most beautifully. The late 1970s recording is also good and the balance convincing within a fairly resonant acoustic.

Milstein's aristocratic and lyrical playing undoubtedly gives pleasure, and he is well supported. The 1961 recording is good, although it could be more expansive and the CD transfer brings a degree of steeliness to the solo violin. At bargain price this might be considered, but it is certainly not a first choice.

Violin concerto No. 1 in G min., Op. 26; Scottish fantasy, Op. 46.
*** BMG/RCA RD 86214 [RCA 6214-2-RC]. Heifetz, New SO of L., Sargent – VIEUXTEMPS: *Concerto No. 5.* ***

Heifetz plays with supreme assurance, and the slow movement shows this fine artist in top romantic form. All lovers of great violin playing should at least hear this coupling, for Heifetz's panache and the subtlety of his bowing and colour bring a wonderful freshness to Bruch's charming Scottish whimsy. Sargent accompanies sympathetically, and it is noticeable that though the soloist is balanced much too closely, there is never any doubt that Heifetz can still produce a true pianissimo.

Violin concerto No. 2 in D min., Op. 44; Scottish fantasy, Op. 46.
**(*) EMI Dig. CDC7 49071-2 [id.]. Perlman, Israel PO, Mehta.

Perlman attractively couples Bruch's two 'next-best' concertante violin works in performances full of characteristic brilliance and panache, recorded in rather bright, aggressive sound at the Mann Auditorium, Tel Aviv. Perlman may be less intimately reflective in both works than he was when he recorded this coupling before with the New Philharmonia, but in the fast movements there are ample compensations in the sharp concentration from first to last.

Kol Nidrei, Op. 47.
*** DG Dig. 427 323-2 [id.]. Matt Haimovitz, Chicago SO, Levine – LALO: *Concerto;* SAINT-SAËNS: *Concerto No. 1.* ***
(B) ** DG 429 155-2; *429 155-4* [id.]. Fournier, LOP, Martinon – DVOŘÁK: *Cello concerto;* BLOCH: *Schelomo.* **(*)

Bruch was not himself Jewish, but his Kol Nidrei sensitively draws on Hebrew melodies associated with the Day of Atonement. Matt Haimovitz, born in Israel, has a natural feeling for the piece and his performance, balancing restraint with expressive intensity, is serenely moving, yet not without romantic feeling. He is subtly accompanied and very well recorded.

Fournier's performance, while not without feeling, is slightly lacking in romantic urgency. The recording is fully acceptable.

Scottish fantasia for violin and orchestra, Op. 46.
*** BMG/RCA Dig. RD 60942. Anne Akiko Meyers, RPO, López-Cobos – LALO: *Symphonie espagnole.* **(*)
(B) **(*) Pickwick IMPX 9031. Campoli, LPO, Boult – MENDELSSOHN: *Violin concerto.* **(*)

Anne Meyers' account is second to none, and she is admirably partnered by López-Cobos and the RPO. The very opening, with its melancholy, sonorous brass, is unforgettable, and the hushed violin entry is to be matched later by most tender playing in the *Andante*, where the response of the RPO is equally warm. The Scherzo and finale both have plenty of Scottish dance-spirit and just before the work's close the soloist makes another magically gentle entry, soliloquizing poetically on just a thread of tone, reaching a poignantly refined climax, so that the brief, ebullient coda is the more effective. First-class Abbey Road recording, expansive and very well balanced.

Campoli made the recordings on this CD in 1958, when he was on peak form. His clean, sweet tone suits the ingenuous simplicity of Bruch's inspiration, and this is a delightful performance. Boult provides a characteristically accomplished account of the orchestral part and the (Decca) recording is vivid, though the CD transfer emphasizes the upper range and reveals some roughness in tuttis. Nevetheless this coupling affords much musical pleasure.

Symphonies Nos. 1 in E flat, Op. 28; 2 in F min., Op. 36; 3 in E, Op. 51. 7 Swedish dances, Op. 63.
** Ph. Dig. 420 932-2 (2) [id.]. Leipzig GO, Masur.

When the first of Bruch's three symphonies is the one that is most striking in its invention and each has its weaknesses, one has to deduce that he was more a symphonist by default than by nature. Yet this collected edition contains much attractive music, beautifully played and recorded, guaranteed to delight anyone wanting undemanding symphonies as alternatives to those of Brahms and Schumann. Masur's performances with the Leipzig Gewandhaus Orchestra are characteristically warm and refined, with smooth recording to match, but sparkle is largely missing. The *Swedish dances*, dating from much later, make an apt and attractive fill-up; but when the disc is not generously filled, it is a pity that only seven from the full set of fifteen are included.

Bruckner, Anton (1824–96)

Symphonies Nos. 1–9.
(M) *** DG 429 648-2 (9) [id.]. BPO, Karajan.
(M) *** DG 429 079-2 (9) [id.]. BPO or Bav. RSO, Jochum.
(M) **(*) HM/BMG GD 60075 (10) [60075-2-RG]. Cologne RSO, Wand.

The reappearance of Karajan's magnificent cycle, long a yardstick by which others were measured – and at mid-price, too – must be warmly welcomed. No. 8, one of the peaks of the cycle, is his 1976 account, which is only marginally less magisterial than his recent Vienna performance. In No. 1, Karajan (like Günther Wand) opts for the 1891 edition, while Jochum gives us the Linz version of 1865–6. We have sung the praises of these recordings loud and long, and in their new format they are outstanding value.

Jochum's DG cycle was recorded between 1958 (No. 5) and 1967 (No. 2), all but four (Nos. 2, 3, 5 and 6) with the Berlin Philharmonic. It enjoys the advantage of accommodating one symphony per disc. No apology need be made for either the performances or the quality of the recorded sound, which wears its years lightly. Readers will be surprised how well the 1957 stereo recording of the *Fifth Symphony* actually sounds. He still has special claims as a guide in this terrain. He communicates a lofty inspiration to his players, and many of these readings can more than hold their own with later rivals.

Günther Wand's more recent survey (1974–81) is with the Cologne Radio Symphony Orchestra. Wand is a dedicated Brucknerian who rarely falters in his majestic progress. His accounts of Nos. 5 and 6 do not match Jochum but elsewhere (in Nos. 2 and 8) he is perhaps to be preferred. The *Eighth* may be the least successful of the Jochum DG set, and the planners were wise to choose Wand's 1979 recording rather than his more recent and less convincing account. Except in No. 6, Wand is never less than perceptive and at times he and his fine orchestra achieve real inspiration.

Symphony No. 0 in D min.; Overture in G min.
**(*) Decca Dig. 421 593-2 [id.]. Berlin RSO, Chailly.

Riccardo Chailly's Bruckner recordings have the merit of clarity and definition but are sometimes short on atmosphere and warmth. His account of the unnumbered *D minor* (the so-called *Die Nullte*), which actually comes between the *First* and *Second Symphonies*, does not have the eloquence of the long-deleted Haitink LP (Philips) but is still eminently acceptable. The Berlin Radio Orchestra respond well to Chailly's direction and, both as a recording and as a performance, this deserves recommendation. There is at present no satisfactory alternative.

Symphony No. 1 in C min.
*** Orfeo Dig. C 145851A [id.]. Bav. State O, Sawallisch.

Symphony No. 1 in C min.; (i) *Te Deum.*
(M) **(*) DG Dig. 435 068-2; *435 068-4* [id.]. Chicago SO, Barenboim; (i) with Jessye Norman, Minton, Rendall, Ramey, Chicago Symphony Ch.

Symphonies Nos. 1 in C min.; 5 in B flat.
**(*) DG 415 985-2 (2) [id.]. BPO, Karajan.

Sawallisch's account of the *First* is probably the best-sounding of the CDs before the public and his interpretation is impressive in its honesty and dignity. There is warmth and some beautiful playing from the fine Bavarian orchestra, which is recorded in a spacious, yet not over-reverberant acoustic.

It makes a generous coupling, having Barenboim's fine version of the *Te Deum* with its starry quartet of soloists and the magnificent Chicago Symphony Chorus as a fill-up for the *Symphony No. 1.* In both works he directs beautifully played, spontaneous-sounding performances that mould Brucknerian lines persuasively, but in the *Symphony* the dramatic tension is less keen, lacking something in concentration. The early digital recording is good but not ideally clear, with a brightness that needs a little taming.

Karajan's versions of Nos. 1 and 5 come yoked together, which saves a disc but may not suit all collectors. No. 1 is digital (1982) but the recording is brightly lit and not always ideally expansive at the bottom end. It is still an incisive and powerful reading. Karajan, like Sawallisch, uses the revised Linz version and here as elsewhere shows a clear-headed concentration, making light of the problems of co-ordinating arguments which in lesser hands can seem rambling. In the *Fifth Symphony* the ear registers a greater resonant warmth in the (1977) analogue sound, for the recording generally is richer and more spacious than its digital companion. The reading is not just poised and polished; it is superbly structured on every level, clear on detail as well as on overall architecture. Karajan takes a patrician view of this great and individual symphonist; even if the slow movement lacks some of the simple dedication which makes Jochum's earlier version with the same orchestra so compelling, the result is undoubtedly satisfying. The playing of the Berlin Philharmonic is magnificent.

Symphony No. 2 in C min.
*** DG Dig. 415 988-2 [id.]. BPO, Karajan.

Karajan's reading is not only powerful and polished, it is distinctive on matters both of tempi and of text. He modifies the Nowak edition by opening out some of the cuts, but by no means all. He starts reticently, only later expanding in grandeur. The scherzo at a fast speed is surprisingly lightweight, the finale relatively slow and spacious. It is a noble reading, not always helped by rather bright digital recording. However, the CD brings a firmer sound-image than the LP, with more weight at the bottom than some in this series, and the strings do not lack amplitude in the *Andante.*

Symphony No. 3 in D min. (original, 1873 version).
**(*) Teldec/Warner Dig. 2292 42961-2 [id.]. Frankfurt RSO, Inbal.

There are in all three versions of the *Third Symphony*: the first completed on the last day of 1873, a second which Bruckner undertook immediately after the completion of the *Fifth Symphony* in 1877, and then, after that proved unsuccessful, a third which he made in 1889. The 1873 is by far the longest version, running to nearly 66 minutes (the first movement alone lasts 24 minutes), and for those who have either of the others it will make far more than a fascinating appendix. The playing of the Frankfurt Radio Orchestra under Eliahu Inbal is very respectable indeed, with a sensitive feeling for atmosphere and refined dynamic contrasts; the recording in its CD format is most acceptable without being top-drawer. This edition has never been recorded before, and the symphony can at last be heard in the form in which it was presented to Wagner.

Symphony No. 3 in D min. (1877 version).
*** Ph. Dig. 422 411-2 [id.]. VPO, Bernard Haitink.
** DG Dig. 431 684-2 [id.]. Dresden State O, Sinopoli.

At the time of writing, Bernard Haitink is the only conductor to have given us a digital version of the 1877 edition of the *Third Symphony*. (He also recorded it on LP with the Concertgebouw in the 1960s.) Karajan, Jochum and Wand all opt for the 1889 revision. Bruckner embarked on this after Hermann Levi had rejected the *Eighth Symphony*, making a number of cuts suggested by the Schalk brothers. Haitink gives us the version favoured by many Bruckner scholars. Questions of edition apart, this is a performance of enormous breadth and majesty, and Philips give it a recording to match. The playing of the Vienna Philharmonic is glorious throughout, and even collectors who have alternative versions should acquire this magnificent issue.

Like Bernard Haitink, Giuseppe Sinopoli opts for the 1877 score, and his performance is generally (though not completely) free from the expressive emphases in which he at times indulges. The playing of the Staatskapelle Dresden is of the highest quality, but the DG recording does not do their resplendent sonority full justice. The balance is recessed and the brass are robbed of some of their warmth and become just a shade shallow and strident. Haitink holds the work together more expertly and the Philips engineers produce an altogether finer sound.

Symphony No. 3 in D min.
*** DG Dig. 421 362-2 [id.]. BPO, Karajan.

Karajan's account of the *Third Symphony* is very impressive indeed. He opts for the Nowak edition of 1888–9. One is awe-struck by the eloquence and beauty of the orchestral playing and the command of architecture here. Karajan achieves a sense of majesty in the opening movement and an other-worldliness and spirituality in the slow movement that cannot fail to move the listener. At the same time, fine though it is, this is not a state-of-the-art recording and it is not as transparent or detailed as, say, Chailly's Bruckner *Seventh* on Decca.

Symphony No. 4 in E flat (Romantic) (original 1874 version).
**(*) Teldec/Warner Dig. 2292 42960-2 [id.]. Frankfurt RSO, Inbal.

Like the *Third*, there are three versions of the *Romantic symphony*, and no one has recorded the original before. The differences are most obvious in the scherzo, a completely different and more fiery movement, but the opening of the finale is also totally different. Inbal's performance is more than adequate – indeed he has a genuine feeling for the Bruckner idiom and pays scrupulous attention to dynamic refinements. The recording is well detailed, though the climaxes almost (but not quite) reach congestion. An indispensable and fascinating issue.

Symphony No. 4 in E flat (Romantic).
(B) *** DG 427 200-2 [id.]. BPO, Jochum.
*** DG 415 277-2 [id.]. BPO, Karajan.
*** Decca Dig. 425 613-2 [id.]. Concg. O, Riccardo Chailly.
*** Denon Dig. C37 7126 [id.]. Dresden State O, Blomstedt.
(B) *** Sony MYK 44871. Columbia SO, Walter.
(M) **(*) EMI Dig. CDD7 63895-2 [id.]. BPO, Tennstedt.
(M) **(*) Sony SBK 47653 [id.]. Phd. O, Ormandy.
** Decca Dig. 430 099-2; *430 099-4* [id.]. Cleveland O, Christoph von Dohnányi.

Jochum's way with Bruckner is unique. So gentle is his hand that the opening of each movement or even the beginning of each theme emerges into the consciousness rather than starting normally. And when it is a matter of leading from one section to another over a difficult transition passage – as in the lead-in to the first-movement recapitulation – no one can match Jochum in his subtlety and persuasiveness. The purist may object that, in order to do this, Jochum reduces the speed far below what is marked, but Jochum is for the listener who wants above all to love Bruckner. The recording from the late 1960s still sounds vivid and firm.

Karajan's opening (on his DG version) also has more beauty and a greater feeling of mystery than almost anyone else on CD. As in his earlier, EMI record, Karajan brings a keen sense of forward movement to this music as well as showing a firm grip on its architecture. His slow movement is magnificent. The DG analogue recording lacks the transparency and detail of the very finest of his records, but there is no doubt that this is a performance of considerable stature.

Chailly's new account has two things in its favour: the incomparable Concertgebouw Orchestra at their most resplendent, and a Decca recording of magnificent opulence. The results are very enjoyable, and Chailly himself is a far from unimpressive Brucknerian, who can evoke a strong sense of atmosphere. Perhaps he does not quite match the greatest of his rivals in strength of personality, but this account has a great deal to commend it and, like his version of the *Seventh*, will have a high priority with those who enjoy sound which, while naturally balanced, is undoubtedly in the demonstration bracket.

Blomstedt opts for the Nowak edition, and the spacious and resonant acoustic in which his version is recorded lends it a pleasing sense of atmosphere. The performance has a certain ardour and conviction that impress. The slow movement has more feeling and poetry than one normally associates with this conductor, and the sumptuous tone produced by the Dresden orchestra is a joy in itself. This is not bright and analytical, but it is a beautiful sound and it suits Bruckner.

Although not quite as impressive as his Bruckner *Ninth*, Bruno Walter's 1960 recording is transformed by its CD remastering, with textures clearer, strings full and brass sonorous. It is not quite as rich as some of the full-price competition, but it is still pretty impressive, and the superbly played 'hunting horn' scherzo is wonderfully vivid. The reading is characteristically spacious; the conductor's special feeling for Bruckner means that he can relax over long musical paragraphs and retain his control of the structure, while the playing has fine atmosphere and no want of mystery.

In Tennstedt's 1982 version the breadth of the recording is admirable, if with a degree of fierceness on fortissimos. This is a reading that combines concentration and a degree of ruggedness; plainness goes with pure beauty and natural strength in the first two movements. The scherzo is urgent, the finale resplendent. With one or two modifications, the Haas edition is used. Not a first choice, but nevertheless compelling.

Eugene Ormandy has never been closely associated with Bruckner on record, yet this reading from 1967 has a warmth and power, a natural expressiveness, which are most persuasive. It is very well played, with opulent Philadelphia string-tone (very different from latterday recordings) and with glorious horns in the hunting motif of the Scherzo. There is some edge on high violins in the transfer, but the recording has plenty of body. The Nowak edition is used.

Christoph von Dohnányi gives a very well-focused and finely detailed presentation of the terrain and draws very precise playing from his magnificent Cleveland Orchestra. In this he is well supported by the Decca engineers, who produce a cleanly balanced and well-lit aural picture. Although the Dohnányi version is scrupulously prepared, there is nothing much more to it. To be frank, it is fundamentally too cool to be a front-runner.

Symphony No. 5 in B flat.
** BMG/RCA Dig. RD 60361; *RK 60361* [60361-2-RC; *60361-4-RC*]. N. German RSO, Wand.

Symphony No. 5 in B flat; (i) *Te Deum.*
*** Ph. Dig. 422 342-2 (2) [id.]. (i) Mattilla, Mentzer, Cole, Holl, Bav. R. Ch., VPO, Haitink.

Bernard Haitink earned his Brucknerian spurs in the Concertgebouw with his late-1960s/early-1970s cycle. One of the most impressive was the *Fifth*, but his new recording with the Vienna Philharmonic is, if anything, even finer. It is superbly recorded and the orchestral playing is predictably of the very highest quality. The only snag, perhaps, is the slow movement, which is rather on the brisk side. He knocks four minutes off Karajan's reading, yet at the same time he succeeds in conveying an unhurried effect. Anyway this is a performance of nobility and it presents undeniably the best sound so far. The *Te Deum* is an added inducement to invest in this set.

Günter Wand's first recording of the *Fifth Symphony* was perhaps one of the less successful in his earlier cycle. This newcomer has better sound than its predecessor and better also than its recently issued companions, Nos. 8 and 9, having been recorded in the Hamburg Musikhalle rather than in the more resonant acoustic of Lübeck Cathedral. His new account is also accommodated on one disc. Wand is never kapellmeister-ish but, at the same time, never inspired either. He tends to move things on just a little too awkwardly at times – the lead into the allegro of the first movement – and the slow movement is not really *sehr langsam*; Karajan takes five minutes longer over it and Jochum four. Wand communicates a sense of awe only intermittently.

Symphony No. 6 in A.
*** Orfeo Dig. C 024821 [id.]. Bav. State O, Sawallisch.
(M) *** EMI CDM7 63351-2 [id.]. New Philh. O, Klemperer.
**(*) DG 419 194-2 [id.]. BPO, Karajan.
**(*) BMG/RCA Dig. RD 60061; *RK 60061* [60061-2-RC; *60061-4-RC*]. N. German RSO, Wand.
**(*) Decca 417 389-2 [id.]. Chicago SO, Solti.

Sawallisch's account of the *Sixth Symphony* is beautifully shaped, spacious yet never portentous or inflated. Tempi – never too slow but never hurried – are beautifully judged, and the Bavarian State Orchestra respond splendidly to his direction. The acoustic has plenty of warmth but is not too reverberant, and the recording sounds excellent.

Starting with a spacious account of the first movement, grandly majestic, sharply architectural, Klemperer directs a characteristically strong and direct reading. It is disarmingly simple rather than expressive in the slow movement (faster than usual) but is always concentrated and strong, and the finale is particularly well held together. Splendid playing from the orchestra and clear, bright recording. Bruckner's massive climaxes are accommodated without strain and the brass is very telling.

Karajan is not as commanding here as in his other Bruckner recordings yet this is still a compelling performance, tonally very beautiful and with a glowing account of the slow movement that keeps it in proportion – not quite the match of the sublime slow movements of Nos. 8 and 9. The transfer of the 1980 analogue recording is well enough managed, although the bright upper range is more noticeable than the lower, which might ideally have been more expansive.

Wand's account of the *Sixth* gets off to a rather heavy-handed start but turns into something really rather imposing. The sense of awe, missing from his *Fifth*, is present here and the architecture of the work unfolds with impressive logic. Haitink has yet to reach this symphony in his second cycle, and it may be worth waiting for. Generally speaking, the *Sixth* has fared unpredictably and has been something of a problem child in Brucknerian circles. This is undoubtedly one of the better ones; the playing of the Hamburg orchestra is very fine indeed, and so is the sound.

Solti offers a strong, rhetorical reading, powerfully convincing in the outer movements and helped by playing and recording of outstanding quality. Where he is less persuasive is in the slow movement, which fails to flow quite as it should; the expressiveness does not sound truly spontaneous. The analogue recording emerges vividly enough in its CD format.

Symphony No. 7 in E.
*** Decca Dig. 414 290-2 [id.]. Berlin RSO, Chailly.
(M) *** Ph. 434 155-2; *434 155-4* [id.]. Concg. O, Haitink.
(M) *** EMI CDM7 69923-2. BPO, Karajan.
*** DG 419 195-2 [id.]. BPO, Karajan.
*** Denon Dig. C37 7286 [id.]. Dresden State O, Blomstedt.
*** Decca Dig. 430 841-2. Cleveland O, Dohnányi.
*** DG Dig. 429 226-2 [id.]. VPO, Karajan.

While Karajan and Haitink both give of their finest in this work, Chailly's account, with its superb Decca digital recording, also ranks among the best available. He obtains some excellent playing from the Berlin Radio Symphony Orchestra and, though he may not attain the warmth and, indeed, the spirituality of Karajan and Jochum, his is a committed performance, and the apparent lack of weight soon proves deceptive. He has a considerable command of the work's architecture and controls its sonorities expertly. The recording, made in the Jesus Christus

Kirche, Berlin, is outstanding in every way. Warm, full tone throughout all the departments of the orchestra, yet a clean and refined sound, which is especially impressive on CD.

Haitink's 1978 version offers considerable competition at mid-price. The Philips remastering is conspicuously more successful than the DG/Karajan disc from the same period. The recording is wide in range and refined in detail, yet retains the ambient warmth of the Concertgebouw. Haitink's reading is more searching than his earlier version, made in the 1960s. The first movement is considerably slower and gains in mystery and atmosphere, and the *Adagio* expands in vision too. The Concertgebouw Orchestra play with their accustomed breadth of tone and marvellously blended ensemble – the closing section of the *Adagio* is wonderfully serene.

Karajan's reading of No. 7 for EMI shows a superb feeling for the work's architecture, and the playing of the Berlin Philharmonic is gorgeous. The recording has striking resonance and amplitude, sounding well if not absolutely refined in its remastered format and making a good alternative medium-price choice for this favourite Bruckner symphony.

In the newer, analogue, DG version, Karajan draws enormously compelling playing from the BPO and this performance shows great power and nobility. This is undoubtedly a great performance, and the recording was one of the best in Karajan's analogue series, with rich strings and sonorous yet biting brass. The digital remastering, however, is not quite as successful in freshening the sound as is Haitink's Philips CD.

A well-shaped account of the *Seventh* comes from Herbert Blomstedt and the Staatskapelle, Dresden. It is not quite as moving as his version of the *Fourth*, but it is still very fine, and the beautiful playing of the Dresden orchestra and the expansive acoustic of the Lukaskirche are strong points in its favour. The reading is totally dedicated and Blomstedt has both strength and imagination to commend him.

Dohnányi secures a magnificent response from the Clevelanders; apart from the expansive sonorities of the work's climaxes, there is some rapt and beautiful pianissimo playing from the strings, especially in the first movement, while the Scherzo has superb rhythmic bite. It is a well controlled reading, rising to climaxes naturally and falling back again, holding the listener in its spell. If there is not quite the same feeling of an inevitably moulded seamless line that one has with Haitink, Dohnányi has the the advantage of a vibrant, modern, digital, Decca recording made within the spacious acoustics of Severance Hall. If both Haitink and Karajan give the impression of having lived with this music all their musical lives, Dohnányi's brings a certain freshness of approach and this performance is undoubtedly very compelling, though not preferable to Chailly's version.

Karajan's digital account of the *Seventh* was his last recording and he secures a marvellous response from the Vienna Philharmonic. This features in the lists without displacing his earlier accounts: in fact the 1977 version has slightly more grip and the 1971 EMI account has a sense of mystery that is also rather special. Those who have either need not make the change.

Symphony No. 8 in C min. (original, 1887 version).
**(*) Teldec/Warner Dig. 2292 43791-2 (2) [id.]. Frankfurt RSO, Inbal.

Eliahu Inbal has strong Brucknerian instincts and, although the Frankfurt Radio Orchestra is not thought of as being in the first bracket, it produces more than acceptable results. There are considerable divergences here from the versions we know, and readers will undoubtedly derive much fascination from comparing them. The recording is very good and, like its companion, No. 3, this is mandatory listening for all Brucknerians.

Symphony No. 8 in C min.
❀ *** DG Dig. 427 611-2 [id.]. VPO, Karajan.
*** Ph. Dig. 412 465-2 (2) [id.]. Concg. O, Haitink – WAGNER: *Siegfried idyll.* ***
**(*) DG Dig. 415 124-2 (2) [id.]. VPO, Giulini.
**(*) BMG/RCA Dig. RD 60364 [60364-2-RC]. N. German RSO, Wand.
(B) **(*) DG 431 163-2; *431 163-4*. BPO, Jochum.

Karajan recorded the *Eighth Symphony* in the late 1950s and again in 1976, on both occasions with the Berlin Philharmonic. His last version is with the Vienna Philharmonic Orchestra and is the most impressive of them all. The sheer beauty of sound and opulence of texture is awe-inspiring but never draws attention to itself: this is a performance in which beauty and truth go hand in hand. We are not far into the first movement when one simply forgets the performance and marvels at the composer's vision. The recording is superior to either of its predecessors in terms of naturalness of detail and depth of perspective, though they were both of good quality. This is quite an experience!

Haitink's is a noble reading of this massive symphony, using the extended Haas edition. Never one to force the pace, Haitink's degree of restraint will please those who find Karajan too powerfully concentrated. The spaciousness of the slow movement brings a rare clarity and refinement; the tempo is relentlessly steady, even slower than Karajan's. On compact disc, the resonant Concertgebouw ambience has all the more atmospheric bloom, as well as fine detail, an aptly beautiful sound.

Giulini elects to use the Nowak edition, which may worry some collectors and incline them towards Haitink or Karajan, who opt for the Haas. If these considerations do not worry you, the Giulini will be a strong contender, for he is a conductor of vision, and the Vienna orchestra give him wonderful support. This reading has undoubted spirituality and power, and the DG recording is spacious and clean. However, the absence of any coupling limits the fullest recommendation.

Günter Wand has exchanged the plainer studio acoustic of his earlier set for the reverberance of Lübeck Cathedral, and his Cologne Radio Orchestra for that of the excellent Hamburg Nord Deutscher Rundfunks. This record is assembled from performances given at the 1987 Schleswig-Holstein Festival and first appeared briefly on EMI before migrating to RCA. There is great breadth and a sense of space here, imposed no doubt by the acoustic, and considerable majesty. However, in climaxes there is an overhanging resonance that might pose problems for some collectors and which prevents this occupying a premier position in what is a highly competitive field.

Jochum uses the Nowak Edition, which involves cuts in the slow movement and finale, and in addition he often presses the music on impulsively in both the outer movements and especially in his account of the *Adagio*, where the climax has great passion and thrust. One is undoubtedly caught up with this, and there is also some marvellously serene playing from the Berlin Philharmonic strings, with a noble contribution from the brass. The combination of the Nowak cuts and Jochum's accelerandos means that the overall playing time is just over 74 minutes, and the symphony fits on to a single bargain-priced CD – which is worth any Brucknerian's money.

Symphonies Nos. 8 in C min. (1890 version); *9 in D min.* (original version).
(B) **(*) EMI CZS7 67279-2 (2) [id.]. VPO, Carl Schuricht.

Carl Schuricht's approach was freely romantic, rather in the manner of Furtwängler or of Eugen Jochum. Yet in both slow movements here, arguably the two greatest that Bruckner ever wrote, his flowing, less spacious manner binds the argument together in warmth of lyricism, rather than bringing out the spiritual depth, as Furtwängler and Jochum did. The rugged power of the allegros comes over splendidly and the early stereo recordings (1963 and 1961 respectively) are vividly atmospheric, if with some constriction in tuttis and an edge on high violins, brought in by the CD transfer.

Symphony No. 9 in D min.
❀ (M) *** Sony MYK 44825 [id.]. Columbia SO, Bruno Walter.
(M) *** DG 429 904-2; *429 904-4* [id.]. BPO, Karajan.
*** Teldec/Warner Dig. 9031 72140-2 [id.]. BPO, Barenboim.
*** DG Dig. 427 345-2 [id.]. VPO, Giulini.
(B) **(*) DG 429 514-2; *429 514-4* [id.]. BPO, Jochum.
**(*) DG 419 083-2 [id.]. BPO, Karajan.
**(*) Decca Dig. 425 405-2 [id.]. Cleveland O, Dohnányi.
**(*) HM/BMG Dig. RD 60365; *RK 60365* [60365-2-RC; *60365-4-RC*]. N. German RSO, Wand.
** EMI Dig. CDC7 54088-2 [id.]; *EL 754088-4*. Rotterdam PO, Jeffrey Tate.
(M) ** Sony SMK 47542 [id.]. NYPO, Bernstein.
*(*) DG Dig. 435 350-2 [id.]. VPO, Bernstein.

Bruno Walter's 1959 recording is a superb achievement. This was one of the most beautiful results of Walter's Indian summer in the CBS studio, and now the results are immeasurably enhanced, with a blend of rich, clear strings and splendidly sonorous brass. Walter's mellow, persuasive reading leads one on through the leisurely paragraphs so that the logic and coherence seem obvious where other performances can sound aimless. Perhaps the scherzo is not vigorous enough to provide the fullest contrast – though the sound here has ample bite – yet it exactly fits the overall conception. The final slow movement has a nobility which makes one glad that Bruckner never completed the intended finale. After this, anything would have been an anticlimax.

This DG Galleria reissue offers a glorious performance of Bruckner's last and uncompleted symphony, moulded in a way that is characteristic of Karajan and displaying a simple, direct nobility that is sometimes missing in this work. Here he seems to find it unnecessary to underline but, with glowing playing from the Berlin Philharmonic and spectacular recording, he gives the illusion of letting the music speak for itself. Even in a competitive field, this 1966 disc stands out at mid-price, to rank alongside Bruno Walter's noble 1959 version.

Daniel Barenboim recorded the *Ninth Symphony* in the 1970s with the Chicago Symphony, and his new version with the Berlin Philharmonic comes from a live concert at the Philharmonie, given in the autumn of 1990. The early performance had considerable warmth and was generally well shaped though the recording itself fell short of a three-star rating. The new account has rather more depth and strength and, of course, the advantage of superb orchestral playing. Moreover the recorded sound has splendid body and transparency and, although it does not displace either of the Karajan accounts or the old Bruno Walter (for which we still retain a strong affection), must be numbered among the strongest newer recommendations.

Giulini's *Ninth* is a performance of great stature, the product of deep thought. As always, there is the keenest feeling for texture and beauty of contour, and he distils a powerful sense of mystery from the first and third movements. The DG recording has a welcome sense of space and transparency of texture. Although this does not displace Walter, it is a record that all Brucknerians should possess.

Jochum's reading has greater mystery than any other and the orchestral playing (at the individual level) reaches a degree of eloquence that disarms criticism. If at times Jochum tends to phrase too affectionately so that consequently the architecture does not emerge unscathed, he is still magnetic in everything he does. The 1966 recording sounds remarkably good and this issue is a genuine bargain, especially if treated as a supplement to Walter's version.

In his later (1977) reading, Karajan clearly wanted to convey a tougher, more majestic impression, and the interpretation concentrates on strength and impact. As before, however, the playing of the Berlin Philharmonic is both technically immaculate and dedicated. The recording balance is closer than before but the digital transfer is not without ambient atmosphere and is truthful in matters of orchestral timbre.

Decca provide the Cleveland Orchestra and Christoph von Dohnányi with a recording of enormous clarity and presence. Dohnányi's reading makes the most of the dramatic tensions inherent in the score – at the expense, perhaps, of its sense of mystery. It gives the impression of a newly cleaned and restored painting, with the colours in bold relief and the drama highlighted.

Günter Wand's account of the *Ninth Symphony*, made with the Hamburg North German Radio Orchestra, is far more expansive than his earlier version. Given the greater length of reverberation of Lübeck Cathedral, Wand naturally adapts his pace to the acoustic and adds about five minutes overall to his earlier account; but the overhang, particularly in tuttis, does muddy the texture at times. Moreover one is not quite sure where one is actually sitting: the brass seem much nearer than the strings and wind. The generous pacing and obvious warmth that Wand secures from his Hamburg forces is impressive, but the performance as a whole does not strike the same note of awe and concentration (particularly in the *Adagio*) that marked his earlier, Cologne reading.

Jeffrey Tate's EMI recording with the Rotterdam Philharmonic is not a strong contender. His first movement has undoubted breadth and dignity and, although they are no match for the Berlin Philharmonic or the Concertgebouw, this fine Dutch orchestra play with dedication. Tate is expansive (at times he even seems discursive) and, although the EMI recording has admirable clarity and detail, the performance itself falls short of the distinction that would prompt a collector to return to it frequently.

Bernstein's 1969 NY version is a warmly felt performance, strongly directed, and very well played. The CBS recording, made at the Lincoln Center, is fuller than usual from this source, with fine sonorous brass sounds, but it is much too forwardly balanced to give the necessary contrast to Bruckner's sustained whispers of pianissimo. However it is on the whole preferable to Bernstein's later record, compiled from performances given in February and March 1990 at the Grosser Saal of the Musikverein. Not that the playing disappoints – on the contrary, the Vienna Philharmonic produce some gloriously sumptuous tone and are well served by the engineers. But the erratic tempi in the first movement (at times terribly slow) and the excessively high emotional temperature of the slow movement are over the top. (He takes over six minutes more than Karajan and some eight minutes more than Walter.) Nothing Bernstein did is without its insights and this is undoubtedly a performance to hear, but it can be recommended only to the very faithful.

CHAMBER MUSIC

String quintet in F.
(M) *** Decca 430 296-2; *430 296-4* [id.]. VPO Quintet with H. Weiss – SCHMIDT: *Piano quintet.* ***

Bruckner's beautiful *Quintet* dates from 1878, immediately after the revision of the *Third* and *Fourth Symphonies*. It is music of substance and depth and has not been better served on records since this account by the Vienna Philharmonic Quintet, recorded in the Sofiensaal in 1974. The Decca engineers were on top form and the quality is full and sweet.

VOCAL MUSIC

(i) *Masses Nos. 1 in D min.; 2 in E min.; 3 in F min.; Motets: Afferentur regi; Ave Maria; Christus factus est pro nobis; Ecce sacerdos magnus; Locus iste; Os justi medititur; Pange lingua; Tota pulchra es, Maria; Vexilla regis; Virga Jesse.* (ii) *Psalm 150; Te Deum.*
(M) **(*) DG 423 127-2 (4) [id.]. (i) Soloists, Bav. R. Ch. & SO; (ii) Soloists, Ch. of German Op., Berlin, BPO; Jochum.

Bruckner's choral music, like the symphonies, spans his musical career. With excellent soloists, including Maria Stader, Edith Mathis, Ernst Haefliger, Kim Borg and Karl Ridderbusch, the performances of the large-scale works have fine eloquence and admirable breadth and humanity and no lack of drama, although other accounts – of the *Te Deum*, for instance – have had more blazing intensity. But that is not Jochum's way, and the concentration of these performances is never in doubt, with much magic distilled, notably in the early *D minor Mass*, a noble and moving account. The original recordings tended to be distanced; in making the sound more present and clear, the CD remastering has lost some of the atmospheric fullness, although the effect is undoubtedly fresher and brighter, if not always absolutely clean on top. The beautiful motets are particularly successful.

Mass No. 2 in E min.
(M) *** Decca 430 365-2; *430 365-4* [id.]. Peter Hall, Schütz Ch. of London, Philip Jones Wind Ens., Norrington – R. STRAUSS: *Deutsche Motette* etc. ***

Roger Norrington's recording of Bruckner's fine *E minor Mass* was the finest of a number of distinguished analogue recordings of the work and now holds an equally strong position in the CD catalogue. It is sung with great feeling and perception and is recorded in a flattering acoustic which produces splendid depth and richness of sonority, the choir wonderfully underpinned by the brass.

Motets: *Afferentur regi; Ave Maria; Christus factus est; Ecce sacerdos magnus; Inveni David; Locus iste; Os justi medititur; Pange lingua; Tota pulchra es, Maria; Vexilla regis; Virga Jesse.*
**(*) Hyp. CDA 66062; *KA 66062* [id.]. Salmon, Corydon Singers, Best; Trotter (organ).

The Corydon Singers under Matthew Best are not quite as well blended or as homogeneous in tone as the Bavarian Radio Chorus, but Best's direction is often imaginative and he achieves a wide tonal range. The motets span the best part of Bruckner's creative life; given their devotional character, though, they are best heard two or three at a time rather than at one sitting.

Motets: *Afferentur regi virgines; Ecce sacerdos magnus; Inveni David; Os justi meditabitur sapientiam; Pange lingua gloriosa.*
(M) *** Decca 430 361-2; *430 361-4* [id.]. St John's College, Cambridge, Ch., ASMF, Guest – BEETHOVEN: *Mass in C.* ***

Although the motets are obviously not the main attraction here, they make a welcome coupling for the Beethoven *C major Mass*. The performances are of the highest quality and the recording is marvellously spacious. Afferentur regi virgines, Inveni David and the splendid *Ecce sacerdos magnus* all have trombones, the remaining two are unaccompanied.

Requiem in D min.; Psalms 112 and 114.
**(*) Hyp. CDA 66245; *KA 66245* [id.]. Rodgers, Denley, Maldwyn Davies, George, Corydon Singers, ECO, Best; T. Trotter (organ).

Matthew Best here tackles the very early setting of the *Requiem* which Bruckner wrote at the age of twenty-five, often gauche in the string-writing, but with a number of pointers to the future, notably in the *Benedictus*. The quality of the writing in the Psalm settings also varies; but with fine, strong performances from singers and players alike, including an excellent team of soloists, this is well worth investigating by Brucknerians. First-rate recording.

Brumel, Antoine (c. 1460 – c. 1520)

Missa, Et ecce terrae motus (in twelve parts); *Sequentia, Dies irae Dies illa.*
❀ *** Sony Dig. SK 46348 [id.]. Huelgas Ens., Paul van Nevel.

Brumel belongs to the same period as Josquin, Isaac, Pierre de la Rue and Obrecht, and was spoken of with veneration by such contemporaries as Rabelais and Glareanus. Born in Chartres, he served at Notre-Dame and at Chambéry in Savoy, before settling in Italy where he succeeded Josquin as maestro di cappella at Ferrara. Morley in his *Plaine and Easie Introduction to Practicall Musicke* wrote that 'only Josquin des Pres and Brumel were able to teach one everything about older canonic techniques'. Lassus himself prepared and took part in a performance of the 12-part Mass, *Et ecce terrae motus*, in Munich in the 1570s, and this recording was made from the manuscript he used – the only copy of the work that survives. It is not just the contrapuntal ingenuity of his music that impresses but the sheer beauty of sound with which we are presented. Not only was Brumel one of the first composers to write a polyphonic requiem but the very first to make a polyphonic setting of the sequence, *Dies irae Dies illa.* This is a more severe work than the glorious 12-part *Mass* which occupies the bulk of this CD, and is written in a more medieval tonal language. The performances by the Huelgas Ensemble under its founder-director, Paul van Nevel, are fervent and eloquent and vividly bring this music back to life (this is its first recording). The recording, made in the ample acoustic of the Irish Chapel in Liège, is resplendent. This will be something of a revelation to those for whom Brumel has been only a name in the history books.

Buller, John (born 1927)

(i) *Proença (Provençal). The Theatre of memory.*
(M) *** Unicorn Dig. UKCD 1049 [id.]. (i) Sarah Walker, Timothy Walker; BBC SO, Mark Elder.

Both these works have a directness and vigour that owes nothing to contemporary '-isms', but simply reflects the individuality of this fascinating late-developer among composers. The more immediately compelling work is *Proença*, exuberant and energetic, a sequence of settings of troubadour songs in the original Provençale, bringing out how modern-seeming the attitudes of the poets were in these poems of 700 years ago. Sarah Walker is the passionately committed soloist, with Timothy Walker on the electric guitar adding a wild, amplified dimension to the sound at climactic points. Though *The Theatre of memory* is more severely controlled, less attractively wild, it too is a substantial work with a clear structure and memorable landmarks. In it Buller ingeniously takes a sixteenth-century concept, based on an actual theatre created for King Francis I of France, which harked back in its use and layouts to the example of ancient Greek drama. So here seven soloists come forward in turn in front of formalized 'chorus' groups. Buller's use of an adventurous but approachable idiom in both works makes this music immediately approachable, yet there is something of the flavour of the latterday Tippett, stretching concepts to the limit. Mark Elder, who conducted the same performers at the Proms première in 1981, here draws passionately committed playing from the BBC orchestra, vividly recorded.

Burgon, Geoffrey (born 1941)

Requiem.
(M) *** Decca Dig. 430 064-2; *430 064-4* [id.]. Jennifer Smith, Murray, Rolfe Johnson, LSO Ch., Woburn Singers, City of L. Sinfonia, Hickox.

Geoffrey Burgon is best known for his incidental music to John le Carré's *Tinker Tailor Soldier Spy* and Evelyn Waugh's *Brideshead Revisited* on television. In idiom his *Requiem* owes much to Benjamin Britten and perhaps early Messiaen. The composer has shown considerable resource in his handling of texture and, though the melodic invention is unmemorable, the overall impression is quite powerful. The work enjoys committed advocacy from these artists and remarkably fine (1981) recorded quality.

At the round earth's imagined corners; But have been found again; Laudate Dominum; Magnificat; Nunc dimittis; A prayer to the Trinity; Short mass; This world; Two hymns to Mary.
**(*) Hyp. Dig. CDA 66123; *KA 66123* [id.]. Chichester Cathedral Ch., Alan Thurlow.

Burgon's famous *Nunc dimittis* is well matched here with the *Magnificat* that he later wrote to complement it and a series of his shorter choral pieces, all of them revealing his flair for immediate, direct communication, and well performed. First-rate recording.

Bush, Geoffrey (born 1920)

(i) *The End of love; Greek love songs;* (ii; iii) *A little love music;* (iii) *3 Songs of Ben Jonson; Song of wonder.*
*** Chan. Dig. CHAN 8830; *ABTD 1053* [id.]. (i) Luxon; (ii) Cahil; (iii) Partridge; composer.

Geoffrey Bush has a particularly sensitive ear for the resonance of the English language and shows no lack of musical resource in their setting. He works within the tradition of John Ireland, with whom he studied, and Benjamin Britten, and his musical language is diatonic yet fresh. The repertoire here ranges from his early Jonson settings (1952) through to the relatively recent cycle, *A little love music* (1976), which are economical in style – the piano is silent – and touching in their directness of utterance. The *Greek love songs* (translated from Meleager, who lived around 160 BC) obviously fire the composer with their heady passion. Here the lover of Heliodora dreams of her kisses and more besides, and fearfully prays that sleep may make his rival impotent. In a bizarre scherzando he sends forth a mosquito to carry his message of ardour, promising the insect rather impractical rewards. *The End of love* has darker imagery, and there is a touching central lament. *The Songs of wonder*, based on children's rhymes but by no means simplistic, make a happy contrast and Ian Partridge relishes their lively character. All these songs are performed with freshness and spontaneity, while the composer , who is an excellent pianist, provides admirable accompaniments. The acoustic is ecclesiastical, but this puts a nice feeling of space behind the performers who are realistically balanced.

Farewell, earth's bliss; 4 Hesperides songs; A Menagerie; (i) *A Summer serenade.*
*** Chan. Dig. CHAN 8864; *ABTD 1479* [id.]. Varcoe, Thompson, Westminster Singers, City of London Sinfonia, Hickox, (i) with Eric Parkin.

Few living composers can match Geoffrey Bush in responding to the rhythms and cadences of English words. His writing for voice regularly combines a Britten-like flexibility of line with the snappy pointing of Walton – like both of them, creating ideas that instantly catch in the mind. This collection of Bush's vocal works has an open freshness stemming from the easy inevitability of the settings, firmly tonal in idiom but not merely derivative. The delightful *Summer serenade* of seven song-settings, written in 1948, five years after Britten's very comparable *Serenade*, has long been his most frequently performed work – a favourite with small choral groups – and this first recording glowingly brings out the sharp contrasts of mood within and between the songs. Bush even manages to give a new slant to words memorably set by Britten in his *Serenade*, Blake's *O rose thou art sick*, making it a funeral procession with chorus. The instrumentation is just as felicitous as the choral writing, with a spiky concertante part for piano played by Eric Parkin. That 20-minute piece is well coupled with a solo song-cycle of comparable length, *Farewell, earth's bliss*, with Stephen Varcoe the baritone soloist; four songs from Herrick's *Hesperides*, also for baritone and strings; and three for unaccompanied voices, including an insistently menacing setting of Blake's *Tyger*. The tenor, Adrian Thompson, not ideally pure-toned, contributes to only two of the *Serenade* songs; otherwise these are near-ideal performances in warm, open sound. Readers unfamiliar with this repertoire should explore it for, quite apart from the vocal line, Bush's string writing is a pleasure in itself.

Busoni, Ferruccio (1866–1924)

Piano concerto, Op. 39.
(M) *** EMI CDM7 69850-2. John Ogdon, Alldis Ch., RPO, Revenaugh.
*** Telarc Dig. CD 80207 [id.]. Garrick Ohlsson, Cleveland O and Men's Ch., Dohnányi.

*** EMI Dig. CDC7 49996-2 [id.]. Peter Donohoe, BBC SO & Singers, Mark Elder.

Busoni's marathon *Piano concerto* is unique, running to 70 minutes, roughly the same time as Beethoven's *Choral Symphony*, with which it has another parallel in its choral finale. With such an ambitious design it must be expected that the music's inspiration will be uneven. Much of the most important material lies with the orchestra, the piano often tending to act more as a poetic obbligato to the work's main argument. John Ogdon's magisterial and powerful advocacy is matched by both his brilliance and his passionate commitment, making the music surge forward, and he is well supported by Daniel Revenaugh and the RPO, with an incandescent contribution from the John Alldis Choir. The EMI recording from the late 1960s sounds bold and immediate in its CD format. This issue makes an outstanding bargain at mid-price.

The full-price alternative from Telarc can be warmly recommended too, even if the first-rate modern digital sound brings fewer advantages than expected, other than highlighting the solo piano. In the choral finale the John Alldis Choir on EMI has far more impact than the men of the Cleveland Orchestra Chorus, making it into a genuine culmination. With extra prominence given to the solo instrument, Garrick Ohlsson's bravura display is very exciting, and the pianist's own enjoyment in virtuosity enhances his electricity and flair.

Peter Donohoe's formidable version was recorded live at the Proms in August 1988. The snag is that the sound, thanks to the acoustic of the Royal Albert Hall, is a little diffuse, reducing the dramatic impact. The chorus in the final movement is rather distant and, inevitably, orchestral ensemble is less clean than in a studio performance. Where it gains is in the surge of excitement that Donohoe builds up from one vast movement to the next, as when his sparklingly volatile account of the scherzo leads into the longest of the five movements, the *Pezzo serioso*. Helpfully, EMI have given separate tracks to the four different sections in that extended third movement. Though this does not replace John Ogdon's classic first-ever recording, it makes an attractive, freely expressive alternative.

Violin sonatas Nos. 1 in E min., Op. 29; 2 in E min., Op. 36a.
*** Chan. Dig. CHAN 8868; *ABTD 1483* [id.]. Lydia Mordkovitch, Victoria Postnikova.

Busoni's two *Violin sonatas* are rarities in the concert hall and though they do not show this master at anywhere his most inspired they deserve more than an occasional hearing. There is no current alternative to the *First* and less interesting of the two, and Lydia Mordkovitch and Victoria Postnikova are impressive advocates of this somewhat uneven piece. Busoni himself thought of his *Second* as a turning point in his development as a composer: here the shades of Brahms certainly fall less heavily. It is a one movement piece, dating from 1898, with a *langsam* opening, a Presto and a most beautiful *Andante* section leading to a set of variations. Mordkovitch and her partner give a more selfless reading than Kremer's older DG account, and with excellent recording this disc should be sought out by admirers of this composer.

Doktor Faust (opera) complete.
(M) *** DG 427 413-2 (3) [id.]. Fischer-Dieskau, Kohn, Cochran, Hillebrecht, Bav. Op. Ch. & R. O, Leitner.

Busoni's epic *Doktor Faust* was left incomplete at the composer's death. Unfortunately, this recording is full of small but tiresome cuts; however, with a magnificent performance from Fischer-Dieskau in the name-part and superb, fierily intense conducting from Leitner, it fully conveys the work's wayward mastery, the magnetic quality which establishes it as Busoni's supreme masterpiece, even though it was finished by another hand. Being offbeat in its layout, the piece works more predictably on record than on stage. The cast is dominated by Fischer-Dieskau, here in 1969 at his very finest; and the only weak link among the others is Hildegard Hillebrecht as the Duchess of Parma. In the CD transfer the vividness of the sound is intensified. Though this is a mid-price set, the documentation is generous, with essays and synopsis and the complete libretto in English translation as well as the original German.

Fantasia contrappuntistica; Fantasia after J. S. Bach; Toccata.
**(*) Altarus AIR-2-9074. John Ogdon.

It is a bizarre thought that Busoni's remarkable *Fantasia contrappuntistica* was begun, as Ronald Stevenson reminds us, on board a transatlantic liner in 1910 and completed in New Orleans. Stevenson calls it a masterpiece and, listening to John Ogdon's performance, one is tempted to agree. The *Fantasia after J. S. Bach* was written a year earlier and is among Busoni's most concentrated and powerful piano works. The balance places Ogdon rather far back and, as the acoustic is somewhat reverberant, the piano sounds a little clangy (for example, at the opening of the *Toccata*).

Butterworth, George (1885–1916)

The banks of green willow.
*** Chan. CHAN 8373 [id.]. Bournemouth Sinf., Del Mar – BANTOCK: *Pierrot of the minute;* BRIDGE: *Suite for strings* etc. ***

The banks of green willow; 2 English idylls; A Shropshire lad (rhapsody).
(M) *** Decca 421 391-2; *421 391-4* [id.]. ASMF, Marriner – BRITTEN: *Variations on a theme of Frank Bridge;* WARLOCK: *Capriol suite.* ***
*** Nimbus Dig. NI 5068 [id.]. E. String O, Boughton – BRIDGE: *Suite;* PARRY: *Lady Radnor's suite.* ***

Butterworth's *Shropshire lad* represents the English folksong school at its most captivatingly atmospheric, and the other works are in a similarly appealing pastoral vein. Marriner's performances with the Academy are stylishly beautiful, without the last degree of finesse but very fine indeed, with vivid, wide-ranging recording quality. The recording dates from 1976 and the CD remastering shows just how good it was.

The four Butterworth pieces, done with tender simplicity in sumptuously atmospheric, digital sound, provide the centrepiece for a Nimbus issue that has become one of that company's best-sellers. As in the Parry and Bridge items, Boughton secures from his Birmingham-based orchestra warm and refined playing in well-paced readings. In an ample acoustic, woodwind is placed rather behind the strings.

On Chandos, Del Mar gives a glowingly persuasive performance of *The banks of green willow*, which comes as part of another highly interesting programme of English music, devoted also to Butterworth's somewhat older contemporaries, Bantock and Frank Bridge. The digital transfer of a 1979 analogue recording has the benefit of even greater clarity without loss of atmosphere.

A Shropshire lad (song-cycle).
(M) *** Decca 430 368-2 [id.]. Benjamin Luxon, David Willison – VAUGHAN WILLIAMS: *Blake songs* etc. ***

Benjamin Luxon gives powerful, dramatic performances of songs which can take such treatment, not quite the miniatures they may sometimes seem. Well-balanced recording and an admirable coupling.

Buxtehude, Diderik (c. 1637–1707)

Trio sonatas: in G; B flat and D min., Op. 1/2, 4 & 6, (BuxWV 253, 255 & 257); in D and G min., Op. 2/2–3, (BuxWV 260–1).
*** ASV/Gaudeamus CDGAU 110; *ZCGAU 110.* Trio Sonnerie.

Make no mistake, this is music of real quality: its invention is fertile and distinguished by a lightness of touch and colour that is quite individual; the melodic lines are vivacious and engaging, and their virtuosity inspiriting. The Trio Sonnerie show real enthusiasm and expertise, and their virtuosity is agreeably effortless and unostentatious. These are most musical performances, and very well recorded, and can be highly recommended, especially to those who regard Buxtehude as merely a name in the musical history books.

Trio sonatas for violin, viola da gamba and harpsichord: in A min., Op. 1/3; in B flat, Op. 1/4; in G min., Op. 2/3; in E, Op. 2/6 (BuxWV 254–5, 261; 264).
(B) *** HM HMA 901089 [id.]. Boston Museum Trio.

The four *Sonatas* on this record come from the two collections published in the composer's lifetime in 1694 and 1696. The Boston Museum Trio are a highly accomplished group and display an exemplary feeling for style. The music is unfailingly inventive and, despite the obvious Italianate elements, distinctive. Not only are the playing, recording and presentation of high quality, but the cost is modest. The CD transfer is immaculate and truthfully reflects the master-tape. A most stimulating concert, only 41 minutes in length, but all of them enjoyable.

Canzona in E min., BuxWV 169; Canzonetta in G, BuxWV 171; Ciacona in E min., BuxWV 160; Chorales: Ach Herr, mich armen Sünder, BuxWV 178; In dulci jubilo, BuxWV 197; Komm, Heiliger Geist, Herre Gott, BuxWV 199; Vater unser im Himmelreich, BuxWV 219; Magnificat primi toni, BuxWV 203; Preludes: in C, BuxWV 137; in D, BuxWV 139.
(*) Chan. Dig. CHAN 0514 [id.]. Piet Kee (organ of St Laurens Church, Alkmaar) – SWEELINCK: *Collection.* *

The splendid Schnitger organ at Alkmaar has recently been restored and it is good to have it in use for fine modern recordings of the music of Buxtehude – for which it is eminently suited – in the hands of an authoritative exponent. Kee's performance of the opening *Magnificat primi toni* is little short of magnificent. In his words, the piece consists of 'a prelude, four fugues with interludes and a sparkling fugal finale', and it is fully worthy to be compared with Bach. The closing *Ciacona in E minor* is pretty impressive too, while the *Canzonetta in G* is deliciously registered, with piping flute colouring. One's reservations, however, concern the presentation of the chorales which, Kee suggests, 'require poetic expression'. Perhaps they do, but they also need to be moved on rather faster; *In dulci jubilo*, in particular, loses much of its character when the pacing is so studied, even though the detail emerges admirably. The Chandos recording is superb.

Canzona in G, BuxWV 170. Chorales: Ach Herr, mich armen Sünder, BuxWV 178; Erhalt uns, Herr, BuxWV 185; Es ist das Heil, BuxWV 186; Gott der Vater, BuxWV 190; Herr Jesu Christ, BuxWV 193; In dulci jubilo, BuxWV 197; Jesus Christus unser Heiland, BuxWV 198; Kommt her zu mir, BuxWV 201; Lobt Gott, ihr Christen allzugleich, BuxWV 202. Fugue in C (Gigue), BuxWV 174; Passacaglia in D min., BuxWV 161; Preludes & fugues: in D, BuxWV 139; in E, BuxWV 141; in F sharp, BuxWV 146.
(M) *** Decca Dig. 430 262-2; *430 262-4.* Peter Hurford (organ of the Church of Our Lady of Sorrows, Toronto).

Hurford's recital subdivides into two sections, each opening with an impressively structured *Prelude and fugue* and the first ending with the *D minor Passacaglia*; the *E major Prelude and fugue* rounds off the second half. In between comes a series of agreeable and mellifluous chorales, obviously a model for Bach, but not imaginatively on a par with the latter's inspired embroidery. What catches the ear most strikingly here are the delightful *Canzona in G* and the captivating *'Gigue' Fugue in C*, uncannily like Bach's *Fugue à la gigue in G*, BWV 577. Hurford's registration here is agreeably apt, giving both pieces a piquant bite to offset the blander sounds he creates for the amiable chorale preludes. A distinguished recital, played with characteristic spontaneity on a splendid organ that is highly suitable for this repertoire.

Chorales: Christ unser Herr zum Jordan kam; Durch Adams Fall ist ganz verderbt; Ein feste Burg ist unser Gott; Erhalt uns Herr bei deinem Wort; Es ist das Heil uns kommen her; Es spricht der unweisen Mund wohl; Gelobet seist du, Jesu Christ; Gott der Vater, wohn uns bei; Magnificat primi toni; 2 Preludes and fugues in A min.; Preludes and fugues in C; F sharp min.
(B) *** HM HMA 90942 [id.]. René Saorgin (Schnitger organ of the Church of St Michel de Zwolle, Holland).

This collection makes an admirable introduction to the organ music of a composer more written about than listened to. The Schitger organ is sensitively and colourfully registered by Saorgin: he is particularly impressive in the serene, reflective chorales, *Durch Adams Fall* and *Es spricht der unweisen Mund wohl*, while the elaborations of the *Magnificat* are finely made. The four *Preludes and fugues* are all interesting: the F sharp minor work opens with a fine flourish and each of these pieces has Buxtehude's characteristic variety of structure. No wonder Bach admired his music. Excellent recording, vividly transferred.

Ciaconas: in C min.; E min., BuxWV 159/60; Passacaglia in D min., BuxWV 161; Preludes and fugues: in D; D min.; E; E min.; BuxWV 139/142; in F; F sharp min., BuxWV 145/146; in G min., BuxWV 149.
(M) *** DG 427 133-2. Helmut Walcha (organ of Church of SS Peter and Paul, Cappel, West Germany).

Buxtehude's organ music has a character of its own: his *Preludes and fugues* are more complex than Bach's straightforward two-part structures. Toccata-like passages and fugal sections alternate, and the writing here and in the *Ciaconas* is often exuberantly florid. Helmut Walcha has the full measure of this repertoire and these performances on the highly suitable Arp

Schnitger organ in Cappel, Lower Saxony, are authoritative and spontaneous. The 1978 recording is excellent and the disc comprises generous measure: 73 minutes.

(i) *Preludes and fugues: in G min.; F ; Chorales: Herr Christ, der einig Gottes Sohn; In dulci jubilo; Lobt Gott, ihr Christen allzugleich; Chorale fantasy: Gelobet seist du, Jesu Christ. Cantatas:* (ii) *In dulci jubilo; Jubilate Domino.*
(B) **(*) HM HMA 90700 [id.]. (i) René Saorgin (organ of St Laurent, Alkmaar); (ii) Alfred Deller, Deller Cons., Perulli, Chapuis.

A good, inexpensive sampler of Buxtehude, dating from 1971. The recording is lively though the transfer seems to give a French accent to the sound of the Alkmaar organ. The opening *Prelude and fugue in G minor* is fully worthy of the young J. S. Bach and, like its companion, is splendidly played by René Saorgin. The chorales are more static and less interesting than Bach's treatment of the same ideas. Of the cantatas, *In dulci jubilo* is a florid piece for four voices with instrumental accompaniment, while *Jubilate Domino* is a solo cantata accompanied by viola da gamba and organ continuo. Deller is in good form throughout.

Cantatas: *An Filius non est Dei, BuxWV 6; Cantata Domino, BuxWV 12; Frohlocket mit Händen, BuxWV 29; Gott fähret auf mit Jauchzen, BuxWV 33; Herr, wenn ich nur Dich habe, BuxWV 39; Heut triumphieret Gottes Sohn, BuxWV 43; Ich bin die Auferstehung, BuxWV 44; Ich habe Lust abzuscheiden, BuxWV 46; Ihr lieben Christen, BuxWV 51; In dulci jubilo, BuxWV 52; Jesus dulcis memoria, BuxWV 56; Jesu meines Lebens Leben, BuxWV 62; Jubilate Deo, BuxWV 64; Mein Gemüt erfreuet sich, BuxWV 72; Nichts soll uns scheiden, BuxWV 77; Nun danket alle Gott, BuxWV 79; Wie wird erneuet, wie wird er freuet, BuxWV 110.*
*** Erato/Warner Dig. 2292 45294-2 (3) [id.]. Schlick, Frimmer, Chance, Jacobs, Prégardien, Kooy, Hannover Knabenchor, Amsterdam Bar. O, Koopman.

It seems possible that Ton Koopman may be planning to do for Buxtehude's cantatas what Harnoncourt and Leonhardt have achieved with Bach on Teldec. There are well over a hundred of them to be explored, and on the evidence of this box they contain much fine music, even if they are not as inspired as Bach's cantatas. All the works here are of a pietist religious character, although the music readily expands into joyously extrovert expressions of praise. Some attractively combine the form of a concerto grosso, with alternating solos and tuttis, and a few are more ambitious, including chorus, trumpets and cornetts, and even trombones, and drums too. The brass writing is inevitably primitive, but highly effective in its stylized way. The work which ends the first disc, *Heut triumphieret Gottes Sohn*, is worthy of Bach and is quite spectacular with its closing *Victoria* and *Allelujah*, and a similar mood prevails at the end of *Jesu meines Lebens Leben*, which opens the second disc. The solo singing is excellent, and the soloists match pleasingly when they sing in duet or trio. René Jacobs has *Jubilate Dominum* effectively to himself, Peter Kooy brings appropriate darkness of timbre to *Ich bin die Auferstehung*, and Barbara Schlick, whose contribution gives much pleasure throughout, has a fine extended solo in *Herr, wenn ich nur Dich habe. Nichts soll uns scheiden von der Liebes Gottes* ('Nought shall take God's love from us') has a delightful opening trio, with the opening Nichts repeated twice, to give an attractively light rhythmic touch. There is plenty to discover here for any collector who enjoys the pre-Bach era. Accompaniments are alive, textures transparent, and the recording balance is altogether excellent.

Byrd, William (1543–1623)

Browning a 5; Fantasia a 3; Fantasia a 3 in C (No. 1); Fantasia a 3 in C (No. 3); Fantasia a 4 in G min; Fantasias a 6 in G min. (Nos 1–2); Pavan & Galliard a 6 in C; Pavana Bray; La Volta.
*** Virgin Dig. VC7 90795-2; *VC 790795-4* [id.]. Fretwork, with Christopher Wilson – DOWLAND: *Lachrimae.* ***

These consort pieces of Byrd have much greater variety of mood and feeling than the unrelieved melancholy of the Dowland *Lacrimae*, with which they are interspersed. They are given performances of both authority and freshness. Good recording, too.

Pavans and galliards (collection).
*** HM HMC 901241/2 [id.]. Davitt Moroney (harpsichord).

On the first of the two discs Davitt Moroney presents the sequence of nine pavans and galliards Byrd composed in the 1570s and '80s, which come from *My Ladye Nevell's Booke*

(1591), and the second creates a second cycle of pieces on the same lines. Between them, Davitt Moroney constructs a sequence of Byrd's finest late pavans, taking care to model it on the same lines of symmetry and contrast that distinguish Byrd's own. Moroney contributes a thorough and scholarly note which sets out the thinking behind his compilation. The playing is totally committed and authoritative though a trifle didactic. His recording, made on an Italian instrument of 1677, is very naturally recorded, though collectors will have to use a very low-level setting to get realistic results. This pair of CDs comprises half of Byrd's output in this field and is a most valuable contribution to the catalogue. The documentation is excellent.

VOCAL MUSIC

Motets in paired settings: *Ave verum corpus* (with PHILIPS: *Ave verum corpus*); *Haec Dies* (with PALESTRINA: *Haec Dies*); *Iustorum animae* (with LASSUS: *Iustorum animae*); *Miserere mei* (with G. GABRIELI: *Miserere mei*); *O quam gloriosum* (with VICTORIA: *O quam gloriosum*); *Tu es Petrus* (with PALESTRINA: *Tu es Petrus*).
(B) *** CfP CD-CFP 4481; *TC-CFP 4481*. King's College, Cambridge, Ch., Sir David Willcocks.

This is an imaginatively devised programme of motets in which settings of Latin texts by Byrd are directly contrasted with settings of the same words by some of his greatest contemporaries. As was the intention, quite apart from adding variety to the programme, the juxtaposition makes one listen to the individual qualities of these polyphonic masters the more keenly, and to register their individuality. The recording emerges with remarkable freshness on CD, and the beauty of the singing is never in doubt.

Cantiones sacrae, Book 1: Aspice Domine; Domine secundum multitudinem; Domine tu iurasti; In resurrectione tua; Ne irascaris Domine; O quam gloriosum; Tristitia et anxiestas; Vide Domine afflictionem; Virgilate.
**(*) CRD Dig. CRD 3420 [id.]. New College, Oxford, Ch., Higginbottom.

Cantiones sacrae, Book 2: Circumdederunt me; Cunctis diebus; Domine, non sum dignus; Domine, salva nos; Fac sum servo tuo; Exsurge, Domine; Haec dicit Dominus; Haec dies; Laudibus in sanctis Dominum; Miserere mei, Deus; Tribulatio proxima est.
**(*) CRD Dig. CRD 3439 [id.]. New College, Oxford, Ch., Higginbottom.

Though the New College Choir under its choirmaster Edward Higginbottom does not sing with the variety of expression or dynamic which marks its finest Oxbridge rivals, it is impossible not to respond to the freshness of its music-making. The robust, throaty style suggests a Latin feeling in its forthright vigour, and the directness of approach in these magnificent *cantiones sacrae* is most attractive, helped by recording which is vividly projected, yet at once richly atmospheric.

The Great Service (with anthems).
*** Gimell Dig. CDGIM 011; *1585T-11* [id.]. Tallis Scholars, Phillips.
*** EMI Dig. CDC7 47771-2. King's College, Cambridge, Ch., Cleobury; Richard Farnes (organ).

Peter Phillips and the Tallis Scholars give a lucid and sensitively shaped account of Byrd's *Great Service*. Theirs is a more intimate performance than one might expect to encounter in one of the great English cathedrals; they are fewer in number and thus achieve greater clarity of texture. Of course, the top lines are sung by women – excellently, too – and the firmer focus will not be seen as a disadvantage by many collectors. The recording is quite excellent: it is made in a church acoustic (the Church of St John, Hackney) and captures detail perfectly. It includes three other anthems, two of which (*O Lord make thy servant Elizabeth* and *Sing joyfully unto God our strength*) are included on the rival EMI disc. This CD will give great musical satisfaction.

Collectors wanting *The Great Service* in a cathedral acoustic will turn to the King's version, which is beautifully recorded on EMI. They have the advantages of boy trebles, a larger complement of singers who can offer more contrast between solo and full verses, and a well-played organ accompaniment, which it probably had in the 1580s. Stephen Cleobury also sets the music in a more authentic liturgical background: he offers the *Kyrie* and puts the two canticles for Evensong into their context with anthems and responses.

Mass for 3 voices; Mass for 4 voices; Mass for 5 voices.
❀ (M) *** Decca 433 675-2 [id.]. King's College, Cambridge, Ch., Willocks.
*** Argo Dig. 430 164-2; *430 164-4* [id.]. Winchester Cathedral Ch., David Hill.
(B) **(*) HM HMA 90211[id.]. Deller Cons.

Masses for 3, 4 and 5 voices; Ave verum corpus.
*** Gimell Dig. CDGIM 345 [id.]. Tallis Scholars, Phillips.

It was the King's College Choir under Sir David Willcocks who pioneered this repertoire on LP and first recordings always have something special about them. This one is no exception and, although later versions of the *Mass for 5 voices* (the first to be recorded at King's, in 1959) have produced singing that is more dramatic and more ardent, the serenity of the King's account with its long, flowing paragraphs remains very appealing, and the power of the words 'Dominus Deus' in the *Sanctus* and the sustained intensity of the closing *Agnus Dei* are very affecting. The performances of the *Masses for 3 and 4 voices*, dating from 1963, remain classics of the gramophone. The latter is particularly fine – just sample the soaring *Sanctus–Benedictus*. Under Willcocks there is an inevitability of phrasing and effortless control of sonority and dynamic that completely capture the music's spiritual and emotional feeling. Byrd remained a Catholic all his life and was generously indulged in his religion by Queen Elizabeth. Even so, it was daring to have the Masses printed (in 1593–5) so that they could be performed in private. The Argo recording – a great tribute to the late Harley Usill – is extraordinarily real: the impression of being in the ante-chapel and listening from that splendid vantage-point to this inspired singing is so vivid that the three decades since these records were made slip away altogether.

Peter Phillips's performances are altogether more ardent than those recorded by Argo at King's, and some might prefer the greater serenity of the latter. But Phillips is a master of this repertoire; undoubtedly these performances have more variety and great eloquence so that, when the drama is varied with a gentler mood, the contrast is the more striking. This enormously rewarding music lends itself to an imaginatively varied treatment, and certainly the sound made by the Scholars in Merton College Chapel is beautiful, both warm and fresh.

David Hill and the Choir of Winchester Cathedral are the latest to offer all three Byrd *Masses* on one CD, and their version can be confidently recommended for those wanting the convenience of all three together on disc. Fine performances that can rate alongside the Tallis Scholars without displacing it. The standard of both singing and recording in this particular repertory remains high.

Whether or not it is historically correct for Byrd's Masses to be sung by solo voices, the great merit of these French Harmonia Mundi performances is their clarity, exposing the miracle of Byrd's polyphony, even though the tonal matching is not always flawless. The *Mass for 5 voices* is particularly impressive, and these were among the finest of the Deller Consort's recordings made in the years before Alfred Deller's death. The 1968 recording is clean and truthful and is faithfully transferred to CD, although it lacks something in ecclesiastical atmosphere.

Mass for 4 voices; Mass for 5 voices.
(M) **(*) EMI Dig. CD-EMX 9505; *TC-EMX 2104* [Ang. CDM 62015]. St John's College, Cambridge, Ch., Guest.

There is no lack of enthusiasm in the performances of the Choir of St John's College, Cambridge, and they can at times be more persuasive than some professional groups. The *Five-part Mass* fares best and is given with genuine fervour. The balance of the recording is rather closer than is usual in this venue, though there is a reasonable glow round the singers.

Mass for 4 voices with Propers for the Feast of Saints Peter and Paul (Gradualia 1607); Motets: Hodie Simon Petrus; Quodcunque ligaveris; Quomodo cantabimus?; Tu es pastor omnium.
*** Virgin Dig. VC7 91133-2; *VC7 91133-4* [id.]. The Sixteen, Harry Christophers.

Mass for 5 voices with Propers for the Feast of All Saints (Gradualia 1605); Motets: Ad dominum cum tribularer; Diliges dominum.
*** Virgin Dig. VC7 90802-2; *VC7 90802-4* [id.]. The Sixteen, Harry Christophers (with: MONTE: *Super flumina Babylonis* ***).

The Byrd *Masses for 3, 4 and 5 voices* can now be (and have been) accommodated on one CD, but the advantage of the two Virgin discs by The Sixteen and Harry Christophers is that the *Masses* are placed in a wider musical context; the *Mass for 4 voices* is contrasted with some of the richer six-part motets from the 1607 Gradualia, including *Quomodo cantabimus?*. Suitably appended is Philippe de Monte's *Super flumina Babylonis*, which the composer had sent Byrd in 1583 and to which the *Quomodo cantabimus?* is a response.

The *Mass for 5 voices* similarly comes with the Propers for the Feast of All Saints, which come from the Gradualia of 1605 and includes the 8-part motet *Ad dominum cum tribularer*, notable for its rich-textured, poignant false relations. The singing is very impressive, the recording excellently focused and the acoustic appropriately spacious.

Anthems: *Praise our Lord, all ye Gentiles; Sing joyfully; Turn our captivity. Motets: Attolite portas; Ave verum corpus; Christus resurgens; Emendemus in melius; Gaudeamus omnes; Justorum animae; Laudibus in sanctis; Non vos relinquam; O magnum mysterium; O quam suavis; Plorans plorabit; Siderum rector; Solve iubente Deo; Veni sancte spiritus; Visita quaesumus Domine.*
*** Coll. Dig. COLCD 110 [id.]. Cambridge Singers, John Rutter.

This is the first of a projected series intended to cover all Byrd's music, so it is not surprising that the beautifully sung *Ave verum corpus* and the jubilant anthem, *Sing joyfully*, were included, alongside much that is less familiar. Officially Byrd wrote for the Anglican Church, but much of his finest music was for the Roman liturgy, at that time officially banned but still performed clandestinely. There is no better example here than *Emendemus in melius*, which was chosen by the composer jointly with Tallis to open their 1575 collection of *Cantiones sacrae*. John Rutter brings a composer's understanding to these readings, which have a simple, direct eloquence, the music's serene spirituality movingly caught; and the atmospheric recording is very faithful, even if detail could be sharper. The programme is divided into four groups, first Anthems, and then Motets: of penitence and prayer; of praise and rejoicing; and for the Church year.

'Songs of sundrie natures': Christ is rising again; Come to me griefe for ever (Funeral songs of Phillip Sydney Knight). Come wofull Orpheus; Elegy on the death of Thomas Tallis: Ye sacred muses. From Virgin's wombe; A carowle for Christmas Day; Have mercy upon me, O God; Lulla, lullaby; Make ye joy to God; Praise our Lord all yee gentiles; Though Amaryllis daunce in greene; Turne our captivitie; Who made thee Hob (Dialogue between two shepherds).
*** EMI Dig. CDC7 47961-2. Hilliard Ens., L. Bar., Hillier.

Although 'naturally disposed to Gravity and Piety', Byrd included a number of livelier pieces in his 1589 collection – but even so, the overall mood here is melancholy. The white, vibratoless tone and a certain uniformity of timbre leave a slightly mannered impression. A special point of interest is that the Hilliard adopt contemporary pronunciation – presumably the speech favoured in the 1590s – and this may to some extent account for a slight feeling of self-consciousness. There is the usual high level of accomplishment about these performances and a beautifully natural recording.

Cage, John (1912–92)

Sonatas and Interludes for prepared piano.
*** Denon Dig. C37 7673 [id.]. Yuji Takahashi.

The sixteen sonatas included here, each in binary form not very different from Scarlatti's, are – by Cage's standards – closely structured, and in their sequence are punctuated by four interludes, very similar in style. One can readily appreciate the attraction of an Eastern performer to this music with its pentatonic passages as well as its odd textures and unexpected sounds – induced by the insertion of bolts, screws, coins, etc., on most of the piano strings. Takahashi's commitment is reinforced by close, rather dry recording, apt for this music.

Campra, André (1660–1744)

Requiem Mass.
**(*) HM HMC 901251; *HMC 401251* [id.]. Baudry, Zanetti, Benet, Elwes, Varcoe, Chapelle Royale Ch. & O, Herreweghe.

André Campra's *Requiem* is a lovely work, with luminous textures and often beguiling harmonies, and its neglect is difficult to understand. Herreweghe's performance, with refined solo and choral singing, makes a good alternative to John Eliot Gardiner's (currently withdrawn) version, for those who prefer a cooler approach to church music of 1700. The recording is refined, to match the performance.

L'Europe galante (opera-ballet).
(M) *** HM/BMG GD 77059 (2) [77059-2-RG]. Yakar, Kweksilber, René Jacobs, La Petite Bande, Leonhardt – LULLY: *Bourgeois gentilhomme.* ***

The sheer tunefulness of *L'Europe galante* has ensured its appeal over the years. This record, the first with period instruments, dates from 1973 and gives us the complete entertainment – and very delightful it is. Like Couperin's *Les Nations*, though in a very different fashion, this enchanting divertissement attempts to portray various national characteristics: French, Spanish, Italian and Turkish. The three soloists all shine and the instrumentalists, directed by Leonhardt, are both expert and spirited. The recording too is well balanced and sounds very fresh on CD. The only snag is that this now comes in harness with Lully's *Le bourgeois gentilhomme*, which is musically much thinner. Full translations are provided.

Idomenée (tragédie lyrique).
**(*) HM HMC 901396/8; *HMC 401396/8* (id.]. Deletre, Piau, Zanetti, Fouchécourt, Boyer, Les Arts Florissants, Christie.

Representing a generation of French opera-composers between Lully and Rameau, André Campra was equally successful writing church music as writing for the stage. One incidental distinction of this opera, *Idomenée*, the fifth of Campra's tragédies lyriques, first given in 1712, is that the libretto by Antoine Danchet was later used as a basis of the libretto for Mozart's great *opera seria* of 70 years later. The big difference is that, where Mozart's opera is made to end happily, Danchet had fate triumphing at the end, when Idomenée in madness slays Idamante, his son. Ilione, the equivalent of Mozart's Ilia, then concludes that the king's punishment will be to go on living. In this first complete recording of any opera by Campra, Christie opts for the later revision of the piece which the composer made for the revival in 1731, eliminating two incidental characters and reworking several scenes. It is a fluent opera in five Acts, preceded by an allegorical prologue. In the manner of the time, it relies on free cantilena rather than formal numbers, with set-pieces kept short and with the chorus often contributing to such brief arias as there are. There are fine processional marches and choruses with a Purcellian flavour, and Christie with his talented Les Arts Florissants team presents the whole work with a taut feeling for its dramatic qualities, though there is nothing here to compare with the big moments in Mozart's opera. The matching of voices to character is closer here than what we would conventionally expect in Mozart. The title-role is given to a wide-ranging bass, the clear-toned if not always steady Bernard Deletre, while Idamante is a high tenor, the expressive Jean-Paul Fouchécourt, on balance the most successful of the soloists. The bright tones of Monique Zanetti as Ilione verge too often on shrillness, and there is an edge too on the warmer soprano voice of Sandrine Piau as Electre. Nevertheless, in the breadth of its span and its frequent hints as to what Purcell might have achieved had he tackled a full-length opera, this is a fascinating work, vividly recorded.

Tancrède (opera); complete.
** Erato/Warner Dig. 2292 45001-2 (2). François Le Roux, Evangelatos, Dubosc, Le Maigat, Reinhart, Alliot-Lugaz, Visse, The Sixteen, La Grande Écurie et la Chambre du Roy, Malgoire.

André Campra had an extraordinary melodic facility (on which Milhaud drew of course in his *Suite provençale*) and collectors who do not have it should seek out the BMG/Harmonia Mundi reissue of his delightful ballet, *L'Europe galante*, written at the end of the seventeenth century (see above). *Tancrède*, the first of his tragédies lyriques, comes at the beginning of the eighteenth: it is very much in the tradition of Lully but is stronger in its blend of lyricism and dance than in dramatic coherence. This recording was made at a performance in Aix-en-Provence in 1986 and, though there are stage noises and at times some less than polished playing, it is well worth investigating, even if the original production at Aix must presumably have taken much longer than the two hours presented here.

Canteloube, Marie-Joseph (1879–1957)

(i) *Chants d'Auvergne: Series 1–5* (complete); (ii) Appendix: *Chants d'Auvergne et Quercy: La Mère Antoine; Lorsque le meunier; Oh! Madelon, je dois partir; Reveillez-vous, belle endormie. Chants paysans Bearn: Rossignolet qui chants. Chants du Languedoc: La fille d'un paysan; Moi j'ai un homme; Mon père m'a plasée; O up!; Quand Marion va au moulin. Chants des Pays*

Basques: Allons, beau rossignole; Comment donc Savoir; Dans le tombeau; J'ai un douce amie; Le premier de tous les oiseaux.
❀ (M) *** Van. 08.8002.72 [OVC 8001/2]. Netania Davrath, O, (i) Pierre de la Roche; (ii) Gershon Kingsley.

It was Netania Davrath who in 1963 and 1966 – a decade before the De los Angeles selection – pioneered a complete recording of Canteloube's delightful song-settings from the Auvergne region of France. While her voice has a lovely, sweet purity and freedom in the upper range, she also brings a special kind of colour and life to these infinitely varied settings. All 30 songs from the five series are included, plus an important appendix of 15 more, collected by Canteloube and admirably scored by Gershon Kingsley, very much in the seductive manner of the others. These include not only additional Auvergne items but songs from other areas too, including the Languedoc and the Basque country. They are quite as delightful as any of the more familiar chants, and some of them are unforgettable. Most memorable of all is *Reveillez-vous, belle endormie*, a Quercy dialogue song of unattainable love, which has a melody that could become as famous as *Baïlèro*, given proper exposure. This ends a programme of two hours of enchanting music which, when dipped into, will give endless pleasure. The accompaniments are freshly idiomatic, warm but not over-upholstered, and the CD transfers retain all the sparkle and atmosphere of the original recordings, made in the agreeable ambience of Baumgartner Hall, Vienna.

Chants d'Auvergne: L'Aio dè rotso; L'Antouèno; Baïlèro; Brezairola; Malurous qu'o uno fenno; Passo pel prat; Pastourelle.
(M) *** BMG/RCA GD 87831 [7831-2-RG]. Anna Moffo, American SO, Stokowski – RACHMANINOV: *Vocalise;* VILLA-LOBOS: *Bachianas Brasileiras No. 5.* ***

Moffo gives radiant performances, helped by the sumptuous accompaniment which Stokowski provides. The result is sweet, seductively so. The recording, from the early 1960s, is opulent to match. With several favourites included, this makes an excellent shorter selection from Canteloube's famous settings, and the couplings are vintage Stokowski.

Chants d'Auvergne: L'Antouèno; Baïlèro; 3 Bourrées; Lou Boussu; Brezairola; Lou coucut; Chut, chut; La Delässádo; Lo Fïolairé; Jou l'pount d'o Mirabel; Malurous qu'o uno fenno; Passo pel prat; Pastourelle; Postouro, sé tu m'aymo; Tè, l'co tè.
❀ (M) *** EMI Dig. CD-EMX 9500; TC-EMX 2075 [Ang. CDM 62010]. Jill Gomez, RLPO, Handley.

Jill Gomez's selection of these increasingly popular songs, attractively presented on a mid-price label, makes for a memorably characterful record which, as well as bringing out the sensuous beauty of Canteloube's arrangements, keeps reminding us, in the echoes of rustic band music, of the genuine folk base. Jill Gomez's voice could not be more apt, for the natural radiance and the range of tone-colour go with a strong feeling for words and sentiment, helped by her intensive study of Provençal pronunciation. Vernon Handley's accompaniments have a directness as well as a warmth which supports the voice admirably, and the recording is outstandingly full and vivid. An ideal purchase for the collector who wants just a selection.

Chants d'Auvergne: L'Antouèno; Baïlèro; 3 Bourrées; 2 Bourrées; Brezairola; La Delaïssádo; Lo Fïolairé; Lou Boussu; Malurous qu'o uno fenno; La pastrouletta è lou chibalie; Passo pel prat; La pastoura als camps; Pastourelle.
*** Decca Dig. 410 004-2 [id.]. Te Kanawa, ECO, Tate.

In Dame Kiri Te Kanawa's recital the warmly atmospheric Decca recording brings an often languorous opulence to the music-making. In such an atmosphere the quick songs lose a little in bite and *Baïlèro*, the most famous, is taken extremely slowly. With the sound so sumptuous, this hardly registers and the result remains compelling, thanks in great measure to sympathetic accompaniment from the ECO under Jeffrey Tate.

Chants d'Auvergne: Baïlèro; 3 Bourrées; Brezairola; Lou Boussu; Lou coucut; Chut, chut; La Délaïssàdo; Lo Fïolairé; Jou l'pount d'o Mirabel; Malurous qu'o uno fenno; Oï ayaï; Pastourelle; La pastrouletta; Postouro, sé tu m'aymo; Tè l'co tè; Uno jionto postouro.
*** Virgin Dig. VC7 90714-2; *VC 790714-4* [id.]. Arleen Augér, ECO, Yan Pascal Tortelier.

Arleen Augér's lovely soprano is ravishing in the haunting, lyrical songs like the ever-popular *Baïlèro*. In the playful items she conveys plenty of fun, though in the more boisterous numbers the recording catches an unexpected edge in her voice. With excellent recording, however, this stands alongside other recommended selections.

Chants d'Auvergne, 4th and 5th series (complete).
(*) Decca 411 730-2 [id.]. Te Kanawa, ECO, Tate – VILLA-LOBOS: *Bachianas Brasileiras No. 5.* *

This second collection of Canteloube folksong arrangements from Kiri Te Kanawa, again with Jeffrey Tate providing richly beautiful accompaniments, presents all remaining items in the five sets of the songs. There is less variety here, partly a question of Dame Kiri's preference for producing a continuous flow of sensuously beautiful sounds rather than giving a folk-like tang.

Cardosa, Frei Manuel (c. 1566–1650)

Requiem: Magnificat; Motets, Mulier quae erat; Non mortui; Nos autem gloriari; Sitivit anima mea.
❀ *** Gimell CDGIM 021; *1585T-21* [id.]. Tallis Scholars, Phillips.

This is quite a discovery. Renaissance music in Portugal is a closed book to most collectors, and unaccompanied choral polyphony continued to flourish there long after Monteverdi had changed the course of music in Italy. Cardosa was a member of the Carmelite order and published five collections of motets and Masses between 1613 and 1648. The Requiem comes from the 1625 Book of Masses and opens in striking and original fashion. The polyphony unfolds in long-breathed phrases of unusual length and eloquence, and both the motets, Mulier quae erat (A woman, a sinner in that city) and the short Nos autem gloriari (Yet should we glory), are rich in texture and have great expressive resplendence. Cardosa's use of the augmented chord at the opening of the Requiem gives his music some of its distinctive stamp. The Tallis Scholars sing with characteristic purity of tone and intonation, and they are splendidly recorded. A glorious issue.

Carissimi, Giacomo (1605–74)

Duos & cantatas: *A piè d'un verde alloro; Bel tempo per me; Così volete, così sarà; Deh, memoria è che più chiedi; Hor che si Sirio; Il mio cor è un mar; Lungi homai deh spiega; Peregrin d'ignote sponde; Rimati in pace homai; Scrivete, occhi dolente (Lettera amorosa); Tu m'hai preso à consumare; Vaghi rai, pupille ardenti.*
(B) *** HM Dig. HMA 901262; HMA 431262 [id.]. Concerto Vocale, René Jacobs.

Carissimi's achievement as a sacred composer has long overshadowed his secular music, whose riches are generously displayed here and whose inspiration and mastery are immediately evident. These are performances of great style and are beautifully recorded. A bargain.

Jepthe; Judicium Salomonis (The Judgement of Solomon); Jonas (oratorios).
*** Mer. Dig. CDE 84132; *KE 77132* [id.]. Coxwell, Hemington Jones, Harvey, Ainsley, Gabrieli Cons. 8 Players, Paul McCreesh.

The present disc collects three of the best known of Carissimi's chamber oratorios. No opening sinfonia survives for *Jepthe* and the editor chooses to preface the oratorio with a Frescobaldi *Toccata*, which works well. *Jepthe* is affectingly presented in this well-prepared and intelligent performance, which is let down only by some vocal insecurities at the very top. The continuo part is imaginatively realized with some pleasing sonorities (organ, double harp, chitarrone, etc.). Despite some undoubted shortcomings, these are most convincing accounts of all three works.

Carlsson, Mark (born 1952)

Nightwings.
*** Crystal Dig. CD 750 [id.]. Westwood Wind Quintet – BARBER: *Summer music;* LIGETI: *Bagatelles;* MATHIAS: *Quintet.* ***

In *Nightwings* the flute assumes the persona of a dreamer, the taped music may be perceived as a dream-world, and the other four instruments appear as characters in a dream. The music is almost wholly diatonic and immediately accessible, but it is not an unimaginative conception. On this evidence, however, the conception is in some respects more interesting than the piece itself. Excellent playing and recording.

Carmina Burana (c. 1300)

Carmina Burana – songs from the original manuscript.
*** O-L Dig. 417 373-2 [id.]. New L. Cons., Pickett.
**(*) HM HMC 90335 [id.]. Clemencic Cons., René Clemencic.

Carmina Burana – songs from the original manuscript, Vol. 2.
*** O-L Dig. 421 062-2 [id.]. New L. Cons., Pickett.

This was the collection on which Carl Orff drew for his popular cantata. The original manuscript comprises more than 200 pieces from many countries, dating from the late eleventh to the thirteenth century, organized according to subject-matter: love songs, moralizing and satirical songs, eating, drinking, gambling and religious texts. The performances on these well-filled Oiseau-Lyre discs have the merit of excellent singing from Catherine Bott and Michael George, and sensitive playing from the instrumentalists under Pickett. The engineering is excellent and strikes a virtually ideal balance between voice and instruments. There is a pleasing acoustic ambience. This makes a clear first choice, given the clarity and warmth of the sound.

René Clemencic's performances, recorded in 1977, have immense spirit and liveliness, and there is much character. The presentation suffers slightly in comparison with its rival from slightly over-reverberant sound, though this at times brings a gain in atmosphere. Most collectors will prefer the better-focused sound of its immediate rival.

Carter, Elliott (born 1908)

Concerto for orchestra; (i) *Violin concerto; Three Occasions.*
*** Virgin Dig. VC7 91503 [id.]. (i) Ole Bohn; L. Sinf., Knussen.

This is the finest, most rewarding disc of Elliott Carter's orchestral music yet, a credit to a British record company and performers. The 1969 *Concerto for orchestra*, in four linked sections plus introduction and coda, marks a watershed in Carter's career, fully establishing his mature style, gritty and uncompromising. Knussen claims for it a seminal status comparable with that of Stravinsky's *Rite of spring* in the 1920s, and his performance reflects that commitment, giving a sense of purpose that minimizes any problems for the listener in this heavily textured, often fragmented music, emphasizing its energy. The other two works are much more recent and more approachable in Carter's later, more lyrical manner. The three sharply contrasted pieces in *Three Occasions* were conceived separately but form a taut, satisfying whole, while the *Violin concerto*, with Ole Bohn the superb soloist, finds Carter encouraging an overtly emotional approach with such markings as 'impulsive' and *angiosciato*, 'anguished'. The composer himself supervised the sessions. The recording is of spectacular range and depth, bringing out the brilliance of the London Sinfonietta's playing.

(i) *Piano concerto. Variations for orchestra.*
*** New World NWCD 347 [id.]. (i) Ursula Oppens; Cincinnati SO, Gielen.

The *Concerto* comes from the mid-1960s and is a densely argued piece, complex in its structure, contrasting an isolated soloist (Ursula Oppens its heroine) whose character is 'free, fanciful and sensitive' with an orchestra that functions as a massive and mechanical ensemble, and with a concertino of seven instruments, surrounding the piano, who act as 'a well-meaning but impotent intermediary'. It is a strange work that seems at first impenetrable but which is undeniably powerful and disturbing. The *Concerto* and the *Variations* date from two different stylistic periods; the *Variations* is an inventive and fascinating work, splendidly played by these Cincinnati forces. The recording was made at concert performances and is excellent.

Carver, Robert (*c.* 1484–*c.* 1568)

10-part Mass, 'Dum sacrum mysterium'; Motets: *Gaude flore Virginali; O bone Jesu.*
*** Gaudeamus Dig. CDGAU 124; *ZCGAU 124* [id.]. Cappella Nova, Alan Tavener.

There is relatively little biographical information to be had about the Scottish composer, Robert Carver – even his dates are uncertain: Kenneth Elliott, the author of his entry in Grove, gave c. 1490–1546, but in his authoritative notes to this disc he tells us that Carver's life was more extended and that he is now known still to have been alive in 1568. This CD and tape, the first in a series of Scottish Renaissance Polyphony, offers three works. The opening piece, the motet *O bone Jesu*, dating from the 1520s, is in 19 parts and is of exceptional luminosity and richness. The 10-part Mass, *Dum sacrum mysterium*, was written at the beginning of the sixteenth century: various dates between 1506 and 1513 are suggested and it is thought that in its final form it was performed at the coronation of the infant James V at Stirling. As the note puts it, among Carver's Masses this is 'undoubtedly the grandest in scope, the most extended in development and the richest in detail'. The motet, *Gaude flore Virginali*, for five voices is of slightly later provenance, perhaps dating from about 1515; though less sumptuous, it has some adventurous modulations. The Cappella Nova under Alan Tavener give a thoroughly dedicated account of all three pieces, though the pitch drops very slightly in the *Gaude flore Virginali*. The recording is very good indeed.

Casadesus, Robert (1899–1972)

Concerto for 3 pianos.
(M) ** Sony MPK 46730 [id.]. Robert, Gaby & Jean Casadesus, Colonne Concerts O, Dervaux – FRANCK: *Symphonic variations;* D'INDY: *Symphonie.* ***

The *Concerto for three pianos*, Op. 65, was written in the mid-1960s for the composer, his wife and his son, Jean, who recorded it with the now defunct Orchestre des Concerts Colonne under Pierre Dervaux. There is a spiky first movement, an *Allegro marziale* which inhabits a no-man's land somewhere between Poulenc, Stravinsky and the Prokofiev of the piano concertos, and there is an atmospheric siciliano middle movement and a vigorous finale. It is an attractive piece whose ideals would harmonize with Les Six, but the thematic substance remains ultimately unmemorable. The recording is a bit on the dry side but not excessively so.

Casken, John (born 1949)

Golem (chamber opera in 2 parts).
*** Virgin Dig. VC7 91204-2 [id.]. Clarke, Hall, Robson, Music Projects London, Richard Bernas.

Golem is based on the well-known Jewish legend of the rabbi, the Maharal, who creates a saviour figure, a Golem, from lifeless clay. The Maharal's altruistic aims are thwarted when the Golem, developing human feelings, refuses to be controlled. It was this score which in 1990 won for Casken the first Britten Award for Composition, with this recording as part of the prize. It is a curious piece but a memorable and atmospheric one, with this splendid performance taken from a brilliantly re-edited version of BBC tapes. The piece is the more involving for the often sinister atmospheric writing, as when at the start of the story, after the flashback opening scene, the orchestra simulates the beating of the wings of a great bird, a frightening sound. Though through the Prelude and five continuous scenes the Maharal's monologues take up a disproportionate share of the whole, that matters little in a recording, particularly when the role is so confidently taken by Adrian Clarke. John Hall as the Golem is equally convincing, and most striking of all is Christopher Robson in the counter-tenor role of Ometh, 'a Promethean figure of hope and conscience'. The meeting between the Golem and Ometh in the final scene brings a tender resolution, when in their halting way they realize that, but for the Maharal's obstruction, their partnership could have brought success, not tragedy.

Castillon, Alexis de (1838–73)

(i) *Piano concerto in D, Op. 12. Esquisses symphoniques, Op. 15.*
(M) *** EMI CDM7 63943-2 [id.]. (i) Ciccolini; Monte Carlo PO, Prêtre.

Alexis de Castillon was intended by his parents for the army. He found his way to music relatively late; in 1868 when he was thirty Duparc introduced him to César Franck and at the première of his *Piano concerto* in 1872 the soloist was Saint-Saëns. The *Concerto* is much indebted to Schumann and Beethoven, influences which are by no means fully assimilated even in the *Esquisses symphoniques*, written not long before his death. The ideas have grace and facility, and there is an elegance and charm about some of the piano writing that offset the occasional infelicitous orchestral tutti. Aldo Ciccolini plays with virtuosity and much poetic feeling, and Georges Prêtre gets good results from the Monte Carlo orchestra. Neither piece has the effortless inventive flow and polish of Saint-Saëns, but they are well worth investigating.

Catalani, Alfredo (1854–93)

La Wally (opera): complete.
(M) *** Decca 425 417-2 (2) [id.]. Tebaldi, Del Monaco, Diaz, Cappuccilli, Marimpietri, Turin Lyric Ch., Monte Carlo Op. O, Fausto Cleva.

This unashamed piece of hokum was much loved by Toscanini, who named his children after characters in it. The title-role prompts Renata Tebaldi to give one of her most tenderly affecting performances on record, a glorious example of her singing late in her career. Her poise and control of line in the celebrated aria, *Ebben? Ne andro lontana*, provide a model for any generation. The work's mixture of sweetness and melodrama has its attractions despite the absurdity of the story. Tebaldi is well matched by a strong cast. Mario del Monaco begins coarsely, but the heroic power and intensity of his singing are formidable, and it is good to have the young Cappuccilli in the baritone role of Gellner. The sound in this late-1960s recording is superbly focused and vividly real, a fine example of Decca recording at a vintage period, with only a touch of over-brightness in the CD transfer. On two discs only (two Acts per disc) with libretto and translation, it will not easily be displaced.

Cavalli, Francesco (1602–76)

Giasone (complete).
*** HM Dig. HMC 901282/4; *HMC 401282/4* [id.]. Chance, Schopper, Dubosc, Deletré, Mellon, Banditelli, Visse, De Mey, Concerto Vocale, Jacobs.

With the brilliant and sensitive counter-tenor, Michael Chance, in the title-role of an opera that roams far away from the authentic tale of Jason and the Argonauts, René Jacobs's recording of Cavalli's opera is a remarkable achievement. Based on a stage production given in Innsbruck, it brings fine, stylish singing and playing which uses period performance positively to communicate with a modern audience. Drawing from no fewer than twelve textual sources, Jacobs drew up a text which necessarily omits much material but still runs for almost four hours of music. In the instrumentation Jacobs adds recorders in particular to the strings, to give greater variety. The admixture of comedy that can be embarrassing in operas of this period is here handled splendidly. The vividly characterful Dominique Visse in particular scores a huge success in the drag-role of the nurse, Delfa, very much in the tradition of Hugues Cuenod's performances for Raymond Leppard in Cavalli at Glyndebourne. It is a pity that none of the others characterize like Visse, beautifully as they sing. Clean, well-balanced sound.

Xerse (complete).
*** HM HMC 901175/8; *HMC 401175/8* [id.]. René Jacobs, Nelson, Gall, Poulenard, Mellon, Feldman, Elwes, De Mey, Visse, Instrumental Ens., Jacobs.

'Ombra mai fù,' sings King Xerxes in the opening scene, addressing a plane tree, and most listeners will have a double-take, remembering Handel's *Largo*, which comes from a later setting of the same libretto. Cavalli's opera, even longer than Handel's Serse but just as brisk in its action, can be presented just as winningly, as here in the first ever recording. Jacobs' presentation is piquant to match the plot, often genuinely funny, sustaining the enormous length very well. As well as directing his talented team, Jacobs sings the title-role, only one of the four counter-tenors, nicely contrasted, who take the castrato roles. The fruity alto of Dominique Visse in a comic servant role is particularly striking, and among the women – some of them shrill at times – the outstanding singer, Agnès Mellon, takes the other servant role, singing delightfully in a tiny laughing song. The three Acts of the opera are preceded by an allegorical prologue. Excellent sound, which consistently allows the fresh, young voices of the principals to make every word plain. Notes and libretto are first rate.

Certon, Pierre (died 1572)

Chansons: *Amour a tort; Ce n'est a vous; C'est grand pityé; De tout le mal; En espérant; Entre vous gentilz hommes; Heilas ne fringuerons nous; Je l'ay aymé; Je neveulx poinct; Martin s'en alla; Plus nu suys; Que n'est auprès de moy; Si ta beaulté; Ung jour que Madame dormait.* Mass: *Sur le pont d'Avignon.*
(B) *** HM 901034 [id.]. Boston Camerata, Joel Cohen.

Pierre Certon is hardly a familiar name, but this engaging Mass and the coupled secular songs give him strong claims to attention. He was active in Paris during the period 1530–70 and held the title of Master of the Choir at the Saint-Chapelle. The *Mass Sur le pont d'Avignon* has genuine appeal, and the chansons also exercise a real charm over the listener. The Mass is performed *a cappella*, and the chansons enjoy instrumental support. In both sacred and secular works the Boston Camerata bring freshness, musical accomplishment and stylistic understanding to bear; the recording, made in a spacious acoustic, creates the most beautiful sounds. This is highly recommended to musical explorers: its rewards are considerable, and it might have been considered for a Rosette had translations been included alongside the French texts of the songs. But the documentation is otherwise good.

Cesti, Antonio (1623–69)

Cantatas: *Amanti, io vi disfido; Pria ch'adori.*
(B) **(*) HM HMA 901011 [id.]. Concerto Vocale – D'INDIA: *Duets, Laments & Madrigals.* **(*)

The career of Antonio Cesti was remarkably diverse. Beginning (at the age of fourteen) as a Franciscan friar, he proceeded to a vocal career in Florence (where he sang in Cavalli's *Giasone*), then went on to become a theatrical producer as well as a secular composer, and he was eventally absolved by Rome from his monastic vows. His 17-minute cantata, *Pria ch'adori*, is a serenata for two voices, after the Monteverdi style, including even a *Lamento d'Arianna* in duet form. *Amanti, io vi disfido* is a much shorter, bravura piece that might almost have come from Monteverdi's *Madrigali guerrieri*, only the invention (as in the longer work) is less individual. The performances by Judith Nelson and René Jacobs are certainly pleasingly fresh, and the distinguished instrumental group includes William Christie providing the continuo. The sound is pleasingly fresh.

Chabrier, Emmanuel (1841–94)

Bourrée fantasque; España (rhapsody); *Gwendoline: Overture. Marche joyeuse; Le Roi malgré lui: Danse slave; Fête polonaise. Suite pastorale.*
(M) *** Mercury 434 303-2 [id.]. Detroit SO, Paray – ROUSSEL: *Suite.* **(*)

The return of this finely played and idiomatically conducted collection of Chabrier's best orchestral pieces does not disappoint. The CD transfer has refined the (basically) 1960 sound-picture and made it seem more natural, without loss of fullness. The bass resonance, which was a characteristic of the hall at Cass Technical High School, is better focused here than it was on LP. It brought a slightly more forward balance than would have been ideal but is most effective in the melodrama of the full-blooded Detroit performance of the *Gwendoline Overture.* Paray's whimsically relaxed and sparkling account of *España* gives great pleasure and his rubato in the

Fête polonaise is equally winning. The *Suite pastorale* is a wholly delightful account, given playing that is at once warm and polished, neat and perfectly in scale, with the orchestra beautifully balanced. The third movement, *Sous bois*, is rather fast, but the finish of the phrasing makes the effect convincing. The *Marche joyeuse* was recorded in Detroit's Old Orchestral Hall a year before the rest of the programme. The *Bourrée fantasque* and the Roussel *Suite* have been added as a bonus; they were made earlier, in the Ford Auditorium in 1957. The eagle ear will detect the acoustic differences.

España (rhapsody); *Suite pastorale.*
*** Chan. Dig. CHAN 8852; ABTD 1469 [id.]. Ulster O, Yan Pascal Tortelier – DUKAS: *L'apprenti sorcier; La Péri.* **(*)

Yan Pascal Tortelier and the excellent Ulster Orchestra give an altogether first-rate account of Chabrier's delightful *Suite pastorale*, distinguished by an appealing charm and lightness of touch. The third movement, *Sous bois*, which was rushed off its feet in the old Decca set, is suitably atmospheric and enchanting. There is a spirited account of *España*, too.

PIANO MUSIC

Bourrée fantasque; Impromptu in C; 10 Pièces pittoresques.
(M) **(*) Pianissimo Dig. PP 10792 [id.]. Richard McMahon.

Franck described Chabrier's *Dix Pièces pittoresques* as 'a bridge between our own times and those of Couperin and Rameau', and Ravel greatly admired *Sous-bois*, which Cortot said was 'full of the quiet rustling of leaves'. This, together with the charming *Idyll, Danse villageoise* and *Scherzo-waltz* were to be orchestrated and form the *Suite pastorale*. Richard McMahon's highly individual rubato catches the impulsive feeling of the opening *C major Impromptu* rather well, and he is equally free in handling the first of the ten pieces, *Paysage*; then he is exquisitely gentle in *Mélancolie.* When he comes to the delicate *Idyll* the accompanimental figure is perhaps rather strongly articulated, yet the same boldness is highly effective in the *Danse villageoise*, with its resolute opening imitation, and in the highly animated *Scherzo-waltz*. The *Bourrée fantasque*, too, is played with much rhythmic vigour. Any minor reservations here are dwarfed by the interest of this attractively enterprising programme, for McMahon certainly brings all this music vividly to life. He is well recorded too. An impressive début record for a new label, specializing in off-beat piano repertoire.

OPERA

L'Étoile (complete).
❀ *** EMI Dig. CDS7 47889-8 (2) [Pathé id.]. Alliot-Lugaz, Gautier, Bacquier, Raphanel, Damonte, Le Roux, David, Lyon Opéra Ch. and O, Gardiner.

This fizzing operetta is a winner: the subtlety and refinement of Chabrier's score go well beyond the usual realm of operetta, and Gardiner directs a performance that from first to last makes the piece sparkle bewitchingly. Central to the story, the star of *L'Étoile* is the pedlar, Lazuli, a breeches role, and Gardiner has been lucky to include in his company at the Lyon Opéra a soprano with just the personality, presence and voice to carry it off, Colette Alliot-Lugaz. Except for Gabriel Bacquier as the Astrologer, Sirocco, the others are not well known either, but all are first rate. The helpful French dialogue adds to the sparkle (just long enough to give the right flavour), and numbers such as the drunken duet between King and Astrologer are hilarious. Outstandingly good recording, with excellent access.

Le roi malgré lui (complete).
(M) *** Erato/Warner 2292 45792-2 (2) [id.]. Hendricks, Garcisanz, Quilico, Jeffes, Lafont, French R. Ch. & New PO, Dutoit.

This long-neglected opera is another Chabrier masterpiece, and Erato (in collaboration with French Radio) is to be congratulated on putting it on record, albeit in flawed form. Ravel said that he would rather have written this piece than Wagner's *Ring* cycle and, though the plot is an impossible muddle, the music makes one understand that extravagant remark. The reluctant king of the title is Henry of Valois, elected to the throne of Poland, who rather sympathizes with those who are plotting against him and adds to the muddle by changing places with his friend, Nangis. The result is a modified Cinderella story, ending happily, which prompts a series of superb numbers, some *España*-like in brilliance (the well-known Waltz of Act II transformed in its choral form) and some hauntingly romantic, with even one sextet suggesting a translation of

Wagner's Rhinemaiden music into waltz-time. The pity is that the linking recitatives have been completely omitted from this recording, and in addition the score has been seriously cut. But Charles Dutoit is a most persuasive advocate. Star among the singers is Barbara Hendricks as the slave-girl Cinderella figure, Minka, who is finally united with Nangis (well sung by the light tenor, Peter Jeffes). Gino Quilico is the king, Isabel Garcisanz (rather shrill-toned) is Alexina, the ambitious wife of the buffo character, Fritelli, who is sung by Jean-Philippe Lafont. The recording is naturally balanced and has plenty of atmosphere. The choral focus is not absolutely sharp, but the soloists are vividly projected, the orchestra has plenty of colour and the CD transfer has not brightened the sound-picture artificially. There is excellent documentation and a clearly printed libretto, and this is undoubtedly a highlight of Erato's 'Affordable opera' series.

Chadwick, George (1854–1931)

Symphony No. 2, Op. 21.
*** New World Dig. NWCD 339 [id.]. Albany SO, Julius Hegyi – PARKER: *Northern Ballad.* ***

George Chadwick's *Second Symphony* (1883–6) breathes much the same air as Brahms and Dvořák; the scoring is beautifully clean and the ideas appealing, if perhaps wanting the distinctive stamp of an original. The scherzo had to be repeated at its first performance – independently of the whole symphony – when one critic noted that it 'positively winks at you'. It is quite delightful. The symphony as a whole is cultivated, well crafted and civilized. Very natural recorded sound and an excellent performance from these New England forces. An interesting disc.

Serenade for strings.
*** Albany Dig. TROY 033-2 [id.]. V. American Music Ens., Hobart Earle – GILBERT: *Suite.* ***

Chadwick's *Serenade*, written in 1890, is here given its European première. It is a delightful work which ought to be much better known. The lyrical feeling of the first movement and the haunting nostalgia of the *Andante* are matched by the expressive warmth of the Minuet which has a genial, Dvořákian intensity and variety of rhythmic style. The finale is hardly less striking in its dancing melodic appeal, and altogether this very well-crafted piece by the so-called 'Boston classicist' gives much pleasure. It is quite beautifully played by this excellent Viennese group, drawn from younger members of the Vienna Symphony Orchestra, who clearly relish its fresh melodic appeal and provide a Viennese lilt in the finale. The sound too is first rate, a successful example of a 'live recording' bringing no loss in realism and a gain in spontaneity.

Chappell, Herbert (born 1934)

Guitar concerto No. 1 (Caribbean concerto).
*** Decca Dig. 430 233-2; 430 233-4 [id.]. Eduardo Fernández, ECO, Barry Wordsworth – ARNOLD: *Guitar concerto;* BROUWER: *Retrats Catalans.* ***

Chappell's warm and vigorous concerto makes a splendid coupling for the Arnold work. Like Arnold a skilled film composer, Chappell has here written a Caribbean-inspired piece which, with few pretensions, vies with the ubiquitous *Concierto de Aranjuez* in immediate colourfulness and with Arthur Benjamin's Caribbean pieces in energy. Unlike most guitar concertos, which keep stopping and starting, this one builds consistently. The slow movement hinges on a simple surging melody not too distant from Khachaturian's *Spartacus Adagio*, and is followed by a riotous finale on Cuban dance rhythms. A winner, brilliantly played and colourfully recorded.

Charpentier, Gustave (1860–1956)

Louise (opera): complete.
(M) *** Sony S3K 46429 (3) [id.]. Cotrubas, Berbié, Domingo, Sénéchal, Bacquier, Amb. Op. Ch., New Philh. O, Prêtre.

This fine, atmospheric recording, the first in stereo, explains why *Louise* has long been a favourite opera in Paris. It cocoons the listener in the atmosphere of Montmartre in the 1890s, with Bohemians more obviously proletarian than Puccini's, a whole factory of seamstresses and an assorted range of ragmen, junkmen, pea-sellers and the like making up a highly individual cast-list. The opera starts with a love-duet and from there meanders along happily, enlivened mainly by the superb crowd scenes. One of them, normally omitted but included here, proves as fine as any, with Louise's fellow seamstresses in their workhouse (cue for sewing-machines in the percussion department) teasing her for being in love, much as Carmen is teased in Bizet's quintet. The love-duets too are enchanting and, although the confrontations with the boring parents are far less appealing, the atmosphere carries one over. Ileana Cotrubas makes a delightful heroine, not always flawless technically but charmingly girlish. Plácido Domingo is a relatively heavyweight Julien and Jane Berbié and Gabriel Bacquier are excellent as the parents. Under Georges Prêtre, far warmer than usual on record, the ensemble is rich and clear, with refined recording every bit as atmospheric as one could want. A set which splendidly fills an obvious gap in the catalogue.

Charpentier, Marc-Antoine (1634–1704)

Concert à 4 (for viols), H.545; Musique de théâtre pour Circé et Andromède; Sonata à 8 (for 2 flutes & strings), H.548.
**(*) HM Dig. HMC 901244; *HMC 401244* [id.]. London Baroque, Medlam.

Marc-Antoine Charpentier's music for Thomas Corneille's *Circé* was written in 1675, and its companion for Pierre Corneille's *Andromède* followed seven years later. The pieces are most expertly played here by the members of London Baroque (though the string sound still does not entirely escape the faint suspicion that it has been marinaded in vinegar) and well reward investigation. As usual in recordings from this source, the sound is excellent.

Le malade imaginaire (incidental music).
*** Erato/Warner Dig. 2292 45002-2 [id.]. Poulenard, Feldman, Ragon, Les musiciens du Louvre, Marc Minkowski.
*** HM Dig. HMC 90-1336; 40-1336 [id.]. Zanetti, Rime, Brua, Visse, Crook, Gardeil, Les Arts Florissants, Christie.

Molière, having fallen out with Lully, dictator of French music in Louis XIV's time and not an agreeable man, turned instead to Charpentier for the music he needed for his last comedy, *Le malade imaginaire*. This sequence of extended prologue and three intermèdes tingles with energy, and is superbly realized on this first recording of the complete incidental music, much of which was lost for three centuries. The extended allegorical prologue works like a miniature comic opera, fresh and speedy, amply confirming that the long-underappreciated Charpentier was a master at least equal to Lully. Eight first-rate soloists and a lively period orchestra are spurred by the consistently animated direction of Marc Minkowski, and the vivid recording adds to the illusion of live performance.

Even next to the outstanding first recording made a little earlier for Erato by Marc Minkowski, this Harmonia Mundi issue brings important advantages, not least the practical ones of a rather more extended treatment and more cueing points. It was recorded after a live stage production, and the acting is somewhat more uninhibited than on the Erato issue, perhaps too much so. With rather less forward and more refined sound, Christie – though he uses percussion just as dramatically as his rival – is lighter in his textures and rhythms, often opting for faster speeds. Whichever version is preferred, this is a masterly example of writing for the stage and, in the vigour and speed of its comic-opera interludes, it makes one wish Charpentier had had more chance to rival Lully. The format is cumbersome, with a single disc contained in a double jewel-case, but the libretto is far more readable.

Motets: *Alma Redemptoris; Amicus meus; Ave regina; Dialogus inter Magdalenam et Jesum; Egredimini filiae Sion; Elevations; O pretiosum; O vere, o bone, Magdalena lugens; Motet du saint sacrement; O vos omnes; Pour le passion de notre Seigneur* (2 settings); *Salve regina; Solva vivebat in antris Magdalena lugens.*
*** HM HMC 901149 [id.]. Concerto Vocale.

Half of the motets on this record are for solo voice and the others are duets. Among the best and most moving things here are the *O vos omnes* and *Amicus meus*, which are beautifully done. Another motet to note is *Magdalena lugens*, in which Mary Magdalene laments Christ's death at the foot of the Cross. Expressive singing from Judith Nelson and René Jacobs, and excellent continuo support. Worth a strong recommendation.

Caecilia, virgo et martyr; Filius prodigus (oratorios); *Magnificat.*
*** HM Dig. HMC 90066 [id.]. Grenat, Benet, Laplenie, Reinhard, Studer, Les Arts Florissants, Christie.

The two works recorded here come from different periods of Charpentier's life: *Caecilia, virgo et martyr* was composed in 1675, when he wrote a number of works on the subject of St Cecilia; the second, on the theme of the Prodigal Son, is later and is richer in expressive harmonies and poignant dissonances. The music's stature and nobility are fully conveyed here. The *Magnificat* is a short piece for three voices and has an almost Purcellian flavour. One thing that will immediately strike the listener is the delicacy and finesse of the scoring. All this music is beautifully recorded; the present issues can be recommended with enthusiasm.

Élévation; In obitum augustissimae nec non piissimae gallorum Reginae lamentum; Luctus de morte augustissimae Mariae Theresiae Reginae Galliae.
(M) *** Erato/Warner Dig. 2292 45339-2 [id.]. Degelin, Verdoodt, Smolders, Crook, Vandersteene, Widmer, Namur Chamber Ch., Musica Polyphonica, Devos.

The music here shows Charpentier at his most inspired, and this CD could well provide an introduction to the composer for many collectors. All three works lament the death in 1683 of Queen Maria Teresa, wife of Louis XIV of France since 1660. Clearly the event moved Charpentier deeply, and each reflects the paradox of the Christian faith in contrasting grief with joy and hope in the life hereafter. *Élévation*, by no means as short as its title, is a motet in the form of a metaphorical duologue between Christ and Hunger, with obvious allusions to the Eucharist; while *Luctus de morte augustissimae* is another imaginatively expressive dialogue in which three male soloists, counter-tenor, tenor and bass, sing individually and together about the Queen's character and majesty in a mourning supplication of considerable intensity. The performance here could hardly be bettered, bringing out all the music's drama, joy and depth of feeling. The recording, made in a spacious acoustic, is also first class in every way. Very highly recommended.

In navitatem Domini nostri Jésus Christi (canticum), H.414; Pastorale sur la naissance de notre Seigneur Jésus Christ, H.483.
*** HM HMC 901082; *HMC 401082.* Les Arts Florissants Vocal & Instrumental Ens., Christie.

This *Canticum* has much of the character of an oratorio (indeed, the word 'canticum' was loosely used to indicate both the motet and the oratorio) and affirms the composer's debt to his master, Carissimi. The invention has great appeal and variety. The *Pastorale* is not new to the gramophone, but the present performance offers music that was not included in the previously recorded Guy Lambert edition. It is a most rewarding piece, and the grace and charm of the writing continue to win one over to this eminently resourceful composer. This collection by William Christie is self-recommending, so high are the standards of performance and recording, and so fertile is Charpentier's imagination. The CD remastering is very successful; the only snag in the presentation is the minuscule print of the accompanying texts.

In navitatem Domini nostri Jésus Christ, H.416; Pastorale sur la naissance de notre Seigneur Jésus Christ.
*** HM HMC 905130 [id.]. Les Arts Florissants Vocal & Instrumental Ens., Christie.

The cantata, *In navitatem*, is one of some 35 which Charpentier composed in this genre (the French call them histoires sacrées). It is one of his grandest, a finely balanced edifice in two complementary halves, separated by an instrumental section, an eloquent evocation of the night. The little pastorale was written in the tradition of the ballet de cour or divertissement. This is enchanting music, elegantly played and excellently recorded.

Leçons de ténèbres.
*** HM HMC 901005 [id.]. Jacobs, Nelson, Verkinderen, Kuijken, Christie, Junghänel.

These *Leçons de ténèbres* are eloquent and moving pieces, worthy of comparison with Purcell and more substantial musically than Couperin's later setting. Since the falsetto tradition was weak, it seems unlikely that any of the music was intended for male alto, a fact that the counter-tenor René Jacobs readily concedes in his notes. Yet his performance (like that of his colleagues) is so authentic in every respect that it is difficult to imagine it being surpassed. The music has depth and these artists reveal its stature to fine effect. The recording is as distinguished as the performances.

Méditations pour le Carême; Le reniement de St Pierre.
*** HM Dig. HMC 905151; *HMC 405151* [id.]. Les Arts Florissants, William Christie.

Le reniement de Saint Pierre is one of Charpentier's most inspired and expressive works and its text draws on the account in all four Gospels of St Peter's denial of Christ. The *Méditations pour le Carême* are a sequence of three-voice motets for Lent with continuo accompaniment (organ, theorbo and bass viol) that may not have quite the same imaginative or expressive resource but which are full of nobility and interest. The performances maintain the high standards of this ensemble, and the same compliment can be paid to the recording.

(i) *Messe de minuit pour Noël (Midnight Mass for Christmas Eve);* (ii) *Te Deum.*
(M) **(*) EMI CDM7 63135-2. (i) Cantelo, Gelmar, Partridge, Bowman, Keyte, King's College Ch., ECO, Willcocks; (ii) Lott, Harrhy, Brett, Partridge, Roberts, King's College Ch., ASMF, Ledger.

There is a kinship between Charpentier's lovely *Christmas Mass* and Czech settings of the Mass that incorporate folk material; and the combination of verse anthems and carol-like pieces is attractive, even the *Kyrie* having a jolly quality about it. The King's performance is warm and musical, but there isn't much Gallic flavour. The organist, Andrew Davis, intelligently uses realizations of the organ interludes – which the composer directs shall be based on the carol themes – by Nicolas Le Bègue. The recording comes from the late 1960s and certainly now has more bite than it did; but reservations remain about the basic style of the singing. The coupling is the best known of the *Te Deum* settings, and this time the King's performance has a vitality and boldness to match the music and catches also its douceur and freshness. The recording, made a decade later than the coupling, is also very successful and has been transferred well to CD.

Miserere, H.219; Motets: *pour la seconde fois que le Saint Sacrament vien au même reposoir, H.372; pour le Saint Sacrement au reposoir, H.346. Motet pour une longue offrande, H.434.*
*** HM Dig. HMC 901185; *HMC 401185* [id.]. Mellon, Poulenard, Ledroit, Kendall, Kooy, Chapelle Royale, Herreweghe.

Charpentier's *Motet pour une longue offrande* is one of his most splendid and eloquent works. There are some poignant dissonances in the *Deus justus et patiens* section. The *Miserere*, the last of four settings Charpentier made of Psalm 50, was written for the Jesuit Church on Rue Saint-Antoine, whose ceremonies were particularly sumptuous. All four works on the disc are powerfully expressive and beautifully performed. The recording, made in collaboration with Radio France, is most expertly balanced.

OPERA

Actéon (complete).
(B) *** HM HMA 901095; *HMA 401095* [id.]. Visse, Mellon, Laurens, Feldman, Paut, Les Arts Florissants Vocal & Instrumental Ens., Christie.

Actéon is a short work in six scenes; the sheer fecundity and, above all, quality of invention take one by surprise – though, by this time, one should take for granted Charpentier's extraordinarily rich imagination. Actéon is particularly well portrayed by Dominique Visse; his transformation in the fourth tableau and his feelings of horror are almost as effective as anything in nineteenth-century opera! Although scholarship is an important ingredient in this undertaking, musicianship and flair are even more important, and these are in welcome evidence. The other singers are first rate, in particular the Diane of Agnès Mellon. Alert playing and an altogether natural recording which is truthfully balanced and sounds splendidly fresh, as well as excellent presentation, make this a most desirable issue and a real bargain.

Les Arts Florissants (opéra et idyle en musique).
(B) *** HM HMA 901083 [id.]. Les Arts Florissants Vocal & Instrumental Ens., William Christie.

Charpentier was kept away from the principal Parisian stage as a result of Lully's monopoly; *Les Arts Florissants*, which he called variously an opera and an 'idyll in music', was composed for Marie of Lorraine, Duchessse de Guise, who maintained a small group of musicians and mounted little chamber operas there. *Les Arts Florissants* is a short entertainment in five scenes;

the libretto tells of a conflict between the Arts who flourish under the rule of Peace, and the forces of War, personified by Discord and the Furies. (In the first performance Charpentier himself sang one of the roles, representing the art of Painting.) This and the little Interlude that completes the music include some invigorating and fresh invention, performed very pleasingly indeed by this eponymous group under the expert direction of William Christie. Period instruments are used, but intonation is always good and the sounds often charm the ear. The recording is excellent as regards both timbre and balance, and the CD transfer is totally natural. A bargain.

David et Jonathas (complete).
(M) *** Erato/Warner 2292 45162-2 [id.]. Esswood, Alliot-Lugaz, Huttenlocher, Soyer, David, Jacobs, Lyon Opera Ch., E. Bar. Festival O, Corbóz.
**(*) HM Dig. HMC 90 1289/90; *HMC 401289/90* [id.]. Lesne, Zanetti, Gardeil, Visse, Les Arts Florissants, Christie.

David et Jonathas comes from 1688, the year after Lully's death had brought to an end his monopoly of the musical stage, and precedes Charpentier's only real opera, *Médée* (1693). Although the formula and the instrumental layout are thoroughly Lullian, Charpentier's music has greater imagination and musical substance than Lully's. The action follows the biblical narrative in broad outline, and much of the music (which is new to the gramophone) is fresh and inventive, remarkably free from period cliché. It confirms the impression, made by many other Charpentier records during the last few years, that in him France has one of her most inspired Baroque masters. The Erato performance is marked by some good singing, though there are passages which would, one feels, benefit from greater finish. But Michel Corbóz gets generally excellent results from his artists and is well recorded. Where on LP the set was extravagantly laid out on three discs, the CD version packages it easily on two, well laid out and with a very comprehensive set of notes. The CD transfer is first class in every way, and this is another worthwhile addition to Erato's 'Affordable opera' series.

The action of *David et Jonathas* follows the biblical narrative in broad outline, and much of the music is fresh and inventive, remarkably free from period cliché. Christie's version on Harmonia Mundi may not always be especially dramatic, but it has a notably sure sense of authentic Baroque style and scale, as well as fine choral singing. However, only one of Christie's soloists is really outstanding, the characterfully distinctive counter-tenor, Dominique Visse, who gives a vivid, highly theatrical performance. The others are relatively colourless; but those who relish authenticity above all else will clearly take to this version, very well recorded.

Medée (complete).
❀ *** HM HMC 901139/41; *HMC 401139/41* [id.]. Feldman, Ragon, Mellon, Boulin, Bona, Cantor, Les Arts Florissants Ch. & O, Christie.

Few records of early Baroque opera communicate as vividly as this, winner in 1985 of the International record critics' award and the Early Music prize in the Gramophone record awards. Despite the classical convention of the libretto and a strictly authentic approach to the performance, Christie's account has a vitality and a sense of involvement which bring out the keen originality of Charpentier's writing, his implied emotional glosses on a formal subject. This was Charpentier's only tragédie-lyrique, and richly extends our knowledge of a long-neglected composer. Les Arts Florissants, in the stylishness of its playing on period instruments, matches any such group in the world, and the soloists are all first rate. Excellent recording.

Chausson, Ernest (1855–99)

Symphony in B flat, Op. 20.
*** Denon Dig. CO 73675 [id.]. Netherlands R. PO, Jean Fournet – FAURÉ: *Pelléas et Mélisande.* ***

Symphony in B flat, Op. 20; Soir de Fête, Op. 32; The Tempest, Op. 18: 2 Scenes.
**(*) Chan. Dig. CHAN 8369; *ABTD 1135* [id.]. Radio-Télévision Belge SO, Serebrier.

Symphony in B flat, Op. 20; Vivianne (symphonic poem), *Op. 9.*
**(*) Erato/Warner 2292 45554-2; 2292 45554-4 [id.]. Basle SO, Jordan.

Jean Fournet's new account of the *Symphony in B flat* is arguably the finest now on the market. Not only is it very well shaped, but the texture in the voluptuous slow movement is heard in excellent focus. Fournet paces all three movements well and gets sensitive results from his players. It is to be preferred to Serebrier's account, though that is more logically coupled with other Chausson pieces, *Soir de Fête* plus two scenes from the incidental music for *The Tempest*. Serebrier's account of the *Symphony* has real conviction and receives good recording, but on balance Fournet is first choice.

Armin Jordan and the Basle orchestra also give a well-shaped account of the Symphony and are thoroughly atmospheric in the Wagnerian slow movement. The orchestral playing is responsive and the recording has an agreeable warmth, with plenty of space round the sound. Jordan is a fine (and much underrated) conductor with an obvious sympathy for this work, and he is thoroughly convincing in both the symphony and *Viviane*. This issue can be recommended alongside (but not in preference to) the Serebrier on Chandos.

Poème (for violin and orchestra), Op. 25.
(M) *** Ph. Dig. 432 513-2. Kremer, LSO, Chailly (with Concert ***).
*** DG Dig. 423 063-2 [id.]. Perlman, NYPO, Mehta – RAVEL: *Tzigane;* SAINT-SAËNS: *Havanaise* etc.: SARASATE: *Carmen fantasy.* ***

Kremer's poetic account of Chausson's *Poème* is part of a highly recommendable concert of French concertante works for violin and orchestra.

Perlman's 1987 digital version is a very fine one and will not disappoint. The sound is immediate and refined in detail, while the balance of the soloist is very slightly less forward. The New York Philharmonic players are undoubtedly responsive under Mehta; yet Chailly displays more feeling for the atmosphere of the piece. In making a choice, some readers will wish to bear in mind that the Perlman disc includes a stunning performance of Sarasate's *Carmen fantasy*.

CHAMBER MUSIC

Concert for piano, violin and string quartet, Op. 21.
(*) Essex CDS 6044. Accardo, Canino, Levin, Batjer, Hoffman, Wiley – SAINT-SAËNS: *Violin sonata No. 1.* *
*** Telarc CD 80046 [id.]. Maazel, Margalit, Cleveland O Qt.
**(*) Decca Dig. 425 860-2; 425 860-4 [id.]. Thibaudet, Bell, Takács Qt – RAVEL: *Piano trio.* **(*)

Salvatore Accardo and Bruno Canino and their four colleagues convey a sense of effortless music-making and of pleasure in making music in domestic surroundings. Accardo is particularly songful in the third movement, light and delicate elsewhere. It is a thoroughly enjoyable account, recorded in a warm acoustic.

It was Telarc who pioneered the first digital recording of Chausson's *Concert* on LP, by the husband-and-wife team of conductor Lorin Maazel (as violin soloist) and Israela Margalit on the piano, together with the excellent Cleveland Quartet. The CD transfer confirms its musical and technical excellence. There is a wide range of dynamics and, though there are times when one would have welcomed more emotional restraint, the performance is both sensitive and accomplished. Maazel's vibrato in the slow movement may not be to all tastes but it would be ungenerous to withhold a star, particularly in view of the spectacular clarity and presence of the recording. However, unlike the competing Essex and Decca records these artists offer no fill-up.

Decca's team comprises Joshua Bell, Jean-Yves Thibaudet and the Takács Quartet, and they give a good account of themselves. Joshua Bell is perhaps a little too forceful and thrustful in tone in the main theme of the first movement, and they are rather on the fast side in the finale and wanting in breadth. These artists do not convey much period feeling or atmosphere and are less inside its sensibility than the artists on the Telarc CD. The recording is bright and well focused.

Piano quartet in A, Op. 30; Piano trio in G min., Op. 3.
(B) **(*) HM HMA 901115 [id.]. Les Musiciens.

The Op. 30 *Piano quartet* of 1896 is one of Chausson's finest works and reinforces the oft-quoted claim that he is the connecting link between Franck and Debussy. Les Musiciens comprise the Pasquier Trio and Jean-Claude Pennetier, but they are recorded rather closely, and their performance is lacking some of the subtlety and colour one knows this ensemble can command. The effect both here and in the early *G minor Trio*, Op. 3, is somewhat monochrome. However, this is enormously civilized music; the playing is both warm and spontaneous, and the ambience of the acoustic is pleasing. This is now inexpensively reissued in the Musique d'Abord series.

Piano trio in G min., Op. 3.
*** Ph. Dig. 411 141-2 [id.]. Beaux Arts Trio – RAVEL: *Trio in A min.* ***

The early *G minor Trio* will come as a pleasant surprise to most collectors, for its beauties far outweigh any weaknesses. There are many glimpses of the promise to come, and the invention is strong. The playing of the Beaux Arts Trio is superbly eloquent and the recording is very impressive on CD, even if the piano looms a little too large in the picture. A distinguished issue.

Chanson perpétuelle, Op. 37.
❀ (M) *** Decca 425 948-2 [id.]. Dame Janet Baket, Melos Ens. (with French song recital *** ❀).

Dame Janet Baker's magical performance of Chausson's setting of the Charles Cros poem – a declaration of passion to a departed lover, with the words inspiring continuous music – is part of a collection of French songs of the greatest distinction. It was originally issued on Oiseau-Lyre in 1967, recorded with the combination of atmosphere and presence for which that label was famous.

(i) *Chanson perpétuelle, Op. 37;* (ii) *Poème de l'amour et de la mer, Op. 19;* (iii) *5 mélodies, Op. 2/2–5 & 7 (Le charme; Le colibri; La dernière feuille; Sérénade italienne; Les papillons).*
*** Erato/Warner 2292 45368-2 [id.]. Jessye Norman, (i) Monte Carlo Qt, Dalberto; (ii) Monte Carlo PO, Jordan; (iii) Michel Dalberto.

Although Jessye Norman's account of the glorious *Poème de l'amour et de la mer* does not wholly eclipse memories of Dame Janet Baker's version, it is still very competitive in its own right. The orchestral texture is splendidly opulent and atmospheric, and Jessye Norman makes an impressive sound throughout. Sometimes her voice seems a bit too big for these pieces – and the closer-than-ideal balance does not help here – but her artistry is never for a moment in doubt. Few will be disappointed with this disc, although its playing time is comparatively short.

Le roi Arthus (opera): complete.
(M) *** Erato/Warner Dig. 2292 45407 (3) [id.]. Zylis-Gara, Quilico, Winbergh, Massis, Fr. R. Ch. & New PO, Jordan.

This first ever recording of *Le roi Arthus* reveals it to be a powerful piece, full of overt Wagnerian echoes. The vigour and panache of the opening suggest *Tannhäuser* and *Walküre* rather than *Tristan*, while the forthright side of *Parsifal* lies behind the noble music for Arthur himself, a more virile figure than King Mark. The love-duets in *Tristan*-style, of which there are several, have a way of growing ever more lusciously lyrical to bring them close to Massenet and Puccini. Armin Jordan directs a warmly committed performance which brings out the full stature of the work, far more than just a radio recording translated. Gino Quilico in the name-part sings magnificently, and the freshness and freedom of Gösta Winbergh's tone are very apt for Lancelot's music. Teresa Zylis-Gara, though not always ideally sweet-toned, is an appealing Guinevere; the recorded sound is generally full and well balanced. This makes a valuable addition to the catalogue and is guaranteed to delight many more than specialists in French opera.

Chávez, Carlos (1899–1978)

Symphonies Nos. 1 (Sinfonia de Antigona); 4 (Sinfonia romantica).
*** ASV Dig. CDDCA 653; *ZCDCA 653* [id.]. RPO, Bátiz – REVUELTAS: *Caminos* etc. ***

The *Sinfonia de Antigona* (1933) was reworked from incidental music Chávez composed for a production of Sophocles' *Antigone*. It is a primitive, highly exotic piece with plenty of colour and a large wind section; the extravagant scoring includes heckelphone, eight horns, two harps and plenty of percussion. The effect is appropriately primeval. The *Fourth Symphony* is perhaps less blatantly exotic but is full of character. Excellent playing from the RPO, offering demonstration sound of great impact, detail and presence.

Cherubini, Luigi (1760–1842)

String quartets Nos 1–6.
(M) *** DG 429 185-2 (3). Melos Qt.

Cherubini's *Quartets* are new to the CD catalogue and here have the advantage of authentic performing texts. No. 2 in C is a reworking of the Symphony in D, though he composed a fresh slow movement. Cherubini's melodic inspiration is often both distinguished and distinctive, although there are times when it falls short of true memorability; but a fine musical intelligence and polished craftsmanship are always in evidence. The Melos Quartet play these works with real commitment and authority, while the remastered recorded sound is well balanced and clear.

String quartet No. 1 in E flat.
*** Collins Dig. 1267-2 [id.]. Britten Qt – VERDI: *Quartet;* TURINA: *La Oración del Torero.* ***

Cherubini's early *First Quartet* (1814) apparently uses ideas borrowed from the symphonies of Méhul, but they are thoroughly absorbed, so that all four movements spring from the same basic material. The Britten Quartet certainly catch the impulsive *Allegro agitato* mood of the ambitious first movement and find great diversity – and an excitingly wide dynamic range – in the set of variations which form the *Larghetto sans lenteur*. There is elegance in the relatively mellow scherzo, which then produces a sudden mood change and a delectable Mendelssohnian lightness in the middle section, bringing a response of gossamer articulation from these highly sensitive players. The finale has a more robust energetic bustle and a most engaging secondary idea. This is a highly rewarding work and one cannot imagine it being better played or recorded. The sound and balance is very realistic indeed and the acoustic perfectly judged.

(i) *Coronation Mass for King Charles X; Marche religieuse.* (ii) *Requiem in C min.;* (iii) *Requiem in D min. for male voices;* (iv) *Solemn mass in G for the Coronation of Louis XVIII.*
(M) *** EMI Dig./Analogue CMS7 63161-2 (4). (i) Philh. Ch. & O; (ii) Amb. S., Philh. O; (iii) Amb. S., New Philh. O; (iv) LPO Ch., LPO; Muti.

Three of these records are digital, the *D minor Requiem* (recorded in 1975) is analogue. They come in a handsome slip-case and, at mid-price, should bring this fine repertoire to a wider audience. The *C minor Requiem*, the best known, was called by Berlioz 'the greatest of the greatest of his [Cherubini's] work', and he went on to claim that 'no other production of this great master can bear any comparison with it for abundance of ideas, fullness of form and sustained sublimity of style'. Muti directs a tough, incisive reading, underlining the drama, to remind one that this was a work also recorded by Toscanini some three decades earlier. Muti is well served both by his orchestra and by the relatively small professional choir; and the full, clear recording is most satisfying.

Requiem.
(M) (**(*)) BMG/RCA mono GD 60272; GK 60272 (2) [60272-RG-2; *60272-RG-4*]. Marshall, Merriman, Conley, Hines, Robert Shaw Ch., NBC SO, Toscanini – BEETHOVEN: *Missa solemnis.* (**(*))

Toscanini, like his latterday disciple, Riccardo Muti, was an admirer of Cherubini's choral music, and though the start of this live performance of 1950 lacks the full Toscanini electricity, the Shaw Chorale, superbly disciplined, quickly responds to the maestro, to produce searingly incisive singing in such movements as the *Dies irae*. It makes a fair coupling for Toscanini's keenly dramatic account of Beethoven's *Missa solemnis*; but it would have been better to have had them separated, as could easily have been arranged. Characteristically dry recording.

OPERA

Lodoiska (complete).
**(*) Sony Dig. S2K 47290 (2) [id.]. Devia, Lombardo, Moser, Corbelli, Shimell, Luperi, La Scala, Milan, Ch. & O, Muti.

Muti as a lifelong devotee of Cherubini's music resurrected this opera in a production at La Scala Milan to celebrate the work's 200th anniversary in 1991, with the Sony engineers recording a series of live performances. The plot and its setting is a prime example of an 'interesting historical curiosity', when with its story of false imprisonment and rescue it profoundly influenced the composer's great admirer, Beethoven. But where in *Fidelio* the heroine rescues her husband, Cherubini's scheme of hero rescuing heroine is far more conventional. The layout of narrative is also most ungainly, so that the heroine arrives only at the very end of the extremely long Act 1 and the villain, Dourlinski, by far the most interesting character, is not heard at all until well into Act 2. Cherubini's score, often urgently dramatic, lacks memorable tunes, as so much of his music does. He also has a disconcerting way at moments of high drama of switching into a major key with crashing banality. Yet Muti's conviction in this live recording brings much to enjoy, suggesting that the piece is more effective on disc when the staging is left to one's imagination. The British baritone, William Shimell, is a splendid Dourlinski, almost making one forget how much more colourful Beethoven's Pizarro is. As Lodoiska herself the soprano, Mariella Devia sounds sweeter and purer than when heard live, and so does Thomas Moser in the heavyweight tenor role of the Tartar chief, Titzikan. In the high tenor role of the hero, Floreski, Bernard Lombardi copes well with the high tessitura, but the voice bleats disagreeably. In the dry acoustic of La Scala the voices have been recorded close, so that there is a lack of atmosphere, and stage noises keep intruding, though the Sony engineers have done well to get such body in the sound. Squeezed on to two well-filled discs, Act 1 on the first, Acts 2 and 3 on the second, the set makes a colourful rarity.

Medea (complete).
*** Hung. HCD 11904/5 [id.]. Sass, Luchetti, Kováts, Takács, Kalmár, Gregor, Hungarian Radio and TV Ch., Budapest SO, Gardelli.
(M) ** EMI CMS7 63625-2 (2) [Ang. CDMB 63625]. Callas, Scotto, Pirazzini, Picchi, La Scala Ch. & O, Serafin – BEETHOVEN: *Ah! perfido.* **

Gardelli conducts a powerful performance of Cherubini's formidable opera, explaining very clearly why Beethoven so admired this composer. This Hungarian set, originally made in 1978 but sounding very fresh and vivid on CD, shows off the formidable strengths of the Hungarian State Opera, and in particular the artistry of Sylvia Sass, who has rarely if ever sounded as impressive on disc as here, full and firm, the tone creamier than it has latterly become, unexaggerated in expression yet intensely dramatic. One hardly misses the extra individuality of a Callas in a consistently gripping performance, helped by fine support from the other principals, not to mention Gardelli and the orchestra. Kolos Kováts as Creon and Klára Takács as Neris are particularly fine, and Veriano Luchetti is stronger and more individual than he has generally been on disc. Well-balanced sound, cleanly transferred.

Callas's 1957 studio recording of *Medea* may not bring out the full expressiveness of her historic reading of a long-neglected opera – live recordings reveal it better – but it is still a magnificent example of the fire-eating Callas. She completely outshines any rival. A cut text is used and Italian instead of the original French, with Serafin less imaginative than he usually was; but, with a cast more than competent – including the young Renata Scotto – it is an enjoyable set. Callas's recording of the Beethoven scena, *Ah! perfido,* makes a powerful fill-up, even though in this late recording (1963/4) vocal flaws emerge the more.

Chopin, Frédéric (1810–49)

(i) *Piano concertos Nos. 1–2. Andante spianato & Grande polonaise brillante; Ballades Nos. 1–4; Barcarolle* (1946 & 1962 recordings); *Berceuse* (1946 & 1962 recordings); *Boléro; Fantaisie in F min.; Impromptus Nos. 1–4; 51 Mazurkas; 19 Nocturnes; 3 Nouvelles-études; 6 Polonaises; Polonaise-Fantaisie; 24 Preludes; Scherzi Nos. 1–4; Sonata No. 2* (1946 & 1961 recordings); *Sonata No. 3; Tarantelle; 14 Waltzes.*
(M) *** BMG/RCA GD 60822 [60822-2-RG] (11). Artur Rubinstein, (i) with London New SO, Scrowaczewski; or Symphony of the Air, Wallenstein.

Rubinstein's principal Chopin oeuvre is offered here on eleven CDs at mid-price. His achievement was unique in this repertoire, and for the most part the remastered recordings are almost worthy of the playing. Alternative versions are offered of several pieces, but most of the recordings listed are discussed below as individual issues, many still at full price.

CONCERTANTE AND ORCHESTRAL MUSIC

Piano concertos Nos. (i) *1 in E min., Op. 11;* (ii) *2 in F min., Op. 21.*
*** DG 415 970-2 [id.]. Zimerman, LAPO, Giulini.
*** Sony Dig. SK44922 [id.]. Perahia, Israel PO, Mehta.

(BB) *** Naxos Dig. 8.550123; *4550123* [id.]. István Székely, Budapest SO, Gyula Németh.
(B) *** DG 429 515-2; *429 515-4* [id.]. Tamás Vásáry, BPO, Semkow or Kulka.
**(*) BMG/RCA RD 85612 [RCA 5612-2-RC]. Rubinstein, London New SO, Skrowaczewski or Symphony of the Air, Wallenstein.
**(*) Olympia OCD 149 [id.]. Yevgeny Kissin, Moscow Philh. Ac. SO, Dmitri Kitaenko.
(M) *(*) Ph. 434 145-2; *434 145-4* [id.]. Arrau, LPO, Inbal.

The CD coupling of Zimerman's performances of the two Chopin *Concertos* with Giulini is also hard to beat. In the *First Concerto* Zimerman is fresh, poetic and individual in his approach; this is a sparkling, beautifully characterized performance. His reading of the *F minor Concerto* has also won much acclaim, and rightly so. Elegant, arisocratic, sparkling, it has youthful spontaneity and at the same time a magisterial authority, combining sensibility with effortless pianism. Both recordings are cleanly detailed. While the balance favours the soloist too much, this coupling leads the field, without question.

Perahia's earlier record of the Chopin *E minor Concerto* was with Mehta and the New York Philharmonic, but this is much finer. His remarkable sensitivity and virtuosity have not been heard to better effect since his Mozart cycle. His effortless brilliance and refinement of touch recall artists like Hoffman and Lipatti. Mehta provides a highly sensitive accompaniment once the soloist enters but is curiously offhand and matter-of-fact (indeed almost brutal) in the orchestral ritornelli. The sound is an improvement on anything else we have had from the Mann Auditorium, Tel Aviv – which it would need to be – though it is still dryish and far from ideal. The three stars are for Perahia's playing, not the sound!

István Székely is particularly impressive in the *E minor Concerto*, but in both works he finds atmosphere and poetry in slow movements and an engaging dance spirit for the finales, with rhythms given plenty of character. Németh accompanies sympathetically, building the uncut opening ritornelli impressively, and the Budapest strings caress Chopin's lyrical melodies affectingly; the orchestral contribution here is quite refined. The recording is resonantly full in the Hungarian manner, not absolutely clear on detail; but the piano image is bold and realistic, and the brilliance of the pianist's articulation is crisply caught. A splendid bargain in every sense of the word.

Vásáry's approach is much more self-effacing: his gentle poetry is in clear contrast with the opulent orchestral sound (especially in No. 1, where the recording is more resonantly expansive than in No. 2). Yet soloist and orchestra match their styles perfectly in both slow movements, which are played most beautifully, and the finales have no lack of character and sparkle. In their way, these performances will give considerable pleasure and, with recording that retains its depth and bloom, this makes a fine bargain coupling.

Rubinstein's performances are no less welcome and there is much that is unforgettably magical in the solo playing. Rubinstein's shaping of the secondary theme of the first movement of the *E minor* is memorable, and in the *Larghetto* his control of colour and rubato are inimitable. Again in the *F minor Concerto*, although the Carnegie Hall sound is less than ideal, Rubinstein's contribution is an object lesson in the delicate playing of Chopin's poetic moments; his rubato is so natural that the music sounds as if it were extemporized. As with nearly all the CD issues of Rubinstein's early recordings, the piano timbre is much fuller and less twangy than it sounded on the original LPs, although the orchestral quality is more variable.

Superb playing from the twelve-year-old Yevgeny Kissin in this extraordinary début recording: these are bold, Romantic readings, full of flair and with a remarkable amount of poetry, too. Kissin's approach is unashamedly extrovert, yet his rubato is ever responsive to the the musical flow. Passage-work is glitteringly alive and the finales of both *Concertos* sparkle with bravura, while there is a winning delicacy in the music's lyrical pages. The playing has all the adrenalin and spontaneity one expects at a live concert, and the orchestra creates positive, full-bodied tuttis, yet does not want for refined feeling, and there is some lovely playing from the strings. A thrilling coupling, given an excellent, well-balanced recording, made in the concert hall of the Moscow Conservatoire. The applause at the end is well justified.

Philips now offer both Arrau performances together on an Insignia reissue, where the documentation is concerned with the artist rather than the music. Perhaps this is appropriate in this instance, since the great Chilean pianist's playing, while immaculately aristocratic, is also self-conscious. His rubato will not convince everyone and his expresssive hesitations do not always grow naturally out of what has gone before. The recordings, made in 1971/2, are of fine Philips quality and are admirably transferred to CD. The balance gives the soloist undue prominence, but the orchestra remains well in the picture and, like Arrau's timbre, is caught truthfully. But this is not Chopin playing to kindle universal enthusiasm.

Piano concerto No. 1.
(BB) **(*) Naxos Dig. 8.550292 [id.]. Székely, Budapest SO, Németh – LISZT: *Concerto No. 1.* **(*)

(i) *Piano concerto No. 1. Andante spianato et Grande polonaise brillante, Op. 22; Waltz No. 1 in E flat (Grande valse brillante), Op. 18.*
(M) *** DG 419 054-2; *419 054-4* [id.]. Krystian Zimerman, (i) Concg. O, Kondrashin.

(i) *Piano concerto No. 1. Ballade No. 1, Op. 23; Nocturnes Nos. 4 & 5, Op. 15/1–2; 7 Op. 27/1; Polonaise No. 6, Op. 53.*
(M) *** EMI CDM7 64354-2 [id.]; *EG 764354-4.* Pollini, (i) Philh. O, Kletzki.

(i) *Piano concerto No. 1. Ballade No. 2 in F, Op. 38; Scherzo No. 4 in E, Op. 54.*
(M) *** DG Analogue/Dig. 431 580-2; *431 580-4.* Krystian Zimerman, (i) with Concg. O, Kondrashin.

Pollini's classic recording still remains the best available of the *E minor Concerto.* This is playing of such total spontaneity, poetic feeling and refined judgement that criticism is silenced. The digital remastering has been generally successful. Orchestral texture is drier and clearer, with slight loss of bass, but there is better definition; the piano timbre is unimpaired. The additional items come from Pollini's first EMI solo recital, and the playing is equally distinguished, the recording truthful.

Zimerman's mid-priced version of the *E minor Concerto* comes from a live performance at the Concertgebouw in 1979. Zimerman gives a characteristically authoritative and poised performance and seems to have established a particularly good rapport with Kondrashin. He is balanced rather forwardly, and there is plenty of spontaneity (particularly in the slow movement and finale). The *Andante spianato* and the *Waltz* are drier and less open in acoustic; otherwise the sound is altogether excellent. This performance has also been reissued with his more recent, digital recording of the *F major Ballade* and the *Scherzo in E major* (which has some breathtaking passages), taken from his début recital, recorded rather dryly by Polskie Nagrania.

Piano concerto No. 2 in F min., Op. 21.
(M) *** Decca 417 750-2 [id.]. Ashkenazy, LSO, Zinman – TCHAIKOVSKY: *Piano concerto No. 1.* ***

Ashkenazy's 1965 recording is a distinguished performance: his sophisticated use of light and shade in the opening movement, and the subtlety of phrasing and rubato, are a constant source of pleasure. The recitativo section in the *Larghetto,* which can often sound merely rhetorical, is here shaped with mastery and there is a delectable lightness of touch in the finale. David Zinman and the LSO are obviously in full rapport with their soloist, and the vintage recording has been remastered most satisfactorily.

Les Sylphides (ballet; orch. Douglas).
❀ (B) *** DG 429 163-2; *429 163-4.* BPO, Karajan – DELIBES: *Coppélia;* OFFENBACH: *Gaîté parisienne.* ***
(M) *** Sony SBK 46550 [id.]. Phd. O, Ormandy – DELIBES: *Coppélia; Sylvia:* suites ***; TCHAIKOVSKY: *Nutcracker suite.* **(*)
(M) **(*) Decca Dig. 430 723-2; *430 723-4* [id.]. National PO, Bonynge – ROSSINI/RESPIGHI: *Boutique fantasque.* **(*)

Karajan conjures consistently beautiful playing with the Berlin Philharmonic Orchestra, and he evokes a delicacy of texture which consistently delights the ear. The woodwind solos are played gently and lovingly, and one can feel the conductor's touch on the phrasing. The upper register of the strings is bright, fresh and clearly focused, the recording is full and atmospheric, and this is one of Karajan's very finest recordings. At bargain price it is unbeatable, coupled on CD with not only *Coppélia* (although the suite is not complete) but also Offenbach's *Gaîté parisienne.*

The Philadelphia strings are perfectly cast in this score and, although the CBS sound is less svelte than the DG quality for Karajan, it is still very good. Ormandy begins gently and persuasively. Later the lively sections are played with irrepressible brilliance, and some might feel that this extrovert approach is almost overdone in the first *Waltz,* where Ormandy gives the upper strings their head. But later the playing has that rich, expansive excitement for which this orchestra is famous. Ormandy's couplings are more generous than the DG alternative, with nearly 76 minutes of ballet music, all equally charismatic.

Bonynge's performance shows a strong feeling for the dance rhythms of the ballet, and the orchestral playing is polished and lively. Bonynge also has the advantage of excellent 1982 digital recording, made in the Kingsway Hall. Even so, Karajan remains unsurpassed in this beautiful score.

CHAMBER MUSIC

Cello sonata in G min., Op. 65.
*** Claves CD 50-703 [CD 703]. Claude Starck, Ricardo Requejo – GRIEG: *Cello sonata.* ***
(M) **(*) EMI CMS7 63184-2. Du Pré, Barenboim – FRANCK: *Cello sonata.* **(*)
(B) **(*) Hung. White Label HRC 171 [id.]. Miklós Perényi, Tibor Wehner – FAURÉ: *Cello sonatas.* ***

(i) *Cello sonata in G min., Op. 65; Introduction and polonaise brillante in C, Op. 3;* (ii) *Ballades Nos. 3 in A flat, Op. 47; 4 in F min., Op. 52.*
(M) *** DG 431 583-2; *431 583-4.* (i) Rostropovich, Argerich; (ii) Sviatoslav Richter.

With such characterful artists as Rostropovich and Argerich challenging each other, this is a memorably warm and convincing account of the *Cello sonata*, Chopin's last published work, a piece which clicks into focus in such a performance. The contrasts of character between expressive cello and brilliant piano are also richly caught in the *Introduction and polonaise*, and the recording is warm to match. Richter's 1961/62 accounts of the two *Ballades* have a commanding individuality, and the recording is remarkably good throughout this disc.

The Claves performance is fluent and well characterized and the recording, if not in the very highest flight, is still eminently truthful. The playing has authority and dedication, and collectors need not hesitate to choose this version if the Grieg coupling is suitable.

The easy romanticism of the *Cello sonata* is beautifully caught by Jacqueline du Pré and Daniel Barenboim. Though the cellist phrases with all her usual spontaneous-sounding imagination, this is one of her more reticent records, while still bringing an autumnal quality to the writing which is very appealing. The recording is excellently balanced.

Though the Hungaroton performance has not the stature of the Rostropovich–Argerich account, it offers playing of quality. Miklós Perényi is not as well served by the engineers as he is in the coupled Fauré sonatas, where his tonal eloquence comes into its own, but he plays with real musical feeling and taste, and his pianist, Tibor Wehner, is excellent.

Piano trio in G min., Op. 8.
*** Teldec/Warner Dig. 2292 43715-2 [id.]. Trio Fontenay – SMETANA: *Piano trio.* **

The Trio Fontenay give a vividly characterized and well-projected account of the Op. 8 *Trio*, written when Chopin was eighteen, and not exactly one of his greatest works. It is well worth hearing, all the same. Good clear recording.

SOLO PIANO MUSIC

Albumblatt in E; Allegro de concert, Op. 46; Barcarolle, Op. 60; Berceuse, Op. 57; Boléro, Op. 19; 2 Bourrées; Cantabile in B flat; Contredanse in G flat; 3 Écossaises, Op. 72/3; Fugue in A min.; Galop marquis; Largo in E flat; Marche funèbre, Op. 72/2; 3 Nouvelles Études; Rondos, Opp. 1, 5, 16 & 73; Sonata No. 1 in C min., Op. 4; Tarantelle, Op. 43; Variations brillantes, Op. 12; Variation No. 6 from Hexameron; Variations on a German National air; Variations (Souvenir de Paganini); (i) *Variations for piano duet.* (i) *Wiosna* from *Op. 74/2.*
*** Decca 421 035-2 (2) [id.]. Vladimir Ashkenazy; (i) with Vovka Ashkenazy.

Many of the shorter pieces presented here are very early, the *Écossaises*, for instance, the *Rondos*, Opp. 1 and 5, and the ingenious *Variations on a German National air (Der Schweizerbub).* Here as elsewhere Ashkenazy's playing is often magical, fresh and direct, full of touches of insight. But there are substantial works too, including the *Barcarolle* and *Berceuse*, both superbly done, as is the *Allegro de concert*. In the *D major Variations* Ashkenazy is joined by his son. The *C major Sonata* is not deeply characteristic, but Ashkenazy makes out a more persuasive account for it than anyone who has recorded it so far. The piano transcription of Chopin's song, *Wiosna*, is particularly fetching. Throughout, Ashkenazy's playing is authoritative and poetic, and the recordings are excellent. A number of venues were used, and while the ear registers the slight differences of balance and acoustics, the quality of the digital remastering offers consistent realism and presence.

Andante spianato et Grande polonaise brillante, Op. 22; Barcarolle in F sharp min., Op. 60; Berceuse in D flat, Op. 57; Bólero in C, Op. 19; Impromptus Nos. 1–4; Fantaisie-impromptu, Op. 66; 3 Nouvelles études, Op. posth.; Tarantelle in A flat, Op. 43.
*** BMG/RCA RD 89911 [RCA 5617-2-RC]. Artur Rubinstein.

In Chopin piano music generally Rubinstein has no superior. The *Andante spianato and Grande polonaise* obviously inspires him, and his clear and relaxed accounts of the *Impromptus* make most other interpretations sound forced by comparison. The magnificent *Barcarolle* and *Berceuse* contain some of Chopin's finest inspirations – and if the *Tarantelle* may appear musically less interesting and not very characteristic, in Rubinstein's hands it is a glorious piece, full of bravura.

Allegro de concert, Op. 45; Ballades Nos. 1–4; Introduction & variations on Je vends des scapulaires, Op. 12.
*** CRD CRD 3360. Hamish Milne.

Ballades Nos. 1–4; Barcarolle, Op. 60; Fantaisie in F min., Op. 49.
*** DG Dig. 423 090-2; *423 090-4* [id.]. Krystian Zimerman.

Ballades Nos. 1–4; Scherzi Nos. 1–4.
*** BMG/RCA RD 89651 [RCD1 7156]. Artur Rubinstein.
*** Decca 417 474-2 [id.]. Vladimir Ashkenazy.
(M) *(**) Teldec/Warner Dig. 9031 74781-2 [id.]. Cyprien Katsaris.

Krystian Zimerman's impressive set of the *Ballades* and the other two works on this disc are touched by distinction throughout and have spontaneity as well as tremendous concentration to commend them. Indeed, readers who elect to have only one set of the *Ballades* would find this an eminently satisfying first choice, for the modern digital recording is of fine DG quality.

Rubinstein's readings are unique and the digital remastering has been highly successful. The performances of the *Ballades* are a miracle of creative imagination, with Rubinstein at his most inspired. The *Scherzi*, which gain most of all from the improved sound (they were originally very dry), are both powerful and charismatic.

Ashkenazy's playing is full of poetry and flair, as the opening *G minor Ballade* readily demonstrates, while the *Ballade in A flat* has exceptional warmth and sonority. The *Scherzi* have characteristic panache and the whole programme is imbued with imaginative insights and a recital-like spontaneity.

Hamish Milne gives thoughtful and individual performances of the *Ballades*. They may initially sound understated, but in their freshness and concentration they prove poetic and compelling. Similarly he plays the two rarities with total conviction, suggesting that the *Allegro de concert* at least (originally a sketch for a third piano concerto) is most unjustly neglected. The recorded sound is first rate.

Cyprien Katsaris is a player with an impressive technique and considerable power. He is a fiery interpreter of Chopin but displays no lack of poetic feeling. The *B minor Scherzo* is very brilliant indeed, though the virtuosity never distracts attention away from composer to interpreter. As piano playing it is certainly very good, at times even distinguished, but the recording as such leaves much to be desired. The acoustic is not really big enough and the climaxes are overwhelming.

Barcarolle, Op. 60; Berceuse, Op. 57; Fantaisie in F min., Op. 49; Impromptu No. 1 in A flat, Op. 29; Impromptu No. 2 in F sharp, Op. 36; Impromptu No. 3 in G flat, Op. 51.
*** Sony Dig. MK 39708 [id.]. Murray Perahia.

Perahia is a Chopin interpreter of the highest order. There is an impressive range of colour and an imposing sense of order. This is highly poetic playing and an indispensable acquisition for any Chopin collection. The CBS recording does him justice.

Barcarolle, Op. 60; Berceuse, Op. 57; Scherzi Nos. 1–4.
**(*) DG Dig. 431 623-2; *431 623-4* [id.]. Maurizio Pollini.

Berceuse, Op. 57; Fantaisie in F min., Op. 49; Scherzi Nos. 1–4.
*** Chan. Dig. CHAN 9018 [id.]. Howard Shelley.

Howard Shelley offers much the same programme as Maurizio Pollini on DG, substituting the *F minor Fantasy* for the *Barcarolle*, giving slightly longer playing time. He emerges unscathed from any comparison; he has the advantage of a more sympathetic recording with less of the close scrutiny to which the DG engineers subject the great Italian pianist. But there is a greater freshness and tenderness about his approach and though he is obviously totally inside this music, he manages to convey the feeling that he is discovering it for the first time. These are performances of no mean quality.

There is no want lack of intellectual power or command of keyboard colour in Maurizio Pollini's accounts of the Chopin *Scherzi*. This is eminently magisterial playing with powerfully etched contours and hard surfaces that inspires more admiration than pleasure. It is very well if somewhat clinically recorded and may well inspire greater warmth among his admirers but it will leave many listeners relatively unmoved.

Barcarolle in F sharp, Op. 60; Berceuse in D flat, Op. 57; Fantaisie in F. min., Op. 49; Nocturne No. 4 in F, Op. 15/1; Polonaise No. 4 in C min., Op. 40/2; Sonata No. 3 in B min., Op. 58.
(B) **(*) Pickwick Dig. PCD 834; *CIMPC 834* [id.]. John Ogdon.

John Ogdon's collection presents fresh and thoughtful performances, not as electrifying as some he recorded earlier in his career but often bold and full of individual insights. His speeds for the slower pieces are at times daringly extreme, but he sustains them well and the delicacy of much that he does is a delight, set in contrast to his natural strength in bravura. Bright, clear, realistic recording, giving the piano a powerful presence.

Études, Op. 10/1–12; Op. 25/1–12; 3 Nouvelles études.
*** Chan. Dig. CHAN 8482 [id.]. Louis Lortie.

Études, Op. 10, Nos. 1–12; Op. 25, Nos. 1–12.
*** Decca 414 127-2 [id.]. Vladimir Ashkenazy.
*** DG 413 794-2 [id.]. Maurizio Pollini.

Louis Lortie's set of the 24 *Études* can hold its own with the best. His playing has a strong poetic feeling and an effortless virtuosity. He is beautifully recorded at The Maltings, Snape (whose acoustic occasionally clouds the texture), but collectors wanting a first-class account of these extraordinary pieces will find that the Chandos disc is the only CD also to include the three *Nouvelles études* of 1839.

Ashkenazy's 1975 version sounds wonderfully vivid in its CD form, and the fine transfer that Decca provide may well make this a first choice for some collectors. However, honours are very evenly divided between these performances and those by Pollini and Lortie, and both those artists have the advantage of modern digital sound.

Pollini's record also comes from 1975 and sounds splendidly fresh in its digitally remastered form. This is playing of much stature. These are vividly characterized accounts, masterly and with the sound eminently present, although not as full in sonority as the more recent versions. However, this recording is available at bargain price if the collector also accepts the *Polonaises* and *Preludes* (see below).

Études, Op. 10/1–12; Op. 25/1–12; Polonaises 1–7; 24 Preludes, Op. 28.
(B) *** DG 431 221-2 (3) [id.]. Maurizio Pollini.

The reissue of these works on three CDs at bargain price makes a most attractive package. Pollini offers playing of outstanding mastery as well as subtle poetry, and the DG engineers have accomplished the remastering with splendid freshness. Pollini has impeccable taste in handling rubato and the firmest sense of line and form. It is a pity, however, that the later *Preludes* are not included.

Mazurkas Nos. 1–51.
*** BMG/RCA RD 85171 (2) [RCA 5614-2-RC]. Artur Rubinstein.
*** Decca 417 584-2 (2) [id.]. Vladimir Ashkenazy.

The *Mazurkas* contain some of Chopin's most characteristic music. All are delightful, even if there is no need to linger very long over some of them. Rubinstein could never play in a dull way to save his life, and in his hands these fifty-one pieces are endlessly fascinating, though on occasion in such unpretentious music one would welcome a completely straight approach. As with the *Ballades* and *Scherzi*, the digital remastering has brought a much more pleasing piano timbre.

Ashkenazy's recordings were made at various times between 1975 and 1985. His are finely articulated, aristocratic accounts and the sound is amazingly fresh and consistent, considering the time-span involved. He includes the posthumously published *Mazurkas* and the recording quality is more modern and more natural than that afforded to Rubinstein, with a believable presence.

Nocturnes Nos. 1–19.
*** BMG/RCA RD 89563 (2) [RCA 5613-2-RC]. Artur Rubinstein.

Nocturnes Nos. 1–21.
*** Decca 414 564-2 (2) [id.]. Vladimir Ashkenazy.
*** Hyp. Dig. CDA 66341/2; *KA 66341/2* [id.]. Lívia Rév.
*** Ph. 416 440-2 (2) [id.]. Claudio Arrau.
(M) **(*) DG Dig. 423 916-2 (2) [id.]. Daniel Barenboim.

Rubinstein in Chopin is a magician in matters of colour; his unerring sense of nuance and the seeming inevitability of his rubato demonstrate a very special musical imagination in this repertoire. The recordings were the best he received in his Chopin series for RCA, and the quality is now finer still in these excellent CD transfers. There is no appreciable background noise.

Ashkenazy's set includes the two posthumously published *Nocturnes*: the performances were recorded over a decade from 1975 to 1985. The disparity in dates seems not to have affected the consistency of sound that the Decca engineers have achieved. The playing is splendidly ruminative and atmospheric. As always, Ashkenazy is completely attuned to Chopin's unique sound-world, though occasionally some may feel that his tone is too big in fortissimo passages for these intimate pieces – as if he is playing in a large concert hall rather than in a late-night salon.

Livia Rév is an artist of refined musicianship and impeccable taste, selfless and unconcerned with display or self-projection. Indeed there are times when she comes too close to understatement. But still these are lovely performances and the recording has great warmth.

Arrau's approach clearly reflects his boyhood training in Germany, creating tonal warmth coupled with inner tensions of the kind one expects in Beethoven. In this he has something in common with Barenboim. With the *Nocturnes* it can be apt to have an element of seriousness, and this is a very compelling cycle, full of poetry, the rubato showing an individual but very communicable sensibility. This is among Arrau's very finest Chopin recordings.

Barenboim's playing is of considerable eloquence, the phrasing beautifully moulded, and he is superbly recorded. His set will still give much pleasure with its relaxed, less than impetuous style, although occasionally there is just a hint of blandness.

Nocturnes Nos. 1–4; 7–10; 12–13; 15; 18–19.
(M) **(*) DG 431 586-2; *431 586-4*. Daniel Barenboim.

Barenboim's selection has been generously expanded for this reissue (72 minutes). The performances, taken from his complete set, are intense, thoughtful and poetic, following rather in the mid-European tradition. Compared with Rubinstein (at full price), they lack a mercurial dimension. The recording is first class.

Polonaises Nos. 1–7.
*** BMG/RCA RD 89814 [RCA 5615-2]. Artur Rubinstein.
*** DG 413 795-2 [id.]. Maurizio Pollini.
(B) ** DG 429 516-2; *429 516-4*. [id.]. Shura Cherkassky.

Master pianist that he was, Rubinstein seems actually to be rethinking and re-creating each piece, even the hackneyed '*Military*' and *A flat* works, at the very moment of performance in this recording, made in Carnegie Hall. His easy majesty and natural sense of spontaneous phrasing gives this collection a special place in the catalogue.

Pollini offers playing of outstanding mastery as well as subtle poetry, and the DG engineers have made a decent job of the transfer. This is magisterial playing, in some ways more commanding than Rubinstein (and rather better recorded) though not more memorable. (This set is also available at bargain price if taken with the *Études* and *Preludes* – see above.)

Shura Cherkassky is sometimes an idiosyncratic artist and his playing has certain eccentricities of style and tempo. Compared with Pollini, he sometimes sounds wilful, and the famous *A major Polonaise* is rather deliberate. But for the most part his playing shows a redeeming spontaneity. The recording is good though not distinguished, bold but a little hard.

24 Preludes, Op. 28.
*** DG 413 796-2 [id.]. Maurizio Pollini.

24 Preludes, Op. 28; Preludes Nos. 25–26; Barcarolle, Op. 60; Polonaise No. 6 in A flat, Op. 53; Scherzo No. 2 in B flat min., Op. 31.
(M) **(*) DG 415 836-2; *415 836-4* [id.]. Martha Argerich.

Preludes, Op. 28; Preludes Nos. 25–26; Berceuse, Op. 57; Fantasy in F min., Op. 4.
*** Hyp. Dig. CDA 66324 [id.]. Lívia Rév.

24 Preludes, Op. 28; Preludes Nos. 25–26; Impromptus Nos. 1–4; Fantaisie-impromptu, Op. 66.
*** Decca 417 476-2 [id.]. Vladimir Ashkenazy.
(M) **(*) Ph. 426 634-2; *426 634-4*. Claudio Arrau.

24 Preludes, Op. 28; Preludes Nos. 25–26; 3 Mazurkas, Op. 59; Scherzo No. 3 in C sharp min., Op. 39.
(M) *** DG 431 584-2; *431 584-4* [id.]. Martha Argerich.

Ashkenazy's 1979 set of the *Preludes* combines drama and power with finesse and much poetic delicacy when called for. The presence of the four *Impromptus* and the *Fantaisie-impromptu* makes this CD even more attractive. There is an aristocratic quality about these excellently recorded performances that is wholly Chopinesque.

Lívia Rév's playing has an unforced naturalness that is most persuasive. She is an artist to her fingertips and, though she may not have the outsize musical personality of some great pianists, she does not have the outsize ego either. A scrupulous musician and a dedicated artist, even if at times one wishes she would let rip. She includes not only the extra *Preludes*, but two other substantial pieces as well.

Pollini's set is also highly distinguished. He has impeccable taste in handling rubato, the firmest sense of line and form, and the reading evinces an effortless and complete mastery. However, the absence of later *Preludes* or of any other additional items is not in this issue's favour. Nevertheless, combined with the *Études* and *Polonaises* in a three-disc bargain-price set – see above – it is well worth considering.

The *Preludes* show Martha Argerich at her finest, spontaneous and inspirational, though her moments of impetuosity may not appeal to all tastes. But her instinct is sure, with many poetic, individual touches. The other pieces are splendidly played. On her alternative CD, the *Mazurkas* are similarly volatile, and the *Scherzo* brings some glitteringly delicate articulation to make one catch one's breath. The recording of the *Preludes*, made in Watford Town Hall in 1977, was among the best she received from DG.

Arrau's *Preludes* date from the mid-1970s and are much admired. He certainly receives a full-bodied recording which does justice to his subtle nuances of tone; every *Prelude* bears the imprint of a strong personality and each appears to spring from an inner conviction, even if the outward results will not have universal appeal. The same thoughts might be applied to the *Impromptus*. Arrau's Chopin is seldom mercurial, but it is never inflexible and has its own special insights. The *Fantaisie-impromptu* is a highlight here, with the richly coloured piano timbre contributing a good deal to the character of its presentation.

Piano sonatas Nos. 1 in C min., Op. 4; 2 in B flat min., Op. 35; 3 in B min., Op. 58; Études, Op. 10/6; Op. 25/3, 4, 10 & 11; Mazurkas Op. 17/1–4.
(B) *** Virgin Dig. VCK7 91501-2 (2) [id.]. Leif Ove Andsnes.

The young Norwegian pianist has the advantage of state-of-the-art piano-sound and his recital comes in one of these slim two-CD packs for the price of one. As such it is splendid value. Andsnes proves as idiomatic an interpreter of Chopin as he has of Grieg. In the two mature sonatas he has the stiffest competition to contend with and comes through astonishingly well. He also makes out a very good case for the early *C minor Sonata*, Op. 4, which is less well represented on disc and which he plays with real conviction and flair. The other pieces generally come off well and collectors can invest in this set with complete confidence.

Sonata No. 2 in B flat min. (Funeral march), Op. 35; Andante spianato et Grande Polonaise brillante, Op. 22; Études, Op. 10/3–4; Nocturne No. 8 in D flat, Op. 27/2.
**(*) Mer. ECD 84070; *KE 77070* [id.]. John Bingham.

John Bingham's account of the *Sonata* is highly sensitive and most musicianly; if it lacks the sense of scale or range of rivals such as Ashkenazy or Rubinstein, it has a special dimension of its own. There is also some most beautiful playing in the *Nocturne* and the two studies. The Meridian recording is not made in an ideal acoustic; but this playing is certainly full of individuality.

Piano sonata No. 2 in B flat min. (Funeral march), Op. 35; Ballades Nos. 1–4.
*** DG Dig. 435 622-2 [id.]. Andrei Gavrilov.

Piano sonatas Nos. 2 in B flat min., Op. 35; 3 in B min., Op. 58.
**(*) Ph. Dig. 420 949-2; *420 949-4* [id.]. Mitsuko Uchida.

Like the three Prokofiev sonatas which appeared not many months before the present CD, Gavrilov's set of the *Ballades*, coupled with the *B flat minor Sonata*, finds him in much better form than he has been for some time. (This is his best record since his Scriabin recital of the early 1980s.) He does both Chopin and his own talents much greater justice than he did on his EMI set from the mid-1980s, which was similarly coupled. We spoke then of some moments of tenderness (not too many, mind you) and found him horribly aggressive in the A minor section of the *F major Ballade*. Here we find finesse and control as well as real poetic feeling. It is good to be able to recommend this without any serious reservation, and to note that the DG engineers produce very good and realistic sound.

Mitsuko Uchida has a large following as a Mozartian but is less often heard in Romantic repertoire. Her Chopin is not quite as successful as her extraordinary set of the Debussy *Études*, though she first came to wider attention with this composer at the Warsaw Chopin Competition, and later at Leeds. She always produces a beautiful sound and there is some particularly refined tone in the slow movements of both sonatas. A very present and realistic piano image, and plenty of sensitive touches, even if she lacks the sweep and power of many rivals.

Piano sonata No. 2; Barcarolle in F sharp, Op. 60; Polonaise No. 6 in A flat (Heroic), Op. 53; Polonaise-fantaisie in A flat, Op. 61.
(M) **(*) DG 431 582-2; *431 582-4* [id.]. Martha Argerich.

Martha Argerich's *B flat minor Sonata* was recorded in 1975 and its combination of impetuosity and poetic feeling is distinctly individual. Her brilliance is admirably suited to the two *Polonaises*, and the *Barcarolle* (the earliest recording here) is also charismatic. The recording still sounds fresh and the CD transfer gives her plenty of presence.

Piano sonatas Nos. 2 in B flat min. (Funeral march), Op. 35; 3 in B min., Op. 58.
*** DG Dig. 415 346-2 [id.]. Maurizio Pollini.
*** Sony CD 76242 [MK 37280]. Murray Perahia.

Piano sonatas Nos. 2 (Funeral march); 3 in B min., Op. 58; Fantaisie in F min., Op. 49.
*** BMG/RCA RD 89812 [RCA 5616-2-RC]. Artur Rubinstein.
*** Decca 417 475-2 [id.]. Vladimir Ashkenazy.

Piano sonata No. 2 in B flat min. (Funeral march), Op. 35; Andante spianato et Grande Polonaise brillante, Op. 22; Ballade No. 3 in A flat, Op. 47; 4 Mazurkas, Op. 24; Variations brillantes, Op. 12.
**(*) Olympia OCD 193 [id.]. Peter Katin.

Piano sonata No. 3 in B min., Op. 58; Ballade No. 4 in F min., Op. 52; Barcarolle, Op. 60; Mazurkas, Op. 59/1–3; Polonaise-Fantaisie, Op. 61.
**(*) Olympia OCD 186 [id.]. Peter Katin.

Rubinstein's readings of the *Sonatas* are unsurpassed, with a poetic impulse that springs directly from the music and a control of rubato to bring many moments of magic. The sound is improved, too, though both Pollini and Ashkenazy gain in this respect.

Pollini's performances are enormously commanding; his mastery of mood and structure gives these much-played *Sonatas* added stature. The slow movement of Op. 35 has tremendous drama and atmosphere, so that the contrast of the magical central section is all the more telling. Both works are played with great distinction, but the balance is just a shade close.

Murray Perahia's technique is remarkable, but it is so natural to the player that he never uses it for mere display; always there is an underlying sense of structural purpose. The dry, unrushed account of the finale of the *B flat Sonata* is typical of Perahia's freshness, and the only pity is that the recording of the piano is rather clattery and close.

Ashkenazy's *B flat minor Sonata* is the version released in 1981. Both this and its companion are impressive, though not necessarily a first choice – if such there can be – in this field. There is a shade less tenderness and vision in the slow movement of the *B minor* than there is in some rival versions, though the *B flat minor* has wonderful panache. An authoritative account of the *F minor Fantasy* provides an excellent makeweight. The recordings still sound first class.

Katin produces a consistently refined sonority throughout the dynamic range and there is much sensitivity and poetic feeling in the *Andante spianato* and *Mazurkas*. His is an essentially ruminative and private approach, and in both the *Ballades* and *Sonatas* one misses a sense of scale and the narrative grip one finds in Rubinstein and Ashkenazy. But there is much that is felicitous and responsive here. Admirers of this fine artist need not hesitate.

(i) *Piano sonata No. 3 in B min., Op. 58;* (ii) *Polonaises Nos. 1 in C sharp min.; 2 in E flat min., Op. 26/1–2;* (i) *3 in A (Military); 4 in C min., Op. 40/1–2.*
(M) **(*) DG 431 587-2; *431 587-4* [id.]. (i) Emil Gilels; (ii) Lazar Berman.

Gilels's account of the *B minor Sonata* is thoughtful and ruminative, seen through a powerful mind and wholly individual fingers, and there is not a bar that does not have one thinking anew about this music. An altogether haunting reading. The two *Polonaises* are also superb: they have majesty, grandeur and poetry, and the 1978 recording, made in the Berlin Jesus-Christus Kirche, is very satisfactory. For the reissue, DG have added the two Op. 26 *Polonaises*, recorded in Munich by Lazar Berman a year later. These readings possess a certain magisterial command and are also well recorded.

Waltzes Nos. 1–14.
*** BMG/RCA RD 89564 [RCD1-5492]. Artur Rubinstein.

Waltzes Nos. 1–14; Barcarolle, Op. 60; Mazurka in C sharp min., Op. 50/3; Nocturne in D flat, Op. 27/2.
❀ (M) (***) EMI CDH7 69802-2. Dinu Lipatti.

Waltzes Nos. 1–16.
(B) **(*) Decca 417 045-2; *417 045-4* [id.]. Peter Katin.

Waltzes Nos. 1–19.
*** Decca 414 600-2 [id.]. Vladimir Ashkenazy.
(M) *(*) Teldec/Warner Dig. 9031 75857-2; *9031 75857-4* [id.]. Cyprien Katsaris.

Lipatti's classic performances were recorded by Walter Legge in the rather dry acoustic of a Swiss Radio studio at Geneva in the last year of Lipatti's short life, and with each LP reincarnation they seem to have grown in wisdom and subtlety. Their appearance on a mid-priced CD, together with the *Barcarolle* and *Nocturne*, recorded in 1947, cannot be too warmly welcomed and the transfer has been accomplished most successfully. The reputation of these meticulous performances is fully deserved.

Ashkenazy's recordings were made over the best part of a decade (1977–85) but, despite the time-span, the sound is expertly matched by the engineers. There is an impressive feeling for line throughout, an ability to make these *Waltzes* seem spontaneous and yet as carefully wrought as a tone-poem.

Rubinstein's performances have a chiselled perfection, suggesting the metaphor of finely cut and polished diamonds, emphasized by the crystal-clear quality of the RCA recording. The digital remastering has softened the edges of the sound-image, and there is an illusion of added warmth. Rubinstein's pacing is always perceptive, his rubato subtle and his phrasing elegant; and now the playing seems less aloof, more directly communicative.

Peter Katin does not play the *Waltzes* in numerical order, as is customary, but in chronological order, which seems eminently sensible. The playing is thoughtful and affectionate, certainly assured and positive, especially in the more brilliant pieces, which are presented with flair. The bright yet quite full recording (from 1972) is very cleanly focused on CD and the piano is given striking presence. An excellent bargain recommendation.

Brilliant but often unsympathetic playing from Cyprien Katsaris, who allows his technical fluency to run away with him. There are moments of poetry, of course, but the aristocratic quality that an Ashkenazy or Lipatti brings to this repertoire is missing here. As with his account of the *Ballades* and *Scherzi*, the sound, despite the benefits of CD, does not compare with the best piano recording from Philips or Decca. The digital recording is brilliant and clear, but rather forward and wanting in sonority.

RECITAL COLLECTIONS

Andante spianato et Grande polonaise brillante, Op. 22; Ballades Nos. 1, Op. 23; 4, Op. 52; Barcarolle, Op. 60; Études: in G flat, Op. 10/5; in C sharp min., Op. 25/7; Polonaise-fantaisie, Op. 61; Waltz in A flat, Op. 69/1.

(M) *** BMG/RCA GD 87752 [7752-2-RG]. Vladimir Horowitz.

All these performances derive from live recitals. The *Andante spianato* (offering wonderful delicacy of articulation) was recorded in 1945 but still sounds well; the remaining performances date from between 1979 and 1982. The sound is modern: the *Polonaise-fantaisie*, the *Ballades* and the *Waltz* are digital, the rest analogue. The performances are fabulous; to the end of his career Horowitz's technique was transcendental and his insights remarkable. There is much excitement – but even more that is unforgettably poetic, and not a bar is predictable. With the sound so realistic, his presence is very tangible.

Ballade No. 1 in G min., Op. 23; Barcarolle, Op. 60; Fantaisie-Impromptu, Op. 66; Mazurkas: in B flat, Op. 7/1; in D, Op. 33/2; Nocturnes: in E flat, Op. 9/2; in F sharp, Op. 15/2; in D flat, Op. 27/2; in G min., Op. 37/1; Polonaises: in A (Military), Op. 40/1; in A flat, Op. 53; Waltzes: in A flat, Op. 34/1; in D flat (Minute); in C sharp min., Op. 64/1–2.
(M) *** BMG/RCA GD 87725 [7725-2-RG]. Artur Rubinstein.

An outstanding mid-priced recital – there is no more distinguished miscellaneous Chopin collection in the catalogue – with fourteen contrasted pieces, well programmed. The recording is surprisingly consistent and Rubinstein's inimitable touch gives much pleasure. The programme ends admirably with the lovely *Nocturne in D flat*, followed by the *G minor Ballade*, coaxing and dazzling by turns.

'Favourites': Ballade No. 1 in G min., Op. 23; Fantaisie-impromptu, Op. 66; Mazurkas: in B flat, Op. 7/1; in D, Op. 33/2; Nocturnes: in E flat, Op. 9/2; in F sharp, Op. 15/2; in B, Op. 32/1; Polonaise in A flat, Op. 53; Scherzo in B flat min., Op. 31; Waltzes: in E flat (Grand valse brillante), Op. 18; in A min., Op. 34/2; in A flat; B min., Op. 69/1–2; in G flat, Op. 70/1.
(M) *** Decca Dig. 417 798-2; *417 798-4*. Vladimir Ashkenazy.

An exceptionally attractive recital, with many favourites, played with Ashkenazy's customary poetic flair and easy brilliance. The digital recordings were made at various times during the early 1980s but match surprisingly well: the sound has striking realism and presence.

Ballade No. 1 in G min., Op. 23; Mazurkas Nos. 19 in B min., 20 in D flat, Op. 30/2–3; 22 in G sharp min., 25 in B min., Op. 33/1 and 4; 34 in C, Op. 56/2; 43 in G min., 45 in A min., Op. 67/2 and 4; 46 in C; 47 in A min., 49 in F min., Op. 68/1–2 and 4; Prelude No. 25 in C sharp min., Op. 45; Scherzo No. 2 in B flat min., Op. 31.
**(*) DG 413 449-2 [id.]. Arturo Benedetti Michelangeli.

Although this recital somehow does not quite add up as a whole, the performances are highly distinguished. Michelangeli's individuality comes out especially in the *Ballade* and is again felt in the *Mazurkas*, which show a wide range of mood and dynamic. The *Scherzo* is extremely brilliant, yet without any suggestion of superficiality. The piano tone is real and lifelike, and has been most realistically transferred to CD.

Ballade No. 3 in A flat, Op. 47; Barcarolle in F sharp, Op. 60; Fantaisie in F min., Op. 49; Fantaisie-impromptu, Op. 66; Nocturnes Nos. 2 in E flat, Op. 9/2; 5 in F sharp, Op. 15/2; Prelude in D flat, Op. 28/15; Waltzes Nos. 7 in C sharp min., Op. 64/2; 9 in A flat, Op. 69/1.
(M) *** Ph. 420 655-2; *420 655-4* [id.]. Claudio Arrau.

A fine recital, showing both poetry and the thoughtful seriousness which distinguishes Arrau's Chopin, which is West rather than East European in spirit. The CD is admirably transferred, bringing the fullness of timbre and natural balance we expect of Philips.

Berceuse in D flat, Op. 57; Études, Op. 10/1–4, 6–7; Op. 25/1, 4, 6 & 7; Nocturnes: in G min., Op. 37/1; in B, Op. 62/1; Scherzo No. 1 in B min., Op. 20; Waltzes: in E flat (Grand valse brillante), Op. 18; in A min., Op. 34/2; in C sharp min., Op. 64/2.
(M) **(*) DG 431 588-2; *431 588-4*. Tamás Vásáry.

An excellent recital compiled from Vásáry's mid-1960s recordings, showing this artist at his most impressive in this repertoire. The opening *Scherzo* is brilliantly and flexibly done and the *Études* are authoritative and commanding, the famous *E major*, Op. 10, No. 3, beautifully done. Perhaps the *Berceuse* is a shade deliberate; but both the *Nocturnes* and *Waltzes* have plenty of colour and their rubato is generally convincing. The layout is satisfyingly conceived, and the recital ends dashingly with the *Grand valse brillante*. The sound is generally very believable, with only a hint of brittleness in the opening *Scherzo*.

'Chopin masterpieces': (i) *Études: Op. 10, Nos. 3 in E; 5 in G flat; 12 in C min. (Revolutionary);* (ii) *Op. 25, No. 9 in G flat;* (iii) *Fantaisie-impromptu, Op. 66; Nocturnes: Nos. 2 in E flat, Op. 9/2;* (ii) *10 in A flat, Op. 32/2;* (iv) *Polonaises: Nos. 3 in A, Op. 40/1;* (v) *6 in A flat (Heroic), Op. 53;* (vi) *Préludes, Op. 28, Nos. 7 in A; 20 in C min.*; (vii) *Waltzes Nos. 1 in E flat (Grande valse brillante), Op. 18; 6 in D flat (Minute); 7 in C sharp min., Op. 64/1–2.*
(B) *** CfP CD-CFP 4501; *TC-CFP 4501* (i) Anievas; (ii) Adni; (iii) Ogdon; (iv) Ohlsson; (v) Pollini; (vi) Orozco; (vii) Malcuzynski.

EMI first made this compilation available in 1974 and it is as successful today as it was then. The programme includes many favourites and the selection has been made with skill. The recital opens and closes with a polonaise (Pollini is in splendid form in the final item). But this excellent roster of pianists never disappoints and the quality is consistently good. Malcuzynski's contribution is among the highlights: his *Grande valse brillante* has a characteristic glitter, while other attractive performances include the *Sylphides Nocturne in A flat* and Daniel Adni's '*Butterfly' Study*, which takes wing with charming grace. The transfers are all well managed.

Piano sonata No. 2 in B flat min., Op. 35; Barcarolle in F sharp, Op. 60; Nocturnes Nos. 5 in F sharp, Op. 15/2; 13 in C min., Op. 48/1; 15 in E, Op. 62/2; 20 in C sharp min., Op. posth.; Scherzo No. 2 in B flat min., Op. 31.
*(**) Virgin Dig. VC7 90738-2; *VC 790738-4.* Mikhail Pletnev.

Pletnev is a master pianist: in his hands the finale of the *Sonata* has a wizardry comparable only with Horowitz and Rachmaninov. However, whatever it *is*, this is not a self-effacing performance, and the expressive posturing will disappoint his growing circle of admirers. Of course there are marvellous things here – the *C minor Nocturne* is one – but on the whole this is masterly pianism first and Chopin second.

Cilea, Francesco (1866–1950)

Adriana Lecouvreur (complete).
*** Decca Dig. 425 815-2; 425 815-4 (2) [id.]. Sutherland, Bergonzi, Nucci, d'Artegna, Ciurca, Welsh Nat. Op. Ch. & O, Bonynge.
(M) **(*) Decca 430 256-2 (2) [id.]. Tebaldi, Simionato, Del Monaco, Fioravanti, St Cecilia, Rome, Ac. Ch. & O, Capuana.

Sutherland's performance in the role of a great tragic actress could not be warmer-hearted. The generosity of Sutherland as an artist, her ability to magnetize as well as to thrill the ear with her distinctive timbre, still full and rich, make this an essential set for all devotees, a recording made right at the end of her career. There are others on record with a more natural feeling for the role but, despite the beat in her voice, Sutherland impresses with her richness and opulence in the biggest test, the aria, *Io son l'umile ancella*, an actress's credo. Sutherland's formidable performance is warmly backed up by the other principals, and equally by Richard Bonynge's conducting, not just warmly expressive amid the wealth of rich tunes, but light and sparkling where needed, easily idiomatic.

Tebaldi's consistently rich singing misses some of the flamboyance of Adriana's personality and in her characterization both *Io son l'umile ancella* and *Poveri fiori* are lyrically very beautiful. But then, this is an opera that relies very largely on its vocal line for its effect. One wishes that Del Monaco had been as reliable as Tebaldi but, alas, there are some coarse moments among the fine, plangent top notes. Simionato is a little more variable than usual but a tower of strength nevertheless. The recording is outstanding for its time (early 1960s), brilliant and atmospheric.

Cimarosa, Domenico (1749–1801)

Double flute concerto in G.
(B) **(*) Decca 421 630-2; 421 630-4. Aurèle and Christiane Nicolet, Stuttgart CO, Münchinger – MOZART: *Flute concertos.* ***

Although not momentous music, Cimarosa's *Concerto for two flutes* has undeniable charm, and its gay final rondo is quite memorable. The only drawback is the composer's emphasis on florid writing, with the two solo instruments playing consistently in thirds and sixths. The performance here is warmly gracious, with a good accompaniment and excellent sound.

Il maestro di cappella (complete).
(M) *** Decca 433 036-2 (2) [id.]. Fernando Corena, ROHCG O, Argeo Quadri – DONIZETTI: *Don Pasquale*. ***
*** Hung. Dig. HCD 12573 [id.]. József Gregor, Boys of Schola Hungarica, Corelli CO, Pál – TELEMANN: *Der Schulmeister*. ***

Corena's classic assumption of the role of incompetent Kapellmeister has been out of the catalogue for too long. The Decca stereo allows his orchestral rehearsal to come over most vividly, with the poor man dashing first to the left then to the right, to one instrument after another, trying to keep each in order. Corena shows complete mastery of the buffo bass style, and he is so little troubled by the florid passages that he can relax in the good humour. The vintage 1960 recording is clear and atmospheric, with the directional effects naturally conveyed, and the CD transfer is quite admirable.

Gregor's firm rich bass goes with a comparably strong personality and a striking ability to act the buffoon in this romp of an intermezzo with its comic conflict between the maestro di cappella and the orchestra. Plainly, Gregor's performance has benefited from stage experience. Though his comic style is on the broad side, his magnetism pulls the piece together very effectively, with Thomás Pál a responsive conductor. It is aptly if ungenerously coupled with the more heavily Germanic Telemann cantata. First-rate recording.

Il pittor parigino (complete).
**(*) Hung. Dig. HCD 12972/3-2 [id.]. Szucs, Kincses, Garino, Gregor, Klietmann, Salieri CO, Pál.

The Parisian painter of the title is the beloved of the heroine, who will lose her inheritance if she marries anyone but a baron she detests. With plenty of misunderstandings and disguises and with some nice touches of parody of operatic tradition in Cimarosa's frothy score, it makes a delightful entertainment in a performance, recorded – rather dryly in the studio – after a stage production given in both Budapest and Monte Carlo. Tamás Pál is an efficient conductor, himself playing harpsichord recitatives, and he draws a lively performance – using modern instruments – from the Salieri Chamber Orchestra. The cast is a strong one, using a number of soloists from the Budapest Opera who are becoming increasingly well-known on record, though Marta Szucs as the heroine, Eurilla, is less sweet on the ear than Veronika Kincses as her scheming cousin, Cintia. The outstanding performance comes from the veteran buffo bass, József Gregor, brilliant as the Baron.

Clarke, Rebecca (1886–1979)

Piano trio.
*** Gamut Dig. GAMCD 518 [id.]. Hartley Trio – BRIDGE: *Phantasie trio;* IRELAND: *Phantasie*. ***

Rebecca Clarke, British-born, a viola-player as well as a composer (pupil of Stanford in his later years) had great success in the United States after the First World War. Her superb *Viola sonata* vied with Bloch's *Viola suite* in a major competition, and she followed that up with this equally striking *Piano trio*, which similarly shows influences from Bloch and Bartók much more than from English sources. The vehemence of the first movement gives way to mystery and melancholy in the slow movement, with the finale drawing on both those contrasting moods. The Hartley Trio gives a passionate, warmly persuasive performance, and if the cello-line is not as strongly projected as the rest, that is largely a question of the recording which otherwise is full and forward. The *Phantasie trios* of Bridge and Ireland make a valuable if not very generous fill-up.

Clemens non Papa, Jacob (*c*. 1510/15–*c*. 1555/6)

Missa Pastores quidnam vidistis; Motets: Pastores quidnam vidistis; Ego flos campi; Pater peccavi; Tribulationes civitatum.
❀ *** Gimell Dig. CDGIM 013; *1585T-13* [id.]. Tallis Scholars, Peter Phillips.

This admirable disc serves as an introduction to the music of Jacob Clement or Clemens non Papa (who was jokingly known as Clemens-not-the-Pope, so as to distinguish him from either Pope Clement VII or the Flemish poet, Jacobus Papa). He was one of the later representatives of the Renaissance Flemish school, following on after Dufay, Ockeghem and Josquin. The beauty of line and richness of texture in the masterly *Missa Pastores quidnam vidistis* are unforgettable in this superb performance by the Tallis Scholars. Tempi are flexible, while the overall momentum is convincingly controlled and Peter Phillips heightens the tension by quickening the pace in the closing phrases of different parts of the Mass, as in *Cum Sancto Spiritu* in the *Gloria* and in *Hosanna in excelsis* which acts as a 'coda' for the *Benedictus*. The programme opens with the parody motet associated with the Mass, which has a glorious eloquence. Of the other motets, *Pater peccavi*, solemnly rich-textured, is especially memorable; but the whole programme is designed to reveal to twentieth-century ears another name hitherto known only to scholars. The recording is uncannily real and superbly balanced. It was made in the ideal acoustics of the Church of St Peter and St Paul, Salle, Norfolk.

Clementi, Muzio (1752–1832)

Keyboard sonatas: in F min., Op. 14/3; in F sharp min., Op. 26/2; in C (quasi concerto), Op. 33/3; in G min., Op. 34/2; Rondo (from Sonata, Op. 47/2).
(M) *** BMG/RCA GD 87753 [7753-2-RC]. Vladimir Horowitz (piano).

These electrifying performances from the 1950s show a Clementi of greater substance and sterner mettle than the composer we thought we knew. In Horowitz's commanding hands these *Sonatas* sound almost worthy of Beethoven and, though the piano sound is shallow by the side of most up-to-date recordings, the quality is a great improvement upon either of the vinyl transfers with which we have compared it.

Piano sonatas: in E flat, Op 24/3; in D, Op. 26/3; in C; in G, Op. 39/1–2.
(B) **(*) Hung. White Lab(HRC 092 [id.]. Donatella Failoni.

Donatella Failoni is a thoughtful and intelligent player, with a clean, direct style. She is particularly persuasive in the *D major Sonata* which in her hands almost has the calibre of Mozart; throughout, she makes a good case for these underrated works and she is given a bold, faithful recording. This is well worth exploring at its reasonable price.

Piano sonatas: in F min., Op. 13/6; in B flat, Op. 24/2; in F sharp min., Op. 25/5; in G, Op. 37/1.
*** Accent ACC 67911D [id.]. Jos van Immerseel.

Very fleet and brilliant performances from Jos van Immerseel, playing on an instrument made by Michael Rosenberger in 1795, recorded at Finchcocks in 1979 – and very well, too. As Horowitz showed us in the 1950s, Clementi is a very considerable composer and possessed a fertile imagination. The slow movements of these sonatas have some considerable expressive depth, and the outer ones are full of a brilliance that is well served by this eminently skilful and excellent artist.

Coates, Eric (1886–1958)

Ballad; By the sleepy lagoon; London suite; The Three Bears (phantasy); *The Three Elizabeths* (suite).
(M) *** ASV Dig. CDWHL 2053; *ZCWHL 2053*. East of England O, Malcolm Nabarro.

One of the most memorable ideas here comes in the central movement of *The Three Elizabeths, Elizabeth of Glamis*, which celebrates the Queen Mother (who is charmingly pictured on the front of the disc) and draws a springtime evocation of Glamis Castle, not missing out the cuckoo. Its delightful main theme, complete with Scottish snap, is given to the oboe, and Gareth Hulse presents it simply but not too ripely, as is suitable for the Scottish climate. Nabarro has the full measure of Coates's leaping allegros: the first movement of the same suite – famous as the TV signature-tune of *The Forsyte Saga* – has admirable rhythmic spirit, and he plays the famous marches with crisp buoyancy. *The Three Bears* sparkles humorously, as it should; only in *By the sleepy lagoon* does one really miss a richer, more languorous string-texture. Excellent, bright recording, and the price is right.

(i) *By the sleepy lagoon;* (ii) *Calling all workers* (march); (iii) *Cinderella* (phantasy); *From meadow to Mayfair: suite; London suite; London again suite;* (i) *The Merrymakers overture;* (iii) *Music everywhere* (march); (iv) *Saxo-rhapsody;* (i) *The Three Bears* (phantasy); (ii) *The Three Elizabeths* (suite); (i) *The three men* (suite): *Man from the sea.* (iii) *Wood nymphs* (valsette).
(B) *** CfP CD-CFPD 4456; TC-CFPD 4456 (2) [id.]. (i) LSO, Mackerras; (ii) CBSO, Kilbey; (iii) RLPO, Groves; (iv) with Jack Brymer.

This collection of the music of Eric Coates with its breezy tunefulness is now issued on a pair of very inexpensive CDs, cleanly transferred. It includes, besides some very lively performances from Sir Charles Mackerras, several outstanding ones from the CBSO under Reginald Kilbey, who proves the ideal Coates conductor. The marches are splendidly alive and vigorous. Although the CDs bring out the brittleness in the upper range, notably in the Groves recordings, the ambient effect helps to prevent too great an imbalance towards the treble.

Songs: *Always as I close my eyes; At sunset; Bird songs at eventide; Brown eyes I love; Dinder courtship; Doubt; Dreams of London; Green hills o'Somerset; Homeward to you; I heard you singing; I'm lonely; I pitch my lonely caravan; Little lady of the moon; Reuben Ranzo; Song of summer; A song remembered; Stonecracker John; Through all the ages; Today is ours.*
*** ASV Dig. CDDCA 567; *ZCDCA 567.* Brian Rayner-Cook, Raphael Terroni.

Eric Coates, as well as writing skilful orchestral music, also produced fine Edwardian ballads, which in many instances transcended the limitations of the genre, with melodies of genuine refinement and imagination. Most date from earlier in his career, prior to the Second World War. Brian Rayner-Cook, with his rich baritone beautifully controlled, is a superb advocate and makes a persuasive case for every one of the nineteen songs included in this recital. The recording is admirably clear.

Coleridge-Taylor, Samuel (1875–1912)

(i) *Clarinet quintet in A;* (ii; iii) *Ballade in D min.* (for violin and piano); (iii) *Petite suite de concert;* arr. of spirituals: *Take Nabandji; Going up; Deep river; Run, Mary, run; Sometimes I feel like a motherless child; The Bamboula.*
** Koch Dig. 3-7056-2 [id.]. (i) Harold Wright, Hawthorne Qt; (ii) Michael Ludwig, (iii) Virginia Eskin.

Coleridge-Taylor is credited with an early *Clarinet quintet in F sharp minor*, a student work first heard at the Royal College of Music in 1895 but played in Berlin by the Joachim Quartet two years later. Whether or not this is the same piece is unclear, for the accompanying notes give no information about it except to quote a New York Times notice by Harold Schonberg of a 1973 performance work describing it accurately as 'an assured piece of writing in the post-Romantic tradition.' It is in no way distinctive; its 12-minute first movement seems a little overlong for its material, but it has a pleasingly wistful *Larghetto affectuoso.* It is very well played here by Harold Wright, the principal clarinet of the Boston Symphony, with a quartet made up of other front-desk players from the orchestra and given a faithful if studioish recording. The *Ballad in D minor* is even less memorable, but is adequately presented. The CD opens with a charmless account of the *Petite suite de concert* in (presumably) a piano arrangement, which is made even less enticing by the clattery piano recording. Why this transcription was chosen for inclusion instead of some of the composer's other piano music is inexplicable. The arrangements of the *Spirituals* are effective enough but overall this 80-minute collection is a disappointment.

Scenes from The Song of Hiawatha (complete).
*** Argo Dig. 430 356-2; 430 356-4 (2) [id.]. Helen Field, Arthur Davies, Bryn Terfel, Welsh Nat. Op. Ch. & O, Kenneth Alwyn.

Coleridge-Taylor's choral trilogy based on Longfellow's epic poem had its first performance under the composer in the Royal Albert Hall in 1900. It took a while to catch on, but every year from 1924 until the outbreak of war in 1939 it was given a staged presentation at the same venue. Often nearly a thousand costumed 'Red Indian' performers came to enjoy themselves hugely, singing under the baton of their tribal chief, Sir Malcolm Sargent. His splendid record of Part One, *Hiawatha's wedding feast* (now withdrawn), remains unsurpassed by the present, complete version, and its ambience is more convincing too. Part One is still regularly performed by choral societies in the north of England, and one wondered about the neglect of Parts Two and Three, *The Death of Minnehaha* and *Hiawatha's departure*. Alas, the reason is made clear: there is a distinct falling-off in the composer's inspiration, so fresh and spontaneously tuneful in Part One; when the main theme of *Hiawatha's wedding feast* returns in Part Three (band 12), with the words *From his place rose Hiawatha*, one realizes how memorable it is, compared with what surrounds it. Of course the choral writing is always pleasingly lyrical and makes enjoyable listening. Part Two has plenty of drama, and towards the end Helen Field has a memorably beautiful solo passage, which she sings radiantly, echoed by the chorus, *Wahonomin! Wahonomin! Would that I had perished for you*. There is also an almost Wagnerian apotheosis at the actual moment of the *Farewell* (band 14), which is sung and played here with compelling grandiloquence. Indeed Kenneth Alwyn is completely at home in this music. He directs a freshly spontaneous account and has the advantage of excellent soloists, though the Welsh Opera Choir seem less naturally at home in the idiom than Sargent's own Royal Choral Society. The recording was made in the rather intractable Brangwyn Hall, Swansea, and the engineers have put their microphones fairly close to the performers. The result, while vivid, lacks the glowing ambient effect of the Royal Albert Hall, which would have been a much better venue.

Cooke, Arnold (born 1906)

Clarinet concerto.
*** Hyp. CDA 66031; *KA 66031* [id.]. Thea King, NW CO of Seattle, Alun Francis – JACOB: *Mini-concerto;* RAWSTHORNE: *Concerto.* ***

Unfairly, Arnold Cooke has for the most of his career been saddled with the label 'pupil of Hindemith' which may be true enough, but which gives little indication of his individuality. His music does contain an element of Hindemithian formalism, carefully crafted, but the slow movement of this concerto soars well beyond. Thea King makes a passionate advocate, brilliantly accompanied by the Seattle Orchestra in excellent 1982 analogue sound, faithfully transferred.

Copland, Aaron (1900–90)

Appalachian spring (ballet; complete original version)
*** Koch Dig. 3-7019-2; 2-7019-4 [id.]. Atlantic Sinf., Schenck – BARBER: *Cave of the heart.* ***

This Koch International issue offers a welcome chance to hear a modern digital recording of *Appalachian spring* in its original form for thirteen instruments. In this it makes a logical coupling to the original Barber *Medea*, also composed for Martha Graham. It sounds very different from the more familiar version and, as in the case of the Barber coupling, a spikier, more Stravinskian character emerges. There are a few differences of text and of sonority but more of character between the two, and the playing of the Atlantic Sinfonietta and the bright, upfront recording present the chamber version in the best possible light. This is a most interesting and stimulating issue.

(i) *Appalachian spring; Billy the Kid; Rodeo* (complete ballets); (ii) *Dance panels.*
(M) *** EMI Dig. CMS7 64315-2 (2) [Ang. CDMB 64315]. (i) St Louis SO, Slatkin; (ii) NY Chamber Symphony, Schwarz.

This two-disc set (offering just short of two hours of Copland's finest music) is particularly valuable in collecting together the complete scores of the three major ballets. *Appalachian spring* is heard, not in its original chamber scoring, but in full orchestral dress and the St Louis playing and acoustic ensure that the colouring is rich-hued, and textures are full. Copland filled in the orchestration in those sections of music which he had omitted from the usual concert suite, at the behest of Eugene Ormandy to persuasive effect. With *Billy the Kid* the complete version means the inclusion of a number of passages which Copland excised solely out of concern for length. *Rodeo* also has substantially more music, including a piano interlude in *Saturday night waltz*. Slatkin conducts strong and colourful performances, very well recorded with plenty of detail as well as bloom. The atmospheric bite in Billy's gun-battle, with its fortissimo timpani, is very impressive. The inclusion of the rare *Dance panels* is also most welcome. Those who enjoy the other ballets will surely respond to this inspired and diverse score, which typically moves with great ease from lyric tonal painting to jazzy dance rhythms. Again performance and recording are to a high standard.

Appalachian spring (ballet) *suite.*
(M) *** DG 431 048-2; 431 048-4 [id.]. LAPO, Bernstein; BARBER: *Adagio* ***; GERSHWIN: *Rhapsody in blue.* **(*)

Bernstein's DG version of *Appalachian spring* was recorded at a live performance, and the conductor communicates his love of the score in a strong, yet richly lyrical reading, and the compulsion of the music-making is obvious. The recording is close but not lacking atmosphere, and it sounds extremely vivid. It is here recoupled with his rather less recommendable second recording of Gershwin's *Rhapsody in blue.*

(i) *Appalachian spring* (ballet) *suite; Billy the Kid: ballet suite;* (ii) *Clarinet concerto;* (i) *Danzón Cubano; Fanfare for the common man; John Henry; Letter from home;* (i; iv) *Lincoln portrait;* (iii) *Music for movies;* (i) *Our Town; An Outdoor overture; Quiet city; Rodeo (4 Dance episodes);* (iii) *El Salón México;* (i) *Symphony No. 3; Las agachadas.*
(M) *** Sony SM3K 46559 (3) [id.]. (i) LSO; (ii) Benny Goodman, Columbia Symphony Strings; (iii) New Philh. O; (iv) with Henry Fonda; (v) New England Conservatory Ch., composer.

Sony here offer a comprehensive anthology of the major orchestral works, ballet suites and film scores dating from Copland's vintage period, 1936–48. The composer directs with unrivalled insight throughout. Alongside the many familiar scores there are three novelties: *John Henry*, the railroad ballad about the black folk hero who was regarded as the finest rail-layer and rock-crusher of his time; the engaging *Letter from home*; and a vocal vignette which, as such, doesn't properly belong here but is very welcome neverthless, *Las agachadas* ('The shake-down song'), an unaccompanied choral piece, sung spiritedly in Spanish. Benny Goodman's instinctively idiomatic account of the *Clarinet concerto*, which he commissioned, is indispensable in such a collection, as is the *Third Symphony*. By the side of Bernstein's vibrant account, the composer's approach seems comparatively mellow – even gentle at times, as in the scherzo. But the natural authority is commanding, and the work's freshness of inspiration communicates anew. The remastering for CD is done most skilfully, retaining the ambience of the originals, while achieving more refined detail.

(i) *Appalachian spring* (ballet) *suite; Billy the Kid* (ballet) complete; (ii) *Danzón cubano; El salón México.*
(M) *** Mercury 434 301-2 [id.]. (i) LSO; (ii) Minneapolis SO, Antal Dorati.

Dorati pioneered the first stereo recording of the complete *Billy the Kid* ballet, and the 1961 Mercury LP caused a sensation on its first appearance for its precision of detail and brilliance of colour, while the generous acoustics of Watford Town Hall added ambient warmth. The gunshots (track 13) were and remain electrifying, with their clean percussive transients, while the LSO playing combines tremendous vitality and rhythmic power with genuine atmospheric tension in the score's evocative sections. The degree of fierceness on the violin timbre is more noticeable in *Appalachian spring*, but again the sound has plenty of colour and atmosphere and the clarity is remarkable. The orchestra's sprung rhythms are very engaging, and the closing section is very touching. For the CD, earlier (1957) Minneapolis versions of the *Danzón cubano* and *El salón México* have been added. Dorati, though always vital, is somewhat inflexible in his treatment of both pieces, which here lack a feeling of complete metrical freedom, even though the Mexican evocation piece has much sensuous charm. The recording is crisp and clean to suit his approach.

Appalachian spring (ballet) *suite; Dance symphony; Fanfare for the common man; Rodeo: 4 dance episodes; El salón México.*
(M) *** Decca Dig. 430 705-2; 430 705-4 [id.]. Detroit SO, Dorati.

Dorati has the full measure of Copland's masterly *Appalachian spring* score, creating a marvellous evocation at the opening and a feeling of serene acceptance at the close; throughout, Dorati finds a balance between the nicely observed interplay of the human characters and the spacious and lonely grandeur of the Appalachian backcloth. The 1984 Decca digital recording is impressive in its range and beauty of texture, and again confirms the excellence of the acoustic of the Old Orchestral Hall, Detroit. The other works on this mid-priced CD were all digitally recorded in the United Artists Auditorium in 1981. They are notable for their bright, extrovert brilliance and the playing demonstrates very clearly the degree of orchestral virtuosity available in Detroit. The only reservation is that Dorati's treatment of jazzy syncopations – an essential element in Copland of this vintage – is very literal, lacking the lift we think of as idiomatic. Nevertheless, as sound this is very impressive and the performances have much vitality.

Appalachian spring (ballet); *3 Latin-American sketches; Quiet city; Short symphony.*
*** DG 427 335-2 [id.]. Orpheus CO.

Appalachian spring (ballet) *suite; Short symphony.*
*** Pro Arte Dig. CDD 140 [id.]. St Paul CO, Russell Davies – IVES: *Symphony No. 3.* ***

With exceptionally vivid sound, bright and immediate, giving a realistic sense of presence, the Orpheus Chamber Orchestra's collection makes for a very distinctive Copland record of four works in which the composer is at his most approachable. The version of *Appalachian spring* here is the shortened text of the suite allied to the original 13-instrument ballet scoring. With strings discreetly augmented, the 'wide-open spaces' freshness of Copland's invention is underlined, with rhythmic bite sharpened. In the *Short symphony* the intimacy underlines the jagged Stravinskian echoes. *Quiet city* on this scale may lack some of its usual misty, evocative qualities, but it is all the more intense. The three *Latin-American sketches* are bitingly colourful, characteristic little squibs of pieces. The performances, immaculately drilled, have a consistent sense of corporate purposefulness, of live communication made the more intense by the realism of the recording.

On Pro Arte, using a smaller ensemble than is usual, Russell Davies conducts fresh and immediate performances of both the *Short symphony* and the well-known suite from *Appalachian spring*, which was originally conceived for chamber orchestra. The recording is bright and forward to match the performances. An excellent and recommendable anthology.

(i) *Billy the Kid* (ballet suite); (ii) *Piano sonata.*
(M) (***) BMG/RCA mono GD 60915 [60915-2]. (i) RCA Victor SO, Bernstein; (ii) Bernstein (piano) – BERNSTEIN: *On the Town: suite* etc. (***)

Bernstein got to know the music of *Billy the Kid* by sitting with the composer and playing the full score on the piano. He also learned the formidable *Sonata* as it was being written in 1941. Both performances are full of nervous energy and must be regarded as definitive. Although the piano is forwardly balanced, no apologies need by made for the late 1940s orchestral sound, which is full and atmospheric throughout; the violin timbre is a bit shrill on top, but fully acceptable. Of couse the gunfight is sonically much less spectacular than Dorati's famous Mercury account, but the venomous bite of the orchestral playing more than compensates.

Ceremonial fanfare; John Henry (A railroad ballad); Jubilee variations; (i) *Lincoln portrait;* (ii) *Old American songs, set 1; An Outdoor overture; The Tender Land: The promise of living.*
*** Telarc Dig. CD 80117 [id.]. Cincinnati Pops O, Kunzel; (i) with Katharine Hepburn (nar.); (ii) Sherrill Milnes.

Katharine Hepburn's remarkable delivery of Abraham Lincoln's words quite transcends any limitations in Copland's *Lincoln portrait* and makes it an undeniably moving experience, and Kunzel, clearly inspired by the authority of her reading, punctuates the text with orchestral comments of singular power. Incidentally there is much fine orchestral writing in this piece before the narration begins, which Kunzel delivers eloquently. The shorter pieces are also given splendid life. Sherrill Milnes's highly infectious performance of the first set of *Old American songs* shows a spirited boisterousness that recalls Howard Keel in *Seven Brides for Seven Brothers*. Altogether a collection that is more than the sum of its parts, given superlative Telarc recording, highly spectacular and realistic, yet with natural balance.

Clarinet concerto.
*** BMG/RCA Dig. RD 87762 [7762-2-RC]. Stolzman, LSO, Leighton Smith – CORIGLIANO: *Concerto;* BERNSTEIN: *Prelude, fugue and riffs.* ***
*** Sony MK 42227 [id.]. Benny Goodman, Columbia SO, composer – BERNSTEIN: *Prelude, fugue and riffs;* GOULD: *Derivations;* STRAVINSKY: *Ebony concerto* ***; BARTÓK: *Contrasts.* (***)
(M) *** EMI Dig. CDM7 64305-2 [id.]. David Shifrin, NY Chamber Symphony, Gerard Schwarz – BARBER: *Violin concerto* ***; GERSHWIN: *Concerto in F.* **
*** Chan. Dig. CHAN 8618; *ABTD 1307* [id.]. Janet Hilton, SNO, Bamert – NIELSEN: *Concerto;* LUTOSLAWSKI: *Dance preludes.* ***

*** ASV Dig. CDDCA 568; *ZCDCA 568* [id.]. MacDonald, N. Sinfonia, Bedford – FINZI: *Concerto;* MOURANT: *Pied Piper.* ***

Copland's splendid *Clarinet concerto* is at last coming into its own, on record at least. Stolzman is effectively cool in the serene opening and catches the work's later quirky jazz elements to perfection; in this he is well matched by Lawrence Leighton Smith and the LSO players, who let their hair down without losing rhythmic sharpness or crispness of ensemble. The finale's flair is exhilarating and, with first-rate RCA recording, this bids to upstage even Benny Goodman in its combination of idiomatic understanding, natural virtuosity and superior sound.

Benny Goodman gives a splendid account of the concerto he commissioned in 1947, and the recording from the early 1960s sounds admirably fresh in remastered form – the slight astringency in the violin timbre suits the music. With the composer directing the accompaniment, this performance is eminently recommendable.

David Shifrin's account is among the best, the opening radiant in timbre and showing a natural fluency of phrasing and the later, jazzy elements also well caught. The recording is vivid with a most attractive ambience, and the couplings are generous.

Janet Hilton's performance is softer-grained and has a lighter touch than Stolzman's, yet she finds plenty of sparkle for the finale and her rhythmic felicity is infectious. She is at her very finest, however, in the gloriously serene opening, where her tender poetic line is ravishing. The performance is attractively spontaneous and the change of mood from lyricism to jaunty extroversion is managed beautifully.

George MacDonald gives a virtuoso performance, not quite as dramatic and full of flair as that of the dedicatee, Benny Goodman, but in many ways subtler in expression and particularly impressive in the long lyrical paragraphs of the first of the two movements.

Piano concerto.

(M) *** Van. 08.4029.71 [OVC 4029]. Earl Wild, Symphony of the Air, composer – MENOTTI: *Piano concerto.* **(*)

Copland has also recorded his *Piano concerto* for CBS, taking the solo role himself, with Leonard Bernstein conducting – see below. That performance, perhaps because of the influence of the conductor, is freer and more persuasive in the passages influenced by jazz. Yet this Vanguard record, with a supreme piano virtuoso providing a glittering account of the piano part, is very recommendable. The 1961 recording, with a vivid projection of the piano, is first rate, hardly showing its age in the crisp new CD transfer. The coupling is a fascinating curiosity.

(i; ii) *Piano concerto;* (iii) *Dance symphony;* (ii) *Music for the theatre;* (iii) *2 Pieces for string orchestra; Short symphony (Symphony No. 2); Statements; Symphonic ode;* (iv; ii) *Symphony for organ and orchestra.*

(M) *** Sony SM2K 47232 (2) [id.]. (i) Composer (piano); (ii) NYPO, Bernstein; (iii) LSO, composer; (iv) with E. Power Biggs.

This second Sony Copland collection covers early orchestral and concertante music written between 1922 and 1935 and is, if anything, more valuable than the first box. The 1923 *Rondino*, the second of his *Two Pieces for string orchestra*, is the earliest work here. It fits remarkably well with the *Lento molto* (which precedes it), written five years later, again conceived for string quartet. The *Lento* is a totally memorable piece which instantly establishes Copland's unique harmonic credentials and so has a familiar flavour. The *Symphony for organ and orchestra* is a powerful and strikingly innovative work, dating from 1924, when Copland was finishing his studies with Nadia Boulanger. The composer subsequently re-scored the piece as his *First Symphony*, but its character and personality stand out best in its original format. It is given an extremely idiomatic and responsive performance by Power Biggs, who is fully sensitive to its atmosphere, and Bernstein balances the overall sounds with great skill and a marvellous feeling for colour. The recording is spectacularly worthy of the playing. The *Piano concerto* (1927) is both abrasive and strongly jazz-influenced. With the composer playing his own piano part with obvious feeling and Bernstein directing brilliantly, the result is a most impressive example of 'symphonic jazz'. The pungently flamboyant *Symphonic ode*, commissioned by the Boston Symphony, helped the orchestra to celebrate its fiftieth anniversary: it was written between 1927 and 1929. The *Dance symphony* was completed that same year. The *Short symphony* dates from 1931–3; both works are full of originality and energy and are tautly constructed. *Statements* (1934–5), as the bald title suggests, is one of Copland's less expansive works, but its six vignettes, *Militant*, *Cryptic*, *Dogmatic*, *Subjective*, *Jingo* and *Prophetic*, reveal a compression of thought and sharpness of idea that are most refreshing. All these performances have a definitive authority combined with total spontaneity of response from the participants which makes them compelling listening, and the recordings – dating from between 1964 and 1967 – are very well engineered, extremely vivid in the excellent CD transfers.

(i) *Connotations;* (ii) *Dance panels; Down a country lane;* (i) *Inscape;* (ii) *3 Latin-American sketches; Music for a great city; Orchestral variations; Preamble for a solemn occasion; The Red Pony* (film score).
(M) *(**) Sony SM2K 47236 (2) [id.]. (i) NYPO, Bernstein; (ii) LSO or New Philh. O, composer.

This third Copland box from Sony is something of a disappointment – not the music, which is even rarer than before and of great interest. *The Red Pony* is vintage Copland, and the *Orchestral variations*, though strictly an orchestral version of the *Piano variations* of 1930, make a unique and impressive contribution to Copland's oeuvre. *Connotations* and to a lesser extent *Inscape*, the major work of the composer's final period, are serially orientated. *Dance panels* is an abstract ballet without a narrative line, and *Music for a great city*, with its jazz influences and nocturnal scene, derives from another film-score (*Something Wild*). The three *Latin-American sketches* are a late attempt by the composer to return to his earlier popular style; *Down a country lane* is an engaging piano piece (commissioned by Life magazine) and subsequently scored for small orchestra, while the *Preamble* is occasional music in the best sense. The performances are all extremely successful, but the CD transfers are over-bright and, for all their vividness of detail, tiring to the ear, particularly the thin violins and the more pungent climaxes of the later works. Moreover, while the documentation is basically admirable, nowhere – except minimally on the labels of the actual discs – is the track layout given.

(i) *Fanfare for the common man;* (ii) *John Henry; Letter from home;* (iii) *Quiet city.*
(M) *** EMI Dig. CDM7 64306-2 [id.]. (i) Mexican City PO, Bátiz; (ii) St Louis SO, Slatkin; (iii) NY Chamber Symphony, Schwarz – BARBER: *Adagio;* THOMSON: *Autumn* etc. ***

No complaints about the Mexican City brass (or percussion) in the famous *Fanfare*, a most vivid and sonorous account. *Letter from home* (commissioned by Paul Whiteman in 1944 but revised in 1962) is a short, nostalgic piece, which yet reaches a passionate climax. It is beautifully played under Slatkin and the warm St Louis acoustics suit it admirably. *John Henry* is more succinctly based on a folk song, about a black railroad construction worker, who pitted his manual skills against a steam hammer in a fierce contest which he won, but at the cost of his life. Copland's urban tone painting, *Quiet city* is also given an evoactive performance, appropriately in New York, with Mark Hill and Neil Balm, the responsive cor anglais and trumpet soloists. Excellent digital sound throughout.

3 Latin-American sketches; The Red Pony (film score): *suite. The Tender land* (opera): *suite.*
**(*) Koch Dig. 3-7092-2 [id.]. Phoenix SO, James Sedares.

It is good to discover that Phoenix, Arizona, has an excellent resident orchestra, certainly on a par with the first rate group in Seattle, and – under James Sadares – they are completely at home in the folksy Mexicana of the *Latin-American sketches*, with rhythms snappy, colours bright-hued. But they are at their very finest in Copland's totally memorable film score for *The Red Pony*, catching the spaciousness of the opening evocation, dreamily touching in *The gift* (of the pony), boisterous in the *Circus music*, and totally winning in the delightfully picaresque *Walk to the Bunkhouse*, a hit if ever there was one. Here the recording is most vivid, approaching the demonstration bracket, and it expands impressively for the exultant *Happy ending*. But in the suite from *The Tender Land*, both in the *Love music* and *The promise of living* the ear craves a rather more sumptuous sonority from the strings (such as one experiences with records made in the auditoriums in St Louis, Dallas and Detroit). It seems possible that on this occasion, the microphone placing has not made the most of the ambience of Phoenix's Symphony Hall. Even so the CD is worth having for *The Red Pony* alone.

(i) *Lincoln portrait. Our Town* (film music) suite; *An Outdoor overture; Quiet city.*
(M) **(*) Van. 08.4037.71 [OVC 4037]. (i) Charlton Heston; Utah SO, Abravanel – GOULD: *Latin American symphonette.* **

Maurice Abravanel has the full measure of this music and the playing of the Utah orchestra is most sympathetic. In the *Lincoln portrait* Charlton Heston's warm, friendly voice is a pleasure to listen to. His delivery of Lincoln's words is slow and strong, more persuasive than Henry Fonda's relatively diffident manner, although there are moments of melodrama, and his repeated 'This is what he said' seems to come too many times. (Katharine Hepburn is far more vibrant than either, but she is at full price.) The sumptuous recorded sound is very beautiful throughout, much richer than the Sony balance, but the Utah reverberation inflates *Quiet city* almost into a trumpet concerto, with William Sullivan's fine solo contribution made to dominate the texture unduly.

Quiet city.
*** Argo 417 818-2 [id.]. ASMF, Marriner – BARBER: *Adagio;* COWELL: *Hymn;* CRESTON: *Rumor;* IVES: *Symphony No. 3.* ***

Marriner's 1976 version is both poetic and evocative, and the playing of the trumpet and cor anglais soloists is of the highest order. The digital remastering has brought added clarity without loss of atmosphere.

Symphony No. 3.
(M) *** EMI Dig. CDM7 64304-2 [id.]. Dallas SO, Mata – HANSON: *Symphony No. 2.* ***

Symphony No. 3; Quiet city.
*** DG Dig. 419 170-2 [id.]. NYPO, Bernstein.

With Bernstein conducting Copland's *Third Symphony*, you appreciate more than with rival interpreters that this is one of the great symphonic statements of American music. He consciously exaggerates the rhetoric, leading up to the fantasy on the *Fanfare for the common man*, which opens the finale. In absolute terms he may be accused of going over the top but, recorded at live concerts, the electricity of the performance is irresistible. The recording is full-bodied and bright, but its brashness is apt for the performance. The hushed tranquillity of *Quiet city*, another of Copland's finest scores, is superbly caught by Bernstein in the valuable fill-up.

Eduardo Mata and the Dallas Symphony Orchestra give a powerful, unexaggerated reading. If Leonard Bernstein (in a work which he has rather made his own) underlines the eloquent rhetoric, the symphonic grandeur of Copland's argument, Mata follows far more closely the composer's indications in the score, not least his often-repeated instruction, 'with simple expression'. He trusts Copland's authority more, and the concentration and cohesiveness of the whole performance bear out his confidence, helped by full and well-balanced recording.

VOCAL MUSIC

(i) *In the Beginning. Help us, O Lord; Have mercy on us, O my Lord; Sing ye praises to our King.*
*** Hyp. Dig. CDA 66219; *KA 66219* [id.]. (i) Catherine Denley; Corydon Singers, Best – BARBER: *Agnus Dei;* BERNSTEIN: *Chichester Psalms.* ***

In the Beginning is a large-scale, fifteen-minute motet for unaccompanied chorus and soprano solo, written in 1947. The open harmonies and clean textures and lines are very characteristic of the composer at his most approachable, and the long span of the work is well structured with the help of the soprano soloist, here the fresh-toned Catherine Denley. The chorus is just as clear and alert in its singing, not just in the big motet but also in the three delightful little pieces which come as an appendix. The last is vigorous, like a carol; but all three bring out Copland's deft use of voices. Vivid recording, full of presence.

Old American songs: Sets 1 and 2 (original versions).
*** Argo Dig. 433 027-2 [id.]. Samuel Ramey, Warren Jones – IVES: *Songs.* ***
*** Chan. Dig. CHAN 8960; *ABTD 1552* [id.]. Willard White, Graeme McNaught (with collection: *'American spirituals; Folk-songs from Barbados and Jamaica'* ***).

Both these discs of the Copland *Old American songs* offer the original versions with piano accompaniment, where most artists on disc have used Copland's orchestral arrangements. Otherwise they are quite distinct from each other. Samuel Ramey and his excellent accompanist treat them far more as art songs, with subtler shading of phrase and tempo, and a more extreme range of speeds within each song. Though the voice is not so smoothly caught as usual, Ramey's focus is much sharper than Willard White's, and it is only in part a question of vocal quality.

Characteristically White's opulent bass comes with a pronounced vibrato which on disc tends to get exaggerated. Yet with its helpful acoustic the Chandos recording captures the richness of his voice most attractively, very characterfully black in its evocations. White's softer-grained readings may not be so detailed, but his resonant singing is both warm and characterful. The songs provide a better match that way with the other items on the disc.

The Tender Land (opera) complete.
*** Virgin Dig. VCD 791113-2 (2) [id.]. Comeaux, Dressen, Soloists, Ch. and O of Plymouth Music Series, Philip Brunelle.

Commissioned by Rodgers and Hammerstein to write a piece to celebrate the thirtieth anniversary of the American League of Composers, Copland wrote as guileless an opera as could be, innocent-seeming in its diatonic harmony, sparing of dissonance, to match the rustic simplicity of the story of a farm family. The graduation from high school of the daughter, Laurie, is being celebrated when two drifters arrive, Martin and Top. Laurie and Martin fall instantly in love, but what follows is not just a story of love's young dream with a happy ending. Copland himself likened *The Tender Land* to the ballet, *Appalachian spring*, but the opera is gentler. The key passage is the big quintet at the end of Act I, *The promise of living*. It brings a simple tune that builds up to a memorable, moving climax, and, though not quoted, fragments of the melody then seem to underpin the rest of the score, with its set-numbers including a square-dance ensemble and a big love-duet. Nothing has quite the sharpness of *Appalachian spring*, but it is an amiable piece, beautifully performed here in a rather lighter style than Copland himself adopted on a much earlier recording of excerpts. Elizabeth Comeaux and Dan Dressen make an affecting pair of lovers, and the recording is open and atmospheric, conveying the stage picture very effectively.

Corelli, Arcangelo (1653–1713)

Concerti grossi, Op. 6/1–12.
*** BMG/RCA Dig. RD 60071 (2) [id.]. Guildhall Ens., Robert Salter.
*** DG Dig. 423 626-2 (2) [id.]. E. Concert, Pinnock.
(BB) *** Naxos Dig. 8.550402/3 [id.]. Capella Istropolitana, Jaroslav Kr(e)chek.
*** HM Dig. HMC 901406/7; *HMC 401406/7* [id.]. Ens. 415, Bancinini, Christensen.
(M) *** HM/BMG GD 77007 (2) [77077-2-RG]. La Petite Bande, Kuijken.
(M) *** Decca 430 560-2 (2) [id.]. ASMF, Sir Neville Marriner.

It does not seem so long ago that the Corelli *Concerti grossi*, Op. 6, were meagrely represented on record: now they even outstrip Handel's Op. 6 and are represented by almost a dozen versions and at almost every price level and – amazingly – very few are less than recommendable. The newest from the Guildhall Ensemble and Robert Salter (RCA) is very fine indeed and is probably a first choice for those who prefer modern instruments. They have the benefit of really excellent recording: immediate and present without being too forward, full-bodied and transparent in detail. The playing is really vital and imaginative and has plenty of warmth and imagination.

The DG performances bring not only an enthusiasm for this music but a sense of its spacious grandeur. The English Concert are entirely inside its sensibility, and the playing of the concertino group (Simon Standage, Micaela Comberti and Jaap Ter Linden) is wonderfully fresh-eyed and alert, yet full of colour. The recordings are bright without being in the least overlit. Collectors wanting an authentic-instrument version can safely choose between the DG and Harmonia Mundi versions.

At super-bargain price, the Naxos set by the Capella Istropolitana under Jaroslav Kr(e)chek represents very good value indeed. Each CD contains well over an hour's music and is available separately, and anyone collecting the one is unlikely to resist the temptation to go on to the other. The players are drawn from the Slovak Philharmonic and have great vitality and, when necessary, virtuosity to commend them. The digital recording is clean and well lit, but not over-bright, and makes their version strongly competitive.

Ensemble 413 is augmented to some 39 musicians and draws on the scholarship of Jesper Christensen who has made a study of performance practice and of the forces used by Corelli himself. In a way, their excellently recorded set must be numbered among the very best of the period-instrument versions. They wear their scholarship lightly and their playing has a zest and taste which are most persuasive. They are totally immersed in the Corellian idiom and, like Pinnock on DG, convey the music's breadth and nobility.

La Petite Bande also offers a useful mid-price alternative to the Pinnock set. Authentic instruments are used to excellent effect, and the playing is always expressive and musical. The 1977 recordings were made in a highly sympathetic acoustic, that of Cedernsaal at Schloss

Kirchheim; besides being splendidly lifelike, they are also impressive in conveying the nobility and grandeur of Corelli.

The older Argo set, now reissued on Decca's Serenata label, was prepared with evident thought and care. The vitality and intelligence of the performances, expertly played by the Academy, is striking and they are given vintage 1973/4 recording, made in the flattering acoustics of St John's, Smith Square. However, for those wanting this music played on modern instruments, the digital Naxos set, with its added economy, takes pride of place.

Concerti grossi, Op. 6/1, 3, 7, 8 (Christmas), 11 & 12.
(M) *** DG Dig. 431 706-2; 431 706-4. E. Concert, Trevor Pinnock.

We have given high praise to the (full-price) complete set from which these performances come. At mid-price, with the *Christmas Concerto* included, this will admirably suit those collectors who want an original-instrument version and who are content with a single-disc selection.

Trio sonatas, Op. 1/1, 3, 7, 9, 11–12; Op. 2/4, 6, 9, 12.
*** DG Dig. 419 614-2 [id.]. E. Concert (members), Pinnock.

Trio sonatas, Op. 1/9, 10 & 12 (Ciacona); Op. 2/4; Op. 3/5; Op. 4/1; Violin sonata, Op. 5/3; Concerto grosso in B flat, Op. 6/5.
**(*) EMI Dig. CDC7 47965-2 [id.]. L. Baroque, Medlam.

Trio sonatas, Op. 1/9; Op. 2/4 & 12 (Ciacona); Op. 3/12; Op. 4/3; Op. 5/3, 11 & 12 (La Follia).
*** Hyp. Dig. CDA 66226 [id.]. Purcell Qt.

Corelli is a composer more praised than played, and the quality of invention in these pieces underlines the injustice of their neglect. The players from the English Concert dispatch them with a virtuosity and panache that is inspiriting, and their evident enthusiasm for this music is infectious. This is a most impressive and rewarding issue – and excellently recorded into the bargain.

The London Baroque collection mixes church and chamber sonatas, with an impeccable feeling for the style of the period and a continuo which includes archlute and organ, appropriately. Ornamentation is judicious and intonation is secure. Though not lacking vitality, the performances here are graceful and comparatively restrained, lighter in feeling and texture than Pinnock and his English Concert, and thus providing a genuine alternative approach.

The Hyperion disc is one of six designed to illustrate the widespread use in the eighteenth century of the famous *La Follia* theme. It includes a varied collection of sonate da chiesa and sonate da camera. Excellent performances from all concerned, and recording to match. The acoustic has warmth and resonance, while the detail is admirably defined. A thoroughly enjoyable issue which deserves wide currency.

Violin sonatas, Op. 5/1, 3, 6, 11 and 12 (La Follia).
*** Accent Dig. ACC 48433D [id.]. Sigiswald & Wieland Kuijken, Robert Kohnen.

When authenticity of spirit goes hand in hand with fine musical feeling and accomplishment, the results can be impressive, as they undoubtedy are here, drawing one into the sensibility of the period. This is a thoroughly recommendable issue which deserves to reach a wider audience than early-music specialists; the recording is natural and the musicianship refined and totally at the service of Corelli.

Corigliano, John (born 1938)

Clarinet concerto.
*** New World Dig. NW 309-2 [id.]. Drucker, NYPO, Mehta – BARBER: *Essay No. 3.* ***
*** BMG/RCA Dig. RD 87762 [7762-2-RC]. Stolzman, LSO, Leighton Smith – COPLAND: *Concerto;* BERNSTEIN: *Prelude, fugue and riffs.* ***

In its slow movement John Corigliano's *Clarinet concerto* pays elegiac tribute to the composer's father, who for more than two decades was concertmaster of the New York Philharmonic; not surprisingly, it shows considerable feeling for orchestral colour. The sonorities are always fascinating, and there are moments of some depth too. The playing both of Stanley Drucker, its dedicatee, and of the orchestra is quite superb, and the recording does them full justice.

Stolzman also gives an outstanding account of the *Concerto*, his richly expressive treatment of the slow movement balanced by superb flair and virtuosity in the finale. This is every bit as good a performance as that offered on the New World disc; and many will prefer Stolzman's couplings, which are distinguished. The RCA recording is first class.

Flute concerto (Pied Piper fantasy); Voyage.
**(*) BMG/RCA Dig. RD 86602 [6602-2-RC]. James Galway, Eastman Philh. O, David Effron.

Galway is at his inimitable best in Corigliano's *Flute concerto*; however, this is a longer and far less concentrated piece than the *Clarinet concerto*. The picaresque qualities of its invention in detailing the Pied Piper narrative are spread thinly in memorability of material, although the closing section when the children are led away into the distance is right up Galway's street. The serene *Voyage* is shorter and more memorable; but in spite of fine playing and excellent recording the main work outstays its welcome.

(i) *Oboe concerto;* (ii; iii) *3 Irish folksong settings: The Sally Gardens; The foggy dew; She moved thro' the fair;* (ii; iv) *Poem in October.*
(M) *** BMG Analogue/Dig. GD 60395 [60395-2-RG]. (i) Humbert Lucarelli, American SO, Kazuyoshi Akiyama; (ii) Robert White; (iii) Ransom Wilson; (iv) Nyfenger, Lucarelli, Rabbai, American Qt, Peress (cond. from harpsichord).

John Corigliano's highly imaginative *Oboe concerto* is an ambitious four-movement piece (26 minutes), requiring great flexibility and virtuosity from its soloist. The work opens ingeniously with the orchestra tuning up, and the music springs fairly naturally from this familiar aleatory pattern of sound. The performance here is outstanding, expert and spontaneous and very well recorded. The three *Folksong settings* are for tenor and flute; the latter's embroidery is effective, without adding anything very significant, but Robert White's headily distinctive light tenor gives much pleasure, as he does in the Dylan Thomas setting, *Poem in October*. White's performance is most beautiful, especially in the poignant closing section. His diction is remarkably clear, but even so the omission of the texts in the accompanying leaflet is unforgivable.

Symphony No. 1.
*** Erato/Warner Dig. 2292 45601-2 [id.]. Stephen Hough, John Sharp, Chicago SO, Barenboim.

This fine, deeply felt work is an elegy for friends of the composer, three in particular who have died of AIDS. The *Symphony* opens with an expression of rage, subsiding to a pianissimo, when from afar you hear Hough on the piano playing Godowsky's arrangement of the Albéniz *Tango*, quoted at length. It is a haunting effect, potentially sentimental but saved from being so by the sharpness of the composer's response: the friend commemorated was a pianist and this is the piece specially associated with him. The tarantella of the second movement is a nightmare development of a trivial piano piece that Corigliano wrote for the second friend; and the third movement, a chaconne, has as a central motif a solo cello theme improvised by the third friend when he recorded a tape with Corigliano years earlier. That third movement develops a web of interweaving themes – each representing a friend who died – first contrapuntally and finally into a funeral march. The brief fourth movement is an epilogue quoting all three movements. Barenboim and the Chicago orchestra bring out the full passionate intensity of the inspiration in this live recording. The sound is immediate and full-bodied, giving full scope to the colourful and often spectacular orchestral writing. This is well worth exploring and very rewarding.

Cornysh, William (c. 1468–1523)

Adieu, adieu my heartes lust; Adieu, courage; Ah Robin; Ave Maria, mater Dei; Gaude, virgo, mater Christi; Magnificat; Salve regina; Stabat Mater; Woefully arrayed.
❀ *** Gimell Dig. CDGIM 014; *1585T-14* [id.]. Tallis Scholars, Phillips.

The nine pieces recorded here all derive from the Eton Choir Book and will surely come as a revelation to collectors unfamiliar with this period and a joy to those who are. Much of Cornysh's music has disappeared, including several Masses, and even the opening section of the *Stabat Mater* lacks treble, counter-tenor and tenor parts (Peter Phillips uses Frank Lloyd Harrison's ingenious reconstruction). The music is quite unlike much other polyphony of the time and is florid, wild, complex and, at times, grave. The Tallis Scholars give a magnificent, totally committed account of these glorious pieces – as usual their attack, ensemble and true intonation and blend are remarkable. For those who do not know this music, this will be one of the discoveries of the year. Excellent recording.

Couperin, François (1668–1733)

L'apothéose de Corelli; L'apothéose de Lully; Concert 'dans le goût théatral'.
*** Erato/Warner Dig. 2292 45011-2 [id.]. Bury, Wilcock, Campbell, E. Bar. Soloists, Gardiner.

Gardiner here presents an ideal Couperin coupling in superb performances, bringing together the two great instrumental works, both called apothéoses, celebrating first Corelli and then, even more grandly, Lully. Each one, in linking its sequence of movements, has a stylized classical programme. In the Corelli work Couperin imagines the composer in communication with the Muses, while the Lully work starts with the composer in the Elysian fields making music with the Lyric Shades, before being abducted to Parnassus. It is all an excuse for inspired music. The disc is completed with a fine *Concerto 'in the theatrical style'*, in which the instrumentation has been realized by Peter Holman. First-rate sound.

Concerts Royaux Nos. 1 in G; 2 in D; 3 in A; 4 in E min.
*** ASV Gaudeamus CDGAU 101; *ZCGAU 101* [id.]. Trio Sonnerie.

The *Concerts Royaux* can be performed in a variety of forms (violin, flute, oboe, viol and bassoon) and in pre-war days they were played in rich chamber-orchestral transcriptions. The Trio Sonnerie give them in the most economical fashion (violin, viola da gamba and harpsichord). Monica Huggett's violin playing in particular is distinguished by subtlety of phrasing and keenness of musical response, and the contribution of all three musicians is unfailingly imaginative. Excellent recording.

Les Goûts-réunis: Nouveaux concerts Nos. 8; 9 (Ritratto dell'amore).
(M) **(*) HM/BMG GD 71968. Kuijken Ens.

The Kuijken Ensemble use original instruments, and one only has to sample the *Overture* of the *Eighth Concert* to find how attractive is their sound-world. The *Ninth Concert* has a linking programme and its eight dance movements contrast the many facets of love. The playing here is idiomatic and pleasing; but the disc offers short measure: there is plenty of room for another Concert.

L'apothéose de Lulli; La Parnasse ou l'apothéose de Corelli; Pièces de clavecin: 9e Ordre: Allemande à deux. 14e Ordre: La Juilliet. 15e Ordre: Muséte de Choisi; Muséte de Taverni. 16e Ordre: La Létiville.
*** HM Dig. HMC 901269; *HMC 401269* [id.]. William Christie, Christophe Rousset (harpsichords).

Couperin's preface explains that he himself played these works on two harpsichords with members of his family and pupils; and William Christie has chosen to follow his example. Surprisingly, they sound rather more exciting in this form than in the more familiar instrumental versions, largely perhaps because of the sheer sparkle and vitality of these performers. The accompanying notes are very informative and helpful, and the two larger pieces are supplemented by four shorter movements from the *Pièces de clavecin*. Hugely enjoyable and stimulating listening, splendidly recorded.

L'Art de toucher le clavecin: Preludes in A, C, B flat, D min., E flat, F, & G min. L'Arlequine; Les Baricades mistérieuses; Suites in C min., Ordre 3; B min., Ordre 8; Suite in A.
❀ *** HM/BMG Dig. RD77219 [77219-2-RC]. Skip Sempé (harpsichord).

Skip Sempé has become something of a cult figure in the last year or two, but don't let that put you off. This is playing of real insight and flair, by far the best Couperin recital to have appeared in recent years and one of the most imaginative. Skip Sempé plays the 3rd and 8th Ordres, interspersing them with half a dozen of the preludes from the Art de toucher le clavecin and a handful of other pieces from the 6th, 15th, 23rd and 24th Ordres. There is expressive freedom about this playing and a poetic vitality that will persuade those who have hitherto found it difficult to come to terms with eighteenth-century French keyboard music. Sempé plays a modern copy by Bruce Kennedy of a Ruckers-Taskin and is very well recorded, though readers will find they will get better results by listening at a slightly lower-level setting than usual. An altogether outstanding issue and an ideal starting point for any collector embarking on Couperin.

Harpsichord suites, Book 1, Ordres 1–5.
(B) *** HM HMA 190351/3 [id.]. Kenneth Gilbert.

Harpsichord suites, Book 2, Ordres 6–12.
(B) *** HM HMA 190354/6 [id.]. Kenneth Gilbert.

Harpsichord suites, Book 3, Ordres 13–19.
(B) *** HM HMA 190357/8 [id.]. Kenneth Gilbert.

Harpsichord suites, Book 4, Ordres 20–27.
(B) *** HM HMA 190359/60 [id.]. Kenneth Gilbert.

The Canadian scholar Kenneth Gilbert has edited the complete keyboard works of Couperin, and his recording of them is made on an exact copy of an instrument by Henry Hemsch (1750) made by Hubbard in Boston. Professor Gilbert's performances are scrupulous in matters of registration, following what is known of eighteenth-century practice in France. There is no want of expressive range throughout the series and Gilbert plays with authority and taste – and, more to the point, artistry. He is also well served by the engineers. Readers should note that the sound throughout the series is of excellent quality and altogether on a par with the performances. Once started, the listener will want to explore this rewarding world more fully, and there is no doubt that Kenneth Gilbert is an eminently authoritative guide. Moreover these records are modestly priced.

Harpsichord suites, Book 2, Ordres 8 & 9.
*** Denon Dig. CO 1719 [id.]. Huguette Dreyfus (harpsichord).

Huguette Dreyfus chooses an eighteenth-century instrument by Jacques Goerman, restored by Mercier-Ythier and tuned in accordance with Marpurg temperament (A = 415). Its colours are rather sombre and subdued, and Huguette Dreyfus plays with her customary authority and restraint. The *Huitième ordre* includes the famous *Passacaille* that Landowska played with such panache and flair. Excellent balance and recording.

Harpsichord suites, Book 2, Ordre 11; Book 3, Ordre 13.
*** Denon Dig. C37 7070 [id.]. Huguette Dreyfus (harpsichord).

For Ordres 11 and 13, Huguette Dreyfus plays a Dowd and shows herself yet again to have great understanding of this style; Mme Dreyfus certainly has the poetic sensibility and the grasp of rubato so necessary in the interpretation of Couperin's art. She is impeccably recorded.

Messe a l'usage ordinaire des paroisses.
(B) *** HM HMA 90714; HMA 43714 [id.]. Michel Chapuis (organ of St Mazimin-en-Var).

Couperin was an organist all his working life, but the two *Organ Masses* which constitute his entire output for the instrument were composed in 1690 when he was twenty-two. Michel Chapuis uses the organ of St Mazimin-en-Var, completed in the 1770s by Jean-Esprit Isnard, a beautiful instrument that sounds excellent in this recording which, dating from 1967, sounds remarkably vivid. The performance has all the scholarship, authority and style one would expect from this fine player, and this makes a good bargain in the Musique d'Abord series.

3 Leçons de ténèbres; Motet pour le jour de Pâques.
*** O-L 430 283-2 [id.]. Nelson, Kirkby, Ryan, Hogwood.

3 Leçons de ténèbres.
(B) *** HM HMA 90210 [id.]. Deller, Todd, Perulli, Chapuis.

The *Trois Leçons de ténèbres* were written for performance on Good Friday and were the only ecclesiastical music Couperin published during his lifetime. Unlike Bach's cantatas, Couperin's settings had female voices in mind and he could barely have hoped for more ethereal timbres than those of Judith Nelson and Emma Kirkby. Purity and restraint rather than warmth and humanity are the keynote of these performances, but few listeners are likely to complain of the results. The recordings are vividly transferred to CD and the balance is very natural; the *Easter motet* is an additional attraction and makes a spirited and happy contrast, aptly following after the Good Friday music.

Deller's account of the *Trois Leçons* is inevitably less authentic, since this music, written for a convent, did not envisage performances by male voices. In every other respect, however, it has a wonderful authenticity of feeling and a blend of scholarship and artistry that gives it a special claim on the attention of collectors. Though less pure than its Oiseau-Lyre rival, Deller has greater insight and no less spirituality. The 1967 recording is beautifully transferred to CD. The two approaches are very different; some may be swayed by the presence of a fill-up on the Hogwood recording; but the Deller reissue has the advantage of economy and, except for those who do not respond to Deller's art, this carries stronger persuasive powers.

Motets: *Domine salvum fac regem; Jacunda vox ecclesiae; Laetentur coeli; Lauda Sion salvatorem; Magnificat; O misterium ineffabile; Regina coeli; Tantum ergo sacramentum; Venite exultemus Domine; Victoria, Christo resurgenti.*
(B) *** HM HMA 901150; HMA 431150 [id.]. Feldman, Poulenard, Reinhart, Linden, Moroney.

The consensus of informed opinion is that the *Tenebrae* represent Couperin's sacred music at its best, but there is much here that is well worth investigating, and the motets on this record cover a wider spectrum of feeling and range of expressive devices than might at first be imagined. The performances are eminently acceptable, with some particularly good singing from Jill Feldman; the recording is made in a spacious and warm acoustic. There is no doubting that this is a collection of special interest to all lovers of French Baroque music and its reissue in the Musique d'Abord series is most welcome.

Couperin, Louis (c. 1626–61)

Suites de pièces and complete harpsichord music.
(B) *** HM 901124/27 (4) [id.]. Davitt Moroney (harpsichord).

Louis Couperin was a pupil of Chambonnières, and his keyboard output comprises enough individual dance pieces to make sixteen suites, as well as other pieces. Couperin did not organize his music into fixed suites, and the Bauyn manuscript groups them in order of ascending tonality; contemporary players would have put together their own suites from this. The most famous of Louis Couperin's pieces are the unmeasured preludes, which Davitt Moroney plays with great idiomatic understanding, as he does the remaining works. Three instruments are used, all tuned to the temperaments in use in France in the middle of the seventeenth century. This comprehensive survey makes out a strong case for this repertoire; readers expecting it to be greatly inferior in quality to the clavecin music of François-le-Grand will be pleasantly surprised – though, of course, there is less of the poetic fantasy of his nephew at his best. The recording is eminently truthful and the CD transfer wholly natural. If the volume level is set judiciously, the illusion of reality is remarkable. This box is impressively presented and at bargain price the set is well worth exploring.

Harpsichord suites: in A min.; in C; in F; Pavane in F sharp min.
(M) *** HM/BMG GD 77058 [77058-2-RG]. Gustav Leonhardt (harpsichord).

Gustav Leonhardt plays a copy by Skowroneck of a 1680 French harpsichord, and the sound is altogether vivid and appealing; the quality of the recording is completely natural and lifelike. Louis Couperin's invention is not always as rich in character as that of his nephew, and it needs playing of this order to show it to best advantage. Leonhardt has such subtlety and panache that he makes the most of the grandeur and refinement of this music to whose sensibility he seems wholly attuned. This is the best introduction to Louis Couperin's keyboard suites now before the public.

Cowell, Henry (1897–1965)

Hymn and fuguing tune No. 10 for oboe and strings.
*** Argo 417 818-2 [id.]. Nicklin, ASMF, Marriner – BARBER: *Adagio;* COPLAND: *Quiet city;* CRESTON: *Rumor;* IVES: *Symphony No. 3.* ***

This likeable *Hymn and fuguing tune*, by a composer otherwise little known, is well worth having and is expertly played and recorded here. The digital remastering has slightly clarified an already excellent recording.

Cowen, Frederick (1852–1935)

Symphony No. 3 in C min. (Scandinavian); The Butterfly's ball: concert overture; Indian rhapsody.
** Marco Polo Dig. 8.220308 [id.]. Czechoslovak State PO (Košice), Adrian Leaper.

As a child Frederick Cowen studied with two Mozart pupils, Attwood and Hummel, before enrolling at the Leipzig Conservatoire where his teachers included Reinecke and Moscheles. He composed six symphonies and some 300 or so songs, and was for a time conductor of the Hallé and the Liverpool Philharmonic. The *Symphony No. 3* (1880) was inspired by a tour he made of the Scandinavian countries as accompanist to the French contralto, Zélia Trebelli. It shows (to borrow Hanslick's judgement) 'good schooling, a lively sense of tone painting and much skill in orchestration, if not striking originality'. But what Cowen lacks in individuality he makes up for in natural musicianship and charm. His best-known work is the *Concert overture, The Butterfly's ball* (1901), which is scored with Mendelssohnian delicacy and skill. The *Indian rhapsody* (1903) with its naïve orientalisms carries a good deal less conviction. The performances are eminently lively, though the upper strings sound a little undernourished. The recording is pleasingly reverberant but somewhat lacking in body.

Creston, Paul (born 1906)

A Rumor.
*** Argo 417 818-2 [id.]. ASMF, Marriner – BARBER: *Adagio;* COPLAND: *Quiet city;* COWELL: *Hymn;* IVES: *Symphony No. 3.* ***

A Rumor is a witty and engaging piece and is played here with plenty of character by the Academy under Sir Neville Marriner. It completes a thoroughly rewarding and approachable disc of twentieth-century American music that deserves the widest currency. The sound is first class.

Symphony No. 2, Op. 35; Corinthians XIII, Op. 82; Walt Whitman, Op. 53.
*** Koch Dig. 37036-2 or KI 7036 [id.]. Krakow PO, David Amos.

It is good that the American symphonists of the 1940s and 1950s are coming back into their own. Paul Creston's music is still neglected outside the United States. His musical language is strongly influenced by French music – one passage from Walt Whitman (1952) sounds as if it has migrated from *Daphnis et Chloé*, and the harmonic language of the first part of *Corinthians* (1963) is also Ravel-derived. Creston's orchestration is both opulent and expert, though some climaxes are overblown. (This is not the sort of music that would appeal to admirers of Elliott Carter.) Creston was championed by such conductors as Ormandy, Monteux and Stokowski and, like Walter Piston and David Diamond, found serial and post-serial techniques foreign to his nature. The *Second Symphony* (1944) opens rather like a Roy Harris symphony but subsequently becomes highly exotic in the manner of a Roussel or a Villa-Lobos, with infectiously vital rhythms and lush textures. It is played with real enthusiasm and affection by these Polish forces and is well very recorded, even though the sound could do with greater transparency in the upper range. This should enjoy wide appeal.

Crusell, Bernhard (1775–1838)

Clarinet concertos Nos 1–3
*** ASV Dig. CDDCA 784; *ZCDCA 784* [id.]. Emma Johnson, RPO/ECO, Herbig; Groves; or Schwarz.

No one brings out the fun in these clarinet concertos by Crusell quite as infectiously as Emma Johnson, and this generous recoupling (74 minutes) bringing all three together is a delight. The sources of the recordings may vary widely in personnel, venues and recording dates, but one would hardly know that from the finished disc. The solo instrument is consistently well focused, with the orchestra in each set in a warmly reverberant acoustic, lacking detail only in the heaviest tuttis. With well-structured first movements, sensuous slow movements and exuberant finales, Johnson establishes her disc as a first choice above all others.

Clarinet concertos Nos. 1 in E flat, Op. 1; 3 in E flat, Op. 11.
*** Hyp. CDA 66055 [id.]. Thea King, LSO, Francis.

Crusell, born in Finland in 1775 but working in Stockholm most of his career, was himself a clarinettist, and these delightful concertos demonstrate his complete understanding of the instrument. There are echoes of Mozart, Weber and Rossini in the music, with a hint of Beethoven, and though the writing is demanding for the soloist, Crusell generally avoided cadenzas. Thea King with her beautiful liquid tone makes an outstanding soloist, well accompanied by Francis and the LSO. The recording is first class, with an attractive ambient effect. However, Emma Johnson offers all three concertos for much the same cost.

Clarinet concerto No. 2 in F min., Op. 5.
❀ *** ASV Dig. CDDCA 559; *ZCDCA 559* [id.]. Emma Johnson, ECO, Groves – BAERMANN: *Adagio;* ROSSINI: *Introduction, theme and variations;* WEBER: *Concertino.* ***
*** Hyp. CDA 66088; *KA 66088* [id.]. Thea King, LSO, Francis – WEBER: *Concerto No. 2.* ***

Crusell's *Second Clarinet concerto* made Emma Johnson a star, and in return she put Crusell's engagingly lightweight piece firmly on the map. Her delectably spontaneous performance is now caught on the wing and this recording sounds very like a live occasion. There is an element of daring in the music-making, the sparkling virtuosity of the outer movements bringing a lilting bravura that has one relishing the sense of risks being taken and brought off with ease, and the songful Andante is no less appealing. Groves is a lively and sympathetic accompanist, and the balance is a natural one.

Thea King's approach makes this *Concerto* seem more serious, suggesting an almost Beethovenian character to the first movement, while the *Andante pastorale* slow movement is played with a wide range of tone-colour to contrast with the jaunty *Allegretto* finale. It is not the obvious coupling for the better-known Weber *Concerto*, but an attractive one. The digital recording is full and atmospheric, with the soloist balanced forward.

Concertino for bassoon and orchestra in B flat; Introduction et air suédois for clarinet and orchestra, Op. 12; Sinfonia concertante for clarinet, horn, bassoon and orchestra, Op. 3.
*** BIS Dig. BIS CD 495 [id.]. Hara, Korsimaa-Hursti, Lanski-Otto, Tapiola Sinf., Vänskä.

The most substantial piece here is the *Sinfonia concertante, for clarinet, horn, bassoon and orchestra* (1808), which was Crusell's most frequently performed work in nineteenth-century Stockholm. It was composed for himself and two of his colleagues – the horn player, Hirschfeltdt, and Conrad Preumayr, bassoon – to play, and the latter subsequently became his son-in-law! The finale is a set of variations on a chorus from Cherubini's opera, *Les deux journées.* The much later *Concertino for bassoon and orchestra*, written for a European tour Preumayr made in 1829–30, is an altogether delightful piece, which quotes at one point from Boieldieu. It is played with appropriate freshness and virtuosity by László Hara. The best-known and most recorded work on the CD is the *Introduction et air suédois for clarinet and orchestra* (1804) which is nicely done by Anna-Maija Korsimaa-Hursti. The Tapiola Sinfonietta, the orchestra of Esspoo, play with enthusiasm and spirit for Osmo Vänskä, and the BIS recording has lightness, presence and body. This is by no manner of means great music, but it has distinct charm.

Introduction, theme and variations on a Swedish air.
*** ASV Dig. CDDCA 585; *ZCDCA 585* [id.]. Emma Johnson, ECO, Yan Pascal Tortelier – DEBUSSY: *Rapsodie;* TARTINI: *Concertino;* WEBER: *Concerto No. 1.* ***

Emma Johnson, a naturally inspirational artist, skates lightly over any banalities in Crusell's *Variations*, giving a carefree performance, often witty, youthfully daring. Well recorded in a helpful acoustic, it makes an attractive item in a mixed collection of concertante pieces which show contrasted sides of a winning young instrumentalist.

Clarinet quartets Nos. 1 in E flat, Op. 2; 2 in C min., Op. 4; 3 in D, Op. 7.
*** Hyp. CDA 66077; *KA 66077* [id.]. Thea King, Allegri Qt (members).

These are captivatingly sunny works, given superb performances, vivacious and warmly sympathetic. Thea King's tone is positively luscious, as recorded, and the sound is generally excellent. The CD transfer is highly successful.

Clarinet quintet in C min., Op. 4.
*** Orfeo C 141861A [id.]. Karl Leister, Pražák Qt – MOZART: *Clarinet quintet.* **(*)

Aptly, Karl Leister plays this extrovert Scandinavian piece with more dash and flair than its Mozart coupling. One feels that he is actually enjoying it – at this stage of his career – more than the Mozart masterpiece.

Divertimento in C, Op. 9.
*** Hyp. CDA 66143 [id.]. Francis, Allegri Qt – KREUTZER: *Grand quintet;* REICHA: *Quintet.* ***

Crusell's music certainly has charm and grace, and the *Divertimento*, Op. 9, is no exception. No one wanting this slight but charming piece and its companions need look further than this nicely played and well-recorded account.

Cui, César (1835–1918)

Suites: (i) *Concertante, Op. 25. Miniature, Op. 20; Petite, Op. 43.*
**(*) Marco Polo Dig. 8.220308 [id.]. (i) Nishizaki; Hong Kong PO, Schermerhorn.

César Cui is the least-known and the least nationalist of the 'Mighty Handful' (Balakirev, Rimsky-Korsakov, Mussorgsky and Borodin), and in some ways the least gifted. He spent his childhood in Vilnius (his mother was Lithuanian, his father French) and studied briefly with Moniuszko before going to St Petersburg where he was drawn into Balakirev's circle. His father had served in Napoleon's army and Cui himself became a lecturer at the Academy of Military Engineering in addition to his composing and writing (he was active as a critic). His output of songs and miniatures is extensive and some of it is of quality. He wrote relatively little for the orchestra, for which (in Rimsky-Korsakov's words) he had 'neither inclination nor ability', but by the 1880s he was not amateurish, as Balakirev had thought when they first met. These pieces have a faded period charm that is very appealing (try the *Petite Marche* and the equally likeable *Impromptu à la Schumann* from the *Suite miniature*) and are very well played by the Hong Kong Philharmonic. Takako Nishizaki is the expert soloist in the *Suite concertante.* An interesting issue that fills a gap in the repertoire, and very decently recorded too.

Czerny, Karl (1791–1857)

Andante e polacca in E for horn and piano, Op. posth.; 3 Fantasias brillante on themes of Schubert for horn and piano, Op. 339.
*** Etcetera Dig. KTC 1121 [id.]. Barry Tuckwell, David Blumenthal.

The *Andante and polacca* is a characteristically ripe piece which is enjoyable enough when played with such aplomb, but the real interest of this recital lies with the three Schubertian *Fantasias.* In effect they are pot-pourris of favourite Schubert songs, with the horn given the vocal melody against a background of glittering piano cascades. Indeed the piano part requires by far the greater bravura and Blumenthal is quite dazzling. But he does not upstage Barry Tuckwell, who plays this series of great melodies with vocal feeling and a fine sense of line. The first *Fantasy* includes *Der Wanderer*, *Erlkönig* and the lilting *Serenade*, the second a soaring *Ave Maria*, *Fischerweise* and a gloriously flowing *Ungeduld.* The third is more adventurous, drawing on the (piano) *Fantasy in F minor*, the *Cavatina* from *Alfonso und Estrella*, *Gute Nacht* from *Winterreise*, but chooses *The Trout* for its end-piece. The performances could hardly be bettered; if you want Schubert Lieder without the words, then the present recording is most pleasing, the resonance flattering to both artists but the focus realistically firm.

Danzi, Franz (1763–1826)

Flute concertos Nos. 1 in G, Op. 30; 2 in D min., Op. 31; 3 in D min., Op. 42; 4 in D, Op. 43.
*** Orfeo Dig. C 00381-2H [id.]. András Adorjan, Munich CO, Stadlmair.

Danzi was an almost exact contemporary of Beethoven. He wrote four *Flute concertos*, all included here, which suggest a style midway between eighteenth-century classicism and the more romantic manner of Weber. The *D minor Concerto*, Op. 31, is an excellent example, with three strongly contrasted movements including an engaging *Polacca* finale. All three performances by

András Adorjan and Stadlmair with his Munich Chamber Orchestra are impeccably stylish and have plenty of vitality, and the recording is both full and transparent and is well balanced.

(i) *Piano quintet in F, Op. 53. Wind quintets, Op. 67/1–3.*
*** BIS Dig. CD 539 [id.]. (i) Love Derwinger; BPO Wind Qt.

Although the bulk of his music was for the stage (he was *Kapellmeister* at Karlsruhe and the mentor of Weber), Franz Danzi is largely remembered nowadays for his instrumental music and in particular his music for wind. Inspired by the pioneering example of Reicha, Danzi was one of the first composers to cultivate the wind quintet, writing no fewer than nine, collected in three sets of three each. The first set, Op. 56 (1821) was indeed dedicated to Reicha, while the remaining two appeared three years later. They are light, diverting pieces of no great musical substance but when played with such distinction and recorded with such great clarity and presence they offer unexpected pleasure. The *Piano quintet*, in which the Berlin quintet are joined by the young Swedish pianist, Love Derwinger, is also pretty empty-headed but rather delightful all the same.

Da Ponte, Lorenzo (1749–1838)

L'ape musicale.
**(*) Nuova Era Dig. 6845/6 (2). Scarabelli, Matteuzzi, Dara, Comencini, Teatro la Fenice Ch. & O, Vittorio Parisi.

This greatest of librettists was no composer, but he was musical enough to devise a pasticcio like *L'ape musicale* ('The musical bee') from the works of others, notably Rossini and Mozart. His first pasticcio under this title was given in 1791 before Mozart died, and Da Ponte went on to use the theme three times more, last of all when he had emigrated to New York. It is that final version which has been reconstructed here by Giovanni Piazza, and it makes a delightful, if offbeat entertainment, generally well sung in a lively performance. The first Act – full of Rossinian passages one keeps recognizing – leads up to a complete performance of Tamino's aria, *Dies Bildnis*, sung in German at the end of the Act. Similarly, Act II culminates in an adapted version of the final cabaletta from Rossini's *Cenerentola*. Documentation is copious but, in translation, not always very explicit, though the various sources of musical material are identified in a classified table (Italian only). The libretto is given in Italian and English texts, the latter (presumably) in the free translation which Da Ponte himself made. The sound is dry, with the voices slightly distanced. The stage and audience noises hardly detract from the fun of the performance.

David, Félicien (1810–76)

Les brises d'Orient; Les minarets.
*(*) Marco Polo Dig. 8.223376 [id.]. Daniel Blumenthal.

Félicien David enjoyed some fame during his day and the admiration of Berlioz and Saint-Saëns. His most admired work was the symphonic ode, *Le Désert* (1844), an evocation of Egypt where he spent some time during the 1830s. Immediately on his return from the Middle East he composed a set of *Mélodies orientales* for piano which enjoyed little immediate success, following them up with a number of other pieces on oriental and exotic subjects, including *Lalla Roukh* and *La Perle du Brésil*. After the success of *Le Désert* he republished his piano pieces in the two volumes recorded here, *Les brises d'Orient* and *Les minarets*. Their exoticism sounds very muted nowadays but they have a certain faded period charm – or would have if the rather claustrophobic acoustic in which they are recorded did full justice to Daniel Blumenthal's advocacy. Primarily of curiosity interest that is soon satisfied, though there are some pieces to which one could imagine oneself becoming attached.

Debussy, Claude (1862–1918)

2 Arabesques; Clair de lune (arr. Caplet); *Estampes: Pagodes* (arr. Grainger); *La Mer; Petite suite; Prélude: La cathédrale engloutie* (arr. Stokowski); (i) *Rhapsody for clarinet and orchestra.*

*** Cala Dig. CACD 1001 [id.]. (i) James Campbell, Philh. O, Geoffrey Simon.

Geoffrey Simon's warm, urgent reading of *La Mer*, very well recorded, comes in coupling with six items originally involving piano. Debussy did his own arrangement of the *Clarinet rhapsody* and approved André Caplet's arrangement of *Clair de lune* as well as Henri Büsser's of the *Petite suite*. Stokowski's freely imagined orchestral version of *La cathédrale engloutie* is effectively opulent, and the most fascinating instrumentation of all comes in Percy Grainger's transcription of *Pagodes*, with an elaborate percussion section simulating a Balinese gamelan.

Berceuse héroïque; Marche écossaise; La Mer; Musiques pour le Roi Lear; Nocturnes; Prélude à l'après-midi d'un faune.
(M) **(*) EMI CDM7 69587-2. French R. & TV Ch. & O, Martinon.

Martinon's account of *La Mer* first appeared in the mid-1970s. It still has plenty of atmosphere and enjoys the idiomatic advantage of fine French orchestral playing. The *Musiques pour le Roi Lear* is a real rarity; the colourful *Fanfare* remains impressive, and *Le sommeil de Lear* is highly evocative. The *Nocturnes* are not quite the equal of the finest versions, but are still beautifully played. This is a fairly competitive recommendation, though in the digital remastering there is a slight edge at the upper end of the range, where the trumpets are shrill.

La Boîte à joujoux (orch. Caplet): complete.
*** Chan. Dig. CHAN 8711; *ABTD 1359* [id.]. Ulster O, Yan Pascal Tortelier – RAVEL: *Ma Mère l'Oye*. ***

Debussy's enchanting ballet score depicts adventures in a children's box of toys, and is full of delights. Although the ballet has its robust moments (often humorous), its essential feeling is impressionistic, like a series of etchings. It is beautifully played by the Ulster Orchestra under Yan Pascal Tortelier, who clearly relishes the witty quotations from Gounod's *Faust* and Debussy's own *Golliwog's Cake-walk*. The subtlety and atmosphere are captured admirably by the splendid Chandos recording, which is in the demonstration class.

Children's corner; Danse: Tarantelle styrienne (arr. Ravel); *Estampes: La soirée dans Grenade* (arr. Stokowski). *L'isle joyeuse; Nocturnes; Préludes: Bruyères; La fille aux cheveux de lin.*
*** Cala CACD 1002 [id.]. Philh. O, Geoffrey Simon.

Geoffrey Simon's version of the three *Nocturnes*, colourful and atmospheric, with nothing vague in *Fêtes*, follows the formula of the companion record. The orchestrations of piano music include Stokowski's vivid realization of *La soirée dans Grenade*, as well as Ravel's magical re-interpretation of *Danse*. Debussy himself approved André Caplet's sensitive orchestration of *Children's corner* ('so gorgeously apparelled', he said), with its reference to *Tristan* in the final *Golliwog's cakewalk* underlined by the orchestration. Full, vivid recorded sound. This is a most stimulating pair of discs.

Children's corner; Petite suite.
*** Chan. Dig. CHAN 8756; *ABTD 1395* [id.]. Ulster O, Yan Pascal Tortelier – RAVEL: *Le tombeau de Couperin* etc. ***

Like Ravel's *Le tombeau de Couperin* and the *Valses nobles*, with which they are coupled, these pieces are for the piano but, unlike them, they were transcribed by other hands. The Ulster Orchestra certainly play very well for Yan Pascal Tortelier and the recording is every bit as good as predecessors in this series. Doubtless choice will rest on the matter of coupling, but no one investing in the present disc will be disappointed.

Danse (orch. Ravel); (i) *Fantaisie for piano and orchestra;* (ii) *La plus que lente;* (iii) *Khamma;* (iv) *Première Rhapsodie for clarinet and orchestra;* (v) *Rhapsodie for saxophone.*
(M) **(*) EMI CDM7 69668-2. (i) Aldo Ciccolini; (ii) John Leach; (iii) Fabienne Boury; (iv) Guy Dangain; (v) Londe; Fr. R. & TV O, Martinon.

The rarity here is *Khamma*, a ballet whose scoring Debussy entrusted to Charles Koechlin. The two *Rhapsodies* are underrated, and although there are alternative versions of all these pieces on CD, few are more generously coupled or more economically priced. Very acceptable performances and recordings.

Danse (Tarantelle styrienne); Sarabande (orch. Ravel).
*** Virgin Dig. VC7 91098-2 [id.]. Lausanne CO, Zedda – MILHAUD: *Création du monde;* PROKOFIEV: *Sinfonietta* etc. ***

Zedda's performances with the Lausanne Chamber Orchestra are neat and polished, full of character and well recorded. But it is the couplings that make his disc specially attractive.

Danses sacrée et profane.
*** Ph. 416 437-2 [id.]. Vera Badings, Concg. O, Haitink – BIZET: *Symphony* etc. ***

A ravishingly beautiful account of Debussy's contrasting *Danses*, matching elegance and refinement with warmth. The sound is suitably warm and glowing, atmospheric rather than sharply defined.

(i) *Danses sacrée et profane;* (ii) *Fantaisie for piano and orchestra;* (iii) *Première rhapsodie for clarinet and orchestra.*
*** Chan. Dig. CHAN 8972 [id.]. (i) Masters; (ii) Queffélec; (iii) King, Ulster O, Y. P. Tortelier – RAVEL: *Intro & allegro* etc. **(*)

A well-filled disc which offers some lush sounds though the *Fantaisie* is really not top-drawer Debussy. It is sensitively played by Anne Queffélec, who has also recorded it on Erato. This is no less fine a performance and the *Première rhapsodie for clarinet and orchestra* is played by Christopher King with a natural unforced eloquence that is very persuasive, and the *Danses sacrée et profane* come off well.

Fantasy for piano and orchestra.
(M) *** Erato/Warner 2292 45086-2 [id.]. Anne Queffélec, Monte Carlo Op. O, Jordan – RAVEL: *Concertos.* ***

Debussy's *Fantasy*, an early work, does not find his musical language fully formed, but it is well worth investigating, for in Anne Queffélec's hands it makes a good impression. The warm recording too is persuasive.

Images.
*** Chan. Dig. CHAN 8850; *ABTD 1467* [id.]. Ulster O, Yan Pascal Tortelier – RAVEL: *Alborada; Rapsodie espagnole.* ***

Images; Jeux; Le Roi Lear (incidental music).
*** EMI Dig. CDC7 49947-2. CBSO, Rattle.

Images; (i) *Nocturnes.*
*** Decca Dig. 425 502-2 [id.]. Montreal SO, Dutoit; (i) with chorus.

Simon Rattle's version of the *Images* is memorably atmospheric. *Gigues* is wonderfully languorous and *Ibéria* is quite intoxicating with its heady perfumes and subtle colourings. In fact some may even find it a trace too exotic and its sensuousness a shade too voluptuous. The *Rondes de printemps* is also very fine. *Jeux*, too, comes off well. Rattle is just a touch more expansive than most rivals, and also more evocative, though he does not depart from the basic metronome markings. Haitink probably remains a first choice in this score, for he has atmosphere and a tauter grip on the music's flow, but Baudo's mid-priced EMI version should not be forgotten either. The *King Lear* excerpts sound splendid. First-rate recording, very vivid but beautifully balanced.

Dutoit and his Montreal Symphony Orchestra give performances of both these great Debussy works which, in their idiomatic expressiveness, echo their achievement earlier in Ravel, helped, as there, by some of the richest and most luminous orchestral sound ever put on disc. In comparison with such rivals as Previn and Rattle in the *Images*, and with Haitink in the *Nocturnes*, Dutoit is freer in his use of rubato, as well as in his warm, espressivo moulding of phrase. His sharp pointing of rhythm, as in the Spanish dances of *Ibéria* or the processional march in *Fêtes*, is also highly characteristic of his approach to French music. Some will prefer a cooler manner in Debussy, but for those who like these impressionistic masterpieces to be presented in full colour, with a vivid feeling for atmosphere, this is an ideal choice, and it has the merit of providing an exceptionally generous coupling.

The idea of coupling Debussy and Ravel, as the Ulster Orchestra and Yan Pascal Tortelier are doing, will inevitably pose problems of duplication for some collectors; but those who have embarked on this journey can collect this newcomer with some confidence. The link between the two discs is the two composers' feeling for and portrayal of Spain – in *Ibéria* in Debussy's case. But even the dank Breton atmosphere of *Gigues* is exquisitely captured, and although *Les parfums de la nuit* is on the fast side it remains highly evocative. The orchestral playing is very good indeed and the recorded sound is of the high quality we have come to expect of this series.

It is not necessarily the best *Images* on the market, if one can speak in such crude terms, but it is certainly among the best. The *Rondes de printemps* has delicacy and freshness in their hands.

Images: Ibéria.
❀ (M) *** BMG/RCA GD 60179 [60179-2-RG]. Chicago SO, Fritz Reiner – RAVEL: *Alborada* etc. *** ❀

Fritz Reiner and the Chicago orchestra give a reading that is immaculate in execution and magical in atmosphere. There have been superb modern accounts since this first appeared, over 30 years ago, but none that are more refined in terms of characterization. This marvellously evocative performance, and the Ravel with which it is coupled, has been underrated by the wider record-loving public over the years and has long been out of circulation. It should not be overlooked now, for the recorded sound with its natural concert-hall balance is greatly improved in terms of body and definition. It is amazingly realistic even without considering its vintage.

Images: Ibéria. La Mer; Nocturnes: Nuages; Fêtes. Prélude à l'après-midi d'un faune.
(M) (**(*)) BMG/RCA mono GD 60265 [60265-2-RG]. NBC SO, Toscanini.

By emphasizing clarity, Toscanini with his electric intensity and sense of purpose consistently compels attention. One thinks of these supreme examples of musical impressionism, not as colour pieces, but as masterly structures of great originality in purely musical terms. Least effective is the account of the first of the *Nocturnes*, where Toscanini's metrical manner is unsympathetic, but *Fêtes* is exhilaratingly fast and brilliant, even if the procession is raced along mercilessly. Clean, bright transfers.

Images: Ibéria. Prélude à l'après-midi d'un faune; (i) *La damoiselle élue.*
*** DG Dig. 423 103-2 [id.]. (i) Maria Ewing, Brigitte Balleys, LSO Ch.; LSO, Abbado.

The London Symphony Orchestra has rarely sounded as sensuously beautiful on record as in Abbado's Debussy collection, bringing together two favourite works, in coupling with the exotic early cantata inspired by Rossetti's *Blessèd Damozel, La damoiselle élue.* With a warm church resonance adding to the bloom not just of the orchestral sound but of the voices, the cantata brings the most distinctive performance, poised and spacious. Maria Ewing has never sounded sweeter on record, and Brigitte Balleys, a touch raw-toned on some notes, sings with attractive freshness. The purely orchestral works bring more urgent, even impulsive performances, marked by a warmly persuasive rubato style. Though balances are not always quite natural, the ambient warmth of All Saints', Tooting, seems ideal for the music, orchestral as well as vocal, and the effect is very vivid and glowing, without loss of detail.

Jeux; Khamma.
*** Chan. Dig. CHAN 8903; *ABTD 1512* [id.]. Ulster O, Tortelier – RAVEL: *Boléro; La valse.* ***

The two Debussy ballets both come from the same period. For *Khamma* (1911), Debussy had no enthusiasm and in the end entrusted its orchestration to Koechlin. It remains a rarity in the concert hall and its neglect extended to the gramophone until Ansermet recorded it in the 1960s. Apart from Martinon's record at mid-price, it is not otherwise available in its orchestral form. Generally speaking the Chandos issue scores over its EMI rival in the refinement and spaciousness of its sound. In the Martinon it is coupled with the *Rhapsodies* for clarinet and saxophone, *La plus que lente*, and the *Fantaisie* for piano and orchestra. Yan Pascal Tortelier has the advantage in the more logical coupling of Debussy's greatest ballet, *Jeux* (1912). He gets some very good playing, too, from the Ulster Orchestra, and though this latter performance is not to be preferred to the magical Haitink account on Philips which still sounds excellent, or either of the EMI versions (Baudo and Rattle), it remains highly competitive and desirable.

Jeux; La Mer; Prélude à l'après-midi d'un faune.
❀ (M) *** EMI Dig. CD-EMX 9502; *TC-EMX 2090* [Ang. CDM 62012]. LPO, Baudo.

Serge Baudo's version of *La Mer* is first class and can be ranked alongside the finest accounts now on disc. The recording is beautifully natural and expertly balanced. The same may be said for his lovely account of *Prélude à l'après-midi d'un faune*, as atmospheric as any in the catalogue and more beautifully shaped than many. In the faster sections, *Jeux* is at times brisker than we are used to and well conveys the sense of the playfulness of the tennis match. Its competitive price makes it even more enticing.

Jeux; (i) *Nocturnes.*
*** Ph. 400 023-2 [id.]. Concg. O, Haitink, (i) with women's Ch. of Coll. Mus.

Haitink's reading of *Jeux* is wonderfully expansive and sensitive to atmosphere. In the *Nocturnes*, the cruel vocal line in *Sirènes* taxes the women of the Collegium Musicum Amstelodamense, but few versions are quite as beguiling and seductive as Haitink's. Add to this an equally admirable recorded quality, with transparent textures, splendidly defined detail and truthful perspective – in short, demonstration sound – and the result is very distinguished indeed.

La Mer.
(M) *** BMG/RCA GD 60875 [60875-2-RG]. Chicago SO, Reiner – RIMSKY-KORSAKOV: *Scheherazade.* ***
(M) **(*) EMI/Phoenixa CDM7 63763-2; *EG 763763-4* [id.]. Hallé O, Barbirolli – RAVEL: *Daphnis et Chloé* etc. **(*)
(M) (**) EMI mono CDH7 69784-2. BBC SO, Toscanini – ELGAR: *Enigma variations.* (***)

La Mer; (i) *Nocturnes.*
(M) *** EMI CDM7 69184-2; *EG 769184-4.* Philh. O, Giulini, with Ch.
(M) *** EMI Dig. CDD7 64056-2 [id.]. LSO, Previn; (i) with Amb. S. – RAVEL: *Alborada* etc. ***
(B) **(*) EMI CZS7 62669-2 (2). O de Paris, Barbirolli; (i) with female Ch. (with Concert: French music ***).
**(*) Ph. Dig. 411 433-2 [id.]. Boston SO, Sir Colin Davis; (i) with Tanglewood Festival Ch.

La Mer; Nocturnes; Prélude à l'après-midi d'un faune.
(B) *** Pickwick Dig. PCD 915; *CIMPC 915.* LSO, Frühbeck de Burgos, with Ch. in Nocturnes.
** Erato/Warner Dig. 2292 45605-2 [id.]. SRO, Armin Jordan.

La Mer; Prélude à l'après-midi d'un faune.
(M) *** DG 427 250-2. BPO, Karajan – RAVEL: *Boléro; Daphnis et Chloé.* ***
(M) *** EMI CDM7 64357-2 (id.]; *EG 764357-4.* BPO, Karajan – RAVEL: *Alborada* etc. ***

After three decades, Karajan's 1964 DG account of *La Mer* is still very much in a class of its own. So strong is its evocative power that one feels one can almost see and smell the ocean, and the superb playing of the Berlin orchestra, for all its virtuosity and beauty of sound, is totally at the service of the composer. The performance of the *Prélude à l'après-midi d'un faune* is no less outstanding, the cool perfection of the opening flute solo matched by ravishing string-playing in the central section.

Reiner's 1960 recording has all the warmth and atmosphere that make his version of *Ibéria*, recorded at about the same time – see above – so unforgettable. The pianissimo opening has enormous evocative feeling and the *Jeux des vagues* has the same haunting sense of colour. Of course the marvellous acoustics of the Chicago Hall contribute to the appeal of this superbly played account: the effect is richer and fuller than in Karajan's remastered DG version, and Reiner's record gives no less pleasure. With Karajan, one could picture the bracing air of the northern Atlantic, whereas with Reiner, although the dialogue of the wind and waves is no less powerful, one senses a more southern latitude.

Giulini's early EMI version of *La Mer* is also very distinguished. The Philharmonia are in splendid form, and the coupled *Nocturnes* are also played with great delicacy of feeling and refinement of detail; if *Nuages* is perhaps a little too dreamy, it is nevertheless full of atmosphere. *Sirènes*, however, is somewhat lacking in a sense of movement, slow to the point of sluggishness. Nevertheless, overall this is an impressive reissue.

Previn's ocean is clearly in the southern hemisphere, with Debussy's orchestral colours made to sound more vividly sunlit. The playing of the LSO is extremely impressive, particularly the ardour of the strings. The recording has glittering detail and expands brilliantly at climaxes (though, even on CD, there is a slight loss of refinement at the very loudest peaks). The *Nocturnes* have even greater spontaneity. Some might feel that the *Sirènes* are too voluptuous but this matches Previn's extrovert approach. The reissue adds a pair of first-class Ravel performances and gives a total playing time of nearly 77 minutes.

Although strong in Mediterranean atmosphere, Frühbeck de Burgos's account of *La Mer* has an underlying grip, helped by the wide dynamic range of the Walthamstow recording. Overall there is plenty of excitement, with the LSO's virtuosity in the finale matched by the rich-toned ardour of the strings when they rise to the emotional peak of Jeux de vagues. There is much subtlety of detail, both here and in the *Nocturnes*, where textures again have the sensuousness of southern climes, while the processional of Fêtes proceeds spectacularly, glittering with colour. The *Prélude à l'après-midi d'un faune* brings lovely delicate flute playing from Paul Edmund-

Davies and a richly moulded string climax. If these are not conventional readings, they are full of impulse and superbly recorded.

Karajan's 1978 analogue re-recording of *La Mer* for EMI may not have quite the supreme refinement of his earlier DG version – partly a question of the warmer, vaguer recording – but it has a comparable concentration, with the structure persuasively and inevitably built. At the very opening of the work the extremes of dynamic and tempo may seem exaggerated, and at times there is a suggestion of the pursuit of beauty of sound for its own sake, but there is never any doubt about the brilliance and virtuosity of the Berlin orchestra. The *Prélude* has an appropriate languor, and there is a persuasive warmth about this performance, beautifully moulded; but again the earlier version distilled greater atmosphere and magic. Detail remains diffuse, but overall the sound is fuller than on the earlier recording. The new Ravel coupling is very generous.

Barbirolli's 1959 Hallé version of *La Mer* readily demonstrates his special feeling for the atmosphere and rhapsodical freedom of Debussy's masterly score. The performance has remarkable grip and becomes increasingly exciting in its closing section. The remastering for CD of the (originally PRT) recording is a great success, cutting down background noise without losing vividness, and simultaneously improving the focus.

The later, French account, recorded in Paris in 1968, is also very sympathetic and certainly does not lack sensuous, evocative feeling. Barbirolli and the Orchestre de Paris are helped by the more modern sound. There is some lack of inner tension about the playing, both here and in the *Nocturnes*, where the close balance of the female chorus in *Sirènes* reduces the ethereal effect, but, as in the earlier, Hallé recording, there is plenty of adrenalin flowing in the closing *Dialogue du vent et de la mer* of the former piece.

The waters that Sir Colin Davis's reading evokes are somewhat cold and grey, and there is always the sense of tremendous power used with restraint. The set of *Nocturnes* is also very fine. Sir Colin's measured approach to *Sirènes* is convincing, marvellously sustained in both feeling and atmosphere. *Nuages* is hardly less concentrated in poetic feeling, slow and ethereal. Both works are sumptuously recorded; the snag is that the acoustics of the Boston Hall tend to blur inner detail, although the definition of the CD is better than that of the original LP.

Armin Jordan and the Orchestre de la Suisse Romande give sensitive, musicianly accounts of all three pieces, and no one investing in it is likely to be disappointed. The orchestra is now in much better shape than it was towards the end of Ansermet's reign; the wind blend well and produce a cultured sound. All the same, these performances have merit rather than stature and, for all the excellence of the Erato recording, it would not be possible to prefer it to such strongly characterized readings as Karajan's 1964 *La mer* or the Giulini coupling from the same period.

Toscanini's 1935 BBC recording of *La Mer* is extremely vivid and the sense of occasion is striking. However, it cannot quite compare with his much later NBC recording (see above) which, with far crisper ensemble, bites harder; the London recording, well handled by the engineers, is seriously marred by audience noises (there are some appalling coughs to disfigure the quiet opening section).

Nocturnes.

** Chan. Dig. CHAN 8914; *ABTD 1518* [id.]. Ulster O, Yan Pascal Tortelier with chorus – RAVEL: *Ouverture de féerie; Shéhérazade.* **

A seductive and strongly characterized account of the *Nocturnes* with some good singing in *Sirènes*, and splendidly refined recording. The *Fêtes* is very powerful and menacing. A competitive account, even if does not displace such recommendations as Haitink, Giulini and Tilson Thomas. The *Shéhérazade* with which it is coupled is not a first recommendation either, which perhaps qualifies its competitiveness, particularly at full price and 55 minutes' playing time.

(i) *Nocturnes; Le Martyre de Saint Sébastien: 2 Fanfares & symphonic fragments; Printemps* (symphonic suite).

❀ (M) *** DG 435 069-2; *435 069-4* [id.]. (i) Ch.; O de Paris, Daniel Barenboim.

This is one of Barenboim's very finest records and in its reissued format (72 minutes) generously includes not only the early *Printemps* and the fragments from *Le Martyre de Saint Sébastien* but also his splendid set of *Nocturnes*. This performance, although highly individual in its control of tempo, has great fervour. *Sirènes* develops a feeling of soaring ecstasy, and the closing pages with the chorus are rapturously beautiful. Comparably in *Le Martyre* Barenboim succeeds in distilling an intense, rapt quality and brings to life its evocative atmosphere in a way that has not been matched since Cantelli's mono HMV recording. If Barenboim does not diffuse the score with quite the same delicacy of feeling that Cantelli secured, he still refrains from any expressive indulgence and allows the music to speak for itself. He is no less persuasive in *Printemps.* This receives a performance as good as any in the catalogue: Barenboim succeeds in balancing intensity with atmospheric feeling, and the result is very persuasive. The 1977/8 recordings, made in either Notre Dame du Liban or the Paris Mutualité, are spacious, rich in texture and well balanced, with good definition and range, and the CD transfer refines detail without reducing the sonic allure.

Prélude à l'après-midi d'un faune.
*(*) Chan. Dig. CHAN 8893 [id.]. Ulster O, Yan Pascal Tortelier – RAVEL: *Daphnis and Chloe* (ballet; complete). **(*)

Yan Pascal Tortelier's sensitively shaped but rather too brisk *Prélude à l'après-midi d'un faune* is the fill-up to a complete *Daphnis* in the intelligently planned Chandos series. The Debussy is not really a strong contender, given the abundant performances of stature in the catalogue.

Rhapsody for clarinet and orchestra.
*** ASV Dig. CDDCA 585; *ZCDCA 585* [id.]. Emma Johnson, ECO, Yan Pascal Tortelier – CRUSELL: *Introduction, theme & variations;* TARTINI: *Concertino;* WEBER: *Concerto No. 1.* ***

Debussy's lovely *First Rhapsody* brings out the most persuasive qualities in Emma Johnson's artistry. The range of expression with extreme contrasts of tone and dynamic makes this an exceptionally sensuous performance, yearningly poetic, and recorded in a helpful acoustic.

CHAMBER MUSIC

(i) *Cello sonata;* (ii) *Danse sacrée et danse profane;* (iii) *En blanc et noir; 6 Épigraphes antiques; Lindajara; Petite suite;* (iv) *Sonata for flute, viola and harp;* (v) *Syrinx;* (vi) *String quartet in G min.;* (vii) *Violin sonata.*
(B) ** EMI CZS7 67416-2 (2) [id.]. (i) Maurice Gendron, Jacques Février; (ii) Annie Challan, Paris Conservatoire O, André Cluytens; (iii) Jean-Philippe Collard, Michel Béroff; (iv; v) Michel Debost; (v) Yehudi Menuhin, Lily Laskine; (vi) Parrenin Qt; (vii) Christian Ferras, Pierre Barbizet.

Nearly two and a quarter hours of music for the price of one CD in performances which are far from negligible and in some cases distinguished. The best part of the second disc is taken up by the music for piano duet or two pianos, stylishly played by Jean-Philippe Collard and Michel Béroff, though their 1983 recording is not altogether ideal. The 1970 Parrenin account of the *String quartet* was much admired at the time and remains a strongly competitive element in this package, as does the recording of the *Danse sacrée et danse profane* under André Cluytens. Maurice Gendron is perhaps better served by the engineers (and for that matter his pianist) in the Philips recording he made of the *Cello sonata* and the 1963 Ferras–Barbizet record of the *Violin sonata* is no match for the Grumiaux on Philips (see below, where a discussion of the Debost–Menuhin–Laskine *Sonata for flute, viola and harp* can be found). Not a bad package by any manner of means, and value for money.

Cello sonata; Petite pièce for clarinet and piano; Première Rapsodie for clarinet and piano; Sonata for flute, viola and harp; Violin sonata; Syrinx for solo flute.
*** Chan. CHAN 8385 [id.]. Athena Ens.

The well-recorded Chandos set from 1981 scores in being generously filled. The most ethereal of these pieces is the Sonata for flute, viola and harp, whose other-worldly quality is beautifully conveyed here; indeed, this version can hold its own with the best in the catalogue. In the case of the other sonatas, there are strong competitors but, as a collection, this is certainly recommendable.

Cello sonata in D min.
*** Decca 417 833-2 [id.]. Rostropovich, Britten – SCHUBERT: *Arpeggione sonata* **(*); SCHUMANN: *5 Stücke.* ***
**(*) ASV Dig. CDDCA 796 [id.]. Bernard Gregor-Smith, Yolande Wrigley – BRIDGE; DOHNÁNYI: *Sonatas.* **(*)
** Virgin Dig. VC7 90812-2 [id.]. Steven Isserlis, Pascal Devoyon – FRANCK; POULENC: *Sonatas.* **

(i) *Cello sonata;* (ii) *Violin sonata.*
(*) Chan. Dig. CHAN 8458; *ABTD 1170* [id.]. (i) Yuli Turovsky; (ii) Rostislav Dubinsky; Luba Edlina – RAVEL: *Piano trio.* *

Like Debussy's other late chamber works, the *Cello sonata* is a concentrated piece, quirkily original. The classic version by Rostropovich and Britten, now restored to the catalogue at premium price, has a clarity and point which suit the music perfectly. The recording is first class, and if the couplings are suitable, this holds its place as first choice.

Bernard Gregor-Smith and Yolande Wrigley enter a crowded market (there are some twenty versions now before the public) but their choice of couplings is distinctly enterprising and exploratory. There is no alternative version of the Dohnányi and the Bridge is not generously represented on CD either. Even disregarding the question of couplings their account of the *Sonata* is highly competitive. They play with great refinement and authority, as well as much sensitivity. They are perhaps too closely balanced but this does not prevent their record being a highly desirable one.

In the *Cello sonata*, Turovsky gives a well-delineated, powerful account, with Luba Edlina, less reticent, perhaps – and, some might feel, less refined in feeling – than some of the great performances of the past. In the *Violin sonata*, Rostislav Dubinsky and Luba Edlina (his wife) are in excellent form, though this is red-blooded Slavonic Debussy rather than the more ethereal, subtle playing of a Grumiaux.

Steven Isserlis and Pascal Devoyon make a well matched partnership, though the latter is ill-served by the engineers. His piano entry sounds pretty thunderous, though both these fine players are exposed to rather too close a scrutiny. Isserlis brings great intensity to the middle movement, and there are many things to admire throughout this extraordinarily concentrated masterpiece, but this is not a first recommendation.

(i) *Cello sonata in D min.;* (ii; iii) *Sonata for flute, viola and harp;* (iv) *Violin sonata in G min.;* (ii) *Syrinx.*
(M) *** Ph. 422 839-2. (i) Gendron, Françaix; (ii) Bourdin; (iii) Lequien, Challan; (iv) Grumiaux, Hajdu.

Though these excellent performances on Philips do not wholly dislodge others from one's affections, for example Rostropovich's account of the *Cello sonata* or Chung's version of the *Violin sonata* on Decca, they are very nearly as fine. Gendron's version of the *Cello sonata* is most eloquent and is splendidly recorded.

Sonata for flute, viola and harp.
*** Koch Dig. 3-7016-2 [id.]. Atlantic Sinf. – JOLIVET: *Chant de Linos;* JONGEN: *Concert.* ***

The three members of the Atlantic Sinfonietta (Bradley Garner, Lois Martin and Gillian Benet) are well balanced and achieve a feeling of repose and mystery. This is the best of the recent recordings of this enormously civilized and ethereal music and comes with a multi-composer coupling, of which the Jongen is an amiable rather than an outstanding piece.

Piano trio in G.
(M) *** Pickwick Dig. MCD 41; *MCC 41* [id.]. Solomon Trio – FAURÉ; RAVEL: *Piano trios.* ***
**(*) Denon Dig. CO 72508 [id.]. Rouvier, Kantorow, Müller – FAURÉ; RAVEL: *Trios.* **(*)
** Chan. Dig. CHAN 9016 [id.]. Borodin Trio – MARTIN; TURINA: *Piano trios.* **

The *G major Trio* was written in 1879, when Debussy was staying with Madame von Meck and playing piano duets with her. His *Trio* undoubtedly shows more promise than fulfilment and is almost entirely uncharacteristic. Since its publication in 1985, it has attracted a half-dozen or so recordings. Lionel Friend, Yonty Solomon and Timothy Hugh give as good an account as any on Pickwick and are very well recorded indeed. They play with considerable finesse and sensitivity, and persuade the listener that this piece is stronger than in fact it is.

Jean-Jacques Kantorow, Philippe Müller and Jacques Rouvier are an accomplished ensemble and give a persuasive account of the piece; they are excellently recorded.

There is nothing wrong with the Borodin Trio's account on Chandos, though these artists are often disinclined to allow the music to speak for itself but coat every phrase with an expressive overlay that at times gets in the way of purity of expression. However theirs is is an agreeable performance which can be recommended if the couplings meet your requirements.

String quartet in G min.
(M) *** Ph. 420 894-2 [id.]. Italian Qt – RAVEL: *Quartet.* ***

(M) *** DG 435 589-2 [id.]. LaSalle Qt – RAVEL: *Quartet.* ***
(BB) **(*) Naxos Dig. 8.550249 [id.]. Kodály Qt – RAVEL: *Quartet* etc. ***
(B) **(*) Hung. White Label HRC 122 [id.]. Bartók Qt – RAVEL: *Quartet* **(*); DVOŘÁK: *Quartet No. 12.* ***
**(*) Denon Dig. C37 7830 [id.]. Nuovo Qt – RAVEL: *Quartet.* **(*)
(BB) **(*) Virgin Dig. VJ7 91569-2 [id.]. Borodin Qt – RAVEL: *Quartet.* **
(M) **(*) Pickwick Dig. MCD 17; *MCC 17.* New World Qt – RAVEL: *Quartet* **(*); DUTILLEUX: *Ainsi la nuit.* ***
** Decca Dig. 430 434-2 [id.]. Ysaÿe Qt – RAVEL: *Quartet.* **

It need hardly be said that the playing of the Italian Quartet is outstanding. Perfectly judged ensemble, weight and tone make this a most satisfying choice, and the recording engineers have produced a vivid and truthful sound-picture, with plenty of impact.

Expert playing, too, on DG by the fine LaSalle Quartet on top form. Their reading takes a place of honour alongside – but not in preference to – the fine account by the Italian Quartet. The 1971 recording was of high quality and the CD transfer in no way degrades its natural balance.

As we know from their Haydn recordings, the Kodály Quartet are an excellent ensemble and they give a thoroughly enjoyable account that can be recommended to those who do not want to spend that bit extra on the mid-priced Quartetto Italiano version. There are moments here (in the slow movement, for example) when the Kodály, too, are touched by distinction. This music-making has the feel of a live performance and is to be preferred to some of the glossier, mechanized accounts at full price: these players also have the benefit of a generous fill-up and very good recorded sound. Excellent value.

The account by the Bartók Quartet is full of character, and the *Andante* is certainly *doucement expressif.* The recording is good, too, and well balanced; with three quartets on offer, this record is a genuine bargain.

The Nuovo Quartet are very musical and there is a natural, unforced quality about their playing that is likeable. There are some moments of affectation and they pull the development section of the first movement around. The scherzo is marvellously delicate and a delight – and their slow movement, too, is appropriately thoughtful and inward-looking. They blend very beautifully and the recording is well focused in an acoustic that has warmth and space. This can be recommended to those seeking a digital version of this coupling.

If one is talking just about perfection of ensemble, purity of intonation and tonal blend, the Borodins' account has to be a three-star recommendation. The opening of the scherzo is quite breathtaking in its body and sheer technical perfection. However, their reading is at times over-sophisticated, with some expressive slides from the leader which will not enjoy universal appeal and a slowing-up for the second group in the first movement. Recording quality is superb, and readers should undoubtedly try to hear this – but the Italians allow the music to speak for itself.

The New World Quartet is Harvard-based and their playing gives undoubted pleasure. The Debussy is very well played but a bit overprojected. The expressive rubato of the leader may pose problems for those with austere tastes. However, most rivals offer only the Ravel *Quartet* whereas these artists add an interesting Dutilleux piece. They are very well recorded.

The Ysaÿe Quartet are musicianly and sensitive players who are all Paris Conservatoire-trained. Their performance has much going for it, for they have excellent rapport and a finely blended corporate tone. Ultimately, however, they do not challenge the very first recommendations in the Debussy in terms of characterization. Unusually for the Decca engineers, the microphones bring us really too close to them for comfort and perhaps to do them the fullest justice.

Violin sonata in G min.
***DG Dig. 415 683-2 [id.]. Shlomo Mintz, Yefim Bronfman – FRANCK; RAVEL: *Sonatas.* ***
*** Collins Dig. 1112-2; *1112-4* [id.]. Lorraine McAslan, John Blakely – RAVEL; SAINT-SAËNS: *Sonatas.* ***
** Virgin Dig. VC 790760-2 [id.]. Dmitry Sitkovetsky, Pavel Gililov – JANÁČEK; R. STRAUSS: *Violin sonatas.* ***

Violin sonata in G min.; Prélude (La fille aux cheveux de lin) arr. Arthur Hartmann.
(M) (**) BMG/RCA mono GD 87871; *GK 87871* [7871-2-RG; *7871-4-RG*]. Heifetz, Bay – MARTINŮ: *Duo* ***; RAVEL: *Trio* etc. (**); RESPIGHI: *Sonata.* (***)

(i) *Violin sonata in G min.;* (ii) *Sonata for flute, viola and harp.*
❀ (M) *** Decca 421 154-2; *421 154-4.* (i) Kyung Wha Chung, Radu Lupu; (ii) Melos Ens. (members) – FRANCK: *Violin sonata;* RAVEL: *Introduction and allegro.* *** ❀

Kyung Wha Chung and Radu Lupu are superbly balanced and most truthfully recorded. Miss Chung plays with marvellous character and penetration, and her partnership with Radu Lupu could hardly be more fruitful. Nothing is pushed to extremes, and everything is in perfect perspective so far as both the playing and the recording are concerned. The *Sonata for flute, viola and harp* and the Ravel *Introduction and allegro* come from a famous Oiseau-Lyre record made in 1962. In both works the playing is wonderfully sensitive and the music's ethereal atmosphere well caught. The recording sounds admirably real.

Shlomo Mintz and Yefim Bronfman give a performance that is difficult to fault and gives much pleasure. They can be recommended alongside – though not in preference to – Chung and Lupu. This is undoubtedly a magnificent account and excellently recorded, too.

Lorraine McAslan gives a very fine account of the Debussy *Sonata*, perhaps not quite as outstanding as the Ravel, where she could well be a first choice, but impressive enough in all conscience. She is well partnered by John Blakely, and the recording is very good indeed, well balanced and truthful.

Dmitry Sitkovetsky and Pavel Gililov are much stronger in the Janáček and Strauss *Sonatas* than they are in the Debussy. They give a responsive performance, but there is a change of perspective which finds the balance favouring the piano, with the result that Sitkovetsky seems all too reticent. Nor do these artists seem to have the same natural feeling for this repertoire that they have for Janáček.

Heifetz's immaculately played account of the *Violin sonata* was recorded in the 1950s and, although the golden tone is glorious, allowances have to be made for the dryish piano timbre – though not, of course, for Emanuel Bay's playing.

MUSIC FOR TWO PIANOS

Danses sacrée et profane; En blanc et noir; Lindaraja; Nocturnes (trans. Ravel); *Prélude à l'après-midi d'un faune.*
*** Hyp. Dig. CDA 66468 [id.]. Stephen Coombs and Christopher Scott.

Stephen Coombs and Christopher Scott made an outstanding début with this fine recording, which leads the field in this repertoire. It now reappears on Hyperion, who seem to have taken over recordings made on the LDR label.

(i) *En blanc et noir* (for 2 pianos); *Petite suite* (for piano, 4 hands). (ii) 2 *Arabesques; Berceuse héroïque; Children's corner; Danse bohémienne; Estampes; Hommage à Haydn; Masques; Mazurka; Le petit nègre; Pour le piano; Rêverie; Suite bergamasque; Valse romantique.*
(B) *** Turnabout 0004 (2). (i) Walter & Beatriz Klien; (ii) Peter Frankl – FAURÉ: *Dolly.* ***

En blanc et noir is a masterpiece and its comparative neglect is unaccountable, while the *Petite suite* is just as charming in its four-handed piano version as it is in full orchestral dress. The playing here from the Klien duo is sensitive and the recording good. The rest of the programme comes from Peter Frankl, who is an eminently stylish Debussy player and is also well recorded. Readers need feel no hesitation in investing in this collection with its appealing Fauré bonus. However, it is a matter for regret that the documentation lists the works played and nothing more.

SOLO PIANO MUSIC

2 Arabesques; Images oubliées; Préludes, Book 1.
*** ASV Dig. CDDCA 720; *ZCDCA 720* [id.]. Gordon Fergus-Thompson.

Ballade; Berceuse héroïque; Danse; Danse bohémienne; D'un cahier d'esquisses; Élégie; Hommage à Haydn; L'isle joyeuse; Masques; Mazurka; Morceau de concours; Nocturne; Page d'album; Le petit nègre; La plus que lente; Valse romantique.
*** ASV Dig. CDDCA 711; *ZCDCA 711* [id.]. Gordon Fergus-Thompson.

Children's corner; Estampes; Images, I & II.
*** ASV Dig. CDDCA 695; *ZCDCA 695* [id.]. Gordon Fergus-Thompson.

Études, Books 1–2; Pour le piano.
*** ASV Dig. CDDCA 703; *ZCDCA 703* [id.]. Gordon Fergus-Thompson.

Préludes. Book 2; Suite bergamasque.
*** ASV Dig. CDDCA 723; *ZCDCA 723* [id.]. Gordon Fergus-Thompson.

Gordon Fergus-Thompson's set of the Debussy *Études* is altogether excellent, both artistically and so far as recording is concerned and, purely on its own merits, can be recommended. It also includes *Pour le piano*, whereas the Uchida CD is uncoupled. However, Lívia Rév's Saga record is even more generous. As far as the remainder of Fergus-Thompson's survey is concerned, he maintains a consistently high standard of artistry. If one places his sets of *Préludes* alongside recordings by Arrau or Gieseking, then they are clearly less individually distinctive, but overall this playing shows a genuine feeling for the Debussy palette and, with fine, modern, digital sound, these records will give considerable satisfaction. The collection of shorter pieces is particularly successful.

2 Arabesques; Berceuse héroïque; D'un cahier d'esquisses; Élégie; L'isle joyeuse; Masques; Nocturne; Pour le piano; Suite bergamasque; Tarentelle styrienne.
** EMI Dig. CDC7 54451-2 [id.]. Aldo Ciccolini.

Ballade; Estampes; Images I & II; Images oubliées; Rêverie; Valse romantique.
** EMI Dig. CDC7 54447-2 [id.]. Aldo Ciccolini.

Children's corner; Études, Books I–II; Étude retrouvée.
**EMI Dig. CDC7 54450-2 [id.]. Aldo Ciccolini.

Préludes, Book 1; La boîte à joujoux.
** EMI Dig. CDC7 54448-2 [id.]. Aldo Ciccolini.

Préludes, Book 2; Danse bohémienne; 6 Épigraphes antiques; Hommage à Haydn; La plus que lente; Le petit nègre; Mazurka; Morceau de concours; Page d'album.
** EMI Dig. CDC7 54449-2 [id.]. Aldo Ciccolini.

As we go to press EMI have issued the complete piano music on five well-filled CDs from the Italian-born pianist, Aldo Ciccolini, who has lived in France since the late 1940s, and has delighted collectors with, among other things, the Satie piano music and the concertos of Saint-Saëns (the latter, alas, now withdrawn). His Debussy was greeted with rapturous acclaim by a critic of *The Times* of London, and there is no doubting both his sensitivity to colour and his refinement of keyboard control. However, our admiration for his artistry can not be unqualified. *Pagodes* and *Poissons d'or* are beautifully shaded and full of atmosphere, but in other pieces – the first movement of the *Images oubliées*, for example – there is too little poetry. (Compare Zoltan Kocsis's beautiful account on Philips.) The opening of the *Suite bergamasque* is less sensitive than it might be, and there are other moments where one feels the need for fresher responses and pianistic finesse. In the *Images*, for all their felicities, he does not really offer a serious challenge to Arrau or Egourov, nor in the *Études* and *Préludes* to Arrau and Lívia Rév, both of whom are recorded much more sympathetically. Indeed reservations about the recorded sound must be registered. The acoustic, that of the Salle de Musique of La Chaux-de-Fonds in Switzerland, is resonant but the balance is curious. In *Pagodes*, for instance, the middle range of the instrument is both close and dryish and the sound lacks real transparency. There are undoubted felicities and insights, as one would expect from this distinguished artist, but, generally speaking, none of these discs would be a first choice.

2 Arabesques; Ballade; Danse bohémienne; Images I–II; Images (1894); Mazurka; Nocturne.
(M) *** Saga SCD 9020. Lívia Rév.

For a long time Lívia Rév was underrated as a pianist; it was these Debussy recordings which established her reputation, receiving wide and just acclaim when they first appeared on LP. This compilation (77 minutes 38 seconds) can hold its own with any in the catalogue. Lívia Rév has sensibility, a finely developed sense of colour, a keen awareness of atmosphere and fleet fingers. She is moreover decently recorded in a spacious acoustic, and the CD transfers are extremely successful.

2 Arabesques; Ballade; Images, Book 1; L'isle joyeuse; La plus que lente; Rêverie; Suite bergamasque.
*** Conifer Dig. CDCF 148; *MCFC 148* [id.]. Kathryn Stott.

After her extremely successful Fauré disc, Kathryn Stott repeats the formula with Debussy, assembling an admirable recital which spans Debussy's composing career from the *Deux*

Arabesques of 1888, through to *La plus que lente* (1910). She is unerringly sensitive to atmosphere, there is no lack of finesse and her impetuosity always sounds spontaneous. This is a very refreshing programme, given excellent realism and presence.

2 Arabesques; Ballade; Images, Book 1: Reflets dans l'eau; Mouvement. Book 2: Poissons d'or. L'isle joyeuse; Préludes, Book 2: Feux d'artifice. Suite bergamasque.
(M) *** EMI CD-EMX 2055-2; *TC-EMX 2055*. Daniel Adni.

This collection dates from 1972 and was a follow-up to a similarly successful Chopin recital which had served as Daniel Adni's gramophone début the previous year and was equally well recorded. It is outstanding in every way: this young Israeli pianist proves himself a Debussian of no mean order. His recital is well planned and offers playing that is as poetic in feeling as it is accomplished in technique.

2 Arabesques; Berceuse héroïque; D'un cahier d'esquisses; Hommage à Haydn; Images Books 1 & 2; L'isle joyeuse; Page d'album; Rêverie.
❀ *** Ph. Dig. 422 404-2 Zoltán Kocsis.

Zoltán Kocsis's Debussy recital is quite outstanding. The recording of the piano is among the most realistic we have heard. Artistically, this new recital is if anything even more distinguished in terms of pianistic finesse, sensitivity and tonal refinement than his earlier, 1983 Debussy collection – see below.

2 Arabesques; Children's corner; Images I and II; Suite bergamasque.
(M) *** Decca 417 792-2. Pascal Rogé.

Pascal Rogé's playing is distinguished by a keen musical intelligence and sympathy, as well as by a subtle command of keyboard colour. Apart from the *Images* with their finesse and highly accomplished pianism, the *Suite bergamasque* is particularly successful, with genuine poetry in the famous *Clair de lune*. The well-defined Decca sound is most realistic. The quality is eminently secure and the bottom end of the piano reproduces in a most lifelike fashion.

2 Arabesques; L'isle joyeuse; Masques; La plus que lente; Pour le piano; Suite bergamasque; Tarantelle styrienne (Danse).
(B) *** DG 429 517-2 [id.]. Tamás Vásáry.

Vásáry is at his very best in the *Suite bergamasque*, and *Clair de lune* is beautifully played, as are the *Arabesques*. *La plus que lente* receives the least convincing performance. Here Vásáry's rubato sounds slightly unspontaneous. But overall this is a satisfying recital and makes an excellent bargain, particularly as the piano is so realistic.

Berceuse héroïque; Children's corner suite; Danse; D'un cahier d'esquisses; Mazurka; Morceau de concours; Nocturne; Le petit nègre; La plus que lente; Rêverie.
*** Denon Dig. C37 7372 [id.]. Jacques Rouvier.

An enjoyable and interesting Debussy recital from Jacques Rouvier, which has the advantage of very truthful recording. This serves as a very useful addition to the catalogue and can be thoroughly recommended.

Berceuse héroïque; Études, Books 1–2; Morceau de concours; Suite bergamasque.
(M) *** Saga SCD 9027. Lívia Rév.

The *Études* are not represented as generously in the catalogue as the *Préludes* or *Images*, so these fine performances are doubly welcome. Lívia Rév is consistently imaginative and her playing has considerable poetic feeling, as well as great technical accomplishment. The *Suite bergamasque* is also highly sensitive. The 1980 recording is excellent and the disc offers 75 minutes of music.

Children's corner; Élégie; Hommage à Haydn; Page d'album; Préludes, Book 1; La plus que lente; Tarantelle styrienne (Danse).
(M) *** Saga SCD 9021. Lívia Rév.

Lívia Rév plays *Children's corner* very well, though without quite the elegance we find in Pascal Rogé's Decca recital. But her performance of the *Préludes* holds its own in terms of sensitivity and atmosphere. Her keyboard mastery is beyond question (just sample *La cathédrale engloutie*) and she is a fine colourist. The recording, too, is first class, full and natural, and admirably transferred to CD. Moreover the playing time of this programme is over 71 minutes.

Children's corner; Images, Sets 1 & 2.
*** DG 414 372-2 [id.]. Michelangeli.

Michelangeli is outstanding in this repertoire. It is a magical and beautifully recorded disc. Michelangeli has made few records, but this is one of his best. It is also among the most distinguished Debussy playing in the catalogue. The remastering of the 1971 recording has been wonderfully successful.

Estampes; Images I & II; Images oubliées (1894); Pour le piano.
*** Denon Dig. CD 1411 [id.]. Jacques Rouvier.

Jacques Rouvier is very well recorded; there is plenty of atmosphere and space round the sound. His account of the *Cloche à travers les feuilles* has great poise and *Et la lune descend sur le temple qui fut* has wonderful atmosphere and repose. In the *Images oubliées* he is not quite as imaginative (or as outstandingly recorded) as Zoltán Kocsis on Philips, but all the same this is an impressive issue.

Estampes; Images, Books 1–2; Préludes, Books 1–2.
(M) *** Ph. 432 304-2 (2) [id.]. Claudio Arrau.

Claudio Arrau's versions of these solo piano works by Debussy, praised by us in the past in their full-price format, have been re-released by Philips at mid-price as part of their Arrau Edition, commemorating the death of the great pianist. The piano timbre in these 1978/9 analogue recordings has a consistent body and realism typical of this company's finest work.

Estampes: La soirée dans Grenade; Jardins sous la pluie. Étude No. 5 pour les octaves. Images, Book 1: Reflets dans l'eau. Préludes, Book 2: La terrasse des audiences du clair de lune; Feux d'artifice.
(M) ** BMG/RCA GD 60415; *GK 60445* [60415-2-RG; *60415-4-RG*]. Van Cliburn – BARBER: *Sonata* **(*); MOZART: *Sonata No. 10.* **

Van Cliburn shows that he is no mean interpreter of Debussy in these sensitive performances, but he is handicapped a little by the lustreless recording. Nevertheless the disc is well worth having for the Barber *Sonata*.

Études, Books 1–2.
❀ *** Ph. Dig. 422 412-2 [id.]. Mitsuko Uchida.

Mitsuko Uchida's remarkable account of the *Études* on Philips is not only one of the best Debussy piano records in the catalogue and arguably her finest recording, but also one of the best ever recordings of the instrument.

Préludes, Books 1–2 (complete).
❀ (M) *** EMI mono CDH7 61004-2 [id.]. Walter Gieseking.
(M) *** Pickwick Dig. MCD 16; *MCC 16*. Martino Tirimo.
(M) (**(*)) Sony mono MPK 45688 [id.]. Robert Casadesus.

In his day, Walter Gieseking was something of a legend as a Debussy interpreter, and this excellent CD transfer testifies to his magic. Background is almost vanquished; our copy produced some very slight noise near the opening, but for the most part this is simply not a problem. Gieseking penetrates the atmosphere of the *Préludes* more deeply than almost any other artist. This is playing of rare distinction and great evocative quality. However, the documentation is concerned solely with the artist and gives no information about the music save the titles and the cues.

No grumbles about value for money or about quality from Martino Tirimo on Pickwick; he accommodates both Books on the same disc. His playing is very fine indeed and can withstand comparison with most of his rivals – and, apart from the sensitivity of the playing, the recording is most realistic and natural. This is first choice for those wanting a modern digital record offering the complete set.

Robert Casadesus's accounts of the *Préludes* are (like Gieseking's before him) legendary. His recordings were made in 1953/4 and the piano sound is faithful, though the second book has a warmer, fuller piano image. The performances of Book 2 show the pianist at his very finest: *Brouillards* and *Feuilles mortes*, for instance, are superbly atmospheric and *Feux d'artifice* glitters with fiery brilliance. At times in Book 1 he is a trifle cool. Nevertheless this is all distinguished playing.

Jacques Rouvier's separate Denon records of Book 1 (C37 7121) and Book 2 (C37 7043), for all their atmosphere and elegance, now seem uncompetitive, while Michelangeli's account of Book 1 (DG 413 450-2), cool and aloof, if distinctive, is also overpriced.

Préludes, Book 2; Images, Set 2; Masques.
**(*) Hyp. Dig. CDA 66487 [id.]. Lívia Rév.

Lívia Rév's new accounts for Hyperion do not banish memories of her fine survey of the 1970s on Saga. Atmosphere is of the essence in this repertoire and there is no lack of that in these performances. She produces sonorities of unfailing refinement but the microphones observe her too closely, and some of the mystery this music evokes is lost. A lower level setting helps but generally speaking despite the freshness of the new Hyperion recording, her earlier performances do possess just a greater sense of magic.

VOCAL MUSIC

Mélodies: (i) *Aimons-nous et dormons;* (ii) *Les Angelus;* (iii) *Ariettes oubliées;* (iv) *3 Ballades de François Villon; Beau soir;* (ii) *La Belle au Bois dormant;* (i) *Calmes dans le demi-jour;* (ii) *3 Chansons de Bilitis;* (iv) *Chanson de France;* (i) *4 Chansons de jeunesse;* (ii) *Les cloches;* (v) *Danse de jardin; L'échelonnement des haies; Fêtes galantes* (1st group); (iv) *Fêtes galantes* (2nd group); (v) *Fleur de blés;* (i) *Jane;* (iv) *Mandoline; La mer est plus belle;* (v) *Noël des enfants qui n'ont plus de maison; Nuit d'étoiles;* (i) *Paysage sentimental;* (ii) *5 Poèmes de Charles Baudelaire;* (v) *3 Poèmes de Stéphane Mallarmé;* (iv) *Le promenoir des deux amants;* (v) *4 Proses lyriques;* (i) *Romance; Rondeau; Rondel chinois;* (iv) *Le son du cor s'afflige;* (i) *Voici que le printemps; Zéphyr.*
(M) *** EMI CMS7 64095-2 (3). (i) Mady Mesplé; (ii) Michèle Command; (iii) Frederica von Stade; (iv) Gérard Souzay; (v) Elly Ameling; all with Dalton Baldwin.

These three generously filled discs at mid-price offer no fewer than 55 of Debussy's songs out of a total of just over 80. Drawn from recordings made between 1971 and 1979, they were all done in the Salle Wagram in Paris with Dalton Baldwin accompanying. Arranged in the order of publication, they give an illuminating idea of the composer's development, from his earliest Fauré-like songs, through his vital discovery of the poet Verlaine as his most consistent source of inspiration, and on to the rarefied atmosphere of the late songs such as the Villon and Mallarmé settings. Charmingly, he followed those last two groups with a little simple song to words he had composed himself, *Noël des enfants qui n'ont plus de maison*, written in 1915 as a heartfelt response to the First World War. Though Mady Mesplé's bright soprano has a flutter in it as recorded, hers is the smallest contribution, and all the others are in splendid voice, with Michèle Command characterfully French and Gérard Souzay at his freshest. The most ravishing singing of all comes from Elly Ameling and Frederica von Stade. The latter sings ecstatically in Debussy's evocative setting of Verlaine's most famous poem, *Il pleure dans mon coeur* (from the *Ariettes oublieées*), with Baldwin bringing out the subtlety of the pattering accompaniment. Well-balanced, clear sound. The booklet provides an essay in English and French, with full texts in French only.

Mélodies: *Beau soir; 3 Chansons de Bilitis; 3 Chansons de France; Les cloches; Fêtes galantes* (2nd group); *Mandoline.*
*** Unicorn DKPCD 9035; *DKPC 9035* [id.]. Sarah Walker, Roger Vignoles – ENESCU: *Chansons* ***; ROUSSEL: *Mélodies.* **(*)

Sarah Walker's Debussy collection makes an outstandingly fine disc of French songs. With deeply sympathetic accompaniment from Roger Vignoles, Sarah Walker's positive and characterful personality comes over vividly, well tuned to the often elusive idiom. Excellent recording in a warm acoustic.

OPERA

Pelléas et Mélisande (complete).
*** DG Dig. 435 344-2 (2) [id.]. Ewing, Le Roux, Van Dam, Courtis, Ludwig, Pace, Mazzola, Vienna Konzertvereingung, VPO, Abbado.
*** Decca Dig. 430 502-2 (2) [id.]. Alliot-Lugaz, Henry, Cachemaille, Thau, Carlson, Golfier, Montreal Ch. & SO, Dutoit.
(M) **(*) Sony SM3K 47265 (3) [id.]. Shirley, Söderström, McIntyre, Ward, Minton, ROHCG Ch. & O, Boulez.

Abbado's outstanding version broadly resolves the problem of a first recommendation in this opera, which has always been lucky on record. If among modern versions the choice has been hard to make between Karajan's sumptuously romantic account, almost Wagnerian, and Dutoit's clean-cut, direct one, Abbado satisfyingly presents a performance more sharply focused than the one and more freely flexible than the other, altogether more urgently dramatic. Hearing Abbado, one registers the developments in the dream-like story more involvingly, and the beauty of the playing of the Vienna Philharmonic outshines even that of Karajan's Berlin Philharmonic, making it one of the most seductive of all Debussy recordings. The casting is excellent, with no weak link. Francois Le Roux as Pelléas sounds younger and more ardent than his rivals, and Maria Ewing makes a fresh, bright-eyed Mélisande, responding girlishly, far more than a wilting medieval heroine. José van Dam – Golaud also for Karajan – repeats his biting yet beautifully sung portrait of this far-from-villainous character. Philippe Courtis is a firm, dark Arkel, and Christa Ludwig a strongly characterful Geneviève, with Patricia Pace convincingly childlike as Yniold. Like the Dutoit version the DG one comes on two discs instead of three, with a better break point in Act 3 between the discs, when Pelléas and Golaud emerge from the cavern into the open air.

In the first complete opera recording made in the warm ambience of St Eustache, Charles Dutoit brings out the magic of Debussy's score with an involving richness typical of that venue which has played so important a part in the emergence of the Montreal orchestra into the world of international recording. This is not the dreamy reading which some Debussians might prefer, but one which sets the characters very specifically before us as creatures of flesh and blood, not mistily at one remove. The first inspiration was to choose Colette Alliot-Lugaz as Mélisande, already well known from her commanding performances in Lyon Opera recordings, notably under John Eliot Gardiner. She presents, not the fey, elfin figure often portrayed, but a bright, characterful heroine, full of girlish fun. With Dutoit choosing his singers most carefully, much is gained from having an entirely French-speaking cast, with Alliot-Lugaz well matched by Didier Henry as Pelléas, light and young-sounding. Gilles Cachemaille, strong and incisive, is young-sounding too as Golaud, not as sinister or sumptuous-toned as some but much more a potential lover, no mere villain.

Boulez's sharply dramatic view of Debussy's atmospheric score is a performance which will probably not please the dedicated Francophile – for one thing there is not a single French-born singer in the cast – but it rescues Debussy from the languid half-tone approach which for too long has been accepted as authentic. Boulez's attitude may initially stem from a searching analysis of the musical structure – Debussy anticipating today's avant garde in so many ways – but the dramatic element has been focused more sharply too, for he sees the characters as flesh and blood, no mere wayward shadows. He is supported by a strong cast; the singing is not always very idiomatic but it has the musical and dramatic momentum which stems from sustained experience on the stage. In almost every way this has the tension of a live performance. The recording, made at EMI's Abbey Road Studios in December 1969 and January 1970, does not allow a true pianissimo, but it is still both vivid and atmospheric; indeed the balance is theatrically more convincing on CD than it was on LP. There is a well-produced booklet with full translation.

Delalande, Michel-Richard (1657–1726)

Symphonies pour les soupers du roy (complete).
*** HM Dig. HMC 901337/40; *HMC 401337/40* (4) [id.]. Ensemble La Simphonie du Marais, Reyne.

Immediately after the war Oiseau Lyre Editions published two 78-r.p.m. records of the *Symphonies pour les soupers du roy* (which RL still has), by the eponymous Oiseau Lyre Ensemble under Roger Désormière. At that time the composer was generally known as Lalande; less well known was the sheer extent of the music he composed for Louis XIV's nocturnal repasts (he ate at ten o'clock in the evening) or the fact that they occupied him over so long a period. The first ten suites took the composer as many years (the 1690s in fact), and in 1713 two more suites were added. Hence in the last years of his life the Sun King could choose from among a dozen suites to accompany his meal. This is the first time all have been committed to disc. Each of these four CDs contains between 36 and 45 individual movements, much of it as charming and inventive as the familiar excerpts. The young members of the Ensemble La Simphonie du Marais, led by Hugo Reyne, give thoroughly fresh and stylish accounts of them. It should naturally be heard with a volume of Elizabeth David or some other appropriate collection of recipes to hand.

Confitebor tibi Domine; Super flumina Babilonis; Te Deum.
*** HM Dig. HMC 901351; *HMC 401351* [id.]. Gens, Piau, Steyer, Fouchécourt, Piolino, Corréas, Les Arts Florissants, Christie.

In all, Delalande was the pre-eminent court musician under Louis XIV and Louis XV and, apart from his celebrated *Symphonies pour les soupers du roy*, he composed no fewer than 75 motets. He brought the French baroque motet to its height. He composed the bulk of them before 1710, spending the last years of his life in revising his earlier music. As he developed it, the motet falls into several sections with contrasting solo and ensemble voices and instruments, and the larger, *grand motet* of his mature years can be in as many as 15 sections. The two motets are recorded here in their original form. *Confitebor tibi Domine* (1699) and *Super flumina Babilonis* (1687) have much expressive writing, and the performances under William Christie are light and airy but not wanting in expressive feeling. At times he is too brisk, as in the final chorus of *Super flumina Babilonis*, where the words are 'O miserable daughter of Babylon! Happy shall he be that taketh and dasheth thy little ones against the stones', which he dispatches in very cavalier fashion. The more familiar *Te Deum* is given as good a performance as any that has appeared in recent years. The sound is airy and spacious and the performances combine lightness and breadth.

Delibes, Léo (1836–91)

Coppélia (ballet): complete.
*** Decca Dig. 414 502-2 (2) [id.]. Nat. PO, Bonynge.
(M) *** Decca 425 472-2 (2). SRO, Richard Bonynge – MASSENET: *Le Carillon.* ***

Bonynge's digital recording of Delibes' sparkling and tuneful complete ballet was made with the National Philharmonic with its personnel of expert British sessions musicians, who bring a polished and spirited ensemble, with the wind solos a constant delight. The only slight drawback is the relatively modest number of violins, which the clarity of the digital recording makes apparent. In moments like the delicious *Scène et valse de la poupée*, which Bonynge points very stylishly, the effect is Mozartian in its grace. But the full body of strings above the stave lacks something in amplitude and the fortissimos bring a digital emphasis on brilliance that is not wholly natural. In all other respects the recording is praiseworthy, not only for its vividness of colour, but for the balance within a concert-hall acoustic (Walthamstow Assembly Hall).

Bonynge secures a high degree of polish from the Swiss Romande Orchestra, with sparkling string and wind textures and sonority and bite from the brass. The Decca recording sounds freshly minted and, with its generous Massenet bonus, little-known music of great charm, this set remains very competitive.

Coppélia: extended excerpts; *Sylvia:* extended excerpts.
(B) *** EMI CZS7 67208-2 (2); *EG 764265-4*. Paris Op. O, Mari.

The complete recordings Jean-Baptiste Mari made of Delibes's *Coppélia* and *Sylvia* ballets in 1977 with the Paris Opéra Orchestra have never been surpassed; it is a pity that (although the complete set of *Coppélia* is available on tape in a chunky, bargain-priced CfP box – TC-CFPD 4712) EMI have chosen to issue only excerpts on CD, rather than pair the complete sets. Having said that, one must also add that 75 minutes is offered from each and (especially in the case of *Sylvia*) virtually all the important music is included. Moreover the two discs are offered for the price of one in the French Rouge et Noir series. The CD transfers are well made, the sound is fresh and the extra brightness of focus brings no attendant edginess. If just a little of the allure of the very beautiful analogue LPs has been sacrificed, these CDs are still highly recommendable. Mari uses ballet tempi throughout, yet there is never any loss of momentum and the long-breathed string phrasing and the felicitous wind solos are a continual source of delight. The telling musical characterization, in *Coppélia* especially (which is the superior score), from the robust peasantry to the deliciously pointed *Music of the Automatons* is vividly memorable, and Mari's natural sympathy and warmth make the very most of the less memorable parts of the score for *Sylvia* (and they are only slightly less memorable). The cassette offers a shorter selection from each ballet but still plays for over 80 minutes.

Coppélia (ballet) suite: excerpts.
(B) *** DG 429 163-2. BPO, Karajan – CHOPIN: *Les Sylphides* *** ❀; OFFENBACH: *Gaîté parisienne.* ***

(i) *Coppélia* (ballet) suite; (ii) *Sylvia* (ballet) suite.
(M) *** Sony SBK 46550 [id.]. Phd. O, Ormandy – CHOPIN: *Les Sylphides* ***; TCHAIKOVSKY: *Nutcracker suite.* **(*)
(BB) *** LaserLight Dig. 15 616. (i) Berlin RSO, Fricke; (ii) Budapest PO, Sandor – GOUNOD: *Faust ballet.* ***

Ormandy and the Philadelphia Orchestra are on top form here. The playing sparkles and has a fine sense of style. Sylvia is particularly successful: the gusto of the opening and closing sections is infectious, with its life-assertive geniality; the more delicate numbers, including the famous *Pizzicato*, are played with affection and polish. The selection of items from *Coppélia* is generous, each strongly characterized. Both suites are done in a continuous presentation but are, unfortunately, not banded. The recording is notably full and brilliant in the CBS manner.

Although the playing of the (East German) Berlin Radio orchestra is not quite as cultured as that of the Berlin Philharmonic under Karajan, it is still very fine, and Fricke displays a lighter touch in the *Csárdás*. He also includes more music, both at the opening and in the delectable *Music of the Automatons*, one of Delibes' most piquant and memorable inspirations. The digital recording is first class, with sparkle and warmth and an attractively warm ambient effect. The Budapest performance of *Sylvia* is also graceful and vividly coloured, and the recording again is first rate. A genuine super-bargain.

Karajan secures some wonderfully elegant playing from the Berlin Philharmonic Orchestra, and generally his lightness of touch is sure. The *Csárdás*, however, is played very slowly and heavily, and its curiously studied tempo may spoil the performance for some. The recording is very impressive; but it is a pity that in assembling the CD the suite had to be truncated (with only 71 minutes' playing time, at least one more number could have been included). As it is, the *Scène et valse de la poupée*, *Ballade de l'épi* and the *Thème slav varié*, all present on the original analogue LP, are omitted here.

Coppélia: suite; *Kassya: Trepak; Le roi s'amuse:* suite; *La Source:* suite; *Sylvia:* suite.
(BB) **(*) Naxos Dig. 8.550080; *4550080* [id.]. Slovak RSO (Bratislava), Ondrej Lenárd.

An attractive hour of Delibes, with five key items from *Coppélia*, including the *Music for the Automatons* and *Waltz*, four from *Sylvia*, not forgetting the *Pizzicato*, and four from *La Source*. Perhaps most enjoyable of all are the six pastiche ancient airs de danse, provided for a ballroom scene in Victor Hugo's play, *Le roi s'amuse*. They are played most gracefully here, and the excerpts from the major ballets are spirited and nicely turned. The brightly lit digital sound has body too, and the acoustics of the Bratislava Concert Hall are not unflattering to Delibes's vivid palette.

La Source (ballet): Act II; Act III, scene i.
*** Decca Dig. 421 431-2 (2). ROHCG O, Bonynge – MINKUS: *La Source* (Act I; Act III, scene ii); DRIGO: *La Flûte magique.* ***

It is not clear why the composition of the music for *La Source* was divided between two composers, the established Minkus and the younger Delibes who had not yet tried his hand in the field of ballet and for whom the commission was a godsend. He begins the Second Act in the elegantly lightweight style of his colleague, but soon his stronger musical personality asserts itself with a romantic horn tune and, later, an even more memorable melody in the strings. His felicitous use of the orchestral palette is readily discernible; but, even so, this is clearly a forerunner for *Coppélia* and *Sylvia* from a composer whose style is not yet fully individualized. However, the ballet was to become a success and establish Delibes' reputation in the field, for Minkus returned to Russia and left the French composer in charge. Bonynge makes the music sparkle throughout, and the warm yet vivid sound is out of Decca's top drawer.

Sylvia (ballet): complete.
(M) *** Decca 425 475-2 (2). New Philh. O, Richard Bonynge – MASSENET: *Le Cid.* ***

If the score for *Sylvia* does not quite brim over with hits in the way that *Coppélia* does, and some of the best tunes are presented more than once, it still contains much delightful music and characteristically felicitous scoring. It is played here with wonderful polish and affection, and the recording is full, brilliant and sparkling in Decca's best manner. The CDs offer a splendid Massenet bonus, another recording out of Decca's top drawer.

OPERA

Lakmé (complete).
(M) *** Decca 425 485-2 (2). Sutherland, Berbié, Vanzo, Bacquier, Monte Carlo Op. Ch. and O, Bonynge.

Lakmé is a strange work, not at all the piece one would expect knowing simply the famous *Bell song*. Predictably enough, at the beginning it has its measure of orientalism, but quickly comedy is introduced in the shape of Britons abroad, and Delibes presents it with wit and charm. This performance (with Monica Sinclair a gloriously outrageous Governess) seizes its opportunities with both hands, while the more serious passages are sung with a regard for beautiful vocal line that should convert anyone. Sutherland swallows her consonants, but the beauty of her singing, with its ravishing ease and purity up to the highest register, is what matters; and she has opposite her one of the most pleasing and intelligent of French tenors, Alain Vanzo. Excellent contributions from the others too, spirited conducting and brilliant, atmospheric recording. Highly recommended in this mid-price reissue which costs little more than the original LPs.

Delius, Frederick (1862–1934)

Air and dance; Fennimore and Gerda: Intermezzo; Hassan: Intermezzo and serenade; Koanga: La Calinda; On hearing the first cuckoo in spring; A Song before sunrise; Summer night on the river; A Village Romeo and Juliet: The Walk to the Paradise Garden.
(M) *** Decca 421 390-2; *421 390-4* [id.]. ASMF, Marriner.

These are lovely performances, warm, tender and eloquent. They are played superbly and recorded in a flattering acoustic. The recording is beautifully balanced – the distant cuckoo is highly evocative – though, with a relatively small band of strings, the sound inevitably has less body than with a full orchestral group.

Air and dance for string orchestra; On hearing the first cuckoo in spring; Summer evening; Summer night on the river.
*** Chan. CHAN 8330 [id.]. LPO, Handley – VAUGHAN WILLIAMS: *Serenade* etc. ***

Handley's refusal to sentimentalize – which can miss some of the more sweetly evocative qualities of the music – goes with the most subtle nuances in performance, fresh as well as beautiful and atmospheric. The tonal richness of the LPO's playing is well caught in the Chandos recording.

American rhapsody (Appalachia); Norwegian suite (Folkeraadet: The Council of the people); Paa Vidderne (On the heights); Spring morning.
** Marco Polo 8.220452 [id.]. Slovak PO, Bratislava, John Hopkins.

A fascinating collection of early Delius, mostly uncharacteristic, but with pre-echoes of his later work. *Paa Vidderne*, the most substantial piece, is rather melodramatic but has a distinct melodic interest. *Spring morning* is shorter and similarly picaresque, but the *Folkeraadet suite* displays a sure orchestral touch and is most attractive in its diversity of invention. The *American rhapsody* is a concise version of *Appalachia* without the chorus, given here in its original 1896 format. John Hopkins brings a strong sympathy and understanding to this repertoire and secures a committed and flexible response from his Czech players in music which must have been wholly unknown to them.

2 Aquarelles (arr. Fenby); *Fennimore and Gerda: Intermezzo. Hassan: Intermezzo and serenade* (all arr. Beecham); *Irmelin: Prelude. Late swallows* (arr. Fenby); *On hearing the first cuckoo in spring; A Song before sunrise; Summer night on the river.*
(M) *** Chan. CHAN 6502; *MBTD 6502* [id.]. Bournemouth Sinf., Norman Del Mar.

There are few finer interpreters of Delius today than Del Mar, once a protégé of Beecham; and this nicely balanced collection of miniatures, now reissued at mid-price, is among the most broadly recommendable of the Delius collections available. The 49-minute concert creates a mood of serene, atmospheric evocation – into which Eric Fenby's arrangement of *Late swallows* from the *String quartet* fits admirably – and the beauty of the 1977 analogue recording has been transferred very well to CD, with all its warmth and bloom retained.

2 Aquarelles; Fennimore and Gerda: Intermezzo. On hearing the first cuckoo in spring; Summer night on the river.
*** DG 419 748-2 [id.]. ECO, Barenboim – VAUGHAN WILLIAMS: *Lark ascending* etc.; WALTON: *Henry V*. ***

Barenboim's luxuriant performances have a gorgeous sensuousness and their warm, sleepy atmosphere should seduce many normally resistant to Delius's pastoralism. The couplings are no less enticing; indeed, some might feel that this music-making has a touch of decadence in its unalloyed appeal to the senses.

Brigg Fair; Dance rhapsody No. 2; Fennimore and Gerda: Intermezzo. Florida suite; Irmelin: Prelude. Marche-caprice; On hearing the first cuckoo in spring; Over the hills and far away; Sleigh ride; Song before sunrise; Summer evening; Summer night on the river; (i) *Songs of sunset.*
❀ *** EMI CDS7 47509-8 (2) [id.]. RPO, Beecham; (i) with Forrester, Cameron, Beecham Ch. Soc.

The remastering of the complete stereo orchestral recordings of Delius's music, plus the choral *Songs of sunset*, is something of a technological miracle, and it fully deserved *Gramophone* magazine's 1987 award for remastering 'historical' material. The result is far from historical in effect, for it brings Beecham's ravishing performances into our own time with an uncanny sense of realism and presence. Beecham's fine-spun magic, his ability to lift a phrase, is apparent throughout. The shorter pieces bring superb wind solos, while the great conductor often conjures a hazy sentient warmth from the strings which no other conductor has matched since. In the *Songs of sunset* the choral focus is soft-grained, but the words are surprisingly audible, and the backward balance of the soloists is made to sound natural against the rich orchestral textures. The CD documentation includes a booklet in which Lyndon Jenkins describes the relationship between the composer and his great interpreter. The gramophone here offers music-making which is every bit as rewarding as the finest live performances.

Brigg Fair; Eventyr; In a summer garden; A Song of summer.
(B) *** CfP CD-CFP 4568; *TC-CFP 4568*. Hallé O, Vernon Handley.

Although the tempi are sometimes controversial, Handley is an understanding and exciting Delian, and these pieces are beautifully played. The woodwind and horn solos in *Brigg Fair* are particularly delectable and the strings throughout make some lovely translucent sounds. The digital recording is of EMI's best quality, matching clarity of definition with ambient lustre and rich colouring. A bargain.

Cello concerto.
*** BMG/RCA RD 70800. Lloyd Webber, Philh. O, Handley – HOLST: *Invocation;* VAUGHAN WILLIAMS: *Fantasia.* ***

Lloyd Webber is inside the idiom and plays the *Cello concerto* with total conviction. Its lyricism is beguiling enough, but the work proceeds in wayward fashion, and the soloist must play every note as if he believes in it ardently – and this Lloyd Webber and his partners do. The RCA balance is ideal and conveys an almost chamber-like quality at times, with great warmth and clarity.

(i) *Cello concerto;* (ii) *Double concerto for violin and cello. Paris, the song of a great city.*
(M) *** EMI Dig. CD-EMX 2185; *TC-EMX 2185*. (i; ii) Rafael Wallfisch; (ii) Tasmin Little; RLPO, Mackerras.

This superb new recording of the *Double concerto*, with soloists who easily outshine their predecessors on record (however distinguished), confirms the strength of a piece which establishes its own logic, with each theme developing naturally out of the preceding one. Though the prevailing speed is leisurely, there is no sense of Delian meandering, with firm, square rhythms generally preferred to the composer's favourite triple or compound-time. The *Cello concerto* was Delius's own favourite among his concertos, another warmly persuasive piece, with a barcarolle-like theme at its heart. Wallfisch is just as persuasive here, and with the authority of Delius's helper and amanuensis, Eric Fenby, he and Mackerras have opted for an unusually fast tempo for the final *Allegramente* section based on a square folk-like melody. Sir Charles proves just as understanding an interpreter of the composer in the big tone-poem, *Paris, the song of a great city*. Though his speeds are relatively fast, he moulds them with unerring persuasiveness, consistently drawing warmly committed playing from the Liverpool orchestra. The recording is comparably full and atmospheric.

Piano concerto in C min.
(B) *** Decca 433 633-2; *433 633-4*. Kars, LSO, Gibson – ELGAR: *Cello concerto* etc. ***

Jean-Rodolphe Kars proves a superb and eloquent advocate of what has previously been thought of as one of Delius's weaker pieces. He plays with much refinement of touch and sensitivity and brings great artistry and imagination to his part. The lovely Grieg-like middle section is beautifully done and his playing has great taste. The LSO under Sir Alexander Gibson provides admirable support, and the 1969 recording preserves an excellent balance between the two. The piano is extremely well captured by the engineers, and the spaciously atmospheric sound-picture is in the best traditions of Decca.

Violin concerto; Légende for violin and orchestra; Suite for violin and orchestra.
*** Unicorn Dig. DKPCD 9040; *DKPC 9040* [id.]. Ralph Holmes, RPO, Handley.

Ralph Holmes gives a strong and beautiful performance of one of Delius's supreme masterpieces, the *Violin concerto*. Holmes and Handley, an ideal partnership, bring out the Delian warmth in their shaping of phrase and pointing of rhythm, while keeping firm control of the overall structure. The *Légende* – long forgotten in this orchestral form – and the early *Suite* make ideal couplings, played with equal understanding. Holmes's beautifully focused playing is nicely balanced, against the wide span of the orchestra behind him, in first-class digital recording.

(i) *Violin concerto. 2 Aquarelles* (arr. Fenby); *Dance rhapsodies 1 and 2; Intermezzo from Fennimore and Gerda; Irmelin prelude; On hearing the first cuckoo in spring; Summer night on the river.*
**(*) Decca Dig. 433 704-2 [id.]. (i) Tasmin Little; Welsh Nat. Op. O, Mackerras.

Tasmin Little in her own note on the Delius *Violin concerto* underlines a remark by the composer himself about 'the sense of flow'. Her superb performance certainly captures it wonderfully, though the bright, forward recording makes her tone sound rather less sweet than usual. Even so, her shading down to hushed pianissimos is ravishing, with the close of the work bringing a moment of total repose, while Mackerras draws strong, sympathetic playing from the orchestra of WNO. When – as Deryck Cooke demonstrated in a brilliant analysis and as the note explains – this is far from just a rhapsodic work, it is a pity that no one thought to mark the separate sections with CD tracks. It is less serious but still inconsiderate for the listener that the sections of the *Dance rhapsodies* are not demarcated either, works which similarly are far from rhapsodic and here receive fresh, taut performances. In the shorter works the woodwind soloists are outstanding, but the forwardness and clarity of the recording tend to make the results less evocative than they might be.

(i) Violin concerto; Dance rhapsody No. 1; (ii) *On the mountains. Song of the high hills.*
(M) (***) EMI mono CDM7 64054-2. (i) Pougnet; (ii) Hart, L. Jones, Luton Ch. Soc.; RPO, Beecham.

Glorious performances whose appearance in this splendidly transferred CD cannot be welcomed too warmly. Apart from the *Dance rhapsody*, which was made in 1952, the recordings all date from 1946 and relatively few allowances need be made for them. Despite the limited, close-focused mono sound, they perfectly capture the mystery of Delius in these evocative works, while conveying a purposeful sense of structure. Jean Pougnet is persuasively sweet-toned in the *Violin concerto* – with the sections marked by separate CD tracks – but it is the *Song of the high hills* that inspires Beecham to a classic performance, growing ever more sensuous in the final climactic section with wordless chorus, even though here the recording calls for more tolerance on sonic grounds than its companions. *On the Mountains* (*Paa vidderne*), another Norwegian inspiration, is a welcome rarity, an early work inspired by an Ibsen poem which dates from 1891. Though there are many authentic Delian fingerprints, it has an outward-going vigour not normally associated with the composer, and was rightly described by Beecham himself as 'an effective showpiece'.

(i) *Dance rhapsody No. 1; Eventyr;* (ii) *Life's dance; North Country sketches; A Song of summer.*
(M) **(*) EMI CDM7 63171-2. (i) RLPO; (ii) RPO, Sir Charles Groves.

This collection contains a virtually unknown piece, *Lebenstanz*, or *Life's dance*, which was written in the 1890s immediately before the tone-poem *Paris*. It presents a fascinating contrast, beginning with an urgency not always associated with this composer. *Song of summer*, a typically evocative piece, comes from the other end of Delius's career. The *North Country sketches*, depicting with Delian impressionism the seasons of the year, are equally welcome, as are the *Dance rhapsody* and *Eventyr.* Groves is a sensitive interpreter, even if he rarely matches the irresistible persuasiveness of a Beecham. The balance is vivid and warm, almost too close in sound to do justice to such delicately atmospheric music, and orchestral textures are not ideally transparent.

Eventyr; Fennimore and Gerda: Intermezzo. Irmelin: prelude. Over the hills and far away; Paris, the song of a great city.
(***) Beecham Trust mono BEECHAM 2. LPO, Sir Thomas Beecham.

These recordings date from between 1935 and 1939. The transfers from the original 78 r.p.m. discs were made by the highly skilled Anthony Griffiths, and the further remastering for CD seems to have been entirely beneficial.

Fennimore and Gerda: Intermezzo. Irmelin: Prelude. Koanga: La Calinda (arr. Fenby). *On hearing the first cuckoo in spring; Sleigh ride; A Song before sunrise; Summer night on the river; A Village Romeo and Juliet: The Walk to the Paradise Garden.*
(B) *** CfP CD-CFP 4304; *TC-CFP 4304.* LPO, Vernon Handley.

This is a successful anthology, with expansive and imaginative phrasing; the woodwind playing of the LPO is particularly fine. Those looking for a bargain collection of Delius should find this very good value, although Handley's approach to *The Walk to the Paradise Garden* is strongly emotional, closer to Barbirolli than to Beecham. The CD brings enhanced clarity, if with slightly less sumptuous violin timbre.

Florida suite; North Country sketches.
*** Chan. Dig. CHAN 8413; *ABTD 1150* [id.]. Ulster O, Handley.

Handley's choice of tempi is always apt and it is fascinating that in the *North Country sketches* which evoke the seasons in the Yorkshire moors a Debussian influence is revealed. The delicious tune we know as *La Calinda* appears in the first movement of the *Florida suite*; elsewhere, the local influences absorbed by the young composer in America bring parallels with Dvořák. But Handley's refined approach clearly links the work with later masterpieces. The recording is superbly balanced within the very suitable acoustics of the Ulster Hall; one's only real criticism is the lack of sumptuous weight to the violins when they have an eloquent musical line in the *Florida suite*; otherwise, tuttis are superbly expansive.

Cello sonata.
*** Chan. Dig. CHAN 8499; *ABTD 1209* [id.]. Raphael and Peter Wallfisch – BAX: *Rhapsodic ballad;* BRIDGE: *Cello sonata;* WALTON: *Passacaglia.* ***

The Delius *Sonata* is a less concentrated, more discursive piece than the Bridge with which it is coupled, but there is a highly personal atmosphere, and these Chandos performers give as strong and sympathetic an account of it as is to be found. They are also excellently recorded.

String quartet.
*** ASV Dig. CDDCA 526; *ZCDCA 526* [id.]. Brodsky Qt – ELGAR: *Quartet.* ***

The Brodsky Quartet give a richly expressive performance of Delius's *String quartet* with its evocative slow movement, *Late swallows.* In this music the ebb and flow of tension and a natural feeling for persuasive but unexaggerated rubato is vital; with fine ensemble but seeming spontaneity, the Brodsky players consistently produce that. First-rate recording.

VOCAL MUSIC

(i) *An Arabesque; Dance rhapsody No. 2; Fennimore and Gerda: Intermezzo.* (i; ii) *Songs of sunset.*
*** Unicorn Dig. DKPCD 9063; *DKPC 9063* [id.]. (i) Thomas Allen; (ii) Sarah Walker, Amb. S., RPO, Fenby.

The present collection follows up Fenby's earlier two-disc set for Unicorn (see below), and brings equally warm, well-sung and well-played performances, atmospherically recorded. What emerges as a Delius masterpiece is *An Arabesque*, a 15-minute work for baritone, mixed chorus and orchestra, setting a Pan-worship poem (in English translation) of the Norwegian poet and biologist, Jens Peter Jacobsen. The emotional thrust of the opening sequence, superbly sung by Thomas Allen and with passionate singing from the chorus too, subsides into characteristic Delian reflectiveness, but with a distinction and sense of purpose to put it among the composer's finest works. The *Songs of sunset* also bring ravishing sounds, with Sarah Walker as deeply expressive as Allen. The *Dance rhapsody No. 2* is crisply sprung in this performance, while the sensuousness of the *Fennimore and Gerda Intermezzo* returns us to gorgeously characteristic orchestral textures. Warm, full sound, yet refined and transparent.

(i) *An Arabesque;* (ii) *Hassan* (incidental music); (iii) *Sea drift.*
(M) (*(**)) Sony mono MPK 47680 [id.]. (i) Nørby; (ii) Fry; (iii) Boyce; BBC Ch., RPO, Beecham.

It is sad that these three Delius recordings, though made between December 1954 and February 1958 after the advent of stereo, were done in mono only. Once that is said, the results are persuasive in a way unsurpassed by any rival Delius interpreter, with the lyrical line of each passage, central to the argument, lovingly drawn out. *An Arabesque*, the least well-known of the three pieces, makes a superb counterpart to the long-recognized masterpiece, *Sea drift*, setting the words of Walt Whitman. Both have a baritone soloist as well as chorus, and it is a pity that the two baritones chosen here sound unsteady, as caught by the microphone. Nevertheless this makes a worthwhile disc for lovers of Delius's music with *Hassan* including his most approachable piece, the famous *Serenade*. The transfers are clear but have some roughness from the original recording.

2 Aquarelles. (i) *Caprice & elegy. Fantastic dance; Irmelin: Prelude. Koanga: La Calinda. A Song of summer.* (ii) *Cynara.* (ii; iii) *Idyll.* (iv) *A late lark.* (v) *Songs of farewell.*
*** Unicorn Dig. DKPCD 9008/9 [id.]. Fenby, with (i) Lloyd Webber; (ii) Allen; (iii) Lott; (iv) Rolfe Johnson; (v) Amb. S.; RPO.

Eric Fenby draws loving, dedicated performances from the RPO. *A Song of summer* is the finest of the works which Fenby took down from the dictation of the blind, paralysed and irascible composer, but the *Songs of farewell* (to words of Whitman) and the love scene entitled *Idyll*, rescued from an abortive opera project, are most beautiful too, with Felicity Lott and Thomas Allen especially impressive in the *Idyll.* These major works were based on earlier sketches, while other items here were arranged by Fenby with the composer's approval. The transfer to CD is expertly managed, with Delius's comparatively thick choral textures here sounding fresh and almost transparent.

Part-songs: *Durch den Wald; Frühlingssanbruch; Midsummer songs; On Craig Ddu; Sonnenscheinlied; The splendour falls; 2 unaccompanied part songs.*
(*) Conifer Dig. CDCF 162; *MCFC 162* [id.]. CBSO Ch., Simon Halsey – GRAINGER: *Part-songs.* *

These Delius part-songs make an apt supplement to the CBSO Chorus's record of Grainger items, warmer and smoother because of full choral treatment but lacking some of the sharpness of performance that comes with one voice per line. Nevertheless Halsey draws crisp, refined singing from his excellent team, helped by atmospheric recording.

4 Old English lyrics. Songs: *Brasil; Indian love song; Love's philosophy; The nightingale; The nightingale has a lyre of gold; Secret love; Sweet Venevil; Twilight fancies.*
**(*) Chan. Dig. CHAN 8539; *ABTD 1247* [id.]. Benjamin Luxon, David Willison – ELGAR: *Songs.* **(*)

Benjamin Luxon aptly chooses a group of Delius songs to couple with his selection of those by Elgar. They are just as delightful in their unpretentiousness, as near a meeting-point between the two sharply contrasted masters as can be found in any genre, and they draw most persuasive performances from Luxon and Willison, sadly marred by the rough tone which has latterly afflicted this fine baritone. Excellent, well-balanced recording.

Song of the high hills. Songs: *The bird's story; Le ciel est pardessus le toit; I-Brasil; Il pleure dans mon coeur; Let springtime come; La lune blanche; To daffodils; Twilight fancies; Wine roses.*
❀ *** Unicorn Dig. DKPCD 9029; *DKPC 9029* [id.]. Lott, Sarah Walker, Rolfe Johnson, Amb. S., RPO, Fenby.

Even among Delius issues, this stands out as one of the most ravishingly beautiful of all. Eric Fenby draws a richly atmospheric performance from Beecham's old orchestra in one of the most ambitious and beautiful, yet neglected, of Delius's choral works. Inspired by the hills of Norway, Delius evocatively conveys the still, chill atmosphere above the snow-line by episodes for wordless chorus, here finely balanced. The coupling of Delius songs in beautiful, virtually unknown orchestral arrangements is ideally chosen, with all three soloists both characterful and understanding.

OPERA

A Village Romeo and Juliet (complete).
*** Argo Dig. 430 275-2 [id.]. Field, Davies, Hampson, Mora, Dean, Schoenberg Ch., Austrian RSO, Mackerras.

(i) *A Village Romeo and Juliet* (opera; complete); (ii) *Sea drift*.
(M) (***) EMI mono CMS7 64386-2 (2) [id.]. (i) Ritchie, Soames, Dowling, Sharp, Bond, Dye; (i; ii) Clinton; Ch. & RPO, Beecham.

This is one of Delius's most beautiful and heart-warming scores, and Sir Charles Mackerras, even more than Sir Charles Groves on the earlier LP recording from EMI, brings that out lovingly. His approach is rather broader and more affectionate, with each scene timed to convey its emotional thrust, however flimsy the story-line. The Argo cast is even finer than the EMI one, with Helen Field and Arthur Davies very sympathetic as the lovers and with the rich-toned Thomas Hampson adding international glamour. Drawing sensuous, refined playing from the Austrian Radio Orchestra, Mackerras brings out the ecstasy of the piece. The spacious, atmospheric recording has the voices cleanly focused, with offstage effects beautifully caught.

Beecham made this complete recording of Delius's evocative opera in the days of 78s in 1948, and though the mono sound is limited in range, it is well focused, and Beecham's ability to mould Delius's melodic lines gives it an extra warmth and magic, even compared with later stereo recordings. The cast is drawn from a representative group of singers of the immediate post-war period, most of whom were too little heard on record, as for example Rene Soames who sings Sali as a man, or Margaret Ritchie who sings Sali as a child. Even less appreciated has been the baritone, Gordon Clinton, who not only sings the role of the Dark Fiddler with clean attack, but is even more impressive in the big baritone solo of *Sea drift*. It is worth any Delian getting this set for that magnificent performance, even warmer than the two other Beecham recordings, early and late, of this most moving setting of Walt Whitman, expansive but tautly held together. This 1951 version was for some reason never issued, and appears for the very first time in this CD Beecham edition, a superb, unexpected memorial not only to the conductor but to a fine, long-unappreciated singer.

Dering, Richard (*c.* 1580–1630)

Motets: *Ardens est cor meum; Ave maria gratia plena: Ave verum corpus; Factum est silentium; Gaudent in coelis; O crux ave spes unica; O bone Jesu; O quam suavis; Quem vidistis, pastores?*.
**(*) EMI Dig. CDC7 54189-2 [id.]; *EL 754189-4*. King's College, Cambridge, Ch., Cleobury – PHILIPS: *Motets*.

As Peter Platt's note reminds us, both Richard Dering and his older contemporary, Peter Philips, were Catholic expatriates who lived in the Spanish-dominated southern Netherlands. Dering was converted to Rome after a visit to Italy and spent the period 1617–25 in Brussels, before returning to England as organist to the Catholic Queen, Henrietta Maria, and musician for the lutes and voices to King Charles I. Like an examination question, this CD contrasts and compares the two composers' settings of the same texts, drawing on Dering's *Cantiones sacrae* of 1617 and the *Cantica sacra* of 1618 and the posthumously published set of 1662. There are some beautiful and expressive settings here, and the disc forms a useful addition to the catalogue. The performances are faithful though sometimes a bit stiff, and the actual sound, though good, is not ideal in focus or blend, partly perhaps but not solely due to the recording. Very recommendable all the same.

Destouches, André (1672–1749)

Première Suite des éléments (ballet music).
*** O-L 421 656-2 [id.]. AAM, Hogwood – REBEL: *Les Élémens*. ***

A few years before Rebel composed his highly original ballet on 'les élémens', André Destouches, even better connected as a court composer, wrote this ballet on the same theme. The result is less original but still well worth hearing, especially in this refreshing performance on original instruments. The vividness of the recording is undoubtedly enhanced on CD but, with 45 minutes' playing time, this reissue is not especially generous.

Dett, R. Nathaniel (1882–1943)

8 Bible vignettes; In the bottoms; Magnolia suite.
**(*) New World Dig. NWCD 367 [id.]. Denver Oldham.

Robert Nathaniel Dett was born in Drummondsville, Quebec, which was populated largely by the descendants of slaves. He showed natural gifts as a pianist, developing his talents while working as a bell-hop in a hotel at Niagara Falls. He graduated from Oberlin Conservatory in 1908, the first Negro to gain a Bachelor of Music degree. His music is full of echoes of Dvořák and MacDowell, as well as the influence of the Negro spiritual. His writing is at times colourful and, though limited in its range of expressive devices, is attractive, particularly so in the suite *In the bottoms*, which evokes the moods and atmosphere of Negro life in the 'river bottoms' of the Deep South. However, this is not a disc to be taken all at once. Denver Oldham is a persuasive enough player and he is decently recorded.

Diamond, David (born 1915)

(i) *Concerto for small orchestra;* (ii) *Symphonies Nos 2; 4.*
*** Delos Dig. D/CD 3093 [id.]. (i) NY CO; (ii) Seattle SO, Gerard Schwarz.

David Diamond first attracted attention in Europe after the Second World War with his *Rounds* for strings, but he was grievously neglected in the 1960s and '70s. The *Fourth Symphony* found its way on to LP, thanks to Leonard Bernstein who had conducted its 1948 première, though it was never released in the UK; however, apart from that and the *Romeo and Juliet* score, his music has remained out in the cold. The writing is very diatonic, tonal, impeccably crafted and sophisticated, qualities that were not highly prized in the 1960s and 1970s. The *Second Symphony* is a large-scale work lasting nearly three-quarters of an hour, written in 1942–3 at the height of the war, and it has great sweep and power. There is a lot of Roy Harris in the opening measures and the music unfolds with a similar sense of inevitability and purpose. Overall his music is less what one might in vulgar journalese call 'macho'. There are also reminders of Shostakovich and of the Copland of *Appalachian spring.* It is beautifully crafted and evinces a continuity of musical thought that defines the real symphonist. The *Concerto for small orchestra* is somewhat earlier, having been written not long after he finished his studies with Nadia Boulanger in Paris in 1939. It is original in form; there are two parts which open and conclude with a Fanfare with two preludes and fugues in between. The Mediterranean-like *Fourth Symphony* with its glowing, luminous textures sounds even more relaxed and lyrical in this performance than in Bernstein's account from the 1960s. Dedicated and expert performances from the Seattle Orchestra under Gerard Schwarz. The acoustic is spacious and well ventilated (some may find it too reverberant) but the balance is very well judged.

(i) *Kaddish for cello and orchestra. Psalm; Romeo and Juliet; Symphony No. 3.*
*** Delos Dig. DE 3103 [id.]. (i) Starker; Seattle SO, Gerard Schwarz.

This is the second instalment of what seems to be a complete survey of Diamond's symphonic output. The *Third Symphony* comes from the same year as the *Fourth* (1945) and is new to the gramophone. It is a four-movement work of no mean power. The *Romeo and Juliet* music is among his better-known (or perhaps one should say less unfamiliar) works – it has been recorded before. It is an inventive score, full of character and atmosphere, which shows him as a real man of the orchestra. Anyone who has invested in the *Second* and *Fourth Symphonies* will know what to expect from this one, and the Seattle Orchestra proves an eloquent advocate. *Kaddish* is a more recent piece and is played here by its dedicatee, Janos Starker.

Dickinson, Peter (born 1934)

4 Auden songs; 3 Comic songs; A Dylan Thomas cycle; An e. e. cummings cycle; Let the florid music praise; 3 Songs from The Unicorns.

*** Conifer Dig. CDCF 154; *MCFC 154* [id.]. Marilyn Hill Smith, Meriel Dickinson, Martyn Hill, Henry Herford, Peter Dickinson, Robin Bowman.

Peter Dickinson's settings of Auden – several of them poems already memorably set by Britten – are crisply rhythmic, not least *Over the heather* from the *Three Comic songs*, also known as *Roman wall blues* as sung by a Roman centurion. The Dylan Thomas songs are aptly rhetorical, while the uncapitalized freedom of e. e. cummings prompts a more abrasive style. The three songs to words by John Heath Stubbs strike a warmer note and together provide a fine emotional climax to the whole sequence. The four soloists make a well-contrasted group. Though not always ideally sweet of tone, they and the piano accompanists are very well recorded.

4 Blues; Blue rose; Concerto rag; Extravagances; Hymn-tune rag; Quartet rag; A red, red rose; So, we'll go no more a roving; Stevie's tunes; Wild rose rag.
**(*) Conifer Dig. CDCF 134; *MCFC 134* [id.]. Meriel Dickinson, Peter Dickinson.

Dickinson's eclectic style and ingenious mind are well illustrated in this collection of miniatures, with musical references and allusions adding to the point of the pieces. His love of American popular music provides a basic element. With the composer accompanying his sister, Meriel, in the songs, it makes an entertaining disc, with clear sound, just a little dry on piano tone.

Diepenbrock, Alphons (1862–1921)

Elektra suite; (i) *Hymn for violin & orchestra. Marsyas suite; Overture: The Birds.*
*** Chan. Dig. CHAN 8821; *ABTD 1446* [id.]. (i) Emmy Verhey; Hague Residentie O, Vonk.

For most non-native collectors, Dutch music is a closed book, save possibly for Pijper and Badings. Diepenbrock was something of a polymath and was self-taught as a composer. The *Birds Overture* (1917), written for a student production of Aristophanes, is rather delightful if very Straussian, with some vaguely Impressionist touches. The *Marsyas music* (1910) is expertly and delicately scored with touches of Strauss, Reger and Debussy. Try also the second movement of *Elektra* (track 9) which has a haunting, melancholy charm that is most appealing. Diepenbrock does not possess a strongly distinctive musical personality but his music is eminently civilized and melodically inviting. Good performances from the Residentie Orchestra under Hans Vonk and eminently truthful recording quality. Recommended.

(i) *Hymne an die Nacht;* (ii) *Hymne;* (i) *Die Nacht;* (iii) *Im grossen Schweigen.*
*** Chan. Dig. CHAN 8878; *ABTD 1491* [id.]. (i) Linda Finnie; (ii) Christoph Homberger; (iii) Robert Holl; Hague Residentie O, Hans Vonk.

If, for most people outside the Netherlands, Diepenbrock is little more than a name, the release in 1990 of a CD of his best-known (or, rather, least unfamiliar) works, *Marsyas* and *Elektra*, came as something of a revelation. This second volume brings four symphonic songs, all of great beauty and with an almost Straussian melancholy. There are touches of Reger and Debussy as well as Strauss, and all four pieces are expertly and delicately scored. Diepenbrock was a multi-faceted artist and was a musician of great culture; this music has languished in neglect far too long and deserves to come in from the cold. Those who have tried and liked the disc above will naturally want this, but others should start here, for it will kindle even greater enthusiasm. Good performances from all three soloists and the Residentie Orchestra under Hans Vonk, and very good recording indeed.

Dittersdorf, Carl Ditters von (1739–99)

(i) *Double-bass concerto in E;* (ii) *Flute concerto in E min.;* (iii) *Symphonies in C & D.*
** Olympia OCD 405 [id.]. (i) Stefan Thomas, Arad PO, Boboc; (ii) Gavril Costea, Cluj-Napoca PO, Cristescu; (iii) Oradea Philharmonic CO, Ratiu.

Dittersdorf spent the years 1765–9 in Oradea, augmenting the bishop's orchestra with imported Viennese instrumentalists and organizing regular concerts. It seems appropriate that the present orchestra of that Transylvanian town should take an interest in his music, and they give lively performances of two of his symphonies. The *C major* is an agreeably conventional three-movement piece; but the *D major* is more elaborate, with an infectious opening movement, an engaging *Chanson populaire d'Elsass* for its *Andante*, a minuet with two trios and a set of variations for its modestly paced finale. The other works are also played by Transylvanian musicians. Both the concertos are attractive and require considerable bravura from their soloists. The double-bass soloist is especially impressive; even if – by the very nature of his instrument – he cannot help sounding lugubrious in the *Adagio*, Stefan Thomas is able to impress us by his easy command in the work's outer movements, especially during the jolly finale. The recorded sound varies somewhat but is always fully acceptable and quite well balanced.

Harp concerto in A (arr. Pilley).
❀ (M) *** Decca 425 723-2; *425 723-4* [id.]. Marisa Robles, ASMF, Iona Brown – BOIELDIEU; HANDEL: *Harp concertos* etc. *** ❀

Dittersdorf's *Harp concerto* is a transcription of an unfinished keyboard concerto with additional wind parts. It is an elegant piece, thematically not quite as memorable as the Boieldieu coupling, but captivating when played with such style. The recording too is from the old Argo catalogue's top drawer. With its additional solo items (see under Boieldieu for details), this collection makes one of the most rewarding anthologies for harp ever issued.

6 Symphonies after Ovid's Metamorphoses.
**(*) Chan. Dig. CHAN 8564/5; *DBTD 2012* (2). Cantilena, Shepherd.

All the *Ovid symphonies* have a programmatic inspiration and relate episodes from the *Metamorphoses* of Ovid, such as *The fall of Phaeton*, which are vividly portrayed. *The rescue of Andromeda by Perseus* is a particularly effective work (it has an inspired *Adagio*) and the slow movement of the *D major*, *The petrification of Phineus and his friends*, is a delight. One well appreciates the contemporary verdict that Ditters 'spoke to the heart'. *The transformation of the Lycian peasants into frogs* could hardly be more graphic and is full of wit. This is inventive and charming music that will give much pleasure, and it is generally well served by Cantilena under Adrian Shepherd. The performances are not outstanding but they are very musical, and the recording, made in a lively and warm acoustic, is very clean and well detailed.

Dohnányi, Ernst von (1877–1960)

Konzertstück for cello and orchestra, Op. 12.
*** Chan. Dig. CHAN 8662 [id.]. Wallfisch, LSO, Mackerras – DVOŘÁK: *Cello concerto.* ***

Dohnányi's *Konzertstück*, in effect a full-scale cello concerto lasting 24 minutes, is a delightful rarity which makes an unusual and attractive coupling for Wallfisch's outstanding version of the Dvořák. It may not be a great work but it has many rich, warm ideas, not least a theme in the slow movement all too close to *Pale hands I loved beside the Shalimar*, and none the worse for that. Wallfisch's performance, as in the Dvořák, is strong, warm and committed, and the Chandos sound is first rate.

(i) *Ruralia hungarica, Op. 32b;* (i; ii) *Variations on a nursery tune, Op. 25;* (iii) *Serenade in C (for string trio), Op. 10.*
(B) *** Hung. White Label HRC 121 [id.]. (i) Budapest SO, Lehel, (ii) with István Lantos; (iii) Kovács, Bársony, Botvay.

Ruralia hungarica, although a cultivated score, still has an element of peasant earthiness. There is also, in its five movements, wide variety of mood, and the music rises to considerable eloquence; it was admired by Bartók for its colourful scoring. György Lehel and the Budapest orchestra successfully convey its exuberance and poetry, and the pianist in the famous *Variations*, István Lantos, is characterful as well as brilliant. To make this record even more attractive, we are offered the *Serenade*, Op. 10, an expressive and inventive piece with a particularly beautiful slow movement. Again the playing here is accomplished and spontaneous. With excellent, well-balanced sound, this is one of the outstanding bargains on Hungaroton's White Label.

Cello sonata in B flat min., Op. 8.
**(*) ASV Dig. CDDCA 796[id.]. Bernard Gregor-Smith, Yolande Wrigley – BRIDGE; DEBUSSY: *Sonatas.* **(*)

Like so much of Dohnányi's early music, the *Cello sonata* (1899) is very Brahmsian in feeling.

It is astonishingly assured with a remarkable grasp of form, and in its handling of its very good if not profoundly original ideas. There is a marvellously inventive scherzo, which leaves no doubt that it is the work of a great pianist-composer. The finale is a theme and variations and what a superb theme it is too. It is a most welcome addition to the catalogue, and is played with great expertise and fine musicianship by this excellent duo partnership. The recording is just a bit too bright and forward to be ideal but with that proviso, the disc can be cordially recommended.

(i) *Piano quintet in C min., Op. 1. String quartet No. 2 in D flat, Op. 15.*
**(*) Chan. Dig. CHAN 8718; *ABTD 1360* [id.]. (i) Wolfgang Manz; Gabrieli Qt.

Manz's performance of the Dohnányi *Quintet* lacks something in fantasy and lightness of touch. But the bigger-boned, somewhat Brahmsian effect of this performance is certainly compelling, if less strong on charm. The scherzo of the *Second Quartet* is reminiscent of the opening of *Die Walküre* and there are reminders of Dvořák and Reger as well as Brahms. It is a strong piece, splendidly played by the Gabrielis and beautifully recorded.

(i) *Variations on a nursery tune, Op. 25. Capriccio in F min., Op. 28.*
*** Chesky CD-13 [id.]. Earl Wild, (i) New Philh. O, Christoph von Dohnányi – TCHAIKOVSKY: *Piano concerto No. 1.* ***

A scintillating account of the piano part from Earl Wild is matched by a witty accompaniment directed by the composer's grandson, who doesn't miss a thing. The New Philharmonia Orchestra plays superbly and obviously relishes the humour: the pompous introduction is not overdone, and the chimerical and eclectic changes of style in the variations are beautifully managed. Splendid vintage analogue recording from the early 1960s, fresh, natural, very well balanced and immaculately transferred to CD. The *Capriccio*, brilliantly played, acts as an encore (before the Tchaikovsky coupling), but the recording is rather recessed.

Donizetti, Gaetano (1797–1848)

Il Barcaiolo; Cor anglais concertino in G; Oboe sonata in F; (Piano) Waltz in C (with PASCULLI: *Concerto on themes from La Favorita; Fantasia on Poliuto.* LISZT: *Réminsciences de Lucia di Lammermoor*).
*** Mer. CDE 84147; *KE 77147* [id.]. Jeremy Polmear, Diana Ambache.

The *Sonata in F* is an agreeable piece with a fluent *Andante* and a catchy finale; and the vignette, *Il Barcaiolo*, is even more engaging. The *Cor anglais concerto* centres on a set of variations which are not unlike the fantasias on themes from his operas by Pasculli. However, these demand the utmost bravura from the soloist. Diana Ambache proves a sympathetic partner and gives a suitably flamboyant account of Liszt's famous *Lucia paraphrase*. The recording, made in Eltham College, London, is a shade too reverberant here, though the resonance is more agreeable in the duos.

String quartet No. 13 in A.
*** CRD CRD 3366 [id.]. Alberni Qt – PUCCINI: *Crisantemi;* VERDI: *Quartet.* ***

This is an endearing work, with a scherzo echoing that in Beethoven's *Eroica*, and with many twists of argument that are attractively unpredictable. It is well coupled here with other works for string quartet by Italian opera composers, all in strong, committed performances and well recorded. The CD transfer is fresh and vivid.

OPERA

Anna Bolena (complete).
*** Decca Dig. 421 096-2 (3) [id.]. Sutherland, Ramey, Hadley, Mentzer, Welsh Nat. Op. Ch. & O, Bonynge.

In this 1987 recording of *Anna Bolena*, Sutherland crowns her long recording career with a commanding performance. Dazzling as ever in coloratura, above all exuberant in the defiant final cabaletta, she poignantly conveys the tragedy of the wronged queen's fate with rare weight and gravity. Ramey as the king is outstanding in a fine, consistent cast. Excellent recording.

Il Campanello (complete).
*** Sony Dig. MK 38450 [id.]. Baltsa, Dara, Casoni, Romero, Gaifa, V. State Op. Ch., VSO, Bertini.

This sparkling one-act piece is based on something like the same story which Donizetti developed later in *Don Pasquale.* Enzo Dara as the apothecary, Don Annibale, and Angelo Romero as the wag, Enrico, are delightful in their patter duet, and Agnes Baltsa is a formidable but sparkling Serafina. Gary Bertini is a sympathetic conductor who paces things well, and the secco recitatives – taking up rather a large proportion of the disc – are well accompanied on the fortepiano. Generally well-balanced recording.

Don Pasquale (complete).
*** EMI Dig. CDS7 47068-2 (2) [Ang. CDCB 47068]. Bruscantini, Freni, Nucci, Winbergh, Amb. Op. Ch., Philh. O, Muti.
(M) *** Decca 433 036-2 (2) [id.]. Corena, Sciutti, Oncina, Krause, V. State Op. Ch. & O, Kertész – CIMAROSA: *Il maestro di cappella.* ***
*** Erato/Warner Dig. 2292 45487-2 (2) [id.]. Bacquier, Hendricks, Canonici, Quilico, Schirrer, Lyon Opera Ch. & O, Ferro.

With sparkle and spring on the one hand and easily flexible lyricism on the other, Muti's is a delectably idiomatic-sounding reading, one which consistently captures the fun of the piece. It helps that three of the four principals are Italians. Freni is a natural in the role of Norina, both sweet and bright-eyed in characterization, excellent in coloratura. The buffo baritones, the veteran Bruscantini as Pasquale and the darker-toned Leo Nucci as Dr Malatesta, steer a nice course between vocal comedy and purely musical values. They sound exhilarated, not stressed, by Muti's challenging speeds for the patter numbers. On the lyrical side, Muti is helped by the beautifully poised and shaded singing of Gösta Winbergh, honey-toned and stylish as Ernesto. Responsive and polished playing from the Philharmonia and excellent studio sound.

Kertész may have been Hungarian and the use of the Vienna State Opera Chorus and Orchestra may bring some moments suggestive rather of operetta than of Italian opera; but the important thing is that high spirits are conveyed all the time. Corena is an attractive buffo, even if his voice is not always focused well enough to sing semiquavers accurately. Juan Oncina, as often on record, sounds rather strained, but the tenor part is very small; and Krause makes an incisive Malatesta. Graziella Sciutti is charming from beginning to end, bright-toned and vivacious, and remarkably agile in the most difficult passages. The 1964 Decca recording is excellent, with plenty of atmosphere as well as sparkle. A splendid bargain version with a generous fill-up.

The Erato version gains enormously from the rhythmic subtlety and affectionate phrasing encouraged by the conductor, Gabriele Ferro. This is a reading with more light and shade than Muti's or Kertész's, not so high-powered but more relaxed, genially capturing the spirit of comedy in this delightful score. The singers live up to that direction, not always so positively characterful as their direct rivals, but always musically imaginative. They also work together as an excellent team, one of the marks of recordings based on the Lyon Opera House. Gabriel Bacquier is a vintage Pasquale, vocally in splendid form, while Louis Quilico sings superbly as Malatesta. Their celebrated patter duet brings a combination of high comedy, formidable agility and fine vocalization. Barbara Hendricks is a charming Norina with her sweet timbre, and Luca Canonici an engaging Ernesto, even if his production is not always perfectly even. The recording has fine atmosphere, though some of the vocal balances are inconsistent. A set that encourages you to go on listening.

L'Elisir d'amore (complete).
*** Decca 414 461-2 (2) [id.]. Sutherland, Pavarotti, Cossa, Malas, Amb. S., ECO, Bonynge.
(M) *** Sony CD 79210 (2) [M2K 34585]. Cotrubas, Domingo, Evans, Wixell, ROHCG Ch. & O, Pritchard.
**(*) Eurodisc 601 097 (3) [RCA ARE3-5411]. Popp, Dvorský, Weikl, Nesterenko, Munich R. Ch. & O, Wallberg.

Joan Sutherland makes Adina a more substantial figure than usual, full-throatedly serious at times, at others jolly like the rumbustious Marie. Malibran, the first interpreter of the role, was furious that the part was not bigger, and got her husband to write an extra aria. Richard Bonynge found a copy of the piano score, had it orchestrated, and included it here, a jolly and brilliant waltz song. Though that involves missing out the cabaletta *Il mio fugor dimentica*, the text of this frothy piece is otherwise unusually complete, and in the key role of Nemorino Luciano Pavarotti proves ideal, vividly portraying the wounded innocent. Spiro Malas is a superb Dulcamara, while Dominic Cossa is a younger-sounding Belcore, more of a genuine lover than usual. Bonynge points the skipping rhythms delectably, and the recording is sparkling to match, with striking presence.

On the Sony reissue delight centres very much on the delectable Adina of Ileana Cotrubas. Quite apart from the delicacy of her singing, she presents a sparkling, flirtatious character to underline the point of the whole story. Plácido Domingo by contrast is a more conventional hero and less the world's fool that Nemorino should be. It is a large voice for the role and *Una furtiva lagrima* is not pure enough in its legato, but otherwise his singing is stylish and vigorous. Sir Geraint Evans gives a vivid characterization of Dr Dulcamara, though the microphone sometimes brings out roughness of tone and this is all the more noticeable with the added projection of CD. Ingvar Wixell is an upstanding Belcore. The stereo staging is effective and the remastered recording bright and immediate. This set remains at full price in the USA.

Wallberg conducts a lightly sprung reading, marked by a charming performance of the role of Adina from Lucia Popp, comparably bright-eyed, with delicious detail both verbal and musical. Nesterenko makes a splendidly resonant Dr Dulcamara with more comic sparkle than you would expect from a great Russian bass. Dvorský and Weikl, both sensitive artists, sound much less idiomatic, with Dvorský's tight tenor growing harsh under pressure, not at all Italianate, and Weikl failing similarly to give necessary roundness to the role of Belcore. Like other sets recorded in association with Bavarian Radio, the sound is excellent, naturally balanced with voices never spotlit.

Emelia di Liverpool (complete). *L'eremitaggio di Liwerpool* (complete).
*** Opera Rara OR 8 (3) [id.]. Kenny, Bruscantini, Merritt, Dolton, George Mitchell Ch., Philh. O, David Parry.

The very name, *Emelia di Liverpool*, makes it hard to take this early opera of Donizetti seriously, described in the score as a '*dramma semi-serio per musica*', which means it ends happily. Yet, as Dame Joan Sutherland showed as long ago as 1957 in concert and broadcast performances, it contains much splendid material. Here in this set, sponsored by the Peter Moores Foundation, we have not only the original version of 1824 but also the complete reworking of four years later, which was given the revised title noted above. Having both versions side by side, very different if comparable, gives searching insights into the composer's methods. Neither version won success, but these discs amply confirm the good impressions from 1957, particularly in the duets and ensembles. Such a veteran as Sesto Bruscantini makes an enormous difference in the buffo role of Don Romualdo in *Emelia*, a character who speaks in Neapolitan dialect. His fizzing duet with Federico (the principal tenor role, superbly sung by Chris Merritt) sets the pattern for much vigorous invention. The baritone, Geoffrey Dolton, sings stylishly, but the microphone catches a pronounced flutter, and even the brilliant Yvonne Kenny's singing is disturbed by occasional unevenness. But with fresh, direct conducting from David Parry this is a highly enjoyable set for all who respond to this composer. The booklet contains the librettos of both versions as well as the spoken dialogue not included on the discs. Good, clear recording.

La Favorita (complete).
(M) **(*) Decca 430 038-2 (3). Cossotto, Pavarotti, Bacquier, Ghiaurov, Cotrubas, Teatro Comunale Bologna Ch. & O, Bonynge.

La Favorita may not have as many memorable tunes as the finest Donizetti operas, but red-blooded drama provides ample compensation. Set in Spain in the early fourteenth century, the story revolves around the predicament of Fernando – strongly and imaginatively sung here by Pavarotti – torn between religious devotion and love for the beautiful Leonora, who (unknown to him) is the mistress of the king. The recording, made in Bologna, is not ideal – showing signs that the sessions were not easy – but the colour and vigour of the writing are never in doubt. The mezzo role of the heroine is taken by Fiorenza Cossotto, formidably powerful if not quite at her finest, while Ileana Cotrubas is comparably imaginative as her confidante Ines, but not quite at her peak. Bacquier and Ghiaurov make up a team which should have been even better but which will still give much satisfaction. Bright recording, vividly transferred, but the effect is not quite out of Decca's top drawer.

La Fille du régiment (complete).
*** Decca 414 520-2 (2) [id.]. Sutherland, Pavarotti, Sinclair, Malas, Coates, ROHCG Ch. & O, Bonynge.

It was with this cast that *La Fille du régiment* was revived at Covent Garden, and Sutherland immediately showed how naturally she takes to the role of Marie, a vivandière in the army of Napoleon. This original French version favoured by Richard Bonynge is fuller than the Italian revision and, with a cast that at the time of the recording sessions was also appearing in the theatre, the performance could hardly achieve higher spirits with keener assurance. Sutherland is in turn brilliantly comic and pathetically affecting, and Pavarotti makes an engaging hero. Monica Sinclair is a formidable Countess, and even if the French accents are often suspect it is a small price to pay for such a brilliant, happy opera set, a fizzing performance of a delightful Donizetti romp that can be confidently recommended both for comedy and for fine singing. Recorded in Kingsway Hall, the CD sound has wonderful presence and clarity of focus.

Lucia di Lammermoor (complete).
*** Decca 410 193-2 (2) [id.]. Sutherland, Pavarotti, Milnes, Ghiaurov, Ryland Davies, Tourangeau, ROHCG Ch. & O, Bonynge.
(M) *** Decca 411 622-2 (2) [id.]. Sutherland, Cioni, Merrill, Siepi, St Cecilia Ac., Rome, Ch. & O, Pritchard.
(M) (***) EMI mono CMS7 63631-2 (2) [Ang. CDMB 63631]. Callas, Di Stefano, Panerai, Zaccaria, La Scala Ch. & O, Karajan.
(M) (***) EMI mono CMS7 69980-2 (2) [Ang. CDMB 69980]. Callas, Di Stefano, Gobbi, Arie, Ch. & O of Maggio Musicale Fiorentino, Serafin.

It was hardly surprising that Decca recorded Sutherland twice in the role with which she is inseparably associated. Though some of the girlish freshness of voice which marked the 1961 recording disappeared in the 1971 set, the detailed understanding was intensified, and the mooning manner, which in 1961 was just emerging, was counteracted. Power is there as well as delicacy, and the rest of the cast is first rate. Pavarotti, through much of the opera not as sensitive as he can be, proves magnificent in his final scene. The sound-quality is superb on CD, though choral interjections are not always forward enough. In this set, unlike the earlier one, the text is absolutely complete.

The 1961 Sutherland version of *Lucia* remains an attractive proposition in the mid-price range. Though consonants were being smoothed over, the voice is obviously that of a young singer and dramatically the performance was close to Sutherland's famous stage appearances of that time, full of fresh innocence. Though the text is not quite as full as the 1971 version, a fascinating supplement is provided in an aria (from *Rosmonda d'Inghilterra*) which for many years was used as a replacement for the big Act I aria, *Regnava nel silenzio*). The recording remains very fresh and vivid, though not everyone will like the prominent crowd noises. Sutherland's coloratura virtuosity remains breathtaking, and the cast is a strong one, with Pritchard a most understanding conductor.

Recorded live in 1955, when Karajan took the company of La Scala to Berlin, for years this finest of Callas's recordings of *Lucia* was available only on pirate issues. Callas was an artist who responded vividly to an audience and an occasion, particularly with a great conductor in charge. Karajan's insight gives a new dimension to the work, even though the usual much-cut text is used. Despite the limited sound, Callas's voice is caught with fine immediacy. Her singing is less steely than in the 1953 studio recording, and far firmer than in the 1959 one (now withdrawn).

Callas's earlier mono set, which dates from 1953, is given an effective remastering which brings out the solo voices well, although the acoustic is confined and the choral sound less well focused. Here, needless to say, is not the portrait of a sweet girl, wronged and wilting, but a formidably tragic characterization. The diva is vocally better controlled than in her later stereo set (indeed some of the coloratura is excitingly brilliant in its own right), and there are memorable if not always perfectly stylish contributions from Di Stefano and Gobbi. As in the later set, the text has the usual stage cuts, but Callas's irresistible musical imagination, her ability to turn a well-known phrase with unforgettable inflexions, supremely justifies the preservation of a historic recording.

Lucia di Lammermoor: highlights.
(M) *** Decca 421 885-2; *421 885-4* [id.] (from above complete recording with Sutherland, Pavarotti; cond. Bonynge).
(M) **(*) EMI CDM7 63934-2 [id.]; *EG 763934-4* (from complete set, with Callas, Tagliavini, Cappuccilli, Ladysz, Philh. Ch. & O, Serafin).

For those who have chosen Callas or Sutherland's earlier, complete set, this 63-minute selection from her later (1971) version should be ideal. It includes the Fountain scene, the sextet, the Mad scene and the great tenor aria in the last scene. The splendid Kingsway Hall recording, produced by Christopher Raeburn and engineered by Kenneth Wilkinson and James Lock, has been transferred admirably to CD.

A satisfactory hour-long selection from Callas's 1959 Kingsway Hall stereo recording, with Callas not as completely in vocal control as she was in her earlier, mono set. However, the present cast is adequate, and Callas's flashing-eyed interpretation remains unique.

Lucrezia Borgia (complete).
(M) *** Decca 421 497-2 (2) [id.]. Sutherland, Aragall, Horne, Wixell, London Op. Voices, Nat. PO, Bonynge.

Sutherland is in her element here. In one or two places she falls into the old swooning style but, as in the theatre, her singing is masterly, not only in its technical assurance but in its power and conviction, making the impossible story of poisoner-heroine moving and even sympathetic. Aragall sings stylishly too, and though Wixell's timbre is hardly Italianate he is a commanding Alfonso. Marilyn Horne in the breeches role of Orsini is impressive in the brilliant *Brindisi* of the last Act, but earlier she has moments of unsteadiness. Thanks to researches by Richard Bonynge, the set also includes extra material for the tenor, including an aria newly discovered, *T'amo qual dama un angelo.* The recording is characteristically full and brilliant.

Maria Stuarda (complete).
(M) *** Decca 425 410-2 (2) [id.]. Sutherland, Tourangeau, Pavarotti, Ch. & O of Teatro Comunale, Bologna, Bonynge.

In Donizetti's tellingly dramatic opera on the conflict of Elizabeth I and Mary Queen of Scots the confrontation between the two Queens is so brilliantly effective that one regrets that history did not actually manage such a meeting between the royal cousins. Here the contrast between the full soprano Maria and the dark mezzo Elisabetta is underlined by some transpositions, with Tourangeau emerging as a powerful villainess in this slanted version of the story. Pavarotti turns Leicester into a passionate Italian lover, not at all an Elizabethan gentleman. As for Sutherland, she is at her most fully dramatic too, and the great moment when she flings the insult *Vil bastarda!* at her cousin brings a superb snarl. In the lovely prayer before the Queen's execution with its glorious melody, Sutherland is richly forthright but does not quite efface memories of Dame Janet Baker. Otherwise she remains the most commanding of Donizetti sopranos, and Richard Bonynge directs an urgent account of an unfailingly enjoyable opera. Unusually for Decca, the score is slightly cut. The recording is characteristically bright and full and the CD transfer first rate.

Mary Stuart (complete, in English).
(M) **(*) EMI Dig. CMS7 69372-2 (2). Dame Janet Baker, Plowright, Rendall, Opie, Tomlinson, E. Nat. Op. Ch. and O, Mackerras.

Mary Stuart was the opera chosen at the ENO just before Dame Janet decided to retire from the opera stage in 1982; happily, EMI took the opportunity to make live recordings of a series of performances at the Coliseum. Though far from ideal, the result is strong and memorable, with Dame Janet herself rising nobly to the demands of the role, snorting fire superbly in her condemnation of Elizabeth as a royal bastard, and above all making the closing scenes before Mary's execution deeply moving. Her performance is splendidly matched by that of Rosalind Plowright, though the closeness of the recording of the singers makes the voice rather hard. The singing of the rest of the cast is less distinguished, with chorus ensemble often disappointingly ragged, a point shown up by the recording balance. The acoustic has the listener almost on stage, with the orchestra relatively distant. It is a valuable and historic set, but the Decca version (in Italian) with Sutherland gives a fuller idea of the work's power.

Mary Stuart: highlights (in English).
(M) **(*) EMI Dig. CDM7 63727-2 [id.]; *EG 763727-4* (from above complete recording; cond. Mackerras).

The highlight of Donizetti's dramatization of the conflict between Elizabeth I and Mary Queen of Scots is the more communicative when the interchange occurs in English, with Dame Janet (as Mary Stuart) and Joan Plowright rising to the challenge superbly. This scene is at the centre of the 61 minutes of highlights from the memorable if uneven ENO performance. Many will enjoy this while not requiring the complete set.

Poliuto (complete).
*** Sony Dig. M2K 44821 (2) [id.]. Carreras, Ricciarelli, Pons, Polgar, V. Singakademie Ch., VSO, Oleg Caetani.

Set in Rome in the early Christian period, *Poliuto* is based on Corneille's tragedy, Polyeucte, a story of martyrdom. Written in 1838, it was originally banned by the censor and was first heard in a version that Donizetti arranged for Paris under the title *Les martyrs*. It is a piece that was revived at various periods, thanks to the advocacy of such tenors as Tamagno and Lauri-Volpi; Maria Callas, attracted to the dramatic role of the heroine, Paolina, appeared opposite Franco Corelli in a revival at La Scala, Milan, in 1960. This version was recorded in the Vienna Konzerthaus in 1986. That was before Carreras's serious illness, and the voice is in splendid form. Ricciarelli as Paolina lacks something in dramatic bite, but she gives the heroine an inward warmth and tenderness. Pons and Polgar are also excellent and, though the piece is not remarkable for any depth of character-drawing, it is well worth investigating for the foretastes it brings of middle-period Verdi, and specifically for one of Donizetti's most inspired ensembles in the Act II finale. The recording is clear and vivid, hardly betraying the fact that it was made live at a concert performance.

Arias from: *Don Pasquale; Don Sebastiano; Il Duca d'Alba; L'elisir d'amore; La Favorita; La Fille du régiment; Lucia di Lammermoor; Maria Stuarda.*
**(*) Decca 417 638-2 [id.]. Luciano Pavarotti with various orchestras & conductors.

A cleverly chosen compilation of Pavarotti recordings of Donizetti from various sources – not just complete sets but previous recital discs. It is good to have one or two rarities along with the favourite numbers, including Tonio's celebrated 'High-C's' solo from the Act I finale of *La Fille du régiment*. Sound from different sources is well co-ordinated. However, this record is overpriced.

Dowland, John (1563–1626)

Consort music: *Captain Digorie Piper, his pavan and galliard; Fortune my foe; Lachrimae; Lady Hunsdon's almain; Lord Souch's galliard; Mistress Winter's jump; The shoemaker's wife (a toy); Sir George Whitehead's almain; Sir Henry Guildford's almain; Sir Henry Umpton's funeral; Sir John Smith's almain; Sir Thomas Collier's galliard; Suzanna.*
*** Hyp. Dig. CDA 66010 [id.]. Extempore String Ens.

The Extempore Ensemble's technique of improvising and elaborating in Elizabethan consort music is aptly exploited here in an attractively varied selection of pieces by Dowland. Performers in turn are each allowed what the jazz musician would recognize as a 'break', and on record, as in concert, the result sounds the more spontaneous. Excellent recording, given added presence on CD.

Lute music: *Almaine; Dowland's first galliard; Earl of Derby, his galliard; Earl of Essex, his galliard; Farewell (fancy); Forlorne hope (fancy); Frog galliard; Lachrimae antiquae; Lachrimae verae; Lady Rich, her galliard; Lord d'Lisle, his galliard; Melancholie galliard; Mrs Vaux's gigge; My Lady Hunsdon's puffe; My Lord Willoughby's welcome home; Piper's pavan; Resolution; Semper Dowland, Semper dolens; The Shoemaker's wife (a toy); Sir Henry Gifford, his almaine.*
*** BMG/RCA RD 89977. Julian Bream (lute).

Julian Bream captures the melancholy (the piece entitled *Semper Dowland, semper dolens* is certainly autobiographical) and the eloquence of these endlessly imaginative miniatures. He produces an astonishing range of colour from the lute: each phrase shows distinction, nothing is in the least routine. The CD gives Bream the most realistic presence, though care should be exercised with the volume control – a lower-level setting is advisable for a truthful image.

First Booke of Songes (1597): 1, Unquiet thoughts; 2, Whoever thinks or hopes; 3, My thoughts are wing'd with hopes; 4, If my complaints; 5, Can she excuse my wrongs; 6, Now, O now I needs must part; 7, Dear, if you change; 8, Burst forth my tears; 9, Go crystal tears; 10, Think'st thou then; 11, Come away, come sweet love; 12, Rest awhile; 13, Sleep wayward thoughts; 14, All ye who love or fortune; 15, Wilt thou unkind; 16, Would my conceit; 17, Come again; 18, His golden locks; 19, Awake, sweet love; 20, Come, heavy sleep; 21, Away with these self-loving lads.
*** O-L 421 653-2 [id.]. Cons. of Musicke, Rooley.

Rooley and the Consort of Musicke he directs have recorded all the contents of the *First Booke of Songes* of 1597 in the order in which they are published, varying the accompaniment between viols, lute with bass viol, voices and viols, and even voices alone. There is hardly any need to stress the beauties of the music itself, which is eminently well served by this stylish ensemble, and beautifully recorded.

Second Booke of Songes (1600): I saw my lady weep; Flow my tears; Sorrow, stay; Die not before thy day; Mourn day is with darkness fled; Time's eldest son; Then sit thee down; When others say Venite; Praise blindness eyes; O sweet words; If floods of tears; Fine knacks for ladies; Now cease my wond'ring eyes; Come, ye heavy states of night; White as lilies was her face; Woeful heart; A shepherd in a shade; Faction that ever dwells; Shall I sue; Toss not my soul; Clear or cloudy; Humour say what mak'st thou here.
*** Decca 425 889-2 [id.]. Kirkby, York Skinner, Hill, D. Thomas, Cons. of Musicke, Rooley.

The *Second Booke* contains many of Dowland's best-known songs, such as *Fine knacks for ladies, I saw my lady weep* and *Flow my tears*. Incidentally, the latter are performed on lute and two voices, the bass line being sung by David Thomas; this is quite authentic, though many listeners will retain an affection for its solo treatment. The solo songs are given with great restraint (sometimes perhaps rather too great) and good musical judgement, while the consort pieces receive expressive treatment. Emma Kirkby gives an excellent account of *Come, ye heavy states of night* and *Clear or cloudy*. Perhaps it is invidious to single her out, as the standard of performance throughout is distinguished. Refined intelligence is shown by all taking part. This will inevitably be the most sought after of all the *Bookes of Songes* since it contains so many of Dowland's finest and most inspired pieces. The recording is of the highest quality.

Third Booke of Songes (1603): *1, Farewell too fair; 2, Time stands still; 3, Behold a wonder here; 4, Daphne was not so chaste; 5, Me, me and none but me; 6, When Phoebus first did Daphne love; 7, Say, Love, if ever thou didst find; 8, Flow not so fast, ye fountains; 9, What if I never speed; 10, Love stood amazed; 11, Lend you ears to my sorrow; 12, By a fountain where I lay; 13, O, what hath overwrought; 14, Farewell unkind; 15, Weep you no more sad fountains; 16, Fie on this feigning; 17, I must complain; 18, It was a time when silly bees; 19, The lowest trees; 20, What poor astronomers; 21, Come when I call.*
**(*) O-L 430 284-2 [id.]. Kirkby, Skinner, Hill, Thomas, Mackintosh, Cons. of Musicke, Rooley.

Although there are certain details with which to quarrel – a general air of sobriety and an excessive restraint in colouring words – there is a great deal of pleasure to be derived from this project. The performers show dedication and accomplishment, and in all cases they are expertly served by the engineers. David Thomas gives an excellent account of himself in *What poor astronomers they are* and Emma Kirkby's voice is also a delight. The whole set is well worth investigation and an impressive achievement; the instrumental support is of high quality, as is the presentation. Apart from a certain reluctance to characterize, this commands much admiration. The CD transfer is absolutely refined and clear: this might almost be a digital recording.

Ayres and Lute-lessons: *Prelude and Galliard; All ye whom love; Away with these self-loving lads; Come again sweet love; Come heavy sleep; Go Christal teares; If my complaints; My thoughts are winged; Rest awhile;* (Lute): *Semper Dowland, semper dolens. A shepherd in a shade; Stay sweet awhile; Tell me, true love; What if I never speede; When Phoebus first did Daphne love; Wilt thou unkind.*
(B) **(*) HM HMA 901076 [id.]. Deller Consort, Mark Deller; Robert Spencer.

Dowland's 'ayres' were designed for a consort of singers as well as for solo singer and lute, and it is good to hear them in this form. This record draws on the First Booke of 1597 and those of 1600, 1603 and 1612, as well as two of the Lute Lessons, excellently played by Robert Spencer. The performances are exemplary, though some might be worried by the tendency to over-colour certain words; but for the most part these give consistent pleasure. The sound is excellent.

Lute songs: *Awake sweet love, thou art returned; Can she excuse my wrongs?; Come again! sweet love doth now invite; Fine knacks for ladies; Flow not so fast, ye fountains; Go, crystal tears; Lady, if you so spite me; Me, me and none but me; Shall I strive with words to move?; Shall I sue?; Sorrow stay; Tell me true love; What is I never speed?; When Phoebus first did Daphne love; Lute lessons: Captain Candish's galliard; Lady Laiton's almain; Preludium and Lachrimae pavan; Semper Dowland; Semper dolens.*

(M) *** Saga SCD 9004. James Bowman, Robert Spencer.

This admirable record contains songs from all three *Bookes* plus two from *A Pilgrim's Solace* (1612). The lute solos, played in exemplary fashion by Robert Spencer, provide two central interludes. This record makes a fine single-disc introduction to Dowland's art. James Bowman brings sensitivity and intelligence to each song and characterizes them tellingly. The recording is very good too, real and present.

Ayres: *Awake, sweet love; Come away, come away sweet love; Come heavy sleep; Fie on this faining; Fine knacks for ladies; Flow my tears; If my complaints could passions move; I saw my lady weep; Love those beames; My thoughts are wingd with with hopes; Say love, if ever thou didst finde; Shall I strive; Shall I sue; Sorrow sorrow stay; Sweete stay awhile; To aske for all thy love; Weep you no more; Were every thought an eye; When Phoebus first; Wilt thou unkind.*
*** Virgin Dig. VC7 90726-2; *VC 790726-4* [id.]. Nigel Rogers, Paul O'Dette.

This Dowland recital, made in 1988, has eluded us until now, and it turns out to be one of the finest of Dowland CDs. Whether or not you like the actual sound Nigel Rogers makes (and voices are a tremendously personal matter), there can be no question of his artistry and taste. This is singing of real style, every word clearly enunciated, every nuance of colour and dynamics beautifully placed. Paul O'Dette's lute playing is hardly less fine, and both artists are beautifully balanced. Strongly recommended.

Ayres: *Can she excuse my wrongs?; Come again, sweet love; Come heavy sleep; Flow not so fast, ye fountains; From silent night; Go nightly cares; In darkness let me dwell; I saw my lady weep; Shall I sue?.* Consort pieces: *Captain Digory Piper's pavane and galliard; The First galliard.* Lute lessons: *Melancholy galliard; Mistess White's nothing; Mistress Winter's jump; My Lady Hunsdon's puff.* Lute duets: *My Lord Chamberlain's galliard; My Lord Willoughby's welcome home.* Lute lessons: *Orlando sleepeth; Sir John Smith's almain; Tarlton's resurrection.*
*** HM HMC 90245 [id.]. Alfred Deller, Consort of Six, Robert Spencer.

Ayres: *Come away, come away sweet love; Flow my tears; If my complaints could passions move; If that a sinner's sighs be angel's food; Lasso, vita mia; Me, me and none but me; O gentle Death; Say, love, if ever thou didst find; Sorrow stay; Weep you no more sad fountain; What if I never speed?; Wilt thou unkind, thus reave me.* Consort pieces: *Can she excuse galliard; Fortune my foe; The Frog galliard; Katherine Darcy's galliard; Lachrimae pavane; The Round battle galliard.* Lute lessons: *Can she excuse galliard; Galliard; The Lady Laiton's almain; Midnight; Mistress White's thing; The Shoemaker's wife (Toy).*
*** HM HMC 90244. Alfred Deller, Consort of Six, Robert Spencer.

Deller's two collections are admirably planned and beautifully recorded. He is in excellent voice and songs like *Come away sweet love, Sorrow stay* and the poignant *Come again, sweet love* (which opens the second disc) suit his special timbre especially well, while variety is provided by interweaving his solos with lute piecs and music for Elizabethan consort of six instruments (two viols, flute, lute, cittern and bandora). The recording is naturally balanced and neither of these recitals outstay their welcome.

Lachrimae, or Seaven Teares.
*** BIS Dig. CD 315 [id.]. Dowland Consort, Jakob Lindberg.

Jakob Lindberg and his consort of viols give a highly persuasive account of Dowland's masterpiece. The texture is always clean and the lute clearly present. The recording is made in the pleasing acoustic of Wik Castle, near Uppsala, and needs to be reproduced at a low-level setting. Beautiful playing, expertly recorded.

Lachrimae or Seaven Teares: excerpts.
*** Virgin Dig. VC7 90795-2 [id.]. Fretwork, with Christopher Wilson – BYRD: *Consort music.* ***

This record differs from rival accounts in that it intersperses the *Lachrimae* (which are unbroken in the fine Jakob Lindberg record) with consort music of Byrd, thus bringing greater variety of mood and feeling. The performances are of undoubted merit and can be recommended as offering an interesting alternative.

Drigo, Riccardo (1846–1930)

La Flûte magique (ballet; complete).
*** Decca Dig. 421 431-2 [id.]. ROHCG O, Bonynge – DELIBES; MINKUS: *La Source.* ***

Drigo's ballet has nothing whatsoever to do with Mozart's opera, but its storyline does have something in common with *The Red shoes*, for, once the hero starts playing his flute, no one can stop dancing. It has a happy ending, and the score is appropriately vivacious, the invention inconsequential but so prettily scored and amiably tuneful that it makes a very agreeable entertainment when played as wittily and elegantly as here. Richard Bonynge is in his element and, with Decca's finest sound, this cannot fail to entertain.

Dukas, Paul (1865–1935)

L'apprenti sorcier (The sorcerer's apprentice).
*** DG Dig. 419 617-2; *419 617-4* [id.]. BPO, Levine – SAINT-SAËNS: *Symphony No. 3.* ***
*** EMI Dig. CDC7 49964-2 [id.]. Oslo PO, Mariss Jansons – RAVEL: *Daphnis* **(*); RESPIGHI: *Feste romane.* ***
(M) *** Sony SBK 46329; *40-46329* [id.]. Phd. O, Ormandy – BERLIOZ: *Symphonie fantastique* **; MUSSORGSKY: *Night.* ***
(*) Decca Dig. 421 527-2 [id.]. Montreal SO, Dutoit (with Concert: '*Fête à la française*' *).
(M) **(*) Chan. CHAN 6503; *MBTD 6503* [id.]. SNO, Gibson – ROSSINI/RESPIGHI: *La boutique fantasque;* SAINT-SAËNS: *Danse macabre.* **(*)
(B) **(*) Pickwick Dig. PCD 921. Nat. Youth O of Great Britain, Christopher Seaman – STRAVINSKY: *Firebird ballet.* **(*)

Levine chooses a fast basic tempo, though not as fast as Toscanini (who managed with only two 78 sides), but achieves a deft, light and rhythmic touch to make this a real orchestral scherzo. Yet the climax is thrilling, helped by superb playing from the Berlin Philharmonic; in the gentle 'epilogue' the picture of a crestfallen apprentice handing the broom back to his master comes readily into the mind's eye. The sound is suitably expansive and its clarity reveals the brilliance of Dukas's scoring. The CD has an amplitude and sparkle which are especially telling.

Although there is just an occasional hint of the self-consciousness affecting *Daphnis et Chloé*, Jansons's account of *L'apprenti sorcier* is brilliant and exhilarating. There is a strong sense of atmosphere, and the playing of the Oslo orchestra in all departments reminds us that it is now among the very finest in Europe.

Ormandy's 1963 recording of Dukas's famous orchestral narrative is played with great orchestral bravura. The pacing is just right, and the imagery of Walt Disney's *Fantasia* springs readily to mind. Spectacular sound too.

Dutoit does not quite match Levine's zest (nor indeed achieves the sense of calamity at the climax that the latter does), but he is genially enjoyable and is featured within a desirable collection, given demonstration-worthy recording – see our Concerts section.

Gibson secures excellent playing from the SNO, if without the sheer panache of his Philadelphia competitors. The recording (made in City Hall, Glasgow, in 1972) is less overtly brilliant than Ormandy's but has plenty of atmosphere. The Chandos disc, however, is ungenerous in playing time (37 minutes).

Under Christopher Seaman, the National Youth Orchestra of Great Britain give a most attractive account of Dukas's orchestral scherzo, with ensemble and commitment that leave little to be desired. There is plenty of impulse here, and the modern digital recording is full and brilliant.

L'apprenti sorcier; La péri.
(*) Chan. Dig. CHAN 8852; *ABTD 1469* [id.]. Ulster O, Yan Pascal Tortelier – CHABRIER: *España* etc. *

It is puzzling that so attractive, colourful and potentionally popular a score as *La péri* is neglected. It seldom figures in the concert hall and this is its only recent recording. Yan Pascal Tortelier takes the opening fanfare much quicker than did Ansermet and Dervaux, and the begining of the ballet proper is oddly balanced: the horn and woodwind interpolations (marked *pp*) are a bit too close by comparison with the strings (also marked *pp*, but almost *ppp* on this disc), and the string line could afford to be more prominent throughout. It is, however, a very good performance indeed with plenty of atmosphere and feeling. The wind and strings are much more naturally proportioned in *L'apprenti sorcier*, which is equally successful as a performance.

Ariane et Barbe-bleue (opera): complete.
(M) *** Erato/Warner Dig. 2292 45663-2 (2) [id.]. Ciesinski, Bacquier, Paunova, Schauer, Blanzat, Chamonin, Command, Fr. R. Ch. & O, Jordan.

Ariane et Barbe-bleue is a rarity and this is its first appearance on CD. It is rich in invention and atmosphere, as one would expect from the composer of *La péri* and *L'apprenti sorcier*, and its vivid colours should ensure its wide appeal. Dukas was enormously self-critical and consigned an earlier opera, *Horn and Rimenhild*, to oblivion, along with much other music. Ariane is, like Debussy's *Pelléas*, set to a Maeterlinck text but there is none of the half-lights and the dream-like atmosphere of the latter. The performance derives from a French Radio production and is, with one exception, well cast; its direction under the baton of Armin Jordan is sensitive and often powerful; the recording is eminently acceptable. The complete libretto is included, and this most enterprising and valuable reissue is strongly recommended.

Duparc, Henri (1848–1933)

Mélodies (complete): *Au pays où se fait la guerre; Chanson triste; Élégie; Extase; La fuite (duet); Le galop; L'invitation au voyage; Lamento; Le Manoir de Rosamonde; Phidylé; Romance de Mignon; Sérénade; Sérénade florentine; Soupir; Testament; La vague et la cloche; La vie antérieure.*
*** Hyp. Dig. CDA 66323 [id.]. Sarah Walker, Thomas Allen, Roger Vignoles.

The Hyperion issue is as near an ideal Duparc record as could be. Here are not only the thirteen recognized songs but also four early works – three songs and a duet – which have been rescued from the composer's own unwarranted suppression. The singers are ideally matched and contrasted, both of them characterful and searching; and the layout of songs on the record is itself most happily devised, with the singers alternating and with the programme framed by Sarah Walker's inspired singing of two of the finest songs of all, both of them settings of Baudelaire, *L'invitation au voyage* and *La vie antérieure*, a late inspiration. Roger Vignoles is the ever-sensitive accompanist; and the recording captures voices and piano beautifully, bringing out the tang and occasional rasp of Walker's mezzo and the glorious tonal range of Allen's baritone.

Dupré, Marcel (1886–1971)

Symphony in G minor for organ and orchestra, Op. 25.
*** Telarc Dig. CD 80136 [id.]. Michael Murray, RPO, Ling – RHEINBERGER: *Organ concerto No. 1.* ***

If you enjoy Saint-Saëns's *Organ symphony* you'll probably enjoy this. The organ's contribution is greater, though it is not a concerto. It is a genial, extrovert piece, consistently inventive if not as memorably tuneful as its predecessor. The performance has warmth, spontaneity and plenty of flair, and the recording has all the spectacle one associates with Telarc in this kind of repertoire.

Chorale and fugue, Op. 57; 3 Esquisses, Op. 41; Preludes and fugues: in B; G min., Op. 7/1 & 3; Le tombeau de Titelouse: Te lucis ante terminum; Placare Christe servulis, Op. 38/6 & 16; Variations sur un vieux Noël, Op. 20.
*** Hyp. Dig. CDA 66205; *KA 66205* [id.]. John Scott (St Paul's Cathedral organ).

An outstandingly successful recital, more spontaneous and convincing than many of the composer's own recordings in the past. Dupré's music is revealed as reliably inventive and with an atmosphere and palette all its own. John Scott is a splendid advocate and the St Paul's Cathedral organ is unexpectedly successful in this repertoire. The reverberation does bring some clouding of detail, but the swirling sounds are always pleasing to the ear, and details focus well at lower dynamic levels.

Duruflé, Maurice (born 1902)

Fugue sur la thème du Carillon des heures de la Cathédrale de Soissons; Prélude, adagio et choral varié sur la thème du Veni Creator; Prélude sur l'Introit de l'Épiphanie; Prélude et fugue sur le nom d'Alain, Op. 7; Scherzo, Op. 2; Suite, Op. 5.
**(*) Delos Dig. D/CD 3047 [id.]. Todd Wilson (Schudi organ of St Thomas Aquinas, Dallas, Texas.

The producer of this record, which contains all Duruflé's organ music, consulted the composer before choosing the present organ, which has recently been modified to make it even more suitable for the purpose. Even so, it possesses a mellifluous palette and, coupled with the cathedral-like reverberation of Dallas's Catholic church, the effect has less reedy bite than that of a typical French instrument. But the performances of Duruflé's often powerful and always engagingly inventive music are of the highest quality, and Todd Wilson builds thrilling climaxes as well as articulating cleanly and showing a fine ear for colour, notably in the *Scherzo*, Op. 2. Obviously, he also relishes the Alain quotations (from *Litanies*) in the ingenious piece that commemorates his name. The account of the closing *Toccata* of the *Suite*, Op. 5, has breathtaking bravura and if here, as elsewhere, detail is not sharply registered, the spontaneity and power of the playing are compulsive. The recording is immensely spectacular in its amplitude and range, although once or twice saturation point seems to be approached at the forceful closing cadences.

Requiem, Op. 9.
(*) EMI Dig. CDC7 49880-2 [id.]. Murray, Bär, King's Coll. Ch., ECO, Cleobury – FAURÉ: *Requiem.* *

Requiem, Op. 9 (3rd version); *4 Motets, Op. 10.*
*** Hyp. Dig. CDA 66191; *KA 66191* [id.]. Ann Murray, Thomas Allen, Corydon Singers, ECO, Best; Trotter (organ).

Using the chamber-accompanied version, with strings, harp and trumpet – a halfway house between the full orchestral score and plain organ accompaniment – Best conducts a deeply expressive and sensitive performance of Duruflé's lovely setting of the *Requiem.* With two superb soloists and an outstandingly refined chorus, it makes an excellent recommendation, well coupled with motets, done with similar freshness, clarity and feeling for tonal contrast. The recording is attractively atmospheric yet quite clearly focused.

It makes a generous and ideal coupling having the Duruflé *Requiem* coupled with the work which it clearly seeks to emulate, the Fauré *Requiem.* Cleobury takes a rather recessive view of the Duruflé, bringing out its meditative repose rather than any dramatic tension. But with beautiful, polished – if very English – singing from the King's Choir, and excellent contributions from the two soloists, this can certainly be recommended – although, considered individually, neither performance would be a first choice.

Dutilleux, Henri (born 1916)

L'Arbre des Songes (Violin concerto).
*** Sony Dig. MK 42449 [id.]. Stern, O Nat. de France, Maazel – MAXWELL DAVIES: *Violin concerto.* ***

In his *Violin concerto* Dutilleux, always the perfect craftsman and consistently writing with refinement, yet shows how taut self-discipline can go with natural expressive warmth. There are passages in this tightly knit structure of seven linked sections which sound very like Walton updated; and the underlying romantic fervour finds Stern playing with warm commitment, strongly accompanied by Maazel and the Orchestre National. First-rate recording.

Symphony No. 1; Timbres, espace, mouvement.
❀ *** HM Dig. HMC 905159 [id.]. O Nat. de Lyon, Serge Baudo.

In Dutilleux's *First Symphony* there is a mercurial intelligence and a vivid imagination at work, and the orchestral textures are luminous and iridescent. What is particularly impressive is its sense of forward movement: you feel that the music is taking you somewhere. *Timbres, espace, mouvement* is a more recent work, dating from 1978. Serge Baudo is an authoritative interpreter of this composer and the Lyon orchestra also serve him well. The engineering is superb: there is plenty of space round the various instruments, and the balance is thoroughly realistic.

Le Loup (ballet): symphonic fragments.
(M) *** EMI CDM7 63945-2 [id.]. Paris Conservatoire O, Prêtre – MILHAUD: *Création du monde;* POULENC: *Les Biches.* ***

Dutilleux's score for *Le Loup*, with its 'Beauty and the Beast' storyline bringing a tragic ending, is dominated by a haunting, bitter-sweet waltz theme of the kind that, once heard, refuses to budge from the memory. But the invention throughout has plenty of colour and variety, and Dutilleux's orchestral palette is used individually to great effect. Prêtre makes a persuasive case for the suite, and this vivid recording is part of a highly attractive triptych of French ballet scores.

Métaboles.
(M) *** Erato/Warner 2292 45689-2 [id.]. French Nat. RO, Munch – HONEGGER: *Symphony No. 4.* ***

Métaboles is a marvellously atmospheric piece, with the fastidious orchestral palette this composer commands: it has something of the rhythmic energy of Stravinsky, the evocative atmosphere of Messiaen, but is wholly individual. It is played in splendid and exhilarating fashion by the Orchestre National de l'ORTF (as the French Radio Orchestra was cumbersomely known in the days of de Gaulle), and the recording could have been made yesterday. Strongly recommended.

Ainsi la nuit.
(M) *** Pickwick Dig. MCD 17; *MCC 17* [id.]. New World String Qt – DEBUSSY: *String quartet;* RAVEL: *String quartet.* **(*)

Dutilleux's score dates from the mid-1970s but, despite its title, the music is not intended to be programmatic in any depictive sense; instead it is meant to conjure up the moods and impressions surrounding the idea of 'night' – not night itself so much as its aura. As so often with this composer, the writing is highly imaginative, and the New World Quartet convey its sense of mystery and its scurrying whispers most effectively. Excellent recording too.

Piano sonata.
**(*) Olympia Dig. OCD 354 [id.]; Archduke MARC 2. Donna Amato – BALAKIREV: *Sonata.* **(*)

The Dutilleux *Sonata* has an almost symphonic breadth and sense of scale; it is tonal – the first movement is in F sharp minor and its centrepiece, a *Lied*, is finely wrought and original, and skilfully linked to the final chorale and variations. Donna Amato, a young American pianist, gives a totally committed and persuasive account of it, and the recording is very truthful; given the interest and rarity of the coupling, this is a most desirable issue.

Dvořák, Antonín (1841–1904)

Carnaval overture, Op. 92; The Golden spinning wheel, Op. 109; Hussite overture, Op. 67; In nature's realm, Op. 91; My home, Op. 62; The Noonday witch, Op. 108; Othello, Op. 93; Symphonic variations, Op. 78; The Water goblin, Op. 107; The Wild dove, Op. 110.
(M) *** DG 435 074-2 (2) [id.]. Bav. RSO, Rafael Kubelik.

Kubelik's performances are among his finest on record and they are superbly played. He is splendidly dashing in *Carnaval*; the two other pieces, Opp. 91 and 93 (all three linked by a recurring main theme) which Dvořák wrote immediately before his first visit to America in 1892, are comparably successful and full of colouristic subtlety. He is superbly passionate in the *Hussite overture*, without overdoing the rhetoric. The opening of *The Golden spinning wheel* is gentle and elfin-like, and there is some bewitching playing from the woodwind throughout this performance; this is matched by tender strings and the noble restraint of the trombones. In both *The Water goblin* and *The Noonday witch* Kubelik's dramatic urgency is most compulsive, with stabbing rhythms in the former and the lyrical sections of the score given with much poignancy. *The Wild dove* is more difficult to bring off, but here – as in the other two – there is magic and lustre in the orchestra, and the atmospheric tension is striking. The *Symphonic variations* opens warmly and graciously, yet Kubelik is obviously determined to minimize the Brahmsian associations; his light touch and apt pacing lead on to the lively finale, which becomes a characteristic mixture of fugato and the spirit of the dance. The recordings, made in the Munich Hercules-Saal between 1973 and 1977, are freshly transferred to CD and generally sound excellent.

Overtures: Carnaval, Op. 92; In Nature's realm, Op. 91; Othello, Op. 93. Scherzo capriccioso, Op. 66.
*** Chan. Dig. CHAN 8453; *ABTD 1405* [id.]. Ulster O, Handley.

Dvořák wrote this triptych immediately before his first visit to America in 1892. Until now, Opp. 91 and 93 have tended to be eclipsed by the just public acclaim for the *Carnaval overture*. Handley's superb performances put the three works in perspective. A splendid issue, superbly recorded in the attractive ambience of Ulster Hall, Belfast.

Overtures: Carnaval, Op. 92; In Nature's realm, Op. 91; Othello, Op. 93; Scherzo capriccioso, Op. 66; Symphonic variations, Op. 78.
*** ASV Dig. CDDCA 794 [id.]. RPO, John Farrer.

John Farrer scores over Handley by including also the *Symphonic variations*, an undervalued work, here given a performance of airy freshness which confounds any Brahmsian associations, and gives the music much lyrical charm, linking the work more closely than usual to the *Slavonic dances*. There is certainly no lack of substance, but the buoyant fugue at the end is wonderfully spirited. The three linked overtures have comparable warmth and delicacy of colouring. There is plenty of drama too, especially in *Othello*, and the only slight disappointment is that *Carnaval*, while vigorous enough, with a richly hued central section, could have been even more exuberant. The *Scherzo capriccio*, is brightly vivacious, with the lilting secondary theme beguilingly subtle in its rhythmic lift. The recording, made at St Barnabas Church, Mitcham is wide ranging and naturally balanced, more transparent less sumptuous in violin timbre than the Chandos alternative.

Cello concerto in B min., Op. 104.
*** DG 413 819-2 [id.]. Rostropovich, BPO, Karajan – TCHAIKOVSKY: *Rococo variations.* ***
*** Chan. Dig. CHAN 8662; *ABTD 1348* [id.]. Wallfisch, LSO, Mackerras – DOHNÁNYI: *Konzertstück.* ***
(M) *** BMG/RCA GD 86531 (6531-2-RG]. Harrell, LSO, Levine – SCHUBERT: *Arpeggione sonata.* ***
(M) *** EMI CDM7 69169-2; *EG 769169-4*. Tortelier, LSO, Previn – TCHAIKOVSKY: *Rococo variations.* ***
(B) *** DG 429 155-2; *429 155-4* [id.]. Fournier, BPO, Szell – BLOCH: *Schelomo;* BRUCH: *Kol Nidrei.* **(*)
(M) (***) EMI CDH7 63498-2 [id.]. Casals, Czech PO, Szell – ELGAR: *Concerto* (**(*)) (with BRUCH: *Kol Nidrei* (***)).
**(*) Ph. 412 880-2 [id.]. Heinrich Schiff, Concg. O, C. Davis – ELGAR: *Concerto.* **(*)
(M) ** Decca Dig. 430 743-2; *430 743-4* [id.]. Lynn Harrell, Philh. O, Ashkenazy – SCHUMANN: *Concerto.* ***
(BB) ** Naxos Dig. 8.550503 [id.]. Maria Kliegel, RPO, Halasz – ELGAR: *Cello concerto.* **
*(*) BMG/RCA Dig. RD 60717 [60717-2-RC]. Starker, St Louis SO, Slatkin – BARTÓK: *Concerto* (arrangement). ***

(i) *Cello concerto; Carnaval overture, Op. 92; Rusalka: Polonaise.*
**(*) Ph. Dig. 422 387-2 [id.]. (i) Julian Lloyd Webber; Czech PO, Neumann.

If Rostropovich can sometimes sound self-indulgent in this most romantic of cello concertos, the degree of control provided by Karajan gives a firm yet supple base, and there have been few recorded accounts so deeply satisfying. The result is unashamedly romantic, with many moments of dalliance, but the concentration is never in doubt. Splendid playing by the Berliners, and a bonus in the shape of Tchaikovsky's glorious *Rococo variations*. The analogue recording dates from 1969 and the original sound was both rich and refined; the effect is certainly enhanced in the first-class CD transfer.

Rafael Wallfisch's is an outstanding version, strong and warmly sympathetic, masterfully played and with fewer expressive distortions than is common, and with its rich Chandos recording full of presence. This is a performance which, in its taut co-ordination between soloist, conductor and orchestra, far more than usual establishes the unity of the work. This is not to say that the soloist lacks individuality but that he is so confident and commanding that rhythms which are usually distorted come out with emphatic precision. The excitement as well as the warmth of the piece comes over as in a live performance, and Wallfisch's tone remains rich and firm in even the most taxing passages. Above all – helped by a natural balance for the solo cello – this is a performance which conveys the deepest expressiveness without any hint of self-indulgence. The orchestral playing, the quality of sound and the delightful, generous and unusual coupling all make it a recommendation which must be given the strongest advocacy.

In Lynn Harrell's first RCA recording, made in the mid-1970s, his collaboration with James Levine in Dvořák's *Cello concerto* proved a powerful and sympathetic one. Richly satisfying accounts of the first and second movements culminate in a reading of the finale which proves the most distinctive of all. The main body of the movement is finely integrated, but it is the *Andante* epilogue which brings the most memorable playing, very expansive but not at all sentimental, with a wonderful sense of repose. The recording is bright and full and has been remastered most successfully for CD.

The richness of Tortelier's reading of Dvořák's *Cello concerto* has long been appreciated on record; his 1978 recording with Previn has a satisfying centrality, not as passionately romantic as Rostropovich's (full-price) recording on DG, but with the tenderness as well as the power of the work held in perfect equilibrium.

Julian Lloyd Webber's version boasts an obvious advantage in having as collaborators the Czech Philharmonic under the Dvořák specialist, Neumann – although not everyone will like the fruity, slightly whiny horn tone in the great second-subject melody when it first appears in the introduction. Some of the advantage is dissipated by the recording, which is agreeable and atmospheric but not ideally clear on inner detail; other versions bring orchestral playing of even sharper intensity. Not that there is any lack of intensity in Lloyd Webber's playing. This is a strong and warmly sympathetic performance, marked by ripe, rich tone and opulent vibrato; but there are places where the stress on the soloist shows in unwanted agogics and uneven rhythms, even in an occasional forced easing of tempo. Only next to the very finest versions does this appear as anything like a flaw, and anyone who fancies the non-cello Dvořák coupling will not be disappointed.

Fournier's reading has a sweep of conception and richness of tone and phrasing which carry the melodic lines along with exactly the mixture of nobility and tension that the work demands. The phrasing in the slow movement is ravishing, and the interpretation as a whole balances beautifully. DG's recording is forward and vivid, with a broad, warm tone for the soloist. Dating from 1962, it sounds newly minted on a single bargain-price CD and tape, coupled with Bloch and Bruch.

Casals plays with astonishing fire and the performance seems to spring to life in a way that eludes many modern artists; the rather dry acoustic of the Deutsches Haus, Prague, and the limitations of the 1937 recording are of little consequence. This disc is one of the classics of the gramophone.

Schiff's reading has an unexaggerated vein of poetry more akin to Yo-Yo Ma, and its range of emotion is satisfying on a smaller scale. It sounds extremely well in its CD transfer and, with a generous and successful Elgar coupling, is well worth considering.

Lynn Harrell's 1982 digital version of the Dvořák *Cello concerto* for Decca, while brilliantly recorded, is relatively disappointing when compared with his fervent, earlier, analogue version with James Levine for RCA. It is now reissued, coupled with a splendid account of the Schumann *Concerto*.

On the Naxos bargain label it makes a generous coupling having the two greatest of all cello concertos. Maria Kliegel is a warmly expressive soloist, generally persuasive, whose tone is yet not ideally opulent, and whose expansive manner – as in the second subject of the first movement – runs to extremes. If the orchestral accompaniment was tauter, the results would be even more convincing. As it is, the reading runs the risk of self-indulgence. Yet with good, modern, digital sound and so generous a coupling, it makes a fair bargain in the lowest price range.

Janos Starker, one of the first great cellists to emerge in the early LP era, still plays with a satisfying fullness and firmness of tone. but with the solo instrument balanced very close, the dynamic range on his RCA digital recording is disappointingly narrow, and the performance lacks the flair which made his earlier record so compelling. If it makes a generous coupling for Starker's unique recording of the Bartók *Viola concerto* in its cello version, there are many far more satisfying accounts of the Dvořák.

Piano concerto in G min., Op. 33.
*** BMG/RCA Dig. RD 60781 [60781-2]. Rudolf Firkušný, Czech PO, Václav Neumann – JANÁČEK: *Concertino; Capriccio.* ***
(*) Decca Dig. 417 802-2 [id.]. András Schiff, VPO, Dohnányi – SCHUMANN: *Introduction and allegro appassionato.* *

Firkušný has played the Dvořák *Piano concerto* in both the original version and that by Vilém Kurz, as well as a *mélange* of the two, and recorded it several times during his long and distinguished career. None were produced under such happy circumstances as the present performance which celebrated his returned to Prague after almost half a century in exile. The recording made in the Spanish Hall of Prague Castle conveys its sunny geniality to good effect, and although the great pianist was seventy-nine when this record was made, the playing still sounds both youthful and aristocratic. For long the partnership of Sviatoslav Richter and Carlos Kleiber has dominated the catalogue. This EMI version has recently been withdrawn, no doubt to reappear at mid-price, but Firkušný now makes an admirable first choice, and his claims are enhanced by the value of the coupling, (and the 73 minutes' playing time of the CD).

Schiff's excellent performance derives from a public concert in the Musikverein, and he is given splendid support from the Vienna Philharmonic under Dohnányi. In the Decca recording, the piano is very up-front and the perspective in this respect is not wholly natural. All the same, this is an excellent performance.

Violin concerto in A min., Op. 53.
(B) *** CfP Dig. CD-CFP 4566; *TC-CFP 4566* [Ang. CDB 62920]. Tasmin Little, RLPO, Handley – BRUCH: *Concerto No. 1.* ***
*** EMI Dig. CDC7 49858-2 [id.]. Kyung Wha Chung, Phd. O, Muti (with *Romance, Op.11*).
*** EMI CDC7 47168-2 [id.]. Perlman, LPO, Barenboim (with *Romance, Op.11*).
(M) *** Ph. 420 895-2. Accardo, Concg. O, C. Davis – SIBELIUS: *Violin concerto.* ***
(***) Sony Dig. MK 44923 [id.]. Midori, NYPO, Mehta (with *Carnaval overture* and *Romance*).
*** DG Dig. 419 618-2 [id.]. Mintz, BPO, Levine (with *Romance*) – SIBELIUS: *Concerto.* **(*)
(B) *** Sup. 110601-2. Josef Suk, Czech PO, Ančerl – SUK: *Fantasy.* ***
(B) **(*) DG Compact Classics 413 844-2 (2) [id.]. Edith Peinemann, Czech PO, Peter Maag – BEETHOVEN: *Romances* ***; BRAHMS: *Violin concerto* **(*); BRUCH: *Violin concerto No. 1.* **

Tasmin Little brings to this concerto an open freshness and sweetness, very apt for this composer, that are extremely winning. The firm richness of her sound, totally secure on intonation up to the topmost register, goes with an unflustered ease of manner, and the recording brings little or no spotlighting of the soloist; she establishes her place firmly with full-ranging, well-balanced sound that co-ordinates the soloist along with the orchestra.

Kyung Wha Chung in her first recording under her exclusive EMI contract gives a heartfelt reading of a work that can sound wayward. The partnership with Muti and the Philadelphia Orchestra is a happy one, with the sound warmer and more open than it has usually been in the orchestra's recording venue. Chung may not always generate the tense excitement of such rivals as Perlman and Midori, with their generally faster speeds, but in each movement she uses the extra elbow-room to bring out subtler detail, more fantasy. So in the first movement, using a warm vibrato, she draws out the Slavonic melancholy to the full, and in the finale she is able to give light and shade to the dance rhythms, with the 'giocoso' element bubbling out in a happy and genial reading. She finds similar concentration in the *Romance*, which is also the coupling on Perlman's and Midori's versions.

Perlman and Barenboim still sound pretty marvellous and show all the warmth and virtuosity one could desire. This CD also has the eloquent and touching *F minor Romance*. Perlman is absolutely superb in both pieces: the digital remastering undoubtedly clarifies and cleans the texture, though there is a less glowing aura about the sound above the stave.

In his Philips recording, Accardo is beautifully natural and unforced, with eloquent playing from both soloist and orchestra. The engineering is altogether excellent, and in a competitive field this must rank high, especially at mid-price.

Midori, still in her teens, gives an astonishing display not merely of virtuosity but of artistic maturity. From the similarities with Perlman's version, not least over tempo, one might have guessed that she too has been guided by the great New York teacher, Dorothy DeLay. Yet, even more than Perlman, Midori finds a vein of tenderness, using a wider range of tone-colour and dynamic; and the finale, at a speed even faster than Perlman's, becomes a bitingly brilliant Slavonic dance, with the passage-work only occasionally showing signs of haste. A most exciting performance. The *Romance* too finds Midori a deeply sympathetic Dvořákian; but collectors should not be swayed too much by the presence of the extra item, the *Carnaval overture*, for the sound is coarse, with brass over-prominent. The recording for the main items is warm and undistracting, if not ideally well defined.

There is dazzling playing from Schlomo Mintz, whose virtuosity is effortless and his intonation astonishingly true. There is good rapport between soloist and conductor, and the performance has the sense of joy and relaxation that this radiant score needs. The digital sound is warmer and more natural in its upper range than the remastered EMI recording.

Suk's earlier performance is back in the catalogue at bargain price, effectively remastered, recoupled with the Suk *Fantasy*. Its lyrical eloquence is endearing, the work is played in the simplest possible way and Ančerl accompanies glowingly.

Edith Peinemann's poetic and pleasingly natural account of Dvořák's *Violin concerto* is the bonus item provided to fill out the pair of Compact Classics CDs, which otherwise match the equivalent DG cassette. She is well partnered by Peter Maag, and the Czech Philharmonic provide a vividly idiomatic accompaniment, especially in the very winning finale.

Romance, Op. 11.
*** Ph. Dig. 420 168-2 [id.]. Zukerman, St Paul CO – BEETHOVEN: *Romances;* SCHUBERT: *Konzertstücke* etc. ***

Zukerman gives a simple, heartwarming performance of this beguiling work within a most attractive concert of short pieces for violin and orchestra, and he is beautifully recorded.

Rondo in G min., Op. 94.
*** ASV Dig. CDRPO 8012; *ZCRPO 8012* [id.]. Tortelier, RPO, Groves – ELGAR: *Concerto* **(*); TCHAIKOVSKY: *Rococo variations.* ***

The Dvořák *Rondo* is one of Tortelier's party-pieces, and its point and humour are beautifully caught here.

Serenade for strings in E, Op. 22.
(*) Virgin Dig. VC7 91165-2; *VC 791165-4.* LCO, Warren-Green – SUK: *Serenade* *; TCHAIKOVSKY: *Serenade.* **(*)
(BB) **(*) Naxos Dig. 8.550419 [id.]. Capella Istropolitana, Kr(e)chek – SUK: *Serenade.* ***

Serenade for strings, Op. 22; Romance, Op. 11.
(B) *** Pickwick Dig. PCD 928; *CIMPC 928.* Laredo, SCO, Laredo – WAGNER: *Siegfried idyll.* ***

Serenade for strings, Op. 22; Serenade for wind in D min., Op. 44.
*** ASV Dig. CDCOE 801; *ZCCOE 801* [id.]. COE, Alexander Schneider.
*** Ph. 400 020-2 [id.]. ASMF, Marriner.
*** Decca Dig. 417 452-2 [id.]. LPO, Hogwood.
(B) **(*) CfP Dig. CD-CFP 4597; *TC-CFP 4597.* (i) ECO, Mackerras; (ii) ECO (without conductor).

The young players of the Chamber Orchestra of Europe give winningly warm and fresh performances of Dvořák's *Serenades.* The distinction of the wind soloists in this fine orchestra has been demonstrated many times on disc, and the *Wind serenade* brings a particularly distinguished performance. Schneider's approach in the *String serenade* is no less persuasive, with the COE string players producing beautifully refined playing, vividly caught in the ASV recording.

Marriner's later, Philips performance is direct without loss of warmth, with speeds ideally chosen and refined, yet spontaneous-sounding and consistently resilient string playing. It still remains very competitive; in the *Wind serenade* the Academy are comparably stylish, with beautifully sprung rhythms, and the recording has a fine sense of immediacy.

A fresh, bright and spring-like account of both works from Hogwood and the LPO in clean, slightly recessed sound. Textually this version of the *String serenade* is unique on record when it uses the original score, newly published, in which two sections (one of 34 bars in the scherzo and the other of 79 bars in the finale), missing in the normal printed edition, are now included. Though these performances are not quite as winning or as rhythmically subtle as those of Schneider or Marriner, they are still very enjoyable, and the inclusion of the extra material brings added interest.

Laredo's performance of Dvořák's lovely *Serenade* is volatile, full of spontaneous lyrical feeling. The recording, made in City Hall, Glasgow, is admirably balanced to give a true concert-hall effect and add ambient lustre to the string timbre. As an encore Laredo takes the solo role in the *F minor Romance*, which he plays with appealing simplicity.

Warren-Green and his excellent London Chamber Orchestra bring their characteristically fresh, spontaneous approach to the Dvořák *Serenade*, with the opening nostalgia not over-indulged and with agreeably light articulation in allegros: the scherzo and finale are exhilarating. If without the winning individuality of the outstanding COE version under Schneider, this is still very enjoyable, and the Suk coupling is outstanding. Excellent sound: the recording was made in All Saints', Petersham, but enjoys acoustic bloom without ecclesiastical blurring.

Fine playing from the Capella Istropolitana on Naxos, and flexible direction from Jaroslav Kr(e)chek. His pacing is not quite as sure as in the delightful Suk coupling, and the *Adagio* could flow with a stronger current, but this is still an enjoyable and well-recorded performance.

Exceptionally clear sound in both works on CfP, although the strings in Op. 22 have a degree of digital edge that some ears may find slightly aggressive. Mackerras is surprisingly direct in the *String serenade* and his seemingly deliberate lack of charm is emphasized by the sound.Those who prefer fresh athleticism rather than ripeness should find this to their taste. The *Wind serenade* is played without a conductor and the result is agreeably crisp and sparkling, with vivid recording.

Serenade for wind, Op. 44.
*** CRD CRD 3410 [id.]. Nash Ens. – KROMMER: *Octet-Partita*. ***

The Nash Ensemble can hold their own with the competition in the *D minor Serenade*, and their special claim tends to be the coupling, a Krommer rarity that is well worth hearing. The CRD version of the Dvořák is very well recorded and the playing is very fine indeed, robust yet sensitive to colour, and admirably spirited.

Slavonic dances Nos. 1–8, Op. 46; 9–16, Op. 72.
*** Decca Dig. 430 171-2 [id.]. Cleveland O, Christoph von Dohnányi.
❀ (M) *** Sony SBK 48161 [id.]. Cleveland O, George Szell.
*** BIS Dig. CD 425 [id.]. Rheinland-Pfalz State PO, Leif Segerstam.
(M) **(*) Decca Dig. 430 735-2; *430 735-4* [id.]. RPO, Dorati.

Dohnányi's rhythmic flexibility and the ebb and flow of his rubato are a constant delight. The changing moods of Nos. 2 and 3 of Op. 46 are winningly handled, and the woodwind delicacy of No. 4 is no less engaging; No. 5 is irresistibly infectious, and the string articulation in No. 6 is deliciously refined, followed by some equally delicate woodwind playing in No. 7. The bustling energy of Nos. 1 and 8 and the opening dance of Op. 72 have plenty of impetus, yet never bring a feeling that the music is pressed too hard; the panache of the playing is simply exilharating. The sweep of the violins in the languorous E minor dance, Op. 72, No. 2, is thrilling, while the gentle melancholy of the D flat major dance (Op. 72/4) and the wistful introduction to the last of this second set are equally well caught. This final dance is done most imaginatively with a musing, improvisatory freedom, almost valedictory in feeling. The recording is superb, very much in the demonstration bracket, with the warm acoustics of the Cleveland Hall ideal in providing rich textures and brilliance without edge.

Szell's exuberant, elegant and marvellously played set of the *Slavonic dances* now returns to the catalogue, absolutely complete (74 minutes), newly remastered by Bejun Mehta and Christopher Herles. Our Rosette recognizes their loving skill alongside Szell's remarkable achievement, for these recordings have never before sounded half as good as this. True, the balance is close (which means pianissimos fail to register) but the charisma of the playing is unforgettable. Just sample the delicacy of articulation at the opening of No. 6 – a joy from beginning to end – or the breathtaking accelerando at the close of No. 3. This is orchestral playing of extraordinary distinction, and for all the racy exuberance one senses a predominant feeling of affection and elegance. There is endless delicate colouristic detail and delectably light rhythmic precision. Szell's constant ebb and flow of rubato is shown so well in the glorious string playing in the famous *No. 10 in E minor*, (Op. 72/2), while the sheer zest of the presentation brims over in the bouncing sparkle of No. 11 (Op. 72/3). Fascinatingly the sessions were spaced over a period of two years, starting in January 1963, and concluding in January 1965. The warm acoustics of Severance Hall ensures the consistency of the orchestral sound, although as it happens the very earliest recordings are among the most successful.

On the BIS collection the sound is full and vivid, the orchestral playing does not lack imaginative touches, and Segerstam's approach is suitably volatile and with plenty of lyrical exuberance, while the opening *Furiant* readily demonstrates the zest of the music-making. There is delicacy of rhythm and colour from both strings and woodwind.

Dorati's performances have characteristic brio, the RPO response is warmly lyrical when necessary, and the woodwind playing gives much pleasure. Sparkle is the keynote and there is no lack of spontaneity. On CD the louder tuttis are not as sweet in the upper range of the strings as one would expect. However, the digital sound is generally superior.

Symphonies Nos. 1–9.
(M) *** Chan. Dig. CHAN 9008/13 [id.]. SNO, Neeme Järvi.

Symphonies Nos. 1–9; Overtures: Carnaval; Hussite; My home; Othello.
(M) **(*) Ph. 432 602-2 (6). LSO, Rowicki.

Symphonies Nos. 1–9; Overtures: Carnaval; In nature's realm; My home. Scherzo capriccioso.
❀ (B) *** Decca 430 046-2 (6). LSO, István Kertész.

Symphonies Nos. 1–9; Carnaval overture; Scherzo capriccioso; The wood dove, Op. 110.
(M) **(*) DG 423 120-2 (6). BPO, Kubelik.

Järvi has the advantage of outstanding, modern, digital recording, full and naturally balanced. The recordings were made between May 1986 and October 1987, in either the SNO Centre or the Henry Wood Hall, Glasgow. The set is offered at upper mid-price, six CDs for the price of four. Only the *Fourth Symphony* is split centrally between discs; all the others can be heard uninterrupted. But there are no fillers, as with Kertész on Decca.

For those not wanting to go to the expense of the digital Chandos Järvi set, Kertész's bargain box, recorded in the Kingsway Hall between 1963 and 1966, is an easy first choice among the remaining collections of Dvořák symphonies. The CD transfers are of Decca's best quality, full-bodied and vivid with a fine ambient effect. Only in the earliest recorded, No. 8, is there a noticeable touch of thinness in the violin timbre, most strikingly in the *Allegretto* third movement; No. 7, one of the more relaxed performances of the cycle, is given greater dramatic impact than on LP. It was Kertész who first revealed the full potential of the early symphonies, and his readings gave us fresh insights into these often inspired works. To fit the symphonies and orchestral works on to six CDs some mid-work breaks have proved unavoidable, and these occur in Nos. 2 (after the first movement) and No. 5 (before the finale); but the set remains a magnificent memorial to a conductor who died sadly young.

Kubelik's set has much to recommend it: first and foremost the glorious playing of the Berlin Philharmonic and the natural warmth that Kubelik brings to his music-making. He seems less convinced by the earliest symphonies than Järvi. In spite of some idiosyncratic but not unidiomatic touches, however, he achieves glowing performances of Nos. 6–9. At mid-price this remains a desirable set; the bonus items are all well played and recorded and are equally idiomatic.

Rowicki's Dvořák cycle is overshadowed by the Kertész series with the same orchestra. Heard as a whole in this mid-price box, Rowicki's readings present a consistent and very satisfying view of Dvořák, slightly understating the expressiveness of slow movements and often in fast movements adding a touch of fierceness. The opening of No. 6, for example, with the syncopated accompaniment very clearly defined, sounds unusually fresh and individual, even if one would not always want to hear it interpreted in that way. The recordings, made between 1965 and 1972, are generally refined, warm and full-bodied in the Philips manner. The CD transfer has opened up the sound: although it is still resonantly weighty, the effect is more vivid than on LP. This is certainly enjoyable listening. However, this set would have been even more attractive at bargain price.

Symphony No. 1 in C min. (The Bells of Zlonice), Op. 3; The Hero's song, Op. 111.
*** Chan. Dig. CHAN 8597; *ABTD 1291* [id.]. SNO, Järvi.

The first of Dvořák's nine symphonies is on the long-winded side. Dvořák never had a chance to revise it, which he certainly would have done, had the score not been lost for over half a century. Yet whatever its structural weaknesses, it is full of colourful and memorable ideas, often characteristic of the mature composer. Järvi directs a warm, often impetuous performance, with rhythms invigoratingly sprung in the fast movements and with the slow movement more persuasive than in previous recordings. Tense and energetic as the SNO performance remains throughout the last two movements, there are some signs of the ensemble growing slacker. The real rarity here is *The Hero's song*, Dvořák's very last orchestral work. It has no specific programme, though the journey from darkness to light in the unspecified hero's life is established clearly enough. Järvi's strongly committed, red-blooded performance minimizes any weaknesses. The recording, warmly atmospheric in typical Chandos style, is among the best in this series, not always clean on detail but firmly focused.

Symphony No. 1 in C min. (The Bells of Zlonice), Op. 3; Legends, Op. 59/1–5.
(BB) *** Naxos Dig. 8.550266 [id.]. Slovak PO, Czecho-Slovak RSO, Gunzenhauser.

Though on a super-bargain label, this Bratislava version rivals any in the catalogue both as a performance and in sound. The ensemble of the Slovak Philharmonic is rather crisper than that on the other modern rival, Järvi's Chandos disc, and the recording, full and atmospheric, has detail less obscured by reverberation. The first five of Dvořák's ten *Legends* make a generous coupling: colourful miniatures, colourfully played.

Symphony No. 2 in B flat, Op. 4; Legends, Op. 59/6–10.
(BB) *** Naxos Dig. 8.550267 [id.]. Slovak PO, Czecho-Slovak RSO, Gunzenhauser.

With speeds more expansive than those of his Chandos rival, Neeme Järvi, Gunzenhauser gives a taut, beautifully textured account, very well played and recorded, a formidable rival in every way, even making no allowance for price. The completion of the set of *Legends* makes a very generous coupling (73 minutes).

Symphony No. 2 in B flat, Op. 4; Slavonic rhapsody No. 3 in A flat, Op. 45.
**(*) Chan. Dig. CHAN 8589; *ABTD 1283* [id.]. SNO, Järvi.

Järvi directs a characteristically warm and urgent performance of this exuberant inspiration of the 24-year-old composer. A jubilant work, it is by far the longest symphony Dvořák ever wrote, and was originally longer still, before the composer revised it. Unfortunately, the Chandos sound, characteristically reverberant but washier than usual, misses the necessary sharpness. The tangy Czech flavour of the music loses some of its bite, and the results are often too smooth; one might easily miss even the entry of the second subject. The generous fill-up, the *Slavonic rhapsody No. 3*, is done with delicious point and humour, and with sound back to Chandos's normally high standard.

Symphony No. 3 in E flat, Op. 10; Carnaval overture; Scherzo capriccioso.
*** Virgin Dig. VC7 90797-2; *VC 790797-4* [id.]. RLPO, Pešek.

Symphony No. 3 in E flat, Op. 10; Carnaval overture, Op. 92; Symphonic variations, Op. 78.
*** Chan. Dig. CHAN 8575; *ABTD 1270* [id.]. SNO, Järvi.

This was the first of Dvořák's symphonies to show the full exuberance of his genius. The music certainly betrays the influence of Wagner, but nowhere do the Wagnerian ideas really conceal the essential Dvořák. Pešek's strong, direct manner in Dvořák here works to bring out the rhythmic freshness of the writing in a most persuasive reading. Pešek gives a radiant account of the lovely second subject and is masterly in controlling the long development section. He has similar concentration in sustaining a very slow speed for the central *Adagio*, keeping it clean and taut, where Järvi, much faster, sounds relatively unsettled. The clarity of the recording, beautifully set against a believable acoustic, adds to the rhythmic freshness, not least in Pešek's urgent performance of the finale. He is warmly sympathetic as well in his account of the *Scherzo capriccioso*, in which he observes the central repeat.

Järvi's is also a highly persuasive reading, not ideally sharp of rhythm in the first movement but totally sympathetic. His account of the *Adagio* blossoms, and the finale effectively combines energy with weight. The recording is well up to the standards of the house and the fill-ups are particularly generous, with an exhilarating performance of *Carnaval* followed by a strongly characterized set of variations, with a rich, lyrical emphasis.

Symphonies Nos. 3 in E flat, Op. 10; 6 in D, Op. 60.
(BB) *** Naxos Dig. 8.550268 [id.]. Slovak PO, Stephen Gunzenhauser.

These exhilarating performances of the *Third* and *Sixth Symphonies* are well up to the standard of earlier records in this splendid Naxos series. Gunzenhauser's pacing is admirably judged through both works, and rhythms are always lifted. Excellent, vivid recording in the warm acoustics of the Bratislava Concert Hall.

Symphony No. 4 in D min.; Othello overture.
** Virgin Dig. VC7 91144-2 [id.]. Czech PO, Libor Pešek.

Symphony No. 4 in D min., Op. 13; (i) *Biblical songs, Op. 99.*
*** Chan. Dig. CHAN 8608; *ABTD 1251* [id.]. SNO, Järvi, (i) with Brian Rayner-Cook.

Järvi's affectionate reading of this early work brings out the Czech flavours in Dvořák's inspiration and makes light of the continuing Wagner influences, notably the echoes of *Tannhäuser* in the slow movement. Allowing himself ample rubato, Järvi completely avoids any *Tannhäuser*-like squareness and, in the bold march-time trio of the *Scherzo* with its jangling cymbal and triangle, edges away from vulgarity in his persuasive rhythmic pointing, as well as giving a delectable swagger to the *Allegro feroce* main section. This is a performance to win converts to a work often underrated. The generous coupling has Brian Rayner-Cook giving positive and clean-cut, if not very Slavonic-sounding, performances of the ten *Biblical songs* which Dvořák wrote in America at the same period as the *Cello concerto*. The recording is well up to the Chandos standard.

The Czech Philharmonic always have something individual to say in this music, and with Pešek they are at their most seductive in the *Othello overture* and in the scherzo of the *Symphony*, with its main theme given an infectious, lolloping rhythmic gait. But Pešek's reading fails to develop sufficient thrust in the first movement; nor does he attempt to disguise the Wagnerian influences which can weight heavily on the slow movement. Fortunately the finale is as racy and vigorous as anyone could want. The recording is good, rather than outstanding, and this is ungenerous measure.

Symphonies Nos. 4–6.
** Sup. Dig. 11 1005-2 (2) [id.]. Czech PO, Václav Neumann.

Neumann's plain Dvořák style has a certain honesty, but lacks charm. His first movement of the *Fourth* is more concentrated than Pešek's, but his underplaying of the Wagnerian passages means that the *Andante* fails to make much impact at all. The Czechs know just how to bring off the vivacious scherzo, but the finale is rhythmically too forceful. In the first movement of the *Fifth* Neumann lets the music unfold simply without coaxing, and his *Andante* has a pleasing warmth. Then one has to change discs for a badly placed break, before the brilliant scherzo. All in all, this is too plainspun to be in any way distinctive and it is only in the *Sixth* that Neumann achieves that degree of flowing spontaneity that distinguishes his best work in the recording studio. The grace of the *Adagio* is matched by the spirited zest of the *Furiant* scherzo, and the finale too has ample vitality and thrust. But this pair of CDs is totally uncompetitive at full price.

Symphonies Nos. 4 in D min., Op. 13; 8 in G, Op. 33.
(BB) **(*) Naxos Dig. 8.550269; *4550269* [id.]. Slovak PO, Stephen Gunzenhauser.

Gunzenhauser's *Fourth* is very convincing. In his hands the fine lyrical theme of the first movement certainly blossoms and the relative lack of weight in the orchestral textures brings distinct benefit in the Scherzo. The slow movement, too, is lyrical without too much Wagnerian emphasis. The naturally sympathetic orchestral playing helps to make the *Eighth* a refreshing experience, even though the first two movements are rather relaxed and without the impetus of the finest versions. The digital sound is excellent, vivid and full, with a natural concert-hall ambience.

Symphony No. 5 in F, Op. 76; Othello overture, Op. 93; Scherzo capriccioso, Op. 66.
❀ *** EMI Dig. CDC7 49995-2 [id.]; *EL 749995-4.* Oslo PO, Jansons.

Symphony No. 5 in F, Op. 75; The water goblin, Op. 107.
*** Chan. Dig. CHAN 8552; *ABTD 1258* [id.]. SNO, Järvi.

Jansons directs a radiant account of this delectable symphony and the EMI engineers put a fine bloom on the Oslo sound. With its splendid encores, equally exuberant in performance, this is one of the finest Dvořák records in the catalogue.

Järvi is also most effective in moulding the structure, subtly varying tempo between sections to smooth over the often abrupt links. His persuasiveness in the slow movement, relaxed but never sentimental, brings radiant playing from the SNO, and Czech dance-rhythms are sprung most infectiously, leading to an exhilarating close to the whole work, simulating the excitement of a live performance. The fill-up is unusual and colourful, a piece based on a gruesome little fairy-story full of sharp dramatic contrasts. It is a highly rewarding piece and a substantial bonus when the advocacy is so strong.

Symphonies Nos. 5 in F, Op. 76; 7 in D min., Op. 70.
(BB) *** Naxos Dig. 8.550270; *4550270* [id.]. Slovak PO, Stephen Gunzenhauser.

Gunzenhauser's coupling is recommendable even without the price advantage. The beguiling opening of the *Fifth*, with its engaging Slovak wind solos, has plenty of atmosphere, and the reading generates a natural lyrical impulse. The *Seventh*, spontaneous throughout, brings an eloquent *Poco adagio*, a lilting scherzo, and a finale that combines an expansive secondary theme with plenty of excitement and impetus.

Symphony No. 6 in D, Op. 60.
*** Decca Dig. 430 204-2; *430 204-4* [id.]. Cleveland O, Dohnányi – JANÁČEK: *Taras Bulba.* ***

Symphony No. 6 in D; The noon witch, Op. 108.
*** Chan. Dig. CHAN 8530; *ABTD 1240* [id.]. SNO, Järvi.

Dohnányi continues his Dvořák series in Cleveland with a superb account of No. 6, coupling it unexpectedly but pointfully with another Czech masterpiece, the Janáček rhapsody. With its obvious echoes of Brahms's *Symphony No. 2* (also in D major), this is a work which gains from the refinement of the playing, with the violin melody at the start of the slow movement given ethereal beauty. Dohnányi even underlines the likeness with the Brahms *Second* at the start of the finale, with the opening given a hushed expectancy before blazing out. But nor does Dohnányi in his warmth and freshness miss the earthy qualities of the writing; and the impact of the performance is greatly enhanced by the fullness and weight of the recording, one of Decca's most vivid. This easily takes precedence over the Järvi version on Chandos, though some will still prefer the latter's rare Dvořák coupling, *The noonday witch.*

Järvi and the Scottish National Orchestra give a highly sympathetic reading of Dvořák's *Sixth*, underlining the direct links with Brahms's *Second Symphony*, notably at the start of the first and fourth movements. The bloom on the Chandos sound adds to the lyrical warmth and sweetness of the slow movement, ripely and relaxedly done but without self-indulgence. The *Furiant*, rhythmically sprung like a jolly dance, leads to a finale taken challengingly fast but with lifted rhythms too, and with sharp contrasts of mood. In the fill-up, Järvi brings out the programmatic story-telling of the piece, with tremolo strings breathtakingly delicate on the entry of the witch. The recording is in the demonstration bracket.

Symphony No. 7; The golden spinning wheel, Op. 109.
*** Chan. Dig. CHAN 8501; *ABTD 1211* [id.]. SNO, Järvi.

We have long praised Carlos Païta's outstanding, inspirational version of Dvořák's *D minor Symphony*, a reading of striking lyrical ardour, matching excitement with warmth. This music-making has the kind of spontaneity one experiences only at the most memorable of live performances, helped by a natural concert-hall balance and the strikingly wide dynamic range of the CD format. However, Païta has his own label; this record has become increasingly difficult to obtain and is only intermittently available (Lodia LOD-CD 782).

Järvi's Chandos version is just a little plain-spun. He secures playing of considerable lyrical ardour from his excellent SNO players, but the articulation of the scherzo misses out that engaging 'comma' which brings added lift to the presentation of the main idea. However, it would be wrong to make too much of this; Chandos offer a very substantial bonus in including one of Dvořák's most memorable symphonic poems. Järvi's account has plenty of drama and atmosphere. The CD brings a fine bloom to a warmly resonant orchestral sound-image.

Symphonies Nos. 7 in D min., Op. 70; 8 in G, Op. 88.
(M) *** Mercury 434 312-2 [id.]. LSO, Antal Dorati.
(M) *** Decca Dig. 430 728-2; *430 728-4* [id.]. Cleveland O, Christoph von Dohnányi.
*** Virgin Dig. VC7 90756-2; *VC 790756-4* [id.]. RLPO, Pešek.
(M) *** Ph. 420 890-2; *420 890-4* [id.]. Concg. O, C. Davis.
**(*) Sup. Dig. 11 0713-2 [id.]. Czech PO, Neumann.

Dorati's coupling brings an extraordinary successful account of No. 7 to rank alongside Barbirolli's Hallé version in its spontaneous feel of a live performance. It is similarly enhanced by the vividly realistic concert hall balance of the (1963) Mercury recording – one of their very finest. The interpretation is free, yet Dorati's strong rhythmic grip on the first movement means that he can relax for the entry of the second subject and again at the beginning of the recapitulation. The passionate climax then makes way for a gentle reprise of the main theme on the horns, with a magical diminuendo. The *Poco Adagio* is similarly impulsive and full of ardour, and the Scherzo lifts off with a sparkle, even though there is no rhythmic nudging of the main theme. The finale has enormous energy and bite, and an exuberant thrust, leading on to a thrilling coda where the tension rises to the highest level, as Dorati broadens the few final bars. The *Eighth Symphony* was recorded four years earlier, with the acoustic of Watford Town Hall again providing a highly convincing ambience. Dorati's reading proves comparably vibrant. Yet he is expansively warm at the opening, and shows himself sensitive to the work's pastoral qualities, making the *Adagio* the kernel of his interpretation. The LSO playing is again very fine, and full of impulse and feeling. The violins are especially pleasing in the graceful third movement, which Dorati takes a little faster than usual, to good effect. The trumpets set the scene of the last movement regally and at the close there is another display of spontaneous combustion, when the symphony storms to its exciting close.

Dohnányi's coupling of Dvořák's *Seventh* and *Eighth Symphonies* with the Cleveland Orchestra is also very attractive indeed. Tempi are all aptly judged. The playing of the Cleveland Orchestra is so responsive that the overall impression is one of freshness, and the recording is in the demonstration class, using the acoustics of the Masonic Auditorium to give a convincingly natural balance, the internal definition achieved without any kind of digital edge.

In Pešek's Dvořák series the opening of the *D minor*, the darkest of the cycle, may lack the ominous and mysterious atmosphere of some performances, but the fresh, direct manner relates it readily to other Dvořák. The slow movement is warm and relaxed, and the scherzo becomes a happy folk-like dance, despite the minor key, while Pešek's speed in the finale also allows him to give a lift to the stamping dance-rhythms. No. 8 receives a similarly refreshing performance, persuasive in a light, relaxed way, with the folk element again brought out, above all in the middle movements. The scherzo is liltingly light; and again the performance benefits from the full, clear sound.

The coupling of Sir Colin Davis's analogue recordings of the *D minor* and *G major Symphonies* is also highly recommendable. The recordings (from 1975 and 1978 respectively) have been remastered most successfully: there is very little loss to the body of the string timbre and the Concertgebouw ambience casts a warm glow on woodwind and horns, while detail is cleaner, with the bass firm. Davis's performances, with their bracing rhythmic flow and natural feeling for Dvořákian lyricism, are appealingly direct, yet have plenty of life and urgency.

The coupling of the *Seventh* and *Eighth Symphonies* also shows Neumann's direct Dvořák manners at their most impressive. The reading of the *Seventh* is strong and purposeful, yet the famous Scherzo has lilting buoyancy. The *Eighth* opens warmly and brings comparable vitality; again the Scherzo and finale have plenty of lift and excitement. The Czech orchestral colour in the lyrical music of the slow movements has a special appeal with even the degree of horn vibrato part of this special palette. The recording is spacious, and if not as glowingly vivid as the sound the Decca engineers achieve in Cleveland, it is fully acceptable. But this reissue has only a limited appeal in the full price bracket.

Symphonies Nos. 7 in D min., Op. 70; 9 (From the New World).
(M) **(*) EMI/Phoenixa CDM7 63774-2; *EG 763774-4* [id.]. Hallé O, Sir John Barbirolli.

Barbirolli's recordings derive from the Pye/Nixa label and date from 1957 and 1959. The remastering has successfully cleaned up the fizzy upper focus of the LP originals. Indeed the *Seventh* emerges totally renewed. Its first movement has fine exhilaration and a superb burst of adrenalin in the closing pages; the *Poco adagio* has an engaging Dvořákian lyrical flow, and the scherzo is contagiously buoyant, after its gently seductive opening. The finale opens powerfully and gathers further momentum to reach a thrilling denouement. In the *New World* Barbirolli achieves memorability by the utmost simplicity of his approach. The first movement unfolds dramatically after a presentation of the second subject which achieves lyrical contrast with very little relaxation of tempo. There is an electrifying tightening of tension towards the end of the movement (an effect which is repeated with equal compulsion in the finale). The *Largo* is sustained with unaffected beauty, and the scherzo is notable for its woodwind colour and especially the delightful trills in the trio. The finale gathers the music's threads together before the exciting close, with a real sense of apotheosis. Altogether this is Barbirolli at his revelatory finest.

Symphony No. 8 in G, Op. 88.
(B) *** Sony MYK 44872 [id.]. Columbia SO, Bruno Walter – WAGNER: *Parsifal* excerpts. ***
(M) (***) EMI mono CDM7 63399-2 [id.]. RPO, Beecham – SIBELIUS: *Symphony No. 2*. (***)
**(*) Sony SK 46670 [id.]. Concg. O, Giulini – RAVEL: *Ma Mère l'Oye*. **(*)

Symphony No. 8 in G; Carnaval overture; The wood dove, Op. 110.
(B) *** DG 429 518-2; *429 518-4* [id.]. BPO or Bav. RSO, Kubelik.

Symphony No. 8 in G; Legends Nos. 4, 6 & 7, Op. 59; Scherzo capriccioso.
❀ (M) *** EMI CDM7 64193-2; *EG 764193-4* [id.]. Hallé O, Sir John Barbirolli.

Symphony No. 8 in G, Op. 88; Scherzo capriccioso; Notturno for strings.
*** Telarc Dig. CD 80206 [id.]. LAPO, Previn.

Symphony No. 8 in G, Op. 88; The wood dove, Op. 110.
*** Chan. Dig. CHAN 8666; *ABTD 1352* [id.]. SNO, Järvi.

Barbirolli's account of this symphony was one of his best Pye records: the reading has immense vitality and forward impetus, the kind of spontaneous excitement that is rare in the recording studio, and yet the whole performance is imbued with a delightful, unforced lyricism. There is, however, a slight lapse in the third movement when the strings take over the main tune of the Trio; here the combination of vibrato and a fruity portamento brings a characteristically indulgent underlining of the lovely melody. But this is a small blemish on an otherwise remarkably good performance. The *Scherzo capriccioso* is warm and very exciting too, and the *Legends* make a colourful bonus. This was always the finest of Barbirolli's late Dvořák symphonies technically, and the EMI documentation reveals why: it was made in 1957/8 in Manchester's recently rebuilt Free Trade Hall by the Mercury recording team, led by Wilma Cozart Fine. In remastered form it is tremendously real and vivid; more than any other of these reissued Barbirolli recordings, it gives the listener an electrifying illusion of sitting in a concert hall listening to a live performance.

Previn and the Los Angeles Philharmonic give a delectable performance of the *Eighth*. Warmth and freshness go with the finest recorded sound yet achieved with this orchestra in Royce Hall, full and with a vivid sense of presence that allows fine inner clarity. Characteristically, Previn's Dvořák style is sharply rhythmic, and his idiomatic use of rubato brings affectionate moulding of phrase and rhythm, generally kept within a steady pulse. The tenderness that Previn brings to the delicate second subject is a fine instance, and the delectable counter-theme in the slow movement with its descending demi-semiquaver scales has rarely been so lightly done. The natural lilt of the first contrasting episode in the scherzo is also a delight, with Previn providing an exuberant pay-off in the *furiant* coda to that movement. Previn's fill-up is equally attractive, with the infectiously sprung account of the *Scherzo capriccioso* scarcely harmed by the omission of the central repeat.

Järvi's highly sympathetic account of the *Eighth* underlines the expressive lyricism of the piece, the rhapsodic freedom of invention rather than any symphonic tautness, with the SNO players reacting to his free rubato and affectionate moulding of phrase with collective spontaneity. Ensemble is excellent, and speeds are never eccentric. The finale is marginally slower than usual, but the changes of mood are made to sound easy and natural. *The Wood dove* makes a good if not generous fill-up, atmospherically telling. The warm Chandos sound has plenty of bloom, with detail kept clear, and is very well balanced.

Kubelik's *Eighth* is appealingly direct, with responsive, polished playing from the Berlin Philharmonic Orchestra. For its reissue, the Bavarian Radio Orchestra provide the substantial encores, which are splendidly done.

Walter's famous account of Dvořák's *Eighth* was recorded in 1962, just before he died. It is a strong yet superbly lyrical reading; but the overall lyricism never takes the place of virility and Walter's mellowness is most effective in the *Adagio*. The sound was always warm and full but now is more naturally clear, the focus of all sections of the orchestra firmer. With its equally inspired coupling of the *Prelude and Good Friday music* from *Parsifal*, this bargain-priced issue ranks high in the CBS legacy.

Beecham always got rousing results, and this is an infectiously spirited and rumbustious performance, but full of glowing Dvořákian lyricism. The 'live' recording comes from 1959 and the Royal Festival Hall acoustics bring a somewhat dry ambience, with a bright sheen on the strings and a less-than-ideal balance for the brass – the trumpet fanfare in the finale is much too close and tuttis can be a bit fierce. Nevertheless the sound is fully acceptable and every bar of the music is alive.

Carlo-Maria Giulini in his mid-seventies expansively brings out an unexpected sensuousness in Dvořák's folk-based writing, justifying the odd coupling by bringing it surprisingly close to the Ravel. The beauty comes not only from Giulini's loving manner, his warmly expressive style and expansive phrasing, but from the glorious playing of the Royal Concertgebouw, above all the incomparable strings. From first to last the ear is caressed, and though in principle the approach is wrong for what is essentially fresh, open-air music, Giulini's concentration and the sense of immediate communication is magnetic. This is very much a record for Giulini-admirers and those with a sweet tooth, helped by warm, atmospheric recording.

Symphonies Nos. 8 in G, Op. 88; 9 in E min. (From the New World).
*** Lodia Dig. LO-CD 789 [id.]. RPO, Païta.
(M) ** EMI CDM7 64325-2 [id.]; *EG 764325-4*. BPO, Karajan.
(B) ** Decca 433 646-2; *433 646-4* [id.]. LAPO, Zubin Mehta.

Païta's generous coupling of Dvořák's two most popular symphonies brings a thrustful new version of No. 8 and an equally positive and fiery account of the *New World*, marked by extreme speeds, slow as well as fast. The full-bodied, larger-than-life recording has a vivid sense of presence, enhancing the dramatic impact of performances which – to judge by the occasional flaw in ensemble – were done in long takes, adding to the sense of spontaneity. The RPO string playing is particularly beautiful in the *Largo* slow movement of the *New World*, taken very slowly but steadily too. Only in the main *Allegro con fuoco* of the finale does Païta's fondness for fast speeds lose some of the music's weight and breadth. But those who have enjoyed Païta's *Seventh Symphony* will find that these performances have much in common with that, even if the balance is less natural in its simulation of the concert hall.

Whereas Karajan's 1977 *New World* for EMI is robust and spontaneous sounding, but refined too, with the cor anglais solo of the *Largo* made fresh, at a nicely flowing tempo, his account of the *G major Symphony* is a disappointment. When he recorded this work earlier for Decca with the VPO, if the reading had moments of self-indulgence, he also projected a consistent degree of affection. In Berlin he is straighter, and in the trio of the scherzo the Berlin strings achieve their portamenti with considerable subtlety. But the *Adagio*, so involving in the Vienna performance, is curiously unaffecting, while the scherzo's coda is rhythmically square. The most attractive part of the performance is near the close of the finale, where the composer recalls his opening material; here Karajan is appealingly nostalgic before dashing away into the coda. The sound is vivid in both works, but tends to fierceness, especially in the G major work.

This 1975 Los Angeles coupling appears generous – although not generous enough for Mehta to include the first-movement exposition repeat in the *New World Symphony*; but then neither does Karajan. The Decca recording is strikingly spectacular and full-blooded. Both performances are vibrant and bold. On the whole the *Eighth* comes off marginally better than the *Ninth*, but the reading is lacking in tenderness and charm – essential qualities, even in this ebullient symphony. The *New World*, brilliantly extrovert, crisply disciplined but lacking grace, misses most of Dvořák's subler shadings, even if it makes a strong impact.

Symphony No. 9 in E min. (From the New World), Op. 95.
(B) *** DG 429 676-2. BPO, Karajan – SCHUBERT: *Symphony No. 8.* ***
(M) **(*) EMI Dig. CDD7 63900-2 [id.]. BPO, Tennstedt – KODÁLY: *Háry János.* ***
**(*) Denon Dig. CO 79728 [id.]. Czech PO, Kubelik – MOZART: *Symphony No. 36.* **(*)
**(*) Decca Dig. 414 421-2 [id.]. Cleveland O, Dohnányi.
(M) (***) BMG/RCA mono GD 60279; *GK 60279* [60279-2-RG; *60279-4-RG*]. NBC SO, Toscanini – KODÁLY: *Háry János*: suite (***); SMETANA: *Má Vlast: Vltava.* (**)
** Virgin Dig. VC7 91476-2 [id.]. Houston SO, Eschenbach – TCHAIKOVSKY: *Francesca da Rimini.* **

(i) *Symphony No. 9 (New World);* (ii) *American suite, Op. 98b.*
(M) *** Decca Dig. 430 702-2; *430 702-4* [id.]. (i) VPO, Kondrashin; (ii) RPO, Dorati.

Symphony No. 9 (New World); Carnaval overture, Op. 92.
**(*) Sup. Dig. 11 0960 2 [id.]. Czech PO, Bělohlávek.

Symphony No. 9 (New World); Carnaval overture; Scherzo capriccioso, Op. 66.
(M) **(*) Decca 417 724-2 [id.]. LSO, Kertész.

Symphony No. 9 (New World); My home overture, Op. 62.
*** Chan. Dig. CHAN 8510; *ABTD 1220* [id.]. SNO, Järvi.

(i) *Symphony No. 9 (New World);* (ii) *Scherzo capriccioso.*
(B) *** DG 427 202-2; *427 202-4* [id.]. (i) BPO; (ii) Bav. RSO, Kubelik.

(i) *Symphony No. 9 (New World);* (ii) *Scherzo capriccioso;* (iii) *Serenade for strings in E, Op. 22* (CD only: (ii) *Carnaval overture; The wood dove*).
(B) *** DG Compact Classics 413 147-2; *413 147-4*. (i) BPO; (ii) Bav. RSO; (iii) ECO; Kubelik.

(i) *Symphony No. 9 (New World);* (ii) *Serenade for strings.*
(M) **(*) Sony SBK 46331; *40-46331* [id.]. (i) LSO, Ormandy; (ii) Munich PO, Kempe.

Symphony No. 9 (New World); Slavonic dances Nos. 1, 3 and 7, Op. 46/1, 3 & 7; 10 and 15, Op. 72/2 & 7.
(M) *** DG 435 590-2; *435 590-4* [id.]. BPO, Karajan.

Symphony No. 9 (New World); Slavonic dances Nos. 6, 8, 10, Op. 46/6 & 8, 72/2.
**(*) Teldec/Warner Dig. 9031 73244-2 [id.]. NYPO, Kurt Masur.

(i) *Symphony No. 9 (New World);* (ii) *Symphonic variations, Op. 78.*
(B) *** CfP Dig. CD-CFP 9006; *TC-CFP 4382*. LPO, Macal.

Kondrashin's Vienna performance of the *New World Symphony* was one of Decca's first demonstration CDs, and its impact remains quite remarkable. Recorded in the Sofiensaal, the range of the sound is equalled by its depth. The ambience of the hall prevents a clinical effect, yet every detail of Dvořák's orchestration is revealed within a highly convincing perspective. Other performances may exhibit a higher level of tension, but there is a natural spontaneity here, with the first-movement exposition repeat fitting naturally into the scheme of things. The cor anglais solo in the *Largo* is easy and songful, and the finale is especially satisfying, with the wide dynamic range adding drama and the refinement and transparency of the texture noticeably effective as the composer recalls ideas from earlier movements. This splendid disc now returns to the top of the list of recommedations as a superb mid-priced bargain, enhanced by the inclusion of Dorati's RPO version of the engaging *American suite*, which also has clear influences from the New World.

Dohnányi's *New World*, superbly played and recorded like the companion recordings of Nos. 7 and 8, should by rights be a first recommendation, but it fails to observe the first-movement exposition repeat. That said, there is much to praise in this grippingly spontaneous performance, generally direct and unmannered but glowing with warmth. In the first movement Dohnányi, without any stiffness, allows himself relatively little easing of tempo for the second and third subjects while the great cor anglais melody in the *Largo* and the big clarinet solo in the finale are both richly done, with the ripe and very well-balanced Decca recording adding to their opulence. The sound is spectacularly full and rich. However, without a coupling this is short measure.

Macal as a Czech takes a fresh and unsentimental view of the *New World Symphony*, with speeds far steadier than usual in the first movement. His inclusion of the repeat balances the structure convincingly. With idiomatic insights there is no feeling of rigidity, with the beauty of the slow movement purified, the scherzo crisp and energetic, set against pastoral freshness in the episodes, and the finale again strong and direct, bringing a ravishing clarinet solo. The *Symphonic variations*, which acts as coupling, is less distinctive but is well characterized. The digital recording is strikingly believable in its natural balance, with body as well as brilliance, and excellent definition. A fine bargain recommendation.

Karajan's 1964 DG recording held a strong place in the catalogue for two decades, and it is certainly far preferable to his digital version. It has a powerful lyrical feeling and an exciting build-up of power in the outer movements. The *Largo* is played most beautifully, and Karajan's element of detachment lets the orchestra speak for itself, which it does, gloriously. The rustic qualities of the scherzo are affectionately brought out, and altogether this is very rewarding. The recording is full, bright and open. This is now reissued at bargain price, generously coupled with Schubert's *Unfinished*, as a sampler for DG's Karajan Symphony Edition. For those who do not require the *Unfinished Symphony* as coupling, DG have reissued Karajan's 1964 version, sounding as good as ever, coupled with five favourite *Slavonic dances*, given virtuoso performances; they remain stylish because of the superbly polished playing. In the dances the recording is overlit but can be tamed.

Kubelik's marvellously fresh account of the *New World*, recorded in the early 1970s, is certainly among the top versions. His accounts of the *Scherzo capriccioso* and *String serenade* have a comparable freshness. The recording is brightly lit and, like the *Symphony*, somewhat dry in the bass, but the transfers are of DG's finest quality. The Compact Classics pair of CDs includes also fine performances of *Carnaval* and *The wood dove*.

Järvi's opening introduction establishes the spaciousness of his view, with lyrical, persuasive phrasing and a very slow speed, leading into an allegro which starts relaxedly, but then develops in big dramatic contrasts. The expansiveness is underlined, when the exposition repeat is observed. The *Largo* too is exceptionally spacious, with the cor anglais player taxed to the limit but effectively supported over ravishingly beautiful string playing. The scherzo is lilting rather than fierce, and the finale is bold and swaggering. *My home* overture is also given an exuberant performance, bringing out the lilt of dance rhythms.

Among earlier analogue accounts Kertész's LSO version stands out, with a most exciting first movement (exposition repeat included), in which the introduction of the second subject group is eased in with considerable subtlety; the *Largo* brings playing of hushed intensity to make one hear the music with new ears. Kertész's exuberant *Carnaval overture* and his brilliant and lilting account of the *Scherzo capriccioso* are as attractive as any in the catalogue.

Tennstedt's is a warm, romantic reading, freely expressive at generally spacious speeds, very much in the German rather than the Czech tradition. The natural, easy warmth of the famous cor anglais solo at the start of the slow movement has a pure felicity that it would be hard to match. The CD adds clarity to the rich, full recording; however, it also adds a degree of shrillness on the treble in fortissimos. The addition of the *Háry János* suite to Tennstedt's *New World* adds greatly to the attractiveness of this budget-price CD.

It is apt that one of the first two recordings made by Kurt Masur in his new role as music director of the New York Philharmonic should be of the *New World Symphony*. Taken from a live concert given in October 1991 in Avery Fisher Hall, the Teldec recording makes light of the hall's notoriously unhelpful acoustic. Though the sound is on the dry side, the engineers have done wonders not only in giving it a fair bloom but in conveying an extreme dynamic range. The slow movement is particularly fine, with pianissimos that have you catching your breath, and with Masur's very straight, simple phrasing conveying a tender intensity. It is a tribute to Masur and the players that a live performance – apparently taken from one concert and not edited from other sources – should achieve a precision of ensemble to rival that of a studio performance. Masur's very direct manner in the fast movements brings strong, dramatic results, but with very forward sound, and with percussion standing out (the timpani almost deafening at times) the results are on the aggressive side. This is not among the warmer readings of this much recorded work, yet with an attractive coupling of three *Slavonic dances* winningly done, ending with the best-known of all, the *G minor Furiant*, Opus 46 no. 8, it makes a worthwhile addition to a long list. However the first choices for this symphony are all at medium price and each also offers an equally generous coupling.

Visiting Prague for a second time after his historic return from exile a year earlier, Rafael Kubelik made this live recording at a concert in October 1991. It captures the emotional intensity of a moving occasion, though the result is hardly a top contender among the many duplications of this ever-popular work. The main allegro is far faster and fiercer here than it was in Kubelik's studio recording for DG of 1973 with the Berlin Philharmonic, though here too he allows himself generous slowing in the second and third subjects. In the slow movement the wind chording at the start is none too precise, and the cor anglais tone sounds constricted. In the scherzo Kubelik again takes a broad view of the first episode and trio, with their lilting rhythms, and the finale like the first movement is challengingly fast. With recording which inevitably falls short of the finest in its balances, this has a certain historical value, linked to a conductor not always given his full due on record.

It is good to welcome from Supraphon a new-generation recording of the *New World* by the Czech Philharmonic under Jiří Bělohlávek, at the time its principal conductor. He is a most sympathetic Dvořákian, less severe than his predecessor, Vaclav Neumann. He is here consistently warmer, drawing a spontaneous-sounding performance from the players, with free expressiveness always sounding idiomatic. In the Czech manner, relying on a note the composer wrote on one of his scores, the performance omits the exposition repeat. The recorded sound is full-bodied, but the reverberation prevents inner detail from coming out quite cleanly enough in heavy tuttis. The other snag is that at full price the disc offers only the *Carnaval overture* as fill-up, though in an outstandingly jolly and exuberant reading.

With speeds consistently fast and the manner clipped, Toscanini's reading of the *New World* is anything but idiomatic, but it still tells us something unique about Dvořák and his perennial masterpiece, presenting a fiery, thrilling experience. The sound is fuller than most from this source and the transfer brings that out, despite the usual dryness.

Under Ormandy the playing of the LSO has life and spontaneity, and the rhythmic freshness of the scherzo (achieved by unforced precision) is matched by the lyrical beauty of the *Largo* and the breadth and vigour of the finale. Perhaps the reading has not the individuality of the finest versions; but the sound is full and firm in the bass to support the upper range's brilliance. For coupling, we are offered an essentially mellow account of the *String serenade*, directed by Kempe with affectionate warmth.

Eschenbach's reading with the Houston Orchestra is strong and often thoughtful, played and recorded with refinement, but it often sounds self-conscious and over-prepared, not at all idiomatic with a very slow tempo indeed for the *Largo*. That brings out the refined beauty of the Houston string tone, and generally ensemble is excellent. It would have been much better to have this under-appreciated orchestra in music less frequently recorded than the *New World*. Hardly a first choice, but perhaps recommendable to those who want the unusual coupling.

CHAMBER AND INSTRUMENTAL MUSIC

Flute sonatina in G min. (trans. Galway).
*** BMG/RCA Dig. RD 87802 [7802-2-RC]. James Galway, Phillip Moll – FELD; MARTINŮ: *Sonatas*. ***

What the flute version of Dvořák's *Sonatina* underlines more than the violin original is how close this tuneful, unpretentious piece, written for the composer's young children, is to the *New World symphony* of the same year, 1893. The skipping *Molto vivace* of the third movement emerges as almost an Irish jig, and similarly the finale might be inspired by the whistling of an errand-boy. Well recorded, with characterful performances and an unusual and attractive coupling of two modern Czech flute works, it makes an excellent recommendation for anyone wanting a Galway record out of the ordinary.

Piano quartets Nos. 1 in D, Op. 23; 2 in E flat, Op. 87.
❀ *** Hyp. Dig. CDA 66287; *KA 66287* [id.]. Domus.

The Dvořák *Piano quartets* are glorious pieces, and the playing of Domus is little short of inspired. This is real chamber-music-playing: intimate, unforced and distinguished by both vitality and sensitivity. As one would expect, the *E flat* is the more mature and concentrated piece, and the playing in the slow movement is quite magical. Domus are recorded in an ideal acoustic and in perfect perspective; they sound wonderfully alive and warm. An altogether outstanding chamber-music record.

Piano quartet No. 2 in E flat, Op. 87.
**(*) BMG/RCA RD 86256 [RCA 6256-2-RC]. Rubinstein, Guarneri Qt – FAURÉ: *Piano quartet No. 1*. **(*)

Rubinstein's recording, made in December 1970, is here enhanced and is now fuller than originally – though not especially transparent – and the close balance prevents a real pianissimo. Nevertheless this is infectious music-making and there is much to enjoy.

Piano quintet in A, Op. 81.
(M) *** Decca 421 153-2. Clifford Curzon, VPO Qt – FRANCK: *Quintet*. ***

This wonderfully warm and lyrical (1962) performance of Dvořák's *Piano quintet* by Clifford Curzon is a classic record, one by which all later versions have come to be judged, and the CD transfer retains the richness and ambient glow of the original analogue master, yet has improved definition and presence. The piano timbre remains full and real.

Piano quintet in A, Op. 81; Piano trio No. 4 in E min. (Dumky), Op. 90.
**(*) Virgin Dig. VC7 90736-2; *VC 790736-4* [id.]. Nash Ens.

(i) *Piano quintet in A, Op. 81; String quartet No. 12 in F (American), Op. 96.*
*** BMG/RCA RD 86263 [6263-2-RC]. (i) Rubinstein; Guarneri Qt.

It is surprising that the obvious coupling of the *Piano quintet* and the *String quartet No. 12* has not been made more often. Both the RCA performances are memorably warm and spontaneous; tempi tend to be brisk, but the lyrical element always underlies the music and the playing has both great vitality and warmth. Needless to say, Rubinstein's contribution to the *Quintet* is highly distinguished. The recordings, made in April 1971 and 1972 respectively, are well balanced, detailed and fairly full, helped by the attractive studio ambience.

The Nash offer a useful alternative coupling of the *Piano quintet* and the *Dumky trio*. Good, musicianly performances that are eminently well recorded and give satisfaction, without being as memorable as such classic accounts as that with Clifford Curzon.

Piano trio No. 1 in B flat, Op. 21.
*** Teldec/Warner Dig. 2292 44177-2 [id.]. Trio Fontenay – BRAHMS: *Piano trio No. 2.* ***

First-class playing and recording from the Trio Fontenay, and a useful coupling as well, of rewarding music.

Piano trio No. 3 in F min., Op. 65.
*** Chan. Dig. CHAN 8320; *ABTD 1207* [id.]. Borodin Trio.

Piano trios No. 3 in F min., Op. 65; 4 in E min. (Dumky), Op. 90.
*** Sony Dig. MK 44527 [id.]. Emanuel Ax, Young-Uck Kim, Yo-Yo Ma.
(M) **(*) Ph. 426 095-2; *426 095-4.* Beaux Arts Trio.

Piano trio No. 4 in E min. (Dumky), Op. 90.
*** Chan. Dig. CHAN 8445; *ABTD 1157* [id.]. Borodin Trio – SMETANA: *Piano trio.* ***
**(*) Ph. Dig. 416 297-2 [id.]. Beaux Arts Trio – MENDELSSOHN: *Piano trio No. 1.* **(*)

The *F minor Trio* is given a powerful yet sensitive performance by the Ax/Kim/Ma trio. There is the occasional moment when one feels that expressive feeling is just a little too explicit, yet on the whole this is a fine performance and, like the *Dumky*, has warmth and freshness. Occasionally Ax, for all his sensitivity, produces too thick a sound in fortissimo passages, but for the most part his playing is full of musical insight. The recording is faithful and natural.

The Beaux Arts' 1969 performances of Op. 65 and the *Dumky* still sound fresh and sparkling, though the recording on CD is a little dry in violin timbre; the *F minor*, arguably the finer and certainly the more concentrated of the two, is played with great eloquence and vitality.

The playing of the Borodin Trio in the *F minor Trio* has great warmth and fire; such imperfections as there are arise from the natural spontaneity of a live performance, for one feels this is what it must have been, with few if any retakes. The pianist, Luba Edlina, is balanced rather forward but otherwise the wide-ranging Chandos recording has transferred with impressive presence to CD; however, this now seems short measure. But in the *Dumky trio* it is the spontaneous flexibility of approach to the constant mood-changes that makes the splendid Borodin performance so involving, as well as the glorious playing from each of the three soloists. The recording here is naturally balanced and the illusion of a live occasion is striking.

The latest digital Beaux Arts performance is rather more assertive than their earlier approach and, although not lacking dramatic contrast and refinement of detail (Menahem Pressler's playing always gives pleasure), has a degree less spontaneity than before. The new recording has striking realism and presence; and for those who like high drama, this version should be very satisfactory.

String quartets Nos. 1–14; Cypresses, B.152; Fragment in F, B.120; 2 Waltzes, Op. 54, B.105.
(M) *** DG 429 193-2 (9). Prague Qt.

Dvořák's *Quartets* span the whole of his creative life: the *A major*, Op. 2, pre-dates the *First Symphony* and the *G major*, Op. 106, comes two years after the *New World*. This set was made in 1973–7 and first appeared on 12 LPs. In the new format, *No. 3 in D* (which, remarkably, takes 69 minutes 42 seconds) can be accommodated complete on one CD. The glories of the mature *Quartets* (Opp. 34, 51, 61, 80, 96 and 105–6) are well known, though it is only the so-called *American* which has achieved real popularity. The beauty of the present set is that it offers seven more *Quartets* (not otherwise available) plus two *Quartet movements*, in *A minor* (1873) and *F major* (1881), plus two *Waltzes* and *Cypresses* for good measure, all in eminently respectable performances and decent recordings.

String quartets Nos. 8 in E, Op. 80; 9 in D min., Op. 34.
**(*) Chan. Dig. CHAN 8755; *ABTD 1394* [id.]. Chilingirian Qt.

String quartets Nos. 10 in E flat, Op. 51; 11 in C, Op. 61.
**(*) Chan. Dig. CHAN 8837; *ABTD 1458* [id.]. Chilingirian Qt.

Recordings of the Dvořák quartets are not so thick on the ground that one can afford to be ungrateful for good new versions. Chandos provide very fine recorded sound for the Chilingirians, who play with sensitivity in all four *Quartets*, though in terms of sonority they are not as full-blooded as, say, the Endellion (Virgin) listed below. These are straightforward, well-paced readings that are eminently serviceable. Some collectors may feel, perhaps, that they fall short of the very highest distinction, but they are unfailingly musicianly and vital.

String quartet No. 12 in F (American), Op. 96.
(B) *** Pickwick Dig. PCD 883; *CIMPC 883* [id.]. Delmé Qt – BRAHMS: *Clarinet quintet.* ***
*** Ph. Dig. 420 803-2 [id.]. Guarneri Qt – SMETANA: *String quartet No. 1.* ***
*** Ph. 420 396-2 [id.]. Orlando Qt – MENDELSSOHN: *String quartet No. 1.* ***
(B) *** Hung. White Label HRC 122 [id.]. Bartók Qt – DEBUSSY; RAVEL: *Quartets.* **(*)

String quartet No. 12 (American); Cypresses.
*** DG Dig. 419 601-2 [id.]. Hagen Qt – KODÁLY: *Quartet No. 2.* ***

The Delmé Quartet on a superbly recorded Pickwick disc at bargain price give a winningly spontaneous-sounding performance, marked by unusually sweet matching of timbre between the players, which brings out the total joyfulness of Dvořák's American inspiration. The exuberant finale in particular has its rhythms sprung with delectable lightness, leading to an exhilarating close. The unusual coupling, a similarly warm reading of the Brahms *Clarinet quintet*, is both attractive and generous.

The Guarneri performance is warmly romantic; the articulation of the lovely secondary theme of the first movement is particularly affectionate, and both here and in the *Largo sostenuto* one notices the rich cello line of David Soyer, within a responsive texture of finely blended lyricism. Of course there is plenty of life too, and the dance-like finale has an agreeable rhythmic lightness. The recording is full in timbre and most natural in balance and presence.

The Hagen Quartet make an uncommonly beautiful sound and their account of this masterly score is very persuasive indeed. Their playing is superbly polished, musical and satisfying, and few will fail to respond. In the finale, for example, they are marvellously spirited, and they play the enchanting *Cypresses*, which Dvořák transcribed from the eponymous song-cycle, with great tenderness. The recording is altogether superb, very present and full-bodied.

The digital remastering of the 1980 Orlando recording brings very striking presence and immediacy; it emphasizes that their approach, while still romantic, has more drama than the Guarneri account. But again the slow movement is beautifully played and the finale has the most sparkling articulation and dash. With such realistic sound, this still ranks among the best versions of the *Quartet*, with the finely balanced and well-blended tone, excellent musical judgement and great sensitivity, and perhaps it will appear soon at mid-price.

A splendidly alive and spontaneous account from the Bartók Quartet too, polished yet with plenty of warmth and lyrical feeling, and with a dance-like sparkle in the scherzo and finale. Good sound, generous couplings and the bargain status of this issue ensure its value.

String quartets Nos. 12 in F (American), Op. 90; 13 in G, Op. 106.
*** ASV Dig. CDDCA 797; *ZCDCA 797.* Lindsay Qt.

The *F major Quartet* (*American*) is abundantly represented on CD and while it is difficult to speak of a 'best version', the Lindsay is certainly among the very best both in terms of performance and recording (perhaps the balance is marginally too close to be ideal but not so close as to iron out their wide dynamic range). The *G major*, Op. 106, was actually completed shortly before the *A flat*, Op. 105, hence its earlier numbering. It, too, is very well played with much the same dedication and sensitivity. An outstanding coupling.

(i) *String quartet No. 12 (American);* (ii) *String quintet in E flat, Op. 97.*
(M) *** Decca 425 537-2; *425 537-4* [id.]. (i) Janáček Qt; (ii) Vienna Octet (members).

The Janáček performance of the *American quartet* is strikingly fresh, while the *Lento* is warmly eloquent. This is virtuosity of a high order put completely at the service of the composer, and the fine 1964 recording has depth as well as realistic definition. The coupled *E flat Quintet*, another of the greatest works of Dvořák's American period, is given a comparably eloquent and characterful performance by members of the Vienna Octet. Again the recording is full, with an attractive ambience, and the focus is firmer than the orginal LP.

String quintet in G, Op. 77; String sextet in A, Op. 48.
(M) **(*) Decca 430 299-2; *430 299-4* [id.]. Vienna Octet (members).

The *Sextet*, Op. 48, is undoubtedly one of the Czech master's most spontaneous and flowing works. The members of the Vienna Octet give it an eloquent performance. The *G major Quintet* is an early work. The Viennese players are especially sympathetic to the lyrical elements in the music: the scherzo lacks something in sparkle. It is not an easy movement to bring off since, although it has a dance-like quality, it is by no means a furiant. The Viennese group catches the gaiety of the finale more readily, although one misses the authentic Czech lilt. The recording, though not outstanding by Decca's high standards – there is a slight degree of edge in the CD focus of the violin timbre – is still fully acceptable.

String quintet in E flat, Op. 97; String sextet in A, Op. 48.
*** Hyp. Dig. CDA 66308; *KA 66308* [id.]. Raphael Ens.

The *E flat major Quintet*, Op. 97, is one of the masterpieces of Dvořák's American years, and it is most persuasively given by the Raphael Ensemble. It is also very well recorded, though we are placed fairly forward in the aural picture.

Slavonic dances Nos. 1–16, Opp. 46 & 72.
**(*) Ara. Dig. Z 6559 [id.]. Artur Balsam, Gena Raps (piano, four hands).
**(*) Hyp. Dig. CDA 66204; *KA 66204* [id.]. Peter Noke, Helen Krizos (piano, four hands).

Generally fine performances from Artur Balsam and Gena Raps, who respond to the music in a spirit of relaxed enjoyment, yet do not miss its brio. The recording too is well balanced in a pleasing acoustic.

Peter Noke and Helen Krizos often play with more dash, but some of the more reflective moments are less sensitively observed here although their impetuous verve is undoubtedly exhilarating at times. The Hyperion recording is more resonant and, coupled to a fairly close microphone placing, the effect is less convincing, although there is no lack of focus.

VOCAL AND CHORAL MUSIC

Mass in D, Op. 86.
(M) *** Decca 430 364-2 [id.]. Ritchie, Giles, Byers, Morton, Christ Church Cathedral Ch., Preston; Cleobury (organ) – LISZT: *Missa choralis.* ***

The *Mass in D* has many delights to offer. In such a beautifully shaped reading it is self-recommending, especially when coupled with a superb performance of Liszt's equally fresh *Missa choralis*. As so often, the CD remastering shows just how good was the original (Argo) recording, which is impeccably balanced.

Requiem, Op. 89.
(M) *** Decca 421 810-2 (2). Lorengar, Komlóssy, Isofalvy, Krause, Amb. S., LSO, Kertész – KODÁLY: *Hymn of Zrinyi; Psalmus Hungaricus.* ***

The *Requiem* reflects the impact on Dvořák of the English musical world of the day and has a good deal of relatively conventional writing in it. Kertész conducts with a total commitment to the score and secures from singers and orchestra an alert and sensitive response. Pilar Lorengar's vibrato is at times a trifle disturbing, but it is the only solo performance that is likely to occasion any reserve. The recording matches the performance: it has a lifelike balance and the CD remastering adds freshness and bite.

(i) *Stabat Mater, Op. 58;* (ii) *Legends, Op. 59.*
(M) *** DG 423 919-2 (2) [id.]. (i) Mathis, Reynolds, Ochman, Shirley-Quirk, Bav. R. Ch. & O; (ii) ECO, Kubelik.

Dvořák's devout Catholicism led him to treat this tragic religious theme with an open innocence that avoids sentimentality. Kubelik is consistently responsive and this is a work which benefits from his imaginative approach. The recording, made in the Munich Herkules-Saal, is of very good quality. There are ten *Legends*, lyrical and romantic equivalents of the *Slavonic dances* but less robust in rhythmic style and more delicately coloured. They are presented here most persuasively and the 1976 recording, made in the London Henry Wood Hall, is pleasingly vivid and atmospheric.

Te Deum, Op. 103.
**(*) Telarc Dig. CD 80287 [id.]. Atlanta Ch. & SO, Robert Shaw – JANÁČEK: *Glagolitic Mass.* **(*)

Dvořák's vigorous, grandly ceremonial setting of the *Te Deum*, written for his very first concert in New York in 1892, is surprisingly neglected on record. Shaw conducts a glowing performance, very well played and sung, though the relatively backward balance of the chorus – a fault of the Janáček recording too – takes away some of the dramatic impact. The orchestral sound is vivid and forward.

OPERA

Rusalka (complete).
*** Sup. Dig. 10 3641-2 (3) [id.]. Beňačková-Čápová, Novak, Soukupová, Ochman, Drobkova, Prague Ch. & Czech PO, Neumann.

Dvořák's fairy-tale opera is given a magical performance by Neumann and his Czech forces, helped by full, brilliant and atmospheric recording which, while giving prominence to the voices, brings out the beauty and refinement of Dvořák's orchestration. Written right at the end of the composer's career in his ripest maturity but with Wagnerian influences at work, the piece has a unique flavour; where on stage it can seem too long for its material, on record it works beautifully. The title-role is superbly taken by Gabriela Beňačková-Čápová. The voice is creamy in tone, characterfully Slavonic without disagreeable hooting or wobbling, and the famous *Invocation to the Moon* is enchanting. Vera Soukupová as the Witch is just as characterfully Slavonic in a lower register, though not so even; while Wieslaw Ochman sings with fine, clean, heroic tone as the Prince, with timbre made distinctive by tight vibrato. Richard Novak brings out some of the Alberich-like overtones as the Watersprite, though the voice is not always steady. The banding could be more generous, but a full translation is included.

Rusalka: highlights.
(B) *** Sup. Dig. 110617-2. Beňačková-Čápová, Novak, Soukupová, Ochman, Drobkova, Prague Ch. & Czech PO, Neumann.

This is a first-class selection, available on a bargain-priced disc and offering an hour of music, although only a synopsis is provided.

Dyson, George (1883–1964)

At the Tabard Inn: overture; (ii) *In honour of the City;* (i; ii) *Sweet Thames run softly.*
*** Unicorn Dig. UKCD 2013; *DKPC 9048* [id.]. RPO with (i) Stephen Roberts; (ii) Royal College of Music Chamber Ch., Willcocks.

There could hardly be a better introduction to Sir George Dyson's music than this collection, with two vigorously sung choral works preceded by the overture based upon themes from his best-known work, *The Canterbury Pilgrims. In honour of the City*, Dyson's setting of William Dunbar, uses a modern translation of Dunbar's Chaucerian English and to fine, direct effect. The third work here shows Dyson at his most spontaneous. *Sweet Thames run softly* has words by Spenser taken from his *Prothalamion*, celebrating a famous marriage of 1596 when the two young daughters of the Earl of Worcester sailed up the Thames as far as the Temple. The score is full of imaginative touches, with a pair of virginal flutes to represent the brides-to-be. With Stephen Roberts an excellent baritone soloist in the more ambitious cantata, these performances, full of life and warmth, could hardly be bettered; and the recording is first class.

(i) *Concierto leggiero* (for piano & strings); *Concerto da camera; Concerto da chiesa* (both for string orchestra).
❀ *** Chan. Dig. CHAN 9076 [id.]. (i) Eric Parkin; City of L. Sinfonia, Hickox.

Until now we have been inclined to think of Dyson as essentially a composer of vocal music, but this splendid Chandos CD rights the balance and brings not only an engagingly light-textured concertante item for piano but also two powerful and eloquent works in the great tradition of English string music. All these pieces belong to the composer's last composing years and date from 1949/51. The writing shows both a strongly burning creative flame as well as new influences from outside, notably – in the string writing – that of Britten's *Variations on a theme of Frank Bridge*. The *Concierto leggiero* is delicately textured, even skittish, yet becomes very passionate indeed in the finale. The opening of the *Concerto da camera*, written in nine parts, is admirably described in Christopher Palmer's accompanying notes as '. . . springy, gutsy, athletic, muscular . . .'. Its *Andante* brings another expressive climax of great intensity and the finale is bursting with vitality. The *Concerto da chiesa* is warmer and more atmospheric. It is written in *concerto grosso* style with a contrasting *concertino* (of four players) and a ripieno. Its hymn-tune basis brings an immediate melodic appeal, especially in the central variations and in the finale which produces an apotheosis of haunting beauty. The performances here are wonderfully fresh and committed and the string recording has plenty of bite and full sonority, while the balance with the piano is quite admirable. Highly recommended.

(Organ) *Fantasia and Ground bass. 3 Choral hymns; Hierusalem; Psalm 150; 3 Songs of praise.*
*** Hyp. CDA 66150; *KA 66150* [id.]. Vakery Hill, St Michael's Singers, Thomas Trotter, RPO, Jonathan Rennert.

In his old age Dyson returned to Winchester, the city where he had spent his happiest years teaching, and there he wrote the two major items here, not only the ecstatic hymn, *Hierusalem*, for soprano, chorus, string quartet and orchestra, but the strongly argued *Fantasia and Ground bass* for organ, beautifully played here by Jonathan Rennert, choirmaster of the St Michael's Singers. Where the organ piece unashamedly builds on an academic model, *Hierusalem* reveals the inner man more surprisingly, a richly sensuous setting of a medieval poem inspired by the thought of the Holy City, building to a jubilant climax. Just under 20 minutes long, it is a splendid work, and is backed here by the six hymns and the Psalm setting, all of them heartwarming products of the Anglican tradition. Performances are outstanding, with Rennert drawing radiant singing and playing from his team, richly and atmospherically recorded.

Benedicite; Benedictus; Evening services in D; Hail, universal Lord; Live forever, glorious Lord; Te Deum; Valour. (i) (Organ) *Prelude; Postlude; Psalm-tune prelude (I was glad); Voluntary of praise* (with HOWELLS: *Dyson's delight*).
*** Unicorn Dig. DKPCD 9065; *DKPC 9065* [id.]. St Catherine's College, Cambridge, Ch., Owen Rees; (i) Owen Rees (organ).

Sir George Dyson's writing may not always be strikingly individual, but every so often its invention soars. There are some well-made organ pieces too (plus an admiring contribution from Herbert Howells based on two themes from Dyson's *Canterbury Pilgrims*), but it is the vocal music that is the more memorable. It is all sung with striking freshness by choristers who, young as some of them may be, seem to have its inflexions in their very being. Excellent recording too, in a properly spacious acoustic, though the words come over well.

The Blacksmiths. The Canterbury Pilgrims: suite. Quo vadis: Nocturne. 3 Rustic songs. Song on May morning; Spring garland; A Summer day; To music.
*** Unicorn Dig. DKPCD 9061; *DKPC 9061* [id.]. Neil Mackie, Royal College of Music Chamber Ch., RPO, Willcocks.

Sir George Dyson spent most of his life teaching in public schools, notably Winchester, finally becoming Principal of the Royal College of Music in London. Yet he came from a humble Yorkshire background, and *The Blacksmiths* – done here with a reduced orchestra (two pianos, timpani, percussion and strings), as suggested by the composer – has an earthiness that sets it apart from the regular English choral tradition. *The Canterbury Pilgrims*, the work for which Dyson is best known, is here represented by a suite assembled by Christopher Palmer, who also acted as record producer, making one want to hear the full work. The other items, most of them more conventional, make up an appealing disc, played and recorded well.

Egk, Werner (1901–83)

The Temptation of St Anthony (cantata).
(M) *** DG 429 858-2 [id.]. J. Baker, Koekert Qt, Bav. RSO (strings), composer – MARTIN: *Everyman; The Tempest.* *** ❀

Werner Egk's song-cycle *The Temptation of St Anthony* comes from 1945 and is a setting for contralto, string quartet and string orchestra of some eighteenth-century verses. It has a certain folk-like simplicity; as a modest makeweight for the Martin *Everyman songs* it is not of comparable distinction. Dame Janet Baker was in particularly good voice at this period in her career and the recording, which dates from the mid-1960s, is very good.

Elgar, Edward (1857–1934)

(i) *Adieu; Beau Brummel: Minuet;* (ii) *3 Bavarian dances, Op. 27; Caractacus, Op. 35: Woodland interlude. Chanson de matin; Chanson de nuit, Op. 15/1–2; Contrasts, Op. 10/3; Dream children, Op. 43; Falstaff, Op. 68: 2 Interludes. Salut d'amour; Sérnade lyrique;* (ii; iii) *Soliloquy for oboe*

(orch. Gordon Jacob); (i) *Sospiri, Op. 70; The Spanish Lady: Burlesco. The Starlight Express: Waltz. Sursum corda, Op. 11.*
(M) *** Chan. CHAN 6544; *MBTD 6544* [id.]. Bournemouth Sinf., (i) George Hurst; (ii) Norman Del Mar; (iii) with Goossens.

The real treasure in this splendid collection of Elgar miniatures is the *Soliloquy* which Elgar wrote right at the end of his life for Leon Goossens. Here the dedicatee plays it with his long-recognizable tone-colour and feeling for phrase in an orchestration by Gordon Jacob. Most of the other pieces in Norman Del Mar's programme are well known but they come up with new warmth and commitment here, and the 1976 recording, made in the Guildhall, Southampton, has an appealing ambient warmth and naturalness. For the CD reissue Chandos have generously added some delightful Elgar rarities recorded by George Hurst a year earlier in Christchurch Priory. The most striking is the *Sursum corda* for organ, brass, strings and timpani (no woodwind). The *Burlesco*, a fragment from the unfinished Elgar opera, is engagingly done, and each of these items has its charms. Again the recording has plenty of fullness, but the CD transfer brings some thinness to the violins than in the Del Mar recording. The disc has an overall playing time of nearly 76 minutes.

Acoustic recordings (1914–25): Abridged or excerpts: *Bavarian dances; Carillon; Carissima; Chanson de nuit; Cockaigne overture;* (i) *Cello concerto;* (ii) *Violin concerto. Enigma variations; In the South; King Olaf; Light of life; Polonia; Pomp and circumstance marches Nos. 1 & 4; Salut d'amour; The Sanguin fan; Symphony No. 2* (complete). (iii) *Fringes of the fleet;* (iv) *Sea pictures;* (iii; v) *Starlight express; Fantasia and Fugue* (Bach, arr. Elgar); *Overture* (Handel, arr. Elgar).
(M) (**(*)) Pearl GEMM CDS 9951/5 (5). (i) Beatrice Harrison; (ii) Marie Hall; (iii) Charles Mott; (iv) Leila Megane; (v) Agnes Nicholls; O or Royal Albert Hall O, cond. composer.

This box of five Pearl CDs gathers together all of Elgar's recordings made in the days of the acoustic gramophone. With players in limited numbers gathered round an acoustic horn, the sounds are limited but have been transferred here with astonishing fidelity. Orchestrations had to be modified to bring out the bass line, and all but the *Symphony No. 2*, among the major works, had to be cut for the medium, often drastically, as when the *Violin concerto* is reduced from 50 to 15 minutes. *Enigma* has only one small cut in *Nimrod*, and it is particularly valuable to have the recordings of music which Elgar never returned to in the days of electrical recording, notably *Sea pictures* and such wartime works as *Fringes of the fleet*, *Polonia*, *Carillon* and *Starlight express*. Speeds here are generally brisker than in his later, electrical recordings, and performances – mostly with an unidentified orchestra but the later ones with the Royal Albert Hall Orchestra – are often flawed. Marie Hall adopts an exaggeratedly portamento style in the *Violin concerto*, and Beatrice Harrison is less assured here than in her electrical recording of the full *Cello concerto*, but Leila Megane proves a formidable contralto soloist in *Sea pictures*. The sense of witnessing historic events is irresistible, with Elgar consistently hypnotic as a conductor.

Caractacus, Op. 35: Woodland interlude. Crown of India (suite), Op. 66; Grania and Diarmid, Op. 42: Funeral march. Light of Life, Op. 29: Meditation. Nursery suite; Severn suite, Op. 87.
(M) **(*) EMI CDM7 63280-2; *EG 763280-4*. RLPO, Groves.

This is all music that Groves understands warmly, and the results give much pleasure. It is interesting to find the patriotic music coming up fresher than the little interlude from *The Light of Life*, beautiful as that is. Both the *Nursery suite* and the orchestral version of the *Severn suite* come from Elgar's very last period, when his inspiration came in flashes rather than as a sustained searchlight. The completely neglected *Funeral march* is a splendid piece. The CD transfer retains the bloom of the original recordings and adds to the vividness.

Cockaigne overture, Op. 40; Enigma variations, Op. 36; Introduction and allegro for strings; Serenade for strings, Op. 20.
❀ *** Teldec/Warner Dig. 9031 73279-2 [id.]. BBC SO, Andrew Davis.

Andrew Davis's collection of favourite Elgar works is electrifying, bringing the most striking evidence yet on disc of the new spirit he has inspired in the BBC Symphony Orchestra. The very opening of *Cockaigne* has rarely been so light and sprightly, and it leads on to the most powerful characterization of each contrasted section. The two string works are richly and sensitively done, with Davis pacing them with total understanding, and with the BBC strings producing the most refined tone in the central *Larghetto* of the Serenade. Similarly the big tonal contrasts in *Enigma* are dramatically brought out, notably in Davis's rapt and spacious reading of *Nimrod*, helped by the spectacular Teldec recording. It is good to have the optional organ parts included in

Cockaigne and in the finale of *Enigma*, discreetly but effectively balanced. This is surely a worthy successor to Barbirolli in this repertoire and is an outstanding disc in every way.

(i) *Cockaigne overture, Op. 40;* (ii) *Froissart overture, Op. 19; Pomp and circumstance marches, Op. 39, Nos* (i) *1 in D;* (ii) *2 in A min.; 3 in C min.;* (i) *4 in G;* (ii) *5 in C.*
(M) *** EMI CDM7 69563-2. (i) Philh. O; (ii) New Philh. O; Barbirolli.

It is good to have Barbirolli's ripe yet wonderfully vital portrait of Edwardian London at last on CD where the recording retains its atmosphere as well as its vividness. *Froissart* is very compelling too, and Barbirolli makes a fine suite of the five *Pomp and circumstance marches*, with plenty of contrast in Nos. 2 and 3 to offset the Edwardian flag-waving of Nos. 1 and 4.

Cello concerto in E min., Op. 85.
❀ *** EMI CDC7 47329-2 [id.]; *TC-ASD 655*. Du Pré, LSO, Barbirolli – *Sea Pictures*. *** ❀
*** Sony Dig. MK 39541 [id.]. Yo-Yo Ma, LSO, Previn – WALTON: *Cello concerto*. ***
(B) *** Pickwick Dig. PCD 930; *IMPC 930* [id.]. (i) Felix Schmidt; LSO, Frühbeck de Burgos – VAUGHAN WILLIAMS: *Tallis fantasia; Greensleeves*. **(*)
(M) *** Decca 421 385-2; *421 385-4* [id.]. Lynn Harrell, Cleveland O, Maazel – WALTON: *Violin concerto*. ***
**(*) Ph. Dig. 412 880-2 [id.]. Heinrich Schiff, Dresden State O, Marriner – DVOŘÁK: *Cello concerto*. **(*)
(*) Virgin Dig. VC7 90735-2; *VC 790735-4* [id.]. Isserlis, LSO, Hickox – BLOCH: *Schelomo*. *
(*) ASV Dig. CDRPO 8012; *ZCRPO 8012* [id.]. Tortelier, RPO, Groves – DVOŘÁK: *Rondo;* TCHAIKOVSKY: *Rococo variations*. *
(M) (**(*)) EMI mono CDH7 63498-2 [id.]. Casals, BBC SO, Boult – DVOŘÁK: *Concerto* (***) (with BRUCH: *Kol Nidrei* (***)).
(BB) ** Naxos Dig. 8.550503 [id.]. Maria Kliegel, RPO, Halasz – DVOŘÁK: *Cello concerto*. **

(i) *Cello concerto;* (ii) *Cockaigne overture, Op. 40; Enigma variations, Op. 36.*
*** Sony MK 76529. (i) Du Pré, Phd. O; (ii) LPO; Barenboim.

(i) *Cello concerto. Elegy for strings, Op. 58; In the South (Alassio), Op. 50.*
(B) **(*) CfP CD-CFP 9003; *TC-CFP 40342*. (i) Robert Cohen; LPO, Del Mar.

(i) *Cello concerto. Enigma variations, Op. 36.*
*** Ph. Dig. 416 354-2; *416 354-4* [id.]. (i) Julian Lloyd Webber; RPO, Menuhin.

(i) *Cello concerto;* (ii) *Introduction and allegro for strings, Op. 47.*
(B) *** Decca 433 633-2; *433 633-4*. (i) Harrell, Cleveland O, Maazel; (ii) ASMF, Marriner – DELIUS: *Piano concerto*. ***

(i) *Cello concerto. Introduction and allegro for strings, Op. 47; Overtures: Froissart, Op. 19; In the South (Alassio), Op. 50.*
(M) **(*) EMI CDM7 69200-2. (i) Tortelier; LPO, Boult.

Jacqueline du Pré was essentially a spontaneous artist, no two performances by her were exactly alike; wisely, Barbirolli at the recording sessions of Elgar's *Cello concerto* encouraged her above all to express emotion through the notes. Her style is freely rhapsodic, but the result produced a very special kind of meditative feeling. The tempi, long-breathed in the first and third movements, are allowed still more elbow-room when du Pré's expressiveness requires it; in the very beautiful slow movement, brief and concentrated, her inner intensity conveys a depth of espressivo rarely achieved by any cellist on record. Brilliant virtuoso playing too in scherzo and finale. CD brings a subtle extra definition to heighten the excellent qualities of the 1965 recording, with the solo instrument firmly placed. This performance is now also available at mid-price, the only reservation being that it comes in a box of two discs, also offering her recordings of Haydn and Beethoven (EMI CMS7 69707-2 – see our Concerts section).

The Philips coupling of the *Cello concerto* and the *Enigma variations*, the two most popular of Elgar's big orchestral works, featuring two artists inseparably associated with Elgar's music, made the disc an immediate bestseller, and rightly so. These are both warmly expressive and unusually faithful readings, the more satisfying for fidelity to the score and the absence of exaggeration. The speeds – as in the flowing *Moderato* in the first movement of the *Concerto* – are never extreme, always well judged, and Julian Lloyd Webber in his playing has never sounded warmer or more relaxed on record, well focused in the stereo spectrum.

Jacqueline du Pré's second recording of the Elgar *Cello concerto* was taken from live performances in Philadelphia in November 1970, and this is a superb picture of an artist in full flight. Here on CBS you have the romantic view of Elgar at its most compelling. The mastery of du Pré lies not just in her total commitment from phrase to phrase but in the feeling for the whole, setting her sights on the moment in the Epilogue where the slow-movement theme returns, the work's innermost sanctuary of repose. Barenboim's most distinctive point in *Enigma* is his concern for the miniature element, giving the delicate variations sparkle and emotional point, while the big variations have full weight, and the finale brings extra fierceness at a fast tempo. *Cockaigne* is comparably lively and colourful. The sound of the CBS transfer lacks something in body and amplitude.

In its rapt concentration Yo-Yo Ma's recording with Previn is second to none. The first movement is lighter, a shade more urgent than the Du Pré/Barbirolli version, and in the scherzo he finds more fun, just as he finds extra sparkle in the main theme of the finale. The key movement with Ma, as it is with du Pré, is the *Adagio*, echoed later in the raptness of the slow epilogue, and there his range of dynamic is just as daringly wide, with a thread of pianissimo at the innermost moment, poised in its intensity. Warm, fully detailed recording, finely balanced, with understanding conducting from Previn.

Felix Schmidt, a young cellist with the widest expressive range, gives a bold, emotionally intense reading which finds a most satisfying middle ground between the romantic freedom typified by the unique Jacqueline du Pré and the steadier way of a Paul Tortelier. Schmidt's hushed, deeply meditative account of the slow movement is among the most moving of all. With his rich, full tone opulently recorded, his account can be recommended beside the very finest versions, depending on preference as to coupling, in this instance an unconventional linking with two of Vaughan Williams's most popular works.

Lynn Harrell's outstanding account with the Cleveland Orchestra on Decca offers a strong challenge. With eloquent support from Maazel and this fine orchestra (the woodwind play with appealing delicacy), this reading, deeply felt, balances a gentle nostalgia with extrovert brilliance. The slow movement is tenderly spacious, the scherzo bursts with exuberance and, after a passionate opening, the finale is memorable for the poignantly expressive reprise of the melody from the *Adagio*, one of Elgar's greatest inspirations. Alongside the mid-price Walton coupling, this is now offered with Marriner's strong but straighter performance of the *Introduction and allegro*. Both recordings are splendidly transferred to CD with fine body of tone and, at bargain price and with an excellent account of the Delius *Piano concerto*, this is strongly recommendable.

On his earlier, EMI recording, Tortelier gives a noble and restrained performance; Boult accompanies with splendid tact and in addition gives fine accounts of the *Introduction and allegro*, the early *Froissart overture* – which combines orchestral links with Brahms with emergent fingerprints of the later Elgar – and *In the South*.

Robert Cohen's performance is firm and intense, with steady tempi, the colouring more positive, less autumnal than usual, relating the work more closely to the *Second Symphony*. Yet there is no lack of inner feeling. Del Mar's accompaniment is wholly sympathetic, underlining the soloist's approach. He also directs an exciting account of *In the South*, recorded in a single take and highly spontaneous in effect. The *Elegy* makes an eloquent bonus. The recording is wide-ranging and well balanced, but shows Cohen's tone as bright and well focused rather than as especially resonant in the bass.

Schiff gives a warm, thoughtful account, at his most successful in the lovely slow movement and the epilogue, both played with soft, sweet tone. The sound is excellent, to match the orchestra's richness.

The most distinctive point about Steven Isserlis's version on Virgin is his treatment of the slow movement, not so much elegiac as songful. Using a mere thread of tone, with vibrato unstressed, the simplicity of line and the unforced beauty are brought out. The very placing of the solo instrument goes with that, rather more distant than is usual, with the refinement of Elgar's orchestration beautifully caught by both conductor and engineers.

Tortelier's latest version of the Elgar, issued on the RPO's own label to celebrate the cellist's seventy-fifth birthday in March 1989, may not be as firm and powerful as his earlier account with Boult. In the finale the septuagenarian shows signs of strain; but the performance has a spontaneity and a new tenderness which make it very compelling.

Casals recorded the Elgar *Cello concerto* in London in 1946, and the fervour of his playing caused some raised eyebrows. A powerful account, not least for Sir Adrian's contribution, even though its eloquence would have been even more telling were the emotion recollected in greater tranquillity. A landmark of the gramophone all the same, and the strongly characterized Max Bruch *Kol Nidrei* makes a fine encore.

Maria Kliegel is at her finest, deeply expressive and intense, in Elgar's miraculously compressed slow movement, and again in the comparably meditative epilogue for the finale. There she runs little risk of sounding self-indulgent within a limited span. The lyrical main theme of the first movement by contrast is pulled around in an unconvincing way, and though the virtuoso writing of the scherzo and the finale demonstrate the soloist's agility, her intonation is at times suspect. Flawed as it is – like the Dvořák with which it is coupled – it makes a fair bargain, well recorded in modern, digital sound.

(i) *Cello concerto in E min., Op. 85;* (ii) *Violin concerto in B min., Op. 61.*
(M) (***) EMI mono CDH7 69786-2. (i) Beatrice Harrison, New SO; (ii) Menuhin, LSO, composer.

The 1932 Menuhin/Elgar recording of the *Violin concerto* emerges on CD with a superb sense of atmosphere and presence. As for the performance, its classic status is amply confirmed: in many ways no one has ever matched – let alone surpassed – the seventeen-year-old Menuhin in this work, even if the first part of the finale lacks something in fire. The response of conductor, soloist and orchestra has extraordinary magic, with great warmth but no self-indulgence. The performance of the *Cello concerto* has nothing like the same inspiration, when Beatrice Harrison's playing is at times fallible, and there are moments which seem almost perfunctory; but there is still much Elgarian feeling. Even with reservations about the *Cello concerto*, this record is indispensable for Menuhin's totally compulsive account of the *Violin concerto*, a very moving experience.

(i) *Cello concerto in E min., Op. 85. Elegy, Op. 58. Enigma variations, Op. 36; Introduction and allegro, Op. 47.*
❀ (M) *** EMI stereo/mono CDM7 63955-2 [id.]; *EG 763955-4*. (i) Navarra, Hallé O, Barbirolli.

This Hallé version of the *Enigma variations* was recorded in the Manchester Free Trade Hall in 1956 by the Mercury team, Wilma Cozart and Harold Lawrence. In its new CD transfer the sound is extraordinarily good, and the performance is revealed as Barbirolli's finest account ever on record. *Nimrod* has never sounded as nobly resonant as here, and the finale is the most exciting of any performance in the catalogue. Barbirolli generates powerful fervour and an irresistible momentum: at the very end, the organ entry brings an unforgettable, tummy-wobbling effect which engulfs the listener thrillingly. The *Introduction and allegro* is mono and, though not quite so impressively recorded, has comparable passion – the recapitulation of the big striding tune in the middle strings has superb thrust and warmth. The concert closes with a moving account of the *Elegy*, simple and affectionate. In between comes Navarra's strong and firm view of the *Cello concerto*. With his control of phrasing and wide range of tone-colour this 1957 perfomance culminates in a most moving account of the Epilogue.

Violin concerto in B min., Op. 61.
❀ (M) *** EMI Dig. EMX 2058; *TC-EMX 2058*. Nigel Kennedy, LPO, Handley.
(M) (***) BMG/RCA mono GD 87966 [7966-2-RG]. Heifetz, LSO, Sargent – WALTON: *Concerto.* (***)
(*) Collins Dig. 1338-2 [id.]. Accardo, LSO, Hickox – WALTON: *Concerto.* *

(i) *Violin concerto in B min., Op. 61; Overture Cockaigne, Op. 40.*
(BB) *** Naxos Dig. 8.550489 [id.]. Dong-Suk Kang, Polish Nat. RSO (Katowice), Adrian Leaper.

Violin concerto in B min.; Salut d'amour; La Capricieuse.
(M) *** Decca 421 388-2; *421 388-4* [id.]. Kyung Wha Chung, LPO, Solti.

This remains Nigel Kennedy's finest achievement on record, arguably even finer than the long line of versions with star international soloists either from outside or within Britain. With Vernon Handley as guide it is a truly inspired and inspiring performance and the recording is outstandingly faithful and atmospheric. At mid-price it is a supreme Elgarian bargain.

Dong-Suk Kang, immaculate in his intonation, plays the Elgar with fire and urgency. This is very different from most latterday performances, with markedly faster speeds; yet those speeds relate more closely than usual to the metronome markings in the score, and they never get in the way of Kang's ability to feel Elgarian rubato naturally, guided by the warmly understanding conducting of Adrian Leaper. The dashing, mercurial quality of the performance in the finale, very exciting, then leads on to a finely sustained account of the long accompanied cadenza. Irrespective of price, this is a keenly competitive version, with excellent, wide-ranging digital sound, if with rather too forward a balance for the soloist. With the bonus of a finely detailed account of *Cockaigne*, it makes an outstanding bargain.

The extra clarity and sense of presence in the CD transfer intensify the impact of Kyung Wha Chung's heartfelt performance, with Solti responding with warmth to the wide-ranging expressiveness of the soloist. Chung's dreamily expansive playing in that middle movement is ravishing in its beauty, not least in the ethereal writing above the stave, and so too are the lyrical pages of the outer movements. The bravura passages draw from her a vein of mercurial fantasy, excitingly volatile, and no other recording brings a wider range of dynamic or tone in the soloist's playing. The two little violin pieces, accompanied by Philip Moll, act as encores.

Heifetz's view of Elgar, with speeds unusually fast, may not be idiomatic, but this recording brings a masterly example of his artistry, demonstrating very clearly that, for all the ease and technical perfection, he is in no way a cold interpreter of romantic music. The mono recording is limited, not helped by a low hum in the transfer, and the solo instrument is balanced very close; but such a historic document should not be missed.

It is refreshing to have as immaculate a violinist as Salvatore Accardo giving a new and thoughtful view of the Elgar concerto. From Hickox's relatively light treatment of the opening onwards, this is a reading that underplays the grandeur of Elgar, with Accardo bringing out the flowing lyricism in each of the movements, while tackling the bravura passages with fresh incisiveness. Such an approach brings out more parallels than usual with the Walton concerto, the exceptionally generous coupling. Brilliant, full recording.

Coronation march, Op. 65; Froissart: concert overture, Op. 19; In the South (Alassio): concert overture, Op. 50; The Light of life: Meditation, Op. 29.
*** ASV Dig. CDDCA 619; *ZCDCA 619* [id.]. RPO, Yondani Butt.

Yondani Butt draws warm and opulent performances from the RPO. Both the overtures have splendid panache, well shaped and with the joins smoothed over; and he brings out the purely musical, non-jingoistic quality of the *Coronation march. The Light of life meditation*, taken very slowly, is prevented from becoming soupy by Butt's direct, simple expressiveness. Warm, atmospheric recording, yet with plenty of brilliance – an excellent Elgar sound, in fact.

Dream children, Op. 43; The Wand of Youth: suites 1–2, Op. 1a/b; (i) *The Starlight Express, Op. 78: songs: O childen, open your arms to me; There's a fairy that hides; I'm everywhere; Wake up, you little night winds; O stars, shine brightly!; We shall meet the morning spiders; My old tunes are rather broken; O, think beauty; Dustman, Laughter, Tramp and busy Sweep.*
**(*) Argo Dig. 433 214-2 [id.]. (i) Alison Hagley, Bryn Terfel; Welsh Nat. Op. O, Mackerras.

Not surprisingly, the brilliant numbers of Elgar's *Wand of youth suites* are played with plenty of dash under Mackerras, yet there is warmth and affection for the more gentle pieces too, and the delicately scored *Dream children*. But why only include the vocal numbers from *The Starlight Express*, charming as they are? They are well sung and, like the orchestral pieces, vividly recorded, but the acoustic of Brangwyn Hall, Swansea is not ideal for this music, which needs a warmer, more intimate acoustic.

Elegy for strings, Op. 58; Introduction and allegro for strings, Op. 47; Serenade for strings in E min., Op. 20; Sospiri, Op. 70; The Spanish Lady; suite (ed. Young).
(M) **(*) Decca 421 384-2 [id.]. ASMF, Marriner – WARLOCK: *Serenade.* ***

Marriner's somewhat stiff manner in the *Introduction and allegro* will not appeal to everyone, but the subtlety and strength of his unique band of string players are never in doubt. The collection has the added interest of including the brief snippets arranged by Percy Young from Elgar's unfinished opera, *The Spanish Lady*. Marriner's version of the *Serenade*, warm and resilient, shows him at his finest. The (1968) sound on CD is fresh and full – but with just a touch of astringency in the violins, which adds to the bite of the *Introduction and allegro*. The Warlock *Serenade* has also been included for this reissue.

Enigma variations (Variations on an original theme), Op. 36.
(M) (***) EMI mono CDH7 69784-2. BBC SO, Toscanini – DEBUSSY: *La Mer.* (**)
(M) (***) BMG/RCA mono GD 60287 [60287-2-RG]. NBC SO, Toscanini – MUSSORGSKY: *Pictures.* (**)
(M) ** Ph. 432 276-2; *432 276-4*. Concg. O, Haitink – STRAUSS: *Ein Heldenleben.* ***

Toscanini's freely expressive BBC reading makes a fascinating contrast with his much later NBC orchestra recording, done live but in much more clinical conditions. Where the American orchestra plays the notes brilliantly but, as it seems, too literally, what is basically the same interpretation comes over with a far greater sense of fantasy, of idiomatic warmth and flair in the electric atmosphere of Queen's Hall, ending with a dazzling account of the finale, which promptly inspires an eruption of joy and excitement from the audience. Though elsewhere audience noises intrude, the sound is astonishingly vivid, especially for a transfer from 78 r.p.m., roughening at times as at the very end of the finale.

It is a pity that Toscanini's sharply focused but warmly expressive NBC reading of *Enigma* should come in a coupling with his severe account of the Mussorgsky. The Elgar, often expansive as well as affectionately phrased, as in the statement of the theme, gives a much more sympathetic view of the taskmaster conductor than most of his late recordings. Though traditionalist Elgarians may not always approve, it makes for an electrifying experience. The transfer is clean but not too aggressive.

Haitink's reading of the *Enigma variations*, while thoughtfully direct and beautifully played, nevertheless lacks the dynamism to weld the separate variations into a unity. The blood never tingles, as it does in the coupling of Strauss's *Ein Heldenleben*. Excellent, refined analogue recording.

(i) *Enigma variations;* (ii) *Falstaff, Op. 68.*
(M) *** EMI CDM7 69185-2. (i) Philh. O, (ii) Hallé O, Barbirolli.
**(*) Decca Dig. 430 241-2; *430 241-4* [id.]. Montreal SO, Charles Dutoit.

Ripe and expansive, Barbirolli's view of *Falstaff* is colourful and convincing; it has fine atmospheric feeling too, and the interludes are more magical here than in the Boult version. *Enigma*, too, was a work that Barbirolli, himself a cellist, made especially his own, with wonderfully expansive string-playing and much imaginative detail; the recording was made when he was at the very peak of his interpretative powers. The massed strings have lost some of their amplitude, but detail is clearer and the overall balance is convincing, with the Kingsway Hall ambience ensuring a pleasing bloom.

Dutoit and the Montreal Symphony may not be as naturally attuned to Elgar as they were to Holst in their recording of *The Planets*, but these are strong and urgent versions of both works, superbly played. At generally brisk speeds, Dutoit is particularly successful with *Falstaff*: it may at times lack a degree of delicacy and tenderness but in its complexity it is held strongly and purposefully together, with an acute feeling for the story-telling. *Enigma* is comparably clean-cut – though, for all the power of the playing, there is a slight lack of emotional commitment, and this may disconcert Elgar devotees. Warm, full recording, though rather more distanced than is usual in the Montreal venue.

Enigma variations, Op. 36; Grania and Diarmid (incidental music), *Op. 42; The Sanguine Fan (ballet; complete), Op. 81;* (i) *There are seven that pull the thread.*
*** Chan. Dig. CHAN 8610; *ABTD 1298* [id.]. LPO, Bryden Thomson, (i) with Jenny Miller.

Bryden Thomson conducts a broad, characterful reading of *Enigma*, warmly expressive but never mannered, leading the ear on persuasively in a purposefully structured whole. He finds all the charm of *The Sanguine Fan* ballet, characterizing it well without inflating it; while the unexpected mixture of Elgar and Celtic twilight in the *Grania and Diarmid* incidental music brings a similarly agreeable response, notably in the fine, measured *Funeral march*. The little Yeats song, *There are seven*, is warmly sung by Jenny Miller, though the microphone exaggerates her generous vibrato. First-class Chandos sound.

Enigma variations; In the South (Alassio); Serenade for strings.
*** Virgin Dig. VC7 90727-2; *VC 790727-4* [id.]. RPO, Andrew Litton.
*** DG Dig. 423 679-2 [id.]. Philh. O, Sinopoli.

Andrew Litton brings a natural flair to this repertoire. His recording of *Enigma* may not be traditional in every detail – *Nimrod* is intense and strong rather than elegiac – but each variation is vividly characterized without eccentricity. *In the South* and the *Serenade* also confirm Litton's innate feeling for Elgarian rubato, phrasing and rhythm, the qualities which are implied rather than specified in the score. The programme is warmly and atmospherically recorded in EMI's St John's Wood studio.

Whatever individual quirks there are in Sinopoli's readings of Elgar, the passion behind them is highly authentic and totally convincing, harking back to the composer's own unashamedly emotional performances. Not that the quirks are as extreme here as in the *Second Symphony*, though some will feel that the *Serenade*, expansive and opulent, is presented on too large a scale. Though Sinopoli avoids the usual speeding-up at the end of *Enigma*, the thrust of that and of all the other climaxes is pressed home passionately. The warmth of *In the South* from an Italian conductor is exceptionally sympathetic. The sound is rich and forward, adding to the dramatic impact, with the Philharmonia, strings in particular, playing superbly. A splendid acquisition for collectors seeking a fresh view of these ageless masterpieces.

Enigma variations; Introduction and allegro for strings, Op. 47; Serenade for strings, Op. 20.
(M) **(*) EMI Dig. CD-EMX 9503; *TC-EMX 2011*. LPO, Vernon Handley.

Vernon Handley's generously full Eminence collection is given brilliantly wide-ranging digital sound. In the string works, the CD makes the emphasis of the upper range at the expense of the middle the more striking; one needs more amplitude here. Handley's strong personal identification with the music brings a consciously moulded style that tends at times to rob the *Enigma variations* of its forward impulse. The performances of the string works are more direct.

(i) *Enigma variations;* (ii) *Pomp and circumstance marches Nos. 1–5, Op. 39.*
(M) *** Chan. CHAN 6504; *MBTD 6504* [id.]. SNO, Sir Alexander Gibson.
(M) *** DG 429 713-2; *429 713-4* [id.]. RPO, Norman Del Mar.
(M) *** EMI CDM7 64015-2 [id.]; *EG 764015-4*. (i) LSO; (ii) LPO, Sir Adrian Boult.

Enigma variations; Pomp and circumstance marches Nos. 1, 2 & 4.
(M) ** Ph. 434 159-2; *434 159-4* [id.]. Concg. O, Marriner.

Sir Alexander Gibson's reading of *Enigma* has stood the test of time and remains very satisfying, warm and spontaneous in feeling, with a memorable climax in *Nimrod*. The 1978 recording, made in Glasgow's City Hall, remains outstanding, with the organ sonorously filling out the bass in the finale, which has real splendour. The *Pomp and circumstance marches*, too, have fine nobilmente and swagger.

In the *Enigma variations* Del Mar comes closer than any other conductor to the responsive rubato style of Elgar himself, using fluctuations to point the emotional message of the work with wonderful power and spontaneity. Recorded in Guildford Cathedral, with plentiful reverberation, this version has the advantage of a splendid contribution from the organ at the end. The RPO plays superbly, both here and in the *Pomp and circumstance marches*, given Proms-style flair and urgency – although some might feel that the fast speeds miss some of the nobilmente. The reverberant sound here adds something of an aggressive edge to the music-making; however, at mid-price this remains a competitive reissue.

Boult's *Enigma* comes from the beginning of the 1970s, but the recording has lost some of its amplitude in its transfer to CD: the effect is fresh, but the strings are less warm. The reading shows this conductor's long experience of the work, with each variation growing naturally and seamlessly out of the music that has gone before. Boult's approach to the *Pomp and circumstance marches* is brisk and direct, with an almost no-nonsense manner in places. There is not a hint of vulgarity and the freshness is most attractive, though it is a pity he omits the repeats in the Dvořák-like No. 2. The brightened sound brings a degree of abrasiveness to the brass.

The Philips collection is a good deal less generous. It was an interesting idea to record Sir Neville Marriner's 1977 *Enigma* with the Concertgebouw Orchestra and his reading is commendably clear-cut. But for all the refinement of their playing the orchestra fails to convey a consistent development of structure and tension and the coupling is limited to only three of the *Pomp and circumstance marches*. The recording is wide ranging, but has some unnaturally close balances. Even so the sound overall gains from the expansive hall acoustic.

(i) *Enigma variations (Variations on an original theme);* (ii) *Pomp and circumstance marches Nos. 1–5;* (iii) *Serenade for strings.*
(B) *** Decca 433 629-2; *433 629-4*. (i) LAPO, Mehta; (ii), LSO, Bliss; (iii) ASMF, Marriner.

This 71-minute bargain Decca collection is worth anyone's money. Sir Arthur Bliss's rumbustiously vigorous accounts of the *Pomp and circumstance marches* have previously been coupled with Monteux's *Enigma*. Now this is exchanged for Mehta's much more modern (1973) recording. Mehta, born and brought up in India, had evidently at that time not rejected all sympathy for the British Raj and its associations, and it was also before his American experience had begun to streamline his interpretations. Here he proves a strong and sensitive Elgarian, and this is a highly enjoyable performance. If there are no special revelations, the transition from the nobly conceived and spacious climax of *Nimrod* to a delightfully graceful *Dorabella* is particularly felicitous. The vintage Decca recording, with the organ entering spectacularly in the finale, is outstanding in its CD transfer, and this is one of Mehta's very finest records, worthy to stand alongside his splendid set of Holst's *Planets*, dating from the same period. Marriner's elegantly played yet highly sensitive account of the *String serenade* makes a fine bonus, although the ASMF strings are rather more brightly lit in the present transfer. The marches, which date from as early as 1958, are strikingly vivid without being edgy.

(i) *Enigma variations;* (ii) *Pomp and circumstance marches Nos. 1 and 3* (CD only: (iii) *Cello concerto in E min.*).
(B) *** DG Compact Classics 413 852-2 (2); *413 852-4* [id.]. (i) LSO, Jochum; (ii) RPO, Del Mar (CD only: (iii) Fournier, BPO, Wallenstein) – HOLST: *Planets.* **(*)

The Compact Classics issue combines Steinberg's exciting and brilliantly recorded complete set of the Holst *Planets* with Eugen Jochum's inspirational reading of *Enigma*, and bringing as a bonus two of Del Mar's extremely spirited *Pomp and circumstance marches*. The equivalent pair of CDs adds Fournier's moving and eloquent account of the *Cello concerto* which, by reason of the forward balance of the soloist, is made to sound more extrovert than usual. It has undoubted fervour and conviction, even if the close microphone placing, besides reducing the dynamic contrast of the solo playing, also obscures some of the orchestral detail. Like others – including Elgar himself – Jochum sets a very slow *adagio* at the start of *Nimrod*, slower than the metronome marking in the score; unlike others, he maintains that measured tempo and, with the subtlest gradations, builds an even bigger, nobler climax than you find in *accelerando* readings. It is like a Bruckner slow movement in microcosm, around which revolve the other variations, all of them delicately detailed, with a natural feeling for Elgarian rubato. The playing of the LSO matches the strength and refinement of the performance. The remastered recording, however, sounds brighter and more vivid than before but has lost some of its richness. CD and tape are closely matched.

Falstaff (symphonic study), *Op. 68; The Sanguine Fan* (ballet), *Op. 81;* BACH, arr. ELGAR: *Fantasia and fugue in C min. (BWV 537), Op. 86.*
(M) *** EMI CDM7 63133-2. LPO, Boult.

Falstaff, Op. 68; Introduction and allegro for strings, Op. 47; arr. of BACH: *Fantasia and fugue in C min., Op. 86.*
(B) *** Pickwick Dig. PCD 934; *CIMPC 934* [id.]. National Youth O of Great Britain, Christopher Seaman.

These works have rarely been given such heartfelt performances as those by Christopher Seaman and the National Youth Orchestra. The weight of string sound, combined with the fervour behind the playing, makes this an exceptionally satisfying reading of the *Introduction and allegro*, while *Falstaff* demonstrates even more strikingly how, working together intensively, these youngsters have learnt to keep a precise ensemble through the most complex variations of expressive rubato. Most Elgarians will enjoy these performances – including the Bach arrangement, also done passionately – far more than cooler ones, however polished. Warm, full, digital recording adds to an outstanding bargain, though irritatingly there is no tracking of sections in *Falstaff*, over half an hour long.

Boult treats *Falstaff* essentially as a symphonic structure. It follows therefore that some of the mystery, some of the delicate sense of atmosphere that impregnates the interludes for example, is undercharacterized. But the crispness of the playing and Boult's unfailing alertness amply compensate for that. The little-known ballet score written during the First World War makes for an unexpected and enjoyable coupling, and Elgar's Bach arrangement is richly expansive. The remastering, as with Boult's other Elgar recordings, clarifies textures without too much loss of ambience and weight.

Falstaff; Symphonies Nos. 1–2; (i) *Dream of Gerontius: Prelude* and excerpts. *The Music makers*: excerpts. *Civic fanfare and National anthem.*
(***) EMI mono CDS7 54560-2 (3). (i) Margaret Balfour, Steuart Wilston, Herbert Heyner, Tudor Davies, Horace Stevens, Royal Ch. Soc., Three Choirs Festival Ch., LSO or Royal Albert Hall O, composer.

It is thrilling in this first volume of EMI's Elgar Edition to find that the recordings, made between 1927 and 1932, have a body and immediacy that give the most astonishing sense of presence. Elgar is with us here and now, providing in these inspired performances an insight beyond that of any other conductor of his music. Consistently these are tough performances, with rhythms pressed sharply home and with speeds generally faster than has become normal today. In addition, Elgar's sense of line, his ability to mould rhythms with natural flexibility, regularly brings an extra emotional thrust and an extra intensity. What is special is the poignancy, the vulnerability conveyed in this music even at its grandest. The recordings of the two symphonies – No. 1 dating from 1930, No. 2 from 1927 – and of *Falstaff* (1931) have a vividness and clarity which allow you to hear more detail than in many modern digital recordings. Any surface hiss is so even that the ear dismisses it at once, particularly when there is such weight and body in the sound. Most thrilling of all is the *First Symphony*, where Elgar modifies some of the markings in the score on speed-changes; and this reading of *Falstaff*, too, has never been surpassed. The *Symphony No. 2* comes with fascinating supplements, including a rehearsal of the Scherzo and an alternative take of the first part of the movement.

Most atmospheric of all are the live recordings of *Gerontius* and the *Music-makers* on the third disc, all recorded live at a time when recording on wax discs in short spans of under five minutes presented almost insoluble problems. The *Gerontius* excerpts are taken from two separate performances in 1927, the one at the Albert Hall (45 minutes of it) even more vivid than the more distantly balanced selection, recorded later in Hereford Cathedral at the Three Choirs Festival. The excerpts from the *Music-makers* were recorded then too, but with better balances and cleaner focus than in *Gerontius*. The brief *Civic fanfare* is a curiosity, the only Elgar first performance preserved on record.

Introduction and allegro for strings, Op. 47; Serenade for strings in E min., Op. 20.
❀ *** Virgin Dig. VCy7 90819-2; *VCy 790819-4* [id.]. LCO, Christopher Warren-Green – VAUGHAN WILLIAMS: *Tallis fantasia* etc. *** ❀

(i) *Introduction and allegro for strings, Op. 47; Serenade for strings, Op. 20;* (ii) *Elegy, Op. 58; Sospiri, Op. 70.*
*** EMI CDC7 47537-2. (i) Sinfonia of L. with Allegri Qt; (ii) New Philh. O, Barbirolli – VAUGHAN WILLIAMS: *Tallis fantasia* etc. ***

Repeating a coupling made famous by Sir John Barbirolli, Christopher Warren-Green, directing and leading his reborn London Chamber Orchestra, could hardly have made a more impressive début. The account of the *Introduction and allegro* has tremendous ardour: the great striding theme on the middle strings is unforgettable, while the fugue has enormous bite and bravura. The whole work moves forward in a single sweep and the sense of a live performance, tingling with electricity and immediacy, is thrillingly tangible. It is very difficult to believe that the group contains only seventeen players (6-5-2-3-1), with the resonant but never clouding acoustics of All Saints' Church, Petersham, helping to create an engulfingly rich body of tone. Appropriately, the *Serenade* is a more relaxed reading yet has plenty of affectionate warmth, with the beauty of the *Larghetto* expressively rich but not overstated.

Barbirolli brings an Italianate ardour and warmth to this music without in any way robbing it of its Englishness; and the response of the string players, full-throated or subtle as the music demands, was matched by superb analogue recording, notable for its combination of clarity and ambient richness. For CD, the *Elegy*, like the *Serenade* showing Barbirolli in more gentle, beguiling mood, and the passionate *Sospiri* have been added for good measure. The CD transfer, however, while retaining the fullness and amplitude, seems more restricted on top and has lost some of the original bite.

Nursery suite; Wand of Youth suites Nos. 1 and 2, Op. 1a and 1b.
*** Chan. Dig. CHAN 8318; *ABTD 1079* [id.]. Ulster O, Bryden Thomson.

Although Boult's performances of the more robust items from the *Wand of Youth* brought marginally more exuberance, the playing in Ulster is attractively spirited; in the gentle pieces (the *Sun dance*, *Fairy pipers* and *Slumber dance*) which show the composer at his most magically evocative, the music-making engagingly combines refinement and warmth. The *Nursery suite* is strikingly well characterized, and with first-class digital sound this is highly recommendable.

Serenade for strings in E min., Op. 20.
(B) *** Pickwick Dig. PCD 861; *CIMPC 861* [id.]. Serenata of London – GRIEG: *Holberg suite;* MOZART: *Eine kleine Nachtmusik* etc. ***

A particularly appealing account of Elgar's *Serenade*, with unforced tempi in the outer movements admirably catching its mood and atmosphere so that the elegiac *Larghetto*, beautifully and sensitively phrased, finds a natural place in the overall scheme. The Serenata of London is led rather than conducted by Barry Wilde; but this is a performance of undoubted personality, and it is recorded with remarkable realism and naturalness. With excellent couplings, this is an outstanding bargain.

Symphony No. 1 in A flat, Op. 55.
❀ (B) *** Pickwick Dig. PCD 956; *CIMPC 956* [id.]. Hallé O, James Judd.
(B) *** CfP CD-CFP 9018; *TC-CFP 4541*. LPO, Vernon Handley.
*** Ph. Dig. 416 612-2 [id.]. RPO, André Previn.

Symphony No. 1 in A flat; Cockaigne overture.
*** Decca Dig. 430 835-2; *430 835-4* [id.]. LSO, Mackerras.
(M) *** Decca 421 387-2; *421 387-4* [id.]. LPO, Solti.

Symphony No. 1 in A flat; Chanson de matin; Chanson de nuit; Serenade for strings, Op. 20.
(M) *** EMI CDM7 64013-2 [id.]; *EG 764013-4*. LPO, Sir Adrian Boult.

Symphony No. 1 in A flat; In the South (Alassio): concert overture, Op. 50.
**(*) BMG/RCA Dig. RD 60380 [60380-2-RC]. LPO, Slatkin.
**(*) Collins Dig. 1269-2 [id.]. ASMF, Marriner.

Symphony No. 1 in A flat; Pomp and circumstance marches Nos. 1, 3 & 4.
**(*) Teldec/Warner Dig. 9031 73278-2 [id.]. BBC SO, Andrew Davis.

Symphony No. 1 in A flat; Pomp and cicumstance marches Nos. 1 & 4.
*** DG Dig. 431 663-2 [id.]. Philh. O, Giuseppe Sinopoli.

James Judd, more than any rival on disc, has learnt directly from Elgar's own recording of this magnificent symphony. He does not copy slavishly but uses his deep understanding of what Elgar achieves on record to enhance the Hallé's performance. So the reading has extra authenticity in the many complex speed-changes (sometimes indicated confusingly in the score), in the precise placing of climaxes and in the textural balances. Like Elgar, he draws out the horns and trombones thrillingly, and the Hallé brass, forwardly balanced, blazes out superbly, with the final coda thrust home magnificently. Above all, Judd outshines others in the pacing and phrasing of the lovely slow movement which in its natural flowing rubato has melting tenderness behind the passion, a throat-catching poignancy not fully conveyed elsewhere but very much a quality of Elgar's own reading. The refinement of the strings down to the most hushed pianissimo confirms this as the Hallé's most beautiful disc in years, recorded with warmth and opulence. Though there is no coupling, the bargain price is ample compensation.

It was with the LSO in 1930 that Elgar himself made his own recording of the *First Symphony*. In its passionate intensity it has never been surpassed since, and the composer at times made important modifications to the markings in the score. Since then, that oldest of London's independent orchestras has done relatively little recording of the central Elgar repertory compared with its rivals, but Mackerras's superb performance rights the balance. It is the most bitingly passionate reading since Elgar's own, brilliantly recorded with the rasp of the brass in particular echoing the sort of sound that Elgar himself plainly preferred. Signs are that Mackerras has studied that Elgar recording, both on the detailed modifications implied and on the way that the composer built and resolved climaxes, using flexible rubato allied to acute timing of the key moment of resolution. So, in the middle section of the finale when the main theme appears in augmentation, Mackerras reserves an extra surge of volume for the climactic violin phrase, and his account of the brassy final coda is the most stirring yet, a thrilling culmination. The *Cockaigne overture*, brilliantly done with high contrasts and incisive attack, makes a generous and welcome fill-up.

Vernon Handley directs a beautifully paced reading which can be counted in every way outstanding, even making no allowance for price. The LPO has performed this symphony many times before but never with more poise and refinement than here. It is in the slow movement above all that Handley scores, spacious and movingly expressive. With very good sound, well transferred to CD, this is a highly recommendable alternative version.

Boult clearly presents the *First Symphony* as a counterpart to the *Second*, with hints of reflective nostalgia amid the triumph. His EMI disc contains a radiantly beautiful performance, with no extreme tempi, richly spaced in the first movement, invigorating in the syncopated march rhythms of the scherzo, and similarly bouncing in the Brahmsian rhythms of the finale. Most clearly distinctive is the lovely slow movement, presented as a seamless flow of melody, less 'inner' than with Handley, and above all glowing with untroubled sweetness. The CD remastering of the 1976 Abbey Road recording, as so often, has lost the exceptionally full-blooded quality of the original LP: the violin timbre is thinner and, although the brass is full, the sharpening of detail is not all gain. This applies also to the 1967 recording of the *Chansons* and the 1972 *Serenade* (recorded, like the finale of the *Symphony*, in Kingsway Hall). Here Boult's simplicity and tenderness are no less effective than a riper view.

Previn's view of the first movement is spacious; his espressivo style tends towards accelerando rather than tenuto, towards fractional anticipation rather than hesitation, which makes for alert allegros and a slow movement that is warm but not self-indulgent. The syncopations of the scherzo/march theme have an almost jazzy swagger, and the reading is crowned by a flowing account of the finale which has the necessary heart-tug. The Philips sound is more refined than the typical Elgar sound from EMI, but there is no lack of richness or bite.

Solti's version of the *First Symphony* is in Decca's mid-price British Collection series, aptly coupled with his sharply dramatic account of *Cockaigne*. The CD transfers bring out the fullness as well as the brilliance of the excellent 1970s sound, and though Solti's thrusting manner will give the traditional Elgarian the occasional jolt, his clearing away of the cobwebs stems from his study of the composer's own recording before he ever attempted to conduct the work at all.

Slatkin's reading for RCA has an even more generous coupling with *In the South*. In his thoughtful and deeply committed readings of Elgar, Slatkin here leans towards relatively extreme speeds, fast as well as slow. The overture is pressed hard and, though it loses something in Italianate warmth, the close is thrust home superbly. In the symphony he sustains his speeds well, and in the first three movements the orchestra's ensemble is tellingly crisp, even in the headlong speed for the scherzo, which yet begins to sound rushed. Anyone specially wanting this coupling should certainly consider this, but the slight distancing of the sound takes away some of the impact, unless volume is turned high.

As in his warm and passionate account of the *Second Symphony*, Sinopoli takes an expansive view of the *First* from his broad account of the motto theme onwards. Though the opening movement is not as dramatic as it can be, it is warm and strong, with extra broadening for some of the subsidiary subjects, in which Sinopoli finds extreme tenderness, as he does too in the slow movement, taken very gently. As in his earlier Elgar recordings he provides a refreshing insight, relating Elgar more closely to Bruckner than usual.

With sound of demonstration quality Andrew Davis conducts a broad, rather plain reading of the Symphony which is yet highly idiomatic and beautifully played. With one important reservation this is almost as fine in its way as Davis's other Elgar record for Teldec of *Enigma* and shorter pieces. Sadly the performance of the symphony falls short at the very end, where the brassy coda fails to blaze as it should.

Marriner and the augmented Academy offer playing of superb precision, with extreme speeds both fast and slow. The fast allegros are exhilarating, but the very slow *Adagio* third movement sags badly. The sound is outstandingly fine, not just in the symphony but in the colourful account of the overture.

Symphony No. 2 in E flat, Op. 63.
(B) *** CfP CD-CFP 4544; *TC-CFP 4544*. LPO, Vernon Handley.
**(*) DG Dig. 423 085-2 [id.]. Philh. O, Sinopoli.

Symphony No. 2; Cockaigne overture, Op. 40.
(M) *** EMI CDM7 64014-2 [id.]. LPO, Sir Adrian Boult.

Symphony No. 2; The Crown of India (suite), *Op. 66.*
(M) *** Chan. CHAN 6523; *MBTD 6523* [id.]. SNO, Gibson.

Symphony No. 2; Serenade for strings.
*** BMG/RCA Dig. RD 60072 [60072-2-RC]. LPO, Slatkin.

Symphony No. 2; Sospiri.
**(*) EMI Dig. CDC7 54192-2 [id.]; *EL 754192*. LSO, Jeffrey Tate.

Handley's is the most satisfying modern version of a work which has latterly been much recorded. What Handley conveys superbly is the sense of Elgarian ebb and flow, building climaxes like a master and drawing excellent, spontaneous-sounding playing from an orchestra which, more than any other, has specialized in performing this symphony. The sound is warmly atmospheric and vividly conveys the added organ part in the bass, just at the climax of the finale, which Elgar himself suggested 'if available': a tummy-wobbling effect. This would be a first choice at full price, but as a bargain CD there are few records to match it.

Gibson's recording shows his partnership with the SNO at its peak, and this performance captures all the opulent nostalgia of Elgar's masterly score. The reading of the first movement is more relaxed in its grip than Handley's, but its spaciousness is appealing and, both here and in the beautifully sustained *Larghetto*, the richly resonant acoustics of Glasgow City Hall bring out the full panoply of Elgarian sound. The finale has splendid nobilmente, with a thrilling reprise, and the relaxation of tension for the closing pages is most sensitively managed. In the *Crown of India* suite Gibson is consistently imaginative in his attention to detail, and the playing of the Scottish orchestra is again warmly responsive, especially in the score's more delicate moments.

Slatkin's account of the *Second Symphony* is splendid, timed beautifully to deliver authentic frissons, and it has extra power in the finale from the addition of pedal notes on the organ, just before the epilogue – as Elgar once suggested to Sir Adrian Boult. Previously, only Vernon Handley had included them on his equally outstanding version for CfP. Though the new Slatkin is much more expensive than that, it also includes a strong account of the *Serenade for strings*. Those looking for a first-class modern digital recording of the symphony should be well satisfied.

For his fifth recording of the *Second Symphony* Sir Adrian Boult, incomparable Elgarian, drew from the LPO the most richly satisfying performance of all. Over the years Sir Adrian's view of the glorious nobility of the first movement had mellowed a degree, but the pointing of climaxes is unrivalled. With Boult more than anyone else the architecture is clearly and strongly established, with tempo changes less exaggerated than usual. The peak comes in the great *Funeral march*, where the concentration of the performance is irresistible. The scherzo has lightness and delicacy, giving more room to breathe. In the finale, Boult gives a radiant account of the lovely epilogue. This is a version to convert new listeners to a love of Elgar, although, even more than in the *First Symphony* the ear notices a loss of opulence compared with the original LP. This is also very striking in *Cockaigne*, which opens the disc, although it serves to emphasize the fresh directness of Boult's approach.

Sinopoli's version lasts an amazing 65 minutes – or some 20 minutes longer than Elgar's own, which admittedly was cramped by 78-r.p.m. side-lengths. The result has consistent spontaneity and conveys emotional thrust; it is true that in the first movement Sinopoli misses the leaping exhilaration which the compound time should ideally have, but that and the slow movement have a glow which endows the score with Brucknerian majesty. The recording is exceptionally beautiful, both full and refined, with the Philharmonia strings playing radiantly.

Jeffrey Tate conducts the LSO in an expansive, warmly expressive reading, which compellingly sustains its exceptionally slow speeds. The recording is warm and slightly diffused to match. The brief string piece, *Sospiri*, makes an attractive but ungenerous coupling. An enjoyable record, but competition is strong and this is not a first choice.

CHAMBER AND INSTRUMENTAL MUSIC

Piano quintet in A min., Op. 84; String quartet in E min., Op. 83.
**(*) Mer. ECD 84082; *KE 77082*. John Bingham, Medici Qt.
*(*) Decca Dig. 433 312-2 [id.]. (i) David Owen Norris; Mistry Qt.

John Bingham and the Medici Quartet play with a passionate dedication and bring an almost symphonic perspective to the *Piano quintet*, and there is no denying their ardour and commitment, particularly in the slow movement. They also give a fine and thoroughly considered account of the *Quartet*, more extrovert in its expressive feeling than with the Chilingirians; and overall their reading is full of perceptive and thought-provoking touches. There will be many who will respond to the higher voltage. Unfortunately they are far too close in the *Quartet* (though less so in the *Quintet*) and it still remains difficult for a real *pp* to register, while tone tends to harden somewhat on climaxes.

Having Elgar's last two chamber works coupled on a single disc is apt and attractive, and the Mistry Quartet with David Owen Norris give warmly committed performances. Yet their playing is not as refined as it might be, and that results in the *Quartet* in particular sounding less convincing than on the finest rival versions. The outer movements seem a little perfunctory and the central slow movement lacks hushed intensity. In the *Quintet* the compulsion of Owen Norris's playing helps, but even the fragmentary opening lacks the hushed anticipation needed, and the beefy energy of much of the rest hardly compensates. The forward balance of the recording tends to expose flaws in ensemble and matching, and to minimize subtlety of expression.

String quartet in E min., Op. 83.
*** Collins Dig. 1280-2 [id.]. Britten Qt – WALTON: *Quartet*. ***
*** Chan. Dig. CHAN 8474; *ABTD 1185* [id.]. Gabrieli Qt – WALTON: *Quartet*. ***

*** ASV Dig. CDDCA 526; *ZCDCA 526* [id.]. Brodsky Qt – DELIUS: *Quartet.* ***

There is a poignancy in this late work which the beautifully matched members of the Britten Quartet capture to perfection. If the piece has often seemed elusive, these young players show the deepest insights, giving a reminder that the slow movement was music that the composer chose to be played at his wife's funeral. Not only do the Britten Quartet bring out the emotional intensity, they play with a refinement and sharpness of focus that gives superb point to the outer movements. With more portamento than one would normally expect today, the result is totally in style. For all the poise and restraint of the central *Piacevole*, they build it to a glorious climax before the final, almost unbearably tender close. Warmly expressive as the Gabrieli Quartet are in the Chandos coupling of these same works, the Brittens are even more searching.

Apart from its intrinsic excellence, the Gabrieli playing has a far-from-autumnal vitality and much eloquence; and the recording, made in the excellent acoustic of The Maltings, Snape, is up to the high standards one expects from this source.

The young players of the Brodsky Quartet take a weightier view than usual of the central, interlude-like slow movement but amply justify it. The power of the outer movements, too, gives the lie to the idea of this as a lesser piece than Elgar's other chamber works. First-rate recording.

Violin sonata in E min., Op. 82.
**(*) ASV Dig. CDDCA 548; *ZCDCA 548* [id.]. Lorraine McAslan, John Blakely – WALTON: *Sonata.* **(*)

Violin sonata in E min., Op. 82; Canto popolare; Chanson de matin, Op. 15/2; Chanson de nuit, Op. 15/1; Mot d'amour, Op. 13/1; Salut d'amour, Op. 12; Sospiri, Op. 70; 6 Easy pieces in the first position.
*** Chan. Dig. CHAN 8380; *ABTD 1099* [id.]. Nigel Kennedy, Peter Pettinger.

At the start of the *Sonata*, Kennedy establishes a concerto-like scale, which he then reinforces in a fiery, volatile reading of the first movement, rich and biting in its bravura. The elusive slow movement, *Romance*, is sharply rhythmic in its weird Spanishry, while in the finale Kennedy colours the tone seductively. As a coupling, Kennedy has a delightful collection of shorter pieces, not just *Salut d'amour* and *Chanson de matin* but other rare chips off the master's bench. Kennedy is matched beautifully throughout the recital by his understanding piano partner, Peter Pettinger, and the recording is excellent.

Though Lorraine McAslan cannot match the virtuoso command and warmth of tone of Nigel Kennedy's Chandos recording of the *Sonata*, hers is an impressive and warm-hearted version, full of natural imagination, helped by the incisive playing of John Blakely, and her coupling is more substantial. Good, forward recording, which gives the violin tone less bloom than it might.

MUSIC FOR WIND

Adagio cantabile (Mrs Winslow's soothing syrup); Andante con variazione (Evesham Andante); 5 Intermezzos; Harmony music No. 1.
(M) *** Chan. CHAN 6553 [id.]. Athena Ens.

4 Dances; Harmony music Nos. 2–4; 6 Promenades.
(M) *** Chan. CHAN 6554 [id.]. Athena Ens.

As a budding musician, playing not only the violin but also the bassoon, Elgar wrote a quantity of brief, lightweight pieces in a traditional style for himself and four other wind-players to perform. He called it 'Shed Music'; though there are few real signs of the Elgar style to come, the energy and inventiveness are very winning, particularly when (as here) the pieces – often with comic names – are treated to bright and lively performances. Excellent recording, with the CD transfers sounding as fresh as new paint.

PIANO MUSIC

Adieu; Carissima; Chantant; Concert allegro; Dream children, Op. 43; Griffinesque; In Smyrna; May song; Minuet; Pastorale; Presto; Rosemary; Serenade; Skizze; Sonatina.
**(*) Chan. Dig. CHAN 8438 [id.]. Peter Pettinger.

This record includes all of Elgar's piano music. He did not have anywhere near the same feeling for the keyboard as many of his contemporaries – and the earlier writing is both derivative and poorly laid out for the instrument. It has not established itself in the piano repertoire but, as Peter Pettinger shows, there are interesting things in this byway of English music (such as the *Skizze* and *In Smyrna*). We get both the 1889 version of the *Sonatina* and its much later revision. Committed playing from this accomplished artist, and a pleasing recording too, with fine presence on CD.

VOCAL AND CHORAL MUSIC

Songs: *After; Arabian serenade; Is she not passing fair; Like to the damask rose; Oh, soft was the song; Pleading; Poet's life; Queen Mary's song; Rondel; Shepherd's song; Song of autumn; Song of flight; Through the long days; Twilight; Was it some golden star?*
**(*) Chan. Dig. CHAN 8539; *ABTD 1164* [id.]. Benjamin Luxon, David Willison – DELIUS: *Songs*. **(*)

Benjamin Luxon seemingly cannot avoid the roughness of production which has marred some of his later recordings, but gives charming freshness to this delightful selection. Such a simple invention as the *Shepherd's song* is hauntingly beautiful. Brilliant and sensitive accompaniment, and a very fine recording balance.

Angelus, Op. 56/1; Ave Maria; Ave maris stella; Ave verum corpus, Op. 2; Ecce sacerdos magnus; Fear not, O land; Give unto the Lord, Op. 74; Great is the Lord, Op. 67; I sing the birth; Lo! Christ the Lord is born; O hearken thou, Op. 64; O salutaris hostia Nos. 1–3.
*** Hyp. Dig. CDA 66313; *KA 66313* [id.]. Worcester Cathedral Ch., Donald Hunt; Adrian Partington.

Though one misses the impact of a big choir in the *Coronation anthem, O hearken thou*, and in the grand setting of Psalm 48, *Great is the Lord*, the refinement of Dr Hunt's singers, their freshness and bloom as recorded against a helpful acoustic, are ample compensation, particularly when the feeling for Elgarian phrasing and rubato is unerring. Most of these fourteen items are more intimate, and the Worcester performances are near ideal, with clean ensemble, fine blending and taut rhythmic control. Vividly atmospheric recording, which still allows full detail to emerge.

The Apostles, Op. 49.
*** Chan. Dig. CHAN 8875/6; *DBTD 2024* (2) [id.]. Hargan, Hodgson, Rendall, Roberts, Terfel, Lloyd, LSO Ch., LSO, Hickox.
(M) *** EMI CMS7 64206-2 (2). Armstrong, Watts, Tear, Luxon, Grant, Carol Case, Downe House School Ch., LPO Ch., LPO, Boult.

Even though Sir Adrian Boult's pioneering first recording of *The Apostles* has reappeared on CD, this passionately committed account from Richard Hickox still has the balance of advantage, not just because of the full, glowing sound but for the extra warmth. Where Boult's reading has four-square nobility, Hickox is far more flexible in his expressiveness, drawing singing from his chorus which far outshines that on the earlier reading. Most of his soloists are preferable too, for example Stephen Roberts as a light-toned Jesus and Robert Lloyd characterful as Judas. Only the tenor, David Rendall, falls short, with vibrato exaggerated by the microphone. By his pacing Hickox brings out the dramatic element in the music, giving many scenes an apt and welcome operatic flavour. The recording, made in St Jude's, Hampstead, is among Chandos's finest, both warm and incandescent, with plenty of detail.

Sir Adrian Boult at eighty-five directed one of his most inspired recordings, an account of Elgar's long-neglected oratorio (the first of a projected trilogy; *The Kingdom* was the second) which must warm the heart of any Elgarian. That the work failed earlier to make the impact it deserves stands as a condemnation of contemporary fashion. Its melodies may not be quite as memorable as those of *Gerontius*, but many of the numbers, like the setting of the Beatitudes, *By the wayside*, show Elgar at his most inspired. The characters of Mary Magdalene and Judas are unexpectedly rounded and sympathetic and the work ends – like *Gerontius* – with a mystic chorus of angels and apostles in heaven – singing glorious floating *Alleluias*. Boult's performance gives the closing scene great power and a wonderful sense of apotheosis, with the spacious sound-balance rising to the occasion. Generally fine singing – notably from Sheila Armstrong and Helen Watts – and a 1973/4 Kingsway Hall recording as rich and faithful as anyone could wish for. The CD transfer refines detail but retains the breadth and the warm ambience. The powerfully lyrical *Meditation* from *The Light of Life* makes a suitable postlude without producing an anticlimax, again showing Boult at his most inspirational.

(i) *Coronation ode, Op. 44; The Spirit of England, Op. 80.*
(M) *** Chan. CHAN 6574 [id.]. Cahill, SNO Ch. and O, Gibson; (i) with Anne Collins, Rolfe Johnson, Howell.

Gibson's performances combine fire and panache, and the recorded sound has an ideal Elgarian expansiveness, the choral tone rich and well focused, the orchestral brass given plenty of weight, and the overall perspective highly convincing. He is helped by excellent soloists, with Anne Collins movingly eloquent in her dignified restraint when she introduces the famous words of *Land of hope and glory* in the finale; and the choral entry which follows is truly glorious in its power and amplitude. *The Spirit of England*, a wartime cantata to words of Laurence Binyon, is in some ways even finer, with the final setting of *For the fallen* rising well above the level of his occasional music. At mid-price this is a real bargain.

The Dream of Gerontius, Op. 38.
*** EMI CDS7 47208-8 (2). Helen Watts, Gedda, Lloyd, John Alldis Ch., LPO, Boult – *The Music Makers.* **(*)
*** Chan. Dig. CHAN 8641/2; *DBTD 2014* (2) [id.]. Palmer, Davies, Howell, LSO Ch. & O, Hickox – PARRY: *Anthems.* ***
**(*) EMI Dig. CDS7 49549-2 (2) [Ang. CDCB 49549]. J. Baker, Mitchinson, Shirley-Quirk, CBSO Ch. & O, Rattle.
**(*) CRD CRD 3326/7; *CRDC 4026/7* [id.]. Tear, Hodgson, Luxon, SNO Ch. & O, Gibson.
(M) **(*) Decca 421 381-2 (2) [id.]. Pears, Minton, Shirley-Quirk, King's College Ch., LSO Ch., LSO, Britten – HOLST: *Hymn of Jesus.* ***

(i) *The Dream of Gerontius. Sea pictures.*
(M) **(*) EMI CMS7 63185-2 (2). Dame Janet Baker, Hallé O, Barbirolli; (i) with Richard Lewis, Kim Borg, Hallé & Sheffield Philharmonic Ch., Amb. S.

Boult's total dedication is matched by his sense of drama. The spiritual feeling is intense, but the human qualities of the narrative are also fully realized. Boult's controversial choice of Nicolai Gedda in the role of Gerontius brings a new dimension to this characterization, and he brings the sort of echoes of Italian opera that Elgar himself – perhaps surprisingly – asked for. He is perfectly matched by Helen Watts as the Angel. The dialogues between the two have a natural spontaneity as Gerontius's questions and doubts find a response which is at once gently understanding and nobly authoritative. It is a fascinating vocal partnership, and it is matched by the commanding manner which Robert Lloyd finds for both his roles. The orchestral playing is always responsive and often, like the choral singing, very beautiful, while the dramatic passages bring splendid incisiveness and bold assurance from the singers. The fine 1976 analogue recording is extremely well balanced and has responded admirably to its CD remastering. There is slight loss of ambience, but the extra clarity adds impact to the big choral climaxes, and the magical opening and closing pages of Part II are not robbed of their atmosphere and sense of mystery. However, in order to make room for *The Music Makers*, a welcome enough bonus, at the end of the first disc Part I of *Gerontius* is broken immediately before the Priest's dramatic *Proficiscere, anima Christiana*, a most unfortunate choice, robbing the listener of the surprise entry of the brass.

Hickox's version outshines all rivals in the range and quality of its sound. Quite apart from the fullness and fidelity of the recording, Hickox's performance is deeply understanding, not always ideally powerful in the big climaxes but most sympathetically paced, with natural understanding of Elgarian rubato. The soloists make a characterful team. Arthur Davies is a strong and fresh-toned Gerontius; Gwynne Howell in the bass roles is powerful if not always ideally steady; and Felicity Palmer, though untraditionally bright of tone with her characterful vibrato, is strong and illuminating. Though on balance Boult's soloists are even finer, Hickox's reading in its expressive warmth conveys much love for this score, and the last pages with their finely sustained closing *Amen* are genuinely moving.

Barbirolli's red-blooded reading of *Gerontius* is the most heart-warmingly dramatic ever recorded; here it is offered, in a first-rate CD transfer, in coupling with one of the greatest Elgar recordings ever made: Dame Janet Baker's rapt and heartfelt account of *Sea pictures.* No one on record can match Dame Janet in this version of *Gerontius* for the fervent intensity and glorious tonal range of her singing as the Angel, one of her supreme recorded performances; and the clarity of CD intensifies the experience. In pure dedication the emotional thrust of Barbirolli's reading conveys the deepest spiritual intensity, making most other versions seem cool by comparison. The recording may have its hints of distortion, but the sound is overwhelming, not least in the great outburst of *Praise to the holiest*, and in the surge of emotion behind the radiant choruses ending each half. Richard Lewis gives one of his finest recorded performances, searching and intense, and, though Kim Borg is unidiomatic in the bass role, his bass tones are rich in timbre, even if his projection lacks the dramatic edge of Robert Lloyd on the full-price Boult set.

Rattle's flamboyant operatic style is certainly not lacking in dynamism and there is much that is moving, but his control of the ebb and flow of tempo and tension is not always convincing. In *Praise to the holiest in the height*, the chorus, while producing gloriously rich and luminous sounds, is pressed into an impetuous accelerando at the close, so that the climax is approached at breakneck speed, in complete contrast to the broad and heavily accented opening section. Similarly the brief but profound orchestral interlude, where the soul of Gerontius goes forward to meet his Maker, is robbed of dignity by a sudden quickening of pace, so that the apocalyptic fortissimo chord conveys the bizarre impression that the Lord has smitten him down for his eagerness. John Mitchinson sings powerfully and dramatically in Part I and Rattle's accompaniment throbs with fervour; but the voice soon develops an uncomfortably wide vibrato under pressure, which is less congenial in Part II. Dame Janet Baker's assumption of the Angel's role is justly famous, but the close microphones are not kind to her high fortissimos; she comes into her own, however, at the work's valedictory close, helped by the rapturously lovely sounds made by chorus and orchestra alike. The recording has the widest possible dynamic range and, with the solo voices recessed and pianissimos having a tendency to recede, it is difficult to achieve a setting which is comfortable in the work's lyrical sections and yet not overwhelming at climaxes.

Gibson's performance is impressively spontaneous and very dramatic. When in his opening section Gerontius (Robert Tear) describes 'this strange innermost abandonment, this emptying out of each constituent', the orchestral response sends a shiver down the spine. The same sense of drama attends the demons (who are forthright rather than sinister), although here the brightness of the CD transfer verges on fierceness. The male soloists match Gibson's urgency, although there is no lack of repose in the dialogue between the Angel (sensitively portrayed by Alfreda Hodgson) and Gerontius at the opening of Part II. With Gibson, the closing pages are sensitively done but lack the magical feeling of blissful infinity that Boult evokes. The CRD recording is generally excellent but, like Rattle's EMI set, it has almost too wide a dynamic range; also the internal cueing is much too limited.

Britten's approach is red-blooded, passionate and urgent and with speeds never languishing – as in this oratorio they can. The LSO Chorus – supplemented by the King's Choir – is balanced backwardly in the warmly atmospheric recording made at The Maltings, but the extra projection and precision of CD bring out how bitingly dramatic the singing is, even if the actual choral sound is not sharply focused. The soloists are a fine, responsive team, with Pears an involving if sometimes over-stressed Gerontius, and Yvonne Minton and John Shirley-Quirk both excellent.

(i) *The Kingdom* (with BACH, arr. ELGAR: *Fantasia and fugue in C min.(BWV 537), Op. 86;* HANDEL, arr. ELGAR: *Overture in D min.* from *Chandos anthem No. 2*).
*** BMG/RCA Dig. RD 87862 (2) [7862-2-RC]. (i) Kenny, Hodgson, Gillett, Luxon, LPO Ch.; LPO, Slatkin.

The Kingdom; Sursum corda; Sospiri.
*** Chan. Dig. CHAN 8788/9; *DBTD 2017* [id.]. Marshall, Palmer, Davies, Wilson-Johnson, LSO Ch., LSO, Hickox.

Hickox is a passionate Elgarian, confident in his dramatic timing and in his use of an expressive rubato which never has any feeling of self-consciousness or over-indulgence. This fine Chandos version provides a strong contrast with the classic Boult recording (currently awaiting reissue), the first ever made and which, above all, brings out the oratorio's nobility. On his RCA version Slatkin, like Hickox, proves a warmly understanding Elgarian, but Hickox's manner is more ripely idiomatic. With a more consistent team of soloists and richer recording, the Chandos is to be preferred – though there is still a strong case for choosing the Boult, which has the finest soloists of all and, in an excellent CD transfer, brings an exceptionally generous coupling. Hickox's soloists make a characterful quartet. Margaret Marshall is the sweet, tender soprano, rising superbly to a passionate climax in her big solo, *The sun goeth down*, and Felicity Palmer is a strong and positive – if not ideally warm-toned – Mary Magdalene. David Wilson-Johnson points the words of St Peter most dramatically, and Arthur Davies is the radiant tenor. The fill-ups are not generous: the intense little string adagio, *Sospiri*, and the early *Sursum corda*; but both similarly reveal Hickox as a deeply understanding Elgarian.

Slatkin's contribution to the RCA set is outstandingly fine, passionate and red-blooded. Slatkin is more daring and less restrained than is Boult in his (currently withdrawn) version;

Slatkin sometimes jumps the gun in unleashing his forces, but he makes nonsense of any suggestion that this is an undramatic, merely meditative piece. Urgent as his view of Elgar is, Slatkin has a natural feeling for Elgarian rubato and is never rigid or breathless. When it comes to the gentler moments, he conveys a hushed dedication surpassing even Boult's. The choral singing is incandescent; but sadly the set falls short in the choice of soloists. All four in varying degrees (Alfreda Hodgson less than the others) sing with uneven production and with noticeable flutter or vibrato amounting to wobble. The sound is full, rich and atmospheric, as it also is in the two ripely characteristic transcriptions of Bach and Handel that come as fill-ups.

The Music Makers, Op. 69.
(*) EMI CDS7 47208-8 (2). Dame Janet Baker, LPO Ch., LPO, Boult – *Dream of Gerontius.* *

It is some measure of the musical material in *The Music Makers* that the passages which stand out are those where Elgar used themes from his earlier works. If only the whole piece lived up to the uninhibited choral setting of the *Nimrod* variation from *Enigma*, it would be another Elgar masterpiece. Dame Janet Baker sings with dedicated mastery, though unfortunately her example is not always matched in Boult's recording by the comparatively dull-sounding choir.

4 Partsongs, Op. 53; 5 Partsongs from the Greek anthology, Op. 45. Choral songs: *Christmas greeting; Death on the hills; Evening scene; The fountain; Fly, singing bird; Goodmorrow; Go, song of mine; The herald; How calmly the evening; Love's tempest; My love dwelt; Prince of sleep; Rapid stream; Reveille; Serenade; The shower; Snow; Spanish serenade; They are at rest; The wanderer; Weary wind of the West; When swallows fly; Woodland stream; Zut! zut! zut!*
*** Hyp. Dig. CDA 66271/2 [id.]. Worcester Cathedral Ch.; Donald Hunt Singers, Hunt; K. Swallow, J. Ballard; R. Thurlby.

Though many of the partsongs, particularly the early ones, show Elgar at his most conventional, they bring many delights and at least one extraordinarily original item in the last of the *Four Partsongs* Opus 53 of 1908, *Owls.* Set to words of Elgar himself, it is dedicated (in Latin) to his daughter Carice's pet rabbit, and presents a weirdly chromatic and pauseful piece, quite unlike the rest. The finest item is the last, in which both choirs join, the eight-part setting of *Cavalcanti* in translation by Rossetti, *Go, song of mine.* It is also fascinating to find Elgar in 1922, with all his major works completed, writing three charming songs for boys' voices to words by Charles Mackay, as refreshing as anything in the whole collection. He was plainly enjoying himself over such trifles. Atmospherically recorded – the secular singers rather more cleanly than the cathedral choir – it is a delightful collection for anyone fascinated by Elgar outside the big works.

Sea pictures (song cycle), *Op. 37.*
❀ *** EMI CDC7 47329-2 [id.]; *TC-ASD 655.* Dame Janet Baker, LSO, Barbirolli – *Cello concerto.* *** ❀

(i) *Sea pictures, Op. 37. Pomp and circumstance marches Nos. 1–5, Op. 39.*
(B) *** CfP CD-CFP 9004; *TC-CFP 40363.* (i) Bernadette Greevy; LPO, Handley.

Sea pictures hardly matches the mature inspiration of the *Cello concerto* with which it is coupled on EMI, but it is heartwarming here none the less. Like du Pré, Baker is an artist who has the power to convey on record the vividness of a live performance. With the help of Barbirolli she makes the cycle far more convincing than it usually seems, with often trite words clothed in music that seems to transform them. On CD, the voice is caught with extra bloom, and the beauty of Elgar's orchestration is enhanced by the subtle added definition.

Bernadette Greevy – in glorious voice – gives the performance of her recording career in an inspired partnership with Vernon Handley, whose accompaniments are no less memorable, and with the LPO players finding a wonderful rapport with the voice. The singer's imaginative illumination of the words is a constant source of delight. In the last song Handley uses a telling *ad lib.* organ part to underline the climaxes of each final stanza. The recording balance is excellent, although the CD suggests that the microphone was rather close to the voice, rich and clear against an orchestral background shimmering with atmospheric detail. The coupled *Marches* are exhilarating, and if Nos. 2 and (especially) 3 strike some ears as too vigorously paced, comparison with the composer's own tempi reveals an authentic precedent.

Scenes from the Bavarian Highlands, Op. 27 (original version).
*** Conifer Dig. CDCF 142; *MCFC 142* [id.]. CBSO Ch, Halsey; Richard Markham – HOLST: *Dirges & Hymeneal* etc. ***

Three movements from this choral version of *Scenes from the Bavarian Highlands* were later to become the *Bavarian dances* for orchestra; but with piano accompaniment this original version is if anything even more charming, particularly when sung as freshly as by the Birmingham choir, vividly recorded.

Eller, Heino (1887–1970)

Dawn (tone poem); (i) *Elegia for harp & strings; 5 pieces for strings.*
*** Chan. Dig. CHAN 8525; *ABTD 1235* [id.]. (i) Pierce; SNO, Järvi – RAID: *Symphony No. 1.* ***

Heino Eller was an Estonian composer and his earliest work here is a tone-poem, *Dawn*, written at the end of the First World War, which is frankly romantic – with touches of Grieg and early Sibelius as well as the Russian nationalists. The *Five Pieces for strings* of 1953 are transcriptions of earlier piano miniatures and have a wistful, Grieg-like charm. The *Elegia for harp and strings* of 1931 strikes a deeper vein of feeling and has nobility and eloquence, tempered by quiet restraint; there is a beautiful dialogue involving solo viola and harp which is quite haunting. Excellent performances and recording, too. Strongly recommended.

Ellington, Edward Kennedy 'Duke' (1899–1974)

Mainly black (suite, arr. Kennedy).
*** EMI Dig. CDC7 47621-2 [id.]. Nigel Kennedy, Alec Dankworth – BARTÓK: *Violin sonata.* ***

As a fascinating and surprisingly apt coupling for the Bartók *Solo Violin sonata*, Nigel Kennedy gives an equally brilliant account of his own free arrangement of Duke Ellington's suite for big band, *Black, Brown and Beige.* With only a double-bass as partner, the haunting beauty of the melody in *Come Sunday* is all the more intense. In other movements the bass sharpens the impact of Kennedy's always vital playing. The sound is outstandingly vivid and full of presence.

Emmanuel, Maurice (1862–1938)

Sonatine bourguignonne; Sonatine pastorale; Sonatine Nos. 3–4; Sonatine No. 5 (Alla francese); Sonatine No. 6.
❀ *** Continuum CCD 1048 [id.]. Peter Jacobs.

A highly recommendable record on three counts. First, it serves to introduce a hitherto virtually unknown French composer of considerable talent, who studied alongside Debussy at the Paris Conservatoire; secondly, the performances are little short of inspired in their spontaneous identification with the composer's world, to say nothing of their remarkable technical command and fluency. Last but not least, they are given a vividly realistic recording, with an analogue source, that has great immediacy in its CD format. Maurice Emmanuel was born in Burgundy and celebrated his native province in the *Sonatine bourgignonne* (1893), drawing on folk tunes as well as featuring the carillon and chimes of the cathedral at Beaune where he was a boy chorister. Later in his career he was to number Messiaen among his pupils and his *Sonatine pastorale* (1897) is inspired by the bird song which fascinated his more famous contemporary, although Emmanuel is comparatively simplistic, more atune with Satie in wittily quoting the coda from the slow movement of Beethoven's *Pastoral symphony* to conclude his portrayal of *Le Rossignol.* The later works are impressionistic, the *Third* (1920) very Debussian, then erupting into a Messiaen-like cascade of brilliance for the finale. The sinuous charms of the *Sonatine Hindous*, written in the same year, contrast with the elegant pastiche of the masterly *Sonatine alla francese* (1926), a 'French suite' in six dance movements of considerable appeal, not so far removed from Ravel's *Tombeau de Couperin.* The *Sixth* and final *Sonatine* is more concise but has a lovely *Adagio* and a finale brimming over with high spirits. It is superbly dispatched by Peter Jacobs, whose clean articulation and vitality throughout the series afford as much pleasure as his feeling for the music's lyricism and atmosphere. Not to be missed.

Enescu, Georges (1881–1955)

Roumanian rhapsody No. 1.
(M) *** Mercury 432 015-2 [id.]. LSO, Dorati – LISZT: *Hungarian rhapsodies Nos. 1–6.* **(*)

Enescu's chimerical *First Roumanian rhapsody* combines a string of glowing folk-derived melodies with glittering scoring to make it the finest genre piece of its kind in laminating Eastern gypsy influences under a bourgeois orchestral veneer. Dorati finds both flair and exhilaration in the closing pages, and the Mercury sound, from the early 1960s, is well up to the standards of the house. The coupling with the Liszt *Hungarian rhapsodies* is entirely appropriate.

Cello sonata, Op. 26/1.
** Marco Polo Dig. 8.223298 [id.]. Rebecca Rust, David Apter – VILLA-LOBOS: *Berceuse* etc. **

Marco Polo enhance their reputation for enterprise with this issue which couples the first of Enescu's two sonatas for cello and piano, Op. 26, with some rarities for the same medium by Villa-Lobos. Despite its late opus number, the *First Cello sonata* is an early work, preceding the *Second violin sonata* (see below) by a few months. It reflects something of the climate of French music at the time (Franck and Fauré in particular) and though it is well wrought and full of interesting ideas, at 37 minutes it rather outstays its welcome. Not mandatory listening, perhaps, but not negligible music either. However it is admirably played by this duo and well recorded too.

Violin sonatas Nos. 2–3; Torso.
**(*) Hyp. Dig. CDA 66484 [id.]. Adelina Oprean, Justin Oprean.

Enescu's *Second violin sonata* is an early work (Op. 6), written in 1899 when he was seventeen and still studying in Paris with Fauré. The *Third* (1926), together with the opera, *Oedipe*, is his masterpiece and shows an altogether different personality; the difference in stylistic development could hardly be more striking and could perhaps be compared to the difference between, say, Bartók's *First Suite for orchestra* and the *Miraculous Mandarin*. Adelina Oprean, a Carl Flesch prize-winner, is thoroughly inside the idiom, as befits a Rumanian and deals with its subtle rubati and quarter-tones to the manner born. She exhibits excellent musical taste but her partner (and brother) is somewhat less scrupulous in his observance of dynamic nuance. The additional *Torso* is a sonata movement from 1911, which was published only in the 1980s.

7 Chansons de Clément Marot.
*** Unicorn Dig. DKPCD 9035; *DKPC 9035* [id.]. Sarah Walker, Roger Vignoles – DEBUSSY: *Songs* ***; ROUSSEL: *Songs.* **(*)

The set of Enescu songs, written in 1908, makes a rare, attractive and apt addition to Sarah Walker's recital of French song. As a Romanian working largely in Paris, Enescu was thinking very much in a French idiom, charming and witty as well as sweetly romantic. Ideal accompaniments and excellent recording.

Oedipe (opera) complete.
*** EMI Dig. CDS7 54011-2 (2) [Ang. CDCB 54011]. Van Dam, Hendricks, Fassbaender, Lipovšek, Bacquier, Gedda, Hauptmann, Quilico, Aler, Vanaud, Albert, Taillon, Orfeon Donostiarra, Monte Carlo PO, Lawrence Foster.

This is an almost ideal recording of a rare, long-neglected masterpiece, with a breathtaking cast of stars backing up a supremely fine performance by José van Dam in the central role of Oedipus. Unlike others who have adapted Sophocles for the opera stage, in his four compressed, vividly atmospheric Acts Enescu attempts to cover the whole story, from Oedipus's birth and the baleful prophecy of his tragic fate through to his exile in Attica. So Act III alone encapsulates the story as told by Stravinsky in *Oedipus Rex*. The idiom is tough and adventurous as well as warmly exotic, with vivid choral effects, a revelation to anyone who knows Enescu only from his *Roumanian rhapsody*. The only reservation is that the pace tends to be on the slow side, but the incandescence of the playing of the Monte Carlo Philharmonic under Lawrence Foster and the richness of the singing and recorded sound amply compensate for that. The veteran, Gabriel Bacquier, is a moving Tiresias, Brigitte Fassbaender characterful as Jocasta, while Maria

Lipovšek's one scene as the Sphinx makes the spine tingle. With such stars as Barbara Hendricks, Nicolai Gedda, John Aler and Gino Quilico in incidental roles, this is a musical feast.

Englund, Einar (born 1916)

Symphonies Nos. 1 (War) (1946); *2 ('Blackbird')* (1948).
**(*) Ondine Dig. ODE 751-2 [id.]. Estonian SO, Peeter Lilje.

Einar Englund was born on the Swedish island of Gotland but settled in Helsinki. His studies were interrupted by the winter war, and the *First Symphony* is in his own words 'an expression of euphoric joy at having – by a sheer miracle – come through four years of hell'. He has a spontaneous and natural gift, and his musical language is probably closer to Shostakovich than to anyone else. The *Second Symphony* presumably acquired its nickname from the apparent evocation of birdsong at the very opening (it is almost reminiscent of the Tippett of *Midsummer marriage*). The slow movement has strong overtones of Shostakovich and Sibelius; the finale has something of the conventional Soviet symphony of the period, though there is one idea which almost suggests Malcolm Arnold. Englund may not be the equal of Tubin but his talents are far from negligible; he knows a thing or two about how to generate musical movement. Good performances and very acceptable (though not outstanding) recorded sound.

Symphonies Nos. 2 ('Blackbird'); (i) *4 for strings and percussion*; (ii) *Epinikia (Triumphal Hymn).*
(M) ** Finlandia FACD 017 [id.]. Helsinki PO, Pertti Pekkanen; (ii) Berglund; (i) Espoo CO, Paavo Pohjola.

This CD offers recordings of these two symphonies made in 1976 and 1980 respectively, together with an earlier piece written for the Olympic Games. There is not a great deal to choose between the two versions of the *Second Symphony*; the analogue recording holds its own against its digital rival and, if anything, the Helsinki performance has the edge over the Estonian CD in terms of intensity. The *Fourth Symphony*, for strings and percussion, was written on commission from the Finnish Radio in homage to Shostakovich, whose death in 1975 prompted its composition. There are some effective percussion effects, bells and ticking string pizzicati, designed – the composer says – to symbolize the brevity of existence; but for all its undoubted ingenuity, the debt to Shostakovich looms far too large. (There is also a brief allusion to *Tapiola.*)

Erkel, Ferenc (1810–93)

Hunyadi László (opera) complete.
*** Hung. HCD 12581/3 [id.]. Gulyás, Sass, Molnár, Dénes, Sólyom-Nagy, Gáti, Hungarian People's Army male Ch., Hungarian State Op. Ch. & O, Kovács.

Like the much later Erkel opera, *Bank ban*, *Hunyadi László* has never been out of the repertory in Hungary, and this recording makes one understand why. The end of Act I even brings a rousing chorus which, like *Va pensiero* in Verdi's *Nabucco*, has all the qualities of a pop tune. Erkel's use of national music may not be as strikingly colourful as Smetana's in Czechoslovakia or Glinka's in Russia – both comparable figures – but the flavour is both distinctive and attractive, strongly illustrating a red-blooded story. Janos Kovács conducts with a vigour suggesting long experience of this work in the opera house. Denes Gulyás is a heroic, heady-toned hero, while Andras Molnár is equally effective as the villainous king, surprisingly another tenor role. Sylvia Sass is excellent as the hero's mother, in this version allowed to sing the beautiful prayer just before Laszlo's execution, excised from the earlier recording. First-rate sound. An excellent, unusual set, full of strong ideas, making easy listening.

Falla, Manuel de (1876–1946)

El amor brujo (original version, complete with dialogue); (i) (Piano) *Serenata; Serenata andaluza; 7 Canciones populares Españolas.*
*** Nuovo Era Dig. 6809 [id.]. Martha Senn, Carme Ens., Luis Izquierdo; (i) Maria Rosa Bodini.

(i) *El amor brujo* (original version); (ii) *El corregidor y la molinara.*
*** Virgin Dig. VC7 90790-2; *VC 790790-4* [id.]. (i) Claire Powell; (ii) Jill Gomez; Aquarius, Cleobury.

By including the dialogue, spoken over music, the Nuovo Era issue provides the complete original conception of *El amor brujo*, rather like a one-act zarzuela, with chamber scoring and a narrative line somewhat different from the ballet we know in its full orchestral dress. This works admirably; a complete translation enables the listener to enjoy the dramatic and musical experience fully. Martha Senn is perfectly cast in the role of the gypsy heroine. She sings flamboyantly and often ravishingly, both here and in the delectable *Canciones populares* and the other two songs offered as coupling, and she is accompanied very sympathetically. Luis Izquierdo directs the main work atmospherically and finds plenty of gusto for the piece we know as the *Ritual fire dance*. He lets the tension slip a little only in the closing sequence, when the coming of dawn should bring a greater sense of exultation. Apart from a rather shrill opening fanfare, the recording is suitably atmospheric and vivid.

The Virgin alternative, by omitting the dialogue, finds room for the original version of the *Three-cornered hat*, also conceived for chamber orchestra, which first appeared as a mime play with music. Much is missing from the ballet we know today, including the glorious opening fanfare, while the finales for both Acts end relatively limply without the extra music which Falla added later. Nevertheless each score is aurally fascinating in its original format. Claire Powell makes an admirable gypsy in *El amor brujo*, while Jill Gomez is equally vibrant in her contributions to the companion work. Nicholas Cleobury concentrates on atmosphere rather than drama and, helped by the transluscent textures of the outstanding Virgin Classics recording, certainly seduces the ear, though his *Ritual fire dance* (here the 'Dance at the end of the day') has less pungency than Izquierdo's.

El amor brujo (ballet): complete.
(M) *** Decca 417 786-2; *417 786-4*. (i) Nati Mistral; New Philh. O, Frühbeck de Burgos – ALBÉNIZ: *Suite española.* ***

(i) *El amor brujo* (ballet; complete); (ii) *Nights in the gardens of Spain.*
❀ (M) *** Decca Dig. 430 703-2; *430 703-4* [id.]. (i) Tourangeau, Montreal SO, Dutoit; (ii) De Larrocha, LPO, Frühbeck de Burgos – RODRIGO: *Concierto.* *** ❀

(i) *El amor brujo* (complete); (ii; iii) *Nights in the gardens of Spain;* (iii) *The Three-cornered hat: 3 dances.*
(M) **(*) Sony mono/stereo MPK 46449 [id.]. Phd. O, with (i) Shirley Verrett, cond. Stokowski; (ii) Philipe Entremont, (iii) Ormandy.

Dutoit's brilliantly played *El amor brujo* has long been praised by us. With recording in the demonstration class, the performance has characteristic flexibility over phrasing and rhythm and is hauntingly atmospheric. The sound in the coupled *Nights in the gardens of Spain* is equally superb, rich and lustrous and with vivid detail. Miss de Larrocha's lambent feeling for the work's poetic evocation is matched by her brilliance in the nocturnal dance-rhythms. There is at times a thoughtful, improvisatory quality about the reading and the closing pages are particularly beautiful. Even if it were not offered at mid-price, with its generous and outstanding Rodrigo coupling, this would still be one of the most attractive compilations of Spanish music in the catalogue.

Raphael Frühbeck de Burgos provides us with an alternative mid-priced version of *El amor brujo*, attractively coupled with Albéniz. The score's evocative atmosphere is hauntingly captured and, to make the most striking contrast, the famous *Ritual fire dance* blazes brilliantly. Nati Mistral has the vibrant open-throated projection of the real flamenco artist. and the whole performance is idiomatically authentic and compelling. Brilliant Decca sound to match.

Stokowski's *El amor brujo* was made in 1960. It is undoubtedly mono, yet the ear could almost be fooled for, though the treble is a bit spiky, the ambient effect is impressive. Stokowski's magnetism is undiluted: the dramatic effects are superbly strong and *El circulo magico* is drawn by a true magician of the orchestra. The vocal interpolations are unforgettably sung by Shirley Verrett with full-throated flamenco fire and darkly resonant timbre. The Philadelphia Orchestra are again at their most flamboyantly expressive in the spectacular 1964 recording of *Nights in the gardens of Spain*. Philip Entremont plays with coruscating brilliance. Ormandy again demonstrates his skill in a concertante work with an essentially extrovert performance which generates much electricity yet which has plenty of atmosphere plus a moulded, expressive diversity. The sound is less opulent in the three dances from *The Three-cornered hat*, but the playing is strong and fiery.

(i) *El amor brujo* (complete); (ii) *Nights in the gardens of Spain; La vida breve: Interlude and dance.*
*** Chan. Dig. CHAN 8457; *ABTD 1169* [id.]. (i) Sarah Walker; (ii) Fingerhut, LSO, Simon.

The brightly lit Chandos recording emphasizes the vigour of Geoffrey Simon's very vital account of *El amor brujo*, and Sarah Walker's powerful vocal contribution is another asset, her vibrantly earthy singing highly involving. In the more atmospheric sections of the score, however, Dutoit finds a degree of extra subtlety, which gives the Montreal performance its distinction. The Simon/Fingerhut version of *Nights in the gardens of Spain* also makes a strongly contrasted alternative to Alicia de Larrocha's much-praised reading. Here the Chandos sound has a sharper focus than the Decca and the effect is more dramatic, with the soloist responding chimerically to the changes of mood, playing with brilliance and power, yet not missing the music's delicacy. The *Interlude and Dance* from *La vida breve* make a very attractive encore.

El amor brujo; The Three-cornered hat (ballet): complete.
❀ *** Decca Dig. 410 008-2 [id.]. Boky, Tourangeau, Montreal SO, Dutoit.

Dutoit provides the ideal and very generous coupling of Falla's two popular and colourful ballets, each complete with vocal parts. Few more atmospheric records have ever been made. Performances are not just colourful and brilliantly played, they have an idiomatic feeling in their degree of flexibility over phrasing and rhythm. The ideal instance comes in the tango-like seven-in-a-bar rhythms of the Pantomime section of *El amor brujo* which is lusciously seductive. The sound is among the most vivid ever; this remains in the demonstration class for its vividness and tangibility.

(i; ii) *Concierto for harpsichord, flute, oboe, clarinet, violin & cello;* (iii; iv) *El amor brujo* (ballet; complete); (v) *Nights in the gardens of Spain;* (iv; vi) *The Three-cornered hat* (ballet; complete); (iv) *La vida breve: Interlude and dance;* (vii; ii) *Psyché;* (vii; viii; ii) *El retablo de Maese Pedro (Master Peter's puppet show).*
(M) *** Decca 433 908-2 (2) [id.]. (i) John Constable; (ii) L. Sinfonia, Rattle; (iii) Marina de Gabarain; (iv) SRO, Ansermet; (v) De Larrocha, LPO, Frübeck de Burgos; (vi) Teresa Berganza; (vii) Jennifer Smith; (viii) with Oliver, Knapp.

Reissued in Decca's 'Musica española' series as part of the Quincentennial celebrations, this is a wholly recommendable set offering 140 minutes of top-quality Falla; it is worth investigating even if some duplication is involved. Ansermet's vivaciously spirited complete *Three-cornered hat* is also available coupled with Alicia de Larrocha's distinguished earlier, analogue version of *Nights in the gardens of Spain* (see below); here we are offered her later, digital account which is finer still. The surprise is the Ansermet mid-1960s *El amor brujo*, glittering with flamenco colour and with a particularly appealing soloist in the vibrant Marina de Gabarain. We had remembered Ansermet's meticulous concern for detail in this ballet but not the degree of evocative persuasion carried by the playing of the Suisse Romande Orchestra, while the brilliance of the sound remains a tribute to Decca engineering of this period. The other recordings derive from a 1980 Argo LP. John Constable proves an admirable interpreter of the *Concierto* and there is no doubting the truth and subtlety of the Argo balance or the excellence of the performance. *Psyché* is a setting of words by Jean Aubry for voice and a small instrumental grouping of the size used in the *Harpsichord concerto*. Jennifer Smith is an excellent soloist and the orchestral response in both works is thoroughly alive and characterful.

Master Peter's Puppet show was commissioned by the Princesse de Polignac for her puppet theatre and first performed in 1923. The instrumental writing, not inappropriately, carries a small influence from Stravinsky's *Petrushka*. The work is not really an opera but a play within a play, both audience and perfomers being puppets. A series of tableaux is presented with The Boy (Jennifer Smith) as MC. He describes the action (which is illustrated instrumentally) in a fascinating, quick recitative style, and at the climax of the story Don Quixote, who is in the 'audience', can contain himself no longer and rushes to save the escaping lovers. It would be difficult to imagine The Boy being better done than it is here, and the other singers, Alexander Oliver (Master Peter) and Peter Knapp (Don Quixote), are also excellent. Simon Rattle shows himself completely at home in the Spanish sunshine and the orchestral playing and recording are matchingly vivid.

(i) *Nights in the gardens of Spain. El amor brujo: Ritual fire dance.*
**(*) BMG/RCA RD 85666. Rubinstein; (i) Phd. O, Ormandy – FRANCK: *Symphonic variations;* SAINT-SAËNS: *Concerto No. 2.* **(*)

Rubinstein's version dates from 1970. His is an aristocratic reading, treating the work as a brilliantly coloured and mercurial concert piece, rather than a misty evocation, with flamenco rhythms glittering in the finale. The two encores which follow are even more arresting.

Nights in the gardens of Spain.
(B) *** DG Compact Classics 413 156-2 (2); *413 156-4* [id.]. Margrit Weber, Bav. RSO, Kubelik – RODRIGO: *Concierto serenata* etc. ** (CD only: BACARISSE: *Concertino* **(*); CASTELNUOVO-TEDESCO: *Concerto* ***).

With Margrit Weber giving a brilliant account of the solo part, particularly in the latter movements, the effect is both sparkling and exhilarating. A little of the fragrant atmosphere is lost, particularly in the opening section (where de Larrocha is gentler), but the performance, with its strong sense of drama, is certainly not without evocative qualities. This Compact Classics cassette is in the main devoted to the music of Rodrigo; and those wanting an inexpensive version of Rodrigo's delightful *Concierto serenata* for harp should not be disappointed with the Falla. The digitally remastered pair of CDs, which acts as an equivalent, also offers concertos by Castelnuovo-Tedesco and Bacarisse.

(i) *Nights in the gardens of Spain;* (ii) *The Three-cornered hat* (ballet): complete; *La vida breve: Interlude and dance.*
(M) *** Decca 417 771-2. (i) De Larrocha, SRO, Comissiona; (ii) SRO, Ansermet.

Alicia de Larrocha's earlier (1971) recording makes an excellent mid-priced recommendation, coupled with Ansermet's lively and vividly recorded complete *Three-cornered hat*; she receives admirable support from Comissiona. The Decca analogue recording entirely belies its age. The *La vida breve* excerpts make an agreeable bonus.

The Three-cornered hat (ballet; complete).
*** Chan. Dig. CHAN 8904; *ABTD 1513* [id.]. Jill Gomez, Philh. O, Yan Pascal Tortelier – ALBÉNIZ: *Iberia.* ***

Yan Pascal Tortelier is hardly less seductive than Dutoit in handling Falla's beguiling dance-rhythms, and the Philharmonia respond to the rhythmic inflexions of the fandango, seguidilla, and more robust farruca as to the manner born. The fine Chandos recording is full and vivid, if rather reverberant – as the opening fanfare immediately demonstrates – and Jill Gomez's contribution floats within the resonance; but the acoustic warmth adds to the woodwind bloom and the strings are beguilingly rich. Tortelier brings out the score's humour as well as its colour and the closing *Jota* is joyfully vigorous.

PIANO MUSIC

Fantasia bética; 4 Piezas españolas.
(M) *** Decca 433 926-2 (2) [id.]. Alicia de Larrocha – ALBÉNIZ: *Iberia* etc. ***

These welcome and attractive couplings for Albéniz's *Iberia* are given exemplary performances and most realistic 1974 recording. The four *Spanish pieces* are each strong in character, the two central movements, *Cubana* and *Montañesa*, darker in colour and atmosphere, the opening *Aragonesa* and sparkling closing *Andaluza* vividly coloured.

OPERA

La vida breve (complete).
(M) **(*) DG 435 851-2 [id.]. Berganza, Nafé, Carreras, Iñigo, Ambrosian Op. Ch., LSO, Navarro.

La vida breve is a kind of Spanish *Cavalleria rusticana* without the melodrama. Teresa Berganza may not have the light-of-eye expressiveness of her compatriot, Victoria de Los Angeles (whose version is currently withdrawn), but she gives a strong, earthy account which helps to compensate for Falla's dramatic weaknesses; and it is good to have so fine a singer as José Carreras in the relatively small tenor role of Paco. Reliant as the piece is on atmosphere above all, it makes an excellent subject for recording and with vivid performances from the Ambrosian Singers and LSO, idiomatically directed, the result here is convincing, even if the balance is not always ideal. However, while this 1978 recording comes in a box with libretto, it is ungenerously reissued at full price.

Farnon, Robert (born 1917)

À la claire fontaine; Colditz march; Derby Day; Gateway to the West; How beautiful is night; 3 Impressions for orchestra: 2, In a calm; 3, Manhattan playboy. Jumping bean; Lake in the woods; Little Miss Molly; Melody fair; Peanut polka; Pictures in the fire; Portrait of a flirt; A Star is born; State occasion; Westminster waltz.
*** Marco Polo Dig. 8.223401 [id.]. Slovak RSO (Bratislava), Adrian Leaper.

The second composer to be featured in Marco Polo's British Light Music series is British only by adoption. He was born and spent his formative years in Canada, came to England in World War II and stayed. His quirky rhythmic numbers, *Portrait of a flirt, Peanut polka* and *Jumping bean* have much in common with Leroy Anderson in their instant memorability; their counterpart is a series of gentler orchestral watercolours, usually featuring a wistful flute solo amid gentle washes of violins. *À la claire fontaine* is the most famous, but *How beautiful is night* and *Pictures in the fire* (which uses a wider range of woodwind colour at the opening) are no less effective. The most ambitious is the evocatively impressionistic *Lake in the woods*, beautifully played here. Then there is the film music, of which the *Colditz march* is rightly famous and the very British genre pieces, written in the 1950s, the familiar *Westminster waltz*, very cockney *Derby Day* and the ceremonial march, *State occasion*, certainly drawing on the Elgar/Walton tradition, but without the Establishment gravitas which usually accompanies ceremonial writing for the Royals. All this music is played by this excellent Slovak orchestra with warmth, polish and a naturalness of idiomatic feeling that is quite astonishing. Their understanding conductor, Adrian Leaper, gives the rhythmic numbers a fine lift and the musicians obviously relish the atmospheric and delicately scored pastoral evocations. The recording is splendid, vivid with the orchestra set back convincingly in a concert hall acoustic.

Fauré, Gabriel (1845–1924)

Ballade for piano and orchestra, Op. 19.
*** Chan. Dig. CHAN 8773; *ABTD 1411* [id.]. Louis Lortie, LSO, Frühbeck de Burgos – RAVEL: *Piano concertos.* **(*)

Louis Lortie's account of the Fauré *Ballade* comes as a fill-up to the Ravel *Concertos* and has the measure of its tenderness and refinement. This young Canadian pianist is a thoughtful artist and his playing has both sensitivity and strength. This is as penetrating and well recorded an account of Fauré's lovely piece as any now available; however, the coupling is not one of the preferred versions of the Ravel Concertos.

(i) *Ballade for piano and orchestra, Op. 19;* (ii) *Requiem, Op. 48; Cantique de Jean Racine, Op. 11.*
(M) **(*) EMI CDM7 69841-2. (i) John Ogdon; (ii) Burrowes, Rayner-Cook, CBSO Ch.; CBSO, Frémaux.

The elusive and delicate essence of Fauré's *Ballade* is not easy to capture, but Ogdon's warmly affectionate approach is enjoyable and is notably sensitive in the central and closing sections of the work. Frémaux has a moulded style in the *Requiem* which does not spill over into too much expressiveness, and there is a natural warmth about this performance that is persuasive. Norma Burrowes sings beautifully; her innocent style is most engaging. The originally reverberant recording has been refocused somewhat and does not lose too much of its warmth.

(i) *Berceuse, Op. 16; Violin concerto;* (ii) *Élégie. Masques et bergamasques: Overture, Op. 112; Pelléas et Mélisande: suite, Op. 80; Shylock: Nocturne, Op. 57.*
** ASV Dig. CDDCA 686; *ZCDCA 686.* (i) Bonucci; (ii) Ponomarev; Mexico City PO, Bátiz.

Fauré's projected *Violin concerto* was composed in the late 1870s; the allegro, which is all that survives, was first performed in 1880. Although it is no masterpiece, it is good to have it on record and students of the composer will certainly want to hear it. Rodolfo Bonucci plays it with affection, as he does the charming *Berceuse* – though his tone above the stave can be a little wiry. Viocheslav Ponomarev produces a big, rich sonority in the celebrated *Élégie*, and Enrique Bátiz plays the orchestral pieces with evident feeling, even if he rather overstates matters at times in the *Nocturne* from *Shylock* and the ravishing *Prélude* of *Pelléas*. Good rather than distinguished recorded sound.

Dolly (suite, orch. Henri Rabaud), *Op. 56; Masques et bergamasques: suite; Pelléas et Mélisande: suite, Op. 80.*
(B) *** EMI CZS7 62669-2 (2). O de Paris, Serge Baudo (with Concert: French music ***).

All three performances here are well observed and are distinguished by eloquent string-playing that can be both passionate and tender. *Dolly* is Beechamesque in its gentle detail. The *Ouverture* of *Masques et bergamasques* has an engaging rhythmic spring. The performance of *Pelléas et Mélisande* is dignified and the beautiful *Prélude* is given with much feeling. The Orchestre de Paris is a fine ensemble, and the warmth of the 1968/69 recording, made in the kindly acoustics of the Salle Wagram, has not been lost, while detail has been refined. This is part of a highly recommendable two-disc concert.

Élégie in C min. (for cello and orchestra), Op. 24.
(B) *** DG 431 166-2; *431 166-4*. Heinrich Schiff, New Philh. O, Mackerras – LALO: *Cello concerto;* SAINT-SAËNS: *Cello concerto No. 1.* ***
** Ph. Dig. 432 084-2; *432 084-4* [id.]. Julian Lloyd Webber, ECO, Yan Pascal Tortelier – D'INDY: *Lied;* HONEGGER: *Concerto;* SAINT-SAËNS: *Concerto* etc. **(*)

Heinrich Schiff gives an eloquent account of the *Élégie*, and he is finely accompanied and superbly recorded. This 1977 performance, coupled with equally enjoyable versions of the Saint-Saëns and Lalo *Cello concertos*, makes an outstanding bargain.

Julian Lloyd Webber plays Fauré's *Élégie* sensitively enough. His account comes, however, on a disc of much interest in that it includes rarities by Honegger and Vincent d'Indy.

Pelléas et Mélisande (suite), Op. 80.
*** Denon Dig. CO 73675 [id.]. Netherlands R. PO, Fournet – CHAUSSON: *Symphony.* ***

The *Prélude* to *Pelléas* must be one of the most beautiful things in all music. Jean Fournet's account has a charm that is essential in this repertoire, and the Netherlands Radio Orchestra plays most sensitively throughout. They are also very well recorded.

CHAMBER MUSIC

(i) *Andante in B flat, Op. 75; Berceuse, Op. 16;* (ii) *Cello sonatas Nos. 1 in D min., Op. 109; 2 in G min., Op. 117; Élégie, Op. 24;* (iii) *Fantaisie, Op. 79; Morceau de concours;* (i) *Morceau de lecture;* (ii) *Papillon, Op. 77;* (i) *Romance, Op. 28;* (ii) *Serenade in B min., Op. 98; Sicilienne, Op. 78;* (i) *Violin sonatas Nos. 1 in A, Op. 15; 2 in E min., Op. 108;* (i; ii) *Trio in D min., Op. 120.*
(B) *** EMI CMS7 62545-2 (2). Jean-Philippe Collard, (i) Augustin Dumay; (ii) Frédéric Lodéon; (iii) Michel Debost.

Piano quartets Nos. (i; ii) *1 in C min., Op. 15;* (i; iii) *2 in G min., Op. 45; Piano quintets Nos. 1 in C min., Op. 89; 2 in D min., Op. 115;* (iii) *String quartet in E min., Op. 121.*
(B) *** EMI CMS7 62548-2 (2). (i) Jean-Philippe Collard; (ii) Augustin Dumay, Bruno Pasquier, Frédéric Lodéon; (iii) Parrenin Qt.

Dumay and Collard bring different and equally valuable insights, and the performances of the *Piano quartets* are masterly. In addition, there are authoritative and idiomatic readings of the two *Piano quintets*, the *Piano trio*, the two *Cello sonatas*, on the first set, above (what a fine player Lodéon is!), and the enigmatic and other-worldly *Quartet*, Fauré's last utterance, plus all the smaller pieces. This is enormously civilized music whose rewards grow with each hearing; however, one has to accept that, because the Paris Salle Wagram was employed for the recordings (made between 1975 and 1978), close microphones have been used to counteract the hall's resonance. The remastering has both increased the sense of presence and brought a certain dryness to the ambient effect, although the string timbres are fresh.

Cello sonatas Nos. 1 in D min., Op. 109; 2 in G min., Op. 117.
(B) *** Hung. White Label HRC 171 [id.]. Miklós Perényi, Loránt Szücs – CHOPIN: *Cello sonata.* **(*)

The distinguished Hungarian cellist Miklós Perényi seems completely attuned to the elusive world of late Fauré, and in both sonatas the engineers do justice to his tone. Loránt Szücs is an excellent partner, and those who want this repertoire will find little cause for complaint. This disc is highly competitive.

Cello sonatas Nos. 1 in D min., Op. 109; 2 in G min., Op. 117; Élégie, Op. 24; Sicilienne, Op. 78.
**(*) CRD CRD 3316 [id.]. Thomas Igloi, Clifford Benson.

Noble performances from the late Thomas Igloi and Clifford Benson that do full justice to these elusive and rewarding Fauré sonatas. Igloi plays with fervour and eloquence within the restrained expressive limits of the music and the recording is clear, if not one of CRD's finest in terms of ambient effect.

Cello sonata No. 2 in G min., Op. 117; Après un rêve, Op. 7, No. 1; Berceuse, Op. 16; Élégie, Op. 24; Papillon, Op. 77; Romance, Op. 69; Sicilienne, Op. 78.
*** Hyp. Dig. CDA 66235; *KA 66235* [id.]. Steven Isserlis, Pascal Devoyon.

Strange that Hyperion did not record both sonatas: the *D minor* could easily have been accommodated; at under 44 minutes, this is as short on quantity as it is strong on quality! But the *G minor* is one of the most rewarding of Fauré's late works and is played with total dedication and eloquence by Steven Isserlis and Pascal Devoyon.

Piano quartet No. 1 in C min., Op. 15.
**(*) BMG/RCA RD 86256 [RCA 6256-2-RC]. Rubinstein, Guarneri Qt – DVOŘÁK: *Piano quartet No. 2.* **(*)

Piano quartets Nos. 1 in C min., Op. 15; 2 in G min., Op. 45.
❀ *** Hyp. CDA 66166; *KA 66166* [id.]. Domus.
*** CRD Dig. CRD 3403 [id.]. Ian Brown, Nash Ens.

Lovely playing from all concerned in this immensely civilized music. Domus have the requisite lightness of touch and subtlety, and just the right sense of scale and grasp of tempi. Their nimble and sensitive pianist, Susan Tomes, can hold her own in the most exalted company. The recording is excellent, too, though the balance is a little close, but the sound is not airless.

The Nash Ensemble's readings are perhaps less inward and searching than the Hyperion team's, but they do not fall short of excellence, and the clarity and presence of the recording very much tell in its favour. A three-star issue then, but the wonderfully responsive Domus performance has something special which gives it preference.

The RCA coupling was recorded in December 1970 and, like other Rubinstein reissues from this period, is affected by a rather close balance which prevents a real pianissimo. The performance is warm and spontaneous and readily conveys the players' highly musical response to this attractive music.

(i) *Piano quartet No. 1 in C min., Op. 15. Piano trio in D min., Op. 120.*
*** Ph. Dig. 422 350-2. Beaux Arts Trio, (i) with Kim Kashkashian.

Collectors of the Fauré chamber music will have to have this, even if it involves duplication. In some ways (notably in subtlety and charm) it surpasses even the Domus account on Hyperion. Theirs has the grace and lightness of youth; the Beaux Arts have the gentle wisdom of maturity. It is almost invidious to say that Menahem Pressler surpasses himself throughout, since he inspires his partners to equal heights. The *Piano trio* has never sounded so persuasive, even in the hands of Dumay, Collard and Lodéon. The recording is absolutely first rate.

Piano quintets Nos. 1 in D min., Op. 89; 2 in C min., Op. 115.
*** Claves Dig. CD 50-8603 [id.]. Quintetto Fauré di Roma.

These two quintets are much less popular than the two piano quartets and inhabit a more private world. These artists have the measure of Fauré's subtle phrasing and his wonderfully plastic melodic lines, and their performances are hard to fault. The pianist is Maureen Jones, and the quartet are members of I Musici. The recording, made in a Swiss church, is warm and splendidly realistic. This music, once you get inside it, has a hypnotic effect and puts you completely under its spell.

Piano trio in D min., Op. 120.
(M) *** Pickwick Dig. MCD 41; *MCC 41* [id.]. Solomon Trio – DEBUSSY; RAVEL: *Piano trios.* ***
**(*) Denon Dig. CO 72508 [id.]. Rouvier, Kantorow, Müller – DEBUSSY; RAVEL: *Trios.* **(*)

The Solomon Trio, comprising Lionel Friend, Timothy Hugh and Yonty Solomon, were formed in 1990. Their account of this subtle and rewarding score, which eludes so many artists, has great finesse and has the advantage of an excellently balanced recording. No one wanting this particular coupling is likely to be disappointed, particularly in view of the price.

A vital performance on Denon of one of Fauré's loveliest and most inward-looking late works which succeeds also in conveying its tendresse, particularly in the slow movement. It is vividly recorded, if rather closely balanced.

Piano trio in D min., Op. 120; (i) *La bonne chanson, Op. 61.*
*** CRD CRD 3389 [id.]. Nash Ens., (i) with Sarah Walker.

The characterful warmth and vibrancy of Sarah Walker's voice, not to mention her positive artistry, come out strongly in this beautiful reading of Fauré's early settings of Verlaine, music both tender and ardent. The passion of the inspiration is underlined by the use of a long-neglected version of the cycle in which the composer expanded the accompaniment by adding string quartet and double-bass to the original piano. Members of the Nash Ensemble give dedicated performances both of that and of the late, rarefied *Piano trio*, capturing both the elegance and the restrained concentration. The atmospheric recording is well up to CRD's high standard in chamber music. In the vocal work the CD quality is a little subdued in the upper range, but that is no real disadvantage: the effect is suitably evocative.

Violin sonatas Nos. 1 in A, Op. 13; 2 in E min., Op. 108.
❀ (M) *** Ph. 426 384-2. Arthur Grumiaux, Paul Crossley – FRANCK: *Sonata.* **(*)
*** Hyp. Dig. CDA 66277; *KA 66277* [id.]. Krysia Osostowicz, Susan Tomes.

The two Fauré *Sonatas* are immensely refined and rewarding pieces, with strange stylistic affinities and disparities. Although they have been coupled before, they have never been so beautifully played or recorded as on the Philips issue. Moreover the two artists sound as if they are in the living-room; the acoustic is warm, lively and well balanced.

Both the Fauré *Sonatas* are also beautifully played by Krysia Osostowicz and Susan Tomes. There is an appealingly natural, unforced quality to their playing and they are completely persuasive, particularly in the elusive *Second Sonata.* The acoustic is a shade resonant but, such is the eloquence of these artists, the ear quickly adjusts.

PIANO MUSIC

Dolly (suite for piano, 4 hands).
(B) *** Turnabout 0004. Walter & Beatriz Klien – DEBUSSY: *En blanc et noir & Collection.* ***

Dolly is highly effective in its four-handed piano version, especially when played as sympathetically and vivaciously as here by the admirable Klien duo. It is well recorded too, and it makes a fine bonus for a generous and valuable Debussy programme.

Solo piano music

Ballade in F sharp, Op. 19; Mazurka in B flat, Op. 32; 3 Songs without words, Op. 17; Valses caprices Nos. 1–4.
*** CRD Dig. CRD 3426 [id.]. Paul Crossley.

Crossley's playing seems to have gone from strength to strength in his series, and he is especially good in the quirky *Valses caprices*, fully equal to their many subtleties and chimerical changes of mood. He is extremely well recorded too.

Ballade in F sharp, Op. 19; Nocturnes Nos. 1–13 (complete); *9 Préludes, Op. 103; Theme and variations in C sharp min., Op. 73.*
(B) *** EMI CMS7 69149-2 (2). Jean-Philippe Collard.

This is glorious music which ranges from the gently reflective to the profoundly searching. The *Nocturnes* offer a glimse of Fauré's art at its most inward and subtle; and they take a greater hold of the listener at each hearing, the quiet-spoken reticence proving more eloquent than one would ever suspect. The *Préludes* are comparably intimate, and this is all music to which Jean-Philippe Collard is wholly attuned. His account of the *Theme and variations* is no less masterly, combining the utmost tonal refinement and sensitivity with striking keyboard authority. The recording is good, though it has not the bloom and body of the very finest piano records.

Barcarolles Nos. 1–13 (complete).
*** CRD CRD 3422 [id.]. Paul Crossley.

Barcarolles Nos. 1–13; (i) *Dolly. Impromptus Nos. 1–5; Mazurka, Op. 32; Pièces brèves Nos. 1–8, Op. 84; Romances sans paroles Nos. 1–3;* (i) *Souvenir de Bayreuth. Valses-caprices Nos. 1–4.*
(B) *** EMI CZS7 62687-2 (2) [id.]. Jean-Philippe Collard, (i) with Rigutto.

The *Barcarolles* contain some of Fauré's most haunting inspiration. The *Impromptus* are rewarding too. The rest of the music here, particularly the *Pièces brèves* and the charming *Dolly suite*, are equally welcome. Jean-Philippe Collard has the qualities of reticence yet ardour, subtlety and poetic feeling to penetrate Fauré's intimate world. The recordings were made in the Salle Wagram but the acoustic sounds confined and, while Collard has exceptional beauty and refinement of tone at all dynamic levels, the only regret is that full justice is not done to it by the French engineers.

Paul Crossley is a fine interpreter of the gentle yet powerful French master. He has a highly sensitive response to the subtleties of this repertoire and is fully equal to its shifting moods. The CRD version was made in the somewhat reverberant acoustic of Rosslyn Hill Chapel, and is more vivid than the 1971 EMI recording of Jean-Philippe Collard. Honours are pretty evenly divided between the two players; both will give pleasure and, if Collard's account is not displaced, the CRD is still a strong challenger.

Barcarolles Nos. 1, 2, 4, Opp. 26, 41, 44; Impromptus Nos. 2 & 3, Opp. 31, 34; Nocturnes Nos. 4 & 5, Opp. 36–7; 3 Romances sans paroles, Op. 17; Valse caprice, Op. 30.
*** Decca Dig. 425 606-2. Pascal Rogé.

Pascal Rogé is ideally suited by temperament and sensibility to this repertoire. It makes an ideal introduction to Fauré's piano music, and anyone wanting to explore this rewarding world could not do better than set out from here. Rogé brings warmth and charm as well as all his pianistic finesse to this anthology, and his artistry is well served by the Decca engineers.

Barcarolles Nos. 1, 4–6; Impromptus 1–3; Nocturnes 1, 4, 6; 3 Romances sans paroles, Op. 17.
*** Conifer Dig. CDCF 138; *MCFC 138* [id.]. Kathryn Stott.

A lovely recital. Kathryn Stott produces not only a wide dynamic range but a rich and subtle variety of colours in this well-chosen Fauré anthology. This is a most intelligently planned and boldly executed recital. She has a strong artistic personality and has thought deeply and to good purpose about this wonderful music. The recording is excellent, and this fine recital would make another highly rewarding introduction for any newcomer to Fauré's piano music.

Barcarolles Nos. 3–5; 7 & 9; Nocturne No. 6 in D flat, Op. 63; 9 Preludes, Op. 103; Valse-caprice No. 4, Op. 62.
** Continuum CCD 1047 [id.]. Peter Jacobs.

Despite the inviting impressionistic painting which graces the front of the disc, this recital is disappointing compared with Peter Jacobs's other issues in this fine Collegium exploratory series, which includes the music of Balfour Gardiner and Maurice Emmanuel. It is not that the planning of a programme covering the music of Fauré's middle period – the 1890s and early 1900s – is at fault, or the playing, which is sensitive to the composer's restrained lyricism. But the recording, made at St Silas's Church, Kentish Town in 1984, sets the piano back in a rather too resonant acoustic, which prevents any real intimacy of effect.

Dolly, Op. 56.
*** Ph. Dig. 420 159-2 [id.]. Katia and Marielle Labèque – BIZET: *Jeux d'enfants;* RAVEL: *Ma Mère l'Oye.* ***

Fauré's touching suite was written for Hélène Bardac, who was known as Dolly and whose mother was Debussy's second wife. The *Kitty waltz* was a gift for her fourth birthday. The Labèque sisters give a beautiful account of it, their playing distinguished by great sensitivity and delicacy. The recording is altogether first class, totally natural and very realistic in its CD format.

Impromptus Nos. 1–5; 9 Préludes, Op. 103; Theme and variations in C sharp min., Op. 73.
*** CRD CRD 3423 [id.]. Paul Crossley.

The *Theme and variations in C sharp minor* is one of Fauré's most immediately attractive works; Paul Crossley plays it with splendid sensitivity and panache, so this might be a good place to start for a collector wanting to explore Fauré's special pianistic world. Crossley never forces the music, yet his purity of style is never chaste, and his concentration and sense of scale demonstrate his full understanding of this repertoire. The recorded sound, too, is extremely well judged, with a most realistic piano image, nicely placed in relation to the listener.

Nocturnes (complete); *Pièces brèves, Op. 84.*
**(*) CRD CRD 3406-7 [id.]. Paul Crossley.

Here the recording is rather closely balanced, albeit in an ample acoustic, but the result tends to emphasize a percussive element that one does not normally encounter in this artist's playing. The beautifully inward *F sharp minor Nocturne*, Op. 104, No. 1, almost loses the intimate, private quality of which Crossley speaks in his excellent notes, and it is not the only one to do so. There is much understanding and finesse, however, and the Pièces brèves are a valuable fill-up.

VOCAL MUSIC

Mélodies (complete): (i) *L'Absent;* (ii) *Accompagnement; Après un rêve; Arpège; Aubade;* (i) *Au bord de l'eau;* (ii) *Au cimetière; Aurore;* (i) *L'aurore; Automne;* (ii) *Barcarolle; Les berceaux; La bonne chanson* (song-cycle), *Op. 61;* (i) *2 Cantiques (En prière; Noël); C'est la paix!; Chanson;* (ii) *Chanson d'amour;* (i) *La chanson d'Ève* (song-cycle), *Op. 95;* (ii) *Chanson du pêcheur; Chanson de Shylock; Chant d'automne; Clair de lune; Dans la forêt de septembre;* (i) *Dans les ruines d'une abbaye;* (ii) *Le Don silencieux;* (i) *2 Duos for 2 sopranos (Puisqu'ici-bas; Tarentelle); La Fée aux chansons; Fleur jetée;* (ii) *La fleur qui va sur l'eau; L'horizon chimérique* (song-cycle), *Op. 118; Hymne; Ici-bas!;* (i) *Les jardins clos* (song-cycle), *Op. 106;* (ii) *Larmes; Lydia; Madrigal de Shylock; Mai; Les matelots;* (i) *Mélisande's song; 5 Mélodies de Venise;* (ii) *Mirages* (song-cycle), *Op. 113;* (i) *Nell;* (ii) *Nocturne;* (i) *Notre amour; Le papillon et la fleur; Le parfum impérissable; Le pays des rêves;* (ii) *Pleurs d'or; Le plus doux chemin; 3 Poèmes de jour; Les présents; Prison; Le ramier; La rançon;* (i) *Rêve d'amour; La rose; Les roses d'Ispahan; Le secret;* (ii) *Sérénade du bourgeois gentilhomme; Sérénade toscane;* (i) *Seule; Soir;* (ii) *Spleen; Sylvie; Tristesse;* (i) *Vocalise-étude;* (ii) *Le voyageur.*
(M) *** EMI CMS7 64079-2 (4). (i) Elly Ameling, (ii) Gérard Souzay; Dalton Baldwin.

The songs were written over the fullest span of Fauré's life, during a period of no less than 60 years, starting with a jolly waltz-song written when the composer was sixteen. The most striking melodies tend to come in the earlier songs – with the second of the four CDs offering many favourite items like *Chanson d'amour* winningly done by Souzay and *Les roses d'Ispahan* bringing a ravishing example of Ameling at her most radiant. Even so, the style is astonishingly consistent throughout. In the late cycles, *La chanson d'Ève*, *Les jardins clos*, *Mirages* and *L'horizon chimérique*, there is an extra subtlety in the composer's restraint; but even in that last period Fauré allowed himself one extrovert return to an earlier style, a simple, jaunty song for soprano celebrating the Armistice of 1918, *C'est la paix!*. Souzay is not quite as even in his vocal production as at the beginning of his career, but no baritone of recent years has surpassed him in this repertory, and Ameling is at her very peak throughout, fresh and even in line with beautiful colourings. The texts of the songs are given only in French.

La bonne chanson, Op. 61; Poème d'un jour, Op. 21; Les berceaux; La chanson d'Ève: Eau vivante; O mort, poussière d'étoiles. Le horizon chimérique; Le jardin clos: Exaucement; Je me poserai sur ton coeur. 5 Mélodies de Venise; Mirages.
(M) *** Ph. 420 775-2 [id.]. Gérard Souzay, Dalton Baldwin.

This is a self-recommending recital. Gérard Souzay had a unique sensibility in this repertoire, and his control of colour and feeling for the words is magical. The songs are drawn from two records, made in 1961 and 1965, and the sound is fresh, with good presence. Baldwin accompanies impeccably and is well in the picture.

La chanson d'Ève, Op. 95; Mélodies: Après un rêve; Aubade; Barcarolle; Les berceaux; Chanson du pêcheur; En prière; En sourdine; Green; Hymne; Des jardins de la nuit; Mandoline; Le papillon et la fleur; Les présents; Rêve d'amour; Les roses d'Ispahan; Le secret; Spleen; Toujours!.
❀ *** Hyp. Dig. CDA 66320; *KA 66320* [id.]. Dame Janet Baker, Geoffrey Parsons.

Starting with the boy Fauré's Opus 1, No. 1, a charming, Gounod-like waltz-song, *Le papillon et la fleur*, Dame Janet Baker gives magical performances of a generous collection of 28 songs, representing the composer throughout his long composing career. The rare song-cycle, *La chanson d'Ève*, represents Fauré's rarefied later style, written long after everything else here; but the youthful composer was a much more striking melodist, and here he is represented by many of his most winning songs. Early copies had a couple of incorrect texts in the booklet, but that does not alter the glowing, magical singing of Dame Janet, still golden-toned at the very period when she announced her retirement from public performance. Geoffrey Parsons is at his most compellingly sympathetic, matching every mood. Many will be surprised at Fauré's variety of expression over this extended span of songs.

Requiem, Op. 48.
(M) *** Pickwick/RPO Dig. CDRPO 7007; *ZCRPO 7007* [id.]. Aled Jones, Stephen Roberts, LSO Ch., RPO, Hickox – BERNSTEIN: *Chichester Psalms.* ***
*** EMI Dig. CDC7 49880-2 [id.]. Murray, Bär, King's College Ch., ECO, Cleobury – DURUFLÉ: *Requiem.* **(*)

Requiem, Op. 48 (1893 version). *Ave Maria, Op. 67/2; Ave verum corpus, Op. 65/1; Cantique de Jean Racine, Op. 11; Maria, Mater gratiae, Op. 47/2; Messe basse; Tantum ergo, Op. 65/2.*
*** Collegium COLCD 109 [id.]. Ashton, Varcoe, Cambridge Singers, L. Sinfonia (members), Rutter.

Requiem, Op. 48 (1893 version); *Ave verum corpus, Op. 65/1; Cantique de Jean Racine, Op. 11; Messe basse; Tantum ergo, Op. 65/2.*
*** Hyp. Dig. CDA 66292 [id.]. Mary Seers, Isabelle Poulenard, Michael George, Corydon Singers, ECO, Matthew Best.

(i) *Requiem, Op. 48; Cantique de Jean Racine, Op. 11;* (ii) *Messe basse.*
(M) *** Decca 430 360-2; *430 360-4* [id.]. (i) Jonathon Bond, Benjamin Luxon; (ii) Andrew Brunt; St John's College, Cambridge, Ch., ASMF, Guest – POULENC: *Mass* etc. ***

Requiem, Op. 48 (1894 version); *Messe des pêcheurs de Villerville.*
*** HM Dig. HMC 90 1292 [id.]. Mellon, Kooy, Audoli, Petits Chanteurs de Saint-Louis, Paris Chapelle Royale Ch., Musique Oblique Ens., Herreweghe.

(i; ii) *Requiem, Op. 48;* (i) *Pavane, Op. 50; Pelléas et Mélisande: suite, Op. 80.*
*** Decca Dig. 421 440-2 [id.]. (i) Kiri Te Kanawa, Sherrill Milnes; (ii) Montreal Philharmonic Ch.; Montreal SO, Dutoit.

John Rutter's inspired reconstruction of Fauré's original 1893 score, using only lower strings and no woodwind, opened our ears to the extra freshness of the composer's first thoughts. Rutter's fine, bright recording now makes a welcome reappearance on the Collegium label with more music added, equally beautifully sung, including the *Messe basse* and four motets, of which the *Ave Maria* setting and *Ave verum corpus* are particularly memorable. The recording is first rate but places the choir and instruments relatively close, with less space round the sound than on the two even more recent rival versions using original instrumentation.

Matthew Best's performance with the Corydon Singers also uses the Rutter edition but presents a choral and orchestral sound that is more refined, set against a helpful church acoustic. In paradisum is ethereally beautiful. Best's soloists are even finer than Rutter's, and he too provides a generous fill-up in the *Messe basse* and other motets, though two fewer than Rutter.

In many ways Philippe Herreweghe scoops both of them in his quest for authenticity, for he has had access to a score which makes use of the recently discovered instrumental parts of the original 1894 performance of the seven-movement version; unlike Rutter and Best, however, he tends to adopt speeds that are a degree slower than those marked. His soloists are more sophisticated than their British rivals, tonally very beautiful but not quite so fresh in expression. What makes the Harmonia Mundi version also particularly attractive is the fill-up, the joint Mass-setting which the young Messager and the young Fauré wrote together over one happy summer holiday in Normandy in 1881. The recording has chorus and orchestra relatively close, but there is a pleasant ambience round the sound.

Richard Hickox also opts for the regular full-scale text of the *Requiem*, yet at speeds rather faster than usual – no faster than those marked – he presents a fresh, easily flowing view, rather akin to John Rutter's using the original chamber scoring on his Conifer issue. Aled Jones sings very sweetly in *Pié Jesu.* With its generous and equally successful coupling, this makes a strong alternative recommendation to the Dutoit version.

Not surprisingly, the acoustics of St Eustache, Montreal, are highly suitable for recording the regular full orchestral score of Fauré's *Requiem*, and the Decca sound is superb. Dutoit's is an essentially weighty reading, matched by the style of his fine soloists, yet the performance has both freshness and warmth and does not lack transparency. The generous coupling of the choral version of the *Pavane* plus a beautifully played and similarly full-textured suite from *Pelléas et Mélisande* adds to the attractiveness of the Decca issue.

The St John's account has a magic that works from the opening bars onwards. Jonathon Bond and Benjamin Luxon are highly sympathetic soloists and the 1975 (originally Argo) recording is every bit as impressive as its digital competitors, while the smaller scale of the conception is probably nearer to Fauré's original conception. Moreover the Decca couplings are exceptionally generous and beautifully sung. This CD has a playing time of 74 minutes.

Following on from John Rutter's and Matthew Best's recordings, the EMI version from King's also uses Rutter's reconstruction of the original 1893 score with limited chamber orchestra. It can also claim ancestry from Sir David Willocks's EMI version of the 1960s using the King's Choir of an earlier generation; now, as then, the refinement and responsiveness of the young King's choristers is unsurpassed among collegiate or cathedral choirs. Like Willcocks, Cleobury uses a boy treble for the *Pié Jesu*, with Richard Eteson clear and bright. Generously coupled with the Duruflé *Requiem*, which was directly inspired by Fauré's example, this makes a worthwhile coupling, although neither performance considered individually would be a first choice.

Feld, Jindrich (born 1925)

Flute sonata.
*** BMG/RCA Dig. RD 87802 [7802-2-RC]. James Galway, Phillip Moll – DVOŘÁK: *Sonatina;* MARTINŮ: *Sonata.* ***

Jindrich Feld writes in a relatively conservative idiom, only occasionally betraying a specifically Czech flavour. What matters is his understanding of the flute, when it prompts Galway to play with characteristic flair. The piece makes an unusual and attractive coupling to the Dvořák and Martinů works, all of them vividly recorded in a relatively dry acoustic.

Ferguson, Howard (born 1908)

(i) *Octet, Op. 4;* (ii; iii) *Violin sonata No. 2, Op. 10;* (iii) *5 Bagatelles.*
*** Hyp. Dig. CDA 66192; *KA 66192* [id.]. (i) Nash Ensemble; (ii) Levon Chilingirian; (iii) Clifford Benson. – FINZI: *Elegy.* ***

This richly satisfying collection is headed by an ensemble piece with few rivals. Ferguson's *Octet* is written for the same instruments as Schubert's masterpiece, a delightful counterpart. From the first seductive clarinet motif onwards, its clean-cut arguments, based on sharply memorable material, emerge naturally and freshly. With echoes of Walton in the idiom, the four compact movements are finely balanced, with a hornpipe scherzo leading to a broadly lyrical slow movement and a jolly jig finale. The other works on the disc display the same gift of easy, warm communication, not just the *Bagatelles* for piano solo but also the darker *Violin sonata No. 2*, written after the Second World War. Finzi's haunting *Elegy for violin and piano*, also played by Levon Chilingirian and Clifford Benson, is an attractive makeweight.

Violin sonata No. 1, Op. 2.
(M) ** BMG/RCA GD 87872; *GK 87872* [7872-2-RG; *7872-4-RG*]. Heifetz, Steuber – CASTELNUOVO-TEDESCO: *Concerto No. 2* (**); FRANÇAIX: *Trio* ***; K. KHACHATURIAN: *Sonata.* **

Howard Ferguson's *First Violin sonata* is beautifully crafted and, though not strongly individual, is a satisfying musical experience, the product of a fastidious intelligence. It was recorded in stereo in 1966, but in a dryish acoustic which does not flatter the bottom-heavy and closely balanced piano of Lillian Steuber. However, it comes in a particularly enterprising compilation and is not otherwise available.

(i) *Partita for 2 pianos, Op. 56. Piano sonata in F min., Op. 8.*
*** Hyp. CDA 66130 [id.]. Howard Shelley, (i) Hilary Macnamara.

Written in memory of his teacher, Harold Samuel, Ferguson's *Sonata* is a dark, formidable piece in three substantial movements, here given a powerful and intense performance. Though Ferguson with rare restraint decided later in life that he would write no more, here his creative urge is never less than purposeful in a romantic sonata that is well constructed with a style which, for all its echoes of Rachmaninov, is quite individual. The *Partita* is set in a neo-classical mould of four movements – overture, courante, sarabande and gigue – but is in no sense shallow in its expression, a large-scale piece, full of good ideas, in which Howard Shelley is joined for this two-piano version by his wife, Hilary Macnamara. Excellent, committed performances and first-rate recording, vividly transferred to CD.

Ferranti, Marco Aurelio Zani de (1801–78)

Exercice, Op. 50/14; Fantaisie variée sur le romance d'Otello (Assisa à piè), Op. 7; 4 Mélodies nocturnes originales, Op. 41a/1–4; Nocturne sur la dernière pensée de Weber, Op. 40; Ronde des fées, Op. 2.

❀ *** Chan. Dig. CHAN 8512; *ABTD 1222* [id.]. Simon Wynberg (guitar) – FERRER: *Collection.* ***

Ferranti, now virtually forgotten, was a famous figure in his day. Let Berlioz sum up the contemporary view of his prowess: 'With a Paganinian technique Zani combines a communicative sensibility and an ability to sing that few, as far as I know, have ever possessed before. He soothes you, magnetizes you; it should be added that he writes excellent music for the guitar and that, to a large degree, the charm of his compositions contributes to the spell over the listener.' Here Simon Wynberg's playing fully enters the innocently compelling sound-world of the Bolognese composer; it is wholly spontaneous and has the most subtle control of light and shade. Ferranti's invention is most appealing, and this makes ideal music for late-evening reverie; moreover the guitar is most realistically recorded.

Ferrer, José (1835–1916)

Belle (Gavotte); La danse de naïades; L'étudiant de Salamanque (Tango); Vals.

*** Chan. Dig. CHAN 8512; *ABTD 1222* [id.]. Simon Wynberg (guitar) – FERRANTI: *Collection.* *** ❀

José Ferrer is a less substantial figure than Ferranti, but these four vignettes (each lasting two to three minutes) are almost as winning as that composer's music. They form a centrepiece in Simon Wynberg's excellent and enterprising recital which is most enjoyable. The recording has striking realism and presence.

Fibich, Zdeněk (1850–1900)

(i) *Symphonies Nos. 2 in E flat, Op. 38;* (ii) *3 in E min., Op. 53.*

**(*) Sup. 11 0657-2 [id.]. Brno State PO, (i) Waldhans; (ii) Bělohlávek.

Fibich's *Second Symphony* is the most often played. At times the music proceeds in a somewhat predictable way, yet the *Adagio* is undoubtedly eloquent, and the scherzo is stirring and colourful. The Brno orchestra under Jiřá Waldhans give a straightforward performance and the 1976 recording is clear, with plenty of body and a convincing ambient effect. In the *Third Symphony* the invention is fresher than that of its predecessor, and the scherzo with its catchy syncopations has great charm. The performance, directed by Jiří Bělohlávek, is sympathetic and alive; the 1981 recording has a concert-hall balance and vividness, while being kinder to the excellent strings of the Brno orchestra than the balance for the *First Symphony*.

Field, John (1782–1837)

Andante in C min.; The Bear dance in E flat (both for four hands); *Grand pastorale in E; Nocturnes Nos. 1–6, 11–12, 14; Sonata No. 1, Op. 1/1; Variations in A min. on a Russian air* (for 4 hands); *Variations in B flat on a Russian air (Kamarinskaya); Variations in D min. on a Russian drinking song.*

** Amon Ra Dig. CD-SAR 48 [id.]. Richard Burnett (various fortepianos); with Lorna Fulford.

Richard Burnett's recital is most likely to appeal to collectors interested in the sound of historic fortepianos. He does not always attempt to articulate the *Nocturnes* to make them sound romantic (although there are one or two exceptions) and the hollow timbre of the various old instruments is perhaps an acquired taste. The famous *Rondo* from the *Sonata in E flat*, Op. 1/1, is presented briskly and deftly but Burnett is at his finest in the sets of variations which suite the more percussive fortepiano timbre very well. Needless to say, his technique and musicianship are in no doubt, and his style in the more sustained writing is very probably what listeners in the early nineteenth century would have expected. Lorna Fulford makes an excellent partner in the four-handed items.

Piano sonatas: Nos. 1 in E flat; 2 in A; 3 in C min., Op. 1/1–3; 4 in B.
**(*) Chan. Dig. CHAN 8787; *ABTD 1422* [id.]. Míceál O'Rourke.

Míceál O'Rorke plays these two-movement *Sonatas* written by his countryman with some flair. He is particularly good in the famous *Rondo* finale of the *First Sonata*, which he plays with real Irish whimsy and sparkling touch. The *Rondos* of all four works are striking and the *Allegretto scherzando* of No. 3 also has hit potential. The opening movements are less uniformly interesting.

Finzi, Gerald (1901–56)

Cello concerto in A min., Op. 40.
*** Chan. Dig. CHAN 8471; *ABTD 1182* [id.]. Wallfisch, RLPO, Handley – K. LEIGHTON: *Veris gratia.* ***

Finzi's *Cello concerto*, perhaps the most searching of all his works, should certainly be in the repertory. Wallfisch's performance is stronger and more direct than that of Yo-Yo Ma, who recorded it on LP for Lyrita at the end of the 1970s. Wallfisch finds all the dark eloquence of the central movement, and the performance overall has splendid impetus, with Handley providing the most sympathetic backing and the Royal Liverpool Philharmonic Orchestra on their finest form. The Chandos recording has an attractively natural balance.

Clarinet concerto, Op. 31.
*** Hyp. CDA 66001; *KA 66001* [id.]. Thea King, Philh. O, Francis – STANFORD: *Concerto.* ***
*** ASV Dig. CDDCA 568; *ZCDCA 568* [id.]. MacDonald, N. Sinfonia, Bedford – COPLAND: *Concerto;* MOURANT: *Pied Piper.* ***

(i) *Clarinet concerto, Op. 31;* (ii) *5 Bagatelles for clarinet and piano.*
*** ASV CDDCA 787; *ZCDCA 787* [id.]. Emma Johnson; (i) RPO, Groves; (ii) Malcolm Martineau – STANFORD: *Clarinet concerto* etc. ***

There is no more delightful disc of British clarinet music than this, with Emma Johnson even more warmly expressive in the concertos than Thea King on her Hyperion disc, and with Sir Charles Groves and the RPO ideally sympathetic accompanists. Finzi's sinuous melodies for the solo instrument are made to sound as though the soloist is improvising them, and with extreme daring she uses the widest possible dynamic, ranging down to a whispered pianissimo that might be inaudible in a concert-hall. Thea King and Michael Collins on Virgin are both less free in their rubato, but no one could accuse Johnson of being self-indulgent or mannered. The recording is full and vivid, though the clarinet is balanced rather close. In the *Bagatelles* too she characterizes each of the five pieces very positively, with the pianist discreet rather than positive. These are all gems, with the languorously beautiful *Romance* – second of the five – sounding like a variation on the spiritual, *Deep river*, and the final *Fughetta* a breezy and witty hornpipe. As in previous recordings for ASV Emma Johnson consistently conveys her own intense joy in the music.

Finzi's *Clarinet concerto* is among his very finest music. The expressive intensity of the slow movement communicates immediately, and the joyous pastoral lyricism of the finale has sharp memorability. On the Hyperion label, Thea King gives a splendid performance, strong and clean-cut. Her characterful timbre, using little or no vibrato, is highly telling against a resonant orchestral backcloth. The accompaniment of the Philharmonia under Alun Francis is highly sympathetic. With Stanford's even rarer concerto, this makes a most attractive issue, and the sound is excellent.

The coupling of Finzi and Copland makes an unexpected but attractive mix, with the Canadian clarinettist, George MacDonald, giving a brilliant and thoughtful performance, particularly impressive in the spacious, melismatic writing of the slow movement. The finale with its carefree 'travelling' theme could be handled more lightly. Refined recording, with the instruments set slightly at a distance.

(i) *Clarinet concerto;* (ii) *Dies natalis; Farewell to arms.*
**(*) Virgin Dig. VC7 90718-2; *VC 790718-4* [id.]. (i) Michael Collins, (ii) Martyn Hill; City of L. Sinfonia, Hickox.

Dies natalis is quintessential Finzi: a setting of words by Traherne, it reflects the composer's preoccupations with the evanescent nature of life and the corruption of innocence by experience. Martyn Hill is set rather far back: his voice is balanced very much as one would expect it to be in real life, and some listeners will want him to be brought further forward. He also suffers from a pronounced vibrato which takes a lot of getting used to, both in *Dies natalis* and in the *Farewell to arms.* The *Clarinet concerto* is brilliantly played by Michael Collins. Throughout all three works Richard Hickox and the City of London Sinfonia give thoroughly sympathetic support, and the Virgin recording is eminently natural and pleasing.

(i) *Clarinet concerto. Love's Labour's Lost: suite; Prelude for string orchestra; Romance for strings.*
*** Nimbus Dig. NI 5101 [id.]. (i) Alan Hacker; E. String O, Boughton.

Alan Hacker's reading of the *Concerto* is improvisatory in style and freely flexible in tempi, with the slow movement at once introspective and rhapsodic. The interpretation finds a release from its essentially elegiac feeling in the songful exhilaration of the finale, with William Boughton's sensitive accompaniment following the changes of mood of his soloist most persuasively. The concert suite of incidental music for Shakespeare's *Love's Labour's Lost* begins with attractive fanfares and a melody in the Bliss/Elgar/Walton tradition, and the rest of the suite is amiably atmospheric and pleasing in invention and in the colour of its scoring. The two string pieces are by no means slight and are played most expressively; the *Romance* is particularly eloquent in William Boughton's hands. The recording, made in the Great Hall of Birmingham University, has the characteristic richness and ambient warmth we associate with Nimbus's fine series of recordings with this group.

(i) *Dies natalis; For St Cecilia;* (ii) *In terra pax; Magnificat.*
(M) *** Decca 425 660-2; *425 660-4.* (i) Langridge, LSO Ch., LSO; (ii) Burrowes, Shirley-Quirk, Hickox Singers, City of L. Sinfonia; Hickox.

Dies natalis is one of Finzi's most sensitive and deeply felt works. *In terra pax* is another Christmas work, this time more direct, opening atmospherically with the baritone's musing evocation of the pastoral nativity scene. Then comes a burst of choral splendour at the appearance of the Angel of the Lord, and after her gentle declaration of the birth of Christ comes another even more resplendent depiction of the 'multitude of the heavenly host', and the music returns to the thoughtful, recessed mood of the opening. The concert ends with the fine *Magnificat* setting from 1951, an American commission. All the performances here are both strong and convincing in their contrasting moods; this generous Decca anthology, taken from vintage Argo recordings made in 1978/9, remains highly recommendable.

Elegy for violin and piano.
*** Hyp. Dig. CDA 66192; *KA 66192* [id.]. Chilingirian, Benson – FERGUSON: *Octet* etc. ***

Finzi's moving little *Elegy for violin and piano* makes an apt fill-up for the record of chamber music by his friend, Howard Ferguson.

Fiorillo, Federigo (1755– after 1823)

Violin concerto No. 1 in F.
*** Hyp. Dig. CDA 66210; *KA 66210* [id.]. Oprean, European Community CO, Faerber – VIOTTI: *Violin concerto No. 13.* ***

Fiorillo's *Concerto* is charmingly romantic; the *Larghetto* is not ambitious, but the finale is agreeably gay. Adelina Oprean's playing can only be described as quicksilver: her lightness of bow and firm, clean focus of timbre are most appealing. She is given a warm, polished accompaniment by this first-class chamber orchestra, conducted with vitality and understanding by Joerg Faerber. The recording, made in the attractive ambience of the London Henry Wood Hall, is eminently truthful and well balanced.

Flotow, Friedrich (1812–83)

Martha (complete).
(M) *** Eurodisc 352 878 (2) [7789-2-RG]. Popp, Soffel, Jerusalem, Nimsgern, Ridderbusch, Bav. R. Ch. and O, Wallberg.

Martha is a charming opera that should be much better known in Britain than it is. The Eurodisc cast is as near perfect as could be imagined. Lucia Popp is a splendid Lady Harriet, the voice rich and full (her *Letzte Rose* is radiant) yet riding the ensembles with jewelled accuracy. Doris Soffel is no less characterful as Nancy, and Siegfried Jerusalem is in his element as the hero, Lionel, singing ardently throughout. Siegmund Nimsgern is an excellent Lord Tristan, and Karl Ridderbusch matches his genial gusto, singing Plunkett's Porter-Lied with weight as well as brio. Wallberg's direction is marvellously spirited and the opera gathers pace as it proceeds. The Bavarian Radio Chorus sings with joyous precision and the orchestral playing sparkles. With first-class recording, full and vivid, this is highly recommended, for the transfer to CD has been managed admirably.

Forqueray, Antoine (1671–1745)

(i) *Pièces de viole;* (ii) *Pièces de clavecin.*
*** HM/BMG Dig. RD 77262 [77262-2]. (i) Jay Bernfield; (ii) Skip Sempé.

Antoine Forqueray was a younger contemporary of Marin Marais and enjoyed a reputation as one of the greatest gamba players of his day, though he responded more favourably to the Italian music of his time (Corelli and Vivaldi) than did Marais. This record contrasts some of his character pieces with the harpsichord transcriptions made by his son, Jean-Baptiste (1699–1782), and published in 1747, two years after his death. The latter was also a formidable player; indeed it has been suggested that the father's denunciation of him to the Paris Police for 'gambling, womanising and theft', when he was beginning to establish himself in the 1720s, was in part motivated by jealousy of his enormous talent! The transcriptions are, as such things should be, re-creations and remarkably free rhythmically. Nor is there a hint of rigidity in Skip Sempé's performances; they have all the expressive freedom and poetic feeling that the music calls for. The music has an intimacy and character that is beguiling, and Jay Bernfeld's playing has a comparable instinctive artistry. Both players are well served by the engineers who do not attempt to make either instrument larger than life. This is one of the most rewarding issues of its kind to appear in recent months.

Pièces de clavecin: Suites in D; G min. (trans. Jean-Baptiste Forqueray).
** Sony Dig. SK 48080 [id.]. Gustav Leonhardt (harpsichord) (with COUPERIN; DUPHLY: *La Forqueray* **).

Played at a normal level-setting Gustav Leonhardt's harpsichord sounds thunderous! It is strange that engineers, presumably fearful of extraneous noises, persistently record both the harpsichord and the clavichord so closely and with scarcely any space round the instrument. Even heard at half the usual volume the sound is overbearing and excessively bottom heavy. The great Dutch musician's approach is scholarly and playing has the requisite flexibility though less spontaneity than his pupil, Sempé whose CD listed above gains immeasurably from a more natural and pleasing recording, and has greater poetic feeling. The disc is completed by two short pieces, too short to warrant separate listing, by François Couperin and Jacques Duphly, both character portraits of Forqueray.

Livre de clavecin de Madame Forqueray, suites Nos. 1, 2 & 5.
** Erato/Warner Dig. 2292 45751-2 [id.]. Ton Koopman.

Ton Koopman plays a generous selection of Jean-Baptiste Forqueray's transcriptions (though it is thought that the second Madame Forqueray, Marie-Rose Dubois, an accomplished harpsichordist, had a hand in them). They are played with a refreshing spontaneity and vitality by Ton Koopman who conveys their range and depth admirably. This is how music of this period should be presented, with imagination and flair. Given the authority of his playing, this should be a strong three-star recommendation but the recording lets it down. Not only is it transferred at a thunderous level (which can up to a point be tamed) but the tone is bottom-heavy and the perspective places the listener standing over the instrument.

Foss, Lucas (born 1922)

Song of Songs.

(M) *** Sony SM2K 47533 [id.]. Jennie Tourel, NYPO, Bernstein – BLOCH: *Sacred service* ***; BEN-HAIM: *Sweet Psalmist of Israel.* **(*)

Too little of of Lucas Foss has been recorded and his main output remains to be discovered. On the evidence of this highly imaginative cantata, it could prove rewarding. Foss was born in Berlin and studied under Hindemith, whose influence can be found in some of the prolix orchestration here. But he is his own man, and this setting of sections of the *Song of Solomon* (first performed by Koussevitzky in 1947) is an attractive mixture of Copland-flavoured sonorities and a wider folk influence, not unlike that found in Canteloube's *Songs of the Auvergne.* The opening section, *Awake O north wind,* with its animated, chirping woodwind introduction, has genuine freshness and vitality, while the second has a pastoral, springlike feeling. But it is in the passionate third setting, *Turn, my beloved* – which has violence as well as passion – that the composer's vivid palette especially fascinates the ear, for the orchestral commentary has plenty to say, and the long powerful postlude, which finally moves into the serene opening mood of the finale, is superbly done here. Jennie Tourel is a strong and compelling soloist, suitably histrionic, but her lyrical singing, especially in the final song which becomes more darkly intense as it unfolds, is memorable. Bernstein secures a bravura accompaniment from his New York players, strongly involved and at their peak in 1958. Like the coupled Bloch *Sacred service,* the remastered sound is suprisingly full and graphic.

Foulds, John (1880–1939)

String quartets Nos. 9 (Quartetto intimo), Op. 89; 10 (Quartetto geniale), Op. 97. Aquarelles, Op. 32.

❀ *** Pearl SHECD 9564 [id.]. Endellion Qt.

The *Quartetto intimo,* written in 1931, is a powerful five-movement work in a distinctive idiom more advanced than that of Foulds' British contemporaries, with echoes of Scriabin and Bartók. Also on the disc is the one surviving movement of his tenth and last quartet, a dedicated hymn-like piece, as well as three slighter pieces which are earlier. Passionate performances and excellent recording, which is enhanced by the CD transfer. A uniquely valuable issue.

Françaix, Jean (born 1912)

L'horloge de flore.

❀ (M) *** BMG/RCA GD 87989. John de Lancie, LSO, Previn (with SATIE: *Gymnopédies Nos. 1 & 3*) – IBERT: *Symphonie concertante;* R. STRAUSS: *Oboe concerto.* ***

*** Nimbus Dig. NI 5330 [id.]. John Anderson, Philh. O, Simon Wright – MARTINŮ; R. STRAUSS: *Concertos.* ***

Inspired by the Linnaeus Flower Clock, *L'horloge de flore* forms a suite of seven characteristically short and mainly gentle movements. The naïvely simple writing is deceptive: this is music of real memorability and much charm. John de Lancie, the sponsor of the piece, plays delightfully, the accompaniment is a model of felicity and good taste, and the recording is just about perfect. The Satie *Gymnopédies,* orchestrated by Debussy, which follows as an encore, are played slowly and gravely and not ineffectively.

John Anderson's performance is hardly less enjoyable in its elegant warmth and finesse; his tone is slightly riper and some will find that John de Lancie's delicacy of timbre is more appealing in the wistful *Cupidone bleue,* second movement and the gently evocative *Belle de nuit,* which blossoms at five in the afternoon. However the newer Nimbus recording is digital and has each movement separately cued. Couplings also come into it, and many will find the Martinů *Concerto* more appealing than the astringent Ibert *Symphonie concertante.*

String trio in C.
(M) *** BMG/RCA GD 87872 [7872-2-RG]. Heifetz, De Pasquale, Piatigorsky – CASTELNUOVO-TEDESCO: *Concerto No. 2* (**); FERGUSON: *Sonata No. 1* **; K. KHACHATURIAN: *Sonata.* **

Jean Françaix's debonair *String trio* of 1933 is a delight, full of sophistication and tenderness. All four movements are far too short, and marvellously played by Heifetz, Joseph de Pasquale and Piatigorsky.

Franck, César (1822–90)

Le chasseur maudit; Les Éolides; Psyché (orchestral sections only).
**(*) Erato/Warner Dig. 2292 45552-2; *2292 45552-4* [id.]. Basle SO, Armin Jordan.

These three underrated works by Franck receive excellent performances from Armin Jordan. There is much fine musicianship in evidence in *Psyché*, and the playing of the Basle orchestra has delicacy and sensitivity. Jordan generates considerable excitement in *Le chasseur maudit*, one of Beecham's favourites; this is a worthy successor to his celebrated account, and both *Les Éolides* and the orchestral movements we are given from *Psyché* show real tendresse. The only thing lacking is real weight of sonority in the lower strings, but the intelligence of the playing makes up for this. Recommended.

(i) *Les Djinns. Psyché* (orchestral sections only); *Symphony in D min.*
**(*) Decca Dig. 425 432-2; *425 432-4* [id.]. (i) Vladimir Ashkenazy (piano/cond.), Berlin RSO.

It is good to have a fine modern recording of *Les Djinns*, Franck's symphonic poem for piano and orchestra. Inspired by Hugo's poem, *Les Orientales*, it is structured as a long crescendo and decrescendo, with the piano in a redemptive rôle, contrasting with the orchestral demonry. The performance is first class, and Ashkenazy is equally at home in the balmy eroticism of *Psyché*. The Decca recording is alluring and more transparent than Barenboim's older DG version. Ashkenazy is less idiomatic in the *Symphony*, playing it with considerable fervour, in the manner of a work in the Russian tradition. With a vivid response from the Berlin Radio Orchestra, he thrusts forward throughout the piece (keeping up a fair momentum in the *Allegretto* while still maintaining its textural delicacy). The orchestral textures do not smooth out the plangent quality of Franck's scoring, and the music-making is undoubtedly exciting; but the reading overall does not resonate in the memory afterwards, as does Monteux's or even Plasson's (see below).

Symphonic variations for piano and orchestra.
❀ (B) *** Decca 433 628-2; *433 628-4* [id.]. Curzon, LPO, Boult – GRIEG: *Concerto* ***; SCHUMANN: *Concerto.* **(*)
(M) *** Sony MPK 46730 [id.]. Robert Casadesus, Phd. O, Ormandy – CASADESUS: *Concerto for 3 pianos* **; D'INDY: *Symphonie.* ***
**(*) BMG/RCA RD 85666. Rubinstein, NY Symphony of the Air, Wallenstein – FALLA: *Nights* etc.; SAINT-SAËNS: *Concerto No. 2.* **(*)

(i) *Symphonic variations for piano and orchestra;* (ii) *Cello sonata* (trans. of *Violin sonata*); (iii) *Piano quintet in F min.*
** ASV Dig. CDDCA 769; *ZCDCA 769* [id.]. Pascal Rogé, (iii) Friedman, Smith, Wellington; (ii; iii) Pople; (i) L. Festival O, cond. Pople.

Clifford Curzon's 1959 recording of the Franck *Variations* has stood the test of time; even after three decades and more, there is no finer version. It is an engagingly fresh reading as notable for its impulse and rhythmic felicity as for its poetry. The vintage Decca recording is naturally balanced and has been transferred to CD without loss of bloom. The Grieg *Concerto* coupling is hardly less desirable.

Casadesus's classic recording of the *Symphonic variations* with the Philadelphia Orchestra comes from 1958 and has been much improved in this transfer. The great French pianist is in masterly form throughout, and no one investing in this disc is likely to be disappointed.

The ASV disc is stronger on quantity (it collects three Franck works and runs to almost 80 minutes) than on quality. Pascal Rogé's account of the *Symphonic variations* is full of felicitous touches but is by no means as well held together as his earlier version with Maazel and the

Cleveland Orchestra (currently out of circulation). Ross Pople produces musical results but there is none of the concentration of Maazel. As always with this pianist, there is never an ugly sound and his playing both here and in the *Sonata* and the *Quintet* is unfailingly sensitive and responsive. In the *Sonata* Ross Pople is musicianly but wanting the ardour and personality of most rivals. Nor is the recording in the very top drawer, either here or in the *Piano quintet*, which gives far too little space round the instruments. Good playing from the quartet and Rogé.

Symphony in D min.
*** Decca Dig. 430 278-2 [id.]. Montreal SO, Dutoit – D'INDY: *Symphonie sur un chant montagnard.* ***
❀ (M) **(*) BMG/RCA GD 86805 [6805-2-RG]. Chicago SO, Monteux – D'INDY: *Symphonie sur un chant montagnard français* **(*) (with BERLIOZ: *Overture: Béatrice et Bénédict* ***).
(M) **(*) EMI CDM7 63396-2 [id.]. O Nat. de l'ORTF, Sir Thomas Beecham – LALO: *Symphony.* **(*)
(B) * DG Compact Classics *413 423-4* [id.]. O de Paris, Barenboim – SAINT-SAËNS: *Symphony No. 3; Danse macabre.* ***

Symphony in D minor; Les Éolides (symphonic poem).
(B) **(*) Pickwick IMPX 9037 [id.]. Cong. O, William Otterloo.

Symphony in D min; (i) *Symphonic variations for piano and orchestra.*
(M) *** EMI Dig. CDD7 63889-2 [id.]. (i) Collard; Capitole Toulouse O, Plasson.
(M) **(*) Decca Dig. 430 744-2; *430 744-4* [id.]. (i) Jorg Bolet; Concg. O, Chailly.

Dutoit's account with the Montreal orchestra is one of the finest to have appeared for many years. It is very well proportioned, almost classical in its approach with the whole being the sum of its parts. It is magnificently played and recorded and though in terms of intensity and vision would not dislodge Monteux, it provides a good choice for those who want a more up-to-date, near-state-of-the-art recording. Doubtless fill-ups play their part in determining choice and the d'Indy *Symphonie cevenole* is also an attraction.

Monteux exerts a unique grip on this highly charged Romantic symphony, and his control of the continuous ebb and flow of tempo and tension is masterly, so that any weaknesses of structure in the outer movements are disguised. The splendid playing of the Chicago orchestra is ever responsive to the changes of mood, and the sound on this new CD is greatly improved; the ingredient of harshness, caused by Franck's scoring of trumpets in his tuttis, now seems hardly a problem, merely adding a degree of pungency and providing a true French accent. The Chicago ambience ensures that the overall effect is properly spacious.

Plasson's 1985 version has conviction and genuine lyrical fervour, equally strikingly in the chromatic secondary theme of the first movement and the impulsive gusto of the finale. This may not seem as individual an account as that by Monteux, but it is certainly both exciting and satisfying, and the recording is much more impressive than RCA's recording for Monteux, even if it is not quite top-drawer EMI. Jean-Philippe Collard's performance of the *Symphonic variations* is characteristically sensitive and full of imaginative colours and is touched by distinction. Those looking for a mid-priced digital version of this coupling should be well satisfied.

Aptly, this Beecham Edition CD couples both the French symphonies he recorded in 1959, not only the *Symphony in D minor* of César Franck but also the *Symphony in G minor* by Franck's close contemporary, Lalo, which is rather less successful. The Franck, much duplicated, has never seemed richer or more powerful on disc. Beecham is masterful in the rhythmic bite he gives to the great syncopated melodies that swagger their way through the outer movements – the second subject in the first movement and the opening theme of the finale. The recording has plenty of body, with a good sense of presence; but the transfer emphasizes an edge on top.

Riccardo Chailly's performance of the *Symphony* is weighty and well considered. He pays scrupulous attention to dynamic shadings and nuances, and the overall effect, particularly in the first movement, is one of seriousness. In its way it is an impressive account, with first-class playing from the Concertgebouw Orchestra and no want of tonal refinement. Jorge Bolet brings a certain majesty and great clarity to the *Symphonic variations*, without having quite the same delicacy as Rubinstein, De Larrocha or Collard. The sound is eminently satisfactory, and the balance on the whole is well judged. Not perhaps a first choice, but certainly among the best. There is a very good tape, with the textures of the *Symphony* not too opulent and the *Variations* very well balanced.

Otterloo's (Philips) recording of the Franck *Symphony* dates from 1964 and has a vivid CD transfer, almost over-brilliant in its string timbre, an unusual feature with Concertgebouw recordings. However, there is no lack of body, and the bright sound suits Otterloo's reading, which has tremendous thrust. Indeed the whole performance moves forward in a single sweep, and its romantic urgency is impossible to resist when the orchestral playing is so assured. A most exciting version, if not strong on subtlety. *Les Éolides* – not otherwise available – is a welcome encore. The composer's holiday experience of the mistral wind in the Rhône valley in 1875 prompted the work's composition. The Aeolids were the breezes which aided Odysseus on his voyage, and here they blow briskly and bring considerable virtuosity from the Concertgebouw strings.

Although he is well recorded, Barenboim's account is disappointing (see above). However, the coupling on the chrome Compact Classics tape brings two of his finest performances on record.

CHAMBER MUSIC

Cello sonata in A (trans. of *Violin sonata*).
**(*) CRD CRD 3391 [id.]. Robert Cohen, Roger Vignoles (with DVOŘÁK: *Rondo*) – GRIEG: *Cello sonata*. **(*)
** Virgin Dig. VC7 90812-2 [id.]. Steven Isserlis, Pascal Devoyon – DEBUSSY; POULENC: *Sonatas*. **

Cohen gives a firm and strong rendering of the Franck *Sonata* in its cello version, lacking a little in fantasy in the outer movements but splendidly incisive and dashing in the second-movement *Allegro*. The Grieg coupling is attractive and apt, but the recording is more limited than one expects from CRD, a little shallow. The addition of the Dvořák *G minor Rondo*, Op. 94, makes a pleasing bonus.

There is some good playing from Steven Isserlis and Pascal Devoyon but the partnership is somewhat let down by a rather overbearing recording which places both artists far too close to the microphone. Although the Franck *Sonata* really does sound better on the violin, these fine players make out as good a case as any for the transcription which the composer himself sanctioned.

Piano quintet in F min.
(M) **(*) Decca 421 153-2. Clifford Curzon, VPO Qt – DVOŘÁK: *Quintet*. ***
* Ph. Dig. 432 142-2 [id.]. Sviatoslav Richter, Borodin Qt – LISZT: *Ave Maria* etc. ***

Not as seductive a performance on Decca as the glorious Dvořák coupling, partly because the sound, though basically full, has a touch of astringency on top; but Curzon and the VPO players are sensitive and firm at the same time. Curzon's playing is particularly fine.

Richter's performance with the Borodin Quartet derives from a public performance in the Pushkin Museum in Moscow. The place was obviously packed and as a result the recorded sound is very dry and two-dimensional. Marvellously concentrated playing from all concerned, but it is difficult to adjust one's ears to the sound.

String quartet in D.
(M) **(*) Decca 425 424-2; *425 424-4*. Fitzwilliam Qt – RAVEL: *Quartet*. **

Franck's *Quartet*, highly ambitious in its scale, contains some of the composer's most profound and compelling thought; and this magnificent performance by the Fitzwilliam Quartet completely silences any reservations. Very well recorded, with the thick textures nicely balanced, this was one of the finest chamber records of the 1980s. However, the CD transfer, in attempting to clarify the sound, has brought a degree of fierceness to the fortissimo violin timbre.

Violin sonata in A.
❀ (M) *** Decca 421 154-2; *421 154-4*. Kyung Wha Chung, Radu Lupu – DEBUSSY: *Sonatas;* RAVEL: *Introduction and allegro* etc. *** ❀
(M) *** DG 431 469-2; *431 469-4*. Kaja Danczowska, Krystian Zimerman – SZYMANOWSKI: *Mythes* etc. *** ❀
*** DG Dig. 415 683-2 [id.]. Shlomo Mintz, Yefim Bronfman – RAVEL; DEBUSSY: *Sonatas*. ***
(M) *** Decca 433 695-2 [id.]. Itzhak Perlman, Vladimir Ashkenazy – BRAHMS: *Horn trio;* SAINT-SAËNS: *Romance;* SCHUMANN: *Adagio and allegro*. ***
(M) **(*) Ph. 426 384-2; *426 384-4*. Arthur Grumiaux, György Sebok – FAURÉ: *Sonatas*. *** ❀
**(*) DG Dig. 429 729-2 [id.]. Gil Shaham, Gerhard Oppitz – RAVEL: *Tzigane;* SAINT-SAËNS: *Sonata No. 1*. **(*)

(BB) ** Naxos Dig. 8.550417 [id.]. Takako Nishizaki, Jenö Jandó – GRIEG: *Violin sonata* etc. **(*)

Kyung Wha Chung and Radu Lupu give a glorious account, full of natural and not over-projected eloquence, and most beautifully recorded. The slow movement has marvellous repose and the other movements have a natural exuberance and sense of line that carry the listener with them. The 1977 recording is enhanced on CD and, with outstanding couplings, this record is in every sense a genuine bargain.

Kaja Danczowska's account of the Franck is distinguished by a fine sense of line and great sweetness of tone, and she is partnered superbly by Krystian Zimerman. Indeed, in terms of dramatic fire and strength of line, this version can hold its own alongside the finest, and it is perhaps marginally better-balanced than the Kyung Wha Chung and Radu Lupu recording. This DG issue has a particularly valuable and interesting coupling and would be worth acquiring for that alone.

On DG, Shlomo Mintz and Yefim Bronfman give a superbly confident account of the *Sonata*. It is impeccably played and splendidly recorded, too. This can rank alongside the best, and it has the advantage of a digital master.

With Perlman and Ashkenazy, the first movement catches the listener by the ears with the thrust of its forward impulse and the intensity of its lyrical flow. Yet there is no lack of flexibility and the sheer ardour of this interpretation makes it a genuine alternative to the Chung/Lupu account. The 1968 analogue recording has been freshly remastered and its added vividness and sharpening of focus brings just a touch of shrillness on the violin at times, although the added edge goes well with the passion of the music-making.

Grumiaux's account, if less fresh than Miss Chung's, has nobility and warmth to commend it. He is slightly let down by his partner, who is not as imaginative as Lupu in the more poetic moments, including the hushed opening bars.

The young American violinist Gil Shaham is obviously a major talent: he was only eighteen when this disc was made. There is great intensity here (at times, one feels it is almost unrelieved) and Gerhard Oppitz partners him with much dexterity. The pianism is perhaps a little too muscular at times, though Oppitz accompanies the opening movement with great sensitivity. Others have moments of greater repose and poetry, but there is no doubt that this is a remarkable début.

Though she is an unfailingly sensitive player, Takako Nishizaki's vibrato is rather wider at the beginning of the sonata than in other of her records that we have heard, even if there is little cause for complaint elsewhere. She has both eloquence and artistry to commend her and Jenö Jandó proves an excellent partner.

Cello sonata in A (transcription of *Violin sonata*).
(M) **(*) EMI CDM7 63184-2. Du Pré, Barenboim – CHOPIN: *Sonata*. **(*)

Du Pré and Barenboim give a fine, mature, deeply expressive reading of a richly satisfying work. They are well balanced, but the effect of the music when transferred to the cello is inevitably mellower, less vibrant.

ORGAN MUSIC

Andantino in E (arr. Vierne); *Cantabile; Choral Nos. 2–3; Pièce héroïque; Prélude, fugue et variation, Op. 18.*
*** Chan. Dig. CHAN 8891; *ABTD 1502* [id.]. Piet Kee (Cavaillé-Coll organ of Basilica de Santa Maria del Coro, Saint Sebastian).

The Dutch composer-organist Piet Kee omits the *Choral No. 1*, for which room could surely have been found, as the playing-time is only 61 minutes 43 seconds, but, apart from this, there can be few grumbles about his record. His instrument is of particular interest, dating as it does from 1862, four years after the organ Cavaillé-Coll built for Franck himself at Sainte Clotilde. It survives virtually in its original state and its effect is much enhanced by the fine acoustic of the Basilica de Santa Maria del Coro in Saint Sebastian which as Piet Kee puts it, gives added lustre to the sound. His notes, incidentally, are extremely thorough and give a bar-by-bar explanation of the registration. His interpretations strike an excellent balance between expressive freedom and scholarly rectitude.

Cantabile; Chorales Nos. 1–3; Maestoso; Noël Angevin; Offertoire; Pièce héroïque; Poco allegretto; Vieux Noël: Maestoso & Andantino.
** Virgin Dig. VC7 91193-2 [id.]. Nicholas Danby (organ of Saint-Omer Cathedral, France).

Nicholas Danby has the advantage of a superbly focused, beautifully balanced recording by Heinz Wildhagen and a fine instrument, the organ of Saint-Omer Cathedral, which Cavaillé-Coll had rebuilt in the mid-1850s. Apart from the *Three Chorals* and the *Pièce heroïque*, he gives us six of the 59 pieces from *L'Organiste* of 1889, which enable one to hear the single stops and the beautiful quiet ranks of the instrument. By comparison with Piet Kee, Nicholas Danby for all his authority seems to extend little expressive flexibility to the bigger pieces and occasionally sounds just a shade business-like. Although organ enthusiasts will doubtless want to sample this for the sake of the instrument, this would probably not be a first choice. The *Third Choral* though far from square or inflexible, is curiously unmoving and uninvolving.

Cantabile; Chorale No. 1; Fantaisie in C; Pièce héroïque; Prélude, fugue and variation.
**(*) Unicorn Dig. DKPCD 9013; *DKPC 9013* [id.]. Jennifer Bate.

Chorale No. 2 in B min.; Fantaisie in C, Op. 16; Grande pièce symphonique, Op. 17.
**(*) Unicorn Dig. DKPCD 9014; *DKPC 9014* [id.]. Jennifer Bate.

Chorale No. 3 in A min.; Final in B flat, Op. 21; Pastorale, Op. 19; Prière in C sharp min., Op. 20.
** Unicorn Dig. DKPCD 9030; *DKPC 9030* [id.]. Jennifer Bate.

Jennifer Bate plays the Danion-Gonzalez organ at Beauvais Cathedral and is given the benefit of an excellent digital recording. The spacious acoustic contributes an excellent ambience to the aural image, and Miss Bate's brilliance is always put at the service of the composer. The *Pièce héroïque* seems rather well suited to the massive sounds which the Beauvais organ can command and all the music in the third volume shows the instrument to good advantage. However, Bate rushes the opening of the *A minor Chorale*, some of whose detail does not register in this acoustic at the speed.

Cantabile; Fantaisie in A; Pièce héroïque; L'Organiste: 8 Pieces.
(M) **(*) Saga SCD 9019. Pierre Cochereau (organ of Notre Dame, Paris).

Cochereau's performances of the *Cantabile* and *Fantaisie* have far more life than usual and the *Pièce héroïque* is suitably massive. The eight miniatures from *L'Organiste* are charming – an adjective one did not expect to apply to Franck's organ music. The recording has the touch of harshness characteristic of a French organ. It is easy to reproduce and does not disappoint in the *Pièce héroïque.* But the playing time is ungenerous.

Chorales Nos. 1–3; Pièce héroïque.
(M) *** Mercury 434 311-2 [id.]. Marcel Dupré (organ of St Thomas's Church, New York) – WIDOR: *Salve Regina* etc. ***

Recorded in October 1957, this was one of the first great organ records of the stereo era. Dupré knows this quartet of Franck's masterpieces better than anybody, yet his interpretations remain fresh and alive from start to finish, and anyone who thinks this music is dull will surely find this CD a revelation. The great French organist exploits the Aeolian Skinner organ in St Thomas's Church on New York's Fifth Avenue, using its wonderful array of colour, with unsurpassed mastery, especially in the *A minor Chorale*, easily the finest of the three. Nearly 9,000 pipes are distributed throughout the instrument, which also controls a trompette-en-chamade beneath the great Rose window, 65 feet above the nave of the church. Mercury have captured the instrument with incredible fidelity, and the stereo sound gives a remarkably vivid aural impression of the spacious building, without a touch of harshness, yet nothing is lost in the way of detail.

Fantaisie in A; Pastorale.
*** Telarc Dig. CD 80096 [id.]. Michael Murray (organ of Symphony Hall, San Francisco) – JONGEN: *Symphonie concertante.* ***

Michael Murray plays these pieces very well, although the San Francisco organ is not tailor-made for them. The Telarc recording is well up to standard.

PIANO MUSIC

Prélude, choral et fugue.
*** Sony Dig. SK 47180 [id.]. Murray Perahia – LISZT: *Années de pèlerinages* etc. ***

Murray Perahia's recording of the *Prélude, choral et fugue* is in a class of its own. Carefully thought out yet apparently spontaneous and highly poetic. Jean-Philippe Collard's authoritative and impressive account, coupled with the *Piano quintet* on EMI, should not be overlooked, but Perahia has the advantage of much fresher and finer recorded sound.

VOCAL AND CHORAL MUSIC

Les Béatitudes.
**(*) Erato/Warner Dig. 2292 45553-2 [id.]. Lebrun, Berbié, Stutzmann, Randall, Jeffes, Vanaud, Loup, Ottevaere, Fr. R. Ch. & Nouvel PO, Armin Jordan.

Les Béatitudes occupied Franck through the 1870s but, despite the revival of interest in his work in recent years, it has never really established itself. There is much writing of quality – as one would expect – but also much that is pedestrian by the standards of the *Symphony*, the *Sonata* or *Psyché*. Also on such a canvas (the score runs to two hours) the invention is curiously deficient in character and in rhythmic variety. The recording was made at a live performance in Paris in 1985 and is sensitively shaped under the baton of Armin Jordan. The solo singers are more than adequate; the choral and orchestral contributions are also admirable, and the sound-picture is very natural.

Frescobaldi, Girolamo (1583–1643)

Capricci, Book 1.
(M) ** HM/BMG GD 77071 [77071-2-RG]. Gustav Leonhardt, Harry Van Der Kamp.

The *Capricci* (the word means 'moods') were published in 1624, written for those interested in 'seriousness of style, a difficult and learned perfection', and were intended not only with didactic ends in mind but as intellectual relaxation for performers and audience. Gustav Leonhardt's analogue recording dates from 1979 and has splendid clarity and warmth. At 73 minutes and at mid-price, this is good value for money, and the music is certainly rewarding. The recording is far too close and wanting in tonal variety; the effect can be improved somewhat by playing at a lower-than-usual level setting.

Keyboard music: *Ancidetemi pur d'Archadelt passaggiato; Canzona quarta; Capriccio di Durezze; Capriccio sopra la Bassa Fiamenga; Cento partite sopra passacagli; Corrrenti Nos. 1–4; Corrente & ciaccona; Gagliarde Nos. 1–5; Partite sopra l'aria della Romanesca; Partite sopra ciaccona; Partita sopra passacagli; Toccata prima; Toccata nona.*
** Dorian Dig. DOR 90124 [id.]. Colin Tilney (harpsichord).

Colin Tilney's survey of Frescobaldi's keyboard music begins and ends with two keyboard elaborations of the vocal style found in the monodic continuo songs of Peri and Caccini and in the madrigals of Monteverdi. Between these two *Toccatas* come a variety of pieces, drawn mostly from the 1620s, in the free style he developed. There is what we would call a transcription of the madrigal *Ancidetemi pur* of 1539 by Arcadelt, and various canzone and passacaglias. Colin Tilney plays an eighteenth-century instrument of unknown derivation and has a persuasive way with him in this repertoire. The only snag is the recording, which is rather closely balanced and needs to be played at a much lower-level setting than usual.

Froberger, Johann (1616–67)

Canzon No. 2; Capriccio No. 10; Fantasia No. 4 sopra sollare; Lamentation faîte sur la mort très douloureuse de Sa Majesté Imperiale, Ferdinand le troisième; Ricercar No. 5; Suites Nos. 2 & 3; Suite No. 14: Lamentation sur ce que j'ay été volé. Toccatas Nos. 9, 10 & 114; Tombeau faict à Paris sur la mort de M. Blancrocher.
*** HM/BMG Dig. RD 77923 [7913-2-RC]. Gustav Leonhardt (harpsichord).

Froberger's contemporaries regarded him as the most important German keyboard composer of the seventeenth century, and his fame extended well into the eighteenth; Bach himself knew and admired his music. He was also one of the most cosmopolitan of north German musicians; his father had introduced him to the music of Josquin and of contemporary German, English and Italian masters, and he also studied for a time in Rome with Frescobaldi, where he met Carissimi. Froberger's music is highly exploratory in idiom and, in works such as the *Tombeau faict à Paris sur la mort de M. Blancrocher* and the *Plainte faite à Londres pour passer la Melancholie*, from the *Suite No. 3*, he reveals great expressive poignancy. There is a searching, thoughtful quality about this music and its composer obviously possessed a strong vein of melancholy. There is rather more space round the instrument than in Leonhardt's Frescobaldi recital and, heard at a low level-setting, it produces very good results. Recommended with enthusiasm.

Fuchs, Robert (1847–1927)

Clarinet quintet, Op. 102.
*** Marco Polo Dig. 8.223282 [id.]. Rodenhäuser, Ens. Villa Musica – LACHNER: *Septet.* ***

Robert Fuchs is probably best known as a teacher: he was a professor at the Vienna Conservatory where his pupils included Mahler, Sibelius, Schreker and Zemlinsky. He was quite a prolific composer, as a glance at the opus number of his *Clarinet quintet* shows; it was composed in 1914, though it could have been written fifty years earlier. It is beautifully crafted and speaks with the accents of Schubert and Brahms rather than with any strong individuality. It is nicely played by the Mainz-based Ensemble Villa Musica whose excellent clarinettist, Ulf Rodenhäuser, is worth a mention. (His name is buried in small print on the inner sleeve.) A curiosity rather than a revelation then, but eminently well recorded.

Gabrieli, Andrea (1520–86)

Laudate Dominum.
(M) **(*) Decca 430 359-2; *430 359-4*. Magdalen College, Oxford, Ch., Wren O, Rose – G. GABRIELI: *Motets* **(*); PERGOLESI: *Miserere II* *** (with BASSANO: *Ave Regina* **(*)).

In modern times the name Gabrieli has usually suggested Giovanni, nephew of Andrea, but in their day they were both held in equal esteem; this fine setting of *Laudate Dominum* for two five-part choirs helps to explain why. Also included is a splendid *Ave Regina* by Andrea's contemporary, Giovanni Bassano, which is laid out for three four-part choirs and brass in a similar polychoral style. Both are are well performed, if without strong individuality, and the recording is magnificently expansive.

Gabrieli, Giovanni (1557–1612)

Hodie Christus natus est; Plaudite; Virtute magna.
(M) **(*) Decca 430 359-2; *430 359-4* [id.]. Magdalen College, Oxford, Ch., Gowman (organ), Wren O, Rose – A. GABRIELI: *Laudate Dominum* **(*); PERGOLESI: *Miserere II.* ***

The Christmas motet, *Hodie Christus natus est*, is justly the most celebrated; but the other pieces too are most beautiful, notably *Plaudite* for three separate choirs. The performances, though finely controlled, could be more positive and dramatic, but they are very well recorded.

Gade, Niels (1817–90)

Symphonies Nos. 1 in C min. (On Sjønland's fair plains), Op. 5; 8 in B min., Op. 47.
*** BIS Dig. CD 339 [id.]. Stockholm Sinf., Järvi.

Mendelssohn conducted the première of Gade's *First Symphony* (1841–2) and, although his influence is all-pervasive, it is a charming piece. Thirty years separate it from his *Eighth* and last symphony, still much indebted to Mendelssohn. Despite this debt, there is still a sense of real mastery and a command of pace. The Stockholm Sinfonietta and Neeme Järvi give very fresh and lively performances, and the recording is natural and truthful.

Symphonies Nos. 2 in E, Op. 10; 7 in F, Op. 45.
**(*) BIS Dig. CD 355 [id.]. Stockholm Sinf., Järvi.

Schumann thought No. 2 'reminiscent of Denmark's beautiful beechwoods'. The debt to Mendelssohn is still enormous here, but it is very likeable, more spontaneous than the *Seventh*, written twenty years later in 1864–5, though this work has a delightful scherzo. Splendid playing from the Stockholm Sinfonietta under Järvi, and good recording too.

Symphonies Nos. 3 in A min., Op. 15; 4 in B flat, Op. 20.
*** BIS Dig. CD 338 [id.]. Stockholm Sinf., Järvi.

The key of Gade's *Third* naturally prompts one's thoughts to turn to Mendelssohn's *Scottish symphony*, composed only five years before it. Yet there is great freshness and a seemingly effortless flow of ideas and pace, and a fine sense of musical proportion. No. 4 was more generally admired in Gade's lifetime, but its companion here is the more winning. It is beautifully played and recorded.

Symphonies Nos. 3 in A min., Op. 15; (i) *5 in D min., Op. 25.*
**(*) Dacapo Dig. DCCD 9004 [id.]. (i) Amalie Malling, Coll. Mus., Copenhagen, Schönwandt.

Michael Schönwandt's performances of these two Gade symphonies are most musical, and distinguished by sensitive phrasing and a fine feeling for line. In the *Fifth Symphony*, the piano is less closely observed than it is in the BIS recording, where it almost assumes a solo rather than a concertante role. Amalie Malling is the more reticent player, too, and plays with taste and grace. However, the 1988 recording though perfectly acceptable is not as good or as fresh sounding as its BIS rival which is on balance to be preferred.

Symphonies Nos. (i) *5 in D min., Op. 35; 6 in G min., Op. 32.*
*** BIS Dig. CD 356 [id.]. Stockholm Sinf., Järvi; (i) with Roland Pöntinen.

Gade's *Spring Fantasy* had been his engagement present to his future wife, the daughter of J. P. E. Hartmann, the leading Danish composer of the day. The *Fifth Symphony* was his wedding present and, appropriately enough, it is a delightfully sunny piece which lifts one's spirits; its melodies are instantly memorable, and there is a lively concertante part for the piano, splendidly played by the young Roland Pontinen. The *Sixth Symphony* is rather more thickly scored and more academic. The recording is very good, though perhaps less transparent and open than others in the series but, given the charm of the *Fifth Symphony* and the persuasiveness of the performance, this coupling must be warmly recommended.

String quartets Nos. 1 in F min., 2 in E min., 3 in D, Op. 63.
*** BIS Dig. CD 516 [id.]. Kontra Qt.

The Kontra Quartet give a thoroughly committed account of the *D major Quartet*, Op. 63 of 1888, published in the year of his death, and also of his earlier essays in the genre, which he did not publish in his lifetime – and which remain in manuscript to this day. They are pleasing works of great facility and are worth hearing particularly in such good performances and recordings as we are given here. However the fact remains that they show (as does so much of Gade's music) too strong a gravitational pull of Mendelssohn. Nevertheless, in terms of invention and craftsmanship, they give a certain pleasure.

Korsfarerne (The Crusaders), Op. 50.
**(*) BIS Dig. CD 465 [id.]. Rorholm, Westi, Cold, Canzone Ch., Da Camera, Kor 72, Music Students' Chamber Ch., Aarhus SO, Frans Rasmussen.

Gade's *Korsfarerne* was composed in 1866, a year after the *Seventh Symphony*. It is in three sections, *In the desert*, *Armida* and *Towards Jerusalem*, and lasts the best part of an hour. The Danish forces assembled here do it proud, as do the BIS recording team, but it is difficult to summon up much enthusiasm for the music itself. It is impeccably crafted, ideas are well paced, and there are moments of real freshness, but the debt to Mendelssohn, say in the *Chorus of the Spirits of Darkness* which opens the second section, overwhelms any feeling of originality.

Gallo, Domenico (c. 1730– ?)

Trio sonatas: No. 2: Moderato; No. 3: Presto I; Presto II; No. 7: Allegro.
*** Decca Dig. 425 614-2 [id.]. St Paul CO, Hogwood – PERGOLESI: *Sinfonia;* STRAVINSKY: *Pulcinella* etc. ***

These tiny movements come as a valuable and delightful appendix to Hogwood's fine recording of Stravinsky's *Pulcinella*, showing how he transformed such sources as these.

Gardiner, Henry Balfour (1877–1950)

Humoresque; The joyful homecoming; Michaelchurch; Noel 5 Pieces; Prelude; Salamanca; Shenadoah and other pieces (suite).
*** Continuum CCD 1049 [id.]. Peter Jacobs.

Balfour Gardiner was a musical contemporary of Cyril Scott, Roger Quilter and Percy Grainger. Like his musical friends he was at his finest in miniatures, and his writing has an attractive simplicity and innocence. The most ambitious piece here is the Grainger-influenced *Michaelchurch*, with its sounding of bells, but the shorter *Salamanca* – which came to the composer in a dream – is even more evocatively colourful. *The Joyful homecoming* (a march), brings further Grainger associations; the whimsical *Noel* (with its closing quotation of a very famous carol) and the *Five pieces*, show the composer at his most disarming. There is an affinity with both Scott and Quilter here. The *Andante* is charming, and *London bridge* (the central number) thoroughly absorbs the flavour of the nursery rhyme. The suite including *Shenadoah* – not to be confused with folk shanty, which has an added 'n' in its title – is also attractive. Most of this music is slight, but its appeal is undeniable when it is presented with such authority and sympathy. It is very well recorded indeed. The source is analogue, but there is no background worth mentioning and the piano image is absolutely real, with a natural presence.

Gaubert, Philippe (1879–1941)

Music for flute and piano: *Sonatas Nos. 1–3; Sonatine. Ballade; Berceuse; 2 Esquisses; Fantaisie; Nocturne et allegro scherzando; Romance; Sicilienne; Suite; Sur l'eau.*
*** Chan. Dig. CHAN 8981/2; *DBTD 2031* [id.]. Susan Milan, Ian Brown.

Older collectors will remember Philippe Gaubert from the days of 78s when he conducted memorable accounts of Debussy and Dukas. He was conductor of the Paris Conservatoire Orchestra during the 1920s and of the Opéra where he conducted the first French performances of many operas including *Ariane et Barbe-bleu* which he brought to Covent Garden in the 1930s. He made his name as a flautist and was a pupil of Taffanel whom he succeeded not only as conductor but also as professor of flute at the Paris Conservatoire. His music for his own instrument (and most of his other composing) was done in the early hours or when on holiday. The *Romance*, the earliest piece in this two-CD set comes from 1905, the last, his *Sonatine* from 1937. Gaubert had a genuine lyrical gift and his music has an elegance and allure that will captivate. He is eminently well served by Susan Milan and Ian Brown, and they are all well balanced by the Chandos engineers. Truthful sound; civilized and refreshing music, not to be taken all at one draught but full of delight. Edward Blakeman's notes are particularly informative and interesting and there are two charming illustrations.

Gay, John (1685–1732)

The Beggar's Opera (arr. Bonynge and Gamley).
*** Decca Dig. 430 066-2 (2) [id.]. Kanawa, Sutherland, Morris, Dean, Mitchell, Hordern, Marks, Lansbury, Resnik, Rolfe Johnson, London Voices, Nat. PO, Bonynge.

This entertaining digital version of *The Beggar's Opera* creates the atmosphere of a stage musical. The spoken prologue comes before the overture (rather in the way some films complete their opening sequence before the main titles appear). With Warren Mitchell and Sir Michael Hordern immediately taking the stage, the listener's attention is caught before the music begins. The musical arrangements are free – including an unashamedly jazzy sequence in Act II, complete with saxophones – but the basic musical material is of vintage quality and responds readily to a modern treatment which is always sparkling and often imaginative. The casting is imaginative too. With Alfred Marks and Angela Lansbury as Mr and Mrs Peacham a touch of humour is assured; if James Morris is not an entirely convincing Macheath, he sings nicely, and Joan Sutherland makes a spirited Lucy. The rest of the participants show themselves to be equally at home with singing and speaking, an essential if the piece is to spring fully to life. Kiri Te Kanawa as Polly undoubtedly steals the show, as well she should, for it is a peach of a part.

She sings deliciously and her delivery of the dialogue is hardly less memorable. The whole show is done with gusto, and the digital recording is splendid, as spacious as it is clear.

Geminiani, Francesco (1687–1762)

Concerti grossi, Op. 2/5–6; Op. 3/3; Op. 7/2; in G min. (after Corelli, *Op. 5/5*); *in D min.* (after Corelli, *Op. 5/12*); *Theme & variations (La Follia).*
(M) *** BMG/RCA Dig. GD 77010 [77010-2-RG]. La Petite Bande, Sigiswald Kuijken.

A more considerable and innovative figure than is generally supposed, the quality of invention in the Geminiani concertos recorded here rises high above the routine. There is considerable expressive depth in some of the slow movements too. La Petite Bande is incomparably superior to many of the period-instrument ensembles; their string-tone is light and feathery, accents are never overemphatic, and there is a splendid sense of movement. Those who are normally allergic to the vinegary offerings of some rivals will find this record a joy. It is beautifully recorded too, and makes an admirable and economical introduction to this underrated and genial composer.

6 Concerti grossi, Op. 3.
*** O-L 417 522-2 [id.]. AAM, Schröder; Hogwood.

Hogwood's approach reveals the vigour and freshness of Geminiani's melodious and resourceful invention. The concerti are given performances of genuine quality by the Academy of Ancient Music under their Dutch leader, and readers normally resistant to the cult of authentic instruments can be reassured that there is no lack of body and breadth here. They are also extremely well recorded (analogue, 1976), although the CD transfer notices some studio noise and there is a curious moment of background hum which comes up suddenly and disappears on track 8 (Op. 3/2).

Concerti grossi: in D min. (*La Folia,* from CORELLI: *Sonata in D min., Op. 5/12*); *in G min., Op. 7/2; Trio sonatas Nos. 3 in F* (from *Op. 1/9*); *5 in A min.* (from *Op. 1/11*); *6 in D min.* (from *Op. 1/12*); *Violin sonatas: in E min., Op. 1/3; in A, Op. 4/12.*
*** Hyp. Dig. CDA 66264 [id.]. Purcell Band & Qt.

This record comes from Hyperion's '*La Folia*' series, though the only piece here using that celebrated theme is the arrangement Geminiani made of Corelli's *D minor Sonata.* Apart from the *G minor Concerto,* Op. 7, No. 2, the remainder of the disc is given over to chamber works. The Purcell Quartet play with dedication and spirit and convey their own enthusiasm for this admirably inventive music to the listener.

6 Cello sonatas, Op. 5.
**(*) O-L 433 192-2 [id.]. Anthony Pleeth, Richard Webb, Christopher Hogwood.

Geminiani's six *Sonatas,* Op. 5, appeared first in Paris in 1746 and in London the following year. The present recording is based on the London edition and uses a replica of an eighteenth-century cello and bow and a 1766 Kirckman harpsichord. The admirable players do their best to reproduce contemporary performance practice, though the absence of vibrato (and the prominence of the cello continuo) may prove drawbacks for some ears, while the harpsichord sometimes seems a little backward. But the music is rewarding and often imaginative, and the recording is most realistic. With the reservations mentioned, this is a refreshing experience, provided the sonatas are taken one at a time.

Gershwin, George (1898–1937)

An American in Paris; Catfish Row (suite from Porgy and Bess); (i) *Piano concerto in F. Cuban overture; 'I got rhythm' variations; Lullaby for string orchestra; Promenade;* (i) *Rhapsody in blue; Second Rhapsody for piano and orchestra.*
(B) *** VoxBox 1154832 (2) [CDX 5007]. (i) Jeffrey Siegel; St Louis SO, Leonard Slatkin.

The orchestral playing in St Louis, projected by bold, vividly forward recording, has a tingling vitality throughout and the *Cuban overture* lifts off marvellously, helped by the exuberant percussive condiment, administered equally beguilingly in the sultry middle section. The same rhythmic effervescence is no less attractive in the *Piano concerto,* a splendid performance, full of verve and colour, with an authentic atmosphere in the Andante. The *Second Rhapsody* and the delightfully witty and affectionate account of the *'I got rhythm' variations* are hardly less appealing, while there is a delicious clarinet solo from George Silfries to open the engaging *Promenade*. It is as persuasively stylish as the *Lullaby*. But above all it is the vibrancy of this music-making which is so telling, with Jeffrey Siegel not as subtle as Leonard Bernstein in the *Rhapsody in blue* but playing with genuine charisma, and Slatkin presents the central melody with an agreeable warmth. *Catfish Row*, Gershwin's own selection from *Porgy and Bess*, is strongly characterized, while Slatkin's vigorous and characterful account of *An American in Paris*, if rhythmically a little mannered at times, is no less potent than the rest of this heady transatlantic mixture. Outstanding value.

(i) *An American in Paris;* (ii) *Piano concerto in F;* (iii) *Rhapsody in blue.*
(B) *** Pickwick Dig. PCD 909; *CIMPC 909*. (ii; iii) Gwenneth Pryor; LSO, Richard Williams.
(M) **(*) Ph. 420 492-2. (ii; iii) Werner Haas; Monte Carlo Op. O, De Waart.
(B) **(*) CfP CD-CFP 9012; *TC-CFP 4413*. (ii; iii) Blumenthal; ECO, Steuart Bedford.
(M) **(*) DG Dig. 427 806-2; *427 806-4*. Bernstein with LAPO – BARBER: *Adagio;* BERNSTEIN: *Candide overture* etc. ***

An American in Paris; (i) *Piano concerto in F; Rhapsody in blue; Variations on 'I got rhythm'*.
(M) **(*) BMG/RCA GD 86519 [RCA 6519-2-RG]. (i) Earl Wild; Boston Pops O, Fiedler.

From the opening glissando swirl on the clarinet, the performance of the *Rhapsody in blue* by Gwenneth Pryor and the LSO under Richard Williams tingles with adrenalin, and the other performances are comparable. The *Rhapsody* has splendid rhythmic energy, yet the performers can relax to allow the big expressive blossoming at the centre really to expand. Similarly in the *Concerto*, the combination of vitality and flair and an almost voluptuous response to the lyrical melodies is very involving. *An American in Paris*, briskly paced, moves forward in an exhilarating sweep, with the big blues tune vibrant and the closing section managed to perfection. The performances are helped by superb recording, made in the EMI No. 1 Studio; but it is the life and spontaneity of the music-making that enthral the listener throughout all three works.

In Monte Carlo the *Concerto* is particularly successful; its lyrical moments have a quality of nostalgia which is very attractive. Werner Haas is a volatile and sympathetic soloist, and his rhythmic verve is refreshing. Edo de Waart's *An American in Paris* is not only buoyant but glamorous too – the big blues melody is highly seductive and, as with all the best accounts of this piece, the episodic nature of the writing is hidden. There is a cultured, European flavour to this music-making that does not detract from its vitality, and the jazz inflexions are not missed, with plenty of verve in the *Rhapsody*. Very good sound.

Daniel Blumenthal gives performances of the two concertante pieces which convincingly combine Ravelian delicacy of articulation with genuine feeling for the jazz-based idiom. The syncopations are often naughtily pointed, to delightful effect, and Bedford and the ECO, unlikely accompanists as they may be, give warm and understanding support. *An American in Paris* is also done warmly but with less panache. For those seeking a cultured flavour in this music, however, this can be strongly recommended as an alternative to Haas.

Earl Wild's playing is full of energy and brio, and he inspires Arthur Fiedler to a similarly infectious response. The outer movements of the *Concerto* are comparably volatile and the blues feeling of the slow movement is strong. At the end of *An American in Paris* Fiedler adds to the exuberance by bringing in a bevy of motor horns. The brightly remastered recording suits the music-making, though the resonant Boston acoustics at times prevent absolute sharpness of focus: ideally, the spectacular percussion at the beginning of the *Concerto* should sound cleaner.

An American in Paris; Cuban overture; (i) *Rhapsody in blue; Porgy and Bess: Symphonic picture* (arr. R. R. Bennett).
**(*) Decca Dig. 425 111-2 [id.]. (i) Louis Lortie; Montreal SO, Charles Dutoit.

An American in Paris; (i) *Rhapsody in blue.*
(M) *** Sony SMK 47529 [id.]. NYPO, Bernstein; (i) Bernstein (piano) – BERNSTEIN: *Candide overture* etc. ***

An American in Paris (revised F. Cambell-Watson); (i) *Rhapsody in blue; Girl crazy*: excerpts (arr. Leroy Anderson); *Porgy and Bess* (suite, arr. R. R. Bennett & A. Courage).
*** Ph. Dig. 426 404-2; *426 404-4* [id.]. (i) Misha Dichter; Boston Pops O, John Williams.

Bernstein's 1958/9 CBS (now Sony) coupling was recorded when (at the beginning of his forties) he was at the peak of his creativity, with *West Side Story* only two years behind him. This record set the standard by which all subsequent pairings of *An American in Paris* and *Rhapsody in blue* came to be judged. It still sounds astonishingly well as a recording; the *Rhapsody* in particular has better piano-tone than CBS often provided in the 1970s. Bernstein's approach is inspirational, exceptionally flexible but completely spontaneous. Although the jazzy element is not masked, it is essentially a concert performance, fully justifying the expanded orchestration, masterly in every way, with much broader tempi than in the composer's piano-roll version, but quixotic in mood, rhythmically subtle and creating a life-enhancing surge of human warmth at the entry of the big central tune. The performance of *An American in Paris* is vividly characterized, brash and episodic; an unashamedly American view, with the great blues tune marvellously timed and phrased as only a great American orchestra can do it. This coupling is newly remastered, the sound slightly brighter and drier in its ambient effect. Fortunately, the piano timbre remains virtually unscathed in the *Rhapsody*. This uniquely desirable pairing now comes in harness with Bernstein's fizzing first recording of the *Overture Candide*, and his *Symphonic dances* from *West Side story*, which are hardly less vibrant.

John Williams is just the man for a programme like this. His touch is light and *An American in Paris* is relaxed in a most appealing way – less 'symphonic' than usual. So is the *Rhapsody in blue*, yet Misha Dichter provides plenty of bravura. When the big tune arrives its blend of wind and string sound is strikingly fresh. The selections from *Girl crazy* (with its two big hits, *Embraceable you*, and *I got rhythm*) is infectious, and each of the eight numbers from *Porgy and Bess* is given its full individual character, rather than being streamlined into an ongoing pot-pourri. The Boston sound is first class, warm, yet transparent, with plenty of bite and sonority from the brass, yet not too agressive. Most enjoyable.

The Montreal players bring a mischievous Gallic flair and an attractively light touch to *An American in Paris* which, if not entirely idiomatic, is certainly infectious. The *Cuban overture* has a comparable racy vitality and the *Rhapsody in blue* is strong in rhythmic feeling. But several more convincing versions of the latter piece exist, and the famous *Symphonic picture from Porgy and Bess* sounds more opulently magical in Dorati's hands. The Decca engineers have sought here to achieve an essentially bright and vivid effect by placing their microphones fairly close, and some of the lustre of the St Eustache ambience has been lost: the result is comparatively brash.

Catfish Row (suite from *Porgy and Bess*).
*** Telarc Dig. CD 80086 [id.]. Tritt, Cincinnati Pops O, Kunzel – GROFÉ: *Grand Canyon suite.* ***

Catfish Row was arranged by the composer after the initial failure of his opera and already existed when in 1941 Fritz Reiner commissioned Robert Russell Bennett's more sumptuous *Symphonic picture*, which uses much of the same material. It includes a brief piano solo, played with fine style by William Tritt in the highly sympathetic Telarc performance which is very well recorded.

Piano concerto in F.
(M) ** EMI Dig. CDM7 64305-2 [id.]. Peter Donohoe, CBSO, Rattle – BARBER: *Violin concerto;* COPLAND: *Clarinet concerto.* ***

It is a pity that this rather cosy British version of the *Concerto in F* is coupled with two fine American performances of concertos by Barber and Copland. Peter Donohoe plays brilliantly and Rattle's coaxing of the jazz rhythms is agreeably affectionate, but a dimension is missing in the over-refined warmth of this approach to Gershwin. The recording, too, could be brighter and clearer.

Porgy and Bess: Symphonic picture (arr. Bennett).
(M) *** Decca 430 712-2; *430 712-4* [id.]. Detroit SO, Dorati – GROFÉ: *Grand Canyon suite.* ***

Robert Russell Bennett's famous arrangement of Gershwin melodies has been recorded many times, but never more beautifully than on this Decca digital version from Detroit. The performance is totally memorable, the opening evocatively nostalgic, and each one of these wonderful tunes is phrased with a warmly affectionate feeling for its character, yet is never vulgarized. The sound is quite superb: on CD the strings have a ravishing, lustrous radiance that stems from the refinement of the playing itself, captured with remarkable naturalness.

Rhapsody in blue (see also above, under *An American in Paris*).
(M) **(*) DG 431 048-2; *431 048-4* [id.]. Bernstein with LAPO – BARBER: *Adagio;* COPLAND: *Appalachian spring.* ***
(M) **(*) DG Dig. 427 806-2; *427 806-4*. Bernstein with LAPO – BARBER: *Adagio;* BERNSTEIN: *Candide overture* etc. ***
(M) **(*) Decca Dig. 430 726-2; *430 726-4* [id.]. Katia & Marielle Labèque, Cleveland O, Chailly – ADDINSELL: *Warsaw concerto;* GOTTSCHALK: *Grand fantasia;* LISZT: *Hungarian fantasia;* LITOLFF: *Scherzo.* ***

In his most recent recording for DG, Bernstein rather goes over the top with his jazzing of the solos in Gershwin. Such rhythmic freedom was clearly the result of a live rather than a studio performance. This does not match Bernstein's inspired 1959 analogue coupling for CBS. This version has been reissued at mid-price on two separate CDs, differently coupled.

There seems no special reason for preferring the two-piano version of the *Rhapsody in blue*, and although the Labèque duo play charismatically their account is made somewhat controversial by the addition of an improvisatory element (more decorative than structural). However, the playing does not lack sparkle and the recording is first class.

Rhapsody in blue; Piano concerto in F: Adagio (versions for 2 pianos); (i) Songs: *Has anyone seen Joe?; I got rhythm; They can't take that away from me; Porgy and Bess: Summertime; I loves you, Porgy.*
(M) ** Ph. 434 158-2; *434 158-4* [id.]. Katia and Marielle Labèque; (i) with Barabara Hendricks.

This reissue draws on two LPs, omitting the outer movements of the *Concerto* from the one and some of the songs from the other, yet it plays for only 55 minutes. This highly accomplished piano duo perform with flawless ensemble and sparkling attack, but one misses the orchestra. Barbara Hendricks is equally at home in the songs. She is especially impressive in the numbers from *Porgy and Bess.* Excellent transfers of first-class recordings, but this is short measure, and few listeners will want the truncated *Concerto.*

Arrangements of songs: *Embraceable you; Fascinatin' rhythm; A foggy day; Funny face; He loves and she loves; I got rhythm; Lady be good; Liza; Love is here to stay; The man I love; Nice work if you can get it; Soon; Summertime; S'wonderful; They all laughed; They can't take that away from me.*
(M) *** EMI CDM7 69218-2 [id.]; *EG 769218-4.* Yehudi Menuhin, Stéphane Grappelli.

This is an attractive re-assembly of the Gershwin numbers taken from the famous Menuhin/Grappelli series of studio collaborations in which two distinguished musicians from different musical backgrounds struck sparks off each other to most entertaining effect. The songs are all famous and the treatments highly felicitous. The sound has excellent presence.

VOCAL MUSIC

'Kiri sings Gershwin': Boy wanted; But not for me; By Strauss; Embraceable you; I got rhythm; Love is here to stay; Love walked in; Meadow serenade; The man I love; Nice work if you can get it; Somebody loves me; Someone to watch over me; Soon; Things are looking up. Porgy and Bess: Summertime.
**(*) EMI Dig. CDC7 47454-2 [id.]; *EL 270574-4.* Kiri Te Kanawa, New Theatre O, McGlinn (with Chorus).

In Dame Kiri's gorgeously sung *Summertime* from *Porgy and Bess,* the distanced heavenly chorus creates the purest kitsch. But most of the numbers are done in an upbeat style, which has the advantage of carrying the vocal introductions before the verse and preventing their sounding superfluous out of stage context. Dame Kiri is at her most relaxed and ideally there should be more variety of pacing: *The man I love* is thrown away at the chosen tempo. But for the most part the ear is seduced by the lovely sounds and the direct rhythmic style of the presentation; however, the pop microphone techniques bring excessive sibilants in the CD format.

Songs: *But not for me; Embraceable you; I got rhythm; The man I love; Nice work if you can get it; Our love is here to stay; They can't take that away from me. Blue Monday: Has anyone seen Joe? Porgy and Bess: Summertime; I loves you, Porgy.*
**(*) Ph. 416 460-2 [id.]. Barbara Hendricks, Katia and Marielle Labèque.

Barbara Hendricks is at her finest in the operatic numbers (*I loves you, Porgy* is particularly eloquent), and the warm beauty of the voice gives much pleasure throughout the programme.

The performances of the songs are lushly cultured, often indulgently slow (even the faster numbers lack something in vitality). The piano arrangements are elaborate; the playing is elegantly zestful, not out of style but giving the presentation a European veneer that in its way is very beguiling. The sound is first class.

OPERA AND MUSICALS *Let 'em Eat Cake; Of Thee I Sing* (musicals).
*** Sony Dig. M2K 42522 (2) [id.]. Jack Gilford, Larry Kert, Maureen McGovern, Paige O'Hara, David Garrison, NY Choral Artists, St Luke's O, Tilson Thomas.

Of Thee I Sing and *Let 'em Eat Cake* are the two operettas that George Gershwin wrote in the early 1930s on a political theme, the one a sequel to the other. Though the aim is satirical in both works, the musical tone of voice has the easy tunefulness of typical Gershwin shows, with only the occasional hint of Kurt Weill to suggest a more international source of inspiration. What the British listener will immediately register is the powerful underlying influence of Gilbert and Sullivan, not just in the plot – with Gilbertian situations exploited – but also in the music, with patter-songs and choral descants used in a very Sullivan-like manner.

In every way these two very well-filled discs are a delight, offering warm and energetic performances by excellent artists under Michael Tilson Thomas, not just a star conductor but a leading Gershwin scholar. Both Larry Kert and Maureen McGovern as his wife make a strong partnership, with Jack Gilford characterful as the Vice-Presidential candidate, Alexander Throttlebottom, and Paige O'Hara excellent as the interloping Diana in *Of Thee I Sing*. With the recording on the dry side and well forward – very apt for a musical – the words are crystal clear, not least from the splendidly disciplined chorus that, for much of the time, is protagonist. The well-produced booklets (one for each operetta) give full words – though, as with many CD sets, you need a magnifying glass to read them.

Porgy and Bess (complete).
❀ *** EMI Dig. CDS7 49568-2; *EX 749568-4* (3) [Ang. CDCC 49568]. Willard White, Cynthia Haymon, Harolyn Blackwell, Cynthia Clarey, Damon Evans, Glyndebourne Ch., LPO, Rattle.

EMI's gloriously rich and colourful recording of Gershwin's masterpiece directly reflects the spectacular success enjoyed by the Glyndebourne production. Simon Rattle here conducts the same cast and orchestra as in the opera house, and the EMI engineers have done wonders in re-creating what was so powerful at Glyndebourne, establishing more clearly than ever the status of *Porgy* as grand opera, not a mere jumped-up musical or operetta. The impact of the performance is consistently heightened by the subtleties of timing that come from long experience of live performances. By comparison, Lorin Maazel's Decca version (414 559-2) sounds a degree too literal, and John DeMain's RCA set (RD 82109 [RCD3 2109]), also associated with a live stage production and dating from the mid-1970s, is less subtle. More than their rivals, Rattle and the LPO capture Gershwin's rhythmic exuberance with the degree of freedom essential if jazz-based inspirations are to sound idiomatic. The chorus is the finest and most responsive of any on the three sets, and the bass line-up is the strongest. Willard White, not as youthful-sounding as for Maazel, but warmer and weightier, is superbly matched by the magnificent Jake of Bruce Hubbard, singing as characterfully as in the role of Joe in the EMI *Show Boat* set, and by the dark and resonant Crown of Gregg Baker. As Sportin' Life, Damon Evans gets nearer than any of his rivals to the original scat-song inspiration without ever short-changing on musical values, heightening them with extra expressive intensity and characterization. The women principals too are first rate, if no more striking than their opposite numbers on Decca and RCA: Cynthia Haymon as Bess movingly convincing in conveying equivocal emotions, Harolyn Blackwell as Clara sensuously relishing Rattle's slow speed for *Summertime*, and Cynthia Clarey an intense and characterful Serena. EMI's digital sound is exceptionally full and spacious. Voices are naturally balanced, not spotlit, so that words are not always as crystal clear as on Decca and RCA; but the atmosphere and sense of presence are the more winning.

Porgy and Bess: highlights.
*** EMI Dig. CDC7 54325-2 [id.]; *EL 754325-4* (from above recording, with White, Haymon; cond. Rattle).

Rattle's highlights disc is most generous (74 minutes) and most comprehensive, with the selection evenly divided between the three Acts and with nearly all the key numbers included. However, not all the tailoring is clean: *Summertime* ends rather abruptly and there is at least one fade.

Girl crazy (musical).
*** Elektra-Nonesuch/Warner Dig. 7559 79250-2; *7559 79250-4*. Judy Blazer, Lorna Luft, David Carroll, Eddie Korbich, O, John Mauceri.

Girl crazy, despite its hit numbers – *Embraceable you, I got rhythm* and *Bidin' my time* – has always been counted a failure; but this lively recording, with an ensemble of distinguished New York musicians conducted by John Mauceri, gives the lie to that. It is an escapist piece, typical of the early 1930s, about a New Yorker, exiled by his rich father to the Wild West, who sets up a dude ranch in an outpost previously bereft of women. The story of love and misunderstanding is largely irrelevant, but the score has point and imagination from beginning to end, all the brighter for having removed the sugar-coating which Hollywood introduced in the much-mangled film version of 1943. The casting is excellent. Judy Blazer takes the Ginger Rogers role of Kate, the post-girl, while Judy Garland's less well-known daughter, Lorna Luft, is delightful in the Ethel Merman part of the gambler's wife hired to sing in the saloon. David Carroll is the New Yorker hero, and Frank Gorshin takes the comic role of the cab-driver, Gieber Goldfarb. The whole score, 73 minutes long, is squeezed on to a single disc, packaged with libretto and excellent notes, the first of a projected Gershwin series. The only serious reservation is that the recording is dry and brassy, aggressively so – but that could be counted typical of the period too.

Strike up the Band (musical).
**(*) Nonesuch/Warner Dig. 7559 79273-2; *7559 79273-4* [id.]. Barrett, Luker, Chastain, Graae, Fowler, Goff, Lambert, Lyons, Sandish, Rocco, Ch. & O, Mauceri.

Dating originally from 1927, *Strike up the Band* was the nearest that George and Ira Gershwin ever came to imitating Gilbert and Sullivan. The very subject is Gilbertian – a satirical story about the United States going to war with Switzerland over the price of cheese. In addition Ira's ingenious lyrics sparked George to write with a rhythmic point that regularly suggests a syncopated Sullivan. Quite apart from the two undoubted hits from the show, *The man I love* and *Strike up the band*, there is a whole sequence of delightful numbers that it is good to have revived in this first really complete recording. Despite the ingenuity and musical imagination, in the end the piece fails to match Gershwin's later political satires, *Of thee I sing* and *Let 'em eat cake*, which, at least until the CBS/Sony recordings conducted by Michael Tilson Thomas, were even more seriously underappreciated. This Elektra Nonesuch recording brings a fresh, crisp performance, rather drily recorded with little bloom on the singing voices and with the spoken dialogue sounding too close. For all its vigour, the performance lacks something of the exuberance which marks the recordings of musicals conducted by John McGlinn for EMI. The scholarly preparation of the score from original and newly rediscovered sources is admirable, but the results in performance too often sound a little too literal rather than spontaneous. It may be correct to observe the dotted rhythms of *The man I love* as precisely as this performance does, but something is lost in the flow of the music, and to latterday ears the result is less haunting than the customary reading. The singers are first rate, but they would have been helped by having at least one of their number with a more charismatic personality. The second disc includes an appendix containing seven numbers used in the abortive 1930 revival.

Gesualdo, Carlo (c. 1561–1613)

Ave, dulcissima Maria; Ave, regina coelorum; Maria mater gratiae; Precibus et meritus beatae Mariae (motets). *Tenebrae responsories for Holy Saturday.*
*** Gimell Dig. CDGIM 015; *1585-T-15* [id.]. Tallis Scholars, Peter Phillips.

The astonishing dissonances and chromaticisms may not be as extreme here as in some of Gesualdo's secular music but, as elaborate as madrigals, they still have a sharp, refreshing impact on the modern ear which recognizes music leaping the centuries. The rule-breaking is akin to the uninhibited self-expression of today's composers, freed from academic rules; and similarly it communicates intensely when genuine emotion lies behind the inspiration. The Tallis Scholars give superb performances, finely finished and beautifully blended, with women's voices made to sound boyish, singing with freshness and bite to bring home the total originality of the writing with its awkward leaps and intervals. Beautifully recorded, this is another of the Tallis Scholars' ear-catching discs, powerful as well as polished.

Leçons de Ténèbres: Responsories for Maundy Thursday.
(B) *** HM HMA 190220 [id.]. Deller Cons., Deller.

The Responses for Holy Week of 1611 are as remarkable and passionately expressive as any of Gesualdo's madrigals, and in depth of feeling they should be compared only with the finest music of the age. The idiom is less overtly chromatic than in the madrigals, yet dissonance is used whenever it can heighten an expressive effect, and one has the same awareness of words that fires Gesualdo in the madrigals. The invention is often unpredictable and nearly always highly original. Now that his sacred music is beginning to attract more attention, it is clear that he poured great feeling into this medium. The Deller Consort bring to this music much the same approach that distinguishes their handling of the madrigal literature. The colouring of the words is a high priority, yet it never oversteps the bounds of good taste to become precious or over-expressive. The consort blends remarkably well and intonation is excellent; the transfer of the 1970 recording is wholly natural. This is temptingly inexpensive and we hope the companion disc will also soon be transferred to CD in the excellent Musique d'Abord series.

Madrigals, Book 5 for 5 voices (1611).
*** O-L Dig. 410 128-2 [id.]. Kirkby, Tubb, Nichols, Cornwell, King, Wistreich, Cons. of Musicke, Rooley.

Gesualdo's reputation as a madrigalist rests largely on the Fifth and Sixth Books, both for five voices and both dating from 1611. They were so successful that they were republished in score form, rather than as part books, only two years later; as David Butchart's note reminds us, contemporaries regarded them as 'outstanding for their artifice, range of harmony and chromaticism'. In performances with such perfect tonal blend and accurate intonation as these, the modulatory audacities and anguished suspensions of Gesualdo's music can register as they should. The record comprises 20 madrigals which are more varied in mood and expressive range than many realize. The documentation and presentation maintain the high standards of this label, and the sound-quality is admirably balanced and truthful. Of the Gesualdo recordings released in the last decade or so, this is easily the most distinguished.

Getty, Gordon (20th century)

The White election (song-cycle).
*** Delos Dig. D/CD 3057 [id.]. Kaaren Erickson, Armen Guzelimian.

The simple, even primitive, yet deeply allusive poetry of Emily Dickinson is sensitively matched in the music of Gordon Getty. Here he tackles a sequence of 32 songs, building them into an extended cycle in four linked parts, lasting in all an hour and a quarter. His style, direct and spare, easy and fluent, has links with the Britten of *Winter words* on the one hand and with the minimalists on the other, but with no hint of mindless repetition. Everything is aimed, in as simple a way as possible, at bringing out the meaning of the poems, which have been selected (as Getty puts it) 'to tell Emily's story in her own words'. He adds that 'The most salient features of Emily's life were taken to be the white election, with its theme of union in death, and her unsuspected poetic genius.' The poet's obsession with the colour white and its many-sided symbolism here prompts the composer to heighten the emotional overtones of a life at once unfulfilled in marriage but secretly fulfilled in her verse. If at times the tinkly tunes seem to be an inadequate response to profound emotions, the total honesty of the writing disarms criticism, particularly in a performance as dedicated and sensitive as this, with Kaaren Erickson a highly expressive artist with a naturally beautiful voice. The pianist too is very responsive.

Gibbons, Christopher (1615–1676)

Cupid and Death (with Matthew Locke).
(M) *** HM/BMG GD 77117 (2). Kirkby, Tubb, King, Wistreich, Thomas, Holden, Cass, Nichols, Cornwell, King, Consort of Musicke, Rooley – BLOW: *Venus and Adonis.* ***

Cupid and Death, 'a masque in four entries', dates from 1653, or nearly 30 years before the better-known Blow work with which it is coupled. Gibbons, the son of Orlando Gibbons and the teacher of Blow, seems to have been the lesser partner in the project, with Matthew Locke providing the bulk of the music for this rustic fantasy on an ancient fable. Each of the five 'entries' or Acts is formally laid out in a set sequence of items – a suite of dances, a dialogue, a song and a chorus – and Rooley's team consistently brings out the fresh charm of the music. For repeated listening, the spoken sections, up to ten minutes long, can easily be programmed out on CD. A welcome reissue at mid-price.

Gibbons, Orlando (1583–1625)

Anthems & Verse anthems: *Almighty and Everlasting God; Hosanna to the Son of David; Lift up your heads; O Thou the central orb; See, see the word is incarnate; This is the record of John. Canticles: Short service: Magnificat and Nunc dimittis. 2nd Service; Magnificat and Nunc dimittis. Hymnes & Songs of the church: Come kiss with me those lips of thine; Now shall the praises of the Lord be sung; A song of joy unto the Lord. Organ fantasia: Fantasia for double organ; Voluntary.*
*** ASV Gaudeamus CDGAU 123; *ZCGAU 123* [id.]. King's College Ch., L. Early Music Group, Ledger; John Butt.

This invaluable anthology was the first serious survey of Gibbons's music to appear on CD. The disc has now reverted to the Gaudeamus label. It contains many of his greatest pieces and accommodates seventeen items in all, including superlative accounts of such masterpieces of the English repertoire as *This is the record of John* and *Almighty and Everlasting God.* Not only are the performances touched with distinction, the recording too is in the highest flight and the analogue sound has been transferred to CD with complete naturalness. Strongly recommended.

(i) Anthems: *Almighty and everlasting God; Hosanna to the Son of David; O clap your hands together – God is gone up; O Lord, increase my faith; O Lord, in thy wrath rebuke me not;* (ii) *Introit: First Song of Moses; Second setting of Preces and Proper Psalm 145 for Whit Sunday; Second Service: Voluntary I & Te Deum; Voluntary II & Jubilate. Short Service: Voluntary I & Magnificat; Voluntary II & Nunc dimittis.* Verse anthems for voices and viols: *Glorious and powerful God; See, see, the word is incarnate; This is the record of John.*
(M) **(*) Decca mono/stereo 433 677-2. King's College, Cambridge, Ch., (i) with Boris Ord; Hugh McLean (organ); (ii) with Jacobean Consort of Viols, Willcocks; Simon Preston (organ).

Orlando Gibbons joined King's College Choir at the age of twelve, and wrote some of his earliest music during his stay, before he moved to London as organist of the Chapel Royal in 1605. The present record occupies a much later position in the history of the choir, but is valuable in providing a link with its distinguished Elizabethan chorister and composer, and at the same time representing two later generations of King's music-making. Of the two groups of recordings, the first (mono) was made under Boris Ord is 1955; the second (stereo) came three years later directed by David Willcocks, but with Thurston Dart lending his influence and leading the consort of viols in the verse anthems (alongside Desmond Dupré).

The mono recordings have plenty of ambience to disguise their lack of antiphony; although the Argo engineers found it more difficult to control the famous chapel resonance, the sound is pleasing, if not so cleanly focused as the later venture. Even here the attempt to simulate antiphonal alternation in the *Psalm* is less sophisticated than in later Argo records. But generally the effect is remarkably real, although the consort of viols is not always very well balanced. Juxtaposing the contents of two separate LPs means that there is plenty of variety and the later stereo collection is imaginatively chosen. There is nothing routine about any of these settings: Gibbons is a major musical personality and it was a happy idea in each case to preface the canticles from the two *Services* with an organ voluntary; it was customary in the early seventeenth century to have such a voluntary before the reading of the first Lesson.

Gilbert, Henry (1868–1928)

Suite for chamber orchestra.
*** Albany Dig. TROY 033-2 [id.]. V. American Music Ens., Hobart Earle – CHADWICK: *Serenade for strings.* ***

Henry Gilbert was born in Somerville, Massachusetts, and studied under MacDowell at the New England Conservatory. He belonged to a time when almost all musical influences came from Europe and the American public did not value the output of its indigenous composers. This recorded live performance represents the European première of the *Suite*, which harmonically is innocuous but which has an agreeable nostalgic languor, while its central movement, Spiritual, makes an early attempt to incorporate local idiomatic influences, without direct quotation. The flavour has something in common with Delius's *Florida suite*, although Gilbert's invention is less indelible. An excellent performance here from members of the Vienna Symphony Orchestra, who are completely at home in the music, as well they might be. The recording is excellent.

Ginastera, Alberto (1865–1936)

(i) *Harp concerto, Op. 25;* (ii) *Piano concerto No. 1; Estancia* (ballet suite), *Op. 89.*
*** ASV Dig. CDDCA 654; *ZCDCA 654* [id.]. (i) Nancy Allen; (ii) Oscar Tarrago; Mexico City PO, Bátiz.

The *Harp concerto* is a highly inventive and rewarding work whose brilliant colours are brought fully to life here by Nancy Allen and the Mexican orchestra. Estancia is a comparably vivid piece of Coplandesque macho, its character also very successfully realized. The *First Piano concerto* is mildly serial but far from unattractive – and very brilliantly (and sensitively) played by Oscar Tarrago. An excellent introduction to this composer, and excellently recorded – perhaps a bit over-bright and up-front, but well balanced all the same – and with plenty of range. Strongly recommended.

12 American preludes, Op. 12; Danzas argentinas, Op. 2; Rondó sobre temas infantiles Argentinos, Op. 19; Sonata; Suite de danzas Criollas, Op. 15.
*** Globe GLO 5006 [id.]. Barbara Nissman.

Barbara Nissman packs a punch and has abundant technical resources, all of which are needed in this high-spirited repertoire. At one time the Ginastera *Sonata* was played by every promising competition pupil, but has recently weakened its hold on the repertoire. Indeed his piano music maintains a relatively low profile in the current CD catalogues The present disc dates from 1981 but has been digitally remastered to good effect, though it is short on playing time.

Giordano, Umberto (1867–1948)

Andrea Chénier (complete).
(M) *** BMG/RCA GD 82046 (2) [RCD-2-2046]. Domingo, Scotto, Milnes, Alldis Ch., Nat. PO, Levine.
**(*) Decca Dig. 410 117-2 (2) [id.]. Pavarotti, Caballé, Nucci, Kuhlmann, Welsh Nat. Op. Ch., Nat. PO, Chailly.

Giordano always runs the risk – not least in this opera with its obvious parallels with *Tosca* – of being considered only in the shadow of Puccini, but this red-blooded score can, as here, be searingly effective with its defiant poet hero – a splendid role for Domingo at his most heroic – and the former servant, later revolutionary leader, Gérard, a character who genuinely develops from Act to Act, a point well appreciated by Milnes. Scotto gives one of her most eloquent and beautiful performances, and Levine has rarely displayed his powers as an urgent and dramatic opera conductor more potently on record, with the bright recording intensifying the dramatic thrust of playing and singing.

Pavarotti may motor through the role of the poet-hero, singing with his usual fine diction but in a conventional barnstorming way; nevertheless, the red-blooded melodrama of the piece comes over powerfully, thanks to Chailly's sympathetic conducting, incisive but never exaggerated. Caballé, like Pavarotti, is not strong on characterization but produces beautiful sounds, while Leo Nucci makes a superbly dark-toned Gérard. A number of veterans have also been brought in to do party turns; Hugues Cuénod as Fléville delightfully apt, Piero de Palma as the informer, Christa Ludwig superb as Madelon, and Astrid Varnay well over the top caricaturing the Contessa di Coigny. Though this cannot replace the Levine set with Domingo, Scotto and Milnes, it is a colourful substitute with its demonstration sound.

Fedora (complete).
(M) **(*) Decca 433 033-2 (2) [id.]. Olivero, Del Monaco, Gobbi, Monte Carlo Nat. Op. Ch. & O, Gardelli – ZANDONAI: *Francesca da Rimini.* **(*)

With Giordano it is significant that this opera, like his most famous one, *Andrea Chénier*, dates from the earliest part of his career. He went on to marry the rich daughter of a hotelier, and prosperity was no doubt the bogey of invention. *Fedora* will always be remembered for one brief aria, the hero's *Amor ti vieta*; but, as this highly enjoyable recording confirms, there is much that is memorable in the score, even if nothing else quite approaches it. The piece is adapted from a Sardou melodrama designed for Sarah Bernhardt (parallel with *Tosca*), with an absurd plot involving a passionate volte-face when the heroine's hatred for the hero (her wicked brother's murderer) suddenly turns to love. Meaty stuff, which brings some splendid singing from Magda Olivero and (more intermittently) from Del Monaco, with Gobbi in a light comedy part. Fine, vintage (1969), atmospheric recording. Well worth trying by anyone with a hankering after verismo, especially given its rare Zandonai coupling, added for the CD reissue.

Giuliani, Mauro (1781–1828)

Duo concertante for violin & guitar, Op. 25; Gran duetto concertante for flute & guitar, Op. 52; Serenade for violin, cello & guitar in A, Op. 19.
**(*) BMG/RCA 09026 60237-2 [60237-2]. Swensen, Galway, Anderson, Yamashita.

Giuliani is an elegant purveyor of ingenuous, pleasing phrases, and these three works show him at his most gallantly generous. The *Gran duetto concertante* for flute and guitar has a simple charm and a catchy *Rondo militaire* finale. The closing *Rondeau* of the *Duo concertante* for violin and guitar is nearly as winning, and the work has an agreeable set of *grazioso* variations as its second movement (in terms of length it is quite ambitious – four movements and 33 minutes of musical amiability). The *Serenade* (like the duo) is half that length, but gains from its succinct layout, and it too, has an infectious finale, an *Alla polacca.* These four artists do the composer proud, playing with warmth and elegance – Joseph Swensen's timbre in the *Duo concertante* is sumptuous (almost too lush), and only in the *Serenade* is the penchant of American engineering – the recordings were made in New York City – for close balancing disturbing, when the violin catches the microphone in the galloping scherzo. No one will mind James Galway being forwardly placed, but the splendid guitarist, Kazuhito Yamashita might reasonably complain – especially as he plays so intimately – that he is always consigned to the background. Even so this concert is easy to enjoy.

Sonata for violin and guitar.
*** Sony MK 34508 [id.]. Itzhak Perlman, John Williams – PAGANINI: *Cantabile* etc.***

Giuliani's *Sonata* is amiable enough but hardly substantial fare; but it is played with such artistry here that it appears better music than it is. The recording is in need of more ambience, but sound is invariably a matter of taste, and there is no reason to withhold a strong recommendation. The CD transfer is admirably managed.

Glass, Philip (born 1937)

Dance Pieces: Glasspieces; In the Upper Room: Dances Nos. 1, 2, 5, 8 & 9.
*** CBS Dig. MK 39539 [id.]. Ens., dir. Michael Riesman.

These two ballet scores bring typical and easily attractive examples of Glass's minimalist technique. *Glasspieces* was choreographed by Jerome Robbins for the New York City Ballet. The scoring features woodwind, piano and strings, often heard in separate groups, plus voices, synthesizer and rhythm. Heard away from the stage, the music seems to have a subliminally hypnotic effect, even though rhythmic patterns often repeat themselves almost endlessly.

OPERA

Akhnaten (complete).
*** CBS M2K 42457 (2) [id.]. Esswood, Vargas, Liebermann, Hannula, Holzapfel, Hauptmann, Stuttgart State Op. Ch., Russell Davies.

Akhnaten, Glass's powerful third opera, is set in the time of Ancient Egypt. Among the soloists, Paul Esswood in the title-role is reserved, strong and statuesque; perhaps a more red-blooded approach would have been out of character – this is an opera of historical ghosts, and its life-flow lies in the hypnotic background provided by the orchestra; indeed the work's haunting closing scene with its wordless melismas is like nothing else in music. It offers a theatrical experience appealing to a far wider public than usual in the opera house, as the English National Opera production readily demonstrated; and here the Stuttgart chorus and orchestra give the piece impressively committed advocacy.

Einstein on the beach (complete).
(***) Sony Dig. M4K 38875 (4) [id.]. Childs, Johnson, Mann, Sutton, Ch., Zukovsky (violin), Philip Glass Ens., Riesman.

As the surreal title implies, *Einstein on the beach* is more dream than drama. In this, his first opera, Glass translated his use of slowly shifting ostinatos on to a near-epic scale. The opera takes significant incidents in Einstein's life as the basis for the seven scenes in three Acts, framed by five 'Knee Plays'. Einstein's life is then linked with related visual images in a dream-like way, reflecting the second half of the title, *On the Beach*, a reference to Nevil Shute's novel with its theme of nuclear apocalypse. Other works of Glass are more communicative than this on record. Dedicated performances and first-rate recording. The booklet gives copious illustrations of the stage production.

Satyagraha (complete).
*** Sony Dig. M3K 39672 (3) [id.]. Perry, NY City Op. Ch. and O, Keene.

The subject here is the early life of Mahatma Gandhi, pinpointing various incidents; and the text is a selection of verses from the *Bhagavadgita*, sung in the original Sanskrit and used as another strand in the complex repetitive web of sound. The result is undeniably powerful. With overtones of Indian Raga at the very start, Glass builds long crescendos with a relentlessness that may anaesthetize the mind but which have a purposeful aesthetic aim. Where much minimalist music in its shimmering repetitiveness becomes static, a good deal of this conveys energy as well as power. The writing for chorus is often physically thrilling, and individual characters emerge in only a shadowy way. The recording, using the device of overdubbing, is spectacular.

Glazunov, Alexander (1865–1936)

Chant du ménestrel (for cello and orchestra), Op. 71.
(M) *** DG 431 475-2; *431 475-4*. Rostropovich, Boston SO, Ozawa – SHOSTAKOVICH: *Cello concerto No. 2;* TCHAIKOVSKY: *Andante cantabile.* ***
*** Chan. Dig. CHAN 8579; *ABTD 1273* [id.]. Wallfisch, LPO, Bryden Thomson – KABALEVSKY; KHACHATURIAN: *Cello concertos.* ***

Glazunov's *Chant du ménestrel* ('Song of the troubadour'), which dates from 1900, shows the nostalgic appeal of 'things long ago and far away'. It is a short but appealing piece and a welcome makeweight on either of these excellently played and recorded CDs.

Violin concerto in A min., Op. 82.
❀ (M) (***) EMI mono CDH7 64030-2 [id.]. Heifetz, LPO, Barbirolli – SIBELIUS: *Violin concerto* (**); TCHAIKOVSKY: *Violin concerto.* (***)
*** BMG/RCA RD 87019 [RCD1-7019]. Heifetz, RCA SO, Hendl – PROKOFIEV: *Concerto No. 2;* SIBELIUS: *Violin concerto.* ***
(B) *** Pickwick Dig. PCD 966; *CIMPC 966* [id.]. Udagawa, LPO, Klein – Concert ***.
*** EMI Dig. CDC7 49814-2 [id.]. Perlman, Israel PO, Mehta – SHOSTAKOVICH: *Violin concerto No. 1.* ***

Heifetz's recording of the Glazunov *Violin concerto* was made in 1934 when the composer was still alive. It has greater expressive breadth and spaciousness than his later record with Walter Hendl and the Chicago orchestra. Here phrases breathe even more naturally and there is great warmth. The recording sounds somewhat opaque and the opening of the cadenza (track 9) finds the soloist suddenly a bit too close. Intonation is incredibly sure and the tone sweet. Surfaces are mostly silent in the CD transfer, though there are two passages where one is aware of background noise. Milstein recorded a superb account in the 1950s but, generally speaking, this first Heifetz version of the concerto has never been surpassed. For those who want more modern, stereo sound, Heifetz is again incomparable; his account is the strongest and most passionate (as well as the most perfectly played) in the catalogue. In his hands the *Concerto*'s sweetness is tempered with strength. It is altogether a captivating performance that completely absolves the work from any charge of synthetic sweetness. The RCA orchestra under Hendl gives splendid support, and, although the 1963 recording is not beyond reproach, the disc with its Sibelius and Prokofiev couplings is another essential part of any representative collection.

The Glazunov also receives a heartfelt performance from Udagawa which is just as compelling as the virtuoso stereo accounts from such master violinists as Heifetz and Perlman. In the finale she may not offer quite such bravura fireworks as they do but, with more open sound, the result is very persuasive in its lilting way. The violin is balanced close but not so close as with Perlman or Heifetz, and there is far more space round the orchestral sound, which is full and warm to match the soloist.

The command and panache of Perlman are irresistible in this showpiece concerto, and the whole performance, recorded live, erupts into a glorious account of the galloping final section, in playing to match that even of the supreme master in this work, Heifetz. The acoustic of the Mann Auditorium in Tel Aviv is not an easy one for the engineers and tuttis are rather rough, but this is more atmospheric than most from that source. It makes an unexpected but rewarding coupling for the more substantial Shostakovich *First Concerto*.

(i) *Violin concerto. The Seasons* (ballet), *Op. 67*.
*** Chan. Dig. CHAN 8596 [id.]. (i) Oscar Shumsky; SNO, Järvi.

Neeme Järvi obtains good results from the Scottish National Orchestra in *The Seasons*, though tempi tend to be brisk. The Chandos acoustic is reverberant and the balance recessed. In the *Violin concerto*, Oscar Shumsky is perhaps wanting the purity and effortless virtuosity of Heifetz, but the disc as a whole still carries a three-star recommendation.

From the Middle Ages, Op. 79; Scènes de ballet, Op. 52.
*** Chan. Dig. CHAN 8804; *ABTD 1432* [id.]. SNO, Järvi (with LIADOV: *A musical snuffbox* ***).

Järvi makes out an excellent case for these charming – though at times rather thickly scored – Glazunov suites. He has the advantage of an excellently balanced and wide-ranging recording and gets good playing from the SNO. Although this music is obviously inferior to Tchaikovksy, Järvi has the knack of making you think it is better than it is. The disc also includes a fine account of Liadov's delightful *A musical snuffbox*.

Raymonda (ballet), *Op. 57:* extended excerpts from Acts I & II.
*** Chan. Dig. CHAN 8447; *ABTD 1159* [id.]. SNO, Järvi.

Järvi chooses some 56 minutes of music from the first two Acts, omitting entirely the Slavic/Hungarian Wedding *Divertissement* of the closing Act, and this contributes to the slight feeling of lassitude. But with rich Chandos recording this is a record for any balletomane to wallow in, even if a Russian performance would undoubtedly have more extrovert fire. There are 24 dividing bands, and it is a pity that they are not directly related to the fairly detailed synopsis.

(i) *Les ruses d'amour* (ballet), *Op. 61;* (ii) *The Sea* (fantasy), *Op. 28;* (iii) *March on a Russian theme*.
**(*) Olympia OCD 141 [id.]. (i) USSR RSO, Ziuraitis; (ii) Provatorov; (iii) USSR Ministry of Defence O, Maltsiev.

There are some 55 minutes of ballet music here, not unlike *Raymonda* though not perhaps quite as fine as *The Seasons*. *The Sea*, though not really memorable, has undoubtedly effective pictorial content and is not too long for its material; the *March* is ingenuous. All are very well played, especially the main work which reveals Algis Ziuraitis as a deft exponent of his compatriot's music. The analogue recording is one of Olympia's better CD transfers, with plenty of body, along with its Russian brightness and colour.

The Sea (fantasy), *Op. 28; Spring, Op. 34*.
*** Chan. Dig. CHAN 8611; *ABTD 1299* [id.]. SNO, Järvi – KALINNIKOV: *Symphony No. 1*. ***

The tone-poem, *Spring*, was written two years after *The Sea* and is infinitely more imaginative; in fact, it is as fresh and delightful as its companion is cliché-ridden. At one point Glazunov even looks forward to *The Seasons*. Persuasive and well-recorded performances from the Scottish National Orchestra under Neeme Järvi. The spacious and vivid recording sounds well.

The Seasons (ballet) *Op. 67.*
*** Decca Dig. 433 000-2 (2) [id.]. RPO, Ashkenazy – TCHAIKOVSKY: *Nutcracker.* ***
(BB) **(*) Naxos Dig. 8.550079; *4550079* [id.]. Czech RSO (Bratislava), Ondrej Lenárd – TCHAIKOVSKY: *Sleeping Beauty suite.* **

The Seasons and Tchaikovsky's *Nutcracker* make a perfect coupling. Both scenarios occupy a fantasy world where frost and snowflakes are glitteringly magical rather than freezing. Ashkenazy's account of Glazunov's delightful ballet is the finest it has ever received. The RPO playing is dainty and elegant, refined and sumptuous. Ashkenazy obviously revels in delicacy and colour of the scoring of the earlier sequences, yet the RPO strings respond vigorously to the thrusting vitality of the Autumnal *Bacchanale.* The Decca engineers, working in Watford Town Hall, provide digital sound of great allure and warmth, very much in the demonstration bracket.

Ondrej Lenárd gives a pleasing account of Glazunov's delightful score, finding plenty of delicacy for the vignettes of Winter: *Frost*, *Ice* and *Snow*, and an appropriate warmth for the *Waltz of the cornflowers and poppies* of *Summer*. The entry of Glazunov's most famous tune at the opening of the *Autumn Bacchanale* is very virile indeed, helped by a slight rise in the recording level. The sound is first class, transparently atmospheric yet with plenty of fullness and weight at climaxes. The ear has an impression of a fairly modest string section, but the sounds they make are pleasing and graceful.

Stenka Razin (symphonic poem), *Op. 13.*
*** Chan. Dig. CHAN 8479; *ABTD 1199* [id.]. SNO, Järvi – RIMSKY-KORSAKOV: *Scheherazade.* ***

Stenka Razin has its moments of vulgarity – how otherwise with the *Song of the Volga Boatmen* a recurrent theme? – but it makes a generous and colourful makeweight for Järvi's fine version of *Scheherazade.* The recording is splendid.

Symphonies Nos. 1 in E, Op. 5; 5 in B flat, Op. 55.
**(*) Orfeo Dig. C 093101A [id.]. Bav. RSO, Järvi.

Symphonies Nos. 1 in E, Op. 5; 7 in F, Op. 77.
*** Olympia Dig. OCD 100 [id.]. USSR MoC SO, Rozhdestvensky.

Glazunov composed his prodigious First Symphony in the early 1880s (it is not only remarkably accomplished but delightfully fresh) and the last in 1906 when he had just turned forty. Rozhdestvensky's persuasive advocacy enhances the appeal of all this music. Under his direction the *First Symphony* sounds even more mature, and its slow movement is eloquently shaped, as is that of the '*Pastoral*' *Seventh.* Throughout, the woodwind playing has an agreeable lyrical lightness. The scherzos, always Glazunov's best movements, are a delight, helped by the sparkling ensemble of this fine Soviet orchestra. The digital recording is very bright but full and vividly detailed, not quite as sophisticated as a Western recording yet not coarsening the sound-picture.

The playing of the Bavarian Radio Symphony Orchestra under Neeme Järvi is highly sympathetic and polished. The music is made to sound cogent and civilized, if perhaps a little bland at times. The Orfeo recording is more naturally balanced and ample in texture but, like the performances, lacks something in glitter, although the scherzos remain highly effective. Overall the Russian performances project more vitality, although in their way Järvi's versions are certainly enjoyable.

Symphony No. 2 in F sharp min., Op. 16; Concert waltz No. 1, Op. 47.
**(*) Orfeo Dig. C 148101A [id.]. Bamberg SO, Järvi.

(i) *Symphony No. 2 in F sharp min., Op. 16; Romantic intermezzo, Op. 69; Stenka Razin, Op. 13.*
**(*) Olympia Dig. OCD 119 [id.]. (i) USSR MoC SO, Rozhdestvensky; USSR RSO, Dimitriedi.

The melodic material of the *Second Symphony* has an unmistakably Slavic feeling and, in Rozhdestvensky's hands, is played with enormous eloquence, with glowingly colourful woodwind solos from this splendid orchestra. The snag is the recording which, although it has a most attractive basic ambience, produces problems at fortissimo levels, where the brass bray fiercely and the violins above the stave lose a good deal of body and tend to shrillness. Both the *Romantic intermezzo*, which also generates considerable fervour, and *Stenka Razin*, which is very exciting indeed, especially in its vulgarly thrilling closing section, are analogue recordings and have considerably more body at climaxes.

Järvi's Orfeo sound is altogether more comfortable, and the music-making is more comfortable too. However, within its boundaries, which are more inhibited than Rozhdestvensky's, this is a very good performance: the playing is eloquent; the scherzo is beautifully cultivated and undoubtedly fresh, although the finale sounds relatively lame without the added histrionics. The recording is full-bodied and naturally balanced, but could do with just a bit more brilliance. The *Concert waltz* makes an attractive encore.

Symphony No. 3 in D, Op. 33.
*** ASV CDDCA 581; *ZCDCA 581* [id.]. LSO, Yondani Butt.

Symphony No. 3; Concert waltz No. 2 in F, Op. 51.
*** Orfeo Dig. C 157101A [id.]. Bamberg SO, Järvi.

Symphony No. 3 in D, Op. 33; Poème lyrique, Op. 12; Solemn procession.
**(*) Olympia Dig. OCD 120 [id.]. USSR MoC SO, Rozhdestvensky.

In Järvi's hands the engaging opening of Glazunov's *Third Symphony*, with its lyrical string melody soaring over throbbing wind chords, is richer and more cultivated than Rozhdestvensky's version, where the entry of the Russian brass coarsens the effect. In the lovely *Andante*, there is some fine woodwind playing and the Bamberg violins are warmly expansive when they are given the melody; the scherzo too is delectably played. The finale has plenty of energy and almost doesn't seem too long, when the momentum is so well sustained. The *Concert waltz* too has a charming elegance.

Butt starts with the disadvantage of having no coupling. But the ASV recording is brighter and more open than the Orfeo, and this gives an added freshness to the textures of the slow movement. The response of the LSO catches both its colour and its gentle melancholy; the scherzo too has an extra sparkle here. Butt's reading lies somewhere between those of Järvi and Rozhdestvensky.

In Rozhdestvensky's performance the very opening has a Mendelssohnian lightness of touch, but when the brazen Russian trombones enter, they take the music into a distinctly Slavic world and the Russian-ness of the lyricism soon asserts itself. Otherwise, the playing of the USSR Ministry of Culture Symphony Orchestra is well up to the excellent standard of this series (particularly in the scherzo of the *Symphony*), with notably fine woodwind solos. Rozhdestvensky is especially good in the *Solemn procession*, which is more optimistic than the title suggests, though again the rather papery sound of the violins above the stave and the edgy brass of the recording are a drawback.

Symphonies Nos. 4 in E flat, Op. 48; 5 in B flat, Op. 55.
*** Olympia Dig. OCD 101 [id.]. USSR MoC SO, Rozhdestvensky.

Symphonies Nos. 4 in E flat, Op. 48; 7 in F, Op. 77.
**(*) Orfeo C 148201A [id.]. Bamberg SO, Järvi.

Glazunov's *Fourth* is a charming and well-composed symphony, full of good things and distinctly Russian in outlook, and held together structurally by a theme which Glazunov uses in all three movements. The *Fifth* is much better known and has a particularly fine slow movement. The string playing confirms the Ministry of Culture Symphony as currently the finest Soviet orchestra. The recording is extremely vivid, among the best in this fine series of recordings which undoubtedly give the strongest advocacy to Glazunov's music.

The *Seventh* with its engaging woodwind writing, notably for the oboe in the first movement, has much to attract the listener. The *Andante* is undoubtedly eloquent in Järvi's performance and the scherzo, marked giocoso, is well up to form. The finale has plenty of bustle, even if here it sounds rather long. The sound, as in the rest of Järvi's series, is full and naturally balanced, lacking something in spectacle.

Symphony No. 6 in C min., Op. 58; Poème lyrique, Op. 12.
*** Orfeo Dig. C 157201 [id.]. Bamberg SO, Neeme Järvi.

Symphony No. 6 in C min., Op. 58; Scènes de ballet, Op. 52.
**(*) Olympia Dig. OCD 104 [id.]. USSR MoC SO or RSO, Rozhdestvensky.

Symphony No. 6 in C min., Op. 58; Serenades Nos. 1, Op. 7; 2, Op. 11; Triumphal march, Op. 40.
*** ASV Dig. CDDCA 699; *ZCDCA 699* [id.]. LSO or RPO, Yondani Butt.

Taken overall, Yondani Butt's is the preferred choice for Glazunov's *Sixth*, although of course couplings do come into the matter. But Butt's performance is marginally fresher than Järvi's, helped by the more open sound of the ASV recording, and the fine wind and brass contributions from the LSO; the brass chorale at the end of the Variations is effectively sonorous. There is some lovely string playing too, and Butt finds an attractive elegance in the *Intermezzo*. The finale generates unflagging energy and even a certain dignity. The two waltz-like *Serenades* have a lilting graciousness and the *March*, an American commission, builds a suitably grandiloquent climax on the song, *John Brown's body*.

Järvi makes more than usual of the first movement of the *Sixth*, building an impressive climax. The *Theme and variations* benefits greatly from the polished playing of the Bambergers, who find plenty of colour both here and in the *Intermezzo*, a slight but agreeable replacement for Glazunov's usual scherzo. The finale produces energy and vigour without too much bombast, for the Bamberg brass is sonorous without being blatant, as happens in Rozhdestvensky's alternative Russian performance. The *Poème lyrique* is full of romantic atmosphere and is beautifully played; the full yet vivid recording, which is admirably detailed but which still possesses rich string textures, seems just right for the music.

Rozhdestvensky directs the work with the kind of thrust and conviction to make the very most of it, and is suitably affectionate in the variations. Here, however, the brass chorale is a bit fierce as recorded, and the upper string sound could ideally be more glamorous. The *Scènes de ballet* is analogue: the recording is still very bright but has slightly more depth. It is characteristic of the composer's favourite genre, assured and often tuneful.

(i) *Symphony No. 8 in E flat, Op. 83; Ballade, Op. 78; Slavonic festival, Op. 26.*
*** Olympia Dig. OCD 130 [id.]. (i) USSR MoC SO, Rozhdestvensky; USSR RSO, Dimitriedi.

Symphony No. 8 in E flat, Op. 83; Overture solennelle, Op. 73; Wedding procession, Op. 21.
**(*) Orfeo C 093201A [id.]. Bav. RSO, Järvi.

Rozhdestvensky provides the most powerful advocacy, particularly in the fine first movement and the expansively eloquent *Mesto*. The scherzo is less charming, more purposive than is usual in a Glazunov symphony; it is splendidly played, and in the finale the brass chorale is without the blatancy one tends to expect from a Russian performance. Indeed this is one of Glazunov's most convincing finales, with an attractive lyrical strain. The two bonuses are well worth having. The *Ballade* contrasts expressively intense writing for the strings with a brass interlude, where again the Russian playing is colourful rather than edgy. The *Slavonic festival* is a most engaging piece, a kaleidoscope of vigorous dance-themes and sparkling orchestration. The recording throughout is more agreeable than many in Rozhdestvensky's cycle, not lacking vividness but fuller and better balanced.

As in the rest of his series, Järvi and the Bavarian players give the piece a cultivated, polished performance of the *Eighth*, not lacking commitment and vigour, and certainly with plenty of colour in the scherzo, but bringing to the music a Schumannesque quality at times. Nevertheless the performance is thoroughly musical and undoubtedly enjoyable, with spaciousness to some extent compensating for passion, when the sound is full and pleasing.

String quartet No. 1 in D, Op. 1.
*** Olympia OCD 157 [id.]. Shostakovich Qt – TCHAIKOVSKY: *Trio.* **(*)

Glazunov's *First Quartet* is extraordinarily assured and inventive. It dates from the year after the *First Symphony*, when its composer was eighteen. With a genuinely eloquent *Andante* – beautifully played here – and an accomplished scherzo, the piece ends appealingly with a moderately paced and tuneful finale. The performance is superb: the immaculate ensemble of the Shostakovich Quartet is matched by their warmth and body of tone. One could not imagine a better account. The recording, made in 1974, is well balanced and immediate.

String quartets Nos. 2 in F, Op. 10; 4 in A min., Op. 64.
*** Olympia OCD 173 [id.]. Shostakovich Qt.

The *Second Quartet* is clearly indebted to Borodin; its scherzo has lots of charm and its slow movement is really quite beautiful. The *Fourth* is far less obviously nationalistic and, though it cannot wholly escape the blandness of contour that often distinguishes this composer, there are undoubted rewards. The Shostakovich Quartet have obvious feeling for this music and play with real conviction; their 1974 recording is very good indeed.

Piano sonatas Nos. 1 in B flat min., Op. 74; 2 in E min., Op. 75; Grand concert waltz in E flat, Op. 41.
**(*) Pearl SHECD 9538 [id.]. Leslie Howard.

The Glazunov *Sonatas* are well worth investigating, particularly in performances as committed and as well recorded as these. Howard does not always make the most of the poetry here and is not always consistent in observing dynamic nuances, but there is more to praise than to criticize. Admirers of Glazunov's art should investigate this issue which sounds extremely impressive in its CD format. The analogue recording is most realistically transferred.

Glière, Reinhold (1875–1956)

(i) *Concerto for coloratura soprano, Op. 82;* (ii) *Harp concerto, Op. 74.*
(M) *** Decca 430 006-2. (i) Sutherland; (ii) Ellis, LSO, Bonynge – with Recital. **(*)

Glière's brilliant *Coloratura concerto* inspires Joan Sutherland to some dreamily beautiful singing. The *Harp concerto* is as easy, unpretentious and tuneful as the vocal concerto, with Osian Ellis performing brilliantly. Excellent 1968 Kingsway Hall recording. For the rest of the collection, see under 'Sutherland' in the Vocal Recitals.

Symphony No. 2 in C min, Op. 25; Zaporozhy Cossacks, Op. 64.
**(*) Chan. Dig. CHAN 9071 [id.]. BBC PO, Downes.

Not even the advocacy of Sir Edward Downes with his magnificent Manchester orchestra can conceal the banality of some of the writing in this early Glière symphony. The first movement often sounds like music for a silent film of a Wild West chase, and though the later movements are less flat-footed – with echoes of Tchaikovsky's *Manfred* in the scherzo, a glorious cor anglais theme at the start of the slow movement, and echoes of Rimsky-Korsakov in the finale – it cannot compare with Glière's later and grander *Symphony No. 3. Zaporozhy Cossacks*, written in the mid-1920s during the Soviet period in Russia, is less ambitious but also contains banalities in illustrating a seventeenth-century story of Cossacks and the Turkish sultan. Excellent performances and outstanding recording.

Symphony No. 3 in B min. (Ilya Murometz), Op. 42.
*** Chan. Dig. CHAN 9041 [id.]. BBC PO, Sir Edward Downes.
** Marco Polo Dig. 8.223358 [id.]. Slovak RSO (Bratislava), Donald Johanas.

Downes and the BBC Philharmonic in magnificent form give an urgently passionate performance of this colourful programme piece, more convincing than any rival in what can easily seem too cumbersome a work. Based on Russian legend, its four large-scale movements can easily fall apart, as they tend to on the rival versions, not so much in the rougher Marco Polo performance as in the earlier and even more expansive Farberman recording on Unicorn Kanchana. Here speeds are so slow that the piece stretches to two discs, and this is now outclassed (UKCD 2014/15). Downes, far tauter and more intense, relates the writing very much to the world of Glière's close contemporary, Rachmaninov, with the brilliant third movement, *At the Court of Vladimir the Mighty Sun*, bringing reminders of Rachmaninov's cantata, *The Bells*. The recording, made in the concert hall of New Broadcasting House, Manchester, is one of Chandos's finest, combining clarity and sumptuousness.

Glinka, Mikhail (1805–57)

Russlan and Ludmilla: Overture.
(B) *** Decca 417 689-2; *417 689-4*. LSO, Solti – MUSSORGSKY: *Khovanshchina prelude; Night;* BORODIN: *Prince Igor*: excerpts. ***
(M) *** BMG/RCA GD 60176 [60176-2-RG]. Chicago SO, Fritz Reiner – PROKOFIEV: *Alexander Nevsky* etc. ***

Solti's electrifying account of the *Russlan and Ludmilla overture* is perhaps the most exciting ever recorded, with the lyrical element providing a balancing warmth, though the sound is very brightly lit.

Reiner's performance is not quite as racy as Solti's, but it is still highly infectious, and the 1959 Chicago sound brings plenty of colour and warmth.

Grand sextet in E flat.
*** Hyp. CDA 66163; *KA 66163* [id.]. Capricorn – RIMSKY-KORSAKOV: *Quintet*. ***

Glinka's *Sextet* is rather engaging, particularly when played with such aplomb as it is here. The contribution of the pianist, Julian Jacobson, is brilliantly nimble and felicitous. The recording has an attractive ambience and, if the balance places the piano rather backwardly for a resonant acoustic, the CD provides good detail and overall presence.

Trio pathétique in D min.
*** Chan. Dig. CHAN 8477; *ABTD 1188* [id.]. Borodin Trio – ARENSKY: *Piano trio*. ***

Glinka's *Trio* is prefaced by a superscription; '*Je n'ai connu l'amour que par les peines qu'il cause*' ('I have known love only through the misery it causes'). It is no masterpiece – but the Borodins play it for all they are worth and almost persuade one that it is. As we have come to expect from this source, the recording is vivid and has excellent presence.

Gluck, Christophe (1714–87)

Alceste (complete).
** Orfeo Dig. C 02782 (3) [id.]. Jessye Norman, Gedda, Krause, Nimsgern, Weikl, Bav. R. Ch. and SO, Baudo.

The French version of *Alceste* in this very well-cast set has Jessye Norman commanding in the title-role, producing gloriously varied tone in every register. What is rather lacking – even from her performance – is a fire-eating quality such as made Janet Baker's performance so memorable and which comes out to hair-raising effect in Callas's recording of *Divinités du Styx*. Here it is beautiful but relatively tame. That is mainly the fault of the conductor, who makes Gluck's score sound comfortable rather than tense. The other principals sing stylishly; however, as a set, this does not quite rebut the idea that in Gluck 'beautiful' means 'boring'. Good, well-focused sound from Bavarian Radio engineers.

Le Cinesi (The Chinese women).
(M) *** HM/BMG Dig. GD 77174 [77174-2-RG]. Poulenard, Von Otter, Banditelli, De Mey, Schola Cantorum Basiliensis O, Jacobs.

Gluck's hour-long opera-serenade provides a fascinating view of the composer's lighter side. In the comedy here one can even detect anticipations of Mozart – though, with recitative taking up an undue proportion of the whole, Gluck's timing hardly compares. More importantly, Gluck, rather like Mozart in *Entführung*, uses jangling and tinkling percussion instruments in the overture to indicate an exotic setting. Otherwise the formal attitudes in Metastasio's libretto – written some twenty years before Gluck set it – are pure eighteenth century.

(i) *La Corona* (complete). (ii) *La Danza* (dramatic pastoral).
**(*) Orfeo Dig. C 135872H (2) [id.]. (i) Slowakiewicz, Gorzynska, Nowicks, Bav. R. Ch; (ii) Ignatowicz, Myriak, Warsaw CO; Bugaj.

Hunting-calls set the scene evocatively in the three-movement sinfonia of *La Corona*, which is followed by six arias (including a particularly brilliant one for Atalanta), a delightful duet and a final quartet. This performance, originally recorded for Bavarian Radio, is fresh and direct, with first-rate singing from the three sopranos. The much shorter fill-up, described as a dramatic pastoral, is less interesting and is less reliably done. It is none the less welcome as an extension of the Gluck repertory.

Iphigénie en Aulide (complete).
***Erato/Warner Dig. 2292 45003-2 (2). Van Dam, Anne Sofie von Otter, Dawson, Aler, Monteverdi Ch., Lyon Op. O, Gardiner.

Following up the success of his recording of the more celebrated *Iphigénie en Tauride*, John Eliot Gardiner here tackles the earlier of the two Iphigénie operas, much more neglected. *Iphigénie en Aulide* was written in 1774 – Gluck's first piece in French – and anticipated the *Tauride* opera in its speed and directness of treatment, so different from the leisurely and expansive traditions of opera seria. Based on Euripides by way of Racine, this does not have quite the emotional variety of the later opera, but it is just as moving. Gardiner here eliminates the distortions of the piece which the long-established Wagner edition created and reconstructs the score as presented in the first revival of 1775. Though the original final chorus was then omitted, Gardiner rightly includes it here, amazingly original, with the bass drum prefacing a number which is less a celebration than a dramatic call to war, very different from the conventional happy ending. The darkness of the piece is established at the very start, with men's voices eliminated, and a moving portrait built up of Agamemnon, here superbly sung by José van Dam, with his extended solo at the end of Act II tellingly contrasted with the brevity and economy of the rest. In the title-role Lynne Dawson builds up a touching portrait of the heroine from the contrasted sequence of brief arias, a character developing in adversity, always vulnerable. Her sweet, pure singing is well contrasted with the positive strength of Anne Sofie von Otter as Clytemnestra, and John Aler brings clear, heroic attack to the tenor role of Achille. The performance is crowned by the superb ensemble-singing of the Monteverdi Choir in the many choruses. Based on a production at the Aix-en-Provence Festival, the recording conveys the tensions of a live performance without the distractions of intrusive stage noise.

Iphigénie en Tauride (complete).
❀ *** Ph. Dig. 416 148-2 (2) [id.]. Montague, Aler, Thomas Allen, Argenta, Massis, Monteverdi Ch., Lyon Op. O, Eliot Gardiner.

Gardiner's electrifying reading of *Iphigénie en Tauride* is a revelation. Anyone who has found Gluck operas boring should hear this dramatically paced performance of an opera that is compact and concentrated in its telling of a classical story. Gardiner is an urgent advocate, bringing out the full range of expression from first to last; though his Lyon orchestra does not use period instruments, its clarity and resilience and, where necessary, grace and delicacy are admirable. The cast is first rate. Diana Montague in the name-part sings with admirable bite and freshness, making the lovely solo *O malheureuse Iphigénie* pure and tender. Thomas Allen is an outstanding Oreste, characterizing strongly – as in his fury aria – but singing with classical precision. John Aler is a similarly strong and stylish singer, taking the tenor role of Pylade, with some fine singers from Gardiner's regular team impressive in other roles. The recording is bright and full, with the balance favouring voices but not inappropriately so.

Orfeo ed Euridice (complete).
*** EMI Dig. CDS7 49834-2 (2). Hendricks, Von Otter, Fournier, Monteverdi Ch., Lyon Opera O, Gardiner.
**(*) Decca 417 410-2 (2) [id.]. Horne, Lorengar, Donath, ROHCG Ch. & O, Solti.
**(*) Capriccio Dig. 60 008-2 (2) [id.]. Kowalski, Schellenberger-Ernst, Fliegner, Berlin R. Ch., C. P. E. Bach CO, Hartmut Haenchen.
(M) **(*) BMG/RCA GD 87896 (2) [7896-2-RG]. Verrett, Moffo, Raskin, Rome Polyphonic Ch., Virtuosi di Roma, Fasano.
**(*) Sony Dig. SX2K 48040 (2) [id.]. Argenta, Chance, Beckerbauer, Stuttgart Chamber Ch., Tafelmusik, Bernius.

Gardiner here cuts through the problem of which text to use in this opera – the original Vienna version with alto in the title-role or the Paris version with tenor – by opting broadly for the Berlioz edition, which aimed at combining the best of both. At Glyndebourne under Raymond Leppard, much the same solution was adopted, and one hopes that Erato will issue on CD its fine recording with Dame Janet Baker from that source. For Gardiner, Anne Sofie von Otter is a superb Orfeo, tougher than Dame Janet, less vulnerable but less feminine too, and dramatically most convincing. The masculine forthrightness of her singing matches the extra urgency of Gardiner's direction; and both Barbara Hendricks as Eurydice and Brigitte Fournier as Amour are also excellent. The chorus is Gardiner's own Monteverdi Choir, superbly clean and stylish. Unlike the Leppard/Glyndebourne production, Gardiner's omits the celebratory ballet at the end of the opera. The recording is full and well balanced.

The surprise of the Decca set is the conducting of Georg Solti, which combines his characteristic brilliance and dramatic bite with a feeling for eighteenth-century idiom which is most impressive. Solti and Horne opt to conclude Act I, not as the Gluck score prescribes, but with a brilliant display aria, *Addio, o miei sospiri*, taken from the contemporary opera, *Tancredi*, by Ferdinando Bertoni. That may sound like cavalier treatment for Gluck, but stylistically Solti justifies not only that course but his whole interpretation, which combines drama with delicacy. Marilyn Horne makes a formidably strong Orfeo, not as deeply imaginative as Dame Janet Baker, but wonderfully strong and secure, with fine control of tone. Pilar Lorengar sings sweetly, but is not always steady, while Helen Donath is charming in the role of Amor. Recording quality is outstandingly fine.

The big attraction of the Capriccio version is the inspired singing of the German counter-tenor, Jochen Kowalski, in the title-role. The main shortcoming can be assessed at the very start, when the washy acoustic obscures rapid figuration in the overture, and the whole scale of the performance seems too big. Haenchen, with a good chamber orchestra using modern instruments, opts for the Vienna version of the opera, using Italian, more compact than the later Paris score; but he provides as an appendix the Paris ballet with its *Dance of the blessed spirits*, an essential item. The extra sharpness of the Vienna score is unfortunately countered not only by the recording and the conductor's occasionally heavy direction, but also by the murkiness of the large-sounding chorus. None of these shortcomings need weigh very heavily against the glories of the solo singing, notably that of Kowalski who, with his firm, characterful voice, generally warm-toned in a masculine way, creates an exceptionally convincing portrait of the bereaved Orpheus. More than usual he brings out the full poignant agony of the hero's situation. *Che farò* is taken effectively fast, but tenderly and with big rallentandos, and his intensity is matched by the fresh vehemence of his Eurydice, Dagmar Schellenberger-Ernst. Having a boy-treble as Amour is more controversial. He comes from the Tölzer Boy Singers, and sings with commendably clean attack, fine rhythmic sense and no hooting.

Clearly, if you have a mezzo as firm and sensitive as Shirley Verrett, then everything is in favour of your using the original Italian version rather than the later, Paris version with tenor. Quite apart from making a sensible decision over the text, Fasano uses the right-sized orchestra (of modern instruments) and adopts an appropriately classical style. Anna Moffo and Judith Raskin match Verrett in clean, strong singing, and the Rome Polyphonic Chorus is far more incisive than most Italian choirs. The recording is vivid and atmospheric, but on CD the close balance of the voices emphasizes the music's dramatic qualities rather than its tenderness. However, this makes a good mid-priced recommendation.

Bernius, a fine Gluck conductor, with his period group, Tafelmusik, opts for the original Vienna version of this operatic landmark, omitting all the material Gluck wrote later for Paris. The impact of the opera is all the sharper, but it is disappointing not to have the *Dance of the Blessed Spirits*. Sony should have included it as a supplement with the rest of the Paris ballet music, as the Capriccio version does. It makes very short measure to have only 83 minutes of music on two full-price discs. Just as the Capriccio set has the outstanding German counter-tenor, Jochen Kowalski, in the title-role, so this one has the leading British counter-tenor, Michael Chance, dominating the whole performance, with his voice full and forward. The focus of the sound is far sharper than on the disconcertingly distanced Capriccio. Nancy Argenta is a sweet-toned Euridice, and Amore is taken by the confident German boy-treble, Stefan Beckerbauer. With such sprightly playing from Tafelmusik, using period instruments, this is an even more stylish version than its Capriccio rival, but the price is very high.

Orfeo ed Eurydice (abridged version, sung in Italian).
(M) (**) Decca mono 433 468-2. Ferrier, Ayars, Vlachopoulos, Glyndebourne Festival Ch., Southern PO, Stiedry.

This much-abridged version of Gluck's opera was recorded soon after the Glyndebourne performances of 1947 and is now valuable only for Kathleen Ferrier's magnificent contribution. Even so, it is obvious that this was only a first attempt by a great artist to scale a formidable part. At that time she was not entirely at ease singing in Italian, and when Fritz Stiedry chose an absurdly fast tempo for the big aria, *Che farò*, she was less impressive – in spite of the vocal freshness – than in the later version with Sargent. That is also included as part of the ten-disc Kathleen Ferrier Edition, with each disc available separately – see under Vocal Recitals below. Decca have little to be proud of in this reissue; apart from Stiedry's imaginative contribution with chorus and orchestra being no more than adequate, the bright transfer is edgy and the sound not always completely secure.

La rencontre imprévue (opéra-comique).
*** Erato/Warner Dig. 2292 45516-2 (2) [id.]. Lynne Dawson, Le Coz, Flechter, Dubosc, Marin-Degor, Guy de Mey, Viala, Lafont, Cachemaille, Dudziak, Lyon Op. O, Gardiner.

This is another of the revelatory recordings of Gluck that John Eliot Gardiner has made with the Lyon Opera. Here he demonstrates that one of Gluck's comic operas – a genre long disparaged for bad timing and poor invention – can come up as freshly as the great reform operas like the two Iphigénie works he previously recorded. It is true that *Les pèlerins de la Mecque* – as Gardiner prefers to call it, rather than using its duller, more usual title, given above – has nothing like the comic timing of Mozart. Yet the brief 'Turkish' overture with its jingles has a breeziness that rivals that of *Entführung*, and all through the brisk sequence of arias and ensembles Gardiner gives the lie to the idea of the score being banal. The story may be disjointed but, with dialogue neatly edited and with some excellent singing, these three 35-minute Acts make delightful entertainment on record. The sweet-toned Lynne Dawson is charming as the heroine, Rezia, and Guy de Mey as the hero, Ali, is one of the few tenors who could cope effortlessly with the high tessitura, even though the voice does not sound quite young enough. Pierre Cachemaille sings powerfully in an incidental role, and other excellent members of the Lyon team include the tenor, Jean-Luc Viala, and the baritone, Francis Dudziak. The Lyon acoustic, as usual, is on the dry side, as recorded, but that has many advantages in comic opera.

Opera arias from *Alceste; Armide; Iphigénie en Aulide; Iphigénie en Tauride; Orfeo ed Euridice; Paride ed Elena; La rencontre imprévue.*
(M) *** Ph. 422 950-2; *422 950-4.* Dame Janet Baker, ECO, Raymond Leppard.

Helped by alert and sensitive accompaniments, Dame Janet Baker's singing of Gluck completely undermines any idea of something square or dull. The most famous arias bring unconventional readings – *Divinités du Styx* from *Alceste* deliberately less commanding, more thoughtful than usual – but the rarities are what inspire her most keenly: the four arias from *Paride ed Elena*, for example, are vividly contrasted in their sharply compact form. Outstanding recording, vividly remastered.

Goehr, Alexander (born 1932)

Metamorphosis/Dance, Op. 36; (i) *Romanza for cello and orchestra, Op. 24.*
(M) *** Unicorn Dig. UKCD 2039. (i) Moray Welsh; RLPO, Atherton.

Goehr wrote the *Romanza*, one of his most lyrical works, with Jacqueline du Pré in mind. Moray Welsh plays warmly and stylishly, but it is a pity that the dedicatee never recorded this piece which, in its serial argument, still requires persuasiveness, with its rhapsodic layout of Aria incorporating scherzo and cadenza. *Metamorphosis/Dance* was inspired by the Circe episode in the *Odyssey*, a sequence of elaborate variations, full of strong rhythmic interest. Not for nothing did the composer describe the piece as an 'imaginary ballet', though he would have done better to have chosen a less daunting title. The performance is excellent.

Goldmark, Karl (1830–1915)

Rustic wedding symphony, Op. 26; Sakuntala overture, Op. 13.
*** ASV Dig. CDDCA 791; *ZCDCA 791* [id.]. RPO, Yondani Butt.

It is good to welcome the highly engaging *Rustic wedding symphony* to the CD catalogue. It was one of the three colourful works – the others being the *Violin concerto No. 1* and the opera, *The Queen of Sheba* – which appeared in quick succession in the mid-1870s, and which together have sustained Goldmark's reputation to the present day. 'Clear-cut and faultless', Brahmns called this large but consciously unpretentious programme symphony, wittily echoing what Schumann had once said to Brahms himself, that 'it sprang into being, a finished thing, like Minerva from the head of Jupiter'. The first movement brings not a sonata-form structure but a simple set of variations with one or two pre-echoes of Mahler in *Wunderhorn* mood. It opens with a distinctly rustic theme on the lower strings, which when taken up by the horns (with woodwind birdsong overhead) is as magical as any passage in the romantic symphonic repertory, not forgetting the beginning of Mahler's *First*. The other movements, include a wistful *Bride's song*, and a delightful *Serenade*, bringing some distinguished RPO woodwind playing and remind us that the symphony was a Beecham favourite. The hazily romantic evocation of a summer garden which forms the slow movement then leads to a boisterous dance finale, with genial injections of fugato. Yondani Butt has the work's full measure and the RPO clearly enjoy themselves. The Brian Culverhouse recording, too, made in London's Henry Wood Hall, is impressive. It has brightly lit violins, but plenty of bloom on the woodwind, and the only miscalculation of balance concerns the trombone entry in the first movement which is too blatant and too loud. Otherwise this is in every way enjoyable. The *Overture Sakuntala* opens impressively but does not quite sustain its 18 minutes, though its themes and atmosphere have much in common with the symphony. Butt presents it with persuasive vigor and lyrical feeling, and does not shirk the melodrama.

Die Königin von Saba (opera).
** Hung. HCD 12179/82 [id.]. Nagy, Gregor, Kincses, Jerusalem, Miller, Takács, Hungarian State Op. Ch. and O, Fischer.

With the Queen of Sheba representing evil and the lovely Sulamit representing good, the theme of this opera has a link with Wagner's *Tannhäuser*, yet in style Goldmark rather recalls Mendelssohn and Gounod, with a touch of Meyerbeer. In the tenor role of Asad, Siegfried Jerusalem gives a magnificent performance, not least in his aria, *Magische Töne*. Klára Takács is dramatic and characterful as the Queen of Sheba, but on top the voice is often raw. Sándor Nagy is an impressive Solomon, and Adam Fischer, one of the talented family of conductors, draws lively performances from everyone. The recording is very acceptable, but even on CD there are many details which do not emerge as vividly as they might. The documentation, too, is poorly produced.

Goldschmidt, Berthold (born 1903)

(i) *String quartets Nos. 2–3;* (ii) *Letzte Kapitel*; *Belsatzar*.
*** Largo Dig. LC 8943 [id.]. (i) Mandelring Qt; (ii) Marks; Ars-Nova Ens., Berlin, Schwarz.

Berthold Goldschmidt was thirty, just establishing himself as a composer and conductor, when he was hounded from Nazi Germany. He settled in London and in 1951 his opera *Cenci* was awarded an Arts Council prize but remained unproduced. During the 1960s he was active as a conductor and directed the first performance of Deryck Cooke's performing version of the sketch of the Mahler *Tenth Symphony*, as well as Nielsen's *Saul and David*. His beautiful *Mediterranean songs*, which should be recorded, reveal a strong lyrical imagination. However, he was one of the victims not only of the Nazis but of the changed climate in the 1960s and gave up composition for a time. This disc collects his *Letzte Kapitel* (1931) for speaker and an instrumental ensemble, very much in the style of Kurt Weill, and the *Second Quartet* (1936), the first work he wrote in exile. It has something of the fluency of Hindemith or other neo-classical figures of the period. It is an excellently fashioned piece with a rather powerful slow movement, an elegy subtitled *Folia*. The CD is completed by two later works, *Beltsazar* (1985), an *a cappella* setting of Heine, and the *Third Quartet* (1989) is a remarkable achievment for an 86-year-old, the product of a cultured and thoughtful musical mind. The performances are dedicated, the recordings satisfactory (there could be a bit more space round the players in the string quartets). The notes are excellent though their type-face is hardly reader-friendly; the durations given of the finale of the *Second Quartet* and of the one-movement *Third* are wildly inaccurate.

Gordon, Gavin (1901–70)

The Rake's Progress (ballet suite).
(M) (***) EMI mono CDH7 63911-2 [id.]. ROHCG O, Constant Lambert – LAMBERT: *Horoscope* etc.; RAWSTHORNE: *Street corner*. (***)

Gavin Gordon wrote his ballet based on Hogarth for the Sadler's Wells company in 1935. In its lively English idiom it had great success; as an attractive period piece the suite now makes a welcome fill-up to the colourful Lambert works. The 1946 mono recording is astonishingly vivid.

Gorecki, Henryk (born 1933)

Symphony No. 3, Op. 36.
*** Elektra Nonesuch Dig. 979282-2 [id.]. Dawn Upshaw, London Sinf., David Zinman.

Written in 1976, Gorecki's *Symphony No. 3* brought a total change of style in this Polish composer's work. After years of experimentation he here simplified his idiom in a way that relates the work on the one hand to minimalism and on the other to the music of John Tavener, similarly drawing inspiration from religious sources. Scored for strings and piano with soprano solo in each of the three movements, all predominantly slow, the work has the subtitle,

Symphony of sorrowful songs. It sets three laments taking the theme of motherhood. The massive first movement, nearly half an hour long, builds up a slow canon in an extended crescendo which rises in pitch as well as in volume. It finally resolves on the central setting of a fifteenth-century text from a monastic collection, with clear reference to the lament of the Virgin Mary at the Cross. The second movement, setting a prayer to the Virgin Mary inscribed by an eighteen-year-old woman prisoner on the wall of the Gestapo headquarters in Zakopane incongruously brings a switch to a sensuously beautiful idiom, sweeter and lighter, with the soprano solo soaring radiantly. The third movement is the setting of a folksong with a two-chord ostinato as accompaniment, persistently repeated, resolving in a concluding passage of total peace, a mother's plea for her lost son to sleep happily. Though the pace is consistently slow, there is an inner momentum in the music which is magnetic in a very similar way to Tavener's. The *Sinfonietta's* fine performance, beautifully recorded, is crowned by the radiant singing of Dawn Upshaw.

Gottschalk, Louis (1829–69)

(i; iii) *Grande fantaisie triumphal on the Brazilian national anthem* (arr. Adler); (i; iv) *Grande tarantelle for piano and orchestra;* (iii) *Marche solennelle* (for orchestra and bands); *Marcha triunfal y final de opera;* (iv) *Symphonies Nos. 1 (A Night in the Tropics)* (ed. Buketoff); *2 (A Montevideo);* (i; iv) *The Union: Concert paraphrase on national airs* (arr. Adler); *Variations on the Portuguese national anthem for piano and orchestra* (ed List). (ii) *5 Pieces* (for piano, 4 hands); (iv; v) *Escenas campestres (Cuban country scenes):* opera in 1 Act.
(B) **(*) VoxBox 1154842 (2) [CDX 5009]. (i) Eugene List; (ii) Cary Lewis & Brady Millican; (iii) Berlin SO, Adler; (iv) V. State Op. O, Buketoff; (v) with Paniagua, Estevas, Garcia.

This Vox Box offers a distinguished anthology, with obvious dedication from editors and executants alike. Eugene List was just the man to choose as soloist. Whether tongue-in-cheek or not, he manages to sound stylish throughout and in The *Union concert paraphrase*, which is outrageous, he is superb. There is no space here to dwell on the felicities of Gottschalk's elegant vulgarity. If you want Lisztian bravura, try the concertante pieces; if you fancy romanticism mixed with popular national dance rhythms, sample the two symphonies. There is also an imitation of Tchaikovsky's *Marche slave* which does not quite come off. The solo piano pieces (very forwardly recorded) are more variable: *La Gallina* is particularly likeable. The programme ends with some attractive vocal music (the *Escenas campestres*), which is vividly sung. The recording is not of the very best quality; at the very opening of the *Grande tarantelle* one notices that the castanets are not quite clean and the upper range of the sound is inclined to be a bit shallow. Yet the effect, if sometimes two-dimensional, is always vivid and sparkling, and the bright, slightly hard piano timbre is not out of place here.

Grand fantaisie triumphal for piano and orchestra.
(M) *** Decca Dig. 430 726-2; *430 726-4* [id.]. Ortiz, RPO, Atzmon – ADDINSELL: *Warsaw concerto* ***; GERSHWIN: *Rhapsody* **(*); LISZT: *Hungarian fantasia* ***; LITOLFF: *Scherzo.* ***

Gottschalk's *Grand fantasia* has naïvety, and a touch of vulgarity too, but the performers here give it an account which nicely combines flair and a certain elegance, and the result is a distinct success.

Le banjo; Berceuse (cradle song); *The dying poet* (meditation); *Grand Scherzo; The last hope* (religious meditation); *Mazurk; Le Mancenillier* (West Indian serenade); *Pasquinade caprice; Scherzo romantique; Souvenirs d'Andalousie; Tournament gallop; The Union: Concert paraphrase de concert on national airs (The Star spangled banner; Yankee Doodle; Hail Columbia).*
*** Nimbus Dig. NI 5014 [id.]. Alan Marks.

Louis Gottschalk was born in New Orleans of mixed German and French parentage. He studied music in Paris under Charles Hallé and then launched himself on a hugely successful career as composer/conductor/virtuoso pianist, appealing to an American and European audience whose musical taste was without pretensions. He became to some extent an isolated figure, cut off from serious musical influences, and his music retained a refreshing naïveté to the last. It is good to have a current exponent of his art who is wholly sympathetic to its ethos. Alan Marks plays with unassuming panache: his *Souvenirs de'Andalousie* glitter with bravura, his felicity of touch and crisp articulation bring much sparkle to the *Grand scherzo* and *Scherzo romantique*, while he sounds like a full orchestra in the *Tournament galop*. Most importantly, he finds simplicity and charm in the delightful *Berceuse* and *Le Mancenillier*, while there is not a hint of sentimentality in *The last hope* or *The dying poet*. He is most realistically recorded in a fairly reverberant acoustic, which suits the flair of his playing.

PIANO MUSIC FOR FOUR HANDS

La Bananier (Chanson nègre), Op. 5; La Gallina (Danse cubaine), Op. 53; Grande Tarantelle, Op. 67; La jota aragonesa (Caprice espagnol), Op. 14; Marche de nuit, Op. 17; Ojos criollos (Danse cubaine – Caprice brillante), Op. 37; Orfa (Grande polka), Op. 71; Printemps d'amour (Mazurka-caprice de concert), Op. 40; Réponds moi (Danse cubaine), Op. 50; Radieuse (Grand valse de concert), Op. 72; La Scintilla (L'Étincelle – Mazurka sentimentale), Op. 21; Ses yeux (Célèbre polka de concert), Op. 66.
**(*) Nimbus Dig. NI 5324 [id.]. Alan Marks & Nerine Barrett (piano, 4 hands).

Alan Marks and Nerine Barrett make an effervescent Gottschalk partnership, playing this repertoire to the manner born. They seem as at home in the Cuban rhythms as in the Spanish: *La jota aragonesa* shimmers with twinkling light, while the *Grande tarantelle* makes a splendid finale. The slight snag is that they are – very realistically – recorded in an empty, resonant hall and, while this brings a perhaps appropriate degree of inflation, it also reduces the subtlety of effect and is more tiring to the ear than a sharper focus.

Gould, Morton (born 1913)

Derivations for clarinet and band.
*** Sony MK 42227 [id.]. Benny Goodman, Columbia Jazz Combo, composer – BARTÓK: *Contrasts;* BERNSTEIN: *Prelude, fugue and riffs;* COPLAND: *Concerto;* STRAVINSKY: *Ebony concerto.* (***)

Gould's *Derivations* is in Gershwinesque mould. The first-movement *Warm-up* is well managed, but the central *Contrapuntal blues* and (especially) the *Rag* are the most memorable of these four miniatures. Benny Goodman is in his element and the accompaniment under the composer is suitably improvisatory in feeling.

Fall River legend (ballet; complete).
*** Albany Dig. TROY 035 [id.]. Brock Peters, National PO, Milton Rosenstock (with recorded conversation between Agnes de Mille and Morton Gould).

This complete recording of *Fall River legend* was associated with the Dance Theatre of Harlem's 1983 production of the ballet. The work opens dramatically with the Speaker for the Jury reading out the Indictment at the trial, and then the ballet tells the story in flashback. Gould's music has a good deal in common with the folksy writing in Copland's *Appalachian spring*, and it is given a splendidly atmospheric performance and recording by the New York orchestra under Rosenstock, the Harlem Dance Theatre's Musical Director. There is also a 26-minute discussion on the creation of the ballet between Agnes de Mille and the composer.

Fall River legend: suite; Spirituals for string choir and orchestra.
(M) *** Mercury 432 016-2 [id.]. Eastman-Rochester SO, Howard Hanson – BARBER: *Medea: suite.* ***

On Mercury comes the composer's orchestral suite from the ballet, vividly played by the Eastman-Rochester Orchestra under the highly sympathetic Howard Hanson, who also gives an outstandingly vibrant account of the *Spirituals*, which resourcefully and wittily uses the massed string choir as an autonomous body in concertante with the rest of the orchestra. The 1959/60 recording has astonishing clarity, range and presence and makes one realize why Mercury engineering established such a high reputation early in the stereo era.

Formations; (i) *Spirituals.*
*** Bay Cities BCD 1016 [id.]. Knightsbridge Symphony Band, Gould; (i) LSO, Susskind – ANTHEIL: *Symphony No. 4.* **

Morton Gould subtitled *Spirituals* (1941) 'for string choir and orchestra' because the plan was to use the strings as if they were a vocal choir. It is an attractive, bright piece in the received Copland tradition, very well laid out for the chosen forces and excellently played by the LSO under Walter Susskind. *Formations* is a later piece (1964), commissioned for either Marching or Concert Band; exhilarating light music and played with real spirit and enthusiasm under the composer's own baton. Good sound too.

Latin American Symphonette.
(M) ** Van. 08.4037.71 [OVC 4071]. Utah SO, Abravanel – COPLAND: *Lincoln portrait* etc. **(*)

Abravanel's performance has plenty of colour and spirit, and is very well played, but the Utah acoustic with its wide reverberation brings problems, at times making the full-blooded scoring sound roisterously over the top. The result is infectious but noisy.

Gounod, Charles (1818–93)

Symphonies Nos. 1 in D; 2 in B flat.
(M) **(*) EMI CDM7 63949-2. Toulouse Capitole O, Plasson.

Gounod's two *Symphonies* sound astonishingly youthful, though they were composed in quick succession in his mid-thirties. When listening to No. 1, the Bizet *Symphony* springs to mind. The effortless flow of first-rate ideas and the mastery, both of the orchestra, which is handled with the greatest expertise, and of symphonic form, are very striking. The *Second Symphony* is very like the *First*, and both receive decent performance from Michel Plasson. The EMI engineers have produced fresh, warm sound and the CD transfer is very successful.

Symphony No. 1 in D; Petite symphonie in B flat for wind instruments.
*** Decca Dig. 430 231-2; *430 231-4* [id.]. Saint Paul CO, Hogwood – BIZET: *L'Arlésienne.* ***

Instead of the *Second Symphony*, Hogwood offers the *Petite symphonie for wind*, which dates from Gounod's later years: he was nearly seventy when he wrote it for one of the celebrated Parisian wind ensembles of the day. The work has impeccable craftsmanship and is engagingly witty and civilized. Hogwood has its full measure and, with his 'authentic' ear for colour, makes the most of its scoring, even noting the composer's fondness for the lowest bassoon note, B flat. The work's lovely *Andante cantabile*, with its memorable flute solo, is played most beautifully, and the outer movements are infectious in their sprung rhythms. The Saint Paul Chamber Orchestra plays on modern instruments, but their crisp, athletic style brings clean textures, and the trumpets in the finale of *Symphony No. 1* are attractively bright and well focused. In the *Petite symphonie* the matching wind timbres have lots of character and the bright horn articulation at the opening of the scherzo is typical of the zest of the playing. Excellent recording and an interesting Bizet coupling.

Messe solennelle de Saint Cécile.
*** EMI Dig. CDC7 47094-2 [id.]. Hendricks, Dale, Lafont, Ch. and Nouvel O Philharmonique of R. France, Prêtre.
(M) *** DG 427 409-2 [id.]. Seefried, Stolze, Uhde, Czech Ch. & PO, Markevitch.

Gounod's *Messe solennelle*, with its blatant march setting of the Credo and sugar-sweet choral writing, may not be for sensitive souls, but Prêtre here directs an almost ideal performance, vividly recorded, to delight anyone not averse to Victorian manners. Prêtre's subtle rhythmic control and sensitive shaping of phrase minimize the vulgarity and bring out the genuine dramatic contrasts of the piece, with glowing singing from the choir as well as the three soloists.

Markevitch's vintage version, recorded in the mid-1960s, still sounds remarkably well in DG's mid-price Dokumente series. In his straight-faced way Markevitch makes the incongruity of Gounod's jolly and vulgar tunes all the more delectable, and soloists, chorus and orchestra are all first rate.

Faust (complete).
*** EMI Dig. CDS7 54228-2 (3) [id.]. Leech, Studer, Van Dam, Hampson, Ch. & O of Capitole de Toulouse, Plasson.
(M) **(*) EMI CMS7 69983-2 (3) [Ang. CDMC 69983]. De los Angeles, Gedda, Blanc, Christoff, Paris Nat. Op. Ch. and O, Cluytens.
**(*) Ph. Dig. 420 164-2 (3) [id.]. Te Kanawa, Araiza, Nesterenko, Bav. R. Ch. and SO, C. Davis.

Recordings of *Faust* have been dogged by ill-luck, with major flaws regularly preventing a full recommendation, but Plasson with his excellent cast headed by three American singers comes nearer than anyone to scotching the jinx. Ironically it is the French-speaking singer among the four principals who might worry traditionalists, for José van Dam's gloriously dark, finely focused bass-baritone yet does not have the heft of a full-blooded bass voice, such as is associated with the role of Mephistopheles. That said, it is a masterly performance, more searching and sinister than almost any, with the singer projecting superbly and consistently exploiting his idiomatic French, so different from the slavonic singers who are his main rivals in the other main sets. The *Calf of gold* solo has a lift in its jolly bouncing rhythms that makes it all the more sinister, and it is good to have as one of the four previously unrecorded offerings in the Appendix on the third disc an early, discarded aria intended for the same point in the opera. All three of the American principals are outstanding stylists, very much in sympathy with the idiom. Cheryl Studer, while exploiting the power of her soprano, conveys the girlishness of Marguerite, managing to lighten her voice, using the widest range of dynamic and colour. In the *Jewel song* she is brighter and jollier than any of her main rivals, helped by Plasson's understanding accompaniment. If Richard Leech's voice, on a par with van Dam's, might in principle seem too lightweight for the role of Faust, the lyrical flow and absence of strain, coupled with fine projection, make his singing consistently enjoyable. As Valentine Thomas Hampson is strongly cast, with his firm, heroic baritone. As for the ensemble and choral writing and Plasson's direction generally he is more successful than any latterday rival in giving a rhythmic lift to Gounod's score, bringing out the jollity of the Kermesse scene, and building the final trio the more compellingly by keeping power in reserve till the final stanza. The sound has a good sense of presence, set in a pleasantly reverberant acoustic which does not obscure necessary detail. In addition to the supplementary numbers – which also include a trio for Faust, Siebel and Wagner as well as a duet for Marguerite and Valentine – the appendix offers the complete ballet music.

In the reissued Cluytens set the seductiveness of De los Angeles's singing is a dream and it is a pity that the recording hardens the natural timbre slightly. Christoff is magnificently Mephistophelian; the dark, rich, bass voice with all its many subtle facets of tone-colour is a superb vehicle for the part, at once musical and dramatic. Gedda, though showing some signs of strain, sings intelligently, and among the other soloists Ernest Blanc has a pleasing, firm voice, which he uses to make Valentin into a sympathetic character. Cluytens's approach is competent but somewhat workaday. He rarely offers that extra spring which adds so much to Gounod's score in sheer charm, and he shows a tendency to over-drive in the more dramatic passages. The recording is well balanced on the whole, although at times some of the soloists are oddly placed on the stereo stage.

Sir Colin Davis, with his German orchestra and with no French singer among his principals, may not always be idiomatic but, with fine singing from most of them, it is a refreshing version. Dame Kiri, more than you might expect, makes a light and innocent-sounding Marguerite, with the *Jewel Song* made to sparkle in youthful eagerness leaping off from a perfect trill. Evgeni Nesterenko as Mephistopheles is a fine saturnine tempter; Andreas Schmidt as Valentin sings cleanly and tastefully in a rather German way; while Pamela Coburn as Siebel is sweet and boyish. The big snag is the Faust of Francisco Araiza, a disappointing hero with the voice, as recorded, gritty in tone and frequently strained. The sound is first rate.

Faust: highlights.
** EMI Dig. CDC7 54358-2 [id.]; *EL 754358-4* (from above recording, with Leech, Studer; cond. Plasson).

The EMI digital selection is not particularly generous at full price (53 minutes), including the key numbers and only the final Trio from Act V.

Faust: ballet music (suite).
(M) **(*) Decca Dig. 430 718-2; *430 718-4* [id.]. Montreal SO, Dutoit – OFFENBACH: *Gaîté parisienne.* **(*)

Gounod's attractive suite is warmly and elegantly played by the Montreal orchestra under Dutoit, although the conductor's touch is not as light as one would have expected. The CD sounds first rate. However, there is also a splendidly 'French' performance conducted by Paul Paray on Mercury in a collection called '*French Opera Highlights*' (Philips/Mercury 432 014-2) – see under Detroit Symphony Orchestra in our Concerts section, below.

Grainger, Percy (1882–1961)

(i) *Air from County Derry (Londonderry air); Country gardens; (ii) Danish folk music suite;* (i) *Handel in the Strand;* (ii) *The immovable 'Do'; In a nutshell suite;* (i) *Mock morris; Molly on the shore; Shepherd's hey;* (Piano) *Knight and shepherd's daughter; Walking tune.* Arrangements: FAURÉ: *Nell, Op. 18/1.* GERSHWIN: *Love walked in; The man I love.*
(M) *** EMI CDM7 63520-2; *EG 763520-4.* (i) Light Music Soc. O, Dunn; (ii) E. Sinfonia, Dilkes; (iii) Daniel Adni.

A useful and very generous Grainger anthology (79 minutes long). The performances are particularly spontaneous and the recording is bright and fresh, perhaps not as sumptuous in the *Londonderry air* as might be ideal. The inclusion of the piano pieces is particularly welcome. Daniel Adni plays them with a combination of sound musical instinct and good taste that gives unfailing pleasure, and he is very well recorded. The curiosities here are the Fauré and Gershwin arrangements, models of their kind.

Blithe bells (Free ramble on a theme by Bach: Sheep may safely graze): Country gardens; Green bushes (Passacaglia); Handel in the Strand; Mock morris; Molly on the shore; My Robin is to the greenwood gone; Shepherd's hey; Spoon River; Walking tune; Youthful rapture.
(M) *** Chan. CHAN 6542; *MBTD 6542* [id.]. Bournemouth Sinf., Montgomery.

Montgomery's anthology of Grainger's music stands out for the sparkling and sympathetic playing of the Bournemouth Sinfonietta and an engaging choice of programme. For those wanting only a single Grainger collection, this could be first choice. Among the expressive pieces, the arrangement of *My Robin is to the greenwood gone* is highly attractive, but the cello solo in *Youthful rapture* is perhaps less effective. Favourites such as *Country gardens, Shepherd's hey, Molly on the shore* and *Handel in the Strand* all sound as fresh as new paint. The 1978 recording, made in Christchurch Priory, has retained all its ambient character in its CD transfer.

Irish tune from County Derry; Lincolnshire Posy (suite); *Molly on the shore; Shepherd's hey.*
(M) *** ASV CDWHL 2067; *ZCWHL 2067.* L. Wind O, Wick – MILHAUD; POULENC: *Suite française.* ***

First class playing and vivid recording, with the additional attraction of delightful couplings, make this very highly recommendable. These Grainger pieces come off excellently and the sound could hardly be better balanced; the full sonorities in the *Londonderry air* are particularly appealing. This is in the demonstration class.

'Dished up for piano', Volume 1: Andante con moto; Arrival platform humlet; Bridal lullaby; Children's march; Colonial song; English waltz; Gay but wistful; The Gum-suckers' march; Handel in the Strand; Harvest hymn; The immovable 'Do'; In a Nutshell (suite); In Dahomey; Mock morris; Pastoral; Peace; Sailor's song; Saxon twi-play; To a Nordic princess; Walking tune.
*** Nimbus Dig. NI 5220 [id.]. Martin Jones.

'Dished up for piano', Volume 2: Arrangements: BACH: *Blithe bells.* BRAHMS: *Cradle song.* Chinese TRAD.: *Beautiful fresh flower.* DOWLAND: *Now, o now, I needs must part.* ELGAR: *Enigma variations: Nimrod.* Stephen FOSTER: *Lullaby; The rag-time girl.* GERSHWIN: *Love walked in; The man I love.* RACHMANINOV: *Piano concerto No. 2: Finale* (abridged). R. STRAUSS: *Der Rosenkavalier: Ramble on the last love-duet.* TCHAIKOVSKY: *Piano concerto No. 1* (opening); *Paraphrase on the Flower waltz.*
**(*) Nimbus Dig. NI 5232 [id.]. Martin Jones.

'Dished up for piano', Volume 3: Folksong arrangements: *The brisk young sailor; Bristol Town; Country gardens; Died for love; Hard-hearted Barb'ra Helen; The hunter in his career; Irish tune from County Derry; Jutish medley; Knight and shepherd's daughter; Lisbon (Dublin Bay); The merry king; Mo Ninghean Dhu; Molly on the shore; My Robin is to Greenwood gone; One more day my John* (2 versions, easy and complex); *Near Woodstock Town; The nightingale and the two sisters; O gin I were where Gowrie rins; Rimmer and goldcastle; The rival brothers; Scotch Strathspey; Shepherd's hey; Spoon River; Stalt vesselil; Sussex mummer's Christmas carol; The widow's party; Will ye gang to the Hielands, Lizzie Lindsay.*
*** Nimbus Dig. NI 5244 [id.]. Martin Jones.

Martin Jones's survey of Grainger's piano music is refreshingly lively and spontaneous.

Volume 1 is particularly attractive, and that is the place to start, for there is not a dull item here. The jolly pieces come off engagingly, but Jones often finds hidden depths in a composer best known for his boisterous and whimsical frivolousness. The *Bridal lullaby* (a delightful miniature), the charming *Colonial song* and the broodingly evocative *Pastoral*, the surprisingly extended, almost profound, last movement of the *In a Nutshell suite*, all show Jones at his most penetratingly thoughtful. This is lovely playing. There is plenty of dash in the folksong arrangements, and charm too, and they display a much greater range than one might have expected. Not all are equally memorable but, with a programme of 68 minutes to choose from, that hardly matters. The transcriptions are the most fascinating of all. The opening of the Tchaikovsky *Piano concerto* – some would say the 'best bit' – is transcribed straightforwardly, with a flamboyant flourish to finish it off, and the purple patch at the end of the Rachmaninov No. 2 cannot fail to make an impact in a performance as brilliant as this. Martin Jones then plays the Gershwin pieces in a beguilingly sultry manner, and he is equally good in the freely composed pastiche on Bach's *Sheep may safely graze* (*Blithe bells*). But he plays *Nimrod* and the *Der Rosenkavalier* excerpts too slowly; such a degree of languor might come off with the orchestra, but on the piano the effect is enervating. In all other respects the collection of transcriptions is most entertaining. The piano is recorded reverberantly in the Nimbus manner – but it rather suits this repertoire, and the image is absolutely truthful.

Duke of Marlborough fanfare; Green bushes (Passacaglia); Irish tune from County Derry; Lisbon; Molly on the shore; My Robin is to Greenwood gone; Shepherd's hey; Piano duet: Let's dance gay in green meadow; Vocal & choral: *Bold William Taylor; Brigg Fair; I'm seventeen come Sunday; Lord Maxwell's goodnight; The lost lady found; The pretty maid milkin' her cow; Scotch strathspey and reel; Shallow Brown; Shenandoah; The sprig of thyme; There was a pig went out to dig; Willow willow.*
(M) *** Decca 425 159-2. Pears, Shirley-Quirk, Amb. S. or Linden Singers, Wandsworth Boys' Ch., ECO, Britten or Steuart Bedford; Britten and V. Tunnard (pianos).

This is an altogether delightful anthology, beautifully played and sung by these distinguished artists. Grainger's talent was a smaller one than his more fervent advocates would have us believe, but his imagination in the art of arranging folksong was prodigious. Vocal and instrumental items are felicitously interwoven, and the recording is extremely vivid, though the digital remastering has put a hint of edge on the voices.

Part songs: *Australian up-country song; Brigg Fair; Danny Deever; Irish tune from County Derry; The lost lady found; Morning song in the jungle; The peora hunt; Shallow Brown; Six dukes went afishin'; Skye boat song; There was a pig.*
*** Conifer Dig. CDCF 162; *MCFC 162* [id.]. CBSO Ch., Simon Halsey – DELIUS: *Part songs.* **(*)

Robust and engaging, these songs emerge just as characterfully when treated chorally, as here, instead of with the sharper focus of single voices. Some of the more evocative gain from this larger-scale treatment, particularly when the CBSO Chorus sings so responsively and with such fine ensemble under Simon Halsey. Atmospheric recording.

Granados, Enrique (1867–1916)

Cuentos de la juventud, Op. 1: Dedicatoria. Spanish dances, Op. 37/4 & 5; Tonadillas al estilo antiguo: La Maja de Goya. Valses poéticos.
❀ *** BMG/RCA RCD 14378 [RCD1 4378]. Julian Bream – ALBÉNIZ: *Collection.* *** ❀

Like the Albéniz items with which these Granados pieces are coupled, these performances show Julian Bream at his most inspirational. The illusion of the guitar being in the room is especially electrifying in the middle section of the famous *Spanish dance No. 5*, when Bream achieves the most subtle pianissimo. Heard against the background silence, the effect is quite magical. But all the playing here is wonderfully spontaneous. This is one of the most impressive guitar recitals ever recorded.

12 Danzas españolas; Allegro de concierto; El Pelele.
(M) *** Decca Analogue/Dig. 433 923-2 (2) [id.]. Alicia de Larrocha – ALBÉNIZ: *Suite española* etc. ***

Alicia de Larrocha has an aristocratic poise to which it is difficult not to respond, and plays with great flair and temperament. There have been other fine accounts of Granados's *Danzas españolas*, but this is undoubtedly the most desirable and best-recorded version in circulation. The transfer of the 1982 analogue master to CD has been very successful and the sound has enhanced presence. *El Pelele* is an appendix to the *Goyescas* collection and comes as one of two brilliant encores (the sparkling *Allegro de concierto* is digitally recorded) to make an attractive bonus. The Albéniz couplings are equally recommendable.

Escenas románticas; Goyescas (complete); *6 Piezas sobre cantos populares españoles.*
❀ (M) *** Decca Dig./Analogue 433 920-2 (2). Alicia de Larrocha – ALBÉNIZ: *Sonata;* SOLER: *8 Sonatas.* ***

Alicia de Larrocha brings special insights and sympathy to the *Goyescas* (given top-drawer Decca sound in 1977); her playing has the crisp articulation and rhythmic vitality that these pieces call for, while she is hauntingly evocative in *Quejas o la maja y el ruisñor*. The overall impression could hardly be more idiomatic in flavour nor more realistic as a recording. The subtle, expressively ambitious *Escenas románticas* again show the surprisingly wide range of Granados's piano music. They were recorded digitally in 1985, as were the *6 Piezas sobre cantos populares españoles*. With the *Preludio* of this set we immediately enter the sound-world of strumming guitars with which Miss de Larrocha has such a natural accord, and under her guidance, experience the soft breezes of the Spanish evening, while the later dance movements, like the closing *Zapateado*, flash with flamenco iridescence.

Graun, Johann Gottlieb (1703–71)

Oboe concerto in C min.
(M) *** DG 431 120-2. Holliger, Camerata Bern, Van Wijnkoop – KREBS: *Double concerto* **(*); TELEMANN: *Concerto.* ***

This Graun was the brother of the better-known composer of the opera *Montezuma*, and the *C minor Concerto* is delectable in its originality. All three movements are highly inventive and the only pity is that this compact disc omits the companion *G minor Concerto*, included on the original CD. There would have been room for it, with a playing time of only 55 minutes. Nevertheless, this is a valuable reissue. All the music is attractive and, with Holliger at his most sparkling and with excellent sound, this is well worth exploring.

Grieg, Edvard (1843–1907)

Piano concerto in A min., Op. 16.
*** Ph. 412 923-2. Kovacevich, BBC SO, Sir Colin Davis – SCHUMANN: *Piano concerto.****
*** Sony Dig. MK 44899 [id.]. Perahia, Bav. RSO, C. Davis – SCHUMANN: *Concerto.* ***
(B) *** CfP Dig. CD-CFP 4574 [id.]; *TC-CFP 4574*. Pascal Devoyon, LPO, Maksymiuk – SCHUMANN: *Piano concerto.* ***
(B) *** Decca 433 628-2; *433 628-4* [id.]. Curzon, LSO, Fjeldstad – FRANCK: *Symphonic variations* *** ❀; SCHUMANN: *Concerto.* **(*)
(M) **(*) Decca 417 728-2 [id.]. Radu Lupu, LSO, Previn – SCHUMANN: *Concerto.* **(*)
(M) (***) EMI mono CDH7 63497-2. Lipatti, Philh. O, Galliera – with: CHOPIN: *Piano concerto No. 1.* (**)
(M) **(*) EMI Dig. CDD7 63903-2 [id.]; *ET 763903-4*. Cécile Ousset, LSO, Marriner – RACHMANINOV: *Piano concerto No. 2.* ***
(M) **(*) Sony/CBS CD 44849; *40-44849*. Fleisher, Cleveland O, Szell – SCHUMANN: *Concerto.* **(*)
(B) **(*) Pickwick IMPX 9041 [id.]. Julius Katchen, LSO, Kertész – SCHUMANN: *Concerto.* **(*)

(i) *Piano concerto in A min. 6 Lyric pieces, Op. 65.*
*** Virgin Dig. VC7 91198-2; *VC7 91198-4* [id.]. Leif Ove Andsnes, (i) Bergen PO, Dmitri Kitaenko – LISZT: *Piano concerto No. 2.* ***

(i) *Piano concerto in A min. Lyric suite, Op. 54; Peer Gynt suite No. 2, Op. 55.*
**(*) Chan. Dig. CHAN 8723; *ABTD 1363* [id.]. (i) Margaret Fingerhut; Ulster O, Vernon Handley.

The freshness and imagination displayed in the coupling of the Grieg and Schumann *Concertos* by Stephen Kovacevich and Sir Colin Davis offers a recording collaboration which continues to dominate the catalogue. Whether in the clarity of virtuoso fingerwork or the shading of half-tone, Bishop-Kovacevich is among the most illuminating of the many great pianists who have recorded the Grieg *Concerto*. He plays with bravura and refinement, the spontaneity of the music-making bringing a sparkle throughout, to balance the underlying poetry. The 1972 recording has been freshened most successfully.

Perahia revels in the bravura as well as bringing out the lyrical beauty in radiantly poetic playing. He is commanding and authoritative when required, with the blend of spontaneity, poetic feeling and virtuoso display this music calls for. The performance gains from having been recorded at a live concert, though there are no intrusive audience noises to betray that, and the sound is as full and well balanced as in most ordinary studio recordings. He is given sympathetic support by Sir Colin Davis and the fine Bavarian Radio Symphony Orchestra. Kovacevich's simpler, even more dedicated manner in the same coupling on Philips is even more moving in the first two movements, but there is no finer version of the Grieg recorded in the digital age than this.

Leif Ove Andsnes was still in his teens when he recorded the Grieg and Liszt *Concertos* in Grieg's home town with the Bergen Philharmonic. Youthful virtuosi are almost two-a-penny nowadays, but Andsnes wears his brilliance lightly. There is no lack of display and bravura here, but no ostentation. Indeed he has great poetic feeling and delicacy of colour, and Grieg's familiar warhorse comes up with great freshness. His piano is in perfect condition (not always the case on records) and is excellently balanced in relation to the orchestra. This is one of the best modern accounts.

The French pianist Pascal Devoyon has never enjoyed the recognition he so richly deserves on record. His account of the Grieg *Concerto* is characteristic of him: aristocratic without being aloof, pensive without being self-conscious, and brilliant without being flashy. He is a poetic artist whose natural musicianship shines through, and this excellent account is very competitive. This is a very fine issue, with excellent playing from the LPO under Jerzy Maksymiuk.

The sensitivity of Clifford Curzon in the recording studio is never in doubt and, like the Franck coupling, his 1959 account of the Grieg *Concerto* sounds as fresh as the day it was made. The sound is bright and open and the recording hardly shows its age in this crisply focused CD transfer. Curzon's approach to Grieg is wonderfully poetic and this is a performance with strength and power as well as lyrical tenderness. This ranks alongside Kovacevich and Perahia and the reading is second to none in distilling the music's special atmosphere.

Radu Lupu's recording dates from 1974 and is now even more brightly lit than it was originally, not entirely to advantage. But the performance is a fine one; there is both warmth and poetry in the slow movement; the hushed opening is particularly telling. The orchestral contribution under Previn is a strong one.

The famous 1947 Lipatti performance remains eternally fresh, and its return to the catalogue is a cause for rejoicing. Although the recording has greater clarity and definition, particularly at the top, put this CD alongside one of the LP transfers of the 1970s and the ear now notices a slightly drier quality and a marginal loss of bloom.

Ousset's is a strong, dramatic reading, not lacking in warmth and poetry but, paradoxically, bringing out what we would generally think of as the masculine qualities of power and drive. The result, with excellent accompaniment recorded in very full sound, is always fresh and convincing. A good choice for anyone wanting this unusual coupling with the Rachmaninov *Concerto No. 2*.

Margaret Fingerhut gives a thoughtful and musicianly reading that holds a fine balance between the virtuosic and poetic elements in the *Concerto*. Her first-movement cadenza shows tenderness as well as brilliance, as indeed does the slow movement. Only in the finale does she fall short of distinction (and, even so, the slow middle section has many felicitous touches). Vernon Handley makes a little too much of the *Peer Gynt suite*, which is occasionally somewhat overblown, but he gets generally sympathetic and responsive playing from the Ulster Orchestra and is well recorded.

Fleisher's performance of the Grieg ranks with the finest, combining strength with poetry in a satisfying balance. The Cleveland Orchestra gives a very positive accompaniment under Szell, with deeply expressive playing in the *Adagio*. There is plenty of sparkle in the outer movements. The recording is bold and clear – bordering on the fierce so far as the upfront orchestral presence is concerned – and tape-hiss seems more obtrusive than usual in the CD transfer.

Katchen's 1963 performance reissued at bargain price on Pickwick is strong and commanding, a minor touch of wilfulness tempered by a natural flexibility and a feeling for the work's poetry. Kertész provides plenty of life in the accompaniment, and the recording hardly sounds its age: indeed it has never sounded better than it does on CD, the sound vivid and spacious in Decca's more spectacular manner. An enjoyable and spontaneous, extrovert alternative to less assertive readings.

2 Elegiac melodies, Op. 34; Erotik; 2 Melodies, Op. 53; 2 Norwegian airs, Op. 63.
(BB) **(*) Naxos Dig. 8.550330; *4550330* [id.]. Capella Istropolitana, Adrian Leaper – SIBELIUS: *Andante festivo* etc. **

Adrian Leaper secures responsive and sensitive playing from the Capella Istropolitana in this Grieg collection and the recording is very good indeed, with the balance natural. There is the very slightest hint of glassiness from the upper strings, but not all systems would be troubled by this.

(i) *2 Elegiac melodies, Op. 34; Holberg suite, Op. 40;* (ii) *Peer Gynt* (incidental music): extended excerpts.
(B) **(*) Decca 433 614-2; *433 614-4* [id.]. (i) National PO, Boskovsky; (ii) RPO, Weller.

This is an attractive and generous (76 minutes) collection. Weller's is a purely orchestral selection from *Peer Gynt*, offering twelve key numbers, very positively characterized and showing the RPO in excellent form. *In the Hall of the Mountain King* is played with fine malignant gusto and *Solveig's cradle song* is touching. The 1978 analogue recording was of Decca's best quality and has lost only marginally in allure in its CD transfer. The Boskovsky items also sound fresh, but the somewhat athletic performances lack something in refinement; Boskovsky's rhythmic flair is less apparent here than in his home repertory.

Holberg suite, Op. 40.
*** DG Dig. 400 034-2 [id.]. BPO, Karajan – MOZART: *Eine kleine Nachtmusik;* PROKOFIEV: *Symphony No. 1.* ***
(B) *** Pickwick Dig. PCD 861; *CIMPC 861* [id.]. Serenata of London – ELGAR: *Serenade;* MOZART: *Eine kleine Nachtmusik.* ***

Karajan's performance of the *Holberg suite* is the finest currently available. The playing has a wonderful lightness and delicacy, with cultured phrasing not robbing the music of its immediacy. There are many subtleties of colour and texture revealed here by the clear yet full digital sound with its firm bass-line.

The performance by the Serenata of London is first class in every way, spontaneous, naturally paced and played with considerable eloquence. The digital recording is most realistic and very naturally balanced. A bargain.

Lyric suite, Op. 54; Norwegian dances, Op. 35; Symphonic dances, Op. 64.
*** DG Dig. 419 431-2 [id.]. Gothenburg SO, Järvi.

Excellent playing from the Gothenburg orchestra under Neeme Järvi. He secures light and transparent textures and finely balanced sonorities throughout. His *Lyric suite* includes *Klokkeklang* ('Bell-ringing'); taken rather slowly, it sounds far more atmospheric than in the piano version, where it is placed last. Very fine, wide-ranging recording, which makes excellent use of the celebrated acoustic of this orchestra's hall.

Lyric suite, Op. 54; Sigurd Jorsalfar (suite), Op. 56; Symphonic dances, Op. 64.
**(*) ASV Dig. CDDCA 722; *ZCDCA 722* [id.]. RPO, Yondani Butt.

The *Symphonic dances* are particularly successful here. They are not easy to bring off, yet Butt and the RPO capture their charm and energy without succumbing to melodrama in No. 4. The *Lyric suite*, too, is fresh and the trolls in the finale have an earthy pungency. However, the outer movements of *Sigurd Jorsalfar* are less successful, with an element of ponderousness. One can too easily overdo the homage in the *Homage march*. Excellent, vivid recording with a nice degree of resonance.

Symphony in C; In Autumn: Overture, Op. 11; Old Norwegian melody with variations, Op. 51; Funeral march in memory of Rikard Nordraak.

*** DG Dig. 427 321-2 [id.]. Gothenburg SO, Järvi.

This is the best recording of the Grieg *Symphony* to appear so far, both as a performance and as a recording. Indeed Järvi produces excellent, fresh accounts of all four works on the disc. Enterprisingly, he includes the orchestral transcription of the Op. 51 *Variations for two pianos* and the arrangement for wind of the *Funeral march for Nordraak*. Most natural and unaffected performances, beautifully balanced.

CHAMBER MUSIC

Cello sonata in A min., Op. 36.

*** Claves CD 50-703 [CD 703]. Claude Starck, Ricardo Requejo – CHOPIN: *Cello sonata.* ***

**(*) CRD CRD 3391 [id.]. Robert Cohen, Roger Vignoles – FRANCK: *Cello sonata.* **(*)

The Grieg *Sonata* is gratefully written for both instruments. Its slow movement is related to the *Homage march* from *Sigurd Jorsalfar*, and the work undoubtedly enriches the cellist's relatively small repertoire. Both Starck and his Spanish partner play with a superb and compelling artistry.

With his clean, incisive style Cohen gives a strong performance of the rarely heard Grieg *Sonata*, sensitively accompanied by Roger Vignoles. In the folk element Cohen might have adopted a more persuasive style, bringing out the charm of the music more, but certainly he sustains the sonata structures well. The last movement is one of Grieg's most expansive. The recording lacks a little in range at both ends of the spectrum but presents the cello very convincingly. It has been most naturally transferred to CD.

String quartet in G min., Op. 27.

** Ph. Dig. 426 286-2 [id.]. Guarneri Qt – SIBELIUS: *Quartet.* **

Grieg's only *Quartet* (apart from a later, unfinished work in two movements) comes from 1878, two years after the first production of *Peer Gynt*, and gave him much trouble. It is cyclic. A theme from his Op. 25 Ibsen setting of *Spillemaend* ('Fiddlers') serves as a unifying motive and also provided a model for Debussy's *Quartet* in the same key. The Guarneri play with splendid ensemble and unanimity but without the fresh innocence and charm this composer ideally calls for. At present there is no CD alternative, and there can be no quarrels with the recording; but it is probably wiser to wait until a more enjoyable performance comes along.

(i) *Violin sonata No. 3 in C min., Op. 45. Lyric pieces: Arietta, Op. 12/1; Berceuse, Op. 38/1; Cradle song, Op. 68/5; Little bird, Op. 43/4; Remembrances, Op. 71/7.*

(BB) **(*) Naxos Dig. 8.550417 [id.]. (i) Takako Nishizaki; Jenö Jandó – FRANCK: *Violin sonata.* **

Takako Nishizaki and her Hungarian partner give a very spirited and vital account of the *Sonata* that is thoroughly enjoyable and very recommendable, given the modest outlay involved. But Jandó proves a most sensitive player in the middle movement. In the *Lyric pieces*, which are heard in transcriptions by Vladimir Godar, the balance is quite different, placing the soloist closer to the microphone.

Ballade, Op. 24; 4 Lyric Pieces: March of the dwarfs; Notturno, Op. 54/3–4; Wedding day at Troldhaugen, Op. 65/6; Peace of the woods, Op. 71/4. Sonata in E min., Op. 7; arr. of songs: *Cradle song; I love thee; The princess; You cannot grasp the wave's eternal course. Peer Gynt: Solveig's song.*

**(*) Olympia OCD 197 [id.]. Peter Katin.

The *Sonata* is not one of Grieg's finest works, but it has a touching *Andante* and is agreeably inventive, if perhaps conventionally so. Katin gives it a clean, direct performance, and he is impressive in the rather dolorous set of variations which forms the *Ballade*. The song arrangements, too, come off well, and the four *Lyric pieces* are presented very appealingly, if without quite the distinction of the much-praised Gilels recital devoted entirely to these works.

Lyric pieces, Books 1–10 (complete).

(M) **(*) Unicorn Dig. UKCD 2033, *UKC 2033* (1–4); UKCD 2034, *UKC 2034* (5–7); UKCD 2035, *UKC 2035* (8–10) [id.]. Peter Katin.

Peter Katin is a persuasive and sensitive exponent of this repertoire, and he has the benefit of a recording of exceptional presence and clarity (though very occasionally it seems to harden in climaxes, when one notices that the microphone is perhaps a shade close). Katin has the measure of Grieg's sensibility and characterizes these pieces with real poetic feeling. His performances are by far the most sensitive and idiomatic survey of the complete set at present on offer.

Lyric pieces: Op. 12/1; Op. 38/1; Op. 43/1–2; Op. 47/2–4; Op. 54/4–5; Op. 57/6; Op. 62/4 and 6; Op. 68/2, 3 and 5; Op. 71/1, 3 and 6–7.
❀ *** DG 419 749-2 [id.]. Emil Gilels.

A generous selection of Grieg's *Lyric pieces*, from the well-known *Papillon*, Op. 43/1, to the less often heard and highly poetic set, Op. 71, written at the turn of the century. With Gilels we are in the presence of a great keyboard master whose characterization and control of colour and articulation are wholly remarkable. An altogether outstanding record in every way. The CD has brought a rather soft-focused piano sound, but the result is ideal for this repertoire.

VOCAL MUSIC

Landkjenning (Recognition of Land): cantata, Op. 31; Olav Trygvason (operatic fragments), *Op. 50:* Scenes 1–3. *Peer Gynt*, Act V: Choral scenes.
(M) *** Unicorn UKCD 2056 [id.]. Hanssen, Hansli, Carlsen, Olso Philharmonic Ch., LSO, Per Dreier.

Grieg was at the height of his fame when these excerpts from *Olav Trygvason* first saw the light of day in 1888. Olav was the Norwegian king (995–1000) who converted his pagan countrymen to Christianity; and these three scenes scored a great success at their first performance. But neither they nor *Landkjenning*, an earlier cantata that portrays the Norwegian king sighting land as he returns from his travels to claim the throne, is vintage Grieg, though as always there are some appealing ideas, particularly in the third scene of *Olav*. The cantata was originally written for organ and was scored some years later. The Norwegian soloists and chorus respond in exemplary fashion to Per Drier – indeed the choral contribution is quite thrilling in its impact, helped by the recording's dramatic range of dynamic. There is also sensitive and idiomatic playing from the LSO. The recording is naturally focused within a convincing perspective, and the CD transfer has undoubtedly enhanced what was originally (in 1978) a most succesful sound-balance in All Saints', Tooting. For a bonus the CD offers three scenes from Act V of *Peer Gynt* for soprano (the admirable Toril Carlsen), chorus and orchestra, *Night scene*, the brief *a cappella* sequence of *Churchgoers singing on the forest path* and the lovely *Solveig's lullaby*. This is Grieg at his most lyrically inspired. Readers with a special interest in this eternally fresh composer need not hesitate.

Peer Gynt (incidental music), *Op. 23* (complete).
(M) *** Unicorn UKCD 2003/4 [id.]. Carlson, Hanssen, Björköy, Hansli, Oslo PO Ch., LSO, Dreier.

Per Dreier achieves very spirited results from his soloists, the Oslo Philharmonic Chorus and our own LSO, with some especially beautiful playing from the woodwind; the recording is generally first class, with a natural perspective between soloists, chorus and orchestra. The Unicorn set includes 32 numbers in all, including Robert Henrique's scoring of the *Three Norwegian dances*, following the revised version of the score Grieg prepared for the 1886 production in Copenhagen. This music, whether familiar or unfamiliar, continues to astonish by its freshness and inexhaustibility.

Peer Gynt (incidental music), *Op. 23* (complete); *Sigurd Jorsalfar* (incidental music), *Op. 56* (complete).
*** DG Dig. 423 079-2 (2) [id.]. Bonney, Eklöf, Sandve, Malmberg, Holmgren; Foss, Maurstad, Stokke (speakers); Gösta Ohlin's Vocal Ens., Pro Musica Chamber Ch., Gothenburg SO, Järvi.

Neeme Järvi's recording differs from its predecessor by Per Dreier in offering the Grieg Gesamtausgabe *Peer Gynt*, which bases itself primarily on the twenty-six pieces he included in the 1875 production rather than the final published score, prepared after Grieg's death by Halvorsen. This well-documented set comes closer to the original by including spoken dialogue, as one would have expected in the theatre. The CDs also offer the complete *Sigurd Jorsalfar* score, which includes some splendid music. The performances by actors, singers (solo and choral) and orchestra alike are exceptionally vivid, with the warm Gothenburg ambience used to creative effect; the vibrant histrionics of the spoken words undoubtedly add to the drama.

Peer Gynt: extended excerpts.
*** DG Dig. 427 325-2 [id.]. Bonney, Eklöf, Malmberg, Maurstad, Foss, Gothenburg Ch. & SO, Järvi.
*** Decca Dig. 425 448-2 [id.]. Urban Malmberg, Mari-Ann Haeggander, San Francisco Ch. & SO, Blomstedt.
*** Sony Dig. MK 44528 [id.]. Hendricks, Oslo PO, Salonen.

(i) *Peer Gynt:* extended excerpts; (ii) *Holberg suite, Op. 40.*
(M) ** Ph. 432 192-2; *432 192-4* [id.]. (i) Ameling, San Francisco SO, De Waart; (ii) ASMF, Marriner.

Neeme Järvi's disc offers more than two-thirds of the 1875 score, and the performance has special claims on the collector who wants one CD rather than two (half the second CD of the set is taken up by *Sigurd Jorsalfar*).

Decca's set of excerpts makes a useful alternative to the Järvi disc. All but about 15 minutes of the complete score is here and the spoken text is included too, all admirably performed. Perhaps the Gothenburg acoustic is to be preferred to the Davies Hall, San Francisco, and there is a marginally greater sense of theatre in the Swedish account. However, there is really not much to choose between them, and the Decca recording approaches the demonstration class.

Salonen's selection is generous too, offering some seventeen numbers: all those included in the suites plus one or two more than have previously been included in single-disc highlights. Anyone investing in this version with Barbara Hendricks and the Oslo Philharmonic is unlikely to be disappointed.

The front of the De Waart/Philips record describes the contents as *Peer Gynt suites Nos. 1 and 2.* Their content is, of course included, but the selection is much fuller than that, with 12 items altogether. The *Wedding march* is not included, but the brief, unaccompanied choral piece, *Song of the churchgoers*, is. The performances are warmly sympathetic with sound to match – not especially brilliant. Marriner's *Holberg suite* is even more beautifully recorded, with plenty of air round the string textures and a natural balance. However the performance is less distinguished. Brisk tempi in the odd-numbered movements (with even a sense of hurry in the *Gavotte*) are not balanced by a compatrable serenity in the *Sarabande* and *Air*, although the account of the latter is not without eloquence. The playing itself is fresh and committed, but overall this reissue remains slightly disappointing. There is no documentation, except for a list of titles.

(i) *Peer Gynt: excerpts. Overture: In Autumn, Op. 11; Symphonic dance No. 2.*
(M) *** EMI CDM7 69039-2 [id.]. (i) Ilse Hollweg, Beecham Ch. Soc.; RPO, Beecham.

Beecham showed a very special feeling for this score, and to hear *Morning*, the gently textured *Anitra's dance*, or the eloquent portrayal of the *Death of Aase* under his baton is a uniquely rewarding experience. Ilse Hollweg makes an excellent soloist. The recording dates from 1957 and, like most earlier Beecham reissues, has been enhanced by the remastering process. The most delectable of the *Symphonic dances*, very beautifully played, makes an ideal encore after *Solveig's lullaby*, affectingly sung by Hollweg. The final item, the *Overture In Autumn*, not one of Grieg's finest works, is most enjoyable when Sir Thomas is so affectionately persuasive.

Peer Gynt (incidental music): *Overture; Suites 1–2. Lyric pieces: Evening in the mountain; Cradle song, Op. 68/5; Sigurd Jorsalfar: suite, Op. 56; Wedding day at Troldhaugen, Op. 65/6.*
(BB) **(*) Naxos Dig. 8.550140; *4550140* [id.]. CSSR State PO, Košice, Stephen Gunzenhauser.

A generous Grieg anthology on Naxos (70 minutes, all but 3 seconds) and the performances by the Slovak State Philharmonic Orchestra in Košice (in Eastern Slovakia) are very fresh and lively and thoroughly enjoyable. There is wide dynamic range both in the playing and in the recording, and sensitivity in matters of phrasing. Their American conductor, Stephen Gunzenhauser, gets very good results and, though there may be more sumptuous recordings at full price, the sound is really very good indeed.

Peer Gynt: (i) *Suite No. 1, Op. 46;* (ii) *Suite No. 2, Op. 55.*
*** DG Dig. 410 026-2 [id.]. BPO, Karajan – SIBELIUS: *Pelléas et Mélisande.* ***

Peer Gynt: suites Nos. 1 & 2; Holberg suite; Sigurd Jorsalfar: suite.
(M) *** DG 419 474-2; *419 474-4* [id.]. BPO, Karajan.

Grieg's perennially fresh score is marvellously played in Karajan's digital recording, though there are small differences between this and his earlier DG version with the same orchestra:

Anitra danced with greater allure though no less elegance in 1972 and there was greater simplicity and repose in *Aase's Death*. The digital recording is one of the best to have emerged from the Berlin Philharmonie.

Karajan's analogue set remains available on a mid-priced DG CD, where the highly expressive performances were played with superlative skill and polish. There is a touch of fierceness on the *Sigurd Jorsalfar* climaxes, but otherwise these performances are given good sound.

(i) *Peer Gynt: suites Nos. 1–2. Lyric suite, Op. 54; Sigurd Jorsalfar: suite.*
(M) *** DG Dig. 427 807-2; *427 807-4* [id.]. (i) Soloists, Ch.; Gothenburg SO, Järvi.

Järvi's excerpts from *Peer Gynt* and *Sigurd Jorsalfar* are extracted from his complete sets, so the editing inevitably produces a less tidy effect than normal recordings of the *Suites*. However, the performances are first class and so is the recording, and this comment applies also to the *Lyric suite*, taken from an earlier, digital orchestral collection.

4 Psalms, Op. 74.
**(*) Nimbus Dig. NI 5171 [id.]. Håkan Hagegård, Oslo Cathedral Ch., Terje Kvam – MENDELSSOHN: *3 Psalms*. **(*)

The *Four Psalms* are based on old Norwegian church melodies. They are rarely heard except on the radio and are dignified, beautiful pieces, very well sung here by the choir and the Swedish baritone, Håkan Hagegård. The recording is eminently faithful, though the pauses between the Psalms are not long enough and, at under 45 minutes, this CD offers short measure.

(i) *Sigurd Jorsalfar, Op. 22: incidental music; Funeral march in memory of Rikard Nordraak* (orch. Halvorsen); (i) *The Mountain spell, Op. 32.*
(M) *** Unicorn UKCD 2019. (i) Kåre Björköy; Oslo Philharmonic Ch., LSO, Per Dreier.

Grieg's *Sigurd Jorsalfar* comprised five movements in all, from which Grieg drew the familiar suite; but there were additional sections as well, most importantly the moving *Funeral march* in memory of Nordraak. Even though it does not claim to be a first recording, *Den Bergtekne* ('The Mountain spell') for baritone, strings and two horns is something of a rarity. *The Mountain spell* (or 'thrall', as it is sometimes translated) is somewhat later than *Sigurd Jorsalfar* and was one of Grieg's favourite pieces. It is a song of great beauty, and is alone worth the price of the CD. The Oslo Philharmonic Choir give a spirited account of themselves, as do the LSO, who play sensitively for Per Dreier. Kåre Björköy is an excellent soloist with well-focused tone. The recording is very good indeed and the perspective is agreeably natural.

Griffes, Charles (1884–1920)

(i) *The Pleasure Dome of Kubla Khan, Op. 8;* (ii) *3 Tone pictures, Op. 5;* (ii; iii) *3 Poems of Fiona Macleod;* (iv) *4 German songs; 4 Impressions; Song of the Dagger.*
** New World NW 273/4 [id.]. (i) Boston SO; (ii) New World CO; Ozawa; (iii) with P. Bryn-Julson; (iv) Stapp, Milnes, Richardson, Spong.

Charles Griffes studied in Berlin with Humperdinck, who persuaded him to concentrate on composition rather than pursue a career as a concert pianist. His early works are Brahmsian but he soon succumbed to the influence of the Russians and Debussy. He wrote most of his music in the free time left over from his teaching at Hackley School in Tarrytown, New York. He was a gifted artist in watercolour and made some fine etchings in copper. The four *German songs* come from the early years of the century when he was much influenced by Brahms; they are well sung here by Sherrill Milnes, but the four *Impressions* (1912–16) are less well served. Ozawa's performance of *The Pleasure Dome* lacks something of the warmth of the old RCA version with Charles Gerhardt but it conveys much of the work's strong atmosphere. By far the most persuasive performance comes from Phyllis Bryn-Julson in the Op. 11 settings of Fiona Macleod. The recordings date from the 1970s and are eminently acceptable.

Fantasy pieces; Legend; The Pleasure Dome of Kubla Khan; 3 Preludes; Rhapsody in B min.; Sonata; 3 Tone pictures.
** Kingdom Dig. KCLCD 2011 [id.]. James Tocco.

The *Sonata* is the most radical and expressionistic work here and *The Pleasure Dome of Kubla Khan* the best known. Like *The White Peacock*, it began life as a piano piece, though it is a little too congested to make its best effect. Griffes was obviously an accomplished pianist (he had originally planned a solo career) and his music makes considerable demands on the performer. The most interesting pieces are the three late *Preludes* (1919), which have a keen sense of mystery and concentration. So, too, have the three *Tone pictures*. James Tocco plays with insight and sensitivity; he meets the virtuoso demands of the *Sonata* and is keenly responsive to the dynamic nuances of these scores. He is not well served by the acoustic, which has far too little space round the aural image and as a result proves tiring on the ear. All the same, such is the interest of the music and the quality of the playing that this shortcoming should not be exaggerated.

Grofé, Ferde (1892–1972)

Grand Canyon suite.
(M) *** Decca 430 712-2; *430 712-4* [id.]. Detroit SO, Dorati – GERSHWIN: *Porgy and Bess.* ***
*** Telarc Dig. CD 80086 [id.] (with additional cloudburst, including real thunder). Cincinnati Pops O, Kunzel – GERSHWIN: *Catfish Row.* ***

Antal Dorati has the advantage of superlative Decca recording, very much in the demonstration class, with stereoscopically vivid detail. Yet the performance combines subtlety with spectacle, and on CD the naturalness of the orchestral sound-picture adds to the sense of spaciousness and tangibility. With its outstanding coupling, and its price advantage, this version is very much in a class of its own.

The Cincinnati performance is played with great commitment and fine pictorial splendour, although Dorati scores at *Sunrise*, where his powerful timpani strokes add to the power of the climax, while at the opening of *Sunset* the Detroit strings have greater body and richness. Yet the Cincinnati *On the trail* has fine rhythmic point and piquant colouring. What gives the Telarc CD its special edge is the inclusion of a second performance of *Cloudburst* as an appendix. Over a period of five years the Telarc engineers had been recording genuine thunderstorms in both Utah and Arizona, and an edited version of their most spectacular successes is laminated into the orchestral recording. The result is overwhelmingly thrilling, except that in the final thunderclap God quite upstages the orchestra, who are left trying frenziedly to match its amplitude in their closing peroration.

Hahn, Reynaldo (1875–1947)

Le bal de Béatrice d'Este (ballet suite).
*** Hyp. Dig. CDA 66347; *KA 66347* [id.]. New London O, Ronald Corp – POULENC: *Aubade; Sinfonietta.* ***

Le bal de Béatrice d'Este is a rather charming pastiche, dating from the early years of the century and scored for the unusual combination of wind instruments, two harps, piano and timpani. It is dedicated to Saint-Saëns and evokes an evening in the palazzo of an Italian noblewoman. Ronald Corp and the New London Orchestra play it with real panache and sensitivity.

Songs: *À Chloris; L'Air; L'Automne; 7 Chansons Grises; La chère blessuré; D'une prison; L'enamourée; Les étoiles; Fêtes galantes; Les fontaines; L'Incrédule; Infidélité; Offrande; Quand je fus pris au pavillon; Si mes vers avaient des ailes; Tyndaris.*
**(*) Hyp. CDA 66045 [id.]. Hill, Johnson.

It is partly because swift or brisk songs are so few here that the classical pastiches of *Chloris* and *Quand je fus pris au pavillon* come as quite a refreshment. If Hahn never quite matched the supreme inspiration of his most famous song, *Si mes vers avaient des ailes*, the delights here are many, the charm great. Martyn Hill, ideally accompanied by Graham Johnson, modifies his very English-sounding tenor to give delicate and stylish performances, well recorded. There is a touch of pallor about this singing, but in general it suits the music.

Halévy, Jacques Fromental (1799–1862)

La juive (opera): complete.
*** Ph. Dig. 420 190-2 (3). Varady, Anderson, Carreras, Gonzalez, Furlanetto, Amb. Op. Ch., Philh. O, Almeida.

La juive (The Jewess), was the piece which, along with the vast works of Meyerbeer, set the pattern for the epic French opera, so popular last century. Eleazar was the last role that the great tenor, Enrico Caruso, tackled, and it was in this opera that he gave his very last performance. Yet in its entirety it was probably never performed on a single night, and the Philips recording is not absolutely complete, even if much more is included here than you will find in the published edition. The cuts are mainly of crowd scenes, drinking choruses and the like, many of which simply hold up the action. As it is, over three hours of music on three CDs makes an attractive package. The greater part of the recording was completed in 1986, but that was just at the time when José Carreras was diagnosed as having leukaemia. The recording was made without him, and it was only in 1989 that he contributed his performance through 'overdubbing'. It is a tribute to the Philips engineers that the results rarely if ever betray that deception, sounding naturally balanced even when Carreras is contributing to the many complex ensembles. He sings astonishingly well, but the role of the old Jewish father really needs a weightier, darker voice, such as Caruso had in his last years. Julia Varady as Rachel makes that role both the emotional and the musical centre of the opera, responding both tenderly and positively. In the other soprano role, that of the Princess Eudoxia, June Anderson is not so full or sweet in tone, but she is particularly impressive in the dramatic coloratura passages, such as her Act III *Boléro*. Ferruccio Furlanetto makes a splendidly resonant Cardinal in his two big solos, and the Ambrosian Opera Chorus brings comparable bite to the powerful ensembles. Antonio de Almeida as conductor proves a dedicated advocate. As a massive music-drama, this is at least as impressive and moving as anything Meyerbeer wrote. As a recording, it is a formidable achievement.

Halvorsen, Johan (1864–1935)

Air Norvégien, Op. 7; Danses Norvégiennes.
(BB) *** Naxos Dig. 8.550329 [id.]. Dong-Suk Kang, Slovak (Bratislava) RSO, Adrian Leaper – SIBELIUS: *Violin concerto;* SINDING: *Légende;* SVENDSEN: *Romance.* ***

Dong-Suk Kang plays the attractive *Danses Norvégiennes* with great panache, character and effortless virtuosity, and delivers an equally impeccable performance of the earlier *Air Norvégien.*

Handel, George Frideric (1685–1759)

Ballet music: *Alcina: overture; Acts I & III: suites. Il pastor fido: suite. Terpsichore: suite.*
(M) *** Erato/Warner Dig. 2292 45378-2 [id.]. E. Bar. Soloists, Gardiner.

Alcina contains a high proportion of lyrical music and the expressive writing here is very appealing; so is the scoring with its felicitous use of recorders. John Eliot Gardiner is just the man for such a programme. He is not afraid to charm the ear, yet allegros are vigorous and rhythmically infectious. The bright and clean recorded sound adds to the sparkle, and the quality is first class. A delightful collection, and very tuneful too.

Amaryllis (suite): *Gavotte; Scherzo. The Gods go a-begging* (ballet): suite. *The Great elopement: Serenade.* (i) *Love in Bath* (complete).
(M) *** EMI CDM7 63374-2; *EG 763374-4*. RPO, Sir Thomas Beecham, (i) with Ilse Hollweg.

This delightful CD collects together many of Beecham's most famous Handel arrangements and – unless you are an out-and-out purist – the result is irresistible. The new name, *Love in Bath*, in fact conceals the identity of Beecham's intended ballet, *The Great elopement*. The earlier ballet, *The Gods go a-begging*, was produced for the stage with choreography by Balanchine, and nine of its eleven numbers are included here; its delectable woodwind scoring is a special feature. Needless to say, the Royal Philharmonic play like angels – if occasionally not perfectly disciplined angels! – and the originally mellow sound has been freshly remastered with great skill: there is greater transparency and little loss of bloom.

Concerto grosso in C (Alexander's Feast); Oboe concertos Nos. 1–2; Organ concerto in D min.; Sonata a 5 in B flat.
(M) **(*) Teldec/Warner 2292 43032-2 [id.]. Schaeftlein, Tachezi, VCM, Harnoncourt.

Jurg Schaeftlein is a fine oboist, but he omits the third concerto (HWV 287) in favour of Herbert Tachezi's spirited performance of a fairly attractive hybrid organ concerto, based on a sonata from the first set of Telemann's *Tafelmusik*. Alice Harnoncourt is the third soloist in the *Sonata a 5*. Good performances, all well recorded and cleanly transferred to CD.

Concerto grosso in C (Alexander's Feast); Oboe concertos Nos. 1–3; Sonata a 5 in B flat.
*** DG Dig. 415 291-2 [id.]. E. Concert, Pinnock.

Rhythms are sprightly, and Pinnock's performance of the *Alexander's Feast concerto* has both vitality and imagination and is as good as any now available. The *B flat Sonata* (HWV 288) is to all intents and purposes a concerto, and it is given with great sensitivity and taste by Simon Standage and his colleagues. David Reichenberg is the excellent soloist in the *Oboe concertos*. Excellently balanced and truthful recording, but the record could have been filled more generously.

Concerti grossi, Op. 3/1–6.
*** DG 413 727-2 [id.]. E. Concert, Pinnock.
*** Ph. Dig. 411 482-2 [id.]. ASMF, Marriner.
(M) *** Ph. 422 487-2; *422 487-4*. ECO, Leppard.

Concerti grossi, Op. 3/1–6; Overtures: Alcina; Ariodante.
(M) *** Decca 430 261-2; *430 261-4* [id.]. ASMF, Sir Neville Marriner.

The six Op. 3 *Concertos* with their sequences of brief jewels of movements find Pinnock and the English Concert at their freshest and liveliest, with plenty of sparkle and little of the abrasiveness associated with 'authentic' performance. For a version on period instruments, this could hardly be better, with its realistic, well-balanced sound. The playing has breadth as well as charm.

In Sir Neville Marriner's latest version with the Academy, tempi tend to be a little brisk, but the results are inspiring and enjoyable. The continuo is divided between organ and harpsichord, though the latter is reticently balanced. Not unexpectedly, textures are fuller here than on Pinnock's competing Archiv recording, and the CD quality is admirably fresh.

Marriner's earlier (1964) Argo set, now reappearing on Decca's Serenata label, remains fully competitive (irrespective of price) for musical scholarship and, what is even more to the point, for musical expressiveness and spontaneity. Flutes and oboes are employed as Handel intended and the final concerto features the organ as a solo instrument, very much conjuring up the composer's spirit hovering in the background. The ASMF was in peak form when this recording was made and the sound is very well balanced and vivid. The two overtures, recorded a decade later, make an acceptable bonus.

Among budget versions of Handel's Op. 3, Leppard's set also stands high. The playing is lively and fresh, and the remastered recording sounds very good. Leppard includes oboes and bassoons and secures excellent playing all round. At times one wonders whether he isn't just a shade too elegant, but in general this CD offers one of the best versions of Op. 3 on modern instruments.

12 Concerti grossi, Op. 6/1–12.
❀ *** Chan. Dig. CHAN 9004/6 [id.]. I Musici de Montréal, Yuli Turovsky.
*** Ph. Dig. 410 048-2 (3) [id.]. ASMF, Iona Brown.
**(*) DG Dig. 410 897-2 (1–4); 410 898-2 (5–8); 410 899-2 (9–12) [id.]. E. Concert, Pinnock.
(M) **(*) Ph. 426 465-2; *426 465-4* (3). ECO, Leppard.
**(*) BMG/RCA Dig. RD 87895 [7895-2-RC] (*Nos. 1–4*); RD 87907 [7907-2-RC] (*Nos. 5–8*); RD 87921 [7921-2-RC] (*Nos. 9–12*). Guildhall String Ens., Robert Salter.

A refreshing and stimulating new set of Handel's Opus 6 – the high water mark of Baroque orchestral music – from Montreal. The group uses modern instruments, and the very first concerto immediately shows the exhilarating vigour and vitality of the playing and demonstrates Yuli Turovsky's worthy aim to seek a compromise between modern and authentic practice, by paring down vibrato in some of the expressive music, with just a hint of squeezing on the melodic line, as when the solo group make their restrained entry in the slow movement. This approach also comes off especially well in the *Largo e piano* of No. 4 and even more so in the closing minuet of No. 5 (*Un poco larghetto*) played simply and lightly. Indeed No. 5 as presented here, with enormous character, might be counted the finest of the twelve with tinglingly animated allegros – the interplay of the central *Presto* is wonderfully crisp in articulation – and the following slow movement sounding poignantly ethereal with its spare texture. The pointed, almost staccato treatment of the famous *Larghetto e piano* movement of No. 12 – one of the composer's most famous tunes – might be counted more controversial, but many will like Turovsky's light touch and gentle grace. The concertino, Eleonora and Natalya Turovsky and Alain Aubut, play impressively, although Catherinne Perrin's harpsichord continuo has a rather recessive profile. The main group (6,3,1,1) produces full, well-balanced tone and Handel's joyous fugues are particularly fresh and buoyant. Ideally one would have liked rather more dynamic contrast between the solo group and the ripieno, but the sound is full-bodied and vividly real. Turovsky paces convincingly and, while not missing Handel's breadth of sonority and moments of expressive grandeur, he achieves a convincing sense of period. This now becomes our first choice for this wonderful music and takes over our Rosette from the ASMF, which remains a distinguished alternative choice.

The young Iona Brown participated at Marriner's late-1960s recording sessions, but the new readings have many new insights to offer and Miss Brown sets her own personality firmly on the proceedings. In the expressive music (and there are some memorable Handelian tunes here) she is freer, warmer and more spacious than Marriner. Where allegros are differently paced, they are often slightly slower, yet the superbly crisp articulation and the rhythmic resilience of the playing always bring added sparkle. On recording grounds, the Philips set gains considerably: the sound is fuller and fresher and more transparent. The contrast between the solo group and the ripieno is even more tangible. This can be recommended strongly.

In his pursuit of authentic performance on original instruments, Pinnock finds a fair compromise between severe principle and sweetened practice. For all its 'authenticity', this is never unresponsive music-making, with fine solo playing set against an attractively atmospheric acoustic. Ornamentation is often elaborate – but never at the expense of line. These are performances to admire and to sample, but not everyone will warm to them. If listened through, the sharp-edged sound eventually tends to tire the ear, and there is comparatively little sense of grandeur and few hints of tonally expansive beauty. The recording is first class and each of the three CDs is available separately.

Leppard's 1967 set sounds splendid in its newly remastered format, not in the least dated. The main group is comparatively full-bodied, which means that his soloists stand out in greater relief. There is grace and elegance here, but rather less gravitas than with Iona Brown and the ASMF. These performances, too, have plenty of spirit and lively rhythmic feeling, while the richer orchestral texture brings added breadth in slow movements. With the sound newly minted, this is excellent value at mid-price, though Leslie Pearson's harpsichord continuo is dwarfed by the tuttis.

The Guildhall String Ensemble offer fresh, modestly scaled performances, with plenty of life about them. Although modern instruments are used, textures are lighter, more transparent, than those of the ASMF. The effect is very real and tangible, with the soloists nicely separated from the ripieno, although their forward balance means that there is not the degree of dynamic contrast that Handel obviously intended. However, tempi are generally apt, and this music-making has a buoyantly rhythmic sparkle and a nicely balanced espressivo feeling in Handel's songful slow movements.

Harp concerto in B flat, Op. 4/5.
(B) *** DG 427 206-2. Zabaleta, Paul Kuentz CO – MOZART: *Flute and harp concerto;* WAGENSEIL: *Harp concerto.* ***

(i) *Harp concerto, Op. 4/6. Variations for harp.*
❀ (M) *** Decca 425 723-2; *425 723-4.* Marisa Robles, (i) ASMF, Iona Brown – BOIELDIEU; DITTERSDORF: *Harp concertos* etc. *** ❀

Handel's Op. 4/6 is well known in both organ and harp versions. Marisa Robles and Iona Brown make an unforgettable case for the latter by creating the most delightful textures, while never letting the work sound insubstantial. The ASMF accompaniment, so stylish and beautifully balanced, is a treat in itself, and the recording is well-nigh perfect. This collection (which also includes solo harp variations by Beethoven and a set attributed to Mozart) amounts to a good deal more than the sum of its parts.

The DG recording sounds clear and immediate and the crystalline stream of sound is attractive. Zabaleta's approach is agreeably cool, with imaginative use of light and shade. The Privilege reissue also includes a set of variations by Spohr.

Oboe concertos Nos 1–3, HWV 301, 302a & 287; Concerto grosso, Op. 3/3; Hornpipe in D, HWV 356; Overture in D, HWV 337/8; Sonata a 5 in B flat, HWV 288.
(M) **(*) Ph. 426 082-2; *426 082-4* [id.]. Heinz Holliger, ECO, Raymond Leppard.

Holliger, being a creative artist as well as a masterly interpreter, does not hesitate to embellish repeats; his ornamentation may overstep the boundaries some listeners are prepared to accept. His playing and that of the other artists in this collection is exquisite, and the recording is naturally balanced and fresh.

Organ concertos, Op. 4/1–6; Op.7/1–6; Second set: Nos. 1 in F; 2 in A; Arnold edition: Nos. 1 in D; 2 in F.
❀ *** Erato/Warner Dig. 2292 45394-2 (3) [id.]. Ton Koopman, Amsterdam Bar. O.

Organ concertos, Op. 4/1–6; in A, HWV 296.
*** DG Dig. 413 465-2 (2) [id.]. Simon Preston, E. Concert, Pinnock.

Organ concertos, Op. 7/1–6; in F (The cuckoo and the nightingale); in D min., HWV 304.
*** DG Dig. 413 468-2 (2) [id.]. Simon Preston, E. Concert, Pinnock.

Organ concertos, Op. 4/1–6; in F (The cuckoo and the nightingale), HVW 295; in A, HWV 296; Sonata in D min. (Il trionfo del tempo a del disinganno), HWV 46a.
(M) *** Decca Dig. 430 569-2 (2). Peter Hurford, Concg. CO, Joshua Rifkin.

Organ concertos, Op. 7/1–6; in D min., HWV 304; in F, HWV 305 & Appendix.
(M) *** Decca Dig. 433 176-2 (2). Peter Hurford, Concg. CO, Rifkin.

It is good to have Ton Koopman's complete set of Handel's *Organ concertos* back in the catalogue. They take precedence over all the competition, both as performances and as recordings. The playing has wonderful life and warmth, tempi are always aptly judged and, although original instruments are used, this is authenticity with a kindly presence, for the warm acoustic ambience of St Bartholomew's Church, Beek-Ubbergen, Holland, gives the orchestra a glowingly vivid coloration, and the string timbre is particularly attractive. So is the organ itself, which is just right for the music. Ton Koopman plays imaginatively throughout and he is obviously enjoying himself: no single movement sounds tired and the orchestral fugues emerge with genial clarity. Koopman directs the accompanying group from the keyboard, as Handel would have done, and the interplay between soloist and ripieno is a delight. The sound is first class and the balance could hardly be better.

Simon Preston's set of the Handel *Organ concertos* comes in two separate packages. In the first, containing the six Op. 4 works, plus the *A major* (the old No. 14), though the balance of the solo instrument is not ideal, the playing of both Preston and the English Concert is admirably fresh and lively. Ursula Holliger is outstanding on a baroque harp in Op. 4, No. 6, and she creates some delicious sounds; however, it seems perverse not to include the organ version of this work, with the harp arrangement already available on other records. The second of the two boxes, containing the six Op. 7 works, plus the '*The cuckoo and the nightingale*' and the old *No. 15 in D minor*, was recorded on the organ at St John's, Armitage, in Staffordshire, and is even more attractive, not only for the extra delight of the works but for the warmth and assurance of the playing, which comes near the ideal for an 'authentic' performance. These are all recordings which positively invite re-hearing, with full, clear sound, all the fresher on CD.

Peter Hurford's 1985 Decca set also comes in two separate CD boxes and features the organ of Bethlehemkerk, Papendrecht, Holland, which has attractively fresh and bright registrations, particularly suited to the Op. 4 set. The highly engaging *The cuckoo and the nightingale concerto* is particularly successful – here Hurford interpolates a Telemann movement instead of improvising, as the composer would have done. The *Sonata* is also attractive and, with splendid recording, fresh and yet not lacking weight where needed, this is very enjoyable indeed. The sound is in the demonstration bracket, and this is highly recommendable. Peter Hurford's Op. 7 set has comparable sparkle, if not being quite as memorable as Op. 4. The effect (especially of the first four concertos) seems a little lightweight. But the digital recording is first class and the considerable bonuses are well worth having. Excellent value.

Organ concertos, Op. 4/1 & 2; Op. 7/1 & 2.
(M) ** Teldec/Warner 2292 43434-2 [id.]. Karl Richter with CO.

Organ concertos, Op. 4/3 & 4; Op. 7/3 & 4.
(M) *** Teldec/Warner 2292 43540-2 [id.]. Karl Richter with CO.

Organ concertos, Op. 4/5 & 6; Op. 7/5 & 6.
(M) *** Teldec/Warner 2292 42412-2 [id.]. Karl Richter with CO.

These Teldec recordings come from a complete set which Karl Richter recorded in 1959. The sound is surprisingly undated and the performances have the merit of exactly the right kind of organ (St Mark's, Munich) and a small, flexible orchestral group which Richter directs from the keyboard. The element of extemporization is a limited feature, at first, especially in Op. 4; but later, in Op. 7, organ *ad libs* are effectively included. Throughout, the playing is attractively buoyant; the full sound of the strings, contrasted with imaginative registration, makes this series increasingly attractive. The second and third discs can be recommended strongly.

Organ concertos, Op. 4/2; Op. 7/3–5; in F (The cuckoo and the nightingale).
(M) *** DG Dig. 431 708-2; *431 708-4* [id.]. Simon Preston, E. Concert, Pinnock.

This is more generous than the previous (full-price) sampler from Preston's series with Pinnock; all the Op. 7 works plus the *The cuckoo and the nightingale* are recorded on the organ at St John's, Armitage, in Staffordshire, which seems particularly well suited to this repertoire. Both performances and sound are admirably fresh.

Overtures: Admeto; Alcina; Ariodante; Esther; Lotario; Orlando; Ottone; Partenope; (i) *Il pastor fido; Poro.*
(M) *** Ph. 422 486-2. ECO or (i) New Philh. O, Leppard.

Overtures: Agrippina; Alceste; Il pastor fido; Samson; Saul (Acts I & II); Teseo.
*** DG Dig. 419 219-2 [id.]. E. Concert, Pinnock.

Trevor Pinnock directs vigorous, exhilarating performances of these Handel overtures, most of them hardly known at all but full of highly original ideas, even in the most formally structured pieces. All are freshly and cleanly recorded.

Characteristically elegant performances from Leppard, richly recorded. The orchestral playing is gracious and polished, and the recording is bright and well balanced.

Music for the Royal Fireworks (original wind scoring).
*** Telarc Dig. CD 80038 [id.]. Cleveland Symphonic Winds, Fennell – HOLST: *Military band suites.* *** ❀

Music for the Royal Fireworks; Concerto grosso in C (Alexander's Feast); Concerti grossi, Op. 6/1 & 6.
(M) *** DG 431 707-2; *431 707-4*. E. Concert, Trevor Pinnock.

Music for the Royal Fireworks (original version); (i) *Coronation anthems* (see also below).
*** Hyp. Dig. CDA 66350 [id.]. (i) New College, Oxford, Ch.; augmented King's Consort, Robert King.

In 1978, in Severance Hall, Cleveland, Ohio, Frederick Fennell gathered together the wind and brass from the Cleveland Symphony Orchestra and recorded a performance to demonstrate spectacularly what fine playing and digital sound could do for Handel's open-air score. The overall sound-balance tends to favour the brass (and the drums), but few will grumble when the result is as overwhelming as it is on the CD, with the sharpness of focus matched by the presence and amplitude of the sound-image.

Pinnock's performance of the *Fireworks music* has tremendous zest; this is not only the safest but the best recommendation for those wanting a period-instrument version. The account of the *Alexander's Feast concerto* has both vitality and imagination and is no less recommendable; for those who already have a complete set of Op. 6, yet who want to experience Pinnock's way with this music, the disc proves a useful sampler.

King provides the first ever period performance of Handel's *Royal fireworks music* to use the full complement of instruments Handel demanded. It was quite an achievement assembling no fewer than 24 baroque oboists ('foreman Paul Goodwin') and 12 baroque bassoonists, nine trumpeters, nine exponents of the hand horn and four timpanists. It all makes for a glorious noise, and for once the fill-up provides what is probably the main attraction. King's Handel style has plenty of rhythmic bounce, and the recording in its warmly atmospheric way gives ample scale. The coupled performances of the four *Coronation anthems* are not as incisively dramatic as some but still convey the joy of the inspiration.

Music for the Royal Fireworks; Water music (complete).
*** Argo 414 596-2 [id.]. ASMF, Marriner.
(BB) *** Naxos Dig. 8.550109; *4550109* [id.]. Capella Istropolitana, Bohdan Warchal.

Marriner directs a sparkling account of the complete *Water music*, using modern instruments. All the well-loved movements we once knew only in the Harty suite come out refreshed, and the rest is similarly stylish. Scholars may argue that textures are too thick; but for many listeners the sounds which reach the ears have a welcome freedom from acerbity. It is a substantial advantage that the CD (for the transfer is very successful) also includes the complete *Fireworks music* – unlike most of its rivals. Here Marriner deliberately avoids a weighty manner, even at the magisterial opening of the overture. But with full, resonant recording, this coupling makes sound sense and the remastered Argo recording still sounds both full and fresh.

Bohdan Warchal directs the Capella Istropolitana in bright and lively performances of the complete *Water music* as well as the *Fireworks music*, well paced and well scaled, with woodwind and brass aptly abrasive, and with such points as double-dotting faithfully observed. Textures are clean, with an attractive bloom on the full and immediate sound. As always with Naxos – but not with all bargain labels – first-rate notes are provided; but the listing of movements fails to distinguish the three separate *Water music* suites. However, this remains a strong bargain recommendation.

Music for the Royal Fireworks (complete); *Concerto a due cori No. 2 in F; Alexander's Feast: Overture; Concerto grosso. Jephtha: Overture; Sinfonia. Solomon: Overture; Arrival of the Queen of Sheba.*
(M) ** Ph. Dig. 434 154-2; *434 154-4* [id.]. E. Bar. Soloists, Gardiner.

John Eliot Gardiner secures an excellent response from his players, and as one would expect from this conductor, rhythms are alive and well articulated, and phrasing is always musical even if there are the usual string bulges. Wind intonation is good, though not always impeccable. In the *Fireworks music* the effect is robustly spectacular and there is some impressive hand horn playing in the *Concerto a due cori*. The other items come from sets: the *Alexander's Feast* items are rather drily recorded, but the *Queen of Sheba's* original dress is agreeably colourful and her pace is sprightly.

Music for the Royal Fireworks: suite; Water music; suite (arr. Harty and Szell); *The Faithful shepherd: Minuet* (ed. Beecham); *Xerxes: Largo* (arr. Reinhardt).
(B) *** Decca 417 694-2; *417 694-4*. LSO, Szell.

Many readers will, like us, have a nostalgic feeling for the Handel–Harty suites from which earlier generations got to know these two marvellous scores. George Szell and the LSO offer a highly recommendable coupling of them on a Decca lower-mid-priced issue, with Handel's *Largo* and the *Minuet* from Beecham's *Faithful shepherd suite* thrown in for good measure. The orchestral playing throughout is quite outstanding, and the strings are wonderfully expressive in the slower pieces. The horns excel, and the crisp new Decca re-transfer makes for a good bargain.

Water music: Suites Nos. 1–3 (complete).
*** DG Dig. 410 525-2 [id.]. E. Concert, Pinnock.
*** ASV Dig. CDDCA 520; *ZCDCA 520* [id.]. ECO, Malcolm.
**(*) Chan. Dig. CHAN 8382; *ABTD 1136* [id.]. Scottish CO, Gibson.
**(*) Delos Dig. D/CD 3010 [id.]. LAPO, Schwarz.

To offer the *Water music* without the *Fireworks music* now seems ungenerous but, for those collectors who already have the former, Pinnock's version on DG Archiv is very enticing. Speeds are consistently well chosen and are generally uncontroversial. One test is the famous *Air*, which here remains an engagingly gentle piece. The recording is beautifully balanced and clear, but with bloom on the sound to balance the CD presence.

Those whose taste does not extend to 'authentic' string textures should be well satisfied with George Malcolm's splendid digital recording for ASV. The playing is first class, articulation is deft and detail admirable. Decoration is nicely judged and the alertness of the music-making, combined with full, vivid sound, makes a strong impact. There is a sense of delight in the music which makes this version especially appealing.

Sir Alexander Gibson's pacing of the allegros is brisk and he points the rhythms with infectious zest. There is fine lyrical playing too, notably from the principal oboe, while the horns are robust. The combination of energy and warmth comes as a welcome relief after prolonged exposure to period instruments. The ample acoustic of the Glasgow City Hall is attractive and this is a very likeable performance which could well be a first choice for many readers.

The Los Angeles performance under Gerard Schwarz is hardly less enjoyable, its character more athletic, with playing that is both polished and sprightly. It has an attractive freshness of spirit, yet is without the abrasiveness of early-instrumental timbres. The sound is first class and the clear detail does not prevent an overall ambient warmth.

CHAMBER MUSIC

Flute sonatas, Op. 1/1b, 5, 6, 8 & 9; & in D. Oboe sonatas Op. 1/8; in B flat (Fitzwilliam); & in F min.
(M) *** HM/BMG Dig. GD 77152 [77152-2-RG]. Camerata Köln.

Recorder sonatas, Op. 1/2, 4, 7 & 11; Recorder sonatas in B flat; in D; in G (Fitzwilliam); Trio sonata in F.
(M) *** HM/BMG Dig. GD 77104 [77104-2-RG]. Camerata Köln.

Flute sonatas, Op. 1/1a; in D; in A min., E min., and B min. (Halle Nos. 1–3).
*** Ph. Dig. 412 606-2 [id.]. Bennett, Kraemer, Vigay.

These two CDs by the Camerata Köln playing on period instruments give very satisfying accounts of this repertoire. What accomplished players they are! The first disc is intelligently planned to give maximum variety of texture. The programme includes everything except Op. 1, No. 1a, an arrangement – not by Handel himself – of No. 1b. Not only is the playing rewarding, but the quality of the 1985 sound has exemplary clarity, yet warmth too.

William Bennett's compact disc comprises the three *Halle sonatas* and two others: one from the Op. 1 set and the other a more recent discovery from a Brussels manuscript. Bennett uses a modern flute very persuasively, and Nicholas Kraemer and Denis Vigay provide admirable support. The recording is most realistic and and present.

Oboe sonatas (for oboe and continuo), *Op. 1/5 and 8; in B flat, HWV 357; Sinfonia in B flat for 2 violins and continuo, HWV 338; Trio sonatas: in E min. for 2 flutes, HWV 395; in F for 2 recorders, HWV 405.*
*** Ph. Dig. 412 598-2 [id.]. ASMF Chamber Ens.

Marvellously accomplished accounts of the three oboe sonatas. Indeed there are no reservations whatsoever about any of the performances or the recording quality, which is among Philips's best.

Recorder sonatas, Op. 1/2, 4, 7, 9 and 11; in B flat.
*** Ph. Dig. 412 602-2 [id.]. Petri, Malcolm, Vigay, Sheen.
*** CRD Dig. CRD 3412 [id.]. L'École d'Orphée.

Michala Petri plays with her accustomed virtuosity and flair, and it would be difficult to imagine her performances being improved upon. She has the advantage of excellent rapport with her continuo players, and the Philips engineers have produced a natural and spacious sound.

The CRD performances have already won much acclaim. There is some elegant and finished playing from the two recorder players, and this makes a rewarding alternative to Petri for those preferring 'authentic' timbres.

Trio sonatas, Op. 2/1–6; Sonatas for 2 violins: in F, HWV 392; in G min., HWV 393.
*** Ph. Dig. 412 595-2 [id.]. ASMF Chamber Ens.

Trio sonatas, Op. 5/1–7; Sonatas for 2 violins: in E, HWV 394; in C, HWV 403.
*** Ph. Dig. 412 599-2 (2) [id.]. ASMF Chamber Ens.

The performances from Michala Petri, William Bennett, Kenneth Sillito, Malcolm Latchem and others are wonderfully accomplished and have a refreshing vigour and warmth. In these sonatas, Handel's invention seems inexhaustible and it is difficult to imagine readers not responding to them. The sound is excellent in every way.

Trio sonatas (for flute and violin), *Op. 2/1;* (for violins), *Op. 2/3; Op. 5/2 & 4; Violin sonata in A, Op. 1/3; Sonata for 2 violins in G min., HWV 393.*
*** DG Dig. 415 497-2 [id.]. E. Concert, Pinnock.

Rhythms are vital, and the playing of the two violinists (Simon Standage and Micaela Comberti) has panache and style – as, for that matter, have the other contributors. The flautist, Lisa Beznosiuk, is particularly expert and imaginative in the *B minor Sonata*, Op. 2, No. 1; the whole enterprise gives pleasure and stimulus and can be recommended even to those normally unresponsive to period instruments or their copies, while the recording has excellent ambience and warmth.

Violin sonatas, Op. 1/3, 6, 10, 12, 13–15; in D min., HWV 359a; in D min., HWV 367a; Fantasia in A, HWV 406.
*** Ph. Dig. 412 603-2 (2) [id.]. Iona Brown, Nicholas Kraemer, Denis Vigay.

Iona Brown plays with vigour and spirit, and there is a welcome robustness about this music-making; many will find it a relief to turn to the modern violin after the Gillette-like strains of the Baroque variety.

KEYBOARD MUSIC

Chaconne in G, HWV 435; Suites Nos. 10 in D min.; 12 in G min., 13 in B flat.
(M) **(*) Saga SCD 9028 [id.]. Robert Woolley (harpsichord).

Robert Woolley uses a 1636 Ruckers, slightly enlarged by Hemsch, but as the soundboard retains its original bracing and barring, it probably sounds much the same today as it did in the eighteenth century. The recording was made in the church associated with the Duke of Chandos (Saint Lawrence, Little Stanmore, Middlesex), where Handel must often have played on the organ. The ambience is agreeable, but it does prevent an absolutely sharp focus. Nevertheless, if the volume control is set carefully, the instrument can be made to seem in scale, and it is rich in timbre. Robert Woolley has the full measure of this repertoire. Perhaps he slightly overdoes the decoration at the very beginning of the massive *Chaconne,* which follows on effectively after the (rather similar) noble *Sarabande* with divisions, which concludes the *D minor Suite*. The *Suite in B flat* includes a splendid set of variations not unlike the famous '*Harmonious Blacksmith*' set. The theme was also used by Brahms in his Handelian variations. All in all, a rewarding disc.

Harpsichord suites Nos. 1–8.
(M) *** DG 427 170-2 (2). Colin Tilney (harpsichord).

Colin Tilney plays two fine period instruments from Hamburg (both pictured in the accompanying booklet). The 1728 Zell (used for *Suites 1, 3, 6* and *7*) has two manuals. The 1710 Fleischer – the oldest surviving harpsichord known to have been made in Hamburg – is played in *Suites 2, 4, 5* (with its famous *Harmonious blacksmith* variations) and *8*; it has only one manual and its elegant design follows English models. Both suit this repertoire extremely well and there are subtle and occasionally striking differences in colour and resonance between the two instruments. Tilney has a fine technique and a firm rhythmic grip and he shows awareness of stylistic problems, even if there are inconsistencies with double-dotting. His approach is direct and thoughtful, not inflexible, and at times has almost a rhapsodic element. Altogether this playing has much to commend it in its vitality and consistency of style.

Suites Nos. 2 in F; 3 in D min.; 5 in E; 6 in F sharp min.; 7 in G min.
**(*) HM HMC 90447 [id.]. Kenneth Gilbert (harpsichord).

Gilbert uses a copy of a Taskin harpsichord by Bédard. He observes most first-half repeats but not the second, and he is as imaginative in the handling of decoration and ornamentation as one would expect. Perhaps some grandeur, some larger-than-life vitality, is missing; but so much else is here that there is no cause for qualifying the recommendation. The recording is much better balanced and more natural than recent rivals.

VOCAL AND CHORAL MUSIC

Acis and Galatea (masque).
*** DG 423 406-2 (2) [id.]. Burrowes, Rolfe Johnson, Martyn Hill, Willard White, E. Bar. Soloists, Gardiner.

(i) *Acis and Galatea;* (ii) *Cantata: Look down, harmonious saint.*
*** Hyp. Dig. CDA 66361/2; *KA 66361/2.* (i; ii) Ainsley; (i) McFadden, Covey-Crump, George, Harre-Jones; King's Cons., Robert King.

Robert King directs a bluff, beautifully sprung reading of *Acis and Galatea* that brings out its domestic jollity. Using the original version for five solo singers and no chorus, this may be less delicate in its treatment than John Eliot Gardiner's reading of the original version on DG Archiv but, at speeds generally a little faster and with warmer, fuller sound, it is if anything even more winning. The soloists are first rate, with John Mark Ainsley among the most stylish of the younger generation of Handel tenors, and the bass, Michael George, characterizing strongly as Polyphemus, yet never at the expense of musical values. Claron McFadden's vibrant soprano is girlishly distinctive. This Hyperion issue scores somewhat on price too and provides a valuable makeweight in the florid solo cantata, thought to be originally conceived as part of *Alexander's Feast*, nimbly sung by Ainsley.

Certain of John Eliot Gardiner's tempi are idiosyncratic (some too fast, some too slow), but the scale of the performance, using original instruments, is beautifully judged, with the vocal soloists banding together for the choruses. The acoustic is rather dry, the balance fairly close, but the soloists are consistently sweet of tone, although the singing is less individually characterful than in some previous versions. Willard White is a fine Polyphemus, but his *O ruddier than the cherry* has not quite the degree of genial gusto that Owen Brannigan brought to it. The authentic sounds of the English Baroque Soloists are finely controlled and the vibrato-less string timbre is clear and clean without being abrasive. A thoroughly rewarding pair of CDs.

(i) *Aci, Galatea e Polifemo.* (ii) *Recorder sonatas in F; C & G* (trans. to *F*).
*** HM Dig. HMC 901253/4; *HMC 401253/4* [id.]. (i) Kirkby, C. Watkinson, Thomas, L. Bar., Medlam; (ii) Michel Piquet, John Toll.

Aci, Galatea e Polifemo proves to be quite a different work from the always popular English masque, *Acis and Galatea*, with only one item even partially borrowed. In effect it is a one-act opera, full of delightful brief numbers, far more flexible in scale and layout than later full-scale Italian operas. Charles Medlam directs London Baroque in a beautifully sprung performance with three excellent soloists, the brightly characterful Emma Kirkby as Aci, Carolyn Watkinson in the lower-pitched role of Galatea (often – a little confusingly – sounding like a male alto), and David Thomas coping manfully with the impossibly wide range of Polifemo's part. The three recorder sonatas are comparably delightful, a welcome makeweight. Excellent sound, full of presence.

Ah, che pur troppo è vero; Mi palpita il cor. Duets: *A miravi io son intento; Beato in ver chi può; Conservate, raddioppiate; Fronda leggiera e mobile; Langue, geme e sospira; No, di voi non vuo fidarni; Se tu non lasci amore; Sono liete, fortunate; Tanti strali al sen; Troppo cruda* (cantatas).
*** Hung. Dig. HCD 12564-5 [id.]. Zádori, Esswood; Falvay, Németh, Ella (cello, flute and harpsichord).

The two vocal soloists, the clear-voiced soprano Maria Zádori and the counter-tenor Paul Esswood, sing delightfully throughout this generous collection of very rare Handel duet cantatas, most of them charmers when the singing is so sweet and accomplished and the coloratura so brilliantly turned. Excellent recording, the voices most naturally focused and the accompaniment sounding very refined, with the harpsichord particularly realistic.

(i) *Alceste* (incidental music); (ii) *Comus* (incidental music).
*** O-L 421 479-2 [id.]. (i) Nelson, Kirkby, Elliott; (i; ii) Cable, Thomas; (ii) Kwella; AAM, Hogwood.

Commissioned to write incidental music for a play by Smollett, the composer was stopped in his tracks by the abandonment of the whole project. Nevertheless there is much to enjoy in what he wrote for *Alceste*, not just solo items but also some simple tuneful choruses, all introduced by an impressive, dramatic overture in D minor. The incidental music for *Comus* makes equally refreshing listening, intended as it was to be an epilogue for a performance of the Milton masque. Performances of all this music have the freshness and vigour one associates with the Academy under Hogwood at their finest. The sound, too, is first rate.

(i) *Alexander's Feast* (complete). (ii) *Harp concerto, Op. 4/6;* (iii) *Organ concerto, Op. 4/1.*
*** Collins Dig. 7016-2 (2). (i) Argenta, Partridge, George, The Sixteen Ch.; (ii) Lawrence-King, Tragicomedia; (iii) Nicholson; (i; iii) The Sixteen O, Christophers.

Alexander's Feast; Concerto grosso in C (Alexander's Feast).
**(*) Ph. Dig. 422 053-2 (2) [id.]. Carolyn Watkinson, Robson, Donna Brown, Stafford, Varcoe, Monteverdi Ch., E. Bar. Soloists, Eliot Gardiner.

Harry Christophers directs a lively, sympathetic account of Handel's extended cantata, very well sung and recorded. The sound effectively sways the balance of advantage between this and

Gardiner's Göttingen version on Philips, which, recorded live, lacks bloom on the voices. The three soloists – Nancy Argenta, Ian Partridge and Michael George – are all first rate, making a more consistent team than the quintet used by Gardiner. The bass, Michael George, is satisfyingly firm and dark in the two big bass arias, both of them among Handel's greatest, *Bacchus ever bright and fair* and *Revenge, Timotheus cries*. Christophers also provides two of the related Opus 4 concertos instead of Gardiner's one.

Gardiner's version of *Alexander's Feast* was recorded live at performances given at the Göttingen Festival. The sound is not distractingly dry, but it is still harder than usual on singers and players alike, taking away some of the bloom. What matters is the characteristic vigour and concentration of Gardiner's performance, which winningly explains how this now neglected piece could, in Handel's lifetime, have been his most frequently performed work after *Messiah* and *Acis and Galatea*. Among the most striking numbers are the two big arias for the bass, both with brilliant brass obbligato: the drinking song *Bacchus ever fair and young* (with two horns) and the Victorian favourite, *Revenge, Timotheus cries* (with trumpet). Stephen Varcoe may lack the dark resonance of a traditional bass, but he projects his voice well. Nigel Robson's tenor suffers more than do the others from the dryness of the acoustic. The soprano, Donna Brown, sings with boyish freshness, and the alto numbers are divided very effectively between Carolyn Watkinson and the soft-grained counter-tenor, Ashley Stafford. The two discs also include the *Concerto grosso in C* that was given with the oratorio at its first performance and which still bears its name.

L'Allegro, il penseroso, il moderato.
*** Erato/Warner 2292 45377-2 (2). Kwella, McLaughlin, Jennifer Smith, Ginn, Davies, Hill, Varcoe, Monteverdi Ch., E. Bar. Soloists, Gardiner.

Taking Milton as his starting point, Handel illustrated in music the contrasts of mood and character between the cheerful and the thoughtful. Then, prompted by his librettist, Charles Jennens, he added compromise in *Il moderato*, the moderate man. The final chorus may fall a little short of the rest (Jennens's words cannot have provided much inspiration), but otherwise the sequence of brief numbers is a delight, particularly in a performance as exhilarating as this, with excellent soloists, choir and orchestra. The recording is first rate.

Alpestre monte; Mi palpita il cor; Tra le fiamme; Tu fedel? Tu costante? (Italian cantatas).
*** O-L Dig. 414 473-2 [id.]. Emma Kirkby, AAM, Hogwood.

The four cantatas here, all for solo voice with modest instrumental forces, are nicely contrasted, with the personality of the original singer by implication identified with *Tu fedel*, a spirited sequence of little arias rejecting a lover. Even 'a heart full of cares' in *Mi palpita il cor* inspires Handel to a pastorally charming aria, with a delectable oboe obbligato rather than anything weighty, and even those limited cares quickly disperse. Light-hearted and sparkling performances to match.

Aminta e Fillide (cantata).
*** Hyp. CDA 66118; *KA 66118* [id.]. Fisher, Kwella, L. Handel O, Darlow.

In writing for two voices and strings, Handel presents a simple encounter in the pastoral tradition over a span of ten brief arias which, together with recitatives and final duet, last almost an hour. The music is as charming and undemanding for the listener as it is taxing for the soloists. This lively performance, beautifully recorded with two nicely contrasted singers, delightfully blows the cobwebs off a Handel work till now totally neglected.

Anthem for the Foundling Hospital; Ode for the birthday of Queen Anne.
*** O-L 421 654-2 [id.]. Nelson, Kirkby, Minty, Bowman, Hill, Thomas, Ch. of Christ Church Cathedral, Oxford, AAM, Preston – HAYDN: *Missa brevis in F.* ***

The *Ode* is an early work, written soon after Handel arrived in England. It has its Italianate attractions, but it is the much later *Foundling Hospital anthem* which is the more memorable, not just because it concludes with an alternative version of the *Hallelujah chorus* (sounding delightfully fresh on this scale with the Christ Church Choir) but because the other borrowed numbers are also superb. An extra tang is given by the accompaniment on original instruments. The CD adds Haydn's early *Missa brevis* as an attractive bonus.

Apollo e Dafne (cantata).
**(*) HM HMC 905157; *HMC 405157* [id.]. Judith Nelson, David Thomas; Hayes, San Francisco Bar. O, McGegan.

Apollo e Dafne is one of Handel's most delightful cantatas, with at least two strikingly memorable numbers, a lovely siciliano for Dafne with oboe obbligato and an aria for Apollo, *Come rosa in su la spina*, with unison violins and a solo cello. Both soloists are first rate, and Nicholas McGegan is a lively Handelian, though the playing of the orchestra could be more polished and the sound more firmly focused.

Athalia (oratorio).
*** O-L Dig. 417 126-2 (2) [id.]. Sutherland, Kirkby, Bowman, Aled Jones, Rolfe Johnson, David Thomas, New College, Oxford, Ch., AAM, Hogwood.

As Queen Athalia, an apostate Baal-worshipper who comes to no good, Dame Joan Sutherland sings boldly with a richness and vibrancy to contrast superbly with the pure silver of Emma Kirkby, not to mention the celestial treble of Aled Jones, in the role of the boy-king, Joas. That casting is perfectly designed to set the Queen aptly apart from the good Israelite characters led by the Priest, Joad (James Bowman in a castrato role), and Josabeth (Kirkby). Kirkby's jewelled ornamentation is brilliant too, and Aled Jones's singing – despite a few moments of caution – is ethereally beautiful, if only a little more remarkable than that of the three trebles from the Christ Church Choir who sing the little trios for Three Virgins at the end of Act II. Christopher Hogwood with the Academy brings out the speed and variety of the score that has been described as Handel's first great English oratorio. The recording is bright and clean, giving sharp focus to voices and instruments alike.

Duets: *Beato in ver; Langue, geme; Tanti strali.* Cantatas: *Parti, l'idolo mio; Sento là che ristretto.*
(B) *** HM HMA 901004; *HMA 431004* [id.]. Judith Nelson, René Jacobs, William Christie, K. Jünghanel.

These Handel duets (two of them very early from his Italian period) and the two cantatas – more substantial works – contain some delightful music, Handel at his most charming. With outstanding solo singing from both Judith Nelson and René Jacobs, they are given very stylish performances, cleanly recorded. A bargain.

Belshazzar (complete).
*** DG Dig. 431 793-2 (3) [id.]. Rolfe Johnson, Augér, Robbin, Bowman, Wilson-Johnson, E. Concert Ch. & O, Pinnock.

After Walton any musical treatment of the ominous writing on the wall is bound to seem tame, but Handel's oratorio, written two years after *Messiah* with the *Messiah's* librettist, Charles Jennens, supplying the words, contains rich inspirations. Handel modified the work over the years, and Pinnock has opted not for the earliest but for the most striking and fully developed text. The cast is starry, with Arleen Augér at her most ravishing as the Babylonian king's mother, Nitocris, Anthony Rolfe Johnson in the title role, James Bowman as the prophet, Daniel, and Catherine Robbin as King Cyrus, all excellent. Full, well-balanced sound.

Brockes Passion.
**(*) Hung. Dig. HCD 12734/6-2 [id.]. Klietmann, Gáti, Zádori, Minter & soloists, Halle Stadtsingechor, Capella Savaria, McGegan.

The relatively crude Passion text by Barthold Brockes prompted a piece of some thirty or so arias, two duets and a trio, most of them brief but full of superb ideas, many of which Handel raided for his later oratorios. Thus, the deeply moving duet between Christ and the Virgin Mary just before the *Crucifixion* later became the duet for Esther and King Ahasuerus in *Esther*. Generally, this degree of depth – worthy to be compared with Bach's Passion music – is missing, but there is still much to enjoy. Nicholas McGegan with the excellent Capella Savaria using period instruments directs a lively, refreshing account of the piece that easily outshines previous versions. The team of soloists has no weak link, and the only comparative reservation concerns the singing of the chorus, fresh but less polished than the rest. The Hungaroton recording is bright and well focused, with a fine sense of presence.

Carmelite Vespers.
*** EMI Dig. CDS7 49749-2 (2) [Ang. CDCB 49749]. Feldman, Kirkby, Van Evera, Cable, Nichols, Cornwell, David Thomas, Taverner Ch. & Players, Parrott.

What Andrew Parrott has recorded here is a reconstruction by Graham Dixon of what might have been heard in July 1707 at the church of the Carmelite Order in Rome for the Festival of Our Lady of Mount Carmel. Dixon has put the motets and Psalm settings in an order appropriate for the service of Second Vespers, noting that it is not the only possible reconstruction. So *Dixit Dominus* is introduced by plainchant and a chanted antiphon, with similar liturgical links between the other Handel settings – in turn *Laudate pueri*, *Te decus Virgineum*, *Nisi Dominus*, *Haec est Regina Virginum*, *Saeviat Tellus* and *Salve Regina*. Of these, the only unfamiliar Handel piece is *Te decus Virgineum* – which makes this not quite the new experience promised but an enjoyable way of hearing a magnificent collection of Handel's choral music. In a liturgical setting in 1707, women's voices would not have been used, but the sopranos and altos of the Taverner Choir produce an aptly fresh sound, as does the fine group of soloists, headed by an outstanding trio of sopranos: Emma Kirkby, Jill Feldman and Emily van Evera. The recording, made in St Augustine's, Kilburn, has a pleasant and apt ambience, which however does not obscure detail.

(i) *Cecilia vogi un sguardo* (cantata); *Silete venti* (motet).
*** DG Dig. 419 736-2 [id.]. Jennifer Smith, Elwes, E. Concert, Pinnock.

These two fine cantatas come from a later period than most of Handel's Italian-language works in this genre. Both reveal him at his most effervescent, a quality superbly caught in these performances with excellent singing and playing, most strikingly from Jennifer Smith whose coloratura has never been more brilliantly displayed on record. Excellent recording.

Chandos anthems Nos. 1: O be joyful in the Lord; 2: In the Lord put I my trust; 3: Have mercy on me, HWV 246/8.
*** Chan. Dig. CHAN 8600; *ABTD 1293* [id.]. Lynne Dawson, Ian Partridge, The Sixteen Ch. & O, Christophers.

Handel based the first *Chandos anthem, O be joyful*, setting the *Jubilate*, Psalm 100, on his *Utrecht Te Deum*; grandly, he uses three soloists as well as chorus. The second, though rather longer, uses tenor alone with chorus, while the third has soprano and tenor, both in solo and duet. The impact of the performances is affected strongly by the recorded sound, set in a warm acoustic characteristic of Chandos but with rather a close balance; that makes the choir sound bigger and with a greater body of weight than on The Sixteen's recording of *Messiah*. Ian Partridge is the radiant-voiced linchpin of these performances and is superbly matched by Lynne Dawson with her gloriously pure, silvery soprano. Michael George's much briefer contribution is also most stylish. The closeness of sound makes the instrumental sonatas which start each *Anthem* more abrasive than they might be, but not uncomfortably so.

Chandos anthems Nos. 4: O sing unto the Lord a new song; 5: I will magnify thee; 6: As pants the hart for cooling streams.
*** Chan. Dig. CHAN 0504; *EBTD 0504* [id.]. Lynne Dawson, Ian Partridge, The Sixteen Ch. & O, Christophers.

The second volume of the Chandos series is hardly less appealing than the first. There are some splendidly vigorous choruses, while in No. 6 there is a lovely adagio chorus, *As pants the hart for cooling streams*, and an equally memorable soprano aria, beautifully sung by Lynne Dawson. Indeed the performances are well up to standard, as is the recording.

Chandos anthems Nos. 10: The Lord is my light; 11: Let God arise.
*** Chan. Dig. CHAN 0509; *EBT 0509*. Lynne Dawson, Ian Partridge, The Sixteen Ch. & O, Christophers.

Although he is framed by some splendidly ambitious choruses, the tenor soloist dominates No. 10, and Ian Partridge sings with his customary style and sweetness of timbre. Lynn Dawson makes her entry on the penultimate number. The two soloists share the honours in No. 11: they have one aria each, and here the chorus is again in exhilarating form, especially in the closing *Alleluja*. The recording is spacious while continuing to preserve the music's intimate feeling.

Coronation anthems (1. Zadok the Priest; 2. The King shall rejoice; 3. My heart is inditing; 4. Let Thy hand be strengthened).
*** DG Dig. 410 030-2 [id.]. Westminster Abbey Ch., E. Concert, Preston; Pinnock (organ).

Coronation anthems (complete); *Judas Maccabaeus; See the conqu'ring hero comes; March; Sing unto God.*
*** Ph. Dig. 412 733-2 [id.]. ASMF Ch., ASMF, Marriner.

(i) *Coronation anthems;* (ii) *Chandos anthem No. 9: O praise the Lord.*
(M) *** Decca 421 150-2. (i) King's College Ch., Willcocks; (ii) with E. Vaughan, A. Young, Forbes Robinson; ASMF, Willcocks.

The extra weight of the Academy of St Martin-in-the-Fields Chorus compared with the Pinnock version seems appropriate for the splendour of music intended for the pomp of royal ceremonial occasions, and the commanding choral entry in *Zadok the Priest* is gloriously rich in amplitude, without in any way lacking incisiveness. The instrumental accompaniments are fresh and glowing. Sir Neville Marriner's direction is full of imaginative detail, and the Philips recording, with its wide dynamic range, is admirably balanced and excitingly realistic in its CD format. The excerpts from *Solomon* are delightful.

Those who prefer sparer, more 'authentic' textures can choose Pinnock where, although the overall effect is less grand, the element of contrast is even more telling. After the lightness and clarity of the introduction to *Zadok the Priest*, to have the choir enter with such bite and impact underlines the freshness and immediacy. The recording gives ample sense of power, and the use of original instruments gives plenty of character to the accompaniments. An exhilarating version.

The reissued 1961 Argo recording of these four anthems makes an admirable mid-priced recommendation, particularly as the extra clarity and presence given to the choir improve the balance in relation to the orchestra. The *Chandos anthem* makes a fine bonus.

Dettingen Te Deum; Dettingen anthem.
*** DG Dig. 410 647-2 [id.]. Westminster Abbey Ch., E. Concert, Preston.

The *Dettingen Te Deum* is a splendidly typical work and continually reminds the listener of *Messiah*, written the previous year. Preston's new Archiv performance from the English Concert makes an ideal recommendation, with its splendid singing, crisp but strong (Stephen Varcoe does the two brief airs beautifully), excellent recording and a generous, apt coupling. This setting of *The King shall rejoice* should not be confused with the *Coronation anthem* of that name. It is less inspired, but has a magnificent double fugue for finale. The recording is first class, although the Westminster Abbey reverberation prevents a sharp choral focus.

Dixit Dominus; Nisi Dominus; Salve Regina.
*** DG Dig. 423 594-2 [id.]. Westminster Abbey Ch. & O, Simon Preston.

Dixit dominus; Nisi dominus; Silete venti.
*** Chan. Dig. CHAN 0517; *EBTD 0517* [id.]. Dawson, Russell, Brett, Partridge, George, The Sixteen Choir & O, Harry Christophers.

Dixit Dominus; Zadok the Priest.
*** Erato/Warner 2292 45136-2. Palmer, Marshall, Brett, Messana, Morton, Thomson, Wilson-Johnson, Monteverdi Ch. and O, Gardiner.

On DG Archiv *Dixit Dominus* is very aptly coupled with fine performances of another – less ambitious – Psalm setting, *Nisi Dominus*, and a votive antiphon, *Salve Regina*, which Handel composed between the two. Preston here draws ideally luminous and resilient singing from the Westminster Abbey Choir, with a fine team of soloists in which Arleen Augér and Diana Montague are outstanding. Their duet together in *Dixit Dominus, De torrente in via bibet*, is ravishingly beautiful, with clashing suspensions made to add emotional depth. The playing of the orchestra of period instrumentalists, led by Roy Goodman, in every way matches the fine qualities of the singing.

Harry Christophers directs lively performances of Handel's two great Psalm-settings using period instruments and a fine team of soloists. In both *Dixit dominus* and *Nisi dominus* his readings come into rivalry with Trevor Pinnock's outstanding DG Archiv disc. Christophers' speeds tend to be more extreme, slow as well as fast, and the recorded sound, though full and well detailed, is less immediate. On balance Pinnock with his rather more bouncy rhythms remains the first choice, but the Chandos issue gains significantly from a much more generous third item. The motet *Silete venti*, with soprano solo, is a substantial piece of nearly half an hour which allows the silver-toned Lynne Dawson to shine even more than in the other items, ending with a brilliant *Alleluia* in galloping compound time.

John Eliot Gardiner catches the music's brilliance and directs an exhilarating performance, marked by strongly accented, sharply incisive singing from the choir and outstanding solo contributions. In high contrast to the dramatic choruses, the duet for two sopranos, *De torrente*, here beautifully sung by Felicity Palmer and Margaret Marshall, is languorously expressive, but stylishly so. However, the Erato coupling is less generous than the two works offered on DG.

Esther (complete).
**(*) O-L Dig. 414 423-2 (2) [id.]. Kwella, Rolfe Johnson, Partridge, Thomas, Kirkby, Elliott, Westminster Cathedral Boys' Ch., Ch. and AAM, Hogwood.

Hogwood has opted for the original 1718 score with its six compact scenes as being more sharply dramatic than the 1732 expansion, and his rather abrasive brand of authenticity goes well with the bright, full recorded sound which unfortunately exaggerates the choir's sibilants. The Academy's own small chorus is joined by the clear, bright trebles of Westminster Cathedral Choir, and they all sing very well (except that the elaborate passage-work is far too heavily aspirated, at times almost as though the singers are laughing). The vigour of the performance is unaffected and the team of soloists is strong and consistent, with Patrizia Kwella sounding distinctive and purposeful in the name-part.

Israel in Egypt (oratorio).
(M) **(*) DG 429 530-2 (2) [id.]. Harper, Clark, Esswood, Young, Rippon, Keyte, Leeds Festival Ch., ECO, Mackerras.

(i) *Israel in Egypt; The Ways of Zion* (funeral anthem).
**(*) Erato/Warner 2292 45399-2 (2) [id.]. (i) Knibbs, Clarkson, Elliot, Varcoe, Monteverdi Ch. & O, Gardiner.

Though the solo singing shared between principals in the chorus is variable on Erato, the choruses are what matter in this work, making up a high proportion of its length, and the teamwork involved brings tingling excitement. It is good to have the moving funeral anthem as an extra item. The DG/Mackerras account may have superior solo contributions but Gardiner's chorus remains the finer.

Mackerras's performance represents a dichotomy of styles, using the English Chamber Orchestra sounding crisp, stylish and lightweight and the fairly large amateur choir, impressively weighty rather than incisive, but given strong projection on CD. Thus the work makes its effect by breadth and grandiloquence rather than athletic vigour. The recording balance also reflects the problems of the basic set-up, with the chorus sometimes virtually drowned by the orchestra in the epic pieces, and then suddenly coming to the fore for the lighter moments of the score. The solo singing is distinguished, but its style is refined rather than earthy and it is the choruses which are the glory of this performance.

Jephtha.
*** Ph. Dig. 422 351-2 (3) [id.]. Robson, Dawson, Anne Sofie von Otter, Chance, Varcoe, Holton, Monteverdi Ch., E. Bar. Soloists, Gardiner.

Whatever Handel's personal trials in writing what, in all but name, is a biblical opera, the result is a masterpiece, containing some magnificent music, not least in the choruses. There are only three *da capo* arias out of ten, and the beautiful accompanied recitatives – not least Jephtha's celebrated *Deeper and deeper still* in Act II – give a cohesion to the whole. John Eliot Gardiner's recording was made live at the Göttingen Festival in 1988 and, though the sound does not have quite the bloom of his finest studio recordings of Handel, the exhilaration and intensity of the performance come over vividly, with superb singing from both chorus and an almost ideal line-up of soloists. Nigel Robson's tenor may be on the light side for the title-role, but in such a lovely aria as *Waft her, angels* the clarity of sound and the sensitivity of expression are very satisfying. Lynne Dawson, with her bell-like soprano, sings radiantly as Iphis; and the counter-tenor, Michael Chance, as her beloved, Hamor, is also outstanding. Anne Sofie von Otter is powerful as Storge, and Stephen Varcoe with his clear baritone, again on the light side, is a stylish Zebul. As for the Monteverdi Choir, their clarity, incisiveness and beauty are a constant delight.

Joshua (complete).
❀ *** Hyp. Dig. CDA 66461/2; *KA 66461/2* [id.]. Kirkby, Bowman, Ainsley, George, Oliver, New College, Oxford, Ch., King's Consort, King.

Written in 1747, five years after *Messiah* first appeared, *Joshua*'s popularity owed much to two numbers which at once gained currency outside the opera house, the chorus *See, the conqu'ring hero comes* and the brilliant soprano aria *O, had I Jubal's lyre.* In the context of the whole oratorio, heard in quick succession in the triumphant third Act, their magnetism is enhanced, with the patriotic chorus atmospherically bringing louder, grander repetitions, and with Emma Kirkby here ideally sparkling and light in the solo. Her Act I aria too is a delight, *Hark, 'tis the linnet*, full of delightful bird noises. She has the role of Achsa, daughter of the patriarchal leader, Caleb (taken here by the bass, Michael George). Her love for Othniel, superbly sung by James Bowman, provides the romantic interest in what is otherwise a grandly military oratorio, based on the Book of Joshua. The brisk sequence of generally brief arias is punctuated by splendid choruses, with solo numbers often inspiring choral comment. The call to arms in Act I is particularly effective, with the brass silent until that moment. Act II then tells the story of the siege of Jericho, leading up to Joshua's stopping of the sun in the astonishingly original *O thou bright orb*. In that final number of the Act for tenor and chorus, first high violins and then the rest of the strings are eerily stilled to represent the miracle, with the chorus finally fading away at the end of the Act. The sounds of victory are then left for Act III. The singing is consistently strong and stylish, with the clear, precise tenor, John Mark Ainsley, in the title-role giving his finest performance on record yet. Robert King and his Consort crown their achievement in other Hyperion issues, notably their Purcell series, with polished, resilient playing, and the choir of New College, Oxford, sings with ideal freshness. Warm, full sound. On two well-packed discs, it makes an exceptionally attractive Handel issue.

Lucrezia (cantata). Arias: *Ariodante: Oh, felice mio core . . . Con l'ali do constanza; E vivo ancore? . . . Scherza infida in grembo al drudo; Dopo notte. Atalanta: Care selve. Hercules: Where shall I fly? Joshua: O had I Jubal's lyre. Rodelinda: Pompe vane di morte! . . . Dove sei, amato bene? Serse: Frondi tenere e belle . . . Ombra mai fù (Largo).*
(M) *** Ph. 426 450-2; *426 450-4*. Dame Janet Baker, ECO, Leppard.

Even among Dame Janet's most impressive records this Handel recital marks a special contribution, ranging as it does from the pure gravity of *Ombra mai fù* to the passionate virtuosity in *Dopo notte* from *Ariodante*. Leppard gives sparkling support and the whole is recorded with natural and refined balance. An outstanding disc, with admirable documentation.

Messiah (complete).
*** DG Dig. 423 630-2 (2). Augér, Anne Sofie von Otter, Chance, Crook, J. Tomlinson, E. Concert Ch., E. Concert, Pinnock.
*** Ph. Dig. 434 297-2 (2) [id.]. Marshall, Robbin, Rolfe Johnson, Brett, Hale, Shirley-Quirk, Monteverdi Ch., E. Bar. Soloists, Gardiner.
*** Hyp. Dig. CDA 66251/2; *KA 66251/2* [id.]. Lynne Dawson, Denley, Maldwyn Davies, Michael George, The Sixteen Ch. & O, Christophers.
*** Chan. Dig. CHAN 0522/3; *EBTD 0522/3* [id.]. Rodger, Della Jones, Robson, Langridge, Terfel, Coll. Mus. 90, Hickox.
(M) *** Ph. 420 865-2; *420 865-4* (2) [id.]. Harper, Watts, Wakefield, Shirley-Quirk, LSO Ch., LSO, C. Davis.
(B) *** EMI CZS7 62748-2 (2) [Ang. CDMB 62748]. Harwood, J. Baker, Esswood, Tear, Herincx, Amb. S., ECO, Mackerras.
(M) *** Erato/Warner 2292 45447-2 (2) [id.]. Palmer, Watts, Davies, Shirley-Quirk, ECO Ch., ECO, Leppard.
*** Decca Dig. 414 396-2 (2) [id.]. Te Kanawa, Gjevang, Keith Lewis, Howell, Chicago Ch. & SO, Solti.
**(*) O-L 411 858-2 (3) [id.]. Nelson, Kirkby, Watkinson, Elliott, Thomas, Christ Church Cathedral Ch., Oxford, AAM, Hogwood.
(B) **(*) CfP CD-CFPD 4718; *TC-CFPD 4718* (2) [id.]. Morison, Thomas, Lewis, Milligan, Huddersfield Ch. Soc., RLPO, Sargent.
** HM Dig. HMU 907050/52 (3); *HMU 407050/52* (3) [id.]. Hunt, Williams, Spence, Minter, Thomas, Parker, U. C. Berkeley Chamber Ch., Philharmonia Baroque O, McGegan.

Pinnock presents a performance using authentically scaled forces which, without inflation, rise to grandeur and magnificence, qualities Handel himself would have relished. With a choir of thirty-two voices, cleanly and powerfully recorded in a warm acoustic, the result is thrilling, not least when timpani decorate the cadences. The fast contrapuntal choruses, such as *For unto us a Child is born*, are done lightly and resiliently in the modern manner, but there is no hint of breathlessness, and Pinnock (more than his main rivals) balances his period instruments to give a satisfying body to the sound. There is weight too in the singing of the bass soloist, John Tomlinson, firm, dark and powerful, yet marvellously agile in divisions. Arleen Augér's range of tone and dynamic is daringly wide and, with radiant purity in *I know that my Redeemer liveth*, she and Pinnock, at a slow tempo, find a vein of tenderness too often lacking in period performance. The contralto aria, *He was despised*, is even more extreme in slowness, yet Anne Sofie von Otter sustains it superbly with her firm, steady voice. Some alto arias are taken by the outstanding counter-tenor, Michael Chance, who in some ways is even more remarkable. The tenor, Howard Crook, is less distinctive but still sings freshly and attractively. With full, atmospheric and well-balanced recording, this is a set not to be missed, even by those who already have a favourite version of *Messiah*.

Gardiner chooses bright-toned sopranos instead of boys for the chorus, on the grounds that a mature adult approach is essential, and conversely he uses, very affectingly, a solo treble to sing *There were shepherds abiding*. Speeds are fast and light, and the rhythmic buoyancy in the choruses is very striking. There is drama and boldness, too. *Why do the nations* and *The trumpet shall sound* (both sung with great authority) have seldom come over more strongly. The soloists are all first class, with the soprano Margaret Marshall finest of all, especially in *I know that my Redeemer liveth* (tastefully decorated). There are times when one craves for more expansive qualities; the baroque string sound can still give cause for doubts. Yet there are some wonderful highlights, not least Margaret Marshall's angelic version of *Rejoice greatly*, skipping along in compound time. The CDs bring most items individually cued and the sound is outstandingly beautiful. Now reissued on two CDs, it remains a top recommendation alongside Pinnock.

Harry Christophers' brilliant and stylish choir, The Sixteen, have also made a highly appealing performance, one of the most attractive ever on disc. The scale is compact – with three extra sopranos added to the regular sixteen singers – but the bloom on the sound of chorus and instruments alike gives them brightness and clean projection with no sense of miniaturization. Christophers consistently adopts speeds more relaxed than those we have grown used to in modern performances and the effect is fresh, clear and resilient. Alto lines in the chorus are taken by male singers; a counter-tenor, David James, is also used for the *Refiner's fire*, but *He was despised* is rightly given to the contralto, Catherine Denley, warm and grave at a very measured tempo. The team of five soloists is at least as fine as that on any rival set, with the soprano, Lynne Dawson, singing with silvery purity to delight traditionalists and authenticists alike. The band of thirteen strings sounds as clean and fresh as the choir. Even the *Hallelujah chorus* – always a big test in a small-scale performance – works well, with Christophers in his chosen scale, through dramatic timpani and trumpets conveying necessary weight. The sound has all the bloom one associates with St John's recordings, but – thanks to the dampening effect of an audience – no clouding from reverberation.

Hickox with the period-style forces of Collegium Musicum 90 offers a fresh, resilient reading, in which the often fast speeds in choruses are never made to sound breathless. The soloists too are allowed full expressiveness, an outstanding team, with Joan Rodgers emerging as one of the very finest and most imaginative sopranos of her generation and the young bass, Bryn Terfel, establishing himself as already an outstandingly characterful artist. Though this does not outshine such a set as Trevor Pinnock's on DG Archiv, those who specially fancy these soloists could well find it an apt first choice, with its excellent Chandos recording.

The Philips LSO recording conducted by Sir Colin Davis has not lost its impact and sounds brightly lit and fresh in its digitally remastered format. Textures are beautifully clear and, thanks to Davis, the rhythmic bounce of such choruses as *For unto us* is really infectious. Even *Hallelujah* loses little and gains much from being performed by a chorus of this size. Excellent singing from all four soloists, particularly Helen Watts who, following early precedent, is given *For He is like a refiner's fire* to sing, instead of the bass, and produces a glorious chest register. The performance is absolutely complete and is excellent value at mid-price.

The EMI/Mackerras set provides a comparable new look, but also a clear alternative in its approach. The choruses on EMI have not quite the same zest as on Philips, but they have a compensating breadth and body. More than Davis, Mackerras adopted Handel's alternative versions, so the soprano aria *Rejoice greatly* is given in its optional 12/8 version, with compound time adding a skip to the rhythm. A male alto is also included, Paul Esswood, and he is given some of the bass arias as well as some of the regular alto passages. Among the soloists, Dame Janet Baker is outstanding. Her intense, slow account of *He was despised* – with decorations on the reprise – is sung with profound feeling. Like Davis, Mackerras includes all the numbers traditionally omitted. The recording is warm and full in ambience and, with the added brightness of CD, sounds extremely vivid.

Raymond Leppard presents a fine, enjoyable account of *Messiah*, which lies somewhere between Sir Colin Davis's earlier Philips set and the Mackerras EMI version. His tempi, unlike Davis's, are never exaggeratedly fast and his ornamentation is less fancy than Mackerras's on

EMI. The closest Leppard comes to eccentricity is in his tempo for *The trumpet shall sound*, very fast indeed, like Davis's with the same baritone; *All we like sheep*, preceded by a delightful flourish from the organ, is even jauntier than Davis's account. Leppard has the same contralto, Helen Watts, as well as the same bass and, if anything, both are in finer form. Felicity Palmer is fresher-toned than she sometimes is on record, while Ryland Davies sings brightly and cleanly. The chorus is admirably resilient and luminous; although the acoustics of St Giles, Cripplegate, prevent an absolutely sharp focus, the fine 1976 Erato recording is obviously fuller and more modern than either the Davis/Philips or Mackerras/EMI sets.

Surprisingly, Sir Georg Solti had never conducted *Messiah* before this recording, but he inspires the most vitally exciting reading on record. The Chicago Symphony Orchestra and Chorus respond to some challengingly fast but never breathless speeds, showing what lessons can be learnt from authentic performance in clarity and crispness. Yet the joyful power of *Hallelujah* and the *Amen chorus* is overwhelming. Dame Kiri Te Kanawa matches anyone on record in beauty of tone and detailed expressiveness, while the other soloists are first rate too, even if Anne Gjevang has rather too fruity a timbre. Brilliant, full sound and great tangibility, breadth and clarity on the CDs.

By aiming at re-creating an authentic version, reproducing a performance of 1754, Christopher Hogwood has achieved a reading which is consistently vigorous and refreshing. The trebles of Christ Church are superb, and though the soloists cannot match the tonal beauty of the finest of their rivals on other sets, the consistency of the whole conception makes for most satisfying results. As to the text, it generally follows what we are used to, but there are such oddities as *But who may abide* transposed for a soprano and a shortened version of the *Pastoral symphony*. The recording is superb, clear and free to match the performance.

It is good to have Sir Malcolm Sargent's 1959 recording now restored to the catalogue in full for, apart from the pleasure given by a performance that brings out the breadth of Handel's inspiration, it provides an important corrective to misconceptions about pre-authentic practice. Sargent unashamedly fills out the orchestration (favouring Mozart's scoring where possible). By the side of Davis, his tempi are measured, but his pacing is sure and spontaneous and, with a hundred-strong Huddersfield group, no one will be disappointed with the weight or vigour of the choruses. There is some splendid singing from all four soloists, and Marjorie Thomas's *He was despised* is memorable in its moving simplicity. The success of the CD transfer is remarkable: the old analogue LPs never sounded as clear as this.

On three discs McGegan offers all of Handel's many alternative versions for different numbers. Those not used in the main running-order are conveniently placed at the end of each CD, so that the listener can conveniently programme whichever alternative is preferred. Even though that involves an extra disc, that is an excellent idea, and much of the singing from the young American soloists and choir is fresh and firm. Sadly, the dryness of the acoustic is both unflattering to the voices, and gives a lacklustre quality to the whole performance, sapping the tension.

Messiah (complete; orch. Sir Eugene Goossens).
❀ (M) *** BMG/RCA GD 61266-20 (3) [61266-2]. Vyvyan, Sinclair, Vicker, Tozzi, RPO Ch. & O, Sir Thomas Beecham.

Beecham's *Messiah* sharply divided opinion when it first appeared in 1960. It recalls a momentous live performance in the 1930s, with the added splendour of a professional chorus, and here the impressive stereo shows that chorus and orchestra are on the same footing. Goossens has tried to achieve in his re-scoring something of the Biblical atmosphere that emerges from the 23rd Psalm, with its praise of many instruments. At first it sounds either shocking or exciting to hear highly anachronistic percussion (cymbals, anvil, triangle), not to mention horns and trombones and a full body of strings. But the scoring undeniably fits the sense of the words and the words come through with a remarkable clarity. This is a performance which at every point radiates the natural flair of the conductor. and Beecham is extraordinarily sensitive to Handel's rhetoric and pathos. The use of the cymbals to cap the choruses *For unto us a child is born* and *Glory to God* is unforgettable, and the latter has a charming coda, complete with delicate flute trill. The use of the heavy brass is also very telling. Beecham's tempi are slower than we expect today, but given his expansive view of Handel, they are convincingly appropriate, with the possible exception of the *Hallelujah chorus*, which gathers speed exuberantly as it nears its end. Plainly the chorus, orchestra and soloists were all inspired by the occasion. Jennifer Vyvyan and Monica Sinclair both sing freshly. Jon Vickers brings to his tenor arias a heroic quality that is often welcome and effective, and his performance of *Thou shall break them* has an unforgettable punch. Yet he can be tender too, and *Thy rebuke hath broken his heart* is very moving. Giorgio Tozzi's English is sound and his management of the tricky bass arias (especially *Why do the nations*) compels admiration. But it is above all Beecham's set, and its sense of exultant glory in the riches of Handel's masterpiece is life enhancing. The 1959 recording of the chorus and orchestra is full and expansive in its CD transfer and the soloists have remarkable presence and immediacy. The ample textures make a wonderful antidote to the meagre sounds sometimes offered in baroque music by the most severe authenticists, whom Beecham would surely have scorned. All in all a stimulating alternative experience, and offered economically too. The third disc with its 17-minute appendix of eight items – normally cut at the time this recording was made – comes as a bonus, as the set is priced as for two mid-range CDs. A full text is provided and the documentation contains Beecham's own eulogy of Handel, and his argued justification of Sir Eugene Goossens' orchestration.

Der Messias (sung in German, arr. Mozart): complete.
(M) **(*) DG 427 173-2 (2). Mathis, Finnilä, Schreier, Adam, Austrian R. Ch. & O, Vienna, Mackerras.
** EMI Dig. CDS7 54353-2 (2). Frimmer, Georg, Prégardien, Schreckenberg, Rheinische Kantorei, Kleine Konzert, Hermann Max.

Mozart's arrangement of *Messiah* has a special fascination. It is not simply a question of trombones being added but of elaborate woodwind parts too – most engaging in a number such as *All we like sheep*, which even has a touch of humour. *Rejoice greatly* is given to the tenor (Peter Schreier sounding too heavy) and *The trumpet shall sound* is considerably modified and shortened. To avoid the use of a baroque instrument, Mozart shares the obbligato between trumpet and horn. Mackerras leads his fine team through a performance that is vital, not academic in the heavy sense. The remastered recording is excellent and a translation is provided.

The EMI Reflexe set offers the first period performance on disc of the Mozart arrangement, filling an important gap. It is well played and sung on an intimate scale, with some first-rate solo singing in the German tradition. Disappointingly, the recording is not clear or transparent enough to allow the individual details of Mozart's instrumentation to be distinguished fully, a vital point if the detailed differences between this and the original are to be properly appreciated. The background notes too are totally inadequate for what has claims to be a scholarly set.

Messiah (sung in English): highlights.
*** Ph. Dig. 412 267-2; *412 267-4* [id.] (from above set, cond. Gardiner).
*** Decca Dig. 417 449-2; *417 449-4* [id.] (from above set, cond. Solti).
(M) *** EMI CDM7 69040-2 [id.]; *EG 769040-4* (from above set, cond. Mackerras).
*** O-L Dig. 440 086-2 [id.] (from above set, cond. Hogwood).
(B) **(*) CfP CD-CFP 9007 (from above set, cond. Sargent).
(B) **(*) Pickwick Dig. PCD 803; *CIMPC 803*. Lott, Finnie, Winslade, Herford, Scottish Philharmonic Singers, Scottish SO, Malcolm.

Here Gardiner's collection reigns supreme with the single caveat that *The trumpet shall sound* is missing. The *Amen* chorus is included, however, and rounds off a satisfying musical experience. Solti's selection is undoubtedly generous, including all the key numbers and much else besides. The sound is thrillingly vivid and full. At mid-price Mackerras is first choice, while the digitally remastered CD of highlights from the Hogwood recording, issued before the complete set, acts as an excellent sampler for it.

As with the complete set, the great and pleasant surprise among the bargain selections is the Classics for Pleasure CD of highlights from Sir Malcolm Sargent's 1959 recording; no one will be disappointed with *Hallelujah*, while the closing *Amen* has a powerful sense of apotheosis.

Beautifully sung by excellent soloists (especially Felicity Lott) and choir, the Pickwick issue makes another good bargain-priced CD, very naturally and beautifully recorded in warmly atmospheric sound, though the performance could at times be livelier.

(i) *Nell'Africaine selve; Nella stagion che, dio viole e rose* (Italian cantatas). Duets: *Quel fior che all'aba ride; No, di voi non vo' fidarmi; Tacete ohimè, tacete!;* Trio: *Se tu non lasci amore.* (ii) *The Alchemist* (incidental music): suite. Theatre songs: *Universal passion: I like the am'rous youth. The Way of the World: Love's but the frailty of the mind. The What d'ye call it: Twas when the seas were roaring.*

*** O-L 430 282-2 [id.]. (i) Kirkby, Nelson, Thomas; Hogwood; Sheppard; (ii) Kwella, Cable, Thomas, AAM, Hogwood.

This attractive reissue combines almost all the contents of two highly recommended analogue LPs recorded in 1980/81. The most ear-catching items among the Italian cantatas are those which Handel later drew on in *Messiah* for such numbers as *His yoke is easy*, *For unto us a child is born* and *All we like sheep*. Emma Kirkby and Judith Nelson sing them brilliantly; and one of the melodically less striking pieces yet prompts an amazing virtuoso display from the bass, David Thomas, who is required to cope with an enormous range of three octaves. In the fast movements Hogwood favours breathtaking speeds (in every sense), yet the result is exciting, not too hectic, and the recording is outstanding. The coupled selection of Handel's theatre music contains more delightful rarities, and the performances by the Academy under Hogwood have all the freshness and vigour one associates with his companion set of Purcell theatre music. The transfers to CD are sophisticated: the sound is first class throughout.

Ode for the birthday of Queen Anne (Eternal source of light divine); Sing unto God (Wedding anthem); Te deum in D (for Queen Caroline).

*** Hyp. Dig. CDA 66315; *KA 66315* [id.]. Fisher, Bowman, Ainsley, George, New College, Oxford, Ch., King's Consort, Robert King.

Handel wrote this *Birthday Ode for Queen Anne* near the beginning of his years in England (before his master, the Elector of Hanover, became George I), combining Purcellian influences with Italianate writing to make a rich mixture. King's performance may not quite match Hogwood's on the rival Oiseau-Lyre disc in vigour (see above), but it is richly enjoyable, with warm, well-tuned playing from the King's Consort and with James Bowman in radiant form in the opening movement. There is excellent singing from the other soloists too. The other two items are far rarer. Though less consistently inspired, they have some charming moments, to make an attractive coupling. Warmly atmospheric recording, not ideally clear on detail.

Ode for St Cecilia's Day.

*** DG Dig. 419 220-2 [id.]. Lott, Rolfe Johnson, Ch. & E. Concert, Pinnock.

*** ASV Dig. CDDCA 512; *ZCDCA 512* [id.]. Gomez, Tear, King's College Ch., ECO, Ledger.

Trevor Pinnock's account of Handel's magnificent setting of Dryden's *Ode* comes near the ideal for a performance using period instruments. Not only is it crisp and lively, it has deep tenderness too, as in the lovely soprano aria, *The complaining flute*, with Lisa Beznosiuk playing the flute obbligato most delicately in support of Felicity Lott's clear singing. Anthony Rolfe Johnson gives a robust yet stylish account of *The trumpet's loud clangour*, and the choir is excellent, very crisp of ensemble. Full, clear recording with voices vivid and immediate.

Those seeking a version with modern instruments will find Ledger's ASV version a splendid alternative. With superb soloists – Jill Gomez radiantly beautiful and Robert Tear dramatically riveting in his call to arms – this delightful music emerges with an admirable combination of freshness and weight. Ledger uses an all-male chorus; the style of the performance is totally convincing without being self-consciously authentic. The recording is first rate, rich, vivid and clear.

La Resurrezione.

*** O-L Dig. 421 132-2 (2) [id.]. Kirkby, Kwella, C. Watkinson, Partridge, Thomas, AAM, Hogwood.

*** Erato/Warner Dig. 2292 45617-2 [id.]. Argenta, Schlick, Laurens, De Mey, Mertens, Amsterdam Bar. O, Ton Koopman.

Though *La Resurrezione* does not have the great choral music which is so much the central element of later Handel oratorios, it is a fine and many-faceted piece. Hogwood directs a clean-cut, vigorous performance with an excellent cast of singers highly skilled in the authentic performance of Baroque music. Emma Kirkby is at her most brilliant in the coloratura for the Angel, Patrizia Kwella sings movingly as Mary Magdalene and Carolyn Watkinson as Cleophas adopts an almost counter-tenor-like tone. Ian Partridge's tenor has a heady lightness as St John, and though David Thomas's Lucifer could have more weight, he too sings stylishly. Excellent recording, well balanced and natural in all respects, with an attractive ambient bloom.

Koopman's recording of this oratorio provides a valuable alternative to the fine Hogwood version on Oiseau-Lyre. Koopman's cast of soloists is just as strong, with Barbara Schlick as the Angel outstandingly fine and Klaus Mertens as Lucifer weightier and stronger than his oppposite number. Koopman's approach is lighter and more resilient, allowing more relaxation, though the recording is less well focused, with voices less full and immediate.

Saul (complete).

*** Ph. Dig. 426 265-2 (3) [id.]. Miles, Dawson, Ragin, Ainslie, Mackie, Monteverdi Ch., E. Bar. Soloists, Gardiner.

Made at the Gottingen festival in 1989, Gardiner's version of this magnificent oratorio offers a live recording far more sympathetic than Harnoncourt's on Teldec (2292 42651-2). Gardiner's performance is typically vigorous in what is rather a Biblical opera than an oratorio. With choruses leavening the sequence of arias and with the confrontation of David and Saul most dramatically treated, it is more obviously approachable for the modern listener than most Handel operas. Completed some three years before *Messiah*, *Saul* had the same librettist, Charles Jennens, and represents Handel's full emergence as a great oratorio composer, with the widest range of emotions conveyed. The alternation of mourning and joy in the final sequence of numbers is startlingly effective. With Derek Lee Ragin in the counter-tenor role of David, with Alastair Miles as Saul, Lynn Dawson as Michael and John Mark Ainslie as Jonathan, it is not likely to be surpassed on disc for a long time.

Solomon.

❀ *** Ph. Dig. 412 612-2 (2) [id]. C. Watkinson, Argenta, Hendricks, Rolfe Johnson, Monteverdi Ch., E. Bar. Soloists, Gardiner.

This is among the very finest of all Handel oratorio recordings. With panache, Gardiner shows how authentic-sized forces can convey Handelian grandeur even with clean-focused textures and fast speeds. The choruses and even more magnificent double-choruses stand as cornerstones of a structure which may have less of a story-line than some other Handel oratorios – the Judgement apart – but which Gardiner shows has consistent human warmth. Thus in Act I, the relationship of Solomon and his Queen is delightfully presented, ending with the ravishing Nightingale chorus, *May no rash intruder*; while the Act III scenes between Solomon and the Queen of Sheba, necessarily more formal, are given extra warmth by having in that role a singer who is sensuous in tone, Barbara Hendricks. Carolyn Watkinson's pure mezzo, at times like a male alto, is very apt for Solomon himself (only after Handel's death did baritones capture it), while Nancy Argenta is clear and sweet as his Queen. In the Judgement scene, Joan Rodgers is outstandingly warm and characterful as the First Harlot, but the overriding glory of the set is the radiant singing of Gardiner's Monteverdi Choir. Its clean, crisp articulation matches the brilliant playing of the English Baroque Soloists, regularly challenged by Gardiner's fast speeds, as in the *Arrival of the Queen of Sheba*; and the sound is superb, coping thrillingly with the problems of the double choruses.

Susanna.

**(*) HM Dig. HMU 907030/2; *HMC 407030/2* [id.]. Hunt, Minter, Feldman, Parker, J & D. Thomas, U. C. Berkeley Chamber Ch., Philh. Bar. O, McGegan.

This is the first ever recording of a superb oratorio, written right at the end of Handel's composing career. The richness of inspiration comes very near to matching that of the other biblical piece he wrote earlier in the summer of 1748, *Solomon*. It is a much more intimate piece and, if it has failed to achieve the impact it deserves, that is largely because choruses are very few, making it unappealing to choral societies. Yet the wealth of arias and the refreshing treatment of the Apocrypha story of Susanna and the Elders make it ideal for records. McGegan's performance does not quite match those of his earlier Handel recordings, made in Budapest. This one was done live with a talented period group from Los Angeles. The main snag is that the dry acoustic brings an abrasive edge to the instrumental sound and takes away bloom from the voices. It also underlines a certain squareness in the rhythmic treatment, with tension often low, even in such a magnificent number as the chromatic chorus which follows the overture. Yet with fine soloists including Lorraine Hunt (Susanna), Drew Minter (Joacim) and Jill Feldman (Daniel), this is far more than a mere stop-gap.

Theodora.

**(*) Teldec/Warner Dig. 2292 46447-2 (2) [id.]. Alexander, Blochwitz, Kowalski, Van Nes, Scharinger, Schönberg Ch., VCM, Harnoncourt.

Theodora, first heard in 1750, was one of the very last of Handel's oratorios, with only *Jephtha* of the major works to come. It badly needed a CD recording, and there is much to enjoy in this lively account, with fresh, clean textures typical of the Concentus Musicus, and with Harnoncourt thrusting in manner, occasionally to the point of being heavy-handed. The Schönberg Choir sings with apt weight and freshness. The jollity of the choruses of heathens is nicely distinguished from the far more solemn choruses for Christians, though words are often unclear. The solo casting is strong, though this team of international singers does not always sound at home, either stylistically or in singing English. Roberta Alexander sings with characteristic warmth in the title-role of the noble Christian, in this story of self-sacrifice in Antioch during the period of persecution under the Romans. Though a purer voice would have been even more apt, she is the finest of the soloists, with the counter-tenor Jochen Kowalski exceptionally warm of tone but hardly sounding Handelian in the role of Didymus, the centurion converted to Christianity. Jard van Nes is warm and fruity as Irene and Hans Peter Blochwitz is light and fresh as Septimius. Bright, full recording.

The Triumph of time and truth.
*** Hyp. CDA 66071/2 [id.]. Fisher, Kirkby, Brett, Partridge, Varcoe, L. Handel Ch. and O, Darlow.

Darlow's performance of Handel's very last oratorio, with the London Handel Choir and Orchestra using original instruments, has an attractive bluffness. This is broader and rougher than the authentic recordings by John Eliot Gardiner, but it is hardly less enjoyable. The soloists all seem to have been chosen for the clarity of their pitching – Emma Kirkby, Gillian Fisher, Charles Brett and Stephen Varcoe, with the honey-toned Ian Partridge singing even more beautifully than the others, but with a timbre too pure quite to characterize 'Pleasure'. Good atmospheric recording; though the chorus is a little distant, the increase in overall immediacy which has come with the CD transfer makes this less striking.

Utrecht Te Deum and Jubilate.
*** O-L 414 413-2 [id.]. Nelson, Kirkby, Brett, Elliot, Covey-Crump, Thomas, Ch. of Christ Church Cathedral, Oxford, AAM, Preston.

Handel wrote the Utrecht pieces just before coming to London, intending them as a sample of his work. Using authentic instruments and an all-male choir with trebles, Preston directs a performance which is not merely scholarly but characteristically alert and vigorous, particularly impressive in the superb *Gloria* with its massive eight-part chords. With a team of soloists regularly associated with the Academy of Ancient Music, this can be confidently recommended.

OPERA

Agrippina (complete).
*** HM Dig. HMU 907063/65; *HMU 407063/65* (3). Bradshaw, Saffer, Minter, Hill, Isherwood, Popken, Dean, Banditelli, Sziláagi, Capella Savaria, McGegan.

Though based, like *Giulio Cesare*, on Roman history, *Agrippina* presents a total contrast with that later opera from Handel's full maturity. Written for Venice in 1710 it is delightfully light-hearted, the astonishingly brilliant inspiration of the young Handel. The libretto by Cardinal Grimani avoids the stiffness of most librettos of the period. That plainly encouraged the adventurous young composer to experiment with an even more fluid, less formalized structure than in most of his later operas for London. There is no number quite so striking as the finest in the later masterpieces, but the opera is magnetic in its fanciful telling of the intrigues between the Emperor Claudius, his wife Agrippina, Nero her son and Poppea, as well as Otho (Ottone) and Pallas (Pallante).

Nicolas McGegan is markedly more sympathetic in his European recordings of Handel with the Budapest-based Capella Savaria than in those he has made in California, supported by a less unhelpfully dry acoustic. *Agrippina* was recorded in the studio at the time of the 1991 Gottingen Festival. With a fine bloom on voices and instruments, notably the brass, the performance is exhilaratingly fresh and alert. The cast is first rate, led by the silvery Sally Bradshaw as Agrippina, the bright Nero of Wendy Hill and the seductive Poppea of Lisa Saffer, all well contrasted in their equally stylish ways.

Alcina (complete).
*** EMI Dig. CDS7 49771-2 (3) [Ang. CDCB 49771]. Augér, Della Jones, Kuhlmann, Harrhy, Kwella, Maldwyn Davies, Tomlinson, Opera Stage Ch., City of L. Bar. Sinfonia, Hickox.

It would be hard to devise a septet of Handelian singers more stylish than the soloists here. Though the American, Arleen Augér, may not have the weight of Joan Sutherland (who in a much-edited text sang the title-role both at Covent Garden and on record), she is just as brilliant and pure-toned, singing warmly in the great expansive arias. Even next to her, Della Jones stands out in the breeches role of Ruggiero, with an extraordinary range of memorable arias, bold as well as tender. Eiddwen Harrhy as Morgana is just as brilliant in the aria, *Tornami a vagheggiar*, usually 'borrowed' by Alcina, while Kathleen Kuhlmann, Patrizia Kwella, Maldwyn Davies and John Tomlinson all sing with a clarity and beauty to make the music sparkle. As for the text, it is even more complete than any known performance ever, when it includes as appendices two charming items that Handel cut even at the première. Hickox underlines the contrasts of mood and speed, conveying the full range of emotion. There are few Handel opera recordings to match this, with warm, spacious sound, recorded at EMI's Abbey Road studio.

Alessandro (complete).
(M) **(*) HM/BMG GD 77110 (3) [77110-2-RG]. Jacobs, Boulin, Poulenard, Nirouët, Varcoe, Guy de Mey, La Petite Bande, Kuijken.

Sigiswald Kuijken directs his team of period-performance specialists in an urgently refreshing, at times sharply abrasive reading of one of Handel's key operas. As a high counter-tenor, René Jacobs copes brilliantly with the taxing role of Alexander himself. His singing is astonishingly free and agile, if too heavily aspirated. Among the others, Isabelle Poulenard at her best sounds a little like a French Emma Kirkby, though the production is not quite so pure and at times comes over more edgily. The others make a fine, consistent team, the more effective when the recording so vividly conveys a sense of presence with sharply defined directional focus. Even though reissued at mid-price, the set is well documented and with full translation.

Amadigi (complete).
*** Erato/Warner Dig. 2292-45490-2 [id.]. Stutzmann, Smith, Harrhy, Fink, Musiciens du Louvre, Minkowski.

Written in 1715, *Amadigi* was the fifth of the Italian operas that Handel wrote for London, following up the success of the first, *Rinaldo*, and rounding off his early period of operatic experimentation. Much of its initial success was owed to the lavishness (by the standards of the time) of the staging but, perhaps surprisingly, it involves only five high voices, with no tenor or bass among the soloists. That hardly limits the variety or vigour of Handel's inspiration, with brilliant arias for Prince Dardano of Thrace in particular, superbly sung by Bernarda Fink. Nathalie Stutzmann sings Amadigi's gentle arias most affectingly, notably the lovely *Sussurate, onde vezzose*, and the two women characters, Amadigi's lover Melissa and Princess Oriana, are well taken by Eiddwen Harrhy and Jennifer Smith. As in his splendid recording of Charpentier's music for *Le malade imaginaire*, Marc Minkowski directs an electrifying performance, which is given greater impact by the closeness of the recording. That also brings an abrasiveness to the period strings, but not disagreeably so; rather, the impression is of a performance on an intimate scale, and the more involving for that.

Atalanta (complete).
*** Hung. Dig. HCD 12612/4 [id.]. Farkas, Bartfai-Barta, Lax, Bandi, Gregor, Polgar, Savaria Vocal Ens. & Capella, McGegan.

The fresh precision of the string playing of the Capella Savaria demonstrates – even without the help of vibrato – what Hungarian string quartets have been proving for generations: a superfine ability to match and blend. This is an opera crammed with dozens of sparkling, light-hearted numbers with no flagging of the inspiration, the opposite of weighty Handel. Led by the bright-toned Katarin Farkas in the name-part, the singers cope stylishly, and the absence of Slavonic wobbles confirms the subtle difference of Magyar voices; Joszef Gregor with his firm, dark bass is just as much in style, for example, as he regularly is in Verdi. First-rate recording.

Flavio (complete).
*** HM Dig. HMC 901312/13; *HMC 401312/13* (2) [id.]. Gall, Ragin, Lootens, Fink, *et al.*, Ens. 415, Jacobs.

Based on a staging of this unjustly neglected Handel opera at the 1989 Innsbruck Festival, René Jacobs' recording vividly captures the consistent vigour of Handel's inspiration. Unlike most Handel operas, this one has principal soloists in all four registers and keeps well within modern ideas of length, with some two and a half hours of music squeezed on to the two CDs. That and the quality of invention make it surprising that *Flavio* has never enjoyed popular success, even in Handel's time. The plot is no stiffer or more improbable than most of the period, and Handel's score was brilliantly written for some of the most celebrated singers of the time, including the castrato, Senesino. His four arias are among the highspots of the opera, all sung superbly here by the warm-toned and characterful counter-tenor, Derek Lee Ragin. The first three are brilliant coloratura arias; but the last, in the rare key of B flat minor, touches a darker, more tragic note. The other tragic aria is for the heroine, Emilia, again in a distant key, F sharp minor; but almost every other aria is open and vigorous, with the whole sequence rounded off in a rousing ensemble. René Jacobs' team of eight soloists is a strong one, with only the strenuous tenor of Gianpaolo Fagotto occasionally falling short of the general stylishness. Full, clear sound.

Giulio Cesare (complete).
*** HM Dig. HMC 901385/7; *HMC 401385/7* [id.]. Larmore, Schlick, Fink, Rorholm, Ragin, Zanasi, Visse, Concerto Köln, Jacobs.

Astonishingly with what is probably Handel's greatest and most popular opera, this is the very first CD version to offer a really complete text. The previous ones were based on theatre productions, seriously cut. The counter-tenor, René Jacobs, now conductor of the German group, Concerto Köln, is a warmly expressive rather than a severe period performer. With a cast of consistently fresh voices, with rhythms sprung infectiously, he also allows the broadest expansion on the great reflective moments. So Caesar's mourning for Pompey in Act 1 brings the most darkly intense account of his aria, *Alma del gran Pompeo*, and the two greatest and most beautiful of Cleopatra's arias, *V'adoro pupille* and *Piangero*, are similarly expansive without being over-romanticized. The casting of the pure, golden-toned Barbara Schlick as Cleopatra proves outstandingly successful, when she compasses so commandingly the sharp contrasts between the heroine's eight arias, bringing out different sides of the character from girlish vivacity to tragic intensity. Jennifer Larmore too, a fine, firm mezzo, with a touch of masculine toughness in the tone, makes a splendid Caesar. Together they crown the whole performance with the most seductive account of their final duet. Others both stylish and characterful include the American counter-tenor, Derek Lee Ragin, excellent in the sinister role of Tolomeo (Ptolemy), Bernarda Fink as Cornelia and Marianne Rorholm as Sesto, with the bass, Furio Zanasi, as Achille. Jacobs' expansive speeds mean that the whole opera will not fit on three CDs, but the fourth disc, at 18 minutes merely supplementary, comes free as part of the package, and includes an extra aria for the servant, Nireno, delightfully sung by the French counter-tenor, Dominique Visse. Firm, well-balanced sound.

Hercules (complete).
*** DG Dig. 423 137-2 (3) [id.]. Tomlinson, Sarah Walker, Rolfe Johnson, Jennifer Smith, Denley, Savidge, Monteverdi Ch., E. Bar. Soloists, Gardiner.

Gardiner's generally brisk performance of *Hercules* using authentic forces may at times lack Handelian grandeur in the big choruses, but it conveys superbly the vigour of the writing, its natural drama. Writing in English, Handel concentrated on direct and involving human emotions more than he generally did when setting classical subjects in Italian. Numbers are compact and memorable, and the fire of this performance is typified by the singing of Sarah Walker as Dejanira in her finest recording yet. John Tomlinson makes an excellent, dark-toned Hercules with florid passages well defined except for very occasional sliding. Youthful voices consistently help in the clarity of the attack – Jennifer Smith as Iole, Catherine Denley as Lichas, Anthony Rolfe Johnson as Hyllus and Peter Savidge as the Priest of Jupiter. Refined playing and outstanding recording quality.

Julius Caesar (complete; in English); see also above, under *Giulio Cesare*.
(M) *** EMI Dig. CMS7 69760-2 (3). Dame Janet Baker, Masterson, Sarah Walker, Della Jones, Bowman, Tomlinson, E. Nat. Op. Ch. & O, Mackerras.

Dame Janet, in glorious voice and drawing on the widest range of expressive tone-colours, shatters the old idea that this alto-castrato role should be transposed down an octave and given to a baritone. Valerie Masterson makes a charming and seductive Cleopatra, fresh and girlish, though the voice is caught a little too brightly for caressing such radiant melodies as those for *V'adoro pupille* (*Lamenting, complaining*) and *Piangero* (*Flow my tears*). Sarah Walker sings with powerful intensity as Pompey's widow; James Bowman is a characterful counter-tenor Ptolemy and John Tomlinson a firm, resonant Achillas, the other nasty character. The ravishing accompaniments to the two big Cleopatra arias amply justify the use by the excellent ENO

Orchestra of modern, not period, instruments. The full, vivid studio sound makes this one of the very finest of the invaluable series of ENO opera recordings in English.

Julius Caesar: highlights (in English).
(M) *** EMI Dig. CDM7 63724-2 [id.]; *EG 63724-4* (from above recording; cond. Mackerras).

A well-selected, generous compilation (68 minutes) for those not wanting the complete set.

Orlando (complete).
*** O-L Dig. 430 845-2 (3) [id.]. Bowman, Augér, Robbin, Kirkby, D. Thomas, AAM, Hogwood.

Hogwood and his fine team made this recording immediately after taking this opera on tour in the United States, giving semi-staged performances. Based on Ariosto's *Orlando furioso* and, more closely, on a libretto earlier used by Domenico Scarlatti, Handel's *Orlando* was radically modified to provide suitable material for individual singers, as for example the bass role of the magician, Zoroastro, specially created for a member of Handel's company. Even so, the title-role seems to have failed to please the celebrated castrato, Senesino, for whom it was intended, probably because of Handel's breaks with tradition, notably in the magnificent mad scene which ends Act II on the aria, *Vaghe pupille*, with the simple ritornello leading to amazing inspirations. That number, superbly done here by James Bowman, with appropriate sound effects, is only one of the virtuoso vehicles for the counter-tenor. This was written in 1732, after Handel had begun to compose English oratorios, and that experience evidently encouraged him to be more adventurous in his handling of operatic form. For the jewelled sequences of arias and duets, Hogwood has assembled a near-ideal cast, with Arleen Augér at her most radiant as the queen, Angelica, and Emma Kirkby characteristically bright and fresh in the lighter, semi-comic role of the shepherdess, Dorinda. Catherine Robbin assumes the role of Prince Medoro strongly, though the recording sometimes catches an unevenness in the voice. Though a weightier bass would be preferable, David Thomas sings stylishly as Zoroastro. Acclaimed as Hogwood's first complete opera set, this is one of his finest achievements on record, taut, dramatic and rhythmically resilient. Vivid, open sound. The three Acts might just have been squeezed on to two discs, but the three-disc layout allows each Act to occupy a single disc, if at considerable extra expense.

Partenope (complete).
(M) *** HM/BMG GD 77109 (3) [77109-2-RG]. Laki, Jacobs, York, Skinner, Varcoe, Müller-Molinari, Hill, La Petite Bande, Kuijken.

By the time he wrote *Partenope* in 1730 Handel was having to cut his cloth rather more modestly than earlier in his career. One problem for Handel was that at this time his company could call on only one each of soprano, tenor and bass; with an excellent team of counter-tenors and contralto, however, this performance makes light of that limitation. With the exception of René Jacobs, rather too mannered for Handel, the roster of soloists is outstanding, with Krisztina Laki and Helga Müller-Molinari welcome additions to the team. Though ornamentation is sparse, the direction of Sigiswald Kuijken is consistently invigorating, as is immediately apparent in the *Overture*. The 1979 recording sounds quite marvellous in its CD format, and the only irritation is that the English translation is printed separately – in an old-style font – from the Italian original.

Il pastor fido (opera) complete.
**(*) Hung. Dig. HCD 12912 (2) [id.]. Esswood, Farkas, Lukin, Kállay, Flohr, Gregor, Savaria Vocal Ens., Capella Savaria, McGegan.

Drawn largely from material originally written for other operas, and revised three times with still more mixing of sources, *Il pastor fido* is an unpretentious pastoral piece, which charms gently rather than compelling attention. Though there is some fussiness in the orchestral playing (on period instruments) in this welcome recording, Nicholas McGegan demonstrates what talent there is in Budapest, among singers as among instrumentalists. Singers better known in much later operatic music translate well to Handel, for example the celebrated bass, József Gregor, but the most stylish singing comes from the British counter-tenor, Paul Esswood, in the castrato role of Mirtillo. Good sound and excellent documentation.

Rodelinda, Regina de Langobardi (complete).
**(*) HM/BMG Dig. RD 771927 (3). Schlick, Schubert, Cordier, Wessel, Prégardien, Schwarz, La Stagione, Schneider.

With *Rodelinda* in February 1725 Handel followed up the enormous success of *Giulio Cesare* a year earlier, using the same librettist, Nicola Francesco Haym. Here too he modified the strict operatic conventions of the time, notably in the most celebrated of the arias, *Dove sei*, inaccurately translated as 'Art thou troubl'd.' That emerges without pause from the accompanied recitative before it, surprising the ear the more with its beauty. On this German recording from Michael Schneider and La Stagione it is tenderly sung with plaintive tone by the British counter-tenor, David Cordier, matching the rest of the excellent, otherwise all-German cast. Barbara Schlick is pure and golden in the title-role and the tenor, Christoph Prégardien, is also outstanding as the hero, Grimoaldo. Schneider is a lively and fresh Handelian not afraid of expressiveness, but often adopting a clipped, abrasive manner. He encourages generous ornamentation in Da capo repeats. Each act fits neatly on a single CD, but inconveniently the libretto prints Italian text and English translation separately. First-rate, clean sound.

Tamerlano (complete).
(M) *** Erato/Warner Dig. 2292 45408-2 (3) [id.]. Ragin, Robson, Argenta, Chance, Findlay, Schirrer, E. Bar. Soloists, Gardiner.

John Eliot Gardiner's live concert performance of *Tamerlano* presents a strikingly dramatic and immediate experience. The pacing of numbers and of the recitative is beautifully thought out and, with a cast notable for clean, precise voices, the result is electrifying. Leading the cast are two outstanding counter-tenors, whose encounters provide some of the most exciting moments: Michael Chance as Andronicus, firm and clear, Derek Ragin in the name-part equally agile and more distinctive of timbre, with a rich, warm tone that avoids womanliness. Nigel Robson in the tenor role of Bajazet conveys the necessary gravity, not least in the difficult, highly original G minor aria before the character's suicide; and Nancy Argenta sings with starry purity as Asteria. The only serious snag is the dryness of the sound, which makes voices and instruments sound more aggressive on CD than they usually do in Gardiner's recordings with the English Baroque Soloists.

COLLECTIONS

Arias: *Alexander's Feast: The Prince, unable to conceal his pain; Softly sweet in Lydian measures. Atalanta: Care selve. Giulio Cesare: Piangero. Messiah: Rejoice greatly; He shall feed his flock. Rinaldo: Lascia ch'io pianga. Samson: Let the bright Seraphim.*
**(*) Delos Dig. D/CD 3026 [id.]. Arleen Augér, Mostly Mozart O, Schwarz – BACH: *Arias.* **(*)

Arleen Augér's bright, clean, flexible soprano is even more naturally suited to these Handel arias than to the Bach items with which they are coupled. The delicacy with which she tackles the most elaborate divisions and points the words is a delight, and the main snag is that the orchestral accompaniment, recorded rather too close, is coarse, though the sound is bright and clear.

Opera arias: *Agrippina: Bel piacere. Orlando: Fammi combattere. Partenope: Funbondo spira il vento. Rinaldo: Or la tromba; Cara sposa; Venti turbini; Cor ingrato; Lascia ch'io pianga. Serse: Frondi tenere; Ombra mai fù.*
(M) **(*) Erato/Warner Dig. 2292 45186-2 [id.]. Marilyn Horne, Sol. Ven., Scimone.

Horne gives virtuoso performances of a wide-ranging collection of Handel arias. The flexibility of her voice in scales and trills and ornaments of every kind remains formidable, and the power is extraordinary down to the tangy chest register. The voice is spotlit against a reverberant acoustic. Purists may question some of the ornamentation, but voice-fanciers will not worry. The recording sounds well.

Arias: *Judas Maccabaeus: Father of heaven. Messiah: O Thou that tellest; He was despised. Samson: Return O God of Hosts.*
❀ (M) (***) Decca 433 474-2; *433 474-4*. Kathleen Ferrier, LPO, Boult – BACH: Arias. (***)

Kathleen Ferrier had a unique feeling for Handel; these performances are unforgettable for their communicative intensity and nobility of timbre and line. She receives highly sympathetic accompaniments from Boult, another natural Handelian. John Culshaw who produced the 1952 LP described this performance of *He was despised* as having 'a beauty and simplicity that I cannot think has been, or will be, surpassed'. On CD the deeply moving closing bars, when the orchestra drops away to leave the voice momentarily unaccompanied in the words 'He was despised . . . rejected', has an uncanny presence. There is, of course, pre-Dolby background noise, but in no way does it detract from the illusion of reality. This is now reissued at mid-price as part of the Kathleen Ferrier Edition.

Hanson, Howard (1896–1981)

(i) *Piano concerto in G, Op. 36; Symphonies Nos. 5 (Sinfonia sacra), Op. 43;* (ii) *7 (A Sea symphony).*
*** Delos Dig. DE 3130 [id.]. (i) Carol Rosenberger; Seattle SO, Schwarz; (ii) with Seattle Symphony Chorale.

Even if none of these works has the concentration of the early symphonies, admirers of the composer will want this collection, for all the music is given ardent advocacy and is superbly recorded. *Mosaics* was written in 1957 for Szell and his Clevelanders. While it is in variation form, it is compressed into an ongoing movement, opening sombrely, but later lightening its atmosphere somewhat, if not its forward-looking perspective. The single movement *Sinfonia sacra* (1955) – inspired by Christ's Passion – is also very succinct (about 15 minutes – three more than the variations). The composer's Nordic inheritance dominates the opening, which is very Sibelian in colour and feeling. There is a pastoral central section, and the work climaxes in a powerful brass chorale, with the intensity then falling away for a brief closing elegy. The *Sea Symphony*, a setting of Walt Whitman, was written as recently as 1977. Comparisons with the Vaughan Williams work are not to Hanson's advantage, but there is some powerful choral writing, and the 81-year-old composer looks back to his most successful piece, the *Romantic Symphony*, in the finale. The four movement *Piano concerto* (1948) is well made, but not one of the composer's most memorable works, although it has a fine slow movement. Carol Rosenberger is an eloquent soloist and is fully up to the bravura demanded by the second movement scherzo, marked *Allegro feroce* and the jollier finale.

Symphonies Nos. 1 in E min. (Nordic); 2 (Romantic); Elegy in memory of Serge Koussevitzky.
*** Delos Dig. D/CD 3073 [id.]. Seattle SO, Gerard Schwarz.

Hanson's *First Symphony* is a sombre, powerful work. Hanson was of Swedish descent and his music has a strong individuality of idiom and colour. The *Second* is warmly appealing and melodically memorable with an indelible theme which permeates the structure. These Seattle performances have plenty of breadth and ardour, and Schwarz's feeling for the ebb and flow of the musical paragraphs is very satisfying. The recording, made in Seattle Opera House, is gloriously expansive and the balance is convincingly natural. This is demonstration sound in the best sense. As a bonus, the record includes the *Elegy* written to commemorate the conductor who commissioned the *Second Symphony* and who gave its first performance in 1930.

Symphonies Nos. 1 in E min. (Nordic), Op. 21; 2 (Romantic), Op. 30; (i) *Song of democracy.*
(M) *** Mercury 432 008-2 [id.]. Eastman-Rochester O, composer; (i) with Eastman School of Music Ch.

Hanson's own pioneering stereo recordings of his two best-known symphonies have a unique thrust and ardour, with the sense of the orchestral musicians being stimulated, both by the composer's direction and by the music's emotional force. The *Song of democracy*, an effective occasional piece setting words by Walt Whitman, has plenty of dramatic impact and is also very well recorded.

Symphony No. 2 (Romantic), Op. 30.
(M) *** EMI Dig. CDM7 64304-2 [id.]. St Louis SO, Slatkin – COPLAND: *Symphony No. 3.* ***

The *Romantic* subtitle is wholly appropriate, for the *Second Symphony* is very much in a post-Rachmaninov vein. Apart from the memorable opening motif which finds its way into all three movements, the melody of the *Andante* is justly renowned in America, where it has been used as theme music for TV. Such incidental use in no way detracts from the appeal of the symphony itself which, if harmonically not breaking any new ground, is structurally sound, imaginatively laid out and by no means lightweight. Slatkin's performance is a very satisfying one, responding to the expressive nostalgia of the slow movement and bringing an exhilarating attack to the finale – there are only three movements. The full, atmospheric recording, beautifully balanced and rich in its washes of string-tone, is a pleasure in itself.

Symphony No. 3; Elegy in memory of my friend Serge Koussevitzky, Op. 44; (i) *Lament for Beowulf.*
(M) *** Mercury 434 302-2 [id.]. Eastman-Rochester O, composer, (i) with Eastman School of Music Ch.

The *Third*, which the composer recorded in 1963 in full, resonant sound, is a powerful work, with strong Nordic feeling in the outer movements. For those familiar with the earlier works, the musical terrain is familiar: the string threnodies surge purposefully forward, there are similar rhythmic patterns and confident rhetorical gestures. This is highly accessible music. This applies also to the *Elegy*, which has considerable lyrical power and variety of colour. The cantata also makes an immediate impression and is very well sung, but is in fact a more conventional piece. However, here as in the orchestral works the 1958 Mercury sound is first rate.

(i) *Symphony No. 4 (Requiem), Op. 34;* (ii) *Lament for Beowulf, Op. 25; Merry Mount: suite, Op. 31;* (iii) *Pastorale for oboe, harp and strings, Op. 38; Serenade for flute, harp and strings, Op. 35.*
*** Delos Dig. DE 3105 [id.]. (i) Seattle SO; (ii) with Symphony Chorale; (iii) NY Chamber Symphony of 92nd Street Y; Gerard Schwarz.

This CD spans Howard Hanson's career from his late twenties through to his maturity. The *Fourth Symphony* (1943) was written in memory of his father, and its four movements have titles taken from the Requiem mass (*Kyrie, Requiescat, Dies irae* and *Lux Aeterna*). Like so much of Hanson, it can be described as neo-Sibelian in the way that many Swedish composers of the period such as Atterberg were – and is more than a touch overblown. The earliest work is the *Lament for Beowulf*, composed in 1925 towards the end of his studies in Italy after winning the Prix de Rome, and in its way an impressive achievement. Gerard Schwarz proves an even more eloquent exponent of the work than the composer, who recorded it for Mercury in the 1950s but he has the benefit of a softer-grained, less glassy recording. The *Pastorale for oboe, harp and strings* and the *Serenade for flute, harp and strings* find Hanson at his best; they are both unpretentious and beautifully fashioned, and do not have the grandiose ambitions of the symphony.

Harbison, John (born 1938)

(i) *Concerto for double brass choir and orchestra;* (ii) *The Flight into Egypt;* (iii) *The Natural world.*
*** New World Dig. 80395-2 [id.]. (i) LAPO, Previn; (ii) Roberta Anderson, Sanford Sylvan, Cantata Singers & Ens., David Hoose; (iii) Janice Felty, Los Angeles Philharmonic New Music Group, Harbison.

These three fine works provide an illuminating survey of the recent work of one of the most communicative of American composers today. The most striking and vigorous is the concerto he wrote as resident composer for Previn and the Los Angeles Philharmonic, and for the orchestra's brass section in particular. The very opening may promise minimalism, nagging and very loud, but that quickly gives way to colourful and energetic writing with plenty of cross-rhythms of the kind loved by Previn. The other two works reveal the more thoughtful Harbison, the one a collection of three songs to nature poems by Wallace Stevens, Robert Bly and James Wright. The text for *The Flight into Egypt* is taken from the St Matthew Gospel in the King James Bible version, a measured and easily lyrical setting of the story of the Holy Family fleeing from King Herod. Sanford Sylvan and the choir sing the main text, with Roberta Anderson interjecting as the Angel. Excellent performances and recording.

Harris, Roy (1898–1979)

(i) *Violin concerto; Symphonies Nos. 1; 5.*
** Albany AR012 [id.]. (i) Gregory Fulkerston; Louisville O, Leighton Smith; Mester or Whitney.

The *Third Symphony* has overshadowed all of Roy Harris's other compositions so that the appearance of the present issue offers a chance of filling out our picture of him. Many people think of him as a one-work composer; although there is some truth in this, in that the *Third* encapsulates Harris's characteristics, there is much else that is fine, including the 1933 symphony, recorded here. No. 1 is strong stuff, hardly less impressive than No. 3, but neither No. 5 nor the *Violin concerto* adds greatly to our picture of him. Gregory Fulkerston gives a persuasive account of the solo part, but the strings of the enterprising Louisville Orchestra are wanting in body and lustre. The recordings are serviceable rather than distinguished.

Epilogue to profiles in courage; When Johnny comes marching home (An American overture).
** Albany TROY 027-2 [id.]. Louisville O, Jorge Mester – BECKER: *Symphonia brevis;* SCHUMAN: *Symphony No. 4* etc. **

Roy Harris's overture, *When Johnny comes marching home*, dates from 1934, and thus precedes the famous *Third Symphony*. It was composed in two clear sections of just under four minutes each with the side-lengths of a 78-r.p.m. record in mind and was one of his first works to be put on record (by Ormandy and the Minneapolis orchestra). It is a fresh and attractive piece and, like most of Harris's music of the 1930s, has a vital impulse which by 1964, when he composed the *Epilogue to profiles in courage*, had slackened into self-imitation. Good performances and rather good recording too (the overture comes from 1978 and the *Epilogue* from 1966).

Symphony No. 3 in one movement.
*** DG Dig. 419 780-2 [id.]. NYPO, Bernstein – SCHUMAN: *Symphony No. 3.* ***

Roy Harris's *Third* is the archetypal American Symphony. There is a real sense of the wide open spaces, of the abundant energy and independent nature of the American pioneers, and an instinctive feeling for form. The music moves forward relentlessly from the very opening bars until the massive eloquence of its coda. Like Samuel Barber's *First*, it is a one-movement work, but it is held together more convincingly, is far less episodic, grander and more deeply original. Bernstein gives a keenly felt but essentially softer-grained account of the work than the famous first Koussevitzky recording. There is no lack of punch or weight, but the ends of some paragraphs are carefully rounded. However, this is a great symphony – splendidly played and well recorded.

Harty, Hamilton (1879–1941)

(i) *Piano concerto in B min.;* (ii) *In Ireland (Fantasy for flute, harp and orchestra); With the wild geese.*
*** Chan. Dig. CHAN 8321; *ABTD 1084* [id.]. (i) Binns, (ii) Fleming, Kelly; Ulster O, Thomson.

Harty's *Piano concerto*, written in 1922, has strong Rachmaninovian influences, but the melodic freshness remains individual and in this highly sympathetic performance the work's magnetism increases with familiarity, in spite of moments of rhetoric. The *In Ireland fantasy* is full of delightful Irish melodic whimsy, especially appealing when the playing is so winning. Melodrama enters the scene in the symphonic poem, *With the wild geese*, but its Irishry asserts itself immediately in the opening theme. Again a splendid performance and a high standard of digital sound.

Violin concerto in D; Variations on a Dublin air.
*** Chan. CHAN 8386; *ABTD 1044* [id.]. Ralph Holmes, Ulster O, Thomson.

Though the *Violin concerto* has no strongly individual idiom, the invention is fresh and often touched with genuine poetry. Ralph Holmes gives a thoroughly committed account of the solo part and is well supported by an augmented Ulster Orchestra under Bryden Thomson. The *Variations* are less impressive though thoroughly enjoyable. These are accomplished and well-recorded performances.

An Irish symphony; A Comedy overture.
*** Chan. Dig. CHAN 8314; *ABTD 1027* [id.]. Ulster O, Thomson.

The *Irish symphony* dates from 1904 and arose from a competition for a suite or symphony based on traditional Irish airs, inspired by the first Dublin performance of Dvořák's *New World symphony*. Harty's symphony won great acclaim for its excellent scoring and good craftsmanship. The scherzo is particularly engaging. It is extremely well played by the Ulster Orchestra under Bryden Thomson, and the overture is also successful and enjoyable. The recording is absolutely first class in every respect.

VOCAL MUSIC

The Children of Lir; Ode to a nightingale.
*** Chan. Dig. CHAN 8387; *ABTD 1051* [id.]. Harper, Ulster O, Thomson.

Harty's setting of Keats's *Ode to a nightingale* is richly convincing, a piece written for his future wife, the soprano, Agnes Nicholls. The other work, directly Irish in its inspiration, evocative in an almost Sibelian way, uses the soprano in wordless melisma, here beautifully sung by Heather Harper. The performances are excellent, warmly committed and superbly recorded.

Haydn, Josef (1732–1809)

Cello concerto in C, Hob VIIb/1.
(B) *** Ph. 422 481-2. Gendron, LSO, Leppard – BOCCHERINI: *Cello concerto.* ***
**(*) EMI CDC7 47614-2. Jacqueline du Pré, ECO, Barenboim – DVOŘÁK: *Concerto.* **(*)

Cello concertos in C and D, Hob VIIb/1–2.
*** Ph. Dig. 420 923-2 [id.]. Heinrich Schiff, ASMF, Marriner.
*** O-L Dig. 414 615-2 [id.]. Christophe Coin, AAM, Hogwood.
(BB) *** Naxos Dig. 8.550059; *4550059* [id.]. Ludovít Kanta, Capella Istropolitana, Peter Breiner – BOCCHERINI: *Cello concerto.* ***
(M) **(*) EMI CDM7 69299-2 [id.]; *EG 769299-4.* Tortelier, Württemberg CO, Faerber.
**(*) Sony MK 36674 [id.]. Yo-Yo Ma, ECO, Garcia.

Cello concerto in D, Hob VIIb/2.
*** EMI CDC7 47840-2 [id.]. Jacqueline du Pré, LSO, Barbirolli – BOCCHERINI: *Concerto.* **(*)

Cello concertos in C and D, Hob VIIb/1–2; in G (arr. of *Violin concerto, Hob VIIa/4*).
**(*) DG Dig. 419 786-2 [id.]. Mischa Maisky, COE.

Even in a competitive field, Heinrich Schiff is a strong contender. His playing has not only an effortless fluency but also a zest for life. As always, he produces a beautiful sound, as indeed do the Academy under Marriner. These are impressively fresh-sounding performances with lyrical and affectionate (but not too affectionate) playing from all concerned. Schiff plays his own cadenzas – and very good they are. The recording has the realistic timbre, balance and bloom one associates with Philips.

Christophe Coin, too, is a superb soloist and, provided the listener has no reservations about the use of original instruments, Hogwood's accompaniments are equally impressive. The style is not aggressively abrasive but gives extra clarity and point to the music, not least in the breathtakingly brilliant account of the finale of the *C major Concerto.* Certainly no fresher or more vital performance of these two works has been put on disc, although Coin's own cadenzas – undoubtedly stylish – are on the long side. Excellent sound.

Kanta is a soloist of quality. The excellent Naxos recording is made in a bright, resonant acoustic in which every detail is clearly registered, though the players are perhaps forwardly placed. The accompaniments are alert and fresh. Kanta plays contemporary cadenzas. This record is a genuine bargain.

Tortelier gives warmly expressive performances of the two *Concertos*, more relaxed than some of his rivals, but not lacking spontaneity. He is sympathetically if not always immaculately accompanied by the Württemberg Chamber Orchestra. Clear yet warm digital sound to match, very pleasingly balanced. At mid-price this remains fully competitive.

Ma's refinement has its own rewards, though some may prefer a bolder approach to music firmly belonging to the classical eighteenth century. Apart from one or two odd points of balance, the recording is clean and full.

Mischa Maisky gives beautifully cultured readings of both concertos, which he also directs himself. He has much warmth and refinement, though his tempi are generally a bit too fast. He adds a bonus in the shape of an arrangement of the *G major Violin concerto.* The recordings, made in the Vienna Konzerthaus, have admirable body and presence, and detail is well placed. Marvellous playing, but not a first choice.

Gendron's account of the *C major Concerto* is highly musical and is sensitively accompanied by Leppard. This coupling with Boccherini shows him at his finest, and the recording is of good Philips quality.

With Barbirolli to partner her, Jacqueline du Pré's performance of the best-known *D major Concerto* is warmly expressive. Though purists may object, the conviction and flair of the playing are extraordinarily compelling, and the romantic feeling is matched by an attractively full, well-balanced recording which belies its age (1969).

In the *C major*, this time in partnership with Barenboim, Du Pré gives a performance of characteristic warmth and intensity. Her style, as in the D major work, is sometimes romantic in a way that, strictly speaking, is inappropriate in this music – yet the very power of her personality is strongly conveyed. This is the sort of music-making that defies cold analysis. Good recording.

(i) *Cello concerto in C, Hob VIIb/1;* (ii; iv) *Horn concertos Nos. 1–2;* (iii; iv) *Trumpet concerto in D.*
(M) *** Decca 430 633-2; 430 633-4 [id.]. (i) Rostropovich, ECO, Britten; (ii) Tuckwell; (iii) Alan Stringer; (iv) ASMF, Marriner.

(i) *Cello concerto in C, Hob VIIb/1;* (ii) *Horn concertos Nos. 1–2 in D, Hob VIId/3–4;* (iii) *Trumpet concerto in E flat.*
(M) *** Ph. Dig. 432 060-2; *432 060-4*. (i) Heinrich Schiff; (ii) Baumann; (iii) Hardenberger; ASMF, Marriner or I. Brown.

A self-recommending collection from Philips. All the solo playing is first class: Schiff is superbly stylish in the *C major Cello concerto*, Baumann's warm tone and fine sense of line in the works for horn are most appealing, and Hardenberger's famous account of the *Trumpet concerto* is unsurpassed. The accompaniments are admirable and the recording is of Philips's best, if rather resonant. There is no more enticing collection of Haydn concertos than this; the only snag is the total absence of information about the music.

Rostropovich's earlier (1964) stereo recording of the *C major Cello concerto* for Decca is undoubtedly romantic, and some may feel he takes too many liberties in the slow movement. But tempi are well judged and with very sympathetic conducting from Britten. The coupling of first-class 1966 versions of both the *Horn concertos* by Tuckwell in peak form and Stringer's 1967 account of the *Trumpet concerto* (all deriving from Argo masters) is certainly tempting. Alan Stringer favours a forthright, open timbre, but he plays the famous slow movement graciously and the orchestral accompaniment, as in the *Horn concertos*, has striking elegance and finesse. All three CD transfers are first class. Another most desirable collection, offering 73 minutes of music.

Cello concerto in C; Violin concerto No. 1 in C, Hob VIIa/1; Double concerto for violin and harpsichord in F, Hob XVIII/6.
**(*) Mer. CDE 84177; *KE 77177* [id.]. William Conway, Malcolm Layfield, David Francis, Goldberg Ens., Layfield.

The gleamingly fresh opening tutti of the *Violin concerto*, full of vitality, is immediately welcoming. Malcolm Layfield makes an appealing soloist, and the *Double concerto* is also enjoyably done and excellently balanced. The *Cello concerto* has vigorous allegros, but the melodic line in the slow movement is rather less convincing. The overall sound is impressive, except for a small amount of background hiss, which suggests a non-digital master.

(i) *Harpsichord concerto in D, Hob XVIII/2;* (ii) *Oboe concerto in C, Hob VIIg/C1;* (iii) *Trumpet concerto in E flat.*
**(*) DG Dig. 431 678-2 [id.]. (i) Trevor Pinnock; (ii) Paul Goodwin; (iii) Mark Bennett; ECO, Pinnock.

The sounds of the 'authentic' oboe and the keyed trumpet are a good deal more robust than their modern equivalents and, for all the expertise of the soloists, there is some loss of finesse. Pinnock understands this and provides accompaniments that are comparably characterful and robust. Paul Goodwin plays with plenty of character in a work that Haydn probably did not write at all, and Mark Bennett gives the most convincing account we have yet experienced on a keyed trumpet of Haydn's greatest concerto, avoiding the throttled timbre that some authenticists manage to produce. But the highlight of the disc is Trevor Pinnock's delightfully fresh account of the *Harpsichord concerto*, beautifully balanced and in perfect scale against the small chamber group.

Horn concerto No. 1 in D, Hob VIId/3.
(M) *** Decca 417 767-2 [id.]. Barry Tuckwell, ASMF, Marriner – MOZART: *Concertos Nos 1–4*. ***

Haydn's *First Horn concerto* is a fine work, technically more demanding than any of the Mozart concertos – especially as played by Barry Tuckwell on Decca, with a profusion of ornaments and trills, witty or decorative. Tuckwell's playing throughout is of the highest order, and Marriner's vintage accompaniments are equally polished and full of elegance and vitality. The remastering is admirably fresh.

Horn concertos Nos. 1 in D, Hob VII/d3; 2 in D, Hob VII/d4.
(M) *** Teldec/Warner Dig. 9031 74790-2 [id.]. Dale Clevenger, Liszt CO, Rolla – M. HAYDN: *Concertino.* ***

Dale Clevenger, principal horn with the Chicago Symphony, gives superb accounts of the two *Horn concertos* attributed to Haydn (the second is of doubtful lineage). The accompaniments are supportive, polished and elegant. These performances have fine spirit and spontaneity and on CD the Telefunken recording, made in a nicely judged and warm acoustic, is in the demonstration class: when Clevenger plays his solo cadenzas, the tangibility of his presence is remarkable, yet the combination with the orchestra is hardly less convincing.

(i) *Horn concertos Nos. 1–2;* (ii) *Trumpet concerto in E flat;* (i) *Divertimento a 3 in E flat.*
**(*) Nimbus NI 5010 [id.]. (i) Thompson; (ii) Wallace; Philh. O, Warren-Green.

In his interesting notes for the Nimbus CD, Michael Thompson suggests that Haydn wrote his *First* and *Second Concertos* for his first and second horn players, Thaddäus Steinmüller and Carl Franz. Yet both works explore the widest range, and it was the *Divertimento*, an attractive bonus, that exploited Steinmüller's ability to slip easily into the stratosphere of the horn register. Thompson manages it too, with aplomb, and he gives bold, confident accounts of the two concertos, with a sprinkling of decoration. John Wallace's trumpet timbre is strikingly brilliant, as recorded, and his playing in the *Trumpet concerto* is full of personality. He too likes to decorate and there are some attractive surprises in the finale. The recording was made in the resonant ambience of All Saints', Tooting, but the CD provides good definition under the circumstances, even if the harpsichord tends to get lost.

Oboe concerto in C, Hob VIIg/C1.
*** Capriccio Dig. 10 308 [id.]. Lajos Lencsés, Stuttgart RSO, Marriner – HUMMEL: *Intro., theme & variations;* MARTINŮ: *Concerto.* ***

Haydn's *Oboe concerto* is of doubtful authenticity and in Lajos Lencsés' hands it is given an almost Italianate sunny grace. The *Andante* is played with appealing delicacy and the Minuet finale has an elegantly light touch. Marriner brings a touch of classical gravitas to the tuttis of the first movement and is altogether a most sympathetic accompanist. The balance is natural and the sound excellent. So are the couplings.

Piano concerto in D, Hob XVIII/2.
(B) **(*) Pickwick Dig. PCD 964; *IMPC 964* [id.]. Gloria d'Arti, ECCO, Aadland – BACH: *Clavier concerto No. 1;* MOZART: *Piano concerto No. 8.* **(*)

It is fascinating to compare this highly musical performance by the talented sixteen-year-old Italian pianist with Trevor Pinnock's harpsichord version – see above. Tempi are remarkably similar, yet the Pinnock version seems lighter and fresher and more transparent. Such is the case for using original instruments! Even so this modern performance has plenty of vitality and is very enjoyable in its own right. It is excellently recorded.

Trumpet concerto in E flat.
❀ *** Ph. Dig. 420 203-2; *420 203-4* [id.]. Håkan Hardenberger, ASMF, Marriner – HERTEL***; HUMMEL***❀; STAMITZ: *Concertos.* ***
*** Delos Dig. D/CD 3001 [id.]. Schwarz, New York 'Y' CO – HUMMEL: *Concerto.* ***
*** Sony CD 37846 [id.]. Marsalis, Nat. PO, Leppard – HUMMEL: *Concerto**** (with L. MOZART: *Concerto* ***).
(B) *** CfP Dig CD-CFP 4589; *TC-CFP 4589.* Ian Balmain, RLPO, Kovacevich – MOZART: *Horn concertos.* ***

The only possible reservation about Hardenberger's vividly recorded version of Haydn's finest concerto is that the acoustic in which the orchestra is set is a shade over-reverberant. The trumpet, however, placed well forward, is right in the room with the listener and its physical presence is highly involving. Hardenberger's playing of the noble line of the *Andante* is no less telling than his fireworks in the finale and, with Marriner providing warm, elegant and polished accompaniments throughout, this is probably the finest single collection of trumpet concertos in the present catalogue.

George Schwarz's account on Delos is hardly less memorable, but the Delos CD now seems distinctly short measure, although the Hummel coupling is equally desirable. Indeed, Schwarz's stylish command, richly gleaming timbre and easy bravura are impossible to resist, and in the lovely *Andante* he adds a little decoration to the melody, played with a warm, serene elegance. The finale combines wit and sparkle. The recording is attractively reverberant without inflating the lively accompaniment which Schwarz himself directs.

Marsalis is splendid too, his bravura no less spectacular, with the finale a *tour de force*, yet never aggressive in its brilliance. He is cooler than Schwarz in the slow movement, but his way with Haydn is eminently stylish, as is Leppard's lively and polished accompaniment. The CBS recording is faithful and the CD gives a very vivid projection, although the orchestral sound is slightly artificial in its immediacy.

With Stephen Kovacevich as conductor, Ian Balmain, principal trumpet with the Royal Liverpool Philharmonic, favours extreme speeds for Haydn's delectable *Trumpet concerto*, playing brilliantly. If not quite as memorable as Hardenberger's version, it makes an apt and attractive coupling for Claire Briggs's fine recordings of all four Mozart *Horn concertos*, very well recorded.

Violin concerto in C, Hob VIIa/1.
(M) *** Teldec/Warner Dig. 9031 74784-2 [id.]. Zehetmair, Liszt CO – M. HAYDN: *Concerto* **(*); SIBELIUS: *Concerto.* **

Haydn's *C major Violin concerto* is given a superb performance by the young Hungarian violinist, Thomas Zehetmair, stylish, strong and resilient. He also directs the accompaniments which are alert and spirited in outer movements and responsive in the lovely *Adagio.*

Violin concertos: in C, Hob VIIa/1; in G, Hob VIIa/4.
(B) *** Ph. 426 977-2; *426 977-4.* Grumiaux, ECO or New Philh. O, Leppard – MOZART: *Adagio; Rondo;* SCHUBERT: *Rondo.* ***

Haydn's *Violin concertos* are early works; the *C major*, with its winding, serenade-like melody in the slow movement, is probably the finer, but the *G major* too has an eloquent *Adagio* and a bustling finale. They make perfect vehicles for Grumiaux's refined classicism. Good mid-1960s sound and alert, gracious support from Leppard.

Sinfonia concertante in B flat; Symphony No. 96 in D (Miracle).
*** DG Dig. 423 105-2 [id.]. COE, Abbado.

Abbado conducts the Chamber Orchestra of Europe in winning performances of both works, lively and sparkling. With outstanding solo contributions – the violinist and cellist just as stylish as their wind colleagues who have already appeared as soloists on several records – this issue of the *Sinfonia concertante* even outshines other excellent versions from Vienna and London with more mature soloists. The symphony too brings some brilliant playing, capturing the fun of Haydn's inspiration without any hint of undue haste or breathlessness. Abbado has rarely made a record as happy as this.

SYMPHONIES

Symphonies Nos. 1–104; A; B.
❀ (M) *** Decca 430 100-2 (32) [id.]. Philharmonia Hungarica, Antal Dorati.

Antal Dorati was ahead of his time as a Haydn interpreter when, in the early 1970s, he made his pioneering recording of the complete Haydn symphonies. Superbly transferred to CD in full, bright and immediate sound, the performances are a consistent delight, with brisk allegros and fast-flowing andantes, with textures remarkably clean. The slow rustic-sounding accounts of Minuets are more controversial, but the rhythmic bounce makes them very attractive too. The packaging is excellent, available either in eight separate boxes or as a complete set, with the sequence kept helpfully in numerical order. The time-length is generous, but it is a pity that no way was found of including the extra and alternative movements which Dorati originally recorded along with the complete cycle. That would make a valuable supplementary disc and could have been given free with the complete set.

Symphonies Nos. 1 in D; 2 in C; 3 in G; 4 in D; 5 in A; 6 in D (Le Matin); 7 in C (Le Midi); 8 in G (Le Soir); 9 in C; 10 in D; 11 in E flat; 12 in E; 13 in D; 14 in A; 15 in D; 16 in B flat.
(M) *** Decca 425 900-2 (4) [id.]. Philharmonia Hungarica, Antal Dorati.

The urgent crescendo which opens *Symphony No. 1* at once establishes the high voltage of inspiration, and from then on there is no suspicion of a power failure. These works – antedated by one or two symphonies that are later in the Breitkopf numbering – come from the early

Esterházy period (1759–63) and show the young, formidably gifted composer working at full stretch. Dorati left these symphonies until well on in his great pioneering recording project, and the combination of exhilaration and stylishness is irresistible.

Symphonies Nos. 1 in D; 2 in C; 3 in G; 4 in D; 5 in A.
*** Hyp. Dig. CDA 66524 [id.]. Hanover Band, Roy Goodman.

Goodman here establishes a winning manner in early Haydn. More than most of his rivals, he conveys the geniality of the inspiration, less abrasive and more relaxed than most period performers. He is helped by a warmly atmospheric acoustic, not as sharply analytical as that in Christopher Hogwood's rival series on L'Oiseau-Lyre Florilegium.

Symphonies Nos. 6 in D (Le Matin); 7 in C (Le Midi); 8 in G (Le Soir).
*** DG Dig. 423 098-2 [id.]. E. Concert, Pinnock.
*** Ph. Dig. 411 441-2 [id.]. ASMF, Marriner.
(B) *** Decca 421 627-2; *421 627-4* [id.]. Philh. Hungarica, Dorati.
*** Hyp. Dig. CDA 66523 [id.]. Hanover Band, Roy Goodman.
**(*) Denon Dig. 8175 79612-2 Lausanne CO, Lopez-Cobos.

These were almost certainly the first works that Haydn composed on taking up his appointment as Kapellmeister to the Esterházys and it seems very likely that their highly imaginative content and frequent use of instrumental solos were designed as much to stimulate the interest of his players as to make a grand effect on his employer. Pinnock's players clearly relish their opportunities here and take them with strong personality. The performances are polished and refined, yet highly spirited, with infectious allegros and expressive feeling. The size of the string group (4.4.2.2.1) is made to seem expansive by the warm acoustics of the Henry Wood Hall and there is certainly weight here, yet essentially this is a bracing musical experience with the genius of these early works fully displayed.

Admirers of Marriner and his Academy should not be disappointed with their (1982) alternative. The ASMF is nothing if not a band of soloists and there is plenty of character throughout this set, fresh and polished and very well balanced and recorded, though the harpsichord is only just distinguishable.

Dorati is at his finest in these relatively well-known named symphonies, with their marvellous solos for members of the Esterházy orchestra. The remastered recording sounds fresh and clear, but just a little of the body has been lost from the strings. A bargain, nevertheless.

Goodman's performances with the Hanover Band are characteristically lively and fresh, bringing out the colour of these three linked works. Allegros are brisk but never sound breathless, and slow movements are relaxed enough to allow a winning expressiveness. The recording is warm without obscuring detail.

The credentials of the Lausanne Chamber Orchestra in Haydn were firmly established through the excellent Philips series of Haydn operas conducted by Antal Dorati. Under Lopoz-Cobos in these early symphonies the playing is comparably fresh and lively. The digital sound is full and firm, rather closely balanced, and anyone wanting performances on modern instruments will find much to enjoy. Winningly they convey the fun as well as the colour of Haydn's early inspirations and prompt some excellent solo work from the orchestra's principals. However, it weighs against this disc that no continuo is used, making the performances seem heavier than either the Dorati or Marriner versions of this favourite triptych.

Symphonies Nos. 17 in F; 18 in G; 19 in D; 20 in C; 21 in A; 22 in E flat (Philosopher) (1st version); *23 in G; 24 in D; 25 in C; 26 in D min. (Lamentatione); 27 in G; 28 in A; 29 in E; 30 in C (Alleluja); 31 in D (Hornsignal); 32 in C; 33 in C.*
(M) *** Decca 425 905-2 (4) [id.]. Philharmonia Hungarica, Antal Dorati.

Because of the idiosyncrasies of the Breitkopf numbering, this sequence of symphonies includes one, *Lamentatione*, that is later than the rest, a transitional work leading into the dark, intense manner of Haydn's middle period. It gives marvellous perspective to the rest, all of them fascinating and many of them masterly. The early festive symphonies, like Nos. 32 and 33, both in C major, with trumpets and timpani, have their individual marks of inspiration, for example in the C minor slow movement of No. 33. As in the rest of the cycle, Dorati's performances, helped by vivid recording, have you listening on from one symphony to the next, compulsively following the composer's career.

Symphonies Nos. 21 in A; 22 in E flat (Philosopher); 23 in G; 24 in D; 28 in A ; 29 in E; 30 in C (Alleluja); 31 in D (Horn Signal); 34 in D min.

**(*) O-L Dig. 430 082-2 (3) [id.]. AAM, Christopher Hogwood.

This first box of Hogwood's projected Haydn cycle on period instruments brings fresh and lively allegros and outstandingly vivid and immediate sound. The classical style of Hogwood and the AAM has perceptibly mellowed since they recorded their Mozart symphony cycle, and the playing itself is even more refined, but there is still a degree of stiffness in slow movements.

Symphonies Nos. 22 in E flat (Philosopher); 63 in C (La Roxelane); 80 in D min.
*** DG Dig. 427 337-2 [id.]. Orpheus CO.

The three symphonies offered here span twenty of Haydn's most creative years, from the highly original *Philosopher* (1764) to the mature D minor work with its serenely beautiful *Adagio* and characteristic interplay of drama and benign yet twinkling humour in the outer movements. *La Roxelane* is so nicknamed because its not-so-slow second movement brings characteristically felicitous variations on an *entr'acte* which Haydn had previously written as part of the incidental music for a play: La Roxelane was its heroine. The rest of the work is typically inventive, and the Orpheus players give all three symphonies with that sense of style, polish and intelligent commitment we have come to expect from them. Pacing, suppleness of phrase and precision of ensemble again demonstrate that for them a conductor isn't necessary, and the DG sound is well up to the previous high standard of their Haydn series.

Symphonies Nos. 26 (Lamentatione), 35, 38–9, 41–2, 43 (Mercury), 44 (Trauer), 45 (Farewell), 46–7, 48 (Maria Theresia), 49 (La passione), 50–52, 58, 59 (Fire), 65.
(M) *** DG Dig. 435 001-2 (6). E. Concert, Trevor Pinnock.

This set lays out in chronological order (not in the normal Hoboken catalogue sequence) the so-called *Sturm und Drang Symphonies*, which Haydn composed during his early years at Eszterháza between 1766 and 1773, but including also Nos. 41, 48 and 65, which are outstanding examples, not of 'storm and stress', but of Haydn's ceremonial application of symphonic form. Pinnock's forces are modest (with 6.5.2.2.1 strings), but the panache of the playing conveys any necessary grandeur. It is a new experience to have Haydn symphonies of this period recorded in relatively dry and close sound, with inner detail crystal clear (harpsichord never obscured) and made the more dramatic by the intimate sense of presence, yet with a fine bloom on the instruments. Some may find a certain lack of charm at times, and others may quarrel with the very brisk one-in-a-bar minuets and – dare one say it! – even find finales a bit rushed. Converts to the authentic school will surely find such misgivings of little import, and certainly the recording is well balanced and extremely vivid.

Symphonies Nos. 26 in D min. (Lamentatione); 52 in C min.; 53 in D (L'Imperiale).
*** Virgin Dig. VC7 90743-2; *VC 790743-4* [id.]. La Petite Bande, Sigiswald Kuijken.

Two of the toughest of Haydn's *Sturm und Drang* symphonies plus one of the celebratory works which he wrote on emerging from that self-questioning period make an excellent coupling in lively and stylish period performances. As recorded in a Haarlem church in the Netherlands, the light-textured string sound is more abrasive than usual and the oboe timbre is both plangent and sonorous; but the ear quickly adjusts. These are fresh, vital, cleanly articulated performances which wear their authenticity lightly and even indulge in speeds for slow movements that are more expansive and affectionate than many purists would allow. The '*Lamentatione*' refers to the Gregorian chant Haydn used in both the first two movements. No. 53 is thought to derive its title from a performance given before the Empress Maria Theresia.

Symphonies Nos. 34 in D min.; 35 in B flat; 36 in E flat; 37 in C; 38 in C (Echo); 39 in G min.; 40 in F; 41 in C; 42 in D; 43 in E flat (Mercury); 44 in E min. (Trauer); 45 in F sharp min. (Farewell); 46 in B; 47 in G.
(M) *** Decca 425 910-2 (4) [id.]. Philharmonia Hungarica, Antal Dorati.

Despite the numbering, this set of symphonies arguably includes the very first symphony of all, *No. 37 in C*, revealing, as H. C. Robbins Landon points out in his absorbing commentary, 'impeccable craftsmanship and enormous energy'. This particular sequence brings us to the frontier in Dorati's interpretations between those using and not using harpsichord continuo. He switches over in the middle of *No. 40 in F* – not illogically, when the finale is a fugue in which continuo would only be muddling. The two named symphonies towards the end of the box (*Trauer* and *Farewell*) lead into the darker intensity of Haydn's so-called *Sturm und Drang* period. Unfailingly lively performances and abiding, brightly vivid sound.

Symphony No. 44 in E min. (Trauer).
(B) *** Pickwick Dig. PCD 820; *CIMPC 820* [id.]. O of St John's, Smith Square, Lubbock – MOZART: *Symphony No. 40.* **(*)

The Orchestra of St John's are on their toes throughout their splendidly committed account of the *Trauersymphonie*. Outer movements are alert and vivacious – the finale has striking buoyancy and spring – and there is some lovely espressivo playing in the beautiful *Adagio* slow movement which brings out the forward-looking qualities of the writing. The recording too is in the demonstration class.

Symphonies Nos. 44 in E min. (Trauer); 88 in G; 104 in D (London).
(BB) *** Naxos Dig. 8.550287; *4550287* [id.]. Capella Istropolitana, Barry Wordsworth.

Symphonies Nos. 45 in F sharp min. (Farewell); 48 in C (Maria Theresia); 102 in B flat.
(BB) *** Naxos Dig. 8.550382; *4550382* [id.]. Capella Istropolitana, Barry Wordsworth.

Symphonies Nos. 82 in C (The Bear); 96 in D (Miracle); 100 in G (Military).
(BB) *** Naxos Dig. 8.550139; *4550139* [id.]. Capella Istropolitana, Barry Wordsworth.

Symphonies Nos. 83 in G min. (The Hen); 94 in G (Surprise); 101 in D (The Clock).
(BB) *** Naxos Dig. 8.550114; *4550114* [id.]. Capella Istropolitana, Barry Wordsworth.

Symphonies Nos. 85 in B flat (La Reine); 92 in G (Oxford); 103 in E flat (Drum Roll).
(BB) *** Naxos Dig. 8.550387 [id.]. Capella Istropolitana, Barry Wordsworth.

Like Barry Wordsworth's recordings of Mozart symphonies, also with the Capella Istropolitana on the Naxos label, this Haydn collection provides a series of outstanding bargains at the lowest budget price. The sound is not quite as clean and immediate as in the Mozart series, a little boomy at times in fact, and Wordsworth's preference for relatively relaxed speeds is a little more marked here than in Mozart, but the varied choice of works on each disc is most attractive. It is good that, in addition to named symphonies, Wordsworth includes two of the undoubted masterpieces among those unnamed, both with supremely beautiful slow movements, *No. 88 in G* and *No. 102 in B flat*. At their modest cost, these are well worth collecting alongside Dorati's Philharmonia Hungarica boxes.

Symphonies Nos. 44 in E min. (Trauer); 77 in B flat.
**(*) DG Dig. 415 365-2 [id.]. Orpheus CO.

Symphonies Nos. 45 in F sharp min.; 81 in G.
**(*) DG Dig. 423 376-2 [id.]. Orpheus CO.

Symphonies Nos. 48 in C (Maria Theresia); 49 in F min. (La Passione).
**(*) DG Dig. 419 607-2 [id.]. Orpheus CO.

This Orpheus series is of high calibre both of playing and of recording, but at full price the offering of two symphonies per full-priced CD now seems ungenerous. However, the orchestra certainly seem to be of one mind in No. 44, which they give with great freshness and spirit. All the players are expert, and so keenly do they listen to each other that they blend, almost as if they had a fine conductor in front of them. They capture the urgency of feeling of the *Trauersymphonie*, and No. 77 is given with a lightness of touch and infectious high spirits. Its humour and vivacity are beautifully realized, and the DG engineers provide excellent recording, too. Strongly recommended; as sound, this CD is especially believable.

They are also at their very finest in their coupling of the *Farewell Symphony* and *No. 81 in G*. Here the opening is rhythmically strong, but the players most appealingly catch the charming touch of melancholy which underlies the first movement's second group, while the bassoon solo that lies at the centre of the Minuet is equally characterful. In the *Farewell symphony*, the tenderly refined *espressivo* of the strings in the *Adagio* is most beautiful, while the departing players in the finale present their solos with personable finesse.

The *Maria Theresia symphony* is a splendidly festive piece and is comparably served here by this excellent conductorless ensemble. They take its first movement very briskly – perhaps a shade too much so. The two horns playing at pitch, rather than an octave lower, give a particularly bright colouring; the Orpheus also omit the trumpets and drums which are of dubious authenticity. *La Passione* makes an excellent foil and these players capture the dark *Sturm und Drang* introspection of the piece.

Symphonies Nos. 45 in F sharp min. (Farewell); 46 in B; 47 in G.
**(*) Hyp. Dig. CDA 66522 [id.]. Hanover Band, Roy Goodman.

With Goodman's Hanover Band, the *Farewell Symphony* is not done as bitingly as one might expect of a work from Haydn's *Sturm und Drang* period in the unexpected key of F sharp minor. The recording is marginally less well focused than the rest, but the actual 'farewell' in the finale with its diminishing orchestra is presented very delicately with a welcome absence of gimmick. The other works here are well up to the high standard of this excellent Hyperion series.

Symphonies Nos. 45 in F sharp min. (Farewell); 48 in C (Maria Theresia).
(M) *** Sony Dig. MDK 46507 [id.]. L'Estro Armonico, Derek Solomons.

The musical marvel of No. 45 in the rare key (for Haydn's time) of F sharp minor brings one of Solomons' finest performances. Solomons keeps his ensemble of period instruments very small, with six violins but only one each of the other stringed instruments, a scale Haydn himself employed at Esterháza, and in the slow movement of the *Farewell* the effect is touchingly graceful, almost ethereal in texture. Special mention must be made of the brilliant horn playing of Anthony Halstead (no concessions here to any technical problems) not only in this work but also in the slow movement of No. 48, again hauntingly beautiful. The invigorating opening movement of that same work, bursting with exuberance and with the first horn, crooked in C alto, shining out over the strings, brings thrilling sound, and the Minuet is no less impressive. Recorded in the pleasingly atmospheric acoustic of St Barnabas Church, Woodside Park, the sense of vibrant yet intimate music-making is most stimulating.

Symphonies Nos. 48 in C (Maria Theresia); 49 in F min. (La Passione); 50 in C; 51 in B flat; 52 in C min.; 53 in D (L'Impériale); 54 in G; 55 in E flat (Schoolmaster); 56 in C; 57 in D; 58 in F; 59 in A (Fire).
(M) *** Decca 425 915-2 (4) [id.]. Philharmonia Hungarica, Antal Dorati.

The nine symphonies which comprise the bulk of this box, from *Maria Theresia* onwards, show Haydn in the full flight of his *Sturm und Drang* period: tense, exhilarating music, full of anguished minor-key arguments that belie the idea of jolly 'Papa' Haydn working patiently for his princely master. The special value of Dorati's box is that it enables the listener to hear the ongoing sequence of nine works and to experience their historical impact in the same way as Prince Esterházy and his court must have done. Such symphonies as *La Passione* and *Maria Theresia* are already quite well known, but the others without sobriquets are no less compelling; and it is impossible to become bored for a moment by the vigorous, committed performances given by Dorati and his orchestra of Hungarian exiles. The CD transfers continue to be outstandingly vivid.

Symphonies Nos. 59 in A (Fire); 100 in G (Military); 101 in D (Clock).
(M) *** Ph. 420 866-2 [id.]. ASMF, Marriner.

Marriner's recordings derive from the mid-1970s and the performances are very satisfactory, as is the remastering. The *Clock* is vital and intelligent, the playing of the Academy very spruce and elegant. There is perhaps not quite the depth of character that informs Sir Colin Davis's performances of this repertoire, but they do display finesse, and the readings are never superficial in expressive terms.

Symphonies Nos. 60 in C (Il Distratto); 61 in D; 62 in D; 63 in C (La Roxolane); 64 in A; 65 in A; 66 in B flat; 67 in F; 68 in B flat; 69 in C (Laudon); 70 in D; 71 in B flat.
(M) *** Decca 425 920-2 (4) [id.]. Philharmonia Hungarica, Antal Dorati.

These middle-period symphonies maintain an amazing standard of invention, with such movements as the Adagio and 6/8 finale of No. 61 endlessly interesting. With the exception of an occasional movement (No. 69/II or No. 70/III), this music is riveting, and even where the actual material is conventional, as in the theatrical first movement of No. 69 (nicknamed *Laudon* after a field marshal), the treatment is sparkling, with many surprising turns. The only serious flaw in Dorati's interpretations – and it is something to note in a few of the symphonies in other boxes too – is his tendency to take minuets rather slowly. In many of them Haydn had already moved half-way towards a scherzo. But the Philharmonia Hungarica maintains its alertness with amazing consistency, never giving the suspicion of merely running through the music, and the dynamic tone of the whole project is re-established with works that had previously been not just neglected but absurdly underrated. The continuing vividness of the playing is matched by the bright CD transfers.

Symphonies Nos. 70 in D, 71 in B flat, 72 in D
*** Hyp. Dig. CDA 66526 [id.]. Hanover Band, Roy Goodman.

Symphonies Nos. 73 in D (La chasse), 74 in E flat, 75 in D.
*** Hyp. Dig. CDA 66520 [id.]. Hanover Band, Roy Goodman.

Symphonies Nos. 76 in E flat, 77 in B flat, 78 in C min.
*** Hyp. Dig. CDA 66525 [id.]. Hanover Band, Roy Goodman.

Every one of Goodman's excellent series for Hyperion can be warmly recommended, and the attractions are all the greater, and rather less confusing to the non-specialist, since each group of three links consecutive works in the usual Mandyczewski numbering. That brings anomalies, when modern scholarship has established new dating for particular symphonies. With the disc containing No. 72 the discrepancy of date is extreme, for that brilliant work, unlike the other two, dates from Haydn's earliest years in Esterhaza. Yet the very contrast with the much later works makes the group all the more refreshing, with No. 72 joyously reflecting the virtuosity of the horns in Haydn's first orchestra. Those in the Hanover Band, led by Anthony Halstead, have a field-day. Horns have a spectacular role too in No. 73, *La chasse*, with its hunt finale. It is well set against the unjustly neglected symphonies adjacent to it. In some ways the most rewarding of all the discs in this group is of Nos 76, 77 and 78, the first set of symphonies since nos 6, 7 and 8 that Haydn explicitly designed as a group of three. The performances of these intensely original works are exhilarating, and very well recorded.

Symphonies Nos. 72 in D; 73 in D (La chasse); 74 in E flat; 75 in D; 76 in E flat; 77 in B flat; 78 in C min.; 79 in F; 80 in D min.; 81 in G; 82 in C (L'Ours); 83 in G min. (La Poule).
(M) *** Decca 425 925-2 (2) [id.]. Philharmonia Hungarica, Antal Dorati.

This collection – apart from No. 72, which is an earlier work, and the two *Paris Symphonies* tacked on at the end – centres on nine symphonies written more or less consecutively over a compact period of just four years (1780–84). Robbins Landon emphasizes that these are much more courtly works than their *Sturm und Drang* predecessors and that at this time Haydn was regarding the symphony as a side concern, being mainly concerned with opera. Even so, what will strike the non-specialist listener is that, whatever the courtly manners of the expositions (and even there moods vary, particularly in the two minor-key symphonies), the development sections give a flashing reminder of Haydn's tensest manner, with kaleidoscopic sequences of minor keys whirling the argument in unexpected directions. At that time Haydn had just made contact with Mozart and though, on chronological evidence, the direct similarities can only be accidental the influence is already clear. The performances achieve an amazing degree of intensity, with alertness maintained throughout.

Symphonies Nos. 73 in D (La chasse); 74 in E flat; 75 in D.
*** Hyp. Dig. CDA 66250; *KA 66250* [id.]. Hanover Band, Roy Goodman.

Symphonies Nos. 78 in C min.; 102 in B flat.
**(*) DG Dig. 429 218-2 [id.]. Orpheus CO.

For Haydn symphonies on modern instruments, there are no more refined or polished performances than those on this disc, one of the Orpheus Chamber Orchestra's series. The underappreciated *No. 78 in C minor*, with its darkly chromatic first movement, comes in coupling with the magnificent No. 102, its slow movement containing one of the most beautiful of all Haydn melodies. These are model performances, yet they provide very short measure for a full CD, and the high polish makes them a little unsmiling.

Symphonies Nos. 80 in D min.; 87 in A; 89 in F.
*** ASV Dig. CDDCA 635; *ZCDCA 635* [id.]. L. Mozart Players, Jane Glover.

Jane Glover conducts the reinvigorated London Mozart Players in strong and energetic performances of these three relatively rare symphonies. No. 87 is the least known of the *Paris symphonies*; but all three of these works show Haydn at his most inventive. *No. 80 in D minor* begins as though it were a throwback to the *Sturm und Drang* period, but then at the end of the exposition Haydn gives a winning smile, as though to say, 'I fooled you!' No. 89 ends with a dance movement which contains delectable *strascinando* (dragging) passages, where the music hesitates before launching into reprises, done with great zest by the LMP. No. 87 has its delights too, notably in the lyrical *Adagio* with lovely flute and oboe solos. Though textures are not as transparent as we are beginning to demand in an age of period performance – largely a question of the ambient recorded sound – these modern-instrument performances are as winning as they are lively.

(Paris) Symphonies Nos. 82 in C (The Bear); 83 in G min. (The Hen); 84 in E flat.
❀ *** Virgin Dig. VC7 90793-2; *VC 790793-4*. O of Age of Enlightenment, Kuijken.

(Paris) Symphonies Nos. 85 in B flat (La Reine); 86 in D; 87 in A.
❀ *** Virgin Dig. VC7 90844-2; *VC 790844-4*. O of Age of Enlightenment, Kuijken.

These two discs, well filled, with three symphonies apiece, together present an outstanding set of Haydn's six *Paris symphonies*, between them offering among the most enjoyable period-performance recordings of Haydn ever. Kuijken and the players of the OAE wear their authenticity lightly and even allow themselves spacious speeds in slow movements, where expansion seems needed, as in the *Andante* of No. 83. There is a warm bloom on the sound, with woodwind well defined but not over-prominent. Textures are airily transparent, even when in the finale of No. 86 Kuijken opts for a very fast *allegro* indeed. Kuijken's one-in-a-bar treatment of the Minuets is a delight, giving them a Laendler-like swing. With dynamic contrasts underlined, the grandeur of Haydn's inspiration is fully brought out, along with the vigour; yet Kuijken gives all the necessary sharpness to the reminiscence of *Sturm und Drang* in the near-quotation from the *Farewell* in the first movement of No. 85, *La Reine*. The magnificence of that movement is underlined by the observance of the second-half repeat. Above all, Kuijken and his players convey the full joy of Haydn's inspiration in every movement.

Symphonies Nos. 82 in C (The Bear); 83 in G min. (The Hen).
*** Ph. Dig. 420 688-2 [id.]. Concg. O, C. Davis.

These splendid performances very much perpetuate the spirit of Sir Thomas Beecham's Haydn in their combination of humanity and elegance and a lively communication of the music's joy. Rhythms are crisp and allegros are energetic without a suspicion of hurry, while slow movements are full of grace. Tempi always seem just right, especially in the minuets which some conductors find elusive. Sir Colin Davis has made no finer record than this, and the Philips engineers capture the seductive Concertgebouw string-textures more transparently than ever, without loss of warmth and weight.

Symphonies Nos. 82 in C (The Bear); 83 in G min. (The Hen); 84 in E flat.
*** Hyp. Dig. CDA 66527; *KA 66527* [id.]. Hanover Band, Roy Goodman.

Goodman continues his outstanding Hyperion series with characteristically brisk and biting versions of the first three *Paris Symphonies*. He provides a strongly contrasted and equally valid view to that of Kuijken and the OAE on their excellent Virgin issue. With their tougher manner Goodman and the Hanover Band find these symphonies much less genial, relating them instead to the sharpness and tensions of the earlier *Sturm und Drang* works, with trumpets and timpani very much to the fore. So, in the *Hen*, one is forcefully reminded that it is in the dark key of G minor, and the hen-clucking noises, though beautifully pointed, come merely as a lighter interlude. Other differences are that Goodman observes significantly more repeats than Kuijken and has his harpsichord continuo (played by himself) more prominently balanced.

Symphonies Nos. 83 in G min. (Hen); 100 in G (Military).
(B) ** Pickwick IMPX 9036 [id.]. VPO, Münchinger.

Münchinger's performances offer orchestral style and phrasing in the best Viennese tradition, but the conductor himself is somewhat straightlaced: his rhythmic pulse is rigid and he does not turn the corners as genially as some conductors. The 1961 recording has a Decca source, and sounds remarkably good in its CD format: the quality is full and clear and the bass is firmer than it was on LP. The balance remains weighty and in the military sections of No. 100 some ears might find the bass drum too exuberant.

Symphonies Nos. 84 in E flat; 85 in B flat (La Reine); 86 in D; 87 in A (Paris Symphonies); 88 in G; 89 in F; 90 in C; 91 in E flat; 92 in G (Oxford); 93 in D; 94 in G (Surprise); 95 in C min.
(M) *** Decca 425 930-2 (4) [id.]. Philharmonia Hungarica, Antal Dorati.

It is a pity that Decca's layout in four-CD groups, and employing a consistent numerical sequence, has meant that Dorati's sets of both the six *Paris* and the first six *London Symphonies* have each had to be split over two separate CD boxes. However, here we have not only the last four of the main *Paris* set (Nos. 84–7) but also the other Paris-based works, all given fresh and stylish performances. Of the three *London Symphonies* included here, No. 93 brings one of the most delightful performances of Dorati's cycle, with a delectable, Ländler-like first movement. No. 95 is the only work in the set which lacks a slow opening section. Its compactness and the C minor tensions, however, recall the *Sturm und Drang* period.

Symphonies Nos. 88 in G; 89 in F; 92 (Oxford).
(B) *** DG 429 523-2; *429 523-4* [id.]. VPO, Boehm.
** Virgin VC7 91499-2 [id.]. La Petite Bande, Kuijken.

Enjoyably cultured performances from Boehm and the Vienna Philharmonic, who play with great polish and tonal refinement. The finale of No. 88 and the Andante of No. 89 are most beautifully done and the slow movement of the former is gravely expansive. The remastering is very successful indeed in freshening the sound without losing its body and depth; some will want a less weighty effect, possible with a smaller group, but Boehm's touch can charm in allegros, as in the sprightly finale of the *Oxford Symphony*.

These performances directed by Kuijken have many of the qualities that made his set of the Haydn *Paris Symphonies*, also on Virgin, so winning. Yet with a gap of two years and a change of players from the Orchestra of the Age of Enlightenment to Kuijken's own group, La Petite Bande, come differences which weigh significantly against this later issue. For these rather later symphonies Kuijken has abandoned the use of harpsichord continuo, and his preference for very measured speeds in slow movements leads him to at least one serious miscalculation. At a funereal pace Kuijken makes the heavenly *Largo* of No. 88 far too heavy, seriously holding up the flow of the great melody with overemphasis and exaggerated pauses, all made the more obtrusive without continuo. The speed is far slower than in Dorati's modern-instrument performance, as are the slow movements in the other two symphonies. Otherwise these are relaxed performances of a nicely balanced group of late symphonies. The sound is warm and generally well balanced, though violins are not always clearly enough defined in tuttis, and overall this is something of a disappointment when compared with Kuijken's earlier achievement.

Symphonies Nos. 88 in G; 92 in G (Oxford).
**(*) DG Dig. 413 777-2 [id.]. VPO, Bernstein.

A warmly glowing account of both symphonies from Bernstein with the full strings of the Vienna orchestra and a richly upholstered recording. Bernstein observes the repeat of the development and restatement in the first movement of No. 88 and gives a romantic and really rather beautiful account of the *Largo*. Both performances emanate from concerts at the Musikvereinsaal.

Symphonies Nos. 88 in G; 104 in D (London).
*** CRD CRD 3370 [id.]. Bournemouth Sinf., Ronald Thomas.

Although the orchestra is smaller than the Concertgebouw or LPO, the playing has great freshness and vitality; indeed it is the urgency of musical feeling that Ronald Thomas conveys which makes up for the last ounce of finesse. They are uncommonly dramatic in the slow movement of No. 88 and bring great zest and eloquence to the rest of the symphony too. In No. 104 they are not always as perceptive as Sir Colin Davis, but this brightly recorded coupling can be recommended alongside his version.

Symphonies Nos. 90 in C; 91 in E flat.
** Virgin Dig. VC7 91141-2; *VC 791141-4* [id.]. La Petite Bande, Kuijken.

Symphonies Nos. 90 in C; 91 in E flat; 92 in G (Oxford).
*** Hyp. Dig. CDA 66521; *KA 66521* [id.]. Hanover Band, Roy Goodman.

Goodman and Kuijken are in direct rivalry over the surprisingly neglected Nos. 90 and 91, two symphonies that come between the *Paris* set and the final *London Symphonies*. On every count Goodman and the Hanover Band are preferable, with their brisker speeds and more resilient rhythms, and their disc also includes the *Oxford Symphony*. Kuijken, so masterly with the Orchestra of the Age of Enlightenment in the *Paris Symphonies*, also on Virgin, is here less lively with La Petite Bande, regularly taking *Andantes* slower than such a traditional rival as Dorati. The recording for Goodman is preferable, pleasantly atmospheric and more cleanly focused than in his earlier recordings for Nimbus.

Symphonies Nos. 91 in E flat; 92 in G (Oxford).
*** Ph. Dig. 410 390-2 [id.]. Concg. O, C. Davis.

The *Oxford* and its immediate predecessor in the canon, No. 91 in E flat, are here given performances that are refreshingly crisp and full of musical life. The sheer joy, vitality and, above all, sanity that these performances radiate is inspiriting and heart-warming. Excellent recorded sound.

Symphonies Nos. 92 in G (Oxford); 94 in G (Surprise); 96 in D (Miracle).
(M) *** Sony SBK 46332 [id.]; *40-46332*. Cleveland O, Szell.

Symphonies Nos. 93 in D; 94 in G (Surprise); 95 in C min.; 96 in D (Miracle); 97 in C; 98 in B flat (London Symphonies).
(M) *** Sony MY2K 45673 (2) [id.]. Cleveland O, Szell.

With superb polish in the playing and precise phrasing it would be easy for such performances as these to sound superficial, but Haydn's music obviously struck a deep chord in Szell's sensibility and there is humanity underlying the technical perfection. Indeed there are many little musical touches from Szell to show that his perfectionist approach is a dedicated and affectionate one. The recordings have been splendidly remastered and the sound is fuller and firmer than it ever was on LP, with the Cleveland ambience well caught. The underlying aggressiveness in the recording still produces a thinness in the violins in No. 95 and, to a far lesser extent, in No. 97. Both Nos. 97 and 98 are strong performances. These are most distinguished reissues, and all collectors should try the disc offering the three named symphonies.

Symphonies Nos. 92 in G (Oxford); 104 in D (London).
(B) *** Pickwick Dig. PCD 916; *CIMPC 916*. E. Sinfonia, Groves.

Sir Charles Groves makes an admirable case for a modern orchestra, especially when it is recorded so faithfully, with agreeable ambient warmth, a bloom on strings and woodwind alike, yet with good definition. The performances are robust yet elegant as well; both slow movements are beautifully shaped, with Haydn's characteristic contrasts unfolding spontaneously. In the last movement of the *Oxford*, the dancing violins are a special delight in what is one of the composer's most infectious finales.

Symphonies Nos. 93–98.
(M) (***) EMI mono CMS7 64389-2 (2) [id.]. RPO, Sir Thomas Beecham.

Symphonies Nos. 99–104.
❀ (M) *** EMI CMS7 64066-2 (2) [id.]. RPO, Sir Thomas Beecham.

Symphonies Nos. 93–104 (London symphonies).
❀ (M) *** Ph. 432 286-2 (4) [id.]. Concg. O, Sir Colin Davis.
(M) **(*) DG Dig. 429 658-2 (4) [id.]. BPO, Karajan.

Symphonies Nos. 93 in D; 94 in G (Surprise); 100 in G (Military).
(M) **(*) DG Dig. 427 809-2; *427 809-4* [id.]. BPO, Karajan.

This Haydn series is one of the most distinguished recordings Sir Colin Davis has given us in recent years, and its blend of brilliance and sensitivity, wit and humanity, gives this box a special claim on the collector. There is no trace of routine in these performances and no failure of imagination. The excellence of the playing is matched by Philips's best recording quality and, with three symphonies to each CD, this is remarkable value too. The recordings were made between 1975 and 1981. Nos. 93, 94 and 96 are digital, the rest analogue, but all have been transferred to CD with fine body and range. For some, this could prove an antidote to the more abrasive Pinnock style in the earlier, *Sturm und Drang Symphonies*.

The art of phrasing is one of the prime secrets of great music-making, and no detail in Beecham's performances of the *London Symphonies* goes untended. They have also great warmth, drama too, and perhaps a unique geniality. They were mostly recorded in the early days of stereo (1958–9) but in the second box (*Symphonies 99–104*) one would hardly guess. The sound throughout is amazingly full and fresh, with plenty of body, sweet violin-timbre and no edge. The first box are mono recordings; they sound admirably full-bodied and have been transferred amazingly successfully. The performances profess an inner life and vitality that put them in a class of their own. The old Breitkopf texts are used. As Lyndon Jenkins comments in the excellent notes, it was the spirit of Haydn that interested Beecham, not the letter: he favoured a large orchestra (to glorious effect) and worked from the same scores he had used all his life. But the whole set is a classic of the gramophone, and the later symphonies offer some of the most beautiful recorded sound in the whole Beecham discography. A treasurable set to put alongside Sir Colin Davis's recordings.

Karajan offers big-band Haydn – but what a band! The sound of the Berlin Philharmonic is itself a joy. This set, we gather, enjoyed the imprimatur of no less an authority than H. C. Robbins Landon; but it inspires admiration rather than affection. But there is often tenderness in slow movements – witness the close of *No. 98 in B flat* – and there is no want of dignity and breadth. As a fine sampler, the triptych of Nos. 93, 94 and 100 can be recommended. First-movement exposition repeats are observed and the playing undoubtedly has distinction. The sound is first class.

Symphonies Nos. 93 in D; 99 in E flat.
❀ *** Decca Dig. 417 620-2 [id.]. LPO, Solti.

In this pairing of Nos. 93 and 99, two favourites of Sir Thomas Beecham, the atmosphere is sunny and civilized; there is no lack of brilliance – indeed the LPO are consistently on their toes – but the music-making is infectious rather than hard-driven. The string phrasing is as graceful as the woodwind articulation is light and felicitous, and pacing is wholly sympathetic. The lovely slow movement of No. 93 has both delicacy and gravitas and that of No. 99 is serenely spacious. The minuets are shown to have quite different characters, but both finales sparkle in the happiest manner. The sound on CD is very much in the demonstration class in its transparency, warmth and naturalness.

Symphonies Nos. 94 in G (Surprise); 96 in D (Miracle).
*** O-L Dig. 414 330-2 [id.]. AAM, Hogwood.

The playing here is superb: polished, feeling, and full of imaginative detail. The oboe solo in the Trio of the third movement of the *Miracle symphony* is a delight, and the sparkle in the finale with its crisp articulation and spirited pacing is matched by the elegance given to the engaging second subject of the first movement. The account of No. 94 is particularly dramatic and in the *Andante* there is not just the one 'surprise' (and that pretty impressive, with the contrast afforded by gentle strings at the opening) but two more *forte* chords to follow at the beginning of each subsequent phrase – a most telling device. The presence of Hogwood's fortepiano can also be subtly felt here, and later the wind solos are full of character. The minuet is fast, but this follows naturally after the drama of the slow movement, while the finale makes a light-hearted culmination. With superb recording, full yet transparent, this is an issue to make converts to the creed of authenticity.

Symphonies Nos. 94 in G (Surprise); 96 in D (Miracle); 100 in G (Military).
(M) *** Decca 417 718-2 [id.]. Philh. Hungarica, Dorati.

These three symphonies, collected from Dorati's historic complete Haydn cycle, make a delightful group. The only controversial speed comes in the *Andante* of the *Surprise*, much faster than usual, but the freshness of the joke is the more sharply presented. Dorati's flair comes out in the bold reading of the military section of the slow movement of No. 100, and though the digital transfer exaggerates the brightness of upper frequencies, the warm acoustic of the hall in Marl, West Germany, where the recordings were done makes the result very acceptable.

Symphonies Nos. 94 in G (Surprise); 101 in D (Clock).
(M) *** DG 423 883-2 [id.]. LPO, Jochum.

Jochum's are marvellously fresh, crisp accounts of both symphonies, elegantly played and always judiciously paced. The sound remains first class, with added clarity but without loss of bloom, the bass cleaner and only slightly drier.

Symphonies Nos. 94 in G (Surprise); 104 in D (London).
(M) *** Ph. Dig./Analogue 434 153-2; *434 153-4* [id.]. Concg. O, Sir Colin Davis.

Davis's *Surprise* was recorded in 1981 and is digital; No. 104 dates from four years earlier and is analogue, but the digital transfer is of high quality. Both performances have breadth and dignity, yet are full of sparkle and character. The Concertgebouw sound has good definition and the warmth and humanity of the readings is especially striking in the slow movements. The documentation, however, concentrates on Davis's biographical details and makes no mention of the music.

Symphonies Nos. 95 in C min; 104 in D (London).
*** Decca Dig. 417 330-2 [id.]. LPO, Solti.

Solti's LPO coupling of the little-known but splendid *No. 95 in C minor* and the *London symphony* is altogether superb and the LPO playing – smiling and elegant, yet full of bubbling vitality – is a constant joy. No. 95 has a striking sense of cohesion and purpose, and there is no finer version of No. 104. Solti uses a full body of strings and all the resources of modern wind instruments with the greatest possible finesse, yet the spontaneity of the music and the music-making is paramount. Top-drawer Decca sound (the record was made in the attractive acoustics of London's Henry Wood Hall) makes this an exceptionally natural-sounding CD.

Symphonies Nos. 96 in D (Miracle); 97 in C; 98 in B flat; 99 in E flat; 100 in G (Military); 101 in D (Clock); 102 in B flat; 103 in E flat (Drum Roll); 104 in D (London). Symphonies A in B flat; B in B flat; Sinfonia concertante in B flat (for oboe, bassoon, violin, cello & orchestra).
(M) *** Decca 425 935-2 (4) [id.]. Philharmonia Hungarica, Antal Dorati.

Dorati and the Philharmonia Hungarica completed their monumental project of recording the entire Haydn symphonic *oeuvre* with not a suspicion of routine. These final masterpieces are performed with a glowing sense of commitment, and Dorati, no doubt taking his cue from the editor, H. C. Robbins Landon, generally chooses rather relaxed tempi for the first movements. In slow movements his tempi are on the fast side and, though an extra desk of strings has been added to each section, the results are authentically in scale, with individual solos emerging naturally against the glowing acoustic, and with intimacy comes extra dramatic force in sforzandos. As an appendix we are given the *Sinfonia concertante* and *Symphonies A* and *B*, which were not included in the numerical list simply because originally they were not thought to be symphonies at all. They are presented with characteristic vitality. Dorati's account of the *Sinfonia concertante* is a performance of few extremes, one which – not surprisingly, given the context – presents the work as a further symphony with unusual scoring, rather than as a concerto-styled work.

Symphonies Nos. 100 in G (Military); 104 in D (London).
*** Ph. 411 449-2 [id.]. Concg. O, C. Davis.
*** O-L Dig. 411 833-2 [id.]. AAM, Hogwood.

Sir Colin Davis's coupling has genuine stature and can be recommended without reservation of any kind. The playing of the Concertgebouw Orchestra is as sensitive as it is brilliant, and Davis is unfailingly penetrating. The performances also benefit from excellent recorded sound, with fine clarity and definition.

Those looking for performances on period instruments will find Hogwood's accounts are uncommonly good ones and offer much better playing than was the case in some of his Mozart cycle. The wind execution is highly accomplished and the strings well blended and in tune. The change in the balance in the orchestral texture is often quite striking, particularly where the bassoon cuts through the lower strings. The 'Turkish' percussion instruments in the *Military symphony* are most effectively placed, and the performances are not only vital but also splendidly paced. The recording has clarity and presence. An altogether impressive issue.

CHAMBER MUSIC

Baryton trios Nos. 71 in A; 96 in B min.; 113 in D; 126 in C.
*** Gaudeamus CDGAU 109 [id.]. John Hsu, Miller, Arico.

Baryton trios Nos. 87 in A min.; 97 in D (Fatto per la felicissima nascita de S:ai:S Principe Estorhazi); 101 in C; 111 in G.
*** Gaudeamus CDGAU 104 [id.]. John Hsu, Miller, Arico.

Prince Esterházy was particularly fond of the baryton, whose delicate sonorities much appealed to him, and was a keen amateur player himself. During his years at Eisenstadt, Haydn composed 126 trios for his delectation. As John Hsu puts it on the sleeve, 'the baryton is a kind of viola da gamba with a broadened neck, behind which is a harp . . . the metal harp-strings are exposed within the open-box-like back of the neck so that they may be plucked by the thumb of the left hand'. These are most beguiling performances which have subtlety and finesse. Natural and well-balanced recorded sound. The second collection is no less desirable than the first.

Duo sonatas for violin and viola Nos. 1–6.
(B) *** Hung. White Label HRC 071 [id.]. Dénes Kovács, Géza Németh.

Haydn composed these six duos some time in the late 1760s. Haydn's diversity of invention seems inexhaustible. The performances here are expert and spontaneous – the players are obviously enjoying the music, and so do we. The recording too is well balanced and has fine presence and realism. Ideal repertoire for a bargain label!

Piano trios (complete).
❀ (M) *** Ph. 432 061-2 (9). Beaux Arts Trio.

The original Beaux Arts set of the complete *Piano trios* was not only awarded a Rosette by us but was also named 1979 Record of the Year by *Gramophone* and went on in 1980 to win the 'Grand Prix International du Disque de l'Académie Charles Cros'. It is not often possible to hail one set of records as a 'classic' in quite the way that Schnabel's Beethoven sonatas can be so described; all too few performances attain that level of artistic insight, and such is the sheer proliferation of material today that records have to struggle increasingly for attention. Yet this set can be described in those terms, for the playing of the Beaux Arts Trio is of the very highest musical distinction. The contribution of the pianist, Menahem Pressler, is little short of inspired, and the recorded sound on CD is astonishingly lifelike. The performances follow the Critical Edition of H. C. Robbins Landon, whose indefatigable researches have increased the number of *Trios* we know in the standard edition from 31 to 43. This is the kind of inflation one welcomes! The CD transfer has enhanced detail without losing the warmth of ambience or sense of intimacy.

Piano trios, Hob XV, Nos. 24–27.
(M) *** Ph. 422 831-2; *422 831-4*. Beaux Arts Trio.

These are all splendid works. No. 25 with its *Gypsy rondos* is the most famous, but each has a character of its own, showing the mature Haydn working at full stretch (they are contemporary with the *London symphonies*). The playing here is peerless and the recording truthful and refined.

String quartets: in E flat, Op. 1/0; Nos. 43 in D min., Op. 42; 83 in B flat, Op. 103.
**(*) Mer. ECD 88117; *CDE 77117* [id.]. English Qt.

This disc explores off-the-beaten-track and rarely played Haydn. The Op. 1, 'No. 0', is no masterpiece but has distinct charm, particularly when it is as well played as it is here. These fine players rise to all the challenges posed by this music, and the recorded sound is eminently truthful. There would have been room for another *Quartet* on this disc, which offers rather short measure at 43 minutes.

String quartets Nos. 1 in B flat, Op. 1/1; 67 in D, Op. 64/5 (Lark); 74 in G min., Op. 74/3 (Rider).
*** DG Dig. 423 622-2 [id.]. Hagen Qt.

The Hagen are supple, cultured and at times perhaps a little overcivilized, but in these three Haydn quartets they play flawlessly and are wonderfully alert and intelligent. This is real chamber-music-making; and the recording, made in the Cologne Radio Sendesaal, is perfectly balanced: in fact it could not be improved upon.

String quartet No. 3 in D, Op. 1/3.
(M) ** Decca 433 691-2 [id.]. Weller Qt – *Quartets Nos. 37–39.* ***

The Weller Quartet are somewhat cool in the opening *Adagio* of this work and, although the performance is accurate and musical, it only really springs to life in the vivacious scherzo, which is admittedly by far the best movement. No complaints about the recording.

String quartets Nos. 17 in F (Serenade), Op. 3/5; 38 in E flat (Joke), Op. 33/2; 76 in D min. (Fifths), Op. 76/2.
(M) *** Decca 425 422-2; *425 422-4*. Janáček Qt.

These performances are strong and dedicated and careful to sense that the style of Haydn is not that of either Beethoven or Mozart. The music itself is highly civilized; whether Haydn or Hoffstetter wrote that delicious tune which forms the slow movement of the *Serenade quartet* seems irrelevant; it is an attractive little work and makes a good foil for the really splendid music of its companions. The recording (mid-1960s vintage) always had good presence; the CD brings even more striking tangibility and plenty of body, within a well-judged ambience.

String quartets Nos. 17 in F (Serenade), Op. 3/5; 63 in D (Lark), Op. 64/5; 76 in D min. (Fifths), Op. 76/2.
(M) *** Ph. 426 097-2; *426 097-4*. Italian Qt.

First-class playing here, although the first movement of the *Lark* is a bit measured in feeling and could do with more sparkle. The *Serenade quartet* is made to sound inspired, its famous slow movement played with exquisite gentleness. The *D minor Quartet* is admirably poised and classical in feeling. This rivals the grouping by the Janáček Quartet on Decca, but the remastered Philips recording, although refined, is drier: the Decca has more bloom and warmth.

String quartets Nos. 32 in C, Op. 20/2; 44 in B flat, Op. 50/1; 76 in D min. (Fifths), Op. 76/2.
*** ASV Dig. CDDCA 622; *ZCDCA 622* [id.]. Lindsay Qt.

Obviously, since these are public performances, one has to accept music-making reflecting the heat of the occasion, the odd sense of roughness (the finale of Op. 76, No. 2), for these artists take risks – and this is perhaps a shade faster than it would be in a studio. There is splendid character in these performances and plenty of musical imagination. These readings have a spontaneity which is refreshing in these days of retakes! The recordings are eminently truthful and audience noise is minimal.

String quartets Nos. 34 in D, Op. 20/4; 47 in C sharp min., Op. 50/4; 77 in C (Emperor), Op. 76/3.
*** ASV Dig. CDDCA 731; *ZCDCA 731* [id.]. Lindsay Qt.

The Lindsay performances were recorded, as were other issues in this series, at public performances, on this occasion in London's Wigmore Hall. The advantages this brings are twofold: higher spontaneity and a greater propensity to take risks. The disadvantages can be the absence of the last ounce of polish, and a tendency to overproject in the concert hall, with a resultant loss of intimacy and, in slower movements, repose. In all three performances the gains outweigh any loss, though the balance tends to cause some coarse-sounding tone in fortissimo passages. An excellent disc and tape, all the same.

String quartets Nos. 37 in B min.; 38 in E flat (Joke); 39 in C (Bird), Op. 33/1–3.
(M) *** Decca 433 691-2 [id.]. Weller Qt – *Quartet No. 3.* **

String quartets Nos. 40 in B flat; 41 in G; 42 in D (How do you do), Op. 33/4–6.
(M) *** Decca 433 692-2 [id.]. Weller Qt – *Quartet No. 83.* **

String quartets Nos. 37–42, Op. 33/1–6.
*** Hung. HCD 11887/8-2 [id.]. Tátrai Qt.

This is exceptionally polished and lively playing, beautifully recorded (the mid-1960s sound, balanced by Erik Smith and Gordon Parry, does not sound in the least dated). If the performances are not as penetrating as the very finest, they are sunny and civilized and always enjoyable. There is a genial touch too, and certain movements – the Trio of the Scherzo in the *Joke quartet*, the first movement of Op. 33/3 – are memorable, while the delightful spiccato playing in the latter work's *Allegretto* shows the character of the music-making. The slow movements are sophisticated in approach yet not unexpressive; the *Largo* of Op. 33/4 is particularly poised. Tempi are generally well considered, even if the finale of the *Joke* is perhaps too fast; on the other hand the last movement of Op. 33/4 is beautifully judged.

The Tátrai recording comes from 1979 and maintains the generally high standard of their cycle; in other words, the playing is unfailingly musical and intelligent, and the recording eminently acceptable.

String quartets Nos. 50–56 (The Seven Last Words of our Saviour on the cross), Op. 51.
*** Olympia Dig. OCD 171 [id.]. Shostakovich Qt.

The Shostakovich Quartet gives an eloquent and thoughtful account of Haydn's score. There is no overstatement and no point-making, yet the playing is tremendously felt – and they are a quartet who produce a beautifully integrated and cultured sound. This present performance sounds totally natural and unforced.

String quartets Nos. 57 in G; 58 in C; 59 in E, Op. 54/1–3.
*** ASV Dig. CDDCA 582; *ZCDCA 582* [id.]. Lindsay Qt.
*** Virgin Dig. VC7 90719-2; *VC 790719-4* [id.]. Endellion Qt.

This is a relatively neglected set, though the second, the *C major* (placed last on this ASV recording), is a profound and searching masterpiece, while the *G major* gives a taste of the high-flying violin writing that distinguishes the set. The playing of the Lindsay Quartet is splendidly poised and vital, and the recording is very fine indeed.

The Endellion Quartet on Virgin are recorded at The Maltings, Snape, which provides the ideal acoustic environment. The playing is bright-eyed, fresh and vital. The overall sound is beautifully integrated and there are many moments of musical insight. Yet the Lindsays' insights go deeper into this movement, even if at times they have marginally less surface polish. All the same, if theirs remains a first preference, the Endellions are so good and so well recorded that they deserve a strong recommendation.

String quartets Nos. 50–56 (The Seven Last Words of Christ); 63–68, Op. 64 1–6 (Tost quartets).
(M) **(*) DG 431 145-2 (3). Amadeus Qt.

It is perhaps a pity that the Amadeus version of *The Seven Last Words of Christ* is linked on CD with Op. 64, for the immaculate Amadeus style, though not lacking in drama, does tend to smooth over the darker side of Haydn. The last six of the twelve *Tost quartets* are another matter. Here the superb ensemble and cultivated playing are always easy on the ear when the recording is so well balanced and natural. There is no lack of life in allegros, for all their neat, spick-and-span precision; if other performances of some of the great slow movements have more intensity, the playing here is still certainly felt, as well as being assured and beautiful, with tempi aptly chosen and well sustained. Indeed, overall these performances give much pleasure.

String quartets Nos. 50–56 (The Seven Last Words of our Saviour on the Cross), Op. 51; 83 in B flat, Op. 103.
(BB) *** Naxos Dig. 8.550346 [id.]. Kodály Qt.

The Kodály Quartet give a memorable performance, strongly characterized and beautifully played, with subtle contrasts of expressive tension between the seven inner slow movements. They also offer an appropriate bonus in Haydn's last, unfinished, two-movement *Quartet*. He was working on this in 1803, at about the same time as he directed his last public concert, which was *The Seven Last Words*. The recording is first rate, vividly present yet naturally balanced, like the other isssues in this attractive Naxos series.

String quartets Nos. 57 in G; 58 in C; 59 in E, Op. 54/1-3.
(BB) *** Naxos Dig. 8.550395; *4550395* [id.]. Kodály Qt.

The present works show Haydn at his most inventive. The Kodály players enter animatedly into the spirit of the music and give a fine, direct account of Op. 54/1; the leader, Attila Falvay, shows himself fully equal to Haydn's bravura embellishments in the demanding first violin writing, both here and in Op. 54/3. The Naxos sound is fresh and truthful, well up to the standard of this excellent super-bargain series.

String quartets Nos. 60 in A; 61 in F min. (Razor); 62 in B flat, Op. 55/1–3 (Tost Quartets).
(BB) **(*) Naxos Dig. 8.550397. Kodály Qt.

Opus 55 brings playing which is undoubtedly spirited and generally polished, but the music-making at times seems plainer than usual in the Naxos series. The recording is bright and clear, with a realistic presence. Incidentally, the origin of the title of the F minor work comes from an anecdote supplied by the English publisher, John Bland. Haydn was supposed to have offered 'his best quartet for a pair of decent razors', and that was how his music was paid for.

String quartet No. 67 in D (Lark), Op. 65/4.
(B) **(*) DG Compact Classics 413 845-2 (2) [id.]. Amadeus Qt – BEETHOVEN: *Ghost trio* ***; MOZART: *Hunt quartet* ***; SCHUBERT: *Trout quintet*. **

This is the bonus (on the CDs only) for this Compact Classics collection of named chamber works. The Amadeus playing has characteristic finesse, and this is an enjoyable performance, although the first movement could ideally be a little more relaxed. The sound is very good, bright and immediate.

String quartets Nos. 69 in B flat; 70 in D; 71 in E flat, Op. 71/1–3; 72 in C; 73 in F; 74 in G min. (Reiter), Op. 74/1–3 (Apponyi quartets).
(BB) *** Naxos Dig. 8.550394 (*Nos. 69–71*); 8.550396 (*Nos. 72–74*) [id.]. Kódaly Qt.
*** Hung. HCD 12246/7-2 [id.]. Tátrai Qt.

The *Apponyi quartets* (so named because their 'onlie begetter' was Count Antal Apponyi) are among the composer's finest. The Naxos recordings by the Kodály Quartet are outstanding in every way and would be highly recommendable even without their considerable price advantage. The performances are superbly shaped, naturally paced and alive; the playing is cultivated, yet it has depth of feeling too, and the group readily communicate their pleasure in this wonderful music. The digital recording has vivid presence and just the right amount of ambience: the effect is entirely natural.

Hungaroton have chosen to issue these performances by the Tátrai Quartet, rather than commission new ones from their expert younger ensembles such as the Eder or the Takács – a wise decision, since these are civilized, selfless readings that never deflect the listener's attention away from Haydn's inexhaustible invention. The sound is natural.

String quartets Nos. 71 in E flat, Op. 71/3; 72 in C, Op. 74/1.
*** Hyp. CDA 66098 [id.]. Salomon Qt.

String quartets Nos. 73 in F; 74 in G min., Op. 74/2–3.
*** Hyp. CDA 66124 [id.]. Salomon Qt.

The Opp. 71 and 74 *Quartets* belong to the same period as the first set of *Salomon symphonies* (1791–2) and are grander and more 'public' than any of their predecessors. The appropriately named Salomon Quartet use period instruments. They are vibrato-less but vibrant; the sonorities, far from being nasal and unpleasing, are clean and transparent. There is imagination and vitality here, and the Hyperion recording is splendidly truthful. Its clarity is further enhanced in the CD transfers.

String quartets Nos. 69 in B flat; 70 in D; 71 in E flat, Op. 71/1–3; 72 in C; 73 in F; 74 in G min. (Reiter), Op. 74/1–3; Op. 77/1–2; in D min., Op. 103.
(M) *** DG 429 189-2 (3). Amadeus Qt.

This excellent set shows the Amadeus on their finest form; there is a sense of spontaneity as well as genuine breadth to these readings. Haydn's late quartets have much the same expansiveness and depth as the symphonies, and here the Amadeus succeed in conveying both their intimacy and their scale. The recordings have a warm acoustic and plenty of presence.

String quartets Nos. 72 in C; 73 in F; 74 in G min., Op. 74/1–3.
*** Virgin Dig. VC7 91097-2; *VC 791097-4* [id.]. Endellion Qt.

The Endellion Quartet are also proving sound guides to this rewarding repertoire; this record can be recommended alongside their comparably well-played and -recorded set of Op. 54.

String quartets Nos. 75 in G; 76 in D min. (Fifths); 77 in C (Emperor); 78 in B flat (Sunrise); 79 in D; 80 in E flat, Op. 76/1–6.
❀ (BB) *** Naxos Dig. 8.550314; *4550314* (*Nos. 75–77*); 8.550315; *4550315* (*Nos. 78–80*). Kodály Qt.
*** Hung. HCD 12812/3-2 [id.]. Tátrai Qt.
(M) **(*) DG 415 867-2 (2) [id.]. Amadeus Qt.

String quartets Nos. 76 (Fifths); 77 (Emperor); 78 (Sunrise), Op. 76/2–4.
❀ (BB) *** Naxos Dig. 8.550129; *4550129* [id.]. Kodály Qt.

Haydn's six *Erdödy quartets*, Op. 76, contain some of his very greatest music, and these performances by the Kodály Quartet are fully worthy of the composer's inexhaustible invention. Their playing brings a joyful pleasure in Haydn's inspiration and a polished refinement than can only come from familiarity over a considerable period. Yet there is not the slightest suspicion of over-rehearsal or of routine: every bar of the music springs to life spontaneously, and these musicians' insights bring an ideal combination of authority and warmth, emotional balance and structural awareness. The group of three familiar named works (recorded in 1988 in the Italian Institute in Budapest) would make an ideal present for any novice coming to this repertoire for the first time. But the other works in the set, those without nicknames, are no less inspired. The recordings of the complete set, made in the Hungaroton Studios in Budapest in 1989, are absolutely natural in balance and combine a sense of intimacy with an admirably realistic projection: the players might well be at the end of one's room. Heard side by side, it is extraordinary how alike the two sets of performances of the three named works are, equally refreshing and spontaneous; and, with the producer (János Mátyás) the same in each instance, the balance and sound too are remarkably similar. Perhaps the acoustics of the Hungaroton Studios are slightly warmer, but there is little in it.

The Tátrai's classic set of the *Erdödy Quartets* is ageless and always much admired. These performances are unforced and natural, as intimate as if they were playing for pleasure, and as authoritative as one could hope for. The splendours of this set are as inexhaustible as those of the Beaux Arts set of the *Trios*. What will surprise many collectors is the quality of the sound. A very strong recommendation on all counts – artistic and technical.

The Amadeus performances are certainly polished but, by the side of the Kodály Quartet, relatively mannered. Norbert Brainin's vibrato is a little tiresome on occasion; but, generally speaking, there is much to reward the listener here; the recordings are vivid and they have enhanced realism and presence in their CD format.

String quartets Nos. 76 in D min. (Fifths); 77 in C (Emperor); 78 in B flat (Sunrise), Op. 76/2–4.
*** Teldec/Warner Dig. 2292 43062-2 [id.]. Eder Qt.

The Eder is a Hungarian quartet whose players command a refined and beautiful tone, with generally excellent ensemble and polish. These are elegant performances that are unlikely to disappoint even the most demanding listener, save perhaps in the finale of the *Emperor*, which they take a little too quickly. But this is unfailingly thoughtful quartet-playing whose internal balance and tonal blend are practically flawless. The recording is altogether excellent.

String quartet No. 77 in C (Emperor), Op. 76/3.
(M) *** Teldec/Warner 2292 42440-2 [id.]. Alban Berg Qt – MOZART: *Quartet No. 17.* ***

Back in the 1970s the Alban Berg displayed admirable polish, but the end-result was without that hint of glossy perfection which poses a problem with some of their more recent recordings. This performance of Haydn's *Emperor quartet*, dating from 1975, has playing of striking resilience and sparkle. The famous slow movement has seldom been put on record with such warmth and eloquence. The sound is bright, clear and well balanced, and the Mozart coupling is even finer.

String quartets Nos. 81 in G; 82 in F, Op. 77/1–2; 83 in D min., Op. 103.
*** Decca Dig. 430 199-2; *430 199-4* [id.]. Takács Qt.
*** Hyp. Dig. CDA 66348 [id.]. Salomon Qt.
(M) **(*) HM/BMG Dig. GD 77106 [77106-2-RG]. Smithson Qt.

The Takács Quartet play with warmth, expressive refinement and vitality. The sound is clean and well focused, with just the right amount of resonance. Those who prefer the usual modern string quartet approach need not hesitate and cassette collectors, who in any event have no choice, need not worry unduly on that count.

The Salomon, recorded in a less ample acoustic, produce an altogether leaner sound but one that is thoroughly responsive to every shift in Haydn's thought. Of the two period-instrument groups they seem to have the greater inner vitality and feeling.

The Smithson Quartet is led by Jaap Schröder and is one of the pre-eminent period-instrument ensembles in America. They are recorded in the generous acoustic of the Evangelical Church of Blumenstein near Berne, which helps to enrich the sonority. Readers who prefer their Haydn quartets with this purer timbre rather than with the traditional greater warmth of the modern string quartet will find much to admire here.

String quartet No. 83 in B flat, Op. 103.
(M) ** Decca 433 692-2 [id.]. Weller Qt – *Quartets Nos. 40–42.* ***

The Weller give an eminently smooth and polished account of the incomplete two-movement quartet of Haydn's old age. The recording is well engineered and makes a good bonus for the the Op. 33 Quartets, even if the performance is slightly less impressive than the Weller's playing of the earlier works.

KEYBOARD MUSIC

Piano sonatas Nos. 32 in G min., Hob XIV/44; 33 in C min., Hob XVI/20; 56 in D, Hob XVI/42; Variations in F, Hob XVII/6.
(M) *** Collins Dig. 3017-2 [id.]. Andrew Wilde.

These performances have a simplicity and directness of approach which is very winning. The playing is unidiosyncratic but does not lack character. It has purpose and a sense of classical proportion and is fresh in its use of colour. Wilde's unassertive approach to the opening of the favourite *C minor Sonata* is particularly appealing, and he is good too in the *Variations.* Moreover the recording is wholly natural and real.

Piano sonatas Nos. 33 in C min., Hob XVI/20; 38 in F, Hob XVI/23; 58 in C, Hob XVI/48; 60 in C, Hob XVI/50.
*** Sony Dig. MK 44918 [id.]. Emanuel Ax.

Emanuel Ax offers four *Sonatas*, two of which duplicate Mikhail Pletnev's remarkable disc. Ax is a fine stylist and his playing is full of colour, without being quite so personal. He brings sparkle, refined musicianship and fluent fingers to these pieces and he is well enough recorded.

There is a faint halo of resonance round the aural image, but the reverberation is not excessive. An enjoyable recital.

Piano sonatas Nos. 33 in C min., Hob XVI/20; 47 in B min., Hob XVI/32; 53 in E min., Hob XVI/34; 50 in D, Hob XVI/37; 54 in G, Hob XVI/40; 56 in D, Hob XVI/42; 58 in C; 59 in E flat; 60 in C; 61 in D; 62 in E flat, Hob XVI/48–52; Adagio in F, Hob XVII/9; Andante with variations in F min., Hob XVII/6; Fantasia in C, Hob XVII/4.
*** Ph. 416 643-2 (4). Alfred Brendel.

This collection offers some of the best Haydn playing on record – and some of the best Brendel, too. There are eleven sonatas in all, together with the *F minor Variations* and the *C major Fantasia* (or *Capriccio*). They have been recorded over a number of years and are splendidly characterized and superbly recorded. The first is analogue, the remainder digital.

Piano sonatas Nos. 33 in C min., Hob XVI/20; 58 in C, Hob XVI/48; 60 in C, Hob XVI/50.
*** Denon Dig. C37 7801 [id.]. András Schiff.

Those who do not respond to Brendel's strong keyboard personality and find his Haydn a shade self-conscious should consider this disc. Schiff plays with an extraordinary refinement and delicacy; he is resourceful and highly imaginative in his use of tone-colour; his phrasing and articulation are a constant source of pleasure. Superb in every way and beautifully recorded, too.

Piano sonatas Nos. 33 in C min., Hob XVI/20; 59 in E flat, Hob XVI/49.
*** Ph. 426 815-2 [id.]. Alfred Brendel.

This is the first of the four Haydn discs Brendel made for Philips and it was recorded in 1979 in very clean, warm, analogue sound. In some ways it is one of his very best: there is no trace of the excessively brittle staccato which has troubled some of his recent Mozart and, although it is obvious that the performances are the product of much thought, there is still a sense of spontaneity. This is well worth acquiring.

Piano sonatas: 33 in C min., Hob XVI/20; 60 in C, Hob XVI/50; 62 in E flat, Hob XVI/52; Andante & Variations in F min., Hob XVII/6.
*** Virgin Dig. VC7 90839-2; *VC 790839-4* [id.]. Mikhail Pletnev.

Pletnev's reading of the *Sonatas* is full of personality and character. The *C major* is given with great elegance and wit, and the great *E flat Sonata* is magisterial. This playing has a masterly authority, and Pletnev is very well recorded. No Haydn collection should be without these thoughtful and individual performances. Three stars for everything in this recital except the *F minor Variations*, which is shorn of repeats and gravitas.

Piano sonatas Nos. 38 in F, Hob XVI/23; 51 in E flat, Hob XVI/38; 52 in G, HobXVI/39.
*** Mer. CDE 84155; *KE 77155* [id.]. Julia Cload.

Julia Cload's cool, direct style is heard at its best in her second group of sonatas. The clean articulation in the first movement of the *F major* is matched by her thoughtfulness in the *Adagio*, and the other performances have the same mixture of boldness and introversion. The piano image is bright and clear, with just a touch of hardness on *fortes*; one wonders, incidentally, why Meridian have not recorded her digitally; there is a degree of background noise here.

Piano sonatas Nos. 47 in B min., Hob XVI/32; 53 in E min., Hob XVI/34; 56 in D, Hob XVI/42; Adagio in F, Hob XVII/9; Fantasia in C, Hob XVII/4.
*** Ph. Dig. 412 228-2 [id.]. Alfred Brendel.

These performances are held together marvellously, self-aware at times, as many great performances are, but inspiriting and always governed by the highest intelligence. The *B minor Sonata* has a *Sturm und Drang* urgency, and Brendel's account has vitality and character. Moreover the recording is splendidly realistic.

Piano sonatas Nos. 50 in D, Hob XVI/37; 54 in G, Hob XVI/40; 55 in B flat, Hob XVI/41; Adagio in F, Hob XVII/9.
*** Mer. ECD 84083; *KE 77083* [id.]. Julia Cload.

Julia Cload's playing is fresh, characterful and intelligent, and will give considerable pleasure. She has the advantage of very truthful recorded sound.

Piano sonatas Nos. 50 in D, Hob XVI/37; 54 in G, Hob XVI/40; 62 in E flat, Hob XVI/52; Andante with variations in F min., Hob XVII/6.

*** Ph. Dig. 416 365-2 [id.]. Alfred Brendel.

Brendel at his finest, and Philips, too: he is splendidly recorded. The playing has a jewelled precision – not perhaps to all tastes (some will find it too self-aware). However, its intelligence and artistry will win over most collectors.

Piano sonatas Nos. 58 in C; 59 in E flat; 60 in C; 61 in D; 62 in E flat, Hob XVI/48–52.
*** BMG/RCA Dig. RD 77160 [77160-2-RC]. Andreas Staier (fortepiano).

Andreas Staier's recital of late sonatas is one of the best Haydn discs on the market. He plays a recent copy by Christopher Clarke of a fortepiano from around 1790 by the Viennese maker, Anton Walter, and proves a highly sensitive and imaginative interpreter. He brings a surprisingly wide dynamic range as well as a diversity of keyboard colour to these pieces and holds the listener throughout. He is very well recorded indeed.

VOCAL MUSIC

The Creation (complete; in English).
*** EMI Dig. CDS7 54159-2 [Ang. CDCB 54159]; *EX 754159-4* (2). Augér, Langridge, David Thomas, CBSO & Ch., Simon Rattle.
*** Decca Dig. 430 397-2; *430 397-4* (2) [id.]. Kirkby, Rolfe Johnson, George, AAM Ch. & O, Hogwood.
(M) **(*) EMI CMS7 69894-2 (2). Harper, Tear, Shirley-Quirk, King's College Ch., ASMF, Willcocks.

Both Rattle and Hogwood use the English text, which Haydn himself recognized as having equal validity with the German. The English version may have its oddities – like the 'flexible tiger' leaping – but it is above all colourful, and Rattle brings out that illustrative colour with exceptional vividness: birdsong, lion-roars and the like. The subtlety of his control of rhythm and phrase gives extra point and more light and shade than the other versions, even Hogwood's using period instruments. Rattle consistently brings out the fun in the writing, as well as the serious purpose, with the grandest of themes given sparkle, thanks to a composer who, more than any, recognized how vital humour can be in music. Rattle has plainly learnt from period performance, not only concerning speeds – often surprisingly brisk, as in the great soprano aria, *With verdure clad* – but as regards style too. The male soloists sound none too sweet as recorded, but they characterize positively; and there is no finer account of the soprano's music than that of Arleen Augér. Fast or not, *With verdure clad* brings heavenly sweetness and purity, with Augér soaring up effortlessly. The weight of the Birmingham chorus is impressive, achieved without loss of clarity or detail in a full, well-balanced recording.

Hogwood defies what has become the custom in period performance and opts for large forces such as Haydn – who during his trips to London was much impressed by large-scale performances of Handel oratorios – would have welcomed. The result, for all its weight, retains fine clarity of detail and an attractive freshness, as in the television performance which used substantially the same numbers. The choir of New College, Oxford, with its trebles adds to the brightness of choral sound, and the trio of soloists is admirably consistent – Emma Kirkby brightly distinctive, and Anthony Rolfe Johnson sweet-toned. Michael George is wonderfully intense in the hushed opening recitative before the blazing outburst on the creation of light, even if later the voice emerges less beautifully. Hogwood may lack some of the flair and imagination of Rattle, but it would be hard to find a period performance to match this. The sound has fine presence and immediacy.

Quite apart from the fact that it is based on Milton, the idea of *The Creation* was first presented to Haydn in the form of an English libretto provided by the impresario Salomon. David Willcocks captures the work's genial, spirited vigour and it is good to have 'the flexible tiger' and 'the nimble stag' so vividly portrayed. Though Heather Harper is not always quite as steady or sweet-toned as usual, this is a first-rate team of soloists, and the choral singing and the playing of the Academy could hardly be more stylish.

The Creation (*Die Schöpfung;* in German).
(M) *** DG 435 077-2 (2). Janowitz, Ludwig, Wunderlich, Krenn, Fischer-Dieskau, Berry, V. Singverein, BPO, Karajan.
*** DG Dig. 419 765-2 (2) [id.]. Blegen, Popp, Moser, Ollmann, Moll, Bav. R. Ch. & SO, Bernstein.
*** Ph. 416 449-2 [id.]. Mathis, Fischer-Dieskau, Baldin, Ch. & ASMF, Marriner.

(B) **(*) CfP CD-CFPD 4444; *TC-CFPD 4444* (2). Donath, Tear, Van Dam, Philh. Ch. & O, Frühbeck de Burgos.
**(*) Erato/Warner Dig. 2292-45449-2 (2) [id.]. Margaret Marshall, Branisteanu, Tappy, Rydl, Huttenlocher, Suisse Romande R. Ch., Pro Arte of Lausanne, Lausanne CO, Jordan.

(i) *The Creation;* (ii) *Mass No. 7 in B flat (Little organ mass): Missa brevis Sancti Johannis de Deo.*
(M) *** Decca 425 968 (2). (i; ii) Ameling; (i) Krenn, Krause, Spoorenberg, Fairhurst; (ii) P. Planyavsky (organ); (i; ii) V. State Op. Ch., VPO, Münchinger.

Among versions of *The Creation* sung in German, Karajan's 1969 set remains unsurpassed and, at mid-price, is a clear first choice despite two small cuts (in Nos. 30 and 32). Here Karajan produces one of his most rapt choral performances; his concentration on refinement and polish might in principle seem out of place in a work which tells of religious faith in the most direct of terms, but in fact the result is outstanding. The combination of the Berlin Philharmonic at its most intense and the great Viennese choir makes for a performance that is not only polished but warm and dramatically strong too. The soloists are an extraordinarily fine team, more consistent in quality than those on almost any rival version. This was one of the last recordings made by the incomparable Fritz Wunderlich, and fortunately his magnificent contribution extended to all the arias, leaving Werner Krenn to fill in the gaps of recitative left unrecorded. The recording quality is both atmospheric and lively in its CD transfer and is far preferable to his later, digital version (410 718-2).

Bernstein's version, recorded at a live performance in Munich, uses a relatively large chorus, encouraging him to adopt rather slow speeds at times. What matters is the joy conveyed in the story-telling, with the finely disciplined chorus and orchestra producing incandescent tone, blazing away in the big set-numbers, and the performance is compulsive from the very opening bars. Five soloists are used instead of three, with the parts of Adam and Eve sung by nicely contrasted singers. So the charming, golden-toned Lucia Popp is a warmly human Eve, to contrast with the more silvery and ethereal Gabriel of Judith Blegen; and Kurt Ollmann as Adam is lighter and less magisterial than his angelic counterpart, Kurt Moll as Raphael who, with his dark bass tone, produces the most memorable singing of all. Bernstein's tenor, Thomas Moser, combines a lyrical enough quality with heroic weight, confirming this as an unusually persuasive version, well recorded in atmospheric sound.

With generally fast tempi Marriner draws consistently lithe and resilient playing and singing from his St Martin's team. There is no lack of weight in the result, although you might count Dietrich Fischer-Dieskau in the baritone role as too weighty, recorded rather close, but his inflexion of every word is intensely revealing. The soprano Edith Mathis is very sweet of tone if not always quite as steady as some of her rivals on record. The one notable snag is that Aldo Baldin's tenor is not well focused by the microphones. Otherwise the 1980 analogue recording still sounds first rate.

Münchinger provides another excellent, mid-price *Creation*. It is a fine performance that stands up well, even in comparison with Karajan's set, and the Decca recording is much better balanced. Münchinger has rarely conducted with such electric tension on record and although his direct style is somewhat square, his soloists make a satisfying team. The set also includes Haydn's *Little organ mass*, so called because the solo organ is used to add colour to the soprano's *Benedictus*, a most delightful setting. Ameling here matches her appealing contribution to the main work and the choral singing is pleasingly crisp. The sound is first class, the remastering highly successful.

Rafael Frühbeck de Burgos directs a genial performance, recorded with fullness and immediacy. Though the early Karajan version has even crisper ensemble in both chorus and orchestra, the easier pacing of Frühbeck provides an alternative which at bargain price remains very good value. The soloists are all excellent, and though Helen Donath is not as pure-toned as Janowitz on DG, with a hint of flutter in the voice, she is wonderfully agile in ornamentation, as in the bird-like quality she gives to the aria, *On mighty pens*. The chorus might gain from a rather more forward balance, but the CD increases the immediacy and has good definition.

Exceptionally among recent versions, Armin Jordan's recording with the Lausanne Chamber Orchestra uses separate soloists for Adam and Eve in the final part, both lighter-toned than their counterparts earlier. With immediate recording which brings soloists and orchestra close together, the impression is of an intimate chamber performance with a substantial chorus set slightly back. With Jordan pointing rhythms lightly and naturally, the joy of the writing is well caught. Though never sluggish, speeds are generally traditional, usually slower than with Rattle, notably in *With verdure clad* (*Nun beut die Flur*). Margaret Marshall is warmly caught but the balance prevents a genuine pianissimo. Eric Tappy is rather tight-toned and Kurt Rydl is a weighty bass soloist.

The Creation: Arias and choruses.
(M) **(*) DG Dig. 429 489-2. Mathis, Murray, Araiza, Van Dam, V. Singverein, VPO, Karajan.
(M) **(*) Decca Dig. 430 739-2; *430 739-4* (from above Chicago set; cond. Solti).

This is a generous disc of excerpts, offering 72 minutes' playing time, but, without the continuity of the complete work, the ear is drawn to notice the contrived balance.

Solti's selection (70 minutes) is only slightly less generous than Karajan's, but the recording is much fuller and better balanced, although the choruses (notably 'The heavens are telling') sound massive in the ample Chicago acoustic. Among the soloists the charming Norma Burrowes easily steals the show.

Mass No. 2 in F (Missa brevis).
*** O-L 421 654-2 [id.]. Kirkby, Nelson, Ch. of Christ Church Cathedral, Oxford, AAM, Preston – HANDEL: *Anthem for Foundling Hospital* etc. ***

Haydn wrote the early *Missa brevis* when he was seventeen. The setting is engagingly unpretentious; some of its sections last for under two minutes and none takes more than three and a half. The two soprano soloists here match their voices admirably and the effect is delightful.

Mass No. 3 in C (Missa Cellensis): Missa Sanctae Caeciliae.
*** O-L Dig. 417 125-2 [id.]. Nelson, Cable, Hill, Thomas, Ch. of Christ Church Cathedral, AAM, Preston.

The *Missa Cellensis* (also known as the *Missa Sanctae Caeciliae*) is Haydn's longest setting of the liturgy; the *Gloria* alone (in seven cantata-like movements) lasts nearly half an hour. Preston directs an excellent performance with fine contributions from choir and soloists, set against a warmly reverberant acoustic.

Masses Nos. (i) *5 in E flat (Missa in honorem Beatissimae Virginis Mariae), Hob XXII/4;* (ii) *6 in G (Missa Sancti Nicolai), Hob XXII/6; Missa rorate coeli desuper, Hob XXII/3.*
*** O-L 421 478-2 [id.]. Christ Church Cathedral Ch., Oxford, AAM, Preston, with (i) Nelson, Watkinson, Hill, Thomas; (ii) Nelson, Minty, Covey-Crump, Thomas.

In the early *E flat Mass* Haydn followed the rococo conventions of his time, dutifully giving weight to the *Gloria* and *Credo* in culminating fugues but generally adopting a style featuring Italianate melody which to modern ears inevitably sounds operatic. One intriguing point is Haydn's use of a pair of cors anglais, which add a touch of darkness to the scoring. The *Missa Sancti Nicolai* dates from 1772 but has a comparable freshness of inspiration. The performance is first rate in every way, even finer than that of the earlier Mass, beautifully sung, with spontaneity in every bar and a highly characterized accompaniment. The little *Missa rorate coeli desuper* was written by Haydn when he was still a choirboy in Vienna, and it may well be his earliest surviving work. Not everything is perfunctory, for the *Agnus Dei* has a touching gravity. The whole work lasts for just under eight minutes. Excellent recording ensures that this CD receives a warm welcome.

Masses Nos. (i) *7 in B flat: Missa brevis Sancti Joannis de Deo (Little organ mass), Hob XXII/7;* (ii) *8 in C (Mariazellermesse): Missa Cellensis, Hob XXII/8;* (iii) *Organ concerto No. 1 in C, Hob XVIII/1.*
(M) *** Decca 430 160-2; *430 160-4* [id.]. (i) J. Smith; Scott; (ii) J. Smith, Watts, Tear, Luxon; (i; ii) St John's College, Cambridge, Ch., Guest; (i–iii) ASMF; (iii) Preston, Marriner.

With excellent singing and fine orchestral playing, this is a very desirable issue in the splendid Guest series, and was originally recorded by Argo in 1977. The CD transfers are admirably fresh and well focused, and for a bonus we are given Simon Preston's persuasive account of an early organ concerto, written about 1756. Preston's vivid registration and Marriner's spirited accompaniment ensure the listener's pleasure, and the fine 1966 recording, sounding cleaner in the bass than in its original LP format, was also made at St John's.

Mass No. 9 in B flat (Heiligmesse): Missa Sancti Bernardi von Offida, Hob XXII/10.
(M) *** Decca 430 158-2 [id.]. Cantelo, Minty, Partridge, Keyte, St John's College, Cambridge, Ch., ASMF, Guest – MOZART: *Litaniae de venerabili.* ***

Of all Haydn's Masses the *Heiligmesse* is one of the most human and direct in its appeal. Its combination of symphonic means and simple vocal style underlines its effectiveness. The name *Heiligmesse* derives from the church song on which Haydn based the *Sanctus*. Like the other records in this series, this is a splendid performance, and the vintage Argo sound has been transferred very successfully to CD. The solo singing is good, if not always equally distinguished, and the choral response is excellent.

Mass No. 10 in C: Missa in tempore belli (Paukenmesse), Hob XXII/9.
(M) *** Decca 430 157-2; *430 157-4* [id.]. Cantelo, Watts, Tear, McDaniel, St John's College, Cambridge, Ch., ASMF, Guest – MOZART: *Vesperae sollennes.* ***

This was the last of the six Haydn late Masses to be recorded by Guest and his St John's forces for Argo, in 1969, and it is well up to the standard previously set. Guest provides a clean, brightly recorded account with good soloists. The Argo performance sounds very fresh in its remastered format. It is now generously coupled with a fine Mozart recording, made a decade later.

Mass No. 11 in D min. (Nelson): Missa in angustiis.
(M) *** Decca 421 146-2. Stahlman, Watts, Wilfred Brown, Krause, King's College, Cambridge, Ch., LSO, Willcocks – VIVALDI: *Gloria.* ***

Mass No. 11 in D min. (Nelson); Te Deum in C, Hob XXIIIc/2.
*** DG Dig. 423 097-2 [id.]. Lott, C. Watkinson, Maldwyn Davies, Wilson-Johnson, Ch. & E. Concert, Pinnock.

The *Nelson Mass* (*Missa in angustiis*: Mass in times of fear) brings a superb choral offering from Trevor Pinnock and the English Concert. Using a larger band of strings than in his highly successful recordings of Baroque instrumental music, Pinnock brings home the high drama of Haydn's autumnal inspiration. The extraordinary instrumentation at the very start, with organ replacing wind, and horns and trumpets made all the more prominent, has never sounded more menacing. With incandescent singing from the chorus and fine matching from excellent soloists (Felicity Lott in exceptionally sweet voice), the exuberance of the *Gloria* is then brought home all the more by contrast. Misplaced accents, almost jazzy, add to the joyful exhilaration. Similarly exuberant syncopations mark the magnificent setting of the *Te Deum*, which comes as a very valuable makeweight. The inspiration of such music leaps forward from the eighteenth century all the more excitingly in an authentic performance such as this. Excellent, full-blooded sound, with good definition.

The CD of the famous Willcocks account, recorded by Argo in 1962, does not quite manage to control the focus of the resonant King's acoustic, but the effect is admirably full-bodied and vivid; those not wanting to stretch to Pinnock's full-priced digital CD will find this a satisfactory alternative with its very generous Vivaldi coupling.

Mass No. 12 in B flat (Theresienmesse), Hob XXII/12.
(M) *** Decca 430 159-2; *430 159-4* [id.]. Spoorenberg, Greevy, Mitchinson, Krause, St John's College, Cambridge, Ch., Guest – M. HAYDN: *Ave Regina;* MOZART: *Ave verum corpus.* ***
(M) *** Sony Dig. SM2K 47522 (2). Popp, Elias, Tear, Hudson, LSO Ch., LSO, Bernstein – BEETHOVEN: *Choral fantasia* etc. ***

The *Theresa Mass* followed on a year after the *Nelson Mass*. It may be less famous but the inspiration is hardly less memorable, and Haydn's balancing of chorus against soloists, contrapuntal writing set against chordal passages, was never more masterly than here. George Guest injects tremendous vigour into the music (as in the *Harmoniemesse*, there is a 'military' conclusion in the *Donna nobis pacem*) and the St John's Choir, in splendid form, makes the very most of this fine work. Good solo singing and brilliant, vivid, 1965 recording.

Bernstein recorded the *Theresienmesse* in 1979 at Henry Wood Hall immediately after a live performance at the Festival Hall, and the grand manner goes with playing and singing of infectious bounce and resilience, typical of this conductor. The soloists are first rate, especially Lucia Popp, and with rounded, not specially analytical digital sound this can be warmly recommended as an enjoyably spontaneous large-scale alternative to Guest's fine version on Decca.

Mass No. 13 in B flat (Schöpfungsmesse).
(M) *** Decca 430 161-2; *430 161-4* [id.]. Cantelo,, Watts, Tear, Forbes Robinson, St John's College, Cambridge, Ch., ASMF, Guest – MOZART: *Mass No. 12 (Spaur).* ***

Guest again draws an outstanding performance from his own St John's College Choir and an excellent band of professionals, a fresh and direct reading to match the others of his highly successful Argo series. The very opening has superb weight and vigour, matched by the *Gloria*, rich with brass, and the exuberant *Credo*; while in the introduction to the *Benedictus* Haydn uses the horns to create a most forward-looking warmth of colour, before the richly textured vocal entry.

Mass No. 14 in B flat (Harmoniemesse), Hob XXII/14.
(M) *** Decca 430 162-2; *430 162-4* [id.]. Spoorenberg, Watts, Young, Rouleau, St John's College, Cambridge, Ch., Guest – MOZART: *Vesperae de Dominica.* ***

Haydn was over seventy when he started writing this Mass, but his freshness and originality are as striking as in any of the earlier works. In particular the last section of the Mass brings a wonderfully memorable passage when, after the genial, life-enhancing *Benedictus*, comes the contrast of a gentle setting of the *Agnus Dei*, with the spirit of Mozart hovering in the background. Then Haydn bursts out with fanfares into a vigorous, even aggressive *Donna nobis pacem*. The fine performance caps the others in this outstanding series. The quartet of soloists is strong, with Helen Watts in particular singing magnificently. The brilliant and well-balanced 1966 recording has been transferred splendidly to CD, which now offers a substantial bonus in the Mozart *Vespers*, recorded at St John's over a decade later.

The Seasons (Die Jahreszeiten; oratorio): complete (in German).
*** DG Dig. 431 818-2 (2). Bonney, Rolfe Johnson, Schmidt, Monteverdi Ch., E. Bar. Soloists, Gardiner.
(M) *** DG 423 922-2 (2) [id.]. Janowitz, Schreier, Talvela, VSO, Boehm.
*** Ph. Dig. 411 428-2 (2) [id.]. Mathis, Jerusalem, Fischer-Dieskau, Ch. & ASMF, Marriner.
**(*) Teldec/Warner Dig. 2292 42699-2 (2) [id.]. Blasi, Protschka, Holl, Schönberg Ch., VSO, Harnoncourt.

As in so many of his choral recordings, Gardiner brushes away any cobwebs from the music in Haydn's last oratorio. If ever after the cosmic splendour of *The Creation*, this more genial piece has seemed an anticlimax, Gardiner completely refutes that. So the howling of the winter wind in the opening prelude makes the arrival of spring all the more warming, and the first chorus, *Come gentle spring*, flows along freshly at an easy jig. Gardiner consistently heightens the contrasts, bringing out Haydn's habitual cheerfulness, but setting it against the moments of repose and pure beauty, notably in the summer episode. The summer storm is then by contrast the more thrilling, close relation of Beethoven's *Pastoral Symphony*. Gardiner here more than ever rejects the idea prevalent among period performers that slow, measured speeds should be avoided, and almost always gets the best of both worlds in intensity of communication, whatever the purists may say. Even more than usual, this studio performance conveys the electricity of a live event. The silver-toned Barbara Bonney and Anthony Rolfe Johnson at his most sensitive are outstanding soloists, and though the baritone, Andreas Schmidt, is less sweet on the ear, he winningly captures the bluff jollity of the role of Simon. Gardiner counters the old, mistaken idea that the earliest performances in Haydn's time were on a large scale, and here with relatively small forces – on what is now thought the original scale – gives the work an extra immediacy and sharpness of focus, with the brass in particular thrillingly full-toned.

Boehm's performance enters totally into the spirit of the music. The soloists are excellent and characterize the music fully; the chorus sing enthusiastically and are well recorded. But it is Boehm's set. He secures fine orchestral playing throughout, an excellent overall musical balance and real spontaneity in music that needs this above all else. The CD transfer of the 1967 recording is admirably managed; the sound overall is a little drier, but the chorus have plenty of body and there is an excellent sense of presence.

Sir Neville Marriner offers (at full price) a superbly joyful performance of Haydn's last oratorio. Edith Mathis and Dietrich Fischer-Dieskau are as stylish and characterful as one would expect, pointing the words as narrative. Siegfried Jerusalem is both heroic of timbre and yet delicate enough for Haydn's most elegant and genial passages. The chorus and orchestra, of authentic size, add to the freshness. The recording, made in St John's, Smith Square, is warmly reverberant, with vivid detail.

Harnoncourt's version is characteristically vibrant and his dramatization of the elements strong, with Robert Holl making a memorable contribution in *Winter*. On the other hand, Protschka's style is lighter than that of Siegfried Jerusalem for Marriner, with his honeyed elegance and heroic ring. Angela Maria Blasi has a sweet, small timbre and is consistently persuasive. The Arnold Schönberg Choir sing with fine bite and fervour and are especially invigorating in the harvest celebrations of *Autumn*. Detail is perceptively observed throughout the work, and Harnoncourt brings his usual powerful rhythmic feeling to the music-making – accents are readily stressed here and the narrative flow is vividly maintained. The Teldec recording is excellent, with good balance and realistic projection, and there is certainly no lack of drama.

The Seasons: highlights.
(M) **(*) Ph. Dig. 432 617-2; *432 617-4*. Mathis, Jerusalem, Fischer-Dieskau, Ch. & ASMF, Marriner.

Marriner's selection is generous (72 minutes) and well chosen, but this Laser Line series, disgracefully, provides no information whatsover about the work from which these excerpts are drawn, not even telling the purchaser from which section each comes.

Stabat Mater.
(M) *** Decca 433 172-2 [id.]. Augér, Hodgson, Rolfe Johnson, Howell, L. Chamber Ch., Argo CO, Laszlo Heltay.
**(*) Erato/Warner Dig. 2292 45181-2 [id.]. Armstrong, Murray, Hill, Huttenlocher, Lausanne Vocal Ens. & CO, Corboz.

Haydn's *Stabat Mater*, one of his first major masterpieces showing him at full stretch, was written in the early years at Esterháza. Scored for strings with oboes, the work is far bigger in aim than this scale might imply, and some of the choruses include harmonic progressions which in their emotional overtones suggest music of a much later period. On record, as in the concert hall, the work is scandalously neglected and it is good that Heltay's reading conveys its essential greatness, helped by excellent soloists and vividly atmospheric recording.

The Erato version offers brisk speeds; but it has an excellent quartet of soloists, fine choral singing of the kind we have come to expect from the Lausanne choir, and first-rate digital recording.

Te Deum in C, Hob XXIIIc/2.
(M) **(*) BMG/RCA GD 86535 [6535-2-RG]. V. Boys' Ch., Ch. Viennensis, VCO, Gillesberger – MOZART: *Requiem mass; Ave verum*. **(*)

A fine, vigorous account of the *Te Deum* by these Viennese forces, very vividly recorded, coupled to a not inconsiderable account of Mozart's *Requiem*. At mid-price it is excellent value.

OPERA

L'anima del Filosofo (Orfeo ed Euridice).
** BMG/RCA Dig. RD 77229 [77229-2] (2). Prégardien, Schmiege, McFadden, Schwarz, Schneider, Netherlands Chamber Ch., La Stagione, Frankfurt, Michael Schneider.

Haydn wrote his Orpheus opera in 1791 for performance in London. He was just completing it after his arrival, when the whole project had to be abandoned. King George III refused to license the theatre when its patron was his son, the Prince of Wales, later King George IV. Though the subject of the Orpheus story failed signally to draw from Haydn the sort of tragic music that it requires, there are many delightful numbers. What one seriously misses too are the big solo numbers for the main characters that no doubt Haydn would have added before the first performance. That would have added dramatic interest, as well as musical substance. This first CD recording is generally well sung, with the clean-toned tenor, Christoph Prégardien, as Orfeo and the warm, expressive Marilyn Schmiege as Euridice and the baritone Gotthold Schwarz a resonant Creonte. Unfortunately, Michael Schneider and La Stagione Frankfurt, lively in the brisk numbers, too often make heavy weather of the broader, more spacious passages. A more crisply focused recording would also have helped in adding bite.

Armida: excerpts; *La vera constanza*: excerpts.
(M) *** Ph. 426 641-2; *426 641-4*. Jessye Norman, Claes Ahnsjö, Lucerne CO, Dorati.

With both these operas currently out of the catalogue, this set of arias and duets is the more attractive, to whet the musical appetite for the complete works. Jessye Norman's voice is superbly captured in fine recording, with Claes Ahnsjö also impressive in two duets. Lively and sympathetic conducting from Dorati.

L'Infedeltà delusa.
**(*) HM/BMG RD 77099 (2) [77099-2-RC]. Argenta, Lootens, Prégardien, M. Schäfer, Varcoe, La Petite Bande, Sigiswald Kuijken.

More than Haydn's other operas, *L'infedeltà delusa* makes one wonder whether Mozart and Da Ponte had access to it before they created their three supreme operatic masterpieces. When the Act III finale is launched by the jealous Vespina slapping her beloved's face, it might almost be Susanna in *Figaro*. As there, the effect is totally refreshing, with sudden realism in the midst of formality. Some of the scenes are very complex for their period too. Musically, the surprises come less in the melodic writing which, in one jolly number after another, is relatively conventional, than in ear-catching twists and striking instrumental effects. Haydn was proud of the Esterházy horns, for example, and they have some marvellous whooping to do. The plot of the opera is unusual for the time in giving the role of the heavy father to the tenor (well taken by Christoph Prégardien), reflecting the fact that it was expressly designed for Karl Friberth, literary adviser to Prince Esterházy as well as a singer. This performance on period instruments nicely captures the flavour of a semi-domestic performance in the prince's country palace. Both the sopranos, Nancy Argenta and Lena Lootens, are agile and precise, if a little edgy. Both tenors, Markus Schäfer as well as Prégardien, are stressed by the range demanded; but, like the bass, Stephen Varcoe, they have clean voices, apt for Haydn on a small scale. The scale of the whole work, much shorter than was common in the late eighteenth century, makes it the more apt for revival today. *L'infedeltà delusa* may be no *Così fan tutte*, but this is a most enjoyable set, even if a reissue of Dorati's pioneering version for Philips using modern instruments, more strongly cast, will be a powerful contender when issued on CD.

Haydn, Michael (1737–1806)

Concertino for horn and orchestra in D.
(M) *** Teldec/Warner Dig. 9031 74790-2 [id.]. Dale Clevenger, Liszt CO, Rolla – J. HAYDN: *Concertos.* ***

Michael Haydn's *Concertino* is in the form of a French overture, beginning with a slow movement, followed by a fast one, and closing with a minuet and Trio in which the soloist is featured in only the middle section. It is played with fine style by Dale Clevenger, whose articulation is a joy in itself. Rolla and his orchestra clearly enjoy themselves and the recording, like the coupled concertos by Josef Haydn, is very realistic indeed. An outstanding coupling.

Violin concerto in B flat.
(M) **(*) Teldec/Warner Dig. 9031 74784-2 [id.]. Zehetmair, Liszt CO – J. HAYDN: *Concerto* ***; SIBELIUS: *Concerto.* **

A *Violin concerto* from Michael Haydn (written in 1760) makes an enterprising coupling for the better-known work by his brother, Josef. The finale is the weakest part, though not lacking in spirit. The performance with Thomas Zehetmair combining roles of soloist and conductor is strongly characterized and very well recorded. One's only reservation concerns a tendency for the phrasing – notably in the slow movement – to have squeezed emphases, so that the melodic line swells out dynamically, though this is not an alternative to the use of vibrato, as in 'authentic' performances.

Symphonies Nos. 19 in C, P.10; 21 in C, P.12; 23 in D, P.43; 26 in G, P.16; 29 in C, P.19; 37 in B flat, P.28; 39 in F, P.30; 41 in F, P.32.
(B) **(*) VoxBox 1155012 (2) [CDX 5020]. Bournemouth Sinf., Harold Fabermann.

It is good that Harold Fabermann is exploring the symphonies of Michael Haydn, and even better that they are being recorded digitally – though at times one would not realize this, for the resonant recording often makes tuttis sound opaque and not too cleanly focused. The composer's inspiration is uneven but the slow movements are always pleasing. P.16 (No. 26) was the symphony which Mozart brought back from Vienna in 1793 and which has long been mistakenly attributed to him (as No. 37, K.444). However, Mozart's score omits the bassoon solo (perhaps he felt it sounded too comic!) so this is the first recording of what Michael Haydn actually wrote. Many of the symphonies are notable for their helter-skelter finales (marked variously *Allegro molto*, *Vivace* or *Fugato-Vivace assai*) which have great energy, responsively generated by the Bournemouth players. The performances are well made and sympathetic, suitably athletic in the allegros; but they lack the final degree of flexibility and imagination in the expressive writing. Probably the finest work in the group included is the last on the second disc, No. 29 (P.19), resourcefully scored for a large classical band: highly inventive in the extended central *Rondeau* and generating real vitality in the outer movements. It is given one of the best performances too, and it ought to be in the repertoire. The documentation with the set is admirable; the Perger numbers, incidentally, realign the symphonies in order of composition.

Symphony in C, P.12.

(M) *** Teldec/Warner Dig. 9031 74788-2 [id.]. Liszt CO, János Rolla – ROSSINI: *String sonatas.* ***

This *Symphony in C major*, if otherwise fairly conventional, contains a strikingly beautiful inspiration, the central elegiac *Andante in A minor* for strings with solo oboe. It is very well played throughout and is freshly recorded.

Divertimenti: in C, P. 98; in C, P. 115.

*** Denon Dig. C37 7119 [id.]. Holliger, Salvatore Qt – J. C. BACH: *Oboe quartet;* MOZART: *Adagio.* ***

Both these *Divertimenti* contain captivating and original inspirations. The longer of the two, P. 98, has a fizzing first movement and a joyful *Presto* finale, while P. 115 brings unexpected timbres. Well coupled and vividly recorded.

Ave Regina.

(M) *** Ph. 430 159-2; *430 159-4* [id.]. St John's College, Cambridge, Ch., Guest – J. HAYDN: *Theresienmesse;* MOZART: *Ave verum corpus.* ***

This lovely antiphon, scored for eight-part double choir, looks back to Palestrina and the Venetian school of the Gabrielis and the young Monteverdi. It is beautifully sung and recorded.

Headington, Christopher (born 1930)

Violin concerto.

❀ *** ASV CDDCA 780; *ZCDCA 780* [id.]. Xue Wei, LPO, Glover – R. STRAUSS: *Violin concerto.* ***

Written in 1959 and dedicated to the late Ralph Holmes, the Headington *Violin concerto* is a warmly lyrical, unashamedly tonal work, in which a fiery central scherzo is framed by two longer, more reflective movements, both with a vein of melancholy which echoes the comparable movements in the violin concertos of Walton and Prokofiev. The finale is a spacious set of variations in which the last and longest acts as a movingly meditative summary. Xue-Wei plays with a passionate commitment to match that in his Brahms and Tchaikovsky recordings, with Jane Glover and the London Philharmonic providing warmly sympathetic accompaniments. Excellent sound. Those looking for twentieth-century music that is accessible, and rewards familiarity need not hesitate.

Heath, Dave (born 1956)

The Frontier.

*** Virgin VC7 91168-2; *VC7 91168-4* [id.]. LCO, Warren-Green – ADAMS: *Shaker loops* *** ❀; GLASS: *Company* etc. ***; REICH: *8 Lines.* ***

Most minimalist composers are American and, although Dave Heath was born in Manchester, the influences on his music are transatlantic, not only from jazz (which he acknowledges) but also with Copland-like whiffs of the barn dance. In *The Frontier* the incisive rhythmic astringency is tempered by an attractive, winding lyrical theme which finally asserts itself just before the spiky close. The work was written for members of the LCO, and their performance, full of vitality and feeling, is admirably recorded.

Hebden, John (18th century)

6 Concertos for strings (ed. Wood).
**(*) Chan. Dig. CHAN 8339 [id.]. Cantilena, Shepherd.

Little is known about John Hebden except that he was a Yorkshire composer who also played the cello and bassoon. These concertos are his only known works, apart from some flute sonatas. Although they are slightly uneven, at best the invention is impressive. The concertos usually feature two solo violins and are well constructed to offer plenty of contrast. The performances here are accomplished, without the last degree of polish but full of vitality. The recording is clear and well balanced, and given good presence.

Henze, Hans Werner (born 1926)

Symphonies Nos. (i) *1–5;* (ii) *6.*
(M) *** DG 429 854-2 (2) [id.]. (i) BPO, (ii) LSO, composer.

The Henze *Symphonies* are remarkable pieces which inhabit a strongly distinctive sound-world. The *First* with its cool, Stravinskyan slow movement is a remarkable achievement for a 21-year-old, though we hear it in a revision Henze made in early 1963. There is a dance-like feel to the *Third* (1950), written while Henze was attached to the Wiesbaden Ballet. It is rich in fantasy. The *Fourth* is among the most concentrated and atmospheric of his works; there is at times an overwhelming sense of melancholy and a strongly Mediterranean atmosphere to its invention. The *Fifth Symphony* comes from the period of the *Elegy for young lovers* and quotes from one of its arias; the language is strongly post-expressionist. The *Sixth Symphony* was composed while Henze was living in Havana. The performances, dating from 1966 and 1972, are excellent and the recorded sound amazingly vivid, even if a comparison between the CD transfer of No. 3 and the original LP reveals some compression in the sense of space occupied by the orchestra. An important and indispensable set, recommended with enthusiasm.

El Cimarron (complete).
** Koch Schwann Dig. 314 030 (2) [id.]. Yoder, Faust, Evers, Ardeleanu.

El Cimarron is one of the most striking of the works that Henze wrote during the period when he was much influenced by extreme left-wing politics, with emphasis on Fidel Castro's communist regime in Cuba. Spanning an hour an half, its 15 episodic sections tell the true story of a runaway Cuban slave, using a vocal soloist – who narrates as well as singing baritone – accompanied by three instrumentalists who play a whole range of instruments. The idiom is simple and direct in an expressionist way, with the percussionist instructed to use some 50 different instruments in combinations requiring virtuoso agility. Similarly the flautist uses a number of different flutes, while the guitarist supplements his part with bongos and woodblocks. The Koch Schwann disc brings the benefit of fine modern digital recording, and the players give a virtuoso performance, but one rather too rigidly controlled for so freely expressive a work. In concentration and animal energy they hardly compare with the performers in the original DG recording directed by the composer, in which the Japanese percussionist, Stomu Yamash'ta, gave an inspired performance.

OPERA

Die Bassariden (The Bassarids).
*** Koch Schwann 314 006-2 (2) [id.]. Tear, Schmidt, Armstrong, Lindsley, Wenkel, Burt, Murray, Berlin RIAS Chamber Ch. & RSO, Albrecht.

In a massive single act of almost two hours Henze's *The Bassarids*, based on the Bacchae of Euripides, is among the most powerful of modern operas. It is not just more deeply emotional than is usual with Henze, it tellingly and involvingly presents a contrast of rival philosophies between the Dionysiac and the Apollonian, the sensual and the intellectual. With its meaty musical argument and consciously symphonic shape, it is an opera that has cried out for a complete recording, and this fine account from Berlin fills the bill well, amply confirming the work's power. With its well-constructed libretto by W. H. Auden and Chester Kallman (who also did *The Rake's Progress* for Stravinsky) it becomes on disc a massive dramatic symphony, full of inventive vigour. The cast is first rate, including Kenneth Riegel, Andreas Schmidt, Robert Tear and Karen Armstrong, and the 1986 sound is full and well balanced, giving weight and warmth to the taut playing of the Berlin Radio Symphony Orchestra. The choral writing adds greatly to the impact, splendidly realized here by the RIAS Choir. One unnecessary snag is that the CDs provide separate tracks only for the four movements (acts), not for individual sections.

Hérold, Ferdinand (1791–1833)

La Fille mal gardée (ballet, arr. Lanchbery): complete.
(M) *** Decca Dig. *430 849-2* (2) [id.]. ROHCG O, Lanchbery – LECOCQ: *Mam'zelle Angot*. ***

Lanchbery himself concocted the score for this fizzingly comic and totally delightful ballet, drawing primarily on Hérold's music, but interpolating the famous comic *Clog dance* from Hertel's alternative score, which must be one of the most famous of all ballet numbers outside Tchaikovsky. There is much else of comparable delight. Here, with sound of spectacular Decca digital fidelity, Lanchbery conducts a highly seductive account of the complete ballet with an orchestra long familiar with playing it in the theatre, now reissued coupled with Gordon Jacob's equally delicious confection, based on the music of Lecocq.

La Fille mal gardée: extended excerpts.
❀ *** EMI Dig. CDC7 49403-2. RLPO, Wordsworth.

Barry Wordsworth's scintillating account of a generous extended selection from the ballet on CD includes all the important sequences. With playing from the Royal Liverpool Philharmonic Orchestra that combines refinement and delicacy with wit and humour, this is very highly recommendable, with the EMI recording in the demonstration bracket.

Herrmann, Bernard (1911–75)

Film scores: *Beneath the Twelve-mile Reef;* (i) *Citizen Kane: suite; Hangover Square:* (ii) *Concerto macabre. On Dangerous Ground: Death hunt. White Witch Doctor: suite.*
(M) *** BMG/RCA GD 80707; *GK 80707* [0707-2-RG; *0707-4-RG*]. Nat. PO, Gerhardt, (i) with Te Kanawa, (ii) Achucarro.

Bernard Herrmann's reputation as a film composer in the grand Hollywood tradition was immediately established with his remarkable 1940 score for *Citizen Kane*. It is well able to stand up on its own and includes a fascinating pastiche aria from a fictitious opera, *Salammbo*, eloquently sung here by Kiri Te Kanawa. The collection opens with an exhilarating example of the composer's ferocious chase music, the *Death hunt* from *On Dangerous Ground*, led by eight roistering horns with the orchestral brass augmented. *Beneath the Twelve-mile Reef* displays Herrmann's soaring melodic gift and his orchestral flair. The Busoni/Liszt-derived *Concerto macabre* is brilliantly played by Joaquin Achucarro, while *White Witch Doctor* offers opportunities for pseudo-exoticism and a wide range of drum effects, introduced with much colouristic skill. Charles Gerhardt and his splendid orchestra obviously relish the hyperbole and the recording is spectacular.

Wuthering Heights (opera): complete.
(M) *** Unicorn UKCD 2050/52 [id.]. Bainbridge, Kelly, Bell, Beaton, Kitchiner, Rippon, Ward, Bowden, Elizabethan Singers, Pro Arte O, composer.

Bernard Herrmann, best known for his film scores and as conductor, spent many years working on his operatic adaption of Emily Brontë's novel, and though it inevitably gives an over-simplified idea of the tensions in the original story, the result is confident and professional. Much of the writing is fittingly atmospheric, though Hermann detracts from the final effect by going on too long (3½ hours) and keeps the pace of the music consistently slow. Though the writing is purely illustrative rather than musically original, this performance, strongly conducted by the composer, makes for a colourful telling of the story. The solo singing is consistently good and the recording beautifully clear. The Elizabethan Singers come in rather incongruously as highly civilized 'carollers from Gimmerton'. Perhaps the whole drama is too civilized to represent stark Brontë emotions, but it is good to have on CD a complete recording of an ambitious modern opera, as yet unstaged.

Hertel, Johann (1727–89)

Trumpet concerto in D.
*** Ph. Dig. 420 203-2; *420 203-4* [id.]. Hardenberger, ASMF, Marriner – HAYDN *** ❀: HUMMEL *** ❀: STAMITZ: *Concertos.* ***

Johann Hertel's *Trumpet concerto* is typical of many works of the same kind written in the Baroque era, with a highly placed solo line, a touch of melancholy in the *Largo* and plenty of opportunities for crisp tonguing in the finale. Håkan Hardenberger clearly relishes every bar and plays with great flair. He is stylishly accompanied and vividly recorded, though the acoustic is a shade resonant.

Hildegard of Bingen (1098–1179)

Ordo virtutum (The Play of the Virtues).
(M) *** HM/BMG Dig. GD 77051 (2) [77051-2-RG; *77051-4-RG*]. Köper, Mockridge, Thornton, Laurens, Feldman, Monahan, Lister, Trevor, Sanford, Smith, Sequentia.

The more one learns about Abbess Hildegard of Bingen, the more astonishing her achievement appears. She was not just a leading poet and composer of the twelfth century, she was a major political figure who not only founded her own Abbey but corresponded with popes and emperors. *Ordo virtutum* is a mystery play, a genre which she may well have created. Where her motets and hymns are more reflective, this 90-minute piece includes strikingly dramatic passages, with the Devil himself intervening. This recording, made in collaboration with West German Radio of Cologne, is outstandingly fine, particularly recommendable for anyone to investigate who already knows the superb collection of shorter pieces recorded by Gothic Voices for Hyperion (at full price). The sound here is equally full, immediate and atmospheric, with the voices beautifully caught.

Hymns and sequences: *Ave generosa; Columba aspexit; O Ecclesia; O Euchari; O Jerusalem; O ignis spiritus; O presul vere civitatis; O viridissima virga.*
*** Hyp. CDA 66039; *KA 66039* [id.]. Gothic Voices, Muskett, White, Page.

This record draws on the Abbess Hildegard of Bingen's collection of music and poetry, the *Symphonia armonie celestium revelationum* – 'the symphony of the harmony of celestial revelations'. These hymns and sequences, most expertly performed and recorded, have excited much acclaim – and rightly so. A lovely CD.

Hindemith, Paul (1895–1963)

(i) *Concert music for brass and strings; Mathis der Maler* (symphony); (ii) *Viola concerto (Der Schwanendreher).*
(M) **(*) DG 423 241-2 [id.]. (i) Boston SO, Steinberg; (ii) Benyamini, O de Paris, Barenboim.

William Steinberg's accounts of *Mathis* and the *Concert music* were recorded in the early 1970s and are first class, even if the balance is a little recessed. Hindemith was a fine violist and *Der Schwanendreher* is his third concerto for the instrument. It is based on folksongs and the unusual title (*The Swan-Turner*) is of the tune he uses in the finale. Benyamini and the Orchestre de Paris under Barenboim give a very full-bodied account of it; Benyamini is rather forwardly balanced, but his rich (almost over-ripe) tone is glorious.

Cello concerto; (i) *Clarinet concerto.*
*** Etcetera KTC 1006 [id.]. Tibor de Machula; (i) George Pieterson; Concg. O, Kondrashin.

The 1940 *Cello concerto* is exhilarating and inventive, and Tibor de Machula proves an excellent protagonist. As always with Hindemith, the musical argument is rich in incident. The *Clarinet concerto* was written in 1947 for Benny Goodman, who gave its première with Ormandy and the Philadelphia Orchestra. It is not, however, jazz-inspired and is lyrical and eventful. The recordings (made in the Concertgebouw, Amsterdam) are public performances and emanate from the Hilversum Radio archives. Rewarding scores in eminently serviceable recordings.

(i) *Violin concerto;* (ii) *Mathis der Maler (Symphony);* (iii) *Symphonic metamorphosis on themes of Weber.*
❀ (M) *** Decca 433 081-2 [id.]. (i) David Oistrakh, LSO, composer; (ii) SRO, Kletzki; (iii) LSO, Abbado.

Oistrakh's performance of the Hindemith *Violin concerto* is a revelation: it can surely never before have blossomed into such rewarding lyricism, with the great violinist providing many moments when the ear is ravished by the beauty of his phrasing and inflection. The composer, clearly inspired by the marvellous contribution of his soloist, provides an overwhelmingly passionate accompaniment and the 1962 recording, produced by Erik Smith in Decca's West Hampstead Studio remains one of the finest ever made of the combination of violin and orchestra. It still sounds extraordinarily vivid and spacious, more brightly lit in its CD format but firmer in focus too, although the upper range of the violin timbre has lost a little of its bloom. The Rosette is for the concerto but the couplings are well chosen, both also offering vintage late 1960s Decca sound. Abbado's *Symphonic metamorphosis on themes of Weber* is second to none. It is a relief to find a conductor content to follow the composer's own dynamic markings and who does not succumb to the temptation to score interpretative points at the music's expense. The stopped notes on the horns at the beginning of the finale, for example, are marked *piano* and are played here so that they add a barely perceptible touch of colour to the texture. The Decca engineers balance this so musically that the effect is preserved. This admittedly unimportant touch is symptomatic of the subtlty of Abbado's approach in a performance that in every respect is of the highest quality. Kletzki's account of *Mathis der Maler* is also impressive, very well prepared and with a similar attention to detail. He, too has the advantage of finely balanced and truthful recording, and even if the Suisse Romande strings cannot produce quite the body of tone of the LSO, the orchestra still plays very well for him. With 77 minutes of music offered, this is an indispensable disc for all Hindemithians, even if some duplication is involved.

(i) *The Four temperaments; Nobilissima visione.*
**(*) Delos Dig. D/CD 1006 [id.]. (i) Carole Rosenberger; RPO, James de Preist.

The Four temperaments, a set of variations on a three-part theme for piano and strings of 1940, is one of Hindemith's finest and most immediate works. Carole Rosenberger gives a formidable reading of this inventive and resourceful score. James de Preist also secures responsive playing from the RPO strings and gives a sober, well-shaped account of the *Nobilissima visione* suite, doing justice to its grave nobility. The recording is natural and well balanced but could be more transparent, particularly at the top end of the spectrum.

Mathis der Maler (symphony).
(M) **(*) Chan. CHAN 6549 [id.]. LSO, Horenstein – R. STRAUSS: *Death and transfiguration.* **

Mathis der Maler (symphony); *Concert music, Op. 50; Symphonic metamorphoses on themes by Weber.*
*** DG Dig. 429 404-2; *429 404-4* [id.]. Israel PO, Bernstein.

Mathis der Maler (symphony); *Symphonic metamorphoses on themes of Carl Maria von Weber; Trauermusik.*
*** Decca Dig. 421 523-2 [id.]. San Francisco SO, Blomstedt.

Blomstedt has a strong feeling for *Mathis der Maler* and presents a finely groomed and powerfully shaped performance, with lucid and transparent textures. The famous *Trauermusik*, written on the death of King George V, has an affecting quiet eloquence and dedication, and is infinitely more responsive to dynamic shading than any previous account: the solo viola, Geraldine Walther, is exceptionally sensitive. Blomstedt's reading of the *Symphonic metamorphoses on themes of Carl Maria von Weber* is appropriately light in touch; and the recording is exemplary in the naturalness of its balance.

High-voltage Hindemith from Bernstein and the Israel Philharmonic; it was recorded live in the Robert Mann Auditorium in Tel Aviv whose dry acoustic is a handicap. However, accepting this limitation, the DG engineers have produced sound of great clarity and presence that reveals every strand in the orchestral texture. Judging from this record, the Israel orchestra is in much better shape than it was some years ago, with first-class strings rich in sonority, and good brass ensemble. In both the *Concert music for brass and strings* and the *Weber metamorphoses* the playing is exhilarating and, though some may find Bernstein a shade too intense at the opening of the *Mathis Symphony*, the performance is thrilling. But these Bernstein performances have a lot going for them all the same.

Horenstein's *Mathis der Maler* was the last record he made, and it has the merit of breadth and weight. The recording, originally issued by Unicorn, has been remastered satisfactorily, and at mid-price this is again competitive.

Symphonic metamorphosis on themes by Weber.
*** Ph. Dig. 422 347-2 [id.]. Bav. RSO, C. Davis – REGER: *Mozart variations.* *** ❀

Sir Colin Davis's account of the *Symphonic metamorphosis on themes by Weber*, which must now be Hindemith's most popular work, is first class, though not perhaps as gutsy as Bernstein (DG). However, the cultured sound produced by the Bavarian Radio Symphony Orchestra is a joy in itself and the reading has plenty of character and enormous finesse. It comes with an altogether masterly reading of Reger's glorious *Variations and fugue on a theme by Mozart* and is given state-of-the art Philips recording. Recommended with enthusiasm.

Symphony in E flat; Overture Neues vom Tage; Nobilissima visione.
*** Chan. Dig. CHAN 9060 [id.]. BBC PO, Tortelier.

Although the *Nobilissima visione* suite has not been neglected on record, and Hindemith's own account of it was recently transferred to CD, the *Symphony in E flat* (1940) is a comparative rarity, though Sony will surely reissue Bernstein's brilliant account of it with the New York Philharmonic in their Royal Edition and there was a fine version from Sir Adrian Boult from the same period. It is an inventive and resourceful score and is well worth investigating. Yan Pascal Tortelier gets excellent results from the BBC Philharmonic (formerly the BBC Northern Symphony Orchestra). The rather thick and bottom-heavy scoring of the symphony is well delineated (though perhaps the very bass end of the spectrum could be more transparent in climaxes). Good, musicianly performances of *Nobilissima visione* and the much earlier *Neues vom Tage* Overture complete an admirable addition to the Hindemith discography.

Octet (for wind and strings).
(M) ** Sony SMK 46250 [id.]. Members of the Marlboro Festival – BARBER: *Summer music* **(*); NIELSEN: *Woodwind quintet.* **

Those unsympathetic to the composer will find Hindemith at his ugliest and most manufactured in the *Octet* (1957–8). The artists recorded here play it more persuasively than most predecessors on disc, and the recording balance places slightly more air round the sound than in the Nielsen. The disc as a whole is well worth investigating.

(i) *Viola sonatas* (for viola and piano) *Op. 11/4; Op. 25/4;* (Unaccompanied) *Viola sonatas: Op. 11/5; Op. 25/1; Op. 31/4.*
*** ECM Dig. 833 309-2 (2) [id.]. Kim Kashkashian, (i) Robert Levin.

Hindemith was himself a distinguished violist and gave the first performance of the Walton *Concerto*. In all, he composed seven sonatas for the viola, four for solo instrument and three for viola and piano. The solo *Sonatas* are all accommodated on the first CD; they are played with superb panache and flair – and, even more importantly, with remarkable variety of colour – by Kim Kashkashian, who has an enormous dynamic range. The performances of the sonatas with piano are hardly less imaginative. Robert Levin is a marvellously sensitive accompanist who is inspired to similarly imaginative heights by his partner; though the piano sound is not absolutely ideal (nor, for that matter, is the instrument itself – there are one or two twangy notes and a slightly tubby bottom end – but too much should not be made of this), the recording is generally good.

Berceuse; In einer Nacht, Op. 15; Kleines Klavierstück; Lied; 1922 Suite, Op. 26; Tanzstücke, Op. 19.
**(*) Marco Polo Dig. 8.223335 [id.]. Hans Petermandl.

Exercise in three pieces, Op. 31/I; Klaviermusik, Op. 37; Series of little pieces, Op. 37/II; Sonata, Op. 17; Two little piano pieces.
** Marco Polo Dig. 8.223336 [id.]. Hans Petermandl.

Ludus Tonalis; Kleine Klaviermusik, Op. 45/4.
** Marco Polo Dig. 8.223338 [id.]. Hans Petermandl.

Piano sonatas Nos. 1–3; Variations.
** Marco Polo Dig. 8.223337 [id.]. Hans Petermandl.

Hans Petermandl is an expert guide in this repertoire and presents it with real sympathy for, and understanding of, the idiom; his performances of some of these smaller pieces, like the beautiful *Lied* (1921), are very persuasive. The three *Sonatas for piano* come from 1936, shortly after Hindemith had established himself firmly with the wider musical public with *Mathis der Maler*. The *First* is an unusual five-movement structure with a powerful march as the second movement replacing a set of variations, which is included as an appendix. Hindemith never published them, though it seems that he thought well of them. The short sonatina-like *Second Sonata* has a charm that this admirable pianist does not wholly communicate. The textures in Hindemith's piano music are often unbeautiful and less than transparent and, although neither the piano nor the acoustic of the Concert Hall of Slovak Radio is outstanding, the sound is perfectly acceptable.

When lilacs last in the dooryard bloom'd (Requiem).
*** Telarc Dig. CD 80132 [id.]. DeGaetani, Stone, Atlanta Ch. & SO, Robert Shaw.
(M) **(*) Sony/CBS MPK 45881. Louise Parker, George London, NY Schola Cantorum, NYPO, composer.

Robert Shaw's record carries special authority, since it was he who commissioned Hindemith to compose this 'Requiem for those we loved' at the end of the 1939–45 war. It is one of the composer's most deeply felt works and one of his best. Hindemith took Whitman's poem in memory of Lincoln and fashioned from it a requiem that is both non-liturgical and highly varied – not just recitatives and arias, but marches, passacaglias and fugue. Robert Shaw gives a performance of great intensity and variety of colour and nuance. Both his soloists are excellent, and there is both weight and subtlety in the orchestral contribution. Splendid recording.

On Sony, Hindemith himself is at the helm, so the performance carries a special authority. The music has surpassing beauty and eloquence. Louise Parker and George London are committed soloists and, though they are too forward in relation to the orchestra, the recording has a full and realistic acoustic and is perfectly acceptable in its CD format, given the interest of the composer's own interpretation.

(i) *Cardillac* (opera) complete; (ii) *Mathis der Maler*: excerpts.
(M) *** DG 431 741-2 (2) [id.]. Fischer-Dieskau, Grobe, (i) Kirschstein, Kohn, Cologne R. Ch. & SO, Keilberth; (ii) Lorengar, Berlin RSO, Ludwig.

Taken from a radio performance, this reissue of *Cardillac* shows Hindemith at his most vigorous. In the story of a Parisian goldsmith who resorts to murder in order to save his own creations, he uses academic forms such as fugue and passacaglia with Bachian overtones in the idiom but to striking dramatic effect. Fischer-Dieskau as the goldsmith has a part which tests even his artistry, and though the other soloists are variable in quality the conducting of Keilberth holds the music together strongly. This is the original, 1926 version of the score, fresher and more effective than Hindemith's later revision. As a generous and ideal coupling, the second disc contains an hour of excerpts from Hindemith's even more celebrated opera, *Mathis der Maler*, again with Fischer-Dieskau taking the lead, and with Donald Grobe in a supporting role. The selection concentrates on Mathis's solos and on his duets with his beloved, Regina, a role beautifully sung by Pilar Lorengar. The 1960s recordings of both operas are excellently transferred, with voices full and fresh. No texts are given, but instead there are detailed summaries of the plots, with copious quotations.

Holst, Gustav (1874–1934)

(i) *Beni Mora (oriental suite), Op. 29/1; A Fugal overture, Op. 40/1; Hammersmith – A Prelude and scherzo for orchestra, Op. 52;* (ii) *Japanese suite;* (i) *Scherzo (1933/4); A Somerset rhapsody, Op. 21.*
*** Lyrita SRCD 222 [id.]. (i) LPO; (ii) LSO; Boult.

This Lyrita collection is consistently successful and generous, with outstanding performances throughout. *Beni Mora* (written after a holiday in Algeria), is an attractive, exotic piece that shows Holst's flair for orchestration vividly. Boult clearly revels in its sinuosity. *The Japanese suite* (composed in 1915, right in the middle of work on *The Planets*!) was commissioned by a

Japanese dancer, Michio Ito, who whistled the tunes on which it might be based to the composer! But the result, if faintly pentatonic, is not very Japanese, although it has much charm, particularly the piquant *Marionette dance* and the innocuous *Dance under the cherry tree*. The most ambitious work here is *Hammersmith*, far more than a conventional tone picture, intensely poetic. Although conceived for military band, it was orchestrated a year later (1931). The *Scherzo*, from a projected symphony that was never completed, is strong, confident music. The *Somerset rhapsody* similarly exploits Holst's mastery over the orchestra and is unpretentious but very enjoyable, and the brief, spiky *Fugal overture* is given plenty of lift and bite to open the concert invigoratingly. As with other records in this Lyrita series the first class analogue recording has been splendidly transferred to CD.

Brook Green suite for string orchestra; (i) *A Fugal concerto, Op. 40/2;* (ii) *Lyric movement for viola and small orchestra; St Paul's suite for string orchestra, Op. 29/2. Arrangements of Morris dance tunes: Bean setting; Constant Billy; Country gardens; How d'ye do; Laudanum bunches; Rigs o'Marlow; Shepherd's hey.*
*** Koch Dig. 3-7058-2 [id.]. New Zealand CO, Nicholas Braithwaite; with (i) Alexa Still, Stephen Popperwell; (ii) Vyvyan Yendoll.

Another first-class Holst anthology offering two attractive works not otherwise available. *The Fugal concerto* – written on the ocean liner, Aquitania when the composer was on his way to an American music festival in 1923 – features concertante solos for flute and oboe and is a beautifully crafted triptych of miniatures; the rather more ambitious *Lyric movement* is hardly less appealing and is warmly played here by Vyvyan Yendoll, who has a fine, rich timbre. The New Zealand Chamber Orchestra is a new and excellent group formed in 1987. They respond sensitively and persuasively to Nicholas Braithwaite who is thoroughly at home in this repertoire. The textures of the *Brook Green suite* are pleasingly light and airy and in the *St Paul's suite* the gutsy opening *Jig* makes a complete contrast with the pianissimo delicacy of the *Ostinati*. The set of country dances is agreeably spontaneous. The recording has plenty of body and is remarkably real and tangible, indeed in the demonstration bracket, even if the soloists are rather closely balanced, and that applies also to the wind players in the work for viola. Most stimulating.

Hammersmith: Prelude and scherzo, Op. 52.
(M) *** Mercury 432 009-2 [id.]. Eastman Wind Ens., Fennell – BENNETT: *Symphonic songs* ***; JACOB: *William Byrd suite* ***; WALTON: *Crown Imperial.* *** ❀

Holst's highly original and characteristically individual piece is scored for 25 individual wind instruments (there is no doubling of parts in this recording). Holst insisted that *Hammersmith* is not programme music, yet he admitted that the ever-flowing Thames nearby was part of his inspiration. The work has an indelible principal theme, its effects are colourful and imaginative, and its range of mood wide. Fennell's pioneering stereo recording is superbly played by these expert students from the Eastman School, and the effect is totally spontaneous. The recording remains demonstration-worthy, though it dates from 1958!

Invocation for cello and orchestra, Op. 19/2.
*** BMG/RCA RD 70800. Lloyd Webber, Philh. O, Handley – DELIUS: *Concerto;* VAUGHAN WILLIAMS: *Folksongs fantasia.* ***

Holst's *Invocation for cello and orchestra* is a highly attractive and lyrical piece, well worth reviving and a valuable addition to the growing Holst discography. Both the performance and recording are of admirable quality. The CD brings increased vividness, yet is strikingly refined. Recommended.

Military band suites Nos. 1–2.
❀ *** Telarc Dig. CD 80038 [id.]. Cleveland Symphonic Winds, Fennell – HANDEL: *Royal Fireworks music.* ***

Holst's two *Military band suites* contain some magnificent music. Frederick Fennell's new versions have more gravitas though no less *joie de vivre* than his old Mercury set. They are magnificent, and the recording is truly superb – digital technique used in a quite overwhelmingly exciting way. Perhaps there is too much bass drum, but no one is going to grumble when the result is so telling. The *Chaconne* of the *First Suite* makes a quite marvellous effect here. The playing of the Cleveland wind group is of the highest quality, smoothly blended and full in slow movements, vigorous and alert and with strongly rhythmic articulation in fast ones.

Military band suites Nos. 1–2. Hammersmith: Prelude and scherzo, Op. 52.
(BB) *** ASV CDQS 6021; *ZCQS 6021*. L. Wind O, Denis Wick – VAUGHAN WILLIAMS: *English folksong suite* etc. ***

The London performances have great spontaneity, even if they are essentially lightweight, especially when compared with the earlier, Fennell versions. In *Hammersmith*, however, the approach is freshly direct rather than seeking to evoke atmosphere. The sound is first class and the Vaughan Williams couplings are no less successful; this reissue is very competitively priced.

The Perfect fool: ballet suite.
*** Collins Dig. 1124-2 [id.]. Philh. O, Barry Wordsworth – VAUGHAN WILLIAMS: *Job*. ***

Wordsworth conducts a colourful, warmly idiomatic performance of these popular ballet movements from Holst's opera, *The Perfect fool,* making an attractive fill-up for Vaughan Williams's *Job*, just as vividly recorded.

The Planets (suite), *Op. 32.*
*** Decca Dig. 417 553-2; *417 553-4* [id.]. Montreal Ch. & SO, Dutoit.
*** Collins Dig. 1036-2 [id.]. LPO & Ch., Hilary Davan Wetton.
(M) *** EMI CDM7 64441-2. Amb. S., LSO, Previn – DUKAS: *Sorcerer's apprentice;* GERSHWIN: *Rhapsody in blue*. ***
(M) *** EMI CDM7 69045-2 [id.]; *EG 769045-4*. LPO, Boult (with G. Mitchell Ch.).
(M) *** Decca 417 709-2 [id.]. V. State Op. Ch., VPO, Karajan.
(B) **(*) DG Compact Classics 413 852-2 (2); *413 852-4* [id.]. Boston Ch. & SO, Steinberg – ELGAR: *Enigma variations; Pomp and circumstance* *** (CD only: *Cello concerto* ***).
**(*) DG Dig. 400 028-2 [id.]. Berlin Ch. & BPO, Karajan.
(M) ** EMI Dig. CDD7 64300-2; *ET 764300-4*. Toronto SO, Andrew Davis – BRITTEN: *Young person's guide*. **
** Collins Dig. 1348-2 [id.]. The Sixteen women's voices, Philh. O, Svetlanov (with RIMSKY-KORSAKOV: *Mlada suite*. **)

(i) *The Planets;* (ii) *Egdon Heath, Op. 47; The Perfect Fool* (suite); *Op. 39.*
(M) **(*) Decca 425 152-2; *425 152-4*. LPO, (i) Solti; (ii) Boult (with LPO Choir).

The Planets; A Fugal overture, Op. 40/1; St Paul's suite, Op. 29.
*** Collins Dig. CDDCA 782; *ZCDCA 782*. (i) St Paul's Cathedral Ch.; L. Festival O, Ross Pople.

(i) *The Planets;* (ii) *The Perfect Fool* (suite).
(B) *** Decca 433 620-2; *433 620-4* [id.]. (i) LAPO, Mehta; (ii) LPO, Boult.
(BB) **(*) Virgin/Virgo Dig. VJ7 91457-2; *VJ7 91457-4* [id.]. RLPO, Mackerras.

Charles Dutoit's natural feeling for mood, rhythm and colour, so effectively used in his records of Ravel, here results in an outstandingly successful version, both rich and brilliant, and recorded with an opulence to outshine all rivals. It is remarkable that, whether in the relentless build-up of *Mars*, the lyricism of *Venus*, the rich exuberance of *Jupiter* or in much else, Dutoit and his Canadian players sound so idiomatic. The final account of *Saturn* is chillingly atmospheric. This marvellously recorded disc is a clear first choice on CD.

Hilary Davan Wetton's set of *Planets* is among the most successful of recent records. It has a superb digital recording, made in All Saints', Tooting, which creates a gripping sense of spectacle in *Mars*, given with a biting attack and forceful rhythms. Pacing is measured, but the wild bursts from the tam-tam add to the ferocity which is hammered home in the powerful final chords. After a delicately translucent *Venus*, combining serenity with restrained ardour, the delicacy of *Mercury* lacks the sharpest definition. But the resonance adds to the impact of *Jupiter* with its ebullient horns, although here the big tune could be more expansive. With potent, measured melancholy, *Saturn* moves to a forceful climax, dominated by the timpani; then *Uranus*, with its ringing brass chords and rollicking horns, makes a dramatic contrast, while *Neptune*'s ethereal chorus returns us to a silent infinity.

Previn's remastered EMI analogue version of 1974 remains very desirable. Though it does not have quite the range of a digital recording, the focus is firm and the realistic perspective gives an admirable illusion of depth. Previn's interpretation is an outstandingly attractive one, with many of Holst's subtleties of orchestral detail telling with greater point than on many other versions. The performance is basically traditional, yet has an appealing freshness. Now reissued in EMI's 'Armchair concerts' series with attractive Gershwin and Dukas couplings, it is very competitive indeed.

Ross Pople's performance with the London Festival Orchestra also stands high. *Mars*, with a spectacular clash on the tam tam near the beginning has plenty of power and malignant bite, and if *Venus* is rather cool *Mercury* flies swiftly and gracefully and is lightly textured, with the closing section particularly nimble. *Jupiter* opens and closes with buoyant rhythmic verve, the big tune built to a rich climax, with trumpets gleaming over the full-bodied strings. *Saturn* has a pervading melancholy without being turned into a dirge and *Uranus*, admirably paced and with superb brass sounds, is comparable with Mehta's fine account in its vigour. *Neptune* has an ethereal sense of space, with pure yet luminous singing from the St Paul's choristers melting into infinity at the close. The sound is splendidly atmospheric, yet has good definition too. However, the break between the end of *Neptune* and the ebulliant *Fugal overture* is too brief (20 seconds). This too is well played and strongly characterized as is the *St Paul's suite*, although here there is an absence of charm, partly caused by the rather drier recorded sound, with the microphones closer. But the neoclassical vitality of these works is well caught and our slight reservations need not inhibit a three star grading for *The Planets*.

It was Sir Adrian Boult who, over sixty years ago, first 'made *The Planets* shine', as the composer put it, and if the opening of *Mars* – noticeably slower than in Boult's previous recordings – suggests a slackening, the opposite proves true: that movement gains greater weight at a slower tempo. *Mercury* has lift and clarity, not just rushing brilliance, and it is striking that in Holst's syncopations – as in the introduction to *Jupiter* – Boult allows himself a jaunty, even jazzy freedom which adds an infectious sparkle. The great melody of *Jupiter* is more flowing than previously but is more involving too, and *Uranus* as well as *Jupiter* has its measure of jollity, with the lolloping 6/8 rhythms delectably pointed. The recording has gained presence and definition with its digital remastering and yet not lost its body and atmosphere. At mid-price, this could well be a first choice for many.

Still competitive is Karajan's Decca version, which still sounds remarkably vivid with its brilliantly remastered recording, now more precise in detail but retaining its atmospheric analogue sound-picture. There are many individual touches, from the whining Wagnerian tubas of *Mars*, *Venus* representing ardour rather than mysticism, the gossamer textures of *Mercury*, and the strongly characterized *Saturn* and *Venus*, with splendid playing from the Vienna brass, now given more bite. The upper range of the strings, however, has a touch of fierceness at higher dynamic levels.

Mehta's set of *Planets* set a new standard for sonic splendour when it was first issued in 1971. The new ADD transfer still provides outstanding sound, but there is a touch more edge on the strings and the quality has lost just a little of its richness and amplitude; though definition is sharper, the background hiss is fractionally more noticeable. Even so, this is a superb disc and a clear first bargain choice. As on the Solti *Planets*, Boult's splendid account of the ballet suite from *The Perfect Fool* has now been added. This was recorded a decade earlier, but the vintage Decca sound remains spectacular, with the LPO brass hardly less resplendent than their colleagues in Los Angeles.

Also recorded in 1971, Steinberg's Boston set of *Planets* was another outstanding version from a vintage analogue period. It remains one of the most exciting and involving versions and now sounds brighter and sharper in outline, though with some loss of opulence. *Mars* in particular is intensely exciting. At his fast tempo, Steinberg may get to his fortissimos a little early, but rarely has the piece sounded so menacing on record. The testing point for most will no doubt be *Jupiter*, and here Steinberg the excellent Elgarian comes to the fore, giving a wonderful nobilmente swagger. In its Compact Classics reissue Steinberg's fine performance is coupled with Jochum's inspirational account of *Enigma* plus a dash of *Pomp and circumstance*. The pair of CDs also include Fournier's ardent reading of Elgar's *Cello concerto* as a substantial bonus.

Karajan's later digital CD (for DG) is undoubtedly spectacularly wide-ranging, while the marvellously sustained pianissimo playing of the Berlin Philharmonic Orchestra – as in *Venus* and the closing pages of *Saturn* – is the more telling against a background of silence. But the 'digital edge' on the treble detracts from the overall beauty of the orchestra in fortissimos. *Jupiter* ideally needs a riper body of tone, although the syncopated opening now erupts with joy and the big melody has a natural flow and nobility. *Venus* has sensuous string phrasing, *Mercury* and *Uranus* have beautiful springing in the triplet rhythms, and the climax of that last movement brings an amazing glissando on the organ.

The Decca recording for Solti's Chicago version is extremely brilliant, with *Mars* given a vivid cutting edge at the fastest possible tempo. Solti's directness in *Jupiter* (with the trumpets coming through splendidly) is certainly riveting, the big tune red-blooded and with plenty of character. In *Saturn* the spareness of texture is finely sustained and the tempo is slow, the detail precise; while in *Neptune* the coolness is even more striking when the pianissimos are achieved with such a high degree of tension. The CD gives the orchestra great presence, and the addition of Boult's classic versions of *Egdon Heath* and *The Perfect Fool* ballet music makes this reissue very competitive.

Mackerras's usual zestful approach communicates readily and the Liverpool orchestra bring a lively response, but the over-reverberant recording tends to cloud the otherwise pungently vigorous *Mars*, and both *Venus* and *Saturn* seem a little straightforward and marginally undercharacterized, while again in the powerful climax of *Uranus* there is some blurring from the resonance. *The Perfect Fool*, with its vivid colouring and irregular rhythms, has much in common with *The Planets* and makes a fine coupling, especially when played with such flair.

Svetlanov's new Collins version is disappointing. *Mars* is very slow and heavy, even if the brass adds a sinister edge in the second part. *Mercury* could be fleeter of foot and the texture more transparent, and *Jupiter* gets bogged down with a lack of rhythmic sparkle in the opening section and the big tune slow, and unexpansive at the climax. Best is *Saturn*, which has an expansive dignity and a deep melancholy – clearly this made a strong impression on Svetlanov's slavic temperament. *Uranus* is treated as an orchestral scherzo and has plenty of life and colour, while in *Neptune* there is radiantly rich singing from the ladies of The Sixteen. The coupled Rimsky-Korsakov *Mlada suite* is successful, but even here the famous *Cortège* could be more animated. Full, atmospheric recording

Andrew Davis recorded *The Planets* with the Toronto orchestra as the first of a series for EMI, taking the players to a new and more helpful venue outside the city. Alas for good intentions, the results do not quite match those achieved in very similar circumstances by the Toronto orchestra's direct rival in Montreal. Though full and firm, the sound is not as open or as atmospheric as that on the finest versions (as, for example, Dutoit's Decca) and Davis's taut control of the music, with fast speeds in *Mars* and *Saturn* diminishing the relentlessness of the argument, makes the result sound just a little inhibited. It is a good, beefy account – but in so strong a field there are many finer versions.

Air and variations; 3 Pieces for oboe & string quartet, Op. 2.
*** Chan. Dig. CHAN 8392; *ABTD 1114* [id.]. Francis, English Qt – BAX: *Quintet;* MOERAN: *Fantasy quartet;* JACOB: *Quartet.* ***

The three pieces here are engagingly folksy, consisting of a sprightly little *March*, a gentle *Minuet* with a good tune, and a *Scherzo*. Performances are first class, and so is the recording.

VOCAL MUSIC

Choral hymns from the Rig Veda (Groups 1–4), *H. 97–100; 2 Eastern pictures for women's voices and harp, H. 112; Hymn to Dionysus, Op. 31/2.*
**(*) Unicorn Dig. DKPCD 9046; *DKPC 9046* [id.]. Royal College of Music Chamber Ch., RPO, Willcocks; Ellis.

The *Choral hymns from the Rig Veda* show Holst writing with deep understanding for voices, devising textures, refined, very distinctively his, to match atmospherically exotic texts. Though performances are not always ideally polished, the warmth and thrust of the music are beautifully caught. The *Hymn to Dionysus*, setting words from the *Bacchae* of Euripides in Gilbert Murray's translation, a rarity anticipating Holst's *Choral symphony*, makes a welcome and substantial fill-up, along with the two little *Eastern pictures*. Beautifully clean and atmospheric recording.

Choral hymns from the Rig Veda (Group 3), *H. 99, Op. 26/3.*
*** Hyp. CDA 66175; *KA 66175* [id.]. Holst Singers & O; Davan Wetton; T. Owen – BLISS: *Lie strewn the white flocks;* BRITTEN: *Gloriana: Choral dances.* ***

The third group of *Choral hymns from the Rig Veda*, like the whole series, reveals Holst in his Sanskritic period at his most distinctively inspired. In this responsive performance, it makes an excellent coupling for the attractive Bliss and Britten items, atmospherically recorded.

The Cloud messenger, Op. 30; The Hymn of Jesus, Op. 37.
*** Chan. Dig. CHAN 8901; *ABTD 1510* [id.]. Della Jones, LSO Ch. & O, Richard Hickox.

Hickox's account of Holst's choral masterpiece, *The Hymn of Jesus*, dramatic and highly atmospheric, easily outshines even Sir Adrian Boult's vintage version for Decca – now on CD in coupling with Britten's reading of Elgar's *Dream of Gerontius* (Decca 421 381-2). Not only does modern digital sound make an enormous difference in a work where the choral sounds are terraced so tellingly, but Hickox secures tauter and crisper ensemble, as well as treating the sections based on plainchant with an aptly expressive freedom. The coupling is ideal. Inspired by Sanskrit literature, the long-neglected choral piece, *The Cloud messenger*, may lack the concentration of *The Hymn of Jesus* but it brings similarly incandescent choral writing. If the measured opening seems rather bland, the atmosphere is transformed when the chorus enters at full force in a thrilling sunburst. Holst's early Wagnerian sympathies bring some echoes of *Parsifal* – apt for a mystic journey with visions of the Himalayas – even if some of the oriental effects are unsubtle. Warmly and positively realized by Hickox and his powerful forces, with Della Jones a fine soloist, it makes a major discovery, whatever its incidental shortcomings. Hickox proves abundantly that it has never deserved the dismissal which followed its unfortunate first performance in 1913. Rich and ample Chandos recording adds to the involvement.

Dirge and Hymeneal, H. 124; 2 Motets, H. 159/60; 5 Part-songs, H. 61.
*** Conifer Dig. CDCF 142; *MCFC 142* [id.]. CBSO Ch., Halsey, R. Markham (piano) – ELGAR: *Scenes from the Bavarian Highlands.* ***

It is fascinating to find among these Holst part-songs the original musical idea that he used later in the *Saturn* movement of *The Planets* suite, with the piano accompaniment pivoting back and forth. That is from the *Dirge and Hymeneal.* The other items – all unaccompanied – bring writing just as hauntingly beautiful and original, not least the most demanding and ambitious of them, the motet *The evening watch*, in eight parts, slow and hushed throughout. Beautiful, refined performances, atmospherically recorded.

The Evening watch, H.159; 6 Choruses, H.186; Nunc dimittis, H.127; 7 Partsongs, H.162; 2 Psalms, H.117.
*** Hyp. Dig. CDA 66329; *KA 66329* [id.]. Holst Singers & O, Hilary Davan Wetton.

Having given us a splendid set of *Planets*, Hilary Davan Wetton now turns to the often more austere but no less inspired choral music. The second of the two Psalm settings, using a very famous tune, has a frisson-creating climax, as affecting as any in the more famous orchestral work. *The Evening watch* creates a rapt, sustained pianissimo until the very closing bars, when the sudden expansion is quite thrilling. The *Six Choruses* for male voices show the composer at his most imaginative, with a characteristically original use of vocal colour, while the comparable *Partsongs* for women, set to words by Robert Bridges, often produce a ravishingly dreamy, mystical beauty. The final song, *Assemble all ye maidens*, is a narrative ballad about a lost love, and its closing section is infinitely touching. The performances are gloriously and sensitively sung and unerringly paced, while St Paul's Girls' School, Hammersmith, is not only an appropriate recording venue but produces a lovely bloom on voices and accompanying strings alike.

Hymn of Jesus, Op. 37.
(M) *** Decca 421 381-2 (2) [id.]. BBC Ch., BBC SO, Boult – ELGAR: *Dream of Gerontius.* **(*)

Boult's superb performance of *The Hymn of Jesus*, a visionary masterpiece that brings some of Holst's most searching inspirations, comes as a generous and apt – if unusual – coupling for Elgar's great oratorio. The spatial beauty of Holst's choral writing is vividly caught with fine presence in the early-1960s recording.

OPERA

(i) *Savitri* (complete); (ii) *Dream city* (song cycle, orch. Matthews).
**(*) Hyp. Dig. CDA 66099 [id.]. (i) Langridge, Varcoe, Palmer, Hickox Singers; (ii) Kwella; City of L. Sinfonia, Hickox.

The simple story is taken from a Sanskrit source – Savitri, a woodcutter's wife, cleverly outwits Death, who has come to take her husband – and Holst with beautiful feeling for atmosphere sets it in the most restrained way. Felicity Palmer is more earthy, more vulnerable as Savitri than Janet Baker was in the earlier Argo recording, her grainy mezzo well caught. Philip Langridge and Stephen Varcoe both sing sensitively with fresh, clear tone, though their timbres are rather similar. Hickox is a thoughtful conductor both in the opera and in the orchestral song-cycle arranged by Colin Matthews (with Imogen Holst's approval) from Holst's settings of Humbert Wolfe poems. Patrizia Kwella's soprano at times catches the microphone rather shrilly.

Holst, Imogen (1907–84)

String quartet No. 1.

*** Conifer Dig. CDCF 196; *MCFC 196*. Brindisi Qt – BRIDGE: *3 Idylls;* BRITTEN: *String quartet No. 2*. ***

Imogen Holst is best known as the author of a study of her father and a book on Byrd, and for her work for Benjamin Britten. She directed the Purcell Singers and collaborated with Britten on his edition of *Dido and Aeneas*. Her two-movement *Quartet* is a shortish work, written in Cornwall in 1946; although not strongly personal, it is full of interest. There is a scurrying scherzo which leaves an impression of Britten's own *Second Quartet*, and there are faint traces of Bartók, Hindemith and Shostakovich – and, in the first movement, a whiff of her own father's late music, such as *Hammersmith* or *Egdon Heath*. Both performance and recording are of high quality.

Honegger, Arthur (1892–1955)

(i) *Concertino for piano and orchestra; Pastorale d'été; Prélude, arioso et fughette sur le nom de Bach* (for strings); *Symphony No. 4 (Deliciae Basilienses).*

* Chan. Dig. CHAN 8993; *ABTD 1575* [id.]. (i) Tamás Vásáry; Bournemouth Sinf., Vásáry.

There are some felicitous moments and some sensitive playing in the *Fourth Symphony*, but generally speaking Tamás Vásáry delivers rather laboured accounts of all the pieces here, with the sole exception of the *Pastorale d'été*. Nowhere is he more laboured than in the delightful *Concertino for piano and orchestra*, which here takes almost twelve minutes as opposed to the eight taken by Eunice Norton in her immensely characterful first recording. The recording is very good indeed but this is very disappointing.

Cello concerto.

**(*) Ph. Dig. 432 084-2; *432 084-4* [id.]. Julian Lloyd Webber, ECO, Yan Pascal Tortelier – FAURÉ: *Élégie* **; D'INDY: *Lied* **(*); SAINT-SAËNS: *Concerto* etc. **(*)

Honegger's pastoral *Concerto* is dedicated to Maurice Maréchal, who recorded it with the composer in the days of 78s; it is a work of immense charm. Although, as recorded, he does not produce a big (or well-focused) tone, Lloyd Webber plays with refined musicianship and conveys the charm and character of this piece very effectively. He is well supported by Yan Pascal Tortelier, and the Philips recording is eminently natural and well balanced.

Symphonies Nos. 1–3.

(M) ** EMI CDM7 64274-2 [id.]. O de Capitole de Toulouse, Michel Plasson.

Symphonies Nos. 4–5; Pacific 231.

(M) *** EMI CDM7 64275-2 [id.]. O de Capitole de Toulouse, Michel Plasson.

Honegger's symphonies are currently much underrated and their scant representation in the concert hall scarcely reflects their artistic standing. The *First* was commissioned by Koussevitzky for the fiftieth anniversary of the Boston Symphony; the *Second* is a probing, intense wartime composition that reflects something of the anguish Honegger felt during the German occupation. The *Third* (*Liturgique*) dates from the end of the war, while the *Fourth*, composed for Paul Sacher, makes use of Swiss folk material. It is perhaps the most underrated of them all, for its delights grow fresher with every hearing and its melodic charm is irresistible. Beneath its smiling surface there is a gentle vein of nostalgia and melancholy, particularly in the slow movement. The finale is sparkling and full of high spirits, though even this ends on a bitter-sweet note. The *Fifth* is a powerful work, inventive, concentrated and vital. Michel Plasson has the advantage of fine recording from the late 1970s and the spacious acoustics of the Toulouse Halle-aux-Grains seem right for the music. The CD transfers are natural in balance and enhance the sound, which has plenty of ambience. However, the performances do not have the panache and virtuosity that make Karajan's coupling of Nos. 2 and 3 so memorable, and at times in the most searing music one feels a lack of grip and emotional intensity. Nevertheless there are some fine moments here and Plasson finds much of the charm of No. 4, even if the Scherzo of the *Fifth Symphony* sounds rather tame. One other point: in the *Symphony for strings* (the *Second*) the trumpet for which Honegger called to strengthen the chorale, but which he did not regard as mandatory, is omitted.

Symphony No. 1; Pastorale d'été; 3 Symphonic movements: Pacific 231; Rugby; No. 3.
*** Erato/Warner Dig. 2292 45242-2 [id.]. Bav. RSO, Dutoit.

Honegger's *First Symphony* is a highly stimulating and rewarding piece. Charles Dutoit gets an excellent response from the Bavarian Radio Symphony Orchestra, who produce a splendidly cultured sound and particularly beautiful phrasing in the slow movement. Dutoit also gives an atmospheric and sympathetic account of the *Pastorale d'été* and in addition offers the *Three Symphonic movements*, of which *Pacific 231* with its robust and vigorous portrait of a railway engine is by far the best known.

Symphonies Nos. 2 & 3 (Symphonie liturgique).
❀ (M) *** DG 423 242-2 [id.]. BPO, Karajan.

This reissue includes arguably the finest versions of any Honegger works ever put on record. In No. 2 the Berlin strings have extraordinary sensitivity and expressive power, and Karajan conveys the sombre wartime atmosphere to perfection. At the same time, there is astonishing refinement of texture in the *Liturgique*, whose slow movement has never sounded more magical. The recording was always one of DG's best, and this transfer brings to life more detail and greater body and range. A great record, completely in a class of its own.

Symphonies Nos. 2; 4 (Deliciae Basiliensis).
**(*) Erato/Warner Dig. 2292 45247-2 [id.]. Bav. RSO, Dutoit.

Symphonies Nos. 2 for strings with trumpet obbligato; 4 (Deliciae Basilienses); Pastorale d'été; Prélude, arioso et fughette sur le nom de Bach (for strings).
*** Virgin Dig. VC7 91486-2 [id.]. Lausanne CO, Jesús López-Cobos.

The *Fourth Symphony* (*Deliciae Basiliensis*) was designed for chamber forces and, unlike Dutoit's coupling of Nos. 2 and 4 on Erato which uses full strings, Jesús López-Cobos and the Lausanne orchestra correspond in scale to the forces used in the first performance by Paul Sacher and his Basle Chamber Orchestra who commissioned it. Both symphonies are given with great sensitivity and atmosphere; and so, too, are the *Pastorale d'été*, a most poetic account, and the *Prélude, arioso et fughette sur le nom de Bach*, a 1936 transcription of a piano piece written four years earlier. Excellent performances which, while they do not displace Karajan in the *Second Symphony* or Munch in the *Fourth*, can be recommended alongside them – no mean compliment! They are superbly recorded.

Dutoit has the advantage of excellent recording. The perspective is completely natural and there is plenty of air around the various instruments, while detail is clean and well focused. He draws very cultured string playing from the Bavarian Radio orchestra in the dark, introspective *Symphony for strings* and his performance is thoroughly meticulous in its observance of detail, but it is just a shade deficient in vitality and drive. The *Deliciae Basiliensis* also has rather measured tempi. In expressive intensity it does not match Karajan's account on DG, coupled with No. 3. However, Dutoit's beautifully recorded performance of No. 4 serves to rekindle enthusiasm for a much-underrated work whose sunny countenance and keen nostalgia unfailingly bring delight.

Symphonies Nos. 2 for strings; 5 (Di tre re).
(M) (***) BMG/RCA mono/stereo GD 60685 [60685-2-RG]. Boston SO, Charles Munch – MILHAUD: *La création du monde* etc. ***

Charles Munch made the first recordings of both *Symphonies*; in fact this transfer of the *Fifth* is one of them. The *Second*, made in 1953, is a bit harder-driven than his later version with the Orchestre de Paris. The performance of the *Fifth* is full of character though the sound is a bit dry. The witty and enigmatic middle movement has never been surpassed on record. Some (but relatively little) allowance needs to be made for the actual sound-quality of the 1952 mono recording.

Symphonies Nos. 3 (Symphonie liturgique); 5 (Di tre re); Chant du joie; Pacific 231; Pastoral d'été.
(M) *** Sup. 11 0667-2. Czech PO, Serge Baudo.

Serge Baudo's 1960s recordings of the *Symphonie liturgique* and the *Fifth* (*Di tre re*) now reappear on the Supraphon Crystal collection. The *Fifth* represents a vast improvement in body and presence over the LP, and it still remains among the very best versions of the work, superior in sonic terms to the Münch and infinitely more vital than the Dutoit. The *Liturgique* is not quite in the Karajan class but it is very good indeed as are the remaining pieces on offer. Given the modest price of this disc plus the generous playing time, this deserves a very strong recommendation.

Symphony No. 4 (Deliciae Basilienses).
(M) *** Erato/Warner 2292 45689-2 [id.]. French Nat. RSO, Munch – DUTILLEUX: *Métaboles.* ***

Munch's 1967 account of the delightful *Fourth Symphony* remains by far the most characterful on disc – it is to be preferred to any of the full-price rivals and has the right blend of energy and atmosphere. The recording is also eminently acceptable, with a decently balanced sound typical of a good broadcast. An additional attraction is the interesting coupling. What this lacks in playing time (it is only 43 minutes) it more than makes up for in quality and musical interest. Strongly recommended.

Jeanne d'Arc au bûcher.
❀ *** DG Dig. 429 412-2 [id.]. Keller, Wilson, Escourrou, Lanzi, Pollet, Command, Stutzman, Aler, Courtis, R. France Ch., Fr. Nat. O, Seiji Ozawa.

This DG account of *Jeanne d'Arc au bûcher* is much more successful than Ozawa's 1970s recording in English for CBS. There is a strong cast of both singers and actors and this newcomer, which has the merit of being given in the original French, is currently the only version available. Honegger's 1935 setting of the Claudel poem is one of his most powerful and imaginative works, full of variety of invention, colour and textures. While many of its episodes make a strong effect, the work is more than the sum of its parts. It is admirably served by these forces, and in particular by the Joan of Marthe Keller. The singers, too, are all excellent and the Choir and the six soloists of the Maîtrise of Radio France are as top-drawer as the orchestra. The DG engineers cope excellently with the large forces and the acoustic of the Basilique de Saint-Denis. There is an excellent perspective, with plenty of detail and presence, as well as a wide dynamic range. In short, a powerful and important work, performed with dedicated artistry and recorded with splendid realism.

Le Roi David (complete).
(M) *** Erato/Warner 2292 45800-2 [id.]. Eda Pierre, Collard, Tappy, Petel, Valere, De Dailly, Philippe Caillard Ch., Ens. Instrumental, Dutoit.
(M) *** Van. 08.4038.71 [OVC 4038]. Davrath, Sorensen, Preston, Singher, Madeleine Milhaud, Utah University Ch., Utah SO, Abravanel.

Charles Dutoit's *Le Roi David* uses the original instrumental forces and not the full orchestra favoured by most of his rivals. In this he has single wind with flute alternating with piccolo, oboe with cor anglais and so on, horn, trumpets and trombone, no strings apart from cello and double-bass, percussion with celeste, organ and piano. The recording comes from 1970, not that anyone coming to it afresh would guess that. It is a compelling performance of strong dramatic coherence.

Listening to the present digital transfer of the Vanguard version, it is difficult to believe that the recording was made in 1961. It is remarkably vivid, well detailed and present, and the playing of the Utah Symphony under Maurice Abravanel is very fine. The recording also stands up well, though one would welcome greater back-to-front perspective and slightly more air round the soloists. Netania Davrath is excellent too, and so is Madeleine Milhaud, the composer's wife, as the Witch of Endor. Thoroughly recommendable.

Howells, Herbert (1892–1983)

Collegium regale: canticles; Behold, O God our defender; Like as the hart; St Paul's service: Canticles. Take him to earth for cherishing. (Organ): *Psalm prelude: De profundis; Master Tallis's testament.*
*** Hyp. Dig. CDA 66260; *KA 66260* [id.]. St Paul's Cathedral Ch., Scott; Christopher Dearnley.

This well-planned programme of Howells's music is framed by the two fine sets of canticles; in between come the organ solos and motets, *Take him to earth for cherishing* being dedicated to

John F. Kennedy. All the music is of high quality and the recording gives it resonance, in both senses of the word, with the St Paul's acoustic well captured by the engineers. A fine representation of a composer who wrote in the mainstream of English church and cathedral music but who had a distinct voice of his own.

Collegium regale: Te Deum and jubilate; Office of Holy Communion; Magnificat and Nunc dimittis. Preces & Responses I & II; Psalms 121 & 122; Take him, earth for cherishing. Rhapsody for organ, Op. 17/3.
❀ *** Decca Dig. 430 205-2 [id.]. Williams, Moore, King's College, Cambridge, Ch., Cleobury.

No composer of the twentieth century has so richly added to the store of Anglican church music as Herbert Howells. Here is an unmatchable collection of the settings inspired by the greatest of our collegiate choirs, King's College, Cambridge, presented in performances of heartwarming intensity in that great choir's 1989 incarnation. Over the years Howells composed *Collegium regale* settings of the three principal Anglican services, for Mattins, for Holy Communion and – most gloriously of all – for Evensong. All of them triumphantly possess what Hugh Ottaway described as Howells' 'spiritualized sensuality' and, more than any previous performances on record, these capture that most movingly. The soaring lines of the *Gloria* at the end of both the Evensong canticles, *Magnificat* and *Nunc dimittis*, have a power and radiance that exactly match the chapel's unique architecture. The boy trebles in particular are among the brightest and fullest ever to have been recorded with this choir. The disc sensitively presents the sequence in what amounts to liturgical order, with the service settings aptly interspersed with responses, psalm-chants, anthems with organ introits and voluntaries all by Howells. Even those not normally attracted by Anglican church music should hear this.

Hymnus Paradisi, An English Mass.
*** Hyp. Dig. CDA 66488 [id.]. Kennard, Ainsley, RLPO Ch., RLPO, Handley.

Here is a recording of Herbert Howells' most ambitious work that at last captures to the full its deep dedication. In a prelude and five substantial choral movements, *Hymnus Paradisi* is a heartfelt expression of grief over the death of the composer's son at the age of nine, and Handley conveys a mystery, a tenderness rather missing from the previous recording, made by Sir David Willcocks for EMI, strong as that is. Handley's soloists may not have the tonal opulence of their predecessors, Heather Harper and Robert Tear, but they bring a moving compassion, as in the haunting setting of the 23rd Psalm which makes up the third movement. The Hyperion digital recording is warmer, fuller and more atmospheric than the EMI analogue, though the choir is more backwardly placed. *Hymnus Paradisi* is generously and aptly coupled with another major Howells work, *An English mass*, simpler yet also hauntingly beautiful.

(Organ) *Psalm prelude, Set 1/1; Paen; Prelude: Sine nomine.* (Vocal): *Behold, O God our defender; Here is the door; Missa Aedi Christi: Kyrie; Credo; Sanctus; Benedictus; Agnus Dei; Gloria. Sing lullaby; A spotless rose; Where wast thou?.*
*** CRD Dig. CRD 3455 [id.]. New College, Oxford, Ch., Edward Higginbottom (organ).

A further collection of the music of Herbert Howells, splendidly sung by Edward Higginbottom's fine choir, while he provides the organ interludes in addition. The opening *Behold, O God our defender* expands gloriously, and the excerpts from the *Missa Aedis Christi* (heard in two groups) are almost equally impressive. Among the shorter pieces, the carol-anthem, *Sing lullaby*, is especially delightful, and the programme ends with the motet, *Where wast thou?*, essentially affirmative, in spite of the question posed at the opening. Beautifully spacious sound makes this a highly rewarding collection.

Requiem. Motets: *The House of the Mind; A Sequence for St Michael.*
*** Chan. Dig. CHAN 9019 [id.]. Finzi Singers, Spicer – VAUGHAN WILLIAMS: *Lord thou hast been our refuge* etc. ***

Howells' *Requiem* is the work which prepared the way for *Hymnus Paradisi*, providing some of the material for it. For unaccompanied chorus, it presents a gentler, compact view of what in the big cantata becomes powerfully expansive. The Finzi singers, 18-strong, give a fresh and atmospheric, beautifully moulded performance, well coupled with two substantial motets with organ by Howells as well as choral pieces by Vaughan Williams.

Hummel, Johann (1778–1837)

Bassoon concerto in F.
*** Denon Dig. CO 79281 [id.]. Werba, V. String Soloists, Honeck – MOZART; WEBER: *Concertos.* ***

A good modern recording of Hummel's engaging *Bassoon concerto* was needed and Michael Weber is a personable and characterful soloist. He is well accompanied and recorded and the couplings are attractive. As usual, Denon index the structural layout of all three concertos included on this CD.

Piano concertos: in A min., Op. 85; B min., Op. 89.
*** Chan. Dig. CHAN 8505; *ABTD 1217* [id.]. Stephen Hough, ECO, Bryden Thomson.

The *A minor* is Hummel's most often-heard piano concerto, never better played, however, than by Stephen Hough on this Chandos disc. The coda is quite stunning; it is not only his dazzling virtuosity that carries all before it but also the delicacy and refinement of colour he produces. The *B minor*, Op. 89, is more of a rarity, and is given with the same blend of virtuosity and poetic feeling which Hough brings to its companion. He is given expert support by Bryden Thomson and the ECO – and the recording is first class.

Trumpet concerto in E.
❀ *** Ph. Dig. 420 203-2; *420 203-4* [id.]. Hardenberger, ASMF, Marriner – HAYDN *** ❀; HERTEL***; STAMITZ: *Concertos.* ***

Trumpet concerto in E flat.
*** Delos Dig. D/CD 3001 [id.]. Schwarz, New York 'Y' CO – HAYDN: *Concerto.* ***
*** Sony CD 37846 [id.]. Marsalis, Nat. PO, Leppard – HAYDN: *Concerto* *** (with L. MOZART: *Concerto* ***).

(i) *Trumpet concerto in E;* (ii) *Introduction, theme and variations for 2 trumpets, Op. 102.*
(M) *** Erato/Warner 2292 45061-2 [id.]. Maurice André; (i) LOP, Mari; (ii) with Raymond André, Paillard CO, Paillard – MOLTER: *Concertos.* **(*)

Hummel's *Trumpet concerto* is usually heard in the familiar brass key of E flat, but the brilliant Swedish trumpeter, Håkan Hardenberger, uses the key of E, which makes it sound brighter and bolder than usual. Neither he nor Marriner miss the genial lilt inherent in the dotted theme of the first movement, yet this seductive element is set off by the brassy masculinity of the actual timbre. The slow-movement cantilena soars beautifully over its jogging pizzicato accompaniment, and the finale captivates the ear with its high spirits and easy bravura; Hardenberger's crisp tonguing and tight trills are of the kind to make you smile with pleasure. This is the finest version of the piece in the catalogue, for Marriner's accompaniment is polished and sympathetic. The recording projects the vibrant trumpet image forward with great presence, and the only slight complaint is that the orchestral recording is a shade too reverberant.

Like Hardenberger, Maurice André plays Hummel's concerto in the bright key of E, and he has the advantage of a splendid accompaniment directed by Jean-Baptiste Mari. They capture the work's *galant* style admirably and the finale is infectious. Good sound too, but the I*ntroduction, theme and variations* (where Maurice is joined by his son, Raymond) is much less interesting music, even though it is presented with flair.

Both Schwarz and Marsalis give fine accounts of Hummel's *Concerto*, but neither player quite catches its full *galant* charm. In matters of bravura, however, neither can be faulted; both artists relish the sparkling finale. If Marsalis is more reserved in the slow movement, he has the advantage of very fine accompaniment from Leppard, and the Sony record includes a substantial extra work.

Introduction, theme and variations in F min./maj., Op. 102.
*** Capriccio Dig. 10 308 [id.]. Lajos Lencsés, Stuttgart RSO, Marriner – HAYDN; MARTINŮ: *Concertos.* ***

Lajos Lencsés – the principal oboe of the Stuttgart orchestra – plays with both poise and an obvious relish for Hummel's engaging invention. His account is relaxed but matches Holliger's in elegance and charm. He is very well recorded and has worthwhile couplings.

Piano quintet in E flat, Op. 87; Piano septet in D min., Op. 74.
(M) *** Decca 430 297-2 [id.]. Melos Ens. – WEBER: *Clarinet quintet.* ***

These two highly engaging works show the composer at his most melodically fecund and his musical craftsmanship at its most apt. It is the ideas themselves (as in all music) that can make or break the structure, and here they are entirely appropriate to music designed in the first instance to entertain. This these works certainly do in such spontaneous and polished performances – just try the opening movement of the *Septet* to sample the composer's felicity. Moreover the 1965 recording sounds absolutely first class in its CD format.

Septet in D min., Op. 74.
*** CRD CRD 3344 [id.]. Nash Ens. – BERWALD: *Septet.* ***

Hummel's *Septet* is an enchanting and inventive work with a virtuoso piano part, expertly dispatched here by Clifford Benson. The *Septet* is full of vitality, and its scherzo in particular has enormous charm and individuality. A fine performance and excellent recording make this a highly desirable issue, particularly in view of the enterprising coupling.

String quartets: in C; in G; in E flat, Op. 30/1–3.
*** Hyp. Dig. CDA 66568 [id.]. Delmé Qt.

Hummel wrote his three *String quartets* – his only contribution to the form – in 1803/4. Three years earlier a fairly complete edition of all Haydn's quartets had been published, and that same year (1801) – a momentous one for the string quartet medium – had seen the arrival of Beethoven's Op.18. Hummel's works are closer to Haydn than Beethoven, though the first of the set in C major with its impressive opening *Adagio e mesto* in the minor key, fine *Adagio*, and brisk, scherzo-like Minuet, with its forward-looking structure, obviously leans towards the influence of the later composer. But Hummel's special flair for diverting the listener is also found in this Opus, notably in the Minuet of Op. 30/2, marked *Allegro con fuoco,* with its serenade Trio, which then reappears charmingly as a coda, to follow the reprise of the Minuet. The dancing triple rhythms of the *Allemande e alternativo* of Op. 30/3 are hardly less engaging, while the audacious quotation of *Comfort ye* from Handel's *Messiah* in the preceding *Andante*, brings yet another example of Hummelian sleight of hand. In short these are fascinating works, highly inventive, and crafted with the composer's usual fluent charm. They are splendidly played by the Delmé group, who match their timbres pleasingly to bring the necessary finesse, yet also provide plenty of vitality and warmth. The Hyperion recording is fresh and believable.

Violin sonatas: in E flat, Op. 5/3; in D, Op. 50; Nocturne, Op. 99.
*** Amon Ra CD-SAR 12 [id.]. Ralph Holmes, Richard Burnett.

Ralph Holmes's violin timbre is bright and the Graf fortepiano under the fingers of Richard Burnett has plenty of colour and does not sound clattery. The *D major Sonata*, which comes first, is a very striking work with hints of early Beethoven; but the *D flat Sonata*, written a decade and a half earlier in 1798, has a memorably eloquent slow movement which shows Ralph Holmes at his finest. Richard Burnett has a chance to catch the ear in the finale of the *D major Sonata* when he uses the quaintly rasping cembalo device (without letting it outstay its welcome). The *Nocturne* is an extended piece (nearly 16 minutes) in variation form, and it is a pity that the CD, while banding the movements of the two sonatas, does not provide more internal cues. A thoroughly worthwhile issue, 'authentic' in the most convincing way, which shows this engaging composer at his most assured and inventive.

Mass in B flat, Op. 77; Tantum ergo (after Gluck).
*** Koch Dig. 3-7117-2 [id.]. Westminster Oratorio Ch., New Brunswick CO, John Floreen.

Hummel wrote his *Mass in B flat* while working for the Esterházys and, although probably composed about five years earlier, it was used to celebrate Prince Nikolaus's name-day in 1810. It is an unpretentious work of great charm and a real discovery. The *Kyrie* is modest but winning, the *Gloria* (with trumpets) refreshingly unpompous. Then, after a rather jolly *Credo*, comes the brief but felt *Sanctus* and, at the words *Hosanna in excelsis*, Hummel breaks into an engaging 6/8 rhythm and this lilting melody dominates the *Benedictus*, while the *Agnus Dei* has a melodic contour that is rather similar to Mozart's *Ave verum* and is quite haunting. After a burst of high spirits, the work closes comparatively gently, with the composer's inventiveness holding out to the very end. The *Tantum ergo* (1806) is a fairly straight arrangement of the *Pantomime* from from Act I of Gluck's *Alceste.* It makes a delightful chorale and has hit potential. The Westminster Choir (from the College of that name in Princeton, New Jersey) give exactly the right kind of modest performance, emphasizing the work's warm lyricism; the conductor, while not lacking vigour, is careful not to be too forceful at climaxes. The orchestral accompaniment is nicely in scale, and the recording, though not crystal clear, has the most agreeable ambience.

Humperdinck, Engelbert (1854–1921)

The Bluebird: Prelude; Star dance. Hänsel und Gretel: Overture. Königskinder: Preludes to Acts II & III. The Sleeping Beauty: suite.
** Virgin Dig. VC7 91494-2 [id.]. Bamberg SO, Karl Rickenbacher.

The Canteen Woman (Die Marketenderin): Prelude. The Merchant of Venice: Love scene. Moorish rhapsody: Tarifa (Elegy of summer); Tangier (A night in a moorish coffe-house); Tetuan (A night in the desert). The Sleeping Beauty: suite.
**(*) Marco Polo Dig. 8.223369 [id.]. Slovak RSO (Bratislava), Martin Fischer-Dieskau.

By far the most memorable piece of music on these two discs is the *Hansel and Gretel overture*, although the Introduction to Act III of *Königskinder* is also very touching, characteristically using horns evocatively to intone the Minstrel's last song. The *Overture* to this same opera is significant in demonstrating Humperdinck's characteristic failing – a prolixity of ideas, none of them quite memorable enough to emerge from the ongoing energy of the writing. His post-Wagnerian orchestration can be too thick and this inhibits his festive pieces, but the lightly scored items have charm, the *Star dance* for instance from *The Blue Bird*, or the *Ballade* from *The Sleeping Beauty*. The *Love scene* from *The Merchant of Venice* ('On such a night') is beautiful, but rather over-extended, and all three sections of the *Moorish rhapsody* are much too long (the composite piece lasts some 32 minutes). The opening of the *Summer elegy* begins with raptly ethereal writing for the violins, but the jolly Moorish coffee-house sequence sounds as if the restaurant is on lease from the owner of a Bavarian Bier-Keller. Rickenbacher secures warm, cultured playing from his Bambergers; the Slovak performances under Martin Fischer-Dieskau (the famous Lieder singer's grandson) are rather less polished but have greater freshness and vitality, while the Marco Polo recording is more open, if less opulent than the Virgin sound.

Hänsel und Gretel (complete).
*** EMI Dig. CDS7 54022-2 (2) [Ang. CDCB 54022]; *EX 754022-2*. Von Otter, Bonney, Lipovšek, Schwarz, Schmidt, Hendricks, Lind, Tölz Boys' Ch, Bav. RSO, Tate.
(M) *** EMI CMS7 69293-2 (2) [Ang. CDMB 69293]. Schwarzkopf, Grümmer, Metternich, Ilsovay, Schürhoff, Felbermayer, Children's Ch., Philh. O, Karajan.
*** Sony M2K 79217 (2) [M2K 35898]. Cotrubas, Von Stade, Ludwig, Nimsgern, Te Kanawa, Söderström, Cologne Op. Children's Ch., Cologne Gürzenich O, Pritchard.

Tate brings a Brucknerian glow to the *Overture*, and then launches into a reading of exceptional warmth and sympathy at speeds generally faster than those in rival versions. Karajan in his vintage EMI recording may be more rapt, finding more mystery in the *Evening hymn* and *Dream pantomime*, but the freshness of Tate avoids any hint of sentimentality, giving the *Evening hymn* the touching simplicity of a children's prayer. He relates the opera to the Wagner of Act II of *Die Meistersinger*, rather than to anything weightier. The Witch of Marjana Lipovšek is the finest of all, firm and fierce, using the widest range of expression and tone without any of the embarrassing exaggerations that mar, for example, Elisabeth Söderström's strong but controversial reading for Pritchard on Sony, and without any of the fruitiness of the conventional readings provided on the other sets. The chill that Lipovšek conveys down to a mere whisper makes one regret, more than usual, that the part is not longer. All the casting matches that in finesse, with no weak link. Barbara Bonney as Gretel and Anne Sofie von Otter as Hänsel are no less fine than the exceptionally strong duos on the rival sets, notably Schwarzkopf and Grümmer on the splendid mid-priced Karajan set and Cotrubas and von Stade on the excellent alternative from Pritchard. The main difference is that Bonney and von Otter have younger, fresher voices. The casting of the parents reflects that young approach too: Hanna Schwarz and Andreas Schmidt. There is only a slight question mark over the use of the Tölzer Boys' Choir for the gingerbread children at the end. Inevitably they sound what they are, a beautifully matched team of trebles, and curiously the heart-tug is not quite so intense as with the more childish-sounding voices in the rival choirs. That is a minimal reservation, however, when the breadth and warmth of the recording add to the compulsion of the performance, giving extra perspectives in focus and dynamic, compared with any other version.

Karajan's classic 1950s set of Humperdinck's children's opera, with Schwarzkopf and Grümmer peerless in the name-parts, is enchanting; this was an instance where everything in the recording went right. The original mono LP set was already extremely atmospheric. In most respects the sound has as much clarity and warmth as rival recordings made in the 1970s. There is much to delight here; the smaller parts are beautifully done and Else Schürhoff's Witch is memorable. The snag is that the digital remastering has brought a curious orchestral bass emphasis, noticeable in the Overture and elsewhere, but notably in the *Witch's ride*.

Beautifully cast, the Pritchard version from CBS was the first in genuine stereo to challenge the vintage Karajan set. Cotrubas – sometimes a little grainy as recorded – and Von Stade both give charming characterizations, and the supporting cast is exceptionally strong, with Söderström an unexpected but refreshing and illuminating choice as the Witch. Pritchard draws idiomatic playing from the Gürzenich Orchestra; the recording is pleasingly atmospheric and very realistically balanced.

Hänsel und Gretel: highlights.
*** EMI Dig. CDC7 54327-2 [id.]; *EL 754327-4* (from above complete recording, with Von Otter & Bonney; cond. Tate).

The highlights disc is generous, well selected to contain more than half of the opera (73 minutes) and most of the key passages, though not the overture.

Königskinder (complete).
(M) *** EMI CMS7 69936-2 (3). Donath, Prey, Dallapozza, Schwarz, Unger, Ridderbusch, Bav. R. Ch., Tolz Boys' Ch., Munich R. O, Wallberg.

The success of *Hänsel und Gretel* has completely overshadowed this second fairy-tale opera of Humperdinck, which contains much fine music. Humperdinck had expanded his incidental music for a play to make this opera, which was given its première in New York in 1910. In a recording as fine as this it is a piece well worth investigation. Both the conducting and the singing of the principals are most persuasive.

Ibert, Jacques (1890–1962)

Divertissement.
*** Chan. Dig. CHAN 9023 [id.]. Ulster O, Yan Pascal Tortelier – MILHAUD: *Le Boeuf; Création;* POULENC: *Les Biches*. ***

Yan Pascal Tortelier provides at last a splendid, modern, digital version of Ibert's *Divertissement*. While memories of Martinon's old Decca version are not entirely eclipsed, especially in the riotous Finale with police whistle, the Ulster performance has much elegance and spirit. The *Cortège* is charming, the *Valse* has deliciously chattering woodwind, great verve from the strings and wonderfully vulgar trombones, while the *Parade* has exactly the right mock pomposity. There is much delicacy of detail, and the coupled suite from Poulenc's *Les Biches* is equally delectable. Marvellous, top-drawer Chandos sound.

Escales (Ports of call).
(M) **(*) Mercury 432 003-2 [id.]. Detroit SO, Paray – RAVEL: *Alborada* etc. ***

Paray's recording catches the Mediterranean exoticism of *Escales* admirably, and the 1962 Mercury recording has plenty of atmosphere as well as glittering detail. The diaphanous strings in the opening *Palermo* are particularly impressive, and only in the loudest tuttis does the sound seem over-brilliant. The Ravel couplings are very impressive too.

Escales; Ouverture de fête; Tropisms pour des amours imaginaires.
(M) *** EMI CDM7 64276-2 [id.]. Fr. Nat. R. O, Jean Martinon.

The well-known *Escales* have genuine atmosphere in Martinon's exemplary performance, and the 1974 recording (balanced with quadraphony in mind) is spacious, at times sensuously so, and pleasingly natural. The strings here have more allure than in Paray's Mercury version. *Tropisms* was Ibert's last work; the manuscript only came to light the year that this recording was made. It has moments of real imagination, as well as others that are less compelling, and is a piece of greater substance than the *Ouverture de fête* which, though it has a striking principal theme, is rather inflated (the reverberant Salle Wagram acoustic is less beneficial to this piece). The *Ouverture* was commissioned by the French government for presentation to Prince

Tugukawa on the occasion of the 2,600th anniversary of the Japanese Empire in 1940. All three performances are expert and the CD transfer is most impressive.

Symphonie concertante (for oboe and string orchestra).
(M) *** BMG/RCA GD 87989. John de Lancie, LSO, Previn – FRANÇAIX: *L'horloge de flore* *** ❀; R. STRAUSS: *Oboe concerto.* ***

Ibert's *Symphonie concertante* was written for Paul Sacher and the Basle Chamber Orchestra in 1948/9. The writing in the outer movements has enormous vitality and impulse and demands great virtuosity from the orchestra; here it produces an exhilarating response from the LSO strings, and the extended *Adagio* has a wan, expressive poignancy. John de Lancie is a first-class soloist. André Previn directs with much conviction and spirit. The sound is very good – its slight lack of opulence suits the music.

d'India, Sigismondo (*c.* 1582–*c.* 1630)

Duets, Laments and Madrigals: *Amico, hai vinto; Ancidetemi pur, dogliosi affanti; Che nudrisce tua speme; Giunto a la tomba; Langue al vostro languir; Occhi della mia vita; O leggiadr' occhi; Quella vermiglia rosa; Son gli accenti che ascolto; Torna il sereno Zefiro.*
(B) **(*) HM HMA 901011 [id.]. Concerto Vocale – CESTI: *Cantatas.* **(*)

Sigismondo d'India was among the vanguard of the new movement founded by Monteverdi at the beginning of the seventeenth century, and his laments show him to be a considerable master of expressive resource. He is highly responsive to the emotions of the poetry, and the harmonies and unpredictable lines make this music fascinating. The performances are authoritative, though there are moments of slightly self-conscious rubato that hold up the flow. The recording is fully acceptable and the coupling is also of considerable interest; so, despite this qualification, this is worth exploring, especially in view of the modest price of the well-transferred CD.

Amico hai vint'io; Diana (Questo dardo, quest' arco); Misera me (Lamento d'Olympia); Piangono al pianger mio; Sfere fermate; Torna il sereno zefiro.
*** Hyp. CDA 66106 [id.]. Emma Kirkby, Anthony Rooley (chitarone) – MONTEVERDI: *Lamento d'Olympia* etc. ***

All these pieces are rarities. They are also of very great interest. Sigismondo d'India's setting of the *Lamento d'Olympia* makes a striking contrast to Monteverdi's and is hardly less fine. This is an affecting and beautiful piece and so are its companions, particularly when they are sung as superbly and accompanied as sensitively as they are here. A very worthwhile CD début.

d'Indy, Vincent (1851–1931)

Diptyque méditerranéan; Poème des rivages (symphonic suite).
(M) **(*) EMI Dig. CDM7 63954-2. Monte Carlo PO, Prêtre.

Neither work represents d'Indy at his most consistently inspired but there are still good things. The comparison often made between the *Diptyque* and the glorious *Jour d'été à la montagne* is not flattering. But the *Soleil matinal* of the *Diptyque* has a blend of the Wagner of *Parsifal* and that quality of conservative impressionism which d'Indy made so much his own after the turn of the century. There are considerable beauties in this piece and in the *Poème* and, though the recording is not top-drawer, string textures are transparent, even diaphanous at gentler moments, and the sound does not lack allure. This is well worth investigating for, despite some unevenness of inspiration, Prêtre holds the music together impressively.

Lied, Op. 19.
**(*) Ph. Dig. 432 084-2; *432 084-4* [id.]. Julian Lloyd Webber, ECO, Yan Pascal Tortelier – FAURÉ: *Élégie* **; HONEGGER: *Concerto* **(*); SAINT-SAËNS: *Concerto* etc. **(*)

There is no alternative recording of Vincent d'Indy's *Lied for cello and orchestra*, and all credit to Julian Lloyd Webber for returning it to currency. It has something of the nobility that always distinguished this composer, and it comes with an interesting coupling in the shape of the Honegger *Concerto.*

Symphonie sur un chant montagnard français (Symphonie cévenole).
*** Decca Dig. 430 278-2 [id.]. Jean-Yves Thibaudet, Montreal SO, Dutoit – FRANCK: *Symphony.* ***
*** Conifer Dig. CDFC 146; *MCFC 146* [id.]. Michel Block, Berne SO, Peter Maag – MARTINŮ: *Rhapsody-Concerto.* ***
(B) *** Hung. White Label HRC 106 [id.]. Gabriella Torma, Budapest PO, Tamás Pál – LALO: *Symphonie espagnole.* **(*)
(M) *** Sony MPK 46730 [id.]. Robert Casadesus, Phd. O, Ormandy – CASADESUS: *Concerto for 3 pianos* **; FRANCK: *Symphonic variations.* ***
(M) **(*) BMG/RCA GD 86805 [6805-2-RG). Nicole Henriot-Schweitzer, Boston SO, Munch – FRANCK: *Symphony.* **(*) ❀

(i) *Symphonie sur un chant montagnard français (Symphonie cévenole);* (ii) *Symphony No. 2 in B flat, Op. 57.*
(M) *** EMI CDM7 63952-2. (i) Ciccolini, O de Paris, Baudo; (ii) Toulouse Capitole O, Plasson.

Aldo Ciccolini gives a good account of himself in the demanding solo part of the *Symphonie*, and the Orchestre de Paris under Serge Baudo give sympathetic support. The music is charming and resourceful and the recording, if not outstanding, is pleasing and with a convincing piano image. The *Second Symphony* (1902–3) is as impressive as it is neglected. Although its cyclic organization betrays its francophilia, there is intellectual vigour, charm (as in the modal, folk-like *Modéré* of the third movement) and nobility in the arching lines of the fugue in the finale. Michel Plasson proves a sympathetic and committed advocate, and his orchestra, though not in the luxury bracket, responds with enthusiasm and sensitivity to his direction. The recording too is spacious, full and well focused. Those who complain about repeated duplications of the Franck *Symphony* should investigate this disc and discover one of the composer's most powerful works.

Jean-Yves Thibaudet's Decca account, with the Montreal orchestra, of d'Indy's *Symphonie sur un chant montagnard*, coming as it does with a splendid version of the Franck *Symphony*, has strong claims on any collector wanting a brand-new version. It is sensitively played and outstandingly well recorded.

Michel Block, a sensitive and intelligent player, gives a sympathetic account of this strange but, in his hands, appealing work. The recording is well balanced and the perspective natural: it could perhaps open out more at climaxes and the very top of the piano is less transparent than is ideal. However, few would regret investing in this thoroughly recommendable issue with its fine Martinů coupling.

A sensitive and atmospheric account from Gabriella Torma and the Budapest Philharmonic under Pál. The Hungaroton recording is warmly atmospheric and the piano is balanced well with the orchestra. There is no lack of vividness here, and these artists show great sympathy for this attractive music. The Lalo coupling is recommendable, too. A bargain.

Casadesus gives a commanding performance and the transfer does greater justice to the sonority of the fabulous Philadelphians than it did in its earlier, LP incarnations. The recording comes from the late 1950s and the transfer has recaptured some of the sumptuousness of the string tone, though the piano timbre is at times lacking in freshness.

Nicole Henriot-Schweitzer and Munch present a fresh and crisp performance which is certainly true to the atmosphere of the composer's inspiration, which he found in the mountains of the Cevennes. Munch's natural affinity and the bright-eyed response of the Boston players make for the happiest results, and Henriot-Schweitzer plays the piano part most sympathetically. The early (1958) stereo recording comes up well.

String quartets Nos. 1 in D, Op. 35; 2 in E, Op. 45.
**(*) Marco Polo Dig. 8.223140 [id.]. Kodály Qt.

In all d'Indy composed three string quartets and was working on a fourth at the time of his death. Even in France they are rarities, though when the *First* (1890) appeared, it was hailed as a masterpiece. It is a large-scale piece, some forty minutes in duration, and beautifully crafted, very much in the style of his revered César Franck. It comes from the time when D'Indy was working on his opera, *Fervaal*, written under the spell of Bayreuth. The *Second* (1897) is hardly less ambitious, fashioned with fastidious craftsmanship and finesse, and showing something of his admiration for late Beethoven. For all the clarity and distinction of mind they evince, neither work has the eloquence or poetry of Fauré's chamber music and the ideas are more beautifully worked out than they are beautiful; it must also be said that greater variety of texture would be welcome. The excellent Kodály Quartet are recorded in the Italian Institute in Budapest, which is kinder to quartets than pianos, but even so the rather close balance tends to iron out dynamic extremes. All the same this Marco Polo recording undoubtedly fills a gap in the repertoire and even if these artists do not sound as if they have played these pieces all their lives, they serve the music well.

Ippolitov-Ivanov, Mikhail (1859–1935)

Caucasian sketches (suite), *Op. 10.*
*** ASV Dig. CDDCA 773; *ZCDCA 773.* Armenian PO, Tjeknavorain – KHACHATURIAN: *Gayaneh* etc. **(*)
** Olympia OCD 107 [id.]. USSR RSO, Fedoseyev – ARENSKY: *Piano concerto* etc. **

Ippolitov-Ivanov was not just a 'one-work composer'; his fames rests on a single movement, the *Procession of the Sardar*, the hit number from the *Caucasian sketches*, which is played by the Armenians with great brio. The other items rely mainly on picaresque oriental atmosphere for their appeal which Tjeknavorian also captures evocatively in this brightly lit recording. The alternative Russian versions under Fedoseyev are hardly less idiomatic and the sound fully acceptable, if the more interesting Arensky couplings are preferred.

Ireland, John (1879–1962)

Piano concerto in E flat.
*** Conifer Dig. CDCF 175; *MCFC 175* [id.]. Kathryn Stott, RPO, Handley – BRIDGE: *Phantasm;* WALTON: *Sinfonia concertante.* ***
*** Unicorn Dig. DKPCD 9056; *DKPC 9056* [id.]. Tozer, Melbourne SO, Measham – RUBBRA: *Violin concerto.* ***

Piano concerto in E flat; Legend for piano and orchestra; Mai-Dun (symphonic rhapsody).
*** Chan. Dig. CHAN 8461; *ABTD 1174* [id.]. Parkin, LPO, Thomson.

John Ireland's only *Piano concerto* has a distinctive melodic inspiration throughout all three movements and its poetic lyricism is in the best traditions of the finest English music. Kathryn Stott gives the most sympathetic reading on record since the original interpreter on disc, Eileen Joyce. Spaciously expressive in the lyrical passages – not least the lovely slow movement – and crisply alert in the jazzy finale, Stott plays with a sense of spontaneity, using freely idiomatic rubato. Generously and aptly coupled with the much more neglected Walton and Bridge works, and very well recorded, this version, the third on CD, makes an easy first choice for the work.

Eric Parkin gives a splendidly refreshing and sparkling performance and benefits from excellent support from Bryden Thomson and the LPO. They are no less impressive in *Mai-Dun* and the beautiful *Legend for piano and orchestra.*

Geoffrey Tozer also gives a characterful account of Ireland's lyrical and often whimsical *Concerto.* It wears well and its charms have not faded in the half-century or more since it was composed. Tozer conveys the poetic feel of the slow movement and, though he takes a rather measured tempo in the finale, the music loses none of its freshness. The recording is a little studio-bound, and a slightly more open acoustic would have been preferable – but too much should not be made of this. Doubtless the coupling will decide matters for most collectors.

A Downland suite; Elegiac meditation; The Holy Boy.
*** Chan. Dig. CHAN 8390; *ABTD 1112* [id.]. ECO, David Garforth – BRIDGE: *Suite for strings.* ***

David Garforth and the ECO play with total conviction and seem wholly attuned to Ireland's sensibility. *A Downland suite* was originally written for brass band, and in 1941 Ireland began to make a version for strings. As was the case with the *Comedy overture* for brass band which he rewrote in 1936, he completely reconceived it. However, his reworking was interrupted and the present version was finished and put into shape by Geoffrey Bush, who also transcribed the *Elegiac meditation.* The recording is first class, clear and naturally balanced.

The Forgotten rite (Prelude); (i) *These things shall be*; (ii) (Piano) *April.*
(M) (***) EMI CDH7 63910-2. Hallé O, Barbirolli; (i) with Parry Jones, Hallé Ch.; (ii) composer – BAX: *Symphony No. 3.* (***)

Barbirolli's account of *The Forgotten rite* has something quite special: there is a quiet, inward-looking quality that has eluded subsequent performers. The 1949 sound may not have the freshness and bloom we expect from modern recording but the performance has both. This is quintessential Ireland. *These things shall be*, written for the 1937 coronation celebrations, is not. In fact it is a rather conventional piece though this stirring account does its best to show it in a positive light. There is a welcome bonus in Ireland himself playing *April.* All these performances make a useful and generous pendant to Barbirolli's impassioned and indispensable account of Bax's *Third Symphony.*

A London overture; Epic march; (i) *The Holy Boy; Greater love hath no man; These things shall be; Vexilla regis.*
*** Chan. Dig. CHAN 8879; *ABTD 1492* [id.]. (i) Bryn Terfel, LSO Ch., LSO, Richard Hickox.

This CD forms as good an introduction as any to John Ireland's music, which has not enjoyed the same revival of interest as his contemporary, Arnold Bax (although, of course, Ireland's splendid *Piano concerto* should also be part of any representative collection). Richard Hickox is a sympathetic interpreter of the composer and obtains sensitive results (and good singing) in *The Holy Boy* and *These things shall be.* He does make heavy weather of the opening of *A London overture* but more than compensates for that in his sensitive phrasing of the second group. The disc is of particular interest in that it brings a rarity, *Vexilla Regis* for chorus, brass and organ, composed when Ireland was nineteen and still a student of Stanford. First-class recorded sound.

Phantasie (trio) in A min.
*** Gamut Dig. GAM CD 518 [id.]. Hartley Trio – BRIDGE; CLARKE: *Trios.* ***

Built on striking material, energetically argued, the Ireland *Phantasie* is one of the finest of the one-movement works prompted by the sponsorship of W. W. Cobbett. One ideally should have a whole disc devoted to the *Piano trios* of Ireland, but this fine work, well played and recorded, makes an excellent fill-up for the similar Bridge *Phantasie* and the splendid *Piano trio* of Rebecca Clarke.

PIANO MUSIC

The Almond tree; Decorations; Merry Andrew; Preludes: (The undertone; Obsession; The Holy Boy; Fire of spring); Rhapsody; Sonata in E min.; Summer evening; The Towing-path.
*** Chan. Dig. CHAN 9056 [id.]. Eric Parkin.

John Ireland's piano music ought to be in the repertoire of some of the great international pianists for his is a voice of undoubted originality. He is not generously represented in the current catalogues so that it is good that Eric Parkin has embarked on another complete survey for Chandos. This new issue serves to reaffirm the positive impression he made in his earlier set on Lyrita in the late 1970s. It goes without saying that he is completely inside the idiom, and brings both dedication and sympathy to this repertoire. Moreover he is far more successfully recorded than he was in the Bax piano music on this label: the sound is clean, well-rounded and pleasing. A most welcome issue.

Isaac, Heinrich (*c.* 1450–1517)

Missa de Apostolis. Motets: *Optime pastor; Tota pulchra es; Regina caeli laetare; Resurrexi et adhuc tecum sum; Virgo prudentissima.*
*** Gimell Dig. CDGIM 023; *1585T23* [id.]. Tallis Scholars, Peter Phillips.

The German contemporary of Josquin des Pres, Heinrich Isaac has not until recently been widely appreciated. Preferring the rich polyphonic textures possible from writing in five or six rather than four parts (Josquin's general choice), Isaac inserts sections of plainchant which to modern ears come as dramatic contrast and refreshment. That makes it surprising that such fine examples of his work as these have remained so little appreciated. The Mass setting is glorious, culminating in an ethereal version of *Agnus Dei*, flawlessly sung by the Tallis Scholars. Among the many striking passages is the opening of the six-part setting of *Virgo prudentissima* for two upper voices only, with women's rather than boys' voices all the more appropriate with such a text. Ideally balanced recording.

Ives, Charles (1874–1954)

Calcium light night; Country band march; Largo cantabile: Hymn; 3 Places in New England; Postlude in F; 4 Ragtime dances; Set for theatre orchestra; Yale–Princeton football game.
*** Koch Dig. 37025-2; *37025-4* [id.]. O New England, Sinclair.

This selection of shorter Ives pieces makes an ideal introduction for anyone wanting just to sample the work of this wild, often maddening, but always intriguing composer. Some of these pieces, like the evocations of college life in the Yale–Princeton football game and *Calcium light night*, encapsulate the kind of raw material Ives developed in bigger works like *Three places in New England*, one of his most colourfully attractive works. Excellent performances and recording.

Central Park in the dark; New England Holidays symphony; The unanswered question (original and revised versions).
*** Sony Dig. MK 42381 [id.]. Chicago Symphony Ch. & O, Tilson Thomas.

The *New England Holidays symphony* comprises four fine Ives pieces normally heard separately. The performance from Michael Tilson Thomas and his Chicago forces is in every way superb, while the wide-ranging CBS recording provides admirable atmosphere for the magical opening of *Washington's birthday* and is fully equal to the complex textures and spectacle of *Decoration Day* and the great climax of the finale. This is now among the most impressive Ives records in the catalogue, for the other pieces – shorter but no less characteristically original works – are made to sound as breathtakingly original as the day they were written.

Symphony No. 1 in D min.
*** Chan. Dig. CHAN 9053; *ABTD 1589* [id.]. Detroit SO, Järvi – BARBER: *Essays 1–3*. ***

Like Barber's *School for Scandal Overture*, Charles Ives's *First Symphony* was a graduation exercise composed during the last months of his student years as a pupil of Horatio Parker. There is a certain freshness about its melodic invention that is appealing; the idiom is polite and generally conservative with Dvořák as perhaps the strongest influence, but there are already glimpses of iconoclasm in the (often queasy) modulatary shifts. Neeme Järvi gives a very persuasive account of it and there is a fresh and unforced virtuosity from the Detroit orchestra. Excellent, very natural recorded sound, excellently balanced.

Symphonies Nos. 1; 4.
**(*) Sony Dig. SK 44939 [id.]. Chicago SO, Michael Tilson Thomas.

Tilson Thomas's strong and brilliant Chicago performances make a generous and apt coupling, the more valuable for providing first recordings of the revised editions of the composer's tangled scores. These may not be the warmest or most concentrated of performances but, with bright, well-detailed sound and superb playing, they can be strongly recommended to those wanting the generous and apt coupling.

Symphony No. 2; Central Park in the dark; The gong on the hook and ladder; Hallowe'en; Hymn for strings; Tone roads No. 1; The Unanswered question.
*** DG Dig. 429 220-2 [id.]. NYPO, Bernstein.

Bernstein's disc brings one of the richest offerings of Ives yet put on record, offering the *Symphony No. 2*, with its array of references and parodies, extravagant even by this wild composer's standards, plus six shorter orchestral pieces. They include two of his very finest, *Central Park in the dark* and *The Unanswered question*, both characteristically quirky but deeply poetic too. In a note on the record, Bernstein explains in plain words the depth of his feelings towards this 'greatly gifted primitive'; and the superb performances, recorded live, consistently reflect that in their electricity and concentration. The *Symphony No. 2* was a work which Bernstein recorded with this orchestra for CBS many years ago, but this DG version with its radiant string-sound is much warmer still. The extra tensions and expressiveness of live performance here heighten the impact of each of the works. The difficult acoustic of Avery Fisher Hall in New York has rarely sounded more sympathetic on record.

Symphonies Nos. 2; 3 (The Camp meeting).
**(*) Sony Dig. SK 46440 [id.]; *40-46440.* Concg. O, Michael Tilson Thomas.

This recoupling is welcome when it so neatly provides a counterpart to Tilson Thomas's Chicago recordings of the other two Ives symphonies. The performances may not have the fervour of a Bernstein in this music – perhaps reflecting the fact that this is not an American orchestra – but they are strong and direct, and in No. 3 the revised edition is used on record for the first time. The recording, though not ideally sharp in its focus, is warm and atmospheric.

Symphony No. 3 (The Camp meeting).
*** Argo 417 818-2 [id.]. ASMF, Marriner – BARBER: *Adagio;* COPLAND: *Quiet City;* COWELL: *Hymn;* CRESTON: *Rumor.* ***
*** Pro Arte Dig. CDD 140 [id.]. St Paul CO, Russell Davies – COPLAND: *Appalachian spring* etc. ***

Symphony No. 3 (The Camp meeting); (i) *Orchestral set No. 2.*
*** Sony Dig. MK 37823 [id.]. Concg. O, Tilson Thomas; (i) with Concg. Ch.

Tilson Thomas's version of Ives's most approachable symphony is the first to use the new critical edition, prepared with reference to newly available Ives manuscripts. Thanks to that and to Tilson Thomas's clear, incisive manner, it avoids any hint of blandness; the *Second Orchestral set*, with its three substantial atmosphere pieces, brings performances of a sharpness to back up the characteristically wordy titles – *An elegy to our forefathers*, *The rockstrewn hills join in the people's outdoor meeting* and *From Hanover Square North at the end of a tragic day the voice of the people again arose.* First-rate recording to match the fine performances.

Russell Davies does not use the new edition of Ives's score; nevertheless, he gives a fine account of this gentlest of Ives's symphonies, with its overtones of hymn singing and revivalist meetings. It makes a good coupling for the fine Copland works. Though the forward, relatively intimate acoustic may not evoke a church atmosphere at all, the beauty of the piece still comes over strongly.

Marriner's account is first rate in every way. It does not have the advantage of a digital master, but the 1976 analogue recording has slightly sharper detail in this remastered format. The performance has plenty of conviction; moreover it comes as part of an anthology that is of unusual interest and merit.

Symphony No. 3; Three places in New England.
(M) *** Mercury 432 755-2 [id.]. Eastman-Rochester O, Howard Hanson – SCHUMAN: *New England triptych* ***; MENNIN: *Symphony No. 5.* **(*)

Ives's quixotic genius is at its most individual in the *Three places in New England.* Written between 1903 and 1914, this music is still able to shock the ear, especially the second movement, *Putnam's Camp, Redding, Connecticut*, with its fantasy images inspired by a child's dream at a site connected with the American War of Independence. Both works are most understandingly presented here under Howard Hanson, who is equally at home in the folksy imagery of *The Camp meeting*, which is the subtitle of the *Third Symphony*, an immediately attractive triptych, full of colourful invention. The acoustics of the Eastman Theatre are less than ideally expansive, but the 1957 recording is remarkably full-bodied and vivid.

Symphony No. 4.
**(*) Chan. Dig. CHAN 8397; *ABTD 1118* [id.]. John Alldis Ch., LPO, Serebrier.

Ives's most intense inspirations came when he limited himself to a single piece; though he was a big enough man to encompass symphony-length, it was difficult for him to fit the pieces together. Even so, no Ives enthusiast should miss this preposterous work, scored for an immense orchestra. José Serebrier acted as subsidiary conductor for Stokowski when he conducted the world première. In this English performance he somehow manages to find his way through multi-layered textures which have deliberately conflicting rhythms. The players respond loyally, and the movement representing *Chaos* is particularly colourful and dramatic in its sharp contrasts of dynamic, brutal but somehow poetic. *Order* is represented by a fugue, and the finale brings an apotheosis: a vivid, gripping work, but perhaps not as great as some American commentators originally thought. For the record collector at least, it provides a store-house of fantastic orchestral sound in a recording as vivid as this.

(i) *Symphony No. 4; Robert Browning Overture;* (ii) Songs: *An Election, Lincoln the great commoner; Majority, They are There!*
(M) *** Sony MPK 46726 [id.]. (i) NY Schola Cantorum; (ii) Gregg Smith Singers; American SO, Stokowski

This reissue of three vintage Stokowski recordings of Ives makes a welcome addition to the Masterworks Portrait series, well transferred to CD. The (originally 1965) recording of the *Fourth Symphony*, made at the same period as the belated première of the work, brings a stunning performance, with sound that is still amazingly full and vivid. Stokowski also brings out the often aggressive vigour of the *Robert Browning Overture*. The choral songs with orchestra provide an attractive makeweight.

Piano trio (1904).
*** Teldec/Warner Dig. 2292 44924-2 [id.]. Trio Fontenay – BRAHMS: *Piano trio No. 1.* ***

The Ives *Trio* is an amazing piece for 1904 and it is excellently played by the Trio Fontenay. Whether collectors wanting Brahms's Op. 8 will want it too is another matter – and vice versa, of course. Anyway, they play it with great spirit and are given eminently clear but not overbright recording.

Songs: *An old flame; At the river; Charlie Rutlage; The children's hour; The circus band; He is there!; In the alley; A night song; Romanzo di Central Park; Slow march.*
*** Argo Dig. 433 027-2 [id.]. Samuel Ramey, Warren Jones – COPLAND: *Old American songs.* ***

In this varied choice of ten Ives songs, an attractive pairing with Copland, Ramey deftly avoids the obvious pitfalls in writing which is only parodistic in part, whether in the overtly sentimental fragments or the rousing songs like *The circus band* and the patriotic First World War song, *He is there!*. It makes an illuminating contrast having Ives's much more idiosyncratic setting of *At the river* as well as Copland's on the disc. Warren Jones's accompaniments are highly sympathetic. Excellent recording.

Songs: *At the river; Charlie Rutledge; The children's hour; The circus band; He is there; In the alley; A night song; An old flame; Romanza di Central Park; Slow march.*
*** Decca Dig. 433 027-2; *433 027-4* [id.]. Samuel Ramey, Warren Jones – COPLAND: *Old American songs.* ***

With some characteristically vigorous songs as well as many that might almost be Edwardian ballads (spiced Ives-style), this group of ten songs, superbly done, makes an ideal and attractive coupling for the colourful Copland settings, very well recorded. A coupling not to be missed.

Songs: *Autumn; Berceuse; The cage; Charlie Rutlage; Down East; Dreams; Evening; The greatest man; The Housatonic at Stockbridge; Immortality; Like a sick eagle; Maple leaves; Memories: 1, 2, 3; On the counter; Romanzo di Central Park; The see'r; Serenity; The side-show; Slow march; Slugging a vampire; Songs my mother taught me; Spring song; The things our fathers loved; Tom sails away; Two little flowers.*
*** Etcetera Dig. KTC 1020 [id.]. Roberta Alexander, Tan Crone.

Roberta Alexander presents her excellent and illuminating choice of Ives songs – many of them otherwise unavailable on record – in chronological order, starting with one written when Ives was only fourteen, *Slow march*, already predicting developments ahead. Sweet, nostalgic songs predominate, but the singer punctuates them with leaner, sharper inspirations. Her manner is not always quite tough enough in those, but this is characterful singing from an exceptionally rich and attractive voice. Tan Crone is the understanding accompanist, and the recording is first rate.

Jacob, Gordon (1895–1987)

Mini-concerto for clarinet and string orchestra.
*** Hyp. CDA 66031; *KA 66031* [id.]. Thea King, NW CO of Seattle, Alun Francis – COOKE; RAWSTHORNE: *Concertos.* ***

Gordon Jacob in his eighties responded to an earlier recording of his music by Thea King by writing this miniature concerto for her, totally charming in its compactness, with not a note too many. The slow movement in particular is a gem. Thea King is the most persuasive of dedicatees, splendidly accompanied by the orchestra from Seattle and treated to first rate 1982 analogue sound, splendidly transferred.

William Byrd suite.
(M) *** Mercury 432 009-2 [id.]. Eastman Wind Ens., Fennell – BENNETT: *Symphonic songs* ***; HOLST: *Hammersmith* ***; WALTON: *Crown Imperial.* *** ❀

Gordon Jacob's arrangement of the music of Byrd is audaciously anachronistic, but it is very entertaining when played with such flair under that supreme maestro of the wind band, Frederick Fennell. The closing number, *The Bells* (*Variations on a ground*), is particularly successful. The recording is up to the usual high Mercury standard in this repertoire.

Divertimento for harmonica and string quartet.
*** Chan. Dig. CHAN 8802; *CBTD 026* [id.]. Tommy Reilly, Hindar Qt – MOODY: *Quintet; Suite.* ***

Gordon Jacob's set of eight sharply characterized miniatures shows the composer at his most engagingly imaginative. The variety of invention, whether in the *Romance* and *Siciliano*, the *Elegy* or the final *Jig*, constantly beguiles the ear, and the performances are deliciously piquant in colour and feeling. The recording could hardly be more successful, for the harmonica's special timbre can blend and yet stand out from the string textures.

Oboe quartet.
*** Chan. Dig. CHAN 8392; *ABTD 1114* [id.]. Francis, English Qt – BAX: *Quintet;* HOLST: *Air and variations* etc.; MOERAN: *Fantasy quartet.* ***

Gordon Jacob's four-movement *Oboe quartet* is the slightest of the four works included in this admirable anthology, but is none the less very welcome. It is well crafted and entertaining, particularly the vivacious final Rondo. The performance could hardly be bettered, and the recording is excellent too.

Janáček, Leoš (1854–1928)

Capriccio for piano left-hand and wind; Concertino for piano and seven instruments.
*** BMG/RCA Dig. RD 60781 [60781-2]. Rudolf Firkušný, Czech PO, Václav Neumann – DVOŘÁK: *Piano concerto in G min.* ***

Authoritative and well recorded performances on BMG/RCA. As a small boy Firkušný studied both composition and the piano with Janáček (from 1921), and so knew the composer before either the *Concertino* or the *Capriccio* came into being. He himself is now older than Janáček when he wrote these remarkable pieces but conveys a youthful fire which seems to burn almost as brightly as the earlier recordings he made with the Philadelphia Wind in the 1950s and the Bavarian Radio with Kubelik on DG in the 1970s. A thoroughly worthwhile coupling with Dvořák.

Mládi.
**(*) DG Dig. 415 668-2 [id.]. Orpheus CO – BARTÓK: *Divertimento* etc. **(*)

Mládi (Youth) is a work of Janáček's old age. On the DG version, the playing is excellent and the recording very realistic. Tempi may at times seem brisker by comparison with some past performances on record, but the music is never made to seem hurried. This makes a fine choice for those wanting the pairing with Bartók.

Sinfonietta.
*** EMI Dig. CDC7 47504-2 [id.]. Philh. O, Rattle – *Glagolitic Mass.* ***
(M) *** Decca 425 624-2 [id.]. LSO, Abbado – *Glagolitic Mass.* ***
*** Chan. Dig. CHAN 8897; *ABTD 1508* [id.]. Czech PO, Bělohlávek – MARTINŮ: *Symphony No. 6;* SUK: *Scherzo.* ***

Sinfonietta; Lachian dances; Taras Bulba.
(BB) *** Naxos Dig. 8.550411 [id.]. Slovak RSO (Bratislava), Ondrej Lenárd.

Sinfonietta; Taras Bulba.
(M) *** Decca Dig. 430 727-2; *430 727-4* [id.]. VPO, Mackerras – SHOSTAKOVICH: *Age of gold.* ***

Mackerras's coupling comes as a superb supplement to his Janáček opera recordings with the Vienna Philharmonic. The massed brass of the *Sinfonietta* has tremendous bite and brilliance as well as characteristic Viennese ripeness, thanks to a spectacular digital recording. *Taras Bulba* too is given more weight and body than is usual, the often savage dance rhythms presented with great energy.

Rattle gets an altogether first-class response from the orchestra and truthful recorded sound from the EMI engineers. The rival Decca recording is a hi-fi spectacular with rather forward placing and a hint of aggression; many collectors may find the EMI sound more pleasing. The Decca has greater clarity and presence in its favour, as well as Mackerras's authority in this repertoire. However, Rattle's coupling with the *Glagolitic Mass* is very attractive indeed and will be first choice for many collectors.

Abbado gives a splendid account of the *Sinfonietta* and evokes a highly sympathetic response from the LSO. His acute sensitivity to dynamic nuances and his care for detail are felt in every bar, without any sense of excessive fastidiousness, and this is thoroughly alive and fresh playing. The recording balance, too, allows the subtlest of colours to register while still having plenty of impact. In its remastered CD format it sounds quite splendid.

Jíři Bělohlávek's exultant and imaginative account of the *Sinfonietta* is one of the best currently on offer and is coupled with an outstanding version of Martinů's *Sixth Symphony*. The players, as one would expect, are entirely inside this repertoire and the recording, made in the Smetana Hall, Prague, is impressive.

On Naxos we have the normal LP coupling of the *Sinfonietta* and *Taras Bulba*, but with the *Lachian dances* thrown in for good measure, all played by musicians steeped in the Janáček tradition – and all at a very modest cost. These are excellent performances and well worth the money involved; the recording, made in a fairly resonant studio, is natural and free from any artificially spotlit balance.

Sinfonietta; Preludes: From the House of the Dead; Jealousy (original *Overture to Jenůfa*); *Katya Kabanova; The Makropulos affair.*
(M) *(**) EMI CDM7 63779-2; *EG 763779-4*. Pro Arte O, Mackerras (with WEINBERGER: *Schwanda the Bagpiper: Polka & fugue;* SMETANA: *Bartered Bride: Overture* ***).

The present (1959) performance has a fire and bite that are not quite matched even by Mackerras himself in his later, Decca record (see above). The playing of the Pro Arte Orchestra is immensely vivid; its lack of the last degree of refinement seems to increase its forceful projection. The brass sonorities (the work uses twelve trumpets) are pungent, and elsewhere the recording has striking detail and colour. The original coupling of the four operatic *Preludes* was an imaginative choice, and similar comments apply to the vibrant playing here. The only snag is that in this bright CD transfer the EMI engineers have rather gone over the top in the upper range, which is very brightly lit indeed to the point of shrillness. The two vivacious encores by Weinberger and Smetana have comparable colour and zest, plus excellent detail, and it is a pity that, even here, the upper range is a bit fierce.

Taras Bulba (rhapsody).
*** Decca Dig. 430 204-2; *430 204-4* [id.]. Cleveland O, Dohnányi – DVOŘÁK: *Symphony No. 6.* ***

Opulently recorded in Decca's finest Cleveland style, like the Dvořák symphony with which it is coupled, Dohnányi's version of *Taras Bulba* provides a generous makeweight on a fine disc. Quite apart from the sound, this brings a more warmly expressive reading than the brilliant rival Decca version from Mackerras and the Vienna Philharmonic. Paradoxically, the Cleveland account is the more Viennese in style, where Mackerras persuades his truly Viennese musicians to sound like Czechs, playing with a sharp attack very apt for this composer's music.

String quartets Nos. 1 (Kreutzer); 2 (Intimate letters).
(M) *** Decca 430 295-2; *430 295-4* [id.]. Gabrieli Qt – SMETANA: *Quartet No. 1.* ***
*** ASV Dig. CDDCA 749; *ZCDCA 749* [id.]. Lindsay Qt (with DVOŘÁK: *Cypresses* ***).

(i) *String quartets Nos. 1–2;* (ii) *On an overgrown path: suite No. 1.*
*** Calliope Dig. CAL 9699 [id.]. (i) Talich Qt; (ii) Radoslav Kvapil.

Janáček's two *String quartets* come from his last years and are among his most deeply individual and profoundly impassioned utterances. The Gabrieli Quartet have the measure of this strikingly original music and give a highly idiomatic and strongly felt account of these masterpieces. They have the advantage of a well-focused and truthfully balanced recording, made in Rosslyn Hill Chapel in 1977, which has transferred well to CD and has maximum clarity and blend as well as considerable warmth. With its generous Smetana coupling, this CD plays for 73 minutes.

Otherwise pride of place must go to the Talich Quartet on Calliope, not because their recording is the best – it is by no means as vivid as the Decca – but because of their extraordinary qualities of insight. They play the *Intimate letters* as if its utterances came from a world so private that it must be approached with great care. Their understanding of and love for this music comes across in every bar, and their insights are deeper than almost any of their predecessors on disc. The disc's value is much enhanced by a fill-up in the form of the *First suite, On an overgrown path.* Radoslav Kvapil is thoroughly inside this repertoire.

The Lindsays on ASV are eminently competitive and have the right blend of sensitivity and intensity. Theirs was apparently the first choice for the BBC's 'Building a Library' series and it must certainly rank very highly among current recommendations. It is played with the same concentration and sensitivity they bring to all they do, and recorded with great naturalness.

Violin sonata.

*** Virgin Dig. VC7 90760-2; *VC 790760-4* [id.]. Dmitry Sitkovestsky, Pavel Gililov – DEBUSSY: *Sonata* **; R. STRAUSS: *Sonata.* ***

(*) DG Dig. 427 351-2 [id.]. Gidon Kremer, Martha Argerich – BARTÓK: *Sonata No. 1;* MESSIAEN: *Theme and variations.* *

Janáček composed two violin sonatas in his youth, neither of which survives. The present work was finalized in 1921. It is a rarity both in the concert hall and on record, and Dmitry Sitkovestsky and Pavel Gililov seem completely attuned to its thoughtful, impulsive, improvisatory idiom. There is excellent rapport between the two players, and the engineers produce a natural, well-balanced sound.

Like the Bartók, with which it is coupled, the Janáček *Sonata* is a powerfully impassioned and original work. It is played with great imaginative intensity and power by Gidon Kremer and Martha Argerich, though it is less selfless here than with Sitkovetsky on Virgin: there is some expressive exaggeration, and those who are at times disturbed by the note of hysteria and narcissism that characterizes Kremer's tone will find evidence of it here. Excellent DG recording.

Piano sonata (1.X.1905); In the mist; 3 Moravian dances; On an overgrown path: Books 1 & 2; A recollection.

*** EMI Dig. CDC7 54094-2 [id.]. Mikhail Rudy.

Piano sonata (1.X.1905); In the mist; On the overgrown path, Book 2; A recollection.

**(*) BMG/RCA Dig. RD 60147 [60147-2-RC]. Rudolf Firkušný.

Piano sonata (1.X.1905); In the mist; On the overgrown path, Book 2; A recollection; Theme & variations.

(M) *** DG 429 857-2 [id.]. Rudolf Firkušný.

Rudolf Firkušný recorded these pieces for DG in the early 1970s and he produces seamless legato lines, hammerless tone and rapt atmosphere. Given its competitive price, many collectors will opt for this anthology, which still sounds very good and also includes the *Zdenka Theme and variations.*

Firkušný brings a special authority and sensitivity to this repertoire. As a small boy he played many of these pieces to the composer, but it is his selfless dedication to this music that tells. His basic approach has not varied greatly since he last recorded these pieces for DG twenty years ago. The three stars are for the marvellous playing; the RCA digital recording does not give us the best piano quality: though it is perfectly acceptable, it is a little biased towards the middle and bass registers.

Mikhail Rudy proves a perceptive and sympathetic guide in this music. His is a fine account of the *Sonata*, and he succeeds in penetrating the world of the *Overgrown path* miniatures to perfection. He conveys their acute sense of melancholy and their improvisatory character with distinction. Rudolf Firkušný has special claims in this repertoire, and this anthology supplements rather than displaces his CD, but it is thoroughly recommendable, and the recorded sound is very natural.

Along an overgrown path: Suite No. 1; In the mists; Sonata: I.X.1905.

*** Virgin Dig. VC7 91222-2 [id.]. Leif Ove Andsnes.

Janáček's piano music is not being neglected and, though neither of Firkušný's recordings (on DG and RCA Gold Seal respectively) is displaced by the Virgin CD featuring the young Norwegian pianist, Leif Ove Andsnes, the fact remains that his is a very well thought-out and imaginatively realized recital. He gives a highly sensitive account of *In the mists*, which is second to none in conveying the pervasive melancholy and evocative atmosphere of these pieces. This is every bit as telling as Mikhail Rudy's EMI account and beautifully recorded.

VOCAL MUSIC

Glagolitic Mass.
*** EMI Dig. CDC7 47504-2 [id.]. Palmer, Gunson, Mitchinson, King, CBSO & Ch., Rattle – *Sinfonietta.* ***
(M) *** Decca 425 624-2 [id.]. Kubiak, Collins, Tear, Schone, Brighton Festival Ch., RPO, Kempe – *Sinfonietta.* ***
**(*) Telarc Dig. CD 80287 [id.]. Atlanta Ch. & SO, Robert Shaw – DVOŘÁK: *Te Deum.* **(*)

Written when Janáček was over seventy, this is one of his most important and most exciting works, full of those strikingly fresh uses of sound that make his music so distinctive. The opening instrumental movement has much in common with the opening fanfare of the *Sinfonietta*, and all the other movements reveal an original approach to the church service. The text is taken from native Croatian variations of the Latin text, but its vitality bespeaks a folk inspiration. Rattle's performance, aptly paired with the *Sinfonietta*, is strong and vividly dramatic, with the Birmingham performers lending themselves to Slavonic passion. The recording is first class. An outstanding coupling.

The Decca recording is an extremely good one. Kempe's reading is broad but has plenty of vitality, and the Brighton chorus sings vigorously. The playing of the Royal Philharmonic is wonderfully committed and vivid, and there is first-rate solo singing, with Teresa Kubiak particularly impressive.

Shaw conducts an incisive, freshly dramatic reading of Janáček's colourful masterpiece, lacking only a little in idiomatic Czech flavour. Though the Telarc recording presents the orchestra (and organ) forwardly and vividly, the chorus is relatively backward, a great pity when the singing is so fine. That flaw in the recording balance need not deter anyone who fancies the unusual but apt coupling.

OPERA

The Cunning little vixen (complete); *Cunning little vixen* (suite, arr. Talich).
*** Decca Dig. 417 129-2 (2) [id.]. Popp, Randová, Jedlická, V. State Op. Ch., Bratislava Children's Ch., VPO, Mackerras.

Mackerras's thrusting, red-blooded reading is spectacularly supported by a digital recording of outstanding, demonstration quality. That Janáček deliberately added the death of the vixen to the original story points very much in the direction of such a strong, purposeful approach. The inspired choice of Lucia Popp as the vixen provides charm in exactly the right measure, a Czech-born singer who delights in the fascinating complexity of the vixen's character: sparkling and coquettish, spiteful as well as passionate. The supporting cast is first rate, too. Talich's splendidly arranged orchestral suite is offered as a bonus in a fine new recording.

(i) *The Cunning Little Vixen* (sung in English); (ii) *Taras Bulba.*
*** EMI CDS7 54212-2 (2) [id.]. (i) Watson, Tear, Allen, ROHCG Ch. & O; (ii) Philh. O; Simon Rattle.

Simon Rattle's recording came as a spin-off – generously sponsored by the Peter Moores Foundation – from the outstanding Covent Garden production of the opera in June 1990. For anyone who wants the work in English, it provides an ideal answer, with Rattle's warmly expressive approach to the score giving strong support to the singers, who equally have gained in expressiveness from singing their roles on stage in the theatre. The cast is outstanding, with Lillian Watson delightfully bright and fresh as the Vixen and Thomas Allen firm and full-toned as the Forester. The characterizations of both humans and animals are all strongly individual – again reflecting stage experience by such individual singers as Robert Tear and Gwynne Howell. Rattle's reading provides a clear-cut contrast with that of Sir Charles Mackerras on the splendid Decca version with the Vienna Philharmonic and a Czech cast. If Mackerras's Janáček style is more angular and abrasive, bringing out the jagged, spiky rhythms and unexpected orchestral colours, Rattle's is more moulded, more immediately persuasive, if less obviously idiomatic.

The English words are splendidly clear, set against a warm, well-balanced recording of the orchestra. Though the EMI booklet is less informative than the exceptionally fine Decca one, the number of CD tracks and their identification are much clearer. The coupling of *Taras Bulba* – taken from Rattle's fine earlier recording with the Philharmonia – is also marginally more generous than the two movements of the so-called *Little Vixen suite* which Mackerras adds.

(i) *From the house of the dead;* (iii) *Mládí* (for wind sextet); (ii; iii) *Říkadla* (for Chamber Ch. & 10 instruments).
*** Decca Dig. 430 375-2 (2) [id.]. (i) Jedlička, Zahradníček, Žídek, Zítek, V. State Op. Ch., VPO, Mackerras; (ii) L. Sinf. Ch.; (iii) L. Sinf., Atherton.

With fine digital recording adding to the glory of the highly distinctive instrumentation, the Decca version of Janáček's last opera outshines even the earlier recordings in Mackerras's series. By rights, this piece – based on Dostoevsky – should be intolerably depressing in operatic form, but in effect, as this magnificent performance amply demonstrates, the mosaic of sharp response, with sudden hysterical joy punctuating even the darkest, most bitter emotions, is consistently uplifting. With one exception the cast is superb, with a range of important Czech singers giving sharply characterized vignettes. The exception is the raw Slavonic singing of the one woman in the cast, Jaroslav Janska as the boy, Aljeja, but even that fails to undermine the intensity of the innocent relationship with the central figure, which provides an emotional anchor for the whole piece. The chamber-music items added for this reissue are both first rate: *Mládí*'s youthful sparkle comes across to excellent effect in the London Sinfonietta's fine version, as does *Říkadla*, a rarity for chamber choir and ten instruments.

Jenůfa (complete).
❀ *** Decca Dig. 414 483-2 (2) [id.]. Söderström, Ochman, Dvorský, Randová, Popp, V. State Op. Ch., VPO, Mackerras.

This is the warmest and most lyrical of Janáček's operas, and it inspires a performance from Mackerras and his team which is deeply sympathetic, strongly dramatic and superbly recorded. After Mackerras's previous Janáček sets, it was natural to choose Elisabeth Söderström for the name-part. Mature as she is, she creates a touching portrait of the girl caught in a family tragedy. The two rival tenors, Peter Dvorský and Wieslav Ochman as the half-brothers Steva and Laca, are both superb; but dominating the whole drama is the Kostelnitchka of Eva Randová. For the first time on record one can register the beauty as well as the power of the writing for this equivocal central figure. Some may resist the idea that she should be made so sympathetic but, particularly on record, the drama is made stronger and more involving.

(i) *The Makropulos affair (Věc Makropulos)*: complete; (ii) *Lachian dances*.
*** Decca 430 372-2 (2) [id.]. (i) Söderström, Dvorský, Blachut, V. State Op. Ch., VPO, Mackerras; (ii) LPO, Huybrechts.

Mackerras and his superb team provide a thrilling new perspective on an opera which is far more than the bizarre dramatic exercise it once seemed, with its weird heroine preserved by magic elixir well past her 300th birthday. In most performances the character of the still beautiful Emilia seems mean beyond any sympathy, but here the radiant Elisabeth Söderström sees it rather differently, presenting from the first a streak of vulnerability. She is not simply malevolent: irritable and impatient rather, no longer an obsessive monster. Framed by richly colourful singing and playing, Söderström amply justifies that view, and Peter Dvorský is superbly fresh and ardent as Gregor. The recording, like others in the series, is of the highest Decca analogue quality. The performance of the *Lachian dances* by the London Philharmonic under the Belgian conductor, François Huybrechts, is highly idiomatic and effective and makes a good bonus.

Osud (complete).
*** EMI Dig. CDC7 49993-2 [Ang. CDC 49993]. Langridge, Field, Harries, Bronder, Kale, Welsh National Op. Ch. & O, Mackerras.

This single-disc recording of Janáček's – most unjustly neglected – opera, richly lyrical, more sustained and less fragmented than his later operas, is not just a valuable rarity but makes an ideal introduction to the composer. It is a piece that was for generations rejected for being unstageable, thanks to the oddities of the libretto; that was until the English National Opera presented it at the Coliseum in London in an unforgettable production by David Pountney. Though this recording, one of the series sponsored by the Peter Moores Foundation, was made with Welsh National Opera forces, its success echoes the ENO production too, with Philip Langridge, as at the Coliseum, superb in the central role of the composer, Zivny, well supported by Helen Field as Mila, the married woman he loves, and by Kathryn Harries as her mother – a far finer cast than was presented on a short-lived Supraphon set. That was done in the original Czech, whereas this performance, following ENO, uses Rodney Blumer's excellent English translation, adding to the immediate impact. Sir Charles Mackerras matches his earlier achievement in the prize-winning series of Janáček opera recordings for Decca, capturing the full gutsiness, passion and impetus of the composer's inspiration, from the exhilarating opening waltz ensemble onwards, a passage that vividly sets the scene in a German spa at the turn of the century. The warmly atmospheric EMI recording, made in Bragnwyn Hall, Swansea, brings out the unusual opulence of the Janáček sound in this work written immediately after *Jenufa*, yet it allows words to come over with fine clarity. With a playing-time of nearly 80 minutes, the single disc comes complete with English libretto and excellent notes.

Joachim, Joseph (1831–1907)

(i) *Violin concerto in the Hungarian manner, Op. 11. Overtures: Hamlet, Op. 4; Henry IV, Op. 7.*
(M) *** Pickwick Dig. MCD 27; *MCC 27.* (i) Elmer Oliveira; LPO, Leon Bottstein.

Joseph Joachim's fame rests as a legendary performer and the dedicatee of the Brahms *Violin concerto*, rather than as a composer. Joachim abandoned composition not long after the *Hungarian Concerto* when he was twenty-three ('Why should one compose while there is a Brahms in the world?'). Nevertheless his concerto is one of the most demanding works written for the instrument in the nineteenth century. Conservative in outlook and indebted to Mendelssohn and Beethoven, it is a very considerable achievement – as, for that matter, is the playing of Elmer Oliveira in this truthful, present and well-balanced recording. The conductor Leon Bottstein also gives committed accounts of the splendid *Henry IV* and *Hamlet Overtures*. An enterprising and rewarding release.

Jolivet, André (1905–74)

(i) *Concertino for trumpet, piano and strings; Trumpet concerto.*
*** Sony Dig. MK 42096 [id.]. Wynton Marsalis, (i) Craig Shepherd, Philh. O, Salonen – TOMASI: *Concerto.* ***

As crossover music goes, this is rather successful, with the brilliant musicianship, dizzy bravura and natural idiomatic feeling of Wynton Marsalis tailor-made for this repertoire. There is not a great deal for Craig Shepherd to do in the duet concertino, but he does it well enough. This is certainly a flamboyant piece – but the solo concerto is the finer work, with the Latin-American dance-rhythms fully laminated to the music itself. The recording is not especially clear, but this does not seem to matter too much, though some ears will detect background hum at times. The CD offers poor value at only 35 minutes.

Chant de Linos.
*** Koch Dig. 3-7016 [id.]. Atlantic Sinf. – JONGEN: *Concert;* DEBUSSY: *Sonata.* ***

The *Chant de Linos* is among the most demanding pieces for flute in the chamber-music repertoire. It was originally composed in 1944 for flute and piano as a competition piece for the Paris Conservatoire, but Jolivet subsequently made this highly effective transcription for flute, violin, viola, cello and harp. It is played with exemplary taste and effortless virtuosity by Bradley Garner and his colleagues of the Atlantic Sinfonietta and is most beautifully recorded. It comes with a poetic and thoughtful account of the Debussy *Trio sonata* and a Jongen rarity.

Jongen, Joseph (1873–1953)

Symphonie concertante, Op. 18.
*** Telarc Dig. CD 80096 [id.]. Murray, San Francisco SO, De Waart – FRANCK: *Fantaisie* etc. ***

Anyone who likes the Saint-Saëns *Third Symphony* should enjoy this. Even if the music is on a lower level of inspiration, the passionate *Lento misterioso* and hugely spectacular closing *Toccata* make a favourable impression at first hearing and wear surprisingly well afterwards. The performance here is undoubtedly persuasive in its verve and commitment, and Michael Murray has all the necessary technique to carry off Jongen's hyperbole with the required panache. He receives excellent support from Edo de Waart and the San Francisco Symphony Orchestra. The huge Ruffatti organ seems custom-built for the occasion and Telarc's engineers capture all the spectacular effects with their usual aplomb. A demonstration disc indeed.

Concert à cinq.
*** Koch Dig. 3-7016-2 [id.]. Atlantic Sinf. – DEBUSSY: *Sonata;* JOLIVET: *Chant de Linos.* ***

The Belgian composer Joseph Jongen was enormously prolific (he reached Opus 241) and self-critical (towards the end of his life he destroyed over 100 of his works). His three-movement *Concert à cinq* for flute, harp and string trio is a civilized piece very much in the post-impressionist style. It remains more pleasing than memorable, though these players do their utmost for it. The record is well worth getting, as it offers an outstandingly sensitive account of the Debussy *Trio sonata* and is beautifully balanced.

Joplin, Scott (1868–1917)

Rags: *Bethena (concert waltz); Cascades rag; Country club (ragtime two-step); Elite syncopations; The Entertainer; Euphonic sounds (A syncopated novelty); Fig leaf rag; Gladiolus rag; Magnetic rag (syncopations classiques); Maple leaf rag; Paragon rag; Pine apple rag; Ragtime dance; Scott Joplin's new rag; Solace (Mexican serenade); Stoptime rag; Weeping willow (ragtime two-step).*
(M) *** Nonesuch Elektra/Warner 7559 79159-2. Joshua Rifkin (piano).

Joshua Rifkin is the pianist whose name has been indelibly associated with the Scott Joplin revival, originally stimulated by the soundtrack music of the very successful film, *The Sting*. His relaxed, cool rhythmic style is at times more subtle than Dick Hyman's more extrovert approach and, although the piano timbre is full, there is a touch of monochrome in the tone colour. The recordings were made in the mid-1970s and are very well transferred to CD. Only four (favourite) numbers here are duplicated on Dick Hyman's RCA CD, so aficionados will undoubtedly want both.

Rags: *A Breeze from Alabama; The Cascades; The Chrysanthemum; Easy winners; Elite syncopations; The Entertainer; Maple leaf rag; Original rags; Palm leaf rag; Peacherine rag; Something doing; The Strenuous life; Sunflower slow drag; Swipesy; The Sycamore.*
(M) *** BMG/RCA GD 87993 [7993-2-RG]. Dick Hyman.

Dick Hyman's playing is first rate. His rhythmic spring (the crisp snap of the main phrase of *Original rags* is a splendid example), clean touch and sensibility in matters of light and shade – without ever trying to present this as concert music – mean that pieces which can easily appear stereotyped remain fresh and spontaneous-sounding throughout. The recording has fine presence; the piano image (not too rich, but not shallow either) seems just right.

Treemonisha (opera: arr. and orch. Schuller): complete.
(M) **(*) DG 435 709-2 (2) [id.]. Balthrop, Allen, Rayam, White, Houston Grand Op. Ch. and O, Schuller.

The tragic story of Scott Joplin's life hinges on his desire to flee from composing the rags which gave him a degree of fame, and to write a full-blown opera. In the end, having completed the score of *Treemonisha*, he managed to sponsor a single performance in an obscure hall in Harlem in 1915, only to be faced with a total flop. He died two years later. Over half a century later, with Joplin's rags suddenly the rage once more, Günther Schuller orchestrated and edited the surviving piano score, and the result was presented on stage in Houston and New York. This well-rehearsed performance on record stems from that live production, and something of a live occasion is conveyed. The deliciously ingenuous score will not appeal to all tastes, with its mixture of choral rags, barber's shop quartets, bits of diluted Gilbert and Sullivan, Lehár and Gershwin, and much that is outrageously corny, but – to some ears – irresistibly so. The story (with libretto by Joplin himself) tells of a black girl who fights with all too ready success against the primitive superstitions of her race. For this to have bitten as it should, one would need a far sharper portrayal of evil. Thus the work has the ethos of the musical rather than of the opera house. But (with the exception of some unlovable singing from Betty Allen as Monisha) the performance and recording are first class and many will find themselves warming to the spontaneity of Joplin's invention.

Josquin des Prés (*c.* 1450–1521)

Motets: *Ave Maria, gratia plena; Ave, nobilissima creatura; Miserere mei, Deus; O bone et dulcissime Jesu; Salve regina; Stabat mater dolorosa; Usquequo, Domine, oblivisceris me.*
*** HM Dig. HMC 901243; *HMC 401243* [id.]. Chapelle Royale Ch., Herreweghe.

A valuable Josquin anthology which gives us the *Miserere*, so much admired by the doyen of Josquin scholars, Edward Lowinsky. The Chapelle Royale comprises some nineteen singers, but they still produce a clean, well-focused sound and benefit from excellent recorded sound. Their account of the expressive *Stabat mater* sounds thicker-textured than the New College forces under Edward Higginbottom, but there is a refreshing sense of commitment and strong feeling. They are well served by the recording engineers.

Antiphons, Motets and Sequences: *Inviolata; Praeter rerum serium; Salve regina; Stabat mater dolorosa; Veni, sancte spiritus; Virgo prudentissima; Virgo salutiferi.*
*** Mer. ECD 84093; *KE 77093* [id.]. New College, Oxford, Ch., Higginbottom.

The Meridian anthology collects some of Josquin's most masterly and eloquent motets in performances of predictable excellence by Edward Higginbottom and the Choir of New College, Oxford. Higginbottom does not shrink from expressive feeling and at the same time secures both purity of tone and clarity of texture. An admirable introduction to Josquin, and an essential acquisition for those who care about this master.

Missa: Faisant regretz; Missa di dadi.
*** O-L Dig. 411 937-2 [id.]. Medieval Ens. of London, Peter and Timothy Davies.

The two Josquin Masses recorded here are both new to the catalogue; both are parody Masses based on English music of the period. The *Missa: Faisant regretz* acquires its name from the fact that its four-note cantus firmus occurs on the words, 'Faisant regretz', in the chanson *Tout a par moy*. They are both ingenious works and, more to the point, very beautiful, particularly when sung with such dedication and feeling as here. Nine singers are used for this recording, the number that would have been available in an average-size choir of one of the smaller religious establishments before the 1480s, the last decade when these Masses could have been composed. The Medieval Ensemble of London sing superbly; they not only blend perfectly but are blessed with perfect intonation. This deserves the strongest recommendation to all with an interest in this period.

Missa – L'homme armé super voces musicales.
*** DG 415 293-2 [id.]. Pro Cantione Antiqua, Bruno Turner – OCKEGHEM: *Missa pro defunctis.* ***

This Mass on the *L'homme armé* theme is both one of the most celebrated of all Mass settings based on this secular melody and at the same time one of Josquin's most masterly and admired works. It was written in the late 1480s or early '90s and is called *super voces musicales* to distinguish it from his *Missa L'homme armé in sexti toni* (in the sixth mode). Jeremy Noble's edition is used in the present (1977) performance, which must be numbered among the very finest accounts not only of a Josquin but of any Renaissance Mass to have appeared on record. On CD, the transparency of each strand in the vocal texture is wonderfully clear and the singers are astonishingly present. An outstanding issue.

Missa Pange lingua.
**(*) HM Dig. HMC 901239 [id.]. Clément Janequin Ens.

Missa Pange lingua; Missa La sol fa re mi.
*** Gimell Dig. CDGIM 009; *1585T-09* [id.]. Tallis Scholars, Peter Phillips.

The Gimell recording of the *Missa Pange lingua* has collected superlatives on all counts and was voted record of the year in the *Gramophone* magazine's 1987 awards. The tone the Tallis Scholars produce is perfectly blended, each line being firmly defined and yet beautifully integrated into the whole sound-picture. Their recording, made in the Chapel of Merton College, Oxford, is first class, the best of the *Missa Pange lingua* and the first of the ingenious *Missa La sol fa re mi*. Not to be missed.

The Clément Janequin Ensemble also can hardly be flawed. They use eight singers but also make considerable use of solo voices. The Mass is interspersed with chant appropriate to the Feast of Corpus Christi, sung by the Organum Ensemble under Marcel Peres; CD players can be programmed to omit some or all of these bands – but, even so, it puts rival versions at something of an advantage when they can accommodate another Mass.

Kabalevsky, Dmitri (1904–87)

Cello concerto No. 1 in G min.
*** Sony Dig. MK 37840 [id.]. Yo-Yo Ma, Phd. O, Ormandy – SHOSTAKOVICH: *Cello concerto No. 1.* ***

Both of Kabalevsky's *Cello concertos* have been recorded before, though neither with such persuasive force as Yo-Yo Ma brings to the *First.* This is an amiable piece and is well crafted and pleasing. The excellence of the performance is matched by a fine recording which adds considerably to the refinement and presence of the sound, and its vividness is such as to seem to add stature to the music itself.

Cello concerto No. 2, Op. 77.
*** Chan. Dig. CHAN 8579; *ABTD 1273* [id.]. Wallfisch, LPO, Thomson – GLAZUNOV: *Chant du ménestrel;* KHACHATURIAN: *Concerto.* ***
*** Virgin Dig. VC7 90811-2; *VC 790811-4* [id.]. Isserlis, LPO, Litton – PROKOFIEV: *Concertino; Cello sonata.* ***

The *Second* is the darker of the two *Cello concertos* and touches on a deeper vein of feeling than one encounters in, say, his more familiar *Second Symphony.* It is played eloquently – and with the greatest virtuosity – by Rafael Wallfisch, who is well supported by Bryden Thomson and the LPO. Excellent recording too.

Steven Isserlis on Virgin gives as compelling and ardent an account of the *Concerto* as does Wallfisch on Chandos and, since the LPO play as well for Andrew Litton as they did for Bryden Thomson, there is little to choose between them. As far as recorded sound is concerned, both are impressive: perhaps Virgin use a slightly less resonant acoustic. The coupling will probably settle matters for most collectors; Isserlis offers two rarities, both new to CD.

Violin concerto in C, Op. 48.
*** Chan. Dig. CHAN 8918; *ABTD 1519* [id.]. Lydia Mordkovitch, SNO, Järvi - KHACHATURIAN: *Violin concerto.* ***
(**) Chant du Monde mono LDC 278883 [id.]. David Oistrakh, USSR Nat. O, composer – KHACHATURIAN: *Violin concerto.* *** ❀

Kabalevsky's *Violin concerto* comes from 1948 and is designed for a young audience. It is slight, lasting no more than a quarter of an hour, but it has a particularly attractive slow movement with a haunting, folk-like idea, perhaps prompted by Zhdanov's decree from earlier that year advocating a populist style. It is most persuasively presented by these artists. Throughout, Lydia Mordkovitch plays with great flair and aplomb and is given first-class Chandos recording.

David Oistrakh's 1955 mono recording is in most ways definitive, with the composer helping to make the delightfully atmospheric slow movement quite memorable. Oistrakh's clean articulation and sparkle in the finale are also outstanding – and it is a pity that so much allowance has to be made for the sound, which is papery, with a shrill solo image and whistly orchestral strings. At a modest volume level, with a top cut, it is listenable, however, and the playing itself is highly rewarding.

The Comedians (suite), *Op. 26.*
(M) *** EMI Dig. CDD7 63893 [id.]. Bav. State O, Sawallisch (with Concert of Russian music ***).

Kabalevsky's suite has a certain brashness in its scoring at times, but the polished playing of the Bavarian State Orchestra adds a touch of elegance and these ten charming vignettes, full of colour and vitality, are made to sound very entertaining indeed. The most famous is the exuberant *Galop*, a knockabout circus piece, complete with xylophone; but the charming *Intermezzo* and the gentle *Little lyrical scene* are just as memorable in their contrasting restraint, while the Scherzo is worthy of Prokofiev. First-class sound, with plenty of ambience, so that the music can be boisterous without vulgarity.

Kalinnikov, Vasily (1866–1901)

Intermezzos Nos. 1 in F sharp min.; 2 in G.
*** Chan. Dig. CHAN 8614; *ABTD 1303* [id.]. SNO, Järvi – RACHMANINOV: *Symphony No. 3.* ***

These two colourful *Intermezzos* with a flavour of Borodin are charming examples of Kalinnikov's work, an attractive if hardly generous fill-up for Järvi's red-blooded account of Rachmaninov's *Third Symphony*.

Symphony No. 1 in G min.
*** Chan. Dig. CHAN 8611; *ABTD 1299* [id.]. SNO, Järvi – GLAZUNOV: *The Sea; Spring.* ***

Some of the fame of Kalinnikov's *First Symphony* must be attributed to the second theme of the first movement which is irresistible and, once heard, is difficult to get out of your head. The symphony contains something akin to the flow and natural lyricism of Borodin, and the second movement has something of the atmosphere and character of early Rachmaninov or his almost exact contemporary, Glazunov. Neeme Järvi and the Scottish National Orchestra seem fired with enthusiasm for this appealing work, and the engineers serve them admirably. Strongly recommended.

Symphony No. 2 in A; The Cedar and the palm; Overture: Tsar Boris.
*** Chan. Dig. CHAN 8805; *ABTD 1433* [id.]. SNO, Järvi.

The *Second Symphony*, though not quite as appealing as No. 1, is played by the Scottish orchestra under Neeme Järvi with enthusiasm and commitment, and the Chandos recording is in the demonstration class. The Tsar to whom the *Overture* alludes is the one celebrated by both Pushkin and Mussorgsky. *The Cedar and the palm* was Kalinnikov's last piece and was inspired by Heine's, which must have enjoyed a vogue at the turn of the century, as Sibelius also planned a work inspired by it. Both these novelties are worth having on disc.

Kern, Jerome (1885–1945)

Showboat (complete recording of original score).
❀ *** EMI Dig. CD-RIVER 1 (3) [Ang. A23 49108]. Von Stade, Hadley, Hubbard, O'Hara, Garrison, Burns, Stratas, Amb. Ch., L. Sinf., John McGlinn.

In faithfully following the original score, this superb set at last does justice to a musical of the 1920s which is both a landmark in the history of Broadway and musically a work of strength and imagination hardly less significant than Gershwin's *Porgy and Bess* of a decade later. Even with spoken scenes cut and dialogue drastically pruned, the recording lasts for almost four hours – and that includes a fascinating appendix of variants and extra items alone lasting over an hour. The original, extended versions of important scenes are included, as well as various numbers written for later productions. In the modern 'crossover' manner, this recording is operatically cast, but with far more concern for idiomatic performance than usual. As the heroine, Magnolia – who dauntingly has to age 37 years between beginning and end – Frederica von Stade gives a meltingly beautiful performance, totally in style, bringing out the beauty and imagination of Kern's melodies, regularly heightened by wide intervals to make those of most of his Broadway rivals seem flat. The first half-hour alone brings a clutch of hit numbers – *Make believe, Ol' man river* and *Can't help loving that man* among them – which one would be lucky to find in a whole season of Broadway musicals today. The London Sinfonietta play with tremendous zest and feeling for the idiom, while tuba bass and banjo regularly add spice to the ensemble; the Ambrosian Chorus sings with joyful brightness and some impeccable American accents. Opposite von Stade, Jerry Hadley makes a winning Ravenal, and Teresa Stratas is charming as Julie, giving a heartfelt performance of the haunting number, *Bill* (words by P. G. Wodehouse). Above all, the magnificent black bass, Bruce Hubbard, sings *Ol' man river* and its many reprises with a firm resonance to have you recalling the wonderful example of Paul Robeson, but for once without hankering after the past. The cast of actors is also distinguished, with Lillian Gish, a star since her first appearance on the silent screen, as an old lady on the levee, right at the end. Beautifully recorded to bring out the piece's dramatic as well as its musical qualities, this is a heart-warming issue.

Khachaturian, Aram (1903–78)

Cello concerto.
*** Chan. Dig. CHAN 8579; *ABTD 1273* [id.]. Wallfisch, LPO, Thomson – GLAZUNOV: *Chant du ménestrel;* KABALEVSKY: *Cello concerto No.2.* ***

The *Cello concerto* is a post-war work, dating from 1946, and although it is true that there are some imaginative moments and expert handling of the orchestra, it is not one of Khachaturian's strongest pieces. Rafael Wallfisch plays with total commitment and has the benefit of excellent and sympathetic support from the LPO under Bryden Thomson. The recording is of the usual high standard we have come to expect from Chandos.

Flute concerto (arr. Rampal/Galway); *Gayaneh: Sabre dance. Masquerade: Waltz. Spartacus: Adagio of Spartacus and Phrygia.*
*** BMG/RCA Dig. RD 87010; *RK 87010.* Galway, RPO, Myung-Whun Chung.

Khachaturian's *Flute concerto* is a transcription of the *Violin concerto* made by Jean-Pierre Rampal, with the composer's blessing. Galway has prepared his own edition of the solo part 'which goes even further in its attempts to adapt the solo line to the characteristics of the flute'. He has the advantage of a modern digital recording, but the resonant acoustic of Watford Town Hall tends to coarsen the orchestral tuttis very slightly, especially the big fortissimo flare-up towards the end of the slow movement, which is fierce. Needless to say, the solo playing is peerless; if in the finale even Galway cannot match the effect Oistrakh makes with his violin, the ready bravura is sparklingly infectious. As encores, he offers three of Khachaturian's most famous melodies. They are marvellously played, with the *Sabre dance* elegant rather than boisterously noisy.

Piano concerto in D flat.
(***) Olympia mono OCD 236 [id.]. Moura Lympany, LPO, Fistoulari – SAINT-SAËNS: *Piano concerto No. 2.* (**(*))

Moura Lympany gave Khachaturian's *Piano concerto* its London première in 1940, and in 1952 she made the present mono recording for Decca with Fistoulari, who was also the conductor of the wartime London première of the *Violin concerto.* The *Piano concerto* is by no means as fine a work but, for all its moments of cheapness, it has an inherent vitality which has kept it in the record catalogues. The Lympany/Fistoulari account has a dash, sparkle and bravura which have never been matched on record since: even the Flexatone warbling in the *Andante* is made to seem convincing, and Khachaturian's melancholy Armenian melodies are given their full character. The recording, first rate in its day, now sounds curiously cavernous, though perfectly acceptable; the sheer élan of the performance soon makes one forget the aural deficiencies.

(i) *Piano concerto in D flat; Gayaneh* (ballet) *suite; Masquerade: suite.*
**(*) Chan. Dig. CHAN 8542; *ABTD 1250* [id.]. (i) Orbelian, SNO, Järvi.

The Chandos recording is splendid technically, well up to the standards of the house. Constantin Orbelian, an Armenian by birth, plays brilliantly and Järvi achieves much attractive lyrical detail. He scores in the slow movement by making the most of the curious whistly overtones of the flexitone, used with great aplomb here. The bass clarinet, too, drools sinuously at the end. Overall it is a spacious account, and though the finale has plenty of gusto, the music-making seems just a shade too easy-going in the first movement. The couplings, sumptuously played, are both generous and appealing, especially *Masquerade* – an attractively romantic account of this rather engaging music. Four famous numbers are included from *Gayaneh*, among the finest music Khachaturian ever wrote, and they are played with considerable panache.

Violin concerto in D min.
❀ *** Chant du Monde LDC 278883 [Mobile Fidelity MFCD 899 with SIBELIUS: *Concerto*]. David Oistrakh, USSR RSO, composer – KABALEVSKY: *Violin concerto.* (**)

*** Chan. Dig. CHAN 8918; *ABTD 1519* [id.]. Lydia Mordkovitch, SNO, Järvi - KABALEVSKY: *Violin concerto.* ***

David Oistrakh, for whom the *Concerto* was written, gave the work its première, and is its dedicatee. He is peerless in its performance, not only in projecting its very Russian bravura, but also in his melting phrasing and timbre in the sinuous secondary theme of the first movement, which returns in the finale, and in the equally haunting melody of the *Andante*. Indeed this quite marvellous performance is unlikely ever to be surpassed. The composer, clearly inspired by the expressive response of his soloist, creates a rapt degree of tension in the slow movement and affectionately caresses the Armenian colour and detail in the very atmospheric orchestral accompaniment. The finale has an irresistible exhilaration, and the return of the big tune on the G string is heart-warming. The (1970) Russian recording is warm and very well balanced, especially in its relationship of soloist with orchestra. The acoustic is resonant in the right way – there is bloom but no muddiness or fierceness. This must be listed among the all too few great stereo recordings in which the composer has been able to participate. The *Concerto* is coupled differently in the USA.

Among more recent performances of this attractively inventive concerto, Lydia Mordkovitch is probably the most competitive. She gives a thoroughly committed account of this popular score and receives sensitive support from Neeme Järvi and the Scottish National Orchestra. She plays with real abandon and fire, and Chandos balance her and the orchestra in a thoroughly realistic perspective. This new version has far superior sound to Oistrakh on Chant du Monde.

Gayaneh (ballet): *suite.*
(B) *** DG Compact Classics 413 155-2 (2) [id.]; *413 155-4.* Leningrad PO, Rozhdestvensky – RIMSKY-KORSAKOV: *Scheherazade* **(*); STRAVINSKY: *Firebird suite* *** (CD only: GLINKA: *Overtures* *(*)).

Gayaneh (ballet): *suite; Masquerade: suite; Spartacus* (ballet): *suite.*
(*) ASV Dig. CDDCA 773; *ZCDCA 773.* Armenian PO, Tjeknavorian – IPPOLITOV-IVANOV: *Caucasian sketches.* *

Gayaneh: suite; Spartacus: suite.
(M) **(*) Decca 417 737-2 [id.]. VPO, composer – PROKOFIEV: *Romeo and Juliet.* ***

No one does the *Sabre dance* like the Russians, and with Rozhdestvensky it makes a sensational opening, exploding into the room at the end of Stravinsky's *Firebird suite.* The performance overall combines excitement with panache, and the originally rather fierce recording has been greatly improved in the CD transfer. The cassette sounds well, too. Rozhdestvensky includes the eight best numbers from the ballet.

The composer's own first selection on Decca was recorded in 1962 and offers five items from *Gayaneh* and four from *Spartacus*, coupled to an intelligent selection from Maazel's complete Cleveland set of Prokofiev's *Romeo and Juliet*, dating from a decade later. Khachaturian achieves a brilliant response from the VPO and everything is most vivid, notably the famous *Adagio* from *Spartacus*, which is both expansive and passionate. It is a pity that the Decca remastering process has brought everything into such strong focus; the presence of the sound certainly makes an impact, but the massed violins now have an added edge and boldness of attack, at the expense of their richness of timbre.

The Armenians clearly relish the explosive energy of this music: the *Sabre dancers* burst into the room, closely pursued by the obviously wildly desirous *Young maidens*, and hard on their heels come the Mountaineers, as if the Cossack cavalry were not far behind. Then we have a brief respite with the charming *Lullaby*, before the *Lezghinka* brings yet another burst of slavic fervour. The *Masquerade suite* relies rather more on charm for its appeal, but Tjeknavorian and his players bring a determined gusto, even to the *Waltz* and certainly to the ebullient closing *Galop*. Then the vibrant Spartacus and his ardent lover Phrygia come on stage with a great flair of passion in a melody that is justly famous. One wishes the recording, which is extremely vivid, were more sumptuous here, but for the most part its burnished primary colours suit the dynamic orchestral style.

Spartacus (ballet): *suites Nos. 1–3.*
*** Chan. Dig. CHAN 8927; *ABTD 1529* [id.]. SNO, Neeme Järvi.

The ripe lushness of Khachaturian's scoring in *Spartacus* narrowly skirts vulgarity. Yet Shostakovich admired the work, and its vitality is undeniable. The most famous number, and rightly so, is the splendidly languorous tune for the *Adagio of Spartacus and Phrygia* (long famous as the theme for BBC TV's *Onedin Line* series); it is presented here with splendid opulence and ardour. The melody returns later, more delicately, in Phrygia's parting scene. Other memorable items are the jolly *Variations of of Aegina*, and there is plenty of gusto in the music for the Merchants and Pirates, while the Gaditianian maidens and the *Dance of the Egyptian girl* bring an exotically decadent, sensuous allure. Järvi and the SNO clearly enjoy the music's tunefulness and primitive vigour, while the warmly resonant acoustics of Glasgow's Henry Wood Hall bring properly sumptuous orchestral textures, smoothing over the moments of crudeness without losing the Armenian colouristic vividness.

Knipper, Lev (1898–1974)

(i) *Concert poem for cello and orchestra; Sinfonietta for strings.*
** Olympia OCD 163 [id.]. (i) Shakhovskaya; Moscow Conservatoire CO, Teryan – MIASKOVSKY: *Symphony No. 7.* **

Lev Knipper was a respected figure in Soviet music and a pupil of Glière in Moscow. This *Sinfonietta* comes from 1953 and is well-fashioned but rather anonymous music, albeit with some moments of beauty. The *Concert poem* opens strikingly and is played magnificently, but is not strongly individual either. The recording is rather forwardly balanced.

Knussen, Oliver (born 1952)

Symphony No. 3.
*** ASV Dig. CDRPO 8023; *ZCRPO 8023* [id.]. RPO, Ashkenazy – BRITTEN: *Serenade;* WALTON: *Symphony No. 2.* ***

This performance of Knussen's powerfully concentrated symphony was recorded live in concerts which took place when Ashkenazy returned to Russia after many years of exile in the West. Though, inevitably, ensemble does not always have pin-point precision in a live performance of a complex score, the warmth of communication is enhanced. Next to the Philharmonia players in Tilson Thomas's studio recording for Unicorn Kanchana, the RPO sounds liberated, bringing out the mystery of the opening far more intensely and regularly revealing the emotional thrust of Knussen's beautiful and complex writing. More expansive in manner, it is a performance to recommend to anyone who as yet does not know this young composer's formidable but deeply rewarding music. This closely argued one-movement symphony, lasting in this performance 16½ minutes, is the work which most clearly reveals his weight as a composer.

Where the Wild Things are (complete).
*** Unicorn Dig. DKPCD 9044; *DKPC 9044* [id.]. Rosemary Hardy, Mary King, Herrington, Richardson, Rhys-Williams, Gallacher, L. Sinf., composer.

Oliver Knussen has devised a one-act opera that beautifully matches the grotesque fantasy of Maurice Sendak's children's book of the same name, with its gigantic monsters or Wild Things which prove to have hearts of gold and make the naughty boy, Max, their king. The record presents the piece with all the bite and energy of a live performance. It helped that the sessions took place immediately after a series of stage performances. The final rumpus music, which Knussen managed to complete only after the rest, here feels like the culmination intended. Rosemary Hardy makes a superb Max, not just accurate but giving a convincing portrait of the naughty child with little or no archness. Mary King sings warmly in the small part of the Mother. The brilliant recording vividly conveys a sense of presence and space.

Kodály, Zoltán (1882–1967)

(i) *Concerto for orchestra; Summer evening;* (ii) *Háry János: suite.*
(M) **(*) DG 427 408-2. (i) Budapest PO, composer; (ii) Berlin RSO, Fricsay.

Kodály's *Concerto for orchestra* does not set out to rival the Bartók *Concerto*, but in its own way it is attractive and easy to listen to. *Summer evening*, a pleasantly rhapsodic pastoral piece, dates from ten years earlier. Kodály's own recordings come from 1960 and originally sounded recessed, with little immediacy of impact. The improvement on CD is dramatic and the performances of both works sound much more vital, even if Kodály does not display the fervour and intensity which Fricsay brings to the *Háry János suite* (recorded a year later), with *The Battle and defeat of Napoleon* made very dramatic indeed. The Berlin Radio orchestra play splendidly and the sound is sparkling and clear.

Dances of Galánta.
*** Ph. 416 378-2 [id.]. Concg. O, Zinman – BARTÓK: *Concerto for 2 Pianos, percussion & celesta.* ***

David Zinman offers an attractively vivid performance of the *Dances of Galánta.* Although this is not a very generous coupling for the Bartók *Concerto*, the recording is very much in the demonstration class. Philips experimentally used simple microphone techniques, and the result brings an uncanny sense of presence and realism, indeed of sitting in the concert hall.

(i) *Dances of Galánta; Dances of Marosszék;* (ii) *Háry János: suite.*
(M) *** Mercury 432 005-2 [id.]. (i) Philharmonia Hungarica; (ii) Minneapolis SO, Dorati – BARTÓK: *Hungarian sketches* etc. ***

Dances of Galánta; Dances of Marosszék; Háry János suite; Variations on a Hungarian folksong (The Peacock).
(M) *** Decca 425 034-2; *425 034-4* [id.]. Philharmonia Hungarica, Dorati.

Dances of Galánta; Háry János: suite.
*** Delos Dig. DE 3083 [id.]. Seattle SO, Garard Schwarz – BARTÓK: *Miraculous Mandarin.* **(*)

From sneeze to finale, the Minneapolis orchestral playing in the *Háry János suite* is crisp and vigorous; the excellent 1956 Mercury stereo, while providing well-integrated tuttis, also gives simple separation for the solos and delicate highlighting of the more subtle percussion effects, especially the cimbalom. Dorati went on to record the other two sets of dances with the Philharmonia Hungarica in 1958. The playing of the woodwind soloists in the slow dances is intoxicatingly seductive, and the power and punch of the climaxes come over with real Mercury fidelity. An outstanding disc, since the Bartók couplings are equally successful.

The Philharmonia Hungarica performances of the *Galánta dances* and the familiar *Háry János suite* are also first class, and the *Peacock variations* – luxuriantly extended, highly enjoyable and deserving of greater popularity – are equally fine. While the older, Mercury performances have a very special electricity of their own, the 1973 Decca recording is more modern and is of vintage quality; many collectors will also prefer to have the *Peacock variations* rather than the Mercury Bartók alternative couplings. The Decca disc plays for nearly 76 minutes.

The Seattle Symphony Orchestra play Kodály's music with great vividness and warmth. The *Háry János suite* is more spaciously romantic in feeling than some versions – helped by the rich acoustics of Seattle Opera House – and there is less surface glitter. But *The Battle and defeat of Napoleon* and the *Entrance of the Emperor and his Court* have all the necessary mock-drama and spectacle, and it is good to hear the cimbalom again balanced so effectively within the orchestra. The *Galánta dances* have splendid dash. The recording is outstandingly real, yet very naturally balanced.

Háry János suite.
(BB) *** Naxos Dig. 8.550142; *4550142* [id.]. Hungarian State O, Mátyás Antal (with Concert: *'Hungarian festival'* ***).
(M) *** EMI Dig. CDD7 63900-2 [id.]. LPO, Tennstedt – DVOŘÁK: *Symphony No. 9.* **(*)
(M) (***) BMG/RCA mono GD 60279; *GK 60279* [60279-2-RG; *60279-4-RG*]. NBC SO, Toscanini – DVOŘÁK: *Symphony No. 9* (***); SMETANA: *Má Vlast: Vltava.* (**)

The Hungarian performance of the *Háry János suite* is wonderfully vivid, with the cimbalom – perfectly balanced within the orchestra – particularly telling. The grotesque elements of *The Battle and defeat of Napoleon* are pungently and wittily characterized and the *Entrance of the Emperor and his Court* also has an ironical sense of spectacle. The brilliant digital sound adds to the vitality and projection of the music-making, yet the lyrical music is played most tenderly.

Tennstedt might seem an unlikely conductor for Kodály's sharply characterized folk-based score, but his performance has sympathy as well as power and brilliance, drawing out the romantic warmth of the *Intermezzo.* Digital sound of the fullest, richest EMI vintage.

There is nothing relaxed about Toscanini's view of *Háry János*. He seems not to realize that a joke is involved; but the intensity of the performance gives the music a new and bigger scale, whether appropriate or not.

(Unaccompanied) *Cello sonata, Op. 8;* (i) *Duo for violin and cello.*
*** Delos D/CD 1015 [id.]. Janos Starker, (i) Josef Gingold.

Starker's version, his fourth, was made in 1970 in Japan. When, not long before the composer's death, Kodály heard him playing it, he apparently said: 'If you correct the ritard in the third movement, it will be the Bible performance.' To judge from this record, his prediction was not far from the truth. The recording is made in a smaller studio than is perhaps ideal, though it has a certain nostalgic attraction since it calls to mind the somewhat boxy sound of his first LP. But generally the sound is good; the *Duo*, impressively played by Starker and Josef Gingold, is made in a slightly more open acoustic. There is a small makeweight in the form of Starker's own arrangement of the Bottermund *Paganini variations*. Authoritative and eloquent playing throughout.

String quartets Nos. 1 and 2.
**(*) Hung. Dig. HCD 12362 [id.]. Kodály Qt.

String quartet No. 2, Op. 10.
*** DG Dig. 419 601-2 [id.]. Hagen Qt – DVOŘÁK: *String quartet No. 12* etc. ***

The two performances from this eponymous quartet make an excellent coupling, warmly committed and spontaneous. Though the playing is not as refined as from the most polished Hungarian quartet groups, the natural understanding brings out the sharply contrasted character of the two works very convincingly. Much the more ambitious and more passionate is the *First*, Kodály's Op. 2, written in 1909; in its luxuriant span it inhabits very much the same world as Bartók's *First Quartet* of the same period, yearningly lyrical but bitingly dramatic too, with its characteristic folk element. The *Second Quartet* of 1918 is altogether simpler and less intense, a delightful, compact piece, which reveals Kodály's own character more clearly, very different from that of his close colleague. Excellent, immediate recording.

The Hagen give a marvellously committed and beautifully controlled performance of the *Second* – indeed as quartet playing it would be difficult to surpass. They might strike some collectors as almost too polished – Hungarian peasants in their best Sunday suits, rather than in everyday attire – but, in range of dynamic response and sheer beauty of sound, this is thrilling playing and welcome advocacy of a neglected but masterly piece. The recording is well balanced and admirably present.

Budavári Te Deum; Missa brevis.
*** Hung. HCD 11397-2 [id.]. Andor, Ekert, Makkay, Mohácsi, Szirmay, Réti, Gregor, Hungarian R. & TV Ch., Budapest SO, Ferencsik.

The *Budavári Te Deum* is predictably nationalist in feeling. The *Missa brevis* is also one of Kodály's strongest works, almost comparable in stature to the *Psalmus Hungaricus*. The performances first appeared on record in the early 1970s but sound remarkably fresh in their CD incarnation. The singing is accurate and sensitive, and the playing of the Budapest orchestra under Ferencsik absolutely first class.

Háry János (musical numbers only).
**(*) Hung. HCD 12837/8-2 [id.]. Sólyom-Nagy, Takács, Sudlik, Póka, Mésozöly, Gregor, Palcsó, Hungarian R. & TV Children's Ch., Hungarian State Op. Ch. and O, Ferencsik.

For the CD transfer the dialogue has been cut out, which means there is no dramatic continuity but, when Kodály's score is so colourful, the piece becomes a rich chocolate-box of delights. Ferencsik's performance with Hungarian singers and players is committedly idiomatic, with strong singing, not always ideally well characterized but very stylish, from some of the most distinguished principals of the Budapest Opera.

(i) *Hymn of Zrinyi;* (ii) *Psalmus Hungaricus.*
(M) *** Decca 421 810-2 (2). (i) Luxon, Brighton Festival Ch., Heltay; (ii) Kozma, Brighton Festival Ch., Wandsworth School Boys' Ch., LSO, Kertész – DVOŘÁK: *Requiem.* ***

Psalmus Hungaricus is Kodály's most vital choral work, and this Decca version comes as close to an ideal performance as one is likely to get. Here, with a chorus trained by a Hungarian musician, the results are electrifying, and the recording is outstandingly brilliant too. The light tenor tone of Lajos Kozma is not ideal for the solo part, but again the authentic Hungarian touch helps. The *Hymn of Zrinyi*, for unaccompanied chorus and baritone solo, celebrates a Magyar hero, and Heltay is persuasive. With first-class remastered sound, this generous coupling with Dvořák is strongly recommended.

(i; ii; v) *Missa brevis;* (ii; v) *Pange lingua;* (iii) *Psalmus Hungaricus;* (iv; v) *Psalm 114.*
❀ (M) *** Decca 433 080-2 [id.]. Brighton Festival Ch. with (i) Gale, Le Sage, Francis, Hodgson, Caley, Rippon; (ii) Bowers-Broadbent (organ); (iii) Kozma, Wandsworth School Boys' Ch., LSO, Kertész; (iv) Weir (organ); (v) cond. Heltay.

This splendid collection essentially celebrates the – one can hardly say unsung, but certainly little-known – work of the Hungarian chorus master of the Brighton Festival Chorus, László Heltay. He directs all the music except the *Psalmus Hungaricus*, which is splendidly vibrant in the hands of István Kertész and there is no doubt that Heltay's meticulous training contributed to the fluency of that outstanding performance, idiomatically presented in Hungarian. Here it is ideally coupled with other fine choral works of Kodály. The *Missa brevis* is literally a short setting of the Mass, not one which omits the *Credo*. The *Pange lingua* is a more searching piece, sung here with glorious tone and great intensity. The short setting of *Psalm 114*, from the Geneva Psalter, is also very moving and shows Kodály's relatively gentle art at its most persuasive. Even more than the other two works, it depends for its interest almost as much on the organ as on the choir, and here Gillian Weir makes an impressive contribution. A highly rewarding 70-minute collection, given vintage Decca sound from the mid- to late 1970s. It was recorded in the Kingsway Hall with Christopher Raeburn and Kenneth Wilkinson in charge, and in its CD transfer still offers demonstration quality.

Koechlin, Charles (1867–1961)

Les Bandar-log (symphonic poem), *Op. 176.*
(M) *** EMI CDM7 63948-2 [id.]. BBC SO, Dorati – BOULEZ: *Le soleil des eaux;* MESSIAEN: *Chronochromie* etc. ***

Les Bandar-log is a symphonic poem based on the Kipling story, but used to satirize the vagaries of twentieth-century composers. Among his monkey tribe, Koechlin finds sham Debussians, sham Schoenbergians and sham neo-classicists; after illustrations from each, the spirit of the forest responds with inspired and beautiful working of the main themes. Koechlin – long neglected outside France – accomplishes his plan with fluent mastery and the score is aurally fascinating, especially in a performance as finely played and dedicated as this and with a 1964 recording which in its CD transfer approaches the demonstration class.

Kokkonen, Joonas (born 1921)

(i) *Cello concerto; Symphonic sketches; Symphony No. 4.*
*** BIS Dig. CD 468 [id.]. (i) Torleif Thedéen, Lahti SO, Osmo Vänskä.

Kokkonen is the leading composer of the older generation in Finland; this is the first CD in a project to record all his orchestral works. The *Fourth Symphony* is the strongest work here: its ideas are symphonic, its structure organic and its atmosphere powerful. The *Cello concerto* is a lyrical piece, very accessible – indeed some may find it insufficiently astringent (there is a slightly sanctimonious streak to the composer). The Swedish cellist, Torleif Thedéen, still in his twenties, gives a performance of great restraint, mastery and sensitivity. Good orchestral playing and recording.

(i) *Cello concerto;* (ii) *Symphony No. 3;* (iii) *Cello sonata.*
(M) **(*) Finlandia FACD 027 [id.]. (i; iii) Noras; (i) Helsinki PO, Freeman; (ii) Finnish RSO, Berglund; (iii) Heinonen.

Kokkonen is perhaps less well established outside his native Finland than Aulis Sallinen but he enjoys the status of a national figure there. To mark his seventieth birthday, BIS have recently embarked on a project to record his complete works which reveal him as a fastidious craftsman and a composer of integrity. There is precious little to choose between Arto Noras's version of the *Cello concerto* and that of the young Swedish cellist, Torleif Thedéen; both play with aristocratic finesse and convey the composer's intentions with admirable fidelity; both were recorded in close collaboration with the composer, though Thedéen on BIS has the advantage of digital recording. Paavo Berglund's excellent recording of the *Third Symphony* was made in the early 1970s and briefly appeared on Decca in the UK. It was this work that served to put the composer on the musical map outside Finland. This Finlandia record has the advantage of economy, but perhaps the BIS record coupling the concerto, the *Fourth Symphony* (1971) and the *Symphonic sketches* (1968) makes the better introduction if you want to represent this composer in your collection in good modern recordings.

(i) *Sinfonia da camera; Il paesaggio* ; (ii) *'... durch einen Spiegel...'* (iii) *Wind quintet.*
*** BIS Dig. CD 528 [id.]. (i; ii) Lahti SO, (i) Vänskä; (iii) Söderblom; (ii) with Tiensuu; (iii) Lahti Sinf. Wind Quintet.

Those coming new to Kokkonen's musical idiom, should try the pretentiously titled but resourceful and imaginative *'... durch einen Spiegel ...'*, subtitled *Metamorphosis* for twelve strings and harpsichord. The title actually refers to 1 Corinthians 13:xii: 'For now we see in a mirror dimly', and alludes to the kind of old mirrors Kokkonen remembered from his youth with their silver backing so poor that one could make out what was on the other side. There are reminders of Ligeti and perhaps Frank Martin but some rewardingly individual sonorities. *Il paessaggio* (1987) is an evocative landscape study and the earlier *Wind quintet* (1971–3) is a lively piece. The early *Sinfonia da camera* is grey general-purpose modern music deriving from Bartókian–Hindemithian roots. Very good performances and splendid recording.

Symphony No. 1; Music for string orchestra; (i) *The Hades of the birds* (song-cycle).
*** BIS Dig. CD 485 [id.]. Lahti SO, Söderblom; (i) Monica Groop.

All three pieces collected here come from the beginning of Kokkonen's career; the *Music for string orchestra* (1957) is a rather powerful piece lasting almost half-an-hour, well-wrought and its invention finely sustained if slightly anonymous. The idiom stems from Hindemith, Bartók and Blomdahl, and the colourings are dark. Söderblom's recording supersedes the rival Finlandia account coupled with the *Sinfonia da camera* made in the early 1980s. *The Hades of the birds* (1958) is a short song-cycle, which shows Monica Groop's talents to strong effect (some may remember her as the 1989 'Cardiff Singer of the World') but it is the *First Symphony* (1958–60) which is the strongest piece on the disc. It is serious in purpose and as far as the orchestra is concerned shows considerable mastery of colour.

Symphony No. 2; Inauguratio; Erekhtheion (cantata); *The Last temptations* (opera): *Interludes.*
**(*) BIS Dig. CD 498 [id.]. Vihavainen, Grönroos, Akateeminen Laulu Ch., Lahti SO, Vanska.

Although he usually turns away from one medium or genre after completing a work, Kokkonen composed his *Second Symphony* (1960–61) almost immediately after the *First*. It is a work of some eloquence and its invention has a certain freshness and quality, even if it remains ultimately unmemorable. The interludes from his opera, *The Last temptations*, make a strong impression. Not an essential purchase for admirers of this composer.

Symphony No. 3; (i) *Opus sonorum;* (ii) *Requiem.*
*** BIS Dig. CD 508 [id.]. Lahti SO, Söderblom; (i) with Ilkka Sivonen; (ii) Iskoski, Grönroos, Savonlinna Op. Festival Ch.

Söderblom's account of the *Third Symphony* is a vast improvement on earlier issues in terms of detail and atmosphere, and the same must be said of the *Requiem.* There are some moving passages in the *Requiem* but the music comes close to mawkishness. In the *Opus sonorum*, written in reaction to the sight of the vast battery of percussion so common in the 1960s, Kokkonen assigns all the percussion part to a piano, played with great delicacy here.

(i) *Piano quintet; String quartets Nos. 1–3.*
*** BIS Dig. CD 458 [id.]. (i) Valsta; Sibelius Ac. Qt.

The *Piano quintet*, Op. 5, comes from 1951–3 when the composer was in his early thirties and beginning to flex his creative muscles. The *First String quartet* followed in the late 1950s, the *Second* in the mid-1960s, just before the composition of the *Third Symphony*, and the *Third* followed a decade later in 1976. The *Quintet* is a slight but not unpleasing work; the *First Quartet*, which sounds like any chamber work of the period, has seriousness. Like its companions it is very well played, but even such eloquent advocacy cannot disguise a certain facelessness. But three stars for the performers and the engineers.

The Last Temptations (opera): complete.
**(*) Finlandia FACD 104 (2) [id.]. Auvinen, Ruohonen, Lehtinen, Talvela, Savonlinna Op. Festival Ch. & O, Söderblom.

The 1977 set of Kokkonen's opera, *The Last Temptations*, was previously available on three LPs from DG. The opera tells of a revivalist leader, Paavo Ruotsalainen, from the Finnish province of Savo and of his inner struggle to discover Christ. The opera is dominated by the personality of Martti Talvela, and its invention for the most part has a dignity and power that are symphonic in scale. Too much of the opera takes place in the same tonal area, but overall the work makes a strong impact. All four roles are well sung, and the performance under Ulf Söderblom is very well recorded indeed.

Koppel, Herman D. (born 1908)

Cello concerto, Op. 56.
*** BIS CD 80 [id.]. Erling Blondal Bengtsson, Danish Nat. RSO, Schmidt – NØRHOLM: *Violin concerto.* ***

Herman D. Koppel is best known to older collectors for his early 78-r.p.m. records and subsequent LPs of Nielsen's piano music. Apart from his activities as a pianist, he is a prolific composer, with seven symphonies, five piano concertos and a good deal of chamber music to his credit. His *Cello concerto* dates from 1952 and has never really made much headway outside his native Denmark. His idiom stems from Stravinsky and Bartók, but the opening has something of the luminous quality of Tippett's *Midsummer Marriage.* This recording emanates from a concert performance in 1976 and originally appeared, coupled with Holmboe's *Cello concerto*, which is promised for reissue. Very good recording of an inventive and original piece that deserves to enter the wider international repertoire. It is more satisfying than either the Kokkonen or Sallinen concertos. The coupling, the *Violin concerto* by Ib Nørholm, is also a rewarding piece.

Korngold, Erich (1897–1957)

Film scores: *The Adventures of Robin Hood* (suite); *Captain Blood: Ship in the Night;* (i) *The Sea Hawk* (suite).
(M) *** BMG/RCA GD 80912; *GK 80912* [0912-2-RG; *0912-4-RG*]. Nat. PO, Charles Gerhardt; (i) with Amb. S. – STEINER: *Film scores.* ***

Korngold was the most distinguished of all the Hollywood film composers, and almost all his music makes agreeable entertainment separated from the screen images. Curiously, although this collection, centring on the swashbuckling movies of Erroll Flynn, is entitled *'Captain Blood'*, only a fragment – if a potent one – is included from Korngold's music for this film. Juxtaposed with the more flamboyant Steiner scores for other Flynn vehicles, this makes for one of the very best of these Hollywood anthologies, for the most part offering extended groups of excerpts and fairly generous measure overall. As in the rest of the series, the dedication of Charles Gerhardt and the superb playing of the National Philharmonic Orchestra, coupled with sumptuous RCA recording, means that these performances communicate strongly.

Film scores: excerpts from: *Another Dawn; Anthony Adverse; Deception:* (i) *Cello concerto in C, Op. 37. Of Human Bondage; The Prince and the Pauper; The Private Lives of Elizabeth and Essex; The Sea Wolf.*
(M) *** BMG/RCA GD 80185; *GK 80185* [0185-2-RG; *0185-4-RG*]. Nat. PO, Gerhardt, (i) with Gabarro.

This second disc, like the first, below, is entirely devoted to Korngold's music. He drew on the attractive, lightweight score for *The Prince and the Pauper* as a basis for the variations in the last movement of the *Violin concerto*, while *Night scene* from *Another Dawn* – very effective in its own right – was to provide the principal theme of the first movement. For *Deception* he invented a miniature cello concerto, which is heard here in its expanded complete format. Nearly all this music is inventively rich and the performances by Gerhardt and the National Philharmonic are as persuasive as ever, with brilliant, spacious recording to match.

Film scores: excerpts from: *Anthony Adverse; Between Two Worlds;* (i) *The Constant Nymph; Deception; Devotion; Escape Me Never; King's Row; Of Human Bondage; The Sea Hawk* (suite); *The Sea Wolf* (suite).
(M) *** BMG/RCA GD 87890 [7890-2-RG]. Nat. PO, Gerhardt; (i) with Procter, Amb. S.

This was the first of the Korngold film collections to be reissued on CD and it makes a good summation of the scope of his achievement, particularly when, as throughout the series, the performances are so persuasively committed and the remastered recording, with its panoply of brass and strings, is attractively full and spacious.

String sextet, Op.10.
*** Hyp. Dig. CDA 66425 [id.]. Raphael Ens. – SCHOENBERG: *Verklaerte Nacht.* ***

The Korngold *Sextet* is an amazing achievement for a seventeen-year-old. Not only is it crafted with musicianly assurance and maturity it is also inventive and characterful. The Raphael Ensemble play it with great commitment and the Hyperion recording is altogether first class. It comes with a very enjoyable recording of *Verklaerte Nacht.*

OPERA

Die tote Stadt (complete).
(M) *** BMG/RCA GD 87767 (2) [7767-2-RG]. Neblett, Kollo, Luxon, Prey, Bav. R. Ch., Tölz Ch., Munich R. O, Leinsdorf.

At the age of twenty-three Korngold had his opera, *Die tote Stadt*, presented in simultaneous world premières in Hamburg and Cologne! It may not be a great work, but in a performance like this, splendidly recorded, it is one to revel in on the gramophone. The score includes many echoes of Puccini and Richard Strauss, but its youthful exuberance carries the day. Here René Kollo is powerful, if occasionally coarse of tone, Carol Neblett sings sweetly in the equivocal roles of the wife's apparition and the newcomer, and Hermann Prey, Benjamin Luxon and Rose Wagemann make up an impressive cast. Leinsdorf is at his finest.

Violanta (complete).
**(*) Sony CD 79229 [MK 35909]. Marton, Berry, Jerusalem, Stoklassa, Laubenthal, Hess, Bav. R. Ch., Munich R. O, Janowski.

Korngold was perhaps the most remarkable composer-prodigy of this century; he wrote this opera at the age of seventeen. It was given its first triumphant performance under Bruno Walter, and even Ernest Newman seriously compared Korngold to Mozart. Though luscious of texture and immensely assured, the writing lets one down by an absence of really memorable melody but, with a fine, red-blooded performance and with Siegfried Jerusalem a youthfully fresh hero, it makes a fascinating addition to the recorded repertory. Eva Marton, not always beautiful of tone, combines power and accuracy in the key role of the heroine, suddenly floating high pianissimos with unexpected purity. The recording is quite full if not especially refined.

Kraft, Anton (1749–1820)

Cello concerto in C, Op. 4.
** BMG/RCA Dig. RD 77757 [7757-2-RC]. Anner Bylsma, Tafelmusik O, Jean Lamon – HAYDN: *Cello concertos.* **

Anton Kraft came from Rokycany, near Pilsen, where his father was a brewer. He studied philosophy but eventually turned to music, joining Haydn's orchestra at Esterháza as a cellist. For a time Haydn's *D major concerto* was attributed to him and, in the interesting notes which acompany this CD, Anner Bylsma argues that Kraft had a hand in its composition. The *Concerto in C*, Op. 4, is a rather delightful piece, full of fun and delight and with some memorable ideas, even if it is bereft of any great depth. Good playing and recording, and generally more perfectly in tune than the Haydn works with which it is coupled.

Krebs, Johann Ludwig (1713–80)

Double concerto in B min. for harpsichord, oboe and strings.
(M) **(*) DG 431 120-2. Jaccottet, Holliger, Camerata Bern, Van Wijnkoop – GRAUN; TELEMANN: *Concertos.* ***

Krebs was a pupil of J. S. Bach; he left Leipzig with a glowing testimonial from the master and one can understand why from this delightful *Double concerto*, which makes a good coupling for the concertos of Graun and Telemann. Holliger as ever plays beautifully, but Christiane Jaccottet adopts too romantically expressive a style. However, this remains well worth hearing, and the recording is first rate.

Chorales: *Es ist gewisslich an der Zeit* (with horn); *Gott der Vater wohn uns bei* (with clarino); *Herr Jesu Christ, meins Lebens Licht* (with oboe); *Herzlich lieb hab ich dich, O Herr; In allen meinen Taten* (both with trumpet); *Jesu meine Freude, meine Seel, ermuntre dich; O Gott, du frommer Gott* (all with oboe); *Treuer Gott, ich muss dir klagen* (with oboe d'amore); *Wachet auf; Fantasia on Wachet auf* (with trumpet); *Wachet auf* (2nd version with clarino; 3rd version with trumpet). *Fantasias: Nos. 1–2 in F; in F min.* (all with oboe); *in C* (flute).
*** Argo Dig. 430 208-2 [id.]. Bennett, Black, Laird, Thompson, Hurford (organ of Gloucester Cathedral).

Here is further proof, if any were needed, that Bach's favourite pupil, Johann Ludwig Krebs, was a considerable musician in his own right and a composer of some individuality. His special innovation was to extend the Bachian organ chorale to feature a solo wind or brass instrument playing the cantus firmus melody against the organ's decorative variants. These could be relatively simple, like *Trauer Gott, ich muss dir klagen*, where the oboe d'amore sings the theme demurely; or more florid, as in the lovely *Herr Jesu Christ, meins Lebens Licht* (with oboe). Sometimes the keyboard figurations might be quite exuberant, as in the opening chorale on this collection, *Gott der Vater wohn uns bei*, where the clarino (high trumpet) plays the tune regally against the organ's lively discourse. Krebs then went further, providing his wind players with freer, more complex concertante parts, as the two *Fantasias in F* (with oboe) demonstrate engagingly. The brass lines remain uncomplicated, yet the full horn timbre in *Es ist gewisslich an der Zeit* and the gleaming trumpet in *Wachet auf* bring added colour and interest to the music. Krebs's intricate invention in the keyboard writing sounds attractively spontaneous in the hands of Peter Hurford, whose registration is, as ever, a joy to the ear. The wind and brass players are all experts and their contributions are distinguished. The organ of Gloucester Cathedral seems eminently suited to this repertoire, and the recording is beautifully balanced and vivid. This is a collection with wide appeal.

Kreisler, Fritz (1875–1962)

Allegretto in the style of Boccherini; Allegretto in the style of Porpora; Caprice viennoise; Cavatina; La Chasse in the style of Cartier; La Gitana; Grave in the style of W. F. Bach; Gypsy caprice; Liebesfreud; Liebesleid; Praeludium and allegro in the style of Pugnani; Recitative and scherzo; Schön Rosmarin; Shepherd's madrigal; Sicilienne et rigaudon in the style of Francoeur; Toy soldiers' march; Viennese rhapsodic fantasia; arr. of *Austrian National Hymn.*
(BB) **(*) ASV CDQS 6039; *ZCQS 6039.* Oscar Shumsky, Milton Kaye.

A generous (67 minutes) and well-varied bargain recital of Kreislerian encores. Oscar Shumsky's combination of technical mastery and musical flair is ideal for this music; and it is a pity that the rather dry recording and forward balance – well in front of the piano – makes the violin sound almost too close.

Caprice viennoise, Op. 2; La Gitana; Liebesfreud; Liebesleid; Polichinelle; La Précieuse; Recitativo and scherzo caprice, Op. 6; Rondo on a theme of Beethoven; Syncopation; Tambourin chinois; Zigeuner (Capriccio). Arrangements: ALBÉNIZ: *Tango, Op. 165/2.* WEBER: *Larghetto.* WIENIAWSKI: *Caprice in E flat.* DVOŘÁK: *Slavonic dance No. 10 in E min.* GLAZUNOV: *Sérénade espagnole.* GRANADOS: *Danse espagnole.*
(M) *** DG 423 876-2; *423 876-4* [id.]. Shlomo Mintz, Clifford Benson.

Shlomo Mintz plays with a disarmingly easy style and absolute technical command, to bring out the music's warmth as well as its sparkle. Try *La Gitana* to sample the playing at its most genially glittering. A very attractive programme, given first-class recording and splendid presence without added edge on CD.

Kreutzer, Joseph (*c.* 1820)

Grand Trio.

*** Mer. Dig. CDE 84199; *KE 77199* [id.]. Conway, Silverthorne, Garcia – BEETHOVEN: *Serenade;* MOLINO: *Trio.* ***

Joseph Kreutzer, thought to be the brother of Rodolphe Kreutzer, dedicatee of Beethoven's *A major Violin sonata*, wrote many works for the guitar, of which this is a delightful example. The guitar, given at least equal prominence with the other instruments, brings an unusual tang to the textures of this charming piece, ending with a rousing *Alla Polacca.* A nicely pointed performance, very well recorded in warm, faithful sound.

Krommer, Franz (Kramar, František) (1759–1831)

Octets for wind instruments in B flat, Op. 78; C, Op. 76; E flat, Op. 71; F, Op. 57.

*** EMI Dig. CDC7 54383-2. Bläserensemble Sabine Meyer.

Krommer (sometimes known by his Czech name Kramar – and even by both, hyphenated) is best known nowadays for his *Harmonien* or Partitas for wind. Hearing them played by the Netherlands Wind Ensemble (who recorded them in the late 1970s) or by the Budapest Wind, who broadcast a number of times in the 1980s, was to be carried away by their delightful high spirits! Now come these captivating performances of four of them by the wind ensemble which the clarinettist, Sabine Meyer, has formed. These pieces owe much to both Haydn and Mozart, but they also have a streak of sophisticated humour that is altogether winning. In terms of ensemble, tonal blend and lightness and crispness of articulation, it is difficult to imagine these performances being surpassed. The recording is made in an ideal acoustic, warm and spacious. A disc guaranteed to lift one's flagging spirits and restore one's faith in mankind.

Kuhlau, Friedrich (1786–1832)

(i) *Concertino for two horns, Op. 45;* (ii) *Piano concerto in C, Op. 7; Overture Elverhøj (The elf's hill), Op. 100.*

*** Unicorn Dig. DKPCD 9110; *DKPC 9110* [id.]. (i) Ib Lansky-Otto, Frøydis Ree Wekre; (ii) Michael Ponti; Odense SO, Othmar Maga.

No one would claim that any of Kuhlau's music has great depth, but there is a freshness and grace about it that engages one's sympathies. The overture *Elverhøj* or *The Elf's Hill* is probably his best-known work and is certainly the finest piece on the disc. The *Piano concerto in C*, Op. 7, is modelled on Beethoven's concerto in the same key and was composed in 1810, before the composer fled his native Germany for Copenhagen to avoid being drafted into the advancing Napoleonic armies. The *Concertino for two horns* (1821) is full of initially engaging, but eventually unmemorable, ideas. Very good performances from all concerned, and satisfactory recording.

Elverhøj (The Elf hill), Op. 100.

** Dacapo Dig. DCCD 8902 [id.]. Gobel, Plesner, Johansen, Danish R. Ch. & SO, John Frandsen.

Kuhlau's incidental music to J. L. Heiberg's play, *Elverhøj*, was composed for a production to mark the marriage of the daughter of King Frederik VI in 1829, and the present CD accommodates 21 numbers from it, including its splendid overture. Unlike his opera *Lulu*, composed five years before, it was an immediate success and has retained its popularity in Denmark down to the present day. The usual influences – Beethoven, Weber, Cherubini, Mendelssohn and so on – are to be found, but the overall impression is endearingly fresh. Not so the recording however. This comes presumably from the 1970s (it was issued on the DMA label – Dansk Musik Antologi) and sounds really rather dryish as if recorded in a fully packed concert hall. The music has great charm and the performance too under John Frandsen is very sympathetic.

Lulu (opera): complete.
*** Kontrapunkt/HM 32009/11 [id.]. Saarman, Frellesvig, Kiberg, Cold, Danish R. Ch. & SO, Schönwandt.

This *Lulu* comes from 1824 and enjoyed some success in its day; it would probably have enjoyed more, but contemporary audiences complained that both the text and the music were too long. They certainly had a point: the spoken passages are omitted here – but, even so, the music takes three hours. The opening of Act II has overtones of the Wolf's Glen scene in *Der Freischutz* and the dance of the black elves in the moonlight is pure Mendelssohn – and has much charm. The invention is generally fresh and engaging, though no one would claim that it has great depth. The largely Danish cast cope very capably with the not inconsiderable demands of Kuhlau's vocal writing, and the title-role, sung by the Finnish tenor, Risto Saarman, is admirable. The weakest member of the cast is Anne Frellesvig's rather white-voiced Princess Sidi. The Danish Radio recording is eminently truthful and vivid, and Michael Schönwandt draws excellent results from the Danish Radio Chorus and Orchestra.

Lachner, Franz (1803–90)

Septet in E flat.
*** Marco Polo Dig. 8.223282 [id.]. Ens. Villa Musica – FUCHS: *Clarinet quintet.* ***

Franz Lachner was a friend of Schubert, and his *Septet* dates from 1824, the same year as the Schubert *Octet*. After completing his studies in Vienna, in 1836 he moved to Munich where he remained until he was forced into early retirement by the arrival of Wagner in 1864. The *Septet* is not great music but has an easy-going charm that is really quite winning, and it is nicely played and well recorded by this Mainz-based group.

Lajtha, László (1892–1963)

(i) *Sinfonietta for strings, Op. 43;* (ii) *Symphonies Nos. 4 (Le Printemps), Op. 52; 9, Op. 67.*
** Hung. HCD 31452 [id.]. (i) Hungarian CO, Tátrai; (ii) Hungarian State O, Ferencsik.

László Lajtha belongs to the same generation as Prokofiev and Martinů. Like Bartók and Kodály he was also active as a scholar in the field of ethnomusicology. As a composer he is relatively little heard outside Hungary, though the BBC broadcast his *Seventh Symphony* many years ago. Lajtha studied with Vincent d'Indy and gained a number of distinctions, such as the Elizabeth Sprague Coolidge Prize for his *Third Quartet*, and he was elected a member of the French Academy of Arts. During the war years he founded a chamber orchestra, which he directed until 1944, two years before the composition of the *Sinfonietta for strings*. As a composer he was prolific: his output includes a good deal of choral music, ballets and much chamber music, including ten quartets. His *Fourth Symphony* (*Le Printemps*) dates from 1951 and, like so much of his music, reflects the combined influences of his native folk culture, neo-classicism and French music. It is far from unappealing, but at the same time one has to admit that it remains ultimately unmemorable, as does the *Ninth Symphony* (1963), his penultimate work. The performances have all previously appeared on LP, and though the sleeve gives no dates of recording they are from the mid-1970s (1979 in the case of the *Sinfonietta*).

Lalo, Eduard (1823–92)

Cello concerto No. 1 in D min., Op. 33.
*** DG Dig. 427 323-2 [id.]. Matt Haimovitz, Chicago SO, Levine – SAINT-SAËNS: *Concerto No. 1;* BRUCH: *Kol Nidrei.* ***
(B) *** DG 431 166-2; *431 166-4.* Heinrich Schiff, New Philh. O, Mackerras – FAURÉ: *Élégie;* SAINT-SAËNS: *Cello concerto No. 1.* ***
(M) **(*) Mercury 432 010-2 [id.]. Janos Starker, LSO, Skrowaczewski – SAINT-SAËNS; SCHUMANN: *Concertos.* ***

An outstandingly impressive début from the young cellist, Matt Haimovitz, just nineteen at the time of making his first recording. Levine's opening flourishes are boldly dramatic, immediately eliciting a warm response, and in the second movement the contrasts are again emphasized; the performance throughout combines vitality with expressive feeling in the most spontaneous manner. The recording is very well balanced indeed and highly realistic. The competition from Yo-Yo Ma is strong, but Haimovitz emerges with flying colours, and many will be attracted by his bonus of Bruch's *Kol Nidrei*.

This was also Heinrich Schiff's début recording in 1977, made when he was still very young. His account of the Lalo *Concerto* is fresh and enthusiastic and very well recorded for its period. With its excellent coupling it makes a real bargain.

Janos Starker's 1962 recording with the LSO under Stanislaw Skrowaczewski sounds remarkably good for its age. Though the tutti chords are brutal and clipped, Starker plays splendidly, and the famous Mercury recording technique lays out the orchestral texture quite beautifully and with remarkable transparency.

Symphonie espagnole (for violin and orchestra), *Op. 21*.
(M) *** DG Dig. 429 977-2 [id.]. Perlman, O de Paris, Barenboim – SAINT-SAËNS: *Concerto No. 3*. ***
*** DG Dig. 427 676-2 [id.]. Mintz, Israel PO, Mehta – SAINT-SAËNS: *Introduction & Rondo capriccioso;* VIEUXTEMPS: *Concerto No. 5*. ***
*** Decca Dig. 411 952-2 [id.]. Kyung Wha Chung, Montreal SO, Dutoit – SAINT-SAËNS: *Concerto No. 1*. ***
(M) **(*) Sony MPK 45555 [MYK 37811]; *40-45555*. Stern, Phd. O, Ormandy – BRUCH: *Concerto No. 1*. **(*)
(B) **(*) Ph. 422 976-2; *422 976-4* [id.]. Szeryng, Monte Carlo Op. O, Van Remoortel – PAGANINI: *Violin concerto No. 3*. ***
(B) **(*) Hung. White Label HRC 106 [id.]. Miklós Szenthelyi, Hungarian State O, Lukács – D'INDY: *Symphonie*. ***
(B) **(*) Sony MBK 44717 [id.]. Zukerman, LAPO, Mehta – BRUCH: *Concerto No. 1*. **(*)
(*) BMG/RCA Dig. RD 60942. Anne Akiko Meyers, RPO, Lópes-Cobos – BRUCH: *Scottish fantasia*. *

Lalo's brilliant five-movement distillation of Spanish sunshine is well served by DG. The strongly articulated orchestral introduction from Barenboim combines rhythmic buoyancy with expressive flair and the lyrical material is handled with great sympathy. The richness and colour of Perlman's tone are never more telling than in the slow movement, which opens tenderly but develops a compelling expressive ripeness. The brilliance of the scherzo is matched by the dancing sparkle of the finale. The recording is extremely lively but fairly dry, and the forward balance of the soloist does not obscure orchestral detail.

Minz, too, plays with much panache; he is highly seductive in the lilting secondary theme of the first movement, and brings a comparable touch of restrained voluptuousness to the habanera rhythms of the *Intermezzo*, while the Scherzo is light as thistledown. Like Perlman, he brings a special kind of Hebrew intensity to the *Andante*, then scintillates in the finale. Mehta opens a bit heavily but provides a satisfactory acccompaniment, while the recording, made live in the Israel Mann Autorium, is acceptable, full, if not ideally transparent. The solo violin is truthfully projected. Very enjoyable, and so are the couplings.

Kyung Wha Chung has the advantage of a first-class Decca digital recording, fuller than the DG alternative, and with a highly effective, natural balance. Hers is an athletic, incisive account, at its most individual in the captivatingly light-weight finale, with an element almost of fantasy. Miss Chung does not have quite the panache of Perlman, but Charles Dutoit's accompaniment is first class and the orchestral characterization is strong throughout.

Stern's version from the late 1960s has all the rich, red-blooded qualities which have made this artist world-famous. Reservations concerning the close solo balance are inevitable (although Ormandy's fine accompaniment is not diminished); nevertheless the playing makes a huge impact on the listener and, although the actual sound-quality is far from refined, the charisma of the performance is unforgettable.

Szeryng's performance brings out the work's Spanish sparkle, especially in the brilliant finale. The accompaniment is less distinctive. Yet Szeryng's flair carries the day, and his Paganini coupling is outstanding too.

On Hungaroton, Miklós Szenthelyi brings an added Hungarian sparkle to this music without losing its seductive Spanish character. He is a fine, full-timbred player and this is an attractively spontaneous performance, well accompanied and with an effervescent finale. Although the resonant recording makes tuttis somewhat bass-heavy, detail is well observed and the slow movement is richly sonorous.

Zukerman's account of Lalo's five-movement *Symphonie espagnole* is first class in every way. The solo playing has real panache, Mehta accompanies vividly, and the recording is transferred well to CD, even if the balance is not ideal in its relationship of the soloist to the orchestra.

Anne Akiko Meyers' account offers a genuine alternative view. Her approach to the first movement's secondary theme has a beguilingly light touch, the seductive Spanish lilt pastel-shaded, and her sense of fantasy brings a similar airy lightness to the Scherzo. She introduces the lovely melody of the *Andante* with magically hushed concentration, and then fines her tone down to a thread of sound, before letting the climax unfold naturally. The finale brings appealing sparkle and delicacy of articulation. López-Cobos, does not quite match his young soloist in concentration and he is a bit heavy with the habanera rhythm of the *Intermezzo*. Although he has a much finer ear for detail than Mehta, he does not match the joyous forward momentum that Barenboim finds for Perlman. However he has the advantage of really first class recording, which makes the opening sound full and expansive in the most inviting way, and throughout provides, warmth, colour and refined internal definition, while achieving a natural balance with the soloist.

Symphony in G min.
(M) **(*) CDM7 63396-2 [id.]. O Nat. de l'ORTF, Sir Thomas Beecham – FRANCK: *Symphony.* **(*)

Symphony in G min.; Rapsodie norvégienne; Le roi d'Ys: overture.
(M) *** Ph. 432 278-2; *432 278-4*. Monte Carlo Opera O, Antonio de Almeida.

Lalo's *G minor Symphony* is not the strongest of nineteenth-century French symphonies but, as this Philips reissue demonstrates, it is worth an occasional airing. The Monte Carlo orchestra is not as impressive an orchestra as Beecham's French group; but Almeida observes the repeat in the first movement and plays the work with evident affection. He is a most convincing advocate, particularly in the *Adagio* and finale. Moreover the 1974 Philips recording is superior to the early Beecham EMI alternative; both the *Rapsodie norvégienne* (especially the exciting *Presto* secondary section) and *Le roi d'Ys* are also very well played. Almeida, though not dull, refuses to go over the top in the latter piece, to good effect.

The *Symphony*'s second-movement scherzo with its delectable flute-writing has the sparkling memorability which has long made Lalo's concertante violin work, the *Symphonie espagnole*, an unfailing success, and that scherzo inspires Beecham to a delectably pointed performance; but he has to work harder with the rest, when the material is thinner, and the argument in the first movement lacks tautness. It has to be conceded that Almeida's account overall is more enjoyable. The EMI recording has good body and presence, but the transfer adds an edge on top.

Le roi d'Ys (complete).
*** Erato/Warner Dig. 2292 45015-2 (2) [id.]. Courtis, Ziegler, Hendricks, Villa, Fr. R. Ch. & PO, Jordan.

The Erato version gains enormously in presenting this opulent score in sumptuous modern sound, with Jordan underlining the colourful dramatic contrasts between the exotic scene-setting and the sharply rhythmic choruses. The women soloists are particularly fine, preferable to those on previous sets. The American mezzo-soprano, Delores Ziegler, is very convincingly cast in what – thanks to the celebrated example of Rosa Ponselle, among others – used to be counted a soprano role. Her dramatic, unfruity voice is perfectly contrasted against the ravishing Rozenn of Barbara Hendricks. Eduardo Villa as the hero, Mylio, may not be as stylish as his recorded predecessors, not delicate enough in the famous *Aubade*, but his heady tenor has no trouble with the high tessitura. Jean-Philippe Courtis as the King, in this improbable Breton legend of medieval chivalry, and Marcel Vanaud as the villain, Karnac, have dark, weighty voices, marred at times by flutter.

Lambert, Constant (1905–51)

Aubade héroïque; (i) *The Rio Grande; Summer's last will and testament.*
❀ *** Hyp. Dig. CDA 66565 [id.]. Sally Burgess, Jack Gibbons, William Shimell, Ch. of Opera North and Leeds Festival, (i) with Jack Gibbons; English N. Philh., Lloyd-Jones.

The Rio Grande, Lambert's jazz-based choral concerto setting a poem by Sacheverell Sitwell, is one of the most colourful and atmospheric works from the 1920s, as much a period-piece as Gershwin's *Rhapsody in blue*, yet with deeper resonances and subtler overtones. David Lloyd-Jones directs a scintillating performance that directly reflects the original recording, conducted by the young composer in 1930 with Sir Hamilton Harty as piano soloist. With Sally Burgess a warmly expressive soloist, sharply dramatic choral singing, and Jack Gibbons the brilliant, keenly responsive pianist, Lloyd-Jones gives a totally idiomatic account of music that requires crisp attack combined with a jazzy freedom of rhythm. It was Lambert's tragedy that, having written that delectable piece at 22 and having achieved phenomenal success at the time, he never caught the public's imagination with his music in the same way again. He turned from composition to conducting and music criticism (as wittily provocative as Shaw's) and, above all, to drinking. Though he put the Sadler's Wells Ballet on the map musically, his decline and death at the age of 46 was a sad anticlimax after the jewelled promise of his early years. Yet Lloyd-Jones demonstrates that the other two works on the disc have comparable mastery in similarly memorable invention. The *Aubade héroïque* is an evocative tone-poem inspired by Lambert's memory of a beautiful morning in Holland in 1940 when, with the Nazi invasion, it was far from certain whether he and his colleagues would be able to get back to England. Inspired by the death of his friend (and alchoholic evil influence) Peter Warlock/Philip Heseltine, *Summer's last will and testament* is a big, 50-minute choral work setting lyrics by the Elizabethan, Thomas Nashe, on the unpromising subject of the threat of plague. Nashe was thinking of a real threat in the London of his time, Lambert of the growing disillusion of himself and others in the 1930s. Christopher Palmer, the perceptive note-writer for the disc, suggests a new relevance for the work as 'A requiem for the AIDS generation', in effect a piece ahead of its time. Lloyd-Jones and his outstanding team, mainly from Opera North, bring out the vitality and colour of the writing, with each of the nine substantial sections based on Elizabethan dance-rhythms. Like the other two works, this is a neglected masterpiece, full of energy, not least in the brilliant orchestral movement, *King Pest*, a dance of death. So far from being an elegy for his friend, this is a statement of defiance. The recording in all three works is full, vivid and atmospheric.

(i) *Piano concerto; Horoscope* (ballet): *suite;* (i; ii) *The Rio Grande.*
*** Argo Dig. 436 118-2 [id.]. (i) Kathryn Stott; (ii) Della Jones, BBC Singers; BBC Concert O, Wordsworth.

This Argo issue of three of Lambert's finest works, like the Hyperion issue which appeared almost simultaneously, makes up for years of neglect. With bright, forward recording this account of *The Rio Grande* is rather more aggressive than the Hyperion one and is a degree more literal, less idiomatic in its interpretation of jazzy syncopations. It is also marginally less warmly expressive, but the power and colour of the writing come across with fine bite and clarity. In the ballet suite from *Horoscope* there is one more movement than Lambert ever recorded, the *Palindromic prelude*, less striking than the other movements but still beautifully written. Here again Wordsworth and the BBC Concert Orchestra are a degree more literal than Lambert himself was in jazz-rhythms. The *Concerto* for piano and nine players has long needed a new recording, and Kathryn Stott with members of the orchestra gives splendid point to the angular, even abrasive, writing. This was written as an elegy for Lambert's friend and fellow-composer, Peter Warlock (Philip Heseltine), but the emotional element is much more severely repressed than in the other works on the disc, or in the oratorio, *Summer's last will and testament*, similarly written in response to Warlock's death. Ironically, the composer who seems closest is Stravinsky, whom Lambert frequently disparaged but whose *Piano concerto* brings striking parallels.

Horoscope (ballet): *suite.*
❀ *** Hyp. CDA 66436; *KA 66436* [id.]. E. N. Philh. O, Lloyd-Jones – BLISS: *Checkmate;* WALTON: *Façade.* ***

Constant Lambert was one of the great characters of British music. He had a major influence on Walton, whose *Façade* is also included in this splendid Hyperion triptych; but Lambert was also a considerable composer in his own right. The music for *Horoscope* is sheer delight, and it seems incredible that the only earlier complete recording of the suite was made in the mid-1950s by Irving for Decca. David Lloyd-Jones is equally sympathetic to its specifically English atmosphere. He wittily points the catchy rhythmic figure which comes both in the *Dance for the followers of Leo* and, later, in the *Bacchanale,* while the third-movement *Valse for the Gemini* has a delectable insouciant charm. Excellent playing and first-class sound, perhaps a shade resonant for the ballet pit, but bringing plenty of bloom.

Horoscope (ballet): *suite:* (i) *Dance for the Followers of Leo;* (ii) *Saraband for the followers of Virgo;* (i) *Valse for the Gemini;* (ii) *Bacchanale;* (i) *Invocation to the moon* and finale. (iii; ii) *The Rio Grande.* (ii) *Ballabile* (Chabrier, arr. Lambert); *Apparitions* (Liszt, arr. Lambert, orch. Jacob): *Galop; Cave scene.*
(M) (***) EMI mono CDH7 63911-2 [id.]. (i) RLPO; (ii) Philh. O; (iii) with Kyla Greenbaum, BBC Ch., Lambert – GORDON: *Rake's progress;* RAWSTHORNE: *Street corner.* (***)

More than any subsequent interpreter, Lambert almost captured the authentic jazz inflexions in his brilliant choral settings of Sacheverell Sitwell's 'Rio Grande', both in the vigorous sequences and in the languidly beautiful ones, often based on tango rhythm. Kyla Greenbaum is the similarly understanding piano soloist. Few British works so vividly capture the atmosphere of the 1920s, and the excerpts from the later ballets are comparably colourful and vigorous. The highly engaging *Horoscope* suite, which is otherwise available only at full price, is made up from 78-r.p.m. recordings made at two different periods. Very good transfers.

Lambert, Michel (*c.* 1610–96)

Airs de cour: *Admirons notre jeune et charmante Déesse; Ah! qui voudra desormais s'engager; C'en est fait, belle Iris; D'un feu secret je me sens consumer; Il faut mourir plutost que le changer; Iris n'est plus, mon Iris m'est ravie; Je suis aymé de celle que j'adore; Ma bergere est tendre et fidelle; Ombre de mon amant; Par mes chants tristes et touchants; Pour vos beaux yeux, Iris; Le repos, l'ombre, le silence; Tout l'univers obéit à l'amour; Trouver sur l'herbette.*
(B) *** HM HMA 901123 [id.]. Les Arts Florissants, William Christie.

Michel Lambert published this collection of *Airs de cour* in 1689 when he was in his late seventies. Grove speaks of his airs as models of elegance and grace, in which careful attention was paid to direct declamation. He gained recognition early during his lifetime as an important singer, teacher and dancer, and during the 1660s collaborated with Lully, his son-in-law, in a number of ballets. In all he composed no fewer than twenty collections of *airs,* most of which are lost. The 300 or so that do survive show his artistry in characterization and dialogue to have been of the highest order. They are beautifully performed and expertly recorded by members of Les Arts Florissants and William Christie and are altogether delightful. They are very competitively priced, too. Unlike some bargain issues, there is excellent documentation with the original texts and translation.

Langlais, Jean (born 1907)

(i) *Messe solennelle;* (i; ii; iii) *Missa Salve regina;* (Organ): (i) *Paraphrases grégoriennes, Op. 5: Te Deum. Poèmes évangéliques, Op. 2: La Nativité. Triptyque grégorien: Rosa mystica.*
*** Hyp. Dig. CDA 66270; *KA 66270* [id.]. Westminster Cathedral Ch., David Hill, (i) with J. O'Donnell; (ii) A. Lumsden; (iii) ECO Brass Ens.

Jean Langlais' organ music owes much to Dupré's example, and the two Masses are archaic in feeling, strongly influenced by plainchant and organum, yet with a plangent individuality that clearly places the music in the twentieth century. The *Missa Salve regina* is scored for male-voice chorus, unison boy trebles, two organs and an octet of brass instruments divided into two groups. The style is wholly accessible and the music enjoys fervent advocacy from these artists, who are accorded sound-quality of the high standard one expects from this label. Those unfamiliar with the music of Jean Langlais should lose no time and try this outstanding collection.

Larsson, Lars-Erik (1908–86)

Symphonies Nos. 1 in D, Op. 2; 2, Op. 17.
**(*) BIS Dig. CD 426 [id.]. Helsingborg SO, Hans-Peter Frank.

Even in his native Sweden, Larsson is not thought of as a symphonist, although he has many important works to his credit, notably the lyrical *Violin concerto* (1952) and *Music for orchestra* (1949). The *First Symphony* is a student work, written when he was nineteen and before his studies with Berg. It is derivative but a work of obvious promise, fluent and well put together. There are obvious echoes of the Russian post-nationalists as well as Nielsen and Sibelius. Much the same could be said of the more mature *Second Symphony* (1936–7), which is genial and unpretentious. After its première the composer withdrew it, allowing only the final *Ostinato* to be published. Good performances and recording, but the music itself is not Larsson at his strongest.

Symphony No. 3 in C min., Op. 34; (i) *Förklädd Gud (A God in disguise), Op. 24.*
** BIS CD 96 [id.]. (i) Nordin, Hagegård, Jonsson, Helsingborg Concert Ch.; Helsingborg SO, Frykberg.

A God in disguise was a production for Swedish Radio, similar in ambition to the Louis MacNeice–Benjamin Britten collaboration in *The dark tower*, and was a choral setting of poems by Hjalmar Gullberg. The choral suite for two soloists and narrator that Larsson fashioned from it has great freshness and charm. This 1978 performance has some fine singing from Håkan Hagegård, and the Helsingborg chorus and orchestra give a serviceable account of the score. Like its predecessor, the *Third Symphony* (1944–5) it was withdrawn after its first performance though, as with the *Second*, Larsson allowed the finale to be published as *Concert overture No. 3*. It is as diatonic as *A God in disguise* and, though not completely successful, is strong enough to deserve rescue.

Lassus, Orlandus (*c.* 1530–94)

De profundis clamavi; Exaltabo te, Domine; Missa octavi toni; Missa qual donna.
*** Nimbus Dig. NI 5150 [id.]. Christ Church Cathedral Ch., Oxford, Stephen Darlington.

The *Missa qual donna* begins this excellent CD: it is a late work, expressive and mellifluous, and very well sung by the choir of Christ Church Cathedral, Oxford. As a pendant, the disc also includes Cipriano de Rore's Petrarch setting, *Qual donna a gloriosa fama*, composed forty years earlier, which the Mass takes as its inspiration. The contrast between this and the *Missa octavi toni*, also known as the *Missa Venatorum* (or *Missa Jäger – Hunting Mass*), could hardly be more striking. The motet, *De profundis clamavi*, one of the great penitential Psalms, is almost the most eloquent and expressive of the pieces here. At times one could wish for more ardent tone from the trebles; but unquestionably these are fine performances that enrich the Lassus discography, and the recording is very good indeed.

9 Lamentationes Hieremiae.
*** HM Dig. HMC 901299; *HMC 40.1299* [id.]. Paris Chapelle Royale Ens., Herreweghe.

9 Lamentationes Hieremiae. Aurora lucis rutilat; Christus resurgens; Magnificat Aurora lucis rutilat; Missa Pro defunctis; Regina coeli; Surgens Jesu.
*** Hyp. Dig. CDA 66321/2 [id.]. Pro Cantione Antiqua, Bruno Turner.

The Harmonia Mundi set of the *Lamentations* enjoys one obvious advantage over its rival on Hyperion in that the nine *Lamentations* are all accommodated on the one disc (or cassette), while Bruno Turner's 1981 digital recording spills over on to two. However, in addition to the *Lamentations* for Maundy Thursday, Good Friday and Holy Saturday, the Hyperion recording offers music for Easter Sunday including the glorious *Aurora lucis rutilat* for two five-part choirs and the *Magnificat* based on the motet. The performances by the Pro Cantione Antiqua under Bruno Turner are very persuasive, expressive and vital, with none of the white, vibrato-less tone that is currently in fashion among some early music groups. The recording too is spacious and warm. So, for that matter, is the Harmonia Mundi recording for the Chapelle Royale and Philippe Herreweghe, whose performances are wholly admirable.

Missa Osculetur me; Motets: *Alma Redemptoris Mater; Ave regina caelorum; Hodie completi sunt; Osculetur me; Regina caeli; Salve Regina; Timor et tremor.*
*** Gimell Dig. CDGIM 018; *1585T-18* [id.]. Tallis Scholars, Peter Phillips.

Lassus learned the technique of double-choir antiphonal music in Italy, for, although eight-part polyphony was widely practised and held in the highest esteem in the Low Countries, the massive sonorities of the Venetian School were alien. The Mass is preceded by the motet, *Osculetur me* (*Let him kiss me with the kisses of his lips*), which provides much of its motivic substance and is glorious in its sonorities and expressive eloquence. The singing of the Tallis Scholars under Peter Phillips is as impressive as it was on their earlier records, and the recording is beautifully present.

Missa, super Bell' Amfitrit' alterna.
(M) **(*) EMI Dig. CD-EMX 2180; *TC-EMX 2180.* St John's College, Cambridge, Ch., Guest – ALLEGRI: *Miserere* **(*); PALESTRINA: *Veni sponsa Christi.* ***

Amphitrite was not only the mythological goddess of the sea but also a nickname for Venice, and this Mass is almost certainly connected with the city rather than with Poseidon's wife. It is a complex and varied piece of remarkable textural diversity, and it is finely sung here, although perhaps a little more Latin fervour would have been in order. The digital recording is first class.

Missa super Bell' Amfitrit' alterna; Psalmus penitentialis VII (Psalm 143); Motets: *Alma redemptoris Mater; Omnes de Saba venient; Salve regina, mater misericordiae; Tui sunt coeli.*
❀ (M) *** Decca 433 679-2 [id.]. Christ Church Cathedral, Oxford, Ch., Simon Preston.

This splendid reissue, taken from the old Argo catalogue, combines the contents of a pair of LPs, missing out only one item. The *Mass* comes from about 1585 and is Venetian in style, scored for double choir, each comprising SATB. The seventh *Penitential Psalm* uses a five-part choir with divided tenors, and at *Sicut erat* expands to a six-part choir with divided trebles. The trebles here are firm in line, strong in tone. Indeed, throughout, the singers produce marvellously blended tone-quality and Simon Preston secures magical results. As if this were not enough, the choir conclude with an offering hardly less magnificent, the four eight-part motets, amazingly rich in texture, including a Christmas motet, *Tui sunt coeli.* Here Lassus's layering of texture is gloriously brought out in rich but never over-dense sound. The acoustic is warm and atmospheric (the recordings were made in Merton College Chapel, Oxford, in 1974/5) and the texture is thus heard to best advantage. These performances have an admirable vitality and plenty of expressive range, though there is not the slightest trace of self-indulgence or excessive fervour. The CD transfer further enhances the sound and the effect is uncannily real and vivid.

Lecocq, Alexandre (1832–1918)

Mam'zelle Angot (ballet, arr. Gordon Jacob).
(M) *** Decca 430 849-2 (2) [id.]. Nat. PO, Bonynge – HÉROLD: *La Fille mal gardée.* ***

La Fille de Madame Angot was a highly successful operetta of the 1870s. The ballet originated for Massine's post-Diaghilev company. It found its definitive form, however, in a later, Sadler's Wells, production, also choreographed by Massine. The narrative line follows the story of the operetta and much of the music is also drawn from that source; however, Gordon Jacob includes excerpts from other music by Lecocq. It is a gay, vivacious score with plenty of engaging tunes, prettily orchestrated in the modern French style. Bonynge offers the first recording of the complete score, and its 39 minutes are consistently entertaining when the orchestral playing has such polish and wit. The Kingsway Hall recording is closely observed: the CD brings sharp detail and tangibility, especially at lower dynamic levels.

Lehár, Franz (1870–1948)

The Merry Widow (Die lustige Witwe; complete, in German).
❀ *** EMI CDS7 47178-8 (2) [Ang. CDCB 47177]. Schwarzkopf, Gedda, Waechter, Steffek, Knapp, Equiluz, Philh. Ch. and O, Matačić.
(M) (***) EMI mono CDH7 69520-2 [id.]. Schwarzkopf, Gedda, Kunz, Loose, Kraus, Philh. Ch. & O, Ackermann.

(M) ** DG 435 712-2 (2) [id.]. Harwood, Strats, Kollo, Hollweg, Keleman, Grobe, Krenn, German Op. Ch., BPO, Karajan (with SUPPÉ: Overtures: *Beautiful Galathea; Jolly robbers; Light cavalry; Morning, noon and night in Vienna; Pique dame; Poet and peasant* ***).

Matačić provides a magical set, guaranteed to send shivers of delight through any listener with its vivid sense of atmosphere and superb musicianship. It is one of Walter Legge's masterpieces as a recording manager. He had directed the earlier *Merry Widow* set, also with his wife Elisabeth Schwarzkopf as Hanna, and realized how difficult it would be to outshine it. But outshine it he did, creating a sense of theatre that is almost without rival in gramophone literature. The CD opens up the sound yet retains the full bloom, and the theatrical presence and atmosphere are something to marvel at. The layout is less than ideal, however, and only two bands are provided on each CD, though there is generous indexing.

It was the mono set, of the early 1950s, which established a new pattern in recording operetta. Some were even scandalized when Schwarzkopf insisted on treating the *Viljalied* very seriously indeed at an unusually slow tempo; but the big step forward was that an operetta was treated with all the care for detail normally lavished on grand opera. Ten years later in stereo Schwarzkopf was to record the role again, if anything with even greater point and perception, but here she has extra youthful vivacity, and the *Viljalied* – ecstatically drawn out – is unique. Some may be troubled that Kunz as Danilo sounds older than the Baron, but it is still a superbly characterful cast, and the transfer to a single CD is bright and clear.

'Brahms's *Requiem* performed to the tunes of Lehár' was how one wit described the Karajan version of *The Merry Widow*, with its carefully measured tempi and absence of sparkle. The reverberant recording has been dried out a little, but this means that the choral focus is not always quite clean, although the solo voices have plenty of presence. Karajan's brilliant recordings of six Suppé overtures are added to fill out the space on the second disc, but DG would have done better to have cut the recording a little, so that it would fit on a single CD.

The Merry Widow (English version by Bonynge): highlights.
(M) **(*) Decca 421 884-2; *421 884-4* [id.]. Sutherland, Krenn, Resnik, Masterson, Ewer, Brecknock, Fryatt, Egerton, Amb. S., Nat. PO, Bonynge.

Although not everyone will take to Sutherland's Widow, this is generally an attractive English version. The exuberantly breezy overture (arranged by Douglas Gamley) introduces all the hits seductively, to set the mood of the proceedings. The chorus sings with great zest and the ensembles are infectious. The whole of the closing part of the disc – the Finale of Act II, *Njegus's aria* (nicely done by Graham Ewer), the introduction of the girls from Maxim's and the famous *Waltz duet* – is certainly vivacious; the Parisian atmosphere may seem a trifle overdone, but enjoyably so. Earlier, Sutherland's *Vilja* loses out on charm because of her wide vibrato, but the *Waltz duet* with Krenn is engaging.

Der Zarewitsch (complete).
*** Eurodisc 610 137 (2). Kollo, Popp, Rebroff, Orth, Hobarth, Bav. R. Ch., Munich R. O, Wallberg.

René Kollo may not have the finesse of a Tauber, but he sings with a freshness and absence of mannerism that bring out the melodic beauty. Lucia Popp as the heroine, Sonya, sings ravishingly, and there is no weak link in the cast elsewhere. With two extra numbers given to the Grand Duke (Ivan Rebroff), both taken from Lehár's *Wo die Lerche singt*, the exhilaration of the entertainment comes over all the more refreshingly in the excellent CD transfer. No text is given, only notes in German.

Leighton, Kenneth (1929–88)

(i) *Cello concerto;* (ii) *Symphony No. 3 (Laudes Musicae).*
*** Chan. Dig. CHAN 8741; *ABTD 1380* [id.]. (i) Wallfisch; (ii) Mackie; SNO, Bryden Thomson.

Belated attention is now being paid to this fine composer, barely known at all outside the UK and rarely featured in public concerts. This splendid CD couples the early *Cello concerto*, written in the mid-1950s, at the time of the composer's studies with Petrassi, and the *Third Symphony*, a BBC commission, written in 1984, four years before his untimely death. The symphony is in part a song-cycle, and its glowing, radiant colours and refined textures are immediately winning. Raphael Wallfisch plays the *Concerto* as if his life depended on it, and the

Symphony draws every bit as much dedication from its performers. The recording is very immediate, and presents every strand in the orchestral texture with stunning clarity and definition.

Veris gratia (for cello, oboe and strings), *Op. 9.*
*** Chan. Dig. CHAN 8471; *ABTD 1182* [id.]. Wallfisch, Caird, RLPO, Handley – FINZI: *Cello concerto.* ***

Finzi is the dedicatee of Kenneth Leighton's *Veris gratia*, and so it makes an appropriate coupling for his *Cello concerto*, more particularly as its English pastoral style nods in his direction. It is in essence a miniature sinfonia concertante, featuring oboe as well as cello, written in 1950. The performance is highly sympathetic, George Caird the excellent oboist, and the naturally balanced recording is first class.

Conflicts, Op. 51; Fantasia contrappuntistica, Op. 24; Household pets, Op. 86; Sonatina No. 1; 5 Studies, Op. 22.
**(*) Abacus Dig. ABA 402-2 [id.]. Eric Parkin.

What a civilized composer Kenneth Leighton was. He was one of the most musical of pianists and wrote beautifully for the instrument. The *Household pets* is a sensitive piece, refined in craftsmanship, and the *Fantasia contrappuntistica* is comparably powerful. Eric Parkin plays it with total sympathy, and the recording, though not in the demonstration bracket, is eminently serviceable.

Lemba, Artur (1885–1960)

Symphony in C sharp min.
*** Chan. Dig. CHAN 8656; *ABTD 1342* [id.]. SNO, Järvi (with Concert: *'Music from Estonia'*: Vol. 2***).

Lemba's *Symphony in C sharp minor* was composed in 1908, the first symphony ever to be written by an Estonian. It sounds as if he studied in St Petersburg: at times one is reminded fleetingly of Glazunov, at others of Dvořák (the scherzo) – and even of Bruckner (at the opening of the finale) and of Elgar. This is by far the most important item in an enterprising collection of Estonian music.

Leoncavallo, Ruggiero (1858–1919)

I Pagliacci (complete).
*** DG 419 257-2 (3) [id.]. Carlyle, Bergonzi, Benelli, Taddei, Panerai, La Scala, Milan, Ch. & O, Karajan – MASCAGNI: *Cavalleria rusticana.* ***
(M) *** BMG/RCA GD 60865 (2) [60865-2]. Caballé, Domingo, Milnes, John Alldis Ch., LSO, Santi – PUCCINI: *Il Tabarro.* **(*)
(***) EMI mono CDS7 47981-8 (3) [Ang. CDCC 47981]. Callas, Di Stefano, Gobbi, La Scala, Milan, Ch. & O, Serafin – MASCAGNI: *Cavalleria rusticana.* (***)
(M) **(*) EMI CMS7 63650-2 (2). Scotto, Carreras, Nurmela, Amb. Op. Ch., Philh. O, Muti – MASCAGNI: *Cavalleria rusticana.* **(*)

Karajan does nothing less than refine Leoncavallo's melodrama, with long-breathed, expansive tempi and the minimum exaggeration. One would expect such a process to take the guts out of the drama, but with Karajan the result is superb. One is made to hear the beauty of the music first and foremost, and that somehow makes one understand the drama more. Karajan's choice of soloists was clearly aimed to help that – but the passions are still there; and rarely if ever on record has the La Scala Orchestra played with such beautiful feeling for tone-colour. Bergonzi is among the most sensitive of Italian tenors of heroic quality, and it is good to have Joan Carlyle as Nedda, touching if often rather cool. Taddei is magnificently strong, and Benelli and Panerai could hardly be bettered in the roles of Beppe and Silvio. As a filler, DG provides a splendid set of performances of operatic intermezzi from *Manon Lescaut*, *Suor Angelica*, Schmidt's *Notre Dame*, Giordano's *Fedora*, Cilea's *Adriana Lecouvreur*, Wolf-Ferrari's *Jewels of the Madonna*, Mascagni's *L'amico Fritz*, plus the *Meditation* from *Thaïs* (with Michel Schwalbé), and the *Prelude* to Act III of *La Traviata*.

For those who do not want that obvious coupling, the RCA set is a first-rate recommendation, with fine singing from all three principals, vivid playing and recording, and one or two extra passages not normally included – as in the Nedda–Silvio duet. Milnes is superb in the Prologue, and though Caballé does not always suggest a young girl, this is technically the most beautiful account of Nedda available on record. The 1971 recording was made at Walthamstow Town Hall and the CD transfer has plenty of atmosphere and increased vividness. A full translation is provided.

It is thrilling to hear *Pagliacci* starting with the Prologue sung so vividly by Tito Gobbi. The bite of the voice and its distinctive timbres are unique. Di Stefano, too, is at his finest, but the performance inevitably centres on Callas. There are many points at which she finds extra intensity, extra meaning, so that the performance is worth hearing for her alone. Serafin's direction is strong and direct. The mono recording is dry, with voices placed well forward but with choral detail blurred, a balance underlined in the clarity and definition of CD, and this set is overpriced.

Under Muti's urgent direction both *Cav.* and *Pag.* represent the music of violence. In both he has sought to use the original text, which in *Pag.* is often surprisingly different, with many top notes eliminated and Tonio instead of Canio delivering (singing, not speaking) the final *La commedia è finita*. Muti's approach represents the antithesis of smoothness, and the coarse rendering of the *Prologue* in *Pag.* by the rich-toned Kari Nurmela is disappointing. Scotto's Nedda goes raw above the stave, but the edge is in keeping with Muti's approach, with its generally brisk speeds. Carreras seems happier here than in *Cav.*, but it is the conductor and the fresh look he brings which will prompt a choice here. The sound is extremely vivid.

I Pagliacci: highlights.
(B) *** DG Compact Classics *427 717-4* [id.] (from complete recording with Joan Carlyle, Bergonzi, Benelli, Taddei, La Scala Milan Ch. & O, Karajan) – MASCAGNI: *Cavalleria rusticana*: highlights. ***
(M) **(*) EMI CDM7 63933-2 [id.]; *EG 763933-2* (from above recording; cond. Muti) – MASCAGNI: *Cavalleria rusticana*: highlights **(*).

Karajan's refined approach to Leoncavallo is matched by fine singing from all the principals and, with all the key items from the opera included, this is a very attractive Compact Classics tape coupling. The sound is excellent, although the choral focus is rather soft-grained.

On EMI, a good sampler of the vibrant Muti set with the key numbers vividly projected (27 minutes). The red-blooded drama is very much to the fore.

Liadov, Anatol (1855–1914)

About olden times, Op. 21b; Baba-Yaga, Op. 56; The enchanted lake, Op. 62; 3 Fanfares; Kikimora, Op. 63; The musical snuff-box, Op. 32; Polonaises, Opp. 49 & 55; 8 Russian folksongs, Op. 58.
**(*) ASV Dig. CDDCA 657; *ZCDCA 657* [id.]. Mexico City SO, Bátiz.

Three stars for the ASV recording by Brian Culverhouse – but the performances under Enrique Bátiz fall just short of that rating: the magical world of the finest of these scores could perhaps be conveyed with a more subtle atmosphere. Bátiz sometimes allows the colours to become almost gaudy, though he draws enthusiastic playing from his Mexican orchestra. However, there is much to enjoy here and the music itself (particularly *Kikimora* and the *Eight Russian folksongs*) is full of enchantment. Recommended.

(i) *Baba Yaga, Op. 56; The enchanted lake, Op. 62; Kikimora, Op. 63;* (ii) *8 Russian folksongs.*
(BB) **(*) Naxos Dig. 8.550328 [id.]. Slovak PO, (i) Gunzenhauser (ii) Kenneth Jean – Concert: *'Russian Fireworks'*.

It is good to have inexpensive recordings of these key Liadov works, particularly the *Russian folksongs*, eight orchestral vignettes of great charm, displaying a winning sense of orchestral colour. The performances are persuasive, and the digital recording is vivid and well balanced. They are part of an attractive concert of Russian music, much of it with a more extrovert appeal.

Ligeti, György (born 1923)

(i) *Chamber concerto for 13 instrumentalists;* (ii) *Double concerto for flute, oboe and orchestra; Melodien for orchestra;* (iii) *10 Pieces for wind quintet.*
(M) *** Decca 425 623-2. (i) L. Sinf., Atherton; (ii) with Nicolet, Holliger; (iii) Vienna Wind Soloists.

Over the last decade or so, Ligeti has developed a technique of micro-polyphony that produces strongly atmospheric and distinctive textures. The *Double concerto* makes great play with micro-intervals, not exactly quarter-tones but deviations. The resulting sonorities will not always please but should consistently interest or even exasperate the unprejudiced listener. The distinguished soloists and the London Sinfonietta give accomplished accounts of these complex scores and the Vienna performances of the wind pieces are hardly less stimulating.

Bagatelles.
*** Crystal CD 750 [id.]. Westwood Wind Quintet – CARLSSON: *Nightwings;* MATHIAS: *Quintet;* BARBER: *Summer music.* ***

Ligeti's folk-inspired *Bagatelles* were originally written for piano and in 1953 were arranged by the composer for wind quintet. They are highly inventive and very attractive; and they are played with dazzling flair and unanimity of ensemble by this American group.

Liszt, Franz (1811–86)

Ce qu'on entend sur la montagne (Bergsymphonie).
**(*) ASV Dig. CDDCA 586; *ZCDCA 586* [id.]. LSO, Yondani Butt – TCHAIKOVSKY: *The Tempest.* **(*)

Ce qu'on entend sur la montagne is the first of Liszt's symphonic poems and the longest (28 minutes). It suffers not only from formal weakness but also from a lack of really interesting material. Yondani Butt gives the work with much conviction, and the LSO respond with some powerful and expressive playing. The recording is appropriately spectacular, with a wide dynamic range on CD. The coupling, an early symphonic poem of Tchaikovsky, more inspired music, is very appropriate.

Piano concertos Nos. 1–2; Fantasia on Hungarian folksongs; Fantasia on themes from Beethoven's 'Ruins of Athens'; Grande fantaisie symphonique on themes from Berlioz's 'Lélio'; Malédiction; Polonaise brillante on Weber's Polonaise brillante in E (L'Hilarité); Totentanz (paraphrase on the *Dies Irae*); SCHUBERT/LISZT: *Wanderer fantasia.*
(B) *** EMI CZS7 67214-2 (2) [id.]. Michel Béroff, Leipzig GO, Kurt Masur.

Michel Béroff has won acclaim for his superb technique and his refined poetic sense, and this generous bargain box, which collects Liszt's output for piano and orchestra, shows him to be a Lisztian of insight and flair. Although the concertos have been recorded in abundance, other works here, such as the *Grande fantaisie on themes from Lélio* and the *Fantasia on themes from Beethoven's Ruins of Athens* are rarities. Béroff's account of the two concertos can hold its own with the best of the competition: here there is nothing routine or slapdash, but instead excitement, warmth and spontaneity. Indeed the sparkle and imagination that distinguish his Prokofiev are in ample evidence, along with his remarkable technical prowess. The Leipzig recording, too, sounds first rate in its remastered form (much more natural than the comparable Prokofiev CD transfers) and the distinguished orchestral playing under Masur is given plenty of body and weight, so that it brings an added gravitas to the music-making, to offset the chimerical brilliance. This is especially satisfying in the Schubert *Wanderer* arrangement, while the opening of the Beethoven and Berlioz *Fantasias* are full of atmosphere. The piano timbre has plenty of body and colour as well as sparkle. This is an exhilarating and rewarding set which can be given the strongest recommendation on all counts.

Piano concerto No. 1 in E flat.
**(*) DG 415 061-2 [id.]. Argerich, LSO, Abbado – CHOPIN: *Concerto No. 1.* **(*)

Martha Argerich seems much less flamboyant than her competitors. Hers is a clear, direct, even fastidious approach. She plays the *Larghetto* meltingly, and there is an excellent partnership with Abbado, who also seeks refinement without reducing the underlying tension. The CD remastering of the 1969 recording is extremely successful, the sound hardly dated at all.

Piano concertos Nos. 1–2.
(M) *** Ph. 434 163-2; *434 163-4* [id.]. Sviatoslav Richter, LSO, Kondrashin (with BEETHOVEN: *Cello sonata No. 2, Op. 5/2* with Rostropovich and Richter ***).

(i) *Piano concertos Nos. 1–2;* (ii) *Les Préludes.*
(M) *** Tuxedo TUXCD 1013 [id.]. (i) Brendel, V. Prom Musica O, Michael Gielen; (ii) Hamburg SO, Hans-Jürgen Walther.

Piano concertos Nos. 1–2; Totentanz.
❀ *** DG Dig. 423 571-2 [id.]. Zimerman, Boston SO, Ozawa.
(M) *** Ph. 426 637-2; *426 637-4*. Alfred Brendel, LPO, Haitink.

Piano concertos Nos. (i) *1 in E flat;* (ii) *2 in A. Années de pèlerinage: Sonetto 104 del Petrarca. Hungarian rhapsody No. 6; Valse oubliée.*
(M) *** Mercury 432 002-2 [id.]. Byron Janis, (i) Moscow PO, Kondrashin; (ii) Moscow RSO, Rozhdestvensky (also with SCHUMANN: *Romance in F sharp; Novellette in F.* FALLA: *Miller's dance.* GUION: *The harmonica player* ***).

Krystian Zimerman's DG recording belongs in illustrious company and can be recommended alongside the Berman, Richter and Arrau versions. His record of the two *Concertos* and the *Totentanz* is altogether thrilling, and he has the advantage of excellent support from the Boston orchestra under Ozawa. It has poise and classicism and, as one listens, one feels this music could not be played in any other way – surely the mark of a great performance! The DG recording places the soloist a fraction too far forward, but the overall sound-quality is excellent. This record is outstanding in every way, and it now makes a first choice for this repertoire.

Sviatoslav Richter's 1961 recordings – after nearly a decade a full price – now return more economically on Philips's Insignia label, thus deprived of any documentation about the music; instead there is a superfluous eulogy of Richter. But the music-making is very distinguished indeed, and the remastering makes the very most of the recording, originally engineered by the Mercury team. Richter's playing is unforgettable and so is his rapport with Kondrashin and the LSO, whose playing throughout is of the very highest order. Rostropovich then joins Richter in Beethoven's *G minor Cello sonata*, a most satisfying encore, given a recording full of presence.

Brendel's Philips recordings from the early 1970s hold their place at or near the top of the list. There is a valuable extra work offered here and the recording is of Philips's best. The performances are as poetic as they are brilliant, and those who doubt the musical substance of No. 2 will find their reservations melt away.

Brendel's earlier performances of the Liszt *Concertos*, made (for Vox) a decade before his Philips versions, are by no means superseded by the later accounts. Indeed, with spacious tempi from Gielen, they have a breadth (and in the case of the opening of the *First*) a majesty not approached by other performances. The orchestral support in No. 2 is not as polished as that provided by Haitink and the LPO, and the recording balance is more artificial, but the piano is richly resonant in the lower register. The playing is strikingly spontaneous, with a musing, improvisatory quality in the lyrical writing, especially in the A major work, and the bravura in both concertos is illuminating as well as exciting. The filler is a strong, slighty melodramatic account of *Les Préludes*, brightly played and somewhat brashly recorded. But the concertos are rather special.

Around the time they were recording Richter's Liszt *Concertos* for Philips in London (1962), the Mercury engineers paid a visit to Moscow to record Byron Janis in the same repertoire, and his is a comparably distinguished coupling. The partnership between the soloist and both his Russian conductors is unusually close. Janis's glittering articulation is matched by his sense of poetry and drama, and there is plenty of dash in these very compelling performances, which are afforded characteristically brilliant Mercury sound, although the piano is too close. The encores which follow the two *Concertos* are also very enjoyable.

Piano concertos Nos. 1–2; Fantasia on Hungarian folk songs (for piano & orchestra).
*** RCA Dig. RD 87916 [7916-2-RC]. Barry Douglas, LSO, Hirokami.

Barry Douglas gives a very creditable account of both *Concertos* and commands a wide variety of keyboard colour. He keeps the flamboyant showmanship in hand and a shows a good deal of poetic feeling; his readings are well thought out and never unimaginative.

Piano concerto No. 2 in A.
*** Virgin Dig. VC7 91198-2; *VC7 91198-4* [id.]. Leif Ove Andsnes, Bergen PO, Dmitri Kitaenko – GRIEG: *Piano concerto* etc. ***
(M) *** Pickwick/RPO Dig. CDRPO 5001 [id.]. Janis Vakarelis, RPO, Rowicki – PROKOFIEV: *Concerto No. 3.* **(*)

Leif Ove Andsnes is a gifted young Norwegian player who is far more than just another boy wonder with dazzling fingers – though he certainly has them. There is no lack of display and bravura in the Liszt but no narcissistic ostentation. Indeed he is a real musician who plays with great tenderness and poetic feeling as well as bravura. Marvellous sound, too, with a piano in perfect condition (not always the case on records) and an excellent balance. The Bergen Philharmonic under their newly appointed Soviet conductor are obviously in good shape and give eminently sympathetic support. This is as good as any version now before the collector.

Janis Vakarelis offers an unusual coupling: the Liszt *A major Concerto* and the Prokofiev No. 3. It has the benefit of a really first-class, modern, digital recording with excellent definition and range. The orchestral playing under the late Witold Rowicki is also of the highest quality. Vakarelis is an accomplished and thoughtful player and he is far from uncompetitive.

Dante symphony.
*** Hung. HCD 11918-2 [id.]. Kincses, Hungarian R. & TV Ch., Budapest SO, Lehel.

Lehel's account is second to none and better than most previous versions. Veronika Kincses is a fine singer, and Lehel gives a strongly characterized performance with well-focused singing and fiery, intense orchestral playing. The Hungaroton recording has plenty of detail and presence, and the acoustic is agreeably warm. Like Lopez-Cobos before him, Lehel offers the *Magnificat* ending, which comes off splendidly in his hands.

2 Episodes from Lenau's Faust: Der nächtliche Zug; Mephisto waltz No. 1 (Der Tanz in der Dorfschenke); 2 Legends; Les Préludes.
(M) **(*) Erato/Warner Dig. 2292 45256-2 [id.]. Rotterdam PO, James Conlon.

James Conlon gives us the original orchestration of the *St Francis Legends* plus the rarely heard and highly imaginative *Der nächtliche Zug.* Conlon secures responsive playing from the Rotterdam orchestra, and the engineering is excellent without being in any way spectacular. There is a good, full-bodied and well-balanced sound-picture.

Fantasia on Hungarian folk tunes for piano and orchestra.
(M) *** Decca Dig. 430 726-2; *430 726-4* [id.]. Bolet, LSO, Ivan Fischer – ADDINSELL: *Warsaw concerto* ***; GERSHWIN: *Rhapsody* **(*); GOTTSCHALK: *Grand fantasia* ***; LITOLFF: *Scherzo.* ***

(i) *Fantasia on Hungarian folk tunes; Hungarian rhapsodies Nos. 2 & 5.*
(B) *** DG 429 156-2 [id.]. (i) Shura Cherkassky; BPO, Karajan (with BRAHMS: *Hungarian dances Nos. 17–20* ***).

(i) *Fantasia on Hungarian folk tunes; Hungarian rhapsodies Nos. 2 & 5; Mephisto waltz.*
(M) *** DG 419 862-2 [id.]. (i) Cherkassky; BPO, Karajan.

Bolet is a masterful soloist and he plays here with characteristic bravura. Like the pianist, the Hungarian conductor is an understanding Lisztian, and the accompaniment from the LSO is first rate, with a recording balance of demonstration quality.

Shura Cherkassky's glittering 1961 recording of the *Hungarian fantasia* is an affectionate performance with some engaging touches from the orchestra, though the pianist is dominant and his playing is superbly assured. The rest of the programme is comparably charismatic, although the *Hungarian rhapsody* described as No. 2 is not the famous orchestral No. 2, but an orchestration of No. 12 for piano. The four Brahms *Hungarian dances* make a scintillating, lightweight encore. The Galleria mid-priced CD duplicates three of the items on the bargain disc. The *Mephisto waltz* is now added, brilliantly played and used to introduce the rest of the programme.

(i) *Fantasia on Hungarian folk tunes. Hungarian rhapsodies; Mazeppa; Mephisto waltz No. 1; Les Préludes; Tasso, lamento e trionfo.*
**(*) DG 415 967-2 (2). (i) Shura Cherkassky; BPO, Karajan.

Here the remastering for CD has improved the range and body of the sound impressively, with firm detail throughout the orchestra. The cellos and basses sound marvellous in the *Fifth*

Rhapsody and *Tasso*, and even the brashness of *Les Préludes* is a little tempered. *Mazeppa* is a great performance, superbly thrilling and atmospheric. A superb achievement, showing Karajan and his Berlin orchestra at their finest. However, this set now seems overpriced.

A Faust symphony.
(M) *** DG 431 470-2; *431 470-4*. Kenneth Riegel, Tanglewood Festival Ch., Boston SO, Bernstein.
(M) *** EMI CDM7 63371-2 [id.]; *EG 763371-4*. Alexander Young, Beecham Ch. Soc., RPO, Beecham.
*** EMI Dig. CDC7 49062-2 [id.]. Winberg, Westminster Ch. College Male Ch., Phd. O, Muti.

Bernstein's was the first modern recording to challenge Beecham's classic account, made in 1959. The DG sound is considerably superior and many will now consider it the best buy for this work, which can be as elusive in the concert hall as in the recording studio. Bernstein seems to possess the ideal temperament for holding together grippingly the melodrama of the first movement, while the lovely *Gretchen* centrepiece is played most beautifully. Kenneth Riegel is an impressive tenor soloist in the finale, there is an excellent, well-balanced choral contribution, and the Boston Symphony Orchestra produce playing which is both exciting and atmospheric. The vividness of the recording overall is most compelling.

Sir Thomas Beecham's classic 1959 recording, well transferred to CD, shows this instinctive Lisztian at his most illuminatingly persuasive. His control of speed is masterly, spacious and eloquent in the first two movements without dragging, brilliant and urgent in the finale without any hint of breathlessness. Though in the transfer string-tone is limited in body, balances are very convincing, and the sound is unlikely to disappoint anyone wanting to enjoy a uniquely warm and understanding reading of an equivocal piece, hard to interpret.

As an ardent Tchaikovskian, Muti shows a natural sympathy for a piece which can readily seem overlong, and he finds obvious affinities in the music with the style of the Russian master. Some might feel that he is too overtly melodramatic in the finale, yet his pacing of the first movement is admirable, finding tenderness as well as red-blooded excitement. In the *Gretchen* movement he conjures the most delicately atmospheric playing from the orchestra and throughout he is helped by the ambience of the Old Met. in Philadelphia which seems especially suitable for this score. The digital recording is brilliant yet full-bodied, and without glare.

Hungarian rhapsodies Nos. 1–6.
(M) **(*) Mercury 432 015-2 [id.]. LSO, Dorati – ENESCU: *Roumanian rhapsody No. 1.* ***

Dorati's is undoubtedly the finest set of orchestral *Hungarian rhapsodies*. He brings out the gypsy flavour and, with lively playing from the LSO, there is both polish and sparkle, but the music does not become urbane. The use of the cimbalom within the orchestra brings an authentic extra colouring. The Mercury recording is characteristically vivid, if not quite as full in the upper range as we would expect today.

Hunnenschlacht (symphonic poem).
** Telarc Dig. CD 80079 [id.]. Cincinnati SO, Kunzel – BEETHOVEN: *Wellington's victory.* **

A direct, unsubtle performance of a rarely recorded piece, not one of Liszt's finest works in the genre. The Telarc sound, however, is highly spectacular, with the organ interpolation adding to the expansiveness of texture. Those wanting the *'Battle' symphony* of Beethoven won't be disappointed with this, although the CD is rather short measure.

Mazeppa; Les Préludes; Prometheus; Tasso, lamento e trionfo.
(BB) *** Naxos Dig. 8.550487 [id.]. Polish Nat. RSO (Katowice), Michael Halász.

Michael Halász has the full measure of this repertoire and this is one of the most successful collections of Liszt's symphonic poems to have emerged in recent years. He draws some remarkably fine playing from the Katowice Radio Orchestra. They are a smaller band, and cannot quite manage the body of tone that the Berlin Philharmonic Orchestra brought to *Mazeppa* under Karajan, but by any standards theirs is an impressive performance, vividly characterized and with a powerful denouement when the Cossack hero, heralded by distant trumpets, returns to lead the Ukranian peasants in their revolt. The brass playing is very impressive throughout, especially the trombones and tuba, who have the epic main theme of *Mazeppa*. but its grandiloquence is no less powerful in *Les Préludes*, weighty and never brash. The strings play beautifully too, especially in the pastoral middle section, and this is a vivid and imaginative performance. But most remarkable is *Tasso*, an extended piece (22 minutes), not easy to hold together. Its sombre opening section anticipates Tchaikovsky's *Francesca da Rimini* and later there is some engaging lyrical writing for woodwind and strings in the court music before the brass return for the triumphant close. *Prometheus* is less inspired, more rhetorical, but still convincingly presented. The recording is spacious, with full natural string textures, but it is the resounding brass one remembers most .

Orpheus; (i) *Psalm 13.*
(M) *** EMI CDM7 63299-2. (i) Beecham Ch. Soc.; RPO, Beecham – R. STRAUSS: *Ein Heldenleben.* ***

Beecham's recording of *Orpheus* remains the most poetic and unaffected yet to be committed to disc. It sounds uncommonly fresh and spacious, and the performance is magical. The performance of *Psalm 13* is hardly less impressive. It is sung in English with the legendary Walter Midgely but is drier and more monochrome. All the same, an indispensable issue.

Les Préludes; Hungarian rhapsody No. 2 in C sharp min.
(B) *** EMI CDZ7 62860-2 [id.]. Philh. O, Karajan – MUSSORGSKY: *Pictures.* ***

Karajan's 1958 *Les Préludes* found much favour in its day, as well it should. It still sounds thrilling now, and demonstrates the fine musical judgement of the original balance engineers. Musically, this is the equal of any modern version. It is now available on EMI's cheapest, Laser label, compled with the *Hungarian rhapsody No. 2* and a splendid version of Mussorgsky's *Pictures at an exhibition.*

Totentanz. SCHUBERT/LISZT: *Wanderer fantaisia* (arr. for piano and orchestra).
(M) *** Decca Dig. 430 736-2; *430 736-4* [id.]. Bolet; (i) LSO, Fischer; (ii) LPO, Solti – RACHMANINOV: *Concerto No. 2.* **

Bolet is a masterful soloist here, and he is well partnered in both works and very well recorded. But the Rachmaninov coupling is much less recommendable, and those content with just Liszt's arrangement of Schubert's *Wanderer fantasia* would do better with Bolet's bargain-priced sampler – see below.

PIANO MUSIC

Complete piano music, Vol. 1: *Albumblatt in waltz form; Bagatelle without tonality; Caprice-valses Nos. 1 & 2; Ländler in A flat; Mephisto waltzes Nos. 1–3; Valse impromptu; 4 Valses oubliées.*
*** Hyp. Dig. CDA 66201; *KA 66201* [id.]. Leslie Howard.

Complete piano music, Vol. 2: *Ballades Nos. 1–2; Berceuse; Impromptu (Nocturne); Klavierstück in A flat; 2 Légendes; 2 Polonaises.*
**(*) Hyp. Dig. 66301; *KA 66301.* Leslie Howard.

Complete piano music, Vol. 3: *Fantasia and fugue on B-A-C-H; 3 Funeral odes: Les morts; La notte; Le triomphe funèbre du Tasse; Grosses Konzertsolo; Prelude on Weinen, Klagen, Sorgen, Sagen; Variations on a theme of Bach.*
** Hyp. Dig. CDA 66302; *KA 66302* [id.]. Leslie Howard.

Complete piano music, Vol. 4: *Adagio in C; Études d'exécution transcendante; Élégie sur des motifs de Prince Louis Ferdinand de Prusse; Mariotte.*
** Hyp. Dig. CDA 66357; *KA 66357* [id.]. Leslie Howard.

Complete piano music, Vol. 5: Concert paraphrases: BERLIOZ: *L'Idée fixe; Overtures: Les Francs-Juges; Le Roi Lear; Marche des pèlerins; Valse des Sylphes.* CHOPIN: *6 Chants polonais.* SAINT-SAËNS: *Danse macabre.*
*** Hyp. Dig. CDA 66346; *KA 66346* [id.]. Leslie Howard.

Complete piano music, Vol. 6: Concert paraphrases: AUBER: *3 Pieces on themes from La muette de Portici.* BELLINI: *Réminiscences de Norma.* BERLIOZ: *Benvenuto Cellini: Bénédiction et serment.* DONIZETTI: *Réminiscences de Lucia di Lammermoor; Marche funèbre et Cavatina (Lucia).* ERNST (Duke of Saxe-Coburg-Gotha): *Tony: Hunting chorus.* GLINKA: *Russlan and Ludmilla: Tscherkessenmarsch.* GOUNOD: *Waltz from Faust.* HANDEL: *Almira: Sarabande and Chaconne.* MEYERBEER: *Illustrations de L'Africaine.* MOZART: *Réminiscences de Don Juan.* VERDI: *Aida: Danza sacra & Duetto finale.* TCHAIKOVSKY: *Eugene Onegin: Polonaise.* WAGNER: *Tristan: Isoldes Liebestod.* WEBER: *Der Freischütz: Overture.*
*** Hyp. Dig. CDA 66371/2 [id.]. Leslie Howard.

Complete piano music, Vol. 7: Chorales: *Crux ave benedicta; Jesu Christe; Meine Seele; Nun danket alle Gott; Nun ruhen all Wälder; O haupt; O Lamm Gottes; O Traurigkeit; Vexilla Regis; Was Gott tut; Wer nur den Lieben; Via Crucis; Weihachtsbaum; Weihnachtslied.*
** Hyp. Dig. CDA 66388; *KA 66388* [id.]. Leslie Howard.

Complete piano music, Vol. 8: *Alleluia and Ave Maria; Ave Marias 1–4; Ave Maria de Arcadelt; Ave Maris stella; Harmonies poétiques et religieuses* (complete); *Hungarian Coronation Mass; Hymnes; Hymne du Pape; In festo transfigurations; Invocation; O Roma nobilis; Sancta Dorothea; Slavimo slavno slaveni!; Stabat mater; Urbi et orbi; Vexilla regis prodeunt; Zum Haus des Herrn.*
** Hyp. Dig. CDA 66421/2 [id.]. Leslie Howard.

Complete piano music, Vol. 9: *6 Consolations; 2 Élégies; Gretchen* (from *Faust Symphony*); *Sonata in B min.; Totentanz.*
** Hyp. Dig. CDA 66429; *KA 66429* [id.]. Leslie Howard (piano).

Complete piano music, Vol. 10: Concert paraphrases: BELLINI: *Hexaméron (Grand bravura variations* on the *March* from *I Puritani).* BERLIOZ: *Symphonie fantastique. Un portrait en musique de la Marquise de Blocqueville.*
**(*) Hyp. Dig. CDA 66433 [id.]. Leslie Howard.

Complete piano music, Vol. 11: *Abschied (Russisches Volkslied); Am Grabe Richard Wagners; Carrousel de Madame P-N; Dem Andenken Petöfis; Epithalium; Klavierstück in F sharp; En Rêve; 5 Klavierstücke; Mosonyis Grabgeleit; Recueillement; Resignazione; Romance oubliée; RW (Venezia); Schlaflos! Frage und Antwort; Sospiri; Toccata; Slyepoi (Der blinde Sänger); Die Trauergondel (La lugubre gondola); Trauervorspiel und Trauermarsch; Trübe Wolken (Nuages gris); Ungams Gott; Ungarisches Königslied; Unstern! -Sinistre; Wiegenlied (Chant de berceau).*
**(*) Hyp. Dig. CDA 66445 [id.]. Leslie Howard.

Complete piano music, Vol. 12: *Années de Pèlerinages, 3rd Year (Italy); 5 Hungarian folksongs; Historical Hungarian portraits.*
** Hyp. Dig. CDA 66448 [id.]. Leslie Howard.

Complete piano music, Vol. 13: Concert paraphrases: ALLEGRI/MOZART: *A La Chapelle Sistine: Miserere d'Allegri et Ave verum corpus de Mozart.* BACH: *Fantasia and fugue in G min.; 6 Preludes and fugues for organ.*
** Hyp. Dig. CDA 66438 [id.]. Leslie Howard.

Complete piano music, Vol. 14: *Christus; Polonaises de St Stanislas; Salve Polonia; St Elizabeth.*
**(*) Hyp. Dig. CDA 66466 [id.]. Leslie Howard.

Complete piano music, Vol. 15: Concert paraphrases of Lieder: BEETHOVEN: *Adelaïde; An die ferne Geliebte; 6 Gellert Lieder; 6 Lieder von Goethe; An die ferne Geliebte.* DESSAUER: *3 Lieder.* FRANZ: *Er est gekommenin Sturm und Regen; 12 Lieder.* MENDELSSOHN: *7 Lieder* including *Auf Flügeln des Gesanges.* CLARA & ROBERT SCHUMANN: *10 Lieder* including *Frülingsnacht; Widmung.*
**(*) Hyp. Dig. CDA 66481/2 [id.]. Leslie Howard.

Complete solo piano music, Vol. 16: Piano transcriptions: DAVID: *Bunte Reihe* (24 character pieces for violin and piano), *Op. 30.*
*** Hyp. Dig. CDA 66506 [id.]. Leslie Howard.

Complete piano music, Vol. 17: Concert paraphrases: DONIZETTI: *Spirito gentil* from *La Favorita; Marche funèbre* from *Don Sebastien.* GOUNOD: *Les Sabéennes (Berceuse)* from *La Reine de Saba.* GRÉTRY: *Die Rose (Romance)* from *Zémire et Azor.* MEYERBEER: *3 Ilustrations du Prophète; Fantasia and fugue* on *Ad nos, ad salutarem undam* on a theme from *Le Prophète.* MOSONYI: *Fantsy on Szép Ilonka* (Mosonyi). WAGNER: *Spinning song and Ballade* from *Der fliegende Holländer; Pilgrims' chorus and O du, mein holder Abendstern* from *Tannhäuser; Valhalla* from *The Ring; Feierlicher Marsch zum heiligen Grail* from *Parsifal.*
**(*) Hyp. Dig. CDA 66571/2 [id.]. Leslie Howard.

Complete piano music, Vol. 18: Concert paraphrases: BEETHOVEN: *Capriccio alla turca; Fantasy* from *Ruins of Athens.* LASSEN: *Symphonisches Zwischenspiel zu Calderons Schauspiel*

über allen Zauber Liebe. MENDELSSOHN: *Wedding march and dance of the elves* from *A Midsummer night's dream.* WEBER: *Einsam bin ich, nicht alleine from La Preciosa.* HEBBEL: *Nibelungen.*
**(*) Hyp. Dig. CDA 66575 [id.]. Leslie Howard.

Leslie Howard's ambitious project to record the complete music of Liszt proceeds apace and at least two of these issues have already collected a Grand Prix du Disque in Budapest (Volumes 5 and 6). The performances are very capable and musicianly, and there are moments of poetic feeling, but for the most part his playing rarely touches distinction. The kind of concentration one finds in great Liszt pianists such as Arrau, Kempff and Richter (and there are many younger artists whose names also spring to mind) rarely surfaces. Howard's technical equipment is formidable but poetic imagination and the ability to grip the listener are here less developed. The series has now reached some eighteen volumes and much of this music is not otherwise available. The very first recital, which collected all of Liszt's original piano pieces that might be described as waltzes, promised well, including a fourth *Valse oubliée* that the pianist himself notionally completed from material long buried, and it is no accident that the prize-winning discs are orchestral or operatic paraphrases, which – alongside the Lieder transcriptions – Howard does impressively. However, his rushed account of the *Sonata* does not really stand up against the current competition. It remains untouched by distinction and he fails to put the listener under his spell. One of the most interesting of recent issues is Volume 16, the *Bunte Reihe* of Ferdinand David (1810–70), a contemporary of Mendelssohn. These are transcriptions of music for violin and piano in which the violin seems hardly to be missed at all. They are pleasingly inventive and some of the lyrical inspirations are very like Mendelssohn's *Songs without words.* Leslie Howard plays them beautifully. Certainly the coverage so far is remarkable and, if this playing rarely takes the breath away either by its virtuosity or poetic insights, it is unfailingly intelligent and the recordings are first class.

Années de pèlerinage, 1st Year (Switzerland).
*** Decca Dig. 410 160-2 [id.]. Jorge Bolet.
*** DG Dig. 415 670-2 [id.]. Daniel Barenboim.

This recording of the Swiss pieces from the *Années de pèlerinage* represents Bolet at his very peak, with playing of magical delicacy as well as formidable power. So *Au bord d'une source* brings playing limpid in its evocative beauty. The piano sound is outstandingly fine, set against a helpful atmosphere.

Barenboim's set is also distinguished, rather warmer in pianistic colour and romantic feeling. Barenboim's approach is freer, more improvisatory at times (though Bolet's poetic mastery in the closing two pieces is undeniable). The DG recording projects an image of striking fullness, yet still not lacking brilliance.

Années de pèlerinage, 2nd Year (Italy) (complete).
*** Decca Dig. 410 161-2 [id.]. Jorge Bolet.
*** Chan. Dig. CHAN 8900; *ABTD 1516* [id.]. Louis Lortie.

The pianistic colourings in this fine instalment in Bolet's Liszt series are magically caught here, whether in the brilliant sunlight of *Sposalizio* or the visionary gloom of *Il penseroso.* The *Dante sonata* brings a darkly intense performance, fresh and original and deeply satisfying.

As with his earlier Chandos issues from The Maltings, Snape, Louis Lortie has been excellently served by the engineers. This is singularly vivid and realistic piano sound, and pretty distinguished playing too. By present-day standards it is (at 48 minutes) a bit short on playing time, but Lortie has impeccable taste and fine musical judgement. Those who have heard him play *Après une lecture de Dante* under concert conditions may find his account wanting in the last ounce of fire and intensity, but this disc nevertheless enhances his growing reputation. Not, perhaps, a first recommendation, but this is still high on the list, and there is certainly no cause to withhold three stars.

Années de pèlerinage, 3rd Year (Italy) (complete).
*** Ph. Dig. 420 174-2 [id.]. Zoltán Kocsis.

Zoltán Kocsis gives the most compelling account of these sombre and imaginative pieces; apart from beautiful pianism, he also manages to convey their character without exaggeration. He has impeccable technical control and can convey the dark power of the music without recourse to percussive tone. He is splendidly recorded by the Philips engineers. Lisztians need not hesitate.

Années de pèlerinage, Book 2; Supplement: Venezia e Napoli (Gondoliera; Canzone; Tarantella); 3rd Year: Les jeux d'eau à la Villa d'Este; Ballade No. 2 in B min.; Harmonies poétiques et religieuses: Bénédiction de Dieu dans la solitude.
*** Decca Dig. 411 803-2 [id.]. Jorge Bolet.

'A dazzling pendant to Liszt's Italian *Années de pèlerinage*', as the sleeve-note describes Bolet's performances; and the recital includes two of Liszt's weightiest conceptions, the *Bénédiction* and the *Ballade*, both spaciously conceived and far too little known. The concentration of the longer works, as well as the magically sparkling textures of the sunny Italian pieces, is masterfully conveyed. Vivid and full piano recording.

Années de pèlerinage: 1st Year: Au bord d'une source; Au lac de Wallenstadt; 3rd Year: Les jeux d'eau à la Villa d'Este. Bénédiction de Dieu dans le solitude; Liebestraum No. 3; Mephisto Waltz No. 1; Hungarian rhapsody No. 12; Variations on B-A-C-H.
❀ (BB) *** Virgo VC7 91458-2; *VC 791458-4* [id.]. Kun Woo Paik.

Kun Woo Paik is an outstanding Lisztian and this 78-minute recital, very realistically recorded and offered in the lowest price range, is in every way recommendable. Whether in the delicacy of Liszt's delightful watery evocations from the *Années de pèlerinage*, the devilish glitter of the upper tessitura of the *Mephisto Waltz*, or the comparable flamboyance of the *Hungarian rhapsody*, this is playing of a high order. The famous *Liebestraum* is presented more gently than usual and the wide range of mood of the *Bénédiction* is controlled very spontaneously; it is only in the climax of the *BACH variations* that perhaps a touch more restraint would have been effective. A most exciting issue and a very real bargain.

Années de pèlerinage, 1st Year: Au bord d'une source; 2nd Year: Sonnetto 104 del Petrarca; 3rd Year: Les jeux d'eau à la Villa d'Este; Supplement: Tarantella. Concert paraphrases of Schubert Lieder: *Auf dem Wasser zu singen; Die Forelle.* Concert studies: *Gnomenreigen; Un sospiro. Liebestraum No. 3.* (i) SCHUBERT/LISZT: *Wanderer fantasia* (arr. for piano and orchestra).
(B) *** Decca Dig. 425 689-2 [id.]. Jorge Bolet; (i) with LPO, Solti.

Intended by Decca as a bargain sampler for Bolet's distinguished Liszt series, this makes a unique recital in its own right. Quite apart from including a splendid version of Liszt's transcription for piano and orchestra of Schubert's *Wanderer fantasia*, the recital demonstrates the composer's wide pianistic range, from the evocation of the *Années de pèlerinage* and the romanticism of *Un sospiro* and *Liebestraum* to the glittering brilliance of *Gnomenreigen*, in which Bolet's playing is breathtakingly assured. The recording is very real and present.

Années de pèlerinage, 1st Year: Au bord d'un source. 2nd Year: Sonetto del Petrarca No. 104. 2 Concert studies: Waldesrauschen; Gnomenreigen. Mephisto waltz No. 1; Rhapsodie espagnole.
*** Sony Dig. SK 47180 [id.]. Murray Perahia – FRANCK: *Prélude, choral et fugue.* ***

Murray Perahia's Liszt shows all the keyboard distinction and poetic insight we associate with him. The beauty and range of sonority he produces and the complete dedication he brings to all he does, is everywhere in evidence. This is memorable and very distinguished Liszt playing, and the Sony engineers do full justice to him.

Années de pèlerinage, 1st Year: Vallée d'Obermann; 2nd Year: Après une lecture du Dante (Dante sonata); Sonetto 104 del Petrarca; 3rd Year: Les jeux d'eaux à la Villa d'Este. Ballade No. 2 in B min.; 6 Chants polonais de Chopin; Concert paraphrases on operas by Verdi; 2 Concert studies: Waldesrauschen; Gnomenreigen. 3 Études de concert; 12 Études d'exécution transcendante; Funérailles; Harmonies poétiques et religieuses: Bénédiction de Dieu dans la solitude; Sonata in B min.; Valse oubliée No. 1 in F sharp.
(M) *** Ph. Dig. 432 305-2 (5) [id.]. Claudio Arrau.

Claudio Arrau's Liszt performances are, generally speaking, in a special class: they combine an aristocratic finesse with just the proper amount of virtuoso abandon. His rubato, which can seem idiosyncratic to some musicians in Chopin or Schubert, is never excessive and always idiomatic. The performances are always completely within the sensibility of the period, yet are completely of our time as well. The excellent Philips recordings do justice to his thoroughly individual sound-world and are admirably balanced, and the set can be recommended without any serious reservation.

Années de pèlerinage, 2nd year: 3 Sonetti di Petrarca (Nos. 47, 104 & 123). Concert paraphrase on the *Quartet* from Verdi's *Rigoletto; Consolations Nos. 1–5; Liebesträume Nos. 1–3.*

(M) *** DG 435 591-2 [id.]. Daniel Barenboim.

Daniel Barenboim was on his finest form when he made these recordings in Berlin in 1978/79. He proves an ideal advocate for the *Consolations* and *Liebestraume*, and he is highly poetic in the *Petrarch sonnets*. His playing has an unaffected simplicity that is impressive and throughout there is a welcome understatement and naturalness, until he arrives at the *Rigoletto paraphrase* which is played with plenty of flair and glitter. The quality of the recorded sound is excellent and the natural balance of the CD transfer does full justice to the lyricism of these interpretations.

Années de pèlerinage, 3rd Year: Tarantella. Harmonies poétiques et religieuses: Pensées des morts; Bénédiction de Dieu dans la solitude; Legend: St Francis of Assisi preaching to the birds. Mephisto waltz No. 1; Rhapsodie espagnole.
*** Virgin Dig. VC7 90700-2; *VC 790700-4* [id.]. Stephen Hough.

Stephen Hough's imaginatively planned Liszt recital on the Virgin Classics label is outstanding in every way. The choice of items is both illuminating and attractive. *St Francis preaching to the birds* is magically poetic in its re-creation of birdsong, while in the *Tarantella* Hough gives an inspired performance, combining power and searing virtuosity with delicate poetry and keen wit. Full, vivid recording. This amply confirms what Hough's prize-winning record of Hummel concertos for Chandos suggested, that he is a natural, magnetic communicator in the recording studio.

Ave Maria (Die Glocken von Rom); Harmonies poétiques et religieuses: Pensées des morts; Andante lagrimoso.
*** Ph. Dig. 432 142-2 [id.]. Sviatoslav Richter – FRANCK: *Piano quintet.* *

The three pieces recorded here show Richter's art at its finest. His playing is very inward and concentrated in atmosphere. The listener is immediately drawn into the music and few will resist the spell he casts. The recording emanates from the Bavarian radio and is very good indeed, and a vast improvement on the unacceptably dry and close sound on the Franck *Quintet* which really cannot be given more than a *very* qualified recommendation.

Concert paraphrases of Schubert Lieder: *Auf den Wasser zu singen; Aufenthalt; Erlkönig; Die Forelle; Horch, horch die Lerch; Lebe wohl!; Der Lindenbaum; Lob der Tränen; Der Müller und der Bach; Die Post; Das Wandern; Wohin.*
*** Decca Dig. 414 575-2 [id.]. Jorge Bolet.

Superb virtuosity from Bolet in these display arrangements of Schubert. He is not just a wizard but a feeling musician, though here he sometimes misses a feeling of fun. First-rate recording, with the CD adding the usual extra sense of presence, and gaining from the silent background.

Concert paraphrase of Verdi's *Rigoletto; Études d'exécution transcendante d'après Paganini: La Campanella. Harmonies poétiques et religieuses: Funérailles. Hungarian rhapsody No. 12; Liebestraum No. 3. Mephisto waltz No. 1.*
*** Decca Dig. 410 257-2 [id.]. Jorge Bolet.

Bolet's playing is magnetic, not just because of virtuosity thrown off with ease (as here in the *Rigoletto* paraphrase) but because of an element of joy conveyed, even in the demonic vigour of the *Mephisto waltz No. 1*. The relentless thrust of *Funérailles* is beautifully contrasted against the honeyed warmth of the famous *Liebestraum No. 3* and the sparkle of *La Campanella*. First-rate recording.

3 Concert studies; 2 Concert studies; 6 Consolations; Réminiscences de Don Juan (Mozart).
*** Decca 417 523-2 [id.]. Jorge Bolet.

In the *Concert studies* the combination of virtuoso precision and seeming spontaneity is most compelling, and the record is particularly valuable for including a splendid account of the *Don Juan* paraphrase, a piece which is neglected on record. The *Consolations* show Bolet at his most romantically imaginative: he plays them beautifully.

Consolation No. 3; Étude: Harmonies du soir; Hungarian rhapsody No. 17; Scherzo and march.
**(*) BMG/RCA Dig. RD 60859; *RK 60859*. Sviatoslav Richter – BRAHMS: *Sonata No. 1.* **(*)

This Richter recital was recorded in Lubeck in 1988 at the Schleswig Holstein Festival, and shows the great pianist has lost none of his wizardry. Here is pianism that makes one sit up, full of character and personality; the music-making has all the excitement of a live occasion with plenty of risks taken. The recording itself is a bit wanting in bloom, but fully acceptable. *Harmonies du soir* has that rapt concentration Richter has always commanded.

Études d'exécution transcendante (complete).
**(*) Ph. 416 458-2 [id.]. Claudio Arrau.
**(*) Decca Dig. 414 601-2 [id.]. Jorge Bolet.

Arrau made this recording in 1977 and it was a formidable achievement for an artist in his seventies. Arrau always plays with great panache and musical insight which more than compensate for the occasional smudginess of the recorded sound. On record, Cziffra brings greater obvious virtuosity to these pieces, but he is of course a much younger man. Arrau's playing is most masterly and poetic, and the recording, if too reverberant, is truthful.

If you are looking principally for pianistic fireworks, Bolet is a little disappointing, lacking a little in demonry; but as a searching interpreter of the composer and his musical argument he has few rivals. The Decca recording presents big-scale piano sound to match the performances.

Hungarian rhapsodies Nos. 1–19.
(M) *** DG 423 925-2 (2) [id.]. Roberto Szidon.

At mid-price, Roberto Szidon's set of the *Hungarian rhapsodies* is highly recommendable. Szidon has been missing from the concert platform in recent years – at least so far as England is concerned – and has made few records. There is plenty of fire and flair here, and much that will dazzle the listener! The recording, too, sounds very good indeed.

Hungarian rhapsodies Nos. 2–3, 8, 13, 15 (Rákóczy march); 17; Csárdás obstinée.
(M) *** Van. 08.4024.71 [OVC 4024]. Alfred Brendel.

Although the Vanguard recording is not a recent one, it sounds very good in this excellent CD transfer, and the playing is very distinguished indeed. The Philips engineers provide Brendel elsewhere with more sonorous piano-tone and a wider dynamic range, but there are no more charismatic or spontaneous accounts of the *Hungarian rhapsodies* available, and there is no doubt about the brilliance of the playing nor the quality of musical thinking that informs it.

Liebesträume Nos. 1–3.
*** DG 415 118-2 [id.]. Daniel Barenboim – MENDELSSOHN: *Songs without words* ***; SCHUBERT: *6 Moments musicaux.* **

Barenboim plays these famous Liszt pieces with unaffected simplicity and, taken as a whole, this is a rewarding CD. But they are also available at mid-price – see above.

Piano sonata in B min.
* DG Dig. 429 391-2; *429 391-4* [id.]. Ivo Pogorelich – SCRIABIN: *Sonata.* **

Piano sonata; Années de pèlerinage, 2nd Year: Il Penseroso; 3rd Year: Les jeux d'eau à la Villa d'Este. Hungarian rhapsody No. 15 (Rákóczy march); Mephisto waltz No. 1.
❀ *** Olympia Dig. OCD 172 [id.]. Mikhail Pletnev.

Piano sonata in B min.; Années de pèlerinage, 2nd Year: Après une lecture de Dante (Dante sonata). Harmonies poétiques et religieuses: Invocation; La lugubre gondola, Nos. 1–2.
(M) *** Ph Dig. 432 048-2; *432 048-4*. Alfred Brendel.

Piano sonata; Années de pèlerinage, 2nd Year: Après une lecture du Dante (Dante sonata). Mephisto waltz No. 1.
*** Denon Dig. C37 7547 [id.]. Dezsö Ránki.

Piano sonata; 3 Concert studies.
*** Chan. Dig. CHAN 8548; *ABTD 1223* [id.]. Louis Lortie.

Piano sonata; Grand galop chromatique; Liebesträume Nos. 1–3; Valse impromptu.
*** Decca Dig. 410 115-2. Jorge Bolet.

Piano sonata; Harmonies poétiques et religieuses: Funérailles. La lugubre gondola II; La notte; Nuages gris.
**(*) DG Dig. 431 780-2 [id.]. Krystian Zimerman.

Mikhail Pletnev has a commanding musical authority, a highly distinctive timbre and an amazing dynamic range and variety of colour. His technique is transcendental and can be compared only with the young Horowitz, and there is a refinement and poetry that are hardly less remarkable. He dispatches the *Sonata* with an awesome brilliance and sense of drama, and his *Mephisto Waltz* is altogether thrilling. While the recording does not do full justice to his highly personal sound-world, it is eminently satisfactory. A most exciting disc.

Brendel's latest account of the *Sonata* has received wide acclaim. It is certainly a more subtle and concentrated account than his earlier version, made in the mid-1960s – brilliant though that was – and must be numbered among the very best now available. There is a wider range of colour and tonal nuance, yet the undoubted firmness of grip does not seem achieved at the expense of any spontaneity. It is most realistically recorded.

Louis Lortie gives almost as commanding a performance of the Liszt *Sonata* as any in the catalogue; its virtuosity can be taken for granted and, though he does not have the extraordinary intensity and feeling for drama of Pletnev, he has a keen awareness of its structure and a Chopinesque finesse that win one over. The Chandos recording is made at The Maltings, Snape, and, though a shade too reverberant, is altogether natural.

The power, imagination and concentration of Bolet are excellently brought out in his fine account of the *Sonata*. With the famous *Liebestraum* (as well as its two companions) also most beautifully done, not to mention the amazing *Grand galop*, this is one of the most widely appealing of Bolet's outstanding Liszt series. Excellent recording.

Dezsö Ránki's account of the *Sonata* is very impressive indeed and can hold its own with almost any of its rivals. The *Mephisto waltz* and the *Dante sonata* are hardly less powerful in the hands of the young Hungarian master, the latter with real fire and a masterly control of dramatic pace. The Denon recording is absolutely first class and has admirable clarity, body and presence. This is one of the best Liszt recital programmes currently available.

Krystian Zimerman's record is quite generously and logically coupled. The playing is not free from expressive exaggeration, but such agogic distortions as are present are very much at the service of Liszt rather than the pianist. Such is his mastery that one is soon under his spell and his playing not only in the *Sonata,* but during the remainder of his programme can only be called magisterial. However the recording balance places one very close indeed to the instrument and the aural glare that results is unpleasing. It diminishes the appeal of what would otherwise be a strong contender.

Pogorelich's account of the *Sonata* is an impressive display of keyboard virtuosity but is full of the expressive distortions and exaggerations that will probably strain the patience of those who know artists like Gilels, Richter, Horowitz, Brendel or Pletnev in this repertoire. All one can say is that if your primary interest lies in Pogorelich's undoubted virtuosity, this CD can be given a qualified recommendation, but if you are interested in the Liszt *Sonata*, you are better advised to turn elsewhere. Even so, the close recording balance (the listener's perspective is that of a page-turner) and the short playing time (another facet of implicit narcissism) make it an unappealing disc.

ORGAN MUSIC

Ave Maria; Prelude and fugue on B-A-C-H; Symphonic poems: *Orpheus* (arr. Jean Guillou); *Prometheus* (arr. Schaab/Liszt).
*** Argo Dig. 430 244-2; *430 244-4* [id.]. Thomas Trotter (Klais organ of Ingolstadt Minster) – REUBKE: *Sonata on Psalm 94.* ***

Évocation à la Chapelle Sixtine; Fantasia and fugue on 'Ad nos, ad salutarem undam'; Orpheus (symphonic poem; arr. Jean Guillou); *Variations on a theme by Bach: 'Weinen, Klagen, Sorgen, Zagen'.*
*** Collins Dig. 1249-2 [id.]. Jane Parker-Smith (Klais organ of Ingolstadt Minster).

Évocation à la Chapelle Sixtine; Fantasia and fugue on 'Ad nos, ad salutarem undam'; Prelude and fugue on B-A-C-H; Variations on a theme by Bach: 'Weinen, Klagen, Sorgen, Zagen'.
**(*) Novalis Dig. 150 069-2; *150 069-4* [id.]. Gunther Kaunzinger (organ of the Stiftsbasilica, Waldsassen).

The Argo and Collins records are complementary not only in terms of repertoire but, because both artists have coincidentally chosen the same organ at Ingolstadt. It is obviously very suitable for this music, with its long reverberation period providing a highly spectacular effect. Both players instinctively calculate for the resonance in their timing. When Jane Parker-Smith opens the *Variations on 'Weinen, Klagen, Sorgen, Zagen'*, the surge of organ-sound is like great rolling breakers of the sea coming in. It is an extraordinary piece, with a continuous descending chromatic motive trickling down constantly in the background. The only work common to both CDs is the arrangement of the symphonic poem, *Orpheus*. Comparing them is to discover the principal differences between the two sets of performances. Thomas Trotter is direct, with a firm forward impulse, Jane Parker-Smith is altogether more imaginative. She has a remarkable sense of fantasy, and the atmospheric writing at the beginning of the piece glows with a haunting aura. The sound of the two recordings is subtly different, with a slightly firmer focus on the Collins CD. There is no doubt that Parker-Smith's performances are inspirational. The *Fantasia and fugue on 'Ad nos, ad salutarem undam'* moves from its sombre opening with growing excitement and animation to its mighty *Maestoso* climax. The *Évocation à la Chapelle Sixtine* draws on Allegri's *Miserere* (but not too explicitly) and quotes Mozart's *Ave verum* gently at the close, a moment of utmost magic here. Thomas Trotter's playing is positive and firm, and his account of the *Prelude and fugue on B-A-C-H* is strongly controlled and very powerful, in contrast to the gently serene *Ave Maria*, which is most delicately registered. Apart from the second symphonic poem, he also offers a very impressive Reubke coupling.

Gunther Kaunzinger on Novalis has a distinct advantage in combining all four of Liszt's major organ works on a single 72-minute CD. The three major sets of variations (in different formats) are given authoritative and commanding performances comparing well with the competition. He has more flair than Trotter, although his style and registration is less imaginative than that of Jane Parker-Smith. Moreover, in the *Évocation à la Chapelle Sixtine* there is some background noise during the gentler moments of the music. Nevertheless this is a splendid organ, very well recorded.

VOCAL MUSIC

Lieder: *Blume und Duft; Der drei Zigeuner; Der du von dem Himmel bist* (2 settings); *Ein Fichtenbaum steht einsam; Es muss ein Wunderbares sein; Es rauschen die Winde; Der Hirt; Ihr Auge; Ihr Glocken von Marling; Freudvoll und leidvoll; Die Loreley; O komm im Traum; Des Tages laute Stimmen schweigen; Über allen Gipfeln ist Ruh; Vergiftet sind meine Lieder.*
*** Capriccio Dig. 10 294 [id.]. Mitsuko Shirai, Hartmut Höll.

Mitsuko Shirai has already established a unique place among Lieder-singers of her generation, and now the voice has darkened to add weight and intensity to her always searchingly perceptive singing. Her accompanist husband, Hartmut Höll, equally has few rivals to match him today, and their partnership in this outstanding Liszt record, as in their previous Capriccio issues, brings one revelation after another. There are few collections of Liszt songs as searchingly persuasive as this, and none more beautiful. Provocatively the record starts with Shirai at her most vehement in *Vergiftet sind meine Lieder* (My songs are poised), written when Liszt's long relationship with the Countess d'Agoult was breaking up. Regrettably, no English translations are provided with the text, only a commentary.

Lieder: *Comment, disaient-ils; Die drei Zigeuner; Ein Fichtenbaum steht einsam; Enfant, si j'étais roi; Es muss ein Wunderbares sein; Oh, quand je dors; S'il est un charmant gazon; Über allen Gipfeln ist Ruh; Vergiftet sind meine Lieder.*
*** DG Dig. 419 238-2 [id.]. Brigitte Fassbaender, Irwin Gage – R. STRAUSS: *Lieder.* ***

This is singing which, in its control of detail, both in word and in note, as well as in its beauty and range of expression, is totally commanding. There are few women Lieder singers in any generation who can match this in power and intensity, with each song searchingly characterized. Fassbaender proves just as much at home in the four Victor Hugo settings in French as in the German songs. Sensitive accompaniment, well-placed recording.

Hungarian Coronation Mass.
*** Hung. HCD 12148-2 [id.]. Kincses, Takács, Gulyás, Polgár, Hungarian R. & TV Ch., Budapest SO, Lehel.

Written for the coronation of Franz Josef I as King of Hungary, this setting of the Mass shows Liszt at his most direct, freely indulging his sympathy with a wide range of sources: operatic, Hungarian (in the *Sanctus*), plainchant and, with the *Graduale*, added later, bringing in Lisztian chromaticism. Sung here with dedication by excellent Hungarian forces under György Lehel, its plain homophonic textures – with the soloists generally used together as a quartet – make a strong impact, and the reverberant recording allows plenty of detail to be heard against an apt church acoustic.

The Legend of St Elisabeth.
*** Hung. Dig. HCD 12694/6-2 [id.]. Marton, Kováts, Farkas, Solyom-Nagy, Gregor, Gáti, Budapest Ch., Hungarian Army Male Ch., Children's Ch., Hungarian State O, Joó.

Though uneven in inspiration, Liszt's oratorio on *The Legend of St Elisabeth* contains some of his finest religious music in its span of six tableaux. Arpad Joó drives the work hard, but never to undermine the expressiveness of chorus and soloists, with Eva Marton as Elisabeth more firmly controlled than she has sometimes been in opera, and with no weak link in the rest of the team of principals.

Missa choralis.
(M) *** Decca 430 364-2 [id.]. Atkinson, Tinkler, Royall, Kendall, Suart, St John's College, Cambridge, Ch., Guest; Cleobury (organ) – DVOŘÁK: *Mass in D.* ***

Missa choralis; Via crucis.
❀ (M) *** Erato/Warner 2292 45350-2 [id.]. Donna Brown, Tantcheff, Alary, Oudor, Piquemal, Audita Nova de Paris Vocal Ens., Jean Sourisse; Marie-Claire Alain.

Fine as is the St John's account of the *Missa choralis* under George Guest, this new Erato performance becomes even more compelling. It is superbly sung and recorded, and the performance has a pulsing Latin ardour that is unforgettable in its spontaneous surges of feeling. It is ideally coupled to the other great ecclesiastical choral work of Liszt's final period, *Via crucis*, a provision of music for the Stations of the Cross, which he wrote between 1876 and 1878. This is even more original and certainly more daring in its spare treatment of the Crucifixion story. The organ intervenes with brief interludes to suggest some of the events, with the chorus continuing the tragic ongoing narrative. The extraordinary moment when Jesus is stripped of his garments, with its bare harmonic simplicity, anticipates Messiaen; then the choral cries of *Crucify him* lead to the wonderfully poignant solo, *My Lord, my Lord, why hast thou abandoned me?*. Liszt's forward-looking setting is most movingly realized here, by chorus, soloists who are excellent throughout both works, and not least, Marie-Claire Alain's restrained yet moving organ contribution. The acoustics of Saint-Antoine, Paris seem quite ideal for this music, and the choral focus is firm and clean, allowing expansive dynamics and a natural projection. Very highly recommended.

Guest provides an impressive and beautifully sung version, with well-blended tone. It has the benefit of spacious and richly detailed (originally Argo) recording. The transfer to CD serves only to enhance the original excellent sound.

Missa solemnis.
**(*) Hung. HCD 11861-2 [id.]. Kincses, Takács, Korondy, Gregor, Hungarian R. & TV Ch., Budapest SO, Ferencsik.

This ambitious setting of the Mass is one of Liszt's finest choral inspirations, full of powerful, dramatic ideas, with thematic links between movements that make it stylistically more consistent than most. Ferencsik's recording, made in the mid-1970s, brings a spacious, powerful performance, well played and sung, with four of Hungary's most distinguished singers as soloists. The analogue recording is not ideal but this remains far more than a stop-gap and is a noble account of a masterly choral work.

OPERA

Don Sanche (complete).
**(*) Hung. Dig. HCD 12744/5-2 [id.]. Garino, Hamari, Gáti, Farkas, Hungarian R. & TV Ch., Hungarian State Op. O, Tamás Pál.

Don Sanche or the Castle of Love was the teenage composer's first essay at a stage work. The piece tells of a magic castle of love ruled over by a sinister magician, and how the knight, Don Sanche, finally wins the love of the disdainful Elzire. The only really Lisztian quality is the way he lights on instruments relatively exotic at the time, loading piccolos and trombones on to writing which suggests Weber or Rossini with dashes of Haydn, Schubert or even an occasional watered-down echo of Beethoven's *Fidelio*. The pity is that, after a promising start, the 90-minute one-acter tails off. Támas Pál conducts a lively performance, with some stylish singing from the lyric tenor, Gerard Garino, in the name-part. Other principals are variable, including Julia Hamari as the hard-hearted heroine; but as long as you keep firmly in mind that this is the work of a thirteen-year-old, it will give much pleasure. The sound is bright and close.

Litolff, Henri (1818–91)

Concerto symphonique No. 4: Scherzo.

(M) *** Decca Dig. 430 726-2; *430 726-4* [id.]. Ortiz, RPO, Atzmon – ADDINSELL: *Warsaw concerto* ***; GERSHWIN: *Rhapsody* **(*); GOTTSCHALK: *Grand fantasia* ***; LISZT: *Hungarian fantasia.* ***

*** Ph. Dig. 411 123-2 [id.]. Misha Dichter, Philh. O, Marriner (with Concert of concertante music***).

Cristina Ortiz's version may lack extrovert brilliance but it has an agreeable elegance. The intimacy of this version is emphasized by the balance, which places the piano within the orchestral group, making the gentle central section especially effective. The Decca couplings are all appealing and the CD is impressively natural.

Misha Dichter gives a scintillating account of Litolff's delicious *Scherzo*, played at a sparklingly brisk tempo. Marriner accompanies sympathetically and the recording is excellent.

Lloyd, George (born 1913)

Piano concerto No. 3.

**(*) Albany Dig. TROY 019-2; *TROY 019-4* [id.]. Kathryn Stott, BBC PO, composer.

The *Third Piano concerto*, also inspired by events during the Second World War, is more amiable than one might expect, after the first two. It is very eclectic in style, with flavours of Prokofiev (with diluted abrasiveness) and even of Khachaturian – minus vulgarity – in outer movements which have a toccata-like brilliance and momentum. Kathryn Stott plays with a pleasing, mercurial lightness and makes the most of the music's lyrical feeling. But the slow movement – which recalls 'the knock on the door at midnight that terrorised the countries occupied by Hitler' – is too long (19½ minutes) and its passionate climax uses material which does not show Lloyd at his best. On the other hand, the wistful tune at the centre of the finale is rather appealing. The composer achieves a fine partnership with his soloist and the performance has undoubted spontaneity. But one wonders whether a virtuoso of the calibre of Kissin or Pletnev would add more force and power to the outer movements.

(i) *Piano concerto No. 4; The lily-leaf and the grasshopper; The transformation of that Naked Ape.*

*** Albany AR 004 [id.]. Kathryn Stott; (i) LSO, composer.

The *Fourth Piano concerto* is a romantic, light-hearted piece with a memorable 'long singing tune' (the composer's words), somewhat Rachmaninovian in its spacious lyricism contrasting with a 'jerky' rhythmic idea. The *Larghetto*, serene in a typical, undemanding, Lloydian way, derives from the material of the first movement, and then there is a good-humoured finale. The performance by Kathryn Stott and the LSO under the composer is ardently spontaneous from the first bar to the last. The first of the two solo pieces ingenuously but endearingly evokes a memory of an evening on the Avon when the composer saw a large lily-leaf come floating past him; on it sat a grasshopper. The second is a six-movement suite inspired by Desmond Morris's book *The Naked Ape*. The style is eclectic but still somehow Lloydian. The recording is first rate.

Symphonies Nos. 1 in A; 12.

*** Albany Dig. TROY 032-2; *TROY 032-4* [id.]. Albany SO, composer.

The pairing of George Lloyd's first and last symphonies is particularly appropriate, as both share a theme-and-variations format. The *First*, written in 1932 but recently revised, is relatively lightweight; it is based on a rhythmically catchy main theme, and the variations fall naturally into three basic sections: fast–slow–fast. The mature *Twelfth* uses the same basic layout but ends calmly with a ravishingly sustained pianissimo, semi-Mahlerian in intensity, that is among the composer's most beautiful inspirations. At the beginning of the work, the listener is soon aware of the noble lyrical theme which is the very heart of the *Symphony*. The Albany Symphony Orchestra gave the work its première and they play it with enormous conviction and eloquence. The concentration of the music-making throughout is that of a live performance, helped by the superb acoustics of the Troy Savings Bank Music Hall, which produces sound of demonstration quality, glowing in warmth and sonority and with the most vivid detail. The symphony is full of attractive orchestral effects and shows Lloyd at his very finest. This record therefore makes an admirable starting point for anyone wishing to begin an exploration of the music of a composer who communicates readily and who has already assembled a growing public of admiring music-lovers who find a great deal of contemporary writing totally inaccessible.

Symphonies Nos. 2 and 9.
*** Albany Dig. TROY 055 [id.]. BBC PO, composer.

Lloyd's *Second Symphony* is a lightweight, extrovert piece, conventional in form and construction, though in the finale the composer flirts briefly with polytonality, an experiment he did not repeat. The *Ninth* (1969) is similarly easygoing; the *Largo* is rather fine, but its expressive weight is in scale, and the finale, 'a merry-go-round that keeps going round and round', has an appropriately energetic brilliance. Throughout both works the invention is attractive, and in these definitive performances, extremely well recorded, the composer's advocacy is very persuasive.

Symphony No. 4.
*** Albany AR 002; *AR 002C* [id.]. Albany SO, composer.

George Lloyd's *Fourth Symphony* was composed during his convalescence after being badly shell-shocked while serving in the Arctic convoys of 1941/2. The first movement is directly related to this period of his life, and the listener may be surprised at the relative absence of sharp dissonance – indeed the violence seems muted by subjective feeling; in the serene second movement the composer is able to recall a pre-war journey up the Norwegian coast as far as the North Cape. After a brilliant scherzo, the infectious finale is amiable, offering a series of quick, 'march-like tunes', which the composer explains by suggesting that 'when the funeral is over the band plays quick cheerful tunes to go home'. Under Lloyd's direction, the Albany Symphony Orchestra play with great commitment and a natural, spontaneous feeling. The recording is superb.

Symphony No. 5 in B flat.
*** Albany Dig. TROY 022-2; *TROY 022-4* [id.]. BBC PO, composer.

The *Fifth Symphony* is a large canvas, with five strong and contrasted movements, adding up to nearly an hour of music. It was written during a happy summer spent living simply on the shore of Lac Neuchâtel, during the very hot summer of 1947. The pastoral scene is well caught in the idyll of the first movement. After a Chorale second movement comes a will-o'-the-wisp Rondo (marked *Delicatamente scherzando*) and then a Lamento, march-like, with a powerful climax. In the finale the composer tells us: 'everything is brought in to make as exhilarating a sound as possible – strong rhythms, vigorous counterpoints, energetic brass and percussion'. The movement is loosely structured and is the least cogent part of a work which is strong in invention and orchestral colour. It is played with much commitment by the BBC Philharmonic under the composer, who creates a feeling of spontaneously live music-making throughout. The recording is first class.

(i) *Symphonies Nos. 6;* (ii) *10 (November journeys);* (i) *Overture: John Socman.*
**(*) Albany Dig. TROY 15-2; *TROY 15-4* [id.]. (i) BBC PO; (ii) BBC PO Brass, composer.

The bitter-sweet lyricism of the first movement of *November journeys* is most attractive (the use of the piccolo-trumpet a piquant added colouring), but the linear writing is more complex than usual in a work for brass. In the finale a glowing *cantando* melody warms the spirit, to contrast with the basic *Energico.* The *Calma* slow movement is quite haunting, no doubt reflecting the composer's series of visits to English cathedrals, the reason for the subtitle. The composer's performance with the BBC players, for whom the work was written, is a good one, if not quite as fine as an earlier version by the London Collegiate Brass (now withdrawn). The *Sixth Symphony* is amiable and lightweight; it is more like a suite than a symphony. Lloyd's performance of No. 6 is attractively spontaneous and well played, and the equally agreeable *John Socman overture* (a prelude for his opera of the same name, commissioned for the Festival of Britain in 1951) also comes off well, although it is rather inconsequential. This is not the record with which to start a Lloyd collection.

Symphony No. 7.
*** Albany Dig. TROY 057 [id.]. BBC PO, composer.

The *Seventh Symphony* is on a larger scale than most of Lloyd's earlier works. It is a programme symphony, using the ancient Greek legend of Proserpine. The slow movement is particularly fine, an extended soliloquy of considerable expressive power. The last and longest movement is concerned with 'the desperate side of our lives – "Dead dreams that the snows have shaken, Wild leaves that the winds have taken",' yet, as is characteristic with Lloyd, the darkness is muted; nevertheless the resolution at the end is curiously satisfying. Again he proves an admirable exponent of his own music. The recording is splendid.

Symphony No. 11.
*** Albany Dig. TROY 060 [id.]. Albany SO, composer.

The urgently dynamic first movement of the *Eleventh* is described by the composer as being 'all fire and violence', but any anger in the music quickly evaporates, and it conveys rather a mood of exuberance, with very full orchestral forces unleashed. The second movement, *Lento*, is a songful interlude; the third, a dance, leads to the fourth, a funeral march that for all its drumbeat rhythms is not really mournful. The finale starts with cheerful carolling trumpets and sets the seal on Lloyd's basic message of optimism. With the orchestra for which the work was commissioned, Lloyd conducts a powerful performance, very well played. The recording was made in the Music Hall of Troy Savings Bank near Albany; it is spectacularly sumptuous and wide-ranging.

PIANO MUSIC

An African shrine; The aggressive fishes; Intercom baby; The road through Samarkand; St Anthony and the bogside beggar.
**(*) Albany Dig. AR 003; *C-AR 003* [id.]. Martin Roscoe.

The most ambitious piece here is *An African shrine*, in which the composer's scenario is linked (not very dissonantly) to African violence and revolution. The music is like a symphonic poem for piano and is effectively diverse in mood, but rather extended (at 23 minutes) for its material. *The road through Samarkand* (1972) has travellers from the younger generation leaving for the East; while *The aggressive fishes* are tropical and violently moody, changing from serenity to anger at the flick of a fin. The two most striking pieces are the picaresque tale of the *Bogside beggar* and the charming lullaby written for a baby whose mother is in another room listening with the aid of modern technology. Martin Roscoe's performances are thoroughly committed and spontaneous, and the recording is first class.

VOCAL MUSIC

The Vigil of Venus (Pervigilium Veneris).
*** Argo Dig. 430 329-2 [id.]. Carolyn James, Thomas Booth, Welsh Nat. Op. Ch. & O, composer.

Following up the success of his recordings of his symphonies, George Lloyd here directs Welsh National Opera forces in this ambitious oratorio. Here, as in the symphonies, he thumbs his nose at fashion in a score which both pulses with energy and cocoons the ear in opulent sounds. Delian ecstasy is contrasted against the occasional echo of Carl Orff, an attractive mixture, even if – for all the incidental beauties – there is dangerously little variety of mood in the nine substantial sections. The composer was not entirely happy with what he was able to achieve in that first recording; even so, his performance certainly does not lack intensity and the recording is excellent, given the inherent problems of the recording venue in Swansea.

Lloyd Webber, Andrew (born 1948)

Requiem.
*** EMI Dig. CDC7 47146-2 [id.]; *EL 270242-4*. Brightman, Domingo, Miles-Kingston, Drew, Winchester Cathedral Ch., ECO, Maazel; J. Lancelot (organ).

This *Requiem* may be derivative at many points, with echoes of Carl Orff – not to mention the *Requiems* of both Verdi and Fauré – but, with Maazel conducting a performance of characteristic intensity, it certainly has a life of its own. The *Pié Jesu* is a model of bridge-building, a melody beautiful and individual by any standard, which yet has all the catchiness of one of Lloyd Webber's tunes in a musical. Plainly the high, bright voice of Sarah Brightman was the direct inspiration, and the beauty of her singing certainly earns her this place alongside Plácido Domingo, contributing in a rather less prominent role. Radiant sounds from the Winchester Cathedral Choir, not least the principal treble, Paul Miles-Kingston. Above all, this is music to which one returns with increasing appreciation and pleasure. The CD gives presence and clarity to the excellent sound.

Lloyd Webber, William (1914–82)

(i) *Missa Sanctae Mariae Magdalenae;* (ii) Arias: *The Divine compassion: Thou art the King. The Saviour: The King of Love. 5 Songs.* (iii; iv) *In the half light (soliloquy); Air varié* (after Franck); (iv) *6 Piano pieces.*
*** ASV Dig. CDDCA 584 [id.]. (i) Richard Hickox Singers, Hickox; I. Watson (organ); (ii) J. Graham Hall; P. Ledger; (iii) Julian Lloyd Webber; (iv) John Lill.

William Lloyd Webber was a distinguished academic, a virtuoso organist and a composer who in a few beautifully crafted works laid bare his heart in pure romanticism. In his varied collection, the *Missa Sanctae Mariae Magdalenae* is both the last and the most ambitious of his works, strong and characterful, building up to moments of drama, as when the organ enters for the first time, not in the opening *Kyrie* but suddenly and unexpectedly in the *Gloria* which follows, to thrilling effect. John Lill is a persuasive advocate of the *Six Piano pieces*, varied in mood and sometimes quirky, and accompanies Julian Lloyd Webber in the two cello pieces, written – as though with foresight of his son's career – just as his second son was born. Graham Hall, accompanied by Philip Ledger, completes the recital with beautiful performances of a group of songs and arias, no more remarkable than many works by talented academics, but well worth hearing. Recording, made in a north London church, is warm and undistracting.

Locatelli, Pietro (1695–1764)

Flute sonatas, Op. 2/2, 6, 7 & 10.
*** Ph. Dig. 416 613-2 [id.]. Hazelzet, Koopman, Van der Meer.

These *Sonatas* come from Locatelli's set of twelve, Op. 2, and were published in 1732. The set was sufficiently admired in its day to sell out and be reprinted, and a generous melodic fertility can be heard in the four recorded here. The performances could hardly be more sympathetic and stylish, while the recording itself, dating from 1980, is very truthful and immediate.

Løvenskiold, Herman (1815–70)

La Sylphide (ballet) complete.
(M) *** Chan. Dig. CHAN 6546; *MBTD 6546* [id.]. Royal Danish O, David Garforth.

La Sylphide (1834) predates Adam's *Giselle* by seven years. It is less distinctive than Adam's score, but it is full of grace and the invention has genuine romantic vitality – indeed the horn writing in the finale anticipates Delibes. The present performance (72 minutes) is based on the current performing edition used by the Royal Danish ballet but includes additional music, with the original Act II *Pas de deux*, hitherto unrecorded, added as an appendix. The wholly sympathetic playing is warm, elegant, lively and felicitous in its detailed delicacy, yet robust when necessary and always spontaneous. A most enjoyable disc, superbly recorded (in 1986) in the well-nigh perfect acoustics of the Old Fellows' Hall, Copenhagen.

Lully, Jean-Baptiste (1632–87)

Atys (opera): complete.
*** HM Dig. HMC 901257/9; *HMC 701257/9* (3). Guy de Mey, Mellon, Laurens, Gardeil, Semellaz, Rime, Les Arts Florissants Ch. & O, Christie.

Christie and his excellent team give life and dramatic speed consistently to the performance of *Atys*, so much so that, though this five-act piece lasts nearly three hours, one keeps thinking of Purcell's almost contemporary masterpiece on quite a different – miniature – scale, *Dido and Aeneas*. Invention is only intermittently on a Purcellian level, but there are many memorable numbers, not least those in the sleep interlude of Act III. Outstanding in the cast are the high tenor, Guy de Mey, in the name-part and Agnès Mellon as the nymph, Sangaride, with whom he falls in love.

Le bourgeois gentilhomme (comédie-ballet; complete).
(M) *** HM/BMG GD 77059 (2) [77059-2-RG]. Nimsgern, Jungmann, Schortemeier, René Jacobs, Tölz Ch., La Petite Bande, Leonhardt – CAMPRA: *L'Europe galante*. ***

Entertainment rather than musical value: in itself, Lully's score offers no great musical rewards. The melodic invention is unmemorable and harmonies are neither original nor interesting; but if the music taken on its own is thin stuff, the effect of the entertainment as a whole is quite a different matter. This performance puts Lully's music into the correct stage perspective and, with such sprightly and spirited performers as well as good 1973 recording, this can hardly fail to give pleasure. The orchestral contribution under the direction of Gustav Leonhardt is distinguished by a splendid sense of the French style.

Lumbye, Hans Christian (1810–74)

Amager polka; Amelie waltz; Champagne galop; Columbine polka mazurka; Copenhagen Steam Railway galop; Dream pictures fantasia; The Guard of Amager (ballet): *Final galop. Helga polka mazurka; Hesperus waltz; Lily polka (dedicated to the ladies); Queen Louise's waltz; Napoli* (ballet): *Final galop. Salute to August Bournonville; Salute to our friends; Sandman galop fantastique.*
❀ *** Unicorn Dig. DKPCD 9089; *DKPC 9089* [id.]. Odense SO, Peter Guth.

It is incredible that the waltzes and polkas of Hans Christian Lumbye – 'the Strauss of the North' as this CD collection rightly proclaims him – are not more widely known and loved. A representative EMI LP appeared in the mid-1960s but did not stay around very long. Now this superb Unicorn collection makes handsome amends, offering 75 minutes of the composer's best music, with wonderfully spontaneous performances demonstrating above all its elegance and gentle grace. It opens with a vigorous *Salute to August Bournonville* (he was Director of the Danish Royal Theatre ballet) and closes with a *Champagne galop* to rival Johann junior's polka; and here the hitherto silent audience joins in with enthusiastic, if undisciplined hand-claps, to recall the *Radetzky march* of Johann senior. In between comes much to enchant, not least the delightful *Amelie waltz* and the haunting *Dream pictures fantasia* with its diaphanous opening textures and lilting main theme. Another charmer is the *Sandman galop fantastique*, a vivacious pot-pourri which never wears out its welcome by becoming too vociferous, while *Queen Louise's waltz* has an appropriate melodic poise. But Lumbye's masterpiece is the unforgettable *Copenhagen Steam Railway galop*. This whimsical yet vivid portrait of a local Puffing Billy begins with the gathering of passengers at the station – obviously dressed for the occasion in a more elegant age than ours. The little engine then wheezingly starts up and proceeds on its journey, finally drawing to a dignified halt against interpolated cries from the station staff. Because of the style and refinement of its imagery, it is much the most endearing of musical railway evocations, and the high-spirited lyricism of the little train racing through the countryside, its whistle peeping, is enchanting. It is interesting, too, that the expansive melodic line of the introduction is sometimes hinted at in the opening paragraphs of Lumbye's other music. This is a superbly entertaining disc, showing the Odense Symphony Orchestra and its conductor, Peter Guth, as naturally suited to this repertoire as are the VPO under Boskovsky in the music of the Strauss family. The recording has a warm and sympathetic ambience and gives a lovely bloom to the whole programme.

Lutoslawski, Witold (born 1916)

Chain II; Partita.
*** DG Dig. 423 696-2 [id.]. Mutter, BBC SO, composer – STRAVINSKY: *Violin concerto*. ***

Chain II, a *Dialogue for violin and orchestra*, follows up the technique which Lutoslawski developed in a work written for the London Sinfonietta, *Chain I*, contrasting fully written sections with *ad libitum* movements, where chance plays its part within fixed parameters. The *Partita* is a development of a piece for violin and piano which Lutoslawski originally wrote for Pinchas Zukerman, with the first, third and fifth movements written for violin and orchestra, the second and fourth '*ad libitum*' for violin and piano alone. With Mutter and the composer the most persuasive advocates, both pieces establish themselves as among the finest examples of Lutoslawski's latterday work, provocative and ear-catching in their fantasy. First-rate sound.

Concerto for orchestra.
*** Decca Dig. 425 694-2. Cleveland O, Dohnányi – BARTÓK: *Concerto for orchestra.* **(*)

Lutoslawski's brilliant showpiece is here played with a thrust and precision to bring out the full colour and energy of the work. If it lacks the thematic memorability of the Bartók, it is just as exuberantly colourful. Dohnányi's dedicated performance makes it a perfect counterpart, an apt coupling, recorded with a fullness and brilliance outstanding even by Decca standards.

Dance preludes (for clarinet and orchestra).
*** Hyp. Dig. CDA 66215; *KA 66215* [id.]. Thea King, ECO, Litton – BLAKE: *Clarinet concerto;* SEIBER: *Concertino.* ***
*** Chan. Dig. CHAN 8618; *ABTD 1307* [id.]. Janet Hilton, SNO, Bamert – COPLAND; NIELSEN: *Concertos.* ***

Lutoslawski's five folk-based vignettes are a delight in the hands of Thea King and Andrew Litton, who give sharply characterized performances, thrown into bold relief by the bright, clear recording. Janet Hilton also emphasizes their contrasts with her expressive lyricism and crisp articulation in the lively numbers. Excellent recording.

Symphony No. 3; (i) *Les espaces du sommeil.*
*** Sony Dig. M2K 42271 (2) [id.]. (i) Shirley-Quirk; LAPO, Salonen – MESSIAEN: *Turangalîla symphony.* **(*)
*** Ph. Dig. 416 387-2 [id.]. (i) Fischer-Dieskau; BPO, composer.

Even next to Lutoslawski's own interpretation, Salonen's brings an extra revelation. This is a deeply committed, even passionate account of a work which may be rigorous in its argument but which is essentially dramatic in one massive, continuous span. In *Les espaces du sommeil*, setting a surreal poem by Robert Desnos, Salonen also presents a different slant from the composer himself, making it – with the help of John Shirley-Quirk as an understanding soloist – much more evocative and sensuous in full and well-balanced sound.

The *Third Symphony* is given an authoritative reading by the composer. The performance of *Les espaces du sommeil* might also be counted definitive, with Lutoslawski joined by the dedicatee, the baritone Dietrich Fischer-Dieskau. Treated to refined, finely analytical recording, these are sharply focused performances, but in warmth and thrust of communication they finally yield to those of Esa-Pekka Salonen on his CBS version.

String quartet.
*** Olympia OCD 328 [id.]. Varsovia Qt – SZYMANOWSKI: *Quartets;* PENDERECKI: *Quartet No. 2.* ***

Lutoslawski tells us that in his *String quartet* he uses 'chance elements to enrich the rhythmic and expressive character of the music without in any way limiting the authority of the composer over the final shape of the piece'. Whatever its merits, it has a highly developed and refined feeling for sonority and balance and, generally speaking, succeeds in holding the listener.

Lyapunov, Sergei (1859–1924)

Hashish, Op. 53; Polonaise, Op. 16; Solemn overture on Russian themes, Op. 7; Zelazowa Wola, Op. 37.
**(*) Olympia OCD 129 [id.]. USSR Ac. SO, Svetlanov – BALAKIREV: *Islamey.* **

The *Solemn overture on Russian themes* is much influenced by Balakirev's examples in this genre, and the spirited *Polonaise* is very much in the processional style of Glinka and Tchaikovsky. The tone-poem, *Zelazowa Wola* (Chopin's birthplace), is a tribute to Chopin and is inspired by the centenary celebrations in 1909 in which both Balakirev and Lyapunov played a part (there is an oblique allusion to the *A minor Mazurka*, Op. 17, No. 4). The intriguingly entitled *Hashish* takes its cue from Balakirev's *Tamara* (beloved of Sir Thomas Beecham) but is colourful stuff. If you respond to Balakirev, you should investigate this attractive music, even if you may feel that Lyapunov's indebtedness to his friend and mentor was too great. Svetlanov is in his element in this kind of repertoire and the playing is very good. The recording, though not top-drawer, is perfectly acceptable, though it comes close to overloading in climaxes.

McCartney, Paul (born 1942) and Carl Davis (born 1936)

Liverpool oratorio.
*** EMI Dig. CDS7 54371-2 (2) [id.]; *EX 754371-4.* Te Kanawa, Burgess, Hadley, White, RLPO Ch. & O, Carl Davis.

Liverpool oratorio (abridged version).
*** EMI Dig. CDC7 54642-2 [id.]; *EL 754642-4* (from above).

Hearing McCartney's *Liverpool oratorio* is rather like a ride in a luxurious train that from time to time behaves like a roller-coaster, as smooth, warm progress suddenly lurches into embarrassment. McCartney remains one of the very greatest tune-writers of our day with an uncanny ability to ensnare the ear with striking melody, regularly using wide, unexpected intervals that yet sound easy and natural. Carl Davis developed McCartney's original ideas and as a skilled professional creates the most sensuous textures, instrumental and above all choral. The big choral climaxes often sound like a cross between a massive Christmas carol and something from *Carousel*, with influences as wide-ranging as could be. Echoes of medieval dance music merge into Caribbean rhythms, Mendelssohn's *Elijah* into neo-Bernstein, with conventional pop relatively distant. What lets things down is McCartney's own book for this large-scale, broadly autobiographical piece, which has some spine-chilling moments of corny melodrama and rhymes of total banality. Happily, the composer's sense of fun emerges periodically, as in a delightful school Spanish-lesson sequence and a tipsy cake-walk, countering any feeling of over-inflation. The recording, made live at the first performance in Liverpool Anglican Cathedral, is persuasively conducted by Davis, with the big melodies beautifully setting off the heady tenor of Jerry Hadley as the central character, Shanty, and with Dame Kiri Te Kanawa singing radiantly as his beloved Mary Dee. Sally Burgess and Willard White are equally strong in various character roles, and the treble, Jeremy Budd, heightens the important sequences for cathedral choristers. Those not insisting on the complete work, could well make do with the 77-minute single-CD abridged version.

MacDowell, Edward (1861–1908)

Piano concertos Nos. 1 in A min., Op. 15; 2 in D min., Op. 23.
❀ *** Olympia Dig. OCD 353 [id.]. Donna Amato, LPO, Paul Freeman.

Of MacDowell's two *Piano concertos* the *First* is marginally the lesser of the two. Liszt's influence is strong (MacDowell studied with him) and there is plenty of dash, but the melodic content, though very pleasing, is slightly less memorable than in the *Second*, which has been recorded before. It is a delightful piece, fresh and tuneful, redolent of Mendelssohn and Saint-Saëns. Donna Amato's scintillating performance is entirely winning, and she is equally persuasive in the *A minor*, which Liszt himself played. This music needs polish and elegance as well as fire, and Paul Freeman's accompaniments supply all three. The recording, made in All Saints', Tooting, has the right resonance for the Lisztian spectacle and agreeable ambient warmth for the music's lyrical side. A highly rewarding coupling in all respects.

(i) *Piano concerto No. 2 in D min., Op. 23. Woodland sketches: To a wild rose, Op. 51/1.*
(M) **(*) BMG/RCA GD 60420; *GK 60420* [60420-2-RG; *60420-4-RG*]. Van Cliburn, (i) Chicago SO, Hendl – SCHUMANN: *Concerto.* **(*)

Edward MacDowell wrote his *Second Piano concerto* in Germany in 1884/5 and it is no accident that – especially in the first movement – Liszt's influence can be felt very strongly in the piano writing. The work has a lyrical, rhapsodical first movement, a short but quite delightful Scherzo as a centrepiece, and a lively finale based on a strong and easily recognizable theme. A slow introduction to the third movement and a reflective middle section take the place of a slow movement. The closing pages are a paean of virtuosity and emerge here in glittering fashion from Van Cliburn's nimble fingers. The pianist is not helped by a recording balance which consistently makes him sound rather too loud; but the performance otherwise has the advantage of warm Chicago acoustics, and Walter Hendl's vigorous and sympathetic support, with its fire and spontaneity, triumph over the technical problems. The Scherzo is superb. MacDowell's most famous solo piano piece makes a pleasing encore, though the performance is a trifle cool.

MacMillan, James (born 1959)

The Confession of Isobel Gowdie; Tryst
*** Koch/Schwann Dig. 3-1050-2 [id.]. BBC Scottish SO, Maksymiuk.

James MacMillan from Glasgow is the most exciting young British composer to have emerged in the 1990s. *The Confession of Isobel Gowdie* is a work which has had an extraordinary impact on audiences far wider than those devoted to new music, not least at the Proms in 1990. Inspired by the horrific execution in 1662 of Isobel Gowdie, tortured into confessing herself a witch, MacMillan has used the story as a metaphor for twentieth-century witch-hunting, including what he sees as resurgent fascism today. That effectively brings together the two profound allegiances he has in his philosophy, both to left-wing socialism and to Roman Catholicism. The result is rather like Vaughan Williams's *Tallis fantasia* updated and then invaded by Stravinsky's *Rite of spring*. It is a slow-moving ritual which erupts with energy in the middle, a powerful example of MacMillan's gift of writing music that is physical, making an immediate emotional impact. The other piece on the disc, *Tryst* – marginally longer at 28 minutes – has similar qualities. In juxtaposition it emerges as the obverse of *Isobel Gowdie*, similarly a massive single movement in arch form. This time the music works from violence at the beginning and end to a long slow meditation in the middle, again with echoes of ecclesiastical chant a basic element. Maksymiuk – who conducted this same orchestra in the Prom performance – proves a dedicated interpreter, but MacMillan himself is a formidable conductor of his own music, and one hopes for another disc which might let him exploit that gift. The only flaw in this Koch issue is that each of these long works comes on a single CD track, when very easily the clearly defined sections could have been separately banded.

Maconchy, Elizabeth (born 1907)

String quartets Nos. 1–4.
*** Unicorn Dig. DKPCD 9080; *DKPC 9080* [id.]. Hanson Qt.

String quartets Nos. 5–8.
*** Unicorn Dig. DKPCD 9081; *DKPC 9081* [id.]. Bingham Qt.

Elizabeth Maconchy has excited the admiration of musicians far and wide from Tovey and Sir Henry Wood to Holst and Vaughan Williams. Hopefully this Unicorn series, planned to include all her *Quartets*, will introduce her to a wider audience. The four recorded by the Hanson Quartet encompass the period 1932–43; while the second disc spans the years 1948–67, and the Bingham Quartet seem equally at home in this rewarding repertoire. All these works testify to the quality of Maconchy's mind and her inventive powers. She speaks of the quartet as 'an impassioned argument', and there is no lack of either in these finely wrought and compelling pieces. Even if there is not the distinctive personality of a Bartók or a Britten, her music is always rewarding. Though the playing may occasionally be wanting in tonal finesse, both groups play with total commitment and are well recorded.

Maderna, Bruno (1920–73)

Aura; Biogramma; Quadrivium.
*** DG 423 246-2 [id.]. N. German RSO, Sinopoli.

This record usefully brings together three of Bruno Maderna's key works, among the last he wrote before his untimely death when still in his early fifties. Earliest is *Quadrivium*, for four orchestral groups, each with percussion, a work designed 'to entertain and to interest, not to shock the bourgeoisie'. In 1972 came *Aura* and *Biogramma*; the former won the composer (posthumously) the city of Bonn's Beethoven prize. Excellent recording for dedicated performances.

Madetoja, Leevi (1887–1947)

Symphony No. 3 in A, Op. 55; Huvinäytelmäalkusoitto (comedy overture), Op. 53; Okon Fuoko: suite No. 1, Op. 58; Pohjalainen sara (The Ostrobothnians): suite, Op. 52.
*** Chan. Dig. CHAN 9036 [id.]. Iceland SO, Petri Sakari.

Leevi Madetoja belongs to the first generation of Finnish composers after Sibelius. Indeed he was briefly one of Sibelius's pupils before studying in Paris and Vienna. His *Second Symphony* regularly featured in BBC programmes in the 1940s and '50s, but as Sibelius's star temporarily waned during the late 1950s, his music fell from view. In recent years Finlandia have recorded his three symphonies, which have been perceptively annotated by the French scholar, Henri-Claude Fantapié. This new version of the *Third* was written in 1925–6 when he was living in Houilles not far from Paris. Its outlook is both Finnish in its modality and melancholy, and Gallic in its clarity of line and elegant orchestration. Its only failing, perhaps, is in its finale where invention flags a little but otherwise it is a first-rate score which ought to enjoy wide appeal. So, too, should the couplings, the delightfully high-spirited and attractive *Comedy Overture* and the imaginative suites. The Iceland orchestra give dedicated and persuasive accounts of both scores and both the overture and the symphony fare better than in the première Finnish recordings made in 1973 and only briefly available in the UK.

Mahler, Gustav (1860–1911)

Symphonies Nos. 1–9.
(B) *** Decca Dig./Analogue 430 804-2 (10). Buchanan, Zakai, Chicago Ch. (in No. 2); Dernesch, Ellyn Children's Ch., Chicago Ch. (in No. 3); Te Kanawa (in No. 4); Harper, Popp, Augér, Minton, Watts, Kollo, Shirley-Quirk, Talvela, V. Boys' Ch., V. State Op. Ch. & Singverein (in No. 8); Chicago SO, Solti.

Symphonies Nos. 1–10.
(M) **(*) DG 435 162-2 (13) [id.]. Hendricks, Ludwig, Wittek, M. Price, Blegen, Zeumer, Baltsa, Schmidt, Reigel, Prey, Van Dam, Brooklyn Boys' Ch., Westminster Ch., N Y Choral Artists, V. Boys' Ch., V. Singverein, V. State Op. Ch., Concg. O, NYPO, or VPO, Bernstein.

Symphonies Nos. 1–10; (i) *Kindertotenlieder.*
(M) **(*) Sony Dig. S14K 48198 (14) [id.]. Marton, Norman, Battle, Sweet, Coburn, Quivar, Fassenbaender, Leech, Nimsgern, Estes, V. Boys' Ch., V. State Op. Konzertvereinigung, Schoenberg Ch.; (i) Baltsa; VPO, Maazel.

Solti's achievement in Mahler has been consistent and impressive, and this bargain reissue on ten discs of a set that had previously been offered on fifteen (most at full price) is a formidable bargain that will be hard to beat. Nos. 1–4 and 9 are digital recordings, Nos. 5–8 are digitally remastered analogue. Solti draws stunning playing from the Chicago Symphony Orchestra, often pressed to great virtuosity, which adds to the electricity of the music-making; if his rather extrovert approach to Mahler means that deeper emotions are sometimes understated, there is no lack of involvement; and his fiery energy and commitment often carry shock-waves in their trail. All in all, an impressive achievement.

It is a measure of Bernstein's greatness as a Mahler interpreter and the electricity he consistently conveys in these edited live recordings that, despite obvious shortcomings, they so readily add up to more than the sum of their parts. Having the cycle as a whole on these 13 CDs has one eager to go on from one symphony to another. The wilfulness of some of the readings, the heaviness of underlining, the exaggeratedly slow speeds, notably in Nos 3 and 9, even seem to enrich the total experience. Not everyone will like the sound of a boy treble in the finale of No. 4, for example, but Bernstein's view is always a fresh and individual one. This is a personal statement by one great musician on another, and represents a monumental achievement.

Maazel's cycle of the Mahler symphonies with the Vienna Philharmonic brings generally broad, spacious readings, digitally recorded and generally well-played. Yet these studio performances tend not to convey the full dramatic impact of these massive works, as they might have done with an audience in the concert-hall. When they are considered as a cycle, that reservation becomes all the more noticeable. On 14 discs it makes an expensive purchase, even though the recorded sound is generally very impressive. The pick of the set is the *Fourth* and that shows Maazel at his most inspirational. Apart from No. 8 these recordings are not now available separately.

Symphony No. 1 in D (1893 version, including *Blumine*).
(M) **(*) EMI CDM7 64137-2 [id.]. New Philh. O, Wyn Morris.

In his 1970 recording, originally made for the short-lived Virtuoso label, Wyn Morris enterprisingly chose to follow the 1893 text of Mahler's *First*, which is the earliest that has survived. It makes the *Blumine* second movement much more consistent here than in rival versions that simply tack that extra movement on to the usual score. Detailed differences include muted horns instead of clarinets for the opening fanfares in the hushed introduction, timpani right at the start of the scherzo, solo cello with double-bass at the start of the slow movement, and quavers instead of crotchets for the falling octave which ends the work. Morris's warmly expressive Mahlerian style works most persuasively, though ensemble is not quite as crisp as in most of his other Mahler recordings. The CD transfer has transformed the sound, which is bright with plenty of presence but with just a touch of harshness in tuttis.

(i) *Symphony No. 1 in D* (1896 version); (ii) *Blumine*.
(M) **(*) Collins Dig. 3005-2 [id.]. (i) LSO; (ii) Philh. O; Jacek Kaspszyk.
(B) **(*) Hung. White Label HRC 077 [id.]. Hungarian State O, Iván Fischer.

Kaspszyk has the advantage of excellent, modern, digital recording with a wide dynamic range and a spacious acoustic. The LSO plays with commitment and drama and responds persuasively to the conductor's rather wayward reading, leading to a tense and exciting finale. The very opening is appealingly atmospheric and the slow movement conveys real warmth, as does the Philharmonia string-playing in *Blumine*, the discarded movement that came second in the composer's original scheme.

The bargain version on Hungaroton White Label also includes the original second movement, *Blumine*, placing it where the composer intended. Fischer's reading of the symphony is spaciously conceived, with relaxed tempi throughout, but the Hungarian State Orchestra sustain his conception with very fine playing, especially from the strings in the last movement. With excellent analogue sound, full and well detailed, this is an inexpensive way to sample Mahler's initial layout.

Symphony No. 1 in D (Titan).
(M) *** DG Dig. 431 036-2; *431 036-4*. Concg. O, Bernstein.
(M) *** Decca 417 701-2 [id.]. LSO, Solti.
*** Decca Dig. 411 731-2 [id.]. Chicago SO, Solti.
*** DG Dig. 429 228-2 [id.]. Philh. O, Sinopoli.
(M) *** Unicorn UKCD 2012. LSO, Horenstein.
(M) **(*) EMI Dig. CDD7 64287-2 [id.]; *ET 764287-4*. Phd. O, Muti.
**(*) Ph. Dig. 420 936-2 [id.]. BPO, Haitink.

Symphony No. 1 in D min.; (i) *Lieder eines fahrenden Gesellen*.
(B) **(*) DG 429 157-2 [id.]. Bav. RSO, Kubelik; (i) with Fischer-Dieskau.

Bernstein and the Concertgebouw Orchestra, recorded live, give a wonderfully alert and imaginative performance of Mahler's *First*, with the opening movement conveying the youthful joys of spring in its Wayfaring lad associations, and the second at a relaxed Ländler tempo made more rustic than usual. In the slow movement the funeral march overtones are underlined, leading easily into what Bernstein calls the raucous 'Jewish wedding' episode. The finale has superb panache. This is among Bernstein's finest Mahler issues, very well recorded, even making no allowance for the extra problems encountered at live concerts.

The London Symphony Orchestra play Mahler's *First* like no other orchestra. They catch the magical opening with a singular evocative quality, at least partly related to the peculiarly characteristic blend of wind timbres, and throughout there is wonderfully warm string-tone. Solti's tendency to drive hard is felt only in the second movement, which is pressed a little too much, although he relaxes beautifully in the central section. The remastering for CD has improved definition without losing the recording's bloom.

Because of the excellence of the 1964 LSO version, which has been a prime choice for many years, it was hard for Solti and the Decca engineers to match his earlier achievement, even with exceptionally high-powered playing from the Chicago orchestra and brilliant, crystal-clear digital recording. Particularly on CD, that very clarity takes away some of the atmospheric magic – the feeling of mists dispersing in the slow introduction, for example – but charm and playfulness in this *Wunderhorn* work emerge delightfully; one of the happiest of Solti's records, tinglingly fresh, with perfectly chosen speeds.

Sinopoli's is a warmly satisfying reading, passionately committed, with refined playing from the Philharmonia. Sinopoli in his fine control allows the fullest expressiveness, with bold, theatrical gestures thrust home purposefully. The sound is rich and refined to match, with the orchestra set at a slight distance, though not enough to lose impact.

Unicorn had the laudable aim of securing a relatively modern recording of Horenstein in Mahler's *First*, and the result has a freshness and concentration which put it in a special category among the many rival accounts. With measured tempi and a manner which conceals much art, Horenstein links the work more clearly with later Mahler symphonies. Fine recording from the end of the 1960s, though the timpani is balanced rather too close.

Muti's version was the first recording made by the Philadelphia Orchestra in a new venue, the Memorial Hall, Philadelphia. The 1984 digital master lights up the sound picture, but at the same time gives a pretty fair idea of the richness of timbre this orchestra can achieve and not at the expense of precision of ensemble. Muti, like other conductors prone to fierceness, manages the springtime awakening of the first movement persuasively and also relaxes for the gentler *Wunderhorn* inventions, contrasted sharply against extrovert outbursts, with rhythms crisply pointed and solo playing exceptionally fine.

The Berlin Philharmonic plays superbly for Bernard Haitink in this, his third recording of Mahler's *First*. There is greater gravity in his view now, to bring out the full weight of this ambitious early work, and a greater freedom of expression, though this conductor is hardly one to wear his heart on his sleeve or even to inject charm into such a passage as the Laendler trio of the second movement. The purity and refinement of the Berlin string-tone is superbly caught. The recorded sound is notably finer than many previous recordings made in the Philharmonie, even if it is not entirely free of cloudiness.

Kubelik gives an intensely poetic reading. He is here at his finest in Mahler, and though, as in later symphonies, he is sometimes tempted to choose a tempo on the fast side, the result could hardly be more glowing. The rubato in the slow funeral march is most subtly handled. In its bargain CD reissue the quality is a little dry in the bass and the violins have lost some of their warmth, but there is no lack of body. In the *Lieder eines fahrenden Gesellen* the sound is fuller, with more atmospheric bloom. No one quite rivals Fischer-Dieskau in these songs and this is a very considerable bonus.

(i) *Symphony No. 1 in D* (with (ii) *Blumine*).
(BB) ** Virgin Dig. VJ7 91570-2 [id.]. (i) RPO, Litton; (ii) Bamberg SO, Rickenbacher.

Andrew Litton's 1988 Virgin recording with the RPO has been reissued at super-bargain price, coupled with Karl Rickenbacher's 1989 account of *Blumine*. Litton's way with Mahler is fresh and generally direct, with well-chosen speeds, but the playing of the RPO strings is not always quite polished or taut enough.

Symphonies Nos. (i) *1;* (ii) *2 (Resurrection).*
(B) *** Sony M2YK 45674. (i) Columbia SO; (ii) Cundari, Forrester, Westminster College Ch., NYPO; Bruno Walter.
(M) **(*) Decca 425 005-2 (2) [id.]. (ii) Harper, Watts, LSO Ch.; LSO, Solti.

Bruno Walter's recordings of Mahler's *Symphonies Nos. 1* and *2* are now economically coupled together on a pair of bargain-price discs with the sound further improved over the previous CD issues. The recording of No. 1 sounds splendid in this new format and Walter is at his most charismatic here. While the recording's dynamic range is obviously more limited than more recent versions, the balance and ambient warmth are entirely satisfying, emphasizing the Viennese character of the reading, with the final apotheosis drawn out spaciously and given added breadth and impact. Even more than the *First Symphony*, the 1958 CBS set of the *Resurrection Symphony* is among the gramophone's indispensable classics. In the first movement there is a restraint and in the second a gracefulness which provide a strong contrast with a conductor like Solti. The recording, one of the last Walter made in New York before his series with the Columbia Symphony Orchestra, was remarkably good for its period and the dynamic range is surprisingly wide. In remastering for CD, the glowing sound brings an evocative haze to the score's more atmospheric moments, and in the finale the balance with the voices gives the music-making an ethereal resonance, with the closing section thrillingly expansive.

Solti's 1964 LSO account of Mahler's *First Symphony* reappears in the Solti Edition, coupled with No. 2 which was also recorded in the Kingsway Hall two years later. This recording remains a demonstration of the outstanding results Decca were securing with analogue techniques at that time, although on CD the sharpness of focus (especially in No. 2) and the brilliance of the fortissimos, emphasized by the wide dynamic range, may not suit all ears. Helen Watts is wonderfully expressive in the chorale, conveying real inner feeling, while the chorus has a rapt intensity that is the more telling when the recording perspectives are so clearly delineated.

Symphony No. 2 in C min. (Resurrection).
❀ *** EMI CDS7 47962-8 (2) [Ang. CDCB 47962]. Augér, J. Baker, CBSO Ch., CBSO, Rattle.
*** Chan. Dig. CHAN 8838/9; *DBTD 2022* [id.]. Felicity Lott, Julia Hamari, Latvian State Ac. Ch., Oslo Ch. & PO, Jansons.
(M) *** EMI CDM7 69662-2 [id.]; *EG 769662-4*. Schwarzkopf, Rössl-Majdan, Philh. Ch. & O, Klemperer.
(M) *** DG 427 262-2 (2) [id.]. Neblett, Horne, Chicago SO Ch. and O, Abbado.
*** Decca Dig. 410 202-2 (2) [id.]. Buchanan, Zakai, Chicago SO Ch. & SO, Solti.
**(*) DG Dig. 423 395-2 (2) [id.]. Hendricks, Ludwig, Westminster Ch., NYPO, Bernstein.
(B) **(*) Pickwick Dig. DPCD 910; *CIMPC 910* (2) [MCA MCAD 11011]. Valente, Forrester, LSO Ch., LSO, Kaplan.

(i) *Symphony No. 2 (Resurrection);* (ii) *Lieder eines fahrenden Gesellen;* (iii) *Lieder und Gesänge (aus der Jugendzeit):* excerpts.
*** DG Dig. 415 959-2(2) [id.]. (i) Fassbaender, Plowright, Philh. Ch.; (ii) Fassbaender; (iii) Weikl; Philh. O, Sinopoli.

Simon Rattle's reading of Mahler's *Second* is among the very finest records he has yet made, superlative in the breadth and vividness of its sound and with a spacious reading which in its natural intensity unerringly sustains generally slow, steady speeds to underline the epic grandeur of Mahler's vision. This comes closer than almost any rival version to creating the illusion of a live performance, its tensions and its drama, while building on the palpable advantage of well-balanced studio sound. Rattle here establishes himself as not merely a good but a great Mahlerian with a strongly individual view, controlling tensions masterfully over the broadest span. The playing of the CBSO is inspired, matching that of the most distinguished international rivals. The choral singing, beautifully balanced, is incandescent, while the heart-felt singing of the soloists, Arleen Augér and Dame Janet Baker, is equally distinguished and characterful. Recorded in Watford Town Hall instead of the orchestra's usual Birmingham venue, the sound is full and clear even in the heavyweight textures of the finale.

Sinopoli's version of the *Resurrection* brings the additional advantage that the two CDs also include two Mahler song-cycles: the *Lieder eines fahrenden Gesellen*, beautifully sung by Brigitte Fassbaender, and the *Songs of Youth* '*aus der Jugendzeit*', skilfully orchestrated by Harold Byrns, well sung by Bernd Weikl, bringing extra anticipations of the mature *Des Knaben Wunderhorn* songs. In the symphony Sinopoli has meticulous concern for detail, yet he still conveys consistently the irresistible purposefulness of Mahler's writing, fierce at high dramatic moments and intense too, rarely relaxed, in moments of meditation, with Urlicht beautifully sung with warmth and purity by Fassbaender. The recorded sound, though not quite as full and vivid as that for Rattle, is among the most brilliant of any in this work. Rosalind Plowright is a pure and fresh soprano soloist, contrasting well with the equally firm, earthier-toned mezzo of Fassbaender.

The crisp attack at the start of the opening funeral march sets the pattern for an exceptionally refined and alert reading of the *Resurrection Symphony* from Jansons and his Oslo orchestra. Transparent textures are beautifully caught by the glowing recording – one of the last big projects of the outstanding recording producer and engineer, Jimmy Burnett. Through the first four movements, this may seem a lightweight reading, but the extra resilience and point of rhythm bring out the dance element in Mahler's *Knaben Wunderhorn* inspirations rather than ruggedness or rusticity. That Jansons intends this is confirmed when, at the finale, the whole performance erupts in an overwhelming outburst for the vision of Resurrection. That transformation is intensified by the breathtakingly rapt and intense account of the song, *Urlicht*, which precedes it. At a very measured speed, with Julia Hamari the warmly dedicated soloist, Jansons secures the gentlest of pianissimos. The chorale for pianissimo trumpets at the start is far more hushed than usual, magically distanced. In the finale, power goes with precision and meticulous observance of markings, when even Mahler's surprising diminuendo on the final choral cadence is observed. With the Oslo Choir joined by singers from Jansons' native Latvia, the choral singing is heartfelt, to crown a version which finds a special place even among the many distinguished readings on a long list.

The transfer of Klemperer's performance – one of his most compelling on record – on to a single CD (playing for over 79 minutes) is a considerable achievement, and the remastered sound is impressively full and clear, with the fullest sense of spectacle in the closing pages. The first movement, taken at a fairly fast tempo, is intense and earth-shaking, and that is surely as it should be in a work which culminates in a representation of Judgement Day itself. Though in the last movement some of Klemperer's speeds are designedly slow, he conveys supremely well the mood of transcendent heavenly happiness in the culminating passage, with chorus and soloists themselves singing like angels. The Last Trump brings a shudder of excitement, and the less grand central movements have their simple charm equally well conveyed.

Abbado's version proves a performance of extremes, with variations of tempo more confidently marked than is common but with concentration so intense there is no hint of self-indulgence. The delicacy of the Chicago orchestra in the second and third movements is as remarkable as its precision, while the great contrasts of the later movements prove a challenge not only to the performers but to the DG engineers, who produce sound of the finest analogue quality. Generally the singing is as splendid as the playing, but if there is even a minor disappointment, it lies in the closing pages which are just a little contained. However, while highly recommendable, this entails two CDs.

In digital sound of extraordinary power Solti has re-recorded with the Chicago orchestra this symphony which with the LSO was one of the finest achievements of his earlier Mahler series. Differences of interpretation are on points of detail merely, with a lighter, more elegant rendering of the minuet-rhythms of the second movement. Though the digital recording is not always as well balanced as the earlier analogue (Isobel Buchanan and Mira Zakai are too close, for example), the weight of fortissimo in the final hymn, not to mention the Judgement Day brass, is breathtaking. Interpretatively too, the outer movements are as fiercely intense as before.

The big advantage of Bernstein's DG version over his previous CBS recording with the LSO lies in the quality of sound. Recorded live in Avery Fisher Hall, New York, the engineers have overcome the acoustic problems to a remarkable degree, presenting a weighty and wide-ranging sound, set against a warm reverberation (superimposed?) not associated with that venue. The expansion for the choral finale is well handled, and it is there in the urgency of the final chorus that Bernstein's interpretation gains over his previous one, recorded in the studio, a shade more intense. Otherwise, like earlier recordings in Bernstein's DG series, the live performance shows the conductor more self-indulgent than before, as well as more expansive, often overlaying Mahler's simplest and most tender melodies with forced expressiveness – even if, as ever, the voltage is high.

Under Gilbert Kaplan the LSO plays with a biting precision and power to shame many an effort on record under a world-renowned conductor. Added to that, the sound is exceptionally brilliant and full, bringing home the impact of the big dramatic moments, which are what stand out in the performance. The second-movement Ländler too is rhythmically heavy-handed, but even there the ensemble is splendid, with fine detail brought out. It is good to have the veteran Canadian mezzo, Maureen Forrester, as soloist, when her voice remains so rich and full. The soprano Benita Valente is less aptly fruity of tone; but she and Forrester as well as the fine chorus sing with a will, crowning a performance that is never less than enjoyable, thanks above all to the playing and to superb sound. The documentation included is exceptionally generous, with a long essay and analysis by Kaplan in one booklet and a fascinating collection of Mahler's letters about the symphony in a second.

Symphony No. 3 in D min.

*** Ph. Dig. 432 162-2 (2) [id.]. Jard van Nes, Tölz Boys' Ch., Ernest-Senff Ch., BPO, Haitink.

*** DG Dig. 410 715-2 (2) [id.]. J. Norman, V. State Op. Ch., V. Boys' Ch., VPO, Abbado.

(M) *** Unicorn UKCD 2006/7 [id.]. Procter, Wandsworth School Boys' Ch., Amb. S., LSO, Horenstein.

**(*) Decca Dig. 414 268-2 (2) [id.]. Dernesch, Glen Ellyn Children's Ch., Chicago Ch. & SO, Solti.

**(*) Denon Dig. C37 7828/9 [id.]. Soffel, Limburger, Domsingknaben, Frankfurter Kantorei, Frankfurt RSO, Inbal.

*(*) Chan. Dig. CHAN 8970/1 [id.]. Anne Gjevang, Copenhagen Boys' Ch., Danish Nat. R. Ch. and SO, Segerstam.

(i) *Symphony No. 3;* (ii) *Das klagende Lied.*
**(*) Ph. 420 113-2 (2) [id.]. (i) Forrester, Netherlands R. Ch., St Willibrod Boys' Ch.; (ii) Harper, Procter, Hollweg, Netherlands R. Ch.; Concg. O, Haitink.

Symphony No. 3; 5 Rückert Lieder.
*** Sony M2K 44553 (2) [id.]. Janet Baker, LSO Ch., LSO, Tilson Thomas.

Michael Tilson Thomas, in one of his first recordings with the LSO since being appointed its principal conductor, directs a powerful account of this challenging symphony. Predictably, he inspires the orchestra to play with bite and panache in the bold, dramatic passages and to bring out the sparkle and freshness of the *Knaben Wunderhorn* ideas; but what crowns the performance is the raptness of his reading of the noble, hymn-like finale, hushed and intense, beautifully sustained. There is a formidable bonus in Dame Janet Baker's searching performances of the five *Rückert Lieder.* She is just as moving here as she was in the classic recording of them she made twenty years earlier with Sir John Barbirolli. Excellent CBS sound, both warm and brilliant.

With the Berlin Philharmonic producing glorious sounds, recorded with richness and immediacy, Haitink conducts a powerful, spacious reading. It culminates in a glowing, concentrated account of the slow finale, which gives the whole work a visionary strength often lacking. Haitink takes a forthright view of the massive first movement, and finely pointed ones of the following instrumental movements. The mystery of *Urlicht* is then beautifully caught by the mezzo soloist Jard van Nes, with fine discipline in the lusty bell song of the fifth movement. An outstanding addition to Haitink's emergent new Mahler cycle.

With sound of spectacular range, Abbado's performance is sharply defined and deeply dedicated. The range of expression, the often wild mixture of elements in this work, is conveyed with extraordinary intensity, not least in the fine contributions of Jessye Norman and the two choirs. The recording has great presence and detail on CD.

More than the earlier issue of Mahler's *First Symphony*, this account of the Mahler *Third* shows Horenstein at his most intensely committed. The manner is still very consistent in its simple dedication to the authority of the score and its rejection of romantic indulgence; but with an extra intensity the result has the sort of frisson-creating quality one knew from live Horenstein performances. Above all the restraint of the finale is intensely compelling. Though the strings are rather backwardly balanced and the timpani are too prominent, the recording quality is both full and brilliant. Fine vocal contributions from Norma Procter, the Ambrosian Singers and the Wandsworth School Boys' Choir.

In Solti's Chicago version the last movement is hushed and intense, deeply concentrated, building up superbly even though the hastening is a shade excessive towards the end. The other movements have brilliance, freshness and clarity, with Helga Dernesch a fine if rather detached soloist. Solti remains a bold Mahler interpreter, missing some of the *Wunderhorn* fun. The virtuoso playing of the Chicago orchestra is brilliantly caught by the wide-ranging recording, though the posthorn of the third movement is placed unatmospherically close.

In a work that can seem over-inflated Haitink's straightforwardness as a Mahlerian makes for a deeply satisfying performance. Though in the first movement his rather fast speed allows for less lift in the rhythm than do some others, he captures to perfection the fresh, wide-eyed simplicity of the second movement and the carol-like quality of the fifth movement, *Bell song.* Best of all is the wonderfully simple and intense reading of the long concluding slow movement, which here is given an inner intensity that puts it very close to the comparable movement of Mahler's *Ninth.* Haitink's soloists are excellent, the playing of the Concertgebouw is refined and dedicated. For CD the symphony has been coupled with *Das klagende Lied,* a much earlier recording but one of high quality, although the performance is not ideal, lacking urgency and a sense of imaginative imagery.

Eliahu Inbal in his Frankfurt version for Denon takes a spacious view, well sustained by very fine playing from the orchestra. This marked the point in the joint project between Denon and Hesse Radio where the intensive planning of a whole Mahler cycle within a two-year span began to deliver extra intensity in the finished results as recorded. The slow speeds are sustained easily and naturally, with the *Wunderhorn* element brought out more prominently than usual. The sound, as in the rest of the series, is excellent in its natural balances; but there are readings which convey the grandeur of Mahler's vision more powerfully.

Segerstam's view of Mahler here conveys little of the darker, neurotic side of the composer. His is a generally clean-cut, often rugged performance, well-recorded, which fails to rise to the full challenge of this massive work. Though he is not afraid to opt for spacious speeds in the long outer movements, the result feels too small-scale. Good singing from the chorus and from the soloist, Anne Gjevang.

Symphony No. 4 in G.
(M) *** EMI Dig. CD-EMX 2139; *TC-EMX 2139*. Felicity Lott, LPO, Welser-Möst.
*** Denon Dig. C37 7952 [id.]. Helen Donath, Frankfurt RSO, Inbal.
*** Decca Dig. 410 188-2 [id.]. Kiri Te Kanawa, Chicago SO, Solti.
(M) *** DG 419 863-2; *419 863-4* [id.]. Edith Mathis, BPO, Karajan.
*** Ph. Dig. 412 119-2 [id.]. Roberta Alexander, Concg. O, Haitink.
**(*) DG Dig. 423 607-2 [MYK 37225]. Helmut Witek (treble), Concg. O, Bernstein.
(M) *(*) Pickwick/RPO Dig. CDRPO 8017; *ZCRPO 8017* [id.]. Yvonne Kenny, RPO, Inoue.

(i) *Symphony No. 4 in G;* (ii) *Lieder eines fahrenden Gesellen.*
❀ (M) *** Sony SBK 46535 [id.]; *40-46535*. (i) Judith Raskin, Cleveland O, Szell; (ii) Frederica von Stade, LPO, Andrew Davis.
**(*) Chan. Dig. CHAN 8951 [id.]. Linda Finnie, RSO, Järvi.

George Szell's 1966 record of Mahler's *Fourth* represented his partnership with the Cleveland Orchestra at its highest peak. The digital remastering for CD brings out the very best of the original recording, making it sound translucently clear, yet without losing the ambient warmth. The performance remains uniquely satisfying: the interpretation has an element of coolness, but the music blossoms, partly because of the marvellous attention to detail (and the immaculate ensemble), but more positively because of the committed and radiantly luminous orchestral response to the music itself. In the finale Szell found the ideal soprano to match his conception: Judith Raskin sings without artifice, and her voice has an open colouring like a child's, yet the feminine quality subtly remains. An outstanding choice, generously coupled. In contrast with most other recorded performances, Frederica von Stade insinuates a hint of youthful ardour into her highly enjoyable account of the *Wayfaring Lad* cycle. If the playing of the LPO under Andrew Davis seems at times to lack refinement, this is partly the fault of close analogue recording.

Welser-Möst's spacious reading of Mahler's *Fourth*, as one of the first recordings he made, makes a formidable offering from so young a conductor. The outer movements are fresh and beautifully shaped, with Felicity Lott a youthful-sounding soloist, and the Laendler second movement clean-cut and crisp, with little concern for Austrian charm. It is the third movement *Adagio* that crowns the performance, hushed and intense from the start, with the emotional outbursts strongly controlled. At mid-price with excellent modern digital sound, spacious like the performance, it makes an outstanding mid-priced recommendation, a fine alternative to Szell, especially now that Maazel's VPO version is now available only within his complete set.

With a rather smaller orchestra than in the other symphonies, the engineers who balanced Inbal's fine Frankfurt series were able to rely entirely on the source drawn from single-point placing of microphones. The result is outstandingly fresh and natural, matching a delightful performance of the symphony, the tone of which is set by the easy, happy and relaxed manner of the opening. There is a pastoral element in Inbal's approach all through, reflecting the *Wunderhorn* basis, and even the spacious slow movement is easily songful rather than ethereal. Helen Donath brings boyish, Hansel-like timbre to her solo in the finale.

With outstandingly refined playing from the Concertgebouw, superlatively recorded, Haitink's reading has a fresh innocence that is most winning. Thus the lovely *Adagio*, rather than conveying the deepest meditation, presents an ecstatic, songful musing in the long paragraphs of the main theme, and Roberta Alexander makes a perceptive choice of soloist for such a reading, both fresh and creamy of tone.

Solti's digital version gives the lie to the idea of his always being fierce and unrelaxed. This sunniest of the Mahler symphonies receives a delightfully fresh and bright reading, beautifully paced and superbly played. The recording is bright, full and immediate in the Decca Chicago manner, without inflating the interpretation. Dame Kiri Te Kanawa sings beautifully in the child-heaven finale.

Karajan's refined and poised, yet undoubtedly affectionate account remains among the finest versions of this lovely symphony, and Edith Mathis's sensitively composed contribution to the finale matches the conductor's meditative feeling. With glowing sound, this makes an outstanding mid-priced recommendation alongside Szell's renowned Cleveland CD.

Bernstein conducts the Concertgebouw in a beautifully refined, generally expansive version which brings one highly controversial point. The subtlety of expression makes Bernstein's CBS version of thirty years earlier seem heavy-handed by comparison; but not everyone will respond to his use of a boy treble, instead of a soprano, for the solo in the child-heaven finale. Helmut Witek of the Tölzer Boys' Choir sings with delightful freshness, but the close balance of the voice tends to bring out the element of rawness. Refined Concertgebouw sound, the more commendable when it is realized that this was edited together from live performances.

Järvi conducts the Royal Scottish National in a warm and robust reading of No. 4, which brings out its amiably rustic qualities. The playing is not as refined as on the finest versions, notably from the strings. The close recording balance does not allow a true hush in the slow movement, while the scordatura solo violin in the Laendler second movement is uncomfortably close. Linda Finnie demonstrates how a mezzo can effectively take the solo in the finale instead of a lyric soprano. She sounds child-like enough, though the high phrases at the end of each stanza are not as easy-sounding as they should be. In the *Wayfaring Lad* songs, which come as a generous fill-up, she and Järvi take a broad view. There is no attempt at a boyish manner, but her tender intensity makes the final song most moving, when in hushed pianissimo Finnie stills her vibrato.

Inoue directs a relaxed and generally restrained reading of No. 4, with Yvonne Kenny a sweet-toned soloist in the child-heaven finale. At mid-price it is hardly competitive, for the playing is not always ideally refined.

(i) *Symphony No. 4 in G;* (ii) *Lieder (aus der Jugendzeit): Ablösung im Sommer; Erinnerung; Frühlingsmorgen; Hans und Grethe; Ich ging mit Lust durch einen grünen Wald; Nicht wiedersehen!; Scheiden und meiden; Starke Einbildungskraft.*
(M) (**) Sony mono MPK 46450 [id.]. (i) NYPO, Bruno Walter; (ii) Desi Halban, Bruno Walter.

Interpretatively, Walter still has much to show any rival, with delicately pointed rhythms and easily flexible speeds that consistently sound idiomatic. He brings out the pure joy behind the inspiration, culminating in the child-heaven finale, performed with delicious jauntiness. The aptly boyish-sounding soloist, Desi Halban, is not well focused in the recording, but she is even less flatteringly recorded in the fill-up, eight of Mahler's 'Youth' songs, *Aus der Jugendzeit*, with Walter accompanying at the piano. Recorded in an unattractively dry acoustic, Halban is made to sound edgy under pressure, and Walter's playing is often rhythmically lumpy, not nearly as persuasive as his conducting.

Symphony No. 5 in C sharp min.
(M) *** EMI Dig. CD-EMX 2164; *TC-EMX 2164.* RLPO, Mackerras.
❀ (M) *** EMI CDM7 69186-2 [id.]; *EG 769186-4.* New Philh. O, Barbirolli.
(M) *** DG Dig. 431 037-2. VPO, Bernstein.
*** EMI Dig. CDC7 49888-2 [id.]. LPO, Tennstedt.
*** DG Dig. 415 476-2 [id.]. Philh. O, Sinopoli.
*** Decca Dig. 425 438-2 [id.]. Cleveland O, Dohnányi.
*** Denon Dig. CO 1088 [id.]. Frankfurt RSO, Inbal.
**(*) Virgin Dig. 7 91445-2 [id.]. Finnish RSO, Saraste.

With brilliant, refined playing from the Liverpool orchestra, in warm, well-detailed sound, the Mackerras version at mid-price on Eminence is a match for any in the catalogue at whatever price, whether in performance or recording. Mackerras in his well-paced reading sees the work as a whole, building each movement with total concentration. There is a thrilling culmination on the great brass chorale at the end, with polish allied to purposefulness. Barbirolli in his classic reading may find more of a tear-laden quality in the great *Adagietto*; but Mackerras, with fewer controversial points of interpretation and superb modern sound, makes an excellent first choice.

Barbirolli's famous 1969 version has been digitally remastered on to one mid-priced CD. On any count it is one of the greatest, most warmly affecting performances ever committed to record, expansive yet concentrated in feeling. A classic version and a fine bargain.

Bernstein's is also an expansive version, characteristic of his latterday Mahler style. The lovely *Adagietto* was the music he conducted at the funeral of President Kennedy, and the tempo this time is just as slow as before and just as elegiac, though the phrasing is less heavily underlined. The whole performance (recorded, in the Bernstein manner, at live concerts) has his personal stamp on it, at times idiosyncratic but luminous and magnetically compelling, one of the best in his new DG Mahler series and one of his finest recent records. The sound is more open and refined than in many of DG's Vienna recordings.

Tennstedt's later, digital recording of the *Fifth* was made live at the Festival Hall at a concert which marked a happy reunion between orchestra and its music director after the conductor's long and serious illness. The emotional tension of the occasion is vividly captured. As a Mahler interpretation, it is at once more daring and more idiosyncratic than Tennstedt's earlier, studio recording, but the tension is far keener. One readily accepts the expressive distortions of the moment, the little hesitations that Tennstedt introduces, when the result communicates so immediately and vividly; and the problems of recording live in this difficult acoustic have been masterfully overcome under the direction of the orchestra's managing director and former EMI recording manager, John Willan. The experience hits one at full force, whether in the exuberant, pointed account of the third-movement scherzo, the deeply hushed, expansive one of the *Adagietto* or the headlong reading of the finale, which, even at thrilling high speed, has irresistible swagger.

Sinopoli's version draws the sharpest distinction between the dark tragedy of the first two movements and the relaxed *Wunderhorn* feeling of the rest. Thus, the opening *Funeral march* is tough and biting, expressive but moulded less than one associates with this conductor; here, as later, Sinopoli seems intent on not overloading the big melodies with excessive emotion. This comes out the more clearly in the central movements, where relaxation is the keynote, often with a pastoral atmosphere. The third-movement Ländler has the happiest of lilts but leads finally to a frenetic coda, before the celebrated *Adagietto* brings a tenderly wistful reading, songful and basically happy, not tragic. The *Wunderhorn* mood returns in full joy in the finale, starting with a magical evocation of the Austrian countryside. Warmly atmospheric recording, not lacking brilliance, but not always ideally clear on detail.

Dohnányi conducts the Cleveland Orchestra in an exceptionally high-powered reading, superbly played and recorded, which can still relax totally in expressive warmth. The toughness of the first two movements – with superb discipline bringing immaculate articulation in the second – gives way to an equally polished but nicely lilting Ländler in the third, finely shaded. Though the hushed *Adagietto* keeps a degree of reserve, the songful freshness and purity are very sympathetic, before the thrustful and dramatic finale, dramatically done. The brilliance of the Cleveland playing is matched by the vivid recorded sound.

As in his accounts of the earlier Mahler symphonies, Inbal brings out the *Wunderhorn* element in the *Fifth* very convincingly, and that applies to all five movements. He may not be as exciting as some rivals, but, with superb playing and beautifully balanced sound, full and atmospheric, it is an exceptionally sympathetic reading. The second and third movements, unusually relaxed, lead to an account of the *Adagietto* that is warmly songful yet hushed and sweet, while the finale conveys the happiness of pastoral ideas leading logically to a joyful, triumphant close.

Saraste and the Finnish Radio Orchestra offer a refined and well-paced reading, which gives a relatively light-weight view of the symphony. Mahlerian neurosis is largely missing, which might be justified in a work that ends in joy. Rhythms are beautifully sprung, and the *Adagietto* is the more tenderly moving for being a degree reticent and understated. Refined recording to match.

Symphony No. 5: Adagietto.
*** Pickwick Dig. Single GSK 1001 [id.]. LSO, Gilbert Kaplan.

Gilbert Kaplan, the American businessman who specializes in conducting Mahler's *Resurrection Symphony*, here extends his repertory in a performance of the *Adagietto* from the *Fifth*, reflecting his detailed research. On the evidence of the earliest recordings and other sources, Mahler intended the movement to be played much faster than has become the norm. That also reflects Kaplan's finding that Mahler intended the piece not as an elegy but as a tender love-token for Alma, his wife. Kaplan's warm, easily flowing reading reflects that approach, convincingly well played and very well recorded on a CD single, costing about half the price of a bargain disc. The CD, charmingly presented, with a deep red rose on the front, even has three internal cues, reflecting the major tempo changes. (Incidentally, the journal *Classic CD* featured this movement within their sampler disc, offered free with their June 1992 issue.)

Symphony No. 5 in C sharp min; Symphony No. 9 in D.
* Arkadia CDGI 754.2 (2) [id.]. BBC SO, Boulez.

The Boulez issue from Arkadia offers live recordings made respectively in 1968 and 1971, with Boulez adopting a far more warmly expressive approach to Mahler than one might have expected. The electricity of the performances makes them compelling, but on disc they are hardly competitive, what with the limited, often scratchy sound and inevitably flawed ensemble. Squeezing the two symphonies on to two discs involves a break half through the final *Adagio* of no. 9.

Symphony No. 6 in A min.
*** DG 415 099-2 (2) [id.]. BPO, Karajan – *5 Rückert Lieder*. **(*)
(M) *** Sony SBK 47654 [id.]. Cleveland O, Szell.
*** Ph. Dig. 426 257-2 [id.]. BPO, Haitink – *Lieder eines fahrenden Gesellen*. ***
(M) *** Unicorn UKCD 2024/5. Stockholm PO, Jascha Horenstein.
*** Decca Dig. 430 165-2 (2) [id.]. Concg. O, Chailly – ZEMLINSKY: *Maeterlinck Lieder*. ***
(M) **(*) Pickwick/RPO CDRPO 9005 (2) [id.]. RPO, Inoue.

Symphony No. 6; Symphony No. 10: Adagio.
*** DG Dig. 423 082-2 (2) [id.]. Philh. O, Sinopoli.

Symphony No. 6 in A min.; Todtenfeier (symphonic poem).
** Chan. Dig. CHAN 8956/7 [id.]. Danish RSO, Leif Segerstam.

Symphony No. 6; (i) *Kindertotenlieder*.
**(*) DG Dig. 427 697-2 (2) [id.]. (i) Thomas Hampson; VPO, Bernstein.

With superlative playing from the Berlin Philharmonic, Karajan's reading of the *Sixth* is a revelation, above all in the slow movement which here becomes far more than a lyrical interlude. It emerges as one of the greatest of Mahler's slow movements and the whole balance of the symphony is altered. Though the outer movements firmly stamp this as the darkest of the Mahler symphonies, in Karajan's reading their sharp focus – with contrasts of light and shade heightened – makes them both compelling and refreshing. The superb DG recording, with its wide dynamics, adds enormously to the impact. Christa Ludwig's set of the *Five Rückert Songs* has been added as a bonus.

Szell's powerful outer movements are masterfully shaped and unerringly paced, with the second-movement scherzo a shade broader than the closely related first, beautifully sprung to bring out the grotesquerie. The *Andante moderato* then brings a uniquely delicate and moving account of an elusive movement. At a whispered pianissimo, flowing easily, the result is hauntingly wistful, tender without a hint of sentimentality. The CD transfer gives a fuller, more atmospheric impression of what the orchestra sounded like in Severance Hall, Cleveland, than most of the studio recordings of the time. At budget price, squeezed on to a single disc, this is buried treasure, a historic issue for everyone, not just Mahlerians, and a fine counterpart to Szell's classic reading of Mahler's *Fourth*.

Sinopoli's version of the *Sixth* presents a strongly individual view, outstandingly convincing in the first two movements which, tough and urgent, are given rhythmic elbow room, but sounding less purposeful in the last two movements, both taken notably slower than usual. In the first movement the swaggering gait of the march rhythm has a power comparable with that of Karajan, but without his clipped militaristic fierceness. In the second-movement scherzo Sinopoli finds a haunted quality. With brass whooping and sprung rhythms, it conveys an even more sinister fantasy than with Karajan. The slow movement, taken very slowly indeed, with agogic hesitations peppered over the phrasing, lacks a warm flow, refined as it is. But, like the finale, it finds the right tensions after opening self-consciously, and overall the breadth of vision makes this one of the most compellingly individual versions of all. The *Adagio* from the *Tenth Symphony* makes a generous fill-up; but Sinopoli's very slow reading, with detail heavily underlined, takes away the dark purposefulness of the argument. The recording of both works is among DG's fullest and most brilliant.

Haitink conducts a noble reading of this difficult symphony, underplaying the neurosis behind the inspiration, but, in his clean-cut concentration and avoidance of exaggeration, making the result the more moving in its degree of reticence. This is a far finer reading than the one he conducted earlier with the Concertgebouw, thanks largely to the playing of the Berlin Philharmonic, beautiful, polished and, above all, intensely committed. Jessye Norman's rich-toned account of *Lieder eines fahrenden Gesellen* makes a powerful bonus. Excellent sound, both full-blooded and refined.

Horenstein's Unicorn-Kanchana set originates from live performances, recorded in Stockholm in April 1966; yet the sound is amazingly faithful and well balanced, with a firm bass, full strings, and a spacious concert-hall perspective. In the first movement Horenstein finds extra weight by taking a more measured tempo than most conductors. It is a sober reading that holds together with wonderful concentration. Not that this view of Mahler lacks flexibility, for the slow movement brings the most persuasive rubato. The finale brings another broad, noble reading. Yet some will feel that 33 minutes is short measure for the second CD, especially when

Horenstein's recorded reminiscences with Alan Blyth, featured in the LP set, are not included here.

Chailly's version with the Concertgebouw offers brilliant playing and spectacular sound in a reading remarkable for the broad, rugged approach in the outer movements. There is relentlessness in the slow speed for the first movement, with expressive warmth giving way to a square purposefulness, tense and effective. The third movement brings a comparably simple, direct approach at a genuine flowing *Andante*. In its open songfulness it rouses *Wunderhorn* echoes. Anyone fancying the unexpected but attractive Zemlinsky coupling need not hesitate.

Bernstein's DG version easily outshines his earlier account for CBS on the vividness of the sound alone. His speed for the military march of the first movement still struts rather uncomfortably fast, but it brings more variety and refinement of expression than before. It is much the same with the other three movements. The special attraction of this version is the fill-up, when on the second disc Bernstein offers a searching performance of the *Kindertotenlieder* with, for once, a male soloist, the deeply responsive, rich-voiced Thomas Hampson.

Next to the finest versions Segerstam's lacks dramatic bite, forthright and sympathetic as it is. The playing is clean and fresh, and the recording is first-rate, but the result is too small-scale, particularly in the long finale with its hammer-blows. *Todtenfeier*, the single-movement symphonic poem that Mahler later used in modified form for the first movement of his *Resurrection Symphony*, makes a generous and valuable coupling.

Inoue's version with the RPO on the orchestra's own mid-price label was recorded live at the Royal Festival Hall in 1988, one of the more successful recordings made in that unhelpful acoustic, full and immediate. The performance, not ideally polished, is warm and spontaneous, with a natural feeling for Mahlerian rubato at well-chosen speeds. Inoue consciously adopts a much slower speed for the Laendler-like second movement than for the thematically-related first. The *Andante* third movement is then most beautifully done, hushed and intense, with beautifully-moulded phrasing.

Symphony No. 7 in E min.
*** DG Dig. 413 773-2 (2) [id.]. Chicago SO, Abbado.
*** DG Dig. 419 211-2 (2) [id.]. NYPO, Bernstein.
*** Denon Dig. CO 1553/4 [id.]. Frankfurt RSO, Inbal.
*** Ph. Dig. 426 249-2; *426 249-4* (2) [id.]. Boston SO, Seiji Ozawa – *Kindertotenlieder*. ***
**(*) Ph. Dig. 410 398-2 (2) [id.]. Concg. O, Haitink.

Abbado's command of Mahlerian characterization has never been more tellingly displayed than in this most problematic of the symphonies; even in the loosely bound finale, Abbado unerringly draws the threads together. The contrasts in all its movements are superbly brought out, with the central interludes made ideally atmospheric, as in the eeriness of the scherzo and the haunting tenderness of the second *Nachtmusik*. The precision and polish of the Chicago orchestra go with total commitment, and the recording is one of the finest DG has made with this orchestra.

Leonard Bernstein's *Seventh* for DG was recorded from live performances. It is a riveting performance from first to last, ending with a searingly exciting account of the finale which triumphantly flouts the idea of this as a weak conclusion. It is a performance to send you off cheering, while the purposeful control of earlier movements also minimizes the obvious objections in principle to wilful exaggerations in phrasing and changes of tempo. This is Mahlerian expression at its most red-blooded, and with fine playing from the New York Philharmonic – marginally finer even than in his CBS version – it is a splendid example of Bernstein's flair in Mahler. The recording, fuller than in his much earlier CBS account, is yet a little harsh at times, next to the finest modern digital sound.

Inbal's account of the *Seventh* is one of the high points of his Mahler series, masterfully paced, relaxed and lyrical where appropriate, but incorporating all the biting tensions that are missing in his version of the *Sixth*, the other dark, middle symphony. Inbal's easy, natural manner is particularly effective in the three middle movements, and the radiant beauty of the second *Nachtmusik*, taken at a flowing speed, has never sounded more Elysian. The easy purposefulness of the finale in its many sections brings a masterly example of his unforced, incisive control, ending exuberantly at full power. The recording is outstandingly fine in its vivid, natural balances.

With the sound forward and immediate, Ozawa directs a warmly persuasive account of Mahler's most problematical symphony. It may lack the purposefulness of Abbado or the rugged strength of Bernstein, but the work has never sounded more beautiful, with the two *Nachtmusik* movements played impressionistically. In the outer movements Ozawa's keen control of tension goes with well-lifted, swaggering rhythms. A powerful bonus is the live recording of *Kindertotenlieder* with Jessye Norman at her most compelling.

Beauty is the keynote of Haitink's newer, digitally recorded version of Mahler's *Seventh*. The superb playing of the Concertgebouw Orchestra is richly and amply caught; however, with spacious speeds to match, tensions have tended to ease since Haitink's earlier account; the vision of darkness is softened a degree. The wide dynamic range is very telling, with detail clarified.

Symphony No. 8 (Symphony of 1000).

❀ *** EMI Dig. CDS7 47625-8 (2) [Ang. CDCB 47625]. Connell, Wiens, Lott, Schmidt, Denize, Versalle, Hynninen, Sotin, Tiffin School Boys' Ch., LPO Ch., LPO, Tennstedt.

*** Decca 414 493-2 (2) [id.]. Harper, Popp, Augér, Minton, Watts, Kollo, Shirley-Quirk, Talvela, V. Boys' Ch., V. State Op. Ch. & Singverein, Chicago SO, Solti.

*** Denon Dig. CO 1564/5 [id.]. Robinson, Cahill, Heichele, Budai, Henschel, Riegel, Prey, Stamm, Bav. N., S. & W. German R. Choirs, RIAS Chamber Ch., Limburg Cathedral Ch., Hesse R. Children's Ch., Frankfurt RSO, Inbal.

** Telarc Dig. CD 80267 [id.]. Voight, Wray, Grant, Ziegler, Simpson, Sylvester, Stone, Cox, Atlanta Boys' Ch., Ohio State University Symphonic Ch., Master Ch. of Tampa Bay, Members of S. Florida Ch., Atlanta SO & Ch., Robert Shaw.

(i) *Symphony No. 8 (Symphony of 1000). Symphony No. 10: Adagio.*

**(*) DG 435 102-2 (2) [id.]. VPO, Bernstein, (i) with Price, Blegen, Zeumer, Schmidt, Baltsa, Riegel, Prey, van Dam, V. Op. Ch., V. Boys' Ch.

Tennstedt's magnificent account of the *Eighth*, long delayed through problems of casting, marks a superb culmination, the finest of his whole cycle. Though it does not always have the searing intensity that marks Solti's overwhelming Decca version, Tennstedt's broader, grander view makes at least as powerful an impact, and with the extra range and richness of the modern EMI recording, coping superbly with even the heaviest textures, for most listeners it will be even more satisfying. Not the least impressive point about the recording is the firm, opulent sound of the Westminster Cathedral organ, dubbed on afterwards but sounding all the better focused for that. Next to this EMI recording, the 1972 Decca sound, for all its vividness, with solo voices made more immediate, sounds a little rough, underlining the fierceness. That said, the contrasting approaches of Tennstedt and Solti make them equally cherishable in their illumination of Mahler. It is the urgency and dynamism of Solti which make his reading irresistible, ending in an earth-shattering account of the closing hymn. Tennstedt, both there and elsewhere, finds more light and shade. His soloists, though a strong, characterful team, are not as consistent as Solti's. Even Felicity Lott as Mater Gloriosa is less pure-toned than she has sometimes been, but her solo is the more moving for being ethereally balanced. The great glory of the set is the singing of the London Philharmonic Choir, assisted by Tiffin School Boys' Choir. The chorus may be rather smaller than in live performance, but diction and clarity are aided, with no loss of power. This was a worthy winner in the orchestral category of the 1987 Gramophone awards.

The exhilaration of Inbal's culminating performance, recorded (like earlier ones) at sessions linked to live performances, comes over vividly. Even with a very large chorus, the sound is superbly detailed as well as full and atmospheric. *Veni creator spiritus* is wonderfully fresh and eager, but the clarity of detail does at times reveal fractional imprecision of ensemble. The refinement of sound gives extra intensity to the meditations of the great second movement, and Inbal's fast speed for the closing hymn makes it all the more purposeful, exuberant in joy. The team of soloists is a strong one but, like Tennstedt's octet, cannot match Solti's in consistency. The sound, naturally balanced and with as little tampering as possible, is extremely fine, not as spectacular as Tennstedt's but deeply satisfying in its warmth and beauty.

When Bernstein died in the autumn of 1990, he had still not recorded the massive No. 8 in order to complete his Mahler symphony cycle for DG. The company was fortunately able to track down this radio recording, made in Salzburg in 1975 with the Vienna Philharmonic and an unmatched team of soloists. Though flawed, it brings a much more compelling reading than the one he did with the LSO for CBS/Sony in 1967 as part of his earlier cycle. The newer recording is full and atmospheric, a credit to the engineers of Austrian Radio.

Robert Shaw's Telarc version, very well recorded, brings the powerful advantage of being fitted on a single disc. As a choirmaster second to none – he won his spurs in charge of the choir for Toscanini – he secures splendid singing from the massed choirs, and offers an outstanding team of soloists, with the tenor taking Dr Marianus exceptionally fine. Yet this is a limited view of a cosmic work, as the very opening suggests, rather matter-of-fact and pedestrian. Shaw's metrical treatment at the start of the long second movement conveys the right chill, but the full drama of this setting of the closing scene from Goethe's *Faust* is still missing.

Symphony No. 9 in D min.
*** DG Dig. 410 726-2 (2) [id.]. BPO, Karajan.
(M) *** EMI CDM7 63115-2 [id.]. BPO, Barbirolli.
*** DG 435 378-2 [id.]. BPO, Leonard Bernstein.
(M) *** EMI CMS7 63277-2 (2) [Ang. CDMB 63277]. New Philh. O, Klemperer – WAGNER: *Siegfried idyll.* **(*)
(M) (**(*)) EMI mono CDH7 63029-2. VPO, Bruno Walter.

Symphony No. 9; Symphony No. 10: Adagio.
*** Nuova Era Dig. 6906/7 (2). Mahler-Jugend O, or European Community Youth O, James Judd.
*** Denon Dig. CO 1566/7 [id.]. Frankfurt RSO, Inbal.
**(*) Virgin Dig. VCDS7 91219-2 (2). RLPO, Libor Pešek.
** EMI Dig. CDS7 54387-2. Cologne RSO, Bertini.
*(*) Ph. Dig. 426 302-2 (2) [id.]. Boston SO, Ozawa.

Symphony No. 9; (i) *Kindertotenlieder.*
*** Ph. 416 466-2 (2) [id.]. Concg. O, Haitink; (i) with Hermann Prey.

Karajan recorded Mahler's *Ninth* twice within a space of two years, and both performances transcended his earlier Mahler. The combination of richness and concentration in the outer movements makes for a reading of the deepest intensity, and in the middle movements point and humour are found, as well as refinement and polish. For his later version he added a new dimension of glowing optimism in the finale, rejecting any Mahlerian death-wish. It is this newer performance which appears on CD, recorded at live performances in Berlin and making it a supreme achievement. Despite the problems of live recording, the sound is bright and full, if somewhat close.

Judd conducts the brilliant young players of the Mahler-Jugend Orchestra in a deeply moving account of the *Ninth*, recorded live in Bratislava in April 1990. With recording of spectacular range and vividness, this makes one of the most appealing of all versions. The searing emotional commitment of the players comes out consistently, and no allowance whatever need be made on technical grounds for their youth. Much more than the live recordings of Ozawa and Bertini, this conveys the bite and tensions of a live event, caught with thrilling immediacy. The first horn, vital in this work, produces gloriously rounded tone, and the exceptionally large complement of strings (22.20.18.14.11) play with magnificent resonance over the widest dynamic range. Having had long experience of working with youth orchestras, Judd focuses the natural expressiveness of the players in a beautifully judged reading, weighty in the outer movements, rhythmically sharp in the middle two. Intensively rehearsed, the players achieve immaculate ensemble even in the most complex rubato, with the slow finale crowning the whole performance in a concentrated, warmly elegiac reading. The performance of the *Adagio* from *No. 10* is not quite so distinguished, though warmly satisfying; it was recorded in August 1987 by the rival band from EEC countries, the European Community Youth Orchestra.

Haitink is at his very finest in Mahler's *Ninth*, and the last movement, with its slow expanses of melody, reveals a unique concentration. Unlike almost all other conductors he maintains his intensely slow tempo from beginning to end. This is a great performance, beautifully recorded and, with the earlier movements performed superbly – the first movement a little restrained, the second pointed at exactly the right speed, and the third gloriously extrovert and brilliant – this will be a first recommendation for many Mahlerians. The CD transfer freshens the 1969 recording, which still sounds highly impressive in its body and natural focus. Hermann Prey's early-1970s version of the *Kindertotenlieder* is added, a fresh, intelligent account, yet lacking something in imagination and intensity of expression.

Barbirolli greatly impressed the Berliners with his Mahler performances live, and this recording reflects the players' warmth of response. He opted to record the slow and intense finale before the rest, and the beauty of the playing makes it a fitting culmination. The other movements are strong and alert too, and the sound remains full and atmospheric, though now more clearly defined. An unquestionable bargain.

The contrast between Bernstein's Berlin version of Mahler's *Ninth*, made live in 1979, and the 1985 Concertgebouw one included in his DG Mahler cycle is fascinating. This was the solitary occasion when he was permitted to conduct Karajan's own orchestra, and the response is electric, with playing not only radiant and refined but also deeply expressive in direct response to the conductor. The result totally transcends the Concertgebouw performance, in which Bernstein's expansiveness was so extreme that he came to sound self-conscious in his exaggerated hesitations and over-moulded phrasing. By contrast, the Berlin performance (which Bernstein never expected would be issued on disc) is far more spontaneous, with measured speeds superbly sustained in a much more tautly concentrated reading, yet one which also conveys a comparably hushed inner quality. Bernstein's New York reading on Sony/CBS seems lacking in intensity next to it.

Klemperer's performance was recorded in 1967 after a serious illness, and his refusal to languish pays tribute to his physical and spiritual defiance. Characteristically, he insisted on a relatively close balance, with woodwind well forward, and the physical power is underlined when the sound is full-bodied and firmly focused. The sublimity of the finale comes out the more intensely, with overt expressiveness held in check and deep emotion implied rather than made explicit. This is one of the very finest of Klemperer's later recordings and it is coupled with the much earlier Philharmonia chamber version of Wagner's *Siegfried idyll*.

Inbal's reading may not have the epic power or the sweeping breadth of Karajan, but his simple dedication brings a performance just as concentrated in its way, simulating the varying tensions of a live performance. The second-movement Ländler brings peasant overtones in the rasping woodwind; the third movement is finely pointed, emphasizing its joyfulness; and the simple gravity of the finale, easily lyrical in the big melodies, leads to a wonderfully hushed culmination, not tragic as with Karajan, but in its rapt ecstasy looking forward to the close, on murmurs of '*Ewig*', of *Das Lied von der Erde*. As a logical fill-up, the *Adagio* from the *Tenth Symphony* brings a similarly natural and warm reading. The sound in both works is excellent in its natural balance, a fine example of the Denon engineers' work.

Recorded live at a concert in the Musikvereinsaal on 16 January 1938, only a few weeks before Hitler invaded Austria, Bruno Walter's version with the Vienna Philharmonic was the first recording of this symphony ever issued. The opening is not promising, with coughing very obtrusive; but then, with the atmosphere of this hall caught more vividly than in most modern recordings, the magnetism of Walter becomes irresistible in music which he was the first ever to perform. Interestingly, his speeds in the great spans of the outer movements are faster than we have latterly grown used to, markedly so in the great *Adagio* finale. Ensemble is often scrappy in the first movement, but intensity is unaffected; and, even at its flowing speed, the finale brings warmth and repose with no feeling of haste.

With the middle two movements exceptionally light and pointed, Libor Pešek in his studio recording draws excellent playing from the Royal Liverpool Philharmonic, very well recorded. The hushed pianissimos are particularly beautiful, but compared with the very finest versions the reading lacks a little in weight and emotional intensity. With a flowing, songful account of the *Adagio* from No. 10 as fill-up, it makes an enjoyable listening experince, but falls short of the finest alternative versions.

The warmth and sweetness at the very start of Gary Bertini's Cologne performance, recorded live, leads logically to a sympathetic reading which underplays Mahlerian neurosis, and with that Mahlerian tensions. This is Mahler on a relatively small scale, with ensemble not ideally crisp, and atmospheric recording that could be sharper in focus.

Ozawa in his persuasively moulded reading draws characteristically warm, smooth playing from the Boston Symphony in a live recording which to a surprising degree lacks the feel of a concert performance with its dramatic tensions. One admires without being moved, not least in the controlled yet easily flowing account of the slow finale. The *Adagio* from the *Symphony No. 10* has similar qualities, though the relative lack of bite is less marked.

Symphony No. 10 in F sharp (Unfinished) (revised performing edition by Deryck Cooke).
*** EMI Dig. CDC7 54406-2 [id.]. Bournemouth SO, Rattle.

With digital recording of outstanding quality, Simon Rattle's vivid and compelling reading of the Cooke performing edition has one convinced more than ever that a remarkable revelation of Mahler's intentions was achieved in this painstaking reconstruction. To Cooke's final thoughts Rattle has added one or two detailed amendments; the finale in particular, starting with its cataclysmic hammer-blows and growing tuba line, is a deeply moving experience, ending not in neurotic resignation but in open optimism. In the middle movements, too, Rattle, youthfully dynamic, has fresh revelations to make. The Bournemouth orchestra plays with dedication, marred only by the occasional lack of fullness in the strings. Now reissued on a single CD, this tends to sweep the board.

Piano quartet movement.
*** Virgin Dig. VC 790739-2 [id.]. Domus – BRAHMS: *Piano quartet No. 2.* ***

Mahler's *Piano quartet movement* comes from his student days. It is in no sense characteristic of the Mahler we know from the symphonies; but even at this early stage there is a sense of scale and shape. Ideas unfold at the right pace and in a way that shows the composer to have mastered the received tradition. Domus play with sensitivity and dedication and, though the acoustic is undeniably reverberant, the sound is far from unpleasing.

LIEDER AND SONG-CYCLES

Kindertotenlieder.
*** Ph. Dig. 426 249-2; *426 249-4* (2) [id.]. Jessye Norman, Boston SO, Seiji Ozawa – *Symphony No. 7.* ***
(M) (***) Decca mono 425 995-2 [id.]. Kathleen Ferrier, Concg. O, Klemperer (with BRAHMS: *Liebeslieder waltzes* (***)).

Kindertotenlieder; Lieder eines fahrenden Gesellen.
** Decca 414 624-2 [id.]. Kirsten Flagstad, VPO, Boult – WAGNER: *Wesendonk Lieder.* ***

(i) *Kindertotenlieder; Lieder eines fahrenden Gesellen;* (ii) *5 Rückert Lieder.*
*** EMI CDC7 47793-2 [id.]. Dame Janet Baker, (i) Hallé O; (ii) New Philh. O, Barbirolli.

Dame Janet Baker's collaboration with Barbirolli represents the affectionate approach to Mahler at its warmest. The Hallé strings are not quite as fine as the New Philharmonia in the *Rückert Lieder*, but this generous recoupling brings results that are still intensely beautiful, full of breathtaking moments. The spontaneous feeling of soloist and conductor for this music comes over as in a live performance, and though a baritone like Fischer-Dieskau can give a stronger idea of these appealing cycles, this brings out the tenderness to a unique degree. The remastering has freshened the sound, but the ambient warmth of the original recording has not been lost. An indispensable CD.

Jessye Norman is supremely moving in Mahler's darkly elegiac cycle. This is a live recording, made in Frankfurt in 1988 when the orchestra was on tour, an intense performance with the soloist at her most spontaneously expressive. A valuable makeweight for a fine reading of the *Seventh Symphony*.

Flagstad sings masterfully in these two most appealing of Mahler's orchestral cycles, but she was unable to relax into the deeper, more intimate expressiveness that the works really require. The voice is magnificent, the approach always firmly musical (helped by Sir Adrian's splendid accompaniment), but this recording is recommendable for the singer rather than for the way the music is presented.

Ferrier's live recording with Klemperer was made at a Concertgebouw concert in July 1951. Though in this radio recording the orchestral sound is thin, the opulence of the voice comes over strongly, with the singer just as intense singing Mahler with this rugged Mahlerian as she is with the more affectionate Bruno Walter. In coupling with a historic radio recording of the Brahms *Liebeslieder waltzes*, it is an essential appendix to the Complete Ferrier Edition for admirers of the singer.

(i) *Kindertotenlieder;* (ii) *Lieder eines fahrenden Gesellen;* (i) *4 Rückert Lieder (Um Mitternacht; Ich atmet' einen linden Duft; Blicke mir nicht in die Lieder; Ich bin der Welt).*
*** DG 415 191-2 [id.]. Dietrich Fischer-Dieskau, (i) BPO, Boehm; (ii) Bav. RSO, Kubelik.

Only four of the *Rückert Lieder* are included (*Liebst du um Schönheit* being essentially a woman's song), but otherwise this conveniently gathers Mahler's shorter and most popular orchestral cycles in performances that bring out the fullest range of expression in Fischer-Dieskau at a period when his voice was at its peak. The CD transfer gives freshness and immediacy to both the 1964 recording with Boehm and the 1970 recording with Kubelik.

Das klagende Lied: complete *(Part 1, Waldmärchen; Part 2: Der Spielmann; Part 3, Hochzeitsstücke).*
*** EMI Dig. CDC 747089-2 [id.]. Döse, Hodgson, Tear, Rea, CBSO and Ch., Rattle.

*** Decca Dig. 425 719-2 [id.]. Susan Dunn, Markus Baur, Fassbaender, Hollweg, Schmidt, Düsseldorf State Musikverein, Berlin RSO, Chailly.
(M) *** Sony SK 45841 [id.]. Hoffman, Söderström, Haefliger, Nienstedt, Lear, Burrows, LSO, Boulez.
**(*) DG Dig. 435 382-2 [id.]. Cheryl Studer, Waltraud Meier, Reiner Goldberg, Thomas Allen, Shin-Yuh Kai Ch., Philh. O, Sinopoli.

Das klagende Lied is the amazing inspiration of a teenage composer. Years after its completion, when Mahler came to revise the work he jettisoned the first of the three sections. Boulez was given the rights to a first recording and in 1970 he promptly added his version of *Waldmärchen* to the other two parts, which he had already recorded using the same orchestra but with different soloists and a different venue, Walthamstow instead of Watford Town Hall. Boulez is a distinctive Mahlerian. His clear ear concentrates on precision of texture, but the atmospheric ambience adds warmth despite the forward balance, which also ensures very little difference in sound between the two recordings. Certainly the chill at the heart of this gruesome story of the days of chivalry and knights in armour is the more sharply conveyed. *Waldmärchen* is less effective than the rest. Good singing from the chorus, less good from the soloists. But with any reservations noted, this excellently remastered CD is well worth exploring.

Rattle brings out the astonishing originality but adds urgency, colour and warmth, not to mention deeper and more meditative qualities. So the final section, *Wedding Piece*, after starting with superb swagger in the celebration music, is gripping in the minstrel's sinister narration and ends in the darkest concentration on a mezzo-soprano solo, beautifully sung by Alfreda Hodgson. The ensemble of the CBSO has a little roughness, but the bite and commitment could not be more convincing.

The strength of the Chailly version lies with the splendid singing of the Düsseldorf Choir and the demonstration-worthy Decca recording, full of presence. While not quite upstaging Simon Rattle in revealing the music's marvellously imaginative detail, Chailly pulls one special trick out of the hat in *Waldmärchen* by using a boy alto (Markus Baur) to represent the voice from the grave, a tellingly sepulchral effect, and again after the off-stage band sequence. Of the soloists, Brigitte Fassbaender is at her most vibrant, but Susan Dunn is at rather less than her very best. Chailly's direction is strong and this version can be recommended alongside, though not necessarily in preference to Rattle, who also has first-rate recording.

Sinopoli's version was recorded live in 1990 when the Philharmonia was on tour in Japan. It offers a keenly dramatic reading, very well played and strongly paced to bring out the narrative flow. A drawback is that the sound has its oddities of balance – notably from the chorus which in its backward balance lacks bite – and there is far less sense of presence than in the studio recordings of Rattle and Chailly. Though the group of soloists is starrier than those on the two modern rival sets, that brings relatively few advantages.

Des Knaben Wunderhorn.
*** EMI CDC7 47277-2. Schwarzkopf, Fischer-Dieskau, LSO, Szell.
*** DG Dig. 427 302-2 [id.]. Lucia Popp, Andreas Schmidt, Concg. O, Bernstein.

In his last years Szell on his visits to Europe made a number of records which reflect a warmth and tenderness in his nature not often revealed in his work in Cleveland. This is one of that superlative group of records, with the most refined control of pianissimo in the orchestra matching the tonal subtleties of the two incomparable soloists. Wit and dramatic point as well as delicacy mark these widely contrasted songs, and the device of using two voices in some of them is apt and effective. The EMI recording has been freshened for CD very satisfactorily.

Bernstein's approach, spacious and measured, often tests his singers sorely, but Lucia Popp – very much the dominant partner of the two soloists – characterizes most appealingly, and though Andreas Schmidt is less positive, his singing is both fresh and unmannered. The sound is spacious and atmospheric, remarkably refined and well balanced for a live recording, with the soloists naturally placed, not spotlit. Bernstein includes *Urlicht*, better known as the fourth movement of the *Symphony No. 2*, in its separate song-form.

Des Knaben Wunderhorn; Lieder eines fahrenden Gesellen; 11 Lieder Aus der Jugendzeit; 4 Rückert Lieder.
(M) **(*) Sony SM2K 47170 (2) [id.]. Christa Ludwig, Walter Berry, Dietrich Fischer-Dieskau, Leonard Bernstein.

Where the *Wunderhorn* songs with Christa Ludwig and Walter Berry keep constantly in touch with the folk-inspiration behind them, the other groups with Fischer-Dieskau bring an even subtler and more sophisticated partnership between pianist and singer. It is true that, even in the *Wunderhorn* songs, Bernstein allows himself the most extreme rubato and tenuto on occasion. With the Fischer-Dieskau performances, both singer and pianist adopt a far more extreme expressive style all through, responding to each other in an almost impressionistic way, notably in the four *Rückert Lieder*, which inspire the singer to velvety legato. The eleven 'Youth' songs sound quite different here from the Halban/Walter recording, with *Scheiden und Meiden* given with exhilarating bounce and with a song such as *Nicht wiedersehen* treated expansively. Taken almost twice as slowly as on the rival version, it evokes a totally different, magical world. These 1968 recordings have not been released before, completing a collection which is a valuable supplement to Bernstein's Mahler recordings as a conductor.

Des Knaben Wunderhorn (excerpts): *Verlor'ne Müh; Rheinlegendchen; Wo die schönen Trompeten blasen; Lob des hohen Verstandes; Aus! Aus!. Lieder: Erinnerung; Frühlingsmorgen; Ich ging mit Lust durch einen grünen Wald; Phantasie aus Don Juan; Serenade aus Don Juan.*
*** DG Dig. 423 666-2 [id.]. Anne Sofie von Otter, Rolf Gothoni – WOLF: *Lieder.* ***

The Mahler half of Anne Sofie von Otter's brilliant recital is just as assured and strongly characterized as the formidable group of Wolf songs. Von Otter's mezzo has an aptly boyish quality in the five *Knaben Wunderhorn* settings – including one of the rarer ones, *Aus! Aus!*; Rolf Gothoni's sparkling and pointed playing, as in the Wolf couplings, makes this a genuinely imaginative partnership, bringing out the gravity as well as the humour of the writing. Excellent, well-balanced recording.

Des Knaben Wunderhorn (excerpts): *Das irdische Leben; Wo die schönen Trompeten blasen; Urlicht. Rückert Lieder: Liebst du um Schönheit; Ich bin der Welt.*
(M) **(*) Ph. 426 642-2; *426 642-4*. Jessye Norman, Irwin Gage – SCHUBERT: *Lieder.* **(*)

Jessye Norman recorded these Mahler songs in 1971, near the beginning of her career, and already the voice was developing magically. There is less detail here than in more recent performances, but the magisterial sustaining of long lines at very measured speeds is impressive. Irwin Gage accompanies sensitively, though he cannot efface memories of the orchestral versions. Good recording for its period, skilfully transferred to CD.

Lieder eines fahrenden Gesellen.
*** Ph. Dig. 426 257-2 [id.]. Jessye Norman, BPO, Haitink – Symphony No. 6. ***

Though the *Lieder eines fahrenden Gesellen* is hardly the Mahler cycle one would associate with the opulent tones of Jessye Norman, this is a joy to the ear, with Haitink, in his accompaniment for the jaunty second song, providing the necessary lightness. The stormy darkness of the third song fits the soloist more naturally, always a magnetic singer. It makes a valuable extra for Haitink's deeply satisfying version of the *Sixth Symphony.*

Lieder eines fahrenden Gesellen; Lieder und Gesänge (aus der Jugendzeit); Im Lenz; Winterlied.
❀ *** Hyp. CDA 66100; *KA 66100* [id.]. Dame Janet Baker, Geoffrey Parsons.

Dame Janet presents a superb collection of Mahler's early songs with piano, including two written in 1880 and never recorded before, *Im Lenz* and *Winterlied*; also the piano version of the *Wayfaring Lad* songs in a text prepared by Colin Matthews from Mahler's final thoughts, as contained in the orchestral version. The performances are radiant and deeply understanding from both singer and pianist, well caught in atmospheric recording. A heart-warming record.

Das Lied von der Erde.
❀ (M) *** Ph. 432 279-2; *432 279-4* [id.]. Dame Janet Baker, James King, Concg. O, Haitink.
(M) *** DG 419 058-2; *419 058-4* [id.]. Ludwig, Kollo, BPO, Karajan.
*** DG Dig. 413 459-2 [id.]. Fassbaender, Araiza, BPO, Giulini.
*** EMI CDC7 47231-2 [id.]. Ludwig, Wunderlich, New Philh. O and Philh. O, Klemperer.
(M) **(*) Sony MYK 45500 [id.]. Mildred Miller, Ernst Haefliger, NYPO, Bruno Walter.
(**) Decca mono 414 194-2. Ferrier, Patzak, VPO, Walter.

The combination of this most deeply committed of Mahler singers with Haitink, the most thoughtfully dedicated of Mahler conductors, produces radiantly beautiful and moving results, helped by refined and atmospheric recording. The concentration over the long final *Abschied* has never been surpassed on record (almost all of it was recorded in a single take). Haitink opens the cycle impressively with an account of the first tenor song that subtly confirms its symphonic shape, less free in tempo than usual but presenting unusually strong contrasts between the main stanzas and the tender refrain, *Dunkel ist das Leben.* James King cannot match his solo partner, often failing to create fantasy, but his singing is intelligent and sympathetic. The balance is realistic; for this CD reissue the sound has been brightened and made more vivid, but not at the expense of the original bloom and warmth. The closing pages remain tellingly atmospheric.

Karajan presents *Das Lied* as the most seductive sequence of atmospheric songs, combining characteristic refinement and polish with a deep sense of melancholy. Karajan conveys the ebb and flow of tension as in a live performance. He is helped enormously by the soloists, both of whom have recorded this work several times, but never more richly than here. The sound on CD is more sharply defined, and some of the ambient effect has gone, but the quality is admirably vivid and does not lack a basic warmth.

Giulini conducts a characteristically restrained reading. With Araiza a heady-toned tenor rather than a powerful one, the line *Dunkel ist das Leben* in the first song becomes unusually tender and gentle, with rapture and wistfulness keynote emotions. In the second song, Fassbaender gives lightness and poignancy rather than dark tragedy to the line *Mein Herz ist müde*; and even the final *Abschied* is rapt rather than tragic, following the text of the poem. Not that Giulini fails to convey the breadth and intensity of Mahler's magnificent concept; and the playing of the Berlin Philharmonic could hardly be more beautiful.

Klemperer's way with Mahler is at its most individual in *Das Lied von der Erde* – and that will enthral some, as it must infuriate others. With slower speeds, the three tenor songs seem initially to lose some of their sparkle and humour; however, thanks to superb expressive singing by the late Fritz Wunderlich, and thanks also to pointing of rhythm by Klemperer himself, subtle but always clear, the comparative slowness will hardly worry anyone intent on hearing the music afresh, as Klemperer intends. As for the mezzo songs, Christa Ludwig sings them with a remarkable depth of expressiveness; in particular, the final *Abschied* has the intensity of a great occasion. Excellent digitally remastered recording (1967 vintage).

Though Bruno Walter's New York version does not have the tear-laden quality in the final *Abschied* that made his earlier Vienna account with Kathleen Ferrier unique, that is its only serious shortcoming. Haefliger sparkles with imagination and Miller is a warm and appealing mezzo soloist, lacking only the last depth of feeling you find in a Ferrier; and the maestro himself has rarely sounded so happy on record, even in Mahler. The remastered recording has been considerably improved for CD and now sounds both warm and vivid.

It is a joy to have the voice of Kathleen Ferrier so vividly caught on CD – not to mention that of the characterful Patzak – in Bruno Walter's classic Vienna recording for Decca. It is also an enormous advantage having silent background with minimum tape-hiss, to be able to appreciate the radiance of the performance, not least in the ecstatic closing pages and the final murmurs of '*Ewig*'. The sad thing is that the violin tone in high loud passages has acquired a very unattractive edge, not at all like the Vienna violins, and this makes for uncomfortable listening.

5 Rückert Lieder.

(*) DG 415 099-2 (2) [id.]. Christa Ludwig, BPO, Karajan – *Symphony No. 6.* *

Christa Ludwig's singing on DG is very characterful, if not as magical as Baker's (see above). The *Rückert Lieder* are fine, positive performances. It is the distinction and refinement of the orchestral playing and conducting that make this reissue valuable, although the microphone conveys some unevenness in the voice. The transfer is clear and clean.

Rückert Lieder: Ich atmet' einen Linden Duft; Ich bin der Welt; Um Mitternacht.

(***) Decca 421 299-2. Kathleen Ferrier, VPO, Bruno Walter – BRAHMS: *Alto rhapsody* etc. (***)

Ferrier's recording of three of Mahler's *Rückert Lieder* was a pendant to her historic recording, also with Bruno Walter and the Vienna Philharmonic, of Mahler's *Song of the earth.* Both heartfelt and monumental, they bring weighty readings, exploratory in the world of Mahler on record, not as delicately expressive as many since, but magnetically intense. While the extra clarity of CD is not kind to the orchestral strings, the voice emerges realistically with good presence.

Rückert Lieder: Ich bin der Welt abhanden gekommen; Ich atmet' einen linden Duft; Um Mitternacht.

(M) (***) Decca mono 433 477-2 [id.]. Kathleen Ferrier, VPO, Bruno Walter – BRAHMS: *Alto rhapsody* etc. (***)

Ferrier's recording of three of Mahler's *Rückert Lieder* was a pendant to her historic recording, also with Bruno Walter and the Vienna Philharmonic, of Mahler's *Song of the earth.* Both heartfelt and monumental, they bring weighty readings, exploratory in the world of Mahler on record, not as delicately expressive as many since, but magnetically intense. While the extra clarity of CD is not kind to the orchestral strings, the voice emerges realistically with good presence. The woodwind, too, is glowingly caught, and one wishes that Decca could have found a way of mitigating the razor-sharp thinness of the violins, which sound worse in this Kathleen Ferrier Edition reissue than they did on the original LP.

Malipiero, Gianfrancesco (1882–1973)

String quartets Nos. 1–8.
*** ASV Dig. CDDCD 457 (2) [id.]. Orpheus Qt.

Malipiero was an important figure in Italian musical life and played a vital role in the revival of Monteverdi, whose works he edited. His eight *String quartets* are all modest in length: the longest being the *First* (*Rispetti e strambotti*) (1920), which runs to twenty minutes, while the *Eighth* (1963–4), written when the composer was in his early eighties, takes only twelve. None fall below a certain level of distinction, all are beautifully crafted and there is much freshness and fertility of invention. Nos. 1, 4 and 8 have been recorded before in the days of LP, but this is the first complete survey on CD, and they are all played with expertise and conviction by the Orpheus Quartet, and very well recorded indeed.

Manzoni, Giacomo (born 1932)

Masse: Omaggio a Edgard Varèse.
*** DG Dig. 423 307-2 [id.]. Pollini, BPO, Sinopoli – SCHOENBERG: *Chamber symphony No. 1.* ***

Masse has nothing to do with church liturgy, but refers to measures or quantities, and in its tribute to Varèse follows up a science-based mode of thought which proves surprisingly dramatic and colourful. Only the piano solo has much in the way of melodic interest, and Pollini exploits it all he can, not least in the elaborate cadenza-like passages. Sinopoli too reveals the feeling for texture and dynamic which so often makes his conducting so memorable.

Marais, Marin (1656–1728)

La Gamme en forme de petit opéra; Sonata à la marésienne.
(B) *** HM HMA 901105; *HMA 431105* [id.]. L. Baroque.

La Gamme is a string of short character-pieces for violin, viole de gambe and harpsichord that takes its inspiration from the ascending and descending figures of the scale. Although it is *en forme de petit opéra*, its layout is totally instrumental and the varied pieces and dramatic shifts of character doubtless inspire the title. It plays without a break of any kind and its continuity is enlivened by much variety of invention and resource. The *Sonata à la marésienne* is less unusual, but it also has variety and character. The London Baroque is an excellent group, and they are well recorded too. Now reissued in the Musique d'Abord series, this is most inviting.

Suites for viols: in D min.; in G; Tombeau de Mr Meliton.
*** HM/BMG Dig. RD 77146 [77146-2-RC]. Kenneth Slowik, Jaap ter Linden, Konrad Junghänel.

The viol music of Marin Marais is, like certain white wines, an acquired taste; however, once acquired, it is quite addictive. The two suites recorded here come from the first of his five books of *Pièces de voile*, containing in all some 600 pieces. The music dates from 1686 when he was 'ordinaire de viole de la musique de la chambre du Roi', and an obvious favourite of Lully, to whom there is a fulsome dedication. The present artists, Kenneth Slowik and Jaap ter Linden, alternate between bass viol and gamba in the two suites, with Konrad Junghänel on theorbo; all three belong to the Smithsonian Institute's chamber group and give vibrant, spirited performances that are most persuasive. The recording needs to be played at a lower than usual level-setting if a realistic result is required, as the balance places the listener rather nearer the players than is ideal.

Marcello, Alessandro (1669–1747)

6 Oboe concertos (La Cetra).
(M) *** DG 427 137-2; *427 137-4* [id.]. Heinz Holliger, Louise Pellerin, Camerata Bern, Füri.

The six concertos of *La Cetra* are concertante exercises rather than concertos in the accepted sense of the word, and they reveal a pleasing mixture of originality and convention; often one is surprised by a genuinely alive and refreshing individuality. These performances are vital and keen, occasionally almost aggressively bright, but full of style and character, and the recording is faithful and well projected.

Marenzio, Luca (1553–99)

Madrigals: *Come inanti de l'alba; Crudele, acerba; Del cibo onde il signor; Giunto a la tomba; Rimanti inpace; Sola angioletta* (sestina); *Strider faceva; Tirsi morir volea; Venuta era; Vezzosi augelli.*
(B) *** HMA 901065 [id.]. Concerto Vocale, René Jacobs.

Luca Marenzio enjoyed an enormous reputation during his lifetime, particularly in England, where his madrigals were introduced by *Musica transalpina.* He corresponded with Dowland. His output includes some 400 madrigals, and this record gives an altogether admirable picture of his breadth and range. There are poignant and expressive pieces such as *Crudele acerba*, from the last year of his life, which is harmonically daring, and lighter pastoral madrigals such as *Strider faceva* and the more ambitious sestina, *Sola angioletta*, which this excellent group of singers, occasionally supported by theorbo and lute, project to striking effect. Fine singing and recording and a modest price serve to make this a most desirable issue.

Marsh, John (1752–1828)

Symphonies Nos. 1 in B flat (ed. Robins); *3 in D; 4 in F; 6 in D; A Conversation Symphony for 2 Orchestras* (all ed. Graham-Jones).
** Olympia Dig. OCD 400 [id.]. Chichester Concert, Ian Graham-Jones.

John Marsh was essentially a musical amateur (in the best sense). As a composer he was largely self-taught, yet he shows a considerable facility both in organizing his musical material and in handling orchestral colour. In a sense he was innovative: because of the continuing influence of Handel, the symphony format was not fashionable in England at that time. Yet Marsh was prolific, writing over two dozen of them, of which nine have survived in published form. For the most part they each consist of three short movements and, while the tunes sometimes have a whiff of Handel, there is a strong element of the English village green. Not surprisingly, the harmonic progressions are not always very sophisticated, but they are well wrought and have a certain robust appeal. The *Conversation Symphony* does not divide into two separate ensembles but makes contrasts between higher and lower instrumental groupings. Five of his works are presented here with enthusiasm by an aptly sized authentic Baroque group; they play well enough and are quite effectively recorded, but one wonders what the extra finesse and vitality of Pinnock and his English Concert could make of them.

Martin, Frank (1890–1974)

(i) *Ballade for piano and orchestra;* (ii) *Ballade for trombone and orchestra;* (iii) *Concerto for harpsichord and small orchestra.*
**(*) Jecklin-Disco JD 529-2. (i) Sebastian Benda; (ii) Armin Rosin; (iii) Christiane Jaccottet; Lausanne CO, composer.

These performances first appeared on LP in the early 1970s. The *Harpsichord concerto* is a highly imaginative and inventive piece, arguably the most successful example of the genre since the Falla *Concerto.* The orchestral texture has a pale, transparent delicacy that is quite haunting, and the atmosphere is powerful – as, indeed, it is in the fine *Ballade.* A disc to which this writer

(R.L.) often returns, and which deserves a strong recommendation in spite of minor sonic limitations. Christiane Jaccottet is a committed advocate and her performance has the authority of the composer's direction.

(i) *Cello concerto. The Four elements.*
(M) *** Preludio PRL 2147 [id.]. (i) Jean Decroos, Concg. O, Haitink.

These two excellent performances come from Dutch Radio tapes, and the sound is unobtrusively natural and the balance beautifully judged, enabling Martin's subtle and expertly judged orchestral sonorities to register. Jean Decroos, from the first desk of the Concertgebouw, gives an impressive account of the *Cello concerto* and Haitink secures excellent playing from the Concertgebouw Orchestra. *The Four elements* is another Martin rarity, rich in invention and imaginative resource: its neglect is little short of scandalous. Both performances were recorded at public concerts in 1965 and 1970 respectively, but audience noise is minimal and the quality first rate.

(i) *Piano concerto No. 2;* (ii) *Violin concerto.*
*(**) Jecklin Disco JD 632-2 [id.]. (i) Badura-Skoda; (ii) Schneiderhan; Luxembourg RSO, composer.

The *Violin concerto* (1951) is a score of great subtlety and beauty. It is scarcely credible that Schneiderhan is the only player to have tackled it on record. Don't be put off by the less-than-lustrous sound, for this is a masterpiece and has the benefit of having Martin himself at the helm. The *Second Piano concerto* (1968–9) was written for Badura-Skoda. It is not as lyrical as the *Violin concerto* but is still worth investigation for its thoughtful slow movement.

Concerto for 7 wind instruments, percussion and strings; Études; (i) *Polyptique for violin and two string orchestras.*
❀ *** DG Dig. 435 383-2 [id.]. (i) Marieke Blankestijn; COE, Thierry Fischer.

This is a remarkable record and quite in a class of its own. The *Polyptique* was written in response to a commission from Menuhin in 1973, the year before Martin's death. It is a work of serene profundity, inspired by a polyptych, a set of very small panels depicting scenes from the Passion which Martin saw in Siena. The six movements also form panels of two, one depicting turbulent emotions and the other serene and inward-looking; the first, *Image des Rameaux*, for example, depicting Christ's entry into Jerusalem on Palm Sunday, its companion, *Image de la Chambre haute*, his farewell to the disciples and their anguished questioning. It is a work of great power and is played with rapt concentration and dedication by Marieke Blankestijn and the European Chamber Orchestra under Thierry Fischer. Good though the Erato version of the *Concerto for seven wind instruments, percussion and strings* undoubtedly is, this new account supersedes it – and all other predecessors. There is a lightness of accent and refinement of tone and dynamics that are quite exceptional, and the *Études pour cordes* similarly outclasses its predecessors. The tone is pure and there is the widest possible range of timbre, colour and dynamics without ever the slightest hint of self-consciousness. Music of great quality, playing of great artistry, and recording to match.

Concerto for 7 wind instruments, timpani, percussion and strings; Études for strings; (i) *Petite symphonie concertante for harp, harpsichord, piano and double string orchestra.*
(M) (***) Decca mono 430 003-2. (i) Jamet, Vauchet-Clerc, Rossiaud, SRO, Ansermet.

Concerto for 7 wind instruments, timpani, percussion and strings; (i) *Petite symphonie concertante for harp, harpsichord, piano and double string orchestra;* (ii) *6 Monologues from Everyman.*
*** Erato Dig. 2292 45694-2. (i) Guibentif, Jaccottet, Ruttimann; (ii) Gilles Cachemaille; OSR, Armin Jordan.

This well-recorded Erato disc serves as an admirable introduction to Martin's music, and newcomers to this composer should almost certainly start here, for the *Petite symphonie concertante* makes an ideal entry point into Martin's world. Armin Jordan's account of the *Concerto for seven wind instruments* is very good indeed; though it does not quite match the COE account under Thierry Fischer, it is still very fine. Jordan's recording of the *Petite symphonie concertante*, however, must now be a first recommendation; it is excellently played and recorded (with Christian Jaccottet, who took part in the first performance) and Gilles Cachemaille proves an impressive and thoughtful exponent of the powerful *Everyman* monologues.

The Decca mono CD contains the pioneering record of Frank Martin's masterpiece, the *Petite symphonie concertante*, one of the very first Decca LPs. This authoritative performance has a concentration and an atmosphere that have rarely been matched since. The three excellent soloists, Pierre Jamet (harp), Germaine Vauchet-Clerc (harpsichord) and Doris Rossiaud (piano) are at no point named in the documentation, but their contribution deserves recognition. The 1951 recording does not sound as spectacular as it seemed at the time, and the string-tone shows its age. No apologies need be made for the remarkably vivid recording of the *Études for strings* and the masterly *Concerto for 7 wind instruments*.

Piano quintet; String quintet (Pavane couleur de temps); String trio; Trio sur des mélodies populaires irlandaises.
*** Jecklin-Disco JD 646-2 [id.]. Zurich Ch. Ens.

The *Piano quintet* has an eloquence and an elegiac dignity that are impressive. Ravel's influence is strongly in evidence in the trio section of the second movement and, for that matter, in the short string quintet, subtitled *Pavane couleur de temps*, from 1920. The title is taken from a fairy story in which a young girl wishes for 'a dress the colour of time'. Like the *Piano quintet*, this is a beautiful piece. In the *Piano trio on Irish popular themes* (1925), 'everything is achieved through rhythm', rather than via any harmonic and contrapuntal ingenuity. It is full of imagination and rhythmic life. The more cerebral *String trio* of 1936 is a tougher nut to crack; its harmonies are more astringent and its form more concentrated. To summarize: altogether a most satisfying disc, offering very good performances. Although the recordings were made in 1989–90 they are analogue, presumably emanating from Swiss Radio, but none the worse for that.

Piano trio on Irish folksongs.
** Chan. Dig. CHAN 9016 [id.]. Borodin Trio – DEBUSSY: *Piano trio* **; TURINA: *Piano trio.* **(*)

Martin's *Piano trio on Irish folksongs* is played with plenty of character by the Borodins though they are no match in terms of finesse or style for the Zurich group on Jecklin. Turovsky's intonation at the beginning of the slow movement is a bit shaky and Brenton Langbein on the Swiss CD produces a purer and more cultured sound than Rostislav Dubinsky throughout. It is an excitable reading, perhaps a bit overheated at times, and those primarily wanting the Martin would be well advised to turn to the Zurich version first.

Der Cornet.
*** Orfeo Dig. S 164881A [id.]. Marjana Lipovšek, Austrian RSO, Zagrosek.

Rilke's celebrated collection of poems, *Die Weise von Liebe und Tod des Cornets Christoph Rilke*, tells of a youthful ensign who in 1660 fell under 'the sabres of the Turks into an ocean of flowers'. Writing in the middle of the Second World War, Frank Martin set all but three of the 26 poems, scoring them for a contralto soloist with a small chamber orchestra. The shadowy, half-real atmosphere often reminds one of *Pelléas*; and Martin's responsiveness to the rhythm and music of the words is thoroughly Debussian (German was not his native tongue). All his fingerprints are there, and the restrained, pale colourings provide an effective backcloth to the vivid outbursts that mark some of the settings. The performance by the contralto, Marjana Lipovšek, is a *tour de force*. Hers is a moving account of the songs, in which every word is expertly and vividly placed; and the orchestral playing under Lothar Zagrosek is highly sympathetic. The recording is very faithful, and the performance puts one completely under the spell of this strongly atmospheric work.

(i) *Golgotha;* (ii) *Mass for unaccompanied double choir.*
*** Erato/Warner Analogue/Dig. 2292 45779-2 (2) [id.]. (i) Staempfli, De Montmollin, Tappy, Mollet, Huttenlocher, Faller Ch. & SO, Robert Faller; (ii) Choeur de Chambre du Midi, Denis Martin.

The *Mass for unaccompanied double choir* is an early and not entirely characteristic work dating from 1922, whose beauties are gaining wider recognition. Towards the end of the war Martin was commissioned by the Swiss Radio to compose a piece for Armistice Day. The result was a religious work, *In Terra Pax*. Shortly after its completion he saw the *Three Crosses* of Rembrandt and it was this event that proved the catalyst for the composition of *Golgotha* (1945–8). It is one of his major works, of greater emotional power than *Le vin herbé*, and arguably the greatest Passion since Bach. 'My intention', wrote Martin, 'was to make the sacred tragedy come to life again before our eyes', and in contradistinction to Bach, the narrative passes freely between the various soloists and the body of the choir. Those who acquired the Erato LPs, when they were briefly available in the early 1970s (the recording dates from 1968), will need no reminding of the eloquence, power and dignity of this music, or the conviction of the performance. The *Mass*, which completes the second CD, is a digital recording from 1990, made in the Église Ste Thérèse de Genève, and the singing of the Choeur de Chambre du Midi under Denis Martin is very good indeed.

Mass for double choir.
*** Koch Bayer Dig. BR 100084 [id.]. Frankfurt Vocal Ens., Ralf Otto – REGER: *Geistliche Gesänge.* ***
(*) Nimbus Dig. NI 5197 [id.]. Christ Church Cathedral Ch., Oxford, Stephen Darlington – POULENC: *Mass in G* etc. *

The *Mass* has great purity and, in the hands of Ralf Otto's fine Frankfurt choir, much eloquence too. They have a great understanding of and feeling for this work, and convey its poignancy and depth. Their performance is quite a powerful and moving experience, and they produce a refined and expressive tonal blend as well as a wide dynamic range, which are well captured by the engineers. At 50 minutes it offers ungenerous playing time but it is not short on quality, for the Reger coupling is music of great simplicity and eloquence.

The Choir of Christ Church Cathedral, Oxford, under Stephen Darlington also give a good account of themselves: their tone is clean and beautifully balanced. The boys' voices are moving in a different way from that of the Frankfurt choir, but the English performance does not add up to quite as impressive or richly imaginative a musical experience. The Nimbus disc is eminently well recorded.

6 Monologues from Everyman; The Tempest: 3 excerpts.
❀ (M) *** DG 429 858-2 [id.]. Fischer-Dieskau, BPO, composer – EGK: *The temptation of St Anthony.* ***

The *Everyman Monologues* is a masterpiece – one of the great song-cycles of the twentieth century. Composed in the wake of *Der Cornet*, it is a setting of six monologues from Hofmannsthal's play on the theme of a rich man dying, and gives expression to both the fear of death and the doctrine of resurrection through love. The music is of extraordinary vision and imaginative power, and this classic performance from Fischer-Dieskau and the composer sounds as vivid and fresh as ever. The three excerpts from *The Tempest* make one long to hear the rest of the opera. The orchestral *Prelude* casts a strong and powerful spell and the two arias, from Act III (*My Ariel! Hast thou, which art but air*) and the Epilogue (*Now my charms are all o'erthrown*), are hardly less magical. This music impresses when one first encounters it, yet its beauties grow with each hearing.

Requiem.
*** Jecklin Disco JD 631-2 [id.]. Speiser, Bollen, Tappy, Lagger, Lausanne Women's Ch., Union Ch., SRO, composer.

Written some three years before the composer's death, this music can only be described as seraphic. It is arguably the most beautiful *Requiem* to have been written since Fauré's and, were the public to have ready access to it, would be as popular. The recording, made at a public performance that the (then 83-year-old) composer conducted in Lausanne Cathedral, is very special. The analogue recording is not in the demonstration class, but this music and performance must have three stars.

Le vin herbé (oratorio).
*(**) Jecklin Disco JD 581/2-2 [id.]. Retchitzka, Tuscher, Comte, Morath, De Montmollin, Diakoff, De Nyzankowskyi, Tappy, Jonelli, Rehfuss, Vessières, Olsen, composer, Winterthur O (members), Desarzens.

Martin's oratorio on the Tristan legend is laid out for a madrigal choir of twelve singers, who also assume solo roles, and a handful of instrumentalists, including the piano, played here by the septuagenarian composer himself. It is powerfully atmospheric and sounds like a distant relative of *Pelléas et Mélisande*, having all the pale, dimly lit but at times luminous colouring of Debussy's world. It is powerful and hypnotic, and there is some fine singing here from Nata Tuscher (Isolde), Eric Tappy (Tristan) and Heinz Rehfuss (King Mark). The instrumental playing, though not impeccable, is dedicated (and the same must be said for the choral singing).

The 1960s sound ideally needs a bit more space round it but is much improved in the CD format. *Le vin herbé* is a masterly and compelling work and is strongly recommended.

Martinů, Bohuslav (1890–1959)

La Bagarre; Half-time; Intermezzo; The Rick; Thunderbolt.
*** Sup. SUP 001669 [id.]. Brno State O, Vronsky.

La Bagarre and *Half-time* are early evocations, the latter a Honeggerian depiction of a roisterous half-time at a football match that musically doesn't amount to a great deal. The three later works are much more interesting – *Intermezzo* is linked to the *Fourth Symphony* – and the collection as a whole will be of great interest to Martinů addicts, if perhaps not essential for other collectors. All the performances are alive and full of character, and the recording is vividly immediate.

(i) *Concerto for double string orchestra, piano and timpani;* (ii) *Concerto for string quartet and orchestra;* (iii) *Sinfonia concertante for oboe, bassoon, violin, cello and orchestra.*
*** Virgin Dig. VC7 91099-2; *VC7 91099-4* [id.]. (i) Alley, Fullbrook; (ii) Endellion Qt; (iii) Daniel, Reay, Watkinson, Orton; City of L. Sinfonia, Hickox.

(i) *Concerto for double string orchestra, piano and timpani;* (ii) *Concerto for string quartet and orchestra;* (i) *3 ricercari (for chamber orchestra with 2 pianos).*
** Erato/Warner Dig. 2292-45499-2. (i) Jean-François Heisser, Alain Planès; (ii) Brandis Qt; Fr. Nat. O, James Conlon.

The *Double concerto* has splendid vitality in Hickox's hands (he is brisker than Jiří Bělohávek) and he has obvious sympathy for this repertoire. The level of transfer throughout is low and, in the slow movement in particular, pianissimos call for a higher than usual volume-setting. The *Sinfonia concertante* was inspired by (and written for the same combination as) the famous Haydn score for which Martinů, rightly, had great affection. It is more rewarding than the neo-Baroque *Concerto for string quartet and orchestra*, which is very manufactured. However, this is a useful addition to the growing Martinů discography, and Richard Hickox is an enthusiastic and expert guide in this terrain.

As in the companion issue in this Erato series, the balance is close and synthetic. One soon becomes aware that the studio is simply not spacious enough. There is plenty of impact, and some vigorous, spirited playing from the strings of the Orchestre National, but overall this is no match, either technically or artistically, for the Czech Philharmonic and Jiří Bělohlávek on Chandos. The *Concerto for quartet and orchestra* is again very forwardly balanced and the perspectives quite unnatural, though the performance by the Brandis Quartet and the French National Orchestra under James Conlon certainly sounds convinced . But the cramped acoustic diminishes the pleasure these performances would otherwise have given.

Concerto for double string orchestra, piano and timpani; 3 Frescoes of Piero della Francesca. (i) *Rhapsody-concerto for viola and orchestra.*
*(**) BIS Dig. CD 501 [id.]. (i) Nobuko Imai; Malmö SO, James DePreist.

Nobuko Imai's performance of the *Rhapsody-concerto* is quite special. It has the feel of live music-making, as if the musicians were all swept along by the current this all generates. She is excellently supported by the Malmö orchestra, who play very well indeed throughout. The *Double concerto* receives a dignified reading, but the acoustic unfortunately lets things down: it is far too reverberant; nor is the balance ideal in the *Frescoes*, where wind and brass come dangerously close to swamping the strings. Those wanting the marvellous *Rhapsody-concerto* should still consider this CD, for Imai's account is the best. For the other two pieces it is better to look elsewhere.

Concerto for double string orchestra, piano and timpani; (i) *Sinfonietta giocosa for piano and orchestra;* (ii) *Rhapsody-concerto for viola and orchestra.*
**(*) Conifer Dig. CDCF 210; *MCFC 210.* Brno State PO, Mackerras; (i) Dennis Hennig, Australian CO, Mackerras; (ii) Rivka Golani, Berne SO, Peter Maag.

Conifer have sensibly recoupled some of their earlier Martinů records to give better value for money. Rivka Golani's unaffected account of the *Rhapsody-concerto*, all the more eloquent for being understated, is now added to the *Double concerto* reviewed below, and the delightful

Sinfonietta giocosa, both previously coupled with music by different composers. The wartime but apparently carefree *Sinfonietta giocosa* gets a delightfully fresh performance and an acceptable recording, though the balance is a bit synthetic with little back-to-front depth.

Concerto for double string orchestra, piano and tympani; Spalíček – ballet suites.
*** Conifer Dig. CDCF 202; *MCFC 202* [id.]. Brno State PO, Mackerras.

The ballet *Spalíček* comes from the early 1930s when Martinů was living in Paris; it is an engaging score, based on traditional Czech fairytale tunes and nursery rhymes. In 1940 he overhauled the score for larger forces (the original was for solo voices, children's choir and small orchestra) and asked Miloš Riha to extract two suites from it. Both are recorded here, though the order of some of the movements differs from that on the première recording by Jiří Waldhans and is closer to the order in which they appeared in the ballet itself. The music is delightful and some of the numbers, particularly the *Dance of the Ladies of Honour*, captivating. If you enjoy the Dvořák of the *Slavonic dances*, you will respond to this fresh and open-hearted music. Mackerras also includes the powerful *Concerto for double string orchestra, piano and tympani*, again well played and recorded, though the pianist produces some less-than-elegant tone at climaxes. Eminently recommendable though in the *Double concerto*, Bělohlávek perhaps gives the more concentrated reading.

Concerto for double string orchestra, piano and tympani; Symphony No. 1.
*** Chan. Dig. CHAN 8950; *ABTD 1544* [id.]. Czech PO, Jiří Bělohávek.

Jiři Bělohlávek's dedicated and imaginative account of the *First Symphony* is very good indeed. Bělohávek is totally inside this music, and the recording, made in the agreeably resonant Spanish Hall of Prague Castle, is very natural. (Järvi's acoustic – see below – is only marginally less resonant and, if anything, his recording reproduces a little more detail.) The *Double concerto* is one of the most powerful works of the present century, and its intensity is well conveyed in this vital, deeply felt performance. Strongly recommended for both works.

Oboe concerto.
*** Nimbus Dig. NI 5330 [id.]. John Anderson, Philh. O, Simon Wright – FRANÇAIX: *L'horloge de flore;* R. STRAUSS: *Concerto.* ***
*** Capriccio Dig. 10 308 [id.]. Lajos Lencsés, Stuttgart RSO, Marriner – HAYDN: *Concerto;* HUMMEL: *Intro., theme & variations.* ***

Not surprisingly, Martinů's *Concerto* is full of individual touches and has plenty of rhythmic interest, particularly in the pulsing energy of the wittily high-spirited finale. The newest Nimbus account, by John Anderson, principal of the Philharmonia, is outstanding in every way, with the *Andante* quite ravishing when the soloist's timbre is so rich. The recording is first class and the couplings particularly attractive.

Lajos Lencsés plays with a rather more plangent timbre than in the Haydn and Hummel couplings, and the unusual *Poco andante* – with its two piano-accompanied improvisatory interludes – is memorable in its bitter-sweet lyricism. Marriner accompanies sympathetically and the recording is first rate.

3 Frescoes of Piero della Francesca; Sinfonietta La Jolla; Toccata e due Canzoni.
** Erato/Warner Dig. 2292-45794-2 [id.]. Fr. Nat. O, James Conlon.

Conlon gets some very good playing from the Orchestre National de France in the *Frescoes*, but the recording balance is variable. In the *Toccata e due Canzoni*, written at the same time as the *Fifth Symphony* in 1946, the piano is very prominent and the effect with close lower strings and percussion is bottom-heavy. The microphones are close and the mix synthetic; the overall effect is overlit. The acoustic of Studio No. 104 in the *Maison de la Radio* in Paris is dryish and there is not enough space round the instruments. In the *Frescoes* the balance is more successful but there is still the aural equivalent of glare. These are marvellously evocative and tuneful scores and deserve better.

Rhapsody-concerto for viola and orchestra.
*** Conifer Dig. CDFC 146; *MCFC 146* [id.]. Golani, Berne SO, Maag – D'INDY: *Symphonie sur un chant montagnard français.* ***

This is not quite a viola concerto: though the elements of dialogue and display we associate with the genre are present, it is primarily gentle and reflective. The *Rhapsody* is free in its formal layout, and the quieter episodes of the *Adagio* have an impressive inner repose. The violist Rivka Golani plays with a gloriously warm tone and much musical insight, and the whole performance is agreeably natural: there is nothing high-powered or overdriven. As admirers of Peter Maag will expect, this is a selfless performance of the old school that allows this music to speak for itself and penetrates deeper below the surface. The sound is that of a very fine broadcast rather than a seat in a concert hall, but detail is kept in an excellent and believable perspective. Very strongly recommended.

Symphonies Nos. 1–6 (Fantaisies symphoniques).
(M) *** Sup. 11 0382-2 (3) [id.]. Czech PO, Václav Neumann.

Symphonies Nos. 1–4.
*** BIS Dig. CD 362-3 [id.]. Bamberg SO, Järvi.

Martinů always draws a highly individual sound from his orchestra and secures great clarity, even when the score abounds in octave doublings. He often thickens his textures in this way, yet, when played with the delicacy these artists produce, they sound beautifully transparent. On hearing the *First*, Virgil Thomson wrote, 'the shining sounds of it sing as well as shine', and there is no doubt this music is luminous and life-loving. The *Fourth* is the most popular and is coupled on BIS with the more highly charged and intensely felt *Third*. It is probably best to start with them; but few, having done so, will be able to resist their companions. The thrilling recording is in the demonstration class yet sounds completely natural, and the performances under Neeme Järvi are totally persuasive and have a spontaneous feel for the music's pulse.

Neumann's complete set of the Martinů symphonies was recorded in the Dvořák Hall of the House of Artists, Prague, between January 1976 (No. 6) and 1978 (No. 5). The transfers to CD are excellently done: the sound is full, spacious and bright; it has greater presence and better definition than the original LPs, yet with no edginess in the strings. The orchestral playing, it hardly needs saying, is first class and Neumann's readings have a spacious intensity, a relaxed grip and a natural feeling for the colour and atmosphere of these works. The *Fifth* is invitingly confident (it is full of brightness and intensity with woodwind chirping and violins gleaming), while its closing pages radiate an almost incandescent quality and a life-enhancing power quite out of tune with the bleak post-war years that gave it birth. The *Sixth* is much later, yet Martinů's orchestration and imaginative design are by no means conservative or backward-looking. The exotic textures still intrigue the ear and must initially, for the composer, have outweighed the musical cogency and sweep of his score, so that he was doubtful of its symphonic status. He subtitled it *Fantaisies symphoniques*, and even briefly asked for it not to be included in his numbered symphonies. Václav Neumann's performance has an impressive spaciousness and, though there could be more urgency and fire in places, the reading has life, colour and impetus, and is thoroughly compelling when the Czech orchestra play so vividly: witness the powerful trumpet solo in the finale.

Symphonies Nos. 1; 3; 5.
*** Multisonic 31 0023-2 (2). Czech PO, Ančerl.

This is the real thing. Whether or not you have modern versions of these Martinů symphonies, you should obtain these powerful, luminous performances; they come from Czech Radio recordings made in 1963, 1966 and 1962 respectively. Two symphonies could easily be accommodated on one disc and it is maddening that the *Third* is split between the first and second CDs. Never mind – these are such superb and convincing readings that readers should not hesitate. The music glows in Ančerl's hands and acquires a radiance that quite belies its date.

Symphonies Nos. 1; 5.
**(*) Chan. Dig. CHAN 8915; *ABTD 1523* [id.]. Royal Scottish O, Bryden Thomson.

In the exhilarating *Fifth Symphony* Bryden Thomson gets very spirited playing from the Royal Scottish Orchestra, who approach the score with obvious enthusiasm, particularly in the finale to which they bring real zest. Occasionally one wishes for greater fantasy and sense of mystery (at the very opening of the first movement), but their directness is very persuasive indeed and the performance very likeable; and the recording reveals great clarity of texture.

Symphonies Nos. 3–4.
*** Chan. Dig. CHAN 8917; *ABTD 1525* [id.]. SNO, Bryden Thomson.

The excellent Bryden Thomson gets thoroughly committed playing from his Scottish players in both symphonies. These are fine performances, even if some of the sense of mystery is missing in the middle movement of the *Third* and the opening of the *Fourth* could with advantage be just a shade faster and lighter. The exhilarating scherzo could not be improved upon and the conductor's affection for this music shines throughout. The Chandos recording is first class, brighter and more sharply defined than is Järvi, though, on balance, the latter remains a first recommendation.

Symphonies Nos. 5; 6 (Fantaisies symphoniques).
*** BIS Dig. CD 402 [id.]. Bamberg SO, Järvi.

The *Fifth*, like its predecessor, has some recourse to sectional repetition and is not as powerfully structured or as profoundly original as the *Sixth*. All the same, it is a glorious piece and Järvi brings to it that mixture of disciplined enthusiasm and zest for life that distinguishes all his work. This is vividly imagined music that enriches and enhances the spirit; it follows the Handelian precept and makes one better! Wonderfully transparent, yet full-bodied sound, in the best BIS manner.

Symphony No. 6 (Fantaisies symphoniques).
*** Chan. Dig. CHAN 8897; *ABTD 1508* [id.]. Czech PO, Bělohlávek – JANÁČEK: *Sinfonietta;* SUK: *Scherzo.* ***

Jíři Bělohlávek's account of the *Fantaisies symphoniques* is probably first choice in the current catalogue. This Chandos reading has the inestimable benefit of the Czech Philharmonic. Moreover the interpretation has greater dramatic strength and is more fully characterized; undoubtedly these players believe in every note. It is an outstanding performance that does full justice to the composer's extraordinarily imaginative vision and is very well recorded.

CHAMBER MUSIC

Cello sonatas Nos. 1–3.
*** Hyp. Dig. CDA 66296; *KA 66296* [id.]. Steven Isserlis, Peter Evans.

Steven Isserlis and Peter Evans have done well to collect all three Martinů *Cello sonatas* on one disc. The slow movement of the *First* is dark and inward-looking; it is a powerful, well-wrought and often moving piece, whose combative outer movements are highly effective. The more familiar *Second sonata* comes from the composer's American years – and one recognizes the kind of thinking and sense of musical pace that were developing in the symphonies. The *Third* is thoroughly characteristic Martinů. Good playing and very acceptable recording.

Duo for violin and cello.
(M) *** BMG/RCA GD 87871; *GK 87871* [7871-2-RG; *7871-4-RG*]. Heifetz, Piatigorsky – DEBUSSY: *Sonata* etc. (**); RESPIGHI: *Sonata* (***); RAVEL: *Trio* etc. (**)

Martinů composed two *Duos*, the first in 1927. A short but powerful piece, it was recorded in 1964 and, though the acoustic is a bit dryish, the playing is fabulous.

Flute sonata.
*** BMG/RCA Dig. RD 87802 [7802-2-RC]. James Galway, Phillip Moll – DVOŘÁK: *Sonatina;* FELD: *Sonata.* ***

With the outer movements generally jolly and extrovert, bringing distinctive Martinů touches, the main weight of the *Flute sonata* comes in the central *Adagio* with its powerful middle section and meditative close. Galway is characteristically individual but without mannerism in his performance, and is most sympathetically accompanied by Moll. Relatively dry recording, with a fine sense of presence.

4 Madrigals for oboe, clarinet and bassoon; 3 Madrigals for violin and viola; Madrigal sonata for piano, flute and violin; 5 Madrigal stanzas for violin and piano.
*** Hyp. Dig. CDA 66133; *KA 66133* [id.]. Dartington Ens.

These delightful pieces exhibit all the intelligence and fertility of invention we associate with Martinů's music. The *Five Madrigal stanzas* of 1943 were written for Albert Einstein, no less, whose duo partner was Robert Casadesus! The playing of the Dartington Ensemble is accomplished and expert, and the recording, though resonant, is faithful. Just try the opening piece of the *Five Madrigal stanzas* to discover how melodically inviting this music is.

Nonet; Trio in F for flute, cello and piano; La Revue de cuisine.
*** Hyp. CDA 66084 [id.]. Dartington Ens.

A delightful record. None of these pieces is otherwise available on CD and all of them receive first-class performances and superb recording. The sound has space, warmth, perspective and definition. *La Revue de cuisine* is very much of its decade and the *Charleston* is most engaging.

The *Trio* is as fresh and inventive as Martinů's very best work and is played deliciously. Its *Andante* deserves to be singled out for special mention: it is a most beautiful movement. The *Nonet*, for string trio plus double-bass, flute, clarinet, oboe, horn and bassoon, is equally life-enhancing. An indispensable issue for lovers of Martinů's music.

Sonata for 2 violins and piano.
(*) Hyp. Dig. CDA 66473 [id.]. Osostowicz, Kovacic, Tomes – MILHAUD: *Violin duo* etc. **(*); PROKOFIEV: *Violin sonata.* *

Martinů's *Sonata for two violins and piano* comes from his Paris years and finds him full of invention and vitality. Krsyia Osostowicz, Ernst Kovacic and Susan Tomes play it with all the finesse and sensitivity you could want and are excellently recorded. The disc would be even more recommendable if it offered repertoire of greater substance and had a longer playing time than 46 minutes.

Violin sonatas Nos. 2–3; 5 Madrigal sonatas.
** Sup. Dig. 11 0099-2 [id.]. Josef Suk, Josef Hála.

The *Second Violin sonata* (1931) dates from Martinů's Paris years and shows something of the influence of Roussel and Stravinsky. It is a short and attractive piece, while the bigger-boned *Third* (1944) speaks much the same language as the symphonies. The *Five Madrigal Stanzas* (1943) were dedicated to Albert Einstein whom Martinů had known as a student and whom he met again when he was teaching at Princeton (the composer and the famous scientist performed them). Josef Suk and Josef Hála give excellent acounts of all three pieces, though the 1987 recording is less than appealingly balanced. The sound is rather synthetic and too close.

Études and Polkas; Fantasy and Toccata; Moderato (Julietta Act II), arr. Firkušný; *Les Ritournelles; Piano sonata No. 1.*
**(*) BMG/RCA Dig. RD 87987 [7987-2-RC]. Rudolf Firkušný.

Firkušný was long associated with Martinů and gave the first performances of most of these pieces. The *Fantasy and Toccata* was written for him in the dark days of 1940 while both musicians were waiting to escape from Vichy France to America. Although he loved the instrument, his piano music is not the finest Martinů, but Firkušný displays it in the best possible light. No doubt had he recorded it when he was younger (he is in his late seventies), the rhythmic contours would be more sharply etched and would have more bite, but it could not be more delicate in its keyboard colouring, more authoritative or refined. Firkušný is a pianist of the old school who never plays to the gallery and is supremely musical. The recording is not made in a large enough acoustic but is otherwise truthful.

The Epic of Gilgamesh (oratorio).
❀ *** Marco Polo Dig. 8.223316 [id.]. Depoltová, Margita, Kusnjer, Vele, Karpílšek, Slovak Ph. Ch. & O, Zdeněk Košler.

The Epic of Gilgamesh comes from Martinů's last years and is arguably his masterpiece: it has vision, depth and power. Like Honegger's *King David*, it is for narrator, soloists, chorus and orchestra, and it similarly evokes a remote and distant world, full of colour and mystery. Gilgamesh is the oldest poem known to mankind: it predates the Homeric epics by 1,500 years, which places it at 7000 BC or earlier. The story survives in fragmentary form and tells, in the first part of Martinů's oratorio, how Gilgamesh, King of Uruk, hears of the great warrior, Enkidu, a primitive who is at home with the world of nature and of animals. The king befriends him, they quarrel and fight, before their friendship is finally sealed. The second part tells of Enkidu's death and of Gilgamesh's grief; and the third addresses the themes of death and immortality, Gilgamesh's plea to the gods and his encounter with Enkidu's spirit. The final pages are awesome, even chilling, and the work abounds with invention of the highest quality and of consistently sustained inspiration. The performance is committed and sympathetic and the recording very natural in its balance. A powerful and gripping work – indeed, one of the most imaginative choral works of the present century.

OPERA

The Greek Passion (sung in English).
*** Sup. Dig. 10 3611/2 [id.]. Mitchinson, Field, Tomlinson, Joll, Moses, Davies, Cullis, Savory, Kuhn Children's Ch., Czech PO Ch., Brno State PO, Mackerras.

Written with much mental pain in the years just before Martinů died in 1959, this opera was the work he regarded as his musical testament. Based on a novel by Nikos Kazantzakis (author of *Zorba the Greek*), it tells in an innocent, direct way of a village where a Passion play is to be presented; the individuals – tragically, as it proves – take on qualities of the New Testament figures they represent. At the very opening there is a hymn-like prelude of diatonic simplicity, and what makes the work so moving – given occasional overtones of Janáček, Mussorgsky and Britten – is Martinů's ability to simplify his message both musically and dramatically. This extraordinarily vivid recording – almost stereoscopic in its clear projection of the participants – was made by a cast which had been giving stage performances for the Welsh National Opera in what in effect is the original language of Martinů's libretto, English. Virtually every word is crystal clear and the directness of communication to the listener is riveting, particularly as the choral perspectives are so tellingly and realistically managed. The combination of British soloists with excellent Czech choirs and players is entirely fruitful. Mackerras makes an ideal advocate, and the recording is both brilliant and atmospheric – for instance, the scena with the accordion in Act III is handled most evocatively. With the words so clear, the absence of an English libretto is not a serious omission, but the lack of any separate cues within the four Acts is a great annoyance. But in its simple way *The Greek Passion* makes a most moving experience, and on CD the projection really does give the listener the impression that the tragedy is being played out 'live' in the area just behind the speakers.

Martucci, Giuseppe (1856–1909)

(i) *Piano concerto No. 1 in D min.;* (ii) *La canzone dei Ricordi.*
** ASV Dig. CDDCA 690; *ZCDCA 690* [id.]. (i) Caramiello; (ii) Yakar; Philh. O, d'Avalos.

The *First Piano concerto* (with Francesco Caramiello a capable soloist) comes from 1878, when Martucci was in his early twenties, and was never performed or published in his lifetime (hence the absence of an opus number). It is inevitably derivative, and it is the song-cycle that is the chief attraction here: Rachel Yakar sings beautifully and is particularly affecting in the Duparc-like *Cantavál ruscello la gaia canzone.* The recording is generally faithful, but is a bit 'up-front' so that climaxes come close to coarseness.

(i) *Piano concerto No. 2 in B flat min., Op. 66. Canzonetta, Op. 55/1; Giga, Op. 61/3; Minuetto, Op. 57/2; Momento musicale, Op. 57/3; Serenata, Op. 57/1; Tempo di gavotta, Op. 55/2.*
** ASV Dig. CDDCA 691; *ZCDCA 691* [id.]. Francesco Caramiello; (i) Philh. O, d'Avalos.

The *Second Piano concerto* is a work of Martucci's maturity. It is a big, 40-minute piece in a Brahmsian mould but is nevertheless full of individual touches. Caramiello copes very successfully with its very considerable demands, and the results all round are eminently acceptable – though, without any disrespect to these artists, it would be good to hear the work in the hands of a soloist and conductor of the very first rank. The fill-ups derive mainly from piano pieces and are wholly delightful. The recording is good, though in the *Concerto* the orchestral texture needs better ventilation and tutti do not have quite enough room in which to expand.

Symphony No. 1 in D min., Op. 75; Notturno, Op. 70/1; Novelletta, Op. 82; Tarantella, Op. 44.
** ASV Dig. CDDCA 675; *ZCDCA 675* [id.]. Philh. O, D'Avalos.

The *First Symphony* is greatly indebted to Brahms, but elsewhere there is a vein of lyricism that is more distinctive. Both the *Novelletta* and the *Notturno* were originally for piano; the latter has the nobility and eloquence of Elgar or Fauré and deserves to be much better known. The present *Symphony* is not the equal of the beautiful *Canzone dei Ricordi* on Hyperion, but it is well worth having on disc. The performances by the Philharmonia under Francesco d'Avalos are serviceable rather than distinguished, but the recording is very truthful and well balanced.

Symphony No. 2 in F, Op. 81; Andante in B flat, Op. 69; Colore orientale Op. 44/3.
** ASV Dig. CDDCA 689; *ZCDCA 689* [id.]. Philh. O, d'Avalos.

The *Second Symphony* is a relatively late work, coming from 1904. Its ideas assume greater potency and individuality the closer one comes to it. Though the performance falls short of distinction, it leaves the listener in no doubt as to Martucci's quality as a composer and the nobility of much of his invention. Let us hope that the appearance of this disc will encourage other conductors to take it up. The *Colore orientale* is an arrangement of a piano piece; the beautiful *Andante*, a work of depth, is a transcription of a piece for cello and piano and has a

Fauréan dignity. The recording is a bit too closely balanced. But there is no mistaking that this is music of some quality which deserves wider dissemination.

Le canzone dei ricordi; Notturno, Op. 70/1.
*** Hyp. Dig. CDA 66290; *KA 66290* [id.]. Carol Madalin, ECO, Bonavera – RESPIGHI: *Il tramonto.* ***

Le canzone dei ricordi is a most beautiful song-cycle and comes from 1886, the year of Mahler's *Lieder eines fahrenden Gesellen*. But Martucci's musical language is closer to that of Fauré or the elegiac Elgar, and its gentle atmosphere and warm lyricism are most seductive. At times Carol Madalin has a rather rapid vibrato, but she sings the work most sympathetically and with great eloquence. The *Notturno* is an inspired piece in similar vein and is beautifully played; there are echoes of Mahler and the Italian verismo school, but the music is free from sentimentality and has great dignity. Recommended with all possible enthusiasm.

Mascagni, Pietro (1863–1945)

Cavalleria rusticana (complete).
*** BMG/RCA RD 83091. Scotto, Domingo, Elvira, Isola Jones, Amb. Op. Ch., Nat. PO, Levine.
*** DG 419 257-2 (3) [id.]. Cossotto, Bergonzi, Guelfi, Ch. & O of La Scala, Milan, Karajan – LEONCAVALLO: *I Pagliacci* *** (also with collection of Operatic intermezzi ***).
**(*) DG Dig. 429 568-2 [id.]. Baltsa, Domingo, Baniewicz, Pons, Mentzer, ROHCG Ch., Philh. O, Sinopoli.
(***) EMI mono CDS7 47981-8 (3) [Ang. CDCC 47981]. Callas, Di Stefano, Panerai, Ch. & O of La Scala, Milan, Serafin – LEONCAVALLO: *I Pagliacci.* (***)
(M) **(*) Decca 425 985-2 [id.]. Tebaldi, Bjoerling, Bastianini, Maggio Musicale Fiorentino Ch. & O, Erede.
(M) **(*) EMI CMS7 63650-2 (2). Caballé, Carreras, Hamari, Manuguerra, Varnay, Amb. Op. Ch., Southend Boys' Ch., Philh. O, Muti – LEONCAVALLO: *I Pagliacci.* **(*)
(M) (***) BMG/RCA mono GD 86510 [RCA 6510-2-RG]. Milanov, Bjoerling, Merrill, Robert Shaw Chorale, RCA O, Cellini.
*(*) Ph. Dig. 432 105-2; *432 105-4* [id.]. Norman, Giocomini, Hvorostovsky, Senn, Paris Ch. & O, Bychkov.

There is far more to recommend about the RCA issue than the fact that it is available on a single CD (libretto included). On balance, in performance it stands as the best current recommendation, with Domingo giving a heroic account of the role of Turiddù, full of defiance. Scotto, strongly characterful too, though not always perfectly steady on top, gives one of her finest performances of recent years, and James Levine directs with a splendid sense of pacing, by no means faster than his rivals (except the leisurely Karajan) and drawing red-blooded playing from the National Philharmonic. The recording is very good, strikingly present in its CD format.

Karajan pays Mascagni the tribute of taking his markings literally, so that well-worn melodies come out with new purity and freshness, and the singers have been chosen to match that. Cossotto quite as much as Bergonzi keeps a pure, firm line that is all too rare in this much-abused music. Not that there is any lack of dramatic bite. The CD transfer cannot rectify the balance, but voices are generally more sharply defined, while the spacious opulence is retained. Karajan's fine performances of various opera-interludes make a welcome filler on the three-CD set.

Highly individual, passionately committed, only occasionally wilful, Sinopoli's reading is quite unlike any other. Traditionalists may well not like it, and they will be able to test that soon enough when the opening prelude, very flexible in its rubato, shows the conductor at his most extreme. This performance has the sort of high emotional tension which marks Sinopoli's readings of Elgar, and he is superbly backed by the Philharmonia, the strings in particular playing with a luminous warmth. Regularly Sinopoli brings out markings in the score that are usually neglected, and among the soloists it is Domingo, the keenest musician, who thrives on them most, giving a superb, imaginative performance, vocally as rich as ever. The characterful timbres of Baltsa's mezzo are not ideally suited to the role of Santuzza: there is little sense of vulnerability in her tough sound, even though her vehemence is apt. Juan Pons as the carter, Alfio, sings well, but there is no snarl in the voice, and Suzanne Mentzer rather lacks sparkle in

Lola's solo. Yet with rich, spacious sound this single disc provides a warm and refreshing experience.

Dating from the mid-1950s, Callas's performance as Santuzza reveals the diva in her finest voice, with edginess and unevenness of production at a minimum and with vocal colouring at its most characterful. The singing of the other principals is hardly less dramatic and Panerai is in firm, well-projected voice. This powerful team is superbly controlled by Serafin, a master at pacing this music, giving it full power while minimizing vulgarity. However, with Callas providing the central focus, the performance seems to centre round the aria, *Voi lo sapete*, wonderfully dark and intense, and one soon adjusts to the rather mushy quality of the opera's opening choruses, brought about by the restricted range; the solo voices, however, are projected vividly. However, this set is overpriced.

The early (1957) Decca recording with Tebaldi offers a forthright, lusty account of Mascagni's piece of blood and thunder and has the distinction of three excellent soloists. Tebaldi is most moving in *Voi lo sapete*, and the firm richness of Bastianini's baritone is beautifully caught. As always, Bjoerling shows himself the most intelligent of tenors, and it is only the chorus that gives serious cause for disappointment. They are enthusiastic and accurate enough when accompanying Bjoerling's superb account of the drinking scene (in Italy no doubt the directions for wine were taken literally), but at other times they are very undisciplined. The CD sound is strikingly bright and lively.

There are fewer unexpected textual points in the EMI *Cav.* than in *Pag.*, but Muti's approach is comparably biting and violent, brushing away the idea that this is a sentimental score, though running the risk of making it vulgar. The result is certainly refreshing, with Caballé – pushed faster than usual, even in her big moments – collaborating warmly. So *Voi lo sapete* is geared from the start to the final cry of *Io son dannata*, and she manages a fine snarl on *A te la mala Pasqua*. Carreras does not sound quite so much at home, though the rest of the cast is memorable, including the resonant Manuguerra as Alfio and the veteran Astrid Varnay as Mamma Lucia, wobble as she does. The recording is forward and vivid.

Though Zinka Milanov starts disappointingly in the *Easter hymn*, the conjunction of three of the outstanding Met. principals of the early 1950s' period brings a warmly satisfying performance. Admirers of Milanov will not want to miss her beautiful singing of *Voi lo sapete*, and in the duet Merrill's dark, firm timbre is thrilling. Bjoerling brings a good measure of musical and tonal subtlety to the role of Turiddù, normally belted out, while Cellini's conducting minimizes the vulgarity of the piece.

Jessye Norman produces glorious sounds, and dominates Bychkov's whole performance. It is almost comic the way that after Bychkov's funereal introduction to *Voi lo sapete* she instantly gets the music moving, adding electricity. Plainly she should have been conducting too. Hvorostovsky produces beautiful sounds as Alfio, but the whip-cracking song is very limp, and Giuseppe Giacomini proves a prosaic, colourless Turiddu. Star-casting here lets the listener down.

Cavalleria rusticana: highlights.
(B) *** DG Compact Classics *427 717-4* [id.] (from complete recording with Cossotto, Bergonzi, Guelfi, La Scala, Milan, Ch. & O, Karajan) – LEONCAVALLO: *Pagliacci:* highlights. ***
(M) **(*) EMI CDM7 63933-3 [id.]; *EG 763933-4* (from above complete recording; cond. Muti) – LEONCAVALLO: *Pagliacci:* highlights. **(*)

This Compact Classics highlights tape includes the key items from Karajan's set of *Cavalleria rusticana*, with both Cossotto and Bergonzi in splendid form. There is some lack of bite in the choruses, but that is caused as much by the orginal recording balance as by the tape transfer, which is otherwise excellent.

With over a half an hour of music, the EMI CD provides an admirable sampler of Muti's pungent, earthy approach to *Cavalleria rusticana*, with the recording ambience providing an atmospheric setting for the vivid projection of the drama.

Iris (complete).
*** Sony Dig. M2K 45526 (2) [id.]. Domingo, Tokody, Pons, Giaiotti, Bav. R. Ch., Munich R. O, Patanè.

Iris is the opera – first given in 1898 – which, with its story of Old Japan and a heroine-victim, prompted the ever-competitive Puccini to turn his attention to the East and write *Madama Butterfly*. It has often been said that, but for *Butterfly*, Iris would have stayed in the repertory – but even as committed a performance as this hardly sustains such an idea. Amid the early plaudits for an opera which aims far higher than *Cavalleria rusticana*, Puccini put his finger on the central weakness: a lack of interesting action. This heroine-as-victim is totally passive, much put upon by everyone. The rich hero, Osaka, makes advances to her in Act II, behaves insensitively and promptly finds himself bored by the reactions of a frightened child. How different that delayed duet is from the love-duet in *Butterfly*. Iris's one positive act is to throw herself to her death down a shaft when even her blind father turns against her – through an implausible misunderstanding, needless to say. Illica as librettist falls sadly short of his achievement for Puccini. Musically, *Iris* brings a mixture of typical Mascagnian sweetness and a vein of nobility often echoing Wagner. So the long symbolic prelude representing night and dawn has obvious echoes of Wagner's dawn music in the prologue to *Götterdämmerung*, and it returns at the end of the opera to represent the dead heroine's transfiguration. The comparison with the dawn interlude in *Butterfly* is also pointful, when Puccini, realistic and unsymbolic, is so much more involving. With a strong line-up of soloists including Domingo, and with Giuseppe Patanè a persuasive conductor, this recording makes as good a case for a flawed piece as one is ever likely to get. Domingo's warm, intelligent singing helps to conceal the cardboard thinness of a hero who expresses himself in generalized ardour. The most celebrated passage from the opera, the Neapolitan-like *Apri la tua finestra*, proves to be just a stylized item in a play within the play, not the hero's personal serenade at all. The Hungarian soprano, Ilona Tokody, brings out the tenderness of the heroine but, with dramatic tone, also expansively makes her into a plausible Butterfly figure, singing beautifully except when under pressure. Juan Pons, sounding almost like a baritone Domingo, is firm and well projected as Kyoto, owner of a geisha-house, and Bonaldo Giaiotti brings an authentically dark Italian bass to the role of Iris's father. Full, atmospheric recording.

Lodoletta (complete).
*** Hung. Dig. HCD 31307/8 [id.]. Maria Spacagna, Kelen, Szilágyi, Polgár, Kálmándi, Hungarian State Op. Children's Ch., Hungarian R. & TV Ch. & State O, Charles Rosekrans.

In vivid sound and with some excellent singing, this valuable first recording from Hungaroton makes a persuasive case for Mascagni's unashamed mixture of charm and sentimentality. The plot, based on *Two little wooden shoes* by Ouida, is so soft-centred that the shrewd Puccini firmly gave up his option to set it, having considered it closely. The scene-setting, as at the very start in Holland, is often delightful, although the melodies rarely stick in the mind. As the little Dutch girl, Lodoletta, Maria Spacagna sings most sensitively, even if the voice is too warm and full to suggest extreme youth. As the dissolute painter who unwittingly drives her to her death Péter Kelen proves a stylish and heady-toned lyric tenor, singing his big Act I solo, the *Song of the flowers*, very beautifully. The American, Charles Rosekrans, makes a very sympathetic conductor, in charge of a strong cast from the Hungarian State Opera.

Mason, Benedict (born 1954)

Lighthouses of England and Wales.
**(*) Collins Dig. Single 2004-2 [id.]. BBC SO, Zagrosek.

Though this provides short measure for a CD single (14 minutes), Mason's piece is more than memorable enough to justify the modest price of Collins' 20th-century Plus series. The piece is based on the distinctively rhythmic light signals of dozens of specific lighthouses (plus a fog-signal or two). It then develops into an evocative seascape, in its way a descendant of Debussy's *La mer*. Lothar Zagrosek directs a finely concentrated performance, and the recorded sound is outstanding.

Massenet, Jules (1842–1912)

Le Carillon (ballet): complete.
(M) *** Decca 425 472-2 (2). Nat. PO, Richard Bonynge – DELIBES: *Coppélia*. ***

Le Carillon was written in the same year as *Werther*. The villains of the story who try to destroy the bells of the title are punished by being miraculously transformed into bronze jaquemarts, fated to continue striking them for ever! The music of this one-act ballet makes a delightful offering – not always as lightweight as one would expect. With his keen rhythmic sense and feeling for colour, Bonynge is outstanding in this repertory, and the 1984 Decca recording is strikingly brilliant and colourful. A fine bonus (37 minutes) for a highly desirable version of Delibes' *Coppélia*.

Le Cid: ballet suite.
(M) *** Decca 425 475-2 (2). Nat. PO, Richard Bonynge – DELIBES: *Sylvia*. ***

Over the years, Decca have made a house speciality of recording the ballet music from *Le Cid* and coupling it with Constant Lambert's arrangement of Meyerbeer (*Les Patineurs*). Bonynge's version is the finest yet, with the most seductive orchestral playing, superbly recorded. Now it comes as an engaging encore for an equally recommendable complete set of Delibes' *Sylvia*, with the remastering for CD adding to the glitter and colour of Massenet's often witty scoring.

Cigale (ballet): complete.
(M) *** Decca 425 413-2 (3). Enid Hartle, Nat. PO, Bonynge – TCHAIKOVSKY: *Swan Lake*. **(*)

A late work, written with Massenet's characteristic finesse. *Cigale* was totally neglected after its première in 1904, until Richard Bonynge revived it in this admirable recording. The ballet recounts the La Fontaine fable about the grasshopper and the ant. The melodic invention does not match Massenet's finest, but the score is charming and colourful and is brightly and atmospherically played and sung and brilliantly recorded; and it makes a considerable coupling for Bonynge's complete set of Tchaikovsky's *Swan Lake*.

(i) *Piano concerto in E flat. Papillons noirs, Papillons blancs; Devant le Madone; 10 Pièces de genre, Op. 10; Eau dormante; Eau courante; Musique pour 'bercer les petits enfants'; Toccata; Valse folle; Valse triste.*
(M) ** EMI CDM7 64277-2 [id.]. Aldo Ciccolini, (i) Monte Carlo Nat. Op. O, Cambreling.

Although he was no virtuoso, the composer of *Werther* was a capable pianist (he won first prize for piano at the Paris Conservatoire in 1859 playing Ferdinand Hiller's *Concerto in F minor*), and he wrote idiomatically for it. Massenet's *Piano concerto in E flat* comes from 1903 and, like the remaining pieces on this well-filled disc – which all first appeared in the late 1970s – is not otherwise available. The concerto has been recorded before though it has understandably never enjoyed much exposure. It has perhaps the manners of the Saint-Saëns but none of the flair, and though some of the genre pieces and certainly the two impromptus, *Eau dormante* and *Eau courante* have a certain charm, this has greater curiosity than musical value. Aldo Ciccolini plays with conviction and is well supported in the concerto by Sylvain Cambreling and the Monte Carlo Opera Orchestra. The sound is a bit shallow, and the piano pieces are recorded rather closely in the Salle Wagram.

Manon (ballet) complete (arr. Lucas).
*** Decca Dig. 414 585-2 (2) [id.]. ROHCG O, Bonynge.

This confection of Massenet lollipops – with the famous *Élégie* returning as an idée fixe – is the work of Leighton Lucas; with characteristically lively and colourful playing from the Covent Garden Orchestra under Richard Bonynge, it makes a delightful issue, the more attractive when, as with other Bonynge recordings of ballet, the Decca engineers deliver sound of spectacular quality.

Orchestral suite No. 1, Op. 13; Cendrillon (opera): *suite. Esclarmonde* (opera): *suite.*
** Marco Polo Dig. 8.223354 [id.]. Hong Kong PO, Kenneth Jean.

The British composer, George Lloyd, recently went to Hong Kong to conduct some of his own music and returned impressed with the versatility and skill of this orchestra. They certainly find a French accent for Massenet's slight but charming genre pieces. The delicate atmosphere of *L'île magique* and *Hymenée* from *Esclarmonde*, and the charming *Nocturne* from the *Suite*, Op. 13, is matched by the vigour of the finales from both, the *Marche et Strette* of Op. 13 and *La Chasse*, with its hunting horns in the operatic suite. The charming *Cendrillon* vignettes also have plenty of sparkle. The playing does not find the degree of Beechamesque finesse that makes for totally memorable results in such repertoire, and the Tsuen Wan Town Hall lacks the glowing ambience of the finest Western recording venues, but this remains an enjoyable collection; although with only 58 minutes, room could have been found for more music, when the CD is in the highest price-range.

OPERA

Cendrillon (complete).

**(*) Sony CD 79323 (2) [M2K 35194]. Von Stade, Gedda, Berbié, Welting, Bastin, Amb. Op. Ch., Philh. O, Rudel.

Julius Rudel directs a winning performance of Massenet's Cinderella opera, very much a fairy story in which the magic element is vital. The Fairy Godmother is a sparkling coloratura (here the bright-toned Ruth Welting) and Cendrillon a soprano in a lower register. Von Stade gives a characteristically strong and imaginative performance, untroubled by what for her is high tessitura. The pity is that the role of the prince, originally also written for soprano, is here taken by a tenor, Gedda, whose voice is no longer fresh-toned. Jules Bastin sings most stylishly as Pandolfe, and the others make a well-chosen team. The recording is vivid, but spacious too. Worth exploring, even at full price.

Le Cid (complete).
** Sony CD 79300 (2) [M2K 34211]. Bumbry, Domingo, Bergquist, Plishka, Gardner, Camp Chorale, NY Op. O, Queler.

The CBS recording is taken from a live performance in New York and suffers from boxy recording quality. Only with the entrance of Domingo in the second scene does the occasion really get going, and the French accents are often comically bad. Even so, the attractions of Massenet's often beautiful score survive all the shortcomings and this makes a valuable addition to the CD catalogue. Domingo, not always as stylish as he might be, is in heroic voice and Grace Bumbry as the proud heroine responds splendidly. The popular ballet music is given a sparkling performance. But this should have been reissued at mid-price.

Don Quichotte (complete).
(M) *** Decca 430 636-2 (2) [id.]. Ghiaurov, Bacquier, Crespin, SRO, Kord.

Massenet's operatic adaptation of Cervantes' classic novel gave him his last big success, written as it was with Chaliapin in mind for the title-role. It is a totally captivating piece with not a jaded bar in it, suggesting that Massenet might have developed further away from his regular romantic opera style. There is genuine nobility as well as comedy in the portrait of the knight, and that is well caught here by Ghiaurov, who refuses to exaggerate the characterization. Bacquier makes a delightful Sancho Panza, but it is Régine Crespin as a comically mature Dulcinée, who provides the most characterful singing, flawed vocally but commandingly positive. Kazimierz Kord directs the Suisse Romande Orchestra in a performance that is zestful and electrifying, and the recording is outstandingly clear and atmospheric.

Esclarmonde (complete).
(M) *** Decca 425 651-2 (3) [id.]. Sutherland, Aragall, Tourangeau, Davies, Grant, Alldis Ch., Nat. PO, Bonynge.

The central role of *Esclarmonde*, with its Wagnerian echoes and hints of both Verdi and Berlioz, calls for an almost impossible combination of qualities. In our generation Joan Sutherland is the obvious diva to encompass the demands of great range, great power and brilliant coloratura, and her performance is in its way as powerful as it is in Puccini's last opera. Aragall proves an excellent tenor, sweet of tone and intelligent, and the other parts, all of them relatively small, are well taken too. Richard Bonynge draws passionate singing and playing from chorus and orchestra, and the recording has both atmosphere and spectacle to match the story, based on a medieval romance involving song-contests and necromancy.

Werther (complete).
*** Ph. 416 654-2 (2) [id.]. Carreras, Von Stade, Allen, Buchanan, Lloyd, Children's Ch., ROHCG O, C. Davis.
(M) *** DG 403 304-2 (2). Domingo, Obraztsova, Augér, Grundheber, Moll, Cologne Children's Ch. and RSO, Chailly.
(M) **(*) EMI CMS7 63973-2 (2) [Ang. CDMB 63973]. Gedda, De los Angeles, Mesplé, Soyer, Voix d'Enfants de la Maîtrise de l'ORTF, O de Paris, Prêtre.

Sir Colin Davis has rarely directed a more sensitive or more warmly expressive performance on record than his account of *Werther*, based on a stage production at Covent Garden. Frederica von Stade makes an enchanting Charlotte, outshining all current rivals on record, both strong and tender, conveying the understanding but vulnerable character of Goethe's heroine. Carreras may not be quite so clearly superior to all rivals, but he uses a naturally beautiful voice freshly and sensitively. Others in the cast, such as Thomas Allen as Charlotte's husband Albert and Isobel Buchanan as Sophie, her sister, are excellent, too. The CD transfer on to a pair of discs has been highly successful, with a single serious reservation: the break between the two CDs is badly placed in the middle of a key scene between Werther and Charlotte, just before *Ah! qu'il est loin ce jour!* Otherwise this is one of the very finest French opera sets yet issued in the new medium.

With a recording that gives fine body and range to the sound of the Cologne orchestra, down to the subtlest whisper from the pianissimo strings, the DG version stands at an advantage, particularly as Chailly proves a sharply characterful conductor, one who knows how to thrust home an important climax as well as how to create evocative textures, varying tensions positively. Plácido Domingo in the name-part sings with sweetness and purity as well as strength, coping superbly with the legato line of the aria *Pourquoi me réveiller?* Elena Obraztsova is richer and firmer than she usually is on record, but it is a generalized portrait, particularly beside the charming Sophie of Arlene Augér. The others make up a very convincing team.

Victoria de los Angeles, who has already given us a delectable portrayal of Manon, is equally attractive portraying Charlotte in *Werther*, and here she has the advantage of stereo. Her golden tones which convey pathos so beautifully are ideally suited to Massenet's gentle melodies and, though she is recorded too closely (closer than the other soloists), she makes an intensely appealing heroine. Though sweetness is the predominant quality, Massenet's adaptation of Goethe is full of fine dramatic strokes. Gedda makes an intelligent romantic hero, though Prêtre's direction could be subtler.

Mathias, William (1934–92)

Lux aeterna, Op. 88.

*** Chan. Dig. CHAN 8695 [id.]. Felicity Lott, Cable, Penelope Walker, Bach Ch., St George's Chapel Ch., Windsor, LSO, Willcocks; J. Scott (organ).

Just as Britten in the *War Requiem* contrasted different planes of expression with Latin liturgy set against Wilfred Owen poems, so Mathias contrasts the full choir singing Latin against the boys' choir singing carol-like Marian anthems, and in turn against the three soloists, who sing three arias and a trio to the mystical poems of St John of the Cross. In the last section all three planes come together when the chorus chants the prayer *Lux aeterna*, and the boys sing the hymn, *Ave maris stella*, leaving the soloists alone at the end in a moving conclusion. Overall, the confidence of the writing makes the work far more than derivative, an attractively approachable and colourful piece, full of memorable ideas, especially in this excellent performance, beautifully sung and played and atmospherically balanced.

Wind quintet.

*** Crystal CD 750 [id.]. Westwood Wind Quintet – CARLSSON: *Nightwings;* LIGETI: *Bagatelles;* BARBER: *Summer music.* ***

Of the five movements of this spirited *Quintet* the scherzo is particularly felicitous and there is a rather beautiful *Elegy*. The playing of the Westwood Wind Quintet is highly expert and committed, though the recording is a little less transparent than in the Barber or Ligeti pieces with which it is coupled. However, it is still very good indeed.

Maw, Nicholas (born 1935)

Odyssey.

*** EMI Dig. CDS7 54277-2 (2) [Ang. CDCB 54277]. CBSO, Simon Rattle.

Spanning an hour and 40 minutes, Nicholas Maw's *Odyssey* has been counted the biggest continuous orchestral piece ever written. The prodigious scale is impressive in itself, matched by the naturally grave tone of voice. Despite the smoothly flowing melodic lines and tonal idiom, it is a tough work to take in, and it is best to rely on the lucid analysis provided in the notes. Then the distinctive beauty and purposefulness of *Odyssey* becomes plain. As in Mahler, if not so readily, one comes to recognize musical landmarks in the six substantial movements. The slow movement alone lasts over half an hour, while the allegros bring a genuine sense of speed, thrusting and energetic. It was at Rattle's insistence that this superb recording was made at live concerts. The result is astonishingly fine, with the engineers totally disguising the problems of recording in Birmingham Town Hall.

Maxwell Davies, Peter (born 1934)

Ave maris stella; Image, reflection, shadow; (i) *Runes from a holy island.*
(M) *** Unicorn UKCD 2038; *UKC 2038.* Fires of London, (i) cond. composer.

This is a CD compilation of key Maxwell Davies works, more generously as well as more aptly coupled than on the original LPs. *Ave maris stella,* essentially elegiac, finds the composer at his most severe and demanding. The second piece, *Image, reflection, shadow,* is a kind of sequel; both of them are extended works for small chamber ensemble, which are played here without conductor. *Runes,* conducted by the composer, is much shorter yet just as intense in its rapt slowness. Ideal performances, well recorded, from the group for which all this music was written.

The Boyfriend; The Devils (film-scores): suites. (i) *Seven in nomine.*
*** Collins Dig. 1095-2; *1095-4* [id.]. (i) Mary Thomas; Aquarius, Nicholas Cleobury.

In 1971 Maxwell Davies did the sharply imagined scores for two Ken Russell films, not only the study in insanity, *The Devils,* but also Sandy Wilson's affectionate Twenties' send-up (with Twiggy as heroine), *The Boyfriend.* Davies's distorting lens works surprisingly well in both. These are the concert suites he drew from the film-scores, the one sparkling, the other creepily atmospheric. Nicholas Cleobury draws alert playing from Aquarius, though in *The Boyfriend* the distant recording takes away some of the necessary bite. From the same crisply economical period *Seven in nomine* is a series of rather severe reworkings of the *In nomine* theme of John Taverner, which somewhat obsessed Maxwell Davies while writing his opera on that Tudor composer. He wrote the piece for his own group, The Fires of London, but the members of Aquarius are just as understanding.

Caroline Mathilde – concert suite
*** Collins Dig. Single 2002-2. BBC PO, composer.

The composer conducts the BBC Philharmonic in a colourful concert-suite from the full-length work he wrote for the Royal Danish Ballet. In these vivid performances, brilliantly recorded, he shows how they completely transcend their stylistic roots as eighteenth-century pastiche. A valuable addition to Collins' 20th-Century Plus series of CD singles.

(i) *Trumpet concerto;* (ii) *Symphony No. 4.*
*** Collins Dig. 1181-2; *1181-4* [id.]. (i) John Wallace, SNO; (ii) SCO; composer.

Inspired by the dazzling and poetic playing of the Philharmonia principal, John Wallace, the soloist on the record, the *Trumpet concerto,* written in 1988, is one of the most rewarding of Maxwell Davies's later works. In three movements lasting a full half-hour, it brings a technical challenge to the soloist which makes for atmospheric poetry as well as dramatic excitement. Another source of inspiration has been St Francis, and the slow movement links with the saint's sermon to the birds, deeply meditative; the final coda in its Messiaenic jangling represents sublime glorification when St Francis receives the stigmata. The power and effectiveness of this work has already occasioned a second recorded performance, from Håkan Hardenberger, equally brilliant and evocative (Philips 432 075-2, coupled with other concertos – see our Concerts section below).

The *Fourth Symphony* of 1984 brings similarly striking landmarks. Though it uses chamber forces, this four-movement work is texturally the thorniest of the composer's symphonies, not an easy piece but one with a powerful physical impact. The playing both of the SNO in the concerto and of the SCO in the symphony (the orchestra of which Davies is the Associate Conductor) is strongly committed, with excellent recorded sound.

Violin concerto.
*** Sony Dig. MK 42449 [id.]. Stern, RPO, Previn: DUTILLEUX: *L'Arbre des songes.* ***

Maxwell Davies wrote his *Violin concerto* specifically with Isaac Stern in mind, and there are parallels here with the Walton *Violin concerto* of over forty years earlier. The composer was inspired to draw on a more warmly lyrical side such as he has rarely displayed. Yet for all its beauties, this is a work which has a tendency to middle-aged spread, not nearly as taut in expression as the Walton or, for that matter, the fine Dutilleux concerto with which it is coupled. Stern seems less involved here than in that other work, though this coupling makes a strong, meaty issue for anyone wanting to investigate the recent development of these characterful composers.

Renaissance and Baroque realisations: (PURCELL: *Fantasia & 2 pavans; Fantasia upon one note.* BACH: *Well-tempered Clavier: Preludes & fugues in C sharp major and min.* (i) GESUALDO: *Tenebrae super Gesualdo.* DUNSTABLE: *Veni sancte – Veni creator spiritus.* KINLOCH: *His fantaisie. 3 Early Scottish motets*).
(M) *** Unicorn UKCD 2044 [id.]. Fires of London, (i) with Mary Thomas; composer.

These pieces make a colourful collection, sounding well in CD transfers of the original bright recordings. They mainly represent the composer in the 1960s abrasively distorting into foxtrot and other dance rhythms pieces by Purcell, Bach, Dunstable and others. It is like painting a moustache on the Mona Lisa, only more fun.

Sinfonia; Sinfonia concertante.
(M) *** Unicorn Dig. UKCD 2026; *UKC 2026* [id.]. SCO, composer.

In his *Sinfonia* of 1962 Peter Maxwell Davies took as his inspirational starting point Monteverdi's *Vespers* of 1610. Except perhaps in the simple, grave beauty of the second of the four movements, where the analogy is directly with *Pulchra es* from the *Vespers*, it is not a kinship which will readily strike the listener, but the dedication in this music, beautifully played by the Scottish Chamber Orchestra under the composer, is plain from first to last. The *Sinfonia concertante* of twenty years later, as the title implies, is a much more extrovert piece for strings plus solo wind quintet and timpani. The balance of movements broadly follows a conventional plan, but in idiom this is hardly at all neo-classical and, more than usual, the composer evokes romantic images, as in the lovely close of the first movement. Virtuoso playing from the Scottish principals, not least the horn. Well-balanced recording.

Sinfonia accademica; (i) *Into the labyrinth.*
(M) *** Unicorn UKCD 2022. (i) Neil Mackie; SCO, composer.

Into the labyrinth, in five movements, might be regarded more as a song-symphony than as a cantata. The words by the Orcadian poet (and the composer's regular collaborator), George Mackay Brown, are a prose-poem inspired by the physical impact of Orkney, with the second movement a hymn of praise to fire, wind, earth and water, and the fourth – after a brief orchestral interlude in the third – bringing the centrepiece of the work, comprising almost half the total length, an intense meditation. The fine Scottish tenor, Neil Mackie, gives a superb performance, confirming this as one of Maxwell Davies's most beautiful and moving inspirations. The *Sinfonia accademica* provides a strong and attractive contrast, with its lively, extrovert outer movements and a central slow movement which again evokes the atmosphere of Orkney. Strong, intense performances under the composer, helped by first-rate recording.

OPERA

The Martyrdom of St Magnus.
*** Unicorn Dig. DKPCD 9100 [id.]. Dives, Gillett, Thomson, Morris, Kelvin Thomas, Scottish Chamber Op. Ens., Michael Rafferty.

Lasting just over 70 minutes, this chamber opera in nine scenes, based on the novel *Magnus* by George Mackay Brown, fits neatly on to a single CD. The five soloists – taking multiple parts – belong to Music Theatre Wales, whose director, Michael McCarthy, was responsible for the stage production which forms the basis of this fine recording, made in the concert hall of the Royal College of Music in London. With Gregorian chant providing an underlying basis of argument, Davies has here simplified his regular idiom. The musical argument of each of the nine compact scenes is summarized in the interludes which follow. The story is baldly but movingly presented, with St Magnus translated to the present century as a concentration camp victim, finally killed by his captors. Outstanding among the soloists is the tenor, Christopher Gillett, taking among other roles that of the Prisoner (or saint).

Mayerl, Billy (1902–1959)

All-of-a-twist; Autumn crocus; Bats in the belfry; The Harp of the winds; Insect oddities: Praying Mantis; Wedding of an ant. Jazzaristrix; The Jazz master; Jill all alone; Look lively; Loose elbows; Marigold; Railroad rhythm; Shallow waters; Sweet William. Arrangements: *Body and soul; Limehouse blues; Peg o' my heart; Phil the Fluter's ball; Smoke gets in your eyes.*
*** Virgin Dig. VC7 90745-2; *VC 790745-4* [id.]. Susan Tomes.

Aquarium suite; Autumn crocus; Bats in the belfry; Four Aces suite: Ace of Clubs; Ace of Spades. 3 Dances in syncopation, Op. 73; Green tulips; Hollyhock; Hop-o'-my-thumb; Jill all alone; Mistletoe; Parade of the sandwich-board men; Sweet William; White heather.
**(*) Chan. Dig. CHAN 8848; *LBTD 028* [id.]. Eric Parkin.

Billy Mayerl believed he had achieved a specially English style of jazz. During the 1920s and 1930s his name was a household word, and 20,000 students enrolled in his mail-order School of Music to learn syncopated piano. He left an indelible legacy of light pieces of high quality, with writing that is often much more complex and sophisticated than the rags of Joplin and his contemporaries. His most famous lyrical numbers, such as *Marigold* and *Autumn crocus* (to quote Susan Tomes) combine 'a blend of elegance, wistfulness, nonchalance and high spirits – qualities which stamped his whole output'. The best of his pieces sound surprisingly undated, and in the hands of this stunning young pianist they emerge with a refreshing spontaneity. The flashing cross syncopations of *Bats in the belfry* and *All-of-a-twist* emerge with dazzling rhythmic freedom, for indeed this brilliant and talented artist has those 'Loose elbows' (readily demonstrable in the infectious piece of that name), which are an essential part of the Mayerl style. The gentle numbers, like *Jill-all-alone* and *Shallow waters* are as winning as the picaresque *Insect oddities.* The transcriptions all emerge magnetically, and the easy, flowing flexibility of the playing is as remarkable as the dash and verve of the bravura, so well displayed in the closing tour de force of *Railroad rhythm.* The recording is splendidly real.

Eric Parkin also obviously enjoys this repertoire and plays the music with much sympathy and vivacious rhythmic freedom, even if his shoulders are not quite so loose as those of Miss Tomes. His programme is well chosen to suit his own approach to Mayerl's repertoire and this Chandos record is certainly very enjoyable, as he, too, is very well treated by the recording engineers.

Medtner, Nikolai (1880–1951)

(i) *Piano concertos Nos. 1 in C min., Op. 33; 2 in C min., Op. 50; 3 in E min. (Ballade), Op. 60.* (Piano) *Sonata-Ballade in F sharp, Op. 27.*
*** Chan. Dig. CHAN 9040 (2) [id.]. Geoffrey Tozer; (i) LPO, Järvi.

(i) *Piano concerto No. 1 in C min., Op. 33; Sonata-Ballade in F sharp, Op. 27.*
*** Chan. Dig. CHAN 9038 [id.]. Tozer, (i) LPO, Järvi.

Piano concertos Nos. 2 in C min., Op. 50; 3 in E min., Op. 60.
*** Hyp. Dig. CDA 66580 [id.]. Nikolai Demidenko, BBC Scottish SO, Jerzy Maksymiuk.
*** Chan. Dig. CHAN 9039 [id.]. Tozer, LPO, Järvi.

Apart from about a hundred songs and a few chamber pieces, Medtner, like Chopin, wrote exclusively for the piano. Long known as the 'Russian Brahms', his music strikes the listener as being rather like Rachmaninov but without the big, surging tunes. The main difference lies, as *Grove* puts it, in 'the strong vein of classicism apparent in its tightly controlled structures and its contrapuntal textures'. Although almost three decades separate the *First* and *Third Concertos*, Medtner's musical language remains consistent and unchanged. As a glance at the numbering shows, Chandos offer the three concertos together as a package or separately. Their soloist is the Australian Geoffrey Tozer, who also plays the *Sonata-Ballade, Op. 27*, for good measure. In the *Second* and *Third* concertos they come into direct competition with Hyperion with Nikolai Demidenko as soloist.

Tozer has obvious feeling for this composer, and his playing has no lack of warmth and virtuosity. He has the advantage over his rival of a richer, more transparent recording and a more sympathetic and responsive accompanist in Järvi and the London Philharmonic. Demidenko, on the other hand, has the greater fire and dramatic flair, and his performance with the BBC Scottish Orchestra under Jerzy Maksymiuk has one very much of the edge of one's chair. This is high voltage playing of great dynamism and brilliance. Demidenko plays with tremendous virtuosity though there is at times a faint suggestion of coolness. He is by no means as well recorded as Tozer, the sound of the piano is shallow, and the orchestra lacks real transparency and is a bit two-dimensional in terms of front-to-back perspective. All the same, many will feel that this is a small price for playing of such thrilling quality and, although the recording is not in the top bracket, it deserves a three-star rating on artistic grounds. His must clearly be the preferred version in Nos. 2 and 3, except for those for whom sound-quality is the prime consideration.

Dithyramb, Op. 10/2; Elegy, Op. 59/2; Skazki (Fairy tales): No. 1 (1915); in E min., Op. 14/2; in G, Op. 9/3; in D min. (Ophelia's song); in C sharp min., Op. 35/4. Forgotten melodies, 2nd Cycle, No. 1: Meditation. Primavera, Op. 39/3; 3 Hymns in praise of toil, Op. 49; Piano sonata in E min. (The Night Wind), Op. 25/2; Sonata Triad, Op. 11/1–3.
*** CRD CRD 3338/9 [id.]. Hamish Milne.

Medtner's art is subtle and elusive. He shows an aristocratic disdain for the obvious, a feeling for balance and proportion, and a quiet harmonic refinement that offer consistent rewards. In Hamish Milne's first two-disc set the most substantial piece is the E minor Sonata (The Night Wind), which should dispel any doubts as to Medtner's capacity to sustain an argument on the grandest scale. Milne also includes the less ambitious single-movement sonatas, Op. 11, which are finely concentrated, elegantly fashioned works. There is hardly a weak piece here, and Milne is a poetic advocate whose technical prowess is matched by first-rate artistry. The recording too is very truthful and vivid.

Improvisation No. 2 (in variation form), Op. 47; Piano sonata in F min., Op. 5.
*** CRD Dig. CRD 3461 [id.]. Hamish Milne.

The F minor Sonata comes from 1905 yet finds the composer as fully formed in personality as he is masterly in his handling of sonata form. The Second Improvisation in variation form is a subtle and original work, and Hamish Milne plays it with the authority that distinguishes all he does.

3 Novelles, Op. 17; Romantic sketches for the young, Op. 54; Piano sonatas in G min., Op. 22; A min., Op. 30; 2 Skazki, Op. 8.
*** CRD Dig. CRD 3460 [id.]. Hamish Milne.

The *G minor Sonata* (1911), which Moiseiwitsch and Gilels recorded, makes a good starting point to discovering Medtner, and there is no better guide than this splendid pianist. Sample *Daphnis and Chloe* (the first of the *Novelles*, Op. 17) or the Op. 30 *Sonata* and you will soon find out how varied and satisfying his world can be. Excellent recording.

Piano sonatas Nos. 5 in G min., Op. 22; 6 in C min. (Sonata-Skazka), Op. 25/1; 7 in E min., Op. 25/2.
* Marco Polo Dig. 8.223371 [id.]. Adám Fellegi.

Piano sonatas Nos. 8 in F sharp (Sonata-Ballada), Op. 27; 10 in A min. (Sonata reminicenza), Op. 38/1; 11 in C min. (Sonata tragica), Op. 39/5; 14 in G (Sonata-Idylle), Op. 56.
* Marco Polo Dig. 8.223372 [id.]. Adám Fellegi.

No one who has heard Moiseiwitsch's records of the *G minor Sonata, Op. 22* or heard Gilels play the *Sonata reminicenza* is likely to be much impressed by these performances. True, Adám Fellegi is not much helped by the unglamorous acoustic in which he is recorded, but his performances give little evidence of real feeling for this repertoire. It is high time that Medtner's own recordings were returned to circulation.

Méhul, Étienne-Nicolas (1763–1817)

Symphonies Nos. 1–4; Overtures: La chasse de jeune Henri; Le trésor supposé.
*** Nimbus Dig. NI 5184/5 [id.]. Gulbenkian Foundation O, Swierczewski.

Méhul was a contemporary of Cherubini and flourished during the years of Napoleon. He was enormously prolific and wrote no fewer than 25 operas in the period 1790–1810. The four symphonies recorded here come from 1808–10 (Nos. 3 & 4 have been discovered only in recent years by David Charlton, who has edited them) and are well worth investigating. The invention is felicitous and engaging, and in *No. 4 in E major* Méhul brings back a motif of the *Adagio* in the finale, a unifying gesture well ahead of its time. The performances are eminently satisfactory even if the strings sound a shade undernourished.

Mendelssohn, Fanny (1805–47)

Piano trio in D, Op. 11.
*** Hyp. Dig. CDA 66331; *KA 66331* [id.]. Dartington Piano Trio – Clara SCHUMANN: *Trio in G min.* ***

The *Piano trio* is a late work which was not published until 1850, three years after her death. Like Clara Schumann's *G minor Trio* with which it is coupled, it has impeccable craftsmanship and great facility. Its ideas are pleasing, though not strongly individual. The Dartington Piano Trio play most persuasively and give much pleasure. Excellent recording.

Mendelssohn, Felix (1809–47)

Capriccio brillant for piano and orchestra, Op. 22.
(M) ** Sony SBK 48166 [id.]. Rudolf Serkin, Phd. O, Ormandy – BRAHMS: *Concerto No. 1;* SCHUMANN: *Intro. and allegro appassionato.* **(*)

Serkin is on good form here. This is a brilliant performance, not without panache, if not especially strong on charm. The recording is a little shallow, but otherwise good.

(i) *Piano concerto in A min. for piano and strings;* (ii) *Piano concertos Nos. 1–2; Capriccio brillant, Op. 22.*
(M) *** Teldec/Warner Dig. 9031 75860-2; *9031 78560-4* [id.]. Cyprien Katsaris; (i) Franz Liszt CO, Rolla; (ii) Leipzig GO, Masur.

It was a happy idea to pair the early *A minor Piano concerto* with the two mature works in this form. The former is an extended piece, lasting over half an hour, far longer than the two numbered concertos, an amazing work for a thirteen-year-old, endlessly inventive. Cyprien Katsaris gives it a fresh, strong reading, marked by delightfully crisp and clean articulation and lacking only the last degree of charm. The orchestral playing is splendid and so is the recording.

In the two numbered concertos it is impossible not to respond to Katsaris's vitality, even if at times there is a feeling of his rushing his fences. He plays with enormous vigour in the outer movements and receives strong support from Masur. There is nothing heavy, yet the music is given more substance than usual, while the central slow movements bring a relaxed lyrical *espressivo* which provides admirable contrast. The sheer vigour and impetus of the finale of the *G minor* with its dashing roulades from Katsaris is exhilarating, although some may feel that all the allegros are pressed on a shade too hard. The full, well-balanced recording has attractive ambience and sparkle.

Piano concertos Nos. 1 in G min.; 2 in D min., Op. 40.
*** Decca Dig. 414 672-2 [id.]. András Schiff, Bav. RSO, Dutoit.

(i) *Piano concertos Nos. 1–2;* (ii) *Capriccio brillant, Op. 22; Rondo brillant, Op. 29.*
(B) **(*) Decca 425 504-2; *425 504-4.* Peter Katin; (i) LSO, Collins; (ii) LPO, Martinon.

(i) *Piano concertos Nos. 1–2. Prelude and fugue, Op. 35/1; Rondo capriccioso, Op. 14; Variations sérieuses, Op. 54.*
*** Sony MK 42401 [id.]. Murray Perahia; (i) ASMF, Marriner.

Perahia's playing catches the Mendelssohnian spirit with admirable perception. There is sensibility and sparkle, the slow movements are shaped most beautifully and the partnership with Marriner is very successful, for the Academy give a most sensitive backing. The recording could be more transparent but it does not lack body, and the piano timbre is fully acceptable. Moreover this CBS issue offers three substantial bonuses from Perahia's admirable digital solo recital.

András Schiff plays marvellously, with poetry, great delicacy and fluency, while his virtuosity is effortless. He is given excellent accompaniments by Dutoit and the Bavarian players, and the Decca recording is first class. By the side of the CBS coupling, this is short measure, but the sound is far more realistic.

Katin's early (1955) coupling of the two *Piano concertos* has come up amazingly freshly on CD; the ambient warmth of the recording disguises its age and the piano recording is excellent. Katin has the full measure of these remarkably similar works. His crisp passage-work prevents the outer movements from becoming either brittle or lifeless, and he offers a pleasingly light touch in the finales. In both slow movements his style is sensitive without sentimentality, a feature mirrored in the excellent accompaniments. The two occasional pieces were recorded much later (1971) and are equally accomplished and enjoyable.

(i) *Piano concerto No. 1 in G min., Op. 25;* (ii) *Violin concerto in E min., Op. 64. Symphony No. 4 in A (Italian).*
**(*) Nimbus Dig. NI 5158 [id.]. (i) Kite; (ii) Hudson; Hanover Band, Goodman.

The *G minor Concerto* works surprisingly well on a fortepiano and, with the fortepiano not spotlit, presents much more of a contest between solo instrument and orchestra, when the original scale is reproduced. The *Violin concerto* is rather less successful when the relative closeness of the solo violin – played by the leader of the Hanover Band, Benjamin Hudson – exaggerates the cutting edge of the instrument, with little or no vibrato used, and each portamento, however authentic, is obtrusive. Yet, with well-chosen speeds – a really flowing *Andante* in the second movement – there is still much to enjoy. If anything, Goodman's performance of the *Italian Symphony*, with string ensemble surprisingly large, is even more sympathetic than Sir Charles Mackerras's earlier period recording for Virgin Classics, when here both speeds and manner are more relaxed, notably in the first two movements.

Double piano concertos: in A flat; in E.
*** Hyp. Dig. CDA 66567 [id.]. Coombs, Munrow, BBC Scottish SO, Maksymiuk.

Mendelssohn's *Double concerto in A flat* is the most ambitious of all his concertante works, and the work in E brings an expansive first movement too. Dating from 1824 and 1823 respectively, they provide formidable evidence of the teenage composer's fluency and technical finesse, even if the musical material cannot match such masterpieces that he was about to write as the *Octet* or the *Midsummer Night's Dream overture*. Stephen Coombs and Ian Munro prove ideal advocates, playing with delectable point and imagination, finding a wit and poetry in the writing that might easily lie hidden, with even the incidental passagework magnetizing the ear. The slow movements and the finales are the ones which most clearly point forward to the mature Mendelssohn, with the dashing polka-like finale of the *A flat Concerto* giving a clear foretaste of the comparable movement in the celebrated solo *Concerto No. 1 in G minor*. The recording of the pianos is on the shallow side, and the string-tone is thin too, but that is not inappropriate for the music.

Violin concertos: in D min. (for violin & strings); in E min., Op. 64.
*** Ph. Dig. 432 077-2; *432 077-4* [id.]. Viktoria Mullova, ASMF, Marriner.

Mendelssohn's early *D minor Violin concerto* was completed when he was thirteen, after he had written the first five *Symphonies for strings*. As a structure it is amazingly accomplished; but only the finale, with its dancing main theme, is really memorable. Purity is the keynote of Mullova's fresh and enjoyable readings of both concertos, the early *D minor* as well as the great *E minor*. Whether influenced by having them in juxtaposition, she refuses to treat the *E minor* as a big warhorse work. Both her refinement and that of the Academy present it on a smaller scale than usual, tenderly expressive rather than flamboyant in the expression of emotion, yet with concentration keenly maintained. So the lovely downward phrase leading into the second subject of the first movement has rarely had more poetry in it, the central *Andante* is sweet and songful and, best of all, the finale, light and fanciful, conveys pure fun in its fireworks. The early work follows a similar pattern, with youthful emotions given full rein and with the finale turned into a headily brilliant Csardas. The Philips recording is admirably natural and beautifully balanced.

Violin concerto in E min., Op. 64.
(M) *** Sony Dig. MDK 44902; *40-44902* [id.]. Cho-Liang Lin, Philh. O, Tilson Thomas – BRUCH: *Concerto No. 1* *** (with encores by SARASATE and KREISLER ***).
*** Decca Dig. 410 011-2 [id.]. Kyung Wha Chung, Montreal SO, Dutoit – TCHAIKOVSKY: *Concerto.* ***
*** DG Dig. 400 031-2 [id.]. Mutter, BPO, Karajan – BRUCH: *Concerto No. 1.* ***
(BB) *** Naxos Dig. 8.550153 [id.]. Nishizaki, Slovak PO, Jean – TCHAIKOVSKY: *Concerto.* ***
(B) *** Ph. 422 473-2; *422 473-4*. Grumiaux, New Philh. O, Krenz – TCHAIKOVSKY: *Concerto.* ***
*** EMI Dig. CDC7 49663-2 [id.]. Nigel Kennedy, ECO, Tate – BRUCH: *Concerto No. 1;* SCHUBERT: *Rondo.* ***

(B) *** Pickwick Dig. PCD 829; *CIMPC 829* [id.]. Jaime Laredo, SCO – BRUCH: *Concerto No. 1*. ***
(M) *** EMI CDM7 69003-2 [id.]; *EG 769003-4*. Menuhin, Philh. O, Kurtz – BRUCH: *Concerto No. 1*. ***
(M) *** DG 419 067-2 [id.]. Milstein, VPO, Abbado – TCHAIKOVSKY: *Concerto*. ***
**(*) BMG/RCA RD 85933 [RCA 5933-2-RC]. Heifetz, Boston SO, Munch – TCHAIKOVSKY: *Concerto* etc. **(*)
*** ASV CDDCA 748; *ZCDCA 748* [id.]. Xue-Wei, LPO, Ivor Bolton – BRAHMS: *Violin concerto*. ***
**(*) Decca Dig. 421 145-2 [id.]. Joshua Bell, ASMF, Marriner – BRUCH: *Concerto No. 1*. **(*)
(B) **(*) Pickwick IMPX 9031. Campoli, LPO, Boult – BRUCH: *Scottish fantasia*. **(*)
(M) **(*) Sony CD 42537 [MYK 36724]. Stern, Phd. O, Ormandy – TCHAIKOVSKY: *Concerto*. **(*)
(M) (***) EMI mono CDH7 69799-2 [id.]. Yehudi Menuhin, BPO, Furtwängler – BEETHOVEN: *Concerto*. (***)
(B) **(*) EMI CDZ7 62519-2; *LZ 762519-4*. Menuhin, LSO, Frühbeck de Burgos – BRUCH: *Concerto No. 1*. **(*)
(M) **(*) BMG/RCA Dig. GD 86536 [RCA 6536-2-RG]. Ughi, LSO, Prêtre – BEETHOVEN: *Concerto*. **(*)
(*) DG 419 629-2 [id.]. Shlomo Mintz, Chicago SO, Abbado (also with KREISLER: *Caprice viennoise; Liebeslied; Liebesfreud*) – BRUCH: *Concerto No. 1*. *
(B) ** CfP CD-CFP 4374; *TC-CFP 4374*. Milstein, Philh. O, Barzin – BRUCH: *Concerto No. 1*. **

Cho-Liang Lin's vibrantly lyrical account now reappears with the Bruch *G minor* (plus some attractive encores) to make an unbeatable mid-priced coupling. These are both immensely rewarding and poetic performances, given excellent, modern, digital sound, and Michael Tilson Thomas proves a highly sympathetic partner in the Mendelssohn *Concerto*.

Chung favours speeds faster than usual in all three movements, and the result is sparkling and happy, with the lovely slow movement fresh and songful, not at all sentimental. With warmly sympathetic accompaniment from Dutoit and the Montreal orchestra, amply recorded, the result is one of Chung's happiest records.

Here even more than in her Bruch coupling, the freshness of Anne-Sophie Mutter's approach communicates vividly to the listener, creating the feeling of hearing the work anew. Her gentleness and radiant simplicity in the *Andante* are very appealing, and the light, sparkling finale is a delight. Mutter is given a small-scale image, projected forward from the orchestral backcloth; the sound is both full and refined.

Takako Nishizaki gives an inspired reading of the *Concerto*, warm, spontaneous and full of temperament. The central *Andante* is on the slow side, but well shaped, not sentimental, while the outer movements are exhilarating, with excellent playing from the Slovak Philharmonic. Though the forwardly placed violin sounds over-bright, the recording is full and warm. A splendid coupling at super-bargain price.

Grumiaux's 1973 account of the Mendelssohn is characteristically polished and refined. He plays very beautifully throughout; the pure poetry of his playing is heard at its most magical in the key moment of the downward arpeggio which introduces the second subject of the first movement.

Kennedy establishes a positive, masculine view of the work from the very start, but fantasy here goes with firm control. The slow movement brings a simple, songful view of the haunting melody, and the finale sparkles winningly, with no feeling of rush. With a bonus in the rare Schubert *Rondo* and clear, warm recording, it makes an excellent recommendation.

Laredo's version on a bargain-price CD brings an attractively direct reading, fresh and alert but avoiding mannerism, marked by consistently sweet and true tone from the soloist. The orchestral ensemble is amazingly good when you remember that the soloist himself is directing. The recording is vivid and clean.

The restrained nobility of Menuhin's phrasing of the famous principal melody of the slow movement has long been a hallmark of his reading with Efrem Kurtz, who provides polished and sympathetic support. The sound of the CD transfer is bright, with the soloist dominating but the orchestral texture well detailed.

Milstein's DG version comes from the early 1970s. His is a highly distinguished performance, very well accompanied. His account of the slow movement is more patrician than Menuhin's, and his slight reserve is projected by DG sound which is bright, clean and clear in its CD remastering.

As one might expect, Heifetz gives a fabulous performance. His speeds are consistently fast, yet in the slow movement his flexible phrasing sounds so inevitable and easy that it is hard not to be convinced. The finale is a tour de force, light and sparkling, with every note in place. The recording has been digitally remastered with success and the sound is smoother than before.

Xue-Wei's version, clean and fresh if a little reticent emotionally, makes a generous and attractive coupling for his equally recommendable version of the Brahms. There are more strongly characterized readings than this but, with its pastel-shaded lyricism, this is undoubtedly satisfying, helped by first-rate recording.

Joshua Bell is given a very forward balance by the Decca engineers; but he can still achieve a genuine pianissimo when he wants to, as at the lead in to the first-movement cadenza, which is a moment of magic. Overall, this is a boldly romantic reading, full of warmth and not without poetry; but the spotlight on the soloist all but masks Marriner's fine accompaniment, a distinct drawback.

Campoli's sweet, perfectly formed tone and polished, secure playing are just right for the Mendelssohn *Concerto*, and this is a delightful performance, notable for its charm and disarming simplicity. The 1958 (originally Decca) recording is brightly lit in the CD transfer, and the vividness is marred by a degree of roughness in the orchestral focus; but no matter, this inexpensive record gives much pleasure and is a fine reminder of a superb violinist.

Stern's performance has great bravura, culminating in a marvellously surging account of the finale. The slow movement too is played with great eloquence and feeling, but when pianissimos are non-existent – partly, but not entirely, the fault of the close recording balance – the poetic element is diminished.

Menuhin's unique gift for lyrical sweetness has never been presented on record more seductively than in his classic, earlier version of the Mendelssohn *Concerto* with Furtwängler. The digital transfer is not ideally clear, yet one hardly registers that this is a mono recording from the early 1950s.

Menuhin's second stereo recording with Rafael Frühbeck de Burgos has its moments of roughness, but it has magic too: at the appearance of the first movement's second subject and in the slow movement. The recording sounds fuller than the earlier account with Kurtz, and this makes a good bargain on EMI's inexpensive Laser label.

Ughi's is a fresh, totally unsentimental reading; both the slow movement and the finale are very successful. Ughi lacks only the final individuality of artists like Lin or Menuhin; but he is highly musical and has the advantage of an excellent digital recording, clean and well balanced and set against a believable atmosphere.

Mintz's version is powerfully conceived, less reticent than Mutter, less spontaneous than Chung. It is not quite the equal of the Bruch coupling, although Abbado gives fine support, as he does for Milstein. DG have added some *morceaux de concert* of Kreisler, which are most winningly played. The sound is good, but this should now be at mid-price.

Milstein is not at his most fervently lyrical in his 1961 performance with the Philharmonia Orchestra. There is a certain quality of detachment here, although he plays the slow movement with much finesse and, for all its fine musicianship (there is some good orchestral playing), this is not as memorable or as characterful as his later, DG version with Abbado. Moreover the CD transfer has brought a touch of steeliness on the violin timbre.

(i) *Violin concerto in E min., Op. 64;* (ii) *Symphony No. 4 in A (Italian), Op. 90;* (iii) *A Midsummer Night's Dream: Overture and incidental music* (CD only: (iv) *Overture: A Calm sea and a prosperous voyage*).
(B) *** DG Compact Classics 413 150-2 (2); *413 150-4.* (i) Milstein, VPO, Abbado; (ii) BPO, Maazel; (iii) Mathis, Boese, Bav. RSO with Ch., Kubelik (CD only: (iv) LSO, Chmura).

This is one of the most attractive compilations in DG's Compact Classics series. Milstein's 1973 account of the *Violin concerto* (see above) is highly distinguished. With excellent recording and balance this is worthy to rank with the best, and it is greatly enhanced by the sensitivity of Abbado's accompaniment. Maazel's *Italian Symphony* offers a fast, hard-driven but joyous and beautifully articulated performance of the first movement and equal clarity and point in the vivacious finale. The Berlin Philharmonic playing is both infectious and superbly polished. The central movements are well sustained, and altogether this is highly enjoyable, the recording resonantly full-timbred. Kubelik's fairly complete version of the incidental music for *A Midsummer Night's Dream* is no less enjoyable and the sound is very good here, too. On the pair of CDs the *Midsummer Night's Dream* selection is extended, and a pleasing performance of the *Calm sea and prosperous voyage overture* is added. The sound on both CDs and tape is fresh and bright but does not lack fullness.

Overtures: Athalia, Op. 74; Calm sea and prosperous voyage, Op. 27; The Hebrides (Fingal's Cave), Op. 26; The Marriage of Camacho, Op. 10; A Midsummer Night's Dream, Op. 21; Ruy Blas, Op. 95.
❀ *** BMG/RCA Dig. RD 87905 [7905-2-RC]. Bamberg SO, Flor.

This is the most desirable collection of Mendelssohn overtures the catalogue has ever offered; the evocatively atmospheric opening of *Calm sea and prosperous voyage*, followed by an allegro of great vitality, is a demonstrable example of the spontaneous imagination of these performances, and there is no finer version of *Fingal's Cave*, with its lyrical secondary theme phrased with memorable warmth. *The Marriage of Camacho*, with its brass opening, reminds us somewhat of *Ruy Blas*, and also a little of Weber: it is a most attractive piece with some engaging writing for woodwind. *Athalia* is very enjoyable too, especially when played with such freshness and polish. The recording, made in the Dominikanerbau, Bamberg, has splendid warmth and bloom and a most attractive hall ambience.

Overtures: *Calm sea and a prosperous voyage, Op. 27; Fair Melusina, Op. 32; The Hebrides (Fingal's Cave), Op. 21; A Midsummer Night's Dream, Op. 21; Ruy Blas, Op. 95; Trumpet overture, Op. 101; Overture for wind instruments, Op. 24.*
*** DG Dig. 423 104-2 [id.]. LSO, Abbado.

Three of these performances were originally released with the symphonies in 1985; the rest are new, recorded in various venues – yet, even on CD, the ear is not troubled by the changing acoustics. Neither the *Overture for wind* (1824) nor the (1826) *Trumpet overture* (more notable for furiously busy strings) are forgotten masterpieces. All the other pieces sound strikingly vivid and spontaneous in Abbado's hands, and the recording, wide in range and always with plenty of ambience, suits the music admirably.

Symphonies for string orchestra Nos. 1 in C; 2 in D; 3 in E min.; 4 in C min.; 5 in B flat; 6 in E flat.
*** Nimbus Dig. NI 5141 [id.]. E. String O, William Boughton.

Symphonies for string orchestra Nos. 7 in D min.; 8 in D; 10 in B min.
*** Nimbus Dig. NI 5142 [id.]. E. String O, William Boughton.

Symphonies for string orchestra Nos. 9 in C; 11 in F; 12 in G min.
*** Nimbus Dig. NI 5143 [id.]. E. String O, William Boughton.

Mendelssohn's twelve *String symphonies*, written for family performance by one of the most brilliant boy-geniuses in the history of music, contain delectable inspirations by the dozen. William Boughton conducts the English String Orchestra in winningly energetic readings of these delightful works, not as polished in ensemble as some rivals, but with warmly atmospheric recording helping to make them very persuasive. The first disc contains the six earliest, all written in 1821; on the second disc, with Nos. 7, 8 and 10, the young composer raises his sights. In No. 7 there are clear signs of a Beethovenian influence in the dramatic sharpness of the argument. The third disc contains Nos. 9, 11 and 12, all products of 1823, when the boy was extending his range still further, the mature Mendelssohn style emerging more and more clearly despite the continuing echoes of Mozart and Haydn.

Symphonies for string orchestra Nos. 4 in C min.; 9 in C; 12 in G.
**(*) Mer. CDE 84131; *KE 77131* [id.]. Guildhall String Ens.

The Guildhall group are very accomplished; they play with a lightness and grace that are very appealing. These are warmly spontaneous performances; if their ensemble in the Scherzo of No. 9 could be more sharply precise, the slow movement has an attractive elegiac feeling. The recording, made in the Church of St Edward the Confessor, Mottingham, Kent, is warm and natural, and detail is not clouded.

Symphonies for string orchestra, Nos. 9 in C min.; 10 in B min.; 12 in G min.
*** Hyp. CDA 66196; *KA 66196* [id.]. L. Festival O, Ross Pople.

Ross Pople achieves performances that are as polished and spirited as they are lyrically responsive. No. 9 has a particularly gracious slow movement following the drama of its opening, but No. 12 with its clear debt to Bach is also most impressive. Excellent sound.

Symphonies Nos. 1–5.
(M) *** DG 429 664-2 (3). Mathis, Rebman, Hollweg, German Op. Ch., BPO, Karajan.

Symphonies Nos. 1–5; Overtures: Calm sea and prosperous voyage; The Hebrides (Fingal's Cave).
(M) *** Decca 421 769-2 (3) [id.]. Soloists, V. State Op. Ch., VPO, Dohnányi.

Symphonies Nos. 1–5; Overtures: Fair Melusina, Op. 32; The Hebrides (Fingal's Cave), Op. 26; A Midsummer Night's Dream, Op. 21; Octet, Op. 20: Scherzo.
*** DG Dig. 415 353-2 (4) [id.]. LSO, Abbado (with Connell, Mattila, Blochwitz and LSO Ch. in Symphony No. 2).

Abbado's is a set to brush cobwebs off an attractive symphonic corner; in the lesser-known symphonies it is his gift to have you forgetting any weaknesses of structure or thematic invention in the brightness and directness of his manner. Instead of overloading this music with sweetness and sentiment, as the Victorians came to do, he presents it more as it must have appeared at the very beginning, when on good evidence the composer himself was known to favour brisk, light allegros and crisp rhythms. So the youthful *First* has plenty of C minor bite. The toughness of the piece makes one marvel that Mendelssohn ever substituted the scherzo from the *Octet* for the third movement (as he did in London), but helpfully Abbado includes that extra scherzo, so that on CD, with a programming device, you can readily make the substitution yourself. Good, bright recording, though not ideally transparent.

Karajan's distinguished set of the Mendelssohn *Symphonies* was recorded in 1971/2 in the Berlin Jesus Christus Kirche. The early C minor work sounds particularly fresh, and the *Hymn of praise* brings the fullest sound of all; the very fine choral singing is vividly caught. The soloists make a good team, rather than showing any memorable individuality; but overall Karajan's performance is most satisfying. The *Scottish Symphony* is a particularly remarkable account and the *Italian* shows the Berlin Philharmonic in sparkling form: the only drawback is Karajan's characteristic omission of both first-movement exposition repeats. The recording is brightly lit but not shrill. There are some reservations to be made about the *Reformation Symphony*, but the sound has been effectively clarified without too much loss of weight.

Dohnányi's Decca set (which includes also two key overtures) brings performances which are fresh and direct, often relying on faster and more flowing speeds than in Abbado's full-price set, more clearly rebutting any idea that this music might be sentimental. The most striking contrast comes in the *Hymn of praise*, where Dohnányi's speeds are often so much faster than Abbado's that the whole character of the music is changed, as in the second-movement scherzo, sharp in one, gently persuasive in the other. Many will prefer Dohnányi in that, particularly when the choral sound is brighter and more immediate too. The Decca engineers produced recording which was among the finest of its period and which still sounds well. The snag of the set is that Dohnányi, unlike Abbado, omits exposition repeats, which in the *Italian Symphony* means the loss of the substantial lead-back passage in the first movement.

Symphonies Nos. 1 in C min., Op. 11; 5 in D (Reformation), Op. 107.
**(*) Teldec/Warner Dig. 2292 44933-2 [id.]. Leipzig GO, Kurt Masur.

Masur's mastery in Mendelssohn is due in good measure to his ability to adopt a relatively fast speed and make it sound easy and relaxed, not hurried and breathless. Mendelssohn himself, when conductor of this great Leipzig orchestra, is reported to have taken such a course in his own performances, and in all the movements of both symphonies Masur is consistently swifter than his principal rivals on record. It affects not only fast movements but slow, so that the *Andante* of No. 1 flows with winning ease and no suspicion of sentimentality, more affectionate than at a slower speed. As recorded, the Leipzig sound is on the heavy side for No. 1, with some clouding of tuttis, but when separate discs of No. 1 are rare, this is a welcome issue, part of Masur's latest Mendelssohn cycle. It is a pity that, unlike Abbado for example, he does not add the arrangement of the scherzo from the *Octet* that Mendelssohn used as an alternative third movement in No. 1.

Symphony No. 2 in B flat (Hymn of praise), Op. 52.
(M) *** DG 431 471-2; *431 471-4*. Mathis, Rebmann, Hollweg, German Op. Ch., BPO, Karajan.
*** DG Dig. 423 143-2 [id.]. Connell, Mattila, Blochwitz, LSO Ch., LSO, Abbado.
(M) *** Decca 425 023-2; *425 023-4* [id.]. Ghazarian, Gruberová, Krenn, V. State Ch., VPO, Christoph von Dohnányi.

We have already praised the 1972 Karajan recording of the *Hymn of praise* within the context of his complete set of Mendelssohn symphonies above. In some ways Abbado's full-price digital version is even finer, if not more clearly recorded, but the Karajan CD has a price advantage and, although he has a less individual team of soloists, it is a very satisfying account, with the chorus vibrantly caught within the spacious acoustics of the Berlin Jesus-Christus Kirche.

Abbado's view of the *Second*, brushing aside all sentimentality, is both fresh and sympathetic, and though the recording is not ideally clear on inner detail the brightness reinforces the conductor's view. The chorus, well focused, is particularly impressive, and the operatic flavour of some of the solo work comes over well, notably *Watchman, what of the night?*. The sweet-toned tenor, Hans-Peter Blochwitz, is outstanding among the soloists, and Elizabeth Connell brings weight as well as purity to the main soprano part.

Dohnányi's version relates the piece more to the choral than to the symphonic tradition. The chorus, not particularly large, yet sings incisively, and the wide-ranging 1976 Decca sound underpins the texture of the finale with resonant and superbly focused organ sound. In refinement and delicacy of shaping Dohnányi yields to a conductor like Karajan, and the 6/8 second movement lacks charm (the tempo is a fraction too fast); but overall this is a refreshing account and it is very well recorded indeed. The chorus makes a splendid impact and the acoustics of the Sofiensaal provide a most attractive overall bloom to the performance; those for whom fine sound is important will probably enjoy this more than the Karajan alternative.

Symphony No. 3 in A min. (Scottish), Op. 56; Overtures; Calm sea and a prosperous voyage; The Hebrides (Fingal's Cave); Ruy Blas.
(BB) **(*) Naxos Dig. 8.550222; *4550222* [id.]. Slovak PO, Oliver Dohnányi.

Symphony No. 3 in A min. (Scottish); Overture: The Hebrides (Fingal's Cave).
(M) *** DG 419 477-2; *419 477-4* [id.]. BPO, Karajan.

Karajan's account of the *Scottish* is very fine indeed. The orchestral playing is superb – the pianissimo articulation of the strings is a pleasure in itself and the conductor's warmth and direct eloquence, with no fussiness, are irresistible. The scherzo is marvellously done and becomes a highlight, while there is no doubt that Karajan's final coda has splendid buoyancy and power. However, the coupling is ungenerous.

– Oliver Dohnányi conducts a joyful account of the *Scottish Symphony* on Naxos, given the more impact by forward recording. Mendelssohn's lilting rhythms in all the fast movements are delightfully bouncy, and though the slow movement brings few hushed pianissimos, its full warmth is brought out without sentimentality. The three overtures, also very well done, not least the underappreciated *Ruy Blas*, make an excellent coupling.

Symphonies Nos. 3 in A min. (Scottish); 4 in A (Italian), Op. 90.
(M) *** DG Dig. 427 810-2 [id.]. LSO, Abbado.
(BB) *** ASV CDQS 6004; *ZCQS 6004*. O of St John's, Lubbock.
*** EMI CDC7 54000-2 [id.]; *EL 754000-4*. L. Classical Players, Norrington.
(M) *** Decca 425 011-2; *425 011-4* [id.]. LSO, Abbado.
**(*) Teldec/Warner Dig. 2292 43463-2 [id.]. Leipzig GO, Masur.

Symphonies Nos. (i) *3 in A min. (Scottish), Op. 56;* (ii) *4 in A (Italian), Op. 90; Overture: The Hebrides, Op. 26.*
(M) **(*) Decca 417 731-2 [id.]. VPO, Christoph von Dohnányi.
(M) **(*) Sony Dig./Analogue SBK 46536 [id.]. (i) Bav. RSO, A. Davis; (ii) Cleveland O, Szell.

Abbado's fine digital recordings of the *Scottish* and *Italian Symphonies*, coupled together from his complete set, make a splendid mid-price bargain. The recording is admirably fresh and bright – atmospheric, too – and the ambience, if not absolutely sharply defined, is very attractive. Both first-movement exposition repeats are included. Allegros are exhilarating, but clean articulation means that the pace never seems forced and Abbado judges the espressivo with his usual combination of warmth and refinement.

Lubbock's coupling of the *Scottish* and *Italian Symphonies* makes an outstanding super-bargain issue, offering performances of delightful lightness and point, warmly and cleanly recorded. The string section may be of chamber size but, amplified by a warm acoustic, the result sparkles, with rhythms exhilaratingly lifted. The slow movements are both on the slow side but flow easily with no suspicion of sentimentality, while the *Saltarello* finale of No. 4, with the flute part delectably pointed, comes close to Mendelssohnian fairy music.

There have been previous recordings of the *Italian Symphony* on period instruments, but this is the first disc to offer the *Scottish* as well. As in his Schumann, Norrington opts for unexaggerated speeds in the outer movements, relatively brisk ones for the middle movements. The reults are similarly exhilarating, particularly in the clipped and bouncy account of the first movement of the *Italian*. The *Scottish Symphony* is far lighter than usual, with no hint of excessive sweetness. The scherzo has rarely sounded happier, and the finale closes in a fast gallop for the 6/8 coda with the horns whooping gloriously. Good, warm recording, only occasionally masking detail in tuttis. Mackerras directing the Orchestra of the Age of Enlightenment is very slightly to be preferred in the *Italian Symphony*, if his coupling of the overture and incidental music to *A Midsummer Night's Dream* is suitable (see below).

Abbado's outstanding Decca *Scottish Symphony* is beautifully played and the LSO responds to his direction with the greatest delicacy of feeling, while the *Italian Symphony* has a comparable lightness of touch, matched with lyrical warmth. The vintage 1968 Kingsway Hall recording is freshly detailed yet full, with glowing wind colour, and is in some ways preferable to the DG sound; however, the absence of the first-movement exposition repeat in the *Scottish Symphony* (though not in the *Italian*) is a drawback.

Masur observes exposition repeats in both symphonies, and his choice of speeds brings out the freshness of inspiration judiciously, avoiding any suspicion of sentimentality in slow movements, which are taken at flowing tempi. Conversely, the allegros are never hectic to the point of breathlessness. The one snag is that the reverberant Leipzig recording tends to obscure detail in tuttis; the scherzo of the *Scottish*, for example, becomes a blur, losing some of its point and charm. Otherwise, the sound of the orchestra has all the characteristic Leipzig bloom and beauty.

Christoph von Dohnányi's mid-priced Decca reissue (part digital, part analogue) also includes a rather slow and romantic reading of *The Hebrides*. It is a refreshing account of the *Italian*, never pushed too hard, though the *Saltarello* is taken exhilaratingly fast; it is a pity that the first-movement exposition repeat is omitted. The *Scottish* too is fresh and alert, and the weighty recording helps to underline the stormy quality that Dohnányi aptly finds in the first movement, although in other movements this is a rather less characterful account.

The CBS digital recording of the *Scottish Symphony*, dating from 1980, is of high quality, and Andrew Davis's reading is freshly straightforward, supported by excellent playing from the Bavarian Radio Orchestra. But the score's pianissimo markings are much less strikingly contrasted here than in some other versions, and this is not just a matter of the forward balance. The scherzo is very successful (helped by the transparent detail of the sound) and the slow movement is memorable, nicely paced and beautifully shaped. The finale is alert and zestful. Szell and his Cleveland Orchestra then appear to present the rest of the programme, and are heard in bravura form in their recording of the *Italian Symphony* from 1962. This was the first stereo recording to include the first-movement exposition repeat, and Szell's approach is dramatic and often exhilarating. The precision of the playing is remarkable and there is never any hint of scurrying. The Cleveland sound is full as well as brilliant.

Symphony No. 3 (Scottish); (i) *Die erste Walpurgisnacht.*
**(*) Telarc Dig. CD 80184 [id.]. (i) Cairns, Garrison, Krause, Cleveland Ch.; Cleveland O, Dohnányi.

In his more recent recording for Telarc, Christoph von Dohnányi conducts the Cleveland Orchestra in a fresh, taut performance of the *Scottish*, at generally brisker speeds in all four movements than in his earlier, Vienna version for Decca. The disc is chiefly important for the coupling, the rare dramatic cantata, *Die erste Walpurgisnacht*. With plenty of vigorous if not highly original choral writing, it makes a very enjoyable piece in a performance as red-blooded as this. Not only the orchestra but the Cleveland Orchestra Chorus are superb: bright, fresh and crisply disciplined. The snag is the solo singing, which is undistinguished.

Symphony No. 4 in A (Italian), Op. 90.
*** DG Dig. 410 862-2 [id.]. Philh. O, Sinopoli – SCHUBERT: *Symphony No. 8.* *** ❀
(M) *** EMI Dig. CDD7 64085-2 [id.]. BPO, Tennstedt – SCHUBERT: *Symphony No. 9.* ***
(M) *** DG 415 848-2 [id.]. BPO, Karajan – SCHUBERT: *Symphony No. 8.* ***
(B) *** DG 429 158-2. BPO, Karajan – SCHUMANN: *Symphony No. 1.* ***
(M) (***) EMI mono CDM7 63398-2 [id.]; *EG 763398-4*. RPO, Beecham – BEETHOVEN: *Symphony No. 8;* SCHUBERT: *Symphony No. 8.* (***)

Sinopoli's great gift is to illuminate almost every phrase afresh. His speeds tend to be extreme – fast in the first movement but with diamond-bright detail, and on the slow side in the remaining three. Only in the heavily inflected account of the third movement is the result at all mannered but, with superb playing from the Philharmonia and excellent Kingsway Hall recording, this rapt performance is most compelling. For refinement of detail, especially at lower dynamic levels, the CD is among the most impressive digital recordings to have come from DG.

Tennstedt's account of the *Italian* is vividly articulated and obviously felt. The quality of the Berliners' playing is superb, with the *Saltarello* finale exhilarating in its witty, polished bravura and the woodwind achieving the lightest possible touch. The central movements are elegant and relaxed, with the *Andante* warmly flowing and gentle horns in the Trio of the Minuet. The digital sound has admirable body and clarity to recommend it and this is certainly a version to be considered if the splendid Schubert coupling is wanted.

Karajan's performance of the *Italian* is superbly polished and well paced. The reading is straighter than usual, notably in the third movement, though the effect of Karajan's slower pace is warm, never bland. The recording is very brightly lit in its remastered transfer and has lost some of its depth. The coupling with Schumann comes at bargain price, the coupling with Schubert at mid-price.

In all four movements of the *Italian* Beecham adopts speeds slower than usual, but only in the third-movement Minuet does that make for even a hint of sluggishness. In the rest – notably the outer movements, which at Beecham's speeds can be given the rhythmic lift and pointing they cry out for – he could not be more persuasive.

Symphony No. 4 (Italian); Overtures: Fair Melusina, Op. 32; The Hebrides (Fingal's Cave), Op. 26; Son and stranger (Die Heimkehr aus der Fremde), Op. 89.
(B) *** Pickwick Dig. PCD 824; *CIMPC 824* [id.]. Berne SO, Peter Maag.

Peter Maag, making a welcome return to the recording studio with his Berne orchestra, here offers a winningly relaxed performance of the *Italian Symphony* (including exposition repeat), plus an attractive group of overtures, which once more confirms him as a supreme Mendelssohnian. With fine ensemble from the Berne Symphony Orchestra – only marginally let down at times by the strings – the forward thrust is more compelling than with the taut, unyielding approach too often favoured today. *The Hebrides* receives a spacious reading and the two rarer overtures are a delight too, particularly *Son and stranger*, which in Maag's hands conveys radiant happiness. At bargain price, with full and brilliant recording, it is first rate.

Symphony No. 4 in A (Italian); A Midsummer Night's Dream: Overture, Op. 21, & orchestral incidental music, Op. 61.
*** Virgin Dig. VC 790725-2 [id.]. O of Age of Enlightenment, Mackerras.

(i) *Symphony No. 4 (Italian);* (ii) *A Midsummer Night's Dream: Overture, Op. 21; Incidental music, Op. 61: Fairy march; Wedding march; Intermezzo; Nocturne; Dance of the Clowns; Scherzo.*
(BB) *** LaserLight Dig. 15 526 [id.]. (i) Philh. O, János Sándor; (ii) Budapest PO, Kovacs.

Mackerras directs fresh, resilient, 'authentic'-style performances of both the *Symphony* and the *Midsummer Night's Dream* music. The middle two movements of the *Symphony* are marginally faster than usual but gain in elegance and transparency, beautifully played here, as is the *Midsummer Night's Dream* music. It is particularly good to have an ophicleide instead of a tuba for Bottom's music in the *Overture*, and the boxwood flute in the *Scherzo* is a delight.

A first-class coupling in the super-bargain range from LaserLight. Sándor gives a fresh and exhilarating account of the *Italian Symphony*, with particularly elegant Philharmonia playing in his warm and nicely paced account of the *Andante*. Outer movements sparkle without being rushed, articulation is light and clean, and the digital sound is excellent. The performance of a generous selection from the *Midsummer Night's Dream incidental music* also shows the Budapest orchestra on top form: this is most beguiling and is recorded in a pleasingly warm acoustic which does not cloud detail.

CHAMBER AND INSTRUMENTAL MUSIC

Cello sonatas Nos. 1 in B flat, Op. 45; 2 in D, Op. 58; Assai tranquillo; Song without words, Op. 109; Variations concertantes, Op. 17.
*** Hyp. Dig. CDA 66478 [id.]. Richard Lester, Susan Tomes.

There are few cello sonatas so exhilarating as the second of the two written by Mendelssohn. Susan Tomes, the inspired pianist of the group, Domus, and her cellist colleague, Richard Lester, give a performance full of flair on this ideally compiled disc of Mendelssohn's collected works for cello and piano, brimming with charming ideas. As well as the works with opus number they include a delightful fragment, *Assai tranquillo*, never previously recorded.

Octet in E flat, Op. 20.
*** Hyp. Dig. CDA 66356; *KA 66356* [id.]. Divertimenti – BARGIEL: *Octet*. ***
(M) **(*) Decca 421 093-2; *421 093-4* [id.]. Vienna Octet (members) – BEETHOVEN: *Septet*. ***
(B) **(*) Decca 421 637-2; *421 637-4*. ASMF – BOCCHERINI: *Cello quintet*. **(*)

Octet in E flat, Op. 20; Symphonies for string orchestra Nos. 6 in E flat; 10 in B min.
*** Denon Dig. CO 73185 [id.]. I Solisti Italiani.

Octet in E flat, Op. 20; String quintet No. 1 in A, Op. 18.
*** EMI Dig. CDC7 49958-2. Hausmusik.

Octet in E flat, Op. 20; String quintet No. 2 in B flat, Op. 87.
*** Ph. 420 400-2 [id.]. ASMF Chamber Ens.

This Philips successor comes from just over a decade after the Academy's earlier record of Mendelssohn's *Octet* and the playing has greater sparkle and polish. The recorded sound is also superior and sounds extremely well in its CD format. The *Second Quintet* is an underrated piece and it too receives an elegant and poetic performance that will give much satisfaction.

Using period instruments, the British-based group, Hausmusik, gives a most refreshing performance of the *Octet* and couples it with another miraculous masterpiece of Mendelssohn's boyhood. The period performance gives extra weight to the lower lines compared with the violins, with the extra clarity intensifying the joyfulness of the inspiration. Most revealing of all is the way that the last two movements of the *Octet*, the feather-light *Scherzo* and the dashing finale, with their similar figuration, are presented in contrast, the one slower and more delicately pointed than usual, the other more exhilarating at high speed.

Divertimenti give a very natural and unforced account of the celebrated *Octet* which, though it may not be the most distinguished in the catalogue, still gives great pleasure. Their disc is of special interest in offering a particularly interesting rarity in the form of Woldemar Bargiel's *Octet in C minor*. Excellent recorded sound.

I Solisti Italiani are none other than the old Virtuosi di Roma, and they play with all the finesse and grace you would expect from them. The *Octet* is delightful and could be a first choice, were the acoustic not quite so resonant. The two early *Symphonies* are given with not only elegance but also a conviction that is very persuasive indeed.

The 1973 Vienna version of the *Octet* is highly competitive at mid-price, coupled with an equally attractive account of Beethoven's *Septet*. The playing is polished and spontaneous and the recording has re-emerged freshly in its CD format, although the upper register of the strings is not quite as cleanly focused as the Beethoven coupling.

The 1968 (originally Argo) performance by the ASMF is fresh and buoyant, and the recording wears its years fairly lightly. It offered fine judgement in matters of clarity and sonority, and the digital remastering has not lost the original ambient bloom, although the violin timbre now has noticeable thinness. A good bargain version.

Piano quartets Nos. 1 in C min.; 2 in F min.; 3 in B min., Op. 1–3.
*** Virgin Dig. VC7 91183-2; *VC7 91183-4* [id.]. Domus.

Although the *Piano quartet No. 3 in B minor* was recorded some years ago by the late Werner Hass and members of the Berlin Philharmonic Octet, these early pieces are rarely encountered on disc. *No. 1 in C minor* comes from 1822, when Mendelssohn was thirteen, and thus predates the symphony in the same key by two years. It was the composer's first published composition and was succeeded the following year by another dedicated to '*Monsieur le Professeur Zelter par son élève Felix Mendelssohn-Bartholdy*', equally fluent and accomplished. However, none of the ideas of this *F minor* work are as remarkable as those of its successor in *B minor* of 1825, dedicated to Goethe (Mendelssohn had made enormous strides in the intervening two years). In any event, all three pieces have charm, vitality and musicianship, particularly in the hands of this ensemble, who play with the taste and discernment we have come to expect from them. Excellent recording.

Piano trio No. 1 in D min., Op. 49.
**(*) Ph. Dig. 416 297-2 [id.]. Beaux Arts Trio – DVOŘÁK: *Piano trio No. 4*. **(*)

Piano trios Nos. 1 in D min., Op. 49; 2 in C min., Op. 66.
**(*) Chan. Dig. CHAN 8404; *ABTD 1141* [id.]. Borodin Trio.
**(*) Teldec/Warner Dig. 2292 44947-2. Trio Fontenay.

The latest Beaux Arts performance essays a rather larger scale than its predecessor but is slightly less spontaneous, particularly in the simple slow movement which has an attractive Mendelssohnian innocence, not entirely captured here. The first movement is emphatic in its drama and the effect can be rather over-forceful. The recording is appropriately full-bodied and present.

The Borodin Trio are recorded in a very resonant acoustic and are rather forwardly balanced. They give superbly committed but somewhat overpointed readings. All the same, there is much musical pleasure to be found here.

The Trio Fontenay are rather brightly recorded and they play with passionate commitment and great virility. Their performances are bigger-boned and more robust than some rivals, and they indulge in some slight (and mostly – though not always – undisturbing) expressive vehemence. Greater delicacy from the pianist in the scherzo movement of the *D minor trio* would have been welcome. Undoubtedly powerful and keenly alive though both performances are, they do not communicate much charm.

String quartet No. 1 in E flat, Op. 12.
*** Ph. 420 396-2 [id.]. Orlando Qt – DVOŘÁK: *String quartet No. 12.* ***

The Orlando performance of Mendelssohn's *E flat Quartet* is one of the very best ever put on record. It is played with lightness of touch, delicacy of feeling and excellent ensemble. The original analogue recording was totally natural and lifelike; the CD transfer has added a touch of glare on the first violin, and the effect is almost too present. However, it responds to the controls and we see no reason to withhold a strong recommendation.

String quartets Nos. 1 in E flat, Op. 12; 2 in A, Op. 13.
*** Hyp. Dig. CDA 66397 [id.]. Coull Qt (with 2 Pieces, Op. 81 ***).

The Coull Quartet on Hyperion give fresh and unaffected accounts of both *Quartets* and have the benefit of very good recorded sound. Their performances will give real pleasure, even if they may not have the unanimity or finesse of some ensembles currently before the public. Tempi are well judged and everything flows naturally. The Coull offer the additional inducement of two of the *Four pieces*, Op. 81, which were published after Mendelssohn's death. The Gabrieli are, if anything, even better recorded on Chandos (CHAN 8827) than the Coull but, moving between one and the other, the greater freshness of the younger group tells.

String quintets Nos. 1 in A, Op. 18; 2 in B flat, Op. 87.
(M) *** Sony/CBS CD 45883. Laredo, Kavafian, Ohyama, Kashkashian, Robinson.

A welcome addition to the catalogue. Laredo and his ensemble achieve good matching of timbre, and they give lively accounts of both these neglected works, lacking neither warmth nor finesse. The 1978 recording has responded well to remastering, and has body and presence.

Violin sonatas: in F min., Op. 4; in F (1838).
*** DG Dig. 419 244-2 [id.]. Shlomo Mintz, Paul Ostrovsky.

Mendelssohn was only fourteen when he composed the *F minor Sonata*, but even so it is not wanting in individuality and is much more than a youthful exercise. The 1838 *Sonata* comes from Mendelssohn's productive Leipzig period. The performances are beyond reproach; the playing of both artists is a model of sensitivity and intelligence, and the recording is absolutely first class. Strongly recommended.

PIANO MUSIC

Andante and rondo capriccioso in E min., Op. 14; Prelude and fugue in E minor/major, Op. 35/1; Sonata in E, Op. 6; Variations sérieuses in D min., Op. 53.
*** Sony Dig. MK 37838 [id.]. Murray Perahia.

Perahia is perfectly attuned to Mendelssohn's sensibility and it would be difficult to imagine these performances being surpassed. In Perahia's hands, the *Variations sérieuses* have tenderness yet tremendous strength, and neither the popular *Rondo capriccioso* nor the *Prelude and fugue* have sounded more fresh or committed on record. The quality of the CBS recording is very good indeed.

Étude in F min.; Preludes & 3 Études, Op. 104; 6 Preludes & fugues, Op. 35; Prelude & fugue in E min.
**(*) Nimbus NI 5071 [id.]. Martin Jones.

Fantasy in F sharp min., Op. 28; 3 Fantaisies et caprices, Op. 16; Fantasy on 'The last rose of summer', Op. 15; Variations: in E flat, Op. 82; in B flat, Op. 83; Variations sérieuses in D min., Op. 53.
**(*) Nimbus NI 5072 [id.]. Martin Jones.

Sonatas: in E, Op. 6; in G min., Op. 105; in B flat, Op. 106; Kinderstücke, Op. 72.
**(*) Nimbus NI 5070]id.]. Martin Jones.

In his collection of Mendelssohn piano music, Martin Jones provides a fascinating slant on the composer, particularly his youthful inspirations. In many ways the disc of sonatas – all three written when he was in his teens – is the most interesting of all, reflecting Mendelssohn's devotion to Beethoven and his sonatas. The *Preludes and fugues* inevitably reflect his even deeper devotion to Bach, then still under-appreciated. Their style is positive and consistent, with sweet Mendelssohnian lyricism as well as dashing bravura marking the *Preludes*, and even the *Fugues* bringing far more than Bachian echoes. The sets of variations on the third disc were mostly written later in his career, examples of his high skill and love of the keyboard, rather than works of genius. Martin Jones is an excellent advocate, playing dedicatedly and persuasively, not always immaculately but without mannerism. The recordings, made in the 1970s, come up very well in the CD transfers, with the atmosphere of a small hall realistically conveyed.

Fantasia in F sharp min. (Sonata écossaise), Op. 28; 3 Fantaisies et caprices, Op. 16; Rondo capriccioso in E, Op. 14; Sonata in E, Op. 6.
**(*) Chan. CHAN 8326; *ABTD 1081* [id.]. Lydia Artymiw.

Lydia Artymiw is highly persuasive in the *Sonata*, as she is in the other, by no means inconsequential works. This is an altogether excellent disc, very well recorded – although it must be said that, fine though Miss Artymiw's playing is, she does not match Perahia in quality of imagination or subtlety of dynamic gradation.

Scherzo from A Midsummer Night's Dream, Op. 61 (trans. Rachmaninov).
*** Hyp. CDA 66009; *KA 66009* [id.]. Howard Shelley – RACHMANINOV: *Variations* etc. ***

Howard Shelley, with fabulously clear articulation and delectably sprung rhythms, gives a performance of which Rachmaninov himself would not have been ashamed. This is a delightful makeweight for an outstanding disc of Rachmaninov variations.

Songs without words, Books 1–8 (complete).
**(*) Hyp. Dig. CDA 66221/2; *KA 66221/2* [id.]. Lívia Rév.

Songs without words, Books 1–8 (complete); *Albumblatt, Op. 117; Gondellied; Kinderstücke, Op. 72; 2 Klavierstücke.*
(M) *** DG 423 931-2 (2) [id.]. Daniel Barenboim (piano).

Songs without words, Op. 19/1; Op. 30/6; Op. 38/6; Op. 62/1 and 6; Spring song, Op. 62/6; Spinning song, Op. 67/4; Op. 67/5; Op. 102/6.
*** DG 415 118-2 [id.]. Daniel Barenboim – LISZT: *Liebesträume* ***; SCHUBERT: *Moments musicaux.* **

This 1974 set of Mendelssohn's complete *Songs without words*, which Barenboim plays with such affectionate finesse, has dominated the catalogue for nearly two decades. For the mid-priced CD reissue, the six *Kinderstücke* (sometimes known as 'Christmas pieces') have been added, plus other music, so that the second of the two CDs plays for 73 minutes. The sound is first class.

Lívia Rév is a thoughtful, sensitive and aristocratic artist. Her survey of the *Songs without words* has charm and warmth, and she includes a hitherto unpublished piece. The set is handsomely presented and the recording is warm and pleasing; it is, however, somewhat bottom-heavy. Yet the slightly diffuse effect suits the style of the playing, and this can be recommended alongside Barenboim.

Songs without words: Op. 19/1, 2, 4, 5 & 6 (Venetian gondola song); Op. 30/3, 4, 5 & 6 (Venetian gondola song); Op. 38/1, 2 & 6; Op. 53/1, 2 & 3; Op. 62/1 & 6 (Spring song); Op. 67/4 (Spinning song) & 6; Op. 85/6; Op. 102/3 & 5.

**(*) Decca Dig. 421 119-2 [id.]. András Schiff.

András Schiff plays the *Songs without words* simply, coolly and directly, his style straighter than Lívia Rév's. The famous *Spring song* shows him at his finest. This is his penultimate item and he ends the recital neatly with the engaging Op. 102, No. 3. The recording is most natural and realistic.

VOCAL MUSIC

Elijah (oratorio), *Op. 70.*
*** Chan. Dig. CHAN 8774/5; *DBTD 2016* [id.]. White, Plowright, Finnie, A. Davies, LSO Ch., LSO, Hickox.

Richard Hickox with his London Symphony Chorus and the LSO secures a performance that both pays tribute to the English choral tradition in this work and presents it dramatically as a kind of religious opera. Though in Victorian times this was an oratorio which was notoriously treated as sentimental, Hickox shows what fresh inspiration it contains, what a wealth of memorable ideas, treated imaginatively, as for example in the way that numbers merge one into the next, with dramatic emphasis given to each incident in the story of the prophet. The choice of soloists reflects that approach. Willard White may not be ideally steady in his delivery, sometimes attacking notes from below, but he sings consistently with fervour, from his dramatic introduction to the overture onwards. Rosalind Plowright and Arthur Davies combine purity of tone with operatic expressiveness, and Linda Finnie, while not matching the example of Dame Janet Baker in the classic EMI recording, sings with comparable dedication and directness in the solo, *O rest in the Lord.* The chorus fearlessly underlines the high contrasts of dynamic demanded in the score. The Chandos recording, full and immediate yet atmospheric too, enhances the drama. The old EMI set should by rights be reissued on CD; even when it is, the modern digital sound as well as the performance here will make this a keen contender.

Infelice; Psalm 42 (As the hart pants), Op. 42.
*** Virgin Dig. VC7 91123-2; *VC7 91123-4* [id.]. J. Baker, LSO Ch., City of L. Sinf., Hickox – BRAHMS: *Alto rhapsody* etc. ***

The scena, *Infelice* – a piece which harks back to an earlier tradition – and the Psalm-setting both have the solos prescribed for soprano, but they suit Dame Janet well, here making a welcome foray out of official retirement for a recording. The voice is in superb condition, with the weight of expressiveness as compelling as ever. The *Psalm* sounds very like an extra item from *Elijah.*

A Midsummer Night's Dream: Overture, Op. 21; Incidental music, Op. 61.
*** EMI CDC7 47163-2 [id.]. Watson, Wallis, Finchley Children's Music Group, LSO, Previn.
*** BMG/RCA Dig. RD 87764 [7764-2-RC]. Popp, Lipovšek, Bamberg Ch. & SO, Flor.
(B) *** CfP Dig. CD-CFP 4593; *TC-CFP 4593.* Wiens, Walker, LPO Ch. & O, Litton.
(M) *** DG 415 840-2 [id.]. Mathis, Boese, Bav. R. Ch. & SO, Kubelik – WEBER: *Overtures: Oberon; Der Freischütz.* ***
(M) *** EMI CMD7 64144-2 [id.]; *EG 764144-4.* Harper, J. Baker, Philh. Ch. & O, Klemperer – LISZT: *Piano concerto No. 1* etc. **(*)
(B) **(*) Hung. White Label Dig. HRC 049 [id.]. Kalmar, Bokor, Jeunesses Musicales Girls' Ch., Hungarian State O, Adám Fischer.
(M) (***) BMG/RCA mono GD 60314. Eustis, Kirk, University of Pennsylvania Women's Glee Club, Phd. O., Toscanini – BERLIOZ: *Romeo and Juliet: Queen Mab scherzo.* (**)

On EMI, Previn offers a wonderfully refreshing account of the complete score; the veiled pianissimo of the violins at the beginning of the Overture and the delicious woodwind detail in the Scherzo certainly bring Mendelssohn's fairies into the orchestra. Even the little melodramas which come between the main items sound spontaneous here, and the contribution of the soloists and chorus is first class. The Nocturne (taken slowly) is serenely romantic and the Wedding march resplendent. The recording is naturally balanced and has much refinement of detail. The CD brings the usual enhancement, with the fairy music in the Overture given a most delicate presence.

Claus Peter Flor's account omits the little melodramas, which is a pity; but for those who require the major items only, this beautiful RCA CD could well be a first choice. Recorded in the warmly resonant acoustics of the Dominikanerbau, Bamberg, the orchestra is given glowingly radiant textures; but Flor's stylish yet relaxed control brings the kind of intimacy one expects from a chamber group. The very opening of the Overture, with its soft flute timbre and diaphanous violins, is agreeably evocative and, later, the Wedding march, played with much vigour and élan, expands splendidly. The lightly rhythmic Scherzo, taken not too fast, is another highlight; and Lucia Popp's vocal contribution is delightful, especially when she blends her voice so naturally with that of Marjana Lipovšek in *You spotted snakes*.

Andrew Litton also includes the melodramas and, like Previn, he uses them most effectively as links, making them seem an essential part of the structure. He too has very good soloists; in the Overture and Scherzo he displays an engagingly light touch, securing very fine wind and string playing from the LPO. The wide dynamic range of the recording brings an element of drama to offset the fairy music. Both the Nocturne, with a fine horn solo, and the temperamental Intermezzo are good examples of the spontaneity of feeling that permeates this performance throughout and makes this disc a bargain.

Although Kubelik omits the melodramas, this makes room for an appropriate coupling of the two finest Weber overtures (both also associated with magic) with *Oberon* drawing an obvious parallel with Mendelssohn. They are marvellously played and the sound and 1965 recording are strikingly fresh.

Klemperer's recording (which dates from 1960) was made when the Philharmonia was at its peak, and the orchestral playing is superb, the wind solos so nimble that even the Scherzo, taken more slowly than usual, has a light touch. The contribution of soloists (Heather Harper and Dame Janet Baker) and chorus is first class and the disc has the advantage of including the *Fairy march* and *Funeral march*. The quality is quite full and fresh, but the coupling with Liszt (plus the *Die Fledermaus* overture) although generous does not seem particularly appropriate.

The Hungaroton CD offers much lovely playing, and fine singing from the soloists too, although many will count it a disadvantage that the vocal numbers are sung in German. While the soft focus is attractively atmospheric, the resonant acoustic has to some extent subdued the sound, although the digital recording is full and natural. There is fine, delicate articulation from the woodwind and strings in the *Scherzo*; but the hint of vibrato on the horn solo of the *Nocturne* will not please all ears, although the playing is very responsive. Fischer includes the more important melodramas but omits Nos. 2, 4, 6 and 10. On Hungaroton's bargain White Label, this is competitive.

Toscanini's Philadelphia recording offers the seven most popular numbers from the *Midsummer Night's Dream* music, including the song with chorus, *You spotted snakes*, and the final melodrama. In sparkling performances it offers a fine example of his more relaxed manners in his one Philadelphia season.

3 Psalms, Op. 78.
**(*) Nimbus Dig. NI 5171 [id.]. Oslo Cathedral Ch., Terje Kvam – GRIEG: *4 Psalms*. **(*)

All three *Psalms* have considerable beauty and dignity, especially the first, a setting of Psalm 11 with its ingenious four-part canon. Good performances by the Oslo Cathedral Choir, and eminently serviceable recording. However, at under 45 minutes, the CD offers short measure.

St Paul, Op. 36.
**(*) Ph. 420 212-2 (2). Janowitz, Lang, Blochwitz, Stier, Polster, Adam, Leipzig R. Ch. & GO, Masur.

Like *Elijah* ten years later, *Paulus* – completed in 1836 – was Mendelssohn's substitute for opera. In youthful zest it erupts in great Handelian choruses, and a Bachian style of story-telling is neatly updated in its choral interjections and chorales, with the soprano joining the traditional tenor in the narration. What reduces the dramatic effectiveness is that Mendelssohn, ever the optimist, comes to his happy resolution of the plot far too quickly and with too little struggle involved. Masur, always a persuasive interpreter of Mendelssohn, here directs a performance which, without inflating the piece or making it sanctimonious, conveys its natural gravity. Theo Adam is not always steady, but otherwise the team of soloists is exceptionally strong, and the chorus adds to the incandescence, although placed rather backwardly. The Leipzig recording is warm and atmospheric.

Mennin, Peter (1923–83)

Symphony No. 5.
(M) **(*) Mercury 432 755-2 [id.]. Eastman-Rochester O, Howard Hanson – IVES: *Symphony No. 3* etc.; SCHUMAN: *New England triptych.* ***

Peter Mennin is not as individual a musical personality as William Schuman, let alone Charles Ives; but the *Canto* central movement of his *Fifth Symphony* has a piercing melancholy which is slightly reminiscent of the Barber *Adagio for strings.* The outer movements develop plenty of polyphonic energy, but the toccata-like linear writing lacks real memorability. Hanson's performance is persuasive and vital, and the 1962 Mercury sound makes the very most of the relatively unexpansive acoustics of the Eastman Theatre.

Menotti, Gian-Carlo (born 1911)

Piano concerto in F.
(M) **(*) Van. 08.4029.71 [OVC 4071]. Earl Wild, Symphony of the Air, Jorge Mester – COPLAND: *Concerto.* ***

Menotti's *Piano concerto,* like most of his music, is easy and fluent, never hard on the ear. Its eclectic style brings a pungent whiff of Shostakovich at the opening, and there are hints of Khachaturian elsewhere. Even if it is unlikely to bear repeated listening, the charisma and bravura of Earl Wild's playing make the music sound more substantial than it is.

Amahl and the Night Visitors (opera): complete.
*** That's Entertainment CDTER 1124; *ZCTER 1124.* Lorna Haywood, John Dobson, Curtis Watson, Christopher Painter, James Rainbird, ROHCG Ch. & O, David Syrus.

Recorded under the supervision of the composer himself, this Royal Opera House production of what was originally a television opera brings a fresh and highly dramatic performance, very well sung and marked by atmospheric digital sound of striking realism. Central to the success of the performance is the astonishingly assured and sensitively musical singing of the boy treble, James Rainbird, as Amahl, purposefully effective even in the potentially embarrassing moments. Lorna Haywood sings warmly and strongly as the Mother, with a strong trio of Kings. The realism of the recording makes the chamber size of the string section sound thin at the start, but the playing is both warm and polished.

Amahl and the night visitors: Introduction; March; Shepherd's dance. Sebastian (ballet): suite.
*** Koch Dig. 3-7005-2; *2-7005-4* [id.]. New Zealand SO, Schenck – BARBER: *Souvenirs.* ***

Menotti composed *Sebastian* in 1944 for the Marquis de Cuevas, and he fashioned this seven-movement suite soon after. It is beautifully crafted and expertly scored music whose attractions are strong even if the ideas are not always as memorable as their presentation. The three movements from *Amahl and the night visitors* recorded here are the charming *Introduction*, the rather Prokofievian *March* and the *Rustic dance*, used to depict the three Shepherds' homage to the Magi, which Balanchine later choreographed. The players under Andrew Schenck, who sound as if they are enjoying themselves, are well recorded, even if the studio acoustic of Symphony House, Wellington, is very slightly dry.

Mercadante, Saverio (1795–1870)

Clarinet concerto in B flat.
*** Claves CD 50-813 [id.]. Friedli, SW German CO, Angerer – MOLTER; PLEYEL: *Concertos.* ***

Mercadante's *Concerto* consists of an *Allegro maestoso* and a galant *Andante with variations.* The music is agreeably fluent and very well played by the soloist. An interesting collection of works, showing the development of the clarinet as a solo instrument.

Flute concertos: in D; E; E min.
*** BMG/RCA Dig. RD 87703 [7703-2-RC]. James Galway, I Solisti Veneti, Scimone.

These three *Flute concertos* show Mercadante to be an excellent craftsman, with a nice turn for lyrical melody in the slow movements with their simple song-like cantilenas. Both the *Andante alla siciliana* of the *D major Concerto* and the *Largo* of the *E minor* are appealing, especially with Galway as soloist, while the *Rondo Russo* or *Polacca* finales are inventively spirited. Scimone makes the most of the often exuberantly florid tuttis of the opening movements and elsewhere accompanies Galway's silvery melodic line, sparkling and delicate by turns, with style and polish. The sound is excellent.

Merikanto, Aarre (1893–1958)

(i) *Violin concertos Nos. 2 & 4;* (ii) *10 Pieces;* (iii) *Genesis.*
*** Finlandia Dig. FACD 387 [id.]. (i) Saatikettu, Helsinki PO, James De Priest; (ii) Avanti CO, Angervo; (iii) Mattila, Savonlinna Op. Festival Ch., Lahti SO, Söderblom.

Merikanto is one of the most interesting figures in Finnish music. Best known for his opera, *Juha*, he was a briefly a pupil of Reger and then went to St Petersburg where he studied with Sergei Vasilenko. His *Second Violin concerto* (1925) is quite a find, a most imaginative work which will appeal to anyone who likes the exoticism of Szymanowski and the nature mysticism of Janáček. The third and last movement begins oddly out of style in quasi-Hindemithian fashion. The expressionist *Ten Pieces* (1930), and in particular the first, the *Largo misterioso* cast a strong spell. In 1945 Merikanto cured himself of his morphine adiction but, generally speaking, his later output – with the exception of the remarkable *Genesis* (1956) – is thought to be less adventurous and significant. The *Fourth Violin concerto* (1954) – he burned the *Third* – has a folksy Prokofiev-like character but has no lack of astringency. Merikanto's works are the product of an extraordinarily rich harmonic and orchestral imagination and emanate from an altogether distinctive sound-world. Very good performances and recording. Strongly recommended.

(i) *Fantasy for orchestra; Largo misterioso;* (ii) *Notturno;* (i) *Pan; Symphonic study.*
*** Finlandia Dig. FACD 349 [id.]. Finnish RSO, (i) Segerstam; (ii) Saraste.

The *Fantasy for orchestra* is a work of an extraordinarily rich imagination and leaves no doubt as to his distinctive orchestral sound-world. Both the *Fantasy* and the tone-poem, *Pan*, are sensitively conducted by Leif Segerstam, who successfully conveys their haunting, other-worldly atmosphere. Merikanto fell an easy victim to discouragement and was a harsh self-critic: he destroyed sections of the *Symphonic study* of 1928, but these have been expertly reconstructed by Paavo Heininen. The *Notturno* and *Largo misterioso* are also beautiful pieces that immediately cast a strong spell.

Juha (opera) complete.
**(*) Finlandia FACD 105 (2) [id.]. Lehtinen, Kostia, Krumm, Kuusoja, Finnish Nat. Op. Ch. and O, Ulf Söderblom.

The musical language of *Juha* reflects the composer's international sympathies and yet the music is far more than merely eclectic. It is atmospheric and highly expert in scoring and, in its way, bears a quite distinctive stamp. This performance derives from the early 1970s and, though it may not be ideal, every detail registers and the words are clearly projected. The singing on the whole is more than respectable, and Matti Lehtinen in the title-role is outstanding. The opera is not long – under two hours – and is very well worth investigating.

Messiaen, Olivier (1908–92)

Des canyons aux étoiles; Couleurs de la cité céleste; Oiseaux exotiques.
*** Sony Dig. MK 44762 [id.]. Paul Crossley, L. Sinf., Salonen.

The power of the writing in Messiaen's vast symphonic cycle, *Des canyons aux étoiles*, comes out vividly in Esa-Pekka Salonen's CBS version, with Paul Crossley as soloist both incisive and deeply sympathetic. Highly evocative in its American inspirations, this is the work which most satisfyingly brings together the contrasting strains in Messiaen's musical ethos, not just Christian meditation and response to the grandeur of the universe, but also the influence of birdsong, meticulously notated. Salonen's performance is not obviously devotional in the first five movements; but then, after Michael Thompson's virtuoso horn solo, in the sixth movement Salonen and his players increasingly find a sharper focus, with the playing of the London Sinfonietta ever more confident and idiomatic. The coupling is generous, with *Oiseaux exotiques* again finding Crossley in inspired form as soloist, and with *Couleurs de la cité céleste* made tough rather than evocative. The recording is sharply focused, but has good presence and atmosphere.

(i) *Chronochromie;* (ii) *Et exspecto resurrectionem mortuorum.*
(M) *** EMI CDM7 63948-2 [id.]. (i) BBC SO, Dorati; (ii) O de Paris & Ens. de Percussion, Baudo – BOULEZ: *Le soleil des eaux;* KOECHLIN: *Les Bandar-log.* ***

Messiaen's *Chronochromie* characteristically has its inspiration in nature, the composer's long-established preoccupation with birdsong, and the culminating *Épode*, very difficult as a musical argument, is immediately and readily understandable as a climactic representation of the birds' dawn chorus. This fine performance and immensely vivid recording are worthy of the music, and for the reissue EMI have added Serge Baudo's excellent 1968 recording of *Et exspecto resurrectionem mortuorum*, the wind-and-percussion work that Messiaen intended for performance in the wide open spaces. Baudo conducted its first performances in Paris and Chartres.

Les offrandes oubliées.
(B) *** EMI CZS7 62669-2 (2). O de Paris, Serge Baudo (with Concert: French music ***).

Les offrandes oubliées ('The forgotten offerings') is an early work, dating from 1930, when Messiaen was twenty-two, yet it is entirely characteristic. The work is played with great feeling for its atmosphere and power and is very well recorded. An excellent introduction to Messiaen's orchestral writing which even anticipates the *Turangalîla Symphony.*

Turangalîla symphony.
(*) Sony Dig. M2K 42271 (2) [id.]. Crossley, Murail, Philh. O, Salonen – LUTOSLAWSKI: *Symphony No. 3* etc. *

(i) *Turangalîla symphony;* (ii) *Quartet for the end of time.*
*** EMI Dig. CDS7 47463-8 [id.] (2). (i) Donohoe, Murail, CBSO, Rattle; (ii) Gawriloff, Deinzer, Palm, Kontarsky.

Simon Rattle conducts a winning performance of *Turangalîla*, not only brilliant and dramatic but warmly atmospheric and persuasive. It is not just that his rendering of the love music is ripely sensuous: in his rhythmic control of the fast dramatic movements he is equally understanding, nudging the syncopations of the fifth movement, *Joie du sang des étoiles*, to bring out the exuberant jazz overtones. The recording is warm and richly co-ordinated while losing nothing in detail. Peter Donohoe and Tristan Murail play with comparable warmth and flair, rhythmically persuasive, and the orchestra responds superbly to the challenge of a virtuoso score. Led by the pianist, Aloys Kontarsky, the German performance of the *Quartet for the end of time* is a strong one. Recorded in 1976, it provides a contrasted approach to Messiaen from Rattle's, when atmospheric warmth is only an incidental.

Esa-Pekka Salonen's account of the *Turangalîla Symphony* minimizes its atmospheric beauty, its sensuousness, and underlines the points which look forward to later composers. This is emphasized by the close balance of the piano and ondes martenot, so the passage-work for piano, beautifully played by Paul Crossley, sounds angular in a very modern way rather than evoking birdsong. Significantly, the syncopated rhythms of the energetic fifth movement are pressed home very literally, at a speed faster than usual, with little or no echo of jazz. The Philharmonia plays brilliantly and the recording underlines the sharp focus of the reading, while giving ample atmosphere.

Quatuor pour la fin du temps.
*** Delos Dig. D/CD 3043 [id.]. Chamber Music Northwest – BARTÓK: *Contrasts.* ***
(M) *** Ph. 422 834-2. Beths, Pieterson, Bylsma, De Leeuw.
(M) **(*) BMG/RCA GD 87835 [7835-2-RG]. Tashi (Kavafian, Sherry, Stoltzman, Peter Serkin).

(i) *Quatuor pour la fin du temps (Quartet for the end of time);* (ii) *Le merle noir.*
(M) *** EMI CDM7 63947-2 [id.]. (i) Gruenberg, De Peyer, Pleeth, Béroff; (ii) Zöller, Kontarsky.

Messiaen's visionary and often inspired piece was composed during his days in a Silesian prison camp. Among his fellow-prisoners were a violinist, a clarinettist and a cellist who, with the composer at the piano, made its creation possible. Messiaen tells us that lack of food gave him nightmares and multi-coloured visions. Certainly the instrumental colouring plays a large part in the *Quatuor* and, besides the visions of 'the Angel who announces the end of time', there are also the composer's beloved birdsongs. The 1968 EMI account, led by Erich Gruenberg and with Gervase de Peyer the inspirational clarinettist, is in the very highest class, the players meeting every demand the composer makes upon them, and the fine, clear Abbey Road recording gives the group striking presence while affording proper background ambience. The bonus, too, is well worth having: *Le merle noir* exploits the composer's love of birdsong even more overtly. It is a delightful piece and is splendidly played and recorded here.

It is good to have a fine modern digital recording of Messiaen's strangely haunting *Quatuor*. We already know the calibre of David Shifrin's playing from his recording of Copland's *Clarinet concerto*. Here, like his colleagues, he fully captures the work's sensuous mysticism, while the solos of Warren Lash (cello) and Williams Doppmann have a wistful, improvistory quality: both *Louange à l'éternité de Jésus* and the closing *Louange à l'immortalité de Jésus* are played very beautifully. The Delos recording is naturally balanced and very realistic, while the ambience is suitably evocative.

The Dutch team on Philips are also given the benefit of very good recording which has transferred well to CD; moreover their account has the merit of outstanding team-work and Reinbert de Leeuw has a keen sense of atmosphere, though he does not dominate the proceedings. There is also some superbly eloquent playing from George Pieterson and Anner Bylsma.

With Peter Serkin at the piano it is not surprising that the RCA performance is a distinguished one. The clarinet solo, *Abyss of the birds*, is played with memorable eloquence by Richard Stoltzman, and the cellist, Fred Sherry, plays very beautifully in his *Praise to the eternity of Jesus*, while Ida Kavafian's long violin melisma has a striking, improvisatory quality. Considerable tension is movingly created in the work's closing section; and if there are minor reservations about the forward balance, the players certainly project as real and tangible.

Theme and variations.

*** DG Dig. 427 351-2 [id.]. Gidon Kremer, Martha Argerich – BARTÓK: *Sonata No. 1* ***; JANÁČEK: *Sonata.* **(*)

Messiaen's *Theme and variations* is an early work, coming from 1932, and is something of a rarity on disc. The distinctive personality is already discernible and the music's fervour is well captured here. Collectors will want this disc for the Bartók, which is marvellously played and excellently recorded.

PIANO MUSIC

Cantéyodjaya; Fantaisie burlesque; 4 études de rythme; Rondeau.

*** Unicorn Dig. DKPCD 9051 [id.]. Peter Hill.

Peter Hill, playing a Bösendorfer, is a sympathetic guide in this repertoire; he has a good feeling for atmosphere and makes out an excellent case for all these pieces, save perhaps for the somewhat repetitive *Fantaisie burlesque* of 1932, which outstays its welcome. The playing is consistently sensitive and has great finesse, and the *Cantéyodjaya* (1948) is particularly refined. The recording is unobtrusively natural.

Catalogue d'oiseaux, Books 1–3.

*** Unicorn Dig. DKPCD 9062; *DKPC 9062* [id.]. Peter Hill.

Catalogue d'oiseaux, Books 4–6: L'alouette calandrelle; La bouscarle; La merle de roche; La rousserolle effarvatte.

*** Unicorn Dig. DKPCD 9075; *DKPC 9075* [id.]. Peter Hill.

These scores derive their inspiration from Messiaen's beloved birdsong. Little of the piano writing is conventional, but there is no question as to the composer's imaginative flair, and the music is vivid and colourful to match the plumage of the creatures which Messiaen depicts so strikingly. Peter Hill prepared this music in Paris with the composer himself and thus has his imprimatur. He has great sensitivity to colour and atmosphere and evokes the wildlife pictured in this extraordinary music to splendid effect. He is recorded with the utmost clarity and definition.

Catalogue d'oiseaux, Book 7; Supplement: La fauvette des jardins.

*** Unicorn Dig. DKPCD 9090; *DKPC 9090* [id.]. Peter Hill.

In addition to the last book of the *Catalogue d'oiseaux* we have here *La fauvette des jardins*, composed in the summer of 1970, which the sleeve annotator describes as the perfect parergon to the cycle. It lasts over half an hour and is as long as *La rousserole effarvatte*. The composer himself has spoken with great warmth of this artist and, given what we hear on this disc, he has every reason to. Peter Hill plays with total dedication and, as was the case with earlier issues in the series, he is recorded with the utmost clarity and definition.

Préludes (complete); *Vingt regards sur l'enfant Jésus*.
(B) **(*) EMI CMS7 69161-2 (2) [id.]. Michel Béroff.

The *Préludes* are early works but, like *Vingt regards*, show Béroff at his most inspired, generating the illusion of spontaneous creation. Even for listeners not wholly attuned to Messiaen's sensibility and language, this can be strongly recommended – and it may even make converts to this original master. Clean, well-focused sound – but, even though the venue was the Salle Wagram, the close balance brings a lack of rich sonority.

Visions de l'Amen.
*** EMI CDC7 54050-2 [id.]. Alexandre Rabinovitch, Martha Argerich.
*** New Albion Dig. NA 045 CD [id.]. Double Edge (Edmund Niemann & Nurit Tilles).

Messiaen's *Visions de l'Amen* for two pianos was composed in 1943 for himself and his future wife, Yvonne Loriod, to play, shortly after his release from a Nazi concentration camp, where he had written the *Quatuor pour le fin du temps*. It is a long, eloquent work in seven sections with a powerful sense of mystery, and is played with uncommon conviction by the Russian pianist-composer, Alexandre Rabinovitch, with Martha Argerich at the second piano. Two pianos are notoriously difficult to balance and tune, but the recording does them justice.

The performance from Edmund Niemann and Nurit Tilles is hardly less arrestingly spontaneous. They capture the work's colour and atmosphere powerfully and evocatively - it is Messiaen at his most compelling - and some may prefer the sound of the New Albion recording. The two pianists are set back in a fairly reverberant but not blurring acoustic, which enhances the work's plangent palette.

ORGAN MUSIC

Complete works for organ: *Apparition de l'Église éternelle; L'Ascension (4 Méditations); La banquet céleste; Le corps glorieux (7 Visions de la vie des ressuscités); Diptyque (Essai sur la vie terrestre et l'éternité religieuse); Livre d'Orgue (Reprises par interversion; Première pièce en trio; Les mains de l'abîme; Chants oiseaux; Deuxième pièce en trio; Les yeux dans les roues; Soixante-quatre durées). Messe de la Pentecôte; La Nativité du Seigneur (9 Méditations).*
(M) *** EMI mono CZS7 67400-2 (4) [id.]. Composer (Cavaillé-Coll organ de L'Église de la Sainte-Trinité, Paris).

In an intensive series of sessions which began at the end of May and continued through June and July 1956, Olivier Messiaen returned to the organ in Sainte-Trinité, with which all his music is associated, and recorded everything he had written and published before that date. These performances not only carry the imprint of the composer's authority, but also the inspiration of the occasion. It is remarkable that the concentration of the playing comes over from the very opening bars of each movement, to grip the listener in its spell; and this applies especially to the more elusive works which create a pervasive atmosphere of spiritual mysticism. Messiaen reigned as principal organist at Sainte-Trinité from 1931 onwards and his technical command at the age of 48 is very impressive indeed; moreover there is a natural freedom and latitude in the playing throughout, which shows he was not in the least intimidated by the experience of recording definitive versions of his own music. His articulation has remarkable clarity, not least in the forward-looking *Livre d'Orgue* (1951), which at its heart offers the most explicit and delightful of all the the representations of his beloved *Chants d'oiseaux* (blackbird, robin, thrush and nightingale are all here). The large-scale works have a grip and compelling atmosphere that are unforgettable. No apologies at all need be made for the range, breadth and faithfulness of the recording, although some must be made for the organ itself, which is not always perfectly tuned. Yet the sounds it can produce are always aurally stimulating, not least in the opening *Reprises par interversion* from the *Livre d'orgue* and in the spectacular *Combat de la mort et de la vie* from *Les corps glorieux* (where the pedals are so telling), producing wondrous orchestral effects, including something like a giant contra-bassoon. There is minor background hiss, which is not troublesome, and technically the CD transfers are a remarkable achievement.

Livre du Saint Sacrement.
*** Unicorn Dig. DKPCD 9067/8; *DKPC 9067/8* [id.]. Jennifer Bate (organ of Saint-Trinité, Paris).

What a sound! This is a quite spectacular recording and carries the composer's imprimatur. The *Livre du Saint Sacrement* was composed in 1984 and consists of eighteen movements of great intensity. Jennifer Bate makes an impressive and compelling case for these hypnotic pieces, and the recording is in the demonstration bracket.

La Nativité du Seigneur (9 meditations).
(M) *** Decca 425 616-2 (2) [id.]. Simon Preston (organ of Westminster Abbey) – *La Transfiguration.* ***

La Nativité du Seigneur (9 meditations); Le banquet céleste.
❀ *** Unicorn Dig. DKPCD 9005; *DKPC 9005* [id.]. Jennifer Bate (organ of Beauvais Cathedral).

'*C'est vraiment parfait!*' said Messiaen after hearing Jennifer Bate's Unicorn recording of *La Nativité du Seigneur*, one of his most extended, most moving and most variedly beautiful works. For the CD issue, *Le banquet céleste* has generously been added, an intense comment on the religious experience which has inspired all of the composer's organ music. The recording of the Beauvais Cathedral organ is of demonstration quality.

Simon Preston is a convinced advocate of this score and conveys its hypnotic power most successfully. The Westminster Abbey organ produces the right kind of veiled colours to evoke the work's mysticism. This performance is by no means second best and makes a very generous bonus for *La Transfiguration.*

VOCAL MUSIC

Chants de terre et de ciel; Harawi (Chants d'amour et de mort). 3 Mélodies (Pourquoi; Le sourire; La fiancée); Poèmes pour Mi.
(M) *** EMI CMS7 64092-2 (2). Michèle Command, Marie-Madeleine Petit.

Michèle Command is here most characterful and firmly focused, with her accompanist just as warmly idiomatic. The three early songs of 1930 lead naturally to the two cycles from the late 1930s, more complex in their melodic lines. It is then that the ambitious Harawi cycle of 1945, subtitled *Chant d'amour et de mort* ('Song of love and death'), in another logical development reveals the full scope of the mature Messiaen's style, with its echoes of birdsong. *Harawi* is the ancient Peruvian word for that concept of love and death. This hour-long cycle belongs to what the composer regarded as his 'Tristan and Isolde' trilogy, along with the *Turangalîla Symphony* and the choral cycle, *Cinq Rechants.* Clear, undistracting sound.

La Transfiguration de Notre Seigneur Jésus-Christ.
(M) *** Decca 425 616-2 (2) [id.]. Sylvester, Aquino, Westminster Symphonic Ch., Loriod, Instrumental Soloists, Washington Nat. SO, Dorati – *La Nativité du Seigneur.* ***

This massive work of fourteen movements, divided into two parallel septenaries, sums up the whole achievement of Messiaen. Dorati holds the unwieldy structures together magnificently, and the brilliance and immediacy of the recording are most impressive. The opening percussion effects are very tangible, while the internal balance between singers and instrumentalists is managed ideally – the blend between chorus and orchestra rich yet transparent in detail – indeed everything is clearly interrelated within a sympathetic ambience.

Meyerbeer, Giacomo (1791–1864)

Les Patineurs (ballet suite, arr. & orch. Lambert).
(M) *** Decca 425 468-2 (3). Nat. PO, Richard Bonynge – TCHAIKOVSKY: *Sleeping Beauty.* **(*)

Les Patineurs was arranged by Constant Lambert using excerpts from two of Meyerbeer's operas, *Le Prophète* and *L'Étoile du Nord.* Bonynge's approach is warm and comparatively easy-going but, with such polished orchestral playing, this version is extremely beguiling. The sound too is first rate.

Il Crociato in Egitto (complete).
*** Opera Rara OR 10 (4). Kenny, Montague, Della Jones, Ford, Kitchen, Benelli, Platt, Geoffrey Mitchell Ch., RPO, David Parry.

This was the sixth and last opera which the German-born Meyerbeer wrote for Italy. It was enthusiastically applauded in Venice in 1824, a work which was credited at the time with breaking Rossini's dominance in Italian opera. It may sound very Rossinian to us today, but there is an extra weight in the orchestral writing which points forward to Verdi and later Italian opera. The musical invention may not often be very distinctive, but the writing is consistently lively, notably in the ensembles. With one exception – Ian Platt, ill-focused in the role of the Sultan – the cast is a strong one, with Dianna Montague outstanding in the castrato role of the Crusader-Knight, Armando. Della Jones, too, in the mezzo role of Felicia, whom Armando has abandoned in favour of Palmide, the Sultan's daughter, sings superbly with agile coloratura and a rich chest register. Yvonne Kenny is brilliant as Palmide. Bruce Ford, with his firm, heroic tone, and Ugo Benelli are very well contrasted in the two tenor roles. Though the chorus is small, the recording is clear and fresh.

Les Huguenots (complete).
(M) *** Decca 430 549-2 (4) [id.]. Sutherland, Vrenios, Bacquier, Arroyo, Tourangeau, Ghiuselev, New Philh. O, Bonynge.

Meyerbeer's once-popular opera of epic length has recently returned to the stage in London, so it is opportune that Bonynge's 1970 set should reappear in the catalogue on CD. In the recording his own passionate belief in the music is amply evident. It is good too to have Sutherland augmenting the enticing sample of the role of the Queen which she gave in one of her earlier recorded recitals (*'The art of the Prima Donna'* – see below). The result is predictably impressive, though once or twice there are signs of a 'beat' in the voice, previously unheard on Sutherland records. The rest of the cast is uneven, and in an unusually episodic opera, with passages that are musically less than inspired, that brings disappointments. Gabriel Bacquier and Nicola Ghiuselev are fine in their roles and, though Martina Arroyo is below her best as Valentine, the star quality is unmistakable. The tenor, Anastasios Vrenios, can easily be criticized in the role of Raoul in that this is too small a voice for a heroic part; but very few other tenors – and certainly not those who have been applauded in stage performances – can cope with the extraordinarily high tessitura and florid diversions. Vrenios sings the notes, which is more than almost any rival could. Fine recording to match this ambitious project, well worth investigating by lovers of French opera. The work sounds newly minted on CD. This is far preferable to the Erato set conducted by Diederich, recorded 'live' in 1988 (2292 45027-2).

Le Prophète (complete).
**(*) Sony M3K 79400 (3) [id.]. Horne, Scotto, McCracken, Hines, Dupony, Bastin, Boys' Ch. of Haberdasher's Aske's School, Amb. Op. Ch., RPO, Henry Lewis.

This recording anticipated the 1977 production at the New York Met. with the same conductor and principal soloists. But the fact that it was recorded before the stage performances meant that the usual spadework for recording a rare opera had to be gone through, and the sessions had more than their share of crises. That is reflected in the finished recording, which lacks the last degree of assurance. None of the soloists is quite at peak form, though they all sing more than competently. Nevertheless, with vigorous direction by Henry Lewis – rather brutal in the Coronation scene – there is much to enjoy. The recording is vividly transferred to CD but would have benefited from a more atmospheric acoustic.

Miaskovsky, Nikolay (1881–1950)

Cello concerto.
*** Ph. Dig. 434 106-2; *434 106-4* [id.]. Julian Lloyd Webber, LSO, Maxim Shostakovich (with SHOSTAKOVICH: The *Limpid Stream: Adagio*) – TCHAIKOVSKY: *Rococo variations.* ***

Miaskovsky's *Cello concerto* is a work of great beauty and its neglect is baffling. Rostropovich's pioneering account with Sargent and the RPO made a brief appearance on CD (with the Prokofiev *Sinfonia concertante*) but at full-price which doubtless inhibited its success. This is only its second recording in the West. It radiates an all-pervasive nostalgia, a longing for a world lost beyond recall. In its predominantly elegiac tone and its gentle resigned melancholy, it recalls the Elgar concerto. There was a time when the latter did not enjoy its current popularity and no doubt future generations will wonder at our long neglect of it. All credit to Julian Lloyd Webber for championing this piece and doing so with eloquence, and to Philips for recording it. It is not perhaps quite as concentrated or as strong a performance as the Rostropovich but that was made when the Russian cellist was at his prime. The Shostakovich *Adagio* makes an attractive and imaginative encore and the Tchaikovsky *Rococo variations* are played in their original form. Highly recommended.

(i) *Violin concerto, Op. 44;* (ii) *Symphony No. 22 in B min., Op. 54.*
**(*) Olympia OCD 134 [id.]. Grigori Feigin, USSR RSO, Dmitriev; (ii) USSR SO, Svetlanov.

The *Violin concerto* has a distinctive personality and a rich vein of lyricism. The ideas flow generously and the architecture is well held together; its slow movement in particular seems to look back nostalgically to a secure, genuinely happy world on whose passing the composer sadly muses. Grigori Feigin is the excellent soloist and plays with the right amount of warmth and virtuosity. The *Symphony* is a more powerful and ambitious piece and far more substantial than its immediate neighbours. Neither recording is new; both were made in 1974.

(i) *Lyric concertino in G, Op. 32, No. 3;* (ii) *Symphony No. 3 in A min., Op. 15.*
**(*) Olympia OCD 177 [id.]. USSR SO; (i) Verbitzky, (ii) Svetlanov.

The *Third Symphony* is an epic, ambitious work, conceived in the grand manner and cast in two long movements; its world is close to that of Glière's *Ilya Mourmetz Symphony*. It is a dark, powerful piece, and Svetlanov is a persuasive advocate. The *Lyric concertino* is less satisfactorily recorded. The playing is a little less polished, too – which is a pity, as there are imaginative and original touches in the slow movement which show that Miaskovsky knew his French music.

(i) *Sinfonietta No. 2 in A min. for strings, Op. 68;* (ii) *Symphony No. 27 in C min., Op. 85.*
** Olympia OCD 168 [id.]. USSR Ac. SO; (i) Verbitzky, (ii) Svetlanov.

The *Symphony*, Miaskovsky's penultimate work, is tuneful; its harmonic vocabulary scarcely embraces a chord that would be out of place in Borodin or Brahms – and the slow movement is particularly Brahmsian. It is an endearingly old-fashioned work, and is very much better played and recorded than the *Sinfonietta*, written in a similar idiom. The recording, which dates from 1980, was made in a warm acoustic; the sound image is in excellent perspective, even if the balance will be too recessed for some tastes.

Symphonies Nos. (i) *5 in D, Op. 18;* (ii) *11 in B flat, Op. 34.*
**(*) Olympia OCD 133 [id.]. (i) USSR SO, Ivanov; (ii) Moscow SO, Dudarova.

Miaskovsky himself called the *Fifth* his 'quiet' symphony; it is also pastoral in feeling and more introspective than Glazunov. The *Eleventh* is also conservative in idiom, yet the language is unpredictable; its distinctive melodic style is particularly evident in the finale. The recording of the *Eleventh Symphony* comes from 1978, and the *Fifth* is probably earlier: if neither is outstanding, they are eminently serviceable and comprise a more than welcome addition to this composer's representation on record.

Symphony No. 6 in E flat min., Op. 23.
**(*) Marco Polo Dig. 8.223301 [id.]. Slovak Nat. Op. Ch., Slovak RSO (Bratislava), Stankovsky.

This is one of the most ambitious of all the Miaskovsky symphonies. Epic in scale, about the same length as Beethoven's *Choral Symphony*, and with a choral finale it was written between 1921 and 1923. The music appears to meet the demands of the Soviet authorities for a monumental celebration of the Revolution, and its irony is certainly more muted than with Shostakovich. But in the finale, after the cheerful carolling opening from the horns, the quotation of the *Dies irae,* and the obvious reference to the 'Fool's theme' from *Boris Godunov* in the chorus, together with the oblique message of the text combine to pass on the message that all is not what it seems. The first movement (22 minutes) with its mixture of *Allegro feroce* and *Molto espressivo* is undoubtedly inflated, though it holds the listener, and the closing section is very touching. The *Andante* section of the scherzo also contains writing of much lyrical beauty (and has a theme which appears to derive from the second part of Stravinsky's *Rite of spring*); the slow movement is eloquent in a specially Russian way. The performance here, if not inspired, is persuasive, with the Slovak National Opera Choir thoroughly at home, and the orchestra responding to Robert Stankovsky's directness of manner. The recording is quite well balanced; the sound could be more sumptuous,especially in the matter of string timbre, but the effect is quite expansive. A thoroughly rewarding CD début.

Symphony No. 7 in B min., Op. 24.
** Olympia OCD 163 [id.]. USSR RSO, Ginsburg – KNIPPER: *Concert poem* etc. **

The *Seventh Symphony* (1922) is one of Miaskovky's finest symphonies, a much shorter work than its vast predecessor; though the influence of Glière and Scriabin are discernible, they are here assimilated. The pastoral writing in the *Andante* movement has great beauty, and the performance under Leo Ginsburg is very persuasive. We suspect an earlier recording date than the 1977 given on the sleeve. However, the sound is very agreeable and better balanced than the Knipper with which it is coupled.

Symphony No. 8 in A, Op. 26.
** Marco Polo Dig. 8.223297 [id.]. Slovak RSO (Bratislava), Robert Stankovsky.

Although the *Eighth* is not one of Miaskovsky's finest symphonies, it is still worth investigating. It is a big four-movement work, dating from 1925–6 and drawing on the legend of *Stepan Razin* for its initial inspiration. There are some characteristic ideas, and initially unfavourable impressions are soon dispelled as one comes closer to it. There are the usual reminders of Scriabin, Glière and Glazunov, and the middle movements are both strong. Neither the performance nor the recording is distinctive, but both are thoroughly acceptable; there is a lack of subtlety here, but not of vitality and commitment.

Symphony No. 12 in G min., Op. 35; Silence (symphonic poem after Poe), *Op. 9.*
**(*) Marco Polo Dig. 8.223302 [id.]. Slovak RSO (Bratislava), Robert Stankovsky.

The *Twelfth Symphony* comes from 1932; it is endearingly old-fashioned and has strong appeal. (Some of it could have been written in the 1880s – though so fresh is much of its invention that it is none the worse for that!) By the early to mid-1930s the adventurous artistic policies of the new Soviet regime were succumbing to the increasing Stalinization of the arts, so that it is perhaps no accident that this symphony is subtitled *Kolkhoz* ('Collective Farm'). Although some of the big rhetorical gestures of the *Sixth Symphony* are to be found in the second movement, there are also some pre-echoes of things to come in the later symphonies. It is highly enjoyable, particularly when it is as well played as it is here by the Bratislava Radio Orchestra under their gifted young conductor, Robert Stankovsky, who was still in his early twenties when this record was made. The tone-poem *Silence* dates from 1909, the year after the *First Symphony*, when Miaskovsky was still studying with Liadov at the St Petersburg Conservatoire. It draws for its inspiration on Edgar Allan Poe's *The Raven* – which must have been enjoying a vogue at this time, for in 1911 Sibelius was also setting it (these ideas eventually found their way into the finale of the *Fourth Symphony*). Silence has a strongly atmospheric quality with a distinctly *fin-de-siècle* air: if you enjoy Rachmaninov's *Isle of the dead* or Glière's *Ilya Murometz Symphony*, you should investigate it. It is perhaps too long, given the strength of its melodic ideas, but is full of incidental interest. The orchestra play with enthusiasm and they are decently recorded.

String quartets Nos. 3 in D min., Op. 33/3; 10 in F, Op. 67/1; 13 in A min., Op. 86.
**(*) Olympia OCD 148 [id.]. Leningrad Taneiev Qt.

The *Thirteenth Quartet* is Miaskovsky's last work, one of fastidious craftsmanship and refined musicianship. It is a beautifully wrought score, in which ideas of great lyrical fervour flow abundantly. The Leningrad Taneiev Quartet, a first-class ensemble, play with dedication in all three works and the recordings, though not of the very highest quality, are very acceptable indeed.

PIANO MUSIC

Piano sonatas Nos. 1 in D min., Op. 6; 2 in F sharp min., Op. 13; 3 in C min., Op. 19; 6 in A flat, Op. 64/2.
**(*) Olympia Dig. OCD 214 [id.]. Murray McLachlan.

The sonatas on this disc are all fairly early; the *First* is the longest. In its way it is an oddity; its opening, like that of the Balakirev *B flat minor Sonata* written two years earlier, is fugal – the theme is of considerable angularity – but much of the second movement is more akin to the early Scriabin sonatas. So, too, is the *Second*, though Taneyev, Glazunov and Medtner also spring to mind. The pianist, Murray McLachlan, is still in his early twenties and possesses a very considerable talent. An enterprising issue in every way, and well recorded on the whole, even though the acoustic ambience is not absolutely ideal.

Piano sonatas Nos. 4 in C min., Op. 27; 5 in B, Op. 64/1; Sonatine in E min., Op. 57; Prelude, Op. 58.
*** Olympia Dig. OCD 217 [id.]. Murray McLachlan.

The middle movement of the *Sonatine*, marked *Narrante e lugubre*, is dark and pessimistic, and quite haunting. McLachlan speaks of the 'enormous tactile pleasure' it gives to the performer, but it also grips the listener. As on the companion disc, this gifted young artist communicates his own enthusiasm for this music, and his playing is both authoritative and persuasive. Perhaps this is the record to try first, since both *Sonatas*, not just the more 'radical' *Fourth*, are of interest and substance. Good recording.

Piano sonatas Nos. 6 in A flat, Op. 62/2; 7 in C, Op. 82; 8 in D min., Op. 83; 9 in F, Op. 84.
**(*) Marco Polo Dig. 8.223178 [id.]. Endre Hegedüs.

Piano sonatas Nos. 7 in C, Op. 82; 8 in D min., Op. 83; 9 in F, Op. 84; Reminiscences, Op. 29; Rondo-Sonata in B flat min., Op. 58; String quartet No. 5: Scherzo (trans. Aliawdina): *Yellowed Leaves, Op. 31.*
**(*) Olympia Dig. OCD 252 [id.]. Murray McLachlan.

The sonatas on the Olympia disc are all from 1949, and thus were written in the wake of the notorious Zhdanov Congress when, along with Shostakovich and Prokofiev, Miaskovsky underwent criticism as mindless as that suffered by the Chinese musicians at the time of the Cultural Revolution. The music is of the utmost simplicity but has an endearing warmth. As in the earlier discs, McLachlan provides scholarly and intelligent notes. The recording is good though the acoustic ambience is perhaps not absolutely ideal.

The Marco Polo disc brings brings the last four sonatas: *No. 6 in A flat* dates from 1944 and shares the same opus number as No. 5. The young Hungarian pianist, Endre Hegedüs, is often the more imaginative interpreter: he colours the second theme of the *Barcarolle* section of the *Eighth Sonata* with greater tenderness and subtlety than Murray McLachlan on Olympia, though the latter has great freshness. Hegedüs is recorded in the Concert Hall of the Liszt Academy. The sound is a little wanting in bloom and his piano is not always in good condition; a technician should have been at hand to correct the tired notes in the second movement of the *Sixth Sonata*. On balance, then, honours are fairly even between these two artists.

Milhaud, Darius (1892–1974)

Le boeuf sur le toit, Op. 58; La création du monde, Op. 81.
*** Chan. Dig. CHAN 9023 [id.]. Ulster O, Yan Pascal Tortelier – IBERT: *Divertissement*; POULENC: *Les Biches*. ***

A most engaging account of *Le Boeuf sur le toit* from Tortelier and his Ulster players, full of colourful detail, admirably flexible, and infectiously rhythmic. Perhaps *La Création du monde* is without the degree of plangent jazzy emphasis of a French performance, but its gentle, desperate melancholy is well caught, and the playing has plenty of colour and does not lack rhythmic subtlety. The Chandos recording, although resonant, is splendid in every other respect, and so are the couplings.

La création du monde.
(M) *** EMI CDM7 63945-2 [id.]. Paris Conservatoire O, Prêtre – DUTILLEUX: *Le Loup*; POULENC: *Les Biches*. ***
*** Virgin Dig. VC7 91098-2; *VC 791098-4* [id.]. Lausanne CO, Zedda – DEBUSSY: *Danse; Sarabande*; PROKOFIEV: *Sinfonietta*. ***

La création du monde; Suite provençale.
(M) *** BMG/RCA GD 60685 [60685-2-RG]. Boston SO, Charles Munch – HONEGGER: *Symphonies Nos. 2 & 5*. (***)

Prêtre's recording of *La création du monde* is unsurpassed in catching both the bitter-sweet sensuousness of the creation scene and the jazzy pastiche of the mating dance – the rhythmic touch is very much in the authentic spirit of 1920s' French jazz. The 1961 sound has been transformed in the CD remastering: it is fresh and vivid, yet admirably atmospheric. The couplings are no less attractive.

Both Munch performances come from the early 1960s and are full of all the style and spirit you would expect from this combination. We enjoyed these performances when they were coupled together on one LP in the early 1960s. Munch's account of *La création du monde* has greater virtuosity and panache, if not more jazz feeling, than the rival mid-priced account from Georges Prêtre and the Paris Conservatoire Orchestra, made at about the same time, though the latter has much greater clarity and detail. The Boston recording always sounded a bit too reverberant, and still does. Milhaud always spoke of himself as a Mediterranean composer (he was born in Aix-en-Provence 100 years ago this year) and the *Suite provençale*, based on tunes by another Provençal composer, André Campra, is one of his most captivating pieces. A thoroughly enjoyable disc and, with two symphonies by his friend and exact contemporary, Honegger, thrown in, even at mid-price it is an outstanding bargain.

Milhaud's ballet, with its mixture of yearning melancholy and jazzy high spirits, comes off splendidly in Alberto Zedda's highly spontaneous account, its witty syncopations and brassy exuberance bringing an unbridled effervescence to offset the restrained blues feeling of the main lyrical theme. The performance doesn't miss the Gershwin affinities, and the very vivid recording makes a bold dynamic contrast between the work's tender and abrasive moments.

Suite française.
(M) *** CDWHL 2067; *ZCWHL 2067.* L. Wind O, Wick – GRAINGER: *Irish tune from County Derry* etc.; POULENC: *Suite française.*

Milhaud scored his *Suite française* for wind as well as full orchestra as he wrote it during his wartime stay in the USA and knew of the performance potential there by concert bands. It is an enchanting piece, full of Mediterranean colour and vitality. It would be difficult to imagine a more idiomatic or spirited performance than this one, which has excellent blend and balance. Vivid recording. This is an extraordinarily appealing work and ought to be far more popular than it is.

Symphonies Nos. 1 (1939); *2* (1944); *Suite provençale.*
❀ *** DG Dig. 435 437-2 [id.]. Toulouse Capitole O, Michel Plasson.

In the inter-war years Milhaud was known for his little three-minute symphonies and it was not until he was in his late forties that he embarked on a full-scale essay in the form. This was in response to a commission from the Chicago Symphony Orchestra and he subsequently recorded the work with the Columbia Broadcast Orchestra in the early days of LP. Those who possess that disc or the LP of the *Second* made by Georges Tzipine will know how richly imaginative, melodically inventive and rewarding these scores are and will be puzzled why they have not entered the repertoire. Sample the fourth movement, *Avec sérénité*, of the *Second* and you will see just how sunny, relaxed and easy-going this music is; try also the slow movement of the *First* for its powerful, nocturnal atmosphere. The Orchestre du Capitole de Toulouse and Michel Plasson play these melodious scores with total commitment and convey their pleasure in rediscovering this music. The recording is very natural with a refined tone and well-balanced perspective, by far the most successful sound to have been captured in the Salle-aux-Grains by any engineering team to date. The delightful *Suite provençale* is as good as a holiday in the south of France – and cheaper!

CHAMBER MUSIC

Duo for 2 violins, Op. 243; (i) *Sonata for 2 violins and piano, Op. 15.*
(*) Hyp. Dig. CDA 66473 [id.]. Osostowicz, Kovacic, (i) Tomes – MARTINŮ: *Violin sonata* **(*); PROKOFIEV: *Violin sonata.* *

Neither Milhaud work is otherwise available. The excellent sleeve-note tells us that Milhaud so disliked his *Sonata for two violins and piano* of 1914 that if he encountered it in a music room he would hide it away. It is beautifully crafted and has a charming slow movement but is very slight. Not so slight, though, as the *Duo*, the first two movements of which were composed at a dinner party given in California by Menuhin at which the violinist Roman Totenberg was also a guest. The finale was written the following morning in time for a dinner party *chez* Milhaud. Musically it is all rather like having *canapés* and *petits fours* and missing out the meal! Elegant performances from Krysia Osostowicz and Ernst Kovacic – and in the *Sonata* Susan Tomes.

Music for wind: *La Cheminée du Roi René, Op. 105; Divertissement en trois parties, Op. 399b; Pastorale, Op. 47; 2 Sketches, Op. 227b; Suite d'après Corrette, Op. 161b.*
(M) **(*) Chan. CHAN 6536; *MBTD 6536* [id.]. Athena Ens., McNichol.

Though none of this is first-class Milhaud, it is still full of pleasing and attractive ideas, and the general air of easy-going, life-loving enjoyment is well conveyed by the alert playing of the Athena Ensemble. One's only quarrel with this issue is the somewhat close balance, which picks up the mechanism of the various keys and which does less than justice to the artists' pianissimo tone. However, this can be remedied a little by a lower-level setting, and there is far too much to enjoy here to inhibit a recommendation; even if the overall playing time is not very generous, this is an excellent entertainment.

Sonatina for clarinet and piano; Sonatina for flute and piano; Sonata for flute, oboe, clarinet and piano; Sonatina for oboe and piano.
*** Orfeo Dig. CO 60831A [id.]. Brunner, Nicolet, Holliger, Maisenberg.

The *Sonata* is an ingenious and delightful piece, most expertly played here. The later *Sonatinas* have no less charm and polish, and are beautifully played and very naturally recorded. A strong recommendation for a very attractive concert.

String quartets Nos. 1, Op. 5; 7 in B flat, Op. 87; 10, Op. 218; 16, Op. 303.
*** Cybella Dig. CY 804 [id.]. Aquitaine National Qt.

The *First Quartet* is a beautifully relaxed, sunny work, rather Debussian in feel. The *Seventh* speaks Milhaud's familiar, distinctive language; its four short movements are delightful, full of melody and colour. The *Tenth* is attractive too, while the *Sixteenth* was a wedding anniversary present for the composer's wife: its first movement has great tenderness and warmth. The recordings are very good, though No. 1 appears to be recorded in a slightly drier acoustic than its companions. Individual movements in the quartets are not indexed. The Aquitaine Quartet has excellent ensemble, intonation is good and their playing is polished. The recording has a wide dynamic range and a spacious tonal spectrum.

String quartets Nos. 5, Op. 64; 8, Op. 121; 11, Op. 232; 13, Op. 268.
*** Cybella Dig. CY 805 [id.]. Aquitaine National Qt.

The *Fifth Quartet* is not one of Milhaud's most inspired; the *Eighth*, on the other hand, has much to commend it, including a poignant slow movement. No. 11 has a splendid pastoral third movement and a lively jazzy finale; No. 13 has overtones of Mexico in its finale and a beguiling and charming *Barcarolle*. Both performance and recording are very good.

Minkus, Léon (1826–1917)

La Source (ballet): Act I; Act III, scene ii.
*** Decca Dig. 421 431-2 (2) [id.]. ROHCG O, Bonynge – DELIBES: *La Source* (Act II; Act III, scene i); DRIGO: *Flûte magique.* ***

Composed in partnership with Delibes, it is the contribution of Minkus that sets the style and atmosphere of *La Source*, very much inherited from Adam, though with less melodrama. The music is attractive, its melodic contours less positive than those characteristic of Delibes; but the writing has distinct charm and its picaresque evocation suits the slight narrative line. The score is beautifully played and Bonynge's affection is obvious; there is both grace and sparkle here. First-class Decca sound, too.

Moeran, Ernest J. (1894–1950)

(i) *Cello concerto. Sinfonietta.*
*** Chan. Dig. CHAN 8456; *ABTD 1167* [id.]. (i) Raphael Wallfisch; Bournemouth Sinf., Del Mar.

Raphael Wallfisch brings an eloquence of tone and a masterly technical address to the *Cello concerto* and he receives responsive orchestral support from Norman Del Mar and the Bournemouth players. The well-crafted *Sinfonietta* is among Moeran's most successful pieces: its invention is delightfully fresh, and there is that earthy, unpretentious musicality that makes Moeran so appealing a composer. The recording is a little on the reverberant side but well balanced and present.

(i) *Violin concerto. 2 Pieces for small orchestra: Lonely waters; Whythorne's shadow.*
*** Chan. Dig. CHAN 8807; *ABTD 1435* [id.]. (i) Lydia Mordkovitch; Ulster O, Vernon Handley.

The *Violin concerto* is a rarity in the concert hall and this is only its second recording. Though less striking than the *Symphony in G minor* (and not as consistent in inspiration), it is strongly lyrical in feeling. The first movement is ruminative and rhapsodic, its inspiration drawn from Moeran's love of the west coast of Ireland; the middle movement makes use of folk music; while the finale, a ruminative elegy of great beauty, is the most haunting of the three. Lydia Mordkovitch plays with great natural feeling for this music and, quite apart from his sensitive support in the *Concerto*, Vernon Handley gives an outstanding (and affecting) account of *Lonely waters*. Superb recording.

Symphony in G min.; Overture for a masque.
*** Chan. Dig. CHAN 8577; *ABTD 1272* [id.]. Ulster O, Vernon Handley.

Moeran's superb *Symphony in G minor* is in the best English tradition of symphonic writing and worthy to rank with the symphonies of Vaughan Williams and Walton. But for all the echoes of these composers (and Holst and Butterworth, too) it has a strong individual voice. Vernon Handley gives a bitingly powerful performance, helped by superb playing from the Ulster Orchestra, totally committed from first to last. With the brass cutting through rich textures with thrilling edge, the whole symphony carries more menace with it than in previous recordings, relating to both the dark nature-music of Sibelius and the pre-war period in which it was written. The *Overture for a masque*, a brash, brassy piece in its fanfare opening and Waltonian cross-rhythms, makes an attractive and generous fill-up. The recording is superb, spacious and full, with a dramatic range of dynamic and the Ulster strings sounding exceptionally sweet.

Serenade in G (complete original score); (i) *Nocturne.*
*** Chan. Dig. CHAN 8808; *ABTD 1436* [id.]. Ulster O, Vernon Handley – WARLOCK: *Capriol suite* etc. ***

The *Serenade in G* is a welcome addition to the catalogue, a work which has a good deal in common with Warlock's *Capriol suite* in its orchestral dress, which is the coupling on the Chandos issue. Both use dance forms from a previous age and transform them with new colours and harmonic touches. Moeran's work is more than twice the length of Warlock's and is mellower, more lyrical in style. Handley and the Ulster Orchestra present it with striking freshness and warmth in its original version. This includes the *Intermezzo* and *Forlana*, charming miniatures which were jettisoned after the first performance at the insistence of the publisher, who thought the piece otherwise too long. Handley proves otherwise. He also offers the lovely *Nocturne*, a setting of a poem by Robert Nichols for baritone solo and eight-part chorus, which inspired Moeran from its very opening line ('Exquisite stillness! What serenities of earth and air!'). It was much admired by Britten, who commented about its obvious debt to Delius, to whom it was posthumously dedicated: 'Of course the *Nocturne* owes much to the shifting harmonies of the senior master, but the twilight, nostalgic beauty of this music is Moeran's own.' It is given a wholly sympathetic performance and recording here, and the resonant acoustics of the Ulster Hall, Belfast, provide a warmly atmospheric ambient glow.

Fantasy quartet for oboe and strings.
*** Chan. Dig. CHAN 8392; *ABTD 1114* [id.]. Francis, English Qt – BAX: *Quintet;* HOLST: *Air and variations* etc.; JACOB: *Quartet.* ***

Moeran's folk-influenced *Fantasy quartet*, an attractively rhapsodic single-movement work, is played admirably here, and the recording is excellent, well balanced too.

(i) *String quartet in A min.;* (ii) *Violin sonata in E min.*
*** Chan. Dig. CHAN 8465; *ABTD 1168* [id.]. (i) Melbourne Qt; (ii) Donald Scotts, John Talbot.

There is a strong folksong element in the *Quartet*, and some French influence too; these pieces are stronger than they have been given credit for. Good performances and recording.

Molino, Francesco (1775–1847)

Trio, Op. 45.
*** Mer. Dig. CDE 84199; *KE 77199* [id.]. Conway, Silverthorne, Garcia – BEETHOVEN: *Serenade;* JOSEPH KREUTZER: *Grand Trio.* ***

Italian-born, Molino first settled in Spain, before going on to London and Paris, where he built a reputation as a violinist and guitarist. Unlike the other two works on the disc, this unpretentious trio brings a Spanish flavour in the guitar writing, pointedly brought out by Gerald Garcia. Undemanding music to complete a charming disc for a rare combination. First-rate playing and recording.

Molter, Johann (1696–1765)

Clarinet concerto in D.
*** Claves CD 50-813 [id.]. Friedli, SW German CO, Angerer – MERCADANTE; PLEYEL: *Concertos.* ***

Molter's *Concerto* is for D clarinet and its high tessitura means that, when heard on a modern version of the instrument for which it was written, the timbre sounds uncannily like a soft-grained trumpet – and very effective, too, especially when the playing is both expert and sympathetic. Here the accompaniment is good rather than outstanding: orchestral detail is not ideally clear, and the harpsichord contribution is only just audible. Nevertheless, this remains a most enjoyable collection, for the coupled works are equally interesting.

(i) *Double trumpet concerto in D (MS 330). 2 Trumpet concertos in D (MS 331 & 333).*
(M) **(*) Erato/Warner 2292 45061-2 [id.]. Maurice André; (i) with Raymond André; Paillard CO, Paillard – HUMMEL: *Concerto.* ***

Johann Molter was very prolific – he wrote 170 symphonies – but is best known for his trumpet concertos. They exploit the instrument's high tessitura, but are otherwise fairly conventional. The *Double concerto* is rather more striking than the solo concertos, but all three works here are very well played and accompanied.

Mompou, Federico (1893–1987)

7 Cançons i dansas; Impresiones intimas; Música callada IV; Preludio VII a Alicia de Larrocha.
❀ (M) *** Decca 433 929-2 (2) [id.]. Alicia de Larrocha – Recital: *'Musica española'.* ***

This is gentle, reflective music which brings peace to the listener. Its quiet ruminative quality finds an eloquent exponent in Alicia de Larrocha, to whom Mompou dedicated one of his preludes. The *Impresiones intimas* date from 1911–14 and is his first work of note. Like Falla and Turina, Mompou was drawn to Paris, and these pieces have absorbed something of the delicacy of Debussy. This is a record to dip into rather than to play all the way through: these pensive musings can easily seem aimless and inconsequential if they are heard in an unsympathetic mood. Each piece needs to be savoured in its own right and in the proper framework before its poetic feeling or its fine detail and well-calculated proportions make their full effect. Alicia de Larrocha plays these poetic miniatures *con amore*, and the Decca recording is quite superb. This is reissued as part of a generous and stimulating recital of piano music by Mompou's Spanish contemporaries.

Mondonville, Jean-Joseph Cassanea de (1711–72)

Titon et L'Aurore (complete).
*** Erato/Warner Dig. 2292 45715-2 (2) [id.]. Fouchecourt, Napoli, Huttenlocher, Smith, Monnoyios, Les Musiciens du Louvre, Minkowski.

Described as a 'heroic-pastoral', *Titon et L'Aurore* was presented in Paris in the mid-eighteenth century as a masthead work by the advocates of opera in French, countering the

Italian-language traditionalists. Mondonville, no heavyweight, fluently pours forth a sequence of crisp ideas in each of the three acts of this formal classical tale of the mortal Titon who has the temerity to fall in love with Aurora, goddess of the dawn. Some of the instrumental effects are most vivid. After a formal Prologue featuring Prometheus, Act 1 opens in total darkness with low bassoons and double-basses in duet, before a sustained crescendo heralds the arrival of the goddess. The three acts then bring a courtly entertainment which may miss the emotional intensity of a Rameau, but which is full of charming ideas, presented with freshness and vigour. Marc Minkowski proves an ideal interpreter, directing a performance of the highest voltage, which yet allows the singers a full range of expressiveness. Jean-Paul Fouchécourt in the almost impossibly high tenor role of Titon proves an outstanding example of the French *haute-contre*, sustaining stratospheric lines with elegance and no strain. Catherine Napoli is bright and clear, if shallow at times as Aurore, while Anne Monnoyios sings with ideal sweetness as L'Amour. Fitting neatly on two CDs, it makes an enticing set, very well recorded.

Monteverdi, Claudio (1567–1643)

Ab aeterno ordinata sum; Confitebor tibi, Domine (3 settings); *Deus tuorum militum sors et corona; Iste confessor Domini sacratus; Laudate Dominum, O omnes gentes; La Maddalena: Prologue: Su le penne de venti. Nisi Dominus aedificaverit domum.*
❀ *** Hyp. Dig. CDA 66021; *KA 66021* [id.]. Kirkby, Partridge, Thomas, Parley of Instruments.

There are few records of Monteverdi's solo vocal music as persuasive as this. The three totally contrasted settings of *Confitebor tibi* (Psalm 110) reveal an extraordinary range of expression, each one drawing out different aspects of word-meaning. Even the brief trio, *Deus tuorum militum*, has a haunting memorability – it could become to Monteverdi what *Jesu, joy of man's desiring* is to Bach – and the performances are outstanding, with the edge on Emma Kirkby's voice attractively presented in an aptly reverberant acoustic. The accompaniment makes a persuasive case for authentic performance on original instruments. The CD sounds superb.

Madrigals, Book 4 (complete).
*** O-L Dig. 414 148-2 [id.]. Cons. of Musicke, Anthony Rooley.

Under Anthony Rooley the fine, well-integrated singers of the Consort of Musicke give masterly performances of this dazzling collection of madrigals which readily encompass not only the vocal pitfalls but the deeper problems of conveying the intensity of emotions implied by both music and words. The flexibility and control of dramatic contrast, conveying consistent commitment, make this one of this group's finest records, helped by atmospheric but aptly intimate recording.

Madrigals, Book 6 (complete).
*** Virgin Dig. VC7 91154-2; *VC7 91154-4* [id.]. Consort of Musicke, Anthony Rooley.

Il sesto libro de madrigali (1614) includes the five-part transcription of the *Lamento d'Arianna* and *Zefiro torno*, and also pieces from Monteverdi's years at Mantua. The Consort of Musicke maintain the high standards of taste and artistry with which we associate them; and collectors building a Monteverdi library are unlikely to be disappointed by this example of their sensitive response to this repertoire. Excellent recording.

Madrigals from Books 7 and 8: *Amor che deggio far; Altri canti di Marte; Chiome d'oro; Gira il nemico insidioso; Hor ch'el ciel e la terra; Non havea Febo ancora – Lamento della ninfa; Perchè t'en fuggi o Fillide; Tirsi e Clori (ballo concertato for 5 voices and instruments).*
(B) *** HM HMA 901068; *HMA 431068* [id.]. Les Arts Florissants, Christie.

The singing of this famous group is full of colour and feeling and, even if intonation is not absolutely flawless throughout, it is mostly excellent. Much to be preferred to the bloodless white tone favoured by some early-music groups. Good recording. A bargain.

Madrigals, Book 8: *Madrigali guerrieri et amorosi (Madrigals of love and war).*
❀ (M) *** Ph. 422 503-2 (2) [id.]. Armstrong, Bostock, Fuller, Harper, Howells, Watson, Hodgson, Collins, Alva, Davies, Oliver, Tear, Wakefield, Dean, Grant, Glyndebourne Ch. (members), ECO, Leppard.

These two records include the *Madrigals of love and war* from Book 8 complete, save for the mini-operas, *Il ballo delle ingrate* and *Il combattimento di Tancredi e Clorinda* which were on a separate CD, just withdrawn as we go to press. This set provided a richly enjoyable start to a magnificent project of the early 1970s, nothing less than the complete recording by Leppard and his varied forces of Monteverdi's enormous total output of madrigals. With his star-studded cast Leppard ensures that there is nothing earnest or pedestrian about the results. Some – used to more acerbic textures – may complain at the warmth and richness, not only of the opening *Sinfonia* but also of the pair of magnificent six-part choruses which open each set (both *guerrieri* and *amorosi*), but here as elsewhere Leppard is demonstrating the enormous variety of expression of the composer's three described musical styles, *concitato*, *temperato* and *molle*, and the string accompaniments on modern instruments sound very much in place. It is fascinating that the opening madrigals of each section mirror the sentiments of the other group in reverse. The *Songs of war* begin with the words, 'Let others sing of Love, the tender archer', while the first *Song of love* suggests 'Let others sing of Mars and his followers'. Stylish, often dramatic, always expressive singing and playing – a delight from beginning to end, and the ear is consistently stimulated by the originality of Monteverdi's rhythmic treatment of his text. First-class, atmospheric recording and CD transfers of the very highest Philips quality.

Madrigals, Book 8: *Madrigali guerrieri e amorosi: Altri canti d'Amor; Altri canti di Marte; Chi vol haver felice; Hor ch'l ciel; Lamento della ninfa; Ninfa che scalza il piede; Su pastorelli; Vago augellato. Ballo: Volgendo il ciel per l'immortal sentiero.*
*** EMI Dig. CDC7 54333-2 [id.]. Taverner Cons. & Players, Parrott.

This collection, *Madrigals of war and love* from Book VIII, includes one of the most magical of all Monteverdi pieces, the haunting *Lamento della ninfa*, also one of the most striking included in the 1937 pioneer recordings directed by Nadia Boulanger. Parrott and his Consort and Players, with Emily van Evera the silver-toned soloist, treat it even more expansively than Boulanger did. Far from letting the idea of period performance undermine the emotional element, they draw out the pathos of the piece to the full with its languishing melody. All nine madrigals make up a splendid collection, ending on the *Ballo, Volgendo il ciel*, which in a long solo for tenor echoes the hero's big sequences in the opera, *Orfeo*. It is welcome to find such scholarly performers allowing such warmth of expressiveness in Monteverdi. Warm, full recording to match.

Madrigals, Book 8: Madrigali amorosi.
*** Virgin Dig. VC7 91157-2; *VC7 91157-4* [id.]. Consort of Musicke, Anthony Rooley.

Monteverdi published his *Eighth Book* in 1638 after a long gap in his madrigal output. (The previous collection dates from 1619.) As Denis Arnold put it in his *Master Musicians* study, this collection, like its companions, is 'never purely fashionable nor artificially difficult or experimental'. One of the very greatest of the songs is *Lamento della ninfa* (which Nadia Boulanger so memorably recorded) in what Monteverdi called the *stile rappresentativo* or theatre style, and that is affectingly done here.

Madrigals: *Addio Florida bella; Ahi com'a un vago sol; E così a poco a poco torno farfalla; Era l'anima mia; Luci serene e chiare; Mentre vaga Angioletta ogn'anima; Ninfa che scalza il piede; O mio bene, a mia vita; O Mirtillo, Mirtill'anima mia; Se pur destina; Taci, Armelin deh taci; T'amo mia vita; Troppo ben può questo tiranno amore.*
(B) *** HM HMA 901084; *HMA 431084* [id.]. Concerto Vocale.

A highly attractive collection of generally neglected items, briskly and stylishly performed. The most celebrated of the singers is the male alto, René Jacobs, a fine director as well as soloist. With continuo accompaniment, the contrasting of vocal timbres is achieved superbly. Excellent recording and very good value.

Madrigals: *Altri canti di Marte; Ardo avvampo; Hor che'l ciel e la terra; Ballo: Movete al mio bel suon; O ciecchi, ciecchi; Questi vaghi concenti.* (i) *Sestina: Lagrime d'amante al sepolcro dell'amata.*
(M) *** Decca 433 174-2 [id.]. Palmer, Holt, Bowen, Evans, Elwes, Thomas, Heinrich Schütz Ch., Norrington; (i) Schütz Cons.

These fine madrigals are given crisp, well-drilled performances by Norrington, not as relaxedly expressive as Leppard's outstanding Philips set, but most refreshing. The ample acoustic of St John's, Smith Square, adds agreeable atmosphere. The eloquent and moving Sestina is added for the CD reissue. One of Monteverdi's most unusual and original extended settings.

Madrigali erotici: Chiome d'oro; Come dolci hoggi l'auretta; Con che saovita; Mentre vaga Angioletta; Ogni amante e guerrier; Ohimè, dov'è il mio ben?; Parlo misero, o taccio; S'el vostro cor, Madonna; Tempro la cetra; Vorrei baciarti o Filli.
*** O-L Dig. 421 480-2 [id.]. Emma Kirkby, Nelson, Holden, Elliot, King, Thomas, Cons. of Musicke, Rooley.

Most of the madrigals on this CD come from the Seventh Book of 1619, very much a watershed in Monteverdi's output. In many instances they are for virtuoso singers and make a break with the past in that they call for instrumental accompaniment. The recording is excellently balanced. Strongly recommended.

Lamento d'Olympia; Maladetto sia l'aspetto; Ohimè ch'io cado; Quel sdengosetto; Voglio di vita uscia.
*** Hyp. CDA 66106 [id.]. Emma Kirkby, Anthony Rooley (chitarone) – D'INDIA: *Lamento d'Olympia* etc. ***

A well-planned recital from Hyperion contrasts the two settings of *Lamento d'Olympia* by Monteverdi and his younger contemporary, Sigismondo d'India. The performances by Emma Kirkby, sensitively supported by Anthony Rooley, could hardly be surpassed; her admirers can be assured that this ranks among her best records.

Motets: *Ego flos campi; Ego sum pastor bonus; Exulta, filia Sion; Fuge, fuge anima mea, mundum; Iusti tulerunt spolia; Lapidabant Stephanum; Lauda, Jerusalem; Laudate Dominum; Nigra sum; O bone Jesu, illumina oculos meos; O bone Jesu, O piissime Jesu; O quam pulchra es; Pulchra es; Salve regina; Spuntava al dì; Sugens Jesus, Dominus noster; Surge propera, amica mea; Veni in hortum meum* (with PICCININI: *Toccata X*).
*** Virgin Dig. VC7 91145-2; *VC7 91145-4* [id.]. Brigitte Lesne, Gérard Lesne, Josep Benet, Josep Cabré, Il Seminario Musicale, Tragicomedia.

The music on this disc encompasses all periods of Monteverdi's career; the earliest comes from his first published collection, the *Sacrae Canticulicae* (1582) composed when he was only fifteen. The three-part motets are all taken from this youthful publication; the solo pieces come from the 1610 *Vespers* music, which show the increasing interest he took in monody during his time in Mantua. Other pieces, such as the *Salve Regina*, come from the *Selva Morale* (1640), while *Pulchra es* and *Nigra sum* are performed on instruments alone. The solo motet *O quam pulchra es* is preceded by a *Toccata* by Alessandro Piccinini about which the excellent notes are silent. Gérard Lesne has sung with various groups including Les Arts Florissants and Hespèrion XX before founding his own group, Il Seminario Musicale; the performances here are expert and totally committed. Excellent recording.

Mass of thanksgiving (Venice 1631).
*** EMI Dig. CDS7 49876-2 (2) [Ang. CDCB 49876]. Taverner Consort, Ch. & Players, Parrott.

Following up the success of his reconstruction of Handel's *Carmelite vespers*, Parrott here presents a similar reconstruction of the *Mass of thanksgiving* as performed in Venice on 21 November 1631. Historical records show that the *Mass* was then celebrated in the grandest possible way in St Mark's in thanks to the Virgin Mary for the deliverance of the city from the plague, which had raged throughout the earlier part of the year. What Parrott and his team have sought to assemble is a likely sequence of music for the liturgy, surrounding it with introits, toccatas, sonatas and recessionals, as well as linking chant. At the heart of the celebration lies Monteverdi's magnificent seven-part *Gloria* from his great collection, *Selva morale e spirituale.* The *Kyrie*, sections of the *Credo* (including an amazing chromatic *Crucifixus*), the *Offertory*, *Sanctus*, *Agnus Dei* and a final *Salve regina* also come from that great collection. The only parts of the actual *Mass* written by another composer are the sections of the *Credo* that Monteverdi did not set. They are by Giovanni Rovetta; other contemporaries of Monteverdi contributing incidental items include Girolami Fantini, Giuseppe Scarani and Francesco Usper, to make a very grand whole. The recording is warmly atmospheric, with the brassy music at the opening and close approaching and receding and with appropriate sound-effects punctuating the ceremony. The performance is superb; the only reservation to make is that with only a little less linking material it would have been possible to fit the whole on to a single CD.

Missa de cappella a 4; Missa de cappella a 6 (In illo tempore); Motets: *Cantate domino a 6; Domine ne in furore a 6.*
*** Hyp. Dig. CDA 66214; *KA 66214* [id]. The Sixteen, Christophers; M. Phillips.

Harry Christophers draws superb singing from his brilliant choir, highly polished in ensemble but dramatic and deeply expressive too, suitably adapted for the different character of each Mass-setting, when the four-part Mass involves stricter, more consistent contrapuntal writing and the six-part, in what was then an advanced way, uses homophonic writing to underline key passages. Vivid, atmospheric recording.

Vespro della Beata Vergine (Vespers).
❀ *** DG Dig. 429 565-2; *429 565-4* (2) [id.]. Monoyios, Pennicchi, Chance, Tucker, Robson, Naglia, Terfel, Miles, H. M. Sackbutts & Cornetts, Monteverdi Ch., London Oratory Ch., E. Bar. Soloists, Gardiner.
*** Hyp. Dig. CDA 66311/2; *KA 66311/2* [id.]. The Sixteen, Harry Christophers.
*** EMI Dig. CDS7 47078-8 [Ang. CDCB 47077] (2). Kirkby, Nigel Rogers, David Thomas, Taverner Ch., Cons. & Players, Canto Gregoriano, Parrott.
*** HM/BMG Dig. RD 77760; *RK 77760* (2) [7760-2-RC; *7760-4-RC*]. Zanetti, Fisher, Cordier, Elwes, Kenmdall, Van der Meel, Kooy, Cantor, Stuttgart Chamber Ch., Cologne Musica Fiata, Bernius.
*** Decca 414 572-2 (2) [id.]. Gomez, Palmer, Bowman, Tear, Langridge, Shirley-Quirk, Rippon, Monteverdi Ch. & O, Salisbury Cathedral Boys' Ch., Jones Brass Ens., Murrow Recorder Cons., Gardiner.

Recorded in conjunction with a video performance for television, Gardiner's second recording of the *Vespers* vividly captures the spatial effects that a performance in the Basilica of St Mark's, Venice, made possible. Instead of being consistently placed close, solo voices are beautifully presented in perspective, heightening the atmosphere. Gardiner made his earlier recording for Decca in 1974 using modern instruments, but since then the art of period performance has developed out of all recognition. Here, with the English Baroque Soloists and a team of soloists less starry but more aptly scaled than in 1974, all of them firm and clear, he directs a performance even more compellingly dramatic. It would be hard to better such young soloists as the counter-tenor Michael Chance, the tenor Mark Tucker and the bass Bryn Terfel. Unlike most period performances, this one does not aim to present the *Vespers* on a small scale in a liturgical context. Unashamedly Gardiner refuses to miniaturize this most magnificent of early choral works. Without inflating the instrumental accompaniment – using six string-players only, plus elaborate continuo and six brass from His Majesties Sackbutts and Cornetts – he combines clarity and urgency with grandeur. The difference this time is less one of scale than of freedom of expression, for, even more than in 1974, he directs with panache. Some will still prefer the more intimate, liturgically based view of Parrott or Christophers; but Gardiner's version more than any other conveys the physical thrill which above all has established this long-neglected work as music for today, bringing it into the central repertory alongside the choral masterpieces of later centuries. Treating it in this way as a concert work, Gardiner (as before) does not include plainchant antiphons, and so has room on the two discs for the superb alternative setting of the *Magnificat*, in six voices instead of seven. Recorded back in England with most of the same forces, that supplement brings sound marginally less spacious but more sharply focused, in another dedicated performance.

The Sixteen's version of Monteverdi's 1610 *Vespers* on Hyperion, beautifully scaled, presents a liturgical performance of what the scholar, Graham Dixon, suggests as Monteverdi's original conception. Dixon noted that this was one of the texts used in the Gonzaga family's traditional celebrations for their patron saint, St Barbara. He infers from this that Monteverdi's first idea was to be a work in her honour. In practice the occasional changes of text are minimal; the booklet accompanying the set even includes an order of tracks if anyone wishes to hear the *Vespers* in traditional form. As it is, with a liturgical approach, the performance includes not only relevant Gregorian chant but antiphon substitutes, including a magnificent motet of Palestrina, obviously relevant, *Gaude Barbara.* The scale of the performance is very satisfying, with The Sixteen augmented to 22 singers (7.4.6.5) and with members of the group taking the eight solo roles. Christophers provides a mean between John Eliot Gardiner's unashamedly grand view with modern instruments and pitch and Andrew Parrott's vital, scholarly re-creation of an intimate, princely devotion.

Though Andrew Parrott uses minimal forces, with generally one instrument and one voice per part, so putting the work on a chamber scale in a small church setting, its grandeur comes out superbly through its very intensity. Far more than usual with antiphons in Gregorian chant it becomes a liturgical celebration. Brilliant singing here by the virtuoso soloists, above all by Nigel

Rogers, whose distinctive timbre may not suit every ear but who has an airy precision and flexibility to give expressive meaning to even the most taxing passages. Fine contributions too from Parrott's chosen groups of players and singers, and warm, atmospheric recording, with an ecclesiastical ambience which yet allows ample detail.

With excellent soloists, choir and players, Frieder Bernius directs an outstandingly fresh reading. In his pursuit of a liturgical approach Bernius is not as comprehensive as Parrott; but in fresh and immediate sound he draws performances from his team which are at once rhythmically lively and beautifully moulded. The moments of waywardness, as in *Laudate pueri*, are few, and even then the result is characterful. It is a pity that the booklet fails to identify which soloist sings what; and the second disc brings short measure; but nevertheless for some this will be a first choice.

Gardiner's earlier Decca recording was made in 1974, before he had been won over entirely to the claims of the authentic school. Modern instruments are used and women's voices, but Gardiner's rhythms are so resilient that the result is more exhilarating as well as grander. Singing and playing are exemplary, and the recording is one of Decca's most vividly atmospheric, with relatively large forces presented and placed against a helpful, reverberant acoustic.

Vespri di S. Giovanni Battista.
*** Ph. Dig. 422 074-2 [id.]. Netherlands Chamber Ch., Ch. Viennensis, Amsterdam Monteverdi Ens., Gustav Leonhardt.

This is a conjectural reconstruction of an actual performance directed by the composer; although the emphasis has to be on the conjectural, both the music itself and the performances are delightful. Apart from Monteverdi's settings of *Dixit Dominus*, *Confitebor tibi*, *Laudate pueri* and *Magnificat*, there are toccatas by Giovanni Gabrieli, a motet by Alessandro Grandi (*c.* 1575–1630), and two sonatas by Dario Castello (whose dates are uncertain). The recording, made in Utrecht in an ideal acoustic, is a model of its kind.

OPERA AND OPERA-BALLET

Il ballo delle ingrate; Sestina: Lagrime d'amante al sepolcro dell'amata.
**(*) HM Dig. HMC 901108; *HMC 401108* [id.]. Les Arts Florissants, Christie.

William Christie directs refreshingly dramatic accounts of both *Il ballo delle ingrate* and the *Sestina*. His singers have been chosen for character and bite rather than for beauty of tone, and the final lament of *Il ballo* is spoilt by exaggerated plaintiveness, but (particularly in the *Sestina*) the boldness of Christie's interpretation makes for very compelling performances, beautifully recorded. The note on the CD version irritatingly omits details of the soloists.

Il combattimento di Tancredi e Clorinda. L'Arianna: Lasciatemi Morire (Ariadne's lament) (with FARINA: *Sonata (La Desperata).* ROSSI: *Sonata sopra l'aria di Ruggiero.* FONTANA: *Sonata a tre violini.* MARINI: *Passacaglia a 4. Sonata sopra la Monica; Eco a tre violini.* BUONAMENTE: *Sonata a tre violini*).
**(*) DG 415 296-2 [id.]. C. Watkinson, Rogers, Kwella, David Thomas, Col. Mus. Ant., Goebel.

Carolyn Watkinson's singing of the *Lament* is finely controlled and certainly dramatic. So too is the performance of the touching and powerfully imaginative narrative about the battle of Tancredi and Clorinda, which understandably moved the audience to tears at its première. The other pieces are of more mixed appeal. Highlights are Fontana's engaging *Sonata for three violins* and Marini's ingenious *Eco a tre violini*, which is performed here to great effect, with the imitations echoing into the distance. Elsewhere, the slightly spiky sounds produced by the string players, with the close microphones bringing a touch of edginess, may not appeal to all tastes.

L'Incoronazione di Poppea.
*** Virgin Dig. VCT7 90775-2; *VCT 790775-4* (3) [id.]. Arleen Augér, Della Jones, Linda Hirst, James Bowman, City of L. Bar. Sinfonia, Hickox.
**(*) HM Dig. HMC 901330/2 [id.]. Borst, Laurens, Köhler, Larmore, Schopper, Lootens, Concerto Vocale, Jacobs.

The tender expressiveness of Arleen Augér in the title-role of Monteverdi's elusive masterpiece goes with a performance from Richard Hickox and the City of London Sinfonia which consistently reflects the fact that it was recorded in conjunction with a stage production. Hickox, following the latest scholarship, daringly uses a very spare accompaniment of continuo instruments, contrasting not just with the opulent score presented at Glyndebourne by Raymond Leppard, but with the previous period performance on record, that of Nikolaus

Harnoncourt and the Concentus Musicus of Vienna, who has a far wider, more abrasive range of instrumental sound. Hickox overcomes the problems of that self-imposed limitation by choosing the widest possible range of speeds. So the exuberant Nero–Lucan duet after the death of Seneca is very fast and brilliant, while the heavenly final duet of the lovers – apparently not by Monteverdi at all – is extremely slow, rapt and gentle. The purity of Augér's soprano may make Poppea less of a scheming seducer than she should be, but it is Monteverdi's music for the heroine which makes her so sympathetic in this oddly slanted, equivocal picture of Roman history, and one that has never sounded subtler or more lovely on record than here. Taking the castrato role of Nero, Della Jones sings very convincingly with full, rather boyish tone, while Gregory Reinhart is magnificent in the bass role of Seneca. James Bowman is a fine Ottone, with smaller parts taken by such excellent young singers as Catherine Denley, John Graham-Hall, Mark Tucker and Janice Watson. Linda Hirst sounds too raw of tone for Ottavia, making her a scold rather than a sympathetic suffering widow. Squeezed on to three well-filled CDs, the opera comes with libretto, translation and excellent notes by Clifford Bartlett.

Like the Virgin set conducted by Richard Hickox, the one directed by René Jacobs was recorded immediately after stage performances. This helps to give it fluency, though neither the characterization nor the timing of dialogue gives quite the same illusion of staging. Danielle Borst as Poppea and the Nerone of Guillemette Laurens are both fresh and stylish, if not quite as sharply distinctive as their counterparts. With the exception of a tremulous counter-tenor as Ottone, this is a strong cast, with such fine singers as Guy de Mey and Dominique Visse in subsidiary roles, and with Jennifer Larmore as the wronged Ottavia far richer and more sympathetic than her opposite number. Jacobs' restoration of instrumental ritornellos between scenes is welcome, even if Hickox's balder treatment often brings extra gravity. Excellent, clear recording.

Orfeo (opera): complete.
*** DG Dig. 419 250-2 (2) [id.]. Rolfe Johnson, Baird, Lynne Dawson, Von Otter, Argenta, Robson, Monteverdi Ch., E. Bar. Soloists, Gardiner.

John Eliot Gardiner very effectively balances the often-conflicting demands of authentic performance – when this pioneering opera was originally presented intimately – and the obvious grandeur of the concept. So the 21-strong Monteverdi Choir conveys, on the one hand, high tragedy to the full, yet sings the lighter commentary from nymphs and shepherds with astonishing crispness, often at top speed. However, Gardiner is strong on pacing. He gives full and moving expansion to such key passages as the messenger's report of Euridice's death, sung with agonizing intensity by Anne Sophie von Otter. Lynne Dawson is also outstanding as the allegorical figure of Music in the *Prologue*, while Anthony Rolfe Johnson shows his formidable versatility in the title-role. This is a set to take you through the story with new involvement. Though editing is not always immaculate, the recording on CD is vivid and full of presence.

Moody, James (born 1907)

(i) *Quintet for harmonica and string quartet;* (ii) *Suite dans le style français.*
*** Chan. Dig. CHAN 8802; *ABTD 1202* [id.]. Tommy Reilly; (i) Hindar Qt; (ii) Skaila Kanga – JACOB: *Divertimento.* ***

James Moody has been Tommy Reilly's pianist for over thirty years and he learned to play the harmonica so that he could compose for his partner. His *Suite in the French style* may be pastiche but its impressionism is highly beguiling, especially when Reilly and Skaila Kanga create such exquisite textures. The *Quintet* is more ambitious, less charming perhaps, but likely to prove even more rewarding on investigation, especially the very diverse theme and variations of the finale, the longest movement. The performance and recording are hardly likely to be bettered.

Moret, Norbert (born 1921)

En rêve (Violin concerto).
** DG Dig. 431 626-2 [id.]. Anne-Sophie Mutter, Boston SO, Seiji Ozawa – BARTÓK: *Violin Concerto No. 2.* *

Norbert Moret is a Swiss composer who studied in Paris with Messiaen, Honegger and René Leibowitz and worked for some time in Vienna with Furtwängler and Clemens Krauss. His three-movement concerto, unaggressively avant-garde, subtitled *En rêve*, was written for Mutter and is a slight but not unattractive piece with plenty of shimmering sonorities and a dazzling solo part. It comes with an essentially overprojected and ultimately cold account of the 1938 Bartók *Concerto*.

Mourant, Walter (born 1910)

The Pied Piper.
*** ASV Dig. CDDCA 568; *ZCDCA 568* [id.]. MacDonald, N. Sinfonia, Bedford – COPLAND; FINZI: *Concertos.* ***

Walter Mourant's *Pied Piper* is a catchy, unpretentious little piece for clarinet, strings and celeste, which in a gently syncopated style effectively contrasts 3/4 and 6/8 rhythms. It makes an attractive filler after the Copland *Concerto*.

Mozart, Leopold (1719–87)

Cassation in G (Toy symphony).
**(*) Ph. Dig. 416 386-2 [id.]. ASMF, Marriner – W. A. MOZART: *Serenade No. 13 (Eine kleine Nachtmusik)* etc.; PACHELBEL: *Canon and Gigue.* **(*)

Cassation in G: Toy symphony (attrib. Haydn). (i) *Trumpet concerto in D.*
*** Erato/Warner Dig. 2292 45199-2. (i) Touvron; Paillard CO, Paillard – W. A. MOZART: *Musical Joke.* ***

One could hardly imagine this *Cassation* being done with more commitment from the effects department directed by Paillard, while the music itself is elegantly played. The Minuet is particularly engaging, with its aviary of bird-sounds plus a vigorous contribution from the toy trumpet; and the finale, with its obbligato mêlée, is dispatched with an infectious sense of fun. After this, the more restrained approach to the excellent two-movement *Trumpet concerto* seems exactly right. The recording has plenty of presence and realism, with the balance very well judged, both for the solo trumpet and for the toy instruments in the *Cassation* – which are properly set back.

With the toy instruments played for all they are worth and more on Philips, the additions to the *Toy symphony* make the strongest contrast with Sir Neville's characteristically elegant and refined performance. This is generally effective, though the raucousness of the grotesquely mismatched cuckoo-whistle is hard to take. A good item in an attractive mixed bag, treated to warm, well-balanced recording.

Mozart, Wolfgang Amadeus (1756–91)

Adagio in E, K.261; Rondo in C, K.373 (both for violin & orchestra).
(B) *** Ph. 426 977-2; *426 977-4.* Grumiaux, New Philh. O, Leppard – HAYDN: *Violin concertos;* SCHUBERT: *Rondo.* ***

These two Mozart movements are far from slight: the *Adagio* is really lovely on Arthur Grumiaux's bow and the *Rondo* sparkles. Excellent, stylish accompaniments and very good sound. This makes a strong contribution to a splendid bargain anthology.

Adagio and fugue in C minor: see also below, in VOCAL MUSIC, under Complete Mozart Edition, Volume 22

Cassations Nos. 1 in G, K.63; 2 in B flat, K.99; 3 Divertimenti for strings, K.136/8. Divertimenti Nos. 1 in E flat, K.113; 2 in D, K.131; 7 in D, K.205; 10 in F, K.247; 11 in D, K.251; 15 in B flat, K.287; 17 in D, K.334. Serenades Nos. 1 in D, K.100; 2 in D, K.131; 3 in D, K.185; 4 in D (Colloredo), K.203; 5 in D, K.204; 6 in D (Serenata notturna), K.239; 7 in D (Haffner), K.250; 8 in D (Notturno for 4 orchestras), K.286; 9 in D (Posthorn), K.320; 13 in G (Eine kleine Nachtmusik), K.525. A Musical joke, K.522.

(M) *** Decca 430 311-2 (8) [id.]. V. Mozart Ens., Willi Boskovsky.

There are many delights in these justly famous Boskovsky performances, recorded in the 1960s and '70s, and this single collection includes nearly all the major *Divertimenti* and *Serenades* which are not intended solely for wind instruments. The invention in the *Divertimenti* usually finds Mozart at his most gracious and smiling. The playing is so totally idiomatic and masterly that one scarcely thinks of the artists at all, only of the music. The *Serenades* are hardly less distinguished and are marvellously alive, with admirable phrasing and feeling for detail. *Eine kleine Nachtmusik* and *A Musical joke* (which, like the *Posthorn Serenade*, are also available separately – see below) are as fine as any in the catalogue. The recordings were made over a decade between 1967 and 1978 in the Sofiensaal, and the remastering throughout is strikingly fresh and vivid, with the warm Viennese ambience bringing bloom to the overall sound. The violins are brightly lit, but generally the transfers are most impressively managed.

Complete Mozart Edition, Volume 3: *Cassations Nos. 1 in G, K.63; 2 in B flat, K.99; Divertimento No. 2 in D, K.131; Galimathias musicum, K.32; Serenades Nos. 1 in D, K.100* (with *March in D, K.62); 3 in D, K.185* (with *March in D, K.189); 4 in D (Colloredo), K.203* (with *March in D, K.237); 5 in D, K.204* (with *March in D, K.215); 6 in D (Serenata notturna), K.239; 7 in D (Haffner), K.250* (with *March in D, K.249); 8 in D (Notturno for 4 orchestras), K.286; 9 in D (Posthorn), K.320* (with *Marches in D, K.335/1–2); 13 in G (Eine kleine Nachtmusik), K.525.*
(M) *** Ph. Dig. 422 503-2 (7) [id.]. ASMF, Sir Neville Marriner.

Marriner and his Academy are at their very finest here and make a very persuasive case for giving these works on modern instruments. The playing has much finesse, yet its cultivated polish never brings a hint of blandness or lethargy; it is smiling, yet full of energy and sparkle. In the concertante violin roles Iona Brown is surely an ideal soloist, her playing full of grace. The novelty is the inclusion of the amazingly mature-sounding *Galimathias musicum*, written in 1766 when the composer was ten years old. The scoring and invention are delightfully fresh and the seventeen movements are engagingly varied, even interpolating a brief chorus in No. 8, presumably meant to be sung by the orchestra, but here performed with considerable refinement. Throughout this set the digital recording brings an almost ideal combination of bloom and vividness, achieving a natural balance without loss of inner definition, even though the acoustic is fairly reverberant.

Cassations Nos. 1 in G, K.63; 2 in B flat, K.99; Adagio and fugue in C min., K.546.
*** Capriccio Dig. 10 192 [id.]. Salzburg Camerata, Végh.

These excellent performances of the early *Cassations*, so full of attractive invention, can be strongly recommended. The playing combines vitality with finesse and the allegros have an attractively light resilience and, to make a proper contrast, the Camerata under Végh find plenty of drama in the *Adagio and fugue*. Very good recording in a warm acoustic.

CONCERTOS

Complete Mozart Edition, Volume 9: (i) *Bassoon concerto;* (ii) *Clarinet concerto;* (iii) *Flute concertos Nos. 1–2; Andante in C for flute & orchestra;* (iii; iv) *Flute and harp concerto;* (v) *Horn concertos Nos. 1–4; Concert rondo in E flat for horn and orchestra;* (vi) *Oboe concerto. Sinfonia concertante in E flat, K.297b; Sinfonia concertante in E flat, K.297b* (reconstructed R. Levin).
(M) **(*) Ph. Dig. 422 509-2 (5) [id.]. (i) Thunemann; (ii) Leister; (iii) Grafenauer; (iv) Graf; (v) Damm; (vi) Holliger; ASMF, Marriner (except (vi) Holliger).

The principal wind concertos here are recent digital versions. They are all well played and recorded, notably the works for flute, while Holliger does not disappoint in the *Oboe concerto* (this is his third recording). However, there is a slightly impersonal air about the accounts of the *Bassoon* and *Clarinet concertos*, well played though they are; and there are more individual sets of the works for horn. The *Sinfonia concertante* is offered both in the version we usually hear (recorded in 1972, with the performance attractively songful and elegant) and in a more modern recording of a conjectural reconstruction by Robert Levin, based on the material in the four wind parts.

Bassoon concerto in B flat.
*** Denon Dig. CO 79281 [id.]. Werba, V. String Soloists, Honeck – HUMMEL; WEBER: *Concertos.* ***

Though not quite as individual as some versions, Michael Weber's account does not lack character or geniality and he is well accompanied and recorded. He features the cadenzas by Eusebius Mandyczewski to good effect. If the couplings are suitable this is recommendable.

(i) *Bassoon concerto in B flat, K.191;* (ii) *Clarinet concerto in A, K.622.*
**(*) Claves Dig. CD 50-8205 [id.]. (i) Thunemann; (ii) Friedli; Zurich CO, Stoutz.

The performances on the Claves CD are first class, fresh and direct, sensitive without affectionate lingering, but with slow movements nicely expressive, and with plenty of vitality elsewhere. Klaus Thunemann's woody bassoon timbre has lots of character (although not all will take to his vibrato). The digital recording is bright, fresh and clean.

(i) *Bassoon concerto in B flat, K.191;* (ii) *Clarinet concerto in A, K.622;* (iii) *Flute concerto No.1 in G, K.313; Andante in C, K.315;* (iii; iv) *Flute and harp concerto in C, K.299;* (v) *Horn concertos Nos. 1–4;* (vi) *Oboe concerto in C, K.314; Sinfonia concertante in E flat, K.197b.*
(M) *** DG Dig. 431 665-2 (3). (i) Morelli; (ii) Neidlich; (iii) Palma; (iv) Allen; (v) Jolley or Purvis; (vi) Wolfgang; Orpheus CO.

Randall Wolfgang's plaintive, slightly reedy timbre is especially telling in the *Adagio* of the *Oboe concerto* and he plays the finale with the lightest possible touch, as does Susan Palma the charming Minuet which closes the *Flute concerto*. The *Sinfonia concertante* for wind has three new soloists (Stephen Taylor, David Singer and Steven Dibner) plus William Purvis, and is pleasingly fresh; the players match their timbres beautifully in the *Adagio*, and again the last movement is delightful with its buoyant rhythmic spirit. All the works are given excellent modern recordings and this is a very persuasive collection, probably a 'best buy' for those wanting all the music in a digital format.

(i) *Bassoon concerto;* (ii) *Clarinet concerto;* (iii) *Oboe concerto, K.314.*
(M) *** DG 429 816-2; *429 816-4* [id.]. (i) Zeman; (ii) Prinz; (iii) Turetschek, VPO, Boehm.
(BB) **(*) Naxos Dig. 8.550345 [id.]. (i) Turnovský; (ii) Ottensamer; (iii) Gabriel, V. Mozart Academy, Wildner.

On DG, Dietmar Zeman gives a highly accomplished account of the *Bassoon concerto*, a distinguished performance by any standards. Prinz's account of the *Clarinet concerto* is also beautifully turned; both deserve a position of honour in the field. Turetschek is eminently civilized in the *Oboe concerto*, though his bright timbre is an individual one. The 1974/5 recordings are truthful and well balanced, with the upper range freshened on CD without being edgy.

In the *Oboe concerto* the soloist on Naxos, Martin Gabriel, is excellent. The clarinettist,Ernst Ottensamer, is also a sensitive player, his slow movement is full of feeling; and there is an accomplished performance of the *Bassoon concerto* from Stepan Turnovský, who has the measure of the work's character and wit. Recommendable, particularly at the price.

(i) *Bassoon concerto in B flat, K.191;* (ii) *Clarinet concerto in A, K.622;* (iii) *Violin concerto No. 3 in G, K.216.*
(M) **(*) EMI stereo/mono CDM7 63408-2 [id.]; *EG 763408-4*. (i) Brooke; (ii) Brymer; (iii) De Vito; RPO, Beecham.

Beecham's romantically expansive reading of the Mozart *Clarinet concerto* with Jack Brymer the glowing soloist is a classic recording, totally individual in every phrase, with conductor and soloist inspiring each other. The account of the *Bassoon concerto* has equal magic, thanks to the comparable partnership between Beecham and Gwydion Brooke. But the surprise here is the equally inspired and highly personal account of the *G major Violin concerto*, with Gioconda de Vito as soloist. She too conveys magic comparable to Beecham's own, with the slow movement again luxuriantly expansive. The 1958 sound in the *Clarinet* and *Bassoon concertos* has fine body and presence, but with some emphasis on the top in the transfer (which has developed since its earlier appearance). The 1949 mono recording of the *Violin concerto* is similar, but with a more limited range.

Clarinet concerto; Flute concerto No. 1, K.313; Andante for flute & orchestra, K.315; Flute & harp concerto; Oboe concerto; Horn concertos Nos. 1–4; Rondo for horn & orchestra, K.371.
(B) *** Ph. 426 148-2 (3). Brymer, Claude Monteux, Ellis, Black, Civil, ASMF, Marriner.

Jack Brymer's recording of the *Clarinet concerto* is the third he has made; in some ways it is his best, for he plays with deepened insight and feeling. The *Flute* and *Oboe concertos* are hardly less recommendable and the *Flute and harp concerto* is delightful, even if the instruments are made to seem jumbo-sized! Alan Civil's third recording of the *Horn concertos* is included, and this is discussed below.

(i) *Clarinet concerto;* (ii) *Flute and harp concerto in C, K.299.*
*** ASV Dig. CDDCA 532 [id.]. (i) Emma Johnson; (ii) Bennett, Ellis; ECO, Leppard.
(B) *** Pickwick Dig. PCD 852; *CIMPC 852* [id.]. (i) Campbell; (ii) Davies, Masters; City of L. Sinfonia, Hickox.
(B) *** Decca 421 023-2; *421 023-4.* (i) Prinz; (ii) Tripp, Jellinek; VPO, Münchinger.

Emma Johnson's account of the *Clarinet concerto* has a sense of spontaneity, of natural magnetism which traps the ear from first to last. There may be some rawness of tone in places, but that only adds to the range of expression, which breathes the air of a live performance. Leppard and the ECO are in bouncing form, as they are too for the *Flute and harp concerto*, though here the two excellent soloists are somewhat on their best behaviour, until the last part of the finale sends Mozart bubbling up to heaven. First-rate recording.

David Campbell's agile and pointed performance of the clarinet work brings fastish speeds and a fresh, unmannered style in all three movements. His tonal shading is very beautiful. The earlier flute and harp work is just as freshly and sympathetically done, with a direct, unmannered style sounding entirely spontaneous.

The Decca coupling dates from 1963. The balance between soloists and orchestra is finely calculated and the performances are admirable, sounding as fresh as the day they were made. Refinement and beauty of tone and phrase are a hallmark throughout, and Münchinger provides most sensitive accompaniments.

(i) *Clarinet concerto in A, K.622;* (ii) *Oboe concerto in C, K.314.*
(BB) **(*) HM/BMG Dig. VD 77509 [Victrola 77509-2-RV]. (i) Heinz Deinzer; (ii) Helmut Hucke; Coll. Aur., Franzjosef Maier.

Anyone looking for a bargain coupling of these concertos played on authentic instruments will find these performances characterful and spontaneous, with both soloists fluently mastering technical difficulties. Helmut Hucke's woody oboe timbre is distinctly appealing; if Deinzer gives a rather straight account of the central *Adagio* of the work for clarinet, this is otherwise an enjoyably fresh performance. The acoustics of the Cedernsaal in the Schloss Kirchheim bring a resonant mellowness to the violins, yet the digital sound has good definition.

(i) *Clarinet concerto in A;* (ii) *Oboe concerto in C, K.314;* (i; ii; iii) *Sinfonia concertante, K.297b.*
*** ASV Dig. CDCOE 814; *ZCCOE 814* [id.]. (i) Richard Hosford; (ii) Douglas Boyd; (iii) O'Neill, Williams; COE, Schneider.

The COE issue is a generous and attractive recoupling of three earlier recordings from the mid-1980s. First on the disc comes the *Oboe concerto*, and it would be hard to imagine a performance that conveys more fun in the outer movements, infectiously pointed and phrased, both by the ever-imaginative Douglas Boyd and by his colleagues. The wind soloists in this live recording of the *Sinfonia concertante* are four COE artists who each know when to take centre stage and when to hold back in turn. The variations of the finale are pure delight. Richard Hosford in his reading of the *Clarinet concerto* uses a basset clarinet with its extended lower range, allowing Mozart's original intentions to be realized. At slowish speeds he leans towards the lyrical rather than the dramatic, even in the first movement, and ends with a delightfully bouncy account of the finale. Alexander Schneider, a friend and associate of these players since the orchestra's formation, ideally draws them out with well-paced speeds and well-sprung rhythms. Full, atmospheric recording.

(i) *Clarinet concerto;* (ii) *Clarinet quintet in A, K.581.*
*** Hyp. Dig. CDA 66199; *KA 66199* [id.]. Thea King, (i) ECO, Tate; (ii) Gabrieli Qt.

Thea King's coupling brings together winning performances of Mozart's two great clarinet masterpieces. She steers an ideal course between classical stylishness and expressive warmth, with the slow movement becoming the emotional heart of the piece. The Gabrieli Quartet is equally responsive in its finely tuned playing. For the *Clarinet concerto* Thea King uses an authentically reconstructed basset clarinet such as Mozart wanted. With Jeffrey Tate an inspired Mozartian, the performance – like that of the *Quintet* – is both stylish and expressive, with the finale given a captivating bucolic lilt. Excellent recording.

(i) *Clarinet concerto, K.622;* (ii) *Clarinet quintet, K.581;* (iii) *Clarinet trio (Kegelstatt), K.498.*
**(*) Mer. CDE 84169; *KE 77169* [id.]. Joy Farrell, (i) Divertimenti, Nicholas Daniel; (ii) Divertimenti members; (iii) Garfield Jackson, Graham Johnson.
(M) (**) Testament mono SBT 1007 [id.]. Reginal Kell; (i) LPO, Sargent; (ii) Philh. Qt; (iii) Kentner, Riddle.

The idea of putting the three major Mozart chamber works featuring the clarinet on one CD is excellent, and it is a pity there are reservations to be made. Joy Farrell is a splendid soloist, phrasing with individuality and creating a full, glowing timbre. In the *Concerto* she uses a basset clarinet, and clearly relishes – often in an agreeably whimsical way – the throaty sounds it makes at the very bottom of its register, which Mozart so wittily contrasts with the rich upper range. The *Adagio* is gloriously sustained, and the finale is appropriately spirited with matching accompaniments. The *Quintet* is a fine performance too, the solo instrument warmly integrated with the strings; again the spacious account of the *Larghetto* is memorable. But the reverberant acoustics of St Edward the Confessor's Church, Mottingham, create a very ample texture and there is a loss of subtlety, even though the effect is easy on the ear. This lack of sharpness of focus is even more noticeable in the *Kegelstatt trio*, given an amiable, if not distinctive performance. While Miss Farrell dominates throughout, the pianist, Graham Johnson, does not show a very strong personality: his diffidence is noticeable at his very opening phrase.

Such is the magic of Kell's playing that it triumphs over CD transfers which – although supervised by Keith Hardwick – leave a good deal to be desired. The 78s date from 1940, 1941 and 1945 respectively; there is a lot of surface noise, particularly noticeable in the finale of the *Concerto*; and pervasive in the *Trio*. Kell's unique clarinet timbre emerges pretty well unscathed, but the orchestral strings sound thin and hollow, and the quartet sound is only acceptable. Astonishingly, within moments the ears adjust, and one revels in the artistry of a player who could nudge a rhythm naughtily, and put his imprint unforgettably on every lyrical phrase.

Flute concerto No. 1 in G, K.313; Andante in C, K.315; (i) *Flute and harp concerto in C, K.299.*
(M) *** BMG/RCA GD 86723; *GK 86723.* James Galway; (i) Lucerne Festival O, Baumgartner; (ii) with Marisa Robles, LSO, Mata.
(M) *** Ph. 420 880-2. Claude Monteux; (i) Ellis; ASMF, Marriner.
*** Ph. Dig. 422 339-2 [id.]. Irena Grafenauer; (i) Maria Graf; ASMF, Marriner.

Flute concertos Nos. (i) *1 in G, K.313;* (ii) *2 in D, K.314.*
(B) *** Pickwick Dig. PCD 871; *CIMPC 871.* Judith Hall, Philh. O, Peter Thomas.
(B) *** Decca 421 630-2; *421 630-4.* William Bennett, ECO, Malcolm – CIMAROSA: *Double flute concerto.* **(*)
(B) *** Pickwick PCD 807; *CIMPC 807.* Galway, New Irish Chamber Ens., Prieur.

Flute concertos Nos. 1 in G, K.313; 2 in D, K.314; Andante in C, K.315.
(BB) **(*) Naxos Dig. 8.550074; *4550074* [id.]. Herbert Weissberg, Capella Istropolitana, Sieghart.

Judith Hall produces a radiantly full timbre. Moreover she is a first-class Mozartian, as she demonstrates in her cadenzas as well as in the line of the slow movements, phrased with a simple eloquence that is disarming. There is plenty of vitality in the allegros, and Peter Thomas provides polished, infectious accompaniments to match the solo playing. The balance is most realistic and the sound overall is in the demonstration bracket.

William Bennett also gives a beautiful account of the *Flute concertos.* Every phrase is shaped with both taste and affection, and the playing of the ECO under George Malcolm is fresh and vital. The recording is clean, well detailed and with enough resonance to lend bloom to the sound.

James Galway's silvery timbre is instantly recognizable. He seems as unlike an original instrument as could possibly be imagined. Galway is well supported by the Lucerne orchestra, rather reverberantly recorded, with the solo flute placed well forward. The coupled *Flute and harp concerto* has seldom sounded more lively than it does here, with an engaging element of fantasy in the music-making, a radiant slow movement and a very spirited finale. Marisa Robles makes a characterful match for Galway and they are well accompanied.

Galway's Pickwick alternative is a bargain. The accompaniments, ably directed by André Prieur, are reasonably polished and stylish, and the recording (although it gives a rather small sound to the violins) is excellent, clear and with good balance and perspective. It might be argued that Galway's vibrato is not entirely suited to these eighteenth-century works and that his cadenzas, too, are slightly anachronistic. But the star quality of his playing disarms criticism.

Exquisite playing on the Philips record (with Claude Monteux) from all concerned. The only reservation is that the solo instruments sound larger than life as balanced. In every other respect this splendidly remastered disc is highly recommendable.

Anyone looking for a new digital recording of Mozart's *Flute and harp concerto* could be very happy with the stylishly conceived version by Irena Grafenauer and Maria Graf. Marriner's tempi are apt and the solo playing is highly sensitive, with Grafenauer's nicely focused timbre the right scale for the music. She plays with equal sensibility in the solo concerto and the *Andante*, K.315, its alternative slow movement. The recording is first class and is beautifully balanced.

The Naxos record by Herbert Weissberg and the Capella Istropolitana under Martin Sieghart can hold its head quite high alongside the competition. Weissberg does not have the outsize personality of some of his rivals but he is a cultured player, and the quality of the recording is excellent. In short, good value for money and very pleasant sound.

Flute concertos Nos. 1–2; (i) *Flute and harp concerto, K.299.*
(M) *** DG 429 815-2; *429 815-4* [id.]. Zöller, (i) Zabaleta; VPO, Boehm.

Karlheinz Zöller is a superb flautist. K.313 is a little cool but is played most elegantly, with pure tone and unmannered phrasing; the charming minuet finale is poised and graceful. The performance of K.314 is more relaxed and smiling. Zöller favours the use of comparatively extended cadenzas, and one wonders whether they will not seem too much of a good thing on repetition. However, the 1974 recording gives him a radiant timbre and he is very persuasive. The admirably played *Flute and harp concerto* is discussed below in its alternative bargain coupling.

Flute and harp concerto in C, K.299.
(B) *** DG 427 206-2. Zöller, Zabaleta, BPO, Märzendorfer – HANDEL; WAGENSEIL: *Harp concertos.* ***

The outer movements of this DG performance have an attractive rhythmic buoyancy. The flautist is a most sensitive player and his phrasing is a constant pleasure, while Zabaleta's poise and sense of line knit the overall texture of the solo-duet together most convincingly. Märzendorfer conducts with warmth yet with a firm overall control. In short, with fresh, clear recorded sound, this is highly successful.

(i) *Flute and harp concerto in C, K.299;* (ii) *Piano concerto No. 9 in E flat (Jeunehomme), K.271.*
(M) **(*) Erato/Warner 2292 45558-2 [id.]. (i) Rampal, Laskine, Paillard CO, Paillard; (ii) Pires, Lisbon Gulbenkian Foundation CO, Guschlbauer.

The cast-list here is strong and anyone who fancies this unusual coupling should not be disappointed. Both performances are distinctive; there is some highly sensitive playing from both soloists in the *Flute and harp concerto*, and the somewhat grave character in the account of the *Andantino* of the *Jeunehomme concerto*, makes a good foil for the finale which is full of sparkle. Good sound, though the 1959 recording of K.299 is obviously less modern than in the piano concerto which was made in 1973.

(i) *Flute and harp concerto, K.299;* (ii) *Piano concerto No. 12 in A, K.414;* (iii) *Violin concerto No. 4 in D, K.218.*
(M) (***) EMI mono CDH7 63820-2 [id.]. (i) Le Roy, Laskine; (ii) Kentner; (iii) Heifetz; (i; iii) RPO; (ii) LPO; Beecham.

This CD assembles three classic performances from the 1940s conducted by Beecham. The *Concerto for flute and harp* has a cool elegance in this 1947 performance with René Le Roy and Lili Laskine; and Louis Kentner's much earlier (1940) record of the *Piano concerto in A major*, K.414, is very enjoyable indeed. The Heifetz is a bit high-powered but marvellously played, of course, and it sparkles; at mid-price, this triptych makes a splendid bargain. The transfers are much smoother than the Beecham/Mozart symphonies, and in the *Piano concerto* Louis Kentner's tone has fine naturalness and colour.

(i) *Flute and harp concerto in C, K.299; Sinfonia concertante in E flat, K.297b.*
(BB) *** Naxos Dig. 8.550159; *4550159* [id.]. (i) Jiri Válek, Hana Müllerová; Capella Istropolitana, Richard Edlinger.

Richard Edlinger's account of the *Flute and harp concerto* is thoroughly fresh and stylish, and the two soloists are excellent. Although the *Sinfonia concertante in E flat*, K.297b, is not quite so successful, it is still very impressive, and it should (and indeed does) give pleasure. Both performances are very decently recorded in a warm, lively acoustic; in the lowest price-range they are a real bargain.

Horn concertos Nos. 1 in D, K.412; 2–4 in E flat, K.417, 447 & 495.
(M) (***) EMI mono CDH7 61013-2 [id.]. Dennis Brain, Philh. O, Karajan.
(M) *** Decca 417 767-2. Barry Tuckwell, LSO, Maag – HAYDN: *Concerto No. 1.* ***
(B) *** CfP Dig. CD-CFP 4589; *TC-CFP 4589.* Claire Briggs, RLPO, Stephen Kovacevich - HAYDN: *Trumpet concerto.* ***
(M) *** Teldec/Warner 2292 42757-2 [id.]. Hermann Baumann (hand-horn), VCM, Harnoncourt.
(M) *** DG 429 817-2; *429 817-4* [id.]. Gerd Seifert, BPO, Karajan.

Horn concertos Nos. 1 in D, K.412 (with alternative versions of Rondo); *2–4 in E flat, K.417, K.447 & K.495; Allegro, K.370b & Concert rondo in E flat* (ed. Tuckwell); *Fragment in E, K.494a.*
*** Collins Dig. 1153-2; *1153-4* [id.]. Barry Tuckwell, Philh. O.

Horn concertos Nos. 1–4; Concert rondo in E flat, K.371 (ed. Civil or E. Smith).
(M) *** EMI CD-EMX 2004. Alan Civil, RPO, Kempe.
(M) *** Ph. 420 709-2; *420 709-4.* Alan Civil, ASMF, Marriner.

Horn concertos Nos. 1–4; Concert rondo, K.371 (ed. Tuckwell); *Fragment, K.494a.*
*** Virgin Dig. VC7 90845-2; VC *790845-4* [id.]. Timothy Brown (hand horn), O of Age of Enlightenment, Kuijken.
(M) *** EMI CDM7 69569-2; *EG 769569-4.* Barry Tuckwell, ASMF, Marriner.

The new Collins CD is Barry Tuckwell's fourth recording of the Mozart *Horn concertos*, and it tends to sweep the board, except for those needing an original instrument performance and they are admirably served by Timothy Brown. Astonishingly, even after giving countless performances over the years, there is not a suspicion of routine in Tuckwell's newest versions. They are fresh, wonderfully musical, and played with rounded tone, and consistently imaginative phrasing. The accounts of Nos. 3 and 4 are particularly beautiful, and his earlier Decca digital record (410 284-2) of Nos. 1–4 alone, is now superseded by this new Collins CD. Tuckwell obviously spent considerable time with the orchestra before beginning to record, for there are many touches of detail in the accompaniments which give added pleasure. The Collins recording is in every way first class. Besides the *Fragment*, K.494a, Tuckwell includes not only the piece familiar as the *Concert rondo*, K.371, but an *Allegro* first movement which was planned to go with it, before Mozart abandoned the piece when he became preoccupied with his forthcoming marriage to Constanze. Tuckwell also includes his own alternative version of the *Rondo* finale of the *Concerto in D*, K.412, which is called No. 1, but was the last to be written. It was completed by Süssmayer, Mozart's pupil, after the composer died, but Tuckwell returned to Mozart's original manuscript for his revised version after discovering that Süssmayr had altered what Mozart had written. The two alternative finales are placed side by side on this 71-minute CD, so that the listener can make his own choice between them.

Those wanting to hear what Mozart heard will be delighted with Timothy Brown's authentic alternative. He uses an open hand horn without valves. Notes in the instrument's harmonic sequence which are not naturally in tune, are 'lipped' into pitch with admirable skill and precision. Other notes which are not available in the harmonic sequence are produced by 'stopping' the bell of the horn with the hand, which simultaneously alters both pitch and timbre. Brown uses stopped notes with especially smart effect in the Rondos, and more sparingly and more subtly in the lyrical music. His control of the upper range of the instrument is remarkably free and even, yet the ear is often subtly aware that certain notes are being contrived. Far from being a drawback, this tends to increase the range of colour. If the effect is inevitably less smooth and polished than with a modern instrument, it has great character. Brown's lyrical line is very persuasive indeed, and he handles the chromatics in slow movements very beautifully. In short these performances sound delightfully fresh, and give constant pleasure, and Kuijken's accompaniments are similarly attractive; indeed, although orchestral textures are light, bright and transparent, so cultivated is the orchestral sound than one wonders if at times the violinists forget they are playing original instruments! Timothy Brown includes the additional *Rondo* and also the *Fragment*, which (like Tuckwell) he leaves in mid-air, at the point at which the composer abandoned his manuscript. With first rate recording this is very highly recommendable; no apologies whatsoever need be made about the 'primitive' nature of the hand horn.

In our last volume we reported that current copies of the EMI reissue of Dennis Brain's famous 1954 record of the concertos with Karajan has been remastered, producing a marked improvement in the string tone. Alas, we are now informed that the remastering was done specifically for the American market, and quite recently copies have come from EMI offering the older transfer with its emaciated, shrill violins. So it is inadvisable to buy this CD without sampling it first. Fortunately, Brain's horn timbre remains unaffected. As for the playing, Brain's glorious tone and phrasing – every note is alive – is life-enhancing in its warmth; the *espressivo* of the slow movements is matched by the joy of the Rondos, spirited, buoyant, infectious and smiling. Karajan's accompaniments, too, are a model of Mozartian good manners and the Philharmonia at their peak play wittily and elegantly.

Tuckwell's first (1960) stereo recording of the *Horn concertos* re-emerges freshly on Decca's mid-price label, now shorn of the *Fragment*, K.494a, but offering instead Haydn's best concerto to make it more competitive. Peter Maag's accompaniments are admirably crisp and nicely scaled, giving his soloist buoyant support, and the vintage recording still sounds astonishingly well. However, EMI have also effectively remastered Tuckwell's second set with Marriner, and the 1972 recording sounds fuller, with slightly more body to the violins. This CD has the advantage of including not only the *Concert rondo* but also the *Fragment in E.*

Alan Civil recorded the concertos three times, but the earliest set, with Kempe, is the freshest and most rewarding. His sensitivity is present in every bar and Kempe accompanies benignly and with great affection. The warm 1967 recording has been cleanly remastered, although the RPO violins sound somewhat thinner above the stave than on the Tuckwell/Marriner recordings.

For those seeking a bargain digital set, Claire Briggs, principal horn of the City of Birmingham orchestra, here gives brilliant performances of all four *Concertos*, with the celebrated finale of No. 4 taken exceptionally fast. Even that is superbly articulated without any feeling of breathlessness, though it lacks some of the fun that others have brought.

Like Timothy Brown, Hermann Baumann successfully uses the original hand-horn, without valves, for which the concertos were written, and the result is not achieved at the expense of musical literacy or expressive content. Baumann lets the listener hear the stopped effect only when he decides that the tonal change can be put to good artistic effect. In his cadenzas he also uses horn chords (where several notes are produced simultaneously by resonating the instrument's harmonics), but as a complement to the music rather than as a gimmick. While the horn is given added presence and tangibility in the digital remastering, the brightness of the strings has brought some roughness of focus, since the original recording was mellow and reverberant.

Alan Civil's most recent set was made in 1973. The recording is obviously more modern and the performances are highly enjoyable, with Sir Neville Marriner's polished and lively accompaniments giving pleasure in themselves. The balance has the effect of making the horn sound slightly larger than life.

Gerd Seifert has been principal horn of the Berlin Philharmonic since 1964, and his velvety, warm tone is familiar on many records. His articulation is light and neat here and his nimbleness brings an effective lightness to the gay Rondos. Karajan almost matches his earlier accompaniments for Dennis Brain, and the orchestral playing is strong in character, although he never overwhelms his soloist. The 1969 recording now brings just a hint of over-brightness on the *forte* violins, but this adds to the sense of vitality without spoiling the elegance.

Oboe concerto in C, K.314.
*** ASV Dig. CDCOE 808; *ZCCOE 808* [id.]. Douglas Boyd, COE, Berglund – R. STRAUSS: *Oboe concerto.* ***

Douglas Boyd is never afraid to point the phrasing individually, spontaneously and without mannerism. Others may be purer in their classicism, but this is a very apt reading next to Strauss. Recorded in Henry Wood Hall, the sound is full and vivid.

Piano concertos

Complete Mozart Edition, Volume 7: (i) *Piano concertos, K.107/1–3;* (ii) *Nos. 1–4;* (iii) *5, 6, 8, 9, 11–27; Concert rondos 1–2;* (iii; iv) *Double piano concertos, K.242 & K.365;* (v) *Triple concerto in F, K.242.*
(M) **(*) Ph. Analogue/Dig. 422 507-2 (12) [id.]. (i) Ton Koopman, Amsterdam Bar. O; (ii)

Haebler, Vienna Capella Academica, Melkus; (iii) Brendel, ASMF, Marriner; (iv) Imogen Cooper; (v) Katia and Marielle Labèque, Bychkov, BPO, Bychkov.

Piano concertos Nos. 1–6; 8–9; 11–27; Rondo in D, K.382.
(M) *** EMI CZS7 62825-2 (10). Daniel Barenboim, ECO.

Piano concertos Nos. 1–6; 8–9; 11–27; Rondos Nos. 1–2, K.382 & 386.
(M) *** Sony Analogue/Dig. SK12K 46441 (12). Murray Perahia, ECO.

By omitting the four early concertos after J. C. Bach, Sony have been able to reissue the Perahia set on twelve mid-priced CDs. The cycle is a remarkable achievement; in terms of poetic insight and musical spontaneity, the performances are in a class of their own. There is a wonderful singing line and at the same time a sensuousness that is always tempered by spirituality. There is one slight snag: about half the recordings are digital and of excellent quality, but the remastering of the earlier, analogue recordings, especially those made in 1976/7, has not enhanced the violin timbre. Nos. 5, 12, 21, 22, 24 and 27 are acceptable, although there is a loss of bloom; but Nos. 8, 11 and especially 20 have varying amounts of edginess or shrillness, while Nos. 9, 13 and 14 have a lesser degree of thinness – which admirers of the authentic school may welcome. Others will prefer the rounder, more natural sound of the digital recordings.

The sense of spontaneity in Barenboim's performances of the Mozart concertos, his message that this is music hot off the inspiration line, is hard to resist, even though it occasionally leads to over-exuberance and idiosyncrasies. On balance, any inconsistencies or romantic touches seem merely incidental to the forward drive. These are as nearly live performances as one could hope for on record, and the playing of the English Chamber Orchestra is splendidly geared to the approach of an artist with whom the players have worked regularly. They are recorded with fullness, and the sound is generally freshened very successfully in the remastering, with the piano tone remaining natural.

The Philips Mozart Edition *Piano concertos* box is based on Brendel's set with the ASMF under Marriner. Throughout, his thoughts are never less than penetrating. The transfers are consistently of the very highest quality, as is the playing of the Academy of St Martin-in-the-Fields under Sir Neville Marriner. To make the set complete, Ingrid Haebler gives eminently stylish accounts of the first four *Concertos* on the fortepiano, accompanied by Melkus and his excellent Vienna Capella Academica; the sound is admirably fresh. However, on disc two the ear gets rather a shock when Ton Koopman presents the three works after J. C. Bach. Convincing though these performances are, it seems a strange idea to offer an authentic approach to these three concertos alone, particularly as at the end of the disc we return to a delightfully cultured performance on modern instruments of the alternative version for three pianos of the so-called *Lodron Concerto*, K.242, provided by the Labèque duo plus Semyon Bychkov, with the Berlin Philharmonic Orchestra accompanying in the most sophisticated modern fashion.

Piano concertos Nos. 1 in F, K.37; 2 in B flat, K.39; 3 in D, K.40; 4 in G, K.41.
*** Sony Dig. MK 39225 [id.]. Murray Perahia, ECO.

The first four concertos which occupy Perahia's present issue date from the spring or summer of 1767, when Mozart was eleven. Of course, they are not the equal of any of his more mature concertos; however, played with such grace and affection as here, they make delightful listening.

Piano concertos (i) *Nos. 1 in F, K.37; 2 in B flat, K.39; 3 in D, K.40; 4 in G, K.41; 5 in D, K.175; 6 in B flat, K.238;* (ii) *Concerto in F for 3 pianos, K.242.*
*** Decca 421 577-2 (2) [id.]. (i) Ashkenazy, Philh. O; (ii) Ashkenazy, Barenboim, Fou Ts'ong, ECO, Barenboim.

The celebrated recording of the *F major Concerto*, K.242, with Barenboim and Fou Ts'ong derives from the mid-1970s, but the others are new – and very good. In many ways these are delightful recordings, well ventilated and full-bodied and, for those who have been collecting Ashkenazy, they can be confidently recommended.

Piano concertos Nos. 5, 6, 8, 9, 11–27; (i) *Double piano concerto, K.365;* (i; ii) *Triple piano concerto, K.242. Concert Rondos 1–2.*
(M) *** DG Dig. 431 211-2 (9) [id.]. Malcolm Bilson (fortepiano), E. Bar. Soloists, Gardiner, (i) with Robert Levin; (ii) Melvyn Tan.

Malcolm Bilson's complete set of the Mozart *Piano concertos* appears on nine mid-price CDs. Bilson is an artist of excellent musical judgement and good taste, and his survey is the only one at present available on the fortepiano, though we gather that one is underway from Melvyn Tan, who features here in the *Triple concerto*. For the most part, there is little to quarrel with here and much to enjoy.

Piano concertos Nos. 5 in D, K.175; 8 in C, K.246. Concert rondos Nos. 1 in D, K.382; 2 in A, K.386.
*** DG Dig. 415 990-2 [id.]. Malcolm Bilson (fortepiano), E. Bar. Soloists, Gardiner.

Bilson's coupling of the two early, lightweight *Concertos* with the two *Concert rondos* demonstrates the advantages of period performance at their most telling. What comes out in these early concertos, perhaps even more pointedly than in later and more individual works, is the expressive tonal range possible on the fortepiano in even the simplest passage-work. Warm, well-balanced recording.

Piano concertos Nos. 5 in D, K.175; 25 in C, K.503.
*** Sony Dig. MK 37267 [id.]. Murray Perahia, ECO.

Murray Perahia has the measure of the strength and scale of the *C major*, K.503, as well as displaying tenderness and poetry; while the early *D major*, K.175, has an innocence and freshness that are completely persuasive. The recording is good, but the upper strings are a little fierce and not too cleanly focused.

Piano concertos Nos. 6 in B flat, K.238; 8 in C, K.246; 19 in F, K.459.
(BB) *** Naxos Dig. 8.550208; *4550208* [id.]. Jenö Jandó, Concentus Hungaricus, Mátyás Antal.

No. 19 in F is a delightful concerto and it receives a most attractive performance, aptly paced, the slow movement gently poised and with fine woodwind playing, the finale crisply sparkling. No. 6 is hardly less successful, the engaging melody of its *Andante un poco adagio* beautifully shaped and the finale most sprightly. If No. 8 seems plainer, it is still admirably fresh. With excellently balanced recording this is a genuine bargain.

Piano concertos Nos. 6 in B flat, K.238; 13 in C, K.415.
*** Sony MK 39223 [id.]. Murray Perahia, ECO.

Perahia brings a marvellous freshness and delicacy to the *B flat Concerto*, K.238, but it is in the *C major*, with its sense of character and subtle artistry, that he is at his most sparkling and genial. Even if the acoustic ambience is less than ideally spacious, the CBS sound is still good.

Piano concerto No. 8 in C, K.246.
(B) **(*) Pickwick Dig. PCD 964; *IMPC 964* [id.]. Paola Bruni, ECCO, Aadland – BACH: *Clavier concerto No. 1;* HAYDN: *Piano concerto in D.* **(*)

Paola Bruni was born in Ravenna in 1964, and studied under Ashkenazy and other famous names. She gives an eminently fresh account of Mozart's early *C major Concerto*, written in 1776 when Mozart was twenty. The ECCO give polished, animated accompaniments and this makes an enjoyable triptych with works by Bach and Haydn. Excellent recording.

Piano concertos Nos. 9 in E flat, K.271; 11 in F, K.413.
*** DG Dig. 410 905-2 [id.]. Malcolm Bilson (fortepiano), E. Bar. Soloists, Gardiner.

Malcolm Bilson here shows himself to be a lively and imaginative artist, well matched by the ever-effervescent and alert Gardiner. The recording on CD catches superbly the lightness and clarity of the textures; the darkness of the C minor slow movement of K.271 is eerily caught. Bilson chooses fast allegros, but never at the expense of Mozart.

(i) *Piano concertos Nos. 9 in E flat, K.271; 14 in E flat, K.449. Fantasia in C min., K.396.*
(M) *** Van. 8.4015.71 [OVC 4015]. Alfred Brendel; (i) I Solisti di Zagreb, Janigro.

Brendel's 1968 performance of No. 9 is quite outstanding, elegant and beautifully precise. The classical-sized orchestra is just right and the neat, stylish string-playing matches the soloist. Both pianist and conductor are sensitive to the gentle melancholy of the slow movement, and in the contrasting middle section of the finale Brendel's tonal nuance is beautifully shaded. The performance of K.449 is also first rate, with a memorably vivacious finale. Altogether this is an outstanding reissue with natural sound which hardly shows its age in the clean remastering. The rather serious account of the *Fantasy*, which comes first on the record, has a much drier acoustic and the forward balance brings a less natural effect.

Piano concertos Nos. 9 in E flat, K.271; 21 in C, K.467.
*** Sony MK 34562 [id.]. Murray Perahia, ECO.

Perahia's reading of K.271 is wonderfully refreshing and delicate, with diamond-bright articulation, urgently youthful in its resilience. The famous *C major Concerto* is given a more variable, though still highly imaginative performance. Faithful, well-balanced recording.

Piano concertos Nos. 11 in F, K.413; 12 in A, K.414; 14 in E flat, K.449.
*** Sony MK 42243 [id.]. Murray Perahia, ECO.

These performances remain in a class of their own. When it first appeared, we thought the *F major*, K.413, the most impressive of Perahia's Mozart concerto records so far, its slow movement wonderfully inward; and the *E flat Concerto*, K.449, is comparably distinguished.

Piano concertos Nos. 11 in F, K.413; 16 in D, K.451.
*** Ph. Dig. 416 367-2 [id.]. Alfred Brendel, ASMF, Marriner.

Brendel's performances are distinguished by wonderful clarity of articulation: the ideas are always finely shaped without ever being overcharacterized. Both recordings are refreshing in sound and to the spirit.

Piano concertos Nos. 12 in A, K.414; 14 in E flat, K.449.
*** DG Dig. 413 463-2 [id.]. Malcolm Bilson (fortepiano), E Bar. Soloists, Gardiner.

Malcolm Bilson's coupling of the *'Little A major'*, K.414, and the tough *Concerto in E flat*, K.449, is one of the finest of the Archiv series. Gardiner and the English Baroque Soloists again prove to be ideal accompanists, matching Bilson's expressiveness on the one hand while on the other relishing the very fast speeds he prefers in finales. The extra clarity of authentic instruments makes the music seem all the stronger in its lean resilience. Fresh, clear recording.

Piano concertos Nos. 12 in A, K.414; 14 in E flat, K.449; 21 in C, K.467.
(BB) *** Naxos Dig. 8.550202; *4550202* [id.]. Jenö Jandó, Concentus Hungaricus, András Ligeti.

In Jandó's hands the first movement of K.449 sounds properly forward-looking; the brightly vivacious K.414 also sounds very fresh here, and its *Andante* is beautifully shaped. Similarly the famous slow movement is most sensitive, with a gently poignant cantilena from the strings. The resonance of the Italian Institute in Budapest, where this series of recordings is made, adds warmth and generally provides fullness and bloom without clouding detail. The excellent orchestral response distinguishes the first movement of K.467: both grace and weight are here, and some fine wind playing. An added interest in this work is provided by Jandó's use of cadenzas provided by Robert Casadesus. Jandó is at his most spontaneous throughout these performances and this is altogether an excellent disc.

Piano concertos Nos. 13 in C, K.415; 15 in B flat, K.450.
*** DG Dig. 413 464-2 [id.]. Malcolm Bilson (fortepiano), E. Bar. Soloists, Gardiner.

Festive with trumpets, K.415 makes a striking impact here, despite the modest-sized forces (5, 4, 2, 2, 1 strings). Though Bilson opts for brisk allegros, which emerge with exceptional clarity, he and Gardiner relax well in the central andante and the two adagio episodes of the finale. K.450 brings woodwind to the fore, and the English Baroque players match their string colleagues in stylishness. The recording is nicely balanced without spotlighting, so vivid you can hear the clicking keys of the wind instruments.

Piano concertos Nos. 14 in E flat, K.449; 15 in E flat, K.450; 16 in D, K.451.
(M) *** EMI CDM7 69124-2 [id.]; *EG 769124-4*. Barenboim, ECO.

Barenboim's playing is spontaneous and smiling, while the orchestra respond with genuine vitality and sparkle. K.451 is particularly enjoyable, with a brisk, jaunty account of the first movement, a flowing, expressive slow movement and an exuberant finale. Good recording throughout, and a sensible price.

Piano concertos Nos. 15 in B flat, K.450; 16 in D, K.451.
*** Sony Dig. MK 37824 [id.]. Murray Perahia, ECO.

Perahia's are superbly imaginative readings, full of seemingly spontaneous touches and turns of phrase very personal to him, which yet never sound mannered. His version of the *B flat Concerto* has sparkle, grace and intelligence; both these performances are very special indeed. The recording is absolutely first rate, intimate yet realistic and not dry, with the players continuously grouped round the pianist.

Piano concertos Nos. 15 in B flat, K.450; 21 in C, K.467.
*** Ph. Dig. 400 018-2 [id.]. Alfred Brendel, ASMF, Marriner.

Brendel's outer movements of K.467 are brisk, but tempo is not in itself a problem. Each detail of a phrase is meticulously articulated, every staccato and slur carefully observed. The finale sounds over-rehearsed, for some of the joy and high spirits are sacrificed in the sense of momentum. However, there is much to delight in both these performances. The playing is very distinguished, and so, too, is the recording.

(i) *Piano concertos Nos. 15 in B flat, K.450;* (ii) *23 in A, K.488; 24 in C min., K.491.*
(M) (***) EMI mono CDH7 63707-2 [id.]. Solomon, Philh. O, (i) Ackermann; (ii) Menges.

These records all come from 1953–5 and have that classical purity and tonal finesse for which Solomon was so famous. They are a model of style and have an extraordinary poise and authority. The recordings come up very well, and no apologies need be made for the sound quality or the recorded balance. Essential listening for all Mozartians.

Piano concertos Nos. 16 in D, K.451; 17 in G, K.453.
*** DG Dig. 415 525-2 [id.]. Malcolm Bilson (fortepiano), E. Bar. Soloists, Gardiner.

In K.451 the gains are greater than usual, with textures so beautifully clarified and the relationship between keyboard and orchestra revealed on record more tellingly than it would be in concert, thanks to shrewd balancing. K.453, as ever, is a delight, with Bilson allowing himself a natural degree of expressiveness within the limits of classical taste. As in the rest of the series, he uses apt ornamentation in the slow movements, in the *Andante* of K.451 adding discreetly to the decorations which Mozart himself wrote out for his sister. Warm, well-balanced recording.

Piano concertos Nos. 16 in D, K.451; 25 in C, K.503; Rondo in A, K.386.
(BB) *** Naxos Dig. 8.550207; *4550207* [id.]. Jenö Jandó, Concentus Hungaricus, Mátyás Antal.

Jenö Jandó gives a very spirited and intelligent account of the relatively neglected *D major Concerto*, K.451, in which he receives sensitive and attentive support from the excellent Concentus Hungaricus under Mátyás Antal. The performance has warmth and conveys a genuine sense of delight. The players sound as if they are enjoying themselves and, although there are greater performances of the *C major Concerto*, K.503, on record, they are not at this extraordinarily competitive price.

Piano concertos Nos. 17 in G, K.453; 18 in B flat, K.456.
*** Sony MK 36686 [id.]. Murray Perahia, ECO.
(BB) *** Naxos Dig. 8.550205; *4550205* [id.]. Jenö Jandó, Concentus Hungaricus, Mátyás Antal.

The *G major Concerto* is one of the most magical of the Perahia cycle and is on no account to be missed. The *B flat*, too, has the sparkle, grace and finesse that one expects from him. Even if you have other versions, you should still add this to your collection, for its insights are quite special.

This is also one of the finest in Jandó's excellent super-bargain series. The finesse of the string playing is immediately apparent at the very opening of K.453, and the final *Allegretto* similarly stylish. Tempi are admirably judged and both slow movements are most sensitively played. The variations which form the *Andante* of K.456 are particularly appealing in their perceptive use of light and shade, while the very lively *Allegro vivace* finale of the same work is infectiously spirited. Jandó uses Mozart's original cadenzas for the first two movements of K.453 and the composer's alternative cadenzas for K.546. Excellent sound.

Piano concertos Nos. 17; 20; 22; 24; 25; Rondo in D, K.382. Piano sonatas Nos. 10, K.330; 11, K.331; Fantasias, K.396 & K.475; Romanze, K.Anh.205; Minuet, K.1.
(M) (***) EMI mono CHS7 63719-2 (3). Edwin Fischer, various orchestras & conductors.

Edwin Fischer's record of the *G major Concerto*, K.453, directed from the keyboard, is among the classics of the gramophone. The first CD couples it with an almost equally magisterial account of the *D minor*, K.466, with the *C major Sonata* as a fill-up. Fischer's pre-war recording of K.482, with Barbirolli and the LPO, on the second CD is hardly less powerful, wonderfully paced, concentrated and alive, as is his *C minor*, K.491, with Lawrance Collingwood and the Barbirolli Chamber Orchestra. The last CD brings us a post-war account of the *C major*, K.503, with the Philharmonia under Josef Krips, not quite of the same stature as K.453 and K.482 but full of illuminating touches and fine musicianship. There is much for any Mozartian to learn throughout this set: Fischer plays his own cadenzas, an object lesson in themselves. Listening to these performances, one understands why this artist is so admired by later generations of Mozartians – pianists like Denis Matthews, Alfred Brendel and Murray Perahia. By comparison with the French LP transfer of K.453 some years back, the sound is a little dried-out but is still generally very good.

Piano concertos Nos. 17 in G, K.453; 21 in C, K.467.
*** Decca 411 947-2 [id.]. Vladimir Ashkenazy, Philh. O.

Ashkenazy's performances combine a refreshing spontaneity with an overall sense of proportion and balance. There is a fine sense of movement, and yet nothing is hurried; detail is finely characterized, but nothing is fussy. Moreover the recording is clear and lucid, with the balance between soloist and orchestra finely judged.

Piano concertos Nos. 17 in G, K.453; 26 in D (Coronation), K.537.
**(*) EMI CDC7 47968-2 [id.]. Daniel Barenboim, ECO.

The *G major Concerto* is phrased most musically and is full of life, but it may be spoilt for some by the unusually brisk tempo Barenboim adopts for the first movement. However, Barenboim's account of the *Coronation concerto* must be counted one of the most successful on disc. Altogether this is a fine record, worth acquiring for the sake of the *D major* alone, and the digital remastering is highly felicitous, adding presence and freshening the orchestral textures.

Piano concertos Nos. 17 in G, K.453; 27 in B flat, K.595.
(M) *** Tuxedo TUXCD 1027 [id.]. Alfred Brendel, V. State Op. O, Paul Angerer.

Brendel was an inspired Mozartian when he made his earlier Mozart recordings for the Vox Turnabout label at the end of the 1950s and beginning of the 1960s; these performances have a radiant freshness and spontaneity which he did not quite match in his later, Philips versions. The recording is on the thin side in the matter of violin timbre, although it has a good ambience, and at Brendel's entry one forgets this fault, for the piano is realistically recorded and very convincingly balanced in relation to the orchestra. Brendel is helped by a vivacious orchestral contribution in both works. No. 27 is very distinguished and can be spoken of in the same breath as Gilels's version. It is beautifully proportioned, the lyrical phrasing is most winning, with Brendel's sure feeling for nuance and tempo lighting up the *Andante* and the final Allegretto engagingly nimble.

Piano concertos Nos. 18 in B flat, K.456; 19 in F, K.459.
(M) *** EMI CDM7 69123-2 [id.]; *EG 769123-4.* Barenboim, ECO.
**(*) DG Dig. 415 111-2 [id.]. Malcolm Bilson (fortepiano), E. Bar. Soloists, Gardiner.

Barenboim's account of K.456 is among the most sparkling of his cycle, full of imaginative touches which have one chuckling with delight. K.459, with its *Figaro* overtones, prompts another remarkable performance, brisk in its march rhythms in the first movement, tender in the Susanna-like sweetness of the *Andante* and strong and resilient in the finale, with its great fugal tutti. Excellent sound.

Malcolm Bilson gives a vivacious account of the *B flat Concerto*, briskly paced but never sounding rushed, and the colour of the fortepiano made enticing in the *Andante*, by subtlety of inflexion and imaginative dynamic shading. The performance of *No. 19 in F* is rather more controversial. Gardiner's fast, crisp tempo in the first movement is initially disconcerting and, with the *Allegretto* marking for the second movement observed to the letter, there is less contrast than usual. But again the sparkle of the finale rounds off a reading that is consistent in its freshness and momentum. The clear, naturally balanced recording adds much to the pleasure of this series.

Piano concertos Nos. 19 in F, K.459; 23 in A, K.488.
❀ *** Sony Dig. MK 39064 [id.]. Murray Perahia, ECO.
(M) *** DG 429 812-2; 429 812-4 [id.]. Pollini, VPO, Boehm.

Murray Perahia gives highly characterful accounts of both *Concertos* and a gently witty yet vital reading of the *F Major*, K.459. As always with this artist, there is a splendidly classical feeling allied to a keenly poetic sensibility. His account of K.488 has enormous delicacy and inner vitality, yet a serenity that puts it in a class of its own. Even in a series of such distinction, this performance stands out. On CD, the sound is particularly fresh and natural.

Pollini is sparkling in the *F major*, and in the *A major* has a superbly poised, vibrant sense of line. Every phrase here seems to speak, and he is given excellent support from Boehm and the Vienna orchestra. Good, well-detailed and finely balanced analogue recording, which has transferred very freshly to CD, make this one of the finest Mozart concerto records DG have given us. Excellent value.

Piano concertos Nos. 19 in F, K.459; 27 in B flat, K.595.
*** Decca Dig. 421 259-2 [id.]. András Schiff, Salzburg Mozarteum Camerata Academica, Végh.

Though Schiff's piano occupies a relatively small space in the aural image, it is not an unrealistic one. Details certainly register and the orchestral playing is a delight. This is agreeably relaxed, leisurely music-making though not in the least lacking in intensity or weight (Sandor Végh is very much the hero of the occasion). Occasionally András Schiff dots his 'i's and crosses his 't's a little too precisely, but his playing for the most part is so musicianly and perceptive that this does not seem important. These two readings can be warmly recommended – with the proviso that the resonant acoustic may trouble some listeners.

Piano concertos Nos. 20 in D min., K.466; 21 in C, K.467.
❀ *** DG Dig. 419 609-2 [id.]. Malcolm Bilson (fortepiano), E. Bar. Soloists, Gardiner.
*** Decca Dig. 430 510-2; *430 510-4* [id.]. Schiff, Salzburg Mozarteum Camerata Academica, Végh.
(M) *** BMG/RCA GD 87967 [7967-2-RG]. Rubinstein, RCA Victor SO, Wallenstein (with HAYDN: *Andante & variations in F min.* ***).

Here, even more than in the earlier masterpieces, the benefits of period performance are striking in the way that, along with the extra transparency, the scale of the argument and its dramatic bite, far from being minimized, are actually reinforced. These are vital, electric performances by Bilson and the English Baroque Soloists, expressive within their own lights, neither rigid nor too taut in the way of some period Mozart, nor inappropriately romantic. This is a disc to recommend even to those who would not normally consider period performances of Mozart concertos, fully and vividly recorded with excellent balance between soloist and orchestra – better than you would readily get in the concert hall.

András Schiff's Mozart cycle with the Salzburg Mozarteum Camerata Academica under Sándor Végh is proving one of the more satisfying of recent years – and arguably the finest since Murray Perahia's cycle of the late 1970s. They are not as well recorded as are Uchida and Tate on Philips (the acoustic is a bit resonant) but their performances generally speaking go deeper. Such is the case here and no one following this excellent series need really hesitate. There is plenty of dramatic fire in the *D minor*, K.466, which is marvellously controlled and the *C major*, K.467, comes up sounding beautifully fresh too.

Rubinstein has seldom been caught so sympathetically by the microphones, and the remastered 1961 recording has the orchestral sound admirably freshened. In each concerto the slow movement is the kernel of the interpretation. Rubinstein's playing is melting. The opening of the first movement of K.466, taken fairly briskly, is full of implied drama. Altogether Wallenstein is an excellent accompanist, for finales have plenty of sparkle. The Haydn *Andante and variations*, a substantial bonus recorded a year earlier, again demonstrates Rubinstein's aristocratic feeling for a classical melodic line: it is played most beautifully.

Piano concertos Nos. 20 in D min., K.466; 23 in A, K.488.
*** EMI Dig. CDC7 54366-2 [id.]. Melvyn Tan, L. Classical Players, Norrington.
(B) **(*) Ph. 422 466-2; *422 466-4*. Kovacevich, LSO, C. Davis.

Fresh from his tour with Beethoven's Broadwood piano, Melvyn Tan is embarking on a survey of the Mozart concertos, albeit on his Derek Adlam copy of an 1814 Nanette Streicher. He radiates infectious delight in what he is doing, and the playing has both imagination and poise. Although the fortepiano may be less able than a modern concert grand to convey the dark *Don Giovanni* colourings of the *D minor Concerto*, K.466, these readings have an impressive flair, and the London Classical Players under Norrington are generally supportive. The EMI recording does justice to their artistry. The slow movements of both concertos could with advantage be broader in tempo but neither is wanting in finesse and intelligence, and few readers will fail to find them stimulating.

If the coupling of the *D minor* and the *A major* from Kovacevich and Davis lacks some of the magic of their earlier pairing of the two *C major Concertos*, it is largely that the playing of the LSO is less polished. Nevertheless the minor-key seriousness of the outer movements of K.466 and the F sharp minor *Adagio* of K.488 come out superbly. It is a token of the pianist's command that, without any expressive exaggeration, the K.488 slow movement conveys such depth and intensity. The recording is full and clear in its new format.

Piano concertos Nos. 20 in D min., K.466; 24 in C min., K.491; Concert rondo No. 1 in D, K.382.
(M) *** Ph. 420 867-2. Alfred Brendel, ASMF, Marriner.

The two minor-key *Concertos* are superbly played by Brendel and the analogue recording is of Philips's best. Perhaps the last ounce of tragic intensity is missing but, at mid-price and with the *D major Rondo* now included, there is nothing to inhibit a three-star recommendation.

Piano concertos Nos. (i) *20 in D min., K.466;* (ii) *27 in B flat, K.595.*
*** Sony MK 42241 [id.]. Murray Perahia, ECO.
(M) **(*) Sony MYK 42533 [id.]. Rudolf Serkin, (i) Columbia SO, Szell; (ii) Phd. O, Ormandy.

Perahia produces wonderfully soft colourings and a luminous texture in the *B flat Concerto*, yet at the same time he avoids underlining too strongly the valedictory sense that inevitably haunts this magical score. In the *D minor Concerto* none of the darker, disturbing undercurrents go uncharted, but at the same time we remain within the sensibility of the period. Not, perhaps, the only way of looking at this work, but a wonderfully compelling one. An indispensable issue, well recorded.

Both of Serkin's performances come from the early 1960s and, although the piano tone sounds a bit shallow, there is nothing shallow about the playing in either concerto. Szell was much (and rightly) admired as a Mozartian, but it is Ormandy who proves an even more sensitive and attentive partner. In the slow movement of the *D minor Concerto*, K.466, Serkin in his anxiety to avoid sentimentality adopts a very flowing tempo, which some may find a shade too fast. Elsewhere, pace is expertly judged, and in the *B flat Concerto* both artists have the measure of the depths of the slow movement and the sparkle of the finale.

Piano concerto No. 21 in C, K.467.
(M) (*(**)) EMI mono CDH7 69792-2. Dinu Lipatti, Lucerne Festival O, Karajan – SCHUMANN: *Concerto.* (***)

Lipatti's performance derives from a broadcast from the 1950 Lucerne Festival and there is some discoloration and, at climaxes, distortion. However, nothing can detract from the distinction of Lipatti's playing or its immaculate control.

Piano concertos Nos. (i) *21 in C, K.467;* (ii) *22 in E flat, K.482; 23 in A, K.488;* (i) *24 in C min., K.491;* (ii) *26 in D (Coronation), K.537; 27 in B, K.595;* (iii) *Double piano concerto in E flat, K.365.*
❀ (M) **(*) Sony SM3K 46519 (3) [id.]. Robert Casadesus, with (i) Cleveland O, Szell; (ii) Columbia SO, Szell; (iii) Gaby Casadesus, Phd. O, Ormandy.

A very distinguished set, effectively transferred to CD. Casadesus's Mozart may at first seem understated, but the imagination behind his readings is apparent in every phrase and the accompaniment could hardly be more stylish. Casadesus takes the finale of No. 21 at a tremendous speed, but for the most part this is exquisite Mozart playing, beautifully paced and articulated. While not scaling the heights of Casadesus's earlier accounts with Bigot and Munch, the present versions with the Cleveland Orchestra still sound pretty marvellous, for all the shortcomings of the recording balance and the sometimes over-tense precision of Szell. In fact the balance is better than we had remembered it. Although the orchestra tends to dwarf the soloist in tuttis, the placing of the piano is very pleasing, and the subtleties of the solo playing are naturally caught. In No. 22, Casadesus is second to none: he has space and proportion on the one hand and a marvellously alive sense of detail and phrasing on the other. He is first rate in the *A major* too, accompanied in this and No. 22 by Szell again but this time with the Columbia Symphony Orchestra. Mozart's last piano concertos inspire two extremely memorable performances, each of them underlining the dramatic contrast of soloist and orchestra, almost as a meeting of heroine and hero. The *Double concerto* is essentially a genial work, and this is the one quality completely missing from Casadesus's performance, which has a matching dry recording. All the solo concertos, however, were recorded in Severance Hall, Cleveland, between 1959 and 1962 (except for No. 23, which dates from 1969) and the hall ambience provides an attractive fullness to the overall sound.

Piano concertos Nos. 21 in C, K.467; 24 in C min., K.491.
(B) *** Sony MYK 42594 [MYK 38523]. Robert Casadesus, Cleveland O, Szell.
(B) *** Pickwick Dig. PCD 832; *CIMPC 832* [id.]. Howard Shelley, City of L. Sinfonia.

Casadesus is on top form: he plays most delectably in the first movement of K.467 and its ravishing central *Andante* has seldom sounded so magical. Both here and in the coupled K.491

(where, unusually, he chooses a cadenza by Saint-Saëns) this is exquisite Mozart playing, beautifully paced and articulated. Szell's precision gives a special character to the accompaniments. The 1965 recording sounds remarkably fresh and full, and this disc should belong in any Mozartian's library.

Howard Shelley gives delightfully fresh and characterful readings of both the popular *C major* and the great *C minor* concertos, bringing out their strength and purposefulness as well as their poetry, never overblown or sentimental. His Pickwick disc makes an outstanding digital bargain, with accompaniment very well played and recorded.

Piano concertos Nos. 21 in C, K.467; 25 in C, K.503.
❀ (B) *** Ph. 426 077-2; *426 077-4*. Kovacevich, LSO, C. Davis.

The partnership of Kovacevich and Davis almost invariably produces inspired music-making, and here their equal dedication to Mozart, their balancing of strength and charm, drama and tenderness, make for performances which retain their sense of spontaneity but which plainly result from deep thought. Never has the famous slow movement of K.467 sounded more ethereally beautiful on record than here, with superb LSO string-tone, and the weight of both these great C major works is formidably conveyed. The 1972 recording is well balanced and refined.

Piano concertos Nos. 21 in C, K.467; 27 in B flat, K.595.
*** Sony Dig. SK 46485; *40-46485* [id.]. Murray Perahia, COE.

Murray Perahia has lost none of his mastery and keenness of sensibility, and gives performances of characteristic understanding and finesse with the Chamber Orchestra of Europe. There are new and different insights into both works though neither reading necessarily displaces his earlier accounts with the ECO, which may have a slight edge on the newcomer in terms of freshness and spontaneity. The COE account is undoubtedly the better recorded but readers who have either concerto in his earlier readings need not feel they need replace them.

Piano concertos Nos. 22 in E flat, K.482; 23 in A, K.488.
*** Ph. Dig. 420 187-2 [id.]. Mitsuko Uchida, ECO, Tate.

In balance, fidelity and sense of presence, few recordings of Mozart piano concertos can match Uchida's fine coupling of the late *E flat*, K.482, with its immediate successor, the beautiful *A major*. It makes a fascinating match, presenting illuminating contrasts rather than similarities, and Uchida's thoughtful manner, at times a little understated, is ideally set against outstanding playing from the ECO with its excellent wind soloists.

Piano concertos Nos. 22 in E flat, K.482; 24 in C min., K.491.
*** Sony MK 42242 [id.]. Murray Perahia, ECO.

Not only is Perahia's contribution inspired in the great *E flat Concerto*, but the wind players of the ECO are at their most eloquent in the slow movement. Moreover the *C minor Concerto* emerges here as a truly Mozartian tragedy, rather than as foreshadowing Beethoven, which some artists give us. Both recordings are improved in focus and definition in the CD transfer.

Piano concertos Nos. 22 in E flat, K.482; 25 in C, K.503.
(M) *** Tuxedo TUXCD 1046. Alfred Brendel, VCO or V. State Op. O, Paul Angerer.

Another unforgettable early Brendel coupling, recorded in 1958 but with the sound very respectable in its CD transfer. The string-tone remains thin, but the *E flat Concerto* is better focused than on LP and the excellent wind playing is well caught. Brendel plays the first movement of K.482 with authority, the *Andante* variations very beautifully and the finale enchantingly. No. 25 shows Brendel at his most commanding, and Angerer sets the scene admirably with an imposing opening, even if the recording focus is less clean in this work. Again the solo phrasing is eminently stylish, the *Andante* classically serene and the finale given the lightest touch.

Piano concertos Nos. 23 in A, K.488; 24 in C min., K.491.
❀ (M) *** DG 423 885-2 [id.]. Kempff, Bamberg SO, Leitner.
(B) *** Decca 430 497-2; *430 497-4*. Clifford Curzon, LSO, Kertész (with SCHUBERT: *Impromptus: in G flat & A flat, D.899/3 & 4* ***).

(i) *Piano concertos Nos. 23 in A, K.488;* (ii) *24 in C min., K.491; Rondo in A, K.511.*
(M) *** BMG/RCA GD 87968 [7968-2-RG]. Rubinstein, RCA Victor SO, (i) Alfred Wallenstein; (ii) Josef Krips.

Kempff's outstanding performances of these concertos are uniquely poetic and inspired, and Leitner's accompaniments are comparably distinguished. The 1960 recording still sounds well, and this is strongly recommended at mid-price.

Rubinstein brings characteristic finesse and beauty of phrasing to his coupling. K.488 is especially beautiful, with Wallenstein providing a most sympathetic accompaniment. In K.491 the crystal-clear articulation is allied to the aristocratic feeling characteristic of vintage Rubinstein: the slow movement is memorable in its poise. Krips's accompaniment, like the solo part, is smoothly cultured and acts as a foil to the tragic tone of this great and wonderfully balanced work. The recordings, from 1958 and 1961 respectively, sound fresh, and the *Rondo*, recorded in 1959, is equally distinguished – much more than just an encore.

Curzon's account of these two concertos is immaculate; no connoisseur of the piano will fail to derive pleasure and refreshment from them. Curzon has the advantage of sensitive support both from Kertész and from the Decca engineers and the remastering has added life and vividness to the music-making. Two of the Schubert Op. 90 *Impromptus*, added as an attractive fill-up, add to the attractiveness of this reissue.

Piano concertos Nos. 23 in A, K.488; 26 in D (Coronation), K.537.
(M) *** Sony MPK 45884 [id.]. Casadesus, Cleveland O, Szell.

Here is a coupling to match that by these artists of Nos. 21 and 24. K.537 inspires Casadesus and Szell to a really outstanding performance. Casadesus is marvellous in No. 23, too; this disc is the pick of the three records included in the box discussed above. Szell's accompaniments could hardly be more stylish.

Piano concertos Nos. 23 in A, K.488; 27 in B flat, K.595.
*** Decca Dig. 400 087-2 [id.]. Vladimir Ashkenazy, Philh. O.
(M) *** Ph. 420 487-2; *420 487-4* [id.]. Alfred Brendel, ASMF, Marriner.

Ashkenazy's *A Major* is beautifully judged, alive and fresh, yet warm – one of the most satisfying accounts yet recorded. No quarrels either with the *B flat*, which is as finely characterized as one would expect. The recording focuses closely on the piano, but nevertheless no orchestral detail is masked and the overall impression is very lifelike and beautiful.

On Philips, two of the best of Brendel's Mozart concertos. Both performances come from the early 1970s and sound wonderfully fresh in these digitally refurbished transfers. But allegiance to Gilels in K.595 remains strong.

Piano concerto No. 23 in A, K.488; Piano sonata No. 13 in B flat, K.333 (K.315c).
**(*) DG Dig. 423 287-2; *423 287-4* [id.]. Vladimir Horowitz, La Scala, Milan, O, Giulini.

With Horowitz there are occasional reminders of the passage of time, but they are astonishingly few, and the artistry remains undiminished. The Busoni cadenza is an unusual (and far from unwelcome) feature of the *Concerto*. As usual, the piano is tuned within an inch of its life, and the slightly shallow sound of the instrument is not solely due to the engineers. This is very much Horowitz's record – and at times in the finale there is not too much of the orchestra, nor is there much sign of rapport between Horowitz and Giulini! Still, this is remarkable piano playing, quite unlike any other, and in the *Sonata* not free from affectation. In the *Concerto*, the recording is synthetic and dryish; the *Sonata* is slightly less constricted but far from first rate.

Piano concertos Nos. 24 in C min., K.491; 25 in C, K.503.
*** EMI Dig. CDC7 54295-2 [id.]. Melvyn Tan (fortepiano), L. Classical Players, Norrington.
**(*) Ph. Dig. 422 331-2 [id.]. Uchida, ECO, Tate.

Melvyn Tan's view of these two Mozart concertos comes divested of any late nineteenth-century overlay. He tries not to see the C minor through Beethovenian eyes, and approaches it both imaginatively and with great freshness. His playing has both poise and grace, and so does that of the London Classical Players too. The fortepiano is less well equipped to penetrate the tragic overtones of the slow movement and here Tan does not help himself by adopting too brisk a tempo. He shapes the finale with subtlety and finesse, and is equally thought-provoking in the *C major Concerto*, K.503. The EMI recording is most naturally and truthfully balanced.

Mitsuko Uchida's cycle with Jeffrey Tate has three-star state-of-the art recording quality but, as with some other earlier releases in her cycle, tonal refinement and delicacy are sometimes in stronger evidence than a sense of scale. She is eminently alive and imaginative though the slow movement of the *C major*, K.503, may strike some listeners as a bit too measured. Tate gives workmanlike rather than inspired support and though as one would expect from two artists of this calibre, there are many felicities, this can only be recommended to collectors of the series. In neither concerto would it be a first choice.

Piano concerto No. 25 in C, K.503.
(M) *** Sony MYK 44832 [MYK 37762]. Leon Fleisher, Cleveland O, Szell – BEETHOVEN: *Piano concerto No. 4.* ***
(M) ** Sony SMK 47519 [id.]. Leonard Bernstein, Israel PO – BEETHOVEN: *Piano concerto No. 1.* **(*)

Fleisher and Szell achieve a memorable partnership in this 1959 recording. The kernel of the performance is the beautiful slow movement, classically serene. The commanding outer movements have great vitality: Fleisher shapes the first movement's second subject most engagingly and is wonderfully nimble in the finale, while Szell's orchestral detail is a constant source of pleasure.

Bernstein's recording was made in the Mann Auditorium in Tel Aviv in 1974 and, although the sound is fuller than on the coupling, it is forwardly balanced and the dynamic range is comparatively narrow, a serious drawback in Mozart. The performance is sympathetic and musical – how could it be otherwise? – but this not one of Bernstein's more vivid recording ventures, and its main interest lies in his own cadenza for the first movement which is rather effective and appealing.

Piano concertos Nos. 25 in C, K.503; 26 in D (Coronation), K.537.
*** DG Dig. 423 119-2 [id.]. Malcolm Bilson (fortepiano), E. Bar. Soloists, Gardiner.
*** Decca Dig. 411 810-2 [id.]. Vladimir Ashkenazy, Philh. O.

With Bilson at his strongest and Gardiner and the English Baroque Soloists taking a dramatic view – biting down sharply on the repeated chords of the first movement – the magnificent scale of the *C major* work is formidably established. The *Coronation concerto* is also presented strongly as well as elegantly, with the authentic timpani cutting dramatically through the textures in the first movement. Full and spacious recording in a helpful acoustic.

Ashkenazy's opening of the *C major Concerto* is on the grandest scale, emphasized by the weighty bass response of the recording; but the interpretation is set in relief by the more delicate feeling of the *Andante*. In the *Coronation concerto* Ashkenazy's approach to the first movement is comparably magisterial, while he produces some exquisitely shaded playing in the *Larghetto*, with the final *Allegretto* hardly less refined. In both works the Decca recording is of the highest quality.

Piano concertos Nos. (i) *26 in D (Coronation), K.537;* (ii) *27 in B flat, K.595.*
(M) *** DG 429 810-2; *429 810-4* [id.]. (i) Vásáry, BPO; (ii) Gilels, VPO, Boehm.

Tamás Vásáry is a fine Mozartian with exemplary taste and judgement, and his account of the *Coronation concerto* has grandeur as well as vitality. The quality of the 1974 sound is very good in this transfer. Gilels's account of K.595 is in a class of its own, and those who do not require his coupling with the *Double piano concerto*, K.365 – see below – will find this a worthwhile alternative.

Piano concerto No. 26 in D (Coronation), K.537; Concert rondos, Nos. 1 in D, K.382; 2 in A, K.386.
*** Sony Dig. MK 39224 [id.]. Murray Perahia, ECO.

Perahia succeeds in making K.537 mean more than do most of his rivals, and the dignity and breadth of his reading are matched in the slow movement by enormous delicacy and sensibility. This is a magical performance in which the level of inspiration runs high. The *Concerto* is coupled with superb accounts of the two *Concert rondos*, K.382 and K.386, which for the first time on record incorporate the closing bars newly discovered by Professor Alan Tyson. The recording is naturally balanced within a fairly resonant ambience.

Piano concerto No. 27 in B flat, K.595; (i) *Double piano concerto in E flat, K.365.*
❀ (M) *** DG 419 059-2; *419 059-4* [id.]. Emil Gilels, VPO, Boehm, (i) with Elena Gilels.

Gilels's is supremely lyrical playing that evinces all the classical virtues. No detail is allowed to detract from the picture as a whole; the pace is totally unhurried and superbly controlled. All the points are made by means of articulation and tone, and each phrase is marvellously alive. This is playing of the highest order of artistic integrity and poetic insight, while Boehm and the Vienna Philharmonic provide excellent support. The performance of the marvellous *Double concerto* is no less enjoyable. Its mood is comparatively serious, but this is not to suggest that the music's sunny qualities are not brought out; the interplay of phrasing between the two soloists is beautifully conveyed by the recording without exaggerated separation. The quality on CD is first class, refining detail yet not losing ambient warmth.

Double piano concerto in E flat, K.365; Triple piano concerto in F (Lodron), K.242 (arr. for 2 pianos).
*** Ph. Analogue/Dig. 416 364-2 [id.]. Alfred Brendel, Imogen Cooper, ASMF, Marriner.

The playing on Philips is cultured and elegant, strikingly poised – particularly in K.242 – combining vigour with tonal refinement. Marriner's accompaniments are comparably polished and the Philips engineers afford the music-making a most natural sound-balance. The analogue recording of K.365 dates from 1977; K.242 is digital and was made in 1984.

(i) *Double piano concerto in E flat, K.365; Triple piano concerto in F (Lodron), K.242* (arr. for 2 pianos); *Fantasia in F min., K.608* (arr. Busoni); *5 Variations in G, K.501.*
*** Sony Dig. SK 44915 [id.]. Murray Perahia, Radu Lupu, (i) ECO.

Murray Perahia and Radu Lupu are in good form in both the *Double concerto*, K.365, and the two-piano arrangement of the *Lodron*. The performances emanate from public concerts at The Maltings, Snape, and have much of the excitement and spontaneity of live music-making. The two pianists are beautifully matched in both pieces, and again in the G major variations, K.501 and Busoni's transcription of the *F minor Fantasy*, which were recorded in the studio. It is possible that some ears may find the otherwise excellent balance a shade too close in the concertos but, generally speaking, this highly rewarding collection will bring only delight.

(i) *Double piano concerto in E flat, K.365. Double piano sonata in D, K.448; Fugue for 2 pianos in C min., K.426.*
❀ (M) *** Tuxedo TUXCD 1028 [id.]. Alfred Brendel, Walter Klien; (i) Vienna State Op. O, Paul Angerer.

Like Brendel, Walter Klien is a very distinguished Mozartian. Their version of the *Double concerto* is second to none, not even that by the Gilels duo; if they do not have the advantage of the VPO, Angerer still provides admirable support, and the mood here is sunnier, and no less authoritative, than the DG version. The stereo places the pianos very positively to the left and the right, and the separation, while not exaggerated, is more positive than it would be in the concert hall. But the interplay between the two artists is a continuous delight, with Klien responding to Brendel in the most engaging way and the rapport between them one of equals. The couplings are an equal success, again displaying these artists' joy in Mozart's genial and skilful antiphonal writing.

Violin concertos

Violin concertos Nos. 1–7; Adagio, K.261; Rondos Nos. 1–2, K.269 & K.373 (all for violin and orchestra).
(BB) *** BMG/Eurodisc VD 69255 (3) [69255-2-RG]. Josef Suk, Prague Chamber O, Libor Hlaváček.

Josef Suk's recordings date from 1972. He includes Nos. 6 and 7 which are almost certainly spurious (although some authorities suggest that No. 7 is largely the work of Mozart). Suk makes a good case for them and throughout the set his performances are highly distinguished. The solo playing has character, warmth and humanity, and its unaffected manner is especially suited to the first two concertos: No. 1 is as fine as any in the catalogue. Hlaváček does not always make enough of the dynamic contrasts and, throughout, this music-making is dominated by Suk. This is partly a matter of the recording balance, with the orchestra set back in a warm acoustic. The digital remastering increases the feeling of the soloist's presence and adds a brighter lighting to his timbre, particularly noticeable at the opening of No. 4. But with any reservations noted, these are delightful performances; and admirers of Suk, among whom we are numbered, should in no way be disappointed by this box, which is extremely competitively priced (even if it includes no notes about the music).

Complete Mozart Edition, Volume 8: (i) *Violin concertos Nos 1–5; 7 in D, K.271; Adagio in E, K.361; Rondo in B flat, K.269; Rondo in C, K.373.* (i; ii) *Concertone, K.190;* (iii; iv) *Double Concerto in D for violin, piano and orchestra, K.315f;* (iii; v; vi) *Sinfonia concertante in A, for violin, viola, cello and orchestra, K.320e.* (iii; v) *Sinfonia concertante in E flat, K.364.*

(M) **(*) Ph. Analogue/Dig. 422 508-2 (4). (i) Szeryng, (ii) with Poulet, Morgan, Jones; New Philh. O, Gibson; (iii) Iona Brown, with (iv) Shelley; (v) Imai; (vi) Orton; ASMF, Marriner.

Volume 8 in the Philips Complete Mozart Edition is even more interesting than most, when it contains very convincing reconstructions of works that Mozart left as fragments. Philip Wilby has not only completed the first movement of an early *Sinfonia concertante for violin, viola and cello* (Mozart's only music with concertante cello) but also, through shrewd detective work, has reconstructed a full three-movement *Double concerto* from what Mozart left as 'a magnificent torso', to use Alfred Einstein's description; it is for violin, piano and orchestra, and Wilby's premiss is that – for reasons which he gives in fair detail – the *Violin sonata in D*, K.306, was in fact a reworking of the *Double concerto* which Mozart said he was writing in 1778 and which he could well have completed. The result here is a delight, a full-scale 25-minute work which ends with an effervescent double-variation finale, alternately in duple and compound time. That is superbly done with Iona Brown and Howard Shelley as soloists; and the other ASMF items are very good too, with Iona Brown joined by Nobuko Imai most characterfully on the viola in the great *Sinfonia concertante*, K.364. What is a shade disappointing – even in a well-filled set at mid-price – is to have Henryk Szeryng's readings of the main violin concertos from the 1960s (also available separately on 422 256-2), instead of the Grumiaux set. Szeryng is sympathetic but a trifle reserved and not as refreshing as Grumiaux.

(i) *Violin concertos Nos. 1 in B flat, K.207;* (ii) *2 in D, K.211;* (iii) *3 in C, K.216;* (ii) *4 in D, K.218;* (i) *5 in A (Turkish), K.219;* (ii) *Adagio in C, K.261; Rondo No. 2 in C, K.373; Haffner Serenade, K.250: Rondo* (all for violin & orchestra); (iv) *Sinfonia concertante in E flat, K.364;* (v) *Divertimento in E flat for string trio (violin, viola & cello), K.563.*
(M) **(*) Sony SM3K 46523 [id.]. Isaac Stern, with (i) Columbia SO, Szell; (ii) ECO, Schneider; (iii) Cleveland O, Szell; (iv) Zukerman, ECO, Barenboim; (v) Pinchas Zukerman, Leonard Rose.

Unlike most sets of the Mozart *Violin concertos*, Stern's recordings were made at different times and with different conductors. It goes without saying that the solo playing is always splendid; it is simply that he is not always as sensitive on detail as his rivals, and this especially applies to No. 1 and rather less so to No. 5 where the accompaniment is provided by the Columbia Symphony Orchestra under Szell. The interpretation of No. 3, however, displays Stern's qualities of sparkling stylishness at their most intense in a very satisfying reading, with a beautifully poised and pointed accompaniment from the same conductor but now with the splendid Cleveland Orchestra. In Nos. 2 and 4, Stern has the benefit of rather fuller recording and his playing, as always, is full of personality. The great *Sinfonia concertante* stands among the finest available and is certainly the jewel in this set, presenting as it does two soloists of equally strong musical personality. The central slow movement is taken at a very expansive *Andante* but the concentration intensifies the beauty, and the finale is sparkling and resilient. Fair, if somewhat aggressive recording, with the two soloists too closely balanced. The trio of famous virtuosi, Stern, Zuckerman and Rose, brings an individually characterized performance of the *Divertimento for string trio* with hushed playing accurately conveyed and the players clearly separated within an atmospheric acoustic, even though the recording is rather close and bright.

Violin concertos Nos. 1–5.
(B) *** Ph. 422 938-2 (2). Arthur Grumiaux, LSO, C. Davis.

Violin concertos Nos. 1 in B flat, K.207; 3 in G, K.216; 5 in A (Turkish), K.219.
(M) *** Decca Dig./Analogue 433 170-2 [id.]. Iona Brown, ASMF.

Violin concertos Nos. 2 in D, K.211; 4 in D, K.218; (i) *Sinfonia concertante in E flat, K.364.*
(M) *** Decca Dig./Analogue 433 171-2 [id.]. Iona Brown, (i) Josef Suk; ASMF.

Grumiaux's accounts of the Mozart *Violin concertos* come from the early 1960s and are among the most beautifully played in the catalogue at any price. The orchestral accompaniments have sparkle and vitality and Grumiaux's contribution has splendid poise and purity of tone. There are many delights here and the music-making has warmth as well as refinement; the recording sounds remarkably good, with clean, fresh string-tone and well-defined bass.

Iona Brown's alternative (originally Argo) set of the Mozart *Violin concertos*, on a pair of mid-priced Decca Serenata discs, has the advantage of including a fine account of the great *Sinfonia concertante*, in which she is joined by Josef Suk. The performances of the solo concertos, too, are first rate. The playing has a freshness and vigour that are winning and the participants convey a sense of pleasure in what they are doing. There is a spring-like feeling about the outer movements of the *G major* (No. 3) and a sultry, Mediterranean warmth in the middle movement, but all these performances have an engaging liveliness and are very well integrated. The recordings are part digital, part analogue (K.216 and K.218), but all produce bright, realistic quality on CD.

Violin concertos Nos. 1 in B flat, K.207; 2 in D, K.211; Rondo No. 1 in B flat, K.269.
*** Denon Dig. C37 7506 [id.]. Jean-Jacques Kantorow, Netherlands CO, Hager.

Violin concertos Nos. 1 in B flat, K.207; 2 in D, K.211; Rondo in B flat, K.269; Andante in F (arr. Saint-Saëns from *Piano concerto No. 21, K.467*).
(BB) **(*) Naxos Dig. 8.550414 [id.]. Takako Nishizaki, Capella Istropolitana, Johannes Wildner.

Kantorow's coupling makes an excellent start to his Mozart series. He is given alert, stylish accompaniments by Leopold Hager and the Netherlands Chamber Orchestra, and the recording is eminently realistic. Kantorow's full personality emerges gradually in K.207, although he plays strongly with a fine classical spirit. The account of K.211 is splendid in all respects. The *B flat Rondo* makes an excellent bonus. Kantorow plays his own cadenzas – and very good they are. Highly recommended.

This was the last disc to be recorded (in 1990) of Takako Nishizaki's fine survey of the violin concertos. The opening movement of K.207 is brisk and fresh, with the bright, digital sound emphasizing the immediacy; although the *Adagio* is played with an agreeable, simple eloquence, this is the least individual of Nishizaki's readings. The *Second Concerto*, K.211, although still admirably direct, has rather more flair, the *Andante* touchingly phrased, and the finale has a winning lightness of touch. The *Rondo* is also an attractively spontaneous performance, and as an encore we are offered Saint-Saëns's arrangement of the famous *'Elvira Madigan'* theme from the *C major Concerto*, K.467.

Violin concertos Nos. 1 in B flat, K.207; 2 in D, K.211; 3 in G, K.216.
(M) **(*) Sony Dig. SBK 46539 [id.]. Zukerman, St Paul CO.

Zukerman's set has the advantage of excellent digital recording and a good balance, the violin forward but not distractingly so. The playing of outer movements is agreeably simple and fresh, and in the slow movements of both the *D major* and *G major Concertos* Zukerman's sweetness of tone will appeal to many, although his tendency to languish a little in his expressiveness, particularly in the *G major*, may be counted a less attractive feature. The St Paul Chamber Orchestra accompanies with stylish warmth.

Violin concertos Nos. 1 in B flat, K.207; 4 in D, K.218; Rondo in B flat, K.269.
*** Sony MK 44503 [id.]. Cho-Liang Lin, ECO, Leppard.

As in his coupling of K.216 and K.219, Lin creates a ready partnership with Leppard and the ECO, and his combination of effervescence and delicacy is matched by the orchestra, with appealing tenderness in both slow movements and plenty of dash in the last movement of K.207. The *Rondo*, K.269, is of course an alternative finale for this work, so the CD listener can easily programme a substitution. Excellent recording, naturally balanced, adds to the attractions of this highly recommendable CBS disc.

Violin concertos Nos. 1 in B flat, K.207; 5 in A (Turkish), K.219; Adagio in E, K.261.
(M) **(*) DG Dig. 427 813-2; *427 813-4* [id.]. Itzhak Perlman, VPO, Levine.

Perlman's version of K.207 is first class in every way and, like the particularly graceful account of the *Adagio*, K.261, receives accompaniments which are beautifully played and perfectly integrated in a recording which is ideally balanced and very truthful. K.219 is treated rather more like a virtuoso showpiece than is common. For some the tone will be too sweet for Mozart, though Levine and the VPO are again in good form.

Violin concertos Nos. 2 in D, K.211; 4 in D, K.218.
*** EMI Dig. CDC7 47011-2 [id.]. Anne-Sophie Mutter, Philh. O, Muti.

Anne-Sophie Mutter is given very sensitive support from the Philharmonia under Muti. Her playing combines purity and classical feeling, delicacy and incisiveness, and is admirably expressive. Its freshness too is most appealing, and she is a strong contender in a very competitive field. The EMI recording is very good; the images are sharply defined, but the balance is convincing.

Violin concertos Nos. 2 in D, K.211; 7 in D, K.271a; Rondo in C, K.373.
*** Sony Dig. SK 44913 [id.]; *40-44913*. Cho-Liang Lin, ECO, Leppard.

Lin's coupling of the early *D major concerto* and the doubtfully attributed K.271a follows the pattern of his earlier Mozart recordings in sweet, elegant playing, beautifully supported by Leppard in a traditional but uninflated style. First-rate recording.

Violin concertos Nos. 3 in G, K.216; 4 in D, K.218; Rondos (for violin & orchestra) Nos. 1 in B flat, K.269; 2 in B flat, K.373.
(M) *** DG Dig. 431 282-2; *431 282-2*. Itzhak Perlman, VPO, Levine.

Perlman likes to be closely balanced, and in K.216 one is very conscious of his virtuosity. In No. 4 the artistic rapport between soloist and orchestra is particularly striking. Once again Perlman's bravura is effortless and even more charismatic, and the orchestral playing is glorious. The perspective of the recording seems rather more natural here. The two engaging *Rondos* are played with fine style.

Violin concertos Nos. 3 in G, K.216; 5 in A (Turkish), K.219.
(M) *** DG 429 814-2; *429 814-4* [id.]. Anne-Sophie Mutter, BPO, Karajan.
(BB) *** Naxos Dig. 8.550063 [id.]. Takako Nishizaki, Capella Istropolitana, Stephen Gunzenhauser.

Violin concertos Nos. 3, K.216; 5 (Turkish); Adagio in E, K.261.
*** Sony Dig. MK 42364 [id.]. Cho-Liang Lin, ECO, Leppard.

Extraordinarily mature and accomplished playing from Anne-Sophie Mutter, who was a mere fourteen years old when her recording was made. The instinctive mastery means that there is no hint of immaturity: the playing has polish, but fine artistry too and remarkable freshness. Karajan is at his most sympathetic and scales down the accompaniment to act as a perfect setting for his young soloist. The recording has been brilliantly transferred to CD; some might feel that the orchestral strings are a shade too brightly lit.

Lin's persuasive style brings out the tenderness of both slow movements. There is an element of youthful lightness running through the performances of both *Concertos*, though there is no lack of bite and point either. Lin is full of fancy and imagination, apt for the music of a teenager, and only the first movement of K.216 brings a performance that is less fresh and sparkling on some details. Leppard and the ECO are the most responsive of partners, and the recording is first rate.

This is the finest of Nishizaki's three discs of the Mozart violin concertos on Naxos. The readings are individual and possess the most engaging lyrical feeling, stemming directly from the lovely solo timbre and the natural response of the soloist to Mozartian line and phrase. A good balance, the soloist forward, but convincingly so, and the orchestral backcloth, always polished and supportive, in natural perspective. A real bargain.

Violin concerto No. 4 in D, K.218; (i) *Sinfonia concertante in E flat, for violin, viola and orchestra, K.364.*
(BB) **(*) Naxos Dig. 8.550332 [id.]. Takako Nishizaki, (i) Ladislav Kyselak; Capella Istropolitana, Stephen Gunzenhauser.

A fine account of No. 4, with Takako Nishizaki's solo playing well up to the high standard of this series and with Stephen Gunzenhauser's perceptive pacing adding to our pleasure. The *Sinfonia concertante* is very enjoyable too, if perhaps slightly less distinctive. It does not lack intensity of feeling from the well-matched soloists; indeed, at their expressive entry at the end of the exposition there is a brief passage of affectionate indulgence. The finale is infectious in its liveliness, its rhythms buoyantly pointed. Again, a good balance and excellent sound.

Violin concertos Nos. 4, K.218; 5 (Turkish), K.219.
*** Nimbus Dig. NI 5009. Oscar Shumsky, SCO, Yan Pascal Tortelier.

Violin concertos Nos. 4 in D, K.218; 5 in A (Turkish), K.219; Adagio in E, K.261; Rondo in C, K.373.
(M) **(*) Sony SBK 46540 [id.]. Zukerman, St Paul CO.

Shumsky's performances with the Scottish Chamber Orchestra have the advantage of being totally unaffected, natural and full of character. Yan Pascal Tortelier secures a very alive and thoroughly musical response from the orchestra, and the players themselves convey enthusiasm and pleasure. The recording is nicely balanced.

Zukerman's account of K.218 is unmannered and stylish, admirably direct in approach, though the *Andante* is taken rather slowly. The pacing of the last movement is somewhat idiosyncratic. His admirers will not be disappointed with K.219. He languishes lovingly in the slow movement (though rather less so than in the *G major*, K.219) and is not always subtle in his expression of feeling. The shorter pieces are played with some flair, the *Adagio* most appealingly.

Violin concerto No. 5 in A (Turkish), K.219.
(M) *** BMG/RCA GD 87869 [7869-2-RG]. Heifetz with CO – *String quintet, K.516* etc. ***

Marvellously exhilarating Mozart from Heifetz, though his actual entry in the first movement is quite ethereal. He directs the accompanying group himself, the only time he did so on record. The early (1954) stereo is fully acceptable and the performance memorable, with the crystalline clarity of articulation matched by warmth of timbre and aristocratic phrasing.

Concertone in C, K.190; Sinfonia concertante in E flat, for violin, viola and orchestra, K.364.
❀ *** DG 415 486-2 [id.]. Perlman, Zukerman, Israel PO, Mehta.
*** Sony Dig. SK 47693 [id.]. Cho-Liang Lin, Jaime Laredo, ECO, Leppard.
*** Chan. Dig. CHAN 8315; *ABTD 1096* [id.]. Brainin, Schidlof, SNO, Gibson.
**(*) Denon Dig. C37 7507 [id.]. Kantorow, Olga Martinova, Vladimir Mendelssohn, Hans Meijer, Netherlands CO, Hager.

The DG version of the *Sinfonia concertante* was recorded in Tel Aviv at the Huberman Festival in December 1982. It is balanced with the soloists a fraction too near the microphones and with orchestral detail not so clearly focused as on Chandos. The performance is in a special class and is an example of 'live' recording at its most magnetic, with the inspiration of the occasion caught on the wing. Zubin Mehta is drawn into the music-making and accompanies most sensitively. The *Concertone* is also splendidly done (with a fine oboe contribution from Chaim Jouval); the ear notices the improvement in the sound-balance of the studio recording of this work. But the *Sinfonia concertante*, with the audience incredibly quiet, conveys an electricity rarely caught on record.

The final issue in Cho-Liang Lin's outstanding Mozart concerto cycle brings a performance of the *Sinfonia concertante* which is mandatory listening. The playing has great finesse and style, and Lin makes a natural partnership with Laredo. Not surprisingly, Leppard accompanies with character and ensures that the music-making has plenty of vitality. Neil Black (oboe) and Charles Tunnell (cello) add to the distinction of the *Concertone*. The recording is reverberant, which brings a large-scale orchestral image, but it is fuller and smoother than the DG alternative, if not as clearly defined as the Chandos disc.

The responsive playing of Norbert Brainin and Peter Schidlof does bring a degree of romanticism to the slow movement of the *Sinfonia concertante*, and their phrasing employs tenutos, at times rather indulgently. Yet there is no lack of vitality in outer movements, and Sir Alexander Gibson's accompaniments are stylish and strong. The *Concertone*, where Schidlof changes from viola to violin, is also very successful, with Neil Black making an elegant contribution in the concertante oboe role. The sound is first class.

Kantorow forms an excellent partnership with Vladimir Mendelssohn in the *Sinfonia concertante*; in the *Concertone*, Olga Martinova, the violinist, and the fine oboist, Hans Meijer, distinguish themselves. In keeping with the style of Kantorow's concerto series, the playing is refined and classical in spirit. With recording which is naturally balanced and realistic this Denon CD offers performances which give much pleasure in their freshness and natural responsiveness.

Dances and Marches

Contredanses: La Bataille, K.535; Das Donerwetter, K.534; Les filles malicieuses, K.610; Der Sieg vom Helden Koburg, K.587; It trionfo delle donne, K.607. Gallimathias musicum (quodlibet), K.32; 6 German dances, K.567; 3 German dances, K.605; German dance: Die Leyerer, K.611. March in D, K.335/1. A Musical joke, K.522.
*** DG Dig. 429 783-2; *429 783-4* [id.]. Orpheus CO.

A splendid sampler of the wit and finesse, to say nothing of the high quality of entertainment, provided by Mozart's dance music, which kept people on their feet till dawn at masked balls in the 1780s and early 1790s. The little *March in D* is full of buoyant rhythmic zest, and the felicity of the characteristic *Contredanses* is a constant delight, with *Les filles malicieuses* the model of elegance and *La Bataille* picaresquely celebrated with trumpet, fife and drum. *Die Leyerer* ('The hurdy-gurdy men') are no less piquantly depicted, but the other *German dances* (of which the most famous is the *Sleigh-ride*, K.605/3) are hardly less inventive in style and colour. The playing of the Orpheus group is winningly polished, flexible and smiling, and they bring off the *Musical joke* with considerable flair, both in the gentle fun of the *Adagio cantabile*, which is exquisitely played, and in the outrageous grinding dissonance of the 'wrong notes' at the end. First-class sound, fresh, transparent and vividly immediate.

Complete Mozart Edition, Volume 6: *La Chasse, KA.103/K.299d; Contredanses, K.101; K.123; K.267; K.269b; K.462; (Das Donnerwetter) K.534; (La Bataille) K.535; 535a; (Der Sieg vom Helden Koburg) K.587; K.603; (Il trionfo delle donne) K.607; (Non più andrai) K.609; K.610; Gavotte, K.300; German dances, K.509; K.536; K.567; K.571; K.586; K.600; K.602; K.605; Ländler, K.606; Marches, K.214; K.363; K.408; K.461; Minuets, K.61b; K.61g/2; K.61h; K.94, 103, 104, 105; K.122; K.164; K.176; K.315g; K.568; K.585; K.599; K.601; K.604; Minuets with Contredanses, K.463; Overture & 3 Contredanses, K.106.*
❀ (M) *** Ph. 422 506-2 (6). Vienna Mozart Ens., Willi Boskovsky.

Much of the credit for this remarkable undertaking should go to its expert producer, Erik Smith, who, besides providing highly stylish orchestrations for numbers without Mozart's own scoring, illuminates the music with some of the most informative and economically written notes that ever graced a record. The CD transfers preserve the excellence of the mid-1960s sound: it is a shade crisper in definition and outline but has not lost its bloom. The layout is historical, with the music grouped into five sections: Salzburg and Italy (1769–77); Paris (1778); Vienna and Salzburg (1782–4); Prague (1787); and Dances for the Redoutensaal (1788–91). The collector might feel that he or she is faced here with an *embarras de richesses* with more than 120 *Minuets*, nearly 50 *German dances* and some three dozen *Contredanses*, but Mozart's invention is seemingly inexhaustible, and the instrumentation is full of imaginative touches. Of course these are records to be dipped into rather than played a whole disc at a time; but there are surprises everywhere, and much that is inspired.

2 Contredanses, K.603; Contredanse, K.610; 19 German Dances, K.571/1–6; K.600/1–6; K.602/1–4; K.605/1–3; Marches: in D, K.335/1; in C & D, K.408/1–3; 10 Minuets, K.599/1–6; K.601/1–4.
(M) *** Decca 430 634-2; *430 634-4* [id.]. V. Mozart Ens., Willi Boskovsky.

A self-recommending single-disc selection from Boskovsky's admirable survey of Mozart's dance music. The selection, of course, includes the famous *Sleigh ride* (within K.605) which has some superb posthorn playing, and there are other special effects, notably the charming hurdy-gurdy of K.602. The disc plays for over 76 minutes – but, delightful as the music is, it is not to be taken all at once! The transfers are impeccable.

6 German dances, K.571; Les petites riens: ballet music, K.299b; Serenade No. 13 (Eine kleine Nachtmusik), K.525.
*** Erato/Warner Dig. 2292 45198-2 [id.]. SCO, Leppard.

An excellent collection in every way. The performance of *Les petites riens* is delightful, spirited and polished, and the *German dances* are no less lively and elegant; the famous *Nachtmusik* is nicely proportioned and very well played. The sound is especially believable on CD, giving a tangible impression of the players sitting together, out beyond the speakers.

12 German dances, K.586; 6 German dances, K.600; 4 German dances, K.602; 3 German dances, K.605.
(BB) *** Naxos Dig. 8.550412 [id.]. Capella Istropolitana, Johannes Wildner.

Fresh, bright, unmannered performances of some of the dance music Mozart wrote right at the end of his life. The very last item here, the third of the K.605 *Dances*, is the most famous with its sleigh-bells and two posthorns and nicknamed *The Sleigh-ride*. The playing is excellent and the recording is bright and full. An excellent super-bargain alternative to the Boskovsky Decca CD.

Complete Mozart Edition, Volume 45: *'Rarities and curiosities': Contredanses in B flat & D* (completed Smith); *The London Sketchbook:* (i) *3 Contredanses in F; 2 Contredanses in G; 6 Divertimenti.* (ii) *Wind divertimenti* arr. from operas: *Don Giovanni* (arr. Triebensee); *Die Enführung aus dem Serail* (arr. Wendt) & (i) *March, K 384.* (i; iii) *Rondo in E flat for horn and orchestra, K 371* (completed Smith); (iv) *Larghetto for piano and wind quintet, K 452a;* (v) *Modulating prelude in F/E min.* (vi) *Tantum ergo in B flat, K 142; in D, K 197;* (vii) *Idomeneo: Scene & rondo.* (viii) *Musical dice game, K.516.*
(M) *** Ph. 422 545-2 (3) [id.]. (i) ASMF, Marriner; (ii) Netherlands Wind Ens.; (iii) Timothy

Brown; cond. Sillito; (iv) Uchida, Black, King, Farrell, O'Neil; (v) Erik Smith (harpsichord); (vi) Frimmer, Leipzig R. Ch. & SO, Schreier; (vii) Mentzler, Hendricks, Bav. RSO, C. Davis; (viii) Marriner & Smith.

The last box in the Philips Complete Mozart Edition contains three CDs, and most of the real curiosities are to be found on the third. The first includes the innocent little piano pieces from the child Mozart's 'London Notebook' (written while his father was ill). Erik Smith has orchestrated them and, if the results may not be important, they charm the ear at least as much as Mozart's early symphonies, with many unexpected touches. Marriner and the Academy are ideal performers and the 1971 recording is warm and refined. Then come the arrangements for wind of selections from two key operas (though why not *Nozze di Figaro* which Johann Wendt also scored and which exists in a Decca recording by the London Wind Soloists?). However, what we are offered, elegantly played by the Netherlands Wind Ensemble, is gracious and satisfying. Finally come the rarities and curiosities, the *Rondo for horn and orchestra* with the missing 60 bars (discovered only in 1989) now added, and the other music made good by Erik Smith: a not very important fragment for piano and wind quintet; two extra *Contredanses* and a pair of *Tantum ergo* settings that may or may not be authentic. There is an extra aria for *Idomeneo*, a March first intended for *Die Entführung* then abandoned, and a curious finale in which Erik Smith and Sir Neville Marriner participate (with spoken comments) in a *Musical dice game* to decide the order of interchangeable phrases in a very simple musical composition. The result, alas, is something of a damp squib.

Divertimenti and Serenades

Complete Mozart Edition, Volume 4: *Divertimenti for strings Nos. 1–3, K.136/8; Divertimenti for small orchestra Nos. 1 in E flat, K.113; 7 in D, K.205* (with *March in D, K.290); 10 in F, K.247* (with *March in F, K.248); 11 in D, K.251; 15 in B flat, K.287; 17 in D, K.334* (with *March in D, K.445); A Musical joke, K.622; Serenade (Eine kleine Nachtmusik), K.525.*
(M) *** Ph. Dig. 422 504-2 (5) [id.]. ASMF CO.

This is one of the most attractive of all the boxes in the Philips Mozart Edition. The music itself is a delight, the performances are stylish, elegant and polished, while the digital recording has admirable warmth and realistic presence and definition.

Divertimenti for strings Nos. 1–2, K.136/7; Serenades Nos. 6 (Serenata notturna), K.239; 13 (Eine kleine Nachtmusik), K.525.
*** Capriccio 10185 [id.]. Salzburg Mozarteum Camerata Academica, Végh.

Divertimenti for strings Nos. 1–3, K.136–8; Serenades Nos. 6 (Serenata notturna); 13 in G (Eine kleine Nachtmusik), K.525.
(M) *** Ph. Dig. 432 055-2; *432 055-4*. I Musici.

The newest digital recording of the Salzburg *Divertimenti* by I Musici is particularly successful, extremely vivid and clean, bringing the players before one's very eyes. Their outstanding recording of the three *String divertimenti* is now joined with their remarkably fresh account of *Eine kleine Nachtmusik*, as fine as any in the catalogue and better than most. A self-recommending mid-priced reissue, except for the lack of any information about the music being included.

Delightfully bold, fresh and characterful performances from the Salzburg group, very well recorded. Only in the slow movement of *Eine kleine Nachtmusik*, taken rather slowly, is the playing a shade less refined. Curiously, Végh changes the regular order of movements in K.137, making it a conventional fast-slow-fast piece, though neither the label nor the note recognizes the change.

Complete Mozart Edition, Volume 5: *Divertimentos for wind Nos. 3 in E flat, K.166; 4 in B flat, K.186; 6 in C, K.188; 8 in F, K.213; 9 in B flat K.240; 12 in E flat, K.252; 13 in F, K.253; 14 in B flat, K.270; 16 in E flat, K.289; in E flat, K.Anh. 226; in B flat, K.Anh. 227; Divertimentos for 3 basset horns, K.439b/1–5; Duos for 2 horns, K.487/1–12; Serenades for wind No. 10 in B flat, K.361; 11 in E flat, K.375; 12 in C min., K.388; Adagios: in F; B flat, K.410–11.*
(M) *** Ph. Analogue/Dig. 422 505-2 [id.]. Holliger Wind Ens. (or members of); Netherlands Wind Ens., De Waart (or members of); ASMF, Marriner or Laird.

Mozart's wind music, whether in the ambitious *Serenades* or the simpler *Divertimenti*, brings a naturally felicitous blending of timbre and colour unmatched by any other composer. It seems that even when writing for the simplest combination of wind instruments, Mozart is incapable of being dull. The works for two horns are conjecturally allocated. The principal role involves some hair-raising bravura; thus it is suggested by some authorities that they were intended for basset horns. But given the kind of easy virtuosity they receive here, from Iman Soeteman and Jan Peeters, they get our vote in favour of horns every time. To afford maximum variety, they are presented in groups of three movements, interspersed with the other divertimenti. The playing of the more ambitious works is admirably polished and fresh, and it is interesting to note that Holliger's group provides a stylishly light touch and texture with the principal oboe dominating, while the blending of the Netherlanders is somewhat more homogeneous, though the effect is still very pleasing.

Divertimenti Nos. 7 in D, K.205; 17 in D, K.334; March in D, K.290.
(B) *** Hung. White Label HRC 080 [id.]. Liszt CO, Rolla or Sándor.

An outstanding bargain coupling of two of Mozart's finest *Divertimenti*, in stylish chamber orchestra versions, elegantly played and truthfully recorded in a most pleasing acoustic. K.205 is scored for string trio, plus horns and bassoon, but Mozart's part-writing skilfully ensures that the basic texture is rich; and in the *Adagio* the interplay between violins and violas is especially felicitous. K.334 is perhaps the most familiar of all Mozart's large-scale works in this form, and its famous Minuet has more natural rhythmic pulse here than in the Decca version by members of the Vienna Octet.

Divertimenti Nos. 10 in F, K.247; 11 in D, K.331.
**(*) Capriccio 10 203 [id.]. Salzburg Mozarteum Camerata Academica, Végh.

The playing, as in Végh's previous issues, has striking freshness and vitality; these are chamber orchestral performances on modern instruments, but the scale is admirable and the resonance adds a feeling of breadth. Detail is well observed – there is some fine oboe playing in K.251 – and tempi are usually apt. Although slow movements tend to be on the slow side, while not lacking grace, allegros sparkle and have dash without ever seeming hurried, even if ensemble isn't always absolutely immaculate.

Divertimenti Nos. 11 in D, K.251; 14 in B flat, K.270; Serenade No. 6 in D (Serenata notturna), K.239.
*** DG Dig. 415 669-2 [id.]. Orpheus CO.

These are wholly admirable performances. Alert, crisply rhythmic allegros show consistent resilience, strong yet without a touch of heaviness, while slow movements are warmly phrased, with much finesse and imaginative use of light and shade. The *Serenata notturna*, which can easily sound bland, has a fine sparkle here, while the *B flat Wind Divertimento* makes an effective contrast. Here the oboe playing is particularly felicitous. Impeccable in ensemble, this playing has no sense of anonymity of character or style. The recording is truthful but rather closely balanced, with a touch of edginess to the violins above the stave.

Divertimento No. 15 in B flat, K.287; Divertimento for strings No. 3, K.138.
*** Ph. Dig. 412 740-2 [id.]. ASMF Chamber Ens.

The K.287 *Divertimento*, composed in Salzburg for the Countess Lodron, is a major six-movement piece, with an attractive theme with variations coming second and a central *Adagio*, led by the first violin, of considerable expressive intensity. The finale is witty and humorously based on a folksong ('The farmer's wife has lost the cat'). The ASMF performance here, with a double bass and two horns added to a string quartet, is admirable and beautifully recorded. The *String divertimento* makes an agreeable filler.

Divertimento No. 17; Divertimento for strings No. 1, K.136.
*** Denon Dig C37 7080 [id.]. Augmented Berlin Philh. Qt.

Divertimento No. 17; Notturno (Serenade) in D, K.286; Serenade No. 13 in G (Eine kleine Nachtmusik), K.525.
(B) *** Decca 430 496-2; *430 496-4*. ASMF, Marriner.

Mozart's innocently tricky *Notturno for four orchestras*, with its spatial interplay, is here played with superb style and is very well recorded. The *Divertimento*, equally, finds the Academy of St Martin's at its peak, relishing the technical problems of co-ordinating music which is often performed by solo strings and playing with great finesse. The analogue recording from the old Argo catalogue of the most popular of Mozart's serenades is delightfully played and wears its years lightly, like the others on this disc.

On Denon, a hardly less successful account from the augmented Berlin Philharmonia Quartet. The music-making is polished, spirited and full of warmth. The *String divertimento* is equally attractive but makes a less substantial encore than the ASMF programme. The digital recording is fresh and believable.

Galimathias musicum (Quodlibet), K.32; Wind divertimenti (arr. from operas by Johann Wendt): *Die Entführung aus dem Serail; Le nozze di Figaro.*
(BB) *** HM/BMG VD 77576 [id.]. Coll. Aur.

It is good to have a fine, inexpensive version of Mozart's engaging *Quodlibet* (written at the tender age of ten), coupled with the entertaining Wendt wind arrangements, which select the best tunes from two favourite operas. *Le nozze di Figaro overture* sounds very personable here, but the *Overture* for *Die Entführung* is cut back to 1½ minutes. The authentic wind instruments bring plenty of character and colour, although the voices are missed in the legato arias, like *Porgi amor.* The account of the *Galimathias musicum* is not quite as finished at that by the Orpheus Chamber Orchestra, but it is pleasingly sprightly. The variety of the scoring in this series of seventeen vignettes is amazing: there is some fine writing for solo oboe and horns, an engaging harpsichord solo, plus a remarkable fugato finale. Good, natural sound.

Complete Mozart Edition, Volume 25: (i) *Idomeneo* (ballet music), *K.367;* (ii) *Les petits riens* (ballet), *K.299b; Music for a pantomime (Pantalon und Colombine), K.446* (completed and orch. Beyer); *Sketches for a ballet intermezzo, K.299c* (completed and orch. Erik Smith); (iii) *Thamos, King of Egypt* (incidental music), *K.345.*
(M) *** Ph. 422 525-2 (2) [id.]. (i) Netherlands CO, David Zinman; (ii) ASMF, Marriner; (iii) Eickstädt, Pohl, Büchner, Polster, Adam, Berlin R. Ch. & State O, Klee.

This volume collects together Mozart's theatre music and makes a particularly enticing package. Zinman and his Netherlanders give a neatly turned account of the ballet from *Idomeneo*, musical and spirited, and the 1974 recording sounds well. Marriner takes over with modern digital sound for *Les petits riens* and the two novelties, and the ASMF playing has characteristic elegance and finesse. The two novelties are almost more enticing. The *Sketches for a ballet intermezzo* survive only in a single-line autograph, but Erik Smith's completion and scoring provide a series of eight charming vignettes, most with descriptive titles, ending with a piquant *Tambourin.* The music for *Pantalon and Columbine* (more mime than ballet) survives in the form of a first violin part, and Franz Beyer has skilfully orchestrated it for wind and strings, using the first movement of the *Symphony*, K.84, as the overture and the last movement of *Symphony*, K.120, as the finale. Beautifully played as it is here, full of grace and colour, this is a real find and the digital recording is first rate. *Thamos, King of Egypt* comes from 1779 when Mozart was commissioned to provide incidental music for Gebler's play; it was eventually used for another play. Some of the choruses look forward to *Zauberflöte*, though in general one is reminded most of *Idomeneo.* In any event, it is marvellous music which it is good to have on record, particularly in such persuasive hands as these. The choral singing is impressive and the orchestral playing is excellent.

Masonic funeral music: see also below, in VOCAL MUSIC, under Complete Mozart Edition, Volume 22

Masonic funeral music, K.477; Overtures: Così fan tutte; The Impresario; Le nozze di Figaro; Die Zauberflöte; Serenade No. 13 (Eine kleine Nachtmusik), K.525.
(B) **(*) Sony MYK 42593 [MYK 37774]. Columbia SO, Bruno Walter.

Walter conducts all this music with evident affection; even if some may feel that he is almost too loving at times, particularly in *Eine kleine Nachtmusik*, there is still something very special about this music-making. His tempi in the overtures are unerringly apt. The account of the *Masonic funeral music* is particularly fine. The recording is warm and full, with an ample bass, but a remarkably fresh upper range, with sweet violins.

A Musical joke, K.522.
*** Erato/Warner Dig. 2292 45199-2 [id.]. Paillard CO, Paillard – L. MOZART: *Cassation* etc. ***

(i) *A Musical Joke, K.522;* (ii) *Notturno for 4 orchestras, K.286; Serenades Nos. 6 (Serenata notturna), K.239;* (iii) *13 in G (Eine kleine Nachtmusik), K.525.*

(M) *** Decca 430 259-2; *430 259-4*. V. Mozart Ens., Boskovsky.
(B) ** Decca 433 634-2; *433 634-4*. (i) V. Mozart Ens., Boskovsky; (ii) LSO, Maag; (iii) Israel PO, Mehta.

A Musical joke, K.522; Serenade No. 13 in G (Eine kleine Nachtmusik), K.525.
*** DG 400 065-2 [id.]. Augmented Amadeus Qt.

This delightful collection from Decca at medium price shows just how good Boskovsky and his Vienna Mozart Ensemble were in their prime. The recordings were made in the Sofiensaal in 1968–9 and 1978 (K.239 and K.286); in remastered form they all sound wonderfully fresh and realistic. We have often praised this version of *Eine kleine Nachtmusik* for its grace and spontaneity – one has the impression that one is hearing the piece for the first time – and the same comment could be applied to the string playing in the *Musical joke* (especially the delectable Minuet and the neat, zestful finale which ends with spectacular dissonance). The *Notturno for four orchestras* is a less inspired piece, but its spatial echoes are ingeniously contrived and their perspective admirably conveyed by the recording.

Happily paired with a high-spirited version of Leopold Mozart's *Toy symphony*, Paillard's account of Mozart's fun piece makes the most of its outrageous jokes, with the horns in the opening movement boldly going wrong and the final discordant clash sounding positively cataclysmic; yet it takes into account the musical values, too. The recording is excellent, the orchestral group being placed within a warm ambience which yet does not cloud inner detail.

Eine kleine Nachtmusik has rarely sounded as refreshing and exhilarating as in this Amadeus chamber performance; the finale in particular is delectably resilient. The musical clowning in the *Musical joke*, which can so often seem heavy and unfunny, is here given charm. The horn players, Gerd Seifert and Manfred Klier, are from the Berlin Philharmonic. The recording is first rate.

Peter Maag, in co-operation with the Decca engineers, was the first to show – in his 1960 recording of the *Notturno* – how the backward perspective and spatial interplay of Mozart's four orchestral groups could be conveyed in stereo and, quite apart from the special effects, his performance is musically most satisfying. The body and fullness of the orchestral sound are as impressive as the alert, gracious playing of the LSO, both here and in the *Serenata notturna*, which sounds uncommonly fresh, even if the timpani are backwardly balanced (perhaps on purpose). Boskovky's account of the *Musical Joke* is second to none, and the bright, 1971 recording is equally attractive. What a pity that these excellent performances have been saddled with Mehta's strong but unrefined 1978 version of *Eine kleine Nachtmusik*, which is not helped by fierce reproduction of the Israeli strings. But without this, there is still fifty minutes of fine music-making here, and the disc is modestly priced.

Notturno for four orchestras, K.286; Serenade No. 6 (Serenata notturna), K.239; Serenade No. 13 (Eine kleine Nachtmusik), K.525.
*** O-L Dig. 411 720-2 [id.]. AAM, Hogwood.

Eine kleine Nachtmusik is usually given in the four-movement form that survives. Christopher Hogwood uses an additional minuet that Mozart composed in collaboration with his English pupil, Thomas Attwood. All the repeats in every movement save one are observed – which is perhaps too much of a good thing. The performance is given one instrument to a part and is sprightly and alive. The *Serenata notturna* and the *Notturno for four orchestras* are for larger forces and are given with considerable panache. Technically, this is first class, with clean and well-defined recorded sound and great presence.

Overtures: *Apollo et Hyacinthus; Bastien und Bastienne; La clemenza di Tito; Così fan tutte; Don Giovanni; Die Entführung aus dem Serail; La finta giardiniera; Idomeneo; Lucio Silla; Mitridate, rè di Ponto; Le nozze di Figaro; Il rè pastore; Der Schauspieldirektor; Die Zauberflöte.*
(BB) *** Naxos Dig. 8.550185; *4550185* [id.]. Capella Istropolitana, Barry Wordsworth.

Wordsworth follows up his excellent series of Mozart symphonies for Naxos with this generous collection of overtures, no fewer than 14 of them, arranged in chronological order and given vigorous, stylish performances. In Italian overture form, *Mitridate* and *Lucio Silla*, like miniature symphonies, have separate tracks for each of their three contrasted sections. Very well recorded, the disc is highly recommendable at super-bargain price.

Serenades Nos. 3 in D, K.185; 4 in D (Colloredo), K.203.
(BB) *** Naxos Dig. 8.550413; *4550413* [id.]. Salzburg CO, Harald Nerat.

Well-played, nicely phrased and musical accounts on Naxos, recorded in a warm, reverberant acoustic, but one in which detail clearly registers. The Salzburg Chamber Orchestra has real vitality, and most readers will find these accounts musically satisfying and very enjoyable. This offers particularly good value in terms of playing time.

Serenades Nos. 6 in D (Serenata notturna), K.239; 7 in D (Haffner), K.250.
*** Telarc Dig. CD 80161 [id.]. Prague CO, Mackerras.
**(*) Erato/Warner 2292 45559-2 [id.]. Saar R. CO, Karl Ristenpart.

In Mackerras's coupling the playing is lively and brilliant, helped by warm recorded sound, vivid in its sense of presence, except that the reverberant acoustic clouds the tuttis a little. The violin soloist, Oldrich Viček, is very much one of the team under the conductor rather than a virtuoso establishing his individual line. By omitting repeats in the *Haffner*, Mackerras leaves room for the other delightful *Serenade*, just as haunting, with the terracing between the solo string quartet (in close focus) and the full string band aptly underlined.

Ristenpart secures some polished and sprightly playing, especially from the strings in the *Haffner Serenade*, and this well recorded 1965 account makes a good coupling with the slightly less memorable *Serenata notturna*. Not a first choice, but well worth considering as the transfer is smooth and vivid.

Serenades Nos. 6 in D (Serenata notturna), K.239; 9 in D (Posthorn), K.320.
*** Novalis Dig. 150 013-2 [id.]. Bav. RSO, C. Davis.

Davis secures consistently spirited and responsive playing from the Bavarian Radio Orchestra, not only from the strings but also from the woodwind in their concertante section. The posthorn soloist is also a very stylish player; his contribution is unusually refined, yet still tonally robust. With apt tempi and a fine sense of spontaneity throughout, this is very refreshing. The *Serenata notturna* is also well done, if without quite the sparkle of K.320 – here the backwardly balanced drums sound a shade too resonant.

Serenades Nos. 6 in D (Serenata notturna), K.239; 13 in G (Eine kleine Nachtmusik), K.525.
(B) *** Pickwick Dig. PCD 861; *CIMPC 861* [id.]. Serenata of London – ELGAR: *Serenade*; GRIEG: *Holberg suite*. ***

The performance of the *Night music* by the Serenata of London is as fine as any available. There is not a suspicion of routine here; indeed the players, for all the excellence of their ensemble, give the impression of coming to the piece for the first time. The *Serenata notturna* is perhaps not quite so inspired a work, but these excellent players make a good case for it and are agreeably sprightly whenever given the opportunity. The recording has striking naturalness and realism; this is an outstanding CD bargain.

Serenade No. 7 in D (Haffner), K.250; March in D, K.249.
*** Ph. Dig. 416 154-2 [id.]. I. Brown, ASMF, Marriner.

A spacious, yet warm and polished account of the *Haffner serenade* from Marriner and his Academy players, with Iona Brown making a superb contribution in the concertante violin role. There is sparkle here as well as expressive grace. The recording is resonant, which increases the impression of a full orchestral performance rather than one on a chamber scale. As usual, the Philips engineers provide a natural sound-balance.

Serenade No. 9 in D (Posthorn), K.320; A Musical joke, K.522.
(BB) *** HM/BMG VD 77544; *VK 77544* [77544-2-RV; *77544-4-RV*]. Coll. Aur., Franzjosef Maier.

(i) *Serenade No. 9 in D (Posthorn);* (ii) *Wind divertimenti: in E flat, K.166; in B flat, K.227.*
(M) **(*) DG 429 807-2; *429 807-4* [id.]. (i) BPO, Boehm; (ii) VPO Wind Ens.

Serenades Nos. 9 in D (Posthorn); 13 (Eine kleine Nachtmusik), K.525.
(B) *** Decca 417 874-2; *417 874-4*. V. Mozart Ens., Boskovsky.
**(*) Telarc CD 10108 [id.]. Prague CO, Mackerras.

Aficionados should certainly not overlook the Collegium Aureum period-instrument version of the *Posthorn Serenade*, particularly as it is now offered at superbargain price. The playing is sensitive and vital and never sounds pedantic. Indeed the woodwind sounds in the first-movement *Allegro con spirito* are full of character and quite delightful in the concertante, *Andante grazioso*. The remastered recording (from 1976), made in the spacious acoustics of

Schloss Kirchheim, brings a brighter sound than in the earlier *Serenades* and gives the players a striking presence. The *Musical joke* (recorded in 1979) is effectively presented on a chamber sextet. The use of one instrument to each part is especially telling in the vivacious finale.

Bargain hunters should also be well pleased with Decca's Weekend reissue of Boskovsky's performance with its natural musicality and sense of sparkle. The newest transfer is a little dry in the matter of string timbre, but there is plenty of bloom on the wind, detail is clean and the posthorn is tangible in its presence. The coupled *Night music* is one of the freshest and most attractive performances of this much-played work in any format, and the small string group is most realistically balanced and vividly projected.

Boehm's 1971 Berlin Philharmonic recording of the *Posthorn Serenade* sounds particularly fresh in its digitally remastered format. The playing is characteristically polished, warm and civilized. Two attractive *Wind divertimenti* are now offered as couplings. Like their companion included with Boehm's *Haffner serenade*, they are sensitively played and well blended, but the digital mastering sounds a bit top-heavy.

The Prague strings have great warmth and Mackerras gets vital results from his Czech forces. Rhythms are lightly sprung and the phrasing is natural in every way. The Telarc acoustic is warm and spacious with a wide dynamic range (some might feel it is too wide for this music), and most ears will find the effect agreeable.

Serenade No. 10 in B flat for 13 wind instruments, K.361.
*** ASV Dig. CDCOE 804; *ZCCOE 804* [id.]. COE Wind Soloists, Schneider.
*** Ph. Dig. 412 726-2 [id.]. ASMF, Marriner.
**(*) Accent ACC 68642D [id.]. Octophorus, Kuijken.
(B) **(*) Hung. White Label HRC 076 [id.]. Hungarian State Op. Wind Ens., Ervin Lukacs.

The brilliant young soloists of the Chamber Orchestra of Europe, inspired by the conducting of Alexander Schneider, give an unusually positive, characterful reading. Right at the start, the flourishes from the first clarinet are far more effective when played as here, not literally, but with Schneider leading them on to the first forte chord from the full ensemble. From then on the individual artistry of the players is most winning. The only controversial point is that where the first *Adagio* – nowadays the most popular movement of all, thanks to the sound-track of the film, *Amadeus* – flows very persuasively rather faster than usual, the second *Adagio*, phrased subtly, sounds rather heavier than usual at a slower, more relaxed speed. The sound is exceptionally vivid and faithful.

The Marriner version fits very stylishly in the Academy's series of Mozart wind works, characteristically refined in its ensemble, with matching of timbres and contrasts beautifully judged, both lively and graceful with rhythms well sprung and speeds well chosen, yet with nothing mannered about the result. Full, warm recording that yet allows good detail.

On period instruments Barthold Kuijken directs his talented team in an authentic performance where the matching is never uncomfortably raw, though the distinctive character of eighteenth-century instruments brings a sparer, lighter texture, as it should. Speeds tend to be on the cautious side but the liveliness of the playing makes up for that. The recording adds to the clarity.

Of the bargain versions of Mozart's large-scale wind serenade the Hungaroton is the other one to go for. The blending of the wind players from the Hungarian State Opera is impressive and their performance has an attractively robust character with buoyant allegros, and plenty of flexibility in slow movements. The sound is excellent, naturally vivid within an attractive ambience.

Serenades Nos. 10 in B flat; 11 in E flat, K.375.
(M) *** Ph. 420 711-2. Netherlands Wind Ens., Edo de Waart.
(M) *** Decca 425 421-2; *425 421-4*. L. Wind Soloists, Jack Brymer.

The Netherlanders' performances are fresh and alive, admirably sensitive both in feeling for line and in phrasing, but never lingering too lovingly over detail. Both works are enhanced by the presence and sonority of the recording.

Brymer's group gives a strong, stylish performance of the large-scale *B flat major Serenade* with plenty of imagination in matters of phrasing. The Decca balance is rather close, but this has always been one of the best versions and now, with an equally fine account of K.375 added for the reissue, it is again very competitive; the digital remastering has great presence.

Serenades for wind Nos. 11 in E flat, K.375; 12 in C min., K.388.
*** ASV Dig. CDCOE 802; *ZCCOE 802* [id.]. COE, Schneider.

With Schneider as a wise and experienced guide, the COE Wind give performances which combine brilliance and warmth with a feeling of spontaneity. Schneider very persuasively encourages the individuality of particular soloists, so that the result is both natural and compelling. K.375 in particular is a delight, as genial as it is characterful, conveying the joy of the inspiration. K.388 might have been more menacing at the C minor opening, but the result is most persuasive, with excellent digital sound set against a warm but not confusing acoustic.

Serenade No. 12 in C min., K.388; Wind divertimenti Nos. 12 in E flat, K.252; 13 in F, K.253; 14 in B flat, K.270; 16 in E flat, K.289.
(M) *** Decca 430 298-2; *430 298-4* [id.]. London Wind Soloists, Jack Brymer.

The playing here is of the very highest order. These artists do not miss the sombre quality of the *C minor Serenade* but they are not intimdated by it, and the *Andante* has a winningly gentle poignancy. The other *Divertimenti* are all minor masterpieces. Throughout, the ear delights in the captivating oboe-playing of Terence MacDonagh (his colleague is James Brown; Brymer and Walter Lear are the clarinettists, Roger Birnstingle and Ronald Waller the bassoonists; and the horn players are Alan Civil and Ian Beers). There are countless felicities: all the finales have a wonderfully light touch, but one remembers especially the engaging three-movement *Divertimento in F*, K.253, with its charming first-movement theme and variations and its slow Minuet with its playful Trio. Excellent recording.

Serenade No. 13 in G (Eine kleine Nachtmusik), K.525.
*** Ph. Dig. 410 606-2 [id.]. I Musici (with concert of Baroque music***).
*** DG Dig. 400 034-2 [id.]. BPO, Karajan – GRIEG: *Holberg suite;* PROKOFIEV: *Symphony No. 1.* ***
(*) Virgin Dig. VC7 90786-2; *VC 790786-4* [id.]. Ac. of L., Richard Stamp – PROKOFIEV: *Peter* * ❀; SAINT-SAËNS: *Carnival.* ***

Serenade No. 13 (Eine kleine Nachtmusik); Adagio and fugue in C min., K.546.
**(*) Ph. Dig. 416 386-2 [id.]. ASMF, Marriner – L. MOZART: *Toy symphony;* PACHELBEL: *Canon and gigue.* **(*)

I Musici play the music with rare freshness, giving the listener the impression of hearing the work for the first time. The playing is consistently alert and sparkling, with the *Romanze* particularly engaging. The recording is beautifully balanced.

Apart from a self-conscious and somewhat ponderous minuet, Karajan's is a very fine performance, the playing beautifully cultured, with finely shaped phrasing and well-sprung rhythms. The digital sound, well detailed and not without bloom, is a little sharp-edged.

In his miscellaneous group of popular classical and Baroque pieces, Marriner gives a polished and elegant account of *Eine kleine Nachtmusik*, clearly designed to caress the ears of traditional listeners wearied by period performance. The second-movement *Romanze* is even more honeyed than usual on muted strings. Beautifully balanced recording. The *Adagio and fugue* makes a curious encore, played quite strongly but in no way distinctive.

Anyone buying Richard Stamp's record for the Prokofiev and Saint-Saëns couplings will find this account of Mozart's *Night music* an enjoyable makeweight, if not really distinctive. It is quite direct and well paced, and the playing has vitality.

Sinfonia concertante in E flat for oboe, clarinet, horn, bassoon and orchestra, K.297b.
**(*) ASV Dig. CDCOE 803; *ZCCOE 803* [id.]. COE, Schneider – BACH: *Double violin concerto;* VIVALDI: *Concerto, RV 556.* **(*)

The team of young wind soloists of the Chamber Orchestra of Europe is exceptional, and though their live recording of the *Sinfonia concertante* brings a performance less immaculate than we expect from them, it is a lively, stylish account with atmospheric if imperfectly balanced sound, not helped by audience noises.

(i) *Sinfonia concertante in E flat for violin, viola and orchestra, K.364;* (ii) *Sinfonia concertante in E flat for oboe, clarinet, horn, bassoon and orchestra, K.297b.*
*** Virgin Dig. VCy 790818-2; *VCy 790818-4* [id.]. (i) Warren-Green, Chase; (ii) Hunt, Collins, Thompson, Alexander; LCO, Warren-Green.

In the ideal coupling of Mozart's paired *Sinfonias concertantes*, Christopher Warren-Green is joined by Roger Chase to provide a characteristically vital account of Mozart's inspired work for violin and viola. The *Andante* is slow and warmly expressive, yet without a trace of sentimentality. This is not quite as inspired as the Perlman/Zukerman account (see above), but it is still very satisfying with its full-timbred sound from soloists and orchestra alike. The coupling, K.297b, is even more delectable and it would be hard to imagine a more persuasive team of wind players than those here. The full-bodied recording has plenty of space and atmosphere and the soloists in both works remain real and tangible.

Complete Mozart Edition, Volume 21: (i) *Sonatas for organ and orchestra (Epistle sonatas) Nos. 1–17* (complete). *Adagio & allegro in F min., K.594; Andante in F, K.616; Fantasia in F min., K.608.*
(M) **(*) Ph. 422 521-2 (2). Daniel Barenboim (organs at Stift Wilhering, Linz, Austria; Schlosspfarrkirche, Obermarchtal, Germany – K.594; K.608); (i) German Bach Soloists, Helmut Winschermann.

The *Epistle sonatas* derive their name from the fact that they were intended to be heard between the Epistle and Gospel in the Mass. Admittedly they are not great music or even first-class Mozart; however, played with relish they make a strong impression. On Philips, the balance folds the organ within the strings, perhaps rather too much so, especially in the later works where the obbligato solo part is more important. The final *Sonata*, K.263, becomes a fully fledged concerto. The set is completed with the other works by Mozart which are usually heard on the organ, and here Barenboim's registration is particularly appealing. Indeed the performances are expert and can be recommended.

SYMPHONIES

Symphonies Nos. 1–47 (including alternative versions); in C, K.35; in D, K.38; in F, K.42a; in B flat, K.45b; in D, K.46a (K.51); in D, K.62a (K.100); in B flat, K.74g (K.216); in F, K.75; in G, K.75b (K.110); in D, K.111a; in D, K.203, 204 & 196 (121); in G, K.425a (K.444); in A min. (Odense); in G (New Lambacher).
(M) *** O-L Analogue/Dig. 430 639-2 (19) [id.]. AAM, Schröder, Hogwood.

The monumental complete recording of the Mozart *Symphonies*, using authentic manners and original instruments, now arrives as a complete set on 19 mid-priced CDs. With Jaap Schröder leading the admirably proportioned string group (9.8.4.3.2) and Christopher Hogwood at the keyboard, this was a remarkably successful joint enterprise. The playing has great style, warmth and polish and, if intonation is not always absolutely refined, that is only to be expected with old instruments. The survey is complete enough to include No. 37 – in fact the work of Michael Haydn but with a slow introduction by Mozart. The *Lambacher* and *Odense Symphonies* are also here, plus alternative versions, with different scoring, of No. 40; while the *Paris Symphony* is given two complete performances with alternative slow movements. These recordings are also available in seven separate boxes of two or (mainly) three CDs, but they are still offered at premium price.

Complete Mozart Edition, Volume 1: *Symphonies Nos. 1 in E in E flat, K.16; 4 in D, K.19; in F, K.19a; 5 in B flat, K.22; 6 in F, K.43; 7 in D, K.45; in G (Neue Lambacher), G.16; in G (Alte Lambacher), K.45a; in B flat, K.45b; 8 in D, K.48; 9 in C, K.73; 10 in G, K.74; in F, K.75; in F, K.76; in D, K.81; 11 in D, K.84; in D, K.95; in C, K.96; in D, K.97; 12 in G, K.110; 13 in F, K.112; 14 in A, K.114; 15 in G, K.124; 16 in C, K.128; 17 in G, K.129; 18 in F, K.130; 19 in E flat, K.132* (with alternative slow movement); *20 in D, K.133; in D, K.161 & 163; in D, K.111 & 120; in D, K.196 & 121; in C, K.208 & 102. Minuet in A, K.61g/1.*
(M) *** Ph. 422 501-2 (6) [id.]. ASMF, Marriner.

The reissue, in the Philips Complete Mozart Edition, of Marriner's recordings of the early symphonies confirms the Mozartian vitality of the performances and their sense of style and spontaneity. There are some important additions, recorded digitally in 1989, notably the *Symphony in F*, K.19a, written when the composer was nine. This reappeared as recently as 1981, when a set of parts was discovered in Munich. Also now included is an alternative Minuet for the Salzburg *Symphony No. 14 in A*, K.114, and another charmingly brief (56 seconds) *Minuet in A*, K.61g/1, previously associated with this work. Modern research suggests that it was written a year earlier (1770), in Italy. The layout remains on six compact discs and the ear is again struck by the naturalness and warm vividness of the transfers. Except perhaps for those who insist on original instruments, the finesse and warmth of the playing here is a constant joy.

Complete Mozart Edition, Volume 2: *Symphonies Nos. 21–36; 37: Adagio maestoso in G, K.44* (Introduction to a symphony by M. Haydn); *38–41; Minuet for a Symphony in C, K.409.*
(M) **(*) Ph. 422 502-2 (6) [id.]. ASMF, Marriner.

As with the early works, the later symphonies in the Marriner performances, as reissued in the Philips Mozart Edition, are conveniently laid out on six mid-priced CDs, offered in numerical sequence, without a single symphony having to be divided between discs. No. 40 is now restored to its expected position, where in the earlier CD box it was out of order. However, the over-resonant bass remains in the recording of this work and also in the *Haffner* (both of which date from 1970, nearly a decade before the rest of the cycle was recorded). Otherwise the transfers are of Philips's best quality, and the performances generally give every satisfaction, even if their style does not show an awareness of the discoveries made – in terms of texture and balance – by the authentic school.

Symphonies Nos. 1 in E flat, K.16; in A min. (Odense), K.16a; 4 in D, K.19; in F, K.19a.
(M) **(*) Unicorn Dig. UKCD 2018. Odense SO, Vetö.

It was in Odense that the lost symphony, K.16a, was discovered by the archivist, Gunnar Thygesen. Alas for everyone's hopes, it seems very unlikely, from stylistic evidence and even the key, A minor, that it is genuine Mozart. It remains a charming work in the *Sturm und Drang* manner, and is well coupled here with an apt group of other early Mozart symphonies, done with warmer tone than those in the Hogwood complete set. First-rate recording.

Symphonies No. 19 in E flat, K.132; 20 in D, K.133; 21 in A, K.134; 22 in C, K.162; 23 in D, K.162b.
*** Telarc Dig. CD 80217 [id.]. Prague CO, Mackerras.

Mackerras, having had great success with his Telarc recordings of the later symphonies, is equally lively in these early works from Mozart's Salzburg period. The surprising thing is how fast his speeds tend to be, not just swifter than a rival such as James Levine – who, with the Vienna Philharmonic, is recorded far more closely in drier sound – but also the Academy of Ancient Music. In one instance the contrast is astonishing, when at a very brisk *Andantino grazioso* Mackerras turns the slow middle movement of No. 23 into a lilting Laendler, quite different from other performances. The recording is reverberant, as in the later symphonies, giving relatively weighty textures; with such light scoring, however, there is ample clarity, with braying horns riding beautifully over the rest. Few will complain – when the five symphonies add up to a disc of over 73 minutes – that Mackerras is less meticulous about observing every single repeat than he was with the later masterpieces.

Symphonies Nos. 21 in A, K.134; 22 in C, K.162; 23 in D, K.181; 24 in B flat, K.182; 25 in G min., K.183.
(B) *** Ph. 426 973-2; *426 973-4*. Concg. O, Josef Krips.

Krips's bargain Concertgebouw sequence of Mozart symphonies leading up to the early masterpiece in G minor (which is done most persuasively) is worth any collector's money. The Dutch players bring the necessary warmth, as well as proving characteristically stylish in phrasing and execution. The 1973/4 sound is full, yet the remastering has brought improved detail and freshness. This is one of the best of the Krips series.

Symphonies Nos. 21 in A, K.134; 23 in D, K.181; 24 in B flat, K.182; 27 in G, K.199.
*** Erato/Warner Dig. 2292 45544-2 [id.]. Amsterdam Bar. O, Koopman.

Koopman's readings of these delightful early symphonies are much less severe than most on period instruments, and are sparklingly recorded. Helped by the sound-quality, Koopman consistently catches the fun of early Mozart, as in the delectable finale of No. 21. He also brings out the lightness and elegance of slow movements. This is one of the most enjoyable of recent Mozart symphony records, a welcome foretaste of Koopman's projected cycle of all the symphonies.

Symphonies Nos. 24–36; 38–41 (Jupiter); Masonic funeral music; Minuet & Trio, K.409.
(M) **(*) EMI Dig. CMS7 63856-2 (6). ASMF, Marriner.

Marriner's third set of Mozart symphony recordings is the most beautifully recorded of all. The playing, too, is graceful and elegant. With bracing rhythms and brisker pacing than in his earlier, Philips set, these readings are positive yet unidiosyncratic. Phrasing is supple and the Mozartian spirit is always alive here. There is not quite the incandescent freshness of his earliest, Argo/Decca series (see below), and there is a degree of disappointment in the *Haffner* and *Jupiter Symphonies*, which are slightly undercharacterized. For the most part, however, this music-making will give a great deal of pleasure. The six individual CDs are offered here at mid-price, in their original jewel-boxes, within a slip-case.

Symphonies Nos. 24 in B flat, K.173; 26 in E flat, K.161a; 27 in G, K.161b; 30 in D, K.202.
*** Telarc Dig. CD 80186 [id.]. Prague CO, Mackerras.

With discreet use of harpsichord continuo, Mackerras's readings are consistently stylish in their refreshing Mozart manners. Where in later symphonies Mackerras chooses more relaxed speeds, here he tends to be more urgent, as in the finale of No. 26 or the *Andantino grazioso* slow movement of No. 27, where he avoids the questionable use of muted strings. The reverberation of the recording gives the impression of a fairly substantial orchestra, without loss of detail, and anyone fancying this particular group of early Mozart symphonies need not hesitate.

Symphonies Nos. 25 in G min., K.183; 26 in E flat, K.184; 27 in G, K.199; 29 in A, K.201; 32 in G, K.318.
(M) *** Decca 430 268-2; *430 268-4*. ASMF, Marriner.

A splendidly generous reissue (70 minutes) which makes a fascinating comparison with Marriner's most recent digital recordings for EMI. Although the remastered Argo sound – which is brighter and with rather more edge to the violins – has something to do with it, there is no doubt that in 1969 and 1971 the Academy playing had greater rhythmic bite than it displays in the late 1980s. With an aptly sized group, very well balanced by the engineers, Marriner secures effervescent performances of the earlier symphonies, especially the little *G minor*, the first of the sequence of really great works. The scale of No. 29 is broad and forward-looking, yet the continuing alertness is matched by lightness of touch, while the imaginative detail of any interpretative freedoms adds positively to the enjoyment. The spacious acoustic is well controlled on CD and, though textures are less glowingly rich than in the EMI series, that doesn't seem aurally disadvantageous.

Symphonies Nos. 25 in G min., K.183; 26 in E flat, K.184; 29 in A, K.201.
*** DG Dig. 431 679-2 [id.]. E. Concert, Pinnock.

Coupling the two finest (and most popular) of the teenage works, Nos. 25 and 29, with an electrifying account of the tiny No. 26, this first English Concert issue of Mozart symphonies could not be more promising, with freshness and clarity married to persuasive expressiveness and vividly immediate recording. The brief No. 26 immediately brings to mind Pinnock's highly enjoyable DG Archiv issues of Haydn symphonies from the *Sturm und Drang* period. With sharp attack and big contrasts it too becomes a *Sturm und Drang* symphony. Pinnock has you registering the often abrasive toughness that must have hit early listeners, yet he also manages to convey the genial side of Mozart, both in the rhythmic bounce which has long characterized the work of the English Concert and in his choice of speeds. These are period performances for the general listener when, as in his Bach, Pinnock is not afraid to choose relaxed speeds in slow movements, and the rhythmic lift in all movements is consistently infectious. In No. 29 his relaxed view of the *Andante* brings out its lyricism most persuasively, and the natural horns are thrillingly bright in this bouncy, ebullient account of the finale.

Symphonies Nos. 25 in G min., K.183; 28 in C, K.200; 29 in A, K.201.
*** Telarc Dig. CD 80165 [id.]. Prague CO, Mackerras.

If you want performances on modern (as opposed to period) instruments, these are at least as fine as any, fresh and light, with transparent textures set against a warm acoustic and with rhythms consistently resilient. The impression is of an aptly scaled orchestra believably set in a conventional concert hall. Mackerras's speeds are always carefully judged to allow elegant pointing but without mannerism, and the only snag is that second-half repeats are omitted in slow movements, and in the finale too of No. 29.

Symphonies Nos. 25 in G min., K.183; 32 in G, K.318; 41 in C (Jupiter), K.551.
(BB) *** Naxos Dig. 8.550113; *4550113* [id.]. Capella Istropolitana, Barry Wordsworth.

Symphonies Nos. 27 in G, K.199/161b; 33 in B flat, K.319; 36 in C (Linz), K.425.
(BB) *** Naxos Dig. 8.550264; *4550264* [id.]. Capella Istropolitana, Barry Wordsworth.

Symphonies Nos. 28 in C, K.200; 31 in D (Paris), K.297; 40 in G min., K.550.
(BB) *** Naxos Dig. 8.550164; *4550164* [id.]. Capella Istropolitana, Barry Wordsworth.

Symphonies Nos. 29 in A, K.201; 30 in D, K.202; 38 in D (Prague), K.504.
(BB) *** Naxos Dig. 8.550119; *4550119* [id.]. Capella Istropolitana, Barry Wordsworth.

Symphonies Nos. 34 in C, K.338; 35 in D (Haffner), K.385; 39 in E flat, K.543.
(BB) *** Naxos Dig. 8.550186; *4550186* [id.]. Capella Istropolitana, Barry Wordsworth.

Symphonies Nos. 40 in G min., K.550; 41 in C (Jupiter), K.551.
(BB) *** Naxos Dig. 8.550299 [id.]. Capella Istropolitana, Barry Wordsworth.

Barry Wordsworth's series of 15 symphonies on the Naxos super-bargain-priced label brings consistently refreshing and enjoyable performances. The Capella Istropolitana consists of leading members of the Slovak Philharmonic Orchestra of Bratislava; though their string-tone is thinnish, it is very much in scale with the clarity of a period performance but tonally far sweeter. The recording is outstandingly good, with a far keener sense of presence than in most rival versions and with less reverberation to obscure detail in tuttis. Very strikingly indeed, the sound here allows a genuine terracing, with the wind instruments, and the horns in particular, rising clear of the string band. Wordsworth observes exposition repeats in first movements, but in the finales only in such symphonies as Nos. 38 and 41, where the movement particularly needs extra scale. In slow movements, as is usual, he omits repeats. Consistently a principal concern with him is clarity of texture. That means he often adopts speeds that are marginally slower than we expect nowadays in chamber-scale performances; but, with exceptionally clean articulation and infectiously sprung rhythms, the results never drag, even if No. 29 is made to sound more sober than usual. In every way these are worthy rivals to the best full-priced versions, and they can be recommended with few if any reservations. Anyone wanting to sample might try the coupling of Nos. 34, 35 and 39 – with the hard-stick timpani sound at the start of No. 39 very dramatic, preferable even to the near-rival, full-price coupling from Tate (of Nos. 32, 35 and 39). The *Linz* too is outstanding. For some, the option of having the last two symphonies coupled together will be useful.

Symphonies Nos. 25 in G min., K.183; 27 in G, K.199; 31 in D, K.297.
*** EMI Dig. CDC7 49998-2 [id.]. ECO, Jeffrey Tate.

Tate's record, coupling the little *G minor* with the once-neglected but increasingly popular No. 27, as well as the *Paris Symphony*, makes an excellent addition to his successful EMI series. In No. 25 Tate is generally smoother in style than Glover, but the characterization is more marked, with fine detail and clean articulation freshening the result. He gives the symphony a bigger scale than usual by observing second-half repeats, making it a full 27 minutes long. In all three works he provides a winning combination of affectionate manners, freshness and elegance. Like Mackerras in his brighter, more thrustful account of the *Paris*, Tate provides the alternative *Andante* slow movement, an interesting curiosity, and on CD you can readily programme whichever you prefer.

Symphonies Nos. 25 in G min., K.183; 29 in A, K.201; 33 in B flat, K.319.
**(*) ASV Dig. CDDCA 717; *ZCDCA 717* [id.]. L. Mozart Players, Jane Glover.

Glover may not quite match Sir Charles Mackerras in his Prague Chamber Orchestra series for Telarc in flair or imagination, but these are very fresh and enjoyable performances of all three symphonies, with the two greatest of the boyhood works, Nos. 25 and 29, attractively coupled with the most unjustly neglected of the later symphonies, No. 33. The recording, made in Fairfield Hall, Croydon, matches the others in the series, refined and not as immediate as, say, the sound for Mackerras in Prague. Second-half repeats are omitted, but there is little disadvantage in that.

Symphonies Nos. 25 in G min., K.183; 29 in A, K.201; Serenade No. 6 in D (Serenata notturna), K.239.
(B) *** Decca 430 495-2; *430 495-4*. ECO, Britten.

It is striking that in many movements Britten's tempi and even his approach are very close to those of Marriner on his early, Argo recordings; but it is Britten's genius, along with his crisp articulation and sprung rhythms, to provide the occasional touch of pure individual magic. Britten's slow movements provide a clear contrast, rather weightier than Marriner's, particularly in the little *G minor*, where Britten, with a slower speed and more expressive phrasing, underlines the elegiac quality of the music. Full, well-balanced recording. The addition of the

Serenata notturna, played most engagingly, serves only to make this analogue collection more desirable.

Symphonies Nos. 26 in E flat, K.184; 27 in G, K.199; 28 in C, K.200; 29 in A, K.201.
(B) *** Ph. 426 974-2; *426 974-4.* Concg. O, Josef Krips.

Krips secures superbly characterful playing from the Concertgebouw Orchestra: the *Molto presto* of No. 26 is bracingly vigorous, yet the work's lyrical counterpart is eminently graceful. Both the previously underrated No. 28 in C and the first great masterpiece in A major are very persuasively done, with apt pacing and almost ethereal delicacy from the strings in the beautiful *Andante* of No. 29, and the horns thrusting exuberantly in the coda of the finale. The CD transfers are exemplary, greatly improving the original LPs' sound.

Symphonies Nos 26 in E flat, K.184; 27 in G, K.199; 28 in C, K.200; 30 in D, K.202; 32 in G, K.318.
*** ASV Dig. CDDCA 762; *ZCDCA 762* [id.]. LMP, Jane Glover.

Glover's generous coupling of five early symphonies brings typically fresh and direct readings, marked by sharp attack and resilient rhythms, at speeds on the fast side. With tuttis a little weightier than with most rivals, these are brightly enjoyable performances very much in line with the others in the series.

Symphonies Nos. 26 in G min., K.183; 28 in in C, K.200; 29 in A, K.201; 30 in D, K.202.
*** EMI Dig. CDC7 54092-2 [id.]. ECO, Jeffrey Tate.

Tate's readings of these four teenage symphonies are characteristically elegant, matching the fresh and warm qualities in his other Mozart recordings. His reading of No. 29, by far the most ambitious of the group and the most popular, begins with a typically relaxed account of the first movement, light and persuasive; but both in the slow movement and, most strikingly, in the finale he is refreshingly brisk. Warm, well-balanced sound, as in the rest of the this EMI series.

Symphonies Nos. 28 in C, K.200; 29 in A, K.201; 35 in D (Haffner).
*** Sony Dig. SK 48063 [id.]. BPO, Claudio Abbado.

Though Abbado's Berlin sound is weighty – more so than in Levine's similarly 'big band' Mozart recordings with the Vienna Philharmonic – the results are not just big-scaled but elegant too, with horns whooping out brightly. Though Abbado is never mannered, his phrasing and pointing of rhythm are delicately affectionate, conveying an element of fun and with speeds never allowed to drag. Slow movements are kept flowing, and finales are hectically fast, but played with such verve and diamond-bright articulation that there is no feeling of breathlessness. On its different scale, there is the same spirit of players enjoying themselves as in Abbado's recordings with the Chamber Orchestra of Europe. For the most part Abbado is generous with repeats, but with the *Haffner* sparing of them, so that No. 29 emerges as by far the longest of the three symphonies here – the young Mozart spreading his wings. The Sony engineers have coped splendidly with the acoustic problems of the Philharmonie to give a full and forward sound, with good presence.

Symphonies Nos. 29–36; 38–41; Divertimento No. 7 in D, K.205; 2 Marches, K.335.
(M) **(*) EMI CZS7 67301-2 (4). ECO, Barenboim.

Barenboim's recordings were made at Abbey Road over a five-year span, between 1966 and 1971. The use of an authentic-sized orchestra of modern instruments ensures that the balance between sections is accurate, although the sound caught by the EMI engineers is forward and full-bodied, with a resonant bass. With fine rhythmic pointing and consistently imaginative phrasing, these performances certainly have a place in the catalogue. Nos. 29 and 34 are particularly successful, and the *Paris* (No. 31) is also given an outstanding performance, the contrasts of mood in the first movement underlined and the finale taken at a hectic tempo that would have sounded breathless with players any less brilliant than the ECO. The later symphonies are also available separately and are discussed below, although they have been remastered again for the present box and the sound is now fuller, especially for the strings, bringing added weight. The box also includes the *D major Serenade*, K.205, which responds well to Barenboim's affectionate treatment, while the two *Marches* are attractively jaunty and colourful.

Symphonies Nos. 29 in A, K.201; 32 in G, K.318; 33 in B flat, K.319; 35 (Haffner), 36 (Linz); 38 (Prague); 39 in E flat, K.543; 40 in G min., K.550; 41 (Jupiter).

(M) *** DG 429 668-2 (3) [id.]. BPO, Karajan.

With Nos. 29, 32 and 33 added to the original LP box, these are beautifully played and vitally alert readings; and the recordings, made between 1966 and 1979, are well balanced and given full, lively transfers to CD. There are details about which some may have reservations, and the opening of the *G minor*, which is a shade faster than in Karajan's earlier, Vienna performance for Decca, many not be quite dark enough for some tastes. But the *Jupiter*, although short on repeats, has weight and power as well as surface elegance.

Symphonies Nos. 29 in A, K.201; 33 in B flat, K.319.
*** Ph. Dig. 412 736-2 [id.]. E. Bar. Soloists, Gardiner.

Although the opening is deceptively gentle, the first movement of John Eliot Gardiner's *A major Symphony* soon develops an athletic strength. Delicacy returns in the *Andante*, nicely proportioned and beautifully played. The account of *No. 33 in B flat* is outstandingly successful, the outer movements a delight, full of rhythmic character. The *Andante* brings some slight squeezing of phrases, but overall this is authenticity with a winning countenance and without the abrasiveness of the Academy of Ancient Music in this repertoire. The recording is fresh and immediate and very well balanced.

Symphonies Nos. 29 in A, K.201; 35 in D (Haffner), K.385; Masonic funeral music, K.477.
(M) **(*) DG 429 803-2; *429 803-4* [id.]. VPO, Karl Boehm.

These performances, which first appeared not long before Boehm's death, are distinguished by finely groomed playing from the Vienna Philharmonic. Although they are weightier than his earlier, complete set with the Berlin Philharmonic, they have a relaxed quality and a glowing resonance which make them endearing, the mature products of octogenarian wisdom. They may sometimes lack drive but they remain compelling. The *Masonic funeral music*, darkly characterful, makes a worthwhile bonus. The orchestral quality is full and naturally balanced within its attractive ambience.

Symphonies Nos. 31 in D (Paris), K.207; 33 in B flat, K.319; 34 in C, K.338.
**(*) Telarc Dig. CD 80190 [id.]. Prague CO, Mackerras.

Mackerras and the Prague Chamber Orchestra give characteristically stylish and refined performances, clean of attack and generally marked by brisk speeds. As in their accounts of the later symphonies, all repeats are observed – even those in the *da capos* of minuets – and the only snag is that the reverberant Prague acoustic, more than in others of the Telarc series, clouds tuttis: the Presto finale of the *Paris* brings phenomenal articulation of quavers at the start, which then in tuttis disappear in a mush. One welcome extra on a well-filled disc is the 3/4 alternative *Andante* slow movement for this symphony, Mozart's second thoughts when his 6/8 *Andante* failed to find favour with the Paris public. Surprisingly, after that, the opportunity has not also been taken to include the *Minuet*, K.409, originally intended for No. 34.

(i) *Symphonies Nos. 31 in D (Paris), K.297; 36 in C (Linz), K.425;* (ii) *Overture: Le nozze di Figaro.*
(BB) *** ASV CDQS 6033; *ZCQS 6033.* (i) LSO; (ii) RPO, Bátiz.

After a sprightly account of the *Figaro overture* from the RPO, the LSO under Bátiz provide two spirited and polished accounts of favourite named symphonies. Tempi in outer movements are brisk, but the *Presto* finale of the *Linz* (for instance) produces some sparkling playing from the strings; and in both slow movements the phrasing is warm and gracious. With excellent digital recording, this makes an enjoyable super-bargain pairing.

Symphonies Nos. 31 in D (Paris), K.297; 36 in C (Linz), K.425; 38 in D (Prague), K.504.
*** ASV Dig. CDDCA 647; *ZCDCA 647* [id.]. L. Mozart Players, Jane Glover.

Jane Glover and the London Mozart Players offer a particularly attractive and generous coupling in the three Mozart symphonies associated with cities. The only penalty is that the first-half repeats in the slow movements of the *Linz* and *Prague* are omitted, perhaps not a great loss. Happily, exposition repeats are observed in the outer movements. The performances are all fresh and vital in traditional chamber style, with little influence from period performance. Tuttis are not always ideally clear on inner detail; but the result is nicely in scale, not too weighty, with the delicacy beautifully light and airy. Speeds are never eccentric, and the feeling of live communication comes over at such a moment as in the final coda of the *Linz*, where Glover gives an extra thrust to the closing bars to seal the whole work in exhilaration.

Symphonies Nos. 31 (Paris); 40 in G min.; 41 in C (Jupiter).
(B) *** DG 427 210-2; *427 210-4* [id.]. BPO, Boehm.

Boehm's way with Mozart is broader and heavier in texture than we are used to nowadays, and exposition repeats are the exception rather than the rule; but these are warm and magnetic performances with refined and strongly rhythmic playing, sounding remarkably vivid in their digital transfer.

Symphonies Nos. 32 in G, K.318; 33 in B flat, K.319; 35 in D (Haffner), K.385; 36 in C (Linz), K.425.
(M) *** DG 435 070-2; *435 070-4* [id.]. BPO, Karajan.

Here is Karajan's big-band Mozart at its finest. Although there may be slight reservations about the Minuet and Trio of the *Linz*, which is rather slow (and the other minuets are also somewhat stately), overall there is plenty of life here and slow movements show the BPO at their most graciously expressive. The remastered sound is clear and lively, full but not over-weighted.

Symphonies Nos. 32 in G, K.318; 35 in D (Haffner), K.385; 36 in C (Linz), K.425.
*** Virgin Dig. VC7 90702-2; *VC 790702-4* [id.]. SCO, Saraste.

More than most other versions on modern instruments, Saraste's accounts reflect the new lessons of period performance. These are more detached, less sostenuto performances than those of, for example, Jeffrey Tate and the ECO in these works and, with all repeats observed, make an excellent alternative. The recording, helpfully reverberant, yet gives lightness and transparency to textures, conveying an apt chamber scale.

Symphonies Nos. 32 in G, K.318; 35 in D (Haffner), K.385; 39 in E flat, K.543.
*** Telarc Dig. CD 80203 [id.]. Prague CO, Mackerras.
(BB) *** ASV CDQS 6071; *ZCQS 6071*. ECO, Mackerras.

Mackerras is fresh rather than elegant, yet with rhythms so crisply sprung that there is no sense of rush. His whirling one-in-a-bar treatment of Minuets may disconcert traditionalists, but brings exhilarating results. The third movements of both the *Haffner* and No. 39 become scherzos, not just faster but fiercer than regular minuets, and in the *Haffner* trumpets and timpani bite through textures dramatically. In the little No. 32, Mackerras is brighter and more urgent than usual in all three sections, and generally his account of No. 39 is as commanding as his outstanding versions of the last two symphonies. The slow introduction is crisply dotted, and the 3/4 Allegro is purposeful rather than easily lyrical. The clanging attack of harpsichord continuo is sometimes disconcerting, but this music-making is very refreshing.

Mackerras's ASV record came a decade after his earlier series of Mozart recordings for CfP. It was recorded digitally, in 1985, before he moved on to make his integral set for Telarc. Mackerras here anticipates the urgent style of the later recordings, especially in the Minuets and, with generally brisk speeds, the ASV readings are attractively fresh and full of momentum. Mackerras rarely seeks to charm, but unfussily presents each movement with undistractingly direct manners. In places the fast speeds imperil ensemble a little, and the recording does not always capture the finest detail. But the strong character of the music-making is in no doubt, and the sound is appealingly bright and vivid; at super-bargain price this undoubtedly remains competitive.

Symphonies Nos. 34 in C, K.388; 35 in D (Haffner), K.385; 39 in E flat, K.543.
*** ASV Dig. CDDCA 615; *ZCDCA 615* [id.]. L. Mozart Players, Jane Glover.

Tackling three major works, Jane Glover provides freshly imaginative performances that can compete with any in the catalogue, given the most vividly realistic recorded sound; Nos. 34 and 39 are especially striking. This collection can be recommended with enthusiasm.

Symphonies Nos. 35 (Haffner); 36 (Linz); 38 (Prague); 39 in E flat; 40 in G min.; 41 (Jupiter).
(B) *** Sony M2YK 45676 (2). Columbia SO, Bruno Walter.

Walter's set of Mozart's last and greatest symphonies comes from the beginning of the 1960s, his final recording period. The sound remains wonderfully fresh and full; some may feel that the bass resonance is occasionally too ample, but the upper range is sweet and clear and there is no imbalance. The performances are crisp and classical, while still possessing humanity and warmth. Slow movements are outstanding for their breadth and the natural flow of the phrasing. Melodic lines are moulded nobly and pacing always seems inevitable. Walter achieves just the right balance of tempi in the two sections of the first movement of the *Prague*, for instance, and draws from the *Andante* all the sweetness and lyrical power he is capable of. Finales are sparkling and brilliant, but never forced. The *G minor Symphony* is given a treasurable performance; in the *Jupiter*, if neither the first-movement exposition nor the finale carries repeats, Walter structures his interpretation accordingly, and the reading wears an Olympian quality.

'The birth of a performance': (recorded rehearsals of *Symphony No. 36*). *Symphonies Nos. 35 (Haffner); 36 (Linz); 38 (Prague); 39 in E flat; 40 in G min.; 41 (Jupiter).*
(M) *** Sony stereo/mono SM3K 46511 (3) [id.]. Columbia SO, Bruno Walter.

This set includes Walter's earlier version of the *Linz*, recorded in mono in New York City in 1955. Also included are the famous rehearsals of the *Linz Symphony*, called 'The birth of a performance', occupying the first disc. The second disc comprises Walter's mono performance of the *Linz* together with the *Prague* and No. 40, while the third disc contains performances of the *Haffner*, No. 39 and the *Jupiter* symphonies. These stereo recordings are all discussed in detail above.

(i) *Symphonies Nos. 35 in D (Haffner), K.385; 36 in C (Linz);* (ii) *Rondo for violin and orchestra in B flat, K.269.*
(M) *** Sony Dig. MDK 44647 [id.]. (i) Bav. RSO, Kubelik; (ii) Zukerman, St Paul CO.

First-class performances from Kubelik and the Bavarian Radio orchestra, well paced and alive in every bar. The *Haffner* is particularly strong, and Kubelik's spacious presentation of the *Linz* is also satisfying. Both slow movements are beautifully played. At the end, Zukerman provides a sparkling encore. The CBS recording is admirable, full, yet clear and well balanced.

Symphonies Nos. 35 (Haffner); 36 (Linz); 38 (Prague).
(B) *** DG 429 521-2; *429 521-4* [id.]. BPO, Boehm.

A splendid bargain triptych showing Boehm on his best form. His Berlin account of the *Linz* is one of his finest Mozart performances, balancing vitality with warmth. The *Haffner* and the *Prague* are also alert and sensitive, and the playing is again of the highest order.

Symphonies Nos. 35 in D (Haffner), K.385; 40 in G min., K.550; 41 in C (Jupiter), K.551.
(M) *** Sony SBK 46333 [id.]; *40-46333*. Cleveland O, Szell.

As in his companion triptych of late Haydn symphonies, Szell and his Clevelanders are shown at their finest here. The sparkling account of the *Haffner* is exhilarating, and the performances of the last two symphonies are equally polished and strong. Yet there is a tranquil feeling to both *Andantes* that shows Szell as a Mozartian of striking sensibility and finesse. He is at his finest in the *Jupiter*, which has great vigour in the outer movements and a proper weight to balance the rhythmic incisiveness; in spite of the lack of repeats, the work's scale is not diminished. Here the sound is remarkable considering the early date (late 1950s), and the remastering throughout is impressively full-bodied and clean.

Symphonies Nos. 36 in C (Linz), K.425; 38 in D (Prague), K.504.
*** EMI Dig. CDC7 47442-2 [id.]. ECO, Tate.

Tate's are very live-sounding performances translated to the studio, and his ear for detail as well as his imagination in rethinking the music gives them wit as well as weight within a scale (woodwind balanced close) which never sounds too big or inflated. One detail to note is the way that – exceptionally – Tate brings out the extraordinary originality of instrumentation in the recapitulation of the central slow movement of the *Prague*, with the widest possible span between exposed flutes, oboes and bassoons (bar 105). That movement, with the repeat observed, is given extra weight, matching the enormous span of the first movement.

Symphonies Nos. 37 in G, K.444: Introduction (completed by M. Haydn); *40 in G min., K.550; 41 in C (Jupiter), K.551.*
*** ASV Dig. CDDCA 761; *ZCDCA 761* [id.]. L. Mozart Players, Jane Glover.

This is an excellent example of Jane Glover's work with the LMP. It is good that in addition to the regular coupling of the last two masterpieces the disc offers the so-called *Symphony No. 37*. Mozart's contribution to that work is limited to the slow introduction. The rest of this compact, three-movement symphony is by Mozart's friend, Michael Haydn, younger brother of Joseph. It is a bright and attractive rarity, even though Mozart's introduction is conventionally elegant rather than distinctive. Anyone who fancies this generous coupling need hardly hesitate, particularly when in the two last Mozart symphonies Glover does not skimp on repeats, as she might have done. She omits them – as most versions do – in the slow movements, but includes exposition repeats in the finales as well as in first movements, particularly important in the *Jupiter*, with its grandly sublime counterpoint. There Glover's speed is exceptionally fast, with ensemble not quite so refined or crisp as in such rival versions as Jeffrey Tate's with the ECO, Mackerras's with the Prague Chamber Orchestra or Menuhin's with the Sinfonia Varsovia, but still making for a strong and enjoyable reading.

Symphony No. 38 in D (Prague), K.504.
**(*) Denon Dig. CO 79728 [id.]. Czech PO, Kubelik – DVOŘÁK: *Symphony No. 9 (New World).* **(*)

Mozart's symphony inspired by Prague makes an unusual but attractive coupling for the most popular of all Czech symphonies. Recorded live in October 1991, this Denon performance formed the first part of Rafael Kubelik's concert in Prague, when he followed up his first return from exile, again drawing an inspired performance from the Czech Philharmonic. The reading is lively in a traditional way. The slow introduction and central *Andante* are both warmly expressive rather than darkly tragic, while the main allegro of the first movement, with light, crisp articulation of strings, goes at a hectic speed, on the verge of being too fast, even for the Czech violins. The finale too is light and genial. With this live recording neither the balance nor the ensemble matches the finest, with strings on the thin side.

Symphonies Nos. 38 in D (Prague), K.504; 39 in E flat, K.543.
*** Virgin Dig. VC7 91078-2; *VC 791078-4* [id.]. Sinfonia Varsovia, Sir Yehudi Menuhin.
(M) *** Sony Dig. MDK 44648 [id.]. Bav. RSO, Rafael Kubelik.
(M) *** DG 429 802-2; *429 802-4* [id.]. BPO, Karajan.
*** ASV Dig. CDCOE 806; *ZCCOE 806* [id.]. COE, Schneider.

Menuhin's Mozart with this hand-picked orchestra – of which he is the Principal Conductor – has a clear place for those who, resisting period instruments, yet want many of the benefits of an authentic approach without sacrificing sweetness of string sound. It may be surprising to some that Menuhin is such a complete classicist here, with speeds on the fast side, notably in the *Andante* of the *Prague*, where he is a shade faster even than Hogwood in his period-performance version. Yet even here Menuhin does not sound at all rushed, giving the movement a free, song-like lyricism. He treats the third-movement trio of No. 39 as a brisk Laendler, almost hurdy-gurdy-like, refusing – after consultation with the autograph – to allow a rallentando at the end. Otherwise the only other oddity is his omission of the exposition repeat in the first movement when as a rule he is generous with repeats. The fresh, immediate sound highlights the refined purity of the string-playing.

Kubelik has the advantage of first-class modern digital recording, and this coupling is well up to the standard of the other two discs in his series of late Mozart symphonies. The playing has verve and is highly responsive. No. 39 is especially invigorating in its racy finale but has plenty of strength too.

Karajan's record, too, is strongly recommended. Generally speaking, the playing is so superlative and the sense of pace so well judged that one surrenders to the sheer quality of this music-making: the impression is one of resilience as well as of strength.

Schneider's might be counted old-fashioned readings of both symphonies, with measured speeds both in allegros and in slow movements, marked by fine pointing and moulding. The string band sounds larger than in some recent versions, and that is partly a question of the recording, set in a warm, helpful acoustic which brings out the sweetness of the COE violins and the bloom on the wind instruments. Schneider shows his allegiance to older fashion by not observing exposition repeats in the first movements or first halves of slow movements; but the consistent rhythmic resilience of Schneider's direction and the superb playing of the COE lightens everything.

Symphonies Nos. 38 in D (Prague), K.504; 40 in G min., K.550.
(B) *** Decca 430 494-2; *430 494-4*. ECO, Britten.

In his perfomance of No. 40, Britten takes all repeats – the slow movement here is longer than that of *Eroica* – but is nevertheless almost totally convincing, with the rich Maltings sound to give added weight and resonance. In the *Prague* as in No. 40, Britten conveys a real sense of occasion, from the weighty introduction through a glowing and resilient account of the *Allegro* to a full, flowing reading of the *Andante*.

Symphonies Nos. 39 in E flat, K.543; 41 in C (Jupiter), K.551.
(BB) *** Virgin/Virgo Dig. VJ7 91461-2; *VJ7 91461-4* [id.]. SCO, Saraste.
** EMI Dig. CDC7 54090-2 [id.]; *EL 754090-4*. London Classical Players, Roger Norrington.

Jukka-Pekka Saraste's bargain issue on the Virgo label offers two of the finest performances of these late symphonies available on any disc: fresh, light and resilient in allegros, elegant in the slow movements and with clean, transparent recording. Wordsworth with the Capella Istropolitana may have more weight in these works, but Saraste has extra polish and refinement, with generally brisker speeds, notably in slow movements and minuets. The accompanying notes, however, are almost unbelievably sparse.

Norrington takes the slow introduction to No. 39 so fast that it is barely recognizable. The result is refreshingly different but totally misses the grandeur which is implicit in the piece at that point. Other speeds are disconcertingly fast too; but those who want period performances of these masterpieces that are characterful rather than purely tasteful may well be attracted.

Symphony No. 40 in G min., K.550.
(B) **(*) Pickwick Dig. PCD 820; *CIMPC 820* [id.]. O of St John's, Smith Square, Lubbock – HAYDN: *Symphony No. 44*. ***
**(*) Linn Dig. CKD 003 [id.]. English Classical Players, Jonathan Brett – SCHUBERT: *Symphony No. 5*. **(*)
(M) (**) BMG/RCA mono GD 60271; *GK 60271* [60271-2-RG; *60271-4-RG*]. NBC SO, Toscanini – BEETHOVEN: *Symphony No. 3*. (***)
(*) Decca mono 425 987-2 [id.]. LPO, Erich Kleiber – BEETHOVEN: *Symphony No. 7* (**).

Lubbock's is a pleasingly relaxed account of Mozart's *G minor Symphony*, well played – the Minuet particularly deft – and nicely proportioned. The last ounce of character is missing from the slow movement, but the orchestra is responsive throughout, and the recording is in the demonstration class.

The English Classical Players are a new London orchestral group, playing on modern instruments, who made their début in June 1990, when this record was made. Their playing is alive and polished, phrasing is graceful and the orchestral blend in Mozart and Schubert very appealing. Jonathan Brett's reading of the *G minor Symphony* is well paced and fresh.

Dating from March 1950, Toscanini's version was recorded in the notoriously dry Studio 8-H in Radio City, New York; though the sound is uncomfortable, the high voltage of the interpretation makes considerable amends, with expressive warmth tempering the conductor's characteristic urgency. The slow movement is elegantly done, and even though the finale brings a measure of fierceness, Toscanini eases lovingly into the second subject.

A very classical reading of the *G minor Symphony* by Kleiber, made in 1949 with the LPO in Kingsway Hall. There is no exposition repeat, as was the custom of the period, and the transfer produces acidulated and scrawny sound. Why cannot the Decca transfer engineers do better than this?

Symphonies Nos. 40 in G min., K.550; 41 in C (Jupiter), K.551.
❀ (M) *** DG Dig. 431 267-2; *431 267-4* [431 040-2; *431 040-4*]. VPO, Leonard Bernstein.
*** Virgin Dig. VC7 91082-2; *VC 791082-4* [id.]. Sinfonia Varsovia, Sir Yehudi Menuhin.
*** EMI Dig. CDC7 47147-2 [id.]. ECO, Tate.
*** Telarc Dig. CD 80139 [id.]. Prague CO, Mackerras.
(M) *** Sony Dig. MDK 44649 [id.]. Bav. RSO, Kubelik.
(B) *** CfP CD-CFP 4253; *TC-CFP 40243*. LPO, Mackerras.
(B) **(*) Decca 433 607-2; *433 607-4*. VPO, Karajan.
(M) **(*) DG 435 592-2; *435 592-4* [id.]. BPO, Karajan.
(M) ** Ph. Dig. 434 149-2; *434 149-4* [id.]. O of 18th Century, Frans Brüggen.

This re-coupling is perhaps the most distinguished of Bernstein's Mozart records. Both recordings were made in the Musikverein Grosser Saal in January 1984 and were edited together from live performances. Bernstein's electrifying account of No. 40 is keenly dramatic, individual and stylish, with the finale delightfully airy and fresh. If anything, the *Jupiter* is even finer: it is exhilarating in its tensions and observes the repeats in both halves of the finale, making it almost as long as the massive first movement. Bernstein's electricity sustains that length, and one welcomes it for establishing the supreme power of the argument, the true crown in the whole of Mozart's symphonic output. Pacing cannot be faulted in any of the four movements and, considering the problems of making live recordings, the sound is first rate, lacking only the last degree of transparency in tuttis.

Recorded in exceptionally vivid, immediate sound, Menuhin's versions of both symphonies with the Sinfonia Varsovia find a distinctive place in an overcrowded field, with playing of precision, clarity and bite which is consistently refreshing, giving a feeling of live music-making. The string tuning and refinement of expressive nuance match that of a fine string quartet, and Menuhin reveals himself again as very much a classicist, preferring speeds on the fast side, rarely indulging in romantic tricks. He is generous with repeats – observing exposition repeats in both first movement and finale of the *Jupiter*, for example. With such vivid sound, this is the best current recommendation for this favourite coupling.

For the general listener Tate's account of the *Jupiter* makes an excellent choice, with an apt scale which yet allows the grandeur of the work to come out. On the one hand it has the clarity of a chamber orchestra performance, but on the other, with trumpets and drums, its weight of expression never underplays the scale of the argument which originally prompted the unauthorized nickname. In both symphonies exposition repeats are observed in outer movements, particularly important in the *Jupiter* finale. Those who like a very plain approach may find the elegant pointing in slow movements excessive, but Tate's keen imagination on detail, as well as over a broad span, consistently conveys the electricity of a live performance. The recording is well detailed, yet has pleasant reverberation, giving the necessary breadth.

With generally fast speeds, so brisk that he is able to observe every single repeat, Mackerras takes a fresh, direct view which, with superb playing from the Prague Chamber Orchestra, is also characterful. The speeds that might initially seem excessively fast are those for the Minuets, which – with fair scholarly authority – become crisp country dances, almost scherzos. The definition of woodwind lines is immaculate, with string textures equally clear despite the warm acoustic, though the bassoon has a distinctly East European tone. On the question of repeats, the doubling in length of the slow movement of No. 40 makes it almost twice as long as the first movement, a dangerous proportion – though it is pure gain having both halves repeated in the magnificent finale of the *Jupiter*.

Like his excellent coupling of the *Haffner* and *Linz Symphonies*, these performances by Kubelik are strong and beautifully played, with well-integrated tempi and highly responsive phrasing – both slow movements are very appealingly shaped. Kubelik favours first-movement exposition repeats, but here he misses the chance of extending the finale of the *Jupiter*, although the performance certainly does not lack weight. The CBS recording is first class, and Kubelik's disc is fully competitive.

On Classics for Pleasure, Mackerras directs excellent, clean-cut performances which can stand comparison with any at whatever price. He observes exposition repeats in the outer movements of the *G minor* but not the *Jupiter*, which is a pity for so majestic a work.

Karajan's Decca Vienna recordings, dating from the early 1960s, now have a documentary value, quite apart from the considerable pleasure they bring. In the *G minor*, every detail is beautifully in place, each phrase elegantly shaped and in perspective. The exposition repeat in the first movement is observed. Beautifully articulate and suave (in the best sense), this performance has genuine dramatic power, even though one feels that it all moves within carefully regulated emotional limits. The reading of the *Jupiter* is a strong one, one of the best things that Karajan did during his short period in the Decca studios, even though this time there is no first-movement exposition repeat. The performance is direct and has breadth as well as warmth. The recording, made in the Sofiensaal, is first rate; apart from a degree of bass resonance (which can easily be attenuated) it has hardly dated at all. A most enjoyable coupling.

Some ears find the DG Karajan recordings made later in Berlin in 1976/7 rather streamlined, and the opening of the *G minor Symphony* is here not as subtle in colour as his earlier version for Decca. But the orchestra plays superbly and the *Jupiter* has weight and power as well as surface elegance. The sound too is wholly admirable in its CD transfer, clear, fresh and with plenty of body. Music-making of such vigour and polish cannot help making a strong impression on the listener. Karajan here includes the first movement exposition repeats of both symphonies; he does not extend the finale of the *Jupiter*, but manages to convey the music's breadth by the sheer calibre of his music-making.

Brüggen's live recording of the *G minor* using period instruments is more warmly communicative than most authentic performances, without losing the benefit of clarity and freshness. Speeds are on the fast side without being stiff or eccentric. Good, atmospheric recording with some exaggeration of bass. His newly coupled account of the *Jupiter*, while the strings play with no vibrato, is fundamentally a romantic reading with unusually slow speeds.

Although the refinement of the playing cannot be gainsaid, moulded more subtly than would even have been possible in the eighteenth century without a conductor, the result tends to be sluggish, failing to find the necessary bite in the moments of the most adventurous inspiration and producing too many accents in the finale. The performance is generous with repeats.

CHAMBER MUSIC

Complete Mozart Edition, Volume 14: (i) *Adagio in C for glass harmonica, K.356;* (i; ii) *Adagio in C min. & Rondo in C for glass harmonica, flute, oboe, viola & cello;* (iii) *Clarinet trio in E flat (Kegelstatt), K.498;* (iv; v) *Piano quartets Nos. 1–2;* (iv) *Piano trios Nos. 1–6; Piano trio in D min., K.442;* (vi) *Piano and wind quintet in E flat, K.452.*
(M) *** Ph. Dig./Analogue 422 514-2 (5) [id.]. (i) Bruno Hoffmann; (ii) with Nicolet, Holliger, Schouten, Decroos; (iii) Brymer, Kovacevich, Ireland; (iv) Beaux Arts Trio, (v) with Giuranna; (vi) Brendel, Holliger, Brunner, Baumann, Thunemann.

It is a comment on the strength of the Philips back catalogue that this compilation of Mozart's chamber music with piano has no weak link. The last three discs contain the complete set of the Mozart *Piano trios* recorded by the Beaux Arts Trio in 1987, a first-rate cycle which includes not only the six completed trios but also the composite work, put together by Mozart's friend, the priest Maximilian Stadler, and listed by Köchel as K.442. It is made up of three unrelated movements that Mozart left unfinished, with an allegro (evidently later than the rest) which is far more inspired. The Beaux Arts' teamwork – with the pianist Menahem Pressler leading the way – brings consistently fresh and winning performances, as it also does in the two great *Piano quartets* where, in recordings made in 1983, they are joined by the viola-player, Bruno Giuranna. The *Piano and wind quintet*, K.452, recorded in 1986, subtly contrasts the artistry of Alfred Brendel at the piano with that of the oboist, Heinz Holliger, leading a distinguished team of wind-players. The only non-digital recordings are those of the *Kegelstatt trio*, characterfully done by Stephen Bishop-Kovacevich with the clarinettist Jack Brymer and the viola-player Patrick Ireland, and of the two shorter works involving glass harmonica. Those last are conveniently included here as an extra, both with Bruno Hoffmann playing that rare instrument, so titillating to the ear if heard in fairly brief spans.

Adagio in C for cor anglais, 2 violins & cello, K.580a.
*** Denon Dig. C37 7119 [id.]. Holliger, Salvatore Qt – M. HAYDN: *Divertimenti;* J. C. BACH: *Oboe quartet.* ***

Though the shortest of the four works on Holliger's charming disc, this Mozart fragment is in a world apart, deeply expressive. Excellent performances and recording.

Adagio in C for cor anglais, 2 violins & cello, K.580a; Oboe quartet in F, K.370; Oboe quintet in C min., K.406.
**(*) Claves Dig. CD 50-8406 [id.]. Ingo Goritzki, Berne Qt (members).

This CD conveniently collects together Mozart's two major chamber works featuring the oboe, plus the haunting *Adagio* for cor anglais which Ingo Goritzki plays very sensitively, if not quite as memorably as Holliger. The *Oboe quartet*, too, is fresh and pleasing, if less winning than some of the finest versions – see below. However, the interesting novelty is the *Quintet*, which derives from Mozart's own arrangement of the *Wind serenade*, K.388. Ingo Goritzki makes a fairly convincing case for the choice of a broken consort and the performance is a good one, with the Berne players giving accomplished, if not highly imaginative, support. The recording is vivid and well balanced.

Canons for strings; Canons for woodwind: see below, under VOCAL MUSIC: Complete Mozart Edition, Volume 23

Complete Mozart Edition, Volume 10: (i; vi) *Clarinet quintet;* (ii) *Flute quartets Nos. 1–4;* (iii; vi) *Horn quintet;* (iv; vi) *Oboe quartet;* (v) *Sonata for bassoon and cello, K.292.* (vi) Fragments: *Allegro in F, K.App. 90/580b for clarinet, basset horn, & string trio; Allegro in B flat. K.App. 91/K.516c for a clarinet quintet; Allegro in F, K.288 for a divertimento for 2 horns & strings; String quartet movements: Allegro in B flat, K.App. 72/464a; Allegro in B flat, K.App. 80/514a; Minuet in B flat, K.68/589a; Minuet in F, K.168a; Movement in A, K.App. 72/464a. String quintet No. 1 in B flat, K.174: 2 Original movements: Trio & Finale. Allegro in A min., K.App. 79 for a string quintet. Allegro in G, K.App. 66/562e for a string trio* (completed, where necessary, by Erik Smith).

(M) *** Ph. Analogue/Dig. 422 510-2 (3) [id.]. (i) Pay; (ii) Bennett, Grumiaux Trio; (iii) Brown; (iv) Black; (v) Thunemann; Orton; (vi) ASMF Chamber Ens.

These are highly praised performances of the major chamber works featuring modern wind instruments (Antony Pay uses a normal clarinet). The *Duo for bassoon and cello* is also very engaging, although the balance somewhat favours the bassoonist, Klaus Thunemann, at the expense of his partner, Stephen Orton. But it is the fragments which make this box particularly enticing. Erik Smith tells us in the notes that, with a single exception, he confined himself to 'filling in the missing instrumental parts without adding any more bars'. The exception is the *Movement in A*, K.464a, planned at the finale for the *String quartet No. 18*, K.464: 'The temptation to complete this extensive fragment and make its lovely music playable proved too strong for me,' says E. S., and he goes on to tell how he ingeniously incorporated a 12-bar sketch of a fugue in G minor, changing the key and building it into the unfinished movement with linking material from elsewhere in the movement. The result is a great success. The rest of the items are by no means inconsequential offcuts but provide music of high quality, notably the *String quartet movement*, K.514a. The *Minuet in B flat*, K.589a, in the rhythm of a polonaise and possibly the first draft for the finale of the *Hunt quartet*, is a real charmer which, had it received more exposure, might well have become a Mozartian lollipop like the famous and not dissimilar Minuet in the *D major Divertimento*, K.334. The two pieces with solo clarinet are also very winning (we have had them before, from Alan Hacker on Amon Ra at full price). The performances here are all polished and spontaneous and beautifully recorded.

Clarinet quintet in A, K.581.
(M) *** EMI CDM7 63116-2 [id.]; *EG 763116-4*. Gervase de Peyer, Melos Ens. – BRAHMS: *Quintet*. ***
(*) Orfeo C 141861A [id.]. Karl Leister, Pražák Qt – CRUSELL: *Clarinet quintet*. *
(B) ** Decca 433 647-2; *433 647-4* [id.]. Peter Schmidl, New Vienna Octet (members) – SCHUBERT: *Trout quintet*. **(*)

Clarinet quintet in A, K.581; Clarinet quintet fragment in B flat, K.516c; (i) *Quintet fragment in F for clarinet in C, basset-horn and string trio, K.580b* (both completed by Duncan Druce).
*** Amon Ra/Saydisc CD-SAR 17 [id.]. Alan Hacker, Salomon Qt, (i) with Lesley Schatzberger.

(i) *Clarinet quintet;* (ii) *Oboe quartet in F, K.370.*
(B) *** CfP CD-CFP 4377; *TC-CFP 4377*. (i) Andrew Marriner; (ii) Gordon Hunt, Chilingirian Qt.
(B) *** Pickwick Dig. PCD 810; *CIMPC 810* [id.]. (i) Puddy; (ii) Boyd, Gabrieli Qt.

Leading the CD versions of the *Clarinet quintet* (alongside Thea King's outstanding coupling with the *Clarinet concerto* on Hyperion – see above) is a superb recording by Alan Hacker with the Salomon Quartet, using original instruments. Anton Stadler, the clarinettist for whom the work was written, possessed a timbre which was described as 'so soft and lovely that nobody who has a heart can resist it'. Alan Hacker's gentle sound on his period instrument has a similar quality, displayed at its most ravishing in the *Larghetto*. He is matched by the strings, and especially by the leader, Simon Standage, who blends his tone luminously with the clarinet. Tempi are wonderfully apt throughout the performance, the rhythms of the finale are infectiously pointed and, following a passage of rhapsodic freedom from the soloist, there is a spirited closing dash. Hacker decorates the reprise of the *Larghetto* affectionately and adds embellishments elsewhere. His chortling roulades in the last movement are no less engaging, the music's sense of joy fully projected. The recording balance is near perfect, the clarinet able to dominate or integrate with the strings at will; and the tangibility of the sound is remarkably realistic. Hacker includes a fragment from an earlier projected *Quintet* and a similar sketch for a work featuring C clarinet and basset-horn with string trio. Both are skilfully completed by Duncan Druce.

Having de Peyer's vintage account of the Mozart *Clarinet quintet* in coupling with his equally inspired reading of the Brahms *Quintet* makes an outstanding bargain on a mid-price disc. This clean, fresh, well-pointed performance with the Melos Ensemble is consistently satisfying, recorded in immediate sound in a relatively dry acoustic.

On the bargain-priced CfP version, recorded in 1981, the young Andrew Marriner's persuasive account occupies the front rank, quite irrespective of price. Marriner's playing in the *Quintet* is wonderfully flexible; it reaches its apex in the radiantly beautiful reading of the slow movement, although the finale is also engagingly characterized. The *Oboe quartet* is delectable too, with Gordon Hunt a highly musical and technically accomplished soloist. The Chilingirian players contribute most sympathetically to both works, and the performances are generous in repeats. The CfP issue was recorded in the Wigmore Hall and the sound-balance is most believable.

The alternative bargain-priced Pickwick CD brings a reading of the *Clarinet quintet* which is clean and well paced and, if lacking the last degree of delicacy in the slow movement, is never less than stylish. The young oboist, Douglas Boyd, then gives an outstanding performance in the shorter, less demanding work, with the lilting finale delectably full of fun. The digital recording is vividly immediate and full of presence, with even the keys of the wind instruments often audible.

It is difficult to fault the playing in the warm and simple account by Peter Schmidl and members of the New Vienna Octet, and the 1978 recording is far richer than the Schubert coupling. But the overall effect is rather bland.

(i) *Clarinet quintet, K.581;* (ii) *Flute quartet No. 1 in D, K.285;* (iii) *Oboe quartet, K.370.*
(M) *** DG 429 819-2; *429 819-4* [id.]. (i) Gervase de Peyer; (ii) Andreas Blau; (iii) Lothar Koch; Amadeus Qt.

Gervase de Peyer gives a warm, smiling account of the *Clarinet quintet*. The performance is matched by the refinement of Koch in the *Oboe quartet*. With creamy tone and wonderfully stylish phrasing he is superb. The inclusion of just one of the four *Flute quartets* seems less than ideal, as most Mozartians will want all four. However, it must be admitted that Andreas Blau's playing is delightful, sprightly and full of grace. The Amadeus accompany with sensibility, and the recordings are flawless.

(i) *Clarinet quintet in A, K.581;* (ii) *Horn quintet in E flat, K.407;* (iii) *Oboe quartet in F, K.370.*
(M) *** Ph. 422 833-2; *422 833-4*. (i) Antony Pay; (ii) Timothy Brown; (iii) Neil Black; ASMF Chamber Ens.

It is a delightful idea to have the *Clarinet quintet*, *Oboe quartet* and *Horn quintet* on a single CD. Here, Antony Pay's earlier account of the *Clarinet quintet*, played on a modern instrument, with the Academy of St Martin-in-the-Fields players must be numbered among the strongest now on the market for those not insisting on an authentic basset clarinet. Neil Black's playing in the *Oboe quartet* is distinguished, and again the whole performance radiates pleasure, while the *Horn quintet* comes in a well-projected and lively account with Timothy Brown. The recording, originally issued in 1981, is of Philips's best.

Complete Mozart Edition, Volume 13: (i) *Divertimento in E flat for string trio, K.563;* (ii) *Duos for violin and viola Nos. 1–2, K.423/4;* (i) *6 Preludes and fugues for string trio, K.404a;* (iii) *Sonata (String trio) in B flat, K.266.*
(M) *** Ph. 422 513-2 (2) [id.]. (i) Grumiaux, Janzer, Szabo; (ii) Grumiaux, Pelliccia; (iii) ASMF Chamber Ens.

Grumiaux's 1967 recorded performance of the *Divertimento in E flat* remains unsurpassed; he is here joined by two players with a similarly refined and classical style. The hushed opening of the first-movement development – a visionary passage – is played with a magically intense half-tone, and the lilt of the finale is infectious from the very first bar. The recording has been remastered again: the balance still favours Grumiaux but he also dominates the performance artistically (as he does also in the *Duos*) and the result is now fully acceptable. In the *Duos*, which are ravishingly played, the balance is excellent, and Arrigo Pelliccia proves a natural partner in these inspired and rewarding works. The *Sonata for string trio* dates from 1777 and has a somewhat bland *Adagio/Andante*, followed by a jaunty Minuet. It is no missing masterpiece but is well played by the ASMF Chamber Ensemble and it has a modern, digital recording. Of the six *Preludes and fugues*, the first three derive from Bach's *Well-tempered clavier*, the fourth combines an *Adagio* from the *Organ sonata*, BWV 527, with *Contrapunctus 8* from the *Art of fugue*, the fifth is a transcription of two movements from the *Organ sonata*, BWV 526, and the sixth uses music of W. F. Bach. Mozart made these arrangements in the early 1780s for Baron Gottfried van Swieten in Vienna, composing *Adagio* introductions for Nos. 1–3 and 6. The performances here are sympathetic and direct, the recorded sound bold, clear and bright.

Divertimento in E flat for string trio, K.563.
*** Sony Dig. MK 39561 [id.]. Kremer, Kashkashian, Ma.

Gidon Kremer, Kim Kashkashian and Yo-Yo Ma turn in an elegant and sweet-toned account on CBS and are excellently recorded. Indeed, the sound is fresh and beautifully realistic. There are many perceptive insights, particularly in the *Adagio* movement which is beautifully done; even if there are one or two narcissistic touches from Kremer, his playing is still most persuasive.

Divertimento in E flat for string trio, K.563; Duos for violin and viola, Nos. 1–2, K.423/4.
(B) **(*) Hung. White Label HRC 072 [id.]. Dénes Kovács, Géza Németh, Ede Banda.

If not quite a match in subtlety for the Grumiaux version, the account of this masterly *Divertimento* by the three Hungarian players is freshly enjoyable, the playing vital, spontaneous and agreeably without mannered idiosyncrasy. Dénes Kovács, the leader, dominates the music-making, both in the *Trio* and in the highly rewarding pair of *Duos* which make the substantial coupling. The Hungaroton recording is forward but better balanced than the Philips disc; it has a pleasing ambience, and this inexpensive CD is well worth its modest cost.

Flute quartets Nos. 1 in D, K.285; 2 in G, K.285a; 3 in C, K.285b; 4 in A, K.298.
(M) *** Van. 08.4001.71 [OVC 4001]. Paula Robinson, Tokyo Qt (members).
(M) *** Ph. 422 835-2. Bennett, Grumiaux Trio.
*** Sony Dig. MK 42320 [id.]. Rampal, Stern, Accardo, Rostropovich.
*** Accent ACC 48225D. Bernhard and Sigiswald Kuijken, Van Dael, Wieland Kuijken.
**(*) Virgin Dig. VC7 90740-2; *VC 79047-4*. Philippa Davies, Nash Ens.

This Vanguard recording of the *Flute quartets* (presumably from the 1960s – no date is given) is most winning. Paula Robinson displays a captivating lightness of touch and her silvery timbre seems eminently suited to Mozart. Needless to say, the Tokyo Quartet provide polished accompaniments which combine warmth with much finesse. Textures are transparent and the recording is most naturally balanced. This is Mozartian spontaneity at its most refreshing.

There also seems to be general agreement about the merits of the William Bennett/Arthur Grumiaux Trio accounts of the *Flute quartets*. They are, to put it in a nutshell, exquisitely played and very well recorded, in every way finer than most other versions which have appeared and disappeared over the years. The freshness of both the playing and the remastered 1971 recording gives very great pleasure.

It would be hard to dream up a more starry quartet of players than that assembled on the CBS disc. But the recording was made in a relatively dry studio, and the acoustic emphasizes the dominance of Rampal's flute in the ensemble, with the three superstar string-players given little chance to shine distinctively except in the finale of K.285. A delectable record none the less.

Readers normally unresponsive to period instruments should hear these performances by Bernhard Kuijken, for they have both charm and vitality; they radiate pleasure and bring one close to this music. This record is rather special and cannot be recommended too strongly. The playing is exquisite and the engineering superb.

Philippa Davies is a nimble, highly musical soloist who has a natural feeling for Mozartian line. She is very well balanced with the Nash players and these are pleasingly warm, intimate performances, nicely turned, if not distinctive. And why did Virgin Classics not tip the balance of appeal for their version by adding some more music to a full priced CD which only plays for 52 minutes?

Piano quartets Nos. 1 in G min., K.478; 2 in E flat, K.493 (see also above, under Complete Mozart Edition, Volume 14).
*** Ph. Dig. 410 391-2 [id.]. Beaux Arts Trio with Giuranna.
(B) *** Hung. White Label HRC 170 [id.]. Gyula Kiss, Tátrai Trio.
*** DG Dig. 423 404-2 [id.]. Bilson (fortepiano), Wilcock, Schlapp, Mason.
(M) **(*) BMG/RCA GD 60406 [60406-2-RC]. Rubinstein, Guarneri Qt.

The Beaux Arts group provide splendidly alive and vitally sensitive accounts that exhilarate the listener, just as does the Curzon–Amadeus set (see below), and they have the advantage of first-class digital recording. The Beaux Arts play them not only *con amore* but with the freshness of a new discovery. Incidentally, both repeats are observed in the first movements, which is unusual on record. The usual high standards of Philips chamber-music recording obtain here; the sound (particularly that of the piano) is exceptionally lifelike.

Rubinstein's bright and invigorating playing with members of the Guarneri Quartet has its brightness and forwardness exaggerated in the recording, and the CD transfer emphasizes the balance. This is not so much a tasteful rendering of two of Mozart's most delectable chamber works as a mercurial recreation at the hands of a master pianist who is nothing if not an individualist. Details matter less than the overall sweep of spontaneous expression. The liveliness of Rubinstein even in his eighties enjoying himself with fellow musicians is ample reason for hearing this coupling.

Gyula Kiss, the pianist, is a fine and characterful Mozartian, and he dominates performances which are convincingly paced and alive, with the Tátrai string group making an excellent partnership. Both slow movements show the pianist at his most sensitive and the finales have a contrasting lightness of touch that is most appealing. Natural sound with good presence yet no edginess on the strings.

Even those who find Malcolm Bilson a little wanting in temperament and too judicious will gain pleasure from these well-recorded accounts of the two *Piano quartets*. The balance between the three stringed instruments and the keyboard is immediately altered when heard on period instruments. The playing is excellent and has both sparkle and grace. The recording is outstandingly natural and lifelike.

(i) *Piano quartets Nos. 1–2;* (i) *Horn quintet in E flat, K.407.*
❀ (M) *** Decca mono 425 960-2 [id.]. (i) Clifford Curzon, Amadeus Qt; (ii) Dennis Brain, Griller Qt.

All versions of the Mozart *Piano quartets* rest in the shadow of the recordings by Clifford Curzon and members of the Amadeus Quartet. No apologies need be made for the 1952 mono recorded sound. An early example of the work of John Culshaw, it may be somewhat two-dimensional but is better balanced than many stereo recordings of chamber music. The performances have a unique sparkle, slow movements are elysian. One's only criticism is that the *Andante* of K.478 opens at a much lower dynamic level than the first movement, and some adjustment of the controls needs to be made. The *Horn quintet* coupling was recorded in 1944 and the transfer to CD is even more miraculous. The slight surface rustle of the 78-r.p.m. source is in no way distracting and the sound is unbelievably smooth and beautiful. Dennis Brain's horn contribution is superbly graduated to balance with the textures created by the string players, matching timbres in the true spirit of chamber music. There is not a suspicion of wiriness from the leader. The performance itself combines warmth and elegance with a spirited spontaneity, and the subtleties of the horn contribution are a continuous delight. A wonderful disc that should be in every Mozartian's library.

(i) *Piano quartets Nos. 1–2. String quartet No. 17 in B flat (Hunt), K.458.*
(M) **(*) Decca 425 538-2; *425 538-4* [id.]. (i) André Previn; V. Musikverein Qt.

Previn's sparkling playing gives these parallel masterpieces – especially the *G minor* – a refreshing spontaneity. For those looking for a modern mid-priced CD, this could well be the answer, particularly as the bonus is a fine version of the *Hunt Quartet*. There is a relaxed, unforced quality about the playing here, though there is no want of brilliance either. Here the CD transfer is more brightly lit, so that the upper string timbre is less smooth.

(i) *Piano quartet No. 1 in G min., K.478. String quartet No. 16 in E flat, K.428;* (ii) *String quintets Nos. 3 in C, K.515; 4 in G min., K.516; 5 in D, K.593.*
(M) (***) EMI mono CHS7 63870-2 (2) [Ang. CDHB 63870]. (i) Schnabel; Pro Arte Qt, (ii) with A. Hobday.

These classic accounts from the 1930s are in some ways unsurpassed and withstand the passage of time. Schnabel was sometimes wanting in the pianistic grace we associate with later Mozartians, but these are among his best chamber music records; and the playing of the Pro Arte has a very special wisdom and humanity. The Pro Arte Quartet and Alfred Hobday find more depth and pathos in the *Adagio* fourth movement of the *G minor Quintet* than any ensemble since, and they bring us very close to the spirit of Mozart. A special issue – even in a year that has been rich in historic Mozartiana.

Piano trios – see also above, under Complete Mozart Edition, Volume 14

Piano trios Nos. 1–6; Piano trio in D min., K.442.
*** Ph. Dig. 422 079-2 (3). Beaux Arts Trio.

Piano trios Nos. 1–6.
*** Chan. Dig. CHAN 8536/7; *DBTD 2008* (2). Borodin Trio.

Apart from including an extra work, the Beaux Arts are more generous with repeats, which accounts for the extra disc. Their performances are eminently fresh and are no less delightful and winning. There is a somewhat lighter touch here compared with the Chandos alternative, thanks in no small degree to the subtle musicianship of Menahem Pressler. The Philips recording is strikingly realistic and present.

The Borodin Trio are slightly weightier in their approach and their tempi are generally more measured than the Beaux Arts', very strikingly so in the *Allegretto* of the *G major*. All the same, there is, as usual with this group, much sensitive playing and every evidence of distinguished musicianship. The balance in the Philips set tends to favour the piano a little; the Chandos, recorded at The Maltings, Snape, perhaps produces the more integrated sound.

Piano and wind quintet in E flat, K.452.
*** Sony Dig. MK 42099 [id.]. Perahia, members of ECO – BEETHOVEN: *Quintet*. ***
*** Ph. Dig. 420 182-2 [id.]. Brendel, Holliger, Brunner, Baumann, Thunemann – BEETHOVEN: *Quintet*. **(*)
(M) *** Decca 421 151-2. Ashkenazy, L. Wind Soloists – BEETHOVEN: *Quintet*. ***
(B) *** Hung. White Label HRC 169 [id.]. Sándor Fálvai, Hungarian Wind Quintet – BEETHOVEN: *Quintet*. ***
(M) *(*) DG 453 593-2 [id.]. Gulda, VPO Wind Ens. (members) – BEETHOVEN: *Piano and wind quintet*. *

An outstanding account of Mozart's delectable *Piano and wind quintet* on CBS, with Perahia's playing wonderfully refreshing in the *Andante* and a superb response from the four wind soloists, notably Neil Black's oboe contribution. Clearly all the players are enjoying this rewarding music, and they are well balanced, with the piano against the warm but never blurring acoustics of The Maltings at Snape.

Brendel and his distinguished companions on Philips convey an impressive concentration and strong personality; in the outer movements there is clarity and finesse, and in the slow movement no want of feeling. Playing of strong personality and a certain didacticism, though one is at times aware of Brendel's slightly exaggerated staccato: his pianism is very different from that of Lupu or Perahia. The recording combines a sense of immediacy with a very natural balance among the five instruments.

Ashkenazy's performance in Mozart's engaging *Quintet* is also outstandingly successful, polished and urbane, yet marvellously spirited. His wind soloists are a distinguished team and their playing comes fully up to expectations. The balance and sound-quality are of the highest order and the CD sounds very natural, although the balance is forward. A first-class mid-priced alternative to the full-price versions led by Perahia and Lupu.

An enjoyably fresh performance from Sándor Fálvai and the excellent Hungarian wind players, given a most natural and realistic sound-balance in a pleasing acoustic. The playing has vitality and finesse, and an attractive degree of robustness too. Yet the *Andante* is appealingly serene and gentle, to act as a foil to the infectious finale.

Gulda's recording with members of the VPO, which dates from 1960 was praised by us when it was first issued, but the remastering for CD is not flattering, in particular making the oboe timbre sound excessively thin. Mozart gives the oboe much to do. The performance is suave and beautifully articulated and the wind intonation is impeccable. In matters of phrasing and style there is still much to enjoy and the players have good presence, but the blending of instruments is affected by the brightness of the oboe tone.

Complete Mozart Edition, Volume 12: *String quartets Nos. 1–23.*
(M) *** Ph. 422 512-2 (8) [id.]. Italian Qt.

The earliest recordings by the Italians now begin to show their age (notably the six *Haydn Quartets*, which date from 1966): the violin timbre is thinner than we would expect in more modern versions. But the quality is generally very satisfactory, for the Philips sound-balance is admirably judged. As a set, the performances have seen off all challengers for two decades or more; one is unlikely to assemble a more consistently satisfying overview of these works, or one so beautifully played. They hold a very special place in the Mozartian discography.

String quartets Nos. 1 in G, K.80; 2 in D, K.155; 3 in G, K.156; 4 in C, K.157; 5 in F, K.158; 6 in B flat, K.159; 7 in E flat, K.160; 8 in F, K.168; 9 in A, K.169; 10 in C, K.170; 11 in E flat, K.171; 12 in B flat, K.172; 13 in D min., K.173; Divertimenti: in G, K.136; in B flat, K.137; in F, K.138.
*** DG Dig. 431 645-2 (3) [id.]. Hagen Qt.

This set of three CDs presents all of Mozart's music for string quartet up to the age of seventeen and, although (with the best will in the world) this cannot be called great music, it is played with such charm and polish that one is almost – but not quite – tempted to believe that it is. Unlike the Quartetto Italiano, the Hagens include the *Divertimenti*, K.136–8. They have already given ample evidence of their artistry and musicianship in their recordings of K.589 and K.590. In this present set they strike an excellent balance between naturalness of utterance and sophistication of tone, and the DG recording is in the very first flight.

String quartets Nos. 1 in G, K.80; 2 in D, K.155; 4 in C, K.157.
(BB) ** Naxos Dig. 8.550541 [id.]. Éder Qt.

String quartets Nos. 3 in G, K.156; 5 in F, K.158; 6 in B flat, K.159; 17 in B flat (Hunt), K.458
(B) ** Naxos Dig. 8.550542 [id.]. Éder Qt.

This new, super-bargain Naxos series of the Mozart *Quartets* has much in its favour. The playing of the Éder Quartet is polished and responsive. Their phrasing is warm and elegant; their ensemble is impressive; allegros are vital and they certainly bring the music to life. The snag is the venue, the Sashalom Reformed Church in Budapest. The ecclesiastical resonance affords the group the most beautiful sound. The *Adagio* opening of K.80, at the beginning of the first disc – the amazing work of a fourteen-year-old – is made to sound remarkably full and rich. But the effect overall is almost orchestral and loses virtually all the intimacy of the medium. This applies especially to the mature *Hunt* quartet, which opens the second CD. It is impossible not to respond to such richly inegrated music-making, but one wishes a different venue had been chosen.

String quartets Nos. 14 in G, K.387; 15 in D min., K.421; 16 in E flat, K.428; 17 in B flat (Hunt), K458; 18 in A, K.464; 19 in C (Dissonance), K.465 (Haydn Quartets).
❀ *** CRD CRD 3362 (*Nos. 14–15*); 3363 (*Nos. 16–17*); 3364 (*Nos. 18–19*) [id.]. Chilingirian Qt.
*** Hyp. Dig. CDS 44001/3 [id.]. Salomon Qt.
(M) (**(*)) Sony mono SM2K 47219 (2) [id.]. Budapest Qt.

The set of six quartets dedicated to Haydn contains a high proportion of Mozart's finest works in the genre. The Chilingirian Quartet plays with unforced freshness and vitality, avoiding expressive mannerism but always conveying the impression of spontaneity, helped by the warm and vivid recording. International rivals in these works may at times have provided more poise and polish but none outshines the Chilingirians in direct conviction, and their matching of tone and intonation is second to none. Unlike most quartets, they never sound superficial in the elegant but profound slow movements. The three CDs are packaged separately and offer demonstration quality. The sound is appealingly smooth and real: there is no lack of immediacy, but the ambient effect ensures a natural balance, with no edginess on top.

The Salomon Quartet has already given us some superb Haydn, and no one sampling their Mozart will be disappointed. It goes without saying that their playing is highly accomplished and has a real sense of style; they do not eschew vibrato, though their use of it is not liberal, and there is admirable clarity of texture and vitality of articulation. There is no want of subtlety and imagination in the slow movements. The recordings are admirably truthful and lifelike, and those who seek 'authenticity' in Mozart's chamber music will not be disappointed by them; they are now available in a three-CD boxed set at a slightly reduced price.

The Budapest players recorded Mozart's *Haydn Quartets* in 1953, with the exception of the *E flat*, K.428, which dates from three years earlier and sounds very good indeed. Although that performance does not have the classic stature of the pre-war Pro Arte set, it is still very fine; though the recording is dry, everything is very clear and well defined. The others offer various felicitous touches and, even if the sound throughout is dryish, it is tonally agreeable. In the early 1950s the Budapest were still in very good form and produced a well-blended sonority.

String quartets Nos. 15 in D min., K.421; 17 in B flat (Hunt), K.458.
*** Denon C37 7003 [id.]. Smetana Qt.

Both these 1982 performances were recorded in the House of Artists, Prague. The Smetana find just the right tempo for the first movement of the *D minor*, unhurried but forward-moving. *The Hunt*, which is placed first on the disc, is given a spirited performance and is rather more polished than most of its CD rivals; it is a pleasure to report with enthusiasm on these well-paced accounts.

String quartets Nos. 16 in E flat, K.428; 18 in A, K.464.
(M) ** Naxos Dig. 8.550540 [id.]. Éder Qt.

Like the earlier issue in this super-bargain Naxos series, the playing of the Éder Quartet can hardly be faulted, with well-matched timbres, fine ensemble and a warm, lively response to Mozart, but the resonant recording, made in a Budapest church, gives almost a string orchestral illusion at times, and robs the music-making of intimacy. In slow movements playing which is rich in tone becomes almost bland, in spite of the players' obvious use of dynamic contrast, while detail spreads across the acoustic to become generalized.

String quartet No. 17 in B flat (Hunt), K.458.
(M) *** Teldec/Warner 2292 42440-2 [id.]. Alban Berg Qt – HAYDN: *Quartet No. 77.* ***
(B) *** DG Compact Classics 413 845-2 (2); *413 845-4* [id.]. Amadeus Qt – BEETHOVEN: *Ghost trio* ***; SCHUBERT: *Trout quintet* ** (CDs only: HAYDN: *Lark quartet* **(*)).

String quartets Nos. 17 in B flat (Hunt), K.458; 19 in C (Dissonance), K.465.
❀ *** Teldec/Warner 2292 43037-2 [id.]. Alban Berg Qt.

The warmest possible welcome must be given to the return of this early Teldec coupling by the Alban Berg Quartet. At that period in their history these players had not yet acquired the glossy surface veneer that sometimes detracts from their more recent digital recordings. Their version of the *Hunt quartet* dates from 1979 and is still possibly the finest account on the market. It is also available coupled with Haydn and has much greater polish and freshness even than the Quartetto Italiano, the Melos or the Amadeus, and well withstands all the competition that has come since. The *Dissonance* is of similar vintage, though it never appeared in the UK at the time. It, too, is first class, with a wonderfully expressive account of the slow movement. Although dynamic gradations are steep, there is no sense of exaggeration – on the contrary, there is only a sense of total dedication about these wholly excellent performances, which are recommended with enthusiasm. No reservations about the transfers.

The earlier Amadeus account of the *Hunt Quartet*, recorded in the mid-1960s, was one of their popular successes – and rightly so. It is the most satisfying performance of the four named works on this Compact Classics reissue. The sound is excellent in both formats (the tape omits the Haydn *Lark Quartet*).

String quartets Nos. 17 in B flat (Hunt), K.458; 19 in C (Dissonance), K.465; 23 in F (Prussian No. 3), K.590.
(M) **(*) Decca 433 694-2 [id.]. Musikverein Qt.

The Musikverein Quartet is drawn from members of the Vienna Philharmonic; their excellent principal violin is Rainer Küchl and, when first issued on LP (in 1976), K.590 was attributed to the Küchl Quartet; by the time the other recordings were made in 1979, the group had changed their name, as given in the listing. They bring an imaginative vitality to bear on these scores so than one can forgive the way in which they succumb to the temptations of their own virtuosity in the outer movements of the *Dissonance*. Elsewhere, a relaxed, unforced quality imbues this playing, which is impressive and there is no want of brilliance either. We gave the recordings high praise when they appeared on LP, but this is a case where Decca's 'on automatic pilot' digital transferring process has not been entirely beneficial, for the leader's timbre now sounds excessively thin at times, although this is slightly more obvious in K.458 and K.465 than in K.590.

String quartets Nos. 18 in A, K.464; 19 in C (Dissonance), K.465.
(M) *** EMI CDM7 69102-2 [id.]. Smetana Qt.

The vintage analogue coupling from the Smetana Quartet is excellent in every way. The playing has impetus and feeling, finesse and vitality, and the sound is well balanced, full and clear. Excellent value at mid-price.

String quartets Nos. 20 in D (Hoffmeister), K.499; 21 in D, K.575; 22 in B flat, K.589; 23 in F, K.590 (Prussian Quartets Nos. 1–3).
*** CRD CRD 3427/8 [id.]. Chilingirian Qt.

The Chilingirian Quartet give very natural, unforced, well-played and sweet-toned accounts of the last four *Quartets* and they are extremely well recorded. Though perhaps not as highly polished as were the Melos on DG (though there is not a great deal in it), there is far more musical interest and liveliness here. They are very well recorded too, with cleanly focused lines and a warm, pleasing ambience; indeed in this respect these two discs are second to none.

String quartets Nos. 20 in D (Hoffmeister), K.499; 22 in B flat, K.589.
*** Virgin Dig. VC7 90772-2; *VC7 90772-4* [id.]. Endellion Qt.

So many present-day quartets play Mozart like a jet taking off: candlelight gives way to strip-lighting. This may not be impeccable quartet-playing when compared to some earlier gramophone performances, but one is undoubtely given the impression that these artists are enjoying themselves. Phrasing is freshly thought out and there is spontaneity as well. Good, truthful recordings.

String quartets Nos. 22 in B flat, K.589; 23 in F (Prussian), K.590.
*** DG Dig. 423 108-2 [id.]. Hagen Qt.

The Hagen Quartet play with great fluency, and it is difficult to resist such perfection of ensemble and refinement of blend. Slow movements in particular do not dig deep, but they have an elegance and homogeneity of tone that are remarkable and, at the present time, possibly unsurpassed. The DG recording does justice to their tonal finesse and subtlety. There is more to Mozart than they find, but what they achieve still excites the keenest admiration.

Complete Mozart Edition, Volume 11: *String quintets Nos. 1–6.*
(M) *** Ph. 422 511-2 (3). Grumiaux Trio, with Gerecz, Lesueur.

String quintets Nos. 1–6.
(M) **(*) DG 431 149-2 (3). Amadeus Qt, with Cecil Aronowitz.
(M) ** DG Dig. 431 694-2 (3) [id.]. Melos Qt with Franz Beyer.

(i) *String quintets Nos. 1–6;* (ii) *Clarinet quintet in A, K.581.*
(M) *** Sony M3YK 45827 (3). (i) Juilliard Qt with John Graham; (ii) Harold Wright, Marlboro Ens. (Alexander Schneider, Isidore Cohen, Samuel Rhodes, Leslie Parnas).

No reservations about the Grumiaux ensemble's survey of the *String quintets*: immensely civilized and admirably conceived readings. Throughout the set the vitality and sensitivity of this team are striking, and in general this eclipses all other recent accounts. The remastering of the 1973 recordings for CD is very successful, and this Philips recording still holds its dominant position in the lists.

While the Grumiaux box remains a first choice, the Juilliard set on the Sony makes a very good alternative. The performances are finely shaped and very alive, and even those who do not always warm to this ensemble will find them both alive and responsive here. There is depth in the slow movements of both the *C major* and *G minor Quintets* and plenty of spirit elsewhere. The first movement of the *D major*, K.593, for example, is a delight. The recordings, which emanate from the late 1970s, have come up very well and the set has the additional inducement of offering a very musical account of the *Clarinet quintet* from 1970 with the Marlboro Ensemble who include Harold Wright as the clarinettist and Alexander Schneider leading the quartet.

DG have now reissued their Amadeus set, recorded between 1968 (K.406, K.515) and 1970 (K.516). The Amadeus is distinguished by fine playing and the recordings are remarkably successful in their CD transfers, with only a slight degree of thinness on top to date the earlier sessions.

The Melos Quartet and their second violist, Franz Beyer, have certain merits, well-judged tempi and articulate rhythms. But if they are sound, they are at the same time not always fresh or imaginative. Their playing is at times rather routine and has too little tenderness.

String quintets Nos. 3 in C, K.515; 4 in G min., K.516; Adagio & fugue in C min., K.546.
** Decca Dig. 430 772-2 [id.]. Takács Qt, György Pauk.

The distinction of these artists arouses high expectations that are not entirely fulfilled. To some extent the close balance militates against them, for pianissimos are unable fully to register. The playing though virile is not always as subtle in colouring or searching as these great works require.

(i) *String quintet No. 4 in G min., K.516;* (i) *Violin sonata No. 26 in B flat, K.378.*
(M) *** BMG/RCA GD 87869 [7869-2-RG]. Heifetz, with (i) Baker, Primrose, Majewski, Piatigorsky; (ii) Brooks Smith – *Violin concerto No. 5.* ***

The illustrious ensemble adopts a very fast pace for the first movement of the *G minor Quintet*, and some might feel that its urgency is over-pressed; yet so fine is the playing that, after a minute or two, one adjusts as at a live performance. There are wonderful moments in the rest of the work, not least the viola playing of William Primrose. The acoustic is a little dry, but the sound itself is full and warmly blended, with good detail. The *Violin sonata* was recorded two years later and shows splendid rapport between the great violinist and his partner, Brooks Smith.

Complete Mozart Edition, Volume 15: *Violin sonatas Nos. 1–34; Sonatinas in C & F, K.46d & 46e; Sonatina in F (for beginners), K.547; Sonata in C, K.403* (completed Stadler); *Adagio in C min., K.396; Allegro in B flat, K.372; Andante & allegretto in C, K.404; Andante in A & Fugue in A min., K.402* (completed Stadler); *12 Variations on 'La bergère Célimène', K.359; 6 Variations on 'Hélas, j'ai perdu mon amant', K.360.*
(M) **(*) Ph. Analogue/Dig. 422 515-2 (7). Gérard Poulet, Blandine Verlet; Arthur Grumiaux, Walter Klien; Isabelle van Keulen, Ronald Brautigan.

The early sonatas, from K.6 through to K.31, were recorded in the mid-1970s by Gérard Poulet with Blandine Verlet on harpsichord. The various fragments, sonatinas, sonatas (K.46d, K.46e, K.403 and K.547) and variations were recorded in 1990 by Isabelle van Keulen and Ronald Brautigan. For the remaining four CDs, Philips have turned to the set by Arthur Grumiaux and Walter Klien, recorded digitally in the early 1980s. There is a great deal of sparkle and some refined musicianship in these performances, and pleasure remains undisturbed by the balance which, in the 1981 recordings, favours the violin. The later recordings, from 1982 and 1983, are much better in this respect.

Violin sonatas Nos. 17–28; 32–4; Sonatina in F, K.547.
(M) *** DG Dig. 431 784-2 (4) [id.]. Itzhak Perlman, Daniel Barenboim.
(M) *** Decca 430 306-2 (4). Szymon Goldberg, Radu Lupu.

Violin sonatas Nos. 17–28; 32–34; Sonatina in F, K.547; 12 Variations on La bergère Célimène, K.359; 6 Variations on Au bord d'une fontaine, K.360.
*** Ph. 416 902-2 (5) [id.]. Henryk Szeryng, Ingrid Haebler.

The Perlman and Barenboim interpretations (and the recordings) have a remarkable consistency and reflect a genuinely creative musical symbiosis and a spontaneous joy in the music. The digital recordings are beautifully balanced, and this will probably be a first choice for most collectors, although Goldberg and Lupu are by no means outclassed.

Both Goldberg and Lupu bring humanity and imagination to their performances. There is no doubt that in these works Goldberg shows a wisdom, born of long experience, that is almost unfailingly revealing. Lupu gives instinctive musical support to his partner; and the recordings, made in the Kingsway Hall in 1975, are expertly balanced and have transferred vividly and realistically to CD.

Ingrid Haebler brings an admirable vitality and robustness to her part. Her playing has sparkle and great spontaneity. Szeryng's contribution is altogether masterly, and all these performances find both partners in complete rapport. The analogue recordings from the mid-1970s provide striking realism and truthfulness, and they have been immaculately transferred to CD. The *Variations* included in the set are managed with charm; an extra set is included, plus the *Sonatina in F*, not offered by Klien and Grumiaux, which accounts for the need for five CDs.

Violin sonatas Nos. 17 in C, K.296; 18 in G, K.301; 25 in F, K.377.
(M) *** DG Dig. 431 276-2; *431 276-4*. Itzhak Perlman, Daniel Barenboim.

Violin sonatas Nos. 21 in E min., K.304; 23 in D, K.306; 24 in F, K.376.
(M) *** DG Dig. 431 277-2; *431 277-4*. Itzhak Perlman, Daniel Barenboim.

The *Sonata in C*, K.296, is the first of what Alfred Einstein described as Mozart's concertante sonatas; even here, however, the piano is dominant, a point reflected in the fact that, for all Perlman's individuality, it is Barenboim who leads. This is playing of a genial spontaneity that conveys the joy of the moment with countless felicitous details. Excellent, vivid recording.

Violin sonatas Nos. 26 in B flat, K.378; 28 in E flat, K.380; 32 in B flat, K.454; Violin sonatina in F, K.457.
*** Olympia OCD 125 [id.]. Igor Oistrakh, Natalia Zertsalova.

Igor Oistrakh has not as assertive a personality as his father, and he makes a very real partnership here with Zertsalova, who is an excellent Mozartian. These are all splendid works and they are played with fine classical feeling and impetus; the Rondo finale of K.380 is a demonstrable example of the sparkle of this music-making. The recording, too, is truthful and well balanced, and the disc costs rather less than full price.

Violin sonatas Nos. 33 in E flat, K.481; 34 in A, K.526; Violin sonatina in F, K.547.
(M) *** Decca 425 420-2. Szymon Goldberg, Radu Lupu.

Goldberg's playing has great depth, though at times his age perhaps begins to show (a slight lack of bloom on his tone); but this does not inhibit the strength of the recommendation, for Lupu is marvellously sensitive. The CD transfer is first class, and this is one of the most rewarding single discs of these *Sonatas*.

PIANO MUSIC

Complete Mozart Edition, Volume 16: (i) *Andante with 5 variations, K.501; Fugue in C min., K.426; Sonatas for piano duet in C, K.19d; D, K.381; G, K.357; B flat, K.358; F, K.497; C, K.521; Sonata in D for two pianos, K.448;* (ii) *Larghetto and Allegro in E flat* (reconstructed Badura-Skoda).
(M) ** Ph. 422 516-2 (2) [id.]. (i) Ingrid Haebler, Ludwig Hoffman; (ii) Jörg Demus, Paul Badura-Skoda.

This two-CD set includes all the music Mozart composed for piano duet or two pianos, in elegant (if at times a little too dainty) performances by Ingrid Haebler and Ludwig Hoffman in recordings dating from the mid-1970s. Also included is a Mozart fragment, the *Larghetto and Allegro in E flat*, probably written in 1782–3 and completed by Paul Badura-Skoda, who recorded it in 1971 for the Amadeo label with Jörg Demus. Despite the occasional distant clink of Dresden china, all these performances give pleasure and are very decently recorded.

Piano duet

Adagio & allegro in F min. (for mechanical organ), *K.594; Andante with 5 variations in G, K.501; Fantasia in F min.* (for mechanical organ), *K.608; Sonatas for piano duet in C, K.19d; B flat, K.358; D, K.381; F, K.497; C, K.521; Sonata in D for 2 pianos, K.448.*
(M) *** DG 435 042-2 (2) [id.]. Christoph Eschenbach, Justus Frantz.

Adagio & allegro in F min., K.594; Andante with variations, K.501; Fantasia in F min., K.608; Sonatas for piano duet in C, K.19b; in B flat, K.358; Sonata for 2 pianos in D, K.381.
(M) *** DG 429 809-2; *429 809-4*. Christoph Eschenbach, Justus Frantz.

The major *Sonatas* are magnificent works. Eschenbach and Frantz play with exemplary ensemble and fine sensitivity. The pieces for mechanical clock show (alongside the *Sonatas*) these artists' care for detail, and here as elsewhere they readily convey their own pleasure in the music. The recordings, made between 1972 and 1975, are clean and well balanced, if occasionally a shade dry.

Double piano sonata in D, K.448.
*** Sony MK 39511 [id.]. Murray Perahia, Radu Lupu – SCHUBERT: *Fantasia in D min.* ***

With Perahia taking the primo part, his brightness and individual way of illuminating even the simplest passage-work dominate the performance, producing magical results and challenging the more inward Lupu into comparably inspired playing. Pleasantly ambient recording made at The Maltings, Snape, and beautifully caught on CD.

Solo piano music

Piano sonatas Nos. 1–18 (complete).
(M) *** EMI CZS7 67294-2 (5). Daniel Barenboim.

Piano sonatas Nos. 1–10.
❀ (B) *** VoxBox (2) [CDX 5026]. Walter Klien.

Piano sonatas Nos.11–18; Fantasy in C min., K.475.
❀ (B) *** VoxBox (2) [CDX 5046]. Walter Klien.

Complete Mozart Edition, Volume 17: *Piano sonatas Nos. 1–18; Fantasia in C min., K.475.*
❀ (M) *** Ph. Dig. 422 517-2 (5) [id.]. Mitsuko Uchida.
(M) *** Decca 430 333-2 (5). András Schiff.

On Philips, Mitsuko Uchida's self-recommending collection, with beautiful and naturally balanced digital recording made in the Henry Wood Hall, London, has now been reissued on 5 mid-priced CDs by omitting the shorter pieces, except for the *C minor Fantasia*. Miss Uchida's set of the Mozart *Sonatas* brings playing of consistently fine sense and sound musicianship. There is every indication that this will come to be regarded as a classic series to set alongside those of Gieseking and Walter Klien. Every phrase is beautifully placed, every detail registers, and the early *Sonatas* are as revealing as the late ones. The piano recording is completely realistic, slightly distanced in a believable ambience.

Klien is an outstanding Mozartian; his playing has consistent freshness and is in exemplary taste. It gives enormous pleasure and is at times slightly more robust in its vitality than the playing of Mitsuko Uchida. There is nothing remotely self-conscious about it; the phrasing is unfailingly musical and every detail is beautifully placed without there being the slightest suggestion of preciosity. The balance is rather forward (the piano seems just behind the speakers and the sound-image is widely spread), but the tone is rounded and full, and the brightness in the treble never becomes brittle. There is a minimum of background, which never becomes obtrusive. The set has been successfully accommodated on four bargain-priced discs. These Vox Boxes still await issue in the UK.

András Schiff's earlier, Decca recordings now also reappear, in a box in the same price-range. Schiff, without exceeding the essential Mozartian sensibility, takes a somewhat more romantic and forward-looking view of the music. His fingerwork is precise, yet mellow, and his sense of colour consistently excites admiration. He is slightly prone to self-indulgence in the handling of some phrases but such is the inherent freshness and spontaneity of his playing that one accepts the idiosyncrasies as a natural product of live performance. The piano is set just a little further back than in the Philips/Uchida recordings, and the acoustic is marginally more open, which suits his slightly more expansive manner.

Barenboim's set is also reissued on five CDs instead of the original six. Barenboim, while keeping his playing well within scale in its crisp articulation, refuses to adopt the Dresden china approach to Mozart's *Sonatas*. Even the little *C major*, K.545, designed for a young player, has its element of toughness, minimizing its 'eighteenth-century drawing-room' associations. Though – with the exception of the two minor-key sonatas – these are relatively unambitious works, Barenboim's voyage of discovery brings out their consistent freshness, with the orchestral implications of some of the allegros strongly established. The recording, with a pleasant ambience round the piano sound, confirms the apt scale.

Piano sonatas Nos. 3 in B flat, K.281; 10 in C, K.330; 13 in B flat, K.333.
(M) **(*) DG 431 274-2; *431 274-4* [id.]. Vladimir Horowitz.

It is sensible to have Horowitz's Mozart sonata recordings gathered together. There have to be slight reservations about the sound: the quality in K.333 is rather dry, while K.281 is the most satisfactory. But this was still just about the best recording he received, apart from his live recitals for RCA, and the playing is remarkable, quite unlike any other. It is not always free from affectation but is never less than elegant.

Piano sonata No. 8 in A min., K.310; Fantasia in C min., K.396; Rondo in A min., K.511; 9 Variations on a Minuet by Duport, K.573.
(M) **(*) Van. 08.4025.71 [OVC 4025]. Alfred Brendel.

Fine, strong performances from Brendel with a particularly good set of Variations, where the care with shaping and detail raises the interest of the listener and the stature of the music. The 1968 recording is firm and full. But the measure (51 minutes) could be more generous.

Piano sonatas Nos. 8 in A min., K.310; 14 in C min., K.457; Fantasia in C min., K.475; Rondo: Alla turca (from *Sonata No. 11, K.331*).
(M) *** DG Dig. 431 275-2; *431 275-4*. Maria João Pires.

Maria João Pires is a stylist and a fine Mozartian, as those who have heard any of her cycle on Denon will know. Pires is always refined but is never wanting in classical feeling, and she has a vital imagination. The performance of the *C minor* is particularly fine and her *Rondo Alla turca* engagingly varied in dynamic range: it begins quite gently. Good, clear piano recording, bright but realistic. If DG plan to give us a complete cycle with her, this is good news.

Piano sonatas Nos. 8 in A min., K.310; 17 in D, K.576; (i) *Double piano sonata in D, K.448. Rondo in A min., K.511.*
(M) **(*) Decca 425 031-2; *425 031-4* [id.]. Vladimir Ashkenazy; (i) with Malcolm Frager.

Ashkenazy shows impeccable judgement and taste in the solo sonatas. His playing is immaculate and fresh, and this collection can be counted among his finest analogue records. The transfers of 1967/8 Kingsway Hall recordings are very well managed. The *Sonata for two pianos*, however, is on a lower level of tension; the end result is less individual. But this is still well worth having for the solo works.

Piano sonatas Nos. 8 in A min., K.310; 18 in D, K.576; Fantasias: in C min.; in D min., K.396/7; 12 Variations on 'Je suis Lindor', K.354.
*** EMI Dig. CDC7 54021-2 [id.]. Melvyn Tan (fortepiano).

Here is Mozart playing of temperament by Melvyn Tan which enhances this young player's growing reputation. As always, he is sure-fingered and brilliant. His rather brisk tempi in Schubert did not always convince, but there are no quarrels with his judgement here. Tempi allow every musical point to be made, and thoughtful musical points there are in plenty. The *A minor Sonata* is outstanding: free, fiery and impassioned, with a clear, well-defined sense of line; and there is some fine legato playing in the slow movement of the *D major*, where some of the rubato is a bit overdone, as it is in the *D minor Fantasia*, K.397. The *Variations on 'Je suis Lindor'* are done with great flair, and the whole programme is most vividly recorded.

Piano sonata No. 10 in C, K.330.
(M) ** BMG/RCA GD 60415; *GK 60415* [60415-2-RG; *60415-4* RG]. Van Cliburn – DEBUSSY: *Estampes* etc. **; BARBER: *Sonata.* **(*)

Van Cliburn's record, made in the mid-1960s, offers intelligent playing but sound that is wanting in timbre and sonority. The Debussy and Barber are better in this respect but still dryish.

Piano sonatas Nos. 12 in F, K.332; 13 in B flat, K.333; 14 in C min., K.457; Fantasy in C min.
*** Sony Dig. SK 46748 [id.]. Andreas Haefliger.

The Swiss-born, Juilliard-trained Andreas Haefliger is still in his twenties and shows himself to be an impressive Mozartian. These are finely poised and well-integrated performances without any touch of Dresden china but with plenty of sensitivity. The Sony recording is very clean and firm. Eminently recommendable.

Complete Mozart Edition, Volume 18: *8 Variations in G, K.24; 7 Variations in D, K.25; 12 Variations in C, K.179; 6 Variations in G, K.180; 9 Variations in C, K.264; 12 Variations in C, K.265; 8 Variations in F, K.352; 12 Variations in E flat, K.353; 12 Variations in E flat, K.354; 6 Variations in F, K.398; 10 Variations in G, K.455; 12 Variations in B flat, K.500; 9 Variations in D, K.573; 8 Variations in F, K.613; Adagio in B min., K.540; Eine kleine Gigue in G, K.574; Fantasia in D min., K.397; Minuet in D, K.355; Rondos: in D, K.485; in A min., K.511; 21 Pieces for keyboard, K.1, K.1a–1d;1f; K.2–5; K.5a; K.33b; K.94; K.312; K.394–5; K.399–401; K.408/1; K.453a; K.460.*
(M) ** Ph. Analogue/Dig. 422 518-2 (5) [id.]. Ingrid Haebler or Mitsuko Uchida (both piano), Ton Koopman (harpsichord).

The first three of the five CDs in this collection are taken from Ingrid Haebler's survey of the complete piano music, recorded in the mid-1970s. Although the gentle clink of Dresden china can occasionally be heard, she is an intelligent and perceptive artist who characterizes these variations with some subtlety. The quality of the sound is very good indeed: there is both warmth and presence. Mitsuko Uchida gives us various short pieces, such as the *A minor Rondo*, K.511, and the *B minor Adagio*, K.540, which she plays beautifully – though at less than 40 minutes her disc offers rather short measure. However, Haebler and Koopman make up for that, the latter offering 21 short pieces, including some juvenilia, which he dispatches with some degree of brusqueness. He is very brightly recorded. Recommended, though there is less musical nourishment on the Koopman disc than on its companions.

VOCAL MUSIC

Complete Mozart Edition, Volume 22: (i) *Adagio and fugue in C min., K.546; Maurerische Trauermusik, K.477.* (ii) *La Betulia liberata* (oratorio), *K.118.* (iii) *Davidde penitente* (cantata), *K.469.* (iv) *Grabmusik (Funeral music), K.42.* (v; i) Masonic music: *Dir, Seele des Weltalls, K.429; Ihr unsre neuen Leiter, K.484; Die ihr unermesslichen Weltalls Schöpfer, ehrt, K.619; Lasst uns mit geschlung'gnen Händen, K.623; Laut verkünde unsre Freude, K.623; Lied zur Gesellenreise, K.468; Lobgesang auf die feierliche Johannisloge, K.148; Die Maurerfreude, K.471; Zerfliesset heut, geliebte Brüder, K.483.* (vi) *Passionslied: Kommet her, ihr frechen Sünder, K.146.* (vii) *Die Schuldigkeit des ersten Gebots* (Singspiel), K.35.

(M) **(*) Ph. Analogue/Dig. 422 522-2 (6) [id.]. (i) Dresden State O, Schreier; (ii) Schreier, Cotrubas, Berry, Fuchs, Zimmermann, Salzburg Chamber Ch. & Mozarteum O, Hagen; (iii) M. Marshall, Vermillion, Blochwitz; (iv) Murray, Varcoe; (v) Schreier, Blochwitz, Schmidt, Leipzig R. Ch.; (vi) Murray; (vii) M. Marshall, Murray, Nielsen, Blochwitz, Baldin; (iii; iv; vi; vii) Stuttgart RSO, Marriner.

The six discs in this volume of the Philips Complete Edition cover choral music from the full range of Mozart's career. The two big oratorios are both early works, *La Betulia liberata* and (even earlier, dating from his twelfth year) *Die Schuldigkeit des ersten Gebots* ('The Duty of the First Commandment'). *Davide penitente* is the cantata largely derived from the torso of the *C minor Mass*, while the sixth disc, in many ways the most inspired of all, contains the Masonic music, vividly done in Dresden under the direction of Peter Schreier. For convenience that disc also includes the purely instrumental Masonic music, the *Mauerische Trauermusik* and the *Adagio and fugue in C minor*. Directed by Leopold Hager, the recording of *La Betulia liberata*, originally recorded by DG in 1978, belongs to the Salzburg Mozarteum series, mainly devoted to the early operas, a plain, well-sung performance that does not quite disguise the piece's excessive length. The orchestral sound is thinner than on the other discs, though voices are well caught. Sir Neville Marriner is the conductor both of *Die Schuldigkeit* and of *Davide penitente*, giving sparkle to the early oratorio and vigour to the cantata, a fine piece. Full texts are given, and informative notes on individual works.

Complete Mozart Edition, Volume 20: (i) *Alma Dei creatoris, K.277;* (ii) *Ave verum corpus, K.618;* (i) *Benedictus sit Deus Pater, K.117; Cibavit eos ex adipe frumenti, K.44;* (iii) *Dixit et Magnificat, K.193;* (i) *Ergo interest, an quis, K.143;* (ii) *Exsultate jubilate, K.165;* (i) *God is our refuge* (motet), *K.20; Inter natos Mulierum, K.72;* (iii) *Litaniae de BMV (Lauretanae), K.109 & K.195;* (i) *Kyries, K.33; K.90–91; K.322–3;* (ii) *Kyrie, K.341;* (iii) *Litaniae de venerabili altaris sacramento, K.125 & K.243;* (i) *Miserere mei, Deus, K.85; Misercordias Domini, K.222; Quaerite primum regnum Dei, K.86; Regina coeli, laetare, K.108; K.127; K.276; Sancta Maria, mater Dei, K.273; Scande coeli limina, K.34; Sub tuum praesidium, K.198; Te Deum laudamus, K.141; Veni, Sancte Spiritus, K.47; Venite, populi, venite, K.260;* (ii) *Vesperae solennes de confessore, K.339;* (iii) *Vesperae solennes de Domenica, K.321.*
(M) *** Ph. 422 520-2 (5) [id.]. (i) Nawe, Reinhardt-Kiss, Schellenberger-Ernst, Selbig, Burmeister, Lang, Büchner, Eschrig, Ribbe, Pape, Polster; (ii) Te Kanawa, Bainbridge, Ryland Davies, Gowell, LSO Ch. & O, Sir Colin Davis; (iii) Frank-Reinecke, Shirai, Burmeister, Riess, Büchner, Polster, (i; iii) Leipzig R. Ch. & SO, Kegel.

The five discs in this volume of the Philips Edition cover the Litanies and Vespers, as well as some shorter pieces. It is fascinating to find that the boy Mozart's very first religious piece is an unaccompanied motet, written in London to an English text, *God is our refuge* – which here the Leipzig singers very forgivably pronounce 'reefuge'. Herbert Kegel with the Dresden Staatskapelle and his Leipzig Radio Choir are responsible for the great majority of the pieces here, fresh and alert if on occasion rhythmically too rigid. The big exception is the great setting of the *Solemn vespers*, K.339, for which Sir Colin Davis's 1971 version has understandably been preferred, when the young Kiri Te Kanawa sings the heavenly soprano setting of *Laudate Dominum* so ravishingly. She is also the soloist in the early cantata *Exsultate jubilate* with its brilliant *Alleluia*. Those 1971 recordings, made in London, are bass-heavy but the voices are still brightly caught. The rest – much of it recorded recently with some excellent soloists – brings very fresh and clean recording, with the choir generally more forwardly placed than in the recordings of Mozart's Masses, made by the same forces.

Complete Mozart Edition, Volume 23: (i) *2 Canons for strings; 14 Canons for woodwind; 10 Interval canons for woodwind;* (ii) *6 Canons for female voices; 3 Canons for mixed voices; 13 Canons for male voices; 4 puzzle canons for mixed voices.* (iii) *53 Concert arias. Aria* (with ornamentation by Mozart) for: J. C. BACH: *Adriano in Siria.* (iv) *8 Vocal Duets, Trios and Quartets.* (v) Alternative arias and duets for: *Così fan tutte; Don Giovanni; Die Entführung aus dem Serail; La finta semplice; Idomeneo; Lucio Silla; Mitridate; Le nozze di Figaro.*
(M) *** Ph. 422 523-2 (8) [id.]. (i) Bav. RSO (members); (ii) Ch. Viennensis, Mancusi or Harrer; (iii) Moser, Schwarz, Popp, Mathis, Gruberová, Sukis, Araiza, Ahnsjö, Lloyd, Berry, Kaufmann, Blochwitz, Lind, Burrows, Eda-Pierre; (iv) Blochwitz, Schariner, Pape, Kaufman, Lind, Jansen, Schreier; (v) Blochwitz, Szmytka, Wiens, Gudbjörnson, Vermillion, Schreier, Mathis, Burrows, Tear, Terfel, Kaufmann, Lind, Scharinger.

Taking three more records than the Decca collection of concert arias (see below), the Philips set offers substantial extras, not just a collection of a dozen or so ensembles and a whole disc of 35 canons (some of them instrumental) but some fascinating alternative versions and substitute arias for different Mozart operas, from *La finta semplice* and *Mitridate* through to the three Da Ponte masterpieces. It is fascinating to have Bryn Terfel, for example, as Figaro in a varied recitative and slightly extended version of the Act I aria, *Non piu' andrai*. Eva Lind is vocally a less happy choice for the items involving Susanna and Zerlina, and generally the sopranos chosen for this collection, stylish Mozartians as they are, have less sumptuous voices than those on the Decca set. Broadly, the arias are presented in chronological order, with full texts, as given in the Decca set, though general essays are provided rather than individual commentaries on each of the many dozens of items.

Complete Mozart Edition, Volume 24: (i) Lieder: *Abendempfindung; Als Luise die Briefe ihres ungetreuen Liebhabers; Die Alte; An Chloe; An die Freude; An die Freundschaft; Die betrogene Welt; Dans un bois solitaire; Geheime Liebe; Der Frühling; Gessellenreise; Die grossmütige Gelassenheit; Ich würd' auf meinem Pfad; Das Kinderspiel; 2 Kirchenlieder (O Gottes Lamm; Als aus Ägypten); Des kleinen Friedrichs Geburtstag; Die kleine Spinnerin; Komm, liebe Zither, komm; Lied der Freiheit; Das Lied der Trennung; Un moto di gioia; Oiseaux, si tous les ans; Ridente la calma; Sehnsucht nach dem Frühling; Sei du mein Trost; Das Traumbild; Das Veilchen; Verdankt sei es dem Glanz der Grossen; Die Verschweigung; Warnung; Wie unglücklich bin ich nit; Der Zauberer; Die Zufriedenheit (2): (Was frag' ich viel nach Geld und Gut; Wie sanft, wie ruhig fühl' ich hier); Die Zufriedenheit im niedrigen Stande.* (ii) *6 Notturni for voices and woodwind, K.346; K.436/9 & K.549.*
(M) *** Ph. 422 524-2 (2) [id.]. Elly Ameling, (i) with Dalton Baldwin (piano or organ) or Benny Ludemann (mandolin); (ii) with Elisabeth Cooymans, Peter van der Bilt, Netherlands Wind Ens. (members).

These two discs, containing not just Mozart's solo songs but the six *Nocturnes* for solo voices and wind, make up one of the most delightful volumes in the Philips Complete Mozart Edition. Elly Ameling is the ideal soprano for such fresh and generally innocent inspirations, with her voice at its purest and sweetest when she made the recordings in 1977. In the 1973 recordings of the *Notturni* (setting Italian texts by Metastasio) she is well matched by her soprano and baritone partners, though these are mostly plainer, less distinctive miniatures. Included are two hymns with organ and two tiny songs with mandolin, while aptly the very last of the series, K.598, is one of the lightest of all, *Children's games*, sparklingly done. The recordings come up with fine freshness and presence.

Lieder: *Abendempfindung; Als Luise die Briefe; An die Einsamkeit; An die Freundschaft; An die Hoffnung; Dans un bois solitaire; Eine kleine deutsche Kantate; Gesellenreise; Die grossmütige Gelassenheit; Die kleine Spinnerin; Das Lied der Trennung; Oiseaux, si tous les ans; Ridente la calma; Sehnsucht nach dem Frühlinge; Das Veilchen; Der Zauberer; Die Zufriedenheit.*
(M) **(*) Saga SCD 9037 [id.]. Jill Gomez, John Constable.

Recorded early in Jill Gomez's career, this collection of Mozart songs offers much fresh and charming singing, with the girlish simplicity of some of the songs delightfully brought out, and with fine shading of tone-colour. For all her beauty of tone, the singer is taxed by some of the more demanding songs like *Abendempfindung*, not always helped by John Constable's accompaniments, less imaginative than usual. Particularly valuable is the rare *Eine kleine deutsche Kantate* with its brief, linked sections. The rather dated sound yet captures the voice vividly.

51 Concert arias (complete).
(M) *** Decca Dig./Analogue 430 300-2 (5) [id.]. Te Kanawa, Berganza, Gruberová, Hobarth, Laki, Winbergh, Fischer-Dieskau, Corena; various orchestras & conductors.

The Decca collection of the Mozart concert arias is based on the set issued in the early 1980s of all the arias for soprano. As in that, the approach has been to give each of the singers a varied group, an attractive arrangement for sequential listening, when each has been shrewdly chosen for Mozartian qualities as well as for characterful and beautiful voice. With most of the recordings made in the Sophiensaal in Vienna – in full-bodied sound, analogue except for the items sung by the tenor, Gösta Winbergh – and with Gyorgy Fischer a warmly sympathetic accompanist in the soprano items, these five well-filled discs make a most attractive set.

Concert arias: *Ah! lo previdi . . . Ah t'invola, K.272; Bella mia fiamma . . . Resta oh cara, K.528; Chi sa, K.582; Nehmt meinen Dank, ihr holden Gönner, K.383; Non più, tutto ascolta . . . Non*

temer, amato bene, K.490; Oh temerario Arbace! . . . Per quel paterno amplesso, K.79/K.73d; Vado, ma dove?, K.583.
(M) *** Decca 417 756-2 [id.]. Kiri Te Kanawa, V. CO, György Fischer.

Kiri Te Kanawa's Decca set of Mozart's concert arias for soprano, recorded in 1982, makes a beautiful and often brilliant recital. Items range from one of the very earliest arias, *Oh temerario Arbace*, already memorably lyrical, to the late *Vado, ma dove*, here sung for its beauty rather than for its drama. Atmospheric, wide-ranging recording, which has transferred well to CD.

Concert arias: *Alma grande e nobil core, K.578; Ch'io mi scordi di te?, K.505; Nehmt meinen Dank, K.383; Vado, ma dove?, K.583.* Lieder: *Abendemfindung; Als Luise die Briefe; Die Alte; An Chloë; Dans un bois solitaire; Im Frühlingsanfang; Das Kinderspiel; Die kleine Spinnerin; Das Lied der Trennung; Oiseaux, si tous les ans; Ridente la calma; Sehnsucht nach dem Frühling; Das Trumbild; Das Veilchen; Der Zauberer; Die Zuhfriedenheit.*
(M) *** EMI mono/stereo CDH7 63702-2 [id.]. Schwarzkopf, Gieseking; Brendel; LSO, Szell.

On an earlier full-price CD (EMI CDC7 47326-2) Schwarzkopf's classic series of the Mozart songs with Gieseking was used incomplete as a fill-up for her recordings of Schubert with Edwin Fischer. In this Schwarzkopf Edition issue at mid-price the missing songs are restored – including the most famous one, *Das Veilchen*. As a generous coupling, the disc also includes Schwarzkopf's much later recordings, with Szell conducting four concert arias – including the most taxing of all, *Ch'io mi scordi di te*, with Brendel playing the piano obbligato! Though the voice is not quite so fresh in the concert arias, the artistry and imagination are supreme, and stereo recording helps to add bloom.

Concert arias: *A questo seno . . . Or che il cielo, K.374; Basta, vincesti . . . An non lasciarmi, K.486a; Voi avete un cor fedele, K.217. Exsultate, jubilate* (motet), *K.165. Litaniae de venerabili altaris sacramento, K.243: Dulcissimum convivium. Vesperae de Dominica, K.321: Laudate dominum.*
(B) *** Ph. 426 072-2; *426 072-4*. Elly Ameling, ECO, Leppard.

Elly Ameling's natural reserve can sometimes bring a coolness to her presentation, but here the singing, besides being technically very secure, has a simple radiance in the phrasing which is very beautiful. She is equally happy in the concert arias, sung with delightful flexibility of phrase, and in the ecclesiastical music, where the style has a serene simplicity, while *Exsultate, jubilate* has an infectious sense of joy.

Ave verum corpus, K.618.
(M) *** Decca 430 159-2; *430 159-4* [id.]. St John's College, Cambridge, Ch., Guest – J. HAYDN: *Theresienmesse;* M. HAYDN: *Ave regina.* ***

This simple and eloquent account of Mozart's choral lollipop is beautifully recorded and, it is to be hoped, may introduce some collectors to the inspired late Haydn Mass with which it is coupled.

Ave verum corpus, K.618; Exsultate, jubilate, K.165; Kyrie in D minor, K.341; Vesperae solennes de confessore in C, K.339.
**(*) Ph. 412 873-2 [id.]. Te Kanawa, Bainbridge, Ryland Davies, Howell, LSO Ch., LSO, C. Davis.

This disc could hardly present a more delightful collection of Mozart choral music, ranging from the early soprano cantata *Exsultate, jubilate*, with its famous setting of *Alleluia*, to the equally popular *Ave verum*. Kiri Te Kanawa is the brilliant soloist in the cantata, and her radiant account of the lovely *Laudate Dominum* is one of the highspots of the *Solemn vespers*. That work, with its dramatic choruses, is among the most inspired of Mozart's Salzburg period, and here it is given a fine responsive performance. The 1971 recording has been remastered effectively, although the choral sound is not ideally focused.

(i; ii) *Ave verum corpus, K.618;* (iii; iv) *Exsultate, jubilate, K.165; Masses Nos.* (i; ii; iii; v) *10 in C (Missa brevis): Spatzenmesse, K.220;* (ii; iii; vi) *16 in C (Coronation), K.317.*
(M) *** DG 419 060-2. (i) Regensburg Cathedral Ch.; (ii) Bav. RSO, Kubelik; (iii) Edith Mathis; (iv) Dresden State O, Klee; (v) Troyanos, Laubenthal, Engen; (vi) Procter, Grobe, Shirley-Quirk, Bav. R. Ch.

Kubelik draws a fine, vivid performance of the *Coronation Mass* from his Bavarian forces and is no less impressive in the earlier *Missa brevis*, with excellent soloists in both works. Then Edith

Mathis gives a first-class account of the *Exsultate, jubilate* as an encore. The concert ends with Bernard Klee directing a serenely gentle account of the *Ave verum corpus* (recorded in 1979). The digital remastering is entirely beneficial.

Exsultate, jubilate, K.165 (Salzburg version); Motets: *Ergo interest, K.143; Regina coeli* (2 settings), *K.108, K.127.*
*** O-L Dig. 411 832-2; *411 832-4* [id.]. Emma Kirkby, Westminster Cathedral Boys' Ch., AAM Ch. and O, Hogwood.

The boyish, bell-like tones of Emma Kirkby are perfectly suited to the most famous of Mozart's early cantatas, *Exsultate, jubilate*, culminating in a dazzling account of *Alleluia*. With accompaniment on period instruments, that is aptly coupled with far rarer but equally fascinating examples of Mozart's early genius, superbly recorded. A most refreshing collection, beautifully recorded.

(i) *Exsultate, jubilate, K.165;* (ii) *Litaniae lauretanae, K.195; Mass No. 16 in C (Coronation), K.137.*
(M) *** Decca 417 472-2. (i) Erna Spoorenberg, Ledger; (ii) Cotrubas, Watts, Tear, Shirley-Quirk, Schola Cantorum of Oxford, ASMF, Marriner.

Marriner's fine 1971 coupling of two of Mozart's most appealing early choral works has been linked with Erna Spoorenberg's radiant and sparkling account of the *Exsultate, jubilate*. In the two more extended works, the solo singing is again outstandingly good, notably the contribution of Ileana Cotrubas; and the Oxford Schola Cantorum are impressively vibrant. The Academy provides the most sensitive and stylish accompaniments and, with the sound full of presence, this reissue must receive the warmest welcome.

Litaniae de venerabili altaris sacramento, K.243.
(M) *** Decca 430 158-2; *430 158-4* [id.]. Marshall, Cable, Evans, Roberts, St John's College, Cambridge, Ch., Wren O, Guest – HAYDN: *Heiligmesse.* ***

Mozart made four settings of the Litany, of which this is the last, written in 1776. It is ambitiously scored for an orchestra of double wind, two horns and three trombones – used to add sonorous gravity to many of the choral passages and to bring point and drama to the choral fugue, *Pignus futurae gloriae*. The opening *Kyrie* and the later *Hostia sancta* integrate the vocal quartet with the chorus almost operatically; among the solo items is a lively, florid tenor contribution to the *Panis vivus*, while in the beautiful *Dulcissimum convivium* the solo soprano is accompanied with flutes added to the orchestra in place of the oboes. It is Mozart at his most imaginative and vital; the artists here rise to the occasion and give a highly responsive performance, with Margaret Marshall outstanding among the soloists. Excellent 1980 sound.

Masonic music

Masonic music: *Masonic funeral music (Maurerische Trauermusik), K.477; Die ihr des unermesslichen Weltals Schöpfer ehrt* (cantata), *K.619; Die ihr einen neuen Grade, K.468; Dir, Seele des Weltalls* (cantata), *K.429; Ihr unsre neuen Leiter* (song), *K.484; Lasst uns mit geschlungnen Händen, K.623a; Laut verkünde unsre Freude, K.623; O heiliges Band* (song), *K.148; Sehen, wie dem starren Forscherange, K.471; Zerfliesset heut', geliebte Brüder, K.483.*
(M) *** Decca 425 722-2; *425 722-4*. Werner Krenn, Tom Krause, Edinburgh Festival Ch., LSO, Kertész.

This Decca reissue is among the most worthwhile of those stimulated by the Bicentenary. It contains the more important of Mozart's masonic music in first-class performances, admirably recorded. Most striking of all is Kertész's strongly dramatic account of the *Masonic funeral music*; the two lively songs for chorus, *Zerfliesset heut'* and *Ihr unsre neuen Leiter*, are sung with warm humanity and are also memorable. Indeed the choral contribution is most distinguished throughout, and Werner Krenn's light tenor is most appealing in the other items which he usually dominates.

Complete Mozart Edition, Volume 19: *Masses Nos. 1 in G (Missa brevis), K.49; 2 in D min. (Missa brevis), K.65; 3 in C ('Dominicus'), K.66; 4 in C min. (Waisenhaus), K.139; 5 in G (Pastoral), K.140; 6 in F (Missa brevis), K.192; 7 in C (Missa in honorem Ssmae Trinitatis), K.167; 9 in D (Missa brevis), K.194; 10 in C (Spatzenmesse; 'Sparrow Mass'), K.220; 11 in C ('Credo'), K.257; 12 in C (Spaur-Messe), K.258; 13 in C ('Organ solo'), K.259; 14 in C (Missa*

longa), K.262; 15 in B flat (Missa brevis), K.275; 16 in C ('Coronation'), K.317; 17 in C (Missa solemnis), K.337; 18 in C min. (Great), K.427; 19 in D min. (Requiem), K.626.
(M) **(*) Ph. Analogue/Dig. 422 519-2 (9) [id.]. Mathis, Donath, M. Price, McNair, Montague, Shirai, Casapietra, Trudeliese Schmidt, Lang, Schiml, Markert, Burmeister, Knight, Schreier, Araiza, Heilmann, Baldin, Ryland Davies, Rolfe Johnson, Ude, Jelosits, Adam, Polster, Andreas Schmidt, Hauptmann, Rootering, Grant, Eder; Leipzig R. Ch.; Monteverdi Ch.; V. Boys' Ch.; John Alldis Ch.; Ch. Viennensis; Leipzig RSO; E. Bar. Soloists; Dresden State O; LSO; VSO; Dresden PO; Kegel; C. Davis; Gardiner; Schreier; Harrer.

One hardly thinks of Mozart as a profoundly religious composer, but these 18 Masses bear witness to the vigour of his inspiration when setting liturgical words, even in his boyhood. Only one Mass, but that the great *C minor*, has period performers. John Eliot Gardiner's inspired reading, with superb soloists as well as his Monteverdi Choir and English Baroque Soloists, has rightly been chosen in preference to others from the Philips catalogue, and the *Requiem* comes in another outstanding modern version, with the Dresden Staatskapelle and Leipzig Radio Choir conducted by Peter Schreier, as imaginative a conductor as he is a tenor. That same choir and orchestra under the choir's regular conductor, Herbert Kegel, is responsible for the great bulk of the rest of the Masses, three of the early works recorded in 1973, but mostly done in the 1980s. With the chorus tending to be placed a little backwardly, it does not always sound its freshest, but performances – with consistently clean-toned soloists, including latterly Mitsuko Shirai – are bright and well sprung. Sir Colin Davis and the LSO in the earliest recording here, dating from 1971, take a weightier view than any in the *Credo Mass*, K.257, with sound bass-heavy, but again his vigour and freshness are very compelling. Two favourite Masses, the *Coronation Mass* and the *Spatzenmesse* (Sparrow Mass), come in performances conducted by Uwe Christian Harrer with the Vienna Symphony Orchestra and the Vienna Boys' Choir; boys also distinctively take the soprano and alto solos. Though Harrer's speeds tend to be slow, the rhythmic buoyancy is most compelling, with choral sound full and forward.

Masses Nos. 2 in D min. (Missa brevis), K.65; 5 in G (Pastoralmesse), K.140; 7 in G (In honorem Santissimae Trinitas), K.167.
*** Ph. Dig. 422 264-2 [id.]. Donath, Markert, Blochwitz, Schmidt, Leipzig R. Ch. & SO, Kegel.

Kegel directs his splendid choir and a full modern orchestra – by latterday standards too large for this music – in fresh, vigorous performances of these three early Masses, well recorded. Nos. 2 and 5, both called *Missa brevis*, are brief to the point of perfunctoriness, but they still contain Mozartian jewels, such as the chromatic duet of K.65. Far finer is the extended setting of K.167 which, with its trumpets and drums, looks forward to later ceremonial works and is crowned by a splendid, finely structured *Credo*.

Mass No. 4 in C min. (Weisenhausmesse), K.139.
(M) *** DG 427 255-2. Janowitz, Von Stade, Moll, Ochman, V. State Op. Ch., VPO, Abbado.

By any standards this is a remarkably sustained example of the thirteen-year-old composer's powers, with bustling allegros in the *Kyrie*, *Gloria* and *Credo*, as well as at the end of the *Agnus Dei*, while the *Gloria* and *Credo* end with full-scale fugues. This far from negligible piece sounds at its very best in Abbado's persuasive hands. His is a most characterful account, and the remastered DG recording sounds admirably lively, with the soloists in good perspective.

Mass No. 12 in C (Spaur), K.258.
(M) *** Decca 430 161-2; *430 161-4* [id.]. Palmer, Cable, Langridge, Roberts, St John's College, Cambridge, Ch., Wren O, Guest – HAYDN: *Schöpfungsmesse.* ***

The *Spaur Mass* is not among Mozart's most inspired, but its directness is appealing and the *Benedictus*, which offers a fine Mozartian interplay of chorus and soloists, is very appealing. In a vigorous performance like this, with trombones justifiably doubling some of the choral lines, it is most enjoyable. Excellent Argo sound, 1979 vintage.

Mass No. 16 in C (Coronation), K.317.
(M) **(*) DG 423 913-2 (2) [id.]. Tomowa-Sintow, Baltsa, Krenn, Van Dam, V. Singverein, BPO, Karajan – BEETHOVEN: *Missa solemnis.* ***

(i) *Mass No. 16 in C (Coronation), K.317;* (ii; iii) *Missa brevis in C (Spatzenmesse), K.220;* (iii) *Ave verum corpus;* (iv) *Exsultate, jubilate, K.165; Vesperae solennes de Confessore, K.339: Laudate Dominum.*
(M) **(*) DG 429 820-2; *429 820-4* [id.]. (i) Tomowa-Sintow, Baltsa, Krenn, Van Dam, V.

Singverein, BPO, Karajan; (ii) Mathis, Troyanos, Laubenthal, Engen; (iii) Regensberger Cathedral Ch., Bav. RSO, Kubelik; (iv) Mathis, Dresden Ch. & State O, Klee.

Karajan's 1976 recording of the *Coronation Mass* is a dramatic reading, lacking something in rhythmic resilience perhaps; but, with excellent solo singing as well as an incisive contribution from the chorus, there is no lack of strength and the score's lyrical elements are sensitively managed. Kubelik draws a fine, lively account of the earlier *Missa brevis*, and again the solo singing is of high quality. Bernard Klee contributes a serene performance of the lovely *Ave verum corpus*, and Edith Mathis offers a first-class account of the *Exsultate, jubilate* and a slightly less appealing *Laudate Dominum* (recorded in 1979, six years after the motet). The remastering is vivid: although the choral focus in the two main works is not absolutely sharp, the sound is otherwise impressive, the ambience agreeably expansive.

Masses Nos. 16 in C (Coronation), K.317; 17 (Missa solemnis), K.337.
**(*) Argo Dig. 411 904-2. Margaret Marshall, Murray, Covey-Crump, Wilson-Johnson, King's College Ch., ECO, Cleobury.

Though rhythmically Cleobury's performance is not as lively as the finest versions of K.317, the coupling can be recommended warmly, with its excellent soloists and fresh choral singing all beautifully recorded.

Mass No. 18 in C min. (Great), K.427.
(M) *** DG Dig. 431 287-2; *431 287-4.* Hendricks, Perry, Schreier, Luxon, V. Singverein, BPO, Karajan.
*** Ph. Dig. 420 210-2 [id.]. McNair, Montague, Rolfe Johnson, Hauptmann, Monteverdi Ch., E. Bar. Soloists, Gardiner.
*** Decca Dig. 425 528-2. Augér, Dawson, Ainsley, D. Thomas, Winchester Cathedral Ch. & Winchester College Quiristers, AAM, Hogwood.

In his 1982 digital recording of the *C minor Mass* Karajan gives Handelian splendour to this greatest of Mozart's choral works and, though the scale is large, the beauty and intensity are hard to resist. Solo singing is first rate, particularly that of Barbara Hendricks, the dreamy beauty of her voice ravishingly caught. Woodwind is rather backward, yet the sound is both rich and vivid – though, as the opening shows, the internal balance is not always completely consistent.

John Eliot Gardiner, using period instruments, gives an outstandingly fresh performance of high dramatic contrasts, marked by excellent solo singing – both the sopranos pure and bright-toned and Anthony Rolfe Johnson in outstandingly sweet voice. Gardiner has made some minor corrections in the *Credo* and rewritten the string parts of *Et incarnatus* in a style closer to Mozart's – to beautiful effect, if at a relaxed speed. With the recording giving an ample scale without inflation, this can be warmly recommended to more than those simply wanting a period performance.

Hogwood's version can be recommended warmly alongside the fine Gardiner account, even though his control of rhythm is less resilient and often squarer. The soloists if anything are even finer, and many Mozartians will prefer having boy trebles in the chorus and German pronunciation of Latin. Hogwood also opts for an edition by Richard Maunder which, among other things, adds appropriate instruments to the incomplete orchestrations of the *Credo* and *Et incarnatus est*. This is particularly impressive in the *Credo*, where trumpets and timpani bring an aptly festive flavour, adding to the panache of the opening. The sound has a vivid sense of presence, with treble tone cutting through very freshly.

Requiem Mass (No. 19) in D min., K.626.
(BB) *** Virgin/Virgo Dig. VJ7 91460-2; *VJ7 91460-4* [id.]. Yvonne Kenny, Alfreda Hodgson, Arthur Davies, Gwynne Howell, N. Sinfonia Ch., LSO Ch., N. Sinfonia, Richard Hickox.
(M) *** DG Dig. 431 288-2; *431 288-4.* Tomowa-Sintow, Müller Molinari, Cole, Burchuladze, V. Singverein, VPO, Karajan.
(M) *** DG 429 821-2; *429 821-4* [id.]. Tomowa-Sintow, Baltsa, Krenn, Van Dam, V. Singverein, BPO, Karajan.
*** Ph. Dig. 411 420-2 [id.]. Margaret Price, Schmidt, Araiza, Adam, Leipzig R. Ch., Dresden State O, Schreier.
(M) **(*) Ph. 420 353-2; *420 353-4* [id.]. Donath, Minton, Ryland Davies, Nienstedt, Alldis Ch., BBC SO, C. Davis.

Requiem Mass, K.626 (completed Eybler/Süssmayr, ed. Robbins Landon).
**(*) Nimbus Dig. NI 5241 [id.]. Janowitz, Bernheimer, M. Hill, D. Thomas, Hanover Band Ch., Hanover Band, Goodman.

Requiem Mass, K.626; Ave verum corpus, K.618.
(M) **(*) BMG/RCA GD 86535 [RCA 6535-2-RG]. Equiluz, Eder, Vienna Boys' Ch., V. State Op. Ch. & O, Gillesberger; or VSO, Froschauer – HAYDN: *Te Deum.* **(*)

Requiem Mass, K.626; Kyrie in D min., K.341.
*** Ph. Dig. 420 197-2 [id.]. Bonney, Von Otter, Blochwitz, White, Monteverdi Ch., E. Bar. Soloists, Gardiner.

John Eliot Gardiner with characteristic panache gives a bitingly intense reading, opting for the traditional course of using the Süssmayr completion but favouring period instruments at lower pitch. The result is one of the most powerful performances ever, for while the lighter sound of the period orchestra makes for greater transparency, the weight and bite are formidable. In particular the heavy brass and the distinctively dark tones of basset horns give the piece an even more lugubrious character than usual, totally apt. The soloists are an outstanding quartet, well matched but characterfully contrasted too, and the choral singing is as bright and luminous as one expects of Gardiner's Monteverdi Choir. The superb *Kyrie in D minor* makes a very welcome and generous fill-up, to seal a firm recommendation.

At super-bargain price, Richard Hickox's excellent version of the *Requiem Mass* on the Virgo label matches any in the catalogue. With generally brisk speeds and light, resilient rhythms, it combines gravity with authentically clean, transparent textures in which the dark colourings of the orchestration, as with the basset horns, come out vividly. All four soloists are outstandingly fine, and the choral singing is fresh and incisive, with crisp attack. The voices, solo and choral, are placed rather backwardly; otherwise the recording is excellent, full and clean to match the performance.

Karajan's 1987 digital version of the *Requiem* is a large-scale reading, but one that is white-hot with intensity and energy. The power and bite of the rhythm are consistently exciting. The solo quartet is first rate, though Helga Müller Molinari is on the fruity side for Mozart. Vinson Cole, stretched at times, yet sings very beautifully, and so does Paata Burchuladze with his tangily distinctive Slavonic bass tone. The close balance adds to the excitement, though the sound, both choral and orchestral, lacks transparency.

Unlike his earlier analogue recording, Karajan's 1976 version also is outstandingly fine, deeply committed. The toughness of his approach is established from the start with incisive playing and clean-focused singing from the chorus, not too large and set a little backwardly. The fine quartet of soloists is also blended beautifully. The remastered recording sounds first class.

Peter Schreier's is a forthright reading of Mozart's valedictory choral work, bringing strong dramatic contrasts and marked by superb choral singing and a consistently elegant and finely balanced accompaniment. The singing of Margaret Price in the soprano part is finer than any other yet heard on record, and the others make a first-rate team, if individually more variable. Only in the *Kyrie* and the final *Cum sanctis tuis* does the German habit of using the intrusive aitch annoy. Altogether this is most satisfying.

The surprise version is Gillesberger's. Using treble and alto soloists from the Vienna Boys' Choir, who sing with confidence and no little eloquence, this performance also has the advantage of a dedicated contribution from Kurt Equiluz. Gillesberger's pacing is well judged and the effect is as fresh as it is strong and direct. The 1982 recording is excellent, vivid yet full, and the result is powerful but not too heavy. Mozart's *Ave verum* is also very well sung.

Davis with a smaller choir gives a more intimate performance than is common, and with his natural sense of style he finds much beauty of detail. But Davis does not provide the same sort of 'bite' that in performances on this scale should compensate for sheer massiveness of tone. Anyone wanting a version on this scale need not hesitate, but this is plainly not the definitive version.

Roy Goodman's Nimbus CD, with the Hanover Band, has the distinction of presenting the new Robbins Landon edition on disc for the first time. As Landon explains in his notes, he 'decided to investigate the very first attempts at reconstruction, even before Süssmayr completed his'. Landon has therefore incorporated the orchestrations completed by another Mozart pupil, Joseph Eybler, where possible, in place of the usual Süssmayr ones, keeping the rest of the text in the Süssmayr edition. The practical differences are less than might be expected. The thickness of some of Süssmayr's orchestration is avoided, though it is disappointing not to have dramatic trombones interjecting at the start of the *Rex tremendae*. The performance, using period instruments on an intimate scale, is first rate, though the reverberant recording does not allow detail consistently to come through.

Requiem mass (No. 19) in D min. (edited Maunder).
**(*) O-L Dig. 411 712-2; *411 712-4* [id.]. Emma Kirkby, Watkinson, Rolfe-Johnson, David Thomas, Westminster Cathedral Boys' Ch., AAM Ch. and O, Hogwood.

Hogwood's version is strictly incomparable with any other, using as it does the edition of Richard Maunder, which aims to eliminate Süssmayr's contribution to the version of Mozart's unfinished masterpiece that has held sway for two centuries. So the *Lacrimosa* is completely different, after the opening eight bars, and concludes with an elaborate *Amen*, for which Mozart's own sketches were recently discovered. This textual clean-out goes with authentic performance of Hogwood's customary abrasiveness, very fresh and lively to underline the impact of novelty. With fine solo singing from four specialists in Baroque performance and bright choral sound, brilliantly recorded, it can be recommended to those who welcome a new look in Mozart.

Vesperae de dominica, K.321.
(M) *** Decca 430 162-2; *430 162-4* [id.]. Marshall, Cable, Evans, Roberts, St John's College, Cambridge, Ch., Wren O, Guest – HAYDN: *Harmoniemesse.* ***

Aptly coupled with Haydn's *Harmoniemesse*, Mozart's vibrant *Vesperae de dominica* opens with a series of brilliant choral settings (with contrasting solo quartet), accompanied by trumpets and strings. Margaret Marshall is appropriately agile in the lively soprano solo of the *Laudate Dominum*, and the work closes with an ambitious *Magnificat* in which all the participants are joined satisfyingly together. The St John's performance is full of vigour and Guest creates a proper sense of apotheosis in the work's closing section. The 1980 recording is full and vivid.

Vesperae solennes de confessore, K.339.
(M) *** Decca 430 157-2; *430 157-4* [id.]. Palmer, Cable, Langridge, Roberts, St John's College, Cambridge, Ch., Wren O, Guest – HAYDN: *Paukenmesse.* ***

Although Guest's version of Mozart's masterpiece does not always match the full-price recording by Sir Colin Davis for Philips (see above under *Ave verum corpus*) – with Felicity Palmer a less poised soloist than Kiri Te Kanawa – the Decca account has the advantage of authenticity in the use of boys in the chorus. Moreover the CD transfer of the 1979 Argo recording is preferable to the less well-defined Philips sound: the Decca remastering is cleanly focused, yet has plenty of warmth and atmosphere.

OPERA

Complete Mozart Edition, Volume 26: *Apollo et Hyacinthus* (complete).
(M) *** Ph. 422 526-2 (2) [id.]. Augér, Mathis, Wulkopf, Schwarz, Rolfe Johnson, Salzburg Chamber Ch. & Mozarteum O, Hager.

This recording was made in Salzburg in 1981. The opera was written when Mozart was eleven, with all but two of the parts taken by schoolchildren. The style of the writing and vocalization is rather simpler than in other dramatic works of the boy Mozart, but the inspiration is still remarkable, astonishingly mature. The orchestration is assured and full of imaginative touches. The performance here is stylish and very well sung. If, as so often in early Mozart, recitatives seem too long, the CD banding allows one to make one's own selection if not requiring the whole opera. Excellent, clear and well-balanced recording, admirably transferred to CD.

Complete Mozart Edition, Volume 30: *Ascanio in Alba* (complete).
(M) **(*) Ph. 422 530-2 (3) [id.]. Sukis, Baltsa, Mathis, Augér, Schreier, Salzburg Chamber Ch., Salzburg Mozarteum O, Hager.

Written when he was fifteen, *Ascanio in Alba* came between the boy composer's two other Milan commissions, *Mitridate* and *Lucio Silla.* At 2¾ hours it is comparably expansive, though it lacks the dramatic qualities of those other imaginative examples of *opera seria.* Though it hardly compares with what Mozart was to do later, it brings one delightful number after another. Interspersed between the arias are choruses of comment, far more so than is usual in an *opera seria.* The final trio leads on, very imaginatively for the time, to a recitative and separate cabaletta, before the final brief chorus. Hager makes an excellent start with an exceptionally lively account of the delightful overture, but then the choruses seem relatively square, thanks to the pedestrian, if generally efficient singing of the Salzburg choir. Hager's speeds are sometimes on the slow side, but the singing is excellent, with no weak link in the characterful cast, though not everyone will like the distinctive vibrato of Lilian Sukis as Venus. The analogue recording, made in collaboration with Austrian Radio in 1976, is full and vivid.

Bastien und Bastienne (complete). Concert arias: *Mentre ti lascio, o figlia, K.513; Misero ! o sogno . . . Aura, che intorno spiri, K.431. Le nozze di Figaro: Giunse alfin il momento . . . Deh vieni; Un moto di gioia.*
*** Sony Dig. SK 45855; *40-45855* [id.]. Gruberová, Cole, Polgar, Liszt CO, Leppard.

Complete Mozart Edition, Volume 27: *Bastien und Bastienne* (complete); Lieder: *Komm, liebe Zither, komm; Die Zufriedenheit.*
(M) *** Ph. Dig. 422 527-2 [id.]. Dominik Orieschnig, Georg Nigl, David Busch, V. Boys' Ch., VSO, Harrer.

Leppard, recently neglected by the record companies, on Sony conducts a near-ideal performance of the eleven-year-old Mozart's charming little one-Acter, very well recorded. The trio of soloists is excellent. Edita Gruberová is delectably fresh and vivacious as the heroine, Vinson Cole is a sensitive and clean-voiced Bastien and Laszlo Polgar is full of fun in the buffo role of Colas. The dialogue is excellently directed, and the Liszt Chamber Orchestra of Budapest plays with dazzling precision, bringing wit to the opening with its anticipation of Beethoven's *Eroica*. As a generous fill-up, the three soloists sing Mozart arias, including the big scena for tenor, *Misero! o sogno*, and a replacement aria for Susanna, especially written for the 1789 production of *Le nozze di Figaro*: *Un moto di gioia*.

On Philips, it is performed by boy trebles instead of the soprano, tenor and bass originally intended. Members of the Vienna Boys' Choir give a refreshingly direct performance under Uwe Christian Harrer, missing little of the piece's charm, though a modern recording with adult singers would still be welcome. The two songs with mandolin accompaniment, also sung by one of the trebles, make an attractive fill-up. First-rate 1986 digital sound.

Complete Mozart Edition, Volume 44: *La clemenza di Tito* (complete).
(M) *** Ph. 422 544-2 (2) [id.]. Dame Janet Baker, Minton, Burrows, Von Stade, Popp, Lloyd, ROHCG Ch. & O, Sir Colin Davis.

La clemenza di Tito (complete).
*** DG Dig. 431 806-2 (2). Rolfe Johnson, Von Otter, McNair, Varady, Robbin, Hauptmann, Monteverdi Ch., E. Bar. Soloists, Gardiner.
(M) *** DG 429 878-2 (2) [id.]. Berganza, Varady, Mathis, Schreier, Schiml, Adam, Leipzig R. Ch., Dresden State O, Boehm.

Sir Colin Davis's superb set is among the finest of his many Mozart recordings. Not only is the singing of Dame Janet Baker in the key role of Vitellia formidably brilliant, with every roulade and exposed leap flawlessly attacked; she actually makes one believe in the emotional development of an impossible character, one who progresses from villainy to virtue with the scantiest preparation. The two other mezzo-sopranos, Minton as Sesto and Von Stade in the small role of Annio, are superb too, while Stuart Burrows has rarely if ever sung so stylishly on a recording as here; he makes the forgiving Emperor a rounded and sympathetic character, not just a bore. The recitatives add to the compulsion of the drama, while Davis's swaggering manner in the pageant music heightens the genuine feeling conveyed in much of the rest, transforming what used to be dismissed as a dry *opera seria*. Excellent recording, which gains in brightness and immediacy in its CD format.

Following the pattern of his prize-winning recording of Mozart's other great *opera seria*, *Idomeneo*, Gardiner's recording was done live at performances in Queen Elizabeth Hall, London. Again with his vitality and bite he turns the piece into a genuinely involving drama. One keeps marvelling how Mozart developed opera seria conventions, not how he was limited by them. Though the team of soloists is not quite so consistent as on Sir Colin Davis's 1977 recording, Anthony Rolfe Johnson is outstanding in the title role, making the wise, forgiving Emperor a rounded character in the mould of Idomeneo. Any blandness in the story is then dispelled by the vivid characterization of both Anne-Sofie von Otter as Sesto, the best friend who rebels, and of Julia Varady as Vitellia, who here becomes the equivalent of the violent Elettra in Idomeneo. Sylvia McNair is an enchanting pure-toned Servilia, and Catherine Robbin a well-matched Annio, though the microphone catches an unevenness in the voice, as it does with Cornelius Hauptmann in the incidental role of Publio. More seriously, DG's vivid, immediate recording picks up a distracting amount of banging and bumping on stage in the Sussmayr recitatives, which with fair judgement are substantially pruned – more so than on the Davis version.

Boehm gave the work warmth and charm, presenting the piece more genially than we have grown used to. The atmospheric recording helps in that, and the cast is first rate, with no weak link, matching at every point that of Sir Colin Davis on his full-price Philips set. Yet, ultimately, even Julia Varady for Boehm can hardly rival Dame Janet Baker for Davis, crisper and lighter in her coloratura. Davis's incisiveness, too, has points of advantage; but, to summarize, any Mozartian can safely leave the preference to his feelings about the two conductors, the one more genial and glowing, the other more urgently dramatic.

Complete Mozart Edition, Volume 42: *Così fan tutte* (complete).
(M) *** Ph. 422 542-2 (3) [id.]. Caballé, Dame Janet Baker, Cotrubas, Gedda, Ganzarolli, Van Allan, ROHCG Ch. & O, Sir Colin Davis.

Così fan tutte (complete).
❀ (M) *** EMI CMS7 69330-2 (3) [Ang. CDMC 69330]. Schwarzkopf, Ludwig, Steffek, Kraus, Taddei, Berry, Philh. Ch. & O, Boehm.
*** Ph. Dig. 422 381-2; *422 381-4* (3) [id.]. Mattila, Von Otter, Szmytka, Araiza, Allen, Van Dam, Amb. Op. Ch., ASMF, Marriner.
❀ (M) (***) EMI mono CHS7 69635-2 (3) [Ang. CDHC 69635]. Schwarzkopf, Otto, Merriman, Simoneau, Panerai, Bruscantini, Philh. Ch. & O, Karajan.
*** EMI Dig. CDS7 47727-8 (3) [id.]. Vaness, Ziegler, Watson, Aler, Duesing, Desderi, Glyndebourne Ch., LPO, Haitink.
(M) *** Erato/Warner 2292 45683-2 (3) [id.]. Te Kanawa, Stratas, Von Stade, Rendall, Huttenlocher, Bastin, Rhine Op. Ch., Strasbourg PO, Lombard.
**(*) O-L Dig. 414 316-2 (3) [id.]. Yakar, Resick, Nafé, Winberg, Krause, Feller, Drottningholm Court Theatre Ch. & O, Östman.
(M) **(*) DG 429 824-2 (2) [id.]. Janowitz, Fassbaender, Grist, Schreier, Prey, Panerai, V. State Op. Ch., VPO, Boehm.
**(*) Teldec/Warner Dig. 9031 71381-2 [id.]. Margiono, Van der Walt, Ziegler, Cachemaille, Steiger, Hampson, Concg. O, Harnoncourt.
(M) (***) EMI mono CHS7 63864-2 (2) [Ang. CDHB 63864]. Souez, Helletsgruber, Nash, Domgraf-Fassbaender, Brownlee, Eisinger, Glyndebourne Festival Ch. & O, Fritz Busch.

First choice remains with Boehm's classic set, reissued on three mid-priced CDs, with its glorious solo singing, headed by the incomparable Fiordiligi of Schwarzkopf and the equally moving Dorabella of Christa Ludwig, a superb memento of Walter Legge's recording genius. It still bears comparison with any other recordings, made before or since.

Marriner directs a fresh and resilient performance, beautifully paced, often with speeds on the fast side, and with the crystalline recorded sound adding to the sparkle. Though the women principals (Karita Mattila a warm Fiordiligi, Anne Sofie von Otter a characterful Dorabella and Elzbieta Szmytka a light, charming Despina) make a strong team, the men are even finer: Francisco Araiza as Ferrando, Thomas Allen as Guglielmo and José van Dam as Alfonso all outstanding. Individual as they are, they work together superbly to produce the crispest possible ensembles so that, though the reading is lighter in weight than those of Boehm, Karajan, Haitink or Davis, it has more fun in it, bringing out the laughter in the score. For those wanting a modern digital recording this could well be a first choice; but the classic Boehm set and Karajan's sparkling mono version both remain indispensable.

Commanding as Schwarzkopf is as Fiordiligi in the 1962 Boehm set, also with the Philharmonia, the extra ease and freshness of her singing in the earlier (1954) version under Karajan makes it even more compelling. Nan Merriman is a distinctive and characterful Dorabella, and the role of Ferrando has never been sung more mellifluously on record than by Leopold Simoneau, ravishing in *Un aura amorosa*. The young Rolando Panerai is an ideal Guglielmo, and Lisa Otto a pert Despina; while Sesto Bruscantini in his prime brings to the role of Don Alfonso the wisdom and artistry which made him so compelling at Glyndebourne. Karajan has never sparkled more naturally in Mozart than here, for the high polish has nothing self-conscious about it. Though the mono recording is not as clear as some others of this period, the subtleties of the music-making are very well caught.

With speeds often more measured than usual, Haitink's EMI version yet consistently conveys the sparkle of live performances at Glyndebourne. The excellent teamwork, consistently conveying humour, makes up for a cast-list rather less starry than that on some rival versions. This is above all a sunny performance, sailing happily over any serious shoals beneath Da Ponte's comedy. Claudio Desderi as Alfonso helps to establish that Glyndebourne atmosphere, with recitatives superbly timed and coloured. If Carol Vaness and Delores Ziegler are rather too alike in timbre to be distinguished easily, the relationship becomes all the more sisterly when, quite apart from the similarity, they respond so beautifully to each other. John Aler makes a headily unstrained Ferrando, beautifully free in the upper register; and Lilian Watson and Dale Duesing make up a strong team. The digital recording gives fine bloom and an impressive dynamic range to voices and orchestra alike.

The energy and sparkle of Sir Colin Davis are set against inspired and characterful singing from the three women soloists, with Montserrat Caballé and Janet Baker proving a winning partnership, each challenging and abetting the other all the time. Cotrubas equally is a vivid Despina, never merely arch. Though Gedda has moments of rough tone and Ganzarolli falls short in one of his prominent arias, they are both spirited, while Richard van Allan sings with flair and imagination. Sparkling recitative, and recording which has you riveted by the play of the action.

Kiri Te Kanawa made her first, Erato recording of *Così* in 1977, more than a decade before her digital set with Levine. Her voice sounds radiant, rich and creamy of tone; she is commanding in *Come scoglio*, and tenderly affecting in *Per pietà*, which is more moving here than with Levine. Lombard is a sympathetic accompanist, if not always the most perceptive of Mozartians; some of his tempi are on the slow side, but his sextet of young singers make up a team that rivals almost any other. Frederica von Stade's Dorabella is distinguished, with fine detail and imaginative phrasing, David Rendall is a fresh-toned tenor and the others, too, give firm, appealing performances. With warm recording of high quality, naturally transferred to CD this is most enjoyable and could be a first choice for any who follow the singers in question.

Except that soloists of international standing have been introduced – an aptly fresh-voiced team, stylishly Mozartian – this Oiseau-Lyre recording aims to reproduce one of the most successful of Arnold Östman's authentic productions in the beautiful little court opera-house at Drottningholm, near Stockholm. The point to marvel at initially is the hectic speed of almost every number, yet Östman refreshingly establishes a valid new view. Few Mozartians would want to hear *Così fan tutte* like this all the time but, with no weak link in the cast and with the drama vividly presented, it can be recommended both to those who enjoy authentic performance and to all who are prepared to listen afresh.

Boehm's third recording makes a delightful memento and, offered on a pair of mid-priced CDs, it is worth considering, despite its obvious flaws. It was recorded live during the Salzburg Festival performance on the conductor's eightieth birthday, and though the zest and sparkle of the occasion come over delightfully, with as splendid a cast as you could gather, the ensemble is not ideally crisp for repeated listening. The balance favours the voices, with stage noises made the more prominent on CD.

As in his other Mozart opera recordings, Harnoncourt, the period-performance specialist, here favours an orchestra of modern instruments, while adopting aspects of period-style. His is a quirkily magnetic reading, with speeds eccentric in both directions, slow as well as fast. Though even the lovely terzetto *O soave sia il vento* is raced along, Fiordiligi's great Act II aria, *Per pietà*, is taken impossibly slowly. Even so, Charlotte Margiono sustains the line immaculately, and she is similarly accommodating over another of Harnoncourt's eccentricities, making the emphatic opening of Fiordiligi's other big aria, *Come scoglio*, into a hushed meditation. With Deon van der Walt sweetly caught as Ferrando and Delores Ziegler an outstanding Dorabella (as she is in Haitink's EMI set), the casting has no weak link, though this remains a performance to hear once rather than repeatedly.

The legendary Glyndebourne performance, the first ever recording of *Così fan tutte*, is the finest of the three pioneering sets recorded on 78s in the mid-1930s with the newly founded Glyndebourne company. The sound in the CD transfer, though limited, is amazingly vivid, with voices very well focused and with a keener sense of presence than on many recordings of the 1990s. Busch at the time was a progressive Mozartian, preferring athletic treatment – occasionally to excess, as in the concluding ensemble of Act I – but this is as efferverscent as any more recent recording, and nowadays even the use of a piano for the recitatives instead of a harpsichord seems less outlandish with the emergence of the fortepiano. John Brownlee as Don Alfonso is very much the English aristocrat, with 'fruffly-fruffly' English vowels instead of Italianate ones, but he is a fine, stylish singer. Ina Souez and Luise Helletsgruber as the two sisters outshine all but the very finest of their successors on record, technically superb; and

Heddle Nash and Willi Domgraf-Fassbaender as their lovers are at once stylish and characterful, with Irene Eisinger as a delightfully soubrettish Despina. Cuts are made in the recitatives according to the custom of the time and, more seriously, four numbers disappear – including, amazingly, Ferrando's *Tradito, schernito* and Dorabella's *E amore un ladroncello*. The bonus is that, with those cuts, the opera fits on to only two mid-price CDs.

Così fan tutte: highlights.
(M) **(*) DG Dig. 431 290-2; *431 290-4* [id.]. Te Kanawa, Murray, McLaughlin, Blochwitz, Hampson, Furlanetto, Concert Group of V. State Op., VPO, Levine.

A generous selection (75 minutes) from Levine's brisk, rather unsmiling full-price *Così*, especially useful for sampling Dame Kiri's Fiordiligi, one of her finest Mozartian performances on record, and Thomas Hampson's characterfully rich portrayal of Guglielmo.

Complete Mozart Edition, Volume 41: *Don Giovanni* (complete).
(M) *** Ph. 422 541-2 (3) [id.]. Wixell, Arroyo, Te Kanawa, Freni, Burrows, Ganzarolli, ROHCG Ch. & O, Sir Colin Davis.

Don Giovanni (complete).
*** EMI CDS7 47260-8 (3) [Ang. CDCC 47260]. Waechter, Schwarzkopf, Sutherland, Alva, Frick, Sciutti, Taddei, Philh. Ch. & O, Giulini.
(M) *** Decca 411 626-2 (3). Siepi, Danco, Della Casa, Corena, Dermota, V. State Op. Ch., VPO, Krips.
*** EMI Dig. CDS7 54255-2 (3) [Ang. CDCC 54255]. Shimell, Studer, Vaness, Ramey, Mentzer, Lopardo, Carolis, Rootering, V. State Op. Konzertvereinigung, VPO, Muti.
*** DG Dig. 419 179-2 (3) [id.]. Ramey, Tomowa-Sintow, Baltsa, Battle, Winbergh, Furlanetto, Malta, Burchuladze, German Op. Ch., Berlin, BPO, Karajan.
(M) (***) EMI mono CHS7 63860-2 (3) [Ang. CDHB 63860]. Siepi, Schwarzkopf, Berger, Grümmer, Dermota, Edelmann, Berry, Ernster, V. State Op. Ch., VPO, Furtwängler.
**(*) Ph. Dig. 432 129-2 (3); *432 129-4* (2) [id.]. Allen, Sweet, Mattila, Alaimo, Araiza, Lloyd, McLaughlin, Otelli, Amb. O Ch., ASMF, Marriner.
**(*) Sony M3K 35192 (3) [id.]. Raimondi, Moser, Te Kanawa, Berganza, Riegel, Van Dam, Paris Op. Ch. & O, Maazel.
(M) **(*) EMI CMS7 63841-2 (3) [Ang. CDMC 63841] Ghiaurov, Watson, Gedda, Ludwig, Berry, Freni, Montarsolo, Crass, New Philh. O & Ch., Klemperer.
**(*) O-L Dig. 425 943-2; *425 943-4* (3) [id.]. Hagegård, Cachemaille, Augér, Della Jones, Van der Meel, Bonney, Terfel, Sigmundsson, Drottningholm Court Theatre Ch. & O, Östman.
(M) (***) EMI mono CHS7 61030-2 (3) [Ang. CDHB 61030]. Brownlee, Souez, Von Pataky, Helletsgruber, Baccaloni, Henderson, Mildmay, Glyndebourne Fest. Ch. & O, Fritz Busch.

The classic Giulini EMI set, lovingly remastered to bring out even more vividly the excellence of Walter Legge's original sound-balance, sets the standard by which all other recordings have come to be judged. Not only is the singing cast more consistent than any other; the direction of Giulini and the playing of the vintage Philharmonia Orchestra give this performance an athletic vigour which carries all before it. Elisabeth Schwarzkopf, as Elvira, emerges as a dominant figure to give a distinctive but totally apt slant to this endlessly invigorating drama. The young Sutherland may be relatively reticent as Anna but, with such technical ease and consistent beauty of tone, she makes a superb foil. Taddei is a delightful Leporello, and each member of the cast – including the young Cappuccilli as Masetto – combines fine singing with keen dramatic sense. Recitatives are scintillating, and only the occasional exaggerated snarl from the Don of Eberhard Waechter mars the superb vocal standards. Even that goes well with his fresh and youthful portrait of the central character.

Sir Colin Davis has the advantage of a singing cast that has fewer shortcomings than almost any other on disc and much positive strength. For once one can listen, untroubled by vocal blemishes. Martina Arroyo controls her massive dramatic voice more completely than one would think possible, and she is strongly and imaginatively contrasted with the sweetly expressive Elvira of Kiri Te Kanawa and the sparkling Zerlina of Mirella Freni. As in the Davis *Figaro*, Ingvar Wixell and Wladimiro Ganzarolli make a formidable master/servant team with excellent vocal acting, while Stuart Burrows sings gloriously as Don Ottavio, and Richard Van Allan is a characterful Masetto. Davis draws a fresh and immediate performance from his team, riveting from beginning to end, and the recording, now better defined and more vivid than before, is still refined in the recognizable Philips manner.

Krips's recording of this most challenging opera has kept its place as a mid-priced version that is consistently satisfying, with a cast of all-round quality headed by the dark-toned Don of Cesare Siepi. The women are not ideal, but they form an excellent team, never overfaced by the music, generally characterful, and with timbres well contrasted. To balance Siepi's darkness, the Leporello of Corena is even more saturnine, and their dramatic teamwork is brought to a superb climax in the final scene – quite the finest and most spine-tingling performance of that scene ever recorded. The 1955 recording – genuine stereo – still sounds remarkably well.

Muti's EMI version is a strong contender, based as it is on the performances he has conducted at Salzburg, though with important changes of casting. It is on a bigger scale than such immediate rivals as Marriner's Philips set or Haitink's EMI, but is refreshingly alert, using a fortepiano continuo. Shimell makes a rather gruff Don, not as insinuatingly persuasive as he might be, and like the others he is not helped by the distancing of voices. With Samuel Ramey, Karajan's chosen Don for his DG recording, convincingly translated here to the role of Leporello, and Cheryl Studer an outstanding Donna Anna, the rest of the casting is strong and satisfying.

Even if ensemble is less than perfect at times in the Karajan set and the final scene of Giovanni's descent to Hell goes off the boil a little, the end result has fitting intensity and power. The very opening may be extraordinarily slow and massive, but the rest of the performance is just as remarkable for fast, exhilarating speeds as for slow. Though Karajan was plainly thinking of a big auditorium in his pacing of recitatives, having Jeffrey Tate as continuo player helps to keep them moving and to bring out word-meaning. The starry line-up of soloists is a distinctive one. Samuel Ramey is a noble rather than a menacing Giovanni, consistently clear and firm. Ferruccio Furlanetto's beautiful timbre as Leporello may not be contrasted quite enough, but both his style of singing – with sing-speech allowed into recitative – and his extrovert acting provide the necessary variation.

The historic Furtwängler performance was recorded live by Austrian Radio at the 1954 Salzburg Festival, barely three months before the conductor's death. Though speeds are often slow by today's standards, his springing of rhythm never lets them sag. Even the very slow speed for Leporello's catalogue aria is made to seem charmingly individual. With the exception of a wobbly Commendatore, this is a classic Salzburg cast, with Cesare Siepi a fine, incisive Don, dark in tone, Elisabeth Schwarzkopf a dominant Elvira, Elisabeth Grümmer a vulnerable Anna, Anton Dermota a heady-toned Ottavio and Otto Edelmann a clear and direct Leporello. Stage noises often suggest herds of stampeding animals, but both voices and orchestra are satisfyingly full-bodied in the CD transfer, and the sense of presence is astonishing.

Marriner has the benefit of outstandingly fine recorded sound, full and well-balanced. His direction is well-paced and resilient, with far keener feeling for dramatic pacing than his earlier recording of *Figaro*. Vocally the star is Thomas Allen as the Don, even more assured than he was for Haitink in his EMI Glyndebourne version. The others make a strong team, with Simone Alaimo an attractive young-sounding Leporello, though Sharon Sweet is occasionally raw-toned as Donna Anna.

Lorin Maazel directs a strong and urgent performance, designed to serve as soundtrack for the Losey film. An obvious strength is the line-up of three unusually firm-toned basses: José van Dam a saturnine Leporello, not comic but with much finely detailed expression; Malcolm King a darkly intense Masetto, and Ruggero Raimondi a heroic Giovanni, not always attacking notes cleanly but on balance one of the very finest on record in this role. Among the women Kiri Te Kanawa is outstanding, a radiant Elvira; Teresa Berganza as a mezzo Zerlina generally copes well with the high tessitura; and though Edda Moser starts with some fearsome squawks at her first entry, the dramatic scale is certainly impressive and she rises to the challenge of the big arias. Unfortunately the recording, made in a Paris church, has the voices close against background reverberation.

Most of the slow tempi which Klemperer regularly adopts, far from flagging, add a welcome breadth to the music, for they must be set against the unusually brisk and dramatic interpretation of the recitatives between numbers. Added to that, Ghiaurov as the Don and Berry as Leporello make a marvellously characterful pair. In this version, the male members of the cast are dominant and, with Klemperer's help, they make the dramatic experience a strongly masculine one. Nor is the ironic humour forgotten with Berry and Ghiaurov about, and the Klemperer spaciousness allows them extra time for pointing. Among the women, Ludwig is a strong and convincing Elvira, Freni a sweet-toned but rather unsmiling Zerlina; only Claire Watson seriously disappoints.

Östman follows up his earlier recordings of *Così fan tutte* and *Le nozze di Figaro* with this period performance of *Don Giovanni*. This time, with a far darker score, he has modified his stance. Though speeds are still often fast, this time they rarely seem breathless. The tough sound of period instruments sharpens the drama, even if scrawny violins are at times a trouble. Exceptionally, some speeds are unusually slow – as for example the rustic ensembles – but rhythms are well sprung and the intimate scale of a Drottningholm production is well caught. Håkan Hagegård as Giovanni could be sweeter-toned, but his lightness and spontaneity, particularly in exchanges with the vividly alive Leporello of Gilles Cachemaille, are most winning, with recitative often barely vocalized. Arleen Augér is a radiant Donna Anna, while two Welsh singers also make fine contributions: Della Jones a full-toned Elvira and Bryn Terfel a resonant Masetto. Understandably, the original Prague text is used, which means that each of the two Acts can be fitted complete on to a single disc, an obvious advantage. Such essential additions as Ottavio's *Dalla sua pace* (beautifully sung by Nico van der Meel) and Elvira's *Mi tradi* are given in an appendix on the third disc.

There are those who still count the early Glyndebourne set the finest of all, with Fritz Busch an inspired Mozartian, pointing the music with a freshness and absence of nineteenth-century heaviness rare at the time. A piano is used for the *secco* recitatives and the chords are played very baldly and without elaboration; but the interplay of characters in those exchanges has never been caught more infectiously on disc. John Brownlee as Giovanni may have a rather British-stiff-upper-lip Italian accent (noticeable for the most part in the recitatives) but his is a noble performance, beautifully sung, and he is brilliantly set against the lively, idiomatically Italian Leporello of Salvatore Baccaloni. The three ladies are both contrasted and well matched, with Audrey Mildmay as Zerlina a delightful foil for the excellent, if otherwise little-known Ina Souez and Luise Helletsgruber. Koloman von Pataky uses his light, heady tenor well as Ottavio, and the British stalwarts, David Franklin and Roy Henderson, are first rate as the Commendatore and Masetto respectively. Altogether this version is a delight, and Keith Hardwick's digital transfers are astonishingly vivid, with very little background noise.

Don Giovanni: highlights.
(M) *** DG Dig. 431 289-2; *431 289-4* (from recording with Ramey, Tomowa-Sintow, Baltsa, Battle, Winbergh, Furlanetto, Malta, Burchuladze, BPO, cond. Karajan).
(M) *** EMI CDM7 63078-2. Waechter, Schwarzkopf, Sutherland, Alva, Frick, Sciutti, Taddei, Philh. Ch. & O, Giulini.
(M) **(*) EMI CDM7 69055-2 [id.] (from above recording, with Ghiaurov, Watson, Freni, Ludwig, Gedda, Berry; cond. Klemperer).
(M) **(*) DG 429 823-2; *429 823-4* [id.]. Milnes, Tomowa-Sintow, Zylis-Gara, Mathis, Schreier, Berry, V. State Op. Ch., VPO, Boehm.
** EMI Dig. CDC7 54323-2 [id.] (from above set, with Shimell, Studer, Ramey; cond. Muti).

A generous selection (66 minutes) from Karajan's digital set, most of the favourite items included and all the principals given a chance to sparkle, in solos, duets and ensembles. The selection opens with the *Overture* and closes with the powerful final scene.

Not surprisingly, the Giulini EMI selection concentrates on Sutherland as Donna Anna and Schwarzkopf as Donna Elvira, so that the Don and Leporello get rather short measure, but Sciutti's charming Zerlina is also given fair due; while Klemperer's set of highlights is well chosen to show his version's many merits, and this is a sampler of a very distinctive performance.

Boehm's DG selection is very generous (76 minutes) and is taken from live performances at Salzburg (recorded in 1977). It makes a welcome representation of a set centring round Sherrill Milnes's unusually heroic assumption of the role of the Don, and he sings with a richness and commitment to match his swaggering stage presence. The rest of the cast give stylish performances without being deeply memorable but, unlike *Così* where ensembles were less than ideally crisp, this live *Giovanni* presents strong and consistently enjoyable teamwork.

The selection from Muti's set is not particularly generous (62 minutes) for a full-priced highlights disc. However, it does include most of the key numbers.

(i) *Don Giovanni:* highlights; (ii) *Die Entführung aus dem Serail:* highlights.
(B) *** DG Compact Classics 431 181-2 (2); *431 181-4* [id.]. (i) Milnes, Tomowa-Sintow, Zylis-Gara, Mathis, Schreier, Berry, V. State Op. Ch., VPO; (ii) Augér, Grist, Schreier, Neukirch, Moll, Leipzig R. Ch., Dresden State O, Boehm.

With sparkling sound, this is one of the finest operatic tape bargains in the DG Compact Classics catalogue. The *Don Giovanni* highlights were recorded live at the 1977 Salzburg

Festival. The strong cast is dominated by a swaggering Don in Sherrill Milnes, and Anna Tomowa-Sintow proves a generally creamy-toned Donna Anna. Teresa Zylis-Gara and Edith Mathis are good too, and Walter Berry is a genial Leporello. The selection is well chosen and it is joined by an equally attractive set of excerpts from Boehm's superb *Entführung*, with Arleen Augér at her very finest in the role of Constanze, Kurl Moll relishing the characterization of Osmin, and the rest of the cast almost equally impressive. Again the transfer is vivid, and both overtures are included. The CDs sound even better and have striking presence, but they include only two extra numbers from *Don Giovanni*, although there are four additional items from *Die Entführung*. Even so, with an overall playing time of only 106 minutes on the pair of CDs, the tape (which costs about a third as much) is far better value.

Complete Mozart Edition, Volume 38: *Die Entführung aus dem Serail* (complete).
(M) ** Ph. 422 538-2 (2) [id.]. Eda-Pierre, Stuart Burrows, Norma Burrowes, Tear, Lloyd, Jürgens, Alldis Ch., ASMF, Sir Colin Davis.
Die Entführung aus dem Serail (complete).
(M) *** DG 429 868-2 (2) [id.]. Augér, Grist, Schreier, Neukirch, Moll, Leipzig R. Ch., Dresden State O, Boehm.
*** Teldec/Warner Dig. 2292 42643-2 (3) [id.]. Kenny, Watson, Schreier, Gamlich, Salminen, Zurich Op. Ch. & Mozart O, Harnoncourt.
**(*) O-L Dig. 430 339-2 (2) [id.]. Dawson, Hirsti, Heilmann, Gahmlich, Von Kannen, Hinze, AAM & Ch., Hogwood.
**(*) Decca Dig. 417 402-2 (2) [id.]. Gruberová, Battle, Winbergh, Zednik, Talvela, V. State Op. Ch., VPO, Solti.

(i) *Die Entführung aus dem Serail* (complete). (ii) Arias from: *La clemenza di Tito; Die Entführung; Idomeneo.*
(M) **(*) EMI stereo/mono CHS7 63715-2 (2). (i) Lois Marshall, Hollweg, Simoneau, Unger, Frick, Beecham Ch. Soc., RPO, Beecham; (ii) Léopold Simoneau.

Boehm's is a delectable performance, superbly cast and warmly recorded. Arleen Augér proves the most accomplished singer on record in the role of Constanze, girlish and fresh, yet rich, tender and dramatic by turns, with brilliant, almost flawless coloratura. The others are also outstandingly good, notably Kurt Moll whose powerful, finely focused bass makes him a superb Osmin, one who relishes the comedy too. Using East German forces, Boehm uncovers a natural, unforced Mozartian expression which carries the listener along in glowing ease. The warm recording is beautifully transferred, to make this easily the most sympathetic version of the opera on CD, with the added attraction of being at mid-price.

Harnoncourt's version establishes its uniqueness at the very start of the overture, tougher and more abrasive than any previous recording, with more primitive percussion effects than we are used to in his Turkish music. It is not a comfortable sound, compounded by Harnoncourt's often fast allegros, racing singers and players off their feet. Another source of extra abrasiveness is the use of a raw-sounding flageolet instead of a piccolo. Once you get used to it, however, the result is refreshing and lively. Slow passages are often warmly expressive, but the stylishness of the soloists prevents them from seeming excessively romantic. The men are excellent: Peter Schreier singing charmingly, Wilfried Gamlich both bright and sweet of tone, Matti Salminen outstandingly characterful as an Osmin who, as well as singing with firm dark tone, points the words with fine menace. Yvonne Kenny as Constanze and Lilian Watson as Blonde sound on the shrill side, partly a question of microphones.

Christopher Hogwood in the first period recording of *Entführung* offers a bonus number, discovered as a result of keen detective work. It is a march which precedes the chorus of janissaries, very useful for producers wanting to get supernumeraries on stage. Hogwood has rarely sounded so relaxed on record, though the excellent cast is let down by one unwise choice, the ill-focused Osmin of Gunther von Kannen. Otherwise Lynne Dawson is a dazzling Konstanze, relying on fine projection rather than weight in the big arias, and contrasting well with the soubrettish Blonde of Marianne Hirsti. The tenor Uwe Heilmann as Belmonte here completely avoids the fluttery tone which mars his performance as Tamino in the Solti set of *Zauberflöte*.

Though Solti's speeds are disconcertingly fast at times – as in Pedrillo and Osmin's drinking duet, *Vivat Bacchus* – and the manner is consequently often too tense to be comic, the performance is magnetic overall, with the big ensembles and choruses electric in their clean, sharp focus. Gruberová makes a brilliant Constanze, but the edge on the voice is not always comfortable. Gösta Winbergh makes an ardent, young-sounding Belmonte, Kathleen Battle a seductive, minxish Blonde and Heinz Zednik a delightfully light and characterful Pedrillo, with Martti Talvela magnificently lugubrious as Osmin. With brilliant recording this makes a fresh and compelling reading, but not one likely to make you smile often.

There is much to treasure in Beecham's vivid but idiosyncratic reading, not least the incomparable portrayal of Osmin by the great German bass, Gottlob Frick, thrillingly dark and firm, characterizing superbly. His aria, *O wie will ich triumphieren*, like the *Overture* and the *Chorus of Janissaries* in Act I, finds Beecham fizzing with energy, spine-tingling in intensity. Léopold Simoneau as Belmonte has rarely been matched on record for mellifluous beauty and flawless line, and Gerhard Unger is a charming Pedrillo, not least in the spoken dialogue. The two women soloists are more variable; Lois Marshall is technically fine as Constanze, but the voice has a hint of rawness, while Ilse Hollweg, bright and clear, could also be more characterful. The oddity of the set lies in the text. Beecham, dissatisfied with the heroine's two big arias following each other so closely, moved the second, heroic one, *Martern aller Arten*, to Act III and he also made an unwarranted cut in *Traurigkeit*. He also moved Belmonte's *Wenn der Freude* to the beginning of Act III, where it replaces *Ich baue ganz*, a curious decision. The transfer of early stereo sound is first rate. The four mono recordings of Mozart arias sung by Simoneau – including the missing *Ich baue ganz* – make an excellent bonus.

Sir Colin Davis, using a smaller orchestra, the St Martin's Academy, than he usually has in his Mozart opera recordings, produces a fresh and direct account, well but not outstandingly sung. There are no performances here which have one remembering individuality of phrase, and even so characterful a singer as Robert Tear does not sound quite mellifluous enough in the role of Pedrillo; while Robert Lloyd as Osmin is outshone by both his rivals, especially by the incomparable Gottlob Frick in the Beecham set. Crisp as the ensembles are, Davis's reading rather lacks lightness and sparkle.

Complete Mozart Edition, Volume 33: *La finta giardiniera* (complete).
(M) *** Ph. 422 533-2 (3) [id.]. Conwell, Sukis, Di Cesare, Thomas Moser, Fassbaender, Ihloff, McDaniel, Salzburg Mozarteum O, Hager.

Complete Mozart Edition, Volume 34: *Die Gärtnerin aus Liebe* (*La finta giardiniera* sung in German) (complete).
(M) **(*) Ph. 422 534-2 (3) [id.]. Unger, Hollweg, Donath, J. Norman, Cotrubas, N. German R. Ch. & SO, Schmidt-Isserstedt.

This is the only *opera buffa* written by Mozart in his youth that can be regarded as a preparation for *Figaro*, particularly as you find Mozart at nineteen confidently using techniques in the extended finales which he was to perfect in the Da Ponte masterpiece.

By the time Leopold Hager came to record the opera in 1980 with Salzburg Mozarteum forces, the text of the recitatives in Italian had been rediscovered and he was able to use the original language. He has a strong vocal team, with three impressive newcomers taking the women's roles – Jutta-Renate Ihloff, Julia Conwell (in the central role of Sandrina, the marquise who disguises herself as a garden-girl) and Lilian Sukis (the arrogant niece). Brigitte Fassbaender sings the castrato role of Ramiro, and the others are comparably stylish. It is a charming – if lengthy – comedy, which here, with crisply performed recitatives, is presented with vigour, charm and persuasiveness. The recording, made with the help of Austrian Radio, is excellent and has been brightly and freshly transferred to CD.

Hans Schmidt-Isserstedt's set was made in Hamburg a decade earlier, and ne was forced to record the version that used the clumsy German Singspiel translation, in use until the discovery of the Italian recitatives. However, though this performance is slow in getting off the ground, it readily makes up for this later, with particularly delightful performances from Eleana Cotrubas and Hermann Prey in the roles of the two servants. The sound too is very pleasing, although the violin tone is a little on the thin side; but the CD transfer does not exaggerate this and retains an attractive ambience.

Complete Mozart Edition, Volume 28: *La finta semplice* (complete).
(M) *** Ph. Dig. 422 528-2 (2) [id.]. Hendricks, Lorenz, Johnson, Murray, Lind, Blochwitz, Schmidt, C. P. E. Bach CO, Schreier.

Peter Schreier draws sparkling playing from the C. P. E. Bach Orchestra of East Berlin, so that, with an excellent cast, this completely new recording in the Philips Complete Mozart Edition is one of the most delectable of all the sets of early Mozart operas. What is astonishing is that the invention of the twelve-year-old Mozart was no less winning than that of anything he wrote in his early teens, starting with an overture guaranteed to raise the spirits. In every way Schreier's version replaces the earlier, Orfeo full-priced set from Leopold Hager, particularly when it comes at mid-price on two discs instead of three. The digital recording is wonderfully clear, with a fine sense of presence, capturing the fun of the comedy. Ann Murray has never sung more seductively in Mozart than here as Giacinta, and the characterful Barbara Hendricks is a delight in the central role of Rosina.

Complete Mozart Edition, Volume 37: *Idomeneo* (complete with ballet music).
(M) ** Ph. 422 537-2 (3) [id.]. Araiza, Mentzer, Hendricks, Allen, Lewis, Alexander, Heilmann, Hollweg, Peeters, Bav. R. Ch. & RSO, Sir Colin Davis.

Idomeneo (complete).
❀ *** DG Dig. 431 674-2 (3) [id.]. Rolfe Johnson, Von Otter, McNair, Martinpelto, Robson, Hauptmann, Monteverdi Choir, E. Bar. Soloists, Gardiner.
(M) *** DG 429 864-2 (3) [id.]. Ochman, Mathis, Schreier, Varady, Winkler, Leipzig R. Ch., Dresden State O, Boehm.
*** Decca Dig. 411 805-2 (3) [id.]. Pavarotti, Baltsa, Popp, Gruberová, Nucci, V. State Op. Ch., VPO, Pritchard.
(M) (***) EMI mono CHS7 63685-2 (2) [Ang. CDHB 63685]. Richard Lewis, Simoneau, Jurinac, Glyndebourne Fest. Ch. & O, Pritchard.

Gardiner's revelatory recording, taken from live performances at Queen Elizabeth Hall in June 1990, is the first on period instruments. With its exhilarating vigour and fine singing it will please many more than period-performance devotees. Using period instruments 'played with gusto', Gardiner says, the result in this opera is 'earthier and emotionally raw'. He also suggests that this is 'the most orchestrally conceived of all Mozart's operas', and the recording substantiates both these claims. Gardiner's aim has been to include all the material Mozart wrote for the original 1781 production, whether it was finally used or not. It is astonishing to find that, with all the variants and amendments, the music for Act III alone lasts an hour and three-quarters, and he recommends the use of the CD programming device for listeners to select the version they prefer, with supplementary numbers put at the end of each disc. The abrasiveness is modified by Gardiner's Mozartian style, well sprung and subtly moulded rather than severe, and his choice of singers puts a premium on clarity and beauty of production rather than weight. Even Hillevi Martinpelto, the young soprano chosen to sing the dramatic role of Elettra, keeps a pure line in her final fury scene, avoiding explosiveness – a passage given in alternative versions. The other principals sing beautifully too, notably Anne Sofie von Otter as Idamante and Sylvia McNair as Ilia, while Anthony Rolfe Johnson, a tenor on the light side for the role of Idomeneo in a traditional performance, is well suited here, with words finely projected. The electrifying singing of the Monteverdi Choir adds to the dramatic bite, and the sound is excellent, remarkably fine for a live performance in a difficult venue.

Boehm's conducting is a delight, often spacious but never heavy in the wrong way, with lightened textures and sprung rhythms which have one relishing Mozartian felicities as never before. As Idomeneo, Wieslaw Ochman, with tenor tone often too tight, is a comparatively dull dog, but the other principals are generally excellent. Peter Schreier as Idamante also might have sounded more consistently sweet, but the imagination is irresistible. Edith Mathis is at her most beguiling as Ilia, but it is Julia Varady as Elettra who gives the most compelling performance of all, sharply incisive in her dramatic outbursts, but at the same time precise and pure-toned, a Mozartian stylist through and through.

More than any previous recorded performance, the Decca version conducted by Sir John Pritchard centres round the tenor taking the name-part. It is not just that Pavarotti has the natural magnetism of the superstar, but that he is the only tenor at all among the principal soloists. Not only is the role of Idamante given to a mezzo instead of a tenor – preferable, with what was originally a castrato role – but that of the High Priest, Arbace, with his two arias is taken by a baritone, Leo Nucci. The wonder is that though Pavarotti reveals imagination in every phrase, using a wide range of tone colours, the result remains well within the parameters of Mozartian style. By any reckoning this is not only the most heroic and the most beautiful but also the best controlled performance of this demanding role that we have on record. Casting Baltsa as Idamante makes for characterful results, tougher and less fruity than her direct rivals. Lucia Popp as Ilia tends to underline expression too much, but it is a charming, girlish portrait. Gruberová makes a thrilling Elettra, totally in command of the divisions, as few sopranos are;

owing to bright Decca sound, the projection of her voice is a little edgy at times. As to Pritchard, he has relaxed a little since his Glyndebourne days – this is a bigger view than before – and (with text unusually complete) more than current rivals brings light and shade to the piece.

The very first 'complete' recording of the opera, recorded in 1955 with Glyndebourne forces under John Pritchard, makes a timely reappearance on CD. Though it uses a severely cut text and the orchestral sound is rather dry, it wears its years well. The voices still sound splendid, notably Sena Jurinac as a ravishing Ilia, Richard Lewis in the title-role, and Léopold Simoneau so delicate he almost reconciles one to the casting of Idamante as a tenor (from Mozart's compromised Vienna revision). The cuts mean that the whole opera is fitted on to two discs.

Sir Colin Davis's second version of Mozart's great *opera seria* comes with the fine qualities of presentation associated with the Philips Complete Mozart Edition; the text aims at completeness, with an appendix on the third disc containing major numbers like Arbace's two arias, omitted in the main text, as well as the ballet music designed to be performed after the drama is over. It also has the advantage over Davis's previous recording that the role of Idamante is given to a mezzo instead of a tenor, following Mozart's original Munich text. Such a number as the great Quartet of Act III benefits much by that – but unfortunately, as in Davis's previous version, there are flaws in the casting; his reading has also grown smoother and less incisive, less fresh than before, if now at times grander. Francisco Araiza's efforts to produce the heroic tone needed often sound strained, and he is not clean enough in his attack; while Barbara Hendricks as Ilia adopts an even less apt Mozartian style, with too much sliding and under-the-note attack, missing the purity needed for this character.

Complete Mozart Edition, Volume 32: *Lucio Silla* (complete).
(M) *** Ph. 422 532-2 (3) [id.]. Schreier, Augér, Varady, Mathis, Donath, Krenn, Salzburg R. Ch. & Mozarteum Ch. & O, Hager.

Lucio Silla (slightly abridged).
*** Teldec/Warner Dig. 2292 44928-2 (2). Schreier, Gruberová, Bartoli, Kenny, Upshaw, Schoenberg Ch., VCM, Harnoncourt.

The sixteen-year-old Mozart wrote his fifth opera, on the subject of the Roman dictator Sulla (Silla), in double quick time. There are many pre-echoes of later Mozart operas, not just of the great *opera seria*, *Idomeneo*, but of *Entführung* and even of *Don Giovanni*. Though the formal limitations inhibit ensembles, there is a superb one at the end of Act I, anticipating the Da Ponte masterpieces. A rousing chorus is interrupted by an agonized G minor lament for the heroine and leads finally to an ecstatic reunion duet. The castrato roles are here splendidly taken by Julia Varady and Edith Mathis, and the whole team could hardly be bettered. The direction of Hager is fresh and lively, and the only snag is the length of the *secco* recitatives. However, with CD one can use these judiciously. The 1975 analogue recording, originally DG, has been taken over for the Philips Mozart Edition and the remastering is vivid and natural, although it is a pity that, in fitting the work on to CD, the first break had to come nine minutes before the end of Act I, in the middle of the scena described above, just before the duet.

What Harnoncourt has done is to record a text which fits on to two generously filled CDs, not just trimming down the recitatives but omitting no fewer than four arias, all of them valuable. Yet his sparkling direction of an outstanding, characterful team of soloists brings an exhilarating demonstration of the boy Mozart's genius, with such marvels as the extended finale to Act I left intact. The Hager version of 1975 with its complete text has been reissued in the Philips Complete Mozart Edition, with just as star-studded a cast as this, but anyone not over-concerned about completeness will find Harnoncourt's two CDs a vivid experience. As in the earlier set, Schreier is masterly in the title-role, still fresh in tone, while Dawn Upshaw is warm and sweet as Celia, and Cecilia Bartoli is full and rich as Cecilio. The singing of Edita Gruberová as Giunia and Yvonne Kenny as Cinna is not quite so immaculate, but still confident and stylish. The Concentus Musicus of Vienna has rarely given so bright and lightly sprung a performance on record. Excellent digital sound.

Complete Mozart Edition, Volume 29: *Mitridate, rè di Ponto* (complete).
(M) **(*) Ph. 422 529-2 (3) [id.]. Augér, Hollweg, Gruberová, Baltsa, Cotrubas, Salzburg Mozarteum O, Hager.

Mozart at fourteen attempted his first full-scale *opera seria* and showed that he could fully encompass the most ambitious of forms. Not all the 22 arias are of the finest quality; some are too long for their material, and the Metastasio libretto is hardly involving dramatically. But a fresh and generally lively performance (the rather heavy recitatives excepted) brings splendid illumination to the long-hidden area of the boy Mozart's achievement. Two of the most striking arias (including an urgent G minor piece for the heroine, Aspasia, with Arleen Augér the ravishing soprano) exploit minor keys most effectively. Ileana Cotrubas is outstanding as Ismene, and the soloists of the Salzburg orchestra cope well with the often important obbligato parts. The recording is bright and fresh, the CD transfer vivid and forward and a little lacking in atmosphere.

Complete Mozart Edition, Volume 40: *Le nozze di Figaro* (complete).
(M) *** Ph. 422 540-2 (3) [id.]. Freni, Norman, Minton, Ganzarolli, Wixell, Grant, Tear, BBC Ch. & SO, Sir Colin Davis.

Le nozze di Figaro (complete).
*** Decca Dig. 410 150-2 (3). Te Kanawa, Popp, Von Stade, Ramey, Allen, Moll, LPO & Ch., Solti.
❀ (B) *** CfP CD-CFPD 4724; *TC-CFPD 4724* (2). Sciutti, Jurinac, Stevens, Bruscantini, Calabrese, Cuenod, Wallace, Sinclair, Glyndebourne Ch. & Festival O, Gui.
(M) *** EMI CMS7 63266-2 (2) [Ang. CDMB 63266]. Schwarzkopf, Moffo, Cossotto, Taddei, Waechter, Vinco, Philh. Ch. & O, Giulini.
(M) **(*) Decca 417 315-2 (3) [id.]. Gueden, Danco, Della Casa, Dickie, Poell, Corena, Siepi, V. State Op. Ch., VPO, Erich Kleiber.
(M) *** DG 429 869-2 (3) [id.]. Janowitz, Mathis, Troyanos, Fischer-Dieskau, Prey, Lagger, German Op. Ch. & O, Boehm.
**(*) EMI Dig. CDS7 49753-2 (3) [Ang. CDCC 49753]. Lott, Desderi, Rolandi, Stilwell, Esham, Korn, Glyndebourne Ch., LPO, Haitink.
(M) (**(*)) EMI mono CMS7 69639-2 (2) [Ang. CDMB 69639]. Schwarzkopf, Seefried, Jurinac, Kunz, Majkut, London, V. State Op. Ch., VPO, Karajan.
** DG Dig. 431 619-2 (3) [id.]. Te Kanawa, Upshaw, Von Otter, Furlanetto, Hampson, Troyanos, NY Met. Op. Ch. & O, Levine.
** Decca Dig. 421 333-2 (3) [id.]. Hagegård, Augér, Salomaa, Bonney, Nafé, Jones, Feller, Gimenez, Drottningholm Theatre Ch. & O, Östman.
*(*) BMG/RCA Dig. RD 60440 (3) [60440-2-RC]. Donath, Varady, Titus, Furlanetto, Schmiege, Bav. R. Ch. & SO, C. Davis.

It is important not to judge Solti's effervescent version of *Figaro* by a first reaction to the overture, which is one of the fastest on record. Elsewhere Solti opts for a fair proportion of extreme speeds, slow as well as fast, but they rarely if ever intrude on the quintessential happiness of the entertainment. Samuel Ramey, a firm-toned baritone, makes a virile Figaro, superby matched to the most enchanting of Susannas today, Lucia Popp, who gives a sparkling and radiant performance. Thomas Allen's Count is magnificent too, tough in tone and characterization but always beautiful on the ear. Kurt Moll as Dr Bartolo sings an unforgettable *La vendetta* with triplets very fast and agile 'on the breath', while Robert Tear far outshines his own achievement as the Basilio of Sir Colin Davis's amiable recording. Frederica von Stade, as in the Karajan set, is a most attractive Cherubino, even if *Voi che sapete* is too slow; but crowning all is the Countess of Kiri Te Kanawa, challenged by Solti's spacious tempi in the two big arias, but producing ravishing tone, flawless phrasing and elegant ornamentation throughout. With superb, vivid recording this now makes a clear first choice for a much-recorded opera. However, in view of the strong competition, Decca should find a way of reducing the price of this set.

The most effervescent performance of *Figaro* on disc, brilliantly produced in early but well-separated stereo, the 1955 Glyndebourne recording makes a bargain without equal on only two CDs from CfP. The transfer on CD brings sound warmer, more naturally vivid and with more body than on many modern recordings. The realistic projection instantly makes one forget any minimal tape-hiss, and the performance, recorded in the studio immediately after a vintage Glyndebourne season, offers not only unsurpassed teamwork, witty in its timing, but also a consistently stylish and characterful cast. Just as Sesto Bruscantini is the archetypal Glyndebourne Figaro, Sena Jurinac is the perfect Countess, with Graziella Sciutti a delectable Susanna and Risë Stevens a well-contrasted Cherubino, vivacious in their scenes together. Franco Calabrese as the Count is firm and virile, if occasionally stressed on top; and the three character roles have never been cast more vividly, with Ian Wallace as Bartolo, Monica Sinclair as Marcellina and the incomparable Hugues Cuenod as Basilio. The only regret is that Cuenod's brilliant performance of Basilio's aria in Act IV has had to be omitted (as it so often is on stage) to keep the two discs each within the 80-minute limit. There is no libretto; instead a detailed synopsis is provided, with cueing points conveniently indicated. But this set costs little more than a third the price of the Decca/Solti version.

Like his set of *Don Giovanni* – also recorded in 1959 – the Giulini version is a classic, with a cast assembled by Walter Legge that has rarely been matched, let alone surpassed. If the fun of the opera is more gently presented by Giulini than by some others, he provides the perfect frame for such a characterful line-up of soloists. Taddei with his dark bass-baritone makes a provocative Figaro; opposite him, Anna Moffo is at her freshest and sweetest as Susanna. Schwarzkopf as ever is the noblest of Countesses, and it is good to hear the young Fiorenza Cossotto as a full-toned Cherubino. Eberhard Waechter is a strong and stylish Count. On only two mid-priced discs instead of the original four LPs, it makes a superb bargain, though – as in the other EMI two-disc version, the Gui on CfP – Marcellina's and Basilio's arias are omitted from Act IV. The break between discs is neatly managed towards the end of the Act II finale. The transfer is excellent, giving a focus and sense of presence often not achieved in modern digital recordings. Unlike many mid-priced opera sets from EMI, this one comes in a slip-case, complete with full libretto and translation, bringing an advantage over the CfP set.

The pacing of Sir Colin Davis has a sparkle in recitative that directly reflects experience in the opera house, and his tempi generally are beautifully chosen to make their dramatic points. Vocally the cast is exceptionally consistent. Mirella Freni (Susanna) is perhaps the least satisfying, yet there is no lack of character and charm. It is good to have so ravishingly beautiful a voice as Jessye Norman's for the Countess. The Figaro of Wladimiro Ganzarolli and the Count of Ingvar Wixell project with exceptional clarity and vigour, and there is fine singing too from Yvonne Minton as Cherubino, Clifford Grant as Bartolo and Robert Tear as Basilio. The 1971 recording has more reverberation than usual, but the effect is commendably atmospheric and on CD the voices have plenty of presence.

Kleiber's famous set was one of Decca's Mozart bicentenary recordings of the mid-1950s. It remains an attractively strong performance with much fine singing. Few if any sets since have matched its constant stylishness. Gueden's Susanna might be criticized but her golden tones are certainly characterful and her voice blends with Della Casa's enchantingly. Danco and Della Casa are both at their finest. A dark-toned Figaro in Siepi brings added contrast and, if the pace of the recitatives is rather slow, this is not inconsistent within the context of Kleiber's overall approach. It is a pity that the Decca remastering, in brightening the sound, has brought a hint of edginess to the voices, though the basic atmosphere remains. Also, the layout brings a less than felicitous break in Act II. In this respect the cassettes were superior – and they had smoother sound, too.

Boehm's version of *Figaro* is also among the most consistently assured performances available. The women all sing most beautifully, with Janowitz's Countess, Mathis's Susanna and Troyanos's Cherubino all ravishing the ear in contrasted ways. Prey is an intelligent if not very jolly-sounding Figaro, and Fischer-Dieskau gives his dark, sharply defined reading of the Count's role. All told, a great success, with fine playing and recording, enhanced on CD.

As in his other Glyndebourne recordings, Haitink's approach is relaxed and mellow. Where in *Così* the results were sunny, here in *Figaro* there is at times a lack of sparkle. There is much lovely singing and fine ensemble from a strong team, yet one which does not quite match the casting of the Solti set.

Recorded in 1950, Karajan's first recording of *Figaro* offers one of the most distinguished casts ever assembled; but, curiously at that period, they decided to record the opera without the secco recitatives. That is a most regrettable omission when all these singers are not just vocally immaculate but vividly characterful – as for example Sena Jurinac, later the greatest of Glyndebourne Countesses, here a vivacious Cherubino. The firmness of focus in Erich Kunz's singing of Figaro goes with a delightful twinkle in the word-pointing, and Irmgard Seefried makes a bewitching Susanna. Schwarzkopf's noble portrait of the Countess – not always helped by a slight backward balance in the placing of the microphone for her – culminates in the most poignant account of her second aria, *Dove sono*. The sound, though obviously limited, presents the voices very vividly.

Levine's DG recording with forces from the Met. in New York brings some outstanding individual performances – notably Anne-Sofie von Otter as a delightful Cherubino – but overall it lacks the effervescence needed for this opera. Dame Kiri Te Kanawa's Countess is far better appreciated in the Solti Decca set, Dawn Upshaw is too pert a Susanna, and Ferruccio

Furlanetto's resonant Figaro is not helped by the roughness of Levine's accompaniment, as in *Non piú andrai*.

Östman's version (based on the production at the Drottningholm Court Theatre) is the first to use period instruments; like his *Così*, it brings generally hectic speeds, but here such treatment undermines both the fun and the dramatic point. Östman refuses to pause or even to broaden for a second in passages which cry out for it; and with such a metrical beat even the most sparkling moments lose their brightness, and charm is far away. Nevertheless the cast is impressive. The Susanna of Barbara Bonney is delightful, and though Petteri Salomaa is rather dry-toned, he makes an engaging young Figaro. Håkan Hagegård is a splendid Count, and Arleen Augér a pure-toned Countess. Among the others, too, there are no weak links at all, and the set is valuable for generously including variant numbers that Mozart incorporated in productions at different times. Full and well-balanced recording.

Sir Colin Davis's RCA version comes as a disappointment after his excellent Philips set, now reissued at mid-price in the Philips Mozart Edition. Though his pointing of Mozart is as finely judged as ever, the result does not sparkle as it did, not helped by the colourless Figaro of Alan Titus. There are some fine individual performances, but this hardly matches the finest versions.

Le nozze di Figaro: highlights.
(M) *** DG 429 822-3 (from above set, cond. Karl Boehm).
** EMI Dig. CDC7 54321-2 [id.]. Margaret Price, Battle, Murray, Allen, Hynninen, Rydl, V. State Op. Ch., VPO, Muti.

Boehm's selection includes many of the key numbers, but with a little over an hour of music it is less generous than its companion highlights discs. Moreover, it is inadequately documented, but the singing is first class and the sound vivid.

The Muti 1987 digital set of *Figaro* with the Vienna Philharmonic (EMI CDS7 47978-8 [Angel CDCC 47978]) is disappointing for the cloudiness of focus in the recording, and the singing too is very variable. Margaret Price is a powerful, firm Countess and Kathleen Battle – not unexpectedly, a sparkling Susanna. But Thomas Allen's Figaro, commanding as he is, lacks the necessary touch of humour, and Ann Murray is an edgy Cherubino. The highlights disc is the best way to sample this recording for admirers of all or any of these artists: it is fairly generous, with a 70-minute playing time.

Complete Mozart Edition, Volume 39: *L'Oca del Cairo* (complete).
(M) *** Ph. Dig. 422 539-2 [id.]. Nielsen, Wiens, Coburn, Schreier, Johnson, Fischer-Dieskau, Scharinger, Berlin R. Ch. (members), C. P. E. Bach CO, Schreier – *Lo sposo deluso*. ***

We owe it to the Mozart scholar and Philips recording producer, Erik Smith, that these two sets of Mozartian fragments, *L'Oca del Cairo* and *Lo sposo deluso*, have been prepared for performance and recorded. Dating from 1783–4, they anticipate the great leap forward in the history of comic opera represented by *Le nozze di Figaro* in 1786. Though it is doubtful whether even Mozart could have developed the ideas they contain into comparable masterpieces, the incidental delights are many. *L'Oca del Cairo* ('The Cairo goose'), containing roughly twice as much music as *Lo sposo deluso*, involves six substantial numbers, most of them ensembles, including an amazing finale to the projected Act I. It is as extended as the comparable finales of *Figaro* and *Così fan tutte*, with contrasted sections following briskly one after the other. The score left by Mozart has the vocal parts virtually complete, as well as the bass line and the occasional instrumental indications. Smith has sensitively filled in the gaps to make a satisfying whole, very well conducted by Peter Schreier, who also takes part as one of the soloists. Dietrich Fischer-Dieskau takes the *buffo* old-man role of Don Pippo, and Anton Scharinger is brilliant in the patter aria in tarantella rhythm for the major-domo, Chichibio, bringing a foretaste of Donizetti. Fresh, bright digital recording.

Complete Mozart Edition, Volume 35: *Il rè pastore* (complete).
(M) **(*) Ph. Dig. 422 535-2 (2) [id.]. Blasi, McNair, Vermilion, Hadley, Ahnsjö, ASMF, Marriner.

Il rè pastore, the last of Mozart's early operas, is best known for the glorious aria, *L'amero*, one of the loveliest he ever wrote for soprano. The whole entertainment is among the most charming of his early music, a gentle piece which works well on record. This version by Marriner and the Academy is completely new, specially recorded for the Complete Mozart Edition with a first-rate cast. Brisk and bright, with plenty of light and shade, and superbly played, it yet does not efface memories of the 1979 DG version conducted by Leopold Hager, which offered even purer singing. Here Angela Maria Blasi, despite a beautiful voice, attacks notes from below, even in *L'amero*. Excellent sound.

Complete Mozart Edition, Volume 36: *Der Schauspieldirektor* (complete).
(M) **(*) Ph. 422 536-2 (2) [id.]. Welting, Cotrubas, Grant, Rolfe Johnson, LSO, Sir Colin Davis – *Zaïde*. ***

Der Schauspieldirektor (*The Impresario*): complete.
(M) *** DG 429 877-2 (3) [id.]. Grist, Augér, Schreier, Moll, Dresden State O, Boehm – *Die Zauberflöte*. **(*)

(i–v; viii) *Der Schauspieldirektor*. Concert arias: (ii; vii; ix) *Misera, dove son!, K.369; Un moto di gioia, K.579; Schon lacht der holde Frühling, K.580.* (i; vii; ix) *Vado, ma dove? oh Dei!, K.583; Bella mia fiamma, addio, K.529; Nehmt meinen Dank, ihr holden Gonner!* (iv; vi; x) *Die Entführung: Ha! Wie will ich triumpheren.* (v; viii) *Le nozze di Figaro: Overture.*
*** Decca Dig. 430 207-2 [id.]. (i) Te Kanawa, (ii) Gruberová, (iii) Heilmann, (iv) Jungwirth; (v) VPO; (vi) Vienna Haydn O; (vii) Vienna CO; (viii) Pritchard; (ix) Fischer; (x) Kertész.

This Decca recording of the four musical numbers from *Der Schauspieldirektor* (presented 'dry' with no German dialogue) was made only six months before Sir John Pritchard died, an apt last offering from him, a great Mozartian. Having two such well-contrasted star sopranos adds point to the contest, and the performances are a delight, though the recorded sound is not as well focused as usual from this source. The *Figaro overture*, also conducted by Pritchard, is another completely new item. The rest is reissue material, with three concert arias each from Gruberová and Dame Kiri, taken from Decca's 1981 boxed set of the collected arias. Manfred Jungwirth's bitingly dark account of Osmin's aria from *Entführung* dates from ten years before that, a welcome extra. The single disc is boxed with texts and notes.

The DG performance of *Der Schauspieldirektor* is without dialogue, so that it is short enough to make a fill-up for Boehm's *Zauberflöte*. Reri Grist's bravura as Madame Herz is impressive, and Arleen Augér is pleasingly fresh and stylish here. The tenor and bass make only minor contributions, but Boehm's guiding hand keeps the music alive from the first bar to the last.

There is no contest whatsoever between the two rival prima donnas presented in the Philips recording. *Ich bin die erste Sängerin* ('I am the leading prima donna'), they yell at each other; but here Ileana Cotrubas is in a world apart from the thin-sounding and shallow Ruth Welting. Davis directs with fire and electricity a performance which is otherwise (despite the lack of spoken dialogue) most refreshing and beautifully recorded (in 1975) in a sympathetic acoustic.

Complete Mozart Edition, Volume 31: *Il sogno di Scipione* (complete).
(M) *** Ph. 422 531-2 (2) [id.]. Popp, Gruberová, Mathis, Schreier, Ahnsjö, Thomas Moser, Salzburg Chamber Ch. & Mozarteum O, Hager.

Il sogno di Scipione presents an allegorical plot with Scipio set to choose between Fortune and Constancy; and in effect it consists of a sequence of 11 extended arias using three tenors and two sopranos. Given the choice of present-day singers, this cast could hardly be finer, with Edita Gruberová, Lucia Popp and Edith Mathis superbly contrasted in the women's roles (the latter taking part in the epilogue merely), and Peter Schreier is joined by two of his most accomplished younger colleagues. Hager sometimes does not press the music on as he might, but his direction is always alive, and the Salzburg Mozarteum Orchestra plays with fine point and elegance – witness the winningly sprightly violins in the *Overture*. With fine recording, vividly and atmospherically transferred to CD, the set is not likely to be surpassed in the immediate future.

Complete Mozart Edition, Volume 39: *Lo sposo deluso.*
(M) *** Ph. 422 539-2 [id.]. Palmer, Cotrubas, Rolfe Johnson, Tear, Grant, LSO, Sir Colin Davis – *L'Oca del Cairo* ***.

The music presented here from *Lo sposo deluso* is the surviving music from an unfinished opera written in the years before *Figaro*, and it contains much that is memorable. The *Overture*, with its trumpet calls, its lovely slow middle section and recaptitulation with voices, is a charmer, while the two arias, reconstructed by the recording producer and scholar, Erik Smith, are also delightful: the one a trial run for Fiordiligi's *Come scoglio* in *Così*, the other (sung by Robert Tear) giving a foretaste of Papageno's music in *The Magic Flute*.

Complete Mozart Edition, Volume 36: *Zaïde.*
(M) *** Ph. 422 536-2 (2) [id.]. Mathis, Schreier, Wixell, Hollweg, Süss, Berlin State O, Klee – *Der Schauspieldirektor*. **(*)

Zaïde, written between 1779 and 1780 and never quite completed, was a trial run for *Entführung*, based on a comparable story of love, duty, escape and forgiveness in the seraglio. It has nothing like the same sharpness of focus dramatically, which may perhaps account for Mozart's failure to complete the piece when within sight of the end. For whatever reason, he left it minus an overture and a finale, but it is simple enough for both to be supplied from other sources, as is done here: the *Symphony No. 32* makes an apt enough overture, and a *March* (K.335/1) rounds things off quickly and neatly. Much of the music is superb, and melodramas at the beginning of each Act are strikingly effective and original, with the speaking voice of the tenor in the first heard over darkly dramatic writing in D minor. Zaïde's arias in both Acts are magnificent: the radiantly lyrical *Ruhe sanft* is hauntingly memorable, and the dramatic *Tiger aria* is like Constanze's *Martern aller Arten* but briefer and more passionate. Bernhard Klee directs a crisp and lively performance, with excellent contributions from singers and orchestra alike – a first-rate team, as consistently stylish as one could want. The 1973 recording is most refined, and the CD transfer retains the appealingly warm ambient atmosphere, making this an attractively compact Mozartian entertainment.

Complete Mozart Edition, Volume 43: *Die Zauberflöte* (complete).
(M) *(*) Ph. Dig. 422 543-2 (3) [id.]. M. Price, Serra, Schreier, Moll, Melbye, Venuti, Tear, Dresden Kreuzchor, Leipzig R. Ch., Dresden State O, Sir Colin Davis.

Die Zauberflöte (complete).
*** Ph. Dig. 426 276-2; *426 276-4* (2) [id.]. Te Kanawa, Studer, Lind, Araiza, Bär, Ramey, Van Dam, Amb. Op. Ch., ASMF, Marriner.
❀ (M) (***) DG mono 435 742-2 (2). Stader, Streich, Fischer-Dieskau, Greindl, Haefliger, Berlin RIAS Ch. & SO, Fricsay.
(M) *** EMI CMS7 69971-2 (2) [Ang. CDMB 69971]. Janowitz, Putz, Popp, Gedda, Berry, Frick; Schwarzkopf, Ludwig, Hoffgen (3 Ladies), Philh. Ch. & O, Klemperer.
(M) *** EMI mono CHS7 69631-2 (2) [Ang. CDHB 69631]. Seefried, Lipp, Loose, Dermota, Kunz, Weber, V. State Op. Ch., VPO, Karajan.
*** EMI Dig. CDS7 47951-8 (3) [Ang. CDCC 47951]. Popp, Gruberová, Lindner, Jerusalem, Brendel, Bracht, Zednik, Bav. R. Ch. & SO, Haitink.
*** Telarc Dig. CD-80302 (2). Hadley, Hendricks, Allen, Anderson, Lloyd, SCO & Ch., Mackerras.
(M) **(*) DG 429 877-2 (3) [id.]. Lear, Peters, Otto, Wunderlich, Fischer-Dieskau, Hotter, Crass, Berlin RIAS Chamber Ch., BPO, Boehm – *Der Schauspieldirektor*. ***
**(*) Decca Dig. 433 210-2 (2). Ziesak, Heilmann, Sumi Jo, Leitner, M. Kraus, Moll, Zednik, V. State Op. Ch., VPO, Solti.
** EMI Dig. CDS7 54287-2 [Ang CDCB 54287]. Upshaw, Hoch, Rolfe Johnson, Schmidt, Argenta, Bär, L. Classical Ch. & Players, Norrington.
(M) (**(*)) Pearl mono GEMMCDS 9371 (2). Lemnitz, Roswaenge, Berger, Hüsch, Strienz, Ch. & BPO, Beecham.
(M) (**) EMI mono CHS7 61034-2 [Ang.CDHB 61024] (cast as above, cond. Beecham).
(M) (*(*)) Nimbus mono NI 7827/28; *NC 7827/28* [id.] (cast as above, cond. Beecham).

Marriner directs a pointed and elegant reading of *Zauberflöte*, bringing out the fun of the piece. It lacks weight only in the overture and finale, and the cast is the finest in any modern recording. Dame Kiri – who could have sounded grand rather than girlish – lightens her voice delightfully, and consistently sings with fine control. Olaf Bär, vividly characterful, brings the Lieder-singer's art to the role of Papageno, as Gerhard Hüsch and Dietrich Fischer-Dieskau did in earlier vintage recordings. Araiza's voice has coarsened since he recorded the role of Tamino for Karajan, but this performance is subtler and conveys more feeling. Cheryl Studer's performance as Queen of the Night is easily the finest among modern recordings; and Samuel Ramey, not quite as rich and firm as usual, yet gives a generous and wise portrait of Sarastro. José van Dam, Karajan's Sarastro, is here a superb Speaker. With spoken dialogue directed by August Everding, this is now the finest digital version, superbly recorded, with the added advantage that it comes on only two discs instead of the three used for most other recent recordings.

From the early LP era Fricsay's is an outstandingly fresh and alert *Die Zauberflöte*, marked by generally clear, pure singing and well-sprung orchestral playing at generally rather fast speeds. In some ways Fricsay anticipates the Mozart tastes of a later generation, even if his approach to ornamentation is hardly in authentic-period style. So the duet, *Bei Männern*, and Pamina's big aria, *Ach, ich fühls*, are taken at flowing speeds, with Maria Stader and Dietrich Fischer-Dieskau phrasing most beautifully. The most spectacular singing comes from Rita Streich as a dazzling Queen of the Night – the finest on record – and the relatively close balance of the voice gives it the necessary power such as Streich generally failed to convey in the opera house. It is this unique contribution which nudges us towards a Rosette; but Ernst Haefliger, too, is at his most honeyed in tone as Tamino, and only the rather gritty Sarastro of Josef Greindl falls short – and even he sings with a satisfyingly dark resonance. This was the first version to spice the musical numbers with brief sprinklings of dialogue, just enough to prevent the work from sounding like an oratorio. Even including that, DG has managed to put each of the Acts complete on a single disc. The transfer of the original 1954 mono recording (made in the Berlin Jesus-Christus-Kirche) is remarkably full-bodied, with a pleasant ambience and sense of presence. There are few CD transfers of mono recordings that approach this in natural realism, and the quality of the production lets one appreciate why DG had such a high reputation for excellence in the early days of mono LP.

Klemperer's conducting of *The Magic Flute* is one of his finest achievements on record; indeed he is inspired, making the dramatic music sound more like Beethoven in its breadth and strength. But he does not miss the humour and point of the Papageno passages, and he gets the best of both worlds to a surprising degree. The cast is outstanding – look at the distinction of the Three Ladies alone – but curiously it is that generally most reliable of all the singers, Gottlob Frick as Sarastro, who comes nearest to letting the side down. Lucia Popp is in excellent form, and Gundula Janowitz sings Pamina's part with a creamy beauty that is just breathtaking. Nicolai Gedda too is a firm-voiced Papageno. The transfer to a pair of CDs, made possible by the absence of dialogue, is managed expertly – the whole effect is wonderfully fresh, the balance strikingly good.

Apart from the Fricsay set with Rita Streich which includes some spoken dialogue, there has never been a more seductive recording of *Zauberflöte* than Karajan's mono version of 1950. The Vienna State Opera cast here has not since been matched on record: Irmgard Seefried and Anton Dermota both sing with radiant beauty and great character, Wilma Lipp is a dazzling Queen of the Night, Erich Kunz as Papageno sings with an infectious smile in the voice, and Ludwig Weber is a commanding Sarastro. There is no spoken dialogue; but on two mid-priced CDs instead of three LPs, it is a Mozart treat not to be missed, with mono sound still amazingly vivid and full of presence.

Haitink directs a rich and spacious account of *Zauberflöte*, superbly recorded in spectacularly wide-ranging digital sound. The dialogue – not too much of it, nicely produced and with sound effects adding to the vividness – frames a presentation that has been carefully thought through. Popp makes the most tenderly affecting of Paminas and Gruberová has never sounded more spontaneous in her brilliance than here as Queen of the Night: she is both agile and powerful. Jerusalem makes an outstanding Tamino, both heroic and sweetly Mozartian; and though neither Wolfgang Brendel as Papageno nor Bracht as Sarastro is as characterful as their finest rivals, their personalities project strongly and the youthful freshness of their singing is most attractive. The Bavarian chorus too is splendid.

Though the recording puts a halo of reverberation round the sound, Mackerras and the Scottish Chamber Orchestra find an ideal scale for the work. His speeds are often faster than usual, not least in Pamina's great aria of lament, *Ach, ich fühls*, but they always flow persuasively. This is the version among recent ones which best conveys the fun of the piece, as well as its power, with the orchestral textures even clearer and more detailed than those of Norrington and his period players. Jerry Hadley makes a delightfully boyish Tamino, with Thomas Allen the most characterful Papageno, singing beautifully. Robert Lloyd is a noble Sarastro, and though June Anderson is a rather strenuous Queen of the Night, it is thrilling to have a big, dramatic voice so dazzlingly agile. Barbara Hendricks is a questionable choice as Pamina, not clean enough of attack, but the tonal quality is golden. Unlike his rivals Mackerras offers in an appendix an extra duet for Tamino and Papageno, though the conductor justifiably pours cold water on its credentials. Among modern recordings this is a set to put beside Haitink's very enjoyable EMI version, despite the reverberant sound.

One of the glories of Boehm's DG set is the singing of Fritz Wunderlich as Tamino, a wonderful memorial to a singer much missed. Fischer-Dieskau, with characteristic word-pointing, makes a sparkling Papageno on record and Franz Crass is a satisfyingly straightforward Sarastro. The team of women is well below this standard – Lear taxed cruelly in *Ach, ich fühl's*, Peters shrill in the upper register (although the effect is exciting), and the Three Ladies do not blend well – but Boehm's direction is superb, light and lyrical, but weighty where necessary to make a glowing, compelling experience. Fine recording, enhanced in the CD set, which has also found room for Boehm's admirable account of *Der Schauspieldirektor*, a very considerable bonus to this mid-priced reissue.

Recorded in Berlin between November 1937 and March 1939, Beecham's recording of *Zauberflöte* was also the first opera set produced by Walter Legge. It brings a classic performance, and though Helge Roswaenge was too ungainly a tenor to be an ideal Tamino, the casting has otherwise been matched in only a few instances on record. Beecham too was at his peak, pacing each number superbly. Like other early recordings of this opera, this one omits the spoken dialogue; but the vocal delights are many, not least from Tiana Lemnitz as a radiant Pamina, Erna Berger as a dazzling Queen of the Night, and Gerhard Hüsch as a delicately comic Papageno, bringing the detailed art of the Lieder-singer to the role. Of the three currently available transfers of this Beecham recording to CD, the Pearl is the one which captures the original 78 recording most naturally, with the keenest sense of presence for the voices, even if it leaves it with plentiful surface hiss. The disappointment of the EMI alternative is the dryness of the sound, with a limited top, little sense of presence and no bloom on the voices. The Nimbus attempt finds that company's re-recording process, using an acoustic gramophone, less effective than it can be. The orchestral sound is made thin, almost disembodied, and though the voices have bloom on them, they often jangle.

The last of Sir Colin Davis's recordings of Mozart's major operas, and the only one made outside Britain, is also the least successful. It is a performance of little sparkle or charm. Thus, although Margaret Price produces a glorious flow of rich, creamy tone, she conveys little of the necessary vulnerability of Pamina in her plight. Luciana Serra sings capably but at times with shrill tone and not always with complete security; while Peter Schreier is in uncharacteristically gritty voice as Tamino, and Mikael Melbye as Papageno is ill-suited to recording, when the microphone exaggerates the throatiness and unevenness of his production. The greatest vocal glory of the set is the magnificent, firm and rich singing of Kurt Moll as Sarastro. The recording is excellent.

Solti directs the Vienna Philharmonic in a well-paced and strong reading of *Zauberflöte* that misses some of the fun. There are snags too in his cast. Though Ruth Ziesak as Pamina and Sumi Jo as Queen of the Night both sing with beguiling sweetness and elegance, and Kurt Moll is gloriously firm and dark as Sarastro, the other leading male principals are disappointing. Both the Tamino of Uwe Heilmann and the Papageno of Michael Kraus are too fluttery and unsteady to give pleasure, though the latter characterizes well. Full, well-balanced Decca sound.

Norrington in his period performance linked his recording with a live concert, but left too long a period between them, so that the sparkle of the live event disappeared. Fast speeds become fierce and unsmiling, when rhythms can no longer be lifted seductively. The cast is strong but not ideal, with Cornelius Hauptmann unstylishly wobbly as Sarastro.

Die Zauberflöte: highlights.
(M) *** EMI CDM7 63451-2; *EG 763451-4* (from above recording, cond. Klemperer).
(M) *** DG Dig. 431 291-2; *431 291-4*. Mathis, Ott, Perry, Araiza, Hornik, Van Dam, German Op. Ch., Berlin, BPO, Karajan.

Those looking for a first-rate set of highlights from *Die Zauberflöte* will find the mid-priced Klemperer disc hard to beat. It makes a good sampler of a performance which, while ambitious in scale, manages to find sparkle and humour too. A synopsis details each individual excerpt, and in this case the inclusion of the *Overture* is especially welcome. The remastered sound has plenty of presence, but atmosphere and warmth too.

The Karajan set of highlights is reasonably generous (61 minutes); it includes the *Overture* and most of the key numbers, including the Papageno/Papagena items, and it demonstrates the overall strength of a generally first-rate cast.

Arias from: *Davidde penitente; Così fan tutte; La clemenza di Tito; La finta giardiniera; Don Giovanni; Die Entführung aus dem Serail; Idomeneo; Le nozze di Figaro; Die Zauberflöte.*
**(*) EMI Dig. CDC7 54329-2; *EL 754329-4* [id.]. Plácido Domingo, Munich R. O, Kohn.

Domingo's years singing Otello and other big heroic roles have taken their toll of his powers of projecting the upper voice gently, however firm and beautiful the sound generally remains. The slight distancing of the voice in the recording spectrum hardly alleviates the problem, and paradoxically, the most enjoyable, happy and relaxed performances here are of the two unheroic 'character' roles. Domingo gives a delicious little portrait of Don Basilio in *Figaro* and as Pedrillo in *Entführung* sings the 'Into Battle' aria with superb contrasts as a miniature heroic piece. There are obvious thrills in Domingo's singing of Idomeneo's big aria, *Fuor del mar*, while the Emperor's brief solo in *La clemenza di Tito* suits his heroic style too. Domingo's sense of line never deserts him, but most of the great items here demand much gentler handling tonally. The welcome rarities are the aria from *La finta giardiniera*, and the tenor aria which Mozart added to his material from the *C minor Mass* for the oratorio, *Davidde penitente*, intending it for the first Belmonte.

Arias: *La clemenza di Tito: S'altro che lagrime. Così fan tutte: Ei parte . . . Sen . . . Per pietà. La finta giardiniera: Crudeli fermate . . . Ah dal pianto. Idomeneo: Se il padre perdei. Lucio Silla: Pupille amate. Il re pastore: L'amerò, sarò costante. Zaïde: Ruhe sanft, mein holdes Leben. Die Zauberflöte: Ach ich fühl's es ist verschwunden.*
*** Ph. Dig. 411 148-2 [id.]. Kiri Te Kanawa, LSO, C. Davis.

Kiri Te Kanawa's is one of the loveliest collections of Mozart arias on record, with the voice at its most ravishing and pure. One might object that Dame Kiri concentrates on soulful arias, ignoring more vigorous ones; but with stylish accompaniment and clear, atmospheric recording, beauty dominates all.

Arias: *Don Giovanni; Die Entführung aus dem Serail; Idomeneo; Le nozze di Figaro; Die Zauberflöte.*
(M) (***) EMI mono CDH7 63708-2. Elisabeth Schwarzkopf (with various orchestras & conductors, including John Pritchard).

Just how fine a Mozartian Schwarzkopf already was early in her career comes out in these 12 items, recorded between 1946 and 1952. The earliest are Konstanze's two arias from *Entführung*, and one of the curiosities is a lovely account of Pamina's *Ach ich fühl's*, recorded in English in 1948. The majority, including those from *Figaro* – Susanna's and Cherubino's arias well as the Countess's – are taken from a long-unavailable recital disc conducted by John Pritchard. Excellent transfers.

ANTHOLOGIES

'The Complete Mozart Edition': highlights. Excerpts from: *Horn concerto No. 4, K.495; Piano concerto No. 5 in D, K.175; Serenade No. 12 in C min., K.388; Symphony No. 29, K.201; Flute quartet No. 1 in D, K.285; Piano trio No. 4 in E, K.542; Allegretto in B flat for string quartet, K.App.68* (completed by Erik Smith); *String quartet No. 22 in B flat, K.589; Violin sonata No. 25 in F, K.377; Piano sonata No. 8 in A min., K.310; Exsultate Jubilate, K.165. Die kleine Spinnerin*. Excerpts from: *Requiem Mass, K.626; La clemenza di Tito; Così fan tutte; Don Giovanni; Die Entführung aus dem Serail; Le nozze di Figaro; Die Zauberflöte.*
(B) *** Ph. Dig./Analogue 426 735-2 [id.]. Various artists.

Issued as a sampler for Philips's Complete Mozart Edition and designed to tempt purchasers to explore further, this is a thoroughly worthwhile anthology in its own right. Rather modestly, Erik Smith suggests in the introduction that his selection cannot claim to represent the Edition very seriously, as twenty other items might be 'just as valid'. But he goes on to explain that 'In general the pieces have been chosen for the delight they can give out of context with their charm and melodiousness', and he notes two exceptions to this: Don Giovanni's dramatic final scene with the Commendatore, and an excerpt from the *Requiem* which includes the opening of the *Lacrymosa*, the last music Mozart wrote. The major novelty, previously unrecorded, is the *Allegretto for string quartet* in polonaise rhythm, of which Mozart completed only the first eight bars but then continued with 68 bars for the first violin alone. Smith reconstructed this himself, and very worthwhile it proves. The rest of the programme fits together uncannily well and includes artists of the calibre of the Beaux Arts Trio, Brendel, Grumiaux, Marriner and Uchida, plus many famous vocal soloists, making a fine and certainly a tempting entertainment. The recording is consistently real and refined in the best Philips manner, and the CD offers some 76 minutes of marvellous music. To make this issue even more of a bargain, the accompanying 204-page booklet offers an excellent potted biography, directly related to Mozart's output, with much about the social background against which his works were composed. Of course it also includes details of the 180 CDs which comprise the 45 volumes of the Edition, and it provides pictures and information about the principal performing artists. Finally, the Index gives a complete Köchel listing of Mozart's works, together with the volume number in which each appears.

'Fifty Years of Mozart singing on record': (i) *Concert arias;* Excerpts from: (ii) *Mass in C min., K.427;* (iii) *La clemenza di Tito;* (iv) *Così fan tutte;* (v) *Don Giovanni;* (vi) *Die Entführung aus*

dem Serail; (vii) *La finta giardiniera;* (viii) *Idomeneo;* (ix) *Le nozze di Figaro;* (x) *Il re pastore;* (xi) *Zaïde;* (xii) *Die Zauberflöte.*

(M) (***) EMI mono CMS7 63350-2 (4) [id.]. (i) Rethberg, Ginster, Francillo-Kaufmann; (ii) Berger; (iii) Kirkby-Lunn; (iv) V. Schwarz, Noni, Grümmer, Hahn, Kiurina, Hüsch, Souez, H. Nash; (v) Vanni-Marcoux, Scotti, Farrar, Battistini, Corsi, Leider, Roswaenge, D'Andrade, Pinza, Patti, Maurel, Renaud, Pernet, McCormack, Gadski, Kemp. Callas; (vi) Slezak, L. Weber, Tauber, Lehmann, Nemeth, Perras, Ivogün, Von Pataky, Hesch; (vii) Dux; (viii) Jurinac, Jadlowker; (ix) Stabile, Helletsgruber, Santley, Gobbi, Lemnitz, Feraldy, Schumann, Seinemeyer, Vallin, Rautawaara, Mildmay, Jokl, Ritter-Ciampi; (x) Gerhart; (xi) Seefried; (xi) Fugère; Wittrisch; Schiøtz, Gedda, Kurz, Erb, Kipnis, Galvany, Hempel, Sibiriakov, Frick, Destinn, Norena, Schöne, Kunz.

This is an astonishing treasury of singing, recorded over the first half of the twentieth century. It begins with Mariano Stabile's resonant 1928 account of Figaro's *Se vuol ballare*, snail-like by today's standards, while Sir Charles Santley in *Non piu andrai* a few tracks later is both old-sounding and slow. The stylistic balance is then corrected in Tito Gobbi's magnificently characterful 1950 recording of that same aria. Astonishment lies less in early stylistic enormities than in the wonderful and consistent purity of vocal production, with wobbles – so prevalent today – virtually non-existent. That is partly the result of the shrewd and obviously loving choice of items, which includes not only celebrated marvels like John McCormack's 1916 account of Don Ottavio's *Il mio tesoro* (breaking all records for breath control, and stylistically surprising for including an appoggiatura), but many rarities. The short-lived Meta Seinemeyer, glorious in the Countess's first aria, Germaine Feraldy, virtually unknown, a charming Cherubino, Johanna Gadski formidably incisive in Donna Anna's *Mi tradi*, Frieda Hempel incomparable in the Queen of the Night's second aria – all these and many dozens of others make for compulsive listening, with transfers generally excellent. There are far more women singers represented than men, and a high proportion of early recordings are done in languages other than the original; but no lover of fine singing should miss this feast. The arias are gathered together under each opera, with items from non-operatic sources grouped at the end of each disc. Helpfully, duplicate versions of the same aria are put together irrespective of date of recording, and highly informative notes are provided on all the singers.

Mundy, William (*c.* 1529–*c.* 1591)

Vox Patris caelestis.

*** Gimell CDGIM 339 [id.]. Tallis Scholars, Phillips – ALLEGRI: *Miserere;* PALESTRINA: *Missa Papae Marcelli.* ***

Mundy's *Vox Patris caelestis* was written during the short reign of Queen Mary (1553–8). The work is structured in nine sections in groups of three, the last of each group being climactic and featuring the whole choir, with solo embroidery. Yet the music flows continuously, like a great river, and the complex vocal writing creates the most spectacular effects, with the trebles soaring up and shining out over the underlying cantilena. The Tallis Scholars give an account which balances linear clarity with considerable power. The recording is first class and the digital remastering for CD improves the focus further.

Mussorgsky, Modest (1839–81)

Night on the bare mountain (original version).

(M) *** Ph. 420 898-2 [id.]. LPO, Lloyd-Jones – RIMSKY-KORSAKOV: *Scheherazade.* ***

Although it uses some of Mussorgsky's basic material, the piece we know as *Night on the bare mountain* is much more the work of Rimsky-Korsakov, who added much music of his own. The original has undoubted power and fascination, but its construction is considerably less polished. David Lloyd-Jones's performance makes a good case for it, bringing out all the crude force of its Satanic vision. The new digital transfer is also first class, and this makes an exciting bonus for an outstanding version of Rimsky-Korsakov's *Scheherazade.*

Night on the bare mountain (orch. Rimsky-Korsakov).
(M) *** Sony SBK 46329; *40-46329* [id.]. Phd. O, Ormandy – BERLIOZ: *Symphonie fantastique* **; DUKAS: *L'apprenti sorcier.* ***
(M) *** Mercury 432 004-2 [id.]. LSO, Dorati – PROKOFIEV: *Romeo and Juliet suites.* ***
(M) **(*) Decca Dig. 430 700-2; *430 700-4* [id.]. Montreal SO, Dutoit – RIMSKY-KORSAKOV: *Capriccio espagnol*; TCHAIKOVSKY: *1812* etc. **(*)

Night on the bare mountain; Khovanshchina: Prelude (both arr. Rimsky-Korsakov).
(B) *** Decca 417 689-2; *417 689-4*. LSO, Solti – BORODIN: *Prince Igor: Overture and Polovtsian dances;* GLINKA: *Russlan overture.* ***

Solti's *Night on the bare mountain* can stand up to all competition in its vintage 1967 recording with its fine amplitude and great brilliance. This remains one of Solti's finest analogue collections, offering also the highly atmospheric *Khovanshchina Prelude*, which is beautifully played.

With virtuoso playing from the Philadelphia Orchestra, Ormandy's 1967 recording has plenty of thrills, with its shrieking banshees and darkly sonorous brass. As in the coupled *Sorcerer's apprentice* of Dukas, the potent imagery of Walt Disney's *Fantasia* springs readily to mind.

Dorati's fine 1960 account of *Night on the bare mountain* comes as an encore for Skrowaczewski's outstanding Prokofiev, and it is interesting at the end of *Romeo and Juliet* to note the subtle shift of acoustic from the Minneapolis auditorium to Wembley Town Hall.

Dutoit's *Night on the bare mountain* is strong and biting, but the adrenalin does not flow as grippingly as in, say, Ormandy's version. The brilliant, atmospheric recording is naturally balanced, with the bloom characteristic of the Montreal sound.

Night on the bare mountain; Khovanshchina: Prelude (both arr. Rimsky-Korsakov); *Pictures at an exhibition* (orch. Ravel).
**(*) Decca Dig. 417 299-2 [id.]. Montreal SO, Dutoit – RIMSKY-KORSAKOV: *Russian Easter festival overture.* **(*)

Dutoit's *Khovanshchina prelude*, with its haunting evocation of dawn over the Moscow River, has sounded more magical in other hands. *A Night on the bare mountain* is strong and biting, but again the playing does not generate the power of, say, Solti's version. Dutoit's *Pictures* have each movement strongly characterized and there is a sense of fun in the scherzando movements. But overall this is less involving than with Karajan, and the brilliant recording is not as sumptuous as some other versions, although it has the bloom characteristic of the Montreal sound.

Night on the bare mountain (original version); *Khovanshchina: Prelude* (orch. Rimsky-Korsakov); *Pictures at an exhibition* (orch. Ravel).
*** Collins EC 1004-2 [id.]. LSO, Kaspryzk.

The LSO performance of the *Pictures* directed by Jacek Kaspryzk is superbly recorded in London's Henry Wood Hall, rivalling the famous Telarc version in its weight and brilliance and its ripe treatment of the orchestral brass: the sound is rather less sumptuous in the spectacular closing *Great Gate of Kiev* but is more sharply focused. The performance, led onwards convincingly by the various Promenades, is strongly characterized, with the nostalgia inherent in *The old castle* carried on to the portrait of the ox-wagon, which yet does not lose its juggernaut power. There is much orchestral virtuosity, exhilarating in *The Tuileries* and in the bustle of the *Limoges market place*, and the brass has subtlety as well as bite in *The hut on fowl's legs*, yet produces a powerful sonority for the *Catacombs* sequence. The spacious closing apotheosis has plenty of weight and power. Rimsky-Korsakov's glowing scoring of the beautiful *Khovanshchina Prelude* is also made radiant by fine orchestral playing, though perhaps ideally Kaspryzk could have moved the music on a little more firmly. He finds plenty of gusto, however, in the bizarre wildness of Mussorgsky's original draft for *Night on the bare mountain* (without the serene closing section).

(i) *Night on the bare mountain* (arr. Rimsky-Korsakov); (ii) *Pictures at an exhibition* (orch. Ravel).
*** DG Dig. 429 785-2; *429 785-4* [id.]. NYPO, Sinopoli – RAVEL: *Valses nobles et sentimentales.* **(*)
*** Telarc Dig. CD 80042 [id.]. Cleveland O, Maazel.
(B) *** DG Compact Classics 413 153-2 (2); *413 153-4* [id.]. (i) Boston Pops O, Fiedler; (ii)

Chicago SO, Giulini – TCHAIKOVSKY: *1812* etc. **(*) (CD only: BORODIN: *In the Steppes of central Asia* **).
(BB) **(*) Naxos 8.550051 [id.]. Slovak PO, Nazareth – BORODIN: *In the Steppes of Central Asia* etc. **(*)

Sinopoli's electrifying New York recording of Mussorgsky's *Pictures at an exhibition* not only heads the list of modern digital versions but also it again displays the New York Philharmonic as one of the world's great orchestras, performing with a epic virtuosity and panache that recall the Bernstein era of the 1960s. The playing of violins and woodwind alike is full of sophisticated touches, so well demonstrated by their colourful, brilliant articulation in *Tuileries Gardens* and *Limoges*, the wittily piquant portrayal of the *Unhatched chicks*, and the firm, resonant line of the lower strings in *Samuel Goldenberg and Schmuyle*. But it is the brass that one rememembers most, from the richly sonorous opening *Promenade*, through the ferocious bite and subtle grotesquerie of *Gnomus*, the bleating trumpet of *Schmuyle*, the stabbing sforzandos at the opening of *Catacombs*, to the malignantly forceful rhythms of *The hut on fowl's legs*, with the playing of the trombones and tuba often assuming an unusual yet obviously calculated dominance of the texture. The finale combines power with dignified splendour, and the bells toll out from their tower to emphasize the Byzantine character of Hartmann's picture of the *Kiev Gate*. *A Night on the bare mountain* is comparably vibrant, with the Rimskian fanfares particularly vivid and the closing pages full of Russian nostalgia. The splendid digital recording, made in New York's Manhattan Center, has breadth and weight, and its fullness comes with a believable overall perspective and excellent internal definition.

The quality of the Telarc Cleveland recording is apparent at the very opening of *Night on the bare mountain* in the richly sonorous presentation of the deep brass and the sparkling yet unexaggerated percussion. With the Cleveland Orchestra on top form, the *Pictures* are strongly characterized; this may not be the subtlest reading available, but each of Mussorgsky's cameos comes vividly to life. The chattering children in the Tuileries are matched in presence by the delightfully pointed portrayal of the cheeping chicks, and if the ox-wagon (*Bydlo*) develops a climax potent enough to suggest a juggernaut, the similarly sumptuous brass in the *Catacombs* sequence cannot be counted as in any way overdramatized. After a vibrantly rhythmic *Baba-Yaga*, strong in fantastic menace, the closing *Great Gate of Kiev* is overwhelmingly spacious in conception and quite riveting as sheer sound, with the richness and amplitude of the brass which make the work's final climax unforgettable. Unfortunately the *Pictures* are not cued separately.

It is interesting that Giulini's memorably successful account of the *Pictures* should use the Chicago orchestra, thus repeating Reiner's success of the early days of stereo. The modern recording, however, is noticeably more refined and detailed, with brilliant percussive effects (a superb bass drum in *The hut on fowl's legs*). With superlative orchestral playing and strong characterization, this is highly recommendable; the new transfer is outstandingly vivid and full-bodied in both CD and tape formats. It is here paired with an excitingly volatile account of *Night on the bare mountain*, directed by Fiedler. Both sound well on this bargain-price Compact Classics issue, generously coupled with Tchaikovsky. The pair of CDs also includes a romantically atmospheric performance of Borodin's *In the Steppes of Central Asia*, very well played by the Dresden State Orchestra under Kurt Sanderling, if with the violins sounding a little undernourished in the CD transfer. Mussorgsky's *Pictures* are also available on a single CD, coupled with Ravel (see below).

The super-baragain Naxos coupling is vividly played and recorded and is well worth its modest price. *A night on the bare mountain* is played flexibly, yet does not lack excitement. The *Pictures*, too, have plenty of character. The climax of *Bydlo* is dramatically enhanced by a fortissimo contribution from the timpanist, and the detail throughout is well observed, from the bleating Schmuyle to the chirping chicks. *Tuileries* and *Limoges* bring lightly etched orchestral bravura, while the closing picture of the Kiev Gate has architectural grandeur and a sense of majesty. Enjoyable, if lacking the last touch of individuality.

(i) *Night on the bare mountain* (arr. Rimsky-Korsakov); *Pictures at an exhibition* (arr. Funtek). (ii) *Songs and dances of death* (arr. Aho).
*** BIS Dig. CD 325 [id.]. (i) Finnish RSO, (i) Leif Segerstam; (ii) Järvi, with Talvela.

This fascinating CD offers an orchestration by Leo Funtek, made in the same year as Ravel's (1922); it is especially fascinating for the way the different uses of colour change the character of some of Victor Hartman's paintings: the use of a cor anglais in *The old castle*, for instance, or the soft-grained wind scoring which makes the portrait of *Samuel Goldenberg and Schmuyle* more sympathetic, if also blander. The performances by the Finnish Radio Orchestra under Leif Segerstam both of this and of the familiar Rimsky *Night on the bare mountain* are spontaneously presented and very well recorded. The extra item is no less valuable: an intense, darkly Russian account of the *Songs and dances of death* from Martti Talvela with the orchestral accompaniment plangently scored by Kalevi Aho.

Pictures at an exhibition (orch. Ravel).
(B) *** DG 429 162-2; *429 162-4* [id.]. BPO, Karajan – STRAVINSKY: *Rite of spring.* ***
*** Sony Dig. SK 45935 [id.]; *40-45935*. BPO, Giulini – STRAVINSKY: *Firebird suite.* **(*)
*** DG Dig. 423 901-2 [id.]. LSO, Abbado – STRAVINSKY: *Petrushka.* ***
(M) *** DG 415 844-2 [id.]. Chicago SO, Giulini – RAVEL: *Ma mère l'Oye; Rapsodie espagnole.* ***
(M) *** EMI Dig. CDM7 64516-2 [id.]; *EG 764516-4*. Phd. O, Muti – STRAVINSKY: *Rite of spring.* ***
(*) DG Dig. 413 588-2 [id.]. BPO, Karajan – RAVEL: *Boléro; Rapsodie espagnole.* *
(B) *** EMI CDZ7 62860-2 [id.]. Philh. O, Karajan – LISZT: *Hungarian rhapsody No. 2* etc. ***
(M) *** Decca Dig. 417 754-2 [id.]. Chicago SO, Solti – BARTÓK: *Concerto for orchestra.* ***
(M) (**) BMG/RCA mono GD 60287 [60287-2-RG]. NBC SO, Toscanini – ELGAR: *Enigma variations.* (***)

Pictures from an exhibition (orch. Ravel); *Khovanshchina: Prelude; Persian dance; Prince Galitsin's departure into exile.*
**(*) Erato/Warner Dig. 2292 45596-2 [id.]. Rotterdam PO, James Conlon.

Karajan's 1966 record stands out. It is undoubtedly a great performance, tingling with electricity from the opening Promenade to the spaciously conceived finale, *The Great Gate of Kiev*, which has real splendour. Other high points are the ominously powerful climax of *Bydlo* as the Polish ox-wagon lumbers into view very weightily, and the venomously pungent bite of the brass – expansively recorded – in the sinister *Catacombs* sequence, which is given a bizarre majesty. Detail is consistently pointed with the greatest imagination, not only in the lighter moments, but for instance in *The hut on fowl's legs*, where the tuba articulation is sharp and rhythmically buoyant. Throughout, the glorious orchestral playing, and especially the brass sonorities, ensnare the ear; even when Karajan is relatively restrained, as in the nostalgic melancholy of *The old castle*, the underlying tension remains. The remastered analogue recording still sounds pretty marvellous.

Giulini's newest account of Mussorgsky's *Pictures* can also be counted among the finest recent versions. Recorded in the Jesus Christus Kirche, Berlin, the sound is rich and spacious, the orchestral playing superb. The reading has a pervading sense of nostalgia which haunts the delicate portrayal of *The old castle* and even makes the wheedling interchange between the two Polish Jews more sympathetic than usual. In the lighter pieces the scherzando element brings a sparkling contrast, with the unhatched chicks cheeping piquantly, and there is sonorous solemnity for the *Catacombs* sequence. A powerful and weighty *Baba Yaga*, yet with the bizarre element retained in the subtle rhythmic pointing of the middle section, leads naturally to a majestic finale, with the Berlin brass full-bloodedly resplendent, and the tam-tam flashing vividly at the climax.

Abbado takes a straighter, more direct view of Mussorgsky's fanciful series of pictures than usual, less consciously expressive, relying above all on instrumental virtuosity and the dazzling tonal contrasts of Ravel's orchestration. He is helped by the translucent and naturally balanced digital recording; indeed, the sound is first class, making great impact at climaxes yet also extremely refined, as in the delicate portrayal of the unhatched chicks. Abbado's speeds tend to be extreme, with both this and *Tuileries* taken very fast and light, while *Bydlo* and *The Great Gate of Kiev* are slow and weighty. This performance is now recoupled with an equally distinguished and spectacularly recorded account of *Petrushka*.

Giulini's 1976 Chicago recording had always been among the front runners. He is generally more relaxed and often more wayward than Karajan, but this is still a splendid performance and the finale generates more tension than Karajan's most recent, digital version, though it is not as overpowering as the earlier, analogue recording. Besides the generous Ravel couplings, there is an alternative Russian programme on Compact Classics – see above.

Muti's reading, given the excellence of its recorded sound, more than holds its own, although the balance is forward and perhaps not all listeners will respond to the brass timbres at the opening. The lower strings in *Samuel Goldenberg and Schmuyle* have extraordinary body and presence, and *Baba-Yaga* has an unsurpassed virtuosity and attack, as well as being of a high standard as a recording. The coupling is no less thrilling. This can be recommended even to those readers who have not always responded to later records from this conductor.

Karajan's 1987 record is also very impressive, very similar in many ways to the earlier account, again with superb Berlin Philharmonic playing and the weight of the climaxes contrasting with the wit of the *Tuileries* and the exhilaration of *The Market at Limoges*. Where the newest version is a shade disappointing, compared with the old, is in the finale. Here Karajan is as spacious as before but, from the beginning, is a little slack when he fails to detach the massive chords, and the culminating apotheosis falls a little short in physical excitement. The digital sound is very wide-ranging, even if the sense of presence is less keen than in his 1960s recording.

Karajan's Philharmonia recording of Mussorgsky's *Pictures* was made in the Kingsway Hall in 1955–6. There is extraordinary clarity and projection, yet no lack of body and ambience, and it is matched by the brilliantly polished detail of the orchestral playing – the Philharmonia offering breathtaking standards of ensemble and bite. The presentation of each picture is outstandingly strong, and *The Great Gate of Kiev* brings a frisson-creating climax of great breadth and splendour, achieved as much by Karajan's dignified pacing as by the spread of the sound.

Solti's performance is fiercely brilliant rather than atmospheric or evocative. He treats Ravel's orchestration as a virtuoso challenge, and with larger-than-life digital recording it undoubtedly has demonstration qualities, and the transparency of texture, given the forward balance, provides quite startling clarity. Now very generously recoupled at mid-price with Solti's outstanding version of Bartók's *Concerto for orchestra*, it makes a formidable bargain.

Conlon uses Ravel's orchestration but makes a few changes in the light of studying Mussorgsky's piano manuscript (to which Ravel had no direct access). The changes are only slightly more than cosmetic, although two extra bars have been added effectively to the coda of the *Ballet of the unhatched chicks* and two – added by Ravel – have been removed from *Baba-Yaga*. But the most striking change is with the vehement performance of *Bydlo* at one unrelenting dynamic level, which may be what Mussorgsky wrote, but in practice works less well than Ravel's opening crescendo. Otherwise this is a strongly characterized, very well played performance, which could have clearer detail, for the acoustic of Rotterdam's empty De Doelen Concert Hall is very resonant. However the closing *Great Gate of Kiev* has much breadth and dignity, even if the tam tam strokes at the end are clouded by the reverberation. The couplings are what makes this record really distinctive, excerpts from *Khovantschina*, orchestrated by Shostakovich, who (unlike Rimsky-Korsakov) leaves Mussorgsky's music untouched. The wonderfully evocative *Prelude* has never sounded more beautiful than here.

Toscanini was no colourist, and his regimented view of the exotic Mussorgsky–Ravel score is at its least sympathetic in the opening statement of the opening *Promenade*, not just rigidly metrical but made the coarser by the cornet-like trumpet tone. Many of the individual movements are done with greater understanding – for example, the *Ballet of the unhatched chicks* – but too often Toscanini's lack of sympathy undermines the character of this rich score. Clean, bright transfer.

(i) *Pictures at an exhibition* (orch. Ravel); (ii) *Pictures at an exhibition* (original piano version).
(M) *** Ph. 420 708-2. (i) Rotterdam PO, Edo de Waart; (ii) Misha Dichter.

Those seeking the natural pairing of the original piano version of Mussorgsky's *Pictures* with Ravel's orchestration will hardly better this analogue Philips CD. The Rotterdam orchestra play splendidly throughout, and Edo de Waart's performance has a natural, spontaneous momentum, with each picture aptly characterized and the final climax admirably paced and excitingly powerful. The 1975 recording is rather resonant, but detail comes through well enough. The surprise here, however, is Misha Dichter's outstanding performance of the original piano score, among the finest on record. Each separate picture is telling and he perceptively varies the mood of each Promenade to provide an appropriate link. After a riveting account of *Baba-Yaga*, demonstrating great keyboard flair, the closing *Great Gate of Kiev* is overwhelmingly powerful, and the piano's sonority is splendidly caught by the Philips recording.

Pictures at an exhibition (orch. Gortchakov).
** Teldec/Warner Dig. 2292 44941-2 [id.]. LPO, Kurt Masur (with PROKOFIEV: *Symphony No. 1* **).

The most strikingly individual picture in the Gortchakov orchestration is the *Ballet of the unhatched chicks*, which is delightfully worthy of Liadov, especially its piquant middle section. *The old castle* features a muted trumpet rather than a saxophone, and *Samuel Goldberg and Schmuyle* mixes up cor anglais, trumpet and strings. *Bydlo* (as with James Conlon's Rotterdam performance of Ravel's version) begins loudly and forcefully, here using trombones. Elsewhere the scoring is sumptuous, with the strings used liberally, especially in the Promenades, and climaxes are well splashed with percussion in *Gnomus* and the *Catacombes* sequence. In *The Great Gate of Kiev* Gortchakov gives the monks' chorale to the brass, reducing the element of dynamic contrast. The final climax is opulent enough, but overall this record serves only to confirm the superiority of the Ravel score. The orchestral playing is first class both in the Mussorgsky and in Prokofiev's *Classical Symphony*, which makes an agreeable if not generous makeweight.

Pictures at an exhibition: (i) orch. Ashkenazy; (ii) original piano version.
**(*) Decca Dig. 414 386-2 [id.]. (i) Philh. O, Ashkenazy; (ii) Ashkenazy (piano).

A side-by-side comparison between Mussorgsky's original piano score and the orchestral version is always instructive; but here the orchestration is Ashkenazy's own, which he made after finding dissatisfaction with Ravel's transcription. His arrangement concentrates on a broader orchestral tapestry – helped by the richness of the Kingsway Hall acoustic – and he does not attempt to match Ravel in subtlety of detail or precision of effect. The character of the pictures is not always very individual, although Ashkenazy finds plenty of Russian feeling in the music itself. The recording is brightly opulent rather than glittering. Ashkenazy's digital solo account of the *Pictures* does not differ in its essentials from his earlier, analogue recording. It is distinguished by spontaneity and poetic feeling but lacks something of the extrovert flair with which pianists like Richter or Berman can make one forget all about the orchestra. The piano focus is clear with fine presence, if not quite natural in balance.

Pictures at an exhibition (original piano version).
❀ *** Virgin Dig. VC7 91169-2; *VC7 91169-4* [id.]. Mikhail Pletnev – TCHAIKOVSKY: *Sleeping Beauty*: excerpts. *** ❀
(M) *** DG 431 170-2; *431 170-4*. Lazar Berman – PROKOFIEV: *Romeo and Juliet*. ***
(*) Collins Dig. 1276-2; *1276-4* [id.]. Vladimir Ovchinikov – SHOSTAKOVICH: *Piano concerto No. 1*. *
(M) (***) Ph. mono 420 774-2. Sviatoslav Richter (with *Recital* (***))
*(*) DG Dig. 431 972-2 [id.]. Nicolas Economou – SCHUMANN: *Kreisleriana*. **

Pictures at an exhibition; 5 Souvenirs d'enfance; The Seamstress.
**(*) Nuova Era Dig. 6826 [id.]. Michele Campanella – BALAKIREV: *Berceuse* etc. **(*)

Pictures at an exhibition (piano version, ed. Horowitz); *Sunless: By the water.*
(M) *** BMG/RCA GD 60449; *GK 60449* [60449-2-RG]. Vladimir Horowitz – TCHAIKOVSKY: *Piano concerto No. 1*. (***)

Some of the finest artists play Mussorgsky's *Pictures* as you can only imagine them in your mind's ear; others, like Horowitz, Richter and Pletnev, play them as you could never imagine them! There are remarkable effects of colour and of pedalling in Pletnev's performance – easily the most commanding to have appeared since Richter and, one is tempted to say, a re-creation rather than a performance. Pletnev does not hesitate to modify the odd letter of the score in order to come closer to its spirit. *The Ballet of the unhatched chicks* has great wit and the *Great Gate of Kiev* is extraordinarily rich in colour. An altogether outstanding issue.

Horowitz's famous 1951 recording, made at a live performance at Carnegie Hall, is as thrilling as it is perceptive. Mussorgsky's darker colours are admirably caught (and this applies also in the pianist's own arrangement of the final song from the *Sunless* cycle, which is played as a sombre encore). The rhythmic angularity, forcefully accented, projects *Bydlo* potently and the lighter scherzando evocations are dazzlingly articulated. But it is the closing pictures which are especially powerful, the pungent *Baba-Yaga*, and the spectacular *Great Gate of Kiev*, where Horowitz has embroidered the final climax to add to its pianistic resplendency. The piano image is bold and clear, somewhat hard but not lacking fullness.

Like Horowitz, Lazar Berman brings an uncompromisingly fast pacing to the opening *Promenade*. One can picture him striding brusquely round the exhibition, hands behind his back. But when he stops, he is strongly involved in each picture, and his playing makes a very direct communication with its arresting power and atmosphere, notably so in *Bydlo*, *Catacombs* and *Cum mortuis*, although the *Ballet of the unhatched chicks* finds him more concerned with articulation (the playing is superb) than with humorous evocation. The *Great Gate of Kiev* makes a riveting climax. The CD transfer brings an impressively realistic piano image.

The Philips reissue offers Sviatoslav Richter's 1958 Sofia recital. The mono recording has been remastered using this company's NoNoise digital background reduction system, but alas this cannot suppress the audience's bronchial afflictions, and a troublesome tape roar also remains. Nevertheless, the magnetism of Richter's playing comes over and his enormously wide dynamic range brings a riveting final climax, even if, with the piano backwardly positioned, some of the pianissimo playing is not too cleanly focused. Besides the Mussorgsky, the recital offers a generous programme, including Schubert *Impromptus* and a *Moment musical*, the Chopin *Étude in E*, Op. 10, No. 3, two Liszt *Valses oubliées* and excerpts from the *Transcendental studies*, all readily demonstrating the Richter magic in spite of indifferent sound.

In his set of the *Pictures*, the Italian pianist Michele Campanella is more logically coupled than many (indeed, most) rivals. The five *Souvenirs d'enfance* of 1865 and *The Seamstress*, written six years laters, are rarities on CD, the latter is not otherwise available. The *Souvenirs d'enfance* is a particularly engaging and affecting set, and Campanella plays it with real feeling. The *Pictures* themselves have an imposing breadth and if they are not as magisterial as Richter, or as full of imaginative colours as Pletnev, they are a cut above some of the recent versions to have reached CD. They want only the last ounce of spontaneous feeling, not always easy to realize in familiar repertoire and under studio conditions. Impressive all the same and very well recorded too.

Vladimir Ovchinikov proves to be a highly cultured guide to this exhibition and he produces a fine reading. The sound is always beautifully rounded and dynamic shadings are most subtle and well thought out. He is not a big barn-storming virtuoso player to put alongside Richter or Horowitz but his performance is most musicianly. Nor does his account have the character or originality of Pletnev's recent (and rather outsize) reading, but its merits are far from inconsiderable and the recording is altogether first class.

Nicolas Economou is an imaginative artist whose remarkable powers are seen to advantage in much virtuoso repertoire. He is not at his best here. Many of his *Pictures* are eccentric; in many instances rushed (the Polish oxwagon of *Bydlo* is in danger of prosecution for speeding) and in others (such as the *Tuileries* movement) touched by routine. Of course there are some good things but not enough of them to make it anywhere near a front-runner. The DG piano sound is rather close and not particularly pleasing.

Pictures at an exhibition (arr. for brass by Elgar Howarth).
(M) *** Decca 425 022-2; *425 022-4* [id.]. Philip Jones Brass Ens., Howarth – SAINT-SAËNS: *Carnival of the animals.* **

Pictures at an exhibition (arr. Howarth); *St John's Night on the bare mountain* (arr. Alan Wiltshire).
*** Collins Dig. 1227-2; *1227-4* [id.]. The Wallace Collection, John Wallace (with KHACHATURIAN: *Spartacus: Adagio of Spartacus and Phrygia* (arr. John Miller) **).

There is no reason why Mussorgsky's famous piano work should not be transcribed for brass as effectively as for a full symphony orchestra, and Elgar Howarth's imaginatively inspired arrangement fully justifies the experiment. There is never any suggestion of limited colour; indeed, in the pioneering 1977 Philip Jones recording (originally Argo), the pictures of the marketplace at Limoges and of the unhatched chicks have great pictorial vividness, and the evocation of the dead (in *Catacombs*) has an almost cinematic element of fantasy. The *Great Gate of Kiev* is as thrilling here as in many orchestral recordings, and the splendidly rich and sonorous Kingsway Hall recording remains in the demonstration bracket in its Decca CD format. If the Saint-Saëns coupling is rather less successful in transcription, that is no fault either of players or of engineers.

The Collins version by the John Wallace Collection brings more modern, digital recording, and the slightly drier acoustics of the Blackheath Concert Hall. Combined with the highly dramatic characterization of the playing, the effect is to increase the brilliance and pungency of the more grotesque portrayals; *Gnomus* and *The hut on fowl's legs* are both given considerable malignant force, *Bydlo* approaches menacingly, and the *Catacombs* sequence is even more powerfully sinister than with Philip Jones. The cheeping chicks, too, are more piquantly vociferous than usual, and the *Great Gate of Kiev* has striking power and impact. What makes this record a collector's item is the inclusion of Alan Wiltshire's dazzling brass arrangement of Mussorgsky's own rather crude original version of what we know as *Night on the bare mountain*.

Wiltshire and Wallace create weirdly barbarous climaxes and some ear-tickling pianissimo effects with muted brass and xylophone, so that the starkness of Mussorgsky's inspiration comes over compellingly. The performance brings much instrumental bravura, but it concentrates on drama and colouristic detail at the expense somewhat of structural cohesion. The famous *Spartacus Adagio*, which is placed between the two Mussorgsky works, has a thrilling climax, but here one misses the string textures, despite the eloquence of the performance.

The Complete Songs.
❀ (M) (***) EMI mono CHS7 63025-2 (3) [Ang. CHS 63025]. Boris Christoff, Alexandre Labinsky, Gerald Moore, French R. & TV O, Georges Tzipine.

Boris Christoff originally recorded these songs in 1958; they then appeared in a four-LP mono set with a handsome book, generously illustrated with plates and music examples, giving the texts in Russian, French, Italian and English, and with copious notes on each of the 63 songs. Naturally the documentation cannot be so extensive in the CD format – but, on the other hand, one has the infinitely greater ease of access that the new technology offers. The Mussorgsky songs constitute a complete world in themselves, and they cast a strong spell: their range is enormous and their insight into the human condition deep. Christoff was at the height of his vocal powers when he made the set with Alexandre Labinsky, his accompanist in most of the songs; and its return to circulation cannot be too warmly welcomed. This was the first complete survey, and it still remains the only one.

OPERA

Boris Godunov (original version; complete).
**(*) Ph. 412 281-2 (3) [id.]. Vedernikov, Arkhipova, Koroleva, Shkolnikova, Sokólov, USSR TV and R. Ch. and SO, Fedoseyev.
** Sony Dig. S3K 45763 (3) [id.]. Ghiaurov, Mineva, Svetlev, Martinovich, Frank, Ghiuselev, Popov, Sofia Nat. O Ch., Sofia Festival O, Tchakarov.

Fedoseyev conducts a powerful performance of Mussorgsky's masterpiece in its original scoring, using the composer's own 1872 revision, as near an 'authentic' solution as one can get with a problematic score that never reached definitive form. The earthy strength of the music comes over superbly. Ideally for records, one needs a firmer singer than the mature Vedernikov as Boris, but this is a searingly intense performance which rises commandingly to the big dramatic moments, conveying the Tsar's neurotic tensions chillingly. Arkhipova is also too mature for the role of Marina, but equally her musical imagination is most convincing. The rest of the cast is a mixed bag, with some magnificent Russian basses but a few disappointing contributions, as from the whining tenor, Vladislav Piavko, as the Pretender. Though the recording was made over a period of years, the sound is full and satisfying, if not always ideally balanced.

Though Ghiaurov gives a magnificent performance as Boris, as fine in its way as his recording for Karajan of 20 years earlier, and Tchakarov brings out the reflective side of the score well, the whole recording seriously lacks power. It is partly a question of backward orchestral and choral balance, partly a lack of bite in the actual performance. Without the necessary earthy quality the score fails to make its full impact. The intensity of Boris's big monologues and above all the death scene, with Ghiaurov singing beautifully, rarely snarling in sing-speech, hardly compensates for such a shortcoming. Among the others Stefka Mineva is typically fruity as Marina, with a pronounced vibrato, and Michail Svetlev as the Pretender, Grigori, produces characteristic Slavonic sound too with his clean, tight-toned tenor. Among the basses Nicola Ghiuselev is magnificent as Pimen, but Dimiter Petkov is a disappointing, unsteady Varlaam. As on the Philips set the 'original' 1872 text is used, but with the 1869 St Basil's Scene provided as a supplement before the death scene. The definitive Kromy Forest scene then comes after that, ending again with the Simpleton. Solo voices come over well, and though the orchestra sounds too distant, the recording allows fine clarity.

Boris Godunov (arr. Rimsky-Korsakov).
*** Decca 411 862-2 (3) [id.]. Ghiaurov, Vishnevskaya, Spiess, Maslennikov, Talvela, V. Boys' Ch., Sofia R. Ch., V. State Op. Ch., VPO, Karajan.

If Ghiaurov in the title-role lacks some of the dramatic intensity of Christoff on the EMI set (CDS7 47993-8 [Ang. CDCC 47993]), Karajan's superbly controlled Decca version, technically outstanding, comes far nearer than previous recordings to conveying the rugged greatness of Mussorgsky's masterpiece. Only the Coronation scene lacks something of the weight and momentum one ideally wants. Vishnevskaya is far less appealing than the lovely non-Slavonic Marina of Evelyn Lear on EMI, but overall this Decca set has much more to offer.

Khovanshchina (complete).
*** DG Dig. 429 758-2 (3) [id.]. Lipovšek, Burchuladze, Atlantov, Haugland, Borowska, Kotscherga, Popov, V. State Op. Ch. & O, Abbado.
**(*) Ph. Dig. 437 147-2 (3) [id.]. Minjelkiev, Galusin, Steblianko, Ohotnikov, Borodina, Kirov Theatre Ch. & O, Gergiev.

Abbado's live recording brings the most vivid account of this epic Russian opera yet on disc, giving cohesion to a sequence of scenes even more episodic than those in *Boris Godunov*. With the text left incomplete and in a fragmentary state at the composer's death, there is no clear answer to the work's textual problems, but Abbado's solution is more satisfying than any other: he uses the Shostakovich orchestration (with some cuts), darker and harmonically far more faithful than the old Rimsky-Korsakov version, now regarded as a travesty by Mussorgskians. Yet Abbado rejects the triumphant ending of the Shostakovich edition and follows instead the orchestration that Stravinsky did for Diaghilev in 1913 of the original subdued ending as Mussorgsky himself conceived it. When the tragic fate of the Old Believers, immolating themselves for their faith, brings the deepest and most affecting emotions of the whole opera, that close, touching in its tenderness, is far more apt. One is left sharing the pain of their stoic self-sacrifice, instead of being brought back to automatic praise of Mother Russia. Lipovšek's glorious singing as Marfa, the Old Believer with whom one most closely identifies, sets the seal on the whole performance. Aage Haugland is a rock-like Ivan Khovansky and, though Burchuladze is no longer as steady of tone as he was, he makes a noble Dosifei. Stage noises sometimes intrude and voices are sometimes set back, but this remains a magnificent achievement.

Though Gergiev's Kirov version is less compelling than Abbado's live Vienna recording, it provides a viable alternative, broader and more rugged, if less persuasive. Gergiev does not disguise the squareness of much of the writing, and such a number as the *Dance of the Persian slave-girls* in Act IV lacks the flair and brilliance of Abbado. Unlike either Abbado or Tchakorov on Sony, Gergiev stays faithful to the Shostakovich version of the score throughout, notably at the very end. There he simply adds a loud repetition of the *Old Believer's chorale* on unison brass, a less subtle ending than either Abbado's fascinating Stravinsky version or Tchakarov's reference back to the *Dawn on the Moscow River prelude*. The soloists from the Kirov may not have such starry names as those on Abbado's version, but they make a fine, consistent team with Olga Borodina magnificent as Marfa, both rich and firm. Nikolai Ohotnikov with his dark bass is splendidly firm too as Dosifei, and though Bulat Minjelkiev as Ivan Khovansky has a pronounced vibrato, its rapidity prevents it from developing into a wobble. The two tenors are very well contrasted – Vladimir Galusin as Andrei lighter and brighter than the weighty Alexei Steblianko as Golitsyn.

Sorochinsky Fair (opera) complete.
*** Olympia OCD 114 A/B (2) [id.]. Matorin, Mishchevsky, Voinarovsky, Klenov, Temichev, Chernikh, Zhakharenko, Stanislavsky Theatre Ch. & O, Esipov – BORODIN: *Petite suite*. ***

This first complete recording of Mussorgsky's unfinished opera uses the edition, prepared by Vissarion Shebalin, in the colourful and vigorous performance by the company of the Stanislavsky Theatre in Moscow. Though the most striking passage, *St John's Night* at the beginning of Act III, is the original choral version of what Rimsky-Korsakov turned into *Night on the bare mountain*, this is not at all a grim piece but a folk-comedy that is full of fun, as charming and attractive as any, its score spiced with characteristically individual Mussorgskian progressions. In this version, the piece ends joyfully with an exhilarating choral version of the famous *Gopak*, here brilliantly sung. The full-ranging Melodiya recording has fine immediacy and presence, though the impression is very much one of a studio rather than of the theatre, with voices sharply focused. That does not diminish the impressiveness of a company who have performed the piece on stage, with the bass, Vladimir Matorin, outstanding as the village elder, Tcherevik. An English translation of the libretto is included in the booklet.

Newman, Alfred (1901–70)

Film music: *20th Century-Fox Fanfare.* Excerpts from: *Airport; Anastasia; Best of Everything; The Bravados; Captain from Castile;* (i) *Conquest. Down to the Sea in Ships; How to Marry a Millionaire (Street scene).* (i; ii) *The Robe.* (ii) *The Song of Bernadette. Wuthering Heights.*
(M) *** BMG/RCA GD 80184; *GK 80184* [0184-2-RG; *0184-4-RG*]. Nat. PO, (i) with Band of the Grenadier Guards; (ii) Amb. S.; Charles Gerhardt.

Alfred Newman was Hollywood's own man. Unlike his émigré colleagues, Korngold, Rózsa and Waxman, he was born in Connecticut, and Hollywoodian hyperbole was an intrinsic part of his musical nature. He was good at rumbustious, rather empty marches (as in *Captain from Castile*) and tended to overscore. The very first piece here (after the famous Twentieth Century-Fox *Fanfare*, which will ensure his immortality) is genuinely memorable. *Street scene*, a Gershwinesque evocation originally written in 1931 for a film of the same name but more recently made familiar by its re-use as an introduction for *How to Marry a Millionaire*, combines strong thematic interest with a real feeling for atmosphere. For the rest, there is sentimentality (Cathy's theme from *Wuthering Heights*), orchestral inflation, the occasional vivid evocation (the vision sequence in *The Song of Bernadette* very effective, even if essentially tasteless) and luscious religiosity (*The Robe*). Charles Gerhardt's committed advocacy and the splendid orchestral playing ensure maximum impact throughout.

Nicolai, Carl Otto (1810–49)

The merry wives of Windsor (Die lustigen Weiber von Windsor): complete.
(M) **(*) EMI CMS7 69348-2 (2) [Ang. CDMB 69348]. Frick, Gutstein, Engel, Wunderlich, Lenz, Hoppe, Putz, Litz, Mathis, Ch. & O of Bav. State Op., Heger.

The great glory of this fine EMI set is the darkly menacing Falstaff of Gottlob Frick in magnificent voice, even if he sounds baleful rather than comic. It is good too to have the young Fritz Wunderlich as Fenton opposite the Anna Reich of Edith Mathis. Though the others hardly match this standard – Ruth-Margret Putz is rather shrill as Frau Fluth – they all give enjoyable performances, helped by the production, which conveys the feeling of artists who have experienced performing the piece on stage. The effectiveness of the comic timing is owed in great measure to the conducting of the veteran, Robert Heger. From the CD transfer one could hardly tell the age of the recording, with the voices particularly well caught.

Nielsen, Carl (1865–1931)

Clarinet concerto, Op. 57.
*** Chan. Dig. CHAN 8618; *ABTD 1307* [id.]. Janet Hilton, SNO, Bamert – COPLAND: *Concerto;* LUTOSLAWSKI: *Dance preludes.* ***

Janet Hilton gives a highly sympathetic account of the Nielsen *Concerto*, but it is characteristically soft-centred and mellower in its response to the work's more disturbing emotional undercurrents than Ole Schill's splendid account on BIS – see below. However, that is coupled with the *Sinfonia espansiva*; those who prefer a record offering other clarinet works will not be disappointed by Janet Hilton's alternative programme. The Chandos recording is first class.

(i) *Clarinet concerto, Op. 57;* (ii) *Flute concerto;* (iii) *Violin concerto, Op. 33.*
*** Chan. Dig. CHAN 8894; *ABTD 1505* [id.]. (i) Thomsen; (ii) Christiansen; (iii) Sjøgren; Danish RSO, Schønwandt.

Niels Thomsen's powerfully intense account of the late *Clarinet concerto* is completely gripping. He is scrupulous in observing every dynamic and expressive marking, and penetrates its character as well as any rival and better than most. Michael Schønwandt gives sensitive and imaginative support, both here and in the two companion works. Toke Lund Christiansen is hardly less successful in the *Flute concerto*. Kim Sjøgren and Schønwandt give a penetrating and thoughtful account of the *Violin concerto*; there is real depth here, thanks in no small measure to

Schønwandt. This is a most useful issue which will save the collector needless duplication; the recording, made in collaboration with Danish Radio, is first class.

(i) *Clarinet concerto, Op. 57;* (ii) *Symphony No. 3 (Sinfonia espansiva). Maskarade overture.*
*** BIS Dig. CD 321 [id.]. (i) Ole Schill; (ii) Pia Raanoja, Knut Skram; Gothenburg SO, Myung-Whun Chung.

The *Third Symphony* (*Sinfonia espansiva*) is an exhilarating and life-enhancing work; it radiates a confidence and well-being soon to be shattered by the First World War. The young Korean conductor secures playing of great fire and enthusiasm from the Gothenburgers, and has vision and breadth – and at the same time no want of momentum. Two soloists singing a wordless vocalise are called for in the pastoral slow movement, and their contribution is admirable. Myung-Whun Chung also gives a high-spirited and sparkling account of the *Overture* to Nielsen's comic opera, *Maskarade*. As for the *Concerto*, Ole Schill brings brilliance and insight to what is one of the most disturbing and masterly of all modern concertos. The BIS recording is marvellous, even by the high standards of this small company.

(i) *Flute concerto; Symphony No. 1; Rhapsody overture (An imaginary journey to the Faroe Islands).*
*** BIS Dig. CD 454 [id.]. (i) Patrick Gallois; Gothenburg SO, Myung-Whun Chung.

Myung-Whun Chung and the Gothenburg orchestra have an instinctive feeling for Nielsen. They play with commendable enthusiasm and warmth, and Chung shapes the *Symphony* with great sensitivity to detail and a convincing sense of the whole. The *Rhapsody overture: An imaginary journey to the Faroe Islands* is not the composer at his strongest (Nielsen called it 'nothing more than a piece of jobbery on my part'), but it has a highly imaginative opening. The *Flute concerto* is given a marvellous performance by Patrick Gallois, quite the most strongly characterized since the pioneering account by its dedicatee, Holger Gilbert-Jespersen (Decca). Gallois makes a glorious sound and eschews excessive vibrato.

Violin concerto, Op. 33.
❀ *** Sony Dig. MK 44548; *40-44548* [id.]. Cho-Liang Lin, Swedish RSO, Salonen – SIBELIUS: *Violin concerto.* *** ❀
(i) *Violin concerto, Op. 33. Symphony No. 5, Op. 50.*
*** BIS Dig. CD 370 [id.]. (i) Dong-Suk Kang, Gothenburg SO, Myung-Whun Chung.

Cho-Liang Lin brings as much authority to Nielsen's *Concerto* as he does to the Sibelius and he handles the numerous technical hurdles with breathtaking assurance. The simple eloquence with which he tackles the closing pages of the introduction is most affecting. His perfect intonation and tonal purity excite admiration, but so should his command of the architecture of this piece; there is a strong sense of line from beginning to end. Salonen is supportive here and gets good playing from the Swedish Radio Symphony Orchestra.

Dong-Suk Kang is more than equal to the technical demands of this concerto and is fully attuned to the Nordic sensibility. He brings tenderness and refinement of feeling to the searching slow movement and great panache and virtuosity to the rest. Who would have forecast at the time of the Nielsen renaissance in the 1950s that, thirty years on, two Korean artists would have produced such completely idiomatic results? The *Fifth Symphony* is hardly less successful and is certainly the best-recorded version now available. Myung-Whun Chung has a natural feeling for Nielsen's language and the first movement has real breadth.

Symphonies Nos. 1–6.
(M) **(*) Unicorn UKCD 2000/2 [id.]. Gomez, Rayner-Cook (in No. 3), LSO, Schmidt.

The performances on Unicorn Kanchana are ablaze with life, warmth and a sense of discovery. The recordings were always a bit rough, but the digital remastering represents an undoubted (though not spectacular) improvement, for the texture still remains coarse in tuttis. However, the brass is less garish and better integrated into the overall aural picture. In No. 2 and the last three symphonies Ole Schmidt is a sure and penetrating guide. Whatever quibbles one might have, his readings have an authentic ring to them, for he has real feeling for this glorious music. They obviously represent good value.

Symphonies Nos. 1 in G min., Op. 7; 2 in B min., Op. 16 (The 4 Temperaments).
*** Chan. Dig. CHAN 8880 [id.]. Royal Scottish O, Bryden Thomson.

Strong, vigorous accounts of both symphonies from the Royal Scottish Orchestra under Bryden Thomson, with a particularly well-characterized reading of *The Four Temperaments.*

The second movement is perhaps a shade too brisk, but in most respects these performances are difficult to flaw. Blomstedt's accounts on Decca have perhaps greater polish but Thomson has directness and an obvious affection for this music and he maintains a sense of momentum that is admirable.

Symphonies Nos. 1 in G min., Op. 7; 6 (Sinfonia Semplice).
*** Decca Dig. 425 607-2; *425 607-4* [id.]. San Francisco SO, Blomstedt.

Blomstedt's record of the *First Symphony* is the best to have appeared for many years. It has vitality and freshness, and there is a good feel for Nielsen's natural lyricism. He inspires the San Francisco orchestra to excellent effect and the lean, well-focused string sound and songful wind playing are lovely. In the *Sixth Symphony* he has no want of intensity, though a broader tempo would have helped generate greater atmosphere in the first movement. Ole Schmidt (Unicorn) is more penetrating here. However, the performance is undeniably impressive and enjoys the advantage of far better recording. Indeed the quality is altogether first class, with good perspective and detail: the acoustic has more clarity than warmth, but the sound has plenty of space and front-to-back depth.

Symphony No. 2 (The Four Temperaments), Op. 16; Aladdin suite, Op. 34.
*** BIS CD 247 [id.]. Gothenburg SO, Myung-Whun Chung.

Symphonies Nos. 2 (The Four Temperaments); (i) *3 (Espansiva), Op. 27.*
*** Decca Dig. 430 280-2; *430 280-4* [id.]. (i) Kromm, McMillan; San Francisco SO, Blomstedt.

This coupling is possibly the finest of Blomstedt's cycle: he finds just the right tempo for each movement and nowhere is this more crucial than in the finale of the *Espansiva*. The two soloists are good and the orchestra play with all the freshness and enthusiasm one could ask for. The recording, though not quite in the demonstration bracket (the Davies Symphony Hall imparts a slight chill to the upper strings), is very fine indeed.

Myung-Whun Chung has a real feeling for this repertoire and his account of the *Second Symphony* is also very fine. The Gothenburg Symphony Orchestra proves an enthusiastic and responsive body of players; Chung, who studied with Sixten Ehrling at the Juilliard, does not put a foot wrong. The recording is impressive, too, and can be recommended with enthusiasm.

Symphony No. 3 (Espansiva), Op. 27; Overture, Maskarade.
**(*) Audiophon Dig. CD 72025 [id.]. Danish Nat. O, Sixten Ehrling.

The Audiophon version derives from a live concert at the Kennedy Center for the Performing Arts in 1984, that was much hailed in America at the time. Rightly so – and particularly for the eloquence of its slow movement and the straightforward, no-nonsense approach of the first, and for the convincing tempo of the finale. All the same, the string sound is a bit opaque and wanting in brilliance. Ehrling's concert also included a spirited account of the *Maskarade Overture*, again very well played but not so special that, with just over 40 minutes' playing time, its claims displace the Blomstedt as a primary recommendation.

Symphonies Nos. 3 (Sinfonia espansiva); 6 (Sinfonia semplice).
*** BMG/RCA Dig. RD 60427 [60427-2-RC]. Royal Danish O, Paavo Berglund.
** Sony Dig. SK 46500 [id.]. Swedish RSO, Salonen.

Paavo Berglund's account of the *Sinfonia espansiva* is the best to appear since Blomstedt's Decca version and is a great improvement on the Salonen coupling. The playing of the Royal Danish Orchestra, in which Nielsen once served, is beautifully prepared and full of vitality; Berglund is faithful to Nielsen's intentions and hardly puts a foot wrong. His two soloists, though unnamed, are very good and the general architecture of the work is well conveyed. In the more problematic *Sixth Symphony* Berglund proves a perceptive guide. His performance matches Blomstedt's in integrity and insight and is obviously the product of much thought. The RCA engineers produce a recording of splendid body and presence, different from but not inferior to the sound Decca gives Blomstedt. In the first movement of the *Sixth* both are brisker than was Jensen in his pioneering 1953 record (he was said to have an exceptionally good feeling for Nielsen's tempo markings, having played under the composer's own baton) and the sense of foreboding underlying the apparently serene opening bars is possibly understated. In any event, Berglund can be strongly recommended alongside (though not necessarily in preference to) Blomstedt.

Esa-Pekka Salonen keeps closer to the score than he has done in most earlier issues in his Nielsen cycle, but the listener is left just a little too aware of surface finesse and tonal sophistication. The broad closing bars of the *Sinfonia espansiva* have rather more bombast than dignity in his hands. The *Sixth Symphony* is generally free from exaggeration but only intermittently conveys the feeling that this music is part of his bloodstream. The sound is decent but not a patch on the Decca or RCA recordings.

Symphony No. 4 (Inextinguishable), Op. 29.
**(*) DG Dig. 413 313-2 [id.]. BPO, Karajan.

Symphony No. 4 (Inextinguishable), Op. 29; An Imaginary journey to the Faroe Islands (Rhapsodic overture); Pan and Syrinx, Op. 49.
(M) **(*) Chan. CHAN 6524; *MBTD 6524* [id.]. SNO, Gibson – SIBELIUS: *The Dryad* etc. ***

By far the best performance of Nielsen's *Fourth* ever recorded comes from Karajan. The orchestral playing is altogether incomparable and there is both vision and majesty in the reading. The strings play with passionate intensity at the opening of the third movement, and there is a thrilling sense of commitment throughout. The wind playing sounds a little over-civilized – but what exquisitely blended, subtle playing this is. It is excellently recorded, too. However, this seems ungenerous measure alongside Blomstedt's Decca coupling.

Sir Alexander Gibson has well-judged tempi and an obvious sympathy for the *Inextinguishable*, and there is no want of commitment from the Scottish players. Perhaps the strings do not have quite the weight that is required, and one misses the last ounce of fire. Yet there is much to admire, including a well-balanced (1979) analogue sound-picture, truthfully transferred to CD. Both *Pan and Syrinx* and the much later *Rhapsodic overture* are given perceptive readings that realize much of the mystery these scores evoke, and the Sibelius couplings bring a similar sensitivity to atmosphere and colour. At mid-price this is worth considering.

Symphonies Nos. 4 (Inextinguishable); 5, Op. 50.
*** Decca Dig. 421 524-2 [id.]. San Francisco SO, Blomstedt.

Symphony Nos. 4 (Inextinguishable), Op. 29; 5, Op. 50; Maskarade: Overture.
**(*) Virgin Dig. VC7 91210-2; *VC7 91210-2* [id.]. BBC SO, Andrew Davis.

The opening of Blomstedt's *Fourth* has splendid fire: this must sound as if galaxies are forming. Blomstedt conveys Nielsen's image about the soaring string-lines in the slow movement ('like the eagle riding on the wind') most strikingly – more so than Karajan. The finale is exhilarating, yet held on a firm rein. The *Fifth Symphony*, too, is impressive: it starts perfectly and is almost as icy in atmosphere as those pioneering recordings of the 1950s. The desolate clarinet peroration also comes off most successfully. The recording balance could not be improved upon: the woodwind are decently recessed, there is an almost ideal relationship between the various orchestral sections and a thoroughly realistic overall perspective.

Andrew Davis and the BBC Symphony Orchestra give fine performances of both symphonies. There is plenty of spirit and enthusiasm here and in No. 4 something of the work's incandescent quality. The strings have a distinctive, full-bodied sound and there is a forceful vigour about the whole orchestra which is invigorating. The *Fifth* is powerfully shaped too, and Davis is completely inside the idiom and has a good feeling for the architecture of this music. The brass are a bit crude at times, but on the whole these are powerful accounts and well recorded.

CHAMBER MUSIC

Canto serioso; Fantasias for oboe and piano, Op. 2; The Mother (incidental music), Op. 41; Serenata in vano; Wind quintet, Op. 43.
**(*) Chan. CHAN 8680 [id.]. Athena Ens.

This reissue gathers together Nielsen's output for wind instruments in chamber form, with everything played expertly and sympathetically. The recording is balanced very close; nevertheless much of this repertoire is not otherwise available, and this is a valuable disc.

Wind quintet, Op. 43.
*** Sony Dig. CD 45996. Ens. Wien-Berlin – TAFFANEL: *Quintet.* ***
(M) ** Sony SMK 46250 [id.]. Members of the Marlboro Festival – BARBER: *Summer music* **(*); HINDEMITH: *Octet.* **

The Ensemble Wien-Berlin gives one of the best accounts of the Nielsen *Wind quintet* to have appeared in years. Their tonal blend and purity of intonation are beyond praise and there are too many felicities of characterization in the variation movement to enumerate. They are meticulous in observing expressive and dynamic shadings and have a good feel for the Nielsen idiom. They are also beautifully recorded, and the only reservation must be that, at 50 minutes, this disc gives short measure. The Taffanel piece is urbane and civilized but inconsequential – however, there can be no grumbles at the distinction of the playing or the recording.

The Marlboro performance of the *Wind quintet* dates from 1971 and is a good one. If it is not an automatic recommendation, this is not because of any artistic reservations but rather because of the recording balance, which places the listener just a little too close to the players. There are some perceptive things here, and these players penetrate the spirit of the poignant preamble that opens the *Theme and variations.*

String quartets Nos. 1 in G min., Op. 13; 2 in F min., Op. 5; 3 in E flat, Op. 14; 4 in F, Op. 44. (i) *String quintet in G* (1888); (ii) *Andante lamentoso (At the bier of a young artist)* (1910).
*** BIS Dig. CD 503/4 [id.]. Kontra Qt, (i) Philipp Naegele; (ii) Jan Johansson.

The Nielsen *Quartets* are all from his first period. The *G minor*, Op. 13, of 1888 has the later opus number as it was published after the *F minor*, Op. 5 (1890). Both pre-date the *First Symphony*, and there is a greater depth and grandeur about the *E flat*, Op. 14 (1898), while the *Fourth* comes from the same year as *Maskarade.* Unlike the symphonies, they have never been particularly well served on disc, even in the days of 78s and mono LPs. The Kontra's set is by far the best to appear since the Copenhagen Quartet recorded them in the mid-1960s for Vox/Turnabout. There is an ardour and temperament to the playing which most listeners will find very persuasive, particularly after the scrawny and inadequate playing of the eponymous Carl Nielsen Quartet on DG which has had to serve until now. Others may find their intensity just a shade too unrelieved, but this does not seriously diminish the warmth with which they can be recommended. In addition we are given by far the finest account yet recorded of the *G major String quintet*, an early work in which the influence of Svendsen is still strong and where they are joined by the American violist Philipp Naegele, and the only current account of the *Andante lamentoso* (*At the bier of a young artist*) in its chamber form. The BIS recordings, made in the Malmö Concert Hall, have plenty of presence and clarity, and are rather forwardly (but not unpleasingly) balanced. Recommended.

VOCAL MUSIC

(i) *Hymnus amoris, Op. 12;* (ii) *3 Motets, Op. 55; The sleep, Op. 18;* (iii) *Springtime in Fünen, Op. 43.*
*** Chan. Dig. CHAN 8853; *ABTD 1470* [id.]. Soloists; (i) Copenhagen Boys' Ch.; (ii–iii) Danish Nat. R. Ch.; (iii) Skt. Annai Gymnasium Children's Ch., Danish Nat. RSO; (i; iii) Segerstam; (ii) Parkman.

Hymnus amoris is an early work from the mid-1890s, full of glorious music whose polyphony has a naturalness and freshness that it is difficult to resist, and which is generally well sung. *Søvnen* ('The Sleep') comes from 1903–4, between *Saul and David* and *Maskarade*, and just after Nielsen had evoked an interest in Reger's music. The harsh dissonances of the middle *Nightmare* section rather shocked Danish musical opinion at the time and still generate a powerful effect. Segerstam gets very good results both here and in the enchanting *Springtime in Fünen*, and the solo singing is good. The three motets, written in the last years of the composer's life for Mogens Wöldike and his Palestrina Choir, actually contain a Palestrina quotation. Generally excellent performances and fine recorded sound make this an invaluable addition to Nielsen's representation on CD.

(i) *Springtime in Fünen. Aladdin suite, Op. 34.*
*** Unicorn Dig. DKPCD 9054; *DKPC 9054* [id.]. (i) Ingo Nielsen, Von Binzer, Klint, Lille Muko University Ch., St Klemens Children's Ch.; Odense SO, Veto.

Springtime in Fünen is one of those enchanting pieces to which everyone responds when they hear it, yet which is hardly ever performed outside Denmark. The engaging Aladdin orchestral suite is well played by the Odense orchestra. This disc is a little short on playing time – but no matter, it is well worth its cost and will give many hours of delight.

OPERA

Maskarade (complete).
**(*) Unicorn DKPCD 9073/4 [id.]. Hansen, Plesner, Landy, Johansen, Serensen, Bastian, Brodersen, Haugland, Danish R. Ch. & SO, Frandsen.

Maskarade is new to the gramophone: only the overture and a handful of interludes have been recorded before. The plot is straightforward and simple, and to recount it would do scant justice to the charm and interest of the opera. *Maskarade* is a buoyant, high-spirited score full of strophic songs and choruses, making considerable use of dance and dance-rhythms, and having the unmistakable lightness of the buffo opera. It is excellently proportioned: no Act seems overlong, one is always left wanting more, and the scoring is light and transparent. The performance here is delightful, distinguished by generally good singing and alert orchestral support. The disappointment is the CD transfer which, in trying to clarify textures, has in fact made the focus less clean.

Saul and David (complete).
❀ *** Chan. Dig. CHAN 8911/12; *DBTD 2026* [id.]. Haugland, Lindroos, Kiberg, Westi, Ch. & Danish Nat. RSO, Järvi.

Nielsen's first opera comes from the same period as the *Second Symphony*; most collectors have known it in the English-language version, made in 1972, with Boris Christoff as Saul and with Jascha Horenstein conducting. This is in every way a vast improvement: the sound is glorious, it is sung in the original language, which is as important with Nielsen as it is with Janáček, and it has the merit of an outstanding Saul in Aage Haugland. The opera centres on Saul: his is the classic tragedy concerning the downfall of a heroic figure through some flaw of character. The remainder of the cast is very strong and the powerful choral writing is well served by the Danish Radio Chorus. The opera is abundant in wonderful and noble music, the ideas are fresh and abundant and full of originality. The opera convinces here in a way that it rarely has before, and the action is borne along on an almost symphonic current that disarms criticism. A marvellous set.

Nørholm, Ib (born 1931)

Violin concerto, Op. 60.
*** BIS CD 80 [id.]. Leo Hansen, Danish Nat. RSO, Herbert Blomstedt – KOPPEL: *Cello concerto.* ***

Ib Nørholm has enjoyed little exposure outside his native Denmark and has fallen very much in the shadow of his contemporary, Per Nørgård. Both are pupils of Vagn Holmboe, some of whose feeling for light shines through this concerto. His *Seventh Symphony* has also been recorded, but this concerto, recorded at a concert performance in 1975, is his sole representation in the UK catalogue. The work was written in response to a commission by the Danish Radio for a concerto for the leader of its orchestra, Leo Hansen, who is the excellent soloist here. It not only evinces considerable imaginative powers but contains some music of real beauty and is expertly laid out for the orchestra. The Danish Radio recording, while not state of the art, is more than acceptable, and it comes with a rewarding coupling.

Novák, Vitězslav (1870–1949)

Pan (symphonic poem), *Op. 43.*
*** Marco Polo Dig. 8.223325 [id.]. Slovak PO, Zdeněk Bílek.

It is difficult to understand the neglect of Novák's music outside Czechoslovakia. His glorious cantata, *The Storm*, is an inspired work but has not made it to CD. His five-movement symphonic poem, *Pan*, comes from much the same period (1910) and has some lovely music in it. Novák belonged to the generation of composers (Delius, Mahler, Debussy, Janáček, Sibelius etc.) for whom Nature was still central, and there is a pantheistic sensibility here. The scoring has great delicacy and imaginative resource, and there is a distinctly Gallic feeling to much of it. There are occasional reminders of Debussy and d'Indy (in particular the latter's *Jour d'été à la montagne*) as well as the opulence of Strauss and Reger. It would be difficult to guess, if one did not already know it, that this score originated in a keyboard work, so masterly is the transcription. Lyrical, often inspired (occasionally a bit overlong – particularly the last movement) and rewarding, this score is beautifully played by the Slovak Philharmonic under Zdeněk Bílek, and no less beautifully recorded.

Ockeghem, Johannes (*c.* 1410–97)

Requiem (Missa pro defunctis).
*** DG 415 293-2 [id.]. Pro Cantione Antiqua, Hamburger Bläserkreis für alte Musik, Turner – JOSQUIN DES PRÉS: *Missa – L'homme armé.* ***

The DG Archiv version of the *Missa pro defunctis* was originally recorded in Hamburg in 1973. The Pro Cantione Antiqua was unmatched at this period (with such artists as James Bowman and Paul Esswood as their counter-tenors, this is hardly surprising), and Bruno Turner's direction has both scholarly rectitude and musical eloquence to commend it. For most of the Requiem, the lines are at times doubled by the excellent Hamburger Bläserkreis für alte Musik. It is an eminently welcome addition to the compact disc catalogue.

Offenbach, Jacques (1819–80)

Cello concerto.
*** BMG/RCA RD 71003. Ofra Harnoy, Cincinnati SO, Kunzel – SAINT-SAËNS: *Concerto No. 1;* TCHAIKOVSKY: *Rococo variations.* ***

Offenbach's *Cello concerto* is a delight, with all the effervescence and tunefulness of his operettas. It is played with verve and brio and a full range of colour by Ofra Harnoy and did much to establish her reputation, while the accompaniment from Kunzel and his Cincinnati players is just as lively and sympathetic. Excellent recording throughout.

Gaîté parisienne (ballet, arr. Rosenthal): complete.
(M) **(*) Decca Dig. 430 718-2; *430 718-4.* Montreal SO, Dutoit – GOUNOD: *Faust: ballet music.* **(*)

Dutoit has the advantage of digital sound that is bright and has good projection, though the acoustic is resonant and detail is not especially clear; but the recording undoubtedly emerges from Decca's top drawer. He opens the music racily and there are many admirable touches, yet as the ballet proceeds there is a hint of blandness in the lyrical moments.

Gaîté parisienne (ballet, arr. Rosenthal): extended excerpts.
(B) *** DG 429 163-2. BPO, Karajan – CHOPIN: *Les Sylphides* *** ❀; DELIBES: *Coppélia: Suite excerpts.* ***

Karajan's selection is generous. On the DG disc, only Nos. 3–5, 7 and 19–21 are omitted. The remastering of the 1972 recording is highly successful. Textures have been lightened to advantage and the effect is to increase the raciness of the music-making, while its polish and sparkle are even more striking.

Gaîté parisienne (ballet music, arr. Rosenthal): excerpts; *Overture: Orpheus in the Underworld.*
(M) ** Sony SMK 47532 [id.]. NYPO, Bernstein (with SUPPÉ: *Overture: Beautiful Galathea* ***) – BIZET: Symphony. **(*).

Bernstein's suite includes a good deal of the raciest part of the score and then closes with the *Barcarolle.* The playing is characteristically effervescent, but the rather hard light of the 1969 CBS sound – the recording was made in the Avery Fisher Hall – makes everything seem brittle, and the ear is easily tired, unless a modest volume level is chosen. The Overtures are characteristically boisterous: Bernstein is warmly elegant as well, in Suppé's *Beautiful Galathea.*

Overtures: *La Belle Hélène; Bluebeard; La Grande-Duchesse de Gérolstein; Orpheus in the Underworld; Vert-vert. Barcarolle from Contes d'Hoffmann.*
**(*) DG Dig. 400 044-2 [id.]. BPO, Karajan.

Other hands besides Offenbach's helped to shape his overtures. Most are on a pot-pourri basis, but the tunes and scoring are so engagingly witty as to confound criticism. *La Belle Hélène* is well constructed by Haensch, and the delightful waltz tune is given a reprise before the end. Karajan's performances racily evoke the theatre pit, and the brilliance is extrovert almost to the point of fierceness. The Berlin playing is very polished and, with so much to entice the ear, this cannot fail to be entertaining; however, the compact disc emphasizes the dryness of the orchestral sound; the effect is rather clinical, with the strings lacking bloom.

Le Papillon (ballet): complete.
(M) *** Decca 425 450-2. LSO, Richard Bonynge – TCHAIKOVSKY: *Nutcracker*. **(*)

Le Papillon is Offenbach's only full-length ballet and it dates from 1860. If the tunes do not come quite as thick and fast as in Rosenthal's confected *Gaîté parisienne*, the quality of invention is high and the music sparkles from beginning to end. In such a sympathetic performance, vividly recorded (in 1974) it cannot fail to give pleasure. Highly recommended to all lovers of ballet and Offenbach.

Cello duos, Op. 54: Suites Nos. 1–2.
(B) *** HM 901043 [id.]. Roland Pidoux and Étienne Péclard.

This Harmonia Mundi issue was an unexpected and delightful surprise when it first appeared in 1980. With a good, natural transfer, the CD is no less appealing. Offenbach was himself a very accomplished cellist, and these two works are bristling with bravura, but tuneful, too, and imaginatively laid out to exploit the tonal possibilities of such a duo. The two works offer plenty of contrast, and Offenbach's natural wit is especially apparent in the *First Suite in E major*. The performances are excellent and so is the recording, although it is rather resonant.

OPERA

Les brigands (complete).
**(*) EMI Dig. CDS7 49830-2 (2). Raphanel, Alliot-Lugaz, Raffalli, Trempont, Le Roux, Lyon Opera Ch. & O, Gardiner.

This is one of Gardiner's delectably frothy French offerings, in which the Lyon Opera Company re-enacts in the studio a stage presentation. *Les brigands* has a Gilbertian plot about brigands and their unlikely association with the court of Mantua, with the carabinieri behaving very like the police in *The Pirates of Penzance*. It may not be quite such a charmer as its predecessor in Gardiner's Lyon sequence, Chabrier's *L'étoile* (EMI), and the tone of the principal soprano, Ghislaine Raphanel, is rather edgily French, but the rest of the team is splendid. Outstanding as ever is the characterful mezzo, Colette Alliot-Lugaz, in another of her breeches roles. Warm, well-balanced recording.

Les Contes d'Hoffmann (The Tales of Hoffmann): complete.
❀ *** Decca 417 363-2 (2) [id.]. Sutherland, Domingo, Tourangeau, Bacquier, R. Suisse Romande and Lausanne Pro Arte Ch., SRO, Bonynge.
** DG Dig. 427 682-2 (2). Domingo, Gruberová, Eder, Schmidt, Bacquier, Morris, Diaz, Ludwig, Rydl, Fr. R. Ch., Fr. Nat. O, Ozawa.

On Decca the sparkling CD transfer makes Offenbach's inspired score sound even more refreshing, with the immediacy of the action even more striking, and the acoustics of Victoria Hall, Geneva, adding fullness and warmth to the vividness. Joan Sutherland gives a virtuoso performance in four heroine roles, not only as Olympia, Giulietta and Antonia but also as Stella in the *Epilogue*, which in this version is given greater weight by the inclusion of the ensemble previously inserted into the Venice scene as a septet, a magnificent climax. Bonynge opts for spoken dialogue, and puts the Antonia scene last, as being the more substantial. His direction is unfailingly sympathetic, while Sutherland is impressive in each role, notably as the doll Olympia and in the pathos of the Antonia scene. As Giulietta she hardly sounds like a *femme fatale*, but still produces beautiful singing. Domingo gives one of his finest performances on record, and so does Gabriel Bacquier. It is a memorable set, in every way, much more than the sum of its parts.

In his autobiography Plácido Domingo devotes special attention in whole chapters to two operatic roles only, not just Otello – which one would expect – but Hoffmann in Offenbach's opera. He finds something of Beethoven and of the mocked hunchback, Rigoletto, in the character; and DG's set conducted by Ozawa justifies itself first and last by the intelligence and strength of Domingo's performance. Yet there is no denying that the voice is no longer as fresh as it was when he recorded the same role for Decca opposite Dame Joan Sutherland, a version which, unlike this, was consistently well cast. Edita Gruberová is one of the few sopranos today who could attempt to match Sutherland's feat of singing all the strongly contrasted heroine roles. Yet even in the coloratura role of the doll, Olympia, which should suit her perfectly, she gives a limited portrait; though she sings strongly and intelligently in the other two roles, the timbre of the voice is no help. The others in the cast are disappointing, even Gabriel Bacquier, who sang all four villain roles for Decca, but here is limited to Coppélius.

Les Contes d'Hoffmann: highlights.
(M) *** Decca 421 866-2; *421 866-4* (from above set, cond. Bonynge).
(M) *** DG Dig 435 402-2 [id.] (from above recording, with Domingo, Gruberová, Bacquier; cond. Ozawa).

The Decca highlights disc is one of the finest compilations of its kind from any opera. With over an hour of music, it offers a superbly managed distillation of nearly all the finest items and is edited most skilfully.

The DG highlights – which is also part of the 'Domingo Edition' – is comparably generous (72 minutes) and includes even more of the Prologue (25 minutes), and well-chosen excerpts from the other three Acts, rounding off with the touching *Malheureux, tu ne comprends donc pas* from the Epilogue. Offered at mid-price, this has the advantage of modern digital sound (though rather a reverberant acoustic), and those who want to sample Gruberová in the three soprano roles should find this a useful appendix to the Decca complete set. Those without the complete opera who want just a selection will still find the admittedly shorter Decca highlights the more rewarding.

Orpheus in the Underworld: highlights of English National Opera production (in English).
**(*) That's Entertainment Dig. CDTER 1134. Kale, Watson, Angas, Squires, Bottone, Pope, Belcourt, Styx, Burgess, E. Nat. Op. Ch. & O, Mark Elder.

The sparkling English National Opera production starts not with the conventional overture but with a prelude, over which the invented character, Public Opinion, delivers a moral in unmistakable imitation of the then Prime Minister. From then on the whole entertainment depends a lot for its fun on the racy new adaptation and translation by Snoo Wilson and the ENO producer, David Pountney. Offenbach devotees should be warned: there is little of Parisian elegance in this version and plenty of good knockabout British fun, brilliantly conveyed by the whole company. For this kind of performance one really needs a video, when even Bonaventura Bottone's hilariously camp portrait of a prancing Mercury is not nearly so much fun when simply heard and not seen. Bright, vivid recording to match the performance.

La Périchole (complete).
(M) *** Erato/Warner 2292 45686-2 (2) [id.]. Crespin, Vanzo, Bastin, Lombard, Friedmann, Trigeau, Rhine Op. Ch., Strasbourg PO, Lombard.

Dating from 1976, this recording of one of Offenbach's most delectable operettas features in the principal roles two of the singers who represent the French tradition at its very finest. Though both Régine Crespin in the title-role and Alain Vanzo as her partner, Piquillo, were past their peak at that time, their vocal control is a model in this music, with character strongly portrayed but without any hint of vulgar underlining. That is strikingly true of Crespin's account of the most famous number, the heroine's tipsy song, *Ah! quel diner*, which makes its point with delectable slyness. Crespin is fresh and pointed too in the letter song in waltz-time, which precedes it, an equally celebrated number. Vanzo, firm and clear and betraying few signs of age, produces heady tone in his varied arias, some of them brilliant. Jules Bastin is charactereful too in the subsidiary role of Don Andres, Viceroy of Peru. Lombard secures excellent precision of ensemble from his Strasbourg forces, only occasionally pressing too hard. The recorded sound is vivid and immediate, and the only disappointment is that spoken dialogue is omitted even in numbers described as *Mélodrame*. Instead, the libretto provides a detailed synopsis of the action between the texts and translations of numbers.

Orff, Carl (1895–1982)

Carmina Burana.
*** Decca Dig. 430 509-2; *430 509-4* [id.]. Dawson, Daniecki, McMillan, San Francisco Boys' & Girls' Choruses, San Francisco Symphony Ch. & SO, Blomstedt.
*** Ph. Dig. 422 363-2 [id.]. Gruberová, Aler, Hampson, Shinyukai Ch., Knaben des Staats & Berlin Cathedral Ch., BPO, Ozawa.
❀ (M) *** Sony SBK 47668 [id.]. Harsanyi, Petrak, Presnell, Rutgers University Ch., Phd. O, Ormandy.
*** EMI CDC7 47411-2 [id.]. Armstrong, English, Allen, St Clement Danes Grammar School Boys' Ch., LSO Ch., LSO, Previn.

(M) *** DG 423 886-2; *423 886-4* [id.]. Janowitz, Stolze, Fischer-Dieskau, Schöneberger Boys' Ch., Berlin German Op. Ch. & O, Jochum.
(M) *** Decca 417 714-2; *417 714-4* [id.]. Burrows, Devos, Shirley-Quirk, Brighton Festival Ch., Southend Boys' Ch., RPO, Dorati.
(B) *** Pickwick Dig. PCD 855 [id.]. Walmsley-Clark, Graham-Hall, Maxwell, Southend Boys' Ch., LSO Ch., LSO, Hickox.
(M) *** BMG/RCA GD 86533 [RCA 6533-2-RG]. Mandac, Kolk, Milnes, New England Conservatory Ch. & Children's Ch., Boston SO, Ozawa.

Blomstedt's is the finest modern version of Orff's exhilaratingly hedonistic cantata. The great *Ave formosissima* has never sounded grander or more opulent at the work's close, punctuated with superb thwacks on the bass drum. Throughout the choral singing, men, boys, and girls, all enjoying themselves hugely – as they should, with such stimulating words to sing – has great passion and energy and all three soloists are equally outstanding. John Daniecki's use of vocal colouring in the role of the roasted swan is entertainingly diverse, while Keven McMillan is a splendidly unctuous Abbot, with his later solo full of lustful yearning. In return Lynne Dawson portrays the girl in the red tunic with seductive innocence, yet with delicate underlying sentience, and her moment of submission climaxing the *Cours d'amours* sequence is ravishingly compliant. Blomstedt's reading is full of imaginative touches of light and shade, yet the flow of passionate energy is paramount. He is helped by the remarkable range and sonority of the Decca recording, very much in the demonstration bracket.

Ozawa's digital recording of Orff's justly popular cantata carries all the freshness and spontaneity of his earlier successful Boston version – still a good mid-priced competitor on RCA – yet is even finer in its overall control, matching exuberance with added breadth. The *Cours d'amours* sequence is the highlight of his reading, with the soprano, Edita Gruberová, highly seductive; and Thomas Hampson's contribution is impressive too, if not quite as imaginative as Thomas Allen's for Previn. The wide dynamic range of the recording makes a spectacular effect throughout, not least in Hampson's *Abbot's song*, where there is a cataclysmic comment from the percussion, but also in the subtly engaging interplay between chorus and semi-chorus in the rural dance-music. Ozawa's trebles are more chaste than Previn's but bring much charm to their *Amor volat undique* ('Love flies everywhere'). Ozawa's infectious rubato in *Oh, oh, oh, I am bursting out all over*, interchanged between male and female chorus towards the end of the work, is wonderfully bright and zestful, with the contrast of the big *Ave formosissima* climax which follows made to sound spaciously grand. Taken overall, this Philips version readily goes to the top of the list alongside Blomstedt, Ormandy and Previn, who has a more robust fervour (his trebles deliciously earthy) which fits the hedonistic medieval poems so perfectly.

Ormandy and his Philadelphians have just the right panache to bring off this wildly exuberant picture of the Middle Ages by the anonymous poets of former days, and there is no more enjoyable version. It has tremendous vigour, warmth and colour and a genial, spontaneous enthusiasm from the Rutgers University choristers, men and boys alike, that is irresistible. *Veni, veni venias* (in *Cours d'amour*) is a tour de force that makes the nape of the neck tingle, while the boys obviously enjoy themselves hugely in *Tempus est iocundum*, and the closing *Ave formosissima* and reprise of *O Fortunata* are quite glorious. The soloists are excellent, especially the baritone, Harvey Presnell, who is outstanding – though the tenor, Rudolf Petrak, is pretty good too, and the lament of the poor roasting swan sounds less strained than usual. The soprano sings her lovely *In trutina* seductively enough, aided by Ormandy, even if her voice sounds a little uncovered in her passionate upward leap of submission later. But it is the chorus and orchestra that steal the show; the richness and eloquence of the choral tone is a joy in itself. The recording was made in 1960 in the Broadwood Hotel, Philadelphia; the resonant acoustic gives the work a wonderful breadth and spaciousness. The reverberation prevents the last degree of sharpness of detail and bite in the choral sound, but the effect is wholly natural and the remastering engineer is to be congratulated that he did not try to provide an artificial brightening. This is quite splendid, one of Ormandy's most inspired recordings and, even if you already have the work in your collection, this exhilarating version will bring additional delights.

Previn's 1975 analogue version, vividly recorded, is even more sharply detailed than Ozawa's. It is strong on humour and rhythmic point. The chorus sings vigorously, the men often using an aptly rough tone; and the resilience of Previn's rhythms, finely sprung, brings out a strain not just of geniality but of real wit. This is a performance which swaggers along and makes you smile. The recording captures the antiphonal effects impressively, better even in the orchestra than in the chorus. Among the soloists, Thomas Allen's contribution is one of the glories of the music-making, and in their lesser roles the soprano and tenor are equally stylish. The digital remastering is wholly successful: the choral bite is enhanced, yet the recording retains its full amplitude. The background hiss has been minimized and is really apparent only in the quieter vocal solos in the latter part of the work. A triumphant success. But this should be reissued at mid-price.

The CD reissue of Jochum's 1968 recording of *Carmina Burana* is outstandingly successful. Originally the choral pianissimos lacked immediacy, but now this effect is all but banished and the underlying tension of the quiet singing is very apparent. The recording has a wide dynamic range and when the music blazes it has real splendour and excitement. Fischer-Dieskau's singing is refined but not too much so, and his first solo, *Omnia sol temperat*, and later *Dies, nox et omnia* are both very beautiful, with the kind of tonal shading that a great Lieder singer can bring; he is suitably gruff in the *Abbot's song* – so much so that for the moment the voice is unrecognizable. Gerhard Stolze too is very stylish in his falsetto *Song of the roasted swan*. The soprano, Gundula Janowitz, finds a quiet dignity for her contribution and this is finely done. The closing scene is moulded by Jochum with wonderful control, most compelling in its restrained power.

Dorati's speeds are generally brisk and the effect is exhilaratingly good-humoured, with the conductor showing a fine rhythmic sense. The characterization of the soloists is less sensuous than in some versions, but John Shirley-Quirk's account of the Abbot's song is very dramatic, with the chorus joining in enthusiastically. Because of Dorati's thrust, this is more consistently gripping than Hickox's otherwise first-rate Pickwick account and, if there are moments when the overall ensemble is less than perfectly polished, the feeling of a live performance is engendered throughout, even though this is a studio recording. No translation is provided and the synopsis is cursory, which earns Decca a black mark.

Richard Hickox, on his brilliantly recorded Pickwick CD, like Previn uses the combined LSO forces, but adds the Southend Boys' Choir who make sure we know they understand all about sexual abandon – their *Oh, oh, oh, I am bursting out all over* is a joy. Penelope Walmsley-Clark, too, makes a rapturous contribution: her account of the girl in the red dress is equally delectable. The other soloists are good but less individual. The performance takes a little while to warm up (Hickox's tempi tend to be more relaxed than Dorati's), but the chorus rises marvellously to climaxes and is resplendent in the *Ave formosissima*, while the sharp articulation of consonants when the singers hiss out the words of *O Fortuna* in the closing section is also a highlight. The vivid orchestral detail revealed by the bright digital sound adds an extra dimension. The documentation provides a vernacular narrative for each band but no translation.

On RCA, Ozawa's strong, incisive performance brings out the bold simplicity of the score with tingling immediacy, rather than dwelling on its subtlety of colour. The soloists, too, are all characterful, especially Sherrill Milnes. The tenor, Stanley Kolk, sounds a little constrained with his *Roast swan*, but otherwise the solo singing is always responsive. Overall this is a highly effective account. The snag is the absence of a translation or of any kind of documentation beyond a listing of the 25 cued sections.

(i) *Die Kluge;* (ii) *Der Mond.*

(M) *** EMI CMS7 63712-2 (2) [Ang. CDMB 63712]. (i) Cordes, Frick, Schwarzkopf, Wieter, Christ, Kusche; (ii) Christ, Schmitt-Walker, Graml, Kuen, Lagger, Hotter; Philh. Ch. & O, Sawallisch.

(M) **(*) BMG/Eurodisc GD 69069 (2) [69069-2-RG]. (i) Stewart, Frick, Popp, Kogel, Schmidt, Nicolai, Gruber; (ii) Van Kesteren, Friedrich, Kogel, Gruber, Kusche, Grumbach, Buchta, Kiermeyer Kinderchor; Bavarian R. Ch., Munich R. O, Kurt Eichhorn.

Sawallisch's pioneering Orff recordings of the mid-1950s were regularly used as demonstration recordings in the early days of stereo; the sound, well balanced, is still vivid and immediate on CD, with such effects as the thunderbolt in *Der Mond* impressive still. Elisabeth Schwarzkopf is here just as inspired in repertory unusual for her as in Mozart, characterful and dominant as the clever young woman of the title in *Die Kluge*. It is good too to hear such vintage singers as Gottlob Frick and Hans Hotter in unexpected roles. Musically, these may not be at all searching works, but both short operas provide easy, colourful entertainment, with Sawallisch drawing superb playing from the Philharmonia. No texts are provided, but the discs are very generously banded.

Eichhorn's Eurodisc version of the early 1970s provides an excellent alternative, with casts equally consistent. *Der Mond* is given in Orff's revised, 1970 version, and the composer himself is credited with having supervised the production of the recordings. Certainly their great merit is the fun and jollity they convey, beautifully timed if not always quite as crisp of ensemble as the EMI versions. The sound as transferred is shriller and brighter than the 1950s EMI, rather wearingly so, with voices not quite so cleanly focused. German texts are given but no translation.

Pachelbel, Johann (1653–1706)

Canon in D.
*** Virgin Dig. VCy 791081-2; *VCy 791081-4* [id.]. LCO, Warren-Green – ALBINONI: *Adagio;* VIVALDI: *Four seasons.* ***
(M) *** Decca 417 712-2; *417 712-4* [id.]. Stuttgart CO, Münchinger – ALBINONI: *Adagio* ***; VIVALDI: *Four Seasons.* **(*)

Canon and Gigue.
**(*) Ph. Dig. 416 386-2; *416 386-4* [id.]. ASMF, Marriner – MOZART: *Serenade: Eine kleine Nachtmusik;* L. MOZART: *Toy symphony.* **(*)

A lovely performance of the *Canon* from Christopher Warren-Green and his excellent London Chamber Orchestra, with a delicately graceful opening and a gorgeous climax and with radiant violins. With splendid sound this is as fine as any version in the catalogue, unless you seek an authentic performance on a much smaller scale, when you should turn to Andrew Parrott and his Taverner Players (EMI CDC7 69853-2 – see our Concerts section, below). Marriner turns the two pieces into a ternary structure by oddly repeating the *Canon* again after the *Gigue*, a tiny concession to the short measure on his CD. Warm, well-balanced recording. Among budget-price recordings, Münchinger's is as good as any; but many other enjoyable performances are listed in the Concerts section.

Pacius, Fredrik (1809–91)

Kung Karls Jakt (King Charles's Hunt) (opera): complete.
(M) *** Finlandia Dig. FACD 107. Törnvist, Lindroos, Krause, Grönroos, Jubilate Ch., Finnish Nat. Op. O, Söderblom.

Fredrik Pacius was German-born and studied with Spohr, before settling in Helsinki. Here he became known as 'the father of Finnish music', for he brought the Finnish capital, then a provincial backwater, into contact with the mainstream of European music. His opera *King Charles's Hunt* was composed in 1851–2 but Pacius made no fewer than three subsequent revisions, the fourth and last version being staged as late as 1880. Although it is hailed as the first Finnish opera, it is by a German and to a Swedish-language text, exhibiting little sign of nationalism except in its choice of subject. Although the second version was staged in Stockholm, it has never entered the repertoire abroad and has maintained no more than a peripheral hold on the stage in Finland itself. The plot is simple and tells of how an attempt on the sixteen-year-old Charles XI of Sweden, on a hunting trip in the Åland islands, is thwarted by a young fisherman's daughter, whose fiancé had shot one of the king's elks (a capital offence) but who is subsequently pardoned. The musical ideas are pretty simple too, some are pleasant but there is little evidence of much individuality; his Danish contemporaries, Hartman and Heise are far more distinctive. There is some fine singing from Pirkko Törnqvist as the fisherman's daughter, Leonora, Peter Lindroos as her fiancé, and from Walton Grönroos as the coup leader, Gustaf Gyllenstjerna. The young King is a speaking role. Much care has been lavished on the production and Ulf Söderblom holds things together admirably. No masterpiece is uncovered but it will be of interest to collectors with a specialist interest in the beginnings of opera in the northern countries.

Padilla, Juan Gutierrez de (c. 1590–1664)

Missa: Ego flos campi. Stabat Mater.
(B) *** Pickwick Dig. PCD 970; *CIMPC 970* [id.]. Mixolydian, Piers Schmidt – VICTORIA: *Missa surge propera* etc. ***

Juan Gutierrez de Padilla's Mass *Ego flos campi* is for double choir, and throughout its *Credo* one choir interrupts the other, constantly punctuating the flow of the words with repetitions of the word 'credo'. His Mass setting is more homophonic than much of his other music, certainly than his motets for five or six voices, which Bruno Turner describes as in a 'thoroughly conservative polyphonic style of great assurance'. The Mass is nevertheless full of interest, though of course the comparison which the sleeve-writer makes between the two composers on the disc is not to Victoria's disadvantage. Padilla's setting of the *Stabat Mater* lacks the expressive depth of that Renaissance master. Dedicated performances and excellent recording.

Paganini, Niccolò (1782–1840)

Violin concerto No. 1 in D, Op. 60.
❀ *** EMI CDC7 47101-2 [id.]. Itzhak Perlman, RPO, Foster – SARASATE: *Carmen fantasy.**** ❀
*** Ph. Dig. 422 332-2 [id.]. Mullova, ASMF, Marriner – VIEUXTEMPS: *Concerto No. 5.* ***
*** DG Dig. 429 786-2 [id.]. Gil Shaham, NYPO, Sinopoli – SAINT-SAËNS: *Concerto No. 3.* ***
** Teldec/Warner Dig. 9031 73266-2 [id.]. Maxim Vengerov, Israel PO, Mehta – SAINT-SAENS: *Havanaise* etc. ***; WAXMAN: *Carmen fantasy.* **(*)

Itzhak Perlman demonstrates a fabulously clean and assured technique. His execution of the fiendish upper harmonics in which Paganini delighted is almost uniquely smooth and, with the help of the EMI engineers who have placed the microphones exactly right, he produces a gleamingly rich tone, free from all scratchiness. The orchestra is splendidly recorded and balanced too, and Lawrence Foster matches the soloist's warmth with an alive and buoyant orchestral accompaniment. Provided one does not feel strongly about Perlman's traditional cuts, there has been no better record of the *D major Concerto*.

Viktoria Mullova's account of the *D major Concerto* is second to none: her virtuosity dazzles and holds one enthralled, and she has the advantage of a bright, modern recording. She copes with all the technical hurdles effortlessly and with great brilliance, and the Academy of St Martin-in-the-Fields under Sir Neville Marriner give sterling support. Splendidly present and vivid recording (though the acoustic is bass-resonant and the timpani is somewhat prominent).

Gil Shaham, the young American violinist, was just eighteen when he made this début recording, and very impressive it is. His technical ease in the histrionics of Paganini's stratospheric tessitura, harmonics and all, is breathtaking, and he can phrase an Italianate lyrical melody – and there are some good ones in this *Concerto* – with disarming charm and ravishing timbre. His dancing spiccato in the finale is a joy, with its light rhythmic touch, and, however high he ascends, there is never a hint of scratchiness. Sinopoli's finely graduated and often dramatic accompaniment could hardly be more sympathetic.

Maxim Vengerov gives a strongly extrovert account. Mehta's fast opening tutti sets the scene without poise, but in spite of this, the solo contribution has much warmth and some infectious fireworks in the finale. But this performance is not distinctive.

Violin concertos Nos. 1 in D, Op. 6; 2 in B min. (La Campanella), Op. 7.
*** DG 415 278-2 [id.]. Accardo, LPO, Dutoit.
*** Denon Dig. CO 77611 [id.]. Kantorow, Auvergne O.
(B) *** DG 429 524-2; *429 524-4* [id.]. Shmuel Ashkenasi, VSO, Esser.

Violin concertos Nos. 3 in E; 4 in D min.
*** DG 423 270-2 [id.]. Accardo, LPO, Dutoit.

Violin concerto No. 5 in A min.; Maestosa sonata sentimentale; La primavera in A.
*** DG 423 578-2 [id.]. Accardo, LPO, Dutoit.

Violin concerto No. 6 in E min., Op. posth.; Sonata with variations on a theme by Joseph Weigl; Le streghe (Variations on a theme of Süssmayr), Op. 8; Variations of Non più mesta from Rossini's La Cenerentola.
*** DG 423 717-2 [id.]. Accardo, LPO, Dutoit.

Paganini's *Concertos* can too often seem sensationally boring, or the scratchy upper tessitura can assault rather than titillate the ear. But Accardo, like Perlman, has a formidable technique, marvellously true intonation and impeccably good taste and style; it is a blend of all these that makes these performances so satisfying and enjoyable. He is accompanied beautifully by the

LPO under Dutoit and the sound is very good, although the transfers seem to have generated some excess of bass resonance. Paganini's *E minor Concerto* is a relatively recent discovery and almost certainly predates the *First Concerto*. Of the additional couplings *La primavera* is a late work; ideas from Haydn turn up in the *Maestosa sonata sentimentale*. The *Variations* provide plenty of violinistic fireworks. The *Witches' dance* (*Le streghe*) is not as diabolical as the composer may have intended, but its difficulties are spectacular, including one ludicrous passage involving left-hand pizzicati. The solo playing here is stunning.

Kantorow plays superbly and he is very naturally recorded (the microphones in exactly the right place). In both concertos his lyrical line is very appealing indeed and the fireworks are dazzling, especially in the *La Campanella* finale of No. 2 In No. 1 he plays a shorter first movement cadenza than Accardo, to advantage and in the *Adagio* of No. 2 the melody soars sweetly over its pizzicato accompaniment to ravishing effect. The Denon recording is digital, but the acoustics have a slightly studio-ish feeling; on DG the spacious ambience of Barking Town Hall gives more ambient colouring but the solo balance is a shade more artificial. Accardo also gains from having a highly imaginative partner in charge of the orchestra, even if the Auvergne Orchestra manage very nicely with their soloist in command. Either of these records will give much pleasure.

At bargain price on CD, Ashkenasi's coupling of the two favourite Paganini *Concertos* is also very good value. He surmounts all the many technical difficulties in an easy, confident style and, especially in the infectious *La Campanella* finale of No. 2, shows how completely he is in control. The microphone is close and he clearly has a smaller sound than Accardo, but his timbre is sweet and the high tessitura and harmonics are always cleanly focused. The digital remastering is smooth and does not make the upper range edgy.

Violin concerto No. 3 in F.
(B) *** Ph. 422 976-2; *422 976-4* [id.]. Szeryng, LSO, Gibson – LALO: *Symphonie espagnole*. **(*)

Henryk Szeryng's performance is dazzling technically, with assured bravura in the spectacular pyrotechnics which the composer kept in reserve for the extended finale. The first movement is even longer – the opening ritornello lasts for four minutes – but, apart from an engaging *Allegro marziale* theme, is not of great musical interest. The best movement is undoubtedly the central *Cantabile spianato*, a brief aria-like piece, its theme engagingly introduced over pizzicatos in the orchestra. Not a lost masterpiece, then, but uncommonly well played here, and given a vivid CD transfer.

Violin and guitar: *Cantabile; Centone di sonate No. 1 in A; Sonata in E min., Op. 3/6; Sonata concertata in A.*
*** Sony MK 34508 [id.]. Itzhak Perlman, John Williams – GIULIANI: *Sonata*. ***

Superb playing from both Perlman and John Williams ensures the listener's attention throughout this slight but very agreeable music. With a good balance, the music-making here gives much pleasure, and this is a generally distinguished disc.

24 Caprices, Op. 1.
(M) *** DG 429 714-2; *429 714-4* [id.]. Salvatore Accardo.
*** EMI CDC7 47171-2 [id.]. Itzhak Perlman.

These two dozen *Caprices* probably still represent the peak of violinistic difficulty, even though more than a century has gone by since their composition. Accardo succeeds in making Paganini's most routine phrases sound like the noblest of utterances and he invests these *Caprices* with an eloquence far beyond the sheer display they offer. There are no technical obstacles and, both in breadth of tone and in grandeur of conception, he is peerless. He observes all the repeats and has an excellent CD transfer; moreover he has a price advantage too.

Perlman's playing is flawless, wonderfully assured and polished, yet not lacking imaginative feeling. Such is the magnetism of his playing that the ear is led on spontaneously from one variation to the next. The 1972 recording is extremely natural and the transfer to CD brings a very convincing illusion of realism, without the microphones seeming too near the violin.

Paine, John Knowles (1839–1906)

Symphony No. 1 in C min., Op. 23; Overture, As you like it.
*** New World Dig. NW 374-2 [id.]. NYPO, Mehta.

Paine's symphonies were milestones in the history of American music, and it is good that at last Mehta's fine recordings of both of them will allow them to be appreciated more widely. No. 1, first heard in 1876, ambitiously follows up the success of the earlier, ambitious *Mass in D.* Here too Paine consciously inspires echoes of Beethoven, with little feeling of dilution – though, after his dramatic C minor opening, he tends to relax into sweeter, more Mendelssohnian manners for his second subject and the three other movements. What is striking is the bold assurance, and the overture – a concert work inspired by Shakespeare, not designed for the theatre – is also full of charming ideas. Mehta is a persuasive advocate, helped by committed playing and full, well-balanced recording.

Symphony No. 2 in A, Op. 34.
*** New World Dig. NW 350-2 [id.]. NYPO, Mehta.

Written four years after the *First Symphony*, this magnificent work is both more ambitious and more memorable than its predecessor. Though for generations Paine was dismissed by Americans as merely an academic who echoed Mendelssohn and Schumann, this work far more remarkably anticipates Mahler. The movingly expressive third-movement *Adagio* starts with the clearest foretaste of the *Adagietto* of Mahler's *Fifth Symphony* and, later, ideas richly follow that up in writing of great warmth. The idiom is notably more chromatic than that of the *First*, and the other movements – introduced by an extended slow introduction – bring an element of fantasy, as in the fragmented rhythms and textures of the scherzo. It is a work that should certainly be revived in the concert hall, and not just in America. Mehta draws a strongly committed performance from the New York Philharmonic, and the sound is first rate.

Paisiello, Giovanni (1740–1816)

Il barbiere di Siviglia (opera): complete.
*** Hung. Dig. HCD 12525/6-2 [id.]. Laki, Gulyás, Gregor, Gati, Sólyom-Nagy, Hungarian State O, Adám Fischer.

Paisiello's *Barbiere di Siviglia* may for many generations have been remembered only as the forerunner of Rossini's, but latterly stage revivals have helped to explain why, before Rossini, the opera was such a success. The musical inspiration may too often be short-winded, but the invention is full of vitality, and that is reflected captivatingly in this Hungarian performance under Adám Fischer. Jószef Gregor is a vividly characterful Bartolo, a role more important here than in Rossini, while István Gati is a strong, robust Figaro. Krisztina Laki is a brilliant Rosina and Dénes Gulyás a clean, stylish Almaviva, relishing his Don Alonso imitation. Full, vivid recording.

Palestrina, Giovanni Pierluigi di (1525–94)

Missa Assumpta est Maria; Missa Sicut lilium.
*** Gimell Dig. CDGIM 020; *1585T-20* [id.]. Tallis Scholars, Peter Phillips.

After the *Missa Papae Marcelli*, the *Missa Assumpta est Maria* is probably the best known of Palestrina's works, though it is of late provenance and was not published in his lifetime. Its companion on this CD is based on the motet, *Sicut lilium inter spinas* ('Like a lily among thorns') which comes from his First Book of Motets (1569). As is their practice, the Tallis Scholars record the *Masses* together with the motets on which they are based, and sing with their customary beauty of sound and well-blended tone. They are superbly recorded in the Church of St Peter and St Paul in Salle, Norfolk.

Antiphon: Assumpta est Maria; Missa: Assumpta est Maria. Antiphon, Motet and Missa: Veni sponsa Christi. Magnificat VI toni.
(M) *** Decca 433 678-2 [id.]. St John's College, Cambridge, Ch., Guest.

The older St John's record of *Assumpta est Maria* dates from 1971, but the (originally Argo) recording sounds splendid on CD, if perhaps not so refined in texture as its digital competitor. This is one of Palestrina's most sublime works and the St John's performance is thoroughly persuasive. The Decca couplings are even more generous (70 minutes) than on the Gimell CD and equally attractive. Some may find the presentation a little lacking in Latin fervour compared with what one would hear on the Continent: the trebles sound distinctly Anglican. But this is fine singing by any standards, and has great purity of tone and beauty of phrasing. The acoustic has atmosphere, yet detail is not lost.

Hodie Beata Virgo; Litaniae de Beata Virgine Maria in 8 parts; Magnificat in 8 parts (Primi Toni); Senex puerum portabat; Stabat Mater.
(M) *** Decca 421 147-2; *421 147-4* [id.]. King's College Ch., Willcocks – ALLEGRI: *Miserere.* ***

This is an exceptionally fine collection dating from the mid-1960s. The flowing melodic lines and serene beauty which are the unique features of Palestrina's music are apparent throughout this programme, and there is no question about the dedication and accomplishment of the performance. Argo's recording is no less successful, sounding radiantly fresh and clear.

Missa Benedicta es (with *Plainchant*).
*** Gimell CDGIM 001; *1585T-01* [id.]. Tallis Scholars, Peter Phillips (with JOSQUIN: *Motet: Benedicta es*).

This recording, made in the resonant acoustic of the Chapel of Merton College, Oxford, comes from 1981 and has been digitally remastered with considerable success. Palestrina's Mass is coupled with the Josquin motet, *Benedicta es*, on which it is based, together with the plainchant sequence on which both drew. The Tallis Scholars and Peter Phillips sing with impressive conviction and produce an expressive, excellently blended sound.

Missa brevis; Missa Nasce la gioia mia (with PRIMAVERA: *Madrigal: Nasce la gioia mia*).
*** Gimell Dig. CDGIM 008; *1585T-08* [id.]. Tallis Scholars, Phillips.

Like the *Missa Nigra sum*, the *Missa Nasce la gioia mia* was included in the 1590 Book of Masses and is a parody Mass, modelled on the madrigal, *Nasce la gioia mia* by Giovan Leonardo Primavera, who was born in Naples in 1540. The Tallis Scholars and Peter Phillips give expressive, finely shaped accounts of both the *Missa brevis* and the *Mass*, which they preface by the madrigal itself. A most rewarding disc: no grumbles about the recording.

Missa Nigra sum (with motets on *Nigra sum* by LHERITIER; VICTORIA; DE SILVA).
*** Gimell Dig. CDGIM 003; *1585T-03* [id.]. Tallis Scholars, Phillips.

Palestrina's *Missa Nigra sum* is another parody Mass, based on a motet by Jean Lheritier and follows its model quite closely. Its text comes from the Song of Solomon ('I am black but comely, O ye daughters of Jerusal: therefore has the king loved me, and brought me into his chambers'). On this record, the plainchant and the Lheritier motet precede Palestrina's *Mass*, plus motets by Victoria and Andreas de Silva, a relatively little-known Flemish singer and composer who served in the Papal chapel and later in Mantua. The music is inspiring and the performances exemplary. This is a most beautiful record and the acoustic of Merton College, Oxford, is ideal.

Missa Papae Marcelli.
*** Gimell CDGIM 339; *1585T-39* [id.]. Tallis Scholars, Phillips – ALLEGRI: *Miserere;* MUNDY: *Vox Patris caelestis.* ***

Missa Papae Marcelli; Tu es Petrus (motet).
*** DG 415 517-2 [id.]. Westminster Abbey Ch., Preston (with ANERIO: *Venite ad me omnes;* NANINO: *Haec dies;* GIOVANNELLI: *Jubilate Deo* ***) – ALLEGRI: *Miserere.* **(*)

The account on DG by the Westminster Abbey Choristers transcends any Anglican stylistic limitations. It is a performance of great fervour, married to fine discipline, rich in timbre, eloquent both at climaxes and at moments of serenity. The singing is equally fine in the hardly less distinctive motet, *Tu es Petrus*. Felice Anerio, Giovanni Bernardino Nanino and Ruggiero Giovannelli represent the following generation of composers in straddling the end of the sixteenth and beginning of the seventeenth century. Their contributions to this collection are well worth having, particularly Giovannelli's *Jubilate Deo* which makes a splendid closing item. The digital recording is first class. All Saints', Tooting, was used, rather than the Abbey, and the acoustics are both intimate and expansive, while detail is beautifully caught.

The Gimell alternative is an analogue recording from 1980, but the digital remastering produces extremely fine sound, firm, richly blended and not lacking internal detail. The acoustics of Merton College, Oxford, are admirably suited to this music; the singing has eloquence, purity of tone, and a simplicity of line which is consistently well controlled.

Missa Papae Marcelli; Stabat Mater.
(B) *** Pickwick PCD 863; *IMPCD 863* [id.]. Pro Cantione Antiqua, Mark Brown.

Pro Cantione Antiqua on the budget-priced Pickwick label bring not only an outstandingly fresh and alert account of Palestrina's most celebrated *Mass* but one which involves keen scholarship. With an all-male choir and no boy trebles, and with one voice per part, this chamber choir yet sings with power and resonance against a warm and helpful church acoustic. The authentic atmosphere is enhanced by the inclusion of relevant plainchants between the sections of the *Mass*. The magnificent eight-part *Stabat Mater* also receives a powerful performance, warm and resonant.

Veni sponsa Christi.
(M) *** EMI Dig. CD-EMX 2180; *TC-EMX 2180*. St John's College, Cambridge, Ch., Guest – ALLEGRI: *Miserere;* LASSUS: *Missa super bella.* **(*)

Every section of the *Veni sponsa Christi Mass* is introduced by the same idea with much subtle variation, and this impressive work ends with two *Agnus Dei* settings, the second with an additional tenor part. It receives an eloquent, imaginatively detailed and finely shaped performance here, and the relative restraint of the Anglican choral tradition suits Palestrina's flowing counterpoint better than it does the Lassus Venetian coupling.

Panufnik, Andrzej (1914–91)

(i) *Arbor Cosmica;* (ii) *Symphony No. 3 (Sinfonia sacra).*
*** Elektra Nonesuch/Warner Dig. 7559 79228-2 [id.]. (i) NY Ch. Symphony; (ii) Concg. O; composer.

The *Sinfonia sacra*, written in 1963 in tribute to Poland's millennium of Christianity and statehood, is one of Panufnik's most warmly and immediately communicative works, and here receives a magnificent performance from the Concertgebouw under the composer. Its two substantial movements aim to reflect the composer's religious and patriotic feelings, the more intense when he had already fled from Poland into exile from the Stalinist excess of the communist regime. The first movement, *Three Visions*, is in three distinct sections, a brassy fanfare, a meditation for strings and a longer dashing allegro, which starts with a dramatic timpani cadenza, and works up to a powerful final climax. As the title implies, *Arbor Cosmica*, written much later in 1983, is one of the many works of Panufnik which directly reflect a visual concept, this time the branches of a tree. The 12 'evocations' are all generated from a single three-note chord, each with the structure mapped out like a tree. The overall length of nearly 40 minutes is well sustained by the sharply defined contrasts between the sections, making it sound like an extended set of variations. The composer draws dedicated performances both from the Concertgebouw and the New York Chamber Symphony, with the former inevitably sounding richer and fuller.

(i) *Autumn music; Heroic overture;* (i, ii) *Nocturne;* (iii) *Sinfonia rustica;* (i) *Tragic overture.*
(M) *** Unicorn UKCD 2016. (i) LSO, Horenstein; (ii) with Anthony Peebles; (iii) Monte Carlo Op. O, composer.

Andrzej Panufnik has made his home in England since the 1950s. The two overtures are early pieces and of relatively little musical interest, but the *Autumn music* and *Nocturne* are worth hearing. They may strike some listeners as musically uneventful, but the opening of the *Nocturne* is really very beautiful indeed and there is a refined feeling for texture and a sensitive imagination at work here. The *Sinfonia rustica* is the most individual of the works recorded here and has plenty of character, though its invention is less symphonic, more in the style of a sinfonietta. The performance under the composer is thoroughly committed. The LSO under Horenstein play with conviction and they are very well recorded.

(i) *Bassoon concerto;* (ii) *Violin concerto;* (iii) *Hommage à Chopin.*
*** Conifer Dig. CDFC 182; *MCFC 182* [id.]. (i) Thompson; (ii) Smietana; (iii) K. Jones; L. Musici, Stephenson.

The *Violin concerto* comes from 1971 and was composed in response to a commission from Menuhin; it is a strongly atmospheric piece and, although some may feel it is let down by a rather thin finale, it is well worth a place in the repertory; it is beautifully played here by Krzysztof Smietana. The *Hommage à Chopin* is an earlier piece which also owes its origin to a commission, this time from Unesco, who asked a number of composers to pay tribute to Chopin at the time of the centenary of his death in 1949. Panufnik composed five vocalises for voice and piano, transcribing them for flute and orchestra in 1966. Highly evocative and sensitive pieces that make use of folk music from Masovia, the central part of Poland where Chopin was born, they could not have more persuasive advocacy than they do from Karen Jones and the London Musici. The *Bassoon concerto* (1985), a darker piece dedicated to the memory of the Polish priest, Jerzy Popieluszko, who was murdered that year, was commissioned by the American player, Robert Thompson, who plays it with great sensitivity. Perhaps the strongest movement is the elegiac *Aria.* The London Musici under Mark Stephenson play with dedication throughout and, as the recording was made in the presence of the composer, it can be assumed to be authoritative. The Conifer sound, very well balanced at The Maltings, Snape, is first class.

(i) *Piano concerto. Symphony No. 9 (Sinfonia della speranza).*
*** Conifer Dig. CDCF 206; *MCFC 206* [id.]. (i) Ewa Poblocka; LSO, composer.

In a massive single movement of 41 minutes Panufnik's *Ninth Symphony* brings a formidable example of the composer's fascination with translating geometric concepts into notes. As he says, his aim is 'to balance a severe, self-imposed technical discipline with an expression of my deeply-felt emotions'. The visual analogy here is with light travelling through a prism, and the accompanying booklet provides a diagram illustrating how the formula works, using a three-note cell refracted in various ways. Whether or not one follows the detailed logic of that, the sense of purpose engendered by such a clear-cut concept makes itself felt to the listener even at a first hearing, particularly in a performance as powerful as this conducted by the composer. The shape and colours of the rainbow then provide a related analogy, dictating the framework of the symphony. It is made up of a series of arcs, each with similar construction but strongly contrasted and clearly distinct, built into a developing whole. The result has similarities with a gigantic passacaglia. The close brings a violent crescendo, with massive strings set against powerful percussion. That shattering conclusion may not immediately suggest the message of hope implied by the Italian title, but there is no denying the symphony's strength, an apt work for celebrating the 175th anniversary of the Royal Philharmonic Society.

Written almost 25 years earlier but recomposed in 1982, Panufnik's *Piano concerto* is not so extended, but carries comparable weight. The opening *Entrata*, the shortest of the three movements, has a neo-classical flavour in its ostinatos for the solo instrument, leading to a bald, spare central slow movement, with Panufnik at his most thoughtful. The mood is rather like that of some of Bartók's night music. The finale by contrast, built on the conflict between the intervals of a major and minor third, is violently rhythmic with jazzy syncopations. Though the piano writing gives the soloist relatively little chance for conventional keyboard display, her playing adds to the power of the composer's purposeful interpretation. The piano tone is a degree too clangy, but otherwise the recording is spacious and full.

(i) *Concerto festivo;* (ii) *Concerto for timpani, percussion and strings; Katyń epitaph; Landscape;* (iii) *Sinfonia sacra (Symphony No. 3).*
(M) *** Unicorn UKCD 2020. (i) LSO, (ii) with Goedicke & Frye; (ii) Monte Carlo Op. O, composer.

This splendidly recorded collection might be a good place for collectors to begin exploring Panufnik's output. The *Concertos* are both readily communicative and the *Katyń epitaph* is powerfully eloquent. The best of this music is deeply felt. The *Sinfonia sacra* serves to demonstrate the spectacular quality of the vividly remastered recording, with its compelling introductory 'colloquy' for four trumpets, followed by a withdrawn section for strings alone. In the finale of the second part of the work, Hymn, the trumpets close the piece resplendently.

Symphony No. 8 (Sinfonia votiva).
*** Hyp. Dig. CDA 66050; *KA 66050* [id.]. Boston SO, Ozawa – SESSIONS: *Concerto for orchestra.* ***

The *Sinfonia votiva* has a strongly formalistic structure, but its message is primarily emotional. It marks the response of the composer not only to the miraculous icon of the Black Madonna in his native Poland but also to the tragedy of contemporary events in that country. It begins with an extended slow movement, which is then daringly balanced against a briskly contrasted finale. Though Panufnik's melodic writing may as a rule reflect the formalism of his thought rather than tapping a vein of natural lyricism, the result is most impressive, particularly in a performance of such sharp clarity and definition as Ozawa's, very well recorded.

Paray, Paul (1886–1979)

Mass for the 500th anniversary of the death of Joan of Arc.
(M) **(*) Mercury 432 719-2 [id.]. Yeend, Bible, Lloyd, Yi-Kwei-Sze, Rackham Ch., Detroit SO, Paul Paray – SAINT-SAËNS: *Symphony No. 3.* ***

An unexpected coupling for the Saint-Saëns *Organ Symphony*, but Paray's harmonic language is comfortable enough for admirers of that work to enjoy his *Mass*, much admired by the composer Florent Schmitt. It could hardly have a more eloquent performance. The soloists are good and the choir are inspired to real fervour by their conductor, who at the close (in a brief recorded speech) expresses his special satisfaction with the singing of the closing, very romantic *Agnus Dei*. Excellent (1957) Mercury stereo, using the Ford Auditorium in Detroit.

Parker, Horatio (1863–1910)

A Northern ballad.
*** New World Dig. NWCD 339 [id.]. Albany SO, Julius Hegyi – CHADWICK: *Symphony No. 2.* ***

Horatio Parker's *Northern ballad* of 1899 was an enormous success in its day and calls both Dvořák and Grieg to mind. It has remained unpublished and unperformed in recent times. Excellent playing and recording. An interesting disc.

Parry, Hubert (1848–1918)

(i) *The Birds: Bridal march;* (ii) *English suite; Lady Radnor's suite* (both for strings); *Overture to an unwritten tragedy; Symphonic variations.*
*** Lyrita SRCD 220 [id.]. (i) LPO; (ii) LSO; Boult.

Since this repertoire was first issued on LP, the representation of Parry in the catalogue has expanded enormously, as can be seen below. These orchestral works are not among his most ambitious, but they are undoubtedly attractive, and should delight any Elgarian wanting to venture into the late Victorian hinterland. The *Bridal march* comes from Parry's equivalent to Vaughan Williams's *Wasps*, a suite of incidental music for *The Birds*, also by Aristophanes. Here the rich, *nobilmente* string melody asserts itself strongly over any minor contributions from the woodwind aviary. The two *Suites* of dances for strings have some charming genre music and the *Overture* is very strongly constructed. But best of all is the set of variations, with its echoes of Brahms's *St Anthony* set and its foretastes of *Enigma*. Shorter than either, it does not waste a note: a big work in a small compass. Boult's advocacy is irresistible. and the CD transfer demonstrates the intrinsic excellence of the analogue recordings, with gloriously full string sound.

Lady Radnor's suite.
*** Nimbus Dig. NI 5068 [id.]. E. String O, Boughton – BRIDGE: *Suite;* BUTTERWORTH: *Banks of green willow* etc. ***

Parry's charming set of pastiche dances, now given an extra period charm through their Victorian flavour, makes an attractive item in an excellent and generous English collection, one of Nimbus's bestsellers. Warm, atmospheric recording, with refined playing set against an ample acoustic.

Symphonies Nos. 3 in C (English); 4 in E min.
*** Chan. Dig. CHAN 8896; *ABTD 1507* [id.]. LPO, Matthias Bamert.

The rehabilitation of Parry is long overdue, and this disc and its companion, both sponsored by the Vaughan Williams Trust, do more than any previous issues to achieve that. Bamert proves a masterly interpreter, bringing out the warmth and thrust of the writing, akin to that of Elgar but quite distinct. No. 3 is the most immediately approachable of the symphonies, with its bold melodies, often like sea-shanties, and its forthright structure. Yet it is No. 4 which proves even more rewarding, a larger-scale and more ambitious work which, amazingly, was never performed at all between the first performance of the revised version in 1910 and the present recording. The bold opening, in its dark E minor, echoes that of Brahms's *First Piano concerto*, leading to an ambitious movement lightened by thematic transformation that can take you in an instant into infectious waltz-time. The elegiac slow movement and jolly and spiky scherzo lead to a broad, noble finale in the major key. The sound is rich and full to match the outstanding playing.

Symphony No. 5 in B min.; Elegy for Brahms; From death to life.
*** Chan. Dig. CHAN 8955; *ABTD 1549* [id.]. LPO, Bamert.

The *Fifth* and last of Parry's symphonies, completed in 1912, is in four linked movements, terser in argument than the previous two in the series and often tougher, though still with Brahmsian echoes. Amazingly, Parry seems to have been influenced in his structure by the example of Schoenberg in his *Chamber Symphony No. 1*, a work which this generous, broad-minded musician greatly admired. Yet after the minor-key rigours of the first movement, *Stress*, there is little in the idiom to link this with the avant-garde writing of the time. The other three movements are comparably subtitled *Love*, *Play* and *Now*, with the scherzo bringing echoes of Berlioz and the optimistic finale opening with a Wagnerian horn-call. The other two works make an apt and rewarding coupling. The *Elegy for Brahms* conveys grief, but its vigour rises above passive mourning into an expression of what might almost be anger. *From death to life* consists of two connected movements – hardly Lisztian, as the title implies – but exuberantly melodic, with a theme in the second which echoes Sibelius's *Karelia*. As with the companion disc, it would be hard to imagine finer, more committed performances or richer sound.

Nonet in B flat.
*** Hyp. Dig. CDA 66291; *KA 66291* [id.]. Capricorn – STANFORD: *Serenade (Nonet)*. ***

Parry's *Nonet* is an early piece, composed in 1877 while he was still in his twenties. It is for flute, oboe, cor anglais and two each of clarinets, bassoons and horns; Parry wrote it as an exercise, having acquired the score of Brahms's *Serenade in A*, and then put it on one side. Although the finale is perhaps a little lightweight, it is a delight from beginning to end. If one did not know what it was, one would think of early Strauss, for it is music of enormous accomplishment and culture as well as freshness. An excellent performance and recording.

Violin sonata in D, Op. 103; Fantasie-sonata in B, Op. 75; 12 short pieces.
*** Hyp. CDA 66157 [id.]. Erich Gruenberg, Roger Vignoles.

The *Fantasie-sonata*, an early work written at high speed just after Parry had left his job at Lloyd's in the City to become a full-time composer, provides a fascinating example of cyclic sonata form, earlier than most but also echoing Schumann. The three-movement *Sonata in D* is another compact, meaty piece, again written fast, the strongest work on the disc. The *Twelve short pieces*, less demanding technically, are delightful miniatures dedicated to Parry's wife and daughters, some of them later providing material for larger-scale works. Gruenberg and Vignoles prove persuasive advocates, and the recording is first rate.

Blest pair of sirens; I was glad (anthems).
*** Chan. Dig. CHAN 8641/2; *DBTD 2014* (2) [id.]. LSO Ch. & O, Hickox – ELGAR: *Dream of Gerontius*. ***

Parry's two finest and most popular anthems make an attractive coupling for Hickox's fine, sympathetic reading of Elgar's *Dream of Gerontius*. The chorus for Parry is rather thinner than in the main work but is very well recorded.

Evening Service in D (Great): Magnificat; Nunc dimittis. Hear my words, ye people; I was glad when they said unto me; Jerusalem; Songs of farewell.

*** Hyp. CDA 66273; *KA 66273* [id.]. St George's Chapel, Windsor, Ch., Christopher Robinson; Roger Judd (organ).

Everyone knows *Jerusalem*, which highlights this collection resplendently; but it is good to see Parry's other choral music being recorded. In the *Songs of farewell* trebles are used and the effect is less robust than in Marlow's version, but undoubtedly very affecting. Perhaps the stirring coronation anthem, *I was glad*, needs the greater weight of an adult choir, but it is still telling here. The excerpts from the *Great Service in D* are well worth having on record, as is the anthem, *Hear my words, ye people*. Excellent recording, the chapel ambience colouring the music without blunting the words.

Songs of farewell.
*** Conifer Dig. CDCF 155; *MCFC 155* [id.]. Trinity College, Cambridge, Ch., Richard Marlow – STANFORD: *Magnificat* etc. ***

Parry's *Songs of farewell* represent his art at its deepest, beautiful inspirations that until now have been neglected on disc, even the relatively well-known setting of Henry Vaughan, *My soul, there is a country*. Finest and most searching of the set is the Donne setting, *At the round earth's imagined corners*, with its rich harmonies poignantly intense and beautiful, deeply emotional behind its poised perfection. Richard Marlow with his splendid Trinity Choir, using fresh women's voices for the upper lines instead of trebles, directs thoughtful, committed performances which capture both the beauty and the emotion. This Parry collection is very well recorded and well coupled with the Stanford items, more contained though just as beautifully written for voices.

The Soul's ransom (sinfonia sacra); The Lotos eaters.
*** Chan. Dig. CHAN 8990; *ABTD 1572* [id.]. Jones, Wilson-Johnson, LPO and Ch., Bamert.

Parry's magnificent choral work, *The Soul's ransom*, described as a 'sinfonia sacra', suffered from a disastrous première in 1906 and stayed in total neglect for over 70 years. This superb performance under Matthias Bamert effectively rights the balance, a splendid supplement to his outstanding series for Chandos of Parry symphonies. Using a Biblical text, with soprano and baritone soloists as well as choir and orchestra, its sequence of solos and choruses form a broadly symphonic four-movement structure with references back not only to Brahms and the nineteenth century but to much earlier choral composers, notably Schütz. This 45-minute piece is generously coupled with another fine Parry work, also neglected. *The Lotos eaters* is a setting for soprano, chorus and orchestra of eight stanzas from Tennyson's choric song of that name, with Della Jones again the characterful soloist. Written in 1892 it strikes a vein of sensuousness rare in the British music of its time, reflecting instead the exoticry of the literary world in the 1890s. Full and atmospheric recording to match the incandescent performances.

Pärt, Arvo (born 1935)

(i) *Arbos* (two performances); (ii) *Pari Intervallo;* (iii) *An den Wassern zu Babel; De Profundis;* (iv; v) *Es sang vor langen Jahren;* (iii) *Summa;* (iii; v; vi) *Stabat Mater.*
*** ECM Dig. 831 959-2 [id.]. (i) Brass Ens., Stuttgart State O, Davies; (ii) Bowers-Broadbent; (iii) Hilliard Ens., Hillier; (iv) Bickley; (v) Kremer, Mendelssohn; (vi) Demenga.

Arvo Pärt was the first Estonian composer to embrace serialism, but he has also taken on board other techniques, ranging from a kind of neo-medievalism to aleatoric practices. All the music recorded here was composed in the period 1976–85 and gives a good picture of Pärt's musical make-up with all its strengths and limitations. *Arbos*, which is heard in two different versions, 'seeks to create the image of a tree or family tree'. It does not modulate and has no development, though pitch and tempi are in proportional relationships. Like the *Cantus in memory of Benjamin Britten*, the *Stabat Mater* (1985) for soprano, counter-tenor, tenor and string trio, commissioned by the Alban Berg Foundation, is distinguished by extreme simplicity of utterance and is almost totally static. This music relies for its effect on minimal means and invites one to succumb to a kind of mystical, hypnotic repetition rather than a musical argument. The artists performing here do so with total commitment and are excellently recorded. This is music that will either infuriate through its lack of perceptible movement or enchant the listener by its strong and austere atmosphere.

Passio Domini Nostrum Jesu Christi secundum Joannem.
*** ECM Dig. 837 109-2 [id.]. Michael George, John Potter, Hilliard Ens., Western Wind Chamber Ch. (Instrumental group), Paul Hillier.

Pärt's *Passion of our Lord Jesus Christ according to St John* was composed in 1982 in a bleak narrative style that reminds one of a mixture of Stravinsky and Schütz. It repeats the same scraps of ideas over and over again; it takes 70 minutes and never seems to leave the Aeolian mode, and it ought to be intolerable; yet in its way it is a strangely impressive experience, albeit not a wholly musical one. Impeccable recording and a dedicated performance.

Penderecki, Krzysztof (born 1933)

The Awakening of Jacob; (i) *Cello concerto No. 2;* (ii) *Viola concerto. Paradise Lost: Adagietto.*
*** Polski Nagrania PNCD 020 [id.]. (i) Monighetti; (ii) Kamasa; Polish Nat. RSO, Antoni Wit.

Penderecki 'returned to melody' in the late 1970s and early '80s after his long advocacy of avant-garde techniques. The *Cello concerto No. 2* was written in 1982 for Rostropovich, and this 1984 recording is impressively played by Ivan Monighetti. The *Viola concerto* is rather like skimmed Bartók; it brings masterly playing from Stefan Kamasa and the Polish Radio Orchestra. One cannot escape the same suspicion one felt of his avant-garde period: that behind the mask of colour and orchestral trickery there is little real substance. However, others may feel differently, and these mid-1980s performances have plenty of ardour and commitment and are well recorded.

String quartet No. 2.
*** Olympia OCD 328 [id.]. Varsovia Qt – SZYMANOWSKI: *Quartets;* LUTOSLAWSKI: *Quartet.* ***

Penderecki's *First quartet* of 1960 lasts seven minutes; the *Second* (1968) is not much longer and is hardly more substantial. It is full of the gimmicks and clichés of the period. Whatever its merit, it is extremely well played.

St Luke Passion.
**(*) Argo 430 328-2; *430 328-4* [id.]. Von Osten, Roberts, Rydl, Warsaw Philharmonic Ch., Polish RSO, composer.

The *St Luke Passion* was the work which first brought Penderecki international fame and popularity. With its bold choral effects, including widely spaced choirs uttering crowd noises, this was one of the very first avant-garde works to make a breakthrough into a wider public. This first CD version is welcome, beautifully recorded by British engineers in Poland; but Penderecki's own reading cannot quite match in intensity the earlier version made under Henryk Czyz in the 1960s. The composer's relatively detached approach exposes a dangerous thinness in the argument, though it remains a powerful and moving piece.

Pergolesi, Giovanni (1710–36)

Sinfonia for cello and continuo.
*** Decca Dig. 425 614-2; *425 614-4* [id.]. Peter Howard, St Paul CO, Hogwood – GALLO: *Trio sonata movements;* STRAVINSKY: *Pulcinella* etc. ***

Though Stravinsky originally thought that all his sources for his ballet, *Pulcinella*, were drawn from Pergolesi, much of the material he used was written by others. Stylishly played here, this charming *Sinfonia for cello* is genuine, providing in its finale the material for the memorable *Vivo* movement, which Stravinsky outrageously scored for trombone and double-bass.

Magnificat.
(M) **(*) Decca 425 724-2; *425 724-4*. Vaughan, J. Baker, Partridge, Keyte, King's College Ch., ASMF, Willcocks – VIVALDI: *Gloria; Magnificat.* **(*)

This Pergolesi *Magnificat* – doubtfully attributed, like so much that goes under this composer's name – is a comparatively pale piece to go with the Vivaldi *Magnificat* and *Gloria*. But the King's Choir gives a beautiful performance, and the recording matches it in intensity of atmosphere. The CD transfer is expertly managed.

Miserere II in C min.
(M) *** Decca 430 359-2; *430 359-4*. Wolf, James, Covey-Crump, Stuart, Magdalen College, Oxford, Ch., Wren O, Bernard Rose – A. and G. GABRIELI: *Motets*. **(*)

Pergolesi's *Miserere* was long listed under doubtful or spurious works, but modern opinion seems to favour its probable authenticity. Whatever the case, this work is both ambitious and moving. It consists of fifteen numbers: seven solo arias, two trios and six choruses. The singers are all of quality, particularly Richard Stuart, and Bernard Rose secures expressive and persuasive results from the Magdalen College Choir and the Wren Orchestra. The (originally Argo) recording, made in Magdalen College Chapel in 1979, is warm and atmospheric and sounds magnificently real and vivid in its CD format.

Stabat Mater.
*** DG 415 103-2; *415 103-4* [id.]. Margaret Marshall, Valentini Terrani, LSO, Abbado.

(i; ii) *Stabat Mater;* (ii) *In coelestibus regnis;* (i) *Salve Regina in A.*
*** Hyp. Dig. CDA 66294; *KA 66294* [id.]. (i) Gillian Fisher; (ii) Michael Chance; King's Consort, Robert King.

Abbado's account brings greater intensity and ardour to this piece than any rival, and he secures marvellously alive playing from the LSO – this without diminishing religious sentiment. Margaret Marshall is an impressive singer; her contribution combines fervour with an attractive variety of colour, while Lucia Valentini Terrani is an excellent foil. The DG recording has warmth and good presence and the perspective is thoroughly acceptable. This is now a clear first choice.

The Hyperion recording makes a very good case for authenticity in this work. The combination of soprano and male alto blends well together yet offers considerable variety of colour. There is purity of timbre here, but also plenty of expressive intensity. The accompanying string group is led by Roy Goodman, thus ensuring a high standard, and the continuo is equally well managed. Each of the soloists is given a separate encore. Gillian Fisher's *Salve Regina* is quite a considerable piece in four sections, whereas Michael Chance's motet is brief but makes an engaging postlude. Excellent sound.

La serva padrona (opera) complete recording (includes alternative ending and insertion arias).
*** Hung. HCD 12846-2 [id.]. Katalin Farkas, József Gregor, Capella Savaria, Németh.

La serva padrona is ideally suited to disc, and on this Hungaroton issue receives a delightful, sparkling performance with the excellent period-performance group, Capella Savaria. József Gregor sings with splendid buffo stylishness, while Katalin Farkas, as Serpina the maid, brings out the fun of the writing, with the shrewishness of the character kept in check. Bright, clean recording.

Pettersson, Allan (1911–80)

(i) *Viola concerto. Symphony No. 5.*
*** BIS Dig. CD 480 [id.]. (i) Nobuko Imai; Malmö SO, Moshe Atzmon.

Allan Pettersson's *Fifth* is a one-movement work and begins well. However, invention flags and the brooding, expectant atmosphere and powerful ostinatos arouse more promise of development than fulfilment. The *Viola concerto* comes from the last year of Pettersson's life and is pretty amorphous, but has rather greater substance than the garrulous, self-pitying symphonies he composed in the 1970s. Both pieces lack the concentration and quality of Tubin or Holmboe. The three stars are for the performers and the recording team.

Pfitzner, Hans (1869–1949)

(i) *Duo for violin, cello and orchestra, Op. 43;* (ii) *Symphony in C, (An die Freunde), Op. 43;* (iii) Songs: *Abbitte; Die Einsame; Der Gärtner; Hast du von den Fischerkindern das alte Märchen vernommen?; Herbstgefühl; Hussens Kerker; In Danzig; Leuchtende Tage; Michaelskirchplatz; Nachts; Säerspruch; Zum Abschied meiner Tochter.*

(***) Preiser mono 90029. (i) Max Strub, Ludwig Hoelscher, Berlin Staatsoper O; (ii) Berlin PO, composer; (iii) Gerhard Hüsch, composer.

This CD collects recordings made by Hans Pfitzner, both as a conductor and as pianist, between 1938 and 1940, when the German record industry was celebrating his seventieth birthday. The most astonishing performances for the younger generation will be Gerhard Hüsch's remarkable accounts of the songs. (He recorded these at much the same time as he sang Papageno in Beecham's legendary *Magic Flute*.) What a voice and what diction! The Preiser CD does not run to the full texts of the songs, let alone a translation, but, sung like this, you don't need them. These Lieder inhabit much the same world as those of Brahms and Strauss and have moments of great poignancy. The simplicity of Pfitzner's setting of Eichendorff's *Der Gärtner* or the opening song on the disc, *Hast du von den Fischerkindern das alte Märchen vernommen?*, have an eloquence all their own. Pfitzner was by this time a better conductor than pianist (he is inclined to overpedal) and his performances of both the *Duo* and the *Symphony in C* have splendid grip. German recording of this period was much admired at the time and, to judge from the quality of the orchestral sound, rightly so.

Palestrina (opera) complete.
(M) *** DG 427 417-2 (3) [id.]. Gedda, Fischer-Dieskau, Weikl, Ridderbusch, Donath, Fassbaender, Prey, Tölz Boys' Ch., Bav. R. Ch. & SO, Kubelik.

Though Pfitzner's melodic invention hardly matches that of his contemporary, Richard Strauss, his control of structure and drawing of character through music make an unforgettable impact. It is the central Act, a massive and colourful tableau representing the Council of Trent, which lets one witness the crucial discussion on the role of music in the church. The outer Acts – more personal and more immediately compelling – show the dilemma of Palestrina himself and the inspiration which led him to write the *Missa Papae Marcelli*, so resolving the crisis, both personal and public. At every point Pfitzner's response to this situation is illuminating, and this glorious performance with a near-ideal cast, consistent all through, could hardly be bettered in conveying the intensity of an admittedly offbeat inspiration. This CD reissue captures the glow of the Munich recording superbly and, though this is a mid-price set, DG has not skimped on the accompanying booklet.

Philips, Peter (*c.* 1561–1640)

Motets: *Ave verum corpus; Ave Maria gratia plena; Ecce vicit Leo; Factum est silentium; Gaudent in coelis; Hodie nobis de coelo; O bone Jesu; O crux ave spes unica; O quam suavis.*
**(*) EMI Dig. CDC7 54189-2 [id.]; *EL 754189-4*. King's College, Cambridge, Ch., Cleobury – DERING: *Motets*. **(*)

Both Peter Philips and his younger contemporary, Richard Dering, were Catholics and spent much of their lives on the Continent. Philips had been a choirboy at St Paul's Cathedral but left London when he was about twenty and settled first in Rome, then in Antwerp, before ending his days at the Chapel Royal of the Archduke Albert in Brussels. His music enjoyed some popularity in its day and much of it was published by the Antwerp publisher, Pierre Phalèse. This CD contrasts and compares the two composers' settings of the same texts, drawing on Philips's *Cantiones sacrae* of 1612 and 1613 and the *Paradisus sacris* of 1628. There are some beautiful and expressive settings among both composers, and the disc forms a useful addition to the catalogue. The performances are faithful but the actual sound falls short of distinction, and is not always perfect in either focus or blend, partly perhaps but not solely due to the recording. The repertoire is not otherwise available.

Pierné, Gabriel (1863–1937)

Les Cathédrales: Prelude (No. 1); Images, Op. 49; Paysages franciscains, Op. 43; Viennoise (suites de valses et cortège blues), Op. 49 bis.
(M) *** EMI CDM7 63950-2. Loire PO, Pierre Dervaux.

Gabriel Pierné was a leading figure in French musical life during the years of Debussy and Ravel. The opening *Prélude* to *Les Cathédrales* (1915) is an evocation of the desolation caused by war; while *Images* is a late work, composed in 1935, only two years before Pierné's death.

The score is full of touches of pastiche – a reference to Dukas's *La Péri* in the opening, an allusion to Debussy's *Gigues*, and so on – and there follows a set of pieces, *Viennoise*, in which Pierné developed two of the numbers in the divertissement as 'valses et cortège blues'. The three picturesque *Paysages franciscains* (1920) betray the composer's love of Italy. All of this is rewarding music in the best French tradition, extremely well played. The 1978 recording has plenty of warmth and atmosphere, and the CD brings a greater sense of transparency without drying out the ambience.

Cydalise et le Chèvre-pied (ballet): *suites Nos. 1–2. Ramuntcho (Overtures on Basque popular theme).*
(M) *** EMI CDM7 64278-2 [id.]. Paris Opéra O, Jean-Baptiste Mari.

Everyone will recognize the piquant opening of *Cydalis et le Chèvre-pied*: as the *Entry of the Little Fauns* it enjoyed great popularity in the 1940s and '50s. Indeed its fame has helped to keep Pierné's name alive and led to the resurgence of interest in him in France. The ballet dates from 1919 and was first produced in 1923. The ideas are fresh, often modal and beautifully fashioned, though ultimately not really distinctive, though the *Pas des apothicaires* is robustly catchy and the *Danses des Esclaves* and *Entreé des suivantes et du Négrillon* have a delicate grace. Nevertheless, when played so elegantly and sympathetically, this is music that deserves the widest circulation; even the *Ramuntcho overture*, an earlier piece dating from 1907, has vitality and charm. The Paris Opéra Orchestra is on its best form here and Mari, who has also given us outstanding Delibes recordings, was an ideal choice for this repertoire. It is a pity that the brief notes fail to relate the ballet's story directly to the 16 excerpts; but the picture, Louis Janmot's *Rayon de soleil*, on the front of the CD is aptly attractive.

Piston, Walter (1894–1976)

(i; ii) *Capriccio for harp and strings;* (ii) *3 New England sketches;* (iii) *Serenata;* (ii) *Symphony No. 4.*
*** Delos Dig. DE 3106 [id.]. (i) Wunrow; (ii) Seattle SO; (iii) NY CO; Gerard Schwarz.

If the *Third Symphony* (once available on Mercury and hopefully destined for reissue during the lifetime of this book) is Piston's most powerfully organic and darkly brooding symphony, the *Fourth* is his most genial. It has an irresistible opening idea and the whole work exudes a lyricism that we do not always associate with this composer. The slow movement is highly imaginative with a strong atmosphere; some passages are quite inspired, almost reminding the listener of a landscape bathed in strong moonlight. It is arguably the finest American symphony, as powerful in its forward sweep as the Harris *Third* and better held together than either Barber's *First* or Copland's *Third*. The remaining pieces, not only the *New England sketches* but also the inventive *Capriccio for harp and strings*, are well worth seeking out. Even if the performance of the *Fourth Symphony* does not banish memories of Ormandy's pioneering mono account with the Philadelphia Orchestra, the natural recording, of somewhat lower level than usual, and Gerard Schwarz's natural and unforced direction makes this a most desirable CD. The slow movement of the *Serenata*, equally well played by New York forces is quite inspired.

The Incredible flutist (complete ballet).
*** Albany TROY 016-2. Louisville O, Jorge Mester (with KAY: *Cakewalk* ***).

The Incredible flutist (ballet; complete); *New England sketches; Symphony No. 6* (1955).
*** BMG/RCA Dig. RD 60798 [60798-2-RC]. St Louis SO, Leonard Slatkin.

The Incredible flutist is Piston's best-known piece, with its appealing melodies and colourful textures. At this time he was still recovering from the heady Gallic influences he had encountered at the feet of Nadia Boulanger in Paris. The most powerful work on Slatkin's disc is the *Sixth Symphony*, written for Charles Munch and the Boston orchestra which he knew so well. At the time Piston wrote rather disarmingly, 'It seemed as though the melodies were being written by the instruments themselves as I just followed along,' and there is an inexorable sense of logic and inevitability. Piston is a cultivated, refined symphonist who does not wear his heart on his sleeve. The playing of the St Louis orchestra under Leonard Slatkin both here and in the *New England sketches* is sensitive and brilliant, and the RCA engineers give them excellent quality.

Walter Piston's ballet *The Incredible flutist* comes from 1938 and is one of the most refreshing and imaginative of all American scores. Hitherto it has been known as a suite, in which the composer selected his more important material, ideas that are instantly memorable. The full score – offered on Troy for the first time in an excellent mid-1970s recording – does bring a degree of dilution but a gain in cohesion. Incidentally, the Flutist does not make his appearance until well into the ballet, which is about the visit of a circus to a sleepy Spanish village. Jorge Mester directs an authoritative account; the Louisville Orchestra are highly sympathetic and play vividly throughout. The CD remastering adds presence, while retaining the original ambience.

Symphony No. 2.
(M) *** DG 429 860-2 [id.]. Boston SO, Tilson Thomas – RUGGLES: *Sun-treader;* SCHUMAN: *Violin concerto.* ***

Walter Piston has greater reticence and refinement than Aaron Copland and is less a prisoner of his own mannerisms than Roy Harris. His wartime *Second Symphony* (1943) makes a good entry point if you are starting to collect his music. It is more than finely crafted: it has a generosity of melodic invention and in the slow movement possesses a nobility that makes a strong impression. Michael Tilson Thomas and the Boston Symphony are very persuasive in its advocacy and the recording from the early 1970s is very good.

Symphonies Nos. 5; (i) 7 and 8.
** Albany AR 011 [id.]. Louisville O, Whitney, (i) Mester.

Walter Piston's symphonies belong among the best that America has ever produced. Some authorities suggest that his music is finely crafted but more worthy than inspired. The opening of the *Fifth Symphony* belies that, and the music has a sureness of purpose and feeling for organic growth that are the hallmark of the true symphonist. The *Seventh* and *Eighth Symphonies*, though not quite the equal of the finest Piston, are powerful and rewarding works which will speak to those who are more concerned with substance than with surface appeal. The Louisville is not in the front rank of American orchestras, but the performances are thoroughly committed and good, without being outstanding. The recordings sound better than they did on LP and serve as a vehicle to acquaint us with a serious and thoughtful composer.

(i) *Piano quintet. Passacaglia; Piano sonata; Toccata.*
**(*) Northeastern/Koch Int. Dig. NR 232-CD [id.]. Leonard Hokanson; (i) Portland Qt.

The *Piano quintet* is a fine work – indeed, it must be numbered among the finest post-Second World War piano quintets. Its claims on the repertoire are every bit as strong as either of the Bloch quintets and, though it does not have as strong a profile or personality as the Shostakovich, it is a work of great vitality and integrity. These artists give a more than respectable account of it, and Leonard Hokanson proves no less convincing and responsive in the early *Piano sonata.* The recording is not three-star, but this should not seriously inhibit a recommendation to those with an interest in this fine composer.

String quartets Nos. 1–3.
** Northeastern/Koch Dig. NR 9001-CD [id.]. Portland Qt.

Piston's five string quartets embrace the period 1933–62 and are finely crafted pieces, sinewy and Hindemithian at times (the first movement of No. 1), thoughtful and inward-looking at others (the Lento opening of No. 2 and the slow movement of No. 3). His music never wears its heart on its sleeve, but if its emotional gestures are restrained there is no real lack of warmth. Some of the faster movements, such as the finale of No. 1, are a bit busy. The Portland Quartet play well, though there is some less than absolutely true intonation in the slow movement of No. 3. The recordings are clear but the acoustic is a little on the small side.

Pizzetti, Ildebrando (1880–1968)

Messa di Requiem. Due composizioni corali: Il giardino di Afrodite; Piena sorgeva la luna. Tre composizioni corali: Cade la sera; Ululate; Recordare, Domine.
*** Chan. Dig. CHAN 8964 [id.]. Danish Nat. R. Chamber Ch., Stefan Parkman.

Like Arnold Bax in England, Ildebrando Pizzetti belongs to what the Italians call the *Generazione dell'Ottanta*, his best-known contemporaries being Malipiero and Casella. Every composer suffers neglect after his death but the trough into which Pizzetti's fortunes have declined has been even deeper than Malipiero's (or Bax's here in the late 1950s and early 1960s). Operas such as *Murder in the Cathedral* and *Il Calzare d'Argento* no longer hold the stage, though off-air LPs of them circulated at one time, and such colourful scores as the *Concerto dell'estate* and the suite *La Pisanella* have disappeared from the catalogue. His *Requiem* (coupled with the Frank Martin *Mass*) was recorded on the Swedish label Proprius, but this Chandos issue is even finer and has the merit of offering two other Pizzetti rarities in performances of high quality by the Danish Radio Chamber Choir. Pizzetti wrote with exceptional sympathy for voices and his *Requiem* (1922–3), in memory of his first wife, is a work of striking beauty and purity of utterance. In his note John Waterhouse speaks of it as occupying something of the same position in Italian music as the Vaughan Williams *Mass in G minor* (1920–21) does in English music. Be that as it may, there is no doubt that this is a most rewarding issue, one of the finest choral records of recent years.

Pleyel, Ignaz (1757–1831)

Clarinet concerto in C.
*** Claves CD 50-813 [id.]. Friedli, SW German CO, Angerer – MERCADANTE: MOLTER: *Concertos.* ***

Pleyel's *Concerto*, written for C clarinet, is obviously post-Mozart, and his debt to that master is obvious. The work is engagingly inventive throughout, with the finale especially attractive. Friedli plays it skilfully and sympathetically and gets good if not outstanding support from Angerer. The CD gives good presence to the soloist; orchestral detail is a little clouded by the resonance, but the overall sound is very pleasing.

Ponce, Manuel (1882–1948)

Folia de España (Theme and variations with fugue).
(M) *** Sony SBK 47669 [id.]. John Williams (guitar) – BARRIOS: *Collection.* ***

Ponce's *Variations on 'Folia de España'* are subtle and haunting, and their surface charm often conceals a vein of richer, darker feeling. This piece, with its fugue, extends for 24 minutes and the writing is resourceful and imaginative. The performance is first rate and the sound admirably clean and finely detailed, yet at the same time warm.

Ponchielli, Amilcare (1834–86)

La Gioconda (complete).
*** Decca Dig. 414 349-2 (3) [id.]. Caballé, Baltsa, Pavarotti, Milnes, Hodgson, L. Op. Ch., Nat. PO, Bartoletti.
*** EMI CDS7 49518-2 (3) [Ang. CDCC 49518]. Callas, Cossotto, Ferraro, Vinco, Cappuccilli, Companeez, La Scala, Milan, Ch. & O, Votto.

The colourfully atmospheric melodrama of this opera gives the Decca engineers the chance to produce a digital blockbuster, one of the most vivid opera recordings yet made. The casting could hardly be bettered, with Caballé just a little overstressed in the title-role but producing glorious sounds. Pavarotti has impressive control and heroic tone. Commanding performances too from Milnes as Barnaba, Ghiaurov as Alvise and Baltsa as Laura, firm and intense all three. Bartoletti proves a vigorous and understanding conductor, presenting the blood and thunder with total commitment but finding the right charm in the most famous passage, the *Dance of the hours*.

Maria Callas gave one of her most vibrant, most compelling, most totally inspired performances on record in the title-role of *La Gioconda*, with flaws very much subdued. The challenge she presented to those around her is reflected in the soloists – Cossotto and Cappuccilli both at the very beginning of distinguished careers – as well as the distinctive tenor Ferraro and the conductor Votto, who has never done anything finer on record. The recording still sounds well, though it dates from 1959.

Porter, Cole (1891–1964)

Ballets: *The Snake in the grass* (from *Fifty million Frenchmen); Within the Quota.* Overtures: *Anything goes; Can-Can; Du Barry was a lady* (with *Gavotte*); *Fifty million Frenchmen; Gay divorce* (with *Night and day*); *Kiss me Kate; Leave it to me; Out of this world; Something for the Boys; You never know.*
*** EMI Dig. CDC7 54300-2 [id.]; *EL 754300-4.* London Sinf., John McGlinn.

A splendid supplement to John McGlinn's series of recordings of American musicals, with 76 minutes of racy vitality and plenty of good tunes. The orchestrations are authentic, most notably that for the ballet, *Within the Quota*, written for Parisian performance in 1923 and orchestrated by no less than Charles Koechlin. The fascinating score has the brittle, jazzy, satirical flavour of its time, and much ecclectic outside influence in its parody of 'the American dream'. It could well have been written for the Ballets Russes. This is its world première recording. The much briefer *Snake in the grass* originally had choreography by Massine. It was intended as an up-market ballet interlude in *Fifty Million Frenchmen*, but was dropped from the show before the New York première. The Overtures were not put together or scored by the composer, but by the professionals of the day, including F. Henry Klickman, Hans Spialek, and Robert Russell Bennett. *As Gay divorce* does not include the most famous number from the show, a separate arrangement of *Night and day* has been included, richly scored by Spialek. The performances here are surely definitive and the bright recording fits the music like a glove.

Anything goes (musical).
*** EMI Dig. CDC7 49848-2 [id.]; EL 749848-2. Criswell, Groenendaal, Von Stade, Ambrosian Ch., LSO, McGlinn.

John McGlinn, with a scholarly concern for original sources comparable to that of a baroque specialist, here reconstructs the original (1934) version of Cole Porter's brilliant score, with the plot following the characters on a liner sailing the Atlantic in the 1930s. McGlinn firmly demonstrates the extra vigour and point of this version over the radical revisions made after the Second World War, when other numbers were introduced and the orchestration was radically altered. McGlinn had the benefit of working with Hans Spialek, one of the original orchestrators, just before he died at the age of 89. In the original production Ethel Merman had her first big Broadway success in the unlikely role of Reno, evangelist-turned-nightclub-singer, and here Kim Criswell proves a superb successor. In the very first number, *I get a kick out of you*, she commandingly establishes her star quality, and she remains the focus of the whole piece, though Frederica von Stade is equally winning as the second heroine, Hope. One of the other hit numbers, *You're the top*, is presented in a clipped way that follows the original rather than what has become traditional practice. The well-filled single disc includes as an appendix three extra numbers cut from the 1934 score, one of them, *There's no cure like travel*, a more elaborate version of the chorus, *Bon voyage*, involving a counter-theme in descant. Full, satisfyingly beefy sound, bringing out the vigour of playing and singing.

Kiss me Kate (musical).
*** EMI Dig. CDS7 54033-2 (2). Barstow, Hampson, Criswell, Dvorsky, Burns, Evans, Amb. Ch., L. Sinf., John McGlinn.

It may seem extravagant for a Cole Porter musical to stretch to two discs but, as in his previous recordings for EMI, McGlinn has delved into the archives and has rescued the originally neglected material, so providing a substantial and fascinating appendix, unearthing such lovely songs as the heroine's *We shall never be younger*. There is also a nicely judged sprinkling of dialogue between numbers. Having two opera-singers, Josephine Barstow and Thomas Hampson, in the principal roles of the ever-argumentative husband-and-wife team who play Kate and Petruchio in *The Taming of the Shrew* also works excellently, both strong and characterful. There is little of the inconsistency of style which made the choice of Dame Kiri Te Kanawa so controversial in *West Side Story*. Kim Criswell is delectable as Lois Lane, brassy but not strident in *Always true to you, darling, in my fashion*. Strong characterization too from George Dvorsky, Damon Evans and Karla Burns, with the London Sinfonietta – as in the prize-winning set of *Show Boat* – playing their hearts out. The recording is full and vivid with enough atmosphere to intensify the sense of presence.

Songs: *Begin the Beguine; Bring me back my butterfly; Bull Dog; Don't fence me in; Drink; Easy to love; A fool there was; How's your romance?; I concentrate on you; In the still of the night; It was written in the stars; I've got you under my skin; My cozy little corner in the Ritz; Night and day; Two little babes in the wood; When I had a uniform on; When my baby goes to town; Who said Gay Paree?*
*** EMI Dig. CDC7 54203-2 [id.]; *EL 754203-4*. Thomas Hampson, Ambrosian Ch., LSO, McGlinn.

As in McGlinn's outstanding recording of Irving Berlin's *Annie get your gun*, Thomas Hampson proves an ideal baritone for this repertory, totally inside the idiom, yet bringing to it a gloriously firm, finely controlled voice. The selection is a delightful one, including not just popular 'standards' but unexpected rarities. Excellent sound.

Poulenc, Francis (1899–1963)

(i) *Les animaux modèles;* (ii; iii) *Les Biches* (complete ballet); (ii) *Bucolique;* (i; iv) *Concerto champêtre (for harpsichord & orchestra);* (i; v) *Double piano concerto in D min.;* (vi) *2 Marches et un intermède (for chamber orchestra); Les mariés de la Tour Eiffel (La baigneuse de Trouville; Discourse du Génal).* (ii) *Matelote provençale; Pastourelle;* (vi) *Sinfonietta; Suite française.*
(B) *** EMI Analogue/Dig. CZS7 62690-2 (2). (i) Paris Conservatoire O; or (ii) Philh. O; (iii) with Amb. S.; (iv) with Van der Wiele, or (v) composer and Février; (vi) O de Paris; all cond. Prêtre.

Les Biches comes here in its complete form, with the choral additions that Poulenc made optional when he came to rework the score. The music is a delight, and so too is the group of captivating short pieces, digitally recorded at the same time (1980): *Bucolique, Pastourelle* and *Matelote provençale.* High-spirited, fresh, elegant playing and sumptuous recorded sound enhance the claims of all this music. The strings have freshness and bloom and there is no lack of presence. The set is worth having for this music alone – we gave it a Rosette when it was first issued on a single LP and cassette.

The *Suite française* is another highlight. It is based on themes by the sixteenth-century composer, Claude Gervaise; they are dance pieces which Poulenc has freely transcribed, and the wind and brass writing is very colourful. It is well played and recorded in a pleasing, open acoustic. Poulenc himself was a pianist of limited accomplishment, but his interpretation (with partner) of his own skittish *Double concerto* is infectiously jolly. In the imitation pastoral concerto for harpsichord, Aimée van de Wiele is a nimble soloist, but here Prêtre's inflexibility as a conductor comes out the more, even though the finale has plenty of high spirits. The *Sinfonietta*, too, could have a lighter touch, but it does not lack personality. *Les animaux modèles* is based on the fables of La Fontaine, with a prelude and a postlude, but here the recording is rather lacking in bloom, and the *Deux Marches* are also a trifle overbright. But for the most part the resonance gives colour and ambience to the transfers from the late 1960s. With nearly 156 minutes' playing time, these CDs are well worth exploring.

Aubade (Concerto choréographique); Piano concerto in C sharp min.; (i) *Double piano concerto in D min.*
*** Erato/Warner Dig. 2292 45232-2 [id.]. Duchable; (i) Collard; Rotterdam PO, Conlon.

The *Aubade* is an exhilarating work of great charm. It dates from the late 1920s and is a send-up of Mozart, Stravinsky, etc. The *Piano concerto* has a most beguiling opening theme and evokes the faded charms of Paris in the '30s. The skittish *Double concerto* is infectiously jolly. One could never mistake the tone of voice intended. The performances of the two solo works by François-René Duchable and the Rotterdam orchestra have a certain panache and flair that are most winning. The *Double concerto* too captures all the wit and charm of the Poulenc score, with the 'mock Mozart' slow movement particularly elegant. The balance is almost perfectly judged. Perhaps in the solo works Duchable is a shade too prominent, but not sufficiently so to disturb a strong recommendation, for the sound is otherwise full and pleasing.

Aubade; Sinfonietta.
*** Hyp. Dig. CDA 66347; *KA 66347* [id.]. New London O, Ronald Corp – HAHN: *Le bal de Béatrice d'Este (ballet suite).* ***

The *Sinfonietta* has enormous charm – at least it has in this winning performance! It is a fluent and effortless piece, full of resource and imagination, and Ronald Corp and the New London Orchestra, making their début on record, do it proud. This performance has a real sense of style and a Gallic elegance that promise well for this ensemble's future. Julian Evans is an alert soloist in the *Aubade*: his is a performance of real character and, though less well balanced than the *Sinfonietta*, he can hold his own artistically with the best. The Hahn rarity with which it is coupled enhances the interest and value of this release.

Les Biches (ballet suite).
*** Chan. Dig. CHAN 9023 [id.]. Ulster O, Yan Pascal Tortelier – IBERT: *Divertissement*; MILHAUD: *Le Boeuf; La Création*. ***
(M) *** EMI CDM7 63945-2 [id.]. Paris Conservatoire O, Prêtre – DUTILLEUX: *Le Loup;* MILHAUD: *Création du monde*. ***

Yan Pascal Tortelier and the Ulster Orchestra give an entirely winning account of Poulenc's ballet suite. Its freshness makes one realize why, when the ballet was first performed by Diaghilev's Ballets Russes, the composer became an overnight star. Here the opening has delightfully keen rhythmic wit, and the playing is equally polished and crisply articulated in the gay *Rag-Mazurka* and infectious *Final*. The lovely *Adagietto* is introduced with tender delicacy, yet reaches a suitably plangent climax. Top-drawer Chandos sound and splendid couplings ensure the overall succes of this admirable compilation.

Prêtre has re-recorded *Les Biches* digitally in its complete format (see above). This 1961 recording of the suite, omitting the chorus, is well worth having in its own right: the racy style of the orchestral playing is instantly infectious in the opening *Rondeau* with its catchy trumpet solo. The remastered sound-picture is one example where the bright vividness of CD is entirely advantageous.

Les Biches (ballet): *suite;* (i) *Piano concerto;* (ii) *Gloria*.
(M) *** EMI CDM7 69644-2. (i) Ortiz; (ii) N. Burrowes, CBSO Ch.; CBSO, Frémaux.

Cristina Ortiz advances an alert and stylish account of Poulenc's disarming *Piano concerto* and is given splendid support from Louis Frémaux and the Birmingham orchestra. The latter's performance of *Les Biches*, too, is good-humoured, even if the opening trumpet tune is almost too fast in its impulsive vigour. In the *Gloria* Frémaux also secures excellent results and he has a sympathetic soloist in Norma Burrowes. The recording is brightly remastered but retains much of its sense of spectacle.

(i) *Concert champêtre for harpsichord and orchestra;* (ii) *Concerto in G min. for organ, strings and timpani.*
(M) *** Erato/Warner Dig. 2292 45233-2 [id.]. (i) Koopman; (ii) Alain; Rotterdam PO, Conlon.

The *Organ concerto* has never come off better in the recording studio than on this Erato recording, made in Rotterdam's concert hall, the Doelen, with its excellent Flentrop organ. Marie-Claire Alain is fully equal to the many changes of mood, and her treatment of the *Allegro giocoso* readily catches the music's rhythmic humour. The balance is very well managed and the CD is in the demonstration bracket in this work. The *Concert champêtre* always offers problems of balance, as it is scored for a full orchestra, but the exaggerated contrast was clearly intended by the composer. Those who like such a strong contrast will not be disappointed, for the performance is most perceptive, with a particularly elegant and sparkling finale. James Conlon provides admirable accompaniments.

(i) *Concert champêtre; Organ concerto in G min.;* (ii) *Gloria*.
(M) *** Decca 425 627-2. (i) Malcolm (hapsichord/organ), ASMF, Iona Brown; (ii) Greenbert, SRO Ch., SRO, Lopez-Cobos.

Organ concerto in G min. (for organ, strings and timpani).
(M) *** Decca 417 725-2 [id.]. George Malcolm, ASMF, Iona Brown – SAINT-SAËNS: *Symphony No. 3*. **(*)

George Malcolm's excellent version of the *Organ concerto* is also available coupled with Saint-Saëns, but pairing it with the *Concert champêtre* is even more attractive. In the latter work the engineers did not succumb to the temptation to make the harpsichord sound larger than life, and on CD the beautifully focused keyboard image contrasts wittily with the designedly ample orchestral tuttis. Some might feel that in the finale Malcolm rushes things a bit but the music effervesces, and in every other respect this is an exemplary account. Lopez-Cobos gives a fine account of the *Gloria*, expansive yet underlining the Stravinskian elements in the score. The sound throughout this CD is in the demonstration bracket.

Suite française.
(M) *** ASV CDWHL 2067; *ZCWHL 2067*. L. Wind O, Wick – GRAINGER: *Irish tune from County Derry* etc.; MILHAUD: *Suite française*. ***

This engaging suite is based on themes by the sixteenth-century composer Claude Gervaise, which Poulenc scored for a small ensemble of wind instruments for a production of a play of Édouard Bourdet called *La Reine Margot*. They are dance pieces which Poulenc has freely transcribed and which come up very freshly in these artists' hands. Excellent recording and couplings. Thoroughly recommended.

Cello sonata.
** Virgin Dig. VC7 90812-2 [id.]. Steven Isserlis, Pascal Devoyon – DEBUSSY; FRANCK: *Sonatas*. **

Steven Isserlis and Pascal Devoyon play most sensitively and are inside this idiom, but the close scrutiny to which the microphone subjects them does them some disservice. Both artists show subtlety and intelligence, and their performance deserves a recommendation.

Élégie for horn and piano; Sextet for piano, flute, oboe, clarinet, bassoon and horn; Clarinet sonata; Flute sonata; Trio for piano, oboe and bassoon.
**(*) Decca Dig. 421 581-2 [id., without *Élégie*]. Portal, Gallois, Bourgue, Rogé, Wallez, Cazalet.

Were the recording as good as the performances, Decca's collection would warrant a Rosette. The playing of Maurice Bourgue in the *Oboe sonata* is both masterly and touching, and all these artists are on top form. These performances have a wonderful freshness and convey a real sense of delight. The *Sextet* has an irresistible charm and, whether in the melting lyrical episode in the first movement or the sparkling articulation of the finale, these artists have an unfailing elegance. Pascal Rogé's pianism throughout is a constant source of pleasure, and the only drawback is the reverberance of the Salle Pleyel. Both the internal balance of the players and that of the recording engineers is excellent, even though they do not overcome the resonant venue. All the same, an enchanting disc.

PIANO MUSIC

Badinage; Bourrée au pavillon d'Auvergne; Feuillets d'album; Française; Humoresque; 6 Impromptus, Nos. 1–5; 15 Improvisations; 3 Intermezzi; Mélancolie; 3 Mouvements perpétuels; Napoli; 8 Nocturnes; 3 Novelettes; Pastourelle; 3 Pièces; Pièce brève sur le nom d'Albert Roussel; Presto in B flat; Promenades; Les soirées de Nazelles; Suite in C; Suite française; Thème varié; Valse in C; Valse-improvisation sur le nom de Bach; Villageoise.
**(*) Sony Dig. M3K 44921 (3). Paul Crossley.

Paul Crossley is a perceptive guide in this repertoire and those wanting so comprehensive a Poulenc collection can safely be directed here. Crossley is fleet-fingered and unfailingly intelligent, though he does not really have the grace and charm of Pascal Rogé. Good recording quality.

Badinage; Les Biches: Adagietto; Intermezzo No. 3 in A flat; 3 Mouvements perpétuels; Napoli; 3 Pièces; Les soirées de Nazelles; Suite in C; Valse-improvisation sur le nom de Bach.
*** Chan. Dig. CHAN 8637; *ABTD 1325* [id.]. Eric Parkin.

Eric Parkin's Poulenc recital competes very successfully and, though Rogé has perhaps just that extra ounce of charm and elegance, Parkin can be said to hold his own – which is some compliment. Decca score in the quality and sound of the piano. The Chandos recording is rather more resonant, though not unacceptably so. However, for anyone wanting a single disc of Poulenc's piano music, the Pascal Rogé recital must have preference.

Capriccio; Élégie; L'embarquement pour Cythère; Sonata for piano, four hands; Sonata for two pianos.
*** Chan. Dig. CHAN 8519; *ABTD 1229* [id.]. Seta Tanyel, Jeremy Brown.

Delightful and brilliant playing that is not to be missed. These two artists have a very close rapport and dispatch this repertoire with both character and sensitivity. They are ebullient and high-spirited when required and also uncover a deeper vein of feeling in the *Élégie* and the *Sonata for two pianos*. The Chandos recording is excellent, very vivid and present.

Humoresque; 15 Improvisations; Intermezzi Nos. 1 in C; 2 in D flat; Mélancolie; 3 Novelettes; Presto in B flat; Suite française d'après Claude Gervaise; Thème varié; Villageoises (Petites pièces enfantines).
*** Chan. Dig. CHAN 8847; *ABTD 1464* [id.]. Eric Parkin.

Eric Parkin is consistently underrated within these shores. He is an artist of instinctive taste and a refined musical intelligence who is completely inside this idiom. Readers who have begun collecting his cycle need not hesitate: he has plenty of spirit and character and abundant sensitivity. Perhaps Rogé has the greater pianistic finesse plus a gamin-like charm, but Parkin too has charm and, in many of the pieces where they overlap, there is often little to choose between them. The Chandos recording is slightly closer than the Decca, but the sound is very present and natural.

Humoresque; Improvisations Nos. 4, 5, 9–11 & 14; 2 Intermezzi; Intermezzo in A flat; Nocturnes; Presto in B flat; Suite; Thème varié; Villageoises.
*** Decca Dig. 425 862-2; *425 862-4* [id.]. Pascal Rogé.

Pascal Rogé's second Poulenc recital is every bit as captivating as his earlier disc, whether in the beguiling *Bal fantôme*, the third of the *Nocturnes*, inspired by Julien Green's *Le Visionnaire* in which an invalid hears the distant strains of a ball from his sick-bed, or in its dazzling, Stravinsky-like successor, evoking the myriads of moths and other winged creatures of the night. As in Rogé's first recital, there is charm and character here. The acoustic is somewhat reverberant but not excessively so. Elegant playing, responsive to all the rapidly changing shifts of tone in Poulenc's music, and strongly recommended.

Improvisations Nos. 1–3; 6–8; 12–13; 15; Mouvements perpétuels; 3 Novelettes; Pastourelle; 3 Pièces; Les soirées de Nazelles; Valse.
❀ *** Decca Dig. 417 438-2; *417 438-4* [id.]. Pascal Rogé.

This music is absolutely enchanting, full of delight and wisdom; it has many unexpected touches and is teeming with character. Rogé is a far more persuasive exponent of it than any previous pianist on record; his playing is imaginative and inspiriting, and the recording is superb.

VOCAL MUSIC

Mélodies: *Allons plus vite; Banalités; Le bestiare; Calligrammes; Chansons galliardes; Dans le jardin d'Anna; Epitaphe; La Grenouillère; Montparnasse; Le Pont; Priez pour paix.*
**(*) Adès 14114-2 & 14115-2 [id.]. Pierre Bernac, composer.

Pierre Bernac and Francis Poulenc were among the most celebrated partnerships in the recital rooms and broadcasting studios of the 1950s. Like his pupil Gérard Souzay, Bernac had enormous charm and great feeling for characterization and, although Poulenc was not the greatest of pianists, he was a sympathetic accompanist. Poulenc's contribution to the literature of French song is second only to that of Debussy and this recital is an invaluable guide to it. These recordings were made in Paris in 1959, when Bernac's vibrato was a little wider than in earlier life but his powers of characterization were undimmed. What a singer he was! The sound is stereo, and very alive and fresh for its period. (An earlier recital, recorded in 1950, can also be found in the Vocal Recitals section, below.)

(i) *Le Bal masqué; Le Bestiaire. Sextet for piano & wind; Trio for piano, oboe & bassoon.*
*** CRD Dig. CRD 3437 [id.]. (i) Thomas Allen; Nash Ens., Lionel Friend.

Thomas Allen is in excellent voice and gives a splendid account of both *Le Bal masqué* and *Le Bestiaire*. The Nash play both the *Trio* and the *Sextet* with superb zest and character. The wit of this playing and the enormous resource, good humour and charm of Poulenc's music are well served by a recording of exemplary quality and definition. Not to be missed.

Mélodies: *Banalités: Hôtel; Voyage à Paris. Bleuet. C; Calligrammes: Voyage. 4 Chansons pour enfants: Nous voulons une petite soeur. Les chemins de l'amour. Colloque; Hyde Park; Métamorphoses; Miroirs brûlants: Tu vois le feu du soir. Montparnasse; 2 Poèmes de Louis Aragon; 3 Poèmes de Louise Lalanne; Priez pour paix; Tel jour, telle nuit; Toréador.*
*** Hyp. Dig. CDA 66147 [id.]. Songmakers' Almanac: Lott, Rolfe Johnson, Murray, Johnson.

Graham Johnson calls his collection *Voyage à Paris*, after the title of the first song, a frothy and exuberant miniature which gets the record off to a flamboyant start. Felicity Lott sings that and the great majority of the remaining 29 songs, joyful and tender, comic and tragic by turns. The other soloists have one song apiece, done with comparable magnetism, and Richard Jackson joins Felicity Lott (one stanza each) in Poulenc's solitary 'song for two voices', *Colloque*, written in 1940 to words by Paul Valéry. Following that is another wartime song, *C*, most moving of all. First-rate recording, though Lott's soprano is not always as sweetly caught as it can be.

Figure humaine; Laudes de Saint Antoine de Padoue; 4 Motets pour le temps de Noël; 4 Motets pour un temps de pénitence; 4 Petites prières de Saint François d'Assise.
*** Virgin Dig. VC7 91075-2 [id.]. The Sixteen, Harry Christophers.

A lovely record which assembles the cantata for double choir, *Figure humaine*, with some of the composer's most celebrated *a cappella* motets. These performances can more than hold their own with most of Poulenc's choral music and is to be strongly recommended both on artistic grounds and for the excellence of the sound.

(i; ii) *Gloria; Ave verum corpus; Exultate Deo;* (ii) *Litanies à la Vierge Noire; 4 Motets pour le temps de Noël; 4 Motets pour un temps de pénitence; Salve regina.*
*** Coll. COLCD 108; *COLC 108*. (i) Donna Deam, Cambridge Singers, (ii) City of L. Sinfonia, John Rutter.

A generous selection of Poulenc's choral music, much of it of great beauty and simplicity, in very fresh-sounding performances and well-focused sound. In the *Gloria*, Donna Deam is not as strong a soloist as was, say, Rosanna Cartori (with Prêtre). However, the general standard of singing is high and the results can be recommended with confidence.

Mass in G; 4 petites prières de Saint François d'Assise; Salve regina.
*** Nimbus Dig. NI 5197 [id.]. Christ Church Cathedral Ch., Oxford, Stephen Darlington – MARTIN: *Mass for double choir*. **(*)

The *Mass in G* comes from 1937, not long after Poulenc's return to Catholicism, and has been described as combining the asceticism of Victoria with the brutality of Stravinsky. It is a work of strong appeal and greater dramatic fire than the *Salve Regina* of 1941 or the more intimate *Quatre petites prières de Saint François d'Assise* (1948) for men's voices. The choir of Christ Church Cathedral, Oxford, under Stephen Darlington sing with clean tone and excellent balance. The boys generally cope well with the demanding writing above the stave, and the Nimbus recording is very good indeed.

(i) *Mass in G. Salve regina.*
(M) *** Decca 430 360-2; *430 360-4* [id.]. (i) Bond; St John's College, Cambridge, Ch., Guest – FAURÉ: *Requiem* etc. ***

As a generous coupling for the Fauré *Requiem*, the choir of St John's College, Cambridge, offers the pre-war *Mass in G* major together with the motet, *Salve regina*, a finely wrought piece, in performances of great finish. The St John's forces cope admirably with the delicacy and sweetness of Poulenc's chromatic harmony, and the recorded sound is eminently realistic and truthful in its CD format.

4 Motets pour un temps de pénitence.
(M) *** Decca 430 346-2. Christ Church Cathedral, Oxford, Ch., L. Sinf., Simon Preston – STRAVINSKY: *Canticum sacrum* etc. ***

These motets are of great beauty and they are vibrantly performed here; indeed Simon Preston's account of them with the Christ Church Catherdral Choir could hardly be improved on, and the 1973 (originally Argo) recording produces rich timbre and a clean focus within an ideal ambience.

(i; iii) *4 Motets pour un temps de pénitence;* (ii; iv–vi) *7 Répons de ténèbres;* (iii, vi) *Sécheresses.*
(M) *** EMI CDM7 64279-2 [id.]. (i) Resnel; (ii) Carpentier; (iii) R. France Ch., (iv) Maîtrise de la Sainte Chapelle, (v) Petits Chanteurs de Chaillot, (vi) R. France New PO, Prêtre.

The three works on this disc were recorded in 1983–4 but were not generally available at that time in the UK. Indeed the current catalogue lists no alternative versions of either *Sécheresses* or the *Sept Répons de ténèbres*. There is a lot of Stravinsky in Poulenc's cantata, *Sécheresses*, composed in 1937 (mind you, so there is in much of his choral music) and it marks a turning point in his creative development; it was his first full-scale piece for voices and orchestra combined, and can in some ways be viewed as a forerunner of the *Stabat mater* and *Gloria*. It is quite a powerful piece and so is the much later *Sept Répons de ténèbres* (1961) for treble, chorus and orchestra; all show us the more serious side of his personality. Indeed its second movement seems almost like a trial run for the *Gloria*. Georges Prêtre gets very good results from his forces, Alexandre Carpentier, the treble gets a little lost in the acoustic of the Salle Wagram, but generally speaking, despite one or two moments of vulnerable choral intonation in the *Sept Répons*, the performances are more than serviceable and give pleasure. The more familiar *Quatre Motets pour un temps de pénitence* from 1938–9 complete a most attractive disc. No texts are provided.

Stabat Mater; Litanies à la vierge noire; Salve Regina.
*** HM Dig. HMC 905149; *HMC 405149* [id.]. Lagrange, Lyon Nat. Ch. and O, Baudo.

Serge Baudo is perhaps a more sympathetic interpreter of this lovely score than was Prêtre in his earlier record, and he gets more out of it. He certainly makes the most of expressive and dynamic nuances; he shapes the work with fine feeling and gets good singing from the Lyon Chorus. Michèle Lagrange has a good voice and is an eminently expressive soloist. The coupling offers the short *Salve Regina* and the *Litanies à la vierge noire*, an earlier and somewhat more severe work. A welcome and worthwhile issue.

Praetorius, Michael (1571–1621)

Dances from Terpsichore (extended suite).
*** Decca Dig. 414 633-2 [id.]. New L. Cons., Philip Pickett.

Dances from Terpsichore (Suite de ballets; Suite de voltes). (i) Motets: *Eulogodia Sionia: Resonet in laudibus; Musae Sionae: Allein Gott in der Höh sei Ehr; Aus tiefer Not schrei ich zu dir; Christus der uns selig macht; Gott der Vater wohn uns bei; Polyhymnia Caduceatrix: Erhalt uns, Herr, bei deinem Wort.*
(M) *** EMI CDM7 69024-2 [Ang. CDM 69024]. Early Music Cons. of L., Munrow, (i) with boys of the Cathedral and Abbey Church of St Alban.

Terpsichore is a huge collection of some 300 dance tunes used by the French-court dance bands of Henri IV. They were enthusiastically assembled by the German composer, Michael Praetorius, who also harmonized them and arranged them in four to six parts; however, any selection is conjectural in the matter of orchestration. One of the great pioneers of the 'authentic' re-creation of early music, David Munrow's main purpose was to bring the music fully to life and, at the same time, imaginatively to stimulate the ear of the listener. This record, made in 1973, is one of his most successful achievements. The sound is excellent in all respects. Munrow's instrumentation is imaginatively done: the third item, a *Bourrée* played by four racketts (a cross between a shawm and comb-and-paper in sound) is fascinating. The collection is a delightful one, the motets reminding one very much of Giovanni Gabrieli.

Philip Pickett's instrumentation (based on the illustrations which act as an appendix to the maestro's second volume of Syntagma Musicum of 1619) is sometimes less exuberant than that of David Munrow before him; but many will like the refinement of his approach, with small instrumental groups, lute pieces and even what seems like an early xylophone! There are also some attractively robust brass scorings (sackbuts and trumpets). The use of original instruments is entirely beneficial in this repertoire; the recording is splendid.

Christmas music: *Polyhymnia caduceatrix et panegyrica Nos. 9–10, 12 & 17. Puericinium Nos. 2, 4 & 5. Musae Sionae VI, No. 53: Es ist ein Ros' entsprungen. Terpsichore: Dances Nos. 1; 283–5; 310.*
*** Hyp. Dig. CDA 66200; *KA 66200* [id.]. Westminster Cathedral Ch., Parley of Instruments, David Hill.

Praetorius was much influenced by the polychoral style of the Gabrielis; these pieces from the *Polyhymnia caduceatrix et panegyrica* and the *Puericinium*, which come from the last years of his life, reflect this interest. The music is simple in style and readily accessible, and its performance on this atmospheric Hyperion record is both spirited and sensitive.

Christmas music: *Polyhymnia caduceatrix et panegyrica Nos. 10, Wie schön leuchtet der Morgenstern; 12, Puer natus in Bethlehem; 21, Wachet auf, ruft uns die Stimme; 34, In dulci jubilo.*
*** EMI Dig. CDC7 47633-2 [id.]. Taverner Cons., Ch. & Players, Parrott – SCHÜTZ: *Christmas oratorio.* ***

This is the finest collection of Praetorius's vocal music in the current catalogue. The closing setting of *In dulci jubilo*, richly scored for five choirs and with the brass providing thrilling contrast and support for the voices, has great splendour. Before that comes the lovely, if less ambitious *Wie schön leuchtet der Morgenstern*, where the opening shows how effectively Tessa Bonner and Emily Van Evera take the place of boy trebles. Both *Wachet auf* and *Puer natus in Bethlehem* are on a comparatively large scale, their combination of block sonorities and florid decorative effects the very essence of Renaissance style. The recording is splendidly balanced, with voices and brass blending and intertwining within an ample acoustic which brings weight and resonance without clouding.

Prokofiev, Serge (1891–1953)

Andante for strings, Op. 50 bis; Autumn (symphonic sketch), *Op. 8; Lieutenant Kijé: suite, Op. 60; The Stone flower: suite, Op. 118; Wedding suite, Op. 126.*
*** Chan. Dig. CHAN 8806; *ABTD 1434* [id.]. SNO, Järvi.

The suite from *Lieutenant Kijé* is the most familiar score here, and it is played with great flair and spirit; indeed, it is as good as any account now available. The *Andante* is a transcription for full strings of the slow movement of the *First String quartet*, made at the suggestion of Miaskovsky, and its eloquence is more telling in this form. *Autumn*, on the other hand, is an early piece, much influenced by Rachmaninov, in particular his symphonic poem, *The Isle of the dead*, and is full of imaginative touches. Järvi takes it at a fairly brisk tempo (it would have gained by a more spacious opening), but it remains appropriately atmospheric. The *Wedding suite* is drawn from *The Stone flower* and complements the Op. 118 suite from Prokofiev's last full-length ballet. Though not the equal of his other full-length ballets, *The Stone flower* has some engaging lyrical invention, and the music recorded here is still full of appeal. The performances and recording are in the best traditions of the house.

Boris Godunov, Op. 70 bis: Fountain scene; Polonaise. Dreams, Op. 6. Eugene Onegin, Op. 71: Minuet, Polka, Mazurka. 2 Pushkin waltzes, Op. 120. Romeo and Juliet (ballet): *suite No. 2, Op. 64.*
*** Chan. Dig. CHAN 8472; *ABTD 1183* [id.]. SNO, Järvi.

Järvi's second suite from *Romeo and Juliet* has sensitivity, abundant atmosphere, a sense of the theatre, and is refreshingly unmannered. Of the rarities, *Dreams* is atmospheric, if derivative, with a fair amount of Debussy and early Scriabin – to whom it is dedicated. A fuller selection of the music Prokofiev wrote for a production of *Eugene Onegin* is available – see below – but what is offered here, plus the *Two Pushkin waltzes*, are rather engaging lighter pieces. All this music is well worth having and the performances are predictably expert. The range of the recording is wide, the balance finely judged and detail is in exactly the right perspective.

Chout (The Buffoon): ballet, *Op. 21.*
**(*) Olympia Dig. OCD 126 [id.]. USSR MoC SO, Rozhdestvensky.

Chout comes from Prokofiev's time in Paris and was the first of his ballets that Diaghilev actually staged, a wonderfully imaginative score, full of colour and resource. Diaghilev never revived the ballet after 1922 and Prokofiev made a concert suite of twelve numbers. Rozhdestvensky gives a very lively account of the complete score and gets good playing from his youthful Moscow orchestra. The recording is as vivid as the music; indeed some may find it a little overbright at the top.

Chout (ballet): *suite, Op. 21a; Love for 3 Oranges: suite, Op. 33a; Le pas d'acier: suite, Op. 41a.*
*** Chan. Dig. CHAN 8729; *ABTD 1369* [id.]. SNO, Järvi.

Chout (ballet) *suite; Romeo and Juliet* (ballet), *Op. 64:* excerpts.
(M) *** Decca 425 027-2; *425 027-4* [id.]. LSO, Claudio Abbado.

It is difficult to see why a well-selected suite from *Chout* should not be as popular as any of Prokofiev's other ballet scores. Abbado's version with the LSO offers a generous part of the score, including some of the loosely written connecting material, and he reveals a sensitive ear for balance of texture. The excerpts from *Romeo and Juliet* include some of the most delightful numbers, which are often omitted from selections, such as the *Dance with mandolins*, the

Aubade and so on. The *Dance of the girls* is very sensuous and rather slow. But Abbado brings it off, and elsewhere there is admirable delicacy and a lightness of touch that are most engaging. The analogue recording, made in the Kingsway Hall in 1966, was a model of its kind; the remastering has brought an added intensity of impact without losing the ambient warmth and colour.

Järvi has a natural affinity for this repertoire and gets splendid results from the SNO; and the recording is pretty spectacular. Although Järvi gives us only a half of *Le pas d'acier*, it is the better half and his is a more refined performance (and infinitely more present recording) than the complete ballet on Olympia.

Cinderella (ballet; complete), Op. 87.
*** Decca Dig. 410 162-2 (2) [id.]. Cleveland O, Ashkenazy.

Compact disc collectors wanting the complete ballet can safely invest in Ashkenazy without fear of disappointment. Some dances come off better in Previn's EMI version (available only in highlights form), and there is an element of swings and roundabouts in comparing them. Detail is more closely scrutinized by the Decca engineers; Ashkenazy gets excellent results from the Cleveland Orchestra. There are many imaginative touches in this score – as magical indeed as the story itself – and the level of invention is astonishingly high. On CD, the recording's wonderful definition is enhanced, yet not at the expense of atmosphere, and the bright, vivid image is given striking projection.

Cinderella (ballet): highlights.
(M) *** EMI Dig.CDD7 64289-2 [id.]; *ET 764289-4*. LSO, Previn.

EMI have not yet seen fit to issue Previn's complete recording on CD but this highlights disc is generous (71 minutes) and well laid out to include the most important numbers from each of the three acts, including the final resolution of the story and Prokofiev's *Amoroso* apotheosis, as the Prince and Princess dance together in their enchanted garden. The playing of the LSO for Previn is extremely alert and beautifully characterized, the wind playing is particularly fine and there is a good sense of theatre. The 1983 Abbey Road recording has a spacious acoustic, while detail is crystal clear; indeed the brilliantly lit sound seems particularly apt for Prokofiev, for there is a pleasingly warm ambience. Yet the moment when midnight strikes is apocalyptic indeed! With 27 numbers offered, and a synopsis relating the action to each of the separate cues this reissue rather sweeps the board.

(i) *Cinderella:* excerpts; (ii) *Romeo and Juliet:* excerpts.
(M) *** EMI CD-EMX 2194; *TC-EMX 2194*. (i) RPO, Irving; (ii) Philh. O, Kurtz.

We have had a soft spot for this Irving/Kurtz coupling since it first appeared on LP. A perceptive and fairly generous selection from both ballets is included. Kurtz's *Romeo and Juliet* comes from the mid-1960s, but Irving's performances are from 1958, yet it would be difficult to guess the dates of either from the sound here, which is admirable in its definition and body. Irving secures very fine playing from the RPO, crisply rhythmic and sympathetic. In *Romeo and Juliet* Kurtz's performances are slightly lacking in dramatic tension in the longer movements, but the shorter dances come off superbly. But what beautifully shaped phrasing the Philharmonia give us and what full timbre. Given the remarkable quality of the transfers, this remains competitive, though it would have been even more so at bargain, rather than mid-price.

Cinderella (ballet): *suites Nos. 1 & 3.*
**(*) Chan. Dig. CHAN 8939; *ABTD 1535* [id.]. SNO, Järvi.

While there are no complaints about either the Järvi performances or the recordings, which mostly emanate from 1986–7 (four numbers were added for this issue), at 55 minutes and full price this is not the most generous of selections. All the same, Neeme Järvi and the Royal Scottish Orchestra are thoroughly persuasive.

Cinderella (ballet): *suites Nos. 1 & 2, Op. 107–8:* excerpts. (i) *Peter and the wolf, Op. 67.*
*** Chan. Dig. CHAN 8511; *ABTD 1221* [id.]. (i) Lina Prokofiev; SNO, Järvi.

Järvi's Prokofiev series here offers a characterful version of *Peter and the wolf.* In time-length it is very slow, but the magnetism of Madame Prokofiev (the composer's first wife), with many memorable lines delivered in her tangily Franco-Russian accent, makes up for that leisurely manner, with beautiful, persuasive playing from the Scottish National Orchestra. The very first mention of the wolf brings an unforgettable snarl, which most children will relish. Järvi's compilation of eight movements from the two *Cinderella suites* has even more persuasive playing, with the sensuousness of much of the writing brought out. Warmly atmospheric recording, with the narration realistically balanced.

Cinderella: suite No. 1, Op. 107; Lieutenant Kijé (suite); The Love for 3 Oranges: March; Scherzo; The Prince and Princess. Romeo and Juliet: Madrigal; Dance of the girls with lilies.
(BB) *** Naxos Dig. 8.550381 [id.]. Slovak State PO, (Košice), Andrew Mogrelia.

The calibre of this excellent Slovak orchestra is well demonstrated here, and its perceptive conductor, Andrew Mogrelia, is at his finest in his gently humorous portrait of *Lieutenant Kijé*, full of fantasy and gentle irony. The admirable selection of the three 'best bits' from *The Love for Three Oranges* brings out Prokofiev's Rimskian inheritance of Russian colour, rather than emphasizing the music's abrasive edge. The charming items from *Romeo and Juliet* are not duplicated in the fuller selection below. Excellent recording.

(i) *Concertino for cello and orchestra, Op. 132* (ed. Rostropovich; orch. Kabalevsky); (Solo) *Cello sonata, Op. 133* (ed. Blok).
*** Virgin Dig. VC7 90811-2; *VC 790811-4* [id.]. Isserlis, (i) LPO, Litton – KABALEVSKY: *Cello concerto No. 2.* ***

Only the first movement of the solo *Cello sonata* survived Prokofiev's death, and that in fragmentary form. Characteristic though much of it is (and the same must be said of the *Concertino*, two movements of which were fully sketched in short score), it is not vintage Prokofiev. Isserlis plays both pieces with great fervour and intelligence: he modifies Kabalevsky's scoring but also includes a rather imaginative cadenza by Olli Mustonen. These are the only recordings of either piece at present on CD and are of obvious interest to admirers of the composer.

(i) *Flute concerto* (orch. Palmer); (ii) *Humoresque scherzo, Op. 12 bis; Overture on Hebrew themes, Op. 34 bis; Sonata for unaccompanied violins, Op. 115; Symphony No. 1 in D (Classical), Op. 25.*
**(*) Conifer Dig. CDCF 173; *MCFC 173* [id.]. (i) Jonathan Snowden; (ii) Alexander, Gatt, Mackie, Orford; L. Musici, Mark Stephenson.

The *Flute concerto* is an arrangement of the *Sonata in D major*, which Prokofiev himself transcribed for violin and piano. It is expertly scored by Christopher Palmer but is in no sense a concerto, the orchestra's role being confined to that of accompaniment, for Prokofiev's piano writing was essentially small-scale and intimate. The *Humoresque scherzo* is one of the Op. 12 piano pieces in Prokofiev's own transcription for four bassoons, and the *Sonata*, Op. 115, so often heard for solo violin, was originally intended to be heard played by violins in unison, and sounds effective in this form. The *Overture on Hebrew themes* in its full orchestral form is well played and recorded, and so is the *Classical Symphony*, though it is rather on the slow side. Jonathan Snowden gives an excellent account of the arrangement of the *D major Sonata* and the recordings are well balanced, natural and realistic.

Piano concertos Nos. 1–5.
*** Chan. Dig. CHAN 8938; *DBTD 2027* (2) [id.]. Boris Berman (in Nos. 1, 4 & 5); Horacio Gutiérrez (in Nos. 2 & 3), Concg. O, Järvi.
(M) **(*) Decca 425 570-2 (2) [id.]. Ashkenazy, LSO, Previn.

Piano concertos Nos. 1 in D flat, Op. 10; 3 in C, Op. 26; 4 in B flat, Op. 53.
(BB) *** Naxos Dig. 8.550566 [id.]. Kun Woo Paik, Polish Nat. RSO (Katowice), Antoni Witt.

Piano concertos Nos. 2 in G min., Op. 16; 5 in G, Op. 55.
(BB) *** Naxos Dig. 8.550565 [id.]. Kun Woo Paik, Polish Nat. RSO (Katowice), Antoni Witt.

(i) *Piano concertos Nos. 1–5;* (ii) *Overture on Hebrew themes. Visions fugitives, Op. 22.*
(B) *** EMI CMS7 62542-2 (2). Michel Béroff; (i) with Leipzig GO, Masur; (ii) with Portal, Parrenin Qt.

The merits of the Berman single discs are discussed below. As a package, its claims are strong, both artistically and in terms of recording quality.

Honours are more evenly divided between Ashkenazy and Béroff than one might expect. Ashkenazy's virtuosity is often challenged by the young Frenchman, and he too plays masterfully; indeed, both sets of performances prove remarkably distinguished on closer acquaintance. However, for some the remastered Decca recording, which now has a top-heavy balance, will be a drawback. There is a fair amount of edginess and the upper strings tend to sound shrill at higher dynamic levels. The balance in the EMI version is slightly better, although the overall sound-picture is not wholly natural. The EMI CD transfer brings a fairly spiky sound to the violins – one would not guess that this was the Leipzig Gewandhaus Orchestra in the opening tutti of the *First Concerto*, which is bright rather than rich-textured. Nevertheless there is plenty of ambience and the somewhat acerbic sounds are not inappropriate for Prokofiev. Slow movements have plenty of atmosphere. Béroff is a pianist of genuine insight, and Masur gives him excellent support. He is free of some of the agogic mannerisms that distinguish Ashkenazy (in the first movement of No. 2 and the slow movement of No. 3) and he has great poetry. Ashkenazy has marvellous panache, of course; Previn is a sensitive accompanist and, for all its too-brilliant lighting, the Decca recording is extremely vivid, although the piano is made stereoscopically prominent. Generous bonuses are offered by the EMI set, which is reissued in their French 'two for the price of one' series. Béroff's account of the *Visions fugitives* is particularly distinguished, and the piano recording gives little cause for complaint.

The first of the two Naxos CDs begins with the *Third concerto*, and at the opening the ear is immediately ravished by the sound of the Polish orchestra's principal clarinet. Then Kun Woo Paik spurts off into the main allegro with enormous dash. His playing throughout these five concertos has exhilarating bravura. Tempi are dangerously fast at times and occasionally he has the orchestra almost scampering to keep up with him, but they do, and the result is often electrifying, not only in the *Allegro tempestoso* finale of No. 2, which these artists respond to quite literally, but in the *Allegro con fuoco Toccata* of No. 5. The *Vivace* finale of the *Fourth concerto* brings some remarkably neat articulation from the Polish strings. The famous theme and variations central movement of the *Third concerto* is played with great diversity of mood and style and the darkly expressive *Larghetto* of No. 5 is very finely done, while the piquant *Moderato ben accentuato* second movement is full of character with some spectacular splashes of sound from the soloist. The *First concerto*, which comes last on the first CD has great freshness and compares well with almost any version on disc. In short, with vivid recording in the Concert Hall of Polish Radio, which has plenty of ambience, this set is enormously stimulating and a remarkable bargain. It has far better sound than the remastered Decca recording for Ashkenazy, and any lack of polish in the playing is more than compensated for by the spontaneous combustion and exuberance of the music-making.

(i) *Piano concerto No. 1 in D flat. Suggestion diabolique, Op. 4/4.*
(M) *** EMI CDM7 64329-2 [id.]; *EG 764329-4*. Gavrilov, (i) LSO, Rattle – BALAKIREV: *Islamey;* TCHAIKOVSKY: *Piano concerto No. 1.* ***

A dazzling account of the *First Piano concerto* from Andrei Gavrilov. This version is second to none for virtuosity and sensitivity: it is no exaggeration to say that this exhilarating account is the equal of any we have ever heard and superior to most. Apart from its brilliance, this performance scores on other fronts too; Simon Rattle provides excellent orchestral support and the EMI engineers offer most vivid recording, while the *Suggestion diabolique* makes a hardly less dazzling encore after the concerto. The coupled Tchaikovsky concerto brings some reservation, but not the accompanying *Theme and variations*, and Balakirev's *Islamey* is pretty stunning. This CD is more than worth its asking price.

Piano concertos Nos. 1 in D flat, Op. 10; 4 in B flat for the left hand, Op. 53; 5 in G, Op. 56.
*** Chan. Dig. CHAN 8791; *ABTD 1424* [id.]. Boris Berman, Concg. O, Järvi.

On Chandos, very fine performances of all three *Concertos* which challenge but perhaps do not displace existing versions, except in terms of recorded quality. Detail is very sharply defined and the orchestral playing is very distinguished, as one would expect from this incomparable Dutch ensemble. Boris Berman has established an enviable reputation as interpreter of this composer, and he plays with great panache and (at times) dazzling virtuosity. He holds the music on a taut rein and has the nervous energy and ebullience this music needs. The superb recording quality will sway many collectors in his favour.

(i) *Piano concertos Nos. 1 in D flat, Op. 10; 3 in C, Op. 26. Piano sonata No. 3 in A min., Op. 28.*
(M) **(*) Sony MYK 44876 [id.]; *40-44876*. Gary Graffman; (i) Cleveland O, George Szell.

These are performances of great virtuosity and stunning brilliance. They have wit and humour too, and the orchestral playing is superb. Just occasionally these artists emphasize the motoric, mechanistic side of Prokofiev, but the lyrical geniality comes over too. The playing has considerable thrust but is never unrelenting. The early-1960s recording has the advantage of the attractive Cleveland ambience and the piano balance is more realistic than in many CBS recordings from this period.

Piano concerto No. 1 in D flat; Piano sonata No. 5 in C, Op. 38.
*** ASV Dig. CDDCA 555; *ZCDCA 555* [id.]. Osorio, RPO, Bátiz – RAVEL: *Left-hand concerto* etc. ***

Jorge Federico Osorio copes splendidly with the *Concerto* and is a thoroughly perceptive interpreter. He is accompanied well by Bátiz, and readers wanting this coupling need not fear that it is second best; they are excellently recorded. ASV offer an interesting fill-up in the form of the Prokofiev *Fifth Sonata*, which Osorio does in its post-war, revised form. It is an interesting piece from the 1920s and a welcome addition to the catalogue.

Piano concertos No. 2 in G min., Op. 16; 3 in C, Op. 26.
*** Chan. Dig. CHAN 8889; *ABTD 1500* [id.]. Horacio Gutiérrez, Concg. O, Neeme Järvi.

Horacio Gutiérrez gives a vital and brilliant account of the solo part of the *Second Piano concerto* and is keenly responsive to the shifting moods and extreme dynamics of Prokofiev's writing. If you think his fortissimo playing too unrelieved in the first-movement cadenza or elsewhere, it is because the composer marks it so. The Concertgebouw Orchestra under Neeme Järvi play magnificently throughout, and though the Chandos recording favours the piano, it does not do so to excess. In terms of recording quality alone, this must rank high in the lists.

Piano concerto No. 3 in C, Op. 26.
*** DG 415 062-2 [id.]. Argerich, BPO, Abbado – TCHAIKOVSKY: *Piano concerto No. 1.* ***
(M) **(*) Pickwick/RPO CDRPO 5001; *ZCRPO 5001* [id.]. Janis Vakarelis, RPO, Rowicki – LISZT: *Concerto No. 2.* ***

There is nothing ladylike about the playing of Martha Argerich but it displays countless indications of feminine perception and subtlety. The *C major Concerto* was once regarded as tough music but here receives a sensuous performance, and Abbado's direction underlines that from the very first, with a warmly romantic account of the ethereal opening phrases on the high violins. This is a much more individual performance of the Prokofiev than almost any other available and brings its own special insights. The recording remains excellent.

The Greek pianist Janis Vakarelis gives a very good account of the Prokofiev *C major Concerto*, though the excellence of the recording and sympathetic orchestral support from the RPO under the late Witold Rowicki would not tip the scales in its favour when put alongside the Argerich version with Abbado. Vakarelis is decidedly on the slow side in the variations movement, where he does not show quite enough tenderness. However, the performance has no lack of brilliance and zest.

(i) *Piano concerto No. 3 in C, Op. 26;* (ii; iii) *Violin concertos Nos. 1–2;* (iii) *Lieutenant Kijé suite;* (iv) *March in B flat, Op. 99; Overture on Hebrew themes;* (iii) *Scythian suite; (iv) Symphony No. 1 (Classical);* (v) *Alexander Nevsky.*
(M) *** DG Analogue/Dig. 435 151-2 (3) [id.]. (i) Argerich, BPO; (ii) Mintz; (iii) Chicago SO; (iv) COE; (v) Obraztsova, LSO Ch., LSO; all cond. Abbado.

Not all of this collection is essential Prokofiev, but the *Hebrew overture* and the ebullient *March* are superbly played, and the *Classical Symphony* is one of the very finest available recorded performances. So is *Alexander Nevsky*, which has great intensity and tragic power as well as refinement of detail. The digital remastering of the 1979 recording is very impressive in its combination of body and bite; and the same could be said of *Lieutenant Kijé* and the *Scythian suite* (both 1977), which have plenty of atmosphere. The earliest recording (1967) is of the *Piano concerto*, and the sound here does show its age a little, but Martha Argerich's performance is outstandingly rewarding and individual, and there is certainly no lack of vividness. Mintz's 1983 versions of the *Violin concertos* hold up well against the full-priced competition and, like all the other performances here, show that Abbado has a special feeling for the composer's sound-world. As with the COE recordings, the sound here is of DG's best digital quality.

(i) *Piano concerto No. 3 in C, Op. 26. Contes de la vieille grand-mère, Op. 31/2 & 3; Étude, Op. 52; Gavotte No. 2, Op. 25; Gavotte No. 3, Op. 32; Paysage, Op. 59; Sonatine pastorale, Op. 59; Sonata No. 4, Op. 29: Andante. Suggestions diaboliques, Op. 4/4; Visions fugitives, Op. 22/3, 5, 6, 9–11, 16–18.*
(M) (***) Pearl mono GEMMCD 9470. Composer, (i) LSO, Piero Coppola.

An invaluable disc that gives us the only recordings Prokofiev ever made of his own music as a pianist. He recorded the *Third Piano concerto* with Piero Coppola and the LSO on three shellac discs in 1932; three years later, he made three more records of his own piano music, all of which are assembled on this disc. Prokofiev's playing has the same wit and character as the music itself and, although interpretatively he is straightforward, there is a really strong musical personality in evidence. The recordings, though a bit monochrome and dry, are good for the period. Not to be missed.

Piano concerto No. 4 in B flat for the left hand, Op. 53.
(M) (***) Sony MPK 46452 [id.]. Rudolph Serkin, Phd. O, Ormandy – REGER: *Piano concerto.* **

Prokofiev's *Fourth Piano concerto* is still the least often played of the five (recordings of it usually come within complete sets). It was commissioned by the one-armed pianist and philosopher, Paul Wittgenstein, but was never played by him; he rejected it on the grounds that it was too aggressively modern and it remained unperformed until 1956, well after the composer's death. Serkin's recording was made only two years later and the performance is not likely to be bettered. His mastery helps to disguise some of the work's defects, though even he cannot quite conceal the fact that the vivace finale is far too short to balance the rest properly. The mono recording is excellent.

Piano concerto No. 5 in G, Op. 55.
*** DG 415 119-2 [id.]. Sviatoslav Richter, Warsaw PO, Witold Rowicki – RACHMANINOV: *Piano concerto No. 2.* ***

Richter's account of the *Fifth Piano concerto* is a classic. It was recorded in 1959, yet the sound of this excellent CD transfer belies the age of the original in its clarity, detail and vividness of colour. In any event it cannot be recommended too strongly to all admirers of Richter, Prokofiev and great piano playing.

Violin concertos Nos. 1 in D, Op. 19; 2 in G min., Op. 63.
*** DG Dig. 410 524-2 [id.]. Mintz, Chicago SO, Abbado.
*** Virgin Dig. VC7 90734-2; *VC 790734-4* [id.]. Sitkovetsky, LSO, C. Davis.
(M) *** Decca 425 003-2; *425 003-4.* Kyung Wha Chung, LSO, Previn – STRAVINSKY: *Concerto.* ***
*** EMI Dig. CDC7 47025-2 [id.]. Perlman, BBC SO, Rozhdestvensky.
*** Chandos Dig. CHAN 8709; *ABTD 1354* [id.]. Mordkovitch, SNO, Järvi.

Mintz's performances are as fine as any; he phrases with imagination and individuality and, if he does not display quite the overwhelming sense of authority of Perlman, there is an attractive combination of freshness and lyrical finesse. He has the advantage of Abbado's sensitive and finely judged accompaniments. In short, this partnership casts the strongest spell on the listener and, with recording on CD which is both refined and full, and a realistic – if still somewhat forward – balance for the soloist, this must receive the strongest advocacy.

Dmitri Sitkovetsky conveys the demonic side of the *First Concerto* more effectively than almost any other player without losing sight of its lyricism or sense of line. His version of the scherzo touches an ironic, almost malignant nerve while he has the measure of the ice-maiden fairy-tale element at the opening. The *Second* is hardly less powerful and has a sympathetic collaborator in Sir Colin Davis. The soloist is rather more forward than is ideal, but orchestral detail is never masked and the internal orchestral balance is very natural.

Kyung Wha Chung gives performances to emphasize the lyrical quality of these *Concertos*, with playing that is both warm and strong, tender and full of fantasy. The melody which opens the slow movement of No. 2 finds her playing with an inner, hushed quality and the ravishing modulation from E flat to B, a page or so later, brings an ecstatic frisson. Previn's acompaniments are deeply understanding. The Decca sound has lost only a little of its fullness in the digital remastering, and the soloist is now made very present.

Perlman's performances bring virtuosity of such strength and command that one is reminded of the supremacy of Heifetz. Though the EMI sound has warmth and plenty of bloom, the balance of the soloist is unnaturally close, which has the effect of obscuring important melodic ideas in the orchestra behind mere passage-work from the soloist. Nevertheless one is left in no doubt that both works are among the finest violin concertos written this century. Apart from the balance, the recording is very fine.

Lydia Mordkovitch enters a hotly contested field and gives readings of strong personality and character. She is well supported by the SNO and Järvi and more than holds her own with rival versions. There are some splendidly malignant sounds in the scherzo of No. 1 and much intensity and panache throughout both pieces. She does not displace Mintz (DG) or Sitkovetzky (Virgin), both of them very special, but both performances make a very satisfying alternative and have first-class sound.

(i) *Violin concerto No. 1 in D, Op. 19;* (ii) *Sinfonia concertante for cello and orchestra, Op. 125.*
(M) **(*) Erato/Warner Dig. 2292 45708-2 [id.]. (i) Mutter, Nat. SO, Washington, Rostropovich; (ii) Rostropovich, LSO, Ozawa.

Anne-Sophie Mutter's must be the most inorganic account of the first movement of Prokofiev's Op. 19 on record: its exposition is highly self-conscious; but she plays with stunning virtuosity and tonal refinement, particularly in the scherzo. In its way this is an exciting performance, and the playing of the Washington orchestra for Rostropovich is very vital and sensitive. However, both artists indulge in some idiosyncratic point-making and some of the fairy-tale innocence of the opening is lost. The recording of the *Sinfonia concertante* (which arose, phoenix-like, from the ashes of Prokofiev's pre-war *Cello concerto in E minor*) is another matter. Rostropovich is in glorious form throughout and Ozawa shows great sensitivity to dynamic nuance. The orchestral balance is excellent, with a truthful overall perspective.

Violin concerto No. 2 in G min., Op. 63.
*** BMG/RCA RD 87019 [RCD1 7019]. Heifetz, Boston SO, Munch – GLAZUNOV; SIBELIUS: *Concertos.* ***

In the arioso-like slow movement, Heifetz chooses a faster speed than is usual, but there is nothing unresponsive about his playing, for his expressive rubato has an unfailing inevitability. In the spiky finale he is superb, and indeed his playing is glorious throughout. The recording is serviceable merely, though it has been made firmer in the current remastering. But no one is going to be prevented from enjoying this ethereal performance because the technical quality is dated.

Divertimento, Op. 43; The Prodigal Son, Op. 46; Symphonic song, Op. 57; Andante (Piano Sonata No. 4).
*** Chan. Dig. CHAN 8728; *ABTD 1368* [id.]. SNO, Järvi.

The *Divertimento* is a lovely piece: its first movement has an irresistible and haunting second theme. It comes from 1929, the same period as *The Prodigal Son*, though two of its movements derive from the ballet, *Trapeze*. Its long neglect is puzzling since it is highly attractive and ought to be popular. So, for that matter, should *The Prodigal Son*, some of whose material Prokofiev re-used the following year in the *Fourth Symphony*. Another rarity is the *Symphonic song*, a strange, darkly scored piece which Miaskovsky told the composer is 'not entirely right for us . . . it lacks a familiar simplicity and breadth of contour'. It does have some interesting and characteristic colours and is more effective than the sonata transcription. The recording is first class – as, indeed, are the performances. An indispensable item in any Prokofiev collection.

The Gambler: 4 Portraits, Op. 49; Semyon Kotko: Symphonic suite, Op. 81 bis.
*** Chan. Dig. CHAN 8803; *ABTD 1431* [id.]. SNO, Järvi.

The interest aroused by the Brussels production of *The Gambler* in 1929 prompted Prokofiev to fashion the *Four Portraits*, which enshrine the best of the opera and are exhilarating and inventive. *Semyon Kotko* was composed after his return to the Soviet Union and, though not top-drawer Prokofiev, is still thoroughly enjoyable. The best of the eight movements are the fourth (*The Southern night*), the sixth (*The Village is burning*) and the seventh (*Funeral*), which find his inspiration flowing at a more characteristic level. The *Suite* has not been recorded since the 1950s, and Järvi gives a thoroughly sympathetic reading in vivid and present sound.

Lieutenant Kijé (incidental music): *suite, Op. 60.*
(M) *** EMI Dig. CDD7 64105-2 [id.]. LPO, Tennstedt – SHOSTAKOVICH: *Symphony No. 10.* ***

Lieutenant Kijé (suite), *Op. 90; The Love for 3 Oranges* (suite); *Symphony No. 1 in D (Classical).*
(M) **(*) Sony Dig. MDK 46502 [id.]. O Nat. de France, Lorin Maazel.

Prokofiev's colourful suite drawn from film music makes an unusual coupling for the Tenth Symphony of Shostakovich. Tennstedt's reading, in repertory with which he is not usually associated, is aptly brilliant and colourful, with rhythms strongly marked. Excellent recording, especially vivid and present in its CD format.

After a brilliant account of the *Classical Symphony*, very well played and brightly lit, Maazel gives exceptionally dramatic and strongly characterized accounts of Prokofiev's two colourful suites. Though he does not miss the romantic allure in the portrait of *The Prince and Princess* from *The Love for three Oranges* or the nostalgia of *Kijé*, it is the Prokofievian sharpness of the rhythms and the crisp pointing of detail that register most strongly, helped by the resonant acoustic, which adds an effective pungency of colour to Prokofiev's bolder scoring. Inner detail registers vividly at all dynamic levels; while Maazel is clearly seeking a strongly presented projection rather than refinement and gentle irony, the committed orchestral response is certainly exhilarating.

(i) *Love for 3 oranges* (suite); (ii) *La pas d'acier: suite, Op. 41 bis;* (i) *Scythian suite, Op. 20.*
(B) (**) EMI mono CZS7 62647-2 (2) [Ang. CDMB 62647]. (i) French Nat. R. O; (ii) Philh. O, Markevitch – STRAVINSKY: *Le baiser de la fée* etc. (***)

Sharply characterized performances from Markevitch, brilliantly played. No apologies need be made for the mono sound, which is both brilliant and atmospheric and is transferred to CD without added edge or thinness. However, it is the Stravinsky coupling which makes this reissue distinctive.

(i) *Love for three oranges (suite), Op. 33a; Scythian suite, Op. 20;* (ii) *Symphony No. 5, Op. 100.*
(M) **(*) Mercury 432 753-2 [id.]. (i) LSO; (ii) Minneapolis SO, Antal Dorati.

Dorati's account of Prokofiev's powerful and atmospheric *Scythian suite* was among the first in stereo; it was recorded at Watford Town Hall in 1957. The remastering confirms the excellence of the original engineering, with the stark brutality of the *Invocation to Veles and Ala* and the nightmarish forcefulness of the evocation of *The Evil God and Dance of the Pagan Monsters* set in bold relief against the winningly atmospheric nocturnal sequence. The suite from the *Love for three oranges* is similarly striking in its characterization and vivid primary colours, with the resonance not blunting the rhythms. The CD is worth considering for these two performances; but the *Fifth Symphony*, recorded in Minneapolis two years later, is less successful. Dorati's reading is similarly forceful but the effect is hard and often unsympathetic.

On the Dnieper (ballet), *Op. 51; Le pas d'acier* (ballet), *Op. 41.*
*** Olympia Dig. OCD 103 [id.]. USSR MoC SO, Rozhdestvensky.

Earlier records of *Le pas d'acier* by Albert Coates and Rozhdestvensky have been of the suite; this gives us the newly published complete score. It is full of vitality and (apart from one or two numbers) highly attractive, very much in the *ballet mécanique* style; *On the Dnieper* is a lyrical work not dissimilar to *The Prodigal Son*. Colourful performances and recordings. Lovers of Prokofiev's ballets should not miss this welcome addition to the discography.

Peter and the wolf, Op. 67 (see also above, under Cinderella).
❀ *** Virgin Dig. VC7 90786-2; *VC 790786-4* [id.]. Gielgud, Ac. of L., Richard Stamp – SAINT-SAËNS: *Carnival* ***; MOZART: *Eine kleine Nachtmusik.* **(*)
*** Telarc Dig. CD 80126 [id.]. André Previn, RPO, Previn – BRITTEN: *Young person's guide* etc. **(*)
(BB) *** ASV CDQS 6017; *ZCQS 6017.* Angela Rippon, RPO, Hughes – SAINT-SAËNS: *Carnival.* ***
(M) **(*) EMI Dig. CD-EMX 2165; *TC-EMX 2165.* William Rushton, LPO, Sian Edwards – BRITTEN: *Young person's guide* ***; RAVEL: *Ma Mère l'Oye.* **
(M) *(**) BMG/RCA GD 86718; *GK 86718.* Boston Pops O, Fiedler – SAINT-SAENS: *Carnival of the animals;* TCHAIKOVSKY: *Nutcracker suite.* **

(i; ii) *Peter and the wolf;* (iii) *Lieutenant Kijé: suite;* (iv) *Love for 3 oranges: suite;* (ii) *Symphony No. 1 in D (Classical).*
❀ (B) *** Decca 433 612-2; *433 612-4* [id.]. (i) Sir Ralph Richardson, (ii) LSO, Sargent; (iii) Paris Conservatoire O, Boult; (iv) LPO, Weller.

(i) *Peter and the wolf, Op. 67. March in B flat, Op. 99; Overture on Hebrew themes, Op. 34b; Symphony No. 1 (Classical), Op. 25.*
**(*) DG Dig. 429 396-2; *429 396-4* [id.]. (i) Sting, COE, Abbado.

Sir John Gielgud's highly individual presentation of Prokofiev's masterly narrative with orchestra brings a worthy successor to our previous favourite version, by Sir Ralph Richardson for Decca; moreover Richard Stamp and the Academy of London have the advantage of a superb, modern, digital recording, warmly atmospheric but with a strikingly wide dynamic range. This is never more effective than when, after a deceptively relaxed opening, the first moment of danger arrives, at the approach of the sinuous feline predator, with Sir John conveying most imaginatively the slinky cunning of the cat and the chirpy high spirits of its elusive prey. At the climax, when the wolf finally catches the duck, there is high drama so the contrast of the plaintive oboe echoing the duck's theme is the more engagingly pathetic. At the end, Sir John, who has presided over these events with a wonderfully benign involvement, becomes Grandfather himself with his restrained moral questioning of Peter's youthful bravado. Throughout, his obvious relish for the colour as well as the narrative flow of the text has been splendidly matched by the detail and impetus of Richard Stamp's accompaniment, with the orchestral soloists making the very most of all their opportunities.

Sir Ralph Richardson brings a great actor's feeling for words to the narrative; he dwells lovingly on their sound as well as their meaning, and this genial preoccupation with the manner in which the story is told matches Sargent's feeling exactly. There are some delicious moments when that sonorous voice has exactly the right coloration, none more taking than Grandfather's very reasonable moral: '. . . and if Peter had not caught the wolf . . . what then?' But of course he did, and in this account it was surely inevitable. Sir Malcolm Sargent's direction of the accompaniment shows his professionalism at its very best, with finely prepared orchestral playing and many imaginative little touches of detail brought out, yet with the forward momentum of the action well sustained. The original coupling, Sargent's amiable, polished account of the *Classical Symphony* has now been restored. All the tempi, except the finale, are slow but Sir Malcolm's assured elegance carries its own spontaneity. The sound is vivid – Sir Ralph Richardson is afforded striking presence – but the remastering has taken some of the bloom from the violins, although the warm ambience remains. Boult's Paris recording of *Lieutenant Kijé* offers more gusto than finesse, but the result is exhilaratingly robust and the very early (1955) stereo comes up remarkably well. Weller's *Love for three oranges* is a different matter, a first-class performance with a rich palette of colour, generating exciting orchestral bravura and given top-drawer 1977 recording. But our Rosette is for *Peter and the wolf*.

André Previn's Telarc version, lightly pointed, lively, colourful and perfectly timed, has the enormous advantage of the conductor's own delightfully informal narration. The arrival of the wolf is marvellously sinister, yet in telling of the swallowing of the duck Previn keeps just a touch of avuncular kindness behind the horror, most delicately done. Vivid recording, with the voice balanced well against the orchestra without too much discrepancy.

Angela Rippon narrates with charm yet is never in the least coy; indeed she is thoroughly involved in the tale and thus also involves the listener. The accompaniment is equally spirited, with excellent orchestral playing, and the recording is splendidly clear, yet not lacking atmosphere. This makes an excellent super-bargain recommendation.

Although narrative and orchestral commentary were recorded separately on the Eminence recording, it is remarkable how well the two fit together. But the flair and professionalism of Sian Edwards meant that William Rushton was able to add his story-telling to a vividly colourful orchestral tapestry which had its momentum already established. He is a personable narrator, adding touches of his own like a 'vast' grey wolf and 'nothing to report' from the bird; but his delivery does not have the relish for the words that makes the version by Sir Ralph Richardson so memorable. However, this remains a direct, sparkling presentation, brightly and realistically recorded, which cannot fail to entertain children of all ages.

Before making his recording, Sting (otherwise Gordon Sumner) listened to other recordings, notably to our own special favourite among modern versions, with Sir John Gielgud benignly presiding over the events of the tale. Sting provides instead what he calls a 'proletarian version', vociferous in its excited involvement and very free in its use of the original text. Abbado obviously enjoys working with such a vigorous narrator and provides an orchestral backing which is both vividly spontaneous-sounding and very polished. Children will undoubtedly respond to this. The account of the *Classical Symphony* is comparably elegant and stylish and it is beautifully played and recorded. But the other items here, though attractive enough, are curiously chosen and not particularly generous.

On BMG/RCA, Sir Alec Guinness joins the pantheon of great actors who have recorded an unforgettable narrative for *Peter and the wolf*. As he begins, one does an aural double take, so fresh and young is the vocal colour; then one discovers that he was recorded in 1952, the year he took the hero's role in the film of Arnold Bennett's *The Card* and five years before *Bridge over the River Kwai.* The orchestral part was laminated on afterwards and can't be said to be distinctive in any way, but Guinness's contribution – not least in the newly written text for the introduction of the characters – has a unique resonance and charm, as if it were 'The Card' himself (Denry Machin) who was telling the story. (How Arnold Bennett would have delighted in that!) The voice is recorded with great presence, the orchestra less vividly, within a reverberant acoustic. The hunter's guns make very little impact at all.

Romeo and Juliet (ballet), *Op. 64* (complete).
*** Decca 417 510-2 (2) [id.]. Cleveland O, Maazel.
*** DG 423 268-2 (2) [id.]. Boston SO, Ozawa.
(B) **(*) CfP CD-CFPD 4452; *TC-CFPD 4452* (2). Bolshoi Theatre O, Zuraitis.
**(*) Ph. 432 166-2 (2) [id.]. Kirov Theatre O, Valery Gergiev.

Maazel will please those who believe that this score should above all be bitingly incisive. The rhythms are more consciously metrical, the tempi generally faster, and the precision of ensemble of the Cleveland Orchestra is little short of miraculous. The recording is one of Decca's most spectacular, searingly detailed but atmospheric too. Both sets have been strikingly successful in their CD transfers and are generously cued.

Immediately at the opening, one notices Ozawa's special balletic feeling in the elegance of the string phrasing and the light, rhythmic felicity. Yet he can rise to the work's drama and in the love-music his ardour is compulsive. At times, one feels, the characterization has less affectionate individuality than Previn's (currently out of the catalogue), whose tempi are always so apt, and the element of pungency which Maazel brings to the score is almost entirely missing in Boston. But this music-making is very easy to enjoy and the actual playing is very fine indeed, while Ozawa has the advantage of outstanding modern digital recording, full of atmosphere.

Zuraitis's 1982 digital bargain version of *Romeo and Juliet* includes an important supplement in addition to the usual complete ballet score. Having studied the original manuscript material, he adds three movements finally omitted in the ballet, the *Nurse and Mercutio* (using familiar material), a sharply grotesque *Moorish dance* and a so-called *Letter scene* which provides a sketch for what eight years later became the scherzo of the *Fifth Symphony*. Zuraitis has scored this last with reference to the symphony. The performance generally may lack something in orchestral refinement, compared with the full-price versions of Ozawa and Maazel, but not Russian feeling. With strikingly bright digital sound of colour and power, not always perfectly balanced, it is excellent value.

Gergiev secures beautifully polished playing from the Kirov Ballet Theatre Orchestra. Indeed it is graceful to the point of being over-cultivated. There is much delicacy of effect, rhythms are crisp and clean and there is plenty of energy, while the brass sonorities are without the rough edges one expects from Russian orchestras. But this is a very romantic view, at its finest in the captivating portrayal of *The young Juliet*, and *Juliet alone*, while the picaresqe numbers like the engaging *Dance with mandolins* and the charming *Aubade* and *Dance of the girls with lillies* are beautifully played. The *Death of Mercutio* certainly brings a moment of red-blooded drama, but when it come to the Balcony scene the lovers' ardour has little sexuality and elsewhere Prokofiev's pungency is muted. The opening of Act 3 is powerful, but the anguish and tragedy of the climax of the story has intensity without stark despair. The recording, made on location in Leningrad by a Philips team, is of the very highest quality, so this is a performance to enjoy primarily for the lyricisim of Prokofiev's inspiration.

Romeo and Juliet (ballet), *Op. 64:* extended excerpts.
**(*) Decca Dig. 430 279-2; *430 279-4* [id.]. Montreal SO, Dutoit.

As a recording, the Dutoit selection is in a class of its own. This is characteristic Decca Montreal sound, very much in the demonstration bracket, vivid in colour, translucent in its delicacy in presenting the pianissimo strings, and with plenty of power and spectacle at climaxes. The playing is polished, sensitive and very refined, yet warm; Dutoit's reading is full of perceptive and affectionate detail. This is greatly enjoyable – but what is missing is the tearing agony of the tragedy; the passionate ardour of the lovers becomes warmly expansive romanticism. But the Decca sound is the finest yet given to Prokofiev's marvellous score: the Montreal acoustic seems tailor-made for this music, and Dutoit offers 75 minutes (24 out of the total of 52 numbers), ideally arranged in narrative order. Even so, Levi, Salonen, Skrowaczewski and Järvi all convey the emotional power of the score more tellingly.

Romeo and Juliet (ballet), *Op. 64:* highlights.
*** Sony Dig. MK 42662 [id.]. BPO, Salonen.

With magnificent playing from the Berlin Philharmonic Orchestra, Esa-Pekka Salonen's set seems marginally a first choice for those wanting merely a full-priced single disc of excerpts from Prokofiev's masterly score. The Berlin Philharmonic playing has an enormous intensity and a refined felicity in the score's more delicate moments. The portrayal of *Juliet as a young girl* is deliciously light in its detail, while the *Folk dance* and *Dance with the mandolins* are full of subtleties of colour and articulation. One is touched and deeply moved by this music-making, while the selection admirably parallels the work's narrative. The recording, made in the Philharmonie, has more resonance and amplitude than the DG engineers usually achieved in this hall for Karajan; indeed it matches sumptuousness with a potent clarity of projection, and the dynamic range is dramatically wide.

Romeo and Juliet (ballet): *suites Nos. 1, 2 & 3.*
*** Chan. Dig. CHAN 8940; *ABTD 1536* [id.]. SNO, Järvi.

These derive from various couplings which appeared between 1985 and 1988. At 78 minutes this is a generous selection of the ballet and eminently competitive. Not necessarily a first choice, but as good as many and better than some. It is unlikely to disappoint.

Romeo and Juliet (ballet): *suites Nos. 1 & 2, Op. 64.*
(M) *** Mercury 432 004-2 [id.]. Minneapolis SO, Skrowaczewski – MUSSORGSKY: *Night.* ***

Skrowaczewski's recording of the two ballet suites was made in 1962. The playing of the Minneapolis orchestra is on a virtuoso level: the string ensemble is superbly assured, the horn playing spectacular, and the wind solos are at one with the special character of Prokofiev's orchestral palette. The crystal-clear acoustic of the hall in Edison High School, with its backing ambience, seems ideally suited to the angular melodic lines and pungent lyricism of this powerful score, to underline the sense of tragedy without losing the music's romantic sweep. There are many marvellous moments here, and the fidelity and spectacle of the Mercury engineering reach a zenith in the powerful closing sequence of *Romeo at Juliet's tomb.* At mid-price this is highly recommendable.

Romeo and Juliet: suites Nos. 1 and 2: excerpts.
*** Telarc Dig. CD 80089 [id.]. Cleveland O, Yoel Levi.

Levi offers one of the finest single discs of excerpts from Prokofiev's masterpiece and he draws wonderfully eloquent playing from his orchestra. He seems to have a special affinity with Prokofiev's score, for pacing is unerringly apt and characterization is strong. There are some wonderfully serene moments, as in the ethereal introduction of the flute melody in the first piece (*Montagues and Capulets*), and the delicacy of the string playing in *Romeo at Juliet's tomb* – which explores the widest expressive range – is touching. The quicker movements have an engaging feeling of the dance and the light, graceful articulation in *The child Juliet* is a delight; but the highlights of the performance are the *Romeo and Juliet love scene* and *Romeo at Juliet's before parting*, bringing playing of great intensity, with a ravishing response from the Cleveland strings leading on from passionate yearning to a sense of real ecstasy. The rich Telarc recording is in the demonstration class, but this offers less music than several of its competitors.

Romeo and Juliet (ballet): suite.
(M) *** Decca 417 737-2; *417 737-4* [id.]. Cleveland O, Maazel – KHACHATURIAN: *Gayaneh; Spartacus.* **(*)

An intelligently chosen selection of six pieces (including *Juliet as a young girl*, the *Balcony scene* and *The last farewell*) makes a generous coupling for Decca's Khachaturian ballet scores.

Scythian suite, Op. 20.
*** DG 410 598-2 [id.]. Chicago SO, Abbado – BARTÓK: *Miraculous Mandarin* etc. ***

Abbado's account of the *Scythian suite* has drive and fire; if it displays less savagery than some previous versions, the Chicago orchestra have no want of power, and Abbado achieves most refined colouring in the atmospheric *Night movement.* The enhancement of the CD remastering is striking: the focus is firmer, yet there is no loss of warmth and body.

(i) *Sinfonia concertante in E min., Op. 125. Romeo and Juliet: suite No. 3, Op. 101.*
**(*) Chan. Dig. CHAN 8508; *ABTD 1218* [id.]. (i) Rafael Wallfisch; SNO, Järvi.

Wallfisch has the measure of the leisurely first movement and gives a thoroughly committed account of the Scherzo and the *Theme and Variations* that follow, and Neeme Järvi lends him every support. It is inevitable that the cello should be given a little help by the microphone (as is the case in the previous versions) but it does seem a shade too forward. The fill-up, the third suite from *Romeo and Juliet*, is an excellent makeweight.

Sinfonietta in A, Op. 48; Symphony No. 1 in D (Classical), Op. 25.
*** Virgin Dig. VC7 91098-2. Lausanne CO, Zedda – DEBUSSY: *Danse* etc.; MILHAUD: *Création du monde.* ***

Prokofiev could not understand why the early *Sinfonietta* failed to make an impression on the wider musical public, and neither can we. Alongside the *Classical Symphony* the *giocoso* outer movements have a more fragile geniality but they are highly delectable, as are the somewhat angular *Andante*, the brief *Intermezzo* and the witty Scherzo. The use of the orchestral palette is as subtle as it is engaging and, with Alberto Zedda's affectionately light touch and fine Lausanne playing, the piece emerges here with all colours flying. The account of the *Classical Symphony* is also highly persuasive, the violins exquisitely gentle at their poised entry in the *Larghetto* and the outer movements spirited, with the finale mercurial in its zestful progress. The fairly resonant sound, with the orchestra slightly recessed, adds to the feeling of warmth without blunting the orchestral articulation.

Symphonies Nos. 1–7.
*** Chan. Dig. CHAN 8931/4 [id.]. SNO, Järvi.

Symphonies Nos. 1–7; Overture russe, Op. 72; Scythian suite, Op. 20.
(M) **(*) Decca 430 782-2 (4). LSO or LPO, Walter Weller.

These Chandos recordings from the mid-1980s are of the highest quality. They have been shorn of their couplings in this box, the only important loss being the delightful *Sinfonietta*. Both versions of the *Fourth Symphony* are included: the 1947 revision appears with the *Classical* on the first disc, while the 1930 original is coupled with the *Third*. Nos. 2 and 6 are on the third disc, and 5 and 7 on the last, so that no side-breaks are involved. As performances, these are the equal of the best.

Weller began his 1970s Kingsway Hall recordings with the LSO (Nos. 1, 5 and 7) then turned to the LPO. The performances are polished and very well played, though at times they are emotionally a little earthbound. The *Classical Symphony* is cultured and elegant but slightly bland, and for some reason the transfer has brought a degree of shrillness to the strings. Elsewhere, any added bite seems advantageous and the violins are full and expansive. Transfers are well managed, though there is some loss of naturalness in the upper range. The finest of the set is No. 2, where the playing of the LPO has great finesse as well as power. No. 3 is less gripping and could do with more thrust, but the playing and sound are both impressive. Weller chooses the revised, 1947 score of No. 4, and this account is distinctly enjoyable, with the work's balletic origins colourfully caught. No. 5 also has undoubted merits, even if the reading is let down by the slow movement, which lacks tautness and forward impetus. In the *Sixth*, too, the bitter tang of Prokofiev's language is again toned down and the hard-etched lines smoothed over. The *Seventh* suits Weller's approach more readily and he catches the atmosphere of its somewhat balletic second movement particularly well. The *Russian overture* has plenty of energy but the *Scythian suite*, too, needs more abrasiveness, and *Night* (the third movement) could be more atmospheric. However, those who normally find Prokofiev's orchestral writing too pungent could well be won over by these performances.

Symphony No. 1 in D (Classical), Op. 25.
*** DG Dig. 423 624-2 [id.]. Orpheus CO – BIZET: *Symphony;* BRITTEN: *Simple symphony.* ***
(M) *** Decca 417 734-2 [id.]. ASMF, Marriner – BIZET: *Symphony;* STRAVINSKY: *Pulcinella.* ***
*** DG Dig. 400 034-2 [id.]. BPO, Karajan – GRIEG: *Holberg suite;* MOZART: *Serenade: Eine kleine Nachtmusik.* ***
*** Delos Dig. D/CD 3021 [id.]. LACO, Schwarz – SHOSTAKOVICH: *Piano concerto No. 1* **(*); STRAVINSKY: *Soldier's tale suite.* ***

Prokofiev wrote his Classical pastiche at the relatively advanced age of twenty-six. But the music has a certain youthful precociousness, and the Orpheus performance has comparable freshness and wit – the droll bassoon solo in the first movement against sparkling string figurations is delightful. In the cantilena of the *Larghetto*, some ears might crave a greater body of violin tone; but the playing has a fine poise, and the minuet and finale have equal flair. Excellent, truthful recording to make this a highly desirable triptych.

Marriner's famous recording has been remastered effectively and sounds very fresh; although there has been some loss of bass response, the ambient warmth ensures that the sound retains its body and bloom. Marriner's tempi are comparatively relaxed, but the ASMF are in sparkling form and play beautifully in the slow movement. Detail is stylishly pointed and the finale is vivacious, yet elegant too.

Karajan's performance is predictably brilliant, the playing beautifully polished, with grace and eloquence distinguishing the slow movement. The outer movements are wanting in charm alongside Marriner. The recording is clearly detailed, though the balance is not quite natural; the upper strings are very brightly lit, with a touch of digital edge, but the ambience is attractive. This is also available at mid-price, coupled with Karajan's superb version of the *Fifth Symphony*.

Schwarz's version, if not quite as brilliant as Karajan's, is a nicely paced performance, the slow movement particularly pleasing in its relaxed lyricism and the finale sparkling with high spirits. It is very well played; the orchestra is naturally balanced within a fairly resonant acoustic which provides plenty of air round the instruments.

Symphonies Nos. 1 in D (Classical); 4 in C, Op. 112 (revised 1947 version).
*** Chan. Dig. CHAN 8400; *ABTD 1137* [id.]. SNO, Järvi.

Prokofiev drastically revised the score of the *Fourth Symphony*. The extent of this overhaul, made immediately after the completion of the *Sixth Symphony*, can be gauged by the fact that the 1930 version takes 23 minutes 8 seconds and the revision 37 minutes 12 seconds. The first two movements are much expanded and the orchestration is richer: among other things, a piano is added. Not all of Prokofiev's afterthoughts are improvements, but Järvi succeeds in making out a more eloquent case for the revision than many of his predecessors. He also gives an exhilarating account of the *Classical Symphony*, one of the best on record. The slow movement has real douceur and the finale is wonderfully high-spirited. On CD, the recording has fine range and immediacy, but in the *Fourth Symphony* the upper range is a little fierce in some of the more forceful climaxes.

Symphonies Nos. 1 in D (Classical), Op. 25; 5 in B flat, Op. 100.
*** Decca Dig. 421 813-2 [id.]. Montreal SO, Dutoit.
*** Ph. Dig. 420 172-2 [id.]. LAPO, Previn.
**(*) Collins Dig. 1064-2 [id.]. Philh. O, Barshai.
*(*) Telarc Dig. CD 80289 [id.]. Atlanta SO, Yoel Levi.

Though at a relatively expansive speed, the lyricism of the first movement of the *Fifth* is given full expressive rein by Dutoit who, with his rhythmic sharpness, balances that against the right degree of spikiness, very necessary in Prokofiev. That sharpness goes with wit in the slow movement, while the third movement, like the first, for all the lushness of the violin sound is more than just a romantic episode, its ominous side brought out potently. The finale, superbly articulated, is fresh and animated, making much of the rough, pawky humour. In the *Classical Symphony* too, Dutoit points the humour infectiously, helped by beautifully sprung rhythms and crisp ensemble. The sound is warm and atmospheric, as well as brilliant.

In the first movement of the *Fifth* Previn's pacing seems exactly right: everything flows so naturally and speaks effectively. The Scherzo is not as high voltage as some rivals, but Previn still brings it off well; and in the slow movement he gets playing of genuine eloquence from the Los Angeles orchestra. He also gives an excellent account of the perennially fresh *Classical Symphony*. The recording is beautifully natural with impressive detail, range and body.

Rudolf Barshai gives a dignified and civilized performance of the *Fifth* with well-chosen, judicious tempi. He gets good, well-disciplined playing from the Philharmonia Orchestra, and if one heard this account on the radio or in the concert hall, it would be with pleasure. However, greater bite and zest are needed, the lines need to sing with greater intensity. The Collins recording more than holds its own with the best; there is abundant detail and outstanding presence at the bottom end of the register.

Were technical brilliance the sole criterion, Yoel Levi's record of the *Fifth Symphony* with the Atlanta Symphony Orchestra would top the lists. This is a demonstration record *par excellence* which has a tonal splendour and presence that are quite remarkable. If the quality is spectacular, the performance is another matter. It is arguably the most leaden and heavy-handed performance now before the public. Tempi are very slow (even the scherzo never gets off the ground) and the music never flows. It must be said that there is nothing idiosyncratic about Levi's reading; everything is carefully and conscientiously prepared, but he is far too literal in both works.

Symphonies Nos. 1 (Classical); 7, Op. 131; Love for 3 oranges (opera): *suite*.
(B) *** CfP CD-CFP 4523; *TC-CFP 4523*. Philh. O, Malko.

Malko's performances were recorded in 1955, and the accounts of the two symphonies were the first stereo EMI ever made. All the performances are quite excellent, and the *Seventh Symphony*, of which Malko conducted the UK première, is freshly conceived and finely shaped. What is so striking is the range and refinement of the recording: the excellence of the balance and the body of the sound are remarkable. No less satisfying is the suite from *Love for three oranges*, an additional bonus making this outstanding value.

Symphony No. 2 in D min., Op. 40; Romeo and Juliet (ballet): *suite No. 1, Op. 64*.
**(*) Chan. Dig. CHAN 8368; *ABTD 1134* [id.]. SNO, Järvi.

The *Second Symphony* reflects the iconoclastic temper of the early 1920s; the violence and dissonance of its first movement betray Prokofiev's avowed intention of writing a work 'made of iron and steel'. In its formal layout (but in no other respect), the symphony resembles Beethoven's Op. 111, with two movements, the second of which is a set of variations. It is this movement that more than compensates for the excesses of its companion. It is rich in fantasy and some of the variations are wonderfully atmospheric. Neeme Järvi produces altogether excellent results from the Scottish National Orchestra; indeed, he has a real flair for this composer. The Chandos recording is impressively detailed and vivid. The *Romeo and Juliet* suite comes off well; the SNO play with real character, though the quality of the strings at the opening of the *Madrigal* is not luxurious.

Symphonies Nos. 2 in D min., Op. 40; 7 in C sharp min., Op. 131.
** DG Dig 435 027-2 [id.]. BPO, Seiji Ozawa.

In Ozawa's coupling the *Second Symphony* fares better than the *Seventh*, though neither performance is touched with distinction. Listening blindfold to the *Seventh*, one would be hard put to recognize this celebrated orchestra. It produces a general-purpose sonority that would not have passed muster in Karajan's days, and the recording is synthetic with little back-to-front perspective. At the very beginning the strings sound curiously wanting in bloom. Frankly, Malko's 1955 record of Nos.1 and 7 sounds more naturally balanced, and the Decca alternative with Walter Weller is infinitely superior with far more air around the instruments. The slow movement of the *Second Symphony* is better, though Ozawa seems cool and only intermittently engaged in these scores.

Symphonies Nos. 3 in C min., Op. 44; 4 in C, Op. 47 (original, 1930 version).
*** Chan. Dig. CHAN 8401; *ABTD 1138* [id.]. SNO, Järvi.

Neeme Järvi's account of the *Third* is extremely successful. He is particularly successful in the *Andante*, which derives from the last Act of the opera, *The Fiery Angel*, and succeeds in conveying its sense of magic and mystery. In the Scherzo, said to have been inspired by the finale of Chopin's *B flat minor Sonata*, he secures a very good response from the SNO strings. In many ways the original of the *Fourth Symphony* seems more like a ballet suite than a symphony: its insufficient tonal contrast tells – yet the Scherzo, drawn from the music for the Temptress in *The Prodigal Son* ballet, is particularly felicitous.

Symphony No. 5 in B flat, Op. 100.
*** Chan. Dig. CHAN 8576 [id.]. Leningrad PO, Jansons.

Symphony No. 5 in B flat, Op. 100; (i) *Lieutenant Kijé (suite), Op. 60.*
** BMG/RCA Dig. RD 60984 [60984-2]. St Petersburg PO, Temirkanov.
*(*) DG Dig. 435 029-2 [id.]. (i) Andreas Schmidt; BPO, Seiji Ozawa.

Symphony No. 5 in B flat, Op. 100; Waltz suite, Op. 110.
*** Chan. Dig. CHAN 8450; *ABTD 1160* [id.]. SNO, Järvi.

Mariss Jansons's reading with the Leningrad Philharmonic was recorded at a live concert in Dublin. Needless to say, the playing is pretty high voltage, with firm, rich string-tone, particularly from the lower strings, and distinctive wind timbre. The wind is not quite as refined as with Western orchestras, but it is good to hear Prokofiev's writing in vivid primary colours. Jansons goes for brisk tempi – and in the slow movement he really is too fast. The Scherzo is dazzling and so, too, is the finale, which is again fast and overdriven. An exhilarating and exciting performance, eminently well recorded too. For special occasions rather than everyday use perhaps, but recommended to those willing to accept the ungenerous measure.

Järvi's credentials in this repertoire are well established and his direction unhurried, fluent and authoritative. His feeling for the music is unfailingly natural. The three *Waltzes* which derive from various sources are all elegantly played. The Chandos recording is set just a shade further back than some of its companions in the series, yet at the same time every detail is clear.

The St Petersburg Philharmonic, as we must now learn to call the great Leningrad ensemble, is still a magnificent orchestra even if it does not produce quite the same special sound one recalls from the days of Mravinsky. In the *Fifth Symphony* pleasure is somewhat diminished by one or two small mannerisms in which Yuri Temirkanov indulges. At the very opening theme things almost come to a stop as early as bar 7, and in the trio section of the scherzo, each four bar phrase is broken up by a disruptive little pause which inhibits the flow of the line. Needless to say there are many good things here but the performance as a whole offers no serious challenge to existing recommendations even though it is very well recorded.

Ozawa's account of *Lieutenant Kijé* restores the singer to his rightful place in the suite, but neither the performance of the *Suite* nor that of the *Fifth Symphony* rises much above routine. It goes without saying that the orchestral playing is excellent and there are moments to which one responds. A well-prepared and business-like reading, but one with little poetic feeling in the closing pages of the slow movement and not much excitement.

Symphony No. 6 in E flat min., Op. 111. Waltz suite, Op. 110, Nos. 1, 5 and 6.
*** Chan. Dig. CHAN 8359; *ABTD 1122* [id.]. SNO, Järvi.

Though it lags far behind the *Fifth* in popularity, the *Sixth Symphony* goes much deeper than any of its companions; indeed it is perhaps the greatest of the Prokofiev cycle. Neeme Järvi has an instinctive grasp and deep understanding of this symphony; he shapes its detail as skilfully as he does its architecture as a whole. At times, however, one longs for greater sonority from the strings, who sound distinctly lean at the top and wanting in body and weight in the middle and lower registers, even in quieter passages – although there is no question that the orchestra play with much commitment. These artists have the measure of the music's tragic poignancy more than almost any of their predecessors on record. The fill-up, as its title implies, is a set of waltzes, drawn and adapted from various stage works: Nos. 1 and 6 come from *Cinderella* and No. 5 from *War and Peace.*

Symphony No. 7 in C sharp min., Op. 131; Sinfonietta in A, Op. 5/48.
*** Chan. Dig. CHAN 8442; *ABTD 1154* [id.]. SNO, Järvi.

Neeme Järvi's account of the *Seventh Symphony* is hardly less successful than the other issues in this cycle. He gets very good playing from the SNO and has the full measure of this repertoire. Enterprisingly, Chandos offer the early *Sinfonietta* as a highly attractive coupling (what a sunny and charming piece it is!). The digital recording has great range and is excellently balanced.

CHAMBER AND INSTRUMENTAL MUSIC

Cello sonata in C, Op. 119.
*** Decca Dig. 421 774-2; *421 774-4* [id.]. Harrell, Ashkenazy – SHOSTAKOVICH: *Sonata* etc. ***
*** Chan. Dig. CHAN 8340 [id.]. Yuli Turovsky. Luba Edlina – SHOSTAKOVICH: *Sonata.* ***

Prokofiev's *Sonata* is the product of his last years and, like the *Sinfonia concertante*, was inspired by the playing of the young Rostropovich. This excellent Decca account displaces earlier recommendations: readers will find Harrell and Ashkenazy wholly satisfying on all counts.

Yuli Turovsky and Luba Edlina are also eloquent advocates of this *Sonata*. A finely wrought and rewarding score, it deserves greater popularity, and this excellent performance and recording should make it new friends. The balance is particularly lifelike on CD.

Overture on Hebrew themes, Op. 34.
** Chan. Dig. CHAN 8924; *ABTD 1522* [id.]. Campbell, Turovsky, Golani, Borodin Trio – ARENSKY: *Piano trio No. 2;* SHOSTAKOVICH: *Seven romances.* *(*)

The Borodin Trio, reinforced by James Campbell, Eleonora Turovsky and Rivka Golani, give a spirited account of Prokofiev's delightful *Overture*, which makes an attractive bonus for their somewhat hybrid (and not wholly successful) programme.

Violin sonata (for solo violin), *Op. 115; Sonata for two violins.*
*** Chan. Dig. CHAN 8988; *ABTD 1570* [id.]. Mordkovitch, Young – SCHNITTKE: *Prelude;* SHOSTAKOVICH: *Violin sonata.* ***

Sonata for 2 violins, Op. 56.
*** Hyp. Dig. CDA 66473 [id.]. Osostowicz, Kovacic – MARTINŮ: *Violin sonata;* MILHAUD: *Violin duo* etc. **(*)

The solo *Violin sonata in D*, Op. 115, is a crisply characteristic piece in three short movements, with no Bachian pretensions at all. The *Sonata in C for two violins*, written much earlier in 1932, is a work designed for corporate performance, but which is just as effective, played – as here – by solo violins. The warmth of Lydia Mordkovitch is well matched by her partner, Emma Young and with couplings by Schnittke and Shostakovich makes an attractive group of Soviet violin works.

The *Sonata for two violins* gives the impression of being vintage Prokofiev, as performed by Krysia Osostowicz and Ernst Kovacic. The slow movement is played with exceptional imagination and poetry. Unfortunately this is not a well-filled disc nor does it contain other music of any great substance, so the couplings don't quite rate three stars. But the performance of this sonata does.

String quartets Nos. 1 in B min., Op. 50; 2 in F, Op. 92.
*** Olympia Dig. OCD 340 [id.]. American Qt.
**(*) Collins Dig. 1189-2; *1189-4.* [id.]. Britten Qt.

String quartets Nos 1-2; (i) *Overture on Hebrew Themes, Op. 34.*
**(*) Hyp. Dig. CDA 66573 [id.]. Coull Qt. (i) with Malmsbury, Petti.

String quartets Nos. 1 – 2; Sonata in C for 2 violins, Op. 56.
*(*) DG Dig. 431 772-2 [id.]. Emerson Qt.

There was a time when the Prokofiev *Quartets* were rarely encountered on record, though the *Second* has always maintained a peripheral hold on the catalogue. Now, perhaps prompted by the centenary celebrations, there is suddenly a wide choice. The *First* comes from 1930 and Prokofiev subsequently arranged its slow movement, an *Andante*, for string orchestra. The American Quartet play it far more persuasively than any earlier version and reveal it to be a work of some appeal as well as substance. The *Second* incorporates folk ideas from Kabarda in the Caucasus, which Taneyev had also studied earlier in the century, but to highly characteristic ends. Although the performance does not have quite the bite and zest of the unforgettable pioneering disc by the Hollywood Quartet, it does not fall far short of it. Apart from one trifling blemish (the image recedes momentarily at one point), the recording is absolutely first class and can confidently be recommended. A rewarding issue.

Among the newer issues are two British contenders, the Coull on Hyperion and the Britten Quartet on Collins. Honours are pretty evenly divided between them; the former has the advantage of offering a fill-up, the *Overture on Hebrew themes*, the latter is available on cassette. Both are very well recorded and both sets of performers are careful in following Prokofiev's dynamic markings. Neither brings quite the ardour and eloquence of the American Quartet, which is very persuasive in both pieces; both are to be preferred to the mechanized perfection of the Emersons. No one investing in either is likely to be disappointed; both ensembles have an excellent grasp of what this music is all about, though the Britten sound a shade too measured in the first movement of No. 2. The Coull produce a clean, well-focused sonority though they do not possess the refinement or beauty of sound of an ensemble like the Hagen Quartet. Both ensembles have much going for them, as have the Chilingirians on Chandos (CHAN 8929), although their playing is somewhat less taut and concentrated. All in all, the Olympia CD remains a clear first choice.

If you like your quartets to sound as if they are composed of people rather than computers, the Emerson Quartet's Prokofiev is not for you. In terms of sheer technical expertise, attack and unanimity of ensemble, and sheer virtuosity, they are, of course, peerless. This is in one sense by far the best-played performance of the *Quartets* – but in another the worst. No phrase is left to speak for itself and there is no feeling of repose in the beautiful slow movement of No. 2. The *Sonata for two violins* is equally glamorized, overnourished and overprojected. Very forward, brightly lit recording.

Violin sonatas Nos. 1 in F min., Op. 80; 2 in D, Op. 94a.
*** DG Dig. 423 575-2 [id.]. Shlomo Mintz, Yefim Bronfman.

Shlomo Mintz made a great impression with his coupling of the two *Concertos*, and his recording of the *Sonatas* is hardly less successful. Mintz has a wonderful purity of line and immaculate intonation, and his partner, Yefim Bronfman, is both vital and sensitive. These are commanding performances, imaginative in phrasing and refined in approach. The DG recording is excellent. This is a clear first choice.

Violin sonata No. 2 in D.
** Ph. Dig. 426 254-2. Viktoria Mullova, Bruno Canino – RAVEL: *Sonata in G;* STRAVINSKY: *Divertimento.* ***

The *Second Sonata* is given a brilliant performance by Mullova and Canino, even if the lyrical charm and tenderness of the first movement elude them and the scherzo is rather rushed. This is musically not as impressive as the Stravinsky or the Ravel with which it is coupled. The recording is quite superb.

PIANO MUSIC

Piano sonata No. 1 in F min., Op. 1; 4 Pieces, Op. 4; Prelude and Fugue in D min. (Buxtehude, arr. Prokofiev); *2 Sonatinas, Op. 54; Gavotte (Hamlet, Op. 77bis); 3 Pieces, Op. 96.*
*** Chan. Dig. CHAN 9017 [id.]. Boris Berman.

Boris Berman's survey of the complete Prokofiev piano music is proving the most satisfactory all-round set of the sonatas so far. This excellent CD brings some transcriptions, including a Buxtehude (Organ) *Prelude and fugue* and the three *Pieces*, Op. 96, which include two dances from his film music to *Lermontov* and a *Waltz* from *War and Peace*. He does not play these with quite the same elegance and distinction that mark the *Sonatinas*, which are beautifully characterized and splendidly recorded.

Piano sonatas Nos. 1 in F min., Op. 1; 4 in C min., Op. 29; 5 in C, Op. 38/135; 9 in C, Op. 103; 10 in E min., Op. 137.
**(*) Olympia Dig. OCD 255 [id.]. Murray McLachlan.

Murray McLachlan proves a sound and generally sympathetic guide to this repertoire. In addition to playing these sonatas (including a fragment – albeit only the few bars that survive – of a *Tenth*), he provides a well-informed and perceptive note. He is totally inside the idiom and makes out a very good case for the revision of the *Fifth Sonata*, though he is less convincing in the *Ninth* and does not obliterate memories of Richter. Its first movement, for example, sounds a little bland and needs greater variety of keyboard colour and a wider dynamic range than is shown here. Taken all round, however, this is accomplished playing and a remarkable feat for a pianist still in his early twenties. The recording – a bit on the close side – falls just short of three stars.

Piano sonatas Nos. 3 in A min., Op. 28; 7 in B flat, Op. 83; 8 in B flat, Op. 84.
*** DG Dig. 435 439-2 [id.]. Andrei Gavrilov.

It is good to find this pianist back on top form. Gavrilov's account of the *Seventh Sonata* is exciting and exhilarating, and in this work totally devoid of any exaggeration. In the *Eighth* he is equally if not more successful, and can withstand the most exalted comparisons. He rushes his fences in the *Third*, though as virtuoso playing it is pretty dazzling. Moreover he is given impressive recorded sound, not perhaps as rounded as the finest EMI and Philips discs but well balanced and not too close.

Piano sonata No. 4, Op. 29; Music for children, Op. 65; 6 Pieces, Op. 52.
*** Chan. Dig. CHAN 8926; *ABTD 1527* [id.]. Boris Berman.

The *Fourth Sonata*, like its predecessor, takes its inspiration from his earlier notebooks, and its thick, bottom-heavy texture gives it less immediate appeal than its immediate neighbours. Its *Andante* was the only sonata movement the composer himself ever recorded and the only one he transcribed for full orchestra. The Op. 52 *Pieces* are transcriptions of movements from other works: the ballet *The Prodigal Son*, the *Andante* from the *First Quartet*, which he also arranged for full strings, and the scherzo from the *Sinfonietta* and one of the *Songs without words*, Op. 35, which is better known in its violin-and-piano form. Berman plays them incisively, with marvellous articulation and wit. The first volume in this project was recorded at The Maltings, Snape, but this venue (St Silas Church in north London) is no less lively and pleasing an acoustic.

Piano sonata No. 5 in C, Op. 38/135; 4 Pieces, Op. 32; Love of three oranges: Scherzo and March; Romeo and Juliet: 10 Pieces, Op. 75.
*** Chan. Dig. CHAN 8851; *ABTD 1468* [id.]. Boris Berman.

Boris Berman is Israeli born and now heads the piano department at Yale. As those who have followed his concert and BBC performances over the last few years will know, he is a pianist of impeccable technique, concentration and intensity, and his temperament is ideally suited to this repertoire. He plays the post-war revision of the *Fifth Sonata*, and its crisp, brittle inner movement is heard to splendid advantage. The other works are presented with equal perception. State-of-the-art recording from Chandos, made at The Maltings, Snape.

Piano sonata No. 6 in A, Op. 82.
❀ *** DG Dig. 413 363-2 [id.]. Pogorelich – RAVEL: *Gaspard de la nuit*. ***

Pogorelich's performance of the *Sixth Sonata* is quite simply dazzling; indeed, it is by far the best version of it ever put on record. It is certainly Pogorelich's most brilliant record so far and can be recommended with the utmost enthusiasm in its CD format.

Piano sonatas Nos. 6 in A, Op. 82; 7 in B flat, Op. 83; 8 in B flat, Op. 84.
** EMI Dig. CDC7 54281-2 [id.]; *EL 754281-4*. Peter Donohoe.

Peter Donohoe recorded the *Sixth Sonata* earlier in his EMI career. This CD collects all the wartime sonatas in straight-from-the-shoulder, powerful, combative performances that have much to recommend them even if none bowls one over. In the finale of the *Seventh* he is curiously lacking in tension and subtlety of articulation. The *Eighth Sonata* is better and he paces the opening excellently, though the *Andante sognando* is a bit short on charm, but this issue has the advantage of very cleanly focused recorded sound.

Piano sonata No. 7 in B flat, Op. 83.
*** DG 419 202-2 [id.]. Maurizio Pollini – Recital. ***

This is a great performance, well in the Horowitz or Richter category. It is part of a generous CD of twentieth-century music, although many readers who respond to Prokofiev and Pollini's outstanding account of Stravinsky's *Three movements from Petrushka* may find the accompanying works of Boulez and Webern less to their taste, fine as the performances are.

Piano sonata No. 7, Op. 83; Sarcasms, Op. 17; Tales of an old grandmother, Op. 31; Visions fugitives, Op. 22.
*** Chan. CHAN 8881; *ABTD 1494* [id.]. Boris Berman.

Boris Berman's account of the *Visions fugitives* is the best since Michel Béroff's of the 1970s. Berman is completely inside the astringent idiom and subtle character of these pieces, and his playing in the *Sarcasms* could scarcely be bettered. He gives altogether outstanding performances of all four works, and the superbly vivid recording greatly enhances the sheer musical satisfaction this disc gives.

Piano sonatas Nos. 7 in B flat, Op. 83; 8 in B flat, Op. 84.
*** Sony Dig. MK 44680 [id.]. Yefim Bronfman.

Yefim Bronfman has a formidable technique, and neither work holds any terrors for him; his clarity of articulation and tonal finesse are unfailingly impressive. The opening of No. 8 has a good sense of forward movement, and this is much to be preferred to the slow, meandering gait favoured by some pianists. Highly accomplished playing throughout, though it is distinctly short measure these days. All the same, it is very recommendable.

Piano sonatas Nos. 7 in B flat, Op. 83; 8 in B flat, Op. 84; 9 in C, Op. 103.
*** ASV Dig. CDDCA 755; *ZCDCA 755* [id.]. John Lill.

This disc, coupling the last three *Sonatas*, offers exceptionally good value and makes a very acceptable alternative to Boris Berman on Chandos. Differences between the two artists are relatively slight and both can be recommended with reasonable confidence. In the slow movement of No. 7, Berman perhaps has the greater intensity and concentration, and the excellent ASV recording, made in Henry Wood Hall, yields to the outstandingly present sound Chandos achieved at The Maltings, Snape. Be that as it may, all three *Sonatas* are performances of high quality and John Lill is never less than a thoughtful and intelligent guide in this repertoire.

Piano sonata No. 8 in B flat, Op. 84; Cinderella: 10 Pieces, Op. 97; 4 Pieces, Op. 3.
*** Chan. Dig. CHAN 8976; *ABTD1565* [id.]. Boris Berman.

In the expansive *Eighth Sonata*, there is more pianistic refinement in Berman's account than in the Donohoe reviewed above, though it is in the ten numbers from *Cinderella* and the Op. 3 *Pieces* that Berman's command of atmosphere and character tells most. Nevertheless this is fine playing and the quality of the recorded sound is excellent.

Romeo and Juliet: suite.
(M) *** DG 431 170-2; *431 170-4*. Lazar Berman – MUSSORGSKY: *Pictures.* ***

Prokofiev made these piano transcriptions of the *Romeo and Juliet* music and played them in public in 1937 before the ballet itself was staged at the Bolshoi. Berman characterizes each piece to excellent effect and is well served by the engineers, who produce bold and well-focused tone. The music's inspiration comes over remarkably well in pianistic colouring.

VOCAL MUSIC

Alexander Nevsky (cantata), Op. 78; Ivan the Terrible, Op. 116 (film music, arr. in oratorio form by Stasevich); *Lieutenant Kijé:* (suite), *Op. 60.*
(B) **(*) VoxBox 1155022 (2) [CDX 5021]. St Louis SO & Ch., Slatkin.

The two-disc bargain VoxBox offers excellent performances of all three of the concert works derived from Prokofiev's film-scores, with Stasevich's arrangement of the *Ivan the Terrible* music taking up the first disc and the other two works the second. No date is given for the analogue recordings but the sound is full, and the chorus too sings incisively and, except in the first two choruses of *Alexander Nevsky*, the balance is not too distant. Vocally, the greatest glory is the darkly expressive singing of Claudine Carlson in the *Lament for the dead* in *Nevsky*, with the chest register revealing a glorious contralto quality. She is the soloist in items from *Ivan the Terrible* too. Very good value.

Alexander Nevsky (cantata), Op. 78.
(M) *** EMI CDM7 63114-2. Anna Reynolds, LSO Ch., LSO, Previn – RACHMANINOV: *The Bells.* ***

(i) *Alexander Nevsky, Op. 78. Lieutenant Kijé (suite), Op. 60.*
*** DG 419 603-2 [id.]. (i) Elena Obraztsova, LSO Ch.; LSO, Abbado.
(M) *** BMG/RCA GD 60176 [60176-2-RG]. (i) Rosalind Elias, Chicago SO Ch.; Chicago SO, Reiner – GLINKA: *Russlan Overture.* ***

(i) *Alexander Nevsky, Op. 78. Scythian suite, Op. 20.*
*** Chan. Dig. CHAN 8584 [id.]. (i) Linda Finnie, SNO Ch.; SNO, Järvi.

Abbado's performance culminates in a deeply moving account of the tragic lament after the battle (here very beautifully sung by Obraztsova), made the more telling when the battle itself is so fine an example of orchestral virtuosity. The chorus is as incisive as the orchestra. The digital remastering of the 1980 recording has been all gain and the sound is very impressive indeed, with great weight and impact and excellent balance. *Lieutenant Kijé* also sounds splendid, and Abbado gets both warm and wonderfully clean playing from the Chicago orchestra.

The bitter chill of the Russian winter can be felt in the orchestra at the very opening of Järvi's reading and the melancholy of the choral entry has real Slavic feeling; later in their call to 'Arise, ye Russian people' there is an authentic good-humoured peasant robustness. His climactic point is the enormously spectacular *Battle on the ice*, with the recording giving great pungency to the bizarre orchestral effects and the choral shouts riveting in their force and fervour. Linda Finnie sings the final lament eloquently and Järvi's apotheosis is very affecting, but at the close Obraztsova and Abbado create an even graver valedictory feeling which is unforgettable. As coupling, Järvi chooses the ballet *Ala and Lolly*, which subsequently became the *Scythian suite*. Its motoric rhythms are characteristic of the composer at his most aggressive, but the lyrical music is even more rewarding.

All the weight, bite and colour of the score are captured by Previn, and though the timbre of the singers' voices may not suggest Russians, they cope very confidently with the Russian text; Previn's direct and dynamic manner ensures that the great *Battle on the ice* scene is powerfully effective. Anna Reynolds sings the lovely *Lament for the dead* most affectingly. The sound is sharply defined, with plenty of bite; just a little of the old analogue ambient fullness has gone.

Reiner's version, recorded in 1959, was another of the astonishingly vivid early achievements of the RCA stereo catalogue. The performance is gripping from the first bar to the last. With choral singing of great fervour and a movingly eloquent contribution from Rosalind Elias in the great *Lament*, one hardly notices that the English-language performance inevitably sounds less idiomatic with an American accent. The *Lieutenant Kijé suite*, recorded two years earlier, is another colourful example of the Chicago orchestra at their peak, the sound again full and atmospheric.

Eugene Onegin (incidental music), *Op. 71; Hamlet* (incidental music), *Op. 77; Lieutenant Kijé* (suite), *Op. 60.*
*** Chant du Monde Dig. LDC 288 027/8 (2) [id.]. Koroleva, Stetsenko, Blagovest Ch., Maly Moscow SO, Vladimir Ponkin.

The piano score for Prokofiev's incidental music for *Eugene Onegin* was rediscovered only in 1973. It was commissioned at the centenary of the death of Pushkin in 1937, and the project was then politically aborted. In due course the work was orchestrated and proves to be a major find, with an inspiration comparable to *Romeo and Juliet* in lyric fervour and melodic sweep. Prokofiev had left detailed indications of his intended orchestration, and there are vocal solos and a splendid *Chorus of the Men of Honour*. Many of the numbers are highly characteristic, and there is Prokofievian grotesquerie as well an an aching elegiac languor for Tatiana's predicament, quite as powerful as Tchaikovsky's operatic response to the same story. *Hamlet* is less ambitious, offering ten vignettes, but including three engaging songs for Ophelia charmingly sung here by Ludmilla Koroleva. The orchestral playing in both scores is fresh and ardent, and the Russian wind and brass playing is suitably vibrant. The performance of *Lieutenant Kijé* brings out the music's laconic melancholy in a specially Russian way, and its more extrovert qualities are also boldly projected. Excellent modern digital recording throughout (though the opening and closing cornet solos in *Kijé* could have benefited from greater distancing). This is an indispensable set for any true Prokofievian.

5 Poems of Anna Akhmatova, Op. 27; 2 Poems, Op. 9; 5 Poems of Konstantin Balmont, Op. 36; 3 Romances, Op. 73.
**(*) Chan. Dig. CHAN 8509; *ABTD 1219* [id.]. Carole Farley, Arkady Aronov.

Rare and valuable repertoire. The two songs of Op. 9 are vaguely impressionistic in feeling, though the first is the more imaginative. Otherwise the piano writing in these songs is thoroughly personal, nowhere more so than in the Op. 36 Balmont settings. The songs are powerful and full of resourceful and imaginative touches. The Akhmatova settings are quite beautiful. The *Three Romances*, Op. 73, to words of Pushkin, are full of the wry harmonic sleights of hand that are so characteristic of his musical speech. The American soprano, Carole Farley, responds to the different moods and character of the poems and encompasses a rather wide range of colour and tone, although at times her voice is rather edgy and uneven in timbre. The accompanying of Arkady Aronov is highly sensitive and perceptive; his playing is a joy throughout. The recording is completely truthful.

OPERA

L'amour des trois oranges (The Love for 3 oranges): complete.
**(*) Virgin Dig. VCD 791084-2; *VCD 791084-4* (2) [id.]. Bacquier, Bastin, Dubosc, Gautier, Viala, Lyon Opera Ch. & O, Kent Nagano.

Previous recordings of Prokofiev's sparkling charade, *The Love for three oranges*, have always been in Russian. Very reasonably, however, Virgin opted for the alternative of French, as being the original language: that was the language used when the opera was given its first, lavish production in Chicago in December 1921. French inevitably brings a degree of softening in vocal texture, but most listeners will understand far more of the words; and the brilliant young conductor, Kent Nagano, and his Lyon Opera House team make up for any loss in knife-edged precision of ensemble. The only star names in the cast are the basses in the two main character-roles, Gabriel Bacquier as the King and Jules Bastin as the monstrous Cook, guardian of the three oranges. They are well matched by the others, including Jean-Luc Viala as an aptly petulant Prince and Catherine Dubosc as a sweetly girlish Princess Ninette. A snag with the recorded sound is that the commenting chorus – very much a part of the action in *commedia dell'arte* style – is focused too vaguely, a pity when the timing is so crisp. Happily, the focus for the solo voices is clearer. On the whole, Virgin's enterprise in going to Lyon and its outstanding new music director – successor to John Eliot Gardiner – has paid off impressively. However, it is irritating that there are so few cueing points on the CDs (just one for each scene), even if this is very much an ensemble opera, with few set solos.

The Fiery Angel (complete).
*** DG Dig. 431 669-2 (2) [id.]. Secunde, Lorenz, Zednik, Moll, Gothenburg SO, Järvi.

Like his even earlier one-Act opera, *Maddalena*, *The Fiery Angel* centres on a neurotically obsessed woman, the tragic Renata, whose hysterical visions finally get her condemned as a witch. Though the story is largely distasteful, the score is masterly, containing passages as rich and warm as anything Prokofiev ever wrote before his return to Soviet Russia, as, for example, some of the duetting in Act III between Renata and her lover, the knight Ruprecht. What reinforces the impact of the work is its compactness, telling a complicated story in five crisply tailored Acts, with the first two Acts on the first CD, the remaining three on the second. Prokofiev's vivid orchestration adds colour and atmosphere, as when in Act IV Mephistopheles is conjured up, along with Faust, and proceeds to eat an offending serving lad – cue for horrific whoopings on the horns. After that the final scene with the Inquisitor (Kurt Moll ever sinister) and chattering nuns does not quite rise to the expected climax. This fine recording easily outshines the only previous version, which was recorded in 1957 with a cast singing in French. Nadine Secunde for Järvi sings passionately as Renata, well supported by Siegfried Lorenz as Ruprecht. With such warm advocacy one can fully appreciate the work's mastery, even if the reasons for its failure to get into the repertory remain very clear.

Maddalena (opera) complete.
**(*) Olympia Dig. OCD 215 [id.]. Ivanova, Martynov, Yakovenko, Koptanova, Rumyantsev, male group of State Chamber Ch., MoC SO, Rozhdestvensky.

Maddalena is an opera which Prokofiev wrote in 1911, two years after graduating, but he then failed to finish the scoring. It was left to the conductor, Edward Downes, to complete the orchestration over 60 years later, revealing a fascinating example of Russian Grand Guignol. Though Prokofiev orchestrated only the first and shortest of the four scenes, Downes's contribution has a true Prokofiev ring, with distinctive colouring. His edition is here adopted by these Russian performers for the first recording. Any disappointment with the work lies more in the relative lack of melodic distinction in the vocal writing which, for the most part, flows in an easy cantilena. Nevertheless, this 50-minute piece very ably tells the horrific story of the predatory Maddalena and her savage way with men. Rozhdestvensky, with his fine orchestra of young players, directs a persuasive performance, even if some of the singing is indifferent. Ivavova is a bright, precise soprano, with Martynov singing splendidly in the tenor role of her wronged husband, Genaro. By contrast, Yakovenko in the baritone role of Maddalena's lover is disappointingly wobbly. Full, forward sound, not always refined. The disc comes with libretto, translation and notes.

War and peace (complete).
❀ (M) *** Erato/Warner 2292 45331-2 (4) [id.]. Vishnevskaya, Miller, Ciesinski, Tumagian, Ochman, Ghiuselev, Smith, Paunova, Petkov, Toczyska, Zakai, Gedda, Fr. R. Ch. & Nat. O, Rostropovich.

Here in the first really complete recording of *War and peace* Rostropovich magnificently fulfils the promise he made to the composer, not long before the latter's death, to do all he could to get this masterpiece fully appreciated. Though the components may suggest too facile a representation of Tolstoi's vast novel, a performance like this shows triumphantly how tautly they cohere to make a comparably epic work of art. Flawed as some of the casting is in this Paris recording, the performance confirms the piece as one of the greatest operas of the century, in which Prokofiev produces one haunting melody after another. The recording is vividly atmospheric, both in the evocative love-scenes and ball-scenes of the first half (Peace) or in the battle-scenes of the second half (War). The emotional thrust is overwhelming, with the energy and warmth of Rostropovich's conducting building to a climax, when the whole work culminates in a great patriotic chorus using the most memorable melody of all, heard first in General Kutuzov's solo after the Council of Fili. The French Radio Chorus sings with fervour both there and elsewhere, notably in the Choral epigraph – telling of the invasion of Russia – which Rostropovich logically places, not at the beginning of the opera, but immediately before the scenes of war. Instead, at the start he includes an optional overture which rehearses some of the main melodies. Though Galina Vishnevskaya was already in her early sixties when she made the recording, she characterizes the young Natasha with wonderful vividness, only occasionally raw in tone. Lajos Miller, not flawless either, is a clear-voiced Andrei, and Wieslaw Ochman is a first-rate Pierre, with the veteran Nicolai Gedda brought in as Kuragin. Katherine Ciesinski is a warm-toned Sonya, but Dimiter Petkov is disappointingly unsteady as Natasha's father, Count Rostov. The small role of Napoleon is strongly taken by Eduard Tumagian, while Nicola Ghiuselev is a noble Kutuzov, in some ways the most impressive of all. Even with a total playing time of over four hours, the opera yet seems compact. It fits neatly on the four CDs, with the first two devoted to the scenes of peace and the last two to the scenes of war, without a single scene being broken in the middle. The booklet contains English, French and German translations, but no transliteration of the original Russian.

Puccini, Giacomo (1858–1924)

Crisantemi for string quartet.
*** CRD CRD 3366 [id.]. Alberni Qt – DONIZETTI: *Quartet No. 13;* VERDI: *Quartet.* ***

Puccini's brief essay in writing for string quartet dates from the late 1880s; three years later he used the main themes in his first fully successful opera, *Manon Lescaut.* The piece is given a warm, finely controlled performance by the Alberni Quartet and makes a valuable makeweight for the two full-scale quartets by fellow opera-composers. The sound is excellent.

(i) *Crisantemi; Minuets 1–3; Quartet in A min.: Allegro moderato; Scherzo in A min.;* (ii) *Foglio d'album; Piccolo tango;* (iii; ii) *Avanti Urania; E l'uccellino; Inno a Diana; Menti all'avviso; Morire?; Salve regina; Sole e amore; Storiella d'amore; Terra e mare.*
*** Etcetera KTC 1050. (i) Raphael Qt; (ii) Tan Crone; (iii) Roberta Alexander.

It is fascinating to find among early, rather untypical songs like *Storiella d'amore* and *Menti all'avviso* a charming little song, *Sole e amore*, written jokingly for a journal, 'Paganini', in 1888, which provided, bar for bar, the main idea of the Act III quartet in *La Bohème* of eight years later. Puccini's melodic flair comes out in such a song as *E l'uccellino*, written in Neapolitan style; and there is a rousing homophonic hymn for his fellow-huntsmen in *Inno a Diana*, while *Avanti Urania!* improbably was written to celebrate the launching of a titled friend's steam-yacht. The two piano pieces are simple album-leaves; among the six quartet pieces, *Crisantemi* is already well known; the rest are student pieces, including a delightful fragment of a Scherzo. Performances are good, though Roberta Alexander's soprano is not ideally Italianate. The recorded sound is vivid and immediate against a lively hall ambience.

Messa di Gloria.
*** Erato/Warner Dig. 2292 45197-2 [id.]. Carreras, Prey, Amb. S., Philh. O, Scimone.

Puccini's *Messa di Gloria* was completed when he was only twenty. The bold secularity of some of the ideas, for example the brassy march for the *Gloria* itself, is very much in the Italian tradition, perilously skirting the edge of vulgarity. Scimone and a fine team are brisker and lighter than their predecessors on record, yet effectively bring out the red-bloodedness of the writing. José Carreras turns the big solo in the *Gratias* into the first genuine Puccini aria. His sweetness and imagination are not quite matched by the baritone, Hermann Prey, who is given less to do than usual, when the choral baritones take on the yearning melody of *Crucifixus.* Excellent, atmospheric sound.

OPERA

La Bohème (complete).
(***) EMI mono CDS7 47235-8 (2) [Ang. CDCB 47235]. De los Angeles, Bjoerling, Merrill, Reardon, Tozzi, Amara, RCA Victor Ch. & O, Beecham.
*** Decca 421 049-2 (2) [id.]. Freni, Pavarotti, Harwood, Panerai, Ghiaurov, German Op. Ch., Berlin, BPO, Karajan.
(M) *** Decca 425 534-2 (2). Tebaldi, Bergonzi, Bastianini, Siepi, Corena, D'Angelo, St Cecilia Ac. Ch. & O, Serafin.
**(*) BMG/RCA RD 80371 [RCD2 0371]. Caballé, Domingo, Milnes, Sardinero, Raimondi, Blegen, Alldis Ch., Wandsworth School Boys' Ch., LPO, Solti.
(***) EMI mono CDS7 47475-8 (2) [Ang. CDCB 47475]. Callas, Di Stefano, Moffo, Panerai, Zaccaria, La Scala, Milan, Ch. & O, Votto.

(M) (**) EMI mono CHS7 63335-2 (2) [Ang. CDHB 63335]. Albanese, Gigli, Poli, Baracchi, Baronti, La Scala, Milan, Ch. & O, Berrettoni.
(M) (**) BMG/RCA GD 60288; *GK 60288* (2) [60288-2-RG; *60288-4-RG*]. Albanese, Peerce, Valentino, McKnight, Moscona, Cehanovsky, NBC Ch., NBC SO, Toscanini.
(M) DG 435 715-2 (2) [id.]. Scotto, Poggi, Gobbi, Meneguzzer, Ch. & O of Maggio Musicale Fiorentino, Votto.

Beecham's is a uniquely magical performance with two favourite singers, Victoria de los Angeles and Jussi Bjoerling, challenged to their utmost in loving, expansive singing. The voices are treated far better by the CD remastering than the orchestra, which is rather thinner-sounding than it was on LP, though as ever the benefits of silent background are very welcome in so warmly atmospheric a reading. With such a performance one hardly notices the recording, but those who want fine modern stereo can turn readily to Karajan.

Karajan too takes a characteristically spacious view of *Bohème*, but there is an electric intensity which holds the whole score together as in a live performance. Karajan unerringly points the climaxes with full force, highlighting them against prevailing pianissimos. Pavarotti is an inspired Rodolfo, with comic flair and expressive passion, while Freni is just as seductive a Mimi as she was in the Schippers set ten years earlier. Elizabeth Harwood is a charming Musetta, even if her voice is not as sharply contrasted with Freni's as it might be. Fine singing throughout the set. The reverberant Berlin acoustic is glowing and brilliant in superb Decca recording, with the clean placing of voices enhancing the performance's dramatic warmth.

Tebaldi's Decca set with Bergonzi dominated the catalogue in the early days of stereo; technically it was an outstanding recording in its day. Vocally the performance achieves a consistently high standard, with Tebaldi as Mimi the most affecting. Carlo Bergonzi is a fine Rodolfo; Bastianini and Siepi are both superb as Marcello and Colline, and even the small parts of Benoit and Alcindoro (as usual taken by a single artist) have the benefit of Corena's magnificent voice. The veteran Serafin was more vital here than on some of his records. The recording, now thirty years old, has its vividness and sense of stage perspective enhanced on CD, with minimal residual tape-hiss, though the age of the master shows in the string timbre above the stave.

The glory of Solti's set of *Bohème* is the singing of Montserrat Caballé as Mimi, an intensely characterful and imaginative reading which makes you listen with new intensity to every phrase, the voice at its most radiant. Domingo is unfortunately not at his most inspired. *Che gelida manina* is relatively coarse, though here as elsewhere he produces glorious heroic tone, and never falls into vulgarity. The rest of the team is strong, but Solti's tense interpretation of a work he had never conducted in the opera house does not quite let the full flexibility of the music have its place or the full warmth of romanticism.

Callas, flashing-eyed and formidable, may seem even less suited to the role of Mimi than to that of Butterfly, but characteristically her insights make for a vibrantly involving performance. Though Giuseppe di Stefano is not the subtlest of Rodolfos, he is in excellent voice here, and Moffo and Panerai make a strong partnership as the second pair of lovers. Votto occasionally coarsens Puccini's score but he directs with energy. The comparatively restricted dynamic range means that the singers appear to be 'front stage', but there is no lack of light and shade in Act II.

The pre-war EMI set conducted by Berrettoni is dominated – as was planned at the time of recording – by the great tenor, Beniamino Gigli, a superstar of his day. The way he spices the role of Rodolfo with little Gigli chuckles is consistently charming. From first to last his facial expression comes over vividly in his strongly characterized singing, and the pity is that he is not well served by the conducting (unimaginative) or the recording. Licia Albanese is tenderly affecting but, thanks to the recording, the voice is recessed. Afro Poli sings firmly, but proves a colourless Marcello, and Tatiana Menotti is an edgy, fluttery Musetta.

Toscanini's 1946 set is taken from the first of his concert performances of opera in New York, recorded in 1946. The sound is even drier than most from this source, but the voices are vivid in their forward placing, and fortunately the singers had been chosen for their clean focus. Albanese, though held in an expressive straitjacket by the conductor, sounds fuller and sweeter as Mimi than in her earlier recording with Gigli; indeed she is delightfully fresh, even though no pianissimos are possible in the NBC acoustic. Jan Peerce as Rodolfo and Francesco Valentino as Marcello are reliable rather than imaginative – not surprising with the conductor such a disciplinarian – and Anne McKnight makes a bright, clear Musetta. Toscanini is heavy-handed and often rigid in his direction, but his love of this score, which he knew from its earliest performances, shines out all through, not least in his loud and endearing vocal obbligatos during the big tunes.

We wonder why DG decided to reissue their Florence recording of *Bohème*, and we list it here in case any collector is tempted by the cast and the medium price. It is, in fact, totally unrecommendable. Even Gobbi is less than a success as Marcello: do we really want to hear a Bohemian snarling? Scotto's voice is not at all well caught, and as for Poggi, he makes the most frightful noises!

La Bohème: highlights.
*** Decca 421 245-2; *421 245-4* [id.] (from above recording with Freni and Pavarotti; cond. Karajan).
(M) **(*) Decca 421 301-2; *421 301-4* (from above complete set with Tebaldi and Bergonzi; cond. Serafin).

It is a pity to cut anything from so taut an opera as *La Bohème*; but those who feel they can make do with a single CD instead of two will find this selection from the Karajan set ideal.

Most collectors will surely want a reminder of the vintage set with Tebaldi and Bergonzi at the height of their powers. The selection is well made, and the disc is competitively priced.

La Fanciulla del West (The Girl of the Golden West) complete.
❀ (M) *** Decca 421 595-2 (2) [id.]. Tebaldi, Del Monaco, MacNeil, Tozzi, St Cecilia Ac., Rome, Ch. & O, Capuana.
**(*) DG 419 640-2 (2) [id.]. Neblett, Domingo, Milnes, Howell, ROHCG Ch. and O, Mehta.
*(*) Sony Dig. S2K 47189 (2) [id.]; *40-47189*. Zampieri, Domingo, Pons, La Scala, Milan, Ch. & O, Maazel.

Like Karajan's classic 1961 Tosca (see below), the Decca set of *La Fanciulla del West* has been remastered for CD with spectacular success. The achievement is the more remarkable when one considers that the original recording was made in 1958; but this is vintage Decca sound, both atmospheric and vivid. Tebaldi gives one of her most warm-hearted and understanding performances on record, and Mario del Monaco displays the wonderfully heroic quality of his voice to great – if sometimes tiring – effect. Cornell MacNeil as the villain, Sheriff Rance, sings with great precision and attack, but unfortunately has not a villainous-sounding voice to convey the character fully. Jake Wallace's entry and the song *Che faranno i viecchi miei* is one of the high spots of the recording, with Tozzi singing beautifully. Capuana's expansive reading is matched by the imagination of the production, with the closing scene wonderfully effective.

Mehta's manner – as he makes clear at the very start – is on the brisk side, not just in the cakewalk rhythms but even in refusing to let the first great melody, the nostalgic *Che faranno i viecchi miei*, linger into sentimentality. Sherrill Milnes as Jack Rance makes that villain into far more than a small-town Scarpia, giving nobility and understanding to the first-Act arioso. Domingo, as in the theatre, sings heroically, disappointing only in his reluctance to produce soft tone in the great aria *Ch'ella mi creda*. The rest of the team is excellent, not least Gwynne Howell as the minstrel who sings *Che faranno i viecchi miei*; but the crowning glory of a masterly set is the singing of Carol Neblett as the Girl of the Golden West herself, gloriously rich and true and with formidable attack on the exposed high notes. Full, atmospheric recording to match, essential in an opera full of evocative offstage effects, but the slight drying-out process of the digital sound adds some stridency in tuttis, readily acceptable with so strong a performance.

After a long gap Maazel here resumes his projected Puccini cycle for Sony/CBS with a live recording of an opera that presents more snags than usual using that technique. Intrusive stage noises from the miners as they charge around, bad balances with voices consistently subordinated to orchestra, and the inconsistent inclusion of applause from the over-enthusiastic audience all prevent this from being a viable competitor with the finest studio recordings. Though the orchestra is placed forward of the voices, it fails to carry the necessary weight at climaxes, and the dry Scala acoustic is unkind to instruments and voices alike, dulling their edge. As a Puccinian Maazel has mellowed since his earlier recordings, and he moulds Puccini melodies affectionately, but the dramatic bite is dulled thanks only in part to the recording. Even Domingo's heroic voice has a slight unevenness exposed at the start, though as ever he rises superbly to the big moments. Even so, his studio recording with Mehta on DG is far preferable. Juan Pons sounds far too gentlemanly and sympathetic to be the unforgiving Sheriff Rance, and in some ways Mara Zampieri fares best with her bright, cleanly projected voice bringing the occasional hint of a hoot. A disappointment.

La Fanciulla del West: highlights.
(M) *** DG 435 407-2; *435 407-4* [id.] (from above recording, with Neblett, Domingo, Milnes; cond. Mehta).

This is most welcome as the only current set of highlights from *Fanciulla del West*, essentially representing the hero (as part of the 'Domingo Edition') but covering the whole opera generously with 75 minutes of music. No libretto, but a good track synopsis.

Madama Butterfly (complete).
*** DG Dig. 423 567-2 (3) [id.]. Freni, Carreras, Berganza, Pons, Amb. Op. Ch., Philh. O, Sinopoli.
**(*) Decca 417 577-2 (3) [id.]. Freni, Ludwig, Pavarotti, Kerns, V. State Op. Ch., VPO, Karajan.
(M) *** BMG/RCA GD 84145 (2) [4145-2-RG]. Moffo, Elias, Valletti, Cesari, Catalani, Rome Op. Ch. & O, Leinsdorf.
(M) *** EMI CMS7 69654-2 (2) [Ang. CDMB 69654]. Scotto, Bergonzi, Di Stasio, Panerai, De Palma, Rome Op. Ch. & O, Barbirolli.
(M) **(*) Decca 425 531-2 (2) [id.]. Tebaldi, Bergonzi, Cossotto, Sordello, St Cecilia Ac. Ch. & O, Serafin.
(M) **(*) EMI CMS7 63634-2 (2) [Ang. CDMB 63634]; *TC-CFPD 4446*. De los Angeles, Bjoerling, Pirazzini, Sereni, Rome Op. Ch. & O, Santini.
(***) EMI mono CDS7 47959-8 (2) [id.]. Callas, Gedda, Borriello, Danieli, La Scala, Milan, Ch. & O, Karajan.

With speeds that in principle are eccentrically slow, Sinopoli's reading is the most idiosyncratic on record, but also one of the most powerful and perhaps the most beautiful of all, certainly in the ravishing orchestral sound. However expansive his speeds, Sinopoli is never sentimental or self-indulgent. Puccini's honeyed moments are given, not sloppily, but with rapt intensity – as at the poignant close of the *Flower duet*, when '*sola e rinnegata*' is recalled from Act I. They are then set the more movingly against the biting moments, from the opening fugato of Act I, sharply incisive, through to the final aria, tough and intense, where the trumpet monotone as Butterfly dies (marked to be played as a solo but rarely done that way) nags the nerves as never before. As she was for Karajan in his classic Decca set, Freni is a model Butterfly; though the voice is no longer so girlish, she projects the tragedy even more weightily than before. José Carreras is similarly presented as a large-scale Pinkerton in this, one of his last opera-recordings before his serious illness. Juan Pons is a virile Sharpless and Teresa Berganza an equally positive, unfruity Suzuki. This is a set which in its spacious but intensely concentrated way brings a unique and unforgettable experience.

Karajan's set is also extravagantly laid out on three discs instead of two as for most of the rival sets – slow speeds partly responsible – and the advantage that each Act is complete on a single disc will not be considered adequate compensation by most collectors. However, Karajan inspires singers and orchestra to a radiant performance which brings out all the beauty and intensity of Puccini's score, sweet but not sentimental, powerfully dramatic but not vulgar. Freni is an enchanting Butterfly, consistently growing in stature from the young girl to the victim of tragedy, sweeter of voice than any rival on record. Pavarotti is an intensely imaginative Pinkerton, actually inspiring understanding for this thoughtless character, while Christa Ludwig is a splendid Suzuki. The recording is one of Decca's most resplendent, with the Vienna strings producing glowing tone.

Anna Moffo's Butterfly proves delightful, fresh and young-sounding. *Un bel dì* has some sliding at the beginning, but the end is glorious, and the *Flower duet* with Rosalind Elias is enchanting. Valletti's Pinkerton has a clear-voiced, almost Gigli-like charm – preferable to most rivals – and with Corena as the Bonze the only blot on the set vocally is the unimaginative Sharpless of Renato Cesari. Leinsdorf is efficient and undistracting and, with vivid recording (balanced in favour of the voices), this makes a first-class mid-priced recommendation, costing less than half the price of the Decca Karajan set with Freni, Ludwig and Pavarotti.

Under Sir John Barbirolli, players and singers perform consistently with a dedication and intensity rare in opera recordings made in Italy, and the whole score glows more freshly than ever. There is hardly a weak link in the cast. Bergonzi's Pinkerton and Panerai's Sharpless are both sensitively and beautifully sung; Anna di Stasio's Suzuki is more than adequate, and Renata Scotto's Butterfly has a subtlety and perceptiveness in its characterization that more than make up for any shortcoming in the basic beauty of tone-colour. It is on any count a highly individual voice, used here with great intelligence to point up the drama to its tragic climax. On

CD the violins have lost a little of their original opulence, but in all other respects the recording combines vividness with atmosphere.

Serafin's reading is sensitive and beautifully paced. Tebaldi is at her most radiant; though she was never the most deft of Butterflies dramatically, her singing is consistently rich and beautiful, sometimes breathtakingly so. The excellence of Decca engineering in 1958 is amply proved in the CD transfer, with one serious exception: the absence of bass at the very opening brings a disagreeably shrill and thin sound, improved once the orchestration grows fuller, with voices very precisely and realistically placed.

Victoria de los Angeles' 1960 recording displays her art at its most endearing, her range of golden tone-colour lovingly exploited. Opposite her, Jussi Bjoerling was making one of his last recordings and, though he shows few special insights, he produces a flow of rich tone to compare with that of the heroine. Mario Sereni is a full-voiced Sharpless, but Miriam Pirazzini is a disappointingly wobbly Suzuki; Santini is a reliable, generally rather square and unimaginative conductor who rarely gets in the way. With recording quality freshened, this fine set is most welcome either on a pair of mid-priced CDs or, still sounding bright and clear, in its CfP cassette format (offered in a chunky box with a synopsis rather than a libretto).

Callas's view, aided by superbly imaginative and spacious conducting from Karajan, gives extra dimension to the Puccinian little woman, and with some keenly intelligent singing too from Gedda as Pinkerton this is a set which has a special compulsion. The performance projects the more vividly on CD, even though the lack of stereo in so atmospheric an opera is a serious disadvantage. Yet the powerful combination of Callas and Karajan – each challenging the other both in expressive imagination and in discipline – makes a powerful effect on the listener; unlike Karajan's later and more sumptuous Decca version with Freni, this one is fitted on to two CDs only.

Madama Butterfly: highlights.
*** Decca 421 247-2; *421 247-4* [id.] (from above recording with Freni and Pavarotti; cond. Karajan).
(M) *** EMI CDM7 63411-2; *EG 763411-4* (from above recording with Scotto and Bergonzi; cond. Barbirolli).
(M) ** Decca 421 873-2; *421 873-4* [417 733-2] (from complete recording, with Tebaldi and Bergonzi; cond. Serafin).

Karajan's disc offers an obvious first choice for a highlights CD from *Butterfly* if you are willing to pay full price.

The EMI selection (54 minutes) offers only slightly more music than the Tebaldi selection, but it does include the essential *Humming chorus.* Scotto's Butterfly was one of her finest recorded performances.

The Tebaldi/Bergonzi Decca set dates from 1958. The magnetism of the singing is very compelling, but the 51 minutes' selection is ungenerous and still omits the *Humming chorus.*

Manon Lescaut (complete).
*** DG Dig. 413 893-2 (2) [id.]. Freni, Domingo, Bruson, ROHCG Ch., Philh. O, Sinopoli.
*** Decca Dig. 421 426-2 (2) [id.]. Kiri Te Kanawa, Carreras, Paolo Coni, Ch. & O of Teatro Comunale di Bologna, Chailly.
(M) (***) BMG/RCA mono GD 60573 (2) [60573-2-RG]. Albanese, Bjorling, Merrill, Rome Op. Ch. & O, Perlea.
(M) (***) EMI mono CDS7 47393-8 (2) [Ang. CDCB 47392]. Callas, Di Stefano, Fioravanti, La Scala, Milan, Ch. and O, Serafin.

With his concern for detail, his love of high dramatic contrasts, and the clear pointing of changes of mood, along with sharp control of tension, Sinopoli presents the plan of each Act with new precision, reflecting the composer's own careful crafting. This is also the most sensuous-sounding reading on record, thanks also to the fine playing of the Philharmonia and a superb contribution from the chorus. Plácido Domingo's portrait of Des Grieux is here far subtler and more detailed, with finer contrasts of tone and dynamic, than in his earlier, EMI recording opposite Caballé. Freni proves an outstanding choice: her girlish tones in Act I rebut any idea that she might be too mature. *In quelle trine morbide*, in Act II, retains freshness of tone with fine concern for word detail, while the long duet and aria of the last Act present a most moving culmination, not feeling like an epilogue. Of the others, a first-rate team, Renato Bruson nicely brings out the ironic side of Lescaut's character, and having Brigitte Fassbaender just to sing the *Madrigal* adds to the feeling of luxury, as does John Tomlinson's darkly intense moment of drama as the ship's captain. The voices are more recessed than is common, but they are recorded with fine bloom, and the brilliance of the orchestral sound comes out impressively.

Dame Kiri, creamier of tone than Mirella Freni on DG, also gives an affecting characterization, at times rather heavily underlined but passionately convincing in the development from innocent girl to fallen woman. Freni's is the subtler performance and, in the final aria, *Sola, perduta, abbandonata*, Sinopoli's ominously steady tread helps to give her the greater intensity, and the playing from Chailly's Bologna orchestra cannot quite match that of the Philharmonia. Yet Chailly is a degree more idiomatic in his pacing. Both tenors are good but Carreras, recorded just before his illness, sounds a little strained at times. The Decca sound, with voices further forward, is the more vivid.

In Perlea's 1954 recording, the mono sound may be limited, but no Puccinian should miss it, when Jussi Bjoerling gives the finest ever interpretation on record of the role of Des Grieux. This is one of Bjoerling's best recordings, passionately committed and gloriously sung; and Robert Merrill too is superb as Manon's brother, giving delightful irony to the closing scene of Act I which has rarely sounded so effervescent. The Manon of Licia Albanese is sensitively sung, but the voice is not at all girlish, even less so than in her two classic recordings as Mimì in *Bohème* – with Gigli in 1939 and in Toscanini's concert performance in 1946.

It is typical of Callas that she turns the final scene into the most compelling part of the opera. Serafin, who could be a lethargic recording conductor, is here electrifying, and Di Stefano too is inspired to one of his finest complete opera recordings. The cast-list even includes the young Fiorenza Cossotto, impressive as the singer in the Act II *Madrigal*. The recording – still in mono, not a stereo transcription – minimizes the original boxiness and gives good detail, but for once the CD medium loses out when a break is involved in Act II between the two discs, whereas LP had that Act complete on one side.

Manon Lescaut: highlights.
(M) *** DG Dig. 435 408-2; *435 408-4* [id.] (from above recording, with Freni, Domingo; cond. Sinopoli).

With 66 minutes of music offered, most of the important music is included, so this selection from the highly recommendable Sinopoli set will certainly tempt collectors who already have another recording of the complete opera. An adequate synopsis with track cues is provided in lieu of a libretto.

La Rondine (complete).
*** Sony Dig. M2K 37852 [id.]. Te Kanawa, Domingo, Nicolesco, Rendall, Nucci, Watson, Knight, Amb. Op. Ch., LSO, Maazel.

La Rondine has never caught on, and a recording like this will almost certainly surprise anyone at the mastery of the piece, with a captivating string of catchy numbers. The story, told in Viennese-operetta style, is based on a watered-down *Traviata* situation, culminating not in tragedy but in a sad-sweet in-between ending such as the Viennese loved. It is not just a question of Puccini taking Viennese waltzes as model, but all kinds of other suitable dances such as tangos, foxtrots and two-steps; but he commandeered them completely, to make the result utterly Puccinian. Maazel's is a strong, positive reading, crowned by a superb and radiant Magda in Dame Kiri Te Kanawa, mature yet glamorous. Domingo, by age too mature for the role of young hero, yet scales his voice down most effectively in the first two Acts, expanding in heroic warmth only in the final scene of dénouement. Sadly, the second pair are far less convincing, when the voices of both Mariana Nicolesco and David Rendall take ill to the microphone.

Il Tabarro (complete).
(M) **(*) BMG/RCA GD 60865 (2) [60865-2]. Leontyne Price, Domingo, Milnes, John Alldis Ch., New Philh. O, Leinsdorf – LEONCAVALLO: *I Pagliacci*. ***

Leontyne Price may not be ideally cast as the bargemaster's wife, but she is fully in character, even though she does not point word-meanings in enough detail. Sherrill Milnes is rather young-sounding for the bargemaster, but he sings memorably in the climactic aria, Nulla silenzio, sustaining an unusually slow termpo. Plácido Domingo makes a fresh-voiced and well-characterized young bargee, while Leinsdorf is at his most sympathetic. The CD transfer increases the sense of presence, yet retains the ambient evocation. A full translation is provided.

Tosca (complete).
❀ *** EMI CDS7 47175-8 (2) [id.]. Callas, Di Stefano, Gobbi, Calabrese, La Scala, Milan, Ch. and O, De Sabata.
*** DG Dig. 431 775-2 (2). Freni, Domingo, Ramey, Terfel, ROHCG Ch., Philh. O, Sinopoli.
(M) *** Decca 421 670-2 (2) [id.]. Leontyne Price, Di Stefano, Taddei, V. State Op. Ch., VPO, Karajan.
*** DG 413 815-2 (2) [id.]. Ricciarelli, Carreras, Raimondi, Corena, German Op. Ch., BPO, Karajan.
*** Ph. 412 885-2 (2) [id.]. Caballé, Carreras, Wixell, ROHCG Ch. and O, C. Davis.
**(*) Decca Dig. 414 597-2 (2) [id.]. Te Kanawa, Aragall, Nucci, Welsh Nat. Opera Ch., Nat. PO, Solti.
(M) (***) EMI mono CHS7 63338-2 (2) [Ang. CDHB 63338]. Caniglia, Gigli, Borgioli, Dominici, Rome Op. Ch. & O, Fabritiis.
(M) ** EMI CMS7 69974-2 (2) [Ang. CDMB 69974]. Callas, Bergonzi, Gobbi, Paris Op. Ch. & Conservatoire O, Prêtre.

There has never been a finer recorded performance of *Tosca* than Callas's first, with Victor de Sabata conducting and Tito Gobbi as Scarpia. One mentions the prima donna first because, in this of all roles, she was able to identify totally with the heroine and turn her into a great tragic figure, not merely the cipher of Sardou's original melodrama. Gobbi too makes the unbelievably villainous police chief into a genuinely three-dimensional character, and Di Stefano as the hero, Cavaradossi, was at his finest. The conducting of De Sabata is spaciously lyrical as well as sharply dramatic, and the mono recording is superbly balanced in Walter Legge's fine production. Though there is inevitably less spaciousness than in a stereo recording, the voices are caught gloriously. Only in the big *Te Deum* scene at the end of Act I does the extra clarity of CD reveal a hint of congestion, and this is minimal. However, this set has recently been remastered, with improvement in the orchestral sound and a layout which places Act I complete on the first CD and Acts II and III on the second. The CDs are now generously cued, and we feel able to restore the Rosette which the performance so richly deserves.

With a trio of soloists that could hardly be more starry, what above all marks out the new DG version as exceptional is the conducting of Sinopoli. Even more than the Puccini operas he has previously recorded – always with spacious, finely moulded treatment – *Tosca* seems to match his musical personality. The big chords of the Scarpia motif at the very start have never come over with greater power than here, helped by DG recording of spectacular weight and range, with an involving sense of immediacy. Sinopoli then sets the mood of each section of the opera very vividly, often pointing rhythms to lighten the texture, as in the Act 1 love duet or in moments when Scarpia affects to conceal his sinister side. Not that Ramey's is a conventional portrait of the evil police-chief. The natural timbre of his glorious bass is noble, with no snarl in it. Inevitably one misses many of the sinister or villainous overtones, but the role has rarely been sung with more sheer beauty, with such a climax as the *Te Deum* at the end of Act 1 sounding thrilling in its firmness and power. Domingo's heroic power is formidable too, and unlike many of his opera recordings for DG this one presents him in close-up, not distanced. Freni's is not naturally a Tosca voice, and her singing here is less firm and even than it was on her earlier Decca recording, but it is still a powerful, heartfelt performance. Among the others the Welsh bass, Bryn Terfel, makes a formidable international recording début as Angelotti, clear-cut and positive.

On Decca, Karajan deserves equal credit with the principal singers for the vital, imaginative performance, recorded in Vienna. Some idea of its quality may be gained from the passage at the end of Act I, just before Scarpia's *Te Deum*. Karajan takes a speed far slower than usual, but there is an intensity which takes one vividly to the Church of San Andrea while at the same time building the necessary tension for the depiction of Scarpia's villainy. Taddei himself has a marvellously wide range of tone-colour, and though he cannot quite match the Gobbi snarl he has almost every other weapon in his armoury. Leontyne Price is at the peak of her form and Di Stefano sings most sensitively. The sound of the Vienna orchestra is enthralling – both more refined and richer than usual in a Puccini opera, and it sounds quite marvellous in its digitally remastered format, combining presence with atmosphere and making a superb bargain at mid-price.

On Karajan's DG version the police chief, Scarpia, seems to be the central character, and his unexpected choice of singer, a full bass, Raimondi, helps to show why, for this is no small-time villain but a man who in full confidence has a vein of nobility in him. Katia Ricciarelli is not the most individual of Toscas, but the beauty of singing is consistent, with *Vissi d'arte* outstanding at a very slow tempo indeed. Carreras is also subjected to slow Karajan tempi in his big arias and, though the recording brings out an unevenness in the voice, it is still a powerful, stylish performance. The recording is rich and full, with the stage picture clearly established and the glorious orchestral textures beautifully caught; the CD transfer improves definition and increases the feeling of spaciousness, putting more air round the voices and adding bloom to the orchestral sound.

Sir Colin Davis rarely if ever chooses idiosyncratic tempi, and his manner is relatively straight; but it remains a strong and understanding reading, as well as a refreshing one. In this the quality of the singing from a cast of unusual consistency plays an important part. With the purity of *Vissi d'arte* coming as a key element in her interpretation, Caballé presents Tosca as a formidable siren-figure. Carreras reinforces his reputation as a tenor of unusual artistry as well as of superb vocal powers. Though Wixell is not ideally well focused as Scarpia, he presents a completely credible lover-figure, not just the lusting ogre of convention. The 1976 analogue recording is full as well as refined, bringing out the beauties of Puccini's scoring. It is given a strikingly successful CD transfer, with three-dimensional placing of voices.

Rarely has Solti phrased Italian melody so consistently *con amore*, his fiercer side subdued but with plenty of power when required. Even so, the timing is not always quite spontaneous-sounding, with transitions occasionally rushed. Scarpia's entry is presented with power but with too little of the necessary menace. Nucci in that role sings strongly but not very characterfully. Aragall as Cavaradossi produces a glorious stream of heroic tone, and the incidental characters are also strongly cast. But the principal *raison d'être* of the set must be the casting of Dame Kiri as the jealous opera-singer. Her admirers will relish the glorious sounds, but the jealous side of Tosca's character is rather muted. Her recognition of the fan shown to her by Scarpia, *E L'Attavanti!*, has no snarl of anger in it, even though she later conveys real pain in her half-tones, as Scarpia's poison begins to work.

'The Gigli *Tosca*' was one of the glories of Puccini representation in the catalogue. The transfer brings astonishingly vivid sound, as in the rasping trombones on the opening Scarpia chords, along with a fine sense of presence. The great tenor dominates the whole performance, his facial expressiveness consistently beaming out through his voice, while Maria Caniglia, not characterful enough to be a memorable Tosca, sings with warmth and total commitment. Armando Borgioli is a young-sounding, virile Scarpia, forceful and upstanding rather than sinister. The conducting of Fabritiis brings far more natural and convincing timing than you find on many a more recent recording.

The Callas stereo *Tosca* is exciting and disappointing in roughly predictable proportions. There are few points of improvement over the old mono set, with Callas in the title-role and De Sabata conducting far more imaginatively than takes place here. When it comes to vocal reliability, the comparison of the new with the old is just as damaging, as an impartial observer might have predicted. Gobbi is magnificent still, but no more effective than he was in the mono recording, and Bergonzi's Cavaradossi, intelligent and attractive, is not helped by a recording balance not in his favour.

Tosca: highlights.
*** DG 423 113-2 [id.] (from above set with Ricciarelli and Carreras; cond. Karajan).
*** EMI Dig. CDC7 54324-2 [id.]; *EL 754324-4*. Scotto, Domingo, Bruson, Amb. Op. Ch., St Clement Danes School Boys' Ch., Philh. O, Levine).
**(*) Decca Dig. 421 611-2 [id.] (from above set with Te Kanawa, Aragall and Nucci; cond. Solti).

The selection from Karajan's powerful, closely recorded Berlin version is welcome. The breadth of Karajan's direction is well represented in the longer excerpts; there is also Tosca's *Vissi d'arte*, but Scarpia's music is under-represented, which is a pity when Raimondi made such a distinctive Scarpia with his dark bass timbre.

Domingo first recorded *Tosca* for EMI rather than DG, and Cavaradossi is one of his most impressive roles. So this selection fits in well with DG's 'Domingo Edition', although (unlike that series of highlights) it is issued at full price and, even so, offers only 65 minutes of excerpts, although all the key items are here.

Dame Kiri Te Kanawa sings gloriously on Solti's set, as does Aragall; but those interested in the opera itself would do better to spend just a little more to obtain the splendid mid-priced Decca Karajan set.

Il Trittico: (i) *Il Tabarro;* (ii) *Suor Angelica;* (iii) *Gianni Schicchi.*
**(*) Sony CD 79312 (3) [M3K 35912]. (i; ii) Scotto, (i; iii) Domingo, (i) Wixell, Sénéchal, (ii) Horne, (ii; iii) Cotrubas, (iii) Gobbi, Amb. Op. Ch., (ii) Desborough School Ch., (i; ii) Nat. PO, (iii) LSO, Maazel.
(M) **(*) RCA/Eurodisc Dig. GD 69043 (3) [7775-2-RC: *Il Tabarro;* 7806-2-RC: *Suor Angelica;* 7751-2-RC: *Gianni Schicchi*]. (i) Nimsgern, Lamberti, Auer, Tokody; (i; iii) Pane; (ii) Popp, Lipovšek, Schimi, Jennings; (iii) Panerai, Donath, Baniewicz, Seifert; Bav. R. Ch., Munich R. O, Patanè.

Il Tabarro may most seriously lack atmosphere in Maazel's version, but his directness is certainly refreshing, and in the other two operas it results in powerful readings; the opening of *Gianni Schicchi*, for example, has a sharp, almost Stravinskian bite. In the first two operas, Scotto's performances have a commanding dominance, presenting her at her finest. In *Gianni Schicchi* the veteran Tito Gobbi gives an amazing performance, in almost every way as fine as his EMI recording of twenty years earlier – and in some ways this is even more compelling. The generally close recording has a full range and the immediacy is increased by the vivid CD transfers. The only snag is the lack of cueing; CBS provide only one track for the whole of *Il Tabarro* and only two each for *Gianni Schicchi* and *Suor Angelica*, the second in each case being used to indicate the main soprano aria.

Patanè directs consistently well-paced, idiomatic performances of all three operas, well played and atmospherically recorded. Neither Lucia Popp as Angelica nor Maria Lipovšek as the vindictive Zia Principessa is ideally cast in the central opera of the triptych – the one overstressed, the other sounding too young – but these are both fine artists who sing with consistent imagination. Nimsgern as Michele in *Tabarro* gives a memorable, well-projected performance, and so does the characterful Rolando Panerai as Schicchi in the comic final opera, both central to the success of the performances. In the USA the three operas are available separately but at premium price.

Turandot (complete).
*** Decca 414 274-2 (2) [id.]. Sutherland, Pavarotti, Caballé, Pears, Ghiaurov, Alldis Ch., Wandsworth School Boys' Ch., LPO, Mehta.
(M) *** EMI CMS7 69327-2 (2) [Ang. CDMB 69327]. Nilsson, Corelli, Scotto, Mercuriali, Giaiotti, Rome Op. Ch. & O, Molinari-Pradelli.
*** DG Dig. 423 855-2 (2) [id.]. Ricciarelli, Domingo, Hendricks, Raimondi, V. State Op. Ch., V. Boys' Ch., VPO, Karajan.
(***) EMI mono CDS7 47971-8 (2) [id.]. Callas, Fernandi, Schwarzkopf, Zaccaria, La Scala, Milan, Ch. & O, Serafin.

The role of Turandot, the icy princess, is not one that you would expect to be in Joan Sutherland's repertory, but here on record she gives an intensely revealing and appealing interpretation, making the character far more human and sympathetic than ever before. Sutherland's singing is strong and beautiful, while Pavarotti gives a performance equally imaginative, beautiful in sound, strong on detail. To set Caballé against Sutherland was a daring idea, and it works superbly well; Pears as the Emperor is another imaginative choice. Mehta directs a gloriously rich and dramatic performance, superlatively recorded, still the best-sounding *Turandot* on CD, while the reading also remains supreme.

The EMI set brings Nilsson's second assumption on record of the role of Puccini's formidable princess. As an interpretation it is very similar to the earlier, RCA performance, but its impact is far more immediate, thanks to the conducting of Molinari-Pradelli. Corelli may not be the most sensitive prince in the world, but the voice is in glorious condition. Scotto's Liù is very beautiful and characterful too. With vividly remastered sound, this makes an excellent mid-priced recommendation, though the documentation, as yet, does not include an English translation.

In Karajan's set, both the Liù of Barbara Hendricks and the Turandot of Katia Ricciarelli are more sensuously feminine than is usual. With her seductively golden tone, Hendricks is almost a sex-kitten, and one wonders how Calaf could ever have overlooked her. This is very different from the usual picture of a chaste slave-girl. Ricciarelli is a far more vulnerable figure than one expects of the icy princess, and the very fact that the part strains her beyond reasonable vocal limits adds to the dramatic point, even if it subtracts from the musical joys. By contrast, Plácido Domingo is vocally superb, a commanding prince; and the rest of the cast presents star names even in small roles. The CD sound is full and brilliant, if at times rather close in the manner of DG engineers working in the Berlin Philharmonie. Ensemble is not always quite as flawless as one expects of Karajan with Berlin forces, though significantly the challenge of the manifestly less inspired completion by Alfano has him working at white heat.

One quickly reads something of Callas's own underlying vulnerability into her portrait of Turandot. With her the character seems so much more believably complex than with others, and this 1957 recording is one of her most thrillingly magnetic performances on disc. It is made the more telling, when Schwarzkopf provides a comparably characterful and distinctive portrait as Liù, far more than a Puccinian 'little woman', sweet and wilting. Even more than usual one regrets that the confrontation between princess and slave is so brief. Next to such sopranos Eugenio Fernandi sounds relatively uncharacterful as Calaf, but his timbre is pleasing enough. By contrast, Serafin's masterly conducting exactly matches the characterfulness of Callas and Schwarzkopf, with colour, atmosphere and dramatic point all commandingly presented. With such a vivid performance, the 1957 mono sound – satisfyingly full-bodied, not boxy – hardly seems to matter, although the choral passages tend to overload at climaxes.

Turandot: excerpts.
(M) (***) EMI mono CDH7 61074-2 [id.]. Dame Eva Turner, Martinelli, Albanese, Favero, Tomei, Dua, ROHCG Ch., LPO, Barbirolli.

The Références issue of Dame Eva Turner in extracts from *Turandot* has live recordings made at Covent Garden during the Coronation season of 1937, with Sir John Barbirolli conducting and with Giovanni Martinelli as a unique Calaf. The excerpts were recorded at two separate performances and fascinatingly duplicate most of the items, with the second performance in each pair marginally more spacious and helpful in sound, and generally warmer and more relaxed as a performance. Martinelli's heroic timbre may be an acquired taste, but he is stirringly convincing, and Dame Eva Turner gloriously confirms all the legends, even more commanding than in her earlier studio accounts of the big aria, *In questa reggia.* Keith Hardwick's excellent transfers, for all the obvious limitations of recording on stage at Covent Garden, give a superb sense of presence.

Turandot: highlights.
*** Decca 421 320-2; *421 320-4* [id.]. Sutherland, Pavarotti, Caballé, Ghiaurov, LPO, Mehta.
(M) *** DG Dig.435 409-2; *435 409-4* [id.] (from above recording, with Ricciarelli, Domingo; cond. Karajan).
(M) **(*) EMI CDM7 63410-2; *EG 763410-4.* Caballé, Carreras, Freni, Plishka, Sénéchal, Rhine Op. Ch., Strasbourg PO, Lombard.

A generous and shrewdly chosen collection of excerpts from the glorious Decca set of *Turandot. Nessun dorma,* with Pavarotti at his finest, is here given a closing cadence for neatness. The vintage Decca sound is outstandingly full and vivid.

Domingo is at his very finest here, and he is exceptionally well represented in this 70-minute selection of highlights (part of the 'Domingo Edition'), as indeed is the chorus. The opera's narrative is cued with track references, which serves instead of a translation.

Caballé's Turandot is well worth having on disc, even if, like the others in EMI's Puccini highlights series, the selection (52 minutes) is far from generous.

Le Villi: complete.
*** Sony MK 76890 [MK 36669]. Scotto, Domingo, Nucci, Gobbi, Amb. Op. Ch., Nat. PO, Maazel.

Maazel directs a performance so commanding, with singing of outstanding quality, that one can at last assess Puccini's first opera on quite a new level. Puccini's melodies may be less distinctive here than they later became, but one can readily appreciate the impact they had on early audiences. Scotto's voice tends to spread a little at the top of the stave but, like Domingo, she gives a powerful performance, and Leo Nucci avoids false histrionics. A delightful bonus is Tito Gobbi's contribution reciting the verses which link the scenes; he is as characterful a reciter as he is a singer. The recording is one of CBS's best.

COLLECTIONS

Arias: *La Bohème: Quando m'en vo' soletta. Gianni Schicchi: O mio babbino caro. Madama Butterfly: Un bel dì. Manon Lescaut: In quelle trine morbide. La Rondine: Chi il bel sogno di Doretta. Tosca: Vissi d'arte. Le Villi: Se come voi piccina.*
*** Sony Dig. MK 37298 [id.]. Kiri Te Kanawa, LPO, Pritchard – VERDI: *Arias.* ***

The creamy beauty of Kiri Te Kanawa's voice is ideally suited to these seven lyrical arias –

including such rarities as the little waltz-like song from *Le Villi*. Expressive sweetness is more remarkable than characterization, but in such music, well recorded and sounding especially believable on CD, who would ask for more?

'Puccini heroines'; La Bohème: Sì, mi chiamano Mimì; Donde lieta uscì; Musetta's waltz song. Edgar: Addio, mio dolce amor. La Fanciulla del West: Laggiù nel Soledad. Gianni Schicchi: O mio babbino caro. Madama Butterfly: Bimba, bimba non piangere (*Love duet,* with Plácido Domingo); *Un bel dì. Manon Lescaut: In quelle trine morbide; Sola, perduta, abbandonata. La Rondine: Ore dolci a divine. Tosca: Vissi d'arte. Turandot: In questa reggia. Le Villi: Se come voi piccina.*
*** BMG/RCA RD 85999 [RCA 5999-2-RC]. Leontyne Price, New Philh. O or LSO, Downes; Santi.

This collection is a formidable demonstration of the art of Leontyne Price at the very peak of her career, still marvellously subtle in control (the end of Tosca's *Vissi d'arte* for example), powerfully dramatic, yet able to point the *Rondine* aria with delicacy and charm. The *Love duet* from *Butterfly* in which she is joined by Domingo is particularly thrilling, and there is much else here to give pleasure. The remastering is extremely vivid and the voice is given fine bloom and presence. A Puccinian feast!

Arias: *La Bohème; Sì, mi chiamano Mimì; Donde lieta uscì. Gianni Schicchi: O mio babbino caro. Madama Butterfly: Un bel dì; Tu, tu piccolo Iddio. Manon Lescaut: In quelle trine morbide; Sola, perduta, abbandonata. La Rondine: Chi il bel sogno di Doretta. Tosca: Vissi d'arte. Turandot: Signore, ascolta!; Tu che di gel sei cinta. Le Villi: Se come voi piccina.*
*** EMI CDC7 47841-2 [id.]. Montserrat Caballé, LSO, Mackerras.

Montserrat Caballé uses her rich, beautiful voice to glide over these great Puccinian melodies. The effect is ravishing, with lovely recorded sound to match the approach. This is one of the loveliest of all operatic recital discs and the comparative lack of sparkle is compensated for by the sheer beauty of the voice. The CD transfer is extremely successful, vivid yet retaining the full vocal bloom.

Purcell, Henry (1659–95)

Sonnatas of 3 parts Nos. 1–7, Z.790–6; Pavans: in A min.; B flat; G min., Z.749, Z.750, Z.752.
*** Chan. Dig. CHAN 8591; *ABTD 1287* [id.]. Purcell Qt.

Sonnatas of 3 Parts Nos. 8–12, Z.797–801; Sonnatas in 4 Parts Nos. 1–2, Z.802–3; Chacony in G min., Z.751; Fantasia on a Ground in D & F; Pavans in A, Z.748; G min., Z.751.
*** Chan. Dig. CHAN 8663; *ABTD 1349* [id.]. Purcell Quartet.

In these *Sonnatas,* which Purcell published when he was twenty-three, he turned from the fantasias for viol consort to the new, concerted style which had been developed in Italy. Interspersed among the *Sonnatas* are three earlier and highly chromatic *Pavans,* composed before Purcell embraced the sonata discipline. If anything, the second volume is more attractive than the first, for it includes the indelible *Chacony in G minor* (based on a song-tune, *Scocca Pur,* by Giovanni Battista Draghi, after whom Purcell named his first-born son). The Purcell Quartet give a first-class account of themselves: their playing is authoritative and idiomatic; and the Chandos recording is of exceptional clarity and definition. The artists are firmly focused in a warm but not excessively reverberant acoustic, and the sound has splendid body. Strongly recommended. The disc also includes the first two of the *Sonnatas of 4 Parts.*

Sonnatas of 4 Parts Nos. 1–10, Z.802–11.
*** O-L 433 190-2 [id.]. Mackintosh, Huggett, Coin, Hogwood (chamber organ or spinet).

Sonnatas of 4 Parts Nos. 3–10, Z.804–811; Prelude for solo violin in G min., Z.773; Organ voluntaries Nos. 2 in D min.; 4 in G, Z.718 & 710.
*** Chan. Dig. CHAN 8763; *ABTD 1401* [id.]. Purcell Quartet.

It is odd that these *Sonnatas,* surely the best of the period, should be relatively neglected both in the concert hall and on record. The Oiseau-Lyre recording made in 1979 pioneered the way and it still sounds excellent in its CD format. It has the advantage of including all the four-part works on a single CD, and the playing is authoritative in style and feeling and the recording exemplary.

The Purcell Quartet are hardly less impressive and have the advantage of modern, digital recording with a firm focus and perhaps slightly more body. They too play with full command of the Purcellian style and, although the first two *Sonnatas* are included on their previous disc, this leaves room for a solo violin *Prelude* and two organ *Voluntaries*, both admirably presented and, like the *Sonnatas*, offering very realistic sound.

(i) *Suites for string orchestra from: Abdelazer; The Gordian knot untied; The married beau; The virtuous wife.* (ii) *12 Lessons from Musick's Handmaid; Harpsichord suite No. 6 in D.*
(M) ** Van. 08.4044.71 [OVC 4071]. (i) Hartford (Connecticut) CO, Fritz Mahler; (ii) George Malcolm.

A mixed bag. The playing of these suites of stage music is competent and lively and the recording good, although the chosen medium – without voices – does not show Purcell's full genius, which did not lie in his use of the limited range of colour possible with the seventeenth-century string orchestra. But there are plenty of good tunes here, and the result is certainly successful within its limitations. However the harpsichord playing of George Malcolm is in a different league, especially in the *Lessons* published in *Musick's Handmaid.* In short he is superb, and well recorded, too.

Harpsichord music (complete): *Suites Nos. 1–8* (with alternative Prelude for *Suite No. 4*). *Abdelazar: Jig. 4 Airs; Canary; Celebrate the festival: Gavotte. Dioclesian: Trumpet tune. The Double Dealer: Air. Hornpipe; The Indian Queen: Trumpet tune. 2 Marches; The Married Beau: March. The Old Bachelor: Hornpipe. Minuet; A New ground; New Irish tune; New minuet; New Scotch tune; Prelude in G min.; Round O; The Queen's dolour; Raise the voice: Minuet. Rigadoon; Saraband with division; Sefauchi's farewell; 2 Song tunes; Suite of 5 Lessons; Timon of Athens: Chaconne. Trumpet tune called The Cibell.*
(M) *** Saga SCD 9009/10. Robert Woolley (harpsichord).

Robert Woolley is a fine player. He was still in his mid-twenties when he made these recordings at the beginning of the 1980s. He plays copies of two eighteenth-century instruments by Benjamin Slade and his pupil, Thomas Hitchcock, and how well they sound! The harpsichord image is very natural and most attractive to the ear. The playing itself is vital and imaginative: Woolley can hold his own against senior and better-known rivals. The selection offers much that is not otherwise available, and Purcell's arrangements include many cherishable miniatures. A good deal of the music, including the *Suites*, derives from *A Choice Collection of Lessons* (published posthumously in 1696); other items are from *A Banquet of Musick* (1688) and many of the transcriptions come from the Second Part of *Musick's-Handmaid*, published by Playford in 1689, and were 'carefully revised and corrected by the same Mr Henry Purcell'. An indispensable set for those interested in English keyboard music.

VOCAL MUSIC

Arise my muse (1690); Now does the glorious day appear (1689) (Odes for Queen Mary's birthday); Ode for St Cecilia's Day: Welcome to all pleasures (1683).
*** Hyp. Dig. CDA 66314; *KA 66314* [id.]. Fisher, Bonner, Bowman, Chance, Daniels, Ainsley, George, Potts, King's Consort, Robert King.

Robert King directs the King's Consort and eight excellent soloists in this triptych of three of Purcell's finest ceremonial odes, including the shorter of the two *St Cecilia odes.* Ensemble could in places be sharper; but it is a delight to hear such superb artists as the counter-tenors James Bowman and Michael Chance in duet. The recording is vividly atmospheric.

Ayres, Theatre music and Sacred songs: *Awake awake, ye dead (Hymn for the Day of Judgement); Birthday ode for Queen Mary: Strike the viol. Dioclesian: O how happy's he; Chaconne. Respighi, The earth trembled (A hymn on our Saviour's Passion). The Fairy Queen: One charming night. How plaisant is this flow'ry plain and grove* (ode). *The Indian Queen: Ye twice ten hundred deities; Wake Quivera. Ode for St Cecilia: Raise, raise the voice; Oedipus: Hear, ye sullen pow'rs below; Come away, do not stay. The Old Bachelor: Thus to a ripe consenting maid. Olinda: There ne'er was so wretched a lover as I* (duet). *Timon of Athens: Hark how the songsters. Pavane and Trio.*
(B) **(*) HM HMA 90214 [id.]. Deller Consort & Ens., Deller.

With the programme revised since the original LP issue, Deller has put together what one might regard as a sampler of Purcell's vocal music, a varied collection which includes some of his finest inspirations. Always fresh and often lovely performances, given good if not outstanding recording.

Benedicte: O all ye works of the Lord. Coronation music for King James II: I was glad. Funeral music for Queen Mary: Man that is born of woman; In the midst of life; Thou knowest, Lord, the secrets of our hearts. Anthems: Blow up the trumpet in Sion; Hear my prayer, O Lord; I will sing unto the Lord; Jubilate; Lord, how long wilt Thou be angry; O God, Thou art my God; O God, Thou hast cast us out; O Lord God of Hosts; Remember not, Lord, our offences; Save me, O God.
*** Conifer Dig. CDCF 152; *MCFC 152* [id.]. Trinity College Ch., Cambridge, Marlow; Matthews; G. Jackson (organ).

Richard Marlow gets good results from his singers; such expressive anthems as *Remember not, Lord, our offences* and *Hear my prayer, O Lord* are eloquently done and beautifully recorded. Dr Peter le Huray reminds us that all the music on this disc, apart from one anthem, was composed before Purcell was twenty-five. What an extraordinary achievement! Excellent performances from all concerned – not least the Conifer recording team.

(i) *Come ye sons of art (Ode on the birthday of Queen Mary, 1694);* Anthems: (ii) *My beloved spake;* (iii) *Rejoice in the Lord alway (Bell anthem);* (iv) *Welcome to all the pleasures (Ode on Cecilia's Day, 1683).*
(M) **(*) Van. 08.8027.71 [OVC 8027]. Alfred Deller, Deller Consort; (i) Mark Deller, Mary Thomas, Bevan, Oriana Concert Ch. & O; (ii) Cantelo, English, Bevan; (iii; iv) Kalmar O; (iii) Thomas, Sheppard, Tear, Worthley; Oriana Concert O. (iv) Cantelo, McLoughlin, English, Grundy, Bevan.

An enjoyable anthology showing Deller at his finest. The other soloists are good too, especially the tenor, Gerald English. The two anthems make a fine centrepiece, responding to the demand of Charles II for composers 'not to be too solemn' and to 'add symphonies, etc., with instruments' to their sacred vocal music. The *Bell anthem* is so called because of the repeated descending scales in the introduction. The warm, expressively played accompaniments are rather different from the effect one would achieve today with original instruments. The recording is closely balanced; although made at either Walthamstow or Cricklewood Church, the effect is not quite as spacious as one would expect, though pleasingly full.

Come, ye sons of art away; Funeral music for Queen Mary (1695).
*** Erato/Warner 2292 45123-2 [id.]. Lott, Brett, Williams, Allen, Monteverdi Ch. and O, Equale Brass Ens., Gardiner.

Come, ye sons of art away; Ode on St Cecilia's Day: Welcome to all the pleasures; Of old when heroes thought it base (Yorkshire Feast song).
*** DG Dig. 427 663-2 [id.]. J. Smith, Priday, Amps, Chance, Wilson, Ainsley, George, Richardson, E Concert Ch., E. Concert, Pinnock.

Come, ye Sons of Art, the most celebrated of Purcell's birthday odes for Queen Mary, is splendidly coupled on Erato with the unforgettable funeral music he wrote on the death of the same monarch. With the Monteverdi Choir at its most incisive and understanding, the performances are exemplary and the recording, though balanced in favour of the instruments, is clear and refined. Among the soloists Thomas Allen is outstanding, while the two counter-tenors give a charming performance of the duet, *Sound the trumpet*. The *Funeral music* includes the well-known *Solemn march* for trumpets and drums, a *Canzona* and simple anthem given at the funeral, and two of Purcell's most magnificent anthems setting the *Funeral sentences*.

Pinnock directs exuberant performances of three of Purcell's most magnificent occasional works, and the dramatic impact is enormously enhanced by the full and immediate recording, which yet has plenty of air round it. The weight and brightness of the choral sound go with infectiously lifted rhythms, making the music dance, as in the first chorus of *Welcome to all the pleasures*, the best known of his *Queen Mary Odes*, the one for 1694. There the line, 'to celebrate this triumphant day', could not come over more infectiously. The soloists are all outstanding, with the counter-tenor duetting of Michael Chance and Timothy Wilson in Sound the trumpet delectably pointed. The coupling is particularly valuable, the neglected *Yorkshire Feast song*, composed in 1690 for an 'otherwise obscure annual gathering of York nobility'. It is full of wonderful inspirations, like the tenor and counter-tenor duet, *And now when the renown'd Nassau* – a reference to the new king, William III.

(i) *Funeral music for Queen Mary* (complete); *Jubilate Deo in D; Te Deum laudamus in D.* (ii) Verse anthems: *I was glad; O give thanks O Lord God of hosts.*
(M) **(*) Decca 430 263-2; *430 263-4.* (i) Bowman, Brett, Partridge, Forbes Robinson, Consort of Sackbuts, ECO; (ii) Esswood, Partridge, Anthony Dawson; (i; ii) St John's College, Cambridge, Ch., George Guest.

The *Funeral music for Queen Mary* consists of far more than the unforgettable *March* for lugrubious sackbuts with punctuating timpani (later repeated without timpani), which still sounds so modern to our ears. In the event, this brings the least effective performance on the 1972 Decca (originally Argo) collection, not as bitingly tragic as it might have been. The rest of the work is beautifully done, and so are the grand ceremonial settings of the *Te Deum* and *Jubilate*, although the solo contributions are a little uneven. The verse anthems – intended for Charles II's Chapel Royal – were recorded three years later. Though their direction could be more flamboyant, the singing is superb, with Paul Esswood and Ian Partridge especially fine among the soloists. The recording is vivid and atmospheric, though the focus on CD is not absolutely sharp.

In guilty night (Saul and the Witch of Endor); Man that is born of woman (Funeral sentences); Te Deum and Jubilate Deo in D.
(B) **(*) HM HMA 90207 [id.]. Deller Consort, Stour Music Festival Ch. & O, Deller.

In guilty night is a remarkable dramatic scene depicting Saul's meeting with the Witch of Endor. The florid writing is admirably and often excitingly sung by Alfred Deller himself as the King and Honor Sheppard as the Witch. The *Te Deum and Jubilate* are among Purcell's last and most ambitious choral works; the *Funeral sentences* from early in his career are in some ways even finer in their polyphonic richness. The chorus here is not the most refined on record but, with sensitive direction, this attractive collection is well worth hearing. The recording is good and has certainly been made more vivid on CD.

Ode on St Cecilia's Day (Hail! bright Cecilia).
*** Erato/Warner Dig. 2292 45187-2 [id.]. Jennifer Smith, Stafford, Gordon, Elliott, Varcoe, David Thomas, Monteverdi Ch., E. Bar. Soloists, Gardiner.
(M) *** DG 427 159-2 [id.]. Woolf, Esswood, Tatnell, Young, Rippon, Shirley-Quirk, Tiffin Ch., Amb. S., ECO, Mackerras.
*** EMI Dig. CDC7 47490-2 [id.]. Kirkby, Chance, Kevin Smith, Covey-Crump, Elliott, Grant, George, Thomas, Taverner Ch. & Players, Parrott.

Gardiner's characteristic vigour and alertness in Purcell come out superbly in this delightful record of the 1692 *St Cecilia Ode* – not as well known as some of the other odes he wrote, but a masterpiece. Soloists and chorus are outstanding even by Gardiner's high standards, and the recording excellent.

A splendid all-male performance of Purcell's joyous *Ode* on DG, with an exceptionally incisive and vigorous choral contribution matched by fine solo singing. Simon Woolf is ideally cast here and the recording is excellent, although the balance between soloists and tutti does not make much distinction in volume between the smaller and the larger groups.

Though Parrott's EMI version lacks the exuberance of Gardiner's outstanding Erato issue, in a more reticent way it brings a performance full of incidental delights, particularly vocal ones from a brilliant array of no fewer than twelve solo singers, notably five excellent tenors. With pitch lower than usual, some numbers that normally require counter-tenors can be sung by tenors. Interestingly, Parrott includes the *Voluntary in D minor* for organ before the wonderful aria celebrating that instrument and St Cecilia's sponsorship of it, *O wondrous machine.* It holds up the flow, but at least on CD it can readily be omitted.

Ode for Queen Mary's birthday (1692); *Ode for St Cecilia's day: Welcome to all pleasures.*
(B) ** HM HMA 90222 [id.]. Deller Consort, Stour Music Festival CO, Deller.

These Odes make an attractive pairing, two works which despite doggerel texts yet inspired Purcell to some striking and memorable ideas, as for example the duet for two counter-tenors, *Sweetness of nature*, in the *St Cecilia Ode*. The performances are not ideal, with rhythms a little heavy, and the recording is limited, though it has been opened up by the CD transfer and is quite acceptable if you fancy the coupling. The price is modest.

Anthems: *O sing unto the Lord; Praise the Lord, O Jerusalem; They that go down to the sea in ships.* Ode: *My heart is inditing; Te Deum and Jubilate Deo in D.*

(M) *** DG 427 124-2; *427 124-4*. Ch. of Christ Church Cathedral, Oxford, E. Concert, Preston.

This mid-priced collection includes, alongside favourite anthems, the big setting of the morning service canticles and the coronation ode, *My heart is inditing*. The performances are full of character, vigorous yet with the widest range of colour and feeling. The recording, made in London's Henry Wood Hall, is both spacious and well detailed.

Duets and solos for counter-tenor: *Bonduca: Sing, sing ye Druids. Come, ye sons of art: Sound the trumpet. Elegy on the death of Queen Mary: O dive custos Auriacae domus. The Maid's last prayer: No resistance is but vain. Ode on St Cecilia's Day: In vain the am'rous flute. O solitude, my sweetest choice. The Queen's epicedium: Incassum, Lesbia rogas. Timon of Athens: Hark how the songsters.*
*** Hyp. Dig. CDA 66253; *KA 66253* [id.]. James Bowman, Michael Chance, King's Consort, King – BLOW: *Ode* etc. ***

It was a happy idea to link an outstanding performance of John Blow's *Ode on the Death of Purcell* to this sparkling collection of solos and duets which show both the composer and these fine artists in inspirational form. The performances are joyous, witty and ravishing in their Purcellian melancholy, with often subtle response to word meanings, and King's accompaniments are both supportive and have plenty of character in their own right. Excellent recording.

Songs and airs: *Bess of Bedlam; Evening hymn; If music be the food of love; Lovely, lovely Albina; Not all my torments; Olinda in the shades unseen; The Plaint; O, Urge me no more; When first Amintas sued for a kiss. Arias: Birthday ode for Queen Mary: Crown the altar. The Fairy Queen: Hark! hark!; O, O let me weep; Ye gentle spirits of the air. The Indian Queen: I attempt from love's sickness to fly. Pausanias: Sweeter than roses. The Tempest: Dear pritty youths. Timon of Athens: The cares of lovers.*
*** O-L Dig. 417 123-2 [id.]. Emma Kirkby, Rooley, Hogwood.

The purity of Emma Kirkby's soprano – as delightful to some ears as it is disconcerting to others – suits this wide-ranging collection of Purcell songs splendidly, though you might argue for a bigger, warmer voice in the *Bess of Bedlam song*. The *Evening hymn* is radiantly done, and so are many of the less well-known airs which regularly bring new revelation. Excellent recording, if with the voice forward, and very present.

Songs: *Come, let us drink; A health to the nut brown lass; If ever I more riches; I gave her cakes and I gave her ale; Laudate Ceciliam; The miller's daughter; Of all the instruments; Once, twice, thrice I Julia tried; Prithee ben't so sad and serious; Since time so kind to us does prove; Sir Walter enjoying his damsel; 'Tis women makes us love; Under this stone; Young John the gard'ner.*
*** HM HMC 90242 [id.]. Deller Cons., Deller.

One section of this charming and stylish collection has a selection of Purcell's catches, some of them as lewd as rugby-club songs of today, others as refined as *Under this stone* – all of which the Deller Consort take in their stride. The final two pieces are extended items; *If ever I more riches*, a setting of Cowley, has some striking passages. The remastering for CD has greatly improved the sound, with voices fresh and first-rate recording of the instruments.

Songs: *The fatal hour comes on apace; Lord, what is man?; Love's power in my heart; More love or more disdain I crave; Now that the sun hath veiled his light; The Queen's Epicedium; Sleep, Adam, sleep; Thou wakeful shepherd; Who can behold Florella's charms.* Arias: *History of Dioclesian: Since from my dear Astrea's sight. Indian Queen: I attempt from love's sickness to fly. King Arthur: Fairest isle. Oedipus: Music for a while. Pausanias: Sweeter than roses. The Rival Sisters: Take not a woman's anger ill. Rule a wife and have a wife: There's not a swain.*
*** Etcetera Dig. KTC 1013 [id.]. Andrew Dalton; Uittenbosch; Borstlap.

Andrew Dalton has an exceptionally beautiful counter-tenor voice, creamy even in its upper register to make the extended 'Hallelujahs' of *Lord, what is man?* and *Now that the sun* even more heavenly than usual. One half has sacred songs, some of them less well known, the other secular, including various favourites. Many of them require transposition, but only in some of the soprano songs such as Fairest isle does that distract. A delightful disc, well recorded.

Songs and dialogues: *Go tell Amynta; Hence fond deceiver; In all our Cinthia's shining sphere; In some kind dream; Lost is my quiet; Stript of their green; What a sad fate is mine; What can we poor females do; Why my poor Daphne, why complaining.* Theatre music: *Amphitryon: Fair Iris*

and her swain. Dioclesian: Tell me why. King Arthur: You say 'tis love; For love every creature is formed by his nature. The Old Bachelor: As Amoret and Thyrsis lay.
*** Hyp. CDA 66056 [id.]. Kirkby, Thomas, Rooley.

This nicely planned Hyperion collection has one solo apiece for each of the singers, but otherwise consists of duets, five of them from dramatic works. The first half is the lighter in tone; the second half brings contrasting gravity, but this is just the sort of inspired material of Purcell that, unfairly, has tended to be forgotten. These near-ideal performances, beautifully sung and sensitively accompanied on the lute, make a delightful record, helped by excellent sound.

STAGE WORKS AND THEATRE MUSIC

Dido and Aeneas (complete).
❀ (M) *** Decca 425 720-2; *425 720-4*. Dame Janet Baker, Herincx, Clark, Sinclair, St Anthony Singers, ECO, Anthony Lewis.
*** Ph. Dig. 416 299-2 [id.]. Jessye Norman, McLaughlin, Kern, Allen, Power, ECO and Ch., Leppard.
*** Chan. Dig. CHAN 0521; *EBTD 0521* [id.]. Kirkby, Thomas, Nelson, Noorman, Rees, Taverner Ch. & Players, Parrott.
(M) (***) EMI mono CDH7 61006-2 [id.]. Flagstad, Schwarzkopf, Hemsley, Mermaid Theatre Singers & O, Geraint Jones.
** HM Dig. HMC 905173 [id.]. Laurens, Cantor, Feldman, Visse, Les Arts Florissants, Christie.
** Erato/Warner 2292 45263-2 [id.]. Troyanos, Stilwell, Palmer, Kern, Langridge, ECO Ch., ECO, Leppard.

Janet Baker's 1962 recording of *Dido* is a truly great performance. The radiant beauty of the voice is obvious enough, but here she goes beyond that to show what stylishness and insight she can command. The emotion is implied, as it should be in this music, not injected in great uncontrolled gusts. Listen to the contrast between the angry, majestic words to Aeneas, *Away, away!*, and the dark grief of the following *But death alas I cannot shun*, and note how Baker contrasts dramatic soprano tone-colour with darkened contralto tone. Even subtler is the contrast between the opening phrase of *When I am laid in earth* and its repeat a few bars later: it is a model of graduated mezza voce. Then with the words *Remember me!*, delivered in a monotone, she subdues the natural vibrato to produce a white tone of hushed, aching intensity. Anthony Lewis chooses fast speeds, but they challenge the ECO (Thurston Dart a model continuo player) to produce the crispest and lightest of playing, which never sounds rushed. The other soloists and chorus give very good support. Herincx is a rather gruff Aeneas, but the only serious blemish is Monica Sinclair's Sorceress. She overcharacterizes in a way that is quite out of keeping with the rest of the production. Like most vintage Oiseau-Lyre recordings, this was beautifully engineered: the remastering thins out the upper range a little, but the effect is to increase the feeling of authenticity, for the ambient bloom remains.

Authenticists should keep away, but Jessye Norman amply proves that this amazingly compressed setting of the epic *Aeneid* story has a dramatic depth and intensity to compare with Berlioz's setting. The opening phrase of *Ah Belinda* brings the most controversial moment, when Norman slows luxuriantly. But from then on the security and dark intensity of her singing make for a memorable performance, heightened in the recitatives by the equally commanding singing of Thomas Allen as Aeneas. The range of expression is very wide – with Norman producing an agonized whisper in the recitative just before *Dido's Lament* – but the inauthentic element must not be exaggerated. Marie McLaughlin is a pure-toned Belinda, Patrick Power a heady-toned Sailor, singing his song in a West Country accent, while Patricia Kern repeats her performance as the Sorceress, using conventionally sinister expression. The warm-toned counter-tenor, Derek Ragin, makes the Spirit Messenger into an eerie, other-worldly figure. Leppard's direction is relatively plain and direct, with some slow speeds for choruses. Excellent recording.

Andrew Parrott's concept of a performance on original instruments has one immediately thinking back to the atmosphere of Josias Priest's school for young ladies where Purcell's masterpiece was first given. The voices enhance that impression, not least Emma Kirkby's fresh, bright soprano, here recorded without too much edge but still very young-sounding. It is more questionable to have a soprano singing the tenor role of the Sailor in Act III; but anyone who fancies the idea of an authentic performance need not hesitate. The CD is exceptionally refined, the sound well focused, with analogue atmosphere yet with detail enhanced.

Though Flagstad's magnificent voice may in principle be too weighty for this music – one might point to the latter-day equivalent of Jessye Norman – she scales it down superbly in her noble reading, which brings beautiful shading and masterly control of breath and tone. Schwarzkopf is brightly characterful as Belinda, and though Thomas Hemsley is not ideally sweet-toned as Aeneas, he sings very intelligently; even in this age of period performance, this traditional account under Geraint Jones sounds fresh and lively still, not at all heavy. The mono sound, obviously limited, yet captures the voices vividly, and this above all is Flagstad's set.

A version of *Dido and Aeneas* such as the Harmonia Mundi issue with a predominantly French cast may seem an oddity but, with trifling exceptions, English accents are more than acceptable; William Christie, as in his recordings of other early operas, provides direction on an authentic chamber scale that makes the results both dramatic and intense. Particularly impressive – and an interesting idea for casting – is having the role of the Sorceress taken by the outstanding French counter-tenor, Dominique Visse. The shortcoming is that Guillemette Laurens makes a disappointing Dido, not strong or positive enough. First-rate recording.

On the Erato disc Leppard directs a consistently well-sprung, well played performance, as one would expect, but the overall impression is disappointing, largely because the climax of the opera fails to rise in intensity as it should. Tatiana Troyanos, stylish elsewhere, misses the tragic depth of the great lament of Dido, and without that focus the impact of the rest falls away. Philip Langridge sings the Sailor's song freshly and the recording is excellent, clear yet full and atmospheric.

Dioclesian; Timon of Athens.
*** Erato/Warner 2292 45327-2; *2292 45327-4* (2) [id.]. Dawson, Fisher, Covey-Crump, Elliot, George, Varcoe, Monteverdi Ch., E. Bar. Soloists, Gardiner.

On his two-disc Erato set John Eliot Gardiner rescues some of the most colourful and memorable of Purcell's theatre music. It is tragic that such inspired writing should by its very format have fallen out of the current repertory, when these pieces illustrate plays that are totally non-viable on the stage today. Like *The Fairy Queen*, *The Prophetess or the History of Dioclesian* is one of Purcell's semi-operas and presents similar problems in modern performance. Gardiner relies purely on musical quality in performing the copious amount of music Purcell wrote for the piece, hardly attempting to give any idea of the dramatic context which these disconnnected arias, ensembles and scenes illustrate. The martial music, shining with trumpets, is what stands out from *Dioclesian*, adapted from a Jacobean play first given in 1622. Gardiner is such a lively conductor, regularly drawing out the effervescence in Purcell's inspiration, that the result is delightfully refreshing, helped by an outstanding team of soloists. The incidental music for *Timon of Athens* offers more buried treasure, including such enchanting inventions as *Hark! how the songsters of the grove*, with its 'Symphony of pipes imitating the chirping of birds', and a fine *Masque for Cupid and Bacchus*, beautifully sung by Lynne Dawson, Gillian Fisher and Stephen Varcoe. Excellent Erato sound.

The Fairy Queen (complete).
*** DG Dig. 419 221-2 (2) [id.]. Harrhy, Jennifer Smith, Nelson, Priday, Penrose, Stafford, Evans, Hill, Varcoe, Thomas, Monteverdi Ch., E. Bar. Soloists, Gardiner.
*** HM Dig. HMC 901308/9; *HMC 401308/9* [id.]. Argenta, Dawson, Daniels, Loonen, Correas, Les Arts Florissants, William Christie.
(M) *** Decca 433 163-2 (2) [id.]. Vyvyan, Bowman, Pears, Wells, Partridge, Shirley-Quirk, Brannigan, Norma Burrowes, Amb. Op. Ch., ECO, Britten.

Gardiner's performance is a delight from beginning to end, for, though authenticity and completeness reign, scholarship is worn lightly and the result is consistently exhilarating, with no longueurs whatever. The fresh-toned soloists are first rate, while Gardiner's regular choir and orchestra excel themselves, with Purcell's sense of fantasy brought out in each succeeding number. Beautifully clear and well-balanced recording, sounding all the fresher on CD, with the silent background especially telling in the light-textured music. The layout places the first three Acts complete on disc one and the remaining two Acts on the second CD.

William Christie made this recording of *The Fairy Queen* immediately after a highly successful production on stage at the Aix-en-Provence Festival, and the robust vigour of his treatment is most compelling. He uses a far bigger team of both singers and instrumentalists than John Eliot Gardiner on the rival, DG Archiv set, allowing a wider range of colours. The drunken poet episode, for example, uses a glissando bassoon so that, in its earthiness, that sequence makes Gardiner's version sound too refined by comparison. The bite of the performance is increased by the relative dryness of the recorded sound. Some of the voices need more air round them to sound their best, and Gardiner's extra elegance goes with warmer, more congenially atmospheric recording. Among Christie's soloists two sopranos, well known in Britain, are outstanding: Nancy Argenta and Lynne Dawson; and the whole team is a strong one. The number of singers in solo roles allows them to be used together as chorus too – an authentic seventeenth-century practice. This makes a vigorous and refreshing alternative to the fine Gardiner set; but the Harmonia Mundi booklet is most inadequate: ingeniously, it has you chasing around in three places instead of one to identify both which number is where and who is singing. Any table of contents should be detailed enough to answer all questions.

Britten's version from the early 1970s used a newly reshaped arrangement of the music made by Britten himself in collaboration with Imogen Holst and Peter Pears. The original collection of individual pieces is here grouped into four satisfying sections: *Oberon's birthday*, *Night and silence*, the *Sweet passion* and the *Epithalamium*. Here the authentic glow of a Maltings performance (1971 vintage) is beautifully conveyed in the playing, the singing and the recording. The cast is consistently satisfying, with Peter Pears and Jennifer Vyvyan surviving from the much earlier mono version of Anthony Lewis on Oiseau-Lyre.

The Indian Queen (incidental music; complete).
*** HM HMC 90243; *HMC 40243* [id.]. Knibbs, Sheppard, Mark and Alfred Deller, Elliot, Bevan, Deller Singers, King's Musick, Deller.
**(*) Erato/Warner 2292 45556-2; *2292 45556-4* [id.]. Hardy, Fischer, Harris, Smith, Stafford, Hill, Elwes, Varcoe, Thomas, Monteverdi Ch., E. Bar. Soloists, Eliot Gardiner.

Deller's group is at its liveliest and most characterful in *The Indian Queen. Ye twice ten hundred deities* is sung splendidly by Maurice Bevan; and the duet for male alto and tenor, *How happy are we* (with Deller himself joined by Paul Elliot), as well as the best-known item, the soprano's *I attempt from love's sickness to fly* (Honor Sheppard), are equally enjoyable.

The reissued Erato version is fully cast and uses an authentic accompanying baroque instrumental group. The choral singing is especially fine, with the close of the work movingly expressive. John Eliot Gardiner's choice of tempi is apt and the soloists are all good, although the men are more strongly characterful than the ladies; nevertheless the lyical music comes off well. The recording is spacious and well balanced, and the performance has many individual felicities. Recommended alongside the Deller set on Harmonia Mundi.

(i) *The Indian Queen* (incidental music); (ii) *King Arthur* (complete).
❀ (M) *** Decca 433 166-2 (2) [id.]. (i) Cantelo, Wilfred Brown, Tear, Partridge, Keyte, St Anthony Singers, ECO, Mackerras; (ii) Morison, Harper, Mary Thomas, Whitworth, Wilfred Brown, Galliver, Cameron, Anthony, Alan, St Anthony Singers, Philomusica of L., Lewis.

The Indian Queen is another of the Purcellian entertainments that fit into no modern category, a semi-opera. The impossible plot matters little, for Purcell's music contains many delights; indeed the score seems to get better as it proceeds. This Decca Serenata (originally Oiseau-Lyre) version dates from 1966 and the recording, from a vintage era, remains first rate. With stylish singing and superb direction and accompaniment (Raymond Leppard's harpsichord continuo playing must be singled out), this is an invaluable reissue. Charles Mackerras shows himself a strong and vivid as well as scholarly Purcellian.

The Rosette, however, is for the pioneering 1959 set (also Oiseau-Lyre) of *King Arthur*, fully worthy to stand alongside the companion recording of *Dido and Aeneas*, made three years later – see above. Here the success of the interpretation does not centre on the contribution of one inspired artist, but rather on teamwork among a number of excellent singers and on the stylish and sensitive overall direction of Anthony Lewis. Oiseau-Lyre's excellent stereo also plays a bit part. This was an early set, but one would never guess it from the pleasing ambience and the sophistication of the antiphonal effects. A very happy example is the chorus *This way, that way*, when the opposing spirits (good and evil) make a joint attempt to entice the King, while the famous freezing aria will surely send a shiver through the most warm-blooded listener. Indeed *King Arthur* contains some of Purcell's most memorable inspiration, not just the items mentioned above and the famous song, *Fairest isle*, but a whole range of lively and atmospheric numbers which are admirably realized here by a very strong cast.

King Arthur (complete).
*** Erato/Warner 2292 45211-2 (2) [id.]. Jennifer Smith, Gillian Fischer, Priday, Ross, Stafford, Elliott, Varcoe, E. Bar. Soloists, Gardiner.

*** DG Dig. 435 490-2 (2) [id.]. Argenta, Gooding, Perillo, MacDougal, Tucker, Bannatyne-Scott, Finley, Ch. & E. Concert, Pinnock.

King Arthur may be cumbersome on stage, but in Gardiner's set its episodic nature matters hardly at all; one can simply relish the wealth of sharply inspired and colourful numbers. Gardiner's solutions to the textual problems carry complete conviction, as for example his placing of the superb *Chaconne in F* at the end instead of the start. Solo singing for the most part is excellent, with Stephen Varcoe outstanding among the men. As the Cold Genius he helps Gardiner to make the Frost scene far more effective than usual. He is also one of the trio who give a delightfully roistering account of *Harvest home. Fairest isle* is treated very gently after that, with Gill Ross, boyish of tone, reserved just for that number. Throughout, the chorus is characteristically fresh and vigorous, and the instrumentalists beautifully marry authentic technique to pure, unabrasive sounds. The recording vividly captures a performance in an aptly intimate but not dry acoustic.

Pinnock opens with the *Chaconne*, which is placed before the *Overture*. His performance is consistently refreshing and can be recommended alongside, though not in preference to Gardiner's. Linda Perillo makes a charming Philidel (one cannot imagine Arthur' soldiers having any doubt about their direction when she leads the famous *Hither, this way* chorus) and later her Sirens duet with Julia Gooding, *Two daughters of this aged stream*, is captivating. Brian Bannatyne-Scott is superb in Aeolus's *Ye blust'ring brethren*, and in his *Frost aria* (where Pinnock's sharply articulated accompaniment anticipates *Winter* in Vivaldi's *Four Seasons*) he achieves an unusual if controversial effect by beginning his series of shakes from slightly under the note. Not surprisingly, Nancy Argenta sings beautifully in the double roles of Cupid and Venus and her *Fairest isle* will not disappoint. The *Harvest home* sequence is every bit as exuberant here as it is with Gardiner, and both chorus and orchestra sing and play throughout with consistent vitality. The DG recording is first class, but why no coupling? The second CD plays for only 39 minutes.

King Arthur: highlights.
(B) ** HM HMA 90200 [id.]. Sheppard, Knibbs, Hardy, Alfred and Mark Deller, Elliot, Nixon, Maurice and Nigel Bevan, Deller Ch., King's Musick, Alfred Deller.

It was sensible of Harmonia Mundi, faced with the competition of Lewis's outstanding complete set, to choose to reissue a bargain disc of highlights from Dellers's 1978 version. This has considerable merit, not least a stylish accompaniment from the King's Musick, using original instruments effectively and not too abrasively, and a spacious recording which has transferred realistically to CD. Deller's solution to performing problems will satisfy almost everyone and, though the solo singing is not always polished, the performance has a refreshing vigour; Deller pioneered the idea of singing the Harvest home' chorus in Act V in a rousing West-country accent. But a highlights disc without the famous opening scene of Act II (*Hither this way*), with its opposing spirits, is almost unbelievably bad planning, when there would have been plenty of room for it.

The Tempest (incidental music; complete).
*** Erato/Warner 2292 45555-2; *2292 45555-4* [id.]. Jennifer Smith, Hardy, Hall, Elwes, Varcoe, David Thomas, Earle, Monteverdi Ch. & O, Eliot Gardiner.

Whether or not Purcell himself wrote this music for Shakespeare's last play (the scholarly arguments are still unresolved), Gardiner demonstrates how delightful it is, a masterly collection, in performances both polished and stylish and with excellent solo and choral singing. At least the *Overture* is clearly Purcell's, and that sets the pattern for a very varied collection of numbers, including three da capo arias and a full-length masque celebrating Neptune for Act V. The recording, full and atmospheric, has transferred vividly to CD.

Theatre music (collection).

Disc 1: *Abdelazar: Overture & suite. Distressed Innocence: Overture & suite. The Gordian Knot Untied: Overture & suite; The Married Beau: Overture & suite. Sir Anthony Love: Overture & suite.*

Disc 2: *Bonduca: Overture and suite. Circe: suite. The Old Bachelor: Overture and suite. The Virtuous Wife: Overture and suite.*

Disc 3: *Amphitrion: Overture and suite; Overture in G min.; Don Quixote: suite.*

Disc 4: *Overture in G min. The Double Dealer: Overture and suite. Henry II, King of England: In vain, 'gainst love, in vain I strove. The Richmond Heiress: Behold the man. The Rival Sisters: Overture; 3 songs. Tyranic Love: Hark my Damilcar!* (duet); *Ah! how sweet it is to love. Theodosius:* excerpts. *The Wives' Excuse:* excerpts.

Disc 5: *Overture in D min.; Cleomenes, the Spartan Hero: No, no, poor suff'ring heart. A Dialogue between Thirsis and Daphne: Why, my Daphne, why complaining?. The English Lawyer: My wife has a tongue:* excerpts. *A Fool's Preferment:* excerpts. *The History of King Richard II: Retir'd from any mortal's sight. The Indian Emperor: I look'd and saw within. The Knight of Malta: At the close of the ev'ning. The Libertine:* excerpts. *The Marriage-hater Match'd: As soon as the chaos . . . How vile are the sordid intregues. The Massacre of Paris: The genius lo* (2 settings). *Oedipus:* excerpts. *Regulus: Ah me! to many deaths. Sir Barnaby Whigg: Blow, blow, Boreas, blow. Sophonisba: Beneath the poplar's shadow. The Wives' excuse:* excerpts.

Disc 6: *Chacony; Pavans Nos. 1–5; Trio sonata for violin, viola de gamba & organ. Aureng-Zebe: I see, she flies me. The Canterbury Guests: Good neighbours why?. Epsom Wells: Leave these useless arts. The Fatal Marriage: 2 songs. The Female Virtuosos: Love, thou art best. Love Triumphant: How happy's the husband. The Maid's Last Prayer:* excerpts. *The Mock Marriage: Oh! how you protest; Man is for the woman made. Oroonoko: Celemene, pray tell me. Pausanius: Song (Sweeter than roses) and duet. Rule a Wife and Have a Wife: There's not a swain. The Spanish Friar: Whilst I with grief.*

(M) *** O-L 425 893-2 (6). Kirkby, Nelson, Lane, Roberts, Lloyd, Bowman, Hill, Covey-Crump, Elliott, Byers, Bamber, Pike, David Thomas, Keyte, Shaw, George, Taverner Ch., AAM, Hogwood.

Most of the music Purcell wrote for the theatre is relatively little heard, and one must remember that the 'suites' assembled here were not originally intended for continuous performance. If in the earlier discs they do not provide the variety and range one would expect from works conceived as a whole, much of the music comes up with striking freshness in these performances using authentic instruments. As well as the charming dances and more ambitious overtures, as the series proceeds we are offered more extended scenas with soloists and chorus, of which the nine excerpts from *Theodosius*, an early score (1680), are a particularly entertaining example. Before that, on Disc 3 we have already had the highly inventive *Overture and incidental music* for *Don Quixote*. Though the music was written at high speed, much of it was attractively lively and it deserves to be resurrected in such stylish performances, with much enchanting singing from both the soprano soloists, Emma Kirkby and Judith Nelson. Disc 4 also includes a delightful duet from *The Richmond Heiress*, representing a flirtation in music. There are other attractive duets elsewhere, for instance the nautical *Blow, blow, Boreas, blow* from *Sir Barnaby Whigg*, which could fit admirably into *HMS Pinafore* (Rogers Covey-Crump and David Thomas) and the jovial *As soon as the chaos* from *The Marriage-hater Match'd*. In *Ah me! to many deaths* from *Regulus*, Judith Nelson is at her most eloquent while, earlier on Disc 5, she sings charmingly the familiar *Nymphs and shepherds*, which comes from *The Libertine*, a particularly fine score with imaginative use of the brass. The equally famous *Music for a while*, beautifully sung by James Bowman, derives from *Oedipus*. The last disc again shows Judith Nelson at her finest in a series of arias, but it also includes a splendidly boisterous *Quartet* from *The Canterbury Guests*. The collection is appropriately rounded off by members of the Academy giving first-class performances of some of Purcell's instrumental music, ending with the famous *Chacony*. The sharpness of inspiration comes over very compellingly on original instruments, though Hogwood tends to prefer tempi faster than one might expect. The discs are comprehensively documented and with full texts included.

Quantz, Joseph Joachim (1697–1773)

Flute concertos: in C; in D (For Potsdam); G; G min.
*** BMG/RCA Dig. RD 60247; *RK 60247* [60247-2-RC; *60247-4-RC*]. James Galway, Württemberg CO, Heilbron, Faerber.

The climax to Joseph Joachim Quantz's career came in 1741 when, as composer, virtuoso flautist and teacher, he was appointed musical major-domo to the Court of Frederick the Great (who, as self-made star, was estimated to have given at least 10,000 performances as flute soloist for the court's daily musical soirées at Sanssouci). C. P. E. Bach was also in attendance, but Bach's pay was one-sixth of Quantz's, for the king found a natural affinity with the latter's musical conservatism. Nevertheless Quantz was a skilled musician and all four concertos here are pleasing, while their slow movements show a genuine flair for melody. The *Arioso mesto* of the *G major* is particularly charming but the *Amoroso* of the *C major* is appealing too. Quantz also wrote well-organized allegros, and the opening *Allegro assai* of the *G major* shows him at his most vigorous, even if perhaps the *Potsdam concerto* is overall the best of the four works here. The thoroughly musical James Galway is most winning in the lyrical cantilenas, and the Württemberg group accompany with polish and much vitality. They play modern instruments, of course, but their athletic style has clearly benefited from the authentic influence in the alert outer movements. Excellent sound, but only one concerto should be played at a time.

Quilter, Roger (1877–1953)

A Children's overture.

(M) ** EMI CDM7 64131-2; *EG 764131-4.* Light Music Society O, Sir Vivian Dunn (with TOMLINSON: *Suite of English folk dances;* HELY-HUTCHINSON: *Carol Symphony;* VAUGHAN WILLIAMS: *Fantasia on Christmas carols* **).

This charming overture, skilfully constructed from familiar nursery rhymes, hitherto has not been available on CD except in an old mono recording. Its neglect is inexplicable. Sir Vivian Dunn gives a good if not remarkable performance and the recording too is pleasing rather than outstanding. But the music itself is a delight. Ernest Tomlinson's suite of six folk-tunes, simply presented and tastefully scored, makes an attractive bonus. Again the sound is acceptable but could be richer. Hely-Hutchinson's *Carol Symphony* has curiosity value and a charming slow movement. But neither this nor the Vaughan Williams *Fantasia* is transferred to CD very successfully, and this recording of the *Children's overture* is at best a stop-gap until the promised Marco Polo CD of Quilter's orchestral music appears.

Rabaud, Henri (1873–1949)

Divertissement sur les chansons russes, Op. 2; Églogue (Poème virgilien), Op. 7; Marouf, Savetier du Caire (Danses); La Procession nocturne.

(M) **(*) EMI CDM7 63951-2 [id.]. O Philharmonique des pays de Loire, Pierre Dervaux.

Henri Rabaud's music is generally neglected, though both *La Procession nocturne* and the opera *Maroûf, Savetier du Caire* were recorded in the LP era. The *Dances* from the opera are an appealing exercise in exoticism; but by far the best pieces are the sensitively scored *La Procession nocturne* and the *Églogue*. Rabaud was a pupil of Massenet, and his musical language belongs far more to the world of Franck and d'Indy than to that of Debussy. Good performances from the Loire orchestra under Pierre Dervaux; they play with evident sympathy and acceptable, if reverberant, recording. An interesting disc for anyone who likes exploring the byways of French music.

Rachmaninov, Sergei (1873–1943)

Caprice bohémien, Op. 12; The Isle of the dead (symphonic poem), *Op. 29; Prince Rostislav* (symphonic poem after Alexei Tolstoy); *The Rock* (fantasy for orchestra), *Op. 7; Scherzo in F; Symphonic dances, Op. 45; Vocalise, Op. 34/14; Youth Symphony;* (i) *The Bells, Op. 35; 3 Russian folksongs, Op. 41; Spring* (cantata), *Op. 20.*

(B) **(*) VoxBox (3) [CD3X 3002]. St Louis SO, Slatkin; (i) with Voketaitis, Christos, Planté & Ch.

This three-disc bargain box brings an invaluable collection of all Rachmaninov's orchestral works other than the symphonies. Recorded in 1979–80, it covers not only the well-established works like *The Isle of the dead* and the magnificent choral symphony, *The Bells*, but also such rarities as the *Caprice bohémien* (one of the less inspired pieces) and youthful works such as the

Scherzo in F major (like Mendelssohn with a Russian accent) and the first-movement structure labelled *Youth Symphony*. At the other end of Rachmaninov's career come the *3 Russian folksongs* (sung rather slackly by the St Louis chorus) and his last work of all, the *Symphonic dances*. The playing of the St Louis Symphony is first rate, with all sections, notably the violins, able to respond to Slatkin's subtle use of rubato and with some excellent individual playing, as in the cor anglais solo in the last movement of *The Bells*. The recording is refined and well detailed but fails to make its full impact when not only is the chorus too distantly balanced – underlining an absence of bite in much of the singing – but the orchestral sound lacks immediacy. Nevertheless this box adds up to more than the sum of its component parts. It still awaits issue in the UK.

Piano concertos Nos. 1–4.
(B) *** EMI CZS7 67419-2 (2) [id.]. Collard, Capitole Toulouse O, Plasson.

Piano concertos Nos. 1–4; Rhapsody on a theme of Paganini.
**(*) Chan. Dig. CHAN 8882/3; *DBTD 2025* (2) [id.]. Howard Shelley, SNO, Bryden Thomson.

(i)Piano concertos Nos. 2–3; Rhapsody on a theme of Paganini. Preludes: in C Sharp min., Op 3/2 in B flat & G min., Op. 23/2 & 5; in B min. & D flat, Op. 32/10 & 13; Etudes–tableaux, Op. 39/1, 2 & 5.
(B)*** Decca 436 386-2 (2) [id.]. Ashkenazy, (i) LSO, Previn. Jean-Philippe Collard's recordings of the four Rachmaninov concertos date from the late 1970s. Collard is completely at home in this repertoire; his account of the *First* has splendid fire and can hold its own with all comers (even Pletnev and Ashkenazy, though the former is incomparable in the slow movement); and much the same goes for its companions. Perhaps the *Third concerto* is the least incandescent in his hands, but readers wanting an inexpensive set (all four concertos for the price of one CD) need look no further, for this is playing of quality, and the recording, though not outstanding, is fully acceptable, and avoids the artificial edginess of the Decca transfers.

Yet this pair of Decca CDs – offered for the cost of a single premium-priced disc – tends to sweep the board in including outstanding performances of Rachmaninov's three greatest concertante works for piano and orchestra, plus five favourite Preludes and three of the Op. 39 *Etudes tableaux*. Unlike the previous complete set (425 576-2), the digital remastering offers first-class transfers, full and well balanced, with the Kingsway Hall ambience casting a pleasing glow over the proceedings. This is very highly recommendable, including as it does Ashkenazy's outstanding version of the *C minor Piano concerto*, where slow movement is memorably beautiful.

Chandos, having had considerable success with their remastered Earl Wild recordings with Horenstein, which remain highly recommendable, were obviously hoping to repeat the trick with this new set from Howard Shelley and the Royal Scottish National Orchestra under Bryden Thomson. They set up their microphones to capture the warm acoustics of Caird Hall, Dundee, and the result is certainly sumptuous, almost overwhelmingly so at climaxes, with rich strings and powerfully resonant brass and a bold, truthful piano image projected way out in front. The performances do not lack adrenalin either, although their ebb and flow of tension is not consistent, and at times the music-making almost tends to run away with itself, notably in the *Third Concerto*. The first-movement climax of the *Second Concerto* is very powerful, and there is some lovely playing from the orchestra at the end of the slow movement. The finales have great dash and much charisma from Shelley, but Bryden Thomson at times seems less assured in the idiom. Just after the opening of the *Rhapsody on a theme of Paganini* he produces a curious echo effect (in which his soloist joins), while his *Eighteenth variation* could have more unbuttoned fervour. In the finale of the *First concerto* his caressing of the lyrical string-tune is too cosy. Moreover he fails to match exactly his soloist's ardour in the big statement of the great melody at the climax of the finale of the *Second Concerto*. The *Fourth Concerto* has some spectacular moments but lacks a really firm profile. Even so, there is much to enjoy here, and Howard Shelley's contribution is consistently distinguished.

Piano concertos Nos. 1 in F sharp min., Op. 1; 2 in C min., Op. 18.
(***) Olympia mono OCD 190 [id.]. Moura Lympany, Philh. O, Nicolai Malko – PROKOFIEV: *Piano concerto No. 1.* **(*)

Piano concerto No. 3 in D min., Op. 30.
(***) Olympia mono OCD 191 [id.]. Moura Lympany, New SO, Anthony Collins – PROKOFIEV: *Piano concerto No. 3.* **(*)

Moura Lympany's recording of the *Third* is the earliest recording and comes from a 1952 Decca LP; it sounds simply amazing for its age. Her EMI account of the *First* yields nothing in terms of virtuosity or panache to many bigger names on the international circuit, and the mono sound is very good for its age, though it is not quite as impressive as in the Decca *Third*. In No. 3, as was the custom in the 1950s, she plays Rachmaninov's later cadenza, the one he himself recorded. These are very fine performances which will give pleasure, and Olympia must be congratulated on restoring them to circulation in such excellent transfers.

(i) *Piano concerto No. 1 in F sharp min., Op. 1;* (ii) *Rhapsody on a theme of Paganini, Op. 43.*
*** Virgin Dig. VC7 90724-2; *VC 790724-4* [id.]. Pletnev, Philh. O, Pešek.
*** Decca Dig. 417 613-2; *417 613-4* [id.]. Ashkenazy, (i) Concg. O; (ii) Philh. O, Haitink.

Mikhail Pletnev's accounts of the *F sharp minor Concerto* and the *Rhapsody on a theme of Paganini* with the Philharmonia Orchestra under Libor Pešek are very fine indeed. He is one of the few pianists whose technique can be (and has been) compared with the young Horowitz. The *Paganini rhapsody* is distinguished not only by quite stunning virtuosity and unobtrusive refinement but also by great feeling. This is playing that is strong in personality and musicianship – an altogether outstanding début that should acquire classic status. The CD sounds especially vivid.

This coupling also finds Ashkenazy in excellent form. The *Paganini variations* are, if anything, even better than his earlier LP with Previn. Haitink gets splendid sound from the Philharmonia in the *Variations* and Decca provides excellent recording. The *First Concerto* is no less impressive, and the Concertgebouw Orchestra under Haitink offer luxurious support.

Piano concerto Nos. 1 in F sharp min., Op. 1; 4 in G min., Op. 40.
(M) **(*) Decca 425 004-2; *425 004-4*. Ashkenazy, LSO, Previn.

Piano concertos Nos. 1 in F sharp min., Op. 1; 4 in G min., Op. 40; Rhapsody on a theme of Paganini, Op. 43.
(M) **(*) Sony SBK 46541 [id.]. Philippe Entremont, Phd. O, Ormandy.

Entremont gives a marvellously dashing account of both early and late concertos, rivalling the composer himself in the sheer effrontery of his bravura. Where Entremont falls short – and he is not helped by the American recordings (dating from 1963 and 1961 respectively) which boosts pianissimos – is in the gentler music, where he could be more affectionate. The recording quality could be sweeter too, and the piano tone is rather clattery. In the *Rhapsody on a theme of Paganini*, recorded in in 1958, Ormandy oversees a strongly directed performance, with Entremont rising excitingly to the challenge. The balance here is rather more natural.

On Decca, the transfers of Nos. 1 and 4 are satisfactory; the brilliance is not too plangent and the performances are certainly exciting.

Piano concerto No. 2 in C min., Op. 18.
*** BMG/RCA RD 85912 [RCA 5912-2-RC]. Van Cliburn, Chicago SO, Reiner – TCHAIKOVSKY: *Concerto No. 1.* ***
*** DG 415 119-2 [id.]. Sviatoslav Richter, Warsaw PO, Wislocki – PROKOFIEV: *Concerto No. 5.* ***
(M) *** EMI Dig. CDD7 63903-2 [id.]; *ET 763903-4*. Cécile Ousset, CBSO, Rattle – GRIEG: *Concerto.* **(*)
**(*) EMI Dig. CDC7 542322 [id.]. Mikhail Rudy, Leningrad PO, Mariss Jansons – TCHAIKOVSKY: *Concerto.* **(*)
(M) ** Decca Dig. 430 736-2; *430 736-4* [id.]. Bolet, Montreal SO, Dutoit – LISZT: *Totentanz* etc. ***

With Reiner making a splendid partner, Van Cliburn's 1958 account of the Rachmaninov *C minor* is second to none. The pacing of the first movement is comparatively measured, but the climax is unerringly placed, remaining relaxed yet enormously telling. The finale too does not seek to demonstrate runaway bravura but has sparkle and excitement, with the lyrical element heart-warming to match the very beautiful account of the central *Adagio*, full of poetry and romantic feeling. The recording is wonderfully rich, with the Chicago acoustic adding a glorious ambient glow, while the piano, though forwardly placed, has an unexpected body and fullness of timbre. In the finale the cymbals demonstrate an excellent upper range, and the enhancement of the digital remastering almost makes this seem as if it were made yesterday. Coupled with an equally splendid version of the Tchaikovsky *B flat minor*, albeit not so richly recorded, this coupling is a world-beater.

Richter has strong, even controversial ideas about speeds in this concerto. The long opening melody of the first movement is taken abnormally slowly, and it is only the sense of mastery that Richter conveys in every note which prevents one from complaining. The slow movement too is spacious – with complete justification this time – and the opening of the finale lets the floodgates open the other way, for Richter chooses a hair-raisingly fast allegro, which has the Polish players scampering after him as fast as they are able. Richter does not, however, let himself be rushed in the great secondary melody, so this is a reading of vivid contrasts. The coupling is Richter's classic account of Prokofiev's *Fifth Concerto*, so this CD combines two of Richter's very finest performances for the gramophone. The sound is very good.

Cécile Ousset gives a powerful, red-blooded performance in the grand manner, warmly supported by Simon Rattle and the CBSO. Her rubato may often be extreme but it never sounds studied, always convincingly spontaneous; and the EMI recording copes well with the range of the playing. Those wanting a coupling with the Grieg *Concerto* will find Ousset's account similarly strong.

As is the case in the Tchaikovsky concerto with which it is coupled, Mikhail Rudy evinces both artistry and taste, and Mariss Jansons and the Leningrad (now St. Petersburg) Philharmonic provide eloquent support. His playing may not have the dazzling brilliance of some of his most famous rivals but there is plenty to admire and relish. Rudy has no want of feeling or technical finesse, and the recording has good if unspectacular sound and a refined balance that does justice to all concerned.

Bolet's version is disappointing. The first movement has a fine climax, but the tension is allowed to ebb away before the end of the movement. The *Adagio*, helped by the glowing Montreal acoustics, is at its finest when Dutoit is in full command, as at the opening and close which are ravishingly romantic, with Bolet embroidering effectively. The finale is very measured and the effect becomes heavy rather than spacious, with the great lyrical melody sounding sluggish. The Decca recording is sumptuously spectacular but, with the Tchaikovsky coupling even less attractive, this is a non-starter.

(i) *Piano concerto No. 2 in C min., Op. 18; Études tableaux, Op. 39/1–2, 4–6 & 9.*
*** BMG/RCA Dig. RD 87982 [7982-2-RC]. Evgeny Kissin, (i) LSO, Valentin Gergiev.

Evgeny Kissin's Rachmaninov shows (as for that matter does his recording of the Chopin concertos) that he is a serious artist who phrases intelligently and resists the temptation to play to the gallery in any way. He produces a beautiful sound throughout and it is a compliment to him that any comparisons that spring to mind are with great pianists. The LSO under Valentin Gergiev give him every support. The six *Études tableaux* are imaginatively played and impressively characterized. The recording is well balanced and truthful. A remarkable CD début.

Piano concertos Nos. 2 in C min., Op. 18; 3 in D min., Op. 30.
(M) *** Chan. CHAN 6507; *MBTD 6507* [id.]. Earl Wild, RPO, Horenstein.

Piano concertos Nos. (i) *2 in C min, Op. 18;* (ii) *3 in D min., Op. 30. Preludes: in C sharp min., Op. 3/2; in E flat, Op. 23/6.*
❀ (M) *** Mercury 432 759-2 [id.]. Byron Janis; (i) Minneapolis SO; (ii) LSO, Antal Dorati.

We have long admired these Mercury performances; coupled together, they make an unbeatable bargain, representing Byron Janis's very finest record. Janis has the full measure of this music: his shapely lyrical phasing and natural response to the ebb and flow of the melodic lines is a constant source of pleasure. The climax of the first movement of the *C minor Concerto* is very exciting, and he is equally tender in the coda of the *Adagio*. Then in the finale there is all the sparkling bravura one could ask for, but the great lyrical tune is made beguilingly poetic. Although the 1960 recording has plenty of ambience, the Minneapolis violins lack the richness of the LSO strings, recorded at Watford in 1961. The simple opening of the *Third Concerto* benefits from the extra warmth, and Janis lets the theme unwind with appealing spontaneity. The romantic glow which Dorati infuses into the blossoming second subject is matched by the atmosphere of the *Adagio*, and in the great closing climax of the finale the passion is built up – not too hurriedly – to the greatest possible tension. Janis makes two cuts (following the composer's own practice), one of about ten bars in the second movement and a rather longer one in the finale. Two favourite *Preludes*, with the *E flat* coming first, most persuasively played, make an excellent encore.

Earl Wild's performances derive from a complete set produced by Charles Gerhardt for RCA and recorded at the Kingsway Hall in 1965. The first movement of the *C minor Concerto* is faster than usual, but the expressive fervour is in no doubt; the *Adagio*, too, blossoms readily. The *Third Concerto* is among the very finest versions of this work on record and, in terms of bravura, is in the Horowitz class. The digital remastering is a great success, the overall balance is truthful and the hall ambience brings a rich orchestral image and plenty of brilliance. However, unfortunately there are three cuts, one in the second movement and two in the third, a total of 55 bars.

Piano concerto Nos. 2 in C min.; 4 in G min., Op. 40.
**(*) Decca Dig. 414 475-2; *414 475-4* [id.]. Ashkenazy, Concg. O, Haitink.

Unfortunately, in the *C minor Concerto* Ashkenazy's new account cannot quite match his poetic earlier reading with Previn. The opening theme is a touch ponderous this time, and elsewhere too the yearning passion of the work is rather muted, even in the lovely reprise of the main theme in the slow movement. Those reservations are relative; Ashkenazy gives a superb account of the *Fourth Concerto*, strong and dramatic and warmly passionate, with Haitink and the Concertgebouw establishing the work as more positively characterful than is often appreciated. Splendid Decca sound, with the Concertgebouw acoustics making a warmly resonant framework.

Piano concerto No. 2 in C min.; Rhapsody on a theme of Paganini, Op. 43.
(M) *** Decca 417 702-2 [id.]. Ashkenazy, LSO, Previn.
(BB) *** Naxos Dig. 8.550117; *4550117* [id.]. Jandó, Budapest SO, Lehel.
(B) *** CfP Dig. CD-CFP 9017; *TC-CFP 4383*. Tirimo, Philh. O, Levi.
(B) *** Decca 433 627-2; *433 627-4*. Katchen, LSO, Solti; or LPO, Boult.
** EMI Dig. CDC7 49966-2 [id.]; *EL 749966-4*. Andrei Gavrilov, Phd. O, Muti.
*(*) EMI Dig. CDC7 54003-2 [id.]. Andrei Gavrilov, RPO, Ashkenazy – TCHAIKOVSKY: *Symphony No. 4*. *

Decca's recoupling of Ashkenazy's earlier recordings with Previn is a very desirable CD indeed. At mid-price it makes a clear first choice. In the *Concerto*, Ashkenazy's opening tempo, like Richter's, is slow, but the tension is finely graduated towards the great climax; and the gentle, introspective mood of the *Adagio* is very beautiful indeed. The finale is broad and spacious rather than electrically exciting, but the scintillating, unforced bravura provides all the sparkle necessary. The *Rhapsody* too is outstandingly successful, the opening variations exhilaratingly paced and the whole performance moving forward in a single sweep, with the eighteenth variation making a great romantic blossoming at the centre. The Kingsway Hall sound is rich and full-bodied in the best analogue sense; unlike the complete set from which this is taken, the digital remastering has here retained all the bloom, especially in the slow movement of the *Concerto*, among the most beautiful on record. Detail is somewhat sharper in the *Rhapsody*; in the *Concerto*, however, atmosphere rather than clarity is the predominating factor, unlike the remastered complete set above, where the focus is much sharper and the quality less sweet.

Outstanding in the Naxos super-bargain series, Jenö Jandó's performances of both works are strongly recommendable. Although the *Concerto* opens modestly, the tempo relatively measured, it moves to a splendid climax, the piano astride the orchestra in a most exciting way. Jandó has the full measure of the ebb and flow of the Rachmaninovian phraseology, and the slow movement is romantically expansive, the reprise particularly beautiful, while the finale has plenty of dash and ripe, lyrical feeling. The *Rhapsody* is played brilliantly, as fine as any performance in the catalogue. The digital recording is satisfyingly balanced, with a bold piano image and a full, resonant orchestral tapestry, although it is a pity that the variations in the *Rhapsody* are not separately cued.

. Concentrated and thoughtful, deeply expressive yet never self-indulgent, Tirimo is outstanding in both the *Concerto* and the *Rhapsody*, making this one of the most desirable versions of this favourite coupling, irrespective of price. Speeds for the outer movements of the *Concerto* are on the fast side, yet Tirimo's feeling for natural rubato makes them sound natural, never breathless, while the sweetness and repose of the middle movement are exemplary. The digital recording is full, clear and well balanced.

Two recordings of Andrei Gavrilov from the same company issued within a year, albeit with different orchestras and conductors, betokens an odd sense of priorities – but the fortunes of the larger record companies are no longer determined by questions of artistic direction. Gavrilov's

Philadelphia recording with Riccardo Muti was made in the studio, while the RPO recording celebrates a live concert given on a visit to Russia by the RPO. The solo playing is distinguished by flamboyant virtuosity and a self-regarding brilliance that is not wholly pleasing. In both performances there is finely shaped and responsive orchestral support, but neither in the concerto, nor in the *Rhapsody on a theme of Paganini* does he bring the aristocratic distinction or naturalness of utterance that he commanded in his earlier recordings.

There is no want of impetuosity in the 1989 Moscow performance, recorded in collaboration with his agent and manager. Presumably the latter thought the result would be a best-seller but the excitement of the *C minor concerto*, like his slightly later version listed above, is rarely more than skin-deep and the slow movement is just a little too self-aware to be touching. It comes in harness with a somewhat lacklustre performance of the Tchaikovsky *Fourth Symphony*. Neither version begins to compare with his account of the *D minor Concerto*, made in the 1970s.

Piano concerto No. 3 in D min., Op. 30.
*(**) BMG/RCA RD 82633 [RCD1 2633]. Horowitz, NYPO, Ormandy.
**(*) Decca Dig. 417 239-2 [id.]. Ashkenazy, Concg. O, Haitink.

(i) *Piano concerto No. 3;* (ii) *Rhapsody on a theme of Paganini, Op. 43.*
(M) **(*) BMG/RCA GD 86524 (RCA 6524-2-RG]. (i) Ashkenazy, Phd. O, Ormandy; (ii) Pennario, Boston Pops O, Fiedler.

(i) *Piano concerto No. 3. Sonata No. 2 in B flat min., Op. 36; Moment musical in E flat min., Op. 16/2; Polka; Prelude in C, Op. 32/5.*
(M) (***) BMG/RCA GD 87754 [7754-2-RC-]. Vladimir Horowitz; (i) with RCA SO, Reiner.

Horowitz's RCA account with Reiner dates from 1951. As a performance it is full of poetry, yet electrifying in its excitement. In spite of its dated sound and a less than ideal balance, its magic comes over and it is to be preferred to his later performance with Ormandy. The *Sonata* comes from live concerts in 1980 and is also pretty electrifying. He plays the conflation he made (and which Rachmaninov approved) of the 1913 original and the 1931 revision plus a few further retouchings he subsequently added. An indispensable part of any Rachmaninov collection which, in its digitally remastered form, sounds better than it has before.

Horowitz's legendary association with Rachmaninov's *D minor Concerto* daunted even the composer. Horowitz made it virtually his own property over half a century. In January 1978 he was persuaded to re-record the work in stereo, this time at a live concert, with Ormandy drawing a committed and romantically expansive accompaniment from the New York Philharmonic Orchestra. Perhaps just a little of the old magic is missing in the solo playing but it remains prodigious, and Horowitz's insights are countless. Not all the playing is immaculate and there is some rhythmic eccentricity in the finale; but the communicative force of the reading is unquestionable. The snag is the recording, which was originally very dry and clinical, the piano timbre lacking bloom. For CD, the remastering has altered the sound-picture radically, considerably softening the focus, to bring a more romantic aura to the music-making. The result is that at lower dynamic levels the image appears to recede. The effect is disconcerting – but one can adjust to it, and certainly the effect is more agreeable than the 'bare bones' of the original LP sound-quality.

Ashkenazy has recorded this concerto four times; as a work, it seems to prove elusive for him. On his Decca digital disc he is beautifully recorded and there is unfailing sensitivity and musicianship, but one needs a greater sense of impact and focus – his very first recording with Fistoulari had more ardour and spontaneity. So too had his 1976 RCA version, recorded in Philadelphia with Eugene Ormandy. If one can adjust to its unflattering piano sound, then the mid-1970s performance has much to offer: it has great charisma, and Ormandy, too, is at his finest. The coupling is a prodigiously brilliant account of the *Rhapsody* from Leonard Pennario and Fiedler which is certainly compulsive; the snag here is that the forward balance, coupled to the bright digital remastering, makes orchestral fortissimos sound shrill.

(i) *Piano concerto No. 3 in D min., Op. 30. Études-tableaux, Op. 33/3 & 8; Op. 39/2.*
** Collins Dig. 12462; *12464* [id.]. Cristina Ortiz, (i) Philh. O, Ivan Fischer.

Were the catalogue less crowded, Cristina Ortiz's version with the Philharmonia Orchestra under Ivan Fischer might have stronger claims on the collector, for her reading is intelligent and imaginative. However she does not command the requisite dramatic address and formidable muscularity this concerto demands. Nor is Ivan Fischer always fully supportive, though the Philharmonia play well enough and are given good recorded sound.

Piano concerto No. 4 in G min., Op. 40 (see also below, under *Monna Vanna*).
❀ *** EMI CDC7 49326-2 [id.]. Michelangeli, Philh. O, Gracis – RAVEL: *Piano concerto in G.* *** ❀

This is one of the most brilliant piano records ever made. It puts the composer's own recorded performance quite in the shade, and the Ravel coupling is equally illuminating. The recording does not quite match the superlative quality of the playing but still sounds pretty good.

Études-tableaux (orch. Respighi).
*** Collins Dig. 1175-2; *1175-4* [id.]. LPO, Rozhdestvensky – BRAHMS: *Piano quartet.* ***

Respighi was a master of the orchestra and his celebrated version of Rachmaninov's *Études-tableaux* sounds splendidly idiomatic. If one did not know them in their piano form, one could be entirely convinced that they were conceived for the orchestra. Rozhdestvensky gets excellent results from the LPO, and the Collins recording is absolutely first class.

The Isle of the dead, Op. 29; Symphonic dances, Op. 45.
(M) *** Decca Dig. 430 733-2; *430 733-4*. Concg. O, Ashkenazy.
(BB) **(*) Naxos Dig. 8.550583 [id.]. RPO, Enrique Bátiz.

Ashkenazy's is a superb coupling, rich and powerful in playing and interpretation. One here recognizes *The Isle of the dead* as among the very finest of Rachmaninov's orchestral works, relentless in its ominous build-up, while at generally fast speeds the *Symphonic dances* have extra darkness and intensity too, suggesting no relaxation whatever at the end of Rachmaninov's career. The splendid digital recording highlights both the passion and the fine precision of the playing.

Bátiz gives the *Symphonic dances* an attractively spontaneous performance, full of lyrical intensity, with some splendid playing from the RPO strings. The vivid recording, made in the Henry Wood Hall, has plenty of ambience and a bright focus. Its spectacle helps to give the feeling that Bátiz almost goes over the top in his extremely passionate climax for *The Isle of the Dead*. The performance certainly does not lack darker feelings, and the RPO playing is powerful, even if Batiz's overall control on the long crescendo and diminuendo is less taut that that of Ashkenazy or Previn. But at super-bargain price this remains well worth considering.

Rhapsody on a theme of Paganini, Op. 43.
** Telarc Dig. CD 80193 [id.]. Gutierrez, Baltimore SO, Zinman – TCHAIKOVSKY: *Piano concerto No. 1.* **

Horacio Gutierrez's fingerwork in the *Rhapsody on a theme of Paganini* and his virtuosity are both impressive. But the best is the enemy of the good, and there are more imaginative and poetic accounts to be had. The Baltimore Orchestra give firm support under David Zinman, but neither here nor in the Tchaikovsky *First Piano concerto* could one point to qualities that would warrant a three-star rating.

Symphonies Nos. 1–3.
(B) **(*) VoxBox (2) [CDX 5034]. St Louis SO, Slatkin.

Symphonies Nos. 1–3; Youth Symphony (1891).
(M) *** Decca Dig. 421 065-2 (3). Concg. O, Ashkenazy.

Ashkenazy's set – offered at mid-price – can be given an unqualified recommendation. The performances, passionate and volatile, are intensely Russian; the only possible reservation concerns the slow movement of the *Second*, where the clarinet solo is less ripe than in some versions. Elsewhere there is drama, energy and drive, balanced by much delicacy of feeling, while the Concertgebouw strings produce great ardour for Rachmaninov's long-breathed melodies. The vivid Decca sound within the glowing Concertgebouw ambience is ideal for the music.

Having all three of Rachmaninov's *Symphonies* in ripely idiomatic performances on two budget-priced VoxBox discs makes an excellent bargain, even if the recording lacks something in immediacy. Recorded between 1976 and 1979, they reveal that already, early in his career as the St Louis music director, Slatkin had welded this second-oldest American orchestra into a most responsive ensemble, able in Rachmaninov's ripest melodies to play with both polish and a warmly flexible expressiveness. The sound in No. 1, presumably recorded last, is rather fuller and more forward than in the other two symphonies, but there is plenty of detail in each. This does not match the digital Decca/Ashkenazy box, but it is excellent value. It is not yet available in the UK.

Symphony No. 1 in D min., Op. 13.
*** Decca Dig. 411 657-2 [id.]. Concg. O, Ashkenazy.

Symphony No. 1 in D min.; The Isle of the dead, Op. 29.
*** Virgin Dig. VC7 90830-2; *VC 790830-4* [id.]. RPO, Andrew Litton.

Symphony No. 1 in D min.; The Rock (fantasy), *Op. 13; Vocalise, Op. 34/14; Aleko: Intermezzo.*
(M) *** DG Dig. 435 594-2 [id.]. BPO, Maazel.

With a darkly intense account of *The Isle of the dead* as a generous fill-up, Litton's version of the *Symphony* brings exceptionally beautiful sound which captures the RPO strings in luminous form. This is a powerful performance, as the very opening indicates, but it is just as remarkable for its refinement and gentler qualities, with Litton persuasive in his free use of rubato. The magisterial fanfares at the start of the finale may be less biting or thrustful than with some others, but the resilience and clarity make the results equally compelling.

Ashkenazy's is also an outstanding version, volatile and extreme in its tempi, with the Concertgebouw players responding in total conviction. The digital recording is most impressive, for the sound is full, atmospheric and brilliant. Though the weight of the opening of the finale is magnificent, the relentless hammering rhythms are presented vividly in scale, where they can easily seem oppressive. The Scherzo at a very fast speed has Mendelssohnian lightness, the flowing *Larghetto* is presented as a lyrical interlude. However, there is no fill-up, and collectors would do better to consider the complete set at mid-price.

It is good to have a mid-priced version of the *First Symphony*. Maazel's is a superb performance in which he characteristically makes Rachmaninov's often thick orchestration beautifully transparent, consistently clarifying detail. He may lack something in Slavonic passion but, with a generous fill-up, the fascinating early fantasy, *The Rock*, the positive strength of the reading stands well against any rival. In the famous opening theme of the finale Maazel is almost genial, where Ashkenazy on the outstanding Decca version makes the music swagger more brazenly. The 1984 recording, drier than Ashkenazy's Decca, was one of the finest that the DG engineers produced in the early years of digital recording in the apparently intractable acoustics of the Philharmonie. For the reissue, the *Vocalise* and *Aleko Intermezzo* have been added from earlier (1983) sessions and the full warmth of lyricism is lacking in the former.

Symphony No. 2 in E min., Op. 27.
(B) *** Pickwick Dig. PCD 904; *CIMPC 904* [id.]. LSO, Rozhdestvensky.
**(*) Decca Dig. 400 081-2 [id.]. Concg. O, Ashkenazy.
**(*) Telarc Dig. CD 80113 [id.]. RPO, Previn.
** Olympia Dig. OCD 237 [id.]. Moscow SO, Dmitri Kitaenko – BALAKIREV: *In Czechia.* **

Symphony No. 2; Vocalise, Op. 34/14.
*** Virgin Dig. VC7 90831-2; *VC 790831-4* [id.]. RPO, Andrew Litton.

Rozhdestvensky gives a very Tchaikovskian reading of Rachmaninov's *E minor Symphony*. There is plenty of vitality, but it is the conductor's affectionate warmth in the secondary material of the first two movements, with the big string melodies blossoming voluptuously, that is especially memorable. The slow movement, after a beguiling opening clarinet solo, has a climax of spacious intensity, and its power is almost overwhelming; the finale is flamboyantly broadened at the end, and the feeling of apotheosis is very much in the Tchaikovsky mould. With the LSO responding superbly, this is a most satisfying account, and the richness, brilliance and weight of the recording, made in All Saints', Tooting, adds to the compulsion of the music-making.

Refinement is the mark of Litton's well-paced reading, with the RPO caught in glowing form by the engineers as in the rest of the cycle. There is power in plenty, and Litton readily sustains his observance of the exposition repeat in the first movement, making it a very long movement indeed at over 23 minutes. But the moments of special magic are those where, as in his lightly pointed account of the Scherzo or, most of all, the lovely clarinet melody of the slow movement, subtlety of expression gives Rachmaninov's romanticism an extra poignancy. Even the red-blooded close of the finale with Litton is more subtly varied than usual, both emotionally and in execution. When the symphony alone lasts so much longer than usual, the *Vocalise*, done equally beautifully, makes a generous fill-up.

Ashkenazy's reading has a romantic urgency and drive that are missing from Previn's Telarc version, with the climaxes of the outer movements far more gripping. In the Scherzo too, the Amsterdam strings are tauter in ensemble; there is a vibrant impulse about the performance as a whole which is very Russian in its intensity. The Decca recording is full-bodied but with a degree of edge on the strings, and this extra bite suits Ashkenazy's approach.

The greater feeling of spaciousness of Previn's 1985 Telarc recording, compared with his earlier, EMI account which is awaiting reissue, is apparent at the very opening. The whole reading is more moderately paced than those of its competitors, with long-breathed phrases moulded flexibly, with far less urgency and none of Ashkenazy's impetuosity. This expansiveness is enhanced by the finely sustained playing of the RPO strings and the sumptuous Telarc recording with its luxuriant resonance. With such superbly rich sound there are some ravishing moments, but in the last resort the lack of electricity brings a degree of disappointment.

The sleeve gives the date of Dmitri Kitaenko's recording with the Moscow Symphony as 1983, a year earlier than the version issued on Chant du Monde with the same conductor and the Moscow Philharmonic. Without now having the Chant du Monde set to hand it is difficult to establish whether they are the same performances but they certainly have the same characteristic: tremendously ardent and expressive string playing. This fervour extends to the other sections of the orchestra, who play with the same virtuosity and intensity that distinguishes Yevgeny Svetlanov's USSR Academic. There are also the same flaws in the orchestral sound; the upper strings have a strident edge, and the brass are pretty raucous, and in climaxes the sound comes close to discoloration. However the performance has plenty of character and the coupling is very attractive.

Symphony No. 3 in A min., Op. 44.
(M) *** EMI CDM7 69564-2; *EG 769564-4*. LSO, Previn – SHOSTAKOVICH: *Symphony No. 6*. ***
*** Chan. Dig. CHAN 8614; *ABT 1303* [id.]. LSO, Järvi – KALLINIKOV: *Intermezzos*. ***
** Olympia Dig. OCD 209 [id.]. Moscow SO, Dmitri Kitaenko. – STRAUSS: *Also sprach Zarathustra*. (*)

Symphony No. 3 in A min., Op. 44; Symphonic dances, Op. 45.
*** Virgin Dig. VC7 90832-2; *VC 790832-4* [id.]. RPO, Andrew Litton.
*(*) Decca Dig. 433 181-2 [id.]. Phd. O, Dutoit.

Previn's EMI CD brings an outstanding performance; the digital remastering brings plenty of body alongside the sharpened detail, even if some of the amplitude has been exchanged for clarity. There is much that is elusive in this highly original structure, and Previn conveys the purposefulness of the writing at every point, revelling in the richness, but clarifying textures. The LSO has rarely displayed its virtuosity more brilliantly in the recording studio, and, with its generous Shostakovich coupling, this is first choice for this symphony.

The gentleness of Litton's treatment of the great second-subject melody in the *Third Symphony* may initially sound cool, but the transparent beauty of Rachmaninov's scoring is brought out superbly by conductor, players and engineers. The slow movement has rarely been done so tenderly, and though the opening of the finale may sound a little cautious, not urgent enough, it is crisply pointed and leads on to a superbly brisk, tense conclusion. The *Symphonic dances* have similarly been given weighty performances, but the refinement and beauty of this last of Rachmaninov's orchestral works here go with sharp, clean attack, making an ideal and generous coupling for the *Symphony*.

Järvi conducts the LSO in a high-powered, red-blooded and not especially subtle performance which, in very full, bright sound, makes its points forcefully and convincingly. In his weighty, purposeful way he misses some of the subtleties of this symphony, but with superb playing from the LSO – linking back to André Previn's unsurpassed reading with them – the intensity is magnetic, with even a very slow *Adagio* for the outer sections of the middle movement made to sound convincing, and with the finale thrusting on at an equivalently extreme tempo.

The full-blooded and responsive playing of the Moscow orchestra is splendidly passionate and authentic in feeling. The recorded sound is acceptable (there is a trace of coarseness and some oddities of balance) and were competition not stronger, this would deserve a less qualified recommendation. Moreover it is encumbered with a less than satisfactory recording of *Also sprach Zarathustra*.

Anyone who has heard the records of the Philadelphia Orchestra playing for Rachmaninov himself, or for Ormandy will find Dutoit's interpretation of the *Third Symphony* a disappointment. The *Symphonic dances* are hardly more memorable. The excellent Decca recording, which surely rates three stars, conveys the sheer size of the Philadelphia sound, but the performance itself is an altogether different matter. There is very little warmth and little of the ardour and lyrical intensity or dramatic fire which Russian conductors like Koussevitzky brought to it. This is very cool indeed; a bloody Mary without the vodka!

CHAMBER AND INSTRUMENTAL MUSIC

Cello sonata in G min., Op. 19; Vocalise, Op. 34/14 (with DVOŘÁK: *Polonaise;* SIBELIUS: *Malinconia*).
**(*) Ph. Dig. 412 732-2 [id.]. Heinrich Schiff, Elisabeth Leonskaja.

Schiff's performance of the *Sonata* with Elisabeth Leonskaja is not extrovert; instead, it has a thoughtful, inward quality that draws the listener to it. Its nostalgia and melancholy are undoubtedly potent. Needless to say, the Philips recording is first class. The Sibelius *Malinconia* is an uncharacteristic piece; it is not very effective, and the Dvořák *Polonaise in A* is altogether more vivid. This is distinctly preferable to the accounts by Turovsky on Chandos (CHAN 8523) and Baillie on Unicorn Kanchana (DKPCD 9083).

Trios élégiaques Nos. 1 in G min., Op. 8; 2 in D min., Op. 9.
*** Chan. Dig. CHAN 8431; *ABTD 1101* [id.]. Borodin Trio.
*** Ph. Dig. 420 175-2 [id.]. Beaux Arts Trio.

The *G minor Trio* is a pensive one-movement piece lasting no more than a quarter of an hour, while Op. 9 is on a much larger scale. They are both imbued with lyrical fervour and draw from the rich vein of melancholy so characteristic of Rachmaninov. The performances by the Borodin Trio are eloquent and masterly, and the recording is admirably balanced and has plenty of warmth.

The Beaux Arts are less overtly intense and eloquent; they leave the music to speak for itself without ever being matter of fact. Their reading is lighter in colouring without being any the less deeply felt. It is difficult to make a clear choice: the Beaux Arts are splendidly aristocratic and have great refinement; the Borodins are red-blooded and ardent; either will give satisfaction.

PIANO MUSIC

Barcarolle in G min., Op. 10/3; Études-tableaux, Op. 39/4 & 6; Humoresque in G, Op. 10/5; Lilacs, Op. 21/5; 5 Morceaux de fantaisie, Op. 3: (Élégie in E flat min.; Prelude in C sharp min.; Mélodie in E; Polichinelle in F sharp min.; Sérénade in B flat min.); Polka de V. R.; Prelude in G min., Op. 23/5. Transcriptions: MUSSORGSKY: *Hopak.* SCHUBERT: *Wohin?.* RIMSKY-KORSAKOV: *Flight of the bumble-bee.* KREISLER: *Liebeslied; Liebesfreud. The Star spangled banner.*
(M) *** Decca 425 964-2 [id.]. Sergei Rachmaninov (Ampico Roll recordings, 1919–29).

Daisies, Op. 38/5; Études-tableaux, Op. 33/2 & 7; Op. 39/6; Humoresque, Op. 10/5; Lilacs, Op. 21/5; Mélodie, Op. 3/5; Moment musical, Op. 16/2; Oriental sketch; Polka de V. R.; Preludes: in C sharp min., Op. 3/2; in G flat, Op. 23/10; in E, F min. & F, Op. 32/3, 6 & 7; Serenade, Op. 3/5. Transcriptions: BACH: *Violin Partita No. 2: Prelude; Gavotte; Rondo; Gigue.* MENDELSSOHN: *Midsummer Night's Dream: Scherzo.* KREISLER: *Liebesfreud.* SCHUBERT: *Wohin?.* MUSSORGSKY: *Hopak.* TCHAIKOVSKY: *Lullaby, Op. 16/11.* RIMSKY-KORSAKOV: *The Flight of the bumble-bee.*
(M) (***) BMG/RCA mono GD 87766 [7766-2-RG]. Sergei Rachmaninov.

These two records make a fascinating comparison. The RCA collection includes virtually all Rachmaninov's electric 78-r.p.m. recordings, made between 1925 and 1942, with most dating from 1940. The second offers the composer's Ampico piano-roll recordings, made during a shorter time-span, between 1919 and 1929, when Rachmaninov was at his technical peak. The Ampico recordings were reproduced on a specially adapted Estonia concert grand in the Kingsway Hall and recorded in stereo in 1978/9. On CD the sound is outstandingly real and the impression on the listener is quite uncanny when the recital opens with the *Élégie in E flat minor*, which was put on roll in October 1928 yet has all the spontaneity and presence of live music-making. A number of items are common to both discs, so it is possible to make direct comparisons. The Ampico system at that time could accurately reflect what was played, including note duration and pedalling, but the *strength* at which the notes were struck had to be edited on to the roll afterwards by a skilled musician/technician, who annotated his score while the artist performed. Wrong notes could also be edited out, and the recording had finally to be approved by the performer after hearing a playback. It can only be said that listening to these Ampico recordings never brings a feeling of any mechanical tone graduation, and in pieces like the *Humoresque in G major* or the *Polka de V. R.* not only does Rachmaninov's scintillating bravura sound absolutely natural, but also his chimerical use of rubato is more convincing on the earlier recordings. On the RCA CD, the opening *Preludes* bring a curiously hollow piano timbre, and the effect throughout is shallow, partly the effect of the dry studio acoustic. Rachmaninov's performances were usually remarkably consistent – witness his sombre account of the famous *Prelude in C sharp minor*, while *The Flight of the bumble-bee*, a *tour de force* of exuberant articulation, brings only one second's difference in playing time between the two versions. However, in the closing *Liebesfreud* on the Decca disc, with its coruscating decorative cascades, his virtuosity is dazzling and the performance takes about a minute less than on the RCA version. It sounds good on both discs, but on the Decca version one has the impression of Rachmaninov sitting at the end of one's room. A remarkable achievement.

Élégie, Op. 13/1; Études-tableaux, Op. 39/3 & 5; Moments musicaux, Op. 16/3–6; Preludes, Op. 23/1, 2, 5 & 6; Op. 32/12.
(M) *** EMI Dig. CDD7 64086-2 [id.]. Andrei Gavrilov – SCRIABIN: *Preludes.* ***

There is some pretty remarkable playing here, especially in the stormy *B flat major Prelude*, while the *G sharp minor* from Op. 32 has a proper sense of fantasy. More prodigious bravura provides real excitement in the *F sharp minor Étude-tableau*, Op. 39/3, and in the *E minor Moment musical*, while Gavrilov relaxes winningly in the *Andante cantabile* of Op. 16/3 and the *Élégie*. Sometimes his impetuosity almost carries him away, and the piano is placed rather near the listener so that we are nearly taken with him, but there is no doubt about the quality of this recital.

Études-tableaux, Op. 33; (i) *Suites for 2 pianos, Nos. 1 (Fantasy), Op. 5; 2, Op. 17.*
(M) *** Decca 425 029-2; *425 029-4* [id.]. Vladimir Ashkenazy; (i) with André Previn.

Ashkenazy's 1981 account of the Op. 33 *Études-tableaux* is very impressive indeed, but it is for the *Suites* that this reissue is especially valuable. The colour and flair of Rachmaninov's writing are captured with wonderful imagination, reflecting a live performance by Ashkenazy and Previn in London in the summer of 1974. The recordings were made in All Saints' Church, Petersham, and the pianos are fairly closely observed against the resonant acoustic; the sound is bold and has striking presence.

Études-tableaux, Opp. 33 & 39.
*** Hyp. CDA 66091; *KA 66091* [id.]. Howard Shelley.
*** EMI Dig. CDC7 54077-2 [id.]. Vladimir Ovchinikov.
**(*) ASV Dig. CDDCA 789; *ZCDCA 789* [id.]. Gordon Fergus-Thompson.

The conviction and thoughtfulness of Shelley's playing, coupled with excellent modern sound, make this convenient coupling a formidable rival to Ashkenazy's classic versions, which in any case are not coupled together on CD.

Impressive and authoritative performances of all the *Études-tableaux* from Vladimir Ovchinikov, whose playing can hardly be faulted at any level and who has the advantage of excellent recorded sound. These were recorded not long after he performed the memorable feat of playing all seventeen pieces straight off in London's Wigmore Hall after having given an equally impressive account of Prokofiev's *Eighth Sonata*.

Nor is there much wrong with the rival ASV account from Gordon Fergus-Thompson who is an artist with a big technique and no mean poetic imagination. His recording, perhaps, yields in quality to the EMI which is a first recommendation.

Études-tableaux, Op. 39, Nos. 1–9; Variations on a theme of Corelli, Op. 42.
*** Decca Dig. 417 671-2 [id.]. Vladimir Ashkenazy.

Superb performances from Ashkenazy make this the most desirable of Rachmaninov issues. The *Corelli variations* is a rarity and a very fine work. The recording is first class.

Moments musicaux, Op. 16; Morceaux de salon, Op. 10.
*** Hyp. Dig. CDA 66184; *KA 66184* [id.]. Howard Shelley.

Howard Shelley has a highly developed feeling for Rachmaninov and distinguishes himself here both by masterly pianism and by a refined awareness of Rachmaninov's sound-world. The recording is eminently realistic and natural.

24 Preludes (complete).
(M) *(*) BMG/RCA Dig. GD 60568 [60568-2-RC]. Alexis Weissenberg.

24 Preludes; Preludes in D min. and F; Morceaux de fantaisie, Op. 3.
*** Hyp. CDA 66081/2; *KA 66081/2* (available separately) [id.]. Howard Shelley.

24 Preludes (complete); *Piano sonata No. 2 in B flat min., Op. 36.*
*** Decca 414 417-2 (2). Vladimir Ashkenazy.

Considering his popularity and their quality, it is odd that Rachmaninov's *Preludes* have not been recorded complete more often. Ashkenazy's were the first to appear on CD, with the excellent recording further enhanced. There is superb flair and panache about this playing. As a bonus, the compact discs offer the *Second Piano sonata*, with Ashkenazy generally following the 1913 original score but with some variants. He plays with great virtuosity and feeling, and the result is a *tour de force*.

Shelley is a compellingly individual interpreter of Rachmaninov. Each one of the *Preludes* strikes an original chord in him. These are very different readings from those of Ashkenazy but their intensity, well caught in full if reverberant recording, makes these readings an essential recommendation alongside those of the Russian pianist.

Alexis Weissenberg is a big pianist with a commanding technique and plenty of it. But he is inattentive to dynamic nuances between *piano* and *pianopianissimo* and this diminishes the pleasure that his playing gives. He is no match for either Ashkenazy or Howard Shelley. In the USA this record is issued at full-price.

Preludes: Op. 3/2; Op. 23/1–2, 4–6; Mélodie, Op. 3/3; Polichinelle, Op. 3/4; Variations on a theme of Corelli, Op. 42.
*** Conifer Dig. CDCF 159; *MCFC 159* [id.]. Kathryn Stott.

Kathryn Stott has a good feeling for Rachmaninov and gives well-considered accounts of all the pieces on this generously filled CD. It would be difficult to fault her sensitive performance of the *Corelli variations*; there is a strong rhythmic grip and her phrasing is keenly articulate. In the recording one is fairly close to the piano, but not unreasonably so.

13 Preludes, Op. 32.
*** DG Dig. 427 766-2 [id.]. Lilya Zilberstein – SHOSTAKOVICH: *Sonata No. 1.* ***

Lilya Zilberstein came to international attention in 1987 when she won the Busoni Competition at Bolzano. She faces rather more formidable competition in the Rachmaninov *Preludes* than in the Shostakovich *Sonata*, but she takes the various hurdles in her stride. She has technique, style and finesse, and the recording is in the very first flight. This is not only a promising début but a valuable addition to the catalogue.

Piano sonatas Nos. 1 in D min., Op. 28; 2 in B flat min., Op. 36 (revised 1931).
*** Hyp. CDA 66047; *KA 66047* [id.]. Howard Shelley.

Howard Shelley offers here the 1931 version of the *B flat Sonata*. He has plenty of sweep and grandeur and withstands comparison with the distinguished competition. He has something of the grand manner and an appealing freshness, ardour and, when required, tenderness. He is accorded an excellent balance by the engineers, which places the piano firmly in focus.

Piano sonata No. 2 in B flat min., Op. 36 (original version); *Fragments in A flat; Fughetta in F; Gavotte in D; Mélodie in E; Morceau de fantaisie in G min.; Nocturnes Nos. 1–3; Oriental sketch in B flat; Piece in D min.; 4 Pieces; Prelude in E flat min.; Romance in F sharp min.; Song without words in D min.*
*** Hyp. CDA 66198; *KA 66198* [id.]. Howard Shelley.

Howard Shelley now gives us the original version of Op. 36 and his performances here show unfailing sensitivity, intelligence and good taste. Most of the shorter pieces are early, and not all are Rachmaninov at his very greatest – but they are persuasively played, as is the *Sonata*; they have the merit of excellent recorded sound. A valuable issue.

Suites Nos. 1–2, Opp. 5 & 17; Symphonic dances, Op. 45.
*** Hyp. Dig. CDA 66375; *KA 66375* [id.]. Howard Shelley, Hilary Macnamara.

Two pianos are notoriously difficult to balance, and the present disc is not as triumphantly successful as, say, the Louis Lortie–Hélène Mercier Ravel recital on Chandos, though it is still pretty good. Howard Shelley and Hilary Macnamara give strong performances of both the *Suites* and the *Symphonic dances*. In the *Suites* their responses are not quite as imaginative as those of Ashkenazy and Previn (see above), and there are moments in the middle movement of the *Symphonic dances* when more subtle and lighter rhythmic accents would not have come amiss. But there is plenty of dramatic fire in the outer movements, and some musicianly playing elsewhere in this generously filled disc.

Transcriptions: *Daisies; Lilacs; Polka de W. R.; Vocalise.* BACH: *Prelude; Gavotte; Gigue.* BIZET: *Minuet from L'Arlésienne.* KREISLER: *Liebesleid; Liebesfreud.* MENDELSSOHN: *Midsummer night's dream: Scherzo.* MUSSORGSKY: *Sorochinsky Fair: Hopak.* RIMSKY-KORSAKOV: *Flight of the bumble-bee.* SCHUBERT: *Wohin?.* TCHAIKOVSKY: *Lullaby.*
*** Hyp. Dig. CDA 66486 [id.]. Howard Shelley.

This is a kind of footnote or *Anhang* to the complete Rachmaninov which Hyperion have recorded with Howard Shelley, and those who have the remainder of his series will need no prompting to add this to their collections. Even those who haven't should consider it, for Shelley plays with an authority and sensitivity that is wholly persuasive and despatches the virtuoso transcriptions to the manner born. The transcription of the *Vocalise* is by Zoltan Kocsis but otherwise all are Rachmaninov's own.

Song transcriptions: *Dreams; Floods of spring; In the silent night; The little island; Midsummer eve; The Muse; O, cease thy singing; On the death of a linnet; Sorrow in springtime; To the children; Vocalise; Where beauty dwells.*
**(*) Dell'Arte CD DBS 7001 [id.]. Earl Wild (piano).

Earl Wild is a pianist all too often taken for granted as a virtuoso pure and simple, rather than the great artist that he is. On this CD he plays twelve masterly transcriptions he has made of Rachmaninov songs, ranging from *In the silent night* from the Op. 4 set of 1890 to *Dreams* of Op. 38 (1916). Of course his virtuosity is dazzling – but so too is his refinement of colour and his musicianship. The recording is not of comparable distinction but is acceptable enough.

Variations on a theme of Chopin, Op. 22; Variations on a theme of Corelli, Op. 42; Mélodie in E, Op. 3/3.
*** Hyp. CDA 66009; *KA 66009* [id.]. Howard Shelley – MENDELSSOHN: *Scherzo.* ***

Rachmaninov's two big sets of variations for solo piano make an excellent coupling, and Howard Shelley gives dazzling, consistently compelling performances, full of virtuoso flair. The *Corelli variations* are the better-known set; but it is the more expansive *Chopin variations* which represent the composer at his most masterly. The grouping of variations brings a kind of sonata balance, with the climax of the final section built superbly by Shelley, helped by first-rate piano sound.

Recital collection

Preludes Nos. 1 in C sharp min., Op. 3/2; 6 in G min.; 11 in G flat, Op. 23/5 & 10; 18 in F, Op. 32/7; 23 in G sharp min., Op. 32/11. Mélodie, Op. 3/3; Variations on a theme of Chopin, Op. 2; Arr. of KREISLER: *Liebeslied; Liebesfreud.*
*** Decca Dig. 421 061-2 [id.]. Jorge Bolet.

Bolet's Rachmaninov recital is one of the finest records he has given us for some time. It has the beautiful pianism of his Chopin, with a much stronger sense of profile. These are all aristocratic performances and eminently well recorded.

VOCAL MUSIC

The Bells, Op. 35.
(M) *** EMI CDM7 63114-2. Sheila Armstrong, Robert Tear, John Shirley-Quirk, LSO Ch., LSO, Previn – PROKOFIEV: *Alexander Nevsky.* ***

The Bells, Op. 35; 3 Russian songs, Op. 41.
*** Decca Dig. 414 455-2 [id.]. Troitskaya, Karczykowski, Krause, Concg. Ch. & O, Ashkenazy.

The Bells, Op. 35; Vocalise, Op. 34/14.
(*) Chan. Dig. CHAN 8476; *ABTD 1187* [id.]. Murphy, Lewis, Wilson-Johnson, SNO Ch. & O, Järvi – TCHAIKOVSKY: *Romeo and Juliet duet* etc. *

Ashkenazy's volatile Russian style is eminently suitable for Rachmaninov's masterly cantata. His tenor soloist has just the right touch of temperament, and in the slow movement Natalia

Troitskaya's contribution combines Slavonic feeling with freshness. The chorus respond readily to the black mood of the Scherzo and bring a melancholy intensity to the finale. The Decca recording is superb, wide in range, spacious and clear.

In *The Bells*, as in Previn's equally fresh and direct account of the other Russian choral work included on his CD, Prokofiev's *Alexander Nevsky*, the LSO Chorus sings convincingly in the original language. The timbre may not be entirely Russian-sounding (cleaner and fresher in fact), but in what amounts to a choral symphony Previn's concentration on purely musical values as much as on evocation of atmosphere produces powerful results, even when the recording as transferred to CD has lost just a little of its ambient warmth in favour of added presence and choral brilliance.

The climaxes expand just as impressively in the Usher Hall, Edinburgh, as in the Decca set, and have great impact too, but detail is less clear and there is less bite. The three soloists all sing eloquently but without the Slavonic character of Ashkenazy's group. In short, the Decca recording has an extra degree of intensity, especially in the vehemence of the Scherzo. Järvi's Tchaikovsky couplings are unique, but Ashkenazy's choice of the *Russian folksongs* seems more apt.

(i) *The Bells, Op. 35;* (ii) *Spring, Op. 20.*
**(*) Chan. Dig. CHAN 8966 [id.]. (i) Ustinova, Westi; (ii) Hynnine; Danish Nat. R. Ch. & O, Dmitri Kitaenko.

The Bells and the *Spring cantata* make an ideal coupling. *Spring* is not a pastoral evocation but a folk tale about a Russian couple who spend a claustrophobic winter confinement in their cottage after the wife has betrayed her husband with a lover. Happily when the 'green rushing tides of spring return', the husband's dark thoughts of revenge turn to forgiveness. Both performances are strongly felt, with really excellent soloists, and the singing of the Danish Radio Chorus conveys their involvement. However the atmospheric acoustic tends to blunt the attack of their singing and obscure the words, while the black climax of the third section of *The Bells* loses much of its ferocity and bite without more abrasive consonants. In this latter work Ashkenazy's version is undoubtedly more powerful, especially in conveying the dark intensity of the third movement.

Vespers, Op. 37.
*** Hyp. Dig. CDA 66460; *KA 66460* [id.]. Corydon Singers, Matthew Best.

Rachmaninov's setting of the *Vespers* – more correctly the 'All-night vigil' – is among his supreme masterpieces, a beautiful and dedicated example of his writing in an idiom totally different from most of his work. Though this British choir lacks the dark timbres associated with Russian choruses and though the result could be weightier and more biting, this is a most beautiful performance, very well sung and recorded in an atmospheric, reverberant setting very apt for such church music.

Vocalise, Op. 34/14 (arr. Dubensky).
(M) *** BMG/RCA GD 87831 [7831-2-RG]. Anna Moffo, American SO, Stokowski – CANTELOUBE: *Songs of the Auvergne;* VILLA-LOBOS: *Bachianas Brasileiras No. 5.* ***

Rachmaninov's *Vocalise* was a favourite showpiece of Stokowski, usually in a purely orchestral arrangement; but here with Moffo at her warmest it is good to have the vocal version so persuasively matching the accompaniment.

OPERA

(i) *Monna Vanna* (incomplete opera: Act I, orch. Buketoff); (ii) *Piano concerto No. 4* (original version).
**(*) Chan. Dig. CHAN 8987 [id.]. (i) Milnes, McCoy, Walker, Karoustos, Thorsteinsson, Blythe; (ii) William Black; Iceland SO, Buketoff.

Monna Vanna is the fragment of an opera based on Maeterlinck which Rachmaninov wrote around the inspired period of his *Second Symphony*. He composed the piano score of Act I complete during an exceptionally happy stay in Dresden in 1907, but was prevented from continuing it at the time by other commitments. Maeterlinck then refused to let him have the rights for setting the play, but Rachmaninov thought so well of the fragment that it was the one score he brought away from Russia after the Revolution. Igor Buketoff, who knew the composer, has rescued this Act I score and orchestrated it very sensitively to make an interesting curiosity. In its ripely romantic manner – very different from Debussy setting Maeterlinck – it may not have big tunes, but the writing has lyrical warmth and flows freely, thrusting home climactic moments with the same sureness as Rachmaninov's symphonies. The snag is the wordy libretto and improbable story. Buketoff's performance with the Iceland Symphony is warmly convincing, but the singing is flawed, with Sherrill Milnes, as Monna Vanna's jealous husband, standing out from an indifferent team, otherwise thin-toned and often wobbly. That enjoyable rarity is unexpectedly but attractively coupled with Buketoff's resurrection of the original score of the *Fourth Piano concerto*, rather more expansive than the text we know. William Black is the powerful soloist, though the piano sound, unlike that of the orchestra, lacks weight.

Raff, Joachim (1822–82)

Symphony No. 5 (Lenore).
(M) *** Unicorn UKCD 2031. LPO, Bernard Herrmann.

Raff left eleven symphonies; No. 5, with its colourful programmatic writing, is generally counted the finest of his cycle. In some ways it is a very naïve work, based as it is on a high romantic ballad by the poet Bürger. A dead soldier-lover calls upon the girl he has left behind, and on a devil's ride he disconcertingly turns into a skeleton. The first two movements merely provide preparation for that dramatic development, while the third depicts the lovers' parting, with the main march heard first in crescendo then diminuendo to represent the arrival and departure of a troop of the lover's regiment – a piece much beloved by the Victorians. A thoroughly enjoyable Mendelssohnian symphony, colourfully performed with clean and vivid recording, given extra projection on CD, especially the percussion.

Raid, Kaljo (born 1922)

Symphony No. 1 in C min.
*** Chan. Dig. CHAN 8525; *ABTD 1235* [id.]. SNO, Järvi – ELLER: *Dawn; Elegia* etc. ***

Raid's *First Symphony* of 1944 was written when he had just passed twenty-one and was still studying with Eller; it shows a genuine feel for form and a fine sense of proportion, even though the personality is not fully formed. Well worth hearing. Neeme Järvi gets very committed playing from the Scottish National Orchestra and the recording is warm and well detailed.

Rameau, Jean Philippe (1683–1764)

Les Boréades: orchestral suite; Dardanus: orchestral suite.
*** Ph. Dig. 420 240-2 [id.]. O of 18th Century, Brüggen.

The orchestral suite from *Les Boréades* occupies the larger part of the disc. The invention is full of resource and imagination, and the playing here of both this and *Dardanus* is spirited and sensitive and will provide delight even to those normally unresponsive to authentic instruments.

Hippolyte et Aricie: orchestral suite.
(M) *** HM/BMG GD 77009 [77009-2-RG]. La Petite Bande, Kuijken.

During Rameau's lifetime there were three productions of *Hippolyte et Aricie*, for which various instrumental additions were made. This record collects virtually all the orchestral music from the three in performances so lively and winning that the disc is irresistible. Sigiswald Kuijken gets delightful results from his ensemble; the melodic invention is fresh and its orchestral presentation ingenious. In every way an outstanding release – and not least in the quality of the sound.

Les Indes galantes: suites for orchestra.
(B) *** HM HMA 901130 [id.]. Chappelle Royale O, Philippe Herreweghe.

Besides the harpsichord arrangements listed below, Rameau also arranged his four 'concerts' of music from *Les Indes galantes* for orchestra (scoring for flutes, oboes and trumpets) and including, in the composer's words, 'the Symphonies, intermingled with some of the sung Airs, as well as the first three entrées'. The result makes nearly three-quarters of an hour of agreeable listening, especially when played so elegantly – and painlessly – on original instruments, and very well recorded (in 1984). This is one of the most attractive reissues in Harmonia Mundi's inexpensive Musique d'Abord series.

KEYBOARD MUSIC

Les Indes galantes: excerpts (harpsichord transcriptions).
*** HM HMC 901028; *HMC 401028*. Kenneth Gilbert.

These transcriptions are Rameau's own, made some time after the success scored by his first opera-ballet, *Les Indes galantes*, in 1735. He grouped a number of items into four suites or '*concerts*', and these included not only dance numbers and orchestral pieces but arias as well. Kenneth Gilbert, playing a fine instrument in contemporary tuning, reveals these miniatures as the subtle and refined studies they are. He could not be better served by the recording engineers, and the CD brings added presence and background quiet.

Music for harpsichord: *Book 1* (1706); *Pièces de clavecin* (1724); *Nouvelles suites de pièces de clavecin* (*c.* 1728); *5 Pièces* (1741); *La Dauphine* (1747).
*** O-L Dig. 425 886-2 (2) [id.]. Christophe Rousset (harpsichord).
(M) *** DG 427 176-2 (2). Kenneth Gilbert (harpischord).

Christophe Rousset has met with wide acclaim in the musical press – and rightly so! This is marvellously persuasive and vital playing. Rousset has much the same blend of imagination, flair and poetic sensitivity that distinguished Skip Sempé's Couperin recital. Rousset's playing is authoritative and scholarly, yet fresh and completely free from the straitjacket of academic rectitude. He provides an interesting note, which rightly pays tribute to Marcelle Meyer and Kenneth Gilbert; and he plays a Hemsch from 1751, in a perfect state of preservation, and a 1988 copy of a 1636 Ruckers harpsichord, modified in 1763 by Hemsch. The sound is excellent – though, as so often with the harpsichord, it should be reproduced at a lower-than-usual level setting.

Rameau's keyboard music is among the finest of the whole Baroque era, and Kenneth Gilbert is not just a scholar but an artist of genuine insight and stature. He uses three harpsichords here, all from the Paris Conservatoire and all from the period: a Goujon (1749), a Hemsch (1761), and a third by Dumont (1679) restored by Pascal Taskin in 1789. They are superb instruments and are excellently recorded too (in 1977); although the CD brings added presence, the instruments remain in a good perspective.

Pièces de clavecin: Suite (No. 1) in A min.; L'Agaçante; La Dauphine; L'Indiscrète; La Livri; La Pantomine: La Timide.
*** CRD CRD 3320; *CRDC 4020* [id.]. Trevor Pinnock.

Trevor Pinnock chose a more mellow instrument here, making his stylish, crisply rhythmic performances even more attractive. The selection includes *La Dauphine*, the last keyboard piece which Rameau wrote, brilliantly performed. Excellent recording.

Harpsichord suites: in A min. (1728); *in E min.* (1724).
*** CRD CRD 3310; *CRDC 4010* [id.]. Trevor Pinnock.

Harpsichord suites: in D min./maj. (1724); *in G maj./min.* (1728).
*** CRD CRD 3330; *CRDC 4030* [id.]. Trevor Pinnock.

Excellent performances. Trevor Pinnock is restrained in the matter of ornamentation, but his direct manner is both eloquent and stylish. The harpsichord is of the French type and is well recorded.

Grand motets: *In convertendo; Quam dilecta laboravi.*
*** HM HM 901078; *HM 401078* [id.]. Gari, Monnaliu, Ledroit, De Mey, Varcoe, Chapelle Royale Ch., Ghent Coll. Vocale, Herreweghe.

These two motets are among Rameau's finest works. The recordings were made in the Carmelite Church in Ghent which has a warm, reverberant acoustic, and the Ghent Collegium Vocale is stiffened by forces from La Chapelle Royale in Paris. They produce excellent results and the soloists are also very fine indeed. The instrumental ensemble includes several members of La Petite Bande and so its excellence can almost be taken for granted.

OPERA-BALLET AND OPERA

Anacréon (complete).

(B) *** HM HMA 90190 [id.]. Schirrer, Mellon, Feldman, Visse, Laplénie, Les Arts Florissants, Christie.

The music here has charm, even if it is not Rameau at his most inventive; the performance is as authoritative and stylish as one would expect from William Christie's group. It is not essential Rameau, but readers with an interest in the period will want it – and it has moments of great appeal. The recording is admirable and this reissue is a genuine bargain.

Platée (complete).
** Erato/Warner Dig. 2292 45028-2 (2) [id.]. Ragon, Jennifer Smith, Guy de Mey, Le Texier, Gens, Ens. Vocale Françoise Herr, Musiciens du Louvre, Minkowski.

Platée, written in 1745, is described as a '*ballet bouffon*', in fact a comic opera comprising a Prologue and three short Acts, based on a classical theme. The central character, the nymph Platée (Plataea), is a drag part taken by a tenor, a favourite comic device of the time, as Raymond Leppard's realization of Cavalli's *La Calisto* brought out. With such a send-up of classical tradition, the performers here understandably adopt comic expressions and voices, which in a recording, as opposed to a stage performance, become rather wearing on the listener. It is like being nudged in the ribs, prompted to laugh, when the joke is not subtle. Also surprisingly, with such stylish singers as the tenor Guy de Mey, almost all the soloists aspirate heavily in florid passages. Within that convention this is a lively, brisk performance, very well conducted by Marc Minkowski, but marred by the dryness of the recording. As a joint project with French Radio, it was made in what sounds like a small Paris studio: though the sense of presence is very vivid, the sound of period instruments reminds one of the abrasiveness of much earlier recordings. Minkowski writes of the distinctive instrumentation that Rameau devised, all top and bottom, and the aggressive acoustic emphasizes that. But as a work, *Platée* certainly provides a fascinating side-glance at Rameau's mastery.

Pygmalion (complete).
(M) **(*) HM/BMG GD 77143 [77143-2-RG]. Elwes, Van der Sluis, Vanhecke, Yakar, Paris Chapelle Royal Ch., La Petite Bande, Leonhardt.

Leonhardt's 1980 account with John Elwes as Pygmalion and Mieke van der Sluis as Céphise is welcome back to the catalogue. Leonhardt's direction is rather leisurely, but his soloists make a good team. The use of period instruments brings attractive transparency of texture and, thanks to the excellence of the original recording, this is enhanced on CD. The documentation (including full translation) is first class.

Zoroastre (complete).
(M) **(*) HM/BMG GD 77144 (3) [77144-2-RG]. Elwes, De Reyghere, Van der Sluis, Nellon, Reinhart, Bona, Ghent Coll. Vocale, La Petite Bande, Kuijken.

Though Kuijken's characteristically gentle style with his excellent authentic group, La Petite Bande, fails to give the piece all the bite and urgency it needs, this is nevertheless a fine presentation of a long-neglected masterpiece, with crisp and stylish singing from the soloists, notably John Elwes in the name-part and Gregory Reinhart as Abramane. The Ghent Collegium Vocale, placed rather close, sing with vigour in the choruses, but the individual voices fail to blend. The five Acts (with Rameau here abandoning the old convention of an allegorical Prologue) are now offered on three mid-priced CDs against the original set on four LPs. The excellent documentation (144 pages, including translations) puts the mid-priced issues of many of the large international companies to shame.

Rautavaara, Einojuhani (born 1928)

Symphonies 1–3.
*** Ondine Dig. ODE 740-2 [id.]. Leipzig RSO, Max Pommer.

Einojuhani Rautavaara first came to attention in the mid-1950s with his *Requiem for our time* for brass instruments. A pupil of Aarre Merikanto in Helsinki, he later continued his studies with Copland, Sessions and Vladimir Vogel. (He is the nephew of the soprano Auliikki Rautavaara whose records and Glyndebourne appearances will be remembered by older collectors.) He is a prolific composer; there are some eight operas or chamber operas, and seven concertos for various instruments. He has been overshadowed outside Finland by Joonas Kokkonen and Aulis Sallinen, but the present disc shows him to be a symphonist to reckon with.

Ideas never outstay their welcome and there is a sense of inevitability about their development. Those with a taste for Shostakovich or Simpson should find these pieces, which date from 1956-61, congenial. Good performances by the Leipzig Radio Orchestra under Max Pommer and very decent recorded sound too.

Ravel, Maurice (1875–1937)

Alborada del gracioso; Une barque sur l'océan; Boléro; (i) *Piano concerto in G; Piano concerto for the left hand. Daphnis et Chloé* (complete ballet); *L'Éventail de Jeanne: Fanfare. Menuet antique; Ma Mère l'Oye* (complete); *Pavane pour une infante défunte; Rapsodie espagnole; Le tombeau de Couperin; La valse; Valses nobles et sentimentales.*
❀ (M) *** Decca 421 458-2 (4). Montreal SO with Ch. and (i) Pascal Rogé; Dutoit.

(i) *Alborada del gracioso;* (ii) *Une barque sur l'océan; Boléro;* (i; iii) *Piano concerto for the left hand;* (ii; iv) *Daphnis et Chloé* (complete ballet); (ii) *Fanfare pour L'Éventail de Jeanne; Menuet antique; Ma Mère l'Oye* (complete ballet); (i) *Pavane pour une infante défunte; Rapsodie espagnole;* (ii) *Shéhérazade: Ouverture de féerie. Le tombeau de Couperin; La valse; Valses nobles et sentimentales.*
(M) **(*) Sony SM3K 45842 (3) [id.]. (i) Cleveland O; (ii) NYPO; Boulez; (iii) with Entremont; (iv) Camerata Singers.

Alborada del gracioso; Une barque sur l'océan; Boléro; Daphnis et Chloé (complete ballet); *L'Éventail de Jeanne; Fanfare; Menuet antique; Ma Mère l'Oye* (complete); *Pavane pour une infante défunte; Rapsodie espagnole; Shéhérazade: Ouverture de féerie; Le tombeau de Couperin; La valse; Valses nobles et sentimetales.*
*** DG Dig. 429 768-2 (3) LSO & Ch., Claudio Abbado.

Anyone coming new to this repertoire will find Dutoit's four-disc mid-price box unbeatable value: the orchestral playing is wonderfully sympathetic and the recording ideally combines atmospheric evocation with vividness of detail. In the concertos, Pascal Rogé finds gracefulness and vitality for the *G major* work and, if there is less dynamism in the *Left-hand concerto*, there is no lack of finesse. The balance is very realistic and the recording throughout is in the demonstration class.

Boulez's distinguished Sony set unfortunately comes into direct competition with Dutoit's outstanding Montreal box of four CDs, also at mid-price. However, Sony do offer very good value. Three CDs are used, yet only the *G major Piano concerto* is missing and instead we are offered a glitteringly iridescent account of the *Ouverture de féerie*, which is omitted by Dutoit. Entrement's account of the *Left-hand concerto* is strong and characterful and not lacking in poetic colour; but the rather forward CBS sound is a little fierce at the orchestral climax and does not altogether flatter the piano timbre. On the whole, however, the remastering makes the most of recordings which were originally among the best of their period (1972–5) from this source, even if they were at times balanced artificially in the interests of internal clarity and strong projection. The *Alborada* is quite brilliant and, throughout, Boulez allows all the music ample time to breathe; gentler textures have the transluscence for which this conductor is admired. *Une barque sur l'océan* has a genuine magic, while the complete *Daphnis et Chloé* has a sense of ecstasy and an ability to transport the listener into the enchanted landscape that this work inhabits, with its wonder, its vivid colours and innocence. Boulez is also at his very best in *Ma Mère l'Oye*: the luminous textures of the gentle music are matched by the glitter and impact of the score's more dramatic moments. Boulez's *Rapsodie espagnole* is equally distinctive: it is beautifully shaped and atmospheric in an entirely different way from Karajan's; Boulez's Spain is brilliant, dry and well lit. Both *Boléro* and *La valse* generate considerable tension and have powerful climaxes. There is no doubt that this music-making with its cleanly etched sound is immensely strong in character, and many listeners will respond to it very positively. There is excellent internal cueing.

Abbado's fastidiously polished and highly sensitive Ravel performances occupy three CDs as opposed to the four of Dutoit on Decca. The Decca includes the two *Piano concertos* with Pascal Rogé, but not the *Shéhérazade Overture*; neither include the song-cycle of that name though, to be fair, Margaret Price's recording of it (with Abbado) was not the unqualified success one might have expected. Abbado's complete *Daphnis* is not quite as vivdly recorded as the Dutoit (in fact the opening is barely audible unless the controls are adjusted to a high-level setting). But Abbado has impeccable taste in this repertoire and it goes without saying that the LSO play gloriously throughout. The mid-price Decca set has just that extra edge over the DG, though musically honours are pretty evenly divided.

However, Sony also offer very good value. Three CDs are used, yet only the *G major Piano concerto* is missing and instead we are offered a glitteringly iridescent account of the *Ouverture de féerie*, which is omitted by Dutoit but not by Abbado. Entrement's account of the *Left-hand concerto* is strong and characterful and not lacking in poetic colour; but the rather forward CBS sound is a little fierce at the orchestral climax and does not altogether flatter the piano timbre. On the whole, however, the remastering makes the most of recordings which were originally among the best of their period (1972–5) from this source, even if they were at times balanced artificially in the interests of internal clarity and strong projection. The *Alborada* is quite brilliant and, throughout, Boulez allows all the music ample time to breathe; gentler textures have the transluscence for which this conductor is admired. *Une barque sur l'océan* has a genuine magic, while the complete *Daphnis et Chloé* has a sense of ecstasy and an ability to transport the listener into the enchanted landscape that this work inhabits, with its wonder, its vivid colours and innocence. Boulez is also at his very best in *Ma Mère l'Oye*: the luminous textures of the gentle music are matched by the glitter and impact of the score's more dramatic moments. Boulez's *Rapsodie espagnole* is equally distinctive: it is beautifully shaped and atmospheric in an entirely different way from Karajan's; Boulez's Spain is brilliant, dry and well lit. Both *Boléro* and *La valse* generate considerable tension and have powerful climaxes. There is no doubt that this music-making with its cleanly etched sound is immensely strong in character, and many listeners will respond to it very positively. There is excellent internal cueing.

Alborada del gracioso; Une barque sur l'océan; Overture, Shéhérazade (1899); (i) *Shéhérazade – song-cycle;* (ii) *Tzigane; La valse.*
*** DG Dig. 427 314-2 [id.]. (ii) Margaret Price; (i) Salvatore Accardo; LSO, Abbado.

Highly sensitive performances of these beautiful scores. Abbado is on excellent form and brings out all the subtle colourings of Ravel's orchestration, in which he is greatly helped by the excellent DG recording. Accardo is superb in *Tzigane*, and Abbado creates delicious sounds in the two transcriptions from *Miroirs* and *La valse*. Margaret Price is a little disappointing: her voice does not float effortlessly over the texture as does Crespin on Decca and she does not seem to be quite inside the sensibility of this music. Abbado includes Ravel's early overture to *Shéhérazade*, which is completely unrelated to the cycle, and is still something of a rarity. Reservations about Price's *Shéhérazade* apart (which not everyone will share), this can be strongly recommended.

Alborada del gracioso; Boléro; Rapsodie espagnole; La valse.
*** Decca 410 010-2 [id.]. Montreal SO, Dutoit.

The playing of the Montreal orchestra under Charles Dutoit is absolutely first class and thoroughly atmospheric, and the recorded sound has a clarity, range and depth of perspective that are equally satisfying. This recording defines the state of the art and, apart from the sumptuous music-making, has impressive refinement and a most musically judged and natural balance.

(i) *Alborada del gracioso;* (ii) *Boléro;* (i) *La valse.*
(M) *** EMI CDM7 64357-2 [id.]; *EG 764357-4*. (i) O de Paris; (ii) BPO; Karajan – DEBUSSY: *La Mer.* ***

Karajan's digitally remastered 1978 EMI Berlin Philharmonic *Boléro* has fine presence and a splendid forward impetus. The Paris *Alborada* and *La valse* have been tacked on for this reissue. They were recorded in 1974 as part of an outstanding French concert of Ravel's orchestral music (see below).

Alborada del gracioso; Daphnis et Chloé (ballet; complete); *Ma Mère l'Oye; Pavane pour une infante défunte; Rapsodie espagnole; Le tombeau de Couperin; Valses nobles et sentimentales.*
(M) (***) Decca mono 425 997-2 (2) [id.]. SRO, Ansermet.

These Ansermet performances are from the early 1950s, not the more familiar versions he recorded a decade later in the early days of stereo, which are included in the Ansermet Edition – see our Concerts section, below. They serve to show why this conductor and his Suisse Romande Orchestra were so highly regarded in the early 1950s and similarly, why Decca had so commanding a lead in the field of recording. His *Rapsodie espagnole* – and in particular the

Feria – is marvellously atmospheric and colourful (almost but not quite the equal of Reiner's 1960s account), and generally speaking, his *Valses nobles* and *Le tombeau de Couperin* suite score over their successors. His complete *Daphnis* of 1952 was the very first to be made, and – like its stereo successor – was something of a disappointment at the time – and remains so. Anyone looking for modern recordings of this repertoire will turn first to the Dutoit or Abbado compilations, but this issue deserves a place of honour in the catalogue and collectors will be surprised at how well these performances sound.

Alborada del gracioso; Fanfare for L'Éventail de Jeanne; Ma Mère l'Oye (complete ballet); *Miroirs: La vallée des cloches* (arr. Percy Grainger); *La valse;* (i) *Shéhérazade* (song-cycle).
*** EMI Dig. CDC7 54204-2 [id.]. (i) Maria Ewing; CBSO, Simon Rattle.

This CD was undoubtedly the Ravel record of 1991 and it missed inclusion in our *Yearbook* by only a hairsbreadth. The recording of the CBSO, made in the Arts Centre of Warwick University, is extraordinarily spectacular, with a state-of-the-art sound-balance of the widest range and amplitude. The impression of a large orchestra in a hall extending beyond the speakers is uncannily tangible. The performances too have great magnetism and electricity, and the orchestral playing is superb. Rattle captures the lambent allure of Percy Grainger's orchestration of the last of the *Miroirs* (the fourth, *Alborada del gracioso*, the composer orchestrated himself) and gives an equally glowing account of *Ma Mère l'Oye*, with delectably refined textures, and the more exotic detail glittering amidst the orchestral warmth. *La valse* sounds gorgeous too, with the misty shadows of the opening slowly clearing so that the climax can blossom and disintegrate with alarming power. At the beginning of the programme, Maria Ewing's *Shéhérazade* immediately follows Ravel's vivid *Fanfare*. The first song, *Asie*, is a performance of unbridled passion, matched in voluptuous intensity by Rattle and his players; then in the aching yearning of *La flûte enchantée* the atmosphere becomes more impressionistic, so that *L'indifférent* ravishes in a rather more subtle manner, with the intensity simmering below the surface. But it is essentially a dramatic performance, and the shimmering *Alborada* is well placed to follow on afterwards.

Alborada del gracioso; Pavane pour une infante défunte; Rapsodie espagnole; Le tombeau de Couperin; La valse.
(M) *** Mercury 432 003-2 [id.]. Detroit SO, Paray – IBERT: *Escales.* **(*)

Paray's Ravel performances enjoyed a high reputation in the 1960s. His *Rapsodie espagnole* can be spoken of in the same breath as the Reiner/RCA and Karajan/EMI versions, with its languorous, shimmering textures and sparkling *Feria.* His *Alborada* glitters and the *Pavane* is glowingly elegiac. *La valse*, too, is impressively shaped and subtly controlled. *Le tombeau de Couperin* has great refinement and elegance: the solo oboist plays beautifully. This last item was recorded in the old Detroit Orchestral Hall, with its mellow acoustic; the rest of the programme was done at Cass Technical High School, and the sound is that bit brighter and more vivid. All have been excellently remastered.

Alborada del gracioso; Pavane pour une infante défunte; Rapsodie espagnole; Valses nobles et sentimentales.
❀ (M) *** BMG/RCA GD 60179 [60179-2-RG]. Chicago SO, Reiner – DEBUSSY: *Ibéria.* *** ❀

These performances are in an altogether special class. In the *Rapsodie espagnole*, the *Prélude à la nuit* is heavy with fragrance and atmosphere; never have the colours in the *Feria* glowed more luminously, while the *Malagueña* glitters with iridescence. In the thirty years since it first appeared, this is the recording we have turned to whenever we wanted to hear this work for pleasure. No one captures its sensuous atmosphere as completely as did Reiner. Its appearance on CD together with its companions is a cause for celebration, and the recorded sound with its natural concert-hall balance is greatly improved in terms of clarity and definition.

Alborada del gracioso; Rapsodie espagnole.
*** Chan. Dig. CHAN 8850; *ABTD 1467* [id.]. Ulster O, Yan Pascal Tortelier – DEBUSSY: *Images.* ***

Yan Pascal Tortelier gives very good performances of both works and has the advantage of excellent Chandos sound. His *Rapsodie espagnole* is not quite as gripping as some celebrated accounts (Reiner, Karajan, Giulini and others) but it is highly atmospheric all the same, and some collectors may be swayed by the claims of the outstanding digital recording.

Alborada del gracioso; Rapsodie espagnole; Le tombeau de Couperin; La valse.
(M) *** EMI CDM7 63526-2; *EG 763526-4* [id.]. O de Paris, Karajan.

These superb performances were recorded just a decade after Karajan's DG analogue *Daphnis et Chloé suite*, one of the best things he ever did for the gramophone. The Orchestre de Paris, while not the Berlin Philharmonic – the horn vibrato, though unobtrusive, may not be appreciated by all ears – responds splendidly to Karajan's sensuous approach to these scores. The dynamic range is very wide and the acoustic somewhat too resonant. The *Alborada* is on the slow side, and doubtless the reverberation prompted this. But, even if the atmospheric quality of these performances is not wholly free from a trace of self-consciousness, there is no doubt about the mastery of *La valse*, which is extremely fine, or of the *Rapsodie espagnole*, the best performance since Reiner's. The remastering for CD is extremely successful.

Alborada del gracioso; Valses nobles et sentimentales.
(M) *** EMI Dig. CDD7 64056-2 [id.]. RPO, Previn – DEBUSSY: *La Mer* etc. ***

Previn's is a provocatively languorous account of the *Valses nobles et sentimentales*, lazy of tempo and affectionately indulgent, and afforded glowing 1985 Abbey Road recording; then the *Alborada* provides a brilliant close to a concert which has already given the listener two outstanding Debussy performances.

Boléro; (i) *Daphnis et Chloë: suite No. 2; Ma Mère l'Oye (suite); Valses nobles et sentimentales.*
(BB) *** Naxos Dig. 8.550173; *4550173* [id.]. (i) Slovak Philharmonic Ch.; Slovak RSO (Bratislava), Kenneth Jean.

The Slovak Radio Orchestra, which is a fine body and is superbly recorded, respond to Kenneth Jean more warmly than they do on their (very good) companion disc reviewed below. At the price, this is very good value indeed; the *Ma Mère l'Oye* can hold its own alongside all but the most distinguished competition: indeed *Les entretiens de la belle et de la bête* is as keenly characterized as either Giulini or Dutoit, both long at mid-price, and *Le jardin féerique* is enchanting. For those wanting these pieces this is a real bargain.

Boléro; Daphnis et Chloé: suite No. 2.
(M) *** DG 427 250-2. BPO, Karajan – DEBUSSY: *La mer; Prélude.* ***

Karajan's 1964 *Boléro* is a very characteristic performance, marvellously controlled, hypnotic and gripping, with the Berlin Philharmonic at the top of its form. The 1965 *Daphnis et Chloé* suite is outstanding, even among all the competition. He has the advantage of the Berlin Philharmonic at their finest and it would be difficult to imagine better or more atmospheric playing. The CD has opened up the sound spectacularly although now there is a touch of glare.

Boléro; (i) *Daphnis et Chloé: suite No. 2; Pavane pour une infante défunte; La valse.*
(M) *** Decca Dig. 430 714-2; *430 714-4* [id.]. Montreal SO, Dutoit; (i) with chorus.

A further permutation of Dutoit's beautifully made Montreal recordings, warmly and translucently recorded at St Eustache, now reissued at mid-price. The *Daphnis et Chloé* suite is drawn from the highly praised complete set. If this programme is suitable, the performances and recordings cannot be bettered.

Boléro; L'éventail de Jeanne: Fanfare; Ma Mère l'Oye (complete ballet); *Pièce en forme de habañera* (arr. Arthur Horérée); *Rapsodie espagnole.*
*** Sony Dig. MK 44800 [id.]. LSO, Tilson Thomas.

Tilson Thomas is wholly attuned to the sensibility of this magical music and Ravel's sumptuous orchestral colours are vividly reproduced. There is a beautifully sultry account of the *Prélude à la nuit* and plenty of atmosphere in the *Rapsodie espagnole*. Ravel's *Vocalise-étude en forme de habañera* has the remarkable John Harle as the saxophone soloist. These are seductive, delicious performances, beautifully recorded.

Boléro; Rapsodie espagnole.
*** DG Dig. 413 588-2 [id.]. BPO, Karajan – MUSSORGSKY: *Pictures.* **(*)

Karajan's later versions of *Boléro* and *Rapsodie espagnole* find the Berlin Philharmonic in characteristically brilliant form, recorded in very wide-ranging digital sound; the thrust of *Boléro* and the sensuousness of the *Rapsodie* are conveyed with unerring power and magnetism.

Boléro; La valse.
*** Chan. Dig. CHAN 8903 [id.]. Ulster O, Yan Pascal Tortelier – DEBUSSY: *Jeux; Khamma.* ***
** Chan. Dig. CHAN 8996; *ABTD 1578* [id.]. Detroit SO, Järvi – ROUSSEL: *Bacchus; Symphony No. 3.* ***

Yan Pascal Tortelier's *Boléro* and *La valse* come as a makeweight to the two ballets Debussy composed not long before the First World War (Ravel's short ballets are both post-war.) Recommendable performances and well recorded in the best traditions of the house. Here is an instance where the desirability of the coupling can safely determine choice.

Neeme Järvi's accounts of *La valse* and *Boléro* are fill-ups to a predominantly Roussel CD. His *La valse* is brisk and not without its moments of exaggeration – indeed affectation unusual in this conductor. Very natural recorded sound, and though not a first choice for either Ravel piece, both performances give pleasure.

Piano concerto in G.
❀ *** EMI CDC7 49326-2 [id.]. Michelangeli, Philh. O, Gracis – RACHMANINOV: *Concerto No. 4.* *** ❀

Michelangeli plays with superlative brilliance which yet has great sympathy for the tender moments. He achieves exactly the right compromise between inflating the work and preventing it from seeming 'little'. The opening whipcrack could have been more biting, but the orchestra generally plays with great vigour. The exquisite playing in the slow movement makes up for any deficiencies of dimensional balance. The recording has been remastered very successfully and is of the highest quality: clear, with bold piano timbre and excellent orchestral detail.

(i) *Piano concerto in G. Gaspard de la nuit; Sonatine.*
(M) *** DG 419 062-2 [id.]. Argerich, (i) BPO, Abbado.

Argerich's half-tones and clear fingerwork give the *G major Concerto* unusual delicacy, but its urgent virility – with jazz an important element – comes over the more forcefully by contrast. The compromise between coolness and expressiveness in the slow minuet of the middle movement is tantalizingly sensual. Her *Gaspard de la nuit* abounds in character and colour, and the *Sonatine* is a similarly telling performance. The *Concerto* balance is very successful and there is crisp detail, while the solo piano has fine presence and no want of colour.

Piano concerto in G; Piano concerto in D for the left hand.
(M) *** Erato/Warner 2292 45086-2 [id.]. Anne Queffélec, Strasbourg PO, Lombard – DEBUSSY: *Fantasy.* ***
(*) Chan. Dig. CHAN 8773 [id.]. Louis Lortie, LSO, Frühbeck de Burgos – FAURÉ: *Ballade.* *

(i) *Piano concerto in G; Piano concerto for the left hand. Une barque sur l'océan; L'éventail de Jeanne: Fanfare; Menuet antique.*
**(*) Decca Dig. 410 230-2. (i) Rogé; Montreal SO, Dutoit.

Anne Queffélec's accounts of both *Concertos* are thoughtful and imaginative. She is a thorough musician with no mean sense of poetry. The excellent Strasbourg orchestra under Alain Lombard give her admirable support, and the well-balanced recording sounds fresher in its CD format. The rare Debussy coupling is also well worth having.

Pascal Rogé brings both delicacy and sparkle to the *G major Concerto*, which he gives with his characteristic musical grace and fluency. He produces unfailing beauty of tone at every dynamic level and brings great poetry and tenderness to the slow movement; but in the *Left-hand concerto* he is a good deal less dynamic. There is a certain want of momentum here, even though there is much to admire in the way of pianistic finesse – and charm. The Decca recording offers excellent performances of three short orchestral pieces as a makeweight, which may tip the scales in its favour for some collectors.

Louis Lortie's account of the two *Concertos* on Chandos has the advantage of altogether outstanding recording, in a field that is itself particularly strong in this respect. In the *G major* he is often highly personal without becoming unduly idiosyncratic. He has remarkable pianism and a fastidious sense of colour at his command and wonderfully clean articulation. In the *Left-hand concerto* he is perhaps less convincing; he really takes his time over the cadenzas and his agogic hesitations are sometimes over-indulgent. Immaculate playing as such, and superb recording, but ultimately not as satisfying as his major rivals, though better recorded than most of them.

(i) *Piano concerto for the left hand. Miroirs: Alborada del gracioso.*
*** ASV Dig. CDDCA 555; *ZCDCA 555* [id.]. Osorio, RPO, Bátiz – PROKOFIEV: *Piano concerto No. 1* etc. ***

Jorge-Federico Osorio's account of the *Left-hand concerto* can hold its own with the best. He also gives a crisp and colourful performance of the *Alborada.*

Daphnis et Chloé (ballet; complete).
❀ *** Decca Dig. 400 055-2. Montreal SO and Ch., Dutoit.
(M) *** BMG/RCA GD 60469 [60469-2-RG]. New England Conservatory Ch., Boston SO, Munch – ROUSSEL: *Bacchus et Ariane.* (***)
**(*) Chan. Dig. CHAN 8893; *ABTD 1504* [id.]. Ulster O, Yan Pascal Tortelier – DEBUSSY: *Prélude à l'après-midi d'un faune.* *(*)

Daphnis et Chloé (complete); *Boléro.*
*** EMI Dig. CDC7 54303-2 [id.]. CBSO, Simon Rattle.

Daphnis et Chloé (complete); *Pavane pour une infante défunte; Rapsodie espagnole.*
(M) *** Decca 425 956-2 [id.]. ROHCG Ch., LSO, Pierre Monteux.

(i) *Daphnis et Chloé* (complete); (ii) *Rapsodie espagnole.*
(M) *** EMI Dig. CDD7 63887-2 [id.]. (i) LSO Ch. & LSO; (ii) RPO, André Previn.

Daphnis et Chloé (complete); *Valses nobles et sentimentales.*
(M) *** EMI CDM7 69566-2; *EG 769566-4.* Paris Op. Ch., O de Paris, Martinon.

Dutoit's performance is sumptuously evocative with his splendid orchestra creating the most ravishing textures. He adopts an idiomatic and flexible style, observing the minute indications of tempo change but making every slight variation sound totally spontaneous. The final *Danse générale* finds him adopting a dangerously fast tempo, but the Montreal players – combining French responsiveness with transatlantic polish – rise superbly to the challenge, with the choral punctuations at the end adding to the sense of frenzy. The digital recording is wonderfully luminous, with the chorus ideally balanced at an evocative half-distance. It is a pity that Decca do not provide cues to guide access to the main sections of the score.

Charles Munch's Boston account is one of the great glories of the 1950s, superior in every way to his later version from the 1960s. The playing in all departments of the Boston orchestra is simply electrifying. The sound here may not be as sumptuous as the Monteux on Decca, but the richness of colour lies in the playing, and there is a heady sense of intoxication that at times sweeps you off your feet. A wonderful, glowing account, recorded before the virtuosity which Munch and his Bostonians commanded had become hard-driven. Spot-on intonation from the choir – the LSO's chorus did not hold their pitch so securely for Monteux. The strings do not have ideal bloom and transparency (this was one of the first stereo recordings) and the sound does not open out. But try the *Danse de supplication de Chloé* (track 15) and the ensuing scene in which the pirates are put to flight, and you will get a good idea of just how dazzling this is and how little the sonic limitations matter.

With rhythm more important than atmosphere, Previn directs a very dramatic performance of *Daphnis et Chloé,* clear-headed and fresh. It is certainly made vivid, full-bodied too, yet with textures sharply defined. The original full-priced issue had very few internal cues, and it is good to see that, for the reissue, EMI have now provided a total of 18. Previn's unashamedly sultry 1985 *Rapsodie espagnole* with the RPO has also been added for good measure. Both recordings were made at Abbey Road, but the balance gives a concert-hall effect, and the glowing ambience in the *Rapsodie* nicely offsets the glitter. (Excellent value: 73 minutes.)

Simon Rattle conducts the CBSO in one of the most warmly expressive readings yet of Ravel's great ballet score. The moulding of phrase and subtle flexibility of rubato bear tribute not only to his feeling for Ravel but to the responsiveness of the Birmingham Orchestra as well as its fine chorus, trained by Simon Halsey. The sensuous beauty of the slow sequences is enhanced by the mistily evocative recording, though the dynamic range is so extreme that it is hard to set the controls at a convenient level to give clarity to pianissimos without making the climaxes too aggressively loud. Such show-piece numbers as the *Danse guerrière* and the final *Danse générale* have a winning resilience and energy, and interestingly Rattle translates his affectionate manner in Ravel to his performance of *Boléro,* relatively slow and easily expressive, not so hard-edged as it can be.

Monteux conducted the first performance of *Daphnis et Chloé* in 1912; Decca's 1959 recording, a demonstration disc in its day, captured his poetic and subtly shaded reading in the most vivid colours within an agreeably warm ambience. The performance was one of the finest things Monteux did for the gramophone. The CD transfer has opened up the sound, with generally impressive results. Perhaps just a little of the atmospheric allure has been lost (though *Daybreak* still sounds ravishing), but the sound generally is more transparent, without loss of body. Decca have added his 1962 recording of the *Pavane*, wonderfully poised and played most beautifully, and the *Rapsodie espagnole*, in which Monteux inspirationally achieves a balance and a contrast between the mood of quiet introspection for the opening and flashing brilliance for the *Feria*.

Martinon's *Daphnis et Chloé* has an intoxicating atmosphere: its sense of ecstasy and Dionysian abandon are altogether captivating. The delicacy of colouring in the *Nocturne*, the naturalness with which every phrase unfolds, and the virtuosity of the Orchestre de Paris are a constant source of delight. The *Valses nobles and sentimentales* are not quite so outstanding – there are preferable versions – but are still enjoyable. The sound, originally luminously opulent, is now clearer with only slight loss of richness.

The Chandos team provide very natural sound for Yan Pascal Tortelier and his fine Ulster Orchestra. The performance soon puts you under its spell and conveys much of the sense of ecstasy and magic of this score, and of colours so richly-hued and vivid that they belong to the world of the imagination rather than reality. Phrasing is sensitive and there are some gorgeous sounds throughout. All the same it does not have the ecstatic quality of the old Münch version, which is perhaps the most choreographic of all, or the Dutoit on Decca.

Daphnis et Chloé: suite No. 2.
(*) EMI Dig. CDC7 49964-2 [id.]. Oslo PO, Mariss Jansons – DUKAS: *L'apprenti sorcier;* RESPIGHI: *Feste romane.* *

Whether played complete or in the familiar second suite of symphonic fragments, Ravel's score for *Daphnis et Chloé* must have magic. Mariss Jansons and the superb Oslo Philharmonic have more magic than some but not quite enough to displace from memory such accounts as the 1965 Karajan – see above, under *Boléro*. The playing is marvellous and at times breathtaking, but there is the occasional moment of self-consciousness, in the *Pantomime* and elsewhere, that invites admiration rather than inspiring that heady intoxication which the greatest interpreters can create in this score.

Daphnis et Chloé: suite No. 2; Ma Mère l'Oye (ballet): *suite; La valse.*
(M) **(*) EMI/Phoenixa stereo/mono CDM7 63763-2; *EG 763763-4* [id.]. Hallé O, Barbirolli – DEBUSSY: *La Mer.* **(*)

Barbirolli's languorous shaping of Ravel's great yearning string phrase in *Daybreak* really tugs at the heartstrings, its sense of ecstasy is profound and unforgettable. He has the advantage of using a chorus, very well balanced into the texture; indeed the 1959 recording is astonishingly full and luminous, more immediate in focus than the Debussy coupling. The flute playing in the *Pantomime* is wonderfully brilliant and sensitive; the *Danse générale* sparkles, with the chorus (not credited in the performance details) contributing very vividly to the climax. *La valse* also has plenty of temperament and excitement, and *Ma Mère l'Oye* great delicacy and innocence; the Hallé textures are ravishing, and the ear could hardly guess that this later recording derives from a 1957 mono master, so transluscent is the sound.

(i) *Introduction and allegro;* (ii) *Tzigane;* (iii) *Don Quichotte à Dulcineé.*
(*) Chan. Dig. CHAN 8972 [id.]. (i) Masters; (ii) Yan Pascal Tortelier; (iii) Roberts; Ulster O, Y. P. Tortelier – DEBUSSY: *Danses sacrée* etc. *

Tortelier directs *Tzigane* from the bow, as it were, and plays very well. Whether or not Ravel approved the use of full strings, the *Introduction and allegro* loses something of its ethereal quality when given in this form, though the playing of the harpist Rachel Masters is impeccable. No grumbles at all about Stephen Roberts's fine singing in the *Don Quichotte* songs either.

Ma Mère l'Oye (complete ballet).
*** Ph. Dig. 400 016-2 [id.]. Pittsburgh SO, Previn – SAINT-SAËNS: *Carnival of the Animals.* ***
*** Chan. Dig. CHAN 8711; *ABTD 1359* [id.]. Ulster O, Yan Pascal Tortelier – DEBUSSY: *Boîte à joujoux.* ***
**(*) Sony SK 46670 [id.]. Concg. O, Giulini – DVOŘÁK: *Symphony No. 8.* **(*)

Ma Mère l'Oye (complete); *Le tombeau de Couperin; Valses nobles et sentimentales.*
❀ *** Decca Dig. 410 254-2 [id.]. Montreal SO, Dutoit.

Ma Mère l'Oye (complete); *Pavane pour une infante défunte.*
(BB) *** Virgin/Virgo Dig. VJ7 91469-2; *VJ7 91469-4* [id.]. SCO, Saraste – BIZET: *Symphony.* **(*)

Ma Mère l'Oye (complete); *Rapsodie espagnole.*
(M) *** DG 415 844-2 [id.]. LAPO, Giulini – MUSSORGSKY: *Pictures.* ***

A few bars of this Decca record leave no doubt as to its excellence. This offers demonstration quality, transparent and refined, with the textures beautifully balanced and expertly placed. The performances too are wonderfully refined and sympathetic. *Ma Mère l'Oye* is ravishingly beautiful, its special combination of sensuousness and innocence perfectly caught.

In Previn's version of the complete *Mother Goose* ballet, played and recorded with consummate refinement, the quality of innocence shines out. The temptation for any conductor is to make the music exotically sensuous in too sophisticated a way, but Previn retains a freshness apt for nursery music. The recording is superb, with the Philips engineers presenting a texture of luminous clarity.

More than usual, Tortelier's performance has a balletic feel to it, bringing out the affinities with *Daphnis et Chloé.* The exotic orchestration associated with *Laideronnette, Empress of the Pagodas* glitters vividly, yet the lovely closing *Jardin féerique*, opening serenely, moves to a joyous climax.

Saraste directs a most sensitive, beautifully scaled and well-paced reading of the complete *Mother Goose* ballet. He catches its fantasy and tenderness as well as its glitter; and the Scottish players produce lovely sounds in the gentler music, yet can flare up vividly when the composer calls for virtuosity. The *Pavane* is serenely spacious and with a very fine horn solo. Generously coupled with the youthful Bizet *Symphony* and given warmly atmospheric recording, this makes an excellent bargain issue. The accompanying notes, however, are totally inadequate.

The Giulini Los Angeles performance conveys much of the sultry atmosphere of the *Rapsodie espagnole.* Indeed some details, such as the sensuous string responses to the cor anglais tune in the *Feria*, have not been so tenderly caressed since the intoxicating Reiner version. The *Ma Mère l'Oye* suite is also sensitively done; though it is cooler, it is still beautiful.

In Ravel, as in the Dvořák symphony with which it is coupled, Giulini's spacious approach goes with beautiful playing from the Concertgebouw, but the tension is less keen. Ravel, even at his most sensuous, really needs a sharper manner, yet Giulini is masterly in the apotheosis of the final movement, *Le jardin féerique*, enfolding us in sensuous sounds. The whole disc remains a very personal offering.

Ma Mère l'Oye (ballet): *suite.*
(B) *** CfP CD-CFP 4086; *TC-CFP 4086.* SNO, Gibson – BIZET: *Jeux d'enfants;* SAINT-SAËNS; *Carnival.* ***
(M) ** EMI Dig. CD-EMX 2165; *TC-EMX 2165.* LPO, Sian Edwards – BRITTEN: *Young person's guide* ***; PROKOFIEV: *Peter and the wolf.* **(*)

Gibson is highly persuasive, shaping the music with obvious affection and a feeling for both the innocent spirit and the radiant textures of Ravel's beautiful score. The orchestral playing is excellent and the recording very good, if perhaps wanting a little in atmosphere. But the CD transfer is well managed and, with excellent couplings, this is very recommendable.

Warm and beautiful orchestral playing from the LPO under Sian Edwards, but Ravel's magical score does not yield all its secrets here; its sense of gentle, innocent ecstasy is missing. Sian Edwards will present this music more perceptively when she has lived with it a little longer. Excellent recording.

Ouverture de féerie; (i) *Shéhérazade*
** Chan. Dig. CHAN 8914; *ABTD 1518* [id.]. (i) Linda Finnie, Ulster O, Yan Pascal Tortelier – DEBUSSY: *Nocturnes.* **

A good account of *Shéhérazade* from Linda Finnie, though it must be admitted that in neither vocal beauty nor interpretative insight does it challenge the Ewing (EMI) or the earlier classic accounts by Danco or Crespin. The *Ouverture de féerie* is very good – but again not superior to current rivals. At 55 minutes length and at full price this is one of the least indispensable of what is an often distinguished series.

Le tombeau de Couperin; Valses nobles et sentimentales.
*** Chan. Dig. CHAN 8756; *ABTD 1395* [id.]. Ulster O, Yan Pascal Tortelier – DEBUSSY: *Children's corner* etc. ***

Yan Pascal Tortelier's accounts of *Le tombeau de Couperin* and the *Valses nobles* have plenty of appeal. They come in harness with two Debussy pieces, also originally composed for the piano though transcribed by other hands; whether you want these performances rather than the many alternatives now on the market will doubtless depend on the matter of coupling. The Ulster Orchestra certainly play very well for Tortelier and the recording is every bit as good as predecessors in this series.

Valses nobles et sentimentales.
(*) DG Dig. 429 785-2; *429 785-4* [id.]. NYPO, Sinopoli – MUSSORGSKY: *Night* etc. *

With Sinopoli Ravel's *Valses nobles et sentimentales* is perhaps a shade too idiosyncratic, even though it is played superbly by the New York Philharmonic. At the beginning Sinopoli is attractively genial in his rhythmic impetus, rather than seeking to overwhelm the listener; but in the last three sections he takes Ravel's markings to an extreme, with the music almost coming to a halt in the middle of the *Moins vif.* Nevertheless the delicacy of the playing and the sensuous radiance of the texture remind one of *Ma Mère l'Oye*, and it is all too easy to be seduced.

Tzigane (for violin and orchestra).
*** DG Dig. 423 063-2; *423 063-4* [id.]. Itzhak Perlman, NYPO, Mehta – CHAUSSON: *Poème;* SAINT-SAËNS: *Havanaise* etc.; SARASATE: *Carmen fantasy.* ***

Perlman's later, digital version is very fine and the recording is obviously modern. The DG collection includes a highly desirable extra Sarasate item. But the earlier EMI (deleted) performance has just that bit more charisma.

CHAMBER MUSIC

(i) *Introduction and allegro;* (ii–iv) *Piano trio;* (v) *Pièce en forme de habanera;* (iii; iv) *Sonata for violin and cello;* (vi) *String quartet in F;* (vii; viii) *Tzigane;* (iii; ii) *Violin sonata;* (ix; viii) *Ma Mère l'Oye* (for piano, 4 hands); (x; xi) *3 Chansons madécasses;* (x; xii) *3 Poèmes de Stéphane Mallarmé.*
(B) ** EMI CZS7 67217-2 (2)[id.]. (i) Challen & Ens.; (ii) Pludermacher, (iii) Jarry, (iv) Tournus; (v) Paul Tortelier, Iwaski; (vi) Parrenin Qt; (vii) Ferras, (viii) Barbizet; (ix) François; (x) Benoit, (xi) & Ens.; (xii) O de Paris Soloists, Jacquillat.

These performances emanate from the French catalogues of the 1970s and, even if few of the performances would be a first choice, in only one instance do they fall below a certain level of accomplishment. Indeed at nearly 80 minutes on each CD (and two CDs for the price of one) they represent very good value for money. The Parrenin's account of the *String quartet* is the best known of the performances and among the finest things here. But the performances of the *Piano trio* by Gérard Jarry, Georges Pludermacher and Michel Tornus and the Jarry/Pludermacher *Violin sonata* are also thoroughly enjoyable. The *Mallarmé Songs* are really far better suited to a soprano and Jean-Christophe Benoit does not convince here or in the *Chansons madécasses*, though he has undoubted taste. The 1965 *Introduction and allegro* is more than acceptable, though it is not superior to the famous (and slightly earlier) Melos set on Decca. The only failure is an insensitive and unimaginative *Ma Mère l'Oye* by Samson François and Pierre Barbizet. There are enough good things here to make it recommendable, particularly at the price.

Introduction and allegro for harp, flute, clarinet and string quartet.
❀ (M) *** Decca 421 154-2; *421 154-4*. Osian Ellis, Melos Ens. – DEBUSSY; FRANCK: *Sonatas.* *** ❀

The beauty and subtlety of Ravel's sublime septet are marvellously realized by this 1962 Melos account. The interpretation has great delicacy of feeling, and the recording hardly shows its age at all.

Piano trio in A min.
*** Ph. Dig. 411 141-2 [id.]. Beaux Arts Trio – CHAUSSON: *Piano trio.* ***
(M) *** Pickwick Dig. MCD 41; *MCC 41* [id.]. Solomon Trio – DEBUSSY; FAURÉ: *Piano trios.****

*** Chan. Dig. CHAN 8458; *ABTD 1170* [id.]. Borodin Trio – DEBUSSY: *Violin and Cello sonatas.* ***
**(*) Denon Dig. CO 72508 [id.]. Rouvier, Kantorow, Müller – DEBUSSY; FAURÉ: *Trios.* **(*)
**(*) Collins Dig. 1040-2 [id.]. Trio Zingara – SHOSTAKOVICH: *Piano trio No. 2.* **(*)
**(*) Decca Dig. 425 860-2; *425 860-4* [id.]. Thibaudet, Bell, Isserlis – CHAUSSON: *Concert.* **(*)

The most recent Beaux Arts account of the Ravel *Trio* is little short of inspired and is even finer than their earlier record of the late 1960s. The recording, too, is of high quality, even if the piano is rather forward.

The Solomon Trio, formed in 1990, comprises Lionel Friend, Timothy Hugh and Yonty Solomon. Their account of the Ravel is very fine indeed and has the advantage of an excellently balanced recording. While they do not displace the Beaux Arts Trio, theirs is thoroughly recommendable and is certainly among the best versions now before the public. It has fine couplings, too, and a price advantage.

The Borodin Trio pair the Ravel with the two Debussy *Sonatas*, which makes a logical and attractive coupling. They are excellently recorded and their playing has great warmth and is full of colour. Some may find them too hot-blooded by the side of the Beaux Arts, whose version is wonderfully poised and cultivated.

Jean-Jacques Kantorow, Philippe Müller and Jacques Rouvier are a highly accomplished team and are excellently recorded; their account gives much pleasure – even though the usually impressive Jacques Rouvier is not as responsive as Menahem Pressler in this work.

A fine account of the *Piano trio* comes from a young group making their début recording. The Trio Zingara was formed in 1978 and has won much acclaim and a number of prizes. Their pianist, Annette Cole, produces some beautiful *pianissimo* tone in the first movement, and the playing of all three is sensitive. If they do not match the Beaux Arts in subtlety and refinement, theirs is a thoroughly enjoyable and impressive performance, and it is recorded with great presence and clarity.

Joshua Bell, Jean-Yves Thibaudet and Steven Isserlis are not a permanent trio like the Beaux Arts (Philips), the Borodin (Chandos) or the Trio Zingara (Collins), but nevertheless they show keen responsiveness in their account of the Ravel. These gifted players are second to none in sensitivity, and both Bell and Isserlis play with great tonal finesse and artistry. They are recorded with great clarity and presence, and those wanting this particular coupling will find much to admire.

(i) *Piano trio in A min.;* (ii) *Sonatine: Menuet.*
(M) (**) BMG/RCA mono GD 87871; *GK 87871* [7871-2-RG; *7871-4-RG*]. Heifetz; (i) Rubinstein, Piatigorsky; (ii) Bay – DEBUSSY: *Sonata* etc. (**); RESPIGHI: *Sonata* (***); MARTINŮ: *Duo.* ***

It goes without saying that the million-dollar trio (Heifetz, Rubinstein and Piatigorsky), recorded in 1950, play the Ravel like a million dollars, yet its inspired opening is curiously lacking in magic and atmosphere. Peerless though the playing is, this is not a version to which one would often be tempted to return when the Beaux Arts is to hand.

String quartet in F.
*** EMI Dig. CDC7 543462 [id.]; *EL 7543462.* Britten Qt – VAUGHAN WILLIAMS: *On Wenlock Edge; Quartet.* ***
(M) *** Ph. 420 894-2. Italian Qt – DEBUSSY: *Quartet.* ***
(M) *** DG 435 589-2 [id.]. LaSalle Qt – DEBUSSY: *Quartet.* ***
(B) **(*) Hung. White Label HRC 122 [id.]. Bartók Qt – DEBUSSY: *Quartet* **(*); DVOŘÁK: *Quartet No. 12.* ***
(M) **(*) Pickwick Dig. MCD 17; *MCC 17* [id.]. New World Qt – DEBUSSY: *Quartet* **(*); DUTILLEUX: *Ainsi la nuit.* ***
**(*) Denon Dig. C37 7830 [id.]. Nuovo Qt – DEBUSSY: *Quartet.* **(*)
** Virgin Dig. VC 791077-2 [id.]. Borodin Qt – DEBUSSY: *Quartet.* **(*)
(M) ** Decca 425 424-2; *425 424-4.* Carmirelli Qt – FRANCK: *Quartet.* **(*)
(BB) ** Virgin Dig. VJ7 91569-2 [id.]. Borodin Qt – DEBUSSY: *Quartet.* **(*)
** Decca Dig. 430 434-2 [id.]. Ysaÿe Qt – DEBUSSY: *Quartet.*

String quartet in F; (i) *Introduction & allegro for harp, flute, clarinet and string quartet.*
(BB) *** Naxos Dig. 8.550249 [id.]. Kodály Qt; (i) with Maros, Gyöngyössy, Kovács – DEBUSSY: *Quartet.* **(*)

The Britten Quartet, one of the most accomplished of the younger generation, provides an outstanding version of the Ravel *Quartet* in a beautifully judged performance very realistically recorded as an unusual coupling for the two Vaughan Williams works for string quartet, written after study with Ravel.

For many years the Italian Quartet held pride of place in this coupling. Their playing is perfect in ensemble, attack and beauty of tone, and their performance remains highly recommendable, one of the most satisfying chamber-music records in the catalogue.

There is little to choose between the DG LaSalle performance and the Italian Quartet on Philips. If the latter have perhaps the greater immediacy and sense of vitality, the former create a superb feeling of atmosphere and bring great freshness and delicacy of feeling to this score. The fine 1971 DG recording has been admirably and naturally transferred to CD: it has body and transparency but no edginess.

The Naxos version can more than hold its own against a number of discs offered at premium price, and those coming fresh to this repertoire are unlikely to be disappointed. Artistically and technically this is a satisfying performance which has the feel of real live music-making. The *Introduction and allegro* is not as magical or as atmospheric as that of the Melos Ensemble from the 1960s, nor is it as well balanced (the players, save for the harp, are a bit forward), but it is still thoroughly enjoyable.

The Bartók Quartet on Hungaroton's cheapest label also give a sympathetic and well-characterized reading, only marginally less perceptive than the Italian version; and they too are well recorded. Moreover they offer an additional work. Those collectors looking for a bargain will not be disappointed here.

The Harvard-based New World Quartet give an admirable account of the Ravel, a shade overprojected at times, and the leader's expressive rubato and that of the violist may not be to all tastes. Well recorded though it is, it does not displace existing recommendations though it offers the inducement of a Dutilleux rarity.

Denon's version by the Nuovo Quartet is a sympathetic and likeable account, by no means as immaculate as the finest now before the public, but for the most part these players make a beautiful sound and show considerable feeling and sensitivity. There is an agreeably unforced quality in the way they let the music unfold. Very enjoyable – despite less than absolutely spot-on intonation – and very well recorded.

It is tempting to pass over the Carmirelli, which is offered as a bonus to the Franck *Quartet.* But this would be unjust, for their playing, if not as distinguished as that of their finest competitors, is still very good, and the recording is perfectly acceptable, even though it dates from the mid-1950s. In its CD transfer it is smoother than the Franck coupling.

The Borodin Quartet make the most sumptuous sound; tonally this group must be in a class of its own. They not only play but seem to think as one person, and their unanimity of ensemble and perfection in matching each other in matters of phrasing is wonderful. But despite the ravishing sounds they produce, their Ravel is not unalloyed pleasure. They pull things out of shape, and they adopt a totally different tempo for the second group of the first movement, which proves most disturbing. They are beautifully recorded but their approach is too mannered to give complete artistic satisfaction. The middle section of the scherzo is disfigured by artificiality and a narcissism one had never associated with this ensemble.

The youthful Ysaÿe Quartet play the *F major Quartet* with evident *tendresse* and a keen feeling for line. They do not however displace top recommendations unless you like to sit in front of or among the players. The Decca balance is too close to allow the work's atmosphere and the players' artistry to register to best effect.

Tzigane.
**(*) DG Dig. 429 729-2 [id.]. Gil Shaham, Gerhard Oppitz – FRANCK: *Sonata;* SAINT-SAËNS: *Violin sonata No. 1.* **(*)

Gil Shaham gives an impressive account of Ravel's celebrated display piece, coupling it with the delightful Saint-Saëns *D minor Sonata* and a fine version of the Franck *Sonata.*

Violin sonata in G.
*** Collins Dig. 1112-2; *1112-4* [id.]. Lorraine McAslan, John Blakely – DEBUSSY; SAINT-SAËNS: *Sonatas.* ***
*** Ph. Dig. 426 254-2. Viktoria Mullova, Bruno Canino – PROKOFIEV: *Sonata* **; STRAVINSKY: *Divertimento.* ***
*** DG Dig. 415 683-2 [id.]. Shlomo Mintz, Yefim Bronman – DEBUSSY; FRANCK: *Sonatas.* ***

Lorraine McAslan is a gifted young player who made a strong impression with her recent record of the Britten *Violin concerto.* She possesses a strong musical personality as well as excellent technique and a wide command of colour and dynamics. She is splendidly partnered by John Blakely, and their account of the *Sonata* is as characterful as any in the catalogue.

Mullova and Canino give a beguiling performance of the Ravel *Violin sonata*, one of the finest to have appeared for many years. It is played with diamond-like precision and great character. The Philips recording is marvellous. However, the couplings are not as successful as McAslan's.

Shlomo Mintz and Yefim Bronman's account of the Ravel comes in harness with Franck and Debussy. Impeccable, highly polished playing, even if it is not so completely inside Ravel's world in the slow movement. The glorious sounds both artists produce are a source of unfailing delight. They are beautifully recorded too.

PIANO DUET

Boléro; Introduction and allegro; Ma Mère l'Oye; Rapsodie espagnole; La valse.
❀ *** Chan. Dig. CHAN 8905; *ABTD 1514* [id.]. Louis Lortie and Helène Mercier.

Louis Lortie has already made a solo Ravel record for Chandos (see below) and has given an impressive account of himself in the two *Concertos*; but his recital for piano (four hands and two pianos) with his Canadian partner, Helène Mercier, is quite magical. As with his solo recital, the acoustic is that of The Maltings, Snape, and the result is quite outstanding sonically: you feel that you have only to stretch out and you can touch the instruments. The transcriptions are, of course, Ravel's own – he was an absolute master of this art – and, given the quality of the playing, one hardly misses the orchestra, whether it be in the *Feria* of the *Rapsodie espagnole* or the mysterious half-colours of the *Prélude á la nuit*; these artists command an exceptionally wide range of colour and dynamic nuance. Probably not all listeners will relish the idea of the *Introduction and allegro* on two pianos, yet Ravel's transcription, particularly in their hands, is stunningly effective, as – even more surprisingly – is *Boléro*, which is omitted in the much-admired disc of Stephen Coombs and Christopher Scott.

Ma Mère L'Oye.
*** Ph. Dig. 420 159-2 [id.]. Katia and Marielle Labèque – FAURÉ: *Dolly;* BIZET: *Jeux d'enfants.* ***

The Labèque sisters give an altogether delightful performance of Ravel's magical score, which he later orchestrated and expanded. The recording could not be more realistic and present.

SOLO PIANO MUSIC

À la manière de Borodine; À la manière de Chabrier; Gaspard de la nuit; Jeux d'eau; Menuet antique; Menuet sur le nom de Haydn; Miroirs; Pavane pour une infante défunte; Prélude; Sérénade grotesque; Sonatine; Le tombeau de Couperin; Valses nobles et sentimentales.
*** CRD Dig. CRD 3383/4 [id.]. Paul Crossley.

Paul Crossley's accounts of all these works are beautifully fashioned and can hold their own with the available competition. He is aristocratic, with an admirable feeling for tone-colour and line, and rarely mannered (the end of *Jeux d'eau* is an exception). His version of *Le tombeau de Couperin* has a classical refinement and delicacy that are refreshing. The CRD recording is very good indeed, and this fine set deserves the warmest welcome.

À la manière de Borodine; À la manière de Chabrier; Gaspard de la nuit; Menuet antique; Menuet sur le nom de Haydn; Miroirs; Prélude; Sonatine.
*** Chan. Dig. CHAN 8647; *ABTD 1333* [id.]. Louis Lortie.

The Canadian pianist, Louis Lortie, gives an impressive account of himself in *Gaspard de la nuit.* His account of *Le gibet* is chilling and atmospheric, and in the *Miroirs* he produces some ravishing pianism. His rhythmic articulation in the *Alborada* is marvellously clean, and throughout the whole set his playing is elegant, virile and sensitive. The recording is made in

The Maltings, Snape, and the closely observed sound perhaps robs *Ondine* and *Scarbo* of some of their sense of enchantment and eeriness respectively, but a lower-than-usual playback level helps restore a little of their mystery. This is a distinguished and stimulating recital.

À la manière de Borodine; À la manière de Chabrier; Menuet antique; Prélude; Le tombeau de Couperin; Valses nobles et sentimentales.
**(*) Nimbus NI 5011 [id.]. Vlado Perlemuter.

Gaspard de la nuit; Jeux d'eau; Miroirs; Pavane.
**(*) Nimbus NI 5005 [id.]. Vlado Perlemuter.

Though Perlemuter's technical command is not as complete as it had been, he gives delightful, deeply sympathetic readings; the sense of spontaneity is a joy. There may be Ravel recordings which bring more dazzling virtuoso displays, but none more persuasive. Nimbus's preference for an ample room acoustic makes the result naturally atmospheric on CD, with light reverberation presenting a halo of sound.

Gaspard de la nuit.
*** DG Dig. 413 363-2 [id.]. Pogorelich – PROKOFIEV: *Sonata No. 6.* *** ❀

Pogorelich's *Gaspard* is out of the ordinary. In *Le gibet*, there is self-conscious striving after effect. We are made conscious of the pianist's refinement of tone and colour first, and Ravel's poetic vision afterwards. But for all that, this is piano playing of astonishing quality. The control of colour and nuance in *Scarbo* is dazzling and its eruptive cascades of energy and dramatic fire have one sitting on the edge of one's seat. The coupling, Prokofiev's *Sixth Sonata*, is quite simply stunning.

VOCAL MUSIC

(i) *Chansons madécasses;* (ii) *Don Quichotte à Dulcinée; 5 mélodies populaires grecques;* (iii) *3 poèmes de Stéphane Mallarmé;* (iv) *Shéhérazade.*
*** Sony Dig. MK 39023 [id.]. (i) Norman, Ens. InterContemporain; (ii) José van Dam; (iii) Jill Gomez; (iv) Heather Harper; BBC SO, Boulez.

With four characterful and strongly contrasted soloists, Boulez's collection of Ravel's songs with orchestra (including arrangements) makes a delightful disc. The *Don Quichotte* and the *Greek popular songs* (both with José van Dam as soloist) are rarely heard in this orchestral form. Van Dam may not be ideally relaxed, but the dark, firm voice is very impressive. Excellent sound, with translations provided.

Chansons madécasses; 3 Poèmes de Stéphane Mallarmé.
❀ (M) *** Decca 425 948-2 [id.]. Dame Janet Baker, Melos Ens. (with *Recital of French songs* *** ❀).

Superb singing from Dame Janet, her voice at its most radiant in 1966, and a wonderfully sympathetic accompaniment from members of the Melos group, matched by a recording which spins a lovely web of atmospheric sound.

2 Mélodies hébraïques; 3 Poèmes de Stéphane Mallarmé; Shéhérazade.
(M) (***) Decca mono 425 988-2 [id.]. Suzanne Danco, SRO, Ansermet – BERLIOZ: *Les nuits d'été.* (***)

The great Belgian-born soprano recorded Ravel's *Shéhérazade* with Ansermet and the Suisse Romande Orchestra in the days of 78s, but her second and hardly less magical recording, made towards the end of 1954, is rightly chosen, for Decca engineering had made remarkable advances in the intervening years. Danco evokes a sense of enchantment in the opening song, *Asie*, and the other-worldly quality of sound she produces is ideal for *La flûte enchantée.* Her performance of the three Mallarmé *Songs* has probably never been surpassed in sheer purity of sound. Ansermet's orchestra was in good shape at this time, and the mono sound is impressively detailed and atmospheric.

Shéhérazade (song-cycle).
*** Decca 417 813-2 [id.]. Régine Crespin, SRO, Ansermet (with *Recital of French songs* ***).

Crespin is right inside these songs and Ravel's magically sensuous music emerges with striking spontaneity. She is superbly supported by Ansermet who, aided by the Decca engineers, weaves a fine tonal web round the voice. As in the Berlioz *Nuits d'été* (the original coupling, which is included here within a fuller recital, offering also Poulenc and Debussy) her style has distinct echoes of the opera house; but the richness of the singer's tone does not detract from the delicate languor of *The enchanted flute*, in which the slave-girl listens to the distant sound of her lover's flute playing while her master sleeps.

OPERA

L'Enfant et les sortilèges (complete).
*** DG 423 718-2 [id.]. Ogéas, Collard, Berbié, Gilma, RTF Ch. & Boys' Ch., RTF Nat. O, Maazel.

L'Heure espagnole (complete).
*** DG 423 719-2 [id.]. Berbié, Sénéchal, Giraudeau, Bacquier, Van Dam, Paris Op. O, Maazel.

Maazel's recordings of the two Ravel one-Act operas were made in the early 1960s and, though the solo voices in the former are balanced too close, the sound is vivid and the performances are splendidly stylish. Neo-classical crispness of articulation goes with refined textures that convey the tender poetry of the one piece, the ripe humour of the other. The CD remastering has been very successful and both performances are given striking presence, without loss of essential atmosphere. Full librettos are included. However, these records are surely now due for mid-price reissue.

Rawsthorne, Alan (1905–71)

Clarinet concerto.
*** Hyp. CDA 66031; *KA 66031* [id.]. Thea King, NW CO of Seattle, Alun Francis – COOKE: *Concerto;* JACOB: *Mini-concerto.* ***

Though the *Clarinet concerto* is an early work of Rawsthorne's it already establishes the authentic flavour of his writing with a certain gritty and angular quality masking the obvious depth of feeling behind. You feel he is about to unleash himself into a grand Waltonian melody, but he never actually does. That constraint makes for musical strength, the more obviously so in a performance as persuasive as this from soloist and orchestra alike. And even Rawsthorne relaxes in the brilliant finale. Excellent 1982 analogue recording, expertly trasnferred to retain the recording's full ambient effect.

Overture: Street corner.
(M) (***) EMI mono CDH7 63911-2 [id.]. Philh. O, Lambert – LAMBERT: *Horoscope* etc.; GORDON: *Rake's progress.* (***)

Street corner, following very much the mood of Walton's comedy overtures, is among Rawsthorne's most colourful and appealing works. It makes a welcome fill-up to the Lambert pieces in this première recording, made in 1946 and sounding astonishingly vivid.

Rebel, Jean-Féry (1661–1747)

Les Élémens (ballet).
*** O-L 421 656-2 [id.]. AAM, Hogwood – DESTOUCHES: *Suite.* ***

Rebel's ballet on the elements emerging out of Chaos can startle even twentieth-century listeners with the massive discord illustrating 'chaos' at the start. The sequence of dances, beautifully performed on original instruments by Hogwood's Academy, is consistently sharp and refreshing, helping to revive an undeservedly neglected name.

Reger, Max (1873–1916)

Ballet suite; Variations on a theme of Hiller, Op. 100.
*** Orfeo C 090841 [id.]. Bav. RSO, C. Davis.

The *Hiller variations* (1907) is one of Reger's greatest works, full of wit, resource and, above all, delicacy. It culminates, as do so many Reger pieces, in a double fugue. The *Ballet suite* is a delightful piece, scored with great clarity and played, as is the *Hiller variations*, with charm and commitment. Sir Colin Davis emerges as a thoroughly *echt*-Reger conductor and the Bavarian orchestra is in excellent form. The recording is first rate, though we have one minor quibble: the individual variations are not indexed.

Piano concerto in F min., Op. 114.
(M) ** Sony MPK 46452 [id.]. Rudolf Serkin, Phd. O, Ormandy - PROKOFIEV: *Piano concerto No. 4*. (***)

Reger's *Piano concerto* is a remarkable and powerful composition. Its dark opening momentarily suggests Shostakovich! No one but Reger, however, could have conceived the rugged, Brahmsian piano writing. The slow movement is a contemplative, rapt piece that touches genuine depths. Less successful, perhaps, is the rhetorical finale. Serkin gives a magisterial performance and is well supported by the Philadelphia Orchestra under Ormandy; this record has considerable documentary value, even though the early-1960s sound is not very inviting and is even rather harsh in its CD transfer (the outstanding mono coupling is much more agreeable!).

Lyrisches Andante.
*** Claves Dig. D 8502 [id.]. Deutsche Kammerakademie Neuss, Goritzki – SCHOECK: *Cello concerto*. ***

Reger's *Lyrisches Andante* is a short, songful and gentle piece for strings; it should make many friends for this much misunderstood composer, particularly in this dedicated performance.

(i) *Symphonic prologue to a tragedy, Op. 108;* (i) *2 Romances for violin and orchestra, Op. 50.*
**(*) Schwann CD311 076. (i) Berlin RSO, Albrecht; (ii) with Maile; cond. Lajovic.

The tragedy in question is Sophocles' *Oedipus Rex*, and Reger's *Symphonic prologue* is one of his very finest and most powerful works. Inspiration runs consistently high and Reger's score, which comes from the period of Strauss's *Elektra* and Mahler's *Das Lied von der Erde*, deserves far more exposure. The violin *Romances* are beautiful pieces and are very well played by Hans Maile and the Berlin Radio Orchestra. Strongly recommended for the sake of the marvellous music; however, it must be said that the 1982 recording is serviceable rather than distinguished (textures at climaxes are inclined to be opaque).

4 Tone poems after Böcklin, Op. 128; Variations on a theme by Hiller, Op. 100.
*** Chan. Dig. CHAN 8794; *ABTD 1426* [id.]. Concg. O, Järvi.

The Swiss symbolist Arnold Böcklin (1827–1901) is best remembered by music-lovers for his painting, *Der Toteninsel* (*The Isle of the dead*), which inspired Rachmaninov's tone-poem as well as the third of Reger's four *Tone poems* of 1913. Those who still think of Reger's music as densely contrapuntal and turgidly scored will be amazed by the delicacy and refinement of his orchestration. Textures in *Der geigende Eremit* (*Hermit playing the violin*) are wonderfully transparent, and *Im spiel der Wellen* has something of the sparkle of the *Jeu de vagues* movement of *La Mer* photographed in sepia; while the *Isle of the dead* is a lovely and often very touching piece. The *Hiller variations* are gloriously inventive, full of that blend of confidence, delicacy of feeling and imagination that characterizes Reger at his best. It is beautifully recorded and Neeme Järvi's performance has the combination of sensitivity and virtuosity that this composer needs.

Variations and fugue on a theme by Mozart, Op. 132.
❀ *** Ph. Dig. 422 347-2 [id.]. Bav. RSO, C. Davis – HINDEMITH: *Symphonic metamorphosis*. ***

It is little short of amazing that Reger's *Variations and fugue on a theme by Mozart* is so little heard in the concert hall, for it deserves great popularity. Sir Colin Davis's account with the Bavarian Radio Symphony Orchestra is the best since Karl Boehm's pioneering pre-war 78s. The playing has great subtlety and the strings produce a particularly cultured sound (though one could reasonably ask how it could be otherwise with this wonderful orchestra). The whole performance has a radiance and glow that does full justice to this masterpiece, which is not only scored with great delicacy but has wit and tenderness in equal measure. The Philips recording is state of the art. Recommended with enthusiasm.

Chorale fantasia on Straf' mich nicht in deinem Zorn, Op. 40/2; Chorale preludes, Op. 67/4, 13, 28, 40, 48; Introduction, passacaglia and fugue in E min., Op. 127.
*** Hyp. Dig. CDA 66223; *KA 66223* [id.]. Graham Barber (organ of Limburg Cathedral).

The *Introduction, passacaglia and fugue*, which takes all of 28 minutes, is bold in conception and vision and is played superbly on this excellently engineered Hyperion disc by Graham Barber at the Klais organ of Limburg Cathedral, an instrument ideally suited to this repertoire. The five *Chorale preludes* give him an admirable opportunity to show the variety and richness of tone-colours of the instrument. The Hyperion recording captures the quality of the king of beasts marvellously on CD.

PIANO MUSIC

Variations and fugue on a theme of Bach, Op. 81.
(BB) **(*) Naxos Dig. 8.550469 [id.]. Wolf Harden – SCHUMANN: *Humoreske.* **(*)

Wolf Harden is a highly talented German pianist in his late twenties. He proves a sensitive and imaginative interpreter of the Schumann *Humoreske*, and his account of the Reger *Variations and fugue on a theme of Bach*, Op. 81, is every bit as fine. Unfortunately there is far less air or sense of space round the piano here and the instrument sounds much drier than in the Schumann. Yet such is the compelling quality of his playing (and the rarity of this remarkable piece on record) that it would be curmudgeonly to withhold a recommendation on this count.

Variations and fugue on a theme by Telemann, Op. 134.
(M) *** Decca 417 791-2. Jorge Bolet – BRAHMS: *Handel variations.* ***

Reger's *Telemann variations*, his last major work for solo piano, makes a challenging and compelling coupling for Bolet's superb account of Brahms's *Handel* set. The virtuosity is phenomenal, not least in the fugue at the end, which was once considered unplayable. Bolet breasts all difficulties with commanding strength. A thrilling experience with first-rate remastered recording.

VOCAL MUSIC

8 Geistliche Gesänge, Op. 138.
*** Koch Bayer Dig. BR 100084. Frankfurt Vocal Ens., Ralf Otto – MARTIN: *Mass for double choir.* ***

These eight spiritual songs are simple homophonic settings of various sacred texts. Only one of them takes longer than three minutes, but all of them are of a substance that belies their length and have a gravely expressive beauty that is conveyed well by this excellent Frankfurt choir, who also offer an outstanding performance of Frank Martin's *Mass for double choir.* Excellent recording.

Reich, Steve (born 1936)

8 Lines.
*** Virgin Dig. VC7 91168-2; *VC7 91168-4* [id.]. LCO, Warren-Green – ADAMS: *Shaker loops* *** ❀; GLASS: *Company* etc. ***; HEATH: *Frontier.* ***

Steve Reich's *8 Lines* (originally called an *Octet*) is minimalism in its most basic form, and, although the writing is full of good-humoured vitality, the listener without a score could be forgiven for sometimes thinking that 'the needle had got stuck in the groove'. The performance is expert and the recording seems admirable.

Tehillim.
** ECM 827 411-2 [id.]. Steve Reich & musicians, George Manahan.

Steve Reich is listed among the percussion players in *Tehillim*, with Manahan conducting, a work completed in 1982. The central focus, in this Hebrew setting of Psalms 19 and 18 (in that order), is on the vocal ensemble of four voices, a high soprano, two lyric sopranos and an alto. The minimalist technique is the same as in the purely instrumental works, but the result – with clapping and drumming punctuating the singing – has an element of charm rare in minimalist music. With jazzy syncopations and Cuban rhythms, the first of the two movements in this half-hour-long work, setting verses from Psalm 18, sounds like Bernstein's *Chichester Psalms* caught in a groove. The second starts slowly but speeds up for the verses of praise to the Lord and the final *Hallelujahs.* Clear, forward, analogue recording.

Variations for winds, strings & keyboard.
*** Ph. 412 214-2 [id.]. San Francisco SO, De Waart – ADAMS: *Shaker loops.* ***

Reich's *Variations*, written for the San Francisco orchestra in 1980, marked a new departure in the writing of this leading minimalist, using a large orchestral rather than a small chamber scale. The repetitions and ostinatos, which gradually get out of phase, are most skilfully used to produce a hypnotic kind of poetry, soothing rather than compelling.

Reicha, Antonín (1770–1836)

Oboe quintet in F, Op. 107.
*** Hyp. CDA 66143 [id.]. Sarah Francis, Allegri Qt – CRUSELL: *Divertimento;* R. KREUTZER: *Grand quintet.* ***

Antonín Reicha's *F major Quintet* is spectacularly unmemorable but always amiable. The present performance is of high quality and very well recorded.

Wind quintets: in E flat, Op. 88/2; in F, Op. 91/3.
*** Hyp. Dig. CDA 66268 [id.]. Academia Wind Quintet of Prague.

Czech wind playing in Czech wind music has a deservedly high entertainment rating and the present performances are no exception. The music itself has great charm and geniality; it is ingenuous yet cultivated, with some delightful, smiling writing for the bassoon. The players are clearly enjoying themselves, yet they play and blend expertly. The sound too is admirable.

Reindl, Constantin (1738–99)

Sinfonia concertante in D for violin, two flutes, two oboes, bassoon, two horns and strings.
*** Novalis Dig. 150 031-2 [id.]. ECO, Griffiths – STALDER: *Symphony No. 5; Flute concerto.* ***

The *Sinfonia concertante* was written in about 1789 at the time of the outbreak of the French Revolution and, though there is nothing revolutionary about it, it is not just bland rococo music; it is fresh and inventive, and the finale has a most attractive (and obstinately memorable) main theme. A delightful performance by the ECO under Howard Griffiths and an excellent, natural and well-balanced recording.

Respighi, Ottorino (1879–1936)

(i) *Adagio con variazioni* (for cello and orchestra); *The Birds; 3 Botticelli pictures;* (ii) *Il tramonto.*
*** Chan. Dig. CHAN 8913; *ABTD 1517* [id.]. (i) Wallfisch; (ii) Linda Finnie; Bournemouth Sinf., Vásáry.

Respighi's *Adagio* is a transcription of an earlier piece for cello and piano, and gains from the added colour. It is pleasant, but not distinctive, though Raphael Wallfisch is very persuasive. *The Birds* is an enchanting aviary of orchestral colour and the lovely playing and luminous recording gives much pleasure. Dorati's Mercury version is not entirely upstaged, but the softer focus of the Chandos digital sound brings added warmth and atmosphere. The lambent Italianite evocation of the *Three Botticelli pictures* is also aurally bewitching, and the orchestral playing again has much allure, with the sound most vivid. But what caps the success of this Chandos Respighi anthology is Linda Finnie's ravishing account of *Il tramonto*, even finer than Carol Madalin's on Hyperion – see below. Her vocal timbre is fresh yet has an element of gentle voluptuousness just right for this ecstatic setting of Shelley. Vásáry, too, finds much magic in the orchestral setting and he shades textures with great subtlety. Again very responsive orchestral playing and the recording, made in the suitably warm acoustics of Wessex Hall at Poole Arts Centre is in the demonstration class throughout this CD.

Ancient airs and dances: suites Nos. 1–3; The Birds (suite).
❀ *** Vanguard/Omega Dig. 08.1007.71. Australian CO, Christopher Gee.

Ancient airs and dances: suites 1–3; 3 Botticelli pictures (Trittico Botticelliano).
*** Telarc Dig. CD 80309 [id.]. Lausanne CO, Jesús López-Cobos.

The reissue of Dorati's Mercury version (uncompetitive without a fill-up – 434 304-2) is upstaged by Christopher Gee's treasurable Omega coupling, now reissued on the parent Vanguard label, at slightly under premium price. The performance of *The Birds* is a complete delight, opening and closing vigorously, yet providing the most refined portraits of the dove, nightingale and cuckoo, with particularly lovely oboe playing in *The dove*. The opening of the first suite of *Ancient airs and dances* has a comparable grace and delicacy of feeling; throughout, Lyndon Gee's response to Respighi's imaginative orchestration is wonderfully fresh, with the oboe (again) and bassoon distinguishing themselves among the many fine wind solos. The strings produce lovely translucent textures at the beginning of the *Third suite*; yet when a robust approach is called for, the players provide it admirably. The bitter-sweet combination of nobility and melancholy that often haunts this music, especially in the *Second suite*, is not missed, and the espressivo playing has an affecting eloquence. The recording, made at the ABC Studio at Chatsworth, Sydney, is in the demonstration class.

Opening brightly and comparatively robustly the Lausanne performance yet has both warmth and finesse. The rhythmic pulse is lively, without being heavy and there is much engaging woodwind detail, with the oboeist playing beautifully in the haunting *Villanella* of the first suite and opening the second beguilingly. López-Cobos does not quite evoke the degree of bitter-sweet nostalgia for the past, which distinguishes the Dorati version, but the Lausanne strings certainly catch the melancholy elegance of the *Campanae parisensis* which follows the perky *Danza rustica*, and at the graceful beginning of the Third suite, textures are agreeably light and transparent. The Telarc recording is first rate and even more impressive in the *Botticelli pictures* with *La primavera* burgeoning with the extravagently exotic spring blossing, and *The birth of Venus* rapt in its radiantly expansive ecstasy. In between *The adoration of the Magi*, with its familiar carol quotation makes a poignantly serene interlude. The wind playing really is outstanding in this triptych and the warm ambience of the Musica Theatre of La Chaux-de-Fonds gives the sound a lovely bloom.

Ancient airs and dances: suite No. 3; The Birds (suite).
*** Ph. Dig. 420 485-2 [id.]. ASMF, Marriner – ROSSINI: *La Boutique fantasque*. **(*)

Ancient airs and dances: suite No. 3; The Fountains of Rome; The Pines of Rome.
*** DG 413 822-2 [id.]. BPO, Karajan.

Karajan's highly polished, totally committed performances of the two most popular Roman pieces are well supplemented by the *Third suite* of *Ancient airs and dances*, brilliantly played and just as beautifully transferred, more impressive in sound than many more recent Karajan recordings. In the symphonic poems Karajan is in his element, and the playing of the Berlin Philharmonic is wonderfully refined. The evocation of atmosphere in the two middle sections of *The Pines of Rome* is unforgettable. In *The Fountains* the tension is rather less tautly held, but the pictorial imagery is hardly less telling when the orchestral response is so magical.

Marriner too gives a very beautiful account of the *Third suite* of *Ancient airs and dances*, with gracious phrasing and luminous string textures. He catches both the music's noble melancholy and its moments of passionate feeling. The performance of *The Birds* is hardly less persuasive, the portrait of *The Dove* particularly tender, and there is much delicacy of texture elsewhere. The ASMF strings are wonderfully responsive and play as one. The sound is excellent too, but the coupling is a curious choice, acting merely as a pleasant filler.

Le astuzie di Colombina; La pentola magica; Sèvres de la vieille France.
*** Marco Polo Dig. 8.223346 [id.]. Slovak RSO (Bratislava), Adriano.

The three ballets recorded here were composed in 1920 in the immediate wake of *La boutique fantasque*, to a commission by Ileana Leonidiva. *Sèvres de la vieille France* is based on seventeenth- and eighteenth-century airs, scored with great elegance and charm; *La pentola magica* makes use of Russian models; Gretchaninov in the Prelude, Arensky in the *Entry of the Tsar with the Bridegrooms*, Anton Rubinstein in the *Dance of the Tartar Bowmen* and Rebikov in the finale. *Le astuzie di Colombina*, described as a 'Scherzo Veneziano', uses popular Venetian melodies among other things. There are reminders of the Strauss of *Le bourgeois gentilhomme*. Respighi never sanctioned further performances and although two of the scores were published after his death, *Le astuzie di Colombina* remains in manuscript. They are not the equal of *Belkis* but do contain some winning and delightful numbers. The *Sèvres de la vieille France* has some very endearing pieces. Not top-drawer by any manner of means but second-class Respighi is better than many other composers at their best. Decent performances and good recording.

Belkis, Queen of Sheba: suite. Metamorphoseon modi XII.
*** Chan. Dig. CHAN 8405; *ABTD 1142* [id.]. Philh. O, Simon.

The ballet-suite *Belkis, Queen of Sheba*, taken from a full-length ballet written in the early 1930s, is just what you would expect: a score that set the pattern for later Hollywood biblical film music; but *Metamorphoseon* is a taut and sympathetic set of variations. It has been ingeniously based on a medieval theme, and though a group of cadenza variations relaxes the tension of argument in the middle, the brilliance and variety of the writing have much in common with Elgar's *Enigma*. Superb playing from the Philharmonia, treated to one of the finest recordings that even Chandos has produced, outstanding in every way. This is very attractive music and the sound is certainly in the demonstration bracket.

(i) *The Birds* (suite); *Brazilian impressions;* (ii) *The Fountains of Rome; The Pines of Rome.*
(M) **(*) Mercury 432 007-2 [id.]. (i) LSO; (ii) Minneapolis SO, Antal Dorati.

This Mercury reissue combines the contents of two analogue LPs, one of which had not previously been issued in the UK, probably because of the established and justly famous RCA/Reiner/Chicago coupling of the same music. This has reappeared on CD in the USA at full price [RCA RCD1-5407] but is still awaited in the UK. The Minneapolis Northrop Auditorium – for all the skill of the Mercury engineers – never produced a web of sound with quite the magical glow which Orchestral Hall, Chicago, could provide in the late 1950s. Nevertheless, in Dorati's hands the opening and closing evocations of the *Fountains of Rome*, cleanly focused as they are by the use of Telefunken 201 microphones, have a unique, shimmering brightness which certainly suggests a sun-drenched landscape, although the turning of the Triton fountain brings a shrill burst of sound that almost assaults the ears. The tingling detail in the companion *Pines of Rome* is again matched by Dorati's powerful sense of atmosphere, so that the sepulchral Catacombs sequence, with its haunting nightingale's song, has a disturbing melancholy, while the finale has an overwhelming juggernaut forcefulness. The coupling of *The Birds* and *Brazilian impressions* was made in the smoother, warmer acoustics of Watford Town Hall in 1957, and here the vividness of detail particularly suits Dorati's spirited account of *The Birds*, bringing pictorial piquancy of great charm and strongly projected dance-rhythms. The liveliness of the LSO playing is most appealing. Resphighi wrote *Brazilian impressions* while spending the summer of 1927 in Rio de Janeiro. The triptych recalls Debussy's *Ibéria*, though it is much less subtle. The second impression invokes the *Dies irae* in sinister fashion; it is named after Butantan, famous for its reptile institute, where poisonous snakes are bred in large numbers for the production of serum. The finale, *Canzone e danza*, certainly glitters in Dorati's hands even if overall this work does not represent Respighi at his finest.

The Birds (suite); The Fountains of Rome; The Pines of Rome.
(B) *** Decca 425 507-2; *425 507-4*. LSO, Istvan Kertész.

Under Kertész *The Birds* is very engaging in its spirited elegance; seldom before has the entry of the nightingale's song been so beautifully prepared in the central section of *The Pines of Rome*, where Kertész creates a magical, atmospheric frisson. The iridescent brilliance of the turning on of the Triton fountain in the companion-piece is matched by the grandeur of the Trevi processional, when Neptune's chariot is imagined to be seen crossing the heavens. In sharpening detail the remastering of the 1969 recording loses only a little of the original ambient warmth and depth.

3 Botticelli pictures; (i) *Aretusa;* (ii) *Lauda per la Nativita del Signore;* (i) *Il Tramonto.*
❀ *** Collins Dig. 1349-2 [id.]. (i) Dame Janet Baker; (ii) Patricia Rosario, Louise Winter, Lynton Atkinson, Hickox Singers; City of L. Sinfonia, Hickox.

This is one of the most heartwarming of all discs of Respighi, bringing together in deeply committed performances the sensuousness of his big orchestral works and his fascination with early music. The collection is crowned by the contributions of Dame Janet Baker in one of her rare post-retirement visits to the recording studio. As on the Virgin recording of *La Sensitiva*, Dame Janet gives ravishing performances of two more of Respighi's warm and sensitive settings of Shelley poems (in Italian translations by R. Ascoli), written at the same period. Being less extended they make their points more directly yet with comparable warmth and intensity. *Aretusa*, composed in 1910, was the first work in which Respighi established his mature style, an exhilarating setting of a poem about the nymph, Arethusa, with lightly surging fountain music that anticipates the *Fountains* and *Pines of Rome*. *Il tramonto* ('The sunset'), written in 1914, evokes a mood remarkably similar to *Beim Schlafengehen* from Strauss's *Four Last Songs* of 30 years later and, with Dame Janet Baker as soloist, is just as beautiful. *Lauda*, a late work written between 1928 and 1930, is a 25-minute nativity cantata which with parts for soprano (the Angel), mezzo (the Virgin Mary), tenor and chorus (shepherds). It touchingly presents the story as a simple pastoral sequence, with the tenderly expressive woodwind accompaniment suggesting rustic pipe music. The *Trittico Botticelliana* is better known, one of Respighi's most delicate scores, establishing its seductiveness in the shimmering sounds at the very opening of the first movement, *Primavera*. Refined playing and recording.

Brazilian impressions; Church windows (Vetrate di chiesa).
*** Chan. Dig. CHAN 8317; *ABTD 1098* [id.]. Philh. O, Simon.

Respighi's set of musical illustrations of church windows is not among his finest works but is well worth having when the recording is impressively spacious and colourful. Geoffrey Simon is sympathetic and he secures very fine playing from the Philharmonia. The superb digital recording and the useful coupling (which avoids duplication with Respighi's more famous works) will be an added incentive to collectors. On CD, the wide dynamic range and a striking depth of perspective create the most spectacular effects.

Burlesca; Overture Carnevalesca; Prelude, chorale & fugue; Suite in E; Symphonic variations.
**(*) Marco Polo Dig. 8.223348 [id.]. Slovak RSO (Bratislava), Adriano.

The present CD collects a number of early works that testify more to Respighi's promise than to his fulfilment! The *Symphonic variations* were written when he was twenty-one and they made a strong impression on Rimsky-Korsakov. Respighi was a violist for two seasons with the Maryinsky Theatre in St Petersburg. The *Prelude, chorale & fugue* was scored while Respighi was still in Russia. The *Symphonic variations* is very well crafted, with a lot of Brahms and Franck – though the scoring already betrays his future expertise (there are parts for cor anglais, two harps and organ!). There are two versions of the *Suite in E major* from 1901 and 1903; the former is actually subtitled *Sinfonia* (indeed in ambition it is closer to the symphony, though Respighi did not turn to the form until his *Sinfinia drammatica* of 1914). The influences are mainly Slavonic; primarily Dvořák and Rimsky-Korsakov, but in the *Burlesca* of 1906 with its whole-tone scale one can discern a whiff of Debussy. The release discovers no masterpieces but does afford a valuable insight into Respighi's creative development. Good performances from Adriano and the Slovak Radio Orchestra and decent recording.

Concerto Gregoriano; Poema autunnale.
**(*) Marco Polo Dig. 8.220152 [id.]. Nishizaki, Singapore SO, Choo Hoey.

The Roman trilogy has overshadowed Respighi's other music to such an extent that many music-lovers are unaware even of the existence of his *Piano* and *Violin concertos*. The *Concerto Gregoriano* (for violin) comes from 1921 and, as its name suggests, is strongly modal in character, though its scoring is fully characteristic and at times lush. The first two movements are linked together and are both slow and ruminative in feeling, while there is a longer and more vigorous finale. Takako Nishizaki and the Singapore orchestra under Choo Hoey give a thoroughly committed account of both this work and the slightly later *Poema autunnale*, though the rather subfusc recording inhibits a totally unqualified welcome.

(i) *Piano concerto in modo misolidio. 3 Preludes on Gregorian themes.*
** Marco Polo Dig. 8.220176 [id.]. Sonya Hanke, (i) with Sydney SO, Myer Fredman.

Respighi's *Piano concerto in modo misolidio* dates from 1925 and was first heard that same year in New York with Respighi himself as soloist and Mengelberg conducting. It is a far from ineffective piece, but the present recording falls short of the ideal: the piano is a bit close and the instrument does not sound in absolutely first-class condition (there are some tired notes). The *Three Preludes on Gregorian themes* for piano were written in 1919 and dedicated to Casella. They were subsequently scored and another movement added to become the more familiar *Vetrate di chiesa*. Good, but not particularly outstanding, playing from the Australian pianist, Sonya Hanke, with the Sydney orchestra.

Feste romane.
*** EMI Dig. CDC7 49964-2 [id.]. Oslo PO, Mariss Jansons – DUKAS: *L'apprenti sorcier* ***; RAVEL: *Daphnis.* **(*)

In *Feste romane* Mariss Jansons gets playing of high voltage and no mean virtuosity from the Oslo Philharmonic. They may not be a first choice but they certainly rank high among the very finest versions, and anyone wanting this particular coupling need not hesitate. The recording is very clean and well detailed, though not wanting in atmosphere.

Feste romane; The Fountains of Rome; The Pines of Rome (symphonic poems).
*** Ph. Dig. 432 133-2; *432 133-4* [id.]. ASMF, Marriner.
(BB) *** Naxos Dig. 8.550539 [id.]. RPO, Bátiz.
*** EMI Dig. CDC7 47316-2 [id.]. Phd. O, Muti.
*** Decca Dig. 410 145-2. Montreal SO, Dutoit.
(M) *** DG 415 846-2 [id.]; *415 846-4*. Boston SO, Ozawa.
(BB) **(*) BMG/RCA VD 60486; *VK 60486*. Phd. O, Ormandy.
(M) (**(*)) BMG/RCA mono GD 60262; *GK 60262* [60262-2-RG; *60262-4-RG*]. NBC SO, Toscanini.
** Chan. Dig. CHAN 8989; *ABTD 1571* [id.]. Philh. O, Yan Pascal Tortelier.

Marriner's set of Respighi's trilogy is the finest modern version by a tiny margin. The ASMF playing is wonderfully alluring, and the central movements of *The Pines* have a radiance matched by the sensuous Italian light of the sunset at the Villa Medici. Similarly the watery detail of the two earlier fountains has a transluscent glitter, and if the climactic heavenly processional of the Triton fountain could have more weight, it remains pretty impressive, as does the Roman military juggernaut in *The Pines of the Appian Way*. In *Feste romane* Marriner achieves a splendid balance between vividness and brashness, between exultant jubilation (in the Twlefth Night celebrations of Epiphany) and wildness, with the popular clamour made riotous without over-the-top vulgarity. The ASMF playing is splendid, polished, warm intense and where necessary providing plenty of exuberance. The Philips recording, too, is in the demonstration bracket.

But then so is the Naxos recording, engineered by Brian Culverhouse in St Barnabas, Mitcham. The climax of *The Fountain of Trevi at mid-day*, when Neptune parades across the heavens, is enormously spectacular, and here a computer organ was used to provide the underlying sustained pedal (the church organ was out of pitch) and effectively clean and weighty it is. The *Pines* and *Fountains* bring extremely fine playing with much warmth and finesse from the RPO, and the gentle evocation is beautifully managed, while the cascading waters of the *Triton fountain* become a positive torrent. The focus of the Naxos recording is slightly sharper than the Philips, and this brings an extra degree of brazen splendour to the tumultuous popular crowd sequences in the *Circus* and *Jubilee* scenes of the *Feste romane*, while at the close of the *October festival* the mandolin serenade emerges more tangibly. This Naxos CD would be recommendable at premium price; in the super-bargain range it is very tempting indeed.

Muti gives warmly red-blooded performances of Respighi's Roman trilogy, captivatingly Italianate in their inflexions. With brilliant playing from the Philadelphia Orchestra and warmly atmospheric recording, far better than EMI engineers have generally been producing in Philadelphia, these are exceptional for their strength of characterization. The CD version clarifies the reverberant recording very effectively, with individual soloists cleanly placed.

Dutoit, as in other brilliant and colourful pieces, draws committed playing from his fine Montreal orchestra. Where many interpreters concentrate entirely on brilliance, Dutoit finds a vein of expressiveness too, which – for example in the opening sequence of *The Pines of Rome* – conveys the fun of children playing at the Villa Borghese. The recorded sound is superlative on CD, where the organ pedal sound is stunning.

Ozawa's CD offering some of his finest performances on record has been digitally remastered for its Galleria reissue and remains very competitive at mid-price; however, while sharpening the focus and refining detail, the brighter treble has brought a hint of harshness to the loudest fortissimos.

Ormandy plays all three works with enormous gusto and panache, and the orchestral virtuosity is thrilling, with the robust vulgarity of *Feste romane* breathtaking in its unbuttoned zest. The cascade at the turning on of the Triton fountain is like a dam bursting, and all the pictorial effects spring vividly to life. The 1973/4 recording is immensely spectacular. It is atmospheric too, but brightly lit to the point of garishness, and not all ears will respond to the tingling brilliance. But the performances make an unforgettable impact.

Toscanini's recordings of the Roman trilogy are in a class of their own; they (and Reiner in the *Pines* and the *Fountains*, still awaited on CD in the UK) are the yardstick by which all others are measured. This is electrifying playing, which comes over well in this transfer – though, to be fair, the old LPs (particularly the German RCA pressings of the *Feste romane*) had a rounder, fuller (less acidulated) tone on the strings above the stave.

Yan Pascal Tortelier certainly secures polished and beautiful playing from the Philharmonia Orchestra, but his readings are altogether more subdued, and the warm acoustics of All Saints, Tooting, although they add allure to the mistier evocations of *The Pines* and *Fountains*, tend to blunt the gaudier effects of the *Roman festival*.

Violin sonata in B min.
*** DG Dig. 427 617-2 [id.]. Kyung Wha Chung, Krystian Zimerman – R. STRAUSS: *Sonata*. ***
(M) (***) BMG/RCA mono GD 87871; *GK 87871* [7871-2-RG; *7871-4-RG*]. Heifetz, Bay – DEBUSSY: *Sonata* (**); RAVEL: *Trio* etc. (**); MARTINŮ: *Duo*. ***

At present Kyung Wha Chung and Krystian Zimerman have the field to themselves in Respighi's fine *Sonata*. Kyung Wha Chung is at her best and has the inestimable advantage of having a great artist as her partner; Krystian Zimerman brings an enormous range of colour and dynamics to the piano part – the clarity of his articulation in the *Passacaglia* is exceptional. This is undoubtedly the finest performance to appear on record since the Heifetz version.

Heifetz and Emanuel Bay recorded this sonata in 1950 and their performance has never been surpassed, not even by the superbly played and sumptuously recorded version by Kyung Wha Chung and Krystian Zimerman at full price. The latter remain the obvious recommendation, for it is difficult to summon up great enthusiasm for the Heifetz–Rubinstein–Piatigorsky Ravel *Trio*. All these performances, save the Martinů, are in mono.

La sensitiva.
*** Virgin VC7 91164-2; *VC7 91164-4* [id.]. J. Baker, City of L. Sinf., Hickox – BERLIOZ: Mélodies (including *Nuits d'été*). ***

Tautly structured over its span of more than half an hour, Respighi's setting of Shelley's poem, *The sensitive plant* (in Italian translation), is a most beautiful piece, which Dame Janet and Richard Hickox treat to a glowing first recording. The vocal line, mainly declamatory, is sweetly sympathetic and the orchestration is both rich and subtle. An unexpected but very enjoyable and generous coupling for the Berlioz items.

Il tramonto.
*** Hyp. Dig. CDA 66290; *KA 66290* [id.]. Carol Madalin, ECO, Bonavera – MARTUCCI: *Le canzone dei ricordi; Notturno*. ***

Respighi's *Il tramonto* (*The sunset*) is a setting of Shelley (in Italian translation) for string quartet or full strings (as heard here). It is a glorious work which at times calls to mind the world of late Strauss. A most lovely record. Recommended with all possible enthusiasm.

OPERA

La Fiamma (complete).
*** Hung. Dig. HCD 12591/3 [id.]. Tokody, Kelen, Takács, Sólyom-Nagy, Hungarian R. and TV Ch., Hungarian State O, Gardelli.

Richly atmospheric, with choruses and ensembles both mysterious and savage, *La Fiamma* makes a fine impact in this excellent first recording, idiomatically conducted by Lamberto Gardelli. The Hungarian cast is impressive, with Ilona Tokody producing Callas-like inflexions in the central role of Silvana, the young wife of the exarch, Basilio. She falls in love with her son-in-law, shocks her husband into falling down dead, and then cannot find tongue to deny a charge of witchcraft. Sándor Sólyom-Nagy is impressive as Basilio, Peter Kelen is aptly light-toned as the son-in-law, but it is the formidable Klára Takács as the interfering Eudossia who personifies the grit in the oyster, providing high melodrama. The playing is warmly committed and, apart from some distancing of the chorus, the sound is first rate, atmospheric but also precisely focused.

Reubke, Julius (1834–58)

Sonata in C min. on Psalm 94.
*** Argo Dig. 430 244-2; *430 244-4* [id.]. Thomas Trotter (organ of Ingolstadt Minster) – LISZT: *Ave Maria; Prelude & fugue on B-A-C-H* etc. ***

Julius Reubke (son of an organ builder) studied under Liszt at Weimar and modelled his *Sonata* on Liszt's *Fantasia and fugue on 'Ad nos, ad salutarem undam'*. He gave its première in 1857 and died the year after, aged only twenty-four. His monothematic piece is powerfully conceived and ingeniously wrought; its three sections can be regarded either as separate movements or as different facets of a single structure. The organ at Ingolstadt has a long reverberation period, which gives plenty of atmosphere to the sombre central *Adagio-Lento*. Trotter's performance is strongly controlled and the Argo recording makes an exciting spectacle of the work's fugal climax.

Revueltas, Silvestre (1899–1940)

Caminos; Musica para charlar; Ventanas.
*** ASV Dig. CDDCA 653; *ZCDCA 653* [id.]. Mexico City PO, Bátiz – CHAVEZ: *Sinfonia de Antigona; Symphony No. 4.* ***

The music on this record is highly colourful, with moments of considerable vulgarity rubbing shoulders with very evocative and imaginative episodes, such as the depiction of *Twilight* in the second *Musica para charlar*. Revueltas is not a major musical personality but a lively and colourful one. Excellent playing from the Mexican orchestra under Bátiz and sound of demonstration quality, with great impact, detail and presence.

Rheinberger, Joseph (1839–1901)

Organ concerto No. 1 in F, Op. 137.
*** Telarc Dig. CD 80136 [id.]. Michael Murray, RPO, Ling – DUPRÉ: *Symphony.* ***

Rheinberger's *Concerto* is well made, its invention is attractive and it has suitable moments of spectacle that render it admirable for a coupling with the Dupré *Symphony*, with its use of the massive Albert Hall organ. The performance here is first rate, as is the large-scale Telarc digital recording. A fine demonstration disc.

Rimsky-Korsakov, Nikolay (1844–1908)

Capriccio espagnol, Op. 34.
(B) *** DG Compact Classics 413 422-2 (2); *413 422-4* [id.]. BPO, Maazel – BIZET: *L'Arlésienne; Carmen;* DUKAS: *L'apprenti sorcier;* CHABRIER: *España.* **(*) (CD only: FALLA: *Three-cornered hat:* dances **).
(M) **(*) Decca Dig. 430 700-2; *430 700-4*. Montreal SO, Dutoit – MUSSORGSKY: *Night;* TCHAIKOVSKY: *1812* etc. **(*)

Maazel's 1960 recording of the *Capriccio espagnol* remains one of the very finest of recorded performances. With gorgeous string and horn playing, and a debonair, relaxed virtuosity in the *Scene e canto gitano* leading to breathtaking bravura in the closing section, every note in place, this is unforgettable. With Claudio Abbado's splendid account of Bizet's *L'Arlésienne* and *Carmen* suites, this is worth acquiring for the car, even if some duplication may be involved with the other items. The pair of CDs also includes excerpts from Falla's *Three-cornered hat* ballet. On both discs and tape the remastered sound is exceptionally vivid.

Dutoit's *Capriccio espagnol* is given a genial rather than an electrifying performance, though one not lacking in brilliance in terms of the orchestral playing. The recording is characteristic of the Montreal acoustic: full and warm, with luminous detail.

Capriccio espagnol, Op. 34; Le coq d'or: suite; Russian Easter festival overture, Op. 34.
(M) *** Mercury 434 308-2 [id.]. LSO, Antal Dorati – BORODIN: *Prince Igor: Polovstian dances.* **(*)

Dorati's 1959 *Capriccio espagnole* brings glittering bravura and excitement from the LSO players (only Maazel's Berlin Philharmonic version, from the same early stereo era is more arresting and has greater sumptuousness) and the *Russian Easter festival overture*, recorded at Walthamstow at the same sessions is equally dynamic and colourful. Even more remarkably, the rich-hued and vibrant *Le coq d'or* dates from as early as 1956, yet hardly sounds dated. The playing has plenty of allure in its evocation of Queen Shemakha, yet in its drama and well defined detail draws ready parallels with Dorati's companion LSO recording of Stravinsky's *Firebird ballet*.

Christmas eve (suite); Le Coq d'or: suite; *Legend of the invisible city of Kitezh:* suite; *May night:* overture; *Mlada:* suite; *The Snow Maiden:* suite; *The Tale of the Tsar Saltan:* suite.
*** Chan. Dig. CHAN 8327/9; *DBTD 3004* (3) [id.]. SNO, Järvi.

There is an essential pantheism in Rimsky's art. The *Prelude* to *The invisible city of Kitezh* is described as a hymn to nature, while the delights of the *Christmas eve suite* (an independent work) include a magical evocation of the glittering stars against a snow-covered landscape and, later, a flight of comets. The plots of his operas, drawn on Gogol and Ostrovsky, are peopled by picaresque human characters, however. In *Le Coq d'or* the bumbling King Dodon has his counterpart in the alluring Queen Shemakha, for whom Rimsky wrote one of his most sensuously languorous melodies. Apart from the feast of good tunes, the composer's skilful and subtle deployment of the orchestral palette continually titillates the ear. Neeme Järvi draws the most seductive response from the SNO; he consistently creates orchestral textures which are diaphanously sinuous. Yet the robust moments, when the brass blazes or the horns ring out sumptuously, are caught just as strikingly. The CDs have much presence, while the focus is bright and sharp, and the listener is assured that here is music which survives repetition uncommonly well.

Christmas eve: suite; Le coq d'or: suite; The Tale of Tsar Saltan: suite; Flight of the bumble bee.
*** ASV Dig. CDDCA 772; *ZCDCA 772* [id.]. Armenian PO, Tjeknavorian.

Tjeknavorian and his fine Armenian Orchestra are completely at home in Rimsky's sinuous orientalism. There is a first rate trumpeter to play the arresting fanfares which open each movement of the *Tsar Saltan suite* and articulate the pungently bizarre warnings of *The Golden cockerel*, while the delicately sensuous portrayal of Queen Shemakha in the latter suite brings lovely, diaphanous string textures, matched elsewhere by glittering, iridescent wind-colouring. The racy vigour and sparkle of the playing brings a jet-setting bumble bee and the carolling horns and bold brass add to the vividness. The music from *Christmas eve* with its charming ballet of stars and comets, and Tchaikovskian *Polonaise* exudes similar sparkling vitality within a glowing palette. In short this is one of the most desirable and generous Rimsky-Korsakov collections in the current catalogue. The ambience of the Khachaturian Hall in Yerevan, Armenia, adds to the appeal of Brian Culverhouse's sound picture, and only a degree of thinness in the violin timbre above the stave prevents the use of the adjective, sumptuous. In all other respects this is in the demonstration bracket.

Le coq d'or: suite. Mlada: suite. The Snow Maiden: suite.
(BB) ** Naxos Dig. 8.500486 [id.]. Slovak RSO (Bratislava), Donald Johanos.

The inexpensive Naxos collection is also well played and enjoyable. It has plenty of colour and picaresque detail (the *Dance of the birds* in the *Snow Maiden* chirps engagingly). But in *Le coq d'or* Queen Shemakha is portrayed more plainly: textures have a less lustrous shimmer, although Rimsky can never fail to sound beguiling here. The music-making is spirited (especially in the boisterous closing *Cortège* from *Mlada*) and given bright digital sound with a concert hall ambience. But this is a much less seductive programme than its ASV competitor.

Scheherazade (symphonic suite), *Op. 35.*
*** EMI CDC7 47717-2 [id.]. RPO, Beecham – BORODIN: *Polovtsian dances.* ***
*** Ph. 400 021-2 [id.]. Concg. O, Kondrashin.
(M) *** BMG/RCA GD 60875 [60875-2-RG]. Chicago SO, Fritz Reiner – DEBUSSY: *La Mer.* ***
(M) *** Ph. 420 898-2 [id.]. LPO, Haitink – MUSSORGSKY: *Night on the bare mountain.* ***
(B) *** CfP CD-CFP 4341; *TC-CFP 4341.* Philh. O, Kletzki – TCHAIKOVSKY: *Capriccio italien.* ***
*** Chan. Dig. CHAN 8479 [id.]. SNO, Järvi – GLAZUNOV: *Stenka Razin.* ***
(M) *** DG 419 063-2; *419 063-4* [id.]. BPO, Karajan – BORODIN: *Polovtsian dances.* ***
(B) **(*) DG Compact Classics 413 155-2 (2); *413 155-4* [id.]. Boston SO, Ozawa – STRAVINSKY: *Firebird suite* ***; KHACHATURIAN: *Gayaneh* *** (CD only: GLINKA: *Overtures* *(*)).

Scheherazade; Capriccio espagnol, Op. 34.
❀ *** Telarc Dig. CD 80208 [id.]. LSO, Sir Charles Mackerras.

Scheherazade, Op. 35; Fairy tale (Skazka), Op. 29; Sadko, Op. 5; Songs of India, from Sadko (arr. Tjeknavorian).

*** ASV Dig. CDDCA 771; *ZCDCA 771* [id.]. Armenian PO, Tjeknavorian.

(i) *Scheherazade;* (ii) *May night overture; Sadko, Op. 5.*
(B) *** Decca 421 400-2. (i) LSO, Monteux; (ii) SRO, Ansermet.

Mackerras is a dynamic interpreter of this vividly Russian score and he has the advantage of a superb Telarc digital recording – produced by Jack Renner, who masterminded the famous Mussorgsky *Pictures at an exhibition* on the same label – which is very much in the demonstration class. Mackerras's reading combines gripping drama with romantic ardour, subtlety of colour with voluptuousness; he is helped, as is Haitink, by a wonderfully beguiling portrait of Scheherazade herself, provided by his orchestral leader, in this case Kees Hulsmann. The solo violin is naturally balanced within the overall orchestral picture, yet Hulsmann's gently alluring image dominates the narrative. Scheherazade's presence is felt at the very opening through the vivid kaleidoscoping colours of the second movement, blossoming in the ravishing slow movement, which recalls Beecham in its elegant sumptuousness. She returns in gentle triumph, at the end of the grippingly thrustful finale with its spectacular climax, to bring a magical closing meditation. The charming closing reverie, with the Sultan lying peacefully satiated in the arms of his young wife, their themes blissfully intermingled, is unforgettable. After an appropriate pause, Mackerras then delivers a thrilling bravura account of *Capriccio espagnol*, lushly opulent in the variations, glittering in the exotic *Scena e canta gitano*, and carrying all before it in the impetus of the closing *Fandango asturiano*.

Beecham's *Scheherazade* was recorded in London's Kingsway Hall in March 1957. It is a performance of extraordinary drama and charisma. Alongside the violin contribution of Stephen Staryk, all the solo playing has great distinction; in the second movement Beecham gives the woodwind complete metrical freedom (notably the bassoon), yet the electricity of the music-making never for a moment flickers; later the brass fanfares have great flair and bite. The sumptuousness and glamour of the slow movement are very apparent, yet a sultry, cultured refinement pervades the languor of the string phrasing. The finale has an explosive excitement, rising to an electrifying climax, which the dynamic range of the digital remastering frees from any restriction. The coupled *Polovtsian dances* have comparable dash and excitement. However, this is surely due for a mid-price reissue.

On ASV a refreshing and totally gripping new-look recording of *Scheherazade* from Eastern Russia, completely slavic in temperament and feeling and very exciting too. Yuri Boghosian, leader of the the Armenian Philharmonic, immediately presents a seductively slight and sinuous image for the heroine-narrator and the first movement brings the strongest attack and thrust from the strings. Throughout the central movements one is made aware of the lustrous oriental character of Rimsky's melodies. The heavy brass blazes in the fanfares near the opening of the second in a way one would not expect in the West, while in the third the graceful allure of *The Young Prince and Princess* contrasts with the glittering rhythmic sparkle of the dance episode, and there is a spontaneous burst of ardour when the main love theme climaxes near the close. The finale, with its spectacular storm and shipwreck has exhilarating animation and bite. Not surprisingly, following his companion CD (including *Le coq d'or*), Tjeknavorian shows great imaginative flair in realizing the vivid orchestral effects in the two shorter folk tales, and as a final exotic sweetmeat offers his own gently luscious arrangement of Rimsky's most famous melody, better known as the *Chant hindue*, which caresses the ear beguilingly. The brilliant recording with its concert-hall balance is undoubtedly truthful and has great vividness and projection, but relatively little sumptuousness. But it suits the performances admirably.

Kondrashin's version with the Concertgebouw Orchestra has the advantage of splendid modern analogue recorded sound, combining richness and sparkle within exactly the right degree of resonance. Hermann Krebbers' gently seductive portrayal of Scheherazade's narrative creates a strong influence on the overall interpretation. The first movement, after Krebbers' tranquil introduction, develops a striking architectural sweep; the second is vivid with colour, the third beguilingly gracious, while in the finale, without taking unusually fast tempi, Kondrashin creates an irresistible forward impulse leading to a huge climax at the moment of the shipwreck.

Reiner's first movement opens richly and dramatically and has a strong forward impulse. The unnamed orchestral leader, naturally balanced, plays most seductively, and the two central movements have beguiling colour, helped by the glowing ambience. Reiner's affectionate individual touches have much in common with Beecham's (full-price) version and sound comparably spontaneous. The third movement is wonderfully languorous and the finale, brilliant and very exciting, has a climax of resounding power and amplitude. The Chicago Hall ambience makes up in body and spaciousness for any lack of internal clarity, and the sound is richer if less refined in detail than the Philips recording for Haitink.

Haitink's LPO record dates from 1974. The recording shows its age just a little in the string timbre, but in all other respects it is exceptionally truthful in both sound and perspective. It is a relief to hear a solo violin sounding its natural size in relation to the orchestra as a whole. Yet Rodney Friend, who plays the solos subtly, dominates the performance with his richly sinuous picture of Scheherazade herself as narrator of each episode. The playing of the LPO is both sensitive and alert, Haitink's interpretation wholly unaffected and totally fresh in impact.

Kletzki's famous recording of Rimsky-Korsakov's orchestral showpiece was a best seller on HMV's Concert Classics LP label for fifteen years. The Kingsway Hall recording has an attractively spacious acoustic, and the Philharmonia solo playing (from a peak period) is superb, with highly distinguished violin solos from Hugh Bean. Kletzki's reading is broad in the first movement (with less bite and thrust than with Tjeknavorian), but he makes the second glow and sparkle (the famous brass interchanges having the most vivid projection). The elegantly sinuous finesse of the Philharmonia string playing in the third movement is matched by the exhilaration of the finale. The admirably balanced recording has been enhanced by the CD transfer and now sounds remarkably firm and realistic: it is difficult to believe that it dates from the end of the 1950s. At bargain price this remains very competitive.

Järvi's version with the SNO may not be the most high-powered or weighty; nor is it as idiosyncratic as, for instance, the Beecham or Karajan versions; but, with the episodic argument strongly held together as in the telling of a story, it is most persuasive. The playing is no less fine than in versions from the most distinguished international orchestras, and the recorded sound is spectacular in the Chandos manner, spacious and refined. Indeed for those looking for a splendid modern digital version, this could well be first choice.

The recordings from Monteux and Ansermet on the Decca Weekend CD come from the earliest days of stereo. Monteux's version of *Scheherazade* is, if anything, even more vivid than Haitink's and the recording remains brilliant and sparkling, the performance sensuous and exciting, full of charisma. Ansermet finds all the colour in the *May night overture* and *Sadko*, an exotic Rimskian fairy-tale with a colourful storm for a climax; while the Decca engineers, working in Geneva, provided both atmosphere and the fullest orchestral palette. In the finale of *Scheherazade* Monteux holds back the climax – another storm – until the last minute and then unleashes his forces with devastating effect. The orchestral playing is not as polished as the LPO under Haitink, but it has tremendous zest and spontaneity, and this makes a fine bargain recommendation, even though the upper range lacks something in opulence.

Karajan's 1967 recording is greatly enhanced in its CD format. The extra vividness brings more life and sparkle to the central movements, which are superbly played, and the brass fanfares in the second have a tingling immediacy. The added presence also increases the feeling of ardour from the glorious Berlin strings in the *Andante*. The outer movements have great vitality and thrust, and the bright percussion transients add to the feeling of zest. Yet Michel Schwalbé's sinuously luxuriant violin solos are still allowed to participate in the narrative. The fill-up is a sizzling account of the Borodin *Polovtsian dances*, with no chorus, but managing perfectly well without.

Ozawa's version, available on Compact Classics, makes a fair bargain alternative if the fine couplings, Maazel's early stereo recording of the *Firebird suite* and Rozhdestvensky's *Gayaneh*, are suitable. It is an attractive performance, richly recorded. The first movement is strikingly spacious, building to a fine climax; if the last degree of vitality is missing from the central movements, the orchestral playing is warmly vivid. The finale is lively enough, if not earth-shaking in its excitement; the reading as a whole has plenty of colour and atmosphere, however, and it is certainly enjoyable. The chrome-tape transfer is sophisticated. The pair of CDs offer a marginal sonic improvement but they cost far more and include as a bonus only relatively undistinguished accounts of two Glinka overtures.

Symphonies Nos. 1 in E min., Op. 1; 2 (Antar), Op. 9; 3 in C, Op. 32; Capriccio espagnol, Op. 35; Russian Easter festival overture, Op. 36.
*** DG Dig. 423 604-2 (2). Gothenburg SO, Järvi.

Whatever Rimsky-Korsakov's symphonies may lack in symphonic coherence they make up for in colour and charm. Some of the material is a little thin but there is some highly attractive invention as well. *Antar*, which is far more of a symphonic suite than a symphony, is not quite as strong as some of its protagonists would have us believe, but it should surely have a stronger presence in the concert and recorded repertoire than it has. The performances under Neeme

Järvi have considerable merit and, although the Gothenburg orchestra is not the equal of the USSR Academic Symphony, it is so excellently recorded that it will be the first choice for most collectors; moreover the addition of the *Capriccio espagnol* and the *Russian Easter festival overture* makes the Chandos set a very attractive proposition.

Symphony No. 2 (Antar), Op. 9.
*** Telarc CD 80131 [id.]. Pittsburgh SO, Maazel – TCHAIKOVSKY: *Symphony No. 2.* ***

Maazel's taut yet sympathetic reading holds together a work which, structurally at least, might more aptly be counted as a suite (as *Scheherazade* is) but which, with strong and colourful yet refined treatment like this, is fittingly regarded as belonging to Rimsky's symphonic canon. Excellent playing – notably in the finale, where the Pittsburgh woodwind excel themselves in delicacy – and brilliant, finely balanced recording.

Tsar Saltan, Op. 57: March.
*** Telarc Dig. CD 80107 [id.]. RPO, Previn – TCHAIKOVSKY: *Symphony No. 5.* ***

The crisp, stylized *March* from *Tsar Saltan*, a fairy-tale piece, makes a delightful *bonne-bouche*, a welcome fill-up for Previn's fine account of the Tchaikovsky *Fifth Symphony*, equally well played and recorded.

Piano and wind quintet in B flat.
*** Hyp. CDA 66163; *KA 66163* [id.]. Capricorn – GLINKA: *Grand Sextet.* ***
*** CRD CRD 3409; *CRDC 4109* [id.]. Ian Brown, Nash Ens. – ARENSKY: *Piano trio No. 1.* ***

Rimsky-Korsakov's youthful *Quintet for piano, flute, clarinet, horn and bassoon* is a thoroughly diverting piece. It is like a garrulous but endearing friend whose loquacity is readily borne for the sake of his charm and good nature. The main theme of the finale is pretty brainless but singularly engaging, and the work as a whole leaves a festive impression. Capricorn's account has great vivacity and is very well recorded. The excellence of the pianist, Julian Jacobson (formerly Dawson Lyall), should be noted: he contributes a rare sparkle to the proceedings.

The Nash Ensemble give a spirited and delightful account of it on CRD that can be warmly recommended for its dash and sparkle and full, naturally balanced sound. The CD transfer retains all the analogue warmth but is not made at a high level; though those used to digital records might like sharper inner definition, the effect is very pleasing with no lack of presence.

Robles, Marisa (born 1937)

Narnia suite.
(M) *** ASV CDWHL 2068; *ZCWHL 2068.* Composer, Christopher Hyde-Smith, Marisa Robles Harp Ens.

This incidental music was commissioned for ASV's integral recording of the C. S. Lewis *Narnia Chronicles*, as read (quite admirably) by Michael Hordern. Even though it consists entirely of a series of miniatures for harp, with the flute of Christopher Hyde-Smith used sparingly but to great effect, the music stands up well away from the narrative. Its freshness and innocence are entirely in keeping with the special atmosphere of C. S. Lewis's narrative. There are indelible leitmotivs for Narnia and Aslan and the writing for *The Voyage of the Dawn Treader*, perhaps the most imaginative of all the tales, is particularly attractive. With the composer so admirably partnered, the music cannot fail to charm the listener, particularly as the digital recording is clear and lustrous. *The Chronicles of Narnia* are available on tape only (including the incidental music) as follows: *The Magician's Nephew* (ASV *ZCSWD 351*); *The Lion, The Witch and The Wardrobe* (*ZCSWD 352*); *The Horse and His Boy* (*ZCSWD 353*); *Prince Caspian* (*ZCSWD 354*); *The Voyage of the Dawn Treader* (*ZCSWD 355*); *The Silver Chair* (*ZCSWD 356*); *The Last Battle* (*ZCSWD 357*).

Rodrigo, Joaquín (born 1902)

A la busca del más allá; (i) *Concierto andaluz* (for 4 guitars); (ii) *Concierto de Aranjuez* (for guitar); (iii) *Concierto de estio* (for violin); (iv) *Concierto en modo galante* (for cello); (v) *Concierto heroico* (for piano); (vi) *Concierto madrigal* (for 2 guitars); (vii) *Concierto pastoral* (for

flute); (viii) *Concierto serenata* (for harp). (ii) *Fantasia para un gentilhombre. Música para un jardín; Per la flor del Iliri blau; 5 Piezas infantiles; Soleriana; Zarabanda lejana y villancico.*
(M) *** EMI Dig. CDZ7 67435-2 (4) [id.]. (i) Moreno, Garibay, López, Ruiz; (ii) Alfonso Moreno; (iii) Agustín Ara; (iv) Robert Cohen; (v) Jorge Osorio; (vi) Moreno, Mariotti; (vii) Lisa Hansen; (viii) Nancy Allen; LSO; Mexico State PO; RPO, Enrique Bátiz.

This admirable reissued collection is surely worthy of Rodrigo's ninetieth-birthday celebrations and is a tribute to Enrique Bátiz, who must have had a hand in organizing the recordings as well as directing them. The only missing pieces are the second *Guitar concerto* (*Concierto para una Fiesta*) which Pepe Romero has recorded for Philips and which is not quite a match for the first, and the later *Cello concerto* (*Concierto como un divertimento*) commissioned by Julian Lloyd Webber, which no doubt will reappear from RCA in due course. The present EMI recordings were made between 1980 and 1985, many of them in Watford Town Hall, and are of excellent quality, although the early digital technique often brings an overlit sound to the treble, perhaps appropriate for music drenched in Spanish sunshine. The *Summer concerto* for violin ('conceived in the manner of Vivaldi') is the composer's own favourite, and Léon Ara catches its neo-classical vitality admirably in the outer movements, with the LSO comparably zestful, articulating cleanly and buoyantly; the central *Sicilienne* with its set of simple variations is most sympathetic. The *Cello concerto* is given a masterly performance by Robert Cohen; he combines elegance of phrasing with warm beauty of timbre in the lovely secondary theme (*in tempo di minuetto galante*) of the first movement and the no less haunting melody which dominates the *Adagietto*. His spirited articulation of the opening ostinato ideas and the lively Zapateado rondo finale is matched by Bátiz, who secures playing of fire and temperament from the LSO. The *Concierto serenata* for harp, a favourite of ours, has an unforgettable piquancy and charm. Nancy Allen is a shade reticent, almost entirely to advantage, however, for Bátiz scales down his support with the RPO to produce a very winning partnership with his soloist, who consistently beguiles the ear with her gentleness (the very opening with its cascade of trickling notes is wonderfully inviting). The *Concierto pastoral* for flute was composed with James Galway in mind in 1978. It is a spikier piece than usual from this composer and its brilliant introduction is far from pastoral in feeling, but Rodrigo's fragmented melodies soon insinuate themselves into the consciousness. The slow movement has a witty scherzando centrepiece framed by the *Adagio* outer sections. Rodrigo's *Piano concerto* was conceived in the early 1930s, but then set aside and the early sketches were lost.The present work dates from 1939. It has a programmatic content, with the four movements written 'under the sign of the Sword, the Spur, the Cross and the Laurel'. But heroism is not a quality one associates with Rodrigo's art; the first movement with its fanfare-like main theme soon becomes merely garrulous; the scherzo outstays its welcome, and the best part is the *Largo* which, seeking a medieval ambience, is attractively atmospheric. The performers give a strong, extrovert account of the piece; perhaps more could be made of it, but the playing here seems to do it justice and certainly does not lack vigour and commitment. The *Concierto Andaluz* has its weaknesses but remains engaging if a trifle inflated, perhaps to match its profusion of soloists. Surprisingly the digital recording does not give a very impressive focus to the four soloists, even if Bátiz draws vivid sounds from the Mexican orchestra. A similar comment might be made about the effect of the duo *Concierto madrigal*, with its set of twelve delightful vignettes, many with a medieval flavour, but part of the reason for this is that the four guitar soloists here do not achieve the strongest profile, and this is also one reason why Alfonso Moreno's account of the famous *Concierto de Aranjuez*, though bright and sympathetic, is in no way outstanding, in spite of the strong projection of the recording. The 77 minutes of orchestral music which occupies the fourth disc is particularly valuable; as it is not otherwise available it surely calls for a separate issue. The symphonic poem, *Ala busca del más allá* ('In search of the beyond'), written as recently as 1976, could easily be dismissed as film music without a film, yet it is evocative and powerfully scored; *Música para un jardín* is a quartet of cradle songs, originally conceived for the piano and scored with all the piquancy at the composer's command. John Duarte in the notes for the original issue described the music as having 'a phantom-like quality; the subtle enchantment lies in its coolness, transparency and lyricism, spiced with a pleasant scattering of harmonic surprises'. The *Five Children's pieces* are delightful, but they were not originally written for piano and later orchestrated (as claimed by the otherwise excellent accompanying notes) but were conceived in orchestral dress, while the two neo-classical evocations of eighteenth-century Spain (*Soleriana*) are also unostentatiously appealing. *Per la flor del Iliri blau* ('For the flower of the blue lily') dates from 1934 and is based on a Valencian legend concerning the search of a prince for a rare flower with miraculous curative qualities; it is needed to aid, not a princess, but his ailing father. He meets his death in an ambush on the way home. The music opens with a medieval fanfare and has something in common with Smetana's famous cycle about his homeland, though Rodrigo is more impressive in moments of gently atmospheric detail than in the melodrama. The *Zarabanda lejana* ('Distant sarabande') was Rodrigo's first work for guitar (1926), written in homage to Luis Milan. He later orchestrated it and added the *Villancico* to make a binary structure, the first part nobly elegiac, the second a gay dance movement with a characteristic touch of harmonic astringency, but having something of the flavour of a carol.

(i) *Concierto Andaluz* (for 4 guitars); (ii) *Concierto de Aranjuez;* (ii; iii) *Concierto madrigal* (for 2 guitars); (ii) *Concierto para una fiesta; Fantasia para un gentilhombre.* Solo guitar pieces: *Bajando de la Meseta; En los Trigales; Fandango; Junto al Generalife; 3 Little Pieces; Romance de Durandarte; Sonata a la española; Tiento antiquo.*
(M) *** Ph. 432 581-2 (3) [id.]. (i) Los Romeros; (ii) Pepe Romero; (iii) Angel Romero; ASMF, Marriner.

This distinguished set gathers together all Rodrigo's major concertante guitar works in first-class performances and adds a rewarding recital of solo works as a postlude, all played with natural spontaneity and complete authority by an artist who feels this music from his innermost being. The *Sonata* is no less strongly Spanish in character and the genre pieces are comparably picturesque in evoking Mediterranean atmosphere and local dance-rhythms. Los Romeros make the very most of the *Concierto Andaluz* with its infectious tunefulness in the outer sections and plenty of romantic atmosphere. The highly engaging *Concierto madrigal*, in which Pepe and Angel Romero duet persuasively, is based on an anonymous Spanish Renaissance melody, treated in variation style. The work is divided into ten titled episodes, of which the first seven are brief and the last three, *Arieta*, *Zapateado* and *Caccia a la española*, are more extended. If the *Concierto para una fiesta* does not quite repeat the success of the *Concierto de Aranjuez*, it still has plenty of Andalusian colour, and Pepe Romero's performance has all the freshness of new discovery. He is equally magnetic in the solo items. Throughout, Marriner and the Academy provide accompaniments which are thoroughly polished and have much warmth, and the Philips sound is most natural and beautifully balanced.

Concierto de Aranjuez (for guitar and orchestra).
❀ (M) *** Decca Dig. 430 703-2; *430 703-4* [id.]. Carlos Bonell, Montreal SO, Dutoit – FALLA: *El amor brujo* etc. *** ❀
*** Sony Dig. CD 37848 [id.]. John Williams, Philh. O, Frémaux.
(M) *** BMG/RCA GD 86525 [6525-2-RG]. Bream, Monteverdi O, Gardiner – VILLA-LOBOS: *Concerto* etc. ***

Concierto de Aranjuez; (i) *Concierto madrigal* (for 2 guitars); *Fantasia para un gentilhombre.*
(M) *** Ph. 432 828-2; *432 828-4* [id.]. Pepe Romero; (ii) Angel Romero; ASMF, Marriner.

Concierto de Aranjuez; Fantasia para un gentilhombre.
(M) *** Decca Dig. 417 748-2 [id.]. Carlos Bonell, Montreal SO, Dutoit (with FALLA: *Three-cornered hat* ***).

(i) *Concierto de Aranjuez; 3 Piezas españolas (Fandango; Passacaglia; Zapateado); Invocation and dance (Homage to Manuel de Falla).*
*** BMG/RCA Dig. RD 84900 [RCD1 4900]. Julian Bream, (i) COE, Gardiner.

Decca have reissued the much-praised Bonell/Dutoit recording of the *Concierto* a second time, now re-coupled with Alicia de Larrocha's splendid digital recording of Falla's *Nights in the gardens of Spain* plus Dutoit's outstanding complete *El amor brujo.* This is a very attractive pairing and the reasons for the success of the Rodrigo performance remain unaltered: an exceptionally clear, atmospheric and well-balanced digital recording plus Bonell's imaginative account of the solo part, and the strong characterization of the orchestral accompaniments by Charles Dutoit and his excellent Montreal orchestra. A feeling of freshness pervades every bar of the orchestral texture. De Larrocha's luminous account of *Nights in the gardens of Spain* is equally distinguished, and this makes one of the most desirable compilations of Spanish music in the catalogue.

The Bonell/Dutoit *Concierto* was originally paired with the *Fantasia para un gentilhombre.* Decca then made this issue even more attractive by adding a bonus of three dances from Falla's

Three-cornered hat (taken from Dutoit's complete set) and by placing the recording on their mid-priced Ovation label. In the *Fantasia*, the balance between warmly gracious lyricism and sprightly rhythmic resilience is no less engaging; here again, the orchestral solo playing makes a strong impression.

Pepe Romero's performance of the *Concierto de Aranjuez* has plenty of Spanish colour, the musing poetry of the slow movement beautifully caught. The account of the *Fantasia* is warm and gracious, with the Academy contributing quite as much as the soloist to the appeal of the performance. Although inner detail is less sharply focused than on the Bonell digital version, it hardly matters, as the warm beauty of the analogue atmosphere emphasizes the Mediterranean feeling. Angel joins Pepe for the Renaissance-inspired duet, *Concierto madrigal*, which is very attractive indeed, making this a very viable alternative to the Decca coupling.

Bream's digital recording of the *Concierto* has a personality all its own. With outer movements offering strong dynamic contrasts and some pungent accents (from orchestra as well as soloist) the music's flamenco associations are underlined and the famous *Adagio* is played in a very free, improvisatory way, with some highly atmospheric wind solos in the orchestra. The balance is more natural than usual, with the guitar set slightly back and heard in a convincing perspective with the orchestra. The only slight snag is that the resonance adds a touch of harshness to the emphatic orchestral tuttis. What makes this issue especially valuable, however, is the inclusion of the *Tres Piezas españolas*, of which the second, *Passacaglia*, is one of Rodrigo's finest shorter works. No less involving is his *Invocation* for Manuel de Falla, with both performances showing Bream at his most inspirationally spontaneous.

John Williams's newest version of the *Concierto* (his third) also has the advantage of first-class digital recording. The acoustic, however, is a little dry compared with the Decca issue, while the woodwind is a shade too forward. Nevertheless, this is technically superior to Williams's previous, analogue partnership with Barenboim and the performance is even finer. The slow movement is wonderfully atmospheric and the finale is light and sparkling with an element of fantasy and much delicacy of articulation in the accompaniment. The performance of the *Fantasia* is no less memorable and this is altogether a most winning coupling, not as extrovert as the Bonell/Dutoit partnership, but no less distinguished.

Bream recorded the *Concierto de Aranjuez* twice in the analogue era; this mid-priced CD is the first of his analogue recordings and it has a little more dash than the later one with Sir Colin Davis, yet the differences are too subtle for easy analysis. Sufficient to say that this is excellent value and that the couplings are also valuable.

PIANO MUSIC

Music for 2 pianos: (i) *5 Piezas infantiles* (piano, 4 hands): *Atardecer; Gran marcha de los subsecretarios; Sonatina para dos Muñecas;* (solo piano): *Air de ballet sur le nom d'une jeune fille; Album de Cecilia; A l'ombre de Torre Bermeja; Bagatela; Berceuse d'automne; Berceuse de printemps; Danza de la Amapola; 3 Danzas de españa; 4 Estampas andaluzas; 3 Evocaciones; Pastorale; 4 Piezas (Caleseras: Homenaje a Chueca; Fandango del Ventorrillo; Plegaria de la Infanta de Castilla; Danza Valenciana); Preludio de Añoranza; Preludio al Gallo mañanero; Serenata española; Sonada de adiós (Hommage à Paul Dukas); 5 Sonatas de Castilla, con Toccata a modo de Pregón: Nos. 1–2 in F sharp min.; 3 in D; 4 in B min. (como un tiento); 5 in A. Suite; Zarabanda lejana.*

❀ *** Bridge BCD 9027 A/B [id.]. Gregory Allen (i) with Anton Nel.

Of all the new piano music that has come our way in the last twelve months, this Rodrigo box has proved among the most stimulating. Very little of Rodrigo's vocal music – repertoire by which he sets great store – is yet recorded, or is even heard in performance outside Spain, and until now his piano writing has been comparably neglected. It is conspicuously absent from the various anthologies recorded by the great Spanish pianist, Alicia de Larrocha, for Decca. The present two-CD set instantly makes amends, offering 2 hours 33 minutes and including all the composer's piano works of any importance. They are played by a brilliant young American pianist, Gregory Allen, winner of the 1980 Rubinstein Competition in Tel Aviv. His recordings carry the composer's imprimatur: 'His magnificent technique and his authentically fine interpretation satisfy me completely'.

Rodrigo, blind from the age of three, after a childhood bout of diphtheria, has spent much of his creative life sitting at the piano keyboard, and he is a consummate master of its technical and colouristic possibilities. He has acknowledged the huge influence of the twentieth-century French school on his piano writing; having studied under Paul Dukas at the École Normale in the late 1920s, he returned with the French idiom deeply embedded in his musical consciousness. He paid eloquent tribute to that French master in his movingly sombre *Sonada de adiós* (1935). In his earliest piano work, the *Suite* of 1923, with its sprightly *Prelude*, cool *Sicilienne* and Satie-ish minuet the link is obvious, while the glittering brilliance of the *Prelude al Gallo mañanero* is unmistakably Debussian in its reminders of *Reflets dans l'eau* and *Feux d'artifice*. If here the influences are unassimilated, later Rodrigo's use of French impressionism is entirely conscious. So the audaciously sardonic *Gran marchas de los subsecretarios* (1941), for all its highly personal sense of fun, recalls Satie's *Sonatine bureaucratique*, while the impressionistic *Tres Evocations* (1980–81) evoke the Debussy of *Nocturnes* and *Iberia*, and its central *Noche en el Guadalquivir* is deeply reminiscent of *La cathédrale engloutie*. The soft melancholy of the last piano piece Rodrigo wrote, in 1987, *Preludio de Añoranza* poignantly recalls the refined delicacy of atmosphere one finds in Ravel. There are other influences too. The *Cinq Sonatas de Castilla* (1950–51), look back further in time and draw continually on the keyboard writing of Scarlatti. But they have great vitality and an entirely individual palette and are spiced with piquant dissonances which the Italian composer would have disowned. Of course much of the other music here has an entirely individual voice. The *Serenata española* of 1931 marks Rodrigo's positive adoption of an overtly Andalusian style, while the *Cuatro Piezas* of 1936–8 and the *Cuatro estampas andaluzas* of 1946–52 are as sharply Spanish in character as any of the similarly picaresque miniatures of Granados or Albéniz. Rodrigo's children's pieces have especial charm: the opening number of the *Cienco piezas infantiles* (1924), transcribed for two pianos, erupts boisterously, while the *Plegaria* (prayer) has a poignant, touching innocence which is to recur in the *Album for* (his daughter) *Cecilia* (1948) – its six movements all ingeniously written in the treble clef. The delectable 1977 *Sonatina para dos Muñecas* (two puppets) was designed for four very small hands, those of his grandchildren, Cecilita and Patty, who gave the première at the tender ages of nine and twelve respectively! Its finale, *Vuelta del cole*, is an irrepressibly vivacious skipping song, written almost entirely in canon between the two parts, interrupted now and then with vigorous childish stamps. The darker side of Rodrigo's nature, sometimes brooding, sometimes nostalgic, is found in the early *Berceuse d'autumne* (1923) but at its most expressive in the nocturne, *Atardecer* (dusk), an ambitious piece for two players (1975); but it also colours some of the miniatures, not least the austere yet deeply felt *Plegaria de la Infanta de Castilla* from the *Cuatro Piezas* of 1936–8. The recording is uncommonly real and has great presence. In the duo works Allen is admirably partnered by Anton Nel.

Roman, Johan Helmich (1694–1758)

(i) *Violin concertos: in D min.; E flat; F min.; Sinfonias: in A; D and F.*
*** BIS Dig. CD 284 [id.]. (i) Nils-Erik Sparf; Orpheus Chamber Ens.

None of the *Sinfonias* here have appeared on disc before – and indeed only one (the *A major*) exists in print. Of the five *Violin concertos* attributed to Roman, the three recorded here are classified by Bengtsson as 'probably authentic'. They are certainly attractive pieces, particularly in such persuasive hands as those of Nils-Erik Sparf and the Orpheus Chamber Ensemble (who are not to be confused with the distinguished American group, but are drawn from the Stockholm Philharmonic). Very stylish and accomplished performances that are scholarly in approach.

The Golovin music.
*** Cap. Dig. CAP 1325. Drottningholm Bar. Ens.

Count Golovin was the Russian Ambassador to the Swedish Court at the time of the coronation of the twelve-year-old tsar, Peter II, in 1728; for the festivities at his residence Roman provided what has been described as 'a generous bouquet of orchestral pieces', 45 movements in all, of which the Drottningholm Baroque Ensemble have recorded two dozen. The music has a good deal of charm; here it is recorded not only on period instruments but in the original acoustic in which the music was first heard. An attractive disc.

(i) *Assaggi for violin in A, in C min. and in G min., BeRI 301, 310 & 320;* (i; ii) *Violin and harpsichord sonata No. 12 in D, BeRI 212;* (ii) *Harpsichord sonata No. 9 in D min., BeRI 233.*
*** Cap. CAP 21344 [id.]. (i) Jaap Schröder; (ii) Johann Sönnleitner.

Assaggio (the singular form of *Assaggi*) means 'essay' in the sense of test-piece or attempt. The

Assaggi recorded here chart an unusual path between the purely virtuosic and the introspective. They often take one by surprise, particularly when played with such imagination as they are by Jaap Schröder. The harpsichord sonata is also more inward-looking than many others of Roman's pieces, and the only work that one could possibly describe as fairly predictable is the opening *Sonata for violin and continuo.* Excellent performances and recording, as well as exemplary presentation.

Rossi, Luigi (1597–1663)

Oratorio per la Settimana Santa; Un peccator pentito (Spargete sospiri).
*** HM Dig. HMC 901297; *HMC 401297* [id.]. Soloists, Les Arts Florissants, William Christie.

William Christie and his talented period-performance group here revive one of the earliest examples of an oratorio. Complete with demons, singing solo and in chorus, it graphically tells the story of Christ's judgment before Pontius Pilate and His Crucifixion. Though most of the 17 sections are brief, the climactic points bring more extended numbers, including a magnificent lament for the Virgin Mary, a vigorous last chorus of demons and a superb final madrigal. The extra item is an equally moving motet setting a poem by Giovanni Lotti. Though a list of soloists is given, there is no indication who sings what. The full and bright recording gives an edge to string tone.

Orfeo (opera; complete).
**(*) HM Dig. HMC 901358/60 (3); *HMC 401358/60* (3) [id.]. Mellon, Zanetti, Piau, Favat, Fouchécourt, Salzmann, Corréas, Deletré, Les Arts Florissants, Christie.

Luigi Rossi's *Orfeo* was written in 1647 exactly 40 years after Monteverdi's pioneering masterpiece on the same subject. It has a much more complex classical story than the Monteverdi, yet in its artificial way it is less effectively dramatic. Even so, it offers such incidental delights as a slanging match between Venus (enemy of Orfeo, when he represents marital fidelity) and Juno. That hint of a classical send-up adds sparkle, contrasting with the tragic emotions conveyed both in Orfeo's deeply expressive solos and in magnificent Monteverdi-like choruses. Rossi, when composing the opera in Paris, heard of the death of his young wife back in Italy, and the bereavement affected what he wrote, even though the serious element is limited in the original libretto. William Christie draws characteristically lively and alert playing from Les Arts Florissants, but his cast is not as consistent as those he usually has in his Harmonia Mundi recordings. Too many of the singers sound fluttery or shallow, and even Agnes Mellon as Orfeo is less even and sweet of tone than usual. Nonetheless, with excellent documentation and first-rate sound, this makes a most welcome recording of an important rarity.

Rossini, Gioacchino (1792–1868)

La boutique fantasque (ballet, arr. Respighi) complete.
❀ (M) *** Sony Dig. MDK 46508 [id.]. Toronto SO, Andrew Davis – BIZET: *L'Arlésienne: suite No. 2* etc. **(*)
(M) **(*) Decca Dig. 430 723-2; *430 723-4* [id.]. National PO, Bonynge – CHOPIN: *Les Sylphides.* **(*)

At last comes a really outstanding complete CD of *La boutique fantasque*, one of the great popular triumphs of Diaghilev's Ballets Russes. In the sympathetic hands of Andrew Davis there is never a dull bar, for Respighi's linking passages (usually omitted) are ingeniously crafted and he leads the ear on affectionately. The Toronto orchestra is on peak form, playing with glittering bravura and warmth; the gentler second half of the ballet is particularly enticing. The digital recording has a spectacularly wide dynamic range; the magical opening (here taken faster than usual) with gentle pizzicato strings evoking gleaming horn chords, at first a mere whisper, then expands gloriously. The vividness of the CBS sound is balanced by a glowing underlying warmth, and this becomes a demonstration disc for the digital era which recalls Ansermet's famous Decca mono LP of the early 1950s, made with the LSO in the Kingsway Hall, London.

Bonynge goes for sparkle and momentum above all in Respighi's brilliant arrangement of Rossini. The Decca recording has great brilliance and the orchestral colours glitter within the

Kingsway Hall ambience. But compare the very opening with Andrew Davis, and here there is much less magic and – more surprisingly – less atmosphere, while the dynamic range of the Toronto recording is much more dramatic.

La boutique fantasque (ballet, arr. Respighi): *suite.*
(M) **(*) Chan. CHAN 6503; *MBTD 6503* [id.]. SNO, Gibson – DUKAS: *L'apprenti sorcier;* SAINT-SAENS: *Danse macabre.* **(*)
(M) **(*) Sony SBK 46340 [id.]; *40-46340.* Phd. O, Ormandy – TCHAIKOVSKY: *Sleeping Beauty:* highlights. **
(*) Ph. Dig. 420 485-2 [id.]. ASMF, Marriner – RESPIGHI: *Ancient airs; The Birds.* *

Gibson's version of the suite is strikingly atmospheric. Helped by the glowing acoustics of Glasgow's City Hall, his performance sounds for all the world as if the Scottish conductor had first listened to Ansermet's famous Decca mono LP. Tempi are similar and the opening has much of the evocation that the Swiss maestro created. The orchestra is on its toes and plays with warmth and zest, and the 1973 recording has transferred vividly to CD. The only snag is the short playing time (37 minutes).

Ormandy presents Respighi's glittering orchestration with much brilliance and dash, and the Philadelphia Orchestra has all the sumptuousness one could ask for. This is more extrovert music-making than Gibson's and it is undoubtedly exhilarating, even if the effect of the recording is less refined. The playing time of the Sony CD is much more generous too, but not everyone will want the rather inflated coupling.

Marriner's suite is insubstantial, offering only about 20 minutes' music, chosen rather arbitrarily. It is elegantly played and warmly recorded.

Introduction, theme and variations in C min. for clarinet and orchestra.
*** ASV Dig. CDDCA 559; *ZCDCA 559* [id.]. Emma Johnson, ECO, Groves – CRUSELL: *Concerto No. 2* *** ❀; BAERMANN: *Adagio* ***; WEBER: *Concertino.* ***

As in all her recordings, Emma Johnson's lilting timbre and sensitive control of dynamic bring imaginative light and shade to the melodic line. Brilliance for its own sake is not the keynote, but her relaxed pacing is made to sound exactly right. Vivid recording.

Overtures: *Armida; Il Barbiere di Siviglia; Bianca e Faliero; La cambiale di matrimonio; La Cenerentola; Demetrio e Poblibio; Edipo a Colono; Edoardo e Cristina;* (i) *Ermione. La gazza ladra; L'inganno felice; L'Italiana in Algeri; Maometto II; Otello.* (i) *Ricciardo e Zoraide. La scala di seta; Semiramide; Le siège de Corinthe; Il Signor Bruschino; Tancredi; Il Turco in Italia; Torvaldo e Dorliska; Il viaggio a Reims; William Tell. Sinfonia al Conventello; Sinfonia di Bologna.*
(M) *** Ph. 434 016-2 (3) [id.]. ASMF, Marriner; (i) with Amb. S.

Marriner's three discs span all Rossini's overtures, but one must remember that the early Neapolitan operas, with the exception of *Ricciardo e Zoraide* and *Ermione*, make do with a simple Prelude, leading into the opening chorus. *Ricciardo e Zoraide*, however, is an extended piece (12 minutes 25 seconds), with the choral entry indicating that the introduction is at an end. *Maometto II* is on a comparable scale, while the more succinct *Armida* is an example of Rossini's picturesque evocation, almost like a miniature tone-poem. Sometimes Rossini used the same overture for more than one opera, and there are extensive quotations of material from one to another. Even so, 24 overtures plus two sinfonias make a delightful package in such sparkling performances, which eruditely use original orchestrations. Rossini's earliest overtures include *Demetrio e Poblibio*, a charmer written when he was only fifteen, and the *Sinfonia al Conventello*, commissioned by Agostino Triossi, a wealthy merchant from Ravenna, to be performed at Conventello, his summer residence. This piece, brief but already characteristic, later provided a theme for *Il Signor Bruschino*, and the 1808 *Sinfonia di Bologna* yet another tune for *L'inganno felice*. Full, bright and atmospheric recording, spaciously reverberant, admirably transferred to CD, with no artificial brilliance.

Overtures: *Il Barbiere di Siviglia; La cambiale di matrimonio; La Cenerentola; La gazza ladra; La scala di seta; Semiramide; William Tell.*
**(*) EMI Dig. CDC7 49155-2 [id.]. ASMF, Marriner.

The highlight here is the sparkling account of *La Cenerentola*, and *William Tell* opens well and ends with great gusto. *La scala di seta* sounds more crisply spontaneous in the splendid Orpheus Chamber Orchestra's compilation on DG. Yet, in its good-humoured way, the

Marriner disc is very enjoyable, the playing is clean and well mannered and the EMI recording full-bodied and clear. It was curious, though, to end with *La cambiale di matrimonio* (which by no means dispels memories of Beecham) rather than the more suitable *William Tell*.

Overtures: *Il Barbiere di Siviglia; La cambiale di matrimonio; L'inganno felice; L'Italiana in Algeri; La scala di seta; Il Signor Bruschino; Tancredi; Il Turco in Italia.*
*** DG Dig. 415 363-2 [id.]. Orpheus CO.

The Orpheus Chamber Orchestra displays astonishing unanimity of style and ensemble in this splendid collection of Rossini overtures, played without a conductor. Not only is the crispness of string phrasing a joy, but the many stylish wind solos have an attractive degree of freedom, and one never senses any rigidity in allegros which are always joyfully sprung. *La scala di seta* is an especial delight, and the opening string cantilena of *Il Barbiere* is agreeably gracious. These are performances that in their refinement and apt chamber scale give increasing pleasure with familiarity. The DG recording is marvellously real with the perspective perfectly judged.

Overtures: *Il Barbiere di Siviglia; La Cenerentola; La gazza ladra; L'Italiana in Algeri; La scala di seta; Semiramide; Il Signor Bruschino; William Tell.*
**(*) Decca Dig. 433 074-2; *433 074-4* [id.]. Montreal SO, Charles Dutoit.

Dutoit achieves spirited, polished playing in eight favourite overtures, and the opening *La scala di seta* demonstrates the crisp elegance of the string articulation. There is not always quite the flair and sheer panache of the very finest versions, and while this is all very agreeable, the rich sound picture brings a rather flowery bouquet to the sound; occasionally the ear craves a touch more astringency and wit.

Overtures: *Il Barbiere di Siviglia; La Cenerentola; La gazza ladra; L'Italiana in Algeri; Le siège de Corinthe; Il Signor Bruschino.*
(M) *** DG 419 869-2; *419 869-4* [id.]. LSO, Abbado.

Brilliant, sparkling playing, with splendid discipline, vibrant rhythms and finely articulated phrasing – altogether invigorating and bracing. There is perhaps an absence of outright geniality here, but these are superb performances and this remains one of the very finest collections of Rossini overtures ever, for the wit is spiced with a touch of acerbity, and the flavour is of a vintage dry champagne which retains its bloom, yet has a subtlety all its own.

Overtures: *Il Barbiere di Siviglia; La Cenerentola; La gazza ladra; La scala di seta; Il Signor Bruschino; William Tell.*
❀ (M) *** BMG/RCA GD 60387 [60387-2-RG]. Chicago SO, Fritz Reiner.

As with the others in RCA's remastered Reiner/Chicago series, the sound-quality has been improved phenomenally; no one could possibly guess that these recordings were made over thirty years ago (in 1958) for, as sound, they are preferable to most digital collections. The blaze of brass tone, supported by a rich orchestral backcloth and resonant bass drum, at the gallop in the *William Tell overture*, is all-engulfing, a thrilling moment indeed. The Chicago Symphony was always famous for its brass department, and this is an excellent reminder of how resplendent the playing could be; at the same time the scurrying violins display the utmost virtuosity. Reiner is equally impressive at the grandiloquent opening of *La gazza ladra*, where the hall acoustics again add a magnificent amplitude to the full orchestral tutti. But it is the sparkle and vivacity of these performances that one remembers above all – and, in *La Cenerentola*, the wit, as well as fizzing orchestral bravura. One would have liked the opening flourish of *La scala di seta* to be neater – it is presented too lavishly here – but this is the solitary reservation over a magnificent achievement.

Overtures: *Il Barbiere di Siviglia; La gazza ladra; L'Italiana in Algeri; La scala di seta.*
(B) *** DG 429 164-2. BPO, Karajan – VERDI: *Overtures and Preludes.* ***

Overtures: *Il Barbiere di Siviglia; La gazza ladra; L'Italiana in Algeri; La scala di seta; William Tell* (CD only: *Semiramide*).
(B) *** DG Compact Classics 431 185-2 (2); *431 185-4* [id.]. BPO, Karajan – VERDI: *Overtures.* ***

Karajan's virtuoso Rossini performances are superbly polished and vivid. *La scala di seta* abandons almost all decorum when played as brilliantly as here, but this music-making is nothing if not exhilarating. The 1971 recordings are crisply transferred with plenty of supporting weight and good ambience. With equally distinguished Verdi for coupling, this is one of the finest of the later Compact Classics tapes. The pair of CDs include only one extra Rossini overture and one of Verdi, so the cassette is far better value. However, the single bargain CD makes amends.

Overtures: *Il Barbiere di Siviglia; La gazza ladra; L'Italiana in Algeri; La scala di seta; Il Signor Bruschino; Semiramide; William Tell.*
❀ *** EMI Dig. CDC7 54091-2 [id.]. L. Classical Players, Norrington.

It is the drums that take a star role in Norrington's Rossini collection. They make their presence felt at the beginning and end of an otherwise persuasively styled reading of *Il Barbiere*; at the introduction of *La gazza ladra*, where the snares rattle spectacularly and antiphonally; creating tension more distinctly than usual at the beginning of *Semiramide*, and bringing tumultuous thunder to the Storm sequence in *William Tell.* Of course the early wind instruments are very characterful too, with plenty of piquant touches: the oboe colouring is nicely spun in *L'Italiana in Algeri* and properly nimble in *La scala di seta*, a particularly engaging performance, mainly because of the woodwind chirpings. The brass also make their mark, with the stopped notes on the hand horns adding character to the solo quartet in *Semiramide*, and both horns and trumpets giving a brilliant edge to the announcement of the galop in *William Tell.* The strings play with relative amiability and a proper sense of line and are obviously determined to please the ear as well as to stimulate; altogether these performances offer a very refreshing new look over familiar repertoire. The recording is first class.

String sonatas Nos. 1–6 (complete).
*** ASV CDDCA 767; *ZCDCA 767* [id.]. Serenata of London (members).
*** Hyp. Dig. CDA 66595 [id.]. O of Age of Enlightenment (members).
(M) **(*) Decca 430 563-2 (2). ASMF, Marriner (with DONIZETTI: *String quartet in D* (arr. for string orchestra); CHERUBINI: *Étude No. 2 for French horn and strings;* BELLINI: *Oboe concerto in E flat* **(*))

String sonatas Nos. 1 in G; 3 in C; 4 in B flat; 5 in E flat.
**(*) DG Dig. 413 310-2 [id.]. Bern Camerata, Füri.

String sonatas Nos. 1 in G; 4 in B flat; 5 in E flat; 6 in D.
(M) *** Teldec/Warner 9031 74788-2 [id.]. Liszt CO, János Rolla – M. HAYDN: *Symphony, P.12.* ***

Almost simultaneously, Serenata of London, working as a string quartet, and a comparably sized group from the Orchestra of the Age of Enlightenment, playing period instruments, each manage to include all six of the *String sonatas* – the astonishingly assured work of the twelve-year-old Rossini – on one CD (timings: 77 minutes 53 seconds and 79 minutes 40 seconds respectively). This is not achieved by super-brisk tempi: the inherent virtuosity in the part-writing would surely preclude that; indeed the pacing of both groups is eminently well judged and the playing is fresh and polished. As might be expected, the Serenata, playing modern instruments and led by the easily brilliant Barry Wilde, give the warmer, more sunny bouquet to Rossini's string textures; their competitors, led by the dazzling Elizabeth Wallfisch, offer a slightly drier vintage, though their approach is by no means unsmiling. Indeed their bass player, ChiChi Nwanoku, brings added sharpness of attack to his moments of bravura, where Michael Brittain, with comparable virtuosity at times sounds rather deadpan. On both discs the recording is truthful and naturally balanced, accurately reflecting the different string timbres, but bringing no unnatural edge in either instance.

We admit that we still have a very soft spot for the sparkle, youthful exuberance and wit of the Marriner performances, made when the ASMF was at an early peak, but the playing time, at fractionally over 80 minutes, means that two CDs have been used. The 1966 recording still sounds well and the encores are expertly chosen (especially the Donizetti *Quartet*, which has an appropriately Rossinian flavour), but with an overall playing time of only 112 minutes this pair of discs now seems relatively uncompetitive, even at mid-price.

The Bern performances, given by a small string ensemble, have an elegance, virtuosity and sparkle that is difficult to beat. The playing is pretty dazzling and they are accorded recording quality of the highest order. The sound is particularly fresh and vividly focused; overall, the balance is very satisfying. This is a record that will give enormous pleasure. However, this disc now seems overpriced.

The merits of the Liszt Chamber Orchestra and János Rolla, who directs from the first desk, are by now well known. They are hardly less virtuosic or less polished than the Bern Camerata, and they have the advantage of very natural digital sound. Moreover the attractive Michael Haydn coupling is considerable compensation for the two missing sonatas, and the disc comes at mid-price.

Cantata: *Giovanna d'Arco.* Songs: *L'âme délaissée; Ariette à l'ancienne; Beltà crudele; Canzonetta spagnuola (En medio a mis colores); La grande coquette (Ariette pompadour); La légende de Marguerite; Mi lagnerò tacendo* (5 settings including *Sorzico* and *Stabat Mater*); *Nizza; L'Orpheline du Tyrol (Ballade élégie); La pastorella; La regata veneziana* (3 songs in Venetian dialect); *Il risentimento; Il trovatore.*
*** Decca Dig. 430 518-2 [id.]. Cecilia Bartoli, Charles Spencer.

The songs of Rossini's old age were not all trivial, and this brilliantly characterized selection – with the pianist as imaginative as the singer – gives a delightful cross-section. The big solo cantata on the theme of Joan of Arc provides a culmination, but it is also fascinating to have five entirely different settings of the same text, *Mi lagnerò tacendo*, each representing a totally different but entirely apt mood. Bartoli's artistry readily encompasses such a challenge, a singer who, even at this early stage of her career, is totally in command both technically and artistically. The recording, too, has splendid presence.

Petite messe solennelle.
*** Eurodisc 610 263 (2). Lovaas, Fassbaender, Schreier, Fischer-Dieskau, Münchner Vokalisten, Hirsch, Sawallisch (pianos), Baffalt (harmonium), Sawallisch.

Rossini's *Petite messe solennelle* must be the most genial contribution to the church liturgy in the history of music. The description '*Petite*' does not refer to size, for the piece is comparable in length to Verdi's *Requiem*; rather it is the composer's modest evaluation of the work's 'significance'. But what a spontaneous and infectious piece of writing it is, bubbling over with characteristic melodic, harmonic and rhythmic invention. The composer never over-reaches himself. 'I was born for *opera buffa*, as well Thou knowest,' Rossini writes touchingly on the score. 'Little skill, a little heart, and that is all. So be Thou blessed and admit me to paradise.' The Sawallisch performance would surely merit the granting of the composer's wish. The soloists are first rate, the contralto outstanding in the lovely *O salutaris* and *Agnus Dei.* Good choral singing and fine, imaginative playing from the two pianists. The (originally Ariola) recording, now available on Eurodisc, dates from the early 1970s and is of high quality.

Stabat Mater.
❀ *** Chan. Dig. CHAN 8780; *ABTD 1416* [id.]. Field, Della Jones, A. Davies, Earle, LSO Ch., City of L. Sinfonia, Hickox.
(M) **(*) Decca 417 766-2. Lorengar, Minton, Pavarotti, Sotin, LSO Ch., LSO, Kertész.

In his setting of *Stabat Mater* Rossini may upset the squeamish by having rip-roaring tunes, like the tenor's rumbustious march-setting of *Cujus animam* or the jaunty quartet setting of *Sancta Mater* with its persistent oom-pah rhythms, but it is a mistake to try and over-refine the piece. Richard Hickox rightly presents it warmly with gutsy strength, but then he makes sure that singing and playing have a point and polish to eliminate vulgarity. This is a most winning account which has one marvelling that a work written piecemeal should have such consistently memorable invention, much of it anticipating – or reflecting – early Verdi. All four soloists here are first rate, not Italianate of tone but full and warm. As ever in Hickox's choral recordings, the London Symphony Chorus – which he has long trained – sings with fine attack as well as producing the most refined pianissimos in the unaccompanied quartet, here as usual given to the full chorus rather than to the soloists. Full-bodied and atmospheric sound.

Kertész's approach brings out an unexpected degree of beauty, notably in the fine choral singing, and even *Cujus anima* is given extra delicacy, with Pavarotti singing most beautifully and linking back to the main theme with a subtle half-tone. Some may feel that Kertész underplays the work in removing the open-hearted vulgarity, but he certainly makes one enjoy the music afresh. Soprano, mezzo and bass may not have all the idiomatic Italian qualities, but their singing matches Kertész's interpretation; and this Decca version also has a price advantage.

OPERA

Armida (complete).
*** Koch Europa Dig. 350211 [id.]. Gasdia, Merritt, Matteuzzi, Ford, Furlanetto, Workman, Amb. Op. Ch., I Sol. Ven., Scimone.

Armida is one of the most distinctive of the serious operas that Rossini wrote for Naples in the years after the *Barber of Seville*. In 1817, when it was first performed, the piece ran into the criticism that it was too 'German', but to modern ears the writing is characteristically Rossinian, with the delights of Armida's magic garden remaining very much in the clear light of Italian day, with no mystery conveyed at all. The ballet at the end of Act II (the only one Rossini included in any of his Italian operas) is bright and jolly, not other-worldly at all. Hardly presented as sinister, the sorceress, Armida, becomes what Richard Osborne in his book on Rossini aptly describes as one of the first great operatic *femmes fatales* of the nineteenth century. She has some marvellous fire-eating moments of display, particularly in the last act, when the knight, Rinaldo finally manages to resist her magic and escape. Her realization of defeat, dramatically conveyed on a repeated monotone, is intensely human. Other remarkable numbers include a quartet in Act I, in which at a key moment Rossini quotes (whether intentionally or not) Caldara's song, *Caro mio ben*. This first studio recording from Europa in every way matches the quality of comparable opera sets from the big international companies, not only in recorded sound but in casting too. As Armida, Cecilia Gasdia may not be strikingly characterful (Maria Callas knew the role) but her singing is both powerful and agile, firm and bold in Rossini's brilliant coloratura. As for the problem of finding three high *bel canto* tenors capable of tackling elaborate ornamentation, Europa offers a trio as fine as any available today. One of the high spots comes in Act III, when Rinaldo is joined by two fellow-knights intent on saving him from Armida, and they sing a radiant ensemble. William Matteuzzi and Bruce Ford more than match Chris Merritt as Rinaldo. Though the principal, he is the least gainly of the three, but still impressive, notably in the love duets with Armida, one of them in Act II introduced by a long romantic cello solo. Ferruccio Furlanetto is excellent in two bass roles, and a fourth tenor, Charles Workman, might well have stood in for any of the others. The three acts are squeezed on to two extremely well-filled CDs. The booklet includes an introduction in English, but no translation of the Italian libretto.

Il Barbiere di Siviglia (complete).
*** Ph. Dig. 411 058-2 (3) [id.]. Baltsa, Allen, Araiza, Trimarchi, Lloyd, Amb. Op. Ch., ASMF, Marriner.
*** Decca Dig. 425 520-2 (3) [id.]. Cecilia Bartoli, Nucci, Matteuzzi, Fissore, Burchuladze, Ch. & O of Teatro Comunale di Bologna, Patanè.
*** EMI CDS7 47634-8 (2) [Ang. CDCB 47634]. Callas, Gobbi, Alva, Ollendorff, Philh. Ch. & O, Galliera.
(M) *** EMI CMS7 64162-2 (2) [id.]; (B) CfP *TC-CFPD 4704*. De los Angeles, Alva, Cava, Wallace, Bruscantini, Glyndebourne Festival Ch., RPO, Gui.
(M) *** BMG/RCA GD 86505 (3) [RCA 6505-2-RG]. Roberta Peters, Valletti, Merrill, Corena, Tozzi, Met. Op. Ch. & O, Leinsdorf.
(M) **(*) Decca 417 164-2 (2) [id.]. Berganza, Ausensi, Benelli, Corena, Ghiaurov, Rossini Ch. & O of Naples, Varviso.

Il Barbiere was Sir Neville's first opera recording and he finds a rare sense of fun in Rossini's witty score. His characteristic polish and refinement – beautifully caught in the clear, finely balanced recording – never get in the way of urgent spontaneity, the sparkle of the moment. Thomas Allen as Figaro – far more than a *buffo* figure – and Agnes Baltsa as Rosina – tough and biting, too – manage to characterize strongly, even when coping with florid divisions, and though Araiza allows himself too many intrusive aitches, he easily outshines latterday rivals, sounding heroic, not at all the small-scale tenorino, but never coarse either. Fine singing too from Robert Lloyd as Basilio.

Patanè is a relaxed Rossinian, generally favouring unrushed speeds, timing the delectably pointed recitatives with a keen concern for stage action. With helpful sound-effects and full and vivid sound, it makes a happy first digital recommendation for a much-recorded opera. What sets it apart is the exciting choice of singer as the heroine, Rosina. Cecilia Bartoli made this recording when she was still in her early twenties, a mezzo with a rich, vibrant voice who not only copes brilliantly with the technical demands but who also gives a sparkling, provocative characterization. In her big Act I aria, *Una voce poco fa*, she even outshines the memorable Agnes Baltsa on the excellent Marriner set. Like the conductor, Bartoli is wonderful at bringing out the fun. So is Leo Nucci, and he gives a beautifully rounded portrait of the wily barber, even though the voice is less firm and less expansive than it was, showing signs of wear. Thomas Allen for Marriner sings much better and gives a more youthful characterization. Burchuladze, unidiomatic next to the others, still gives a monumentally lugubrious portrait of Basilio, and the

Bartolo of Enrico Fissore is outstanding, with the patter song wonderfully articulated at Patanè's sensible speed.

Gobbi and Callas were here at their most inspired and, with the recording quality nicely refurbished, the EMI is an outstanding set, not absolutely complete in its text, but so crisp and sparkling it can be confidently recommended. Callas remains supreme as a minx-like Rosina, summing up the character superbly in *Una voce poco fa*. In the final ensemble, despite the usual reading of the score, Rosina's verse is rightly given premier place at the very end. Though this was not among the cleanest of Philharmonia opera recordings, the early stereo sound comes up very acceptably on a pair of CDs, clarified to a degree, presenting a uniquely characterful performance with new freshness and immediacy. The highlights disc offers most of the key solo numbers from Act I, while in Act II it concentrates on Rossini's witty ensembles, including the extended Second Act *Quintet*. The *Overture* is included and, while it is stylishly played, it would have been better to have offered more of the vocal music.

Victoria de los Angeles is as charming a Rosina as you will ever find: no viper this one, as she claims in *Una voce poco fa*. Musically it is an unforceful performance – Rossini's brilliant *fioriture* done lovingly, with no sense of fear or danger – and that matches the gently rib-nudging humour of what is otherwise a 1962 recording of the Glyndebourne production. It does not fizz as much as other Glyndebourne Rossini on record but, with elaborate stage direction in the stereo production and with a characterful line-up of soloists, it is an endearing performance which in its line is unmatched. The recording still sounds well. Tape collectors should be very well satisfied with the CfP equivalent, issued at bargain price on two cassettes in a chunky box, with synopsis instead of libretto. The transfer is kind to the voices and generally vivid, and this costs about half as much as the CDs.

Roberta Peters is a sparkling Rosina, a singer too little known in Europe, who here lives up to her high reputation at the Met., dazzling in coloratura elaborations *in alt*. Robert Merrill may not be a specially comic Figaro, but the vocal characterization is strong, with the glorious voice consistently firm and well focused. Valletti, Corena and Tozzi make up a formidable team, and Leinsdorf conducts with a lightness and relaxation rare for him on record. Good, clear sound of the period, set against a reverberant, helpful acoustic.

Vocally the Decca set, with Teresa Berganza an agile Rosina, is very reliable, and Silvio Varviso secures electrifying effects in many of Rossini's high-spirited ensembles. Manuel Ausensi as Figaro himself is rather gruff but Ugo Benelli is charming as the Count, a free-voiced 'tenorino', though he sounds nervous in his first aria. Corena's fine Dr Bartolo is well known, and Ghiaurov sings with characteristic richness as Basilio. This version is very well recorded – the 1964 sound is noticeably fuller than the earlier, RCA version.

Il Barbiere di Siviglia: highlights.
*** Ph. Dig. 412 266-2 [id.] (from above set, cond. Marriner).
(M) *** EMI CDM7 63076-2; *EG 763076-4* (from complete set with Callas; cond. Galliera).
(M) *** BMG/RCA GD 60188; *GK 60188* [60188-2-RG; *60188-4-RG*] (from above recording with Peters, Valletti, Merrill; cond. Leinsdorf).

The Marriner highlights are well chosen and admirably reflect the qualities of the complete set, while on EMI Callas remains supreme as a minx-like Rosina. The disc offers most of the key solo numbers from Act I, while in Act II it concentrates on Rossini's witty ensembles, including the extended Second Act *Quintet*. The *Overture* is included and, while it is stylishly played, it would have been better to have offered more of the vocal music.

The selection from the Leinsdorf *Barber* is very generous (71 minutes) and well chosen, and the documentation relates the excerpts to an excellent synopsis. The 1958 recording sounds a little shrill in the treble (the violins in the *Overture* are thin), but it responds to the controls.

Il Barbiere di Siviglia: highlights; *La Cenerentola:* highlights.
(B) **(*) DG Compact Classics 427 714-2 (2); *427 714-4* [id.] (from complete recordings, with Berganza, Alva, Prey, Capecchi, Amb. Op. Ch. or Scottish Op. Ch., LSO, Abbado).

Abbado's 1972 recordings of two favourite Rossini operas have a pleasing freshness. Both overtures are included, and the lack of theatrical feeling matters less in highlights; certainly Teresa Berganza, with her agile coloratura, and the stylish Luigia Alva together lead a reliable cast, with Herman Prey as Figaro in *The Barber* and Renato Capecchi as Dandini in *Cenerentola* bringing plenty of sparkle to their performances. The tape reproduces the voices most naturally and has plenty of sparkle. The pair of CDs are attractively transferred but include only five bonus items, with an extra playing time of about 20 minutes. Both operas from which these excerpts are taken are still available but are not among our top recommendations.

La Cenerentola (complete).
*** Ph. Dig. 420 468-2 (2) [id.]. Baltsa, Araiza, Alaimo, Raimondi, Amb. Op. Ch., ASMF, Marriner.
(M) (***) EMI mono CMS7 64183-2 (2). Gabarain, Oncina, Bruscantini, Noni, Glyndebourne Festival Ch. & O, Gui.

Marriner's set of *Cenerentola*, following the pattern of his first opera recording of *Il Barbiere di Siviglia*, conveys Rossinian fun to the full. As in *Il Barbiere*, the role of heroine is taken by the formidable Agnes Baltsa – not so aptly cast this time in a vulnerable Cinderella role – and that of the hero by Francisco Araiza, sweet and fresh of tone, though still allowing too many aspirants in passage-work. Ruggero Raimondi's commanding and resonant singing as Don Magnifico is very satisfying, and there is no weak link in the rest of the cast. The sound is first class in all respects, nicely resonant with plenty of atmosphere.

Dating from 1953, Gui's recording of *Cenerentola* has mono sound of amazing clarity and immediacy. Sadly the text is seriously cut, but the effervescence of Gui's live performances at Glyndebourne has been infectiously caught, making this – at mid-price – a viable alternative to the really complete versions. Juan Oncina produces the most sweet-toned singing as the Prince, with the vintage baritone, Sesto Bruscantini, a vividly characterful Dandini, almost another Figaro. The title role is sung by the Spanish mezzo, Marina de Gabarain, a strikingly positive singer with a sensuous flicker in the voice, very much in the style of the legendary Conchita Supervia.

Le Comte Ory (complete).
❀ *** Ph. Dig. 422 406-2 (2) [id.]. Sumi Jo, Aler, Montague, Cachemaille, Quilico, Pierotti, Lyon Op. Ch. & O, Gardiner.
(M) (***) EMI mono CMS7 64180-2 (2). Oncina, Roux, Jeannette & Monica Sinclair, Glyndebourne Festival Ch. & O, Gui.

This is the piece which tells of the wicked Count Ory's attempt to seduce the virtuous Countess Adèle while her husband is away at the Crusades. In it Rossini deftly uses much of the brilliant material he had written for the occasional celebration opera, *Il viaggio a Reims*. In this re-using Rossini even introduces extra point – not surprising when the hilarious complications of the plot involve such farcical situations as the Count, disguised as a nun, believing he is addressing Countess Adèle, when it is in fact his page (played by a woman), who is himself (herself) in love with the Countess. Rossini handles such complications with unrivalled finesse. With musical argument more sustained than in other comic pieces of the period, *Le Comte Ory* stands out even among Rossini operas, as frothy as any, helped by the witty, unconventional plot. Rossini's mastery is matched by the performance here, beautifully and sparklingly sung and with ensembles finely balanced, as in the delectable Act II trio. Gardiner tends to be rather more tense than Gui was, with speeds on the fast side, and he allows too short a dramatic pause for the interruption to the Nuns' drinking choruses. But the precision and point are a delight, with not a single weak link in the casting, which is more consistent than Glyndebourne's. Though John Aler hardly sounds predatory enough as the Count, the lightness of his tenor is ideal, and Sumi Jo as Adèle and Diana Montague as the page, Isolier, are both stylish and characterful. So is the clear-toned Gino Quilico as the tutor, Raimbaud. With the cuts of the old Glyndebourne set opened out and with good and warm, if not ideally crystal-clear, recording, this set takes its place as a jewel of a Rossini issue.

Gui's classic recording of *Le Comte d'Ory*, with the same Glyndebourne forces who gave this sparkling opera on stage, has claims to being the most indispensable of all Rossini opera recordings, bringing pure delight. In limited but clearly focused mono sound, Gui conveys an extra sparkle and resilience, even over Gardiner's brilliant Philips version. There is a natural sense of timing here that regularly has you laughing in joy, as in the dazzling finale of Act I, one of the most infectiously witty of all recordings of a Rossini ensemble. Gui even more than Gardiner capitalizes on the great asset of this piece even against Rossini's Italian comic operas, the extended numbers, often almost as complex as Mozart's finales for the da Ponte operas. The farcical story offers character as well as wit, with such incidental delights as the *Nuns' drinking chorus* of Act II, when the wicked Count Ory and his followers in disguise penetrate the Countess Adele's castle. Juan Oncina in his prime as the Count, the Hungarian Sari Barabas as the Countess Adele and Michel Roux as the Count's friend are superbly matched by Monica

Sinclair as the Countess's housekeeper and Ian Wallace as the Count's tutor. Some 10 minutes of text have been cut, but that allows the complete opera to be fitted on two CDs, each containing a complete act.

La Donna del Lago (complete).
*** Sony Dig. M2K 39311 (2) [id.]. Ricciarelli, Valentini Terrani, Gonzalez, Raffanti, Ramey, Prague Philharmonic Ch., COE, Pollini.

Maurizio Pollini, forsaking the keyboard for the baton, draws a fizzing performance from the Chamber Orchestra of Europe, suggesting fascinating foretastes not just of Donizetti but of Verdi: of the *Anvil chorus* from *Il Trovatore* in the Act I *March* and of the trombone unisons of *La forza del destino* later in the finale. Katia Ricciarelli in the title-role of Elena, Lady of the Lake, has rarely sung so stylishly on record, the voice creamy, with no suspicion of the unevenness which develops under pressure, and very agile in coloratura. Lucia Valentini Terrani with her warm, dark mezzo is no less impressive in the travesti role of Elena's beloved, Malcolm; while Samuel Ramey as Elena's father, Douglas, with his darkly incisive singing makes you wish the role was far longer. Of the two principal tenors, Dalmacio Gonzalez, attractively light-toned, is the more stylish; but Dano Raffanti as Rodrigo Dhu copes with equal assurance with the often impossibly high tessitura. The recording is clear and generally well balanced and given added immediacy in the new format.

Elisabetta Regina d'Inghilterra (complete).
(M) *** Ph. 432 453-2 (2) [id.]. Caballé, Carreras, Masterson, Creffield, Benelli, Jenkins, Amb. S., New Philh. O, Masini.

The first surprise in this lively operatic setting of the Elizabeth and Leicester story comes in the overture, which turns out to be the one which we know as belonging to *Il Barbiere di Siviglia*. It is one of a whole sequence of self-borrowings which add zest to a generally delightful score. When Queen Elizabeth's big aria in Act II wanders into music which we know as the cabaletta to Rosina's *Una voce poco fa*, it may seem strange to have the formidable Tudor monarch associated with comedy, but in their different ways both ladies were certainly vipers. There are passages where Rossini's invention is not at its peak and the libretto is typically unconvincing, but in a well-sprung performance like this, with beautiful playing from the LSO and some very fine singing, it is a set for any Rossinian to investigate. Of the two tenors, José Carreras proves much the more stylish as Leicester, with Ugo Benelli, in the more unusual role of a tenor-villain, singing less elegantly than he once did. Caballé produces some ravishing sounds, though she is not always electrifying. Lively conducting and splendid recording.

Ermione (complete).
(M) *** Erato/Warner Dig. 2292 45790-2 (2) [id.]. Gasdia, Zimmermann, Palacio, Merritt, Matteuzzi, Alaimo, Prague Philharmonic Ch., Monte Carlo PO, Scimone.

Ermione is the one Rossini opera never revived after its first production. First given in Naples in 1819, this *opera seria* is an adaptation of Racine's great tragedy, *Andromaque*; as the title suggests, it is slanted with Hermione at the centre and Andromaque (Andromaca in Italian) taking the subsidiary mezzo role. It begins very strikingly with an off-stage chorus, introduced in the slow section of the overture, singing a lament on the fall of Troy. The use of dramatic declamation, notably in the final scene of Act II, also gives due weight to the tragedy; however, not surprisingly, Rossini's natural sparkle keeps bursting through, often a little incongruously. The piece is interesting too for its structure, working away from the set aria towards more flexible treatment, allowing, for example, Oreste's cavatina in the third scene to have a duetting commentary from the principal tenor's companion, Pilade. That makes three important tenor roles in the opera, Pirro (Pyrrhus) and Pilade as well as Oreste, reflecting the abundance of tenors in the Naples opera at the time.

The formidable technical demands of the writing for tenor present the principal stumbling block for performance today. Though the three tenors in this Monte Carlo set from Erato are good by modern standards – Ernesto Palacio (Pirro), Chris Merritt (Oreste) and William Matteuzzi (Pilade) – they are uncomfortably strained by the high tessitura and the occasional stratospheric top notes. Cecilia Gasdia makes a powerful Ermione, not always even enough in her production but strong and agile; while Margarita Zimmermann makes a firm, rich Andromaca. Scimone, not always imaginative, yet directs a strong, well-paced performance. On this showing, *Ermione* certainly does not deserve the century and a half of neglect it has received, with brickbats even from Rossini specialists who should have known better. Rossini himself, asked to explain the poor audiences for *Ermione* in Naples, said it was written for posterity. Now at last, thanks to Erato, posterity can fully judge. The recording is rather dry on the voices, but the hint of boxiness is generally undistracting. The break between the two discs comes before the final scene of Act I. Reissued in Erato's 'Affordable opera' series this set is a must for true Rossinians. Besides the excellent libretto, there is a second booklet documenting the opera's history and structure.

Guglielmo Tell (*William Tell:* complete, in Italian).
*** Decca 417 154-2 (4) [id.]. Pavarotti, Freni, Milnes, Ghiaurov, Amb. Op. Ch., Nat. PO, Chailly.

Rossini wrote his massive opera about William Tell in French, but Chailly and his team here put forward a strong case for preferring Italian, with its open vowels, in music which glows with Italianate lyricism. Chailly's is a forceful reading, particularly strong in the many ensembles, and superbly recorded. Milnes makes a heroic Tell, always firm, and though Pavarotti has his moments of coarseness he sings the role of Arnoldo with glowing tone. Ghiaurov too is in splendid voice, while subsidiary characters are almost all well taken, with such a fine singer as John Tomlinson, for example, ripely resonant as Melchthal. The women singers too are impressive, with Mirella Freni as the heroine Matilde providing dramatic strength as well as sweetness. The recording, made in 1978 and 1979, comes out spectacularly on CD. The *Pas de six* is here banded into its proper place in Act I.

Guillaume Tell (William Tell) (sung in French).
(M) **(*) EMI CMS7 69951-2 (4). Bacquier, Caballé, Gedda, Mesplé, Hendrikx, Amb. Op. Ch., RPO, Gardelli.

The interest of the 1973 EMI set is that it is sung in the original French. Gardelli proves an imaginative Rossini interpreter, allying his formidable team to vigorous and sensitive performances. Bacquier makes an impressive Tell, developing the character as the story progresses; Gedda is a model of taste, and Montserrat Caballé copes ravishingly with the coloratura problems of Mathilde's role. While Chailly's full-price Decca set puts forward a strong case for using Italian with its open vowels, this remains a fully worthwhile alternative, with excellent CD sound. The one considerable snag is that no English translation is provided.

L'Italiana in Algeri (complete).
❀ *** DG 427 331-2 (2) [id.]. Baltsa, Raimondi, Dara, Lopardo, V. State Op. Konzertvereinigung, VPO, Abbado.
*** Sony Dig. M2K 39048 (2) [id.]. Valentini Terrani, Ganzarolli, Araiza, Cologne R. Ch., Capella Coloniensis, Ferro.
(M) *** Erato/Warner 2292 45404-2 (2) [id.]. Horne, Palacio, Ramey, Trimarchi, Battle, Zaccaria, Prague Ch., Sol. Ven., Scimone.
(M) *** Decca 417 828-2 (2). Berganza, Alva, Corena, Panerai, Maggio Musicale Fiorentino Ch. & O, Varviso.

Abbado's brilliant version was recorded in conjunction with a new staging by the Vienna State Opera, with timing and pointing all geared for wit on stage to make this the most captivating of all recordings of the opera. Agnes Baltsa is a real fire-eater in the title-role, and Ruggero Raimondi with his massively sepulchral bass gives weight to his part without undermining the comedy. The American tenor, Frank Lopardo, proves the most stylish Rossinian, singing with heady clarity in superbly articulated divisions, while both buffo baritones are excellent too. This has all the sparkle of Abbado's scintillating live recording of *Il viaggio a Reims*, plus first-rate studio sound. Like the CBS set, it uses the authentic score, published by the Fondazione Rossini in Pesaro.

The fine CBS version not only uses the critical edition of the score, it goes further towards authenticity in using period instruments including a fortepiano instead of harpsichord for the recitatives (well played by Georg Fischer). Though Ferro can at times be sluggish in slow music (even in the opening of the overture), he is generally a sparkling Rossinian, pacing well to allow a rhythmic lift to be married to crisp ensemble. The set also gains from forward and bright digital recording. Lucia Valentini Terrani here gives her finest performance on record to date, with her seductively rich, firm voice superbly agile in coloratura. Francisco Araiza as Lindoro peppers the rapid passage-work with intrusive aitches – but not too distractingly – and the strength of the voice makes the performance heroic with no suspicion of the twittering of a tenorino.

Ganzarolli treats the role of the Bey, Mustafa, as a conventional buffo role, with a voice not ideally steady but full of character; the rest of the cast is strong, too.

Scholarship as well as Rossinian zest have also gone into Scimone's highly enjoyable version, beautifully played and recorded with as stylish a team of soloists as one can expect nowadays. The text is complete, the original orchestration has been restored (as in the comic duetting of piccolo and bassoon in the reprise in the overture) and alternative versions of certain arias are given as an appendix. Marilyn Horne makes a dazzling, positive Isabella, and Samuel Ramey is splendidly firm as Mustafa. Domenico Trimarchi is a delightful Taddeo and Ernesto Palacio an agile Lindoro, not coarse, though the recording does not always catch his tenor timbre well. Nevertheless the sound is generally very good indeed, and the fullness and atmosphere come out the more vividly on CD.

Under Varviso the opera has Rossinian sparkle in abundance and the music blossoms readily. Teresa Berganza makes an enchanting Italian girl, and the three principal men are all characterful. The recording is vintage Decca, vividly remastered, and adds greatly to the sparkle of the whole proceedings. With excellent documentation this is a fine bargain, even if many may still opt for the later and more complete Scimone version which is also now available at mid-price.

L'Italiana in Algeri: highlights.
*** DG Dig. 429 414-2 [id.] (from complete set, with Baltsa and Raimondi; cond. Abbado).

This 67-minute selection of highlights provides an admirable and sparkling sampler with well-chosen excepts; but this is surely a case where the complete recording in one of the mid-priced versions would prove an even better investment, and it would involve only one more CD.

Maometto II (complete).
*** Ph. Dig. 412 148-2 (3) [id.]. Anderson, Zimmermann, Palacio, Ramey, Dale, Amb. Op. Ch., Philh. O, Scimone.

Claudio Scimone's account of *Maometto II* has Samuel Ramey magnificently focusing the whole story in his portrait of the Muslim invader in love with the heroine. The nobility of his singing makes Maometto's final self-sacrifice all the more convincing, even if the opera is made the less tense dramatically from having no villain. The other singing is less sharply characterized but is generally stylish, with Margarita Zimmermann in the travesti role of Calbo, June Anderson singing sweetly as Anna, not least in the lovely prayer which comes as an interlude in a massive Trio or Terzettone in Act I. Laurence Dale is excellent in two smaller roles, while Ernesto Palacio mars some fresh-toned singing with his intrusive aitches. Excellent recording.

Mosè in Egitto (complete).
(M) *** Ph. 420 109-2 (2) [id.]. Raimondi, Anderson, Nimsgern, Palacio, Gal, Fisichella, Amb. Op. Ch., Philh. O, Scimone.

For a century and more it was assumed that Rossini's later thoughts on the subject of a Moses opera – his expanded version for Paris – were the ones to be preferred. It is good that Scimone took scholarly advice, and in a direct and understanding reading, presents the second and far preferable of the two Italian versions. So here the last and briefest of the three acts is strongly expanded with a big ensemble based on Moses' prayer to make it almost a forerunner of another great chorus for the Children of Israel, *Va pensiero* from Verdi's *Nabucco*. Other Verdian parallels come out, for some of the ceremonial writing suggests a much later Egyptian opera, *Aida*, as well as a masterpiece written at that same period, the *Requiem*. Clearly Scimone justifies his claim that the 1819 version is dramatically more effective than both the earlier Italian one and the later Paris one.

Among the soloists, Raimondi relishes not only the solemn moments like the great invocation in Act I and the soaring prayer of Act III, but the rage aria in Act II, almost like Handel updated if with disconcerting foretastes of Dr Malatesta in Donizetti's *Don Pasquale*. The writing for the soprano and tenor lovers (the latter the son of Pharaoh and in effect the villain of the piece) is relatively conventional, though the military flavour of their Act I cabaletta is refreshingly different. Ernesto Palaccio and June Anderson make a strong pair, and the mezzo, Zehava Gal, is another welcome newcomer as Pharoah's wife. Siegmund Nimsgern is a fine Pharoah, Salvatore Fisichella an adequate Arone (Aaron). The well-balanced recording emerges most vividly on CD.

Otello (complete).
(M) *** Ph. 432 456-2 (2) [id.]. Carreras, Von Stade, Condò, Pastine, Fisichella, Ramey, Amb. S., Philh. O, Lopez-Cobos.

Quite apart from the fact that the libretto of Rossini's *Otello* bears remarkably little resemblance to Shakespeare – virtually none at all until the last act – the layout of voices is odd. Not only is Otello a tenor role, so is Rodrigo (second in importance), and Iago too. It is some tribute to this performance, superbly recorded, and brightly and stylishly conducted by Lopez-Cobos, that the line-up of tenors is turned into an asset, with three nicely contrasted soloists. Carreras is here at his finest – most affecting in his recitative before the murder, while Fisichella copes splendidly with the high tessitura of Rodrigo's role, and Pastine has a distinct timbre to identify him as the villain. Frederica von Stade pours forth a glorious flow of beautiful tone, well-matched by Nucci Condò as Emilia. Samuel Ramey is excellent too in the bass role of Elmiro. Otello, Rossini-style is an operatic curiosity, but this recording helps to explain why it so ensnared such a sensitive opera-lover as the novelist Stendhal.

Semiramide (complete).
(M) *** Decca 425 481-2 (3) [id.]. Sutherland, Horne, Rouleau, Malas, Serge, Amb. Op. Ch., LSO, Bonynge.

The story of *Semiramide* is certainly improbable, involving the love which almost all the male characters bear for the Princess Azema, a lady who rather curiously appears very infrequently in the opera. Instead, Rossini concentrates on the love of Queen Semiramide for the Prince Arsace (a mezzo-soprano), and musically the result is a series of fine duets, superbly performed here by Sutherland and Horne (in the mid-1960s when they were both at the top of their form). What a complete recording brings out, however, is the consistency of Rossini's drama, the music involving the listener even when the story falls short. In Sutherland's interpretation, Semiramide is not so much a Lady Macbeth as a passionate, sympathetic woman and, with dramatic music predominating over lánguorous cantilena, one has her best, bright manner. Horne is well contrasted, direct and masculine in style, and Spiro Malas makes a firm, clear contribution in a minor role. Rouleau and Serge are variable but more than adequate, and Bonynge keeps the whole opera together with his alert, rhythmic control of tension and pacing. The vintage Decca recording has transferred brilliantly to CD.

Tancredi (complete).
** Sony M3K 39073 (3) [id.]. Horne, Cuberli, Palacio, Zaccaria, Di Nissa, Schuman, Ch. and O of Teatro la Fenice, Weikert.

The chief glory of this live recording from Venice is the enchanting singing of Lella Cuberli as the heroine, Amenaide. The purity and beauty of her tone, coupled with immaculate coloratura and tender expressiveness, make it truly memorable. Marilyn Horne, though not quite as fresh-sounding as earlier in her career, gives a formidable performance in the breeches role of Tancredi, relishing the resonance of her chest register, but finding delicacy too in her big aria, *Di tanti palpiti*. Ernesto Palacio is an accomplished Rossini tenor, commendably agile in the role of Argirio, but the tone tends to grow tight; and Ernesto Zaccaria as Orbazzano sings with fuzzy, sepulchral tone. The conducting is efficient rather than inspired, failing to make the music sparkle or to bring the drama to life. The recording gives a realistic idea of a dryish theatre acoustic.

Il viaggio a Reims (complete).
❀ *** DG Dig. 415 498-2 (2) [id.]. Ricciarelli, Valentini Terrani, Cuberli, Gasdia, Araiza, Gimenez, Nucci, Raimondi, Ramey, Dara, Prague Philharmonic Ch., COE, Abbado.

This DG set is one of the most sparkling and totally successful live opera recordings available, with Claudio Abbado in particular freer and more spontaneous-sounding than he generally is on disc, relishing the sparkle of the comedy. The piece has virtually no story, with the journey to Rheims never actually taking place, only the prospect of it. The wait at the Golden Lily hotel at Plombières provides the opportunity for the ten star characters each to perform in turn: and one hardly wonders that after the first performances Rossini refused ever to allow a revival, on the grounds that no comparable cast could ever be assembled. Instead, he used some of the material in his delectable comic opera, *Le comte Ory*, and it is fascinating here to spot the numbers from it in their original form. Much else is delightful, and the line-up of soloists here could hardly be more impressive, with no weak link. Apart from the established stars the set introduced two formidable newcomers in principal roles, Cecilia Gasdia as a self-important poetess (a nice parody of romantic manners) and, even finer, Lella Cuberli as a young fashion-crazed widow. The rich firmness and distinctive beauty of Cuberli's voice, coupled with amazing flexibility, proclaims a natural prima donna. Abbado's brilliance and sympathy draw the musical threads compellingly together with the help of superb, totally committed playing from the young members of the Chamber Orchestra of Europe.

Zelmira (complete).
*** Erato/Warner Dig. 2292 45419-2 (2) [id.]. Gasdia, Fink, Matteuzzi, Merritt, Amb. S., Sol. Ven., Scimone.

Zelmira, the last-but-one opera that Rossini wrote in Italy before going off to live in Paris, has always had a bad press, but this recording, well sung (with one notable exception) and very well recorded, lets us appreciate that Rossinian inspiration had certainly not dried up, even if the plot's absurdities make it hard to imagine a modern staging. Scimone conducted the recording immediately after a concert performance in Venice, and that obviously helped to give vitality to the substantial sequences of accompanied recitative. He takes a generally brisk view of both the arias and the ensembles but never seems to race his singers. Though the story of murders and usurpations in the royal family of Lesbos is too ill-motivated to be involving, it gives some splendid excuses for fine Rossini arias. There is precious little distinction in musical tone of voice between the goodies and baddies in the story, with the usurping Antenore given some of the most heroic music, for example the first aria. That is a tenor role, more robust than that of Ilo, husband of the wronged heroine, Zelmira. In this performance the choice of singers underlines the contrast between the two principal tenor-roles. Chris Merritt combines necessary agility with an almost baritonal quality as the scheming Antenore, straining only occasionally, and William Matteuzzi sings with heady beauty and fine flexibility in florid writing as Ilo. Star of the performance is Cecilia Gasdia in the name-part, projecting words and emotions very intensely in warmly expressive singing. She is well matched by the mezzo, Barbara Fink, as her friend, Emma, and only the wobbly bass of José Garcia as the deposed Polidoro mars the cast. On two generously filled CDs, with libretto in four languages and first-rate notes, this makes an attractive set for Rossinians, not least because of the fine ensembles such as the two quintets, one at the end of Act I, the other at the climax of Act II.

COLLECTIONS

L'assedio de Corinto: Avanziam' . . . Non temer d'un basso affetto! . . . I destini tradir ogni speme . . . Signormche tutto puio . . . Sei tu, che stendi; L'ora fatal s'appressa . . . Giusto ciel. La Donna del lago: Mura Felici; Tanti affetti. Otello: Assisa a pie d'un salice. Tancredi: Di tanti palpiti.
❀ (M) *** Decca 421 306-2 [id.]. Marilyn Horne, Amb. Op. Ch., RPO, Henry Lewis.

Marilyn Horne's generously filled recital disc in Decca's mid-price Opera Gala series brings one of the most cherishable among all Rossini aria records ever issued. The voice is in glorious condition, rich and firm throughout its spectacular range, and is consistently used with artistry and imagination, as well as brilliant virtuosity in coloratura. By any reckoning this is thrilling singing, the more valuable for covering mostly rarities – which, with Horne, makes you wonder at their neglect. The sound is full and brilliant, showing its age hardly at all.

Arias: *La Cenerentola: Non piu mesta. La Donna del Lago: Mura felici . . . Elena! O tu, che chiamo. L'Italiana in Algeri: Cruda sorte! Amor tiranno! Pronti abbiamo . . . Pensa all patria. Otello: Deh! calma, o ciel. La Pietra del Paragone: Se l'Italie contrade . . . Se per voi lo care io torno. Tancredi: Di tanti palpiti. Stabat Mater: Fac ut portem.*
*** Decca Dig. 425 430-2; *425 430-4* [id.]. Cecilia Bartoli, A. Schoenberg Ch., V. Volksoper O, Patanè.

Cecilia Bartoli is one of the most exciting coloratura mezzo-sopranos to have arrived in many years, a successor to Berganza, Horne and Baltsa. She is the more remarkable for having achieved so much so young. The voice is full, warm and even in its richness, which yet allows extreme flexibility. This first recital of Rossini showpieces brings a formidable demonstration not only of Bartoli's remarkable voice but of her personality and artistry. As yet, she is not so much a sparkler as a commander, bringing natural warmth and imagination to each item without ever quite making you smile with delight. That may well follow, but in the meantime there are not many Rossini recitals of any vintage to match this. Vocally, the one controversial point to note is the way that Bartoli articulates her coloratura with a half-aspirate, closer to the Supervia 'rattle' than anything else, but rather obtrusive. Accompaniments under the direction of Patanè in one of his last recordings are exemplary, and Decca provided the luxury of a chorus in some of the items, with hints of staging. Full, vivid recording. Recommended.

'Rossini heroines': Arias from: *La donna de lago; Elisabetta, Regina d'Inghilterra; Maometto II; Le nozze di Teti e Peleo; Semiramide; Zelmira.*
*** Decca Dig. 436 075-2; *435 075-4* [id.]. Cecilia Bartoli, Ch. & O of Teatro la Fenice, Marin.

Cecilia Bartoli follows up the success of her earlier Rossini recital-disc with this second brilliant collection of arias, mostly rarities. The tangy, distinctive timbre of her mezzo goes with a magnetic projection of personality to bring to life even formal passage-work, with all the elaborate coloratura bright and sparkling. The portrait of Queen Elizabeth I in the final scene from *Elisabetta, Regina d'Inghilterra* is fierce and commanding, with the lighter and more vulnerable sides of the character presented rather less effectively. The rarest item of all is an aria for the goddess Ceres from the classically based entertainment, *Le nozze di Teti e Peleo*, making a splendid showpiece. The collection is crowned by a formidably high-powered reading of *Bel raggio* from *Semiramide*, with Bartoli excitingly braving every danger. A characterful disc from an artist who, though still young, is already among the most positive operatic mezzos of today.

Rott, Hans (1858–84)

Symphony in E.
*** Hyp. Dig. CDA 66366; *KA 66366* [id.]. Cincinnati Philh. O, Gerhard Samuel.

Hans Rott, a pupil of Bruckner, spent the last four years of his short life a victim of hallucinatory insanity and succumbed to tuberculosis in his mid-twenties. During a train journey, when a fellow-traveller lit a cigar he brandished a revolver, declaring that Brahms had filled the train with dynamite. Although his *Symphony* owes much to Wagner as well as to Brahms, to whom allusion is made in the finale, it struck strong resonances in his fellow student, Gustav Mahler. It is astonishing to encounter in their pristine form ideas that took root in Mahler's *First* and *Fifth Symphonies*. Mahler wrote that 'his innermost nature is so much akin to mine that he and I are like two fruits from the same tree, produced by the same soil, nourished by the same air'. None of Rott's music has been published and we owe the present work to Dr Paul Banks, who edited it from the incomplete autograph and a set of parts that were prepared for a planned performance by Hans Richter. Structurally the work is original, each movement getting progressively longer, the finale occupying nearly 25 minutes. But the music is full of good ideas and, anticipations of Mahler apart, has a profile of its own. The Cincinnati Philharmonia is a student orchestra who produce extraordinarily good results under Gerhard Samuel. The recording sounds a trifle opaque on certain equipment but is nevertheless good. Readers should investigate this issue without delay.

Roussel, Albert (1869–1937)

Bacchus et Ariane (ballet): *suite No. 2.*
(B) *** EMI CZS7 62669-2 (2) [Ang. CDMB 62647]. O de Paris, Serge Baudo (with Concert: *French music* ***).
(M) (***) BMG/RCA mono GD 60469 [60469-2-RG]. Boston SO, Munch – RAVEL: *Daphnis et Chloé.* ***

Many collectors will rest content with a suite from Roussel's vivid ballet. Serge Baudo achieves a performance of striking colour and intensity. The music's passion is projected as vehemently as its rhythmic feeling, and the Salle Wagram in Paris again provides an acoustic which brings out the rich colours as well as the evocation of the haunting introduction. The CD transfer of the 1969 recording is first class.

The Boston orchestra was still under Koussevitzky's spell in 1952 when the memorable RCA account of the second suite of Roussel's ballet was made. Munch re-recorded it twice during the 1960s but never with greater virtuosity than here. The recording is mono and the playing quite electrifying. A few bars are missing, perhaps due to the original tapes being damaged, or Munch himself may have made a cut in performance.

Suite in F, Op. 33.
(M) **(*) Mercury 434 303-2 [id.]. Detroit SO, Paul Paray – CHABRIER: *Bourrée fantasque* etc. ***

The outer movements of Roussel's *Suite in F* have a compulsive drive which also infects the harmonically complex, bittersweet central *Sarabande*. The scoring is rich (some might say thick), and the resonance of the Detroit Ford Auditorium makes it congeal a little. It is well played and alive, with Paray at his best in the closing *Gigue*.

Symphonies Nos. 1 in D min. (Le Poème de la forêt), Op. 7; 3 in G min., Op. 42.
*** Erato/Warner Dig. 2292 45253-2; *2292 45253-4* [id.]. O Nat. de France, Dutoit.

The *First Symphony* is subtitled *Le Poème de la forêt* and, unlike its successors, it is relatively loosely held together. The first movement, *Forêt d'hiver*, is a kind of prelude, though the winter would be gentle and warm to northern ears, and the closing bars have some of the balminess of a Mediterranean night. The *Third* is both Roussel's most concentrated and his best-known symphony. Dutoit gets first-class playing from the Orchestre National and the recording is excellent. The delicate colourings of *Le Poème de la forêt* are heard to great advantage and there is altogether admirable range, body and definition.

Symphonies Nos. 2 in B flat, Op. 23; 4 in A, Op. 53.
*** Erato/Warner Dig. 2292 45254-2; *2292 45254-4* [id.]. O Nat. de France, Dutoit.

The *Second Symphony* (1919–21) is the product of an abundantly resourceful musical mind and a richly stocked imagination, eminently well served by the finely developed feeling for craftsmanship Roussel had acquired from d'Indy. The scoring has some of the opulence of the first two Bax symphonies, particularly in the lower wind, and in some of the work's brooding, atmospheric slow sections. While recordings of the *Third* come and go, the *Fourth Symphony* of 1934 has been relatively neglected: it is a delightful score and has Roussel's most infectiously engaging Scherzo. Again, in this and the captivating finale, Dutoit and the French National Orchestra are in excellent form. CD does particular justice to the opulence of Roussel's scoring and is particularly imposing in the definition of the bottom end of the register.

Symphony No. 3 in G min., Op. 42; Bacchus et Ariane (ballet): *suite No. 2, Op. 43;.*
*** Chan. Dig. CHAN 8996; *ABTD 1578* [id.]. Detroit SO, Järvi – RAVEL: *Boléro; La valse.* ***

Neeme Järvi's account of the *Third Symphony* has an engaging vitality and character, and the playing of the Detroit orchestra is highly responsive. In the slow movement which he takes rather faster than Dutoit he indulges in a rather steep *accellerando* after the fugal section (5 minutes 50 seconds in). Likewise his finale feels too fast. But it is a committed performance. His account of the second suite from *Bacchus et Ariane* is both vivid and atmospheric, and in a way it is a pity that Chandos could not persuade Järvi to record more Roussel, the whole ballet, or failing that, the *Fourth Symphony* rather than giving us a hybrid offering. Some may find the acoustic a shade too resonant, given the complexity of Roussel's textures but the overall balance is very natural and pleasing. Dutoit (Erato) is more logically coupled with the *First Symphony* (*Le Poème de la forêt*) and remains a first choice, but readers who are attracted by this particular coupling need not hesitate.

(i) *Sérénade, Op. 30. String trio, Op. 58;* (ii) *Trio for flute, viola and cello, Op. 40.*
** Erato/Warner Dig. 2292 45009-2. Paris String Trio, (i) with Frédérique Cambreling; (ii) Patrick Gallois.

At full price this offers short measure at 46 minutes and the performance of the relatively familiar and highly imaginative *Sérénade* for flute, violin, viola, cello and harp is not really superior to those by the Melos or Prometheus Ensembles. Both the *Flute trio* (1929) and the *String trio* (1937) are rarities; the latter is a powerfully argued and astringent piece with a strong central movement. They are well played and not badly recorded, though the balance is not really ideal; there needs to be more space round the instruments.

Doute; 3 Pièces; Prélude & fugue, Op. 46; Rustiques, Op. 5; Segovia, Op. 29; Sonatine; Suite in F sharp min., Op. 14.
*** Chan Dig. CHAN 8887; *ABTD 1498* [id.]. Eric Parkin.

Eric Parkin's record gives an infinitely more favourable impression of Roussel's piano music than Françoise Petit's LP of the *Sonatine*, Op. 16, the *Suite in F sharp minor* and the *Trois Pièces*, Op. 49, written for Casadesus, which was his sole representation in the catalogue for years. Eric Parkin is a sensitive and sympathetic advocate, and he is excellently recorded at The Maltings, Snape. Roussel's keyboard textures are sometimes thick, as in the *Retour de fête* movement from the early *Rustiques*, written at the time of the *First Symphony*. The *Prélude et Fugue* and the *Trois Pièces* are both late and speak with the same accents as the *Fourth Symphony* and *Bacchus et Ariane*.

(i) *2 Idylls, Op. 44; Jazz dans la nuit; 4 Mélodies de Henri de Régnier;* (ii) *2 Mélodies, Op. 19; 2 Mélodies, Op. 20;* (i; iii) *2 Mélodies, Op. 50;* (iv) *2 Mélodies, Op. 55; La Menace;* (ii) *O bon vin, où as-tu crû?; Odes anacréontiques, Opp. 31–2;* (i; iv) *2 Poèmes chinois, Op. 12;* (i) *2 Poèmes chinois, Op. 35; 2 Poèmes chinois, Op. 47;* (i; iii; iv) *4 Poèmes de Régnier, Op. 8;* (iv) *2 Poèmes de Ronsard, Op. 26; Les rêves;* (i) *Vocalise No. 1;* (iv) *Vocalise No. 2.*
*** EMI Dig. CDS7 49271-2 (2) [Ang. CDCB 49272]. (i) Mesplé; (ii) Van Dam; (iii) Ollmann; (iv) Allioz-Lugaz; Dalton Baldwin.

This is the kind of issue you should snap up immediately; the likelihood of its remaining in circulation for long is very limited. Although such songs as *Le bachalier de Salamanque* and the *Sarabande* feature in recitals, most of these imaginative and very beautiful songs are rarities. Roussel is one of the most intelligent and resourceful of all French composers, and these generously filled CDs include many treasures. There are many good performances here – not to be missed by lovers of French song.

Songs: *Jazz dans la nuit; Mélodie, Op. 19/1: Light; 2 Mélodies, Op. 20; 2 Poèmes chinois, Op. 35.*
(*) Unicorn DKPCD 9035; *DKPC 9035* [id.]. Sarah Walker, Roger Vignoles – DEBUSSY; ENESCU: *Songs.* *

Sarah Walker may not plumb the full emotions of some of the deceptively deep songs in her Roussel group – *Light* for example – but the point and charm of *Jazz dans la nuit* are superbly caught, and the group makes an attractive and generous coupling for the Debussy and Enescu songs, all superbly recorded, with Vignoles a most sensitive accompanist.

Rubbra, Edmund (1901–86)

Violin concerto, Op. 103.
*** Unicorn Dig. DKPCD 9056; *DKPC 9056* [id.]. Carl Pini, Melbourne SO, Measham – IRELAND: *Piano concerto.* ***

If the centrepiece of the *Concerto* is its reflective slow movement, the two outer movements are hardly less impressive. As always with this composer, the music unfolds with a seeming inevitability and naturalness and a strong sense of purpose. Carl Pini is the capable soloist; the Melbourne orchestra under David Measham play with a conviction that more than compensates for the somewhat unventilated recording, which makes textures sound thicker than they in fact are.

Sinfonietta (for strings), Op. 163; 4 Medieval Latin lyrics, Op. 32; 5 Spenser sonnets, Op. 42; Amoretti: 5 Spenser sonnets, 2nd series, *Op. 43.*
*** Virgin Dig. VC 790752-2 [id.]. Martyn Hill, Wilson-Johnson, Endellion Qt, City of L. Sinfonia, Schönzeler.

The *Sinfonietta for strings* is Rubbra's last work and alone is worth the price of the record. It is short but concentrated and is eloquently played by the City of London Sinfonia under Hans-Hubert Schönzeler. The songs are all much earlier and are rewarding pieces. Altogether a valuable contribution to the all-too-small Rubbra discography. Excellent recording.

Symphonies Nos. 3, Op. 49; 4, Op. 53; Resurgam overture, Op. 149; A Tribute, Op. 56.
*** Lyrita Dig. SRCD 202 [id.]. Philh O, Norman Del Mar.

Neither symphony has been recorded before and both are strong works. Indeed the opening of the *Fourth* (1942) is of quite exceptional beauty and has a serenity and quietude that silence criticism. Although the scoring in climaxes is sometimes opaque, there is a consistent elevation of feeling and continuity of musical thought. Rubbra's music is steeped in English polyphony and, though his writing is resolutely diatonic and conservative in idiom, it could not come from any time other than our own. Unquestionably both symphonies have a nobility and spirituality that is rare in any age. The fine *Resurgam overture* is a late work.

Symphony No. 5 in B flat, Op. 63.
(M) *** Chan. CHAN 6576 [id.]. Melbourne SO, Schönzeler – BLISS: *Checkmate* ***; TIPPETT: *Little music.* **(*)

Rubbra's *Fifth Symphony* is a noble work which grows naturally from the symphonic soil of Elgar and Sibelius. Although the Melbourne orchestra is not in the very top division, they play this music for all they are worth, and the strings have a genuine intensity and lyrical fervour that compensate for the opaque effect of the octave doublings. The introduction is grander and more spacious here than in Barbirolli's pioneering record with the Hallé, made in the early 1950s, and the finale has splendid lightness of touch. More attention to refinement of nuance would have paid dividends in the slow movement, whose brooding melancholy does not quite emerge to full effect. Altogether, though, this is an imposing performance which reflects credit on all concerned. The recording is well balanced and lifelike; but the ear perceives that the upper range is rather restricted. The Tippett bonus for this mid-priced reissue is welcome.

Symphonies Nos. 6; 8 (Hommage à Teilhard de Chardin); (i) *Soliloquy for cello, two horns and strings.*
*** Lyrita SRCD 234 [id.]. Philh. O, Del Mar; (i) De Saram, LSO, Handley.

The *Sixth* is one of Rubbra's most admired symphonies – and rightly so – and its slow movement is arguably the most beautiful single movement in all Rubbra (save, perhaps, for the first movement of the *Fourth*). As always in Rubbra there is a strong sense of linear continuity and suppleness of line. The *Eighth Symphony*, subtitled *Hommage à Teilhard de Chardin*, has something of the mystical intensity that was to surface again in the *Ninth* (arguably his masterpiece, which still awaits recording). There are reminders that Rubbra was a pupil of Holst, just as the opening of the *Sixth* reminds us of his admiration for Sibelius. Rohan de Saram gives a splendid account of the *Soliloquy*, a kind of miniature cello concerto, written for the composer's friend and colleague of the Rubbra–Gruenberg–Pleeth Trio, though the recording is not as fresh-sounding as its companions. However, no praise can be too high for Norman Del Mar's accounts of the symphonies. They were recorded in the early 1980s and sound very impressive. The CD transfer has further enhanced the quality of the recordings. Rubbra's music speaks with directness and without artifice and is eminently well served here.

Symphony No. 10 (Sinfonia da camera), Op. 145; Improvisations on virginal pieces by Giles Farnaby, Op. 50; A tribute to Vaughan Williams on his 70th birthday (Introduction and danza alla fuga), Op. 56.
*** Chan. CHAN 8378 [id.]. Bournemouth Sinf., Schönzeler.

Rubbra's *Tenth Symphony* is for chamber orchestra; it is a short one-movement work, whose opening has a Sibelian seriousness and a strong atmosphere that grip one immediately. Schönzeler is scrupulously attentive to dynamic nuance and internal balance, while keeping a firm grip on the architecture as a whole. The 1977 recording has been impressively remastered. It has a warm acoustic and reproduces natural, well-placed orchestral tone. The upper range is crisply defined. The *Farnaby variations* is a pre-war work whose charm Schönzeler uncovers effectively, revealing its textures to best advantage. *Loath to depart*, the best-known movement, has gentleness and vision in this performance. Strongly recommended.

Rubinstein, Anton (1829–94)

Piano sonatas Nos. 1 in F min., Op. 12; 3 in F, Op. 41.
*** Hyp. Dig. CDA 66017 [id.]. Leslie Howard.

Piano sonatas Nos. 2 in C min., Op. 20; 4 in A min., Op. 100.
*** Hyp. Dig. CDA 66105 [id.]. Leslie Howard.

Leslie Howard copes with the formidable technical demands of these *Sonatas* manfully. He proves highly persuasive in all four works, though the actual invention is scarcely distinguished enough to sustain interest over such ambitious time-spans. Rubinstein wrote these pieces for himself to play, and doubtless his artistic powers and strong personality helped to persuade contemporary audiences. The 1981 recordings sound excellent.

Ruders, Poul (born 1949)

(i) *Concerto for clarinet and twin orchestra;* (ii) *Violin concerto No. 1;* (iii) *Drama trilogy No. 3 for cello and orchestra 'Polydrama'.*

*** Unicorn Dig. DKPCD 9114 [id.]. (i) Thomsen; (ii) Hirsch; (iii) Zeuten; Odense SO, Tamás Vetö.

Poul Ruders is one of the most naturally talented of the younger Danish composers. The three works on this well-engineered CD are all from the 1980s. His *Violin concerto* (1981), inspired by a visit to Italy, is scored for strings, harp and harpsichord and is a tribute to the sunny atmosphere of Italian baroque music in general and Vivaldi's *Four Seasons* in particular. Apart from its neo-classicism there is a whiff of minimalism about much of it. The *Clarinet concerto* (1985) is strong stuff; to quote Ruders himself, the soloist is a 'Pierrot-like *vox humana* caught in a vice of orchestral onslaught', and the effect is often disturbing and almost surrealistic. He is an imaginative composer with a vein of lyrical feeling and melancholy that surfaces in the *Cello concerto* (1988). A rewarding and interesting figure.

Ruggles, Carl (1876–1971)

Sun-treader.
(M) *** DG 429 860-2 [id.]. Boston SO, Tilson Thomas – PISTON: *Symphony No. 2;* SCHUMAN: *Violin concerto.* ***

Carl Ruggles belongs to the same generation as Ives, whose exploratory outlook he shared, though not his carefree folksiness. Ruggles's music is expressionist and powerful, and he always structures finished works of art. *Sun-treader* takes its inspiration from Browning and, like so much of Ruggles's music, is uncompromising and it makes tough but rewarding listening. Tilson Thomas and the Boston orchestra make out a very good case for it.

Rutter, John (born 1943)

(i; ii) *The Falcon;* (ii) *2 Festival anthems: O praise the Lord in heaven; Behold, the tabernacle of God;* (ii; iii) *Magnificat.*
*** Coll. Dig. COLCD 114; *COLC 114* [id.]. (i) St Paul's Cathedral Choristers; (ii) Cambridge Singers, City of L. Sinfonia; (iii) with Patricia Forbes; all cond. composer.

The Falcon (1969) was Rutter's first large-scale choral work. Its inspiration was a medieval poem, which is linked to the Crucifixion story, and the composer tells us his interpolation of Gregorian chant (beautifully sung here by the St Paul's Choristers) was influenced by his participating as a boy treble in Britten's own recording of his *War Requiem. The Falcon* is in three sections, performed without a break, the first a setting of Psalm 98, but the core of the piece is the mystical central *Lento*. The *Magnificat* was written as recently as 1990 and has the usual Rutter stylistic touches, with a syncopated treatment of the opening *Magnificat anima mea*, and a joyous closing *Gloria Patri*. Not all the writing in between is as striking as this, although the overlapping phrases of *Et misericordia* are highly effective, and there is much to enjoy and admire. The two anthems are characteristically expansive and resplendent with brass. Fine performances and recording in the best Collegium tradition.

(i) *Gloria;* (ii) Anthems: *All things bright and beautiful; For the beauty of the earth; A Gaelic blessing; God be in my head; The Lord bless you and keep you; The Lord is my Shepherd; O clap your hands; Open thou my eyes; Praise ye the Lord; A prayer of St Patrick.*
*** Collegium Dig. COLCD 100; *COLC 100* [id.]. Cambridge Singers, (i) Philip Jones Brass Ens.; (ii) City of L. Sinfonia, composer.

John Rutter is one of those British composers who have quietly gone on composing traditional English church music without recourse to atonalism or barbed wire. He has a genuine gift of melody and his use of tonal harmony is individual and never bland. The resplendent *Gloria* is a three-part piece, and Rutter uses his brass to splendid and often spectacular effect. The anthems are diverse in style and feeling and, like the *Gloria*, have strong melodic appeal – the setting of *All things bright and beautiful* is delightfully spontaneous. It is difficult to imagine the music receiving more persuasive advocacy than under the composer, and the recording is first class in every respect: the CD adds an extra dimension to the brass and organ in the *Gloria*.

3 Musical fables: (i) *Brother Heinrich's Christmas;* (ii) *The Reluctant Dragon; The Wind in the Willows.*

**(*) Coll. COLCD 115; *COLC 115* [id.]. City of L. Sinf.; with (i) Brian Kay, Cambridge Singers, composer; (ii) Richard Baker, King's Singers, Hickox.

John Rutter's name is readily associated with carols, and *Brother Heinrich's Christmas* is a musical narrative with choir, telling the story of how one of the most famous of all carols was introduced late at night by the angels to Brother Heinrich, just in time for it be included in the monks' Christmas Day service. Brother Heinrich also has a donkey who is a member of the monastery choir, even though he can only sing two notes; but thereby hangs the tale. It is all highly ingenuous (Brian Kay has just the right avuncular approach) but engagingly presented, and should appeal to young listeners who have enjoyed Howard Blake's *The Snowman*. The settings of the two famous Kenneth Grahame stories are no less tunefully communicative, if blander and without the benefit of a famous tune as a central pivot. They lie halfway between cantata and dramatized narrative, with Gilbert and Sullivan undertones, and including simulations of pop music of the 1940s (among other derivations), notably a Rodgers-style ballad which sentimentalizes the end of *The Wind in the Willows* episode, after Toad's escape from prison. All the music is expertly sung and played and blends well with the warmly involving narrative, splendidly done by Richard Baker.

(i) *Requiem; I will lift up mine eyes*.
*** Collegium Dig. COLCD 103; *COLC 103* [id.]. (i) Ashton, Dean; Cambridge Singers, City of L. Sinfonia, composer.

John Rutter's melodic gift, so well illustrated in his carols, is here used in the simplest and most direct way to create a small-scale *Requiem* that is as beautiful and satisfying in its English way as the works of Fauré and Duruflé. The *Sanctus* has a pealing-bell effect (so like the carols) and the *Agnus Dei* is both intense and dramatic. The penultimate movement, a ripe setting of *The Lord is my Shepherd*, with a lovely oboe obbligato, sounds almost like an anglicized Song of the Auvergne, while the delightful *Pié Jesu* – which Caroline Ashton sings with the purity of a boy treble – melodically is nearly as catchy as the similar movement in the Lloyd Webber *Requiem*; it makes one reflect that these two works would make a marvellous concert double bill. The performance is wonderfully warm and spontaneous, most beautifully recorded on CD, and *I will lift up mine eyes* makes a highly effective encore piece.

Saint-Saëns, Camille (1835–1921)

Carnival of the animals.
*** Virgin Dig. VC7 90786-2; *VC 790786-4* [id.]. Anton Nel, Keith Snell, Ac. of L., Richard Stamp – PROKOFIEV: *Peter* *** ❀; MOZART: *Eine kleine Nachtmusik*. **(*)
*** Ph. Dig. 400 016-2 [id.]. Villa, Jennings, Pittsburgh SO, Previn – RAVEL: *Ma Mère l'Oye*. ***
(B) *** CfP CD-CFP 4086; *TC-CFP 4086*. Katin, Fowke, SNO, Gibson – BIZET: *Jeux d'enfants;* RAVEL: *Ma Mère l'Oye*. ***
(BB) *** ASV CDQS 6017; *ZCQS 6017*. Goldstone, Brown, RPO, Hughes – PROKOFIEV: *Peter*. ***
(M) ** BMG/RCA GD 86718; *GK 86718*. Litwin and Lipman, Boston Pops O, Fiedler – PROKOFIEV: *Peter* *(**); TCHAIKOVSKY: *Nutcracker suite*. **

Richard Stamp directs an outstanding version of Saint-Saëns's witty zoology, full of affectionate humour. There is much to beguile: the *Tortoises* bringing a lethargic dignity to Saint-Saëns's geriatric treatment of Offenbach's *Can-can* and Stephen Williams's solo double-bass portrayal of *The Elephant* contrasting with the clattering, brilliant skeletal *Fossils*. After Robert Bailey's gentle, slightly recessed image of *The Swan*, the finale bursts on the listener with infectious vigour, the two pianists producing flourishes of great bravura and some telling marcato emphases for the buoyant rhythmic outlines of the *Grand parade*. Throughout, one responds to the polished overall presentation and sense of fun; although some may feel that the recording is rather resonant, it adds a genial warmth to the vitality of the proceedings.

Previn's version makes a ready alternative. The music is played with infectious rhythmic spring and great refinement. It is a mark of the finesse of this performance – which has plenty of bite and vigour, as well as polish – that the great cello solo of *Le Cygne* is so naturally presented. The shading of half-tones in Anne Martindale Williams's exquisitely beautiful playing is made all the more tenderly affecting. Fine contributions too from the two pianists, although their image is rather bass-orientated, within a warmly atmospheric recording.

On CfP the solo pianists, Peter Katin and Philip Fowke, enter fully into the spirit of the occasion, with Gibson directing his Scottish players with affectionate, unforced geniality. The couplings are attractive and the CD transfer confirms the vivid colourfulness and presence of the mid-1970s recording.

The two pianists on ASV also play with point and style, and the accompaniment has both spirit and spontaneity. *The Swan* is perhaps a trifle self-effacing, but otherwise this is very enjoyable, the humour appreciated without being underlined. The recording is excellent, and this makes a good super-bargain CD recommendation.

There is nothing special about the 1961 Boston Pops account, although it has warmth and quite effective characterization, and the two pianists, Leo Litwin and Samuel Lipman, make a lively contribution. *The Swan* (cello) song is very well played by Martin Hubermann, but he is distantly balanced, in a slightly too resonant acoustic. The main interest of this reissue is Alec Guinness narrating *Peter and the wolf.*

Carnival of the animals; Piano trio in F, Op. 18; Septet in E flat, for trumpet, strings & piano, Op. 65.
*** Virgin Dig. VC7 90751-2; *VC 790751-4* [id.]. Nash Ens.

A generously filled disc. Saint-Saëns wrote the first of his two *Piano trios* in his late twenties and, in the Nash's expert hands, its charms are heard here to best advantage. This is a highly persuasive account of the work, while the Nash Ensemble capture the humour of the *Septet* and the *Grand fantaisie zoölogique* excellently. The acoustic has warmth and the balance between the instruments, particularly in the *Carnival of the animals*, is admirably judged.

(i) *Carnival of the animals;* (ii) *Danse macabre, Op. 40; Suite algérienne, Op. 60: Marche militaire française. Samson et Dalila: Bacchanale.* (ii; iii) *Symphony No. 3 in C min., Op. 78.*
(M) *** Sony SBY 47655 [id.]. (i) Entremont, Gaby Casadesus, Régis Pasquier, Yan-Pascal Tortelier, Caussé, Yo-Yo Ma, Lauridon, Marion, Arrignon, Cals, Cerutti; (ii) Phd. O, Ormandy; (iii) with E. Power Biggs.

It would be churlish to bracket the third star for this very generous collection (75 minutes 35 seconds) because the *Carnival of the animals* – performed in its original chamber version – strikes the listener as somewhat lacking in lustre at the opening. The ear adjusts to the rather dry effect. The evocations of the *Hens and Cocks* and *Wild asses* seem a bit clinical. But then things pick up. The tortoises are gently lugubrious, the elephantine double-bass solo is agreeably gruff, the aquarium delectably watery, and no one could complain that *Les oiseaux* fail to chirp merrily in their *Volière*, even if later the *Pianists* are bit stoical. It is a starry cast: Yo-Yo Ma personifies *The Swan* gently and gracefully, and the finale is extremely spirited. Ormandy and his splendid orchestra play the other orchestral lollipops with fine panache – the exuberance at the end of the *Samson et Dalila Bacchanale* is overwhelming, with thundering drums. The catchy *French military march* also goes with a swing, though the CD transfer makes the brass sound a bit coarse at the climax. No complaint about the 1962 sound in the *Symphony*. The performance is fresh and vigorous, with the conductor's affection fully conveyed. The alert, polished Philadelphia playing brings incisive articulation to the first movement and scherzo, while the *Poco Adagio* is warmly expressive without being sentimentalized. E. Power Biggs has the full measure of the hall's Aeolian-Skinner organ, and he makes a spectacular contribution to the finale, which Ormandy structures most excitingly.

(i) *Carnival of the animals;* (ii) *Symphony No. 3 in C min.*
(M) **(*) Decca Dig. 430 720-2; *430 720-4* [id.]. (i) Rogé, Ortiz, L. Sinf.; (ii) Peter Hurford, Montreal SO; Dutoit.

Dutoit's *Carnival of the animals*, given a crisp and clean digital recording, is a sad disappointment. At almost every point the Gibson CfP version is superior in detailed characterization and lightness of touch, and *The Swan* is here played in a very matter-of-fact way. However, this may be regarded as merely a bonus for a fine performance of the *Organ Symphony.* Here Dutoit brings his usual gifts of freshness and a natural sympathy to Saint-Saëns's attractive score. The recording is very bright, with luminous detail, the strings given a thrilling brilliance above the stave. One notices a touch of digital edge, but there is a balancing weight. The reading effectively combines lyricism with passion. In the finale, Hurford's entry in the famous chorale melody is more pointed, less massive than usual, although Dutoit generates a genial feeling of gusto to compensate. With its wide range and bright lighting, this is a performance to leave one tingling, after Dutoit's final burst of adrenalin.

Carnival of the animals (arr. for brass by Peter Reeve).
(M) ** Decca 425 022-2; *425 022-4* [id.]. Philip Jones Brass Ens., Jones – MUSSORGSKY: *Pictures*. ***

A promising idea which proves disappointing in the execution, despite superb sound and plenty of colour – if very different from the original. But the pianists are sorely missed and a horn solo is no substitute for the cello in capturing the grace of Saint-Saëns's portrayal of *The Swan*. The wit, too, is coarsened, even if the geniality of the playing is evident.

Cello concerto No. 1 in A min., Op. 33.
*** DG Dig. 427 323-2 [id.]. Matt Haimovitz, Chicago SO, Levine – LALO: *Concerto;* BRUCH: *Kol Nidrei*. ***
*** BMG/RCA Dig. RD 71003. Harnoy, Cincinnati SO, Kunzel – OFFENBACH: *Concerto;* TCHAIKOVSKY: *Rococo variations*. ***
(M) *** Mercury 432 010-2 [id.]. Janos Starker, LSO, Dorati – LALO: *Concerto* **(*); SCHUMANN: *Concerto*. ***
(B) *** DG 431 166-2; *431 166-4*. Heinrich Schiff, New Philh. O, Mackerras – FAURÉ: *Élégie;* LALO: *Cello concerto*. ***
**(*) Ph. Dig. 432 084-2; *423 084-4* [id.]. Julian Lloyd Webber, ECO, Yan Pascal Tortelier – FAURÉ: *Élégie* **; D'INDY: *Lied* **(*); HONEGGER: *Concerto*. **(*)

Haimovitz and Levine open the *Concerto* with a vigorous surge of passionate feeling, and the second subject is tenderly contrasted, with lovely warm timbre from Haimovitz. This strongly characterized account, full of spontaneity, competes well with the considerable competition from Ma – see below. Moreover it is extremely realistically recorded, with the balance between cello and orchestra nigh on perfect.

Ofra Harnoy's is also a first-rate account, the opening full of fervour and impulse, played with full tone, while later the timbre is beautifully fined down for the *Adagietto* minuet. The orchestral response is equally refined here; and this well-recorded account is in every way recommendable for its unexpected and attractive Offenbach coupling.

The Mercury CD brings three concertos in performances of striking quality. Starker plays the Saint-Saëns *A minor* with charm and grace, and Dorati provides first-class support. The 1964 recording comes up amazingly well and is excellently (and naturally) balanced, while the orchestral texture is beautifully clean without being in the least overlit or analytical.

Schiff was very young at the time of this recording (1977), but there are no signs of immaturity here. He gives as eloquent an account of this concerto as any on record. He sparks off an enthusiastic response from Mackerras, and the recorded sound and balance are excellent. At bargain price, this deserves the strongest recommendation.

Julian Lloyd Webber plays both Saint-Saëns pieces with considerable virtuosity, though he does not command the range of sonority or colour possessed by some of his rivals listed in our main volume. He has the advantage of first-class accompaniment from Yan Pascal Tortelier and the ECO, impressively natural recorded sound and couplings of special interest.

(i) *Cello concerto No. 1 in A min., Op. 33;* (ii) *Piano concerto No. 2 in G min., Op. 22;* (iii) *Violin concerto No. 3, Op. 61.*
❀ (M) *** Sony/CBS Dig. MDK 46506 [id.]. (i) Yo-Yo Ma, O Nat. de France, Maazel; (ii) Cécile Licad, LPO, Previn; (iii) Cho-Liang Lin, Philh. O, Tilson Thomas.

Three outstanding performances from the early 1980s are admirably linked together in this highly desirable CBS mid-price reissue. Yo-Yo Ma's performance of the *Cello Concerto* is distinguished by fine sensitivity and beautiful tone while the Orchestre National de France respond with playing of the highest quality throughout. Cécile Licad and the LPO under Previn turn in an eminently satisfactory reading of the *G minor Piano concerto* that has the requisite delicacy in the Scherzo and seriousness elsewhere. It is a satisfying and persuasive performance of strong contrasts, with both power and thoughtfulness in the opening movement and a toccata-like brilliance of articulation in the finale. Cho-Liang Lin's account of the *B minor Violin concerto* with the Philharmonia Orchestra and Michael Tilson Thomas is exhilarating and thrilling; indeed, this is the kind of performance that prompts one to burst into applause. Like Ma and Licad, he is given excellent recording from the CBS engineers and, in terms of both virtuosity and musicianship, his version is certainly second to none and is arguably the finest yet to have appeared.

Piano concertos Nos. 1–5.
*** Decca 417 351-2 (2) [id.]. Rogé, Philh. O, LPO or RPO, Dutoit.

Played as they are here, these *Concertos* can exert a strong appeal: Pascal Rogé brings delicacy, virtuosity and sparkle to the piano part and he receives expert support from the various London orchestras under Dutoit. Altogether delicious playing and excellent piano sound from Decca, who secure a most realistic balance.

Piano concerto No. 2 in G min., Op. 22.
**(*) BMG/RCA RD 85666. Rubinstein, Phd. O, Ormandy – FRANCK: *Symphonic variations;* FALLA: *Nights* etc. **(*)
(**(*)) Olympia mono OCD 236 [id.]. Moura Lympany, LPO, Jean Martinon – KHACHATURIAN: *Piano concerto.* (***)

Rubinstein's version was made in 1970, and he is partnered by that most understanding of accompanists, Eugene Ormandy. Rubinstein's secret is that, though he appears sometimes to be attacking the music, his phrasing is full of little fluctuations so that his playing never sounds stilted. The recording of the piano is rather dry, even hard at times, but the glitter seems just right for the centrepiece.

Moura Lympany's 1951 account of Saint-Saëns's *Second Piano concerto* is a delight from the ruminative opening to the coruscating brilliance of the finale, with the wonderfully nimble scherzo a central highlight. She is very well accompanied by Martinon, and it is a pity that the transfer of the (originally Decca) mono recording is so cavernous. Moreover there is a serious pitch fluctuation in the first movement (7 minutes 49 seconds).

Piano concertos Nos. 2 in G min., Op. 22; 4 in C min., Op. 44.
*** EMI CDC7 47816-2 [id.]. Jean-Philippe Collard, RPO, Previn.

Jean-Philippe Collard brings panache and virtuosity to these two concertos, as well as impressive poetic feeling. Apart from the sheer beauty of sound, he commands a wide dynamic range and a subtle tonal palette, and the Royal Philharmonic under Previn give him splendid support. Although allegiance to Pascal Rogé on Decca remains unshaken, Collard with his greater dynamic range and authority makes even more of this music.

Piano concertos Nos. 3 in E flat, Op. 29; 5 in F (Egyptian), Op. 103.
*** EMI Dig. CDC7 49051-2 [id.]. Jean-Philippe Collard, RPO, Previn.

The *Third Concerto* of 1869 is not the equal of its predecessor; but there is much ingenuity in the piano writing, and it could hardly be heard to more persuasive effect than it is in Jean-Philippe Collard's hands. The *Fifth* is much better known; it was composed on a visit to Egypt just over a quarter of a century later. There is no doubting Saint-Saëns's skill in exploiting the genius of the piano to suggest Eastern sonorities. At one point Collard makes his instrument sound exactly like an Arab *qunan*, or zither. He plays throughout with superb control and finish, and Previn and the RPO are sensitive and sympathetic accompanists. The sound is very good too, slightly more transparent than the Decca for Rogé.

Violin concerto No. 1 in A, Op. 30.
*** Decca Dig. 411 952-2 [id.]. Kyung Wha Chung, Montreal SO, Dutoit – LALO: *Symphonie espagnole.* ***

Saint-Saëns's *First Violin concerto* is a miniature. Kyung Wha Chung makes the most of the lyrical interludes and is fully equal to the energetic bravura of the outer sections. With a clear yet full-bodied digital recording and an excellent accompaniment from Charles Dutoit, this is persuasive.

Violin concerto No. 3 in B min., Op. 61.
(M) *** DG Dig. 429 977-2; *429 977-4* [id.]. Perlman, O de Paris, Barenboim – LALO: *Symphonie espagnole.* ***
*** DG Dig. 429 786-2 [id.]. Gil Shaham, NYPO, Sinopoli – PAGANINI: *Concerto No. 1.* ***
*** ASV Dig. CDDCA 680; *ZCDCA 680* [id.]. Xue Wei, Philh. O, Bakels – BRUCH: *Concerto No. 1.* ***

On DG, Perlman achieves a fine partnership with his friend Barenboim, who provides a highly sympathetic accompaniment in a performance that is both tender and strong, while

Perlman's verve and dash in the finale are dazzling. The forward balance is understandable in this work, but orchestral detail could at times be sharper.

One only has to sample the delectable way Gil Shaham presents the enchanting *Barcarolle*, which forms the principal theme of Saint-Saëns's *Andante*, to discover the distinction of this performance. Sinopoli, who proves a splendid accompanist, is equally impressive when he introduces, very quietly and evocatively, the almost equally memorable chorale tune that plays such a major role in the finale and which, after Shaham has relished it with fine lyrical warmth, is to reappear, boldly resplendent on the brass. This is a performance which balances elegant *espressivo* with great dash and fire: the very opening bars of the *Concerto* are commanding indeed, and neither soloist nor conductor lets even the slightest suspicion of routine into a performance which dazzles and charms in equal measure. The recording is first class.

Xue Wei's account is full of flair from the very first entry onwards. The orchestral accompaniment is strongly characterized as well: the brass chorale has a splendidly bold resonance, while the soloist creates an ideal mixture of ruminative lyricism and dash, especially in the slow movement with its delicate pianissimo near the close. The finale has plenty of vitality and the sound is vivid, even if the balance, within a church acoustic, seems artificially contrived.

Danse macabre, Op. 40.
*** Denon Dig. DC 8097 [id.]. Tokyo Metropolitan SO, Jean Fournet – BERLIOZ: *Symphonie fantastique.* ***
(M) **(*) Chan. CHAN 6503; *MBTD 6503* [id.]. SNO, Gibson – DUKAS: *L'apprenti sorcier;* ROSSINI/RESPIGHI: *La boutique fantasque.* **(*)

Jean Fournet's 1987 performance of *Danse macabre* comes as a fill-up to a thoroughly recommendable account of the *Symphonie fantastique* and it is a very persuasive reading, well recorded.

Gibson's performance is also well played and vividly recorded, but this CD offers rather short measure (37 minutes), even at mid-price.

Danse macabre, Op. 40; (i) *Havanaise, Op. 83; Introduction and rondo capriccioso, Op. 28. Le jeunesse d'Hercule, Op. 50; Marche héroïque, Op. 34; Phaéton, Op. 39; Le rouet d'Omphale, Op. 31.*
(M) *** Decca 425 021-2; *425 021-4* [id.]. (i) Kyung Wha Chung, RPO; Philh. O; Charles Dutoit.

A splendidly conceived anthology. The symphonic poems are beautifully played, and the 1979 Kingsway Hall recording lends the appropriate atmosphere. Charles Dutoit shows himself an admirably sensitive exponent, revelling in the composer's craftsmanship and revealing much delightful orchestral detail in the manner of a Beecham. *La jeunesse d'Hercule* is the most ambitious piece, twice as long as its companions; its lyrical invention is both sensuous and elegant. The *Marche héroïque* is flamboyant but jolly, and *Phaéton*, a favourite in Victorian times, is engagingly dated but not faded. It is the delightful *Omphale's spinning wheel* and the familiar *Danse macabre* that show Saint-Saëns at his most creatively imaginative. To make the collection more generously attractive, Decca have now added Kyung Wha Chung's equally charismatic and individual 1977 accounts of what are perhaps the two most inspired short display-pieces for violin and orchestra in the repertoire.

Havanaise, Op. 83.
(M) *** Decca 417 707-2 [id.]. Kyung Wha Chung, RPO, Dutoit – BRUCH: *Concerto No. 1;* TCHAIKOVSKY: *Concerto.* ***

Havanaise, Op. 83; Introduction and rondo capriccioso, Op. 28.
*** DG Dig. 423 063-2 [id.]. Perlman, NYPO, Mehta – CHAUSSON: *Poème;* RAVEL: *Tzigane;* SARASATE: *Carmen fantasy.* ***
*** Teldec/Warner Dig. 9031 73266-2 [id.]. Maxim Vengerov, Israel PO, Mehta – PAGANINI: *Concerto No. 1* **; WAXMAN: *Carmen fantasy.* **(*)

Kyung Wha Chung shows rhythmic flair and a touch of the musical naughtiness that gives the *Havanaise* its full charm. Dutoit accompanies most sympathetically, and the recording is excellent.

Perlman's later, DG recordings are hardly less appealing. They have the advantage of an excellent digital sound-balance and the orchestral texture is fuller. Perhaps the early performances are a shade riper, but the closing pages of the *Havanaise* are particularly felicitous on DG. This disc also includes the Sarasate *Carmen fantasy* as a winning extra item.

Maxim Vengerov really shows his mettle in these Saint-Saëns *morceaux de concert*. He plays with disarming simplicity and charm, much finesse, and dazzles with his easy fireworks; the *Havanaise* in particular produces ravishing tone, yet no over-indulgence. Mehta stands back and gives his young soloist his head.

Introduction and Rondo capriccioso.
*** DG Dig. 427 676-2 [id.]. Mintz, Israel PO, Mehta – LALO: *Symphonie espagnole;* VIEUXTEMPS: *Concerto No. 5.* ***

Mintz dazzles the ear with Saint-Saëns's fireworks, yet playing with elegance and finesse. Mehta accompanies attentively and the live recording, made in Israel, is fully acceptable, the balance making a showcase for the soloist.

Romance for horn and piano, Op. 67.
(M) *** Decca 433 695-2 [id.]. Barry Tuckwell, Vladimir Ashkenazy – BRAHMS: *Horn trio;* FRANCK: *Violin sonata;* SCHUMANN: *Adagio & allegro.* ***

Saint-Saëns's unexpectedly sombre *Romance* is beautifully played by Tuckwell and Ashkenazy who find exactly the right element of restraint. Excellent 1974 Kingsway Hall recording.

Symphonies in A; in F (Urbs Roma); Symphonies Nos. 1–3.
(B) *** EMI CZS7 62643-2 (2) [Ang. CDMB 62643]. French Nat. R. O, Martinon (with Bernard Gavoty, organ de l'église Saint-Louis des Invalides in *No. 3*).

Martinon was the most persuasive advocate of Saint-Saëns, and this complete set of the five *Symphonies*, recorded in Paris between 1972 and 1975, is very welcome to the CD catalogue. The A and F major works were totally unknown and unpublished at the time of their recording and have never been dignified with numbers. Yet the A major, written when the composer was only fifteen, is a delight and may reasonably be compared with Bizet's youthful work in the same genre. Not surprisingly, it betrays the influence of Mozart as well as Mendelssohn (who is very 'present' in the first movement) and, consciously or not, Saint-Saëns uses a theme from the *Jupiter Symphony*. Scored for strings with flute and oboe, the charming scherzo survived the early ban as a separate piece and, with its delectable *moto perpetuo* finale, the whole work makes delightful gramophone listening. More obviously mature, the *Urbs Roma Symphony* came six years later, postdating the official No. 1. The writing is perhaps a shade more self-conscious, but more ambitious too, showing striking imagination in such movements as the darkly vigorous scherzo and the variation movement at the end.

The first of the numbered symphonies was written when Saint-Saëns was eighteen. It is a well-fashioned and genial piece, again much indebted to Mendelssohn, and to Schumann too, but with much delightfully fresh invention. The *Second*, written much later, in 1878, is full of excellent ideas and makes a welcome change from the familiar *Third*. Martinon directs splendid performances of the whole set, well prepared and lively; one can sense the pleasure of the French orchestral players in their discovery of the early works. The account of the *Third* ranks with the best: freshly spontaneous in the opening movement, then comes a spacious *Poco adagio*, a rumbustious scherzo and the threads are knitted powerfully together at the end of the finale. Here the recording could do with rather more sumptuousness, for the remastering has lost some of the original amplitude. Elsewhere the quality is bright and fresh, with no lack of body, and it suits the Saint-Saëns textures very well.

Symphony No. 2 in A min., Op. 55; Phaéton, Op. 39; Suite algérienne, Op. 60.
*** ASV Dig. CDDCA 599; *ZCDCA 599* [id.]. LSO, Butt.

The *Second Symphony* is full of excellent ideas, with a fugue delivered with characteristic aplomb in the first movement; the Scherzo is sparklingly concise and the similarly high-spirited *Tarantella* finale has something in common with Mendelssohn's *Italian symphony*. It is very well played here with the freshness of an orchestra discovering something unfamiliar and enjoying themselves; Yondani Butt's tempi are apt and he shapes the whole piece convincingly. He is equally persuasive in the picaresque *Suite algérienne*, the source of the justly famous *Marche militaire française*, and indeed in *Phaéton*. Warmly atmospheric recording

Symphonies Nos. 2 in A min., Op. 55; (i) *3 in C min., Op. 78.*
*** Chan. Dig. CHAN 8822; *ABTD 1447* [id.]. Ulster O, Yan Pascal Tortelier; (i) with Gillian Weir.

Yan Pascal Tortelier's performances are very enjoyable and very well recorded. But in the *Second Symphony* Yondani Butt's account has greater freshness, and the slightly less reverberant

ASV recording contributes to this. If your interest is primarily in this work, Butt's version is first choice, but if you need both *Symphonies* on one CD, then the Chandos issue has much in its favour. Certainly the hall resonance suits the *Organ symphony* and Tortelier's account of it is affectionate, well paced and alive, with plenty of vitality in the opening movement. The resonance helps the *Poco Adagio*, which begins a little soberly, to expand to a fully romantic climax; yet it does not cloud the detail of the scherzo, and Gillian Weir's organ entry in the finale is a truly impressive moment. The theme is strong in outline, yet the organ sound itself is suitably massive. The work moves to an impressive dénouement and at the end the Ulster Hall embraces the brass sonorously, and the closing moments knit together powerfully.

Symphony No. 3 in C min., Op. 78 (see also under *Carnival of the animals*).
*** DG Dig. 419 617-2 [id.]. Simon Preston, BPO, Levine – DUKAS: *L'apprenti sorcier.* ***
(B) *** Pickwick Dig. PCD 847; *CIMPC 847* [id.]. Chorzempa, Berne SO, Maag.
(M) *** Mercury 432 719-2 [id.]. Marcel Dupré, Detroit SO, Paray – PARAY: *Mass.* **(*)
**(*) ASV Dig. CDDCA 665; *ZCDCA 665* [id.]. Rawsthorne, LPO, Bátiz.
(M) **(*) Decca 417 725-2 [id.]. Priest, LAPO, Mehta – POULENC: *Organ concerto.* ***

(i) *Symphony No. 3;* (ii) *Danse macabre, Op. 40.*
(B) *** DG Compact Classics *413 423-4* [id.]. (i) Litaize, Chicago SO; (ii) O de Paris, Barenboim – FRANCK: *Symphony.* *

(i) *Symphony No. 3;* (ii) *Danse macabre; Le Déluge: Prélude, Op. 45; Samson et Dalila: Bacchanale.*
(M) *** DG 415 847-2 [id.]. (i) Litaize, Chicago SO, Barenboim; (ii) O de Paris, Barenboim.

Symphony No. 3; Phaeton, Op. 39.
** Telarc Dig. CD 80274 [id.]. Michael Murray, RPO, Christian Badea.

Symphony No. 3; Suite algérienne, Op. 60.
** Sup. Dig. 11 0971-2 [id.]. Jan Hora, Prague RSO, Válek.

With the Berlin Philharmonic in cracking form, Levine's is a grippingly dramatic reading, full of imaginative detail. The great thrust of the performance does not stem from fast pacing: rather it is the result of incisive articulation. After the exhilarating fervour of the first movement, the *Poco Adagio* has a mood of sombre nobility, the organ subtly underpinning the string sonority, yet leading to a climax of great intensity. The Scherzo bursts upon the listener, full of exuberance from the Berliners, bows tight on strings, and in the engaging middle section the clarity of the digital recording allows the pianistic detail to register crisply. The thunderous organ entry in the finale makes a magnificent effect, and the tension is held at white heat throughout the movement. At the close Levine draws the threads together with a satisfying final quickening.

Barenboim's inspirational 1976 version has long dominated the catalogue. Among the reissue's three attractive bonuses is an exciting account of the *Bacchanale* from *Samson et Dalila*. The performance of the *Symphony* glows with warmth from beginning to end. In the opening 6/8 section the galloping rhythms are pointed irresistibly, while the linked slow section has a poised stillness in its soaring lyricism which completely avoids any suspicion of sweetness or sentimentality. A brilliant account of the Scherzo leads into a magnificently energetic conclusion, with the Chicago orchestra excelling itself with radiant playing in every section. The digital remastering, as so often, is not wholly advantageous: while detail is sharper, the massed violins sound thinner and the bass is drier. In the finale, some of the bloom has gone, and the organ entry has a touch of hardness. The Compact Classics tape offers the *Symphony* uninterrupted in a transfer made from the original analogue master, and includes a fine account of *Danse macabre*; even if the coupled Franck *Symphony* is a much less attractive proposition, this is well worth considering for the car.

Maag's extremely well-recorded Berne performance has a Mendelssohnian freshness and the sprightly playing in the Scherzo draws an obvious affinity with that composer. The first movement has plenty of rhythmic lift and the *Poco Adagio* is eloquently elegiac, yet no one could be disappointed with the organ entry in the finale, which is certainly arresting, while the rippling delicacy of the piano figurations which follow is most engaging. The closing pages have a convincing feeling of apotheosis and, although this is not the weightiest reading available, it is an uncommonly enjoyable one in which the sound is bright, full and suitably resonant.

The fine Paray/Mercury recording dates, astonishingly, from 1957. The early date brings just a hint of shrillness to the violins in the first movement, which Paray presents engagingly with a skittishly light touch; otherwise the sound remains bold, full and remarkably well detailed; it is very successfully remastered for CD. The organ is well balanced in the slow movement, which Paray treats very affectionately (if perhaps a shade indulgently), before a light, brilliantly energetic performance of the scherzo. Then comes Marcel Dupré's weighty organ entry and a finale which is powerfully co-ordinated, building to an impressive climax. However, not everyone may want the coupling, enjoyable as it is.

Bátiz's ASV version was the first digital success for this work, although originally the CD transfer had an unattractive digital edge. Now it has been remastered and sounds spectacularly ample, with the organ almost overwhelmingly resonant in the coda. Under an inspirational Bátiz, the orchestral playing is exhilarating in its energy and commitment, while the *Poco Adagio* balances a noble elegiac feeling with romantic warmth. After the vivacious Scherzo, the entry of the organ in the finale is a breathtaking moment, and the sense of spectacle persists, bringing an unforgettable weight and grandeur to the closing pages. However, without couplings this now seems less competitive.

Mehta draws a well-disciplined and exuberant response from all departments. The slow movement cantilena sings out vividly on the strings, helped by the brightened recording. The digital remastering produces a less sumptuous effect than on the original 1979 LP, and in the finale the focus of the more spectacular sounds is not absolutely clean; even so, this is very enjoyable.

Neither of the newest recordings of the Saint-Saëns *Organ Symphony* measures up to the best of the present competition. Válek's Prague performance has plenty of vitality, the first movement infectious and buoyant, the slow section warm and expansive, and the finale has plenty of thrust and excitement. The recording, too, is one of the most impressive yet to come from Supraphon. But the snag is the balance of the solo instruments. In the scherzo the important piano parts are blurred by the resonance of the Dvořák Hall in the House of Artists, Prague, and the organ entry arrives entirely without dramtic impact, as it is all too plainly at the back of the hall. This drawback is the more disappointing when the account of the *Suite algérienne,* with its ebullient closing *Marche militaire français* has plenty of flair.

There is nothing technically wrong with the Telarc recording, indeed it is a demonstration spectacular. But the performance is good-natured rather than gripping, even though there is no lack of warmth. Moreover the orchestral part of the score was recorded first at Walthamstow, and the organ later in Naples, Florida. When the two were edited together too long a pause was left at the end of the linking passage from the scherzo, and thus the effect of surprise, with the thunderous C major chord bursting in, is lost. Maybe this can be put right, but until it is, this CD is a non-starter.

Violin sonata No. 1 in D min., Op. 75.
*** Essex CDS 6044 [id.]. Accardo, Canio – CHAUSSON: *Concert.* ***
*** Collins Dig. 1112-2; *1112-4* [id.]. Lorraine McAslan, John Blakely – DEBUSSY; RAVEL: *Sonatas.* ***
**(*) DG Dig. 429 729-2 [id.]. Gil Shaham, Gerhard Oppitz – FRANCK: *Sonata;* RAVEL: *Tzigane.* **(*)

The performance by Accardo and Canio is marvellously played, selfless and dedicated. The recording too is very good, and this can be recommended strongly, if the coupling is suitable.

Lorraine McAslan and her fine pianist give a good account of themselves in Saint-Saëns's entertaining *D minor Sonata*, and their reading can hold its head high in the current catalogue. Doubtless couplings will settle the matter, but this player has a wide range of colour and dynamics and has personality. Both the Debussy and Ravel are well played, and the latter is quite outstanding. The recording is very good indeed, well balanced and truthful.

The very talented young American violinist Gil Shaham was only eighteen when this record was made; he is still studying at the Juilliard with Dorothy DeLay. He produces a big and varied range of tone in the engaging *D minor Sonata* and has plenty of temperament. Gerhard Oppitz partners him with great dexterity but could perhaps have brought greater lightness of touch.

Samson et Dalila (opera): complete.
(M) **(*) DG 413 297-2 (2). Obraztsova, Domingo, Bruson, Lloyd, Thau, Ch. & O de Paris, Barenboim.
**(*) Ph. Dig. 426 243-2; *426 243-4* (2) [id.]. Carreras, Baltsa, Estes, Burchuladze, Bav. R. Ch. & RSO, C. Davis.

Barenboim proves as passionately dedicated an interpreter of Saint-Saëns here as he did in the

Third Symphony, sweeping away any Victorian cobwebs. It is important, too, that the choral passages, so vital in this work, be sung with this sort of freshness, and Domingo has rarely sounded happier in French music, the bite as well as the heroic richness of the voice well caught. Renato Bruson and Robert Lloyd are both admirable too; sadly, however, the key role of Dalila is given an unpersuasive, unsensuous performance by Obraztsova, with her vibrato often verging on a wobble. The recording is as ripe as the music deserves.

When the role of Samson is not one naturally suited to Carreras, it is amazing how strong and effective his performance is, even if top notes under stress grow uneven. Particularly after his near-fatal illness, the very strain seems to add to the intensity of communication, above all in the great aria of the last Act, when Samson, blinded, is turning the mill. Unevenness of production is more serious with Agnes Baltsa as Dalila. The microphone often brings out her vibrato, turning it into a disagreeable judder, and the changes of gear between registers are also underlined. She remains a powerful, characterful singer, but hers is hardly the seductive portrait required in this role, and it is a shortcoming that, like the rest of the cast, she is not a native French-speaker. Both Burchuladze as the Old Hebrew and Simon Estes as Abimelech equally seem intent on misusing once-fine voices, but Jonathan Summers as the High Priest of Dagon is far more persuasive. Despite all these reservations, the inspired conducting of Sir Colin Davis, coupled with refined, atmospheric recording, makes this preferable to the old EMI set conducted by Georges Prêtre, also seriously flawed. In particular the new recording gains from splendid choral singing, vital in this work.

Salieri, Antonio (1750–1825)

Double concerto for oboe, flute and orchestra in C.
(B) *** DG 427 211-2 [id.]. Holliger, Nicolet, Bamberg SO, Maag – MOZART: *Flute concertos.* **

(i) *Double concerto for flute, oboe and orchestra;* (ii) *Piano concerto in B flat.*
(M) *** Erato/Warner 2292 45245-2 [id.]. (i) Hoogendoorn, Borgonovo; (ii) Badura-Skoda; Sol. Ven., Scimone (with Franceso SALIERI: *La Tempesta di Mare (Sinfonia in B flat* ***).

Antonio Salieri has been given a certain notoriety by his role as arch-villain in the film, *Amadeus*, but at least it has reawakened interest in his music. He is no Mozart, but in the outer movements of the *Double concerto* the flute and oboe chatter together quite winningly and the central *Largo* is gracious. The performance here is persuasive. The *Piano concerto* is a typical *galant* piece, and Paul Badura-Skoda, playing on a period fortepiano, has its full measure. The accompaniments are first class, animated and polished, and I Solisti Veneti are at their finest in *La Tempesta di Mare.* This work is closest to Mozart in spirit and craftsmanship, an attractive three-movement Italian Overture. But the manuscript suggests it was written by Antonio's elder brother, Francesco, about which nothing is known, not even his dates. With excellent recording, this collection is worth exploring.

Heinz Holliger and Aurèle Nicolet form an expert and sensitive partnership in their earlier version of Salieri's *Double concerto.* The recording is fresh.

Les Danaïdes (complete).
*** EMI Dig. CDS7 54073-2 (2). Margaret Marshall, Gimenez, Kavrakos, Stuttgart RSO, Gelmetti.

This recording, the first ever of a tragic Salieri opera, offers a piece written for Paris in 1784 to a libretto originally intended for Gluck. The result is very Gluckian in the racy way it sets a classical subject, rejecting the formality of *opera seria* in favour of a much freer structure. Though the language is French and the composer Italian, there is a Germanic feel to much of the writing, in the often surprising 'symphonic' modulations and in the line of many of the arias, which at times are almost Schubertian. The five Acts last a mere hour and three-quarters, centring on the conflict of loyalty felt by the heroine, Hypermnestre, between her love for Lyncee and the command from her father, Danaus, that in line with her sisters she must slaughter her husband. The speed masks the enormity of the story, with brisk exchanges in accompanied recitative, brief set numbers – including some charming duets – and, above all, powerful comment from the chorus. Margaret Marshall as the heroine surpasses all she has done so far on record. She sings with superb attack and brilliant flexibility, as well as with tender intensity when Hypermnestre pleads with her father. Dimitri Kavrakos is not always adequately sinister-sounding as Danaus, but the voice is warmly focused. Raul Gimenez in the tenor role of

Lyncee is first rate too, straining only occasionally, and so is Clarry Bartha as one of Danaus's younger daughters. Gelmetti secures a crisp, stylish performance from the Stuttgart Radio Orchestra and the excellent South German Radio Choir. The booklet contains notes in English but no translation of the French libretto.

Falstaff (opera): complete.
*** Hung. Dig. HCD 21789/91 [id.]. Gregor, Zempléni, Gulyás, Gáti, Pánczél, Csura, Vámossy, Salieri Chamber Ch. & O, Tamás Pál.

Like Verdi, Salieri and his librettist ignore the Falstaff of the histories. They tell the story (minus the Anne and Fenton sub-plot and without Mistress Quickly) within the framework of the conventional two-Act opera of the period. Though the opera is long, the speed is fast and furious, with the set numbers bringing many delights, as in the charming little duet, *La stessa, stessissima*, for the two wives reading their identical letters, or Falstaff's first aria, swaggering and jolly, introduced by a fanfare motif, and a delightful laughter trio in Act II. None of the ideas, however charming or sparkling, is developed in the way one would expect in Mozart, but it is all great fun, particularly in a performance as lively and well sung as this. József Gregor is splendid in the name-part, with Dénes Gulyás equally stylish in the tenor role of Ford. Maria Zempléni as Mistress Ford and Eva Pánczél in the mezzo role of Mistress Slender (not Page) are both bright and lively. The eponymous chorus and orchestra also perform with vigour under Tamás Pál; the recording is brilliant, with a fine sense of presence.

Sallinen, Aulis (born 1935)

(i) *Cello concerto, Op. 44; Shadows (Prelude for Orchestra), Op. 52; Symphony No. 4, Op. 49.*
*** Finlandia Dig. FACD 346 [id.]. (i) Arto Noras; Helsinki PO, Kamu.

The *Cello concerto* of 1977 is the most commanding piece here. It is oddly laid out, its long, expansive first movement taking almost twenty minutes and its companion only five. Yet Sallinen's ideas and his sound-world resonate in the mind. Arto Noras has its measure and plays with masterly eloquence. The *Fourth Symphony* is a three-movement work but was composed, as it were, backwards, the first movement on which Sallinen began work eventually becoming the finale. The middle movement is marked *Dona nobis pacem*; throughout the finale, bells colour the texture, as is often the case in his orchestral writing. *Shadows* is an effective short piece which reflects or 'shadows' the content of the opera, *The King goes north to France*. The performances under Okko Kamu are very impressive and the recording quite exemplary.

(i) *Symphonies Nos. 1; 3;* (ii) *Chorali;* (iii) *Cadenze for solo violin;* (iv) *Elegy for Sebastian Knight;* (v) *String quartet No. 3.*
*** BIS CD 41 [id.]. (i) Finnish RSO, Kamu; (ii) Helsinki PO, Berglund; (iii) Paavo Pohjola; (iv) Frans Helmerson; (v) Voces Intimae Qt.

The *First Symphony*, in one movement, is diatonic and full of atmosphere, as indeed is the *Third*, a powerful, imaginative piece written on an island in the Baltic which appears to be haunted by the sounds and smells of nature. The performances under Okko Kamu are excellent and this music with its subtle colourings benefits greatly from the absence of background noise. *Chorali* is a shorter piece, persuasively done by Paavo Berglund; and there are three chamber works, albeit of lesser substance. The recordings are from the 1970s and are all very well balanced. Highly recommended.

(i) *Symphony No. 5 (Washington mosaics), Op. 57;* (ii; iii) *Chamber music III: The Nocturnal dances of Don Juanquixote* (for cello & orchestra), *Op. 58;* (iii) (Solo) *Cello sonata, Op. 26.*
**(*) Finlandia Dig. FACD 370 [id.]. (i) Helsinki PO, or (ii) Finlandia Sinfonietta, Kamu; (iii) Arto Noras.

The success of Sallinen's short but powerful *Shadows*, which is related in atmosphere to the opera, *The King goes forth to France*, prompted Rostropovich to commission a new symphony. The result was *Washington mosaics*, a five-movement work in which the outer movements form the framework for three less substantial but highly imaginative intermezzi. There are Stravinskian overtones in the first movement, though momentum is intermittent. The three intermezzi cast a strong spell, and those who respond to the *First* and *Third Symphonies* will find comparable feeling for nature and a keen sense of its power. There are the same passing reminders of Britten and Shostakovich and the orchestral sonorities are unfailingly resourceful:

the first intermezzo even has expressionistic overtones mildly reminiscent of Berg or of Sallinen's countryman, Aarre Merikanto. The performance is dedicated and the recording is in the first flight. An impressive achievement. Not so *The Nocturnal dances of Don Juanquixote*, which is pretty thin stuff. It incorporates nostalgic recollections of Sallinen's days working in a restaurant band, and the juxtaposition of such disparate elements does not really work. It is impeccably played by Arto Noras, but not even his art can persuade one of its merits. The main idea is irredeemably cheap; and the solo *Cello sonata* of 1971 is hardly a substantial makeweight, even though Noras is a masterly advocate. However, the *Symphony* is an important and rewarding work and carries a strong recommendation.

Sammartini, Giovanni Battista (1700–75)

Symphonies in D; G; String quintet in E.

(B) *** HM HMA 901245; *HMA 431245* [id.]. Ens. 145, Banchini – Giuseppe SAMMARTINI: *Concerti grossi* etc. ***

Giovanni Battista was the younger of the two Sammartini brothers; he spent his whole life in Milan. On this record, the Ensemble 145, led by Chiara Banchini, offer two of his symphonies (he composed over eighty); although neither attains greatness, they have genuine appeal. Good recording.

Sammartini, Giuseppe (*c.* 1693–1750)

Concerti grossi Nos. 6 & 8; (i) *Recorder concerto in F.*

(B) *** HM HMA 901245; *HMA 431245* [id.]. (i) Conrad Steinmann; Ens. 145, Banchini – Giovanni SAMMARTINI: *Symphonies* etc. ***

Giuseppe settled in England in the 1720s and, though influenced by the rather conservative English taste, he was a refined and inventive composer. The Ensemble 145 is a period-instrument group; they produce a firmly focused sound, even though the textures are light and the articulation lively. Excellent playing from Conrad Steinmann in the *Recorder concerto*. This is now reissued in the bargain Musique d'Abord series.

Sarasate, Pablo (1844–1908)

Carmen fantasy, Op. 25.

❀ *** EMI CDC7 47101-2 [id.]. Itzhak Perlman, RPO, Foster – PAGANINI: *Concerto No. 1.**** ❀

*** DG Dig. 423 063-2; *423 063-4* [id.]. Itzhak Perlman, NYPO, Mehta – CHAUSSON: *Poème;* RAVEL: *Tzigane;* SAINT-SAËNS: *Havanaise* etc. ***

Sarasate's *Fantasy* is a selection of the most popular tunes from *Carmen*, with little attempt made to stitch the seams between them. Played like this on EMI, with superb panache, luscious tone and glorious recording, the piece almost upstages the concerto with which it is coupled. The recording balance is admirable, with the quality greatly to be preferred to many of Perlman's more recent digital records.

Perlman has re-recorded this work for DG in a fine new digital version, and it is generously coupled with other famous showpieces. The new performance is beyond criticism – but the earlier one was just that bit riper and more beguiling.

(i) *Carmen fantasy;* (ii) *Zigeunerweisen, Op. 20.*

(M) *** EMI CDM7 63533-2. Perlman, (i) RPO, Foster; (ii) Pittsburgh SO, Previn – *Concert.* ***

Perlman's superb 1972 account of the *Carmen fantasy* is one of his most dazzling recordings. On the mid-priced EMI record, *Zigeunerweisen* (recorded with Previn five years later) is added for good measure, and again the playing is both virtuosic and idiomatic. Here the microphone balance is rather too close, but Perlman can survive any amount of scrutiny.

Zigeunerweisen, Op. 20.
*** DG Dig. 431 815-2 [id.]. Gil Shaham, LSO, Lawrence Foster – WIENIAWSKI: *Violin concertos Nos. 1 & 2* etc. ***

Gil Shaham plays Sarasate's sultry and dashing gypsy confection with rich timbre, languorous ardour and a dazzling display of fireworks at the close. Lawrence Foster opens the proceedings with a fine orchestral flourish, and then accompanies with precision and flair. The solo violin is (understandably) forwardly balanced, but the orchestra remains well in the picture.

Sarum Chant

Missa in gallicantu; Hymns: A solis ortus cardine; Christe Redemptor omnium; Salvator mundi, Domine; Veni Redemptor omnium.
*** Gimell Dig. CDGIM 017; *1585T-17* [id.]. Tallis Scholars, Peter Phillips.

Filling in our knowledge of early church music, the Tallis Scholars under Peter Phillips here present a whole disc of chant according to the Salisbury rite – in other words *Sarum chant* – which, rather than the regular Gregorian style, was what churchgoers of the Tudor period and earlier in England heard at their devotions. The greater part of the record is given over to the setting of the First Mass of Christmas, intriguingly entitled *Missa in gallicantu* or *Mass at cock-crow*. Though this is simply monophonic, the men's voices alone are used, it is surprising what antiphonal variety there is. The record is completed with four hymns from the Divine Offices of Christmas Day. Ivan Moody's note helpfully presents the background of church practice from the thirteenth century through to the abandonment of the Latin rite in England. The record is warmly atmospheric in the characteristic Gimell manner.

Satie, Erik (1866–1925)

Les aventures de Mercure (ballet); *La belle excentrique: Grand ritournelle. 5 Grimaces pour 'Un songe d'une nuit d'été'; Gymnopédies Nos. 1 & 3; Jack-in-the-box* (orch. Milhaud); *3 Morceaux en forme de poire; Parade* (ballet); *Relâche* (ballet).
(M) **(*) Van. 8.4030.71 [OVC 4030]. Utah SO, Maurice Abravanel.

A generous budget collection of Satie's orchestral music, well played and given full, vivid recording from the beginning of the 1970s. The Utah Symphony Orchestra made a number of adventurous excursions into European repertoire at that time and, if Abravanel fails to throw off some of the more pointed music with a fully idiomatic lightness of touch, these are still enjoyable performances; the ballet scores have plenty of colour and rhythmic life.

(i) *Les aventures de Mercure;* (ii) *Gymnopédies 1 & 3* (orch. Debussy); (iii) *Les pantins dansent;* (iv) *Choses vues à droite et à gauche (sans lunettes);* (v; i) *Geneviève de Brabant* (orch. Desormière); (vi) *Messe des pauvres;* (v; vii; iii) *Le piège de Méduse* (comédie lyrique); (viii; i) *Socrate* (drame symphonique).
(B) *(**) EMI CZS7 62877-2 (2). (i) O de Paris, Dervaux; (ii) Paris Conservatoire O, Auriacombe; (iii) LOP, Ciccolini; (iv) Yan-Pascal Tortelier, Ciccolini (piano); (v) Mesplé, Benoit, Paris Op. Ch.; (v) Pierre Bertin (nar.); (vi) René Duclos Ch. (members); Gaston Litaize (organ de l'Église Saint François-Xavier); (vii) Deschamps, Falcucci, Laurence; (viii) Millet, Guiot, Esposito, Mesplé.

In Auriacombe's account of the familiar *Gymnopédies* the burden of expressiveness is carried by the fine Paris woodwind soloists rather than the conductor, but Dervaux (although hampered a little by the resonant acoustic) brings reasonable spirit and no lack of warmth to the engagingly scored *Les aventures de Mercure*. He finds the necessary elegance for the *Danses des grâces* in the Second Tableau and real *tendresse* for the charming *Nouvelle danse* in the Third. Later Ciccolini, taking over the conductor's baton, is suitably sprightly in the quirkily rhythmic *Les patins dansent*. There is some fine singing in *Socrate*; the performance catches well the calm, expressive serenity of the melodic lines. But no libretto or translation is provided either here or in the two works with narrator, *Le piège de Méduse* and *Geneviève de Brabant*. This latter cantata opens with a narration lasting nearly 12 minutes before the music begins and, although Pierre Bertin is eloquent as only a Frenchman can be, the non-French-speaker will be dismayed to find that the entry of the the music is not even cued! Yet there is much that is attractive in Satie's piquant word-settings, both here and in the cabaret-styled *Le piège de Méduse* (with its reminders of Offenbach); however, without the written words or separating tracks, the listener's patience will be sorely tried. The *Messe des pauvres* is a lively Rosicrucian organ Mass, often forcefully played on a bold, grainy-sounding organ, with soprano and bass voices *ad lib.* interrupting the opening *Kyrie* and *Dixit Dominus*. The three brief *Choses vues à droite et à gauche* are scored for violin and piano. Here Yan-Pascal Tortelier joins Ciccolini (who moves over to the piano) to present them with engaging finesse and wit. The recordings were all made in the Salle Wagram between 1967 and 1974, and the transfers are of excellent quality.

PIANO MUSIC

Aperçus désagréables; La belle excentrique (fantaisie sérieuse) (both for 4 hands); *Croquis et agaceries d'un gros bonhomme en bois; Descriptions automatiques; Embryons desséchés; En habit de cheval* (for 4 hands); *Le fils des étoiles, wagnerie kaldéenne du Sar Peladan; 6 Gnossiennes; 3 Gymnopédies; Jack-in-the-box; 3 Mouvements en forme de poire* (for 4 hands); *3 Nocturnes; Peccadilles importunes; 3 Petites pièces montées* (for 4 hands); *Pièces froides; Préludes flasques (pour un chien); Première pensée et sonneries de la Rose Croix; 3 Sarabandes; Sonatine bureaucratique; Sports et divertissements; 3 Valses distinguées du précieux dégoûté.*
(B) **(*) EMI CZS7 67282-2 (2). Aldo Ciccolini.

Although Satie's achievement is sometimes overrated by his admirers, about much of this music there is a desperate melancholy and a rich poetic feeling which are altogether unique. The *Gymnopédies*, *Gnossiennes*, *Sarabandes* and *Piéces froides* show such flashes of innocence and purity of inspiration that criticism is disarmed, while the wit of the sharper vignettes is most engaging. Aldo Ciccolini is widely praised as a Satie interpreter, and he plays here with unaffacted sympathy. He certainly understands the *douloureux* feeling of the famous *Gymnopédies*, with which his recital opens, and he also finds the '*conviction et tristesse rigoureuse*' of the *Gnossiennes*. There is a noble, aristocratic dignity expressed in the *Première pensée et sonneries de la Rose Croix*, yet *La belle excentrique* is thrown off with great dash and élan. In the works where (by electronic means) Ciccolini provides all four hands, the percussive edge of the pianism seems somewhat accentuated by the recording (and this occasionally happens with the bolder articulation in some of the solo pieces too), but generally the piano recording is most realistic, and the CD transfer has plenty of colour and sonority. Altogether this 158-minute collection forms an excellent introduction to Satie's world.

Avant-dernières pensées; Chapitres tournés en tous sens; Croquis et agaceries d'un gros bonhomme en bois; Danses gothiques; Descriptions automatiques; Embryons desséchés; Enfantillages pittoresques; 3 Gnossiennes; 3 Gymnopédies; Heures séculaires et instantanées; Menus propos enfantins; 5 Nocturnes; Ogives; Les pantins dansent; Passacaille; Peccadilles importunes; Pièces froides; 4 Préludes; Prélude en tapisserie; Préludes de la porte héroïque du ciel; Premier menuet; Rêverie de l'enfance de Pantagruel; 3 Sarabandes; Sonatine bureaucratique; Sports et divertissements; 3 Valses distinguées du précieux dégoûté; Veritables préludes flasques; Vieux séquins et vieilles cuirasses.
(B) **(*) VoxBox 1154862 [CDX 5011]. Frank Glazer.

Vox offers a great deal of Satie's solo piano music on two CDs in excellent performances by Frank Glazer, and this VoxBox scores over the EMI competition by offering slightly more music (though, curiously, not the last three *Gnossiennes*). Glazer seems to penetrate the character of each of these aphoristic and haunting miniatures with genuine flair and insight. In some ways his are more searching and sympathetic performances than those of Aldo Ciccolini, and the recording, although rather reverberant and a little veiled in the treble, is full-bodied and faithful. The Vox CD transfer slightly enhances the original piano-sound and there is no drying-out of timbre or ambience. However, in the numbers requiring very pointed articulation, Ciccolini's more percussive style brings a degree more sparkle, even if the actual piano-tone is harder, less easy on the ear. Some of these pieces are insubstantial, but those attracted to the idiom of the music will find this a safe investment.

Avant-dernières pensées. Chapitres tournés en tous sens. Croquis et agaceries d'un gros bonhomme en bois; Descriptions automatiques; Deux rêveries nocturnes; Heures séculaires et instantanées; Nocturnes Nos. 1-3, 5; Nouvelles pièces froides; Pièces froides; Prélude de la porte héroïque du ciel. Les trois valses distinguées d'un précieux dégoûté. Véritables préludes flasques.
*** Decca Dig. 421 713-2 [id.]. Pascal Rogé.

Pascal Rogé's first Satie recital (see below) was a great success; those who have it will need no prompting to invest in its successor. His choice of repertoire on this well-filled disc ranges from the Rose-Croix pieces through to the *Nocturnes* of 1919 (No. 4 was on the earlier disc). As with the earlier recital, his playing has an eloquence and charm that are altogether rather special, and the recorded sound is very good indeed though not quite as full and realistic as that which Virgin provide for Anne Queffélec.

Avant-dernières pensées. Chapitres tournés en tous sens; Embryons desséchés; 6 Gnossiennes; 3 Gymnopédies; Heures séculaires et instantanées; Je te veux; Le Picadilly; Sonatine bureaucratique; Sports et divertissements; Pièces froides; Véritables préludes flasques; Vieux séquins et vieilles cuirasses.
*** Virgin Dig. VC7 90754-2; *VC 790754-4* [id.]. Anne Queffélec.

Anne Queffélec is exceptionally well served by the engineers, who produce as good a piano sound as any to have appeared on CD: it is firm, clean and fresh with a splendid tonal bloom. Their dedication is not misplaced, for her playing has great tonal subtlety and character. With the exception of the celebrated *Gnossiennes* and *Gymnopédies*, most of the music dates from the period of the First World War and is dispatched with great character and style. Nor does she possess less charm than Pascal Rogé. A most delightful issue with an excellent equivalent tape.

Avant-dernières pensées; Embryons desséchés; 6 Gnossiennes; 3 Gymnopédies; Pièces froides; Sarabande No. 3; Sonatine bureaucratique; 3 Valses distinguées du précieux dégoûté; 3 véritables préludes flasques (pour un chien).
*** BIS Dig. CD 317 [id.]. Roland Pöntinen.

Roland Pöntinen is a young Swedish pianist, still in his early twenties when this recording was made. He seems perfectly in tune with the Satiean world, and his playing is distinguished by great sensibility and tonal finesse. He is very well recorded too.

Embryons desséchés; 6 Gnossiennes; 3 Gymnopédies; Heures séculaires et instantanées; Nocturnes Nos. 1-5; Sonatine bureaucratique; Sports et divertissements.
*** Hyp. Dig. CDA 66344; *KA 66344* [id.]. Yitkin Seow.

The Singapore-born pianist Yitkin Seow is a good stylist; his approach is fresh and his playing crisp and marked by consistent beauty of sound. Seow captures the melancholy of the *Gymnopédies* very well and the playing, though not superior to Rogé or Queffélec in character or charm, has a quiet reticence that is well suited to this repertoire. The recording is eminently truthful.

Embryons desséchés; 6 Gnossiennes; 3 Gymnopédies; Je te veux; Nocturne No. 4; Le Picadilly; 4 Préludes flasques; Prélude en tapisserie; Sonatine bureaucratique; Vieux séquins et vieilles cuirasses.
*** Decca Dig. 410 220-2. Pascal Rogé.

Rogé has real feeling for this repertoire and conveys its bitter-sweet quality and its grave melancholy as well as he does its lighter qualities. He produces, as usual, consistent beauty of tone, and this is well projected by the recording. Very well recorded, this remains the primary recommendation on CD for this repertoire, together with its companion above – alongside Anne Queffélec's recital (even more vividly recorded).

Gnossiennes Nos. 1, 4 & 5; 3 Gymnopédies; Nocturne No. 1; Parade; Ragtime parade; Pasacaille; Sarabandes Nos. 1 & 3; Sonatine bureaucratique; Sports et divertissements; Véritables préludes flasques; Vieux sequins et vieilles cuirasses. 6 Pieces published posthumously: *Désespoir agréable; Effronterie; Poésie; Prélude canin; Profondeur; Songe creux.*
(M) **(*) Saga SCD 9041. John McCabe.

This is an attractive anthology and is especially interesting in including six brief but highly characteristic pieces (not necessarily left in complete form) found in Satie's notebooks, and not previously published. John McCabe is an intelligent and sympathetic exponent of this repertoire. He finds the quirky character of the *Sports et divertissements* and is very sympathetic in the *Nocturne* and cool *Sarabandes*; only the famous *Gymnopédies* sound curiously metronomic and deliberate. He makes up in the *Rag-time parade* (extracted and arranged from the ballet by Hans Ourdine) which is played with a nicely relaxed rythmic lilt. Good, though not outstanding recording and an hour of music included in the recital.

Saxton, Robert (born 1953)

Chamber symphony (Circles of light); Concerto for orchestra; The Ring of eternity; The Sentinel of the rainbow.
*** EMI Dig. CDC7 49915-2. BBC SO or L. Sinf., Knussen.

Robert Saxton is one of the most immediately communicative of the younger generation of British composers, using the orchestra with a panache that plainly reflects his own pleasure in rich and colourful sound. These four works, all written between 1983 and 1986, bring fine examples, notably the *Concerto for orchestra*, first given at the Proms in 1984. Its four linked sections broadly follow a symphonic shape, as do those of the *Chamber symphony* of 1986, which uses smaller forces, with solo strings. That later work has the title *Circles of light* and was inspired by a quotation from Dante, when in the *Divine Comedy* he looks into the eyes of his beloved, Beatrice, and links what he sees to the movement of the heavens. The other two works, both lasting around 15 minutes, also have evocative titles and are linked in the composer's mind to the *Concerto for orchestra* to form a sort of trilogy. Oliver Knussen draws intense, committed playing both from the BBC Symphony Orchestra in the *Concerto for orchestra* and *The Ring of eternity*, and from the London Sinfonietta in the chamber-scale works. Full, warm recording.

(i) *In the Beginning;* (ii) *Music to celebrate the resurrection of Christ.*
*** Collins Dig. Single 2003-2. (i) BBC SO, Bamert; (ii) ECO, Bedford.

In the Beginning offers three compact movements, ending with an exhilarating *Dance of joy*. It is well coupled with another deeply felt, religiously inspired work, previously available on a disc otherwise devoted to Britten. A generous offering for a CD single, very well recorded, in Collins's enterprising 20th-century Plus series.

Music to celebrate the resurrection of Christ.
*** Collins Dig. 1102-2; *1102-4* [id.]. ECO, Bedford – BRITTEN: *Piano concerto* etc. ***

Positive and colourful, to reflect wonder in the subject, Saxton's piece makes an unusual but valuable fill-up to Bedford's disc of Britten rarities.

Caritas (opera; complete).
*** Collins 1350-2 (id.]. Eirian Davies, Jonathan Best, Christopher Ventris, Linda Hibberd, Roger Bryson, David Gwynne, E. N. Philh. O, Diego Masson.

Coming from a Jewish background, Robert Saxton yet finds regular inspiration from Christian ritual. From outside the church his music echoes religious experience, often as here in the most complex way. Arnold Wesker's play of the same name sets up an intricate web of sympathies and associations, faithfully reflected in Saxton's score. Wesker directly relates the intolerance of the medieval church to the reactionary politics of the English monarchy in brutally putting down the Peasants' Revolt in 1381. It tells the story of Christine, the daughter of a carpenter, who became an anchoress. The opening scene with its monastic choruses shows her as she is walled up in her cell. Only then does she find out too late that she has no vocation. Amid incidental developments of stomach-turning brutality, her pleas to be freed from her confinement are rejected, and madness finally takes over. It is as disagreeable a plot as could be imagined, with the kinship between extreme religious practice and sexual perversion brought home. Yet thanks to Saxton's approachable, evocative and generally well-paced score, it is a highly involving piece. It is the more disturbingly pointful for its political overtones set alongside the religious, making it finally an opera of protest. Saxton subtly differentiates his echoes of early church music to heighten individual characterization. The recording was made live at the 1991 Huddersfield Festival, with Diego Masson directing the English Northern Philharmonia and an excellent cast, movingly headed by Eirian Davies as Christine, the anchoress. The whole piece is the more telling, when Saxton's scheme is so compact, with an hour-long first act in 12 brisk scenes followed without a pause by a second act of 20 minutes devoted to the painful last monologue of Christine. The stereo sound is of spectacular range and spread, adding greatly to the work's impact.

Scarlatti, Alessandro (1660–1725)

Concerti grossi Nos. 1 in F min.; 2 in C min.; 3 in F; (i) *Sinfonie di concerti grossi for flute and strings Nos. 7 in G min.; 8 in G; 9 in G min.; 10 in A min.; 11 in C; 12 in C min.*
(M) *** Ph. Dig./Analogue 434 160-2; *434 160-4* [id.]. (i) William Bennett; I Musici.

This record has appalling documentation (or lack of it!), of which Philips should be thoroughly ashamed. One assumes it is to be the first reissue of a pair, with the second following to complete both sets of works. We are offered the first three of six *Concerti grossi* (described here as *Concertos* – with the typographical layout giving the impression that they include a solo flute). In fact these noble and elevated works – worthy to be compared with comparable *concerti* of Corelli and Handel – were first published by Benjamin Cooke in 1740, fifteen years after Scarlatti's death. Though not radical in style, they have invention of real quality to commend them. I Musici give performances of much eloquence and warmth and great transparency; the latter is welcome in the fugal movements, especially as the 1979 analogue recording is of the very first rank. The *Sinfonie di concerti grossi* do indeed feature a flute soloist, in this instance the excellent William Bennett, who plays fluently and in fine style. The first on the disc (No. 7) opens winningly, with an elegant minuet, and this is also entertainingly inventive music; the performances are lively and attractive, and eminently freshly recorded in Philips's best digital sound.

Dixit Dominus.
*** DG Dig. 423 386-2 [id.]. Argenta, Attrot, Denley, Ashley Stafford, Varcoe, Ch. & E. Concert, Pinnock – VIVALDI: *Gloria.* ***

Of the four settings of *Dixit Dominus* (Psalm 107) that Alessandro Scarlatti composed, the one chosen by Trevor Pinnock has until now been the least well known. Pinnock, as so often, inspires his performers to sing and play as though at a live event. This Scarlatti Psalm-setting, very well recorded, makes an attractive coupling for the better known of Vivaldi's settings of the *Gloria.*

Il giardino di amore (*The garden of love:* cantata).
(M) *** DG 431 122-2; *431 122-4.* Gayer, Fassbaender, Munich CO, Stadlmair.

Scarlatti called this delightful work a '*serenata*', for there are only two characters and the orchestra is basically a string group with colourful obbligatos for recorder, violin and trumpet. Here the (originally castrato) role of Adonis is attractively sung by a soprano, Catherine Gayer, with Brigitte Fassbaender providing a foil in her portrayal of Venus. The two voices are well matched and the singing has both charm and character. There are some delightful pictorial touches in Scarlatti's word-settings and they are imaginatively realized. The nightingale song (with recorder obbligato) is especially memorable, as is the aria *Con battaglia die fiero tormento,* which has a trumpet obbligato worthy of Handel. The excellent 1964 recording has transferred vividly to CD, and the documentation includes a full translation.

La Giuditta (oratorio).
*** Hung. Dig. HCD 12910 [id.]. Zadori, Gemes, Gregor, Minter, De Mey, Capella Savaria, McGegan.

La Giuditta, telling the biblical story of Judith, is a fascinating example of pre-Handelian oratorio as it was developing in Italy at the end of the seventeenth century. Nicholas McGegan, who has made several successful period-performance recordings for Hungaroton, here directs a fresh and stylish account, with three Hungarian principals joined by the soft-grained but agile American counter-tenor, Drew Minter, as Holofernes, and the excellent French tenor, Guy de Mey, as the Captain. The two main principals, Maria Zadori as Judith and Katalin Gemes as Prince Ozias, both have attractively bright, clear voices. Very well recorded in clean, immediate sound and with libretto and notes included in the package, it makes a most attractive disc, generously filled.

(i) *St Cecilia Mass;* (ii) *Motets: Domine, refugium factus et nobis; O magnum mysterium.*
(M) *** Decca 430 631-2; *430 631-4* [id.]. (i) Harwood, Eathorne, Cable, Eans, Keyte, St John's College Ch., Wren O, Guest; (ii) Schütz Ch. of L., Norrington.

This is far more florid in style than Scarlatti's other Masses and it receives from Guest a vigorous and fresh performance. The soloists cope with their difficult fioriture very confidently and they match one another well. The 1978 recording is atmospheric, yet sets choir and orchestra firmly in place. The two motets are fine pieces that show how enduring the Palestrina tradition was in seventeenth-century Italy. They are noble in conception and are beautifully performed under Roger Norrington.

Scarlatti, Domenico (1685–1757)

Keyboard sonatas (complete).
*** Erato/Warner 2292 45309-2 (34) [id.]. Scott Ross, Huggett, Coin, Henry, Vallon.

Scott Ross's highly distinguished survey of Scarlatti's keyboard music is welcome back to the catalogue. This project, sponsored by the Gulbenkian Foundation, was initiated by the tercentenary of Domenico Scarlatti's birth, prompting the production of an integral recording of Scarlatti's 555 *Keyboard sonatas*, including the three intended for organ, others for violin and continuo, and two for the unlikely combination of violin and oboe in unison. Scott Ross, who, with the participation of Monica Huggett (violin), Christophe Coin (cello), Michel Henry (oboe) and Marc Vallon (bassoon), is primarily responsible, plays five different harpsichords plus the organ, and he is very well recorded throughout in varying acoustics. Scarlatti's invention shows an inexhaustible resourcefulness, and Ross's playing is fully worthy: he is lively, technically assured, rhythmically resilient and, above all, he conveys his enjoyment of the music, without eccentricity. We cannot claim to have heard all thirty-four CDs, but all the evidence of sampling suggests that for the Scarlatti addict they will prove an endless source of satisfaction. The documentation is ample, providing a 200-page booklet about the composer, his music and the performers.

Keyboard sonatas: Kk. 7, 33, 49, 54, 87, 96, 105–7, 159, 175, 206–7, 240–41, 347–8, 380–81, 441–4, 518–19, 524–5.
*** HM HMC90 1164/5 [id.]. Rafael Puyana (harpsichord).

Rafael Puyana gives eminently red-blooded performances of these *Sonatas*, which are refreshing and invigorating, very much in the robust fashion of Landowska, though not always with quite the fiery imagination she brought to bear on them. Where appropriate, he presents them in pairs, as recommended by Kirkpatrick. He uses a three-manual harpsichord from 1740 by Hass of Hamburg, restored by Andrea Goble, which makes a splendidly rich sound, present and lively. Authoritative playing, though he tends, with some exceptions, to concentrate on the more outgoing and brilliant rather than the inward-looking *Sonatas*.

Keyboard sonatas, Kk. 32, 95, 99, 107, 158, 162–4, 193, 208, 210, 213, 215, 246–7, 262, 304, 318, 378–80, 394, 443, 461, 474, 481, 484, 500, 513, 531, 540, 550.
(M) **(*) Collins Dig. 3016-2 [id.]. Fou Ts'ong (piano).

This is the most generous Scarlatti recital in the catalogue, with 32 sonatas included and 73 minutes of music. Fou Ts'ong is not the first name to spring to mind in connection with this repertoire and, not unexpectedly, his approach is at times rather wayward, though stopping short of being overtly romantic. The very first sonata on the disc, the *D minor Sonata* (Kk. 31), has a rather appealing, ruminative quality, and the following *D major Sonata* (Kk. 164) is measured and thoughtful. But in those numbers in which keen articulation is called for (Kk. 484 in D and Kk. 378 in F, for instance) the playing is agreeably fresh, the ornamentation crisp and not fussy. The recording was produced by Fou Ts'ong himself and recorded at St John's Polish Roman Catholic Church, London, in 1984. The ambience is attractive, but the microphones are perhaps a shade too close to the piano (especially noticeable at the very opening).

Keyboard sonatas: Kk. 39, 54, 96, 146, 162, 198, 209, 332, 335, 380, 424, 455, 466, 474, 525, 531.
(M) (***) Sony MK 42410 [id.]. Vladimir Horowitz (piano).

Recorded at various times between 1962 and 1968, the playing is of extraordinary elegance and refinement, and Horowitz's virtuosity is altogether remarkable. Unfortunately the improvement in sound-quality is minimal: the timbre is still dry and papery – so the three stars are exclusively for the playing.

Keyboard sonatas, Kk. 46, 87, 99, 124, 201, 204a, 490–92, 513, 520–21.
*** CRD CRD 3368; *CRDC 4068* [id.]. Trevor Pinnock (harpsichord).

No need to say much about this: the playing is first rate and the recording outstanding in its presence and clarity. There are few better anthologies of Scarlatti in the catalogue, although the measure is not particularly generous.

Keyboard sonatas, Kk 108, 118–19; 141; 198; 203; 454–5; 490–92, 501–2; 516–19.
*** HM/BMG Dig. RD 77224 [77224-2]. Andreas Staier (harpsichord).

We welcomed Andreas Staier's Haydn sonata recital with much enthusiasm. He seems equally at home with the music of Scarlatti and he characterizes each of these Scarlatti sonatas vividly and with real imagination. This CD is presumably the first of an integral version intended to match Scott Ross's marathon that appeared on Erato some years ago. In any event playing (and recording) of this quality has no need to fear even the most exalted comparisons. A strongly recommended issue.

Keyboard sonatas: Kk. 115–16, 144, 175, 402–3, 449–50, 474–5, 513, 516–17, 544–5.
**(*) Decca Dig. 421 422-2 [id.]. András Schiff (piano).

Exquisite and sensitive playing, full of colour and delicacy. As always, András Schiff is highly responsive to the mood and character of each piece. At times one wonders whether he is not a little too refined: in some, one would have welcomed more abandon and fire. However, for the most part this is a delightful recital, and the Decca recording is exemplary in its truthfulness.

Stabat Mater.
*** Erato/Warner Dig. 2292 45219-2 [id.]. Monteverdi Ch., E. Bar. Soloists, Gardiner – Concert: *'Sacred choral music'*. ***

The *Stabat Mater* shows Scarlatti to be a considerable master of polyphony; though it falls off in interest towards the end, it still possesses eloquence and nobility – and it is far less bland than Pergolesi's setting. Gardiner's fine performance couples three motets of interest, by Cavalli, Gesualdo and Clément, which are also splendidly done. The recording is very good indeed, notably fresh in its CD format.

Schmelzer, Johann (*c.* 1620–80)

Balletto di centauri ninfe e salvatici; Balletto di spiritelli; Sonata I à 8; Sonata à 7 flauti; Sonata con arie zu der kaiserlichen Serenada.
*** O-L Dig. 425 834-2 [id.]. New L. Cons., Pickett – BIBER: *Sonatas*. ***

Johann Schmelzer made his reputation initially as a virtuoso violinist ('the famous and nearly most distinguished in all Europe', suggested a contemporary accolade); as a climax to his career, he was apppointed Vice-Kapellmeister to the Viennese Imperial Court, and in 1679 he became Kapellmeister – almost too late, for he died of the plague a year later. One of his tasks was the provision of ballet music for use in pageants, and much of this survives. The two brief scores included here last for about five minutes each, with an average of a movement per minute, but these vignettes have considerable charm. The *Balletto di spiritelli* is scored for recorders and curtal (an ancestor of the bassoon), violins and viols, and the *Balletto di centauri* uses cornetts and sackbuts, as well as recorders, strings and continuo. The even more robust *Sonata con arie zu der kaiserlichen Serenada* (with three trumpets, timpani plus a string ensemble and continuo) has six movements, including two *Arias* and a *Canario*, but still only lasts seven minutes. Philip Pickett himself leads the consort of recorders in the *Sonata à 7*, which is a fairly ambitious continuous piece, longer than either of the ballets, and the *Sonata à 8* highlights a trumpet duo against a group of violins and viols. This is agreeably inventive music, which is brought refreshingly to life by Pickett's instrumental ensemble, using original instruments to persuasive effect. The recording is both clear and spacious.

Schmidt, Franz (1874–1939)

Symphony No. 2 in E flat.
*** Chan. Dig. CHAN 8779; *ABTD 1415* [id.]. Chicago SO, Järvi.

The *Second Symphony* owes much to Strauss and Reger. It calls for huge orchestral forces (five clarinets, eight horns, and so on) and if it is not as individual as his later works, like the noble

Fourth Symphony, it shows the fertility of his invention and his command of the orchestra. (The writing for the wind is particularly felicitous.) The variations comprising the second movement are a little prolix, but by and large this is a rewarding piece with many hints of what is to come. The Chicago orchestra play magnificently for Järvi and are very well recorded. It enjoys a distinct lead over the rival version made in the town of his birth, Bratislava, under Lajos Rajter.

Symphony No. 4 in C.
(M) **(*) Decca 430 007-2. VPO, Mehta – SCHOENBERG: *Chamber symphony No. 1.* **(*)

Schmidt's noble *Fourth Symphony* is much loved in Vienna, as the playing of the VPO on this Decca recording readily testifies. The work is given the intensity of Mahler, without the hint of hysteria, and the breadth and spaciousness of Bruckner – though it is very different from either: Mehta finds also a dignity that reminds one a little of Elgar. The brightened recording gains in vividness in its CD transfer but loses a little of its fullness, though the Vienna ambience remains very telling.

Piano quintet in G (arr. Wührer).
(M) *** Decca 430 296-2; *430 296-4* [id.]. Eduard Mrasek, VPO Qt – BRUCKNER: *String quintet.* ***

Franz Schmidt's *Piano quintet in G* is the first of three that he wrote for Paul Wittgenstein, the one-armed pianist for whom Ravel and Prokofiev both composed concertos. The quintets were subsequently arranged for two hands by Friedrich Wührer. This is rewarding music, full of unexpected touches; it also possesses a vein of genuine nobility, as one would expect from the composer of the *Fourth Symphony*. The performance is elegant and was beautifully recorded in the Sofiensaal in 1974. The CD retains the fullness and the natural, well-judged balance.

Quintet in A for clarinet, piano and strings.
*** Marco Polo Dig. 8.223414 [id.]. Jánoska, Mucha, Lakatos, Slávik, Ruso.
**(*) Preiser 93357 [id.]. Vienna Kammermusiker.

The *Quintet in A major for clarinet, piano and strings* was written in the last year of the composer's life with the pianist Paul Wittgenstein in mind. Its layout is unusual: it begins like some mysterious other-worldly scherzo which immediately introduces a pastoral idea of beguiling charm. The second movement is a piano piece in ternary form; there is a longish scherzo, full of fantasy and wit, and there is an affecting trio, tinged with the melancholy of late Brahms. The fourth sets out as if it, too, is going to be a long, meditative piano piece, but its nobility and depth almost put one in mind of the Elgar *Quintet*. The fifth is a set of variations on a theme of Josef Labor, and is sometimes played on its own. In all, the piece takes an hour and, of the two performances now before the public, the Slovak account on Marco Polo is the one to go for, although there is not a great deal to choose between the two and perhaps the clarinet playing of Christophe Eberle is marginally more imaginative than that of his Slovak colleague, Aladár Jánowska. The Marco Polo recording has greater freshness and bloom, though both could benefit from a bigger recording venue. This is a glorious work.

Das Buch mit sieben Siegeln (The Book with 7 seals): oratorio.
**(*) Orpheus Dig. C 143862H (2). Schreier, Holl, Greenberg, Watkinson, Moser, Rydl, V. State Op. Ch., Austrian RSO, Zagrosek.

Das Buch mit sieben Siegeln has much music of substance and many moments of real inspiration. Peter Schreier's St John is one of the glories of this set, and there are fine contributions from some of the other soloists. This performance was recorded in the somewhat unappealing acoustic of the ORF studios and is wanting in the transparency that the score deserves. Detail is less vivid than it might be and the dynamic range is somewhat compressed; however, the sound is more than acceptable.

Schnittke, Alfred (born 1934)

(i) *Cello concerto No. 2. In memoriam . . .*
*** Sony Dig. SK 48241 [id.]. (i) Rostropovich; LSO, Ozawa.

Readers with an interest in Schnittke's music are well served at present. BIS are currently engaged on an ambitious project to record his complete output and anyone strongly drawn to his music can investigate this with confidence. We hope to explore more of these records in our next edition. Schnittke has a strong feeling for the cello, and his *Second Cello concerto* is a recent work and a strong and powerful one. It was written in 1990 after he had moved from the then Soviet Union to settle in Hamburg where he now teaches. It was composed for Rostropovich whom Schnittke long regarded as a beacon pointing the way in contemporary music. It is conceived on a large scale, the main emotional weight residing in the fifth and last movement, a passacaglia lasting a quarter of an hour, whose theme comes from a film score he composed in the early 1970s for Elem Klimov's *The Agony*. Its powerful, concentrated atmosphere resonates long in the mind and leaves what one could describe as a strong aftertaste. So, for that matter, does *In memoriam . . .*, a transcription and re-working of the *Piano quintet* (1972–6), written on the death of his mother, made at the request of Gennady Rozhdestvensky. Something of the very private grief and spare, hollow textures of the quintet is lost but there are gains in colour in the highly imaginative use of the orchestra. The recording has exceptional richness, detail and depth and the performance of the concerto has all the authority and panache one might expect.

Violin concertos Nos. 1–2.
*** BIS Dig. CD 487 [id.]. Mark Lubotsky, Malmö SO, Eri Klas.

The *First Violin concerto* was composed in 1956, when Schnittke was still a student, but was revised in 1963. It inhabits a post-romantic era: in the composer's own words, its 'sound world is dominated by Tchaikovsky and Rachmaninov, overshadowed by Shostakovich and adorned with the orchestral conventions of the day'. Its lyricism is profoundly at variance with its successor of 1966, commissioned by Mark Lubotsky, the soloist on this record. Here the central concept is what Schnittke calls 'a certain drama of tone colours', and there is no doubt that much of it is vividly imagined and strongly individual. The double-bass is assigned a special role of a caricatured 'anti-soloist'. The 12-note series serves as the thematic foundation, but there is nevertheless a centre of gravity, a constantly recurring note which sometimes lends the music an illusion of tonality. There is recourse to the once fashionable aleotoric technique, but this is all within carefully controlled parameters. The Malmö orchestra under Eri Klas play with evident feeling in both works and are very well recorded. This is an altogether highly satisfactory coupling.

(i) *Gogol suite* (compiled Rozhdestvensky); *Labyrinths.*
*** BIS Dig. CD 557 [id.]. Malmö SO, Lev Markiz; (i) with Anton Kontra.

The *Gogol suite* was compiled by Rozhdestvensky from the music Schnittke composed to a commission for an unusual Gogol spectacle by Yuri Lyubimow. Its eight movements are resourceful in their evocation of character and handling of pastiche, and the ideas, mainly contained in pretty slight music, survive the transformation to concert use successfully. There is a surrealistic quality to it, reminiscent of Gogol's own words quoted in Jürgen Köchel's note, 'The world hears my laughter; my tears it does not see nor recognise'. *Labyrinths* is a ballet score composed in 1971, thin in development and musical ideas but sufficiently strong in atmosphere to survive the transition from stage to concert hall. The Malmö Orchestra under Lev Markiz play very well and the recording is in the demonstration class.

Cello sonata.
*** BIS Dig. CD 336 [id.]. Torleif Thedéen, Roland Pöntinen – STRAVINSKY: *Suite italienne;* SHOSTAKOVICH: *Sonata.* ***

The *Cello sonata* is a powerfully expressive piece, its avant-garde surface enshrining a neo-romantic soul. Torleif Thedéen is a refined and intelligent player who gives a thoroughly committed account of this piece with his countryman, Roland Pöntinen.

Prelude in memoriam Shostakovich (for 2 solo violins).
*** Chan Dig. CHAN 8988; *ABTD 1570* [id.]. Mordkovitch, Young – PROKOFIEV; SHOSTAKOVICH: *Violin sonatas.* ***

The Schnittke *Prelude* for two solo violins is the shortest of the works on Lydia Mordkovitch's excellent disc of Soviet violin music, but it is among the most moving in its intense, elegiac way. She is well matched by her partner, Emma Young.

Violin sonata No. 1; Sonata in the olden style.
*** Chan. Dig. CHAN 8343; *ABTD 1089* [id.]. Dubinsky, Edlina – SHOSTAKOVICH: *Violin sonata.* ***

Schnittke's *First sonata* dates from 1963 when he was still in his late twenties; it is a well-argued piece that seems to unify his awareness of the post-serial musical world with the tradition of Shostakovich. On this version it is linked with a pastiche of less interest, dating from 1977. Excellent playing from both artists, and very good recording too.

Schoeck, Othmar (1886–1957)

Cello concerto, Op. 61.
*** Claves Dig. D 8502 [id.]. Goritzki, Deutsche Kammerakademie Neuss – REGER: *Lyrisches Andante.* ***

The chamber-like scoring of the *Cello concerto* gives it a rather special, private quality and, although it has its longueurs, its atmosphere is at times strong and haunting. No doubt there is an over-reliance on sequence; however, there are times when a quiet voice speaks – and one with powerful resonances. The performance is sensitive and totally dedicated, and the recording is very natural.

(i) *Violin concerto, Op. 21; Serenade, Op. 1; Suite in A flat, Op. 59.*
*** Novalis Dig. 150070-2; *150070-4.* (i) Ulf Hoelscher, ECO, Howard Griffiths.

Schoeck's *Violin concerto* comes from 1911–12 and was inspired, like Bartók's *First concerto* (1908) by Stefi Geyer, with whom both composers were in love. The *Concerto*'s neglect on record is really unaccountable: it has great warmth and enormous appeal and would doubtless enjoy wide popularity if only the public could find a way to it. The ideas are fresh and memorable, and there is an autumnal melancholy about the slow movement almost reminiscent of Elgar. Ulf Hoelscher and the English Chamber Orchestra under Howard Griffiths play this movement – and, for that matter, the whole work – as if they were in love with it (as indeed they should be). The *Serenade* of 1907 has some of the charm of late Strauss, and the *Suite for strings* (1945) is a work of strong character: it has the same luminous quality and sad, gentle ambience as the pastoral intermezzo, *Summer night*, written the same year (see our main volume). Occasionally one feels the need for a richer string sonority, but the performance is dedicated and the recording is well balanced and has both clarity and warmth. Strongly recommended.

Das Stille Leuchten, Op. 60.
**(*) Claves Dig. CD 50-8910 [id.]. Dietrich Fischer-Dieskau, Hartmut Höll.

Das Stille Leuchten (The Silent Light or Illumination) is an altogether magnificent work and, although this record is less than ideal, collectors should seek it out. Many of the 24 songs which make up the cycle are touching and some are really inspired. Like late Strauss, they often convey a feeling of regret at life's evanescence and are full of a resigned but poignant melancholy; yet at times they also bring a great variety and range of mood. Dietrich Fischer-Dieskau sings with all his old artistry and imagination, although the voice has now lost some of its bloom and colour. Hartmut Höll is an inspired pianist.

Schoenberg, Arnold (1874–1951)

Chamber symphony No. 1, Op. 9.
*** DG Dig. 423 307-2 [id.]. BPO, Sinopoli – MANZONI: *Mass.* ***
*** Teldec/Warner Dig. 2292 46019; *2292 46019-4* [id.]. COE, Holliger – BERG: *Chamber concerto.* ***
(M) **(*) Decca 430 007-2. LAPO (members), Mehta – SCHMIDT: *Symphony No. 4.* **(*)

A fine performance of Schoenberg's Op. 9 from Sinopoli. He links it positively back to the high romanticism of Richard Strauss, with the Berlin Philharmonic producing glorious sounds. Full recording to match.

Schoenberg's *Chamber Symphony No. 1* makes an apt coupling for the fine COE version of the Berg, played with equal warmth and thrust, with complex textural problems masterfully solved. It is also given a rich performance under Mehta, arguably too fast at times but full of understanding for the romantic emotions which underlie much of the writing. The 1969 recording is appropriately brilliant, but the CD transfer is very brightly lit.

Chamber symphonies Nos. 1, Op. 9; 2, Op. 38; Verklärte Nacht.
*** DG Dig. 429 233-2 [id.]. Orpheus CO.

Excellent value from the Orpheus Chamber Orchestra who couple their fine account of *Verklärte Nacht* with the two *Chamber symphonies* of 1906 and 1939 respectively. Their *Verklärte Nacht* is swift-moving and a bit overheated; it does not have the subtle range of colouring and dynamics that marks the classic Karajan version. Both the *Chamber symphonies* come off well and the disc is worth acquiring solely for their sake. The *Second* is an underrated piece and the Orpheus play as if they believed in every note. A rather brightly lit but very good recording.

(i) *Piano concerto in C, Op. 42;* (ii) *Violin concerto, Op. 36.*
(M) **(*) DG 431 740-2. (i) Brendel; (ii) Zeitlin; Bav. RSO, Kubelik – BERG: *Violin concerto.* ***

More than usual in these relatively late works, the thick textures favoured by Schoenberg obscure the focus of the argument rather than making it sweeter on the ear. Brendel – who made a recording for Vox very early in his career – remains a committed Schoenbergian, and Zeitlin is impressive too. Though even the CD transfer does not manage to clarify the thorny textures completely, the sound, as transferred, is very good.

Pelleas und Melisande (symphonic poem), *Op. 5.*
*** DG 423 132-2 [id.]. BPO, Karajan – BERG: *Lyric suite: 3 Pieces.* ***
**(*) Chan. Dig. CHAN 8619 [id.]. SNO, Bamert – WEBERN: *Passacaglia.* **(*)

The Straussian opulence of Schoenberg's early symphonic poem has never been as ravishingly presented as by Karajan and the Berlin Philharmonic in this superbly recorded version. The gorgeous tapestry of sound is both rich and full of refinement and detail, while the thrust of argument is powerfully conveyed.

Matthias Bamert gives a finely shaped account that operates at a slightly lower emotional temperature than its distinguished rival, and is none the worse for that. The playing is admirable (though the strings are not, of course, in the same class as those of the Berlin Philharmonic for Karajan) and the sound is well blended, if a bit recessed.

Pelleas und Melisande, Op. 5; Variations for orchestra, Op. 31; Verklaerte Nacht (orchestral version), *Op. 4.*
(M) *** DG 427 424-2 (3) [id.]. BPO, Karajan – BERG: *Lyric suite; 3 Pieces;* WEBERN: *Collection.* ***

These are superb performances which present the emotional element at full power but give unequalled precision and refinement. *Pelleas und Melisande*, written at the same time as the Debussy opera but in ignorance of the rival project, is in its way a Strauss-like masterpiece, while the Op. 31 *Variations*, the most challenging of Schoenberg's orchestral works, here receives a reading which vividly conveys the ebb and flow of tension within the phrase and over the whole plan. Superb recording, excellently remastered.

5 Pieces for orchestra, Op. 16.
*** EMI Dig. CDC7 49857-2 [id.]. CBSO, Rattle – BERG: *Lulu: suite;* WEBERN: *6 Pieces.* ***
*** DG Dig. 419 781-2 [id.]. BPO, Levine – BERG: *3 Pieces;* WEBERN: *5 Pieces.* ***
(M) *** Mercury 432 006-2 [id.]. LSO, Dorati – BERG: *3 Pieces; Lulu suite;* WEBERN: *5 Pieces.* ***

Rattle and the CBSO give an outstanding reading of this Schoenberg masterpiece, bringing out its red-blooded strength, neither too austere nor too plushy. With sound of demonstration quality and an ideal coupling, it makes an outstanding recommendation, even over Levine's similar collection of equivalent masterpieces by other leaders of the Second Viennese School.

The colour and power of Schoenberg's Opus 16 *Pieces* also come over superbly in Levine's purposeful, concentrated reading. This is an interpretation designed to relate Schoenberg to his predecessors rather than to the future. Warm, full-toned recording, with some spotlighting.

Dorati, in his pioneering coupling with other works written at the same period by Schoenberg's emergent pupils, used the version the composer made in 1949, with a slightly reduced orchestra. The performance is strong and vivid; the 1962 sound is admirably vivid and clear.

Variations for orchestra, Op. 31; Verklaerte Nacht, Op. 4.
❀ *** DG 415 326-2 [id.]. BPO, Karajan.

Verklaerte Nacht, Op. 4.
** Decca Dig. 421 182-2 (2) [id.]. Berlin RSO, Chailly – MAHLER: *Symphony No. 10.* **(*)

Karajan's version of *Verklaerte Nacht* is altogether magical and very much in a class of its own. There is a tremendous intensity and variety of tone and colour: the palette that the strings of the Berlin Philharmonic have at their command is altogether extraordinarily wide-ranging. Moreover on CD the sound is firmer and more cleanly defined.

Chailly's version is very well played and recorded, but is in no way distinctive.

Verklaerte Nacht, Op. 4 (string sextet version).
*** Hyp. Dig. CDA 66425; *KA 66425* [id.]. Raphael Ens. – KORNGOLD: *Sextet*. ***

The Raphael Ensemble have the advantage of very good recorded sound and give a fine account of Schoenberg's score. They convey its atmosphere without indulging in overstatement or its reverse. They have, too, the advantage of a rarity in their coupling, the youthful *Sextet* of Korngold.

Suite (for E flat clarinet, clarinet, bass clarinet, violin, viola, cello & piano), *Op. 29; Wind quintet, Op. 26.*
(M) *** Decca 433 083-2 [id.]. L. Sinf. (members), David Atherton.

In his *Suite*, Op. 29, Schoenberg deliberately found inspiration in Viennese dance-rhythms, and modelled the structure on the serenades and divertimentos of the Mozart/Haydn period. But those associations are misleading, for Schoenberg was virtually incapable of producing genuine light music, and this piece only nags at one if one tries to treat it trivially. Even if the third movement bases its variations on a folk-theme (*Ännchen von Tharau*), introduced on the bass clarinet, the effect is meant to be sardonic rather than light-hearted. These recordings by the London Sinfonietta were made in 1973/4 in conjunction with a series of centenary concerts at London's Queen Elizabeth Hall. Happily the recording venue was All Saints' Church, Petersham, and the uncompromising and massive *Wind quintet*, though forwardly balanced, is given plenty of space. It is played with great commitment and bravura, and if not even these players can make the humour of the *Suite* anything but Germanic, the combination of fine playing and lively sound makes this generous 74-minute coupling highly recommendable.

Piano music: *3 Pieces, Op. 11; 6 Small Pieces, Op. 19; 5 Pieces, Op. 23; 3 Pieces, Op. 33a & b; Suite, Op. 25.*
(M) *** DG 423 249-2 [id.]. Maurizio Pollini.

This CD encompasses Schoenberg's complete piano music. Pollini plays with enormous authority and refinement of dynamic nuance and colour, making one perceive this music in a totally different light from other performers. He is accorded excellent sound (very slightly on the dry side), extremely clear and well defined.

VOCAL MUSIC

(i) *The Book of the Hanging Gardens, Op. 15;* (ii) *Pierrot Lunaire, Op. 21.*
*** Nonesuch/Warner 7559 79237-2 [id.]. Jan DeGaetani; (i) Gilbert Kalish; (ii) Contemporary Chamber Ens., Arthur Weisberg.

The Nonesuch New York performance of *Pierrot Lunaire* has long been admired for steering a splendidly confident course among all the many problematic interpretative points. Now it comes coupled with another equally impressive recording of *The Book of the Hanging Gardens*. Jan DeGaetani is a superbly precise soloist, but there is no feeling whatever of pedantry in her performances which, more than most, allow a welcome degree of expressiveness, while keeping a sharp focus and projecting a strong sense of drama.

Erwartung, Op. 17.
*** Decca Dig. 417 348-2 (2) [id.]. Anja Silja, VPO, Dohnányi – BERG: *Wozzeck*. ***

Schoenberg's searingly intense monodrama makes an apt and generous coupling for Dohnányi's excellent version of Berg's *Wozzeck*. As in the Berg, Silja is at her most passionately committed. The sound under pressure may be raw, but the self-tortured questionings of the central character come over grippingly, and the digital sound is exceptionally vivid.

Gurrelieder.
*** Decca Dig. 430 321-2; *430 321-4* (2) [id.]. Jerusalem, Dunn, Fassbaender, Brecht, Haage, Hotter, St Hedwig's Cathedral Ch., Berlin, Düsseldorf State Musikverein, Berlin RSO, Chailly.
*** Ph. 412 511-2 (2) [id.]. McCracken, Norman, Troyanos, Arnold, Scown, Tanglewood Festival Ch., Boston SO, Ozawa.

Chailly's magnificent recording of Schoenberg's massive *Gurrelieder* effectively supplants all existing versions, even Ozawa's impressive Boston set, recorded live. This Berlin recording not only brings richer, fuller, more detailed and better-balanced sound, but it conveys a natural dramatic tension not easy to find in studio conditions. Chailly has a finer team of soloists than on any rival set, with Siegfried Jerusalem as Waldemar not only warmer and firmer of tone than his rivals but more imaginative too. Susan Dunn makes a sweet, touchingly vulnerable Tove, while Brigitte Fassbaender gives darkly baleful intensity to the message of the Wood-dove. Hans Hotter is a characterful Speaker in the final section. The impact of the performance is the more telling with sound both atmospheric and immediate, bringing a fine sense of presence, not least in the final choral outburst.

Ozawa directs a gloriously opulent reading of Schoenberg's *Gurrelieder.* The playing of the Boston Symphony has both warmth and polish and is set against a resonant acoustic; among the soloists, Jessye Norman gives a performance of radiant beauty, at times reminding one of Flagstad in the burnished glory of her tone-colours. As the wood-dove, Tatiana Troyanos sings most sensitively, though the vibrato is at times obtrusive; and James McCracken does better than most tenors at coping with a heroic vocal line without barking. The luxuriant textures are given a degree more transparency, with detail slightly clearer on CD.

Music for chorus: *2 Canons; 3 Canons, Op. 28; Dreimal Tausend Jähre, Op. 50a; Friede auf Erden, Op. 13; 3 Folksongs, Op. 49; 3 German folksongs; Kol Nidre, Op. 39; 4 Pieces, Op. 27; 6 Pieces, Op. 35; Psalm 130, Op. 50b; Modern Psalm No. 1, Op. 50 C; A Survivor from Warsaw, Op. 46.*
(M) *** Sony S2K 44571 (2) [id.]. John Shirley-Quirk, Günther Reich, BBC Singers, BBC SO, Pierre Boulez.

With passionately committed performances from the BBC Singers, this superb collection of choral music explodes any idea that Schoenberg was a cold composer. In his choral pieces, particularly when inspired by a Jewish theme, as in the magnificent *Kol Nidre* of 1938 for narrator, mixed chorus and orchestra, his full romanticism broke out. His adoption of an idiom far removed from abrasive atonality in most of these pieces makes this one of the most approachable of Schoenberg sets, with the use of a narrator in three of the works adding spice to the mixture. The early motet, *Friede auf Erden*, very taxing for the chorus, is here made to sound mellifluous, and only the little middle-period *Pieces*, Opp. 27 and 28, show anything like the full rigour of Schoenbergian argument. The later works, written in America, use twelve-note technique with astonishingly warm, rich results. First-rate recording over the series, all done in the BBC's Maida Vale Studio. Translations are given of the full texts.

Ode to Napoleon.
** DG Dig. 415 982-2 [id.]. Kenneth Griffiths, LaSalle Qt – WEBERN: *Quintet* etc. ***

Written in 1942, the *Ode to Napoleon* sets the words of Byron in Schoenbergian *Sprechstimme* as a heartfelt protest against Nazi tyranny. With hatred at its core, it represents the composer at his most deeply committed, and that bedrock of passion is strongly brought out in the playing of the pianist, Stefan Litwin, and the LaSalle Quartet; sadly, the declamation is harshly recorded in what sounds like another acoustic.

Pierrot Lunaire, Op. 21 (see also above, under *The Book of the Hanging Gardens*).
(M) *** Chan. CHAN 6534; *MBTD 6534* [id.]. Jane Manning, Nash Ens., Rattle – WEBERN: *Concerto.* ***

Jane Manning is outstanding among singers who have tackled this most taxing of works, steering a masterful course between the twin perils of, on the one hand, actually singing and, on the other, simply speaking. As well as being beautifully controlled and far more accurate than is common, her sing-speech brings out the element of irony and darkly pointed wit that is an essential too often missed in this piece. In a 1977 recording originally made for the Open University, Rattle draws strong, committed performances from the members of the Nash Ensemble and, apart from some intermittently odd balances, the sound is excellent.

(i) *Pierrot lunaire, Op. 21;* (ii) *Serenade, Op. 24* (for clarinet, bass clarinet, mandolin, guitar, violin, viola, cello and bass voice); *Die eiserne Brigade* (march for string quartet and piano).
(M) *** Decca 425 626-2. (i) Mary Thomas; (ii) Shirley-Quirk; L. Sinf., Atherton.

These performances derive from David Atherton's distinguished 1973 survey of Schoenberg's chamber music, including vocal works. *Pierrot lunaire* is among the most incisive and dramatic yet recorded and, although not even these performers can make the humour of the *Serenade* anything but Teutonic, the performance remains compelling.

OPERA

Moses und Aron.
*** Decca Dig. 414 264-2 (2) [id.]. Mazura, Langridge, Bonney, Haugland, Chicago Ch. and SO, Solti.

Solti gives Schoenberg's masterly score a dynamism and warmth which set it firmly – if perhaps surprisingly – in the grand romantic tradition. Solti instructed his performers to 'play and sing as if you were performing Brahms', and here Solti's broad romantic treatment presents a reading which in its great variety of mood and pace underlines the drama, yet finds an element of fantasy and, in places – as in the *Golden Calf* episode – a sparkle such as you would never expect from Schoenberg. It is still not an easy work. The Moses of Franz Mazura may not be as specific in his sing-speech as was Gunter Reich in the two previous versions – far less sing than speech – but the characterization of an Old Testament patriarch is the more convincing. As Aaron, Philip Langridge is lighter and more lyrical, as well as more accurate, than his predecessor with Boulez, Richard Cassilly. Aage Haugland with his firm, dark bass makes his mark in the small role of the Priest; Barbara Bonney too is excellent as the Young Girl. Above all, the brilliant singing of the Chicago Symphony Chorus matches the playing of the orchestra in virtuosity. More than ever the question-mark concluding Act II makes a pointful close, with no feeling of a work unfinished. The brilliant recording has an even sharper focus on CD.

Schreker, Franz (1878–1934)

(i) *Chamber symphony for 23 solo instruments;* (ii) *Nachtstück;* (i) *Prelude to a drama;* (ii) *Valse lente.*
**(*) Koch Int. Dig. CD 311 078. Berlin RSO, (i) Gielen, (ii) Rickenbacher.

Schreker's *Chamber symphony* is quite magical, scored with great delicacy and feeling for colour. Perhaps it is slightly over-perfumed, but it is marvellously evocative and imaginative music. There are reminders of Debussy, Strauss, Szymanowski and Puccini, but there is still an individual personality here. The other works are not quite so seductive but they, too, have a heady art-nouveau atmosphere. A most rewarding disc, with good performances and very acceptable, though not out of the ordinary, recording. But don't miss this issue.

Der Schatzgräber (opera): complete.
**(*) Capriccio Dig. 60010-2 (2) [id.]. Protschka, Schnaut, Stamm, Haage, Hamburg State O, Gerd Albrecht.

Completed at the very end of the First World War, *Der Schatzgräber* (The treasure-digger) had phenomenal success in the six years following, being given in Germany and Austria many hundreds of times. The attractions of Schreker's sweet-sour treatment of a curious morality fairy-story then waned. Schreker was forced by the Nazis to resign from his Berlin posts in 1933, and he died the following year. In idiom the comedy scenes owe much to the Wagner of *Meistersinger*, only with fewer tunes. The love music is more freely lyrical, with Schreker giving his central character, Elis – a roving minstrel with magical powers – a series of charming ballads. In Act III, before the great night of love between Elis and the heroine, Els – an innkeeper's daughter with a knack for dispatching unwanted suitors – Schreker has the temerity to have her quote her mother's simple cradle-song, a moment almost too sweet for comfort, and maybe an indication that Freudian motivation had hardly entered the composer-librettist's mind, either there or elsewhere. This first recording was made live at the Hamburg State Opera in 1989, though there are very few signs of the audience's presence, with no applause, even at the end. Josef Protschka sings powerfully as Elis, hardly ever over-strenuous, but Gabriele Schnaut finds it hard to scale down her very bright and powerful soprano and seems happiest when she is scything your ears with loud and often unsteady top notes; yet she is certainly dramatic in this equivocal role. Outstanding among the others is Peter Haage as the court jester, who in the end is the only one to take pity on the disgraced Els, even though Elis is finally persuaded to sing a ballad as she dies. *Der Schatzgräber* may be hokum, but it is enjoyable hokum, and, with Albrecht drawing committed performances from the whole company, this well-made recording is most welcome.

Schröter, Johann (1752–88)

Piano concerto in C, Op. 3/3.
*** Sony Dig. MK 39222 [id.]. Murray Perahia, ECO – MOZART: *Piano concertos Nos. 1–3, K.107.* ***

Johann Samuel Schröter eventually succeeded J. C. Bach as music master to the queen in 1782, six years before his death. He was a highly accomplished pianist, and this sparkling little *Concerto* explains why he was so successful. Murray Perahia gives it all his care and attention without overloading it with sophistication. His account is delightful in every way, and beautifully recorded.

Schubert, Franz (1797–1828)

Konzertstücke in D, D.935; Polonaise in B flat, D.580; Rondo in A, D.438.
*** Ph. Dig. 420 168-2 [id.]. Zukerman, St Paul CO – BEETHOVEN: *Romances;* DVOŘÁK: *Romance.* ***

This was the nearest Schubert came to writing a violin concerto. The engaging *Polonaise* is used separately as a foil between Beethoven and Dvořák, while the *Konzertstücke* and *Rondo* are happily linked to round off a particularly satisfying collection of short concertante works for violin and orchestra.

Rondo in A for violin and strings, D.438.
(B) *** Ph. 426 977-2; *426 977-4.* Grumiaux, New Philh. O, Leppard – HAYDN: *Violin concertos;* MOZART: *Adagio; Rondo.* ***
*** EMI Dig. CDC7 49663-2 [id.]. Nigel Kennedy, ECO, Tate – BRUCH; MENDELSSOHN: *Concertos.* ***

Schubert's *Rondo* has never danced more engagingly than on Grumiaux's bow, and Leppard captures the music's rhythmic lilt equally pleasingly. Excellent 1967 sound. A bargain.

The ideas in Schubert's *Rondo* also flow very sweetly with Kennedy, making this an attractive bonus to the usual Bruch–Mendelssohn coupling.

Symphonies Nos. 1–6; 8 (Unfinished); 9 (Great).
(M) **(*) DG 419 318-2 (4). BPO, Karl Boehm.

Symphonies Nos. 1–6; 8 (Unfinished); 9 (Great); Overtures: Fierabras; In the Italian style in C; Des Teufels Lustschloss.
(B) **(*) Decca 430 773-2 (4). VPO, István Kertész.

Symphonies Nos. 1–6; 8–9; Grand Duo in C, D.812 (orch. Joachim); *Rosamunde overture (Die Zauberharfe), D.644.*
*** DG Dig. 423 651-2 (5) [id.]. COE, Abbado.

Symphonies Nos 1–6; 8–9; Rosamunde: Overture and incidental music.
(M) **(*) BMG/RCA Dig./Analogue GD 60096 (5); [60096-2-RG]. Cologne RSO, Wand.

Abbado's is an outstanding set. Rarely has he made recordings of the central Viennese classics which find him so naturally sunny and warm in his expression. Speeds are often on the fast side but never feel breathless, and the recording is refined, with fine bloom on the string-sound. Textually too, the Abbado set takes precedence over its rivals. Abbado asked one of the orchestra, Stefano Mollo, to carry out research on the original source-material in Vienna for the symphonies not yet included in the *Neue Schubert-Ausgabe.* As a result of his work, there are certain fascinating differences from what we are used to. The slip-case holds the five CD jewel-cases with a separate booklet in each. They are now also available separately – see below.

Performing honours between the Boehm and Kertész sets are fairly evenly divided. Boehm's recordings were made over a decade between 1963 and 1973. Although he does not always smile as often as Schubert's music demands, he is always sympathetic, and the Berlin Philharmonic plays with striking warmth and finesse throughout. Certainly the Berlin wind are a joy to listen to in most of these symphonies, and in Nos. 6, 8 and 9 Boehm is the best of Schubertians. It is only in the early symphonies that he does not quite capture the youthful sparkle of these delightful scores, although in its way No. 1 is brightly and classically done. The remastered sound is remarkably fine, fresh and clear and without loss of bloom. But with no fillers this set is overpriced.

Kertész, too, recorded these works over a fairly long period (between 1963 and 1971). He began with Nos. 8 and 9 and the overtures (which are well worth having), and these two symphonies are the finest performances in the cycle. The *Ninth* is fresh, dramatic and often very exciting, the *Unfinished* highly imaginative and comparably dramatic in its wide dynamic contrasts. In the two early symphonies Kertész scores with the spirited VPO playing and a light touch, and this also applies to Nos. 3 and 6, even if they are without the last ounce of character and distinction. The playing of the VPO is beyond reproach throughout, and if Kertész's Schubert manner is less coaxing than Beecham's, less affectionate than Boehm's, it has a pervading freshness, helped by the transparent yet full Decca sound.

The freshness and bluff honesty of Gunter Wand in Schubert shine through all his performances. Now collected on five mid-price CDs, his cycle offers first-rate sound, engineered by West German Radio. Nos. 3, 5 and 6 as well as the *Rosamunde* music are the only digital recordings. Note that the Boehm set takes only four mid-price CDs, but has no makeweight, and is less generous over repeats.

Symphonies Nos. 1–3; 4 (Tragic); 5–7; 8 (Unfinished); 9 in C (Great); 10 in D, D.936a; Symphonic fragments in D, D.615 and D.708a (completed and orch. Newbould).
*** Ph. Dig. 412 176-2 (6) [id.]. ASMF, Marriner.

Marriner's excellent set gathers together not only the eight symphonies of the regular canon but two more symphonies now 'realized', thanks to the work of Professor Brian Newbould of Hull University. For full measure, half a dozen fragments of other symphonic movements are also included, orchestrated by Professor Newbould. Those fragments include the four-movement outline of yet another symphony – Scherzo complete, other movements tantalizingly cut off in mid-flight. Newbould's No. 7 is based on a sketch which quickly lapsed into a single orchestral line, now devotedly filled out. That work proves less rewarding than 'No. 10', written in the last months of Schubert's life, well after the *Great C major*, which now appears to have been written a year or so earlier. The set brings sparkling examples of the Academy's work at its finest, while the bigger challenges of the *Unfinished* (here completed with Schubert's Scherzo filled out and the *Rosamunde B minor Entr'acte* used as finale) and the *Great C major* are splendidly taken. These are fresh, direct readings, making up in rhythmic vitality for any lack of weight. The recordings, all digital, present consistent refinement and undistractingly good balance. But this set now seems expensive.

Symphonies Nos. 1 in D, D.82; 2 in B flat, D.125.
*** DG Dig. 423 652-2 [id.]. COE, Abbado.

The coupling of the two earliest *Symphonies* brings bright and sparkling performances, reflecting the youthful joy of both composer and players. Even when he adopts a brisk speed, as in the bouncing, one-in-a-bar account of the third-movement *Allegretto* of No. 1, Abbado brings out the sunny relaxation of the writing, most exhilaratingly of all in the light-hearted finales. The recording of both captures the refined playing of the COE very vividly.

Symphonies Nos. 3 in D, D.200; 4 in C min. (Tragic), D.417.
*** DG Dig. 423 653-2 [id.]. COE, Abbado.

Crisp, fast and light, No. 3 is given a delectable performance by Abbado, with the *Presto* finale taken at a hectic speed which all the same sounds bright and easy, not at all breathless. In No. 4, the *Tragic*, Abbado makes the slow C minor introduction bitingly mysterious before a clean, elegant *Allegro*, and with this conductor the other movements are also elegant and polished as well as strong. Textually, No. 4 is particularly interesting, when the scholarly revisions by Stefano Mollo, inspired by the conductor, not only bring the excision of misread diminuendo markings (giving new sharpness to the third movement in particular) but eliminate the extra bars in the slow movement which had been inserted originally by Brahms. The slow movement is outstandingly beautiful, with the oboe solo – presumably COE's Douglas Boyd – most tenderly expressive.

Symphonies Nos. 3 in D, D.200; 5 in B flat, D.485; 6 in C, D.589.
❀ (M) *** EMI CDM7 69750-2. RPO, Beecham.

Symphonies Nos. 3 in D, D.200; 5 in B flat, D.485; Overture in C in the Italian style.
**(*) Nimbus Dig. NI 5172 [id.]. Hanover Band, Roy Goodman.

Beecham's are magical performances in which every phrase breathes. There is no substitute for imaginative phrasing and each line is shaped with affection and spirit. The *Allegretto* of the *Third Symphony* is an absolute delight. The delicacy of the opening of the *Fifth* is matched by the simple lyrical beauty of the *Andante*, while few conductors have been as persuasive as Beecham in the *Sixth* 'little' *C major Symphony*. The rhythmic point and high spirits of the first movement and scherzo are irresistible, and the finale, taken rather more gently than usual, is wonderfully graceful and delectably sprung. The sound is now just a shade drier in Nos. 3 and 6 than in their last LP incarnation but is generally faithful and spacious. This is an indispensable record or tape for all collections and a supreme bargain in the Schubert discography.

As in the Hanover Band's cycle of the Beethoven symphonies, Roy Goodman presents period performances of these two favourites among Schubert's earlier symphonies which are fresh, light and resilient. The *Overture in C* makes an attractive bonus on top of the regular coupling. The Nimbus recording is characteristically reverberant and the balance between strings and wind is less well judged than on many earlier recordings. But even with that balance, the sparkle of the performances in both *Symphonies* and *Overture* is most winning.

Symphonies Nos. 3 in D, D.200; 8 in B min. (Unfinished), D.759.
(B) *** Pickwick Dig. PCD 848; *CIMPC 848* [id.]. City of L. Sinfonia, Hickox.

Hickox's coupling makes a first-rate bargain recommendation on the Pickwick label. These are fresh and direct readings, never putting a foot wrong, very well recorded, with a chamber orchestra sounding full and substantial. Others may find more individuality and charm, but the crisp resilience of the playing is consistently winning.

Symphony No. 5 in B flat, D.485.
❀ (M) **(*) Sony SMK 46246 [id.]. Marlboro Festival O, Casals – BEETHOVEN: *Symphony No. 4.* **
(M) *** EMI CDM7 63869-2 [id.]; *EG 763869-4*. Philh. O, Klemperer – DVOŘÁK: *Symphony No. 9.* **
**(*) Linn CKD 003 [id.]. English Classical Players, Jonathan Brett – MOZART: *Symphony No. 40.* **(*)

The Casals account is a concert performance, recorded at the Marlboro Festival in Vermont in 1970, and it is very special indeed. The reading is spacious and unhurried, eminently straightforward and unaffected, yet unfailingly illuminating. There are some extraneous noises at the beginning of the slow movement (and elsewhere), though they do not deflect attention from either the musical imagination that illumines the playing or the tenderness of the phrasing. The recording inhibits an unreserved recommendation; the string-tone needs more bloom and tutti are a bit rough-grained – but never mind, the performance is full of insight.

More charm here than one might have expected from Klemperer, but basically his conception is stronger than most, so that something like an ideal balance is kept between Schubert's natural lyricism and the firmness of sonata form. The Philharmonia Orchestra is on top form, and rarely has Klemperer recorded a more exhilarating performance than this 1963 version. Recording excellent.

As with his Mozart coupling, Jonathan Brett is generous with repeats, so the overall playing time of this Schubert performance by the excellent English Classical Players is 29 minutes. Brett moves the *Andante con moto* on nicely and, thoughout, the light orchestral touch is very pleasing, especially so in the engagingly Schubertian finale, which is the highlight of the performance, very spirited yet admirably graceful. The recording, made in the London Henry Wood Hall, is most naturally balanced.

Symphonies Nos. 5 in B flat, D.485; 6 in C, D.589.
*** DG Dig. 423 654-2 [id.]. COE, Abbado.

Abbado has rarely sounded more relaxed and winning. He brings out the happy songfulness of the slow movements in these works, as well as the rhythmic resilience of the *Allegros*. As in No. 4, so also in No. 6 Abbado eliminates the extra bars added by Brahms in his original Schubert Edition. Excellent recording, with fine bloom and good, natural contrasts.

Symphonies Nos. 5 in B flat, D.485; 8 in B min. (Unfinished), D.759.
(M) *** Decca Dig. 430 439-2; *430 439-4* [id.]. VPO, Solti.

(M) *** Sony MK 42048 [id.]. Columbia SO or NYPO, Bruno Walter.

As with Solti's fresh, resilient and persuasive (full-price) reading of the *Great C major* with the Vienna Philharmonic, his coupling of Nos. 5 and 8 brings one of his most felicitous recordings. There have been more charming versions of No. 5 but few that so beautifully combine freshness with refined polish. The *Unfinished* has Solti adopting measured speeds but with his refined manner keeping total concentration. Excellent recording.

Walter brings special qualities of warmth and lyricism to the *Unfinished*. Affection, gentleness and humanity are the keynotes of this performance; while the first movement of the *Fifth* is rather measured, there is much loving attention to detail in the *Andante*. The recording emerges fresh and glowing in its CD format and, like the rest of the Walter series, completely belies its age.

Symphonies No. 5 in B flat, D.485; 8 in B min. (Unfinished) (completed and orch. Newbould).
(M) *** Ph. Dig. 432 045-2; *432 045-4*. ASMF, Marriner.

The balance in the *Fifth Symphony* is not quite ideal in the relationship between wind and strings, and the recording is not as clearly defined internally as one might expect. Nevertheless this remains a highly desirable performance, among the finest in Marriner's series. The *Unfinished* is here completed, with Schubert's Scherzo filled out and the *Rosamunde B minor Entr'acte* used as finale. Given a fresh, direct performance, the work becomes fully convincing in its own right.

Symphonies Nos. 5 in B flat, D.485; 9 in C, D.944 (The Great).
(M) (**) BMG/RCA mono GD 60291 [60291-2-RG]. NBC SO, Toscanini.

Harvey Sach's note reminds us that Toscanini first conducted the *Great C major* in 1896! He made three commercial recordings, one with the Philadelphia Orchestra when he was in his mid-seventies, the second (offered here in harness with a 1953 *Fifth* on this disc) recorded in Carnegie Hall in 1947, and a third when he was nearly 86! Not for him the expansive, late-romantic view favoured by Barbirolli, Furtwängler and Bruno Walter. In his 1947 performance Toscanini is tauter and faster than either his earlier or later recording. A useful antidote for it serves to remind one that Schubert was still a young man when this was composed with what was a bright future ahead and that the valedictory halo which came to surround it was a nineteenth-century phenomenon.

Symphony No. 8 in B min. (Unfinished), D.759.
❀ (M) *** DG Dig. 427 818-2; *427 818-4* [id.]. Philh. O, Sinopoli – SCHUMANN: *Symphony No. 3.* ***
❀ *** DG Dig. 410 862-2 [id.]. Philh. O, Sinopoli – MENDELSSOHN: *Symphony No. 4.* ***
(B) *** DG 429 676-2. BPO, Karajan – DVOŘÁK: *Symphony No. 9 (New World).* ***
(M) *** DG 415 848-2; *415 848-4* [id.]. BPO, Karajan – MENDELSSOHN: *Symphony No. 4.* ***
(M) (***) EMI mono CDM7 63398-2 [id.]; *EG 763398-4*. RPO, Beecham – BEETHOVEN: *Symphony No. 8;* MENDELSSOHN: *Symphony No. 4.* (***)

Sinopoli secures the most ravishingly refined and beautiful playing; the orchestral blend, particularly of the woodwind and horns, is magical. It is a deeply concentrated reading of the *Unfinished*, bringing out much unexpected detail, with every phrase freshly turned in seamless spontaneity. The contrast, as Sinopoli sees it, is between the dark – yet never histrionic – tragedy of the first movement, relieved only partially by the lovely second subject, and the sunlight of the closing movement, giving an unforgettable, gentle radiance. The exposition repeat is observed, adding weight and substance. This takes its place among the recorded classics. The warmly atmospheric recording, made in Kingsway Hall, is very impressive. As well as the original coupling with Mendelssohn, this is also available at mid-price, coupled with a superb account of Schumann's *Rhenish symphony*.

Karajan's 1965 DG recording of the *Unfinished* sounds fresher still in remastered form, yet has not lost its fullness and warmth of bass response. Its merits of simplicity and directness are enhanced by the extraordinary polish of the orchestral playing, lighting up much that is often obscured. The first movement is extremely compelling in its atmosphere; the slow movement too brings tinglingly precise attack and a wonderful sense of drama. A superb bargain in its coupling with Dvořák's *New World Symphony*.

Beecham's 1951 mono recording brings a magical example of his work. Though the first movement is taken relatively fast, a genuine allegro, Beecham's moulding of phrase and line could hardly be more persuasive. The build-up during the development section is thrilling, with the rasp of trombones vividly caught; and the slow movement is sweet and spacious, even though the RPO strings are not at their purest.

Symphony No. 8 in B min. (Unfinished); Grand Duo in C, D.812 (orch. Joachim).
*** DG Dig. 423 655-2 [id.]. COE, Abbado.

Abbado's outstandingly refined and sensitive version comes with an unusual and valuable coupling, the orchestral arrangement of the piano-duet *Grand Duo* made by Joachim, once erroneously thought to be the missing *Symphony No. 7*. The second subject in the *Unfinished* brings some slightly obtrusive agogic hesitations at the beginning of each phrase; but with such responsive playing they quickly sound fresh and natural. Abbado's choice of speeds and crisp control of dramatic contrasts are exemplary, bringing out the sunshine of Schubert as well as the darkness.

Symphony No. 9 in C (Great), D.944.
*** Virgin Dig. VC 790708-2 [id.]. O of Age of Enlightenment, Mackerras.
(M) *** Decca 430 747-2; *430 747-4* [id.]. VPO, Solti.
(M) *** EMI Dig. CDD7 64085-2 [id.]. BPO, Tennstedt – MENDELSSOHN: *Symphony No. 4*. ***
(M) *** DG 419 484-2 [id.]. Dresden State O, Boehm.
(M) **(*) Decca 425 957-2 [id.]. LSO, Josef Krips – SCHUMANN: *Symphony No. 4*. **
(B) **(*) Sony MYK 44828 [id.]. Columbia SO, Bruno Walter.
**(*) EMI Dig. CDC7 49949-2. L. Classical Players, Norrington.

Symphony No. 9 in C (Great); Rosamunde: Overture (Die Zauberharfe), D.644.
*** DG Dig. 423 656-2 [id.]. COE, Abbado.

Symphony No. 9 in C (Great); Symphonic fragments in D, D.615.
(M) *** Ph. Dig. 434 218-2; *434 218-4* [id.]. ASMF, Sir Neville Marriner.

Though the COE is by definition an orchestra of chamber scale, the weight of Abbado's version, taken from his complete cycle, is ample, while allowing extra detail to be heard, thanks also to the orchestra's outstandingly crisp ensemble. Speeds are very well chosen, and the expressive detail is consistently made to sound natural. This version is important too for including textual amendments, following the scholarly researches of one of the players, Stefano Mollo. There is a striking difference in the middle of the oboe melody of the first subject in the slow movement, and the scherzo has four extra bars that were originally cut by Brahms in his early edition. The sound is beautifully refined, to match the point and polish of the playing. The *Rosamunde* (*Zauberharfe*) *overture* makes a valuable and generous fill-up.

In the first recording to use period instruments, Sir Charles Mackerras and the Orchestra of the Age of Enlightenment on the Virgin Classics label give a winning performance, one that will delight both those who prefer conventional performance and devotees of the new authenticity. The characterful rasp and bite of period brass instruments and the crisp attack of timpani are much more striking than any thinness of string tone. It is a performance of outstanding freshness and resilience. Except in the first-movement allegro, speeds are on the fast side, with characteristically light, clean articulation, and with rhythms delectably sprung, making for extra clarity. With every single repeat observed, the heavenly length is joyfully as well as powerfully sustained, and the warm, atmospheric recording gives a fine sense of presence.

Sir George Solti is not the first conductor one thinks of as a Schubertian, but the *Great C major symphony* prompted him to one of the happiest and most glowing of all his many records, an outstanding version, beautifully paced and sprung in all four movements and superbly played and recorded. It has drama as well as lyrical feeling, but above all it has a natural sense of spontaneity and freshness, beautifully caught by the richly balanced recording, confirming the Vienna Sofiensaal as an ideal recording location. Now reissued at mid-price to celebrate his eightieth birthday, this is an unbeatable bargain and would be first choice, irrespective of cost, for I.M.

Tennstedt's is an incandescent reading that brings home afresh how Schubert, even in this last and grandest of his symphonies, was still youthfully energetic. With superb playing from the Berlin Philharmonic Orchestra this is also among the very finest versions available, irrespective of price, and, coupled with an equally exhilarating account of Mendelssohn's *Italian Symphony*, makes a clear digital first choice in the lower price ranges. The 1983 sound is not quite as cleanly focused as the Mendelssohn, but it has fine body, a natural warmth and plenty of presence.

Boehm's Dresden performance is more volatile than the glowing one included in his cycle of the Schubert symphonies, with a notable relaxation for the second subject in the first movement and extreme slowing before the end. The slow movement is fastish, with dotted rhythms crisply pointed and a marked slowing for the cello theme after the great dissonant climax. The Scherzo is sunny and lilting, the finale fierce and fast. It may not be quite as immaculate as the studio-recorded version, but it is an equally superb document of Boehm's mastery as a Schubertian, and the recording, though a little edgy on brass, has fine range.

Taken from his collected edition of Schubert symphonies, Sir Neville Marriner's account of the *Great C major* makes up for any lack of weight with the fresh resilience of the playing, consistently well sprung. Though all repeats are observed, bringing the timing of the *Symphony* to over an hour, an attractive fill-up is provided in the little two-movement fragment, D.615, orchestrated by Brian Newbould. Written just after the *Sixth Symphony*, it consists of a slow introduction and first-movement exposition, plus a fragment of a sonata-rondo finale, which similarly breaks off. First-rate recording.

Josef Krips never made a finer record than his 1956 account of Schubert's *Great C major*. The performance has a direct, unforced spontaneity which shows Krips's natural feeling for Schubertian lyricism at its most engaging. The playing is polished yet flexible, strong without ever sounding aggressive. In the final two movements Krips finds an airy exhilaration which makes one wonder how other conductors can ever keep the music earthbound as they do. The pointing of the Trio in the scherzo is delectable, and the feathery lightness of the triplets in the finale makes one positively welcome every one of its many repetitions. As a whole, this reading represents the Viennese tradition at its finest. The recording, outstanding in its day, retains the glowing bloom over the orchestra; but the remastering has, alas, brought a degree of stridency to fortissimos.

Bruno Walter's 1959 CBS recording has been impressively enhanced on CD; the warm ambience of the sound – yet with no lack of rasp on the trombones – seems ideal for his very relaxed reading. The performance has less grip than Furtwängler's, but in the gentler passages there are many indications of Walter's mastery, not least in the lovely playing at the introduction of the second subject of the *Andante*.

Roger Norrington's version is by far the most provocative of the period-performance versions of the *Great C major*, presenting the same sort of challenge in very fast speeds that one finds in his Beethoven, but this time without the backing-up of metronome markings, when Schubert was never able to prepare or hear a performance. Here again, the surprise is quickly modified, and one simply enjoys with new ears. The first movement brings splendid snap and swagger, exhilaratingly presented with Mendelssohnian lightness. But it will take most listeners some time to adjust to the total absence of the usual slowings in the final coda, which here sounds perfunctory. Yet in his crisp, brisk reading of the slow movement Norrington does allow himself a relaxation in the cello melody after the big climax, rightly so. Only in the finale is the speed relatively conventional, with triplets clarified. The Mackerras version with the Orchestra of the Age of Enlightenment on Virgin remains a safer choice of period performance, but those who have enjoyed Norrington in Beethoven may well prefer this, with its challenge made sharper by the recording. All repeats are observed, even those in the da capo return of the Scherzo.

CHAMBER AND INSTRUMENTAL MUSIC

Arpeggione sonata, D.821 (arr. for cello).

*** Ph. Dig. 412 230-2 [id.]. Maisky, Argerich – SCHUMANN: *Fantasiestücke* etc. ***

(M) *** BMG/RCA GD 86531 [RCA 6531-2-RG]. Lynn Harrell, James Levine – DVOŘÁK: *Cello concerto*. ***

(*) Decca 417 833-2 [id.]. Rostropovich, Britten – DEBUSSY: *Sonata;* SCHUMANN: *5 Stücke*. *

(M) (**(*)) EMI mono CDH7 64250-2 [id.]. Emanuel Feuermann, Gerald Moore – BEETHOVEN: *Cello sonata in A* etc. (**)

The *Arpeggione* enjoyed too brief a life for it to have an extensive literature, and Schubert's *Sonata* is about the only work written for it that survives in the repertoire. Mischa Maisky and Martha Argerich make much more of it than any of their rivals. Their approach may be relaxed, but they bring much pleasure through their variety of colour and sensitivity. The Philips recording is in the very best traditions of the house.

Lynn Harrell's account of the *Arpeggione* with James Levine makes an excellent medium-price choice. He is refreshingly unmannered and yet full of personality. Vital, sensitive playing excellently recorded, though the digitally remastered sound is rather light in bass.

Rostropovich gives a curiously self-indulgent interpretation of Schubert's slight but amiable *Arpeggione sonata.* However, the record is particularly valuable for the sake of the couplings.

Feuermann's record of the *Arpeggione sonata* with Gerald Moore does him greater justice than his virtuoso, rather driven account of the Beethoven *A major Cello sonata* with which it is coupled. There is a much greater spontaneity and warmth here.

Arpeggione sonata, D.821 (arr. in G min. for clarinet & piano).
*** Chan. Dig. CHAN 8506; *ABTD 1216* [id.]. Gervase de Peyer, Gwenneth Pryor – SCHUMANN: *Fantasiestücke; 3 Romances;* WEBER: *Silvana variations.* ***

So persuasive is the performance of Gervase de Peyer and Gwenneth Pryor that the listener is all but persuaded that the work was actually written for this combination. With rich timbre and affectionate phrasing, de Peyer brings out all its Schubertian charm. He is beautifully recorded.

Arpeggione sonata in A min. (arr. for flute); *Introduction and variations on Trock'ne Blumen* from *Die schöne Müllerin; Schwanengesang: Ständchen, D.957/4.*
**(*) BMG/RCA Dig. RD 70421. James Galway, Phillip Moll.

The *Arpeggione sonata* also transcribes surprisingly well for the flute and is played with skill and some charm by this partnership. The *Introduction and variations on Trock'ne Blumen* are as neatly played. Not distinctive, but a pleasing and well-recorded recital.

Octet in F, D.803.
❀ *** EMI Dig. CDC7 54118-2. Hausmusik.
*** Chan. Dig. CHAN 8585; *ABTD 1276* [id.]. ASMF Chamber Ens.
*** O-L Dig. 425 519-2 [id.]. AAM Chamber Ens.
*** ASV Dig. CDDCA 694; *ZCDCA 694* [id.]. Gaudier Ensemble.
*** Teldec/Warner Dig. 2292 44195-2 [id.]. Berlin Soloists.

Hausmusik's performance of Schubert's *Octet* on period instruments is so winning that it can be recommended warmly even to those who do not normally follow the authenticity cult. This talented ensemble even outshines its achievement in the earlier EMI recording of Mendelssohn's *Octet.* This time the group includes such imaginative wind-players as the clarinettist, Antony Pay – playing the opening solo of the *Adagio* slow movement with heavenly phrasing – and the horn-player, Anthony Halstead. Speeds are rarely extreme, allowing full, open expressiveness, as in that *Adagio*; and allegros are generally easy enough to allow a delectable rhythmic spring. The pointing is the more infectious when period string-playing allows textures to be so transparent. There are few Schubert records that so consistently convey the joys of spring.

The new Chandos version brings a performance just as delightful as the earlier one by the ASMF, less classical in style, a degree freer in expression, with Viennese overtones brought out in Schubert's sunny invention. In the *Adagio*, Andrew Marriner's clarinet solo is most delicately floated, and the dance rhythms of other movements are delightfully pointed, leading to a strong and urgent account of the finale. It has the benefit of excellent modern digital sound, cleaner on detail than before.

The Academy's Chamber Ensemble using period instruments brings out the open joyfulness of Schubert's inspiration, with excellent matching and vivid recording. The reading is not at all stiff or pedantic, but personal and relaxed, with the clarinettist, Antony Pay, the obvious leader, playing his solos with yearning beauty, notably in the second-movement *Andante*, which has heavenly gentleness and repose. Lightness is the keynote, with speeds never eccentrically fast.

The Gaudier Ensemble come from the front desks of the Chamber Orchestra of Europe and the ECO, and they take their name from the brilliant French sculptor, Henri Gaudier-Brzeska, killed at the age of 25 in the First World War. They give an entirely winning account of the *Octet*, essentially spontaneous yet very relaxed and catching all the ingenuous Schubertian charm. Richard Hosford, the clarinettist, plays very gently indeed in his lovely solo which opens the *Adagio*, yet he contributes some marvellously exuberant roulades to the finale, which opens with an operatic sense of drama and then chortles along infectiously, capping the easy style of the whole performance. Excellent sound, vivid yet well balanced within a pleasing acoustic which gives a feeling of intimacy. An ideal record for a warm summer evening.

The Berlin Soloists give a strong and stylish performance which, on a bigger scale than most, designedly brings out the symphonic power of a piece lasting over an hour. Every single repeat is observed, and with such distinguished playing that length is readily sustained. This is very well characterized, not just in the big, symphonic movements but in the charming *Andante variations* too. Though the sound is not always ideally sweet on string-tone, the recording is full and clear.

Piano quintet in A (Trout), D.667.
*** Decca Dig. 411 975-2 [id.]. András Schiff, Hagen Qt.
*** Ph. 400 078-2 [id.]. Brendel, Cleveland Qt.
(B) **(*) Decca 433 647-2; *433 647-4* [id.]. Clifford Curzon, Vienna Octet (members) – MOZART: *Clarinet quintet*. **
(B) ** DG Compact Classics 413 845-2 (2); *413 845-4* [id.]. Demus, Schubert Qt – BEETHOVEN: *Ghost trio* ***; MOZART: *Hunt quartet* *** (CD only: HAYDN: *Lark quartet* **(*)).
(M) ** Ph. 434 146-2; *434 146-4* [id.]. Beaux Arts Trio (augmented) – BEETHOVEN: *Piano trio No. 5*. ***

(i) *Piano quintet (Trout); String quartet No. 12 (Quartettsatz).*
**(*) DG 413 453-2 [id.]. (i) Gilels; Amadeus Qt (augmented).

(i) *Piano quintet in A (Trout);* (ii) *String quartet No. 14 (Death and the Maiden).*
(M) **(*) Decca 417 459-2; *417 459-4* [id.]. (i) Curzon, Vienna Octet (members); (ii) VPO Qt.
(M) **(*) Sony SBK 46343 [id.]; *40-46343*. (i) Horszowski, Budapest Qt (members), Julius Levine; (ii) Juilliard Qt.

(i) *Piano quintet in A (Trout);* (ii) *String trios, D.471 & D.581.*
(M) *** Ph. 422 838-2; *422 838-4*. (i) Haebler, Grumiaux, Janzer, Czako, Cazauran; (ii) Grumiaux String Trio.

(i) *Piano quintet in A (Trout);* (ii) *Die Forelle;* (iii) *Der Hirt auf dem Felsen.*
**(*) ASV Dig. CDDCA 684; *ZCDCA 684* [id.]. (i) Yitkin Seow, Prometheus Ens.; (ii; iii) Ann Mackay; (iii) Christopher Craker.

(i) *Piano quintet in A (Trout);* (ii) *Der Hirt auf dem Felsen.*
(B) **(*) Pickwick PCD 868; *CIMPC 868* [id.]. (i) Nash Ens.; (ii) Lott, Collins, Brown.

András Schiff and the Hagen Quartet give a delectably fresh and youthful reading of the *Trout quintet*, full of the joys of spring, but one which is also remarkable for hushed concentration, as in the exceptionally dark and intense account of the opening of the first movement. Schiff, unlike many virtuosi, remains one of a team, emphatically not a soloist in front of accompanists; the recording balance confirms that, with the piano rather behind the strings but firmly placed. The Scherzo brings a light, quick and bouncing performance, and there is extra lightness too in the other middle movements. Unlike current rivals, this version observes the exposition repeat in the finale, and with such a joyful, brightly pointed performance one welcomes that.

The Brendel/Cleveland performance may lack something in traditional Viennese charm, but it has a compensating vigour and impetus, and the work's many changes of mood are encompassed with freshness and subtlety, with Brendel at his most persuasive. The recording is well balanced and truthful. The sound is smooth and refined, but lacks something in upper range and sharpness of detail.

Clifford Curzon's 1958 recording of the *Trout* sounds its age in the thin violin timbre, although the piano tone has plenty of colour and it has a warm ambience. It remains a classic performance, with a distinguished account of the piano part and splendidly stylish support from the Vienna players. Schubert's warm lyricism is caught with remarkable freshness. Some might find the brilliant Scherzo a little too fierce to match the rest of the performance, but such vigorous playing introduces an element of contrast at the centre of the interpretation and makes possible a relaxed account of the last movement. The Vienna Philharmonic performance treats *Death and the Maiden* with comparable affection; the playing is peerless, Boskovsky, the leader, showing all his skill and musicianship in the variations. Both recordings have a pleasingly warm ambience and, in the *Trout*, the piano timbre is appealingly full in colour, but here the upper range is noticeably thin; in the string quartet the upper range is fuller. Readers will note that Curzon's version of the *Trout* is also available at bargain price, coupled with a rather bland account of Mozart's *Clarinet quintet*.

There is some admirably unassertive and deeply musical playing from Miss Haebler and from the incomparable Grumiaux; it is the freshness and pleasure in music-making that render this account memorable. These artists do not try to make 'interpretative points' but are content to let the music speak for itself. The balance is not altogether perfect, but the quality of the recorded sound is good. As an extra enticement, Philips have added a pair of *String trios*, given characteristically refined performances by Grumiaux and his companions, delightful music superbly played.

Horszowski's contribution to the *Trout* is undoubtedly distinguished and his clean, clear playing dominates the performance which, although full of imaginative detail, is a little on the cool side – though refreshingly so, for all that. The Juilliard Quartet are far from cool in the *Death and the Maiden quartet*. They begin the famous slow movement with a rapt pianissimo, and the variations are played with great feeling and the widest range of expression and dynamic. The finale is infectiously alert and vigorous, the unanimity of ensemble consistently impressive. A fine performance overall, among the best in the catalogue. In both works the sound is a little dry, but not confined.

The Prometheus Ensemble turn in a very enjoyable and fresh account of the *Trout* on ASV which, though not a first choice, will give much pleasure to those who chance upon it. There are two bonuses in the shape of the equivalent song, charmingly done by Ann Mackay, and *The Shepherd on the rock*. The playing in the *Quintet* is alert and well shaped, and well recorded, too. There is a rather long hiatus just before the A flat section in the second movement (at about 3 minutes 30 seconds in), which is puzzling. Yitkin Seow plays with grace and finesse.

In the DG *Trout* there is a masterly contribution from Gilels, and the Amadeus play with considerable freshness. The approach is very positive, not as sunny and springlike as in some versions, but rewarding in its seriousness of purpose, and the balance is convincing.

The earlier account by the Nash Ensemble on CRD is restored to circulation now (with the *Notturno* on CRD 3352) but this is still at full price. The newer Pickwick issue also brings a fill-up in the shape of *The Shepherd on the rock*. They are rather forwardly recorded here and their account is just a little wanting in the spontaneity that distinguishes the finest of the current versions. Ian Brown is, as always, a sensitive artist.

A very agreeable if not distinctive performance on Compact Classics with Demus dominating, partly because the piano recording and balance are bold and forward, and the string timbre is thinner. Nevertheless the transfer brings very acceptable sound (in both formats) and there is – as befits the eponymous quartet – a real feeling for Schubertian lyricism here and the performance has spontaneity. The first movement is especially arresting and the *Theme and variations* are well shaped.

The Beaux Arts *Trout* is a delightfully fresh performance. Every phrase is splendidly alive, there is no want of vitality or sensitivity, and the recording is basically well balanced. The snag is the digital remastering, which gives undue prominence to Isidore Cohen's violin, lighting it up brightly and thinning down the timbre.

(i; ii) *Piano quintet in A (Trout);* (i; iii) *Piano trios Nos. 1 in B flat, D.898; 2 in E flat, D.929; Notturno in E flat, D.897; Sonata in B flat, D.28* (both arr. for piano trio).
(B) **(*) EMI CZS7 62742-2 (2) [id.]. (i) Hephzibah Menuhin; (ii) Amadeus Qt & J. Edward Merret; (iii) Sir Yehudi Menuhin & Maurice Gendron.

The Hephzibah Menuhin/Amadeus *Trout* was one of the first in stereo, dating from 1958. Like the other performances here, it has a pleasingly domestic sense of scale and considerable charm. Hephzibah seeks simplicity rather than subtlety of colour, but the effect is refreshing, even though the bright recording creates a balance in favour of the upper register of the piano and the upper strings. The three members of the Amadeus Quartet (Norbert Brainin, Peter Schidlof and Martin Lovett) play with nicely judged feeling, and the double-bass contribution of J. Edward Merrett is properly telling. Intimacy is also the keynote of the works for piano trio, and the slighter *Sonata* and engaging *Notturno* come off quite as effectively as the two major works. In the *Trios* Menuhin relaxes with his pianist sister and cellist friend to produce delightfully spontaneous-sounding performances. These may lack some of the power and purposefulness of rival versions, but they have a special place for those who think of the music as gentle and friendly rather than as formidably public. Not that the Menuhin performances lack energy or Schubertian joy. The atmosphere of the *Second Trio* is caught perceptively and the unassertive music-making captures the music's spirit very appealingly. These recordings were made a decade later than the *Quintet* and are cleanly remastered; the sound lacks something in fullness but the focus is natural and the balance realistic. Menuhin's violin is truthfully caught. This inexpensive box is well worth exploring.

Piano trio No. 1 in B flat, D.898.
** Chan. Dig. CHAN 8308; *ABTD 1064* [id.]. Borodin Trio.

Piano trio No. 1 in B flat; Notturno in E flat, D.897.
(M) **(*) Ph. 422 836-2; *422 836-4*. Beaux Arts Trio.

Piano trio No. 1 in B flat; Notturno in E flat; Sonata movement in B flat, D.28.
*** EMI Dig. CDC7 49165-2. Jean-Philippe Collard, Augustin Dumay, Frédéric Lodéon.

Piano trio No. 1 in B flat; Sonata movement in B flat.
(BB) **(*) Naxos Dig. 8.550131; *4550131* [id.]. Stuttgart Piano Trio.

Jean-Philippe Collard, Augustin Dumay and Frédéric Lodéon give a very good account of the sublime *B flat Trio*; not only is each a splendid performer in his own right, a fully integrated ensemble is created that sounds as if the players enjoy chamber music at home every evening, and the recording, made in a decent concert-hall acoustic, is eminently realistic.

The Beaux Arts performance has impeccable ensemble, with the pianist, Menahem Pressler, always sharply imaginative and the string playing sensitive in both line and phrase. The performance is perhaps on the lightweight side, although the slow movement has a disarming simplicity. The *Notturno*, eloquently played, makes an attractive bonus. The recording, from the late 1960s, sounds fresh, although its age shows a little in the timbre of the violin.

The Stuttgart Piano Trio are a well-respected ensemble who have now been in existence almost a quarter of a century. Their Schubert may be at budget price but it is not a bargain-basement performance; the playing is musicianly and intelligent. First-movement exposition repeats are observed and there are many sensitive touches. The recording was made in the Tonstudio Van Geest in Heildelberg – not a venue which inspires confidence, given the quality of some of the Naxos piano recordings made there. But the engineer on this occasion has succeeded in getting rather more acceptable results. Although the sound is still less than ideal, there is slightly more air round the three instruments.

The Borodin Trio gives a warm and characterful interpretation, with natural expressiveness only occasionally overloaded with rubato. The impression is very much of a live performance, though in fact this is a studio recording marked by full and open sound, although the microphone balance is a little close.

Piano trio No. 2 in E flat, D.929.
**(*) Chan. Dig. CHAN 8324 [id.]. Borodin Trio.

Piano trio No. 2 in E flat; Sonata in B flat (for piano trio), *D.28.*
(M) **(*) Ph. 426 096-2; *426 096-4* [id.]. Beaux Arts Trio.

The Beaux Arts Trio's ensemble is superbly polished here, and the pianist's contribution is consistently imaginative, with the cellist, Bernard Greenhouse, bringing simple dedication to such key passages as the great slow-movement melody of the *E flat Trio*. The extra item gives this disc an added appeal. The 1967 recording has fine freshness and immediacy, but the CD remastering brings a degree of dryness to the upper range.

The Borodin Trio gives a strong and understanding performance of the *B flat Trio*, generally preferring spacious tempi. The outer movements are made the more resilient, and only in the Scherzo does the reading lack impetus. The speed for the slow movement is aptly chosen to allow a broad, steady pulse. The pianist is not always at her most subtle, but there is a sense of enjoyment here to which one responds. The compact disc is lifelike and present.

String quartets Nos. 1–15.
(M) ** DG 419 879-2 (6) [id.]. Melos Qt of Stuttgart.

The early quartets have an altogether disarming grace and innocence, and some of their ideas are most touching. The Melos are an impressive body whose accounts of this repertoire are unmannered and on the whole sympathetic. They are let down by recording quality that is less than distinguished, but the remastering has brought added presence.

String quartets Nos. 8 in B flat, D.112; 13 in A min., D.804.
*** ASV Dig. CDDCA 593; *ZCDCA 593* [id.]. Lindsay Qt.

In the glorious *A minor* the Lindsays lead the field. It would be difficult to fault their judgement in both these works so far as tempi and expression are concerned. Every phrase seems to arise naturally from what has gone before, and dynamics are always the result of musical thinking. The recording team has done them much credit.

String quartets Nos. 9 in G min., D.173; 13 in A min., D.804.
**(*) Teldec/Warner 2292 43205-2 [id.]. Alban Berg Qt.

The Alban Berg recorded this account of the *A minor* in 1975 and – despite the more generous coupling (*Death and the Maiden*) offered in their more recent, EMI version – this is to be preferred. It matches the latter in tonal finesse and perfection of ensemble and surpasses it in terms of spontaneity. The *G minor Quartet* is fine; on balance, both are better played here than by the Melos Quartet of Stuttgart, whose complete set is now available on CD.

String quartets Nos. 11 in E, D.353; 15 in G, D.887.
(M) *** Decca 433 693-2 [id.]. Allegri Qt.

The Allegri are recorded in a somewhat reverberant acoustic (the Church of St George the Martyr, London) but their account of the *G major Quartet* is most rewarding. They observe the first movement exposition repeat and are not given to extremes of tempo. The playing is both alive and sensitive. The E major, composed a decade earlier, is if anything even finer, fresh and spontaneous and with excellent judgement in the matter of tempi. The analogue recordings date from the late 1970s and have been most realisically transferred to CD.

String quartets Nos. 12 in C min. (Quartettsatz), D.703; 14 in D min. (Death and the Maiden), D.810.
*** ASV Dig. CDDCA 560; *ZCDCA 560* [id.]. Lindsay Qt.
(BB) **(*) Naxos Dig. 8.550221; *4550221* [id.]. Mandelring Qt.

String quartet No. 14 in D min. (Death and the Maiden), D.810.
*** DG Dig. 431 814-2 [id.]. Hagen Qt – BEETHOVEN: *Quartet No. 16.* **(*)
(M) *** Ph. 420 876-2. Italian Qt – DVOŘÁK: *Quartet No. 12* *** (with BORODIN: *Nocturne* *).

The Lindsays' intense, volatile account of the first movement of the *Death and the Maiden quartet*, urgently paced, played with considerable metrical freedom and the widest range of dynamic, is balanced by an equally imaginative and individual set of variations. The finale has a winning bustle and energy; and the *Quartettsatz*, which acts as the usual filler, is unusually poetic and spontaneous in feeling. The recording is excellent.

The Hagen Quartet enhance their reputation with a vital, well-shaped and sensitive account of *Death and the Maiden*, they are generous in matters of repeats, and produce consistent beauty of sound. They are fully alive to the darker side to the work yet rarely exaggerate. Even if they are perhaps a bit self-aware and rather overdo the pianissimo markings, reducing them to the faintest whisper in the slow movement, this remains one of the best accounts of the piece to appear recently and is highly competitive. It is very well recorded too, and has a very generous coupling – even if the Beethoven performance is less searching than the Schubert.

The Italian Quartet offer a fine coupling with Dvořák, and the Borodin *Nocturne* is thrown in for good measure. They bring great concentration and poetic feeling to this wonderful score, and they are free of the excessive point-making to be found in some rival versions. The sound of the reissue is vivid and clear.

The Mandelring Quartet, from Germany, are a young family group (two brothers and one sister, plus a violist). They are very good indeed. The performances are sensitively and sensibly played and very decently recorded and, though the playing is not as polished as, say, the Quartetto Italiano's *Death and the Maiden*, anyone tempted by this Naxos disc will not be disappointed for so modest an outlay.

String quartets Nos. 13 in A min., D.804; 14 in D min. (Death and the Maiden), D.810.
(M) *** Ph. 426 383-2; *426 383-4* [id.]. Italian Qt.
**(*) EMI Dig. CDC7 47333-2 [id.]. Alban Berg Qt.

The Italians omit the exposition repeat in the first movement of the *A minor Quartet*; the slow movement is spacious – some may feel it is a bit too slow – and has an impressive command of feeling. Their account of *Death and the Maiden* is also very fine. Here the slow movement is particularly telling, showing a notable grip in the closing pages. Technically the playing throughout is quite remarkable. The recordings are well balanced and truthful, sounding a little dryer now in their CD remastering.

The EMI issue by the Alban Berg Quartet is, marvellously played and cleanly recorded, and the only loss is the exposition repeat in the first movement of *Death and the Maiden*. The *A minor Quartet* is beautifully played, though the slow movement (with the theme of the *Rosamunde entr'acte*) is very fast indeed. The playing is breathtaking in terms of tonal blend, ensemble and intonation, but one is not always totally involved, except perhaps in the minuet and trio of the *A minor*. The clear, clean recording is very brightly lit in its CD format, with a slightly aggressive feeling on fortissimos.

String quartets Nos. 13 in A min.; 14 in D min. (Death and the Maiden); 15 in G, D.887.
*** Nimbus NI 5048/9 [id.]. Chilingirian Qt.

In their two-disc set of the last three *Quartets*, the Chilingirians give strongly committed, characterful and spontaneous-sounding readings, warmly recorded and full of presence. On the upper-mid-priced Nimbus label, they make a most attractive recommendation.

String quartet No. 14 in D min. (Death and the Maiden), arr. Mahler.
*** BMG/RCA Dig. RD 60988 [60988-2]. Moscow Soloists, Bashmet – BEETHOVEN: *String quartet No. 11.* ***

If you want the Mahler transcription for full strings this is a more brilliant and sensitive account than the earlier EMI rival. Dynamic and other expressive markings are a bit exaggerated but there is much beauty of tone and excellent recording. But even as well played and recorded as it is here, it is difficult to imagine music lovers returning to this very often in preference to the original.

String quartets Nos. 14 in D min. (Death and the Maiden); 15 in G.
(M) (***) EMI (mono) CDH7 69795-2 [id.]. Busch Qt.

The Busch Quartet's account is more than fifty years old, but it brings us closer to the heart of this music than any other. The slow movement of the *Death and the Maiden quartet* is a revelation, and the same must be said of the *G major*, which has enormous depth and humanity and a marvellous eloquence. For its age, the sound is still amazing, and the musical wisdom is timeless.

String quintet in C, D.956.
*** ASV Dig. CDDCA 537; *ZCDCA 537* [id.]. Lindsay Qt with Douglas Cummings.
❀ (M) *** Saga SCD 9011. Aeolian Qt with Bruno Schreker.
**(*) Sony MK 39134 [id.]. Cleveland Qt with Yo-Yo Ma.
**(*) EMI Dig. CDC7 47018-2 [id.]. Alban Berg Qt with Heinrich Schiff.

String quintet in C, D.956; String trio in B flat, D.581.
(BB) *** Naxos Dig. 8.550388 [id.]. Villa Musica Ens.

The Lindsay version gives the impression that one is eavesdropping on music-making in the intimacy of a private concert. They observe the first-movement exposition repeat and the effortlessness of their approach does not preclude intellectual strength. The Lindsays do the amazing first movement justice, as indeed they do the ethereal *Adagio*. Here they effectively convey the sense of it appearing motionless, suspended, as it were, between reality and dream, yet at the same time never allowing it to become static. Their reading must rank at the top of the list; it is very well recorded.

The augmented Aeolian Quartet give a strong, virile performance of what is arguably Schubert's greatest chamber work. Their style is direct with no mannerisms whatsoever. It might seem bald, were it not for the depth of concentration that the players convey in every bar. The finale, for example, is fresh and rustic-sounding, not because of its pointing of the rhythm but because of the very simplicity of utterance. In the slow movement the Aeolians daringly adopt the slowest possible *Adagio*, and the result might have seemed static but for the inner tension which holds one breathless through hushed pianissimos of the most intense beauty. Never before on record, not even in Casals's old Prades (mono) version had the profundity of this music been so compellingly conveyed. The analogue recording, though not of the clearest in terms of individual definition of instruments, has been transferred to CD with remarkable presence and the engineers have resisted the temptation to sharpen the imagery so that the body of tone has not been lost. This is a clear first bargain choice, and there are few premium-priced issues which approach, let alone match, its intensity.

The Ensemble Villa Musica is a group, based on Mainz, which on this showing is of the highest quality. Not only do these performances offer polish and refinement, with immaculate matching and intonation, but also a satisfying thrust of attack. The great *C major Quintet*, completed in the last months of Schubert's life, is among the most taxing of chamber works, and the Villa Musica players tackle it with a freshness and concentration that are consistently compelling, even if the finale is neat and clean rather than urgently dramatic. The little *String trio*, written when the composer was twenty, makes an attractive and generous fill-up, another assured and stylish performance. With clear, well-balanced recording this super-budget issue makes an outstanding bargain and offers an excellent alternative to the Saga version for those wanting digital sound.

The Cleveland Quartet and Yo-Yo Ma have won golden opinions for their account of the *Quintet* on CBS. They are scrupulous in observing dynamic markings (the second subject is both restrained and *pianissimo*) and they also score by making all repeats. Their performance has feeling and eloquence, as well as a commanding intellectual grip. Moreover they are admirably recorded and thus present a strong challenge.

Few ensembles offer timbre as full-bodied or as richly burnished as that produced by the Alban Berg and Heinrich Schiff and, given the sheer polish and gorgeous sound that distinguish their playing, theirs must rank high among current recommendations. The performance is strongly projected and they have the advantage of excellent recording. However, unlike the Lindsays, they do not observe the first-movement exposition repeat.

Duo in A, D.574; Violin sonatina, D.385; Fantaisie in C, D.934.
(M) **(*) Decca 425 539-2; *425 539-4*. Szymon Goldberg, Radu Lupu.

There is an unaffected, Schubertian feeling in the Goldberg/Lupu performances that is most appealing. Indeed Goldberg is vulnerable in that he almost undercharacterizes the line, and at times one could do with a greater variety of dynamic nuance and tonal colour. Yet the presence of Radu Lupu ensures that these performances give much pleasure: his playing has a vitality and inner life that are consistently rewarding. The remastered recording also sounds full and natural, and is very realistically balanced.

PIANO MUSIC

Allegretto in C min., D.915; Moments musicaux Nos. 1–6, D.780; 2 Scherzi, D.953; 12 Valse nobles, D.969.
(M) **(*) DG 435 072-2; *435 072-4*. Daniel Barenboim.

Some of the finest playing here comes in the two *Scherzi*. In the first, Barenboim's pointing is a delight, and he is equally persuasive in the Trio of the second. The *Allegretto in C minor* is given an effective, improvisatory quality, but the twelve *Valses nobles* are played too forcefully for their full charm to be revealed. In the *Moments musicaux* there is much to admire: Barenboim's mood is often thoughtful and intimate; at other times we are made a shade too aware of the interpreter's art and there is an element of calculation that robs the impact of freshness. There are good things, of course, but this does not challenge Lupu's set (see below). The piano-tone on DG has impressive presence and weight and seems firmer than on LP, though it lacks something in ultimate richness.

Fantasia in C (Wanderer), D.760.
*** Sony Dig. MK 42124 [id.]. Murray Perahia – SCHUMANN: *Fantasia in C*. ***
*** EMI CDC7 47967-2. Sviatoslav Richter – DVOŘÁK: *Piano concerto*. ***
(M) *** Ph. 420 644-2. Alfred Brendel – *Sonata No. 21*. ***
*** DG 419 672-2 [id.]. Maurizio Pollini – *Sonata No. 16*. ***

Murray Perahia's account of the *Wanderer* stands alongside the finest. In his hands it sounds as fresh as the day it was conceived, and its melodic lines speak with an ardour and subtlety that breathe new life into the score. The recording is more than acceptable, even if it does not wholly convey Perahia's wide range of sonority and dynamics.

Richter's 1963 performance is masterly in every way. The piano timbre is real and the remastering gives the great pianist a compelling presence; the coupling is hardly less outstanding.

Brendel's playing is of a high order, and he is truthfully recorded and coupled with what is perhaps Schubert's greatest *Sonata*, so this is excellent value at mid-price.

Pollini's account is outstanding and, though he is not ideally recorded and the piano timbre is shallow, the playing still shows remarkable insights. Moreover the coupling is equally fine.

Fantasia in C (Wanderer), D.760; Impromptus, D.899/3 & 4; Piano sonata No. 21 in B flat, D.960.
❀ *** BMG/RCA RD 86257 [RCA 6257-2-RC]. Artur Rubinstein.

Rubinstein plays the *Wanderer fantasia* with sure magnificence. The extended structure needs a master to hold it together and, particularly in the variations section, Rubinstein is electrifying. The two *Impromptus* are played with the most subtle shading of colour and delectable control of rubato, and the superb account of the *Sonata* shows Rubinstein as a magically persuasive Schubertian. The first movement is very relaxed yet the effect is wonderfully luminous, and a similar inspired and ruminative spontaneity infuses the essentially gentle *Andante*. Then the articulation in the final two movements is a joy, light and crisp in the Scherzo, bolder but never heavy in the finale. The 1965 sound is remarkably real, with fine presence and almost no shallowness.

Fantasia in D min., D.940.
*** Sony Dig. MK 39511 [id.]. Murray Perahia, Radu Lupu – MOZART: *Double piano sonata.* ***

Recorded live at The Maltings, the performance of Lupu and Perahia is full of haunting poetry, with each of these highly individual artists challenging the other in imagination. Where in the Mozart coupling Perahia plays primo, here it is the more recessive Lupu adding to the mellowness of this most inspired of all piano duet works. Warmly atmospheric recording.

Impromptus Nos. 1–4, D.899; 5–8, D.935.
*** Sony Dig. MK 37291 [id.]. Murray Perahia.
*** Ph. 411 040-2 [id.]. Alfred Brendel.
*** Decca Dig. 411 711-2 [id.]. Radu Lupu.
*** Ph. Dig. 422 237-2 [id.]. Alfred Brendel.

Perahia's account of the *Impromptus* is very special indeed and falls barely short of greatness. Directness of utterance and purity of spirit are of the essence here. As one critic has put it, Perahia's vision brings the impression of a tree opening out, whereas Brendel's suggests the moment of full bloom. The CBS recording is very good, truthful in timbre, with an increase in firmness on CD and added presence.

Brendel's analogue set of *Impromptus* is also magical. It is difficult to imagine finer Schubert playing than this; to find more eloquence, more profound musical insights, one has to go back to Edwin Fischer – and even here comparison is not always to Brendel's disadvantage. The piano image is warm and full but slightly diffuse.

Lupu's account of the *Impromptus* is of the same calibre as the Perahia and Brendel analogue versions, and he is most beautifully recorded on CD. Indeed, in terms of natural sound this is the most believable image of the three. Lupu brings his own special insights to these pieces. Perahia displays a fresher innocence; Brendel is more direct and wonderfully warm; but Lupu is compelling in his own way, and these performances yield much that is memorable.

Alfred Brendel's digital set of the *Impromptus* can also be confidently recommended to his admirers. It offers many insights and has the benefit of immaculate recorded sound. In some respects his earlier, analogue recordings of these pieces for Vox (on LP) and Philips (as above) were more affecting; not that this is lacking in warmth, but there is an element of didacticism. Recommended – but not in preference to Perahia or Lupu.

Impromptus Nos. 1–4, D.889; Piano sonata No. 21 in B flat, D.960.
*** Calliope Dig. CAL 9689 [id.]. Inger Södergren.

Inger Södergren's account of the first four *Impromptus* belongs in exalted company, and the *B flat Sonata* is hardly less fine. She is little known even in her native Sweden but enjoys a considerable following in France, where she is spoken of alongside the great pianists of the day – and, on the strength of this record, rightly so. Her playing is marked throughout by sensitivity and a selfless and unostentatious dedication to Schubert. The *Sonata* was recorded in 1983 and reproduces at a lower level than the *Impromptus*. The recording is acceptable rather than outstanding.

4 Impromptus, D.899; Impromptu in B flat, D.935/3; Moments musicaux, D.780/1, 2 & 6.
(B) *** LaserLight Dig. 15609 [id.]. Jenö Jandó.

At last Jenö Jandó is heard, recorded in an acoustic that does justice to his talent. The sound, at least in the opening *B flat major Impromptu* of D.935, is fresh and truthful, the ambience is warm, and the playing is very good. The balance is not as good in the three *Moments musicaux* or in the D.899 *Impromptus*: it is closer and marginally drier. There is probably a very good reason why Jandó didn't record all four of D.935 or all six of the *Moments musicaux*, but the incompleteness diminishes the attractiveness of a good recital.

Moments musicaux Nos. 1–6, D.780.
** DG 415 118-2 [id.]. Daniel Barenboim – LISZT: *Liebesträume;* MENDELSSOHN: *Songs without words.* ***

Barenboim's mood is often thoughtful and intimate; at other times we are made a shade too aware of the interpreter's art, and there is an element of calculation that robs the impact of freshness. The recording is excellent, with fine presence in its CD format.

Moments musicaux, D.780; 2 Scherzi, D.593; Piano sonata No. 14 in A min., D.784.
*** DG Dig. 427 769-2 [id.]. Maria João Pires.

Maria João Pires gives masterly accounts of the *Moments musicaux* and the *A minor Sonata* that are as good as any in the catalogue. Her playing is distinguished throughout by thoughtful and refined musicianship, and she is fully aware of the depth of feeling that inhabits the *Moments musicaux*, without ever indulging in the slightest expressive exaggeration. The digital recording is exceptionally present and clear.

Piano sonatas Nos. 1 in E, D.157; 2 in C, D.279; 3 in E, D.459; 4 in A min., D.537; 5 in A flat, D.557; 6 in E min., D.566; 7 in E flat, D.568; 9 in B flat, D.575; 11 in F min., D.625; 13 in A, D.664; 14 in A min., D.784; 15 in C, D.840 (Relique); 16 in A min., D.845; 17 in D, D.850; 18 in G, D.894; 19 in C min., D.958; 20 in A, D.959; 21 in B flat, D.960.
(M) *** DG 423 496-2 (7) [id.]. Wilhelm Kempff.

Wilhelm Kempff's cycle was recorded over a four-year period (1965–9) and elicited much admiration in our earlier editions. DG has now collected the sonatas into a seven-CD box and those wanting a comprehensive survey of this repertoire need look no further at present. There have been performances of comparable stature: Gilels in the *A minor*, D.784, and *D major*, D.850, Lupu (*G major*, D.894), Perahia (*A major*, D.960) and Richter, but there is no individual overview of the whole cycle that has been musically as consistently satisfying as Kempff's. The recordings are not state of the art (there is an occasional hint of shallowness) but they are very acceptable indeed and there is a wisdom about his playing which puts it in a special category.

Piano sonatas Nos. 1 in E, D.157; 14 in A min., D.784; 20 in A, D.959.
(M) *** Decca 425 033-2; *425 033-4* [id.]. Radu Lupu.

The early *E major Sonata* was written in 1815. Its finale was never composed and only three movements survive. Lupu is sensitive and poetic throughout and he effectively turns the lively Minuet into a brilliant closing movement. He is no less searching in the later *A minor Sonata*. In the *A major* work he strikes the perfect balance between Schubert's classicism and the spontaneity of his musical thought, and at the same time he leaves one with the impression that the achievement is perfectly effortless. The scherzo has great sparkle and delicacy, and the slow movement has an inner repose and depth of feeling that remain memorable long after the record has ended. Yet the strength of the interpretation lies in its sensitivity to detail and appreciation of the structure as a whole. Excellent vintage Decca recording, made in the Kingsway Hall in the late 1970s.

Piano sonata No. 4 in A min., D.537.
** DG Dig. 400 043-2 [id.]. Michelangeli – BRAHMS: *Ballades.* ***

Michelangeli's Schubert is less convincing than the Brahms coupling. He rushes the opening theme and rarely allows the simple ideas of the first movement to speak for themselves. Elsewhere his playing, though aristocratic and marvellously poised, is not free from artifice, and the natural eloquence of Schubert eludes him. Splendid recording.

Piano sonatas Nos. 14–21; German dances; Impromptus; Moments musicaux; Wanderer fantasia.
*** Ph. Dig. 426 128-2 (7) [id.]. Alfred Brendel.

Piano sonatas Nos. 14 in A min., D.784; 17 in D, D.850.
*** Ph. Dig. 422 063-2 [id.] Alfred Brendel.

Piano sonatas Nos 15 in C (Relique), D.840; 18 in G, D.894.
*** Ph. Dig. 422 340-2 [id.]. Alfred Brendel.

Piano sonata No. 16 in A min., D.845; 3 Impromptus, D.946.
*** Ph. Dig. 422 075-2 [id.]. Alfred Brendel.

Piano sonata No. 19 in C min., D.958; Moments musicaux Nos. 1–6, D.780.
*** Ph. Dig. 422 076-2 [id.]. Alfred Brendel.

Piano sonata No. 20 in A, D.959; Allegretto in C min., D.915; 16 German dances, D.783; Hungarian melody in B min., D.817.

**(*) Ph. Dig. 422 229-2 [id.]. Alfred Brendel.

Piano sonata No. 21 in B flat, D.960; Wanderer fantasia, D.760.
*** Ph. Dig. 422 062-2 [id.]. Alfred Brendel.

Brendel's new digital set is perhaps more intense than his last cycle of recordings for Philips, though there was a touching freshness in the earlier set, and he has the benefit of clean, well-focused sound. Generally speaking, these are warm performances, strongly delineated and powerfully characterized, which occupy a commanding place in the catalogue. Their separate availability is also noted, and all of them can be confidently recommended to Brendel's admirers.

Piano sonatas Nos. 14 in A min., D.784; 18 in G, D.894; 12 Waltzes, D.145.
(M) *** Decca 425 017-2; *425 017-4* [id.]. Vladimir Ashkenazy.

This is a recoupling for CD. Ashkenazy's account of the *A minor Sonata* surpasses the pianist's own high standards. There is an astonishing directness about this performance, a virility tempered by tenderness that is very compelling indeed. On the other hand, the *G major Sonata* (which comes first on the disc) is altogether more controversial. The first movement should certainly be leisurely if it is to convey the self-communing as well as the sense of peace that lies at its heart. But Ashkenazy is very slow indeed: he robs it of its normal sense of momentum. If further hearings prove more convincing, this is largely because Ashkenazy's reading is so totally felt and, equally, perceptive. He succeeds in making the piano sound exceptionally expressive. This is a most searching and poetic account, and both sonatas are given highly realistic recording, the *G major* slightly fuller in the bass. The *Waltzes* make an attractive and generous encore.

Piano sonata No. 15 in C (Relique), D.840.
*** Ph. 416 292-2 [id.]. Sviatoslav Richter.

Richter's approach to Schubert's unfinished *Sonata* is both dedicated and strong. He treats the opening movement very spaciously indeed and the following *Andante* is comparably thoughtful; the work ends abruptly where the composer stopped, leaving the rest to the listener's imagination. The recording was made at a live performance and captures the spontaneity of the occasion and the full range of the pianist's dynamic. However, this is not very generous measure.

Piano sonatas Nos. 15 in C (Unfinished), D.840; 19 in C min., D.958; 16 German Dances, D.783.
(M) *** Van. 08.4026.71 [OVC 4026]. Alfred Brendel.

Brendel was at his finest and most spontaneous in the 1960s, after his Vox contract was terminated. There is a freshness in his approach to Schubert here that is not absolutely consistent in his later Schubert recordings for Philips. The *C minor Sonata* is particularly fine, with no sense of agogic distortion of the flow, rather a thoughtful, improvisatory feeling in the slow movement which is consistently illuminating. The two-movement *C major Sonata* also has a memorable *Andante*, and the *German Dances* are an endless delight, lilting in their rhythms and full of imaginative touches. The recording is full and bold and gives every satisfaction, even if it does not bring such a naturally wide range of dynamic as his later, Philips records.

Piano sonata No. 16 in A min., D.845.
*** DG 419 672-2 [id.]. Maurizio Pollini – *Fantasia in C (Wanderer).* ***

Pollini's account of the *A minor Sonata* is searching and profound. He is almost without rival in terms of sheer keyboard control, and his musical insight is of the same order. The piano sound as such could do with slightly more body, but the recording is musically balanced.

Piano sonatas Nos. 16 in A min., D.845; 18 in G, D.894.
❀ *** Decca 417 640-2 [id.]. Radu Lupu.

Radu Lupu's version of the *A minor Sonata* of 1825 is searching and poetic throughout. He brings tenderness and classical discipline to bear on this structure and his playing is musically satisfying in a very Schubertian way. The coupling is hardly less fine, a superb reading, relatively straight in its approach but full of glowing perception on points of detail; moreover, the exposition repeat is observed in the first movement. The analogue recordings date from 1975 and 1979 respectively and are of Decca's finest, with timbre of warm colour yet with a striking sense of presence overall.

Piano sonatas Nos. 17 in D, D.850; 20 in A, D.959; 21 in B flat, D.960; March in E, D.606; Moments musicaux, D.780.
(M) (***) EMI mono CHS 764259-2 (2) Artur Schnabel.

No need in this day and age to extol the merits of Schnabel's Schubert. It was thanks to his championship that the *Piano sonatas* re-entered the repertory for they were rarities in the recital rooms of the 1920s and early 1930s. This EMI compilation offers his pioneering and magisterial accounts of the *D major*, *A major* and *B flat Sonatas*, made between 1937 and 1939 plus the *Moments musicaux*. All Schnabel's Schubert appeared some years ago on the Arabesque label in the United States in very good transfers (straight, with no attempt to take out too much surface noise). Direct comparison of the *D major Sonata* is very much to the advantage of the EMI; the sound is lighter and brighter, and seems to have a couple of octaves more brilliance but there is the same naturalness. Both the *A major* and *B flat Sonatas* sound as well they are ever likely to, for neither was state-of-the-art piano-sound, and there is less surface noise than in the Arabesque versions without any loss of such higher frequencies as there were. The *Moments musicaux* sound remarkably full-bodied. The playing is full of characteristic insights, though it must be admitted that later recordings of the *B flat* from Kempff and Curzon surpassed Schnabel technically. But as always with this artist there is imagination of a remarkable order. These recordings are now fifty years old, but some of the playing Schnabel offers – at the opening of the *B flat* and in the slow movements of all three *Sonatas* – will never be less than special.

Piano sonata No. 19 in C min., D.958; Moments musicaux Nos. 1–6, D.780.
(M) *** Decca Dig. 417 785-2; *417 785-4* [id.]. Radu Lupu.

Lupu's performance has a simple eloquence that is most moving. His *Moments musicaux* are very fine indeed. The Decca recording is very natural and, at mid-price, this is extremely competitive.

Piano sonatas Nos. 19 in C min., D.958; 20 in A, D.959.
*** DG Dig. 427 327-2 [id.]. Maurizio Pollini.

Piano sonata No. 21 in B flat, D.960; Allegretto in C min., D.915; Klavierstücke, D.946.
*** DG Dig. 427 326-2 [id.]. Maurizio Pollini.

In Pollini's hands these emerge as strongly structured and powerful sonatas, yet he is far from unresponsive to the voices from the other world with which these pieces resonate. Perhaps with his perfect pianism he does not always convey a sense of human vulnerability in the way that some of the greatest Schubert interpreters have. The *Sonatas* were recorded at different venues; in the *A major*, for example, the sound is not always completely natural. However, this is playing of some distinction.

Piano sonata No. 20 in A, D.959.
*** Sony Dig. MK 44569 [id.]. Murray Perahia – SCHUMANN: *Piano sonata No. 2.* ***

Perahia's combination of intellectual vigour and poetic insight shows that awareness of proportion and feeling for expressive detail which distinguish the greatest interpreters. As always with this artist, every phrase speaks and each paragraph breathes naturally.

Piano sonata No. 21 in B flat, D.960 (see also under *Fantasia (Wanderer)*).
(M) *** Ph. 420 644-2. Alfred Brendel – *Wanderer fantasia.* ***

Piano sonata No. 21 in B flat; Impromptu in A flat, D.935/2; 6 Moments musicaux, D.780.
❀ *** Decca 417 642-2 [id.]. Clifford Curzon.

Piano sonata No. 21 in B flat; Impromptus, D.899/2–3.
**(*) Denon Dig. C37 7488 [id.]. Dezsö Ránki.

Curzon's tempi are aptly judged, and everything is in fastidious taste. Detail is finely drawn but never emphasized at the expense of the architecture as a whole. It is beautifully recorded, and the piano sounds very truthful in timbre. For the reissue, the coupling has been extended to include the *Moments musicaux*. The digital remastering brings just a hint of hardness at fortissimo levels to a basically warm, full tone; some slight background remains.

Brendel's earlier analogue performance is as impressive and full of insight as one would expect. He is not unduly wayward, for his recording has room for the *Wanderer fantasy* as well, and he is supported by excellent Philips sound.

Dezsö Ránki's performance must be counted controversial in that he begins with a very expansive pacing of the opening theme, far slower than his basic speed later, and he consistently returns to this slow tempo when the famous melody recurs. The effect is to make the first movement unusually volatile, but it is also spontaneous, and he has clearly thought deeply about this approach. The slow movement is intensely poetic and, with a nimbly articulated Scherzo and a finale which balances sparkle with strength, this is a very considerable reading, matched by the two *Impromptus* which are beautifully played and nicely characterized.

VOCAL MUSIC

Lieder Vol. 1: *Der Alpenjäger; Amalia; An den Frühling; An den Mond; Erster Verlust; Die Ewartung; Der Fischer; Der Flüchtling; Das Geheimnis; Der Jüngling am Bache; Lied; Meeres Stille; Nähe des Geliebten; Der Pilgrim; Schäfers Klagelied; Sehnsucht; Thekla; Wanderers Nachtlied; Wonne der Wehmut.*
*** Hyp. Dig. CDJ 33001 [id.]. Dame Janet Baker, Graham Johnson.

Hyperion's complete Schubert song edition, master-minded by the accompanist, Graham Johnson, is planned to mix well-known songs with rarities, and that is what Dame Janet's first collection of 19 items does, demonstrating what jewels lie among unknown and insignificant songs. The whole collection is devoted to Schiller and Goethe settings, above all those he wrote in 1815, an exceptionally rich year for the 18-year-old; one marvels that, after writing his dedicated, concentrated setting of *Wanderers Nachtlied*, he could on that same day in July write two other equally memorable songs, *Der Fischer*, robustly folk-like and tuneful, and *Erster Verlust* (*First loss*), astonishingly deep for a teenager. Dame Janet is in glorious voice, her golden tone ravishing in a song such as *An den Mond* and her hushed tone caressing the ear in *Meeres Stille* and *Wanderers Nachtlied.* Presented like this, the project becomes not a marathon but a voyage of discovery.

Lieder Vol. 2: *Am Bach im Frühling; Am Flusse; Auf der Donau; Fahrt zum Hades; Fischerlied* (two settings); *Fischerweise; Der Schiffer; Selige Welt; Der Strom; Der Taucher; Widerschein; Wie Ulfru fischt.*
*** Hyp. Dig. CDJ 33002 [id.]. Stephen Varcoe, Graham Johnson.

In the accompaniments to Schubert songs, the inspiration of water is a recurrent theme and, for this second Hyperion instalment, Graham Johnson with the baritone, Stephen Varcoe, devises a delightful collection of men's songs, culminating in the rousing strophic song, *Der Schiffer*, one of the most catchily memorable that Schubert ever wrote, here exhilaratingly done. Otherwise the moods of water and wave, sea and river, are richly exploited, from the darkly brooding *Journey to Hades* (*Fahrt zum Hades*) and the urgently threatening journey to the abyss in *Der Strom*, on to the calm of *Am Bach im Frühling.* The last 28 minutes of the collection are devoted to the extended narrative, *Der Taucher* (*The Diver*), setting a long poem of Schiller which is based on an early version of the Beowulf saga. Varcoe and Johnson completely explode the long-accepted idea that this is overextended and cumbersome, giving it a thrilling dramatic intensity.

Lieder Vol. 3: *Abschied; An die Freunde; Augenlied; Iphigenia; Der Jüngling und der Tod; Lieb Minna; Liedesend; Nacht und Träume; Namenstagslied; Pax vobiscum; Rückweg; Trost im Liede; Viola; Der Zwerg.*
*** Hyp. Dig. CDJ 33003 [id.]. Ann Murray, Graham Johnson.

This is one of Ann Murray's finest records with the intimate beauty of the voice consistently well caught and with none of the stress that the microphone exaggerates on record. Graham Johnson has plainly helped in that, not only with his consistently supportive accompaniments but in a selection of songs specially suited to this sensitive, intelligent singer. Like the songs that Johnson chose for Ann Murray's husband, Philip Langridge, these too represent Schubert in his circle of friends, with their poems his inspiration, including a long flower ballad, *Viola*, by his close friend, Franz von Schober, which Murray and Johnson sustain beautifully.

Lieder Vol. 4: *Alte Liebe rostet nie; Am See; Am Strome; An Herrn Josef von Spaun (Epistel); Auf der Riesenkoppe; Das war ich; Das gestörte Glück; Liebeslauschen; Liebesrausch; Liebeständelei; Der Liedler; Nachtstück; Sängers Morgenlied* (2 versions); *Sehnsucht der Liebe.*
*** Hyp. Dig. CDJ 33004 [id.]. Philip Langridge, Graham Johnson.

Philip Langridge's contribution to Hyperion's great enterprise of recording all Schubert songs brings a collection chosen by Graham Johnson to illustrate his setting of words by poets in his immediate circle, ending with *Epistel*, a tongue-in-cheek parody song addressed to a friend who had left Vienna to become a tax collector, extravagantly lamenting his absence. It is Johnson's presentation of such rarities, complete with witty and highly illuminating as well as scholarly notes, that makes the series such a delight. With his inspired accompaniments, Johnson also draws the very finest from his singers. Langridge has rarely sounded so fresh and sparkling on record.

Lieder Vol. 5: *Die Allmacht; An die Natur; Die Erde; Erinnerung; Ferne von der grossen Stadt; Ganymed; Klage der Ceres; Das Lied im Grünen; Morgenlied; Die Mutter Erde; Die Sternenwelten; Täglich zu singen; Dem Unendlichen; Wehmut.*
*** Hyp. Dig. CDJ 33005 [id.]. Elizabeth Connell, Graham Johnson.

Elizabeth Connell's big soprano might have sounded ungainly in Schubert Lieder but, thanks in part to Johnson's choice of songs and to his sensitive support at the piano, Connell has rarely sounded so sweet and composed on record, yet with plenty of temperament. The collection of 14 songs, like others in this outstanding Hyperion series, centres round a theme, this one, Schubert and the countryside, suggested by the most popular song of the group, *Das Lied im Grünen*. As ever with this series, the joy of the record is enhanced by Johnson's brilliant, illuminating notes.

Lieder Vol. 6: *Abendlied für die Entfernte; Abends unter der Linde* (two versions); *Abendstern; Alinde; An die Laute; Des Fischers Liebesglück; Jagdlied; Der Knabe in der Wiege (Wiegenlied); Lass Wolken an Hügeln ruh'n; Die Nacht; Die Sterne; Der Vater mit dem Kind; Vor meiner Wiege; Wilkommen und Abschied; Zur guten Nacht.*
*** Hyp. Dig. CDJ 33006 [id.]. Anthony Rolfe Johnson, Graham Johnson (with chorus).

The theme of Anthony Rolfe Johnson's contribution to the Hyperion Schubert edition is 'Schubert and the Nocturne', making a much more varied collection than you might expect, extending even to the delectable lute-song, *An die Laute*. Two items include a small male chorus, a group of individually named singers. *Jagdlied* is entirely choral, and the final *Zur guten Nacht*, a late song of 1827, has the 'Spokesman' answered by the chorus, ending on a gentle *Gute Nacht*. As ever, Johnson's imagination in devising the programme presents the singer at his most warmly sympathetic. Rolfe Johnson's voice has never sounded more beautiful on record, and the partnership of singer and accompanist makes light even of a long strophic song like *Des Fischers Liebesglück*, beautiful and intense.

Lieder Vol. 7: *An die Nachtigall; An den Frühling; An den Mond; Idens Nachtgesang; Idens Schwanenlied; Der Jüngling am Bache; Kennst du das Land?; Liane; Die Liebe; Luisens Antwort; Des Mädchens Klage; Meeres Stille; Mein Gruss an den Mai; Minona oder die Kunde der Dogge; Naturgenuss; Das Rosenband; Das Sehnen; Sehnsucht* (2 versions); *Die Spinnerin; Die Sterbende; Stimme der Liebe; Von Ida; Wer kauft Liebesgötter?.*
*** Hyp. Dig. CDJ 33007 [id.]. Elly Ameling, Graham Johnson.

Graham Johnson for this seventh volume of his great Schubert series has chosen an extraordinarily rewarding sequence of 24 songs, all written in the composer's *annus mirabilis*, 1815. Many of the more celebrated songs from that year have already been included in other volumes, but the relative rarities here yield extraordinary riches. With Ameling both charming and intense, Johnson's robust defence in his ever-illuminating notes of the first and longest of the songs, *Minona*, is amply confirmed, a richly varied ballad. Here too is a preliminary setting of *Meeres Stille*, less well-known than the regular version, written a day later, but just as clearly a masterpiece, sung by Ameling in a lovely intimate half-tone at a sustained pianissimo. It is fascinating too to compare the two contrasted settings of Mignon's song, *Sehnsucht*, the first of five he ultimately attempted. Singer and accompanist-annotator consistently have you involved with Schubert the man, as well as his songs.

Lieder Vol. 8: *Abendlied der Fürstin; An Chloen; An den Mond; An den Mond in einer Herbstnacht; Berthas Lied in der Nacht; Erlkönig; Die frühen Gräber; Hochzeitslied; In der Mitternacht; Die Mondnacht; Die Nonne; Die Perle; Romanze; Die Sommernacht; Ständchen; Stimme der Liebe; Trauer der Liebe; Wiegenlied.*
*** Hyp. Dig. CDJ 33008; *KJ 33008* [id.]. Sarah Walker, Graham Johnson.

Sarah Walker, always a most characterful artist, has never made a more beautiful record than this, with her perfectly controlled mezzo at its most sensuous. The theme is 'Schubert and the Nocturne', leading from the first, lesser-known version of the Goethe poem, *An den Mond*, to two of the best-loved of all Schubert's songs, the delectable *Wiegenlied*, 'Cradle-song', and the great drama of *Erlkönig*, normally sung by a man, but here at least as vividly characterized by a woman's voice.

Lieder Vol. 9: *Blanka; 4 Canzonen, D.688; Daphne am Bach; Delphine; Didone abbandonata; Gott! höre meine Stimme; Der gute Hirte; Hin und wieder Fliegen Pfeile;* (i) *Der Hirt auf dem Felsen. Ich schleiche bang und still (Romanze). Lambertine; Liebe Schwärmt auf allen Wegen; Lilla an die Morgenröte; Misero pargoletto; La pastorella al prato; Der Sänger am Felsen; Thekla; Der Vollmond strahlt (Romanze).*
*** Hyp. Dig. CDJ 33009; *KJ 33009* [id.]. Arleen Augér, Graham Johnson; (i) with Thea King.

'Schubert and the theatre' is the theme of Arleen Augér's contribution to the great Hyperion project, leading up to the glories of his very last song, the headily beautiful *Shepherd on the rock*, with its clarinet obbligato. That solo is all the more atmospheric for being played here with gentle reticence by Thea King, with Augér firm as a rock over the widest leaps. The *Romanze, Ich schleiche bang* – adapted from an opera aria – also has a clarinet obbligato. As ever in illustrating a theme, Graham Johnson has chosen a delightfully wide range of items, most of them little-known. Notable are the lightweight Italian songs that the young Schubert wrote for his master, Salieri, and a lovely setting, *Der gute Hirt*, ('The good shepherd') in which the religious subject prompts a melody which anticipates the great staircase theme in Strauss's *Arabella.*

Lieder Vol. 10: *Adelwold und Emma; Am Flusse; An die Apfelbäume, wo ich Julien erblickte; An die Geliebte; An Mignon; Auf den Tod einer Nachtigall; Auf einen Kirchhof; Harfenspieler I; Labetrank der Liebe; Die Laube; Der Liebende; Der Sänger; Seufzer; Der Traum; Vergebliche Liebe; Der Weiberfreund.*
*** Hyp. Dig. CDJ 33010; *KJ 33010* [id.]. Martyn Hill, Graham Johnson.

Graham Johnson's themes in the Hyperion Edition never fail to illuminate Schubert in new ways. Here he correlates the year 1815, an *annus mirabilis* for the teenage composer in his exuberant song-writing, with what has been documented of his life over those twelve months, which is remarkably little. So the songs here form a kind of diary, outlined in Johnson's revealing liner-notes. The big item, overtopping everything else, is the astonishing 38-stanza narrative song, *Adalwold and Emma*. It was an item that Fischer-Dieskau refused to consider in his great recorded cycle for DG; with Hill ranging wide in his expression, it proves a fascinating piece here. It is almost half an hour long, from the bold march-like opening to the final happy resolution.

Lieder Vol. 11: *An den Tod; Auf dem Wasser zu singen; Auflösung; Aus 'Heliopolis' I & II; Dithyrambe; Elysium; Der Geistertanz; Der König in Thule; Lied des Orpheus; Nachtstück; Schwanengesang; Seligkeit; So lasst mich scheinen; Der Tod und das Mädchen; Verklärung; Vollendung; Das Zügenglöcklein.*
*** Hyp. Dig. CDJ 33011; *KJ 33011* [id.]. Brigitte Fassbaender, Graham Johnson.

There is no more vibrantly characterful Lieder-singer today, man or woman, than Brigitte Fassbaender, and her disc in the Hyperion Schubert Edition is electrifying. Starting with a chilling account of *Death and the maiden*, the theme of the disc is Death and the composer. Fassbaender's ability precisely to control her vibrato brings baleful tone-colours, made the more ominous by the rather reverberant, almost churchy, acoustic. Yet the selection imaginatively ranges wide in mood, illustrating Johnson's argument in his brilliant essay that, with the average life-span often shorter, death in Schubert's time was ever-present, and not just a matter for gloom. So in *Auf dem Wasser zu singen* the lightly fanciful rippling-water motif presents the soul gliding gently 'like a boat' up to heaven, and the selection ends astonishingly with what generally seems one of the lightest of Schubert songs, *Seligkeit*. This, as Johnson suggests, returns the listener from heaven back to earth, when the last stanza dismisses the idea of staying in heaven so as to go on enjoying the smiles of the beloved Laura. In this, as elsewhere, Fassbaender sings with thrilling intensity, with Johnson's accompaniment comparably inspired.

Lieder, Vol. 12: *Adelaide; An Elise; An Laura, als sie Klopstocks Auferstehungslied sang; Andenken; Auf den Sieg der Deutschen; Ballade; Die Betende; Don Gayseros I, II, III; Der Geistertanz; Lied an der Ferne; Lied der Liebe; Nachtgesang; Die Schatten; Sehnsucht; Trost; Trost in Tränem; Der Vatermörder.*
** Hyp. Dig. CDJ 33012 [id.]. Adrian Thompson, Graham Johnson.

Adrian Thompson's disc brings the only disappointment so far in Graham Johnson's outstanding Schubert series. As recorded, the voice sounds gritty and unsteady, with the tone growing tight and ugly under pressure. With Thompson consistently responsive to his ever-perceptive accompanist, this collection of early songs, all teenage inspirations written between 1811 and 1814, still illuminates the genius of Schubert at this earliest period of his career. But it is a pity a sweeter voice was not used.

Lieder, Vol, 13: (i) *Eine altschottische Ballade. Ellens Gesang I, II & III (Ave Maria); Gesang der Norna; Gretchen am Spinnrade; Gretchens Bitte; Lied der Anna Lyle; Die Männer sind mechant; Marie; Das Marienbild;* (i) *Norman's Gesang; Szene aus Faust. Shilrik und Vinvela; Die Unterscheidung.*
*** Hyp. Dig. CDJ 33013 [id.]. Marie McLaughlin, Graham Johnson; (i) with Thomas Hampson.

Though the theme for Marie McLaughlin's contribution to the Hyperion Schubert edition is not as clear-cut as most – broadly, a survey of Schubert's inner conflicts and contradictions – the majority of songs are drawn from two major sources, some from Goethe's poems inspired by Gretchen in *Faust*, and others from Scottish ballad poetry. So the Goethe settings are crowned by one of the most celebrated of all Schubert songs, *Gretchen am Spinnrade*. McLaughlin gives a fresh and girlish portrait, tenderly pathetic rather than tragic. Fascinatingly the selection also includes *Gretchens Bitte*, an extended song that Schubert left unfinished and for which Benjamin Britten in 1943 provided a completion of the final stanzas. The translations of Scottish ballads cover a wide range, starting with a jauntily simple setting of the poem best known through Loewe's powerful song, *Edward*. Schubert, like Brahms 50 years later, set it as a duet and called it simply *Eine altschottische Liede*. That is one of the three dramatic items involving the baritone, Thomas Hampson, which also include a sinister dialogue for Gretchen and an evil spirit, *Szene aus Faust*. McLaughlin's voice comes over sweetly, with brightness and much charm.

Lieder, Vol. 14: *Amphiaraos; An die Leier;* (i) *Antigone und Oedip. Der entsühnte Orest; Freiwilliges Versinken; Die Götter Griechenlands; Gruppe aus dem Tartarus; Fragment aus dem Aeschylus;* (i) *Hektors Abschied. Hippolits Lied; Lied eines Schiffers an die Dioskuren; Memnon; Orest auf Tauris; Philoktet; Uraniens Flucht; Der Zürnenden Diana.*
*** Hyp Dig. CDJ 33014 [id.]. Thomas Hampson, Graham Johnson; (i) with Marie McLaughlin.

Thomas Hampson's baritone has rarely sounded so rich and varied, both in tone and expression, as in his magnificent contribution to the Hyperion Schubert series. The theme is Schubert and the classics, mainly Ancient Greece. Matching the hushed intensity of the opening song, *Die Götter Griechenlands*, singer and accompanist give a rapt performance, and Hampson's ecstatically sweet tone, with flawless legato, contrasts with the darkly dramatic timbre – satisfyingly firm and steady – that he finds for later songs and dialogues, including the finale *Hektors Abschied*. In that dialogue Marie McLaughlin sings the part of Andromache to Hampson's Hector. The performances are enhanced by the keenly effective ordering of the songs, heightening the dramatic contrast.

Lieder: *Die schöne Mullerin: Wohin?; Des Baches Wiegenlied. Schwanengesang: Liebesbotschaft. Winterreise: Die Post; Frühlingstraum. An die Geliebte; An die Musik; An die Nachtigall; An mein Klavier; Auf dem Wasser zu singen; Ave Maria; Das sie hier gewesen; Du bist die Ruh'; Der Einsame; Des Fischers Liebesglück; Fischerweise; Die Forelle* (2 versions); *Frühlingsglaube; Geheimes; Gretchen am Spinnrade; Heidenröslein; Das Heimweh;* (i) *Der Hirt auf dem Felsen; Im Abendrot; Die junge Nonne; Der Jüngling an der Quelle; Der Jüngling und der Tod; Lachen und Weinen; Liebhabner in allen Gestalten; Das Lied im Grünen; Litanei; Das Mädchen; Der Musensohn; Nacht und Träume; Nachtviolen; Nahe des Geliebten; Nur wer die Sehnsucht kennt; Der Schmetterling; Seligkeit; So lasst mich scheinen; Ständchen; Schweizerlied; Die Vögel; Wiegenlied. Claudine von Villa Bella, D.239: Hin und wieder fliegen Pfeile* (2 versions); *Liebe schwärmt. Rosamunde, D.797: Der Vollmond strahlt.*
(M) (***) EMI mono CHS7 63040-2 (2) [Ang. CDHB 63040]. Elisabeth Schumann (various pianists); (i) Reginald Kell.

The irresistible charm and pure, silvery tones of Elisabeth Schumann make this collection of Schubert songs a delight from first to last. On the two CDs are collected 49 songs, with *Der Hirt auf dem Felsen* (*The Shepherd on the rock*) given separate billing on the cover. The recordings were made between 1927 and 1949, but mostly come from Schumann's vintage period in the 1930s. Transfers capture the voice well but, with a brighter top than on LP, the piano sound has less body. What matters is the vivid personality of the singer, never more sparkling than in such favourite songs as *Wohin?* (one of the earliest, made in 1927), *Heidenröslein* (from 1932) or *Die Forelle*, with a fascinating contrast between the brisk 1936 account and the more cautious but more delicate version of ten years later.

Lieder: *Alinde; Am Tage aller Seelen; An die Entfernte; An die Laute; Auf dem Wasser zu singen; Auf der Riesenkoppe; Die Bürgschaft; Du bist die Ruh'; Der Fischer; Der Fischers Liebesglück; Fischerweise; Die Forelle; Die Götter Griechenlands; Greisengesang; Heidenröslein; Das Heimweh; Im Walde; Der Jüngling an der Quelle; Der Jüngling und der Tod; Lachen und Weinen; Lied des gefangenen Jägers; Das Lied im Grünen; Nachtgesang; Nachtstück; Nähe des Geliebten; Normans Gesang; Der Schiffer; Sei mir gegrüsst; Seligkeit; Das sie hier gewesen; Ständchen; Strophe aus Die Götter; Der Strom; Der Tod und das Mädchen; Der Wanderer; Der Winterabend; Das Zügenglöcklein; Der zürnende Barde.*
(M) *** EMI CMS7 63566-2 (2) [Ang. CDMB 63566]. Dietrich Fischer-Dieskau, Gerald Moore; Karl Engel.

Dating from 1965, most of the items in this collection of Schubert songs superbly represent the second generation of Fischer-Dieskau recordings with Gerald Moore, deeper and more perceptive than his mono recordings, yet with voice and manner still youthfully fresh. Like this, there is no male Lieder-singer to match him. The contrast is fascinating, if subtle, between that main collection and the last nine songs on the second disc: they were recorded six years earlier, with three of them accompanied by Karl Engel, and with the voice still younger but presented in drier sound. With favourite songs comprising a substantial proportion of the programme, this delightful selection makes a valuable basic Lieder collection.

Lieder: *Die Allmacht; An die Natur; Auf dem See; Auflösung; Erlkönig; Ganymed; Gretchen am Spinnrade; Der Musensohn; Rastlose Liebe; Suleika I; Der Tod und das Mädchen; Der Zwerg.*
*** Ph. Dig. 412 623-2 [id.]. Jessye Norman, Philip Moll.

Jessye Norman's characterization of the four contrasting voices in *Erlkönig* is powerfully effective, and the reticence which once marked her Lieder singing has completely disappeared. The poignancy of *Gretchen am Spinnrade* is exquisitely touched in, building to a powerful climax; throughout, the breath control is a thing of wonder, not least in a surpassing account of *Ganymed*. Fine, sympathetic accompaniment from Philip Moll, and first-rate recording.

Am Grabe Anselmos; An die Musik; An die Nachtigall; An Sylvia; Auf dem See; Auf dem Wasser zu singen; Dass sie hier gewesen; Die Forelle; Die junge Nonne; Du bist die Ruh'; Ganymed; Geheimes; Gretchen am Spinnrade; Heidenröslein; Lachen und Weinen; Der Musensohn; Rastlose Liebe; Sei mir gegrüsst; Seligkeit; Ständchen; Suleika I & II; Wiegenlied.
**(*) Virgin Dig. VC7 91195-2; *VC7 91195-4* [id.]. Arleen Augér, Lambert Orkis.

The distinctive point about Arleen Augér's collection of Schubert songs – which includes a high proportion of favourites – is that the accompaniment is played by Lambert Orkis on a fortepiano. Though Augér's voice is caught most beautifully, with the tone consistently sweet and pure, the scale of the accompaniment intensifies a lightweight feeling, with beauty of tone given higher priority than word-meaning. Though in intensity and concern for detail this cannot match Augér's fine disc in Graham Johnson's Schubert series for Hyperion, it clearly has its place.

Lieder: *Am See; Auf dem Wasser zu singen; Auflösung; Die Forelle; Der Fluss; Ganymed; Die Gebüsche; Im Abendrot; Im Frühling; Klage der Ceres. Das Lied im Grünen; Nacht und Träume; Die Rose; Die Vögel; Wehmut.*
** DG Dig. 431 773-2 [id.]. Cheryl Studer, Irwin Gage.

Cheryl Studer is always an intelligent singer, but her attractive choice of songs here brings too many where she fails to scale down her operatic manner, with the melodic line too often disturbed by gustily uneven tone.

Lieder: *An die Entfernte; Auf dem Wasser zu singen; Du bist die Ruh'; Der Erlkönig; Die Forelle; Heidenröslein; Das Heimweh; Der Jüngling an der Quelle; Der Jüngling und der Tod; Das Lied im Grünen; Litanei auf das Fest Aller Seelen; Nachtgesang; Der Schiffer; Sei mir gegrüsst; Ständchen; Der Strom; Der Tod und das Mädchen; Der Wanderer; Der Winterabend; Das Zügenglöcklein; Der zürnende Barde.*
(M) *** EMI CDM7 69503-2 [id.]; *EG 769503-4*. Dietrich Fischer-Dieskau, Gerald Moore.

EMI's mid-price collection of vintage Fischer-Dieskau recordings makes an ideal sampler of favourite Schubert songs. Early in his career the voice was at its freshest and most beautiful and, though the comparably early stereo recording is less atmospheric than on more recent issues, there is a face-to-face immediacy which with such an artist could not be more revealing. A bargain.

Lieder: *An die Musik; An Sylvia; Auf dem Wasser zu singen; Ave Maria; Du bist die Ruh'; Die Forelle; Ganymed; Gretchen am Spinnrade; Heidenröslein; Im Frühling; Die junge Nonne; Litanei; Mignon und der Harfner; Der Musensohn; Nacht und Träume; Sei mir gegrüsst; Seligkeit.*
(B) *** Pickwick Dig. PCD 898; *CIMPC 898* [id.]. Felicity Lott, Graham Johnson.

At bargain price, Felicity Lott's collection brings an ideal choice of songs for the general collector. With Graham Johnson the most imaginative accompanist, even the best-known songs emerge fresh and new. Though Lott's voice loses some of its sweetness under pressure, the slight distancing of the recording gives a pleasant atmosphere, and gentle songs like *Litanei* are raptly beautiful.

Lieder: *An die Musik; An Sylvia; Auf dem Wasser zu singen; Ganymed; Gretchen am Spinnrade; Im Frühling; Die junge Nonne; Das Lied im Grünen; Der Musensohn; Nachtviolen; Nähe des Geliebten; Wehmut.*
(M) (***) EMI mono CDH7 64026-2 [id.]. Elisabeth Schwarzkopf, Edwin Fischer.

Schwarzkopf at the beginning of her recording career and Fischer at the end of his make a magical partnership, with even the simplest of songs inspiring intensely subtle expression from singer and pianist alike. Though Fischer's playing is not immaculate, he left few records more endearing than this, and Schwarzkopf's colouring of word and tone is masterly. The mono sound has been freshened, with the voice given a touch more aural mascara than on the original CD version which sounded even more natural – if more limited – than this.

Lieder: *An die Laute; An Silvia; An die Musik; Der Einsame; Im Abendrot; Liebhaber in allen Gestalten; Lied eines Schiffers an die Dioskuren; Der Musensohn; Ständchen.*
(M) *** DG 429 933-2 [id.]. Fritz Wunderlich, Hubert Giesen – BEETHOVEN: *Lieder* **(*); SCHUMANN: *Dichterliebe.* ***

Few tenors have matched the young Wunderlich in the freshness and golden bloom of the voice. The open manner could not be more appealing here in glowing performances well coupled with other fine examples of this sadly short-lived artist's work.

Lieder: *An die Nachtigall; An mein Klavier; Auf dem Wasser zu singen; Geheimnis;* (i) *Der Hirt auf dem Felsen; Im Abendrot; Ins stille Land; Liebhaben in allen Gestalten; Das Lied im Grünen; Die Mutter Erde; Romanze; Der Winterabend.*
*** HM Orfeo C 001811 A [id.]. Margaret Price, Sawallisch; (i) with H. Schöneberger.

Consistent beauty of tone, coupled with immaculately controlled line and admirably clear diction, makes Margaret Price's Schubert collection a fresh and rewarding experience. Sawallisch as ever shows himself one of the outstanding accompanists of the time, readily translating from his usual role of conductor. The rather reverberant recording gives extra bloom to the voice.

(i; ii) Duets: *Antigone und Oedip; Cronnan; Hektors Abschied; Hermann und Thusnelda; Licht und Liebe (Nachtgesang); Mignon und der Harfner; Selma und Selmar; Sing-Übungen;* (vi) *Szene aus Goethes Faust.* (ii; iii; iv; v) Trios: *Die Advokaten; Gütigster, Bester, Weisester; Die Hochzeitsbraten; Kantata zum Geburtstag des Sängers Johann Michael Vogl; Punschlied; Trinklied; Verschwunden sind die Schmerzen (a cappella).* (i–iv) Quartets: *An die Sonne; Gebet; Die Geselligkeit (Lebenslust); Gott der Weltschöpfer; Gott im Ungewitter; Hymne an den Undenlichen; Nun lasst uns den Leib begraben (Begräbnislied); Des Tages Weihe; Der Tanz.*
(M) *** 435 596-2 (2) [id.]. (i) Dame Janet Baker; (ii) Fischer-Dieskau; (iii) Ameling; (iv) Schreier; (v) Laubenthal; Gerald Moore; (vi) with Berlin RIAS Chamber Ch.

Not all these duets are vintage Schubert – some of the narrative pieces go on too long – but the artistry of Baker and Fischer-Dieskau makes for magical results, above all in a fascinating wordless melisma (*Sing-Übungen*) written as an exercise. Gerald Moore, who is at his finest throughout the set, relishes the magic too. The trios are domestic music in the best sense. Schubert wrote them at various periods of his career for his friends and colleagues to perform. Specially delightful are the two contrasted drinking songs, but *The wedding feast (Die Hochzeitsbraten)* is even more remarkable, a 10½ minute scena in the style of *opera buffa*. Bride (full of misgivings) and groom venture into the woods to poach a hare for their nuptial feast and are caught in the act by the gamekeeper, who is duly bribed and offers to join them at the wedding and bring the roast with him. The quartets, like the trios, were written for various domestic occasions, but the use of four voices seems to have led the composer regularly to serious or religious subjects. These are sweet and gentle rather than intense inspirations, but one could hardly ask for more polished and inspired performances than these. Fine recording from 1973/4, giving the singers a vivid presence on CD.

Lieder: *Ave Maria; Jäger, ruhe von der Jagd; Raste Krieger!; Schwestergruss; Der Zwerg.*
(M) **(*) Ph. 426 642-2; *426 642-4.* Jessye Norman, Irwin Gage – MAHLER: *Des Knaben Wunderhorn* etc. **(*)

These five Schubert songs come as fill-ups to Jessye Norman's early (1971) recordings of songs from Mahler's *Des Knaben Wunderhorn*, plus two *Rückert Lieder*, all sensitively done, if with less detail than she would later have provided. Good recording for its period, well transferred.

Deutsche Messe with Epilogue (The Lord's prayer), D.872; Mass in G, D.167; Psalms Nos. 23, D.706; 92, D.953; Salve Regina in F, D.379.
*** EMI CDC7 47407-2 [id.]. Popp, Fassbaender, Dallapozza, Fischer-Dieskau, Bav. R. Ch. and SO, Sawallisch.

Though this does not contain the most imaginative and original music from the first volume of Sawallisch's collection of Schubert's choral music, it is a pleasing selection, easy and undemanding and superbly sung and recorded. Some of the items, such as the setting of Psalm 23, have piano accompaniment by Sawallisch.

Masses Nos. (i) *5 in A flat, D.678;* (ii) *7 in C, D.961.*
(M) **(*) Decca 430 363-2; *430 363-4.* (i) Eathorne, Greevy, Evans, Keyte, St John's College, Cambridge, Ch., ASMF, Guest; (ii) Bryn-Johnson, De Gaetani, Rolfe Johnson, King, L. Sinf. Ch., L. Sinf., Atherton.

The *A flat Mass* has many beauties and in a fervently inspired reading can sound most impressive. Guest's performance is faithful but just lacks the distinction that marked his earlier recordings of the Haydn *Masses*; neither the singing nor the playing is in the least routine but they lack the personality that these musicians brought to the Haydn and the late *E flat* Schubert *Mass* (see below). Schubert's *C major Mass* setting is less deeply inspired but, in a lively performance like Atherton's, this last of the four early *Masses* has refreshment to offer. The recording in both works is very impressive, full and atmospheric, and admirably transferred to CD.

(i) *Mass No. 6 in E flat, D.950;* (ii; iii) *Gesang der Geister über den Wassern, D.714;* (ii) *Eine kleine Trauermusik: Minuet and finale in D for wind, D.79.*
(M) *** Decca 430 362-2; *430 362-4.* (i) Palmer, Watts, Bowen, Evans, Keyte, St John's College, Cambridge, Ch., ASMF, Guest; (ii) L. Sinf. Ch.; (iii) L. Sinf. (members), Atherton.

In every way this Mass is a richly rewarding work, product of the last year of Schubert's short life. The freshness of the singing here (the chorus far more important than the soloists) and the resilient playing of the Academy make this a delightful performance, given superb 1974 (Argo) sound. As a coupling, secular music brings equally memorable inspiration, above all in Schubert's last setting of Goethe's *Song of the spirits over the water*, a magical piece. The mourning music is very early indeed, remarkable for its solemn brass writing. The 1979 recording is pleasingly atmospheric and the CD transfer has improved the focus.

Rosamunde Overture (Die Zauberharfe, D.644) and incidental music, D.797 (complete).
*** DG Dig. 431 655-2(id.]. Anne Sofie von Otter, Ernst Senff Ch., COE, Abbado.

As a superb supplement to their masterly set of the Schubert symphonies, Abbado and COE give joyful performances of this magical incidental music. It is a revelation to hear the most popular of the entr'actes played so gently: it is like a whispered meditation. Even with a slow speed and affectionate phrasing, it yet avoids any feeling of being mannered. Glowing recording to match. Anne Sofie von Otter is an ideal soloist.

Die schöne Müllerin (song cycle), *D.795.*
*** DG 415 186-2 [id.]. Dietrich Fischer-Dieskau, Gerald Moore.
*** Decca Dig. 430 414-2; *430 414-4* [id.]. Peter Schreier, András Schiff.
*** Capriccio Dig. 10 082 [id.]. Josef Protschka, Helmut Deutsch.

(M) *** Ph. 420 850-2 [id.]. Gérard Souzay, Dalton Baldwin.
*** EMI Dig. CDC7 47947-2 [id.]. Olaf Bär, Geoffrey Parsons.

With an excellent digital transfer to CD barely giving an indication of its analogue source back in 1972, Fischer-Dieskau's classic version on DG remains among the very finest ever recorded. Though he had made several earlier recordings, this is no mere repeat of previous triumphs, combining as it does his developed sense of drama and story-telling, his mature feeling for detail and yet spontaneity too, helped by the searching accompaniment of Gerald Moore. It is a performance with premonitions of *Winterreise*.

Not since Benjamin Britten accompanied Peter Pears has a pianist played Schubert accompaniments with such individuality as András Schiff. He brings new illumination in almost every phrase, to match the brightly detailed singing of Schreier, here challenged to produce his most glowing tone. So in *Wohin?* Schiff transforms the accompaniment into an impressionistic fantasy on the flowing stream, and his rhythmic pointing regularly leads the ear on, completely avoiding any sense of sameness in strophic songs. Schreier, matching his partner as he did in their earlier, prize-winning recording of *Schwanengesang* (see below), transcends even his earlier versions of this favourite cycle, always conveying his response so vividly that one clearly registers his changes of facial expression from line to line. At times the voice develops a throaty snarl, purposely so for dramatic reasons. Outstandingly warm and well-balanced recording.

Josef Protschka gives an intensely virile, almost operatic reading, which is made the more youthful-sounding in the original keys for high voice. As recorded, the voice, often beautiful with heroic timbres, sometimes acquires a hint of stridency, but the positive power and individuality of the performance make it consistently compelling, with all the anguish behind these songs caught intensely. The timbre of the Bösendorfer piano adds to the performance's distinctiveness, well if rather reverberantly recorded.

Souzay made this recording in his prime in 1965; his lyrical style is beautifully suited to this most sunny of song-cycles. Souzay's concentration on purely musical values makes for one of the most consistently attractive versions available, with the words never neglected and Dalton Baldwin giving one of his most imaginative performances on record. The sound belies the recording's age.

Olaf Bär, with Geoffrey Parsons an attentive partner, gives an attractively fresh, boyish-sounding reading of *Schöne Müllerin*. This may not have the dramatic variety of Fischer-Dieskau's strongly characterized readings but, with the songs following each other with hardly a break, it is one full of presence.

Song-cycles: *Die schöne Müllerin, D.795; Schwanengesang, D.957; Winterreise, D.911.* Lieder: *Du bist die Ruh'; Erlkönig; Nacht und Träume.*
(M) (***) EMI mono CMS7 63559-2 (3) [Ang. CDMC 63559]. Dietrich Fischer-Dieskau, Gerald Moore.

Fischer-Dieskau's early mono versions may not match his later recordings in depth of insight, but already the young singer was a searching interpreter of these supreme cycles, and the voice was at its freshest and most beautiful, so that one misses stereo remarkably little. Gerald Moore was, as ever, the most sympathetic partner.

Schwanengesang (Lieder collection), *D.957;* Lieder: *An die Musik; An Sylvia; Die Forelle; Heidenröslein; Im Abendrot; Der Musensohn; Der Tod und das Mädchen.*
*** DG 415 188-2 [id.]. Dietrich Fischer-Dieskau, Gerald Moore.

Schwanengesang. Am Fenster; Bei dir allein; Herbst; Der Wanderer an den Mond.
*** Decca Dig. 425 612-2. Peter Schreier, András Schiff.

Schwanengesang; 5 Lieder: *Am Fenster; Herbst; Sehnsucht; Der Wanderer an den Mond; Wiegenlied, D.867.*
❀ *** DG Dig. 429 766-2 [id.]. Brigitte Fassbaender, Aribert Reimann.

Schwanengesang. Im Freien; Der Wanderer an den Mond; Das Zügenglücklein.
*** EMI Dig. CDC 749997-2. Olaf Bär, Geoffrey Parsons.

Brigitte Fassbaender gives a totally distinctive and compelling account of *Schwanengesang*, defying the convention that this is a cycle for male singers and proving stronger and more forceful than almost any rival. She turns what was originally a relatively random group of late songs into a genuine cycle, by presenting them in a carefully rearranged order and adding five other late songs. Her magnetic power of compelling attention, bringing home every word, is intensified by her sharply rhythmic manner, heightened in turn by the equally positive accompaniment of Aribert Reimann. After starting with a bouncily urgent account of *Der Taubenpost* – published as the last of the *Schwanengesang* songs – she adds the five extra songs early in the sequence, amplifying the other settings of Johann Seidl and Ludwig Rellstab. So the Seidl group includes the haunting lesser-known one of Schubert's cradle-songs, shaded down at the end to the gentlest pianissimo. The celebrated Schubert *Serenade* to words by Rellstab is far more than just a pretty tune, rather a passionate declaration of love; and Fassbaender builds her climax to the cycle round the final Heine settings, heightening their dramatic impact by the new ordering. Her aim is to follow 'the line of suffering' of the poet in love, from the lighthearted wooing of *Das Fischermädchen* through deepening hopelessness, on to a final cry of defiant misery in *Der Atlas*, a song that has never seemed more shattering. This is a unique recording which may well upset traditionalist lovers of Lieder but which brings home the power of the genre to communicate with new intensity.

Fischer-Dieskau's DG version with Moore, though recorded ten years before his CD with Brendel (currently withdrawn), brings excellent sound in the digital transfer, plus the positive advantages, first that the voice is fresher, and then that the disc also contains seven additional songs, all of them favourites. These performances represent a high-water mark in his recording of Schubert.

Schreier's voice may no longer be beautiful under pressure, but the bloom on this Decca recording is far kinder to him than most recent recordings, and the range of tone and the intensity of inflexion over word-meaning make this one of the most compelling recordings ever of *Schwanengesang*. Enhancing that are the discreet but highly individual and responsive accompaniments of András Schiff. Like Bär on his fine EMI version, Schreier makes up a generous CD-length by including not just the 14 late songs published together as *Schwanengesang*, but four more, also from the last three years of Schubert's life. The 14 original songs were never intended as a cycle, anyway. The recording is vividly real, bringing out Schreier's confidential directness in communicating, his mastery in conveying facial expression as he sings. For sample, try his chillingly intense account of *Der Doppelgänger*.

Olaf Bär also amplifies the collection of late songs posthumously published as *Schwanengesang* with well-chosen extra items from the same period, notably (like Schreier) *Der Wanderer an den Mond*. Where Schreier is confidential in that song at a brisk speed, Bär brings out the agony and weariness of the traveller addressing the moon. A similar contrast marks many of the other songs too – even the celebrated serenade, *Ständchen*: where Schreier is light and charming, Bär is strong and passionate. Schreier and Schiff are regularly more individual, but Bär and Parsons are the weightier and more beautiful, very well recorded too.

Schwanengesang excerpts: *Abschied; Am Meer; Der Döppelganger; Das Fischermädchen; Liebesbotschaft; Ständchen; Die Taubenpost. Winterreise* excerpts: *Frühlingstraum; Gefrorne Tränen; Gute Nacht; Die Krähe; Der Leiermann; Der Lindenbaum; Die Post; Wasserflut; Der Wegweiser*. Lieder: *Im Abendrot; Nacht und Träume; Der Wandrer; Der Wanderer an der Mond.*
(M) **(*) Ph. Dig. 432 053-2; *432 053-4* [id.]. Dietrich Fischer-Dieskau, Alfred Brendel.

Some 75 minutes of Schubert Lieder, compiled from three highly praised, full-priced CDs featuring the combined artistry of Fischer-Dieskau and Brendel, and given Philips's high-quality recording, this must be a bargain, even if the documentation – as usual with this series – is disgracefully non-existent. The excerpts from the two song cycles are given in proper order, with the opening and closing song used in each case to frame the others.

Winterreise (song cycle), *D.911.*
*** DG 415 187-2 [id.]. Dietrich Fischer-Dieskau, Gerald Moore.
*** Ph. Dig. 411 463-2; *411 463-4* [id.]. Dietrich Fischer-Dieskau, Alfred Brendel.
❀ (M) *** Decca 417 473-2 [id.]. Peter Pears, Benjamin Britten.
*** EMI Dig. CDC7 49334-2 [id.]. Olaf Bär, Geoffrey Parsons.
*** EMI Dig. CDC7 49846-2 [id.]. Brigitte Fassbaender, Aribert Reimann.

Winterreise (song cycle), *D.911; Piano sonata No. 15 in C, D.840.*
*** Ph. Dig. 416 289-2 (2) [id.]. Peter Schreier, Sviatoslav Richter.

In the early 1970s Dietrich Fischer-Dieskau's voice was still at its freshest, yet the singer had deepened and intensified his understanding of this greatest of song-cycles to a degree where his finely detailed and thoughtful interpretation sounded totally spontaneous, and this DG version is now freshened on CD. However, the collaboration of Fischer-Dieskau with one of today's great Schubert pianists, Alfred Brendel, brings endless illumination in the interplay and challenge between singer and pianist, magnetic from first to last. With incidental flaws, this may not be the definitive Fischer-Dieskau reading, but in many ways it is the deepest and most moving he has ever given. The recording is excellent.

Schubert's darkest song-cycle was in fact originally written for high voice, not low; quite apart from the intensity and subtlety of the Pears/Britten version, it gains enormously from being at the right pitch throughout. When the message of the poems is so gloomy, a dark voice tends to underline the sombre aspect too oppressively, whereas the lightness of a tenor is even more affecting. That is particularly so in those songs where the wandering poet in his despair observes triviality – as in the picture of the hurdy-gurdy man in the last song of all. What is so striking about the Pears performance is its intensity. One continually has the sense of a live occasion and, next to it, even Fischer-Dieskau's beautifully wrought singing sounds too easy. As for Britten, he re-creates the music, sometimes with a fair freedom from Schubert's markings, but always with scrupulous concern for the overall musical shaping and sense of atmosphere. The sprung rhythm of *Gefror'ne Tränen* is magical in creating the impression of frozen teardrops falling, and almost every song brings similar magic. The recording, produced by John Culshaw, was made in the Kingsway Hall in 1963, and the CD transfer is exceptionally successful in bringing a sense of presence and realism.

Bär's is a version of this greatest of song-cycles with all the merits. The singer offers not only a beautiful voice, used with consummate artistry, but an ability to bring out with equal conviction the contrast within the cycle between the poet's ardour and the pain of rejection on the one hand, and the darker, more philosophical element. So Bär, with Geoffrey Parsons a masterly accompanist, is both intensely dramatic and deeply reflective, while finding a beauty of line and tone to outshine almost anyone. The darkness of the close is given the intensity of live communication, and the sound is outstanding, with voice and piano given intimacy in a helpful atmosphere.

Brigitte Fassbaender gives a fresh, boyishly eager reading of *Winterreise*, marked by a vivid and wide range of expression; she demonstrates triumphantly why a woman's voice can bring special illumination to this cycle, sympathetically underlining the drama behind the tragic poet's journey rather than the more meditative qualities. Reimann, at times a wilful accompanist, is nevertheless spontaneous-sounding like the singer. Excellent sound.

Recorded live in 1985, Schreier's is an inspired version, both outstandingly beautiful and profoundly searching in its expression, helped by magnetic, highly individual accompaniment from Richter, a master of Schubert. Speeds are not always conventional – indeed are sometimes extreme – but that only adds to the vivid communication which throughout conveys the inspiration of the moment. Rarely has the agonized intensity of the last two songs been so movingly caught on record; it is a small price to pay that the winter audience makes so many bronchial contributions. A more serious snag is that the cycle spreads over on to a second CD, thanks to the slow speeds.

Winterreise (song-cycle), *D.911;* Lieder: *Erlkönig; Ganymed; Im Abendrot; Nachtgesang; Wanderers Nachtlied.*
(B) *** DG Compact Classics *427 724-4*. Dietrich Fischer-Dieskau, Gerald Moore.

It might be argued that this 1972 account is the finest of all Fischer-Dieskau's recorded performances of the cycle. Moore exactly matches the hushed concentration of the singer, consistently imaginative. This Compact Classics tape is very smoothly transferred and adds five other favourite Lieder for good measure, to make a genuine bargain.

OPERA

Fierrabras (complete).
*** DG Dig. 427 341-2 (2) [id.]. Protschka, Mattila, Studer, Gambill, Hampson, Holl, Polgár, Schoenberg Ch., COE, Abbado.

Few operas by a great composer have ever had quite so devastatingly bad a press as *Fierrabras*. However, in Vienna in 1988 Claudio Abbado conducted for a staging which, against all the odds, proved a great success; and the present recording was taken live from that. As with so many operas, the libretto is the main problem, absurd and cumbersome even by operatic standards. Yet the relationships between the central characters are clear enough, in this story from the days of chivalry. Schubert may often let his musical imagination blossom without considering the dramatic effect, so that there are jewels in plenty in this score; for example, the tenor *Romance* for Eginhard, the second hero, at the start of the Act I finale magically turns from minor to major when his beloved, Emma, takes over the tune. Later in Act II the other heroine, Florinda, transforms an already lovely melody by adding a mezzo-soprano descant. Many solos and duets develop into delightful ensembles, and the influence of Beethoven's *Fidelio* is very striking, with spoken melodrama and offstage fanfares bringing obvious echoes. By the standards of 1823 this was an adventurous opera, and it is sad that Schubert never saw it staged, so that he might have learnt to time the drama more effectively. A recording is the ideal medium for such buried treasure, and Abbado directs a performance as electrifying as his earlier one of Rossini's *Viaggio a Reims*, also with the Chamber Orchestra of Europe. Both tenors, Robert Gambill and Josef Protschka, are on the strenuous side, but have a fine feeling for Schubertian melody. Cheryl Studer and Karita Mattila sing ravishingly, and Thomas Hampson gives a noble performance as the knight, Roland, who finally wins Florinda. Only Robert Holl as King Karl (Charlemagne) is unsteady at times. The sound is comfortably atmospheric, outstanding for a live recording.

Schuman, William (1910–92)

Violin concerto.

(M) *** DG 429 860-2 [id.]. Zukofsky, Boston SO, Tilson Thomas – PISTON: *Symphony No. 2;* RUGGLES: *Sun-treader.* ***

William Schuman's *Violin concerto* is a tough but thoughtful piece with moments of characteristic dramatic intensity and poignant lyricism. Paul Zukofsky rises to its considerable technical demands with imposing virtuosity.

Judith; New England triptych; Symphony for strings; Variations on America.

*** Delos Dig. DE 3115 [id.]. Seattle SO, Gerard Schwarz.

This CD is called 'A Tribute to William Schuman' and appears in the immediate wake of his death. The composer himself heard these performances and spoke of their combination of 'intellectual depth, technical superiority and emotional involvement' and who are we to dissent! However, earlier in his career after a broadcast of his *Second Symphony*, a listener wrote to complain that hearing this work made him 'lose faith in the power of the aspirin'. There is no need to have recourse to any palliatives here. The *Symphony for strings*, his Fifth, is one of his strongest and most beautiful works. And although we must expect Sony to reissue Bernstein's classic account with the New York Philharmonic from the 1960s, this Seattle account makes an admirable alternative and has the advantage of fresher recorded sound. In some ways it benefits from being a more *natural* performance. The longest work on the disc is the ballet, *Judith: a choreographic poem*, written for Martha Graham in 1950. Powerful and atmospheric music, here given a performance with both these qualities. The *New England triptych* (1956) makes use of New England themes by the Bostonian William Billings (1746-1800) whose music served to fuel the cause of the American Revolution. This present account is superior to the version by Howard Hanson on Mercury, though that remains indispensable as it offers the only available version of Peter Mennin's *Fifth Symphony*. Let us hope Gerard Schwarz and his Seattle team go on to record the *Third* and *Sixth Symphonies*.

New England triptych.

(M) *** Mercury 432 755-2 [id.]. Eastman-Rochester O, Howard Hanson – IVES: *Symphony No. 3* etc. ***; MENNIN: *Symphony No. 5.* **(*)

A powerful and appropriate coupling for Ives's masterly *Three places in New England* and *Third Symphony*. William Schuman is not as outrageously original as Ives, but his sound-world is individual and wholly American. This work is drawn from what Schuman describes as the 'spirit of sinewy ruggedness, deep religiosity and patriotic fervour' which characterizes the music of an earlier American composer, William Billings (1746–1800). Each of the three pieces is an orchestral anthem, the first a thrustingly vibrant *Hallelujah*; the second is in the form of a round, and the finale features a marching song. Splendidly alive playing and excellent (1963) Mercury recording, admirably transferred to CD.

Symphony No. 3.

*** DG Dig. 419 780-2 [id.]. NYPO, Bernstein – HARRIS: *Symphony No. 3.* ***

The *Third* of William Schuman's ten symphonies has an authentic American feel to it: it certainly creates a sound-world all its own, but the world it evokes is urban. The chorale movement is particularly evocative, full of nocturnal introspection and wholly original. Schuman is also one of the few modern composers to use fugue both individually and effectively. An impressive performance. The New York Philharmonic play with excellent discipline and are well recorded. Strongly recommended.

Symphony No. 4; Prayer in time of war.
** Albany TROY 027-2 [id.]. Louisville O, Jorge Mester – BECKER: *Symphonia Brevis;* HARRIS: *Epilogue to profiles in courage* etc. **

The *Fourth* is perhaps just a bit of a disappointment after the vital and exhilarating *Third* or the marvellous *Symphony for strings* (No. 5). By far the best (and most characteristic) sections are the eloquent and thoughtful central movement and the exhilarating finale. The work opens promisingly, with a powerful ground bass, but lapses into something very close to note-spinning. All the same, the more inspired passages leave a stronger impression in the memory than the passages of manufactured writing. *Prayer in time of war* comes from 1942, the period of the *Third Symphony*. It is a deeply felt piece, well played here by the Louisville forces. The recordings date from 1968 and 1972 respectively but have come up well.

Schumann, Clara (1819–96)

Piano trio in G min., Op. 17.
*** Hyp. Dig. CDA 66331 [id.]. Dartington Piano Trio – Fanny MENDELSSOHN: *Trio.* ***

In her authoritative study of the composer, Joan Chissell speaks of the *Piano trio* of 1845 as 'an outstanding testimonial to Clara's creative potential, well-proportioned and free from all procrustean strain in its use of extended forms'. It moves within the Mendelssohn–Schumann tradition with apparently effortless ease and, when played as persuasively as it is here, makes a pleasing impression. If it does not command the depth of Robert, it has a great deal of charm to commend it. Excellent recording.

Schumann, Robert (1810–56)

Cello concerto in A min., Op. 129.
(M) *** Mercury 432 010-2 [id.]. Janos Starker, LSO, Skrowaczewski – LALO: *Concerto* **(*); SAINT-SAËNS: *Concerto.* ***
(M) *** Decca Dig. 430 743-2; *430 743-4* [id.]. Lynn Harrell, Cleveland O, Marriner – DVOŘÁK: *Cello concerto.* **

The Schumann *Cello concerto* is not generously represented at the mid-price or bargain end of the catalogue; Janos Starker gives a persuasive account of it that is thoroughly sensitive to the letter and spirit of the score. Skrowaczewski accompanies with spirit and without the rather explosive, clipped tutti chords that rather disfigure the Lalo with which it is coupled. The 1962 recording is amazing for its age: people make great claims for these early Mercury recordings and, judging from this expertly engineered disc, rightly so!

Harrell's is a big-scale reading, strong and sympathetic, made the more powerful by the superb accompaniment from the Cleveland Orchestra. Its controversial point is that he expands the usual cadenza with a substantial sequence of his own. The digital recording is outstandingly fine.

(i) *Cello concerto in A min., Op. 129;* (ii) *Adagio and allegro in A flat, Op. 70; 5 Stücke im Volkston, Op. 102; Fantasiestücke, Op. 73.*
*** Sony Dig. MK 42663 [id.]. Yo-Yo Ma, (i) Bav. RSO, C. Davis; (ii) Emanuel Ax.

Yo-Yo Ma offers the whole of Schumann's music for the cello and piano. As always, Ma's playing is distinguished by great refinement of expression and his account of the *Concerto* is keenly affectionate, although at times he carries tonal sophistication to excess and drops suddenly into *sotto voce* tone and near-inaudibility. Both he and Sir Colin Davis are thoroughly attuned to the sensibility of this composer. The balance, both between soloist and orchestra and within the various departments of the orchestra, blends perfectly. The three pieces for cello and piano are well projected and full of feeling, with sensitive and well-characterized playing from Emanuel Ax.

Piano concerto in A min., Op. 54.
*** Ph. 412 923-2 [id.]. Kovacevich, BBC SO, C. Davis – GRIEG: *Concerto.* ***
*** Sony Dig. MK 44899 [id.]. Perahia, Bav. RSO, C. Davis – GRIEG: *Concerto.* ***
*** CfP Dig. CD-CFP 4574; *TC-CFP4574.* Pascal Devoyon, LPO, Maksymiuk – GRIEG: *Piano concerto.* ***
*** Ph. 412 251-2 [id.]. Brendel, LSO, Abbado – WEBER: *Konzertstück.* ***
*** Decca 417 555-2 [id.]. Ashkenazy, LSO, Segal – TCHAIKOVSKY: *Concerto No. 1.* ***
(M) (***) EMI mono CDH7 69792-2. Lipatti, Philh. O, Karajan – MOZART: *Piano concerto No. 21.* (*(**))
(M) **(*) Decca 417 728-2 [id.]. Radu Lupu, LSO, Previn – GRIEG: *Concerto.* **(*)
(M) **(*) BMG/RCA GD 60420; *GK 60420* [60420-2-RG; *60420-4-RG*]. Van Cliburn, Chicago SO, Reiner – MACDOWELL: *Concerto No. 2.* **(*)
(BB) **(*) Pickwick PWK 1148. Friedrich Gulda, VPO, Andrae – TCHAIKOVSKY: *Piano concerto No. 1.* ***
(B) **(*) Decca 433 628-2; *433 628-4* [id.]. Gulda, VPO, Andrae – FRANCK: *Symphonic variations* *** ❀; GRIEG: *Concerto.* ***
(M) **(*) Sony/CBS CD 44849; *40-44849* [id.]. Fleisher, Cleveland O, Szell – GRIEG: *Concerto.* **(*)
(B) **(*) Sony MYK 44771 [id.]. Istomin, Columbia SO, Bruno Walter – BRAHMS: *Double concerto.* **(*)
(*) Chesky CD 52 [id.]. Malcolm Frager, RPO, Horenstein – BEETHOVEN: *Violin concerto.* *
(B) **(*) Pickwick IMPX 9041 [id.]. Julius Katchen, Israel PO, Kertész – GRIEG: *Concerto.* **(*)

(i) *Piano concerto in A min. Arabeske in C, Op. 18.*
(M) *** Mercury 432 011-2 [id.]. Byron Janis, Minneapolis SO, Skrowaczewski – TCHAIKOVSKY: *Piano concerto No. 1.* **(*)

Our primary recommendation for this favourite Romantic concerto remains with the successful symbiosis of Stephen Kovacevich and Sir Colin Davis, who give an interpretation which is both fresh and poetic, unexaggerated but powerful in its directness and clarity. More than most, Kovacevich shows the link between the central introspective slow movement and the comparable movement of Beethoven's *Fourth Concerto*; and the spring-like element of the outer movements is finely presented by orchestra and soloist alike. The sound has been admirably freshened for its reissue and the 1972 recording date is quite eclipsed. Even though this remains at full price, it is worth it.

Perahia's version benefits – like the classic Philips account from Stephen Kovacevich – from having the guiding hand of Sir Colin Davis directing the orchestra. The recording is taken live from performances Perahia gave in Munich, and no allowance whatever has to be made for the sound, with audience noises not at all apparent. The confident bravura in the performances presents Perahia in a rather different light from usual. He is never merely showy, but here he enjoys displaying his ardour and virtuosity as well as his ability to invest a phrase magically with poetry. In the last resort, Kovacevich's simpler and more intimate manner is even more affecting in the first two movements but, with its full and spacious sound, the Perahia is the finest recent version of this favourite coupling.

Pascal Devoyon, now in his mid-thirties, is at last gaining some of the recognition he so richly deserves. Like the Grieg with which it is coupled, his Schumann *Concerto* is aristocratic without being aloof, pensive without being self-conscious, and brilliant without being flashy. Natural musicianship and artistry are always in evidence and though his account does not challenge such a marvellously fresh performance as that by Kovacevich, at bargain price it still remains competitive, with excellent playing from the LPO under Jerzy Maksymiuk.

Byron Janis's Schumann *Concerto* is a lovely performance, and the 1962 recording sounds amazingly improved over its previous incarnations, especially in regard to the orchestra. The piano is full and firm, if forward, and the orchestral sound has body as well as range. Janis's reading finds an almost perfect balance between the need for romantic ardour and intimacy in the *Concerto* – the exchanges between the piano and the woodwind soloists in the first movement are most engagingly done. Skrowaczewski provides admirable support throughout, and this is highly recommendable – a first choice at mid-price.

Brendel's is a thoroughly considered, yet fresh-sounding performance, with meticulous regard to detail. There is some measure of coolness, perhaps, in the slow movement, but on the whole this is a most distinguished reading. The orchestral playing under Abbado is good, and the recorded sound is up to the usual high standards of the house.

Ashkenazy's performance, balancing the demands of drama against poetry, comes down rather more in favour of the former than one might expect, but it is a refined reading as well as a powerful one, with the finale rather more spacious than usual. The recording from the late 1970s has been remastered most successfully. Those wanting a coupling with Tchaikovsky will find this a worthwhile record.

Dinu Lipatti's celebrated EMI recording has acquired classic status and will more than repay study. The transfer is excellent. A splendidly aristocratic account in very acceptable sound.

Lupu's clean boldness of approach to the first movement is appealingly fresh, but the fusing together of the work's disparate masculine and feminine Romantic elements has not been solved entirely. The digital CD transfer is especially telling in the quieter moments, but tuttis are less transparent than with a digital recording.

Van Cliburn's performance is very persuasive, the first movement rhapsodical in feeling, certainly poetic but exciting too. The *Intermezzo* is pleasingly fresh and the finale admirably buoyant and spirited. Altogether this is most attractive, and so is the unusual MacDowell coupling.

Gulda's account is refreshingly direct yet, with light, crisp playing, never sounds rushed. The *Intermezzo* remains delicate in feeling, with nicely pointed pianism. The finale is just right, with an enjoyable rhythmic lift. This performance has not the distinction of its Franck and Grieg couplings, but it is enjoyably spontaneous and the early stereo (1956), though a little dated, is fully acceptable. It is also available on Pickwick, paired with Tchaikovsky.

Fleischer's 1960 account with Szell is also distinguished, the reading combining strength and poetry in a most satisfying way, yet with a finale that sparkles. In the first movement Szell relaxes the tempo for the famous piano and woodwind dialogues, and the effect is beguilingly intimate, in spite of a very bold, upfront orchestral recording, which tends to sound a little fierce.

Istomin's performance attractively combines strength and poetry, with bold contrasts in the first movement, a nicely lyrical *Intermezzo* and a fluent, well-paced finale. Bruno Walter's directing personality is strong and the recording sounds remarkably fine in its digital remastering, the warm ambience preventing any feeling of aggressiveness being generated by the dramatic tuttis.

Frager's spontaneously bright reading matches the forceful direction of the veteran conductor, Jascha Horenstein. Characteristically, the interlude of the slow movement is fresh and direct, poetic but totally unsentimental. Made in 1967, the recording brings a very sour oboe at the start, thanks to tape 'wow', but otherwise the sound is clean and satisfying. A generous coupling for the Beethoven *Violin concerto.*

Katchen's opening movement has a number of tempo changes and sounds more rhapsodical than usual, but the performance is admirably fresh and the *Intermezzo* has distinct grazioso charm. The finale is suitably brilliant and the whole performance is animated in a pleasingly spontaneous way. This is essentially a virtuoso reading but it is by no means hard driven. The 1963 (Decca) sound is remarkably good and bright, and well balanced in a spacious acoustic.

Violin concerto in D min., Op. posth.

(M) **(*) EMI Dig. CDD7 63894-2 [id.]. Gidon Kremer, Philh. O, Muti – SIBELIUS: *Violin concerto.* **(*)

The Schumann *Violin concerto,* with its vein of introspection, seems to suit Gidon Kremer, who gives a generally sympathetic account of it and has very good support from the Philharmonia Orchestra under Riccardo Muti. It is not Schumann at his most consistently inspired, but there are good things in it, including a memorable second subject and a characteristic slow movement. The recording is full-bodied and vivid, balanced in favour of the soloist. It is good to have this recording reissued at mid-price, as it may tempt collectors to try the work.

Introduction and allegro appassionato in G, Op. 92.

*** Decca Dig. 417 802-2 [id.]. András Schiff, VPO, Dohnányi – DVOŘÁK: *Piano concerto.* **(*)
(M) **(*) Sony SBK 48166 [id.]. Rudolf Serkin, Phd. O, Ormandy – BRAHMS: *Concerto No. 1* **(*); MENDELSSOHN: *Capriccio brillant.* **

The *Introduction and allegro appassionato in G major* brings the full flowering of Schumann's romanticism. Schiff and Dohnányi play it with dedication and commitment, and the recording, while favouring the soloist, is more realistic in balance than for the Dvořák coupling.

Serkin plays this somewhat elusive work with his accustomed panache and he is given excellent support from Ormandy. The piano tone could be fuller in timbre, but the overall effect has considerable warmth and those looking for a recording of this relatively unfamiliar piece will find much here to arrest them. The Brahms coupling also shows Serkin at his finest.

Overture, Scherzo and Finale in E, Op. 52.
(B) *** DG 431 161-2; *431 161-4*. BPO, Karajan – BRAHMS: *Symphony No. 1*. ***

This serves merely as a bonus for Karajan's fine 1964 recording of the Brahms *First Symphony* and this performance is second to none.

Symphonies Nos. 1–4.
(M) *** DG 429 672-2 (2) [id.]. BPO, Karajan.

Symphonies Nos. 1 in B flat (Spring), Op. 38; 4 in D min., Op. 120; Overture, scherzo and finale, Op. 52.
(M) *** EMI CDM7 69471-2 [id.]; *EG 769471-4*. Dresden State O, Sawallisch.

Symphonies Nos. 2 in C, Op. 61; 3 in E flat (Rhenish), Op. 97.
(M) *** EMI CDM7 69472-2 [id.]; *EG 769472-4*. Dresden State O, Sawallisch.

The Dresden CDs of the Schumann *Symphonies* under Sawallisch are as deeply musical as they are carefully considered; the orchestral playing combines superb discipline with refreshing naturalness and spontaneity. Sawallisch catches all Schumann's varying moods, and his direction has splendid vigour. These recordings have dominated the catalogue, alongside Karajan's, for some years and they are most welcome on CD. Although the reverberant acoustic brought a degree of edge to the upper strings, the sound-picture has the essential fullness which the Karajan transfers lack, and the remastering has cleaned up the upper range to a considerable extent.

Karajan's interpretations of the Schumann *Symphonies* stand above all other modern recordings. No. 1 is a beautifully shaped performance, with orchestral playing of the highest distinction; No. 2 is among the most powerful ever recorded, combining poetic intensity and intellectual strength in equal proportions; and No. 3 is also among the most impressive versions ever commited to disc: its famous fourth-movement evocation of Cologne Cathedral is superbly spacious and eloquent, with quite magnificent brass playing. No. 4 can be classed alongside Furtwängler's famous record, with Karajan similarly inspirational, yet a shade more self-disciplined than his illustrious predecessor. However, the reissued complete set brings digital remastering which – as with the Brahms symphonies – has leaner textures than before, while in tuttis the violins above the stave may approach shrillness. Nos. 1 and 3 are also available separately – see below.

Symphonies Nos. 1 in B flat (Spring), Op. 38; 3 in E flat (Rhenish), Op. 97.
(BB) *** ASV Dig. CDQS 6073; *ZCQS 6073* [id.]. RLPO, Janowski.

Janowski's pairing of the *Spring* and *Rhenish symphonies* is particularly successful, coupling the finest performances from his complete Liverpool cycle. The pacing throughout both symphonies is most convincing, with a good deal of the inspirational pull that makes the Karajan readings so telling. The song-like lyricism of the *Larghetto* of the *First Symphony* is matched by the serenity of the slow movement of the *Third*, and both Scherzos are very strongly characterized. In the Cologne Cathedral evocation of the *Rhenish*, the Liverpool brass rise sonorously to the occasion and the recording is altogether first class, bright, clear and full, with a concert hall ambience. At super-bargain price, this is strongly competitive.

Symphony No. 1 in B flat (Spring), Op. 38.
(B) *** DG 429 158-2 [id.]. BPO, Karajan – MENDELSSOHN: *Symphony No. 4*. ***

Symphonies Nos. 1 (Spring); 4 in D min., Op. 120.
(M) **(*) Ph. Dig. 432 059-2; *432 059-4*. Concg. O, Haitink.
**(*) DG Dig. 415 274-2 [id.]. VPO, Bernstein.

Haitink conducts thoughtful and unexaggerated readings of the *First* and *Fourth Symphonies*, beautifully paced and with refined playing from the Concertgebouw Orchestra. His chosen speeds are never controversial, and the playing is both polished and committed, to make these consistently satisfying performances. The only snag is the recording quality which, with works that from the start are thick in their orchestration, is too reverberant. Karajan's bargain version of No. 1 is cleaner and clearer and has weight too.

Bernstein's VPO versions of Nos. 1 and 4 have the extra voltage which comes with live music-making at its most compulsive; it is a pity that Bernstein, who displays a natural response to Schumann, seeks to impose personal idiosyncrasies on the performances that are not as convincing as Furtwängler's. The first movement of the *Spring symphony* is pushed very hard, while the outer movements of No. 4 are not allowed to move forward at a steady pulse. The big transitional climax before the finale of the *Fourth* is massively conceived, yet does not have the spine-tingling sense of anticipation that Furtwängler generated at this point. Even so, with splendid orchestral playing and much engaging detail, there is a great deal to admire here. The recording has an attractive ambience and is full and well balanced, with the woodwind attractively coloured.

Symphony No. 2 in C, Op. 61.
(M) *** DG 435 067-2; *435 067-4* [id.]. BPO, Karajan – BRAHMS: *Symphony No. 2.* ***

Karajan's powerful account of Schumann's *C major Symphony* has great eloquence and is marvellously played. The recording here sounds rather more expansive than in the boxed set.

Symphony Nos. 2; 3 in E flat (Rhenish), Op. 97.
*** DG Dig. 423 625-2 [id.]. BPO, Levine.
(B) *** DG 429 520-2 [id.]. BPO, Kubelik.

Levine conducts warm and positive readings of both *Symphonies,* drawing superb playing from the Berlin Philharmonic. The crispness of the violin articulation in his fast, athletic account of the second-movement scherzo of No. 2 is a marvel, and he gives the *Rhenish* all the rhythmic bounce it needs. Though the Berlin recording is warm and full to match – allowing thrilling crescendos in the Cologne Cathedral movement of the *Rhenish* – the inner textures are not ideally clear. The compensation is that the modern digital recording gives a satisfyingly full body to the sound.

An excellent bargain coupling from Kubelik. No. 2 is beautifully played and eloquently shaped, and in the *Rhenish* Kubelik's straightforward, unmannered approach, coupled to a natural warmth, provides a musical and thoroughly enjoyable account. The remastering of the 1964/5 recordings is most successful: they have more body and warmth than the Karajan complete set.

Symphony No. 3 in E flat (Rhenish), Op. 87.
(M) *** DG Dig. 427 818-2; *427 818-4* [id.]. LAPO, Giulini – SCHUBERT: *Symphony No. 8 (Unfinished).* *** ❀

Giulini's *Rhenish* is completely free of interpretative exaggeration and its sheer musical vitality and nobility of spirit are beautifully conveyed. The Los Angeles players produce a very well-blended, warm and cultured sound that is a joy to listen to in itself. The recording is extremely fine, too. Now recoupled with Sinopoli's inspired version of Schubert's *Unfinished*, this makes an excellent primary recommendation.

Symphonies Nos. 3 in E flat (Rhenish); 4 in D min., Op. 120.
*** EMI CDC7 54025-2 [id.]; *EL 754025-4.* L. Classical Players, Norrington.

With Schumann's orchestration usually accused of being too thick, there is much to be said for period performances like this. Norrington not only clarifies textures, with natural horns in particular standing out dramatically, but, at unexaggerated speeds for the outer movements – even a little too slow for the first movement of No. 3 – the results are often almost Mendelssohnian. Middle movements in both symphonies are unusually brisk, turning slow movements into lyrical interludes. Warm, atmospheric recording.

Symphony No. 4 in D min., Op. 120.
(M) **(*) Decca 425 957-2 [id.]. LSO, Josef Krips – SCHUBERT: *Symphony No. 9.* ***

Krips's lyrical manner suits the inner movements better than the outer ones. However, the work is well played and the brightly remastered 1956 Kingsway Hall recording makes more impact than the original LP.

CHAMBER MUSIC

Abendlied, Op. 85/2; Adagio and allegro in A flat, Op. 70; Fantasiestücke, Op. 73; 3 Romances, Op. 94; 3 Pieces in Folk style, Op. 102/2–4.
(M) *** Ph. 426 386-2; *426 386-4.* Heinz Holliger, Alfred Brendel.

On this delightful record Heinz Holliger gathers together pieces written in 1849, the most fruitful of composing years for Schumann. The three *Romances* are specifically for oboe, but Holliger – pointing out that Schumann never heard any of the pieces except on the violin – suggests that the others too are suitable for oboe, since the composer himself gave different options. One misses something by not having a horn in the *Adagio and allegro*, a cello in the folk-style pieces, or a clarinet in the *Fantasiestücke* (the oboe d'amore is used here); but Holliger has never sounded more magical on record and, with superbly real recording and deeply imaginative accompaniment, the result is an unexpected revelation.

Adagio and allegro for horn and piano, Op. 30.
(M) *** Decca 433 695-2 [id.]. Barry Tuckwell, Vladimir Ashkenazy – BRAHMS: *Horn trio;* FRANCK: *Violin sonata;* SAINT-SAËNS: *Romance.* ***

Schumann's *Adagio and allegro* requires ripe romantic feeling and considerable virtuosity from the horn soloist (much more, for instance, than is needed for the Mozart concertos). Needless to say, both these requirements are readily met here, and these artists create a fine artistic partnership. The 1974 Kingsway Hall recording camnnot be faulted.

(i) *Andante and variations for 2 pianos, 2 cellos and horn in B flat;* (ii) *Ballszenen, Op. 109; 6 Impromptus (Bilder aus dem Osten), Op. 66; Kinderball, Op. 130; 12 Pieces for little and big children, Op. 85;* (iii) *Studies for the pedal piano, Op. 56; 8 Polonaises, Op. 111; Sketches for the pedal piano, Op. 58.*
(B) **(*) VoxBox (3) [CD3X 3001]. Peter Frankl; (i; ii) András Schiff; with (i) Halstead, Varga, Hegedüs; (iii) A. Frankl.

Not all the music is inspired, but enough of it is to make this a thoroughly enjoyable set. Moreover these artists make out the best possible case for it: the *Andante and variations for two pianos, cellos and horn in B flat*, which is a transcription of the Op. 46 two-piano piece, has rarely sounded more eloquent. The other pieces on this three-disc set are no less persuasive. Despite the close balance, the recordings yield pleasing results, for the studio has a warm, natural acoustic. The bulk were made in London in 1978; the pieces for pedal piano, Opp. 56 and 58, recorded in a small Paris studio by Peter and Annie Frankl, sound far less pleasing, thanks to the cramped acoustic. However, the whole set is well worth having. It is not yet available in the UK.

Fantasiestücke, Op. 73; 3 Romances, Op. 94.
*** Chan. Dig. CHAN 8506; *ABTD 1216* [id.]. Gervase de Peyer, Gwenneth Pryor – SCHUBERT: *Arpeggione sonata;* WEBER: *Silvana variations.* ***

The artistry of Gervase de Peyer is heard to splendid effect in these late works of Schumann. With warmth of tone and much subtlety of colour, he gives first-class performances and is well supported by Gwenneth Pryor. The recording is most realistic.

Fantasiestücke, Op. 73; 5 Stücke in Volkston, Op. 102.
*** Ph. Dig. 412 230-2 [id.]. Maisky, Argerich – SCHUBERT: *Arpeggione sonata.* ***

Mischa Maisky and Martha Argerich give relaxed, leisurely accounts of these pieces that some collectors may find almost self-indulgent. Others will luxuriate in the refinement and sensitivity of this playing.

Märchenbilder, Op. 113.
**(*) Chan. Dig. CHAN 8550; *ABTD 1256* [id.]. Imai, Vignoles – BRAHMS: *Viola sonatas.* **(*)

The *Märchenbilder* are pleasing miniatures, persuasively played here by Nobuko Imai and Roger Vignoles. The recording acoustic is not ideal, but this does not seriously detract from the value of this coupling, especially as there is no alternative account of these pieces.

Piano quartet in E flat, Op. 47; (i) *Piano quintet in E flat, Op. 44.*
*** Ph. 420 791-2 [id.]. Beaux Arts Trio, Rhodes, (i) with Bettelheim.
**(*) CRD CRD 3324; *CRDC 4024* [id.]. Rajna, members of the Alberni Qt.

The Beaux Arts Trio (with associates) give splendid performances of both these fine chamber works. The vitality of inspiration is consistently brought out, whether in the *Quintet* or the relatively neglected *Quartet*, and with that goes the Beaux Arts' characteristic concern for fine ensemble and refined textures. The recording is beautifully clear and clean, if less atmospheric than before.

Though not quite so flawlessly polished in their playing, Rajna and the Alberni give performances that in their way are as urgent and enjoyable as those on the Philips disc. The recording is brighter and crisper, which gives an extra (and not unlikeable) edge to the performances.

Piano quintet in E flat, Op. 44.
(BB) *** Naxos Dig. 8.550406; *4550406* [id.]. Jenö Jandó, Kodály Qt – BRAHMS: *Piano quintet.* ***

A strongly characterized performance of Schumann's fine *Quintet* from Jenö Jandó and the Kodály Quartet. Jandó has the right kind of personality for this work and he forms a genuine partnership with his colleagues. One notices the warm tone of the cellist in the first movement's secondary theme. This is robust music-making, romantic in spirit, and its spontaneity is well projected by a vivid recording, made in an attractively resonant acoustic. With its comparable Brahms coupling, this makes an excellent bargain.

Piano trios Nos. 1 in D min., Op. 63; 2 in F, Op. 80; 3 in G min., Op. 110; Fantasiestücke in A min., Op. 88.
**(*) Chan. Dig. CHAN 8832/3; *DBTD 2020* (2) [id.]. Borodin Trio.

It is good to have all three of Schumann's *Piano trios* in one two-CD set with the *Fantasiestücke*, Op. 88, thrown in for good measure. These are full-hearted performances that give undoubted pleasure – and would give more, were it not for some swoons from Rostislav Dubinsky who, at the opening of the *D minor Trio*, phrases with a rather ugly scoop. While too much should not be made of this, greater reticence would have been more telling throughout. There are excellent notes by Joan Chissell and the Chandos recording is vivid and faithful. But no one can say that this playing is cool and uninvolved.

Piano trio No. 1 in D min., Op. 63.
**(*) CRD CRD 3433; *CRDC 4133* [id.]. Israel Piano Trio – BRAHMS: *Piano trio No. 2.* **(*)

The Israel Piano Trio give a powerfully projected account of the *D minor Trio*; the pianist is at times rather carried away, as if he were playing a Brahms concerto. The Scherzo is too emphatically – indeed, almost brutally – articulated. There are, however, some sensitive and intelligent touches, and the recording is first class.

Funf Stücke (5 Pieces) im Volkston (for cello and piano).
(M) *** Decca 417 833-2 [id.]. Rostropovich, Britten – SCHUBERT: *Sonata* **(*); DEBUSSY: *Sonata.* ***

Though simpler than the Debussy *Sonata* with which it is coupled, this is just as elusive a work; but in the hands of masters these *Five Pieces in folk style* have a rare charm, particularly the last, with its irregular rhythm. Excellent recording.

String quartets Nos. 1–3.
**(*) DG Dig. 423 670-2 (3). Melos Qt – BRAHMS: *String quartets 1–3* **(*).

The Melos performances are far from negligible and are generally well shaped. However, for all their ardour they do not seem completely at one with Schumann's world: there is a certain want of tenderness and introspection. Perhaps the brightly lit and forward recording militates against them, and at present they come linked only with Brahms.

String quartets Nos. 1 in A min.; 2 in F, Op. 41/1–2.
*** CRD CRD 3333; *CRDC 4033* [id.]. Alberni Qt.

The *String quartets* are not Schumann at his greatest, but they still offer many rewards. These well-recorded and sympathetic performances by the Alberni Quartet have plenty of finesse and charm and are guided throughout by sound musical instinct. Recommended.

Violin sonatas Nos. 1 in A min., Op. 105; 2 in D min., Op. 121.
*** DG Dig. 419 235-2 [id.]. Gidon Kremer, Martha Argerich.

The *Violin sonatas* both date from 1851 and are 'an oasis of freshness' in his last creative period. Kremer and Argerich are splendidly reflective and mercurial by turn and have the benefit of an excellent recording.

PIANO MUSIC

Albumblätter, Op. 99; Arabeske, Op. 18; Études symphoniques, Op. 13.
(BB) *** Naxos Dig. 8.550144 [id.]. Stefan Vladar.

The young Austrian pianist, Stefan Vladar, is recorded in the cramped acoustic of the Tonstudio van Geest in Heidelberg; it says much for his artistry that, except at climaxes, he almost (but not completely) makes one forget this unsuitable venue. He intersperses the additional studies that Schumann published as an appendix into the *Études symphoniques*. His account is quite simply superb in every respect and deserves recording of comparable excellence. There are some tired notes on the instrument itself during the course of the music-making. His account of the *Albumblätter* is hardly less masterly. Artistically this rates three stars, with the compelling quality of the playing transcending the sonic limitations of the recording.

Arabesque in C, Op. 18; Blumenstück, Op. 19; Carnaval, Op. 9; Davidsbündlertänze, Op. 6; Fantasia in C, Op. 17; 8 Fantasiestücke, Op. 12; 3 Fantasiestücke, Op. 111; Faschingsschwank aus Wien, Op. 26; Humoresque in B flat, Op. 20; Kinderszenen, Op. 15; 4 Nachtstücke, Op. 23; Novelettes, Op. 21; Papillons, Op. 2; 3 Romances, Op. 28; Piano sonatas Nos. 1 in F sharp min., Op. 11; 2 in G min., Op. 22; Waldszenen, Op. 82.
(M) **(*) Ph. 402 308-2 (7) [id.]. Claudio Arrau.

Philips's handsomely packaged commemorative collection of Claudio Arrau's recordings of Schumann has a great deal to commend it. The playing has warmth, poise and the distinctive, aristocratic finesse that graced everything this artist touched. Arrau has the measure of Schumann's impulsive temperament and is almost always perfectly attuned to his sensibility. There is the cultured, full-bodied depth and beauty of sonority one expects from this great artist as well as the impeccable control of colour. Not all the rubati ring true and there are moments that seem a little self-conscious. But there is a very great deal to admire in this compilation, and few collectors will be greatly disappointed.

Arabeske in C, Op. 18; Études symphoniques, Op. 13.
*** DG Dig. 410 916-2 [id.]. Maurizio Pollini.

Pollini's account has a symphonic gravitas and concentration: it also has the benefit of excellent recorded sound. Pollini includes the five additional variations that Schumann omitted from both the editions published during his lifetime, placing them as a group between the fifth and sixth variations.

Arabeske, Op. 18; Études symphoniques, Op. 13; Papillons, Op. 2.
*** Decca Dig. 414 474-2 [id.]. Vladimir Ashkenazy.

Impressive playing, and well recorded too – yet Ashkenazy's *Études symphoniques* have a breadth and splendour that are not entirely in tune with Schumann's sensibility. The *Arabeske* and *Papillons*, however, must be numbered among Ashkenazy's most impressive contributions to this repertoire.

Carnaval; Faschingsschwank aus Wien, Op. 26; Kinderszenen, Op. 15.
(B) *** DG 431 167-2; *431 167-4*. Daniel Barenboim.

Barenboim's 1979 reading of *Carnaval* is one of his finest recording achievements in his role as pianist rather than as conductor. His lively imagination lights on the fantasy in this quirkily spontaneous sequence of pieces and makes them sparkle anew. It is as if he were in the process of improvising the music, yet his liberties of expression are never too great. He may allow himself free rubato in such a piece as *Valse noble*, but the result remains noble, not sentimental. The 'Masked ball' piece (*Carnival jest from Vienna*) is more problematic, but the challenge inspires Barenboim, and here too he is at his most imaginative and persuasive, bringing out the warmth and tenderness as well as the brilliance. The recital opens with a tender and charismatic reading of *Kinderszenen*, sensitive yet unmannered, and with the gentle opening bringing the lightest touch and the closing *Der Dichter sprich* wonderfully serene. The 1979 recording is bold and truthful, but the CD transfer has lost a little of the fullness in the bass.

5 Études, Op. posth.; Études symphoniques, Op. 13; Papillons, Op. 2.
**(*) Sony CD 76635 [MK 34539]. Murray Perahia.

Murray Perahia has a special feeling for the *Symphonic studies* and he makes every expressive point in the most natural and unfussy way. He plays the additional five studies, which Schumann omitted from the published score, as an addendum. The *Papillons* are unlikely to be surpassed. The engineers give Perahia too close a balance to be ideal; the sound is of acceptable quality, but fortissimos are rather clattery.

Études symphoniques.
*** Ph. Dig. 432 093-2; *432 093-4* [id.]. Alfred Brendel – BEETHOVEN: *Variations.* ***

Brendel's new account of the *Études symphoniques* is one of his best records for a long time. Even those who find his recent playing, particularly in Mozart sonatas, a shade too self-conscious can put any anxieties to rest. This is ardent, beautifully controlled playing which is also given first-class sound.

Fantasia in C, Op. 17.
*** Sony Dig. MK 42124 [id.]. Murray Perahia – SCHUBERT: *Wanderer fantasia.* ***

Murray Perahia's account of the *C major Fantasy*, perhaps the most powerful and deeply felt of all Schumann's piano works, has few peers. It is a performance of vision and breadth, immaculate in its attention to detail and refinement of nuance. The recording is good, even if it does not wholly convey the fullest range of sonority and dynamics.

Fantasia in C, Op. 17; Fantasiestücke, Op. 12.
*** Ph. Dig. 411 049-2 [id.]. Alfred Brendel.

As the very opening of the *Fantasiestücke* demonstrates, this is magically spontaneous playing, full of imaginative touches of colour, strong as well as poetic. The actual sound is rather forward, but it serves Brendel well and truthfully conveys the depth of timbre.

Fantasia in C, Op. 17; Kreisleriana, Op. 16.
*** BMG/RCA RD 86258 [RCA 6258-2-RC]. Artur Rubinstein.

Rubinstein's account of the *Fantasia in C* is wonderfully subtle in its control of tempo and colour, and the poetry of the outer sections is quite magical. In spite of the close balance, Rubinstein achieves exquisite gradations of tone; the recording, made in 1965, is among the best he received during this period. *Kreisleriana* is hardly less compelling, with the great pianist at his most aristocratic, although the impetuous opening is rather shallowly recorded.

Fantasia in C, Op. 17; Piano sonata No. 1 in F sharp min., Op. 11.
*** DG 423 134-2 [id.]. Maurizio Pollini.

This is among the most distinguished Schumann records in the catalogue. Pollini's playing throughout has a command and authority on the one hand and deep poetic feeling on the other that hold the listener spellbound. The recording is good but not outstanding – it is rather hard in its digitally remastered form.

Humoreske in B flat, Op. 20.
(BB) **(*) Naxos Dig. 8.550469 [id.]. Wolf Harden – REGER: *Variations.* **(*)

Wolf Harden's performance of the Schumann *Humoreske* is highly imaginative, idiomatic and full of sensitive touches. The actual sound is also vastly superior to many of the other piano recordings emanating from this source. There is plenty of air round the aural image.

Kinderszenen, Op. 15; Sonata No. 1 in F sharp min., Op. 11; Waldszenen, Op. 82.
*** Decca Dig. 421 290-2 [id.]. Vladimir Ashkenazy.

Ashkenazy's account of the *F sharp minor Sonata* is held on a less taut rein than Pollini's. If, in purely pianistic terms, Ashkenazy may not be so totally commanding or authoritative, nevertheless he still has his finger(s) on the pulse of Schumann's inspiration. The playing is very natural and all the more impressive for that. He proves a sound guide in the *Waldszenen*, and his *Kinderszenen* is one of the most appealing in the catalogue, again with a naturalness and directness that are attractive. The Decca recording is excellent, though the balance is closer in the *Sonata*.

Kreisleriana.
** DG Dig. 431 972-2 [id.]. Nicolas Economou – MUSSORGSKY: *Pictures at an exhibition.* **

Kreisleriana, Op. 16; Novelette, Op. 21/8; Piano sonata No. 2 in G min., Op. 22.
**(*) Decca Dig. 425 940-2 [id.]. Vladimir Ashkenazy.

Vladimir Ashkenazy turns in a very fervent account of *Kreisleriana*, which is probably the best thing on this CD. He conveys both the spontaneity and impulsiveness of this music to great effect, and those who are collecting his Schumann cycle can aquire this with some confidence. In the *G minor Sonata, Op. 22* he is also highly charged, though he does not plumb its poetic depths and richness of fantasy to the same extent as did Perahia. Decca's sound, however, is of very good quality.

Economou's *Kreisleriana* comes in harness with a not wholly convincing reading of the Mussorgsky *Pictures*, but even if it were more logically coupled from a collector's viewpoint, it still has some way to go before competing with some of the outstanding performances in the catalogue. He is not lacking in poetic feeling and certainly not in technical address but it is difficult to think of any reason for preferring it to many of its rivals.

Piano sonata No. 2 in G min., Op. 22.
*** Sony Dig. MK 44569 [id.]. Murray Perahia – SCHUBERT: *Piano sonata No. 20.* ***

Perahia's account of the Schumann *G minor Sonata* is fresh, ardent and vital; every phrase is beautifully moulded yet somehow seems spontaneous in feeling – and spontaneity was the essence of Schumann's youthful genius. As always, Perahia's is the art that conceals art, and it is only at the very end that one realizes what total concentration he brings to this (and what concentration it demands). The recording places the listener fairly near the piano but is eminently truthful.

VOCAL MUSIC

Lieder from *Album für die Jugend, Op. 79; Gedichte der Königen Maria Stuart, Op. 135; Myrthen Lieder, Op. 25:* excerpts. *Abends am Strand; Die Kartenlegerin; Ständchen; Stille Tränen; Veratine Liebe.*
*** CRD CRD 3401 [id.]. Sarah Walker, Roger Vignoles.

Sarah Walker's 1982 Schumann collection is most cherishable, notably the five Mary Stuart songs which, in their brooding darkness, are among Schumann's most memorable. The voice is a little weighty for some of the lighter songs from the *Myrthe* collection but, with superb accompaniment and splendid recording, this is an outstanding issue.

Dichterliebe, Op. 48.
(M) *** DG 429 933-2 [id.]. Fritz Wunderlich, Hubert Giesen – BEETHOVEN: *Lieder* **(*); SCHUBERT: *Lieder.* ***

Wunderlich, had he lived, would no doubt have surpassed this early recording of a favourite Schumann song-cycle but, even with an often unimaginative accompanist, his freshness here is most endearing, irresistible with so golden a voice.

Dichterliebe, Op. 48; Liederkreis, Op. 39.
*** Ph. Dig. 416 352-2 [id.]. Dietrich Fischer-Dieskau, Alfred Brendel.
*** EMI CDC7 47397-2 [id.]. Olaf Bär, Geoffrey Parsons.

More than in his previous versions of Schumann's *Dichterliebe*, Fischer-Dieskau's latest one, done in inspired collaboration with Alfred Brendel, brings an angry, inconsolable reading, reflecting the absence of fulfilment in the poet's love – though Fischer-Dieskau's voice has more grit in it than before. The Op. 39 *Liederkreis* also brings inspired, spontaneous-sounding performances, with the voice here notably fresher.

Olaf Bär's performances are finely detailed and full of insight, but relatively reticent in expressive style. These are not such strongly characterized readings as those of Fischer-Dieskau; but in their fresher, more youthful manner they are outstandingly successful. Excellent recording on CD.

Dichterliebe (song-cycle), *Op. 48; Liederkreis* (song-cycle), *Op. 39; Myrthen Lieder, Op. 25.*
*** DG 415 190-2 [id.]. Dietrich Fischer-Dieskau, Christoph Eschenbach.

An outstandingly fine *Dichterliebe* plus the magnificent Op. 39 *Liederkreis*, made the more attractive on CD by the generous addition of seven of the *Myrthen* songs. Though a thoughtfully individual artist in his own right, Eschenbach here provides consistently sympathetic support for the singer. He is imaginative on detail without ever intruding distractingly. Very good sound for the period.

Frauenliebe und Leben (song-cycle), *Op. 42.*
❀ (M) *** Saga SCD 9001 [id.]. Dame Janet Baker, Martin Isepp (with Lieder recital ***).

Janet Baker's range of expression in her earlier, Saga recording of the Schumann cycle runs the whole gamut from a joyful golden tone-colour in the exhilaration of *Ich kann's nicht fassen* through an ecstatic half-tone in *Süsser Freund* (the fulfilment of the line *Du geliebter Mann* wonderfully conveyed) to the dead, vibrato-less tone of agony at the bereavement in the final song. Martin Isepp proves a highly sensitive and supportive partner, and the recording balance – originally curiously artificial – has been immeasurably improved by the CD transfer.

Das Paradies und das Peri, Op. 50 (oratorio: complete).
**(*) Erato/Warner Dig. 2292 45456-2 (2). Edith Wiens, Sylvia Herman, Ann Gjevang, Robert Gambill, Christophe Prégardien, SRO Ch. & O, Armin Jordan.

Schumann described this oratorio as 'my greatest and, I hope, my best work'. Though in the modern repertory it has almost sunk without trace, it is an important pioneering venture: as the first fully romantic oratorio using a secular text, it marked a breakthrough. Based on a quest poem by Thomas Moore, it centres on the heroine's search for gifts as a passport to heaven. From this fine recording one can understand both why the composer was so excited and why the piece has failed to gain a foothold. This was the work which rounded off Schumann's extraordinary period of creative activity prompted by his marriage to Clara, starting with the miraculous 'Year of Song', 1840. The richness and the fluency of the writing carry you on with no let-up, strongly argued, but the melodic invention is less striking than in Schumann's songs, with themes plain rather than memorable. Armin Jordan draws first-rate singing and playing from his Suisse Romande forces, helped by warmly atmospheric recording. The soloists are reliable, but not very distinctive – Edith Wiens, Ann Gjevang, Robert Gambill and Christophe Prégardien.

Requiem in D flat, Op. 148; Requiem für Mignon, Op. 98b.
*** EMI Dig. CDC7 49164-2. Donath, Lindner, Andonian, Soffel, Georg, Gedda, Fischer-Dieskau, Düsseldorf Musical Soc. Ch., Düsseldorf SO, Klee.

Like Mozart, Schumann was unable to shake off the conviction that the *Requiem* was for himself. The opening *Requiem aeternam* is affecting and dignified, and the final *Benedictus* has a haunting eloquence. Bernhard Klee extracts a very sympathetic response from his distinguished team of soloists and the fine Düsseldorf chorus and orchestra. They also give an attentive and committed account of the 1849 *Requiem for Mignon*, Op. 98b. The EMI recording is natural and well balanced.

Scenes from Goethe's Faust.
❀ (M) *** Decca 425 705-2 (2). Harwood, Pears, Shirley-Quirk, Fischer-Dieskau, Vyvyan, Palmer, Aldeburgh Fest. Singers, ECO, Britten.

Britten made this superb recording of a major Schumann work, long neglected, in 1973, soon after a live performance at the Aldeburgh Festival. Though the reasons for neglect remain apparent – this episodic sequence of scenes is neither opera nor cantata – the power and imagination of much of the music, not least the delightful garden scene and the energetic setting of the final part, are immensely satisfying. Britten inspired his orchestra and his fine cast of singers to vivid performances, which are outstandingly recorded against the warm Maltings acoustic. The CD mastering has effectively retained the ambience yet added to the projection of both solo voices and chorus. This is magnificent music, and readers are urged to explore it – the rewards are considerable.

Schütz, Heinrich (1585–1672)

Christmas oratorio (Weinachtshistorie).
*** EMI Dig. CDC7 47633-2 [id.]. Kirkby, Rogers, Thomas, Taverner Cons., Taverner Ch., Taverner Players, Parrott – PRAETORIUS: *Christmas motets.* ***

There is no sense of austerity here, merely a sense of purity, with the atmosphere of the music beautifully captured by these forces under Andrew Parrott. One is soon gripped by the narrative and by the beauty and simplicity of the line. Apart from a rather nasal edge on the violin tone, it is difficult to fault either this moving performance or the well-balanced and refined recording.

(i) *Christmas oratorio (Historia der Geburt Jesu Christi);* (ii) *Deutsche Magnificat;* Motets for double choir: *Ach, Herr, straf mich nicht* (Psalm 6); *Cantate Domino* (Psalm 96); *Herr unser Herrscher* (Psalm 8); *Ich freu mich des* (Psalm 122); *Unser Herr Jesus; Wie lieblich* (Psalm 84).
(M) **(*) Decca 430 632-2; *430 632-4* [id.]. (i) Partridge, soloists, Schütz Ch., Instrumental Ens., Philip Jones Brass Ens.; (ii) Schütz Ch., Symphoniae Sacrae Chamber Ens.; Norrington.

Norrington's Argo recording of the *Christmas oratorio* was made before he espoused the cause of original instruments. It offers some extremely fine singing from Ian Partridge as the Evangelist, while the Heinrich Schütz Choir phrases with great feeling and subtlety; indeed, some may feel that their singing is a little too self-consciously beautiful for music that is so pure in style. The instrumental accompaniment on modern instruments may also strike some listeners as too much of a good thing: the brass has more than a suspicion of heaviness at times and textures are ample. For all that, however, this version offers much to admire, and the 1970 recording has great detail and sonority. A similar comment might be made about the Motets: again, the choral singing is impressively firm and undoubtedly moving, and here the brass, though sonorous, has more edge, while the recording does full justice to the antiphonal effects. The *Deutsche Magnificat* is given with admirable authority, and this splendid example of Schütz's last years (he was eighty-five when he wrote it) is one of the best things in a very generous (75 minutes) and rewarding collection.

Christmas oratorio; The Resurrection (Historia der Auferstehung Jesus Christi).
*** Sony Dig. SK 45943 [id.]. Prégardien, Van der Sluis, Egeler, Kendall, Müller, Robson, Spägele, Stuttgart Chamber Ch., Musica Fiata Köln, Stuttgart Bar. O, Bernius.

The latest account of the *Weinachtshistorie* enjoys the advantage of another Schütz coupling, and a very good one too: the *Historia der Auferstehung Jesus Christi.* This is more strongly projected and dramatic than the more inward and reposeful performance by René Jacobs and the Concerto Vocale. Christoph Prégardien is an excellent Evangelist and Frieder Bernius has the advantage of some first-rate soloists in Mieke van der Sluis, Andrea Egeler and Mona Spägele. Christoph Robson's Jesus is also moving. Bernius maintains an excellent sense of pace, and both the singers and the instrumentalists are excellently balanced and recorded. The *Weinachtshistorie* is equally well projected.

Italian Madrigals (complete).
(B) *** HM HMA 901162; *HMA 431162* [id.]. Concerto Vocale, René Jacobs.
(M) *** HM/BMG Dig. GD 77118 [77118-2-RG]. Consort of Musicke, Rooley.

Schütz's first and only *Book of Italian Madrigals* reflects his encounter with the music of Giovanni Gabrieli and Monteverdi. Composed when he was in his mid-twenties, these madrigals do not represent the mature Schütz but are rather sophisticated examples of the genre modelled on Gabrieli. The Concerto Vocale, led by the counter-tenor, René Jacobs, employ a theorbo which provides added variety of colour, and at times they offer great expressive and tonal range. They omit the very last of the madrigals, the eight-part *Vasto mar.*

Anthony Rooley and the Consort of Musicke are perhaps less varied (no instruments are used) but style and intonation are impeccable. The 1985 digital recording has admirable clarity though there are occasionally discrepancies of pitch between some madrigals; the fifth, for example, *Cos mori debbio* sounds slightly flatter than its predecessor, *Alma affita che fai.*

Musicalische Exequien. Motets: *Auf dem Gebirge; Freue dich des Weibes Jugend; Ist nicht Ephraim mein teurer Sohn; Saul, Saul, was verfolgst du mich.*
*** DG Dig. 423 405-2 [id.]. Monteverdi Ch., E. Bar. Soloists, His Majesties Sagbutts & Cornetts, Gardiner.

Schütz's *Musical Exequien* contains music that is amazing for its period (the first half of the sixteenth century). The Monteverdi Choir responds with fiery intensity, making light of the complex eight-part writing in the second of the three *Exequies.* Four more superb motets by Schütz make an ideal coupling, with first-rate recorded sound.

The Resurrection; Meine Seele erhebt den Herren.
**(*) HM Dig. HMC 901311; *HMC 401311* [id.]. Concerto Vocale, René Jacobs.

René Jacobs's account of Schütz's *Historia der Auferstehung Jesus Christi* with the Concerto Vocale is a performance of great accomplishment and taste, and quite beautifully recorded. This performance still gives great pleasure, as does the lively account of *Meine Seele erhebt den Herren* from the second Book of the *Symphoniae sacrae* (1647). Recommended but not in preference to the excellent new account under Frieder Bernius.

Scriabin, Alexander (1872–1915)

(i) *Piano concerto in F sharp min., Op. 20;* (ii) *Poème de l'extase, Op. 54;* (i) *Prometheus – The poem of fire, Op. 60.*
*** Decca 417 252-2 [id.]. (i) Ashkenazy, LPO; (ii) Cleveland O; Maazel.

Ashkenazy plays the *Piano concerto* with great feeling and authority, and the Decca recording has both clarity and luminosity. Moreover Maazel accompanies most sympathetically throughout. *Prometheus* too, powerfully atmospheric and curiously hypnotic, is given a thoroughly poetic and committed reading and Ashkenazy copes with the virtuoso obbligato part with predictable distinction. Given such outstanding recording and performance, this makes a splendid starting point for any Scriabin collection. Decca have added Maazel's 1979 Cleveland recording of *Le Poème de l'extase.* This is a shade too efficient to be really convincing. The playing is often brilliant and the recording is very clear but the trumpets are rather forced and strident. However, it can be regarded as a bonus for the other two works.

(i) *Piano concerto; Symphony No. 3 in C min. (Le divin poème).*
*(**) BIS Dig. CD 475 [id.]. (i) Roland Pöntinen, Stockholm PO, Leif Segerstam.

Roland Pöntinen has a particularly strong affinity for Scriabin, and his playing here in the *Piano concerto* strikes the right blend of musing intimacy and display. He is given sensitive support from Leif Segerstam and the Stockholm Philharmonic. Perhaps Segerstam overdoes things in the opening of the second movement, where the string pianissimos are just a little self-conscious, but both here and in the *Third Symphony* he shows great finesse in matters of phrasing and tonal colour. Unfortunately these players are badly handicapped by the excessive reverberation of the hall; this muddies the texture and limits the pleasure these performances should give.

Symphonies Nos. 1–3; Poème de l'extase; (i) *Prometheus.*
*** EMI CDS7 54251-2 (3) [id.]. Toczyska, Myers, Westminster Ch. (in *No. 1*), Phd. O, Muti, (i) with Alexeev.

Muti's complete set of the Scriabin *Symphonies* can be recommended almost without reservation. True, in No. 3 the recording could be more refined, but overall the sound is as vivid and richly coloured as the performances. With the two additional symphonic poems (*Le poème de l'extase* white-hot with passionate intensity, yet masterfully controlled) now added, in the place of the original, less appropriate Tchaikovsky couplings, this is an impressive achievement.

Symphony No. 1 in E, Op. 26.
*** Olympia Dig. OCD 159 [id.]. Gorokhovskaya, Pluzhnikov, Glinka State Ac. Ch. of Leningrad, USSR RSO, Fedoseyev.

The new digital recording from the Soviet Union is relaxed and unforced; the orchestral playing is excellent, though the brass are not as refined as those of the Philadelphia; and the two soloists, Yevgenia Gorokhovskaya and Konstantin Pluzhnikov, are every bit as fine as their EMI rivals, Stefania Toczyska and Michael Myers. This can be recommended with confidence, and it has a slight price advantage.

Symphony No. 2 in C min., Op. 29.
*** Chan. Dig. CHAN 8462; *ABTD 1176* [id.]. SNO, Järvi.

Plenty of atmosphere here in Järvi's performance and a splendid orchestral response from his Scottish players. Although it is less amorphous than its predecessor, the *Symphony* needs the most fervent advocacy if the listener is to be persuaded. This splendid account from Järvi, with its richly detailed Chandos recording, can be recommended strongly.

Symphony No. 3 in C min. (Le divin poème), Op. 43.
*** Chan. Dig. CHAN 8898; *ABTD 1509* [id.]. Danish Nat. RSO, Järvi – ARENSKY: *Silhouettes.* ***
*** Etcetera KTC 1027 [id.]. Concg. O, Kondrashin.

Symphony No. 3 (Le divin poème); Le Poème de l'extase, Op. 54.
**(*) DG Dig. 427 324-2 [id.]. NYPO, Sinopoli.

Symphony No. 3 (Le divin poème); Le Poeme de l'extase, Op. 54; Rêverie, Op. 24.
*** Decca Dig. 430 843-2 [id.]. Berlin RSO, Ashkenazy.

Scriabin's mammoth *Third Symphony* calls for vast forces, but there is no doubt that it is original, both in layout and in substance. An excellent performance of this somewhat overblown score comes from Neeme Järvi and the Danish Radio Orchestra. There is something refreshingly unforced and natural about Järvi's version which puts this score in a far better light than those conductors who play it for all they are worth. The performance is carefully prepared and can hold its own among the best now on offer. One of the special attractions of the Chandos issue is its rather endearing coupling, Arensky's *Silhouettes*, which are not otherwise available.

Vladimir Ashkenazy has the advantage of the more logical coupling, an all-Scriabin programme, and good engineering from the Decca team. The Berlin Radio forces are very good (the wind intonation is occasionally impure) and there is a highly charged feel to the performances, particularly that of *Le Poème de l'extase*. Ashkenazy's account is not wholly free from the odd exaggeration – but then Scriabin is not a composer who benefits from understatement.

Kondrashin and the Concertgebouw Orchestra recorded the *Third Symphony* at a public concert in 1976, and the performance has a special authority and intensity, and is well recorded.

Sinopoli's coupling offers another bloom from the hothouse in the form of the *Poème de l'extase*. He has a good feeling for the atmosphere of the *Third Symphony* and draws responsive playing from the New York Philharmonic. However, the recording does not open out too well in climaxes. The *Poème de l'extase* is sensitively shaped and is splendidly performed. Sinopoli's version is certainly not to be dismissed, and those tempted by the coupling may feel these reservations of less importance.

Études, Op. 8/7 & 12; Op. 42/5. Preludes, Op. 11/1, 3, 9, 10, 13, 14, 16; Op. 13/6; Op. 15/2; Op. 16/1 & 4; Op. 27/1; Op. 48/3; Op. 51/2; Op. 59/2; Op. 67/1. Sonatas Nos. 3, Op. 23; 5, Op. 53.
(M) (***) BMG/RCA mono/stereo GD 86215 [6215-2-RC]. Vladimir Horowitz.

The RCA engineers have done wonders to these recordings from the 1950s though there is naturally a limit to what they can accomplish, and some of the original shallowness and clatter remains. The *Preludes* and the legendary account of the *Third Sonata* come from 1956 and give the impression of greater range and firmer focus than in their last vinyl incarnation. The *Fifth* is much later, coming from the mid-1970s, and has more bloom. The performances are obviously three star and form an essential part of any good Horowitz collection.

Preludes, Op. 11, Nos. 2, 4–6, 8–14, 16, 18, 20, 22 & 24.
(M) *** EMI Dig. CDD7 64086-2 [id.]. Andrei Gavrilov – RACHMANINOV: *Élégie* etc. ***

Gavrilov's selection from Opus 11 is arbitrary. At times his approach is impetuous, and dynamics can be exaggerated, but playing of this order is still pretty remarkable. The balance is not too close, yet the CD brings a tangible presence and the piano timbre is well caught.

Piano sonatas Nos. 1–10.
(M) *** Decca 425 579-2 (2) [id.]. Vladimir Ashkenazy.

Piano sonatas Nos. 1–10; Piano sonata in E flat min. (1887–9); Sonata fantaisie in G sharp min.
(M) **(*) DG 431 747-2 (3). Roberto Szidon.

The Scriabin *Piano sonatas* encompass two decades, the first dating from 1892 when he was twenty, while the last five were composed in quick succession from 1911 to 1913. It is good to have all ten in Vladimir Ashkenazy's commanding and authoritative performances, recorded between 1972 and 1984, all on two medium-priced discs. Ashkenazy is clearly attuned to this repertoire, though he is at his finest in the earlier sonatas. The last three are given with brilliance and vision, and there is no lack of awareness of the demonic side of Scriabin's musical personality. In Nos. 9 and 10 Horowitz had more abandon and intensity without losing any of his imperious control. However, these are fine performances and are well recorded.

Roberto Szidon recorded all ten sonatas as well as the two early sonatas and the Op. 28 *Fantasy* in 1971, and this DG reissue offers the whole set. Szidon seems especially at home in the later works. His version of the *Black Mass sonata* (No. 9) fares best and conveys real excitement. At medium price this is an attractive reissue and can be considered alongside Ashkenazy's series. The DG recording is good but not ideal and the tone tends to harden at climaxes.

Piano sonata No. 2 in G sharp min. (Sonata-Fantaisie), Op. 19.
** DG Dig. 429 391-2; *429 391-4* [id.]. Ivo Pogorelich – LISZT: *Sonata.*

Pogorelich's account of the *G sharp minor Sonata-Fantaisie, Op. 19* comes as a make-weight to the Liszt *Sonata* making a very scantily filled CD (48 minutes) which at full price is scarcely competitive. Pogorelich is ideal in this repertoire, having all the refinement of keyboard colour one could ask for, and much of the self-aware quality that Scriabin himself possessed. This is playing of quality let down by an ill-ventilated and unacceptably close balance.

Piano sonata No. 3 in F sharp min., Op. 23; 2 Poems, Op. 32; Vers la flamme, Op. 72.
**(*) Kingdom Dig. KCLCD 2001; *CKCL 2001.* Gordon Fergus-Thompson – BALAKIREV: *Piano sonata.* **(*)

Gordon Fergus-Thompson gives a splendid account of Scriabin's overheated *F sharp minor Sonata* and sensitive, atmospheric performances of the other pieces here. A reverberant but good recording, but the piano does not always sound perfectly fresh.

Piano sonatas Nos. 4, Op. 30; 5, Op. 53; 9 (Black Mass), Op. 68; 10, Op. 70. Étude in C sharp min., Op. 2/1; 8 Études, Op. 42.
**(*) ASV Dig. CDDCA 776; *ZCDCA 776* [id.]. Gordon Fergus-Thomson.

This is the first in an ASV project to record all of Scriabin's piano music with Gordon Fergus-Thomson. All the performances here recorded show a high level of accomplishment and finesse, and the ASV engineers have produced a very decent sound. Fergus-Thomson is thoroughly inside this idiom. At the same time it must be conceded that his performances are not as manic or high-voltage as those of Richter and Horowitz and in the cruelly competitive world of the recorded music would not be a first choice. Nevertheless there is much musical nourishment here to satisfy the collector.

Piano sonatas Nos. 8, Op. 66; 9, Op. 68; 10, Op. 70; 2 Danses, Op. 73; 2 Poèmes, Op. 69; 2 Poèmes, Op. 71; 2 Preludes, Op. 67; 5 Preludes, Op. 74; Vers la flamme, Op. 72.
*(**) Altarus Dig. AIR-CD 9020 [id.]. Donna Amato.

Donna Amato has already given us an impressive record of the *Piano sonata* of Balakirev (coupled with Dutilleux). This new CD reinforces her credentials as an authoritative interpreter of the Russian repertoire. She seems wholly attuned to Scriabin's sensibility and plays all his late music (Opp. 66–74), including the last three *Sonatas*, to the manner born. Scriabin's world is claustrophobic – but unfortunately so is the recording, which sounds as if it was made in a small acoustic environment but with some echo added. (It may well have been a large hall with the instrument hemmed in by screens.) The sound-quality diminishes the pleasure this CD gives but not of course Amato's artistry. There are excellent notes but, unusually these days, no timings of individual pieces or even of complete works.

Seiber, Matyas (1905–60)

Clarinet concertino.
*** Hyp. Dig. CDA 66215; *KA 66215* [id.]. Thea King, ECO, Litton – BLAKE: *Concerto;* LUTOSLAWSKI: *Dance preludes.* ***

Matyas Seiber's highly engaging *Concertino* was sketched during a train journey (in 1926, before the days of seamless rails) and certainly the opening *Toccata* has the jumpy, rhythmic feeling of railway line joints and points. Yet the haunting slow movement has a touch of the ethereal, while the Scherzo has a witty jazz element. Thea King has the measure of the piece; she is accompanied well by Litton, and very well recorded. Recommended.

Servais, Adrien-François (1807–66)

Caprice sur des motifs de l'opéra, Le Comte Ory; Caprices, Op. 11/2 & 4; Grand duo de concert sur deux airs nationaux anglais; Grand fantaisie, Op. 20; Souvenir de Bade; Souvenir de Spa, Op. 2.
*** HM/BMG Dig. GD 77108; [77108-2-RG]. Bylsma, Smithsonian Chamber Players.

Servais was a virtuoso who was hailed by Berlioz as 'the Paganini of the cello'. He composed two concertos and a number of *Souvenirs* and *Caprices*, which are presented here on Servais' own instrument, a Stradivarius from 1701. His music is entertaining stuff, particularly the *Grand duo de concert sur deux airs nationaux anglais*, written in collaboration with his colleague, Hubert Léonard. Somewhat unexpectly the second '*air anglais*' turns out to be *Yankee doodle dandy*! The Servais cello is currently in use at the Smithsonian Institute, and so it is appropriate that six expert string-players of the Smithsonian group, plus harmonium, perform this music for us, providing a delightful entertainment – best not heard all at once, for the music is of spectacular triviality. But it is great fun, and very well recorded too.

Sessions, Roger (born 1896)

Concerto for orchestra.

*** Hyp. Dig. CDA 66050; *KA 66050* [id.]. Boston SO, Ozawa – PANUFNIK: *Symphony No. 8.* ***

Sessions's *Concerto for orchestra* finds him at his thorniest and most uncompromising, with lyricism limited to fleeting fragments of melody; but the tapestry of sound presents its own logic with its contrasts of mood – the playful opening leading one on finally to a valedictory close – sharply defined. Ozawa makes a powerful advocate, helped by superb playing from the Boston orchestra.

Symphony No. 4; Symphony No. 5; Rhapsody for orchestra.

*** New World Dig. NWCD 345 [id.]. Columbus SO, Badea.

Roger Sessions shares with Walter Piston, his tonal contemporary (who also composed eight symphonies), a highly developed sense of structure and an integrity that remained unshaken by changes of fashion. His musical language is dense and his logic is easier to sense than to follow. The performances by the Columbus Symphony Orchestra under Christian Badea appear well prepared, and there is no doubt as to their commitment and expertise. The sound ideally needs a larger acoustic, but every strand in the texture is well placed and there is no feeling of discomfort.

Shchedrin, Rodion (born 1933)

The Frescoes of Dionysius.

** Olympia Dig. OCD 108 [id.]. Bolshoi Theatre Soloists' Ens., Lazarev – BIZET/SHCHEDRIN: *Carmen ballet.* **(*)

A quite effective miniature, fairly static in feeling, owing something to minimalism in structure, inspired by the frescos of Ferapontov Monastery, near Kirilov. It is well played and recorded.

Sheppard, John (*c.* 1515–*c.* 1559)

Christe Redemptor omnium; In manus tuas; Media vita; Reges Tharsis; Sacris solemniis; Verbum caro.

*** Gimell Dig. CDGIM 016; *1585T-16* [id.]. Tallis Scholars, Peter Phillips.

Little is known about John Sheppard save for the bare fact that he was at Magdalen College, Oxford (1543–8), and at the Chapel Royal from 1552 onwards. All the music here is based on chant, and much of it is for the six-part choir of treble, mean (or middle part), two countertenors, tenor and bass, which produces a particularly striking sonority. The *Media vita* ('In the midst of life we are in death') is a piece of astonishing beauty, and it is sung with remarkable purity of tone by the Tallis Scholars under Peter Phillips. There are false relations as expressive as any in his Tudor contemporaries. Glorious and little-known music: the recording could hardly be improved on.

Gaude virgo Christiphera; In manus tuas; Libera nos, salva 1–2; Reges Tharsis.

*** Proudsound Dig. PROUCD 126; *PROU 126* [id.]. Clerkes of Oxenford, David Wulstan – TYE: *Mass Euge bone.* ***

The Clerkes of Oxenford under David Wulstan produce a very different sonority from the

Tallis group, wonderfully blended and balanced, with a tonal sophistication that is remarkable. They overlap only minimally with the Gimell disc, so both can be recommended to the enthusiast. They are placed rather more distantly than the Tallis Scholars but are splendidly recorded in a spacious but not over-reverberant acoustic.

Motets: *Filiae Hierusalem venite; Haec dies; In manus tuas Domine I; In pacem in idipsum; Justi in perpetuum vivent; Lauden dicite Deo; Libera nos, salva nos I; Paschal Kyrie; Regis Tharsis et insulae; Spiritus sanctus procedens I; Verbo caro factum est.*
❀ *** Hyp. Dig. CDA 66259; *KA 66259* [id.]. The Sixteen, Christophers.

It was merely an accident of twentieth-century scholarship – and sudden lack of funds – that prevented the Tudor Music Edition from reaching the volume on Sheppard and with it a wider dissemination of his music. Here in eleven superb responsories The Sixteen consistently convey the rapturous beauty of Sheppard's writing, above all in ethereal passages in the highest register, very characteristic of him. Even there The Sixteen's sopranos seem quite unstressed by the tessitura. There are not many more beautiful records of Tudor polyphony than this.

Shostakovich, Dmitri (1906–75)

(i; ii; iii) *The Adventures of Korzinkina* (film music): *suite, Op. 59;* (iv; ii) *Alone* (film music): *suite, Op. 26;* (v) *La Comédie Humaine* (incidental music to Balzac), *Op. 37;* (i; ii) *Scherzos: in F sharp min., Op. 1; in E flat, Op. 7; Theme & variations in B flat, Op. 3;* (vi) *Spanish songs, Op. 100.*
**(*) Olympia OCD 194 [id.]. (i) USSR MoC SO, (ii) Rozhdestvensky; (iii) with Ch.; (iv) Soloists, Ens. of USSR Ac. SO; (v) Leningrad CO, Gurdzhi; (vi) Artur Eisen, A. Bogdanova.

None of the music on this record is familiar or without interest to admirers of this composer; indeed most of it appears for the first time. The first two pieces are wholly uncharacteristic. The Op. 7 *Scherzo* is more characteristic – there is a prominent part for the piano and there is already evidence of Shostakovich's special kind of wit. The *Spanish songs* come from 1956 and are more substantial; they are splendidly sung by Artur Eisen. The film scores are from the 1930s and uncover no masterpieces. Though the recordings were made during the 1980s and are not top-drawer, this disc is still well worth investigating.

The Age of gold: suite, *Op. 22.*
(M) *** Decca Dig. 430 727-2; *430 727-4* [id.]. LPO, Haitink – JANÁČEK: *Sinfonietta* etc. ***

The joky *Age of gold* suite makes an unexpected if attractive makeweight for the vibrant Mackerras Janáček performances. The performances combine wit and feeling and are brilliantly recorded.

Chamber symphony in C min. Op. 110a (arr. Barshai from *String quartet No. 8); Symphony for strings, Op. 118a* (arr. Barshai from *String quartet No. 10).*
*** DG Dig. 429 229-2. COE, Rudolf Barshai.

The *Chamber symphony* is an arrangement for full strings of the *Eighth Quartet*, and the *Symphony for strings* is a similar transcription of the *Tenth*. Both were made by Rudolf Barshai who, in a note on his long friendship with the composer, tells how these arrangements came to be made; and he directs them both with the authority of the composer and bears his imprimatur. The young players of the Chamber Orchestra of Europe excel themselves in the tonal beauty, refinement and responsiveness of their playing, here recorded for the first time in their new home, the smaller Philharmonie Hall in Berlin. But inevitably, with such a rich string-sound, some of the darkness of the music disappears: the chill of much of the writing in No. 8, inspired by memories of the war and the bombing of Dresden. In compensation, the weight of sound gives extra impact to such movements as the *Allegro molto* in Opus 110a. These are strong performances of real eloquence and power, which are excellently recorded. It is undoubtedly the best and most authoritative version of both scores now on the market and can be confidently recommended to those who prefer the dark, brooding transcriptions to the inward-looking originals.

Cello concerto No. 1 in E flat, Op. 107.
*** Sony Dig. MK 37840 [id.]. Yo-Yo Ma, Phd. O, Ormandy – KABALEVSKY: *Cello concerto No. 1.* ***

*** Chan. Dig. CHAN 8322 [id.]. Raphael Wallfisch, ECO, Geoffrey Simon – BARBER: *Cello concerto.* ***
(M) *** EMI CDM7 63020-2. Tortelier, Bournemouth SO, Berglund – WALTON: *Concerto.* ***

(i) *Cello concerto No. 1, Op. 107;* (ii) *Symphony No. 5.*
(M) *** Sony Dig. MYK 44903 [id.]. (i) Ma, Phd. O, Ormandy; (ii) NYPO, Bernstein.

Yo-Yo Ma on CBS brings an ardent musical imagination to the *First Cello concerto.* He plays with an intensity that compels the listener and the Philadelphia Orchestra give eloquent support. The CBS recording has ample presence and warmth, with the balance slightly favouring the soloist, but very well judged overall. This has now also been reissued at mid-price, generously coupled with Bernstein's exciting 1979 account of the *Fifth Symphony*, recorded in Tokyo when Bernstein and the New York Philharmonic were on tour there. Unashamedly Bernstein treats the work as a Romantic symphony. The very opening makes an impact rarely possible in the concert hall; then, exceptionally, in the cool and beautiful second-subject melody Bernstein takes a slightly detached view – though as soon as that same melody comes up for development, after the exposition, the result is altogether more warmly expressive. The *Allegretto* becomes a burlesque, but its Mahlerian roots are strongly conveyed. The slow movement is raptly beautiful, and the finale is brilliant and extrovert, with the first part dazzlingly fast and the conclusion one of unalloyed triumph, with no hint of irony. On CD, the bass is made to sound full and rich, and the slight distancing of the sound (compared with many CBS recordings) places the orchestra within a believable ambience.

Wallfisch handles the first movement splendidly, though there is not quite the same sense of momentum as in Yo-Yo Ma's account. However, he gives a sensitive account of the slow movement and has thoughtful and responsive support from the ECO. The Chandos recording is outstandingly fine.

Tortelier's reading of the first of Shostakovich's two *Cello concertos* does not always quite match the example of the dedicatee and first performer, Rostropovich (see below), in sheer precision of bravura passages, but Tortelier does match the Russian master in urgency and attack. Berglund and the Bournemouth orchestra provide colourful and committed accompaniment, and the recording has retained its fullness and is even more vivid on CD.

Cello concertos Nos. 1 in E flat, Op. 107; 2, Op. 126.
*** Ph. Dig. 412 526-2 [id.]. Heinrich Schiff, Bav. RSO, Maxim Shostakovich.
**(*) BMG/RCA Dig. RD 87918 [7918-2-RC]. Natalia Gutman, RPO, Temirkanov.

Schiff's superbly recorded account does not displace Yo-Yo Ma in the *First*, but it can hold its own, and interest inevitably centres on its companion. The *Second Concerto* offers fewer overt opportunities for display. It is a haunting piece, essentially lyrical; it is gently discursive, sadly whimsical at times and tinged with a smiling melancholy that hides deeper troubles. The recording is enormously impressive.

Natalia Gutman enjoys an almost legendary reputation in the Soviet Union and the Scandinavian countries, though she has made relatively few appearances in the UK and her representation in the CD catalogue is slender. Her thoughtful account of the two Shostakovich *Concertos* with the RPO and Yuri Temirkanov should satisfy collectors on most counts: the recording itself is first class and the playing has both eloquence and refinement. All the same, given the competition it is probably not a first choice.

(i) *Cello concerto No. 1 in E flat, Op. 107; Piano concertos Nos.* (ii) *1 in C min., Op. 35;* (iii) *2 in F, Op. 101.*
(M) *** Sony MPK 44850 [id.]. (i) Rostropovich, Phd. O, Ormandy; (ii) Previn; (iii) Bernstein; NYPO, Bernstein.

Rostropovich made this recording of the *Cello concerto No. 1* within a few months of the first performance in Russia. Shostakovich himself attended the recording session in Philadelphia and gave his approval to what is a uniquely authoritative reading. Ormandy and the Philadelphia Orchestra accompany superbly, with a precision and warmth rare with new scores. The recording is clear and spacious but the balance places the soloist too prominently. Sony have now shrewdly made an attractive triptych for CD by including Bernstein's radiant account of the *Second Piano concerto*, along with Previn's equally striking account of No. 1. Though these New York performances bring somewhat dated recording, both pianists have a way of turning a phrase to catch the imagination, and a fine balance is struck between Shostakovich's warmth and his rhythmic alertness.

Cello concerto No. 2, Op. 126.
(M) *** DG 431 475-2; *431 475-4* [id.]. Rostropovich, Boston SO, Ozawa – GLAZUNOV: *Chant du ménestrel;* TCHAIKOVSKY: *Andante cantabile.* ***

Shostakovich's *Second Cello concerto* is completely different from its predecessor. At first it appears to lack density of musical incident and seems deceptively rhapsodic, but closer acquaintance reveals its strength; indeed it is an evocative and haunting work. Rostropovich plays with beautifully controlled feeling, and Seiji Ozawa brings sympathy and fine discipline to the accompaniment, securing admirably expressive playing from the Boston orchestra. The analogue recording is first class; if Rostropovich is forward in the aural spectrum, the balance is otherwise impeccably judged and the most is made of the spacious and warm acoustic.

Piano concerto No. 1 in C min., for piano, trumpet and strings, Op. 35.
*** Olympia Dig. OCD 179 [id.]. Kissin, Moscow Virtuosi, Spivakov – *Symphony No. 15.* ***
*** Collins Dig. 1276-2; *1276-4* [id.]. Vladimir Ovchinikov, John Wallace (trumpet), Philh. O, Maxim Shostakovich – MUSSORGSKY: *Pictures.* **(*)
(*) Delos Dig. D/CD 3021 [id]. Rosenberger, Burns, LACO, Schwarz – PROKOFIEV: *Symphony No. 1;* STRAVINSKY: *Soldier's tale.* *

Yevgeny Kissin gives a first-class account of the *First Piano concerto* with the Moscow Virtuosi under Vladimir Spivakov and featuring Vladimir Kafelnikov in the important trumpet solos. With precocious mastery Kissin brings out both the youthful brightness of the outer movements and the yearning expressiveness of the slow movement.

Vladimir Ovchinikov's record of the *Concerto for piano, trumpet and strings* is cultivated and musical and has the advantage of some excellent playing from John Wallace and the Philharmonia Orchestra under Maxim Shostakovich. It is rather softer-edged and perhaps more thoughtful than some earlier readings on record, and some may feel that these artists over-beautify the slow movement. There is, however, no want of bite or wit in the finale. The recorded balance between the two soloists and orchestra is altogether excellent.

There have been more witty accounts of the *First Concerto* than Rosenberger's, but the extra degree of gravitas in the first movement adds an unexpected depth to the music, and the *Lento* is beautifully played, with a fine expressive response from the strings of the Los Angeles Chamber Orchestra. The finale, taken fast, makes a brilliant contrast.

Piano concertos Nos. 1–2; The Unforgettable year 1919, Op. 89; The Assault on beautiful Gorky (for piano and orchestra).
(B) *** CfP Dig. CD-CFP 4547; *TC-CFP 4547.* Alexeev, Philip Jones, ECO, Maksymiuk.

Alexeev is a clear first choice in both *Concertos*, and his record would sweep the board even at full price. The digital recording is excellent in every way and scores over its rivals in clarity and presence. Artistically he has more personality than most of his rivals and he has the advantage of sensitive and idiomatic support from the ECO and Jerzy Maksymiuk. There is a fill-up in the form of a miniature one-movement *Concerto* from a film-score called *The Unforgettable year 1919.* Given the quality of both the performance and the sound, this record should make new friends for the two *Concertos*, particularly at such an attractive price.

(i) *Piano concerto No. 2 in F, Op. 102;* (ii) *Violin concerto No. 1 in A min., Op. 77.*
*** Decca Dig. 425 793-2; *425 793-4* [id.]. (i) Ortiz; (ii) Belkin; RPO, Ashkenazy.

Though there are finer versions of both concertos, there are none better recorded, and anyone who wants this unusual coupling can safely invest in this unexpected instalment in the Ashkenazy Shostakovich series. Cristina Ortiz gives a sparkling account of the jaunty first movement of the *Piano concerto No. 2,* and she also brings out the fun and wit of the finale with fluent, finely pointed playing, not least in the delicious interpolated bars of 7/8. The central *Andante*, taken rather more slowly than usual, is both warm and refined, avoiding sentimentality in the haunting main theme, which here more than ever is like Rachmaninov slimmed down to the bare bones.

Boris Belkin in the first and more popular of the violin concertos plays immaculately and with consistently sweet, pure tone, but he misses some of the work's darker, deeper undertones, whether in the meditative *Nocturne* of the first movement or in the solo leading into the cadenza in the third movement. Decca sound is full and well balanced, not as distanced as other recordings in Ashkenazy's series.

Violin concertos Nos. 1 in A min., Op. 77; 2 in C sharp min., Op. 129.
*** Virgin Dig. VC7 91143-2; *VC 791143-4* [id.]. Sitkovetsky, BBC SO, Andrew Davis.
*** Chan. Dig. CHAN 8820; *ABTD 1445*. Lydia Mordkovitch, SNO, Järvi.

Virgin's coupling by Sitkovetsky and the BBC Symphony Orchestra under Andrew Davis is even more impressive and rather more intense than its competitor on Chandos. Those who acquired the Mordkovitch/Järvi set need not (and will not) feel they should have waited, but there is no doubt as to the excellence of the newcomer, which has tremendous bite. It is also splendidly recorded, and takes its place at the top of the list.

Mordkovitch's concentrated reading of No. 2, so much sparer than No. 1 and less immediately effective, explodes any idea that it marks a disappointing sequel. From her hushed, withdrawn account of the lyrical first theme through all three movements she is matched by Järvi and the orchestra in their total commitment. She even outshines the work's dedicatee and first interpreter, David Oistrakh, in the dark reflectiveness of her playing, even if she cannot quite match him in bravura passages. In the better-known concerto (No. 1) she is hardly less impressive, providing not a second-best, but a very valid alternative to the finest versions available. Here again, the meditative intensity of her playing is magnetic, with a fullness and warmth of tone that have not always marked her playing on record before.

Violin concerto No. 1 in A min., Op. 99.
*** EMI Dig. CDC7 49814-2 [id.]. Perlman, Israel PO, Mehta – GLAZUNOV: *Violin concerto.* ***

Perlman's version of the Shostakovich *First Violin concerto* was recorded live in the Mann Auditorium in Tel Aviv, and though that involves some roughness in the sound, particularly in tuttis, the flair and electricity of this modern wizard of the violin are most compellingly caught. Excitement is the keynote: Perlman and Mehta put the work in the light of day and, in the two fast movements and the cadenza, that brings tremendous dividends. There is no violinist in the world who in sheer bravura can quite match Perlman, particularly live, and the ovation which greets his dazzling performance of the finale is richly deserved. Yet some of the mystery and the fantasy which Russian interpreters have found – from David Oistrakh onwards – is missing, and the close balance of the solo instrument, characteristic of Perlman's concerto recordings, undermines hushed intensity. However, this is not as aggressive a recording as some from this source, and anyone who fancies this unusual coupling will not be disappointed.

Five days, five nights (suite), Op. 111a; Hamlet (suite), Op. 116a (film music); *King Lear (suite), Op. 137.*
*** BMG/RCA RD 87763 [7763-2-RC]. Belgian R. O, Serebrier.

Hamlet obviously generates powerful resonances in Shostakovich's psyche and prompts responsive and committed playing from the Belgian Radio Orchestra, while much of the score for *Five days, five nights* inhabits the bleak world of the *Eleventh Symphony*. In every way a more powerful issue than its companion (see below), this should not be passed over by collectors with an interest in either Shostakovich or the cinema.

The Gadfly (film music): *Suite, Op. 97a.*
(B) **(*) CfP CD-CFP 4463; *TC-CFP 4463*. USSR Cinema SO, Emin Khachaturian.

The score for *The Gadfly* was turned into a twelve-movement suite, published in 1960 and recorded two years later. At times the music is quite pleasing but at others is wholly uncharacteristic. On CfP, a musically committed and well-recorded issue, although the brightening of the sound in the digital remastering has lost some of the smoothness of the original LP.

Symphonies Nos. 1 in F min., Op. 10; 6 in B min., Op. 54.
*** Chan. Dig. CHAN 8411; *ABTD 1148* [id.]. SNO, Järvi.
**(*) Decca Dig. 425 609-2 [id.]. RPO, Ashkenazy.

Symphonies Nos. 1 in F min., Op. 10; 9 in E flat, Op. 70.
*** Decca Dig. 414 677-2 [id.]. LPO, Haitink.

Haitink's reading of the brilliant *First Symphony* may lack something in youthful high spirits, but it is a strong, well-played performance none the less, and it is coupled with a superb account of No. 9. Without inflation Haitink gives it a serious purpose, both in the poignancy of the waltz-like second movement and in the equivocal emotions of the outer movements. The recording is outstandingly clean and brilliant.

Järvi's account of the *First Symphony* is strikingly more volatile than Haitink's in the outer movements – there is no lack of quirkiness in the finale, while the *Largo* is intense and passionate. The *Sixth* has comparable intensity, with an element of starkness in the austerity of the first movement. The Scherzo is skittish at first but, like the finale, has no lack of pungent force. In both symphonies this is emphasized by the reverberant acoustics of Glasgow City Hall, bringing an element of brutality to climaxes (which are spectacularly expansive).

Ashkenazy's coupling of Nos. 1 and 6 is a mixed bag, with the distancing of sound which has marked earlier issues in the series seriously undermining the impact of the *Sixth*. The ominous, slow first movement lacks necessary bite, and it leads to an account of the central scherzo which, at a hectic speed, becomes conventionally spiky instead of wryly comic. The finale is also taken fast, again losing some of its humour. No. 1 is far more successful, with the lightness of much of the scoring beautifully caught in a performance which captures both the spiky humour and the emotional intensity, notably in the melancholy of the slow movement. For this coupling, Järvi's Chandos disc is preferable.

Symphonies Nos. 2 (October Revolution), Op. 14; 3 (The First of May), Op. 20. The Age of gold (suite), Op. 22.
*** Decca Dig. 421 131-2 [id.]. LPO Ch. & O, Haitink.

Shostakovich was still in his early twenties when he composed these symphonies, neither of which shows him at his most inspired. Admirable performances and excellently balanced sound with great presence and body. The joky *Age of gold* suite makes an unexpected if attractive makeweight for the CD, recorded with comparable brilliance.

Symphonies Nos. 2 (October Revolution), Op. 14; 12 in D min. (1917), Op. 112.
**(*) Olympia OCD 200 [id.]. USSR MoC SO, Rozhdestvensky.

Rozhdestvensky's coupling of Nos. 2 and 12 could not be more apt, both of them inspired by the 1917 Russian Revolution but written over thirty years apart. There have been more atmospheric readings of the out-and-out programme symphony, No. 12, than Rozhdestvensky's, but the rugged strength of the writing – not merely illustrative – comes over powerfully. The bright, sometimes coarse recording is typical of the Olympia series.

Symphony No. 4 in C min., Op. 43.
*** Chan. Dig. CHAN 8640; *ABTD 1328* [id.]. SNO, Järvi.
**(*) Decca Dig. 425 693-2 [id.]. RPO, Ashkenazy.

(i) *Symphony No. 4 in C min., Op. 43;* (ii) *Jazz suite No. 1, Op. 38.*
**(*) Olympia Dig. OCD 156 [id.]. (i) USSR MoC SO, Rozhdestvensky; (ii) Soloists Ens.

Järvi gives a characteristically weighty account of this difficult work, which captures the full power and bitterness of the writing, as well as its vein of irony. He draws from the SNO playing which is both rugged and expressive, consistently conveying the emotional thrust of the piece and making the enigmatic ending, with its ticking rhythm, warmer than usual, as though bitterness is finally evaporating. He is helped by exceptionally rich, full recording.

With Rozhdestvensky the humour as well as the concentrated power of the work comes over tellingly, even if in the first movement he does nothing to mitigate rhythmic squareness, and the playing is not ideally refined. The second movement also has its slack moments, but the result is highly idiomatic, as it is in the slow, Mahlerian funeral march of the finale. The little *Jazz suite* makes a delightful extra with its *Waltz*, *Polka* and *Foxtrot*.

Ashkenazy gives a performance of high contrasts, very well recorded but not as bitingly intense as some. He is not helped by choosing an exceptionally fast speed for the first movement, which consequently loses some of its thrust and weight, as well as some ironic overtones. The finale too is not as ominous as it might be; but, for anyone collecting the Ashkenazy series, the version is still worth considering.

Symphony No. 5 in D min., Op. 47 (see also under *Cello concerto No. 1*).
(M) *** BMG/RCA GD 86801 [6801-2-RG]. LSO, Previn (with RACHMANINOV: *The Rock* ***).
*** EMI Dig. CDC7 49181-2 [id.]. Oslo PO, Jansons.
(M) *** Erato/Warner 2292 45752-2 [id.]. Leningrad PO, Mravinsky.
**(*) Decca Dig. 410 017-2 [id.]. Concg. O, Haitink.

Symphony No. 5 in D min.; The Bolt: Ballet suite No. 5.
*** Chan. Dig. CHAN 8650. SNO, Järvi.

Symphony No. 5 in D min.; 5 Fragments, Op. 42.
*** Decca Dig. 421 120-2 [id.]. RPO, Ashkenazy.

Ashkenazy's reading of Shostakovich's most popular symphony brings one of his finest records yet as a conductor. This is an exceptionally searching and intense reading, bitingly dramatic, yet finding an element of wry humour in the second and fourth movements to outshine any rival. Ashkenazy conveys in the slow movement's spareness a rare sense of desolation, more hushed and refined than immediate rivals, with the woodwind solos adding to the chill. Unlike most versions, the Decca issue has a fill-up, the very rare *Five Fragments*, sharp little inventions, like the main work given demonstration sound quality.

Previn's RCA version, dating from early in his recording career (1965), remains at the top of the list of bargain recommendations. This is one of the most concentrated and intense readings ever, superbly played by the LSO at its peak. What has always marked out Previn's reading is the spaciousness of the first and third movements, held together masterfully. In the third movement he sustains a slower speed than anyone else, making it deeply meditative in its dark intensity; and the purity and beauty of the Previn version have never been surpassed, notably in the long-legged second subject, while his build-up in the central development section brings playing of white heat. The bite and urgency of the second and fourth movements are also irresistible. Only in the hint of analogue tape-hiss does the sound fall short of the finest modern digital recordings – and it is more vividly immediate than most. Those wanting a mid-priced digital recording should consider Bernstein's fine account, coupled with Yo-Yo Ma's version of the *First Cello concerto* – see above.

Jansons' EMI version with the Oslo orchestra on top form brings a tautly incisive, electrically intense reading, marked by speeds notably faster than usual that yet have the ring of authenticity. The development section in the first movement for example builds up bitingly into a thrilling climax, with the accelerando powerfully controlled. Not a first choice, but an exciting one.

Mravinsky conducted the première of the *Fifth Symphony* in 1937, and so brings a special authority to this work. The Erato account emanates from a concert performance, almost a half-century later (in 1984) and like his recording made at the 1978 Vienna Festival, briefly available in a 4LP EMI set, is far from impeccable. The former suffered from some vulnerable woodwind intonation and the present version is not free from the odd untidiness but there is still evidence of a commanding personality, and even though the recording itself is not in the luxury bracket, this CD must figure high on any list.

One big merit of the Järvi version is the interest of the coupling, a half-hour suite from his early ballet, full of wry, quirky ideas typical of the young Shostakovich. That suits Järvi perfectly, and in the *Symphony* too he gives a warmly committed performance, even if – as in the great span of the second subject on exposed violins – the playing of the SNO is not as refined as in the finest versions. Otherwise the emotional intensity and spiky humour are very well caught indeed, and the recording is full and warm in the Chandos manner.

Haitink is eminently straightforward, there are no disruptive changes in tempo, and the playing of the Concertgebouw Orchestra and the contribution of the Decca engineers are beyond praise. There could perhaps be greater intensity of feeling in the slow movement, but, whatever small reservations one might have, it is most impressive both artistically and sonically.

Symphonies Nos. 5 in D min.; 9 in E flat, Op. 70.
(BB) *** Naxos Dig. 8.550427 [id.]. Belgian R. & TV O, Alexander Rahbari.
*** Olympia Dig. OCD 113 [id.]. USSR MoC SO, Rozhdestvensky.

Both in the hushed intensity of the lyrical passages and in the vigour and bite of Shostakovich's violent allegros Rahbari's reading is most convincing, with dramatic tensions finely controlled in a spontaneous-sounding way. In No. 9 Rahbari opts for a controversially slow *Moderato* second movement but sustains it well, and the outer movements are deliciously witty in their pointing. The playing of all sections is first rate, and the sound is full and brilliant. An outstandingly generous coupling makes this a most attractive issue, even with no allowance made for the very low price.

The *Ninth* in particular suits Rozhdestvensky's personality ideally, with the element of wit and humour brilliantly presented, and with the darker, more emotional elements emerging strongly and committedly. The Ministry of Culture Orchestra demonstrates in that work that it is second to none in Moscow, though the playing is less polished in No. 5, where violin-tone in the exposed passages is sometimes lacking fullness. Warm, vivid recording, with the players set fairly close against a reverberant acoustic.

Symphonies Nos. 5 in D min.; 10 in E min., Op. 73; 15 in A, Op. 141; Festive overture; The Gadfly (film music): *Suite, Op. 97a.*
** Collins 7012-2 (2) [id.]. LSO, Maxim Shostakovich.

On the face of it three key Shostakovich symphonies conducted by the composer's son, well played and excellently recorded, should be an attractive proposition. Moreover Maxim conducted a very good account of the *Fifth Symphony* in the 1970s and the première recording of the *Fifteenth*. Yet these accounts with the LSO are curiously low voltage. Phrases are sensitively shaped and the architecture is well held together but the epic scale and dramatic sweep of this music is not fully conveyed.

Symphony No. 6 in B min., Op. 54.
(M) *** EMI CDM7 69564-2; *EG 769564-4*. LSO, Previn – RACHMANINOV: *Symphony No. 3.* ***
(***) Dell'Arte mono DA 9023 [id.]. Phd. O, Stokowski – SIBELIUS: *Symphony No. 4* etc. (**)

Here Previn shows his deep understanding of Shostakovich in a powerfully drawn, unrelenting account of the opening movement, his slow tempo adding to the overall impact. After that the offhand wit of the central Scherzo comes over the more delicately at a slower tempo than usual, leaving the hectic finale to hammer home the deceptively joyful conclusion to the argument. Excellent recording, impressively remastered.

There is usually something special about first recordings. Stokowski's *Sixth* was made in 1940, only a few months after the work was premièred, and it brings one face to face not only with this symphony but also with the bleak, harsh times during which it came into being. It is powerfully atmospheric, the lines wonderfully sustained and the playing at times frighteningly intense. Tempi are perfectly judged and the virtuosity of the Philadelphia Orchestra is remarkable. This performance has a special ring of authenticity. Later recordings, including Mravinsky (1965) and Stokowski's Chicago recording (1970), have different claims, but readers should not neglect this excellent transfer.

Symphonies Nos. 6 in B min.; 11 in G min. (1905), Op. 103; Overture on Russian and Kirghiz folk themes, Op. 115.
**(*) Decca Dig. 411 939-2 (2) [id.]. Concg. O, Haitink.

Haitink's performances of the *Symphonies* are characteristically refined and powerful. With superb playing from the Concertgebouw, particularly the strings, the textures have an extra transparency, helped also by the brilliant and atmospheric Decca recording. Haitink's structural control, coupled with his calm, taut manner, also brings out the weight and power of the big slow movements which open both works; the *Largo* of No. 6 is particularly impressive. Nevertheless Haitink seems almost detached, marginally lacking the concentrated tension of a genuine performance.

Symphonies Nos. 6 in B min.; 12 in D min. (The Year 1917), Op. 112.
*** Olympia Dig. OCD 111 [id.]. USSR MoC SO, Rozhdestvensky.

No. 6 is a work that Rozhdestvensky responds to with exceptional warmth, giving weight and intensity to the magnificent opening slow movement and bringing out the spark of dark humour in the Scherzo and finale while giving them necessary bite and power. He is also most persuasive in the programmatic No. 12 with its picture of the events of the 1917 Revolution, bringing out the atmosphere and drama. Unfortunately, the disc has the full span of the work, over 40 minutes of continuous music, with no separating bands for the various sections. First-rate playing from the Ministry of Culture Orchestra and full-bodied, warm recording.

Symphony No. 7 in C (Leningrad), Op. 60.
*** Chan. Dig. CHAN 8623; *ABTD 1312* [id.]. SNO, Järvi.
**(*) Olympia Dig. OCD 118 [id.]. USSR MoC SO, Rozhdestvensky.
(M) (***) BMG/RCA mono GD60293 [60293-2-RG]. NBC SO, Toscanini.
*(*) Erato/Warner Dig. 2292 45414-2. Nat. SO, Rostropovich.

When the *Leningrad Symphony* first appeared at the height of the war, various conductors, Stokowski and Koussevitzky among them, competed for the right to première the work in the

United States. The score was given high priority (given wartime conditions), dispatched via Iran and then by air to New York. The honour of its first performance fell to Toscanini and the NBC Orchestra, whose electrifying broadcast now appears on CD. There is an urgency and fervour that is altogether special and an intensity that shines through the primitive recorded sound. There is a special feeling of authenticity similar to that of Stokowski's 1940 78 records of the *Sixth Symphony* that conveys the flavour of the period and the vividness of the experience more effectively than many modern recordings. Be warned, however, the 1942 sound does call for some tolerance.

Järvi's is a strong, intense reading, beautifully played and recorded, which brings out the full drama of this symphony in a performance that consistently gives the illusion of spontaneity in a live performance, as in the hushed tension of the slow, expansive passages. There have been more polished versions than this, but, with its spectacular Chandos sound, it makes an excellent choice as a single-disc version.

Rozhdestvensky's view of the *Leningrad symphony*'s controversial first movement is unusually broad. It is undeniably powerful but runs the risk of overplaying the element of banality in the notorious *ostinato*. Many will prefer a brisker and more polished reading, but the ruggedness here is certainly authentic; the other movements too bring warmly expressive, spontaneous-sounding performances, which lack only the last degree of subtlety. The sound is full and satisfying but grows coarse at the biggest climaxes.

Rostropovich's account is eminently well-prepared and springs from undoubted feeling, though he is often a bit heavy-handed. He rarely lets the music speak for itself and the overall effect is studied. The engineers provide him with a recording of impressive dynamic range. However well schooled the playing may be, there is a literal feeling here (all i's are dotted and t's crossed).

Symphonies Nos. 7 (Leningrad); 12 (The Year 1917), Op. 112.
**(*) Decca Dig. 412 392-2 (2). LPO or Concg. O, Haitink.

With Haitink, the long first-movement *ostinato* – now revealed as having quite different implications from the descriptive programme suggested by the Soviet propaganda-machine in the war years – is almost an interlude in a work which otherwise in its deep seriousness challenges comparison with the other wartime symphony, the epic *Eighth*. The CD includes also the *Twelfth Symphony*, but the use of two full-price compact discs makes this an expensive investment.

Symphony No. 8 in C min., Op. 65.
*** Ph. Dig. 422 442-2 [id.]. Leningrad PO, Mravinsky.
*** Decca Dig. 411 616-2 [id.]. Concg. O, Haitink.
*(*) Collins Dig. 1271-2 [id.]. LSO, Maxim Shostakovich.

Symphony No. 8 in C min., Op. 65; (i) *3 Satires from Op. 109.*
*** Olympia Dig. OCD 143 [id.]. USSR MoC SO, Rozhdestvensky; (i) with Bogacheva.

Mravinsky's CD is a memorial issue, a live recording in full, clear, digital sound made in 1982. It gives a superb idea of the magnetism of his reading, the way that in the massive slow first movement with its shattering climaxes he built tensions inexorably, demonstrating the firm structural strength while plumbing the deep personal emotions in this stressed wartime inspiration. Equally, a live recording maintains necessary tensions more clearly in the balancing span of the last three linked movements. Most significantly, Mravinsky's flowing speed for the elusive *Allegretto* finale makes the close of the work less equivocal than usual. It is a great performance and, though ensemble is inevitably not always quite as polished as in the finest studio recordings, discrepancies are minimal.

Rozhdestvensky conducts a thrustful and incisive reading of the *Eighth* with electrically intense playing that both holds the enormous structure together and brings out the element of fantasy which literal performances underplay. The spontaneity which Rozhdestvensky conveys regularly in his recordings is here combined with sharpness of focus. The digital recording is full-bodied and wide-ranging, growing a little coarse only in the biggest climaxes. The *Three Satires* are orchestral arrangements of songs from a cycle of poems by Sasha Cherny. Irina Bogacheva, a strong, very Slavonic mezzo, gives characterful performances, though she is closely balanced.

Haitink characteristically presents a strongly architectural reading of this war-inspired symphony, at times direct to the point of severity. After the massive and sustained slow movement which opens the work, Haitink allows no lightness or relief in the Scherzo movements, and in his seriousness in the strangely lightweight finale (neither fast nor slow) he provides an unusually satisfying account of an equivocal, seemingly uncommitted movement.

Maxim Shostakovich enjoys the benefit of a first-class recording but the expectations his name arouses are disappointed. The performance is lacking direction and intensity.

Symphony No9 in E flat, Op. 70. **(*) Decca Dig. 430 505-2; *430 505-4* [id.]. VPO, Solti – BEETHOVEN: *Symphony No. 5.* **(*)

Symphony No. 9 in E flat, Op. 70; Festive overture, Op. 96; Katerina Ismailova (Lady Macbeth of Mtsensk): 5 Entr'actes. Tahiti trot (arr. of Youmans's *Tea for two*), *Op. 16.*
*** Chan. Dig. CHAN 8567; *ABTD 1279* [id.]. SNO, Järvi.

Järvi's version of the *Ninth* brings a warmly expressive, strongly characterized reading in superb, wide-ranging sound. The point and wit of the first movement go with bluff good humour, leading on to an account of the second-movement *Moderato* that is yearningly lyrical yet not at all sentimental. The weight and gravity of the fourth-movement *Largo* are then similarly contrasted with the fun and jokiness of the final *Allegretto.* The mixed bag of fill-up items is both illuminating and characterful, ending with the jolly little chamber arrangement that Shostakovich did in the 1920s of Vincent Youmans's *Tea for two*, the *Tahiti trot.*

The jollity and fun of Solti's performance in the outer movements, as well as in the third movement Scherzo, is most winning, bringing a lighter touch than one might have expected. He keeps the second movement *Moderato* flowing easily, observing that marking exactly, instead of turning it into a full slow movement, and the brief fourth movement *Largo* is rich and weighty with brass. This strongly characterized reading, recorded live in May 1990, makes an attractive supplement to Solti's studio recordings, with its unexpected Beethoven coupling.

Symphonies Nos. (i) *9 in E flat;* (ii) *10 in E min.*
(M) (***) Sony mono MPK 45698 [id.]. NYPO, (i) Efrem Kurtz; (ii) Dmitri Mitropoulos.

Dmitri Mitropoulos's pioneering account of the *Tenth Symphony* with the New York Philharmonic was for many years the yardstick by which later versions were judged. It still is. In spite of the inevitable sonic limitations, it penetrates more deeply into the heart of this score than any of the recent newcomers; only Karajan's mid-1960s version can be put alongside it. It comes with Efrem Kurtz's 1949 version of the *Ninth* (not quite pioneering, since Koussevitzky had beaten him to it) with the same orchestra, playing with great virtuosity. The sound is remarkably good for its period (an edit has removed one note from the opening phrase of the scherzo), but apart from that hiccup this is a stunning performance. Two great performances on one disc must represent one of the real bargains in the Shostakovich discography.

Symphony No. 10 in E min., Op. 93.
*** DG Dig. 413 361-2 [id.]. BPO, Karajan.
(M) *** EMI CDD7 64105-2 [id.]. LSO, André Previn – PROKOFIEV: *Lieutenant Kijé.* ***
(B) *** Pickwick Dig. PCD 955; *IMPC 955* [id.]. Hallé O, Skrowaczewski.
(M) (***) Saga mono SCD 9017 [id.]. Leningrad PO, Mravinsky.
(M) **(*) Erato/Warner 2292 45753-2 [id.]. Leningrad PO, Mravinsky.
(M) **(*) DG 429 716-2; *429 716-4* [id.]. BPO, Karajan.

Symphony No. 10 in E min., Op. 93; Ballet suite No. 4.
*** Chan. Dig. CHAN 8630; *ABTD 1319* [id.]. SNO, Järvi.

(i) *Symphony No. 10 in E min., Op. 93;* (ii) *Hamlet* (incidental music), *Op. 32: Fragments.*
**(*) Olympia OCD 131 [id.]. (i) USSR MoC SO, Rozhdestvensky; (ii) Leningrad CO, Serov.

Already in his 1967 recording Karajan had shown that he had the measure of this symphony; this newer version is, if anything, even finer. In the first movement he distils an atmosphere as concentrated as before, bleak and unremitting, while in the *Allegro* the Berlin Philharmonic leave no doubts as to their peerless virtuosity. Everything is marvellously shaped and proportioned. The *allegro* section of the finale is taken up to a speed much faster than most other rivals. The digital sound is altogether excellent, and this must now rank as a first recommendation.

Järvi, too, conducts an outstandingly strong and purposeful reading in superb sound, full and atmospheric. In the great span of the long *Moderato* first movement he chooses an ideal speed, which allows for moments of hushed repose but still builds up relentlessly. The curious little *Ballet suite No. 4*, with its sombre *Prelude* leading to a bouncy *Waltz* and a jolly *Scherzo tarantella*, makes a delightful bonus.

Previn's is a strong and dramatic reading marked by a specially compelling account of the long first movement, which steers an ideal course between expressive warmth and architectural strength. At marginally slower speeds than usual, Previn's rhythmic lift both in the scherzo and in the finale brings exhilarating results, sparkling and swaggering. The digital recording is early (1982) but strikingly full and firm, less aggressive-sounding than Karajan's analogue version.

Recorded in full, brilliant and weighty sound, Skrowaczewski's version of the *Tenth* is also a top recommendation. The second-movement scherzo has a sharply dramatic intensity that fully brings out its barbaric thrust and, after the hushed introduction to the fourth movement, the final allegro has point and bite in plenty. Above all, the spacious *moderato* of the long first movement has a natural power and concentration which put it among the finest versions, with the Hallé brass superbly focused at the great climaxes. This is one of Skrowaczewski's most memorable recordings with the Hallé.

Mravinsky conducted the work's première, but his mono LP was originally let down by dim recording. The sound has been improved on CD: the violins still sound thin but detail is cleaner and there is a firmer outline and more body overall. In the long first movement Mravinsky captures the doleful melancholy of the opening and he moves to the bitter desperation of the climax with great eloquence. The Leningrad Philharmonic plays the scherzo with staggering virtuosity and the work is satisfyingly resolved in the finale.

Mravinsky's Erato/Warner recording was made at a 1976 concert performance, and it has no want of intensity and power. The recording is somewhat crude and does not displace his earlier (1954) record, now available in much-improved sound on Saga. All the same, it is a performance to reckon with.

Karajan's 1967 reading is superbly moulded, with genuine tragic feeling and authenticity. The Berlin Philharmonic play magnificently and the 1967 recording combines ambient atmosphere with a fierce brilliance to project the score's climaxes pungently – indeed, some may feel that the CD is too brightly lit in the violins.

Following the pattern of his Shostakovich series, Rozhdestvensky conducts a strong and spontaneous-sounding reading of the *Tenth*, not as portentous or intense as some but with a vein of spikiness that is totally idiomatic. Though the digital sound is full and bright, the bass tends to be boomy and rather vague, with internal textures coarsened at climaxes.

Symphony No. 11 (The Year 1905), Op. 103.
**(*) DG Dig. 429 405-2 [id.]. Gothenburg SO, Järvi.

Neeme Järvi's account of the *Eleventh Symphony* has much to recommend it, including good orchestral playing and very fine recorded sound. Good though it is, the performance misses the last ounce of intensity that made the old LP accounts of Mravinsky and Stokowski so extraordinarily powerful. For the moment, the Chandos is the best recommendation for this work, *faute de mieux.*

Symphony No. 12 in D min. (The Year 1917), Op. 112.
(M) *** Erato/Warner 2292 45754-2 [id.]. Leningrad PO, Mravinsky.

Symphony No. 12 (The Year 1917); Age of Gold: suite, Op. 22; Hamlet (suite for small orchestra).
** DG Dig. 431 688-2 [id.]. Gothenburg SO, Järvi.

The *Twelfth Symphony* is one of Shostakovich's more problematic essays in the genre, an example of poster art rather than the more searching symphonic portraiture of its immediate predecessor. Of course there are characteristic passages in the *Razliv* movement but for the most part one is left with the impression that bombast has to serve for substance. However when a conductor of Mravinsky's quality is at the helm, and drawing playing of electrifying intensity from the Leningrad Philharmonic, that impression is almost dispelled. Mravinsky's first version appeared in the early 1960s and long reigned supreme, but this Erato account, taken from a concert performance in 1984, is even higher in voltage and the recording does ample justice to their playing. It offers relatively short measure even at mid-price, but playing of this calibre is very special and no other reading approaches it.

On DG and at full price but with the additional inducements of the *Age of Gold* and *Hamlet* suites, the Gothenburg Orchestra give a good account of themselves under Neeme Järvi and criticisms of the recording have been exaggerated. It admittedly does not have quite the transparency and sharpness of focus of some other recordings made in this famous hall. If it is to come off, this music has to be played with 200 percent conviction and panache, and Järvi's performance does not really challenge Mravinsky in this respect.

Symphony No. 13 in B flat min. (Babi-Yar), Op. 113.
*** Decca Dig. 417 261-2 [id.]. Rintzler, Concg. Male Ch. and O, Haitink.
**(*) Chan. Dig. CHAN 8540; *ABTD 1248* [id.]. Storojev, CBSO, Kamu.

The often brutal directness of Haitink's way with Shostakovich works well in the *Thirteenth Symphony*, particularly in the long *Adagio* first movement, whose title, *Babi-Yar*, gives its name to the whole work. That first of five Yevtushenko settings boldly attacking anti-semitism in Russia sets the pattern for Haitink's severe view of the whole. Rintzler with his magnificent, resonant bass is musically superb but, matching Haitink, remains objective rather than dashingly characterful. The resolution of the final movement, with its pretty flutings surrounding a wry poem about Galileo and greatness, then works beautifully. Outstandingly brilliant and full sound, remarkable even for this series.

With a Russian bass soloist adding an extra touch of dark authenticity, Okku Kamu conducts a strong and sympathetic account of No. 13, well played and very well recorded. His degree of relaxation in the more pointed passages – such as the second movement, *Humour* – adds to the idiomatic feeling, though in weight and dark intensity he cannot always match Haitink, with a bass chorus rather light-toned.

Symphony No. 14; Chamber symphony, Op. 110a.
* Virgin Dig. VC7 91434-2 [id.]. Kasrashvili, Krutikov, Lausanne CO, Lazarev.

(i) *Symphony No. 14 in G min., Op. 135;* (ii) *King Lear (musical fragments), Op. 58a.*
*** Olympia Dig. OCD 182 [id.]. (i) Kasrashubili, Safiulin, USSR MoC SO, Rozhdestvensky; (ii) Romanova, Leningrad CO, Serov.

(i) *Symphony No. 14, Op. 135;* (ii) *6 Poems of Marina Tsvetaeva, Op. 143a.*
*** Decca Dig. 417 514-2 [id.]. (i) Julia Varady, Fischer-Dieskau; (ii) Ortrun Wenkel; Concg. O, Haitink.

The *Fourteenth* is Shostakovich's most sombre and dark score, a setting of poems by Lorca, Apollinaire, Rilke, Brentano and Küchelbecker, all on the theme of death; Haitink's version gives each poem in its original language. It is a most powerful performance, and the outstanding recording is well up to the standard of this fine Decca series. The song-cycle, splendidly sung by Ortrun Wenkel, makes a fine bonus.

The Ministry of Culture Orchestra's performance is magnetic in drawing the sequence together; sadly, however, the booklet does not include texts, only a summary of each poem. The full, bright, digital sound is more atmospheric than some in the Olympia series. Though the voices are balanced close, their characterful Slavonic timbre will delight rather than offend Western ears. The colourful but lightweight *King Lear* pieces, recorded in warm, full, analogue sound, make a useful coupling.

The Lausanne Chamber Orchestra play at times with some intensity for Alexander Lazarev though neither Makvala Kasrashvili nor Mikail Krutikov are ideal soloists. Kasrashvili has a somewhat unpleasing vibrato wobble. Not a strong recommendation, though more acceptable than its companion, the so-called *Chamber Symphony* (a transcription for full strings of the *Eighth String Quartet* made by Rudolf Barshai at the behest of the composer). This performance is intolerably sluggish: the piece normally runs to just over 20 minutes but Lazarev drags it out to very nearly 28!

Symphony No. 15 in A, Op. 141.
*** Olympia Dig. OCD 179 [id.]. USSR MoC SO, Rozhdestvensky – *Piano concerto No. 1.* ***

Symphony No. 15 in A, Op. 141; October, Op. 131; Overture on Russian Kirghiz folk tunes, Op. 115.
**(*) DG Dig. 427 616-2 [id.]. Gothenburg SO, Neeme Järvi.

(i) *Symphony No. 15 in A, Op. 141;* (ii) *From Jewish folk poetry* (song-cycle), *Op. 79.*
✿ *** Decca 417 581-2 [id.]. (i) LPO; (ii) Söderström, Wenkel, Karcykowski, Concg. O; Haitink.

Early readings of the composer's last symphony seemed to underline the quirky unpredictability of the work, with the collage of strange quotations – above all the *William Tell* gallop, which keeps recurring in the first movement – seemingly joky rather than profound. Haitink by contrast makes the first movement sound genuinely symphonic, bitingly urgent. He underlines the purity of the bare lines of the second movement; after the Wagner quotations which open the finale, his slow tempo for the main lyrical theme gives it heartaching tenderness, not the usual easy triviality. The playing of the LPO is excellent, with refined tone and superb attack, and the recording is both analytical and atmospheric. The CD includes a splendidly sung version of *From Jewish folk poetry*, settings which cover a wide range of emotions including tenderness, humour and even happiness as in the final song. Ryszard Karcykowski brings vibrant Slavonic feeling to the work, which with its wide variety of mood and colour has a scale to match the shorter symphonies.

Rozhdestvensky as an interpreter of Shostakovich is particularly good at tapping the vein of wry humour in all the symphonies, a quality which comes to the fore in the equivocal *Fifteenth*. With its full, bright recording, this is one of the most recommendable of Rozhdestvensky's series with the Ministry of Culture Orchestra, particularly when it has for coupling one of the very first recordings made by the teenage prodigy, Yevgeny Kissin, soloist in a fine performance of the *Piano concerto No. 1*.

Neeme Järvi has a good feeling for the composer and, of the digital accounts of the *Fifteenth Symphony*, his should certainly be considered; it has personality and is played characterfully by the Gothenburg orchestra. *October* is a powerful work, written for the fiftieth anniversary of the Revolution in 1967, at about the same time as the *Second Violin concerto*. Very good sound.

CHAMBER AND INSTRUMENTAL MUSIC

Cello sonata in D min., Op. 40.
*** Chan. Dig. CHAN 8340; *ABTD 1372* [id.]. Turovsky, Edlina – PROKOFIEV: *Sonata.* ***
*** BIS Dig. CD 336 [id.]. Thedéen, Pöntinen – SCHNITTKE: *Sonata;* STRAVINSKY: *Suite italienne.* ***

Cello sonata, Op. 40; Moderato.
*** Decca Dig. 421 774-2; *421 774-4* [id.]. Harrell, Ashkenazy – PROKOFIEV: *Sonata.* ***

Lynn Harrell and Vladimir Ashkenazy give a convincing account of the *Sonata*, though they slow down rather a lot for the second group of the first movement. All the same, their brisk tempo and their freedom from affectation are refreshing. Harrell and Ashkenazy also include a short *Moderato* for cello and piano that came to light only five years ago in the Moscow State Archives and which could at some stage have been intended for the *Sonata* itself, though its brevity and its quality both make one doubtful.

Yuli Turovsky and Luba Edlina play the *Cello sonata* with great panache and eloquence, if in the finale they almost succumb at times to exaggeration in their handling of its humour – no understatement here.

The Swedish cellist, Torleif Thedéen, has a real feeling for its structure and the vein of bitter melancholy under its ironic surface. Roland Pöntinen gives him excellent support and the BIS recording does justice to this partnership.

Cello sonata in D min., Op. 40; (i) *Piano trio No. 2 in E min., Op. 67.*
**(*) Sony Dig. MK 44664 [id.]. Yo-Yo Ma, Emanuel Ax; (i) with Isaac Stern.

The *Trio* receives a deeply felt performance, one which can hold its own with any issue, past or present. The *Sonata* is another matter; the playing is as beautiful as one would expect, but here Ma's self-communing propensity for reducing his tone is becoming a tiresome affectation. Ax plays splendidly and the CBS recording is very truthful.

Piano quintet in G min., Op. 57.
(*) CRD CRD 3351; *CRDC 4051* [id.]. Clifford Benson, Alberni Qt – BRITTEN: *Quartet No. 1.* *

Piano quintet, Op. 57; Piano trio No. 2 in E min., Op. 67.
**(*) Chan. Dig. CHAN 8342; *ABTD 1088* [id.]. Borodin Trio, Zweig, Horner.
**(*) ASV ZCALH 929 [id.]. Music Group of London.

Until the Ashkenazy/Fitzwilliam recording on Decca returns to the catalogue, there is no clear first choice for the *Piano quintet*. This is a particularly painful and anguished work, dedicated to the memory of a close friend, Ivan Sollertinsky, who died in the year of its composition. The Chandos version is bolder in character and more concentrated in feeling than its main rival. The Music Group of London show rather less panache but are still impressive, and in their hands the *Trio* is played affectingly.

Alternatively, there is a vigorous and finely conceived account from Clifford Benson and the Alberni Quartet, vividly recorded; if the Britten coupling is wanted, this will be found fully satisfactory.

Piano trio No. 2 in E min., Op. 67.
**(*) Collins Dig. 1040-2 [id.]. Trio Zingara – RAVEL: *Piano trio in A min.* **(*)

The *E minor Piano trio* is extremely well played by the Trio Zingara on what is their début recording. Theirs is an assured and accomplished account, extremely well recorded and sensitively phrased. One quarrel: they take the slow movement slower than marked and, as a result, do not fully sustain its atmosphere and concentration. The CBS version with Isaac Stern, Emanuel Ax and Yo-Yo Ma (see above) conveys more of the anguish and pain of this powerful score. However, those who want this particular coupling will derive much musical satisfaction from it.

String quartets Nos. 1–15.
(M) *** Decca 433 078-2 (6). Fitzwilliam Qt.

Shostakovich concentrated on the symphony earlier in his career; the *First Quartet* was not written until 1938, a year after the *Fifth Symphony*, but into this medium he poured some of his most private and inspired musical thinking. Here perhaps more than in the symphonies is the record of the real man. The Fitzwilliam Quartet played to Shostakovich himself and gave the UK premières of his last three quartets and they bring to the whole cycle complete and total dedication. They are splendid players and their accounts of these works have won wide acclaim and a number of awards, well deserved. One has only to sample the first two quartets to discover the sustained and often hushed intensity of this playing which so consistently has the spontaneity of live music-making. They are given first-class recording too, with great presence and natural body. The recordings were made in All Saints Church, Petersham, Surrey between 1955 and 1957; a rather forward balance was chosen, perhaps because of the ecclesiastical acoustic, and this is slightly emphasized by the CD transfer, yet there is a natural transparency and a firm focus throughout. There are minor criticisms, but they are too trivial to weigh in the balance, for this set is by any standards a formidable achievement.

String quartets Nos. 1 in C, Op. 49; 9 in E flat, Op. 117; 12 in D flat, Op. 133.
*** EMI CDC7 49266-2 [id.]. Borodin Qt.

String quartets Nos. 4 in D, Op. 83; 6 in G, Op. 101; 11 in F min., Op. 122.
*** EMI CDC7 49268-2 [id.]. Borodin Qt.

String quartets Nos. 5 in B flat, Op. 92; 15 in E flat min., Op. 144.
*** EMI CDC7 49270-2 [id.]. Borodin Qt.

String quartets Nos. 10 in A flat, Op. 118; 13 in B flat min., Op. 138; 14 in F sharp, Op. 142.
*** EMI CDC7 49269-2 [id.]. Borodin Qt.

The Shostakovich *Quartets* thread through his creative life like some inner odyssey and inhabit terrain of increasing spiritual desolation. This is the Borodin Quartet's second complete cycle. Two of the performances derive from concerts. The present set, which has suffered from the deletions axe and is currently incomplete, is made in a generally drier acoustic than its predecessors, and the recordings from 1984, particularly No.5 in B flat, suffer in this respect. However, the ear quickly adjusts and the performances can only be described as masterly, while the sheer quality of the playing on this set is unlikely to be surpassed. The Borodin Quartet have something very special to offer in this repertoire.

String quartets Nos. 1 in C, Op. 49; 3 in F, Op. 73; 4 in D, Op. 83.
*** Teldec/Warner Dig. 2292 46009-2 [id.]. Brodsky Qt.

The Brodskys are a young quartet of real accomplishment who give well-prepared and intelligent performances of these quartets, the first of what is to be a complete cycle. They are very attentive to detail and need not fear competition, if the playing is all going to be as fine as this. The recordings are rather close, but this need not inhibit a strong recommendation for those wanting separate digital versions of these works.

String quartets Nos. 4 in D, Op. 83; 8 in C min., Op. 110; 11 in F min., Op. 112.
*** ASV Dig. CDDCA 631; *ZCDCA 631* [id.]. Coull Qt.

The *Fourth quartet* is a work of exceptional beauty and lucidity, one of the most haunting of the cycle; the *Eleventh Quartet* is a puzzling, almost cryptic work in seven short movements. The Coull is not a high-powered group; they sound as if they are playing in domestic rather than public surroundings. They are one of the most gifted of the younger British quartets and give eminently creditable accounts of all three pieces. A very good (if slightly overlit) recording on CD.

String quartet No. 8, Op. 110.
(M) **(*) Decca 425 541-2; *425 541-4* [id.]. Borodin Qt – BORODIN; TCHAIKOVSKY: *Quartets.* **(*)

As the central motif of this fine *Quartet* Shostakovich used a group of four notes derived, cipher-like, from his own name. It proves at least as fruitful as the famous one in the name 'Bach', and the argument throughout this impressive work is most intense. The Borodins' performance is outstanding and the recording real and vivid, although the balance means that in the CD transfer the effect is very forward, almost too boldly immediate.

Viola sonata, Op. 147.
*** EMI Dig. CDC7 54394-2 [id.]. Tabea Zimmermann, Hartmut Höll – BRITTEN: *Lachrymae;* STRAVINSKY: *Élégie.* ***

Shostakovich's *Viola sonata* is perhaps his most bleak and comfortless work, a true song of sorrow, ruminating on the imminence of death. Tabea Zimmermann and her partner, Hartmut Höll, give as powerful and chilling an account of it as one could imagine. In its intensity it even challenges the pioneering record by Fyodor Druzhinin, the violist of the Beethoven Quartet, for whom it was written. The recording is of striking clarity and presence.

Violin sonata, Op. 134.
*** Chan. Dig. CHAN 8988; *ABTD 1570* [id.]. Mordkovitch, Benson – PROKOFIEV: *Sonatas;* SCHNITTKE: *In memoriam.* ***
*** Chan. Dig. CHAN 8343; *ABTD 1089* [id.]. Dubinsky, Edlina – SCHNITTKE: *Sonata No. 1* etc. ***

Lydia Mordkovitch follows up her award-winning disc of the two Shostakovich *Violin concertos* with this Shostakovich *Sonata*, a sort of pendant to the *Violin concerto No. 2*, written a year earlier, also for David Oistrakh. Textures are even balder than in the concerto, with the piano writing often in simple octaves. Even more than the concerto, it can seem a dry piece but Mordkovitch's natural intensity, her ability to convey depth of feeling without sentimentality, transforms it. Clifford Benson is the understanding pianist. In first-rate sound it makes a fine central offering for Mordkovitch's well-planned disc of Soviet violin music.

Rostislav Dubinsky's account is undoubtedly eloquent, and Luba Edlina makes a fine partner. The recording is excellent too, although it is balanced a shade closely.

Piano sonata No. 1.
*** DG Dig. 427 766-2 [id.]. Lilya Zilberstein – RACHMANINOV: *Preludes.* ***

The early *Sonata* was written in the immediate wake of the *First Symphony*. As is the case with the *Trios*, Shostakovich did not return to the medium until the Second World War. It is a radical piece, with something of the manic, possessed quality of Scriabin and the harmonic adventurousness of Berg. Lilya Zilberstein rises triumphantly to its formidable demands, and she makes a strong case for it; she is recorded with striking immediacy and impact. As piano sound, this is state of the art.

24 Preludes, Op. 34.
*** Decca Dig. 433 055-2 [id.]. Olli Mustonen – ALKAN: *25 Preludes.* ***

Of the recordings of the Shostakovich *Preludes*, Op. 34, currently listed in the catalogue the Decca version by the young Finnish pianist, Olli Mustonen, is the strongest contender both artistically and technically, and it scores further over its rivals in offering an Alkan rarity, the *25 Preludes*, Op. 34, some 47 minutes of highly interesting music. A Chant du Monde disc from Varvarova comes with the two piano concertos; another Finnish soloist, Folke Gräsbeck, on Bluebell offers the *Concerto for piano, trumpet and strings*, Op. 35, and the *Chamber Symphony*, perhaps more logical couplings but still less satisfying overall than the Decca release. This is the best record of the *Preludes* since Menahem Pressler's old LP from the 1950s.

24 Preludes and fugues, Op. 87.
❀ *** Hyp. Dig. CDA 66441/3 [id.]. Tatiana Nikolaieva.

In this repertoire, the first choice must inevitably be Tatiana Nikolaieva, 'the onlie begetter', as it were, of the *Preludes and fugues*. It was when he heard her playing Bach in Leipzig in 1950 that Shostakovich conceived the idea of composing his cycle and, during the process of gestation, he telephoned Nikolaieva almost every day to discuss its progress. If Nikolaieva served as both its inspiration and midwife, her association with the work has been lifelong, and this shows. Her reading has enormous concentration and a natural authority that is majestic. There is wisdom and humanity here, and she finds depths in this music that have eluded most other pianists who have offered samples. When heard in its entirety over a couple of evenings, the whole cycle has a cumulative effect much greater than its individual parts. No grumbles about the Hyperion recording, which is very natural.

7 Romances by Alexander Blok, Op. 127.
*(*) Chan. Dig. CHAN 8924; *ABTD 1522* [id.]. Nadia Pelle, Borodin Trio – ARENSKY: *Piano trio No. 2* *(*); PROKOFIEV: *Overture on Hebrew themes.* **

Nadia Pelle makes an appropriately authentic sound in the settings of Alexander Blok; though she is not always totally in tune (nor for that matter is the violinst), too much should not be made of these deficiences. This does not seriously challenge the Decca version with Söderström and Ashkenazy.

Lady Macbeth of Mtsensk (complete).
❀ *** EMI CDS7 49955-2 (2) [Ang. CDCB 49955]. Vishnevskaya, Gedda, Petkov, Krenn, Tear, Amb. Op. Ch., LPO, Rostropovich.

Rostropovich, in his finest recording ever, proves with thrilling conviction that this first version of Shostakovich's greatest work for the stage is among the most original operas of the century. In text *Lady Macbeth* may not be radically different from the revised version, *Katerina Ismailova*, but it has an extra sharpness of focus that transforms what is much more than just a sordid love-story involving three murders by the heroine. Here the brutality of the love affair between the rich merchant's wife and Sergei, the roving-eyed workman, has maximum punch; and Rostropovich, helped by superlative recording, all the more vivid on CD, gives a performance of breathtaking power. Vishnevskaya is inspired to give an outstanding performance and provides moments of great beauty alongside aptly coarser singing; and Gedda matches her well, totally idiomatic. As the sadistic father-in-law, Petkov is magnificent, particularly in his ghostly return, and there are fine contributions from Robert Tear, Werner Krenn, Birgit Finnilä and Alexander Malta.

Sibelius, Jean (1865–1957)

Academic march; Finlandia (arr. composer); *Har du mod? Op. 31/2; March of the Finnish Jaeger Battalion, Op. 91/1;* (i) *The origin of fire, Op. 32; Sandels, Op. 28; Song of the Athenians, Op. 31/3.*
** BIS CD 314 [id.]. (i) Sauli Tilikainen, Laulun Ystävät Male Ch., Gothenburg SO, Järvi.

The origin of fire is by far the most important work on this record. Sauli Tilikainen is very impressive indeed, and the playing of the Gothenburg Symphony Orchestra under Neeme Järvi has plenty of feeling and atmosphere. None of the other pieces are essential Sibelius. The singing of the Laulun Ystävät is good rather than outstanding, and the Gothenburg orchestra play with enthusiasm. Fine recording in the best BIS traditions.

Autrefois (Scène pastorale), Op. 96b; The Bard, Op. 64; Presto in D for strings; Spring song, Op. 16; Suite caractéristique, Op. 100; Suite champêtre, Op. 98b; Suite mignonne, Op. 98a; Valse chevaleresque, Op. 96c; Valse lyrique, Op. 96a.
*** BIS Dig. CD 384 [id.]. Gothenburg SO, Järvi.

A mixed bag. *The Bard* is Sibelius at his greatest and most powerful, and it finds Järvi at his best. He penetrates its intimate musings and sounds its depths to great effect. The remaining pieces are all light: some of the movements of the *Suite mignonne* and *Suite champêtre* could come straight out of a Tchaikovsky ballet, and Järvi does them with great charm. The last thing that the *Suite*, Op. 100, can be called is *caractéristique*, while the three pieces, Op. 96, find Sibelius in Viennese waltz mood. The rarity is *Autrefois*, which has a beguiling charm and is by far the most haunting of these pastiches. Sibelius introduces two sopranos and their *vocalise* is altogether captivating. The *Presto in D major for strings* is a transcription – and a highly effective one – of the third movement of the *B flat Quartet*, Op. 4. Excellent recording, as one has come to expect from BIS.

Belshazzar's Feast (suite), Op. 54; Dance intermezzo, Op. 45/2; The Dryad, Op. 45/1; Pan and Echo, Op. 53; Swanwhite, Op. 54.
*** BIS Dig. CD 359 [id.]. Gothenburg SO, Neeme Järvi.

Belshazzar's Feast, a beautifully atmospheric piece of orientalism, and the incidental music for Strindberg's *Swanwhite* may not be Sibelius at his most powerful but both include many characteristic touches and some haunting moments. Neeme Järvi's collection with the Gothenburg orchestra is first class in every way.

Cassazione, Op. 6; Preludio; The Tempest: Prelude & suites 1–2, Op. 109; Tiera.
*** BIS Dig. CD 448 [id.]. Gothenburg SO, Järvi.

Sibelius's incidental music to *The Tempest*, written for a particularly lavish Copenhagen production in 1926, was his penultimate work and one of his most imaginative scores. Järvi's recording is the first to have appeared for a decade – and very good it is, too. It is the finest and most atmospheric since Beecham and, though it does not surpass the latter in pieces like *The Oak-tree* or the *Chorus of the winds*, it is still impressive and offers first-class modern recording. Järvi also includes the *Prelude*, omitted on Beecham's disc. The *Cassazione* comes from 1904 and is thus later than its early opus number. Sibelius never published it and intended to revise it (in character it resembles the *King Christian II* music), but it is well worth having on disc. Neither *Tiera* nor the *Preludio*, both from the 1890s, is of great interest or particularly characteristic.

Violin concerto in D min. (1903–4 version); *Violin concerto in D min., Op. 47* (1905; published version).
*** BIS Dig. CD 500 [id.]. Leonidas Kavakos, Lahti SO, Osmo Vänskä.

Although the main ideas for the *Violin concerto* came to him much earlier, the work occupied Sibelius for much of 1903–4. Its first performance left him dissatisfied and he immediately withdrew it for revision. This CD presents Sibelius's initial thoughts so that for the first time we can see the familiar final version struggling to emerge from the chrysalis. The differences are considerable (though not by any means as extensive as those in the 1915 and 1919 versions of the *Fifth Symphony*, of which paired recordings are planned by this company). Comparison of the two concertos makes a fascinating study: the middle movement is the least affected by change, but the outer movements are both longer in the original score, and the whole piece takes almost 40 minutes. Very early on one is brought up with a start by an assertive rhythmic figure in the orchestra which Sibelius subsequently removed; and there is some solo writing of enormous difficulty, including a complete and demanding cadenza. Sibelius purified the concerto's form, deleting unnecessary ornament. A rather lovely idea which looks forward to the lighter palette of the *Humoresques* was also removed: the ability to sacrifice good ideas in the interests of structural coherence is one of the hallmarks of a great composer. But though there is some regret at the losses, the overall gain leaves one in no doubt as to the correctness of Sibelius's judgement. The Greek violinist, Leonidis Kavakos, proves more than capable of handling the hair-raising difficulties of the 1904 version and is an idiomatic exponent of the definitive concerto. The Lahti orchestra under Osmo Vänskä give excellent support and the balance is natural and realistic, with the soloist occupying the kind of aural space you would expect in the concert hall. An issue of exceptional interest and value.

Violin concerto in D min., Op. 47.
❀ *** Sony Dig. MK 44548 [id.]. Cho-Liang Lin, Philh. O, Salonen – NIELSEN: *Violin concerto.* *** ❀
*** BMG/RCA RD 87019 [RCD1 7019]. Heifetz, Chicago SO, Hendl – GLAZUNOV: *Concerto;* PROKOFIEV: *Concerto No. 2.* ***
*** Ph. Dig. 416 821-2 [id.]. Mullova, Boston SO, Ozawa – TCHAIKOVSKY: *Concerto.* **(*)
(M) *** Ph. 420 895-2. Accardo, LSO, C. Davis – DVOŘÁK: *Violin concerto.* ***
*** EMI CDC7 47167-2 [id.]. Perlman, Pittsburgh SO, Previn – SINDING: *Suite.* ***
*** EMI Dig. CDC7 54127-2 [id.]; *EL 7754127-4.* Nigel Kennedy, CBSO, Rattle – TCHAIKOVSKY: *Concerto.* **(*)
(M) (***) EMI mono CDH7 61011-2. Ginette Neveu, Philh. O, Susskind – BRAHMS: *Concerto.* (***)
(M) **(*) Sony SMK 47540 [id.]. Francescatti, NYPO, Bernstein – BRAHMS: *Concerto.* **(*)
(BB) *** Naxos Dig. 8.550329; *4550329* [id.]. Dong-Suk Kang, Slovak (Bratislava) RSO, Adrian Leaper – HALVORSEN: *Air Norvégien* etc.; SINDING: *Légende;* SVENDSEN: *Romance.* ***

(M) **(*) EMI Dig. CDD7 63894-2 [id.]. Gidon Kremer, Philh. O, Muti – SCHUMANN: *Concerto*. **(*)
(M) (**) EMI mono CDH7 64030-2 [id.]. Heifetz, LPO, Beecham – GLAZUNOV *Violin concerto* (***) ❀; TCHAIKOVSKY: *Violin concerto*. (***)
(M) ** Teldec/Warner Dig. 9031 74784-2 [id.]. Zehetmair, Leipzig GO, Masur – J. HAYDN: *Concerto* ***; M. HAYDN: *Concerto*. **(*)

Cho-Liang Lin's playing is distinguished not only by flawless intonation and an apparently effortless virtuosity but also by great artistry. He produces a glorious sonority at the opening, which must have been exactly what Sibelius wanted, wonderfully clean and silvery, and the slow movement has tenderness, warmth and yet restraint with not a hint of the over-heated emotions which one encounters all too often. Erik Tawaststjerna makes much of the aristocratic quality which Sibelius looked for in interpreters of the *Concerto*, and there is no lack of aristocratic finesse here. At the same time, however, there is more to the *Concerto* than that, and Lin encompasses the extrovert brilliance of the finale and the bravura of the cadenza with real mastery. The Philharmonia Orchestra rise to the occasion under Esa-Pekka Salonen, and the recording is first class.

Heifetz's stereo performance of the Sibelius *Concerto* with the Chicago Symphony Orchestra under Walter Hendl set the standard by which all other versions have come to be judged. It is also one of his finest recordings; in remastered form the sound is vivid, with the Chicago ambience making an apt setting for the finely focused violin line. The purity and luminous beauty of the violin tone at the opening put the seal on this as an interpretation of unusual depth, consummate technique and supreme artistry. There is some dryness added to the sound, which is very bright, but good results can be obtained by use of the controls.

Viktoria Mullova's account has a certain warmth, though it is mercifully free of the *zigeuner* element one so often encounters in performance. Mullova captures its magical element right from the very opening; the slow movement has a cool dignity that is impressive. The recording is excellent.

Of the mid-price versions, Salvatore Accardo and Sir Colin Davis would be a first choice. There is no playing to the gallery, and no schmaltz – and in the slow movement there is a sense of repose and nobility. The finale is exhilarating, and there is an aristocratic feeling to the whole which is just right.

Itzhak Perlman plays the work as a full-blooded virtuoso showpiece and the Pittsburgh orchestra under André Previn support him to the last man and woman. In the first movement his tempo is broader than that of Heifetz, and he is at his stunning best in the first cadenza and makes light of all the fiendish difficulties in which the solo part abounds. He takes a conventional view of the slow movement, underlining its passion, and he gives us an exhilarating finale. The sound is marvellously alive and thrilling, though the forward balance is very apparent.

Nigel Kennedy's account of the *Violin concerto* is quite superbly balanced; the violin is in exactly the right perspective. Throughout, his intonation is true and he takes the considerable technical hurdles of this concerto in his stride. There is a touch of the *zigeuner* throb in the slow movement, but on the whole he plays with real spirit and panache. This can be confidently recommended if the coupling with the Tchaikovsky, a rather more indulgent performance, is suitable. The playing of the Birmingham orchestra is excellent throughout as, indeed, is the EMI recording.

The magnetism of Neveu in this, her first concerto recording, is inescapable from her opening phrase onwards, warmly expressive and dedicated, yet with no hint of mannerism. The finale is taken at a speed which is comfortable rather than exciting, but the extra spring of the thrumming dance-rhythms, superbly lifted, is ample compensation, providing a splendid culmination.

Francescatti's account is stunning in its immediacy and impact. With Bernstein fully matching the intensity of his soloist this is a performance impossible to forget. Francescatti's richness of tone is immediately evident in the opening theme and dominating the impassioned reading of the slow movement. Under such emotional stress the soloists's technique holds up with amazing security and if this reading does not quite convey the noble assurance that Heifetz offers supremely, the reading has understanding as well as power. The snag is the brightly lit recording, made in the Avery Fisher Hall in 1963, which the remastering serves only to emphasize, with the solo violin artificially balanced well out in front, in a spotlight.

Dong-Suk Kang gave a commanding performance of the Sibelius *Violin concerto* at a 1990 (televised) BBC Prom. and is familiar to both concert and radio audiences on both sides of the

Atlantic. He chooses some popular Scandinavian repertoire pieces, such as the charming Svendsen *Romance in G*, as makeweights. Although this newcomer is very fine, he is perhaps a little wanting – albeit only a little – in tenderness as opposed to passion in the slow movement, but there is splendid virtuosity in the outer movements. The orchestral playing is decent rather than distinguished. In the bargain basement, this enjoys a strong competitive advantage, but even if it were at full price it would feature quite high in the current lists.

Kremer presents the *Concerto* essentially as a bravura showpiece and his is a vibrantly extrovert reading. While the recording balance places the soloist well forward, the orchestral texture has plenty of impact and good detail, and the fortissimo brass blaze out excitingly. There is undoubted poetry in the slow movement, and throughout Muti gives his soloist splendid support. This is hardly a first choice, but it is now much more competitive at mid-price, and it has an interesting coupling.

Heifetz's mono recording was first issued in an HMV Sibelius Society edition of seven 78-r.p.m. discs, so that it never gained the same currency as the post-war account by Ginette Neveu and Dobrowen. Although many first recordings have something special that stands out, the Heifetz/Beecham Sibelius *Violin concerto*, marvellous though it is, excites admiration rather than affection. And despite Sir Thomas's direction, Heifetz gave the more powerful account of it in his later, Chicago recording with Walter Hendl in the early days of stereo. (The reverse was the case with the Glazunov.) A good transfer nevertheless, and well worth having.

Zehetmair is obviously a fine player, though there are one or two zigeuner-like slides that are controversial. Given the richness and distinction of the competition, this is not a strong contender, although it is certainly enjoyable if the couplings by Josef and Michael Haydn are of interest.

The Dryad, Op. 45/1; En Saga, Op. 9.
(M) *** Chan. CHAN 6524; *MBTD 6524* [id.]. SNO, Gibson – NIELSEN: *Symphony No. 4* etc. **(*)

Sir Alexander Gibson's analogue recordings of the Sibelius tone-poems date from the late 1970s and were originally issued by RCA. The recordings have been digitally remastered with great success; the slightly distant sound-balance is admirably suited to the music, with the spacious acoustic of Glasgow City Hall generally flattering the orchestra and creating a suitable ambient atmosphere. Gibson's affinity with the Sibelius idiom is at its most convincing here, particularly in an elusive piece like *The Dryad*, although *En Saga*, which opens the collection, is also evocative and shows an impressive overall grasp. At mid-price and offered coupled with the Nielsen *Fourth*, these versions make rewarding listening.

En Saga, Op. 9; Finlandia, Op. 26; Karelia suite, Op. 11; Legend: The Swan of Tuonela, Op. 22/2; Tapiola, Op. 112.
(M) **(*) EMI Analogue/Dig. EMI CDM7 64331-2 [id.]; *EG 764331-4*. BPO, Karajan.

This was Karajan's third recording of *Tapiola* but his first of *En Saga*, in which he is a brisk story-teller, more concerned with narrative than with atmosphere at the beginning; but the climax is very exciting and the *lento assai* section and the coda are quite magical. Here as in *Finlandia*, which is superbly played, the digital remastering gives a full bodied sound-picture. *Tapiola* is broader and more expansive than the first DG version; at the storm section, the more spacious tempo is vindicated and again the climax is electrifying. But both are great performances and totally committed. *The Swan of Tuonela* is most persuasively done. These recordings date from 1977. The later, digital recording of *Karelia* has been added for the current reissue. Here, in the outer movements, which Karajan paces deliberately, the rather weighty bass detracts somewhat from the freshness of the presentation.

En Saga, Op. 9; Finlandia, Op. 26; Karelia suite, Op. 11; Tapiola, Op. 112.
(M) *** Decca Dig. 417 762-2 [id.]. Philh. O, Ashkenazy.

These are all digital recordings of the first order – Decca sound at its very best. The performances are among the finest available, especially *En Saga* which is thrillingly atmospheric, while the *Karelia suite* is freshly appealing in its directness. The climax of *Tapiola* is almost frenzied in its impetus – some may feel that Ashkenazy goes over the top here; but this is the only real criticism of a distinguished collection and a very real bargain.

En Saga, Op. 9; Scènes historiques, Opp. 25, 66.
*** BIS Dig. CD 295 [id.]. Gothenburg SO, Järvi.

Järvi has the advantage of modern digital sound and the Gothenburg orchestra is fully inside the idiom of this music and plays very well indeed. Järvi's *En saga* is exciting and well paced.

Finlandia; Karelia suite, Op. 11. Kuolema: Valse triste. Legends: Lemminkäinen's return, Op. 22/4; Pohjola's daughter, Op. 49.
(M) **(*) EMI CDM7 69205-2 [id.]. Hallé O, Barbirolli.

Although the orchestral playing is not as polished as that of a virtuoso orchestra, it is enthusiastic and has the advantage of excellent recording from the mid-1960s. *Pohjola's daughter* is extremely impressive, spacious but no less exciting for all the slower tempi. *Lemminkäinen's return* is also a thrilling performance. Overall, a desirable introduction to Sibelius's smaller orchestral pieces, with admirable stereo definition.

(i) *Finlandia, Op. 26; Karelia suite, Op. 11; Kuolema: Valse triste, Op. 44; Legend: The Swan of Tuonela, Op. 22/2;* (ii) *Tapiola, Op. 112.*
(B) ** Decca 433 602-2; *433 602-4* [id.]. (i) New Philh. O, Kazimierz Kord; (ii) VPO, Maazel.

Maazel's 1968 recording of *Tapiola* was one of the finest of the analogue era. It is not as atmospheric as Karajan's at the outset, but it grows in power and impact as it proceeds. Maazel takes the famous storm section far more slowly than almost any other version and it gains immeasurably by his so doing (Kajanus did the same in his famous old recording for the Sibelius Society). The recording is of Decca's best vintage. The rest of the programme under Kord is an altogether more routine affair. It was recorded in Decca's closely balanced Phase 4 system, and the opening of *Finlandia* brings richly sonorous brass sounds, but the performance is too heavy, almost laboured. Kord is at his best in the lighter-textured pieces, *Valse triste* and *The Swan of Tuonela*, which has plenty of atmosphere, but the *Karelia suite*, although played well, needs a stronger profile than this, especially the central *Ballade*.

Finlandia, Op. 26; Karelia suite, Op. 11; Scènes historiques: Festivo, Op. 25/3; The Chase; Love song; At the drawbridge, Op. 66/1–3; The Tempest (incidental music): *suites Nos. 1–2, Op. 109.*
❀ (M) (***) EMI mono CDM7 63397-2 [id.]. RPO, Beecham.

Beecham's mono performance of the incidental music for *The Tempest* is magical – no one has captured its spirit with such insight. A pity that he omits the *Prelude*, which he had done so evocatively on 78s, though the last number of the second suite covers much of the same ground. The four *Scènes historiques* are beautifully done, with the most vivid orchestral colouring: *The Chase* is particularly delectable. No apologies whatsoever need be made about the sound here, though in the *Intermezzo* from *Karelia* (which has a 78-r.p.m. source) the quality is curiously crumbly at the opening and close: surely a better original could have been found. The *Alla marcia* is better, although no one would buy this record for *Finlandia*.

Finlandia, Op. 26; Kuolema: Valse triste, Op. 44; Legends: The Swan of Tuonela, Op. 22/2; Tapiola, Op. 112.
*** DG Dig. 413 755-2 [id.]. BPO, Karajan.

This is Karajan's fourth and undoubtedly greatest account of *Tapiola*, for he has the full measure of its vision and power. Never has it sounded more mysterious or its dreams more savage; nor has the build-up to the storm ever struck such a chilling note of terror: an awesomely impressive musical landscape, while the wood-sprites weaving their magic secrets come vividly to life. *The Swan*, Karajan's third account on record, is powerful and atmospheric; and the remaining two pieces, *Valse triste* and *Finlandia*, reinforce the feeling that this Berlin/Karajan partnership has never been equalled.

Finlandia, Op. 26; Legend: The Swan of Tuonela, Op. 22/2; The Oceanides, Op. 73; Pohjola's daughter, Op. 49; Tapiola, Op. 112.
(M) **(*) Chan. CHAN 6508; *MBTD 6508* [id.]. SNO, Gibson.

Gibson has a real feeling for Sibelius, and these very well-played performances are given an atmospheric and convincingly balanced analogue recording which makes a very realistic impression. *The Oceanides* is particularly successful and, if Karajan finds even greater intensity in *Tapiola*, Gibson's account certainly captures the icy desolation of the northern forests. He is at his most persuasive in an elusive piece like *The Dryad*, although *En Saga* is also evocative, showing an impressive overall grasp. The SNO are at the peak of their form throughout these performances.

(i) *6 Humoresques, Opp. 87 & 89. Rakastava, Op. 14; Pelléas et Mélisande – Suite, Op. 46.*
** Finlandia Dig. FACD 381 [id.]. (i) Leonidas Kavakos, Espoo CO, Juhani Lamminmäki.

The young Greek violinist, Leonids Kavakos, made a very positive impression with his account of the 1903–4 version of the *Violin concerto* for BIS, but he is less convincing in the lovely *Humoresques*. Here he is mannered and is no match for his rival Dong-Suk Kang. *Rakastava* would also benefit from less sophistication though it is not a bad performance. Nor is the Espoo account of the suite from *Pelléas et Mélisande* but, given the opposition from such artists as Beecham and Karajan, the Finlandia issue is not a strong contender.

(i) *6 Humoresques, Opp. 87 & 89; 2 Serenades, Op. 69; 2 Serious melodies, Op. 79; Ballet scene* (1891); *Overture in E* (1891).
*** BIS Dig. CD 472 (i) Dong-Suk Kang, Gothenburg SO, Neeme Järvi.

The *Humoresques* are among Sibelius's most inspired smaller pieces. They are poignant as well as virtuosic and have a lightness of touch, a freshness and a sparkle that make one wonder why they are not in the repertoire of every violinist of standing. The two *Serenades* have great poetic feeling and a keen Nordic melancholy. They are wonderfully played by this distinguished Korean artist, who has impeccable technical address and is beautifully accompanied. The two orchestral works are juvenilia which predate the *Kullervo Symphony*. There are some characteristic touches (the second group of the *Overture* is very much in the *Karelia* idiom), but Sibelius himself did not think well enough of them to permit their publication. All the violin pieces, however, are to be treasured, and the recording is top class. A rewarding and indeed indispensable disc in its way, and not only for Sibelians.

4 Legends, Op. 22 (Lemminkäinen and the maidens of Saari; The Swan of Tuonela; Lemminkäinen in Tuonela; Lemminkäinen's return).
*** BIS Dig. CD 294 [id.]. Gothenburg SO, Järvi.

4 Legends, Op. 22; The Bard, Op. 64; (i) *Luonnatar, Op. 70.*
(M) *** Chan. CHAN 6586 [id.]. SNO, Gibson, (i) with Phyllis Bryn-Johnson.

Järvi has the advantage of fine, modern digital sound and a wonderfully truthful balance. How good it is to hear solo violins sounding so naturally life-size. The bass drum sounds impressively realistic, too. Järvi gives a passionate and atmospheric reading of the first *Legend* and his account of *The Swan of Tuonela* is altogether magical, one of the best in the catalogue. He takes a broader view of *Lemminkäinen in Tuonela* than many of his rivals and builds up an appropriately black and powerful atmosphere, showing the Gothenburg brass to excellent advantage. The slight disappointment is *Lemminkäinen's homeward journey* which, though exciting, hasn't the possessed, manic quality of Beecham's very first record, which sounded as if a thousand demons were in pursuit.

Gibson, however, is at mid-price; he also offers sensitive performances of *The Bard*, which has fine atmosphere and delicate textures, and *Luonnatar*, where the soprano voice is made to seem like another orchestral instrument. The Scottish orchestra play freshly and with much commitment. *The Swan of Tuonela* has a darkly brooding primeval quality, and there is an electric degree of tension in the third piece, *Lemminkäinen in Tuonela*. The two outer *Legends* have ardent rhythmic feeling, and altogether this is highly successful. The recorded sound is excellent.

4 Legends, Op. 22; En Saga, Op. 9.
*(*) Sony Dig. SK 48067 [id.]. Los Angeles PO, Salonen.

Essentially slick performances of both *En Saga* and the *Four Legends* from Esa-Pekka Salonen and the Los Angeles Orchestra. Salonen places the third legend, *Lemminkäinen in Tuonela* second, thus maximizing the contrast between it and *Lemminkäinen's Homeward Journey*. Save for a very good *Swan of Tuonela*, these are very fast, razzle-dazzle performances. They are well recorded (though the bass drum is far too prominent), but there is more Salonen than Sibelius here. There are some very good effects (the lower strings at the opening of *Lemminkäinen in Tuonela* are quite striking) but both Neeme Järvi and Sir Alexander Gibson (on Chandos) are less flashy and bring one closer to this music. So, of course, did Ormandy, whose CD should be reissued on mid-price without delay.

The Oceanides, Op. 73; Pelléas et Mélisande: suite, Op. 46; Symphony No. 7 in C, Op. 105; Tapiola, Op. 112.

(M) *** EMI CDM7 63400-2 [id.]. RPO, Beecham.

The Oceanides, recorded at the composer's behest, is one of Beecham's greatest performances on record and is a must. It is Sibelius's most poetic evocation of the sea, and this marvellous playing captures every nuance of the score. The *Pelléas et Mélisande suite* was a yardstick by which all others have been measured ever since. Only Karajan matches it, and even the Berlin Philharmonic textures do not sound more luminous and magical than here, for the CD transfer is wonderfully refined. However, Beecham omits the *By the sea* movement. *Tapiola* is also very impressive: it has all the requisite brooding power and must be numbered among the very finest accounts committed to disc. Only the *Seventh Symphony* disappoints – and that only relatively speaking.

Pelléas et Mélisande: suite.
*** DG Dig. 410 026-2 [id.]. BPO, Karajan – GRIEG: *Peer Gynt suites 1 & 2.* ***

At last a version of Sibelius's subtle and atmospheric score that can compare with the classic Beecham version; indeed in certain movements, *By the spring in the park* and the *Pastorale*, it not only matches Sir Thomas but almost surpasses him. There is also plenty of mystery in the third movement, *At the seashore*, omitted from the Beecham set. The recording is very striking indeed, with great clarity and presence.

Rakastava (suite), *Op. 14; Scènes historiques, Opp. 25, 66; Valse lyrique, Op. 96/1.*
*** Chan. CHAN 8393 [id.]. SNO, Gibson.

Written for a patriotic pageant, the *Scènes historiques* are vintage Sibelius. In the *Love song* Gibson strikes the right blend of depth and reticence, while elsewhere he conveys a fine sense of controlled power. Convincing and eloquent performances that have a natural feeling for the music. Gibson's *Rakastava* is beautifully unforced and natural, save for the last movement, which is a shade too slow. The *Valse lyrique* is not good Sibelius, but everything else certainly is. Gibson plays this repertoire with real commitment and the recorded sound is excellent, with the orchestral layout, slightly distanced, most believable.

Scaramouche, Op. 71; The Language of the birds: Wedding march.
*** BIS Dig. CD 502 [id.]. Gothenburg SO, Neeme Järvi.

Sibelius undertook the composition of the ballet-pantomime *Scaramouche* – which was commissioned by the Danish publisher, Wilhelm Hansen – with the greatest reluctance and tried to extricate himself from the contract. The score which he delivered in 1913 is the longest musical sequence he ever wrote: it runs to some 65 minutes without a break. Although some of the invention is thin, much more of it, particularly in the first Act, is inspired. Indeed those who know only the suite, which Sibelius's son-in-law, Jussi Jalas, compiled and recorded in the 1970s, will have little idea of its quality. It is scored for relatively small forces, including piano (not unlike Strauss's music for *Le bourgeois gentilhomme* of which one is perhaps reminded); at its best it reminds one of the luminous colourings of the *Humoresques* of five years later. There are interesting glimpses, too, of themes that were forming in the composer's mind, including an idea that was to surface the following year in *The Oceanides*, while the solo viola and cello figure (in Act I, scene viii) foreshadows the *Seventh Symphony*. A wistful, gentle and haunting score, slightly let down by its uneventful second Act. Sibelius did not think highly enough of the *Wedding march* to Adolf Paul's play, *The Language of the birds*, to give it an opus number but it is in fact quite an attractive miniature. The playing of the Gothenburg orchestra under Neeme Järvi is altogether excellent and so, too, is the BIS recording.

Symphonies Nos. 1–7.
(M) *** Decca Dig. 421 069-2 (4). Philh. O, Ashkenazy.
(M) **(*) Decca 430 778-2 (3). VPO, Maazel.
(M) **(*) Chan. Dig. CHAN 6559 (3). SNO, Sir Alexander Gibson.

(i) *Symphonies Nos. 1–7;* (ii) *Night ride and sunrise;* (i) *The Oceanides; Scene with cranes.*
(M) **(*) EMI CMS7 64118-2; *EX 764118-4* (4). (i) CBSO, (ii) Philh. O, Simon Rattle.

Ashkenazy's Sibelius series makes a rich and strong, consistently enjoyable cycle. Ashkenazy by temperament brings out the expressive warmth, colour and drama of the composer rather than his Scandinavian chill, reflecting perhaps his Slavonic background. The recordings are full and rich as well as brilliant, most of them of demonstration quality, even though they date from the early digital period. On four CDs at mid-price, the set makes a most attractive first recommendation.

Simon Rattle's performances with the City of Birmingham Symphony Orchestra are available both as a four-CD boxed set and as individual discs. The best advice is probably to opt for the individual disc for the *Fourth* and *Sixth*, coupled together. They are both impressive, as is his *Seventh*, coupled with the *Fifth* and the highly atmospheric *Scene with cranes*. Also on the same disc is his Philharmonia recording of *Night ride and sunrise* – grievously neglected in the concert hall but powerful in his hands. He swoons a little towards the end of the slow movement of the *First Symphony* and the scherzo is a bit too measured, but this comes with an absolutely superb *Oceanides* – the best since Beecham's. Similarly the *Second*, which is a bit overblown and has a self-indulgent slow movement, comes with a generally excellent *Third*. As a set the box is worth considering, but it would not be first choice.

By far the best of Maazel's performances are the *First* and *Fourth Symphonies* which are, of course, available on a separate disc. The latter is a reading of great power, one of the most intense and uncompromising since the celebrated 1937 Beecham version. The *Seventh Symphony*, too, is another landmark in the Sibelius discography and, apart from the occasional sweetness of the string vibrato, which may worry some more than it does us, has great majesty and breadth. The *Second* is also successful, but the *Fifth* and, more particularly, the *Sixth* do not come off as well. He sounds uninvolved in both works: the *Third* has a very good first movement but a faster-than-ideal second. The Decca analogue sound is excellent and is vividly transferred, and readers need not hesitate on that score.

Sir Alexander Gibson has been a doughty champion of Sibelius over the years and has recorded Nos. 1, 2 and 5 no fewer than three times, and Nos. 3 and 7 twice. His Sibelius cycle with what was the Scottish National and is now the Royal Scottish Orchestra was made over the period 1982–4. It is impressive, both musically and from an engineering point of view; there are no weak spots anywhere. (Indeed, one respected critic chose Gibson's version of No. 1 as his first choice on a BBC 'Record Review' some years ago.) At the same time it must be conceded that the peaks do not dwarf, say, the Maazel *Fourth* or *Seventh*. The performances are eminently sane, sound and reliable, and no one investing in the set is likely to be at all disappointed. Taken individually, none would be an absolute first choice.

Symphonies Nos. 1-3; 5; Belshazzar's Feast (incidental music), *Op. 51; Karelia suite; Pohjola's Daughter, Op. 49; Tapiola, Op. 112.*
(M) (***) Finlandia mono FACD 81234 (3). LSO, Robert Kajanus.

Robert Kajanus was Sibelius's most faithful advocate and conducted the first performances of many of his works. It was Kajanus's *Aino Symphony* that prompted Sibelius to embark on his *Kullervo Symphony*, and it was Kajanus who commissioned *En Saga*. When the Finnish government sponsored recordings of the first two symphonies in 1930, Sibelius insisted on having Kajanus as the most authentic interpreter. These performances were all made in 1930 and 1932 and sound amazingly good for the period. The celebrated storm in *Tapiola*, taken at a much slower and more effective tempo than is now usual, still has the power to terrify despite the inevitable sonic limitations, and no conductor has ever given a more spell-binding and atmospheric account of the suite from *Belshazzar's Feast*. The broader, more leisurely view Kajanus takes of the *Third Symphony* comes as a refreshing corrective to the later, more hurried accounts by Anthony Collins and Lorin Maazel. No performer, save Beecham in the *Fourth* and *Sixth* symphonies, came closer to Sibelius's intentions. Essential listening for all Sibelians.

Symphony No. 1 in E min., Op. 39.
**(*) DG Dig. 435 351-2 [id.]. VPO, Bernstein.

Symphony No. 1 in E min.; En Saga, Op. 9.
*** Collins Dig. 1093-2; *1093-4* [id.]. RPO, Sir Alexander Gibson.

Symphony No. 1 in E min.; Finlandia, Op. 26; Karelia suite, Op. 11.
❀ *** EMI Dig. CDC7 54273-2 [id.]. Oslo PO, Mariss Jansons.

Symphony No. 1 in E min.; The Oceanides.
(M) **(*) EMI Dig. CDM7 64119-2 [id.]; *EG 764119-4*. CBSO, Simon Rattle.

Mariss Jansons's account of the *First Symphony* is the finest to have appeared since Maazel's in the 1960s. The Oslo Philharmonic is on peak form, playing with thrilling virtuosity both in the *Symphony*, *Finlandia* and in the *Karelia suite*. Norway has neglected Sibelius at least on record though Oslo (or Christiania as it was then known) was among the first cities to hear the symphony; Sibelius himself conducted it there in 1900. Tempi are well judged, the players are responsive to every dynamic nuance, phrasing is beautifully shaped and the overall architecture of the piece is splendidly realized. A very exciting performance, which has you on the edge of your seat, and very vividly recorded too.

Sir Alexander Gibson has recorded the symphony twice before, but this new Collins version is undeniably the best. He gets very good playing from the RPO, not quite as high-voltage or virtuosic as the Oslo Philharmonic for Jansons but still very committed. As one would expect from a conductor of such strong Sibelian instincts, there are no idiosyncratic eccentricities and the music is borne along on a sturdy current. The recording is excellent (the same engineer recorded the Oslo performance) and the strings have greater transparency than in the EMI performance. Gibson's account of *En saga* is a bit fast, but there is no want of atmosphere.

If the whole symphony was as fine as the first movement in Rattle's hands, this would be a clear first recommendation. He has a powerful grasp of both its structure and character and elicits an enthusiastic response from his players. The slow movement is for the most part superb, with excellent playing from the wind and brass of the Birmingham orchestra; but he makes too much of the commas at the end of the movement, which are so exaggerated as to be disruptive. The Scherzo has splendid character but is a good deal slower than the marking. The Oceanides were the nymphs who inhabited the waters of Homeric mythology, and the opening of the piece has an atmosphere that is altogether ethereal. Simon Rattle has its measure and conveys all its mystery and poetry. This is a subtle and masterly performance.

Another outstanding new version comes from DG to join a catalogue already well stocked with three-star recordings. Leonard Bernstein gets some electrifying playing from the Vienna Philharmonic and he is superbly recorded at live concerts in the Grosser Saal of the Musikverein in February 1990. Of course there is some expressive self-indulgence, but this is by far the best of Bernstein's recent Sibelius cycle with the Vienna orchestra. However, uncoupled and at full price with only 40 minutes of playing time, it is uncompetitive, particularly when Karajan's excellent 1982 account (coupled with his superb reading of the *Sixth*) and Maazel's Vienna account (coupled with the *Fourth*) are both available at mid-price. All the same, Bernstein's is a version to hear.

Symphonies Nos. 1 in E min.; 3 in C, Op. 52.
(B) **(*) DG 429 526-2. Helsinki R. O, Kamu.

Kamu's Helsinki version of the *First Symphony* does not lack excitement, but it is not distinctive. The *Third*, however, is among the finest ever put on disc and this bargain reissue is well worth exploring on its account alone. Tempi are invariably well judged and the atmosphere is thoroughly authentic, particularly in the slow movement, whose character seems to have eluded so many distinguished conductors. The recording is excellent, but the digital remastering, in seeking to clarify further a full-bodied sound, rich in ambience, gives an occasional hint of minor congestion.

Symphonies Nos. 1 in E min.; 4 in A min., Op. 63.
(M) *** Decca 417 789-2; *417 789-4*. VPO, Maazel.
(M) **(*) Chan. Dig. CHAN 6555; *MBTD 6555* [id.]. SNO, Sir Alexander Gibson.

Maazel's VPO performance of the *First Symphony* has freshness of vision to commend it, along with careful attention to both the letter and the spirit of the score. The Vienna Philharmonic responds with enthusiasm and brilliance and the Decca engineers produce splendid detail (except for the important timpani part in the first movement echoing the main theme, which might have been more sharply defined). The climaxes of the outer movements are very exciting. The *Fourth* is equally impressive. The orchestral tone is less richly upholstered than in some more modern versions; but the players make the closest contact with the music, and Maazel's reading brings great concentration and power: the first movement is as cold and unremitting as one could wish. A fine bargain.

The Scottish orchestra is excellently recorded in the warm acoustics of the Glasgow SNO Centre and one of the hallmarks of the set is Gibson's instinctive northern feeling for Sibelian colour and texture. The fine (1982/3) digital sound brings a natural concert-hall balance. No. 1 does not have the tension and power of, say, Ashkenazy or Maazel, and in the closing pages Gibson draws the music together expansively. The playing of the Scottish orchestra is always committed and, if it lacks something in refinement both here and in the *Fourth*, the impact and authenticity of the latter reading is never in doubt.

Symphonies Nos. 1 in E min.; 6 in D min., Op. 104.
(M) *** EMI Dig. CDD7 63896-2 [id.]; *ET 763896*. BPO, Karajan.

In the *First Symphony* Karajan, a great Tchaikovsky interpreter, identifies with the work's inheritance. But there is a sense of grandeur and vision here, and the opulence and virtuosity of the Berliners helps to project the heroic dimensions of Karajan's performance. The early digital recording (1981) is not top-drawer: the bass is overweighted, but the full upper strings sing out gloriously with the richest amplitude in the finale, which has an electrifying climax; the brass is comparably rich and resonant. Karajan's version of the *Sixth* was made in 1981 and it brings to life the other-worldly quality of this score: the long white nights of the northern summer and their 'fragile melancholy', that the slow movement conjures up. Even though this is a spacious account, we are never unaware of the sense of forward movement. In short, this is Karajan at his finest: not even Beecham made the closing pages sound more magical. This recording is better than its predecessor, and the EMI team have achieved a more spacious acoustic ambience.

Symphonies Nos. 1 in E min.; 7 in C, Op. 105.
(M) *** Decca Dig. 425 028-2; *425 028-4* [id.]. Philh. O, Ashkenazy.

Ashkenazy's digital coupling of the *First* and *Seventh Symphonies*, recorded in 1982 and 1984 respectively, is outstandingly successful; at mid-price, it will become a ready first choice for many collectors. The performance of the *First* is held together well and is finely shaped. Ashkenazy is exactly on target in the Scherzo. The resultant sense of momentum is exhilarating and here, as when echoing the main theme of the first movement, the timpani make a riveting effect. Throughout, the sheer physical excitement that this score engenders is tempered by admirable control. Only at the end of the slow movement does one feel that Ashkenazy could perhaps have afforded greater emotional restraint, but the big tune of the finale is superbly handled. The recording has splendid detail and clarity of texture, and there is all the presence and body one could ask for, with the bass-drum rolls particularly realistic. The *Seventh Symphony* is also very fine. Ashkenazy does not build up this work quite as powerfully as some others do, but he has the measure of its nobility and there is much to admire – indeed, much that is thrilling in his interpretation. As in the *First Symphony*, the playing of the Philharmonia Orchestra, like the recording, is of the very first order.

Symphony No. 2 in D, Op. 43.
**(*) Chesky/New Note CD-3 [id.]. RPO, Barbirolli.
(M) (***) EMI mono CDM7 63399-2 [id.]. BBC SO, Beecham – DVOŘÁK: *Symphony No. 8.* (***)

Symphony No. 2 in D; Finlandia, Op. 26.
*(*) Chan. Dig. CHAN 9020 [id.]. Danish RSO, Segerstam.

Symphony No. 2 in D; Finlandia, Op. 26; Karelia suite, Op. 11.
(M) *** Decca Dig. 430 737-2; *430 737-4* [id.]. Philh. O, Ashkenazy.

Symphony No. 2 in D; Finlandia, Op. 26; Pohjola's daughter, Op. 49; The Swan of Tuonela, Op. 22/2.
(M) (**(*)) BMG/RCA mono GD 60294. NBC SO, Toscanini.

Symphony No. 2 in D; Kuolema, Op. 44: Scene with cranes; Valse triste; Nightride and sunrise, Op. 55.
*** BMG/RCA Dig. RD 87919 [7919-2-RC]. Finnish RSO, Saraste.

Symphony No. 2 in D; Romance for strings in C, Op. 42.
*** BIS Dig. CD 252 [id.]. Gothenburg SO, Järvi.

Symphony No. 2 in D; Legend: The Swan of Tuonela, Op. 22/2.
(B) **(*) Pickwick Dig. PCD 927; *CIMPC 927* [id.]. LSO, Mackerras.

Järvi is very brisk in the opening *Allegretto*: this Gothenburg version has more sinew and fire than its rivals, and the orchestral playing is more responsive and disciplined than that of the SNO on Chandos. Throughout, Järvi has an unerring sense of purpose and direction and the momentum never slackens. Of course, there is not the same opulence as the Philharmonia under Ashkenazy on Decca, but the BIS performance is concentrated in feeling and thoroughly convincing. The *Romance for strings* is attractively done.

Although Saraste's account of the *Second Symphony* is not a first choice, it is still highly recommendable. He has a good feeling for the shape of a phrase and for colour, and has the measure of this symphony's breadth. He can also handle a Sibelian climax, and there is no lack of power here. Although Rattle casts a stronger spell in the *Scene with cranes*, Saraste gets very good results both here and in *Nightride and sunrise*. The recording is well detailed and the whole disc remains strongly competitive.

Ashkenazy's is a passionate, volatile reading, in many ways a very Russian view of Sibelius, with Ashkenazy finding a clear affinity with the Tchaikovsky symphonies. At the very opening, the quick, flexible treatment of the repeated crotchet motif is urgent, not weighty or ominous as it can be. Ashkenazy's control of tension and atmosphere makes for the illusion of live performance in the building of each climax, and the rich digital sound adds powerfully to that impression. Yet some listeners may find it more difficult to respond positively to this reading; like R.L., they may feel the performance is wanting in firmness of grip, especially in the slow movement, with the dramatic pauses lacking spontaneity and unanimity of response. Ashkenazy's performances of *Finlandia* and the *Karelia suite* are as fine as any and, like the symphony are afforded first class Decca sound. The *Symphony* and *Finlandia* were recorded at the Kingsway Hall (1979/80) and *Karelia* at Walthamstow (1985).

Barbirolli's version with the RPO is a performance of stature and is by far the finest of the four versions he committed to disc. There is a thrilling sense of live music-making here and a powerful sense of momentum. A high-voltage account, then, and very well recorded, though the upper strings are slightly drier than they were in the LP version on RCA. It retails at full price, which reduces its competitiveness, particularly as it comes without a fill-up. The sleeve has some howlers: Rapallo, where Sibelius started working on it, is not 'an art-laden town south of Benice' but on the other side of Italy, to the east of Genoa; and the work's dedicatee, Axel Carpelan, was far from 'wealthy'. All the same, this performance is powerful and must rank among the best currently before the public.

Sir Charles Mackerras gives an eminently well-judged account of the *Second Symphony*. The tempo of the first movement is apt, a real allegretto, fast but without going to quite the same extreme as Järvi on BIS. There is no lack of tenderness and he shapes phrases with sensitivity. The fill-up, too, has no lack of atmosphere. The recording, made in the EMI Abbey Road studios, is bright and clean.

Beecham's performance comes from a BBC tape of serviceable quality made at London's Royal Festival Hall in 1954. It is a pretty incandescent performance and the BBC orchestra, spurred on by various vocal exhortations from the conductor, play with great enthusiasm. Beecham admirers will not want to be without it.

Three recordings of the *Second Symphony* survive from Toscanini's baton: one from his BBC season in 1938, a second from 1939 and the present issue from 1940. All offer some superb playing but are a shade hard-driven. The account of *Pohjola's daughter* is arguably the most powerful and exciting ever committed to disc and in its elemental power even surpasses Kajanus and Koussevitzky.

Leif Segerstam's account of the *Second Symphony* is broadly expansive and warm-hearted but not a little self-indulgent, particularly in the slow movement whose climax he italicizes heavily. (Segerstam takes over five minutes longer than Järvi, and well over eight minutes longer than Beecham or Toscanini.) The recording has a pleasing warmth but could do with greater transparency in climaxes.

Symphonies Nos. 2 in D; 3 in C, Op. 52.
(M) *** EMI CDM7 64120-2 [id.]; *EG 7644120-4*. CBSO, Simon Rattle.

In No. 2 the CBSO play with fervour and enthusiasm except, perhaps, in the first movement where the voltage is lower – particularly in the development, which is not easy to bring off. The slow movement is full-bodied and gutsy, convincing even when Rattle arrests the flow of the argument by underlining certain points. The Scherzo is bracing enough, though in the Trio the oboe tune is caressed a little too much; however, the transition to the finale is magnificent and Rattle finds the *tempo giusto* in this movement. The Birmingham strings produce a splendidly fervent unison both here and elsewhere. Rattle's account of the *Third* is vastly superior to his *First* and *Second*. He is convincing not only in his pacing but also in his capacity to relate the parts to the whole. The slow movement is particularly fine; few have penetrated its landscape more completely, and the movement throughout is magical. The way in which he gradually builds up the finale is masterly and sure of instinct. The recording, made in the Warwick Arts Centre, sounds very well balanced, natural in perspective and finely detailed.

Symphonies Nos. 2 in D; 5 in E flat, Op. 82.
(M) *** Chan. Dig. CHAN 6556; *MBTD 6556* [id.]. SNO, Sir Alexander Gibson.

The *Second* is among the best of Gibson's cycle and scores highly, thanks to the impressive clarity, fullness and impact of the 1982 digital recording. Gibson's reading is honest and straightforward, free of bombast in the finale. Tempos are well judged: the first movement is neither too taut nor too relaxed: it is well shaped and feels right. Overall this is most satisfying, as is the *Fifth*, which has similar virtues: at no time is there any attempt to interpose the personality of the interpreter, and the finale has genuine weight and power. The interpretation has the authenticity which comes from the conductor being constantly immersed in these scores since the early 1960s.

Symphony No. 3 in C, Op. 52; King Kristian II suite, Op. 27.
*** BIS Dig. CD 228 [id.]. Gothenburg SO, Järvi.

With the *Third Symphony* there is a sense of the epic in Järvi's hands and it can hold its own with any in the catalogue. In Gothenburg, the slow movement is first class and the leisurely tempo adopted here by the Estonian conductor is just right. Järvi's coupling is the incidental music to *King Christian II*; his account is splendidly committed throughout and free from the literalness that seems at times to distinguish this conductor. This is very beautifully played and recorded.

Symphonies Nos. 3 in C; 6 in D min., Op. 104; 7 in C, Op. 105.
(M) *** Chan. CHAN 6557; *MBTD 6557* [id.]. SNO, Sir Alexander Gibson.

With three symphonies offered, some 74 minutes overall, this is a fine bargain and an excellent way to experience Gibson's special feeling for this composer. The SNO is in very good form. The first movement of the *Third* has real momentum and the Scottish orchestra play with genuine fire and enthusiasm. The *Andantino* is fast, faster than the composer's marking. One feels that Gibson has learned this symphony from Anthony Collins's famous mono Decca version. Such a tempo, while it gives the music-making fine thrust, means that Gibson, like Collins before him, loses some of the fantasy of this enigmatic movement. But there is more here to admire than to cavil at. The *Sixth* is impressive too, with plenty of atmosphere and some radiant playing from the Scottish violin section; as in the *Third*, the Chandos recording is vivid, full and well detailed. The *Seventh* has a rather relaxed feeling throughout, but it does not lack warmth and, as in No. 1, Gibson draws the threads together at the close with satisfying breadth.

Symphony No. 4 in A min., Op. 63; The Bard, Op. 64; En saga, Op. 9; In memoriam, Op. 59 Kuolema – Valse triste; Legend: Lemminkäinen's return, Op. 22/4.
* Koch Legacy mono 3-7061-2 [id.]. LPO, Sir Thomas Beecham.

Symphony No. 4 in A min.; The Bard, Op. 64; The Oceanides, Op. 73; Pohjola's Daughter, Op. 49.
*** RCA Dig. RD 60401 [60401-2-RC]. Finnish RSO, Saraste.

Symphony No. 4 in A min.; Kuolema: Valse triste. The Tempest, Op. 109: Berceuse.
(**) Dell'Arte mono DA 9023 [id.]. Phd. O, Stokowski – SHOSTAKOVICH: *Symphony No. 6.* (***)

Saraste's *Fourth* is a useful addition to the catalogue. His disc offers three other essential Sibelius works in very good performances. The *Symphony* too is well played and has plenty of atmosphere and power; though not all details are perfect (sufficient attention is not paid to dynamics at the opening of the finale), his is basically a convincingly shaped reading which penetrates well inside this dark, elusive world. He rightly uses the glockenspiel in the *Symphony* and follows Sibelius's instructions (in a letter to Leslie Heward) recommending tubular bells for *The Oceanides*, the only conductor to do so. Quite apart from that, his reading is very fine indeed, and there is nothing much wrong with *The Bard* or *Pohjola's daughter* either – and a lot that is right. The Finnish Radio Orchestra plays well for him and the recording is both present and full-bodied.

Stokowski's 1932 account of the *Fourth Symphony* was the first ever made. It is a good performance, even if the finale is a bit too measured, but it does not have the same bleak concentration that distinguishes the Beecham. The *Berceuse* from *The Tempest* has a wonderful allure, but the principal interest of this record is the coupling.

The Koch International Beecham transfer is not quite as full-bodied as the EMI version, and the presence of *En saga, In memoriam* and *Valse triste* does not outweigh the absence of the *Sixth Symphony*. Moreover the Koch CD is uncompetitively priced by comparison.

Symphony No. 4 in A min.; Canzonetta, Op. 62/1; The Oceanides, Op. 73.
**(*) BIS Dig. CD 263 [id.]. Gothenburg SO, Järvi.

Neeme Järvi takes a very broad view of the first movement – and conveys much of its brooding quality. The Scherzo has a splendid strength, even if Järvi allows the pace to slacken far too much towards the end. Both Järvi and Karajan portray the bleak yet other-worldly landscape of the slow movement to excellent effect, but the tension between phrases in the Karajan makes his the more powerful experience. In the finale Järvi opts for the tubular bells rather than the glockenspiel, which Sibelius wanted. As a fill-up, he gives us the *Canzonetta for strings*, Op. 62a, which derives from the music to *Kuolema*. It has great allure and charm and is beautifully played by the Gothenburg strings. *The Oceanides* is a very fine performance, too, though less subtle than Rattle's, particularly in its observance of dynamic nuances.

Symphonies Nos. 4 in A min.; 5 in E flat, Op. 82.
*** Decca Dig. 425 858-2; *425 858-4* [id.]. San Francisco SO, Herbert Blomstedt.

Blomstedt's accounts of the *Fourth* and *Fifth Symphonies* are the finest to have appeared for some years. He allows the music to unfold naturally and conveys a real sense of space. At no point is one ever aware of the barline. The *Fourth Symphony*, some of whose ideas began life as a quartet, has the intimacy of chamber music and yet communicates a strong feeling of the Nordic landscape. Blomstedt is particularly attentive to dynamic shading and gets playing of great tonal refinement from the San Francisco orchestra. He uses tubular bells in the finale of the *Fourth* (Sibelius asked for glockenspiel, and for tubular bells in *The Oceanides*) but no one makes the closing bars of the finale sound more affecting. The *Fifth Symphony* is also wonderfully spacious. Some may find the accellerando between the two sections of the first movement a shade steep, but there is a powerful sense of mystery in the development section.

Symphonies Nos. 4 in A min.; 6 in D min.
*** DG 415 108-2 [id.]. BPO, Karajan.
(M) *** EMI CDM7 64121-2 [id.]; *EG 764121-4*. CBSO, Simon Rattle.

Karajan's 25-year-old recording of the *Fourth Symphony* is only marginally less powerful than Ashkenazy's on Decca, and his performance is of real stature. Although one is bowled over by the Ashkenazy at first, it is the Karajan that has the greater concentration and tension. DG also offer his glorious account of the *Sixth Symphony*, which remains almost unsurpassed among recent accounts. Although this DG transfer does not quite have the range and body of the BIS and Decca versions, it sounds more vivid than on its earlier appearances and, like that of No. 4, the performance is a great one.

Simon Rattle's account of the *Fourth* with the Birmingham orchestra is also one of the best to have appeared in recent years. He invokes a powerful atmosphere in its opening pages: one is completely transported to its dark landscape with its seemingly limitless horizons. The string-tone is splendidly lean without being undernourished and achieves a sinisterly whispering pianissimo in the development. The slow movement is magical. The finale is hardly less masterly: Rattle builds up most convincingly to the final climax and the enigmatic, almost resigned coda. His account of the *Sixth* is almost equally fine. In the slow movement Rattle does not have the tremendous grip that Karajan's DG version commands or quite the concentration that he achieves elsewhere; but that is still awaiting reissue, and – make no mistake – Rattle's is still a *Sixth* to reckon with and its closing bars are memorably eloquent.

Symphonies Nos. (i) *4 in A min.;* (ii) *6 in D min., Op. 104;* (i) *The Bard, Op. 64; Lemminkaïnen's return, Op. 22/4; The Tempest: Prelude.*
❀ (M) (***) EMI mono CDM7 64027-2 [id.]. (i) LPO, (ii) RPO, Sir Thomas Beecham.

In its colour Beecham's account of the *Fourth Symphony* reflects his feeling that, far from being an austere work, as is often claimed, it is ripely romantic. No performance brings one closer to the music, while the recording, made over fifty years ago, sounds astonishingly fresh and bleak in this excellent transfer. The sound is well rounded, with plenty of body and presence. To judge from the composer's correspondence, this performance comes very close to his wishes, and there is a concentration, darkness and poetry that few rivalled. Beecham's 1947 account of the *Sixth Symphony* was said to be Sibelius's favourite recording of all his symphonies. Its eloquence is no less impressive. In the three shorter works on the disc – also taken from the old Beecham Society volumes on 78-r.p.m. discs – Beecham's rhythmic sharpness and feeling for colour vividly convey the high voltage of Sibelius's strikingly original writing. *Lemminkäinen's homeward journey* is positively electrifying, with the horse galloping at frenzied speed and excitement, while the *Prelude* to *The Tempest* is every bit as awesome an evocation of a storm as we had remembered. No subsequent performance is as chilling. All these performances except the *Sixth Symphony* come from the late 1930s, but few allowances need be made, for they spring vividly to life in these remarkable transfers. Indispensable for all Sibelians.

Symphony No. 5 in E flat, Op. 82; En saga, Op. 9; Tapiola, Op. 112.
*** BMG/RCA Dig. RD 87822 [7822-2-RC]. Finnish RSO, Saraste.

Jukka-Pekka Saraste offers an excellently shaped and well-thought-out reading of the *Fifth Symphony*. He handles in masterly fashion the climax at the transition to the scherzo and manages the transition extremely well, as does Rattle in his Philharmonia recording. Saraste conveys much of its breadth; his pace is measured, but the reading has weight and power. Saraste's *En saga* is no less telling in drawing the listener into its atmosphere; his *Tapiola*, on the other hand, is not so successful: this music must really chill the blood in performance – and this does not.

Symphonies Nos. 5 in E flat; 7 in C, Op. 105.
**(*) DG 415 107-2 [id.]. BPO, Karajan.

Symphonies Nos. 5 in E flat; 7 in C; Kuolema: Scene with cranes. Night ride and sunrise.
(M) *** EMI CDM7 64122-2 [id.]; *EG 764122-4*. CBSO, Simon Rattle.

Symphonies Nos. 5 in E flat; 7 in C; Kuolema: Valse triste, Op. 44/1.
** Chan. Dig. CHAN 9055 [id.]. Danish Nat. RSO, Segerstam.

Simon Rattle's record of the *Fifth Symphony* has collected numerous prizes in Europe – and deserves them all. From the very outset one feels that he has found the right tempo. Rattle is scrupulous in observing every dynamic nuance to the letter and, one might add, spirit. What is particularly impressive is the control of the transition between the first section and the scherzo element of the first movement. This relationship is ideally balanced and enables Rattle to convey detail in just the right perspective. There is a splendid sense of atmosphere in the development and a power unmatched in recent versions, save for the Karajan. The playing is superb, with recording to match. The *Seventh* is hardly less powerful and impressive: its opening is slow to unfold and has real vision. This is one of the finest *Sevenths* of recent years. With the addition of an imaginative and poetic account of the *Scene with cranes* from the incidental music to *Kuolema* and a good, if less distinctive, *Night ride and sunrise*, this is a record not to be missed, the finest single disc in Rattle's Birmingham cycle.

Such is the excellence of the classic Karajan DG *Fifth* that few listeners would guess its age. It is a great performance, and this 1964 version is indisputably the finest of the four he has made. Impressive though it is, his *Seventh* is not quite in the same class, and must yield both technically and even artistically to the Ashkenazy, which is very powerful and coupled with an impressive *Tapiola*.

In Segerstam's hands the first movement of the *Fifth Symphony* never really flows; nor is the slow movement allowed to speak for itself. The finale virtually grinds to a halt at letter N; *un pochettino largamente* becomes very molto indeed. The *Seventh* gets pulled about too, though the majestic ending comes off very well. Good recording but not a strong recommendation.

Symphony No. 6 in D min., Op. 104; En saga, Op. 9; Pohjola's daughter, Op. 49.
** Chan. Dig. CHAN 8965. Danish Nat. RSO, Leif Segerstam.

Symphony No. 6 in D min.; Pelléas et Mélisande: suite, Op. 46.
**(*) BIS Dig. CD 237 [id.]. Gothenburg SO, Järvi.

The response of the Gothenburg orchestra to Järvi's direction is whole-hearted; one warms to the eloquence of the opening string polyphony and the impassioned finale. Järvi takes the main section very fast. There are one or two overemphatic gestures in the closing paragraphs of the slow movement, but on the whole this is well thought out and often impressive. It can hold its own with most competition and can be recommended. Järvi produces a very atmospheric account of *Pelléas et Mélisande*, in particular the brief but concentrated *By the sea*. Yet it would be idle to pretend that it can be preferred to Karajan's performance.

Leif Segerstam is, as always, attentive to detail and conveys a strong sense of atmosphere. Towards the end of the first movement he abruptly pulls back, but the passage leading up to that (letter 'M' in the score) is most imaginatively done. As in his account of the *Fourth*, there are many insights and it is good to hear the slow movement played at a really leisurely pace (even though Segerstam perhaps overdoes it). The insights generally outweigh the moments of wilfulness, and the playing of the Danish Radio Orchestra is sensitive and responsive. The recording is not ideally balanced; the strings on which so much of the musical argument depends are occasionally swamped by the wind and brass. Things are better in *Pohjola's daughter* and *En saga* but, good though this is, it would not be a first choice.

Symphony No. 7 in C, Op. 105; Canzonetta, Op. 62a; Kuolema: Valse triste; Scene with cranes, Op. 44. Night ride and sunrise, Op. 55; Valse romantique, Op. 62b.
*** BIS Dig. CD 311 [id.]. Gothenburg SO, Järvi.

Neeme Järvi and the Gothenburg orchestra bring great energy and concentration to the *Seventh Symphony*. Järvi is a sympathetic and authoritative guide in this terrain. The only disappointment is the final climax, which is perhaps less intense than the best versions. However, it is a fine performance, and the music to *Kuolema* is splendidly atmospheric; *Night ride* is strongly characterized. The recording exhibits the usual characteristics of the Gothenburg Concert Hall and has plenty of body and presence.

CHAMBER MUSIC

(i) *Piano quintet in G min.; Piano trio in C (Lovisa); String quartet in E flat.*
*** Finlandia FACD 375 [id.]. Sibelius Ac. Qt, (i) with Tawaststjerna.

(i) *Piano quintet in G min.; String quartet in D min. (Voces intimae), Op. 56.*
*** Chan. Dig. CHAN 8742; *ABTD 1381* [id.]. (i) Anthony Goldstone; Gabrieli Qt.

The last few years have seen an impressive opening up of the Sibelius repertoire. Now comes the *Piano quintet* he composed for Busoni in 1890; it was inspired by Sinding's *E minor Quintet*, which he had heard Busoni play with the Brodsky Quartet in Leipzig. It is a long and far from characteristic piece in five movements, of which only two were played in his lifetime. Anthony Goldstone and the Gabrielis reverse the order of the second and third movements so as to maximize contrast. It is far from being the 'absolute rubbish' Sibelius declared it to be, but it is no masterpiece either. The first movement is probably the finest and Anthony Goldstone, an impressive player by any standards, makes the most of Sibelius's piano writing to produce a very committed performance. The *Voces intimae Quartet* is given a reflective, intelligent reading, perhaps at times wanting in momentum but finely shaped. Good recording.

The early *Quartet* is Haydnesque and insignificant, and the *Lovisa trio*, so called because it was written in that small town in the summer of 1888, offers only sporadic glimpses of things to come. The *Piano quintet* is given a fine performance on Finlandia, and there is little to choose between it and the more expansive Goldstone/Gabrieli account on Chandos.

String quartets: in E flat (1885); *A min.* (1889); *B flat, Op. 4* (1890); *D min. (Voces intimae), Op. 56.*
(M) *** Finlandia Dig. FACD 522092 (2). Sibelius Ac. Qt.

The *E flat Quartet* is a student piece of little personality, very much influenced by the Viennese classics, above all Haydn. The *A minor Quartet* is another matter. Long thought to be lost, as only the first violin part survived, the remaining parts were discovered some years ago and were published both in score and in this performance. It proves a delightful surprise with something of the freshness of Dvořák and Schubert. Sibelius obviously had ambivalent feelings towards the *B flat Quartet*: he thought sufficiently well of it to allot it an opus number but never published it and discouraged its performance. Its second movement bears a slight resemblance to a theme from *Rakastava*, which appeared in its original choral form in 1894. Both are well worth resurrecting even if they do not, of course, match the mature *Voces intimae quartet* in artistry. The playing of the Sibelius Academy Quartet is exemplary and the recordings good: three are digital; *Voces intimae* dates from 1980 and is analogue.

VOCAL MUSIC

Songs with orchestra: *Arioso; Autumn evening (Höstkväll); Come away, Death! (Kom nu hit Död); The diamond on the March snow (Diamanten på marssnön); The fool's song of the spider (Sången om korsspindeln); Luonnotar, Op. 70; On a balcony by the sea (På verandan vid havet); The Rapids-rider's brides (Koskenlaskian morsiammet); Serenade; Since then I have questioned no*

further (Se'n har jag ej frågat mera); Spring flies hastily (Våren flyktar hastigt); Sunrise (Soluppgång).
*** BIS CD 270 [id.]. Jorma Hynninen, Mari Anne Häggander, Gothenburg SO, Panula.

This record collects all the songs that Sibelius originally composed for voice and orchestra, together with those for voice and piano that he himself subsequently orchestrated. Jorma Hynninen is a fine interpreter of this repertoire: his singing can only be called glorious. Mari-Anne Häggander manages the demanding tessitura of *Arioso* and *Luonnotar* with much artistry, and her *Luonnotar* is certainly to be preferred to Söderström's. Jorma Panula proves a sensitive accompanist and secures fine playing from the Gothenburg orchestra. In any event, this is indispensable.

Arioso, Op. 3; Narcissus; Pelleas and Melisande: The three blind sisters. 7 Songs, Op. 17; 6 Songs, Op. 36; 5 Songs, Op. 37; 6 Songs, Op. 88. Souda, souda, sinisorsa.
*** BIS Dig. CD 457 [id.]. Anne Sofie von Otter, Bengt Forsberg.

Presumably Decca will restore to circulation their complete set of the Sibelius *Songs* by Tom Krause and Elizabeth Söderström in due course, but this lovely recital by Anne Sofie von Otter will do very nicely in the meantime. In fact it marks the start of a BIS project to record all the songs; if the remaining issues are as good as this, the set will be a distinguished addition to the Sibelius discography. Miss von Otter always makes a beautiful sound, but she has a highly developed sense of line and brings great interpretative insight to such songs as *Men min fågel märks dock icke* (*My bird is long in homing*) and *Bollspele and Trianon* (*Tennis at Trianon*) which has even greater finesse than Söderström's. And what a good accompanist Bengt Forsberg is. The recording is good if a bit reverberant.

Finlandia (version for orchestra and mixed chorus), *Op. 26; Homeland (Oma maa), Op. 92; Impromptu, Op. 19;* (i) *Snöfrid, Op. 29. Song to the earth, (Maan virsi), Op. 95; Song to Lemminkäinen, Op. 31; Väinö's song, Op. 110.*
** Ondine Dig. ODE 754-2 [id.]. (i) Stina Rautelin (reciter), Finnish Nat. Op. Ch. & O, Eri Klas.

While most of Sibelius's songs are to Swedish texts, the choral music is predominantly Finnish. *Oma maa* ('Homeland') comes from the period of the Finnish civil war when Sibelius was still wrestling with the *Fifth Symphony*. It is a dignified and euphonious work and includes a magical evocation of the wintry nights with Aurora borealis and the white nights of midsummer. But both *Snöfrid* and the *Impromptu*, Op. 19, are to texts by the Swedish poet, Rydberg. There are many characteristic touches, though neither shows Sibelius at his greatest. Nor for that matter does the strophic *Song to Lemminkäinen* (1896). *Väinö's Song* is an appealing piece which bears an opus number between *The Tempest* and *Tapiola* – though it is not really fit to keep them company. *Maan virsi* ('Song to the Earth') is an attractive piece. The performances and the recording are decent rather than distinguished.

Kullervo Symphony, Op. 7.
** BIS Dig. CD 313 [id.]. Mattila, Hynninen, Laulun Ystävät Male Ch., Gothenburg SO, Järvi.

The *Kullervo symphony* is an ambitious five-movement work for two soloists, male-voice choir and orchestra, which Sibelius wrote at the outset of his career in 1892. It brought him national fame and a commission from Kajanus that resulted in *En Saga*. After its first performance Sibelius withdrew the score and it was never performed in its entirety until 1958, a year after his death. It is revealed as an impressive work, full of original touches, particularly in its thoroughly characteristic opening. BIS accommodate the whole work on a single CD, no mean feat considering the wide dynamic range involved. Järvi is so fast that he almost robs the symphony of its epic character and its breadth. The central movement is the high point of this performance, thanks to the superb singing of Karita Mattila and Jorma Hynninen. If only the pace were less headlong, this would have been a strong recommendation. The Gothenburg recording does justice to the large forces involved: the brass is marvellously rich and present as usual and the balance between the singers and orchestra excellently judged. But we hope EMI will restore Berglund's fine version to the catalogue during the lifetime of this book.

The Maiden in the tower (opera). *Karelia suite, Op. 11.*
*** BIS Dig. CD 250 [id.]. Häggander, Hynninen, Hagegård, Kruse, Gothenburg Ch. and SO, Järvi.

The Maiden in the tower falls into eight short scenes and lasts no longer than 35 minutes. Its short *Prelude* is not unappealing but does not promise great things – any more than the ensuing scene delivers them. But the orchestral interlude between the first two scenes brings us the real Sibelius, and the second scene is undoubtedly impressive; there are echoes of Wagner, such as we find in some of the great orchestral songs of the following decade. All the same, Sibelius's refusal to permit its revival was perfectly understandable, for it lacks something we find in all his most characteristic music: quite simply, a sense of mastery. Yet there are telling performances here from Mari-Anne Häggander and Jorma Hynninen and the Gothenburg orchestra. Neeme Järvi's account of the *Karelia suite* is certainly original, with its opening rather impressive in its strange way. It is difficult to imagine a more spacious account of the *Intermezzo*, which is too broad to make an effective contrast with the ensuing *Ballade*.

Simpson, Robert (born 1921)

Energy; Introduction & allegro on a theme by Max Reger; The Four Temperaments; Volcano; Vortex.
*** Hyp. Dig. CDA 66449 [id.]. Desford Colliery Caterpillar Band, James Watson.

There is some extraordinary music here, including one masterpiece, *The Four Temperaments* (1983), which packs quite a punch. This is a four-movement, 22-minute symphony of great imaginative power, and ingeniously laid out for the band. Simpson played in brass bands as a boy and this is doubtless where he acquired some of his expertise in writing for them. Yet he did not write his first mature band piece until he was fifty: this was *Energy* which came in response to a commission from the World Brass Band Championships. The *Introduction and allegro on a theme by Max Reger* is based on a figure that occurs in Reger's *Fantasia and fugue in D minor*, Op. 135b, for organ and is every bit as awesome and impressive as the annotator claims. Together with *Volcano* and his most recent piece, *Vortex*, this makes up his entire output in this medium. The Desford Colliery Caterpillar Band under James Watson play with all the expertise and virtuosity one expects, and the recording has admirable clarity and body, though the acoustic is on the dry side. All the same, this is not to be missed, particularly by those who imagine that they don't like the medium.

(i) *Symphony No. 3;* (ii) *Clarinet quintet.*
(M) *** Unicorn UKCD 2028. (i) LSO, Jascha Horenstein; (ii) Bernard Walton (clarinet), Aeolian Qt.

The *Third Symphony* is in two long movements: the first hammering home in a developed sonata structure the contrast of adjacent tonal centres, B flat against C; the second combining the functions of slow movement, scherzo and finale in a gradually accelerating tempo. There is something Sibelian about the way that, in the first movement, Simpson gradually brings together fragments of musical ideas; but generally this is a work which (within its frankly tonal idiom) asks to be considered in Simpson's own individual terms. The *Clarinet quintet* is a thoughtful, searching piece, dating from 1968 and among Simpson's profoundest utterances. It is played with total commitment here. Both works are given extremely vivid sound.

Symphonies Nos. 6; 7.
*** Hyp. Dig. CDA 66280; *KA 66280* [id.]. RLPO, Handley.

Not surprisingly – since Robert Simpson has distinguished medical forebears and was originally intended for medicine – the *Sixth* is inspired by the idea of growth: the development of a musical structure from initial melodic cells in much the same way as life emerges from a single fertilized cell in nature. The *Seventh*, scored for the same chamber orchestral forces as his remarkable *Second Symphony*, is hardly less powerful in its imaginative vision and sense of purpose. Both scores are bracingly Nordic in their inner landscape and exhilarating in aural experience. The playing of the Liverpool orchestra under Vernon Handley could hardly be bettered, and the recording is altogether first class.

Symphony No. 9.
❀ *** Hyp. Dig. CDA 66299; *KA 66299* [id.]. Bournemouth SO, Vernon Handley (with talk by the composer).

What can one say about the *Ninth* of Robert Simpson – except that its gestures are confident, its control of pace and its material are masterly; it is a one-movement work, but at no time in its 45 minutes does it falter – nor does the attention of the listener. The CD also includes a spoken introduction to the piece that many listeners will probably find helpful. The music is a most powerful experience: concentrated, awesome, and as mysterious as some astronomical phenomenon. It is played superbly by the Bournemouth Symphony Orchestra under Vernon Handley, and is no less superbly recorded.

String quartets Nos. 1; 4.
*** Hyp. Dig. CDA 66419; *KA 66419* [id.]. Delmé Qt.

The *First Quartet* comes from the same year as Simpson's *First Symphony*, and is a remarkable piece. This is not its first appearance on record but is decidedly the best. It opens in as innocent a fashion as the Haydn *Lark Quartet* or Nielsen's *E flat* but, the better one comes to know it, the more it is obvious that Simpson is already his own man. The second movement is a palindrome (most modern composers do not know how to write forwards, let alone backwards as well) but its ingenuity is worn lightly. The *Fourth* is part of the trilogy which Simpson conceived as a kind of commentary on Beethoven's *Rasumovsky quartets* (Simpson suggests that 'if these works enhance the understanding of the genius of Beethoven at their own expense, their purpose will be served'.) Yet they live very much in their own right. Excellent performances from the Delmé, and fine recording too.

String quartets Nos. 3 and 6; String trio (Prelude, Adagio & fugue).
*** Hyp. Dig. CDA 66376 [id.]. Delmé Qt.

The *Third Quartet* is a two-movement piece from 1953–4, so it comes between the *First* and *Second Symphonies.* Its finale is a veritable power-house with its unrelenting sense of onward movement which, like the *Grosse Fuge*, almost strains the medium (small wonder that the composer subsequently arranged it for full strings). Its first movement is a deeply felt piece that has a powerful and haunting eloquence. The *Sixth* (1975) is the third of a set which Simpson tells us constitute a close study of Beethoven's three *Razumovsky quartets*, and is further evidence of his remarkable musical mind. The *String trio* (1987) is a marvellously stimulating and thoughtful piece. Dedicated performances and excellent recording.

String quartets Nos. 7 and 8.
*** Hyp. Dig. CDA 66117 [id.]. Delmé Qt.

The *Seventh Quartet* has a real sense of vision and something of the stillness of the remote worlds it evokes. It is dedicated to Susi Jeans, the organist and widow of the astronomer, and reflects the composer's own passion for astronomy; he speaks of the universe, 'quiet and mysterious yet pulsating with energy'. The *Eighth* turns from the vastness of space to the microcosmic world of insect-life. Indeed this provides a superficial link with Bartók, but, as with so much of Simpson's music, there is a concern for musical continuity rather than beauty of incident. Excellent playing from the Delmé Quartet, and very good recorded sound too.

String quartet No. 9 (32 Variations & fugue on a theme of Haydn).
*** Hyp. Dig. CDA 66127 [id.]. Delmé Qt.

What an original and, in its way, masterly conception the *Ninth Quartet* is! It is quite unlike anything in the literature of chamber music: a set of thirty-two variations and a fugue on the minuet of Haydn's *Symphony No. 47.* Like the minuet itself, all the variations are in the form of a palindrome; some of the earlier ones derive from an early piano work, thus finding an even more natural habitat in the quartet medium. Many will find it a tough nut to crack, and it certainly calls for – and repays – concentrated study. It is a mighty and serious work, argued with all the resource and ingenuity one expects from this composer. A formidable achievement in any age, and a rarity in ours. The Delmé Quartet cope with its difficulties splendidly, and the performance carries the imprimatur of the composer. The recording sounds very good in its CD format.

String quartets Nos. 10 (For Peace); 11.
*** Hyp. Dig. CDA 66225; *KA 66225* [id.]. Coull Qt.

Robert Simpson's *Tenth* and *Eleventh quartets* form a pair. The subtitle *For Peace* of No. 10 refers to 'its generally pacific character' and aspires to define 'the condition of peace which excludes aggression but not strong feeling'. Listening to this *Quartet* is like hearing a quiet, cool voice of sanity that refreshes the troubled spirit after a long period in an alien, hostile world. The one-movement *Eleventh* draws on some of the inspiration of its predecessor. It is a work of enormous power and momentum. Excellent performances and recording.

String quartet No. 12 (1987); (i) *String quintet* (1987).
*** Hyp. Dig. CDA 66503. Coull Qt, (i) with Roger Bigley.

Robert Simpson's *Twelfth Quartet* is a masterly and absorbing score. Here is a composer with a sense of scale and one who can sustain a musical argument in a way that grips the listener. His *String quintet*, written in response to a BBC commission for its Lunchtime Concerts at St John's, Smith Square, is another work of sustained inventive power. The sleeve annotator hails it as the finest example of the genre since the Brahms – and arguably he is right. We are unlikely to get another recording, so this is self-recommending; but it must be noted that the heroic demands this score makes on the players keep them fully stretched. The intonation and tone of the leader is not always impeccable, but the playing has commitment and intelligence.

Sinding, Christian (1856–1941)

Légende, Op. 46.
(BB) *** Naxos Dig. 8.550329 [id.]. Dong-Suk Kang, Slovak (Bratislava) RSO, Adrian Leaper – HALVORSEN: *Air Norvégien* etc.; SIBELIUS: *Violin concerto;* SVENDSEN: *Romance.* ***

Dong-Suk Kang plays Sinding's *Légende* with great conviction and an effortless, songful virtuosity. It is by no means as appealing as the Halvorsen and Svendsen pieces but makes a good makeweight for an excellent collection in the lowest price range.

Suite, Op. 10.
*** EMI CDC7 47167-2 [id.]. Perlman, Pittsburgh SO, Previn – SIBELIUS: *Concerto.* ***

Heifetz recorded this dazzling piece in the 1950s, and it need only be said that Perlman's version is not inferior. Its blend of archaism and fantasy sounds distinctively Scandinavian of the 1890s, yet altogether fresh – and quite delightful. Such is the velocity of Perlman's first movement that one wonders whether the disc is playing at the right speed. Stunning virtuosity and excellent recording.

Smetana, Bedřich (1824–84)

Má Vlast (complete).
*** Sup. Dig. 11 1208-2 [id.]. Czech PO, Rafael Kubelik.
(M) *** Ph. Dig. 432 196-2; *432 196-4* [id.]. Concg. O, Antal Dorati.
*** Telarc CD 80265 [id.]. Milwaukee SO, Zdenek Macal.
*** DG Dig. 431 652-2 [id.]. VPO, James Levine.
*** Virgin Dig. VC7 91100-2; *VC 791100-4* [id.]. RLPO, Pešek.
(M) **(*) Teldec/Warner Dig. 9031 74778-2 [id.]. Frankfurt RSO, Eliahu Inbal.
(M) **(*) DG 429 183-2; *429 183-4* [id.]. Boston SO, Rafael Kubelik.
(B) **(*) Decca 433 635-2; *433 635-4* [id.]. Israel PO, Walter Weller.

In 1990 Rafael Kubelik returned to his homeland after an enforced absence of 41 years to open the Prague Spring Festival with this vibrant performance of *Má Vlast*. He had recorded the work twice before in stereo, first for Decca in the 1950s and then again for DG, the latter a particularly fine performance. But this Czech version is special, imbued with passionate national feeling, yet never letting the emotions boil over. At the bold opening of *Vyšehrad*, with the harp strongly profiled, the intensity of the music-making is immediately projected, and the dominating chorale representing the castle on its rocky precipice is particularly poignant at its last appearance, near the close of the piece. The trickling streams which are the source of *Vltava* have a delicacy almost of fantasy, but the main lyrical theme on the strings moves on briskly and, after the relaxation for the moonlit sequence, one realizes that the return of the chorale as the river flows past Vyšehrad is a key point in Kubelik's reading. *Šárka*, with its bloodthirsty tale of revenge and slaughter, is immensely dramatic, contrasting with the pastoral evocations of the following piece. While the vehement patriotism of the last two sections of the score is conveyed with great fervour – the opening of *Tábor* is particularly arresting – the Slavonic lilt of the music's lighter moments brings the necessary contrast and release. The recording is vivid and full but not sumptuous, yet this suits the powerful impulse of Kubelik's overall view, with the build-up to the exultant close of *Blaník* producing a dénouement of great majesty.

Dorati's is also an extremely fine account of Smetana's cycle, avoiding most of the pitfalls with a reading which brings both vivid drama and orchestral playing of the finest quality. For those who put quality of recording as of prime importance, this could be first choice, particularly considering its cost. The music making has a high adrenalin level throughout, yet points of detail are not missed. The bold accents of the opening *Vyšehrad* may seem too highly stressed to ears used to a more mellow approach to this highly romantic opening piece, and *Vltava* similarly moves forward strongly. In *From Bohemia's woods and fields* the fugato for the strings is paced briskly but, because of the high level of tension, this also falls into place. In the closing *Blaník*, Dorati finds dignity rather than bombast and the pastoral episode is delightfully relaxed, with a fine rhythmic bounce to the march theme which then leads to the final peroration. The Philips sound is splendid, with a wide amplitude and a thrilling concert-hall presence. The sound, within the expansive Amsterdam acoustics, is even richer and more glowing than DG provide for Levine, and Dorati's performance is just as exciting and, if anything, even more spontaneous. The only disadvantage is the absence of any kind of documentation, except a list of titles.

Macal's new Telarc version offers the finest recording of all; indeed it approaches the demonstration bracket. As with his version of Dvořák's *New World Symphony*, he provides a highly spontaneous and enjoyable performance, imaginatively conceived and convincingly paced. The very opening of *Vyšehrad*, with its relatively gentle harp roulades, sets the atmospheric mood of the reading; other accounts, notably Kubelik's, have greater slavic fire and find a more red-bloodedly patriotic feeling, but Macal's approach does not lack vigour and commitment and the excellent orchestral playing is responsive to his less histrionic view. The Milwaukee strings play the string theme of *Vltava* gracefully and warmly, the village wedding has charm and later the moonlight gleams evocatively. *Šárka* has a folksy flavour, the melodrama good-humoured, while in *From Bohemia's woods and fields*, after the radiant high string passage, the horns steal in magically with their chorale. Throughout the brass are full and sonorous, mitigating any rhetorical bombast in the last two symphonic poems; indeed one relishes the rich sounds in *Tábor,* while in *Blaník* the central pastoral idyll brings some delightful woodwind detail and a poetic interplay between oboe and horn. And Macal's Czech nationality ensures that the performance has idiomatic feeling.

DG have remastered James Levine's outstanding complete *Má Vlast* on to a single CD (76 minutes). But he is now upstaged by Dorati on Philips, who has a considerable price advantage plus the glorious acoustic of the Concertgebouw. Levine's performance is full of momentum and thrust, aptly paced, with much imaginative detail. The opening *Vyšehrad* immediately shows the impulse of the music-making, yet it is warmly romantic too; while the two most famous pieces, *Vltava* and *From Bohemia's woods and fields*, are full of flair and most beautifully played. In *Tábor* and *Blaník* the VPO play with great vigour and commitment, and these patriotic pieces have both fervour and plenty of colour. The sound is full-bodied, with a wide amplitude and range, but it is less sumptuous and slightly less atmospheric than the Philips version.

Libor Pešek's set also fits conveniently on to a single disc and, although the recording is not quite as opulent as Levine's VPO version, it still offers very good sound, convincingly balanced in the Liverpool Philharmonic Hall. Pešek's reading does not miss the music's epic patriotic feeling, yet never becomes bombastic. There is plenty of evocation, from the richly romantic opening of *Vyšehrad*, to the more mysterious scene-setting in *Tábor* while the climax of *Sárka*, with its potent anticipatory horn-call, is a gripping piece of melodrama. The two key sections of the work, *Vltava* and *From Bohemia's woods and fields*, are especially enjoyable for their vivid characterization, while at the very end of *Blaník* Pešek draws together the two key themes – the *Vyšehrad* motif and the Hussite chorale – very satisfyingly.

The Teldec digital recording of *Má Vlast* is outstandingly fine, and this is music where colourful, richly spacious yet naturally balanced sound can be especially telling. The orchestral playing is first class, too, and Inbal's reading is very dramatic. The progress of the *Vltava* river is vividly detailed with expansive orchestral climaxes and *From Bohemia's woods and fields* has plenty of strong contrasts. Šárka is certainly exciting and if, here and in the last two pieces, the patriotic fervour brings powerful accenting and bold brass, the balancing pastoral folk idiom in *Blaník* is atmospherically caught. This is not as powerful a performance as Kubelik's new Czech version, but it is certainly compelling.

Kubelik's 1971 recording with the Boston Symphony Orchestra has much in its favour. Kubelik is careful to temper the bombast which too readily comes to the surface in the later sections of the work, and his skill with the inner balance of the orchestra brings much felicitous detail. *Vltava* and *From Bohemia's woods and fields* are very successful. The DG recording, however, has been brightly remastered – cymbal clashes sound very metallic – and one could have wished for more ample orchestral textures, although the sound is fully acceptable.

Weller's set is given top-quality 1978 Decca analogue sound which is strikingly full and lively, basically richer than Kubelik's DG recording. But the characteristically dry Tel Aviv acoustic means that the opening of *Vyšehrad* is not as evocative as it might be, and at times climaxes are not ideally expansive. *Vltava* has attractive detail and plenty of drama and a flowing current worthy of a great river. *From Bohemia's woods and fields* brings some fine string playing, and Weller is at his best in the later, more patriotically melodramatic pieces which he presents strongly, yet without going over the top. The orchestral response is persuasive, and at bargain price this has its place in the catalogue.

Má Vlast: Vltava.
(M) (**) BMG/RCA GD 60279; *GK 60279* [60279-2-RG; *60279-4-RG*]. NBC SO, Toscanini – DVOŘÁK: *Symphony No. 9;* KODÁLY: *Háry János suite.* (***)

Recorded several years earlier than the other two items on Toscanini's disc, *Vltava* has painfully dry and close sound; but the intensity of Toscanini's performance still makes it a valuable document.

Má Vlast: Vltava; From Bohemia's woods and fields; Vyšehrad. The Bartered Bride: Overture and dances.
*** DG Dig. 427 340-2 [id.]. VPO, Levine.

Taken from Levine's recommended complete set, the three most popular symphonic poems from *Má Vlast* plus the *Overture* and *Dances* from *The Bartered Bride* add up to a very attractive single CD. But this needs a mid-price reissue.

Piano trio in G min., Op. 15.
*** Chan. Dig. CHAN 8445; *ABTD 1157* [id.]. Borodin Trio – DVOŘÁK: *Dumky trio.* ***
** Teldec/Warner Dig. 2292 43715-2 [id.]. Trio Fontenay – CHOPIN: *Piano trio.* ***

Writing the *Trio* was a cathartic act, following the death of the composer's four-year-old daughter, so it is not surprising that it is a powerfully emotional work. Although it has an underlying melancholy, it is by no means immersed in gloom: there is serenity too, and the powerful finale ends with a sense of lyrical release. The writing gives fine expressive opportunities for both the violin and cello, which are taken up eloquently by Rostislav Dubinsky and Yuli Turovsky, and the pianist, Luba Edlina, is also wonderfully sympathetic. In short, a superb account, given a most realistic recording balance. Highly recommended.

The Trio Fontenay take a more extrovert view of the *G minor Trio* than do earlier rivals and tend rather to dramatize its emotions. It is good to hear it played as if they believe every note, but they protest too much and do not allow this dignified, elegiac quality to speak as naturally as it might. Good recording.

String quartet No. 1 in E min. (From my life).
*** Ph. Dig. 420 803-2 [id.]. Guarneri Qt – DVOŘÁK: *String quartet No. 12.* ***
(M) *** Decca 430 295-2; *430 295-4* [id.]. Gabrieli Qt – JANÁČEK: *String quartets Nos. 1–2.* ***

Smetana's *E minor Quartet* is autobiographical, its heart in the glorious slow movement in which the composer recalls the happiness of his first love. The Guarneri performance of this movement is wonderfully warm, romantic without a trace of sentimentality, with rich playing from the cellist, David Soyer. The happiness of the second-movement *Polka* ('Reminiscences of youth') is nicely caught and the finale is contrasted dramatically, with the catastrophic onset of deafness heralded by a high-pitched whistle on the first violin; the performance ends in a mood of touching elegiac reverie. The Philips recording is full-textured and most naturally balanced, with unexaggerated presence.

Artistically, the Gabrieli performance of Smetana's autobiographical *First Quartet* is first class; technically, it offers vivid and well-balanced 1977 recorded sound, although the upper range of the violin timbre is marginally less smooth than in the Janáček coupling, even though it was recorded at the same time in the warm acoustics of Rosslyn Hill Chapel.

String quartet No. 1 (From my life) – orchestral version by George Szell. *The Bartered Bride: Overture and dances.*
*** Chan. Dig. CHAN 8412; *ABTD 1149* [id.]. LSO, Geoffrey Simon.

The Czech feeling of Szell's scoring is especially noticeable in the *Polka*, but overall there is no doubt that the fuller textures add a dimension to the music, though inevitably there are losses as well as gains. The powerful advocacy of Simon and the excellent LSO playing, both here and in the sparkling excerpts from *The Bartered Bride*, provide a most rewarding coupling. The recording is well up to the usual high Chandos standards.

OPERA

The Bartered Bride (complete in Czech).
*** Sup. Dig. 10 3511-2 (3) [id.]. Beňaácková, Dvorský, Novák, Kopp, Jonášová, Czech Philharmonic Ch. and O, Košler.

The digital Supraphon set under Košler admirably supplies the need for a first-rate Czech version of this delightful comic opera. The recording acoustic may be rather reverberant for comedy, but the orchestral sound is warm and the voices are given good presence, while the performance sparkles from beginning to end, with folk rhythms crisply enunciated in an infectiously idiomatic way. The cast is strong, headed by the characterful Gabriela Beňaácková as Mařenka and one of the finest of today's Czech tenors, Peter Dvorský, as Jeník. Miroslav Kopp in the role of the ineffective Vašek sings powerfully too. As Kecal the marriage-broker, Richard Novák is not always steady, but his swaggering characterization is most persuasive. The CDs offer some of the best sound we have yet had from Supraphon, fresh and lively. The voices are placed well forward in relation to the orchestra and there is occasionally just a hint of digital edge on the vocal peaks, but the effect overall has fine presence. The discs are fairly generously banded, but this could now be fitted on a pair of CDs, so the set is unnecessarily expensive. The libretto, however, has been improved and is clear and easy to use.

Smyth, Ethel (1858–1944)

Mass in D; March of the Women; Boatswain's mate: Mrs Water's aria.
*** Virgin Dig. VC7 91188-2; *VC7 91188-4* [id.]. Harrhy, Hardy, Dressen, Bohn, Ch. & O of Plymouth Music Series, Minnesota, Philip Brunelle.

Written in the early 1890s in devotion to a young woman friend who was a Catholic, Ethel Smyth's *Mass in D* is one of her most ambitious works, a piece that boldly seeks to echo Beethoven's great *Missa solemnis* in its moods and idiom. Though Smyth's invention is less memorable than Beethoven's, the drive and the vehemence of her writing make this a warmly rewarding piece, with Brahms's *Requiem* another, if less marked, influence. Daringly, Smyth makes the *Christe eleison* into a bitingly insistent sequence, an urgent plea to Christ, which leads to a fortissimo return of the *Kyrie* on an idea originally presented in meditative counterpoint. The composer herself counted the *Gloria*, the longest and most energetic movement, as the finest and prescribed that it should be performed, not in the usual liturgical sequence, but last, as a happy ending, as is done here. Brunelle, first heard in the Virgin set of Britten's *Paul Bunyan*, here comparably resurrects a forgotten British work with great success, drawing fine playing and singing from the members of the Plymouth Music Series. Smyth's once-celebrated suffragette march is done with polish rather than feminist fervour, and Eiddwen Harrhy makes a characterful soloist in the extended aria from Smyth's best-known opera. First-rate sound.

Soler, Vicente Martín y (1754–1806)

(i) *Concerto No. 3 in G for 2 solo harpsichords. Fandango. Sonatas: in C min.; C sharp min.; D; D min.; D flat; F sharp.*
(M) *** Ph. 432 830-2 [id.]. Rafael Puyana (harpsichord); (i) with Genoveva Gálvez.

This recital concentrates on the solo harpsichord sonatas, although as a grand finale we do have one of the concertos played by Puyana and Gálvez. Another fascinating addition to the repertoire is Soler's *Fandango*, a brilliant and lively dance written for a double-keyboard instrument. Since the original version is rather lengthy and repetitive, Puyana has made some cuts which seem to work perfectly well and with no loss of the climactic sense of the composition as a whole, which readily evokes the strumming of guitars. There is a vast amount of intriguing music in the sonatas too, and the brilliantly sympathetic performances here will convince many listeners that Soler's music is well worth further exploration. Puyana is nothing if not a robust player, and the harpsichord is recorded at a rather high level, but this makes the contrast with the gentler movements the more striking. Excellent late-1960s sound, admirably transferred to CD.

Keyboard works: *Sonatas Nos. 1 in A; 3 in B flat; 24–5 in D min.; 28–9 in C; 30–31 in G; 96 in E flat; 118 in A min. Prelude No. 1 in D min.*
(**) Astrée Dig. E 8768 [id.]. Bob van Asperen (harpsichord).

Keyboard works: *Sonatas Nos. 7–9 in C; 20–21 in C sharp min.; 95 in A. Prelude No. 3 in C.*
(**) Astrée Dig. E 8769 [id.]. Bob van Asperen (harpsichord).

Keyboard works: *Sonatas Nos. 10 in B min.; 11 in B; 12–14 in G; 52 in E min.; 73–4 in D; 92 in D (Sonata de clarines); 106 in E min.; Allegro pastoril; Prelude No. 6 in G.*
(**) Astrée Dig. E 8770 [id.]. Bob van Asperen (harpsichord).

Keyboard works: *Sonatas Nos. 37 in D; 46 in D; 56 in F; 98 in B flat min.; 100 in C min.; 103 in C min.; 108 in C; 109 in F; 112 in D; Fandango No. 146; Prelude No. 5 in D.*
(**) Astrée Dig. E 8771 [id.]. Bob van Asperen (harpsichord).

An ambitious venture to record the complete keyboard output of Antonio Soler with Bob van Asperen is let down by insensitive engineering. He plays with plenty of vitality but the value of the enterprise is diminished by the oppressively close balance of the recording – admittedly not quite so bottom-heavy as Ton Koopman's Forqueray record for Erato. However ingenious and varied in colour the registration of the distinguished Dutch harpsichordist, the effect is reduced to an unrelieved and uniform dynamic level which produces aural fatigue. The music is so characterful and the playing so fresh that these discs must be recommended, but readers will want to listen at low level and only to one or two pieces at a time. Moreover the documentation is too generalized for such an important project, with essays about the composer, the performer, the project research, and a cursory discussion of the music, repeated with each CD. Information is not given about individual works and no attempt is made to differentiate between the single movement sonatas and the occasional more ambitious three and four movement combinations, like Nos. 92 and 98, in which Soler created composite works from movements of the same tonality but diverse character. The spectacular thirteen-minute *Fandango* which opens the fourth disc is presented without comment.

Keyboard sonatas, S.R. 15, 21, 42, 84–7, 89.
(M) *** Decca 433 920-2 (2) [id.]. Alicia de Larrocha – ALBÉNIZ: *Sonata* ***; GRANADOS: *Goyescas* etc. *** ❀

Vital performances of eight sonatas by Soler, who, although not the equal of Domenico Scarlatti, is still a rewarding enough composer to warrant attention. Like Scarlatti's music, with an advocate of this calibre, these works are quite as pleasing heard on the piano rather than the harpsichord. Excellent, truthful 1981 recording.

Keyboard sonatas Nos. 18 in C min.; 19 in C min.; 41 in E flat; 72 in F min.; 78 in F sharp min.; 84 in D; 85 in F sharp min.; 86 in D; 87 in G min.; 88 in D flat; 90 in F sharp; Fandango.
*** Virgin Dig. VC7 91172-2; *VC7 91172-4* [id.]. Maggie Cole (harpsichord or fortepiano).

Maggie Cole plays a dozen Soler pieces, eleven *Sonatas* and the celebrated *Fandango*, half of them on the harpsichord and the remainder on the fortepiano; she gives altogether dashing performances on both. The fortepiano is a Derek Adlam copy of a Viennese instrument of the 1790s by Anton Walther and the harpsichord is a Goble. Good pieces to sample are *No. 87 in G minor* (track 5) and, on the harpsichord, *No. 86 in D major* (track 9) or the *Fandango* itself. The playing is all very exhilarating and inspiriting. Played at a normal level-setting, both instruments sound a bit thunderous but, played at a lower level, the results are very satisfactory.

Sor, Fernando (1778–1839)

Les Adieux; Études, Op. 6/4, 6 & 8; Op. 29/23; Op. 35/16–17; Fantasie élégiaque; Sonatas: in C, Op. 15/2; in C min., Op. 25.
*** Decca Dig. 425 821-2 [id.]. Eduardo Fernández (guitar).

This fine recital offers a comprehensive and rewarding approach to the music of Fernando Sor, who in his day was renowned, not only as composer/guitar virtuoso, but also for his orchestral ballet music (notably *Cendrillon*, premièred in London in 1822). Born in Barcelona the Catalan musician travelled widely, but spent the last part of his life in Paris, where he wote the *Fantasia élégiaque*, and where most of the music on this disc was published. Apart from that deeply felt work, with its *Marche funèbre*, which Fernadez plays with appealing restrained eloquence, much of his writing has a melancholy trait. The one-movement *Sonata in C* is thoroughly classical, but the *C minor Sonata*, a more ambitious piece, opens darkly, and has an appealingly lyrical theme and variations for its finale. Both *Les Adieux* and the *Grand solo* open in a mood of characteristic thoughtful reverie. The *Études* are entertainingly diverse: Opus 6, No. 8 and especially, Opus 35, No. 17, with its folk flavour, have hit potential, given sufficient exposure. Fernández's playing is technically commanding and enjoyably spontaneous, and he is realistically recorded, with fine presence.

Fantaisies, Opp. 7 and 30; Variations on a theme by Mozart, Op. 9.
**(*) BMG/RCA Dig. RD 84549 [RCD1 4549]. Julian Bream (guitar) – AGUADO: *Adagio* etc. **(*)

Both Sor *Fantaisies* are ambitious and each has a central set of variations. Bream's approach is spacious and his deliberation – for all the variety and skill of the colouring – means that the listener is conscious of the music's length, although it is all agreeable enough. The more concise Mozartian *Variations* remain Sor's most famous piece, and the variety and flair of the playing demonstrate why. The studio recording, made in New York, is eminently truthful.

Sousa, John Philip (1854–1932)

Marches: *The Ancient and Honorable Artillery Company; The Black Horse Troop; Bullets and bayonets; The Gallant Seventh; Golden jubilee; The Glory of the Yankee Navy; The Gridiron Club; High school cadets; The Invincible eagle; The Kansas Wildcats; The Liberty Bell; Manhattan Beach; The National game; New Mexico; Nobles of the mystic shrine; Our flirtation; The Piccadore; The Pride of the Wolverines; Riders for the flag; The Rifle Regiment; Sabre and spurs; Sesqui-centennial exposition; Solid men to the front; Sound off.*
(M) *** Mercury 434 300-2 [id.]. Eastman Wind Ens., Frederick Fennell.

Fennell's collection of 24 Sousa marches (73 minutes) derives from vintage Mercury recordings of the early 1960s. The performances have characteristic American pep and natural exuberance. Clearly Fennell is a master of this repertoire. It must be said, however, that while the progamme is adventurous, including rare repertoire, many of these examples are 'marching' marches, rather than music to sit and listen to; however the zest of the playing always carries the day. One of the more striking items is *The Ancient and Honorable Artillery Company*, which incorporates *Auld lang syne* as its middle section. The sound, is, of course, first class. (NB. The listing on the outside of the box misses out one march, but it is present!)

Spohr, Ludwig (1784–1859)

Clarinet concertos Nos. 1 in C min., Op. 26; 4 in E min.
**(*) Orfeo C 088101A [id.]. Leister, Stuttgart RSO, Frühbeck de Burgos.

Clarinet concertos Nos. 2 in E flat, Op. 57; 3 in F min.
**(*) Orfeo C 088201A [id.]. Leister, Stuttgart RSO, Frühbeck de Burgos.

The four *Clarinet concertos* of Spohr – the *Fourth* much grander than the other three – make up an attractive pair of discs, particularly when they are as beautifully played as by the long-time principal of the Berlin Philharmonic, Karl Leister. His smooth tone, the ease and agility with which he tackles virtuoso passage-work and his ability to bring out the smiling quality of much of the inspiration make for delightful performances. The radio recording has relatively little stereo spread, but is undistractingly natural.

(i) *Violin concerto No. 8 in A min. (In modo d'una scena cantate), Op. 47;* (ii) *Double quartet in D min., Op. 65.*
(M) (***) BMG/RCA mono GD 87870; *GK 87870* [7870-2-RG; *7870-4-RG*]. Heifetz, with (i) RCA Victor O, Izler Solomon; (ii) Baker, Thomas, Piatigorsky, Amoyal, Rosenthal, Harshman, Lesser – BEETHOVEN: *Serenade.* **

Spohr's *Gesangszenekonsert* is in mono and dates from 1954. A dazzling performance which, in sheer beauty and refinement of tone, remains unsurpassed. Although the recording acoustic could with advantage have been more ample, this is still very good sound for its period and in some ways is more appealing than the dryish, 1968 stereo recording of the *D minor Double quartet*, Op. 65. The first violin dominates the texture, a reminder both of Spohr's prowess as a violinist and – certainly – of Heifetz's. His distinctive timbre and glorious tone shine through.

Symphonies Nos. 6 in G (Historical), Op. 116; 9 in B min. (The Seasons), Op. 143.
** Orfeo C 094841A [id.]. Bav. RSO, Rickenbacher.

Spohr's *Sixth Symphony*, written in 1839, reminds us of the Mikado's Gilbertian quip about 'Spohr interwoven with Bach and Beethoven'. The first movement sets a Baroque atmosphere, with fugal Bach contrasting genially with a Handelian pastoral style. Karl Rickenbacher has the full measure of it and the Bavarian orchestra play it most engagingly. The element of pastiche continues throughout, but the other movements are less successful. Schumann's influence is strong in the *Ninth Symphony*'s *Spring* movement (which comes second). The finale, with its echoes of the hunt, suffers from Rickenbacher's easy-going manner. A more alert, vivacious approach might have brought these two symphonies more fully to life, although the playing of the Bavarian Radio Orchestra is always responsive and cultured, and the attractive ambience of the recording gives pleasure in itself.

Nonet in F, Op. 31; Octet in E, Op. 32.
*** CRD CRD 3354; *CRDC 4054* [id.]. Nash Ens.

Spohr's *Octet* is a work of great charm; the variations on Handel's *Harmonious blacksmith* which form one of the central movements offer that kind of naïveté which (when played stylishly) makes for delicious listening. The *Nonet* is also very attractive. Spohr's invention is again at its freshest and his propensity for chromaticism is held reasonably in check. Both works are very elegantly played here and the recording throughout is natural and lifelike. This is civilized music, well worth having.

Piano trios Nos. 1 in E min., Op. 119; 2 in F, Op. 123.
** Kingdom Dig. KLCD 2004; *CKLC 2004*. Beethoven Broadwood Trio.

These performances are alive and committed but lack the last degree of polish; consequently they are without that touch of urbanity which gives Spohr's music its charm. The players are not helped by being fairly closely miked in a resonant acoustic (the Church of St John-at-Hackney, London) and the effect is not flattering to the violinist, Frances Mason, although Joy Hall's firm cello line (often very important to the textural balance) is caught well. Michael Freyhan plays a Broadwood Grand of 1823 similar to the instrument Beethoven knew, and it gives the overall sound an authentic feel. With a warmer acoustic glow, these performances would have been even more rewarding; even as it is, however, this coupling is well worth exploring by admirers of the composer. Both works have an impressive scale (the disc plays for 66 minutes overall) and their standard of invention is high.

Piano and wind quintet in C min., Op. 52; Septet in A min. for flute, clarinet, horn, bassoon, violin, cello and piano, Op. 147.
*** CRD CRD 3399; *CRDC 4099* [id.]. Ian Brown, Nash Ens.

These two pieces are among Spohr's most delightful, both the sparkling *Quintet* and the more substantial but still charmingly lighthearted *Septet*. Ian Brown at the piano leads the ensemble with flair and vigour, and the recording quality is outstandingly vivid.

String quartets Nos. 3 in D min., Op. 11; 4 in E flat, Op. 15/1; 6 in G min., Op. 27.
** Marco Polo Dig. 8.223254 [id.]. New Budapest Qt.

These three quartets, dating from 1804, 1808 and 1812 respectively, do not show any marked development, rather a difference in adopted styles. The *D minor* is a 'Quatuor brillant' with the focus permanently on the first violin, and the other three players taking very subsidiary roles. It needs rather more polish and easy bravura than it receives here, but is nevertheless a lively, well integrated performance, if not one which suggests that the players had been living with the music for some time before recording it.The *Adagio* with its distinct leaning towards Mozartian opera is rather engaging, as are the dotted rhythms of the closing rondo. The *E flat Quartet*, although still requiring a great deal of virtuosity from the leader, especiallly in the first movement, is written very much in the spirit of Haydn, especially the minuet and finale, and it has a gentle semi-funeral march for its *Andante*. *Quartet No. 6 in G minor* is the most ambitious work here and its long first movement (12 minutes 37 seconds) has a very characteristic main theme. It needs rather more grip than these players achieve, while the the *Adagio*, too, might have achieved more expressive intensity. The Minuet's contrasts and the spirited finale are well managed. Good recording. Listening to these works, with their fluency, craftsmanship, and ready fund of melodic interest, one can understand why Spohr's music, which communicates immediately in its easy-going way, was so successful in its day.

String quartets Nos. 7 in E flat; 8 in C, Op. 29/1–2.
**(*) Marco Polo Dig. 8.22355 [id.]. New Budapest Qt.

The Op. 29 *Quartets* are associated with Johann Tost (dedicatee of Haydn's Opp. 54/5 and 65). He offered to pay Spohr for any chamber music he wrote in Vienna at the time (1813–15) in return for a first call on the music for a limited period. The result is two of the composer's finest works in this format. Both are written in his friendly, accomplished style; the first ingeniously bases its opening movement on a two-note motto theme and has an outstanding set of variations for its slow movement, surely worthy of Haydn. The tender *Adagio* of the *C major* is even finer, daring in its expressive chromaticism, while the second subject of the first movement (*con molto espressione*) has already indicated that the writing is to be harmonically adventurous. As in the *E flat Quartet*, the Minuet has plenty of character and the finale is elegant and animated. Both performances are spontaneous and the players seem inside the music. If the very last ounce of finesse is missing, this is still vibrant, felt quartet-playing, without artifice, and the recording is lively and present.

String quartets Nos. 27 in D min.; 28 in A flat, Op. 84/1–2.
**(*) Marco Polo Dig. 8.223251 [id.]. New Budapest Qt.

These two works, written in 1831–2, exemplify Spohr's smooth, finely integrated quartet-writing at its most characteristic. The slow movement, sustaining a mood of serene simplicity, is the most memorable in each case, although the lyrical finale of the *A flat major Quartet* is also rather appealing. Good performances, lively enough, but capturing the suaveness of the idiom. The recording is truthful.

String quartets Nos. 29 in B min., Op. 84/3; 30 (Quatuor brillant) in A, Op. 93.
**(*) Marco Polo Dig. 8.223252 [id.]. New Budapest Qt.

In many ways *No. 29 in B minor* is the finest of the Op. 84 set, with its touch of melancholy in the first movement, a lively minuet and a pensive slow movement. Op. 93, written in 1835, is more extrovert in atmosphere in the first movement (after a sombre introduction), but it offers another thoughtfully intense slow movement and a very jolly finale. It brings out the best in these players – and there is plenty of bravura for the first violin – and, again, good tonal matching plus a smooth, warm recording combine effectively for this slightly suave music.

VOCAL MUSIC

Lieder: *An Mignon; 6 German Lieder, Op. 103; 6 Lieder, Op. 154; Lied beim Runetanz; Schlaflied; Scottische Lied; Vanitas!; Zigeuner Lied.*
*** Orfeo Dig. C 103841A [id.]. Julia Varady, Dietrich Fischer-Dieskau, Sitkovetsky, Schoneberger, Hartmut Holl.

The amiable inspiration of Spohr in his songs is delightfully presented in this collection from Dietrich Fischer-Dieskau and Julia Varady. It is characteristic of the composer that, even in his setting of *Erlkönig*, he jogs along rather than gallops, and fails to use the violin dramatically, just giving it an ordinary obbligato. The most attractive songs are the set sung by Varady with clarinet obbligato, but those sung by Fischer-Dieskau are also all highly enjoyable, as long as you do not compare them with the finest of the genre. Excellent recording.

Spontini, Gasparo (1774–1851)

Olympie (opera): complete.
**(*) Orfeo Dig. C 137862H (3) [id.]. Varady, Toczyska, Tagliavini, Fischer-Dieskau, Fortune, Berlin RIAS Chamber Ch., German Op. Male Ch., Berlin RSO, Albrecht.

In Spontini's *Olympie*, based on an historical play by Voltaire about the daughter of Alexander the Great, the principal characters are Olympie, Alexander's daughter, and Statire, his widow, with rival suitors for Olympie's hand setting off the dramatic conflict: the tenor, Cassandre, as the goody and the baritone, Antigone, as the baddy. The writing is lively and committed and, despite flawed singing, so is this performance. Julia Varady is outstanding in the name-part, giving an almost ideal account of the role of heroine, but Stefania Toczyska is disappointingly unsteady as Statire and Franco Tagliavini is totally out of style as Cassandre. Even Dietrich Fischer-Dieskau is less consistent than usual, but his melodramatic presentation is nevertheless most effective. The text is slightly cut.

Stainer, John (1840–1901)

The Crucifixion.
(B) *** CD-CFP 4519; *TC-CFP 4519.* David Hughes, John Lawrenson, Guildford Cathedral Ch., Barry Rose; Gavin Williams.

(i) *The Crucifixion. Come thou long-expected Jesus* (hymn); *I saw the Lord* (anthem).
(B) *** Decca 436 146-2; *436 146-4* [id.]. (i) Richard Lewis, Owen Brannigan, St John's College, Cambridge, Ch., Guest.

All five hymns in which the congregation is invited to join are included on the Decca (originally Argo) record. Owen Brannigan is splendidly dramatic and his voice makes a good foil for Richard Lewis in the duets. The choral singing is first class and the 1961 recording is of Argo's best vintage, even finer than its CfP competitor. Moreover the Decca disc includes two bonuses: a hymn set to the words of Charles Wesley and a fine eight-part anthem, *I saw the Lord*, both of which are equally well sung.

The Classics for Pleasure version (from the late 1960s) is of high quality and, although one of the congregational hymns is omitted, in every other respect this can be recommended. John Lawrenson makes a movingly eloquent solo contribution and the choral singing is excellent. The remastered recording sounds first class, but the Decca version is finer still. There is also a newer, digital version, made in St Paul's Cathedral and well sung by the Cathedral Choir under John Scott. It offers smooth, realistic sound, but the solo singing is less attractive than on either of the bargain alternatives (Conifer CDCF 193; *MCFC 193*).

Stalder, Joseph Franz Xaver (1725–65)

(i) *Flute concerto in B flat; Symphony No. 5 in G.*
*** Novalis Dig. 150 031-2 [id.]. (i) William Bennett; ECO, Griffiths – REINDL: *Sinfonia concertante in D.* ***

Though Joseph Stalder is not quite as interesting a composer as his younger compatriot, Reindl, both the short *G major Symphony* and the *Flute concerto* have freshness and charm and well repay investigation, particularly in such excellent performances and recording.

Stamitz, Johann (1717–57)

Trumpet concerto in D (arr. Boustead).
*** Ph. Dig. 420 203-2; *420 203-4* [id.]. Hardenberger, ASMF, Marriner – HAYDN; HUMMEL: *Concertos* *** ❀; HERTEL: *Concerto.* ***

This recently discovered concerto was written either by Stamitz or by a composer called J. G. Holzbogen. The writing lies consistently up in the instrument's stratosphere and includes some awkward leaps. It is quite inventive, however, notably the finale which is exhilarating on the lips of Håkan Hardenberger. There is no lack of panache here and Marriner accompanies expertly. Good if reverberant recording, with the trumpet given great presence.

Stanford, Charles (1852–1924)

Clarinet concerto in A min., Op. 80.
*** Hyp. CDA 66001; *KA 66001* [id.]. King, Philh. O, Francis – FINZI: *Concerto.* ***

(i) *Clarinet concerto in A min.* (for clarinet and strings) *Op. 80;* (ii) *3 Intermezzi* (for clarinet and piano).

*** ASV Dig. CDDCA 787; *ZCDCA 787* [id.]. Emma Johnson; (i) RPO, Groves; (ii) Martineau – FINZI: *Clarinet concerto* etc. ***

In three linked sections the *Clarinet concerto* shows Stanford characteristically fastidious in developing his ideas; the clarinet repertory is not so rich that such a well-written piece should be neglected, particularly as the final section throws inhibition aside and presents more sharply memorable themes in a warm, late-romantic manner. Thea King's crisp-toned playing is most stylish and the accompaniment thoroughly sympathetic. The recording is reverberant but full and vivid, with just a hint of edge on the upper strings.

The Stanford *Clarinet concerto*, less ambitious in scale than the Finzi with which it is coupled, finds Emma Johnson similarly inspired, again even freer and more fluent than Thea King on the rival Hyperion disc. It is a delight how Johnson can edge into a theme with extreme gentleness. So her first entry in the slow movement, taxingly high, seems to emerge ethereally from nowhere, while Thea King's firmer, sharper attack is less poetic. In the finale too King is strong and forthright, but Johnson is warmer and more personal with her cheekily witty treatment of the first solo. As in the Finzi, Sir Charles Groves and the RPO are warmly sympathetic accompanists, very well recorded, though the solo instrument is rather too close. It is an obvious advantage too that ASV provide substantial fill-ups in shorter pieces by the same composers, though it is conceivable that Hyperion might recouple what was one of its early CD issues, adding more material by Finzi and Stanford already recorded by the same soloist. With Michael Martineau a helpful, relatively unassertive accompanist, Emma Johnson characterizes each of the *Intermezzi* very vividly, using extreme tonal contrasts.

(i) *Piano concerto No. 2 in C min., Op. 126;* (ii) *Becket, Op. 48: The Martydom (Funeral march);* (iii) *The Fisherman of Lough Neagh and what he saw (Irish rhapsody No. 4), Op. 141.*
*** Lyrita SRCD 219 [id.]. (i) Malcolm Binns, LSO; (ii–iii) LPO; (i; iii) Nicholas Braithwaite; (ii) Sir Adrian Boult.

Stanford's *Second Piano concerto*, although in three rather than four movements, is a work on the largest scale, recalling the Brahms *B flat Concerto*. Yet Stanford asserts his own melodic individuality and provides a really memorable secondary theme for the first movement. The piece is enjoyable and uninflated, especially when played with such spontaneous freshness. The recording is surely a demonstration of just how a piano concerto should be balanced: it is well night perfect, and the ambience is just right. The *Funeral march* comes from incidental music commissioned at the request of Tennyson for Irving's production of his tragedy, *Becket*. It has an arresting opening but otherwise is a fairly straightforward piece, strongly melodic in a Stanfordian manner. Like the more familiar *Irish rhapsody*, it is splendidly played and recorded.

Symphony No. 3 in F min. (Irish), Op. 28; Irish rhapsody No. 5, Op. 147.
*** Chan. Dig. CHAN 8545; *ABTD 1253* [id.]. Ulster O, Handley.

This *Third* and most celebrated of the seven symphonies of Stanford is a rich and attractive work, none the worse for its obvious debts to Brahms. The ideas are best when directly echoing Irish folk music, as in the middle two movements, a skippity jig of a Scherzo and a glowing slow movement framed by harp cadenzas, while the finale gives an attractive forward glance to Stanford's pupils, Holst and Vaughan Williams. The *Irish rhapsody No. 5* dates from 1917, reflecting perhaps in its martial vigour that wartime date. Even more characteristic are the warmly lyrical passages, performed passionately by Handley and his Ulster Orchestra, matching the thrust and commitment they bring also to the *Symphony*.

Symphony No. 5 in D (L'Allegro ed il Penseroso), Op. 56; Irish rhapsody No. 4 in A min. (The Fisherman of Loch Neagh and what he saw), Op. 141.
*** Chan. Dig. CHAN 8581; *ABTD 1277* [id.]. Ulster O, Handley.

Stanford's *Fifth Symphony* is colourfully orchestrated and full of easy tunes, illustrating passages from Milton's *L'Allegro* and *Il Penseroso*. The essentially jolly first movement leads to a charming, gentle pastoral movement in an easy Laendler rhythm. The last two movements more readily live up to Stanford's reputation as a Brahmsian, representing the *Penseroso* half of the work, and the slow epilogue brings reminders of Brahms's *Third*. The ease and confidence of the writing makes it a winning work in a performance as committed and full of flair as this. The *Irish rhapsody* is more distinctive of the composer, bringing together sharply contrasted, colourful and atmospheric Irish ideas under the title *The Fisherman of Loch Neagh and what he saw*. Excellent recording of the finest Chandos quality.

Symphony No. 6 in E flat (In memoriam G. F. Watts), Op. 94; Irish rhapsody No. 1 in D min., Op. 78.
*** Chan. Dig. CHAN 8627; *ABTD 1316* [id.]. Ulster O, Vernon Handley.

Stanford's *Sixth Symphony* is not the strongest of the set, but it has a rather lovely slow movement, with a pervading air of gentle melancholy. The first movement has some good ideas but the finale is too long, in the way finales of Glazunov symphonies tend to overuse their material. Nevertheless Vernon Handley makes quite a persuasive case for the work and an even better one for the enjoyable *Irish rhapsody No. 1* which features and makes rather effective use of one of the loveliest of all Irish tunes, the *Londonderry air*. Excellent sound.

Serenade (Nonet) in F, Op. 95.
*** Hyp. CDA 66291; *KA 66291* [id.]. Capricorn – PARRY: *Nonet.* ***

The *Serenade* is for flute, clarinet, bassoon, horn, string quartet and double-bass, and comes from the same period (1905) as the *Sixth Symphony*. Like the Parry *Nonet*, with which it is coupled, it is an inventive and delightful piece, its discourse civilized and the scherzo full of charm. Capricorn play this piece with evident pleasure and convey this to the listener. The recording is very natural and truthfully balanced.

Magnificat in B flat, Op. 164; 3 Motets, Op. 38; Motet: Eternal Father, Op. 135.
*** Conifer Dig. CDCF 155; *MCFC 155* [id.]. Trinity College, Cambridge, Ch., Marlow – PARRY: *Songs of farewell.* ***

These fine Stanford motets and canticles, Anglican Church music at its most assured, make a welcome and attractive coupling for the moving and beautiful Parry choral songs. The *Three Motets*, early works, are settings of Latin hymns; *Eternal Father* is an elaborate setting of Robert Bridges; while the big-scale unaccompanied *Magnificat* for double choir makes a magnificent culmination. Immaculate performances and beautifully balanced, atmospheric recording.

Magnificat and Nunc dimittis in A, Op. 12; Anthems: *For lo I raise up, Op. 145; Ye choirs of new Jerusalem, Op. 123; The Lord is my Shepherd; 3 Motets, Op. 38; Motets, Op. 135/1 & 3; Motet: O living will.*
**(*) Hyp. CDA 66030; *KA 66030* [id.]. Worcester Cathedral Ch., Hunt; Trepte (organ).

This characteristic collection of Stanford's church music brings uneven inspiration – with even some overtones of operetta – but there are more than enough pieces which represent the Anglican tradition at its most compelling, even in easy-going performances like these. The essentially mellow recording has a fair degree of bite and presence in its CD format.

Stanley, John (1712–86)

6 Organ concertos, Op. 10.
*** CRD CRD 3365 [id.]. Gifford, N. Sinfonia.

These bouncing, vigorous performances, well recorded as they are on the splendid organ of Hexham Abbey, present these *Concertos* most persuasively. No. 4, with its darkly energetic C minor, is particularly fine. The recording is natural in timbre and very well balanced. The CD gives the attractive organ sounds added tangibility; it has now been remastered and sounds better than ever; moreover, separate movements have now been cued.

Steiner, Max (1888–1971)

Film scores: *The Adventures of Don Juan; Dodge City; They Died With Their Boots On* (suites).
(M) *** BMG/RCA GD 80912; *GK 80912* [0912-2-RG; *0912-4-RG*]. Nat. SO, Charles Gerhardt (with WAXMAN: *Objective Burma!: Parachute Drop.* FRIEDHOFER: *The Sun Also Rises: Prologue; The Lights of Paris* ***) – KORNGOLD: Film scores. ***

Max Steiner, Viennese born, emigrated to the USA in 1914 and, after working as a conductor/arranger/pianist on the East Coast, was lured out West with the coming of the talkies in 1929. He worked first for RKO (providing music for some 135 pictures), then moved to the Selznick studio and on to Warner Brothers, where he wrote scores for 155 more films. Selznick borrowed him back for *Gone with the Wind*. His style is unashamedly eclectic, but his writing never sounds thin in ideas. The first disc, which Steiner shares with Korngold and others, concentrates on swashbuckling Errol Flynn movies. Sumptuous and exuberant orchestration and attractive lyrical ideas bring the use of orchestral colour in the most spectacular Hollywood tradition. *They Died With Their Boots On* (which whitewashes General Custer) is generous with trumpet calls but also develops the most luscious romanticism, again bringing gloriously full textures from the National Philharmonic violins. The brief Waxman item is as dramatic as its title suggests, and Friedhofer's bitter-sweet waltz theme for *The Sun Also Rises* makes a gentle interlude after the strongly motivated action-sequences of the other contributors.

Film scores: *All This and Heaven too; Beyond the Forest; Dark Victory; In This Our Life; Jezebel; The Letter; Now Voyager; A Stolen Life.*
(M) **(*) BMG/RCA GD 80183; *GK 80183* [0183-2-RG; *0183-4-RG*]. Nat. PO, Charles Gerhardt (with KORNGOLD: *The Private Lives of Elizabeth and Essex: Elizabeth. Juarez: Carlotta.* WAXMAN: *Mr Skeffington: Forsaken.* NEWMAN: *All About Eve: Main title.* ***)

As can be guessed from the titles above, this collection concentrates on the highly charged Bette Davis dramas for which Steiner appropriately wrote emotionally drenched string themes. The disc opens with the big tune from *Now Voyager* (included again below) and, while the *Waltz* from *Jezebel* brings a lighter and more frivolous mood, the prevailing mood is mostly melodramatic. The two vignettes from Korngold have more subtlety (his portrait of Queen Elizabeth I is most winning), while Alfred Newman's introduction to *All About Eve* has characteristic vitality. Many of the excerpts here are brief, and the overall selection at around 40 minutes could have been more generous.

Film scores: *The Big Sleep* (suite); *The Charge of the Light Brigade: The charge; The Fountainhead* (suite). (i) *Four Wives: Symphonie moderne.* (ii) *The Informer* (excerpts). *Johnny Belinda* (suite); *King Kong* (excerpts); *Now Voyager* (excerpts); *Saratoga Trunk: As long as I live. Since you went away:* Title sequence.
(M) *** BMG/RCA GD 80136; *GK 80136* [0136-2-RG; *0136-4-RG*]. National PO, Charles Gerhardt, with (i) Earl Wild; (ii) Amb. S.

Steiner could always produce a good tune on demand, with the luscious themes for *Now Voyager* and *As long as I live* from *Saratoga Trunk* almost approaching the famous *Gone with the Wind* melody in memorability; and a dulcet touch was available for the wistful portrayal of *Johnny Belinda. King Kong* and *The Big Sleep* introduce appropriate elements of menace, and in *The Informer* the Ambrosian Singers provide a characteristic outpouring of Hollywood religiosity at the final climax (the death of the principal character). Charles Gerhardt is a master of the grand orchestral gesture and presents all this music with enormous conviction and with care for atmospheric detail.

Gone with the Wind (film score).
(M) *** BMG/RCA GD 80452; *GK 80452* [0452-2-RG; *0452-4-RG*]. National PO, Charles Gerhardt.

It was sensible of Steiner not to associate his most potent musical idea in *Gone with the Wind* with one or more of the principal characters, but instead to centre it on Tara, the home of the heroine. It says something for the quality of Steiner's tune that its ability to haunt the memory is not diminished by its many reappearances. The rest of the music is professionally tailored to the narrative and makes agreeable listening, although the quality of the lyrical invention inevitably becomes more sentimental as the film nears its close. As ever, Charles Gerhardt is a splendid advocate. The recording, too, is both full and brilliant.

Stenhammar, Wilhelm (1871–1927)

(i) *Piano concerto No. 1 in B flat min., Op. 1; Late summer nights, Op. 33.*
**(*) Sterling CDS1004-2. (i) Irene Mannheimer; Gothenburg SO, Dutoit.

(i) *Piano concerto No. 1 in B flat min., Op. 1;* (ii) *Florez och Blanzeflor, Op. 3;* (iii) *Two Sentimental Romances, Op. 28.*
*** BIS Dig. CD 550 [id.]. (i) Love Derwinger; (ii) Peter Mattei; (iii) Ulf Wallin, Malmö SO, Paavo Järvi.
Stenhammar's *First Piano concerto*, his very first opus, was recorded in 1977 by Irène Mannheimer on the Sterling label in Kurt Atterberg's orchestral reconstruction. It is full of

beautiful ideas and the invention is fresh; even if it is too long (at nearly 50 minutes), admirers of the composer will find much to reward them. It is well played, as are the charming, Brahmsian *Late summer nights*.

In the 1890s and the first decade of the present century Stenhammar toured Europe with his youthful concerto (which owes much to Saint-Saëns, Schumann and Brahms), the orchestral material always being sent ahead by train. At one time the orchestral parts were lost and the composer, Kurt Atterberg, who had often heard the work, made a conjectural (and remarkably skilful) reconstruction of the full score. However, a copy of the original autograph was recently discovered by Dr Allen Ho in the Library of Congress (the concerto's US première took place in 1898). The work is as long as the Brahms *B flat Concerto* (Stenhammar himself was a noted Brahms interpreter) but is less concise than its better-known successor. The inner movements are by far the most satisfying. Love Derwinger proves an impressive and sympathetic intepreter and gets good support from Järvi *fils*. Stenhammar's ballad, *Florez och Blanzeflor* ('Flower and Whiteflower'), Op. 3, is a beautiful piece despite its somewhat Wagnerian overtones, and is sensitively sung by the young Swedish baritone Peter Mattei of whom we shall surely hear more.

Serenade in F, Op. 31 (with the *Reverenza* movement).
*** BIS Dig. CD 310 [id.]. Gothenburg SO, Järvi.

The *Serenade for orchestra* is undoubtedly Stenhammar's most magical work, and this version restores the second movement, *Reverenza*, which the composer had removed, to its original place. It is thoroughly characteristic, yet it has some of the melancholy charm of Elgar, as well as an occasional reminder of Reger in its modulatory patterns and its delicacy of texture. Its presence enriches rather than diminishes the effect of the work as a whole. Glorious music, sensitively played and finely recorded. However, this record offers no couplings.

Serenade in F, Op. 31; Chitra (incidental music), *Op. 43;* (i) *Midwinter, Op. 24.*
**(*) Cap./Musica Sveciae Dig. MSCD 626 [id.]. Swedish RSO, (i) with Ch.; Salonen.

The *Serenade* is Stenhammar's masterpiece and Salonen plays it for all it is worth – and more! There are some moments of exaggeration and he dawdles over and sentimentalizes the glorious *Romanza*. The orchestral playing is highly polished and there is great refinement of colour. The recording balance is good though not in the demonstration class: the orchestral textures could be more transparent. The incidental music to Tagore's play, *Chitra*, is a late work, which Hilding Rosenberg arranged for concert use. It is full of atmosphere and indeed is quite magical at times. Salonen gives a robust and intelligent account of *Midwinter*. In the *Serenade* Järvi remains a first choice and is better recorded. He also adds the *Reverenza* movement that Stenhammar suppressed.

Symphony No. 1 in F.
*** BIS Dig. CD 219 [id.]. Gothenburg SO, Järvi.

The *First Symphony* displays sympathies with such composers as Brahms, Bruckner, Berwald and, in the slow movement, even an affinity with Elgar. The composer intended to revise it but never got around to doing so. Nevertheless there is plenty of originality in it. The recording has complete naturalness and truthfulness of timbre and perspective, and on CD there is additional presence and range, particularly at the bottom end of the register.

Symphony No. 2 in G min., Op. 34.
*** Cap. CAP 21151 [id.]. Stockholm PO, Westerberg.

Symphony No. 2; Overture, Excelsior!, Op. 13.
*** BIS CD 251 [id.]. Gothenburg SO, Järvi.

This is a marvellous symphony. It is direct in utterance; its ideas have splendid character and spirit, and there is a sense of forward movement; the melodic invention is fresh and abundant, and the generosity of spirit it radiates is heart-warming. The Stockholm Philharmonic under Stig Westerberg play with conviction and eloquence; the strings have warmth and body, and they sing out as if they love playing this music. The wind are very fine too. The recording is vivid and full-bodied even by the digital standards of today: as sound, this record is absolutely first class.

Neeme Järvi takes an altogether brisker view of the first movement than Westerberg, but the playing is spirited and the recording very good indeed, though not quite as distinguished as on the Caprice rival. The special attraction of this issue, however, is the *Overture, Excelsior!* It is an opulent but inventive score in the spirit of Strauss and Elgar and is played with enormous zest. *Excelsior!* improves enormously on acquaintance and deserves to become a repertoire work.

String quartets Nos. 1 in C, Op. 2; 2 in C min., Op. 14; 3 in F, Op. 18; 4 in A min., Op. 25; 5 in C (Serenade), Op. 29; 6 in D min., Op. 35.
*** Cap. CAP 21337/9 [id.]. Fresk Qt; Copenhagen Qt; Gotland Qt.

Stenhammar was an active chamber musician as well as conductor and solo pianist. The *First Quartet* shows him steeped in the chamber music of Beethoven and Brahms, though there is a brief reminder of the shadow of Grieg; the *Second* is far more individual and one can detect the ardent voice of the real Stenhammar. By the *Third* and *Fourth*, arguably the greatest of the six, the influence of Brahms and Dvořák is fully assimilated and the *Fourth* reflects that gentle melancholy which lies at the heart of Stenhammar's sensibility. The *Fifth* is the shortest; the *Sixth* comes from the war years when the composer was feeling worn out and depressed, though there is little evidence of this in the music. The Copenhagen Quartet play this marvellously. Performances are generally excellent, as indeed is the recording. These quartets are the product of a cultivated mind and a refined sensibility, but their reticence is well worth overcoming.

Lodolezzi sings: suite, Op. 39; (i) *Midwinter, Op. 24;* (ii) *Snöfrid, Op. 5; The Song* (interlude).
*** BIS Dig. CD 438 [id.]. (i; ii) Gothenburg Concert Hall Ch., (ii) with Åhlén, Nilsson, Zackrisson, Enoksson; Gothenburg SO, Järvi.

Snöfrid is an early cantata from 1891, based on a celebrated poem of Viktor Rydberg, which Sibelius also set. The young composer was completely under the spell of Wagner at this time and, like *Florez och Blanzeflor* (*Flower and whiteflower*), offers only occasional glimpses of the mature Stenhammar. *Midwinter* comes from 1907 when the composer was working in Florence on the *Second Piano concerto* and the *Fourth Quartet.* It is a kind of folk-music fantasy or pot-pourri on the lines of Alfvén's *Midsummer vigil,* though not quite so appealing. *Lodolezzi sings* is a play by Hjalmar Bergman, for which Stenhammar provided incidental music in 1919. He had a particularly soft spot for it – as well he might, for it has much innocent charm. None of this is great Stenhammar but it is well worth hearing; the performances under Neeme Järvi are very sympathetic, and the recording is natural and present.

(i) *The Song (Sången), Op. 44;* (ii) *Two sentimental romances, Op. 28;* (iii) *Ithaca, Op. 21.*
*** Cap. CAP 21358 [id.]. (i) Sörenson, von Otter, Dahlberg, Wahlgren, State Ac. Ch., Adolf Fredrik Music School Children's Ch., (ii) Arve Tellefsen, (iii) Håkan Hagegård, Swedish RSO; (i) Blomstedt; (ii) Westerberg; (iii) Ingelbretsen.

The first half of *The Song* has been described as 'a great fantasy' and is Stenhammar at his best and most individual: the choral writing is imaginatively laid out and the contrapuntal ingenuity is always at the service of poetic ends. The second half is less individual, masterly in its way, a lively choral allegro in the style of Handel. The solo and choral singing is superb and the whole performance has the total commitment one might expect from these forces. The superbly engineered recording does them full justice. The *Two sentimental romances* have great charm and are very well played, and Hagegård is in fine voice in another rarity, *Ithaca*.

30 Songs.
*** Caprice MSCD 623. Von Otter, Hagegård, Forsberg, Schuback.

A delightful record. These songs cover the whole of Stenhammar's career: the earliest, *In the forest*, was composed when he was sixteen, while the last, *Minnesang*, was written three years before his death. This is the most comprehensive anthology yet to appear. The songs are unpretentious and charming, fresh and idyllic, nearly all are strophic. Hagegård sings the majority of them with his usual intelligence and artistry, though there is an occasional hardening of timbre. Anne Sofie von Otter is in wonderful voice and sings with great sensitivity and charm. Bengt Forsberg and Thomas Schuback accompany with great taste, and the recording is of the highest quality.

Sterndale Bennett, William (1816–75)

Piano concertos Nos. 1 in D min., Op. 1; 3 in C min., Op. 9.
❀ *** Lyrita Dig. SRCD 204 [id.]. Malcolm Binns, LPO, Nicholas Braithwaite.

Sterndale Bennett earned the admiration of both Mendelssohn and Schumann and was briefly the white hope of English music. Perhaps it was hearing Mendelssohn play his *G minor Concerto* in 1832 that prompted the young sixteen-year-old, who had just embarked on his studies with

Cipriano Potter, to write his Opus 1, a concerto in D minor and a work of extraordinary fluency and accomplishment. David Byers, who has edited the concertos, speaks of Bennett's 'gentle lyricism, the strength and energy of the orchestral tuttis, and the appropriateness and economy of the scoring'; and they are in ample evidence, both here and in the *Third Piano concerto*, composed when he was eighteen. No praise can be too high for the playing of Malcolm Binns whose fleetness of finger and poetic sensibility are a constant source of delight, and for the admirable support he receives from Nicholas Braithwaite and the LPO. If the Danes can revive all the symphonies of Gade, there is no reason why the British should be shy in advancing the claims of Sterndale Bennett's concertos. The engineers produce sound of the highest quality. A most enjoyable disc.

Piano concertos Nos. 2 in E flat, Op. 4; 5 in F min.; Adagio.
*** Lyrita Dig. SRCD 205 [id.]. Malcolm Binns, Philh. O, Nicholas Braithwaite.

This coupling is hardly less successful than its companion, reviewed above. Sterndale Bennett made his Philharmonic Society début when he was in his seventeenth year with the *Second concerto* (1833). It was dedicated to his teacher, Cipriano Potter, and it proves to be a work of great facility and charm. It takes as its model the concertos of Mozart and Mendelssohn, and the brilliance and delicacy of the keyboard writing make one understand why the composer was so highly regarded by his contemporaries. As was the case with both Chopin and Beethoven, there is some confusion in the numbering of the *F minor concerto* of 1836, which was composed before No. 4, and is also in F minor. It, too, is eminently civilized music with lots of charm; the *Adagio*, which completes the disc, is thought to be an alternative slow movement for Bennett's *Third Concerto* (1837). Whether or not this is the case, it is certainly a lovely piece. Malcolm Binns, surely this country's most underrated pianist – his masterly playing really is worth the hype expended on lesser talents – plays with great artistry, and the accompaniment by the Philharmonia Orchestra and Nicholas Braithwaite is equally sensitive. First-class recording.

(i) *Piano concerto No. 4 in F min.; Symphony in G. min.;* (i) *Fantasia in A, Op. 16.*
(M) *** Unicorn Dig. UKCD 2032; *UKC 2032.* (i) Binns; Milton Keynes CO, Hilary Wetton.

William Sterndale Bennett's eclectical *Fourth Piano concerto* reflects Chopin rather more than Mendelssohn and is agreeable and well structured. Its lollipop slow movement is a winner, an engaging *Barcarolle*. The *Symphony* is amiable, not unlike the Mendelssohn string symphonies. Overall it is very slight, but enjoyable enough. Both performances are uncommonly good ones. There is nothing whatsoever second rate about the Milton Keynes Chamber Orchestra; the string ensemble is spirited and clean and the wind playing is first class. Malcolm Binns is a persuasive advocate of the *Concerto*, while Hilary Wetton paces both works admirably and clearly has much sympathy for them. The solo *Fantasia* has been added for the CD issue, which offers excellent sound and a good balance.

Stevens, Bernard (1916–83)

(i) *Cello concerto; Symphony of liberation.*
*** Mer. CDE 84124. (i) Baillie, BBC PO, Downes.

Bernard Stevens came to wider notice at the end of the war when his *Symphony of liberation* won a *Daily Express* competition. What a fine work it proves to be, though the somewhat later *Cello concerto* is even stronger. Dedicated performances from Alexander Baillie and the BBC Philharmonic. Good recording.

(i) *Violin concerto; Symphony No. 2.*
*** Mer. CDE 84174 [id.]. (i) Ernst Kovacic; BBC PO, Downes.

The *Violin concerto* was a wartime commission by Max Rostal and was hailed in the 1940s as the equal of the Britten or Walton *Concertos* – which it is not. However, it is a good piece and well worth investigating. Stevens has not the strong personality of, say, Rawsthorne or quite the depth of Rubbra, but he is far from anonymous. Indeed he is a composer of real substance, and the *Second Symphony* (1964) is impressive in its sustained power and resource. Ernst Kovacic is persuasive in the *Concerto* and Downes and the BBC Philharmonic play well. Good (but not spectacular) recording.

Stockhausen, Karlheinz (born 1928)

Stimmung (1968).
*** Hyp. CDA 66115 [id.]. Singcircle, Gregory Rose.

Gregory Rose with his talented vocal group directs an intensely beautiful account of Stockhausen's 70-minute minimalist meditation on six notes. Though the unsympathetic listener might still find the result boring, this explains admirably how Stockhausen's musical personality can magnetize, with his variety of effect and response, even with the simplest of formulae. Excellent recording.

Donnerstag aus Licht (complete).
**(*) DG 423 379-2 (4). Soloists, Cologne RSO Ch., Hilversum R. Ch. & O, W. German R. Ens., Ens. InterContemporain, composer; Eötvös.

This Thursday episode from Stockhausen's seven-day operatic cycle, sharply eventful, has obvious concentration in its direct musical expression. The central character is the Archangel Michael, with Act I devoted to his childhood, 'moon-eve' and examination, Act II to his journey round the Earth (with trumpet and orchestra), and Act III to the return home, representing finally Judgement Day and the end of time. The recording is hardly a substitute for the full visual experience, but the originality of Stockhausen's aural imagination, not least in his use of voices, is brilliant. The complete text is omitted, and the synopsis is not always detailed enough for the action to be followed fully, a pity in a work which is baffling enough already.

Stradella, Alessandro (1644–82)

San Giovanni Battista (oratorio).
❀ *** Erato/Warner Dig. 2292 45739-2 [id.]. Bott, Batty, Lesne, Edgar-Wilson, Huttenlocher, Musiciens du Louvre, Minkowski.

Stradella's oratorio on the Biblical subject of John the Baptist and Salome is an amazing masterpiece. Written in 1675 by this notorious libertine of a composer, its compact structure of 37 sections lasting just over an hour offers unashamedly sensuous treatment of the story. Insinuatingly chromatic melodic lines for Salome (here described simply as Herodias' daughter) are set against plainer, more forthright writing for the castrato role of the saint, a seventeenth-century equivalent of Richard Strauss. There is one amazing phrase for Salome, gloriously sung here by Catherine Bott, which starts well above the stave and ends after much twisting nearly two octaves below with a glorious chest-note, a hair-raising moment. Salome's brief arias cover an extreme range of moods, both vigorous and pathetic, and there is one beautiful trio she has with her mother and the tenor Counsellor which brings striking echoes of Monteverdi's *Lamento della ninfa*, one of the most languorously beautiful of all madrigals. Herod's anger arias bring reminders of both Purcell and Handel, and at the end Stradella ingeniously superimposes Salome's gloating music and Herod's expressions of regret, finally cutting off the duet in mid-air as Charles Ives might have done, bringing the whole work to an indeterminate close. Quite apart from Catherine Bott's magnificent performance, at once pure and sensuous in tone and astonishingly agile, the other singers are most impressive, with Gerard Lesne a firm-toned counter-tenor in the title-role and Philippe Huttenlocher a clear if sometimes gruff Herod. Marc Minkowski reinforces his claims as an outstanding exponent of period performance, drawing electrifying playing from Les Musiciens du Louvre, heightening the drama. Excellent sound. Not to be missed!

Strauss, Johann Snr (1804–49)

Strauss, Johann Jnr (1825–99)

Strauss, Josef (1827–70) Strauss, Eduard (1835–1916)

(All music listed is by Johann Strauss Jnr unless otherwise stated)

Le Beau Danube (ballet, arr. Désormière); *Cinderella* (*Äschenbrodel;* ballet, rev. and ed. Gamley); *Ritter Pásmán* (ballet music).
(M) **(*) Decca Dig./Analogue 430 852-2 (2) [id.]. Nat. PO, Richard Bonynge.

Johann Strauss did not live to finish his only full-length ballet, *Äschenbrodel.* Most of Act I was completed, but the rest was pieced together by other hands. The music is felicitously scored, but the most memorable moment is when the *Blue Danube* is quoted as a barrel-organ effect but sounding piquantly like an ocarina. Decca provide digital sound of spectacular excellence and Bonynge does his utmost to engage the listener, securing warm, elegant and sparkling playing. But as the *Ritter Pásmán* ballet suite, which is rather more memorable, shows, Strauss's setting of the Cinderella story is inconsequential, though pleasing enough as wallpaper music. *Le beau Danube* is another matter. Désormière draws on vintage Strauss material for *Le beau Danube* and, although his score is not chosen as adroitly as Dorati's *Graduation Ball* (which we urgently need on CD), it opens racily and is very entertaining. Bonynge presents it all with effervescent sparkle and the Decca analogue recording is first class.

(i) *Overtures: Die Fledermaus;* (ii) *Waldmeister.* (iii) *Perpetuum mobile.* Polkas: (iv) *Annen;* (v) *Auf der Jagd;* (vi) *Leichtes Blut;* (iv) *Pizzicato* (with Josef); (vii) *Tritsch-Tratsch;* (iv) *Vergnügungszug.* (viii) *Quadrille on themes from Verdi's 'Un ballo in maschera'.* Waltzes: (ix) *Accelerationen;* (x) *An der schönen blauen Donau;* (xi) *Du und Du;* (iv) *Frühlingsstimmen;* (vi) *Geschichten aus dem Wienerwald;* (xii) & (xiii) & (v) *Kaiser;* (iii) *Rosen aus dem Süden;* (ii) *Wein, Weib und Gesang.* Josef STRAUSS: (iv) *Dorfschwalben aus Österreich;* (v) *Sphärenklänge.* (iv) Johann STRAUSS, Snr: *Radetzky march.*
(M) *** DG mono/stereo 435 335-2 (2). VPO, (i) Maazel; (ii) Boskovsky; (iii) Boehm; (iv) Clemens Krauss; (v) Karajan; (vi) Knappertsbusch; (vii) Mehta; (viii) Abbado; (ix) Josef Krips; (x) Szell; (xi) Erich Kleiber; (xii) Bruno Walter; (xiii) Furtwängler.

This delectable compilation for the 150th anniversary of the Vienna Philharmonic brings recordings of Strauss made between 1929 and 1990. Surprisingly, only four of the 23 items are from DG sources, with the rest borrowed from rival companies, notably from EMI, whose recordings of Erich Kleiber, Clemens Krauss and George Szell (made in the late 1920s and early 1930s) are particularly atmospheric, very well transferred. Other Clemens Krauss performances, plus more by Boskovsky and Knappertsbusch, come from the Decca label, justly famous in this repertoire. It is fascinating to compare Bruno Walter (1937), Wilhelm Furtwängler (1950) and Karajan (1987), all in the *Emperor waltz.* Karajan's other major contribution dates from 1949 (*Sphärenkläange*), and the many well-known favourites are well spiced with a few charming rarities.

Banditen-Galopp; Kaiser Franz Joseph I: Rettungs-Jubel-Marsch; Russischer Marsch. Polkas: *Champagner; Eljen a Magyar!; Neue Pizzicato; Unter Donner und Blitz.* Waltzes: *Künstlerleben; Liebeslieder; Morgenblätter; Wiener Blut; Wiener Bonbons.* Josef STRAUSS: *Auf Ferienreisen polka; Dorfschwalben aus Österreich (Village swallows) waltz.*
(M) *** Decca 425 428-2. VPO, Boskovsky.

Egyptischer Marsch. Polkas: *Annen; Auf der Jagd; Pizzicato* (with Josef); *Tritsch-Tratsch.* Waltzes: *An der schönen blauen Donau; Carnevals-Botschafter; Frühlingsstimmen.* Josef STRAUSS: Polkas: *Feuerfest; Jockey; Polka-mazurka: Die Schwätzerin.* Waltzes: *Dynamiden; Sphärenklänge.* Eduard STRAUSS: *Fesche Geister waltz.* Johann STRAUSS Snr: *Wettrennen-Galopp.*
(M) *** Decca 425 425-2. VPO, Boskovsky.

Persischer Marsch. Polkas: *Bitte schön; Leichtes Blut; 'S gibt nur a Kaiserstadt; Tik-Tak; Vergnügungszug.* Waltzes: *Acccelerationen; Kaiser; Rosen aus dem Süden; Schneeglöckchen.*

Johann STRAUSS Snr: *Loreley-Rhein-Klänge waltz*. Josef STRAUSS: *Die Emancipirte polka-mazurka; Delirien waltz*. Eduard STRAUSS: *Mit Extrapost polka*.
(M) *** Decca 425 429-2. VPO, Boskovsky.

Perpetuum mobile; Spanischer Marsch. Polkas: *Demolirer; Stürmisch in Lieb' und Tanz*. Waltzes: *Du und Du; Freuet euch des Lebens; Geschichten aus dem Wienerwald; Lagunen*. Josef STRAUSS: *Brennende Liebe polka mazurka; Eingesendet polka; Aquarellem waltz*. Eduard STRAUSS: *Bahn frei! polka; Frauenherz polka mazurka*. Johann STRAUSS Snr: *Radetzky march. Piefke und Pufke polka*.
(M) *** Decca 425 426-2. VPO, Boskovsky.

The cream of the Strauss family repertoire is here, and that includes some memorable items from Josef. Eduard, too, offers some memorable pieces, of which the most famous is the infectious *Bahn frei!* with its opening whistle. Each CD is introduced by a famous waltz from Johann and is attractively programmed to alternate other waltzes with polkas, while the charming polka-mazurkas and marches offer further variety. The recordings date from between 1958 and 1976 but their age is partly disguised, since the warm acoustics of the Vienna Sophienbad-Saal (where many of the recordings were made) are agreeably flattering. The performances remain unsurpassed.

'The world of Johann Strauss': Egyptischer Marsch; Perpetuum mobile; Polkas: *Auf de Jagd; Pizzicato* (with Josef); Waltzes: *An der schönen blauen Donau; Frühlingsstimmen; Geschichten aus dem Wienerwald; Rosen aus dem Süden; 1001 Nacht; Wiener Blut*.
(B) *** Decca 430 501-2; *430 501-4*. VPO, Boskovsky.

A further generous and inexpensive Decca permutation of the justly famous Boskovsky/VPO recordings, which still dominate the Strauss family listings. If the programme suits, this is excellent value.

Napoleon-Marsch. Polkas: *Annen; Explosionen; Tritsch-Tratsch*. Waltzes: *An der schönen blauen Donau; Morgenblätter; 1001 Nights; Wein, Weib und Gesang; Wiener Bonbons*. Josef STRAUSS: *Dorfschwalben aus Österreich*. Johann STRAUSS Snr: *Radetzky march*.
(B) *** Decca 433 609-2; *433 609-4*. VPO, Willi Boskovsky.

A particularly enjoyable concert of Boskovsky repertoire, chosen and ordered with skill, opening with the *Blue Danube* and closing with the rousing *Radetzky march*. Boskovsky presents the long introduction to *Wine, women and song* very engagingly, and then the waltz has a splendid lift, while the *Napoleon march* which follows brings both wit and zest. The VPO are on their toes throughout: Josef's *Village swallows* has great charm, followed by *1001 Nights* which has another enticing introduction. The recording dates range from 1958 to 1976; some are spikier than others in the upper range, but the warm Sofiensaal ambience is always flattering.

New Year's Day concert (1979): Polkas: *Auf der Jagd* (with encore); *Bitte schön! Leichtes Blut; Pizzicato* (with Josef); *Tik-Tak*. Waltzes: *An der schönen blauen Donau; Bei uns zu Haus; Wein, Weib und Gesang*. Josef STRAUSS: *Moulinet polka; Sphärenklänge waltz*. Johann STRAUSS, Snr: *Radetzky march*.
(M) **(*) Decca Dig. 430 715-2; *430 715-4*. VPO, Boskovsky.

Decca chose to record Boskovsky's 1979 New Year's Day concert in Vienna for one of their very first digital issues on LP. The clarity, immediacy and natural separation of detail are very striking throughout, although the upper strings of the Vienna Philharmonic are very brightly lit indeed and there is some lack of bloom at the top. The CD does not include the whole concert. The music-making gains much from the spontaneity of the occasion, and the electricity is very apparent; it reaches its peak when the side-drum thunders out the introduction to the closing *Radetzky March*, a frisson-creating moment which, with the audience participation, is quite electrifying.

'1987 New Year Concert in Vienna': Overture: *Die Fledermaus*. Polkas: *Annen; Pizzicato* (with Josef); *Unter Donner und Blitz; Vergnügungszug*. Waltzes: *An der schönen blauen Donau;* (i) *Frühlingsstimmen*. J. STRAUSS S: *Beliebte Annen* (polka); *Radetzky march*. Josef STRAUSS: *Ohne Sorgen polka;* Waltzes: *Delirien; Sphärenklänge*.
❀ *** DG Dig. 419 616-2 [id.]. VPO, Karajan; (i) with Kathleen Battle.

In preparation for this outstanding concert, which was both recorded and televised, Karajan re-studied the scores of his favourite Strauss pieces; the result, he said afterwards, was to bring an overall renewal to his musical life beyond the scope of this particular repertoire. The concert itself produced music-making of the utmost magic. With a minimum of gesture he coaxed the Viennese players into performances of the utmost warmth and freshness; familiar pieces sounded almost as if they were being played for the first time. Kathleen Battle's contribution to *Voices of spring* brought wonderfully easy, smiling coloratura and much charm. *The Blue Danube* was, of course, an encore, and what an encore! Never before has it been played so seductively on record, with the VPO, in Karajan's words, 'demonstrating that their feeling for waltz rhythms is absolutely unique'. In the closing *Radetzky march*, wonderfully crisp yet relaxed, Karajan kept the audience contribution completely in control merely by the slightest glance over his shoulder. The recording is superbly balanced and the acoustics of the Musikverein bring natural warmth to every department of the orchestra, but particularly to the strings. This indispensable collection makes an easy first choice among any Strauss compilations ever issued; it was an occasion when everything was right – and the only grumble is the almost unbelievable lack of accompanying documentation.

'1989 New Year Concert in Vienna': Overture: *Die Fledermaus*. Csárdás: *Ritter Pasman*. Polkas: *Bauern; Eljen a Magyar!; Im Krapfenwald'l; Pizzicato* (with Josef). Waltzes: *Accelerationen; An der schönen blauen Donau; Frühlingsstimmen; Künstlerleben*. Josef STRAUSS: Polkas: *Jockey; Die Libelle; Moulinet; Plappermäulchen*. Johann STRAUSS, Snr: *Radetzky march*.
**(*) Sony/CBS CD 45938 [id.]. VPO, Carlos Kleiber.

In style this is very similar to Kleiber's controversial complete recording of *Fledermaus*, for though he allows all the rhythmic flexibility a traditionalist could want – and sometimes more – his pursuit of knife-edged precision prevents the results from sounding quite relaxed enough, with the Viennese lilt in the waltzes analysed to the last micro-second instead of just being played as a dance. In the delicious polka, *Im Krapfenwald'l*, the cheeky cuckoo-calls which comically punctuate the main theme are made to sound beautiful rather than rustic, and fun is muted elsewhere too. But in one or two numbers Kleiber really lets rip, as in the Hungarian polka, *Eljen a Magyar!* ('Hail to Hungary!'), and in the *Ritter Pásmán Csárdás*. This concert now reappears on a single full-price disc, playing for 76 minutes and omitting just one waltz, *Bei uns zu Haus*. Not everyone responds positively to Kleiber's rather precise style with Viennese rhythms, but this is still an enjoyably spontaneous concert, made the more attractive by the warm, full recording, with the presence of the audience nicely implied without getting in the way.

'1990 New Year Concert': *Einzugsmarsch* (from *Der Zigeunerbaron*). Polkas: *Explosionen; Im Sturmschritt; Tritsch-tratsch*. Waltzes: *An der schönen blauen Donau; Donauweibchen; Geschichten aus dem Wienerwald; Wiener Blut*. Josef STRAUSS: Polkas: *Eingesendet; Die Emancipirte; Sport; Sympathie*. Johann STRAUSS S: *Indianer galop. Radetzky march*.
*** Sony Dig. SK 45808; *40-45808* [id.]. VPO, Zubin Mehta.

A worthy successor to Karajan's wonderful 1987 concert, not *quite* its equal but offering many delights of its own. After the invigorating *Entrance march* from *Zigeunerbaron*, Mehta braves the conservatism of the Viennese audience by presenting a programme of mainly novelties. The first really well-known piece (*Wiener Blut*, splendidly played) finally arrives as item number 7! Before then the applause is grudging, but the listener at home must delight in hearing so much fresh music of high quality superbly played, with all the stimulation of a live occasion. This is Mehta's finest record for years; he conjures a magical response from the VPO and is just as persuasive in the famous waltzes. In the *Blue Danube* he hardly needs forgiveness for indulging himself (as Karajan sometimes did, only slightly more so) with a gentle, rather mannered reprise of one of the subsidiary melodies, and he conjures a moment of sheer kitsch from the Vienna strings. But elsewhere his easy warmth and relaxed rhythmic style are beyond criticism. The recording is superb: the engineers capture the orchestra with complete naturalness within the glowing acoustic bloom of the Grosser Musikvereinsaal.

Overture: *Die Fledermaus*. Polkas: *Annen; Auf der Jagd; Explosionen*. Waltzes: *Frühlingsstimmen; Rosen aus dem Süden; Wein, Weib und Gesang; Windsor echoes*. Josef STRAUSS: *Feuerfest polka* (with ZIEHRER: *Kissing polka*).
(B) *** Pickwick PCD 902; *CIMPC 902* [id.]. LSO, Georgiadis.

Entitled '*An Evening in Vienna*', the performances have nevertheless a British flavour – which is not to say that there is any lack of lilt or beguiling warmth in the waltzes; they are beautifully done, while the polkas all go with an infectious swing. There are no superimposed sound-effects in the *Explosions polka*; one waits until the very end, when there is a spectacular 'collapse' of the whole percussion department. The sound is very good indeed, well balanced with a pleasing ambient bloom. This is very enjoyable and is John Georgiadis's best record to date.

Pappacoda polka; Der lustige Kreig (quadrille); *Klug Gretelein* (waltz). Josef STRAUSS: *Defilir marsch;* Polkas: *Farewell; For ever.* Eduard STRAUSS: *Weyprecht-Payer marsch;* Polkas: *Mädchenlaune; Saat und Ernte;* Waltzes: *Die Abonnenten; Blüthenkranz Johann Strauss'scher.* J. STRAUSS III (son of Eduard): *Schlau-Schlau polka.*
*** Chan. Dig. CHAN 8527. Johann Strauss O of V., Rothstein, with M. Hill-Smith.

Volume 1 of *'Vienna première'* is a concert involving other composers besides the Strauss family; it was sponsored, like the present collection (Volume 2), by the Johann Strauss Society of Great Britain. This programme is admirably chosen to include unfamiliar music which deserves recording; indeed, both the *Klug Gretelein waltz*, which opens with some delectable scoring for woodwind and harp and has an idiomatic vocal contribution from Marilyn Hill-Smith, and *Die Abonnenten* (by Eduard) are very attractive waltzes. *Blüthenkranz Johann Strauss'scher*, as its title suggests, makes a pot-pourri of some of Johann's most famous melodies. The polkas are a consistent delight, played wonderfully infectiously; indeed, above all this is a cheerful concert, designed to raise the spirits; the CD sound sparkles.

Polka: *Unter Donner und Blitz.* Waltzes: *An der schönen blauen Donau; Kaiser; Künsterleben; Morgenblätter; Rosen aus dem Süden; Schatz; Wiener Blut.* Josef STRAUSS: Waltzes: *Dorfschwalben aus Österreich; Mein Lebenslauf ist Lieb' und Lust.*
(M) *** BMG/RCA GD 60177 [60177-2-RG]. Chicago SO, Reiner.

Reiner's collection was recorded in 1957 and 1960, and the sound is voluptuous with the warmth of the Chicago Hall ambience. The performances are memorable for their lilting zest and the sumptuous richness of the Chicago strings, although the *Thunder and lightning polka* has an unforgettably explosive exuberance. Reiner – Budapest born – fully understands how this music should be played and conveys his affection in every bar. A fine appendix for the Boskovsky series – it will give equal pleasure.

Waltzes: *An der schönen blauen Donau; Carnevals-Botschafter; Donauweibchen; Du und du; Feuilleton; Flugschriften; Die Leitartikel; Morgenblätter; Wein, Weib und Gesang; Wiener Frauen.*
(M) **(*) EMI Dig. CDD7 64108-2; *ET 764108-4*. Johann Strauss O of Vienna, Boskovsky.

These recordings date from 1982 and 1984. The fuller digital sound is obviously more modern than that on Boskovsky's remastered VPO records made for Decca; but the effect is for the music-making to sound more robust, though the playing is warm and stylish and there is a genuine Viennese lilt. The *Blue Danube* is a splendid performance, Boskovsky at his finest; *Morning papers* is very enjoyable too, and the novelties sound admirably fresh, especially the two concerning the ladies, *Donauweibchen* and *Wiener Frauen*. This collection is generous (78 minutes) and is thoroughly worthwhile; if the playing does not have quite the magic of Boskovsky's finest VPO performances, it is still very easy to enjoy.

Die Fledermaus (opera): complete (gala performance).
**(*) Decca 421 046-2 (2) [id.]. Gueden, Köth, Kmentt, Waechter, Berry, Zampieri (with guest artists: Nilsson, Tebaldi, Corena, Sutherland, Simionato, Welisch, Berganza, Leontyne Price), V. State Op. Ch., VPO, Karajan.

Die Fledermaus (complete).
*** Ph. Dig. 432 157-2; *432 157-4* (2) [id.]. Kiri Te Kanawa, Gruberová, Leech, Wolfgang Brendel, Bär, Fassbaender, Göttling, Krause, Wendler, Schenk, V. State Op. Ch., VPO, Previn.
(M) (***) EMI mono CHS7 69531-2 (2) [Ang. CDHB 69531]. Schwarzkopf, Streich, Gedda, Krebs, Kunz, Christ, Philh. Ch. & O, Karajan.
(M) *** EMI CMS7 69354-2 (2) [Ang. CDMB 69354]. Rothenberger, Holm, Gedda, Fischer-Dieskau, Fassbaender, Berry, V. State Op. Ch., VSO, Boskovsky.
(B) **(*) CfP CD-CFPD 4702; *TC-CFPD 4702* (2) [Ang. CDMB 62566]. Lipp, Scheyrer, Ludwig, Dermota, Terkal, Waechter, Berry, Philh. Ch. & O, Ackermann.

André Previn has a special relationship with the Vienna Philharmonic, and the collaboration works here to produce an enjoyably idiomatic account of Strauss's masterpiece, yet one which is tautly controlled. This may be a plainer reading than some, avoiding a few traditional hesitations and accelerations when the score plainly indicates '*a tempo*', but it is one which consistently conveys the work's exuberant high spirits. Dame Kiri Te Kanawa's portrait of

Rosalinde brings not only gloriously firm, golden sound but also vocal acting with star quality, and the fact that her German accent is less than perfect is turned to advantage. She becomes an Anglo-Saxon Rosalinde, with the occasional phrase or two of English slipped deftly into the dialogue. Brigitte Fassbaender is the most dominant Prince Orlofsky on disc; for her alone it is worth hearing this set. Singing with a tangy richness and firmness, she emerges as the genuine focus of the party scene, no effete dandy but a tough figure. Her spoken dialogue, throatily delivered, has all the command of Marlene Dietrich in her prime. Edita Gruberová is a sparkling, characterful and full-voiced Adele, stunningly brilliant in her Act III Couplets. The men soloists are vocally just as strong as the women, though not as characterful. Wolfgang Brendel as Eisenstein and Olaf Bär as Dr Falke both sing very well indeed, though their voices sound too alike. Richard Leech as Alfred provides heady tone and a hint of parody, and the odd opera snippets he trots out in Acts I and III are not overdone. Tom Krause makes a splendid Frank, the more characterful for no longer sounding young. Anton Wendler as Dr Blind and Otto Schenk as Frosch the jailer give vintage Viennese performances, with Frosch's cavortings well tailored and not too extended.

This now goes to the top of the list of latterday *Fledermaus* recordings, though with one serious reservation. The Philips production in Act II adds a layer of crowd noise as background throughout the Party scene, even during Orlofsky's solos. Such a host would have been furious at being ignored so blatantly, with women shrieking behind. Strauss's gentler moments are then seriously undermined by the sludge of distant chatter and laughter, as in the lovely chorus *Bruderlein und Schwesterlein*, yearningly done. The only number exempted from background chatter is Rosalinde's great *Heimat* solo and Csárdás, with Dame Kiri soaring expansively. Otherwise the recorded sound is superb, with brilliance and bite alongside warmth and bloom, both immediate and well balanced. The spoken dialogue is well edited and briskly delivered. Like Kleiber on DG, Previn avoids having a series of party-songs in Act II, whether from visitors or principals, and similarly opts for the *Thunder and lightning polka* instead of the ballet.

The mono recording of Karajan's 1955 version has great freshness and clarity, along with the polish which for many will make it a first favourite. Tempi at times are unconventional, both slow and fast, but the precision and point of the playing are magical and the singing is endlessly delightful. Schwarzkopf makes an enchanting Rosalinde, not just in the imagination and sparkle of her singing but also in the snatches of spoken dialogue (never too long) which leaven the entertainment. As Adèle, Rita Streich produces her most dazzling coloratura; Gedda and Krebs are beautifully contrasted in their tenor tone, and Erich Kunz gives a vintage performance as Falke. The original recording, crisply focused, has been given a brighter edge but otherwise left unmolested.

The Boskovsky version, recorded with the Vienna Symphoniker instead of the Philharmonic, now heads the CD list of stereo *Fledermice*. Rothenberger is a sweet, domestic-sounding Rosalinde, relaxed and sparkling, while among an excellent supporting cast the Orlofsky of Brigitte Fassbaender must be singled out as quite the finest on record, tough and firm. The entertainment has been excellently produced for records, with German dialogue inserted, though the ripe recording sometimes makes the voices jump between singing and speaking. The remastering is admirably vivid.

On a pair of CfP CDs, with a synopsis rather than a libretto, comes a vintage *Fledermaus* from 1960. It makes a superb bargain, for the singing is consistently vivacious. Gerda Scheyrer's Rosalinde brings the only relative disappointment, for the voice is not ideally steady; but Wilma Lipp is a delicious Adèle and Christa Ludwig's Orlofsky is a real surprise, second only to Brigitte Fassbaender's assumption of a breeches role that is too often disappointing. Karl Terkal's Eisenstein and Anton Dermota's Alfred give much pleasure, and Erich Kunz's inebriated Frosch in the finale comes off even without a translation. Ackermann's direction has not the sparkle and subtlety of Karajan, but the final result is polished and with a real Viennese flavour. The sound has come up remarkably vividly – there is a nice combination of atmosphere and clarity.

The Karajan 'Gala performance' of 1960 featured various artists from the Decca roster appearing to do their turn at the 'cabaret' included in the Orlofsky ball sequence. The performance of the opera itself has all the sparkle one could ask for. If anything, Karajan is even more brilliant than he was on the older mono issue, and the Decca recording is scintillating in its clarity. Where it does fall short, alas, is in the singing. Hilde Gueden is deliciously vivacious as Rosalinde, a beautifully projected interpretation, but vocally she is not perfect, and even her confidence has a drawback in showing how tentative Erika Köth is as Adèle, with her wavering vibrato. Waldemar Kmentt has a tight, German-sounding tenor, and Giuseppe Zampieri as

Alfred (a bright idea to have a genuine Italian for the part) is no more than adequate. The rest of the cast are very good.

Strauss, Richard (1864–1949)

An Alpine Symphony, Op. 64.
*** DG Dig. 400 039-2 [id.]. BPO, Karajan.
*** Ph. Dig. 416 156-2 [id.]. Concg. O, Haitink.
*** BMG/RCA Dig. RD 69012 [id.]. Bamberg SO, Horst Stein.
(M) *** Decca 417 717-2 [id.]. LAPO, Mehta.

An Alpine symphony, Op. 64; Don Juan, Op. 20.
*** Decca Dig. 421 815-2. San Francisco SO, Blomstedt.

An Alpine symphony; Till Eulenspiegel.
**(*) Decca Dig. 425 112-2 [id.]. Cleveland O, Ashkenazy.

An Alpine symphony, Op. 64; (i) *Songs with orchestra: Das Bächlein; Freundlich Vision; Meinem Kinde; Morgen!*
**(*) Chan. Dig. CHAN 8557; *ABTD 1263* [id.]. SNO, Järvi; (i) with Felicity Lott.

As is shown by his *Heldenleben* (as well as by some of his other Dresden records on Denon, like the Bruckner *Fourth* and *Seventh Symphonies*), Blomstedt has developed into a conductor of real stature who knows how to pace a work and relate climaxes to one another. His *Alpine symphony* is superbly shaped and has that rare quality of relating part to whole in a way that totally convinces. He gets scrupulously attentive playing from the San Francisco orchestra and a rich, well-detailed Decca recording.

Karajan's account is recorded digitally, but orchestral detail is less than ideally clear and there is a slight edge to the upper strings. But it would be wrong to give the impression that the DG sound is less than first class and, as a performance, the Karajan is in the highest flight. It is wonderfully spacious, beautifully shaped and played with the utmost virtuosity. This is certainly one of the finest versions now available.

Haitink's account on Philips is a splendid affair, a far more natural-sounding recording than the Karajan on DG, and strongly characterized throughout. The offstage horns sound suitably exciting, the perspective is excellent, and there is plenty of atmosphere, particularly in the episode of the calm before the storm. Above all, the architecture of the work as a whole is impressively laid out and the orchestral playing is magnificent. This does not quite displace Karajan, but it can hold its own with the best.

The Bamberg orchestra also produce a fine performance, and RCA provide an exceptionally good recording with plenty of detail and a spacious, warm, well-focused aural image. The Bamberg now sounds a much bigger and finer body than it did in the 1960s and '70s – though, as this CD is a co-production with Bavarian Radio, it might well be reinforced. All the same, this is not to be preferred to Blomstedt (who offers a fine *Don Juan* as well).

Those wanting a medium-priced version of the *Alpine Symphony* could hardly do better than turn to Mehta, whose performance is among the best Strauss he has given us, and the vintage 1976 recording is successful in combining range and atmosphere with remarkable detail. It is more brightly lit in its digital transfer, but the Decca engineers let every strand of the texture tell without losing sight of the overall perspective. The effect remains spectacular.

The Cleveland Orchestra commands as rich a sonority and as much virtuosity as any of its illustrious rivals. Ashkenazy gives a generally well-controlled and intelligently shaped reading of the score that has much to recommend it. However, it is not quite as strong in personality as the very finest versions.

Järvi's reading brings a roundly enjoyable performance, ripely recorded in a helpfully reverberant acoustic. Though the performance of the main work is not as electrically taut or crisp of ensemble as, say, Karajan's, tending to give too much too soon, it takes a warm, genial view of the composer's mountain-climb and its incidents. Felicity Lott is at her finest in the four songs, gentle inspirations in which the sweet purity of her voice is never disturbed.

Also sprach Zarathustra.
(*) Olympia Dig. OCD 209 [id.]. Moscow SO, Dmitri Kitaenko – RACHMANINOV: *Symphony No. 3.* **

Also sprach Zarathustra, Op. 30; Le bourgeois gentilhomme: Suite, Op. 60. Der Rosenkavalier: Waltzes.
(M) *** BMG/RCA 09026 60930-2 [60930-2]. Chicago SO, Reiner.

For some collectors (certainly for R.L.) Reiner's 1954 account of *Also sprach Zarathustra* was their introduction to stereo and the impressive feeling of space it conveyed. Later reissues have improved on its definition but none has done so with such stunning success as the present transfer. Indeed, although modern digital techniques eradicate background hiss, they rarely have music-making as incandescent as this to convey. A wonderful performance that ranks alongside the very best ever committed to disc. The same goes for the suite from *Le bourgeois gentilhomme* – possibly the finest ever, and sounding marvellously fresh considering its date (1956).

In these days of spectacular recordings Dmitri Kitaenko's 1985 recording suffers the handicap of uncompetitive sound. The balance is pretty synthetic and there is some coarseness at climaxes. After the blazing C major chord on the organ in the opening section, the recording goes dead. The strings are obviously making a glorious sound but have an unpleasing shrillness above the stave. The performance itself is far from undistinguished.

(i) *Also sprach Zarathustra, Op. 30;* (ii) *Aus Italien: excerpt: On the shores of Sorrento;* (iii) *Death and transfiguration;* (iv) *Don Quixote;* (v) *Ein Heldenleben.*
(M) (***) BMG/RCA mono 09026 60929-2 (2) [60929-2]. (i) Boston SO, Koussevitzky; (ii) Chicago SO, Stock; (iii) Phd. O, Stokowski; (iv) Wallenstein, NYPO, Beecham; (v) NYPO, Mengelberg.

Here is a set that no dedicated Straussian and no one interested in the history of the gramophone will want to be without. To have *Ein Heldenleben* conducted by its dedicatee seems almost miraculous, recorded in 1928 – only 30 years after its composition – in what was exceptionally good quality for the period. And what a performance it is, and what playing the New York Orchestra could produce in those days! It was widely and rightly acclaimed when it reappeared on LP. If Mengelberg's account was not the very first recording of the work, Koussevitzky's 1935 Boston account of *Also sprach Zarathustra* was. It was for long the only version in the catalogue. Of course some allowances have to be made for the quality by comparison with modern performances, though on the other hand some allowances have to be made for most modern performances by comparison with the standards the Boston achieved under Koussevitzky. Beecham's New York account of *Don Quixote* with Alfred Wallenstein as soloist, made in 1932, the year before Strauss's own with Mainardi is another reading of enormous character (though the transfer has a slightly more strident top than we remember from the LP reissue). Stokowski's *Death and transfiguration* shows the Philadelphia Orchestra with similar opulence of tone and virtuosity.

Also sprach Zarathustra; Death and transfiguration, Op. 24; Don Juan, Op. 20.
*** Telarc Dig. CD 80167 [id.]. VPO, Previn.

Also sprach Zarathustra; Don Juan.
*** DG Dig. 410 959-2 [id.]. BPO, Karajan.
*** Denon Dig. CO 2259 [id.]. Dresden State O, Blomstedt.

Karajan's later (1984) version (coupled with an exciting account of *Don Juan*) has the advantage of digital technology and can offer great dynamic range and presence, particularly at the extreme bass and treble. As a performance, this newest version will be very hard to beat and could well be first choice. The playing of the Berlin Philharmonic is as glorious as ever; its virtuosity can be taken for granted, along with its sumptuous tonal refinement, and in Strauss, of course, Karajan has no peer. As a recording it is very good indeed, though it does not offer the spectacular definition and transparency of detail of the Dorati CD version on Decca.

As a recording the Denon CD could hardly be more impressive. The sound is rich, the acoustic is resonant but never clouds detail, and the range and presence are really quite stunning. The performance has all the sense of architecture and authority we have come to expect from Blomstedt, whose Strauss is always distinctive. The Denon disc also contains a very good *Don Juan*.

Previn draws magnificent playing from the Vienna Philharmonic in powerful, red-blooded readings of both symphonic poems, and the recording is among Telarc's finest. Previn's sharp, rhythmic control at speeds that never languish brings out the structural strength of both works, yet Straussian warmth is never underplayed. Strongly recommended for anyone wanting this particular coupling, and enjoying voluptuous sound-quality.

(i) Also sprach Zarathustra; (ii) *Don Juan; Till Eulenspiegel.*
(M) *** Collins Dig. 3002-2 [id.]. LSO, Jacek Kaspszyk.
(M) *** EMI Dig. CDD7 64106-2 [id.]. (i) Phd. O, Ormandy; (ii) VPO, André Previn.

Choice between the new Collins mid-priced CD and the EMI alternative of this favourite Richard Strauss triptych is not easy. The Collins disc has the advantage of the very finest modern digital recording, with the orchestra set back naturally in a concert-hall acoustic. Perhaps Ormandy's reading of *Zarathustra* is detailed slightly more individually, but Kaspszyk's LSO account has fine breadth and momentum, with the LSO consistently on their toes, and with a memorable contribution from the leader, John Georgiadis, in the violin solos. The strings play with affecting sensuality – radiantly sumptuous when they soar above the stave – and this applies to *Don Juan* too, a performance which combines tenderness and passion with the excitement of the chase. *Till* is portrayed with an enjoyably genial vitality. Detail is wittily observed, the trial and execution scene very dramatic, making the epilogue the more touching. The recording throughout is very much in the demonstration bracket: all Strauss's spectacular effects are extravagantly realized, and the climax of *Also sprach Zarathustra* makes just as powerful an impression as the famous opening.

Ormandy's 1979 *Also sprach Zarathustra* is one of his very finest records. The performance unleashes enormous ardour and the superb playing of the Philadelphia Orchestra, especially the strings, is consistently gripping in its extrovert passion. This can be spoken of in the same breath as the Karajan versions, although its emotional feeling is more unbridled. The early recording was made in the Old Met., Philadelphia; on the original LP it was excessively brightly lit, but the balance has been improved vastly and there is now no want of opulence. The climax at the very opening is superbly graduated, the sound immensely spectacular, while the closing section, too, is memorably sustained. Previn's *Don Juan* and *Till Eulenspiegel* were made a year later in the Musikverein, and their style is quite different. This was the conductor's first recording with the VPO and plainly their response is wholehearted. But these are not at all Viennese-type performances: they are relatively direct, strong and urgent, rather than affectionate, refreshing rather than idiomatic. The sound is full and bright but not as open and brilliant as the Philadelphia recording.

Also sprach Zarathustra, Op. 30; (i) *Don Quixote, Op. 35.*
(M) **(*) Sony SBK 47656 [id.]. Phd. O, Ormandy; (i) with Lorne Munroe.

Ormandy's 1963 Sony *Also sprach Zarathustra,* if not as overwhelming as the later, EMI version (see above), has much virtuoso orchestral playing to commend it and many felicities of characterization. His (1961) *Don Quixote* will also give considerable pleasure. Although there are more sumptuous recordings on the market, the Sony remastering is more than acceptable. There is some marvellous orchestral playing and the two soloists play splendidly with plenty of character but without the 'star soloist' approach favoured by so many record companies. A very competitive coupling – perhaps not a first choice, but very good value for money and thoroughly enjoyable.

Also sprach Zarathustra, Op. 30; Ein Heldenleben.
(M) *** Ph. Dig. 432 197-2; *432 197-4* [id.]. Boston SO, Ozawa.

Ozawa's 1981 recording of *Also sprach Zarathustra* became one of the first demonstration records for compact disc, and even for today's ears the depth and unforced firmness of the organ pedal sound leading on to an extraordinary crescendo cannot fail to bring a shiver to the nape of the listener's neck. The solo strings are balanced rather close, but otherwise this is a wonderfully warm and natural sound, with both a beguiling bloom and fine inner clarity. Ozawa as a Strauss interpreter goes for seductive phrasing and warmth rather than high drama or nobility, but this remains one of his finest achievements at Boston. Ozawa's view of *Heldenleben* is similarly free-flowing, lyrical and remarkably unpompous. He consistently brings out the joy of the virtuoso writing, and though the playing of the Boston orchestra is not quite as immaculate as in the companion version of *Zarathustra,* the richness and transparency are just as seductive, superbly caught by the Philips engineers. There is a remarkable sense of presence and reality.

Also sprach Zarathustra; Till Eulenspiegel; Salome: Salome's dance.
(M) *** DG 415 853-2; *415 853-4* [id.]. BPO, Karajan.

Karajan's 1974 DG analogue version of *Also sprach Zarathustra* is coupled with his vividly characterized performance of *Till Eulenspiegel* plus his powerfully voluptuous account of *Salome's dance*. This account of *Also sprach* has long held sway and at mid-price generally makes a strong recommendation. The Berlin Philharmonic plays with great fervour (the timpani strokes at the very opening are quite riveting) and creates characteristic body of tone in the strings, although the digital remastering has thrown a much brighter light on the violins, only just short of glare.

Aus Italien, Op. 16; Die Liebe der Danae (symphonic fragment); *Der Rosenkavalier: waltz sequence No. 2.*
(BB) *** Naxos Dig. 8.550342 [id.]. Slovak PO, Zdenék Košler.

Aus Italien, Op. 16; (i) Songs: *Befreit; Meine Auge; Das Rosenband; Winterweihe.*
*** Chan. Dig. CHAN 8744 [id.]. SNO, Järvi; (i) with Felicity Lott.

Aus Italien is early Strauss and does not do him the fullest justice; but it does have marvellous moments, including the beautiful slow movement. The finale quotes a famous Neapolitan tarantella by Denza but does not make a great deal of it. Järvi takes a spacious view of the work and his recorded sound is full-bodied, with a natural perspective, and there is plenty of warmth. The Scottish orchestra seems at home in the score, giving the finale a certain Celtic lilt. The four songs, sung simply and eloquently but not always very colourfully by Felicity Lott, make an agreeable postlude. However, the Naxos version costs much less and is more enterprisingly coupled.

It is a very well-recorded and vividly detailed account of *Aus Italien* with an excellent sense of presence. The orchestra plays very well for Zdenék Košler both here and in the ten-minute symphonic fragment Clemens Krauss made from *Die Liebe der Danae* and in the *Rosenkavalier* waltz sequence. The Slovak Philharmonic is a highly responsive body, with cultured strings and wind departments and, given the quality of the recorded sound, this represents a real bargain.

Le bourgeois gentilhomme: suite, Op. 60; Dance suite after keyboard pieces by Couperin.
**(*) ASV Dig. CDCOE 809; *ZCCOE 809* [id.]. COE, Erich Leinsdorf.

Leinsdorf is perhaps not quite as subtle or as light of touch as Tate in *Le bourgeois gentilhomme*, but he gives a very good account of the score and, for that matter, a fairly good one of the *Dance suite*, although occasionally he is a bit heavy-handed. But this is delightful music, well worth having. The recording is acceptable enough, though not very rich, but it is clean and well detailed. A generally recommendable disc.

Le bourgeois gentilhomme (suite), *Op. 60:* excerpts; (i) *Don Quixote, Op. 35.*
(M) (***) EMI mono CDH7 63106-2. (i) Tortelier; RPO, Beecham.

Tortelier and Beecham recorded their *Don Quixote* in 1947 during Strauss's visit to London. The playing is pretty electrifying, with the newly formed RPO on their best form. Tortelier had performed the work under Strauss himself and here plays for all the world as if his life depended on it. There is great delicacy in *Le bourgeois gentilhomme* and some delicious playing from the RPO's then leader, Oscar Lampe.

Le bougeois gentilhomme: suite, Op. 60; Metamorphosen for 23 solo strings.
*** EMI Dig. CDC7 47992-2 [id.]. ECO, Jeffrey Tate.

Tate's ECO disc provides an unusual but attractive coupling of the much-neglected incidental music to *Le bourgeois gentilhomme* and the more frequently recorded late masterpiece, *Metamorphosen*. He is a warmly expansive Straussian, building *Metamorphosen* powerfully but not letting the sparkling suite grow too heavy – quite a danger, when it is on the long side. Good EMI sound with plenty of bloom.

Burleske, Op. 11; Parergon, Op. 73; Stimmungsbilder, Op. 9.
**(*) Ara. Dig. Z 6567 [id.]. Ian Hobson, Philh. O, Del Mar.

(i) *Burleske in D min.; Sinfonia domestica, Op. 53.*
*** Sony MK 42322 [id.]. (i) Barenboim; BPO, Mehta.

Mehta's version of the *Sinfonia domestica* is, generally speaking, the best Richard Strauss record he has given us for some years. His account is humane and relaxed and has great warmth; he certainly gets pretty sumptuous playing from the Berlin Philharmonic and has the advantage of very good sound. As its fill-up, it has the *Burleske* for piano and orchestra, given with great brilliance and panache by Daniel Barenboim in a beautifully balanced recording. A highly recommendable disc.

Ian Hobson's account of the *D minor Burleske* is less dazzling than Barenboim's and he takes fewer risks. Nevertheless, on its own terms it is eminently satisfactory, and he is well supported by Norman Del Mar and the Philharmonia, and is well recorded. The *Parergon* for left hand is again very well played. The *Stimmungsbilder* are early, rather Schumannesque pieces, written in 1884: Hobson gives a rather touching account of *Träumerei*, and though one can imagine a performance of the *Intermezzo* with greater charm, there is still much to admire here. Decent recording.

Horn concertos Nos 1 in E flat, Op. 11; 2 in E flat.
**(*) Ph. Dig. 412 237-2 [id.]. Baumann, Leipzig GO, Masur.

(i) *Horn concertos Nos. 1 in E flat, Op. 11; 2 in E flat;* (ii) *Oboe concerto in D;* (iii) *Duet concertino for clarinet, bassoon, strings and harp.*
(M) *** EMI CDM7 69661-2. (i) Peter Damm; (ii) Manfred Clement; (iii) Manfred Weise, Wolfgang Liebscher; Dresden State O, Kempe.

Peter Damm's performances of the *Horn concertos* are second to none and although his use of a (judicious) degree of vibrato may be a drawback for some ears, his tone is gloriously rich. Similarly, while Manfred Clement's *Oboe concerto* is a sensitive reading, his creamily full timbre may not appeal to those brought up on Goossens. There can be no reservations whatsoever about the *Duet concertino*, where the sounds from bassoon and clarinet are beguilingly succulent, while the intertwining of both wind soloists with the dancing orchestral violins of the finale has an irresistible, genial finesse. Throughout, the superb playing of the Dresden orchestra adds an extra dimension to the music-making. Kempe's benign control of the music's ebb and flow shows him always a warmly understanding Straussian. The remastered recording, made in the Dresden Lukaskirche, retains an agreeable ambient glow which greatly pleases the ear.

Baumann's broad stream of tone and consummate technique bring much pleasure throughout both works, and the florid finale of the *Second Concerto* is articulated with enviable ease. But this easy-going quality also brings some relaxation of normal tensions. The bold contrasting episode at the centre of the slow movement of Op. 11 ideally needs a kind of *Don Juan*-like fervour to make its best effect, as Dennis Brain demonstrated. The soloist here is most truthfully caught, but the orchestra, slightly recessed in the reverberant Leipzig acoustic, loses some of its edge in the brilliant tuttis, while inner detail is not sharp.

(i) *Horn concertos Nos. 1–2; Capriccio:* Introduction to the final scene. (ii) *Andante for horn and piano, Op. posth.; Introduction, theme and variations in E flat for horn and piano;* (ii; iii) *Alphorn for soprano, horn and piano, Op. 15/3.*
** Decca Dig. 430 370-2 [id.]. Barry Tuckwell; (i) RPO, Ashkenazy; (ii) Ashkenazy (piano); (iii) with Marie McLaughlin.

A generous but disappointing collection. Barry Tuckwell has recorded the Strauss *Horn concertos* before, and here he has no greater success with them than he had the first time. Ashkenazy over-romanticizes the opening movement of the *First concerto*, which has a certain neo-classical character directly inherited from Mozart, and in the virile striding tune of the *Andante*, Tuckwell overdoes the accents. In the opening movement of the *Second concerto* Ashkenazy's orchestral tapestry lacks ripeness and grip. The finales of both works, however come off splendidly, as they did on the previous occasion. The shorter pieces are well enough played but hardly memorable, and Marie McLaughlin doesn't make a great deal of her contribution to the *Alphorn* piece. The Walthamstow recording is full-blooded and vivid.

Oboe concerto.
*** Nimbus Dig. NI 5330 [id.]. John Anderson, Philh. O, Simon Wright – FRANÇAIX: *L'horloge de flore;* MARTINŮ: *Concerto.* ***
(M) *** BMG/RCA Dig. GD 87989. John de Lancie, CO, Max Wilcox – FRANÇAIX: *L'horloge de flore* *** ❀; IBERT: *Symphonie concertante.* ***
*** ASV Dig. CDCOE 808; *ZCCOE 808* [id.]. Douglas Boyd, COE, Berglund – MOZART: *Oboe concerto.* ***

In the summer of 1945 a young American musician/GI (who before the war had been an oboist with the Pittsburgh Symphony Orchestra) was stationed in the Bavarian Alps; on several occasions he visited the ageing Richard Strauss at his home in Garmisch-Partenkirchen (a photo within the notes of this CD records the meeting). He suggested that Strauss write an oboe concerto, and only months later the eighty-one-year-old composer produced his famous work and, mixing up the cities, inscribed the score as 'inspired by an American soldier (oboist from Chicago)'. That same oboist, John de Lancie, recorded it in 1987, playing persuasively and with much finesse. The chamber accompaniment could ideally sound riper, but the balance is realistic and the sound real.

John Anderson, principal oboe of the Philharmonia, gives a ravishing acount of the Strauss's delectable concerto, his timbre slightly riper than that of the concerto's dedicatee, and the Nimbus digital recording that bit more modern. But John de Lancie's account is very enjoyable too and has the advantage of economy; both artists also offer Françaix's delectable *L'horloge de flore*, so choice can rest with the other coupling: many will prefer the Martinů *Concerto* to the more astringent Ibert *Symphonie concertante*.

Douglas Boyd winningly brings out the happy glow of Strauss's inspiration of old age, and the ebb and flow of his expression with its delicate touching-in of the characteristic flourishes in the solo line sounds totally spontaneous. His warm oboe tone, less reedy than some, equally brings out the *Rosenkavalier* element in this lovely concerto. With warm, well-balanced recording, the gentle contrast of romantic and classical in this work is conveyed delectably.

(i) *Oboe concerto; Metamorphosen for 23 solo strings;* (ii) *4 Last songs (Vier letzte Lieder).*
(M) **(*) DG 423 888-2 [id.]. (i) Koch; (ii) Janowitz; BPO, Karajan.

Karajan's 1971 account of the *Metamorphosen* sounds excellent in its remastered format, full yet better defined. In the *Four last songs* Gundula Janowitz produces a beautiful flow of creamy soprano tone, at the same time leaving the music's deeper and more subtle emotions underexposed. Lothar Koch's oboe timbre is creamy, too: he is forwardly balanced, but Karajan's accompaniment is relatively athletic.

Violin concerto in D min., Op. 8.
*** ASV Dig. CDDCA 780; *ZCDCA 780* [id.]. Xue Wei, LPO, Glover – HEADINGTON: *Violin concerto.* *** ❀

With Jane Glover and the LPO warmly sympathetic accompanists Xue Wei makes a very persuasive case for this very early work of Strauss's, with its echoes of Mendelssohn and Bruch. In style it may be uncharacteristic of the mature composer, but it makes a sweetly attractive rarity.

Death and transfiguration, Op. 24.
(M) **(*) EMI Dig. CDD7 64290-2; [id.]; *ET 764290-4*. LPO, Tennstedt – *4 Last songs* ***; WAGNER: *Götterdämmerung* excerpts. **(*)
(M) (***) BMG/RCA mono GD 60312. Phd. O, Toscanini – TCHAIKOVSKY: *Symphony No. 6.* (***)
(M) ** Chan. CHAN 6549 [id.]. LSO, Horenstein – HINDEMITH: *Mathis der Maler.* **(*)

Tennstedt's 1982 Abbey Road account of *Death and Transfiguration* is a direct yet impressively spacious performance, very well played and recorded, and the CD transfer is both full and clear.

Toscanini's characteristically taut control of tension goes with what was for him a more warmly expressive style than usual, thanks to the influence of the Philadelphia Orchestra. With the transfer giving good body to the limited sound, it is comparable with his equally intense reading of Tchaikovsky's *Pathétique* from the same period.

Horenstein's account of *Death and transfiguration* is spacious and the recorded sound, already vivid, is even more so in its digitally remastered format. Horenstein would not displace Karajan, but at mid-price this coupling is now more competitive.

Death and transfiguration; Don Juan; Till Eulenspiegel.
(M) *** DG Dig. 429 492-2; *429 492-4*. LSO, Abbado.

The performances under Claudio Abbado have plenty of dash and their brilliance is tempered with sensitivity. Some may feel that *Don Juan* veers too much towards the exuberant showpiece and vehicle for display, but both this and *Till Eulenspiegel* must be numbered among the best available. *Death and transfiguration* has a marvellously spacious opening. The strings produce some splendidly silky tone and there is much sensitive wind playing too. The DG upper range is less than smoothly natural, but Abbado's CD now has a price advantage.

Death and transfiguration; Don Juan; Metamorphosen for 23 solo strings; Salome: Dance of the 7 veils.

(M) *** EMI CDM7 63350-2 [id.]. Philh. O, Klemperer.

This generous CD admirably assembles Klemperer's Richard Strauss recordings in convenient form. In his hands it is the *Metamorphosen* and *Death and transfiguration* that excite the greatest admiration. With Klemperer the work for strings has a ripeness that exactly fits Strauss's last essay for orchestra, while *Death and transfiguration* is invested with a nobility too rarely heard in this work. Not everyone will respond to Klemperer's spacious treatment of the other works. His account of *Salome's dance* is splendidly sensuous and *Don Juan* is clearly seen as 'the idealist in search of perfect womanhood'. But with marvellous Philharmonia playing and a recording (made in the Kingsway Hall in 1960/61) which still sounds full-bodied and in the case of *Metamorphosen* has added refinement of detail, this collection is certainly not lacking in strength of characterization.

Death and transfiguration; Metamorphosen for 23 solo strings.
❀ *** DG Dig. 410 892-2 [id.]. BPO, Karajan.

Karajan's new digital account of *Metamorphosen* has even greater emotional urgency than the 1971 record he made with the Berlin Philharmonic and there is a marginally quicker pulse. The sound is fractionally more forward and cleaner but still sounds sumptuous, and the account of *Death and transfiguration* is quite electrifying. The recording balance has no lack of vividness, and the playing of the Berliners is superbly committed. It would be difficult to improve on this coupling by the greatest Strauss conductor of his day.

(i) *Don Quixote, Op. 35; Death and transfiguration.*
(M) *** DG 429 184-2 [id.]. (i) Fournier; BPO, Karajan.

Don Quixote, Op. 35; Salome (opera): *Salome's dance.*
(B) *** Hung. White Label HRC 081 [id.]. Perényi, Hungarian State O, János Ferencsik.

Fournier's partnership with Karajan is outstanding. His portrayal of the Don has no less nobility than previous rivals and compares well with more recent versions. He brings great subtlety and (when required) repose to the part. The finale and Don Quixote's death are very moving in Fournier's hands, while Karajan's handling of orchestral detail is quite splendid. Although Fournier is forwardly balanced, in every other respect the 1966 recording is of DG's very finest quality and (given its price) this can be strongly recommended, more particularly since the disc includes Karajan's superlative 1973 analogue version of *Death and transfiguration*. Textures sound leaner than originally, but the quality is both vivid and refined in detail.

János Ferencsik's account of *Don Quixote*, with Miklós Perényi and László Bársony as the excellent soloists and the Hungarian State Orchestra, can be recommended with confidence. It is in the old, humane tradition of conductors like Clemens Krauss and Rudolf Kempe, full of human insights and with orchestral virtuosity worn lightly. The sound is very good indeed. It does not displace the Fournier and Karajan partnership but can be recommended alongside that fine version.

Ein Heldenleben, Op. 40.
*** Denon Dig. C37 7561 [id.]. Dresden State O, Blomstedt.
(M) *** Ph. 432 276-2; *432 276-4*. Concg. O, Haitink – ELGAR: *Enigma variations.* **
(M) *** EMI CDM7 63299-2. RPO, Beecham – LISZT: *Orpheus* etc. ***
**(*) DG Dig 415 508-2 [id.]. BPO, Karajan.

Ein Heldenleben; Don Juan, Op. 20.
(M) *** DG 429 717-2 [id.]. BPO, Karajan.

Ein Heldenleben; Till Eulenspiegel.
*** Sony Dig. MK 44817 [id.]. LSO, Tilson Thomas.

Among the many fine CDs of *Ein Heldenleben*, the Blomstedt disc with the Dresden Staatskapelle for Denon comes close to the sound we used to associate with DG in the analogue era: warm, with articulate detail, but great tonal homogeneity. Blomstedt shapes his performance with both authority and poetry. One can tell from the outset that this is the real thing, for there is a genuine heroic stride and a sense of dramatic excitement here, while the Dresden orchestra, which has a long Strauss tradition, creates glorious Straussian textures and the whole edifice is held together in a way that commands admiration. In these respects, Blomstedt's account is the most completely satisfying CD.

Haitink's 1970 version of *Ein Heldenleben* is one of his finest records. He gives just the sort of performance, brilliant and swaggering but utterly without bombast, which will delight those who normally resist this rich and expansive work. With a direct and fresh manner that yet conveys consistent urgency, he gives a performance that makes even such fine rival versions as Karajan's 1959 recording sound just a little lightweight. In the culminating fulfilment theme, a gentle, lyrical 6/8, Haitink finds a raptness in restraint, a hint of agony within joy, that links the passage directly with the great Trio from *Der Rosenkavalier*. The Philips sound is admirably faithful and skilfully remastered.

Karajan's 1959 *Heldenleben* on DG still sounds amazingly fresh. It is a superb performance, and at mid-price it can certainly be recommended, in harness with *Don Juan*. Playing of great power and distinction emanates from the Berlin Philharmonic and, in the closing section, an altogether becoming sensuousness and warmth. The remastering has plenty of ambient atmosphere, combined with excellent detail; *Don Juan*, made over a decade later, brings only a marginal difference in body and none in breadth.

Beecham's valedictory *Heldenleben* sounds fabulous. He liked to work on a large scale and his 1961 performance is immensely vigorous but tender and sensuous when the music calls for it. There is also an excellent solo contribution from the leader, Steven Staryk. The recording is quite full and has a transparency of texture inherent in the original balance. Beecham's magic exercises its own special pull and this reissue is a classic of the gramophone.

Karajan's digital *Heldenleben* has tremendous sweep and all the authority and mastery we have come to expect – and, indeed, take for granted. Nor is the orchestral playing anything other than glorious – indeed, in terms of sheer virtuosity the Berlin players have never surpassed this. There is also a dramatic fire and virtuosity that are quite electrifying. However, the recording falls short of the highest of present-day standards, though it has no want of firmness and body: the upper strings are a little lacking in bloom and are a shade congested.

Michael Tilson Thomas's account is also a performance of genuine authority and no less well laid out than other outstanding versions. His interpretation has an epic breadth and humanity that are impressive. If it does not displace its rivals, it can be recommended with complete confidence alongside them, and moreover it has the additional attraction of *Till Eulenspiegel*.

Josephslegende (ballet): *suite, Op. 63; Sinfonia domestica, Op. 53.*
**(*) Delos Dig. DE 3082 [id.]. Seattle SO, Gerard Schwarz.

Strauss composed the *Josephslegende* for Diaghilev on the grandest scale for a large orchestra. Although the neglect of the score in the theatre is understandable on practical grounds, it contains enough good music to be of interest to Straussians. Indeed there are many felicities, the *Dance of the Turkish Boxers* a good example, while there are delicious touches in the fourth scene, *Joseph's dance*. Gerard Schwarz gives us the suite from the ballet (about half an hour's music) in addition to a very idiomatic account of the *Sinfonia domestica*. There is very good playing from the Seattle orchestra: cultured, thoroughly idiomatic and with splendid sweep; the recording, too, is splendidly detailed, if perhaps just a bit too brightly lit to be ideal.

Schlagobers (ballet), *Op. 70:* complete.
** Denon Dig. CO 73414 [id.]. Tokyo Met. SO, Wakasugi.

Schlagobers is a two-act ballet, lasting 75 minutes, whose action is set in a Viennese *Konditorei* (pâtisserie), full of children fresh from their confirmation ceremony. The work comes from the early 1920s (Strauss conducted its first performance for his sixtieth-birthday celebrations), but it is held in low esteem by most Strauss scholars. There are some delights, such as the *March and military exercises of marzipan, Plum soldiers and honey cakes* and the *Dance of the tea cakes* in Act I; but elsewhere his inspiration lapses into routine, as in the *Whipped cream waltz*. Hiroshi Wakasugi gets good results from the Tokyo Metropolitan Orchestra and the recording is more than acceptable, though insufficiently transparent in climaxes.

Sinfonia domestica, Op. 53.
(M) *** EMI CDM7 69571-2. BPO, Karajan.

Sinfonia domestica; (i) *Death and transfiguration.*
(M) **(*) BMG/RCA stereo/mono GD 60388 [60388-2-RG]. Chicago SO; (i) (mono) RCA Victor O; Fritz Reiner.

Sinfonia domestica, Op. 53; Till Eulenspiegel. (i) Songs: *Die heiligen drei Könige aus Morgenland; Zueignung.*

**(*) Chan. Dig. CHAN 8572; *ABTD 1267* [id.]. SNO, Järvi; (i) with Felicity Lott.

Strauss's much-maligned *Sinfonia domestica* is quite admirably served by this mid-priced CD of Karajan's 1973 recording. The playing is stunningly good and the Berlin strings produce tone of great magnificence. The remastered recording demonstrates the wide range of the original; detail is better focused and the ambient atmosphere remains.

Reiner's account of the *Sinfonia domestica* comes from 1956, the earliest days of stereo, and is a wonderful performance, a reading of stature, worthy to rank alongside the Karajan alternative. The Chicago orchestra play with warmth and virtuosity; the recording is inevitably lacking a little in upper range, but it still sounds remarkably good for its age. *Death and transfiguration* is a 1950 mono recording, and it was perverse of RCA not to include his marvellous 1957 Vienna Philharmonic version (in surprisingly good stereo even now).

Järvi's is a strongly characterized, good-natured account, not as refined in ensemble as some past rivals but gutsy and committed to remove any coy self-consciousness from this extraordinarily inflated but delightful musical portrait of Strauss's family life. The performance of *Till* brings out the joy of the work, too; and Felicity Lott's performance of two of Strauss's most delightful songs makes a generous coupling. Warm, rich recording to compensate for any occasional thinness in the SNO's violin tone.

Symphony for wind in E flat (The happy workshop).
** Orfeo C 004821A [id.]. Munich Wind Ac., Sawallisch.

Strauss's *Wind symphony*, as suggested by the subtitle, is essentially a genial piece, though the finale opens sombrely before the mood lightens. This comes off quite well, as does the nicely played *Andantino*, but the focus of the first movement is less sure and the music-making often lacks a necessary smiling quality. The recording, though full and homogeneous in texture, does not display the inner clarity one would expect from a digital source and the CD is poor value, playing for only 38½ minutes.

Cello sonata in F, Op. 6.
**(*) Sony Dig. MK 44980 [id.]. Yo-Yo Ma, Emanuel Ax – BRITTEN: *Sonata.* **(*)

Yo-Yo Ma and Emanuel Ax give a generally fine account of the *Cello sonata*, although there are moments when Ax's fortissimos overpower the cellist and Ma is not wholly free from self-consciousness. The recording is reasonably truthful, though the constraints of the CBS acoustic produce a very slightly synthetic character.

String quartet in A, Op. 2.
**(*) Hyp. Dig. CDA 66317; *KA 66317* [id.]. Delmé Qt – VERDI: *Quartet.* **(*)

The Strauss *Quartet* is early and derivative, as one might expect from a sixteen-year-old, but it is amazingly assured and fluent. The Delmé version is well played; however, although the basic acoustic is pleasing, the sound-balance remains a little on the dry side.

Violin sonata in E flat, Op. 18.
*** DG Dig. 427 617-2 [id.]. Kyung Wha Chung, Krystian Zimerman – RESPIGHI: *Sonata.* ***
*** Virgin Dig. VC7 90760-2; *VC 790760-4* [id.]. Dmitry Sitkovetsky, Pavel Gililov – DEBUSSY: *Sonata* **; JANÁČEK: *Sonata.* ***

In this formidable sonata, Kyung Wha Chung and Krystian Zimerman bring an impressive eloquence and commanding artistry. Collectors wanting their coupling need look no further. Among modern versions Kyung Wha Chung is *primus inter pares*, and her version of the Strauss scores over rivals also in the power and sensitivity of Krystian Zimerman's contribution and the excellence of the DG recording. This *Sonata* needs the best possible advocacy if it is to persuade the uncommitted; in the hands of these artists it is heard at its best.

Dmitry Sitkovetsky is also a passionate and characterful player, who gives a powerful account of the Strauss. Musically, his coupling is more rewarding in that the Debussy and Janáček *Sonatas* are of greater substance than the Respighi which Chung and Zimerman offer. However, theirs is a very special performance and, though Pavel Gililov is a perceptive artist, his playing is not quite the equal of Zimerman's.

VOCAL MUSIC

8 Lieder, Op. 10; 5 Lieder, Op. 15; 6 Lieder, Op. 17; 6 Lieder, Op. 19; Schlichte Weisen, Op. 21; Mädchenblumen, Op. 22; 2 Lieder, Op. 26; 4 Lieder, Op. 27; Lieder, Op. 29/1 & 3; 3 Lieder, Op. 31; Stiller Gang, Op. 31/4; 5 Lieder, Op. 32; Lieder, Op. 36/1–4; Lieder, Op. 37/1–3 & 5–6; 5

Lieder, Op. 39; Lieder, Op. 41/2–5; Gesänge älterer deutscher Dichter, Op. 43/1 & 3; 5 Gedichte, Op. 46; 5 Lieder, Op. 47; 5 Lieder, Op. 48; Lieder, Op. 49/1 & 2; 4–6; 6 Lieder, Op. 56; Krämerspiegel, Op. 66; Lieder, Op. 67/4–6; Lieder, Op. 68/1 & 4; 5 kleine Lieder, Op. 69; Gesänge des Orients, Op. 77; Lieder, Op. 88/1–2; Lieder ohne Opuszahl.
(M) *** EMI CMS7 63995-2 (6). Dietrich Fischer-Dieskau, Gerald Moore.

Fischer-Dieskau and Moore made these recordings of the 134 Strauss songs suitable for a man's voice between 1967 and 1970, tackling them in roughly chronological order. With both artists at their very peak, the results are endlessly imaginative, and the transfers are full and immediate, giving fine presence to the voice. Compared with the later recordings of many of these songs which Fischer-Dieskau recorded for DG with Wolfgang Sawallisch accompanying, these readings are less volatile and more intimate, with the voice a degree fresher and sweeter. As in the original LP set, the booklet contains full texts and translations, as well as a perceptive essay by the singer on Strauss and his songs; yet it would have been helpful to have had a more detailed chronology of the songs.

Lieder: *Allerseelen; Ach Lieb ich muss nun Scheiden; Befreit; Du meines Herzens Krönelein; Einerlei; Heimliche Aufforderung; Ich trage meine Minne; Kling!; Lob des Leidens; Malven; Mit deinen blauen Augen; Die Nacht; Schlechtes Wetter; Seitdem dein Aug; Ständchen; Stiller Gang; Traume durch die Dämmerung; Wie sollten wir geheim; Wir beide wollen springen; Zeltlose.*
*** Ph. Dig. 416 298-2 [id.]. Jessye Norman, Geoffrey Parsons.

Jessye Norman's recital of Strauss brings heartfelt, deeply committed performances, at times larger than life, which satisfyingly exploit the unique glory of the voice. Quite apart from such deservedly popular songs as *Heimliche Aufforderung*, it is good to have such a rarity as Strauss's very last song, *Malven*, sung so compellingly. Some of the songs bring extreme speeds in both directions, with expression underlined in slow songs and *Ständchen* given exhilarating virtuoso treatment at high speed. But the magnetism of the singer generally silences any reservations, and Geoffrey Parsons is the most understanding of accompanists, brilliant too. Good, natural recording.

Lieder: *Allerseelen; All' mein Gedänken; Befreit; Cäcilie; Du meines Herzens Krönelein; Freundliche Vision; Heimliche Aufforderung; Ich schwebe; Kling!; Morgen; Die Nacht; Ruhe, meine Seele; Seitdem dein Aug' in meines schaute; Ständchen; Wiegenlied; Winterweihe; Zueignung.*
*** EMI Dig. CDC7 47948-2 [id.]. Margaret Price, Wolfgang Sawallisch.

Margaret Price's Strauss recital brings a rich variety of mood, colour and expression, helped by exceptionally sensitive and imaginative accompaniments from Sawallisch. The evenness of her production, opening out gloriously in *Zueignung*, is typical, and so it is too in *Freundliche Vision*, well contrasted with the lightness of such a song as *All' mein Gedänken*. If maternal tenderness is missing in *Wiegenlied*, the beauty and precision with which Price follows every marking in the music is a delight, all done with seeming spontaneity. The recording captures the voice with fine bloom.

Lieder: *Des Dichters Abendgang; Freundliche Vision; Heimliche Aufforderung; Ich trage meine Minne; Liebeshymnus; Morgen!; Das Rosenband; Ständchen; Traum durch die Dämmerung; Verführung; Waldseligkeit; Zueignung.*
(M) (***) Ph. Dig. 432 614-2; *432 614-4*. Siegfried Jerusalem, Leipzig GO, Masur.

Starting with an account of *Heimliche Aufforderung* that is both heroic and glowingly beautiful, Siegfried Jerusalem's collection of Strauss Lieder in orchestral arrangements provides a male counterpart to Jessye Norman's magnificent disc, also recorded with Masur and the Leipzig Gewandhaus Orchestra. The shading of tone which Jerusalem commands is most sensitive, as in *Morgen* or a delicate rendering of *Ständchen*. Naturally balanced recording, warmly reverberant to bring out the ravishing beauty of Strauss's orchestrations. However, the reissue has no documentation whatsoever apart from a list of titles.

Deutsche Motette, Op. 62; Hymne, Op. 34/1.
(M) *** Decca 430 365-2; *430 365-4* [id.]. Cash, Temperley, Evans, Varcoe, Schütz Ch. of L., Norrington – BRUCKNER: *Mass No. 2.* ***

Strauss's *German motet*, with sixteen chorus lines, has the sopranos soaring to top D flat and staying there, while at one point the basses go down to bottom B, and the shifting harmonies make one's head reel. The *Hymn*, too, is written in sixteen parts and has a remarkably expressive range. But what matters is that, in superb performances like these, the music is richly poetic, quite distinctive within the whole choral repertory, with glowing reminders of some of Strauss's loveliest music. The CD transfer confirms the gloriously rich quality of the (originally Argo) recording.

Four Last songs (Vier letzte Lieder).
(M) *** EMI Dig. CDD7 64290-2 [id.]; *ET 764290-4*. Lucia Popp, LPO, Tennstedt – *Death and transfiguration*; WAGNER: *Götterdämmerung* excerpts. **(*)

Four last songs; Lieder: *Allerseelen; All' mein Gedanken; Begegnung; Cäcilie; Die Nacht; Hat gesagt – bleibt's nicht dabei; Madrigal; Malven; Morgen; Muttertändelei; Schlechtes Wetter; Ständchen; Zueignung.*
**(*) Decca Dig. 430 511-2; *430 511-4* [id.]. Kiri Te Kanawa, VPO, Solti; or Solti (piano).

Four last songs; Lieder: *Das Bächlein; Befreit; Cäcilie; Freundliche Vision; Die heiligen drei Könige aus Morgenland; Mein Auge; Meinem Kinde; Morgen; Muttertändelei; Ruhe, meine Seele!; Walseligkeit; Wiegenlied.*
**(*) Chan. Dig. CHAN 9054 [id.]. Felicity Lott, SNO, Järvi.

Four Last songs; Lieder: *Befreit; Morgen; Muttertändelei; Ruhe, meine Seele; Wiegenlied; Zueignung.*
**(*) Sony MK 76794 [id.]. Kiri Te Kanawa, LSO, Andrew Davis.

Four Last songs; Lieder: *Cäcilie; Meinem Kinde; Morgen; Ruhe, meine Seele; Wiegenlied; Zueignung.*
❀ *** Ph. Dig. 411 052-2 [id.]. Jessye Norman, Leipzig GO, Masur.

Four Last songs. Die heiligen drei Könige. Capriccio (opera): *Moonlight music and monologue* (closing scene).
**(*) DG Dig. 419 188-2 [id.]. Anna Tomowa-Sintow, BPO, Karajan.

Four Last songs; Arabella: excerpts; *Ariadne auf Naxos: Ariadne's lament; Capriccio:* Closing scene.
(M) (**) Decca mono 425 959-2 [id.]. Lisa della Casa, VPO, Boehm, Moralt, Hollreiser.

(i) *Four Last songs.* (ii) *Arabella* (opera): excerpts. (i) *Capriccio* (opera): Closing scene.
(M) (***) EMI mono CDH7 61001-2 [id.]. Elisabeth Schwarzkopf, (i) Philh. O, Ackermann; (ii) Metternich, Gedda, Philh. O, Von Matačić.

Strauss's publisher Ernest Roth says in the score of the *Four Last songs* that this was a farewell of 'serene confidence', which is exactly the mood Jessye Norman conveys. The start of the second stanza of the third song, *Beim Schlafengehen*, brings one of the most thrilling vocal crescendos on record, expanding from a half-tone to a gloriously rich and rounded forte. In concern for word-detail Norman is outshone only by Schwarzkopf, but both in the *Four Last songs* and in the orchestral songs the stylistic as well as the vocal command is irresistible, with *Cäcilie* given operatic strength. The radiance of the recording matches the interpretations.

Lucia Popp, too, gives a ravishingly beautiful performance of the *Four Last songs.* With the voice given an ethereal glow, naturally balanced in a warmly atmospheric digital recording, the radiance of texture is paramount. This is an orchestral performance rather than a deeply illuminating Lieder performance, and that matches the coupling, the early tone-poem on death which is quoted by the dying composer in the last of the songs. Tennstedt is a direct rather than a persuasive Straussian. The beauty of sound is unfailing. For this mid-priced reissue an exciting Berlin Philharmonic account of *Siegfried's Rhine journey and Funeral music* has been added to follow the songs, and the programme concludes with *Death and transfiguration*.

Schwarzkopf's 1953 version of the *Four Last songs* comes on the mid-price Références label with both its original coupling, the closing scene from *Capriccio*, also recorded in 1953, and the four major excerpts from *Arabella* which she recorded two years later. The *Four Last songs* are here less reflective, less sensuous, than in Schwarzkopf's later version with Szell, but the more flowing speeds and the extra tautness and freshness of voice bring equally illuminating performances. Fascinatingly, this separate account of the *Capriccio* scene is even more ravishing than the one in the complete set, and the sound is even fuller, astonishing for its period.

Felicity Lott's disc brings together a whole series of recordings of Strauss songs in their orchestral versions, which originally appeared as couplings for Järvi's discs of the Strauss symphonic poems. She sings them beautifully, though the voice is not always caught at its most golden, notably in the *Four Last Songs*, which yet are movingly done. Warm, full orchestral sound.

Dame Kiri Te Kanawa gives an open-hearted, warmly expressive reading of the *Four Last songs*. If she misses the sort of detail that Schwarzkopf uniquely brought, her commitment is never in doubt. Her tone is consistently beautiful, but might have seemed even more so if the voice had not been placed rather too close in relation to the orchestra. The orchestral arrangements of other songs make an excellent coupling and Andrew Davis directs most sympathetically.

Though Dame Kiri Te Kanawa's performance in the Solti version of the *Four Last Songs* is weightier than on her early CBS/Sony reading, it has less refinement of detail and so emerges rather heavily. The coupling has Dame Kiri accompanied by Sir Georg, not as conductor but as pianist, a sensitive partner. This may not match the very finest Strauss song records, but these are all characterful, warm-toned performances, generally well recorded.

Karajan directs a ravishing performance, with one of his favourite sopranos responding warmly and sympathetically, if without the final touch of individual imagination that such inspired music cries out for. Tomowa-Sintow's lovely, creamy-toned singing tends to take second place in the attention. The orchestral version of Strauss's nativity-story song makes an attractive if hardly generous extra item. Warm recording, lacking a little in sense of realism and presence.

Lisa della Casa with her creamily beautiful soprano was a radiant Straussian, as these precious excerpts demonstrate. Her account of the *Four Last songs* (given in the original order, not that usually adopted) has a commanding nobility. *Ariadne's lament* also receives a heartfelt performance, soaring to a thrilling climax, and the *Arabella* duets with Gueden, Schoeffler and Poell are hauntingly tender. Sadly, in the transfer the Decca historic issue falls far short of the EMI, with the voice not as forward and vivid, and with the orchestra shrill and papery, lacking the body of the original LPs.

OPERA

Die Ägyptische Helena (complete).
(M) **(*) Decca 430 381-2 (2) [id.]. Dame Gwyneth Jones, Hendricks, Kastu, Detroit SO, Dorati.

Hofmannsthal's device of mingling two Helen legends has an element of jokiness in it, but Ancient Greece, as so often with Strauss, prompted some heavyweight orchestral writing (echoes of *Elektra*), and Dorati, using the original Dresden version of the score, draws magnificent sounds from the Detroit orchestra, richly and forwardly recorded. The vocal sounds are less consistently pleasing. Gwyneth Jones has her squally moments as Helen, though it is a commanding performance. Matti Kastu manages as well as any Heldentenor today in the role of Menelaus, strained at times but with a pleasing and distinctive timbre. The others too are not always helped by the closeness, but this remains a richly enjoyable as well as a valuable set.

Arabella (complete).
*** Orfeo Dig. C 169882H (2). Varady, Fischer-Dieskau, Donath, Dallapozza, Schmidt, Berry, Bav. State Op. Ch. & O, Sawallisch.
*** Decca Dig. 417 623-2 (3) [id.]. Te Kanawa, Fontana, Grundheber, Seiffert, Dernesch, Guttstein, ROHCG Ch. & O, Tate.
(M) **(*) Decca 430 387-2 (2) [id.]. Della Casa, Gueden, London, Edelmann, Dermota, V. State Op. Ch., VPO, Solti.

This Orfeo set of *Arabella* has an immediate advantage over the Decca version with Kiri Te Kanawa in being a digital recording on two CDs against the three for the Decca. Moreover the recording is splendid in every way, not just in sound but in the warmth and understanding of Sawallisch, the characterful tenderness of Julia Varady as the heroine, and Fischer-Dieskau's fine-detailed characterization of the gruff Mandryka, *der Richtige* (Mr Right) according to the heroine's romantic view. Helen Donath too is charming as the younger sister, Zdenka, though the voice might be more sharply contrasted. If there are unappealing elements in an opera which would reach a happy ending far too quickly but for uncongenial twists of plot, this recording clothes them with an entirely Straussian glow of richness and charm. Highly recommended.

Dame Kiri Te Kanawa, in the name-part, gives one of her very finest opera performances on record. She even outshines the most famous of recorded Arabellas, Lisa della Casa, not only in the firm beauty of her voice, but in the word-pointing and detailed characterization. It is a radiant portrait, languorously beautiful, and it is a pity that so unsuited a soprano as Gabriele

Fontana should have been chosen as Zdenka next to her, sounding all the more shrill by contrast. Franz Grundheber makes a firm, virile Mandryka, Peter Seiffert a first-rate Matteo, while Helga Dernesch is outstandingly characterful as Arabella's mother. Though Tate's conducting is richly sympathetic, bringing out the sumptuousness of the score – helped by brilliant Decca recording – his speeds at times are dangerously slow, which might possibly worry established Straussians, if hardly anyone else.

Della Casa soars above the stave with the creamiest, most beautiful sounds and constantly charms one with her swiftly alternating moods of seriousness and gaiety. One moment one thinks of in particular is where in Act I she sees the stranger through her window, *der Richtige* ('Mr Right'), later to appear as Mandryka. Della Casa conveys wonderfully the pain and disappointment of frustrated young love as the man turns away and passes on. Perhaps Solti does not linger as he might over the waltz rhythms, and it may be Solti too who prevents Edelmann from making his first scene with Mandryka as genuinely humorous as it can be, with the Count's *Teschek, bedien'dich* as he goggles at Mandryka's generosity. Edelmann otherwise is superb, as fine a Count as he was an Ochs in the Karajan *Rosenkavalier*. Gueden, too, is ideally cast as Zdenka and, if anything, in Act I manages to steal our sympathies from Arabella, as a good Zdenka can. George London is on the ungainly side, but then Mandryka is a boorish fellow anyway. Dermota is a fine Matteo, and Mimi Coertse makes as much sense as anyone could of the ridiculously difficult part of Fiakermilli, the female yodeller. The sound is most brilliant, but one wishes that some of the effects could have been more realistic, such as the bells of Elemer's sleigh outside the hotel, but that is a small complaint.

Ariadne auf Naxos (complete).

❀ (M) (***) EMI mono CMS7 69296-2 (2) [Ang. CDMB 69296]. Schwarzkopf, Schock, Rita Streich, Dönch, Seefried, Cuenod, Philh. O, Karajan.

*** Ph. Dig. 422 084-2 (2) [id.]. Jessye Norman, Varady, Gruberová, Asmus, Bär, Leipzig GO, Masur.

(M) **(*) Decca 430 384-2 (2) [id.]. Leontyne Price, Troyanos, Gruberová, Kollo, Berry, Kunz, LPO, Solti.

Elisabeth Schwarzkopf makes a radiant, deeply moving Ariadne, giving as bonus a delicious little portrait of the Prima Donna in the Prologue. Rita Streich was at her most dazzling in the coloratura of Zerbinetta's aria and, in partnership with the harlequinade characters, sparkles engagingly. But it is Irmgard Seefried who gives perhaps the supreme performance of all as the Composer, exceptionally beautiful of tone, conveying a depth and intensity rarely if ever matched. Rudolf Schock is a fine Bacchus, strained less than most, and the team of theatrical characters includes such stars as Hugues Cuenod as the Dancing Master. The fine pacing and delectably pointed ensemble add to the impact of a uniquely perceptive Karajan interpretation. Though in mono and with the orchestral sound a little dry, the voices come out superbly. Though the absence of a translation in the libretto is to be regretted, the many index-points on CD, cued to the synopsis, can be used almost as easily as a translation alongside the original German words.

Jessye Norman's is a commanding, noble, deeply felt performance, ranging extraordinarily wide; if she does not quite find the same raptness, the inner agony that still makes Elisabeth Schwarzkopf's performance unique, she yet provides the perfect focus for a cast as near ideal as anyone could assemble today. Julia Varady as the Composer brings out the vulnerability of the character, as well as the ardour, in radiant singing. The Zerbinetta of Edita Gruberová adds an extra dimension to previous recordings in the way she translates the panache of her stage performance into purely aural terms for recording. It is a thrilling performance and, even if the voice is not always ideally sweet, the range of emotions Gruberová conveys, as in her duet with the Composer, is enchanting. Paul Frey is the sweetest-sounding Bacchus on record yet, while Olaf Bär as Harlekin and Dietrich Fischer-Dieskau in the vignette role of the Music-Master are typical of the fine team of artists here in the smaller character parts. Masur proves a masterly Straussian and he is helped by the typically warm Leipzig recording, with sound rich and mellow to cocoon the listener, yet finely balanced to allow you to hear the interweaving of the piano as never before, in twentieth-century imitation of a continuo.

Brilliance is the keynote of Solti's set of *Ariadne*. This extraordinary confection has so many elements that within its chosen limits this reading is most powerful and compelling, with very lively playing and recording as well as some strong singing. What the performance is short of is charm and warmth. Everything is so brightly lit that much of the delicacy and ternderness of the writing tends to disappear. Nevertheless the concentration of Solti in Strauss is never in doubt, and though Leontyne Price has given more beautiful performances on record, she makes a strong central figure, memorably characterful. Tatiana Troyanos is affecting as the composer, and Edita Gruberová establishes herself as the unrivalled Zerbinetta of her generation, though here she is less delicate than on stage. René Kollo similarly is an impressive Bacchus. The Decca CD transfer is characteristically vivid.

Capriccio (complete).
(***) EMI mono CDS7 49014-8 (2) [id.]. Schwarzkopf, Waechter, Gedda, Fischer-Dieskau, Hotter, Ludwig, Moffo, Philh. O, Sawallisch.
*** DG 419 023-2 (2) [id.]. Janowitz, Fischer-Dieskau, Schreier, Prey, Ridderbusch, Troyanos, Bav. R. O, Boehm.

In the role of the Countess in Strauss's last opera, Elisabeth Schwarzkopf has had no equals. This recording, made in 1957 and 1958, brings a peerless performance from her, full of magical detail both in the pointing of words and in the presentation of the character in all its variety. Not only are the other singers ideal choices in each instance, they form a wonderfully co-ordinated team, beautifully held together by Sawallisch's sensitive conducting. Even such a vignette role as that of the Italian soprano is taken by Anna Moffo. As a performance this is never likely to be superseded, and it comes as one of the most cherishable of operatic reissues on CD. The mono sound presents the voices with fine bloom and presence, but the digital transfer makes the orchestra a little dry and relatively backward by comparison.

Janowitz is not as characterful and pointful a Countess as one really needs (and no match for Schwarzkopf), but this DG alternative is a most beautiful performance of a radiant score, well cast, beautifully sung, finely recorded and lovingly conducted. There is full documentation, including translation.

Daphne (complete).
*** DG 423 579-2 (2) [id.]. Gueden, King, Wunderlich, Schoffler, Little, V. State Op. Ch., VPO, Boehm.

On record, this amiable telling of the story of the nymph Daphne wooed by Apollo and finally turned into a tree makes delightful entertainment. The DG set is a live recording, made during the 1964 Vienna Festival, and it proves an enticing account. It could hardly be better cast, with the tenors James King as Apollo and Fritz Wunderlich as Leukippos both magnificent. Hilde Gueden makes a delectable Daphne and gives one of her finest performances on record, while Karl Boehm, the opera's dedicatee, brings out the work's mellowness without any loss of vitality. The DG documentation includes a full translation.

Elektra (complete).
*** Decca 417 345-2 (2) [id.]. Nilsson, Collier, Resnik, Stolze, Krause, V. State Op. Ch., VPO, Solti.
** Ph. Dig. 422 574-2 (2) (id.]. Behrens, Ludwig, Secunde, Ulfung, Hynninen, Tanglewood Festival Ch., Boston SO, Ozawa.

Nilsson is almost incomparable in the name-part, with the hard side of Elektra's character brutally dominant. Only when – as in the Recognition scene with Orestes – she tries to soften the naturally bright tone does she let out a suspect flat note or two. As a rule she is searingly accurate in approaching even the most formidable exposed top notes. One might draw a parallel with Solti's direction – sharply focused and brilliant in the savage music which predominates, but lacking the languorous warmth one really needs in the Recognition scene, if only for contrast. The brilliance of the 1967 Decca recording is brought out the more in the digital transfer on CD, aptly so in this work. The fullness and clarity are amazing for the period.

Ozawa's version of *Elektra* was recorded at live performances of the opera in Boston in 1988, using the stage cuts. Its great glory is the singing of Hildegard Behrens in the name-part, perhaps finer here than she has ever been on record. Hers is a portrayal that movingly brings out the tenderness and vulnerability in this character as well as the unbalanced ferocity. She it is – with Christa Ludwig a marvellous foil as Klytemnestra, searingly intense, letting out a spine-chilling off-stage scream at her murder – who provides the performance's dramatic tension, rather than the conductor. Though this is a live recording, it lacks the very quality which may justify the inevitable flaws in such a project: an underlying emotional thrust. The tension-building passage leading to Elektra's recognition of Orestes is plodding and prosaic and, against radiant singing from Behrens in the carol of joy which follows, the orchestra might as well be playing a Bruckner slow movement, with no emotional underpinning of this supreme moment of fulfilment after pain. The other soloists are disappointing, even Jorma Hynninen who is dry-toned and uningratiating as Orestes. Ragnar Ulfung as Aegisth is also dry-toned, aptly if unpleasantly so, and Nadine Secunde is far too wobbly as Chrysothemis. Voices are well caught, but the orchestral sound is too dry to bring out the glory of Strauss's orchestration.

(i) *Elektra: Soliloquy; Recognition scene; Finale. Salome: Dance of the seven veils; Finale.*
(M) *** BMG/RCA GD 60874 [60874-2-RG]. Inge Borkh, Chicago SO, Fritz Reiner; (i) with Schoeffler, Yeend, Chicago Lyric Theatre Ch.

Inge Borkh never sang *Elektra* at the Met., but this 40-minute group of excerpts, made in 1956, gives a tantalizing indication of what such a performance might have been like. With Borkh singing superbly in the title-role alongside Paul Schoeffler and Francis Yeend, this is a real collectors' piece. Reiner provides a superbly telling accompaniment; the performance of the Recognition scene and final duet are as ripely passionate as Beecham's old 78-r.p.m. excerpts and outstrip the complete versions. By no means does the balance project the singers at the expense of orchestral detail, and the orchestral sound is thrillingly rich, the brass superbly expansive. For the reissue, Reiner's full-blooded account of *Salome's dance* has been added, and Borkh is comparably memorable in the finale scene. Here the 1955 recording is slightly less sumptuous, the voice less flattered on top, but the sound is still characteristically full and vivid. No Straussian should miss this disc.

Die Frau ohne Schatten (complete).
❀ *** Decca Dig. 436 243-2 (3). Behrens, Varady, Domingo, Van Dam, Runkel, Jo, VPO, Solti.
*** DG 415 472-2 (3) [id.]. Nilsson, Rysanek, Hesse, King, Berry, V. State Op. Ch. & O, Boehm.

Claimed to be the first single recording project to have cost £1 million, Solti's set of *Die Frau ohne Schatten*, one of his favourite operas, is as much a landmark in his career as his historic first recording of Wagner's *Ring* cycle, still unsurpassed. One reason for the extraordinary expense was that Solti and his Decca colleagues waited patiently until they could assemble what was felt to be the ideal cast. So the Heldentenor role of the Emperor is taken by Plácido Domingo and, as in Solti's recording of Wagner's *Lohengrin*, the superstar tenor gives a performance that is not only beautiful to the ear beyond previous recording but which has an extra feeling for expressive detail, deeper than that which was previously recorded. Similarly, Solti was willing to delay the recording sessions so as to secure Hildegard Behrens as the Dyer's wife, the woman without a shadow of the opera's title. Vocally that choice is a huge success. What has at times limited her as Brünnhilde in Wagner's *Ring* cycle, her very feminine vulnerability, is here a positive strength, and the voice has rarely sounded so beautiful on record. Julia Varady as the Empress is even more imaginative than the excellent Cheryl Studer on the rival EMI recording under Sawallisch, with a voice even more beautiful, and José van Dam with his clean, dark voice brings a warmth and depth of expression to the role of Barak, the Dyer, which goes with a satisfyingly firm focus. Though Reinhild Runkel in the key role of the Nurse is not as firm as Hanna Schwarz on EMI, she is more in character, with her mature, fruity sound. Eva Lind is shrill in the tiny role of the Guardian of the Threshold, but there is compensation in having Sumi Jo as the Voice of the Falcon. With the players of the Vienna Philharmonic, 120-strong, surpassing themselves, and the big choral ensembles both well disciplined and warmly expressive, this superb recording is unlikely to be matched, let alone surpassed, for many years. Solti himself is inspired throughout. For him this opera is the peak of Strauss's genius. He feels deeply that though the symbolism in Hofmannsthal's libretto is dauntingly complex, the basic human relationships are universal and direct, and that is reflected in the warmth of his conducting. Alongside the characteristically high voltage of the whole performance, there is an irresistible emotional thrust and a moving tenderness. This is a recording, with full and vivid sound of demonstration quality, that should at last secure the recognition it has long deserved for Strauss's own favourite among his operas.

Boehm's live recording of Strauss's most ambitious, most Wagnerian opera provides a magnificent reminder of the conductor at his very finest. It is a performance to love rather than just to admire, with the opera-house acoustic handled persuasively by the engineers of Austrian Radio to give the solo voices plenty of bloom without losing precision. Inevitably there are stage noises and the balance of the singers varies, but this is outstanding among live recordings. The stage cuts are an irritation, but at least they allow each of the hour-long Acts to be accommodated on a single CD. The cast is an excellent one, with Birgit Nilsson making the Dyer's Wife a truly Wagnerian character. Leonie Rysanek sings strongly in the role of the other heroine, the Empress, musically almost as demanding. Barak the Dyer is sung by Walter Berry, searchingly expressive; and James King in the Heldentenor role of the Emperor is just as remarkable for his finely shaded pianissimo singing as for heroic moments, where he is occasionally strained. On CD the perspectives are impressively caught at all levels of dynamic.

Guntram (complete).
*** Sony Dig. M2K 39737 (2) [id.]. Goldberg, Tokody, Sólyom-Nagy, Gati, Bándi, Hungarian Army Ch. & State O, Queler.

Strauss's very first opera suffers from an undramatic libretto written by the composer. Even when he consciously adopts a Wagnerian stance, the music quickly turns sweet, often anticipating the more lyrical side of *Salome*. Heading the cast as the eponymous knight is Rainer Goldberg, reliable and open-toned, only occasionally strained. Otherwise the cast is Hungarian, with Ilona Tokody strong and firm, if rarely beautiful, in the taxing role of the heroine, Freihild. Warmly sympathetic conducting from Eve Queler. The recording acoustic too is attractively rich.

Intermezzo (complete).
*** EMI CDS7 49337-2 (2) [Ang. CDCB 49337]. Popp, Brammer, Fischer-Dieskau, Bav. RSO, Sawallisch.

The central role of *Intermezzo* was originally designed for the dominant and enchanting Lotte Lehmann; but it is doubtful whether even she can have outshone the radiant Lucia Popp, who brings out the charm of a character who, for all his incidental trials, must have consistently captivated Strauss and provoked this strange piece of self-revelation. The piece inevitably is very wordy, but with this scintillating and emotionally powerful performance under Sawallisch, with fine recording and an excellent supporting cast, this set is as near ideal as could be, a superb achievement. The CD transfer is well managed but – unforgivably in this of all Strauss operas – no translation is given with the libretto, a very serious omission.

Der Rosenkavalier (complete).
*** EMI Dig. CDS7 54259-2 (3). Kiri Te Kanawa, Anne Sofie von Otter, Rydl, Grundheber, Hendricks, Dresden Op. Ch., Dresden Boys' Ch., Dresden State O, Haitink.
❀ *** EMI CDS7 49354-8 (3) [id.]. Schwarzkopf, Ludwig, Stich-Randall, Edelmann, Waechter, Philh. Ch. & O, Karajan.
**(*) DG Dig. 423 850-2 (3) [id.]. Tomowa-Sintow, Baltsa, Moll, Perry, Hornik, VPO Ch. & O, Karajan.
** Decca 417 493-2 (3) [id.]. Crespin, Minton, Jungwirth, Donath, Wiener, V. State Op. Ch., VPO, Solti.
(M) (**(*)) Decca mono 425 950-2 (3) [id.]. Reining, Weber, Jurinac, Gueden, V. State Op. Ch., VPO, Erich Kleiber.

Haitink's EMI set, recorded in Dresden, brings a satisfyingly rich Strauss sound, helped by the widest frequency range, even if the voices, forward but not aggressively so, sometimes merge with the instruments. That matches the conductor's beautifully paced reading, dramatic without a hint of vulgarity, bringing out the nobility of the music. Vocally the biggest triumph is the Octavian of Anne Sofie von Otter, not only beautifully sung but acted with a boyish animation to make most rivals sound very feminine by comparison. The ardent young lover of Act I, the protector of Sophie in Act II, smitten by her beauty, and the larking boy of Act III, who is first embarrassed and then achingly appreciative of the Marschallin's generosity – all these facets of the character are played out with total conviction. Not that the Rose Knight of the title becomes the centre of the opera, any more than Octavian ever does. If the first great – and predictable – glory of Dame Kiri's assumption of the role of the Marschallin is the sheer beauty of the sound, the portrait she paints is an intense and individual one, totally convincing. Though, not surprisingly, she yields to Schwarzkopf (Karajan) or Crespin (Solti) in detailed inflection of word meaning, this is a performance, often animated, which in its clear element of tender, feminine vulnerability brings new lights in each scene. In the great Act III Trio, Dame Kiri's poise makes for a glorious launch of the main melody in pure, creamy tone, and a sense that with the great renunciation made, the Marschallin is now smiling with vicarious happiness over her former young lover, with her own sadness only hinted at.

The portrait of Sophie from Barbara Hendricks is a warm and moving one, but less completely satisfying, if only because her voice is not quite so pure as one needs for this young, innocent girl. Yet in the presentation of the silver rose the sense of wonder at the start is vividly conveyed, and Hendricks's picture of the prattling girl of the second half of the scene is a delight. Kurt Rydl with his warm and resonant bass makes a splendid Baron Ochs, not always ideally steady, but giving the character a magnificent scale and breadth. With a marvellous Viennese accent he gives a rounded characterization, not overdoing the comedy, so that one can register the genuine anger of the Baron in Act II at his bride playing him up – for the moment in no mood for trifling. Other portraits are just as colourfully presented, notably the sharply detailed Valzacchi of Graham Clark and the Duenna of Julia Faulkner, fruity yet firm. Franz Grundheber makes a convincing toady of Faninal, Richard Leech with golden tone hints at a send-up in the Italian Tenor's aria, and Claire Powell, though not always quite steady, is a formidably characterful Annina. Whatever the detailed reservations over the singing, it is mainly due to Bernard Haitink, and his long experience conducting this opera at Covent Garden and elsewhere, which makes this the most totally convincing and heartwarming recording of *Rosenkavalier* since Karajan's 1956 set. The Staatskapelle are not just brilliant throughout, but warmly idiomatic, ever responsive to Haitink's well-chosen speeds, relatively brisk in Act I, broader in the other two acts. This recording unlike the Karajan opens out the small stage cuts sanctioned by the composer.

The glory of Karajan's 1956 version, one of the greatest of all opera recordings, shines out the more delectably on CD. Though the transfer in its very clarity exposes some flaws in the original sound, the sense of presence and the overall bloom are if anything more compelling than ever. As to the performance, it is in a class of its own, with the patrician refinement of Karajan's spacious reading combining with an emotional intensity that he has rarely equalled, even in Strauss, of whose music he remains a supreme interpreter. Matching that achievement is the incomparable portrait of the Marschallin from Schwarzkopf, bringing out detail as no one else can, yet equally presenting the breadth and richness of the character, a woman still young and attractive. Christa Ludwig with her firm, clear mezzo tone makes an ideal, ardent Octavian and Teresa Stich-Randall a radiant Sophie, with Otto Edelmann a winningly characterful Ochs, who yet sings every note clearly.

Karajan's digital set brings few positive advantages, not even in recorded sound: for all the extra range of the modern recording, the focus is surprisingly vague, with the orchestra balanced too far behind the soloists. One advantage there certainly is: the Vienna Philharmonic, having been brought up with a natural feeling for waltz rhythm, is a degree more idiomatic in providing a genuine Viennese lilt, if it is also at times less precise. For the principal role Karajan chose Anna Tomowa-Sintow; the refinement and detail in her performance present an intimate view of the Marschallin, often very beautiful indeed, but both the darker and more sensuous sides of the character are muted. The Baron Ochs of Kurt Moll, firm, dark and incisive, is outstanding, and Agnes Baltsa as Octavian makes the lad tough and determined, if not always sympathetic. Janet Perry's Sophie, charming and pretty on stage, is too white and twittery of tone to give much pleasure.

The CD transfer of Solti's version is one of the more disappointing reissues from Decca. The brilliance of the original recording is exaggerated, with some of the compensating body in the sound removed, making the result too aggressive for this gloriously ripe score. Crespin is here at her finest on record, with tone well focused; the slightly maternal maturity of her approach will for many appear ideal. Manfred Jungwirth makes a firm and virile, if not always imaginative Ochs, Yvonne Minton a finely projected Octavian and Helen Donath a sweet-toned Sophie. Solti's direction is fittingly honeyed, with tempi even slower than Karajan's in the climactic moments. The one serious disappointment is that the great concluding *Trio* does not quite lift one to the tear-laden height one ideally wants.

Decca's set with Erich Kleiber was the first ever complete recording of *Rosenkavalier*, and it has long enjoyed cult status. It has many glories, quite apart from the inspired conducting of Kleiber senior. Sena Jurinac is a charming Octavian, strong and sympathetic, and Hilde Gueden a sweetly characterful Sophie, not just a wilting innocent. Ludwig Weber characterizes deliciously in a very Viennese way as Ochs; but the disappointment is the Marschallin of Maria Reining, very plain and lacking intensity, even in the great scene with Octavian at the end of Act I. She is not helped by Kleiber's refusal to linger; with the singers recorded close, the effect of age on what was once a fine voice is very clear, even in the opening solo of the culminating trio. And though the Vienna Philharmonic responds in the most idiomatic way to the waltz rhythms, ensemble is not good, with even the prelude to Act I a muddle. On the prelude more than anywhere, the CD transfer brings out a shrillness and lack of body in the orchestral sound, though voices are well caught.

Der Rosenkavalier: highlights.
(M) *** EMI CDM7 63452-2; *EG 763452-4.* Schwarzkopf, Ludwig, Stich-Randall, Edelmann, Waechter, Philh. Ch. & O, Karajan.

On EMI we are offered the Marschallin's monologue to the end of Act I (25 minutes); the Presentation of the silver rose and finale from Act II; and the Duet and Closing scene, with the Trio from Act III, flawlessly and gloriously sung and transferred most beautifully to CD.

Salome (complete).
*** DG. Dig. 431 810-2 (2) [id.]. Studer, Rysanek, Terfel, Hiestermann, German Opera, Berlin, Ch. & O, Sinopoli.
*** Decca 414 414-2 (2) [id.]. Nilsson, Hoffman, Stolze, Kmentt, Waechter, VPO, Solti.
*** EMI CDS7 49358-8 (2) [id.]. Behrens, Bohme, Baltsa, Van Dam, VPO, Karajan.
(M) *** BMG/RCA GD 86644 (2) [6644-2-RG]. Caballé, Richard Lewis, Resnik, Milnes, LSO, Leinsdorf.
** Sony Dig. S2K 46717 (2) [id.]. Marton, Fassbaender, Lewis, Zednik, Weikl, Holl, BPO, Mehta.

The glory of Sinopoli's DG version is the singing of Cheryl Studer as Salome, producing glorious sounds throughout. She builds her interpretation so that the final scene conveys total evil, while keeping a semblance of girlishness. Her voice is both rich and finely controlled, with delicately spun pianissimos that chill you the more for their beauty, not least in Salome's attempted seduction of John the Baptist. If this is Studer's finest opera-recording yet, it might be counted Sinopoli's finest too. His reading is often unconventional in its speeds, but it is always positive, thrusting and full of passion, the most opulent account on disc, matched by full, forward recording. As Jokanaan, Bryn Terfel makes a compelling recording debut, strong and noble, though the prophet's voice as heard from the cistern sounds far too distant. Among modern sets this makes a clear first choice, though Solti's vintage Decca recording remains the most firmly focused, with the keenest sense of presence.

Birgit Nilsson is splendid throughout; she is hard-edged as usual but, on that account, more convincingly wicked: the determination and depravity are latent in the girl's character from the start. Of this score Solti is a master. He has rarely sounded so abandoned in a recorded performance. The emotion swells up naturally even while the calculation of impact is most precise. Waechter makes a clear, young-sounding Jokanaan. Gerhardt Stolze portrays the unbalance of Herod with frightening conviction, and Grace Hoffman does all she can in the comparatively ungrateful part of Herodias. The vivid CD projection makes the final scene, where Salome kisses the head of John the Baptist in delighted horror (*I have kissed thy mouth, Jokanaan!*), all the more spine-tingling, with a close-up effect of the voice whispering almost in one's ear.

Hildegard Behrens is also a triumphantly successful Salome, a singer who in the early scenes has one actively sympathizing with the girlish princess, and who keeps that sympathy and understanding to a point where most sopranos have been transformed into raging harpies. The sensuous beauty of tone is conveyed ravishingly, but the recording is not always fair to her fine projection of sound, occasionally masking the voice. All the same, the feeling of a live performance has been captured well, and the rest of the cast is of the finest Salzburg standard. In particular José van Dam makes a gloriously noble Jokanaan, and in the early scenes his offstage voice from the cistern at once commands attention. Karajan – as so often in Strauss – is at his most commanding and sympathetic, with the orchestra, more forward than some will like, playing rapturously. This is a performance which, so far from making one recoil from perverted horrors, has one revelling in sensuousness. If the full and warm recording cannot match the vintage Decca in brilliance or atmospheric precision, it suits Karajan's ripe reading very well.

Montserrat Caballé's formidable account of the role of Salome was recorded in 1968, utterly different from that of Birgit Nilsson on Decca and much closer to the personification of Behrens on the Karajan set on EMI (both at full price). For some listeners Caballé might seem too gentle, but in fact the range of her emotions is even wider than that of Nilsson. There are even one or two moments of fantasy, where for an instant one has the girlish skittishness of Salome revealed like an evil inverted picture of Sophie. As for the vocalization, it is superb, with glorious golden tone up to the highest register and never the slightest hesitation in attack. Lewis, Resnik and Milnes make a supporting team that matches the achievement of the Decca rivals, while Leinsdorf is inspired to some of his warmest and most sympathetic conducting on record. The sound has not the pin-point atmosphere of the Decca, but is nearer to the EMI set in its fullness and vivid projection. The price advantage, too, makes this well worth considering.

Mehta's set brings a supreme performance from Brigitte Fassbaender as Herodias, dominating all her scenes. Otherwise performance and recording are disappointing. Above all the wobbly, ill-focused singing of Eva Marton in the title role puts the set out of court except for her devotees. In the theatre the sheer volume might make her performance exciting, but on disc the microphone is unforgiving in showing up the unevenness of vocal production. She conveys a compelling lasciviousness in the final scene, but even there Cheryl Studer and Birgit Nilsson are more involving. Bernd Weikl is disappointing too as Jokanaan, sounding too old, and even the glorious sounds of the Berlin Philharmonic are dimmed by the distancing of the recording, blunting the impact of this highly charged work.

Salome (complete; sung in French).
**(*) Virgin Dig. VCD7 91477-2 (2) [id.]. Huffstodt, Van Dam, Viala, Dupouy, Jossoud, Lyon Opera Ch. & O, Kent Nagano.

Nagano's version is unique. Adventurously, he has revived the adaptation of the vocal line which Strauss himself made to accommodate the original Oscar Wilde text in French. It was never used even in France, but the result is most distinctive, with Nagano drawing finely textured playing from his Lyon Opera Orchestra. Karen Huffstodt is the sensuous soprano who sings Salome, occasionally over-strained. In the final scene the phrase, *Ah! j'ai baisé ta bouche, Jokanaan*, seems all the more dissolute in French. The drawback of the adaptation is that it makes the whole drama seem smaller-scale than in the original German, and that is heightened by the closeness of the voices in the relatively intimate Lyon acoustic. The transparency and resilience of Nagano's reading of the score adds to that impression too, and there is little sense of horror at the tensely pauseful moment of the prophet's execution when Strauss has a solo double-bass play a high harmonic – what should be a chilling effect. Even in the biting drama of the final scene Nagano brings out the lilting dance rhythms. Yet at the end the big moments of climax are shattering, notably when the head of John the Baptist is held high by the executioner. José van Dam sings with characteristic nobility as Jokanaan, though sounding a little old for the role. Jean Dupouy with rather throttled tenor tone sounds aptly decadent as Herod.

Salome: Dance of the 7 veils; Closing scene. Lieder: *Cäcilie; Ich liebe dich; Morgen; Wiegenlied; Zueignung.*
(M) **(*) DG 431 171-2; *431 171-4* [id.]. Caballé, Fr. Nat. O, Bernstein – BOITO: *Mefistofele.* **(*)

One of Caballé's earliest and most refreshingly imaginative opera sets was Strauss's *Salome* with Leinsdorf conducting. This version of the final scene, recorded over a decade later with a very different conductor, has much of the same imagination, the sweet and innocent girl still observable next to the bloodthirsty fiend. The remainder of the recital is less recommendable, partly because Caballé underlines the expressiveness of works that remain Lieder even with the orchestral accompaniment. Bernstein too directs an over-weighted account of the *Dance of the seven veils*. The recording is warm and full.

Arias from: *Die Ägyptische Helena; Ariadne auf Naxos; Die Frau ohne Schatten; Guntram; Der Rosenkavalier; Salome.*
(M) *** RCA GD 60398; *GK 60398* [60398-2-RG; *60398-4-RG*]. Leontyne Price, Boston SO or New Philh. O, Leinsdorf; LSO, Cleva.

Leontyne Price gives generous performances of an unusually rich collection of Strauss scenes and solos, strongly accompanied by Leinsdorf (or Cleva in *Ariadne*), always at his finest in Strauss. Recorded between 1965 and 1973, Price was still at her peak, even if occasionally the voice grows raw under stress in Strauss's heavier passages. It is particularly good to have rarities as well as such regular favourites as the Marschallin's monologue from *Rosenkavalier*, the closing scene from *Salome* and Ariadne's lament. Among the luscious items are the solos from *Guntram* and *Die Ägyptische Helena* and the Empress's awakening from *Die Frau ohne Schatten*, one of the finest of all the performances here.

Stravinsky, Igor (1882–1971)

The Stravinsky Edition: Volume 1, Ballets, etc.: (i) *The Firebird;* (i) *Fireworks;* (iii) *Histoire du soldat;* (i) *Pétrushka;* (iv, iii) *Renard the fox;* (i) *The Rite of spring;* (i) *Scherzo à la russe;* (ii) *Scherzo fantastique;* (v) *The Wedding* (*Les Noces*).

Volume 2, Ballets etc.: (vi) *Agon;* (i) *Apollo;* (i) *Le baiser de la fée;* (i) *Bluebird (pas de deux);* (vii) *Jeux de cartes;* (viii) *Orphée;* (ix, i) *Pulchinella;* (ii) *Scènes de ballet.*

Volume 3, Ballet suites: (i) *Firebird; Pétrouchka; Pulchinella.*

Volume 4, Symphonies: (i) *Symphony in E;* (ii) *Symphony in C;* (i) *Symphony in 3 movements;* (x, ii) *Symphony of Psalms;* (i) Stravinsky in rehearsal: *Apollo; Piano concerto; Pulchinella; Sleeping beauty; Symphony in C; 3 Souvenirs.*

Volume 5, Concertos: (xi, i) *Capriccio for piano and orchestra* (with Robert Craft); *Concerto for piano and wind;* (xii, i) *Movements for piano and orchestra;* (xiii, i) *Violin concerto in D.*

Volume 6, Miniatures: (i) *Circus polka; Concerto in D for string orchestra; Concerto in E flat for chamber orchestra;* (ii) *4 Études for orchestra;* (i) *Greeting prelude;* (ii) *8 Instrumental miniatures; 4 Norwegian moods; Suites Nos. 1–2 for small orchestra.*

Volume 7, Chamber music and historical recordings: (iii) *Concertino for 12 instruments;* (xiv, xv) *Concerto for 2 solo pianos;* (xv, xvi) *Duo concertant for violin and piano;* (xvii, xviii) *Ebony Concerto (for clarinet and big band);* (iii) *Octet for wind;* (xix, iii) *Pastorale for violin and wind quartet;* (xv) *Piano rag music;* (xviii) *Preludium;* (xx, iii) *Ragtime* (for 11 instruments); (xv) *Serenade in A;* (iii) *Septet;* (xii) *Sonata for piano;* (xxi) *Sonata for 2 pianos;* (xviii) *Tango;* (xxii) *Wind symphonies.*

Volume 8, Operas and songs: (xxiii, iii) *Cat's cradle songs;* (xxiii, xxiv) *Elegy for J. F. K.;* (xxv, ii) *Faun and shepherdess;* (xxvi,iii) *In memoriam Dylan Thomas;* (xxvii, iii) *3 Japanese Lyrics* (with Robert Craft); (xxvii, xxix) *The owl and the pussycat;* (xxvii, iii) *2 poems by K. Bal'mont;* (xxx, i) *2 poems of Paul Verlaine;* (xxiii,i) *Pribaoutki (peasant songs);* (xxiii, i) *Recollections of my childhood;* (xxviii, xxxi) *4 Russian songs;* (xxxvii) *4 Russian peasant songs;* (xxiii, iii) *3 songs from William Shakespeare;* (xxvii, i) *Tilim-Bom (3 stories for children);* (xxxii) *Mavra;* (xxxiii) *The Nightingale.*

Volume 9: (xxxiv) *The Rake's progress.*

Volume 10, Oratorio and melodrama: (xxxv, i) *The Flood* (with Robert Craft); (i) *Monumentum pro Gesualdo di Venosa (3 madrigals recomposed for instruments);* (vii) *Ode;* (xxxvi) *Oedipus Rex;* (xxxvii, xxxviii, i) *Perséphone.*

Volume 11, Sacred works: (x) *Anthem (the dove descending breaks the air);* (x) *Ave Maria;* (xxxix, x, i) *Babel;* (xxviii, xxvi, x, iii) *Cantata;* (xl) *Canticum sacrum;* (x, ii) *Credo;* (x, iii) *Introitus (T. S. Eliot in Memoriam);* (xli) *Mass;* (x, i) *Pater noster;* (xlii, i) *A Sermon, a narrative & a prayer;* (xliii, i) *Threni;* (x, i) *Chorale: Variations on: Vom Himmel hoch, da komm ich her* (arr.); *Zvezdoliki.*

Volume 12, Robert Craft conducts: (xliv, i) *Abraham and Isaac;* (iii) *Danses concertantes;* (xlv) *Double canon: Raoul Dufy in memoriam;* (xlvi) *Epitaphium;* (i) *Le chant du rossignol* (symphonic poem); (i) *Orchestral variations: Aldous Huxley in memoriam;* (xlvii) *Requiem canticles;* (i) *Song of the nightingale (symphonic poem).*

(M) *** Sony SX 22K 46290 (22) [id.]. (i) Columbia SO; (ii) CBC SO; (iii) Columbia CO; (iv) Shirley, Driscoll, Gramm, Koves; (v) Allen, Sarfaty, Driscoll, Samuel Barber, Aaron Copland, Lukas Foss, Roger Sessions, American Chamber Ch., Hills, Columbia Percussion Ens.; (vi) Los Angeles Festival SO; (vii) Cleveland O; (viii) Chicago SO; (ix) Jordan, Shirley, Gramm; (x) Festival Singers of Toronto, Iseler; (xi) Philippe Entremont; (xii) Charles Rosen; (xiii) Isaac Stern; (xiv) Soulima Stravinsky; (xv) Igor Stravinsky; (xvi) Szigeti; (xvii) Benny Goodman; (xviii) Columbia Jazz Ens.; (xix) Israel Baker; (xx) Tony Koves; (xxi) Arthur Gold, Robert Fizdale; (xxii) N. W. German RSO; (xxiii) Cathy Berberian; (xxiv) Howland, Kreiselman, Russo; (xxv) Mary Simmons; (xxvi) Alexander Young; (xxvii) Evelyn Lear; (xxviii) Adrienne Albert; (xxix) Robert Craft; (xxx) Donald Gramm; (xxxi) Di Tullio, Remsen, Almeida; (xxxii) Belinck,

Simmons, Rideout, Kolk; (xxxiii) Driscoll, Grist, Picassi, Smith, Beattie, Gramm, Kolk, Murphy, Kaiser, Bonazzi, Washington, D. C., Op. Society Ch. & O; (xxxiv) Young, Raskin, Reardon, Sarfaty, Miller, Manning, Garrard, Tracey, Colin Tilney, Sadler's Wells Op. Ch., John Baker, RPO; (xxxv) Laurence Harvey, Sebastian Cabot, Elsa Lanchester, John Reardon, Robert Oliver, Paul Tripp, Richard Robinson, Columbia SO Ch., Gregg Smith; (xxxvi) Westbrook (nar.), Shirley, Verrett, Gramm, Reardon, Driscoll, Chester Watson Ch., Washington, D. C., Op. Society O; (xxxvii) Gregg Smith Singers, Gregg Smith; (xxxviii) Zorina, Molese, Ithaca College Concert Ch., Fort Worth Texas Boys' Ch.; (xxxix) John Calicos (nar.); (xl) Robinson, Chitjian, Los Angeles Festival Ch. & SO; (xli) Baxter, Albert, Gregg Smith Singers, Columbia Symphony Winds & Brass; (xlii) Verrett, Driscoll, Hornton (nar.); (xliii) Beardslee, Krebs, Lewis, Wainner, Morgan, Oliver, Schola Cantorum, Ross; all cond. composer. (xliv) Richard Frisch; (xlv) Baker, Igleman, Schonbach, Neikrug; (xlvi) Anderson, Bonazzi, Bressler, Gramm, Ithaca College Concert Ch., Gregg Smith; cond. Robert Craft.

On these 22 discs, a revised and remastered version of the 1982 CBS set originally issued on LP, you have the unique archive of recordings which Stravinsky left of his own music. Presented in a sturdy plastic display box that enhances the desirability of the set, almost all the performances are conducted by the composer, with a few at the very end of his career – like the magnificent *Requiem canticles* – left to Robert Craft to conduct, with the composer supervising. In addition there is a handful of recordings of works otherwise not covered, mainly chamber pieces. With some recordings of Stravinsky talking and in rehearsal (included in the box devoted to the symphonies) it makes a vivid portrait.

Stravinsky may not have been a brilliant conductor, but in the recording studio he knew how to draw out alert, vigorous performances of his own music, and every one of these items illuminates facets of his inspiration which other interpreters often fail to notice. There are few if any rival versions of the *Rite of spring* – nowadays, astonishingly, his most frequently recorded work – to match his own recording of 1960 in its compelling intensity and inexorable sense of line.

Nevertheless, there are some disappointments in the set. It is a pity that Stravinsky's earlier, mono version of *Oedipus Rex* (with Jean Cocteau as narrator and Peter Pears in the title-role) was not preferred to his much less taut, stereo remake, and sadly the spoken items fail to include his intensely memorable talk, *Apropos le sacre*, originally issued with his 1960 recording of *The Rite*. It ends unforgettably with the thought: 'I was the vessel through which *Le sacre* passed.' But transfers have been done very well, clarifying and refining the original analogue sound.

The two volumes containing the major ballets are now also available separately, and are discussed below, also the *Symphonies* (Volume 4) and *The Rake's Progress* (Volume 9). Stravinsky began his other opera *Le rossignol* (The Nightingale) in 1909, but when Diaghilev commissioned *The Firebird* he put it aside and did not take it up again until after *Petrushka* and *The Rite of spring*. Much has been made of the stylistic discrepancy which resulted, but one doubts if many listeners would object if they did not already know the history of the work's composition. It is unashamedly exotic in a way that sets it aside from almost every other work Stravinsky has ever written, even *The Firebird*. It is perhaps surprising that Stravinsky wanted to record it, but his handling shows that what can seem over-exotic acquires an almost barbaric strength in his hands. The singing is not always on a par with the conducting, but it is always perfectly adequate and the recording is brilliant and immediate. *Mavra* is sung in Russian and, as usual the soloists who are good are too closely balanced, but the performance has punch and authority and on the whole the CD quality is fully acceptable.

The iron-fingered touch of Philippe Entremont has something to be said for it in the *Capriccio for piano and wind*, with the bright echoes of cake-walk and early jazz, and even in the Bach-like florid writing in the slow movement, but this performance conveys too little of the music's charm. The *Movements for piano and orchestra* are far more formidable. Here serial technique is applied strictly, and even Stravinsky admitted that the work's harmony is more complex than anything he had previously attempted. Despite the fearsome idiom, however, one really *wants* to understand the argument, and the composer's conducting could hardly be more compelling. Stravinsky wrote the *Concerto for piano and wind* to play himself on his concert tours. A strange work which at first seems brittle and arid, this performance reveals a steely strength. Sometimes conductor and soloist are over-dramatic – but then Stravinsky himself is – and firmness and vitality are the main essentials. The recording is excellent. Stern's account of the *Violin concerto in D* adds a romantic perspective to the framework, and at one time, no doubt, Stravinsky would have objected. But an expressive approach to Stravinsky is permissible in a soloist, when the composer is there to provide the bedrock under the expressive cantilena. Plainly this has the forthright spontaneity of a live performance.

The collection of Stravinsky's shorter pieces begins with the very brief prelude on 'Happy birthday to you' which Stravinsky wrote for Pierre Monteux. Most of the suites were adapted from piano-duet works written for children. The *Circus polka* was written for a Barnum & Bailey elephant and erupts magnificently into a distortion of Schubert's *Marche militaire*. The *Dumbarton Oaks concerto* with its obvious echoes of Bach's *Brandenburgs* is one of the most warmly attractive of Stravinsky's neo-classical works, all beautifully played and acceptably recorded. The *Octet for wind* of 1924 comes out with surprising freshness and, throughout, the unexpected combination of neo-Bach and neo-Pop is most refreshing. The *Ragtime* dates from the end of Stravinsky's Russian period, when he was beginning to dabble in the exotic sounds of Western music. The performance could be more lighthearted, but Stravinsky gives the impression of knowing what he wants. The *Ebony concerto*, in this version conducted by the composer, may have little of 'swung' rhythm, but it is completely faithful to Stravinsky's deadpan approach to jazz.

Of the piano music, the *Concerto for two pianos* was written for the composer and his son to play, yet it presents formidable technical difficulties. It is a taut, four-movement work that deserves to be better known. The *Sonata* is much easier, musically and technically, and the *Eight easy pieces* are better known in their later transformation into the two *Suites for orchestra*.

The songs represent a fascinating collection of trifles, chips from the master's workbench dating from the earliest years. There are many incidental delights, not least those in which the magnetic Cathy Berberian is featured.

The *Mass* is a work of the greatest concentration, a quality that comes out strongly if one plays this performance immediately after *The Flood*, with its inevitably slack passages. In 1951 when it first appeared, the *Mass* was criticized by some for its perfunctory treatment of the words of the service. What this performance under the composer shows conclusively is that there is a difference between unseemly haste and genuine concentration. As with other Stravinsky works – the *Wind symphonies* and *Movements for piano and orchestra* – the argument is so concentrated that it is almost a musical shorthand. This is a microcosm of a *Mass*. As directed in the score, trebles are used here, and it is a pity that the engineers have not brought them further forward: their sweet, clear tone is sometimes lost among the lower strands. Otherwise the quality is up to the standard of CBS's other Stravinsky recordings. In *The Flood*, originally written for television, it is difficult to take the bald narrations seriously, particularly when Laurence Harvey sanctimoniously keeps talking of the will of 'Gud'. The Disneyland hill-billy style of narration quite destroys enjoyment and it is difficult to know what its dramatic aim was, fascinating though the work is. *Perséphone* is full of that cool lyricism that marks much of Stravinsky's music inspired by classical myths. As with many of these vocal recordings, the balance is too close, and various orchestral solos are highlighted.

The *Cantata* of 1952 is a transitional piece between Stravinsky's tonal and serial periods. However, of the two soloists, Alexander Young is much more impressive than Adrienne Albert, for her voice is entirely unsuitable, with an unformed choirboy sound somehow married to wide vibrato. For the sake of Stravinsky one endures her. The *Canticum sacrum* dates from the mid-1950s and includes music that some listeners might find tough (the strictly serial choral section). But the performance is a fine one and the tenor solo from Richard Robinson is very moving. The Bach *Chorale variations* has a synthetic modernity that recalls the espresso bar, though one which still reveals underlying mastery. The *Epitaphium* and the *Double canon* are miniatures, dating from the composer's serial period, but the *Canon* is deliberately euphonious.

Of the items recorded by Robert Craft, the *Requiem canticles* stands out, the one incontrovertible masterpiece among the composer's very last serial works and one of the most deeply moving works ever written in the serial idiom. Even more strikingly than in the *Mass* of 1948, Stravinsky conveys his religious feelings with a searing intensity. The *Aldous Huxley variations* are more difficult to comprehend but have similar intensity. Valuable, too, are the ballad *Abraham and Isaac* and the brief *Introitus for T. S. Eliot*.

Stravinsky Edition, Volume 2: Ballets etc.: *Agon; Apollo; Le baiser de la fée; Jeux de cartes; Orpheus;* (i) *Pulcinella. Scènes de ballet;* arr. of Tchaikovsky: *Bluebird pas de deux.*

(M) *** Sony SM3K 46292 [id.]. Columbia SO, LASO, Cleveland O, CBC SO, Chicago SO, composer; (i) with Jordan, Shirley, Gramm.

Stravinsky Edition, Volume 1: Ballets, etc.: *The Firebird; Fireworks; Histoire du soldat (The soldier's tale)*: suite; *Les Noces (The Wedding); Petrushka* (original 1911 score); *Renard the fox; The Rite of spring; Scherzo à la russe; Scherzo fantastique.*
(M) *** Sony SM3K 46291 (3) [id.]. American Concert Ch., Columbia SO, CBC SO, Columbia Chamber Ens., Columbia Percussion Ens., composer.

Of the major ballets, *Petrushka* and *The Firebird* are valuable, but *The Rite* is required listening: it has real savagery and astonishing electricity. The link between *Jeu de cartes* from the mid-1930s and Stravinsky's post-war opera, *The Rake's Progress*, is striking and Stravinsky's sharp-edged conducting style underlines it, while the curiously anonymous-sounding *Scènes de ballet* certainly have their attractive moments. *Orpheus* is a post-war score, written for Balanchine, and has a powerful atmosphere, although one of Stravinsky's most classically restrained works. A good performance, with the composer's own authority lending it special interest. However, its invention is less memorable and distinguished than *Apollo*, one of Stravinsky's most gravely beautiful scores. *Agon* is one of the most stimulating of Stravinsky's later works. Again composed for Balanchine, all the pieces are modelled on a French dance manual of the mid-seventeenth century. The sonorities are as individual and astringent as one expects, and the performance and recording are both of a high order. The orchestra respond with tremendous alertness and enthusiasm to Stravinsky's direction. The recording of *Le baiser de la fée* is a typical CBS balance with forward woodwind. However, if the recorded quality does not inspire too much enthusiasm, the performance of this enchanting score, based on themes by Tchaikovsky, certainly does. It was Diaghilev who suggested to Stravinsky that he might orchestrate some of Pergolesi's music and the result was *Pulcinella*, with the fragile musical fragments turned into something tougher than was expected, if still engaging. Diaghilev did not approve, and Stravinsky tells us that he 'went about for a long time with a look that suggested The Offended Eighteenth Century'. Stravinsky's recording of the whole ballet includes the vocal numbers, which, when well sung, add to the variety and sparkle of the piece, while in the orchestra the clowning of the trombone and the humour generally is strikingly vivid and never too broad. A limited orchestra of 33 players is used, and the close-up sound is less troublesome than in *Baiser de la fée*. Similarly the chamber scoring of the suite from *The Soldier's tale* brings clean yet atmospheric sound, while the crisp, clear reading brings out the underlying emotion of the music with the nagging, insistent little themes given an intensity that is almost tear-laden. There is a ruthlessness in the composer's own reading of *Les Noces* which exactly matches the primitive robustness in this last flowering of Russian nationalism in Stravinsky. It must be a long time since four distinguished composers paid such a tribute as this in playing the work of a fifth. The earlier parts are perhaps too rigid, but as the performance goes on so one senses the added alertness and enthusiasm of the performers. The recording is good, but the balance favours the voices. *Renard* is a curious work, a sophisticated fable which here receives too unrelenting a performance. The voices are very forward and tend to drown the instrumentalists.

Apollo (Apollon Musagète): ballet (complete).
*** DG 415 979-2 [id.]. BPO, Karajan – *Rite of spring.* ***

Though Stravinsky tended to disparage Karajan's approach to his music as not being rugged enough, here is a work where Karajan's moulding of phrase and care for richness of string texture make for wonderful results. This neo-classical score is strong enough to stand such individual treatment, and the writing is consistently enhanced by the magnificent playing of the Berlin Philharmonic Orchestra. The recording dates from 1973 and sounds excellent in its CD format.

Apollo (Apollon Musagète) ballet (complete); *The Firebird* (ballet) complete.
(M) **(*) Decca Dig. 430 740-2; *430 740-4* [id.]. Detroit SO, Antal Dorati.

Dorati's performance of *Apollo* has an attractive vitality, while the variations of Terpsichore and Apollo are genially characterized and the splendid *Pas de deux* – one of Stravinsky's most memorable inspirations – is warmly played. The recording is first class. Dorati's Detroit *Firebird* also has the benefit of spectacular digital recording. The clarity and definition of dark, hushed passages is amazing, with the contra-bassoon finely focused, never sounding woolly or obscure, while string tremolos down to the merest whisper are uncannily precise. There is plenty of space round woodwind solos, and only the concertmaster's violin is spotlit. The performance is very precise, too; though Dorati's reading has changed little from his previous versions with London orchestras, there is just a little more caution. Individual solos are not so characterful and *Kaschei's dance* lacks just a degree in excitement, but overall this is a strong and beautiful reading, even if the Mercury LP account, an electrifying example of 1960s analogue engineering, is not entirely superseded. The somewhat literal quality of the Decca performance, lacking a touch of magic and intensity, is brought out the more on CD, though the vividness and impact of the sound are most impressive.

Apollo; Orpheus (ballets).
*** ASV CDDCA 618 [id.]. O of St John's, Lubbock.

The ASV issue offers an ideal and generous coupling, with refined performances and excellent recording. The delicacy of the rhythmic pointing in *Apollo* gives special pleasure, and there is a first-rate solo violin contribution from Richard Deakin. This is one of Stravinsky's most appealing later scores, as readily accessible as the more famous ballets of his early years.

Apollo (Apollon Musagète): complete; *The Rite of spring* (complete).
**(*) EMI Dig. CDC7 49636-2 [id.]; *EL 749636-4*. CBSO, Rattle.

Rattle gives a relaxed reading of *Apollo*, at once refined and easy-going, but lacking something of the bite one expects with Stravinsky (and with Rattle) even in this amiably neo-classical work. That goes with a reading of *The Rite of spring* which has more joy in it than barbarism. The EMI sound is full and rich against a warm acoustic, not ideally sharp enough but with plenty of body and with good detail. Speeds are often broad, at times diminishing the bite of the performance in favour of warmth and high spirits. This is not quite the supreme version one might have expected after Rattle's youthful recording with the National Youth Orchestra, made in the late 1970s (well worth considering at bargain price on ASV, coupled with Dorati's complete *Firebird* with the RPO – see below).

Le baiser de la fée (ballet; complete). TCHAIKOVSKY, arr. STRAVINSKY: *Sleeping Beauty: Bluebird pas de deux*.
*** Chan. CHAN 8360; *ABTD 1123* [id.]. SNO, Järvi.

Le baiser de la fée is a remarkable symbiosis of Tchaikovskian tuneful charm (as instanced by the unforgettable rhythmic theme for the horns, taken from a piano piece) and Stravinskian twentieth-century neo-classicism. The scoring here is a constant delight, much of it on a chamber-music scale; and its delicacy, wit and occasional pungency are fully appreciated by Järvi, who secures a wholly admirable response from his Scottish orchestra. The ambience seems exactly right, bringing out wind and brass colours vividly. The condensation of the scoring of the *Sleeping Beauty Pas de deux*, made for a wartime performance when only limited forces were available, also shows Stravinsky's orchestral individuality – he even introduces a piano.

Le baiser de la fée (Divertimento); The Firebird: suite (1919 version); *Pulcinella: suite*.
**(*) BMG/RCA Dig. RD 60394 [60394-2-RC]. RPO, Yuri Temirkanov.

An enjoyable and generous (73 minutes) triptych. The RPO are on top form, and Yuri Temirkanov has a feel for balletic nuance and a fine ear for orchestral detail. The performance of *Le baiser de la fée* is particularly attractive, with the lightest touch in the *Scherzo* and *Pas de deux* reminding us that this delectably scored music is as much Tchaikovsky as Stravinsky. The Rimskian colours in the *Firebird* emerge vividly, yet King Kastchei and his entourage are as malignantly pungent as anyone could wish, and the finale expands gloriously. Perhaps in *Pulcinella* the warm acoustics of Watford Town Hall are a little too amiable for the dances of Pergolesi focused through Stravinsky's harmonic and rhythmic distorting lens, but otherwise the recording is first class.

(i) *Le baiser de la fée (Divertimento);* (ii) *Petrushka:* excerpts: *(Danse russe; Chez Petrushka; La fête populaire);* (i) *Pulcinella: suite;* (ii) *The Rite of spring* (complete ballet).
(B) (***) EMI mono CZS7 62647-2 (2) [Ang. CDMB 62647]. (i) French Nat. R. O; (ii) Philh. O, Markevitch – PROKOFIEV: *Love for three oranges* etc. (**)

Markevitch's electrifying 1959 stereo recording of *The Rite of spring* has long been famous, even though the documentation suggests that it is mono. The Philharmonia playing is superbly exciting, and the conductor's rhythmic vitality and ruthless thrust are matched by an amazingly spectacular recording which hardly sounds dated even now. One of the highlights of the performance is the dramatic use of the tam-tam, and in Part 2 the drums are thrillingly crisp and make a powerful impact. The elegant *Divertimento*, which Stravinsky culled from his Tchaikovskian ballet *Le baiser de la fée*, was made famous by Ansermet's mono recording, but the French orchestral playing here has rather more finesse: the horns in their attractive ostinato (taken from a Tchaikovsky piano piece) articulate buoyantly, and the whole performance has flair. The three excerpts from *Petrushka* are similarly lively and colourful, and only *Pulcinella* is slightly disappointing: the trombones blow rasberries in their famous *Vivo* duet with the double basses, and elsewhere Markevitch dilutes the music's charm by his forcefulness. However, in EMI's 'two for the price of one' French series this is certainly value for money.

Le baiser de la fée (Divertimento); The Soldier's tale: suite; Suites for orchestra Nos. 1–2; Octet.
(M) *** Decca Dig. 433 079-2 [id.]. L. Sinf., Chailly.

This is one of the most attractive collections of shorter Stravinsky pieces in the catalogue. Ansermet made a famous mono LP (1951) of the four-movement *Divertimento*, which Stravinsky distilled from the complete ballet in 1934. The Swiss conductor re-recorded it later in stereo, but the second account proved rhythmically less taut and was not so well played. Chailly's version, admirably fresh, cannot be criticized on either of these counts. It is superbly played and Decca's recording is in the finest traditions of the house, especially in its CD format. After the gently nostalgic opening, Chailly's approach to the *Sinfonia* is dramatic and strong: clearly, he sees this movement in terms of the concert hall, rather than the ballet theatre. Stravinsky's dominance over the music is emphasized; later and especially in the Scherzo and *Pas de deux* the Tchaikovskian influences rise more readily to the surface. Chailly's pacing throughout is splendidly judged, rhythms are resilient – the pointing of the lighter rhythmic patterns is especially effective – and the espressivo playing is at once responsive and slightly cool, a most engaging combination. The two *Orchestral suites*, vivid orchestrations of *'Easy' pieces* for piano, provide a kaleidoscopic series of colourful vignettes. Unfortunately, on CD the individual movements are not banded.

A fine modern version of the 1922 *Octet* is most welcome, a considerable piece for flute, clarinet, two bassoons – used to great effect – two trumpets, trombone and bass trombone. It is given a performance of infectious virtuosity, with individual bravura matched by polished ensemble and fine tonal blending. The second-movement *Theme and variations*, with its bizarre quotations of the *Dies irae*, is particularly memorable. The surprisingly little-recorded concert suite from *The Soldier's tale*, added for this reissue, makes an impressive finale. The performance has great flair (witness the brilliantly spiky cornet rhythms of James Watson in the *Royal march*), intimacy (the Devil's violin keeps a relatively low profile until his final triumphant march), and finds sardonic humour in the combination of *Tango, Waltz* and *Ragtime* in the sparkling sixth movement. Throughout the programme, the CD is very much in the demonstration class, with the tangibility and presence of the imagery enhanced by the background silence (the bass drum featured with rare subtlety). The overall bloom, without any clouding, again testifies to the ideal acoustic properties of London's Kingsway Hall.

(i) *Capriccio for piano and orchestra* (1929, rev. 1949); *Concerto for piano and wind* (1924, rev. 1950); *Movements for piano and orchestra.* (Piano): *8 Easy pieces on 5 notes; 4 Études; 3 Movements from Petrushka; Piano rag music; Scherzo; Serenade in A; Sonata in F sharp min.* (1903/4); *Sonata* (1924); *Souvenir d'une marche bouche; Tango; Valse pour les enfants; Waltz for children.*
(B) *** EMI CZS7 67276-2 (2) [id.]. Michel Béroff; (i) O de Paris, Seiji Ozawa.

Michel Béroff was still in his early twenties when he made the concerto recordings in the somewhat reverberant acoustic of the Salle Wagram. They are still better than those of most rivals and certainly better than those in the Sony *Stravinsky Edition*. The *Petrushka* excerpts are wonderfully alert and vital, and splendidly characterized. There is occasionally a very slight glare about the piano sound, recorded in the 1970s, but, among bargain, mid- and full-price discs, this is a first choice for this repertoire.

Le Chant du rossignol (symphonic poem).
*** Erato/Warner 2292 45382-2; *2292 45382-4* [id.]. French Nat. O, Boulez – *Pulcinella.* **(*)
*** Decca Dig. 417 619-2 [id.]. Montreal SO, Dutoit – *Petrushka* etc. ***
**(*) Delos Dig. D/CD 3051 [id.]. Seattle SO, Schwarz – *Firebird.* **(*)

The symphonic poem that Stravinsky made from the material of his opera, *Le Rossignol*, with its extraordinarily rich fantasy and vividness of colouring, deserves a more established place in the concert repertoire. The Boulez performance is masterly; the French National Orchestra on Erato capture detail vividly and have the advantage of a first-class 1982 recording.

Dutoit's account is full of colour and atmosphere and has the advantage of marvellous

Montreal sound. The couplings too are particularly apt, and this is a very desirable disc in all respects.

The Delos Schwarz recording has the most brilliantly etched detail, yet remains reasonably atmospheric. The extremely vivid and well-focused internal detail makes for the kind of record that will thrill audiophiles with equipment capable of making the most of its projection and clarity.

Concerto in D for strings; Danses concertantes; Dumbarton Oaks concerto in E flat; (i) *Cantata on old English texts.*
(M) *** Decca 425 622-2. ECO, Sir Colin Davis; (i) with Kern, Young, St Anthony Singers.

Stravinsky himself admitted that the *Brandenburgs* were his starting point for the *Dumbarton Oaks concerto*. Sir Colin Davis brings enormous vitality as well as the right degree of dry humour to these works, and the 1962 recording sounds as fresh as the day it was made in this very successful CD transfer. Detail is crisp and the ambience is exactly right for the music. The *Cantata* (recorded a year later) has a much cooler atmosphere, its chilling setting of the *Lye-Wake Dirge* more relentless than Britten's; but the sharp originality of the concept makes its inspiration readily felt in a performance that so strikingly captures its harsh mood and strange beauty. Both soloists are excellent and the chorus is vividly caught.

Ebony concerto.
*** Sony MK 42227 [id.]. Benny Goodman, Columbia Jazz Ens., composer – COPLAND: *Concerto;* BARTÓK: *Contrasts;* BERNSTEIN: *Prelude, fugue and riffs;* GOULD: *Derivations.* (***)

The *Ebony concerto* sounds strikingly vivid in an apt compilation centred on Benny Goodman's other comparable recordings.

Violin concerto in D.
(M) *** Decca 425 003-2; *425 003-4.* Kyung Wha Chung, LSO, Previn – PROKOFIEV: *Concertos 1–2.* ***
*** Denon Dig. CO 73325 [id.]. Kantorow, LPO, Bryden Thomson – TCHAIKOVSKY: *Concerto.* **(*)
*** DG Dig. 423 696-2 [id.]. Mutter, Philh. O, Sacher – LUTOSLAWSKI: *Chain II; Partita.* ***
*** DG 413 725-2 [id.]. Perlman, Boston SO, Ozawa – BERG: *Concerto.* ***

Kyung Wha Chung is at her most incisive in the spikily swaggering outer movements, which with Previn's help are presented here in all their distinctiveness, tough and witty at the same time. In the two movements labelled *Aria*, Chung brings fantasy as well as lyricism, less overtly expressive than Perlman (at full price) but conveying instead an inner, brooding quality. Brilliant Decca recording, the soloist diamond-bright in presence, but with plenty of orchestral atmosphere.

Kantorow gives a clean and classical account of the *Violin concerto*, crisply accompanied and very well recorded. It can be highly recommended for anyone wanting the unexpected Tchaikovsky coupling.

Mutter gives a strikingly characterful reading of the Stravinsky *Concerto*, neither brittle nor over-romanticized, with playing and recording of the very finest. There is no more recommendable version, and the coupling – an invigorating rather than a popular choice – is equally fine.

Perlman's precision, remarkable in both concertos on this disc, underlines the neo-classical element in the outer movements of the Stravinsky. The two *Aria* movements are more deeply felt and expressive, presenting the work as a major twentieth-century concerto. The balance favours the soloist, but no one will miss the commitment of the Boston orchestra's playing, vividly recorded.

Danses concertantes; Pulcinella (ballet): *suite.*
*** Chan. Dig. CHAN 8325 [id.]. ECO, Gibson.

Gibson and the ECO are very well recorded on Chandos and give highly enjoyable accounts of both works. The *Pulcinella* suite does not quite eclipse the Marriner (see below), but it is still very lively, and the *Danses concertantes* scores even over the composer's own in terms of charm and geniality. The CD is especially impressive in its firmness of detail.

The Firebird (ballet; complete).
**(*) Delos Dig. D/CD 3051 [id.]. Seattle SO, Schwarz – *Chant du rossignol.* **(*)

(B) **(*) Pickwick Dig. PCD 921; *CIMPC 921*. Nat. Youth O of Great Britain, Christopher Seaman – DUKAS: *L'apprenti sorcier*. **(*)

The Firebird (complete); *Le chant du rossignol; Fireworks; Scherzo à la russe.*
❀ (M) *** Mercury 432 012-2 [id.]. LSO, Dorati.

The Firebird (ballet; complete); *4 Études; Scherzo à la russe.*
**(*) EMI Dig. CDC7 49178-2. CBSO, Rattle.

The Firebird (ballet; complete); *Fireworks, Op. 4; Scherzo fantastique, Op. 3.*
*** Decca Dig. 414 409-2 [id.]. Montreal SO, Dutoit.

The CD transfer of Dorati's electrifying, 1960 Mercury version of *The Firebird* with the LSO makes the recording sound as fresh and vivid as the day it was made; the brilliantly transparent detail and enormous impact suggest a modern digital source rather than an analogue master made over 30 years ago. The stereo has remarkable atmosphere too, and the balance is very natural. The performance sounds completely spontaneous and the LSO wind playing is especially sensitive. Only the sound of the massed upper strings reveals the age of the original master, although this does not spoil the ravishing final climax; the bite of the brass and the transient edge of the percussion are thrilling. The recording of Stravinsky's glittering symphonic poem, *The song of the nightingale*, is hardly less compelling, with sparkle in the upper range and an impressive bass drum. Dorati's reading is urgent and finely pointed, yet is strong, too, on atmosphere. The other, shorter pieces also come up vividly. On CD one can order the programme to taste, and this remains one of the most stimulating Stravinsky compilations in the catalogue.

Dutoit's version brings a characteristically colourful and atmospheric reading of Stravinsky's brilliant ballet score, ideally and generously coupled with the two early orchestral pieces which led Diaghilev to spot the young composer's talent. Thanks in part to Decca's sensuously beautiful Montreal recording, this is a reading that brings out the light and shade of the writing, so that even *Kaschei's dance* is not just a brilliant showpiece but part of the poetic and dramatic scheme. The pianissimos are of breathtaking delicacy – very vital in this work: the hushed introduction to the final scene with its lovely horn solo brings a sense of wonder. The fill-ups are sparklingly done, making this a clear first choice.

Strong, clean and well played, Rattle's CBSO version of *The Firebird* is forthright and positive rather than atmospheric, looking forward to the *Rite of spring* rather than back to Russian nationalism, and it is not one of his most inspired recordings. The two versions of the *Scherzo à la russe* (one for jazz band, one for full orchestra) are both given with all Rattle's usual flair, infectiously bouncy. The *Four studies* provide another light-hearted makeweight.

The Delos version brings brilliant, exceptionally clean ensemble from the Seattle Symphony, showing its paces impressively under its music director, Gerard Schwarz. The recording is brilliant and strikingly sophisticated in its detail.

On Pickwick, *Firebird* is a work which inspires the young players of the current National Youth Orchestra to phenomenal feats of virtuosity. This is played at least as brilliantly as most versions by fully professional orchestras, with ensemble just as precise. Only in *Kaschei's dance*, taken a little cautiously, does the weight of the challenge show itself. The popular Dukas piece makes an attractive fill-up, and the modern digital recording is full and brilliant.

(i) *The Firebird* (complete); (ii) *The Rite of spring* (complete).
(BB) *** ASV CDQS 6031; *ZCQS 6031*. (i) RPO, Dorati; (ii) Nat. Youth O of Great Britain, Simon Rattle.

The ASV CD coupling of the two complete ballets is made possible because Dorati's tempi in the *Firebird* are comparatively fast. But this matches his dramatic approach, as does a recording balance which is rather close, although there is no serious lack of atmosphere in the score's gentler pages of evocation. Not surprisingly with Simon Rattle at the helm, the performance of the National Youth Orchestra in the once-feared showpiece coupling is not just 'good considering', but 'good absolute'; the youngsters under their young conductor (the recordings here date from 1976/7) produce warm and spontaneous playing, and the penalty of having a few imprecisions and errors is minimal.

(i) *The Firebird suite* (1910 score); (ii) *Pulcinella* (suite); *Scherzo fantastique;* (iii) *Suites Nos. 1–2 for small orchestra.*

(M) ** Sony SMK 45843 [id.]. (i) BBC SO; (ii) NYPO (members); (iii) Ensemble InterContemporain, Boulez.

An atmospheric and highly colourful account of *The Firebird suite* from Boulez; the BBC Symphony Orchestra plays with genuine responsiveness and the performance places this among Boulez's more successful earlier records, even though there is not the atmospheric magic found by Maazel in his DG Berlin recording of this music. The 1967 CBS recording is a little overlit and glamorous; the perspective is not absolutely natural (even though Walthamstow Town Hall was used), but the tonal quality is satisfactory and most listeners will not find the spotlighting of wind instruments close enough to be distracting. Boulez uses the comparatively rare 1910 score, including more than usual of the Firebird's opening scene and ending abruptly after *Kashchei's dance*. *Pulcinella* was recorded at the New York Manhattan Center eight years later and is less impressive altogether. Here Boulez misses much of the neo-classical point and the charm; but the early Rimskian *Scherzo fantastique* is very successful and brilliantly done. Best of all are the engaging miniature *Orchestral suites*, given distinct charm by the cool, precise wind playing.

The Firebird: suite (1919 version).
(B) *** DG Compact Classics 413 155-2 (2); *413 155-4* [id.]. Berlin RSO, Maazel – KHACHATURIAN: *Gayaneh* ***; RIMSKY-KORSAKOV: *Scheherazade* **(*) (CD only: GLINKA: *Overtures* *(*)).
(*) Sony SK 45935 [id.]; *40-45935*. Concg. O, Giulini – MUSSORGSKY: *Pictures*. *
(*) Telarc Dig. CD 80039 [id.]. Atlanta SO, Shaw – BORODIN: *Prince Igor*: excerpts. *

Maazel's reading of the *Firebird suite* is in every way outstanding. It has an enjoyable éclat and he has the advantage of the most beautiful woodwind playing; indeed the Berlin Radio Orchestra is consistently on top form. The recording dates from 1960 and betrays its age only marginally by the sound of the massed upper strings. Overall the sound is remarkably warm and atmospheric, and the effect is lustrous and full of magic in both formats.

The Concertgebouw acoustic – as anyone who has experienced live music-making there will know – is less than ideal for fast-moving, sharply dissonant twentieth-century music. Its wide reverberation tends to blur the transients, as here in *Kashchei's dance* which, however, does not lack malignancy. It also brings a voluptuous weight to the richly scored finale, perhaps unmatched on record. Giulini secures wonderfully refined playing in the gentler music, but the lack of rhythmic bite minimizes the balletic feeling and makes the suite seem more symphonic than usual.

Robert Shaw, a thoroughly musical conductor, achieves an atmospheric and vivid reading of Stravinsky's famous suite. The *Round dance of the princesses* is played very gently to maximize the shock of the entry of Kaschei. The very wide dynamic range of the digital recording achieves the most dramatic impact both here and in the closing pages of the finale.

The Firebird: suite (1919 version); *Pulcinella: suite; Scènes de ballet*.
** DG Dig. 435 595-2 [id.]. Israel PO, Bernstein.

Bernstein's versions of Stravinsky's *Firebird* and *Pulcinella* recorded live (with the Israel PO) prove something of a disappointment. The dryness of the acoustic is all too evident at the end of the opening *Sinfonia* of *Pulcinella*, though less disturbing in *Firebird*. The performances are neither as well executed nor as fully characterized as his earlier, highly atmospheric accounts with the New York Philharmonic. The Israel Philharmonic is not in the same league, and the strings in the *Tarantella* of the *Pulcinella suite* sound pretty scrappy and lacklustre. The results in the *Scènes de ballet*, recorded two years earlier, are rather more pleasing. This is a charming and underrated piece which the Israel Philharmonic Orchestra play with something approaching elegance. The CD draws the ear to the unventilated dryness of the recording, but the upper range is clear and clean and not edgy.

The Firebird suite (1919 version); *The Rite of spring*.
(M) *** DG 415 854-2; *415 854-4* [id.]. LSO, Abbado.

Abbado's *Firebird suite* is a performance of great vitality and sensitivity; the conductor's feeling for colour and atmosphere is everywhere and the CD transfer loses nothing of the evocation of the analogue original. There is a degree of detachment in *The Rite of spring*; but on points of detail it is meticulous. There is a hypnotically atmospheric feeling at the opening of Part Two, emphasizing the contrast with the brutal music which follows. The drama is heightened by the wide dynamic range of the recording, and the effect is forceful without ever becoming ugly.

Jeux de cartes (ballet) complete; (i) *Pulcinella* (ballet after Pergolesi) complete.
(M) *** DG 423 889-2 [id.]. (i) Berganza, Davies, Shirley-Quirk; LSO, Abbado.

Abbado gives a vividly high-powered reading of the neo-classical score of *Pulcinella*. If he is in danger of over-colouring, the bite and flair are entirely and convincingly Stravinskian, with rhythms sharply incisive. Not just the playing but the singers too are outstandingly fine. *Jeux de cartes*, recorded five years earlier, sounds somewhat drier than it did originally, but the detail, presence and impact remain very telling. The LSO plays with superb virtuosity and Abbado's feeling for atmosphere and colour is everywhere in evidence, heard against an excellently judged perspective.

Petrushka (ballet; 1911 score) complete.
*** DG Dig. 423 901-2 [id.]. LSO, Abbado – MUSSORGSKY: *Pictures*. ***

Petrushka (1911 score); *4 Études*.
*** Decca Dig. 417 619-2 [id.]. Montreal SO, Dutoit – *Chant du rossignol*. ***

Dutoit in his Montreal version, benefiting from superb, atmospheric but well-detailed sound, gives a sparkling performance that brings out the light and shade of *Petrushka*, its poetry and its rhythmic effervescence. As in other brilliant showpieces, the refinement of Montreal pianissimos adds to the atmospheric thrill, but there is no lack of either power or bite in this subtle telling of the story. The coupling of *Le Chant du rossignol* and the *Four Studies* is both generous and apt.

Abbado combines refinement and a powerful sense of dramatic atmosphere (he is especially sympathetic in the central tableaux) with a kaleidoscopic brilliance. The recording has impressive range and colour, but there is a degree of digital edge on the upper strings which is certainly not entirely natural. It is now reissued, generously coupled with an equally impressive account of Mussorgsky's *Pictures at an exhibition*, and holds its competitive place in the current listings of both works.

Petrushka (1911 version); *The Rite of spring*.
(M) *** Ph. 434 147-2; *434 147-4* [id.]. LPO, Haitink.

(i) *Petrushka* (1911 version); (ii) *The Rite of spring;* (ii; iii) *Le Roi des étoiles* (cantata).
(M) **(*) DG 435 073-2; *435 073-4* [id.]. (i) LSO, Dutoit; (ii) Boston SO, Tilson Thomas, (iii) with New England Conservatory Ch.

Haitink's 1974 *Petrushka* has been remastered with great success. It is a very involving account, with detail imaginatively delineated. The rhythmic feeling is strong, especially in the Second Tableau and the finale, where the fairground bustle is vivid. The LPO wind playing is especially fine; the recording's firm definition and the well-proportioned and truthful aural perspective make it a joy to listen to. The natural, unforced quality of Haitink's *Rite* also brings real compulsion. Other versions may hammer the listener more powerfully, thrust him or her along more forcefully; but the bite and precision of the playing here is most impressive.

Charles Dutoit's brilliantly realized *Petrushka* is triumphantly spontaneous, with rhythms that are incisive yet beautifully buoyant, and a degree of expressiveness in the orchestral playing that subtly underlines the dramatic atmosphere and is especially magical in the Third Tableau. The recording is vivid, the only fault of balance being the prominence of the concertante piano soloist, Tamás Vásáry. The pairing is Tilson Thomas's lively account of the *Rite of spring* (also available on a Compact Classics tape, differently coupled – see below), reverberantly recorded but now given most of the needed bite by the digital remastering. The brief makeweight is the rare motet of the same period as *The Rite*, unperformed for several decades, but here shown as an intensely imaginative and evocative choral work. The overall playing time of this issue is nearly 76 minutes. However, this is by no means a first choice for *The Rite of spring*.

Petrushka (1947 version); *The Rite of spring*.
(M) *** Collins Dig. 3033-2 [id.]. LSO, Frühbeck de Burgos.

Among modern digital versions of this coupling, the Collins mid-priced disc is hard to beat. Frühbeck de Burgos's *Rite of spring* may go over the top a bit in its high-flying histrionics but, if the reading has less firmness of grip than Haitink's, the result is much more thrilling, with the forward balance of the drums bringing a thundering impact to an already spectacular recording. The LSO are clearly on their toes and their playing in *Petrushka* is even more impressive. The bite of the strings and edge on the brass gives the piece great rhythmic vitality; the pathos of

Petrushka's predicament in his cell is the more striking, contrasted with the animated jollity of the *Danse russe*, and there is a galaxy of colour in the vibrant Shrovetide fair sequences. The digital recording, made at Walthamstow Town Hall, approaches the demonstration bracket.

Petrushka (1947 version); *Symphony in 3 movements.*
*** EMI Dig. CDC7 49053-2 [id.]. CBSO, Rattle.

Using the revised, 1947 scoring, Rattle gives a reading which brings out powerfully the sturdy jollity of the ballet, contrasting it with the poignancy of the puppet's own feelings. The full and brilliant recording is beefy in the middle and bass, but Rattle and his players benefit in clarity from the 1947 scoring, finely detailed to bring out many points that are normally obscured. The *Symphony in three movements*, done with comparable power, colour and robustness, makes an unusual but attractive coupling. With his jazz training, Rattle brings out the syncopations and pop references with great panache.

Pulcinella (ballet) complete.
(*) Erato/Warner 2292 45382-2 [id.]. Murray, Rolfe Johnson, Estes, Ens. InterContemporain, Boulez – *Le Chant du rossignol.* *

(i) *Pulcinella* (ballet; complete); *Danses concertantes.*
*** Virgin Dig. VC 790767-2 [id.]. (i) Murray, David Thomas, Hill; City of L. Sinfonia, Richard Hickox.

(i) *Pulcinella* (ballet; complete); *Dumbarton Oaks concerto.*
*** Decca Dig. 425 614-2 [id.]. Bernadette Manca di Nissa, Gordon, Ostendorf, Howard, St Paul CO, Hogwood – GALLO: *Trio sonata movements;* PERGOLESI: *Sinfonia.* ***

(i) *Pulcinella* (complete); *Renard. Ragtime; Octet.*
*** Sony Dig. SK 45965 [id.]. (i) Kenny, Aler, Tomlinson, Robson, Wilson-Johnson; L. Sinf., Esa-Pekka Salonen.

Richard Hickox emphasizes the colour in *Pulcinella*, to bring this neo-classical work rooted in the eighteenth century into the full light of the twentieth. So with sound that gives weight and body as well as plenty of detail he relishes the joke behind the *Vivo*, for example, with its trombone raspberries and lumbering double-bass. Equally he gives plenty of balletic bounce to the allegro movements and expressive warmth to the vocal numbers, phrasing in a romantic rather than a classical way. Among the soloists the tenor, Martyn Hill, stands out, though all are good. Hickox similarly gives a strong reminder that the *Danses concertantes* are, above all, ballet music, colourful and vigorous. Warm, full sound.

Christopher Hogwood has here not just gone back to Stravinsky's own score, in order to iron out various inconsistencies with the diligence of a classical scholar, but has also investigated Stravinsky's own sources. The composer used material from 21 different sources, all of them attributed to Pergolesi at the time, but in fact written by five different composers. As a delightful appendix, Hogwood adds some of the originals. The Pergolesi *Sinfonia* provides in its finale the idea for the *Vivo*, while the four movements from *Trio sonatas* by Domenico Gallo provide the themes for the opening overture, among other things. In keeping with this approach, Hogwood directs refined, deliberately lightweight performances of the two Stravinsky works, as much classical as neo-classical. Yet comparison with the eighteenth-century originals consistently makes you understand how Stravinsky's additions transform rather plain ideas. Of the three vocal soloists in *Pulcinella* the most striking is the firm-toned mezzo-soprano, Bernadette Manca di Nissa.

The complete *Pulcinella* on Sony is coupled with three other characteristic works from the years following the First World War, with Salonen taking every opportunity to point the music with wit. He may be less objective than some rivals, but not only is the fun behind much of this music delightfully brought out, he moulds it sufficiently to suggest a warmth behind neo-classical forms and, frequently, a debt to jazz. That is so not just in *Ragtime* but also in such a work as the delightful *Octet* of 1922–3. When *Pulcinella* is here given with voices, it is good to have another early example of music-theatre in *Renard*, necessarily a rarity in concert, with the Russian folk-tale presented with bluff good humour. Warm recording to match.

Boulez secures superb playing from the Ensemble InterContemporain, and his singers are first class in every way. His is a fine performance, but his pacing is more extreme than some versions, with contrasts between movements almost overcharacterized. However, some may like the periodic added edge, and the Erato recording has been excellently transferred to CD.

Pulcinella (ballet): *suite.*
(M) *** Decca 417 734-2 [id.]. ASMF, Marriner – BIZET; PROKOFIEV: *Symphonies.* ***

Those wanting merely the orchestral suite can rest content with Marriner's vintage version, one of the first recordings by which the Academy spread its wings in the music of the twentieth century. The results are superb and the sound of the digitally remastered CD has all the bite one could ask for. It remains a demonstration disc with its sharp separation of instruments, particularly the trombones against double basses in the *Vivo.*

The Rite of spring (complete ballet) (see also above, under *Petrushka*).
(B) *** DG 429 162-2; *429 162-4* [id.]. BPO, Karajan – MUSSORGSKY: *Pictures.* ***
*** DG 415 979-2 [id.]. BPO, Karajan – *Apollo.* ***
(M) *** EMI Dig. CDM7 64516-2 [id.]; *EG 764516-4.* Phd. O, Muti – MUSSORGSKY: *Pictures.* ***
(M) **(*) Decca 430 709-2; *430 709-4.* Cleveland O, Chailly (with MUSSORGSKY: *Pictures* **).

The Rite of spring; Circus Polka; Fireworks, Op. 4; Greeting prelude (Happy birthday).
(M) **(*) EMI Dig. CD-EMX 2188; *TC-EMX 2188.* LPO, Mackerras.

The Rite of spring; 4 Études; Scherzo à la russe.
** Teldec/Warner Dig. 2292 44938-2; *2292 44938-4* [id.]. Philh. O, Inbal.

The Rite of spring; Symphony in 3 movments.
** Sony Dig. SK 45796 [id.]; *40-45796.* Philh. O, Esa-Pekka Salonen.

Both of Karajan's DG stereo recordings are now available on CD and make a fascinating comparison. The earlier, 1966 version (now offered at mid-price, coupled with Mussorgsky's *Pictures*) came in for criticism from the composer, who doubted whether Berlin Philharmonic traditions could encompass music from so different a discipline. Yet listening to the vibrant sounds coming from the remastered CD, one cannot fully accept the composer's response. Certainly the playing of the Berlin Philharmonic is marvellously polished and civilized, yet it is not without bite or excitement, and the lack of malignancy serves to increase the feeling of symphonic strength, while the beauty of the sound created in the lyrical sections brings a potent nostalgia. Nevertheless, in his 1977 version (coupled with *Apollo*), tougher, more urgent, less mannered, Karajan goes a long way towards rebutting Stravinsky's complaints, and the result is superb, above all powerfully dramatic.

Muti's *Rite of spring* offers a performance which is aggressively brutal yet presents the violence with red-blooded conviction. Muti generally favours speeds a shade faster than usual, and arguably the opening bassoon solo is not quite flexible enough, for metrical precision is a key element all through. The recording, not always as analytically clear as some rivals, is strikingly bold and dramatic, with brass and percussion caught exceptionally vividly. At mid-price, coupled with an equally outstanding version of Mussorgsky's *Pictures*, this is very competitive indeed.

Chailly's version was chosen as a prime recommendation in a recent survey made by Michael Stewart for 'The *Gramophone* Collection'. It is coupled with a curiously metrical version of Mussorgsky's *Pictures at an exhibition* which is singularly unspontaneous, despite superb Decca Cleveland recording. The sound for *The Rite of spring* is even more spectacular. The bass drum, so important in this work, leaps out with a power, precision and resonance to startle the listener. Chailly's reading is taut and urgent, but the fast speeds in Part Two provide less contrast than usual, before the onslaught of the final sacrificial dance. But the impact of the superb Cleveland playing is considerable and anyone wanting to startle friends with the sound will be well pleased.

Mackerras's version is at mid-price on the Eminence label and brings a powerful, often spacious performance, recorded in opulent and finely textured, if slightly distanced sound. The weight of the recording adds powerfully to the dramatic impact, though it is a pity that timpani are backward and less sharply focused than they might be. Though short measure, the three little orchestral trifles are done by Mackerras with delectable point and wit.

Salonen couples his colourful but idiosyncratic reading of the *Rite* with an involvingly larger-than-life account of the *Symphony in three movements*. The playing in the *Symphony* is vivid and intense, with the jazz rhythms of the outer movements bitingly effective and with the central *Andante* moulded at an unusually slow speed. But, quite apart from the interpretative quirks, the *Rite* is given a softer-grained performance, partly a question of the playing, partly of the recording.

Inbal was also highly recommended by Michael Stewart in *Gramophone*. Yet he takes a very metrical view of the *Rite* which, in principle, may be totally valid but which in practice here makes the music sound too safe, lacking excitement. The sound too is full and smooth rather than brilliant, and the coupling is ungenerous.

The Rite of spring (orchestral & pianola versions).
(M) *** Pickwick Dig. MCD 25; *MCC 25*. Boston PO, Zander.

The most fascinating of the recent recordings of Stravinsky's *Rite of spring* is Benjamin Zander's live recording with the Boston Philharmonic, full and vivid if slightly confined in sound. It brings a hard-hitting, colourful performance, directly related to the pianola version with which it is coupled. Stravinsky himself in the 1920s supervised the original Pleyela piano roll recording, which Rex Lawson 'plays' very effectively on a resonant Bösendorfer Imperial. The speeds at which everything is presented remain predetermined and unalterable; and here the most striking point on speed is the very fast tempo for the opening of the final *Sacrificial dance*, markedly faster even than Stravinsky's own on the last – and finest – of his three recordings. With tracks correlated between the two performances, it is very easy to make illuminating comparisons. Zander suggests (and he offers additional documentary evidence) that Stravinsky intended a faster pacing for the ballet's finale and that he modified the tempo only when he discovered that orchestras could not cope with the music at his intended speed (even his own 1960 recording contains inaccuracies). There is no doubt that, played up to this faster tempo, the *Danse sacrale* is electrifying and, once experienced, the slower speed to which we are all accustomed seems comparatively restrained. It is a final irony that the first recording of the suggested intended 'original' tempo is presented on CD by a semi-professional group (of considerable excellence) which now projects rhythms with biting confidence that defeated professionals 70 years earlier!

The Soldier's Tale (complete).
*** Nimbus Dig. NI 5063 [id.]. Christopher Lee, SCO, Lionel Friend.

With the actor Christopher Lee both narrating and taking the individual parts, the Nimbus issue brings an attractively strong and robust reading, lacking the last degree of refinement but with some superb solo playing – from the violinist, for example. The recording is vivid and full of presence, with the speaking voice related to instruments far better than is usual. For a version in English, it makes an excellent investment.

The Soldier's tale (suite).
(M) *** Van. 08.8013.71 [OVC 8013]. Instrumental Ens., Leopold Stokowski – THOMSON: *Film scores*. ***
*** Delos Dig. D/CD 3021 [id.]. LACO, Schwarz – PROKOFIEV: *Symphony No. 1* ***; SHOSTAKOVICH: *Piano concerto No. 1*. **(*)

Stokowski works his magic upon this surprisingly neglected score, making the most of its lyrical warmth as well as the more abrasive Devil's music which has plenty of rhythmic bite. The septet of expert instrumentalists is naturally recorded in a studio acoustic, but one which has plenty of ambience. The solo violinist (Charles Tarack) and the trumpeter (Theodore Weis) are fully up to the considerable demands placed on them. This disc comes at upper-mid-price in the USA.

The Delos acoustic is ideal for the music and the sound is wonderfully realistic and present. The performance makes a nice balance between pungency and the underlying lyricism; there is some splendid solo playing from Paul Shure (violin) and the superb trumpeter, Tony Plog, whose easy virtuosity and fine timbre add much to the music's appeal. Recommended, especially as the couplings are imaginative.

Stravinsky Edition, Volume 4: *Symphony in E flat; Symphony in C; Symphony in 3 movements;* (i) *Symphony of Psalms*. Stravinsky in rehearsal; Stravinsky in his own words.
(M) *** Sony SM2K 46294 (2) [id.]. Columbia SO or CBC SO; (i) Toronto Festival Singers, composer.

In the early *Symphony in E flat*, Op. 1, the young Stravinsky's material may be comparatively conventional and the treatment much too bound to the academic procedures taught him by his master, Rimsky-Korsakov, but at least in this performance the music springs to life. Each movement has its special delights to outweigh any shortcomings. The performance is obviously as near definitive as it could be. The composer's account of the *Symphony in three movements* is an object lesson for every conductor who has tried to perform this work. Stravinsky shows how, by vigorous, forthright treatment of the notes, the emotion implicit is made all the more compelling. The Columbia Symphony plays superbly and the recording is full and brilliant. Stravinsky never quite equalled the intensity of the pre-war 78-r.p.m. performance of the *Symphony of Psalms*. That had many more technical faults than his later, stereo version, and it is only fair to say that this new account is still impressive. It is just that, with so vivid a work, it is a shade disappointing to find Stravinsky as interpreter at less than maximum voltage. Even so, the closing section of the work is very beautiful and compelling. The CD transfers of the American recordings are somewhat monochrome by modern standards but fully acceptable.

Symphony in C; Symphony in 3 movements.
*** Decca Dig. 414 272-3 [id.]. SRO, Dutoit.
(M) *** Chan. Dig. CHAN 6577 [id.]. Royal Scottish O, Sir Alexander Gibson.

Symphony in C; Symphony in 3 movements; Le chant du rossignol.
**(*) Virgin Dig. VC7 91495-2 [id.]. Finnish RSO, Saraste.

Although the Suisse Romande Orchestra is not in the very first rank, the brilliant recording it now receives from the Decca team and the alert direction of Charles Dutoit make this a very winning coupling. These are both exhilarating pieces and Dutoit punches home their virile high spirits and clean-limbed athleticism.

Even when compared with the composer's own versions, these performances by the Royal Scottish Orchestra – in excellent form – stand up well. The vivid naturalness of the splendid 1982 digital recording compensates for any slight lack of bite, and the inner movements of both works are beautifully played. The cool, almost whimsical beauty of the *Andante* of the *Symphony in three movements* is most subtly conveyed, and altogether this is very enjoyable.

Saraste is amiably easy-going at generally broad speeds in the two symphonies. He may lack something in bite but, with such refined, beautifully sprung playing from the orchestra, the results are most persuasive, and *Le chant du rossignol*, also crisp and refined, makes an attractive and generous coupling. The recording is refined to match.

CHAMBER AND INSTRUMENTAL MUSIC

Divertimento.
*** Ph. Dig. 426 254-2 [id.]. Viktoria Mullova, Bruno Canino – PROKOFIEV: *Sonata No. 2 in D* **; RAVEL: *Sonata in G.* ***

The *Divertimento* is an arrangement Stravinsky made in 1933 of his orchestral score, *Le Baiser de la fée*. Quite simply, it is played marvellously by Viktoria Mullova and Bruno Canino and most vividly and naturally recorded.

Élégie, for solo viola.
*** EMI CDC7 54394-2 [id.]. Tabea Zimmermann – BRITTEN: *Lachrymae;* SHOSTAKOVICH: *Viola sonata.* ***

Stravinsky's solo *Elégie* comes from 1944 and was commissioned by the violist, Germain Prévost, to honour the memory of Alphonse Onnou of the celebrated pre-war Pro Arte Quartet. It is finely played and recorded here and comes with moving accounts of the Britten *Lachyrmae* and Shostakovich's deeply felt *Sonata*.

Suite italienne.
*** BIS Dig. CD 336 [id.]. Torleif Thedéen, Roland Pöntinen – SCHNITTKE: *Sonata;* SHOSTAKOVICH: *Sonata.* ***

Stravinsky made several transcriptions of movements from *Pulcinella*, including the *Suite italienne* for violin and piano. The performances by Torleif Thedéen and Roland Pöntinen, Swedish artists both in their mid-twenties, are felicitous and spontaneous, and they are afforded strikingly natural recording.

3 Movements from Petrushka.
*** DG 419 202-2 [id.]. Maurizio Pollini – *Recital.* ***

Staggering, electrifying playing from Pollini, creating the highest degree of excitement. This is part of an outstandingly generous recital of twentieth-century piano music.

VOCAL MUSIC

(i) *Canticum sacrum;* (ii) *Mass;* (iii) *Symphony of Psalms.*

(M) *** Decca 430 346-2. Christ Church Cathedral, Oxford, Ch., Simon Preston; with (i) Morton, Creed; (i; iii) Philip Jones Ens.; (iii) N. Jones, Giles, Cave, Lindley, Herron, L. Sinf. – POULENC: *Motets*. ***

It is fascinating to hear Stravinsky's rapt and masterly *Symphony of Psalms* in a performance with boys' voices, as the composer said he had in mind. The *Canticum sacrum*, more taxing still in its serial austerity, brings another superb example of the artistry of these youngsters. Here again Stravinsky's markings suggest that he may have had such a tone-colour in mind. The *Symphony* lacks some of the weight and bite of larger-scale performances but, with atmospheric, resonant yet well focused sound, the effect is most moving. The comparably spare but very beautiful *Mass* for voices and instruments, given a direct, classical reading, is hardly less impressive and is equally well transferred to CD. The recordings (originally Argo) date from 1973/4.

(i) *Mass;* (ii) *Les Noces.*
(M) *** DG 423 251-2 [id.]. (i) Trinity Boys' Ch., E. Bach Festival O; (i, ii) E. Bach Festival Ch.; (ii) Mory, Parker, Mitchinson, Hudson; Argerich, Zimerman, Katsaris, Francesch (pianos), percussion; cond. Bernstein.

Bernstein reinforces the point that both the *Mass* and the much earlier ballet illustrating a folk wedding ceremony are intensely Russian in their inspiration. In the *Mass* the style is overtly expressive, with the boys of Trinity Choir responding freshly, but it is in *Les Noces* that Bernstein conveys an electricity and a dramatic urgency which give the work its rightful stature as one of Stravinsky's supreme masterpieces, totally original and – even today – unexpected, not least in its black-and-white instrumentation for four pianos and percussion. The star pianists here make a superb, imaginative team. The atmospheric recording now sounds even more vivid in its CD format.

4 Cat's cradle songs; 4 Chants; Elegy for JFK; In memoriam Dylan Thomas; 3 Japanese lyrics; Pastorale; 2 Poems by Konstantin Bal'mont; 2 Poems by Paul Verlaine; Pribaoutki (4 songs); *Recollections of childhood* (3 songs); *2 Sacred songs* (from WOLF: *Spanish Lieder Book*); *3 Shakespeare songs; 4 Songs; Tilim-bom; Mavra: Parasha's aria.*
(M) *** DG 431 751-2 [id.]. Bryn-Julson, Murray, Tear, Shirley-Quirk, Ens. InterContemporain, Boulez.

Anyone who thinks a Stravinsky song could not be utterly charming should try the first item of this recital, the *Pastorale*, a song without words for voice and four wind instruments: Phyllis Bryn-Julson's performance is captivating. Practically all of Stravinsky's songs are accommodated on this useful CD. The early songs occupy more than half of the collection: he wrote the bulk of his vocal output before or during the First World War, after which there is a long gap (1919–53) during which he abandoned the medium. (The *Chanson de Parasha* from *Mavra* was published as a separate song, but that is the sole exception.) All the singing here is very persuasive and well characterized. The Verlaine songs are, oddly enough, given in Russian (Stravinsky originally set them in French), but Shirley-Quirk makes them sound very appealing nevertheless. The record also includes a 1968 transcription of two of Wolf's Spanish songs, his very last opus. The CD transfer is immaculate, with natural, well-focused sound, and translations are provided where necessary.

Oedipus Rex (opera-oratorio).
*** Sony Dig. SK 48057 [id.]. Cole, Von Otter, Estes, Sotin, Gedda, Chéreau, Eric Ericson Chamber Ch., Swedish RSO & Ch., Salonen.
(M) **(*) Decca 430 001-2. McCowen (narrator), Pears, Meyer, McIntyre, Dean, Ryland Davies, Luxon, John Alldis Ch., LPO, Solti.

Salonen with his Swedish forces and an outstanding cast, more consistent than any previous one, conducts the strongest performance yet on disc of this landmark of modern opera. He offers an ideal combination of rugged power and warmth, delivered expressively but without sentimentality. The pinpoint precision of ensemble of the choruses, substantial but not so big as to impair sharpness of focus, does more than anything else to punch home the impact of this so-called opera-oratorio, with its powerful commentary, Greek-style. The singing of the two principals, Vinson Cole as Oedipus and Anne Sofie von Otter as Jocasta, then conveys the full depth of emotion behind the piece. Cole's is a lyrical view of the title-role rather than a big heroic one, with the taxing solos strain-free and sung with both precision and depth of feeling. He sings *Invidia fortunam odit* more poignantly than any predecessor, and also Oedipus' final solo, ending on *Lux facta est* ('All is made clear'). Von Otter as Jocasta readily surpasses her precedecessors on record with her firm detail and expressive singing. Simon Estes as Creon and Hans Sotin as Tiresias are both firm and resonant, with Nicolai Gedda still strong as the Shepherd. With recorded sound both dramatically immediate and warm, and with splendid narration in French from Patrice Chéreau, echoing that of the librettist, Jean Cocteau, this displaces all rivals, even the composer's own American version.

Solti's view of this highly stylized work is less sharp-edged than one would expect, and the dominant factor in the performance is not so much the conductor's direction as the heartfelt singing of Peter Pears in the title-role. Here the crispness and clarity of his delivery go with an ability to point the key moments of deep emotion with extraordinary intensity. The rest of the vocal team is good, if not outstanding, and the narration (in English) of Alec McCowen is apt and undistracting. The transfer to CD is outstandingly vivid and brilliant.

(i) *Perséphone. The Rite of spring.*
(M) *** Virgin Dig. VCK7 91511-2 (2) [id.]. (i) Anne Fournet, Rolfe Johnson, Tiffin Boys' School Ch., LPO Ch.; LPO, Kent Nagano.

Stravinsky's two great evocations of spring make fascinating partners, but with the two works adding up to 83 minutes of music, Virgin has had to devise an ingenious answer to the problem of time-length. So it is that two separate discs are offered at mid-price in a single slim jewel-case, an attractive package when the performances have a refinement and rhythmic resilience which regularly marks Nagano's conducting. The only rival version of *Perséphone* – with its spoken narration described by the librettist, André Gide, as a 'melodrama in three scenes' – is the composer's own, and the contrasts are extreme. Where Stravinsky himself – at speeds consistently more measured than Nagano's – takes a rugged, square-cut view, Nagano, much lighter as well as more fleet, makes the work a far more atmospheric evocation of spring. The playing and singing are consistently more refined, and the modern digital recording gives a warm bloom, while the sung French sounds far more idiomatic from everyone. The narrration of Anne Fournet brings out all the beauty of Gide's words, with Anthony Rolfe Johnson free-toned in the taxing tenor solos. Nagano's reading of *The Rite of spring* has similar qualities. If it is less weightily barbaric than many, the springing of rhythm and the clarity and refinement of instrumental textures make it very compelling, with only the final *Danse sacrale* lacking something in dramatic bite.

(i) *Renard. The Soldier's tale;* (ii) *3 Pieces for clarinet solo; Ragtime;* (iii) *3 Japanese lyrics.*
(B) *** Hung. White Label HRC 078. Budapest Chamber Ens., András Mihály, (i) Gulyás, Keonch, Polgar, Bordas; (ii) Berkes; (iii) Adrienne Csengery.

Mihály's well-planned Stravinsky collection, colourfully performed and recorded, makes an outstanding bargain in Hungaroton's White Label series. The oddity is that *The Soldier's tale* has the full text of the entertainment, over half an hour long, but without any dramatic dialogue. Both in the dramatic scena, *Renard* – with four excellent soloists – and in *Ragtime*, the cimbalom plays a prominent part and, aptly in Budapest performances, Marta Fabian's brilliant, idiomatic playing of that Hungarian instrument is put well to the fore. The clear, silvery soprano, Adrienne Csengery, gives delightful performances of the *Japanese lyrics* and Kálmán Berkes is an agile clarinettist in the unaccompanied pieces.

OPERA

Stravinsky Edition, Volume 9: *The Rake's progress* (complete).
(M) *** Sony SM2K 46299 (2) [id.]. Young, Raskin, Reardon, Sarfaty, Miller, Manning, Sadler's Wells Op. Ch., RPO, composer.

The Rake's progress (complete).
**(*) Decca Dig. 411 644-2 (2) [id.]. Langridge, Pope, Walker, Ramey, Dean, Dobson, L. Sinf. Ch. & O, Chailly.

The Rake of Alexander Young is a marvellous achievement, sweet-toned and accurate and well characterized. In the choice of other principals, too, it is noticeable what store Stravinsky set by vocal precision. Judith Raskin makes an appealing Anne Trulove, sweetly sung if not particularly well projected dramatically. John Reardon too is remarkable more for vocal accuracy than for striking characterization, but Regina Sarfaty's Baba is marvellous on both counts. The Sadler's Wells Chorus sings with even greater drive under the composer than in the theatre, and the Royal Philharmonic play with a warmth and a fittingly Mozartian sense of style to match Stravinsky's surprisingly lyrical approach to his score. The CDs offer excellent sound, with the words remarkably clear and a nice balance between ambient atmosphere and clear projection of the singers.

Riccardo Chailly draws from the London Sinfonietta playing of a clarity and brightness to set the piece aptly on a chamber scale without reducing the power of this elaborately neo-classical piece. Philip Langridge is excellent as the Rake himself, very moving when Tom is afflicted with madness. Samuel Ramey as Nick, Stafford Dean as Trulove and Sarah Walker as Baba the Turk are all first rate, but Cathryn Pope's soprano as recorded is too soft-grained for Anne. Charming as the idea is of getting the veteran Astrid Varnay to sing Mother Goose, the result is out of style. The recording is exceptionally full and vivid but the balances are sometimes odd: the orchestra recedes behind the singers and the chorus sounds congested, with little air round the sound.

Suk, Josef (1874–1935)

Asrael Symphony, Op. 27.
❀ *** Chan. Dig. CHAN 9042; *ABTD 1593* [id.]. Czech PO, Bělohlávek.
*** Virgin VC7 91221-2; *VC7 91221-4* [id.]. RLPO, Pešek.

It is astonishing that a work of this stature has been so neglected outside Czechoslovakia. In its organization it owes a good deal to the 'cyclic' principle, fashionable at the end of the last century. A sense of numbness in the face of grief comes across, yet there is much that is fiery, vigorous and exciting. Asrael is the Angel of Death – hence the title – and touches real depths; but it is more than a moving human document, it is a great work.

Jiri Bělohlávek, the new principal conductor of the Czech Philharmonic, draws powerfully expressive playing from the orchestra in a work which in its five large-scale movements is predominantly slow. Next to Pešek's fine Liverpool performance, the speeds flow a degree faster and more persuasively, and the ensemble, notably of the woodwind, is even crisper, phenomenally so. It helps too that the sound is warmer, closer and more involving than the refined but more distant Virgin recording.

Pešek's Liverpool version has altogether greater sensitivity and imagination than the earlier Supraphon account from Vaclav Neumann, and the sympathy of the Liverpool players is very apparent, but there is no doubt that Bělohlávek's gutsier Czech performance has a greater sense of thrust and power, and for those coming new to this fine work it will be a revelation. Our previous Rosette, which was as much for the music as the earlier Virgin Classics performance, now passes on naturally to the splendid new Chandos disc.

A Fairy-tale, Op. 16; Praga (symphonic poem), Op. 26.
*** Sup. Dig. 10 3389-2 [id.]. Czech PO, Libor Pešek.

Suk's *A Fairy-tale* is a concert suite drawn from the incidental music to Julius Zeyer's fairy-tale drama, *Raduz and Nahulena.* The invention is full of charm and originality, and it is persuasively played here. On this compact disc it is coupled with *Praga*, a patriotic tone-poem reflecting a more public, out-going figure than *Asrael*, which was to follow it. Libor Pešek secures an excellent response from the Czech Philharmonic; the recordings, which date from 1981–2, are reverberant but good.

Fantasy in G min. (for violin and orchestra), *Op. 24.*
(B) *** Sup. 110601-2. Josef Suk, Czech PO, Ančerl – DVOŘÁK: *Violin concerto.* ***

Suk's *Fantasy* is a brilliant piece which relates to the traditional essays in violin wizardry as well as to the Czech nationalist tradition. The work has music of characteristic fantasy, though the rhetorical brilliance is equally strong. Suk's playing is refreshing and the orchestral accompaniment under Ančerl is no less impressive. Good remastered 1960s sound.

Fantastic Scherzo, Op. 25.
*** Chan. Dig. CHAN 8897; *ABTD 1508* [id.]. Czech PO, Bělohlávek – MARTINŮ: *Symphony No. 6;* JANÁČEK: *Sinfonietta.* ***

This captivating piece has invariably turned up as a fill-up for other Suk works, and this may have limited its dissemination. The playing of the Czech Philharmonic under Bělohávek is even finer than any of the earlier performances and it cannot be too strongly recommended, particularly in view of the excellence of the coupling.

Serenade for strings in E flat, Op. 6.
(BB) *** Naxos 8.550419 [id.]. Capella Istropolitana, Kr(e)chek – DVOŘÁK: *String serenade.* **(*)
*** Virgin Dig. VC7 91165-2; *VC 791165-4* [id.]. LCO, Warren-Green – DVOŘÁK; TCHAIKOVSKY: *Serenades.* **(*)

On Naxos an entirely delightful account of Suk's *Serenade*, which ought to be far better known. The innocent delicacy of the opening is perfectly caught and the charm of the dance movement which follows is just as winning. The *Adagio* is played most beautifully and then, with a burst of high spirits (and excellent ensemble), the finale bustles to its conclusion with exhilarating zest. The recording is first class, fresh yet full-textured, naturally balanced and transparent.

Warren-Green and his LCO also give a wonderfully persuasive account of Suk's *Serenade*, making obvious that its inspiration is every bit as vivid as in the comparable works of Dvořák and Tchaikovsky. One readily feels the added intensity, which this group's leader and conductor believes comes from performing (even in the recording studio) standing up. The gleaming radiance of tone in the opening *Andante* is matched by the sparkle of the following *Allegro ma non troppo e grazioso* which has much charm, the haunting nostalgia of the *Adagio* and the spirited joy of the closing *Allegro giocoso*. The recording, made in All Saints', Petersham, is well up to the standard of previous records from this group, fresh, full and natural without blurring from the ecclesiastical acoustic.

PIANO MUSIC

About Mother, Op. 28; Lullabies, Op. 33; 4 Piano pieces, Op. 7; Spring, Op. 22a; Summer, Op. 22b; Things lived and dreamed, Op. 30.
*** Chan. Dig. CHAN 9026/7 [id.]. Margaret Fingerhut.

This generous two-disc selection from Suk's piano music gives a delightfully varied idea of his musical personality. It is striking how the earliest works have a carefree, sweetly lyrical character, gentler than Dvořák but typically Czech. Then, after the death in 1904 and 1905 of his mentor, Dvǒrák, and his wife (Dvǒrák's daughter), even these fragmentary inspirations, like the massive *Asrael Symphony*, become sharp, sometimes even abrasive. The second disc brings the finest and most ambitious of the suites in which Suk generally collected his genre pieces, *Things lived and dreamed.* Lasting nearly 40 minutes, it consists of ten very varied, strikingly imaginative pieces in two groups of five. Each group ends with an elegy but also includes charmingly trivial pieces. Margaret Fingerhut proves a devoted advocate, playing with point and concentration, helped by full-ranging Chandos sound.

Sullivan, Arthur (1842–1900)

The Merchant of Venice (suite); *The Tempest* (incidental music).
(M) *** EMI CMS7 64412-2 (2). CBSO, Sir Vivian Dunn – *Ruddigore.* ***

The longer orchestral work, the suite of incidental music for *The Tempest*, dates from 1861, when the student composer was only nineteen. Not surprisingly it made him an overnight reputation, for it displays an astonishing flair and orchestral confidence. The *Introduction* may be melodramatic but it is memorably atmospheric too, and although some of the other items are conventional, the *Banquet dance* is charmingly scored and the *Dance of the Nymphs and Shepherds* is already anticipating *Iolanthe*. The shorter *Merchant of Venice* suite was composed five years later, and almost immediately the writing begins to anticipate the lively style which was so soon to find a happy marriage with Gilbert's words. The performance here is highly infectious, and the sound is first class, bright yet with plenty of depth and a spacious ambience. This makes a very sizeable bonus for a splendid account of *Ruddigore.*

(i) *Overtures: Cox and Box; Princess Ida; The Sorcerer;* (ii) *Overture in C (In Memoriam).*
(M) **(*) EMI CMS7 764409-2 (2). (i) Pro Arte O, Sargent; (ii) RLPO, Groves – *The Pirates of Penzance.* ***

This collects together the overtures from the operas not recorded by Sargent in his EMI series. The performances are characteristically bright and polished. *In Memoriam* is a somewhat inflated religious piece written for the 1866 Norwich Festival.

Overture Di Ballo.
(M) *** EMI CMS7 64400-2 (2). RLPO, Groves – *Iolanthe.* ***

Sullivan's gay, Italianate overture, felicitously scored, is nicely played by Grove and the Royal Liverpool Orchestra to makes a good bonus for Sargent's *Iolanthe*.

Overtures: *Di ballo; The Gondoliers; HMS Pinafore; Iolanthe; Patience; The Pirates of Penzance; Princess Ida; Ruddigore; The Sorcerer; The Yeomen of the Guard* (all arr. Geoffrey Toye).
*** Nimbus Dig. NI 5066 [id.]. SCO, Alexander Faris.

A well-played and well-recorded collection of Sullivan overtures. Mostly they are little more than pot-pourris, but *The Yeomen of the Guard* is an exception, and the gay *Di Ballo* is vivacious and tuneful and shows Sullivan's scoring at its most felicitous.

(i) *Pineapple Poll: ballet music* (arr. Mackerras); (ii) *Savoy dances* (arr. Robinson); (i) *Overtures: Iolanthe; Mikado.*
(M) **(*) EMI CDM7 63961-2; *EG 763961-4.* Pro Arte O, (i) John Hollingsworth; (ii) Stanford Robinson.

Hollingsworth offers a lively reading of *Pineapple Poll*, supported by good orchestral playing, and the slightly brash recorded quality quite suits the ebullience of the score. The upper register is over-bright but can be smoothed out. With its tuneful bonuses more smoothly done, this is enjoyable and quite good value for money.

Symphony in E (Irish).
(M) *** EMI CMS7 64406-2 (2). RLPO, Groves – *Patience.* ***

It seems a curious idea to couple *Patience* with Sullivan's *Irish symphony*. Yet it is a pleasing work, lyrical, with echoes of Schumann as much as the more predictable Mendelssohn and Schubert. The jaunty *Allegretto* of the third movement with its 'Irish' tune on the oboe is nothing less than haunting. Groves and the Royal Liverpool Philharmonic give a fresh and affectionate performance, and the CD transfer of the 1968 recording is generally well managed.

Songs: *The absent-minded beggar; The Dove song; Gone!; Let me dream again; The lost chord; The Marquis de Mincepie; Mary Morison; The moon in silent brightness; Shakespeare songs: O mistress mine; Orpheus with his lute; Willow song; St Agnes' Eve; Sweethearts; What does the little birdie say?; Winter.*
*** Conifer Dig. CDCFC 156; *MCFC 156* [id.]. Jeanne Ommerle, Sanford Sylvan, Gary Wedow.

It has taken a pair of American singers (with a pianist who is also chorus master of the Sante Fe Opera) to discover the delights of these Sullivan songs and bring them to our attention in an admirably planned recital which offers singing to catch their style superbly. The ballads have all the melodic resource of the Savoy Operas and the duet *Sweethearts* could almost have come from *Patience*, although it has an appropriate link with Victor Herbert in its added sentimentality. The Shakespeare settings are memorable, particularly the unexpected soaring line of *Orpheus with his lute*, though the gentle *Willow song* is equally lovely. *What does the little birdie say?* is a children's lullaby, while the splendid Kipling narrative of *The absent-minded beggar* reminds one of the repertoire Peter Dawson made famous. Jeanne Ommerle sings with full involvement with the words and her voice gives consistent pleasure in her simplicity of line and tonal beauty. Sanford Sylvan is very good, too, and, after opening restraint in *The lost chord*, then builds a resplendent climax, aided and abetted by spectacular accompaniment from the pianist, Gary Wedow; one understands how the Victorians could be bowled over by the sheer eloquence of the piece. Elsewhere the reverberant acoustic of the recording is less than ideal, but the words come over clearly and certainly there is plenty of bloom on the voices. A most involving and entertaining collection without one dull number.

OPERAS

As can be seen below, the two basic sets of recordings of the major Savoy operas, nearly all from Godfrey (on Decca) and Sargent (on EMI) are now back in the catalogue at mid-price. The Decca series usually has the advantage (or disadvantage, according to taste) of including the dialogue. EMI offers some orchestral bonuses and, in the case of *HMS Pinafore*, add *Trial by Jury* as well (as was the practice in the theatre in the heyday of the D'Oyly Carte Opera Company). Godfrey's Decca *Trial by Jury* is saved for inclusion with their outstanding *Yeomen of the Guard*. The Sargent version of *Trial by Jury* (with George Baker as the Judge) is by general consensus the best there is, if only by a small margin, and the EMI version of *Pinafore* is wonderfully fresh too, beautifully sung throughout, while the whole of the final scene is musically quite ravishing.

But the 1960 Godfrey set of this opera is very special indeed, and *HMS Pinafore* is in our view the finest of all the D'Oyly Carte stereo recordings. While Owen Brannigan, on EMI, without the benefit of dialogue conveys the force of Dick Deadeye's personality remarkably strongly, Donald Adams's assumption of the role on Decca (which does have the dialogue) is little short of inspired, and his larger-than-life characterization underpins the whole piece. The rest of the cast make a splendid team: Jean Hindmarsh is a totally convincing Josephine – she sings with great charm – and John Reed's Sir Joseph Porter is a delight. The choral singing is excellent, catching the music's full briny quality, and Isidore Godfrey conducts with marvellous spirit and lift. However, for those who opt for the EMI set – for the sake of *Trial by Jury* – there is an excellent, vivid set of highlights from the Decca recording which would make an essential supplement.

The D'Oyly Carte set of *The Gondoliers*, which suffered from fierce, edgy sound on its early transfer to CD, has now, we understand, been remastered and the quality brought up to Decca's usual high standard. The solo singing throughout is consistently good, the ensembles have plenty of spirit and the dialogue is for the most part well spoken. As a performance this is on the whole preferable to the Sargent account, if only because of the curiously slow tempo Sargent chooses for the *Cachucha*. However, on EMI there is still much to captivate the ear, and Owen Brannigan, a perfectly cast Don Alhambra, sings a masterly *No possible doubt whatever*. The age of the 1957 recording shows in the orchestra but the voices sound fresh and there is a pleasing overall bloom.

With *Iolanthe*, choice between the two alternatives is a case of swings and roundabouts. The 1960 Decca set was given added panache by the introduction of the Grenadier Guards Band into the *March of the Peers*. Mary Sansom is quite a convincing Phyllis, and if her singing has not the sense of style that Elsie Morison brings to the part, she is completely at home with the dialogue. Her discourse with the two Earls – portrayed to perfection by Donald Adams and Thomas Round – is sheer delight. Also Alan Styler makes a vivid and charming personal identification with the role of Strephon, an Arcadian shepherd, whereas John Cameron's dark timbre on EMI seems much less suitable for this role, even though he sings handsomely. However, on EMI the climax of Act I, the scene in which the Queen of the Fairies lays a curse on members of both Houses of Parliament, shows most excitingly what can be achieved with the 'full operatic treatment': this is a dramatic moment indeed. George Baker, too, is very good as the Lord Chancellor: the voice is fuller, more baritonal than John Reed's dryly whimsical delivery, yet he provides an equally individual characterization. Godfrey's conducting is lighter and more infectious than Sargent's in the Act I finale, but both performances offer much to delight the ear in the famous Trio of Act II with the Lord Chancellor and the two Earls.

The 1973 stereo remake of *The Mikado* by the D'Oyly Carte Company directed by Royston Nash is a complete success in every way and shows the Savoy tradition at its most attractive. It is a pity no dialogue is included, but the choral singing is first rate, and the glees are refreshingly done, polished and refined, yet with plenty of vitality. John Reed is a splendid Ko-Ko, Kenneth Sandford a vintage Pooh-Bah and Valerie Masterson a charming Yum-Yum. John Ayldon as the Mikado provides a laugh of terrifying bravura, and Lyndsie Holland is a formidable and commanding Katisha. The CD transfer is very fresh, like a coat of new paint; although the bright lighting has brought more sibilance, the words are exceptionally clear. The Sargent set, with its grand operatic style, brings some fine moments, especially in the finales to both Acts. Owen Brannigan is an inimitable Mikado and Richard Lewis sings most engagingly throughout as Nanki-Poo, while Elsie Morison is freshly persuasive as his young bride-to-be. All in all, there is much to enjoy here, but this remains very much a second choice.

Owen Brannigan was surely born to play the Sergeant of Police in *The Pirates of Penzance*, and he does so unforgettably in both the Decca and EMI sets. On Decca there is a considerable advantage in the inclusion of the dialogue, and here theatrical spontaneity is well maintained. Donald Adams, as the Pirate King, has a splendid gift for Gilbertian inflexion and some of his lines give as much pleasure as his powerfully characterized singing. John Reed's portrayal of the Major General is one of his strongest roles, while Valerie Masterson is an excellent Mabel. Her duet with Frederick, *Leave me not to pine alone*, is enchanting, sung very gently. Godfrey's conducting is as affectionate as ever, and one can hear him revelling in the many added touches of colour that are made possible when he has the RPO to play for him. The CD transfer has vividness and presence, even if there is a slight degree of edge on the voices at times. Sargent's version is great fun, too. Its star is George Baker, giving a new and individual portrayal of the

Major General. The opera takes a little while to warm up, but there is a much to enjoy here. On balance, the Decca set is to be preferred, for Brannigan is especially vivid, and the dialogue undoubtedly adds an extra the sense of the theatre.

Patience and *Ruddigore* were the two greatest successes of the Sargent series. Although there is no dialogue in *Patience*, there is more business than is usual in these EMI productions and a convincing theatrical atmosphere. Elsie Morison's Patience, George Baker's Bunthorne and John Cameron's Grosvenor are all admirably characterized, and the many concerted numbers beguile the ear. The extra card in the D'Oyly Carte hand is the dialogue, so important in this opera above all, with its spoken poetry; if Mary Sansom does not quite match her EMI counterpart, both Bunthorne and Grosvenor are well played, while the military numbers, led by Donald Adams in glorious voice, have an unforgettable vigour and presence. At the moment the Decca *Ruddigore* is out of the catalogue, but in any case the EMI set is musically superior. The whole performance is beautifully sung and Sargent's essentially lyrical approach emphasizes the associations of this delightful score with the music of Schubert. Pamela Bowden is a first-class Mad Margaret and her duet – after she has reformed – with Owen Brannigan has an irresistible gentility. The drama of the score is well managed too, and the CD transfer is first class. There is even an interesting bonus in Sullivan's Shakespearean incidental music. But here there is competition from the That's Entertainment set, which includes the original finale – see below.

Both recordings of *The Yeomen of the Guard*, Decca's and EMI's, are conducted by Sir Malcolm Sargent. Each has many merits. On EMI, all the solo singing is very persuasive indeed, and the presence of Owen Brannigan as Wilfred is very much a plus point, while Monica Sinclair is a memorable Dame Carruthers. In both versions the trios and quartets with which this score abounds are most beautifully warm and polished. But the later Decca account has marginally the finer recording and Sir Malcolm's breadth of approach is immediately apparent in the *Overture*. Both chorus and orchestra (the RPO) are superbly expansive and there is again consistently fine singing from all the principals (and especially from Elizabeth Harwood as Elsie). This Decca *Yeomen* is unreservedly a success, with its brilliant and atmospheric recording. In any case, the trump card is the inclusion of Godfrey's immaculately stylish and affectionate *Trial by Jury* with John Reed as the Judge.

The Gondoliers (complete; with dialogue).
(M) *** Decca 425 177-2 (2). Reed, Skitch, Sandford, Round, Styler, Knight, Toye, Sansom, Wright, D'Oyly Carte Op. Ch., New SO of L., Godfrey.

The Gondoliers (complete; without dialogue).
(M) **(*) EMI CMS7 64394-2 (2). Evans, Young, Brannigan, Lewis, Cameron, Milligan, Monica Sinclair, Graham, Morison, Thomas, Watts, Glyndebourne Festival Ch., Pro Arte O, Sargent.

HMS Pinafore (complete; with dialogue).
❀ (M) *** Decca 414 283-2; *414 283-4*. Reed, Skitch, Round, Adams, Hindmarsh, Wright, Knight, D'Oyly Carte Op. Ch., New SO of L., Godfrey.

HMS Pinafore (complete; without dialogue); *Trial by Jury*.
(M) *** EMI CMS7 64397-2 (2). George Baker, Cameron, Lewis, Brannigan, Milligan, Morison, Thomas, M. Sinclair, Glyndebourne Festival Ch., Pro Arte O, Sargent.

HMS Pinafore: highlights.
(B) *** Decca 436 145-2; *436 145-4* (from above D'Oyly Carte Opera recording; cond. Godfrey).

Iolanthe (complete; with dialogue).
(M) *** Decca 414 145-2; *414 145-4* (2). Sansom, Reed, Adams, Round, Sandford, Styler, Knight, Newman, D'Oyly Carte Op. Ch., Grenadier Guards Band, New SO, Godfrey.

Iolanthe (complete; without dialogue).
(M) *** EMI CMS7 64400-2 (2). George Baker, Wallace, Young, Brannigan, Cameron, M. Sinclair, Thomas, Cantelo, Harper, Morison, Glyndebourne Festival Ch., Pro Arte O, Sargent – *Di Ballo overture*. ***

The Mikado (complete; without dialogue).
(M) *** Decca 425 190-2 (2). Ayldon, Wright, Reed, Sandford, Masterson, Holland, D'Oyly Carte Op. Ch., RPO, Nash.
(M) **(*) EMI CMS7 644403-2 (2). Brannigan, Lewis, Evans, Wallace, Cameron, Morison, Thomas, J. Sinclair, M. Sinclair, Glyndebourne Festival Ch., Pro Arte O, Sargent.

The Mikado (complete, but without Overture).
❀ *** Telarc Dig. CD 80284 [id.]. Donald Adams, Rolfe Johnson, Suart, McLaughlin, Palmer, Van Allan, Folwell, Welsh Nat. Op. Ch. and O, Mackerras.

It is apt that Sir Charles Mackerras, who 40 years ago with his Sullivan-based ballet, *Pineapple Poll*, brought a breath of fresh air into the then copyright-bound world of G & S, should here offer the most scintillating recording of a Gilbert and Sullivan operetta ever put on disc. With the overture omitted (not Sullivan's work) and one of the stanzas in Ko-Ko's 'little list' song (with words unpalatable today), the whole fizzing performance is fitted on to a single, very well-filled disc. The full and immediate sound is a credit to Telarc's American engineers. The cast, with no weak link, is as starry as those in EMI's 'Glyndebourne' series of G and S recordings of thirty years ago, yet far more than Sir Malcolm Sargent on those earlier recordings, Mackerras is electrically sharp at brisk speeds, sounding totally idiomatic and giving this most popular of the G and S operettas an irresistible freshness at high voltage. The tingling vigour of Sullivan's invention is constantly brought out, with performances from the WNO Chorus and Orchestra at once powerful and refined. With that sharpness of focus Sullivan's parodies of grand opera become more than just witty imitations. So Katisha's aria at the end of Act II, with Felicity Palmer the delectable soloist, has a Verdian depth of feeling. It is good too to hear the veteran Savoyard, Donald Adams, as firm and resonant as he was in his D'Oyly Carte recording made no less than 33 years earlier. Let us hope this is to be the first of a series.

The Mikado: highlights.
(B) *** Decca 433 618-2; *433 618-4* [id.] (from above D'Oyly Carte Opera recording; cond. Nash).

Patience (complete; with dialogue).
(M) *** Decca 425 193-2 (2). Sansom, Adams, Cartier, Potter, Reed, Sandford, Newman, Lloyd-Jones, Toye, Knight, D'Oyly Carte Op. Ch. & O, Godfrey.

Patience (complete; without dialogue).
(M) *** EMI CMS7 64406-2 (2). Morison, Young, George Baker, Cameron, Thomas, M. Sinclair, Harper, Harwood, Glydebourne Festival Ch., Pro Arte O, Sargent – *Symphony*. ***

The Pirates of Penzance (complete; with dialogue).
(M) *** Decca 425 196-2; *414 286-4*. Reed, Adams, Potter, Masterson, Palmer, Brannigan, D'Oyly Carte Op. Ch., RPO, Godfrey.

The Pirates of Penzance (complete; without dialogue).
(M) *** EMI CMS7 64409-2 (2). George Baker, Milligan, Cameron, Lewis, Brannigan, Morison, Harper, Thomas, Sinclair, Glyndebourne Festival Ch., Pro Arte O, Sargent – *Overtures*. **(*)

Ruddigore (complete recording of original score; without dialogue).
*** That's Entertainment CDTER2 1128; *ZCTED 1128* [MCA MCAD2 11010]. Hill Smith, Sandison, Davies, Ayldon, Hillman, Innocent, Hann, Ormiston, Lawlor, New Sadler's Wells Op. Ch. & O, Simon Phipps.

What is exciting about the New Sadler's Wells production of *Ruddigore* is that it includes the original finale, created by the logic of Gilbert's plot which brought *all* the ghosts back to life, rather than just the key figure. The opera is strongly cast, with Marilyn Hill Smith and David Hillman in the principal roles and Joan Davies a splendid Dame Hannah, while Harold Innocent as Sir Despard and Linda Ormiston as Mad Margaret almost steal the show. Simon Phipps conducts brightly and keeps everything moving forward, even if his pacing is not always as assured as in the classic Sargent version. The recording is first class, with fine theatrical atmosphere.

Ruddigore (complete; without dialogue).
(M) *** EMI CMS7 64412-2 (2). Lewis, George Baker, Brannigan, Blackburn, Morison, Bowden, M. Sinclair, Harwood, Rouleau, Glyndebourne Festival Ch., Pro Arte O, Sargent – *Merchant of Venice; Tempest:* incidental music. ***

The Yeomen of the Guard (complete; without dialogue).
(M) *** EMI CMS7 64415-2 (2). Dowling, Lewis, Evans, Brannigan, Morison, M. Sinclair, Glyndebourne Festival Ch., Pro Arte O, Sargent.

(i) *The Yeomen of the Guard* (complete; without dialogue); (ii) *Trial by Jury*.
(M) *** Decca 417 358-2; *417 358-4*. Hood, J. Reed, Sandford, Adams, Raffell; (i) Harwood, Knight; (ii) Round; D'Oyly Carte Op. Ch.; (i) RPO, Sargent; (ii) ROHCG O, Godfrey.

'A Gilbert and Sullivan Gala': Arias, duets and trios from: *The Gondoliers; The Grand Duke; Haddon Hall; HMS Pinafore; Iolanthe; The Mikado; Patience; The Pirates of Penzance; Ruddigore; The Sorcerer; The Yeomen of the Guard.*
(M) *** EMI CDM7 64393-2 [id.]. Masterson, Armstrong, Tear, Luxon, Bournemouth Sinf., Alwyn; or N. Sinf., Hickox.

This superb collection combines the best part of two recitals of G & S, the first made by Valerie Masterson and Robert Tear with Kenneth Alwyn in 1982 and recorded at the Guildhall, Southampton, and the second, where the balance is even more realistic, in EMI's No. 1 Studio at Abbey Road, with Sheila Armstrong, Tear and Benjamin Luxon under the direction of Richard Hickox in 1984. The result is one of the most successful (and generous – nearly 73 minutes) anthologies of this repertoire ever put on disc. Quite apart from the excellence of the singing and the sparkling accompaniments, the programme is notable for the clever choice of material, with items from different operas engagingly juxtaposed instead of being just gathered together in sequence. The singing from the first group is particularly fine. Valerie Masterson's upper range is ravishingly fresh and free. It is a pity her *Pinafore* number had to be omitted, but the final cadence of *Leave me not to pine alone* (*Pirates*) is very touching, and she sings Yum-Yum's famous song from *The Mikado, The sun, whose rays*, with a captivating, ingenuous charm. Robert Tear too is in excellent form and his *A wandering minstrel* is wonderfully stylish, while *A magnet hung in a hardware shop* has fine sparkle. The *Prithee, pretty maiden* duet (also from *Patience*) is hardly less endearing. In the second recital it is the ensemble items that score, notably the duets from *Ruddigore, The Gondoliers* and the vivacious *Hereupon we're both agreed* from *The Yeomen of the Guard*; the star here is Benjamin Luxon. He is splendid in the principal novelty, *I've heard it said*, from *Haddon Hall*, a vintage Sullivan number even if the words are not by Gilbert, and he is left to end the concert superbly with a bravura account of *My name is John Wellington Wells* from *The Sorcerer*, and a splendidly timed, beguilingly relaxed account of *When you find you're a broken-down critter* from *The Grand Duke*, in which Richard Hickox and the Northern Sinfonia make the very most of Sullivan's witty orchestral comments.

'The best of Gilbert & Sullivan': excerpts from: *The Gondoliers; HMS Pinafore; Iolanthe; The Mikado; The Pirates of Penzance.*
(B) *** EMI CDZ7 62531-2; *LZ 762531-4*. Morison, Graham, Sinclair, Marjorie Thomas, Lewis, Young, George Baker, Cameron, Brannigan, Sir Geraint Evans, Milligan, Wallace, Glyndebourne Festival Ch., Pro Arte O, Sargent.

With a maximum amount of music included, this makes a fine bargain sampler for Sargent's (currently withdrawn) G & S series on EMI. The longest selection comes from *The Mikado* (with nine items included), not the strongest of the performances but with many felicities. The slow tempo for the *Cachucha* remains a curious drawback in the excerpts from *The Gondoliers*; but the items from *Iolanthe, The Pirates* and *Pinafore* have plenty of zest, and the lyrical singing is a pleasure throughout when the cast is so strong. The transfers are fresh and clear, with an abundance of ambience.

'Gilbert and Sullivan spectacular': Highlights from *The Gondoliers; HMS Pinafore; The Mikado; The Pirates of Penzance.*
(B) *** Pickwick PWK 1157 [id.]. Marion Studholme, Jean Allister, Edmund Bohan, Ian Wallace, English Chorale, L. Concert O, Marcus Dodds.

Though it is obviously not brand-new, and no hard information is provided about its provenance in the otherwise adequate documentation, we do not recall hearing this well-chosen 50-minute selection before. It is very enjoyable indeed. The artists are vividly projected in a theatrical ambience and words are crisp and clear, yet there is plenty of atmosphere. The performances are delightful, traditional yet individual. Marion Studholme sings very freshly, and her duet with the equally excellent tenor, Edmund Bohan, *Leave me not to pine alone* is very touching. The ensembles are sparkling and the small chorus is lively. But it is Ian Wallace who almost steals the show: as the Sergeant of Police in *Pirates* and Ko-Ko in *The Mikado* he is a delight and his beautifully articulate *When I was a lad* from *HMS Pinafore* is wonderfully full of wit. This disc is well worth having in its own right.

Highlights from: *The Gondoliers; HMS Pinafore; Iolanthe; The Mikado; The Pirates of Penzance; The Yeomen of the Guard.*
(B) **(*) CfP CD-CFP 4238; *TC-CFP 4238* [id.]. Soloists, Glyndebourne Festival Ch., Pro Arte O, Sargent.

Another attractive selection of highlights offering samples of six of Sargent's vintage EMI recordings. There is some distinguished solo singing and, if the atmosphere is sometimes a little cosy, there is a great deal to enjoy. The recordings have transferred well.

'The world of Gilbert and Sullivan': excerpts from: (i) *The Gondoliers; HMS Pinafore; Iolanthe;* (ii) *The Mikado;* (i) *The Pirates of Penzance;* (iii) *The Yeomen of the Guard.*
(B) *** Decca 430 095-2; *430 095-4.* Soloists, D'Oyly Carte Op. Co., New SO or RPO, (i) Godfrey; (ii) Nash; (iii) Sargent.

A quite admirable selection from the vintage series of Decca D'Oyly Carte recordings, with John Reed shining brightly as Koko. His 'Little list' song is wonderfully relaxed, and *Tit willow* is charming. He is equally good as Sir Joseph Porter, KCB, in *Pinafore*, where his splendid *I am the monarch of the sea* is preceded by some highly atmospheric stage business. Owen Brannigan's unforgettable portrayal of the Sergeant of Police is demonstrated in the excerpts from *The Pirates of Penzance* (as is Valerie Masterson's charming Mabel), and two of the most delectable items are the Second Act trios from *Pinafore* and *Iolanthe*, both liltingly infectious. The recording has fine atmosphere and presence throughout; *The Gondoliers*, however, betrays the same slightly degraded treble response of the complete recording. But overall, with 62 minutes of music offered, this is a real bargain which will give much delight.

Suppé, Franz von (1819–95)

Overtures: (i) *Beautiful Galatea;* (ii) *Boccaccio; Fatinitza;* (i) *Jolly robbers; Light cavalry; Morning, noon and night in Vienna; Poet and peasant; Pique dame.*
(M) ** EMI CDM7 64196-2; *EG 764196-4.* (i) Hallé O, Barbirolli (stereo); (ii) LPO, Sir Adrian Boult (mono).

Overtures: *Beautiful Galatea; Boccaccio; Light cavalry; Morning, noon and night in Vienna; Pique dame; Poet and peasant.*
(M) *** Mercury 434 309-2 [id.]. Detroit SO, Paul Paray – AUBER: *Overtures.* *** ❀

These two collections of favourite Suppé overtures make a fascinating comparison. Both were recorded by Mercury engineers in the mid- and late 1950s, the Hallé in the Manchester Free Trade Hall, the LPO (in excellent, 1955 mono, but sounding very like early stereo) at Walthamstow, and the Detroit Symphony at Cass Technical High School, producing not so warmly flattering a sound as the Old Orchestra Hall, but still offering sophisticated quality, brightly detailed yet quite full, as remastered by Wilma Cozart Fine. The EMI remastering of the Hallé recordings is altogether brasher, but then Barbirolli's presentation, with adrenalin running free is brasher too. The orchestra is alert and displays considerable virtuosity at times, but the immediacy of the sound exposes the sometimes mannered string vibrato and playing which is not always immaculate.There is a great deal of excitement of course, and the conductor's sense of style (in the shaping of the *Galatea* waltz for instance) avoids vulgarity. But Boult's mellower approach to *Boccaccio* and *Fatinitza* brings a greater degree of finesse from the LPO.

When one turns to Paray, however, one discovers a verve and exhilaration that are wholly Gallic in spirit. His chimerical approach to *Beautiful Galatea* (with a wonderfully luminous passage from the Detroit strings near the very opening) is captivating, and the bravura violin playing in *Light Cavalry* is remarkably deft. With its splendid Auber coupling this is one of Mercury's most desirable reissues.

Overtures: *Beautiful Galathea; Fatinitza; Flotte Bursche; Jolly robbers; Light Cavalry; Morning, noon and night in Vienna; Pique dame; Poet and peasant. March: O du mein Österreich.*
(BB) **(*) LaserLight Dig. 15 611 [id.]. Hungarian State Op. O, János Sándor.

Sándor's LaserLight collection is very generous and the Hungarian State Opera Orchestra know just how to play this repertoire: the zigeuner section in the middle of *Light Cavalry* is most winning, while the cello solo in *Morning, noon and night* has an attractive, romantic simplicity. There is plenty of sparkle and the small group of first violins ensures that the ensemble is clean and agile in the music's racier moments. Sándor offers two extra novelties in *Flott Bursche* (which brings an amiable quotation of *Gaudeamus igitur*) and a vivid Viennese-style march. The digital recording is basically full-bodied but has brilliance too, and this is a real bargain.

Overtures: *Beautiful Galathea; Fatinitza; Jolly robbers; Light cavalry; Morning, noon and night in Vienna; Pique dame; Poet and peasant.*
*** Decca Dig. 414 408-2 [id.]. Montreal SO, Dutoit.

Dutoit's pacing is splendid, combining warmth and geniality with brilliance and wit, as in the closing *galop* of *Fatinitza.* The orchestral playing is admirably polished, the violins sounding comfortable even in the virtuoso passages of *Light cavalry*, one of the most infectious of the performances here. It is difficult to imagine these being bettered, while the Decca sound is superb, well up to the usual Montreal standards.

Overtures: *Beautiful Galathea; Jolly robbers; Light cavalry; Morning, noon and night in Vienna; Pique dame; Poet and peasant.*
*** BMG/Eurodisc RD 69037. RPO, Gustav Kuhn.

Kuhn's performances are like no others. He takes this music very seriously indeed, lavishing care over every detail. Tempi are spacious, consistently slower than normal, but the effect is not to rob the music of vitality, merely to add to its stature. In the lyrical sections he conjures the most beautiful, expansive playing from the RPO, yet he can be racy in the galops, while not rushing the music off its feet. *Beautiful Galathea* is a striking example of this approach, with the gentle waltz theme played with great elegance, yet retaining its light, rhythmic lilt. *Morning, noon and night* is superb and the opening of *Poet and peasant* sounds wonderfully rich and sonorous, and it has a remarkable dignity too. It is a pity that the programme is not generous, but this disc makes up in quality for anything it may lack in quantity. The richly upholstered recording, made in St Barnabas' Church, London, seems exactly right for the music-making.

Overtures: *Fatinitza; Die Frau Meisterin; Der Gascogner; Die Irrfahrt um's Glück; Juanita; Das Modell; Wiener-Jubel.*
*** BMG/RCA Dig. RD 69226. RPO, Gustav Kuhn.

Gustav Kuhn's second collection of Suppé overtures is as distinctive as the first. It is also made more attractive by its concentration on novelties, with three items entirely new to the CD catalogue. With several others it conflicts with Marriner's even more desirable collection, but for many the fact that it duplicates none of the 'famous four' included on virtually every Suppé disc, will be an added enticement. As before Kuhn seeks to remove any suggestion of cheapness from the music, and these are performances of breadth and stature. While they do not have the unbuttoned gusto of some, there is no lack of vitality and much delicacy of detail. *Fatinitza* develops a delectable lilt in its main theme and in *Wiener-Jubel* Kuhn underlines the contrast between the jovial brass and the delicate flute passage which soon follows. He is in his element in the powerfully solemn opening of *Die Irrfahrt um's Glück*, with its magical/mystical portents, and he finds much to charm in the ladies, *Donna Juanita* and *Das Modell*, the score of which was found in the composer's effects after his death. Full, resonant sound, made at Abbey Road, but so strong is the influence of the conductor that this is very like a German recording, made say, in the Leipzig Gewandhaus.

Overtures: *Die Frau Meisterin; Die Irrfahrt um's Glück; Light cavalry; Morning, noon and night in Vienna; Pique Dame; Poet and Peasant; Tantalusqualen; Wiener-Jubel (Viennese Jubilee).*
❀ *** EMI Dig. CDC7 54056-2 [id.]; *EL 754056-4.* ASMF, Marriner.

Marriner's new collection of Suppé *Overtures* goes straight to the top of the list. It is expansively recorded in EMI's No. 1 Studio and, played up to concert volume on big speakers, it produces the most spectacular demonstration quality. The sound has bloom, a wide amplitude, plenty of sparkle and a natural presence. This is just the disc to confound those who decry digital recording – there is all the opulence of the best analogue sound, with more realistic definition. The performances have tremendous exuberance and style: this is one of Marriner's very best records. The established warhorses come up splendidly: the introductions are given plenty of breadth and dignity, *Poet and Peasant* especially. *Pique Dame* has fine, gutsy excitement, while in the similarly lively *Light cavalry*, Marriner halves the tempo at the end to bring the fanfare tune back very broadly. The novelties are delightful. *Die Irrfahrt um's Glück* – concerned with magical goings-on – has a massively portentous opening, superbly realized here; *Die Frau*

Meisterin produces a deliciously jiggy waltz tune, and *Wiener-Jubel*, after opening with resplendent fanfares, is as racy as you could wish. Not to be missed.

Overtures: *Light cavalry; Morning, noon and night in Vienna; Poet and peasant.*
**(*) DG 415 377-2 [id.]. BPO, Karajan – ROSSINI: *Overtures.* **(*)

Karajan's performances are taken from a 1970 collection and are coupled with four Rossini overtures. The playing is swaggeringly brilliant, but the sound is just a little fierce at fortissimo level, although the overall balance is warm and natural.

Svendsen, Johan Severin (1840–1911)

Romance in G, Op. 26.
(BB) *** Naxos Dig. 8.550329 [id.]. Dong-Suk Kang, Slovak (Bratislava) RSO, Adrian Leaper – HALVORSEN: *Air Norvégien* etc.; SIBELIUS: *Violin concerto;* SINDING: *Légende.* ***

Svendsen's once-popular *Romance in G* is otherwise available only in Grumiaux's version from the 1960s. Dong-Suk Kang plays it without sentimentality but with full-hearted lyricism. The balance places him a little too forward, but the recording is very satisfactory.

Symphonies Nos. 1–2; 2 Swedish folk-melodies, Op. 27.
*** BIS Dig. CD 347 [id.]. Gothenburg SO, Neeme Järvi.

Svendsen excelled (where Grieg did not) in the larger forms and, as befits a conductor, was a master of the orchestra. Listening to the two symphonies, one can't help feeling regret that his creative fires burned themselves out and that, after the famous *Romance* for violin and orchestra, he became what we would call nowadays a 'star' conductor. The *D major Symphony* is a student work of astonishing assurance and freshness, in some ways even more remarkable than the *B flat*. Neeme Järvi is a splendid guide to this terrain; these are first-class performances, sensitive and vital, and the excellent recordings earn them a strong recommendation.

Sviridov, Yuri (born 1915)

Oratorio pathétique.
(*) Koch Dig. 3-7017-2 [id.]. Vassilev, Bulgarian R. & TV Ch. & O, Andreev – SHOSTAKOVICH: *Execution of Stepan Razin.* (*)

Yuri (or Georgy) Sviridov was a favourite pupil of Shostakovich and his uneventful *Oratorio pathétique* (1959), to words of Mayakovsky, enjoyed some success in the Soviet Union in the 1960s and was recorded on LP. It disappointed then, and the passage of time has not improved it. Very thin and insubstantial stuff, which is neither performed nor recorded particularly persuasively.

Sweelinck, Jan (1562–1621)

Ballo del Granduca; Echo fantasia; Engelsche Fortuyn; Puer nobis nascitur.
*** Chan. Dig. CHAN 0514; *EBTD 0514* [id.]. Piet Klee (organ of St Laurens Church, Alkmaar) – BUXTEHUDE: *Collection.* ***

It is fascinating to have Sweelinck's music, played on a superb Dutch organ, juxtaposed with that of Buxtehude, who was born sixteen years after Sweelinck died and was a direct onward link with Bach. Sweelinck lived during the Dutch Golden Age and was a contemporary of Rembrandt. His music is colourful and appealing, and it could hardly be better represented than in this engaging 'suite' of four contrasted pieces, three of which are based on melodies by others. The first as played here derives from an English ballad, *Fortune my foe*, and will sound familiar to many ears. Piet Klee is a very sympathetic advocate and he is given a recording of demonstration standard.

Szymanowski, Karol (1882–1937)

Symphonies Nos. 1 in F min., Op. 15; 2 in B flat, Op. 19.
** Marco Polo Dig. 8.223249 [id.]. Polish State PO, Stryja.

Neither of Szymanowski's early symphonies is characteristic. The *First* dates from 1906–7 and is incomplete: only the outer movements, an allegro lasting about 11 minutes and a finale of about 9½, survive. As Jim Samson says in his fine monograph on Szymanowski's music, the problem is not simply the intricacy of the contrapuntal working itself but Szymanowski's apparent compulsion to saturate the texture with further elaborate accompaniments. It is undoubtedly a congested and derivative score – as, for that matter, is the more familiar *Symphony No. 2*, which leaves no doubt as to the composer's interest in Strauss and Reger. The Dorati recording (Decca) does greater justice to the complex textures of this score, but nevertheless this is well balanced and well played.

Symphonies Nos. 2, Op. 19; (i) *3 (Song of the night), Op. 27.*
(M) *** Decca Dig. 425 625-2 [id.]. (i) Ryszard Karczykowski, Jewell Ch.; Detroit SO, Dorati (with BARTÓK: *2 Pictures* ***).

The *Second* is not as rewarding a score as the *Third*, but it is unusual formally: there are only two movements, the second being a set of variations culminating in a fugue. The influences of Strauss and Scriabin are clearly audible and not altogether assimilated. *The Song of the night* is one of the composer's most beautiful scores, and much of its heady, intoxicated – and intoxicating – atmosphere is captured here, together with its extraordinarily vivid colouring and sense of rapture; the detail and opulence of the orchestral textures are fully revealed and the chorus is clear and well balanced. A most valuable reissue, and the Bartók coupling is apt, though here the recording has an analogue master.

(i) *Symphony No. 3 (Song of the Night);* (ii) *Symphony No. 4 (Sinfonia concertante); Concert overture.*
**(*) Marco Polo Dig. 8.223290 [id.]. (i) Ochman, Polish State Philharmonic Ch.; (ii) Taduesz Zmudzinski, Katowice Polish State PO, Karol Stryja.

The Marco Polo version of the *Third Symphony* (but not the *Fourth*) has the advantage of good, well-detailed sound in a resonant hall. The recordings are very recent (1988–9) and Karol Stryja succeeds in getting plenty of atmosphere in No. 3 (not as much as Rowicki but more than Dorati). He, too, uses a tenor rather than a soprano, but his choir is not first class. The *Sinfonia concertante* is not ideally balanced as a recording (the acoustic is too reverberant and the image is not always well focused) but the pianist, Taduesz Zmudzinski, is at least not too forward and he plays with refinement and sensitivity, as witness the opening of the *Andante*, which is quite magical. This is the best stereo *Sinfonia concertante* to date. The Straussian *Concert overture* makes a useful makeweight, though the recording is over-resonant and the balance synthetic.

String quartets Nos. 1 in C, Op. 37; 2, Op. 56.
❀ *** Denon Dig. CO 79462 [id.]. Carmina Qt – WEBERN: *Slow movement for string quartet.* *** ❀
*** Olympia OCD 328 [id.]. Varsovia Qt – LUTOSLAWSKI: *Quartet;* PENDERECKI: *Quartet No. 2.* ***

Ten years separate the two Szymanowski *String quartets*, whose neglect on record over the years by non-native Polish quartets has been grievous. Amends are amply made by this newcomer, played by the Carmina Quartet. This is outstanding music-making and is recorded with the utmost realism and fidelity. The opening of the *Second* has always seemed like being in a magical moonlit landscape listening to the Ravel quartet in the distance, and the Carmina succeed in evoking this whispered dreamlike quality to perfection.

The *First Quartet* is a beautifully wrought three-movement piece. It has a great deal of exposed and demanding writing, which the Varsovia Quartet play with impeccable intonation and splendid sonority. Theirs is a subtle and deeply felt performance, and the same must be said of their account of No. 2. Again the heady perfume and exotic luxuriance of the *Third Symphony* and the two *Violin concertos* can be discerned in this more monochrome medium; however, the finale has slight overtones of Bartók. There are glorious things in both works, and the Varsovia play marvellously throughout. However, the Carmina performances are finer still.

Mythes, Op. 30; Kurpian folk song; King Roger: Roxana's aria (both arr. Kochanski).
❀ (M) *** DG 431 469-2; *431 469-4*. Kaja Danczowska, Krystian Zimerman – FRANCK: *Violin sonata*. ***

The violinist Kaja Danczowska, a pupil of Eugenia Uminska and David Oistrakh, brings vision and poetry to the ecstatic, soaring lines of the opening movement of *Mythes*, *The Fountains of Arethusa*. Her intonation is impeccable, and she has the measure of these other-worldly, intoxicating scores. There is a sense of rapture here that is totally persuasive, and Krystian Zimerman plays with a virtuosity and imagination that silence criticism. An indispensable issue.

Violin sonata in D min., Op. 9; Mythes, Op. 30; Nocturne and tarantella, Op. 28.
*** Chan. Dig. CHAN 8747; *ABTD 1386* [id.]. Lydia Mordkovitch, Marina Gusk-Grin.

Violin sonata in D min., Op. 9; Berceuse; Chant de Kurpie; Chant de Roxane; Danse des Montagnards; Mythes; Romance in D.
** Chant du Monde LDC 278 997 [id.]. Krzysztof Janocicz, Krystyna Borucinska.

The *Violin sonata in D minor* is an early work, very much in the received tradition; but with the *Mythes* and the *Nocturne and tarantella* the world of Brahms and Franck has completely gone and we are in a totally different and wholly individual sound-world. Lydia Mordkovitch is ideally attuned to this sensibility and plays both the *Sonata* and the later works beautifully, and she is sensitively partnered by Marina Gusk-Grin. This can be recommended, though this account of the *Mythes* does not displace Kaja Danczowska and Krystian Zimerman; moreover there would have been room for the *Romance in D major*, Op. 23, and the Konchański transcriptions.

Krzysztof Janocicz and Krystyna Borucinska on Chant du Monde offer a more generous programme. These are thoughtful and intelligent performances, rather let down by an unglamorous and unsympathetic recording acoustic.

PIANO MUSIC

Études, Op. 4; Fantasy, Op. 14; Masques, Op. 34; Métopes, Op. 29.
*** Hyp. Dig. CDA 66409; *KA 66409* [id.]. Dennis Lee.

Études, Op. 4; Masques, Op. 34; Mazurkas, Opp. 50 & 62.
* Delos D/CD 1002 [id.]. Carol Rosenberger.

There is something in the oriental sensibility which responds to Szymanowski, and the Malaysian-born pianist Dennis Lee not only encompasses the technical hurdles of *Masques* and *Métopes* with dazzling virtuosity but also provides the keenest artistic insights. His Hyperion CD is quite simply the finest record of Szymanowski's piano music to have appeared to date; he conveys the exoticism and hothouse atmosphere of these pieces and commands all the refinement of colour and sensitivity to dynamic nuance that this repertoire calls for; moreover he handles the early Chopinesque *Études* and the *Fantasy* with much the same feeling for characterization and artistry. The Hyperion sound is very good indeed.

Carol Rosenberger's Delos collection is not in this league either artistically or as a recording. The recording comes from the 1970s and is not particularly good.

VOCAL MUSIC

(i) *Demeter, Op. 37b; Litany to the Virgin Mary, Op. 59;* (ii) *Penthesilea, Op. 18;* (iii) *Stabat Mater;* (iv) *Veni Creator, Op. 57.*
*** Marco Polo Dig. 8.223293 [id.]. (i) Roma Owsinska; (ii) Anna Malewicz-Madej; (iii) Jadwiga Gadulanka, Krystina Szostek-Radkova, Andrzej Hiolski; (iv) Barbara Zagórzanka; Polish State PO & Ch., Katowice, Karol Stryja.

Szymanowski's *Stabat Mater* is not only one of his greatest achievements but one of the greatest choral works of the present century. This welcome account has the advantage of highly sensitive conducting and an excellent response from the orchestra, but some of the solo singing is less distinguished, and Jadwiga Gadulanka's intonation is less than perfect. The *Litany to the Virgin Mary* is another late work of great poignancy; but *Demeter*, composed not long after the *Violin concerto* and the *Third Symphony*, has the same exotic, almost hallucinatory textures that distinguish these works. It is all heady and intoxicating stuff, and not to be missed by those with a taste for this wonderful composer.

(i) *3 Fragments of the poems by Jan Kasprowicz, Op. 5;* (ii) *Love songs of Hafiz, Op. 24;* (iii) *Songs of the fairy-tale princess, Op. 31;* (iv) *Songs of the infatuated muezzin, Op. 42.*
*** Schwann Dig. CD 314 001 [id.]. (i) Krystyna Szostek-Radkova; (ii) Krystyna Rorbach; (iii) Izabella Klosińska; (iv) Barbara Zagórzanka, Polish Nat. Op. O, Satanowski.

Szymanowski's vocal output has been virtually ignored until quite recently. It is really well worth taking the trouble to explore it. The Schwann and Marco Polo discs have the advantage of presenting these songs in their orchestral form. In the *Songs of the fairy-tale princess*, one feels that Szymanowski must have known Stravinsky's *Le Rossignol* – Izabella Klosińska certainly sings like one. All the singing is very good, but Barbara Zagórzanka in the imaginative *Songs of the infatuated muezzin* deserves special mention. Satanowski achieves marvellously exotic and heady atmosphere throughout, and the recording is excellent.

(i) *3 Fragments of the poems by Jan Kasprowicz, Op. 5;* (ii) *Love songs of Hafiz, Op. 24;* (iii) *Songs of the fairy-tale princess, Op. 31;* (iv) *Songs of the infatuated muezzin, Op. 42;* (v) *King Roger: Roxana's Song.*
**(*) Marco Polo Dig. 8.223294. (i) Anna Málewicz-Madej; (ii & iv) Ryszard Minkiewicz; (iii) Jadwiga Gadulanka; (v) Barbara Zagórzanka; Katowice Polish State PO, Karol Stryja.

On Marco Polo, both the *Songs of the infatuated muezzin* and the *Love songs of Hafiz* are sung by a tenor (Ryszard Minkiewicz) with impressive insight, but the 1989 recording is more resonant and does not flatter him. Jadwiga Gadulanka is hardly less impressive than Klosińska in the extraordinary *Songs of the fairy-tale princess* and one would be hard put to choose between them. What fantastic pieces they are, and how well Stryja and the Katowice orchestra support her. Barbara Zagórzanka sings the famous *Chant de Roxane* beautifully, and both she and Anna Málewicz-Madej in the Kasprowicz songs are very well balanced.

STAGE WORKS

(i) *Harnasie, Op. 55;* (ii) *Mandragora, Op. 43.*
*** Schwann Musica Mundi/Koch Dig. 311064. (i) Jozef Stépień; (ii) Paulus Raptus; (i) Polish Nat. Op. Ch.; Polish Nat. Op. O, Robert Satanowski.

Robert Satanowski's version of Szymanowski's choral ballet, *Harnasie*, is the best so far. It is an opulent score and, like the Op. 50 *Mazurkas*, is the product of the composer's encounter with the folk music of the Gorá mountains. It occupied Szymanowski for the best part of a decade but is rarely heard outside Poland, for it calls for large musical forces, a tenor soloist, chorus and orchestra – and a large *corps de ballet*, all for 35 minutes. It is richly coloured and luxuriant in texture and has a powerfully heady atmosphere. Full justice is done to its opulence and character in this excellent performance. *Mandragora* is a much slighter and less characteristic piece, dating from 1920. It is a harlequinade for chamber forces, designed for a performance of Molière's *Le bourgeois gentilhomme*, not dissimilar in character to the Prokofiev of *Love for three oranges*. The performance is far more persuasive than the earlier version by Antoni Wit that appeared in the centenary year. Both works are very well served by the engineers. A most valuable addition to the catalogue.

(i) *King Roger* (opera; complete); (ii) *Harnasie (The Highland Robbers)* (ballet pantomime), *Op. 55.*
*** Olympia OCD 303A/B [id.]. (i) Hiolski, Rumowska, Nikodem, Pustelak, Dabrowski, Malewicz-Madey, Polish Pathfinders' Union Children's Ch.; (ii) Bachleda; (i; ii) Warsaw Nat. Op. House Ch. & O; (i) Mierzejewski; (ii) Wodiczko.

These two CDs accommodate Szymanowski's masterpiece, the opera *King Roger*, and his last stage-work, the ballet *Harnasie*. Both recordings date from the mid-1960s; they first appeared here, on the Muza label, in very inferior LPs which sounded as if they were made from dog biscuits. The present transfer has made a magnificent job of the originals, which sound strikingly detailed and rich. *King Roger* is the product of Szymanowski's fascination with eastern mysticism and Arab culture. It is set in twelfth-century Sicily and its opening scene, at Mass in the Cathedral of Palermo, is music of awesome beauty. The sense of ecstasy he evokes is intoxicating, and the complex textures and unparalleled wealth of colour he has at his command are impressive by any standards. The Dionysiac atmosphere will be familiar to those who know *The Song of the night* and the *First Violin concerto*. Andrzej Hiolski is a more than adequate Roger and Hanna Rumowska an excellent Roxane. The whole cast is dedicated and the extensive forces involved, including a children's choir and a large orchestra and chorus, respond to the direction of Mieczyslaw Mierzejewski with fervour. It is a pity that Rowicki's later account of *Harnasie*, made in the mid-1970s, could not have been chosen in preference to this earlier version, which runs to about 25 minutes, whereas the whole ballet takes about 34. Not that there are any serious inadequacies here, for the playing and singing are totally committed and do justice to its hedonistic nationalism. An indispensable set for all lovers of this composer.

Taffanel, (Claude) Paul (1844–1908)

Wind quintet in G min.
*** Sony Dig. CD 45996. Ens. Wien-Berlin – NIELSEN: *Wind quintet.* ***

Taffanel played an important part in the rehabilitation of the flute in late nineteenth-century French music; he composed a good deal of polished music for wind instruments. This quintet is an urbane, expertly fashioned piece by a musician of obvious culture who knows how to pace the flow of his ideas. The Ensemble Wien-Berlin play it with the utmost persuasion and charm, but this is a very lightweight companion to the Nielsen masterpiece.

Tallis, Thomas (c. 1505–85)

Anthems: *Blessed are those that be undefiled; Christ, rising again; Hear the voice and prayer; If ye love me; A new commandment; O Lord, in Thee is all my trust; O Lord, give thy holy spirit; Out from the deep; Purge me; Remember not, O Lord God; Verily, verily I say: 9 Psalm Tunes for Archbishop Parker's Psalter.*
*** Gimell Dig. CDGIM 007; *1585T-07* [id.]. Tallis Scholars, Phillips.

This disc collects the complete English anthems of Tallis and is thus a valuable complement to the discs listed below. Here, of course, women's voices are used instead of boys', but the purity of the sound they produce is not in question, and the performances could hardly be more committed or more totally inside this repertoire. Strongly recommended.

Absterge Domine; Candidi facti sunt; Nazareri; Derelinquat impius; Dum transsiset sabbatum; Gaude gloriosa Dei Mater; Magnificat and Nunc dimittis; Salvator mundi.
*** CRD CRD 3429; *CRDC 4129* [id.]. New College, Oxford, Ch., Higginbottom.

The performances by the Choir of New College, Oxford – recorded in the splendid acoustic of the College Chapel – are eminently well prepared, with good internal balance, excellent intonation, ensemble and phrasing. The *Gaude gloriosa* is one of Tallis's most powerful and eloquent works. It has been suggested that it was intended to glorify Queen Mary as well as the Virgin Mary. An invaluable addition to the Tallis discography, and excellently recorded.

Derelinquat impius; Ecce tempus idoneum; In jejunio et fletu; In manus tuas; O nata lux; Salvator mundi; (ii) *Sancte Deus;* (i) *Spem in alium* (40-part motet); *Te lucis ante terminum I & II; Veni Redemptor gentium;* (ii) *Videte miraculum; Organ lesson.*
(M) **(*) Decca 433 676-2 [id.]. King's College, Cambridge, Ch., Willcocks; (i) with Cambridge University Musical Society; Langdon; (ii) Andrew Davis.

The King's College Choir are in their element for this music, written for Waltham Abbey and the Chapel Royal. The highlight of the programme is the magnificent forty-part motet, *Spem in alium*, in which the Cambridge University Musical Society joins forces with Kings. But the simpler hymn settings are no less impressive. The two other motets, *Sanctus Deus* and *Videte miraculum*, like *Spem in alium*, organ accompanied, are less well balanced, giving over prominence to the trebles, but the young Andrew Davis provides an excellent performance of the *Lesson* for organ. The recording is natural and atmospheric, but the inner strands of the forty-part motet are just a little blurred by the King's acoustic.

Audivi vocem de celo a 4; Candidi facti sunt Nazarei eius a 5; Dum transisset sabbatum a 5; Hodie nobis celorum rex a 4; Homo quidam fecit cenam magnam a 6; Honor, virtus et potestas a 5; In pace in idipsum a 4; Loquebantur variis linguis a 7; Spem in alium a 40; Videte miraculum a 6.
*** EMI Dig. CDC7 49555-2 [id.]. Taverner Ch. and Cons., Andrew Parrott.

Gaude gloriosa Dei Mater a 6; In jejunio et fletu a 5; Lamentations of Jeremiah I and II a 5; Miserere nostri a 7; O nata lux de lumine a 5; O sacrum convivium a 5; Salvator mundi I and II a 5; Suscipe, quaeso Domine a 7; Te lucis ante terminum (Procol recedant somnia) I a 5.
*** EMI Dig. CDC7 49563-2 [id.]. Taverner Ch. and Cons., Andrew Parrott.

Parrott's two discs of the Latin church music of Tallis are warmly recommendable, a superb collection. The Taverner style is brighter and more abrasive than we are used to in this often ethereal music, but, quite apart from the scholarly justification, the polyphonic cohesion of the writing comes out the more tellingly. The first of the two discs is the obvious one to investigate initially, containing as it does Tallis's most elaborate and most celebrated choral-piece, the 40-part motet, *Spem in alium*, as well as *Videte miraculum* and *Dum transisset sabbatum* – almost as extended in argument. The second of the two discs has the two magnificent *Lamentations of Jeremiah*, as well as an even more expansive motet which Tallis wrote early in his career, *Gaude gloriosa Dei Mater.*

Gaude gloriosa; Loquebantur variis linguis; Miserere nostri; Salvator mundi, salva nos, I and II; Sancte Deus; Spem in alium (40-part motet).
❀ *** Gimell CDGIM 006; *1585T-06* [id.]. Tallis Scholars, Phillips.

Within the admirably suitable acoustics of Merton College Chapel, Oxford, the Tallis Scholars give a thrilling account of the famous 40-part motet, *Spem in alium*, in which the astonishingly complex polyphony is spaciously separated over a number of point sources, yet blending as a satisfying whole to reach a massive climax. The *Gaude gloriosa* is another much recorded piece, while the soaring *Sancte Deus* and the two very contrasted settings of the *Salvator mundi* are hardly less beautiful. The vocal line is beautifully shaped throughout, the singing combines ardour with serenity, and the breadth and depth of the sound is spectacular.

Lamentations of Jeremiah. Motets: *Absterge domine; Derelinquat impius; In jejunio et fletu; In manus tuas; Mihi autem nimis; O sacrum convivium; O nata lux de lumine; O salutaris hostia; Salve intemerata virgo.*
*** Gimell Dig. CDGIM 025; *1385T-25* [id.]. Tallis Scholars, Peter Phillips.

With purity their watchword, the Tallis Scholars, using women singers in the upper parts, have established their distinctive style built on flawless ensemble and matching. This, the third of their discs devoted to their eponymous composer, is centred on the two great settings of the *Lamentations*. They have often been recorded before, but never more beautifully than here, performances that give total security. As well as the eight fine motets, the collection also has a rare Marian antiphon, *Salve intemerata*, that is among Tallis's most sustained inspirations. Duets, trios and sections for full choir are freely varied over the span of nearly 20 minutes. Clear, atmospheric recording of striking tangibility.

Taneyev, Sergei (1856–1915)

Symphony No. 4 in C min., Op. 12; Overture The Oresteia, Op. 6.
*** Chan. Dig. CHAN 8953 [id.]. Philh. O, Järvi.

Taneyev wrote four symphonies, nine string quartets and two string quintets, but his masterpiece is his opera, *The Oresteia*, whose overture is included here. The *Fourth Symphony*, sometimes known as the *First* as it was the first to be published in his lifetime, is a long piece of 42 minutes; some of its gestures are predictable, to say the least! Its best movement is the delightful scherzo which betrays his keenness of wit. Elsewhere neither his ideas nor their working out are quite as fresh or as individual as in such pieces as, say, the *Piano quintet*. Neeme Järvi gets very good playing from the Philharmonia and his performance supersedes both the earlier version from Rozhdestvensky from the late 1970s, and the Marco Polo coupling with the *Second Symphony*, an unfinished work, orchestrated after the composer's death, laden down with academic devices.

Piano quartet in E, Op. 20.
**(*) Pro Arte Dig. CDD 301 [id.]. Cantilena Chamber Players.

The *Piano quartet* is a finely wrought and often subtle work. Its language is closer to that of Brahms or Fauré than to the Russians, though Taneyev's piano writing is highly original. What a superbly sensitive pianist the Cantilena Chamber Players have in the person of Frank Glazer!

The performance is altogether first rate, though the acoustic in which it is recorded is not quite big enough.

Piano quintet in G min., Op. 30.
*** Ara. Dig. Z 6539 [id.]. Jerome Lowenthal, Rosenthal, Kamei, Thompson, Kates.

The *Piano quintet* is a powerfully made and ambitious score running to nearly 43 minutes. Not only is it well structured and its motivic organization subtle, its melodic ideas are strong and individual. It is arguably the greatest Russian chamber work between Tchaikovsky and Shostakovich. The recording is not in the demonstration bracket, but it is very good; and the playing, particularly of the pianist Jerome Lowenthal, is excellent. Strongly recommended.

Piano trio in D, Op. 22.
*** Chan. Dig. CHAN 8592; *ABTD 1262* [id.]. Borodin Trio.

This *Trio* is a big, four-movement work: the first is in the usual sonata form, though Taneyev restates the themes in reverse order in the recapitulation; the second is a scherzo which also includes a set of variations; then an *Andante espressivo* leads into the finale. The invention is attractive – and so, too, is the excellent performance and recording. Strongly recommended.

String quartets Nos. 8 in C; 9 in A.
**(*) Olympia OCD 128 [id.]. Leningrad Taneyev Qt.

Both these *Quartets* are large-scale works in the classical mould, and both are beautifully crafted, though they are not strongly personal. The minuet of No. 8 and the scherzo of No. 9 are highly attractive. They are well played, though the violin tone above the stave has a tendency to harden.

String quintet in D, Op. 14.
*** Olympia OCD 138 [id.]. Leningrad Taneyev Qt with Benjamin Morozow – BORODIN: *String quartet No. 2.* ***

This *String quintet* reveals a strong and resourceful musical mind. It is beautifully proportioned, in three movements, the last of which is a theme and variations. (One of them is quite magical and has enormous delicacy and atmosphere.) The performance by the eponymous quartet and the cellist, Benjamin Morozow, is extremely fine and so, too, is the recording. A rewarding disc.

The Oresteia (opera): complete.
**(*) Olympia OCD 195 A/B [id.]. Chernobayev, Galushkina, Bukov, Dubrovin, Belorussian State Ch. & O, Kolomizheva.

Taneyev's reputation as an academic must be reassessed in the light of this piece, for this is not only a finely wrought work; it is full of imaginative touches and effective musical drama. Rimsky-Korsakov spoke of its 'pages of unusual beauty and expressiveness'. This performance, recorded in 1978, was briefly available on DG in a rather smoother transfer than on these Olympia CDs, vivid though they are. There are some splendid singers. There is a tendency for the sound to coarsen on climaxes, though some of the blame for this must be laid at the feet of the orchestra. A most worthwhile issue.

Tarrega, Francisco (1852–1909)

Music for guitar: *Adelita; La Cartagenera; Columpio; Danza mora; Endecha; Estudio de velocidad; Estudio en forma de minuetto; Jota; Lagrima; La Mariposa; Minuetto; Oremus; Pavana; Preludio in G; Recuerdos de la Alhambra; Sueno.*
*** DG Dig. 410 655-2 [id.]. Narciso Yepes.

Although much of Tarrega's music is slight, he was a key figure in the movement to restore the guitar to its rightful place as a concert instrument, and stands as the link between Sor and the composers of the early part of our own century. Narciso Yepes made a special study of Tarrega's manuscripts (there is more than one version of each piece) and plays them very persuasively. The recording has fine definition on CD.

Tartini, Giuseppe (1692–1770)

Cello concerto in A.
(M) *** DG 429 098-2; *429 098-4*. Rostropovich, Zurich Coll. Mus., Sacher – BOCCHERINI; VIVALDI: *Concertos*. ***

As with the other works in this fine 1978 collection, Rostropovich's view of Tartini's *A major Concerto* is larger than life; but the eloquence of the playing disarms criticism, even when the cellist plays cadenzas of his own that are not exactly in period. The lively accompaniment is matched by bright, vivid recording that sounds splendid on CD.

Violin concertos: in E min., D.56; in A, D.96; in A min., D.113.
(M) *** Erato/Warner Dig. 2292 45380-2 [id.]. Uto Ughi, Sol. Ven., Scimone.

Tartini is a composer of unfailing originality, and the three violin concertos on this record are all very rewarding. The *Concerto in A major*, which comes last on the disc, has an additional (probably) alternative slow movement, a *Largo Andante* which is particularly beautiful. Uto Ughi's performances are distinguished by excellent taste and refinement of tone, and I Solisti Veneti are hardly less polished. The harpsichord continuo is somewhat reticent but otherwise the recording is exemplary. Highly recommended.

Concertino for clarinet (arr. Jacob).
*** ASV Dig. CDDCA 585; *ZCDCA 585* [id.]. Emma Johnson, ECO, Yan Pascal Tortelier – CRUSELL: *Introduction, theme and variations;* DEBUSSY: *Rapsodie;* WEBER: *Concerto No. 1*. ***

Gordon Jacob's arrangement of sonata movements by Tartini as a brief, four-movement *Clarinet concerto* is a delightful oddity. Inevitably it seems strange to have such baroque ideas associated with clarinet tone; but, with sprightly, characterful playing, it is an attractive and unusual makeweight in Emma Johnson's mixed collection of concertante pieces, well recorded.

Tavener, John (born 1944)

(i) *The Protecting veil* (for cello and orchestra); *Thrinos*.
*** Virgin Dig. VC7 91474-2 [id.]. Steven Isserlis, (i) LSO, Rozhdestvensky – BRITTEN: *Cello suite No. 3*. ***

This recording of Tavener's extended (45-minute) concertante work for cello and strings, *The Protecting veil*, did the impossible for a demanding modern work and stayed in the British classical top ten for months, even reaching the No. 1 slot. In the inspired performance of Steven Isserlis, dedicatedly accompanied by Rozhdestvensky and the LSO, it has an instant magnetism, at once gentle and compelling. Tavener's simplicity of idiom is of quite a different order from the easy-pleasing of minimalism. He has you escaping at once into a spiritual world, sharing his visions. The eight substantial sections in a continuous span are predominantly slow and mellifluous, with the solo cello consistently lyrical; yet in a performance such as this there is no feeling of sameness, of putting the mind to sleep. The 'protecting veil' of the title refers to the Orthodox Church's celebration of a tenth-century vision, when in Constantinople the Virgin Mary appeared and cast her protecting veil over the Christians who were being attacked by the Saracen armies. Tavener, himself a Russian Orthodox convert, echoes the cadences of Orthodox chant, ending each section with passages of heightened lyricism for the soloist. Each time that leads the ear persuasively on into the next section, with the sequence leading from the *Nativity of the Mother of God* by way of the Annunciation and the Incarnation to the final Dormition or passing. The fifth section, the *Lament of the Mother of God at the Cross*, is an unaccompanied meditation for the solo cello, a moving threnody leading at the end to the work's one sharply dramatic moment, when a sudden surge represents Christ's Resurrection. It is as dramatic as the sudden eruption of *Et resurrexit* in Bach's *B minor Mass*, after the darkness of *Et crucifixus*. As in so much of his music, Tavener is not just talking to the converted here, but is bringing equivalent consolation to the non-believer. Much is owed to the performance, with Isserlis a commanding soloist. He is just as compelling in the other two works on the disc, not just the Britten but also the simple lyrical lament, *Thrinos*, which Tavener wrote especially for him. Excellent recording.

The Repentant thief.
*** Collins Dig. Single 2005-2. Andrew Marriner, LSO, Tilson Thomas.

In this memorable work for clarinet and orchestra (Andrew Marriner the keenly responsive soloist) Tavener creates a sharply defined structure, contrasting visionary intensity with rhythmic urgency in alternating *Dances*, *Laments* and *Refrains*. Like other major Tavener works, it makes an immediate physical impact, a fine addition to Collins's enterprising 20th-century Plus series on CD singles.

Funeral Ikos; (i) *Ikon of Light. Carol: The Lamb.*
*** Gimell CDGIM 005; *1585T-05* [id.]. Tallis Scholars, (i) Chilingirian Qt (members), Phillips.

Both the major works on the disc, *Funeral Ikos* and *Ikon of Light*, represent Tavener's more recent style at its most compelling, simple and consonant to the point of bareness but with sensuous overtones. *Ikon of Light* is a setting of Greek mystical texts, with chant-like phrases repeated hypnotically. The string trio provides the necessary textural variety. More concentrated is *Funeral Ikos*, an English setting of the Greek funeral sentences, often yearningly beautiful. Both in these and in the brief setting of Blake's *The Lamb*, the Tallis Scholars give immaculate performances, atmospherically recorded in the chapel of Merton College, Oxford.

Taverner, John (*c.* 1495–1545)

Missa Corona Spinea; Votive antiphon: O Wilhelme pastor bone.
**(*) ASV Dig. CDGAU 115; *ZCGAU 115* [id.]. Christ Church Cathedral Ch., Francis Grier.

Francis Grier's pursuit of authenticity leads him to direct his choir – as finely disciplined as it was under his predecessor, Simon Preston – to sing this superb setting of the Mass a third higher than modern concert pitch. The result is a strain, both on the boy trebles and on listeners' ears. A degree of abrasiveness seems a necessary ingredient of authentic performances, but greater ease in those high mellifluous lines would be more in character. The digital recording is admirably clear as well as atmospheric, but one still has lingering doubts about the correctness of Grier's pitching of the melodic line.

Missa gloria tibi Trinitas; Audivi vocem (responsory); ANON.: *Gloria tibi Trinitas.*
*** Hyp. CDA 66134 [id.]. The Sixteen, Harry Christophers.

Missa gloria tibi Trinitas; Dum transisset sabbatum; Kyrie a 4 (Leroy).
*** Gimell Dig. CDGIM 004; *1585T-04* [id.]. Tallis Scholars, Phillips.

This six-voice setting of the Mass is richly varied in its invention (not least in rhythm) and expressive in a deeply personal way very rare for its period. Harry Christophers and The Sixteen underline the beauty with an exceptionally pure and clear account, superbly recorded and made the more brilliant by having the pitch a minor third higher than modern concert pitch.

Peter Phillips and the Tallis Scholars give an intensely involving performance of this glorious example of Tudor music. The recording may not be as clear as on the rival Hyperion version, but Phillips rejects all idea of reserve or cautiousness of expression; the result reflects the emotional basis of the inspiration the more compellingly. The motet, *Dum transisset sabbatum*, is then presented more reflectively, another rich inspiration.

Missa Mater Christi; Motets: *Mater Christi; O Wilhelme, pastor bone.*
*** Nimbus Dig. NI 5218 [id.]. Christ Church Cathedral Ch., Stephen Darlington.

This is a liturgical reconstruction by Andrew Carwood for the Feast of the Annunciation of Our Lady, at Eastertide, which intersperses Taverner's *Missa Mater Christi* with the appropriate chant. The disc also includes the Motet *Mater Christi*, on which the Mass itself is built, and the antiphon, *O Wilhelme, pastor bone*, composed in honour of St William of York (Wolsey's archbishopric). It was Wolsey who founded Cardinal (later Christ Church) College, at which Taverner was Master of the Choristers. The singing under Stephen Darlington is first class, and the recording made, not at Christ Church, but at Dorchester Abbey, Oxfordshire, is difficult to fault: it is well focused and excellently balanced with a firm image. There are helpful and scholarly notes by John Caldwell.

Mass, O Michael; Dum transisset sabbatum; Kyrie a 4 (Leroy).
*** Hyp. Dig. CDA 66315; *KA 66315* [id.]. The Sixteen, Harry Christophers.

Taverner was the most important figure in English music during the first part of the sixteenth century and recent years have seen a welcome increase in his representation on record. Although the bulk of his music was written during his period at Tattersall and then Cardinal (now Christ Church) College, Oxford, in the 1520s, Taverner continued composing after Wolsey's fall. The Sixteen and Harry Christophers are continuing their ambitious project to record all his festal Masses. The *Missa O Michael* is an ambitious six-part Mass lasting nearly 40 minutes which derives its name from the respond, *Archangeli Michaelis interventione*, which prefaces the performance. The chant on which the Mass is built appears no fewer than seven times during its course. The sleeve-note inclines to the view that the Mass dates from 1519, when the feast of St Michael fell on a Sunday. The so-called Leroy *Kyrie* (the name thought to be a reference to *le roi* Henry) fittingly precedes it: the *Missa O Michael* has no Kyrie. The Easter motet, *Dum transisset sabbatum*, completes an impressive disc.

Missa sancti Wilhelmi; Dum transisset Sabbatum; Ex eius tumba; O Wilhelme, pastor bone.
*** Hyp. Dig. CDA 66427 *KA 66427* [id.]. The Sixteen, Harry Christophers.

Those who have invested in earlier issues in this series will need no prompting to acquire the present CD. This offers the *Missa Sancti Wilhelmi* (known as 'Small Devotion' in two sources and possibly a corruption of *S. Will devotio*), prefaced by the antiphon, *O Wilhelme, pastor bone*, written in a largely syllabic, note-against-note texture, and the second of his two five-part settings of the Easter respond, *Dum transisset Sabbatum*, and washed down, as it were, by the Matin responds for the Feast of St Nicholas, *Ex eius tumba*, and believed to be the only sixteenth-century setting of this text. St Nicholas was the patron saint of Cardinal College, though *Ex eius tumba* would seem to belong to Taverner's period at Tattersall. The singing of The Sixteen under Harry Christophers is expressive and ethereal, and the recording impressively truthful. Recommended with confidence.

Tchaikovsky, Peter (1840–93)

Andante cantabile for cello and orchestra, Op. posth.
(M) *** DG 431 475-2; *431 475-4* [id.]. Rostropovich, BPO – GLAZUNOV: *Chant du ménestrel;* SHOSTAKOVICH: *Cello concerto No. 2.* ***

The composer himself arranged the *Andante cantabile* for cello and orchestra. Rostropovich indulges himself affectionately in the work, and the balance – all cello with a discreet orchestral backing – reflects his approach. The sound is warm and pleasing.

Andante cantabile, Op. 11; Chant d'automne, Op. 37/10; Nocturne, Op. 19/4 (all arr. for cello & orchestra); *Pezzo capriccioso, for cello & orchestra, Op. 62; Sérénade mélancolique, Op. 26; Valse sentimentale, Op. 51/6* (both arr. for cello & orchestra); *Variations on a rococo theme for cello & orchestra, Op. 33; Eugene Onegin: Lensky's aria* (arr. for cello & orchestra).
**(*) BMG/RCA Dig. RD 60758. Ofra Harnoy, LPO, Mackerras.

Ofray Harnoy plays with much lightness and grace in this Tchaikovsky programme, managing to embrace almost every conceivable item which might be transcribed for cello and orchestra. Yet instead of the two song-transcriptions favoured by Wallfisch, she plays an arrangement by the record's producer, Jacob Harnoy, of the *Sérénade mélancholique*, originally for violin and sounding just a little lugubrious transposed down for the cello. As it so happens, the most successful performance here is *Lenski's aria* from *Eugene Onegin* which Harnoy plays with gentle lamenting ardour, with the orchestral wind soloists decorating the vocal line with affectionate sensibility. There is one moment when the bassoon takes over the melody almost imperceptibly, so subtle is the change of colour. The famous *Variations on a rococo theme* are presented in a similar way – using the published score – and though at times Harnoy fines the melodic line down seductively to just a thread of tone, at others one craves a slightly more robust effect. But in the rest of the programme this delicacy and refinement work well enough, although the pervading half-light and sense of melancholy mean that this is not a concert to take all at one sitting. Mackerras accompanies very sensitively and the LPO playing is quite lovely, while the recording balance is ideal, within a pleasingly warm ambience.

Andante cantabile, Op. 11; Nocturne, Op. 19/4; Pezzo capriccioso, Op. 62 (1887 version); *2 Songs: Legend; Was I not a little blade of grass; Variations on a rococo theme, Op. 33* (1876 version).

*** Chan. Dig. CHAN 8347; *ABTD 1080* [id.]. Wallfisch, ECO, Simon.

This delightful record gathers together all of Tchaikovsky's music for cello and orchestra – including his arrangements of such items as the famous *Andante cantabile* and two songs. The major item is the original version of the *Rococo variations* with an extra variation and the earlier variations put in a more effective order, as Tchaikovsky wanted. Geoffrey Simon draws lively and sympathetic playing from the ECO, with Wallfisch a vital if not quite flawless soloist. Excellent recording, with the CD providing fine presence and an excellent perspective.

Andante cantabile, Op. 11; Nocturne, Op. 19/4 (both arr. for cello & orchestra); *Pezzo capriccioso, Op. 62; Variations on a rococo theme, Op. 33* (original versions).
(*) Virgin Dig. VC7 91134-2; *VC7 91134-4* [id.]. Isserlis, COE, Gardiner (with GLAZUNOV: *2 Pieces, Op. 20; Chant du ménestrel, Op. 71.* RIMSKY-KORSAKOV: *Serenade, Op. 37.* CUI: *2 Morceaux, Op. 36* *).

The Virgin collection omits the song arrangements, offering instead an attractive bonus recital of Russian concertante lollipops, all of considerable charm. Isserlis's playing has slight reserve but also an elegant delicacy which is appealing, although it suits Glazunov and Cui rather better than it does Tchaikovsky's *Andante cantabile.* John Eliot Gardiner provides gracefully lightweight accompaniments and the Virgin recording is faithfully balanced, fresh in texture and warm in ambience. Some listeners may find this music-making lacking in extrovert feeling; others may feel that its lightness of touch makes a special appeal.

Capriccio italien, Op. 45.
(BB) *** BMG/RCA Dig. VD 87727 [7727-2-RV]. Dallas SO, Mata (with *Concert* ***).
(B) *** CfP CD-CFP 4341; *TC-CFP 4341* [id.]. Philh. O, Kletzki – RIMSKY-KORSAKOV: *Scheherazade.* ***

On Mata's Dallas disc the concert-hall effect of the recording is very impressive indeed, with the opening fanfares sonically as riveting as the silences when the reverberation dies away naturally. The performance is colourful and exciting, and the piece is issued within an attractive compilation of favourite orchestral showpieces (see Concerts section, below).

Kletzki's performance is very enjoyable. It offers superb Philharmonia playing (the opening bugle call is most arresting) and is very well recorded indeed for its period (late 1950s). Not a first choice, but a good bonus for an outstanding version of *Scheherazade.*

Capriccio italien, Op. 45; 1812 Overture; Marche slave, Op. 31; Romeo and Juliet (fantasy overture).
(BB) *** Naxos Dig. 8.550500; *4550500* [id.]. RPO, Adrian Leaper.

Like Sian Edwards, Adrian Leaper is a natural Tchaikovskian; whether in the colourful extravagance of the composer's memento of his Italian holiday, the romantic ardour and passionate conflict of *Romeo and Juliet*, the sombre expansiveness of *Marche slave* with its surge of adrenalin at the close, or in the extrovert celebration of *1812*, he produces playing from the RPO that is spontaneously committed and exciting. The brilliantly spectacular recording, with plenty of weight for the brass, was made in Watford Town Hall, with realistic cannon and an impressively resonant imported carillon to add to the very exciting climax of *1812*. A splendid disc that would still be recommendable if it cost far more.

Capriccio italien, Op. 45; Élégie for strings; Francesca da Rimini, Op. 32; Romeo and Juliet (fantasy overture).
*** Decca Dig. 421 715-2 [id.]. RPO, Ashkenazy.

Capriccio italien is superb, spectacular, elegant and possessed of exhilarating impetus. *Romeo and Juliet* takes a little while to generate its fullest excitement with the love-theme introduced a little coolly, but its climax has great ardour. *Francesca da Rimini* is very exciting too, with much fine wind-playing from the RPO in the lyrical central section. Ashkenazy does not quite match Stokowski in depicting the lovers' frenzied passion, but his demonic closing evocation of the whirlwinds of Hell is overwhelming in impact. Then the programme ends with Tchaikovsky's haunting *Élégie*, a lovely, wistful string melody played with a wonderful feeling of nostalgia. What makes this concert especially successful is the superb recording. It is a real Tchaikovskian sound, as fine as any on record.

Capriccio italien, Op. 45; Nutcracker suite, Op. 71a; Sleeping Beauty (ballet) *suite, Op. 66a.*
(M) *** DG 431 610-2; *431 610-4* [id.]. BPO, Rostropovich.

We have given the highest praise (and a Rosette) to the Rostropovich triptych combining the three Tchaikovsky ballet suites, which added *Swan Lake* to the two listed here (see below) and that still seems the most appropriate coupling; but anyone whose collection has room for *Capriccio italien* rather than *Swan Lake* will find the present reissue hardly less rewarding. Here the vulgarity inherent in the principal theme evaporates, so decoratively elegant is the playing of the Berlin Philharmonic, especially the violins. The finale, too, has an attractive burst of exuberance, and the bright CD transfer lightens any hint of rhythmic heaviness in the fully scored reprise of the main tune. These were among the finest recordings the DG engineers made in the Philharmonie in the late 1970s.

Piano concerto No. 1 in B flat min., Op. 23.
❀ (M) (***) BMG/RCA mono GD 87992 [7792-2-RG]. Horowitz, NBC SO, Toscanini – BEETHOVEN: *Piano concerto No. 5.* (***)
*** BMG/RCA RD 85912 [RCA 5912-2-RC]. Van Cliburn, RCA SO, Kondrashin – RACHMANINOV: *Concerto No. 2.* ***
*** Chesky CD-13 [id.]. Earl Wild, RPO, Fistoulari – DOHNÁNYI: *Variations on a nursery tune* etc. ***
*** DG 415 062-2 [id.]. Martha Argerich, RPO, Dutoit – PROKOFIEV: *Concerto No. 3.* ***
(M) *** Decca 417 750-2 [id.]. Ashkenazy, LSO, Maazel – CHOPIN: *Concerto No. 2.* ***
*** Decca 417 555-2 [id.]. Ashkenazy, LSO, Maazel – SCHUMANN: *Concerto.* ***
(BB) *** Pickwick PWK 1148. Peter Katin, LSO, Eric Kundell – SCHUMANN: *Concerto.* **(*)
(M) **(*) Mercury 432 011-2 [id.]. Byron Janis, LSO Menges – SCHUMANN: *Concerto.* ***
(M) (***) BMG/RCA mono GD 60449; *GK 60449.* Horowitz, NBC SO, Toscanini – MUSSORGSKY: *Pictures.* ***
**(*) EMI Dig. CDC7 54232-2 [id.]. Mikhail Rudy, Leningrad PO, Mariss Jansons – RACHMANINOV: *Concerto.* **(*)
*(*) Telarc Dig. CD 80193 [id.]. Gutierrez, Baltimore SO, Zinman – RACHMANINOV: *Rhapsody on a theme of Paganini.* *(*)

(i) *Piano concerto No. 1. Suite No. 4 (Mozartiana).*
*(*) Chan. Dig. CHAN 8777 [id.]. (i) Orbelian; Philh. O, Järvi.

(i) *Piano concerto No. 1 in B flat min., Op. 23. Theme and variations, Op. 19/6.*
(M) *** EMI CDM7 64329-2 [id.]; *EG 764329-4.* Gavrilov, (i) Philh. O, Muti – BALAKIREV: *Islamey*; PROKOFIEV: *Concerto No. 1.* ***

Horowitz's famous account of the *B flat minor Concerto*, recorded at a concert in Carnegie Hall in 1943 with his father-in-law conducting, has dwarfed almost every record of the work made since. Somehow the alchemy of the occasion – which raised eleven million dollars in War Bonds! – was unique, and the result is unforgettable. The recording of the orchestra is confined and lacks body, some surface rustle remains from the 78-r.p.m. pressings, while the violins need a judicious degree of filtering, and even then don't sound very rich. But the piano itself is gloriously full and bold. Such is the magnetism of the playing, however, that the ear forgets the sonic limitations within moments. Toscanini's accompaniment is remarkable not only for matching the adrenalin of his soloist but for the tenderness he finds for the lyrical passages of the first movement. The powerful cadenza becomes its climax, wonderfully varied in colour, and with one passage in which there almost seem to be two pianists in duet, rather than just one pair of human hands. Toscanini's moments of delicacy extend to the *Andantino*, which is truly *simplice* (as the composer indicated), even when accompanying the coruscating pianistic fireworks of the central section. The finale carries all before it, with Horowitz's riveting octave passage-work leading on to a tremendously exciting restatement of the big tune and then storming off furiously to the coda. The applause at the end is welcome for once, if only as a release of tension.

The Van Cliburn is also one of the most brilliant recordings of this work ever made. The young American pianist lives up to his reputation as Moscow Prize-winner with playing which has great virtuosity, but much else besides. There is spontaneity and a natural feeling for the phrasing which usually comes only with long experience. Van Cliburn and the Soviet conductor Kondrashin in short give an inspired performance with as much warmth as glitter. The 1958 recording is forward and could do with more atmosphere, but the digital remastering has brought a firmer orchestral image, and the piano timbre is also improved. Coupled with an equally outstanding version of the Rachmaninov *C minor*, this is a very distinguished reissue indeed, even if the piano timbre here is shallower than in the coupling.

Even in the shadow of Horowitz, the spectacular reissue by Earl Wild with the RPO under Fistoulari stands as one of the finest accounts ever of this much-recorded work. The recording was originally made for Reader's Digest by RCA engineers in the early 1960s and has had a chequered career, lying in the RCA vaults for many years. Now it re-emerges on the enterprising Chesky label, and one's only complaint is the premium price. However, it is certainly a premium performance and needs no apology for its sound, which is vintage quality of that period, although the violins have become a little drier with the digital remastering for CD. But this compares favourably with many modern recordings and the piano tone is bold and natural. From the first sweep of the opening the reading is distinguished by its feeling of directness and power, yet the lyrical side of the music (the first movement's second subject, the outer sections of the *Andantino*) brings a comparable sensitivity. In the first movement there are some wholly spontaneous bursts of bravura from the soloist which are quite electrifying; and in the big cadenza one is equally reminded of Horowitz when Wild, by impetuous tempo changes in the imitative passages, makes himself sound almost like a piano duo. The finale too, taken with crackling bravura, again recalls the famous Horowitz/Toscanini live Carnegie Hall recording. Fistoulari, splendidly assured throughout, produces a vivid orchestral response (the flute and piccolo interjections in the finale are as dashing as the solo playing) and makes a superb final climax.

Argerich's 1971 recording of the Tchaikovsky *First Piano concerto* with Dutoit remains a strong recommendation. The sound is firm, with excellent presence, and its ambience is more attractive than the later version. The weight of the opening immediately sets the mood for a big, broad performance, with the kind of music-making in which the personalities of both artists are complementary. Argerich's conception encompasses the widest range of tonal shading. In the finale she often produces a scherzando-like effect; then the orchestra thunders in with the Russian dance theme to create a real contrast. The tempo of the first movement is comparatively measured, but satisfyingly so; the slow movement is strikingly atmospheric, yet delicate, its romanticism light-hearted.

Ashkenazy's performance is offered in alternative couplings: the Chopin is the more attractive, being at mid-price. The soloist refuses to be stampeded by Tchaikovsky's rhetoric, and the biggest climaxes of the first movement are made to grow naturally out of the music. In the *Andantino* too, Ashkenazy refuses to play flashily. The finale is very fast and brilliant, yet the big tune is broadened at the end in the most convincing way. The remastering is highly successful: the piano sounds splendidly bold and clear while the orchestral balance is realistic.

Peter Katin's performance from the beginning of the 1970s is alive and direct, the opening big tune taken fast but with a fine sweep which continues through the first movement. The *Andantino* is played very stylishly, and the finale has plenty of bravura. With vintage Decca sound this is an enjoyable bargain, and the coupled Schumann *Concerto* is equally characterful.

Byron Janis's account is in many ways as dazzling as his Rachmaninov recordings. Menges is not as strong an accompanist as Dorati, most noticeably so in the finale. But this remains a memorable performance, with much dash and power from the soloist in the outer movements and the *Andantino* agreeably delicate. There are plenty of thrills, not least Janis's final stormy octaves before the bold restatement of the great tune in the finale. The Mercury sound is excellent, full and resonant, with a big piano image up front.

Horowitz's earlier version, coupled with the Mussorgsky, was made in Carnegie Hall, in 1941, under studio conditions. The recording is altogether better balanced than the live performance by the same artists, and the orchestral sound is much fuller; indeed the quality brooks no real criticism. The performance has all the thrills and electricity of the 1943 version and the playing is prodigious in its bravura. But throughout one feels that Toscanini – with his soloist responding readily – is forcing the pace, creating enormous urgency. This is an exhilarating listening experience; but the sense of occasion of the live performance created a really great performance which is undoubtedly more satisfying despite its sonic limitations.

Gavrilov is stunning in the finale of the *Concerto*; however, the final statement of the big tune is broadened so positively that one is not entirely convinced. Similarly in the first movement, contrasts of dynamic and tempo are extreme, and the element of self-consciousness is apparent. The *Andante* is full of tenderness and the *prestissimo* middle section goes like quicksilver, displaying the vein of spontaneous imagination that we recognize in Gavrilov's other records. The recording is full and sumptuous with a big, bold forward piano-image, so that the work's famous opening makes an immediate impact. In the *Variations*, Op. 19, Tchaikovsky's invention has great felicity. Gavrilov's playing is stylishly sympathetic here, and the Balakirev and Prokofiev couplings are dazzling.

As always, Mikhail Rudy exhibits much artistry and taste in his eloquent account with the Leningrad (now St Petersburg) Philharmonic coupled with the Rachmaninov *Second concerto*. His playing may not have the breath-taking virtuosoity and command of some of the finest rivals (Horowitz, Gilels, Richter, Pletnev, etc.) and he is perhaps not quite in their league, but there is no want of poetic feeling or technical finesse, and the orchestral playing under Mariss Jansons has enormous character and personality. A distinguished issue with good sound and a refined balance that does admirable justice to both soloist and orchestra.

Horacio Gutierrez and the Baltimore Orchestra under David Zinman also offer a Rachmaninov coupling, in this case the *Rhapsody on a theme of Paganini*. Gutierrez has a dazzling technique and there is no questioning his effortless virtuosity. At the same time there is a certain lack of freshness and spontaneity, and the razzle-dazzle brilliance of the pianist and the routine responses of the conductor do not make for a front recommendation. No quarrels with the recorded sound provided by the Telarc engineers.

Constantine Orbelian's account has many merits though one misses the imaginative shaping of the phrase which distinguish greater artists. There is none of the compelling personality that insists on one listening to the very end of the work. Very good orchestral playing from the Philharmonia under Neeme Järvi and it is their account of Tchaikovsky's *Mozartiana*, which is the chief attraction of this disc. As usual from this source the recorded sound is very natural.

(i) *Piano concerto No. 1 in B flat min., Op. 23;* (ii) *Violin concerto in D, Op. 35.*
(BB) *** BMG/RCA VD 60491; *VK 60491* [60491-2-RV; *60491-4-RV*]. (i) John Browning; (ii) Erick Friedman, LSO, Ozawa.
(M) *** Erato/Warner 2292 45674-2 [id.]. (i) Devoyon; (ii) Amoyal; Philh. O, Dutoit.
(B) **(*) DG 429 166-2; *429 166-4* [id.]. (i) Lazar Berman; (ii) Christian Ferras, BPO, Karajan.
(M) **(*) Sony Dig. MDK 44643 [id.]. (i) Gilels, NYPO; (ii) Zukerman, Israel PO; Mehta.

Browning's mid-1960s interpretation of the solo role in the *Piano concerto* is remarkable, not only for power and bravura but for wit and point in the many *scherzando* passages. His slow movement has an attractively cool simplicity, and in the finale he adopts a fast and furious tempo to compare with Horowitz. Erick Friedman, Heifetz's pupil, is a thoughtful violinist who gives a keenly intelligent performance of the companion work, imbued with a glowing lyricism and with a particularly poetic and beautiful account of the slow movement. There is plenty of dash and fire in the finale, and Ozawa gives first-rate support to both soloists. The recording is excellent. Two performances to match those of almost any rival; moreover this disc is in the lowest price-range.

Devoyon's performance of the *Piano concerto* is the very opposite of barnstorming. It opens and closes spaciously and, even in the big final statement of the finale, the participants hold back from unleashing a torrent of rhetoric. The result is refreshing. There is no lack of spontaneity and the first movement unfolds grandly, its lyrical impulse fully realized. With Dutoit in charge, the Philharmonia playing is predictably polished and committed, and the soloist is persuasive too, refusing to be stampeded at any point. While there are fewer switchback thrills here than usual, there is much that is satisfying. About Amoyal's account of the *Violin concerto* there can be no reservations. He plays with passionate commitment, his slow movement is particularly beautiful, and he is extremely sensitively accompanied. Dutoit gets exciting results from the Philharmonia and the analogue recording from the early 1980s is first class.

Berman's 1976 recording with Karajan makes a formidable bargain issue, well coupled with Christian Ferras's much earlier version of the *Violin concerto*. This is one of the most exciting readings of the *Piano concerto* ever put on record. It is not just a question of massive bravura but of extreme delicacy too, so that in the central scherzando of the slow movement it almost sounds as though Berman is merely breathing on the keyboard, hardly depressing the notes at all. The ripe playing of the Berlin Philharmonic backs up the individuality of Berman's reading, and the recording is massively brilliant to match. Ferras's characteristic tone, with its rather close vibrato in lyrical passages, will not be to all tastes. But his is a well-conceived reading, with Karajan shaping the work as a whole very convincingly. The recording is excellent, rather warmer and more atmospheric than that provided for the *Piano concerto*.

On CBS there are more reservations about the Gilels performance than the Zukerman. The former offers less than first-class orchestral playing and not very distinguished sound, but Gilels's own playing is masterly. In Israel, the sound is much better, and Mehta secures generally good results from the Israel orchestra. The soloist is balanced closely and is made very tangible; Zukerman's warmth is most attractive, and the performance overall has both excitement and spontaneity.

(i) *Piano concerto No. 1;* (ii) *Violin concerto in D, Op. 35;* (iii) *Serenade for strings: Waltz* (CD only: *Serenade for strings:* complete). (iv or v) *Variations on a rococo theme, Op. 33.*
❀ (B) *** DG Compact Classics 413 161-2 (2); *413 161-4.* (i) Argerich, RPO, Dutoit; (ii) Milstein, VPO, Abbado; (iii) BPO, Karajan (cassette only: (iv) Rostropovich, Leningrad PO, Rozhdestvensky; CD only: (v) Rostropovich, BPO, Karajan).

This extended-length chrome tape was the jewel in the crown of DG's Walkman series (now renamed Compact Classics), always generous but here exceptionally so, both in quality of performances and recording, as well as in the amount of music offered. We awarded it a Rosette as the outstanding Tchaikovsky bargain compilation. Now for their 2-CD equivalent, DG have gone one better by replacing Karajan's elegant and polished *Waltz* from the *String serenade* (which remains on the tape) with the remastered analogue performance of the work from which it was drawn. Moreover, on CD Rostropovich's later recording of the *Rococo variations*, with Karajan, is substituted for his earlier version with Rozhdestvensky. Rostropovich and Karajan find a splendid symbiosis, and this performance is superb in every way, and very well recorded. Yet tape collectors need not feel deprived, for Rostropovich's earlier (1961) version also offers playing with just the right amount of jaunty elegance as regards the theme and the first few variations; and when the virtuoso fireworks are let off, they are brilliant, effortless and breathtaking in their éclat. Indeed Rostropovich needs no superlatives, and Rozhdestvensky shows a mastery all his own. Argerich's account of the *B flat minor Piano concerto* is second to none; Milstein's (1973) performance of the *Violin concerto* is equally impressive, undoubtedly one of the finest available, while Abbado secures playing of genuine sensitivity and scale from the Vienna Philharmonic.

Piano concerto No. 2 in G (complete); *Piano sonata No. 1 in G (Grande sonate), Op. 37.*
*** Teldec/Warner Dig. 9031 72296-2 [id.]. Elisabeth Leonskaja; (i) Leipzig GO, Kurt Masur.

A splendid new version of Tchaikovsky's *G minor Piano concerto*, weightier and more expansive (more German!) than the famous Donohoe version and certainly compelling. The red-blooded orchestral tuttis are matched by Leonskaja's (forwardly balanced) bold pianism, and if the slow movement misses some of the delicacy of feeling that Donohoe finds, and the extended solos for violin and cello have rather less individuality than with Kennedy and Isserlis, there is much lyrical ardour. The finale, too, is not chimerical but forceful in its exuberance, powerful and exciting, and the rich Leipzig recording matches the style of the performance. The coupling of Tchaikovsky's *Grand Sonata* in the same key is surely an ideal one. Leonskaja has the full measure of the rhetoric of the first movement and she plays the *Andante* with an appealing spontaneity and freshness, and range of colour. After the brief scherzo, the finale brings more flamboyance, and again the bold, full piano-image is right for the music.

Piano concertos Nos. 2 in G, Op. 44; 3 in E flat, Op. 75.
❀ *** EMI Dig. CDC7 49940-2 [id.]; *EL 749940-4.* Donohoe, Bournemouth SO, Barshai.
*** Ara. Dig. Z 6583 [id.]. Jerome Lowenthal, LSO, Comissiona.
**(*) Virgin Dig. VC7 91202-2; *VC7 91202-4* [id.]. Mikhail Pletnev, Phil. O, Vladimir Fedoseyev.

Donohoe's much-praised recording of Tchaikovsky's *Second Piano concerto* now returns to the catalogue, coupled with his excellent account of the *Third.* This latter is almost equally distinctive, with its volatile qualities well recognized. This superb recording of the full, original score of the *Second* in every way justifies the work's length and the unusual format of the slow movement, where the piece temporarily becomes a triple concerto, with its extended solos for violin and cello; these are played with beguiling warmth by Nigel Kennedy and Steven Isserlis. Barshai's pacing is not only perfectly calculated but he gives the opening tune an engaging rhythmic lift. The whole movement goes with a splendid impetus, yet the central orchestral episode is broadened effectively. The slow movement has one of Tchaikovsky's very best tunes, and the performance is a delight from beginning to end. Peter Donohoe plays marvellously in the first two movements – he is quite melting in the *Andante* – and in the finale he is inspired to bravura which recalls Horowitz in the *B flat minor Concerto.* The main theme, shooting off with the velocity of the ball in a pinball machine, is exhilarating, and the orchestral response has a matching excitement. The coda, with its cascading octaves, is a *tour de force* and brings one to the edge of one's seat in admiration. The recording has a fine, spacious ambience and is admirably realistic and very well balanced. Tchaikovsky's work has never before received such convincing advocacy on record.

In an obviously attractive coupling of two unjustly neglected works, the energy and flair of Lowenthal and Comissiona combine to give highly spontaneous performances, well balanced and recorded. If the *G major Concerto* has not quite the distinction of the EMI version, it is still satisfyingly alive; the soloist brings an individual, poetic response as well as bravura. With very good sound, this is well worth investigating, as the account of the *Third Concerto* is comparably spontaneous.

Commanding playing from Mikhail Pletnev, whose exceptional affinity for the composer is much in evidence. In the *Second Piano concerto* his handling of the second group of the first movement has great tenderness, and his seemingly effortless virtuosity is little short of breathtaking. He also has the advantage of totally idiomatic string soloists in the slow movement where, unfortunately, a few bars are cut. (Why do artists detract from a recording in this way?) It would be difficult to improve on the *Third*, which is strongly and interestingly characterized. Not only is the pianism of the highest voltage but the orchestral playing is highly charged too. The recording is very good but performs rather better on high-grade and sophisticated equipment than it does on more modest machines, where climaxes can give the impression of discoloration.

(i) *Piano concerto No. 2 in G, Op.44* (arr. Siloti); (ii) *Concert fantasia in G, Op. 56.*
*** Olympia OCD 229 [id.]. (i) Gilels, USSR Ac. SO, Svetlanov; (ii) Zhukov, USSR Ac. SO, Kitaenko.

The Russian recording of the abridged Siloti version, made at a public concert in the Moscow Conservatoire in 1972, is hugely exciting and, taken on its own merits, is a great success. Gilels's playing is masterly and Svetlanov brings plenty of vigour to the first movement, and the performance has all the excitement and spontaneity one would expect of a live occasion. The orchestral soloists make the most of the section of concertante music which is left to them, and in the finale the glittering brilliance of Gilels's articulation is matched by his witty restraint in the treatment of the secondary material. The recording balances the piano well forward, but the orchestra remains in the picture and the piano timbre is bold and full. The coupling is a splendid account of the *Concert fantasia*, an engaging and much underrated piece, demanding comparable technical virtuosity from its soloist, which Igor Zhukov provides in full measure. He is sympathetically accompanied, and this is another exciting and involving performance, given very good (1979) sound. The remastering for CD is highly effective.

Violin concerto in D, Op. 35.
*** Decca Dig. 410 011-2 [id.]. Kyung Wha Chung, Montreal SO, Dutoit – MENDELSSOHN: *Concerto.* ***
(M) *** Decca 417 707-2 [id.]. Kyung Wha Chung, LSO, Previn – BRUCH: *Concerto No. 1;* SAINT-SAËNS: *Havanaise.* ***
(BB) *** Naxos Dig. 8.550153; *4550153* [id.]. Takako Nishizaki, Slovak PO, Kenneth Jean – MENDELSSOHN: *Concerto.* ***
(B) *** Ph. 422 473-2; *422 473-4.* Grumiaux, New Philh. O, Krenz – MENDELSSOHN: *Concerto.* ***
(M) *** DG 419 067-2 [id.]. Milstein, VPO, Abbado – MENDELSSOHN: *Concerto.* ***
*** Decca Dig. 421 716-2 [id.]. Joshua Bell, Cleveland O, Ashkenazy – WIENIAWSKI: *Violin concerto No. 2.* ***
(M) (***) EMI mono CDH7 64030-2 [id.]. Heifetz, LPO, Barbirolli – GLAZUNOV: *Violin concerto* (***) 🏵; SIBELIUS: *Violin concerto.* (**)
(BB) **(*) Pickwick PWK 1145 [id.]. Campoli, LSO, Argenta.
(*) Ph. Dig. 416 821-2 [id.]. Mullova, Boston SO, Ozawa – SIBELIUS: *Concerto.* *
(B) **(*) Sony CD 42537 [MYK 36724]. Stern, Phd. O, Ormandy – MENDELSSOHN: *Concerto.* **(*)
(*) EMI Dig. CDC7 54127-2 [id.]; *EL 754127-4.* Nigel Kennedy, LPO, Kamu – SIBELIUS: *Concerto.* *
*(*) Collins Dig. 1128-2; *1128-4* [id.]. Kurt Nikkanen, LPO, Simonov – GLAZUNOV: *Concerto.* **(*)

Violin concerto in D; Sérénade mélancholique, Op. 26; Souvenir d'un lieu cher, Op. 42/3: Mélodie. Valse-scherzo, Op. 34.

*** ASV Dig. CDDCA 713; *ZCDCA 713* [id.]. Xue-Wei, Philh. O, Accardo.

Violin concerto in D; Sérénade mélancolique; String serenade: Waltz.
**(*) BMG/RCA RD 85933 [RCA 5933-2-RC]. Heifetz, Chicago SO, Reiner, or CO – MENDELSSOHN: *Concerto.* **(*)

Chung is engagingly volatile as a performer, responding to the inspiration of the moment, yet she is a deeply thoughtful interpreter. Here, as in her earlier version with Previn, she refuses to sentimentalize the central *Canzonetta*, choosing a flowing, easily songful speed. The result is the more tenderly affecting, though this time the violin is balanced more closely than before. The finale has, if anything, even more exhilaration, with technical problems commandingly overcome at a very fast speed.

Those happy with the coupling with Bruch and Saint-Saëns should be well satisfied with Chung's 1970 version, which is still among the finest in the catalogue and in which Previn's accompanying is highly sympathetic and responsive. This has warmth, spontaneity and discipline; every detail is beautifully shaped and turned without a trace of sentimentality. Chung refuses to sentimentalize the central *Canzonetta*, choosing a flowing, easily songful speed. The result is the more tenderly affecting. The recording is well balanced and detail is clean, though the acoustic is warm.

Xue-Wei gives a warmly expressive reading of this lovely concerto, lacking some of the fantasy and mystery that Kyung Whà Chung for one finds; but, with rich, full tone, he brings out the sensuousness of the work, while displaying commanding virtuosity. With the central *Canzonetta* turned into a simple song without words, not over-romanticized, this is a performance that confirms all the qualities displayed in Xue-Wei's first concerto disc for ASV of Bruch and Saint-Saëns. The coupling will be ideal for many, consisting of violin concertante pieces by Tchaikovsky, not just the *Sérénade mélancolique*, but the *Valse-scherzo* in a dazzling performance, and *Mélodie*, the third of the three pieces that Tchaikovsky grouped as *Souvenir d'un lieu cher*, freely and expressively done. The orchestral playing under another great violin virtuoso is warmly sympathetic but could be crisper, not helped for detail in tuttis by the lively acoustic of St Barnabas Church, Mitcham. However, this makes a very enjoyable collection.

Takako Nishizaki gives a warm and colourful reading, tender but purposeful and full of temperament. As in the Mendelssohn with which this is coupled, the central slow movement is on the measured side but flows sweetly, while the finale has all the necessary bravura, even at a speed that avoids breathlessness. Unlike many, Nishizaki opens out the little cuts which had become traditional. With excellent playing and recording, this makes a first-rate recommendation in the super-bargain bracket.

Grumiaux's playing has the usual aristocratic refinement and purity of tone to recommend it. His reading, too, is beautifully paced and has a particularly fine slow movement, less overtly emotional than some; both here and in the brilliant finale he shows superb aplomb and taste. With an excellent accompaniment from Krenz, this ranks among the finest budget versions, for the 1970s recording has a wide range and is firmly focused in its CD format.

Milstein's fine 1973 version with Abbado is here coupled with the Mendelssohn *Concerto* and remains one of the best mid-price reissues.

Joshua Bell plays with an expressive warmth which is generally kept within a relatively steady pulse. The symphonic strength of the work is brought out without any loss of excitement, rather the opposite. Bell may not have quite the fantasy of a version like Chung's, but it is an outstanding account nevertheless, very recommendable if you fancy the unusual coupling of Wieniawski. In the finale of the Tchaikovsky, Bell does not open out the tiny cuts in the passage-work that until recently have been traditional. Full, brilliant recording, with the soloist well balanced.

Heifetz's first (mono) recording of the Tchaikovsky *Violin concerto*, made in 1937, has tremendous virtuosity and warmth. The sound is opaque by modern standards but the ear quickly adjusts, and the performance is special even by Heifetz's own standards. The playing has even greater freshness and poetic feeling than his later recording with Reiner – though that, too, has a humanity that one does not always associate with this great violinist. The transfer, too, is very good and, coming as it does with a classic account of the Glazunov and a fascinating Sibelius, is a real bargain.

Campoli's performance has a lyrical simplicity and a natural warmth and spontaneity that are very appealing. Ataulfo Argenta accompanies with much sensitivity and shows his feeling for Tchaikovsky's orchestral colouring – especially in the *Canzonetta*, which has much wistful charm – as well as creating plenty of excitement and contrast in the tuttis. The finale brings fireworks from all concerned. The 1958 Decca recording, outstanding in its day, hardly shows its age. In today's marketplace a CD of this work, playing for 34 minutes and offering no coupling, can hardly be considered competitive, but anyone buying this super-bargain disc on impulse could well be surprised at the pleasure which it offers.

With the upper range of the 1957 recording smoothed and the orchestral presence enhanced, the magic of Heifetz can now be enjoyed more fully. There is some gorgeous lyrical playing and the slow movement marries deep feeling and tenderness in ideal proportions, while the finale scintillates. Reiner accompanies understandingly, producing fierily positive tuttis. A fine performance of the *Sérénade mélancolique* makes an attractive encore.

Viktoria Mullova's performance of the Tchaikovsky *Concerto* is immaculate and finely controlled – as is the coupling – but she does not always succeed in achieving the combination of warmth and nobility that this score above all requires. However, her playing has an undeniable splendour and an effortless virtuosity. Ozawa and the Boston orchestra give excellent support and the recording is exemplary.

Stern was on peak form when he made his first stereo recording with Ormandy, and it is a powerfully lyrical reading, rich in timbre and technically immaculate. The playing has undoubted poetry but is not helped by the very close balance of the soloist, so that pianissimos consistently become mezzo fortes. The orchestral sound is vivid but lacks amplitude.

Nigel Kennedy gives a warmly romantic reading of the Tchaikovsky *Concerto*, full of temperament, with one of the most expansive readings of the first movement ever put on disc. Though the sound is ample, his idiosyncrasies will not please everyone. For all his many *tenutos* and *rallentandos*, however, Kennedy is not sentimental, and his range of tone is exceptionally rich and wide, so that the big moments are powerfully sensual. Okku Kamu and the LPO do not always match their soloist; the accompaniment sometimes sounds a little stiff in tuttis, though the final coda is thrilling.

Kurt Nikannen is still in his twenties; after studies with Roman Totenberg he went to the Juilliard where, like so many of the prominent virtuosi of our day, he became a pupil of Dorothy DeLay. He is a gifted player with a strong technique and a particularly sweet tone. However, among the fifty-odd recordings of this concerto now before the public, this would not be in the first dozen despite the excellence of the orchestral playing under Yuri Simonov and the truthfulness of the Collins recording. Nikkanen's interpretation is, to put it mildly, far from selfless; he pulls the melodic line out of shape in a way that might be acceptable in the concert hall but which will not do on record. The Glazunov coupling enters a less competitive field and as a performance is stronger and less ego-centred.

1812 Overture; Francesca da Rimini, Op. 32.
(M) **(*) Decca Dig. 430 700-2; *430 700-4* [id.]. Montreal SO, Dutoit – MUSSORGSKY: *Night;* RIMSKY-KORSAKOV: *Capriccio espagnol.* **(*)

1812 Overture; Francesca da Rimini; Marche slave; Romeo and Juliet (fantasy overture).
(M) *** EMI Dig. CD-EMX 2152; *TC-EMX 2152.* RLPO, Sian Edwards.

1812 Overture; Hamlet (fantasy overture), *Op. 67; The Tempest, Op. 18.*
*** Delos Dig. D/CD 3081 [id.]. Oregon SO, James DePreist.

(i) *1812 Overture;* (ii) *Marche slave;* (iii) *Romeo and Juliet* (CD only: (iv) *Capriccio italien*).
(B) **(*) DG Compact Classics 413 153-2 (2); *413 153-4.* (i) Boston Pops O, Fiedler; (ii) BPO, Karajan; (iii) San Francisco SO, Ozawa; (iv) BPO, Rostropovich – MUSSORGSKY: *Pictures* etc. ***

(i) *1812 Overture; Romeo and Juliet;* (ii) *Eugene Onegin: Polonaise; Waltz; Écossaise. The Oprichnik: Dances.*
*** Ph. 411 448-2 [id.]. (i) Boston SO, with Tanglewood Festival Ch. (in *1812*); (ii) ROHCG O; C. Davis.

The control of the emotional ebb and flow of *Francesca da Rimini* shows Sian Edwards as an instinctive Tchaikovskian, moving through the work surely and compulsively, after the doom-laden opening stroke of the tam-tam has created an impending sense of nemesis. Francesca's clarinet entry is melting and the work's middle section has a Beechamesque sense of colour. The passionate climax, representing the discovery of the lovers, falls only just short of the vehement force of the Stokowski version, while the spectacular recording gives great impact to the closing whirlwind sequence and the despair-laden final chords, where the tam-tam makes its presence felt very pungently. *1812* is also very enjoyable indeed, full of vigour and flair, with the lyrical

Russian folk melodies on strings and woodwind relished colourfully, and a majestic final sequence with superbly resounding cannon. In *Romeo and Juliet*, the love-theme is ushered in very naturally and blossoms with the fullest ardour, while the feud music combined with the Friar Lawrence theme reaches a very dramatic climax. *Marche slave*, resplendently high-spirited and exhilarating, makes a perfect foil. The full-bodied recording is well balanced and thrilling in the proper Tchaikovskian way, with plenty of sonority and weight from the brass and a full string patina.

The Oregon orchestra show their paces in this vividly colourful triptych, and James DePreist is a highly sympathetic Tchaikovskian. Moreover the Arlene Schnitzer Hall in Portland has excellent acoustics for this repertoire, giving the orchestra fine depth and resonance and a true, unexaggerated brilliance. In *1812*, the cannon are perfectly placed and their spectacular entry is as precise as it is commanding. The performance overall is highly enjoyable, energetic but with the pacing unforced, though the ritenuto before the final peroration is not quite convincing. The performances of both *Hamlet* and *The Tempest* are passionately dramatic, the latter generating more intensity (and more melodrama) than Yondani Butt's ASV version, the former approaching yet not quite equalling Stokowski's account in imaginative vividness. But overall this is an impressive CD début.

Sir Colin Davis is not renowned as a Tchaikovskian, yet here he provides one of the most satisfying versions of *1812* ever recorded. Though he departs from the original score – to great effect – by including a chorus, it is musical values rather than any sense of gimmickry that make this version so successful. Men's voices alone are used to introduce the Russian hymn softly at the opening, with the ladies freshening the reprise. In the closing spectacle, the chorus soars above the bells; the effect is exhilarating and the very believable cannon are superbly placed. *Romeo and Juliet* is a slightly reserved performance, but one which in its minor degree of introversion misses neither the noble passion of the lovers nor the clash of swords in the feud sequences. The elegiac closing pages are particularly telling. The colourful operatic dances are a generous makeweight and are played with élan, even if the recording balance has lost just a degree of sparkle in the upper range with the removal of virtually all the background noise.

Fiedler's account of *1812* has plenty of adrenalin and is brilliantly recorded, with the effective display of pyrotechnics at the end adding spectacle without drowning the music. The direct manner of the performance does all Tchaikovsky asks, if with no special individuality. Nevertheless, with Karajan's *Marche slave* plus Ozawa's excellent *Romeo and Juliet*, and first-class sound throughout, this Compact Classics chrome tape, coupled with Mussorgsky, is certainly good value. The pair of CDs add Kurt Sanderling's idiomatic and romantic version of Borodin's *In the Steppes of Central Asia*, which suffers a little from thin violin tone, plus Rostropovich's splendid BPO version of the *Capriccio italien* (see above) which is in every way recommendable.

Dutoit's performances are individually characterized and by no means conventional in approach. *1812*, complete with cannon provided by the 22nd Regiment of Quebec, is exciting without making one sit on the edge of one's seat. The sound is refined and luminous but lacks the sumptuous weight which is needed to give Tchaikovsky's climaxes a physical thrill. *Francesca da Rimini* has both weight and strength, backed up by a recording of spectacular range, but with less variation of tension than in the very finest versions.

Festival coronation march in D; (i) *Romeo and Juliet:* duet (orch. Taneyev).
*** Chan. Dig. CHAN 8476; *ABTD 1187* [id.]. (i) Murphy, Lewis, Wilson-Johnson; SNO, Järvi – RACHMANINOV: *The Bells* etc. **(*)

Tchaikovsky's *Festival coronation march* was written for open-air performance before the Tsar in 1883. It is suitably grandiloquent but has a rather engaging trio, plus a whiff of the Tsarist hymn we recognize from *1812*. It is very well played here and superbly recorded. The vocalization of *Romeo and Juliet*, with the music drawn from the famous fantasy overture, was left in the form of posthumous sketches, which Taneyev completed and scored. The effect is more like a symphonic poem with vocal obbligatos, rather than operatic. It is well sung here but is mainly of curiosity value.

Festival overture on the Danish national anthem, Op. 15; (i) *Hamlet: Overture and incidental music, Op. 67 bis. Mazeppa: Battle of Poltava and Cossack dance; Romeo and Juliet* (fantasy overture; 1869 version); *Serenade for Nikolai Rubinstein's saint's day.*
❀ *** Chan. Dig. CHAN 8310/11; *DBTD 2003* (2) [id.]. LSO, Simon, (i) with Janis Kelly, Hammond-Stroud.

Tchaikovsky himself thought his *Danish Festival overture* superior to *1812*, and though one cannot agree with his judgement it is well worth hearing. The *Hamlet* incidental music is another matter. The overture is a shortened version of the *Hamlet fantasy overture*, but much of the rest of the incidental music is unknown, and the engaging *Funeral march* and the two poignant string elegies show the composer's inspiration at its most memorable. Ophelia's mad scene is partly sung and partly spoken, and Janis Kelly's performance is most sympathetic, while Derek Hammond-Stroud is suitably robust in the *Gravedigger's song*. The music from *Mazeppa* and the tribute to Rubinstein make engaging bonuses, but the highlight of the set is the 1869 version of *Romeo and Juliet*, very different from the final, 1880 version we know so well. It is fascinating to hear the composer's early thoughts before he finalized a piece which was to become one of the most successful of all his works. The performances here under Geoffrey Simon are excitingly committed and spontaneous; the orchestral playing is nearly always first rate, and the digital recording has spectacular resonance and depth to balance its brilliance. Edward Johnson, who provided the initial impetus for the recordings, writes the excellent notes and a translation of the vocal music, which is sung (as the original production of *Hamlet* was performed) in French.

Francesca da Rimini.
** Virgin Dig. VC7 91476-2 [id.]. Houston SO, Eschenbach – DVOŘÁK: *Symphony No. 9.* **

Eschenbach's performance of *Francesca da Rimini* has similar qualities to those in the Dvořák symphony, with which it is coupled. With clean textures and ensemble, with rhythms crisply resilient and with the brass section gloriously ripe, it is a refreshing performance which yet lacks Tchaikovskian passion. It makes a generous and unusual fill-up for the *New World Symphony*.

Francesca da Rimini, Op. 22; Marche slave, Op. 31; Serenade for strings, Op. 48.
*(*) Erato/Warner Dig. 2292 45629-2 [id.]. USSR MoC SO, Rozhdestvensky.

A disappointment. One can hardly believe this is a Russian orchestra in *Francesca da Rimini*. Rozhdestvensky pushes on hard after the opening, but there is a lack of underlying fervour, the middle section of the piece is bland and the climax brings no feeling of despairing, unbridled passions and the stark punishment of Hell. The *Serenade for strings* is also a very low-key performance; the first movement is far too slack, and the rhythms of the finale are heavy rather than buoyant. The best thing here by far is the ebullient *Marche slave*.

Manfred Symphony, Op. 58.
❀ *** Chan. Dig. CHAN 8535; *ABTD 1245* [id.]. Oslo PO, Jansons.
*** EMI Dig. CDC7 47412-2 [id.]. Philh. O, Muti.
(M) *** Collins Dig. 3001-2 [id.]. LSO, Yuri Simonov.

Jansons' performance of *Manfred* with the Oslo Philharmonic crowns his outstanding series in an electrifying account of this difficult, unconventionally structured work. Except in a relatively relaxed view of the *vivace* second movement, Jansons favours speeds flowing faster than usual, bringing out the drama but subtly varying the tensions to press each climax home to the full and always showing his mastery of Tchaikovskian rubato: his warmly expressive phrasing never sounds self-conscious when it is regularly given the freshness of folksong. The performance culminates in a thrilling account of the finale, leading up to the entry of the organ, gloriously resonant and supported by luxuriant string sound. The Chandos recording is among the finest in the Oslo series, atmospheric but with fine inner detail.

Muti's reading is forceful and boldly dramatic throughout. His Scherzo has a quality of exhilarating bravura, rather than concentrating on delicacy; the lovely central melody is given a sense of joyous vigour. The *Andante*, after a refined opening, soon develops a passionate forward sweep; in the finale the amplitude and brilliant detail of the recording, combined with magnificent playing from the Philharmonia Orchestra, brings a massively compulsive projection of Tchaikovsky's bacchanale and a richly satisfying dénouement. The CD adds to the weight and definition of the recording, but the result is slightly less sumptuous than the original LP, and sonically the new Decca version is even more spectacular.

Although Simonov's tempi overall are spacious rather than thrusting (the very opening could have more rhythmic point) and the recording balance is a little recessed, this is still a highly involving and romantically powerful account of what is perhaps the most difficult of all Tchaikovsky's major works to bring off successfully. But Simonov has its measure and his reading reaches its climax with the massive organ entry in the finale, a moment of great drama. The pastoral *Andante* also has a fine lyrical warmth, and the scherzo is lilting and colourful.

The Nutcracker (ballet), *Op. 71* (complete).
*** Decca Dig. 433 000-2 (2) [id.]. Finchley Children's Music Group. RPO, Ashkenazy – GLAZUNOV: *Seasons.* ***
*** Telarc Dig. CD 8137 (2) [id.]. LSO & Ch., Mackerras.
*** Sony Dig. M2K 42173 (2) [id.]. Philh. O & Ch., Tilson Thomas.
(M) **(*) Decca 425 450-2 (2) [id.]. Nat. PO, Richard Bonynge – OFFENBACH: *Le Papillon.* ***
(*) ROH Dig. ROH 304/5 [id.]. ROHCG O, Mark Ermler – ARENSKY: *Variations.* *

(i) *The Nutcracker* (ballet) complete; (ii) *Serenade for strings in C, Op. 48.*
(M) *** Mercury 432 750-2 (2). (i) LSO; (ii) Philharmonia Hungarica, Antal Dorati.

The Nutcracker (complete); *Sleeping Beauty* (ballet): suite.
**(*) Ph. Dig. 435 619-2 (2) [id.]. American Boychoir, Boston SO, Ozawa.

(i) *The Nutcracker* (ballet) complete; (ii) *Swan Lake* (ballet): highlights.
(B) **(*) Pickwick DUET 20 CD [MCAD2 9801]. (i) LPO, Artur Rodzinski; (ii) Utah SO, Abravanel.

The Nutcracker (ballet) complete; *Eugene Onegin: Introduction; Waltz; Polonaise.*
*** Ph. Dig. 420 237-2 (2) [id.]. BPO, Bychkov.

Although Dorati's justly famous Mercury set remains highly competitive at mid-price, Ashkenazy's digital *Nutcracker* now takes its place fairly easily at the top of the list. It is ideally coupled with Glazunov's *Seasons*, a no less enticing performance, and has the benefit of Walthamstow acoustics and state-of-the-art Decca digital sound, glowingly warm, with much colour and bloom for the woodwind. The silkiness of the strings is immediately apparent in the *Miniature overture*, and there is much delicacy of texture elsewhere. The whole party sequence, handled by Ashkenazy with great flexibility, is totally beguiling and there are some good special effects when the children receive their toys. After the church clock strikes midnight the magic begins, and the mock battle and the glorious melody of the children's journey through the pine forest is beautifully managed. The *Snowflakes* choral *waltz* has warmth as well as charm and the famous characteristic dances of the Act II Divertissement match elegance and character with a multi-hued palette of colour. Ideally the recording could be more generously cued in the accompanying documentation, and the narrative needs to be better related to the music in the notes, but for the music-making and recording there can only be the highest praise.

The Telarc set was recorded in Watford Town Hall, bringing the extra resonance of the concert hall, which adds a little glamour to the violins and a glowing warmth in the middle and lower range. When the magic spell begins, the spectacularly wide dynamic range and the extra amplitude make for a physical frisson in the climaxes, while the glorious climbing melody, as Clara and the Prince travel through the pine forest, sounds richly expansive. Before that, the battle has some real cannon-shots interpolated but is done good-humouredly, for this is a toy battle. In the earlier party scene, Mackerras presses forward more than Previn and this creates added intensity in Act I; but in the Act II *Divertissement* Mackerras's sparkling vivacity is sometimes less telling than Previn's easy elegance, and here the latter is preferable. Yet the great *Pas de deux* brings the most sumptuous climax, with superb sonority from the brass on the Telarc version. The Telarc presentation, too, with a detailed synopsis, is far superior to the much more meagre EMI documentation.

Undoubtedly Dorati's LSO version is the finest of the mid- and bargain-priced analogue *Nutcrackers.* The engineering is sophisticated, with a natural balance; the hall ambience provides warmth and bloom, yet detail is characteristically refined. The party sequence of Act I can often sound flat, but not here: Dorati relishes every detail, his characterization is strong, and the playing is full of life and elegance. The *Journey through the pine forest* expands magnificently while the choral delicacy of the *Waltz of the snowflakes* is full of charm. In Act II the characteristic dances have much colour and vitality. Altogether a great success. The *Serenade for strings* is less compelling. The slightly dry effect does not capture quite enough of the hall ambience and turns a close scrutiny on ensemble from the Philharmonia Hungarica, who could at times be more polished. It is an affectionate performance, but not an especially vital one. On the other hand, the relaxed close of the *Élégie* leading on to the gentle opening of the bustling finale is rather effective. In any case, however, this set is worth having for the ballet performance alone. Excellent documentation.

Semyon Bychkov has the services of the Berlin Philharmonic (an orchestra that always identifies readily with Tchaikovsky) and they offer superlative playing, of striking flair and character. Although a concert-hall ambience is favoured, the strings seem more forward, inner detail is very clear and the cymbals have a thrilling metallic clash. There is some superbly stylish playing in the *Divertissement*, and there are many moments when the extra vividness of the Berlin recording is especially compelling; and, of course, Bychkov offers a bonus, for the *Eugene Onegin* excerpts are brilliantly done. The Philips notes are extensive but not so conveniently matched to the CD cues.

Michael Tilson Thomas also has the advantage of fine Philharmonia playing, recorded in rather similar acoustics to the EMI set. The CBS balance is very good too, and this account lies between those of Previn and Mackerras, with a touch more spectacle than the former. Tempi are generally a fraction brisker on CBS, but the brighter rhythmic feeling often pays dividends. Generally, however, this would not be a first choice and the CBS documentation is inadequate, with only a brief synopsis.

Rodzinski's *Nutcracker* derives from the old Westminster label and dates from the earliest days of stereo. The tingling vitality of the playing brings infectious zest to the party scene of Act I – and a smile to the face of the listener, when the clock striking midnight to herald the beginning of the magic is recognized, incongruously, as none other than Big Ben! Later the gorgeous *Journey through the pine forest* brings a frisson of pleasure in its breadth and intensity, while the great Act II *Pas de deux* has even greater passion. The studio recording has a glowing richness of string texture, so effective in the lilting *Waltz of the flowers*. The rather robust contribution of the chorus robs the *Waltz of the snowflakes* of some of its essential delicacy; yet the whole performance is so grippingly involving that reservations are of less moment, with the set in the bargain range. Fortunately the coupling has comparable vividness and excitement; the recording here is less opulent, brighter and with better internal definition. In a generous selection from *Swan Lake* Abravanel produces often electrifying playing from his splendid Utah orchestra – the *Scène final* is thrilling, yet there is much that is elegant and stylish too, not least the charming *Dance of the little swans* and the eloquently played violin/cello duet in the *Danse des cygnes*.

Bonynge's set is made the more attractive by its rare and substantial Offenbach coupling. His approach is sympathetic and the orchestral playing is polished, even if in the opening scene he misses some of the atmosphere. With the beginning of the magic, as the Christmas tree expands, the performance becomes more dramatically involving, and in the latter part of the ballet Bonynge is at his best, with fine passion in the Act II *Pas de deux* and plenty of colour in the characteristic dances. The Decca recording is brilliant and vivid.

Ozawa's light ballet touch produces playing of much elegance and grace, and the Philips recording is remarkably transparent as well as warm and full. The performance of the opening party scene is most felicitously controlled; here the conductor's superb technical control brings immaculate polish without loss of spontaneity. The journey through the pine forest is rich-textured and there is plenty of orchestral virtuosity in the Battle sequence. However the usual special effects are absent, as are the clock's midnight chimes. The dances which make up the Divertissement of Act II, have plenty of finesse, but lack something in individuality and the same comment applies to the *Sleeping Beauty suite* which is the unimaginative fill-up. The sound cannot be faulted, but this is no match for Ashkenazy.

Mark Ermler's version was recorded as one of the first issues on the new Royal Opera House label. As in the companion recording of *Swan Lake*, the players respond warmly and idiomatically to Tchaikovsky's ballet music, but the orchestral ensemble is not quite so crisp here, and the warmly reverberant recording tends to inflate the performance, undermining the piece's delicacy, its fairy-tale atmosphere. Detail is obscured too, notably in rapid string passage-work, with heavy brass putting a gauze over the whole ensemble. It is an enjoyable version nevertheless, recommendable to those who expressly want the engaging Arensky coupling.

The Nutcracker (ballet): excerpts, *Op. 71*.
(M) *** Sony Dig. MDK 44656 [id.]. Amb. S., Philh. O, Tilson Thomas.
*** Telarc Dig. CD 80140 [id.]. Tiffin School Boys' Ch., LSO, Mackerras.

On the face of it, the Tilson Thomas CD would seem to be the strongest recommendation: it offers considerably more music (70 minutes) than the Telarc disc; the bright-eyed Philharmonia playing is always alive and zestful; and the CBS recording is brilliant and well balanced. Moreover the selection is offered at mid-price.

But when one turns to the Telarc disc, which plays for some 55 minutes only, one enters a different, more expansive Tchaikovskian sound-world: the flair of the Battle sequence between the Nutcracker and the Mouse King immediately captures the imagination. Mackerras misses out much of Act I, but not the famous *Marche* nor the sequence called *The Magic Spell begins*, which is superbly expansive. Similarly, the *Scene in the Pine Forest* with Tchaikovsky's great climbing, scaling melody has a frisson-creating tension, and the *Waltz of the snowflakes* sets the mood for the famous characteristic dances of Act II, all splendidly done, and recorded in Telarc's most spectacular manner. Nevertheless the CBS disc is undoubtedly a bargain in its own way.

Nutcracker suite, Op. 71a.
(M) **(*) Sony SBK 46550 [id.]. Phd. O, Ormandy – CHOPIN: *Les Sylphides;* DELIBES: *Coppélia; Sylvia: Suites.* ***
(M) ** BMG/RCA GD 86718; *GK 86718.* Boston Pops O, Fiedler – PROKOFIEV: *Peter* *(**); SAINT-SAËNS: *Carnival.* **

The Philadelphia Orchestra made this wonderful music universally famous in Walt Disney's *Fantasia* and they know how to play it just as well under Ormandy in 1963 as they did under Stokowski. Perhaps there is less individuality in the characteristic dances, but the music-making has suitable moments of reticence (as in the neat *Ouverture miniature*) as well as plenty of flair. In the *Waltz of the flowers* Ormandy blots his copybook by taking the soaring violin tune an octave up on its second appearance, both at the beginning and in the reprise, but the Philadelphia violins make such a brilliant effect that one can almost forgive the excess.

Fiedler's 1956 Boston Pops account is well played and the early stereo is pleasing. This is enjoyable, if not distinctive, but the main interest of this disc is Sir Alec Guinness's narration of *Peter and the wolf.*

(i) *The Nutcracker; Sleeping Beauty; Swan Lake:* excerpts.
(B) **(*) EMI CZS7 62816-2 (2) [id.]. LSO, André Previn, (i) with Amb. S.

By the use of two CDs, offering some 148 minutes of music, this EMI box (issued in the 'two for the price of one' series) covers a substantial proportion of the key numbers from all three ballets. *The Nutcracker* selection is particularly generous in including, besides virtually all the most famous characteristic dances, the 13-minute episode in Act I starting with the Battle sequence, continuing with the magical Pine forest journey and finishing with the delightful choral *Waltz of the snowflakes.* Previn and the LSO provide vivacious, charismatic playing and the recording is full, bright and vivid. The remastering, however, loses some of the smoothness and refinement of focus of the original, analogue recordings in the interest of a lively upper range. But this remains very enjoyable and excellent value.

The Nutcracker; Sleeping Beauty; Swan Lake: highlights.
(M) *** EMI Dig. CDD7 641109-2 [id.]; *ET 764109-4.* Philh. O, Lanchbery.
(B) *** EMI CDZ7 62861-2; *LZ 762861-4.* Philh. O, Efrem Kurtz.

Those wanting a single disc of highlights from Tchaikovsky's three major ballets will surely find Lanchbery's selection fits the bill readily enough. Although it is perhaps a pity that the whole *Nutcracker suite* was not included, the favourite items are here, and there are eight popular excerpts from *Swan Lake* and seven from the *Sleeping Beauty* score. There are 79 minutes of music in all, played with great flair, warmth and polish, and given EMI's top-drawer digital sound.

At bargain price, the alternative collection from Kurtz, with the Philharmonia at its absolute peak, is also very recommendable. The early (late 1950s) stereo sounds astonishingly full, and the performances combine elegance and finesse with sparkle and colour. Here all of the *Nutcracker suite* is included except the *Chinese dance*, an inexplicable omission that would have nicely fitted on, as the programme plays for 77 minutes 39 seconds.

Nutcracker suite, Op. 71a; Romeo and Juliet (fantasy overture); Swan Lake suite, Op. 20.
(M) *** Decca Dig. 430 707-2; *430 707-4.* Chicago SO, Solti.

Solti's digital recording of the *Swan Lake suite* comes in an attractive triptych, given Decca's best standard Chicago recording. *Romeo and Juliet* has an unexpected element of restraint and the love-theme, very tender and gentle when it first appears on the cor anglais, finds a yearning passion without histrionics; the battle sequences have plenty of bite in the strings, and at the climax the trumpets ring out resplendently. The *Nutcracker suite* produces marvellously characterful solo playing and much subtle detail.

Nutcracker suite; Sleeping Beauty: suite; Swan Lake: suite.
❀ (M) *** DG 429 097-2; *429 097-4* [id.]. BPO, Rostropovich.

(M) *** EMI CDM7 64332-2; *EG 764332-4*. LSO, Previn.

Rostropovich's triptych of Tchaikovsky ballet suites is very special. His account of the *Nutcracker suite* is enchanting: the *Sugar plum fairy* is introduced with ethereal gentleness, the *Russian dance* has marvellous zest and the *Waltz of the flowers* combines warmth and elegance with an exhilarating vigour. The *Sleeping Beauty* and *Swan Lake* selections are hardly less distinguished. There is plenty of Slavonic intensity in the sweeping climaxes, and in the former the glorious *Panorama* melody is floated over its gently syncopated rocking bass with magical delicacy. Equally, the whimsical portrait of the cats is matched by the sprightly fledgling swans. The 1979 recording, with full strings and a lustrous ambience, expands spectacularly at climaxes, the CD remastering entirely beneficial, combining bloom with enhanced detail. 69 minutes of sheer joy, and at mid-price too.

The digital remastering has been very successful on the EMI disc, freshening the sound of the excellent recordings, taken from Previn's analogue complete sets (which means that the *Dance of the sugar plum fairy* in *The Nutcracker* has the longer coda rather than the ending Tchaikovsky devised for the *Suite*). The performances are at once vivid and elegant, warm and exciting. Previn's panorama from *Sleeping Beauty* is hardly less beguiling than Rostropovich's and the recording has comparable warmth. There is nearly 73 minutes of music here, and this version can be strongly recommended alongside the DG disc; it is a most enjoyable record.

Nutcracker suite, Op. 71a; Symphony No. 4 in F min., Op. 36.
(M) (***) EMI mono CDM7 63380-2 [id.]. RPO, Sir Thomas Beecham.

Beecham himself praised the balance in the *Nutcracker suite*, one of his own favourite records. Endearingly, the tambourine player in the characteristically zestful account of the *Trépak* almost gets left behind at the end. The performance overall has a Mozartian elegance; the *Dance of the flutes*, seductively slow, is ravishing and so is the closing *Waltz of the flowers*. Sir Thomas allowed his performance of the *Fourth Symphony* to be recorded in mono, though it was made as late as 1957/8. Even so, the sound is outstandingly vivid, and the ear could easily be fooled into thinking it was stereo, so full are the strings and so rich the brass, with their glorious depth of sonority. The performance is unforgettably full of charisma. In the famous rocking crescendo in the first movement, Beecham manages to be urbane while at the same time building up the tension spontaneously; the account is second to none in generating excitement, with the thrilling coda of the last movement creating all the adrenalin of a live occasion.

Serenade for strings in C, Op. 48 (see also below, under *Symphonies Nos. 3 and 5*).
(*) Virgin Dig. VC7 91165-2; *VC7 91165-4*. LCO, Warren-Green – DVOŘÁK: *Serenade* **(*); SUK: *Serenade.* *

Serenade for strings; Suite No. 4 (Mozartiana), Op. 61; Andante cantabile, from Op. 11.
*** ASV Novalis Dig. 150 057-2; *150 057-4* [id.]. ECO, James Judd.

Serenade for strings; Suite No. 4 (Mozartiana); Elegy in G (in remembrance of Ivan Samarin); Andante cantabile (arr. Serebrier); *The Sleeping Beauty: Variations of the Lilac Fairy; Entr'acte* (both orch. Stravinsky).
**(*) ASV Dig. CDDCA 719; *ZCDCA 719* [id.]. SCO, José Serebrier.

In considering new versions of the *Serenade*, readers should bear in mind that Karajan's 1980 digital recording, with marvellously polished playing from the Berlin Philharmonic on their finest form, has been reissued at mid-price. If the coupling, with an equally impressive account of the *Third Symphony*, is suitable, this makes an obvious first choice.

James Judd's performances have a natural flow and an appealing directness and spontaneity. Tempi are never pressed too hard; if, in the *Serenade*, the *Waltz* is a little lacking in romantic ripeness, its simplicity fits in well with the overall conception. The slow movement has pleasing ardour and the finale, nicely prepared, brings plenty of energetic bustle. The *Mozartiana suite* sounds equally fresh: the vividness of Tchaikovsky's scoring is well caught by the excellent recording, the nineteenth-century feeling in the central movements is tastefully handled, and an elegant spirit pervades the music-making throughout. The *Andante cantabile* has a comparable sensibility and is most stylishly presented, while retaining its warmth.

Serebrier offers much more music (77 minutes, against 64 from Judd) and the Scottish Chamber Orchestra play warmly for him. He opens the *Serenade* spaciously and provides an enjoyably easy-going reading, with neat if not sharply focused detail and with no lack of elegance; the *Waltz* here has more seductive feeling than with either Judd or Bashmet. The finale is buoyant and light-hearted. Serebrier also presents the *Mozartiana suite* very winningly, but before that comes the valedictory *Elegy* with its bitter-sweet melancholy. The SCO play it tenderly, with wistful *espressivo*, and are equally sympathetic in Serebrier's arrangement of the *Andante cantabile*. His concert ends with two attractive novelties, orchestrations of two numbers from *The Sleeping Beauty*, made by Stravinsky from the piano score and commissioned by Diaghilev when the ballet was staged in London in 1921. Serebrier's programme is certainly generous and all the music is easy to enjoy, for the recording is full and pleasing; but other versions of the *Serenade* have a stronger profile.

Not surprisingly, Christopher Warren-Green's reading with his excellent LCO players is full of individuality. The first movement's secondary idea has an appealing feathery lightness, and when the striding opening theme reappears at the end of the movement it brings a spontaneous-sounding burst of expressive intensity characteristic of this group. The *Waltz* lilts gently, with the tenutos nicely observed, the *Élégie* has delicacy as well as fervour, and the finale has plenty of energy. This may not be quite as polished or as romantically powerful as Karajan's outstanding version (now an amazing bargain in its pairing with the *Polish Symphony*) but, with an outstanding coupling of the Suk, and enjoyable Dvořák too, this Virgin Classics triptych, very naturally recorded, will give pleasure for its freshness and natural impetus.

Serenade for strings; Souvenir de Florence, Op. 70.
(BB) **(*) Naxos Dig. 8.550404 [id.]. Vienna CO, Philippe Entremont.

Entremont's performances of Tchaikovsky's two major string works communicate above all a feeling of passionate thrust and energy. The *Waltz*, with its neatly managed tenutos, has a nice touch of romantic feeling and, after the ardour of the *Élégie*, the finale steals in persuasively, again producing an unflagging impetus, with dance-rhythms bracing and strong. The unaccountably neglected *Souvenir de Florence* has comparable momentum and eagerness. The dashing main theme of the first movement swings along infectiously, while the wistful secondary idea also takes wing. Entremont brings out the charm and responds easily to the variety of mood, both here and in the *Allegretto*, permeated with a flavour of Russian folksong. Throughout, the commitment and ensemble of the VCO bring the most persuasive advocacy and make one wonder why the *Souvenir* does not have a more central place in the string repertoire.

(i) *Serenade for strings, Op. 48;* (ii) *Invocation to sleep* (for choir and orchestra); *Legend: Christ has a garden* (for unaccompanied choir), *Op. 54/5*.
*(*) Opus Dig. OPS 57-9203 [id.]. (i) Byelorussian CO, Poliansky – ARENSKY: *Variations.* **

Considering the players are Russian, Poliansky's account of the *Serenade* is extraordinarily lacking in vitality. Even the *Elegy* lacks real fervour and the opening to the first movement is impossibly sluggish. The star is for the two almost unknown choral items, well sung, acceptably if not especially clearly recorded.

The Sleeping Beauty (ballet), *Op. 66* (complete).
(M) **(*) Decca 425 468-2 (3). Nat. PO, Richard Bonynge – MEYERBEER: *Les Patineurs.* ***
** ROH Dig. ROH 306/8; *ROHMC 306/8* (3). ROHCG O, Mark Ermler.

Bonynge secures brilliant and often elegant playing from the National Philharmonic Orchestra and his rhythmic pointing is always characterful. As recorded, however, the upper strings lack sumptuousness; otherwise, the sound is excellent and there is much to give pleasure, notably the drama of the awakening scene and the Act III *Divertissement*. The Decca sound has a fine sparkle here, and the solo violin (Mincho Minchev) and cello (Francisco Gabarro) provide most appealing solo contributions.

The account by the Royal Opera House Orchestra, playing very elegantly under Mark Ermler, runs to three full-priced CDs, indicating that tempi are often relaxed and leisurely. Although the performance is not without drama, the combination of amiable warmth in the music-making with a body of orchestral sound that is little short of voluptuous inevitably brings an element of blandness. Although it is easy to sit back and wallow in Tchaikovsky's richly coloured scoring and melodic fecundity, rival versions offer a greater feeling of vitality.

Sleeping Beauty (ballet): highlights.
**(*) ROH Dig. ROH 003; *ROHMC 003* [id.] (from above recording, cond. Ermler).
(M) ** Sony SBK 46340 [id.]; *40-46340*. Phd. O, Ormandy – ROSSINI: *Boutique fantasque.* **(*)

Those wishing to sample the Ermler set will find this disc contains 72 minutes of well-chosen key items. One can certainly appreciate the polish and grace of the orchestral playing here, when the recording – made in St Jude-on-the-Hill, Hampstead – is so flattering.

Ormandy provides a sumptuously glossy selection, with nearly an hour's music (the CD plays for 76 minutes overall). Superbly polished and often exciting playing but, with a forward balance, the effect is somewhat overwhelming. The sound is opulently brilliant rather than refined.

Sleeping Beauty (ballet): *Suite.*
(BB) ** Naxos Dig. 8.550079; *4550079* [id.]. Czech RSO (Bratislava), Ondrej Lenárd – GLAZUNOV: *The Seasons.* **(*)

The Czech Radio Orchestra under Ondrej Lenárd play Tchaikovsky's ballet suite with spirit and colour, and the recording has plenty of weight and ambience and no lack of brilliance. The *Waltz* goes especially well, but before that the *Panorama* is disappointing, taken fast and with a lack of subtlety in the rocking bass rhythm.

(i) *Sleeping Beauty: suite;* (ii) *Swan Lake, Op. 20:* excerpts.
(B) **(*) DG Compact Classics 413 430-2 (2); *413 430-4* [id.]. (i) BPO, Rostropovich; (ii) Boston SO, Ozawa – PROKOFIEV: *Romeo and Juliet* *** (CD only: *Love for 3 oranges:* suite **(*)).

Rostropovich's *Sleeping Beauty suite* is highly distinguished, as fine as any in the catalogue, and the collection of *Swan Lake* excerpts from Ozawa is generous. Here the sophistication of playing and recording, within the warm Boston acoustic, is impressive; while the individual items have less individuality of approach than with Rostropovich, the orchestral response is first class and the final climax expands magnificently. Combined with an excellent selection from Prokofiev's *Romeo and Juliet*, this Compact Classics tape is very good value. The pair of CDs include also a less magnetic account of the *Love for three oranges suite.*

Suites Nos. 1 in D min., Op. 45; 4 (Mozartiana), Op. 61.
*** Olympia Dig. OCD 109 [id.]. USSR Academic SO, Svetlanov.

Tchaikovsky's *Orchestral suites* are directly descended from the dance suites of the Baroque era. Svetlanov shows his understanding of this link by his engagingly light touch. He is particularly successful in *Mozartiana*, where Tchaikovsky's neat scoring is always respectful of the music. Even so, the *Preghiera*, based on Mozart's *Ave verum*, can sometimes sound too opulent, but not here. The *Variations* which end the suite are a delight. The highlight of the earlier D minor work is a deliciously orchestrated *Marche miniature* which tends to dwarf everything else, except perhaps the *Introduction* where Tchaikovsky's innate melancholy at the opening is effectively dispersed by the following fugato. With such sympathetic playing and excellent digital sound, this is a prime recommendation for all keen Tchaikovskians.

(i) *Suites Nos. 2 in C, Op. 53; 4 in G (Mozartiana), Op. 61;* (ii) *Sérénade mélancolique, Op. 26; Mélodie, Op. 42/3.*
(M) **(*) Sony/CBS Dig. MDK 46503 [id.]. (i) Philh. O, Tilson Thomas; (ii) Zukerman, Israel PO, Mehta.

Michael Tilson Thomas makes a very good case for Tchaikovsky's *Mozartiana suite.* The Philharmonia's response is first class, and the *Second Suite* is also played with great vitality. The bright, slightly dry, early digital recording (made in EMI's No. 1 Studio at Abbey Road), which suits *Mozartiana* rather well, makes the more extrovert, fully scored first movement of the *Second*, *Jeu de sons*, seem a little aggressive in its brilliance, although the sharp focus is just right for the *Scherzo burlesque*, bustling with its accordions. The fill-ups, if brief, are scarcely apt but are tenderly played and very appealing. Zukerman is closely balanced and his G string tone in the *Sérénade mélancolique* is ravishing without being too schmaltzy. This is a very good disc, and reservations about the recording are not serious; there is no lack of basic ambience.

(i) *Suite No. 2 in C, Op. 53;* (ii) *Symphony No. 2 in C min. (Little Russian), Op. 17.*
*** Olympia OCD 153 [id.]. (i) USSR Academic SO, Svetlanov; (ii) USSR RSO, Fedoseyev.

Svetlanov's inspirational recording of the *Second Suite* is doubly distinctive for making the listener realize that this is a far more substantial and attractive work than was previously thought. The *Scherzo burlesque* has a part for accordions in its central section, but here they are covered with folksy woodwind sounds: the effect is highly piquant. The finale is a vivacious *Danse baroque* where the energy of the performance bubbles right over. The Russian orchestral playing is full of character and affection throughout, and the vivid recording is a joy in projecting this multi-coloured music.

Fedoseyev's version of the *Little Russian symphony* may not be the most brilliant available: the finale is paced in a very relaxed way and the further broadening at the end is overdone. But the very Russian character of the woodwind and the bright, clean string articulation give the music-making plenty of character and impulse.

Suite No. 3 in G, Op. 55.
*** Olympia Dig. OCD 106 [id.]. USSR Academic SO, Svetlanov – ARENSKY: *Violin concerto.* ***

Svetlanov treats Tchaikovsky's finest suite very freely, supported by the most eloquent response from one of the premier Soviet orchestras. The first movement is lyrically rhapsodic, then comes a bitter-sweet *Valse mélancolique*, its nostalgia curiously dark for all its grace and lightness of form; the Scherzo, deliciously scored, is almost too purposefully gay; but the work is capped by the masterly final theme and variations, which quite outbalances the structure, but justifies itself by its inspired melodic invention and in its unsurpassed use of orchestral colour. Here some of Svetlanov's tempi are unexpected, and the finale *Polacca* is less overwhelming than in some previous versions, Svetalanov emphasizing its dance rhythms rather than seeking to be grandiose. With excellent, vivid digital recording and an attractive concert-hall ambience, this is highly recommendable, particularly in view of the tempting Arensky coupling.

Swan Lake (ballet), *Op. 20* (complete).
(B) *** CfP Dig. CD-CFPD 4727; *TC-CFPD 4727* (2). Philh. O, John Lanchbery.
**(*) ROH Dig. ROH 301/3 [id.]. ROHCG O, Mark Ermler.
(M) **(*) Decca 425 413-2 (3) [id.]. Nat. PO, Richard Bonynge – MASSENET: *Cigale.* ***

Lanchbery's 1982 *Swan Lake* makes a superb bargain and, at this price, must now be a clear first choice among available versions. The CfP reissue on a pair of CDs, which play for 79 minutes and 75 minutes respectively, accommodates Acts I and II on the first disc and Acts III and IV on the second. Though two numbers are cut, the set includes the extra music (a *Pas de deux*) which Tchaikovsky wrote to follow the *Pas de six* in Act III, when Siegfried dances with Odile, mistakenly believing her to be Odette. The EMI recording, made at Abbey Road, is very fine indeed: spacious, vividly coloured and full, with natural perspective and a wide (but not uncomfortably wide) dynamic range. The orchestral playing is first class, with polished, elegant string phrasing matched by felicitous wind solos. Lanchbery's rhythmic spring is a constant pleasure; everything is alert, and there is plenty of excitement at climaxes. The score's marvellous detail is revealed with long theatrical experience. The documentation is good, with an adequate synopsis of the narrative, but without linking track cues.

Released from the Covent Garden pit to record in the warm acoustic of All Saints', Tooting, the players have responded to Ermler's deeply sympathetic direction with both refinement and red-blooded commitment, and one is constantly aware of the idiomatic feeling born of long acquaintance. The sound is exceptionally full and open, with the brass in particular giving satisfying weight to the ensemble without hazing over the detail. Ermler's speeds are often – though by no means always – on the slow side, but it is a pity that the decision was taken to stretch the work on to an extra CD, three instead of two, making it far less competitive. Nor does that bring any advantage in breaks between the discs, with the division between the second and third discs coming distractingly in the middle of the Act III *Pas de six*. Nevertheless Ermler's broad speeds consistently convey, more than most rivals', the feeling of an accompaniment for dancing, as in the great andante of the Act I *Pas de deux*. This is a set to have you sitting back in new enjoyment of a gorgeous score.

Bonynge's approach is essentially strong and vigorous, bringing out all the drama of the score, if less of its charm. The forward impulse of the music-making is immediately striking. As in the other sets of his Decca Tchaikovsky series, the string timbre is somewhat leonine; overall there is fullness without sumptuousness. The brass sounds are open and vibrant and the upper range is brightly lit. The balance is managed well although the (very well-played) violin solos sound rather larger than life. While this lack of ripeness may not appeal to all ears, there is a consistent freshness here, and the moments of spectacle often make a thrilling impact.

Swan Lake (ballet), *Op. 20:* highlights.
(B) *** CfP CD-CFP 4296 [Ang. CDB 62713]. Sir Yehudi Menuhin, Philh. O, Efrem Kurtz.

A fine bargain selection on CfP with Menuhin present for the violin solos. He finds a surprising amount to play here. The 1960 recording matches the exuberance which Kurtz brings to the music's climaxes with an expansive dynamic range, and it has atmosphere as well as brilliance. The Philharmonia are on top form and the woodwind acquit themselves with plenty of style, while the string playing is characteristically elegant.

SYMPHONIES

Symphonies Nos. 1–6.
(M) *** DG 429 675-2 (4) [id.]. BPO, Karajan.
(B) *** Ph. 426 848-2 (4) [id.]. LSO, Markevitch.

Symphonies Nos. 1–6; Capriccio italien; Manfred Symphony.
❀ (M) *** Chan. Dig. CHAN 8672/8; *DBTD 7001* (7) [id.]. Oslo PO, Jansons.

Symphonies Nos. 1–6; Romeo and Juliet (fantasy overture).
(M) *** EMI CZS7 67314-2 (4) [Ang. CDMB 67314]. Philh. O, Muti.
(B) *** Decca 430 787-2 (4) [id.]. VPO, Lorin Maazel.

Jansons' outstanding Tchaikovsky series, which includes *Manfred*, is self-recommending. The full romantic power of the music is consistently conveyed and, above all, the music-making is urgently spontaneous throughout, with the Oslo Philharmonic Orchestra always committed and fresh, helped by the richly atmospheric Chandos sound. The seven separate CDs offered here are packaged in a box priced as for five premium discs, with cassette equivalents.

Muti recorded his Tchaikovsky cycle over a period of six years in the late 1970s. It represented not only the high point of his recording partnership with the Philharmonia Orchestra but also the peak of his interpretative career. It is a measure of Muti's success that even the first of the series to be recorded, No. 1, brings a performance as refined and persuasive as it is exciting, and the three early symphonies all bring orchestral playing which is both sophisticated and colourful. Throughout the cycle, and especially in the strong, urgent No. 4, Muti's view is brisk and dramatically direct, yet never lacking in feeling or imagination. In No. 5 he underlines the symphonic strength of the first movement rather than the immediate excitement. The finale then presents a sharp contrast, with its fast tempo and controlled excitement. In the *Pathétique* tempi are again characteristically fast, yet the result is fresh and youthful, with the flowing first-movement second subject given an easy expressiveness. The March, for all its urgency, never sounds brutal and the finale has satisfying depth and power. The sound generally is well up to EMI's best analogue standard of this period, and it has been transferred to CD very impressively, with the focus firm and no lack of body and weight. The layout involves just one break between discs in the middle of a symphony and the final CD offers the *Pathétique* plus Muti's superb analogue *Romeo and Juliet*, one of the finest available, and full of imaginative touches.

Karajan's set, however, offers a quite outstanding bargain. Without *Manfred* (a work he never recorded), the six symphonies are fitted on to four mid-priced CDs, the only drawback being that Nos. 2 and 5 are split between discs. From both a performance and a technical point of view, the accounts of the last three symphonies are in every way preferable to his later, VPO digital versions; all offer peerless playing from the Berlin Philharmonic which the Oslo Philharmonic cannot always quite match, for all their excellence.

Maazel's performances from the mid-1960s have been remastered and reissued on four CDs, necessitating a break only at the centre of No. 4. The recordings come from a vintage Decca period and are remarkably full and vivid. In the early symphonies the hint of edge in the digital remastering (and it is very minimal) increases the bite and sense of urgency at the expense of charm (this is not a strong feature of Nos. 2 and 3 anyway). But in Nos. 4–6 (and especially in No. 4) the performances, always grippingly spontaneous, sound newly minted, helped by the freshness of the VPO, playing in their first complete cycle in the recording studio and obviously relishing the experience. Maazel's readings are well judged and clearly thought out. Perhaps No. 5 lacks the fullest expansive qualities, but there are few more effective accounts of the March/Scherzo from the *Pathétique. Romeo and Juliet* is exciting too, with plenty of romantic flair.

The admirable Philips set represents the least expensive way to acquire first-class versions of the six Tchaikovsky *Symphonies*. The recording is resonant and full-bodied; the CDs retain the ambient bloom on the strings and provide a fine weight and sonority for the brass. The layout on four CDs means that *Symphonies Nos. 2* and *5* are centrally divided between movements, but the other four works are uninterrupted. Markevitch is a genuine Tchaikovskian and his readings have fine momentum and plenty of ardour. In the *First Symphony* he finds the Mendelssohnian lightness in his fast pacing of the opening movement. In the *Little Russian Symphony* the opening horn solo is full of character and the allegro tautly rhythmic. The finale is striking for its bustling energy rather than its charm. The *Polish Symphony* has a comparably dynamic first movement, but the central movements are expansively warm, the ballet-music associations not missed. No. 4 is as exciting as almost any available. It has a superb, thrusting first movement. The close of the movement, like the coda of the finale, brings the highest degree of tension and a real sense of triumph over adversity. No. 5 has a less flexible first movement, and some might feel that here the forward momentum is too hard pressed to let the secondary material really blossom, and the final statement of the big tune in the finale is slow and rather stolid. But Markevitch is fully back on form in the *Pathétique* with a deeply felt performance of the finale, where the second subject is introduced with great tenderness. The close of the symphony has an elegiac quality to complete a reading which has a wide emotional range and is gripping from first to last.

Symphonies Nos. 1–3.
(M) *** Ph. 420 751-2 (2). Concg. O, Haitink.

Haitink's readings are satisfyingly consistent and they have genuine symphonic strength. His special advantage, in addition to the superb Concertgebouw playing, is the Philips recording, which sounds splendid in its remastered form: rich yet fresh, refined in detail and not lacking weight. Haitink's choice of speeds, though not always conventional, always seems apt and natural, and in the *Little Russian* the solemn nobility of the opening introduction has nothing of pomposity about it and, in the finale, the long and loud coda is given genuine joyfulness, with no blatancy. The *Polish Symphony* has a disarmingly direct freshness of approach.

Symphony No. 1 in G min. (Winter daydreams), Op. 13.
*** Chan. Dig. CHAN 8402; *ABTD 1139* [id.]. Oslo PO, Jansons.

Refreshingly direct in style, Jansons with his brilliant orchestra gives an electrically compelling performance of this earliest of the symphonies. The focus is sharp, both of the playing and of the recording, which is both brilliant and atmospheric, not least in the lyrical outpouring of the slow movement. Structurally strong, the result tingles with excitement, most of all in the finale, faster than usual, with the challenge of the complex fugato passages taken superbly. The recording is highly successful.

Symphony No. 1 (Winter daydreams), Op. 13; Nutcracker suite, Op. 71a.
**(*) Sony Dig. SK 48056 [id.]. Chicago SO, Claudio Abbado.

Abbado does not miss the Mendelssohnian lightness at the opening, but in the first movement the resonant Chicago acoustic and high powered playing, brings the feeling that climaxes are inflated, although both here and in the finale there is no lack of power and excitement. The *Adagio*, warm and refined, brings a glorious climax when the horns take over the tune, but does not otherwise sustain the highest level of tension, and in the Scherzo Giulini seems determined not to stress the waltz feeling in favour of registering Tchaikovsky's delicately colourful woodwind decoration. In the the peroration of the finale it is always difficult to avoid a sense of rhetoric, and the closing bars here do not quite solve this problem. The *Nutcracker suite* is beautifully and intimately played; the warm resonance makes the *Sugar plum fairy* and the *Mirlitons* glow radiantly, and the *Waltz of the flowers* has much elegance.

Symphony No. 1 in G min. (Winter daydreams), Op. 13; (i) *Variations on a rococo theme for cello and orchestra, Op. 33.*
(M) *** DG 431 606-2; *431 606-4* [id.]. BPO, Karajan; (i) with Rostropovich.

Karajan's performance of the *Winter daydreams symphony* is second to none and the playing of the Berlin Philharmonic is quite marvellous. Although he takes the opening *Allegro tranquillo* of the first movement quite fast, there is no feeling of breathlessness: it is genuinely *tranquillo*, though the rhythmic bite of the syncopated passages, so important in these early symphonies, could hardly be sharper. The last movement is given classical strength and the final peroration has regality and splendour. Rostropovich's account of the published score of the *Rococo variations* is hardly less distinguished, and Karajan accompanies him warmly. Both analogue recordings are among DG's best. Neither is lacking in brilliance or fullness, and both have a realistic ambience.

Symphonies Nos.1 (Winter Daydreams); 2 (Little Russian).
*** Virgin Dig. VC7 91119-2; *VC7 91119-4* [id.]. Bournemouth SO, Andrew Litton.

In their Tchaikovsky series for Virgin, Litton and the Bournemouth orchestra here come up with a clear winner, giving urgently spontaneous performances of both symphonies. Not only is this ideal coupling of the first two symphonies exceptionally generous (a few seconds under 80 minutes), but the performances in every way rival any in the catalogue. With warm and full recording, less distanced than many on this label, the disc earns the strongest recommendation. A relaxed, atmospheric view of the opening introduction of No. 1 leads into an exhilarating account of the main first-movement allegro. In this movement and elsewhere Litton reveals himself as a volatile Tchaikovskian, free with accelerandos and slowings, yet never sounding self-conscious or too free. The hushed pianissimos of the Bournemouth strings in the slow movement of No. 1 are ravishing, and the *Second Symphony* too brings a beautifully sprung reading which allows plenty of rhythmic elbow-room in the jaunty account of the syncopated second subject in the finale.

Symphony No. 2 in C min. (Little Russian), Op. 17 (original 1872 score).
*** Chan. Dig. CHAN 8304; *ABTD 1071* [id.]. LSO, Simon.

This is the first recording of Tchaikovsky's original score of the *Little Russian symphony* and probably the first performance outside Russia, prompted by the enterprising enthusiasm of Edward Johnson, who provides an admirably exhaustive sleeve-note. Although the original format gained considerable success at its early performances, it gave the composer immediate and serious doubts, and so in 1879 Tchaikovsky retrieved the score and immediately set to work to rewrite the first movement. He left the *Andante* virtually unaltered, touched up the scoring of the Scherzo, made minor excisions and added repeats, and made a huge cut of 150 bars (some two minutes of music) in the finale. He then destroyed the original. (The present performance has been possible because of the surviving orchestral parts.) There can be no question that he was right. The reworked first movement is immensely superior to the first attempt, and the finale – delightful though it is – seems quite long enough shorn of the extra bars. However, to hear the composer's first thoughts (as with the original version of *Romeo and Juliet*) is fascinating, and this is an indispensable recording for all Tchaikovskians. Geoffrey Simon secures a committed response from the LSO, and the recording is striking in its inner orchestral detail and freshness, although the lower range is without the resonant richness of some CDs.

Symphony No. 2 in C min. (Little Russian), Op. 17 (see also above, under *Suite No. 2*).
*** Telarc Dig. CD 80131 [id.]. Pittsburgh SO, Maazel – RIMSKY-KORSAKOV: *Antar.* ***

Symphony No. 2 (Little Russian); Capriccio italien, Op. 45.
*** Chan. Dig. CHAN 8460; *ABTD 1173* [id.]. Oslo PO, Jansons.

Symphony No. 2 (Little Russian); The Tempest, Op. 18.
**(*) Sony Dig. MK 39359 [id.]. Chicago SO, Abbado.

Like other conductors who learned their craft in the Soviet Union, Jansons prefers a fastish speed for the *Andantino* second movement, but what above all distinguishes this version is the joyful exuberance both of the bouncy Scherzo – fresh and folk-like in the Trio – and of the finale. Jansons' handling of the syncopated idea in the development section of that movement is a delight, and the final coda brings a surge of excitement, making most others seem stiff. The coupling is a fizzing performance of the *Capriccio italien*, bringing a gloriously uninhibited account of the coda with its deliberately vulgar reprise of the Neapolitan tune. With some edge on violin tone, this is not the finest of the Chandos Oslo recordings, but is still fresh and atmospheric.

Maazel's slow introduction is weightier and much more measured than with his competitors. From then on, he believes in treating Tchaikovsky directly and without sentimentality, incisive of attack, refined of texture. The undistracting freshness of his view – never too tense – is enhanced by excellent, well-balanced recording. If the fine *Antar* coupling is suitable, this is thoroughly worth while.

The advantage of Abbado's CBS version over direct rivals is the interest of its fill-up, Tchaikovsky's large-scale *Fantasy* on Shakespeare's *The Tempest*. In that work, Abbado's performance, dramatic and passionate as well as evocative in the opening seascape, is likely to be unrivalled on record; in the *Symphony*, too, he is most persuasive, with virtuoso playing from the Chicago orchestra. With speeds generally faster than usual, he conveys lightness and sparkle, so that in the Scherzo the cross-rhythms are incisively sprung. Only in the finale does he adopt a restrained basic speed; effectively so, except that he slows perceptibly in the jaunty syncopated counter-subject. The recording is warm with the sound a little distanced, natural and undistracting but not ideally clear on detail, with the lower range not too well focused and the bass drum balanced too prominently at times. There are no dividing bands for individual movements.

Symphonies Nos. (i) *2 (Little Russian), Op. 17;* (ii) *4 in F min.*
❀ (B) *** DG 429 527-2; *429 527-4.* (i) New Philh. O; (ii) VPO, Claudio Abbado.
❀ (M) *** DG 431 604-2; *431 604-4.* (i) New Philh. O; (ii) VPO, Abbado.
(BB) *(*) Naxos Dig. 8.850488 [id.]. Polish RSO (Katowice), Adrian Leaper.

Abbado's coupling of Tchaikovsky's *Second* and *Fourth Symphonies* is one of the supreme bargains of the current catalogue. His account of the *Little Russian Symphony* is very enjoyable, although the first movement concentrates on refinement of detail and is a shade too deadpan. The *Andantino* is very nicely done and the scherzo is admirably crisp and sparkling. The finale is superb, with fine colour and thrust and a memorably spectacular stroke on the tam-tam before the exhilarating coda. The 1967 recording still sounds excellent. But this is merely a bonus for an unforgettable account of the *Fourth Symphony*, unsurpassed on record and sounding marvellous in its remastered CD format, brilliant yet atmospheric, with a balancing resonance and depth. Abbado's control of the structure of the first movement is masterly. The *Andantino*, with its gentle oboe solo, really takes wing in its central section. Its delectable reprise is followed by a wittily crisp scherzo, while the finale has sparkle as well as power, epitomizing the Russian dance spirit which was Tchaikovsky's inspiration. It was recorded in 1975 in the Musikverein and still sounds very good indeed. At the time of going to press, the bargain Privilege issue is still available. Should it disappear, however, the second listing above is more than worth its slightly higher price, although the insert leaflet still includes nothing about the music!

Adrian Leaper's coupling comes on the Naxos super-bargain label, but until the last movement of No. 4 the performances are too relaxed to convey the drama and passion contained in the music. Speeds are generally slow, and in such a movement as the *Andantino marziale* of No. 2 the light rhythmic pointing is very effective, but too often, with ensemble not always crisp, the results suggest studio run-throughs rather than live performances. The big exception comes in the finale of the *Fourth Symphony*, where the players of the Polish National Radio Orchestra of Katowice respond with panache. Full-ranging digital sound, but overall this does not begin to compare with Abbado.

Symphony No. 3 in D (Polish), Op. 29.
*** Chan. Dig. CHAN 8463; *ABTD 1179* [id.]. Oslo PO, Jansons.

Symphony No. 3 in D (Polish); Capriccio italien; Eugene Onegin: Polonaise.
*** Virgin Dig. VC 790761-2 [id.]. Bournemouth SO, Litton.

Symphony No. 3 in D (Polish), Op. 29; Serenade for strings in C, Op. 48.
❀ (M) *** DG Analogue/Dig. 431 605-2; *431 605-4* [id.]. BPO, Karajan.

Karajan's version of the *Polish Symphony* ranks with the finest, and no other version offers more polished orchestral playing. The first movement is full of flair, and in the central movements Karajan is ever conscious of the variety of Tchaikovsky's colouring. In the finale the articulation of the *Polacca* is both vigorous and joyful and it brings a sense of symphonic strength often lacking in other versions. The 1979 analogue recording is bold, brilliant and clear, with the ambience of the Philharmonie well conveyed. The *String Serenade* is equally compelling, with taut, alert and superbly articulated playing in the first movement, a passionately intense *Élégie* and a bustling, immensely spirited finale. And no group plays the Waltz with more panache and elegance than the Berlin Philharmonic. The digital recording is early (1980), but satisfyingly well balanced, with a firm, resonant bass-line to balance the bright upper range.

Tchaikovsky's *Third* is given a clear, refreshingly direct reading by Jansons, totally unsentimental, yet conveying the warmth as well as the exuberance of Tchaikovsky's inspiration. The likeness with *Swan Lake* in the first movement is delectably pointed, but it is the irresistible sweep of urgency with which Jansons builds the development section that sets his performance apart, with the basic tempo varied less than usual. The second movement is beautifully relaxed, the *Andante elegiaco* heartwarmingly expressive, tender and refined, and the Scherzo has a Mendelssohnian elfin quality; but it is the swaggering reading of the finale, always in danger of sounding bombastic, which sets the seal on the whole performance. Even the anthem-like second subject has a lightness of touch, avoiding any sense of squareness or coarseness. Though the recording does not convey a genuinely hushed pianissimo for the strings, it brings full, rich and brilliant sound.

Andrew Litton elected to start his Tchaikovsky cycle for Virgin Classics with the most equivocal and intractable of the symphonies, and the results are impressive. In the outer movements he challenges the players to the limit in his fast speeds, but the clean, purposeful manner is very satisfying, weighty without coarseness, even if some other versions spring rhythms more infectiously. Litton's finesse comes out impressively in the *Andante elegiaco*, where he chooses a flowing speed which needs no basic modification for the broad melody which follows. He then moulds that with satisfyingly Elgar-like nobility. In the *Capriccio italien*, the playing and recording display to the full the dramatic contrasts of texture and dynamic, while the *Eugene Onegin Polonaise* brings an even more infectiously rhythmic performance.

Symphonies Nos. 4–6.
** DG Dig. 435 356-2 (2) [id.]. VPO, Karajan.

Symphonies Nos. 4–6; Manfred symphony.
(M) *** Decca 425 586-2 (3) [id.]. Philh. O, Ashkenazy.

Ashkenazy's set is highly competitive on three mid-priced discs, although the CD layout splits No. 5 between the second and third movements. Apart from the emotional power and strong Russian feeling of the readings, the special quality which Ashkenazy conveys is spontaneity. The freshness of his approach, his natural feeling for lyricism on the one hand and for drama on the other, is consistently compelling, even if at times the orchestral ensemble is not as immaculate as with Karajan. The inclusion of the superb, inspirational account of *Manfred* sets the seal on his achievement. The remastering has brought just a degree of digital brightening to the fortissimo violins but adds to the transparency and tangibility of the sound picture overall. The recording quality remains outstandingly full and atmospheric, with the brass gloriously sonorous and a satisfying weight in the bass.

After living with and constantly recording the last three Tchaikovsky symphonies throughout his career, directing both the Philharmonia and Berlin Philharmonic Orchestras, Karajan turned in 1985 to the VPO for his digital swansong in this repertoire. The results are sadly disappointing. The *Fourth* is the most successful of the three. Although the playing of the Vienna orchestra does not match that of the Berlin Philharmonic in polish, the freer control of tempo in the first movement brings a more relaxed second-subject group, while in the *Andantino* the Vienna oboist is in some ways fresher (though the timbre is edgier) than his Berlin counterpart. The scherzo is attractively bright, if less precise, and the finale has both urgency and excitement. With the extra depth in the bass that modern digital recording can provide, the sound is fuller than before, even if the warmly resonant acoustic means that detail is less sharply defined. But overall the 1977 account has a more consistently spontaneous forward thrust. The *Fifth* is also characteristically strong and expressive in Vienna, but here neither the playing nor the recorded sound matches his 1976 Berlin record. In the *Pathétique* the Vienna ensemble is noticeably slacker than the Berliners, and though the reading is not without intensity or spontaneity it lacks the grip of earlier versions. DG would have done better to have reissued this two-disc set at mid-price.

Symphonies Nos. 4–6; The Nutcracker; Sleeping Beauty; Swan Lake: ballet suites.
(M) (***) EMI mono/stereo CMS7 63460-2 (3) [Ang. CDMC 63460]. Philh. O, Karajan.

The Philharmonia in the early 1950s was an extraordinary body, and these early records are worth having even if you already possess Karajan's later accounts with the Berlin Philharmonic. Nos. 4 and 5 are mono, but the 1959 *Pathétique* is stereo. Exhilarating performances that still sound amazing for their period.

Symphony No. 4 in F min., Op. 36.
*** Chan Dig. CHAN 8361; *ABTD 1124* [id.]. Oslo PO, Jansons.
(M) *** Decca 425 972-2. LSO, Szell – BEETHOVEN: *Egmont.* ***
**(*) Telarc Dig. CD 80047 [id.]. Cleveland O, Maazel.
* EMI Dig. CDC7 54003-2 [id.]. RPO, Ashkenazy – RACHMANINOV: *Piano concerto No. 2.* *(*)

Symphony No. 4; Andante cantabile; Marche slave, Op. 31.
(M) *** EMI CDM7 63960-2 [id.]. Hallé O, Barbirolli (with rehearsal sequence).

Symphony No. 4; Capriccio italien.
(M) *** DG 419 872-2 [id.]. BPO, Karajan.

Symphony No. 4; Francesca da Rimini.
*** DG Dig. 429 778-2; *429 778-4* [id.]. NYPO, Bernstein.

Symphony No. 4; Romeo and Juliet: fantasy overture.
(M) *(*) Decca Dig. 430 745-2; *430 745-4* [id.]. Chicago SO, Solti.

Jansons conducts a dazzling performance of the *Fourth*, unusually fresh and natural in its expressiveness, yet with countless subtleties of expression, as in the balletic account of the second-subject group of the first movement. So idiomatic-sounding is Jansons' handling that the transitions between sections are totally unobtrusive, with steady rather than fluctuating speeds. The *Andantino* flows lightly and persuasively, the Scherzo is very fast and lightly sprung, while the finale reinforces the impact of the whole performance: fast and exciting, but with no synthetic whipping-up of tempo. That is so until the very end of the coda, which finds Jansons pressing ahead just fractionally as he would in a concert, a thrilling conclusion made the more so by the wide-ranging, brilliant and realistic recording in which the reverberant background brings warmth of atmosphere and little or no obscuring of detail. The CD adds impressively to the orchestra's sense of presence within the characterful ambience of the Oslo Philharmonic Hall.

Szell's white-hot performance is one of the very finest ever put on disc. At the sessions in 1962 the irascible conductor was in an angry mood, and John Culshaw deliberately prodded him still further by having the first playback in dull sound. Szell then unleashed a force in the subsequent takes that has to be heard to be believed. It now sounds superb on CD, clean, forward and full, with thrillingly immediate brass, and the interpretation at ideally chosen speeds has a freshness rarely matched. The *Egmont* fill-up is odd but attractive, and is very well recorded in the Sofiensaal.

As with others in EMI's Phoenixa series of Barbirolli's recordings from the end of the 1950s and early 1960s, the sound has been immeasurably improved, and one can appreciate the sheer power and drive of the performance which has much in common with Szell's version in its highly charged romanticism. The outer movements are electrifying in their excitement, and the elegantly structured *Andantino* has many characteristic touches of individuality. After the *Symphony* comes a complete contrast in a refined and delicate account of the *Andante cantabile*; then comes a thrilling *Marche slave*, although here the recording is somewhat shrill. The disc ends with a rehearsal sequence, made during the preparation of the *Symphony*, not especially illuminating but valuable in letting us hear the way Barbirolli communcated with his orchestra who so often approached greatness under his baton.

Karajan's 1977 version is undoubtedly more compelling than his previous recordings and is in most respects preferable to the newer Vienna version too. It is the vitality and drive of the performance as a whole that one remembers, although the beauty of the wind playing at the opening and close of the slow movement can give nothing but pleasure. The CD transfer is extremely vivid. The ubiquitous *Capriccio italien* is offered as a filler.

The third of Leonard Bernstein's recordings of the late Tchaikovsky symphonies for DG brings eccentric speeds in the first two movements comparable to those in the *Fifth* and the *Pathétique*, but the electricity is of a quite different order. This is not a performance to compare with any other: it is one that came from an interpreter of genius at a particular moment, white-hot and compelling. The fanfare motto theme at the opening is very grand indeed, with big rallentandos and big pauses. Most surprisingly, in a live recording from Avery Fisher Hall in New York, one of the most difficult for engineers, the sound is aptly big and fruity. The recording may not match what we have on the finest versions, thick rather than clean, but it certainly allows the power and warmth of Bernstein's reading to be fully appreciated. The last two movements are taken at speeds that no one would regard as unconventional. The pizzicato scherzo is not ideally precise of ensemble but it is infectiously sprung and, in Bernstein's big, bold account of the finale, his slowing for the second subject (the *Birch tree* theme) is extreme but persuasive. The close is predictably exciting, with an unashamed accelerando in the closing bars, though without applause and obviously recorded at an editing session. The fill-up, *Francesca da Rimini*, brings a comparably spacious and big-scale performance.

Maazel's Telarc Cleveland disc established a reputation for sound of spectacular depth and brilliance within natural concert-hall acoustics. Maazel's reading is very similar to his very successful 1965 Decca record, and only in the finale does the new version differ markedly from the old, by seeking amplitude and breadth in preference to uninhibited extrovert excitement. Maazel's approach generates a strong forward momentum in the first movement and is consistently involving in its directness. Yet he lightens the tension effectively (like Jansons) by his balletic approach to the second-subject group. The slow movement, with a plaintive oboe solo, is distinctly appealing, and at the *Più mosso* Maazel makes a swift, bold tempo change. In the finale the Cleveland Orchestra produces a thrillingly rich body of timbre in the upper strings and the fullest resonance from the lower strings and brass.

Solti's basic speed for the first movement is surprisingly slow, yet it remains a clear-headed, straightforward reading rather than an affectionate one. The *Andantino* is then slow to the point of sounding sluggish, while in the third and fourth movements, taken very fast, he finally goes for brilliance at all costs. In brilliant sound, lacking a little in depth and perspective, emphasized on CD, it is not a version to warm to. Solti's *Romeo and Juliet* is unexpectedly restrained, with the love theme tenderly intimate, the coda elegiac, to make a strong contrast with the vibrant battle sequences.

Ashkenazy's recording of the *Fourth Symphony* was made when the RPO were visiting Moscow in 1989. Whatever its merits (or those of Andrei Gavrilov's Rachmaninov's *Second Piano concerto*, with which it is paired), they are insufficient to earn it much of a place in the catalogue. It is distinctly low voltage, an account which would not arouse great enthusiasm if one heard it in the concert hall and to which one would seldom return on record. Not a patch on his earlier studio account with the Philharmonia Orchestra for Decca.

Symphony No. 5 in E min., Op. 64.
*** Chan. Dig. CHAN 8351; *ABTD 1111* [id.]. Oslo PO, Jansons.
*** Telarc Dig. CD 80107 [id.]. RPO, Previn – RIMSKY-KORSAKOV: *Tsar Saltan: March.* ***
*** Olympia OCD 221 [id.]. Leningrad PO, Mravinsky (with LIADOV: *Baba Yaga, Op. 56.* MUSSORGSKY: *Khovanshchina: Prelude.* WAGNER: *Tristan: Prelude and Liebstod****).

(i) *Symphony No. 5;* (ii) *Marche slave.*
(M) *** DG 419 066-2; *419 066-4* [id.]. BPO, Karajan.

(i) *Symphony No. 5;* (ii) *Marche slave, Op. 31; Eugene Onegin: Waltz and Polonaise.*
(M) **(*) Mercury 434 305-2 [id.]. (i) LSO; (ii) Minneapolis SO; Antal Dorati.

(i) *Symphony No. 5;* (ii) *Serenade for strings in C, Op. 48.*
(M) *** EMI CDM7 63962-2 [id.]; *EG 763962-4*. (i) Hallé O; (ii) LSO, Barbirolli.

Symphony No. 5 in E min.; The Tempest, Op. 18.
**(*) Virgin Dig. VC7 91140-2; *VC7 91140-4* [id.]. Bournemouth SO, Andrew Litton.

Symphony No. 5; (i) *Eugene Onegin: Tatiana's letter scene.*
❀ (M) *** EMI Dig. CD-EMX 2187; *TC-EMX 2187*. LPO, Sian Edwards; (i) with Eilene Hannan.

Sian Edwards has already given us a truly memorable account of *Francesca da Rimini*; now she conducts an equally electrifying and warm-hearted reading of Tchaikovsky's *Fifth*. With refined playing from the LPO and brilliant recording, it matches any version in the catalogue, particularly when it comes with an unusual and exceptionally attractive fill-up, Tchaikovsky's greatest inspiration for soprano, *Tatiana's letter scene*. That is freshly and dramatically sung, in a convincingly girlish impersonation, by the Australian, Eilene Hannan. Sian Edwards's control of rubato is exceptionally persuasive, notably so in moulding the different sections of the first movement of the symphony, while the great horn solo of the slow movement is played with exquisite delicacy by Richard Bissell. The Waltz third movement is most tenderly done, as though for a ballet, while the finale brings a very fast and exciting allegro, challenging the orchestra to brilliant, incisive playing. The booklet includes a transliteration of the Russian text of the vocal item, together with an English translation.

This was the first symphony to be recorded in an outstanding Tchaikovsky series, in which Jansons, Leningrad-trained, revealed something of the debt he owed to the example of Yevgeny Mravinsky, a master among Russian interpreters. Jansons is notably less wilful than Mravinsky tended to be but is no less intense and electrifying. In the first movement, Jansons' refusal to linger never sounds anything but warmly idiomatic, lacking only a little in charm. The slow movement again brings a steady tempo, with climaxes built strongly and patiently but with enormous power, the final culmination topping everything. In the finale, taken very fast, Jansons tightens the screw of the excitement without ever making it a scramble, following Tchaikovsky's notated slowings rather than allowing extra rallentandos. The sound is excellent, specific and well focused within a warmly reverberant acoustic, with digital recording on CD reinforcing any lightness of bass.

Previn's fine concern for detail is well illustrated by the way that the great horn melody in the slow movement (superbly played by Jeff Bryant) contains the implication of a quaver rest before each three-quarter group, where normally it sounds like a straight triplet. In the first movement, rhythms are light and well sprung, and the third movement is sweet and lyrical yet with no hint of mannerism, for Previn adopts a naturally expressive style within speeds generally kept steady, even in the great climax of the slow movement which then subsides into a coda of breathtaking delicacy. The finale, taken very fast indeed, crowns an outstandingly satisfying reading. The Telarc recording is full and wide-ranging, not as detailed as some, but very naturally balanced.

Mravinsky's Olympia recording of Tchaikovsky's *Fifth* was recorded in Leningrad in 1973; the remaining pieces come from a concert at the Moscow Conservatoire. If anything, the *Symphony* is even more electrifying than either of the earlier DG versions. Climaxes are still somewhat rough on this version – but this is easily overlooked, given the excitement of the playing. Another factor prompting a strong recommendation is the other material on the disc. Liadov's *Baba Yaga* is given a virtuoso performance and is also well recorded; the Mussorgsky is predictably atmospheric, and the Wagner leaves no doubt that Mravinsky must have been a great interpreter of this composer.

Karajan's 1976 recording stands out from his other recordings of the *Fifth*. The first movement is unerringly paced and has great romantic flair; in Karajan's hands the climax of the slow movement is grippingly intense, though with a touchingly elegiac preparation for the horn solo at the opening. The Waltz has character and charm too – the Berlin Philharmonic string playing is peerless – and in the finale Karajan drives hard, creating a riveting forward thrust. The remastered recording brings a remarkable improvement.

Barbirolli's urgent, thrustfully romantic reading of the *Fifth* has an irresistible forward momentum which springs from the very essence of the music. Tempi are unerrringly apt, not only in themselves but also in the way they interrelate. The reading has passion and drama, and the energy of the finale is matched by the nobility with which Barbirolli invests the great main tune when it is introduced in the strings; yet, at its final appearance in the coda, the blazing trumpets have no inhibition whatsoever. EMI have recoupled this Pye reissue with one of their own recordings of the *Serenade for strings* (made in 1964), characteristically ripe and romantic, especially in the *Élégie*. In the first movement Barbirolli is surprisingly metrical when the second subject arrives, but the effect is not in the least heavy. He is naturally expressive in the Waltz and prepares the bustling finale with subtle, loving anticipation. A suberb disc: any lack of refinement in the recording is forgotten when the playing is so consistently involving.

Dorati's recording of the *Fifth* was made in 1961 in Watford Town Hall. The reading is individual and steers a course midway between uninhibited excitement and lyricism. The first movement opens darkly and is especially successful in maintaining tension without frenzy, but the slow movement, again opening rather sombrely, is at a lower general temperature, bursting into excitement at the two climaxes and especially the second. It is beautifully played, with a fine horn solo, as is the *Waltz* which has attractive elegance. The finale (with a steady pace for the allegro) makes only a moderate impact when the brass are silent, but is a positive blaze of colour when they enter. The is a burst of adrenalin at the very end and on the whole this is a satisfying performance that bears repetition well. The vintage Mercury sound is impressive too. The other pieces were recorded in Minneapolis in 1958 and have a brighter, sharper presence. The *Marche Slave*, paced slowly and grandly but with an arresting climax and coda, contrasts with the well lifted, vivacious rhythms of the two dance movements from *Eugene Onegin*.

Litton is surprisingly slow and steady in the first movement of the *Fifth*. There is a case – as Klemperer and Boehm both showed in their diffent ways – for taking a squarely symphonic view, but Litton's reading lacks the high voltage of his finest Tchaikovsky performances. The other three movements are first rate. The slow movement brings a beautiful horn solo, with the sound exquisitely distanced and with Litton sustaining his slow *Andante* well. At a well-judged speed, the Waltz third movement is then delightfully fresh and delicate in a simple way, and the finale, again on the broad side, is warm rather than ominous, with very clean articulation in the playing and fine detail. Atmospherically recorded with slightly distanced sound in the Virgin manner, and transferred at a lower level than the rival issues, this version certainly has its attractions, despite that first movement, particularly when it has so rare and generous a fill-up. The Shakespearean symphonic fantasy, *The Tempest* – not to be confused with the much less ambitious overture of the same name, written for Ostrovsky's play – is given a glowing performance, passionately committed yet refined, to suggest a forgotten masterpiece.

Symphony No. 6 in B min. (Pathétique), Op. 74.
*** Chan. Dig. CHAN 8446; *ABTD 1158* [id.]. Oslo PO, Jansons.
(M) (***) DG 419 486-2 [id.]. BPO, Karajan.
(M) (***) BMG/RCA mono GD 60312. NBC SO, Toscanini – R. STRAUSS: *Death and transfiguration.* (***)

Symphony No. 6 (Pathétique); Capriccio italien; Eugene Onegin: Waltz & Polonaise.
(M) **(*) Sony SBK 47657 [id.]. Phd O, Ormandy.

(i) *Symphony No. 6 (Pathétique);* (ii) *Hamlet* (fantasy overture), *Op. 67a.*
(B) *** Ph. 422 478-2. (i) LSO, (ii) New Philh. O, Markevitch.

Symphony No. 6 in B min., (Pathétique); Marche slave, Op. 31.
❀ *** Virgin VC7 91487-2; *VC 791487-4* [id.]. Russian Nat. O, Mikhail Pletnev.

Symphony No. 6 (Pathétique); Romeo and Juliet (fantasy overture).
**(*) DG Dig. 429 740-2; *429 740-4* [id.]. Philh. O, Sinopoli.
(M) (***) BMG/RCA mono GD 60920. Boston SO, Koussevitzky.

The *Pathétique* is Mikhail Pletnev's début on record as a conductor with the Russian National Orchestra that has been formed for him. It has been greeted with wide press acclaim and not just in the CD periodicals, and comparisons have been made with the most exalted predecessors including Mravinsky, Karajan and even the celebrated pre-war Furtwängler account. There is no doubt that this is among the most vividly dramatic accounts of this symphony to have appeared for some years. The way in which Pletnev launches us into the development of the first movement still takes one aback, even when one knows what to expect. His hand-picked orchestra is as virtuosic as Pletnev himself can be on the keyboard. The scherzo may seem too fast for some people but it is marked *Allegro molto vivace* and Koussevitzky (see below) is not much slower. There is a stirring account of *Marche slave* too, and a very fine recording, perfectly balanced, although the effect is a little recessed.

Mariss Jansons and the Oslo Philharmonic crown their magnetically compelling Tchaikovsky series with a superbly concentrated account of the last and greatest of the symphonies. It is characteristic of Jansons that the great second-subject melody is at once warm and passionate yet totally unsentimental, with rubato barely noticeable. The very fast speed for the third-movement *March* stretches the players to the very limit, but the exhilaration is infectious, leading to the simple dedication of the slow finale, unexaggerated but deeply felt. Fine, warm recording as in the rest of the series.

If one divides interpreters of this *Symphony* into those who tend to press ahead in stringendo and those who hold back in ritenuto, Sinopoli – perhaps surprisingly after his Elgar *Second* – is firmly in the former group. What is similar to that Elgar performance is the passion of the playing of the Philharmonia, recorded with the most satisfying opulence. Sinopoli is not always as electric as Jansons in his fine Oslo reading, adopting slow basic speeds for the middle two movements but sustaining them well, with the 5/8 rhythm of the second brought even closer than is common to the feeling of a waltz. In the march of the third movement, many will prefer Sinopoli's broader view, with a slight easing on the big swaggering fortissimo entries. The big advantage Sinopoli has over Jansons is that it is generously coupled with *Romeo and Juliet.* There Sinopoli's reading is not quite so spontaneous-sounding, with a hint of self-consciousness at the first entry of the big love-theme, though with plenty of uninhibited passion on the later repeats.

Ormandy's fine 1960 performance is a reading of impressive breadth, dignity and power, with no suggestion of routine in a single bar. The orchestra makes much of the first-movement climax and plays with considerable passion and impressive body of tone in both outer movements; yet there is an element of restraint in the finale which prevents any feeling of hysteria. The 5/4 movement has an attractive, melancholy warmth, the repeats effectively taken; the scherzo combines weight with sparkle (the march theme emerges as a real march). In short, this is most satisfying, a performance to live with; the CD transfer, while brightly lit, avoids glare in the upper range. Ormandy's panache and gusto give the *Capriccio italien* plenty of life without driving too hard, and the dances are rhythmically infectious.

For many, Karajan's 1976 version is the finest of his five recordings – but the current issue on CD of this performance must be treated with extreme caution. The bright recording has been remastered fiercely and the upper range is so sharp-edged as to make the ear cringe in the louder passages. Undoubtedly the impact of Tchaikovsky's climaxes – notably those of the first and third movements – is tremendously powerful, the articulation of the Berlin players precise and strong. In the 5/4 movement Karajan allows the middle section to increase the elegiac feeling, against a background of remorseless but distanced drum-beats, like a tolling bell. The finale has great passion and eloquence, with two gentle sforzandos at the very end to emphasize the finality of the closing phrase. We must hope that DG will consider a further remastering of this recording.

Markevitch brings great intensity to his account of the first movement. The effect is undoubtedly powerful but, with a touch of harshness to the recording, some might feel that Markevitch is too aggressive, even though the performance is always under emotional control. The second movement has both warmth and elegance, and the march is treated broadly, providing suitable contrast before a deeply felt performance of the finale, where the second subject is introduced with great tenderness. The performance of *Hamlet* is exciting, with a particularly telling closing section. The portrayal of Ophelia is rather striking, but the remastered recording produces less than ideal fullness for the massed violins.

Koussevitzky's account of the *Pathétique* comes from 1930 but though the sound may lack the vivid colouring of present day recording, the performance certainly doesn't. What sonority Koussevitzky drew from his players and with what intensity they played! This is another version of outsize personality that will have you on the edge of your chair for it is tremendously high voltage. Lukas Foss, who was the Boston Symphony's pianist towards the end of Koussevitzky's reign, says in his note that with him 'everything mattered', nothing was blasé, and under his baton one heard the great nineteenth-century musical literature as if for the first time. Not that it is free from the odd mannerism: he italicizes the passage immediately after the explosive fortissimo that opens the development in the first movement and – believe it or not – passes a brief moment of vulnerable intonation in the finale. The 1936 *Romeo and Juliet* was issued in an RCA Boston Symphony compilation in the 1970s, and ranks as one of the most impassioned accounts of the piece made in that era. The RCA engineers have done their best with the sound, which in spite of some discoloration in climaxes, is more than acceptable.

Toscanini's Philadelphia version of the *Pathétique* glows with the special magic that developed between him and the orchestra over the winter season of 1941–2. Though far more disciplined than most readings, it is altogether warmer than his NBC recording, with the great second-subject melody of the first movement tender in its emotions, not rigid in its easy rubato. He even eases the tempo sympathetically for the fortissimo entries of the march in the third movement. Alongside a magnificent account of the Strauss – an apt link, with death the theme – it makes a superb historical document.

Symphony No. 7 in E flat (reconstructed Bogatyryev); (i) *Variations on a rococo theme for cello and orchestra, Op. 33.*
(M) ** Sony MPK 46453 [id.]. Phd. O, Ormandy; (i) with Leonard Rose.

In 1892 Tchaikovsky began a new symphony, but he was not satisfied with the way his ideas were working out and decided that the material was more suitable for a piano concerto. The sketches for the symphony as originally planned were not destroyed and it was to these that the Soviet musicologist, Bogatyryev, turned. As there was no scherzo, one was provided from a set of piano pieces written in 1893. The finale, however, is bizarre and here sounds rumbustious, blatant, even vulgar, with the reprise of the main theme against a side-drum in no way characteristic of Tchaikovsky's symphonic writing. Ormandy's performance has great fervour and is superbly played; but the recording, although spectacular, also has the harshness one associates with this source. Leonard Rose's warm and elegant account of the *Rococo variations* comes like balm to the ears after the noisy finale of the symphony. However, this CD does have distinct curiosity value.

The Tempest (fantasy), *Op. 18* (see also above, under *Symphony No. 2*).
**(*) ASV Dig. CDDCA 586; *ZCDCA 586* [id.]. LSO, Yondani Butt – LISZT: *Ce qu'on entend sur la montagne.* **(*)

The Tempest is a comparatively early work (1873) but its opening seascape, with its highly evocative horn passage, is matched later by the passionate intensity of Miranda and Ferdinand's love-theme, with its soaring upward leap. Yondani Butt gives an impressively controlled performance, holding back for the final climax, and on CD the spectacular digital recording produces some thrilling sounds within its resonant acoustic – the effect is not unlike a Telarc recording.

Variations on a rococo theme for cello and orchestra (original version).
*** Ph. Dig. 434 106-2; *434 106-4* [id.]. Julian Lloyd Webber, LSO, Maxim Shostakovich – MIASKOVSKY: *Cello concerto.* ***

At last the composer's own version of the *Variations on a rococo theme* is coming into its own. This is the third recording of it to have appeared in recent years. The work was written for the German cellist, Wilhelm Fitzenhagen, who also taught at the Moscow Conservatoire, during 1876, a difficult period in his life, and the composer did not contest the various changes he made both in the order of the variations and in some other details. A scholarly edition appeared as long ago as 1941, but the corrupt edition retained its hold on the repertory. Lloyd Webber's approach is both leisurely and, aided no doubt by the exemplary Philips recording, he produces a pleasingly cultured sound. Not as virtuosic in outlook or as strongly profiled as Rostropovich's version of the corrupt score, but very musical and refreshingly enjoyable.

Variations on a rococo theme for cello and orchestra, Op. 33.
*** DG 413 819-2 [id.]. Rostropovich, BPO, Karajan – DVOŘÁK: *Concerto.* ***
(M) *** EMI CDM7 69169-2 [id.]; *EG 769169-4.* Paul Tortelier, N. Sinfonia, Yan Pascal Tortelier – DVOŘÁK: *Concerto.* ***
(M) *** Decca 425 020-2; *425 020-4* [id.]. Harrell, Cleveland O, Maazel – BRUCH: *Kol Nidrei* ***; DVOŘÁK: *Cello concerto.* ***
*** BMG/RCA Dig. RD 71003. Ofra Harnoy, Victoria SO, Freeman – OFFENBACH: *Concerto;* SAINT-SAËNS: *Concerto No. 1.* ***
*** ASV Dig. CDRPO 8012; *ZCRPO 8012* [id.]. Tortelier, RPO, Groves – ELGAR: *Concerto***(*); DVOŘÁK: *Rondo.* ***

No grumbles about Rostropovich's performance in partnership with Karajan. He plays as if this were one of the greatest works for the cello, and he receives glowing support from Karajan and the Berlin Philharmonic. Rostropovich (in common with all his competitors here) uses the published score, not Tchaikovsky's quite different, original version as played by Wallfisch on Chandos (see above, under *Andante cantabile*). The recording is rich and refined and sounds fresh in its digitally remastered form.

A finely wrought account from Tortelier *père*, accompanied by the Northern Sinfonia under Tortelier *fils*. This is very enjoyable, if perhaps not quite so distinguished as Rostropovich on DG. Well worth considering at mid-price.

An assured, vividly characterized set of *Variations* from Lynn Harrell, with plenty of matching colour from the Cleveland woodwind. The analogue recording is bright and colourful, with the Cleveland ambience adding warmth and the cellist given a spotlight.

Ofra Harnoy's scale is smaller, the style essentially elegant, not missing its colour or ardour but never forgetting the word 'rococo' in the title. It is a considerable performance, stylish yet emotionally responsive, and Paul Freeman's accompaniment is first class, too. The CD gives a forward balance to the cello, but this is more than acceptable when the playing is so enticing.

Tortelier's version on the RPO label is warm and red-blooded, if technically not as flawless as his earlier reading, but the recording is pleasantly atmospheric, slightly distanced so that the tenderness of the performance is brought out the more.

CHAMBER AND INSTRUMENTAL MUSIC

Album for the young, Op. 39: (i) original piano version; (ii) trans. for string quartet by Dubinsky.
*** Chan. CHAN 8365; *ABTD 1129* [id.]. (i) Luba Edlina; (ii) augmented Borodin Trio.

These twenty-four pieces are all miniatures, but they have great charm; their invention is often memorable, with quotations from Russian folksongs and one French, plus a brief reminder of *Swan Lake*. Here they are presented twice, in their original piano versions, sympathetically played by Luba Edlina, and in effective string quartet transcriptions arranged by her husband, Rostislav Dubinsky. The Borodin group play them with both affection and finesse. The CD has plenty of presence.

Piano trio in A min., Op. 50.
(*) Delos Dig. DE 3056 [id.]. Cardenes, Solow, Golabek – ARENSKY: *Trio No. 1.* *
(*) Olympia OCD 157 [id.]. Leningrad Philharmonic Trio – GLAZUNOV: *String quartet No. 1.* *
*(*) Chan. Dig. CHAN 8975 [id.]. Borodin Trio – ALIABIEV: *Piano trio.* *(*)

The Cardenes group do not always seem absolutely at home in the repetitive rhetoric of the first movement, but in all other respects theirs is an appealing performance, polished and warmly spontaneous. In the strongly characterized set of variations they lead the listener on most communicatively; they include the *Fugue*, and they make a good case for it. Very attractively coupled, this is well worth considering, particularly as the recording is naturally balanced and realistic.

The balance of the Leningrad trio is very well integrated, with the piano placed among the strings rather than taking a concertante role. While Tamara Fidler can play boldly when required, she does not strongly dominate the tuttis. But the intimacy of the performance has its own appeal – the very opening is enticing – and this is a real performance, albeit much more relaxed in the first movement. The *Variations* are done with sparkle and a good deal of charm, and the *Fugue* is not left out. The recording is modern (1986), balanced a shade closely but truthful, and it does not make the strings sound edgy. With its handsome Glazunov coupling, this is excellent value.

Nothing particularly special from the Borodin Trio on Chandos who rather wear their hearts on their sleeves. In their earlier recording the Borodin Trio omitted the rather bombastic Variation 7 in the second movement (as they did in their public performances); here they include it, though they do not restore the repetitive section whose removal Tchaikovsky himself sanctioned. Their fill-up, the charming Aliabiev *Piano trio* in the same key may attract some collectors, though the Borodins are not to be preferred to their mid-price rivals on Olympia.

Souvenir de Florence, Op. 70.
** Mer. Dig. CDE 84211; *KE 77211* [id.]. Arienski Ens. – ARENSKY: *String quartet No. 2* ***; BORODIN: *Sextet movements.* **

A very good rather than a distinguished performance of Tchaikovsky's eloquent *Souvenir de Florence*, very decently recorded. The strength of the issue lies in the interest of its coupling, an Arensky rarity, the *A minor Quartet*, from which the well-known *Variations on a theme of Tchaikovsky* derive, and two Mendelssohnian movements from the Borodin *Sextet.*

String quartets Nos. 1 in D, Op. 11; 2 in F, Op. 22; 3 in E flat min., Op. 30; (i) *Souvenir de Florence* (string sextet), *Op. 70.*
*** EMI Dig. CDS7 49775-2 (2). Borodin Qt, (i) with Y. Bashmet, N. Gutman.

This set assembles all three Tchaikovsky *Quartets* together with the glorious *Souvenir de Florence.* Given performances of this distinction and music of this quality of inspiration, the set is self-recommending. The digital recording is very nearly as outstanding as the performances, and there is no reason to qualify the strength and warmth of our recommendation.

String quartet No. 1 in D, Op. 11.
(M) **(*) Decca 425 541-2; *425 541-4* [id.]. Gabrieli Qt – BORODIN; SHOSTAKOVICH: *Quartets.* **(*)

The coupling of Tchaikovsky's *D major Quartet* (including the famous *Andante cantabile*) with the Borodin work containing the comparable *Nocturne* is good planning, especially with Shostakovich added to provide a touch of twentieth-century acerbity. The Gabrielis give a finely conceived performance of the Tchaikovsky, producing well-blended tone-quality, and the 1977 recording is clean and alive; but ideally the upper range could be less forcefully projected.

PIANO MUSIC

The Seasons, Op. 37a.
**(*) Chan. Dig. CHAN 8349; *ABTD 1070* [id.]. Lydia Artymiw.

Tchaikovsky's twelve *Seasons* (they would better have been called 'months') were written to a regular deadline for publication in the St Petersburg music magazine, *Nuvellist.* They are lightweight but attractively varied in character and style. It is the gentler, lyrical pieces that are most effective in the hands of Lydia Artymiw, and she plays them thoughtfully and poetically. Elsewhere, she sometimes has a tendency marginally to over-characterize the music. The digital recording is truthful, and on CD the fairly close balance (pedal noises are faintly audible) gives striking presence to the piano which might ideally have been a little further back; but the image is real.

Sleeping Beauty (excerpts) arr. Pletnev.
❀ *** Virgin Dig. VC7 91169-2; *VC7 91169-4* [id.]. Mikhail Pletnev – MUSSORGSKY: *Pictures at an exhibition.* *** ❀

When he was twenty-one and had just won the Tchaikovsky prize, Pletnev made transcriptions of the *Nutcracker suite* and of scenes from Shchedrin's ballet, *Anna Karenina*, which were of such extraordinary pianistic colour and virtuosity that one barely noticed the absence of the orchestra. In the present transcription he gives us about 30 minutes of *The Sleeping Beauty* in an equally dazzling transcription. In sheer clarity of articulation and virtuosity this is pretty remarkable – also in poetry and depth of feeling. Let us hope that the *Nutcracker* transcription is restored to circulation soon. An altogether outstanding issue and in every way a *tour de force*. (It is reported that, concerning the *Nutcracker*, Horowitz told Pletnev in Moscow, 'There are only two people who can play this – you and me!' But we don't think he can have heard Kissin! – see our Recitals section, below.)

CHORAL MUSIC

The Snow Maiden (Snegourotchka): complete incidental music.
**(*) Chant du Monde LDC 278 904 [id.]. Simonova, Martinov, Elnikov, Lomonossov, USSR R. & TV Ch. & O, Provatorov.

This single disc conveniently and generously includes all the 80 minutes of incidental music Tchaikovsky wrote for *The Snow Maiden*, and much of it is vintage material, very delightful, bringing reminders of *Eugene Onegin* in the peasant choruses and some of the folk-based songs, and of the later Tchaikovskian world of *The Nutcracker* in some of the dances. It is true that Tchaikovsky's *Dance of the tumblers* cannot quite match the one from Rimsky-Korsakov's opera in memorability, but, with fine, idiomatic performances, this work is a most cherishable rarity. The soloists are characterfully Slavonic, better caught in the recording than the chorus, which is not helped by backward balance; the bite of their fine singing does not come over fully. Though the digital recording is bright and full-bodied, there is occasional coarseness in the orchestral sound too.

OPERA

Eugene Onegin (complete).
*** Decca 417 413-2 (2) [id.]. Kubiak, Weikl, Burrows, Reynolds, Ghiaurov, Hamari, Sénéchal, Alldis Ch., ROHCG O, Solti.
**(*) DG Dig. 423 959-2 (2) [id.]. Freni, Allen, Von Otter, Schicoff, Burchuladze, Sénéchal, Leipzig R. Ch., Dresden State O, Levine.

Solti, characteristically crisp in attack, has plainly warmed to the score of Tchaikovsky's colourful opera, allowing his singers full rein in rallentando and rubato to a degree one might not have expected of him. The Tatiana of Teresa Kubiak is most moving – rather mature-sounding for the *ingénue* of Act I, but with her golden, vibrant voice rising most impressively to the final confrontation of Act III. The Onegin of Bernd Weikl may have too little variety of tone, but again this is firm singing that yet has authentic Slavonic tinges. Onegin becomes something like a first-person story-teller. The rest of the cast is excellent, with Stuart Burrows as Lensky giving one of his finest performances on record yet. Here, for the first time, the full range of musical expression in this most atmospheric of operas is superbly caught, with the Decca CDs capturing every subtlety – including the wonderful off-stage effects.

The DG version brings a magnificent Onegin in Thomas Allen. The voice may be on the noble side for the role, hardly implying caddishness; however, not only the sheer beauty and firmness of sound but also the range of detailed expression, the facial communication implied, make this the most satisfying account of the title-role yet recorded. It is matched by the Tatiana of Mirella Freni, even at a late stage in her career readily conveying girlish freshness in her voice. The maturing of the character is most convincingly conveyed. The other parts are also strongly taken. The tautened-nerves quality in the character of Lensky comes out vividly in the portrayal by Neil Schicoff, and Anne Sofie von Otter with her firm, clear mezzo believably makes Olga a younger sister, not the usual over-ripe character. Paata Burchuladze is a satisfyingly resonant Gremin and Michel Sénéchal, as on the Solti set, is an incomparable Monsieur Triquet. What welds all these fine components into a rich and exciting whole is the conducting of James Levine with the Dresden Staatskapelle: passionate, at times even wild in Slavonic excitement, yet giving full expressive rein to Tchaikovskian melody, allowing the singers to breathe. The Leipzig Radio Choir sings superbly as well. The snag is that the DG recording is unevocative and studio-bound, with sound close and congested enough to undermine the bloom on both voices and instruments. In every way the more spacious acoustic in the Solti set is preferable.

Eugene Onegin: highlights.
(M) **(*) DG 431 611-2; *431 611-4* [id.] (from recording with Freni, Thomas Allen, Schicoff, Von Otter, Burchuladze, cond. Levine).

This 68-minute selection from the Levine DG set makes an admirable entertainment. It includes the *Letter scene* (with Freni a freshly charming Tatiana), the *Waltz* and *Polonaise* scenes (with the excellent Leipzig Radio Chorus), other key arias, all strongly characterized, and the entire closing scene (11 minutes). The recording, made in the Dresden Lukaskirche, is too closely balanced and surprisingly unexpansive; but this still makes an impressive sampler.

Pique Dame (complete).
**(*) Sony Dig. S3K 45720 [id.]. Dilova, Evstatieva, Toczyska, Konsulov, Ochman, Masurok, Bulgarian Nat. Ch., Sofia Festival O, Tchakarov.

Tchakarov in his Sony series of Russian operas conducts a fresh, expressive and alert account of *Queen of Spades*, very well recorded. Wieslaw Ochman makes an impressive Herman, amply powerful and only occasionally rough. Yuri Masurok is a superb Yeletsky, and the duet of Lisa and her companion, Pauline, is beautifully done by Stefka Evstatieva and Stefania Toczyska, one of Tchaikovsky's most magical inspirations. As the old Countess, Penka Dilova has a characteristically fruity Slavonic mezzo, very much in character, if with a heavy vibrato. The Countess's famous solo is taken very slowly indeed but is superbly sustained. Ensembles and chorus work are excellent, timed with theatrical point. Conveniently, each Act is fitted on a single CD. When DG issues its Paris version conducted by Rostropovich, on CD, that will outshine this one in the solo singing, but the Bulgarian performance is the more idiomatic.

Arias from: *The Enchantress; Eugene Onegin; Iolantha; Mazeppa; Queen of Spades.*
*** Ph. Dig. 426 740-2; *426 740-4* [id.]. Dmitri Hvorostovsky, Rotterdam PO, Gergiev – VERDI: *Arias.* ***

Hvorostovsky, a golden boy among young baritones, made his recording début in the West with Tchaikovsky arias which ideally exhibit both the magnificent dark voice which won him the title of 'Cardiff Singer of the World' and also his way with Russian words. He presents an eager, volatile Onegin, a passionate Yeletski in *Queen of Spades* and an exuberant Robert in *Iolantha*. One can only hope that he will be guided well, to develop such a glorious instrument naturally, without strain.

Telemann, Georg Philipp (1681–1767)

Concertos: for 2 chalumeaux in D min.; for flute in D; for 3 oboes, 3 violins in B flat; for recorder & flute in E min.; for trumpet in D; for trumpet & violin in D.
*** DG Dig. 419 633-2 [id.]. Soloists, Col. Mus. Ant., Goebel.

As Reinhard Goebel points out, Telemann 'displayed immense audacity in the imaginative and ingenious mixing of the colours from the palette of the baroque orchestra', and these are heard to excellent effect here. Those who know the vital *B flat concerto* – or, rather, A major, for that is how it actually sounds – for three oboes and violins, from earlier versions, will find the allegro very fast indeed and the slow movement quite thought-provoking. The chalumeau is the precursor of the clarinet, and the concerto for two chalumeaux recorded here is full of unexpected delights. Marvellously alive and accomplished playing, even if one occasionally tires of the bulges and nudges on the first beats of bars.

Concerto for flute, oboe d'amore and viola d'amore in E; Concerto polonois; Double concerto for recorder and flute in E min.; Triple trumpet concerto in D; Quadro in B flat.
*** O-L Dig. 411 949-2 [id.]. AAM with soloists, Hogwood.

'An attentive observer could gather from these folk musicians enough ideas in eight days to last a lifetime,' wrote Telemann after spending a summer in Pless in Upper Silesia. Polish ideas are to be found in three of the concertos recorded here – indeed, one of the pieces is called *Concerto polonois*. As always, Telemann has a refined ear for sonority, and the musical discourse with which he diverts us is unfailingly intelligent and delightful. The performances are excellent and readers will not find cause for disappointment in either the recording or presentation.

Horn concerto in D; Double horn concerto in D; Triple horn concerto in D; Suite in F for 2 horns and strings; Tafelmusik, Book 3: *Double horn concerto in E flat.*

*** Ph. Dig. 412 226-2 [id.]. Baumann, Timothy Brown, Hill, ASMF, Iona Brown.

The *E flat Concerto* comes from the third set of *Tafelmusik* (1733) and is the best-known of the four recorded here. The playing here and in the other concertos is pretty dazzling, not only from Hermann Baumann but also from his colleagues, Timothy Brown and Nicholas Hill. Mention should also be made of the concertante contributions from the two violinists. Telemann's invention rarely fails to hold the listener, and the recording has warm ambience and excellent clarity.

Oboe concertos: in C min.; D; D min.; E min.; F min.
*** Ph. Dig. 412 879-2 [id.]. Holliger, ASMF, Iona Brown.

The *C minor Concerto* with its astringent opening dissonance is the most familiar of the concertos on Holliger's record, and the *E minor* has also been recorded before, but the remaining three are all new to the catalogue. Telemann was himself proficient on the oboe and wrote with particular imagination and poignancy for this instrument. The performances are all vital and sensitively shaped and a valuable addition to the Telemann discography. Well worth investigation.

Oboe d'amore concerto No. 2 in A.
(M) *** DG 431 120-2; *431 120-4*. Holliger, Camerata Bern, Füri – GRAUN: *Concerto* ***; KREBS: *Double concerto.* **(*)

Telemann's *Oboe d'amore concerto* is in four engaging movements, opening with a lovely Siciliana which Holliger plays beautifully. It is a highly inventive work throughout, and this excellent performance and recording make the very most of it.

Recorder concertos in C; in F; Suite in A min; (i) *Sinfonia in F.*
**(*) Hyp. Dig. CDA 66413; *KA 66413* [id.]. Peter Holtslag, Parley of Instruments, Peter Holman or (i) Roy Goodman.

The three solo concertos here are a delight. Just try the *Affettuoso* opening of the *F major concerto* and you will surely be seduced. Both this and the *C major* are quite substantial pieces, too, with four movements apiece. Peter Holtslag's piping treble recorder is truthfully balanced, in proper scale with the authentic accompaniments, which are neat, polished, sympathetic and animated. The *Sinfonia* is curiously scored, for recorder, oboe, solo bass viol, strings, cornett, three trombones and an organ, with doubling of wind and string parts. Even with Roy Goodman balancing everything expertly the effect is slightly bizarre, if stimulating. About the great *Suite in A minor* we have some reservations: it is played with much nimble bravura and sympathy on the part of the soloist, but the orchestral texture brings a degree of anorexia; after hearing how grand this piece can sound on a modern string group, the results here are faintly dispiriting.

Recorder concerto in C; (i) *Double concerto for recorder and bassoon.*
*** BIS Dig. CD 271 [id.]. Pehrsson, (i) McGraw; Drottningholm Bar. Ens. – VIVALDI: *Concertos.* ***

Clas Pehrsson and Michael McGraw are most expert players, as indeed are their colleagues of the Drottningholm Baroque Ensemble; the recordings are well balanced and fresh.

Double concerto in F, for recorder, bassoon & strings; Double concerto in E min., for recorder, flute & strings; Suite in A min., for recorder & strings.
*** Ph. Dig. 410 041-2 [id.]. Petri, Bennett, Thunemann, ASMF, Iona Brown.

The *E minor Concerto* for recorder, flute and strings is a delightful piece and is beautifully managed, even though period-instrument addicts will doubtless find William Bennett's tone a little fruity. The playing throughout is highly accomplished and the *Suite in A minor*, Telemann's only suite for treble recorder, comes off beautifully. Excellently played and recorded throughout. The compact disc brings out the forward balance of the soloists in the *Double concerto*, but the effect is not unattractive. The orchestral focus is not absolutely clean, though quite agreeable.

(i) *Viola concerto in G;* (ii) *Suite in A min. for recorder and strings; Tafelmusik,* Part 2: (iii) *Triple violin concerto in F;* Part 3: (iv) *Double horn concerto in E flat.*
❀ (BB) *** Naxos Dig. 8.550156; *4550156* [id.]. (i) Kyselak; (ii) Stivín; (iii) Hoelblingova, Hoelbling, Jablokov; (iv) Z. & B. Tylšar, Capella Istropolitana, Richard Edlinger.

Our Rosette is awarded for enterprise and good planning – to say nothing of good music-making. It is difficult to conceive of a better Telemann programme for anyone encountering this versatile composer for the first time and coming fresh to this repertoire, having bought the inexpensive Naxos CD on impulse. There must be a vibrant musical life in Bratislava, for the excellent Capella Istropolitana consists of members of the Slovak Philharmonic, which is based there, and the soloists here are drawn from its ranks. Ladislav Kyselak is a fine violist and is thoroughly at home in Telemann's splendid four-movement concerto; Jiři Stivín is an equally personable recorder soloist in the masterly *Suite in A minor*; his decoration is a special joy. The *Triple violin concerto* with its memorable *Vivace* finale and the *Double horn concerto* also show the finesse which these musicians readily display. Richard Edlinger provides polished and alert accompaniments throughout: he is especially good at pacing the eight diverse movements of the *Suite*, which has so much in common with Bach's similarly scored *Suite in B minor*. The digital sound is first class.

Darmstadt overtures (suites): in C, TWV 55: C 6; in D, TWV 55: D 15; in D min., TWV 55: D 3; in G min., TWV 55: G 4; Tafelmusik, Part 1: *Overture (suite) in E min.; Concerto in A for flute and violin;* Part 2: *Overture (suite) in D; Concerto for three violins in F;* Part 3: *Overture (suite) in B flat. Concerto for 2 horns in E flat.*
(M) *** Teldec/Warner 2292 42723-2 (3) [id.]. Concerto Amsterdam, Brüggen; VCM, Harnoncourt.

What strikes one with renewed force while listening to these once again is the sheer fertility and quality of invention that these works exhibit. This is music of unfailing intelligence and wit and, although Telemann rarely touches the depths of Bach, there is no lack of expressive eloquence either. Renewing acquaintance with this music has been a pleasure, for it is easy to forget how rewarding these pieces are. The performances are light in touch and can be recommended with real enthusiasm. This would make an excellent start to any Telemann collection.

Tafelmusik (Productions 1 – 3) complete.
*** Teldec/Warner Dig. 2292 44688-2 (4). VCM, Harnoncourt.
*** DG Dig. 427 619-2 (4) [id.]. Col. Mus. Ant., Reinhard Goebel.

When it first appeared in the 1960s, the complete *Tafelmusik* (or 'Banqueting music') filled six LPs, and two eminently recommendable sets dominated the catalogue (August Wenzinger with the Schola Cantorum Basiliensis, and Frans Brüggen's Concerto Amsterdam). With the arrival of the present recordings we are faced with much the same dilemma, though the work now requires four CDs. Harnoncourt's Vienna Concentus Musicus and Goebel's Musiqua Antiqua, Köln, each have a devoted following for whom choice will be a foregone conclusion: at present the Musiqua Antiqua enjoys cult status in Early Music circles. For collectors with allegiance to neither group, choice will be more difficult. Moving from one to the other, it is tempting to think it is a matter of swings and roundabouts: the playing of the Musiqua Antiqua is distinguished by the highest order of virtuosity and unanimity of ensemble and musical thinking. They also have the advantage of very vivid and fresh recording quality; the balance is close and present without being too forward and there is a pleasing acoustic ambience.

Harnoncourt has a slightly more distant, less analytical balance, and his recording has the added poignancy of offering the last performances by the oboists, Jürg Schaeftlein and David Reichenberg (the set bears a dedication to their memory). It also offers distinguished playing, perhaps less virtuosic than the Cologne ensemble but no less sensitive. However, the greater breadth of the Harnoncourt set tells in its favour: Reinhard Goebel and his Cologne players opt for breathlessly quick tempi in which liveliness becomes headlong and there are some self-conscious dynamic exaggerations and expressive bulges. At times one's attention momentarily strays to their polish rather than staying with Telemann's unfailingly inventive resource. All the same, there is much to relish and few coming to this music afresh will be disappointed by either set. Incidentally for older collectors the two LP sets hold up rather well against these newcomers and, were they to be reissued on a bargain label, they would still be quite competitive.

Tafelmusik: Overtures (suites): in E min. (from Part 1); *in D* (from Part 2); *in B flat* (from Part 3).
(M) *** Teldec/Warner 2292 43546-2 [id.]. Concerto Amsterdam, Brüggen.

Essentially, these works are made up of French dance-movements of considerable diversity, and the *E minor Suite* is engagingly scored for a pair of recorders with strings; although it has no *Badinerie*, its sound is not unlike Bach's B minor work; while Telemann's *D major*, with its forthright use of a trumpet, similarly reminds one of the Bach *Third Suite*, even though its invention has nothing in it as memorable as Bach's famous *Air*. The third suite here is perhaps the most agreeable of all, using two oboes with considerable flair. All this music is expertly played by the Concerto Amsterdam under Frans Brüggen, and the remastered 1970 recording is fresh and full, so that the disc sounds hardly dated at all. Offered at mid-price, it represents first-rate value.

Tafelmusik, Production 3: *Overture in B flat; Quartet in E min.;* Production 2: *Concerto in F; Trio sonata in E flat; Solo (Violin) sonata in A; Conclusion in B flat.*
*** DG Dig. 429 774-2 [id.] (from above set, directed Goebel).

For those not wanting a complete set, this arbitrary but well-chosen 75-minute selection may prove useful. Goebel (quoting from writings of Telemann's time) suggests that the 'unforced merriment' of the French pastoral idyll, represented by the descriptive dance movements from the *Overture*, contrasts with the learning, the 'German diligence' of the following *Quartet*. Then after the *Concerto*, where the opening movement has something of the melodic and rhythmic zest of Handel's *Arrival of the Queen of Sheba*, comes 'something gratifying' from Italy in the four-movement *Trio sonata*, followed by the *Solo sonata for violin and continuo*. The recording is faithful, though the edginess of Goebel's violin timbre will not suit all tastes.

Water Music (Hamburg Ebb and Flow); Concertos in A min.; B flat; F.
*** DG Dig. 413 788-2 [id.]. Col. Mus. Ant., Goebel.

Telemann's *Water Music* was written for the centenary celebrations of the Hamburg Admiralty in 1723, and this lively and inventive suite was performed during the festivities. It is one of Telemann's best-known works and, save for the opening *overture*, is given a very lively performance, with sprightly rhythms and vital articulation. The eccentric opening is less than half the speed of Marriner's (deleted) version on Argo or Wenzinger's famous old Archiv account. Of particular interest are the three *Concertos* which form the coupling, two of which (in F major and A minor) are new to records. The invention is of unfailing interest, as is the diversity of instrumental colouring. The balance is admirably judged and the recording excellent.

CHAMBER MUSIC

Der getreue Musik-Meister: Nos. 4, 7, 13, 20, 28, 31, 35, 50, 53, 59, 62.
*** Denon Dig. C37 7052 [id.]. Holliger, Thunemann, Jaccottet.

This compact disc offers three of the most important works from *Der getreue Musik-Meister* for oboe and continuo, two *Sonatas* and a *Suite*, as well as the *F minor Sonata*, designated for recorder or bassoon and played here by Klaus Thunemann. They are interspersed with various miniatures, all well played and recorded. Holliger's playing is unusually expressive and his eloquence alone makes this selection worth having.

Sonatas for two recorders Nos. 1–6.
*** BMG/RCA Dig. RD 87903. Michala Petri and Elisabeth Selin.

Sonatas for two recorders Nos. 1–6; Duetto in B flat.
*** BIS Dig. CD 334 [id.]. Clas Pehrsson, Dan Laurin.

Canon sonatas Nos. 1–6; Duettos Nos. 1–6.
*** BIS Dig. CD 335 [id.]. Clas Pehrsson, Dan Laurin.

All the *Duet sonatas* are in four movements, the second being a fugue; the *Canon sonatas* are for two flutes, violins or bass viols. Needless to say, listening to two recorders for longer than one piece at a time imposes a strain on one's powers of endurance, however expert the playing – and expert it certainly is.

The RCA and BIS versions can be recommended alongside each other, although the BIS disc does contain one extra work. The playing of Michala Petri and Elisabeth Selin is particularly felicitous and the recording first class. However, although it is good to have the two treble recorders blending so well together, a clearer degree of separation would have been advantageous in the imitative writing.

VOCAL MUSIC

(i) *Ino (cantata); Ouvertüre in D (suite).*
*** DG Dig. 429 772-2 [id.]. (i) Barbara Schlick, Col. Mus. Ant., Reinhard Goebel.

Both the cantata *Ino* and the delightful seven-movement *Ouvertüre* or *Suite in D* were written in 1765 during what Peter Czornyi's excellent essay calls Telemann's Indian Summer. *Ino* has been out of the catalogue for some years; rediscovering it serves as a reminder that Telemann is still underrated, even following the pioneering work of the DG-Archiv label in the 1950s and 1960s. Listening to the effortless flow of remarkable invention, one can almost understand the disappointment of the Leipzig burghers that they could not entice Telemann into their service. Barbara Schlick is a delightful soloist, just a little lacking in fire and colour, but certainly lacking nothing in charm; and the wind players of the Musica Antiqua, Köln, have a delicacy and virtuosity that are irresistible. The *Réjouissance* in the *Ouvertüre* is – as so often with this ensemble – uncomfortably rushed (the internal-combustion engine had not been invented in the 1760s, let alone Concorde!), but there is so much that is right and thought-provoking about their playing, both here and in this remarkable cantata, that criticism must be muted. The balance captures just the right perspective between soloist and players, and there is a pleasingly warm acoustic.

(i) *St Matthew Passion;* (ii) *Magnificat in C.*
(M) ** Ph. 432 500-2 (2) [id.]. (i) Jurinac, Altmeyer, Günter, Crass, Lucerne Festival Ch., Swiss Festival O; (ii) Giebel, Malaniuk, Altmeyer, Rehfuss, Reuter-Wolf, Choeur des Jeunes, Lausanne, Munich Pro Arte O, Redel.

Telemann was even more prolific than Bach, and this *Passion* does not always show him at his most inspired. The narrative proceeds at an even emotional pace (with Altmeyer the smoothly lyrical Evangelist) and the choruses are for the most part a series of simple chorales, so that the sudden pungent cry of 'Barabbas!' and 'Let Him be crucified' when Pilate forces the mob to make their choice is the more forcefully dramatic. The other memorable feature, which is also interesting historically, is the series of interpolations in the gospel story. The first of these comes from the bass, Franz Crass, who comments powerfully on the 'Foolish knavery' and 'scheming guile' of Judas; but the highlight of the whole work is the series of poignant soliloquies from the soprano – Sena Jurinac in glorious voice – on the pathos of Christ's predicament, climaxed by an unexpectedly cheerful affirmation at the moment of crucifixion: 'Rejoice deeply for his most lamentable passing brings delight . . . with the joys of heaven . . . and destroys the torment of Hell'. Then at the very close of the story she sings a radiant postlude to Jesus, 'Sleep softly in Thy chamber'. The performance overall, directed by Kurt Redel, is hardly vibrant, but the 1964 recording is musically balanced, if not exactly vivid.

Like Bach and Buxtehude, Telemann was also willing to make use of Latin liturgical texts when the occasion or commission demanded, as in the *C major Magnificat* which is impressively scored for soloists, chorus and a fairly large orchestra, including trumpets. The piece is adequately performed so far as chorus and orchestra are concerned, though Kurt Redel is still essentiallty *kapellmeister*ish. Giebel, Altmeyer and Reuter-Wolf produce finely controlled lines, but Malaniuk and Rehfuss are less pleasing to the ear because of their tendency to wobble. The recording, as in the *St Matthew Passion*, is spacious and resonant.

(i) *Der Tag des Gerichts (The Day of Judgement;* oratorio): complete; (ii) *Pimpinone* (opera): complete; (iii) *Paris quartets Nos. 1 & 6.*
(M) **(*) Teldec/Warner 2292 42722-2 (3) [id.]. (i) Landwehr-Herrmann, Canne-Meijer, Equiluz, Van Egmond, soloists from Vienna Boys' Ch., Hamburg Monteverdi Ch., VCM, Harnoncourt; (ii) Spreckelsen, Nimsgern, Tachezi, Florilegium Musicum Ens., Hirsch; (iii) Amsterdam Qt.

Pimpinone anticipates *La Serva padrona* and offers music of great tunefulness and vivacity. The opera, here given uncut at 70 minutes, has only two characters, no chorus whatever, and a small orchestra. Yet its music is as witty as its libretto. Uta Spreckelsen and Sigmund Nimsgern are perfectly cast, and there is both charm and sparkle, while Hirsch accompanies in suitably spirited fashion. Excellent (1975) recording, with the voices given good presence. *The Day of Judgement* – the last of Telemann's great oratorios, coming from 1761–2 – is less convincing. Although there are moments of considerable inspiration in a work subtitled 'a poem for singing in four contemplations', one feels that Telemann was far too urbane a master to measure himself fully against so cosmic a theme. But the performers give it so persuasive and musical an advocacy and are, moreover, given the advantage of well-balanced recording. The 1966 sound has been effectively remastered and, although the choral focus is not always completely clean, the overall effect is vivid. Since it runs to some 84 minutes' length, the last contemplation is placed on a separate CD, and two of the highly inventive *Paris quartets* are used as the fill-up; and here a high order of virtuosity is put at the service of the composer. The snag is the close recording, vivid enough but with dynamic contrast relatively limited. The other drawback is the absence of translations – only the German words are given.

Die Tageszeiten.
*** HM/BMG RD 77092 [77092-RC-2]. Bach, Georg, Blochwitz, Mannov, Freiburg Vocal Ens. & Coll. Mus., Wolfgang Schäfer.

Telemann's cantata, *Die Tageszeiten* (1759), is a work of great freshness and inventive resource. Its four sections portray the various times of day (*Morning, Midday, Evening* and *Night*) and are full of imaginative ideas. Yet, fairly soon after its first appearance on LP in the early 1960s in an excellent performance from Helmut Koch and the Berlin Chamber Orchestra (DG), it returned to obscurity. This new version, recorded with period instruments and four excellent soloists, makes a different but almost equally strong impression. The strings prompt a fleeting nostalgia for the more robust timbre of modern forces, and the playing under Wolfgang Schäfer could afford to be more full-bodied. But there is some excellent singing, and the recording is clean and well balanced. An enjoyable disc.

Thomson, Virgil (1896–1989)

(i) *Autumn (Concertino for harp, strings and percussion); The Plow that broke the plains* (film music): *suite.*
(M) *** EMI CDM7 64306-2 [id.]. (i) Ann Mason Stockton; LAPO, Marriner – BARBER: *Adagio;* COPLAND: *Fanfare* etc. ***

Virgil Thomson is probably best known for his film-score to Flaherty's *Louisiana Story* and his opera, *Four Saints in Three Acts*, as well as his criticism in the *New York Herald Tribune*. These pieces are often quite appealing, even if none of them is really first rate. The *Autumn suite* has a cool yet distinctly American flavour, and many readers will find it highly attractive. The playing of the Los Angeles orchestra is altogether excellent, and the recording from the late 1970s has admirable space and realism.

Film scores: *The Plow that broke the Plains; The River* (suites).
(M) *** Van. 08.8013.71 [OVC 8013]. Symphony of the Air, Leopold Stokowski – STRAVINSKY: *Soldier's Tale.* ***

Virgil Thomson's orchestral music may be sub-Copland (he too uses cowboy tunes like *Old paint*), but in Stokowski's charismatic hands these two film scores emerge with colours glowing and their rhythmic, folksy geniality readily communicating. The recording is resonantly atmospheric, but vivid too. Most enjoyable, and with a worthwhile coupling. This is at upper mid-price in the USA.

Tiomkin, Dimitri (1894–1979)

Film music: *The Fall of the Roman Empire: Overture: Pax Romana. The Guns of Navarone: Prologue-Prelude; Epilogue. A President's country. Rhapsody of steel. Wild is the wind.*
**(*) Unicorn DKPCD 9047; *DKPC 9047* [id.]. Royal College of Music O, Willcocks; D. King (organ).

Dimitri Tiomkin was one of a number of émigré musicians who made a considerable contribution to the music of Hollywood. He contributed scores to some of the most famous movies of all time, for Hitchcock and Frank Capra among others. But it was Carl Foreman's *High noon* that produced his most memorable idea, and he quotes its famous theme, among others, in *A President's country*, a well-crafted medley used as background music for a documentary about President Johnson's Texas. *Wild is the wind* is another familiar melody; Christopher Palmer's arrangement makes a tastefully scored showcase. The latter has arranged and orchestrated all the music here except *Rhapsody of steel*, a complex pseudo-symphonic score written for another documentary, which lasts some 22 minutes. The music of *Pax Romana* has the robust character of a typical Hollywood epic costume spectacular, featuring a bold contribution from the organ. All the music is played with obvious enjoyment by the Orchestra of the Royal College of Music; no apologies need be made for their technique, which is fully professional. Sir David Willcocks conducts with understanding of the idiom and great personal conviction. The recording is very impressive too, though the balance gives brass and percussion rather too much prominence.

Tippett, Michael (born 1905)

(i) *Concerto for double string orchestra;* (ii) *Fantasia concertante on a theme of Corelli;* (iii; iv) *Piano concerto;* (v) *String quartet No. 1;* (iii) *Piano sonatas Nos. 1–2.*
(M) *(**) EMI CMS7 63522-2 (2). (i) Moscow CO & Bath Festival O, Barshai; (ii) Y. Menuhin, Masters, Simpson, Bath Festival O, composer; (iii) John Ogdon; (iv) Philh. O, Sir Colin Davis; (v) Edinburgh Qt.

This is a useful and interesting compilation (provided with the composer's own notes on the music), and it is a pity that reservations have to be expressed concerning the sound of the CD transfers. Tippett's eloquent *Concerto for double string orchestra* is well served by Barshai's performance, which has both warmth and vitality. The recording is lively but a shade dry in the upper range. The string textures are clear but not ideally expansive. The *Fantasia concertante,* written for the 1953 Edinburgh Festival, is not as immediately striking as its predecessor but, with the composer in charge and Menuhin as principal soloist, its inventiveness and expressive feeling are never in doubt. Again, the sound is clear and vivid but could be more sumptuous. The *Piano concerto* dates from around the same period and again represents Tippett's complex-textured and starkly conceived earlier style. Ogdon gives it a fine performance, although he does not rescue it from waywardness, while the recording, if not ideal, now sounds clearer than originally. The *First String quartet* is not difficult to come to grips with, although it is the outer movements which are most characteristic, and the *Molto lento e tranquillo* seems less striking. It is played rather slackly here; the sound is on the thin side. Ogdon plays the two *Piano sonatas* well and is especially convincing in the *First.* This is undeniably a work of power and originality, even though its relentless diatonicism may strike some listeners as limiting. The work has a vitality of invention that it is easy to admire, even if as piano writing it is not as effective in the traditional sense as Tippett's later essay in this form. This is much more compressed in its argument, and though a more uninhibited approach can bring out the point of Tippett's scheme better, Ogdon displays his usual integrity, as well as virtuosity. The recording is faithful but a shade hard.

Concerto for double string orchestra; Fantasia concertante on a theme of Corelli. (i) *Songs for Dov.*
*** Virgin Dig. VC7 90701-2; *VC 790701-4* [id.]. SCO, composer; (i) Nigel Robson.

It is particularly valuable to have the *Concerto for double string orchestra,* which Tippett had never previously recorded himself. Interpreting his own youthful inspiration, the octogenarian gives delightfully pointed readings of the outer movements, bringing out the jazzy implications of the cross-rhythms, not taking them too literally, while the lovely melody of the slow movement has never sounded more warmly expressive. The Scottish Chamber Orchestra plays with comparable passion in the *Fantasia concertante,* a related work from Tippett's middle period, while Nigel Robson is a wonderfully idiomatic and convincing tenor soloist in the difficult vocal lines of the three *Songs for Dov.* Warm, full recording.

Little music for string orchestra.
(M) **(*) Chan. Dig. CHAN 6576 [id.]. Soloists of Australia, Ronald Thomas – BLISS: *Checkmate*; RUBBRA: *Symphony No. 5.* ***

Tippett's *Little music* was written in 1946 for the Jacques Orchestra. Its contrapuntal style is stimulating but the music is more inconsequential than the *Concerto for double string orchestra.* It receives a good if not distinctive performance here and, truthfully recorded, makes a good encore for the music of Bliss and Rubbra.

Praeludium for brass, bells & percussion; Suite for the birthday of Prince Charles; The Midsummer marriage: (i) *Ritual dances;* (ii) *Sosostris's aria.*
**(*) Nimbus Dig. NI 5217 [id.]. (i; ii) Alfreda Hodgson, (i) Ch. of Opera North; E. N. Philh. O, Tippett.

Tippett in his eighties draws a committed performance from the English Northern Philharmonia, well rehearsed to play this showpiece as part of the Opera North production. This is not the most brilliant account but, quite apart from the composer's insight, it brings an obvious advantage in including the vocal parts in the fourth dance. *Sosostris's aria* makes another good concert item, but the soloist, Alfreda Hodgson, like the chorus, is balanced much too far behind the orchestra. The *Praeludium* is a sustained ceremonial piece, marked by sharp contrasts of dynamic and texture, wayward and distinctive. The *Prince Charles suite* offers another example of Tippett's occasional music, idiosyncratically bringing together echoes of Elgar, Vaughan Williams and Holst in a very Tippett-like way. The composer's direction is rather less persuasive in the *Praeludium* than in the rest, but with warm, atmospheric recording this is more than just an invaluable document.

Symphonies Nos. (i) *1–2;* (ii; iii) *3; 4; Suite for the birthday of Prince Charles.*
(M) *** Decca 425 646-2 (3) [id.]. (i) LSO, C. Davis; (ii) Chicago SO, Solti; (iii) Heather Harper.

All the symphonies have previously been available separately, the *First* and *Third* on Philips, the *Second* on Argo and the *Fourth* on Decca. The Polygram merger permits all four to be accommodated in a box of three CDs (since possessing the *First* and *Fourth* originally involved duplication, as they were both coupled with the *Suite for the birthday of Prince Charles*, this new format is obviously attractive). The transfers are splendidly vivid.

String quartet No. 4.
*** ASV Dig. CDDCA 608; *ZCDCA 608* [id.]. Lindsay Qt – BRITTEN: *Quartet No. 3.* ***

Tippett's *Fourth Quartet* develops even more rigorously the birth-to-death theme of his *Fourth Symphony*, written at about the same time. The emotional core lies in the slow and still abrasive movement which comes third, bringing no easy solution. The Lindsay Quartet give a powerful, deeply committed reading of music far thornier than the late Britten *Quartet* with which it is coupled. Fine, vivid recording, with the players presented rather close, so that extraneous playing noises sometimes intrude.

Piano sonatas Nos. 1 (Fantasy sonata); 2–4.
*** CRD Dig. CRD 34301; *CRDC 4130/1* (2) [id.]. Paul Crossley.

More than two decades separate the first two sonatas, and the remaining two have appeared at ten-year intervals. The *Fantasy sonata* is one of Tippett's very first published works and was written in 1937. The two middle sonatas are related to other Tippett works: the *Second* (1962) to the opera, *King Priam*, from which it quotes; and the *Third* (1973) comes from the same world as the *Third Symphony*. Paul Crossley has been strongly identified with the Tippett sonatas; he recorded the first three for Philips in the mid-1970s: indeed, No. 3 was written for him. The *Fourth* and most recent (1983–4) started life as a set of five bagatelles. Crossley contributes an informative and illuminating note on the sonata and its relationship with, among other things, Ravel's *Miroirs*; his performance has all the lucidity and subtlety one would expect from him. These masterly accounts supersede the earlier recording and their excellence is matched by truthful and immediate sound-quality on CD, with chrome cassettes of high quality.

VOCAL MUSIC

A Child of our time (oratorio).
*** Collins Dig. 1339-2. Robinson, Walker, Garrison, Cheek, CBSO Ch. & SO, composer.
**(*) Ph. 420 075-2 [id.]. Norman, J. Baker, Cassilly, Shirley-Quirk, BBC Singers, BBC Ch. Soc., BBC SO, C. Davis.
**(*) ASV Dig. CDRPO 7012; *ZCRPO 7012* [id.]. Armstrong, Palmer, Langridge, Shirley-Quirk, Brighton Festival Ch., RPO, Previn.

Sir Michael Tippett in his mid-eighties may not secure the best-disciplined performance on record of this earliest of his oratorios, but it is generally the most moving. In a work inspired by the events which led up to the Nazi pogrom on the notorious Kristalnacht in 1938, the emotional element is basic. The spirituals which punctuate the story like chorales in a Bach Passion have a heart-easing expressiveness, warmly idiomatic. *Steal away* and *Deep river*, respectively concluding the first and third parts, are incandescent, while the lightness and resilience of *Nobody knows* allows the syncopations to be pointed with winning jazziness. Next to Sir Colin Davis's taut, tough reading on Philips this may be relatively slack, taking a full five minutes longer overall, but the Collins sound is fuller and warmer than that of rival versions. The soloists are placed well forward, an outstandingly characterful team of singers specially associated with Tippett's music – Faye Robinson, Sarah Walker, Jon Garrison and John Cheek. There are many more helpful cueing points on the CD than on rival versions. On the whole this must be counted first choice.

Davis's speeds tend to be on the fast side, both in the spirituals (taking the place which Bach gave to chorales) and in the other numbers. He may miss some of the tenderness; by avoiding all suspicion of sentimentality, however, the result is incisive and very powerful, helped by excellent solo and choral singing. The CD transfer of 1975 analogue sound is fuller and more atmospheric than the much later Previn recording.

Previn's is a colourful and winning performance, warmer and more expressive than Davis's, predictably helped by the conductor's natural understanding of jazz rhythms. This is a reading which leaves you in no doubt as to the depth of emotion felt by the composer; but ensemble is not always ideally crisp, the chorus is set rather backwardly and the soloists, a less polished if just as characterful team as Davis's, have uneven moments. The digital recording is unobtrusively natural, if slightly recessed.

The Ice-break.
*** Virgin Dig. VC7 91448-2 [id.]. Sylvan, Harper, Wilson-Johnson, Page, Tear, Clarey, Randle, L. Sinf., Atherton.

Produced at Covent Garden in 1976, *The Ice-break* daringly sets the opening act in an airport-lounge. That and the quickly dated slang in the composer's own libretto suggest a trendiness which originally distracted attention from the universal elements in the story. This recording, made with similar forces to those used in a highly successful concert performance at the Proms in 1990, presents the piece more as a modern dramatic oratorio than as an opera. Characteristically full of ideas, it is a work for which the listener can readily provide the imaginary settings. The three acts between them last just under 75 minutes, but that brevity makes the piece feel taut, not shortwinded. The music has the physical impact characteristic of later Tippett, but with less of the wildness that developed in his works of the eighties. Centrally in Act II comes a lament for one of the principal black characters, the nurse Hannah (beautifully sung by Cynthia Clarey). In its bald simplicity that solo provides a vital, touching moment of repose, warmly emotional, to contrast with the tensions of a plot that centres on the cold-war period, with violence, racial conflict and student demonstrations part of the scheme.

David Atherton directs an electrically tense performance, with the American baritone, Sanford Sylvan, singing superbly in the central role of Yuri, a second-generation immigrant, set against Heather Harper as his mother, Nadia, full-voiced and characterful, and David Wilson-Johnson as Lev, the father who in the first scene arrives after 20 years of prison and exile. The single disc comes boxed with libretto and excellent notes by Meirion Bowen.

The Mask of Time.
*** EMI Dig. CDS7 47707-8 (2). Robinson, Sarah Walker, Tear, Cheek, BBC Singers, BBC Ch., BBC SO, Andrew Davis.

The Mask of Time is a piece bursting with exuberant invention. There is richness, generosity and overwhelming vigour in this Seven Days of Creation for a Nuclear Age, astounding in a composer who was nearing eighty when he wrote it. With his BBC forces, Andrew Davis brilliantly clarifies and sharpens the ever-busy score, and the fine discipline brings out a creative, purposeful control behind the wildness, while the poetry of the piece emerges the more intensely, culminating in the lovely setting for soprano and humming chorus of lines by Anna Akhmatova in *Hiroshima, mon amour*. The final wordless chorus then projects the role of music into eternity, under the title, *The singing will never be done*. Davis draws incandescent singing from the BBC Symphony Chorus and attendant professionals. The quartet of soloists too is outstanding, three of them in the original Boston performance. No finer recording has ever been made in the difficult acoustics of the Royal Festival Hall.

King Priam (complete).
*** Decca 414 241-2 (2) [id.]. Tear, Allen, Bailey, Palmer, Minton, Langridge, Robert, Harper, L. Sinf. Ch., L. Sinf., Atherton.

In this superb performance under David Atherton, with an outstanding cast and vivid, immediate recording, the power of Tippett's opera, offbeat as the treatment often is, both musical and dramatic, comes over from first to last. Norman Bailey, thanks to his long association with Wagner, sounds agedly noble to perfection. Robert Tear is a shiningly heroic Achilles and Thomas Allen a commanding Hector, vocally immaculate, illuminating every word.

Tishchenko, Boris (born 1939)

Symphony No. 5.
*** Olympia OCD 213 [id.]. USSR MoC SO, Rozhdestvensky.

Boris Tishchenko's *Fifth Symphony* was composed in 1976, the year of Shostakovich's death, and is a grave, serious – and often painful – work. It opens with a long cor anglais monologue and it pays tribute to Shostakovich not only in the various quotations but at a deeper level; throughout these strong resonances Tishchenko still speaks his own language. A powerful document, this is played with enormous conviction by the Ministry of Culture Symphony Orchestra under Gennady Rozhdestvensky, and is vividly recorded.

Tomasi, André (1901–71)

Trumpet concerto.
(*) Sony MK 42096 [id.]. Wynton Marsalis, Philh. O, Salonen – JOLIVET: *Concertos.* *

Like the Jolivet couplings, this is essentially crossover music, if with a neo-classical flavour. The structure is chimerical, but not without spontaneity and, with Wynton Marsalis offering scintillating bravura throughout and an easy affinity with the swiftly changing moods, the result is quite attractive. In playing time, however, this issue is singularly ungenerous.

Tomkins, Thomas (1572–1656)

The Great service (No. 3); When David heard; Then David mourned; Almighty God, the fountain of all wisdom; Woe is me; Be strong and of a good courage; O sing unto the Lord a new song; O God, the proud are then risen against me.
*** Gimell Dig. CDGIM 024; *1585T-24* [id.]. Tallis Scholars, Phillips.

Living on into his mid-eighties, Tomkins has had both good and bad luck at the hands of posterity. His son, Nathaniel, an amateur musician, ensured the survival of a larger proportion of his church music than with many of his contemporaries, by publishing a big collection, *Musica Deo Sacra*, in 1668. Even so, Tomkins by living on through following generations has generally failed to receive his true measure of appreciation, compared with his direct contemporaries and fellow-pupils of Byrd, such as Gibbons and Weelkes. He is a madrigalist and fluent contrapuntist in the Elizabethan manner who found his highest fulfilment in church music like the magnificent examples contained on this Gimell disc. The *Great Service*, in no fewer than ten parts, sets the four canticles – *Te Deum*, *Jubilate*, *Magnificat* and *Nunc dimittis* – with a grandeur rarely matched, using the most complex polyphony. The following motets bring comparable examples of his mastery. *When David heard*, the best known, is beautifully contrasted with the more agonizing lament, *Then David mourned*, with its clashing dissonances. These complex pieces bring the flawless matching and even tone for which the Tallis Scholars are celebrated, and with recording to match. Admirers of previous Gimell issues will enjoy these, but it is a pity that the choir's manner remains constant and the pulse generally even through settings of some of the most glorious texts in the English language. Surely *O sing unto the Lord a new song* should bring some clearer expression of joy.

Tomlinson, Ernest (born 1924)

An English overture; 3 Gaelic sketches: Gaelic lullaby. Kielder Water; Little serenade; Lyrical suite: Nocturne. Nautical interlude; 3 Pastoral dances: Hornpipe. Silverthorne suite; 2nd Suite of English folk dances; Sweet and dainty. arr. of Coates: *The fairy coach; Cinderella waltz.*
*** Marco Polo Dig. 8.223413 [id.]. Slovak RSO (Bratislava), the composer.

Ernest Tomlinson is the third composer to be represented in Marco Polo's excellent series devoted to British light orchestral music. Lancashire born and bred, he studied at the Royal Manchester College of Music and eventually became (additionally) a Fellow of the Royal College of Organists. Yet there is nothing remotely organ-like about his orchestral pieces. They charm by the very lightness of their being, with scoring as frothy as lace. The delicately winning *Little serenade*, which opens the disc, is the most famous piece, but the gentle, evocative *Kielder Water*, the captivating *Canzonet* from the *Silverthorn suite* and the *Nocturne* are hardly less appealing. *Love-in-a-mist* is as intangible as it sounds, with the most fragile of oboe solos, and it is not surprising that *Sweet and dainty* has been used for a TV commercial. Of course there is robust writing too, in the *Folk song suite* – but not too robust, although the jolly *English Overture* begins with *Here's a health unto His Majesty* and certainly does not lack vitality. The arrangements of music from Eric Coates's *Cinderella phantasy*, commissioned for a BBC Christmas radio play, even brought forth a Leroy Anderson-style galop called *The fairy coach*. The music is played with much grace and the lightest possible touch by the remarkably versatile Slovak Radio Orchestra under the composer, and the vivid recording has delightfully transparent textures, so vital in this repertoire.

Tosti, Francesco (1846–1916)

Songs: *L'alba sepàra della luce l'ombra; Aprile; 'A vucchella; Chanson de L'adieu; Goodbye; Ideale; Malia; Marechiare; Non t'amo; Segreto; La serenata; Sogno; L'ultima canzone; Vorrei morire.*
(M) *** Ph. 426 372-2. José Carreras, ECO, Muller.

Tosti (knighted by Queen Victoria for his services to music) had a gently charming lyric gift in songs like these, and it is good to have a tenor with such musical intelligence – not to mention such a fine, pure voice – tackling once-popular trifles like *Marechiare* and *Goodbye*. The arrangements are sweetly done, and the recording is excellent.

Tubin, Eduard (1905–82)

(i) *Balalaika concerto; Music for strings; Symphony No. 1.*
*** BIS Dig. CD 351 [id.]. (i) Sheynkman; Swedish RSO, Järvi.

The opening of the *First Symphony* almost puts one in mind of Bax, and there is a Sibelian breadth; but for the most part it is a symphony apart from its fellows. The quality of the musical substance is high and the feeling for form is every bit as strong; its presentation is astonishingly assured for a young man still in his twenties; indeed, the scoring is quite masterly. The *Balalaika concerto* was written for Nicolaus Zwetnow, not only a leading exponent of the balalaika but professor of neurosurgery in Oslo! Emanuil Sheynkman's account with Neeme Järvi is first class, both taut and concentrated. Excellent recording.

(i) *Ballade for violin and orchestra;* (ii) *Double-bass concerto;* (i) *Violin concerto No. 2; Estonian dance suite; Valse triste.*
*** BIS Dig. CD 337 [id.]. (i) Garcia; (ii) Ehren; Gothenburg SO, Järvi.

The repertoire for double-bass is hardly over-endowed, but Tubin's highly imaginative *Concerto* must surely be numbered as one of the most successful ever written for this intractable instrument. The work has an unflagging sense of momentum and is ideally proportioned; the ideas never outstay their welcome and one's attention is always held. The *Second Violin concerto*, though not the equal of his finest symphonies, is of much greater substance than its predecessor. It has an appealing lyricism, is well proportioned and has a strong sense of forward movement. The *Ballade* is a work of gravity and eloquence; it is never static, moves purposefully and holds the listener's interest throughout. *Valse triste* is a short and rather charming piece, while the *Dance suite* is the Estonian equivalent of the *Dances of Galánta*. Splendid performances from both soloists in the *Concertos* and from the orchestra under Järvi throughout, and excellent recording.

Symphonies Nos. 2 (The Legendary); 6.
*** BIS CD 304 [id.]. Swedish RSO, Järvi.

The opening of the *Second Symphony* is quite magical: there are soft, luminous string chords that evoke a strong atmosphere of wide vistas and white summer nights, but the music soon gathers power and reveals a genuine feeling for proportion and of organic growth. If there is a Sibelian strength in the *Second Symphony*, the *Sixth*, written after Tubin had settled in Sweden, has obvious resonances of Prokofiev – even down to instrumentation – and yet Tubin's rhythmic vitality and melodic invention are quietly distinctive. The Swedish Radio Symphony Orchestra play with great commitment under Neeme Järvi, and the engineers have done a magnificent job.

Symphonies Nos. 3; 8.
*** BIS Dig. CD 342 [id.]. Swedish RSO, Järvi.

The first two movements of the wartime *Third Symphony* are vintage Tubin, but the heroic finale approaches bombast. The *Eighth* is his masterpiece; its opening movement has a sense of vision and mystery, and the atmosphere stays with you. This is the darkest of the symphonies and the most intense in feeling, music of real substance and importance. Järvi and the Swedish orchestra play it marvellously and the recording is in the demonstration bracket.

Symphonies Nos. (i) *4 (Sinfonia lirica);* (ii) *9 (Sinfonia semplice); Toccata.*
❀ *** BIS Dig. CD 227 [id.]. (i) Bergen SO, (ii) Gothenburg SO, Järvi.

The *Fourth* is a highly attractive piece, immediately accessible, the music well argued and expertly crafted. The opening has a Sibelian feel to it but, the closer one comes to it, the more individual it seems. The recording comes from a concert performance and has an exceptionally well-behaved audience. The *Ninth Symphony* is in two movements: its mood is elegiac and a restrained melancholy permeates the slower sections. Its musical language is direct, tonal and, once one gets to grips with it, quite personal. If its spiritual world is clearly Nordic, the textures are transparent and luminous, and its argument unfolds naturally and cogently. It is strong in both concentration of feeling and melodic invention; the playing of the Gothenburgers under Järvi is totally committed in all sections of the orchestra. The performances are authoritative and the recording altogether excellent.

Symphony No. 5 in B min.; Kratt (ballet suite).
*** BIS Dig. CD 306 [id.]. Bamberg SO, Järvi.

The *Fifth* makes as good a starting point as any to investigate the Tubin canon. Written after he had settled in Sweden, it finds him at his most neo-classical; the music is finely paced and full of energy and invention. The ballet suite is a work of much character, tinged with folk-inspired ideas and some echoes of Prokofiev.

Symphony No. 7; (i) *Concertino for piano and orchestra; Sinfonietta on Estonian motifs.*
*** BIS Dig. CD 401 [id.]. (i) Roland Pöntinen; Gothenburg SO, Järvi.

The *Seventh* is a marvellous work, powerfully conceived and masterly in design, and it receives a concentrated and impressive reading. As always with Tubin, the music has great sureness of purpose and a firm sense of direction: you are never in doubt that this is a real symphony which sets out purposefully and reaches its goal. The ideas could not be by anyone else and the music unfolds with a powerful logic and inevitability. Neeme Järvi inspires the Gothenburg orchestra with his own evident enthusiasm. The *Concertino for piano and orchestra* has some of the neo-classicism of the *Fifth Symphony*. In the course of the three interlinked movements there is the same distinctive sense of momentum one finds in all his best music. Roland Pöntinen gives a dashing account of the solo part. The *Sinfonietta* is a fresh and resourceful piece, a Baltic equivalent of, say, Prokofiev's *Sinfonietta*, with much the same lightness of touch and inventive resource. Superb recording – a quite indispensable disc.

Symphony No. 10; (i) *Requiem for fallen soldiers.*
*** BIS Dig. CD 297 [id.]. Gothenburg SO, Järvi; (i) with Lundin, Rydell, Hardenberger, Lund Students' Ch., Järvi.

Tubin's *Requiem*, austere in character, is for two soloists (a contralto and baritone) and male chorus. The instrumental forces are merely an organ, piano, drums, timpani and trumpet. The simplicity and directness of the language are affecting and the sense of melancholy is finely controlled. The final movement is prefaced by a long trumpet solo, played here with stunning control and a masterly sense of line by the young Håkan Hardenberger. It is an impressive and dignified work, even if the quality of the choral singing is less than first rate. The *Tenth Symphony* is a one-movement piece that begins with a sombre string idea, which is soon interrupted by a periodically recurring horn call – and which resonates in the mind long afterwards. The recordings are absolutely first class and in the best traditions of the house.

Complete piano music: *Album leaf; Ballad on a theme by Maat Saar; 3 Estonian folk-dances; 4 Folksongs from my country; A little march for Rana; Lullaby; 3 Pieces for children; Prelude No. 1; 7 Preludes; Sonatas Nos. 1–2; Sonatina in D min.; Suite on Estonian shepherd melodies; Variations on an Estonian folk-tune.*
*** BIS Dig. CD 414/6 [id.]. Vardo Rumessen.

Tubin's first works for piano inhabit a world in which Scriabin, Ravel and Eller were clearly dominant influences but in which an individual sensibility is also to be discerned. The first disc comprises the charming six *Preludes* and the *First Sonata*, as well as a number of miniatures. The second offers the resourceful *Variations on an Estonian folk-tune*, a lovely work that deserves a place in the repertoire, and the *Sonatina in D minor* where the ideas and sense of momentum are on a larger scale than one would expect in a sonatina. The third disc includes the *Seven Preludes* (which bring harmonic fingerprints familiar from the later symphonies) and, most importantly, the *Second Sonata*, a key work in Tubin's development. It opens with a shimmering figure in free rhythm, inspired by the play of the aurora borealis, and is much more concentrated than his earlier piano works. Vardo Rumessen makes an excellent case for it, and even if the work is not as powerful as, say, the very finest of the symphonies, it is impressive stuff. The performances are consistently fine, full of understanding and flair, and the recording is very natural.

Turina, Joaquin (1882–1949)

Danzas fantásticas, Op. 22; La procesión del Rocio, Op. 9; Ritmos, Op. 43; Sinfonia sevillana, Op. 23.
*** BMG/RCA Dig. RD 60895. Bamberg SO, Antonio de Almeida.

La procesión del Rocio (1913) was Turina's first great success in picaresque Spanish tone-painting, corruscating with *seguidilla* and *garrotín* dance-rhythms in the animated opening *Triana*, suggesting an ageless quality with the arrival of the procession itself, gently led by flute and tabor and ending with a gaudy, Latin, religious celebration. We are more than familiar with the three equally exotic *Danzas fantásticas* (1918), with the opening shaft of bright sunlight of *Exaltación* leading to chimerical mood-changes, and evening bells in *Ensueño*. The closing *Orgía*, for all its flamenco vigour, later also brings dreamlike imagery of floral perfumes drifting on the night air. The three-movement *Sinfonia sevillana* is no less descriptive, beginning with a *Panorama* (though the dance spirit soon reappears), then suggesting the river which runs through the centre of Seville and ending with an exuberant *Fiesta*. *Ritmos* (1928), subtitled '*Fantasia coreografica*', is a series of sharply characterful vignettes, ear-tickling in their tunefulness and the diversity of their orchestral palette. The Bambergers clearly relish the southern sunshine, balmy nocturnal breezes and glittering flamenco dances and, with Almeida directing persuasively, they respond with distinction to this evocative repertoire. The playing has great vitality, finesse and warmth, and the Mediterranean colouring is as vivid as the ear could wish. The recording too is spacious, with the necessary resonance hardly clouding the more garish tuttis and bringing lustrously transluscent strings and glowing wind.

CHAMBER MUSIC

La Oración del Torero.
*** Collins Dig. 1267-2 [id.]. Britten Qt – CHERUBINI; VERDI: *Quartets.* ***

Turina's seductively gentle evocation was conceived with lutes in mind, but quartet playing of this calibre makes the string medium seem exactly right for the music, and brings a refined ravishing of the senses. The performance is full of lush Andalusian atmosphere, yet has an element of restraint and never becomes over-ripe, helped by superb recording and a most sympathetic acoustic. The '*delicadísimo*' close is quite magical.

Piano trio No. 1, Op. 35.
**(*) Chan. Dig. CHAN 9016 [id.]. Borodin Trio – DEBUSSY: MARTIN: *Piano trios.* **

Piano trios Nos. 1, Op. 35; 2, Op. 76; Circulo, Fantasia for piano trio, Op. 91.
*** Calig. Dig. CAL 50902 [id.]. Munich Piano Trio.

Turina's *First Piano trio* comes from the mid-1920s and maintains a delicate balance between national Spanish elements and classical forms – prelude and fugue, theme and variations and so on. To be frank honours are fairly evenly divided between the two versions listed above, and choice will doubtless be resolved by the coupling. Both are highly accomplished performances. The Borodin Trio take the more expansive view; their playing is always sensitive and although they are occasionally a little too highly charged or overheated, they give consistent pleasure and are very well recorded.

The Munich Piano Trio are tauter and take four minutes less. They have plenty of temperament and make the most of character contrasts without ever exaggerating them. The quality of the piano tone sounds at first marginally less bright than in the Chandos but that may be too close for some tastes. On the whole the Munich Trio would be a first choice; the Chandos are less inclined to allow the music to speak for itself. Although neither the *Second Piano trio* (1933) nor the later *Circulo* (1936) is a masterpiece, both are well wrought and the latter has some very appealing ideas. Both works are persuasively presented by this ensemble.

Tye, Christopher (*c.* 1505–*c.* 1572)

Mass: Euge bone; Peccavimus patribus nostris.
*** Proudsound Dig. PROUCD 126; *PROU 126* [id.]. Clerkes of Oxenford, David Wulstan – SHEPPARD: *Collection.* ***

Christopher Tye was a clerk at King's College, Cambridge, before moving on to Ely Cathedral in the 1540s. Mass settings of the period were often based on a setting of a votive antiphon, using the opening to provide a motto for each Mass section. Tye's *Euge bone* belongs to this genre, and Paul Doe surmises that it was composed at about the time of Edward VI's accession. It is a work of great beauty not otherwise available on CD; it is sung here with characteristic tonal sophistication by the Clerkes of Oxenford under David Wulstan, and splendidly recorded in a spacious but not over-reverberant acoustic.

Vaňhal, Jan (1739–1813)

(i) *Double bassoon concerto in F; Sinfonias: in A min.; F.*
**(*) BIS CD 288 [id.]. (i) Wallin, Nilsson; Umeå Sinf., Saraste.

The best thing here is the *Concerto*, which is an arresting and inventive piece. The opening allegro is conceived on a broader canvas than one expects, and the slow movement has real distinction, touching a deeper vein of feeling than anything else on this record. It is not too fanciful to detect in some of the harmonic suspensions the influence of Gluck, with whose music Vaňhal came into contact in the late 1760s. The two *Sinfonias* are less musically developed but far from uninteresting: the minuet of the *F major* has a distinctly '*Sturm und Drang*' feel to it: Vaňhal's symphonies may well have paved the way for Haydn at this period; they were certainly given by Haydn while Kapellmeister at the Esterhazy palace. The recording is good, as one has come to expect from this source, even if the acoustic is on the dry side. The playing of the Umeå ensemble is eminently respectable. The balance is well judged, though perhaps the accomplished young soloists are placed just a little too forward.

Varèse, Edgar (1883–1965)

Ameriques; Arcana; Density 21.5; Intégrales; Ionisation; Octandre; Offrandes.
(M) *** Sony Analogue/Dig. SK 45844 [id.]. Yakar, NYPO, Ens. InterContemporain, Boulez.

In the inter-war period Varèse was regarded as a wild man of the avant-garde in writing a work like *Ionisation* for percussion alone and abandoning conventional argument in favour of presenting blocks of sound. Yet performances like these show what a genius he had – not for assaulting but for tickling the ear with novelty. Boulez brings out the purposefulness of his writing, not least in the two big works for full orchestra, the early *Ameriques* and *Arcana*, written for an enormous orchestra in the late 1920s. Those two works are here played by the New York Philharmonic and are not digitally recorded. The selection recorded more recently in digital sound covers his smaller but just as striking works for chamber ensembles of various kinds, with Rachel Yakar the excellent soprano soloist in *Offrandes*.

Vaughan Williams, Ralph (1872–1958)

Concerto grosso; (i) *Oboe concerto; English folksongs suite; Fantasia on Greensleeves;* (ii) *Romance* (for harmonica and strings).

(M) **(*) Decca 421 392-2; *421 392-4*. (i) Nicklin; (ii) Reilly; ASMF, Marriner.

A somewhat mixed bag of lightweight Vaughan Williams. Celia Nicklin gives a most persuasive account of the elusive *Oboe concerto*, while the *Concerto grosso* is lively and polished. The atmospheric *Romance* is not one of the composer's most inspired works, but it is still worth having on disc. The recordings generally sound well, if with a touch of astringency in the string timbre.

(i) *Oboe concerto;* (ii) *The Lark ascending.*
*** DG 419 748-2 [id.]. (i) Neil Black; (ii) Zukerman, ECO, Barenboim – DELIUS: *Aquarelles* etc.; WALTON: *Henry V*. ***

Neil Black's creamy tone is particularly suited to Vaughan Williams's *Oboe concerto* and he gives a wholly persuasive performance of what is not one of the composer's strongest works. Zukerman's account of *The Lark ascending* is full of pastoral rapture – even if perhaps not totally idiomatic, the effect is ravishing. The recordings from the late 1970s have not lost their allure or atmospheric warmth in the digital remastering.

(i) *Concerto for 2 pianos in C; Symphony No. 5 in D.*
*** Virgin Dig. VC7 90733-2 [id.]. (i) Markham, Broadway; RPO, Menuhin.

VW's arrangement of his thornily inspired *Piano concerto* of 1931 for two pianos and orchestra has never sounded so convincing as here, thanks to the inspired duo of Ralph Markham and Kenneth Broadway, making light of the technical problems of piano writing that rarely fits under the fingers and gives few lyrical rewards. In the *Fifth Symphony* Sir Yehudi Menuhin, rather than dwelling on pastoral Englishry, takes a thrustful, purposefully symphonic view, with little lingering yet with warm expressiveness in each movement and with climaxes pressed home with satisfying power. It is an individual version, superbly recorded.

(i) *Piano concerto; Symphony No. 9 in E min.*
*** Chan. Dig. CHAN 8941; *ABTD 1537* [id.]. (i) Howard Shelley, LPO, Bryden Thomson.

Bryden Thomson's survey of the Vaughan Williams symphonies has been one of Chandos's many successes; each has been paired with a concerto or another major work. Whether or not you are collecting the whole series, this is a particularly valuable issue since it couples the little-known *Piano concerto* with the dark and much underrated *Ninth Symphony*. The *Concerto* had a long period of gestation: the first two movements were written in 1926, before *Job*, and the finale in 1931–2, although this was revised after the first performance in 1933. Perhaps the most strikingly original of the three movements is the imaginative and inward-looking *Romanza*, which has some of the angularity of line one finds in *Flos campi*, while the finale presages the *Fourth Symphony*. The work's neglect may be due to the absence of big themes; if the overt display to which the public is accustomed in bravura concertos is not obvious here, the piece abounds in difficulties of the most demanding nature, which Howard Shelley addresses with flair and brilliance. He makes light of the disconcerting cragginess of the piano writing and consistently brings out both the wit and the underlying emotional power.

Bryden Thomson conducts a powerful performance of the last of Vaughan Williams's symphonies, written when the composer was in his mid-eighties. Though the playing may not be as crisply incisive as that on Previn's 1971 version with the LSO, it brings out an extra warmth of expression, confirming that this is far more than the playful and noisy outburst of an old man. Both performances are greatly helped by the richness and weight of the Chandos sound, warmly atmospheric but with ample detail and a fine sense of presence.

(i) *Violin concerto in D min.;* (ii) *Flos campi.*
(M) (***) EMI mono CDH7 63828-2. (i) Yehudi Menuhin, LPO; (ii) William Primrose (viola), Philh. O; Boult – WALTON: *Viola concerto* etc. (***)

Though the 1946 mono sound inevitably limits the atmospheric beauty of *Flos campi*, this première recording of a masterpiece brings revelatory playing from Primrose, as well as deeply understanding conducting from Boult. Though there have been more immaculate performances on record since, none matches this in its heartfelt intensity, whether in the thrust and vigour of the outer movements or, most of all, in the yearning lyricism of the central *Adagio*, here revealed as among the composer's most tenderly beautiful slow movements. The recording, made in 1952 but never issued at the time, is also limited; but with excellent CD transfers and equally valuable Walton works as a generous coupling, this is a historic CD to cherish.

English folksongs suite; Fantasia on Greensleeves; In the Fen Country; (i) *The Lark ascending; Norfolk rhapsody No. 1;* (ii) *Serenade to music.*
(M) *** EMI CDM7 64022-2 [id.]; *EG 764022-4.* LPO, LSO or New Philh. O, Sir Adrian Boult; (i) with Hugh Bean; (ii) 16 soloists.

An attractive coupling of four works that originally appeared as fill-ups to Boult versions of the symphonies, all beautifully performed and recorded. Hugh Bean understands the spirit of *The Lark ascending* perfectly and his performance is wonderfully serene. For the CD reissue two other works have been added, the colourful *English folksongs suite* and *Greensleeves.* The transfers are fresh and pleasing; in the lovely *Serenade* (which Boult does in the original version for 16 soloists) the voices are given greater presence, yet the overall balance remains convincing.

English folksongs suite; Toccata marziale.
(BB) *** ASV CDQS 6021; *ZCQS 6021.* London Wind O, Denis Wick – HOLST: *Military band suites* etc. ***

As in the Holst suites, the pace of these performances is attractively zestful, and if the slow movement of the *English folksongs suite* could have been played more reflectively, the bounce of *Seventeen come Sunday* is irresistible. The first-class analogue recording has been transferred vividly to CD.

Fantasia on Greensleeves; Fantasia on a theme of Thomas Tallis.
*** EMI CDC7 47537-2 [id.]. Sinf. of L., Allegri Qt, Barbirolli – ELGAR: *Introduction and allegro; Serenade.* ***
(B) **(*) Pickwick Dig. PCD 930; *CIMPC 930* [id.]. LSO, Frühbeck de Burgos – ELGAR: *Cello concerto.* ***

When it first appears in full after the pizzicato introduction, the rich projection of the Tallis theme on which Vaughan Williams based his *Fantasia* sets the seal on Barbirolli's outstanding performance of one of the great masterpieces of all music. The wonderfully ethereal and magically quiet playing of the second orchestra is another very moving feature of this remarkable performance. On CD the sound retains its warmth, amplitude and bloom, but the disposal of background has also taken off a little of the recording's upper range, which is slightly restricted. The delightful *Greensleeves fantasia* makes an attractive bonus, and here the quality is pleasingly fresh.

Though Frühbeck is rather heavy-handed in his treatment of these Vaughan Williams favourites, the playing of the LSO is refined and the recording first rate. On the bargain-price Pickwick label, it makes an unconventional coupling for Felix Schmidt's outstanding reading of the Elgar *Cello concerto.*

Fantasia on Greensleeves; Fantasia on a theme of Thomas Tallis; In the Fen country; (i) *The lark ascending. Partita for double string orchestra.*
** ASV Dig. CDDCA 779; *ZCDCA 779* [id.]. L. Festival O, Ross Pople; (i) with Richard Friedman.

Fantasia on Greensleeves; Fantasia on a theme by Thomas Tallis; (i) *The Lark ascending.*
❀ *** Virgin Dig. VCy 790819-2; *VCy 790819-4* [id.]. (i) Christopher Warren-Green; LCO, Warren-Green – ELGAR: *Introduction and allegro* etc. *** ❀

Fantasia on Greensleeves; Fantasia on a theme of Thomas Tallis; Five variants of Dives and Lazarus; (i) *Flos Campi.*
(M) *** Van. 08.4053.71 [OVC 4071]. (i) Sally Peck, Utah University Ch.; Utah SO, Maurice Abravanel.

To Barbirolli's famous EMI coupling of English string music Christopher Warren-Green and his newly re-formed London Chamber Orchestra have added a radiant account of *The Lark ascending*, in which Warren-Green makes a charismatic solo contribution, very free and soaring in its flight and with beautifully sustained true pianissimo playing at the opening and close. For the *Tallis fantasia*, the second orchestra (2.2.2.2.1) contrasts with the main group (5.4.2.2.1) and here, though the effect is beautifully serene, Warren-Green does not quite match the ethereal, other-worldly pianissimo that made Sir John's reading unforgettable. But that is a minor quibble; the performance overall has great ardour and breadth, almost to match the coupled *Introduction and allegro* of Elgar in its intensity. The recording, made at All Saints' Church,

Petersham, is quite ideal in its resonant warmth and atmosphere, yet has good definition. This is an altogether superb disc.

On Vanguard the string works are given broad, lyrical performances and the warm, spacious, 1968 recording matches them. *Greensleeves* is slow and gracious, and there are more passionate versions of the *Tallis fantasia* available; but the noteworthy point is the way Abravanel catches the inner feeling of the music. The second orchestra makes a luminous sound and the contrasts are well made. Both here and in *Dives and Lazarus* the full strings create a gloriously rich sonority, and the only criticism in the latter variations is that the balance does not position the harp so that its contribution (not a concertante one) emerges very clearly. Sally Peck, the violist, is also placed with her colleagues rather than as a soloist in *Flos Campi* (following the composer's expressed intention), yet her personality still emerges well. Abravanel, always a warm, energetic conductor, displays real understanding, allowing the music to relax as it should in this evocation of the Song of Solomon, but never letting it drag either. The CD transfer is excellent, retaining the naturalness of the original recording.

Good but not distinctive performances on ASV, though not lacking ardour. The *Partita* receives most passionate advocacy, but such ardour only confirms the fact that the work is uneven in inspiration. The *Tallis fantasia*, too, reaches a powerful climax but the earlier interchanges between the main string body and the solo group seem rather static. Richard Friedman proves a sensitive Lark, but both this and *In the Fen country* are more evocative in the Boult recordings. Excellent sound.

Fantasia on a theme of Thomas Tallis; Five variants of Dives and Lazarus; In the Fen Country; Norfolk rhapsody.
*** Chan. Dig. CHAN 8502; *ABTD 1212* [id.]. LPO, Bryden Thomson.

The Chandos collection is generous. It offers a well-recorded anthology of (save for the *Tallis fantasia*) lesser-known Vaughan Williams. Boult recorded *In the Fen Country* and the *Norfolk rhapsody* successfully, but neither is otherwise available in modern digital sound. Bryden Thomson is a thoroughly persuasive guide in all this repertoire, and in the other two pieces more than holds his own with most of the opposition.

Fantasia on Sussex folk tunes for cello and orchestra.
*** BMG/RCA Dig. RD 70800. Lloyd Webber, Philh. O, Handley – DELIUS: *Cello concerto;* HOLST: *Invocation.* ***

The *Fantasia on Sussex folk tunes* has lain neglected since its first performance by Casals, and it proves something of a discovery. This is a highly appealing work, most persuasively performed too. The recording is first class.

Five variants of Dives and Lazarus; (i) *The Lark ascending; The Wasps: Overture and suite.*
(M) *** EMI Dig. CD-EMX 9508; *TC-EMX 2082.* (i) David Nolan; LPO, Handley.

The immediacy of the recording allows no mistiness in *The Lark ascending*, but it is still a warm, understanding performance. The overture is spaciously conceived and it leads to charming, colourful accounts of the other, less well-known pieces in the suite, tuneful and lively. The *Five Variants of Dives and Lazarus* finds Vaughan Williams using his folksong idiom at its most poetic, here superbly played and recorded. The sound is fresh and clear, if rather brightly lit.

Job (A masque for dancing)
*** Collins Dig. 1124-2 [id.]. Philh. O, Wordsworth – HOLST: *The Perfect Fool.* ***

Job (A masque for dancing); Variations for orchestra (orch. Jacob).
*** EMI Dig. CDC7 54421-2 [id.]. Bournemouth SO, Richard Hickox.

The claims of Barry Wordsworth's version are strong, even in competition with the excellent accounts of Richard Hickox and Vernon Handley (the latter currently withdrawn but to be reissued shortly, with extra music added). The Collins recording is the brightest and fullest of all, spectacularly vivid and with tremendous impact in some of the great brass passages. Though, relatively speaking, Wordsworth misses some of the music's hushed intensity, his is the most warmly expressive reading, with excellent playing from the Philharmonia. Typically he characterizes Job's comforters more positively than his rivals, making the saxophone solo whine and sneer. With a comparably colourful Holst coupling, this will for many be a first choice.

Richard Hickox conducts a strong and spacious account of Vaughan Williams's biblical ballet-score, warmly recorded. In its fine pacing it brings out the spiritual intensity of the music, while presenting dramatic contrasts at full power. Though many of his speeds for slow sections are broad, Hickox persuasively brings out the dance element in such numbers as the *Galliard for the Sons of the Morning*. The coupling is a welcome rarity, one of the very last works that the composer completed only a year before he died. He scored it for brass band, but here it is given in the fine orchestral arrangement by Gordon Jacob, a fresh and colourful little work, sharply structured. Both *Job* and the *Variations* sections are copiously indicated with CD tracks.

(i) *Suite for viola and orchestra;* (ii) *Flos campi;* (iii) *Hymn-tune preludes Nos. 1 & 2; Overture: The poisoned kiss; The running set.*
(M) **(*) Chan. CHAN 6545 [id.]. Bournemouth Sinf., (i) with Riddle, cond. Del Mar, (ii) with Ch.; (iii) cond. Hurst.

None of the works here are over-familiar, and the evocation of the Song of Solomon contained in *Flos campi* shows Vaughan Williams at his most rarefied and imaginative. The *Suite* is lightweight but engaging, unpretentious music to be enjoyed, with its charming *Carol* and quirky *Polka mélancolique*. Frederick Riddle is an eloquent soloist, even if the playing is not always technically immaculate, and Norman Del Mar directs sympathetically. The overture to the opera *The poisoned kiss* is merely a pot-pourri, but it is presented most persuasively here. *The running set* is an exhilarating fantasy on jig rhythms. Fine performances under George Hurst.

Symphonies Nos. 1–9; English folksongs suite; Fantasia on Greensleeves; Fantasia on a theme by Thomas Tallis; In the Fen Country; The Lark ascending; Norfolk rhapsody No. 1; Serenade to music; The Wasps: Overture and suite.
(M) *** EMI CMS7 63098-2 (7). LPO, New Philh. O or LSO, Boult.

Boult's approach to Vaughan Williams was firmly symphonic rather than evocative, and his cycle of the symphonies for EMI, here supplemented by many of the shorter orchestral pieces, brings warm and mature readings, which benefit from full-bodied, well-focused sound. EMI's mid-price offer gathers in a box the seven full-price CDs as originally issued, without any modification of format. Between them they present a comprehensive portrait of the composer, unmatched by any other single issue.

A Sea Symphony (No. 1).
(M) **(*) EMI Dig. CD-EMX 2142. Rodgers, Shimell, Liverpool PO Ch., RLPO, Handley.
(BB) *** Virgin Dig. VJ7 59687-2; *VJ 759687-4*. Margaret Marshall, Stephen Roberts, LSO Ch., Philh. O, Richard Hickox.
*** EMI Dig. CDC7 49911-2 [id.]. Lott, Summers, LPO Ch. & O, Haitink.
(M) *** BMG/RCA GD 90500 [60580-2-RG]. Harper, Shirley-Quirk, LSO Ch., LSO, Previn.
(M) *** EMI CDM7 64016-2 [id.]. Armstrong, Carol Case, LPO Ch., LPO, Boult.
(M) (***) Decca mono 425 658-2. Baillie, Cameron, LPO Ch., LPO, Boult.

Vernon Handley conducts a warmly idiomatic performance, which sustains relatively slow speeds masterfully. The emotional thrust of the work is caught powerfully from the very start, both in the big dramatic moments and in the tenderness of the quieter passages. The reading is crowned by Handley's rapt account of the slow movement, *On the beach at night alone*, as well as by the long duet in the finale, leading on through the exciting final ensemble, *Sail forth*, to a deeply satisfying culmination in *O my brave Soul!*. Joan Rodgers makes an outstandingly beautiful soprano soloist, with William Shimell drier-toned but expressive. There are two reservations: the first section of that long finale is less tense than the rest of the performance, and the recording, full and warm, presents problems in its extreme dynamic range, while placing the two soloists rather distantly. Yet to have such a performance in modern digital sound on a mid-price issue is self-recommending.

Richard Hickox directs a strong, warmly expressive reading, more urgent in its speeds than most latterday versions. His relatively brisk speeds and his ability to mould melodic lines with an affectionate rubato – notably with the bright-toned finely drilled LSO chorus – never sounds breathless, and he relishes the sea-sounds that Vaughan Williams gives to the orchestra. The different sections in the longer, outer movements are given strong cohesion, and the finale, *The Explorers*, ends in warmth rather than mystery on *O my brave soul!*. Margaret Marshall is a bright, fresh soprano soloist, but Stephen Roberts lacks some of the weight needed for the baritone solos, thoughtful and well detailed as his singing is. Nevertheless this is a genuine bargain.

As in the rest of his Vaughan Williams series, Bernard Haitink takes what to traditional English ears may seem a very literal view, not at all idiomatic but strong and forthright, to present this colourful work with its Whitman text as a genuine symphony, not just as a colourful cantata. Speeds are almost all unusually spacious, making this (at well over 70 minutes) the slowest version on record; but Haitink sustains that expansive manner superbly. The reading loses in atmosphere, but in its ruggedness it presents an exceptionally strong musical experience. It is the nobility of the writing, rather than its emotional warmth, that is paramount. The final calm epilogue, *O my brave Soul!*, after the excitement of the chorus, *Sail forth*, may be less affectionate and less hushed than in some other versions, lacking a sense of homecoming, but in its more detached way it makes a fine culmination. The recording is the fullest and weightiest yet given to this work, with the orchestra well defined in front of the chorus. Felicity Lott and Jonathan Summers are both excellent.

Previn's nervous energy is obvious from the very start. He does not always relax even where, as in the slow movement, he takes a rather measured tempo. The Scherzo is lighter and cleaner, holding more in reserve. The finale similarly is built up over a longer span, with less deliberate expressiveness. The culminating climax is not allowed to be swamped with choral tone, but has the brass and timpani still prominent. The *Epilogue* may not be so deliberately expressive, but it is purer in its tenderness and exact control of dynamics. Previn has clear advantages in his baritone soloist and his choir. The rich ambience remains, with the performers set slightly back.

Boult's stereo version is a warm, relaxed reading of Vaughan Williams's expansive symphony. Boult, often thought of as a 'straight' interpreter, here demonstrates his affectionate style, drawing consistently expressive but never sentimental phrasing from his singers and players. John Carol Case's baritone does not sound well on disc with his rather plaintive tone-colour, but his style is right, and Sheila Armstrong sings most beautifully. The set has been remastered with outstanding success. There is a vivid impact and the words are remarkably clear. There is no finer version.

It is good also to have Boult's 1954 Decca mono recording of the *Sea Symphony* back again on CD. It has not lost its power to surprise in the famous opening sequence. As for the performance, Boult was at his most inspired. However diffuse the argument may be, conveyed here is the kind of urgency one normally gets only at a live performance. Vaughan Williams was present at the recording sessions.

A London Symphony (No. 2); (i) *Concerto accademico; The Wasps: Overture.*
(M) *** BMG/RCA GD 90501 [60581-2-RG]. LSO, Previn; (i) with James Buswell.

A London Symphony (No. 2); Concerto grosso.
*** Chan. Dig. CHAN 8629; *ABTD 1318* [id.]. LSO, Bryden Thomson.

A London Symphony (No. 2): Fantasia on a theme of Thomas Tallis.
(M) *** EMI CDM7 64017-2; *EG 764017-4*. LPO, Boult.
*** EMI CDC7 49394-2 [id.]. LPO, Haitink.

A London Symphony (No. 2); (i) *The Lark ascending.*
*** Telarc Dig. CD 80158 [id.]. RPO, Previn; (i) with Barry Griffiths.

A London Symphony (No. 2); Partita for double string orchestra.
(M) (**(*)) Decca mono/stereo 430 366-2. LPO, Sir Adrian Boult.

Previn's Telarc version brings an exceptionally spacious reading, marked by a vivid and refined sound-balance. The atmospheric beauty of this lovely score has rarely been brought out more intensely, and the slow movement in particular brings a radiant, deeply poetic performance, caressing the ear. The faster movements consistently bring out the conductor's natural idiomatic feeling for this music, with rhythms nicely sprung – not least the sharp syncopations – and with melodies warmly moulded, though without sentimentality. Barry Griffiths' account of *The Lark ascending* is a welcome bonus, but it is not as instinctively rapturous a performance as those by Iona Brown or Warren-Green.

On RCA, though the actual sonorities are subtly and beautifully realized by Previn, the architecture is presented equally convincingly, with the great climaxes of the first and last movements powerful and incisive. Most remarkable of all are the pianissimos which here have great intensity, a quality of frisson as in a live performance. The LSO play superbly and the digitally remastered recording, made in Kingsway Hall, still sounds well with its wide range of dynamic. The fill-ups are welcome, especially James Buswell's fine account of the *Concerto*.

The sound remains spacious on Boult's splendid 1970 version and the orchestral playing is outstandingly fine. The outer movements are expansive, less taut than in his much earlier mono version for Decca; but here, as in the slow movement, the orchestra produces lovely sounds, the playing deeply committed; and criticism is disarmed. The Scherzo is as light as thistledown and the gentle melancholy which underlies the solemn pageantry of the finale is coloured with great subtlety. With Boult's noble, gravely intense account of the *Tallis fantasia* offered as a coupling, this remains an attractive alternative to Previn. The new CD transfer is remarkably successful.

Like Haitink's other readings of British music, this one is more literal in its rhythmic manners, less obviously idiomatic; but many will find it the more refreshing for that, and the incisiveness certainly makes a powerful impact. In jaunty themes Haitink's straight manner at times brings an unexpected Stravinskian quality, and the expansively serene handling of the lovely melodies of the slow movement brings elegiac nobility rather than romantic warmth. Syncopated themes at times sound a little stiff with this treatment, and the *Lento* sections in the last movement are taken dangerously slowly; but that is set against a fast, intense treatment of the allegro, and the tension is powerfully maintained. In the *Tallis fantasia* the straight rhythmic manners make the result sound somewhat unidiomatic too, but very powerful in its monumental directness. The recording has spectacular range, though it is not quite as transparent or as atmospheric as Previn on Telarc.

Bryden Thomson draws superb playing from the LSO in the *London symphony*, sustaining spacious speeds with a natural feeling for phrasing and rubato that leads the ear on. This is a warmly expressive reading rather than a strongly structural one, helped by the characteristically rich Chandos recording, which in moments of biting attack may be too reverberant for some. The most controversial speed is the one which Thomson chooses for the third-movement Scherzo, subtitled *Nocturne*. Taken slowly like this, it becomes a jolly galumphing dance. The *Concerto grosso* makes a worthwhile coupling, and the LSO's immaculate string section under Thomson's persuasive direction here shows in glowing sound how its easy, unforced inspiration can transcend its utilitarian background and bring it close to the world of the *Tallis fantasia*.

Boult's 1952 recording of the *London Symphony* has great atmosphere and intensity, bringing the feeling of a live performance. The mono sound is spacious and basically full, but the violins sound thin and edgy above the stave, and the remastering has not improved matters, especially in the glorious slow movement. But such is the magnetism of the music-making that the ear readily adjusts. The *Partita* was recorded in the earliest days of stereo in 1956. It does not inspire Boult as does the symphony; but it is well played and the string sound here is more agreeable, if not outstanding.

A London Symphony (No. 2); Symphony No. 8 in G min.
(M) *** EMI CDM7 64197-2; *EG 764197-4* [id.]. Hallé O, Sir John Barbirolli.

Barbirolli's 1957 recording of the *London Symphony* was an inspirational performance, entirely throwing off the fetters of the studio. The reading gathers power as it proceeds and the slow movement has great intensity and eloquence, with the Hallé strings surpassing themselves; its climax sounds surprisingly full. Indeed the recording, besides having a wide dynamic range, has plenty of atmosphere and warmth. The digital remastering is wholly successful, with the background subdued. The new coupling of the *Eighth Symphony* makes the CD doubly attractive. 'Glorious John' (the composer's appreciative description of the work's dedicatee) gave its première, and this record was made (by Mercury engineers) just a month afterwards. It is a robust performance rather than a subtle one, but full of character and feeling, matched by most vivid sound. For many, this will be regarded as a first choice for both these works.

(i) *A Pastoral symphony (No. 3);* (ii) *Oboe concerto.*
**(*) Chan. Dig. CHAN 8594; *ABTD 1289* [id.]. (i) Yvonne Kenny; (ii) David Theodore; LSO, Bryden Thomson.

Bryden Thomson's version of the *Pastoral* is finely paced and powerfully argued. There is no danger here of thinking that VW's predominantly measured writing is merely evocative or rambling. The menace behind it, as well as the implied poignancy, is tellingly conveyed; but the warmly reverberant recording places the orchestra rather close, so undermining the delicacy of pianissimos; and the offstage soprano soloist in the finale is a fraction too close, too specific rather than disembodied, with a hint of vibrato that is distracting. David Theodore's plangent tones in the *Oboe concerto* effectively bring out the equivocal character of this highly original work, making it far more than just another pastoral piece, sharply emphasizing the contrasts of mood and manner.

(i) *A Pastoral Symphony (No. 3); Symphony No. 4 in F min.*
(M) *** BMG/RCA GD 90503 [60583-2-RG]. (i) Heather Harper; LSO, Previn.

(M) *** EMI Dig. CD-EMX 2192; *TC-EMX 2192*. RLPO, Vernon Handley.

Previn draws an outstandingly beautiful and refined performance from the LSO, the bare textures sounding austere but never thin, the few climaxes emerging at full force with purity undiminished. In the third movement the final coda – the only really fast music in the whole work – brings a magic tracery of pianissimo in this performance, light, fast and clear. In the *F minor Symphony* only the somewhat ponderous tempo Previn adopts for the first movement lets it down. But on the whole this is a powerful reading, and it is vividly recorded.

Vernon Handley's coupling of these two strongly contrasted symphonies is another excellent ofering in his Vaughan Williams series for EMI Eminence. Though his speeds are relatively fast – as those of his mentor, Boult tended to be – he has the benefit of refined modern digital recording to help bring out the element of mystery in the *Pastoral symphony*. Even so, with a transfer at relatively low level the results are not as biting as those of the vintage versions by Boult, or even more relevantly by Previn, who in RCA's mid-priced series offers the same coupling as here. The extra bite and warmth of expressiveness in Previn's view brings even greater dividends in the *Fourth Symphony*, when he sustains generally slower speeds. Handley's approach is lighter and less violent. But in a symphony that is less brutal than was originally thought, there is a case for this sympathetic alternative approach.

(i) *A Pastoral Symphony (No. 3);* (ii) *Symphony No. 5 in D.*
(M) *** EMI CDM7 64018-2. (i) Margaret Price, New Philh. O; (ii) LPO, Boult.
(M) (***) Decca mono 430 060-2 [id.]. (i) Margaret Ritchie; LPO, Boult.

On EMI, in the *Pastoral Symphony* Boult is not entirely successful in controlling the tension of the short but elusive first movement, although it is beautifully played. The opening of the *Lento moderato*, however, is very fine, and its close is sustained with a perfect blend of restraint and intensity. Boult gives a loving and gentle performance, easier and more flowing than some rivals', and some may prefer it for that reason, but the emotional involvement is a degree less intense, particularly in the slow movement. Both recordings have been very successfully remastered, retaining the fullness and atmosphere (while refining detail) to help the tranquil mood which is striking in both works.

It is good to have the earlier Kingsway Hall recordings back in the catalogue. They were made in 1952/3 with the composer present; although allowances have to be made for the pinched sound of the upper string climaxes, the recording is basically full and luminous. The translucent textures Boult creates in the *Pastoral Symphony* (the opening is hauntingly ethereal) and his essential delicacy of approach are balanced by his intensity in the *Fifth*, where the climax of the first movement has wonderful breadth and passion.

Symphony No. 4 in F min.
(**) Koch mono 3-7018-2; *2-7018-4* [id.]. BBC SO, composer – HOLST: *Planets*. (**)

Symphony No. 4 in F min.; Concerto accademico.
**(*) Chan. Dig. CHAN 8633; *ABTD 1322* [id.]. LSO, Bryden Thomson.

Bryden Thomson conducts a powerful, individual reading of the *Fourth*, rugged rather than biting in the dramatic opening movement, wistful rather than tragic in the second, and cheeky rather than malevolent in the scherzo. Where many performances of the *Concerto accademico* make the composer's neo-classical manner sound like Stravinsky with an English accent, Thomson and Sillito find a rustic jollity in the outer movements, very characteristic of Vaughan Williams, and a delicate, withdrawn quality in the central slow movement. The recording of both *Concerto* and *Symphony* is warm and full in the Chandos manner.

Vaughan Williams made his recording of the *Fourth Symphony* in 1937, not long after the ink had dried on the score. It is a performance of blazing intensity in which he made no attempt to smooth over any rough edges, while the BBC Symphony Orchestra played as if their very lives depended on it. Theirs is a reading which is intent on capturing the spirit rather than the letter of the work and, although there have been more impressive recordings from Sir Adrian Boult and others, this performance carries a unique and powerful charge. It remains thrilling and makes a stronger impression than almost any modern recording because of its high voltage and despite the handicap of rather dry recorded sound. The transfer is less full-bodied than the LP version which appeared in the 1970s (the upper strings are lacking in timbre), but this should not deter collectors from acquiring it, particularly in view of the interest of the coupling.

Symphonies Nos. 4 in F min.; 6 in E min.
(M) **(*) EMI CDM7 64019-2 [id.]. New Philh. O, Sir Adrian Boult.

In the *Fourth Symphony* Sir Adrian procures orchestral playing of the highest quality from the New Philharmonia, and the slow movement, one of the composer's finest inspirations, is particularly successful. The recording, too, is first class; in this remastered form it sounds admirably fresh and combines body and clarity with spaciousness. There is plenty of bite in the sound, and this increases the sense of attack in the first movement of the powerful *Sixth Symphony*. Here Boult's performance is without the high voltage of his first mono recording for Decca with the composer present, and the reading is not as searching as that earlier account. The strange finale is played beautifully, with its finely sustained pianissimo enhanced on CD, and the atmosphere is not without a sense of mystery, but a greater degree of underlying tension is needed.

Symphony No. 5 in D; The England of Elizabeth: 3 Portraits (arr. Mathieson).
(M) *** BMG/RCA GD 90506 [60586-2-RG]. LSO, Previn.

Symphony No. 5 in D; (i) *Flos campi* (suite).
❀ (M) *** EMI Dig. CD-EMX 9512; TC-EMX 2112 [Ang. CDM 62029]. RLPO, Handley; (i) with Christopher Balmer & Liverpool Philharmonic Ch.

Symphony No. 5 in D; The Lark ascending.
**(*) Chan. Dig. CHAN 8554; *ABTD 1260* [id.]. LSO, Bryden Thomson.

Vernon Handley's disc is outstanding in every way, a spacious yet concentrated reading, superbly played and recorded, which masterfully holds the broad structure of this symphony together, building to massive climaxes. The warmth and poetry of the work are also beautifully caught. The rare and evocative *Flos campi*, inspired by the Song of Solomon, makes a generous and attractive coupling, equally well played, though the viola solo is rather closely balanced. The sound is outstandingly full, giving fine clarity of texture.

In this most characteristic – and, many would say, greatest – of the Vaughan Williams symphonies, Previn refuses to be lured into pastoral byways. His tempi may be consistently on the slow side, but the purity of tone he draws from the LSO, the precise shading of dynamic and phrasing, and the sustaining of tension through the longest, most hushed passages produce results that will persuade many not normally convinced of the greatness of this music. This is an outstanding performance, very well transferred to CD. Previn's later, Telarc version with the RPO does not match this in raptness and emotional thrust. The *England of Elizabeth suite* is a film score of no great musical interest but is undoubtedly pleasant to listen to.

Thomson's version with the LSO, very beautifully played and recorded in spacious sound, brings out the darkness behind this work, inspired by, and dedicated to, Sibelius. It may be less warm and sympathetic than more outward-going readings, less beautiful than others, but it stands as a strong, refreshing reading, superbly recorded, if not quite as cleanly as the very finest. Michael Davis makes a rich-toned soloist in *The Lark ascending*, presented as more than a pastoral evocation.

Symphonies Nos. 5 in D; 6 in E min.
**(*) BMG/RCA Dig. RD 60556 [60556-2-RD]. Philh. O, Leonard Slatkin.

Slatkin in his generous coupling of Nos 5 and 6 is not helped by the recording, which in its distancing prevents the big dramatic moments from having their full impact. Except in the third movement *Romanza* of No. 5 and the pianissimo finale of No. 6 Slatkin opts for speeds on the fast side, yet with his preference for keeping a very steady beat, he remains a restrained interpreter of RVW. The big climaxes of the *Preludio* in No. 5 and of the *Romanza* lack the emotional weight they can have, and the second movement of No. 6 with its insistent anapaestic interruptions lacks menace. Yet there is still much to enjoy in these performances, with refined and intensely beautiful string playing from the Philharmonia.

Symphony No. 6 in E min.; Fantasia on a theme of Thomas Tallis; (i) *The Lark ascending.*
*** Teldec/Warner Dig. 9031 73127-2 [id.]. (i) Tasmin Little; BBC SO, Andrew Davis.

Andrew Davis's reading of the *Sixth* is taut and urgent, with emotions kept under firm control. The two shorter works which come as supplement are given more warmly expressive, exceptionally beautiful performances, with Tasmin Little an immaculate soloist in *The Lark ascending*. Teldec's wide-ranging sound, setting the orchesta at a slight distance, slightly blunts the impact of the symphony in the first three movements, but then works beautifully in the chill of the hushed pianissimo meditation of the finale, as it does too in the fill-ups.

Symphonies Nos. 6 in E min.; 9 in E min.
(M) *** BMG/RCA GD 90508 [60588-2-RG]. LSO, Previn.

The *Sixth Symphony*, with its moments of darkness and brutality contrasted against the warmth of the second subject or the hushed intensity of the final other-worldly slow movement, is a work for which Previn has a natural affinity. In the first three movements his performance is superbly dramatic, clear-headed and direct, with natural understanding. His account of the mystical final movement with its endless pianissimo is not, however, on the same level, for the playing is not quite hushed enough, and the tempo is a little too fast. The *Ninth*, Vaughan Williams's last symphony, stimulates Previn to show a freshness and sense of poetry which prove particularly thought-provoking and rewarding. The RCA recording is highly successful, and the string-tone is expansive and well balanced in relation to the rest of the orchestra.

Sinfonia Antartica (No. 7).
*** EMI Dig. CDC7 47516-2 [id.]. Sheila Armstrong, LPO Ch., LPO, Haitink.

(i) *Sinfonia Antartica (No. 7); Serenade to music.*
(M) *** EMI Dig. CD-EMX 2173; *TC-EMX 2173*. (i) Alison Hargan; RLPO and Ch., Vernon Handley.

Sinfonia Antartica (No. 7); The Wasps (incidental music): *Overture and suite.*
(M) **(*) EMI CDM7 64020-2 [id.]; *EG 764020-4*. LPO, Sir Adrian Boult.

With stunningly full and realistic recording, Haitink directs a revelatory performance of what has long been thought of as merely a programmatic symphony. Based on material from VW's film music for *Scott of the Antarctic*, the symphony is in fact a work which, as Haitink demonstrates, stands powerfully as an original inspiration in absolute terms. Only in the second movement does the 'penguin' music seem heavier than it should be, but even that acquires new and positive qualities, thanks to Haitink.

Vernon Handley's is a most satisfyingly symphonic view of a work that can seem merely illustrative. As in his other Vaughan Williams recordings, Handley shows a natural feeling for expressive rubato and draws refined playing from the Liverpool orchestra. At the end of the epilogue Alison Hargan makes a notable first appearance on disc, a soprano with an exceptionally sweet and pure voice. In well-balanced digital sound it makes an outstanding bargain, particularly when it offers an excellent fill-up, the *Serenade to music*, though in this lovely score a chorus never sounds as characterful as a group of well-chosen soloists. This can be recommended alongside Haitink but costs much less.

Sir Adrian gives a stirring account and is well served by the EMI engineers. There is not really a great deal to choose between this and Previn's version as performances: both are convincing. Perhaps the EMI recording has slightly greater range and a more natural balance; certainly the CD transfer brings an attractively firm focus. However, the inclusion of Vaughan Williams's Aristophanic suite, *The Wasps*, with its endearing participation of the kitchen utensils plus its indelibly tuneful *Overture*, is a bonus for the Boult issue, although in the *Overture* the upper strings sound a bit thin.

(i) *Sinfonia Antartica (No. 7); Symphony No. 8 in D min.*
(M) *** BMG/RCA GD 90510 [60590-2-RG]. (i) Heather Harper, Ralph Richardson, LSO Ch.; LSO, Previn.

In the *Sinfonia Antartica* Previn's interpretation concentrates on atmosphere rather than drama in a performance that is sensitive and literal. Because of the recessed effect of the sound, the portrayal of the ice-fall (represented by the sudden entry of the organ) has a good deal less impact than on Vernon Handley's version. Before each movement Sir Ralph Richardson speaks the superscription written by the composer on his score. Previn's account of the *Eighth* brings no reservations, with finely pointed playing, the most precise control of dynamic shading, and a delightfully Stravinskian account of the bouncing Scherzo for woodwind alone. Excellent recording, which has been opened up by the digital remastering and made to sound more expansive.

Symphony No. 8 in D min.; Fantasia on Greensleeves; 2 Hymn-tune Preludes: (Eventide; Dominus regit me); Partita for double string orchestra.
**(*) Chan. Dig. CHAN 8828; *ABTD 1453* [id.]. LSO, Bryden Thomson.

In a warm and generally easy-going performance of No. 8, Bryden Thomson underlines the work's pastoral element at relatively slow speeds in three of the four movements. The exception is the third-movement *Cavatina*, which at a flowing speed is similarly easy-going, rather lacking the searching undertones which some other readings find. That approach leads on naturally to *Greensleeves* and the *Hymn-tune Preludes*, similarly pastoral in tone; but then the *Partita* finds the composer in more abrasive mood, less easily sympathetic. This curiously angular work sounds more convincing in a more purposeful performance than this, but in the *Fantasia* finale – a replacement movement that VW wrote after the rest – Thomson effectively brings out the foretastes of the dark first movement of the *Sixth Symphony*. The string sound has more edge on it than in most Chandos issues with Thomson, but that may reflect the LSO rather than the recorded sound, which is full and with plenty of body.

Symphonies Nos. 8 in D min.; 9 in E min.
(M) *** EMI CDM7 64021-2 [id.]. LPO, Sir Adrian Boult.

Boult's account of the *Eighth* is an essentially genial one. It may not be as sharply pointed as Previn's version, but some will prefer the extra warmth of the Boult interpretation with its rather more lyrical approach. The *Ninth* contains much noble and arresting invention, and Boult's performance is fully worthy of it. He draws most committed playing from the LPO, and the recording is splendidly firm in tone. The digital remastering is well up to the high standard EMI have set with these reissues of Boult's recordings.

The Wasps: Overture. Serenade to music (orchestral version).
*** Chan. CHAN 8330; *ABTD 1106* [id.]. LPO, Handley – DELIUS: *Collection.* ***

Exceptionally well recorded and vividly impressive on CD, Handley's readings of the *Wasps overture* and the *Serenade to music* in its orchestral version are most sympathetically done. The *Overture* is more urgent here than in Handley's more recent version for Eminence (as part of the complete suite), and though the *Serenade* inevitably lacks a dimension without voices, this is most persuasive, beautifully played by the LPO.

String quartet in G min; (i) *On Wenlock Edge.*
*** EMI Dig. CDC7 543462 [id.]; *EL7 543462.* Britten Qt; (i) with Philip Langridge & Howard Shelley – RAVEL: *Quartet.* ***

Vaughan Williams wrote his *G minor String quartet* in 1909, soon after completing a period of study with Ravel in Paris. The textures may have owed something to his lessons, but the Vaughan Williams idiom could hardly be more distinctive. It provides a fascinating parallel having it next to Ravel's own quartet, most beautifully played and recorded. The Britten Quartet, one of the most talented of the new generation, is then joined by the tenor, Philip Langridge, and the pianist, Howard Shelley, for another Vaughan Williams work of the same period, the Housman cycle, *On Wenlock Edge.* With the Britten Quartet bringing out the eerily evocative colourings in the string-writing, Langridge gives a most dramatic account. In the third song, *Is my team ploughing*, he makes the most extreme and effective contrast between the ghostly voice of the questioner – with vibrato stilled – and the living friend and betrayer who answers. A distinctive coupling, with the beauty of the recording matching the performances.

6 Studies in English folksong for clarinet and piano.
*** Chan. Dig. CHAN 8683; *ABTD 1078* [id.]. Hilton, Swallow – BAX: *Sonata* **(*); BLISS: *Quintet.* ***

These *Folksong studies*, which Vaughan Williams published in arrangements for the viola and cello, come from the mid-1920s and are really very beautiful; they can be recommended even to those normally allergic to this kind of repertory. They are played with the utmost sensitivity by Janet Hilton and Keith Swallow.

VOCAL MUSIC

(i) *10 Blake songs* (for voice and oboe); (ii) *Songs of travel.* Songs: *Linden Lea; Orpheus with his lute; The water mill; Silent noon.*
(M) *** Decca 430 368-2. Robert Tear; (i) Neil Black; (ii) Philip Ledger – BUTTERWORTH: *Shropshire lad.* ***

Robert Tear, recorded in 1972, cannot match Ian Partridge in his wonderfully sensitive account (currently withdrawn) of the *Blake songs*, but his rougher-grained voice brings out a different kind of expressiveness, helped by Neil Black's fine oboe playing. The *Songs of travel*, here presented complete with the five extra songs published later, are also most welcome, as are the other four songs, notably *Silent noon*, added for this reissue. Ledger is a most perceptive accompanist.

Dona nobis pacem; (i) *5 mystical songs.*
*** Chan. Dig. CHAN 8590; *ABTD 1297* [id.]. Wiens, (i) Rayner-Cook, LPO Ch., LPO, Bryden Thomson.

The *Dona nobis pacem* is powerful music and it is well performed on this Chandos disc by Edith Wiens and Bryan Rayner-Cook. The latter gives an eloquent account of the much earlier *Five mystical songs.* Bryden Thomson seems to be assuming the mantle of Sir Adrian Boult and gets playing of total commitment from the London Philharmonic Orchestra. The recording is made in an appropriately resonant acoustic and the orchestral detail registers well.

(i) *Fantasia on Christmas carols;* (ii) *Flos Campi;* (i) *5 Mystical songs;* (iii) *Serenade to music.*
*** Hyp. Dig. CDA 66420; *KA 66420* [id.]. (i) Thomas Allen, (ii) Imai & Corydon Singers; (iii) 16 soloists; ECO, Best.

This radiant record was designed to celebrate the tenth anniversary of the foundation of the Hyperion label by Ted Perry, one of the best loved and most admired figures in the record world. It centres round the *Serenade to music*, one of the great celebratory works of the century, specially composed for the jubilee of Sir Henry Wood in 1938. As in the original performance, sixteen star soloists are here lined up and, though the team of women does not quite match the stars of 1938 – who included Dame Eva Turner and Dame Isobel Baillie – the men are generally fresher and clearer. Above all, thanks largely to fuller, modern recording, the result is much more sensuous than the original, with ensemble better matched and with Matthew Best drawing glowing sounds from the English Chamber Orchestra. The other items are superbly done too, with Nobuko Imai a powerful viola soloist in the mystical cantata, *Flos campi*, another Vaughan Williams masterpiece. Thomas Allen is the characterful soloist in the five *Mystical songs.* Warmly atmospheric sound to match the performances.

Fantasia on Christmas carols; Hodie.
**(*) EMI Dig. CDC7 54128-2 [id.]. Gale, Tear, Roberts, LSO Ch. & O, Hickox.

Though the three soloists cannot match the original trio in Sir David Willcocks's pioneering version (on EMI CDM7 69872-2), Hickox directs a more urgent and more freely expressive reading of the big Christmas cantata, *Hodie*, helped by more refined and incisive choral singing. As on the earlier disc, the *Christmas carol fantasia* proves an ideal coupling, also warmly done.

Lord Thou hast been our refuge; Prayer to the Father of Heaven; A vision of aeroplanes.
*** Chan. Dig. CHAN 9019 [id.]. Finzi Singers, Spicer – HOWELLS: *Requiem* etc. ***

These three choral pieces make an apt coupling for the Howells choral works on the Finzi Singers' disc. *A vision of aeroplanes* improbably but most imaginatively uses a text from Ezekiel.

Mass in G min.; Te Deum in C.
*** Hyp. CDA 66076; *KA 66076* [id.]. Corydon Singers, Best – HOWELLS: *Requiem.* ***

Matthew Best and the Corydon Singers give a highly committed account of the *Mass* and, despite the spacious acoustic, there is admirable clarity of texture.

The Shepherds of the Delectable Mountains; 3 Choral hymns; Magnificat; A Song of thanksgiving; Psalm 100.
*** Hyp. Dig. CDA 66569 (id.]. Gielgud, Dawson, Kitchen, Wyn-Rogers, Ainsley, Bowen, Thompson, Opie, Terfel, Best, Corydon Singers, L. Oratory Jun. Ch., City of L. Sinf., Best.

Matthew Best here follows up the brilliant success of his earlier Hyperion disc of Vaughan Williams with a comparably varied group of works with voices, less well known. Best is particularly successful in defying the idea of *A Song of thanksgiving* as merely an occasional work, written for the victory celebrations at the end of the Second World War in 1945. With Sir John Gielgud as narrator and Lynne Dawson as the sweet-toned soprano soloist, Best gives it a tautness and sense of drama, bringing out the originality of the writing, simple and stirring in its grandeur, not for a moment pompous. The *Magnificat* brings more buried treasure, a massive setting designed not for liturgical but for concert use. Written in 1932, it has links with Vaughan Williams's bigger choral works as well as the inter-war symphonies, heartfelt music from an agnostic composer inspired to some of his highest flights by religious texts. With its haunting ostinatos it is also closer to Holst's choral music than most Vaughan Williams. The *Three Hymns* and the setting of *Psalm 100* are comparably distinctive in their contrasted ways, and though the Bunyan setting of *The Shepherds of the Delectable Mountains* found its rightful place as part of the opera, *The Pilgrim's Progress*, it is good to have a recording of what was originally a separate piece, written much earlier. Most of the solo singing is excellent, and the chorus is superb, helped by warmly atmospheric recording.

Songs of travel; The House of Life (6 sonnets); *4 Poems by Fredegond Shove; 4 Last songs: No. 2, Tired;* Songs: *In the spring; Linden Lea.*
**(*) Chan. Dig. CHAN 8475; *ABTD 1186* [id.]. Benjamin Luxon, David Williams.

Though Benjamin Luxon's vibrato is distractingly wide, the warmth and clarity of the recording help to make his well-chosen collection of Vaughan Williams songs very attractive, including as it does not only the well-known Stevenson travel cycle but the Rossetti cycle, *The House of Life* (including *The Water mill*), as well as the most famous song of all, *Linden Lea.*

The Pilgrim's progress (incidental music, ed. Palmer).
*** Hyp. CDA 66511; *KA 66511* [id.]. Sir John Gielgud, Richard Pasco, Ursula Howells, Corydon Singers, City of L. Sinfonia, Best.

Vaughan Williams had a lifelong devotion to Bunyan's great allegory, which fired his inspiration for at least five major musical projects. The last was the full-scale opera of 1951. Before that, in 1942 when he was completing the *Fifth Symphony* – another Bunyan inspiration – he wrote incidental music for a BBC radio adaptation of the complete *Pilgrim's Progress.* Much of the material, but not all, then found a place in the opera. Christopher Palmer, who, with equal flair, adapted Walton's *Henry V* film score into a similar mixture of speech and music, has here devised a sequence of twelve movements, which – overlapping with the opera and the symphony – throws up long-buried treasure. Matthew Best draws warmly sympathetic performances from his singers and players, in support of the masterly contributions of Sir John Gielgud, taking the role of Pilgrim as he did on radio in 1942, and Richard Pasco as the Evangelist.

OPERA

The Pilgrim's Progress.
(M) *** EMI CMS7 64212-2 (2). Burrowes, Armstrong, Noble, Herincx, Carol Case, Shirley-Quirk, Keyte, LPO Ch., LPO, Boult.

The appearance on CD of this glowing performance under Boult should effectively ensure that this inspired opera, one of the composer's culminating life-works, is at last given its due. Though Vaughan Williams was right in insisting that it is not an oratorio (his description was 'a morality'), the choral writing frames it, sung with heartfelt warmth by the London Philharmonic Choir. What comes out in a recorded performance is that, so far from being slow and undramatic, the score is crammed full of delectable ideas one after the other, and the drama of the mind – as in the book – supplements more conventional dramatic incident. John Noble gives a dedicated performance in the central role of Pilgrim, and the large supporting cast is consistently strong. Much of the material of Act I was also used in the *Fifth Symphony*, and like that masterpiece this opera stands at the heart of the composer's achievement. Vanity Fair may not sound evil here, but Vaughan Williams's own recoil is vividly expressed, and the jaunty passage of Mr and Mrs By-Ends brings the most delightful light relief. Boult underlines the virility of his performance with a fascinating and revealing half-hour collection of rehearsal excerpts, placed at the end of the second CD. The outstanding recording quality of the recording, made in Kingsway Hall at the end of 1970 and the beginning of 1971, is confirmed by the CD transfer, which shows few signs of the passing of two decades. The booklet provides the English words, although they emerge clearly anyway.

Verdi, Giuseppe (1813–1901)

Ballet music, Overtures and Preludes: *Aida* (prelude and ballet); *Un ballo in maschera* (prelude); *La forza del destino* (overture); *Macbeth* (ballet); *Nabucco* (overture); *La Traviata* (Preludes to Acts I & III); *I vespri siciliani* (overture).
*** Collins Dig. 1072-2; *1072-4* [id.]. Philh. O, Jacek Kaspszyk.

Jacek Kaspszyk omits *Luisa Miller* but includes the *Prelude* to *Un ballo in maschera* and the *La Traviata Preludes* which, alongside the delicate introduction to *Aida*, are admirably refined in phrasing and beautifully played. Indeed all the performances here are first class and have an exhilarating spontaneity. There is drama – *Nabucco* is particularly successful in this respect – and the ballet music has an engaging rhythmic sparkle. What makes this Collins disc especially enjoyable is the full, resonant sound and the realistic balance within the pleasing acoustics of London's Henry Wood Hall.

Overtures and Preludes: *Aida* (prelude); *Un ballo in maschera* (prelude); *La forza del destino* (overture); *Nabucco* (overture); *La Traviata* (prelude to Act I); *I vespri siciliani* (sinfonia).
(B) *** DG 429 164-2. BPO, Karajan – ROSSINI: *Overtures.* ***

Overtures and Preludes: *Un ballo in maschera* (prelude); *La Battaglia di Legnano; Il Corsaro* (sinfonias); *Ernani* (prelude); *La Forza del destino; Luisa Miller* (overtures); *Macbeth; I Masnadieri* (preludes); *Nabucco* (overture); *Rigoletto; La Traviata* (preludes); *I vespri siciliani* (sinfonia).
(M) *** DG 419 622-2; *419 622-4* [id.]. BPO, Karajan.

Make no mistake, this playing is in a class of its own and has an electricity, refinement and authority that sweep all before it. Some of the overtures are little known (*Il Corsaro* and *La Battaglia di Legnano*) and are given with tremendous panache and virtuosity. These are performances of real spirit and are vividly recorded, even if the climaxes could expand more.

Overtures and Preludes: *Aida; Il Corsaro; Luisa Miller; Macbeth; Rigoletto; La Traviata (Act I); I vespri siciliani* (CD only: *Nabucco*).
(B) *** DG Compact Classics 431 185-2 (2); *431 185-4* [id.]. BPO, Karajan – ROSSINI: *Overtures.* ***

Not a predictable collection on this excellently transferred Compact Classics cassette. Karajan is in his element, with the polished BPO players producing both elegance (in the *Traviata Prelude*) and plenty of high drama. Most enjoyable! The pair of CDs include only one extra item – but an important one.

String quartet in E min.
*** Collins Dig. 1267-2 [id.]. Britten Qt – CHERUBINI: *Quartet No. 1;* TURINA: *La Oración del Torero.* ***
*** CRD CRD 3366 [id.]. Alberni Qt – DONIZETTI: *Quartet No. 13;* PUCCINI: *Crisantemi.* ***
**(*) Hyp. Dig. CDA 66317; *KA 66317* [id.]. Delmé Qt – R. STRAUSS: *Quartet.* **(*)

A quite outstanding performance of Verdi's only *String quartet* from the Britten group. They match polished energy in the outer movements with much warmth and elegance in the inner ones, particularly the charming Neapolitan serenade theme at the centre of the miniature scherzo. With full, immediate, yet transparent sound this is very impressive indeed.

The Alberni Quartet's performance is also strong and compelling, and it is most imaginatively and attractively coupled with the Puccini and Donizetti pieces. The excellent recording has transferred vividly to CD.

The Delmé are not a 'high-powered', jet-setting ensemble and they give a very natural performance of the Verdi which will give much pleasure: there is the sense of music-making in the home among intimate friends, and it is refreshingly unforced, even if the sound is just a shade on the dry side.

Requiem Mass.
**(*) Decca 411 944-2 (2) [id.]. Sutherland, Horne, Pavarotti, Talvela, V. State Op. Ch., VPO, Solti.
(M) (**(*)) EMI mono CDH7 63341-2 [id.]. Caniglia, Stignani, Gigli, Pinza, Rome Op. Ch. & O, Serafin.
**(*) DG Dig. 415 091-2 (2) [id.]. Tomowa-Sintow, Baltsa, Carreras, Van Dam, V. State Op. Concert Assoc. Ch., Sofia Nat. Op. Ch., VPO, Karajan.

(i) *Requiem Mass;* (ii) *4 Sacred pieces.*
**(*) EMI CDS7 47257-8 (2) [Ang. CDCB 47257]. (i) Schwarzkopf, Ludwig, Gedda, Ghiaurov; (ii) J. Baker; Philh. Ch. & O, Giulini.
(M) (***) DG mono 429 076-2 (2). Stader, Dominguez, Carelli, Sardi, St Hedwig's Cathedral Ch., Berlin RIAS Chamber Ch. & RSO, Fricsay.

(i) *Requiem Mass*. Choruses from: *Aida; Don Carlo; Macbeth; Nabucco; Otello*.
❀ *** Telarc Dig. CD 80152 (2) [id.]. (i) Dunn, Curry, Hadley, Plishka; Atlanta Ch. & SO, Shaw.

Robert Shaw, who first made his name in the recording world as the chorus-master for some of Toscanini's finest recordings, here in the finest of his Atlanta recordings reflects consistently what he learned from the great maestro in the Verdi *Requiem*. It may not have quite the same searing electricity as Toscanini's rough old NBC recording, but it regularly echoes it in power and the well-calculated pacing. In the *Dies irae* for example, like Toscanini he gains in thrust and power from a speed marginally slower than usual. With sound of spectacular quality, beautifully balanced and clear, the many felicities of the performance, not least the electricity of the choral singing and the consistency of the solo singing, add up to an exceptionally satisfying reading, more recommendable than those of even the most eminent conductors. Only the Giulini has choral singing that might be counted finer; and Shaw also has the advantage of outstanding modern digital recording. Though none of the singers are international stars, their clear, fresh, well-focused voices are beautifully suited to recording, and they make a fine team. The fill-up of five Verdi opera choruses is not as generous as Giulini's but is more colourful, and again brings superb choral singing. This is a fine tribute to Shaw's training with this chorus and orchestra over twenty years. An outstanding issue.

By its side Giulini's EMI set is technically rather less satisfactory as a recording. Yet Giulini's combination of refinement and elemental strength remains totally memorable. What Giulini proves is that refinement added to power can provide an even more intense experience than the traditional Italian approach. In this concept a fine English chorus and orchestra prove exactly right: better disciplined than their Italian counterparts, less severe than the Germans. The array of soloists could hardly be bettered. Schwarzkopf caresses each phrase, and the exactness of her voice matches the firm mezzo of Christa Ludwig in their difficult octave passages. Gedda is at his most reliable, and Ghiaurov with his really dark bass actually manages to sing the almost impossible *Mors stupebit* in tune without a suspicion of wobble. Giulini's set also finds space to include the *Four Sacred pieces* and there is no doubt that in a performance as polished and dramatic as this the element of greatness in these somewhat uneven works is magnified. The CD transfer does its best to freshen the sound and is successful enough in the *Sacred pieces*; but it tends to emphasize the occasional roughness of the heavy climaxes in the *Requiem*, even though generally the quality is fully acceptable.

Fricsay's version (not to be confused with his studio recording of 1950) is of a live performance given in 1960, the very last he conducted before his untimely death. It is a commanding account, often at measured speeds but with a biting sense of drama and a gravity that plainly reflect the conductor's own emotions during his last illness. Like him, the two male soloists are Hungarian, and both are first rate, with the tenor, Gabor Carelli, pleasingly Italianate of tone. Maria Stader, also Hungarian-born, sings with a pure, clear tone, very occasionally suffering intonation problems. Oralia Dominguez is the fruity mezzo, and the chorus is superbly disciplined, with the mono recording remarkably full and spacious. The *Four Sacred pieces* were also recorded live, but ten years earlier. Fricsay gives another dedicated performance.

There is little or nothing reflective about Solti's account, and those who criticize the work for being too operatic will find plenty of ammunition here. The team of soloists is a very strong one, though the matching of voices is not always ideal. It is a pity that the chorus is not nearly as incisive as the Philharmonia on the EMI set – a performance which conveys far more of the work's profundity than this. But if you want an extrovert performance, the firmness of focus and precise placing of forces in the Decca engineering of 1967 make for exceptionally vivid results on CD.

Serafin's classic 1939 recording brings a glowing performance, beautifully shaped, warm and dramatic without drawing attention to itself. Maria Caniglia was not the most sensitive of Italian sopranos, but she ends here with a powerful *Libera me*, while the others could not be more characterful. Ebe Stignani and Ezio Pinza have never been surpassed in this music and Gigli, for all his stylistic peccadillos, is unique in his persuasiveness and honeyed tone. The choral singing is strong and dramatic, but the CD transfer requires some knob-twiddling if it is not to sound dull.

Though Karajan's smooth style has altered relatively little since he recorded this work before for DG, the overall impression is notably fresher – and would be even more so, were the recording more sharply focused and more consistent. The lack of brilliance in the recording also diminishes the element of Italian fire, so that the *Dies irae* is less sharply dramatic than in the finest versions. Soloists are good, naturally and warmly expressive. Though Tomowa-Sintow's un-Italian soprano timbre sometimes brings a hint of flutter, she sings most beautifully in the final rapt account of *Libera me*.

(i; ii) *Requiem Mass;* (iii; iv) *Inno delle nazione;* (ii) *Te Deum;* (iii) *Luisa Miller: Quando le sere al placido.* (iv) *Nabucco: Va pensiero.*
(M) (***) BMG/RCA mono GD 60299; *GK 60299* (2) [60299-RG-2; *60299-RG-4*]. (i) Nelli, Barbieri, Di Stefano, Siepi; (ii) Robert Shaw Ch.; (iii) Jan Peerce; (iv) Westminster Ch.; NBC SO, Toscanini.

Toscanini's account of the *Requiem* brings a supreme performance, searingly intense. The opening of the *Dies irae* has never sounded more hair-raising, with the bass-drum thrillingly caught, despite the limitation of dry mono recording. And rarely has the chorus shone so brightly in this work on record, with the Robert Shaw Chorale balanced well forward in sharp focus. Nelli sings well with clear, Italianate purity, while the others are near-ideal, a vintage team – Fedora Barbieri, the young Giuseppe di Stefano and Cesare Siepi. The other works make fascinating listening, too. The *Te Deum* was one of Toscanini's very last recordings, a performance more intense than usual with this work, and it is good to have the extraordinary wartime recording of the potboiling *Hymn of the Nations*. The *Internationale* is added to Verdi's original catalogue of national anthems, to represent the ally, the USSR.

OPERA

Aida (complete).
(M) *** EMI CMS7 69300-2 (3) [Ang. CDMC 69300]. Freni, Carreras, Baltsa, Cappuccilli, Raimondi, Van Dam, V. State Op. Ch., VPO, Karajan.
(M) *** Decca 414 087-2 (3) [id.]. Tebaldi, Simionato, Bergonzi, MacNeil, Van Mill, Corena, V. Singverein, VPO, Karajan.
*** Decca 417 416-2 (3) [id.]. Leontyne Price, Gorr, Vickers, Merrill, Tozzi, Rome Op. Ch. & O, Solti.
** Decca Dig. 417 439-2 (3). Chiara, Pavarotti, Dimitrova, Nucci, Burchuladze, La Scala, Milan, Ch. & O, Maazel.
(M) (***) BMG/RCA mono GD 86652 (3) [6652-2-RG]. Milanov, Bjoerling, Barbieri, Warren, Christoff, Rome Op. Ch. & O, Perlea.
(M) (**) BMG/RCA mono GD 60300; *GK 60300* (3/2) [60300-RG-2; *60300-RG-4*]. Nelli, Gustavson, Tucker, Valdengo, Robert Shaw Ch., NBC SO, Toscanini.
(**) EMI mono CDS7 49030-8 (3) [Ang. CDCC 49030]. Callas, Tucker, Barbieri, Gobbi, La Scala, Milan, Ch. & O, Serafin.

On EMI, Karajan's is a performance of *Aida* that carries splendour and pageantry to the point of exaltation. Yet for all the power of the pageantry, Karajan's fundamental approach is lyrical. Arias are often taken at a slow speed, taxing the singers more, yet Karajan's controversial choice of soloists is amply justified. On record at least, there can be little question of Freni lacking power in a role normally given to a larger voice, and there is ample gain in the tender beauty of her singing. Carreras makes a fresh, sensitive Radames, Raimondi a darkly intense Ramphis and Van Dam a cleanly focused King, his relative lightness no drawback. Cappuccilli here gives a more detailed performance than he did for Muti on EMI, while Baltsa as Amneris crowns the whole performance with her fine, incisive singing. Despite some overbrightness on cymbals and trumpet, the Berlin sound for Karajan, as transferred to CD, is richly and involvingly atmospheric, both in the intimate scenes and, most strikingly, in the scenes of pageant, which have rarely been presented on record in greater splendour.

On Decca, as on EMI, Karajan was helped by having a Viennese orchestra and chorus; but most important of all is the musicianship and musical teamwork of his soloists. Bergonzi in particular emerges here as a model among tenors, with a rare feeling for the shaping of phrases and attention to detail. Cornell MacNeil too is splendid. Tebaldi's creamy tone-colour rides beautifully over the phrases and she too acquires a new depth of imagination. Vocally there are also flaws: notably at the end of *O patria mia*, where Tebaldi finds the cruelly exposed top notes too taxing. Among the other soloists Arnold van Mill and Fernando Corena are both superb, and Simionato provides one of the very finest portrayals of Amneris we have ever had in a complete *Aida*. The recording has long been famous for its technical bravura and flair. CD enhances the overall projection and helps the pianissimos register in a recording with a very wide dynamic range for its period (late 1950s), but the brightness on top at times strikes the ear rather too forcibly. Nevertheless this remains a remarkable technical achievement.

Leontyne Price is an outstandingly assured Aida on Decca, rich, accurate and imaginative, while Solti's direction is superbly dramatic, notably in the Nile Scene. Merrill is a richly secure Amonasro, Rita Gorr a characterful Amneris, and Jon Vickers is splendidly heroic as Radames. Though the digital transfer betrays the age of the recording (1962), making the result fierce at times to match the reading, Solti's version otherwise brings full, spacious sound, finer, more open and with greater sense of presence than most versions since.

Based on a production at La Scala, the Decca set conducted by Maazel conveys surprisingly little of the feeling of operatic drama. Its great glory is the singing of Luciano Pavarotti, his first recording of the role of Radames. The voice is magnificent, and the superstar tenor's pointing of word-meaning consistently adds illumination, with the character strongly projected. He dominates the performance. Sadly Maazel, adopting speeds on the slow side, is often disappointingly square and metronomic, lacking Verdian warmth and forward thrust. Nevertheless, with a strong cast there is much to enjoy besides Pavarotti. Maria Chiara uses her lovely soprano with fine feeling for Verdian line, even if the characterization is generalized. Gena Dimitrova is a dull Amneris, and Leo Nucci a reliable Amonasro, helping to make the Nile scene the most animated sequence of the whole set. Paata Burchuladze sings with sepulchral darkness, but with little feeling for the Italian language. The recording is not ideally spacious in the big ensembles, but it is still full and brilliant in the Decca manner, the best sound accorded to any recent digital set.

All four principals on the historic RCA set are at their very finest, notably Milanov, whose poise and control in *O patria mia* are a marvel. Barbieri as Amneris is even finer here than in the Callas set, and it is good to hear the young Christoff resonant as Ramfis. Perlea conducts with great panache.

Toscanini's 1949 performance of *Aida* is the least satisfying of his New York opera recordings. Richard Tucker sings well but makes a relatively colourless Radames, and Herva Nelli lacks weight as Aida, neatly though she sings and with some touching moments. Nancy Gustavson's Amneris lacks all menace, and Valdengo as Amonasro is the only fully satisfying principal. Yet Toscanini is so electrifying from first to last that his admirers will accept the limited, painfully dry recording.

The Nile Scene has never been performed more powerfully and characterfully on record than in this vintage La Scala set. Though Callas is hardly as sweet-toned as some will think essential for an Aida, her detailed imagination is irresistible, and she is matched by Tito Gobbi at the very height of his powers. Tucker gives one of his very finest performances on record, and Barbieri is a commanding Amneris. The mono sound is more than acceptable.

Aida: highlights (scenes & arias).
(M) *** Decca 417 763-2 [id.] (from above set, with Tebaldi, Bergonzi, cond. Karajan).

Aida: highlights.
(M) (***) BMG/RCA mono GD 60201 [60201-2-RG] (from above recording with Milanov, Bjoerling; cond. Perlea).
(M) *** Decca 421 860-2; *421 860-4* [id.] (from above recording, with Leontyne Price, Gorr, Vickers, Merrill, Tozzi; cond. Solti).
(M) **(*) DG Dig. 435 410-2; *435 410-4* [id.]. Ricciarelli, Domingo, Obraztsova, Nucci, Raimondi, Ghiaurov, La Scala, Milan, Ch. & O, Abbado.
**(*) Decca Dig. 433 162-2; *433 162-4* (from above set with Chiara, Pavarotti; cond. Maazel).

By far the most interesting compilation is the Decca 'Scenes and arias' from John Culshaw's Karajan recording from the early stereo era. The RCA highlights disc is valuable above all for providing a sample of one of Milanov's most compelling performances on record, poised and commanding. There is also a fairly generous mid-priced reminder of Solti's excellent full-price set, with Price an outstandingly assured Aida.

However, a 65-minute selection from the Abbado set is welcome, with cued synopsis rather than a libretto. It is issued as part of DG's 'Domingo Edition' and the selection – although it includes the Triumphal scene and does not neglect Aida or Amneris – rather concentrates on Domingo's contribution.

Those wanting to have a reminder of Pavarotti's magnificently vibrant assumption of the role of Radames will probably find the Decca set of highlights is a better investment than Maazel's complete set. It is good, too, to have a rare representation of Maria Chiara singing in a major recording, and she, too has some fine moments, although the voice is not quite as fresh as on her famous 1972 début recital, which showed such irresistible promise. The 72-minute selection is generous and includes the *Nile scene*. However this CD would have been even more attractive at mid-price.

Alzira (complete).
*** Orfeo CO 57832 (2) [id.]. Cotrubas, Araiza, Bruson, George, Bonilla, Bav. R. Ch., Munich R. O, Gardelli.

Alzira is the shortest of the Verdi operas, but its concision is on balance an advantage on record. In musical inspiration it is indistinguishable from other typical early operas, with Verdian melodies less distinctive than they became later, but consistently pleasing. Gardelli is a master with early Verdi, and the cast is strong, helped by warm and well-balanced recording supervised by Munich Radio engineers.

Aroldo (complete).
** Sony CD 79328 [M2K 39506] (2). Caballé, Cecchele, Lebherz, Pons, NY Oratorio Soc., Westminster Ch. Soc., NY Op. O, Queler.

Aroldo is Verdi's radical revision of his earlier unsuccessful opera, *Stiffelio*: he translated the story of a Protestant pastor with an unfaithful wife into this tale of a crusader returning from the Holy Land. Less compact than the original, it contains some splendid new material such as the superb aria for the heroine, beautifully sung by Caballé. The final scene too is quite new, for the dénouement is totally different. The storm chorus (with echoes of *Rigoletto*) is most memorable – but so are the rum-ti-tum choruses common to both versions. This recording of a concert performance in New York is lively, though the tenor is depressingly coarse.

Attila (complete).
(M) *** Ph. 426 115-2 (2). Raimondi, Deutekom, Bergonzi, Milnes, Amb. S., Finchley Children's Music Group, RPO, Gardelli.

With its dramatic anticipations of *Macbeth*, the musical anticipations of *Rigoletto* and the compression which (on record if not on the stage) becomes a positive merit – all these qualities, helped by a fine performance under Gardelli, make this Philips version of *Attila* an intensely enjoyable set. Deutekom, not the most sweet-toned of sopranos, has never sung better on record, and the rest of the cast is outstandingly good. The 1973 recording is well balanced and atmospheric, but the remastering for CD has been able to make only a marginal improvement in definition, with the chorus less sharply focused than one would expect on a modern digital set.

Un ballo in maschera (complete).
*** Decca Dig. 410 210-2 (2) [id.]. Margaret Price, Pavarotti, Bruson, Ludwig, Battle, L. Op. Ch., Royal College of Music Junior Dept Ch., Nat. PO, Solti.
*** DG Dig. 427 635-2 (2) [id.]. Domingo, Barstow, Nucci, Quivar, Sumi Jo, V. State Op. Konzertvereinigung, VPO, Karajan.
*** DG 415 685-2 (2) [id.]. Ricciarelli, Domingo, Bruson, Obraztsova, Gruberová, Raimondi, La Scala, Milan, Ch. & O, Abbado.
(M) *** BMG/RCA GD 86645 (2) [6645-2-RG]. L. Price, Bergonzi, Merrill, Grist, Verrett, Flagello, RCA Italiana Op. Ch. & O, Leinsdorf.
(M) *** EMI CMS7 69576-2 (2) [Ang. CDMB 69576]. Arroyo, Domingo, Cappuccilli, Grist, Cossotto, Howell, ROHCG Ch., New Philh. O, Muti.

Shining out from the cast of Solti's set of *Ballo* is the gloriously sung Amelia of Margaret Price in one of her richest and most commanding performances on record, ravishingly beautiful, flawlessly controlled and full of unforced emotion. The role of Riccardo, pushy and truculent, is well suited to the extrovert Pavarotti, who swaggers through the part, characteristically clear of diction, challenged periodically by Price to produce some of his subtlest tone-colours. Bruson makes a noble Renato, Christa Ludwig an unexpected but intense and perceptive Ulrica, while Kathleen Battle is an Oscar whose coloratura is not just brilliant but sweet too. Solti is far more relaxed than he often is on record, presenting a warm and understanding view of the score. The recording is extremely vivid within a reverberant acoustic.

Recorded in Vienna early in 1989, *Un ballo in maschera* was Karajan's last opera recording. It was done in conjunction with the new production at that year's Salzburg Festival, which Karajan was scheduled to conduct. He died only days before the first night, while the production was already in rehearsal. The recording makes a fitting memorial, characteristically rich and spacious, with a cast – if not ideal – which still makes a fine team, responding to the conductor's single-minded vision. Karajan's underlining of dynamic contrasts in the final assassination scene, for example, is thrilling, demonstrating his undiminished sense of drama. Standing out vocally is the Gustavo of Plácido Domingo, strong and imaginative, dominating the whole cast. He may not have the sparkle of Pavarotti in this role, but the singing is richer, more refined and more thoughtful. Karajan's unexpected and controversial choice of Josephine Barstow as Amelia certainly makes for a striking and characterful performance, even if vocally it is flawed, with the tone growing raw under pressure. Nevertheless this is Barstow's finest achievement on record, and dramatically she is most compelling. Leo Nucci, though not as rough in tone as in some of his other recent recordings, is over-emphatic, with poor legato in his great solo, *Eri tu*. Sumi Jo, a Karajan discovery, gives a delicious performance as Oscar, the page, coping splendidly with Karajan's slow speed for her Act I solo. Florence Quivar produces satisfyingly rich tone as Ulrica. Though the sound is not as cleanly focused as in the Decca recording for Solti, it is warm and full.

Abbado's powerful reading, admirably paced and with a splendid feeling for the sparkle of the comedy, remains highly recommendable. The cast is very strong, with Ricciarelli at her very finest and Domingo sweeter of tone and more deft of characterization than on the Muti set of five years earlier. Bruson as the wronged husband Renato (a role he also takes for Solti) sings magnificently, and only Obraztsova as Ulrica and Gruberová as Oscar are less consistently convincing. The analogue recording clearly separates the voices and instruments in different acoustics, which on CD is distracting only initially and after that brings the drama closer.

The reissued RCA set makes a fine bargain. All the principals are in splendid voice, and Leinsdorf's direction – too often inflexible in Italian opera – here has resilience as well as brilliance and urgency. Leontyne Price is a natural for the part of Amelia and, with one notable reservation, hers comes near to being a model interpretation, spontaneous-sounding and full of dramatic temperament. Only in the two big arias does Price for a moment grow self-conscious, and there are one or two mannered phrases, overloaded with the wrong sort of expressiveness. Robert Merrill, sometimes thought of as an inexpressive singer, here seems to have acquired all sorts of dramatic, Gobbi-like overtones to add to the flow of firm, satisfying tone. Bergonzi is a model of sensitivity, while Reri Grist makes a light, bright Oscar, and the Ulrica of Shirley Verrett has a range of power, richness and delicacy coupled with unparalleled firmness that makes this one of her most memorable recorded performances. Excellent recording, hardly showing its age, with the voices rather forward.

On EMI the quintet of principals is also unusually strong, but it is the conductor who takes first honours in a warmly dramatic reading. Muti's rhythmic resilience and consideration for the singers go with keen concentration, holding each Act together in a way he did not quite achieve in his earlier recording for EMI of *Aida*. Arroyo, rich of voice, is not always imaginative in her big solos, and Domingo rarely produces a half-tone, though the recording balance may be partly to blame. The sound is vivid, but no translation is provided for this mid-price reissue.

Un ballo in maschera: highlights.
*** DG Dig. 429 415-2 [id.] (from above complete recording, with Domingo, Barstow; cond. Karajan).
(M) *** DG 435 411-2; *435 411-4* [id.] (from above set, with Ricciarelli, Domingo; cond. Abbado).

This highlights selection from Karajan's version is generous (71 minutes), following through the opera's narrative with both Acts well represented.

The selection from the Abbado version, which includes the *Prelude* and opens brightly with *S'avanza il conte,* makes a good choice for a highlights disc, with a cued narrative for the listener to follow the action. The excerpts are well chosen (as part of the 'Domingo Edition') to represent this artist, but Ricciarelli's splendid contribution is not neglected. The CD transfer faithfully reflects the qualities of the complete set.

La Battaglia di Legnano (complete).
(M) *** Ph. 422 435-2 (2). Ricciarelli, Carreras, Manuguerra, Ghiuselev, Austrian R. Ch. & O, Gardelli.

La Battaglia di Legnano is a compact, sharply conceived piece, made the more intense by the subject's obvious relationship with the situation in Verdi's own time. One weakness is that the villainy is not effectively personalized, but the juxtaposition of the individual drama of supposed infidelity against a patriotic theme brings most effective musical contrasts. Gardelli directs a fine performance, helped by a strong cast of principals, with Carreras, Ricciarelli and Manuguerra all at their finest. Excellent recording, with the depth of perspective enhanced on CD.

Il Corsaro (complete).
(M) *** Ph. 426 118-2 (2). Norman, Caballé, Carreras, Grant, Mastromei, Noble, Amb. S., New Philh. O, Gardelli.

By the time he had completed the score, Verdi had fallen out of love with his subject, an adaptation of Byron. Only latterly has the composer's own poor view of *Il Corsaro* been revised in the light of closer study, and Piave's treatment of Byron turns out to be not nearly so clumsy as had been thought. Though the characterization is rudimentary, the contrast between the two heroines is effective, with Gulnara, the Pasha's slave, carrying conviction in the *coup de foudre* which has her promptly worshipping the Corsair, an early example of the Rudolph Valentino figure. The rival heroines are taken splendidly here, with Jessye Norman as the faithful wife, Medora, actually upstaging Montserrat Caballé as Gulnara. Gardelli, as in his previous Philips recordings of early Verdi, directs a vivid performance, with fine singing from the hero, portrayed by José Carreras. Gian-Piero Mastromei, not rich in tone, still rises to the challenge of the Pasha's music. Excellent, firmly focused and well-balanced Philips sound.

Don Carlos (complete).
(M) *** EMI CMS7 69304-2 (3) [Ang. CDMC 69304]. Carreras, Freni, Ghiaurov, Baltsa, Cappuccilli, Raimondi, German Op. Ch., Berlin, BPO, Karajan.
*** EMI CDS7 47701-8 (3) [Ang. CDCC 47701]. Domingo, Caballé, Raimondi, Verrett, Milnes, Amb. Op. Ch., ROHCG O, Giulini.
**(*) DG Dig. 415 316-2 (4) [id.]. Ricciarelli, Domingo, Valentini Terrani, Nucci, Raimondi, Ghiaurov, La Scala, Milan, Ch. & O, Abbado.
**(*) Decca 421 114-2 (3) [id.]. Tebaldi, Bumbry, Bergonzi, Fischer-Dieskau, Ghiaurov, ROHCG Ch. & O, Solti.

Karajan opts firmly for the later, four-Act version of the opera, merely opening out the cuts he adopted on stage. The results could hardly be more powerfully dramatic, one of his most involving opera performances, comparable with his vivid EMI *Aida*. The *Auto da fé* scene is here superb, while Karajan's characteristic choice of singers for refinement of voice rather than sheer size consistently pays off. Both Carreras and Freni are most moving, even if *Tu che le vanità* has its raw moments. Baltsa is a superlative Eboli and Cappuccilli an affecting Rodrigo, though neither Carreras nor Cappuccilli is at his finest in the famous oath duet. Raimondi and Ghiaurov as the Grand Inquisitor and Philip II provide the most powerful confrontation. Though the sound is not as analytically detailed as the earlier, EMI version with Giulini, it is both rich and atmospheric, giving great power to Karajan's uniquely taut account of the four-Act version.

Giulini conducts the same orchestra as Solti directed in the earlier, Decca set and predictably he is more affectionate in his phrasing, while conveying the quiet, dramatic intensity which made his direction so irresistible in the opera house. There is extra joy in the *Auto da fé* scene as it is pointed by Giulini. Generally the new cast is a little stronger than the old, but each is admirably consistent. The only major vocal disappointment among the principals lies in Caballé's account of the big aria *Tu che le vanità* in the final Act. Like the Decca set, this one uses the full, five-Act text. The CD transfer of the 1971 analogue recording brings astonishing vividness and realism, a tribute to the original engineering of Christopher Parker. Even in the big ensembles of the *Auto da fé* scene, the focus is very precise, yet atmospheric too, not just analytic. The extra bite of realism enhances an already fine version to make it the finest, irrespective of age.

For the dedicated Verdian, Abbado's set brings new authenticity and new revelation. This is the first recording to use the language which Verdi originally set, French; in addition to the full five-Act text in its composite 1886 form including the Fontainebleau scene (recorded twice before), there are half a dozen appendices from the original 1867 score, later cut or recomposed. By rights, this should be the definitive recording of the opera for, as has often been promised, the French text brings an apt darkening of tone compared with the open sounds of Italian, and Abbado is a masterly interpreter of Verdi. The first disappointment lies in the variable quality of the sound, with odd balances, so that although the Fontainebleau opening, with its echoing horns, is arrestingly atmospheric, the *Auto da fé* scene lacks bite, brilliance and clarity. In addition, large-scale flair and urgency are missing; once that is said, however, the cast of singers is a strong one. Domingo easily outshines his earlier recording with Giulini (in Italian), while Katia Ricciarelli as the Queen gives a tenderly moving performance, if not quite commanding enough in the Act V aria. Ruggero Raimondi is a finely focused Philip II, nicely contrasted with Nicolai Ghiaurov as the Grand Inquisitor in the other black-toned bass role. Lucia Valentini Terrani as Eboli is warm-toned if not very characterful, and Leo Nucci makes a noble Posa.

The Decca version includes the important passages often excised, notably the Fontainebleau scene, and that may underline the one major deficiency of the set, that the dramatic temperature fails to rise as it should until the duet between Philip and Rodrigo at the end of Act II (Act I in the four-Act version). Tebaldi in this most exacting Verdian role warms up well and gives a magnificent account of *Tu che le vanità*. Bumbry and Bergonzi both sing splendidly, and after some rather gritty singing early on, Fischer-Dieskau rises fittingly to Rodrigo's great death scene, sounding almost (but not quite) as moving as Gobbi in the old EMI set (mono). Ghiaurov as Philip brings a nobility, a sense of stoic pride, that is most compelling. The recording is of Decca's usual high standard, and though with such a marvellous array of talent one might feel the result should be still more overwhelming, there is no doubt that this version has a great deal to commend it.

Don Carlos: highlights.
(M) *** EMI CDM7 63089-2; *EG 763089-4* (from above recording with Domingo, Caballé; cond. Giulini).
(M) **(*) DG Dig. 435 412-2; *435 412-4* [id.] (from above recording, with Ricciarelli, Domingo; cond. Abbado).

Giulini's disc of highlights can be highly recommended. In selecting from such a long opera, serious omissions are inevitable; nothing is included here from Act III, to make room for the *Auto da fé* scene from Act IV – some 37 minutes of the disc is given to this Act. With vivid sound this is most stimulating; the only reservation concerns Caballé's *Tu che le vanità*, which ends the selection disappointingly.

For those with another complete version, the highlights from the Abbado set, sung in French, will be especially worthwhile, even though there are reservations about the recording. Excerpts from all five acts are given briefly detailed cues in the synopsis. As it is part of DG's 'Domingo Edition', that artist is generously represented, but he is in excellent form, and Leo Nucci's contribution is also striking in this 68 minutes selection.

I due Foscari (complete).
(M) *** Ph. 422 426-2 (2). Ricciarelli, Carreras, Cappuccilli, Ramey, Austrian R. Ch. & SO, Gardelli.

I due Foscari brings Verdian high spirits in plenty, erupting in swinging cabalettas and much writing that anticipates operas as late as *Simon Boccanegra* (obvious enough in the Doge's music) and *La forza del destino* (particularly in the orchestral motifs which act as labels for the principal characters). The cast here is first rate, with Ricciarelli giving one of her finest performances in the recording studio to date and with Carreras singing tastefully as well as powerfully. The crispness of discipline among the Austrian Radio forces is admirable, but there is less sense of atmosphere here than in the earlier, London-made recordings in the series; otherwise the Philips sound is impressively present and clear.

Ernani (complete).
(M) **(*) BMG/RCA GD 86503 (2) [6503-2-RG]. Leontyne Price, Bergonzi, Sereni, Flagello, RCA Italiana Op. Ch. & O, Schippers.
**(*) EMI Dig. CDS7 47083-2 (3) [Ang. CDC 47082]. Domingo, Freni, Bruson, Ghiaurov, La Scala, Milan, Ch. & O, Muti.

At mid-price in RCA's Victor Opera series on two CDs instead of three LPs, Schippers' set, recorded in Rome in 1967, is an outstanding bargain. Leontyne Price may take the most celebrated aria, *Ernani involami*, rather cautiously, but the voice is gloriously firm and rich, and Bergonzi is comparably strong and vivid, though Mario Sereni, vocally reliable, is dull, and Ezio Flagello gritty-toned. Nevertheless, with Schippers drawing the team powerfully together, it is a highly enjoyable set, with the digital transfer making voices and orchestra sound full and vivid.

The great merit of Muti's set, recorded live at a series of performances at La Scala, is that the ensembles have an electricity rarely achieved in the studio, even if the results may not always be so precise and stage noises are often obtrusive. The singing, generally strong and characterful, is yet flawed. The strain of the role of Elvira for Mirella Freni is plain from the big opening aria,

Ernani involami, onwards. Even in that aria there are cautious moments. Bruson is a superb Carlo and Ghiaurov a characterful Silva, but his voice now betrays signs of wear. As Ernani himself, Plácido Domingo gives a commandingly heroic performance, but under pressure there are hints of tight tone such as he rarely produces in the studio. The recording inevitably has odd balances which will disturb some more than others. The CD version gives greater immediacy and presence, but also brings out the inevitable flaws of live recording the more clearly.

Falstaff (complete).
*** DG Dig. 410 503-2 (2) [id.]. Bruson, Ricciarelli, Nucci, Hendricks, Egerton, Valentini Terrani, Boozer, LA Master Ch., LAPO, Giulini.
*(**) EMI CDS7 49668-2 (2) [Ang. CDCB 49668]. Gobbi, Schwarzkopf, Zaccaria, Moffo, Panerai, Philh. Ch. & O, Karajan.
(M) (***) BMG/RCA mono GD 60251; *GK 60251* (2) [60251-RG-2; *60251-RG-4*]. Valdengo, Nelli, Merriman, Elmo, Guarrera, Stich-Randall, Robert Shaw Ch., NBC SO, Toscanini.

Giulini's reading combines the tensions and atmosphere of live performance with a precision normally achieved only in the studio. This was Giulini's first essay in live opera-conducting in fourteen years, and he treated the piece with a care for musical values which at times undermined the knockabout comic element. On record that is all to the good, for the clarity and beauty of the playing are caught superbly on CD, and though the parallel with Toscanini is an obvious one – also recorded at a live performance – Giulini is far more relaxed. Bruson, hardly a comic actor, is impressive on record for his fine incisive singing, giving tragic implications to the monologue at the start of Act III after Falstaff's dunking. The Ford of Leo Nucci, impressive in the theatre, is thinly caught, where the heavyweight quality of Ricciarelli as Alice comes over well, though in places one would wish for a purer sound. Barbara Hendricks is a charmer as Nannetta, but she hardly sounds fairy-like in her Act III aria. The full women's ensemble, though precise, is not always quite steady in tone, though the conviction of the whole performance puts it among the most desirable of modern readings.

This earlier (1956) Karajan recording presents not only the most pointed account orchestrally of Verdi's comic masterpiece (the Philharmonia Orchestra at its very peak) but the most sharply characterful cast ever gathered for a recording. If you relish the idea of Tito Gobbi as Falstaff (his many-coloured voice, not quite fat-sounding in humour, presents a sharper character than usual), then this is clearly the best choice, for the rest of the cast is a delight, with Schwarzkopf a tinglingly masterful Mistress Ford, Anna Moffo sweet as Nannetta and Rolando Panerai a formidable Ford. Unfortunately the digital remastering has been mismanaged. While the precision and placing of voices on the stereo stage, a model even today, comes out the more clearly on CD, the transfer itself, at a low level and with high hiss, has lost the bloom and warmth of the original analogue master which was outstanding for its time.

Toscanini's fizzing account of Verdi's last masterpiece has never been matched on record, the most high-spirited performance ever, beautifully paced for comedy. Even without stereo, and recorded with typical dryness, the clarity and sense of presence in this live concert performance set the story in relief. The cast is excellent, led by the ripe, firm baritone, Giuseppe Valdengo. Such singers as Nan Merriman as Mistress Page, Cloe Elmo as a wonderfully fruity Mistress Quickly and Frank Guarrera as Ford match or outshine any more recent interpreters. Toscanini's favourite soprano in his last years, Herva Nelli, is less characterful as Mistress Ford, rather over-parted but still fresh and reliable.

La Forza del destino (complete).
*** DG Dig. 419 203-2 (3) [id.]. Plowright, Carreras, Bruson, Burchuladze, Baltsa, Amb. Op. Ch., Philh. O, Sinopoli.
*** BMG/RCA RD 81864 (3) [RCD3-1864]. Leontyne Price, Domingo, Milnes, Cossotto, Giaiotti, Bacquier, Alldis Ch., LSO, Levine.
(M) *** BMG/RCA GD 87971 (3) [4515-2-RG]. Leontyne Price, Tucker, Merrill, Tozzi, Verrett, Flagello, Foiani, RCA Italiana Op. Ch. & O, Schippers.

Sinopoli's is an exceptionally spacious view of *Forza*, in many ways akin to the similarly distinctive reading of *Il Trovatore* recorded for DG by Giulini. Sinopoli draws out phrases lovingly, sustaining pauses to the limit, putting extra strain on the singers. Happily, the whole cast seems to thrive on the challenge, and the spaciousness of the recording acoustic not only makes the dramatic interchanges the more realistic, it brings out the bloom on all the voices, above all the creamy soprano of Rosalind Plowright. Though José Carreras is sometimes too conventionally histrionic, even strained, it is a strong, involved performance. Renato Bruson is a thoughtful Carlo, while some of the finest singing of all comes from Agnes Baltsa as Preziosilla and Paata Burchuladze as the Padre Guardiano, uniquely resonant. Though the speeds will not please all Verdians, Sinopoli's is a distinctive, deeply felt view which in its breadth conveys the epic nobility of the piece with great authority.

James Levine directs a superb performance of an opera which in less purposeful hands can seem too episodic. The results are electrifying, and rarely if ever does Levine cut across the natural expressiveness of an outstanding cast. Leontyne Price recorded the role of Leonora in an earlier RCA version made in Rome in 1956, but the years have hardly touched her voice, and details of the reading have been refined. The roles of Don Alvaro and Don Carlo are ideally suited to the regular team of Plácido Domingo and Sherrill Milnes so that their confrontations are the cornerstones of the dramatic structure. Fiorenza Cossotto makes a formidable rather than a jolly Preziosilla, while on the male side the line-up of Bonaldo Giaiotti, Gabriel Bacquier, Kurt Moll and Michel Sénéchal is far stronger than on rival sets. In a good, vivid transfer of the mid-1970s sound, this strong, well-paced version will for many provide a safe alternative to Sinopoli, with an exceptionally good and consistent cast.

No soprano of her generation had natural gifts more suited to the role of Leonora in *Forza* than Leontyne Price. The voice in 1964 was fresher and more open; though the clearer, less ambient recording from the Rome studio exposes it in greater detail, on balance this is a more tender and delicate performance than the weightier one she recorded with Levine. Richard Tucker as Alvaro is here far less lachrymose and more stylish than he was earlier in the Callas set, producing ample, heroic tone, if not with the finesse of a Domingo. Robert Merrill as Carlo also sings with heroic strength, consistently firm and dark of tone; while Shirley Verrett, Giorgio Tozzi and Ezio Flagello stand up well against any rivalry. The sound is remarkably full and vivid for its age, with a fine illusion of presence which quickly makes one forget any analogue hiss.

La Forza del destino (slightly abridged).
(***) EMI mono CDS7 47581-8 (3) [Ang. CDCC 47581]. Callas, Tucker, Tagliabue, Clabassi, Nicolai, Rossi-Lemeni, Capecchi, La Scala, Milan, Ch. & O, Serafin.

Callas was at her very peak when she took the role of Leonora in the Scala recording. Hers is an electrifying performance, providing a focus for an opera normally regarded as diffuse. Though there are classic examples of Callas's raw tone on top notes, they are insignificant next to the wealth of phrasing which sets a totally new and individual stamp on even the most familiar passages. Apart from his tendency to disturb his phrasing with sobs, Richard Tucker sings superbly; but not even he – and certainly none of the others (including the baritone Carlo Tagliabue, well past his prime) – begin to rival the dominance of Callas. Serafin's direction is crisp, dramatic and well paced, again drawing the threads together. The 1955 mono sound is less aggressive than many La Scala recordings of this vintage and has been freshened on CD.

Un giorno di regno (complete).
(M) *** Ph. 422 429-2 (2). Cossotto, Norman, Carreras, Wixell, Sardinero, Ganzarolli, Amb. S., RPO, Gardelli.

Un giorno di regno may not be the greatest comic opera of the period, but this scintillating performance under Gardelli clearly reveals the young Verdi as a potent rival even in this field to his immediate predecessors, Rossini and Donizetti. The Rossinian echoes are particularly infectious, though every number reveals that the young Verdi is more than an imitator, and there are striking passages which clearly give a foretaste of such numbers as the duet *Si vendetta* from *Rigoletto*. Despite the absurd plot, this is as light and frothy an entertainment as anyone could want. Excellent singing from a fine team, with Jessye Norman and José Carreras outstanding. The recorded sound is even more vivid on CD.

I Lombardi (complete).
(M) *** Ph. 422 420-2 (2). Deutekom, Domingo, Raimondi, Amb. S., RPO, Gardelli.

If you are looking for sophisticated perfection, *I Lombardi* is not the opera to sample, but the directness of Verdi's inspiration is in no doubt. *Otello* is anticipated in the arias, with Pagano's evil *Credo* and the heroine Giselda's *Salve Maria*. The work reaches its apotheosis in the famous *Trio*, well known from the days of 78-r.p.m. recordings. By those standards, Cristina Deutekom is not an ideal Verdi singer: her tone is sometimes hard and her voice is not always perfectly under control, yet there are also some glorious moments and the phrasing is often impressive. Domingo as Oronte is in superb voice, and the villain Pagano is well characterized by Raimondi. Among the supporting cast Stafford Dean and Clifford Grant must be mentioned, and Gardelli conducts dramatically. The recording's atmosphere is well transferred and the action projects vividly.

(i) *I Lombardi, Act III: Trio.* (ii) *Rigoletto, Act IV* (complete).
(M) (**) BMG/RCA mono GD 60276; *GK 60276* (2); [60276-2-RG; *60276-4-RG*]. (i) Della Chiesa, Peerce, Moscona; (ii) Warren, Milanov, Peerce, Moscona, Merriman, All City Highschool Ch. & Glee Clubs, NBC SO, Toscanini – BOITO: *Mefistofele: Prologue.* (***)

These two fascinating Verdi items are wartime recordings, even more limited in sound than most of Toscanini's in his last years. The *Lombardi Trio* finds the acoustic of the notorious Studio 8H in Radio City at its driest, but the conductor's love for the music still dominates. It is interesting to find a little-known singer, Vivian della Chiesa, emerging strongly alongside Jan Peerce and Nicola Moscona. Equally impressive is the dazzling performance of the NBC Orchestra's concert-master, Mischa Mischakoff, in the virtuoso violin solo of the introduction. The last Act of *Rigoletto* was given in a wartime fund-raising concert in Madison Square Garden and, though the brittleness of sound is at times almost comic and the tautness of Toscanini's control was unrelenting, the performances of the principals are formidable, with Zinka Milanov at her most radiant. With Toscanini's searing account of the *Mefistofele Prologue*, this makes a generous compilation.

Luisa Miller (complete).
*** Sony Dig. S2K 48073 (2) [id.]. Domingo, Millo, Chernev, Rootering, Quivar, Plishka, Met. Op. O and Ch., Levine.
*** Decca 417 420-2 (2) [id.]. Caballé, Pavarotti, Milnes, Reynolds, L. Op. Ch., Nat. PO, Maag.
*** DG 423 144-2 (2) [id.]. Ricciarelli, Obraztsova, Domingo, Bruson, ROHCG Ch. & O, Maazel.
(M) *** BMG/RCA GD 86646 (2) [6646-2-RG]. Moffo, Bergonzi, Verrett, MacNeil, Tozzi, Flagello, RCA Italiana Op. Ch. & O, Cleva.

Levine conducts his forces from the Met. in a red-blooded, exceptionally high-powered reading of this elusive opera, distinguished by the first major recording of the remarkable Russian baritone, Vladimir Chernev. In the role of Miller, the heroine's father, Chernev is even more characterful and musically more individual than either of his main rivals on the other sets, with the power of his singing brought home by the close balance of the voice. That balance is typical of a Sony New York recording which for all its wide-ranging digital sound is limited by the acoustic of the Manhattan Center, less spacious than those on the rival Decca and DG recordings made in the 1970s. Though the sound tends to make Levine's direction seem less subtle than it is, less elegant than Maag on Decca, less refined in texture than Maazel on DG, the impact of the score is brought home formidably. Consistently the reading benefits from the pacing and control that becomes natural to players and singers over a series of live performances in the theatre. Maazel's recording was comparably made in conjunction with live performances at Covent Garden, but it does not make the point nearly as strongly as Levine. It is significant how Plácido Domingo, who takes the role of the hero Rodolfo both for Maazel and for Levine, sings with much greater animation in the New York recording. Among the others Jan-Henrik Rootering, Florence Quivar and Paul Plishka all sing powerfully, even if all three suffer from occasional unsteadiness. The snag is the variable quality of Aprile Millo's singing in the title role. She has the right Verdian timbre, more girlish-sounding than her rivals, but in Act I the coloratura taxes her severely, pushing her into gusty, inelegant moments. From there she markedly improves, so that by the final act she produces some lovely singing with some beautifully floated high pianissimos. It is in that final act that the extra dramatic bite of Levine's reading tells most in its impact. Curiously, the final trio brings rather less close balance for the voices than earlier, but the power is no less intense.

On Decca, Caballé, though not as flawless vocally as one would expect, gives a splendidly dramatic portrait of the heroine and Pavarotti's performance is full of creative, detailed imagination. As Federica, Anna Reynolds is distinctly preferable to Obraztsova, and Maag's sympathetic reading, by underlining the light and shade, consistently brings out the atmospheric qualities of Verdi's conception. Vividly transferred, this Decca recording remains highly competitive.

Though taut in his control, Maazel uses his stage experience of working with these soloists to draw them out to their finest, most sympathetic form. Ricciarelli gives one of her tenderest and most beautiful performances on record, Domingo is in glorious voice and Bruson as Luisa's father sings with velvet tone. Gwynne Howell is impressive as the Conte di Walter and

Wladimiro Ganzarolli's vocal roughness is apt for the character of Wurm. The snag is the abrasive Countess Federica of Elena Obraztsova.

In many ways the RCA set provides a performance to compete with the full-price versions and is just as stylish, with Moffo at her very peak, singing superbly, Carlo Bergonzi unfailingly intelligent and stylish, and Verrett nothing less than magnificent in her role as a quasi-Amneris. MacNeil and Tozzi are also satisfyingly resonant, and Fausto Cleva tellingly reveals his experience directing the opera at the Met. Good recording.

Luisa Miller: highlights.
(M) *** DG 435 413-2; *435 413-4* [id.] (from above recording, with Ricciarelli, Domingo; cond. Maazel).

As it opens with the *Overture*, collectors will welcome this, the only current set of highlights from *Luisa Miller*, vividly transferred to CD. The cues are satisfactorily related to the action in the documentation of the 67-minute selection. As this is part of DG's 'Domingo Edition', Rodolfo tends to dominate the chosen excerpts, but Ricciarelli's moving contribution is also strongly featured. Excellent sound.

Macbeth (complete).
*** Ph. Dig. 412 133-2 (3) [id.]. Bruson, Zampieri, Shicoff, Lloyd, German Op. Ch. & O, Berlin, Sinopoli.
*** DG 415 688-2 (3) [id.]. Cappuccilli, Verrett, Ghiaurov, Domingo, La Scala, Milan, Ch. & O, Abbado.
(M) **(*) BMG/RCA GD 84516 (2) [4516-2-RG]. Warren, Rysanek, Bergonzi, Hines, Met. Op. Ch. & O, Leinsdorf.

Even more than his finest rivals, Sinopoli presents this opera as a searing Shakespearean inspiration, scarcely more uneven than much of the work of the Bard himself. In the Banqueting scene, for example, Sinopoli creates extra dramatic intensity by his concern for detail and his preference for extreme dynamics, as in the vital stage-whispered phrases from Lady Macbeth to her husband, marked *sotto voce*, which heighten the sense of horror and disintegration over the appearance of the ghost. Detailed word-meaning is a key factor in this, and Renato Bruson and Mara Zampieri respond vividly. Zampieri's voice may be biting rather than beautiful, occasionally threatening to come off the rails, but, with musical precision an asset, she matches exactly Verdi's request for the voice of a she-devil. Neil Schicoff as Macduff and Robert Lloyd as Banquo make up the excellent quartet of principals, while the high voltage of the whole performance clearly reflects Sinopoli's experience with the same chorus and orchestra at the Deutsche Oper in Berlin. CD adds vividly to the realism of a recording that is well balanced and focused but atmospheric.

At times Abbado's tempi are unconventional, but with slow speeds he springs the rhythm so infectiously that the results are the more compelling. Based on the Giorgio Strehler production at La Scala, the whole performance gains from superb teamwork, for each of the principals – far more than is common – is meticulous about observing Verdi's detailed markings, above all those for *pianissimo* and *sotto voce*. Verrett, hardly powerful above the stave, yet makes a virtue out of necessity in floating glorious half-tones, and with so firm and characterful a voice she makes a highly individual, not at all conventional Lady Macbeth. As for Cappuccilli, he has never sung with such fine range of tone and imagination on record as here, and Plácido Domingo makes a real, sensitive character out of the small role of Macduff. Excellent, clean recording, impressively remastered for CD.

On two mid-price discs in the Victor Opera series, the Leinsdorf version makes a good bargain, bringing a large-scale performance featuring three favourite principals from the Met. Leonie Rysanek here gives one of her finest performances on record, producing her firmest, creamiest sound for the Sleepwalking scene, even though the coloratura taxes her severely. Leonard Warren, much admired in this part before his untimely death (on stage, singing Don Carlo in *La forza del destino*), gives a strong, thoughtful reading, marred by the way the microphone exaggerates his vibrato. Carlo Bergonzi is a stylish, clear-toned Macduff. Good sound for its period.

Macbeth: highlights.
(M) *** Decca 421 889-2 [id.]. Fischer-Dieskau, Suliotis, Pavarotti, Ghiaurov, Ambrosian Op. Ch., LPO, Gardelli.

(M) *** DG 435 414-2; *435 414-4* [id.] (from above set, with Cappuccilli, Verrett, Domingo; cond. Abbado).

On Decca a generous selection (75 minutes) from a finely dramatic set, splendidly recorded in the Kingsway Hall in 1971 and flawed only by the variable singing of Suliotis. This is arguably Fischer-Dieskau's finest Verdi performance on record and the cast includes a young Pavarotti as Macduff.

Although the 62-minute set of excerpts from Abbado's *Macbeth* is issued as part of DG's 'Domingo Edition', its compilers recognize that Macduff is only a supporting role, and the principal participants, Cappuccilli and Verrett as Macbeth and Lady Macbeth respectively, are well represented. The witches, too, are not forgotten, and the disc opens with their chorus (*Che faceste?*), and includes the scene of the apparitions from Act III. Splendid sound, vividly atmospheric.

I Masnadieri (complete).
(M) *** Ph. 422 423-2 (2). Caballé, Bergonzi, Raimondi, Cappuccilli, Amb. S., New Philh. O, Gardelli.

As this excellent Philips recording makes plain, the long neglect of *I Masnadieri* is totally undeserved, despite a libretto which is a bungled adaptation of a Schiller play. Few will seriously identify with the hero-turned-brigand who stabs his beloved rather than lead her into a life of shame; but, on record, flaws of motivation are of far less moment than on stage. The melodies may only fitfully be out of Verdi's top drawer, but the musical structure and argument often look forward to a much later period with hints of *Forza*, *Don Carlo* and even *Otello*. With Gardelli as ever an urgently sympathetic Verdian, and a team of four excellent principals, splendidly recorded, the set can be warmly welcomed.

Nabucco (complete).
*** DG Dig. 410 512-2 (2) [id.]. Cappuccilli, Dimitrova, Nesterenko, Domingo, Ch. & O of German Op., Berlin, Sinopoli.
*** Decca 417 407-2 (2) [id.]. Gobbi, Suliotis, Cava, Previdi, V. State Op. Ch. & O, Gardelli.

Sinopoli makes Verdi sound less comfortable than traditional conductors, but he never lets the 'grand guitar' accompaniments of early Verdi churn along automatically. One keeps hearing details normally obscured. Even the thrill of the great chorus *Va, pensiero* is the greater when the melody first emerges at a hushed pianissimo, as marked, sound almost offstage. Strict as he is, Sinopoli encourages his singers to relish the great melodies to the full. Dimitrova is superb in Abigaille's big Act II aria, noble in her evil, as is Cappuccilli as Nabucco, less intense than Gobbi was on Gardelli's classic set for Decca, but stylistically pure. The rest of the cast is strong too, including Domingo in a relatively small role and Nesterenko superb as the High Priest, Zaccaria. Bright and forward digital sound, less atmospheric than the 1965 Decca set with Gobbi and Suliotis, conducted by Gardelli.

The vividly real and atmospheric sound in the 1965 Decca recording comes up very three-dimensionally on CD, even though tape-hiss is at a higher level than usual. There is more presence than in Sinopoli's DG, but that digital recording copes better with big ensembles. The Viennese choral contribution was less committed than one would ideally like in a work which contains a chorus unique in Verdi's output, *Va, pensiero*; but in every other way this is a masterly performance, with dramatically intense and deeply imaginative contributions from Tito Gobbi as Nabucco and Elena Suliotis as the evil Abigaille. Gobbi was already nearing the end of his full career, but even he rarely recorded a performance so full of sharply dramatic detail, while Suliotis made this the one totally satisfying performance of an all-too-brief recording career, wild in places but no more than is dramatically necessary. Though Carlo Cava as Zaccaria is not ideally rich of tone, it is a strong performance, and Gardelli, as in his later Verdi recordings for both Decca and Philips, showed what a master he is at pointing Verdian inspiration, whether in the individual phrase or over a whole scene, simply and naturally, without ever forcing.

Nabucco: highlights.
(M) *** DG Dig. 435 415-2; *435 415-4* [id.] (from above recording, with Cappuccilli, Dimitrova, Domingo; cond. Sinopoli).
(M) *** Decca 421 867-2; *421 867-4* (from above recording with Gobbi; cond. Gardelli).

The 64-minute selection of highlights from the Sinopoli set has now been reissued at mid-price as part of the 'Domingo Edition', even though Domingo has only the minor role of

Ismaele. Even so, he is distinctive and, while the major items in which he appears are included, the fine contributions of Cappuccilli, Dimitrova and Nesterenko are well represented, alongside the famous chorus, *Va, pensiero*. The *Overture* is also included.

Suliotis's impressive contribution is well represented on the Decca highlights disc, and there are fine contributions too from Gobbi. Needless to say, the chorus *Va, pensiero* is given its place of honour and the selection runs for 58 minutes. The 1965 recording sounds splendid.

Oberto (complete).
*** Orfeo C 105843 F (3) [id.]. Dimitrova, Bergonzi, Panerai, Baldani, Bav. R. Ch., Munich R. O, Gardelli.

In every way this issue matches the success of Gardelli's earlier, Philips recordings, despite the change of venue to Munich. There is much in *Oberto* that reflects the manners and style of Donizetti, but the underlying toughness regularly provides a distinctive flavour. Gardelli successfully papers over the less convincing moments, helped by fine playing from the orchestra, an outstanding chorus and first-rate principals. Ghena Dimitrova makes a very positive heroine, powerful in attack in her moment of fury in the Act I finale, but also gently expressive when necessary. Only in cabalettas is she sometimes ungainly. The veterans, Carlo Bergonzi and Rolando Panerai, more than make up in stylishness and technical finesse for any unevenness of voice, and Ruza Baldani is a warm-toned Cuniza, the mezzo role. First-rate recording.

Otello (complete).
*** BMG/RCA RD 82951 (2) [RCD2-2951]. Domingo, Scotto, Milnes, Amb. Op. Ch., Nat. PO, Levine.
*** Decca Dig. 433 669-2; *433 669-4* (2) [id.]. Pavarotti, Te Kanawa, Nucci, Rolfe Johnson, Chicago SO & Ch., Solti.
(M) *** BMG/RCA GD 81969 (2) [1969-2-RG]. Vickers, Rysanek, Gobbi, Rome Op. Ch. & O, Serafin.
(M) *** EMI CMS7 69308-2 (2) [Ang. CDMB 69308]. Vickers, Freni, Glossop, Ch. of German Op., Berlin, BPO, Karajan.
**(*) EMI Dig. CDS7 47450-8 (2) [Ang. CDCB 47450]. Domingo, Ricciarelli, Diaz, La Scala, Milan, Ch. & O, Maazel.
(M) (**(*)) BMG/RCA mono GD 60302 (2) [60302-2-RG]. Vinay, Valdengo, Nelli, Merriman, Assandri, NBC Ch. & SO, Toscanini.

Levine's is the most consistently involving *Otello*; on balance, it has the best cast and is superbly conducted as well as magnificently sung. Levine combines a Toscanini-like thrust with a Karajan-like sensuousness, pointing rhythms to heighten mood, as in the Act II confrontation between hero and heroine over Cassio. Domingo as Otello combines glorious heroic tone with lyrical tenderness. Scotto is not always sweet-toned in the upper register, and the big ensemble at the end of Act III brings obvious strain; nevertheless, it is a deeply felt performance which culminates in a most beautiful account of the all-important Act IV solos, the *Willow song* and *Ave Maria*, most affecting. Milnes too is challenged by the role of Iago. His may not be a voice which readily conveys extremes of evil, but his view is far from conventional: this Iago is a handsome, virile creature beset by the biggest of chips on the shoulder. In the digital transfer for CD of the 1977 analogue original, the voices are caught vividly and immediately and with ample bloom. The orchestral sound too is fuller and cleaner than in many more recent versions, though there is an occasional hint of roughness in big tuttis.

Solti's Chicago Symphony recording was made in the spring of 1991 from a series of live performances both in Chicago and New York, which marked the close of his long period as music director of the orchestra. With a superstar cast it ran the risk of being merely a media vehicle, but proves a triumph, not quite a first recommendation but a thrilling realization of a supreme masterpiece. Solti, recovering from illness like most of the cast, has never sounded more warmly communicative in Verdi. The fast speeds never seem too taut or breathless, but simply add to the high voltage of the drama. Leo Nucci, taking the role of Iago for the first time, is sound rather than inspired, warmly Italianate in timbre but lacking in menace. *Era la notte*, fast like much else, becomes a simple narrative, hardly conveying evil. Dame Kiri Te Kanawa, in a role she has sung many times, produces consistently sumptuous tone, unaffected by the closeness of microphone balance. The *Willow song* is glorious with the last cries of 'Salce!' reduced to a precisely pitched whisper, before she launches up to a fearless top A sharp fortissimo. The key element is the singing of Pavarotti as Otello, like Nucci new to his role. Following the pattern of the whole performance, he often adopts faster speeds than usual. He is less meditative, less weighty than his great rival Domingo, so that such a passage as *Ora e per sempre* makes the hero sound like Radames in *Aida*. He then conveys pure anger rather than irony in his big Act III duet with Desdemona. The cries of 'Sangue!' before the Oath duet with Iago do not ring out as with Domingo and others, but they are genuinely sung, not shouted. Whatever the detailed reservations this is a memorable reading heightened by Pavarotti's detailed feeling for the words and consistently golden tone. With such close microphone balance, he like the others is prevented from achieving genuine pianissimos, but above all he offers a vital, animated Otello, not a replacement for Domingo but a magnificent alternative. The impact of the whole is greatly enhanced by the splendid singing of the Chicago Symphony Chorus, helped by digital sound fuller and more vivid than on any rival set.

No conductor is more understanding of Verdian pacing than Serafin and, with sound that hardly begins to show its age (1960), it presents two of the finest solo performances on any *Otello* recording of whatever period: the Iago of Tito Gobbi has never been surpassed for vividness of characterization and tonal subtlety; while the young Jon Vickers, with a voice naturally suited to this role, was in his prime as the Moor. Leonie Rysanek is a warm and sympathetic Desdemona, not always ideally pure-toned but tender and touching in one of her very finest recorded performances. The sense of presence in the open, well-balanced recording is the more vivid on CD, thanks to a first-rate transfer.

Karajan directs a big, bold and brilliant account, for the most part splendidly sung and with all the dramatic contrasts strongly underlined. There are several tiny, but irritating, statutory cuts, but otherwise on two mid-price CDs this is well worth considering. Freni's Desdemona is delightful, delicate and beautiful, while Vickers and Glossop are both positive and characterful, only occasionally forcing their tone and losing focus. The recording is clarified on CD, with better focus and more bloom than on the much more recent EMI set under Maazel.

Maazel's version, used as soundtrack for the Zeffirelli film but with the text uncut (unlike that of the film), brings a fine performance from Domingo and taut, subtle control from Maazel, particularly good in the spacious, tenderly emotional treatment of the final scene. In many ways Domingo shows how he has developed since he made his earlier recording with Levine; but with a disappointingly negative, unsinister Iago in Justino Diaz, the result often loses in dramatic bite, and Maazel's direction occasionally sags, as in the closing pages of Act II at the end of the oath duet. Ricciarelli, though not the ideal Desdemona, sings most affectingly, with pianissimos beautifully caught in the *Willow song* and *Ave Maria*. One snag is the sound, which is curiously recessed, with the voices often not quite in focus and with little sense of presence.

Recorded in December 1947 at rehearsals and radio performances in the notorious Studio 8H, Radio City, in New York, Toscanini's historic reading suffers more than usual from dry, limited sound but in magnetic intensity it is irresistible, bringing home the biting power of Verdi's score as few other recorded performances ever have. Toscanini's speeds are often fast, but his feeling for Verdian line is most persuasive, and above all he controls tension to have one experiencing the drama afresh. Ramon Vinay makes a commanding Otello, baritonal in vocal colouring but firm and clear, with a fine feeling for words. Giuseppe Valdengo had few rivals among baritones of the time in this role, strong, animated and clean in attack, though the vocal differentiation between hero and villain is less marked than usual. Herva Nelli is sweet and pure if a little colourless as Desdemona. The recording prevents her from achieving a really gentle pianissimo, and Toscanini, for all his flowing lines fails to allow the full repose needed.

Otello: highlights.
(M) *** EMI CDM7 63454-2; *EG 763454-4* [id.] (from above recording, cond. Karajan.).

The Karajan highlights disc offers a generally well-managed selection (though of less than an hour). The sound is full, appropriately weighty in the score's more spectacular moments.

Rigoletto (complete).
*** Ph. Dig. 412 592-2 (2) [id.]. Bruson, Gruberová, Shicoff, Fassbaender, Lloyd, St Cecilia Ac., Rome, Ch. & O, Sinopoli.
*** Decca 414 269-2 (2) [id.]. Milnes, Sutherland, Pavarotti, Talvela, Tourangeau, Amb. Op. Ch., LSO, Bonynge.
(***) EMI mono CDS7 47469-8 (2) [Ang. CDCB 47469]. Gobbi, Callas, Di Stefano, Zaccaria, La Scala, Milan, Ch. & O, Serafin.
**(*) DG 415 288-2 (2) [id.]. Cappuccilli, Cotrubas, Domingo, Obraztsova, Ghiaurov, Moll, Schwarz, V. State Op. Ch., VPO, Giulini.

(M) **(*) BMG/RCA GD 86506 (2) [6506-2-RG]. Merrill, Moffo, Kraus, Elias, Flagello, RCA Italiana Op. Ch. & O, Solti.
** Decca Dig. 425 864-2 (2) [id.]. Nucci, Anderson, Pavarotti, Ghiaurov, Verrett, Ch. & O of Teatro Comunale di Bologna, Chailly.

Sinopoli has close concern for his singers here, with full potential drawn from each in what is the most consistent cast yet on record. Edita Gruberová might have been considered an unexpected choice for Gilda, remarkable for her brilliant coloratura rather than for deeper expression, yet here she makes the heroine a tender, feeling creature, emotionally vulnerable yet vocally immaculate. As a stickler for the text, Sinopoli eliminates a top note or two, as in *Caro nome*. Similarly, Renato Bruson as Rigoletto does far more than produce a stream of velvety tone, detailed and intense, responding to the conductor and combining beauty with dramatic bite. Even more remarkable is the brilliant success of Neil Shicoff as the Duke, more than a match for his most distinguished rivals. Here the *Quartet* becomes a genuine climax as it rarely has been in complete recordings. Brigitte Fassbaender as Maddalena is sharply unconventional but vocally most satisfying. Sinopoli's speeds, too, are unconventional at times, but the fresh look he provides makes this one of the most exciting of recent Verdi operas on disc, helped by full and vivid recording, consistently well balanced.

Just over ten years after her first recording of this opera, Sutherland appeared in it again – and this set was far more than a dutiful remake. From the very start Richard Bonynge shows his feeling for the resilient rhythms; the result is fresh and dramatic, underlining the revolutionary qualities in the score which nowadays we tend to ignore. Pavarotti is an intensely characterful Duke: an unmistakable rogue but an unmistakable charmer, too. Thanks to him and to Bonynge above all, the *Quartet*, as on the Sinopoli set, becomes a genuine musical climax. Sutherland's voice has acquired a hint of a beat, but there is little of the mooning manner which disfigured her earlier assumption, and the result is glowingly beautiful as well as being technically supremely assured. Milnes makes a strong Rigoletto, vocally masterful and with good if hardly searching presentation of character. The digital transfer is exceptionally vivid and atmospheric, underlining the excellence of the original engineering with its finely judged balances, but also enhancing the superimposed crowd noises and the like, which not everyone will welcome.

There has never been a more compelling performance of the title-role in *Rigoletto* than that of Gobbi on his classic Scala set of the 1950s. At every point, in almost every single phrase, Gobbi finds extra meaning in Verdi's vocal lines, with the widest range of tone-colour employed for expressive effect. Callas, though not naturally suited to the role of the wilting Gilda, is compellingly imaginative throughout, and Di Stefano gives one of his finer performances. The transfer of the original mono recording is astonishingly vivid in capturing the voices, which are sharply focused and given a fine sense of presence, so that you miss stereo spread remarkably little.

Giulini, ever thoughtful for detail, directs a distinguished performance. He seems determined to get away from any conception of *Rigoletto* as melodrama; however, in doing that he misses the red-blooded theatricality of Verdi's concept, the basic essential. Although it may be consistent with Giulini's view, it further reduces the dramatic impact that Cappuccilli (with his unsinister voice) makes the hunchback a noble figure from first to last, while Domingo, ever intelligent, makes a reflective rather than an extrovert Duke. Cotrubas is a touching Gilda, but the close balance of her voice is not helpful, and the topmost register is not always comfortable. The recording, made in the Musikverein in Vienna, has the voices well to the fore, with much reverberation on the instruments behind, an effect emphasized by the CD transfer.

Anna Moffo makes a charming Gilda in the Solti set of 1963. Solti at times presses too hard, but this is a strong and dramatic reading, with Robert Merrill producing a glorious flow of dark, firm tone in the name-part. Alfredo Kraus is as stylish as ever as the Duke, and this rare example of his voice at its freshest should not be missed. A good bargain, though there are statutory cuts in the text.

Chailly's new digital version has the benefit of full and vivid Decca sound, but the performance cannot match the finest existing versions. Pavarotti, recorded very close, undermines the vivacity of his singing by coarse vocal tricks. His earlier recording opposite Sutherland is far preferable. June Anderson makes a strong Gilda but the voice, as recorded, often sounds too heavy; and Leo Nucci, well below form, is far too rough of tone in the title-role, with the voice often unsteady. Chailly's direction is sympathetic, but lacks the individuality of such Italian rivals as Giulini or Sinopoli.

Rigoletto: highlights.
(M) *** DG 435 416-2; *435 416-4* [id.] (from above complete set, with Cappuccilli, Cotrubas, Domingo; cond. Giulini).
*** Decca 421 303-2 [id.] (from above recording, cond. Bonynge).
(M) **(*) Ph. Dig. 432 619-2; *432 619-4* [id.] (from above recording, cond. Sinopoli).

Two useful and generous sets of highlights for those who do not want to go to the expense of a complete set. On Decca it was a pity that *Questa o quella* had to be given an edited fade. The 61-minute DG collection gets round this problem by including the following number, *Partite? Crudele.* This is now reissued at mid-price as part of the 'Domingo Edition' and makes a clear first choice.

Sinopoli's generous (71 minutes) and vividly recorded set of highlights is flawed. Unfortunately and disgracefully, the CD offers no notes or translation, instead wasting a dozen or so pages on listing other reissues in the digital Laser Line series!

Rigoletto (highlights; in English).
(M) **(*) EMI Dig. CDM7 63726-2. Rawnsley, Field, Davies, Tomlinson, Rigby, E. Nat. Op. Ch. & O, Mark Elder).

Unlike the ENO *Otello*, *Rigoletto* was recorded in the studio (also in 1983), but there is no lack of intensity and, even if you normally resist opera in English, this 63 minutes of excerpts is well worth trying. Excellent, vivid sound and a libretto provided, although the words are admirably clear.

Simon Boccanegra (complete).
❀ *** DG 415 692-2 (2) [id.]. Cappuccilli, Freni, Ghiaurov, Van Dam, Carreras, La Scala, Milan, Ch. & O, Abbado.
** Decca Dig. 425 628-2 (2) [id.]. Nucci, Te Kanawa, Burchuladze, Aragall, La Scala, Milan, Ch. & O, Solti.
(M) (***) EMI mono CMS7 63513-2 (2) [Ang. CDMB 63513]. Gobbi, Christoff, De los Angeles, Campora, Monachesi, Dari, Rome Op. Chor & O, Santini.

Abbado's 1977 recording of *Simon Boccanegra*, directly reflecting the superb production which the La Scala company brought to London at the time, is one of the most beautiful Verdi sets ever made, and the virtual background silence of the CDs enhances the warmth and beauty of the sound, the orchestra fresh and glowing in ambient warmth, the voices vivid and the perspectives always believable. From this, one can appreciate not just the vigour of the composer's imagination but also the finesse of the colouring, instrumental as well as vocal. Under Abbado the playing of the orchestra is brilliantly incisive as well as refined, so that the drama is underlined by extra sharpness of focus. The cursing of Paolo after the great Council Chamber scene makes the scalp prickle, with the chorus muttering in horror and the bass clarinet adding a sinister comment, here beautifully moulded. Cappuccilli, always intelligent, gives a far more intense and illuminating performance than the one he recorded for RCA earlier in his career. He may not match Gobbi in range of colour and detail, but he too gives focus to the performance; and Ghiaurov as Fiesco sings beautifully too. Freni as Maria Boccanegra sings with freshness and clarity, while Van Dam is an impressive Paolo. With electrically intense choral singing as well, this is a set to outshine even Abbado's superb *Macbeth* with the same company.

The glory of Solti's set is the singing of Dame Kiri Te Kanawa as Amelia, a beautiful, touching performance. The freedom and absence of strain in the voice go with an almost Straussian quality in her characterization, with the widest dynamic and expressive range. Giacomo Aragall makes a strong, unforced Gabriele, but the others are less distinguished. As a cast, this line-up hardly matches that of Abbado on his rival DG set. That was also recorded with forces from La Scala, Milan, but in conjunction with a celebrated stage production. Leo Nucci is most disappointing, with the voice showing signs of wear, not nearly steady enough. He sings powerfully, but Boccanegra's solo in the great Council Chamber scene finds the voice spreading. Burchuladze also is surprisingly less steady than usual, and Paolo Coni as Paolo is capable but undistinguished. What also makes this a less compelling reading compared with the DG is Solti's obsession with observing the metronome markings in the score very precisely, laudable in theory but often questionable in practice; so the great recognition scene between Boccanegra and his daughter is powerfully dramatic at a speed far faster than usual, but it lacks tenderness and fails to convey the joy of recognition, which Abbado finds so readily and affectingly. The sound of the DG analogue version is preferable, though less wide-ranging, with the voices more realistically focused.

Tito Gobbi's portrait of the tragic Doge of Genoa is one of his greatest on record, and it emerges all the more impressively when it is set against equally memorable performances by Boris Christoff as Fiesco and Victoria de los Angeles as Amelia. The Recognition scene between father and daughter has never been done more movingly on record; nor has the great ensemble, which crowns the Council Chamber scene, been so powerfully and movingly presented, and that without the help of stereo recording. The transfer is full and immediate, giving a vivid sense of presence to the voices, though tape-hiss is on the high side.

Stiffelio (complete).
(M) *** Ph. 422 432-2 (2). Carreras, Sass, Manuguerra, Ganzarolli, V. ORF Ch. & SO, Gardelli.

Coming just before the great trio of masterpieces, *Rigoletto*, *Il Trovatore* and *La Traviata*, *Stiffelio* was a total failure at its first performance in 1850. To make *Aroldo* six years later, the score was in effect destroyed, and only through the discovery of two copyists' scores in the 1960s was a revival made possible. Though it lacks some of the beauties of *Aroldo*, *Stiffelio* is still a sharper, more telling work, largely because of the originality of the relationships and the superb final scene in which Stiffelio reads from the pulpit the parable of the woman taken in adultery. Gardelli directs a fresh performance, at times less lively than Queler's of *Aroldo* but with more consistent singing, notably from Carreras and Manuguerra. First-rate recording from Philips, typical of this fine series.

La Traviata (complete).
*** Decca Dig. 430 491-2; *430 491-4* (2) [id.]. Sutherland, Pavarotti, Manuguerra, L. Op. Ch., Nat. PO, Bonynge.
**(*) DG Dig. 415 132-2 (2) [id.]. Cotrubas, Domingo, Milnes, Bav. State Op. Ch. & O, Carlos Kleiber.
(M) **(*) Decca 411 877-2 (2) [id.]. Sutherland, Bergonzi, Merrill, Ch. & O of Maggio Musicale Fiorentino, Pritchard.
(M) (*(**)) EMI mono CMS7 63628-2 (2) [Ang. CDMB 63628]. Callas, Di Stefano, Bastianini, La Scala Ch. & O, Giulini.
(**) EMI mono CDS7 49187-8 (2) [Mov. Musica 051-021]. Callas, Kraus, Sereni, Ch. & O of San Carlos Op., Lisbon, Ghione.

Sutherland's second recording of the role of Violetta has a breadth and exuberance beyond her achievement in the earlier version of 1963, conducted by John Pritchard. Some of the supremely tender moments of her earlier recording – *Ah dite alla giovine* in the Act II duet with Germont, for example – are more straightforward this time, but the mooning manner is dispelled, the words are clearer, and the richness and command of the singing put this among the very finest of Sutherland's later recordings. Pavarotti too, though he overemphasizes *Di miei bollenti spiriti*, sings with splendid panache as Alfredo. Manuguerra as Germont lacks something in authority, but the firmness and clarity are splendid. Bonynge's conducting is finely sprung, the style direct, the speeds often spacious in lyrical music, generally undistracting. The digital recording is outstandingly vivid and beautifully balanced but the CD booklet is not ideal.

For some, Cotrubas makes an ideal heroine in this opera; but what is disappointing in the DG recording is that the microphone-placing exaggerates technical flaws, so that not only is her breathing too often audible but also her habit of separating coloratura with intrusive aitches is underlined, and the vibrato becomes too obvious at times. Such is her magic that some will forgive the faults, for her characterization combines strength with vulnerability. But Carlos Kleiber's direction is equally controversial, with more than a hint of Toscanini-like rigidity in the party music, and an occasionally uncomfortable insistence on discipline. The characteristic contributions of Domingo and Milnes, both highly commendable, hardly alter the issue. The recording suggests over-reliance on multi-channel techniques, and the closeness of the microphone-placing, spotlighting not only the soloists but members of the orchestra, is the more apparent on CD, underlining the fierce side of Kleiber's conducting which contrasts strongly with his ripely romantic side.

In Sutherland's 1963 recording of *La Traviata*, it is true that her diction is poor, but it is also true that she has rarely sung on record with such deep feeling as in the final scene. The *Addio del passato* (both stanzas included and sung with an unexpected lilt) merely provides a beginning, for the duet with Bergonzi is most winning, and the final death scene, *Se una pudica vergine*, is overwhelmingly beautiful. This is not a sparkling Violetta, true, but it is vocally closer to perfection than almost any other in a complete set. Bergonzi is an attractive Alfredo and Merrill an efficient Germont. Pritchard sometimes tends to hustle things along with too little regard for shaping Verdian phrases, but the recording quality is outstandingly good in its CD format.

Callas's version with Giulini was recorded in 1955, three years before the Ghione Lisbon set, when the voice was fresher. In the presence of a great conductor, one who often challenged her with unusually slow speeds, Callas responded with even greater depth of expression. There is no more vividly dramatic a performance on record than this, unmatchable in conveying Violetta's agony; sadly, the sound, always limited, grows crumbly towards the end. It is sad too that Bastianini sings so lumpishly as Germont père, even in the great duet of Act II, while di Stefano also fails to match his partner in the supreme test of the final scene. The transfer is fair, though in places it sounds as though an echo-chamber has been used.

Recorded at a live performance in March 1958, Callas's Lisbon-made version, far more than in her earlier Cetra recording of this opera, lets one appreciate the intensity which made this one of her supreme roles, conveying fleeting emotions even in such an obvious passage as the *Brindisi*. Kraus is a fresh, stylish Alfredo, Sereni a positive Germont, more characterful than in the (deleted) EMI set with De los Angeles. However, the extraneous noises in this live recording – like the prompter's constant groaning – as well as the tape background and the crumbling at climaxes, are made all the clearer on CD.

La Traviata: highlights.
(M) *** EMI CDM7 63088-2; *EG 763088-4*. Scotto, Kraus, Bruson, Amb. Op. Ch., Philh. O, Muti.
(M) **(*) DG 435 417-2; *435 417-4* [id.] (from above recording, with Cotrubas, Domingo, Milnes; cond. Carlos Kleiber).

Muti's complete set is at full price and it isn't a first choice, so many will be glad to have this fairly generous (61 minutes) mid-price disc of highlights, including both the Act I and Act III *Preludes* and a well-balanced selection from each of the three Acts, with most of the key numbers included.

Carlos Kleiber's set is flawed in several ways – see above – so a highlights disc seems an ideal way to approach it. It comes as part of DG's 'Domingo Edition' and the 61-minute selection covers most of the key passages.

La Traviata (complete, in English).
(M) **(*) EMI CMS7 63072-2 (2). Masterson, Brecknock, Du Plessis, E. Nat. Op. Ch. & O, Mackerras.

Mackerras directs a vigorous, colourful reading which brings out the drama, and Valerie Masterson is at last given the chance on record she has so long deserved. The voice is caught beautifully, if not always very characterfully, and John Brecknock makes a fine Alfredo, most effective in the final scene. Christian Du Plessis' baritone is less suitable for recording. The conviction of the whole enterprise is infectious – but be warned, Verdi in English has a way of sounding on record rather like Gilbert and Sullivan.

La Traviata (sung in English): highlights.
(M) **(*) EMI CDM7 63725-2 [id.] (from above complete recording; cond. Mackerras).

Those wanting to sample this excellent performance in English will find that the 63-minute selection is fairly evenly divided over the three Acts and it is vividly transferred.

Il Trovatore (complete).
❀ *** BMG/RCA RD 86194 (2) [6194-2-RC]. Leontyne Price, Domingo, Milnes, Cossotto, Amb. Op. Ch., New Philh. O, Mehta.
*** DG Dig. 423 858-2 (2) [id.]. Plowright, Domingo, Fassbaender, Zancanaro, Nesterenko, Ch. & O of St Cecilia Academy, Rome, Giulini.
(***) EMI CDS7 49347-2 (2) [Ang. CDCB 49347]. Callas, Barbieri, Di Stefano, Panerai, La Scala, Milan, Ch. & O, Karajan.
(M) (***) BMG/RCA mono GD 86643 (2) [6643-2-RG]. Milanov, Bjoerling, Warren, Barbieri, Robert Shaw Ch., RCA Victor O, Cellini.

The soaring curve of Leontyne Price's rich vocal line (almost too ample for some ears) is immediately thrilling in her famous Act I aria, and it sets the style of the RCA performance, full-bodied and with the tension consistently held at the highest levels. The choral contribution is superb; the famous *Soldiers'* and *Anvil choruses* are marvellously fresh and dramatic. When *Di quella pira* comes, the orchestra opens with tremendous gusto and Domingo sings with a ringing, heroic quality worthy of Caruso himself. There are many dramatic felicities, and Sherill Milnes is in fine voice throughout; but perhaps the highlight of the set is the opening section of Act III, when Azucena finds her way to Conte di Luna's camp. The ensuing scene with Fiorenza Cossotto is vocally and dramatically quite electrifying. The CDs are transferred vibrantly to make one of the most thrilling of all early Verdi operas on record.

In an intensely revelatory performance, one which is richly red-blooded but which transforms melodrama into a deeper experience, Giulini flouts convention at every point. The opera's white-hot inspiration comes out in the intensity of the playing and singing, but the often slow tempi and refined textures present the whole work in new and deeper detail, product of the conductor's intense study of the work afresh. Inspired casting presents Rosalind Plowright triumphantly in her first international opera recording. Sensuous yet ethereal in *Tacea la notte*, she masterfully brings together the seemingly incompatible qualities demanded, not just sweetness and purity but brilliant coloratura, flexibility and richly dramatic bite and power. Plácido Domingo sings Manrico as powerfully as he did in the richly satisfying Mehta set on RCA, but the voice is even more heroic in an Otello-like way, only very occasionally showing strain. Giorgio Zancanaro proves a gloriously firm and rounded Count di Luna and Evgeny Nesterenko a dark, powerful Ferrando, while Brigitte Fassbaender, singing her first Azucena, finds far greater intensity and detail than the usual roaring mezzo, matching Giulini's freshness. The recording is warm and atmospheric with a pleasant bloom on the voices, naturally balanced and not spotlit. Now on a pair of CDs, it sounds all the firmer and more vivid.

The combination of Karajan and Callas is formidably impressive. There is toughness and dramatic determination in Callas's singing, whether in the coloratura or in the dramatic passages, and this gives the heroine an unsuspected depth of character which culminates in Callas's fine singing of an aria which used often to be cut entirely – *Tu vedrai che amore in terra*, here with its first stanza alone included. Barbieri is a magnificent Azucena, Panerai a strong, incisive Count, and Di Stefano at his finest as Manrico. On CD the 1957 mono sound, though dry and unatmospheric, is one of the more vivid from La Scala at that period.

Though dating from 1952, using a cut text as in the Met. production, the Cellini version brings a vivid reminder of that great opera house at a key period. Milanov, though at times a little raw in Leonora's coloratura, gives a glorious, commanding performance, never surpassed on record, with the voice at its fullest. Bjoerling and Warren too are in ringing voice, and Barbieri is a superb Azucena, with Cellini – rarely heard on record – proving an outstanding Verdian.

Il Trovatore: highlights.
(M) *** DG Dig. 435 418-2; *435 418-4* [id.] (from above recording, with Plowright, Domingo, Fassbaender; cond. Giulini).
(M) (***) RCA mono GD 60191 [60191-2-RG] (from above recording; cond. Cellini).
(M) **(*) Decca 421 310-2; *421 310-4*. Sutherland, Pavarotti, Horne, Wixell, Ghiaurov, L. Op. Ch. & Nat. PO, Bonynge.

Those who have the earlier RCA set in which Domingo participated should consider these highlights from Giulini's unconventional but highly compelling performance, especially as the CD is offered at mid-price (as part of the DG 'Domingo Edition'). It is generous at 67 minutes, and Domingo is again splendid, as are his excellent supporting cast.

For many, a highlights CD will be the ideal way to approach this outstanding 1952 RCA recording, much admired in its day. Two dozen excerpts (68 minutes) span the opera very effectively.

The selection from Bonynge's Decca set is especially valuable as a reminder of Sutherland's Leonora. Pavarotti may be stretched by the role of Manrico, but he is nearly always magnificent. Horne is represented by her powerful *Stride la vampa*, Wixell by an undernourished *Il Balen*.

I vespri siciliani (complete).
**(*) EMI CDS7 54043-2 (3) [Ang. CDCC 54043]; *EX 754043-4*. Merritt, Studer, Zancanaro, Furlanetto, Ch. & O of La Scala, Milan, Muti.
** BMG/RCA RD 80370 (3) [0370-2-RC]. Arroyo, Domingo, Milnes, Raimondi, Ewing, Alldis Ch., New Philh. O, Levine.

This opera has been sadly neglected on record; it is a cumbersome, five-Act piece, written for Paris, and, for all the rousing ensembles and elaborate spectacle, not to mention the big half-hour ballet in Act III, it generally lacks the melodic individuality which marks even the lesser-known Verdi operas. Yet it contains many riches over its span of nearly three and a half hours, and it is good to have a modern recording. This is the most successful yet of the live recordings made by Muti at La Scala, Milan, plagued by a difficult acoustic which is dispiritingly dry for the engineers. The atmosphere is well caught and, though Muti can be too tautly urgent a Verdian, his pacing here is well geared to bring out the high drama. Outstanding in the cast is Cheryl Studer as the heroine, Elena, singing radiantly; while the tenor Chris Merritt as Arrigo sounds less coarse and strained than he has in the past. Giorgio Zancanaro also responds to the role of Monforte – the governor of Sicily, discovered to be Arrigo's father – with new sensitivity, and though Ferruccio Furlanetto as Procida lacks the full weight to bring out the beauty of line in the great aria, *O tu Palermo*, his is a warm performance too.

The work's great merit is not so much its grandeur as its searching portrayal of the father–son relationship between Monforte, the tyrannical governor of Sicily, and Arrigo, the son he has never known. Their Act II duet, using a melody well known from the overture, is nothing short of magnificent, with Domingo and Milnes at their very peak. The rest of the singing is good, if rarely inspired, and though James Levine's direction is colourful and urgent, such a score needs more persuasiveness. Good recording, vividly remastered.

COLLECTIONS

Arias: *Aida: Celeste Aida. Un ballo in maschera: La rivedrà; Di, tu se fedele; Ma se m'è forza perderti. I due Foscari: Dal più remote esilio. Luisa Miller: Quando le sere. Macbeth: Ah, la paterna mano. Rigoletto: Questa o quella; Parmi veder; La donna è mobile. La Traviata: De' miei bollenti. Il Trovatore: Di quella pira.*
(M) *** Decca 417 570-2. Luciano Pavarotti (with various orchestras & conductors).

Taken mainly from a recital which Pavarotti recorded early in his career with Edward Downes and the Vienna State Opera Orchestra, this Verdi collection on the mid-price Opera Gala label can be warmly recommended, a generous collection of favourite items, plus one or two rarer arias.

Arias: *Aida: Ritorna vincitor. Un ballo in maschera: Ecco l'orrido campo. Don Carlos: Tu che le vanità. Ernani: Ernani involami. I Lombardi: O Madre dal cielo. Macbeth: Nel di della vittoria; La luce langue una macchia. Nabucco: Anch'io dischiuso un giorno. I vespri siciliani: Arrigo! Oh parli.*
*** EMI CDC7 47730-2 [id.]. Maria Callas, Philh. O, Rescigno.

In this first of two Verdi recital records issued to commemorate the tenth anniversary of Callas's death, the great soprano is at her most commanding, not flawless but thrilling, both in her creative musicianship and in her characterizations, powerfully Shakespearean in the Lady Macbeth arias presented as a sequence, and holding tension masterfully in the long *Don Carlos* scene. Both those performances date from the late 1950s, when the voice was still in fine condition. Though the later items here come from a period when the voice had deteriorated (done in the 1960s but issued only in 1972), Aida's *Ritorna vincitor*, vehemently done, is magnificent for one. Generally good transfers and clean sound.

Arias from: *La battaglia in maschera; Un ballo in maschera; Il Corsaro; I due Foscari; Ernani; Un giorno di regno;* (i) Duet from *I Lombardi*. Arias from: *Luisa Miller; Rigoletto; Stiffelio; Il Trovatore.*
(M) **(*) Ph. Analogue/Dig. 434 151-2; *434 151-4* [id.]. Jose Carreras; (i) with Katia Ricciarelli, Ambrosian Op. Ch.; various orchestras and conductors.

Admirers of José Carreras will find him in excellent voice in this series of excerpts from his complete sets recorded between 1973 and 1981. He was miscast as Manrico in *Il Trovatore* and his *Di quella pira* is the only disappointment; however, the somewhat similar *Odio solo, ed odio atroce* from *I due Foscari* is much more successful, and the programme is made the more attractive by all the rare material included here, in which he sounds uncommonly fresh. As it so happens, the highlight is the scena from *I Lombardi* (*Dove sola m'inoltro? . . . Per dirupi e per foreste*) to which Katia Ricciarelli makes a splendid contribution. The one great drawback is the absence of translations or any information about the music: the notes of this 60-minute Insignia collection (as with the rest of this badly produced series) are all biographical. The sound, however, is first rate.

Arias: *Don Carlo: Son io, mio Carlo . . . Per me giunto . . . O Carlo, ascolta. Luisa Miller: Sacra la scelta. Macbeth: Perfidi! All'anglo contra me v'unite . . . Pietà, rispetto, amore. La Traviata: Di Provenza il mar. Il Trovatore: Tutto è deserto . . . Il balen.*

*** Ph. Dig. 426 740-2; *426 740-4* [id.]. Dmitri Hvorostovsky, Rotterdam PO, Gergiev – TCHAIKOVSKY: *Arias.* ***

With a glorious voice, dark and characterful, and with natural musical imagination and film-star good looks, Dmitri Hvorostovsky, 'Cardiff Singer of the World' in 1989, on this disc made his recording début in the West not just in Tchaikovsky arias, but here in Verdi, stylishly sung. With a voice of such youthful virility, he hardly sounds like the father-figure of the *Traviata* and *Luisa Miller* items, but the legato in Macbeth's Act IV aria is most beautiful. He also brings the keenest intensity to Posa's death-scene aria from *Don Carlo.*

Arias: *Don Carlos: Tu che le vanità. La Traviata: Ah fors'è lui. Il Trovatore: Timor di me.*
*** Sony Dig. MK 37298 [id.]. Kiri Te Kanwa, LPO, Pritchard – PUCCINI: *Arias.* ***

The Verdi part of Kiri Te Kanawa's Verdi–Puccini recital brings three substantial items, less obviously apt for the singer, but in each the singing is felt as well as beautiful. The coloratura of the *Traviata* and *Trovatore* items is admirably clean, and it is a special joy to hear Elisabetta's big aria from *Don Carlos* sung with such truth and precision. Good recording, enhanced on CD.

Arias & duets: *Un ballo in maschera: Teco io sto. Il Corsaro: Egli non riede ancora! Don Carlos: Non pianger, mia compagna. Giovanna d'Arco: Qui! Qui! Dove più s'apre libero il ciela; O fatidica foresta. Jérusalem: Ave Maria. I Masnadieri: Dall'infame banchetto io m'involai; Tu del mio; Carlo vive. Otello: Già nella notte densa; Ave Maria. Il Trovatore: Timor di me; D'amor sull'ali rosee; Tu vedrai che amor in terr. I vespri siciliani: Arrigo! Ah, parli a un cor.*
(M) *** BMG/RCA GD 86534 (6534-2-RG]. Katia Ricciarelli, Plácido Domingo, Rome PO or St Cecilia Ac. O, Gavazzeni.

At mid-price this collection of Verdi arias and duets from two star singers, both in fresh voice, makes a good bargain. The inclusion of rarities adds to the attractions, and though the sound is not the most modern, it is more than acceptable in the digital transfer. The quality is very bright; although the orchestral timbre is a bit thin, both voices are given a good presence.

Choruses from: *Aida; Un ballo in maschera; Don Carlo; I Lombardi; Macbeth; I Masnadieri; Nabucco; Otello; Rigoletto; La Traviata; Il Trovatore. Requiem Mass: Sanctus.*
*** Decca Dig. 430 226-2; *430 226-4* [id.]. Chicago Symphony Ch. & SO, Solti.

The Solti collection is not drawn from the maestro's previous complete opera sets but is a first-class studio production, recorded in Orchestra Hall, Chicago, with Decca's most resplendent digital sound. The choral balance is forward, but there is plenty of depth too, and the wide dynamic range emphasizes, for instance, the dramatic contrast at the repeated cries of '*Gerusalem!*' from *I Lombardi* (a thrilling moment), while the gentle opening of *Va pensiero* from *Nabucco* (which was sung spontaneously by the crowds in the streets of Milan as Verdi's funeral cortège passed by) is beautifully focused. Solti is on top form. Besides the many exciting histrionic moments there are many refined touches too, notably in the stylish *La Traviata* excerpt, with soloists from the chorus, and the flashing fantasy of *Fuoco di gioia* from *Otello.* The Brigands in *I Masnadieri* sing of 'plunder, rape and arson' with great good humour, and the concert closes with the joyous *Sanctus* from the *Requiem* which, like the rest of the 70-minute programme, demonstrates the refined excellence of the Chicago Chorus, so splendidly prepared by their founder and director, Margaret Hillis. Full translations are included.

Choruses from: *Aida; La Battaglia di Legnano; Don Carlo; Ernani; La forza del destino; Macbeth; Nabucco; Otello; La Traviata; Il Trovatore.*
(BB) *** Naxos Dig. 8.550241 [id.]. Slovak Philharmonic Ch. & RSO, Oliver Dohnányi.

The super-bargain Naxos collection by the excellent Slovak Philharmonic Choir, trained by Marian Vach, brings very realistic sound and the slightly recessed choral balance in the Bratislava Radio Concert Hall is very natural: it certainly does not lack impact and, in the *Fire chorus* from Otello, detail registers admirably. Under Oliver Dohnányi's lively direction the chorus sings with admirable fervour. *Patria oppressa* from *Macbeth* is particularly stirring, and *Va, pensiero,* with a well-shaped line, is movingly projected. The *Soldiers' chorus* from *Il Trovatore* has a jaunty rhythmic feeling, the two novelties from *La Battaglia di Legnano* were well worth including: the second, *Giuramento,* includes four impressive male soloists. The collection ends resplendently with the Triumphal scene from *Aida,* omitting the ballet but with the fanfare trumpets blazing out on either side most tellingly. With a playing time of 56 minutes this is excellent value in every respect.

Victoria, Tomás Luis de (*c.* 1548–1611)

Ascendens Christus (motet); *Missa Ascendis Christus in altum; O Magnum mysterium* (motet); *Missa O Magnum mysterium.*
*** Hyp. Dig. CDA 66190; *KA 66190* [id.]. Westminster Cathedral Ch., David Hill.

Missa Ave maris stella; O quam gloriosum est regnum (motet); *Missa O quam gloriosum.*
❀ *** Hyp. CDA 66114; *KA 66114* [id.]. Westminster Cathedral Ch., David Hill.

The Latin fervour of the singing is very involving; some listeners may initially be surprised at the volatile way David Hill moves the music on, with the trebles eloquently soaring aloft on the line of the music. *Ave maris stella* is particularly fine, Hill's mastery of the overall structure producing a cumulative effect as the choir moves towards the magnificent closing *Agnus Dei.* On the companion disc the spirited presentation of the motet *Ascendens Christus in altum* prepares the way for a performance of the Mass that is similarly invigorating. The spontaneous ebb and flow of the pacing is at the heart of David Hill's understanding of this superb music. The recording balance is perfectly judged, with the Westminster acoustic adding resonance (in both senses of the word) to singing of the highest calibre, combining a sense of timelessness and mystery with real expressive power. Throughout, the choral line remains firm without clouding.

Ave Maria; Ave Maris stella (hymn). *Missa Vidi speciosam. Ne timeas, Maria; Sancta Maria, succurre miseris; Vidi speciosam* (motets).
*** Hyp. Dig. CDA 66129; *KA 66129* [id.]. Westminster Cathedral Ch., David Hill.

An outstanding collection of some of Victoria's most beautiful music celebrating the Virgin Mary. The four-part *Ave Maria* may not be authentic, but the composer would surely not be reluctant to own it; and the hymn *Ave maris stella* is also a memorable setting. *Vidi speciosam* derives from the Song of Songs and its secular language inspires a special kind of expressive radiance which could only come from a Latin composer. The Westminster Choir again show their flexibly volatile response to this music with that special amalgam of fervour and serenity that Victoria's writing demands. The acoustics of Westminster Cathedral add the right degree of resonance to the sound without clouding, and the choral textures are gloriously rich and yet refined too.

Magnificat primi toni; Misa and Motet: O quam gloriosum; Missa pro defunctis (Requiem for 6 voices).
(M) ** Decca 430 267-2 [id.]. St John's College, Cambridge, Ch., George Guest.

This CD draws together excerpts from a pair of Argo CDs made at St John's in 1967 and 1969. The Choir sing well in tune but their performances are a little variable. The *Magnificat primi toni* and the Mass with its paired motet, *O quam gloriosum* are generally well sung, if one accepts the fact that the choir lacks the harsh line drawn by the firmer-toned Spanish bodies. But the 1605 *Requiem* fares less well. The choirboys sound rather flabby in tone, while the men have big vibratos and these two elements never really mix. Good vivid sound, though not as smooth as some CD transfers from the Argo catalogue.

Officium defunctorum.
*** Gimell Dig. CDGIM 012; *1585T-12* [id.]. Tallis Scholars, Phillips (with LOBO: Motet: *Versa est in luctum* ***).
*** Hyp. Dig. CDA 66250; *KA 66250* [id.]. Westminster Cathedral Ch., David Hill.

Victoria's *Officium defunctorum* was his last publication; it comprises his *Requiem for six voices*, the Responsory *Libera me* and two motets. He spoke of it in his dedication as a swan-song, not in regard to his own composing but for the dedicatee – though in fact he died only six years later. It is a work of great serenity and beauty. Honours are fairly evenly divided between the Westminster Cathedral Choir on Hyperion and the Tallis Scholars under Peter Phillips. The Westminster Choir has the advantage of boys' voices and larger forces; they are recorded in a warmer, more spacious acoustic. By comparison with the Gimell recording, the sound seems a little less well focused, but on its own terms it is thoroughly convincing. They permit themselves greater expressiveness, too. Moreover the *Requiem* is set in the wider liturgical context by the use of some chants.

The Tallis Scholars achieve great clarity of texture; they are twelve in number and, as a result, the polyphony is clearer and so, too, are their words. The lines are slightly harder-etched, as indeed are those of Spanish choirs, and their intonation is always true. There are no chants but they offer a short and deeply felt motet by Alonso Lobo (*c.* 1555–1617). The recording has a warm, glowing sound which almost persuades you that you are in the imperial chapel.

Missa Surge propera; Stabat Mater.
(B) *** Pickwick Dig. PCD 970; *CIMPC 970* [id.]. Mixolydian, Piers Schmidt – PADILLA: *Missa Ego flos campi* etc. ***

Tomás Luis de Victoria was undoubtedly Spain's greatest Renaissance master, while Juan Gutierrez de Padilla is relatively little known or performed. Whatever Padilla's merits (and he is a musician of both substance and interest), this disc serves to underline Victoria's stature as a composer of rich, expressive feeling and a powerful musical mind. Listen to the *Agnus Dei* from the Mass *Surge propera* and you will have few doubts as to his stature or the quality of his invention. The *Missa Surge propera* is a five-voiced parody Mass, published in 1583, the only one of his works to be based on Palestrina. It is a beautiful work and is very well sung by Mixolydian under Piers Schmidt and recorded with exemplary skill.

Responsories for Tenebrae.
*** Hyp. Dig. CDA 66304; *KA 66304* [id.]. Westminster Cathedral Ch., David Hill.
** Gimell Dig CDGIM 022; *1385T-22* [id.]. Tallis Scholars, Peter Phillips.

The *Tenebrae Responses* are an essential element in any collection of Renaissance polyphony and they have been well represented on record over the years. Memories of George Malcolm's famous LP from the late 1950s are not dislodged by any of these newcomers. The Tallis Scholars sound absolutely perfect in both blend and intonation but are curiously uninvolving. They are beautifully recorded and technically immaculate but convey little real intensity of feeling. The Westminster Cathedral Choir under David Hill on Hyperion find far more atmosphere in this music and bring a sense of spontaneous feeling to their performance. Of recent versions, this can be welcomed without reservation.

Vierne, Louis (1870–1937)

Pièces en style libre, Op. 31/11, 14, 15, 19, 20, 21 & 24; Pièces de fantaisie, Op. 53/2 & 5; Op. 54/2.
*(**) Unicorn Dig. DKPCD 9064; *DKPC 9064* [id.]. Jennifer Bate (organ of Beauvais Cathedral).

Jennifer Bate makes a perceptive selection from Vierne's two sets of organ pieces, mixing popular items with others less familiar; and her playing is particularly appealing in the gentle numbers such as the *Berceuse*, Op. 31/19, and the *Arabesque*, Op. 31/15, which are registered with subtlety and charm. However, in the more complex pieces – the opening and very noisy *Carillon de Longpont*, for instance, or the fleeting *Scherzetto*, Op. 31, Nos. 21 and 14 respectively – her bravura is seriously muddied by the wide Beauvais reverberation.

Suite No. 3, Op. 54: Carillon de Westminster.
*** DG Dig. 413 438-2 [id.]. Simon Preston (organ of Westminster Abbey) – WIDOR: *Symphony No. 5.* ***

The Vierne *Carillon de Westminster* is splendidly played by Simon Preston and sounds appropriately atmospheric in this spacious acoustic and well-judged recording. It makes an attractive makeweight to the Widor *Fifth Symphony.*

Symphonies Nos. 1–4.
*** Erato Dig. 2292 45485-2 (2). Marie-Claire Alain (Cavaillé-Coll organ of the Abbey of St-Étienne de Caen).

Marie-Claire Alain is here in her element. In terms of registration, pacing and overall grip these performances are very authoritative indeed, and the Cavaillé-Coll organ at St-Étienne de Caen is perfectly suited to this repertoire. Its reedy colouring combined with plenty of underlying sonority in the pedals is especially effective in the *Final* movements, notably that for No. 1, although curiously the sound on the second CD (containing *Symphonies Nos. 1* and *3*) is slightly smoother and better balanced than on its companion.

Symphonies Nos. 1 in D min., Op. 14; 2 in E min., Op. 20.
*** Mer. CDE 84192 [id.]. David Sanger (organ of La Chiesa Italiana di San Pietro, London).

David Sanger's recordings of the Vierne *Organ symphonies* are highly rewarding and can be strongly recommended alongside those of Marie-Claire Alain on Erato. Indeed some listeners are likely to prefer the very appealing patina of the San Pietro organ.

The *D minor Symphony* dates from the turn of the century and was dedicated to Guilmant. Its sense of power and its quiet originality make it well worth having. The *Second* is a finely wrought piece, perhaps more concentrated than its predecessor. Both are played with much sympathy by David Sanger and the recording has excellent depth and range.

Symphonies Nos. 3 in F sharp min., Op. 28; 4 in G min., Op. 32.
*** Mer. CDE 84176; *KE 77176* [id.]. David Sanger (organ of La Chiesa Italiana di San Pietro, London).

In the *Third Symphony*, which is both technically and musically demanding, David Sanger again proves the equal of the challenge on this remarkably attractive organ. Though this is not generally as dark a work as the wartime *Fourth*, it is distinguished by moments of genuine depth. Sanger's feeling for colour in his choice of registration gives special pleasure, especially in the inner movements, the engaging *Intermezzo* from No. 3, for instance, or the equivalent in No. 4, a disarmingly simple minuet. There is no cause to complain of the sound quality, which maintains the high standards Meridian have set themselves: the resonance of the pedals is very telling without muddying the overall sound-picture.

Symphonies Nos. 5 in A min., Op. 47; 6 in B min., Op. 59.
*** Mer. CDE 84171; *KE 77171* [id.]. David Sanger (organ of La Chiesa Italiana di San Pietro, London).

David Sanger's No. 5 was originally coupled with the Op. 31 *Pièces en style libre*, but this CD offers the splendid *Sixth Symphony* instead. Sanger has genuine commitment to this repertoire and though he is playing an instrument somewhat removed from the Cavaillé-Coll sound-world – the effect is sweeter but not bland – he succeeds in conveying an authentic feeling. The recording is vivid and the impressive finales of both works are spectacular.

Vieuxtemps, Henri (1820–81)

Violin concerto No. 5 in A min., Op. 37.
*** DG Dig. 427 676-2 [id.]. Mintz, Israel PO, Mehta – LALO: *Symphonie espagnole;* SAINT-SAËNS: *Intro & Rondo capriccioso.* ***
*** Ph. Dig. 422 332-2 [id.]. Mullova, ASMF, Marriner – PAGANINI: *Concerto No. 1.* ***
*** BMG/RCA RD 86214 [RCA 6214-2-RC]. Heifetz, New SO of L., Sargent – BRUCH: *Concerto No. 1; Scottish fantasia.* ***

Minz's performance has enormous dash, and real lyrical magic too, both in the lovely secondary theme of the first movement and in his meltingly ethereal playing of the Grétry theme (from the opera, *Lucile*) which Vieuxtemps happily borrowed for the beautiful *Adagio*. Mehta, obviously caught up in the inspiration of the solo playing, provides an excellent accompaniment and this is another example of a a memorable live performance recorded 'on the wing'. It was made in the Mann Auditorium, Tel Aviv, and if the acoustic is not especially flattering, the sound is obviously truthful and well balanced.

Like her Paganini No. 1, Viktoria Mullova's account of the *A minor Concerto* is remarkable for its breathtaking virtuosity and its great fire and style. Sir Neville Marriner and the Academy are supportive and the Philips recording, though a bit bass-resonant, is first class and very vivid and present.

The quicksilver of Heifetz is well suited to the modest but attractive *Fifth Concerto* of Vieuxtemps, and Sir Malcolm provides a musical and well-recorded accompaniment. The balance of the soloist is rather close, but the digital remastering is successful and the couplings are both attractive and generous.

Villa-Lobos, Heitor (1887–1959)

Bachianas brasileiras Nos. 1–9; Chôros Nos. 2 (for flute & orchestra); *5* (for piano, Alma Brasileira); *10* (for chorus & orchestra); (i) *11* (for piano & orchestra). *2 Chôros (bis)* (for violin &

cello); (i) *Piano concerto No. 5; Descobrimento do Brasil; Invocação em defesa da Patria;* (i) *Momoprecoce* (fantasy for piano & orchestra); *Symphony No. 4. Qu'est-ce qu'un Chôros?* (Villa-Lobos speaking).
(M) (**(*)) EMI mono CZS7 67229-2 (6). De los Angeles, Kareska, Basrentzen, Braune, Tagliaferro, Du Frene, Plessier, Cliquennois, Bronschwak, Neilz, Benedetti; (i) Blumental; Chorale des Jeunesses Musicales de France, Fr. Nat. R. & TV Ch. & O, cond. composer.

From 1954, over the five years till he died, Villa-Lobos used his regular visits to Paris each spring to record his own works for Pathé-Marconi, the French branch of EMI. This six-CD box offers the fruits of those visits. It is a colourful, warm-hearted collection, not helped by dull mono recordings and ill-disciplined performances, but full of a passionately surging intensity that plainly reflects the personality of a composer of obvious charisma, if of limited ability as a conductor. Endearingly, there is a 10-minute track spoken in French by Villa-Lobos himself, 'What is a *Choros*?' – one of the musical forms he invented for himself. There are four examples of a *Choros* recorded here, including the ambitious *Choros No. 11*, a massive fantasia for piano and orchestra, at 65 minutes over twice as long as most of his regular piano concertos. The *Choros No. 10* is the most attractive, with wild jungle-noises at the end for the men in the chorus, set against a characteristically surging melody. The personal genre for which Villa-Lobos will obviously be remembered is the *Bachianas brasileiras*, relating his love for native Brazilian music to neo-classical Bachian forms, if often rather distantly. All nine of them are recorded here, including the celebrated No. 5 for soprano and eight cellos, with Victoria de los Angeles a radiant soloist. That recording is already well known, but most of the others have had very limited circulation. They make an enjoyable collection for, despite the dull sound, the warmth of the writing never fails to come over.

Bachianas Brasileiras Nos. (iii) *1;* (i; iii) *5;* (i; ii) *Suite for voice and violin.* (iii) arr. of BACH: *The Well-tempered clavier: Prelude in D min., BWV 583; Fugue in B flat, BWV 846; Prelude in G min., BWV 867; Fugue in D, BWV 874.*
*** Hyp. Dig. CDA 66257; *KA 66257* [id.]. (i) Jill Gomez, (ii) Peter Manning, (iii) Pleeth Cello Octet.

Jill Gomez is outstanding in the popular *Fifth Bachianas Brasileiras* and with the violinist, Peter Manning, in the *Suite* (1923). Villa-Lobos' favourite 'orchestra of cellos' produce sumptuous sounds in both the *Bachianas Brasileiras*, and an added point of interest is the effective transcriptions for cellos of unrelated Bach preludes and fugues. An eminently attractive introduction to this most colourful of composers.

Guitar concerto; 5 Preludes.
(M) *** BMG/RCA GD 86525; *GK 86525* [6525-2-RG]. Bream, LSO, Previn – RODRIGO: *Concierto.* ***

Bream's highly distinguished account of the *Guitar concerto* with Previn has now been reissued at mid-price, coupled with Rodrigo, an excellent idea.

Piano concertos Nos. 1–5.
**(*) Decca Dig. 430 628-2 (2)[id.]. Cristina Ortiz, RPO, Gómes-Martínez.

The first and most ambitious of Villa-Lobos's *Piano concertos* dates from 1945, written relatively late in his career, while the fifth and last was completed in 1954. No. 3 is the maverick: though it was begun in 1952, it was not completed until five years later, only two years before the composer died. In his note on the cycle Simon Wright, author of a new book on the composer, points out that the series began in the very year when Villa-Lobos started to travel the world after the Second World War. It was a period when the colourful, romantic piano concerto was even more in vogue than usual, and he enjoyed exploiting that. What emerges from the series, as played by Cristina Ortiz here, is that the first two are the most immediately identifiable as Brazilian in their warm colouring and sense of atmosphere, as in the wide-open-spaces music of the slow movement of No. 1, with its exotic textures. Those two are longer than the others and better sustained, even though the eclectic borrowings are often more unashamed than later, with many passages suggesting Rachmaninov with a Brazilian accent. Nos. 3, 4 and 5 – also in four movements each, like the first two, and contained on the second disc – then follow a very similar pattern. In each of them allegro outer movements frame a slow movement and scherzo with cadenza. No. 3, the work Villa-Lobos found it hard to complete, tends to sound bitty in its changes of direction. No. 4, more crisply conceived, has one or two splendid tunes, but it is in No. 5 that Villa-Lobos becomes most warmly convincing again, returning unashamedly to more echoes of Rachmaninov. With Ortiz articulating crisply, there is much to enjoy from such colourful, undemanding music, brilliantly recorded and sympathetically performed, if with a less than ideal thrust of conviction and power. It is a pity in the booklet that Wright was not given more space to analyse the five works separately, instead of treating the series as a whole.

Berceuse, Op. 50; Divigačao; O canto do capadócio; O canto do cisne negro; O canto do nossa terra; Sonhar, Op. 14.
** Marco Polo Dig. 8.223298 [id.]. Rebecca Rust, David Apter – ENESCU: *Cello sonata.* **

These pieces are all new to the catalogue and are well played and recorded, but they are a bonus for the Enescu *First Violin sonata*, some 37 minutes long, which may not hold the attention of all listeners to the last bar!

PIANO MUSIC

Alma brasileira, Bachiana brasileira No. 4; Ciclo brasileiro; Chôros No. 5; Valsa da dor (Waltz of sorrows).
*** ASV Dig. CDDCA 607; *ZCDCA 607* [id.]. Alma Petchersky.

Alma Petchersky is a refined player who produces a wide range of colour and tone, and her articulation is eminently clean. Villa-Lobos's piano music is not generously represented on CD at present, but this issue is as good as any. The sound is very well focused, though there could have been a little more space round the instrument. Alma Petchersky's style is more romantic than that of Cristina Ortiz, and some might find her thoughtful deliberation in the *Preludio* of the *Bachianas Brasileira No. 4* overdone. Her very free rubato is immediately apparent in the *Valsa da dor* which opens the recital. Yet she clearly feels all this music deeply, and the playing is strong in personality and – with fuller piano than on the Decca collection – her timbre is often richly coloured. She is at her finest in the *Brazilian cycle.* The recording is first class, with more body and resonance than in the Decca collection.

As três Maria; Bachianas Brasileiras No. 4; Caixinha de música quebrada; Ciclo Brasileiro; Cirandas Nos. 4 & 14; Cuia prático; Poema singelo; Saudades das selvas Brasileiras No. 2; Valsa da dor.
*** Decca Dig. 417 650-2 [id.]. Cristina Ortiz.

Cristina Ortiz, herself Brazilian, is a natural choice for this repertoire. Her anthology embraces the piano version of the *Bachianas Brasileiras No. 4* and a well-chosen collection of other pieces, the main work on her well-filled disc being the *Ciclo Brasileiro.* She has a good ear for sonority and her phrasing is subtle and sensitive. The piano sound is clean and bright.

VOCAL MUSIC

Bachianas Brasileiras No. 5 for soprano and cellos.
*** Decca Dig. 411 730-2 [id.]. Te Kanawa, Harrell and instrumental ens. – CANTELOUBE: *Songs of the Auvergne.* **(*)
(M) *** BMG/RCA GD 87831 [7831-2-RG]. Anna Moffo, American SO, Stokowski – CANTELOUBE: *Chants d'Auvergne;* RACHMANINOV: *Vocalise.* ***

The Villa-Lobos piece makes an apt fill-up for the Canteloube songs completing Kiri Te Kanawa's recording of all five books. It is, if anything, even more sensuously done, well sustained at a speed far slower than one would normally expect. Rich recording to match.

Anna Moffo gives a seductive performance of the most famous of the *Bachianas Brasileiras*, adopting a highly romantic style (matching the conductor) and warm tone-colour.

Magdalena.
*** Sony Dig. SK 44945 [id.]. Kaye, Rose, Esham, Gray, Hadley, O, Evans Haile.

Until this disc appeared, not many remembered that Villa-Lobos had written a Broadway musical. The promoters of *Song of Norway*, the musical based on Grieg's music, wanted to follow it up with a comparable one on South America, as being 'as far from the fjords of Norway as an author could possibly get'. They thought to use the music of Villa-Lobos, but the composer, much to everyone's surprise, took control of the project, to make it his own, rather than anyone else's, score. It is a colourful, vigorous piece, alas lacking the big tunes you really need in a musical, but full of delightful ideas. It tells the sort of story that Lehár might have chosen, only translated to South America. Sadly, in spite of an enthusiastic response from everyone, it closed on Broadway in 1948 after only eleven weeks. The present recording was prompted by a concert performance to celebrate the Villa-Lobos centenary, a splendid, well-sung account of what is aptly described as 'a musical adventure'.

Viotti, Giovanni Battista (1755–1824)

Violin concerto No. 13 in A.
*** Hyp. Dig. CDA 66210; *KA 66210* [id.]. Oprean, European Community CO, Faerber – FIORILLO: *Violin concerto No. 1.* ***

Viotti wrote a great many violin concertos in much the same mould, but this is one of his best. Its first movement has agreeable facility; the charming central *Andante* is more ambitious than that in the coupled Fiorillo *Concerto*, and the jaunty rondo/polonaise finale is quite infectious, having much in common with a Paganini finale. Adelina Oprean's quicksilver style and light lyrical touch give much pleasure – she has the exact measure of this repertoire and she is splendidly accompanied and well recorded. The measure, though, is short.

Vivaldi, Antonio (1675–1741)

L'Estro armonico (12 Concertos), Op. 3.
*** DG Dig. 423 094-2 (2) [id.]. Standage & soloists, E. Concert, Trevor Pinnock.
*** O-L 414 554-2 (2) [id.]. Holloway, Huggett, Mackintosh, Wilcock, AAM, Hogwood.
(M) *** Decca 430 557-2 (2) [id.]. ASMF, Sir Neville Marriner.
(M) **(*) DG 435 599-2 (2) [id.]. Spierer, Brandis, BPO (members).

Vivaldi's *L'Estro armonico* was published in 1711. The set includes some of his finest music and had great influence. This new chamber version from Pinnock (with one instrument to a part) seems instinctively to summarize and amalgamate the best features from past versions: there is as much sparkle and liveliness as with Hogwood, for rhythms are consistently resilient, ensemble crisp and vigorous. Yet in slow movements there is that expressive radiance and sense of enjoyment of beauty without unstylish indulgence that one expects from the ASMF. The only aspect that one might cavil at is the use of harpsichord continuo throughout (Hogwood uses organ as well; Marriner additionally featured the lute). However, this is a small point; everything else here gives delight, not least the sound itself, which is totally free from vinegar. The recording was made in EMI's Abbey Road studios and the balance and ambient effect are judged perfectly: there is bloom and internal clarity and a realistic but not exaggerated sense of presence.

There is no question about the sparkle of Christopher Hogwood's performance with the Academy of Ancient Music. The captivating lightness of the solo playing and the crispness of articulation of the accompanying group bring music-making that combines joyful vitality with the authority of scholarship. Textures are always transparent, but there is no lack of body to the ripieno (even though there is only one instrument to each part). Hogwood's continuo is first class, varying between harpsichord and organ, the latter used to add colour as well as substance. The balance is excellent, and the whole effect is exhilarating. The extra range that the compact disc can encompass helps to give the aural image the impression of greater definition.

For those wanting a performance using modern instruments, the ASMF provide a ready answer together with the advantage of economy. As so often, Marriner directs the Academy in radiant and imaginative performances. The delightful use of continuo – lute and organ as well as harpsichord – the sharing of solo honours and the consistently resilient string-playing of the ensemble make for compelling listening. The early 1970s' (originally Argo) recording is superb, rich in timbre, yet with excellent detail and presence.

The Berlin Philharmonic set is also unexpectedly stimulating. The first-class recording, made in the Berlin Jesus Christus Kirche in 1978/9, has been splendidly transferred to CD and the string sounds are gleamingly resilient. The playing is both responsive – often touching – and superbly polished without being glossy. Rhythms are firm (some might feel a shade too firm at times) and slow-movement cantilenas expressively shaped. The players are clearly responding strongly to the music. But this remains a German view. The continuo lacks creative importance and there is a recurring impression that one is listening to Telemann rather than Vivaldi.

L'Estro armonico (12 Concertos), Op. 3.
(M) *** Ph. 426 932-2 (2) [id.]. Michelucci, Gallozzi, Cotogni, Vicari, Colandrea, Altobelli, Garatti, I Musici.

La Stravaganza (12 Concertos), Op. 4.
(M) *** Ph. 426 935-2 (2) [id.]. Ayo, Gallozzi, Altobelli, Garatti, I Musici.

These Philips reissues draw on recordings made (mostly in the highly suitable acoustics of La Chaux-de-Fonds, Switzerland) in 1962/3. The transfers to CD are admirable. These are refreshing and lively performances; melodies are finely drawn and there is little hint of the routine which occasionally surfaces in I Musici – and, for that matter, in Vivaldi himself. Maria Teresa Garatti's continuo features a chamber organ as well as harpsichord in Op. 4, to excellent effect.

La Stravaganza, Op. 4 (complete).
❀ (M) *** Decca 430 566-2 (2) [id.]. ASMF, Sir Neville Marriner.
*** O-L Dig. 417 502-2 (2) [id.]. Huggett, AAM, Hogwood.
** Ph. Dig. 426 280-2 (2) [id.]. Agostini, I Musici.

It has been held that, like *La Cetra, La Stravaganza* does not match the invention of *L'Estro armonico*; but Marriner's performances make the music irresistible. The solo playing of Carmel Kaine and Alan Loveday is superb and, when the Academy's rhythms have such splendid buoyancy and lift, it is easy enough to accept Marriner's preference for a relatively sweet style in the often heavenly slow movements. As usual, the contribution of an imaginatively varied continuo (which includes cello and bassoon, in addition to harpsichord, theorbo and organ) adds much to the colour of Vivaldi's score. The recording, made in St John's, Smith Square, in 1973/4, is of the very highest quality and the CD transfers are in the demonstration class.

Five of the concertos of Op. 4 look, not to the concerto grosso form of Corelli, but to the true solo concerto form of Torelli and Albinoni, which Vivaldi himself presaged in *L'Estro armonico.* Monica Huggett brings not only virtuosity but also considerable warmth to the solo concertos, and the Academy of Ancient Music are both spirited and sensitive. Those who think of Vivaldi's music as predictable will find much to surprise them in *La Stravaganza*; his invention is unflagging and of high quality. Strongly recommended.

I Musici bring their characteristic sonority and fine musicianship to these concertos, and the digital recording is warm and natural. But alongside Marriner the effect is bland.

6 Violin concertos, Op. 6.
(M) **(*) Ph. 426 939-2 [id.]. Pina Carmirelli, I Musici.

These concertos are not otherwise available and, while their invention is more uneven than in the named sets, their rarity will undoubtedly tempt keen Vivaldians. The 1977 performances, with Pina Carmirelli a stylish and responsive soloist, are polished and with well-judged tempi, if with no special imaginative flair. Excellent sound.

12 Concertos (for violin or oboe), Op. 7.
(M) *** Ph. 426 940-2 (2) [id.]. Accardo or Holliger (Opp. 7/1 & 7), I Musici.

The Op. 7 set is relatively unfamiliar and is certainly rewarding. The playing of Accardo and Holliger is altogether masterly, and they have fine rapport with their fellow musicians in I Musici. The 1975 sound-balance is first class (the acoustically sympathetic venue is La Chaux-de-Fonds, Switzerland) and the two CDs are economically priced. This is among the most desirable of the boxes in the Philips Vivaldi Edition.

The Trial between harmony and invention (12 Concertos), Op. 8.
(M) **(*) Ph. 426 943-2 (2) [id.]. Felix Ayo, Garatti, I Musici.
**(*) O-L Dig. 417 515-2 (2) [id.]. Bury, Hirons, Holloway, Huggett, Mackintosh, Piguet, AAM, Hogwood.
(M) **(*) Sony M2YK 46465 (2) [id.]. Pinchas Zuckerman, Neil Black, ECO, Philip Ledger.

The first four concertos of Op. 8 are a set within a set, forming what is (understandably) Vivaldi's most popular work, *The Four Seasons.* Their imaginative power and their eloquence and tunefulness tend to dwarf the remaining eight concertos, but there is some splendid music throughout the complete work, well worth exploring.

Op. 8 is available in comparative abundance, and Ayo's *Four Seasons* (which are the first four concertos of the set) date from as early as 1959. The recording still sounds well, though, with the warm, resonant sound disguising its age. Ayo produces lovely tone throughout and he plays as stylishly as ever, but the accompaniment is short on imaginative detail. At times the ensemble is a shade heavy-handed in the remaining concertos; but Ayo's contribution has both polish and vitality, and there is still a great deal to enjoy in these performances. The later concertos were recorded in 1961/2 and are transferred vividly.

There is no want of zest in the Academy of Ancient Music's accounts of Op. 8. These are likeable and, generally speaking, well-prepared versions and differ from some rivals in choosing the oboe in two of the concertos, where Vivaldi has indicated an option. There are moments where more polish would not have come amiss, and intonation is not above reproach either. However, admirers of the Academy will find much to enjoy here – as, indeed, will those who are not always in tune with period-instrument performances. In *The Four Seasons*, Pinnock is not displaced, however. The recordings are well up to standard and are given fine presence, complete on a pair of CDs.

Zuckerman's solo playing is distinguished throughout, and the ECO provide unfailingly alert and resilient accompaniments. In *Concerto No. 9 in D min.* oboist Neil Black takes the solo position and provides a welcome contrast of timbre – Vivaldi designed this concerto as optionally for violin or oboe, but it probably sounds more effective on the wind instrument. The recording throughout is lively, with a close balance for the soloists. The sound is attractive on CD and does not lack fullness.

The Four Seasons, Op. 8/1–4.
*** Virgin Dig. VCy 791081-2; *VCy 791081-4* [id.]. Christopher Warren-Green with LCO – ALBINONI: *Adagio;* PACHELBEL: *Canon.* ***
*** ASV Dig. CDDCA 579; *ZCDCA 579* [id.]. José Luis Garcia, ECO (with HANDEL: *Water music: suite No. 1 in F* ***).
**(*) Argo 414 486-2 [id.]. Alan Loveday, ASMF, Marriner.
**(*) DG Dig. 400 045-2 [id.]. Simon Standage, E. Concert, Pinnock.
**(*) BIS Dig. CD 275 [id.]. Nils-Erik Sparf, Drottningholm Bar. Ens.
**(*) EMI Dig. CDC7 49557-2 [id.]. Nigel Kennedy, ECO.
**(*) DG Dig. 419 214-2 [id.]. Stern, Zukerman, Mintz, Perlman, Israel PO, Mehta.
(B) **(*) Pickwick Dig. PCD 800; *CIMPC 800* [id.]. Jaime Laredo, SCO.
**(*) Ph. Dig. 410 001-2 [id.]. Pina Carmirelli, I Musici.
**(*) O-L Dig. 410 126-2 [id.]. Hirons, Holloway, Bury, Mackintosh, AAM, Hogwood.
(M) *** DG 431 479-2; *431 479-4.* Schneiderhan, Lucerne Festival Strings, Baumgartner (with ALBINONI: *Adagio;* PACHELBEL: *Canon & Gigue;* PURCELL: *Chacony;* BACH: *Suite No. 3, BWV 1068: Air* ***).
(M) **(*) DG 431 172-2; *431 172-4.* Gidon Kremer, LSO, Abbado.
(M) **(*) Decca 417 712-2; *417 712-4* [id.]. Konstanty Kulka, Stuttgart CO, Münchinger – ALBINONI: *Adagio* ***; PACHELBEL: *Canon.* ***

The Four Seasons, Op. 8/1–4 (with sonnets in Italian and English).
*** Helios/Hyp. CDH 88012; *KH 88012* [id.]. Bruni, Edwards (readers), Adelina Oprean, European Community CO, Faeber.

The Four Seasons, Op. 8/1–4; L'Estro armonico: Concertos in A min.; in D, Op. 3/6 & 9.
(B) *** Ph. 422 479-2; *422 479-4.* Henryk Szeryng, ECO.

(i) *The Four Seasons, Op. 8/1–4;* (ii) *Violin concertos: L'Estro armonico: in A min., Op. 3/6. La Stravaganza: in A, Op. 4/5. Concerto in C min. (Il sospetto), RV 199.*
(M) *** EMI CDM7 64333-2; *EG 764333-4.* Perlman, (i) LPO; (ii) Israel PO.

(i) *The Four Seasons, Op. 8/1–4;* (ii) *L'Estro armonico: Double violin concerto in A min., Op. 3/8;* (iii) *Double trumpet concerto in C, RV 537.*
(BB) *** Virgin/Virgo Dig. VJ7 91463-2; *VJ7 91463-4* [id.]. (i) Andrew Watkinson, (ii) with Nicholas Ward; (iii) Crispian Steele-Perkins, Michael Meeks; City of L. Sinfonia, Watkinson.

The Four Seasons, Op. 8/1–4; La Stravazanza: Concerto in A min., Op. 4/4. Concerto in E min., RV 278.
*** BMG/RCA Dig. RD 60369; *RK 60369* [60369-2-RC; *60369-4-RC*]. Vladimir Spivakov, Moscow Virtuosi.

(i) *The Four Seasons; Concerto funèbre; Concerto per l'orchestra di Dresda; Concerto per la Solennità di San Lorenzo.*

**(*) Decca Dig. 430 697-2; *430 697-4* [id.]. (i) Franco Gulli; I Filarmonici de Teatro Comunale di Bologna, Chailly.

The Four Seasons, Op. 8/1–4; Concerto in G min. per l'orchestra di Dresda, RV 577.
*** Ph. Dig. 420 216-2; *420 216-4* [id.]. Viktoria Mullova, COE, Abbado.

The Four Seasons, Op. 8/1–4; Triple violin concerto in F, RV 551; Quadruple violin concerto in B min., RV 580.
❀ *** Ph. Dig. 422 065-2; *422 065-4* [id.]. Accardo and soloists with CO.

(i) *The Four Seasons;* (ii) *Flute concertos, Op. 10/1–3.*
(M) *** BMG/RCA GD 86553. (i) La Petite Bande, Kuijken; (ii) Brüggen, O of 18th Century.

There are almost countless recordings of Vivaldi's *Four Seasons* and it seems to us that those versions offered without fill-ups in a crowded marketplace have become less competitive. However, Salvatore Accardo's is a version with a difference. Recorded in live performances at the 1987 Cremona Festival, it is of particular interest in that Accardo uses a different Stradivarius for each of the four concertos – period instruments with a difference! Thanks to this aristocrat of violinists, the sounds are of exceptional beauty, both here and also in the two multiple concertos which are added as a bonus. The performances are much enhanced, too, by the imaginative continuo playing of Bruno Canino. The recording itself is a model of fidelity and has plenty of warmth; it must rank very high in the Vivaldi discography.

Christopher Warren-Green makes a brilliantly charismatic soloist, with the re-formed London Chamber Orchestra providing delectably pointed bird-imitations in *Spring* and *Summer*. Tempi of allegros are very brisk, but the effect is tinglingly exhilarating when the soloist's bravura is so readily matched by the accompanying ensemble. Certainly this account of Vivaldi's *Four Seasons* is memorable, and its sheer brio is impossible to resist. Slow movements offer the widest contrast, with delicate textures and subtle use of the continuo, as in *Winter* where Leslie Pearson makes a delightful surprise contribution to the finale, having already embroidered the opening allegro and prevented it from being too chilly. Needless to say, the storms approach gale force, while the peasants are hardly less rumbustious, enjoying their autumn hunting and bacchanal. The recording, made in All Saints' Church, Wallington, has plenty of ambient fullness but remains bright and fresh. With its equally attractive couplings, this can be recommended to those who like their Vivaldi to be dashing and vital, and yet imaginatively pictorial at the same time.

On the bargain Virgo label Andrew Watkinson directs the City of London Sinfonia from the solo violin in one of the very finest versions available of Vivaldi's *Four Seasons*, superbly played and beautifully recorded with clean, forward sound. Anyone wanting a version on modern instruments cannot do better than this, with fresh, resilient playing in allegros, reflecting lessons learnt from period performance, and with sweet, unsentimental expressiveness in slow movements. The two double concertos provide a valuable makeweight, though the orchestra is more backwardly balanced in the *Concerto for two trumpets*. The documentation is poor.

The ASV version of *The Four Seasons*, with José Luis Garcia as soloist and musical director, was chosen on BBC Radio 3 as ideal for 'Building a Record Library'. That was before many of the current versions listed above made their appearance, but one can understand the reasons for its choice. The recording acoustic (All Hallows Church, London) is particularly pleasing, with the violins of the accompanying group sweetly fresh and the soloist nicely balanced. The overall pacing is beautifully judged, and each movement takes its place naturally and spontaneously in relation to its companions. The effects are well made, but there are no histrionics and, although the continuo does not always come through strongly, the unnamed player makes a useful contribution to a performance that is very easy to live with. The one drawback to this issue is that there is only one track for each of the *Four Seasons*. However, there is an attractive Handel bonus.

Marriner's 1970 Academy of St Martin-in-the-Fields version with Alan Loveday still remains near the top of the list of recommended compact discs. It was made during a vintage Argo recording period and the digital remastering has been completely successful, retaining the fullness and bloom of the original, besides slightly refining its inner detail. The performance is as satisfying as ever, and will surely delight all but those who are ruled by the creed of authenticity. It has an element of fantasy that makes the music sound utterly new; it is full of imaginative touches, with Simon Preston subtly varying the continuo between harpsichord and organ. The opulence of string tone may have a romantic connotation, but there is no self-indulgence in the interpretation, no sentimentality, for the contrasts are made sharper and fresher, not smoothed over. But without any coupling this now calls for reissue on a lower-priced label.

The Archiv version by Simon Standage with the English Concert, directed from the harpsichord by Trevor Pinnock, has the advantage of using a newly discovered set of parts found in Manchester's Henry Watson Music Library – which has additionally brought the correction of minor textual errors in the Le Cène text in normal use. The Archiv performance also (minimally) introduces a second soloist and is played on period instruments. The players create a relatively intimate sound, though their approach is certainly not without drama, while the solo contribution has impressive flair and bravura. The overall effect is essentially refined, treating the pictorial imagery with subtlety. The result is less voluptuous than with Marriner and less vibrant than Christopher Warren-Green, but it finds a natural balance between vivid projection and atmospheric feeling. The digital recording is first class. Authenticists should be well satisfied.

The BIS recording by Nils-Erik Sparf and the Drottningholm Baroque Ensemble is in a rather special category. As a recording, it has astonishing clarity and presence; and as playing, it is hardly less remarkable in its imaginative vitality. These Swedish players make the most of all the pictorial characterization without ever overdoing anything: they achieve the feat of making one hear this eminently familiar repertoire as if for the very first time.

Perlman's finesse as a great violinist is evident from first to last. Though some will demand more reticence in baroque concertos, Perlman's imagination holds the sequence together superbly, and there are many passages of pure magic, as in the central *Adagio* of *Summer*. The digital remastering of the 1976 recording is managed admirably, the sound firm, clear and well balanced, with plenty of detail. Now this record has been made much more competitive by the addition of three extra violin concertos, all fine works. Perlman scales down the virtuoso display, and those who enjoy sweet, modern solo string timbre and warmth in slow movements will find these performances a very agreeable bonus. Although the acoustic is somewhat dryish, this does not prevent these extra works from sounding very good. Their recording is digital, and this brings a trace of hardness in tuttis.

Viktoria Mullova's Philips record with the Chamber Orchestra of Europe under Claudio Abbado is well worth considering. As one would expect, she is vibrant and vital in the outer movements and imaginative and eloquent in the slow movements. She is given excellent support by Abbado and his players, and the recording, as always from this source, is very well balanced. There is a bonus in the form of the *G minor concerto*, RV 577, one of two Vivaldi composed for Dresden, whose orchestra boasted a strong wind department.

Vladimir Spivakov's highly enjoyable account of Vivaldi's *Four seasons* is made the more attractive by opening with two of Vivaldi's most imaginative concertos. The *E minor* begins with swirling strings, yet there is an immediately tender response, to make a movement of striking contrasts, while the *Largo*, with its plangent orchestral ritornello, delays the entry of the soloist until almost half-way through. The *A minor* (from *La Stravaganza*) brings a delectable central movement, where the soloist is accompanied very simply by a wistful texture of violins and violas. Both are very well played indeed by soloist and orchestra alike, as is the more famous main work, given an essentially chamber-style account, yet one not lacking its robust moments. Characterization is strong, and Spivakov's sweet, classically focused timbre is particularly melting in the sleepy sentience of the gentle episode of the first movement of *Autumn* and in the beguiling somnambulance of the central *Adagio*. *Winter* opens in a suitably frosty style, and the rain falls in the *Largo* with a gentle, soft quality that any Irishman would recognize. There is plenty of vigour for the summer storms and *Spring* is tinglingly fresh, with its central movement played with contrasting gentle delicacy. Altogether this is highly successful, with the vivid, well-balanced recording achieving excellent presence against the background ambience of L'Église du Liban, Paris.

The novelty of the Helios issue is the inclusion of the sonnets which Vivaldi placed on his score to give his listeners a guide to the illustrative detail suggested by the music. Before each of the four concertos, the appropriate poem is read, first in a romantically effusive Italian manner and then in BBC English (the contrast quite striking). On CD, of course, one can programme out these introductions; one would hardly want to hear them as often as the concertos. The performances are first class, full of energy and with wide dynamic contrasts used to increase the drama. The difference between the gently inebriated, somnolent peasants in the slow movement of *Autumn* and the hunting music of the finale is very striking; while similarly the opening of *Winter* is *sotto voce*, leaving room for later expansion. Adelina Oprean is an excellent soloist, her reading full of youthful energy and expressive freshness; her timbre is clean and pure, her technique assured. Faeber matches her vitality, and the score's pictorial effects are boldly characterized in a vividly projected sound-picture. The sound is first rate: the violins of the accompanying group have the right Italianate gleam.

On RCA, La Petite Bande (soloist unnamed, but presumably Kuijken) offer an authentic version of considerable appeal. Although the accompanying group can generate plenty of energy when Vivaldi's winds are blowing, this is essentially a small-scale reading, notable for its delicacy. But this issue offers not just the four concertos of Op. 8 but also three favourite *Flute concertos* from Op. 10: *Tempesta di mare*, *La notte* and *Il gardinello*. With the master-instrumentalist, Frans Brüggen, playing a period instrument and directing the Orchestra of the 18th Century, the excellence of these performances, vividly recorded, can be taken for granted.

Kennedy's account is certainly among the more spectacular in conveying its picaresque imagery; only *Autumn* brings a degree of real controversy, however, with weird special effects, including glissando harmonics in the slow movement and percussive applications of the wooden part of the bow to add rhythmic pungency to the hunting finale. There is plenty of vivid detail elsewhere. The continuo includes lute (delicately evocative in the slow movement of *Spring*) as well as harpsichord; the overall balance places everything in reasonable perspective, within the flattering ambience of the Church of St John-at-Hackney, in East London. The ECO's playing is always responsive, to match the often very exciting bravura of its soloist, and allegros have an agreeable vitality. However, at 41 minutes, with no fillers, this is not generous and it would not be our first choice for repeated listening.

The recording made under Mehta at the 1982 Huberman Festival in Tel Aviv took the opportunity offered by a stellar gathering of fiddlers to give each of the four concertos to a different soloist. The result is an unqualified success, with each artist revelling in writing that offers equal opportunities for bravura and espressivo playing, plus a chance for the imagination to find a similar balance between the musical and pictorial aspects of Vivaldi's remarkable conception. Again, however, no other music is offered.

The Philips digital recording with Pina Carmirelli is the third out of the four made in stereo by I Musici, and it is undoubtedly the finest of all. Musical values as ever are paramount; this time, however, there is more vitality and the programmatic implications are more strikingly realized (indeed, the bark of the shepherd's dog in *Spring* is singularly insistent). Yet Carmirelli's expressive playing maintains the lyrical feeling and beauty of tone for which I Musici versions are remembered and combines it with attractively alert and nimble bravura in the allegros. The gentle breezes are caught as effectively as the summer storms, and the slow movement of *Autumn* (helped by especially atmospheric recording) makes an elegiac contrast. The opening of *Winter* is certainly chilly. The recording is outstandingly natural.

The newest digital Decca version from Chailly with an assured and highly musical soloist in Franco Gulli, has the advantage of top-drawer sound, and brings performances that are warmly animated and well characterized (without exaggeration), using modern instruments to pleasing effect. The Bologna Philharmonic accompanies spiritedly, if without the very last degree of polish. Curiously, *The Four Seasons* start at band 8 of the CD, and the programme opens with the three other works, as imaginative as anything in the vast Vivaldi repertory. They are very well played too. Enjoyable though this is, it cannot however rise to the very top of a crowded list.

Jaime Laredo's performance has great spontaneity and vitality, emphasized by the forward balance which is nevertheless admirably truthful. The bright upper range is balanced by a firm, resonant bass. Laredo plays with bravura and directs polished, strongly characterized accompaniments. Pacing tends to be on the fast side; although the reading is extrovert and the lyrical music – played responsively – is made to offer a series of interludes to the vigour of the allegros, the effect is exhilarating rather than aggressive. However, there is no extra music.

With a different soloist for each of the four concertos, Hogwood directs the Academy of Ancient Music in lively performances with exceptionally imaginative use of continuo contrasts, guitar with harpsichord in *Spring* and *Autumn*, lute and chamber organ in *Summer* and *Winter*. These performances have a high place among authentic versions, a shade more abrasive than most; however, they cannot quite match the subtly responsive approach of Trevor Pinnock's Archiv set with the English Concert. The CD has striking presence – a state-of-the-art transfer.

Schneiderhan's 1959 version of *The Four Seasons* re-emerges, as fresh as paint, now well buttressed by Pachelbel's *Canon*, Purcell's *Chacony* and the famous Bach *Air* all sounding serenely spacious, while the Albinoni/Giazotto *Adagio* also has a certain refined dignity. These 1966/7 recordings are pleasingly warm and full, yet not too opulent. The *Four Seasons*, too, have a firmer focus than before, and Schneiderhan's timbre, pure and sweetly classical, suits Vivaldi very well indeed. The aptly chamber-scaled performance, with brisk tempi and alert orchestral playing, is full of life, with the pictorial detail emerging naturally but without being overcharacterized.

Kremer's version of *The Four Seasons* with Abbado is an enormously vital one, full of pictorial drama. The summer storms have never raged with more fury than here, yet the delicacy of the gentle zephyrs is matched by the sensuous somnolence of the slow movement of *Autumn*. The brilliant recording suits the music-making, but this version has no fill-up.

Another first-rate bargain version comes from Szeryng, and the only reservation is that the very soft-grained tone of the harpsichord in the continuo does not come through readily because of the reverberation; the chamber proportions of the recording are retained however, and the digital remastering has improved definition. As a bonus, Szeryng offers two concertos from Op. 3, also played immaculately.

On Decca, Kulka gives a first-class solo performance, while Münchinger and the Stuttgart Chamber Orchestra, whose early LPs did so much to reawaken interest in Vivaldi, bring a stylish and lively manner to the accompaniments. This was always a strong recommendation in the mid-price range but, with digital remastering, the brightly lit recording has become vivid to the point of astringency in its CD format, and the ear is drawn to this when the bonus items sound much mellower.

The Four Seasons, Op. 8/1–4 (arr. for flute and strings).
(M) *** BMG/RCA GD 60748; *GK 60748* [60748-2-RG; *60748-4-RG*]. James Galway, Zagreb Soloists.

James Galway's transcription is thoroughly musical and so convincing that at times one is tempted to believe that the work was conceived in this form. The playing itself is marvellous, full of detail and imagination, and the recording is excellent, even if the flute is given a forward balance, the more striking on CD.

(i) *The Trial between harmony and invention, Op. 8: Violin concertos Nos. 5 in E flat (La tempesta di mare); 6 in C (Il piacere), Op. 8/5–6;* (ii) *Bassoon concertos: in C, RV 472; in C min., RV 480; in A min., RV 498; in B flat, RV 504.*
(M) *** Chan. CHAN 6529; *MBTD 6529* [id.]. (i) Ronald Thomas, Bournemouth Sinf.; (ii) Robert Thompson, L. Mozart Players, Ledger.

The two concertos included here from *The Trial between harmony and invention* were among the best of the complete set recorded by Ronald Thomas in 1980. The use of modern instruments does not preclude a keen sense of style, and the balance is convincing. The bassoonist Robert Thompson turns a genial eye on his four concertos. He is rather forwardly projected but the performances are direct and personable and, like the sound, agreeably fresh, among the most attractive accounts of Vivaldi's bassoon concertos available on CD. An enjoyable collection.

La Cetra (12 Violin concertos), Op. 9.
*** O-L Dig. 421 366-2 (2) [id.]. Standage, AAM, Hogwood.
(M) **(*) Ph. 426 946-2 (2) [id.]. Ayo, Cotogni (in Op. 9/9), Altobelli, Garatti, I Musici.

La Cetra (The Lyre) was the last set of violin concertos Vivaldi published. Simon Standage gives an attractive and fluent account of the set, and the recording is excellent, slightly dry but very clean.

I Musici's *La Cetra* dates from 1964 and is again recorded at La Chaux-de-Fonds, which ensures a realistic and pleasing sound-balance. With Felix Ayo the principal soloist, the playing is spirited, characterful and expressively rich, though the overall effect is less individual than in the finest versions from the past. One drawback is that solo passages are given no continuo support, though Maria Teresa Garatti provides an organ continuo for the ripieno. Overall this is good value at mid-price.

6 Flute concertos, Op. 10.
*** DG Dig. 423 702-2 [id.]. Liza Beznosiuk, E. Concert, Pinnock.
*** O-L 414 685-2 [id.]. Stephen Preston, AAM.
*** Ph. 412 874-2 [id.]. Michala Petri, ASMF, Marriner.
(M) *** Ph. 422 260-2; *422 260-4*. Gazzelloni, I Musici.
(M) *** Ph. 426 949-2 [id.]. Gazzelloni, I Musici.
(B) *** Pickwick Dig. PCD 961; *CIMPC 961* [id.]. Judith Hall, Divertimenti of L., Paul Barritt.

There is some expressive as well as brilliant playing on the DG Archiv CD, which should delight listeners. Try track 8 (the *Largo* movement of *Concerto No. 2 in G minor, La Notte*) for an example of the beautifully refined and cool pianissimo tone that Liza Beznosiuk can produce – and almost any of the fast movements for an example of her virtuosity. Her playing in *Il gardellino* is a delight, and Trevor Pinnock and the English Concert provide unfailingly vital and, above all, imaginative support. The DG recording is exemplary in its clarity. Recommended with enthusiasm: this goes to the top of the list.

Stephen Preston also plays a period instrument, a Schuchart, and the Academy of Ancient Music likewise play old instruments. Their playing is eminently stylish, but also spirited and expressive, and they are admirably recorded, with the analogue sound enhanced further in the CD format.

Michala Petri uses a modern recorder and plays with breathtaking virtuosity and impeccable control, and she has the advantage of superb recording. In the slow movements – and occasionally elsewhere – there is more in the music than she finds, but the sheer virtuosity of this gifted artist is most infectious. She uses a sopranino recorder in three of the concertos.

Severino Gazzelloni's version of the six *Concertos*, Op. 10, has been in circulation throughout the 1970s and its merits are well established; it is a safer recommendation for the general collector than the authentic rivals, good though the best of these is.

Judith Hall's record of the Op. 10 *Flute concertos* is fresh and brightly recorded. She plays with considerable virtuosity and a great deal of taste. The Divertimento of London is a modern-instrument group and the players are both sensitive and alert. The recording is so clean and forward that one would at times welcome greater atmosphere. But there's plenty of sensitivity and atmosphere about the performances.

6 Violin concertos, Op. 11.
(M) *** Ph. 426 950-2 [id.]. Salvatore Accardo, I Musici.

6 Violin concertos, Op. 12.
(M) *** Ph. 426 951-2 [id.]. Salvatore Accardo, I Musici.

More rare repertoire here. The Opp. 11 and 12 concertos are perhaps of uneven quality, but the best of them are very rewarding indeed and, played so superlatively by Salvatore Accardo, they are likely to beguile the most unwilling listener. Recorded in 1974/5, these two individual CDs are among the most desirable of the Philips Vivaldi Edition, and their CD transfers are among the best in the series.

37 Bassoon concertos (complete).
(M) *** ASV Dig. CDDCX 625 (6). Daniel Smith, ECO, Ledger; Zagreb Solists, Ninić.

Bassoon concertos: in C, RV 466; in C, RV 467; in F, RV 486; in F, RV 491; in A min., RV 499; in A min., RV 500.
**(*) ASV Dig. CDDCA 565; *ZCDCA 565* [id.]. Daniel Smith, ECO, Ledger.

Bassoon concertos in C, RV 469; in C, RV 470; in C, RV 474; in C, RV 476; in F, RV 487; in G, RV 494.
**(*) ASV Dig. CDDCA 571; *ZCDCA 571* [id.]. Daniel Smith, ECO, Ledger.

Bassoon concertos: in C, RV 472; in C, RV 477; in C, RV 479; in D min., RV 481; in F, RV 488; in B flat (La notte), RV 501.
**(*) ASV Dig. CDDCA 662; *ZCDCA 662* [id.]. Daniel Smith, ECO, Ledger.

The bassoon seems to have uncovered a particularly generous fund of inspiration in Vivaldi, for few of his 37 concertos for that instrument are in any way routine. Daniel Smith's achievement in recording them all is considerable, for he plays with constant freshness and enthusiasm. His woody tone is very attractive and he is very well caught by the engineers. This set can be welcomed almost without reservation and, dipped into, the various recordings will always give pleasure. We have listened to every one of these concertos and come up smiling. Daniel Smith is a genial and personable player and he has considerable facility; even if some of the more complicated roulades are not executed with exact precision, his playing has undoubted flair. He is balanced well forward, but the orchestral accompaniment has plenty of personality and registers well enough. The second volume has brought the juxtaposition of several works in the same key. Even so, this is enjoyably spontaneous music-making, although the concertos should be approached singly, a facility which CD readily provides. The striking work of the third volume is *La notte*, RV 501, which is quite a different piece from the concerto with the same sobriquet for flute and bassoon in G minor. This is a highly original piece, opening with an almost operatic recitative, as if Vivaldi was clearing his throat. Next comes a *Presto* (*Ghosts*), followed by *Sleep* and *Dawn*, all highly evocative in the best *Four Seasons* manner. Smith and Ledger are obviously taken with it and provide an outstandingly characterful performance. Elsewhere the solo playing is spontaneously vigorous and expressive, making up in flair for any final lack of polish. The accompaniments are alert and the recording very lively.

Bassoon concertos: in C, RV 471; in C, RV 475; in F, RV 490; in G, RV 492; in G min., RV 495; in G min., RV 496.
*** ASV CDDCA 734; *ZCDCA 734* [id.]. Daniel Smith, Zagreb Soloists, Tonko Ninić.

For the last three CDs of the series the Zagreb Soloists take over the accompaniments and offer alert, vivacious playing that adds to the pleasure of the performances. Daniel Smith too, responds with more vigour and polish and overall there is plenty of affectionate warmth. The *C major Concerto*, RV 475, opens the disc with a very striking orchestral ritornello and this concerto also has an agreeably pensive *Adagio*; a similar contrast arrives in the *G minor*, RV 495, where the bassoon's staccato figurations of the opening movement make a good foil for the melancholy *Largo* which follows. The *C major*, RV 471, begins in a mood of great good humour and then the *Larghetto* brings a highly imaginative interplay between the bassoon and the expressive string line. But there is plenty of interest throughout and the recording is well balanced and realistic.

Bassoon concertos: in C, RV 473; in C, RV 478; in E flat, RV 483; in F, RV 485; in A min., RV 497; in A min., RV 498; in B flat, RV 502.
**(*) ASV CDDCA 752; *ZCDCA 752* [id.]. Daniel Smith, Zagreb Soloists, Tonko Ninić.

For some reason the Zagreb violins here sound brighter and edgier, giving almost a feeling of original instruments. The quality is also slightly less full. But most of these concertos are well up to form. Vivaldi seems to have ensured that the opening movements are full of character, while the *F major*, RV 485 has a particularly fine central *Largo*. The *E flat major, RV 483* has an opening section marked *Presto* which demands much bravura from the soloist, and the following *Larghetto* has that special vein of melancholy which Vivaldi reserved for this oeuvre. RV 473 *in C* brings a graceful Minuet for its finale instead of the usual allegro.

Bassoon concertos: in C min., RV 480; in E min., RV 484; in F, RV 489; in G, RV 493; in B flat, RV 503; in B flat, RV 504.
*** ASV Dig. CDDCA 751; *ZCDCA 751* [id.]. Daniel Smith, Zagreb Soloists, Tonko Ninić.

This is the record to begin with if you intend sampling this enterprising ASV series. Almost all the works here show Vivaldi at his most inventively spontaneous. The *F major*, RV 489, gets the collection off to a good start with a vigorously rhythmic opening and a genial soloist, while the following *Adagio* is gentle and touching. The bravura of the opening movement of the *G major*, RV 493, stretches Daniel Smith to the limit, and again the following *Largo* is gently poignant. The *Andante* of the *E minor*, RV 484, is also strikingly expressive, while the *B flat major*, RV 504, brings a jolly finale with invigorating staccato triplets from the bassoon. The first movement of the *C minor*, RV 480, again shows Vivaldi at his most vital and the passage-work here has a flavour of Bach. The following *Andantino* (*quasi Menuetto*) is droll in its sentiment and the finale is another bravura movement with the soloist's running semi-quavers going like the wind. The last concerto on the disc brings another of Vivaldi's best lyrical ideas in the first movement and is altogether a most attractive work. Smith and the Zagreb group rise to the occasion and the recording is pleasingly vivid.

Bassoon concertos: in C, RV 473; in E flat, RV 483; in F, RV 485; in G, RV 492; in A min., RV 497; in B flat, RV 503.
*** Ph. Dig. 416 355-2 [id.]. Klaus Thunemann, I Musici.

None of the six *Bassoon concertos* recorded on Philips is second rate: they are all inventive, fresh and at times inspired, and Klaus Thunemann and I Musici give most appealing accounts of them. No complaints either about the quality or balance of the Philips recording. Even those not usually responsive to Vivaldi will find these refreshing and original.

Bassoon concertos: in C, RV 473; in F, RV 490; in G, RV 493; in G min., RV 496; in A min., RV 497; in B flat (La notte), RV 501.
(B) **(*) Hung. White Label HRC 043 [id.]. Gábor Janota, Liszt CO, Budapest, Frigyes Sándor.

Very good playing from Gábor Janota and lively and sensitive support from the Liszt Chamber Orchestra under Frigyes Sándor. The (presumably 1970s) recording is well balanced, with both soloist and orchestra present or pleasingly forward and with no lack of bloom and freshness to the sound. At about an hour's music, good value.

Bassoon concerto in F, RV 485; (i) *Double concerto in G min., for recorder and bassoon (La Notte), RV 104.*
*** BIS Dig. CD 271 [id.]. McGraw, (i) Pehrsson, Drottningholm Bar. Ens. – TELEMANN: *Concertos.* ***

The concerto subtitled *La Notte* exists in three versions: one for flute (the most familiar), RV 439; another for bassoon, RV 501; and the present version, RV 104. Clas Pehrsson, Michael McGraw and the Drottningholm Baroque Ensemble give a thoroughly splendid account of it, and the *Bassoon concerto in F major* also fares well. Excellent recording.

Cello concertos: in C, RV 398; in G, RV 413.
(M) *** DG 429 098-2; *429 098-4.* Rostropovich, Zurich Coll. Mus., Sacher – BOCCHERINI; TARTINI: *Concertos.* ***

Performances of great vigour and projection from Rostropovich. The playing is superbly brilliant and immensely strong in character; it may be somewhat large-scale for Vivaldi's two quite short concertos, but undoubtedly every bar comes fully to life. Spendidly lively accompaniments and excellent CD transfers, bright and clean with no lack of depth. Like Tortelier's collection – see below – with which there is no conflict of repertoire, this is for those who primarily care about the communication of joy in great music.

Cello concertos: in C, RV 400; C min., RV 401; B min., RV 424; for (i) *2 cellos in G min., RV 531;* (i; ii) *violin & 2 cellos in C, RV 561.*
(M) *** EMI CDM7 69835-2; *EG 769835-4.* Paul Tortelier, with (i) Maude Tortelier, (ii) Jacques Manzone; L. Mozart Players, Ledger.

This is one of Tortelier's finest records. The performances here are strong and alive, the slow movements expressive without being over-romanticized. Philip Ledger directs the full-bodied accompanying group and provides a continuo with some flair. The playing is undoubtedly stylish, though the overall effect is not aimed at the 'authentic' lobby, rather at those who seek primarily a warmly understanding response to the composer's inspiration and readily communicated musical enjoyment. The sound is excellent, with the CD remasterings highly successful.

Cello concertos: in C, RV 399; in C min., RV 401; in D min., RV 405; in B flat, RV 423; in F, RV 538; Largo. (i) *Concerto in E min. for cello and bassoon, RV 409.*
*** BMG/RCA Dig. RD 87774 [7774-2-RC]. Harnoy, (i) McKay, Toronto CO, Robinson.

Ofra Harnoy's are traditional performances with modern instruments, and none the worse for that; she plays with style, impeccable technique and eloquence: in short, she is a first-class artist with a good lyrical sense. Three of the concertos recorded here are new to the catalogue. One is an arrangement for cello and bassoon of a concerto for two horns. She is given good support from the Toronto Chamber Orchestra under Paul Robinson, and very well recorded.

Cello concertos: in C min., RV 402; in D, RV 403; in D min., RV 406; in F, RV 412; in G, RV 414; in A min., RV 422; in B min., RV 424.
*** BMG/RCA Dig. RD 60155 [60155-2-RC]. Ofra Harnoy, Toronto CO, Paul Robinson.

There are 27 *Cello concertos*, and the present CD is the second volume in Ofra Harnoy's survey with the Toronto Chamber Orchestra. Her strength lies not so much in her tone, which is not big, but in her selfless approach to this repertoire. She does not regard this music as a vehicle for her own personality but plays it with an agreeable dedication and a delight in its considerable felicities. Again three of the concertos are new to records.

Flute concertos: in A min., RV 108; in F, RV 434; Double flute concerto in C, RV 533; Sopranino recorder concertos: in C, RV 443 & RV 444; in A min., RV 445.
(BB) *** Naxos Dig. 8.550385; *4550385* [id.]. Jálek, Novotny, Stivin, Capella Istropolitana, Oliver Dohnányi.

The Capella Istropolitana, who are drawn from the excellent Slovak Philharmonic, play with vitality and sensitivity for Oliver Dohnányi and the soloists show appropriate virtuosity and flair. As always, there are rewards and surprises in this music, but readers are not recommended to listen to the last nine tracks without a break (or an aspirin), since three consecutive sopranino recorder concertos are too much of a good thing, despite Jiří Stivin's undoubted artistry. The sound is very good indeed, and so is the balance.

Flute concertos in D, RV 427; in D (Il gardellino), RV 428; in D, RV 429; in G, RV 436; in G, RV 438; in A min., RV 440; (i) *in C, for 2 flutes, RV 533.*
*** HM Dig. HMC 905193; *HMC 405193* [id.]. Janet See, (i) S. Schultz; Philh. Bar. O, McGegan.

Janet See is not only a first-class player but also a real artist whose phrasing is alive and imaginative. Her good musical judgement and taste are matched by a splendid technique and control. Moreover the Philharmonia Baroque Orchestra, a West Coast American group, give her excellent support under Nicholas McGegan, who allows the music to unfold at a natural, unforced pace. Vivaldi also deserves some of the credit for all this, too. The diversity and range of these pieces is astonishing. Highly enjoyable.

Concertos for flute, oboe, violin, bassoon and continuo: in C, RV 88; in D (Il gardellino), RV 90; in D, RV 94; in F, RV 99; in G min., RV 107; Concerto for flute, violin, bassoon and continuo, RV 106.
*** Unicorn Dig. DKPCD 9071; *DKPC 9071* [id.]. Magyer, Francis, Stevens, Jordan, London Harpsichord Ens., Sarah Francis.

A highly engaging group of chamber concertos, suitable for the late evening. Vivaldi's felicitous interplay of wind-colours is ever imaginative. In RV 88, 90 and 106, the flute predominates, while RV 94 creates a partnership between flute and violin; in its central *Largo* the oboe rests while the two main participants recall the slow movement of *Winter* from *The Four Seasons. Il gardellino* (The goldfinch) has similar pictorial evocations to that famous work which are charmingly effective here. The players persuasively work together as a team, creating a most attractive intimacy, and the truthful and well-balanced recording adds to the listener's pleasure in nearly an hour of music in which the composer's invention never flags.

Guitar concertos: in D, RV 93; in A min. (from Op. 3/6), RV 356; in C, RV 425. Double guitar concerto in G, RV 532; Quadruple guitar concerto in B min. (from Op. 3/10), RV 580.
**(*) Ph. Dig. 412 624-2; *412 624-4* [id.]. Los Romeros, ASMF, Iona Brown.

Two of these concertos are transcriptions from *L'Estro armonico* and, though they are in themselves pleasing, they are probably more enjoyable in their original form, particularly the slow movements with their sustained melodic lines. The other concertos for lute and mandolin come off excellently. Probably not an issue that would have high priority in a Vivaldi collection, but none the less enjoyable. The *Largo* of RV 93, which ends the programme, is particularly haunting.

Guitar concertos in D, RV 93; in B flat, RV 524; in G min., RV 531; in G, RV 532. Trios: in C, RV 82; in G min., RV 85.
*** DG Dig. 415 487-2 [id.]. Söllscher, Bern Camerata, Füri.

Four of these works are for two mandolins (RV 532) or lute (RV 82, 85, 93), and the other two are for two violins (RV 524) and two cellos (RV 531). Göran Söllscher further enhances his reputation both as a master-guitarist and as an artist on this excellently recorded issue, in which he has first-class support from the Camerata Bern under Thomas Füri. In RV 532, Söllscher resorts to technology and plays both parts. The DG balance is admirably judged.

Mandolin concerto in C, RV 425; Double mandolin concerto in G, RV 532; (Soprano) Lute concerto in D, RV 93; Double concerto in D min. for viola d'amore and lute, RV 540. Trios: in C, RV 82; in G min., RV 85.
*** Hyp. CDA 66160; *KA 66160* [id.]. Jeffrey, O'Dette, Parley of Instruments, Goodman and Holman.

These are chamber performances, with one instrument to each part, and this obviously provides an ideal balance for the *Mandolin concertos.* There are other innovations, too. An organ continuo replaces the usual harpsichord, and very effective it is; in the *Trios* and the *Lute concerto* (but not in the *Double concerto*, RV 540) Paul O'Dette uses a gut-strung soprano lute. This means that in passages with the lute doubling the violin, the two instruments play in unison and the effect is piquant, with the lute giving a delicate edge to the more sustained string articulation. The delightful sounds here, with all players using original instruments or copies, are very convincing. Certainly the mandolin concertos are more telling (plucked with a plectrum) than they are in guitar transcriptions. The recording is realistically balanced within an attractively spacious acoustic.

Violin concertos, Op. 8, Nos. 5 in E flat (La Tempesta di mare), RV 253; 6 in C (Il Piacere), RV 180; 10 in B flat (La Caccia), RV 362; 11 in D, RV 210; in C min. (Il Sospetto), RV 199.
(B) *** CfP Dig. CD-CFP 4522; *TC-CFP 4522.* Sir Yehudi Menuhin, Polish CO, Jerzy Maksymiuk.

Menuhin's collection of five concertos – four of them with nicknames and particularly delightful – brings some of his freshest, most intense playing in recent years. Particularly in slow movements – notably that of *Il Piacere* ('Pleasure') – he shows afresh his unique insight in shaping a phrase. Fresh, alert accompaniment and full digital recording.

(i) *Violin concertos: in A min., Op. 9/5; in E min. (Il favorito), Op. 11/2; in G min., Op. 12/1; in E min. (L'amoroso), RV 271. Orchestral concertos (con molti stromenti) in C, RV 558; in G min., RV 576.*
(M) *** Ph. 432 281-2; *431 281-4.* (i) Arthur Grumiaux; Dresden State O (members), Vittorio Negri.

Arthur Grumiaux never disappoints, and this is one of the most attractive collections of Vivaldi's *Violin concertos* in the catalogue. The *G minor*, Op. 12/1, is a particularly fine work and brings a highly imaginative response; and his playing is hardly less engaging in *L'amoroso*, full of lightness and grace. Negri accompanies sympathetically and the 1973 sound is excellent though fuller in texture than we would expect today. But the solo playing offers endless pleasure. What makes this reissue doubly attractive is the inclusion of the orchestral concertos *con molti stromenti*. The *G minor* work was dedicated to its Dresden performers, though not the present group! The performances are full of life and colour, and the 1970 recording is excellent.

Violin concertos: in D min. (Senza cantin), RV 243; in E (Il riposo), RV 270; in E min. (Il favorito), RV 277; in F (Per la solennità di San Lorenzo), RV 286.
(B) **(*) CfP Dig. CD-CFP 4536; *TC-CFP 4536.* Accardo, I Solisti delle Settimane Musicali Internazionali di Napoli.

Salvatore Accardo plays each of the four concertos on this record on a different instrument from the collection of the Palazzo Communale, Cremona. He plays the *E major*, *Il riposo*, on the Niccolo Amati, *Il favorito* on the Cremonose of 1715, the darker-hued *Concerto senza cantin* ('without using the E string') on the Guarnieri del Gesù, and the *Concerto per la solennità di San Lorenzo* on the Andrea Amati of Charles IX of France. But this is more than a record for violin specialists: it offers playing of the highest order by one of the finest violinists of our time. Accardo himself directs the excellent ensemble, and the EMI recording is very vivid and clear but also rather dry in the manner of some early digital recordings. We would expect a warmer, more ample string-sound today. These are distinguished performances, but not all ears will respond to the relative lack of bloom.

Triple concerto for 2 violins and cello in C min. (San Lorenzo), RV 556.
**(*) ASV Dig. CDCOE 803; *ZCCOE 803* [id.]. COE, Schneider – BACH: *Double concerto;* MOZART: *Sinfonia concertante.* **(*)

Vivaldi's *San Lorenzo concerto* for two violins and cello makes an attractive makeweight for the two other multiple concertos on the Chamber Orchestra of Europe's disc. In a performance recorded live at St John's, Smith Square, the outer movements are inflated in scale but bring winningly resilient playing.

Double concerto for violin and oboe in G min., RV 576; Violin concerto in D (per la S.S.ma Assontione di Maria Vergine), RV 582.
(*) Ph. Dig. 411 466-2 [id.]. Holliger, Kremer, ASMF – BACH: *Double concerto* and *Sinfonia.* *

As in the Bach coupling, Holliger dominates the performance of the *Double concerto*, especially in the slow movement where Kremer's timbre is less expressively expansive. But Kremer comes into his own in the delightful *D major concerto*, showing Vivaldi at his most inspired and imaginative. This features a double orchestra in the accompaniment, sometimes used antiphonally, and, although the effects are brought off well here, the stereo separation is not as clear as might have been expected. Otherwise the sound, clear and resonant, is finely judged; Kremer's sparkling articulation in the allegros is balanced by his serenely beautiful playing in the delicate cantilena of the central *Largo*.

MISCELLANEOUS CONCERTO COLLECTIONS

Bassoon concerto in A min., RV 498; Cello concerto in C min., RV 401; Oboe concerto in F, RV 455; Concerto for strings in A, RV 158; Violin concerto in E min., RV 278; Concerto for 2 violins and 2 cellos, RV 575.
*** Novalis Dig. 150016-2; *150016-4* [id.]. Camerata Bern.

The majority of the concertos on this disc are not otherwise available, and most of them are highly inventive. The Camerata Bern is an excellent ensemble, playing on modern instruments with great expertise and a sure sense of style. There is some particularly good playing from the bassoon soloist in the *A minor Concerto*, RV 498; but throughout the disc there is much to divert and delight the listener, and there is no cause for complaint so far as the recording is concerned.

Bassoon concerto in B flat, RV 502; Cello concerto in C min., RV 401; Oboe concerto in C, RV 447; Double trumpet concerto in C, RV 537. L'Estro armonico: Double violin concerto in A min., RV 522; Quadruple violin concerto in B min., RV 580; Op. 3/8 & 10. Triple violin concerto in F, RV 551.
*** Virgin Dig. VC7 91167-2; *VC 791167-4* [id.]. Soloists, LCO, Christopher Warren-Green.

Christopher Warren-Green and his LCO seldom disappoint and this generous (75 minutes) collection, offering seven of Vivaldi's most appealing concertos, is another fine example of their vividly spontaneous music-making. The record opens brightly with the *Double trumpet concerto* and, in the works for oboe and bassoon, both soloists (Gordon Hunt and Merrick Alexander respectively) play with much character and elegance and, in the case of the latter, also a touch of humour. The lovely slow movement of the *C minor Cello concerto* is warmly sympathetic on Andrew Schulman's bow. For some reason a continuo is used only in the two woodwind concertos. The harpsichord swirls are rather effective in the first movement of the *Oboe concerto* and in the *Largo* of the *Bassoon concerto* a chamber organ piquantly introduces the solo entry. The excerpts from *L'Estro armonico* are gleamingly strong and expressive, and again one senses an added energy, possibly deriving from the musicians standing while they play. Excellent recording, made in All Saints', Petersham, yet with the resonance never becoming oppressive.

Bassoon concerto in E min., RV 484; Flute concerto in G, RV 436; Concerto for oboe and bassoon in G, RV 545; Concerto for strings in A, RV 159; Concerto for viola d'amore and lute in D min., RV 540; Violin concerto in E (L'Amoroso), RV 271.
*** DG Dig. 419 615-2 [id.]. Soloists, E. Concert, Pinnock.

Entitled '*L'Amoroso*' after the fine *E major Violin concerto* which is one of the six varied concertos on the disc, this collection brings lively, refreshing performances with fine solo playing from wind and string players alike, using period instruments in the most enticing way. The *Concerto for oboe and bassoon* is particularly engaging. The recording is well balanced within a pleasingly warm acoustic.

Bassoon concerto in A min., RV 498; Flute concerto in C min., RV 441; Oboe concerto in F, RV 456; Concerto for 2 oboes in D min., RV 535; Concerto for 2 oboes, bassoon, 2 horns and violin in F, RV 574; Piccolo concerto in C, RV 444.
(M) *** Decca 417 777-2; *417 777-4*. ASMF, Marriner.

The playing here is splendidly alive and characterful, with crisp, clean articulation and well-pointed phrasing, free from overemphasis. The *A minor Bassoon concerto* has a delightful sense of humour. Well-balanced and vivid recording; this is highly recommendable for all those who do not insist on original instruments in this repertoire.

Double cello concerto in G min., RV 531; Flute concerto in C min., RV 441; Concerto in G min., for flute and bassoon (La notte), RV 104; Concerto in F for flute, oboe and bassoon (La Tempesta di mare), RV 570; Guitar concerto in D, RV 93; Concerto in F for 2 horns, RV 539; Concerto in B flat for violin and cello, RV 547.
*** ASV Dig. CDDCA 645; *ZCDCA 645* [id.]. Soloists, ECO, Malcolm.

With George Malcolm in charge it is not surprising that this 65-minute collection of seven diverse concertos is as entertaining as any in the catalogue. *La Tempesta di mare* has plenty of descriptive energy, with the interplay of flute (William Bennett), oboe (Neil Black) and the genial bassoon of Robin O'Neill bringing an attractive range of colour. The ear is struck by the spacious acoustic at the opening of the work for violin and cello, RV 547, while the more intimate *Guitar concerto* makes a nice contrast. The pair of horns (Frank Lloyd and Tony

Chidell) sound gloriously robust in sonority in RV 539, while William Bennett chirps cheekily in his bird-like decorations of the solo line in the *C minor Flute concerto*. Perhaps most striking of all is the *Double cello concerto*, vigorously energetic in outer movements, but with a short, serene central *Largo*, with overlapping phrases at the beginning, to remind one of the slow movement of Bach's *Double violin concerto*. The concert ends with the duet version of *La notte*, which has much to charm the ear. Accompaniments are sympathetic and stylish, and the whole programme beams with vitality and conveyed enjoyment. The digital sound is vivid and realistic.

Double concertos: for 2 cellos in G min., RV 531; 2 flutes in C, RV 533; 2 oboes in D min., RV 535; 2 mandolins in G, RV 532; 2 trumpets in C, RV 537; 2 violins, RV 523.
(M) *** Ph. 426 086-2; *426 086-4*. I Musici.

This makes an attractively diverse collection. Most of these concertos are admirably inventive and the performances show I Musici at their very best, on sparkling form. The sound is good too.

Double cello concerto in G min., RV 531; Double flute concerto in C, RV 533; Concertos for strings in D min. (Madrigalesco), RV 129; in G (Alla rustica), RV 151; Double trumpet concerto in C, RV 537; Concerto for 2 violins and 2 cellos in D, RV 564.
*** O-L 414 588-2 [id.]. AAM, Hogwood.

Not everything in this issue is of equal substance: the invention in the *Double trumpet concerto*, for example, is not particularly strong; but for the most part it is a rewarding and varied programme. It is especially appealing in that authenticity is allied to musical spontaneity. The *Concerto for two flutes* has great charm and is dispatched with vigour and aplomb. Performances and recording alike are first rate, with added clarity and presence on CD.

Double cello concerto in G min., RV 531; Lute (Guitar) concerto in D, RV 93; Oboe concerto in F, F.VII, No. 2 (R.455); Double concerto for oboe and violin; Trumpet concerto in D (trans. Jean Thilde); *Violin concerto in G min., Op. 12/1; RV 317.*
(BB) *** Naxos Dig. 8.550384; *4550384* [id.]. Capella Istropolitana, Jaroslav Kr(e)chek.

This is a recommendable disc from which to set out to explore the Vivaldi concertos, especially if you are beginning a collection. Gabriela Krcková makes a sensitive contribution to the delightful *Oboe concerto in F major*, F.VII, No. 2 (R.455), and the other soloists are pretty good too. Should this programme meet your particular needs, there is no need for hesitation. The fresh, well-balanced recorded sound makes this attractive CD well worth its modest cost.

Concertos: for 2 cellos in G min., RV 531; 2 mandolins in G, RV 532; recorder in C min., RV 441; in C, RV 443; Trio for violin, lute & continuo in G min., RV 85.
(M) *** DG Dig. 427 824-2; *427 824-4*. Demenga, Häusler, Söllscher, Copley, Camerata Bern, Füri.

An excellent mid-priced digital collection, assembled from various records made by the Camerata Bern, which will especially suit those who like their Vivaldi on original instruments. Söllscher's account of the *Duet concerto* for mandolins (in which he takes both solo roles) is quite outstanding, and there is some breathtaking virtuosity from Michael Copley in the *Recorder concertos*. Further variety is provided by the *Trio* which is also an attractive work. The well-balanced recording has splendid presence and realism.

Double cello concerto in G min., RV 531; Concertos for strings: in G (Alla rustica), RV 151; in A, RV 158; in B min. (Al santo sepolcro), RV 177; Double violin concerto in B flat, RV 524; Triple violin concerto in F, RV 551.
(M) *** Decca 433 169-2; *433 169-4* [id.]. Soloists, Lucerne Festival Strings, Baumgartner – BOCCHERINI: *Symphony in C.* **

Although all these works are well represented in the current catalogue, readers coming new to Vivaldi may well choose this brightly recorded collection. The playing is splendidly alert and vigorous, and the overall impression is enormously fresh. The solemn *Concerto, Al santo sepolcro* is particularly characterful. Baumgartner is not always the most resilient of conductors, but on this occasion the Lucerne orchestra were clearly on their toes throughout. The soloists are excellent too, and it is good to hear the more robust sound of modern instruments in the concerto for a pair of cellos. The *Triple violin concerto*, incidentally, is the only violin work (out of some 280 which Vivaldi composed for one or more violins) which actually features three; it has a fine, melancholy central *Largo* which is reminiscent of *The Four Seasons*.

L'Estro armonico: Quadruple violin concerto in D; Double violin concerto in D min., Op. 3/1 & 11; Bassoon concerto in E min., RV 484; Flute concerto in G min. (La notte), Op. 10/2; Double mandolin concerto in G, RV 532; Oboe concerto in B flat, RV 548; Orchestral concerto (con molti stromenti) in C, RV 558; Concerto for strings in G (Alla rustica), RV 151.
(M) *** DG Dig. 431 710-2; *431 710-4* [id.]. Soloists, E. Concert, Trevor Pinnock.

This collection of very varied works shows Pinnock and the English Concert at their liveliest and most refreshing, although not always so strong on charm. (The account of the *Bassoon concerto* is perhaps an unintentional exception, for the solo timbre has a certain bovine character.) The *Concerto for four violins* is very lithe, and throughout the concert the solo playing is predictably expert. The *Orchestral concerto* involves an astonishing array of instruments; it is also available as listed above, played on modern instruments by the Dresden orchestra, but authenticists will prefer the spicier timbres displayed here. Excellent recording, giving a most realistic impression on CD.

L'Estro armonico: Quadruple violin concerto in B min., Op. 3/10; La Stravaganza: Violin concerto in B flat, Op. 4/1; Cello concerto in C min., RV 401; Double horn concerto in F, RV 539; Concerto in F for 2 oboes, bassoon, 2 horns and violin, RV 569; Double trumpet concerto in C, RV 537.
(M) *** Decca 425 721-2; *425 721-4*. ASMF, Marriner.

Another excellent collection from the considerable array of Vivaldi concertos recorded by Marriner and his ASMF (on modern instruments) between 1965 and 1977. The soloists are all distinguished, offering playing that is constantly alert, finely articulated and full of life and imagination. Accompaniments are predictably stylish, and the recordings still sound admirably fresh in their CD transfers, with only a touch of shrillness on the *Double trumpet concerto*.

L'Estro armonico: Quadruple violin concerto in D, Op. 3/1; Flute concerto in D (Il gardellino), Op. 10/3; Oboe concerto in C, RV 446; Double concerto in G for oboe & bassooon, RV 545; Concerto for strings in B flat, RV 166; Viola d'amore concerto in D, RV 392; Double concerto in F for violin, organ and strings, RV 542.
(M) *** Ph. Dig. 432 059-2; *432 059-4*. Carmirelli, Nicolet, Holliger, Thunemann, Paris, Perez, Garatti, I Musici.

A generous and well-planned collection, drawn from different sources but given a convincing overall relationship by all being digitally recorded in the excellent acoustics of La Chaux-de-Fonds, Switzerland. With distinguished names among the soloists the performances are predictably fresh, and they all show Vivaldi's amazing fecundity of invention appealingly, not least the miniature *Concerto for strings and continuo*. The work for four violins is also very successful, and Holliger and Thunemann are as expressively appealing as they are nimble. The only slight reservation concerns Aurèle Nicolet's bird imitations in *Il gardellino*, engaging enough, but stylistically somewhat over the top.

(i) *Flute concerto in F (La Tempesta di mare), Op. 10/1;* (ii) *Oboe concertos: in C (from Op. 8/12), RV 449; in D min., RV 454;* (i) *Recorder concerto in C, RV 444; Concertos for strings: in D min., RV 127; in A, RV 158.*
**(*) Chan. Dig. CHAN 8444; 6ABTD 1156 [id.]. (i) Hutchins, (ii) Baskin; I Musici di Montreal, Turovsky.

I Musici di Montreal are recorded in the resonant acoustic of St Madeleine's Church, Montreal, and the balance produces a fresh, bright sound from the fourteen strings, just a shade lacking in body. Their spirited musicianship brings plenty of life to the two attractive string concertos, while the rather beautiful *Largo* of the *A major*, RV 158, enjoys a nicely judged, expressive response. The programme opens buoyantly with Timothy Hutchins's brilliant account of *La Tempesta di mare*, expertly presented on a sopranino recorder; but the highlight of the concert is the pair of oboe concertos, beautifully played by Theodore Baskin. Like Hutchins, he is a principal of the Montreal Symphony. The recording places him realistically in relation to the accompaniment; allowing for the reverberation, the sound is first class.

Double flute concerto in C, RV 533; Double horn concerto in F, RV 539; Double mandolin concerto in G, RV 536; Double oboe concerto in A min., RV 536; Concerto for oboe and bassoon in G, RV 545; Double trumpet concerto in D, RV 563.
*** Ph. Dig. 412 892-2 [id.]. Soloists, ASMF, Marriner.

Apart from the work for two horns, where the focus of the soloists lacks a degree of sharpness, the recording often reaches demonstration standard. On CD, the concerto featuring a pair of mandolins is particularly tangible, with the balance near perfect, the solo instruments in proper scale yet registering admirable detail. The concertos for flutes and oboes are played with engaging finesse, conveying a sense of joy in the felicity of the writing. Throughout, the accompaniments are characteristically polished and especially imaginative in their use of light and shade in alternating phrases. Once again Marriner makes a very good case for the use of modern wind instruments in this repertoire.

Double flute concerto in C, RV 533; Double oboe concerto in D min., RV 535; Double horn concerto in F, RV 539; Double trumpet concerto in C, RV 537; Concerto for 2 oboes, 2 clarinets and strings, RV 560.
(B) **(*) Pickwick Dig. PCD 811; *CIMPC 811* [id.]. Soloists, Scottish CO, Laredo.

An attractive bargain-priced compilation, with soloists and orchestra set back in good perspective in a believable acoustic. The resonance tends to make the trumpet timbre spread, but otherwise the sound is very good. The solo playing is accomplished, although rather more light and shade between phrases would have made the performances even more enticing, while Jaime Laredo's direction of the slow movements is not especially imaginative.

Double concerto for oboe and violin in B flat, RV 548; Triple concerto in C for violin, oboe and organ, RV 554; Double concertos for violin and organ: in D min., RV 541; in C min. & F, RV 766–7.
*** Unicorn Dig. DKPCD 9050; *DKPC 9050* [id.]. Francis, Studt, Bate, Tate Music Group, Studt.

An engaging clutch of concertos, two of which (RV 766–7) are first recordings. The works featuring the organ in a concertante role are in the concerto grosso tradition and are notable for their imaginative juxtaposition of colours – which is not to say that they lack vitality of invention. The recording is very attractive in ambience and the balance is admirable, with the sound first class.

Concertos for strings: in D min. (Concerto madrigalesco), RV 129; in G (Alla rustica), RV 151; in G min., RV 157. (i) Motet: *In turbato mare irato, RV 627;* Cantata: *Lungi dal vago volto, RV 680. Magnificat, RV 610.*
*** Hyp. Dig. CDA 66247; *KA 66247* [id.]. (i) Kirkby, Leblanc, Forget, Cunningham, Ingram, Tafelmusik Ch. & Bar. O, Lamon.

Mingling vocal and instrumental items, and works both well-known and unfamiliar, Jean Lamon provides a delightful collection, with Emma Kirkby a sparkling, pure-toned soloist in two items never recorded before: the motet, *In turbato mare irato*, and the chamber cantata, *Lungi dal vago volto*. The performance is lively, with fresh choral sound. The Tafelmusik performers come from Canada, and though the use of period instruments has some roughness, their vigour and alertness amply make up for that. Good, clear recorded sound.

CHAMBER MUSIC

Cello sonatas Nos. 1–9, RV 39/47.
*** CRD Dig. CRD 3440 [id.] (*Nos. 1–4*); CRD 3441 [id.] (*Nos. 5–9*). L'École d'Orphée.

Cello sonatas Nos. 1–6, RV 40–41, 43, 45–7.
*** O-L Dig. 421 060-2 [id.]. Christophe Coin, Hogwood, Zweistra, Ferre, Finucane.

All nine *Sonatas* are given highly musical performances on CRD; they do not set out to impress by grand gestures but succeed in doing so by their dedication and sensitivity. Susan Sheppard is a thoughtful player and is well supported by her continuo team, Lucy Carolan and Jane Coe. The CRD recording is well focused and very present.

On Oiseau-Lyre, Coin and Hogwood offer only six of the nine *Sonatas*: the half-dozen that were collected together and published in 1740, towards the end of Vivaldi's life, as Op. 14. Compared to the CRD version, Coin is the more authoritative player, whose technique is effortless, and the continuo support is more varied in colour. In addition to Christopher Hogwood's harpsichord, there is baroque guitar and an archlute to lend a diversity of colour and texture that is most welcome. The Oiseau-Lyre sound is excellent.

Cello sonatas: in E min., RV 40; in F, RV 41; in A min., RV 43; in B flat, RV 45–7.
(M) **(*) Erato/Warner 2292 45658-2 [id.]. Paul Tortelier, Robert Veyron-Lacroix.

These performances of the Op. 14 *Cello sonatas* come from 1964 and, unlike some other Erato reissues in the '*Hommage à Paul Tortelier*' series, have the benefit of altogether fresh and well-ventilated sound. Tortelier's playing has predictable warmth and a strong sense of line; the balance very much favours the cellist (in the *A minor Sonata*, RV 43, unacceptably so), but this is nevertheless far more recommendable than the Bach *Viola da gamba sonatas* or the Schumann *Trios* he has also recorded.

12 Sonatas for 2 violins & continuo, Op. 1.
(M) *** Ph. 426 926-2 (2) [id.]. Accardo, Gulli, Canino, De Saram.

12 Violin sonatas, Op. 2.
(M) *** Ph. 426 929-2 (2) [id.]. Accardo, Canino, De Saram.

It is unlikely that Salvatore Accardo's performances, so ably supported by Bruno Canino and Rohan de Saram (and in Op. 1 by Franco Gulli), could be surpassed in terms of sympathetic fluency, musicianship and sheer beauty of tone. Textures are fuller and warmer than would be the case with original instruments, yet the recording balance brings admirable transparency, with the harpsichord coming through naturally. The shadow of Corelli still hangs over the earlier set, yet slow movements often have those specially memorable Vivaldian harmonic inflexions (sample the *Adagio* third movement of Op. 1/1, the *Grave* introduction of Op. 1/2 or the Adagio of the last of the set, Op. 1/6). The dance movements are genially vigorous and the invention is remarkably pleasing and fresh. Collectors will find unexpected rewards in both sets, and the CD transfer of recordings made in 1977 are completely natural yet vivid in Philips's best manner.

Violin sonatas (for violin and continuo), *Op. 2/1, 2, 4, 6, 8, 9, 11–12 (RV 1, 9, 16, 20, 23, 27, 31 & 32).*
(B) *** Hung. White Label HRC 062 [id.]. Dénes Kovács, János Sebestyén, Mária Frank.

Readers who are looking for a group of these sonatas, very well played on modern instruments and decently recorded, will find these accounts by the Hungarian violinist, Dénes Kovács, give much pleasure. He is a player of aristocratic quality and good musical judgement; his continuo support is excellent and the analogue recordings, which presumably date from the 1970s, (the label would have us believe 1987) have warmth and freshness.

6 Violin sonatas, Op. 5.
(M) **(*) Ph. 426 938-2 [id.]. Accardo, Gazeau (in Op. 5/5–6), Canino, De Saram.

Warm, mellifluous playing from Salvatore Accardo in the Op. 5 *Sonatas* of 1716–17, four being solo works with continuo and the remainder *Trio sonatas*. The music is not quite as interesting or inventive as Opp. 1 and 2, but those collecting this Edition will still find much that is rewarding. The 1977 sound is well up to the excellent standard of this series.

VOCAL MUSIC

Beatus vir, RV 597; Credo, RV 592; Magnificat, RV 610.
(M) *** Ph. 420 651-2. Soloists, Alldis Ch., ECO, Negri.

Beatus vir, RV 598; Dixit Dominus in D, RV 594; Introduzione al Dixit: Canta in prato in G, RV 636 (ed. Geigling); *Magnificat in G min., RV 611* (ed. Negri).
(M) *** Ph. 420 649-2. Lott, Burgess, Murray, Daniels, Finnie, Collins, Rolfe Johnson, Holl, Alldis Ch., ECO, Negri.

Crediti propter quod, RV 105; Credo, RV 591; Introduction to Gloria, RV 639; Gloria, RV 588; Kyrie, RV 587; Laetatus sum, RV 607.
(M) *** Ph. 420 650-2. M. Marshall, Lott, Finnie, Rolfe Johnson, Alldis Ch., ECO, Negri.

Dixit dominus, RV 595; In exitu Israel, RV 604; Sacrum, RV 586.
(M) *** Ph. 420 652-2. Alldis Ch., ECO, Negri.

Introduction to Gloria, RV 642; Gloria in D, RV 589; Lauda Jerusalem in E min., RV 609; Laudate Dominum in D min., RV 606; Laudati pueri Dominum in A, RV 602.
(M) *** Ph. 420 648-2. Marshall, Lott, Collins, Finnilä, Alldis Ch., ECO, Negri.

Beatus vir, RV 597; Canta in prato, RV 636; Credo, RV 591; Dixit dominus (2 settings), *RV 594 & RV 595; Gloria* (2 settings), *RV 588 & RV 589; In furore, RV 626; Kyrie, RV 587; Lauda Jerusalem, RV 609; Magnificat, RV 610; Nisi dominus, RV 608; Nulla in mundo pax sincera; O qui caeli, RV 631; Stabat mater, RV 621.*

(M) **(*) Erato/Warner 2292 45716-2 (4) [id.]. Soloists; Lausanne Vocal Ens. & CO; Lisbon Gulbenkian Foundation Ch. & O; E. Bach Festival Ch. & Baroque O; Corboz.

These Philips recordings come from the late 1970s. Vittorio Negri does not make use of period instruments, but he penetrates as deeply into the spirit of this music as many who do. When they first appeared, we found them lively, stylish performances, beautifully recorded – and they come up splendidly in their new format, digitally refurbished. Any lover of Vivaldi is likely to be astonished that not only the well-known works but the rarities show him writing with the keenest originality and intensity. There is nothing routine about any of this music, or any of the performances either.

Whereas Negri's recordings are conveniently offered on a series of individual CDs, the Corboz collection is grouped in a box, even though the recordings come from three different sources. Those from the English Bach Festival, which include the *Gloria*, RV 588 (shorn of the three-movement *Introduction* on a non-liturgical text), and *Nisi Dominus* (beautifully sung by Helen Watts), offer baroque orchestral playing on authentic instruments. The *Gloria*, RV 589, *Kyrie*, *Credo*, *Beatus vir*, *Magnificat* and the motets *Lauda Jerusalem* and *Nulla in mundo pax sincera* come from Lausanne and modern instruments are used to produce a warm, well-focused sound; the acoustic is spacious and the performances vital and musical. The professional singers of the Lausanne Choir are generally admirable and the soloists are sweet-toned. The *Magnificat* is given in its simpler, first version, on a relatively small scale with the chorus singing the alto solo, *Fecit potentiam*. The *Kyrie*, with its double chorus, double string orchestra plus four soloists, makes a fine contrast in its magnificence. The *Dixit dominus*, RV 594, and *Stabat Mater* (a most affecting piece, thought to have been composed at great speed) were recorded in Lisbon, and here the performances are pleasingly old-fashioned, with robust tone and modern instruments. In spite of the woolly acoustic here, the solo singers and instrumentalists are fairly well focused. There is much to enjoy within these four CDs and the transfers are well managed, but the stylistic contrasts suggest that in the long term Negri on Philips will prove the more satisfying investment.

Beatus vir, RV 597; Dixit dominus, RV 594.
*** Argo Dig. 414 495-2 [id.]. Buchanan, Jennifer Smith, Watts, Partridge, Shirley-Quirk, King's College Ch., ECO, Cleobury.

Dixit dominus cannot fail to attract those who have enjoyed the better-known *Gloria*. Both works are powerfully inspired and are here given vigorous and sparkling performances with King's College Choir in excellent form under its latest choirmaster. The soloists are a fine team, fresh, stylish and nimble, and the reverberant recording remains atmospheric, without detail becoming clouded. There is plenty of clean articulation from the choristers, nicely projected in the CD format with its extra sharpness of definition.

Dixit dominus, RV 594; Gloria in D, RV 589.
*** DG Dig. 423 386-2 [id.]. Argenta, Attrot, Denley, Stafford, Varcoe, E. Concert & Ch., Pinnock.

Pinnock's versions of the better-known of Vivaldi's two settings of the *Gloria* and the grander of his two settings of the psalm, *Dixit dominus* (the one for double chorus), make an attractive and strong coupling. His fresh, vigorous performances, beautifully recorded, add impressively to his developing reputation as a choral conductor on record, with first-rate playing and singing.

Gloria in D, RV 589.
(M) *** Decca 421 146-2. Vaughan, J. Baker, King's College, Cambridge, Ch., ASMF, Willcocks – HAYDN: *Nelson Mass.* ***
*** O-L 414 678-2 [id.]. Nelson, Kirkby, Watkinson, Christ Church Cathedral Ch., AAM, Preston – BACH: *Magnificat.* ***
*** DG Dig. 423 386-2 [id.]. Argenta, Attrot, Denley, Ch. & E. Concert, Pinnock – A. SCARLATTI: *Dixit Dominus.* ***

The CD remastering of the stylish 1962 Willcocks recording of Vivaldi's *Gloria* is strikingly vivid and, with excellent choral and solo singing, this makes a fine and generous bonus for the Haydn *Nelson Mass.*

The freshness and point of the Christ Church performance of the *Gloria* are irresistible; anyone who normally doubts the attractiveness of authentic string technique should sample this, for the absence of vibrato adds a tang exactly in keeping with the performance. The soloists too keep vibrato to the minimum, adding to the freshness, yet Carolyn Watkinson rivals even Dame

Janet Baker in the dark intensity of the Bach-like central aria for contralto, *Domine Deus, Agnus Dei.* The choristers of Christ Church Cathedral excel themselves, and the recording is outstandingly fine.

Trevor Pinnock directs a bright, refreshing account of the grander and better known of Vivaldi's *Gloria* settings, with excellent playing and singing from the members of the English Concert. Unlike many advocates of period performance, Pinnock is not afraid to give spacious treatment to slow and reflective movements, bringing out the marked contrasts between the twelve movements. Unusually but attractively coupled with the rare Scarlatti setting of *Dixit Dominus*, and very well recorded, it makes a first-rate alternative recommendation.

Gloria in D, RV 588; Gloria in D, RV 589.
*** Argo Dig. 410 018-2 [id.]. Russell, Kwella, Wilkens, Bowen, St John's College, Cambridge, Ch., Wren O, Guest.

The two settings of the *Gloria* make an apt and illuminating coupling. Both in D major, they have many points in common, presenting fascinating comparisons, when RV 588 is as inspired as its better-known companion. Guest directs strong and well-paced readings, with RV 588 the more lively. Good, warm recording to match the performances.

Gloria in D, RV 589; Kyrie in G min., RV 587.
(M) *** DG 427 142-2. Regensburg Cathedral Ch., V. Capella Academica, Schneidt – BACH: *Motets.* ***

In the superb setting of the *Kyrie*, and the well-known *Gloria*, Schneidt with his fresh-toned Regensburg Choir (the celebrated Domspatzen, 'cathedral sparrows') brings out what may seem a surprising weight for an 'authentic' performance. The use of semi-chorus for solo numbers is questionable, but no one hearing these performances is likely to dismiss the music as trivial. The excellent 1977 recordings have been transferred to CD most effectively.

Gloria in D, RV 589; Kyrie, RV 587 and Credo, R 591; Magnificat, RV 610.
*** Erato/Warner 2292 45122-2 [id.]. Jennifer Smith, Staempfli, Rossier, Schaer, Lausanne Vocal & Instrumental Ens., Corboz.

(i) *Gloria in D, RV 589;* (ii) *Magnificat, RV 610.*
(M) **(*) Decca 425 724-2; *425 724-4.* (i) Vaughan, J. Baker; (ii) Castle, Cockerham, King; King's College Ch., ASMF; (i) Willcocks; (ii) Ledger – PERGOLESI: *Magnificat.* **(*)

Michel Corboz, a fine choral conductor, gives a lively performance of the *Gloria*, and his version is aptly coupled with three other richly rewarding liturgical settings by Vivaldi. The *Magnificat* is given in its simpler first version on a relatively small scale, with the chorus singing the alto solo, *Fecit potentiam.* The *Kyrie* with its double chorus and double string orchestra, plus four soloists, makes a fine contrast in its magnificence. The professional singers of the Lausanne choir are generally admirable, and the soloists are sweet-toned. Good, clear recording.

The Willcocks version of the *Gloria* uses comparatively small forces and, save for the occasional trace of preciosity, it is very stylish. It has excellent soloists and is very well recorded, though some might feel that the exaggerated consonants are tiresome. Ledger also offers the small-scale setting of the *Magnificat* and opts for boys' voices in the solos such as the beautiful duet, *Esurientes*; though the singers are taxed by ornamentation, the result has all the accustomed beauty of this choir's recordings. Excellent transfers.

(i; ii) *Gloria in D, RV 589; Magnificat in G min., RV 610/611;* (ii) *Salve Regina in C min., RV 616* (with ANON.: (i; ii) *Te Deum in D, RV App. 38*).
(M) **(*) Ph. 426 952-2 (2). (i) Giebel; (ii) Höffgen; La Fenice di Venezia Ch. & O, Negri.

This acts a pendant to Negri's fine choral series with the John Alldis Choir and the ECO, although the recordings were made a decade earlier in 1964/5. They have been effectively remastered, however, and though not as cleanly focused as the later set, they have an agreeable spaciousness and atmosphere. The choral singing in Venice is less refined than the London group, but Negri secures performances that are vigorously committed and always alive. The recordings were made in San Marco, where traditionally the performers were dispersed in separate groups, thus achieving both a polychoral and polyinstrumental effect. Thus in the robust account of the famous *Gloria in D*, not only the chorus, but the duet, *Laudamus te,* for soprano and contralto, is arranged antiphonally. The double choir *G minor Magnificat* brings richly spread string sonorities, parts intertwining, and its closing *Gloria patri* is spectacular indeed. To the double string orchestra used to accompany the *Salve regina,* Vivaldi adds both a pair of recorders and a flute to the first string group, featuring them in separate numbers. Throughout the San Marco acoustics bring the richest orchestral textures (no suspicion of original instruments here) and the choral sound is comparably full. Even though inner detail is not sharp, the antiphony is highly effective and the results sonically sumptuous. Of the soloists Agnes Giebel is preferable to Marga Höffgen, but the latter rises to the occasion in her solo *Salve Regina*, singing with eloquence and full tone. The *Te Deum in D* is spurious, a lighter piece, though effectively using trumpets in the orchestra. Listening to the *Judex crederis*, where the antiphonal interplay is especially effective, one can understand its mistaken attribution to Vivaldi.

Juditha triumphans (oratorio) complete.
(M) *** Ph. 426 955-2 (2). Finnilä, Springer, Hamari, Ameling, Burmeister, Berlin R. Soloists Ch. & CO, Negri.

Described as a 'military' oratorio, *Juditha triumphans* demonstrates its martial bravado at the very start, as exhilarating a passage as you will find in the whole of Vivaldi. The vigorous choruses stand as cornerstones of commentary in a structure which, following convention, comes close to operatic form, with recitatives providing the narrative between formal *da capo* arias. Though Vivaldi fell into routine invention at times, the wonder is that so much of this music is so vividly alive, telling the story from the Apocrypha of Judith cutting off the head of the enemy general, Holofernes. As the cast-list will suggest, this Philips version rightly gives the castrato roles to women, with a generally stylish line-up of singers. It is a pity that the role of Judith is taken by one of the less interesting singers, Birgit Finnilä, and that Elly Ameling takes only a servant's role, though that is one which demands more brilliant technique than any. Overall, however, this is a considerable success.

Laudate pueri dominum, RV 601; Nisi Dominus, RV 608.
*** Mer. Dig. CDE 84129; *KE 77129* [id.]. Lynne Dawson, Christopher Robson, King's Consort, Robert King.

The present setting of Psalm 113, RV 601, is a strong work whose inspiration runs at a consistently high level; Lynne Dawson sings with an excellent sense of style and is given splendid support. The coupling, the *Nisi Dominus*, a setting of Psalm 126, is much better known but makes an attractive makeweight. It is also given an excellent performance by Christopher Robson. Good recording.

(i) *Nisi Dominus (Psalm 126), RV 608; Stabat Mater, RV 621; Concerto for strings in G min., RV 153.*
**(*) O-L Dig. 414 329-2 [id.]. AAM, Hogwood; (i) with Bowman.

These performances are vital enough and there is no want of stylistic awareness. James Bowman is a persuasive soloist. The *Concerto* is an engaging work whose charms benefit from the authentic instruments. The CD is altogether excellent; the sound is marvellously fresh and present.

OPERA

L'Olimpiade: highlights.
(B) **(*) Hung. White Label HRC 078 [id.]. Kováts, Takács, Zempleni, Miller, Horvath, Kaplan, Gati, Budapest Madrigal Ch., Hungarian State O, Szekeres.

In the inexpensive White Label series of Hungaroton recordings, a generous collection of highlights from Vivaldi's opera, *L'Olimpiade*, is well worth investigating. An early delight in this selection is the work's most attention-grabbing number, a choral version of what we know as *Spring* from *The Four Seasons*. Ferenc Szekeres' conducting of the Hungarian State Orchestra is too heavy by today's standards, now that we are attuned to period performance, but the singing of soloists and choir is good, and the recording is brightly focused, with clean directional effects.

Orlando Furioso (complete).
*** Erato/Warner 2292 45147-2 (3) [id.]. Horne, De los Angeles, Valentini Terrani, Gonzales, Kozma, Bruscantini, Zaccaria, Sol. Ven., Scimone.

Scimone has heavily rearranged the order of items as well as cutting many, but, with stylish playing and excellent recording, it is a set well worth a Vivaldi enthusiast's attention. Outstanding in a surprisingly star-studded cast is Marilyn Horne in the title-role, rich and firm of tone, articulating superbly in divisions, notably in the hero's two fiery arias. In the role of

Angelica, Victoria de los Angeles has many sweetly lyrical moments, and though Lucia Valentini Terrani is less strong as Alcina, she gives an aptly clean, precise performance. The remastering has somewhat freshened a recording which was not outstanding in its analogue LP form.

Wagenseil, George (1715–77)

Harp concerto in G.

(B) *** DG 427 206-2. Zabaleta, Paul Kuentz CO – HANDEL: *Harp concerto;* MOZART: *Flute and harp concerto.* ***

Wagenseil's *Harp concerto* is a pleasant example of the *galant* style; the felicity of the writing in the first two movements is capped by a very jolly finale. Both performance and recording here can be commended and the remastering is fresh and clear.

Wagner, Richard (1813–83)

Siegfried idyll.

(B) *** Pickwick Dig. PCD 928; *CIMPC 108.* SCO, Jaime Laredo – DVOŘÁK: *String serenade* etc. ***

(M) **(*) EMI CMS7 63277-2 (2) [Ang. CDMB 63277]. Philh. O, Klemperer – MAHLER: *Symphony No. 9.* ***

A beautiful performance from Jaime Laredo and the Scottish Chamber Orchestra, warm and poised and ending serenely, yet moving to a strong central climax. The recording, made in Glasgow City Hall, has a pleasingly expansive ambience, yet textures are clear.

Klemperer favours the original chamber-orchestra scoring and the Philharmonia players are very persuasive, especially in the score's gentler moments. However, the balance is forward and, although the sound is warm, the ear craves a greater breadth of string tone at the climax.

Siegfried idyll. Der fliegende Holländer: Overture. Lohengrin: Prelude to Act I. Die Meistersinger: Overture. (i) *Tannhäuser: Overture and Venusberg music.*

(M) *** Sony MPK 45701 [id.]. Columbia SO, Bruno Walter, (i) with Occidental College Ch.

Bruno Walter draws a lovingly warm account of the *Siegfried idyll* from his players, and the poise of the opening of the *Pilgrims' chorus* is equally full of quiet tension, while the reprise of this famous melody, before the introduction of the Venusberg section, is wonderfully gentle. With the central section thrillingly sensuous, the closing pages – the Occidental College Choir distantly balanced – bring a radiant hush. The *Lohengrin Prelude* is rather relaxed but beautifully controlled. With fine orchestral playing throughout, this stands among the most rewarding of all available compilations of Wagnerian orchestral excerpts.

Siegfried idyll. Der fliegende Holländer: Overture. Lohengrin: Preludes to Acts I and III. Die Meistersinger: Overture.

*** DG Dig. 419 169-2 [id.]. NYPO, Sinopoli.

Superbly spacious performances from Sinopoli, with *Der fliegende Holländer* seeming less melodramatic than usual, yet played with free rubato in the most effective way. The emotional arch of the *Lohengrin* Act I *Prelude* is superbly graduated, with the New York violins finding radiant tone for the closing pianissimo. *Die Meistersinger* is massively stately. Sinopoli opens and closes the *Siegfried idyll* with the greatest delicacy, and the end is wonderfully serene and romantic; the middle section is fast and volatile, moving to its climax with passionate thrust.

Siegfried idyll. Lohengrin: Preludes to Acts I & III. Die Meistersinger: Prelude to Act I. Parsifal: Prelude to Act I. Tristan und Isolde: Prelude and Liebestod.

(M) *** Ph. 420 886-2. Concg. O, Haitink.

The addition of Haitink's simple, unaffected reading of the *Siegfried idyll* to his 1975 collection of *Preludes* enhances the appeal of a particularly attractive concert. The rich acoustics of the Concertgebouw are surely ideal for *Die Meistersinger*, given a memorably spacious performance, and Haitink's restraint adds to the noble dignity of *Parsifal.* The *Lohengrin* excerpts are splendidly played. The digital remastering is almost entirely beneficial.

Siegfried idyll. Lohengrin: Prelude to Acts I & III. Die Meistersinger: Overture. Die Walküre: Ride of the Valkyries; (i) *Wotan's farewell and Magic fire music.*
*** ASV Dig. CDDCA 666; *ZCDCA 666* [id.]. Philh. O, Francesco d'Avalos, (i) with John Tomlinson.

Francesco d'Avalos may not be a Furtwängler, but his pacing of this attractively assembled Wagner concert is most convincing. The opening *Siegfried idyll* has all the requisite serenity and atmosphere; here, as elsewhere, the Philharmonia play most beautifully. The boldly sumptuous recording brings a thrilling resonance and amplitude to the brass, especially trombones and tuba, and in the expansive *Meistersinger overture*, and again in *Wotan's farewell* the brass entries bring a physical frisson. John Tomlinson's noble assumption of the role of Wotan, as he bids a loving farewell to his errant daughter, is very moving here, and the response of the Philharmonia strings matches the depth of feeling he conveys. With the Valkyries also given a splendid sense of spectacle, this collection should have a wide appeal.

Siegfried idyll. Tannhäuser: overture. (i) *Tristan: Prelude and Liebestod.*
*** DG Dig. 423 613-2 [id.]. (i) Jessye Norman; VPO, Karajan.

This superb Wagner record was taken live from a unique concert conducted by Karajan at the Salzburg Festival in August 1987. The *Tannhäuser overture* has never sounded so noble, and the *Siegfried idyll* has rarely seemed so intense and dedicated behind its sweet lyricism; while the *Prelude and Liebestod*, with Jessye Norman as soloist, bring the richest culmination, sensuous and passionate, but remarkable as much for the hushed, inward moments as for the ineluctable building of climaxes. The recording gives little or no idea of a live occasion, thanks to rather close balance, but the glow of the Vienna Philharmonic at its peak is beautifully captured.

ORCHESTRAL EXCERPTS FROM THE OPERAS

Der fliegende Holländer: Overture. Götterdämmerung: Siegfried's Rhine journey and Funeral music. Die Meistersinger: Preludes to Acts I & III. Parsifal: Preludes to Acts I & III; Good Friday music; Transformation scene (Act I); Das Rheingold: Entry of the Gods into Valhalla. Siegfried: Forest murmurs. Tannhäuser: Overture; Grand march. Tristan und Isolde: Preludes to Acts I & III. Die Walküre: Ride of the Valkyries.
(M) ** EMI CZS7 62539-2 (2). LPO, LSO or New Philh. O, Sir Adrian Boult.

Sir Adrian Boult is not remembered primarily as a Wagnerian, yet betweeen 1971 and 1974 he made four LPs of orchestral excerpts at Abbey Road. As the CDs show, the sound was good, particularly the sonorous recording of the brass and the rich horn tone, memorable in the *Tannhäuser Grand march* and the *Prelude to Act III* of *Die Meistersinger*, two of the finest performances here. The tuba solo in the *Overture* of the same opera is particularly telling, and this too is a spaciously weighty account, yet lacking the expansive glow of the very finest recorded versions. The *Lohengrin Prelude to Act III* is properly ebullient, and the *Ride of the Valkyries* is genuinely exciting in a genially extrovert way. Elsewhere the orchestral playing is not always immaculate, nor is the concentration held at the highest level, as in the excerpts from *Parsifal*, although there is some fine, radiant string-playing in the *Tristan Prelude*, well caught by the recording. Sometimes elsewhere the resonance clouds the focus of inner detail, notably in the *Flying Dutchman overture* and *Siegfried's Funeral music*. Admirers of Boult will find a good deal to relish here and the measure is generous – some 150 minutes over the two CDs. The transfers are generally very successful.

Der fliegende Holländer: Overture. Lohengrin: Prelude to Act I. Die Meistersinger: Overture. (i) *Tannhäuser: Overture and Venusberg music. Tristan: Prelude and Liebestod.*
(M) *** EMI CDM7 64334-2 [id.]; *EG 764334-4*. BPO, Karajan; (i) with German Op. Ch.

All the music here is played excellently, but the *Overture and Venusberg music* from *Tannhäuser* (Paris version, using chorus) and the *Prelude and Liebestod* from *Tristan* are superb. In the *Liebestod* the climactic culmination is overwhelming in its sentient power, while *Tannhäuser* has comparable spaciousness and grip. There is an urgency and edge to the *Flying Dutchman overture*, and *Die Meistersinger* has weight and dignity, but the last degree of tension is missing. Moreover the digitally remastered sound produces a touch of fierceness in the upper range of these pieces; the *Tannhäuser* and *Tristan* excerpts are fuller, though some of the original bloom has gone.

Götterdämmerung: Dawn and Siegfried's Rhine journey; Siegfried's death and funeral music.
(M) **(*) EMI Dig. CDD7 64290-2 [id.]; *ET 764290-4.* BPO, Tennstedt – R. STRAUSS: *Death and transfiguration* **(*); *4 Last songs.* ***

These excerpts are drawn from EMI's first (1980) digital orchestral collection from *The Ring*, and the demonstrably brilliant recording has some lack of amplitude and resonance in the bass, and a degree of fierceness on top. However, there is no lack of weight: the climax of *Siegfried's Funeral music* has massive penetration. The orchestral playing is of the finest quality and Tennstedt's readings have plenty of tension and grip.

Götterdämmerung: Dawn and Siegfried's Rhine journey; Funeral march. Lohengrin: Preludes to Acts I & III. Die Meistersinger: Overture; Dance of the apprentices. Die Walküre: Ride of the Valkyries.
(B) *** CfP Dig. CD-CFP 9008. LPO, Rickenbacher.

Karl Anton Rickenbacher, formerly principal conductor with the BBC Scottish Symphony Orchestra, here makes an impressive recording début. He secures first-class playing from the LPO with the strings at their peak in the radiant opening of the *Lohengrin Prelude.* Rickenbacher's tempi are far from stoically Teutonic and he presses the music on convincingly, yet retains a sense of breadth. Some might feel his pacing of the *Die Meistersinger overture* is fractionally fast. The CD improves remarkably on the sound of the original LP: the sound is firmer and fuller, with a more expansive bass response; indeed the *Prelude to Act III* of *Lohengrin* makes a splendid demonstration recording; an exciting performance, particularly vividly projected.

Götterdämmerung: Dawn and Siegfried's Rhine journey; Siegfried's death and funeral march. Das Rheingold: Entry of the gods into Valhalla. Siegfried: Forest murmurs. Die Walküre: Ride of the Valkyries; Wotan's farewell and Magic fire music.
(M) **(*) Decca 417 775-2; *417 775-4.* Nat. SO of Washington, Dorati.

Dorati's selection from *The Ring* is essentially dramatic. The *Ride of the Valkyries* comes off especially well, as do the three excerpts from *Götterdämmerung* (with a superbly played horn solo in *Siegfried's Rhine journey*). But in the final scene from *Die Walküre* the lack of richness and body of the string-tone that this orchestra can produce limits the effect of Dorati's eloquence.

Götterdämmerung: Dawn and Siegfried's Rhine jorney; Siegfried's death and funeral march; (i) *Brünnhilde's immolation. Siegfried: Forest murmurs. Die Walküre: Ride of the Valkyries.*
*** Erato/Warner Dig. 2292 45786-2 [id.]. (i) Deborah Polaski; Chicago SO, Barenboim.

Here Barenboim dons his Furtwänglerian mantle to splendidly spacious effect. Even with tempi measured, he secures playing of great concentration and excitement from the Chicago orchestra, and the recording is one of the finest made in Chicago's Orchestra Hall for many years. With resplendently sonorous brass – yet with plenty of bite in the hammered chords of despair of the powerful funeral sequence – and rich, expansive violins, this is very compelling indeed. Without artificial brilliance but with plenty of weight, the *Ride of the Valkyries* opens the programme vigorously; then *Forest murmurs* brings glowing atmospheric magic. Deborah Polaski makes a bold, passionate Brünnhilde, and if her voice is not flattered by the microphones, and under pressure her vibrato widens and there is a loss of focus at the climax of the *Immolation scene*, this is still histrionically thrilling, and Barenboim and the orchestra provide an overwhelming final apotheosis.

Götterdämmerung: Dawn and Siegfried's Rhine journey; Siegfried's death and funeral music. Die Meistersinger: Prelude. Das Rheingold: Entry of the Gods into Valhalla. Siegfried: Forest murmurs. Tristan und Isolde: Prelude & Liebestod. Die Walküre; Wotan's farewell and Magic fire music.
❀ (M) *** SBK 48175 [id.]. Cleveland O, Szell.

The orchestral playing here is in a very special class. Its virtuosity is breathtaking. Szell generates the greatest tension, particularly in the two scenes from *Götterdämmerung*, while the *Liebestod* from *Tristan* has never been played on record with more passion and fire. The *Tristan* and *Meistersinger* excerpts (from 1962) have been added to the contents of the original LP, which contained the *Ring* sequences made later (in 1968), and the improvement in quality with the latest remastering for CD is little short of miraculous. The remastering engineers, Bejun Mehta and Christopher Heries, seem to have found a lower octave in the recording which was never apparent on LP, and the sound has far more depth and weight, underpinning the performances and giving them greater amplitude and impact. Like the similarly remastered Dvořák *Slavonic dances*, this is reasonably worthy of Szell's extraordinary achievement in Cleveland in the 1960s, even if the forward balance of the recording places a limit on the dynamic range.

Götterdämmerung: Dawn and Siegfried's Rhine journey; Siegfried's death and funeral music. Die Meistersinger: Overture. Das Rheingold: Entry of the Gods into Valhalla. Siegfried: Forest murmurs. Die Walküre: Ride of the Valkyries.
(B) **(*) Decca 433 639-2; *433 639-4*. LSO, Leopold Stokowski.

The collection of *Ring* excerpts here was first issued in 1966 and was not one of Decca's most successful Phase 4 recordings. There is superficial brilliance and patches of roughness in the highly modulated recording – but no matter, this is vintage Stokowski. He is at his most electrifying in *Siegfried's Rhine journey*, while the Gods enter Valhalla like a procession of Roman juggernauts. The opening *Ride of the Valkyries* is all but ruined by the top-heavy balance (though the flute and piccolo detail is aurally fascinating), but *Forest murmurs* with its chirruping birds has never sounded more atmospherically potent. The *Mastersingers overture* was recorded 'live' at the London Festival Hall in 1972; again the orchestra is made to seem much too close and the lack of refinement persists, but the overall balance is better. The performance is full of adrenalin but has warmth and grandeur too, with some glorious playing from the LSO strings. The applause is justified.

Götterdämmerung: Siegfried's Rhine journey & Funeral music. Parsifal: Prelude to Act I. Siegfried: Forest murmurs. Tristan und Isolde: Prelude & Liebestod. Die Walküre: Ride of the Valkyries.
*** Collins Dig. 1207-2; *1207-4* [id.]. Philh. O, Yuri Simonov.

If you want a spectacular, modern, digital recording of Wagnerian orchestral excerpts, this one is hard to beat. The magnificent account of *Siegfried's Rhine journey* (with a splendid horn solo) is followed by a performance of the *Funeral music* which has blazing drama and enormously expansive sound, with the brass biting venomously at Siegfried's betrayal. The *Prelude and Liebestod* from *Tristan* brings playing of great ardour from the Philharmonia strings, while – at a very spacious tempo – they find considerable intensity in the *Parsifal Prelude*. The *Valkyries* come in at a fine canter, nostrils flaring yet not driven too hard.

Die Meistersinger: Prelude to Act III. Tannhäuser: Overture and Venusberg music. Tristan und Isolde: Prelude and Liebestod.
**(*) DG Dig. 413 754-2 [id.]. BPO, Karajan.

In Karajan's digital concert the orchestral playing is altogether superlative; artistically there need be no reservations here. But the upper strings lack an ideal amount of space in which to open out and climaxes are not altogether free. The overall effect is slightly clinical in its detail, instead of offering a resonant panoply of sound. But Brangaene's potion still remains heady, and the playing is eloquent and powerful.

Parsifal: Prelude and Good Friday music.
(B) *** Sony MYK 44872 [id.]. Columbia SO, Bruno Walter – DVOŘÁK: *Symphony No. 8*. ***

A glorious account of the *Prelude* and *Good Friday music* from Walter, recorded in 1959, but with the glowingly rich recording never hinting at its age. The digital remastering is a superb achievement.

VOCAL MUSIC

Wesendonk Lieder.
*** Decca 414 624-2 [id.]. Kirsten Flagstad, VPO, Knappertsbusch – MAHLER: *Kindertotenlieder; Lieder eines fahrenden Gesellen*. **

Wesendonk Lieder. Tristan und Isolde: Prelude und Liebestod.
**(*) Ph. 412 655-2 [id.]. Jessye Norman, LSO, C. Davis.

Flagstad's glorious voice is perfectly suited to the rich inspiration of the *Wesendonk Lieder*. *Im Treibhaus* is particularly beautiful. Fine accompaniment, with the 1956 recording sounding remarkable for its vintage, and skilfully remastered.

The poised phrases of the *Wesendonk Lieder* drew from Jessye Norman in this 1976 recording a glorious range of tone-colour, though in detailed imagination she falls short of some of the finest rivals on record. Though the role of Isolde would no doubt strain a still-developing voice, and this is not the most searching of *Liebestods*, it is still the vocal contribution which crowns this conventional linking of first and last in the opera. Good, refined recording.

Wesendonk Lieder: Der Engel; Stehe still; Im Treibhaus; Schmerzen; Träume. Götterdämmerung: Starke Scheite schichet mir dort. Siegfried: Ewig war ich. Tristan: Doch nun von Tristan?; Mild und leise.
(M) (***) EMI mono CDH7 63030-2 [id.]. Kirsten Flagstad, Philh. O, Furtwängler, Dobrowen.

Recorded in the late 1940s and early '50s, a year or so before Flagstad did *Tristan* complete with Furtwängler, these performances show her at her very peak, with the voice magnificent in power as well as beautiful and distinctive in every register. Not that there is as much bloom on the voice here as in the complete *Tristan* recording. The *Liebestod* (with rather heavy surface noise) may be less rapt and intense in this version with Dobrowen than with Furtwängler but is just as expansive. For the *Wesendonk Lieder* she shades the voice down very beautifully, but this is still monumental and noble rather than intimate Lieder-singing. Like other Références issues, this single CD gives no texts or even notes on the music.

Der fliegende Holländer: Senta's ballad. Götterdämmerung: Immolation scene. Tannhäuser: Elisabeth's greeting; Elisabeth's prayer. Tristan und Isolde: Prelude and Liebestod.
*** EMI Dig. CDC7 49759-2 [id.]. Jessye Norman, Amb. Op. Ch., LPO, Tennstedt.

As a Wagnerian, Tennstedt tends to take a rugged view, and it is a measure of his characterful, noble conducting that his contribution is just as striking as that of the great soprano who is the soloist in these items. After a poised and measured account of *Isolde's Liebestod*, Norman is at her most commanding as Elisabeth, both in the outburst of the *Greeting* and in the hushed, poised legato of the *Prayer*. *Senta's ballad* is also superb, and Brünnhilde's *Immolation scene* brings thrilling singing over a daringly wide range of tone and dynamic, conveying feminine warmth, vulnerability and passion, as well as nobility.

OPERA

Die Feen (complete).
*** Orfeo Dig. C062833 (3) [id.]. Gray, Lovaas, Laki, Studer, Alexander, Hermann, Moll, Rootering, Bracht, Bav. R. Ch. & SO, Sawallisch.

Wagner was barely twenty when he wrote *Die Feen*. The piece is composed continuously in what had become the new, advanced manner, and even when he bows to convention and has a buffo duet between the second pair of principals, the result is distinctive and fresh, delightfully sung here by Cheryl Studer and Jan-Hendrik Rootering. This first complete recording was edited together from live performances. Sawallisch gives a strong and dramatic performance, finely paced; central to the total success is the singing of Linda Esther Gray as Ada, the fairy-heroine, powerful and firmly controlled. John Alexander as the tenor hero, King Arindal, sings cleanly and capably; the impressive cast-list boasts such excellent singers as Kurt Moll, Kari Lovaas and Krisztina Laki in small but vital roles. Ensembles and choruses – with the Bavarian Radio Chorus finely disciplined – are particularly impressive, and the recording is generally first rate.

Der fliegende Holländer (complete).
*** Ph. Dig. 416 300-2 (2) [id.]. Estes, Balslev, Salminen, Schunk, Bayreuth Festival (1985) Ch. & O, Nelsson.
**(*) Decca 414 551-2 (3) [id.]. Bailey, Martin, Talvela, Kollo, Krenn, Isola Jones, Chicago SO Ch. & O, Solti.
(M) ** Decca 417 319-2 (2) [id.]. London, Rysanek, Tozzi, ROHCG Ch. & O, Dorati.

Woldemar Nelsson, with the team he had worked with intensively through the season, conducts a performance even more glowing and responsively paced than those of his starrier rivals. The cast is more consistent than any, with Lisbeth Balslev as Senta firmer, sweeter and more secure than any current rival, raw only occasionally, and Simon Estes a strong, ringing Dutchman, clear and noble of tone. Matti Salminen is a dark and equally secure Daland and Robert Schunk an ardent, idiomatic Erik. The veteran, Anny Schlemm, as Mary, though vocally overstressed, adds pointful character, and the chorus is superb, wonderfully drilled and passionate with it. Though inevitably stage noises are obtrusive at times, the recording is exceptionally vivid and atmospheric. On two discs only, it makes an admirable first choice.

What will disappoint some who admire Solti's earlier Wagner sets is that this most atmospheric of the Wagner operas is presented with no Culshaw-style production whatever.

Characters halloo to one another when evidently standing elbow to elbow, and even the Dutchman's ghostly chorus sounds very close and earthbound. But with Norman Bailey a deeply impressive Dutchman, Janis Martin a generally sweet-toned Senta, Martti Talvela a splendid Daland, and Kollo, for all his occasional coarseness, an illuminating Erik, it remains well worth hearing. The brilliance of the recording is all the more striking on CD, but the precise placing so characteristic of the new medium reinforces the clear impression of a concert performance, not an atmospheric re-creation.

The outstanding quality of Dorati's set is the conducting and the general sense of teamwork. Both orchestra and chorus are on top form, the recording is splendidly clear and vivid and the reissue is offered on two mid-price CDs. George London's Dutchman is the drawback; the voice is comparatively ill-defined, the phrasing sometimes clumsy. Rysanek is not always the steadiest of Sentas but she sings with character, and the rest of the cast is vocally reliable.

Der fliegende Holländer: highlights.
(M) **(*) Ph. Dig. 434 216-2; *434 216-4*. Estes, Balslev, Salminen, Schunk, Bayreuth Festival (1985) Ch. & O, Nelsson.

Here is another digital set of highlights on the Philips Laser Line label which has been issued without proper documentation, synopsis or translation. The 76-minute selection gives an admirable survey of the opera.

Götterdämmerung (complete).
*** Decca 414 115-2 (4) [id.]. Nilsson, Windgassen, Fischer-Dieskau, Frick, Neidlinger, Watson, Ludwig, V. State Op. Ch., VPO, Solti.
*** DG 415 155-2 (4) [id.]. Dernesch, Janowitz, Brilioth, Stewart, Kelemen, Ludwig, Ridderbusch, German Op. Ch., BPO, Karajan.
*** Ph. 412 488-2 (4) [id.]. Nilsson, Windgassen, Greindl, Mödl, Stewart, Neidlinger, Dvořáková, Bayreuth Festival (1967) Ch. & O, Boehm.
(M) **(*) RCA/Eurodisc Dig. GD 69007 (4) [69007-2-RG]. Altmeyer, Kollo, Salminen, Wenkel, Nocker, Nimsgern, Sharp, Popp, Leipzig R. Ch., Berlin R. Ch., Dresden State Op. Ch., Dresden State O, Janowski.

In Decca's formidable task of recording the whole *Ring* cycle under Solti, *Götterdämmerung* provided the most daunting challenge of all; characteristically, Solti, and with him the Vienna Philharmonic and the Decca recording team under John Culshaw, were inspired to heights even beyond earlier achievements. Solti's reading had matured before the recording was made. He presses on still, but no longer is there any feeling of over-driving, and even the *Funeral march* is made into a natural, not a forced, climax. There is not a single weak link in the cast. Nilsson surpasses herself in the magnificence of her singing: even Flagstad in her prime would not have been more masterful as Brünnhilde. As in *Siegfried*, Windgassen is in superb voice; Frick is a vivid Hagen, and Fischer-Dieskau achieves the near impossible in making Gunther an interesting and even sympathetic character. As for the recording quality, it surpasses even Decca's earlier achievement, and the CDs bring added weight to balance the brilliant upper range.

Recorded last in Karajan's *Ring* series, *Götterdämmerung* has the finest, fullest sound, less brilliant than Solti's on Decca but glowing in the CD transfer to match the relatively lyrical approach of the conductor, with Helga Dernesch's voice in the Immolation scene given satisfying richness and warmth. Karajan's singing cast is marginally even finer than Solti's, and his performance conveys the steady flow of recording sessions prepared in relation to live performances. But ultimately he falls short of Solti's achievement in the orgasmic quality of the music. Karajan is a degree less committed, beautifully as the players respond, and warm as his overall approach is. Dernesch's Brünnhilde is warmer than Nilsson's, with a glorious range of tone. Brilioth as Siegfried is fresh and young-sounding, while the Gutrune of Gundula Janowitz is far preferable to that of Claire Watson on Decca. The matching is otherwise very even.

Boehm's urgently involving reading of *Götterdämmerung*, very well cast, is crowned by an incandescent performance of the final Immolation scene from Birgit Nilsson as Brünnhilde. It is an astonishing achievement that she could sing with such biting power and accuracy in a live performance, coming to it at the very end of a long evening. The excitement of that is matched by much else in the performance, so that incidental stage noises and the occasional inaccuracy, almost inevitable in live music-making, matter hardly at all. This recording has been transformed in its CD version. The voices are well forward of the orchestra, but the result gives a magnetically real impression of hearing the opera in the Festspielhaus, with the stage movements adding to that sense of reality. Balances are inevitably variable, and at times Windgassen as Siegfried is treated less well by the microphones than is Nilsson. Generally his performance for Solti is fresher – but there are points of advantage, too. Josef Greindl is rather unpleasantly nasal in tone as Hagen, and Martha Mödl as Waltraute is unsteady; but both are dramatically involving. Thomas Stewart is a gruff but convincing Gunther and Dvořáková, as Gutrune, strong if not ideally pure-toned. Neidlinger as ever is a superb Alberich.

With sharply focused digital sound, Janowski's studio recording hits refreshingly hard, at least as much so as in the earlier *Ring* operas. Speeds rarely linger but, with some excellent casting – consistent with the earlier operas – the result is rarely lightweight. Jeannine Altmeyer as Brünnhilde rises to the challenges not so much in strength as in feeling and intensity, ecstatic in Act I, bitter in Act II, dedicated in the Immolation scene. Kollo is a fine heroic Siegfried, only occasionally raw-toned, and Salminen is a magnificent Hagen, with Nimsgern again an incisive Alberich on his brief appearances. Despite an indifferent Gunther and Gutrune and a wobbly if characterful Waltraute, the impression is of clean vocalization matched by finely disciplined and dedicated playing, all recorded in faithful studio sound with no sonic tricks. On the four CDs the background silence adds to the dramatic presence and overall clarity, which is strikingly enhanced, and this mid-priced reissue is well worth considering.

The Twilight of the Gods (*Götterdämmerung:* complete; in English).
(M) *** EMI CMS7 64244-2 (5) [id.]. Hunter, Remedios, Welsby, Haugland, Hammond-Stroud, Curphey, Pring, E. Nat. Op. Ch. & O, Goodall.

Goodall's account of the culminating opera in Wagner's tetralogy may not be the most powerful ever recorded, and certainly it is not the most polished, but it is one which, paradoxically, by intensifying human as opposed to superhuman emotions, heightens the epic scale. The very opening may sound a little tentative (like the rest of the Goodall English *Ring*, this was recorded live at the London Coliseum), but it takes no more than a few seconds to register the body and richness of the sound. The few slight imprecisions and the occasional rawness of wind tone actually seem to enhance the earthiness of Goodall's view, with more of the primeval saga about it than the magnificent polished studio-made Ring cycles. Both Rita Hunter and Alberto Remedios give performances which are magnificent in every way. In particular the golden beauty of Remedios's tenor is consistently superb, with no Heldentenor barking at all, while Aage Haugland's Hagen is giant-sounding to focus the evil, with Gunther and Gutrune mere pawns. The voices on stage are in a different, drier acoustic from that for the orchestra, but considering the problems the sound is impressive. As for Goodall, with his consistently expansive tempi he carries total concentration – except, curiously, in the scene with the Rhinemaidens, whose music (as in Goodall's *Rhinegold* too) lumbers along heavily.

The Twilight of the Gods (Götterdämmerung): Act III: excerpts in English.
*** Chan. CHAN 8534; *ABTD 1244* [id.]. Rita Hunter, Alberto Remedios, Norman Bailey, Grant, Curphey, Sadler's Wells Opera Ch. & O, Goodall.

This single Chandos CD brings an invaluable reminder of Reginald Goodall's performance of the *Ring* cycle when it was in its first flush of success, covering the closing two scenes. In many ways it possesses an advantage over even the complete live recording of the opera, made at the Coliseum five years later, when Rita Hunter and Alberto Remedios are here obviously fresher and less stressed than at the end of a full evening's performance. Fresh, clear recording, not as full as it might be.

Lohengrin (complete).
❀ *** Decca Dig. 421 053-2 (4) [id.]. Domingo, Norman, Nimsgern, Randová, Sotin, Fischer-Dieskau, V. State Op. Concert Ch., VPO, Solti.
*** EMI CDS7 49017-2 (3) [Ang. CDCC 49017]. Jess Thomas, Grümmer, Fischer-Dieskau, Ludwig, Frick, Wiener, V. State Op. Ch., VPO, Kempe.

With its massive ensembles, *Lohengrin* presents special problems, and the engineers here excel themselves in well-aerated sound that still has plenty of body. Solti presents those ensemble moments with rare power and panache, but he also appreciates the chamber-like delicacy of much of the writing, relaxing far more than he might have done earlier in his career, bringing out the endless lyricism warmly and naturally. It is Plácido Domingo's achievement singing Lohengrin that the lyrical element blossoms so consistently, with no hint of Heldentenor barking; at whatever dynamic level, Domingo's voice is firm and unstrained. In the Act III aria, *In fernem Land*, for example, he uses the widest, most beautiful range of tonal colouring, with ringing heroic tone dramatically contrasted against a whisper of head voice, finely controlled. Jessye Norman, not naturally suited to the role of Elsa, yet gives a warm, commanding performance, always intense, full of detailed insights into words and character. Eva Randová's grainy mezzo does not take so readily to recording, but as Ortrud she provides a pointful contrast, even if she never matches the firm, biting malevolence of Christa Ludwig on the Kempe set. Siegmund Nimsgern, Telramund for Solti as for Karajan, equally falls short of Fischer-Dieskau, his rival on the Kempe set; but it is still a strong, cleanly focused performance. Fischer-Dieskau here sings the small but vital role of the Herald, while Hans Sotin makes a comparably distinctive King Henry. Radiant playing from the Vienna Philharmonic, and committed chorus work too. This is one of the crowning glories of Solti's long recording career.

Kempe's is a rapt account of *Lohengrin* which has been surpassed on record only by Solti's Decca set and which remains one of his finest monuments in sound. After all, Kempe looked at Wagner very much from the spiritual side, giving *Lohengrin* perspectives deeper than is common. The intensity of Kempe's conducting lies in its very restraint, and throughout this glowing performance one senses a gentle but sure control, with the strings of the Vienna Philharmonic playing radiantly. The singers too seem uplifted, Jess Thomas singing more clearly and richly than usual, Elisabeth Grümmer unrivalled as Elsa in her delicacy and sweetness, Gottlob Frick gloriously resonant as the king. But it is the partnership of Christa Ludwig and Fischer-Dieskau as Ortrud and Telramund that sets the seal on this superb performance, giving the darkest intensity to their machinations in Act II, their evil heightening the beauty and serenity of so much in this opera. Though the digital transfer on CD reveals roughness (even occasional distortion) in the original recording, the glow and intensity of Kempe's reading come out all the more involvingly in the new format. The set is also very economically contained on three CDs instead of the four for all rivals, though inevitably breaks between discs come in the middle of Acts.

Die Meistersinger von Nürnberg (complete).

*** DG 415 278-2 (4) [id.]. Fischer-Dieskau, Ligendza, Lagger, Hermann, Domingo, Laubenthal, Ludwig, German Op. Ch. & O, Berlin, Jochum.

**(*) Decca 417 497-2 (4) [id.]. Bailey, Bode, Moll, Weikl, Kollo, Dallapozza, Hamari, Gumpoldskirchner Spatzen, V. State Op. Ch., VPO, Solti.

(M) **(*) Ph. 432 573-2 (4) [id.]. Ridderbusch, Bode, Sotin, Hirte, Cox, Stricker, (1974) Bayreuth Festival Ch. & O, Varviso.

Jochum's is a performance which, more than any, captures the light and shade of Wagner's most warmly approachable score, its humour and tenderness as well as its strength. With Jochum the processions at the start of the final Festwiese have sparkling high spirits, not just German solemnity, while the poetry of the score is brought out radiantly, whether in the incandescence of the Act III *Prelude* (positively Brucknerian in hushed concentration) or the youthful magic of the love music for Walther and Eva. Above all, Jochum is unerring in building long Wagnerian climaxes and resolving them – more so than his recorded rivals. The cast is the most consistent yet assembled on record. Though Caterina Ligendza's big soprano is a little ungainly for Eva, it is an appealing performance, and the choice of Domingo for Walther is inspired. The key to the set is of course the searching and highly individual Sachs of Fischer-Dieskau, a performance long awaited. With detailed word-pointing and sharply focused tone he gives new illumination in every scene, and Horst Laubenthal's finely tuned David matches this Sachs in applying Lieder style. The recording balance favours the voices, but on CD they are made to sound slightly ahead of the orchestra. There is a lovely bloom on the whole sound and, with a recording which is basically wide-ranging and refined, the ambience brings an attractively natural projection of the singers.

The great glory of Solti's set is not the searing brilliance of the conductor but rather the mature and involving portrayal of Sachs by Norman Bailey. The set is well worth investigating for his superb singing alone, but there is much else to enjoy, not least the bright and detailed sound which the Decca engineers have obtained with the Vienna Philharmonic. Kurt Moll as Pogner, Bernd Weikl as Beckmesser and Julia Hamari as Magdalene are all excellent, but the shortcomings are comparably serious. Both Hannelore Bode and René Kollo fall short of their far-from-perfect contributions to earlier sets, and Solti for all his energy gives a surprisingly square reading of this most appealing of Wagner scores, pointing his expressive lines too heavily and failing to convey real spontaneity. It remains an impressive achievement for Bailey's marvellous Sachs, and the Decca sound comes up very vividly on CD.

The Bayreuth performance, recorded during the Festival of 1974, is flawed; but the Swiss conductor Silvio Varviso still proves the most persuasive Wagnerian, one who inspires the authentic ebb and flow of tension, who builds up Wagner's scenes concentratedly over the longest span and who revels in the lyricism and textural beauty of the score. With one exception, the singing is very enjoyable indeed, with Karl Ridderbusch a firmly resonant Sachs and the other Masters, headed by Klaus Hirte as Beckmesser and Hans Sotin as Pogner, really singing their parts. Jean Cox is a strenuous Walther, understandably falling short towards the end; Hannelore Bode as Eva brings the one serious disappointment but she is firmer here than on Solti's later (and full-price) set. For all the variability, the recording, retaining its atmosphere in the CD transfer, gives enjoyment, even if the stage noises are the more noticeable.

Die Meistersinger: excerpts.
(M) *** DG 435 406-2; *435 406-4* [id.] (from above set, with Fischer-Dieskau, Ligendza, Domingo; cond. Jochum) – WEBER: *Oberon* excerpts. ***

Instead of a normal set of highlights for this reissue in the 'Domingo Edition', DG have sensibly concentrated on the items featuring Domingo as Walther. The selection runs for nearly 40 minutes and, while some of the excerpts involve fades, sometimes at both ends, the effect is not too distracting. The sound is first rate and the coupling with excerpts from Weber's *Oberon* an equally happy choice.

Parsifal (complete).
❀ *** DG Dig. 413 347-2 (4) [id.]. Hofmann, Vejzovic, Moll, Van Dam, Nimsgern, Von Halem, German Op. Ch., BPO, Karajan.
*** Decca 417 143-2 (4) [id.]. Kollo, Ludwig, Fischer-Dieskau, Hotter, Kelemen, Frick, V. Boys' Ch., V. State Op. Ch., VPO, Solti.
**(*) DG 435 718-2 (3) [id.]. James King, Gweneth Jones, Stewart, Ridderbusch, McIntyre, Crass, Bayreuth Festival Ch. & O (1970), Boulez.
**(*) Ph. Dig. 416 842-2 (4) [id.]. Hofmann, Meier, Estes, Sotin, Salminen, Mazura, Bayreuth Festival (1985) Ch. & O, Levine.
(M) **(*) Erato/Warner Dig. 2292 45662-2 (4) [id.]. Goldberg, Lloyd, Minton, Haugland, Tschammer, Schöne, Prague Philharmonic Ch., Monte Carlo PO, Jordan.
**(*) Ph. 416 390-2 (4). Jess Thomas, Dalis, London, Talvela, Neidlinger, Hotter, Bayreuth Festival (1962) Ch. & O, Knappertsbusch.

Communion, musical and spiritual, is what this intensely beautiful Karajan set provides, with pianissimos shaded in magical clarity and the ritual of bells and offstage choruses heard as in ideal imagination. The playing of the Berlin orchestra is consistently beautiful; but the clarity and refinement of sound prevent this from emerging as a lengthy serving of Karajan soup. Kurt Moll as Gurnemanz is the singer who, more than any other, anchors the work vocally, projecting his voice with firmness and subtlety. José van Dam as Amfortas is also splendid. The Klingsor of Siegmund Nimsgern could be more sinister, but the singing is admirable. Dunja Vejzovic makes a vibrant, sensuous Kundry who rises superbly to the moment in Act II when she bemoans her laughter in the face of Christ. Only Peter Hofmann as Parsifal leaves any disappointment; at times he develops a gritty edge on the voice, but his natural tone is admirably suited to the part and he is never less than dramatically effective. He is not helped by the relative closeness of the solo voices, but otherwise the recording is near the atmospheric ideal, a superb achievement. The four CDs are still among DG's finest so far.

Solti's singing cast could hardly be stronger, every one of them pointing words with fine, illuminating care for detail; and the complex balances of sound, not least in the *Good Friday music*, are beautifully caught; throughout, Solti shows his sustained intensity in Wagner. There remains just one doubt, but that rather serious: the lack of a rapt, spiritual quality. The remastering for CD, as with Solti's other Wagner recordings, opens up the sound, and the choral climaxes are superb, although the break between the second and third discs could have been better placed. Cueing is generous but the libretto is poor, the typeface minuscule and in places no pleasure to read.

Boulez's recording, made live at Bayreuth in 1970, was only the third version ever issued, yet it has remained the most radical of all. The speeds are so consistently fast that in the age of CD it has brought an obvious benefit in being fitted – easily – on three discs instead of four, yet Boulez's approach, with the line beautifully controlled, conveys a dramatic urgency rarely found in this opera, and never sounds breathless. Traditional Wagnerians may well resist, and certainly Boulez misses the spiritual intensity of a Karajan or a Knappertsbusch, but those listeners less committed will find the results refreshing, with textures clarified in a way characteristic of

Boulez. Even the flower-maidens sing like young apprentices in *Meistersinger* rather than seductive beauties. James King is a firm, strong, rather baritonal hero, Thomas Stewart a fine tense Amfortas, and Gwyneth Jones as Kundry is in strong voice, only occasionally shrill, though Franz Crass is disappointingly unsteady as Gurnemanz. The live Bayreuth recording is most impressively transferred to CD.

Of all the Wagner operas, this is the one that gains most and loses least from being recorded live at Bayreuth, and the dedication of Levine's reading comes over consistently, if not with quite the glow that so marks Karajan's inspired studio performance. Unfortunately the singing is flawed. Peter Hofmann, in far poorer voice than for Karajan, is often ill-focused, and even Hans Sotin as Gurnemanz is vocally less reliable than usual. The rest are excellent, with Franz Mazura as Klingsor, Simon Estes as Amfortas and Matti Salminen as Titurel all giving resonant, finely projected performances, well contrasted with each other. Waltraud Meier is an outstanding Kundry here. The recording, though not the clearest from this source, captures the Bayreuth atmosphere well.

Jordan's 1981 recording with Monte Carlo forces, clean and fresh but lacking in weight and spiritual depth, was used for the controversial film of the opera. Its great merit is the singing of Reiner Goldberg in the name-part. Though the voice is not always well focused, Robert Lloyd's Gurnemanz brings fine singing too, more youthful-sounding than usual. Aage Haugland's Klingsor has nothing sinister in it, but rather masculine nobility, and Yvonne Minton makes a fine, vehement Kundry. This is the only digital mid-priced set of this opera. It has full, natural sound, vivid yet warmly atmospheric in its CD format, and is certainly recommendable to those who liked the film. However, it comes on four CDs against Boulez's three. The documentation is good, with a clear libretto, but the cues are relatively ungenerous.

Knappertsbusch's expansive and dedicated reading is caught superbly in the Philips set, arguably the finest live recording ever made in the Festspielhaus at Bayreuth, with outstanding singing from Jess Thomas as Parsifal and Hans Hotter as Gurnemanz. Though Knappertsbusch chooses consistently slow tempi, there is no sense of excessive squareness or length, so intense is the concentration of the performance, its spiritual quality; and the sound has undoubtedly been further enhanced in the remastering for CD. The snag is that the stage noises and coughs are also emphasized, with the bronchial afflictions particularly disturbing in the *Prelude*. However, the recording itself is most impressive, with the choral perspectives particularly convincing and the overall sound warmly atmospheric.

Das Rheingold (complete).

*** Decca 414 101-2 (3). London, Flagstad, Svanholm, Neidlinger, VPO, Solti.

**(*) DG 415 141-2 (3) [id.]. Fischer-Dieskau, Veasey, Stolze, Kelemen, BPO, Karajan.

**(*) Ph. 412 475-2 (2) [id.]. Adam, Nienstedt, Windgassen, Neidlinger, Talvela, Böhme, Silja, Soukupová, Bayreuth Festival (1967) Ch. & O, Boehm.

(M) **(*) RCA/Eurodisc Dig. GD 69004 (2) [69004-2-RG]. Adam, Nimsgern, Stryczek, Schreier, Bracht, Salminen, Vogel, Buchner, Minton, Popp, Priew, Schwarz, Dresden State O, Janowski.

** EMI Dig. CDS7 49853-2 (2) [Ang. CDCB 49853]. Morris, Lipovšek, Zednik, Adam, Haage, Bav. RSO, Haitink.

The first of Solti's cycle, recorded in 1958, *Rheingold* remains in terms of engineering the most spectacular on CD. The immediacy and precise placing are thrilling, while the sound-effects of the final scenes, including Donner's hammer-blow and the Rainbow bridge, have never been matched since. The effect remains of demonstration quality, to have one cherishing all the more this historic recording with its unique vignette of Flagstad as Fricka. Solti gives a magnificent reading of the score, crisp, dramatic and direct. He somehow brings a freshness to the music without ever overdriving or losing an underlying sympathy. Vocally, the set is held together by the unforgettable singing of Neidlinger as Alberich. He vocalizes with wonderful precision and makes the character of the dwarf develop from the comic creature of the opening scene to the demented monster of the last. Flagstad learned the part of Fricka specially for this recording, and her singing makes one regret that she never took the role on the stage. Only the slightest trace of hardness in the upper register occasionally betrays her, and the golden power and richness of her singing are for the rest unimpaired. As Wotan, George London is sometimes a little rough, but this is a dramatic portrayal of the young Wotan. Svanholm could be more characterful as Loge, but again it is a relief to hear the part really sung. An outstanding achievement.

Karajan's account is more reflective than Solti's; the very measured pace of the *Prelude* indicates this at the start and there is often an extra bloom on the Berlin Philharmonic playing.

But Karajan's very reflectiveness has its less welcome side, for the tension rarely varies. One finds such incidents as Alberich's stealing of the gold or Donner's hammer-blow passing by without one's pulse quickening as it should. There is also no doubt that the DG recording managers were not as painstaking as John Culshaw's Decca team, and that too makes the end result less compellingly dramatic. On the credit side, however, the singing cast has hardly any flaw at all, and Fischer-Dieskau's Wotan is a brilliant and memorable creation, virile and expressive. Among the others, Veasey is excellent, though obviously she cannot efface memories of Flagstad; Gerhard Stolze with his flickering, almost *Sprechstimme* as Loge gives an intensely vivid if, for some, controversial interpretation. The 1968 sound has been clarified in the digital transfer, but generally the lack of bass brings some thinness.

Boehm's preference for fast speeds (consistently through the whole cycle) here brings the benefit that the whole of the *Vorabend* is contained on two CDs, a considerable financial advantage. The pity is that the performance is marred by the casting of Theo Adam as Wotan, keenly intelligent but rarely agreeable on the ear, at times here far too wobbly. On the other hand, Gustav Neidlinger as Alberich is superb, even more involving here than he is for Solti, with the curse made spine-chilling. It is also good to have Wolfgang Windgassen as Loge; among the others, Anja Silja makes an attractively urgent Freia. Though a stage production brings nothing like the sound-effects which make Solti's set so involving, the atmosphere of the theatre in its way is just as potent.

In Marek Janowski's digital recording, the studio sound has the voices close and vivid, with the orchestra rather in the background. Donner's hammer-blow in the Eurodisc set comes up with only a very ordinary 'ping' on an anvil, and the grandeur of the moment is missing. Theo Adam as Wotan has his grittiness of tone exaggerated here, but otherwise it is a fine set, consistently well cast, including Peter Schreier, Matti Salminen, Yvonne Minton and Lucia Popp, as well as East German singers of high calibre. Complete on two mid-priced CDs, it is certainly good value.

Haitink's version of *Rheingold*, the second instalment in his EMI *Ring* cycle made in conjunction with Bavarian Radio, follows the same broad pattern as the first to be issued, *Die Walküre*, strong and expansive rather than dramatic, with tension often not quite keen enough. Vocally too the performance has its flaws. Marjana Lipovšek makes a superb Fricka, rich and well projected, but James Morris – also the Wotan in the rival Levine cycle for DG – sounds grittier than before; the fascinating choice of a noted Wotan of the past for the role of Alberich, Theo Adam, proves a mixed blessing. The often unconventional characterization is magnetic, but Adam can no longer sustain a steady note. One powerful point in favour of the EMI set is that it requires only two CDs instead of the usual three. The recording is warm and full rather than brilliant or well focused.

The Rheingold (complete, in English).
(M) **(*) EMI CMS7 64110-2 (3). Bailey, Hammond-Stroud, Pring, Belcourt, Attfield, Collins, McDonnall, Lloyd, Grant, English Nat. Op. O, Goodall.

Goodall's slow tempi in *Rheingold* bring an opening section where the temperature is low, reflecting hardly at all the tensions of a live performance, even though this was taken from a series of Coliseum presentations. Nevertheless the momentum of Wagner gradually builds up so that, by the final scenes, both the overall teamwork and the individual contributions of such singers as Norman Bailey, Derek Hammond-Stroud and Clifford Grant come together impressively. Hammond-Stroud's powerful representation of Alberich culminates in a superb account of the curse. The spectacular orchestral effects (with the horns sounding glorious) are vividly caught by the engineers and impressively transferred to CD, even if balances (inevitably) are sometimes less than ideal.

Rienzi (complete).
(M) ** EMI CMS7 63980-2 (3) [id.]. Kollo, Wennberg, Martin, Adam, Hillebrand, Vogel, Schreier, Leipzig R. Ch., Dresden State Op. Ch., Dresden State O, Hollreiser.

It is sad that the flaws in this ambitious opera prevent the unwieldy piece from having its full dramatic impact. This recording is not quite complete, but the cuts are unimportant and most of the set numbers make plain the youthful, uncritical exuberance of the ambitious composer. The accompanied recitatives are less inspired, and no one could count the Paris-stye ballet music consistent with the rest, delightful and sparkling though it is. Except in the recitative, Heinrich Hollreiser's direction is strong and purposeful, but much of the singing is disappointing. René Kollo at least sounds heroic, but the two women principals are poor. Janis Martin in the breeches role of Adriano produces tone that does not record very sweetly, while Siv Wennberg as the heroine, Rienzi's sister, slides most unpleasantly between notes in the florid passages. Despite good recording, this can only be regarded as a stop-gap.

Der Ring des Nibelungen (complete).
❀ (M) *** Decca 414 100-2 (15) [id.]. Nilsson, Windgassen, Flagstad, Fischer-Dieskau, Hotter, London, Ludwig, Neidlinger, Frick, Svanholm, Stoltze, Böhme, Hoffgen, Sutherland, Crespin, King, Watson, Ch. & VPO, Solti.
(M) *** DG 435 211-2 (15) [id.]. Veasey, Fischer-Dieskau, Stolze, Kelemen, Dernesch, Dominguez, Jess Thomas, Stewart, Crespin, Janowitz, Vickers, Talvela, Brilioth, Ludwig, Ridderbusch, BPO, Karajan.
(M) *** Ph. 420 325-2 (14) [id.]. Nilsson, Windgassen, Neidlinger, Adam, Rysanek, King, Nienstedt, Esser, Talvela, Böhme, Silja, Dernesch, Stewart, Hoeffgen, Bayreuth Festival (1967) Ch. & O, Boehm.
(M) *** BMG/RCA Dig. GD 69003 (14) [69003-2-RG]. Altmeyer, Kollo, Adam, Schreier, Nimsgern, Vogel, Minton, Wenkel, Salminen, Popp, Jerusalem, J. Norman, Moll, Studer, Leipzig R. Ch., Dresden State Op. Ch. & O, Janowski.
(M) (***) EMI mono CZS7 67123-2 (13) [Ang. CDZM 67123]. Suthaus, Mödl, Frantz, Patzak, Neidlinger, Windgassen, Konetzni, Streich, Jurinac, Frick, RAI Ch. & Rome SO, Furtwängler.

Solti's was the first recorded *Ring* cycle to be issued. Whether in performance or in vividness of sound, it continues to set standards three decades after Decca's great project was completed. As for the casting, that too has never been surpassed, certainly not by latter-day studio recordings. Even the role of the Woodbird in *Siegfried* is uniquely cast, with the young Joan Sutherland outshining all rivals. Nilsson and Windgassen as Brünnhilde and Siegfried may not be as spontaneous-sounding in this studio performance as in their live, Bayreuth recording for Boehm, but the freshness and power are even greater. Solti's remains the most electrifying account of the tetralogy on disc, sharply focused if not always as warmly expressive as some. Solti himself developed in the process of making the recording, and *Götterdämmerung* represents a peak of achievement for him, commanding and magnificent. Though CD occasionally reveals bumps and bangs inaudible on the original LPs, this is a historic set that remains as central today as when it first appeared.

Karajan's recording of *The Ring* followed close on the heels of Solti's for Decca, providing a good alternative studio version which equally stands the test of time. The manner is smoother, the speeds generally broader, yet the tension and concentration of the performances are maintained more consistently than in most modern studio recordings. Though the recordings were linked with stage productions in Salzburg and at the Met. in New York, they preceded the stagings and bring a broadly contemplative rather than a searingly dramatic view of Wagner. Casting is not quite consistent between the operas, with Régine Crespin as Brünnhilde in *Walküre*, but Helga Dernesch at her very peak in the last two operas. The casting of Siegfried is changed between *Siegfried* and *Götterdämmerung*, from Jess Thomas, clear and reliable, to Helge Brilioth, just as strong but sweeter of tone. The original CD transfers are used without change for this mid-price compilation. The recording, pleasantly reverberant, is not as immediate or involving as Solti's Decca, with fewer dramatic sound effects.

Anyone who prefers the idea of a live recording of the *Ring* cycle can be warmly recommended to Boehm's fine set, more immediately involving than any. Recorded at the 1967 Bayreuth Festival, it captures the unique atmosphere and acoustic of the Festspielhaus very vividly. Birgit Nilsson as Brünnhilde and Wolfgang Windgassen as Siegfried are both a degree more volatile and passionate than they were in the Solti cycle, recorded earlier for Decca, with Nilsson at her most incandescent in the final Immolation scene, triumphant at the end of her long performance. Gustav Neidlinger as Alberich is also superb, as he was too in the Solti set; and the only major reservation concerns the Wotan of Theo Adam, in a performance searchingly intense and finely detailed but often unsteady of tone even at that period. Boehm's preference for urgent speeds, never letting the music sag, makes this an exciting experience, and in *Rheingold* it brings the practical advantage that the Vorabend comes on only two CDs instead of three, bringing the total for the set to 14 instead of 15 discs. The sound, only occasionally constricted, has been vividly transferred.

Dedication and consistency are the mark of the Eurodisc *Ring*, a studio recording made with German thoroughness by the East German record company, VEB. Originally packaged cumbersomely by Eurodisc on 18 CDs, RCA here reissue it on 14 mid-price discs, to make it much more attractive. Voices tend to be balanced well forward of the orchestra, but the digital sound is full and clear to have one concentrating on the words, helped by Janowski's direct approach to the score. Overall this is a good deal more rewarding than many of the individual sets that have been issued at full price over the last five years.

When in 1972 EMI first transferred the Italian Radio tapes of Furtwängler's studio performances of 1953, the sound was disagreeably harsh, making sustained listening unpleasant. In this digital transfer, the boxiness of the studio sound and the closeness of the voices still take away some of the unique Furtwängler glow in Wagner, but the sound is acceptable and actually benefits in some ways from extra clarity. Furtwängler gives each opera a commanding sense of unity, musically and dramatically, with hand-picked casts including Martha Mödl as a formidable Brünnhilde, Ferdinand Frantz a firm-voiced Wotan and Ludwig Suthaus (Tristan in Furtwängler's recording) a reliable Siegfried. In smaller roles you have stars like Wolfgang Windgassen, Julius Patzak, Rita Streich, Sena Jurinac and Gottlob Frick.

The Ring 'Great scenes': Das Rheingold: Entry of the Gods into Valhalla. Die Walküre: Ride of the Valkyries; Magic fire music. Siegfried: Forging scene; Forest murmurs. Götterdämmerung: Siegfried's funeral march; Brünnhilde's immolation scene.
(M) *** Decca 421 313-2. Nilsson, Windgassen, Hotter, Stolzel, VPO, Solti.

These excerpts are often quite extended – the *Entry of the Gods into Valhalla* offers some 10 minutes of music, and the *Forest murmurs* from *Siegfried* starts well before the orchestral interlude. Only *Siegfried's funeral march* is in any sense a 'bleeding chunk' which has to be faded at the end; and the disc closes with 20 minutes of Brünnhilde's Immolation scene.

Der Ring: excerpts: *Das Rheingold: Zur Burg führt die Brucke* (scene iv). *Die Walküre: Ein Schwert verhiess mir der Vater; Ride of the Valkyries; Wotan's farewell and Magic fire music. Siegfried: Notung!; Brünnhilde's awakening. Götterdämmerung: Brünnhilde, heilige Braut! Siegfried's death and Funeral music.*
(B) *** DG 429 168-2; *429 168-4* (from complete recording; cond. Karajan).

The DG producer of this record has managed to assemble 70 minutes of key items, mostly nicely tailored, with quick fades. The one miscalculation was to end with *Siegfried's funeral march* from *Götterdämmerung*, which leaves the listener suspended; it would have been a simple matter to add the brief orchestral postlude which ends the opera. Nevertheless there is much to enjoy, and this makes a genuine sampler of Karajan's approach to the *Ring* – even the *Ride of the Valkyries* is comparatively refined. The late-1960s sound is excellent.

Siegfried (complete).
*** Decca 414 110-2 (4). Windgassen, Nilsson, Hotter, Stolze, Neidlinger, Böhme, Hoffgen, Sutherland, VPO, Solti.
*** Ph. 412 483-2 (4) [id.]. Windgassen, Nilsson, Adam, Neidlinger, Soukupová, Köth, Böhme, Bayreuth Festival (1967) Ch. & O, Boehm.
**(*) EMI Dig. CDS7 54290-2 (4) [Ang. CDCD 54290]. Jerusalem, Marton, Morris, Haage, Adam, Rydl, Te Kanawa, Bav. RSO, Haitink.
(M) **(*) RCA/Eurodisc Dig. GD 69006 (4) [69006-2-RG]. Kollo, Altmeyer, Adam, Schreier, Nimsgern, Wenkel, Salminen, Sharp, Dresden State O, Janowski.
** DG 415 150-2 (4) [id.]. Dernesch, Dominguez, Jess Thomas, Stolze, Stewart, Kelemen, BPO, Karajan.
** DG Dig. 429 407-2 (4) [id.]. Goldberg, Behrens, Morris, Zednik, Wlaschiha, Moll, Battle, NY Met. O, Levine.

Siegfried has too long been thought of as the grimmest of the *Ring* cycle, with dark colours predominating. It is true that the preponderance of male voices till the very end, and Wagner's deliberate matching of this in his orchestration, gives a special colour to the opera, but a performance as buoyant as Solti's reveals that, more than in most Wagner, the message is one of optimism. Each of the three Acts ends with a scene of triumphant optimism – the first Act in Siegfried's forging song, the second with him in hot pursuit of the woodbird, and the third with the most opulent of love duets. Solti's array of singers could hardly be bettered. Windgassen is at the very peak of his form, lyrical as well as heroic. Hotter has never been more impressive on record, his Wotan at last captured adequately. Stolze, Neidlinger and Böhme are all exemplary, and predictably Joan Sutherland makes the most seductive of woodbirds. Only the conducting of Solti leaves a tiny margin of doubt. In the dramatic moments he could hardly be more impressive, but that very woodbird scene shows up the shortcomings: the bird's melismatic carolling is plainly intended to have a degree of freedom, whereas Solti allows little or no lilt in the music at all. With singing finer than any opera house could normally provide, with masterly playing from the Vienna Philharmonic and with Decca's most vivid recording, this is a set likely to stand comparison with anything the rest of the century may provide. The CD transfer is of outstanding quality.

The natural-sounding quality of Boehm's live recording from Bayreuth, coupled with his determination not to let the music lag, makes his account of *Siegfried* as satisfying as the rest of his cycle, vividly capturing the atmosphere of the Festspielhaus, with voices well ahead of the orchestra. Windgassen is at his peak here, if anything more poetic in Acts II and III than he is in Solti's studio recording, and vocally just as fine. Nilsson, as in *Götterdämmerung*, gains over her studio recording from the extra flow of adrenalin in a live performance; and Gustav Neidlinger is unmatchable as Alberich. Erika Köth is disappointing as the woodbird, not sweet enough, and Soukupová is a positive, characterful Erda. Theo Adam is at his finest as the Wanderer, less wobbly than usual, clean and incisive.

It is sad that both the modern digital recordings made by big rival companies should be seriously flawed. In *Siegfried*, as much as in the other Ring operas, Haitink has the advantage. His speeds are generally a degree faster, with a sharper dramatic sense, and the choice of Siegfried Jerusalem in the title role of Siegfried is far preferable to that of the seriously flawed Reiner Goldberg. Jerusalem more than any Heldentenor since Wolfgang Windgassen sings the notes with a beauty and clarity of focus that allows the lyrical strength as well as the detailed meaning of Wagner's words to come over. James Morris is the Wanderer in both recordings, rather sweeter on the ear in the EMI set. Neither Eva Marton for Haitink nor Hildegard Behrens for Levine sings steadily as Brünnhilde. Behrens is better focused, but she seems just as overstressed as the loud and gusty Eva Marton on EMI. The weighty Theo Adam makes an unsteady Alberich, vocally far less impressive than Wlaschiha for Levine, but the long-experienced Adam conveys far more of the dramatic bite. Overall Levine is markedly less successful than Haitink at conveying the feeling of a live dramatic performance, which is surprising when his version was directly based on the stage production at the Met in New York. Neither recording is as firmly focused as those in the pioneering Solti set on Decca, but Haitink's EMI has more atmosphere with a keener sense of presence.

With Janowski, direct and straight in his approach and securing superb playing from the Dresdeners, the RCA/Eurodisc set lacks a degree of dramatic tension, for he does not always build the climaxes cumulatively. Thus the final scene of Act II just scurries to a close, with Siegfried in pursuit of a rather shrill woodbird in Norma Sharp. The singing is generally first rate, with Kollo a fine Siegfried, less strained than he has sometimes been, and Peter Schreier a superb Mime, using Lieder-like qualities in detailed characterization. Siegmund Nimsgern is a less characterful Alberich, but the voice is excellent; and Theo Adam concludes his portrayal of Wotan/Wanderer with his finest performance of the series. The relative lightness of Jeannine Altmeyer's Brünnhilde comes out in the final love-duet more strikingly than in *Walküre*. Nevertheless the tenderness and femininity are most affecting as at the entry of the idyll motif, where Janowski in his dedicated simplicity is also at his most compelling. Clear, beautifully balanced digital sound, with voices and instruments firmly placed.

When Siegfried is outsung by Mime, it is time to complain, and though the DG set has many fine qualities – not least the Brünnhilde of Helga Dernesch – it hardly rivals the Solti or Boehm versions. Windgassen on Decca gave a classic performance, and any comparison highlights the serious shortcomings of Jess Thomas. Even when voices are balanced forward, the digital transfer helps little to make Thomas's singing as Siegfried any more acceptable. Otherwise, the vocal cast is strong, and Karajan provides the seamless playing which characterizes his cycle. Recommended only to those irrevocably committed to the Karajan cycle.

Siegfried (complete, in English).
(M) *** EMI CMS7 63595-2 (4). Remedios, Hunter, Bailey, Dempsey, Hammond-Stroud, Grant, Collins, London, Sadler's Wells Op. O, Goodall.

More tellingly than in almost any other Wagner opera recording, Goodall's spacious direction here conveys the genuine dramatic crunch that gives the experience of hearing Wagner in the opera house its unique power, its overwhelming force. In the *Prelude* there are intrusive audience noises, and towards the end the Sadler's Wells violins have one or two shaky moments; but this is unmistakably a great interpretation caught on the wing. Remedios, more than any rival on record, conveys not only heroic strength but clear-ringing youthfulness, caressing the ear as well as exciting it. Norman Bailey makes a magnificently noble Wanderer, steady of tone, and Gregory Dempsey is a characterful Mime, even if his deliberate whining tone is not well caught on record. The sound is superbly realistic, even making no allowances for the conditions. Lovers of opera in English should grasp the opportunity of hearing this unique set. The transfer is remarkably vivid and detailed, kind to the voices and with a natural presence so that the words are clear, yet there is no edge or exaggeration of consonants.

Tannhäuser (Paris version; complete).
*** DG. Dig. 427 625-2 (3) [id.]. Domingo, Studer, Baltsa, Salminen, Schmidt, Ch. & Philh. O, Sinopoli.
*** Decca 414 581-2 (3) [id.]. Kollo, Dernesch, Ludwig, Sotin, Braun, Hollweg, V. State Op. Ch., VPO, Solti.

Following up his fine Lohengrin with Solti for Decca, Plácido Domingo here makes another Wagnerian sortie, bringing balm to ears wounded by the general run of German heroic tenors. Pressured as he is by the jet-set life of a superstar, it is amazing that he can produce sounds of such power as well as such beauty. In the narration of Act III, it is a joy to hear such a range of tone, dynamic and expression, even if he cannot match his rival, René Kollo, on Solti's Decca set in the agony of the culminating word, '*verdammt*', 'damned'. Following up his experience conducting this opera at Bayreuth (though that was the Dresden, not the Paris, version) Giuseppe Sinopoli here makes his most passionately committed opera recording yet, warmer and more flexible than Solti's Decca version, always individual, with fine detail brought out, always persuasively, and never wilful. Recorded not with Bayreuth forces but in the studio with his own Philharmonia Orchestra, the extra range and beauty of the sound brings ample compensation for a recording that does not attempt to create the sound-stage of Solti's version. Agnes Baltsa is not ideally opulent of tone as Venus, but she is the complete seductress. Cheryl Studer – who sang the role of Elisabeth for Sinopoli at Bayreuth – gives a most sensitive performance, not always ideally even of tone but creating a movingly intense portrait of the heroine, vulnerable and very feminine. Matti Salminen in one of his last recordings makes a superb Landgrave and Andreas Schmidt a noble Wolfram, even though the legato could be smoother in *O star of Eve*.

Solti provides an electrifying experience, demonstrating beyond a shadow of doubt how much more effective the Paris revision of *Tannhäuser* is, compared with the usual Dresden version. The differences lie mainly – though not entirely – in Act I in the scene between Tannhäuser and Venus. Wagner rewrote most of the scene at a time when his style had developed enormously. The love music here is closer to *Walküre* and *Tristan* than to the rest of *Tannhäuser*. Solti gives one of his very finest Wagner performances to date, helped by superb playing from the Vienna Philharmonic and an outstanding cast, superlatively recorded. Dernesch as Elisabeth and Ludwig as Venus outshine all rivals; and Kollo, though not ideal, makes as fine a Heldentenor as we are currently likely to hear. The compact disc transfer reinforces the brilliance and richness of the performance. The sound is outstanding for its period (1971), and Ray Minshull's production adds to the atmospheric quality, with the orchestra given full weight and with the placing and movement of the voices finely judged.

Tannhäuser (Dresden version; complete).
**(*) Ph. 420 122-2 (3) [id.]. Windgassen, Waechter, Silja, Stolze, Bumbry, Bayreuth Festival (1962) Ch. & O, Sawallisch.

Sawallisch's version, recorded at the 1962 Bayreuth Festival, comes up very freshly on CD. Though the new medium brings out all the more clearly the thuds, creaks and audience noises of a live performance (most distracting at the very start), the dedication of the reading is very persuasive, notably in the Venusberg scene where Grace Bumbry is a superb, sensuous Venus and Windgassen – not quite in his sweetest voice, often balanced rather close – is a fine, heroic Tannhäuser. Anja Silja controls the abrasiveness of her soprano well, to make this her finest performance on record, not ideally sweet but very sympathetic. Voices are set well forward of the orchestra, in which strings have far more bloom than brass; but the atmosphere of the Festspielhaus is vivid and compelling throughout.

Tannhäuser (Paris version): highlights.
(M) *** DG Dig. 435 405-2; *435 405-4* [id.] (from above complete recording, with Domingo, Studer, Baltsa; cond. Sinopoli).

As this 'Domingo Edition' CD readily demonstrates, Tannhäuser was the Spanish tenor's finest Wagnerian role. These highlights also give a bird's-eye picture of Sinopoli's overall achievement and, by using groups of sequential excerpts, edited fades are minimal. The *Grand march* scene could have been cut off after its final cadence, but it was probably better to use also the following brass link. However, the last item, *Dahin zog's mich, wo ich der Wonn und Lust*, lacks any kind of finality.

Tristan und Isolde (complete).
(M) *** EMI CMS7 69319-2 (4) [Ang. CDMD 69319]. Vickers, Dernesch, Ludwig, Berry, Ridderbusch, German Op. Ch., Berlin, BPO, Karajan.
*** DG 419 889-2 (3) [id.]. Windgassen, Nilsson, Ludwig, Talvela, Waechter, Bayreuth Festival (1966) Ch. & O, Boehm.
(M) *** Decca 430 234-2 (4) [id.]. Uhl, Nilsson, Resnik, Van Mill, Krause, VPO, Solti.
**(*) Ph. Dig. 410 447-2 (5) [id.]. Hofmann, Behrens, Minton, Weikl, Sotin, Bav. R. Ch. & SO, Bernstein.
(***) EMI mono CDS7 47322-8 (4) [Ang. CDC47321]. Suthaus, Flagstad, Thebom, Greindl, Fischer-Dieskau, ROHCG Ch., Philh. O, Furtwängler.
**(*) DG Dig. 413 315-2 (4) [id.]. Kollo, Margaret Price, Fassbaender, Fischer-Dieskau, Moll, Dresden State O, Carlos Kleiber.

Karajan's is a sensual performance of Wagner's masterpiece, caressingly beautiful and with superbly refined playing from the Berlin Philharmonic. He is helped by a recording (not ideally balanced, but warmly atmospheric) which copes with an enormous dynamic range. Dernesch as Isolde is seductively feminine, not as noble as Flagstad, not as tough and unflinching as Nilsson; but the human quality makes this account if anything more moving still, helped by glorious tone-colour through every range. Jon Vickers matches her, in what is arguably his finest performance on record, allowing himself true pianissimo shading. The rest of the cast is excellent too. Though CD brings out more clearly the occasional oddities of balance, the 1972 sound has plenty of body, making this an excellent first choice, with inspired conducting and the most satisfactory cast of all.

Boehm's Bayreuth performance, recorded at the 1966 Festival, has a cast that for consistency has seldom been bettered on disc. Now on only three CDs, one disc per Act, the benefit is enormous in presenting one of the big Wagner operas for the first time on disc without any breaks at all, with each Act uninterrupted. Boehm is on the urgent side in this opera and the orchestral ensemble is not always immaculate; but the performance glows with intensity from beginning to end, carried through in the longest spans. Birgit Nilsson sings the *Liebestod* at the end of the long evening as though she was starting out afresh, radiant and with not a hint of tiredness, rising to an orgasmic climax and bringing a heavenly pianissimo on the final rising octave to F sharp. Opposite Nilsson is Wolfgang Windgassen, the most mellifluous of Heldentenoren; though the microphone balance sometimes puts him at a disadvantage to his Isolde, the realism and sense of presence of the whole set have you bathing in the authentic atmosphere of Bayreuth. Making up an almost unmatchable cast are Christa Ludwig as Brangaene, Eberhard Waechter as Kurwenal and Martii Talvela as King Mark, with the young Peter Schreier as the Young Sailor.

Solti's performance is less flexible and sensuous than Karajan's, but he shows himself ready to relax in Wagner's more expansive periods. On the other hand the end of Act I and the opening of the Love duet have a knife-edged dramatic tension. Birgit Nilsson responds superbly to Solti's direction. There are moments when the great intensity that Flagstad brought to the part is not equalled, but more often than not Nilsson is masterly in her conviction and – it cannot be emphasized too strongly – she never attacks below the note as Flagstad did, so that miraculously, at the end of the Love duet the impossibly difficult top Cs come out and hit the listener crisply and cleanly, dead on the note; and the *Liebestod* is all the more moving for having no soupy swerves at the climax. Fritz Uhl is a really musical Heldentenor. Only during one passage of the Love duet (*O sink' hernieder*) does he sound tired, and for the most part this is a well-focused voice. Dramatically he leaves the centre of the stage to Isolde, but his long solo passages in Act III are superb and make that sometimes tedious Act into something genuinely gripping. The Kurwenal of Tom Krause and the King Mark of Arnold van Mill are both excellent and it is only Regina Resnik as Brangaene who gives any disappointment. The production has the usual Decca/Culshaw imaginative touch, and the recording matches brilliance and clarity with satisfying co-ordination and richness.

Bernstein's five-disc set is not only expensive but cumbersome in five separate 'jewel-boxes'. Nevertheless, the fine quality of the recording is all the more ravishing in the transfer, the sound rich, full and well detailed, a tribute to the Bavarian engineers working in the Herkulessaal in Munich. The surprise is that Bernstein, over-emotional in some music, here exercises restraint to produce the most spacious reading ever put on disc, more expansive even than Furtwängler's. His rhythmic sharpness goes with warmly expressive but unexaggerated phrasing, to give unflagging concentration and deep commitment. The love-duet has rarely if ever sounded so sensuous, with supremely powerful climaxes. Nor in the *Liebestod* is there any question of Bernstein rushing ahead, for the culmination comes naturally and fully at a taxingly slow speed. Behrens makes a fine Isolde, less purely beautiful than her finest rivals but with reserves of power giving dramatic bite. The contrast of tone with Yvonne Minton's Brangaene (good, except for flatness in the warning solo) is not as great as usual, and there is likeness too between Peter Hofmann's Tristan, often baritonal, and Bernd Weikl's Kurwenal, lighter than usual. The King Mark of Hans Sotin is superb. However, this set needs remastering on to four discs.

It was one of the supreme triumphs of the recording producer, Walter Legge, when in 1952 with his recently formed Philharmonia Orchestra he teamed the incomparable Wagnerian, Wilhelm Furtwängler, with Kirsten Flagstad as the heroine in *Tristan und Isolde*. The result has an incandescent intensity, typical of the conductor at his finest. The concept is spacious from the opening *Prelude* onwards, but equally the bite and colour of the drama are vividly conveyed, matching the nobility of Flagstad's portrait of Isolde. The richly commanding power of her singing and her always distinctive timbre make it a uniquely compelling performance. Suthaus is not of the same calibre as Heldentenor, but he avoids ugliness and strain, which is rare in Tristan. Among the others, the only remarkable performance comes from the young Fischer-Dieskau as Kurwenal, not ideally cast but keenly imaginative. One endearing oddity is that – on Flagstad's insistence – the top Cs at the opening of the love-duet were sung by Elisabeth Schwarzkopf. The Kingsway Hall recording was admirably balanced, catching the beauty of the Philharmonia Orchestra at its peak. The CDs have opened up the original mono sound and it is remarkable how little constriction there is in the biggest climaxes, mostly shown in the *fortissimo* violins above the stave.

Kleiber directs a compellingly impulsive reading, crowned by the glorious Isolde of Margaret Price, the most purely beautiful of any complete interpretation on record. Next to more spacious readings, Kleiber's at times sounds excitable, almost hysterical, with fast speeds tending to get faster, for all his hypnotic concentration. But the lyricism of Margaret Price, feminine and vulnerable, is well contrasted against the heroic Tristan of Kollo, at his finest in Act III. Kurt Moll makes a dark, leonine King Mark, but Fischer-Dieskau is at times gritty as Kurwenal and Brigitte Fassbaender is a clear but rather cold Brangaene.

Tristan und Isolde (slightly abridged).
(M) (***) EMI mono CHS7 64037-2 (3). Melchior, Flagstad, Herbert Janssen, Margarete Klose/Sabine Kalter, Sven Nilsson/Emanuel List, ROHCG Ch., LPO, Beecham/Reiner.

What was originally promised as a complete recording of Beecham conducting *Tristan* at Covent Garden in the Coronation season of 1937 proved to be a mixture of recordings made, not only then, but in the previous year as well. In both recordings Melchior and Flagstad take the title-roles, with Herbert Janssen as Kurwenal, three legendary singers in those roles, but the parts of King Mark and Brangane were sung by different singers in each year – and, above all, Fritz Reiner was the conductor in the 1936 recordings. It says much that the end result, a jig-saw of pieces lovingly put together by Keith Hardwick, is so consistent. It is astonishing to find that the warmly expansive account of Act I is the work of Reiner, while it is Beecham who is responsible for the urgent view of Act II with its great love duet – part of it cut following the manner of the day. Act III is divided between Beecham in the first part, Reiner in the second. Whatever the inconsistencies, the result is a thrilling experience, with Flagstad fresher and even more incisive than in her studio recording with Furtwängler of 15 years later, and with Melchior a passionate vocal actor, not just the possessor of the most freely ringing of all Heldentenor voices. Though the orchestral sound is mostly dim and distant, the voices come over vividly and it is easy to forget the limitations. Each Act – with cuts in Act III as well as in Act II – is fitted conveniently and economically on a single disc.

Die Walküre (complete).
*** Decca 414 105-2 (4) [id.]. Nilsson, Crespin, Ludwig, King, Hotter, Frick, VPO, Solti.
*** Ph. 412 478-2 (4) [id.]. King, Rysanek, Nienstedt, Nilsson, Adam, Burmeister, Bayreuth Festival (1967) Ch. & O, Boehm.
(M) (***) EMI mono CHS7 63045-2 (3) [Ang. CHS 63045]. Mödl, Rysanek, Frantz, Suthaus, Klose, Frick, VPO, Furtwängler.

(M) *** RCA/Eurodisc Dig. GD 69005 (4) [69005-2-RG]. Altmeyer, Norman, Minton, Jerusalem, Adam, Moll, Dresden State O, Janowski.
**(*) EMI Dig. CDS7 49534-2 (4) [Ang. CDCD 49534]. Eva Marton, Studer, Morris, Goldberg, Salminen, Meier, Bav. RSO, Haitink.
**(*) DG 415 145-2 (4) [id.]. Crespin, Janowitz, Veasey, Vickers, Stewart, Talvela, BPO, Karajan.

Solti's conception is more lyrical than one would have expected from his recordings of the other three *Ring* operas. He sees Act II as the kernel of the work, perhaps even of the whole cycle, with the conflict of wills between Wotan and Fricka making for one of Wagner's most deeply searching scenes. That is the more apparent when the greatest of latterday Wotans, Hans Hotter, takes the role, and Christa Ludwig sings with searing dramatic sense as his wife. Before that, Act I seems a little underplayed. This is partly because of Solti's deliberate lyricism – apt enough when love and spring greetings are in the air – but also (on the debit side) because James King fails both to project the character of Siegmund and to delve into the word-meanings as all the other members of the cast consistently do. Crespin has never sung more beautifully on record, but even that cannot cancel out the shortcoming. As for Nilsson's Brünnhilde, it has grown mellower, the emotions are clearer, and under-the-note attack is almost eliminated. Some may hesitate in the face of Hotter's obvious vocal trials; but the unsteadiness is, if anything, less marked than in his EMI recordings of items done many years ago.

When Siegmund pulls the sword, Nothung, from the tree – James King in heroic voice – the Sieglinde, Leonie Rysanek, utters a shriek of joy to delight even the least susceptible Wagnerian, matching the urgency of the whole performance as conducted by Boehm. Rarely if ever does his preference for fast speeds undermine the music; on the contrary, it adds to the involvement of the performance, which never loses its concentration. Theo Adam is in firmer voice here as Wotan than he is in *Rheingold*, hardly sweet of tone but always singing with keen intelligence. As ever, Nilsson is in superb voice as Brünnhilde. Though the inevitable noises of a live performance occasionally intrude, this presents a more involving experience than any rival complete recording. The CD transfer transforms what on LP seemed a rough recording, even if passages of heavy orchestration still bring some constriction of sound.

Except for those totally allergic to mono sound even as well balanced as this, the EMI Références set is very strongly recommendable, when not only Furtwängler but an excellent cast and the Vienna Philharmonic in radiant form match any of their successors. Even more than in *Tristan*, Ludwig Suthaus proves a satisfyingly clear-toned Heldentenor, never strained, with the lyricism of *Wintersturme* superbly sustained. Neither Léonie Rysanek as Sieglinde nor Martha Mödl as Brünnhilde is ideally steady, but the intensity and involvement of each is irresistible, classic performances both, with detail finely touched in and well contrasted with each other. Similarly, the mezzo of Margarete Klose may not be very beautiful, but the projection of words and the fire-eating character match the conductor's intensity. Rather in contrast with the women soloists, both bass and baritone are satisfyingly firm and beautiful. Gottlob Frick is as near an ideal Hunding as one will find, sinister but with the right streak of arrogant sexuality; while the Wotan of Ferdinand Frantz may not be as deeply perceptive as some, but to hear the sweep of Wagner's melodic lines so gloriously sung is a rare joy. The 1954 sound is amazingly full and vivid, with voices cleanly balanced against the inspired orchestra. The only snag of the set is that, to fit the whole piece on to only three CDs, breaks between discs come in mid-Act.

Janowski's direct approach matches the relative dryness of the acoustic, with voices fixed well forward of the orchestra – but not aggressively so. That balance allows full presence for the singing from a satisfyingly consistent cast. Jessye Norman might not seem an obvious choice for Sieglinde, but the sound is glorious, the expression intense and detailed, making her a superb match for the fine, if rather less imaginative Siegmund of Siegfried Jerusalem. The one snag with so commanding a Sieglinde is that she overtops the Brünnhilde of Jeannine Altmeyer who, more than usual, conveys a measure of feminine vulnerability in the leading Valkyrie even in her godhead days. Miss Altmeyer may be slightly overparted, but the beauty and frequent sensuousness of her singing are the more telling, next to the gritty Wotan of Theo Adam. With its slow vibrato under pressure, his is rarely a pleasing voice, but the clarity of the recording makes it a specific, never a woolly sound, so that the illumination of the narrative is consistent and intense. Kurt Moll is a gloriously firm Hunding, and Yvonne Minton a searingly effective Fricka.

Haitink's is a broad view, strong and thoughtful yet conveying monumental power. That goes with searching concentration and a consistent feeling for the detailed beauty of Wagner's writing, glowingly brought out in the warm and spacious recording, made in the Herkulessaal in Munich. The outstanding contribution comes from Cheryl Studer as Sieglinde, very convincingly cast, giving a tenderly affecting performance to bring out the character's vulnerability in a very human way. At *Du bist der Lenz* her radiant singing brings an eagerly personal revelation, the response of a lover. Despite some strained moments Rainer Goldberg makes a heroic Siegmund, far finer than most today; and Eva Marton is a noble, powerful Brünnhilde, less uneven of production than she has often been on record. Waltraud Meier makes a convincingly waspish and biting Fricka and Matti Salminen a resonant Hunding. James Morris is a fine, perceptive Wotan, and the voice, not an easy one to record, is better focused here than in Levine's rival DG version of this opera from the Met.

The great merits of Karajan's version are the refinement of the orchestral playing and the heroic strength of Jon Vickers as Siegmund. With that underlined, one cannot help but note that the vocal shortcomings here are generally more marked, and the total result does not add up to quite so compelling a dramatic experience: one is less involved. Thomas Stewart may have a younger, firmer voice than Hotter, but the character of Wotan emerges only partially; it is not just that he misses some of the word-meaning, but that on occasion – as in the kissing away of Brünnhilde's godhead – he underlines too crudely. A fine performance, none the less; and Josephine Veasey as Fricka matches her rival, Ludwig, in conveying the biting intensity of the part. Gundula Janowitz's Sieglinde has its beautiful moments, but the singing is ultimately a little static. Crespin's Brünnhilde is impressive, but nothing like as satisfying as her study of Sieglinde on the Decca set. The voice is at times strained into unsteadiness, which the microphone seems to exaggerate. The DG recording is good, but not quite in the same class as the Decca – its slightly recessed quality is the more apparent in the CD transfer – and the bass is relatively light.

The Valkyrie (complete; in English).
(M) *** EMI CMS7 63918-2 (4). Hunter, Remedios, Curphey, Bailey, Grant, Howard, E. Nat. Op. Ch. & O, Goodall.

The glory of the ENO performance lies not just in Goodall's spacious direction but in the magnificent Wotan of Norman Bailey, noble in the broadest span but very human in his illumination of detail. Rita Hunter sings nobly too, and though she is not as commanding as Nilsson in the Solti cycle she is often more lyrically tender. Alberto Remedios as Siegmund is more taxed than he was as Siegfried in the later opera (lower tessituras are not quite so comfortable for him) but his sweetly ringing top register is superb. If others, such as Ann Howard as Fricka, are not always treated kindly by the microphone, the total dramatic compulsion is irresistible. The CD transfer increases the sense of presence and at the same time confirms the relative lack of sumptuousness.

Die Walküre, Act I (complete).
(M) (***) EMI mono CDH7 61020-2 [id.]. Lehmann, Melchior, List, VPO, Bruno Walter.
(M) **(*) Decca 425 963-2 [id.]. Flagstad, Svanholm, Van Mill, VPO, Knappertsbusch.

Though in the days of 78-r.p.m. discs the music had to be recorded in short takes of under five minutes, one is consistently gripped by the continuity and sustained lines of Walter's reading, and by the intensity and beauty of the playing of the Vienna Philharmonic. Lotte Lehmann's portrait of Sieglinde, arguably her finest role, has a depth and beauty never surpassed since, and Lauritz Melchior's heroic Siegmund brings singing of a scale and variety – not to mention beauty – that no Heldentenor today begins to match. Emanuel List as Hunding is satisfactory enough, but his achievement at least has latterly been surpassed.

Flagstad may not have been ideally cast as Sieglinde, but the command of her singing with its unfailing richness, even after her official retirement, crowns a strong and dramatic performance, with Svanholm and Van Mill singing cleanly. The early stereo still sounds vivid.

Die Walküre: Act III (complete).
(M) *** Decca 425 986-2 [id.]. Flagstad, Edelmann, Schech, VPO, Solti.

This recording was made in 1957. Flagstad came out of retirement to make it, and Decca put us eternally in their debt for urging her to do so. She sings radiantly. The meticulousness needed in the recording studio obviously brought out all her finest qualities, and there is no more than a touch of hardness on some of the top notes to show that the voice was no longer as young as it had been. Edelmann is not the ideal Wotan but he has a particularly well-focused voice, and when he sings straight, without sliding up or sitting under the note, the result is superb and he is never wobbly. But it is Solti's conducting that prevents any slight blemishes from mattering. Not surprisingly, the recording too is remarkably vivid, anticipating the excellence of the great *Ring* project which was to follow.

Die Walküre: highlights.
(M) *** Decca 421 887-2 [id.] (from above complete set with Nilsson, King, Crespin, Hotter; cond. Solti).

The mid-priced Solti highlights disc is not as generous as some (54 minutes) but is spectacularly well recorded. The items chosen, opening with Siegmund's (James King) *Winterstürme wichen dem Wonnemond*, ravishingly lyrical, and including the *Ride of the Valkyries*, make a particularly satisfying reminder of some of the finest moments in the set. Recommendable to those who cannot stretch to the full opera.

VOCAL COLLECTIONS

'Wagner singing on record': Excerpts from: (i) *Der fliegende Holländer;* (ii) *Götterdämmerung;* (iii) *Lohengrin;* (iv) *Die Meistersinger von Nürnberg;* (v) *Parsifal;* (vi) *Das Rheingold;* (vii) *Siegfried;* (viii) *Tannhäuser;* (ix) *Tristan und Isolde;* (x) *Die Walküre.*
(M) (***) EMI mono/stereo CMS7 640082 (4) [id.]. (i) Hermann, Nissen, Endrèze, Fuchs, Beckmann, Rethberg, Nilsson, Hotter; (ii) Austral, Widdop, List, Weber, Janssen, Lawrence; (iii) Rethberg, Pertil, Singher, Lawrence, Spani, Lehmann, Lemnitz, Klose, Wittrisch, Rosavaenge; (iv) Schorr, Thill, Martinelli, Bockelmann, Parr, Williams, Ralf, Lemnitz; (v) Leider, Kipnitz, Wolff; (vi) Schorr; (vii) Nissen, Olszewska, Schipper, Leider, Laubenthal, Lubin; (viii) Müller, Lorenz, Janssen, Hüsch, Flagstad; (ix) Leider, Marherr, Larsen-Todsen, Helm, Melchior, Seinemeyer, Lorenz; (x) Lawrence, Journet, Bockelmann.

This collection, compiled in Paris as '*Les Introuvables du Chant Wagnerien*', contains an amazing array of recordings made in the later years of 78-r.p.m. recording, mostly between 1927 and 1940. In 49 items, many of them substantial, the collection consistently demonstrates the reliability of the Wagner singing at that period, the ability of singers in every register to produce firm, well-focused tone of a kind too rare today. Some of the most interesting items are those in translation from French sources, with Germaine Lubin as Isolde and Brünnhilde and with Marcel Journet as Wotan, both lyrical and clean-cut. The ill-starred Marjorie Lawrence, a great favourite in France, is also represented by recordings in French, including Brünnhilde's Immolation scene from *Götterdämmerung.* Not only are such celebrated Wagnerians as Lauritz Melchior, Friedrich Schorr, Frida Leider, Lotte Lehmann and Max Lorenz very well represented, but also singers one might not expect, including the Lieder specialist, Gerhard Husch, as Wolfram in *Tannhäuser* and Aureliano Pertile singing in Italian as *Lohengrin.* Significantly, Meta Seinemeyer, an enchanting soprano who died tragically young, here gives lyric sweetness to the dramatic roles of Brünnhilde and Isolde; and among the baritones and basses there is none of the roughness or ill-focus that marks so much latter-day Wagner singing. It is a pity that British-based singers are poorly represented, but the Prologue duet from *Götterdämmerung* brings one of the most impressive items, sung by Florence Austral and Walter Widdop. First-rate transfers and good documentation.

Arias: *Götterdämmerung:* (i) *Zu neuen Taten; Starke Scheite schichter mire dort. Lohengrin: Euch Lüften mein Klagen. Parsifal:* (i) *Ich sah' das King. Tristan: Mild und leise. Die Walküre: Du bist der Lenz; Ho-jo-ho!.*
(M) (***) RCA mono GD 87915 [87915-2-RG]. Flagstad, (i) with Melchior, San Francisco Op. O, or Victor SO (both cond. Edwin McArthur); Phd. O, Ormandy

Recorded for RCA in America between 1935 and 1940, this first generation of Wagner recordings by Flagstad reveals the voice at its noblest and freshest, the more exposed in consistently close balance on the 78s of the period. It is a pity that only two of the shortest items – from *Lohengrin* and *Walküre* – have Ormandy conducting. Most of the rest are conducted by Flagstad's protégé, Edwin McArthur, including the two longest, the big duet for Parsifal and Kundry and Brünnhilde's Immolation scene. Yet the grandeur of Flagstad's singing is never in doubt, the commanding sureness, and, though the orchestral sound is unflatteringly dry, the voice is gloriously caught in clean transfers.

Choruses from: *Der fliegende Holländer; Lohengrin; Die Meistersinger; Parsifal; Tannhäuser.*
(M) *** Decca 421 865-2 (from complete sets, cond. Solti).

Solti's choral collection is superb, with an added sophistication in both performance and recording – especially in the subtle use of ambience and perspectives – to set it apart from the DG Bayreuth disc, good though that is. The collection opens with a blazing account of the *Lohengrin* Act III *Prelude*, since of course the *Bridal chorus* grows naturally out of it. But the *Pilgrims' chorus*, which comes next, creates an electrifying pianissimo and expands gloriously, while the excerpts from *Die Meistersinger* and *Parsifal* show Solti's characteristic intensity at its most potent.

Walton, William (1902–83)

Anniversary fanfare; Crown imperial; March for the history of the English-speaking peoples; Orb and sceptre; A Queen's fanfare; (i) *Antiphon; 4 Christmas carols: All this time; King Herod and his cock; Make we now this feast; What cheer?. In honour of the City of London; Jubilate Deo; Where does the uttered music go?.*
*** Chan. Dig. CHAN 8998; *ABTD 1580* [id.]. (i) Bach Ch.; Philh. O, Willcocks.

Sir David Willcocks' version of the cantata, *In honour of the City of London*, in the Chandos Walton series offers opulent Chandos sound, compensating for singing from the Bach Choir not as incisive as that on Richard Hickox's brisker EMI version with the London Symphony Chorus, currently unlisted but very likely to be reissued soon. Not that comparisons are important, when the Chandos disc offers so rich an array of other Walton items for coupling. Sir David Willcocks conducts performances of the two *Coronation marches* full of panache, with the brass superbly articulated and inner detail well caught. Also the *March for the history of the English-speaking peoples*. The *a cappella* choral items are very well done too, if less intimately than on the Conifer disc of Walton choral music from Trinity College Choir. With the original organ parts orchestrated, the *Jubilate* and *Antiphon* gain greatly from having full instrumental accompaniment. The brief fanfares, never previously recorded, are a welcome makeweight, with the *Anniversary fanfare* (written for EMI's 75th anniversary in 1973) designed to lead directly into *Orb and sceptre*, which is what it does here.

Capriccio burlesco; Coronation marches: Crown imperial; Orb and sceptre. Funeral march from Hamlet; Johannesburg festival overture; Richard III: Prelude & suite; Scapino overture; Spitfire prelude & fugue.
(M) **(*) EMI CDM7 63369-2; *EG 763369-4*. RLPO, Sir Charles Groves.

The 1969 collection of Walton's shorter orchestral pieces now seems slightly over-bright with its digital remastering. The sound tends to polarize, with a lack of opulence in the middle range, so necessary in the *nobilmente* of the big tunes of the stirring *Spitfire Prelude and fugue* and *Crown imperial*. The Shakespearean film music was recorded much later (1984) and the quality is fuller, more warmly atmospheric. Although the two *Coronation marches* could do with a little more exuberance, Groves is otherwise a highly sympathetic interpreter of this repertoire, and the playing of the Liverpool orchestra is excellent.

Capriccio burlesco; The First shoot (orch. Palmer); *Granada* (Prelude for orchestra); *Johannesburg festival overture; Music for children. Galop finale* (orch. Palmer); *Portsmouth Point: overture; Prologo e fantasia; Scapino.*
*** Chan. Dig. CHAN 8968; *ABTD 1560* [id.]. LPO, Bryden Thomson.

With Walton's three brilliant comedy overtures providing the cornerstones, this makes a delightful collection of miscellaneous orchestral pieces, another welcome addition to Chandos's Walton series. You might even count the *Capriccio burlesco* as a fourth comedy overture. It was originally written for the New York Philharmonic on their 125th anniversary in 1968, and started life with the title, 'Philharmonic Overture, N.Y. '68'. It may not be as scintillating as the regular overtures, but it is ravishingly orchestrated, with some apt echoes of Gershwin. With *Scapino* commissioned for Chicago and the *Capriccio burlesco* for New York, the *Prologo e Fantasia* completes an American group, a commission from Rostropovich for the National Symphony Orchestra of Washington. First given in 1982, a year before Walton died, it was his last work, in some ways pointing to the development of a simpler, more direct Walton style.The *Granada* Prelude, written for the television company, taps Walton's patriotic march vein in a jaunty way. The other two items bring premier recordings. *The First shoot* comes in Christopher Palmer's brilliant orchestration of the brass band suite which Walton developed in 1981 from a short ballet written for a C.B. Cochran revue in 1935. The opening *Giocoso* is a re-run of *Old Sir Faulk*, and the other movements bring more echoes of *Façade*. As for the other novelty, the ten brief movements of *Music for children*, crisply orchestrated versions of pieces for piano-duet, are here supplemented by a *Galop final*. Longer than the other pieces, it was completed too late to be included in the ballet version presented in Paris, but Palmer has here orchestrated the piano score. Though the opulent Chandos recording tends to take some of the bite away from Walton's jazzily accented writing, the richness of the orchestral sound is consistently satisfying. Thomson makes a strong case for speeds a little more relaxed than usual, notably in the overtures, bringing out the humour all the more infectiously.

(i) Capriccio burlesco; (ii) *Music for children; Portsmouth Point overture*; (i) *The Quest* (ballet suite); *Scapino overture*; (ii) *Siesta*; (i; iii) *Sinfonia concertante*.
*** Lyrita SRCD 224 [id.]. (i) LSO or (ii) LPO, composer; (iii) with Peter Katin.

For the enterprising Lyrita label around 1970 Walton recorded his own interpretations of these varied works, which otherwise he never put on record in the age of LP. Drawn from three separate issues, they make an attractive and generous compilation on CD, a very valuable addition to the Walton discography, particularly when the sound is among the finest of its period. Not that the performances are ideal. When Walton made these recordings, he was in his late sixties, and his speeds had grown a degree slower and safer. *Portsmouth Point* loses some of its fizz at so moderate a speed. In *Scapino* Walton also adopts a relatively slow speed, taking a full minute longer than on his own earlier 78-r.p.m. version (see below). By contrast with the earlier comedy overture it suffers hardly at all from the slower speed, rather the opposite, with the opening if anything even jauntier and the big cello melody drawn out more expressively. *Siesta* too takes a full minute longer than it does in its 78 counterpart, bringing out the piece's romantically lyrical side, rather than making it a relatively cool intermezzo. The *Capriccio burlesco* is delightfully done, rather lighter and wittier in its spiky rhythms than the Bryden Thomson version on Chandos, and with the analogue recording sounding even fuller and richer. The ten little pieces of the *Music for children* are delightful too, with the subtleties of the instrumentation beautifully brought out. Much the biggest work here is the *Sinfonia concertante*, and in the outer movements the performance lacks the thrust that Walton himself gave it in his very first wartime recording, in which Phyllis Sellick was a scintillating soloist. In those movements the Conifer version with Vernon Handley and Kathryn Stott is also preferable, using the original, as opposed to the revised scoring, as here. Yet Peter Katin is a very responsive soloist too, and the central slow movement is much warmer and more passionate than on Conifer, with orchestral detail rather clearer. It is good too to have the only available recording of the suite which Vilem Tausky drew from Walton's wartime ballet based on Spenser's 'Faerie Queene', *The Quest*, only a fraction of the whole but bright and colourful. Walton in his late sixties may have been a more relaxed conductor than he had been earlier, but with his feeling for rhythm and line he regularly provides refreshing insights, so that this generous collection becomes more than the sum of its parts.

Cello concerto.
(M) *** EMI CDM7 63020-2. Tortelier, Bournemouth SO, Berglund – SHOSTAKOVICH: *Cello concerto No. 1.* ***
*** Sony MK 39541 [id.]. Yo-Yo Ma, LSO, Previn – ELGAR: *Concerto.* ***

Tortelier's version of Walton's *Cello concerto* is openly extrovert in its emotional response, offering a highly involving approach. After the haunting melancholy of the first movement, the central scherzo emerges as a far weightier piece than with Ma and Previn (both at full price), while the final variations are developed with a strong sense of compulsion. With full, vivid recording, Tortelier's reading remains very competitive.

Yo-Yo Ma and Previn give a sensuously beautiful performance. With speeds markedly slower than usual in the outer movements, the meditation is intensified to bring a mood of ecstasy, quite distinct from other Walton, with the central allegro becoming the symphonic kernel of the work, far more than just a scherzo. In the excellent CBS recording, the soloist is less forwardly and more faithfully balanced than is common. The CD is one of CBS's most impressive.

(i; ii) *Cello concerto;* (ii) *Improvisations on an impromptu of Benjamin Britten; Partita for orchestra;* (i) *Passacaglia for solo cello.*
*** Chan. Dig. CHAN 8959; *ABTD 1551* [id.]. (i) Rafael Wallfisch; (ii) LPO, Bryden Thomson.

Wallfisch's reading is individual. He is more clearly stretched than Yo-Yo Ma in the jagged central scherzo; but his playing is just as searching and passionate, with the finale even bringing echoes of Bloch's *Schelomo*. With its all-Walton coupling, this is plainly the version to recommend to those primarily concerned with the composer rather than with the cello. With his rich, even tone, Wallfisch is just as warm and purposeful in the solo *Passacaglia* Walton wrote at the end of his life for Rostropovich, while Thomson relishes the vivid orchestral colours in both the *Improvisations*, here wider-ranging in expression than usual, and the brilliant *Partita*. Excellent Chandos sound.

(i) *Cello concerto;* (ii; iii) *Belshazzar's feast;* (iii) *Coronation Te Deum.*
(M) **(*) Chan. CHAN 6547 [id.]. (i) Kirshbaum; (ii) Milnes; (iii) SNO Ch.; SNO, Gibson.

Gibson's view of Walton's brilliant oratorio turns towards brisk speeds but is no less dramatic for that. At medium price it is strongly competitive, particularly with so magnificent a baritone as Sherrill Milnes as soloist. The *Cello concerto*, however, is disappointing, lacking the warmth, weight and expressiveness that so ripe an example of late Romanticism demands. Good CD transfers.

(i) *Viola concerto;* (ii) *Sinfonia concertante.*
(M) (***) EMI mono CDH7 63828-2. (i) William Primrose, Philh. O; (ii) Phyllis Sellick, CBSO; composer – VAUGHAN WILLIAMS: *Violin concerto* etc. (***)

In the inter-war period William Primrose set new standards of virtuosity on the viola and here gives a formidable account of the greatest of viola concertos, with the composer conducting. Recorded in 1946, the mono sound fails to capture a genuine pianissimo, but otherwise the combination of romantic warmth tempered by classical restraint provides a lesson to some more recent interpreters. Unlike them, Primrose adopts an aptly flowing speed for the opening *Andante comodo*, refusing to sentimentalize it. The scherzo is phenomenally fast, sometimes sounding breathless, but the virtuosity is astonishing; and the spiky humour of the finale is delightfully pointed, leading to a yearning account of the epilogue. The *Sinfonia concertante* is another historic recording well deserving study, made in 1945, the first ever of this work. Phyllis Sellick readily matches the composer-conductor in the thrusting urgency and romantic power of the performance. Excellent transfers of both concertos, generously coupled with the two Vaughan Williams works.

Viola concerto; Violin concerto.
*** EMI Dig. CDC7 49628-2 [id.]. Nigel Kennedy, RPO, Previn.

Few works written this century can match Walton's two pre-war string concertos in richness and warmth of melody. Kennedy's achievement in giving equally rich and expressive performances of both works makes for an ideal coupling, helped by the unique insight of André Previn as Waltonian. Kennedy on the viola produces tone as rich and firm as on his usual violin. His double-stopping is wonderfully firm and true, and though in the first movement of the *Viola concerto* he opts for a dangerously slow tempo, drawing the lovely first melody out more spaciously than the score would strictly allow, he justifies it with his concentration at a steady, undistorted pace. The Scherzo has never been recorded with more panache than here, and the finale brings a magic moment in the return of the main theme from the opening, hushed and intense. In the *Violin concerto* too, Kennedy gives a warmly relaxed reading, in which he dashes off the bravura passages with great flair. He may miss some of the more searchingly introspective manner of Chung in her 1971 version, but there are few Walton records as richly rewarding as this, helped by warm, atmospheric sound.

Violin concerto.
(M) *** Decca 421 385-2; *421 385-4* [id.]. Kyung Wha Chung, LSO, Previn – ELGAR: *Cello concerto.* ***
*** Collins Dig. 1338-2 [id.]. Accardo, LSO, Hickox – ELGAR: *Violin concerto.* **(*)
(M) (***) BMG/RCA mono GD 87966 [7966-2-RG]. Heifetz, Philh. O, composer – ELGAR: *Concerto.* (***)

In the brooding intensity of the opening evocation, Kyung Wha Chung presents the first melody with a depth of expression, tender and hushed, that has never been matched on record, not even by Heifetz. With Previn as guide and with the composer himself a sympathetic observer at the recording sessions, Chung then builds up a performance which must remain a classic, showing the *Concerto* as one of the greatest of the century in this genre. Outstandingly fine recording, sounding the more vivid in its CD format.

Salvatore Accardo proves a most sympathetic interpreter of British music in this generous coupling of the Walton and Elgar *Violin concertos*. He seems even more in sympathy with the acid romanticism of Walton than he is with the broader Elgarian brand. His is a bitingly intense performance that brings sensuous treatment of the big romantic melodies and sparkling virtuosity in the bravura writing designed for Heifetz. Richard Hickox draws powerful playing from the LSO, and the recording is full and brilliant.

It was Heifetz who commissioned the Walton *Concerto* and who gave the first performances, as well as making a wartime recording in America. This is the later version, first issued in 1951, which Heifetz made with Walton conducting, using the revised score. Speeds are often hair-raisingly fast, but few Heifetz records convey as much passion as this. The mono recording is dry, with a distracting hum in the transfer, but the high-voltage electricity has never been matched in this radiant music.

Crown Imperial (concert band version).
❀ (M) *** Mercury 432 009-2 [id.]. Eastman Wind Ens., Fennell – BENNETT: *Symphonic songs;* HOLST: *Hammersmith;* JACOB: *William Byrd suite.* ***

Paced with dignity, yet with joyously crisp articulation, Fennell's splendidly paced performance is part of a highly recommendable collection of music for concert band; the entry of the organ at the climax brings a frisson-creating dynamic expansion which is unforgettably exciting. The coda, too, is quite superb. The Mercury sound, from the late 1950s, remains in the demonstration bracket.

Façade (complete, including *Façade 2*).
**(*) ASV Dig. CDDCA 679; *ZCDCA 679* [id.]. Prunella Scales, Timothy West, L. Mozart Players (members), Jane Glover.
**(*) Chan. Dig. CHAN 8869; *ABTD 1484* [id.]. Lady Susana Walton, Richard Baker, City of L. Sinfonia (members), Richard Hickox.

Jane Glover and the London Mozart Players in unaccustomed repertory match the wit of the agile and characterful reciters in a pointed account of the *Façade* entertainment, well recorded, though with the usual bias in favour of the voices. Scales and West as a husband-and-wife team are inventive in their shared roles, and generally it works well. *Scotch rhapsody* is hilariously done as a duet, with West intervening at appropriate moments, and with sharply precise Scots accents. Regional accents may defy Edith Sitwell's original prescription – and her own example – but here, with one exception, they add an appropriate flavour. The exception is *Popular song*, where Prunella Scales's cockney accent clashes horribly with the allusive words, with their 'cupolas, gables in the lakes, Georgian stables'. For fill-up the reciters have recorded more Sitwell poems, but unaccompanied.

Susana Walton, widow of the composer, makes a bitingly characterful reciter, matching with her distinctive accent – she was born in Argentina – the exoticry of many numbers. Richard Baker, phenomenally precise and agile in enunciating the Sitwell poems, makes the perfect foil, and Hickox secures colourful and lively playing from members of the City of London Sinfonia, who relish in particular the jazzy inflexions. *Façade 2* consists of a number of poems, beyond the definitive series of 21, which for various reasons, at different stages of the work's emergence in the 1920s, were omitted. Some of them were early inspirations and others overlapped with those in the *Façade* entertainment as we know it. All of them are fun and make an apt if not very generous coupling for the regular sequence. Warm sound, rather too reverberant for so intimate a work.

(i) *Façade* (complete); (ii) *Siesta; Overtures: Portsmouth Point; Scapino.*
❀ (M) *** Decca mono 425 661-2; *425 661-4* [id.]. (i) Sitwell, Pears, E. Op. Group Ens., Collins; (ii) LPO, Boult – ARNOLD: *English dances.* (***)

Anthony Collins's 1954 recording of *Façade* is a gramophone classic, sounding miraculously vivid and atmospheric in a CD transfer that seems almost like modern stereo. Dame Edith Sitwell had one of the richest and most characterful of speaking voices, and here she recites her early poems to the masterly, witty music of the youthful Walton with glorious relish. Peter Pears is splendid too in the fast poems, rattling off the lines like the *grande dame* herself, to demonstrate how near-nonsense can be pure poetry. Of course there are flaws in Dame Edith's contribution over rhythm. She has no idea whatever of offbeat accentuation or jazz syncopation in *Old Sir Faulk*, but even so the voice itself is incomparable. The Boult mono versions of *Scapino* and *Siesta* make a valuable coupling, although *Portsmouth Point* misses some of the rhythmic bite of his first 78-r.p.m. disc. Malcolm Arnold's own première recording of his masterly *English dances*, full of exuberance and colour, completes a fascinating programme that no lover of English music should miss.

Façade: suites 1 & 2.
*** Hyp. Dig. CDA 66436; *KA 66436* [id.]. E. N. Philh. O, Lloyd-Jones – BLISS: *Checkmate* ***; LAMBERT: *Horoscope.* *** ❀

Brilliantly witty and humorous performances of the two orchestral suites which Walton himself fashioned from his 'Entertainment'. This is music which, with its outrageous quotations, can make one chuckle out loud. Moreover it offers, to quote Constant Lambert, 'one good tune after another', all scored with wonderful felicity. The playing here could hardly be bettered, and the recording is in the demonstration bracket with its natural presence and bloom.

(i) *Façade: suites 1 & 2;* (ii) *Henry V: 2 pieces for strings;* (iii) *Scapino* (comedy overture); (i) *Siesta;* (iv) *Spitfire prelude and fugue* (film music); (v) *Belshazzar's feast.*
(M) (***) EMI mono CDH7 63381-2 [id.]. (i) LPO; (ii) Philh. String O; (iii) Philh. O; (iv) Hallé O; (v) Dennis Noble, Huddersfield Choral Soc., Liverpool Philh. O; all cond. composer.

This very generous compilation covers all the recordings Walton made for EMI in the days of 78 except for the *Viola concerto* with William Primrose and the *Sinfonia concertante* with Phyllis Sellick (both issued separately), as well as the music for the film, *Henry V.* The composer's recording of *Belshazzar's feast*, made at the height of the Second World War, was an astonishing achievement. Recorded in a mere two sessions on two Sundays in Liverpool Philharmonic Hall in January 1943, it still sounds amazingly full and clear, very well transferred, though inevitably with some surface noise. The percussion comes out most vividly, and here even more compellingly than in his later stereo recording Walton establishes the claims of speeds far faster than have latterly become common in this work. The chorus, *Babylon was a great city*, goes at an astonishing pace, but the incisiveness of playing and singing makes it intensely exciting and not merely breathless. Ensemble is not always perfect, and the final chorus brings some untidiness at the end, but the magnetic building of tension over the whole work makes this more compelling than almost any version since. It will be a revelation to all who love the work, with Dennis Noble living up to his surname. The other items bring vintage performances too, and in the transfer the most remarkable example of sound well in advance of its time is in the *Façade suites*. It is scarcely credible that the recordings were made as early as 1936. The least good sound and the least good playing come in the *Spitfire prelude and fugue*, recorded in 1943 just before Barbirolli took over the Hallé. Flawed as it is, it offers a stirring performance. The least ancient recording is of *Scapino*, made in 1951 at the time Walton was recording the *First Symphony*.

Film scores

As you like it; Hamlet.
*** Chan. Dig. CHAN 8842; *ABTD 1461* [id.]. Catherine Bott, Sir John Gielgud, ASMF, Marriner.

Next to his two other great film-scores for Sir Laurence Olivier, Walton's music for *Hamlet* has been poorly treated, both on record and in concert performance; now, thanks to the diligence of Christopher Palmer, this fine disc in Chandos's Walton series gathers together some 40 minutes of music, most of it previously unrecorded. Some proves to be relatively slight – *The Ghost* for example is little more than bogey-bogey atmosphere-making – and nothing quite matches the magnificent *Funeral march*, but this is still a rich and colourful suite, superbly played and recorded, and much enhanced by the contribution of Sir John Gielgud in two of Hamlet's soliloquies, 'O that this too, too solid flesh' and 'To be or not to be'. The selection of music from the pre-war film of *As you like it* makes a valuable fill-up. It omits four tiny passages, previously recorded by Carl Davis on his EMI disc of Walton film music, but adds the splendid setting of *Under the greenwood tree* in a radiant performance by Catherine Bott, a most valuable addition. Marriner and the Academy draw out all the romantic warmth of both scores, and the sound is richly atmospheric to match.

The Battle of Britain (suite); Escape me never (suite); The First of the Few: Spitfire prelude and fugue; Three Sisters; A Wartime sketchbook.
*** Chan. Dig. CHAN 8870; *ABTD 1485* [id.]. ASMF, Marriner.

This heartwarming record gathers together many of the fragments of film music that constituted what Walton regarded as his 'war work'. It occupied him so completely at the time that he produced no major concert piece over that period. *The Spitfire prelude and fugue*, from *The First of the Few*, was immediately turned into a highly successful concert-piece, but we owe it to Christopher Palmer that there is the 'Wartime Sketchbook', drawing material from three of the wartime films, plus scraps that Colin Matthews did not use in the suite from the much later *Battle of Britain* film music. On this showing Walton was at least the equal of Elgar in writing patriotic march tunes, repeatedly matching the achievement of the two well-known coronation marches, not least in the stirring theme from the credits of the film, *Went the day well*. The brief suite from the music for Olivier's film of Chekhov's *The Three Sisters*, from much later, brings more than one setting of the *Tsar's Hymn* and a charming imitation of *Swan Lake*. Earliest on the disc is *Escape me never*, the first of Walton's film-scores, written in 1935 in a more popular idiom; but the war-inspired music is what this delightful disc is really about. Marriner and the Academy give richly idiomatic performances, full of panache, of pieces ripe for performance at the Last Night of the Proms. Aptly opulent recording.

Henry V: A Shakespeare scenario (arr. Christopher Palmer).
*** Chan. Dig. CHAN 8892; *ABTD 1503* [id.]. Christopher Plummer (nar.), Westminster Cathedral Ch., ASMF, Marriner.

Few film-scores can match Walton's for the Olivier film of *Henry V* in its range and imagination. Christopher Palmer has here managed to include over 90 per cent of the music Walton wrote for the film, omitting little more than disconnected fragments, and with speeches and narrations interpolated, using discreetly edited texts, the whole lasting just over an hour. The most controversial change is to 'borrow' the first section of the march which Walton wrote much later for a projected television series on Churchill's *History of the English-speaking Peoples*; otherwise, the chorus's call to arms, *Now all the youth of England is on fire*, would have had no music to introduce it. As an appendix, three short pieces are included which Walton quoted in his score. Sir Neville Marriner caps even his previous recordings in this series, with the Academy producing heartfelt playing and singing in sumptuous sound. The only reservation is over the very slow speed for the *Passacaglia*, illustrating Falstaff's death. Christopher Plummer makes an excellent substitute for Olivier, unselfconsciously adopting a comparably grand style.

Henry V: Passacaglia; The Death of Falstaff; Touch her soft lips and part.
*** DG 419 748-2 [id.]. ECO, Barenboim – DELIUS: *Aquarelles* etc.; VAUGHAN WILLIAMS: *Lark ascending; Oboe concerto.* ***

These two fine Walton string pieces make an admirable complement to a sensuously beautiful collection of English music, with Barenboim at his most affectionately inspirational and the ECO very responsive, and with the 1975 recording retaining its warmth and bloom.

Macbeth: Fanfare & march. Major Barbara (suite); Richard III (Shakespeare scenario).
*** Chan. Dig. CHAN 8841; *ABTD 1460* [id.]. Sir John Gielgud (nar.), ASMF, Marriner.

The music for *Richard III* may not quite rival *Henry V* in its scope and imagination – with Bosworth Field hardly a match for Agincourt – but this is a much meatier offering than the music for the other Olivier/Shakespeare film, *Hamlet*. Disappointingly, Sir John Gielgud underplays Richard III's great 'Now is the winter of our discontent' speech, but working to the underlying music – much of it eliminated in the film – may have cramped his style. The performance generally has all the panache one could wish for, leading up to the return of the grand Henry Tudor theme at the end. The six-minute piece, based on Walton's music for Gielgud's wartime production of *Macbeth*, is much rarer and very valuable too, anticipating in its Elizabethan dance-music the *Henry V* film-score. *Major Barbara* also brings vintage Walton material. Marriner and the Academy give performances just as ripely committed as in their previous discs in the series, helped by sonorous Chandos sound.

The Quest (ballet): complete; *The Wise Virgins* (ballet): suite.
*** Chan. Dig. CHAN 8871; *ABTD 1486* [id.]. LPO, Bryden Thomson.

Walton's two wartime ballet-scores make an attractive coupling, particularly when the greater part of *The Quest*, based on Spenser's *Faerie Queene*, remained unheard for almost half a century. Far more than what is contained in the suite deserves to be preserved, with anticipations of Walton's film music and the *Second Symphony*, as well as echoes of *Scapino*. Walton, even in a hurry, could not help creating memorable ideas and, with the help of Constant Lambert – not to mention Christopher Palmer, who has expanded the instrumentation in line with the suite – the orchestral writing is often dazzling. As in most ballets, there are substantial sequences of purely illustrative music, but the *Variations on the Seven Deadly Sins* form a strong, substantial movement, and the final *Passacaglia* is the more magnificent for being almost twice as long as in the suite. The start brings an effective crib from the slow movement of Vaughan Williams's *Fourth Symphony*, bitonal in a similarly eerie way. Quite apart from the dramatic power of the performance, the recording is superb, among the fullest and clearest from Chandos. The sound for *The Wise Virgins* is more reverberant and the performance has less electricity, though Walton's distinctive arrangements of Bach cantata movements – including *Sheep may safely graze* – remain as fresh as ever.

Sinfonia concertante for piano & orchestra (original version).
*** Conifer Dig. CDCF 175; *MCFC 175* [id.]. Kathryn Stott, RPO, Handley – BRIDGE: *Phantasm;* IRELAND: *Piano concerto.* ***

It is high time that Walton's *Sinfonia concertante* was treated to a good modern recording, and Kathryn Stott, warmly and strongly accompanied by Vernon Handley and the RPO, gives an outstanding reading, the more interesting for bringing the first ever recording of the work's original version. It was in 1943, just before making the very first recording with Phyllis Sellick as soloist – also a superb performance – that Walton revised the score, simplifying the solo part and thinning the orchestration. Responding to a remark that Walton made not long before he died (suggesting that his initial conception was perhaps superior to the revision) and with the active agreement of Lady Walton, Stott and Handley opted to go back to the original, and the result seems to strengthen what is a consistently memorable work, built from vintage Walton material. This was his first full-length piece using orchestra, and – with each movement characterizing one of the three Sitwells, Walton's early sponsors, in turn Osbert, Edith and Sacheverell – it stands up remarkably well, even next to Walton's later masterly concertos for viola, violin and cello. First-rate recorded sound, and a coupling both generous and apt.

Symphony No. 1 in B flat min..
(M) *** BMG/RCA GD 87830 [7830-2-RG]. LSO, Previn (with VAUGHAN WILLIAMS: *Wasps overture* ***).

Symphony No. 1; Varii Capricci.
*** Chan. Dig. CHAN 8862; *ABTD 1477* [id.]. LPO, Bryden Thomson.

On RCA Previn gives a marvellously biting account of the magnificent *First Symphony*. His fast tempi may initially make one feel that he is pressing too hard, but his ability to screw the dramatic tension tighter and tighter until the final resolution is most assured, and certainly reflects the tense mood of the mid-1930s, as well as the youthful Walton's own personal tensions at that time. '*Presto con malizia*' says the score for the scherzo, and malice is exactly what Previn conveys, with the hints of vulgarity and humour securely placed. In the slow movement Previn finds real warmth, giving some of the melodies an Elgarian richness; and the finale's electricity here helps to overcome any feeling that it is too facile, too easily happy a conclusion. The bright recording – made by Decca engineers in the vintage 1960s – has splendid focus in its CD remastering, yet does not lack body. Previn has rarely made a record as powerfully intense as this, and as a performance it is unsurpassed and greatly preferable to his later, Telarc recording.

Any fear that Thomson – who takes a rather relaxed and expansive view of the *Second Symphony* – would not convey the full bite of the *First*, the searingly intense inspiration of Walton's pre-war years, proves totally unfounded. His is a warmly committed, understandingly idiomatic account of the work, weighty and rhythmically persuasive, which brings out the full emotional thrust. In the slow movement his tender expressiveness goes with a flowing speed, well judged to avoid exaggeration. This is a work which builds tensions relentlessly, regularly working towards climaxes which are then dramatically resolved. In that process the extra impact at the moment of thrust, brought about by an agogic hesitation or a slight pressing forward, can be crucial, notably in the hammered repetitions so characteristic of Walton, and Thomson is masterly in judging that. If the scherzo is a degree less demonic than it might be, at a speed fractionally slower than usual, it is infectiously sprung. Previn's famous RCA version of the *Symphony* has a unique, biting intensity, but Thomson's performance, helped by the splendid modern sound, is very satisfying in its own right, and leads all the modern digital recordings. The Chandos coupling is not as generous as some but is very welcome when it brings the first recording of *Varii capricci*, the orchestral suite in five compact movements which Walton developed from his set of guitar *Bagatelles*, written for Julian Bream. The outer movements are typically spiky, with guitar textures turned into ripe orchestral sound. The three middle movements are relaxed and relatively slow, the third a sensuously scored *Alla cubana*, with haunting tango rhythms, while the fourth with its tremolos *sul ponticello* might be subtitled 'Nights in the gardens of Ischia'. With a brilliant performance and sumptuous sound, it makes a fine supplement.

Symphony No. 2.
*** ASV Dig. CDRPO 8023; *ZCRPO 8023* [id.]. RPO, Ashkenazy – BRITTEN: *Serenade;* KNUSSEN: *Symphony No. 3.* ***

Symphony No. 2; Partita for orchestra; Variations on a theme by Hindemith.
❀ (M) *** Sony MPK 46732 [id.]. Cleveland O, Szell.

In a letter to the conductor, Walton expressed himself greatly pleased with Szell's performance of the *Second Symphony*: 'It is a quite fantastic and stupendous performance from every point of view. Firstly it is absolutely right musically speaking, and the virtuosity is quite staggering, especially the Fugato; but everything is phrased and balanced in an unbelievable way.' Listening to the splendidly remastered CD of this 1961 recording, one cannot but join the composer in responding to the wonderfully luminous detail in the orchestra, while the *Lento assai* is very moving, with richly sombre brass playing. In the first-movement allegro, the violins above the stave are miraculously firm and radiant, and the orchestral playing has an exhilarating flair and impulse. Szell's performance of the *Hindemith variations* is no less praiseworthy. Again the music-making is technically immaculate, and under Szell there is not only a pervading warmth, but each fragment is perfectly set in place. Finally comes the *Partita*, which was commissioned by the Cleveland Orchestra and given its première a year before the recording was made. The infectious writing is typical of the composer's earlier style. The recordings are bright, in the CBS manner, but the ambience of Severance Hall brings a backing warmth and depth, and these are technically among the finest of Szell's recordings in this venue. This Cleveland disc occupies a very special place in the Walton discography.

In the concerts that Vladimir Ashkenazy gave with the RPO on his return to Russia in 1989 after 26 years in exile, he included two outstanding British symphonies, the fine Knussen work and this, the more neglected of Walton's two symphonies. In this live recording, ensemble is inevitably less crisp than in most studio performances – as in the fugato of the finale – but the power and passion of Ashkenazy's reading amply compensate. He is somewhat brisker and more urgent than either Previn or Mackerras in the outer movements, bringing out the scherzando element in the finale even more effectively. He then most tellingly draws out the lyrical warmth of the central slow movement at a marginally slower speed. It could hardly be more sensuous, helped by sound that is amazingly good, considering the problems of live recording, atmospheric with plenty of detail and, on the whole, a natural balance.

CHAMBER MUSIC

Passacaglia for solo cello.
*** Chan. Dig. CHAN 8499; *ABTD 1209* [id.]. Raphael Wallfisch – BAX: *Rhapsodic ballad;* BRIDGE: *Cello sonata;* DELIUS: *Cello sonata.* ***

William Walton's *Passacaglia* for solo cello was composed in the last year of his life. It has restraint and eloquence, and Raphael Wallfisch gives a thoroughly sympathetic account of it. Excellent recording.

(i) *Piano quartet; String quartet in A min.*
**(*) Mer. Dig. CDE 84139; *KE 77139* [id.]. John McCabe, English Qt.

The *Piano quartet* is a work of Walton's immaturity, though there are many indications of what is to come. It is coupled with the mature *String quartet*; this is a substantial piece with stronger claims on the repertoire. McCabe and the English Quartet give a convincing enough account of the early piece, but the latter's account of the *String quartet* does not present a strong challenge to that of the Gabrielis on Chandos. If you want this particular coupling rather than the Elgar, however, this is certainly worth investigating.

Piano quartet; Violin sonata.
*** Chan. Dig. CHAN 8999 [id.]. Sillito, Smissen, Orton, Milne.

This performance of the *Piano quartet* with Hamish Milne as pianist makes one marvel that such music could have been the inspiration of a 16-year-old. Admittedly Walton revised the piece, but here is music which instantly grabs the ear, with striking ideas attractively and dramatically presented in each movement. The finale in particular, marked by sharply percussive Bartokian cluster chords, gives clear indications in its rhythmic energy of the mature Walton. His melodic tone of voice generally anticipates the future too. This is a more sharply focused reading than the rival Meridian one, both in the performance and in the recorded sound, with speeds generally flowing more freely and strongly and the string sound more satisfyingly resonant. The two principal performers from the quartet make a warmly sympathetic rather than high-powered duo for the *Violin sonata* of 1949. With its two long movements, both around 13 minutes, a lyrical sonata-form and a set of variations, it makes a difficult work to hold together, more waywardly argued than most Walton. Yet the combination of Sillito's ripely persuasive style and Milne's incisive power, clarifying textures and giving magic to the phrasing, keeps tensions sharp. The satisfyingly full sound helps too.

String quartet No. 1 (ed. Christopher Palmer); *String quartet in A min.*
*** Chan. Dig. CHAN 8944; *ABTD 1540* [id.]. Gabrieli Qt.

Coupled ideally with the mature *String Quartet in A minor*, completed in 1946, is the atonal quartet, long thought to be lost, which Walton wrote when an undergraduate at Oxford. Discovered in the Walton archive and edited by Christopher Palmer, it proves an astonishing work not just for a 21-year-old but for any British composer writing in the early 1920s. Despite the composer's inexperience, the *Quartet* was chosen as one of the three representative British works to be played at the very first ISCM Festival in Salzburg in August 1923. The performance was a fiasco – badly performed at the end of a long programme, with the cellist getting her spike stuck in the catch for a trap-door, so that to everyone's mirth she started sinking below the stage. Ernest Newman pronounced the piece 'horrible', but Alban Berg thought well enough of it to take his young British colleague to see Schoenberg. Soon afterwards Walton withdrew the work. As first conceived in 1919 by the 17-year-old composer, it consisted only of a compact sonata-form Moderato and a massive fugue. After an initial performance in 1921, Walton added a formidable central Scherzo. The result is hardly recognizable as Walton at all but is full of fire and imagination. The composer himself later described this *Quartet* as consisting of 'undigested Schoenberg and Bartók', yet it is far more than merely derivative, in some ways very close to the atonal *Quartet No. 3* that Frank Bridge wrote three years later. One might describe the idiom of the first movement as 'pastoral-atonal', lyrical in its counterpoint, and the scherzo, built on vigorously rhythmic motifs and jagged ostinatos, has much more of Bartók in it than of Schoenberg, while the fugue of the finale seeks to emulate Beethoven's *Grosse Fuge* in its complexity and massive scale, alone lasting almost 16 minutes. The performance, recorded in 1991 by the reconstituted Gabrieli Quartet (leader John Georgiadis), brings out all the latent power and lyrical warmth, often implying an underlying anger. It provides a fascinating contrast with the highly civilized *A minor* work of 25 years later. That comes in a red-blooded Gabrieli recording of 1986 (leader Kenneth Sillito) earlier available in coupling with the Elgar *Quartet*. Both recordings were made in the warm, rich acoustic of The Maltings, Snape, with little discrepancy between them.

String quartet in A min.
*** Collins Dig. 1280-2 [id.]. Britten Qt – ELGAR: *Quartet.* ***
*** Chan. Dig. CHAN 8474; *ABTD 1185* [id.]. Gabrieli Qt – ELGAR: *String quartet.* ***
*** Virgin Dig. VC7 91196-2 [id.]. Endellion Qt – BRIDGE: *String quartet No. 3.* ***

As in the Elgar, the Britten Quartet capture the full poignancy of this work. Walton's *Quartet in A minor* was written at a time when he knew that his then-partner of many years, Lady Wimborne, was dying of cancer. The Britten Quartet bring out the emotional intensity, playing with refinement and sharp focus, finding a repose and poise in the slow movement that brings it close to late Beethoven. Not since the original recording by the old Hollywood Quartet (led by Leonard Slatkin's father, Felix) has the piece been played on record with such polish and refinement. The contrasts of wistful lyricism and scherzando bite in the first movement make most other versions seem clumsy by comparison, and the incisiveness of Walton's jaggedly rhythmic writing is a delight. Warmly expressive as the Gabrieli Quartet are in the Chandos coupling of these same works, the Brittens are even more searching.

Walton's only *String quartet* must rank as one of his best works and, in hands such as those of the Gabrieli Quartet, sounds far more effective than in the version for full strings that he made in the early 1970s. The performance was given at The Maltings, Snape, and the excellence of both the playing and the recorded sound must earn this a strong recommendation on CD, which is in the demonstration bracket.

The contrast between haunting melancholy and spiky wit in this *Quartet* of 1947, Walton's first major work after a long gap during the Second World War, exactly suits the Endellion players. The warmth of their understanding culminates in an outstanding performance of the *Lento* slow movement, superbly sustained at a very measured speed. The marked difference of style and mood here between this work and the other fine quartet on the disc is beautifully brought out, the Walton resigned, the Bridge angry in a way that Walton had rather left behind in his pre-war work. Excellent, warm sound.

Violin sonata.
**(*) ASV Dig. CDDCA 548; *ZCDCA 548* [id.]. Lorraine McAslan, John Blakely – ELGAR: *Sonata.* **(*)

Lorraine McAslan gives a warmly committed performance of Walton's often wayward *Sonata.* The romantic melancholy of the piece suits her well, and though the recording does not make her tone as rounded as it should be, she produces some exquisite pianissimo playing. John Blakely is a most sympathetic partner, particularly impressive in crisply articulated scherzando passages.

CHORAL MUSIC

All this time; Cantico del sole; Jubilate Deo; King Herod and the cock; A Litany; Magnificat and Nunc dimittis; Make we joy now in this feast; Missa brevis; Set me as a seal (antiphon); *The Twelve; What cheer?; Where does the uttered music go?.*
*** Conifer Dig. CDCF 164; *MCFC 164* [id.]. Trinity College Ch., Richard Marlow.

Richard Marlow conducts his Cambridge choir of mixed voices in a delectable collection of Walton's sacred choral music, both unaccompanied and with organ. Item after item – the majority from late in the composer's career – brings home how brightly the spirit of *Belshazzar* still burned in his writing right to the end. The *Missa brevis* for Coventry Cathedral in its spareness strikes a darker, deeper note. The *Cantico del sole*, idiomatically setting Italian words of St Francis, is warmly distinctive, and the longest piece, *The Twelve*, to words specially written by W. H. Auden, is far more than an occasional piece. Marlow draws phenomenally responsive singing from his talented choir, with matching and ensemble that approach the ideal. The recording is just as alive and immaculate.

Belshazzar's Feast; Coronation Te Deum; Gloria.
**(*) Chan. Dig. CHAN 8760 [id.]. Howell, Gunson, Mackie, Roberts, Bach Ch., Philh. O, Willcocks.

(i) *Belshazzar's Feast; Henry V* (film score): *suite.*
*** ASV Dig. CDRPO 8001 [id.]. (i) Luxon, Brighton Festival Ch., L. Coll. Mus., RPO, Previn.

(i) *Belshazzar's Feast. Henry V: 2 Pieces for strings. Partita for orchestra.*
(M) **(*) BMG/RCA Dig. RD 60813 [60813-2-RC]. (i) Allen, LPO Ch.; LPO, Slatkin.

André Previn's new digital version of Walton's oratorio brings a performance in some ways even sharper and more urgent than his fine earlier version for EMI with the LSO. The recording is very clear, revealing details of Walton's brilliant orchestration as never before. The chorus, singing with biting intensity, is set realistically behind the orchestra, and though that gives the impression of a smaller group than is ideal, clarity and definition are enhanced. Benjamin Luxon – who earlier sang in Solti's Decca version – is a characterful soloist, but his heavy vibrato is exaggerated by too close a balance. The five-movement suite from Walton's film-music for *Henry V* makes an attractive coupling. Previn was the first conductor on record since Walton himself to capture the full dramatic bite and colour of this music, with the cavalry charge at Agincourt particularly vivid.

Willcocks's version of *Belshazzar's Feast* came as the first issue in Chandos's big Walton series, a very promising start. He scores over most rivals in his pacing which, far more than is common, follows the example set by the composer himself in his two recordings. Speeds tend to be a degree faster, as in *By the waters of Babylon* which flows evenly yet without haste. The soloist, Gwynne Howell, firm and dark of tone, is among the finest of all exponents but, with the Bach Choir placed rather more distantly than in most versions, this is not as incisive as its finest rivals. The *Coronation Te Deum* receives a richly idiomatic performance, and Willcocks also gives weight and thrust to the *Gloria*, with the tenor, Neil Mackie, outstanding among the soloists. The microphone unfortunately catches an unevenness in Ameral Gunson's mezzo. The recording is warmly reverberant, not ideally clear on choral detail but easy to listen to.

Leonard Slatkin conducts the briskest of all modern versions of *Belshazzar*, bringing reminders of the composer's own very first, wartime recording, far faster in most of its speeds than has become the custom. In the final chorus, *Then sing, sing aloud*, Slatkin is even fractionally faster than Walton, but the syncopated jollity of the music is then diminished. Despite some questionable intonation, the choral ensemble is first rate, and the singing of the baritone soloist, Thomas Allen, is superb, covering the broadest tonal and expressive range. Sadly, the recording places him, like the chorus, rather at a distance, with too little feeling of presence. Though the percussion leaps out at you very dramatically, the recording as a whole lacks the biting impact the work needs. The distancing of sound affects the major item in the coupling too, the *Partita* which Walton wrote for George Szell and the Cleveland Orchestra. Slatkin directs a splendidly rumbustious performance of the opening *Toccata*, and the final *Giga burlesca*, with its snappy cross-rhythms, is exuberantly done, even if this account hardly replaces the original Szell version. In the two little string-pieces from the *Henry V* music Slatkin sustains very slow speeds well. Despite the incidental reservations, those who want the coupling should not be seriously disappointed.

(i) *Christopher Columbus (suite of incidental music);* (ii) *Anon in love;* (iii) *4 Songs after Edith Sitwell: Daphne; Through gilded trellises; Long steel grass; Old Sir Faulk; A Song for the Lord Mayor's table. The Twelve (an anthem for the Feast of any Apostle).*
*** Chan. Dig. CHAN 8824; *ABTD 1449* [id.]. (i) Linda Finnie, Arthur Davies; (ii) Martyn Hill; (iii) Jill Gomez; Westminster Singers, City of L. Sinfonia, Hickox.

The composer's own orchestral versions of his song-cycles *Anon in love* (for tenor) and *A Song for the Lord Mayor's table* (for soprano) are so beautifully judged that they transcend the originals, which had, respectively, guitar and piano accompaniments. The strength and beauty of these strongly characterized songs is enormously enhanced, particularly in performances as positive as these by Martyn Hill and Jill Gomez. The anthem, *The Twelve*, which Walton wrote for his old college, Christ Church, Oxford, to words by W. H. Auden, also emerges far more powerfully with orchestral instead of organ accompaniment. The four Sitwell songs were orchestrated by Christopher Palmer, who also devised the suite from Walton's incidental music to Louis MacNeice's wartime radio play, *Christopher Columbus*, buried for half a century. It is a rich score which brings more happy anticipations of the *Henry V* film-music in the choral writing, and even of the opera *Troilus and Cressida*, as well as overtones of *Belshazzar's Feast*. Warmly committed performances, opulently recorded.

Ward, John (1571–1638)

Madrigals: *Come sable night; Cruel unkind; Die not, fond man; Hope of my heart; If heaven's just wrath; If the deep sighs; I have retreated; My breast I'll set; Oft have I tender'd; Out from the vale; Retire, my troubled soul; Sweet Philomel.*
*** Hyp. Dig. CDA 66256; *KA 66256* [id.]. Consort of Musicke, Anthony Rooley.

Ward's music speaks with a distinctive voice, free from the self-conscious melancholy that afflicts some of his contemporaries. This is not to say that his output is wanting in depth of feeling or elegiac sentiment, but rather that his language is freer from artifice. He chooses poetry of high quality and his music is always finely proportioned and organic in conception. These settings appeared at the end of the period in which the madrigal flourished (in 1613, to be exact) and can be regarded as representing the tradition at its finest. These new performances have a distinct tonal blend; such is the quality of this music and the accomplishment with which it is presented that collectors who respond to this repertoire should not hesitate.

Ward, Robert (born 1917)

(i) *Symphony No. 6;* (ii) *Appalachian ditties and dances;* (iii) *Dialogues;* (iv) *Lamentation and Scherzo.*
** Bay Cities BCD 1015 [id.]. (i) St Stephen's CO, Lorenzo Muti; (ii) Stephen Shipps; (ii; iv) Eric Larsen; (iii) Amadeus Trio.

Now in his mid-seventies, Robert Ward studied at the Eastman School with Howard Hanson and Bernard Rogers and went on to a distinguished academic career at the Juilliard School and, later, the University of North Carolina. His idiom is tonal and unproblematic and his music is impeccably crafted. Having heard (and been impressed by) one of his earlier symphonies, the prospect of hearing some of his more recent works such as the *Symphony No. 6* (1989) for chamber orchestra, and the *Appalachian ditties and dances* (1988) or the slightly earlier *Dialogues* (1984) seemed promising. However, this disc is a disappointment: the *Symphony* is pretty anonymous, with none of the freshness one recalls from his earlier music, and there are few strong or individual ideas in the remaining pieces. Generally goodish performances and recording.

Warlock, Peter (1894–1930)

Capriol suite for strings.
(M) *** Decca 421 391-2; *421 391-4* [id.]. ASMF, Marriner – BRITTEN: *Variations on a theme of Frank Bridge;* BUTTERWORTH: *Banks of green willow* etc. ***

The playing of the St Martin's Academy under Marriner is lively, polished and stylish here and readily reveals the freshness of Warlock's invention, based on Elizabethan dances. The recording is first rate.

Capriol suite (orchestral version); *Serenade for strings (for the sixtieth birthday of Delius).*
*** Chan. Dig. CHAN 8808; *ABTD 1436* [id.]. Ulster O, Vernon Handley – MOERAN: *Serenade* etc. ***

The *Capriol suite* exists in piano-duet form, a very familiar version for strings (both from 1926), and the present full orchestral score, which followed in 1928. The effect is to rob the music of some of its astringency. A dryish wine is replaced with one with the fullest bouquet, for the wind instruments make the textures more rococo in feeling as well as increasing the colour. There are losses as well as gains, but it is good to have Handley's fine performance, made to sound opulent by the acoustics of Ulster Hall, Belfast. The lovely *Serenade*, for strings alone, is also played and recorded very beautifully.

Serenade for strings (for the sixtieth birthday of Delius).
(M) *** Decca 421 384-2 [id.]. ASMF, Marriner – ELGAR: *Elegy for strings* etc. **(*)

Warlock's gentle *Serenade*, written for Delius, is beautifully played and recorded here, an unjustly neglected work receiving its due.

Songs: *As ever I saw; Autumn twilight; The bachelor; The bayly berith the bell away; Captain Stratton's fancy; First mercy; The fox; Hey, trolly, loly lo; Ha'nacker Mill; I held love's head; The jolly shepherd; Late summer; Lullaby; Milkmaids; Mourne no more; Mr Belloc's fancy; My gostly fader; My own country; The night; Passing by; Piggesnie; Play-acting; Rest, sweet nymphs; Sleep; Sweet content; Take, o take those lips away; There is a lady sweet and fair; Thou gav'st me leave to kiss; Walking the woods; When as the rye; The wind from the west; Yarmouth Fair.*
*** Chan. Dig. CHAN 8643 [id.]. Benjamin Luxon, David Willison.

A remarkably generous recital of 32 Warlock songs, ranging wide, from the melancholy and drama to 'hey-nonny-nonny' Elizabethan pastiche. Songs like *Autumn twilight*, the powerfully expressive *Late summer* and *Captain Stratton's fancy* are appealing in utterly different ways, and there is not a single number in the programme that does not show the composer either in full imaginative flow or simply enjoying himself, as in *Yarmouth Fair*. Luxon's performances are first class and David Willison provides sensitive and sparkling accompaniments. The recording is first class.

Waxman, Franz (1906–67)

Carmen fantasy.
(*) Teldec/Warner Dig. 9031 73266-2 [id.]. Maxim Vengerov, Israel PO, Mehta – PAGANINI: *Concerto No. 1* **; SAINT-SAËNS: *Havanaise* etc. *

Franz Waxman's *Carmen fantasy* is less imaginatively compiled than Sarasate's similar confection, but it invites the flamboyance that the young Russian émigré, Maxim Vengerov, can readily provide. He dazzles and seduces the ear by turns, and even if he is forwardly balanced, the orchestral backing is well in the picture.

Film scores: *Bride of Frankenstein: Creation of the female monster; Old Aquaintance: Elegy for strings. Philadelphia Story: Fanfare; Main title; True love. A Place in the Sun: suite. Prince Valiant: suite. Rebecca: suite. Sunset Boulevard: suite. Taras Bulba: suite.*
❀ (M) *** BMG/RCA GD 80708; *GK 80708* [0708-2-RG; *0708-4-RG*]. Nat. PO, Charles Gerhardt.

Of the many European musicians who crossed the Atlantic to make careers in Hollywood, Franz Waxman was among the most distinguished. His first important score was for James Whale's *Bride of Frankenstein*, a horror movie to which many film buffs give classic status. His marvellously evocative music for *The creation of the female monster* was restored by the conductor, mainly from listening to the film sound-track, as the orchestral parts are lost. Waxman stayed on to write for 188 films over 32 years. The opening of the first item on this CD and tape, the *Suite* from *Prince Valiant*, immediately shows the vigour of Waxman's invention and the brilliance of his Richard Straussian orchestration, and this score includes one of those sweeping string tunes which are the very epitome of Hollywood film music. Perhaps the finest of these comes in *A Place in the Sun*, and in the *Suite* it is used to preface an imaginative rhapsodical movement for solo alto sax (brilliantly played here by Ronnie Chamberlain). The collection ends with *The ride to Dubno* from *Taras Bulba* (Waxman's last film-score), which has thrilling impetus and energy and is scored with great flair. All the music here is of high quality, and for any movie buff this is desert-island material. It nostalgically includes the famous MGM introductory title fanfare, which Waxman wrote as a backcloth for Leo the Lion. The orchestral playing throughout is marvellously eloquent, and the conductor's dedication is obvious. The recording is rich and full, with no lack of brilliance in this very successful transfer to compact disc.

Weber, Carl Maria von (1786–1826)

Bassoon concerto in F, Op. 75.
*** Denon Dig. CO 79281 [id.]. Werba, V. String Soloists, Honeck – HUMMEL; MOZART: *Concertos.* ***

Michael Werba's performance of the Weber concerto completes an attractive triptych. Both he and the accompanying group under Rainer Honeck capture the grand operatic flourishes of the first movement and the geniality of the finale. The recording is well balanced and vivid.

Clarinet concertino in C min., Op. 26.
*** ASV Dig. CDDCA 559; *ZCDCA 559* [id.]. Emma Johnson, ECO, Groves – CRUSELL: *Concerto No. 2* *** ❀; BAERMANN: *Adagio* ***; ROSSINI: *Introduction, theme and variatons.* ***

Emma Johnson is in her element in Weber's delightful *Concertino*. Her phrasing is wonderfully beguiling and her use of light and shade agreeably subtle, while she finds a superb lilt in the final section, pacing the music to bring out its charm rather than achieve breathless bravura. Sir Charles Groves provides an admirable accompaniment, and the recording is eminently realistic and naturally balanced.

Clarinet concerto No. 1 in F min., J.114.
*** ASV Dig. CDDCA 585; *ZCDCA 585* [id.]. Emma Johnson, ECO, Yan Pascal Tortelier – DEBUSSY: *Rapsodie;* CRUSELL: *Introduction, theme and variations;* TARTINI: *Concertino.* ***
(M) **(*) BMG/RCA GD 60035 [60035-2-RG]. Stolzman, Mostly Mozart Festival O, Schneider (with ROSSINI: *Theme and variations in C* ***; MOZART: *Andante in C, K.315* **).

In this fine, inspired version of the Weber *First Concerto* the subtlety of Emma Johnson's expression, even in relation to most of her older rivals is astonishing, with pianissimos more daringly extreme and with distinctively persuasive phrasing in the slow movement, treated warmly and spaciously. In the sparkling finale she is wittier than almost any, plainly enjoying herself to the full, and is given natural sound, set in a helpful acoustic.

Stolzman's account of the *F minor Clarinet concerto* displays plenty of character, an easy bravura and a succulent tone in the *Adagio*. Here too the orchestra accompanies warmly. Although the *Introduction* is a shade bland, the coupled Rossini *Variations* sparkle operatically once they get fully underway; but the Mozart *Andante*, conceived for the flute, needs a lighter touch if it is to be heard on the clarinet.

Clarinet concertos Nos. 1 in F min., Op. 73; 2 in E flat, Op. 74; Clarinet concertino in E flat, Op. 26.
❀ *** Denon Dig. CO 79551 [id.]. Paul Meyer, RPO, Günther Herbig.
*** Virgin Dig. VC7 90720-2; *VC 790720-4* [id.]. Antony Pay, O of Age of Enlightenment.
(BB) *** Naxos Dig. 8.550378 [id.]. Ernst Ottensamer, Slovak State PO (Košice), Johannes Wildner.

Clarinet concerto No. 2.
*** Hyp. CDA 66088 [id.]. Thea King, LSO, Francis – CRUSELL: *Concerto No. 2.* ***

The brilliant twenty-year-old Paul Meyer, having already won numerous international awards, shows his prowess here in scintillating accounts of these three Weberian showpieces. He takes every risk in the book, using the widest possible dynamic range, at one moment using a robust cutting edge to his tone, at another fining it down to a magical *sotto voce.* In the slow movement of the *F minor Concerto* he blends delicately with the horn chorale and then, after a beautifully controlled diminuendo, dashes off, chortling through the finale with great glee. He is fortunate in having an excellent accompanist in Günther Herbig, and the RPO provides admirable support: the opening tutti of the *E flat Concerto* is particularly impressive. But it is the solo playing that continually captivates the ear with its wit, while caressing the lyrical melodies with the most subtle control of colour. The *Concertino* is sheer delight from beginning to end, particularly the liltingly infectious finale. With fine recording this record is in a class of its own. As usual with this thoughtful Japanese company, there are helpful index points throughout, to identify the structure of each individual movement.

Antony Pay and the Orchestra of the Age of Enlightenment offer period-instrument performances. Pay uses a copy of a seven-keyed clarinet by Simiot of Lyons from 1800. The sonority is cleaner and less bland than can be the case in modern performances, and the solo playing is both expert and sensitive. A further gesture to authenticity is the absence of a conductor; however, the ensemble might have been even better and the texture more finely judged and balanced had there been one. The recording is vivid and truthful.

Neither the soloist nor the conductor on Naxos is a household name. Ernst Ottensamer is a highly sensitive clarinettist, who has played with the major Viennese orchestras and is a member of the Vienna Wind Ensemble. His account of the two *Clarinet concertos* can hold its own against nearly all the competition in the current catalogue in any price category. The Košice orchestra also responds well to Johannes Wildner's direction, and the recorded sound is very natural and well balanced. A real bargain.

Thea King with her beautiful range of tone-colours gives a totally delightful account of the *Second Concerto*, particularly lovely in the G minor slow movement and seductively pointed in the *Polacca* rhythms of the finale, never pressed too hard. She is accompanied admirably by Alun Francis and the LSO in a warmly reverberant recording that CD makes very realistic indeed.

Horn concertino in E min., Op. 45.
*** Ph. Dig. 412 237-2 [id.]. Baumann, Leipzig GO, Masur – R. STRAUSS: *Horn concertos.* **(*)

Baumann plays Weber's opening lyrical melody so graciously that the listener is led to believe that this is a more substantial work than it is. At the end of the *Andante* Baumann produces an undulating series of chords (by gently singing the top note as he plays) and the effect is spine-tingling, while the easy virtuosity of the closing *Polacca* is hardly less breathtaking. Masur's accompaniment has matching warmth, while the Leipzig Hall adds its usual flattering ambience.

Konzertstück in F min., Op. 79.
*** Ph. 412 251-2 [id.]. Brendel, LSO, Abbado – SCHUMANN: *Piano concerto.* ***

This Philips version of Weber's programmatic *Konzertstück* is very brilliant indeed, and finds the distinguished soloist in his very best form: Brendel is wonderfully light and invariably imaginative. In every respect, including the recording quality, this is unlikely to be surpassed for a long time. On CD, Weber emerges in brighter, firmer focus than on LP; collectors wanting this delightful work in the new format need not hesitate.

Overtures: *Abu Hassan; Der Beherrscher der Geister; Euryanthe; Der Freischütz; Oberon; Peter Schmoll; Invitation to the dance* (orch. Berlioz), *Op. 65.*

❀ *** Nimbus Dig. NI 5154 [id.]. Hanover Band, Roy Goodman.
(M) *** DG 419 070-2 [id.]. BPO, Karajan.

Goodman and the Hanover Band give delectable performances of the six Weber overtures plus *Invitation to the dance* in Berlioz's arrangement. This is among the most persuasive records of period performance, likely to convert even those who resist new-style authenticity. The rasp of trombones at the start of *Euryanthe* has a thrilling tang, and the warm acoustic ensures that the authentic string-players sound neither scrawny nor abrasive, yet present rapid passage-work with crystal clarity. Of feathery lightness, the scurrying of violins in the *Abu Hassan overture* is a delight, and each item – including a rarity in *Der Beherrscher der Geister* – brings its moments of magic, with Goodman, both fresh and sympathetic, securing consistently lively and alert playing from his team.

Karajan's performances have great style and refinement. Weber's overtures are superbly crafted and there are no better examples of the genre than *Oberon* and *Der Freischütz*, both epitomizing the spirit of the operas which they serve to introduce. Needless to say, the Berlin horn playing is peerless in these two pieces. Karajan's stylish performance of another Weberian innovation, the *Invitation to the dance* (in Berlioz's orchestration), makes a valuable bonus. On CD the sound is drier and brighter than originally, with a loss of weight in the bass.

Overtures: *Der Freischütz; Oberon.*
(M) *** DG 415 840-2 [id.]. Bav. RSO, Kubelik – MENDELSSOHN: *Midsummer Night's Dream.* ***

Kubelik offers Weber's two greatest overtures as a fine bonus for his extended selection from Mendelssohn's *Midsummer Night's Dream* incidental music. The playing is first class and compares favourably with the Karajan versions.

Symphonies Nos. 1 in C; 2 in C.
*** ASV Dig. CDDCA 515; *ZCDCA 515* [id.]. ASMF, Marriner.

Curiously, both Weber's *Symphonies* are in C major, yet each has its own individuality and neither lacks vitality or invention. Sir Neville Marriner has their full measure; these performances combine vigour and high spirits with the right degree of gravitas (not too much) in the slow movements. The orchestral playing throughout is infectiously lively and catches the music's vibrant character. The recording is clear and full in the bass, but the bright upper range brings a touch of digital edge to the upper strings.

CHAMBER AND INSTRUMENTAL MUSIC

Clarinet quintet in B flat, Op. 34.
(M) *** Decca 430 297-2 [id.]. Gervase de Peyer, Melos Ens. – HUMMEL: *Piano quintet* etc. ***

Clarinet quintet; Flute trio in G min., Op. 63 (for flute, cello and piano).
*** CRD CRD 3398; *CRDC 4098* [id.]. Nash Ens.

(i) *Clarinet quintet;* (ii) *Grand Duo concertante, Op. 48; 7 Variations on a theme from Silvana, Op. 33.*
**(*) Chan. Dig. CHAN 8366; *ABTD 1131* [id.]. Hilton, (i) Lindsay Qt; (ii) Keith Swallow.

Weber's *Quintet* is delightful music as well as being a willing vehicle for the soloist's immaculate display of pyrotechnics. Gervase de Peyer is in his element here and the strings give him admirable support. The 1959 (originally Oiseau-Lyre) recording is first class; it is vivid, with plenty of atmosphere, and does not sound at all dated.

On the CRD version, Antony Pay makes the very most of the work's bravura, catching the exuberance of the *Capriccio* third movement (as unlike a classical minuet as could possibly be managed) and the breezy gaiety of the finale. The Nash players provide an admirable partnership and then adapt themselves readily to the different mood of the *Trio*, another highly engaging work with a picturesque slow movement, described as a *Shepherd's lament*. The recording is first class, vivid yet well balanced.

Janet Hilton plays with considerable authority and spirit though she is not always as mellifluous as her rivals. This version does not entirely sweep the board even though it is very good indeed. However, Janet Hilton's account of the *Grand Duo concertante* is a model of fine ensemble, as are the *Variations on a theme from Silvana* of 1811, in both of which Keith Swallow is an equally expert partner. At times the acoustic seems almost too reverberant in the two pieces for clarinet and piano, but the sound in the *Quintet* is eminently satisfactory.

Grand Duo concertante in E flat, Op. 48.
*** Virgin Dig. VC 791076-2. Michael Collins, Mikhail Pletnev – BRAHMS: *Clarinet sonatas.* ***

Michael Collins and Mikhail Pletnev play the *Grand Duo concertante* with the greatest delicacy. It makes a refreshingly contrasting makeweight to their masterly accounts of the two Brahms *Sonatas.*

7 Variations on a theme from Silvana in B flat, Op. 33.
*** Chan. Dig. CHAN 8506; *ABTD 1216* [id.]. Gervase de Peyer, Gwenneth Pryor – SCHUBERT: *Arpeggione sonata;* SCHUMANN: *Fantasiestücke* etc. ***

These engaging Weber *Variations* act as a kind of encore to Schubert's *Arpeggione sonata* and with their innocent charm they follow on naturally. They are most winningly played by Gervase de Peyer who is on top form; Gwenneth Pryor accompanies admirably. The recording is first class.

Piano sonatas Nos. 1 in C, Op. 24; 2 in A flat, Op. 39.
(M) *** Pianissimo Dig. PP 20792 [id.]. Martin Jones.

Piano sonatas Nos. 1–2; Rondo brillante in E flat (La Gaîté), Op. 52; Invitation to the dance, Op. 65.
*** CRD Dig. CRD 3485 [id.]. Hamish Milne.

These two Weber *Sonatas* are not easy to bring off, with their classical heritage and operatic freedom of line. Both first movements are ambitious in design yet at the same time histrionically florid. The *Adagio* of the *C major* moves from certain classical serenity to a highly emotional core; the *Andante* of No. 2 is even more striking, begining as a gentle, semi-staccato march, on which Weber builds an imaginative set of variations. There follows a super-brilliant, quicksilver scherzo, to match the formidable moto perpetuo brilliance of the finale of the *First Sonata.* (That earlier work's dedicatee was heard to complain that it was too difficult for her, and Weber commented that if she were not a Grand Duchess he would have agreed with her.) Martin Jones is clearly at home in both works, pacing the music so that it never sounds brittle, revealing an unexpected depth where some pianists would find only opportunities for surface display. He is particularly impressive in the *A flat major* work, concluding the Rondo finale with a fine balance between virtuosity and grazioso feeling. The recording, made in the resonant but not too-resonant acoustic of the Concert Hall of Cardiff University, is admirable and seems just right for his relatively grand manner.

Hamish Milne's style is less overtly expansive, more chimerical, and his performances have a lightness of touch that is most appealing, without ever being superficial. He gives a scintillating account of the finale of the *C major Sonata* (more crisply and neatly articulated than the Jones account, which has just a suspicion of hurry) and his playing in the slow movements has attractive lyrical feeling. If you want added gravitas, turn to Jones, but Milne's readings are equally truthful to the composer's intentions. Moreover he also provides a sparkling account of the *Rondo brilliante* and, as a final encore, a totally captivating account of the charming *Invitation to the dance*, making it sound every bit as appealing on the piano as in Berlioz's orchestration. He is realistically recorded in the BBC Studios at Pebble Mill in Birmingham, where there is slightly less ambient spread than in the Cardiff venue.

Piano sonata No. 2 in A flat, Op. 39.
*** Ph. Dig. 426 439-2 [id.]. Alfred Brendel – BRAHMS: *4 Ballades.* ***

Masterly playing from Alfred Brendel, who makes out a strong case for the Weber *Sonata* which in his hands has seriousness and strength as well as charm. Everything is thoroughly thought out, and one feels that the slightest hesitation is carefully calculated. If there is a certain want of spontaneity, there is no want of mastery. Brendel is recorded in sound of marvellous presence and clarity.

Piano sonata Nos. 3 in D min., Op. 49; 4 in E min., Op. 70; Polacca brillante in E (L'Hilarité) (with LISZT: *Introduzione (Adagio)).*
*** CRD Dig. CRD 3486 [id.]. Hamish Milne.

Hamish Milne here completes his admirable survey of the Weber *Piano sonatas* with a sterner approach to the opening *Allegro feroce* of *No. 3 in D minor*, cast in an almost Beethovenian mould. But Weber was always himself, and operatic feeling inevitably creeps into the lyrical material as well as the passage-work. The variation slow movement is by no means conventional in treatment and is certainly dramatic, while the closing Rondo has wit as well as bravura. The last sonata is more introspective in its colouring and feeling, even in the powerfully energetic Minuet, but the mood lightens in the *Andante consolante* and the work then concludes with a ruthless Tarantella, driven on by its own restless energy. The *Polacca brillante* returns to the world of dazzling articulation and sparkling display. It is heard here with a slow introduction which Liszt arranged from the *Grande Polonaise* of 1808. Hamish Milne's playing is thoroughly inside Weber's world and technically equal to the composer's prodigious demands. He is very well recorded.

OPERA

Der Freischütz (complete).
(M) *** EMI CMS7 69342-2 (2). Grümmer, Otto, Schock, Prey, Wiemann, Kohn, Frick, German Op. Ch., Berlin, BPO, Keilberth.
*** DG 415 432-2 (2) [id.]. Janowitz, Mathis, Schreier, Adam, Vogel, Crass, Leipzig R. Ch., Dresden State O, Carlos Kleiber.

Keilberth's is a warm, exciting account of Weber's masterpiece which makes all the dated conventions of the work seem fresh and new. In particular the *Wolf's glen* scene on CD acquires something of the genuine terror that must have struck the earliest audiences and which is far more impressive than any mere scene-setting with wood and cardboard in the opera house. The casting of the magic bullets with each one numbered in turn, at first in eerie quiet and then in crescendo amid the howling of demons, is superbly conveyed. The bite of the orchestra and the proper balance of the voices in relation to it, with the effect of space and distance, helps also to create the illusion. Elisabeth Grümmer sings more sweetly and sensitively than one ever remembers before, with Agathe's prayer exquisitely done. Lisa Otto is really in character, with genuine coquettishness. Schock is not an ideal tenor, but he sings ably enough. The Kaspar of Karl Kohn is generally well focused, and the playing of the Berlin Philharmonic has plenty of polish. The overall effect is immensely atmospheric and enjoyable.

The DG set marked Carlos Kleiber's first major recording venture and this fine, incisive account of Weber's atmospheric and adventurous score fulfilled all expectations. With the help of an outstanding cast, excellent work by the recording producer, and transparently clear recording, this is a most compelling version of an opera which transfers well to the gramophone. Only occasionally does Kleiber betray a fractional lack of warmth, but the full drama of the work is splendidly projected in the enhanced CD format.

Oberon (complete).
(M) *** DG 419 038-2 (2) [id.]. Grobe, Nilsson, Domingo, Prey, Hamari, Schiml, Bav. R. Ch. & SO, Kubelik.

We owe it to Covent Garden's strange ideas in the mid-1820s as to what English opera should be that Weber's delicately conceived score is a sequence of illogical arias, scenas and ensembles strung together by an absurd pantomime plot. Although, even on record, the result is slacker because of that loose construction, one can appreciate the contribution of Weber, in a performance as stylish and refined as this. The original issue included dialogue and a narrative spoken by one of Oberon's fairy characters. In the reissue this is omitted, cutting the number of discs from three to two, yet leaving the music untouched. With Birgit Nilsson commanding in *Ocean, thou mighty monster*, and excellent singing from the other principals, helped by Kubelik's ethereally light handling of the orchestra, the set can be recommended without reservation, for the recording remains of excellent quality.

Oberon: excerpts.
(M) *** DG 435 406-2; *435 406-4* [id.] (from above complete set, with Nilsson, Domingo; cond. Kubelik) – WAGNER: *Meistersinger excerpts.* ***

As with the coupled excerpts from Wagner's *Meistersinger*, the present selection – part of DG's 'Domingo Edition' – sensibly concentrates on the items featuring Domingo as Hüon. Even so (apart from the stirring introduction to *Von Jugend auf in dem Kampfgefild*) room is found to demonstrate Weber's penchant for brass writing in the third act *March*, using themes familiar in the *Overture* (which is not included).

Webern, Anton (1883–1945)

(i) *Concerto for nine instruments, Op. 24; 5 Movements for string quartet* (orchestral version), *Op. 5; Passacaglia, Op. 1; 6 Pieces for large orchestra, Op. 6; 5 Pieces for orchestra, Op. 10; Symphony, Op. 21; Variations for orchestra, Op. 30.* Arrangements of: BACH: *Musical offering: Fugue* (1935). (ii) SCHUBERT: *German dances* (for small orchestra), *Op. posth.* Chamber music: (iii) *6 Bagatelles for string quartet, Op. 9; 5 Movements for string quartet, Op. 5;* (iv; v) *4 Pieces for violin and piano, Op. 7;* (v; vi) *3 Small pieces for cello and piano, Op. 11;* (v; vii) *Quartet, Op. 22* (for piano, violin, clarinet & saxophone); (iii) *String quartet, Op. 28; String trio, Op. 20;* (v) *Variations for piano, Op. 27.* (Vocal) (viii; i) *Das Augenlicht, Op. 26;* (ix; x) *5 Canons on Latin texts, Op. 16;* (viii; ix; i) *Cantata No. 1, Op. 29;* (viii; ix; xi; i) *Cantata No. 2, Op. 31;* (viii) *Entflieht auf leichten Kähnen, Op. 2;* (ix; x) *5 Sacred songs, Op. 15;* (xii; v) *5 Songs, Op. 3; 5 Songs, Op. 4;* (xii; x) *2 Songs, Op. 8;* (xii; v) *4 Songs, Op. 12;* (xii; x) *4 Songs, Op. 13; 6 Songs, Op. 14;* (ix; x; xiii) *3 Songs, Op. 18;* (viii; i) *2 Songs, Op. 19;* (xii; v) *3 Songs, Op. 23;* (ix; v) *3 Songs, Op. 25;* (ix; x) *3 Traditional rhymes, Op. 17.*
(M) *** Sony SM3K 45845 (3) [id.]. (i) LSO (or members), Pierre Boulez; (ii) Frankfurt R. O, composer (recorded December 1932); (iii) Juilliard Qt (or members); (iv) Stern; (v) Rosen; (vi) Piatigorsky; (vii) Majeske, Marcellus, Weinstein; (viii) John Alldis Ch.; (ix) Lukomska; (x) with Ens., Boulez; (xi) McDaniel; (xii) Harper; (xiii) with John Williams. Overall musical direction: Boulez.

These three CDs contain all Webern's works with opus numbers, as well as the string orchestra arrangements of Op. 5 and the orchestration of the *Fugue* from Bach's *Musical offering.* A rare recording of Webern himself conducting his arrangement of Schubert dances is also included. Though the recording quality varies somewhat, the CD transfers are remarkably consistent, considering that the items included were made over a period of eleven years. What Pierre Boulez above all demonstrates in the orchestral works (including those with chorus) is that, for all his seeming asceticism, Webern was working on human emotions. The spareness of the writing lets us appreciate how atonality can communicate tenderly, evocatively, movingly, not by any imitation of romantic models (as Schoenberg's and Berg's music often does) but by reducing the notes to the minimum. The Juilliard Quartet and the John Alldis Choir convey comparable commitment; though neither Heather Harper nor Halina Lukomska is ideally cast in the solo vocal music, Boulez brings out the best in both of them in the works with orchestra. Rarely can a major composer's whole *oeuvre* be appreciated in so compact a span. There are excellent notes, every item is cued, and perhaps it is carping to regret that the *Passacaglia* and *Variations for orchestra* were not indexed.

Concerto for 9 instruments, Op. 24.
(M) *** Chan. CHAN 6534; *MBTD 6534* [id.]. Nash Ens., Simon Rattle – SCHOENBERG: *Pierrot Lunaire.* ***

This late Webern piece, tough, spare and uncompromising, makes a valuable fill-up for Jane Manning's outstanding version of Schoenberg's *Pierrot Lunaire*, a 1977 recording originally made for the Open University. First-rate sound and a beautifully clean CD transfer.

5 Movements, Op. 5; Passacaglia, Op. 1; 6 Pieces for orchestra, Op. 6; Symphony, Op. 21.
(M) *** DG 427 424-2 (3) [id.]. BPO, Karajan – BERG: *Lyric suite; 3 Pieces;* SCHOENBERG: *Pelleas und Melisande; Variations; Verklaerte Nacht.* ***
(M) *** DG 423 254-2 [id.]. BPO, Karajan.

Available either separately or within Karajan's three-CD compilation, this collection, devoted to four compact and chiselled Webern works, is in many ways the most remarkable of all. Karajan's expressive refinement reveals the emotional undertones behind this seemingly austere music, and the results are riveting – as for example in the dramatic and intense *Funeral march* of Op. 6. Opus 21 is altogether more difficult to grasp, but Karajan still conveys the intensity of argument even to the unskilled ear. Indeed, if Webern always sounded like this, he might even enjoy real popularity. Karajan secures a highly sensitive response from the Berlin Philharmonic, who produce sonorities as seductive as Debussy. Incidentally, he plays the 1928 version of Op. 6. A strong recommendation, with excellent sound.

Passacaglia, Op. 1.
**(*) Chan. Dig. CHAN 8619; *ABTD 1308* [id.]. SNO, Bamert – SCHOENBERG: *Pelleas und Melisande.* **(*)

An eminently serviceable account of Webern's relatively lush *Passacaglia*, harnessed to Matthias Bamert's version of *Pelleas* with the Scottish National Orchestra. Excellent playing and good, if somewhat recessed, recording.

5 Pieces for orchestra, Op. 10.
(M) *** Mercury 432 006-2 [id.]. LSO, Dorati – BERG: *3 Pieces; Lulu suite;* SCHOENBERG: *5 Pieces.* ***

Webern's *Five pieces*, Op. 10, written between 1911 and 1913, mark a radical point in his early development. Their compression is extreme. What we have now gradually come to appreciate, thanks to such performances as this, is that, like so much of Berg and Schoenberg, they have their emotional point to make. The couplings could hardly be more fitting, and the whole record can be strongly recommended to anyone wanting to explore the early work of Schoenberg and his followers before they formalized their ideas in twelve-note technique. Bright, clear, 1962 recording to match the precision of the writing.

6 Pieces for orchestra, Op. 6.
*** EMI Dig. CDC7 49857-2 [id.]. CBSO, Rattle – SCHOENBERG: *5 Pieces;* BERG: *Lulu: suite.* ***
*** DG Dig. 419 781-2 [id.]. BPO, Levine – BERG: *3 Pieces;* SCHOENBERG: *5 Pieces.* ***

Rattle and the CBSO bring out the microcosmic strength of the six Webern *Pieces*, giving them weight and intensity without inflation. Warmth is rightly implied here, but no Mahlerian underlining. This superb performance, given sound of demonstration quality, comes ideally coupled with equally compelling performances of two equivalent masterpieces by Webern's two Second Viennese School colleagues. An outstanding issue in every way.

Levine brings out the expressive warmth of Webern's writing, with no chill in the spare fragmentation of argument and with much tender poetry. With the longest of the six tiny movements, the *Funeral march*, particularly powerful, it complements the other works on the disc perfectly. Ripe recording, with some spotlighting of individual lines.

Im Sommerwind.
*** Decca Dig. 430 324-2; *430 324-4* [id.]. Concg. O, Chailly – BRAHMS: *Symphony No. 2.* ***

Im Sommerwind, written by Webern when he was only twenty, is an evocative 'idyll for large orchestra', inspired by a poem of Bruno Wille. It is a vividly atmospheric musical picture of a summer day in woods and fields. In idiom it recalls Delius more than anyone else, and it is given a warmly understanding performance, refined in its textures, by the Concertgebouw under Chailly. It makes an unexpected but very attractive coupling for Chailly's Brahms, superbly recorded.

6 Bagatelles for string quartet, Op. 9; 5 Movements for string quartet, Op. 5; Slow movement for string quartet (1905); *String quartet* (1905); *String quartet, Op. 28.*
(M) *** Ph. 420 796-2 [id.]. Italian Qt.

Readers who quail at the name of Webern need not tremble at the prospect of hearing this record. The early music in particular is most accessible, and all of it is played with such conviction and beauty of tone that its difficulties melt away or at least become manageable. The recording is of outstanding vividness and presence, and it is difficult to imagine a more eloquent or persuasive introduction to Webern's chamber music than this.

(i) *Piano quintet; String trio, Op. 20; Movement for string trio, Op. posth.; Rondo.*
*** DG Dig. 415 982-2 [id.]. Stefan Litwin, LaSalle Qt – SCHOENBERG: *Ode to Napoleon.* **

The LaSalle Quartet's collection of miscellaneous chamber works makes a valuable supplement to the Philips record of the quartet music. The *String trio* is one of Webern's strongest and most characteristic chamber works. The *Movement* of 1927 was written in preparation for the full-scale *Trio*; while the two early works are fascinating too, particularly the single-movement *Piano quintet*, in a powerful, post-romantic style. The LaSalle performance brings out the emotional thrust without compromise, but the commitment of the players in all these pieces will immediately help the new listener to respond. First-rate recording.

Slow movement for string quartet (1905).
❀ *** Denon Dig. CO 79462 [id.]. Carmina Qt – SZYMANOWSKI: *String quartets Nos. 1 & 2.* *** ❀

Webern's early quartet movement is beautifully played here and comes as a pendant to an altogether outstanding performance and recording of the two Szymanowski quartets.

Weill, Kurt (1900–1950)

(i) *Violin concerto; Kleine Dreigroschenmusik* (suite for wind orchestra from *The Threepenny Opera*).
(M) *** DG 423 255-2 [id.]. (i) Lidell; L. Sinf., Atherton.

Weill's *Concerto* for violin and wind instruments is an early work, resourceful and inventive, the product of a fine intelligence and a good craftsman. The style is somewhat angular (as was that of the young Hindemith) but the textures are always clear and the invention holds the listener's attention throughout. It is splendidly played by Nona Lidell and the wind of the London Sinfonietta, and well recorded too. The *Suite* from *The Threepenny Opera* is given with good spirit and élan.

Theatre songs: *Aufstieg und Fall der Stadt Mahagonny: Alabama song; Wie man sich bettet. Das Berliner Requiem: Zu Potsdam unter den Eichen. Die Dreigroschenoper: Die Moritat von Mackie Messer; Salomon song; Die Ballade von der sexuellen Hörigkeit. One Touch of Venus: I'm a stranger here myself. Der Silbersee: Ich bin eine arme Verwandte; Rom war eine Stadt; Lied des Lotterieagenten.* Songs: *Je ne t'aime pas; Nannas-Lied; Speak low; Westwind.*
*** Decca Dig. 425 204-2 [id.]. Ute Lemper, Berlin R. Ens., John Mauceri.

Ute Lemper is nothing if not a charismatic singer, bringing a powerful combination of qualities to Weill: an ability to put over numbers with cabaret-style punch as toughly and characterfully as Lotte Lenya herself, as well as a technical security that rarely lets her down. The choice of items is both attractive and imaginative, bringing together popular favourites and relative rarities like the brilliant *Lied des Lotterieagenten* from *Der Silbersee.* Lemper is not the least troubled with singing in English as well as in German, and the recording vividly captures the distinctive timbre of her voice. Many will find her singing more seductive than that of Lotte Lenya, and the accompaniments are a pleasure in themselves, most atmospherically recorded.

The Ballad of Magna Carta; Der Lindberghflug.
*** Capriccio Dig. 60012-1 [id.]. Henschel, Tyl, Calaminus, Clemens, Cologne Pro Musica Ch. & RSO, Latham-König; Wirl, Schmidt, Feckler, Minth, Scheeben, Berlin R. Ch. & O, Scherchen.

Der Lindberghflug ('The Lindbergh Flight') is a curiosity. While collaborating for the first time on the *Mahagonny* Songspiel Weill and Bertolt Brecht conceived the idea of a radio entertainment on the subject which was then (in 1927) hitting the headlines: the first solo flight across the Atlantic by Charles Lindbergh. Brecht wrote the text, and Weill started on the music, but for the Baden-Baden Festival it was diplomatic to ask Hindemith to set some of the numbers, and that is how it first appeared. Only later did Weill set the complete work, and that is how it is given in this excellent Cologne recording. As a curiosity, a historic 1930 performance of the joint Weill–Hindemith version, conducted by Hermann Scherchen, is given as an appendix, recorded with a heavy background roar but with astonishingly vivid voices. One can understand why Weill was so enthusiastic about the fine, very German tenor who sang Lindbergh in 1930, Erik Wirl. The tenor in the new recording is not nearly so sweet-toned, and the German narrator delivers his commentary in a casual, matter-of-fact way, where in 1930 they had well-delivered narrations in French and English as well as in German. Otherwise the performance under Jan Latham-König fully maintains the high standards of Capriccio's Weill series; and the other, shorter item, *The Ballad of Magna Carta*, another radio feature, written in America in 1940 to fanciful doggerel by Maxwell Anderson, is most enjoyable too, a piece never recorded before. The sharp style is again very characteristic of Weill, though the choruses tend to soften into his Broadway idiom. Clear, if rather dry, recording with voices vivid and immediate.

Die Dreigroschenoper (The Threepenny Opera): complete.
*** Decca Dig. 430 075-2; *430 075-4* [id.]. Kollo, Lemper, Milva, Adorf, Dernesch, Berlin RIAS Chamber Ch. & Sinf., Mauceri.

*** Sony MK 42637 [id.]. Lenya, Neuss, Trenk-Trebisch, Hesterberg, Schellow, Koczian, Grunert, Ch. & Dance O of Radio Free Berlin, Brückner-Rüggeberg.

By cutting the dialogue down to brief spoken links between numbers and omitting instrumental interludes which merely repeat songs already heard, Decca's all-star production is fitted on to a single, generously filled CD. The aim has been to return to the work as conceived before Brecht exaggerated its propagandist political overtones. As recorded, with John Mauceri drawing incisive playing from the RIAS Sinfonietta and with bright, full, close-up sound, its saltiness and bite are enhanced, together with its musical freshness. The opening is not promising, with the Ballad-singer's singing voice – as opposed to his tangy spoken narration – sounding very old and tremulous. There are obvious discrepancies too between the opera-singers, René Kollo and Helga Dernesch, and those in the cabaret tradition, notably the vibrant and provocative Ute Lemper (Polly Peachum) and the gloriously dark-voiced and characterful Milva (Jenny). That entails downward modulation in various numbers, as it did with Lotte Lenya, but the changes from the original are far less extreme. Kollo is good – but even more compelling is Dernesch, whose *Ballad of sexual obsession* in Act II is the high spot of the whole entertainment. A pity the third verse had to be omitted for reasons of space, though it was also cut before the first (1928) stage performance. The co-ordination of music and presentation makes for a vividly enjoyable experience, even if committed Weill enthusiasts will inevitably disagree with some of the controversial textual and interpretative decisions.

The CBS alternative offers a vividly authentic recording of *The Threepenny Opera*, Weill's most famous score, darkly incisive and atmospheric, with Lotte Lenya giving an incomparable performance as Jenny. All the wrong associations, built up round the music from indifferent performances, melt away in the face of a reading as sharp and intense as this. Bright, immediate, real stereo recording, made the more vivid on CD.

Happy End (play by Brecht with songs); *Die sieben Todsünden (The Seven deadly sins).*
(M) *** Sony mono/stereo MPK 45886 [id.]. Lotte Lenya, male quartet & O, Ch. & O, Brückner-Rüggeberg.

Originally recorded in mono in the mid-1950s, the CBS performance of *The Seven deadly sins*, with the composer's widow as principal singer, underlines the status of this distinctive mixture of ballet and song-cycle as one of Weill's most concentrated inspirations. The rhythmic verve is irresistible and, though Lenya had to have the music transposed down, her understanding of the idiom is unique. The recording is forward and slightly harsh, though Lenya's voice is not hardened, and the effect is undoubtedly vivid. *Happy end* was made in Hamburg-Harburg in 1960. Lenya turned the songs into a kind of cycle (following a hint from her husband), again transposing where necessary, and her renderings in her individual brand of vocalizing are so compelling they make the scalp tingle. Many of these numbers are among the finest that Weill ever wrote. The excellent notes by David Drew are preserved with the CD, but the texts are printed out in German without any translations. The sound is again forwardly balanced, but the CD transfer still provides a backing ambience.

The Rise and fall of Mahagonny (complete).
**(*) Sony MK 77341 (2) [M2K 37874]. Lenya, Litz, Gunter, Mund, Gollnitz, Markworth, Saverbaum, Roth, Murch (speaker), NW German R. Ch. and O, Brückner-Rüggeberg.

Though Lotte Lenya, with her metallic rasping voice, was more a characterful *diseuse* than a singer, and this bitterly inspired score had to be adapted to suit her limited range, it remains a most memorable performance. The recording lacks atmosphere, with voices (Lenya's in particular) close balanced. Yet even now one can understand how this cynical piece caused public outrage when it was first performed in Leipzig in 1930.

Der Silbersee (complete).
*** Capriccio Dig. 60011-2 (2) [id.]. Heichele, Tamassy, Holdorf, Schmidt, Mayer, Korte, Thomas, Cologne Pro Musica Ch., Cologne RSO, Latham-König.

Till now *Der Silbersee*, containing some of Weill's most inspired theatre music and many memorable tunes, has been known on record through the 'recomposed' version in English which was prepared for the New York City Opera in 1980, incorporating material from other Weill sources. This restoration of the original, written just before Weill left Nazi Germany, aims to cope with the basic problem presented by having his music as adjunct, not to a regular music-theatre piece, but to a full-length play by Georg Kaiser. Between Weill's numbers a smattering of the original dialogue is here included to provide a dramatic thread and the speed of delivery adds to the effectiveness. Led by Hildegard Heichele, bright and full-toned as the central character, Fennimore, the cast is an outstanding one, with each voice satisfyingly clean-focused, while the 1989 recording is rather better-balanced and kinder to the instrumental accompaniment than some from this source, with the voices exceptionally vivid. Particularly telling is the finale with its haunting slow waltz bearing a timely 'green' message. The Overture and Act I are complete on the first disc, Acts II and III on the second. Libretto, notes and background material are first rate, as in the rest of Capriccio's Weill series.

Street scene (opera): complete.
*** TER Dig. CDTER2 1185 (2) [id.]. Kristine Ciesinski, Janis Kelly, Bonaventura Bottone, Richard Van Allan, ENO Ch. and O, Carl Davis.
** Decca Dig. 433 371-2 (2) [id.]. Barstow, Ramey, Reaux, Hadley, Augér, Bonney, Dickinson, Scottish Op. Ch. & O, Mauceri.

Street scene was Kurt Weill's attempt, late in his Broadway career, to write an American opera as distinct from a musical. It has few if any of the easy, catchy tunes of most musicals or earlier Weill, and though it presents the events over 24 hours in a Manhattan tenement house with brilliant control of timing and tension, the piece falls far short of *Porgy and Bess* as an American opera. The TER set was made with the cast of the ENO production at the Coliseum, and the idiomatic feeling and sense of flow consistently reflect that. Some of the solo singing in the large cast is flawed, but never seriously, and the principals are all very well cast – Kristine Ciesinski as the much-put-upon Anna Maurrant, Richard van Allan as her sorehead husband, Janis Kelly sweet and tender as the vulnerable daughter, and Bonaventura Bottone as the diffident young Jewish neighbour who loves her. Those are only a few of the sharply drawn characters, and the performance on the discs, with dialogue briskly paced, reflects the speed of the original ENO production. Warm, slightly distanced sound.

Though the starry Decca version, issued simultaneously with the TER, has a cast with many more international names, and the recording has a firmness and sharpness of focus beyond the TER, it cannot match its rival in flow and idiomatic feeling for Weill's score. Too often the performance sounds too literal, failing to flow, with speeds occasionally dragging. Samuel Ramey is too noble-voiced to sound fully convincing as the crusty Frank Maurrant, and others too are less characterful than their rivals, though Josephine Barstow brings telling weight to the role of the mother, Anna.

Der Zar lässt sich Photographieren (complete).
**(*) Capriccio Dig. 60 007-1 [id.]. McDaniel, Pohl, Napier, Cologne R. O, Latham-König.

This curious one-act *opera buffa*, first heard in 1928, is Weill's first comic opera, but his last theatre-piece that is through-composed. With the playwright Georg Kaiser, his collaborator on several previous pieces, he produced a wry little parable about assassins planning to kill the Tsar when he has his photograph taken. Angèle, the photographer, is replaced by the False Angèle, but the Tsar proves to be a young man who simply wants friendship, and the would-be assassin, instead of killing him, plays a tango on the gramophone, before the Tsar's official duties summon him again. Jan Latham-König in this 1984 recording directs a strong performance, though the dryly recorded orchestra is consigned to the background. The voices fare better, though Barry McDaniel is not ideally steady as the Tsar.

Weiss, Silvius (1686–1750)

Overture in B flat; Suite in D min.; Suite No. 17 in F min.
(M) *** BMG/RCA GD 77217 [77217-2-RG]. Konrad Junghänel (lute).

The Silesian composer Silvius Leopold Weiss was an almost exact contemporary of J. S. Bach and was regarded in his day as the greatest lutenist of the Baroque. He composed about 100 works, none of which was published in his lifetime: his preferred form was the cyclic suite. Konrad Junghänel's excellently focused recording comes from 1984. He plays a Baroque 13-string lute by Nico van der Waals with splendid authority and musicianship, though, as so often with recordings of soft-spoken instruments like the lute or the clavichord, the level is too high and best results are obtained by playing this at a lower volume setting. There are long and interesting presentation notes.

Widor, Charles-Marie (1844–1937)

Salve regina; Symphony No. 6: 1st movt.
(M) *** Mercury 434 311-2 [id.]. Marcel Dupré (organ of St Thomas's Church, NY City) – FRANCK: *3 Chorales* etc. ***

These are each movements from symphonies, as the composer later interpolated his *Salve regina* into his *Second.* In both Marcel Dupré displays those qualities of musicianly fervour for which the older generation of French organists was noted, and this recording, made on an exceptionally fine instrument, cannot fail to impress even the most casual listener.

Organ symphony No. 5 in F min., Op. 42/1.
*** DG Dig. 413 438-2 [id.]. Simon Preston (organ of Westminster Abbey) – VIERNE: *Carillon de Westminster.* ***

Organ symphonies No. 5 in F min., Op. 42/1 (complete); *6 in B. Op. 42/2: 1st movt; 8 in B, Op. 42/4: 4th movt (Prelude).*
(M) *** Saga SCD 9048 [id.]. David Sanger (organ of St Peter's Italian Church, Clerkenwell, London).

David Sanger's account of the Widor *Symphony No. 5* is first class in every respect and is recorded with fine bloom and clarity. His restraint in registering the central movements prevents Widor's cosy melodic inspiration from sounding sentimental, and the finale is exciting without being overblown. The other symphonic movements are well done but serve to confirm the conclusion that the famous *Toccata* from No. 5 was Widor's masterpiece.

Simon Preston also gives a masterly account of the Widor *Fifth Symphony*, with a fine sense of pace and command of colour; there is a marvellous sense of space in this DG recording. Detail seems far more sharply focused and one benefits from the wider dynamic range that CD encompasses.

Symphony No. 5: Toccata in F.
*** Argo Dig. 410 165-2 [id.]. Hurford (organ of Ratzeburg Cathedral) – *Recital.* ***
(M) *** EMI CDM7 64192-2 [id.]; *EG 764192-4.* Ralph Downs (Festival Hall organ) – BACH: *Collection.* *(**)

Those wanting the *Toccata* alone could not do better than choose Peter Hurford's exhilarating version, recorded with great presence and impact on a most attractive organ, and giving demonstration quality.

Ralph Downes's recording dates from 1958; it was in the demonstration class then and still sounds spectacular. The blaze of sound at the close is riveting, and the stereo readily conveys the wide spatial displacement of the organ.

Symphonies Nos. 5, Op. 42/1: Adagio & Toccata; 6, Op. 42/2: 1st movt: Allegro; 8, Op. 42/4: Moderato cantabile; Allegro; 9 (Symphonie gothique), Op. 70 (complete); *3 Nouvelles pièces, Op. 87.*
*** Argo Dig. 433 152-2; *433 152-4* [id.]. Thomas Trotter (Cavaillé-Coll organ of Saint-François-de-Sales, Lyon).

A single-CD anthology of this kind is a good way of sampling Widor's other symphonies. No single movement elsewhere approaches the famous *Toccata* from No. 5 in sheer memorability, but the inner movements of the *Symphonie gothique* are attractive and the finale undoubtedly inventive – it is essentially in variation form with an extended coda. The excerpts from the *Eighth Symphony* are also very agreeable. Thomas Trotter is an impressive advocate and he is splendidly recorded on an organ highly suited to this repertoire.

Wieniawski, Henryk (1835–80)

Violin concertos Nos. 1 in F sharp min., Op. 14; 2 in D min., Op. 22; Légende, Op. 17.
*** DG Dig. 431 815-2 [id.]. Gil Shaham, LSO, Lawrence Foster – SARASATE: *Zigeunerweisen.* ***

Listening to Gil Shaham's new DG record, it becomes even more mystifying that Wieniawski's *First Violin concerto* should always be upstaged by the *Second*, which is so often recorded. The first movement of the *F sharp minor* has a fine, lyrical secondary theme (with which Shaham ravishes the ear), and the slow movement *Preghiera* is meltingly long-breathed, while the dancing finale is highly infectious. The Paganinian pyrotechnics in the first movement can be made to dazzle, as Shaham readily demonstrates and Lawrence Foster makes a good deal of the orchestral part. Both soloist and orchestra are equally dashing and lyrically persuasive in the better known *D minor Concerto*, and make an engaging encore out of the delightful *Légende*. With first-class DG recording this record is very recommendable.

Violin concerto No. 2 in D min., Op. 22.
*** Decca Dig. 421 716-2 [id.]. Joshua Bell, Cleveland O, Ashkenazy – TCHAIKOVSKY: *Violin concerto.* ***

Joshua Bell gives a masterly performance, full of flair, even if he does not find quite the same individual poetry in the big second-subject melody or in the central *Romance* as Itzhak Perlman did in his currently deleted version. Excellent recording, brilliant and full.

Wikmanson, Johan (1753–1800)

String quartet No. 2 in E min., Op. 1/2.
*** CRD CRD 33123 (2) [id.]. Chilingirian Qt – ARRIAGA: *String quartets Nos. 1–3.* ***

Although he did not possess the natural inborn talents of an Arriaga, with whom he is coupled here, Wikmanson was a cultured musician. Little of his music survives, and two of his five *Quartets* are lost. The overriding influence here is that of Haydn and the finale of the present quartet even makes a direct allusion to Haydn's *E flat Quartet*, Op. 33, No. 2. The Chilingirian make out a persuasive case for this piece and are very well recorded.

Wirén, Dag (1905–86)

(i) *Violin concerto, Op. 23;* (ii) *String quartet No. 5, Op. 41;* (iii) *Triptych, Op. 33;* (iv) *Wind quintet, Op. 42.*
** Cap. Dig./Analogue CAP 21326. (i) Nils-Erik Sparf, Stockholm PO, Comissiona; (ii) Saulesco Qt; (iii) Stockholm Sinf., Wedin; (iv) Stockholm Wind Quintet.

This release offers a cross-section of Dag Wirén's music not previously available on CD. Wirén is a 'one-work composer', and little of his music is widely known or shares the celebrity of the *Serenade for strings*. The best piece here is probably the post-war *Violin concerto* whose first two movements are often imaginative and inventive; it is very well played by Nils-Erik Sparf and the Stockholm Philharmonic under Sergiu Comissiona. Only the finale is a let-down. The other three pieces, the *Triptych*, the *Fifth String quartet* and the *Wind quintet*, are all disappointingly thin and scrappy. The motivic ideas are short-breathed and rarely take creative flight: it is as if Wirén were constantly running out of steam. The *Quartet* and the *Triptych* are analogue recordings, the other two come from the mid-1980s and are digital. Excellent performances and recordings all the same.

Wolf, Hugo (1860–1903)

*Goethe-Lieder: Anakreons Grab; Erschaffen und Beleben; Frech und Froh I; Ganymed; Kophtisches Lied I & II; Ob der Koran; Der Rattenf*änger; Trunken müssen wir alle sein. Mörike-Lieder: Abschied; An die Geliebte; Auf ein altes Bild; Begegnung; Bei einer Trauung; Denk' es, O Seele!; Er ist's; Der Feuerreiter; Fussreise; Der Gärtner; In der Frühe; Jägerlied; Nimmersatte Liebe; Selbstgeständnis; Storchenbotschaft; Der Tambour; Verborgenheit.
*** DG 415 192-2 [id.]. Dietrich Fischer-Dieskau, Daniel Barenboim.

This collection of seventeen of Wolf's Mörike songs and nine Goethe settings was issued on CD to celebrate the singer's sixtieth birthday, a masterly example of his art. Barenboim's easily spontaneous style goes beautifully with Fischer-Dieskau's finely detailed singing, matching the sharp and subtle changes of mood. The mid-1970s analogue recording has been transferred very well, with the voice vividly immediate.

Lieder: *Frage nicht; Frühling übers Jahr; Gesang Weylas; Kennst du das Land? (Mignon); Heiss mich nicht reden (Mignon I); Nur wer die Sehnsucht kennt (Mignon II); So lasst mich scheinen (Mignon III); Der Schäfer; Die Spröde.*
*** DG Dig. 423 666-2 [id.]. Anne Sofie von Otter, Rolf Gothoni – MAHLER: *Das Knaben Wunderhorn* etc. ***

It is astonishing that so young a singer can tackle even the most formidable of Wolf's *Mignon* songs, *Kennst du das Land?*, a culminating peak of Lieder for women, with such firm, persuasive lines. Her gradation of the climaxes in the three successive stanzas is masterly – even though she will doubtless be finding even greater insights in a few years' time. The gravity of such a song is then delightfully contrasted against the delicacy of *Frühling übers Jahr* or *Die Spröde*. Eight of the songs are Goethe settings, the ninth, the haunting *Gesang Weylas*, to a Mörike poem. The sensitivity and imagination of Rolf Gothoni's accompaniment add enormously to the performances in a genuine two-way partnership. Well-balanced recording.

Italienisches Liederbuch (Italian Song-book, Parts 1 and 2): complete.
(M) *** EMI CDM7 63732-2 [id.]. Elisabeth Schwarzkopf, Dietrich Fischer-Dieskau, Gerald Moore.
(M) **(*) DG 435 752-2 [id.]. Irmgard Seefried, Dietrich Fischer-Dieskau, Erik Werba; Dietrich Fischer-Dieskau, Joerg Demus.

The 46 songs of Wolf's *Italienisches Liederbuch* were published in two parts, in 1892 and 1896. All of them are here, on a CD playing for two seconds over 79 minutes, generous measure indeed at mid-price. These songs show the composer at his most captivatingly individual. Many of them are very brief fragments of fantasy, which call for the most intense artistry if their point is to be fully made. No one today can match the searching perception of these two great singers in this music, with Fischer-Dieskau using his sweetest tones and Schwarzkopf ranging through all the many emotions inspired by love. Note particularly the little vignette, *Wer rief dich denn?*, the song Schwarzkopf was rehearsing when she first met her husband-to-be, Walter Legge, and which she interprets more vividly than anyone else: scorn mingling with hidden heartbreak. Gerald Moore is at his finest, and Walter Legge's translations will help bring the magic of these unique songs even to the newcomer. The well-balanced 1969 recording has been admirably transferred, giving the artists a fine presence.

For some reason there are two pianists in this 1958 DG set, one for each artist, and the impression at the end is one of less than total unity of idea and expression. Is not one really first-rate pianist better than two who, though very capable musicians and accompanists, do not show themselves here to be in that class? There is a similar division of approach in the interpretations of Seefried and Fischer-Dieskau. He shows himself by far the greater artist in this repertory, and his warm, rich-sounding baritone brings a remarkably wide range of colour and emotion. Seefried, in contrast, sounds rather hard, which is suitable for some of the lighter songs but shows up the long sustained lines of *Mir ward gesagt*. All the same this was the first complete recording of the *Italian Song-book* in stereo and as such will have considerable interest, both for Wolf enthusiasts and admirers of Fischer-Dieskau, who looks so youthful in the photograh illustrating the front of the CD.

6 Lieder für eine Frauenstimme. Goethe-Lieder: Die Bekehrte; Ganymed; Kennst du das Land?; Mignon I, II & III; Philine; Die Spröde. Lieder: *An eine Aeolsharfe; Auf einer Wanderung; Begegnung; Denk es, o Seele; Elfenlied; Im Frühling; Sonne der Schlummerlosen; Wenn du zu den Blumen gehst; Wie glänzt der helle Mond; Die Zigeunerin.*
(M) **(*) EMI CDM7 63653-2. Elisabeth Schwarzkopf, Gerald Moore or Geoffrey Parsons.

This is a superb collection, issued as part of Schwarzkopf's 75th birthday edition, representing the peak of her achievement as a Lieder singer. It is disgraceful that no texts or translations are provided as this will seriously reduce its appeal for some collectors; but the selection of items could hardly be better, including many songs inseparably associated with Schwarzkopf's voice, like *Mausfallen spruchlein* and, above all, *Kennst du das Land?*. That supreme Lied may not be quite as intensely moving in this studio recording as in Schwarzkopf's two live recordings, also issued by EMI, but it is commanding in its perfection.

Spanisches Liederbuch (complete).
(M) *** DG 423 934-2 (2) [id.]. Schwarzkopf, Fischer-Dieskau, Moore.

In this superb CD reissue the sacred songs provide a dark, intense prelude, with Fischer-

Dieskau at his very finest, sustaining slow tempi impeccably. Schwarzkopf's dedication comes out in the three songs suitable for a woman's voice; but it is in the secular songs, particularly those which contain laughter in the music, where she is at her most memorable. Gerald Moore is balanced rather too backwardly – something the transfer cannot correct – but gives superb support. In all other respects the 1968 recording sounds first rate, the voices beautifully caught. A classic set.

Wood, Haydn (1882–1959)

Apollo overture; A Brown bird singing (paraphrase for orchestra); *London cameos:* suite (*Miniature overture: The City; St James's Park in the spring; A State ball at Buckingham Palace); Mannin Veen* (Manx tone-poem); *Moods* (suite): *Joyousness* (concert waltz). *Mylecharane* (rhapsody); *The Seafarer (A nautical rhapsody); Serenade to youth; Sketch of a Dandy.*
*** Marco Polo Dig. 8.22340-2. Slovak RSO (Bratislava), Adrian Leaper.

Haydn Wood was Christian-named after the great Austrian composer (although here it is pronounced 'Hayden'), as his Yorkshire father had been to a performance of *The Creation* not long before his son arrived. H.W. was an almost exact contemporary of Eric Coates and nearly as talented. He was a violinist whereas Coates was a violist, but both had much orchestral experience and both developed great skills in orchestration, especially for modest-sized ensembles. Wood spent his childhood on the Isle of Man, and much of his best music is permeated with Manx folk-themes (original or simulated), which often bring a Celtic flavour to his invention. He wrote for the multitude of small orchestras which played on piers and in spas during the Edwardian era and up to the 1940s, but had his greatest success with a series of popular ballades which were much heard (often on portable wind-up gramophones of the time) in the trenches during the First World War. *Roses of Piccardy* alone earned him an estimated £100,000, a huge sum for those days. (Another favourite, *A Brown bird singing*, is heard here in a (slightly overlong) orchestral paraphrase.) Now most of his output is all but forgotten, although military bands in the parks stay faithful to him, and I.M. in his bandstand days remembers often playing *Mannin Veen* ('Dear Isle of Man'), a splendid piece based on four Manx folksongs. The companion rhapsody, *Mylecharane*, also uses folk material if less memorably, and *The Seafarer* is a wittily scored selection of famous shanties, neatly stitched together. The only failure here is *Apollo*, which uses less interesting material and is over-ambitious and inflated. But the English waltzes are enchanting confections, and one, regally allotted to a *State Ball at Buckingham Palace*, climaxes the *London Cameos suite*, which is worthy of Eric Coates, with its bustling picture of *The City*, opening with carolling horns, and the charming reminder of what St James's Park is like on a spring day. This generous collection (69 minutes) opens with a most engaging miniature, *Sketch of a Dandy*, endearingly dated but deliciously frothy and elegant, and played here with an ideal lightness of touch. Adrian Leaper is obviously much in sympathy with this repertoire and knows just how to pace it; his Czech players obviously relish the easy tunefulness and the sheer craft of the writing (as do all orchestral musicians, anywhere). With excellent recording in what is surely an ideal acoustic, this is very highly recommendable.

Wood, Hugh (born 1932)

(i) *Cello concerto;* (ii) *Violin concerto.*
(M) *** Unicorn UKCD 2043. (i) Parikian; (ii) Welsh; RLPO, Atherton.

Wood is a composer of integrity who has steeped himself in the music of Schoenberg and Webern, yet emerged richer for the experience – in contrast to many post-serial composers. His music is beautifully crafted and far from inaccessible. Here he is given the benefit of good recording, and the performances are thoroughly committed. Those who like and respond to the Bartók concertos or even to the Walton should try this. Excellently balanced recording, well transferred to CD.

Wordsworth, William (1908–88)

Symphonies Nos. 2 in D, Op. 34; 3 in C, Op. 48.
*** Lyrita Dig. SRCD 207 [id.]. LPO, Nicholas Braithwaite.

William Wordsworth was a direct descendant of the poet's brother, Christopher; on the evidence of this disc, he was a real symphonist: he composed eight in all, the most recent in 1986, two years before his death. The *Third* enjoyed some measure of exposure in the 1950s (Barbirolli conducted it no fewer than eight times in its first year), but the encouragement its composer received from the BBC in the 1950s was not continued into the 1960s, and his music was relegated to the outermost fringes of the repertoire, while the somewhat embittered composer migrated to the solitude of the Scottish Highlands. The *Second*, dedicated to Tovey, has a real sense of space; it is distinctly Nordic in atmosphere and there is an unhurried sense of growth. It is serious, thoughtful music, both well crafted and well laid out for the orchestra. At times it almost suggests Sibelius or Walter Piston in the way it moves, though not in its accents, and the writing is both powerful and imaginative. The long first movement in particular is sustained impressively. The *Third* is less concentrated and less personal in utterance, but all the same this is music of integrity, and readers who enjoy, say, the symphonies of Edmund Rubbra should sample the *Second Symphony*. Nicholas Braithwaite gives a carefully prepared and dedicated account of it, and the recording is up to the usual high standard one expects from this label.

Ysaÿe, Eugène (1858–1931)

6 Sonatas for solo violin, Op. 27.
*** Chan. Dig. CHAN 8599; *ABTD 1286* [id.]. Lydia Mordkovich.

The six *Sonatas* were all written for the great virtuosi of the time (Szigeti, Thibaud, Enescu and so on) and make cruel demands on the player – and, one is often tempted to add, the listener. Not in this instance, however, for Lydia Mordkovich plays with great character and variety of colour and she characterizes No. 4 (the one dedicated to Kreisler, with its references to Bach and the *Dies Irae*) superbly. These *Sonatas* can seem like mere exercises, but in her hands they sound really interesting. Natural, warm recorded sound. Recommended.

Zandonai, Riccardo (1883–1944)

Francesca da Rimini: excerpts from Acts II, III & IV.
(M) **(*) Decca 433 033-2 (2) [id.]. Olivero, Del Monaco, Monte Carlo Op. O, Rescigno – GIORDANO: *Fedora*. **(*)

Magda Olivero is a fine artist who has not been represented nearly enough on record, and this rare Zandonai selection, like the coupled set of Giordano's *Fedora*, does her some belated justice. Decca opted to have three substantial scenes recorded rather than snippets and, though Mario del Monaco as Paolo is predictably coarse in style, his tone is rich and strong and he does not detract from the achievement, unfailingly perceptive and musicianly, of Olivero as Francesca herself. Excellent, vintage 1969, Decca sound.

Zelenka, Jan (1679–1745)

Capriccios Nos. 1–5; Concerto in G; Hipocondrie in A; Overture in F; Sinfonia in A min..
✿ (M) *** DG 423 703-2 (3) [id.]. Camerata Bern, Van Wijnkoop.

In this superb orchestral collection, as in the companion Archiv issue of Zelenka *Sonatas* (see below), this long-neglected composer begins to get his due, some 250 years late. On this showing he stands as one of the most distinctive voices among Bach's contemporaries, and Bach himself nominated him in that role, though at the time Zelenka was serving in a relatively humble capacity. As in the sonata collection, it is the artistry of Heinz Holliger that sets the seal on the performances, but the virtuosity of Barry Tuckwell on the horn is also a delight, and the music itself regularly astonishes. One of the movements in the *Capriccio No. 5* has the title *Il furibondo (The angry man)* and, more strikingly still, another piece has the significant title *Hipocondrie* and sounds amazingly like a baroque tango. What comes out from this is that, in this period of high classicism, music for Zelenka was about emotion, something one recognizes clearly enough in Bach and Handel but too rarely in lesser composers. And in his bald expressiveness Zelenka often comes to sound amazingly modern, and often very beautiful, as in the slow *Aria No. 2* of the *Fourth Capriccio*. Superb recording, to match Van Wijnkoop's lively and colourful performances, makes these CDs very welcome indeed.

6 Sonatas for 2 oboes and bassoon with continuo.
❀ (M) *** DG 423 937-2 (2) [id.]. Holliger, Bourgue, Gawriloff, Thunemann, Buccarella, Jaccottet.

This second outstanding DG Archiv collection offers yet more music by the remarkable contemporary of Bach, Jan Dismas Zelenka, born in Bohemia but who spent most of his musical working life in Dresden. In these *Trio sonatas* it is almost as though Zelenka had a touch of Ives in him, so unexpected are some of the developments and turns of argument. The tone of voice is often dark and intense, directly comparable to Bach at his finest; and all through these superb performances the electricity of the original inspiration comes over with exhilarating immediacy. Fine recording, admirably remastered. Another set to recommend urgently to any lover of Baroque music.

Lamentationes Jeremiae Prophetae (Lamentations for Holy Week).
(M) *** HM/BMG GD 77112 [77112-2-RG]. Jacobs, De Mey, Widmer, Instrumentalists of the Schola Cantorum Basiliensis, Jacobs.

These solo settings of the six *Lamentations* for the days leading up to Easter reinforce Zelenka's claims as one of the most original composers of his time. The spacious melodic lines and chromatic twists in the harmonic progressions are often very Bachian, but the free-flowing alternation of arioso and recitative is totally distinctive. This mid-price issue of René Jacobs's 1983 recording for Deutsche Harmonia Mundi follows close on a very recommendable full-price version on the Hyperion label with the Chandos Baroque Players. Here, too, all three soloists are excellent, with the least-known, the baritone Kurt Widmer, easily matching the other two in his exceptionally sweet and fresh singing. But, quite apart from price, this BMG disc has the advantage of focusing the voices more cleanly and offering a rather less abrasive instrumental accompaniment, with speeds generally more flowing. Unlike the Hyperion issue, however, this one has separate tracks only for the six different *Lamentations*, not for each section.

Missa dei Filii; Litaniae Laurentanae.
*** HM/BMG Dig. RD 77922 [7922-2-RC]. Argenta, Chance, Prégardien, Gordon Jones, Stuttgart Chamber Ch., Tafelmusik, Bernius.

This fine set offers not only one of Zelenka's late Masses, but also a splendid *Litany* too, confirming him – for all the obscurity he suffered in his lifetime – as one of the most inspired composers of his generation. The *Missa dei Filii* (Mass for the Son of God), is a 'short' mass, consisting of *Kyrie* and *Gloria* only. Some of the movements into which the sections are divided are brief to the point of being perfunctory, but the splendid soprano solo of the *Christe eleison* points forward to the magnificent setting of the *Gloria*, in which the first two sections and the last are wonderfully expansive, ending with a sustainedly ingenious fugue. It seems that Zelenka never heard that Mass, but his *Litany*, another refreshing piece, was specifically written when the Electress of Saxony was ill. Zelenka, like Bach, happily mixes fugal writing with newer-fangled concertato movements. Bernius provides well-sprung support with his period-instrument group, Tafelmusik, and his excellent soloists and choir.

Requiem in C min.
**(*) Claves Dig. CD 50-8501 [id.]. Brigitte Fournier, Balleys, Ishii, Tüller, Berne Chamber Ch. and O, Dahler.

This record of the *Requiem in C minor*, like the settings of the *Lamentations of the Prophet Jeremiah* which Supraphon recorded in the late 1970s, confirms Zelenka's originality. *The Last Trump*, for example, is a thoughtful soprano solo without any of the dramatic gestures one might expect; and the *Agnus Dei* is quite unlike any other setting of his period – or of any other – austere, intent and mystical. There is hardly a moment that is not of compelling interest here; the only minor qualification that needs to be made concerns the balance, which places the solo singers too forward. The performance is well prepared and thoroughly committed. On CD one might have expected the choral focus to be sharper, but in all other respects the sound is very good, with the ambience nicely judged.

Zeller, Carl (1842–98)

Der Vogelhändler (complete).
(M) *** EMI CMS7 69357-2 (2). Rothenberger, Holm, Litz, Dallapozza, Berry, Unger, Forster, Dönch, V. Volksoper Ch., VSO, Boskovsky.

Boskovsky's vivacious and lilting performance of Zeller's delightfully tuneful operetta is in every way recommendable. The cast is strong; Anneliese Rothenberger may be below her best form as Princess Marie, but Renate Holm is a charmer as Christel, and Adolf Dallapozza sings the title-role with heady virility. There are many endearing moments, and the combination of infectious sparkle and style tempts one to revalue the score and place it, alongside *The Merry Widow* and *Die Fledermaus*, among the finest and most captivating of all operettas. For English-speaking listeners some of the dialogue might have been cut, but this is an international set and it is provided with an excellent libretto translation (not always the case in this kind of repertoire). The recording is excellent, combining atmosphere with vividness and giving lively projection of the principal characters.

Zemlinsky, Alexander von (1871–1942)

Die Seejungfrau (The Mermaid); (i) *Psalm 13, Op. 24.*
*** Decca Dig. 417 450-2 [id.]. (i) Ernst Senff Chamber Ch.; Berlin RSO, Chailly.

Zemlinsky's three-movement symphonic fantasy, based on the Hans Andersen story of the little mermaid, is comparable with Schoenberg's high-romantic *Pelleas and Melisande*, written at the same period, an exotic piece full of sumptuous orchestral writing. It is beautifully performed here, with ample recording to match. The choral setting of Psalm 13 dates from three decades later, but still reveals the urgency of Zemlinsky's inspiration – never a revolutionary in the way Schoenberg was, but always inventive and imaginative. The choral sound is not as full as that of the orchestra.

Symphony No. 2 in B flat; (i) *Psalm 23.*
*** Decca Dig. 421 644-2 [id.]. (i) Ernst Senff Chamber Ch.; Berlin RSO, Chailly.

Relatively conservative as the idiom is, this *Symphony* is a striking and warmly expressive work that richly deserves revival, particularly in a performance as strong, committed and brilliantly recorded as this. The slow introduction, with Wagnerian echoes from *Siegfried's funeral march*, leads to a bold *Allegro* based on strong and colourful themes, bringing hints of Brahms in Hungarian mood along with touches of Dvořák. The jagged rhythms of the scherzo are delightfully kaleidoscopic, and the slow movement is then relatively conventional in warm, solid, Brahmsian style, before the 45-minute work is rounded off with a *Passacaglia* paying obvious tribute to Brahms's *Fourth Symphony*. The piece inspires Chailly and the Berlin Radio Symphony Orchestra to one of their finest performances on record, helped by vivid sound, full of presence. The setting of *Psalm 23* – placed first on the disc – dates from later in Zemlinsky's career; it is in a rather more advanced harmonic idiom but is just as warm in expression, airy and beautiful. But do not expect a religious atmosphere: this is sensuous music, beautifully played and sung, which uses the much-loved words of the Psalm as an excuse for musical argument, rather than illuminating them.

String quartets Nos. 1, Op. 4; 2, Op. 15; 3, Op. 19; 4, Op. 25.
(M) *** DG Dig. 427 421-2 (2). LaSalle Qt.

None of the four Zemlinsky *Quartets* is in the least atonal: the textures are full of contrapuntal interest and the musical argument always proceeds with lucidity. There is diversity of mood and a fastidious craftsmanship, and the listener is always held. The musical language is steeped in Mahler and, to a lesser extent, Reger, but the music is undoubtedly the product of a very fine musical mind and one of considerable individuality. Collectors will find this a rewarding set: the

LaSalle play with polish and unanimity, and the recording is first class, as is the admirable documentation.

VOCAL MUSIC

Gesänge Op. 5, Books 1–2; Gesänge (Waltz songs on Tuscan folk-lyrics), Op. 6 ; Gesänge, Opp. 7–8, 10 & 13; Lieder, Op. 2, Books 1–2; Op. 22 & Op. 27.
*** DG Dig. 427 348-2 (2) [id.]. Barbara Bonney, Anne Sofie von Otter, Hans Peter Blochwitz, Andreas Schmidt, Cord Garben.

Thanks to recordings, the art of Alexander von Zemlinsky is coming to be ever more widely appreciated, and this two-disc DG collection of songs can be warmly recommended for the fresh tunefulness of dozens of miniatures. When in the 1890s he first got to know his future brother-in-law, Schoenberg, he was writing songs that would hardly have shocked Schubert; and even later, so far from following Schoenberg, he adopted in his songs a more conservative style than in his orchestral works or operas. With Cord Garben accompanying four excellent soloists, the charm of these chips from the workbench comes over consistently. Best of all is von Otter, more sharply imaginative than the others, making the one consistent cycle that Zemlinsky ever wrote, the six Maeterlinck Songs, Opus 13, the high point of the set.

Lyric symphony, Op. 18.
*** DG Dig. 419 261-2 [id.]. Varady, Fischer-Dieskau, BPO, Maazel.

Zemlinsky's *Lyric symphony* is essentially a symphonic song-cycle, modelled on *Das Lied von der Erde* and based on Eastern poetry; its lush textures and refined scoring make it immediately accessible. The idiom is that of early Schoenberg (*Verklaerte Nacht* and *Gurrelieder*), Mahler and Strauss. Yet it is not just derivative but has something quite distinctive to say. Its sound-world is imaginative, the vocal writing graceful and the orchestration masterly. Both soloists and the orchestra seem thoroughly convinced and convincing, and Maazel's refined control of texture prevents the sound from cloying, as does his incisive manner. Varady and Fischer-Dieskau make an outstanding pair of soloists, keenly responsive to the words, and the engineering is first class, the voices being well balanced against the orchestra.

6 Maeterlinck Lieder, Op. 3.
*** Decca Dig. 430 165-2 (2) [id.]. Jard van Nes, Concg. O, Chailly – MAHLER: *Symphony No. 6.* ***

Beautifully sung by Jard van Nes in her finest recording to date, these ripely romantic settings of Maeterlinck make an unusual but valuable fill-up for Chailly's rugged and purposeful reading of the Mahler symphony. This is very much the world of medieval chivalry which inspired *Pelleas and Melisande*, and Zemlinsky responds wholeheartedly. The rich, vivid recording captures van Nes's full-throated singing with new firmness.

Eine florentinische Tragödie (opera; complete).
*** Schwann Dig. CD 11625 [id.]. Soffel, Riegel, Sarabia, Berlin RSO, Albrecht.

A Florentine Tragedy presents a simple love triangle: a Florentine merchant returns home to find his sluttish wife with the local prince. Zemlinsky in 1917 may have been seeking to repeat the shock tactics of Richard Strauss in *Salome* (another Oscar Wilde story) a decade earlier; but the musical syrup which flows over all the characters makes them far more repulsive, with motives only dimly defined. The score itself is most accomplished; it is compellingly performed here, more effective on disc than it is in the opera house. First-rate sound.

Der Gerburtstag der Infantin (opera; complete).
*** Schwann Dig. CD 11626 [id]. Nielsen, Riegel, Haldas, Weller, Berlin RSO, Albrecht.

The Birthday of the Infanta, like its companion one-Acter, was inspired by a story of Oscar Wilde, telling of a hideous dwarf caught in the forest and given to the Infanta as a birthday present. Even after recognizing his own hideousness, he declares his love to the princess and is casually rejected. He dies of a broken heart, with the Infanta untroubled: 'Oh dear, my present already broken.' Zemlinsky, dwarfish himself, gave his heart to the piece, reproducing his own rejection at the hands of Alma Mahler. In this performance, based on a much-praised stage production, Kenneth Riegel gives a heartrendingly passionate performance as the dwarf declaring his love. His genuine passion is intensified by being set against lightweight, courtly music to represent the Infanta and her attendants. With the conductor and others in the cast also experienced in the stage production, the result is a deeply involving performance, beautifully recorded.

Collections

A selective list – we have included only the outstanding compilations from the many which are available

Concerts of Orchestral and Concertante Music

Academy of St Martin-in-the-Fields, Sir Neville Marriner

Concert: WAGNER: *Siegfried idyll.* SUPPÉ: *Overture Light Cavalry.* GRIEG: *2 Elegiac melodies, Op. 34.* TCHAIKOVSKY: *Andante cantabile.* DVOŘÁK: *Nocturne, Op. 40.* PONCHIELLI: *La Gioconda: Dance of the hours.* NICOLAI: *Overture The Merry Wives of Windsor.* FAURÉ: *Pavane, Op. 50.* BOCCHERINI: *Minuet* (from *Op. 13/5*).
(M) *** EMI Dig. CDD7 64107-2 [id.].

This is a demonstration concert for those who have to think of their neighbours. Many of the pieces here are relatively gentle and they are given radiant performances, recorded in digital sound with ravishingly vivid results. As in his previous Decca/Argo version of the *Siegfried idyll*, Marriner uses solo strings for the gentle passages, a fuller ensemble for the climaxes, here passionately convincing. Other items which are especially beautiful are the Grieg, Dvořák and Tchaikovsky string pieces, while the *Dance of the hours* sparkles with colour and élan. The programme plays for 75 minutes, and both sound and performances are quite exceptional.

'Armchair concert': MOZART: *Serenade: Eine kleine Nachtmusik, K.525. Symphony No. 40 in G min., K.550.* HAYDN: *Cello concerto in D, Hob VIIb/1–2* (with Lynn Harrell, cello).
(M) **(*) EMI CDM7 64447-2 [id.].

An interesting EMI venture, primarily aimed at the novice collector, here brings the first of a series of concerts – each rather more than an hour long – from artists of high calibre, offering a balanced programme of popular repertoire. Marriner and his elegant ensemble are thoroughly at home in the *Night music* and at their best in the *G minor Symphony*, which balances drama and warm lyrical feeling very successfully. Harrell's bravura account of the best-known Haydn *Cello concerto* makes a strong impression, although there are more refined versions available. Good, vivid sound.

'The French connection': RAVEL: *Le Tombeau de Couperin.* DEBUSSY: *Danses sacrée et profane* (with Ellis, harp). IBERT: *Divertissement.* FAURÉ: *Dolly suite, Op. 56.*
*** ASV Dig. CDDCA 517; *ZCDCA 517* [id.].

An excellent collection. The spirited account of Ibert's *Divertissement* is matched by the warmth of Fauré's *Dolly suite* in the Rabaud orchestration. The remainder of the record is hardly less appealing. Ravel's *Le Tombeau de Couperin* is nicely done, as is the Debussy *Danses sacrée et profane.* One would welcome more space round the orchestra and, considering the disc was made in Studio One, Abbey Road, greater use could have been made of the location's ambience. This apart, however, everything is very clear, with the sound even more refined and present on CD.

'The English connection': ELGAR: *Serenade for strings, Op. 20.* TIPPETT: *Fantasia concertante on a theme of Corelli.* VAUGHAN WILLIAMS: *Fantasia on a theme of Thomas Tallis; The Lark ascending* (with Iona Brown).
**(*) ASV Dig. CDDCA 518; *ZCDCA 518* [id.].

Sir Neville Marriner's newer performances of the Elgar *Serenade* and the *Tallis Fantasia* are less intense (and less subtle) than his earlier, Decca versions; the highlight of this concert is Iona

Brown's radiant account of *The Lark ascending*. The sound is rich and very well defined, especially in its CD format.

'English music for strings': HOLST: *St Paul's suite*. DELIUS (arr. Fenby): *2 Aquarelles*. PURCELL: *Chacony*. VAUGHAN WILLIAMS: *Rhosymedre: Prelude*. WALTON: *Henry V* (film music): *Death of Falstaff; Touch her soft lips and part*. BRITTEN: *Simple Symphony, Op. 4*.
(M) *** EMI CD-EMX 2170; *TC-EMX 2170*.

This attractively varied concert brings playing at once refined and resilient, delicately strong and warmly expressive by turns. Britten's *Simple Symphony* seems to be on a more impressive scale than usual; Holst's *St Paul's suite* brings wonderfully pointed rhythms in all four movements, while the Vaughan Williams and the Walton are finely atmospheric, against the sympathetic acoustic of EMI's Abbey Road Studio. The Delius too, atmospheric music *par excellence*, prepares the way for the bold and comparative astringency of the magnificent Purcell *Chacony*, which has never sounded more convincing on modern instruments. The remastered (1972) recording has refined detail and provides a somewhat firmer focus.

Trumpet concertos (with (i) Alan Stringer; (ii) John Wilbraham): (i) HAYDN: *Concerto in E flat*. (ii) HUMMEL: *Concerto in E flat*. ALBINONI: *Concerto in C*. L. MOZART: *Concerto in D*. TELEMANN: *Concerto in D*.
(M) *** Decca 417 761-2.

Alan Stringer favours a forthright, open timbre for the Haydn *Concerto*, but he plays the famous slow movement graciously. John Wilbraham is superbly articulate and stylish in the rest of the programme, and his partnership with Marriner in the captivating Hummel *Concerto* makes for superb results. Albinoni's *Concerto* divides the spotlight between trumpet and three supporting oboes to add textural variety, and both the Leopold Mozart and Telemann works are among the finest of their genre. Throughout, the orchestral accompaniments have striking elegance and finesse, and plenty of vitality too; and the recording is bright, with plenty of presence for the soloists.

VAUGHAN WILLIAMS: *Fantasia on Greensleeves; English folksongs suite*. ELGAR: *Serenade for strings in E min., Op. 20*. BUTTERWORTH: *The Banks of green willow*. WARLOCK: *Capriol suite*. DELIUS: *On hearing the first cuckoo in spring. A Village Romeo and Juliet: The walk to the Paradise Garden*.
(M) *** Decca 417 778-2; *417 778-4*.

All these vintage performances are available in other formats and couplings, many discussed within these pages. If the present assembly is attractive, there are no grounds for withholding a strong recommendation, for the recordings are first class and the digital remastering most successful.

Adler, Larry (harmonica)

'Larry Adler in Concert' (with (i) Pro Arte O, Francis Chagrin or Eric Robinson; (ii) Gerald Moore; (iii) LSO, Basil Cameron; (iv) Gritton, BBC SO, Sargent): (i) ENESCU: *Rumanian rhapsody No. 1*. GERSHWIN: *Rhapsody in blue*. (ii) *Porgy and Bess: It ain't necessarily so*. (i) BIZET arr. Adler: *Carmen fantasy*. RAVEL: *Boléro*. GRANADOS: *Spanish dance No. 5*. BENJAMIN: *Jamaican rumba;* (iii) *Harmonica concerto*. (i) CHAGRIN: *Roumanian fantasy*. (iv) VAUGHAN WILLIAMS: *Romance for harmonica with strings and piano*.
(M) *** EMI stereo/mono CDM7 64134-2 [id.]; *EG 764134-4* [id.].

It was Larry Adler who, more than anyone else, established the harmonica – or mouth-organ, as he always prefers to call it – as a respectable instrument. When in 1952 Vaughan Williams wrote his *Romance* for Adler, he expanded the expressive range of the instrument; and the Arthur Benjamin *Concerto* of the following year similarly brings a surprising range of expression. Both those works were recorded almost at once in the early 1950s in these outstanding performances, and they and the shorter items (for the most part recorded in stereo in 1957) consistently bring out Adler's artistry, his ability to transcend the limitations of the instrument and his creative feeling for phrasing. Indeed this whole programme reflects what Jascha Heifetz said of the mouth-organ: that it comes closer than other instruments to the human voice.

André, Maurice (trumpet)

Trumpet concertos (with LPO, López-Cobos): HAYDN: *Concerto in E flat.* TELEMANN: *Concerto in F.* ALBINONI: *Concerto in D min.* MARCELLO: *Concerto in C min.*
(M) *** EMI CDM7 69189-2 [id.]; *EG 769189-4.*

Maurice André's cultured playing gives much pleasure throughout this collection. Slow movements are elegantly phrased and communicate an appealing, expressive warmth. The stylishness and easy execution ensure a welcome for the Albinoni and Marcello works, which are transcriptions but are made thoroughly convincing in this format. Excellent, lively accompaniments from the LPO under López-Cobos, and good sound, the more vivid on CD.

Trumpet concertos (with (i) ECO, Mackerras; (ii) Munich Bach O, Karl Richter; (iii) Munich CO, Stadlmair): (i) VIVIANI: *Sonata for trumpet & organ in C* (with Hedwig Bilgram). VIVALDI: *Double trumpet concerto in C, RV 537.* TELEMANN: *Concerto-Sonata in D.* (ii) HANDEL: *Concerto in G min.* (arr. from *Oboe concerto No. 3*). (iii) M. HAYDN: *Trumpet concerto in D.* J. HAYDN: *Trumpet concerto in E flat.*
(M) *** DG 419 874-2; *419 874-4.*

The only transcription included here is from a Handel *Oboe concerto*, and that is reasonably effective. Michael Haydn's *Concerto*, a concertante section of a seven-movement *Serenade*, has incredibly high tessitura but, characteristically, Maurice André reaches up for it with consummate ease. He is completely at home in all this repertoire: his version of the Joseph Haydn *Concerto* is stylish and elegant, with a memorably eloquent account of the slow movement, the line gracious and warmly serene. The *Sonata for trumpet and organ* by Giovanni Buonaventura Viviani (1638–*c.* 1692) is also an attractive piece, comprising five brief but striking miniatures, each only a minute or so in length. In the Vivaldi *Double concerto* André plays both solo parts.

Concertos: HAYDN: *Concerto in E flat* (with Bamberg SO, Guschlbauer). L. MOZART: *Concerto in D* (with Paillard CO, Paillard). W. MOZART: *Concerto in C, K.314.* ANON.: *Concerto in C* (both with Liszt CO, Sandor).
(M) ** Erato/Warner 2292 45059-2 [id.].

Maurice André plays the Haydn concerto brilliantly and with style. Unfortunately Theodor Guschlbauer's accompaniment is nothing to write home about, but this is still enjoyable, as is the two-movement work by Leopold Mozart. André clearly relishes its melodic line, which lies in the highest register and Paillard gives good support. The other two works are transcriptions of oboe concertos, and the arrangement of Mozart is of doubtful appeal, though André plays it with much finesse.

'Trumpet voluntary' (with Württemberg CO, Faerber; ASMF, Marriner): CLARK: *Prince of Denmark's march.* FISCHER: *Concerto in C.* KREBS: *Fantasy in F min.* PURCELL: *Sonata in D.* TELEMANN: *Concerto in D.* HANDEL: *Concerto in G min.* BACH: *Concerto in F.*
(M) *** Erato/Warner 2292 45060-2 [id.].

Opening with a flourish, Maurice André introduces this programme with a lively, gleaming account of what the backing-slip describes as 'Purcell's *Trumpet voluntary*', although the notes indicate it is by Jeremiah Clark. The highlights here are the Telemann concerto and the Purcell sonata (both actually written for trumpet). But the Fischer and the Krebs works are attractive too, the former with a lovely pastoral *Adagio*, and the arrangement of a Handel oboe concertos and the amalgam of Bach cantata movements both obviously contain splendid music. André plays everything with his customary confidence and easy, stylish line and the accompaniments are polished. No complaints about the sound either.

Italian Baroque concertos: (with Paillard CO, Paillard; ASMF, Marriner; Franz Liszt CO, Sandor): VIVALDI: *Double trumpet concerto in C* (with Marcel LaGorge); *Concerto in A flat.* TARTINI: *Concerto in D.* ALBINONI: *Concerto in B flat; Double trumpet concerto in C* (with Lionel André). ZIPOLI: *Suite in F.* BELLINI: *Concerto in E flat.*
(M) **(*) Erato/Warner 2292 45062-2 [id.].

The documentation here is inadequate and the sources of these concertos are not identified. The Tartini and Albinoni works are almost certainly transcriptions, and probably the Bellini, too. But this is all attractive music, Maurice André's advocacy is stylishly assured and the performances are generally well accompanied. The programme runs for 72 minutes and the transfers are well made.

'La belle époque' (with (i) O d'Harmonie des Gardiens de la Paix de Paris, Claude Pichaureau; (ii) Monte Carlo Opéra O, Marc Soustrot): (i) ARBAN: *Variations on The Carnival of Venice; Fantaisie brillante; Variations on themes from Verdi's La Traviata.* PETIT: *Goutte d'eau; Fête militaire; Myrto pola; Madelleine.* (ii) LEHÁR: *Land of smiles: Prince Sou-chong's aria.* DELIBES: *Lakmé: Bell song.* BIZET: *Pêcheurs de perles: Romance de Nadir.*
(M) *** Erato/Warner 2292 45185-2 [id.].

An entertaining collection of what the writer of the French notes calls *gaîetés* and *surprises champêtres* played on the cornet as well as the trumpet. L'Orchestre d'Harmonie des Gardiens de la Paix de Paris is in fact a police military band and they accompany with Gallic gusto in the first part of the programme, and the Monte Carlo orchestra is equally lively in the rest. If you have a taste for airs with variations without any purpose but to tickle the ear and show just how many notes can be played to the second, then you won't go wrong here. Good recording.

'The Trumpet and the 20th Century': JOLIVET: *Trumpet concerto No. 2; Concertino for trumpet, string orchestra and piano* (with Annie D'Arco, LOP, composer). TOMASI: *Concerto* (with Radio Luxembourg CO, Froment). AROUTOUNIAN: *Concerto* (with ORTF PO, Maurice Suzan).
(M) *** Erato/Warner 2292 45775-2 [id.].

This is the most interesting and worthwhile of the Erato compilations reissued as part of the 'Maurice André Edition'. Jolivet is a composer of strong personality. His style is jazzy to the point of wildness but when played like this the writing is invigoratingly alive. The exuberant *Concertino* is in fact the first concerto, and is in variation form, yet within the variations is a three movement layout with a strongly expressive centrepiece. Although it opens mysteriously, the *Second concerto* is equally uninhibited. Its *Grave* central movement is appropriately named, but the riotous *Giocoso* finale soon dispels the quiet, nostalgic serenity. Tomasi's *Concerto* also has a blues flavour, and its turbulence is good natured; again the haunting *Nocturne* makes a central point of repose, and the finale is infectiously witty. Aroutounian's work is more garrulous, but such is André's virtuosity that one accepts its extravagance: the playing both in the main first allegro and in the finale is breathtaking. These performances can surely be regarded as definitive, and the 1964 recordings are transferred to CD with great vividness.

Trumpet concertos: TELEMANN: *Concerto for 3 trumpets and 2 oboes in D* (with Guy Touvron & Lionel André (trumpet), Daniel Arrignon & Jean-Philippe Chavana (oboe), O de Paris Ens., Wallez); *Sonata in D* (with V. Soloists). *Concerto for trumpet and 2 oboes in D.* FASCH: *Concerto for trumpet and 2 oboes in D* (with Pierre Pierlot & Jacques Chambon (oboe)). M. HAYDN: *Trumpet concerto in D* (all three concertos with Paillard CO, Paillard).
(M) **(*) Erato/Warner 2292 45776-2 [id.].

There is agreeable variety of texture here and all the works are inventive, the Fasch concerto the most conventional. Michael Haydn's attractive two-movement piece soars immediately up into the stratosphere, but André manages the upper tessitura with consummate ease. The Telemann *Sonata* is an arrangement but, effective enough. Good accompaniments and very acceptable recording.

Australian Chamber Orchestra, Richard Tognetti

JANÁČEK: *Kreutzer sonata for strings* (arr. Tognetti). BARBER: *Adagio, Op. 11.* WALTON: *Sonata for strings.*
*** Sony Dig. SK 48252 [id.].

The Australian Chamber Orchestra, formed in 1975, is led from the front desk by Richard Tognetti, who has also – somewhat controversially – arranged Janáček's *First String quartet* for full string ensemble. The players match its quixotic changes of mood with fine, expressive spontaneity, but perhaps – unlike the Walton – this is a work which is too intimate to be ideally realized with more expansive textures. Walton himself arranged his *Sonata* from the *String quartet in A minor*, and very effective it is. It is splendidly played here, the second-movement presto admirably lively and the lento movingly poignant. Barber's *Adagio* is intensely expressive, slow and elegiac rather than passionate. Most realistic sound.

Bavarian State Orchestra, Wolfgang Sawallisch

Russian orchestral music: KABALEVSKY: *The Comedians* (suite), *Op. 26.* RIMSKY-KORSAKOV: *Capriccio espagnole, Op. 34.* GLINKA: *Overture: Russlan and Ludmilla.* BORODIN: *In the steppes of Central Asia.* MUSSORGSKY (arr. Rimsky-Korsakov): *Night on the bare mountain.* PROKOFIEV: *The Love for 3 Oranges, Op. 33: March & Scherzo.*
(M) *** EMI Dig. CDD7 63893-2 [id.].

This splendid concert of Russian music was included in EMI's first reissued release of mid-priced digital repertoire, although it had not appeared before in the UK. It was made in the Herkulessaal, Munich, in 1987. The sound is splendid, resonantly full, coloured by the attractive ambient bloom characteristic of this famous hall, yet vivid and lively too. Apart from offering the best-ever version of the winning Kabalevsky suite, the Rimsky-Korsakov performance is comparably memorable for its sophisticated and brilliant orchestral playing and for sustaining warmth and excitement throughout without ever going over the top. The Glinka and Mussorgsky pieces are similarly distinctive and *In the steppes of Central Asia* is particularly appealing, not overtly romantic but refreshingly direct. The programme ends with Prokofiev, sparkling and witty, but not too abrasive, like the Kabalevsky at the opening.

Bergen Philharmonic Orchestra, Dimitri Kitayenko

'The Sorcerer's apprentice': DUKAS: *The sorcerer's apprentice.* RAVEL: *Ma Mère l'Oye: suite.* DEBUSSY: *Prélude à l'après-midi d'un faune.* RAVEL: *Boléro.* MUSSORGSKY: *A Night on the bare mountain* (original version).
(BB) *** Virgo Dig. VJ7 91471-2; *VJ 791471-4.*

This is an enjoyable concert, vividly played and given first-class digital recording. It is an inexpensive way to get to know Mussorgsky's original scheme for *Night on the bare mountain* before Rimsky-Korsakov laminated his own ideas (including an interpolated brass fanfare) on to the score. It is crude, rambling and repetitive, but it sounds strikingly primitive and bizarrely individual. The opening Dukas showpiece is glowingly animated, and the other works come off well too. The performances are direct and atmospheric, while *Boléro* moves steadily forward to produce a strong climax. Excellent value, but inadequate documentation.

Berlin Philharmonic Orchestra, Herbert von Karajan

'Armchair concert': J. STRAUSS, Jnr: *Die Fledermaus overture.* MOZART: *Flute and harp concerto in C* (with James Galway, Fritz Helmis); SCHUBERT: *Symphony No. 8 (Unfinished).*
(M) **(*) CDM7 64442-2 [id.].

Though this is shorter measure than others in the series, Karajan and the Berliners are well represented in the 'Armchair Concert' series with Karajan's rapt and spacious account of the *Unfinished*, as well as the warmly elegant Mozart, recorded when Galway was principal flute of the BPO.

GRIEG: *Holberg suite, Op. 40.* SIBELIUS: *Finlandia, Op. 26.* SMETANA: *Má Vlast: Vltava.* LISZT: *Les Préludes.*
(M) *** DG Dig. 427 808-2; *427 808-4.*

Four characterful performances, digitally recorded, superbly played and showing the Karajan charisma at its most impressive. At mid-price this is self-recommending, although Karajan's earlier, EMI recording of the Liszt symphonic poem is even more telling.

Boskovsky Ensemble, Willi Boskovsky

'Viennese bonbons': J. STRAUSS, Snr: *Chinese galop; Kettenbrücke Waltz; Eisele und Beisele Sprünge. Cachucha galop.* J. STRAUSS, Jnr: *Weine Gemüths waltz; Champagne galop; Salon polka.* LANNER: *Styrian dances; Die Werber & Marien waltzes; Bruder halt galop.* MOZART: *3 Contredanses, K.462; 4 German dances, K.600/1 & 3; K.605/1; K.611.* SCHUBERT: *8 Waltzes & Ländler.*

(M) *** Van. 8.8015.71 [OVC 8015].

This is a captivating selection of the most delightful musical confectionery imaginable. The ensemble is a small chamber group, similar to that led by the Strausses, and the playing has an appropriately intimate Viennese atmosphere. Not surprisingly, Boskovsky shows a strong personality as leader and soloist, and this colourful writing bubbles with good spirits and attractive melodies. The programme is made up almost entirely of rare repertoire and it makes one realize what an inexhaustible wealth of rare vintage there is in the Viennese musical cellars. The transfer is impeccable and the recording from the early 1960s, made in the Baumgarten Hall, Vienna, is fresh, smooth and clear, with a nice bloom on sound which is never too inflated.

Boston Pops Orchestra, John Williams

'That's entertainment': excerpts from: *That's Entertainment; Fiddler on the Roof; A Little Night Music; Chorus Line; Annie; Evita; Gigi.* RODGERS: *Waltz medley.*
*** Ph. Dig. 416 499-2 [id.].

This is music John Williams does splendidly and there are plenty of really memorable tunes here which many will enjoy in full orchestral dress, not least those by Richard Rodgers and Stephen Sondheim.

'The very best of the Boston Pops Orchestra': COURAGE: *Star Trek* (TV) *theme.* GERSHWIN: *Girl crazy*: selection (arr. Leroy Anderson). KANDER: *New York, New York.* arr. COURAGE: *A Salute to Fred Astaire.* HAMLISCH: *A Chorus line: Overture.* Duke ELLINGTON (arr. Burns): *Sophisticated ladies* (A tribute). WILLIAMS: *Superman: Love theme.* arr. STEVENS: *Pops salutes the Oscars: (When you wish upon a star; Swingin' on a star; Moon River; Raindrops keep fallin' on my head; The way we were; The shadow of your smile.* ROGERS: *Waltzes* (arr. Leroy Anderson).
*** Ph. Dig. 432 802-2; *432 802-4.*

This excellent CD not only represents the very best of the Boston Pops Orchestra under John Williams, but also the very best record of its kind in the catalogue. Not surprisingly Williams is a superb exponent of this repertoire. Moreover, the orchestrations are a joy, and the orchestral playing is wonderfully polished and spirited; it also has a very special kind of affectionate finesse. There are over two dozen hit tunes here, all of the kind that make one smile with pleasure at their sheer memorability. *New York, New York*, has a marvellous rhythmic lift in the brass (and manages admirably without Sinatra) and when the glorious Boston strings gently introduce *When you wish upon a star*, the effect is quite ravishing. The sound is all it should be, warm, full, transparent with splendid resonant ambience, and this record would have received a Rosette if it were not for the appalling lack of documentation, quite unforgiveable with a full-priced CD. But there is just over an hour of musical magic here.

Boston Symphony Orchestra, Serge Koussevitzky

COPLAND: *El Salón México.* FOOTE: *Suite in E min., Op. 63.* HARRIS: *Symphony (1933); Symphony No. 3.* MCDONALD: *San Juan Capistrano – Two Evening Pictures.*
(M) (***) Pearl mono GEMMCD 9492.

For many collectors, the Boston Symphony has never produced as fine a sonority or as consummate a virtuosity as it did for Koussevitzky. His performance of the Roy Harris *Third Symphony* has never been equalled in intensity and fire – even by Toscanini or Bernstein – and Copland himself never produced as exhilarating an *El Salón México*. Older collectors who cherish special memories of these electrifying performances will find that they are better even than they remembered. The Arthur Foote *Suite* is unpretentious and has great charm. Sonic limitations are soon forgotten, for these performances have exceptional power and should not be missed.

Brüggen, Frans (recorder)

Recorder concertos (with VCM, Harnoncourt): VIVALDI: *Concerto in C min., RV 441.* SAMMARTINI: *Concerto in F.* TELEMANN: *Concerto in C.* NAUDOT: *Concerto in G.*
(M) *** Teldec/Warner 2292 43547-2 [id.].

Frans Brüggen is an unsurpassed master of his instrument, and he gives the four assorted concertos his keen advocacy on this excellent record, reissued from 1968. (In the Vivaldi he even takes part in the tutti.) In his hands, phrases are turned with the utmost sophistication, intonation is unbelievably accurate and matters of style exact. There is spontaneity too and, with superb musicianship, good recording and a well-balanced orchestral contribution, this mid-priced CD can earn nothing but praise.

Burns, Stephen (trumpet)

'Music for trumpet and strings' (with Ensemble): PURCELL: *Sonata No. 1 in D.* STANLEY: *Trumpet voluntary* (from *Organ Voluntary, Op. 6/5*, arr. Bergler). CLARKE: *Suite in D.* CORELLI: *Sonata in D.* BALDASSARE: *Sonata in F.* TORELLI: *Sonata a cinque in D, G.1.*
*** ASV Dig. CDDCA 528; *ZCDCA 528* [id.].

Stephen Burns plays a rotary piccolo trumpet in the East German style by Scherzer, and his freedom and smoothness of timbre in the instrument's highest tessitura are breathtaking. With crisp ornamentation (often florid, in short, decorative bursts of filigree), the playing is attractively stylish: the timbre gleams and the exhilarating articulation of the allegros is balanced by a natural expressive lyricism in slow movements. Whether in the beautiful *Grave* sections of the Corelli and Torelli *Sonatas* or in the faster movements of the latter piece, this is playing to delight the ear with its combination of sensitivity and bravura, and the Purcell and Clarke works are equally persuasive. The recording balances the soloist well forward and the CD projects him almost into the room, although it also emphasizes the rather insubstantial sound of the accompaniment and the ineffective harpsichord balance. But this collection is Stephen Burns' triumph, and it would be churlish to withhold the fullest recommendation.

Chicago Symphony Orchestra, Barenboim

SMETANA: *Má Vlast: Vltava.* DVOŘÁK: *Slavonic dances, Op. 46/1 and 8.* BRAHMS: *Hungarian dances Nos. 1, 3 & 10.* BORODIN: *Prince Igor: Polovtsian dances.* LISZT: *Les Préludes.*
(M) *** DG 415 851-2.

The *Polovtsian dances* have splendid life and impetus. Indeed one hardly misses the chorus, so lively is the orchestral playing. Both *Vltava* and *Les Préludes* show Barenboim and the Chicago orchestra at their finest. The Brahms and Dvořák *Dances* make attractive encores. The only slight snag is that, in the digital remastering, the recording has lost some of its original glow and the strings sound thinner above the stave. But this is striking only in the violin timbre of the big tune of *Vltava.*

Cincinnati Pops Orchestra, Erich Kunzel

'Time warp': DORSEY: *Ascent.* R. STRAUSS: *Also sprach Zarathustra: Opening.* GOLDSMITH: *Star Trek the Movie: Main theme. The Alien: Closing title.* COURAGE: *The Menagerie: suite.* PHILIPS: *Battlestar Galactica: Main theme.* WILLIAMS: *Superman: Love theme. Star Wars: Throne room and end-title.* J. STRAUSS Jnr: *Blue Danube waltz.* KHACHATURIAN: *Gayaneh: Adagio.*
*** Telarc Dig. CD 80106 [id.].

This sumptuously recorded CD is well established as a demonstration disc *par excellence* and needs no fillip from us. Sufficient to say that the playing is first class and the sound superb, the rich ambient effect just right for this music, with particularly gorgeous string and brass timbres, Telarc's concert-hall balance at its most impressive. There are plenty of indelible tunes too and John Williams's music for *Superman* and *Star Wars* (the latter in the Elgar/Walton nobilmente tradition) has never been recorded to more telling effect. The collection opens with an electronic spectacular to put the Cincinnati orchestra in orbit.

'Orchestral spectaculars': RIMSKY-KORSAKOV: *Mlada: Procession of the nobles. Snow Maiden: Dance of the Tumblers.* DUKAS: *L'apprenti sorcier.* WEINBERGER: *Svanda the Bagpiper: Polka and fugue.* SAINT-SAËNS: *Samson et Dalila: Bacchanale.* LISZT: *Les Préludes.*
**(*) Telarc Dig. CD 80115 [id.].

The title is not belied by the sound, which has a sparkling but not exaggerated percussive constituent. The side drum which introduces the colourful Rimsky *Procession of the nobles* is strikingly well focused, and this clarity comes within a believable overall perspective. There is much fine orchestral playing, with the string detail in the *Svanda Polka and fugue* particularly pleasing, and the horns sounding agreeably strong and rich-timbred in the introductory Rimsky-Korsakov piece. The Saint-Saëns *Bacchanale* has plenty of adrenalin, with the timpani and bass drum adding to the climax without swamping it. The account of *Les Préludes* is lightweight until the end, which is almost solemn in its spacious broadening. The one disappointment is *The Sorcerer's apprentice*, here bright and well paced but lacking cumulative excitement.

'The Stokowski sound' (orchestral transcriptions): BACH: *Toccata and fugue in D min., BWV 565; Fugue in G min., BWV 578.* BOCCHERINI: *Quintet in E: Minuet.* DEBUSSY: *Suite bergamasque: Clair de lune; Prélude: La cathédrale engloutie.* BEETHOVEN: *Piano sonata No. 14 (Moonlight): 1st movement.* ALBÉNIZ: *Sevilla.* RACHMANINOV: *Prelude in C sharp min., Op. 3/2.* MUSSORGSKY: *Night on the bare mountain.*
❀ *** Telarc Dig. CD 80129 [id.].

Stokowski began his conducting career in Cincinnati in 1909, moving on to Philadelphia three years later; so a collection of his orchestral transcriptions from his first orchestra is appropriate, particularly when the playing is so committed and polished and the recording so sumptuous. Indeed, none of Stokowski's own recordings can match this Telarc disc in sheer glamour of sound. The *'Little' G minor Fugue* of Bach hardly sounds diminutive here, matching the famous *D minor Toccata and fugue* at its resplendent climax. By contrast, Boccherini's *Minuet* is played as a miniature, tenderly and gracefully. Spectacle is paramount in the Albéniz and Rachmaninov pieces, the latter vulgarly larger than life but irresistible. Schoenberg apparently thought Stokowski's sentient arrangement of *Clair de lune* so convincing that he decided it was Debussy's original version; no wonder he liked it, with its element of ecstasy, complete with shimmering vibraphone. The arrangement of *La cathédrale engloutie* is very free and melodramatically telling. Most interesting is *Night on the bare mountain*, which has a grandiloquent brass chorale added as a coda. Any admirer of Stokowski should regard this superbly engineered CD as an essential purchase.

'Pomp and Pizazz': J. WILLIAMS: *Olympic fanfare.* SUK: *Towards a new life.* ELGAR: *Pomp and circumstance march No. 1.* IRELAND: *Epic march.* TCHAIKOVSKY: *Coronation march.* BERLIOZ: *Damnation de Faust: Hungarian march.* J. F. WAGNER: *Under the Double Eagle.* FUČIK: *Entry of the gladiators.* SOUSA: *The Stars and Stripes forever.* HAYMAN: *March medley.*
*** Telarc Dig. CD 80122 [id.].

As enjoyable a march collection as any available, with characteristically spectacular and naturally balanced Telarc recording, with its crisp transients and wide amplitude. The performances have comparable flair and sparkle. The inclusion of John Ireland's comparatively restrained *Epic march* and the Tchaikovsky *Coronation march*, with its piquant trio and characteristic references to the Tsarist national anthem, makes for attractive contrast, while the Hayman medley (including *Strike up the band, 76 Trombones, South Rampart Street Parade* and *When the Saints go marching in*) makes an exuberant, peppy closing section. By comparison the Berlioz *Rákóczy march* is quite dignified. The sound is in the demonstration class. Most entertaining.

'Symphonic spectacular': SHOSTAKOVICH: *Festival overture, Op. 96.* WAGNER: *Die Walküre: Ride of the Valkyries.* FALLA: *El amor brujo: Ritual fire dance.* BIZET: *L'Arlésienne: Farandole.* JÄRNEFELT: *Praeludium.* CHABRIER: *España.* TCHAIKOVSKY: *Marche slave, Op. 31.* HALVORSEN: *Entry of the Boyars.* ENESCU: *Rumanian rhapsody No. 1, Op. 11.* KHACHATURIAN: *Gayaneh: Sabre dance.*
*** Telarc Dig. CD 80170 [id.].

With spectacular recording, well up to Telarc's best standards, this is a highly attractive collection of orchestral lollipops. Everything is played with the special flair which this orchestra and conductor have made their own in this kind of repertoire. Most entertaining, and technically of demonstration standard.

City of Birmingham Symphony Orchestra, Simon Rattle

'Armchair concert': BRITTEN: *Canadian carnival.* RACHMANINOV: *Rhapsody on a theme of Paganini* (with Cécile Ousset, piano). SIBELIUS: *Symphony No. 5 in E flat.*
(M) *** EMI Dig. CDM7 64440-2 [id.].

The Rattle 'Armchair Concert' offers digital sound fuller and more modern than others in the series, as well as a rather less conventional programme. The Britten rarity makes an unusual opener for the powerful performances of the Rachmaninov and Sibelius, both among the finest in the catalogue. Excellent value.

Cleveland, Royal Philharmonic or Philharmonia Orchestras, Vladimir Ashkenazy

'Capriccio italien': TCHAIKOVSKY: *Capriccio italien.* DEBUSSY: *Prélude à l'après-midi d'un faune; Nocturnes: Fêtes.* SIBELIUS: *Finlandia.* R. STRAUSS: *Salome's dance.* BRUCH: *Kol Nidrei.* RIMSKY-KORSAKOV: *Flight of the bumble-bee.* BORODIN: *Prince Igor: Polovtsian dances* (with London Opera Ch.).
(M) *** Decca 430 730-2; *430 730-4* [id.].

This highly succesful compilation offers Decca's top-quality digital sound throughout; the recordings were made in different venues between 1980 and 1988, yet every piece is in the demonstration bracket. The opening *Capriccio italien* is superb, spectacular, elegant and possessed of exhilarating impetus. *Finlandia* is hardly less exciting, and the performance of the *Polovtsian dances* carries all before it, yet also produces some richly lyrical singing from the chorus. *Salome's dance* has great sensuous feeling and a powerful dénouement, while Lynn Harrell provides a contrasting, mellower interlude with Bruch's *Kol Nidrei.* Ashkenazy's Debussy is unconventional, the *Prélude à l'après-midi d'un faune* freely rhapsodical and given a will-o'-the-wisp delicacy by the transparency of the Cleveland recording, while the climax of *Fêtes* is grippingly extrovert.

Cleveland Symphonic Winds, Fennell

'Stars and stripes': ARNAUD: *3 Fanfares.* BARBER: *Commando march.* LEEMANS: *Belgian Paratroopers.* FUČIK: *Florentine march, Op. 214.* KING: Barnum and Bailey's favourite. ZIMMERMAN: *Anchors aweigh.* J. STRAUSS S: *Radetzky march.* VAUGHAN WILLIAMS: *Sea songs; Folk songs suite.* SOUSA: *The Stars and stripes forever.* GRAINGER: *Lincolnshire posy.*
*** Telarc Dig. CD 80099 [id.].

This vintage collection from Frederick Fennell and his superb Cleveland wind and brass group is one of the finest of its kind ever made. Severance Hall, Cleveland, has ideal acoustics for this programme and the playing has wonderful virtuosity and panache. What is unusual about the programme is its variety. Both the Barber and Leemans pieces mix subtlety with spectacle; the Barnum and Bailey circus march is predictably exuberant, while *The Stars and stripes* is not overblown, with the piccolo solo in natural perspective. Add to all this digital engineering of Telarc's highest calibre, and you have a very special issue, with the Grainger and Vaughan Williams suites adding just the right amount of ballast.

Dallas Symphony Orchestra, Eduardo Mata

TCHAIKOVSKY: *Capriccio italien, Op. 45.* MUSSORGSKY: *Night on the bare mountain.* DUKAS: *L'apprenti sorcier.* ENESCU: *Rumanian rhapsody No. 1.*
(BB) *** BMG/RCA Dig. VD 87727 [7727-2-RV].

One of the outstanding early digital orchestral demonstration CDs. The acoustic of the Dallas Hall produces a thrilling resonance without too much clouding of detail. The Mussorgsky piece is rather lacking in menace when textures are so ample. *The Sorcerer's apprentice* is spirited and affectionately characterized, yet there is no sense of real calamity at the climax. But the Tchaikovsky and Enescu are richly enjoyable, even if the latter lacks the last degree of unbuttoned exuberance in its closing pages. A very real bargain in the lowest price-range, with really marvellous sound.

Detroit Symphony Orchestra, Paul Paray

'French opera highlights': HÉROLD: *Overture: Zampa.* AUBER: *Overture: The Crown diamonds.* GOUNOD: *Faust: ballet suite; Waltz* (from Act II). SAINT-SAËNS: *Samson et Dalila: Bacchanale.* BIZET: *Carmen: Danse bohème.* BERLIOZ: *Les Troyens: Royal hunt and storm.* MASSENET: *Phèdre overture.* THOMAS: *Mignon: Gavotte.*
(M) *** Mercury 432 014-2 [id.].

Paul Paray's reign at Detroit tempted the Mercury producers to record a good deal of French music under his baton, and here is a good example of the Gallic verve and sparkle that were achieved. The two overtures combine colour and flair with high spirits, while the highly animated *Faust ballet music* has much elegance, with the famous *Waltz* joyfully following at the end, with superb rhythmic lift. The *Danse bohème* from *Carmen* has comparable dash. The only disappointment is the unslurred horn phrasing at the magical opening and close of the *Royal hunt and storm.* This may be authentic but, under Beecham and Munch, the gently moulded effect is much more evocative. However, this piece does not lack excitement, and one's only other complaint is that the deliciously polished account of the very Parisian *Gavotte* from *Mignon*, which acts as a bonne-bouche at the end, makes one wish for the whole overture instead.

Du Pré, Jacqueline (cello)

'Impressions': ELGAR: *Cello concerto in E min., Op. 85* (with LSO, Barbirolli). HAYDN: *Cello concerto in C* (with ECO, Barenboim). BEETHOVEN: *Cello sonata No. 3 in A, Op. 69* (with Barenboim): *Piano trio No. 5 in D (Ghost), Op. 70/1* (with Barenboim and Zukerman).
(M) *** EMI CMS7 69707-2 (2).

A medium-priced anthology that is self-recommending if the mixed programme is of appeal. The chamber-music performances have the same qualities of spontaneity and inspiration that have made Du Pré's account of Elgar's *Cello concerto* come to be treasured above all others; if some find her approach to Haydn too romantic, it is nevertheless difficult to resist in its ready warmth. The sound-quality is fairly consistent, for all the remastered transfers are successful.

East of England Orchestra, Malcolm Nabarro

'Robin Hood country': KORNGOLD: *The Adventures of Robin Hood* (film score): *suite.* COATES: *From the countryside (suite): In the meadows; Among the poppies* (only). *Men of Trent march* (orch. Nabarro). NABARRO: *Lincoln Green (A fantasia on Lincolnshire folksongs).* GOODWIN: *City of Lincoln march.* CURZON: *Robin Hood suite.*
(M) ** CDWHL 2069; *ZCWHL 2069.*

After the success of the first record from this orchestra (concentrating on the music of Eric Coates), the present concert, though ingeniously centred on Robin Hood, is disappointing. The Korngold suite lacks the kind of flair and opulence that makes the Gerhardt recording so attractive on RCA. Nabarro's own rhapsody is a cross between the styles of Butterworth and Vaughan Williams and not especially memorable either, and neither Goodwin's march or the bulk of the Curzon suite is distinctive. The most striking item is the Coates *Men of Trent*, written for Nottingham Police Band and skilfully arranged for orchestra by the conductor.

Eastman-Rochester Orchestra, Howard Hanson

American orchestral music: BARBER: *Capricorn concerto, Op. 21* (with Joseph Mariano (flute), Robert Sprenkle (oboe), Sidney Mear (trumpet)). PISTON: *The Incredible flutist* (ballet suite). GRIFFES: *Poem for flute and orchestra.* MCCAULEY: *5 Miniatures for flute and strings* (all with Jospeh Mariano (flute)). BERGSMA: *Gold and the Señor Commandante* (ballet suite).
(M) *** Mercury 434 307-2 [id.].

A first-rate concert of pioneering recordings, made between 1957 and 1963. The collection is worth having for Barber's *Capricorn concerto* alone, a less characteristic work than say any of the

Essays for orchestra, or the solo concertos. It has a neo-classical Stravinskian bite to it, an impression that is accentuated somewhat by the slightly dry, spiky recording, which, with its clear detail suits the vital, well shaped performance. Walter Piston's ballet *The Incredible flutist* comes from 1938 and the suite is one of the most refreshing and imaginative of all American scores. Its ideas are instantly memorable and their charm remains durable. It was composed some years after the composer's studies with Nadia Boulanger in Paris and the very opening is distinctly gallic in atmosphere. Griffes' *Poem* with its gentle, shimmering textures is also French in feeling but is thoroughly worthwhile in its own right. Joseph Mariano is an excellent soloist as he is in the more simplistic but engaging *Miniatures* of the Canadian, William McCauley (born 1917). Kent Kennan's *Three Pieces* are subtitled *Promenade, Nocturne* and *The field of flowers*. The first is a 'pompous grand march'. It doesn't outstay its welcome, and has a Copland-like open air quality in the orchestration; the remaining two pieces are clearly influenced by the ballet music of Stravinsky. Bergsma's ballet is rather noisy at times, and fails to be memorable, though brightly scored. Excellent performances throughout and typically vivid Eastman Rochester sound.

American orchestral music II: MCPHEE: *Tabuh-Tabuhan (Toccata for orchestra)*. SESSIONS: *The Black maskers (suite)*. V. THOMSON: *Symphony on a hymn tune; The Feast of love* (with David Clatworthy).
(M) *** Mercury 434 310-2 [id.].

McPhee's *Tabuh-Tabuhan*, written in 1936 uses Balinese music for its main colouring and rhythmic background. The work is in three movements: *Ostinatos*, *Nocturne* and *Finale*; and its style has much in common with more recent minimalist techniques. The writing in the outer sections has plenty of rhythmic vitality, but throughout the melodic contribution is spare and used very economically. However the composer's rich palette certainly intrigues the ear, when the recording is so vivid. Roger Sessions' *Black maskers suite* was written as incidental music for a play by Andreyev about devil worship and the Black Mass. No doubt in performance the music underlines the evil drama of the theme, but it is not in the same class as, say, Prokofiev's *Scythian suite* and seems in no way memorable. This is no fault of the performance or recording. The Virgil Thomson music is altogether more rewarding. The *Symphony*, dating from 1928, although based on hymn-like material, is attractively quirky (reflecting the composer's Parisian years, the influence of Les Six, and Satie in particular). The music is highly inventive and individual, notably the memorable *Andante* and the strong finale. The cantata dates from 1964, 36 years after the *Symphony* and could hardly be more contrasted in its warmly flowing lyricism, a heady setting of an anonymous Latin love poem which Thomson translated himself. The poet revels in the erotic joys of love, linking the pleasures of human physical passion with the imagery of nature bursting out at springtime, and the composer and his excellent soloist are obviously delighted by the voluptuous feeling of the words. As always the vintage Mercury sound is vivid with colour.

Eastman Wind Ensemble, Frederick Fennell

GRAINGER: *Lincolnshire posy. Hill song No. 2*. PERSICHETTI: *Symphony No. 6 for band*. KHACHATURIAN: *Armenian dances*. W. HARTLEY: *Concerto for 23 winds*. B. ROGERS: *3 Japanese dances*.
(M) **(*) Mercury 432 754-2 [id.].

Marvellous playing and fine recording (incredibly, dating from as early as 1958/9) but the music is of varying interest. Grainger's folksy six-movement *Lincolnshire posy*, wittily and strongly characterized, and the *Hill song* are the highlights. Persichetti's *Symphony* also seems to have a folk element and is brilliantly conceived for the idiom. Its first movement offers some original effects, while the central *Adagio* and *Allegretto* are fairly attractive. But the work falls off at the end. Walter Hartley's *Concerto* is also striking in its blending of colours and it has a cool *Lento* which is rather agreeable. The *Japanese dances* of Bernard Rogers (1893–1968) are ingenuously pentatonic, yet the scoring titillates the ear, especially when so well caught by the recording; but Khachaturian's pair of *Armenian dances* are run-of-the-mill and thin in invention.

Eastman Wind Ensemble, Donald Hunsberger

'Live in Osaka': BACH: *Toccata and fugue in D min., BWV 565* (arr. Hunsberger); *Jesu joy of man's desiring* (arr. Renshaw). HOLST: *Suite No. 1 in E flat.* SCHWANTNER: *... and the mountains rising nowhere.* GRAINGER: *Lincolnshire posy; The Lads of Wamphray.* IVES: *Country band march.* SHOSTAKOVICH: *Festive overture in A, Op. 96* (arr. Hunsberger). RIMSKY-KORSAKOV: *Flight of the bumble bee* (both arr. Hunsberger). MIYAMA: *Glory of Catalonia.* SOUSA: *The Stars and Stripes forever.*
** Sony Dig. SK 47198 [id.].

This record provides excellent evidence that the Eastman Wind Ensemble – presumably still a student group – are still around and vigorous. The bravura of their playing remains as striking as in the great Fennell/Mercury days – just sample the dazzling *Flight of the bumble bee.* Unfortunately this concert has the drawback of a close balance and dry acoustic and the rich sonorities of the great Holst *Suite* tend to evaporate. In any case Donald Hunsberger cannot match Fennell's earlier performances in gravitas, and he mistimes the final cadence of the first movement with a bass drum that sounds relatively puny here. The Bach T*occata and fugue*, too, seems very lightweight, brightly vivid certainly, but with little majesty, while *Jesu joy of man's desiring* is very mannered in phrasing. Other parts of the programme are much more successful, notably the bright-eyed Grainger pieces and the Marches of Ives and Sousa, the one with its ear-tickling dissonance, the other with pleasingly perky piccolos. As for Joseph Schwater's *... and the mountains rise nowhere*, with its exotic effects, use of multiple percussion, water glasses and 'celestial choir' – the players are expected to sing and hum along and whistle too – no one could say the result is unspectacular.

English Chamber Orchestra, Raymond Leppard

ALBINONI: *Sonata a 5 in A, Op. 2/3; Sonata a 5 in G min., Op. 2/6.* VIVALDI: *Concertos: in D, P.175; in G min., P.392; Sonata in E flat (Al Santo sepolcro), P.441.* CORELLI: *Concerto grosso in F, Op. 6/9.*
(B) *** CfP CD-CFP 4371; *TC-CFP 4371.*

An outstanding collection of Italian string concertos, recorded in 1970 and sounding first class in digitally remastered form: there is fullness, yet everything sounds fresh. The two Albinoni *Sonatas* are particularly attractive: the four contrasted movements of Op. 2, No. 3, are individually characterized, with the richness of the five-part ensemble obvious in the two slow movements and the fugal allegros sprightly and resilient, and with Leppard adding some witty harpsichord comments in the finale. The Corelli *Concerto grosso* has six equally diverse movements and, while Vivaldi's *Al Santo sepolcro* has only two, they are strongly contrasted. The standard of invention throughout the concert is high and the playing is polished and committed. Except for those who can accept only original instruments, this is a fine concert for the late evening.

English Concert, Pinnock

PACHELBEL: *Canon and gigue in D.* VIVALDI: *Sinfonia in G min., RV 149.* ALBINONI: *Concerto a 5 in D min. for oboe and strings, Op. 9/2.* PURCELL: *Chacony in G min.* HANDEL: *Solomon: Arrival of the Queen of Sheba.* AVISON: *Concerto grosso No. 9 in A min.* HAYDN: *Concerto for harpsichord in D, Hob. XVIII/2.*
*** DG Dig. 415 518-2; *415 518-4* [id.].

There are many good things here, particularly the Albinoni *Concerto* (with David Reichenberg the eloquent soloist) and the Avison. Although there are popular items too, such as Handel's *Arrival of the Queen of Sheba* from *Solomon* and the Pachelbel *Canon*, there are others of considerable substance: the Purcell *Chacony* and Haydn's *D major Concerto* brilliantly played on the harpsichord by Trevor Pinnock. The performances are crisp and thoroughly alive, and beautifully recorded, and these vital accounts will give unalloyed pleasure.

English Concert Orchestra, Richard Bonynge

'Ballet gala': MINKUS: *Paquita: Grand pas; Don Quixote: Pas de deux.* PUGNI: *Pas de quatre* (all arr. P. March). OFFENBACH: *Le Papillon.* DRIGO: *Le Corsaire: Pas de deux* (arr. Lanchbery). *Diane et Actéon: Pas de deux* (arr. P. March). AUBER: *Pas classique.* AUBER/LAMBERT: *Les Rendez-vous.* D. SCARLATTI/TOMMASINI: *The Good-humoured ladies.* THOMAS: *Françoise de Rimini.*
**(*) Decca Dig. 421 818-2 (2).

Richard Bonynge is a master of this repertoire, but the music by Minkus, Pugni and Drigo on the first disc is conventional pre-Delibes stuff and will be of more interest to balletomanes than to the average collector. The highlight is undoubtedly a suite from Offenbach's charming *Le Papillon*, which Bonynge has recorded complete (Decca 425 450-2, coupled with Tchaikovsky's *Nutcracker*). The second disc deserves a separate issue, for it includes not only Auber's jolly *Pas classique* (with some fine horn playing) but also Lambert's arrangement of more Auber tunes (mainly drawing on *L'enfant prodigue*), with witty, plangent scoring in the manner of his Meyerbeer ballet, *Les Patineurs.* It was compiled in 1933 for Markova and choreographed by Frederick Ashton for the young Vic-Wells Ballet. Also included is the charming *Good-humoured ladies,* a Diaghilev ballet. It was the great impresario himself who suggested drawing on Domenico Scarlatti's keyboard sonatas and he helped to choose the 23 movements, which were then felicitously transcribed by Vincenzo Tommasini. The suite from Thomas's opera *Françoise de Rimini* is also attractive and well worth having on disc. Lively, alert orchestral playing throughout, typically bright Decca sound, vividly recorded in London's Henry Wood Hall; at times, however, the ear craves a more voluptuous effect in the Kingsway Hall mannner.

English Sinfonia, Sir Charles Groves

'Entente cordiale': FAURÉ: *Masques et bergamasques, Op. 112; Pavane, Op. 50.* ELGAR: *Chanson de nuit; Chanson de matin, Op. 15/1–2.* DELIUS: *On hearing the first cuckoo in spring.* RAVEL: *Pavane pour une infante défunte.* WARLOCK: *Capriol suite.* BUTTERWORTH: *The Banks of green willow.* SATIE: *Gymnopédies Nos. 1 & 3* (orch. Debussy).
(B) *** Pickwick Dig. PCD 926; *CIMPC 926.*

Having given us some attractive Haydn recordings with the English Sinfonia, Sir Charles Groves then offered a happy juxtaposition of French and British music. He opens with a performance of Fauré's *Masques et bergamasques* which is sheer delight in its airy grace, and later he finds passion as well as delicacy in the Butterworth rhapsody, very effectively followed by Debussy's languorous orchestrations of the Satie *Gymnopédies.* Groves's approach to Warlock's *Capriol* dances is essentially genial (Marriner's version has more zest); but all this music-making is easy to enjoy. The playing is polished and spontaneous and the recording, made at Abbey Road, quite splendid.

English String Orchestra or English Symphony Orchestra, William Boughton

'The spirit of England': ELGAR: *Overture Cockaigne; Introduction and allegro, Op. 47; Sospiri, Op. 70.* DELIUS: *Summer evening.* BUTTERWORTH: *The banks of green willow; A Shropshire lad.* FINZI: *Suite from Love's Labour's Lost; Clarinet concerto* (with Alan Hacker). VAUGHAN WILLIAMS: *The lark ascending* (with Michael Bochmann); *Oboe concerto* (with Maurice Bourgue); *Fantasia on a theme of Thomas Tallis; Fantasia on Greensleeves.* PARRY: *Lady Radnor's suite.* BRIDGE: *Suite for string orchestra.* HOLST: *St Paul's suite.* WARLOCK: *Capriol suite.* BRITTEN: *Variations on a theme of Frank Bridge, Op. 10.*
❀ (B) *** Nimbus Dig. NI 5210/3 [id.].

The Birmingham-based English String and Symphony Orchestras under William Boughton is completely at home in this repertoire. One has only to sample the excitingly animated account of Holst's *St Paul's suite* (which also has much delicacy of feeling), the ideally paced Warlock *Capriol suite,* or the vibrant account of Britten's *Frank Bridge variations,* to discover the calibre of this music-making. The recordings were made in the Great Hall of Birmingham University which, with its warm reverberation, gives the strings a gloriously rich body of tone, supported by sumptuous cello and bass sonorities. The Elgar *Introduction and allegro* expands wonderfully at its climax (yet the fugue is not blurred) and in Vaughan Williams's *Lark ascending*, where the violin solo is exquisitely played with wonderful purity of tone by Michael Bochmann, the closing pianissimo seems to float in the still air. The work most suited to such an expansive acoustic is Vaughan Williams's *Tallis fantasia*, a deeply expressive performance which gives the listener the impression of sitting in a cathedral, with the solo string group, perfectly matched and blended in timbre, evoking a distant, ethereal organ. The lovely Butterworth pieces are tenderly sympathetic, and Alan Hacker's rhapsodically improvisatory account of Finzi's *Clarinet concerto* is full of colour and warmth. Perhaps Maurice Bourgue's oboe is balanced a little too closely in Vaughan Williams's *Oboe concerto* but the ear adjusts. On the other hand, the flutes melt magically into the strings in the famous *Greensleeves fantasia*. Delius's *Summer evening*, an early work, is quite memorable, and the suites of Parry and Finzi are full of colourful invention. The Bridge *Suite for strings* brings a lively response, with sumptuous textures. Only the opening *Cockaigne overture* of Elgar is a little lacking in profile and drama – and even here Boughton's relaxed, lyrical approach is enjoyable, for he broadens the final climax very satisfyingly. Very reasonably priced, this box makes an outstanding bargain.

Equale Brass

'Baccanales': WARLOCK: *Capriol suite* (arr. Gout). POULENC: *Suite* (arr. Jenkins): *Mouvement perpétuel No. 1; Novellette No. 1 in C; Impromptu No. 3; Suite française*. ARNOLD: *Brass quintet*. F. COUPERIN: *Suite* (arr. Wallace). BARTÓK: *4 Hungarian pictures* (arr. Sears).
*** Nimbus NI 5004 [id.].

This offers sound of striking presence and realism, and the programme is certainly imaginative. The arrangements are cleverly scored and produce highly diverting results. Warlock's *Capriol suite* and the music of François Couperin seem unlikely to adapt well for brass, yet they are the highlights of the programme, alongside the engaging Poulenc *Mouvement perpétuel* and the colourful Bartók *Hungarian pictures*. The Equale Brass is a quintet (two trumpets, horn, trombone and tuba); besides immaculate ensemble, their playing is infectiously spirited and readily conveys the enjoyment of the participants, so that the music-making has the atmosphere of a live concert. Each of the twenty-one items is banded. A demonstration issue.

Galway, James (flute)

'The Concerto collection' (with various orchestras & conductors): BACH: *Concertos in A min., BWV 1056; in E min., BWV 1059*. VIVALDI: *Concertos, Op. 10/1–3*. Karl STAMITZ: *Concerto in G*. MOZART: *Concertos Nos. 1–2, K.313/4*. MERCADANTE: *Concerto in E min*. REINECKE: *Concerto in D, Op. 283*. MAYER: *Concerto (Mandala ki Raga Sangeet: A circle of Raga music)*. RODRIGO: *Concierto pastoral*. KHACHATURIAN: *Concerto* (arr. from *Violin concerto* by Rampal/Galway). IBERT: *Concerto*. NIELSEN: *Concerto*.
*** BMG/RCA Analogue/Dig. RD 60450 (4) [60450-2-RC].

Four CDs of flute concertos may seem indigestible, but with James Galway's consistent artistry, remarkable bravura and distinct charisma always put at the service of the music – which covers a remarkably wide stylistic range – these records will give much pleasure. Most of the recordings are analogue (the Khachaturian, Mayer, Mercadante, Nielsen and Vivaldi are digital) but nearly all the transfers bring first-class sound. The Mozart concertos (among Galway's earliest recordings) are a bit fierce in the orchestra; they have recently been available on Pickwick CD at bargain price, and their inclusion makes one reflect that this box is expensive, even though its excellence is undeniable and it includes much fascinating repertoire that is not otherwise available. Some might feel that in Bach, Mozart and Vivaldi Galway's vibrato is stylistically inappropriate; yet his ability to charm is irresistible: he plays the famous slow-movement cantilena of Bach's BWV 1056 (the *F minor Harpsichord concerto*) as beautifully as one would expect, and his virtuosity in Vivaldi allegros is dazzling. His accounts of the charmingly spiky Rodrigo *Concierto pastoral* (which he commissioned) with its lovely contrasting central *Adagio*, and the delectably high-spirited Ibert piece (with its cool *Andante*) are unlikely to be bettered. When the Mayer *Concerto* was first issued on LP, we gave Galway's record a Rosette. Musical collusions between the cultures of East and West can easily become collisions, but not so here. John Mayer, Calcutta born, spices his five-movement concertante piece with Indian idioms, albeit westernized, and in Galway's hands the result is refreshingly spontaneous. There are perhaps finer versions of the Nielsen *Concerto* available, but Galway's is still a considerable one. Throughout the lesser works the star quality of his presentation makes second-rate music seem much better than it is. The Stamitz (Karl, not Johann), Reinecke and Mercadante are all most winning here. The Mercadante is quite dramatic, and in its *Largo* the orchestra ushers in the plaintive flute cantilena with a distinctly operatic flourish, while the Rondo has a catchy Russian theme. The slow movement of the Reinecke is also portentous at the opening but yields a rhapsodic melody that soars easily on Galway's silver flute, followed by a Weberian finale. The Stamitz is quite an ambitious piece, and Galway makes its elegance sound almost Mozartian. Throughout these discs he is given expert accompaniments; if the solo balance is usually rather forward, the orchestra is always well in the picture. There are fully adequate notes.

'Annie's song and other Galway favourites' (with Nat. PO, Charles Gerhardt): MARAIS: *Le basque.* VILLA-LOBOS: *Bachianas brasileiras No. 5: Aria.* KREISLER: *Liebesfreud.* FAURÉ: *Dolly: Berceuse.* MOZART: *Piano sonata in C, K.545* 1st movt. DENVER: *Annie's song.* HASSE: *Tambourin.* DEBUSSY: *La plus que lente.* TRAD.: *Brian Boru's march* (with Robles Harp Ens.); *Belfast hornpipe* (with Kevin Conneff (bodhran)); *Spanish love song.* BIZET (arr. Borne): *Carmen fantasy.*
(M) **(*) BMG/RCA GD 60747; *GK 60747.*

Apart from the melodic potency of the title number by John Denver (written for Galway's wife), *Le Basque* is as engaging a lollipop as you will find in many a long day's march with Brian Boru. Its simple moto perpetuo charm remains in the memory long after the concert has finished. There is nothing else here as indelible as that, and in the – otherwise effective – ten-minute *Carmen fantasy*, the flute needs all Galway's considerable charisma to substitute for a dark, throaty mezzo voice. But the Fauré piece has charm, the Debussy is gently sultry, and the famous Villa-Lobos cantilena transcribes for flute quite readily. Generally good, bright sound, with a spotlight on the soloist.

'The magic flute of James Galway' (with (i) Nat. PO, Gerhard; (ii) Marisa Robles (harp) & COE; (iii) Philip Moll (piano); (iv) RPO, Myung-Whun Chung): (i) HANDEL: *Solomon: Arrival of the Queen of Sheba.* RACHMANINOV: *Vocalise.* BACH: *Sonata in C min.: Allegro.* (ii) DEBUSSY: *Le petit nègre; Le petit berger.* (iii) SCHUBERT: *Serenade, D.957.* (i) MENDELSSOHN: *Midsummer Night's Dream: Scherzo.* SCHUMANN: *Kinderszenen: Träumerei.* KHACHATURIAN: *Masquerade: Waltz.* (iv) GOSSEC: *Tambourin.* (i) CHOPIN: *Variations on a theme from Rossini's La Cenerentola.* KREISLER: *Schön Rosmarin.* DVOŘÁK: *Humoresque.* BRICCIALDI: *Carnival of Venice.*
(M) *** BMG/RCA GD 60918; *GK 60918.*

Galway's gift for making transcriptions sound as if the music had been originally conceived for the flute almost succeeds in the freshly vivacious *Arrival of the Queen of Sheba*, and his exuberant roulades in the Chopin *Rossini variations* and (especially) the *Carnival of Venice* are very fetching. The *Midsummer Night's Dream scherzo* has an iridescent sparkle and, among the lyrical items, Schumann's *Träumerei* is beautifully phrased. The flair and sparkle of Galway's bravura never fails to astonish, though the Bach *Allegro* is outrageously fast. The two Debussy items, Schubert's *Serenade* and the Khachaturian have been added to the original collection for the CD issue and bring further variety of musical style. The recording balances the flute well forward, and the CD transfer increases the sense of a spotlight on the soloist.

Gothenburg Symphony Orchestra, Neeme Järvi

'Intermezzo': Intermezzi from: MASCAGNI: *Cavalleria Rusticana; L'amico Fritz.* CILEA: *Adriana Lecouvreur.* PUCCINI: *Manon Lescaut; Suor Angelica.* LEONCAVALLO: *Pagliacci.* WOLF-FERRARI: *Jewels of the Madonna.* SCHMIDT: *Notre Dame.* MUSSORGSKY: *Khovanshchina.* MASSENET: *Thaïs: Méditation.* VERDI: *La Traviata: Preludes to Acts I & III.* OFFENBACH: *Contes d'Hoffmann: Barcarolle.* PONCHIELLI: *La Gioconda: Dance of the hours.*
(M) *** DG Dig. 429 494-2; *429 494-4* [id.].

At mid-price this has obvious attractions, though the modern digital sound could ideally be more sumptuous. But these are distinctive performances: there is plenty of temperament in the more passionate interludes and a balancing restraint in the splendidly shaped *Traviata Preludes.* The vivacious excerpt from *The Jewels of the Madonna* sparkles, and only the *Dance of the hours* gives cause for raised eyebrows with some curiously mannered, hesitant rhythmic distortions.

Russian music (with (i) Gothenburg Symphony Ch.; (ii) Gothenburg Symphony Brass Band): BORODIN: *In the Steppes of Central Asia.* (i) *Prince Igor: Polovtsian dances.* RIMSKY-KORSAKOV: *Capriccio espagnol, Op. 34; Russian Easter festival overture, Op. 36.* TCHAIKOVSKY: (i; ii) *Overture 1812, Op. 49; Marche slave, Op. 31.*
*** DG Dig. 429 984-2; *429 984-4* [id.].

Järvi's Russian programme is generous in content (76 minutes); it is splendidly recorded and brings performances of all these favourite showpieces which are as fine as any available. Järvi finds both romance and poetry in Borodin's evocation of the Russian steppes and is equally impressive in the *Polovtsian dances* from *Prince Igor*, with lovely lyrical singing from the Gothenburg Chorus and a spirited but controlled conclusion. It is a pity that the percussion-led opening *Dance of the Polovtsi maidens* is omitted, but in the *General dance* (the one with the strenuous whacks on the bass drum) Torgny Sporsen makes a brief but effective contribution as the Khan. Both Rimsky-Korsakov pieces are brilliantly played: the close of the *Capriccio espagnol* is exhilarating in its unbuttoned exuberance, and the changing moods of the *Russian Easter festival overture*, whether solemn, ecstatic or bursting with energy, are combined impressively in an account which is unsurpassed in the current catalogue. *1812* is exciting too, and not just for the added Gothenburg brass and artillery, and for the fervour of the chorus at the opening. Järvi clearly knows how to structure the piece, and he obviously enjoys the histrionics, and so do we. *Marche slave* has a comparable Slavonic grandeur, its touch of melancholy offset by the quirky rhythmic feeling in the middle section with its nicely placed horn obbligato, and an exultant surge of adrenalin at the close.

'Greensleeves'

English music (with (i) Sinfonia of L. or Hallé O, Barbirolli; (ii) New Philh. O, LPO or LSO, Boult; (iii) Williams, Bournemouth SO, Berglund; (iv) E. Sinfonia, Dilkes): (i) VAUGHAN WILLIAMS: *Fantasia on Greensleeves.* (ii) *The Lark ascending* (with Hugh Bean). (iii) *Oboe concerto in A min.* (ii) *English folksongs suite.* (i) DELIUS: *A Village Romeo and Juliet: Walk to the Paradise Garden. On hearing the first cuckoo in spring.* (iv) BUTTERWORTH: *The Banks of green willow.* (ii) ELGAR: *Serenade for strings, Op. 20.* (iii) MOERAN: *Lonely waters.*
(B) *** EMI *TC2-MOM 104.*

Looking at the programme and artists' roster, the reader will hardly need the confirmation that this is a very attractive tape anthology. Performances never disappoint, the layout is excellent, and for the car this is ideal. On domestic equipment the sound is a little variable, although the tape has been remastered since its first issue and now sounds pleasantly smooth on top. Often the quality is both vivid and rich, as in the title-piece and the Elgar *Serenade.* Vaughan Williams's *Oboe concerto*, stylishly played by John Williams, is admirably fresh. This is excellent value.

Hallé Orchestra, Sir John Barbirolli

'Armchair Concert': NICOLAI: *Overture The Merry Wives of Windsor.* MAHLER: *Lieder eines fahrenden Gesellen* (with Dame Janet Baker). BRAHMS: *Symphony No. 4.*
(M) *** EMI CDM7 64444-2 [id.].

Dame Janet Baker's EMI recording of the Mahler from her earlier years brings a heart-felt performance which has an emotional depth and a weight of expression rarely matched. As 'concertante' centrepiece in this Barbirolli 'Armchair Concert' disc, it comes with a warm, lyrical reading of the Brahms *Fourth* (which is both individual and highly satisfying), as well as the Nicolai overture. Recordings of different vintages are well transferred.

Hallé Orchestra, Maurice Handford

'Hallé encores': COPLAND: *Fanfare for the Common Man.* KHACHATURIAN: *Spartacus: Adagio of Spartacus and Phrygia.* GOUNOD: *Mors et Vita: Judex.* MACCUNN: *Overture: Land of the*

Mountain and the Flood. SATIE: *Gymnopédies Nos. 1 and 3* (orch. Debussy). MASSENET: *Thaïs: Méditation.* TRAD.: *Suo Gan.* BARBER: *Adagio for strings.*
(B) *** CfP CD-CFP 4543; *TC-CFP 4543.*

Maurice Handford and the Hallé offer an exceptionally attractive collection of miscellaneous pieces, beautifully recorded. Many of the items have achieved popularity almost by accident through television and the other media (how else would the MacCunn overture have come – so rightly – to notice?), but the sharpness of the contrasts adds to the charm. The Hallé violins sound a little thin in Barber's beautiful *Adagio*, but otherwise the playing is first rate. What is particularly attractive about this concert is the way the programme is laid out so that each piece follows on naturally after its predecessor. The CD transfer is vivid.

Hardenberger, Håkan (trumpet)

Trumpet concertos (with LPO, Elgar Howarth): M. HAYDN: *Concerto No. 2 in C.* HERTEL: *Concerto No. 1 in E flat.* MOLTER: *Concerto No. 1 in D.* L. MOZART: *Concerto in D.* F. RICHTER: *Concerto in D.*
*** Ph. Dig. 426 311-2; *426 311-4* [id.].

Edward Tarr's excellent note begins by saying that the works recorded here 'testify to the high level of trumpet-playing after the death of Bach' – which might well be modified to read the astonishing level of trumpet-playing attained by Håkan Hardenberger. This young Swedish virtuoso makes everything sound completely effortless and, although none of these pieces is an imperishable masterpiece, he plays them all as if they were. Hugely enjoyable and beautifully recorded, with just the right amount of resonance, presence and bloom. Strongly recommended.

Twentieth-century trumpet concertos (with BBC PO, Elgar Howarth): HARRISON BIRTWISTLE: *Endless parade.* MAXWELL DAVIES: *Trumpet concerto.* BLAKE WATKINS: *Trumpet concerto.*
*** Ph. 432 075-2 [id.].

All three works here offer considerable difficulties for the everyday music-lover to approach, but the performances are of a superlative standard, and a record of this calibre gives one the chance to explore their musical intricacies at leisure. Hardenberger commented on the high concentration at the recording sessions for Harrison Birtwistle's aptly named *Endless parade*, where textures and ideas, dynamics and colour all continually vary, as in a kaleidoscope. The trumpet leads throughout, often playing within the aura of a solo vibraphone. Maxwell Davies's *Concerto* (at 31 minutes) is even more ambitious, and the music moves through a series of changing patterns and tempi, using a plainsong, *Franciscus pauper et humilis*, as a basis, centrally evoking the idea of St Francis preaching to the birds. There is no question as to the evocative power of this work, in spite of its cryptic format. Michael Blake Watkins's *Concerto* may have an apparently more conventional layout, but its argument is complex; at one point the soloist has a heated dialogue with the three orchestral trumpets. The recording is outstandingly vivid.

Harle John (saxophone), Bournemouth Sinfonietta, Ivor Bolton

BRYARS: *The green ray.* NYMAN: *Where the bee dances.* WESTBROOK: *Bean rows and blues shots.*
*** Decca Dig. 433 847-2 [id.].

As with other issues of minimalist or near-minimalist music, this one relies above all on the individual magic of the principal performer. John Harle is a magnetic artist, who consistently turns his ugly duckling of an instrument into a swan. His collection starts sensuously with Gavin Bryars' *The green ray*, a work inspired by a rare trick of light as the sun is setting. Harle's playing makes one wallow in the experience. Michael Nyman's *Where the bee dances* oscillates between slow passacaglia-like passages and ever more hectic jazzy ostinatos, ending near hysteria. The Mike Westbrook piece is the longest and least interesting. It overdoes the jazzy ostinatos, but lets Harle shine both in bravura playing and in bluesy sensuousness, well-supported by Ivor Bolton and the Bournemouth Sinfonietta.

Harvey, Richard (recorder)

'Italian recorder concertos' (with L. Vivaldi O, Huggett): VIVALDI: *Concerto in C min., RV 441; Concerto in C, RV 444.* SAMMARTINI: *Concerto in F.* A. SCARLATTI: *Sinfonia di concerto grosso No. 3.*
*** Gaudeamus CDGAU 111; *ZCGAU 111* [id.].

Richard Harvey plays with persuasive style and flair. Moreover the accompaniments are unusually authentic and in exactly the right scale. The Sammartini *Concerto* is a charmer and, of the two Vivaldi works, RV 444, for sopranino recorder, is especially engaging. The Scarlatti *Sinfonia* in five movements is hardly less winning. The recording has excellent presence and a good balance. Highly recommended.

Haskil, Clara (piano)

Concertos (with various orchestras & conductors): MOZART: *Piano concertos Nos. 9 in E flat, K.271; 20 in D min., K.466; 23 in A, K.488; 24 in C min., K.491.* CHOPIN: *Piano concerto No. 2 in F min., Op. 21.* FALLA: *Nights in the gardens of Spain.* SCHUMANN: *Piano concerto in A min., Op. 54.* (Solo piano) *Kinderszenen, Op. 15; Waldszenen, Op. 82.*
(B) *** Ph. 426 964-2 (4) [id.].

These celebrated performances have come up well: they made their first reappearance in a five-LP box and the recording quality largely belies their years. The *D minor* (K.466) and *C minor* (K.491) *Concertos*, with Markevich and the Lamoureux Orchestra, are remarkably fresh for 1960 and offer beautifully rounded quality. Though she does no more than hint at the darker dramatic fires of the *D minor*, K.466, Haskil never beautifies the piano writing or reaches for the Dresden china. The Chopin and Falla, again both with Markevich, come from 1960, the last year of her life, and they serve as a reminder that she had a stronger temperament and a wider command of keyboard than her reputation as a Mozartian showed. Her Schumann *Concerto*, recorded in The Hague in 1951 under Willem van Otterloo, is particularly sympathetic, though the piano sound is not quite so fresh on this last disc. The solo Schumann pieces, recorded in the early 1950s, are entirely inside the composer's sensibility. Not only is this set a welcome tribute to an artist of vision and gentleness that her admirers will want to collect, it is one that will give much quiet musical satisfaction.

Heifetz, Jascha (violin)

'The Acoustic Recordings 1917–1924' (with André Benoist; Samuel Chotzinoff; O, Pasternak): SCHUBERT: *Ave Maria.* DRIGO: *Valse bluette.* ELGAR: *La Capricieuse, Op. 17.* SARASATE: *Malagueña, Habanera, Op. 21/1 & 2; Introduction and tarantelle, Op. 43; Zapateado, Op. 23/2; Zigeunerweisen, Op. 20/1; Carmen fantasy, Op. 25.* BAZZINI: *La ronde des lutins.* BEETHOVEN: *Ruins of Athens: Chorus of Dervishes; Turkish march.* WIENIAWSKI: *Scherzo-Tarantelle, Op. 16; Concerto No. 2, Op. 22: Romance.* ACHRON: *Hebrew melody, Op. 33; Hebrew lullaby, Hebrew dance, Op. 35; Stimmung, Op. 32.* PAGANINI: *Moto perpetuo; Caprices, Nos. 13 & 20.* KREISLER: *Minuet; Sicilienne et Rigaudon.* GLAZUNOV: *Meditation; Valse.* MOSZKOWSKI: *Guitarre, Op. 45/2.* CHOPIN: *Nocturnes, Op. 9/2; Op. 27/2.* TCHAIKOVSKY: *Souvenir d'un lieu cher: Scherzo, Op. 42/2. Serenade: Valse, Op. 48/2. Concerto, Op. 35: Canzonetta. Sérénade mélancolique, Op. 26.* MENDELSSOHN: *On wings of song, Op. 34/2; Concerto in E min.: finale.* DVOŘÁK: *Slavonic dances, Op. 46/2; Op. 72/2 & 8.* SCHUMANN: *Myrthen: Widmung, Op. 25/1.* LALO: *Symphonie espagnole, Op. 21: Andante.* MOZART: *Divertimento No. 17, K.334: Minuet. Haffner Serenade, K.250: Rondo.* D'AMBROSIO: *Serenade, Op. 4.* JUON: *Berceuse, Op. 28/3.* GOLDMARK: *Concerto in A min., Op. 28: Andante.* GODOWSKY: *Waltz in D.* BRAHMS: *Hungarian dance No. 1 in G min.* HAYDN: *Quartet (Lark), Op. 64/5: Vivace.* GRANADOS: *Danzas españolas, Op. 37/5; Andaluza.* BOULANGER: *Nocturne in F; Cortège.* SCOTT: *The gentle maiden.* SAINT-SAËNS: *Havanaise, Op. 83.*
(M) (***) BMG/RCA mono GD 80942 [0942-2-RG] (3).

These recordings serve as a salutary reminder of Heifetz's extraordinary powers. The earliest records come from the year of the Russian Revolution, when Heifetz was still sixteen and only five years after he had made his début in St Petersburg. As always with Heifetz, even the highest expectations are surpassed: his effortless technical mastery is dazzling, the golden tone strong and pure, the accuracy of his intonation almost beyond belief and his taste impeccable. The collector will also be agreeably surprised by the quality of sound; the earliest was made only two weeks after his Carnegie Hall début, when the art of recording was still relatively primitive, and the original 78-r.p.m. disc was single-sided. Seventy or more years later, his brilliance remains undimmed. The recordings are arranged in chronological order, though the differences during the period are relatively small. This set is a mandatory purchase for all who care about the art of violin playing.

American concertos (with (i) LAPO, Wallenstein; (ii) Dallas SO, Hendl; (iii) Piatigorsky and CO; (iv) RCA Victor SO, Voorhees): (i) KORNGOLD: *Violin concerto, Op. 35.* (ii) RÓZSA: *Violin concerto, Op. 24;* (iii) *Theme and variations, Op. 29a.* (iv) WAXMAN: *Fantasy on Bizet's 'Carmen'.*
(M) *** BMG/RCA mono/stereo GD 87963 [7963-3-RD].

Heifetz's playing in this 1953 mono recording of the Korngold *Violin concerto* is dazzling, the lyrical music sounds gorgeous and the material, drawn from film scores, is always appealing – and especially when presented like this. The Rózsa *Concerto* is slightly less memorable but still worth hearing in such a performance. In the *Theme and variations* he is joined by Piatigorsky, also in very good form. Waxman's *'Carmen' fantasy* is simply a string of Bizet's hit tunes, and they are presented with a panache that is little short of astonishing. Few reservations have to be made about the recording; the Rózsa pieces are in stereo, but the Korngold mono sounds just as good.

Concertante works (with RCA Victor SO, William Steinberg or Izler Solomon): LALO: *Symphonie espagnole, Op. 21.* SAINT-SAËNS: *Havanaise, Op. 83; Introduction and Rondo capriccioso, Op. 28.* SARASATE: *Zigeunerweisen, Op. 20.* CHAUSSON: *Poème.*
(M) (***) BMG/RCA mono GD 87709 [7709-2-RG].

These recordings come from 1951–2 and are inevitably limited in range and body. Heifetz plays the Lalo *Symphonie espagnole* without the central *Intermezzo* movement, as was the custom before the war – and how he plays it! The virtuosity is dazzling and quite transcends the period sound. The Chausson *Poème*, in which the conductor is Izler Solomon, is quite unlike other versions: stripped of sentimentality, it is curiously affecting.

Holliger, Heinz (oboe)

Concertos (with (i) Frankfurt RSO, Inbal; (ii) ECO, Leppard): (i) BELLINI: *Oboe concerto in E flat.* MOLIQUE: *Oboe concertino in G min.* MOSCHELLES: *Concertante in F for flute and oboe* (with Aurèle Nicolet). RIETZ: *Konzertstück in F min., Op. 33.* (ii) FIALA: *Cor anglais concerto in E flat.* HUMMEL: *Adagio, theme and variations in F.*
(B) **(*) Ph. 426 972-2; *426 972-4.*

The playing here is of high quality and the measure generous: six concertante works with a playing time of 76 minutes. The recording is very good too, if rather resonantly inflated orchestrally, and the cost is modest. So perhaps this collection (mostly recorded in the mid-1970s) may be acquired for the two-movement Bellini concerto which is delightful, and the Moschelles double concerto is attractively inventive too, with a very fetching tune in the Rondo finale. The other works are more conventional and rather anonymous; although the Fiala is agreeable enough, the main theme of the Hummel sounds a trifle faded in its intended charm.

Oboe concertos (with I Musici): MARCELLO: *Concerto in D min.* SAMMARTINI: *Concerto in D.* ALBINONI: *Concerto a 5 in G min., Op. 9/8.* LOTTI: *Concerto in A.* CIMAROSA (arr. Benjamin): *Concerto in C.*
*** Ph. Dig. 420 189-2.

A collection like this is self-recommending, with five concertos offered, all of them attractive. The Lotti has a very agreeable extended *Affettuoso* slow movement, and the *Adagio* of the Sammartini is richly memorable too, while the central movement of Albinoni's Op. 9, No. 8, is wonderfully serene here. The Cimarosa–Benjamin concoction is an unalloyed delight. Holliger's timbre is enticingly coloured throughout and his phrasing is always supple and sensitive; some might feel that his ornamentation is at times a shade prolix, but this is a small point. I Musici accompany with characteristic finesse and Italian warmth.

Hollywood Bowl Orchestra, John Mauceri

'Hollywood dreams': SCHOENBERG: *Fanfare for a Bowl concert.* ROGERS: *Carousel: Heaven effect; Carousel waltz.* STEINER: *Gone with the Wind:* Main title. STRAVINSKY: *Firebird suite: Lullaby; Finale.* NEWMAN: *Twentieth Century Fox fanfare; Overture: How to marry a millionaire.* WAXMAN: *A Place in the sun: suite* (with Kenneth Radnonsky, alto sax). BERNSTEIN: *On the Waterfront: Love theme.* ARLEN: *The Wizard of Oz*: suite (with chorus). PROKOFIEV: *Semyon Kotko: The southern night.* KORNGOLD: *The Adventures of Robin Hood: Fanfare and Love scene; Battle, victory and Epilogue.* GORE: *Defending your life: Finale.* BARRY: *Dances with wolves: John Dunbar theme.* WILLIAMS: *E.T.*
** Ph. Dig. 432 109-2; *432 109-4* [id.].

A much-hyped CD when it appeared, and one which appears to have everything going for it, not least John Mauceri in charge of an imaginatively chosen 76-minute programme. Yet the results are curiously disappointing. The recordings were made on Culver City Sound Stage (where the original sound track of *The Wizard of Oz* was done), and the clean, slightly dry acoustic, while creating a sound ideal for a cinema auditorium (which needs extra clarity to counter the audience-absorption) means there is no feeling of glowing sumptuousness. Reproduced at a high level, the orchestra is certainly spectacular, but the brilliance becomes a bit wearing, and comparing the Max Steiner, Alfred Newman and Franz Waxman selections with the Charles Gerhardt RCA CDs is not to John Mauceri's advantage either. Gerhardt brings an uninhibited flair to his Hollywoodiana that Mauceri often misses. Although the *Tara theme* from *Gone with the Wind* cannot fail to make an impact, the Waxman concertante suite for alto saxophone and strings, from *A Place in the Sun*, which sounds wonderfully luscious on the Gerhardt recording, here is too refined and delicate by half. The Schoenberg and Prokofiev items are suitably pungent, but Mauceri's rhythmic treatment of the finale from Stravinsky's *Firebird ballet* is curiously unsympathetic. The eleven-minute pot-pourri from *The Wizard of Oz*, complete with chorus, is wittily orchestrated, but serves to show that *Over the Rainbow* was the film's only hit. Best are John Barry's spacious open-air theme for *Dances with Wolves* and John Williams's exuberant *Flying sequence* from *E.T.* which is indestructible. The documentation is a model of just how it should be done, nicely laid out with stills from every film featured in the programme, including fascinating Hollywood photographs of Schoenberg, Stravinsky and Prokofiev.

Hungarian State Orchestra, Mátyás Antal

'Hungarian festival': KODÁLY: *Háry János: suite.* LISZT: *Hungarian rhapsodies for orchestra Nos. 1, 2 & 6* (arr. Doeppler). HUBAY: *Hejre Kati* (with Ferenc Balogh). BERLIOZ: *Damnation de Faust: Rákóczy march.*
(BB) *** Naxos Dig. 8.550142; *4550142* [id.].

The Hungarian State Orchestra are in their element in this programme of colourful music for which they have a natural affinity. There is no more characterful version of the *Háry János suite* (we have already mentioned it in the Composer index) and Hubay's concertante violin piece, with its gypsy flair, is similarly successful, even if the violin soloist is not a particularly strong personality. The special interest of the Liszt *Hungarian rhapsodies* lies in the use of the Doeppler orchestrations, which are comparatively earthy, with greater use of brass solos than the more sophisticated scoring most often used in the West. The performances are suitably robust and certainly have plenty of charisma. The brilliant digital recording is strong on primary colours but has atmosphere too, and produces plenty of spectacle in the Berlioz *Rákóczy march.*

(Philip) Jones Brass Ensemble

'Lollipops': LANGFORD: *London miniatures.* RIMSKY-KORSAKOV: *Flight of the bumble bee.* ARBAN: *Variations on a Tyrolean theme.* KOETSIER: *Little circus march, Op. 79.* GRIEG: *Norwegian dance, Op. 35/2.* JOPLIN: *Bethena.* PARKER: *A Londoner in New York.* TRAD. (arr. Iveson): *Song of the Seahorse.*

*** Claves CD 50 8503 [id.].

Recorded in St Luke's Church, Hampstead, this Claves CD makes an ideal demonstration showcase for the superb British group that is in some ways the brass equivalent of the Academy of St Martin-in-the-Fields. Offering music written or arranged specifically for these players, the concert is admirably framed by two suites of descriptive miniatures, both considerable additions to the brass repertoire. In between come many entertaining examples of musical bravura, including Rimsky's descriptive piece, sounding like a jumbo-sized bumble-bee on John Fletcher's incredibly nimble tuba, and Arban's more conventional, but no less breathtaking *Variations on a Tyrolean theme*, where Frank Lloyd is the featured horn player, while Jan Koetsier's *Kleiner Zirkusmarsch* has wonderfully deft articulation from the whole group. Gordon Langford's set of six *London miniatures* shows this composer at his most inventive and Jim Parker's *A Londoner in New York* provides a transatlantic mirror-image in his five-movement suite, with lively jazzy imagery. Tony Faulkner, the recording producer, deserves a credit for the wonderful tangibility of the sound-balance, which combines bite and clarity with fine, rich sonority. The presence of the instrumentalists on CD is very real.

'PJBE Finale': PREVIN: *Triolet for brass.* M. BERKELEY: *Music from Chaucer.* LUTOSLAWSKI: *Mini overture.* DURKÓ: *Sinfonietta.* RAUTAVAARA: *Playgrounds for angels.*
*** Chan. Dig. CHAN 8490; *ABTD 1190* [id.].

As usual, the Jones Brass play these complex scores with superb musicianship and with often breathtaking freedom from any suggestion of technical problems. The writing of both the avant-garde works, Zsolt Durkó's *Sinfonietta*, and Einojuhani Rautavaara's *Playgrounds for angels*, with its separate clustering of different brass textures, is very complex; but both are presented with an easy virtuosity which is most compelling. The Previn *Triolet*, in eight, often brief sections, is amiably diverse. The finale of Berkeley's *Music from Chaucer* is even catchier, and this too is very agreeably inventive. The recording is very much in the demonstration bracket.

'Baroque brass': BIBER: *Sonata a 7.* ANON.: *Sonata from Die Bankelsangerlieder.* M. FRANCK: *Intrata.* HASSLER: *Intrada V.* SPEER: *Sonata for trumpet & 3 trombones; Sonata for 3 trombones; Sonata for 4 trombones; Sonata for 2 trumpets and 3 trombones.* SCHEIDT: *Canzona a 10.* BACH: *Chorale: Nun danket alle Gott. Capriccio on the departure of a beloved brother, BWV 992: Aria & fugue in imitation of the postillion's horn (arr. Breuer). Cello suite No. 1: Menuetto & Courante* (arr. Fletcher for solo tuba). D. SCARLATTI: *Keyboard sonatas, Kk.380; Kk.430; Kk.443* (arr. Dodgson). C. P. E. BACH: *March.*
(M) *** Decca 425 727-2; *425 727-4.*

An imaginative and highly rewarding programme, among the best of the Philip Jones anthologies. The music of Daniel Speer is strikingly inventive and the Bach and Scarlatti arrangements are highly engaging – the latter with no attempt at miniaturization. The C. P. E. Bach *March* makes a superbly vigorous coda. If the Baroque idiom and the sound of modern brass instruments combine easily in your aural consciousness, this can be recommended, though not to be taken all at once. The recording is first class.

British music for brass (directed by Elgar Howarth, John Iveson & Howard Snell): BLISS: *Antiphonal fanfare for 3 brass choirs; Greetings to a city (Flourish for 2 brass orchestras); Fanfare for the Lord Mayor of London.* BRITTEN: *Fanfare: The Eagle has two heads. Russian funeral; Fanfare for St Edmondsbury.* ARNOLD: *Symphony, Op. 123; Quintet.* TIPPETT: *Fanfare.* BAX: *Fanfare for the wedding of Princess Elizabeth (1947).* BRIAN: *The Cenci: Fanfare.* WALTON, arr. Howarth: *Spitfire prelude & fugue.*
(M) *** Decca 430 369-2; *430 369-4* [id.].

Not everything here is as original and arresting as the three Britten pieces, especially the (1936) *Russian funeral*, based on a theme also used by Shostakovich in his *Eleventh Symphony*. But the Arnold *Quintet* has real wit and the *Symphony* is a considerable piece, essentially serious. There is plenty of traditional brass splendour from Bliss and Bax, and Elgar Howarth's transcription of Walton's film music for *The First of the Few* is spectacularly vivid. Expert playing throughout and brilliant, sonorous sound of Decca's best analogue quality.

'Virtuoso brass': CLARKE: *Trumpet voluntary.* PURCELL: *Trumpet tune and air.* G. GABRIELI: *Canzona: Sol, sol, la sol; Sonata pian' e forte* (both ed. Gardiner). SUSATO: *Suite* (arr. Iveson). BYRD: *Earl of Oxford's march.* LOCKE: *Music for His Majesty's sackbuts and cornetts.* TRAD.: *Greensleeves.* HANDEL: *La Rejouissance.* SCHEIDT: *Battle suite.* C. P. E. BACH: *March.*

(B) *** Decca 433 640-2; *433 640-4.*

For those who like superbly alive and polished brass-playing and spectacular sonorities, this collection of Baroque and Renaissance music on Decca's Headline bargain label should prove excellent value. The recordings are taken from various anthologies made for Argo/Decca, and the remastering is bright and clean. There are some striking antiphonal effects, as in the *Galliard battaglia* of Scheidt and C. P. E. Bach's *March*, and the melodic invention of the programme is consistently striking. The notes, too, are excellent.

Kaufman, Louis (violin)

'Louis Kaufman plays' ((i) with LSO, Bernard Herrmann): (i) PISTON: *Violin concerto No. 1.* COPLAND: *Violin sonata.* RUSSELL BENNETT: *Hexapoda.* MCBRIDE: *Aria and toccata in swing.* STILL: *Blues from Lennox Avenue Suite.* KERN: *The song is you; Smoke gets in your eyes.*
(***) Bay Cities mono BCD 1019 [id.].

Louis Kaufman has had a long and distinguished career, both as a soloist in the concert hall and in Hollywood, and has been an eloquent champion of American music. The *First Violin concerto* (1939) is typical Piston, fertile in invention and finely crafted. Its sole representation so far has been an American LP (on the Mace label) by Hugo Kohlberg, but Kaufman's eloquent and fervent performance makes out an even stronger case for it. The ideas are memorable, beautifully fashioned and with a strong lyric impulse and a keen sense of momentum. This version comes from a concert given by the LSO and Bernard Herrmann, broadcast in 1956 from the BBC's Maida Vale Studios. The Copland *Violin sonata*, with the composer at the piano, is an even earlier recording, from 1948, originally on the Concert Hall label. The *Sonata* is vintage Copland, with some reflective and tender slow music. The other pieces, by Richard Russell Bennett, William Grant Still and Jerome Kern, all testify to the nervous energy and strong personality of this fine player. The recordings are naturally of variable quality (there is some occasional surface noise in the Copland and Piston pieces), but lovers of American music and of the violin should not be put off by this.

Kremer, Gidon (violin)

Concert (with (i) LSO, Chailly; (ii) Elena Bashkirova): CHAUSSON: (i) *Poème, Op. 25.* MILHAUD: *Le Boeuf sur le toit;* (ii) *Le printemps.* SATIE: (i) *Choses vues à droite et à gauche (sans lunettes).* VIEUXTEMPS: (i) *Fantasia appassionata.*
(M) *** Ph. Dig. 432 513-2; *432 513-4.*

One of Kremer's best records, this has stood up well to repetition. The repertoire is enticing. He plays the Milhaud and Satie pieces with charm, and the Chausson has poetic feeling. Kremer can often seem a self-conscious and narcissistic player but here he is heard at his very best. The 1980–81 recording is altogether excellent.

Laubin, Hannes, Wolfgang and Bernard (trumpets)

Trumpet concertos (with ECO, Simon Preston): TELEMANN: *Concerto in D for 3 trumpets and 2 oboes. Triple trumpet concerto in D.* RATHBERGER: *Concerto in E flat for 2 trumpets and 2 violins.* FRANCESCHINI: *Sonata in D for 2 trumpets and strings.* ALBINONI: *Trumpet concerto in B flat.* VIVALDI: *Double trumpet concerto in C.*
*** DG Dig. 431 817-2 [id.].

There are many collections of trumpet concertos, not least the profusion offered by the Maurice André Edition, but this one really is different. It features a very gifted family of trumpeters and all the works here except one, involve at least two members playing together, as they do with obvious rapport. Moreover these works are fascinatingly textured. In the first by Telemann two oboists from the ECO join the trumpets up front, and what a splendid piece it proves to be, with the composer making the very most of the interplay of colour, especially in the effervescing third movement. But the work by Rathberger which features two concertante violins is equally delectable, with its engaging *Adagio*, where the two trumpets play in thirds above the organ continuo. The four-movement mini-sonata by Franceschini has another agreeable *Adagio* and brings stimulating imitation from the soloists in the finale. The Albinoni is a transcription of an oboe concerto, but both the Vivaldi and Telemann *Double concertos* are authentic and pleasingly inventive, if not as enticing as those with more complex scoring. Simon Preston directs animated, polished and sympathetic accompaniments from the harpsichord or chamber organ and this is baroque music at its most spirited, played on modern instruments, but sounding absolutely authentic and stylish. The recording is excellent.

Lipatti, Dinu (piano)

(with Nadia Boulanger; Philh. O, Zürich Tonhalle O, Lucerne Festival O; Galliera, Ackermann, Karajan): BACH: *Chorale, Jesu, joy of man's desiring* (arr. Hess, from BWV 147); *Chorale preludes, BWV 599 & 639* (both arr. Busoni); *Partita No. 1, BWV 825; Siciliana* (arr. Kempff, from BWV 1031). D. SCARLATTI: *Sonatas, Kk. 9 & 380.* MOZART: *Piano concerto No. 21 in C, K.467; Piano sonata No. 8 in A min., K.310.* SCHUBERT: *Impromptus Nos. 2–3, D.899/2 & 3.* SCHUMANN: *Piano concerto in A min., Op. 54.* GRIEG: *Piano concerto in A min., Op. 16.* CHOPIN: *Piano concerto No. 1 in E min., Op. 11; Barcarolle, Op. 60; Études, Op. 10/5 & 25/5; Mazurka No. 32, Op. 50/3; Nocturne No. 8, Op. 27/2; Piano sonata No. 3 in B min., Op. 58; Waltzes Nos. 1–14.* LISZT: *Années de pèlerinage, 2nd Year: Sonnetto 104 del Petrarca.* RAVEL: *Alborada del gracioso.* BRAHMS: *Waltzes* (4 hands), *Op. 39/1–2, 5–6, 10, 14–15.* ENESCU: *Piano sonata No. 3 in D, Op. 25.*
❀ (M) (***) EMI CZS7 67163-2 (5).

This set represents Lipatti's major recording achievements. Whether in Bach (*Jesu, joy of man's desiring* is unforgettable) or Chopin – his *Waltzes* seem to have grown in wisdom and subtlety over the years – Scarlatti or Mozart, these performances are very special indeed. The remastering is done well, and this is a must for anyone with an interest in the piano.

Little Orchestra of London, Leslie Jones

Scandinavian music: GRIEG: *Elegiac Melodies, Op. 34; Holberg Suite, Op. 40.* NIELSEN: *Little Suite, Op. 1.* SIBELIUS: *Rakastava, Op. 14.*
(M) **(*) Unicorn UKCD 2047 [id.].

These performances from the late 1960s are totally unaffected and natural. The sound is a bit dated (the strings above the stave are a bit wanting in freshness) but the playing is plain but sensitive and musical. The performances are totally devoid of glamour and all the more refreshing for being so! Not a first choice in any of the pieces, but as a collection it gives considerable pleasure all the same.

Lloyd Webber, Julian (cello)

'Encore: Travels with my cello (with RPO, Cleobury): GERSHWIN: *Bess, you is my woman.* DEBUSSY: *Clair de lune.* MOZART: *Turkish Rondo.* TAUBE: *Nocturne.* BIZET: *Habañera.* LEHÁR: *You are my heart's delight.* VANGELIS: *Après-midi.* BACH: *Jesu, joy of man's desiring.* BERNSTEIN: *Somewhere.* MCCARTNEY: *When I'm sixty-four.* RIMSKY-KORSAKOV: *Song of India*, etc.
*** Ph. Dig. 416 698-2.

If anything, Julian Lloyd Webber's second travel album is even more attractive than the first (412 231-2). His warm, singing cantilena always gives pleasure and there are some effective crossover items, notably Vangelis's synthesized *Un après-midi* and the McCartney song. The orchestra clearly enjoy themselves, and the recording is suitably vivid and atmospheric. Very entertaining of its kind.

London Classical Players, Roger Norrington

'Early Romantic overtures': WEBER: *Oberon.* MENDELSSOHN: *The Hebrides (Fingal's Cave), Op. 26.* BERLIOZ: *Les Francs-juges, Op. 3.* SCHUMANN: *Genoveva, Op. 81/5.* SCHUBERT: *Rosamunde (Die Zauberharfe).* WAGNER: *Der fliegende Holländer.*
**(*) EMI Dig. CDC7 49889-2 [id.].

In these performances of six high-Romantic overtures, Norrington and his orchestra of period instrumentalists bring out the same tangy qualities as in earlier music. Even if Mendelssohn's *Hebrides* lacks atmospheric magic, there are many compensations, and Wagner's *Flying Dutchman* is the most ear-catching item of all, with its braying horns, using the 1841 text. One reservation is that Norrington, having once chosen a speed, is reluctant to modify it. This is not for everyone but is fascinating nevertheless. Sound that is characteristic of EMI engineers working at Abbey Road.

London Collegiate Brass, Stobart

ELGAR: *Severn suite, Op. 87* (arr. Geehl and Brand). VAUGHAN WILLIAMS: *Henry V overture.* HOLST: *A Moorside suite.* IRELAND: *A comedy overture.*
*** CRD Dig. CRD 3434; *CRDC 4134* [id.].

Elgar's *Severn suite* is heard in an edition that takes into account the composer's own revisions made for his orchestral arrangement. The result is very convincing, and here the opening theme is given a swagger and feeling of pageantry that remain obstinately in the memory. The rest of the work is also impressive, though the quality of the music is uneven. Vaughan Williams's *Henry V overture* stirringly quotes both French and English traditional melodies. Holst's *Moorside suite* demonstrates the composer's usual mastery when writing for wind and brass; while John Ireland's jaunty *Comedy overture*, played with striking rhythmic felicity, also shows the composer at his finest. The performances here (by a group drawn mainly from the London music colleges, and using trumpets rather than cornets, French horns rather than the tenor horns of the brass band world) produce a fine rich sonority and the execution has impressively polished ensemble. CRD's recording is spacious and realistic, although the upper range at times seems not absolutely clean, probably an effect created by the reverberation.

WALTON: *The First shoot.* TIPPETT: *Festal brass with blues.* BRITTEN: *Russian funeral music.* IRELAND: *A Downland suite.*
*** CRD Dig. CRD 3444; *CRDC 4144* [id.].

Only the John Ireland suite is (deservedly) well known. Walton's *First shoot*, a mock ballet originally part of a C. B. Cochran review, is characteristically witty – the composer made the brass arrangement not long before he died. In spite of its title, the Tippett piece is stronger and more ambitious; and Britten's *Funeral music* makes a good foil. All the music is played expertly and with considerable intensity, if not always with the greatest subtlety. The recording is excellent.

London Gabrieli Brass Ensemble

'The splendour of baroque brass': SUSATO: *La Danserye: suite.* G. GABRIELI: *Canzona per sonare a 4: La Spiritata.* SCHEIDT: *Suite.* PEZEL: *Ceremonial brass music.* BACH: *The Art of fugue: Contrapunctus IX.* CHARPENTIER: *Te Deum: Prelude in D.* arr. James: *An Elizabethan suite.* CLARKE: *The Prince of Denmark's march.* HOLBORNE: *5 Dances.* STANLEY: *Trumpet tune.* LOCKE: *Music for His Majesty's sackbutts and cornetts.* PURCELL: *Trumpet tune and ayre. Music for the funeral of Queen Mary* (with Chorus).
❀ (BB) *** ASV CDQS 6013; *ZCQS 6013.*

This is one of the really outstanding brass anthologies, and the digitally remastered analogue recording is very realistic. The brass group is comparatively small: two trumpets, two trombones, horn and tuba; and that brings internal clarity, while the ambience adds fine sonority. The opening Susato *Danserye* is splendid music, and the Scheidt *Suite* is similarly inventive. Pezel's *Ceremonial brass music* is also in effect a suite – it includes a particularly memorable *Sarabande*; while Matthew Locke's *Music for His Majesty's sackbutts and cornetts* opens with a very striking *Air* and offers six diverse movements overall. With the Gabrieli *Canzona*, Purcell's *Trumpet tune and ayre* and the Jeremiah Clarke *Prince of Denmark's march* (better known as the *Trumpet voluntary*) all familiar, this makes a superb entertainment to be dipped into at will. The closing *Music for the funeral of Queen Mary* brings an eloquent choral contribution. Introduced by solemn drum-beats, it is one of Purcell's finest short works and the performance here is very moving. The arrangements throughout the concert (usually made by Crispian Steele-Perkins, who leads the group both sensitively and resplendently) are felicitous and the documentation is excellent. This is a very real bargain.

London Gabrieli Brass Ensemble, Christopher Larkin

Original 19th-century music for brass: BEETHOVEN: *3 Equales for 4 trombones.* CHERUBINI: *Trois pas redoublés et la première marche; Trois pas redoublés et la seconde marche.* DAVID: *Nonetto in C min.* DVOŘÁK: *Fanfare.* LACHNER: *Nonet in F.* RIMSKY-KORSAKOV: *Notturno for 4 horns.* SIBELIUS: *Overture in F min; Allegro; Andantino; Menuetto; Praeludium.*
*** Hyp. Dig. CDA 66470 [id.].

'From the steeples and the mountains': IVES: *From the steeples and the mountains; Let there be light.* BARBER: *Mutations for brass.* HARRIS: *Chorale for organ and brass.* Virgil THOMSON: *Family portrait.* COWELL: *Grinnell fanfare; Tall tale; Hymn and fuguing tune No. 12.* GLASS: *Brass sextet.* RUGGLES: *Angels.* CARTER: *A Fantasy upon Purcell's Fantasia upon one note.*
*** Hyp. Dig. CDA 66517 [id.].

It is difficult to decide which of these two programmes is the more enterprising and the more rewarding. If you are responsive to brass sonorities and you acquire one of them, you will surely want its companion. Beethoven's *Equales* were used at the composer's funeral. They are brief, but noble and dignified. The Sibelius suite, is folksy, uncharacteristic writing, but has genuine charm. The two *Nonets* are equally inventive, with David's the more ambitious, while Rimsky's *Notturno* is short, but finds time to quote from *Scheherazade*. The Cherubini *Trois pas redoublés* are most infectious, essentially providing an interplay between trumpets and horns.

The second concert opens and closes with the always stimulating music of Charles Ives. *From the steeples to the mountains* is scored for four sets of bells, trumpet and trombones, and its effect is clanguorously wild! Elliot Carter's Purcell arrangement also has tolling bells, and is quite haunting. Of the other pieces the most striking is the Barber *Mutations*, which draws on the chorale, *Christe du Lamm Gottes* with highly individual effect. Virgil Thomson is characteristically quirky with his five *Family portraits*, and all four Cowell pieces are very rewarding, especially the catchy *Grinnell fanfare*. Glass wrote his *Sextet* as a postgraduate exercise, and has since disowned it. If simplistic, compared with the composer's later minimalist excursions, it is real music. Most passionate of all is Ruggles' pungently compressed, muted brass *Angels*, yet the piece is marked 'Serene'! The brass playing throughout the two discs is as communicative as it is expert and the recording is splendidly realistic and present.

London Philharmonic Orchestra Brass, Jorge Mester

'Fanfares for the common man': COPLAND: *Fanfare for the common man; Ceremonial fanfare; Inaugural fanfare.* HANSON: *Chorale & fanfare; Fanfare for the Royal Signal Corps.* HARRIS: *Fanfare for the forces.* COWELL: *Fanfare for Latin allies.* WAGENAAR: *Fanfare for airmen.* GOULD: *Fanfare for freedom; Columbian fanfares.* DEEMS TAYLOR: *Fanfare for Russia.* BERNSTEIN: *Fanfares 1–2; Shivaree.* FULEIHAN: *Fanfare for the Medical Corps.* Virgil THOMSON: *Fanfare for France.* PISTON: *Ceremonial fanfare; Fanfare for the Fighting French.* CRESTON: *Fanfare for paratroopers.* E. GOOSSENS: *Fanfare for the Merchant Marine.*
*** Koch Dig. 37012-2; *27012-4* [id.].

This collection – although not to be taken at a single sitting – offers more musical variety than might be expected. It is centred on a series of commissions made by the late Sir Eugene Goossens between 1931 and 1946. At that time he was Musical Director of the Cincinnati Symphony Orchestra and also a particular devotee of fanfares. A dozen of the items included here were among the nineteen he brought into being, including his own which genially interpolates famous traditional melodies like *The roast beef of Old England* and a rather grand version of *Heart of oak*. The most famous of the other commissions is the title-piece by Copland (here played majestically), and the other two contributions by this composer are only marginally less popular in appeal. Walter Piston, however, offers the toughest brass polyphony; Morton Gould unashamedly increases the range of colour possible by introducing woodwind, while Bernstein's mood is uninhibited, especially in his Ivesian *Shivaree*. Hanson's ambitious three-part *Chorale and Fanfare* expands to a thrilling climax which will appeal to all who enjoy his *Romantic Symphony*. Virgil Thomson combines the style of a classic French military march with witty quotations of *Frère Jacques* and *Yankee doodle dandy*, and Deems Taylor draws on a Russian folksong (*Dubinushka*). The LSO brass playing is polished and spectacular, and the recording, made in St John's, Smith Square, is well balanced and sonorously brilliant.

London Philharmonic Orchestra, Klaus Tennstedt

'Armchair concert': BEETHOVEN: *Egmont overture; Symphony No. 6 (Pastoral).* R. STRAUSS: *Four Last Songs* (with Lucia Popp).
(M) *** EMI Dig. CDM7 64439-2 [id.].

In EMI's 'Armchair Concert' series it is good to have Tennstedt's fresh and alert performances of the Beethoven *Sixth Symphony* and *Egmont overture* representing an underappreciated area of his recording work with the LPO. Lucia Popp is light and lyrical in the Strauss in performances that are more urgent and less weighty than most. A most enjoyable programme.

London Symphony Orchestra, André Previn

'Armchair concert': HOLST: *The Planets (suite).* DUKAS: *The Sorcerer's apprentice.* GERSHWIN: *Rhapsody in Blue* (with Previn, piano).
(M) *** CDM7 64441-2 [id.].

This is the pick of EMI's 'Armchair Concert' series; Previn's outstanding, complete version of the Holst *Planets* – still unsurpassed as a performance and superbly recorded – comes with a generous coupling. Though the account of the Dukas is rather too relaxed, it is still enjoyably colourful, and Previn is at his most persuasive directing the Gershwin from the piano. Many live concerts fail to provide more music than this, and few would offer a really good seat for the modest cost of this CD.

Ma, Yo-Yo (cello)

'Great cello concertos': HAYDN: *Concerto in D, Hob VIIb/2* (with ECO, Garcia). SAINT-SAËNS: *Concerto No. 1, Op. 33* (with O Nat. de France, Maazel). SCHUMANN: *Concerto in A min., Op. 129* (with Bav. RSO, C. Davis). DVOŘÁK: *Concerto in B min., Op. 104* (with BPO, Maazel). ELGAR: *Concerto in E min., Op. 85* (with LSO, Previn).
(M) *** Sony Dig./Analogue M2K 44562 (2) [id.].

An enticing mid-priced package, offering at least two of the greatest of all cello concertos, in Yo-Yo Ma's characteristic and imaginatively refined manner. Only the performance of the Haydn gives cause for reservations and these are slight; many will enjoy Ma's elegance here. He is also lucky in his accompanists, and the CBS sound gives no reasons for complaint. The account of the Saint-Saëns has wonderful finesse, and his Schumann is warmly affectionate, even if at times his range of dynamic seems almost hypersensitive. In the Elgar his rapt concentration brings a performance as intense as it is poised, while the Dvořák concerto combines ardour with much subtlety of colour. Here the partnership with the more extrovert Maazel works strikingly well.

Marsalis, Wynton (trumpet), Edita Gruberová (soprano)

'Let the bright Seraphim' (with ECO, Leppard): FASCH: *Concerto for trumpet and 2 oboes in D.* TORELLI: *2 Sonatas for trumpet and strings a 5.* HANDEL: *Samson: Let the bright Seraphim. Birthday Ode for Queen Anne: Eternal source of Light divine.* PURCELL: *Come ye sons of art: Sound the trumpet; Chaconne. Indian Queen: Trumpet overture; Intrada; Air. King Arthur: Trumpet tune.* MOLTER: *Concerto No. 2 in D.*
*** Sony Dig. MK 39061 [id.].

Although Edita Gruberová makes an important contribution to the success of this anthology, it must be listed here, rather than in the vocal section, for Wynton Marsalis is clearly the star. His superb, sometimes slightly restrained virtuosity is ideal for this programme and his cool sense of classical style brings consistently memorable results. Marsalis scales down his tone superbly to match the oboes in the delightful Fasch *Concerto* (especially as they are backwardly balanced), and he plays the *Sonatas* of Torelli and the sharply characterized Purcell miniatures with winning finesse. With Edita Gruberová he achieves a complete symbiosis in *Sound the trumpet* from *Come ye sons of art*, with the voice and instrumental melismas uncannily imitative; and he forms a comparable partnership in the two Handel arias, where Gruberová's agile and beautifully focused singing is hardly less admirable. The recording balance is excellent and its presence makes the trumpet very tangible, especially in the upper tessitura of the Molter *Concerto*, where the solo playing makes the hairs at the nape of one's neck tingle.

Messiter, Malcolm (oboe), Guildhall String Ens.

Baroque oboe concertos: VIVALDI: *Concertos: in C, RV 447; in D min., RV 454.* HANDEL: *Concerto No. 3 in G min., HWV 287.* MARCELLO: *Concerto in D min.* J. S. BACH: *Concerto in G min., BWV 1056.* ALBINONI: *Concerto in D min., Op. 9/2.*
*** BMG/RCA Dig. RD 60224; *RK 60224* [60224-2-RC].

Although authenticists will resist the warm string textures, this is a generous collection with solo playing of great finesse. Messiter's timbre and phrasing in slow movements are quite ravishing, notably in the Marcello, the Vivaldi, RV 454, and in the Albinoni, but also in the superb central cantilena of the Bach transcription.

Montreal Symphony Orchestra, Charles Dutoit

'Fête à la française': CHABRIER: *Joyeuse marche; España* (rhapsody). DUKAS: *L'apprenti sorcier.* SATIE: *Gymnopédies 1 and 2.* SAINT-SAËNS: *Samson et Dalila: Air and Danse bacchanale.* BIZET: *Jeux d'enfants.* THOMAS: *Overture: Raymond.* IBERT: *Divertissement.*
*** Decca Dig. 421 527-2 [id.].

A nicely organized programme, opening vivaciously with Chabrier's *Joyeuse marche* and closing with a gloriously uninhibited account of the finale of Ibert's *Divertissement*, police-whistle and all. *L'apprenti sorcier* has a genial warmth rather than the last degree of excitement, although no one could complain that Saint-Saëns's *Bacchanale* lacked adrenalin. The *Gymnopédies* have a wistfully gentle melancholy, and Bizet's *Jeux d'enfants* a fine sense of style; while Thomas's *Raymond Overture* has all the gusto of the bandstand. The performance of *España* does not erase memories of Sir Thomas Beecham, but it certainly does not lack rhythmic élan. First-class Decca sound, brightly vivid to suit the music.

'Famous overtures': MENDELSSOHN: *The Hebrides (Fingal's Cave); A Midsummer Night's Dream.* SUPPÉ: *Light cavalry; Poet and peasant.* BERLIOZ: *Le Corsaire.* RIMSKY-KORSAKOV: *Russian Easter festival overture.* GERSHWIN: *Cuban overture.*
(M) *** Decca Dig. 430 741-2; *430 741-4* [id.].

The acoustics of Saint-Eustache in Montreal are ideal for Mendelssohn's dancing strings and luminous woodwind in *A Midsummer Night's Dream overture* and *Fingal's Cave* is suitably romantic. Dutoit finds dignity for the opening of *Poet and peasant* and plenty of dash for *Light cavalry*; Gershwin's *Cuban overture*, too, is appropriately racy. His account of the *Russian Easter festival overture* is strong with a fine climax. Here the colourful Montreal sound brings iridescent orchestral detail but the music's Russian ardour does not blossom so expansively here as in some versions. Nevertheless this collection is generous and the sound undoubtedly in the demonstration class.

I Musici

ALBINONI: *Adagio in G min.* (arr. Giazotto). BEETHOVEN: *Minuet in G, WoO 10/2.* BOCCHERINI: *Quintet in E, Op. 11/5: Minuet.* HAYDN (attrib.): *Quartet, Op. 3/5; Serenade.* MOZART: *Serenade No. 13 in G* (*Eine kleine Nachtmusik*), *K.525.* PACHELBEL: *Canon.*
*** Ph. Dig. 410 606-2 [id.].

An exceptionally successful concert, recorded with remarkable naturalness and realism. The compact disc is very believable indeed. The playing combines warmth and freshness, and the oft-played Mozart *Night music* has no suggestion whatsoever of routine: it combines elegance, warmth and sparkle. The Boccherini *Minuet* and (especially) the Hofstetter (attrib. Haydn) *Serenade* have an engaging lightness of touch.

BARTÓK: *Rumanian folk dances* (with R. Michelucci). BRITTEN: *Simple Symphony, Op. 4.* HINDEMITH: *Trauermusik for viola and strings* (with Cino Ghedin). MARTIN: *Études.* NIELSEN: *Little Suite, Op. 1.* ROUSSEL: *Sinfonietta, Op. 52.*

(M) **(*) Ph. 426 669-2; *426 669-4* [id.].

A valuable anthology. The Britten *Simple Symphony*, recorded in 1962, is perhaps the least convincing and needs more tonal bloom, but otherwise few qualifications need be made. The Frank Martin *Studies* are played marvellously: tone is always in focus and everyone is in the middle of the note, so that the timbre is particularly rich and full. I Musici play these and most of the other pieces with tremendous virtuosity; the Hindemith *Funeral music*, written in a few hours on the death of King George V, is given with real feeling. The first movement of the Nielsen is a bit on the fast side, but otherwise this record gives much pleasure, especially the attractive account of the Roussel *Sinfonietta*. The recordings are mostly from 1968 and come up very well indeed.

National Philharmonic Orchestra, Leopold Stokowski

'Stokowski showcase': Overtures: BEETHOVEN: *Leonora No. 3.* MOZART: *Don Giovanni* (arr. Stokowski). SCHUBERT: *Rosamunde (Die Zauberharfe).* BERLIOZ: *Le carnaval romain.* ROSSINI: *William Tell.* TCHAIKOVSKY: *Solitude, Op. 73/6.* SOUSA: *The Stars and Stripes forever* (both arr. Stokowski). CHABRIER: *España.* SAINT-SAËNS: *Danse macabre.* IPPOLITOV-IVANOV: *Caucasian sketches: Procession of the Sardar.*
(M) *** EMI CDM7 64140-2.

Stokowski's collection of overtures dates from just before his ninety-fourth birthday – yet the electricity crackles throughout and his charisma is apparent in every bar. The Beethoven is immensely dramatic – the distanced trumpet especially effective – while *Rosamunde* combines high romanticism with affectionate warmth. Dissatisfied with Mozart's ending to *Don Giovanni*, Stokowski extends this piece to include music from the opera's finale. The pacing in *William Tell* is fast, but here as elsewhere the players obviously relish the experience and, if ensemble slips a little, the music-making is enjoyably infectious. The extra items, added for the 76-minute CD programme, were recorded at about the same time and are just as charismatic, especially *Danse macabre* (with Sidney Sax the seductive violin soloist) and the exhilarating *Stars and Stripes forever*, re-scored by the conductor to include an *ad lib.* xylophone. Full, resonant sound.

NBC Symphony Orchestra, Arturo Toscanini

French music: FRANCK: *Symphony in D min.* DEBUSSY: *Marche écossaise.* MEYERBEER: *Prologue Dinorah.* ROUSSEL: *Le festin de l'araignée, Op. 17.*
(***) Dell'Arte mono CD DA 9021 [id.].

The recording of the Franck *Symphony* comes from 1946; an earlier account in the Franklyn Mint Toscanini LP edition gave two movements from a 1940 performance, but the present version is making its first appearance, at least on this side of the Atlantic. The Roussel comes from the same year; the Meyerbeer and Debussy are earlier, from 1938 and 1940 respectively, and we are offered the *Prologue* to the Meyerbeer rather than a straightforward overture, as it includes extensive passages for chorus. The playing is pretty dazzling throughout, though the Roussel is rather spoilt by too hurried a tempo for the first animated section (the *Entry of the Ants*) and then again at the *Funeral of the Day-Fly*. The Franck is a marvellously strong performance. As always with these dry NBC recordings, the sound calls for a tolerance that is well worth extending for the sake of music-making which has much charisma.

'The Toscanini collection': BEETHOVEN: *Leonora overture No. 3.* VERDI: *Nabucco: Va pensiero* (with Westminster Ch.). SMETANA: *Má Vlast: Vltava.* BERLIOZ: *Roméo et Juliette: Queen Mab scherzo.* BRAHMS: *Academic festival overture.* WAGNER: *Die Walküre: Ride of the Valkyries.* PUCCINI: *La Bohème: Ehi! Rodolfo!; O soave fanciulla* (with Albanese, Peerce, Cehanovsky, Moscona, Valentino). ROSSINI: *William Tell: Overture.*
(BB) (**(*)) BMG/RCA VD 60340; *VK 60340* [60340-2-RV; *60340-4-RV*].

This generous limited-edition super-bargain sampler for the BMG/RCA Toscanini Edition offers 68 minutes of Toscanini recordings. It is one of the tragedies of recording history that the great Italian maestro did not have a producer with the strength of personality of a Walter Legge to supervise his recordings. (Indeed, Elisabeth Schwarzkopf has recounted the occasion when her husband and Toscanini eventually met and – to her dismay – Legge fearlessly criticized the

Toscanini recorded legacy. Toscanini's response was surprisingly positive, and he agreed, almost ruefully, that perhaps he had needed someone of Legge's calibre as his producer.) However, we have to accept what there is and that includes the execrably dry sounds afforded by the notorious Studio 8-H, which is used for the Beethoven and Brahms *Overtures* and the *La Bohème* excerpt, totally without atmosphere. Verdi's *Va pensiero*, with its clear chorus, and Smetana's *Vltava* sound rather better, although the latter has some distortion. The Carnegie Hall recordings are more attractive, notably the marvellously played *Queen Mab scherzo* and the brilliantly charismatic *William Tell overture.*

New York Trumpet Ensemble, 'Y' Chamber Orchestra, Schwarz

'The sound of trumpets': ALTENBURG: *Concerto in D for 7 trumpets.* VIVALDI: *Double trumpet concerto, RV 537.* BIBER: *Sonata (Sancti Polycarpi).* TORELLI: *Sonata a 5.* TELEMANN: *Concerto in D.*
**(*) Delos Dig. D/CD 3002 [id.].

As we know from his outstanding version of the Haydn *Trumpet concerto*, Gerard Schwarz is an accomplished soloist and musician, and both the Telemann and Vivaldi performances (where he is joined by Norman Smith) are first class. The Altenburg *Concerto* features seven soloists, the Biber *Sonata* eight in two antiphonal groups. Both come off splendidly, neither being too long to outstay its welcome. The balance places the brass well forward, but the chamber orchestra is backward, and detail might have been better defined. Otherwise the sound is very good.

Orchestra of the Age of Enlightenment & LPO

(orchestral members)

'Glyndebourne wind serenades' (cond. (i) Jonathan Dove; (ii) Anthony Pay; (iii) Andrew Parrott): Arrangements of MOZART: (i) DOVE: *Figures in the garden (Le nozze di Figaro).* (ii) OSBORNE: *Arabian nights (Così fan tutte).* (iii) HARVEY: *Serenade in homage to Mozart (Die Zauberflöte).* OLIVER: *Character pieces for wind octet derived from Metastasio's La clemenza di Tito.* SAXON: *Paraphrase on Mozart's Idomeneo.*
*** EMI Dig. CDC7 54424-2 [id.].

These five wind serenades were commissioned for alfresco performance at Glyndebourne before each of the Mozart operas being given there in Mozart bicentenary year, 1991. Each of the composers takes an individual line, with Saxton providing a brilliant encapsulation of *Idmoneneo*, sharply characterized in 16 tiny sections, lasting in all only 10 minutes. Stephen Oliver does much the same with *La clemenza di Tito* only more grittily, while Jonathan Harvey provides a freer reflection on *Zauberflöte.* Nigel Osborne's *Arabian nights* could hardly be farther removed from the world of *Così fan tutte*, but at Glyndebourne the serenade that worked by far the best as pre-Mozartian entertainment was Jonathan Dove's *Figures in the garden*, evoking *Figaro.* The longest and lightest of the serenades, involving seven crisply constructed movements, it wittily hit the right targets amid the popping of champagne corks, and it works well on record too. The others are valuable more as visiting cards for their respective composers. They are all beautifully performed by the original players, members of OAE for the Dove and Osborne, the London Philharmonic in the rest.

L'Orchestre de la Suisse Romande, Ernest Ansermet

Ernest Ansermet Edition: DEBUSSY: *La Mer; Rhapsody for clarinet and orchestra* (with Robert Gugholz (clarinet)). *Suite bergamasque: Clair de lune; Petite suite. Prélude à l'après-midi d'un faune; Jeux* (433 711-2). *Images pour orchestre; Printemps; Nocturnes* (with chorus) (433 712-2). BERLIOZ: *Symphonie fantastique; Overtures: Le Corsaire; Le carnaval romain. Damnation de Faust: Danse des Sylphes; Marche hongoise* (433 713-2). DUKAS: *L'apprenti sorcier; La péri* (with *Fanfare*). DEBUSSY: *La boîte à joujoux* (433 714-2). CHAUSSON: *Symphony in B flat.* FAURÉ: *Pelléas et Mélisande* (suite); *Pénélope: Prélude. Masques et bergamasques* (433 715-2). RAVEL: *Boléro; Valses nobles et sentimentales; Rapsodie espagnole. Pavane pour une infante*

défunte; Ma Mère l'Oye (suite) (433 716-2). *Daphnis et Chloé* (complete ballet; with SRO Ch.); *Alborada del gracioso; La valse* (433 717-2). FRANCK: *Symphony in D min.; Le chasseur maudit; Les Éolides.* BERLIOZ: *Overture Béatrice et Bénédict* (433 718-2). ROUSSEL: *Le festin de l'araignée; Symphonies Nos. 3 in G min., Op. 42; 4 in A, Op. 53* (433 719-2). CHABRIER: *España. Suite pastorale; Joyeuse marche; Le Roi malgré lui: Danse slave; Fête polonaise.* LALO: *Rapsodie pour orchestre; Scherzo pour orchestre; Le Roi d'Ys: Overture* (433 720-2). BIZET: *Symphony in C; Jeux d'enfants; La jolie fille de Perth (suite).* RAVEL: *Le tombeau de Couperin* (433 721-2). BIZET: *Carmen: extended suite; L'Arlésienne: suites Nos. 1–2. Overture: Patrie* (433 722-2).
(M) **(*) Decca 433 803-2 (12) [id.].

In the LP era and the early days of stereo – the 1950s and 1960s – Ansermet was a top recording star. He had begun his career with Diaghilev's Ballets Russes and it was no accident that his celebrated mono *Petrouchka* made an enormous first impression, as much for the crystalline clarity of the orchestral sound as for the actual performance. During the following years a unique creative partnership was established between the Swiss mathematician/conductor and the various Decca recording teams, which produced an astonishing series of successful records in the Victoria Hall, Geneva. By good fortune this had just the right acoustics for the Ansermet sound, just as St Eustache in Montreal was to prove an ideal ambience for the work of Charles Dutoit in the CD era of the 1980s. Ansermet's achievement in terms of commercial and (usually) critical success – at least in Germany and the English-speaking countries – might be compared to that of Marriner and the ASMF who, in their halcyon days, almost never received a bad notice. Although one of his dazzling first mono LPs (Rossini/Respighi's *La boutique fantastique*), made with the LSO in Kingsway Hall, London, demonstrated what marvellous results he could obtain with a really crack orchestra, Ansermet, endearingly, stayed faithful to the players of L'Orchestra de la Suisse Romande, even if in terms of finesse and polish of ensemble they were unable to match the refinement of the greatest international ensembles. But what they could do – with Ansermet at the helm – was to bring every score to tingling life, usually with the tension sustained from the first note to the last. In his introduction to the Ansermet Edition, François Hudry, summing up the conductor's achievement, notes 'the extraordinary feeling he shows for tempo, his rhythmic energy, his precise sense of orchestral colour and his acute ear for musical form'. Ansermet himself described his interpretations as a search for 'the correct feeling'. All the music included here is French, repertoire about which he cared deeply, yet French critical opinion, which – like the Latin countries – found his music-making cold, summed up his art more clinically as '*le poésie de l'exactitude*'. But that is to miss the point: above all, he achieves spontaneity and conveys commitment, plus a special kind of dedication.

We have enjoyed listening through these records in sequence (although they are all available separately): the advantage of so doing is that one quickly adjusts to the characteristic thinness on the high violins which afflicts many early Decca stereo records; in every other way they sound remarkably modern. Among the Debussy recordings, *La boîte à joujoux* (1957) stands out for its imaginative detail, and as this is coupled with Dukas's *La Péri* (1958), which Ansermet also does very sympathetically (including the vibrant introductory *Fanfare*), plus the first-class 1963 *L'apprenti sorcier*, this disc can certainly be individually recommended. The third of the conductor's three *La Mer*s (1964) was an unfortunate choice: it is not as well played as the second, though naturally the orchestral sound is fuller, with a resonant bass. The performance is straightforward but the horns are not perfectly in tune, and the cello melody in *De l'aube à midi* is an unhappy moment from the point of view of true intonation. *Printemps* is more successful, direct and unmannered, while *Jeux* has plenty of atmosphere and is one of Ansermet's finest Debussy performances; the *Nocturnes* are perfectly acceptable, though *Sirènes* is a bit lack-lustre. There must also be reservations about the *Petite suite*, where the weakness of intonation may be found distracting, although the performance is winningly characterful. This comment might also apply to the *Images* (not as subtle as his earlier, mono version) and with some poor wind intonation in *Rondes de printemps*, but full of vitality.

One of the surprises was the 1967 *Symphonie fantasque*, a much more convincing and exciting performance than we had remembered, and stunningly recorded. Indeed the *Marche au supplice* has great impact and in the finale the abrasively pungent woodwind sounds that the SRO produces have a demonic potency. The overtures, too, are impressively vivid (the brass in the jubilant coda of *Le carnaval romain* is very arresting indeed), but the SRO do not quite command the requisite virtuosity and élan this music calls for. Ansermet's account of Chausson's only *Symphony* is warmly sympathetic and the 1967 recording sounds well; the

Fauré couplings show the conductor and his orchestra at their finest, with sympathetic and stylish accounts of the charming *Masques et bergamasques* and the *Pelléas* incidental music, while the noble *Prélude* to *Pénélope* is hardly less impressive. This was recorded earlier (1961) but the ear would hardly guess.

The Ravel is something of a mixed bag. The complete *Daphnis et Chloé*, although spectacularly engineered, misses the rapture and magic of the very finest versions. Elsewhere the playing lacks the last ounce of polish and refinement, although the 1963 *Boléro* has splendid impetus (and sound), as has the excellent *La valse*. The *Rapsodie espagnole* is early (1957) but, despite thin violins, has – like *Ma Mère l'Oye* – that translucent clarity of texture for which the conductor was famous. The Franck *Symphony* is dramatic enough, although tension does tend to be relaxed between climaxes and the orchestral playing is wanting in finesse. *Le chausseur maudit* is splendidly vibrant and *Les Éolides* also comes off well. The Roussel collection is one of the most valuable discs of all. *Le festin de l'araignée* ('The spider's feast') is astonishingly successful stereo although it dates from 1964, and the playing has plenty of character and atmosphere. The two *Symphonies* are even stronger. Again the recording is genuine early stereo (1956) and remarkably good for its date. The performances are suitably abrasive, with the odd scruffy edges, but thoroughly convincing. The Chabrier/Lalo coupling (75 minutes) is hardly less valuable. The 1964 Chabrier recordings are extremely brilliant and, if *España* has not quite the insouciant rhythmic life of Beecham and Paray, the rest of the programme is attractively bright-eyed, with the *Danse slave* particularly invigorating. The *Suite pastorale* is strongly characterized and the restrained *Sous bois* has more lambent atmosphere than with Paray. Anyone joining Lalo's *Rapsodie* just after the opening would think themselves in the world of Rimsky-Korsakov. It is an attractively exotic piece and the *Scherzo* has plenty of character too. Ansermet has their measure and the 1966/68 recording sounds full and clean.

The Bizet recordings are also attractive, particularly the CD including the *Symphony*, where the first movement is characteristically neat and precise, the slow movement cool and poised and the finale animated, if without Marriner's champagne-like gaiety. Both *La jolie fille de Perth* and *Jeux d'enfants* are very nicely done, with clean string-playing and vivid wind-colours, and the 1960 recording is full, with a crisp focus. The *L'Arlésienne* and *Carmen* recordings are earlier (1958) and the violins have a touch of glare. There is plenty of personality in the characterization, but the brash sound affects the livelier *Carmen* items, and Ansermet's percussion player (only too clearly reproduced) gets left behind once or twice.

Orchestre de Paris, (i) Sir John Barbirolli or (ii) Serge Baudo

'French music': (i) DEBUSSY: *La Mer; Nocturnes* (with female chorus). (ii) RAVEL: *Ma Mère l'Oye: suite*. FAURÉ: *Dolly, Op. 56. Masques et bergamasques; Pelléas et Mélisande: suite*. ROUSSEL: *Bacchus et Ariane: suite*. MESSIAEN: *Les offrandes oubliées*.
(B) *** EMI CZS7 62669-2 (2) [Ang. CDMB 62669].

As can be seen, Serge Baudo has the lion's share of this highly recommendable collection, admirably recorded in the Paris Salle Wagram in 1968–9 and now available in EMI's very competitive French 'two for the price of one' series. His performances are perceptive and sensitive and the Orchestre de Paris plays beautifully. Barbirolli's music-making has plenty of sensuous warmth too, but his earlier, Hallé version of *La Mer* has more grip. Nevertheless the Fauré, Messiaen and Roussel items (all discussed separately under their individual composers) make this concert well worth having. Incidentally, the French documentation by Jean Roy is worth taking the trouble to translate: it is more colourful and often has more of interest to say about the music than the English notes by Barry Millington.

Osipov State Russian Folk Orchestra, Vitaly Gnutov

'Balalaika favourites': BUDASHIN: *Fantasy on two folk songs*. arr. GORODOVSKAYA: *At sunrise*. KULIKOV: *The Linden tree*. OSIPOV: *Kamarinskaya*. MIKHAILOV/SHALAYEV: *Fantasy on Volga melodies*. ANDREYEV: *In the moonlight; Under the apple tree; Waltz of the faun*. SOLOVIEV/SEDOY: *Midnight in Moscow*. TCHAIKOVSKY: *Dance of the comedians*. SHISHAKOV: *The living room*. arr. MOSSOLOV: *Evening bells*. arr. POPONOV: *My dear friend, please visit me*. RIMSKY-KORSAKOV: *Flight of the bumble-bee*.

❀ (M) *** Mercury 432 000-2 [id.].

The Mercury recording team visited Moscow in 1962 in order to make the first recordings produced in the Soviet Union by Western engineers since the Revolution. Wilma Cozart Fine, the recording director, recalls that every morning, more in hope than expectation, they would set up their equipment (although they lacked official permission from the bureaucracy, because of arguments over royalty rights), and every morning the musicians would appear, arriving in all kinds of conveyances and carrying balalaikas plus other instruments; and, full of enthusiasm, the sessions would begin. The spirit of that unique occasion is captured wonderfully here – analogue atmosphere at its best. The rippling waves of balalaika sound, the accordion solos, the exhilarating accelerandos and crescendos that mark the style of this music-making: all are recorded with wonderful immediacy. Whether in the shimmering web of sound of *The Linden tree* or *Evening bells*, the sparkle of the folksongs or the sheer bravura of items like *In the moonlight*, which gets steadily faster and louder, or in Rimsky's famous piece (sounding like a hive full of bumble-bees), this is irresistible, and the recording is superbly real in its CD format.

Oslo Philharmonic Orchestra, Mariss Jansons

Concert: TCHAIKOVSKY: *Overture 1812, Op. 49.* DUKAS: *L'apprenti sorcier (The sorcerer's apprentice).* SMETANA: *Má Vlast: Vltava.* DVOŘÁK: *Scherzo capriccioso, Op. 66.* MUSSORGSKY: *Night on a bare mountain* (completed & orch. Ravel).
(M) *** EMI Dig. CDD7 64191-2 [id.]; *ET 764291-4.*

A splendid collection. Five top orchestral favourites – and deservedly so – all given performances as fine as any in the catalogue (and better than most) and top-drawer EMI sound. The opening *1812* combines brilliance with a dignified grandiloquence and the canon are superbly focused at the close. The Dukas is among our top choices for this ever-fresh masterpiece; it is splendidly paced and really exciting, while Smetana's *Vltava* and the Mussorgsky/Rimsky-Korsakov *Night on a bare mountain* are full of evocation and colour. The *Scherzo capriccioso* has great élan and a particularly affectionate central episode played most beautifully; the recording is superb, as it is in the Dukas and Mussorgsky with their spectacular climaxes. This record would be a splendid gift for a relative newcomer to classical music, but will equally satisfy the experienced collector.

Paris Conservatoire Orchestra

Paris Conservatoire Orchestra (conducted by (i) Piero Coppola, (ii) Philippe Gaubert, (iii) André Messager, (iv) Bruno Walter, (v) with Paris Conservatoire Ch.): DEBUSSY: (i; v) *Nocturnes;* (ii) *Nuages et Fêtes;* (i) *Le martyre de St Sébastien;* (i) *La mer.* CHAUSSON: (i) *Symphony.* DUKAS: (ii) *La péri; L'apprenti sorcier.* FAURÉ: *Pelléas et Mélisande: Sicilienne.* HANDEL: *Concerto grosso in B min., Op. 6/12.* D'INDY: (i) *Istar.* LALO: (i) *Namouna – Suite No. 1.* MOZART: Overtures: (i) *Le nozze di Figaro;* (iv) *Die Zauberflöte.* RAVEL: (i) *Daphnis et Chloë: suite no 2; Ma Mère l'Oye: suite;* (ii) *La valse.* RIMSKY-KORSAKOV: (ii) *Sheherazade.* SAINT-SAËNS: (iii) *Le rouet d'Omphale. Overture Le Déluge.* SCHUMANN: (iv) *Symphony No. 4.* WAGNER: (i) *Die Meistersinger: Overture.* WEBER: (iv) *Die Freischütz: Overture.*
(M) (***) Vogue Contrepoint mono 665001 (6) [id.].

This is a set that could easily be overlooked in the flood of historical reissues. It is of quite exceptional interest to all who care about French music and its tradition. The six CDs encompass the period in between the two wars; the first is André Messager's 1918 record of the overture to Saint-Saëns's oratorio *Le Déluge*, the last are Coppola's *Nocturnes* and Bruno Walter's Handel, both 1938. Those who know the Paris Conservatoire in its post-war days will have no idea of its earlier quality. Piero Coppola's performances of the *Nocturnes*, *Le martyre* and *La mer* are quite thrilling; the orchestra was obviously a virtuoso body in 1932 when the latter was made. Amazingly, there is not all that much to choose between it and Toscanini's celebrated 1935 BBC account. *Le martyre* is more concentrated in atmosphere than almost any successor – with the possible exception of Cantelli's Philharmonia disc. Alas, neither his *Valses nobles et sentimentales* nor his *Alborada del gracioso* are included – nor, for that matter, his evocative account of *Ibéria*. Philippe Gaubert's account of Dukas's *Poeme dansé*, *La péri* (minus the *Fanfare*) is certainly more atmospheric than the celebrated Ansermet record and sounds remarkably good for its age too. His *Sheherazade*, however, is not in the same class. Bruno

Walter was a great admirer of this orchestra, who gave him a haven from Nazi persecution, and he gets a beautifully silky, aristocratic tone from them in the Handel *B minor Concerto grosso.* The set even affords an opportunity of comparing Gaubert and Coppola, recorded ten years apart, in the first two Debussy *Nocturnes.* The presentation though adequate, does not do the set the fullest justice.

Parley of Instruments, Roy Goodman

'Purcell's London': KELLER: *Trumpet sonata No. 1 in D.* MATTEIS: *Divisions on a ground in D min.* BALTZAR: *Pavan and Galliard in C.* BLOW: *Chaconne a 4 in G.* ECCLES: *The Judgement of Paris: Symphony for Mercury.* CROFT: *The Twin rivals:* suite. PURCELL: *Trumpet tune in C (Cibell).* ANON.: *Sonata in D (con concertino).*
*** Hyp. Dig. CDA 66108; *KA 66108* [id.].

All this music emerged in London towards the close of the seventeenth century and the fascinating titles do not disappoint: Croft's suite is most attractive, as is Eccles' *Symphony for Mercury.* Purcell makes his own appearance in a characteristic trumpet piece, splendidly played (as is the Keller *Sonata*) by Crispian Steele-Perkins. The Matteis variations are highly inventive and Blow's *Chaconne* is equally individual. All in all a diverse and entertaining mix, very well presented, though the recording could be better defined in the bass.

Perahia, Murray (piano)

'The art of Murray Perahia': BARTÓK: *Sonata for 2 pianos & percussion.* BRAHMS: *Variations on a theme by Haydn* (for 2 pianos), *Op. 60* (with Solti, Corkhill & Glennie). BEETHOVEN: *Piano concerto No. 5 (Emperor)* (with Concg. O, Haitink); *Piano sonatas Nos. 7 in D, Op. 10/3; 23 (Appassionata).* BRAHMS: *Piano quartet No. 1 in G min., Op. 15* (with members of Amadeus Qt); *Rhapsody in B min., Op. 79/1.* CHOPIN: *Piano sonatas Nos. 2 in B flat min. (Funeral march); 3 in B min., Op. 48.* GRIEG: *Piano concerto in A min.* SCHUMANN: *Piano concerto in A min.* (both with Bavarian RSO, C. Davis). MENDELSSOHN: *Piano concertos Nos. 1–2* (with ASMF, Marriner); *Prelude & fugue, Op. 35/1; Rondo capriccioso, Op. 14; Variations sérieuses, Op. 54; Piano sonata, Op. 61.* SCHUBERT: *Wanderer fantasia, Op. 15; Impromptu in E flat, D.899/2.* SCHUMANN: *Fantasia in C, Op. 17; Études symphoniques, Op. 13,* with posthumous *Études; Papillons, Op. 2; 3 Fantasiestücke, Op. 12.* LISZT: *Consolation No. 3; Rapsodie espagnole.*
(M) *** Sony Dig./Analogue SX11K 48153 (11).

This box offers many of Perahia's most distinguished recordings, nearly all of them digital (the Chopin *Sonatas*, Mendelssohn *Concertos* and the major Schumann pieces are analogue but here the sound is always fully acceptable, with the CD transfers adding presence without degrading the quality). Of the eleven CDs, ten are simple reissues in their original packaging (which means that we get three Mendelssohn piano works twice!), and there is a bonus recital disc which, apart from including only a single movement from Beethoven's *Tempest Piano sonata*, Op. 31/2, is an attractive mixture, obviously intended to tempt the listener into exploring further among Perahia's recordings. The set is offered at upper mid-price but this is a limited edition; we are assured that it should remain available during the lifetime of this book, but prospective purchasers should not delay too long.

Perlman, Itzhak (violin)

Spanish music: SARASATE: *Carmen fantasy* (with RPO, Foster); *Zigeunerweisen* (with Pittsburgh SO, Previn). *Danzas españolas: Malagueña; Habanera, Op. 21/1–2; Playera and Zapateado, Op. 23; Spanish dance, Op. 26/8. Caprice basque, Op. 24; Romanza andaluza, Op. 22.* FALLA, arr. KOCHANSKI: *Suite populaire espagnole.* GRANADOS: *Spanish dance.* HALFFTER: *Danza de la gitana.* ALBÉNIZ: *Malagueña, Op. 165/5* (all with Samuel Sanders, piano).
(M) *** EMI CDM7 63533-2.

Perlman's dazzling account of Sarasate's *Carmen fantasy* is offered here with a collection of popular Spanish pieces. Perlman demonstrates a delight in virtuosity in the most joyful way, but some may feel that the balance is a shade too close, and this effect is emphasized somewhat on CD.

Petershof Orchestra, St Petersburg, Leo Korkin

'Music at Pavlovsk Station: The Birth of the Russian orchestra': DARGOMIZHSKY: *Kazatchok.* TCHAIKOVSKY: *Nocturne; Humoresque.* GUNGL: *Onward march; Polka.* LABITZKY: *Idyll.* ALIABIEV: *Morning and evening overture.* GLINKA: *Valse-Fantasy.* RUBINSTEIN: *Melody.* J. STRAUSS, Jnr: *Horse guard march; The Neva polka; The farewell to St Petersburg.*
*** Opus Dig. OPS 58 9204 [id.].

The motivation for Tchaikovsky's hurried entry into the newly opened St Petersburg Conservatoire to play Glinka's *Russlan and Ludmilla overture* through on the piano, in order to ensure that it was the first music heard in the building, is readily shown by this interesting and entertaining concert. Before Glinka (who is represented here by the charming *Valse-Fantasy*) there was virtually no Russian orchestral music. Pavlovsky station was the terminus of a newly built line from St Petersburg which the Tsar inaugurated in 1838 with the construction of a Russian 'Vauxhall' pleasure gardens, where on Sundays the first Russian orchestral concerts were given. The orchestra soon became the principal attraction, and Gungl and, later, Johann Strauss came to conduct there. It was Russia's only professional group of musicians until the St Petersburg Conservatoire opened in 1861. Here is a typical Sunday concert which might have been heard in Pavlosky in the 1840s and 1850s. Tchaikovsky is indelibly represented by the delightfully catchy *Humoresque* (later to be used by Stravinsky in *Le baiser de la fée*), and all this music is readily tuneful, played with a fine sense of style and admirably recorded.

Petri, Michala, (recorder) ASMF

Recorder concertos (directed I. Brown): VIVALDI: *Sopranino recorder concerto in C, RV 443.* SAMMARTINI: *Descant recorder concerto in F.* TELEMANN: *Treble recorder concerto in C.* HANDEL: *Treble recorder concerto in F* (arr. of *Organ concerto, Op. 4/5*).
*** Ph. 400 075-2 [id.].

Michala Petri plays her various recorders with enviable skill, and her nimble piping creates some delightful sounds in these four attractively inventive concertos. This is not a record to be played all at once; taken in sections, it has unfailing charm; the sound is of demonstration quality. The CD retains the analogue ambient warmth, while detail seems marginally cleaner.

'English concertos' (directed K. Sillito): BABEL: *Concerto in C for descant recorder, Op. 3/1.* HANDEL: *Concerto in B flat for treble recorder and bassoon, Op. 4/6* (with G. Sheene). BASTON: *Concerto No. 2 for descant recorder in D.* JACOB: *Suite for treble recorder and strings.*
❀ *** Ph. Dig. 411 056-2 [id.].

The *Concerto* by William Babel (*c.* 1690–1723) is a delight, with Petri's sparkling performance of the outer movements full of good humour and high spirits, matched by Kenneth Sillito's alert accompaniments. The Handel is yet another arrangement of Op. 4/6, with the organ part felicitously re-scored for recorder and bassoon. The two instruments are nicely balanced and thus a familiar work is given an attractive new look. John Baston's *Concerto* has individuality and charm, and the finale is quirkily infectious. Gordon Jacob's *Suite* of seven movements balances a gentle bitter-sweet melancholy in the lyrical writing with a rumbustious, extrovert quality in the dances. Altogether a highly rewarding concert, beautifully played and recorded.

Philadelphia Orchestra, Leopold Stokowski

'Fantasia': BACH, orch. Stokowski: *Toccata and Fugue in D min.* DUKAS: *L'apprenti sorcier.* MUSSORGSKY, arr. Stokowski: *A Night on the Bare Mountain.* STRAVINSKY: *The Rite of spring.* TCHAIKOVSKY: *Nutcracker Suite.*
(M) (***) Pearl mono GEMMCD 4988.

A self-recommending disc for the older generation – and, given the excellently refurbished VHS video of the Disney film, the younger generations too. (Incidentally, the early stereo CDs of the soundtrack are disappointingly shrill.) *The Rite of spring* comes from 1929–30 and the

Nutcracker from as early as 1926, though one would never believe it. Everything Stokowski did at this period was full of character, and the engineers obviously performed miracles. The latest recording is Stokowski's amazing arrangement of *A Night on the Bare Mountain*, which dates from 1940. Such is the colour and richness of sonority Stokowski evokes from the fabulous Philadelphians that surface noise and other limitations are completely forgotten. The performances are too familiar to need detailed comment, though it is worth recalling that his *Rite* was infinitely more masterly and even more exciting than Stravinsky's own account, made at much the same time. Collectors with wide-ranging equipment (and even those without) will be surprised how much sense of presence the Victor engineers managed to get on to wax in those days. The transfers are very good.

Philharmonia Orchestra, Herbert von Karajan

BARTÓK: *Concerto for Orchestra; Music for strings, percussion and celesta.* BRITTEN: *Variations on a theme of Frank Bridge.* DEBUSSY: *La Mer.* HANDEL arr. HARTY: *Water music.* KODÁLY: *Háry János suite.* RAVEL: *Rapsodie espagnol.* SIBELIUS: *Finlandia; Symphonies Nos. 4, 6 & 7; Tapiola.* VAUGHAN WILLIAMS: *Fantasia on a theme of Thomas Tallis.*
❀ (M) (***) EMI mono CMS7 63464-2 (4).

Of the many Karajan/Philharmonia recordings published by EMI this is the one you should on no account miss. The Vaughan Williams and the Britten have hardly ever been played more beautifully, and they are recorded marvellously. Karajan's mid-1950s Sibelius is leaner and more austere than his later versions with the Berlin orchestra (and earned the composer's plaudits). Only No. 7 disappoints, and it is a pity that his earlier No. 5 did not replace it. Also there is something special about the Bartók, which was almost (but not quite) a first recording: Harold Byrns just beat him to it; but, like the Bartók *Concerto*, it has the excitement of discovery.

Philharmonia Orchestra, Otto Klemperer

'Armchair concert': MOZART: *Die Zauberflöte: Overture.* SCHUMANN: *Piano concerto in A min.* (with Annie Fischer). MENDELSSOHN: *Symphony No. 4 (Italian).*
(M) *** EMI CDM7 64448-2 [id.].

It is particularly good to have Annie Fischer's long-buried reading of the Schumann *Piano concerto* as the concertante centrepiece of the Klemperer disc in EMI's 'Armchair Concert' series. Soloist and conductor combine clarity and strength with poetry, and Klemperer's resilient and purposeful reading of the *Italian Symphony* (one the finest and most revealing of all his recorded performances) is equally refreshing, clean and well pointed at measured speeds that are never sluggish. The Philharmonia playing is peerless and the sound very good.

Philharmonia Orchestra, Efrem Kurtz

'Famous marches' (or (i) O de Liège, Paul Strauss): VERDI: *Aida: Triumphal march.* PROKOFIEV: *Love for 3 oranges: March.* RIMSKY-KORSAKOV: *Le coq d'or: Bridal procession.* MEYERBEER: *Le Prophète: Coronation march.* BERLIOZ: *Damnation de Faust: Marche hongroise.* SOUSA: *Stars and Stripes forever.* SCHUBERT (arr. Guiraud): *Marche militaire.* BEETHOVEN: *The Ruins of Athens: Turkish march.* CHABRIER: *Joyeuse marche.* J. STRAUSS Snr: *Radetzky march.* TCHAIKOVSKY: *Marche slave.* (i) BORODIN: *Prince Igor: Polovtsian march.* SAINT-SAËNS: *Suite algérienne: Marche militaire française.* BIZET: *Carmen: Marche des contrabandiers.* ELGAR: *Pomp and circumstance march No. 1.* PIERNÉ: *Marche des petits soldats de plomb.* MENDELSSOHN: *Midsummer night's dream: Wedding march.*
(B) *** EMI CDZ7 67252-2; *LZ 767252-4.*

This is as fine a collection of concert marches as any in the catalogue. The bulk of the programme was recorded at Abbey Road by Peter Andry and Neville Boyling in July 1959, and the sound is unbelievably real and present: the brass in the *Aida Triumphal march* are tangible in their splendour. The Philharmonia playing is peerless, and the whole programme emerges with wonderful freshness and sparkle. Whether in Schubert's *Marche militaire*, which succeeds in being forthright and graceful at the same time, thanks to polished ensemble, or Sousa's *Stars and*

Stripes – where the piccolos sound as cheeky as Cockney sparrows – there is a happy blend of stylishness and exuberance, and the closing *Marche slave* of Tchaikovsky is marvellously done, the coda especially witty. Then the Orchestre de Liège take over for some mainly French repertoire. They are particularly vivid in the Saint-Saëns and the engaging Pierné miniature (with its piquant opening fanfares). Then they add a boisterous French accent to Elgar, taking the big tune slowly and spaciously, but with the brass adding a Gallic edge to the grand reprise to match the fervour of of *La Marseillaise*. The recording, made nearly two decades later, sounds suitably brilliant, but is less refined than the earlier Philharmonia sessions.

Philharmonia Orchestra, Riccardo Muti

'Armchair concert': VERDI: *Overture: La forza del destino* (with New Philh. O). MOZART: *Violin concerto No. 4 in D, K.218* (with Anne-Sophie Mutter (violin)). TCHAIKOVSKY: *Symphony No. 4 in F min., Op. 36.*
(M) *** EMI Analogue/Dig. CDM7 644443-2 [id.].

Muti was at the peak of his career with EMI when he made these recordings between 1977 and 1982 (the Mozart is digital), and the EMI engineers never served him better. The Verdi *Forza del destino overture* is characteristically red-blooded, so that Anne-Sophie Mutter's account of the Mozart *Concerto*, refreshing in its classical simplicity and beautifully accompanied, comes as balm to the senses. Then Muti's urgency in the Tchaikovsky brings a performance of the utmost excitement, one that has vivid colouring and a fine lyrical sweep. The finale is riveting, particularly as the sound is both forward and rich, more satisfying in sonority than most of his more recent digital recordings, made in Philadelphia.

Primavera Chamber Orchestra, Paul Manley

'Music for strings': ROUSSEL: *Sinfonietta, Op. 52.* VAUGHAN WILLIAMS: *Fantasia on Greensleeves; Fantasia on a theme of Thomas Tallis.* ELGAR: *Serenade for strings, Op. 20.* DEBUSSY: *Danses sacreé et profane* (with Aline Brewer, harp).
(M) ** Collins Dig. 3006-2 [id.].

A vibrant account of Roussel's *Sinfonietta*, with clean string textures catching the textural astringency and the finale bright and witty. The *Danses sacrée et profane* go quite well too, but the music's radiance is not fully caught. In the Elgar *Serenade* the same directness of manner fails to coax the gentle charm and full lyrical richness out of this engaging score. The *Tallis fantasia*, too, could ideally be more expansive. Vivid sound, but there are more enticing collections available offering this repertoire.

Ragossnig, Konrad (lute), Ulsamer Collegium, Ulsamer

'Terpsichore': Renaissance dance music by: ATTAINGNANT; DALZA; PETRUCCI; NEUSIDLER; SUSATO; GERVAISE; PHALESE. Early Baroque dance music by: MAINERIO; RESARD; MOLINARO; DA VENOSA; CAROSO; CAROUBEL; HOLBOURNE; DOWLAND; SIMPSON; GIBBONS; PRAETORIUS; HAUSSMANN.
*** DG 415 294-2 [id.].

There are in all 43 items on this compact disc which collects material from the recordings made by this ensemble, issued on two LPs in 1971 and 1972. Although on the face of it this music is of specialist interest, it is in fact highly attractive and could (and should) enjoy wide appeal. The performances are crisp and vital, and the DG engineers have made a first-class job of the digital remastering. Readers who recall the originals will not hesitate, and newcomers will find it full of delights.

Rampal, Jean-Pierre (flute)

'The Great Flute Concertos' (with (i) Sol. Ven., Claudio Scimone; (ii) Prague Ars Redeviva O, Milan, Munclinger; (iii) Jerusalem Music Centre CO; (iv) Israel PO, Zubin Mehta; (v) Marielle Nordmann (harp), Franz Liszt CO, János Rolla): (i) VIVALDI: *Flute concertos: in F (La tempesta di mare), RV 433; in D (Il gardellino), RV 428, Op. 10/1 & 3.* (ii) BACH: *Concertos in C and G*

min., BWV 1055/56. (iii) TELEMANN: *Suite in A min. for flute and strings.* (iv) MOZART: *Flute concertos Nos. 1 in G; 2 in D, K.313/4;* (v) *Flute and harp concerto in C, K.299.*
(M) **(*) Sony Dig./Analogue SM2K 48184 (2) [id.].

Those collectors who would like to celebrate Rampal's seventieth birthday fairly modestly should find these performances generally to their taste. His charisma and beautiful tone (usually helped by forward recording) are well in evidence. The Bach concertos, Mozart's *Concerto for flute and harp* and the Telemann *Suite* show him at his artistic best, and the Vivaldi concertos with nicknames readily demonstrate his easy bravura, even if they are not strong on period authenticity. Reliably good sound and an excellent, 76-page biographical booklet, with plenty of photographs.

'The Art of Jean-Pierre Rampal': BACH: *Flute concertos, BWV 1055/56; Concertos arr. from Cantatas Nos. 35; 209: Sinfonia* (as above). *Flute sonatas, BWV 1020; BWV 1030/35; Partita, BWV 1013* (with Trevor Pinnock (harpsichord), Roland Pidoux (cello)). HAYDN: *London trios Nos. 1–4; Divertissements in G and D* (with Isaac Stern and Mstislav Rostropovich). MOZART: *Flute quartets Nos. 1–4* (with Stern, Rostropovich & Salvatore Accardo); *Flute concertos Nos. 1–2; Andante, K. 315; Rondo, K. 184; Flute and harp concerto* (as above); *Sinfonia concertante in E flat, K.297b* (with Pierre Pierlot (oboe), Ab Koster (horn), Marcel Allard (bassoon)). TELEMANN: *Suite for flute and strings in E min.; Concertos: in D, G & E min.* (with Franz Liszt CO, Rolla). VIVALDI: *6 Concertos, Op. 10* (as above). BENDA: *Concerto in E min.* QUANTZ: *Concerto in C min.* FREDERICK THE GREAT: *Concerto in D: Adagio* (only) (all three with O de Paris, Jean-Pierre Wallez). *Concerto movements* by VIVALDI; CIMAROSA; ROMANO & MOZART *(Concertone). Variations* by REICHA; ROSSINI; BORNE. BEETHOVEN: *Adagio, WoO 33/1* (with various artists).
(M) **(*) Sony Dig./Analogue SX11K 48200 (11) [id.].

Extraordinarily, the 76-page booklet offered with the two-disc celebration of Rampal's seventieth birthday is not included here. What we are given is 10 CDs in the original packaging, held together in a slip case, plus an eleventh which offers a series of agreeable lollipops not otherwise available. Many of these CDs are available separately at full price. Here there is a considerable reduction in cost, but you have to take the lot. It is a limited edition so aficionados should not delay. Highlights include the Bach *Flute concertos* (mostly arranged from keyboard works), the charming Haydn *London Trios* and Mozart *Flute quartets* (with the same artists common to both) and the Telemann anthology which includes some attractive solo concertos not otherwise available. Sony normally ensure that the spotlight of close microphones usually rests on their star soloist and this spoils the balance in the otherwise highly musical Bach *Flute sonatas.* There is no added documentation.

Reilly, Tommy (harmonica), ASMF Chamber Ensemble

'Serenade: MOODY: *Bulgarian wedding dance; Sonata* (arr. from HANDEL: *Flute sonatas*). FAURÉ: *Pavane, Op. 50; Romance; Au bord de l'eau, Op. 8/1.* GRIEG: *Norwegian dance, Op. 35/2.* MARTIN: *Adagietto.* D. REILLY: *Aviator.* T. REILLY: *Serenade.* DEBUSSY: *Bruyères.* MENDELSSOHN: *On wings of song.* TRAD.: *My Lagen love.* MCCARTNEY: *2 Beatle girls: Eleanor and Michelle.*
*** Chan. Dig. CHAN 8486; *ABTD 1202* [id.].

The slightly acerbic edge of the harmonica can add piquancy to a romantic programme like this, and Tommy Reilly is a very stylish player. Moody's two contributions are particularly engaging and so is Reilly's own *Serenade*, while all the other light pieces are predictably appealing, if you like the harmonica timbre, projected against a small accompanying group. The effect is consistently refined (even in the Handel arrangement, which is the very opposite of 'authentic') and the pleasingly atmospheric sound makes this a very agreeable concert.

VAUGHAN WILLIAMS: *Romance.* TAUSKY: *Concertino.* MOODY: *Little suite.* Gordon JACOB: *5 Pieces.*
*** Chan. CHAN 8617; *ABTD 1306* [id.].

The atmospheric sound certainly suits the Vaughan Williams, not thematically one of the composer's strongest works but quite haunting in its way. The Tausky *Concertino* is extremely well made, and it is seductively played; in the last analysis it is not really memorable. James Moody's *Little suite* consists of five lightweight miniatures, nicely conceived and expertly scored; but the highlight of the collection is the Gordon Jacob *Suite*, also offering five vignettes: the quality of invention here is of a consistently high standard. Throughout the concert the playing and recording balance are wholly admirable and the remastered sound retains all the bloom of the original recording, made by Decca engineers in St John's, Smith Square.

Richter, Sviatoslav (piano)

'Sviatoslav Richter plays': GRIEG: *Concerto in A min., Op. 16.* SCHUMANN: *Concerto in A min., Op. 54* (with Monte Carlo Opera O, Matačić). MOZART: *Concerto No. 22 in E flat, K.482.* BEETHOVEN: *Piano concerto No. 3 in C min., Op. 37* (with Philh. O, Muti). *Sonatas Nos. 1 in F min., Op. 2/1; 7 in D, Op. 10/3; 17 in D min. (Tempest), Op. 31/2.* SCHUBERT: *Wanderer fantasy, D.760; Sonata No. 13 in A, D.664.* SCHUMANN: *Faschingsschwank aus Wien, Op. 26.*
(B) **(*) EMI CZS7 67197-2 (4).

Some reservations have to be expressed here, of course: the performances of the Grieg and Schumann *Concertos* are very wilful, but the commanding mastery of this playing is truly remarkable. The standard of the recorded sound, too, is often very realistic, particularly the solo recordings Peter André made of Schubert and Schumann from recitals in Paris and Italy. They need to be reproduced at a high volume level; then the artist's presence is uncanny, while the playing here shows Richter at his most poetically charismatic: the slow movement of the Schubert *A major* is unforgettable. The Beethoven *Sonatas* are pretty impressive too, and can be ranked alongside the versions of Gilels. In the concertos Richter is never less than illuminating; and overall this box has many insights to offer and much musical stimulation.

Piano concertos (with var. orchestras & conductors): MOZART: *Concerto No. 20 in D min., K.466.* BEETHOVEN: *Concerto No. 3 in C min., Op. 37; Rondo for piano & orchestra in B flat, G.151.* RACHMANINOV: *Concerto No. 2 in C min., Op. 18.* TCHAIKOVSKY: *Concerto No. 1 in B flat min., Op. 54.* SCHUMANN: *Piano concerto in A min., Op. 54.* PROKOFIEV: *Concerto No. 5 in G min., Op. 55.*
(B) **(*) DG 429 918-2 (3).

Although there are severe reservations about the Tchaikovsky *Concerto*, where Richter and Karajan fail to see eye to eye over choice of tempi, and though the Beethoven does not show the great pianist at his very best, there are some outstanding performances here, not least the Prokofiev, which is a classic of the gramophone. At bargain price this is quite tempting.

Rimon, Meir (horn), Israel Philharmonic Orchestra

Horn concertos: HANDEL: *Double horn concerto in F* (arr. Rimon). BARSANTI: *Concerto grosso in D for 2 horns, timpani and strings, Op. 3/4.* HAENSEL: *Double horn concerto in F, Op. 80.* FRANZ: *Concert piece in F, for 2 horns and orchestra, Op. 4.* HÜBLER: *Concerto in F for 4 horns and orchestra.* SCHUMANN: *Konzertstück in F for four horns and orchestra, Op. 86.*
(M) *** Pickwick MCD 31; *MCC 31.*

There is much that is new and fascinating to discover in this almost entirely winning collection of horn music, in which Meir Rimon – with digital, electronic assistance – not only plays all the solo horn lines with remarkable virtuosity but also conducts the orchestra with aplomb. The result is the finest existing recording of the Schumann *Konzertstück*, full of exhilarating bravura, climaxing a programme which is rewarding throughout. The Handel *Double concerto* includes outer movements familiar from the *Water music*, but Rimon has interpolated an effective slow movement with a stately melody to make a satisfying whole. The Barsanti *Concerto grosso* combines a winning interplay between the horns and the ripieno with a quite beautiful central *Adagio* for strings alone. The subtitle for Oscar Franz's *Concert piece*, 'In a happy mood', is an apt description for an infectious piece with its melodic line taken from the operetta theatre, yet post-Weberian in manner; however, the musical fabric of Haensel's *Double concerto* is altogether less distinguished. However, Hübler's *Concerto for 4 horns* is another matter. Obviously inspired by the Schumann *Konzertstück*, which was written only five years earlier, it is ripely romantic, splendidly written for the four solo instruments and with an unforgettably exuberant finale. The recording is fully worthy of this highly spontaneous music-making. A most appealing disc in every respect.

Royal Philharmonic Orchestra, Alan Barlow

'This England': ELGAR: *Serenade for strings, Op. 20.* DELIUS: *Irmelin: Prelude. On hearing the first cuckoo in spring; Summer night on the river.* HOLST: *St Paul's suite, Op. 29/2; Brook Green suite.* WARLOCK: *Capriol suite.*
(BB) *** ASV Dig. CDQS 6070; *ZCQS 6070.*

A very enjoyable concert mainly of string music, well played and given first-class natural recording, approaching demonstration standard. The performances are all freshly spontaneous. The Delius pieces have agreeably flowing lines and the *Capriol suite*, if not as chimerical as Marriner's version, is nevertheless strongly characterized and enjoyable in a more robust way. At super-bargain price this is highly recommendable.

Royal Philharmonic Orchestra, Sir Thomas Beecham

French music: BIZET: *Carmen suite No. 1.* FAURÉ: *Pavane, Op. 60; Dolly suite, Op. 56.* DEBUSSY: *Prélude à l'après-midi d'un faune.* SAINT-SAËNS: *Le rouet d'Omphale.* DELIBES: *Le Roi s'amuse* (ballet suite).
❀ (M) *** EMI CDM7 63379-2 [id.].

No one conducts the *Carmen Prelude* with quite the flair of Sir Thomas, while the last movement of the *Dolly suite*, *Le pas espagnole*, (in Rabaud's orchestration) has the kind of dash we associate with Beecham's Chabrier. But for the most part the ear is beguiled by the consistently imaginative and poetic phrasing that distinguished his very best performances. The delicacy of string textures and wind playing (notably the flute) in *Le rouet d'Omphale* and the other *Dolly* numbers – the *Berceuse*, *Le jardin de Dolly* and *Tendresse* – is exquisite, and Debussy's *Prélude à l'après-midi d'un faune* brings a ravishingly diaphanous web of sound. Delibes' pastiche ballet-score, *Le Roi s'amuse*, is given the special elegance that Sir Thomas reserved for music from the past unashamedly rescored to please the ear of later generations. The remastering is marvellously managed and all the recordings (from between 1957 and 1961) sound wonderfully vivid and fresh.

'French favourites' (with (ii) O Nat. de l'ORTF; (iii) LPO): (ii) CHABRIER: *Overture Gwendoline;* (iii) *España* (rhapsody). (i) GOUNOD: *Faust: ballet music.* GRÉTRY: *Zémir et Azor: ballet music.* (i) MASSENET: *Cendrillon: Waltz. La Vierge: The last sleep of the Virgin.* BIZET: *Roma: Carnaval à Roma. Patrie overture.*
(M) (***) EMI mono CDM7 63401-2 [id.].

A programme of French music which Sir Thomas loved so well and played incomparably, derives from a number of (mainly late-1950s) sources, with the supercharged *Gwendoline Overture* recorded in Paris, the seven numbers of the elegantly vivacious *Faust ballet music* in Walthamstow, along with most of the other pieces, except the two most famous items, the delectably fragile *Last sleep of the Virgin* of Massenet (Abbey Road) and the incomparably effervescent *España* in Kingsway Hall. These latter two items derive from 78s, and Michael Dutton's transfers have remarkable realism and brilliance; the upper range of *España* only slightly pinched and the percussive condiment glittering. Incredibly, this absolutely spontaneous LPO performance was recorded in two parts (in 1939), with the sessions three weeks apart. The *Patrie Overture*, even though it is played by the RPO, is as ebulliently Gallic as *La Marseillaise.* Most delectable of all is the wonderfully graceful ballet music from *Zémire et Azor*, especially the *Pantomime*, a lollipop if ever there was one. In this suite the sound is so impressive it is difficult to believe it is not stereo.

'Lollipops': TCHAIKOVSKY: *Eugene Onegin: Waltz.* SIBELIUS: *Kuolema: Valse triste.* BERLIOZ: *Damnation of Faust: Menuet des follets; Danses des sylphes. Les Troyens: Marche.* DVOŘÁK: *Legend in G min., Op. 59/3.* DEBUSSY: *L'enfant prodigue: Cortège et Air de danse.* CHABRIER: *Marche joyeuse.* GOUNOD: *Roméo et Juliette: Le sommeil de Juliette.* VIDAL: *Zino-Zina: Gavotte.* GRIEG: *Symphonic dance No. 2 in A, Op. 64/2.* DELIUS: *Summer evening.* SAINT-SAËNS: *Samson et Dalila: Danse des prêtresses de Dagon; Bacchanale.* MOZART: *Thamos, King of Egypt: Entr'acte. Divertimento in D, K.131: Minuet. March in D (Haffner), K.249.*
(M) **(*) EMI CDM7 63412-2 [id.]; *EG 763412-4.*

It was Beecham who first used the word 'lollipop' to describe his brand of succulent encore pieces. In this selection of 17 examples, Beecham's devotion to French music shines out, with over half of the items by French composers. They include not just three pieces by Berlioz and two by Saint-Saëns but also a delectable rarity by the little-known Paul Vidal (1863–1931), a *Gavotte* from the ballet *Zino-Zina*. Items by Mozart, Dvořák, Sibelius and his special favourite, Delius, also conform to the Beecham definition of a lollipop as a musical sweetmeat; but the account of the *Waltz* from Tchaikovsky's *Eugene Onegin* chosen to start the disc is totally untypical of Beecham, with its metrical, unlilting rhythms. The transfers generally convey a good sense of presence but tend to emphasize an edge on top, which is an unfortunate addition to previous incarnations of this music on disc.

'Armchair concert': BRAHMS: *Academic festival overture.* MOZART: *Clarinet concerto* (with Jack Brymer). BEETHOVEN: *Symphony No. 7 in A.*
(M) *** EMI CDM7 64446-2 [id.].

In the Beecham 'Armchair Concert' it is welcome to have him represented not only by his highly characteristic, warmly expansive reading of the Mozart – with Brymer playing ravishingly – but also in central repertory he did not often tackle. The Brahms is chirpy and resilient, the Beethoven light and exhilarating.

Royal Philharmonic Orchestra, Sir Charles Groves

'An English celebration': ELGAR: *Serenade for strings, Op. 20.* BRITTEN: *Variations on a theme of Frank Bridge, Op. 10.* VAUGHAN WILLIAMS: *Fantasia on a theme by Thomas Tallis.* TIPPETT: *Fantasia concertante on a theme of Corelli.*
❀ (B) *** Pickwick/RPO Dig. CDRPO 5005 [id.].

With gloriously full and real recording, providing the most beautiful string textures, this is one of Sir Charles Groves's very finest records and it makes a worthy memorial to the achievement of the closing decade of his long career. The RPO players give deeply felt, vibrant accounts of four great masterpieces of English string music. The Elgar *Serenade* is almost voluptuous in its warmth, yet the slow movement has a disarmingly simple eloquence and the finale flows gracefully, while Groves readily finds the rich vein of romantic expressive feeling that underpins the Tippett *Corelli fantasia*. Vaughan Williams's *Tallis Fantasia*, too, is movingly spacious, with the acoustics of St Barnabas, Mitcham allowing an ethereal yet full-timbred three-dimensional placing of the solo group, to ravishing effect, while the climaxes bring the impression of sunlight streaming through cathedral stained glass. The Britten *Frank Bridge variations* are played with enormous flair and commitment, so that the changing melodic character of each is vividly contrasted and the poignant *Funeral march* and the deep melancholy of the closing reprise of Bridge's *Idyll* are very moving.

Royal Philharmonic Orchestra, Adrian Leaper

'Orchestral spectacular': CHABRIER: *España.* RIMSKY-KORSAKOV: *Capriccio espagnol.* MUSSORGSKY: *Night on the bare mountain* (arr. Rimsky-Korsakov). BORODIN: *Prince Igor: Polovtsian dances.* RAVEL: *Boléro.*
(BB) *** Naxos Dig. 8.550501; *4550501* [id.].

Recorded in Watford Town Hall by Brian Culverhouse, this concert would be highly recommendable even if it cost far more. All these performances spring to life, and the brilliant, full-bodied sound certainly earns the record its title. The brass in the Mussorgsky/Rimsky-Korsakov *Night on the bare mountain* has splendid sonority and bite, and in the *Polovtsian dances* the orchestra 'sings' the lyrical melodies with such warmth of colour that the chorus is hardly missed. Leaper allows the *Capriccio espagnol* to relax in the colourful central variations, but the performance gathers pace towards the close. Chabrier's *España* has an attractive rhythmic lilt, and in Ravel's ubiquitous *Boléro* there is a strong impetus towards the climax, with much impressive playing on the way (the trombone solo, with a French-style vibrato, is particularly strong).

St Louis Symphony Orchestra, Leonard Slatkin

'American portraits' (with (i) St Louis SO Ch.; (ii) H. Norman Schwarzkopf): COPLAND: *Fanfare for the common man.* SCHUMAN: *New England triptych: Be glad, then, America.* BUCK: (i) *Festival overture on The Star Spangled Banner.* BAGLEY: *National emblem march.* V. THOMSON: *Fugue and chorale on Yankee Doodle.* V. HERBERT: *American fantasia.* SOUSA: *El Capitan.* STEFFE: (i) *Battle Hymn of the Republic* (arr. Ringwald). HAYMAN: *Servicemen on parade.* COPLAND: (ii) *Lincoln portrait.*
*** BMG/RCA 09026 60983-2 [60983-2; *60983-4*].

Here is the perfect American counterpart to Baroness Thatcher's version of the *Lincoln portrait* (see below). Just as the British version is accompanied by patriotic British repertoire, so Schwarzkopf's performance comes as a climax to a highly compelling programme of Americana. The parade ground marches are superbly played and full of pep (*National Emblem* has an unforgettable tuba line) and the pieces by William Schuman and Virgil Thomson are agreeably imaginative. But it is the superb contribution of the St Louis Symphony Orchestra Chorus that brings a special frisson, first in the thrilling vocal climax to Dudley Buck's *Festival overture on The Star Spangled Banner*, and then in the very moving account of *The Battle Hymn of the Republic*, paced with gentle dignity, and gaining much from the superbly spacious acoustic of Powell Symphony Hall. This sets the stage perfectly for the entry of Norman Schwarzkopf to repeat the words of Abraham Lincoln. He speaks clearly and directly and with simple dignity. His articulation and diction are flawless; he is not an actor, but his delivery is refreshingly free from histrionics. Throughout, the recording is very much in the demonstration bracket. The finest version of the *Lincoln portrait* is Katherine Hepburn's inspirational account (see under Copland in the Composer index). But the now retired General Schwarzkopf's obvious, heartfelt sincerity will do any future political aspirations no harm at all.

'Classic marches': BERLIOZ: *Damnation de Faust: Rákóczy march.* BEETHOVEN: *Ruins of Athens: Turkish march.* MEYERBEER: *Le Prophète: Coronation march.* MENDELSSOHN: *Midsummer Night's Dream: Wedding march.* IPPOLITOV-IVANOV: *Caucasian sketches: Procession of the Sardar.* J. STRAUSS S: *Radetzky march.* PIERNÉ: *Marche des petits faunes.* TCHAIKOVSKY: *Nutcracker suite: March.* ELGAR: *Pomp and circumstance march No. 1.* VERDI: *Aida: Triumphal march.* GOUNOD: *Funeral march of a marionette.* PROKOFIEV: *Love of three oranges: March.* SIBELIUS: *Karelia: Alla marcia.* HERBERT: *Babes in Toyland: March of the Toys.* GANZ: *St Louis Symphony march.* SOUSA: *Stars and stripes forever.*
**(*) BMG/RCA Dig. RD 87716 [7716-2-RC].

A generously varied collection of concert marches, with the lighter novelties like the Pierné and Victor Herbert items especially welcome. Slatkin's approach is essentially serious and his spacious tempi (rather too spacious in the Prokofiev and Gounod pieces, which need a touch more bite and wit) seek the grand manner which, coupled to the resonant large-scale recording, suits the more expansive pieces by Meyerbeer, Mendelssohn and Elgar best.

(i) St Louis Symphony Orchestra, Leonard Slatkin

(ii) Dallas Symphony Orchestra, Eduarda Mata

'Great American showpieces': (i) BERNSTEIN: *Overture: Candide; On the Town (3 dance episodes).* GERSHWIN: *An American in Paris; Cuban overture.* BARBER: *Overture: The School for Scandal.* (ii) COPLAND: *El salón México; Danzóon cubano.*
(M) **(*) EMI Dig. CDM7 64303-2 [id.].

Slatkin is at his finest in Barber's *Overture to The School for Scandal*, the composer's graduation exercise, a youthful work of consummate skill. What an inspired piece it is and what a marvellous second subject! Bernstein's *Candide Overture* is played both infectiously and with a jaunty elegance, less hard-driven than the composer's own version, though in *On the Town* Slatkin cannot match Bernstein in the flair he brings to his jazzier inspirations, and the effect is a shade metrical. In Gershwin's *Cuban overture* some of the gutsy feeling is lost; while with *An American in Paris* Slatkin often disguises the seams, he could at times be more extrovert. It is partly that the gloriously ample acoustic of the Lowell Hall, St Louis, makes everything sound opulent, and certainly on sonic grounds no one should be disappointed with Slatkin's contribution to this collection. The two exotic Copland dance pieces are given a vivid palette by Mata in Dallas, and he too has the advantage of a flattering acoustic, although he is less subtle in nudging the rhythms than the composer in his own less ample versions on Sony.

Savijoki, Pekka (saxophone), New Stockholm Chamber Orchestra, Panula

LARSSON: *Concerto for saxophone and string orchestra, Op. 14.* GLAZUNOV: *Concerto in E flat, Op. 109.* PANULA: *Adagio and allegro for string orchestra.*
*** BIS CD 218 [id.].

The find here for most collectors outside Scandinavia will be Lars-Erik Larsson's *Saxophone concerto.* It is a very fine and inventive work; the slow movement with its beautiful canonic opening is of particular distinction. The Glazunov, written at the same time, is more original and imaginative than it at first appears. Accomplished performances and good recording.

Scandinavian Brass Ensemble, Jorma Panula

HALLBERG: *Blacksmith's tune.* HOLMBOE: *Concerto for brass, Op. 157.* MADSEN: *Divertimento for brass and percussion, Op. 47.* GRIEG: *Funeral march.* ALMILA: *Te Pa Te Pa, Op. 26.* DANIELSSON: *Suite No. 3.*
*** BIS Dig. CD 265 [id.].

The sound is quite spectacular and has superb presence and body: in short, a demonstration disc. However, not all the music is spectacular, but the collection is worth having for Holmboe's *Concerto*, a short but finely wrought piece that towers over everything else here. Grieg's *Funeral march* was originally intended for piano, though Grieg arranged it for military band. The Norwegian Trygve Madsen's piece begins attractively enough with some lively syncopation but turns out to be pretty cheap. Christer Danielsson is a Swedish trombonist of note and his *Suite* is craftsmanlike and musicianly.

Scottish Chamber Orchestra, Laredo

'String masterpieces': ALBINONI: *Adagio in G min.* (arr. Giazotto). HANDEL: *Berenice: Overture. Solomon: Arrival of the Queen of Sheba.* BACH: *Suite No. 3, BWV 1068: Air. Violin concerto No. 1 in A min., BWV 1041: Finale.* PACHELBEL: *Canon.* PURCELL: *Abdelazer: Rondo. Chacony in G min.*
(B) *** Pickwick Dig. PCD 802; *CIMPC 802.*

An excellent issue. The playing is alive, alert, stylish and committed without being overly expressive, yet the Bach *Air* has warmth and Pachelbel's *Canon* is fresh and unconventional in approach. The sound is first class, especially spacious and convincing on CD, well detailed without any clinical feeling. The Purcell *Rondo* is the tune made familiar by Britten's orchestral guide; the *Chaconne* is played with telling simplicity.

Scottish Ensemble, Jonathan Rees

Baroque music: ALBINONI: *Adagio for strings and organ* (arr. Giazotto). PACHELBEL: *Canon and gigue for 3 violins and continuo.* VIVALDI: *The Trial between harmony and invention: Violin concerto in B flat (La Caccia), Op. 8/10; L'Estro armonico: Concerto for 2 violins and cello in D min., Op. 3/11.* PURCELL: *Chacony* (arr. Britten). CORELLI: *Concerto grosso in D, Op. 6/4.* BACH: *Suite No. 3 in D: Air.* LOCATELLI: *Concerto grosso, Op. 1/11.*
(BB) *** Virgo Dig. VJ7 91464-2; *VJ 791464-4* [id.].

A most refreshing concert. The Scottish strings play their allegros with bracingly resilient vigour and slow movements with an appealingly refined espressivo. Thus Albinoni's ubiquitous *Adagio* is serene but not too lush, and Pachelbel's *Canon* has vitality, with textures more refined than usual. The soloists, Jonathan Rees, Jane Murdoch and Caroline Dale, are first class in the two highly individual Vivaldi concertos. The Britten arrangement of Purcell is given the strongest possible profile, while the famous Bach *Air* makes a gentle interlude. Excellent sound, generous measure (65 minutes), but totally inadequate back-up documentation.

'Music for strings': GRIEG: *Holberg suite, Op. 40: 2 Elegiac melodies, Op. 34.* DELIUS: *Air and Dance.* ELGAR: *Serenade for strings, Op. 20.* WARLOCK: *Capriol suite.* HOLST: *St Paul's suite, Op. 29/2.*
(B) *** Virgo VJ7 91565-2; *VJ 791565-4* [id.].

The bracing Scottish air suits nearly all this repertoire. The Scottish Ensemble is a relatively small chamber group, and perhaps Grieg's two *Elegiac melodies* need more expansive tone. But the vigorous athleticism suits the *Holberg suite* very well indeed, as it does Warlock's *Capriol*. Both combine robust allegros with much delicacy in the gentler music and in the same way the gossamer pianissimo of the *Ostinato* second movement of Holst's *St Paul's suite* tickles the ear engagingly. The Elgar *Serenade*, too, is given a degree of innocence alongside its freshness and grace. Fine playing and realistic sound, combining body with transparency make this super-bargain Virgo collection a genuine alternative to more opulent recordings of this repertoire.

Scottish National Orchestra, Gibson

'Land of the mountain and the flood': MENDELSSOHN: *The Hebrides overture (Fingal's Cave), Op. 26.* BERLIOZ: *Waverley overture, Op. 2.* ARNOLD: *Tam O'Shanter overture.* VERDI: *Macbeth: Ballet music.* MACCUNN: *Overture: Land of the Mountain and the Flood.*
**(*) Chan. Dig. CHAN 8379 [id.].

The MacCunn overture here provides an attractive foil for the Scottish National Orchestra's collection of short pieces inspired by Scotland. These performances are not as refined as the best available versions – significantly, the most dashing performance is of Arnold's difficult and rumbustious overture – but make an attractive recital. On CD, the spectacularly vivid orchestration of *Tam O'Shanter* produces sound that is in the demonstration bracket; and the MacCunn piece is pretty impressive, too. The Berlioz is vivid, and Gibson's approach to *Fingal's Cave* attractively romantic.

Scottish National Orchestra, Neeme Järvi

Music from Estonia, Vol. 2: LEMBA: *Symphony in C sharp min.* TOBIAS: *Julius Caesar overture.* ELLER: *Twilight.* TORMIS: *Overture No. 2.* PÄRT: *Cantus in memoriam Benjamin Britten.*
*** Chan. Dig. CHAN 8656; *ABTD 1342* [id.].

Easily the best thing here is Lemba's *Symphony* (already mentioned under its composer); it is astonishingly accomplished for a 23-year-old: the invention is fresh and memorable and it is played here with evident enthusiasm. The Heino Eller piece is less impressive than his *Elegy*; the *Julius Caesar overture* by Rudolf Tobias (1873–1918) – the very first Estonian orchestral piece – is of less interest, as is the repetitive Tormis work (inspired by the opening of Tubin's *Fifth Symphony*). The Pärt is an effective and haunting little work. But these works are all short and the *Symphony* is long (40 minutes) and altogether delightful. Strongly recommended.

'Serenade for strings'

Serenades (with (i) Philh. O, C. Davis; (ii) LSO, Barbirolli; (iii) N. Sinfonia, Tortelier; (iv) RPO, Sargent; (v) E. Sinfonia, Dilkes; (vi) Bournemouth Sinf., Montgomery; (vii) LPO, Boult): (i) MOZART: *Serenade No. 13 in G (Eine kleine Nachtmusik), K.525.* (ii) TCHAIKOVSKY: *String serenade, Op. 48: Waltz.* (iii) GRIEG: *Holberg suite, Op. 40. Elegiac melody: Heart's wounds, Op. 34/1.* (iv) DVOŘÁK: *String serenade, Op. 11: 1st & 2nd movts.* (v) WARLOCK: *Capriol suite.* (vi) WIRÉN: *String serenade, Op. 11: March.* (vii) ELGAR: *Introduction and allegro for strings, Op. 47.*
(B) *** EMI *TC2-MOM 108.*

This was the finest of EMI's first release of 'Miles of Music' tapes with an attractive programme, good (and sometimes distinguished) performances and consistent sound-quality, slightly restricted in the upper range, but warm, full and clear. Tortelier's Grieg and Boult's complete version of Elgar's *Introduction and allegro* are obvious highlights, and this certainly makes an attractive background for a car journey, yet can be enjoyed at home too.

Serkin, Rudolf (piano)

'The First recordings' (with (i) Adolph Busch; (ii) Busch Chamber Players): BACH: (i) *Violin Sonata in G, BWV 1021.* BEETHOVEN: *Piano sonata No. 23 in F min., Op. 57;* (i) *Violin sonata in E flat, Op. 12/3.* GEMINIANI, arr. Busch: *Sonata in C min.* MOZART: (ii) *Piano concerto No. 14 in E flat, K449;* (i) *Violin sonata in F, K.377.* REGER: *Violin sonata in F sharp min. Op. 84;* SCHUMANN: *Violin sonata in A min., Op. 105.* (ii) VIVALDI, arr. Busch: *Suite in A.*
(***) EMI mono CDS7 54374-2 (3).

All these performances were recorded before Serkin developed some of his less pleasing mannerisms (such as pedal stamping and ugly ends of phrases): indeed his account of the *E flat Concerto*, K.449, with the Busch Chamber Players is wonderfully sensitive and fresh, and arguably the finest account of the work until Perahia's version in the 1970s. The Busch/Serkin partnership produced playing of the most vital and imaginative character, and both the Mozart sonata and the Schumann *A minor sonata*, Op. 105, have comparable eloquence and intensity. Oddly enough, the Mozart concerto was never reissued in the days of LP and this is its first appearance since the 1930s. Having long cherished the 78s, it is good to have it in more durable form. Strongly recommended.

Slovak Philharmonic Orchestra

'Russian Fireworks' (cond. (i) Richard Hayman; (ii) Kenneth Jean; (iii) Stephen Gunzenhauser; (iv) Michael Halász): (i) IPPOLITOV-IVANOV: *Caucasian sketches: Procession of the Sardar.* (ii) LIADOV: *8 Russian folksongs.* KABALEVSKY: *Comedian's galop.* MUSSORGSKY: *Sorochinski Fair: Gopak. Khovanshchina: Dance of the Persian slaves.* (iii) LIADOV: *Baba Yaga; The enchanted lake; Kikimora.* (iv) RUBINSTEIN: *Feramor: Dance of the Bayaderes; Bridal procession. The Demon: Lesginka.* (ii) HALVORSEN: *Entry of the Boyars.*
(BB) *** Naxos Dig. 8.550328 [id.].

A vividly sparkling concert with spectacular digital sound, more than making up in vigour and spontaneity for any lack of finesse. The Liadov tone-poems are especially attractive and, besides the very familiar pieces by Ippolitov-Ivanov, Halvorsen and Mussorgsky, it is good to have the Rubinstein items, especially the *Lesginka* which has a rather attractive tune.

Smedvig, Rolf (trumpet)

Trumpet concertos (with Scottish CO, Jahja Ling): HAYDN: *Concerto in E flat.* TARTINI: *Concerto in D.* HUMMEL: *Concerto in E flat.* TORELLI: *Concerto in D.* BELLINI: *Concerto in E flat.*
*** Telarc Dig. CD 80232 [id.].

Rolf Smedvig, a native of Seattle, joins the ranks of international virtuosi who offer outstanding versions of the Haydn and Hummel *Concertos*. The easy elegance of his style and his warm phrasing of slow-movement cantilenas is a constant pleasure to the ear, and in the finales the bravura is almost self-effacing in its natural command. Yet in the Haydn *Rondo* he changes his articulation imaginatively when a phrase is repeated. The performances are not quite as exciting as those of Hardenberger (whose projection has rather more extrovert sparkle), but he plays the Hummel in the key of E major, which adds to its brilliance of effect. One of the highlights of the present disc is the wholly engaging Tartini work, a transcription of a violin concerto, which is so effective that one is tempted to dismiss the original as second-best. Bellini's *Concerto*, originally conceived for oboe, is also a delight, heard on the trumpet, when the playing is so sophisticated and so readily catches its operatic feeling. Accompaniments by the SCO under Jahja Ling are admirably cultivated, if with an occasional suspicion of blandness. But that is partly the effect of the richly resonant acoustics of City Hall, Glasgow, where this record was made, with the natural realism characteristic of the Telarc label.

Solomon (piano)

'Great recordings of the century' (with (i) Liverpool PO, Boult; (ii; iii) Philh. O; (ii) Dobrowen; (iii) Susskind): (i) BLISS: *Piano concerto.* (ii) SCRIABIN: *Piano concerto in F sharp min., Op. 20.* (iii) LISZT: *Hungarian fantasia.*
(M) (***) EMI mono CDH7 63821-2.

Solomon's pioneering account of the Bliss *Piano concerto* was made during the war. Solomon, of course, plays marvellously and the disc is important in offering us what would have been the first recording to be issued of the Scriabin *Piano concerto in F sharp minor* had Solomon and Dobrowen passed it for release. It is a lovely reading, every bit as poetic and polished as one would expect, and the sound is not bad for its period. It was made in 1949, at the same time as Solomon recorded the Tchaikovsky, which EMI must surely reissue soon. The Liszt *Hungarian fantasia* accompanied the Bliss when it came out on LP, and it is a pretty dazzling performance. The sonic limitations cannot diminish the sheer aristocratic finesse of this great pianist.

Spanish music for the Quincentennial: 'Música clásica de España'

'Música clásica de España' (played by: (i) O de Conciertos de Madrid, cond. by (ii) Pedro de Freitas Branco; (iii) José Buenagu; (iv) Odon Alonso; (v) Jesús Arámbarri; (vi) José Maria Franco Gil; (vii) Spanish Nat. O, Jesús López Cobos; (viii) Alicia de Larrocha (piano); (ix) Ernesto Bitetti (guitar)): FALLA: (i; ii) *The Three-cornered hat: suites 1–2.* (vii) *El amor brujo* (complete, with Rocio Jurado). (i; ii) RODRIGO: *Concierto de Aranjuez: Adagio* (with Ernesto Bitetti, guitar). (i; iii) TURINA: *La Procesión del rocio; Danzas fantásticas: Orgia* (only). (viii): ALBÉNIZ: *Iberia: Triana. Suite española: Sevilla. Puerta de tierra. Cantos de españa: Sequidillas. Rumores de la caleta (Malaguena).* FALLA: *La vida breve: Danza.* GRANADOS: *Goyescas: El fandango decandil; El Pelele.* (i; v) GURIDI: *Amorosa.* (ix) TÁRREGA: *Recuerdos de la Alhambra.* ANON.: *Romance.* ALBÉNIZ: *Asturias; Mallorca* (both. arr. Segovia). (i; vi) SARASATE: *Zapateado.*
(M) ** EMI Analogue/Dig. CMS7 64241-2 (2).

This collection draws on the Spanish EMI Odeon label, featuring many unknown names, but artists who clearly have this music in their bones, having lived their lives drenched in Spanish sunshine. The suites from *The Three-cornered hat* and the complete *El amor brujo* are particularly strong on local colour. The former has an engagingly genial and bucolic *Miller's dance*, and the latter – digitally recorded – has a flamenco vocal soloist (Rocio Jurado) with a uniquely potent guttural, throaty delivery which is quite riveting. Alicia de Larrocha provides a characteristically distinguished brief recital; unfortunately the piano sound here is ill-focused and not a patch on her Decca recordings. Ernesto Bitetti then proffers some justly famous solo guitar pieces and also gives us a haunting account of Rodrigo's famous concertante *Adagio*. The Orquesta de Conciertos de Madrid under various conductors plays vividly in music of Turina and ends the concert with a glittering if rather flimsy version of Sarasate's *Zapateado*. This music-making has a special character and the sound is more than acceptable. However, it seems likely that this set will have only a limited catalogue life in the UK.

Spanish music for the Quincentennial: 'Viva España'

'Viva España' (played by (i) Paris Conservatoire O, cond. by (ii) Pierre Dervaux; (iii) Rafael Frühbeck de Burgos; (iv) André Cluytens; (v) Nat. O of Spain; (vi) Philh. O, cond. by (vii) André Vandernoot; (viii) Carlo Maria Giulini): (i; ii) CHABRIER: *España.* (i; iii) ALBÉNIZ: *Iberia: Évocation; Fête-dieu à Seville; Triana* (orch. Arbos). (i; iv) RAVEL: *Rapsodie espagnole.* (i; iii) TURINA: *3 Danzas fantásticas.* (v; iii) RODRIGO: *Concierto de Aranjuez* (with Alirio Diaz (guitar)). (i; iii) FALLA: *La vida breve: Dance.* (vi; vii) *L'amor brujo* (complete; with Oralia Dominguez); (i; iii) *Nights in the gardens of Spain* (with Gonzalo Soriano (piano)). (vi; viii) *The Three-cornered hat (suite).*
(M) ** EMI CZS7 67474-2 [id.].

These performances have been around for some time, all dating from the 1960s, except for

Vandernoot's highly animated complete *El amor brujo* (with Oralia Dominguez's darkly intense vocal contribution) and Giulini's vibrant suite from *The Three-cornered hat*, both with the Philharmonia at its early peak and recorded in the Kingsway Hall in the late 1950s. The CD transfers are well managed and have vivid colours and plenty of atmosphere. The playing throughout is thoroughly idiomatic. Dervaux's *España* is exciting if not distinctive, but Frühbeck de Burgos's alluring Albéniz and Turina have rich, bright Mediterranean colouring, and their spectacle shows how good the original recordings were. Soriano makes a perceptive soloist in *Nights in the gardens of Spain* although he does not efface memories of Alicia de Larrocha. Diaz is equally at home in the ubiquitous Rodrigo *Concierto de Aranjuez* and no one could complain about a lack of vitality in either work. Cluytens captures the perfumed evening breezes and the glitter of Ravel's Spanish evocation especially well. Good value when the two discs (152 minutes) are offered for the price of one.

Steele-Perkins, Crispian (trumpet)

'Mr Purcell's trumpeter': (with City of L. Baroque Sinfonia, Hickox): PURCELL: *The Indian Queen: incidental music. Trumpet sonata in D. King Arthur: Act V tunes. Suite in C.* CLARKE: *Ayres for the theatre: Cebel; Trumpet song; 3 Minuets; Round-O (Prince of Denmark's march); Serenade: Gigue.* ANON.: *(Mr Shore's tunes): Shore's trumpet; Trumpett; Prince Eugene's march; Song (Prince Eugene's march into Italy); Shore's tune.* FINGER: *Trumpet and oboe sonata in C* (with A. Robson, oboe). BIBER: *Sonata in G min. for trumpet, violin and 2 violas* (with D. Woodcock, R. Nalden & M. Kelly).
(M) *** EMI Dig. CDM7 63931-2; *EG 763931-2.*

The title of this collection celebrates Purcell's trumpeter, John Shore, and some of the repertoire comes from Shore's personal collection. Both the *Sonatas* of Biber and Gottfried Finger are excellent works; and the programme is agreeably diverse, including an engaging account of *Shore's Tune*, allotted to the treble recorder. The famous *Trumpet voluntary* by Jeremiah Clarke is stirringly done and, with excellent accompaniments from Hickox and fine recording, this record is highly recommendable for trumpet fanciers.

Six Trumpet concertos (with ECO, Anthony Halstead): HAYDN: *Concerto in E flat.* TORELLI: *Concerto in D.* M. HAYDN: *Concerto No. 2 in C.* TELEMANN: *Concerto for trumpet, two oboes and strings.* NERUDA: *Concerto in E flat.* HUMPHRIES: *Concerto in D, Op. 10/12.*
(B) *** Pickwick PCD 821; *CIMPC 821.*

Collectors who have relished Håkan Hardenberger's famous full-price collection of trumpet concertos might well go on to this equally admirable concert, which duplicates only the Haydn – and that in a performance hardly less distinguished. Crispian Steele-Perkins has a bright, gleaming, beautifully focused timbre and crisp articulation, with easy command of the high tessitura of the Michael Haydn work and all the bravura necessary for the sprightly finales of all these concertos. His phrasing in the slow movement of Joseph Haydn's shapely *Andante* is matched by his playing of the *Largo* of the Neruda and the *Adagio–Presto–Adagio* of the Torelli, another fine work. Anthony Halstead with the ECO gives him warmly sympathetic support. The recording balance gives the soloist plenty of presence, but the orchestra is recorded rather reverberantly, an effect similar to that on the Hardenberger record.

Stinton, Jennifer (flute)

'20th-century flute concertos' ((i) with Geoffrey Browne; SCO, Steuart Bedford): HONEGGER: (i) *Concerto da camera for flute, cor anglais and strings.* IBERT: *Flute concerto.* NIELSEN: *Flute concerto.* POULENC, arr. Berkeley: *Flute sonata.*
*** Collins Dig. 1210-2; *1210-4.*

Jennifer Stinton's record is called '20th-century flute concertos' – which, strictly speaking, it is not; only two works here can accurately be so described. Honegger's *Concerto da camera for flute, cor anglais and strings* is a duo concertante piece, and the Poulenc is a transcription by Lennox Berkeley of the *Sonata for flute and piano* (1957). Not that this matters, given the quality of the solo playing. The Nielsen is a fine performance although its contrasts could be more strongly made. But Ibert's charming and effervescent piece comes off very well, though the orchestral playing is not particularly subtle. Honegger's *Concerto da camera* comes from the same period as the *Fourth Symphony* and the slow movement is strongly reminiscent of it. It is very nicely played, as is the Poulenc, and beautifully recorded; though the orchestral contribution falls short of real distinction, this remains a very enjoyable recital, which deserves its third star.

Stockholm Sinfonietta, Esa-Pekka Salonen

'A Swedish serenade': WIRÉN: *Serenade for strings, Op. 11.* LARSSON: *Little serenade for strings, Op. 12.* SÖDERLUNDH: *Oboe concertino* (with A. Nilsson). LIDHOLM: *Music for strings.*
**(*) BIS Dig. CD 285 [id.].

The most familiar piece here is the Dag Wirén *Serenade for strings.* By far the best movement of Lille Bror Söderlundh's *Concertino for oboe and orchestra* is the lovely *Andante*, whose melancholy is winning and has a distinctly Gallic feel to it. By contrast, the finale is rather thin and naïve, but the piece is still worth hearing and is certainly played with splendid artistry by Alf Nilsson and the Stockholm Sinfonietta, one of the best small chamber orchestras in the Nordic countries. The Lidholm *Music for strings* is somewhat grey and anonymous though it is expertly wrought. Esa-Pekka Salonen gets good results from this ensemble and the recording lives up to the high standards of the BIS label. It is forwardly balanced but has splendid body and realism.

Stockholm Sinfonietta, Jan-Olav Wedin

'Swedish pastorale': ALFVÉN: *The Mountain King, Op. 37: Dance of the Cow-girl.* ATTERBERG: *Suite No. 3 for violin, viola and string orchestra.* BLOMDAHL: *Theatre Music: Adagio.* LARSSON: *Pastoral suite, Op. 19; The Winter's Tale: Four vignettes.* ROMAN: *Concerto in D, for oboe d'amore, string orchestra and harpsichord, BeRI 53.* ROSENBERG: *Small piece for cello and string orchestra.*
*** BIS Dig. CD 165 [id.].

A charming record. The Stockholm Sinfonietta is an expert ensemble and play with sensitivity under Jan-Olav Wedin. In addition to affectionate accounts of the *Pastoral suite* and the charming vignettes for *The Winter's Tale*, they include Atterberg's *Suite No. 3*, which has something of the modal dignity of the Vaughan Williams *Tallis fantasy*. It has real eloquence and an attractive melancholy, to which the two soloists, Nils-Erik Sparf and Jouko Mansnerus, do ample justice. The Blomdahl and Roman works are also given alert and sensitive performances; they make one think how delightful they are. Hilding Rosenberg's piece is very short but is rather beautiful. A delightful anthology and excellent (if a trifle closely balanced) recording. Confidently recommended.

Stuttgart Chamber Orchestra, Karl Münchinger

PACHELBEL: *Canon and gigue.* ALBINONI: *Adagio* (arr. Giazotto). BACH: *Jesu, joy of man's desiring; Sheep may safely graze; Suite No. 3: Air. Fugue in G min., BWV 542.* BOCCHERINI: *Minuet* from *Op. 13/5.* HOFSTETTER: *Serenade.* HANDEL: *Concerto grosso, Op. 6/6: Musette. Solomon: Arrival of the Queen of Sheba. Organ concerto, Op. 4/4. Overture: Berenice.*
(M) **(*) Decca 417 781-2; *417 781-4* [id.].

The recording quality of Münchinger's analogue concert is first class and the programme generous; the performances will suit those who prefer their Baroque lollipops played expansively on modern instruments. The balance is close, which does not permit much dynamic contrast in the Pachelbel *Canon*, although the *Gigue* certainly sounds gracious. The Boccherini *Minuet* and the famous *Serenade* once attributed to Haydn are pleasingly done, and among the Handel items the *Organ concerto* (with Ulrich Bremsteller) is nicely registered. The other Handel excerpts produce rich textures from the strings, and the Albinoni *Adagio* is sumptuous. Those who prefer something more authentic can turn to the Taverner Players on EMI – see below.

Taverner Players, Andrew Parrott

PACHELBEL: *Canon and gigue.* HANDEL: *Solomon: Arrival of the Queen of Sheba. Harp concerto in B flat, Op. 4/6* (with A. Lawrence-King, harp). PURCELL: *3 Parts upon a ground; Suite of*

Theatre music. BACH: *Sinfonias from Cantatas 29, 31, 106, 156, 174* and *Christmas oratorio. Cantata 147: Jesu, joy of man's desiring.*
(M) *** EMI Dig. CDM7 69853-2.

This really outstanding collection of Baroque favourites shows that authentic performance can produce both charm and charisma: there is not a whiff of sterile, scholarly rectitude here. Indeed Pachelbel's famous *Canon* sounds delightfully fresh, heard in its original chamber scoring, while Handel's *Queen of Sheba* arrives in exhilarating fashion. The *Harp concerto*, too, sounds delectable when the effect is so neat and stylish. The Bach *Sinfonias* are varied in content (that from No. 29 includes a bravura organ obbligato, played with considerable flair by John Toll), with No. 174 bringing a real novelty in being a different version of Bach's *Brandenburg concerto No. 3*, attractively expanded in scoring to include horns and oboes. First-class digital recording makes this a highly desirable compilation at a very reasonable price.

Thames Chamber Orchestra, Michael Dobson

'The baroque concerto in England' (with Black, Bennett): ANON. (probably HANDEL): *Concerto grosso in F.* BOYCE: *Concerti grossi: in E min. for strings; in B min. for 2 solo violins, cello and strings.* WOODCOCK: *Oboe concerto in E flat; Flute concerto in D.*
*** CRD CRD 3331; *CRDC 4031* [id.].

A wholly desirable collection, beautifully played and recorded. Indeed the recording has splendid life and presence and often offers demonstration quality – try the opening of the Woodcock *Flute concerto*, for instance. The music is all highly rewarding. The opening concerto was included in Walsh's first edition of Handel's Op. 3 (as No. 4) but was subsequently replaced by another work. Whether or not it is by Handel, it is an uncommonly good piece, and it is given a superbly alert and sympathetic performance here. Neil Black and William Bennett are soloists of the highest calibre, and it is sufficient to say that they are on top form throughout this most enjoyable concert.

Thatcher, Baroness, with LSO, Wyn Morris

'Salute to Democracy': COPLAND: *Lincoln portrait; Fanfare for the common man* (Mexico SO, Bátiz). BARBER: *Adagio for strings* (LSO, Previn). SOUSA: *Stars and Stripes forever* (Nat. PO, Stokowski). ELGAR: *Pomp and Circumstance marches Nos. 1 & 4; Enigma variations: Nimrod.* HOLST: *The Planets: Jupiter* (LPO, Boult).
** EMI CDC7 54539-2; *EL 754539-4* [id.].

Though Copland's *Lincoln portrait* is his most frequently played work in the United States, it has not fared well outside America, what with its message about Abraham Lincoln addressed specifically to 'fellow-citizens'. Sir Edward Heath in the 1970s gave a live performance with Maazel and the Cleveland Orchestra, but, unlike this one with Margaret Thatcher as narrator, it was never recorded. Having an English voice has its oddity, but the ex-Prime Minister copes well with the repetitious and heavily stylized cadences of the Carl Sandburg commentary, which frames celebrated quotations from Lincoln himself, culminating in the Gettysburg address. Lady Thatcher varies her pacing and tone cleverly, with much more of the Queen Mother than of the fishwife in her delivery. Musically this is not the most high-powered of readings, and it is more likely to appeal to British admirers of Lady Thatcher than to anyone else. The coupling of patriotic music from both sides of the Atlantic comes in vintage versions from the EMI catalogue. The American items include Stokowski's marvellously flamboyant account of the Sousa march, complete with xylophone glissandos. The British items are all taken from Boult recordings – but what a pity it was that Elgar's *Cockaigne overture* was not also included in Edward Heath's live recording with the LSO, an outstanding version . . . but perhaps there was a veto on that.

Tuckwell, Barry (horn)

'Baroque horn concertos from the Court of Dresden' (with ASMF, Iona Brown): KNECHTL: *Concerto in D.* REINHARDT: *Concerto in E flat.* QUANTZ: *Concertos Nos. 3 in E flat; 9 in E flat.* GRAUN: *Concerto in D.* ROLLIG: *Concertos Nos. 14 in E flat; 15 in D.*

*** Decca Dig. 417 406-2 [id.].

None of this is great music, but it is all played by a master-soloist, and electricity is readily created from the bravura demands of the writing, so easily met by Barry Tuckwell. There is plenty of high tessitura (as in the Knechtl and both the Rollig *Concertos*) while Reinhardt's florid writing, with leaps as well as prolix textures, is very testing indeed. This *Concerto*, like those of Quantz and Rollig, favours a *siciliano* slow movement, which brings lyrical contrast. Probably the best works here are the Graun, short and strong in character (particularly the finale with its crisp decoration), and Quantz's No. 9. This features a concertante oboe soloist, who echoes the horn's solo line most appealingly. Polished and stylish accompaniments from the Academy under Iona Brown, and bright, clear recording, with the overall balance managed well and the harpsichord continuo not lost.

Udagawa, Hideko (violin)

Concertante works (with LPO, Klein): GLAZUNOV: *Violin concerto in A min., Op. 82.* TCHAIKOVSKY: *Souvenir d'un lieu cher, Op. 42.* CHAUSSON: *Poème, Op. 25.* SARASATE: *Romanze andaluza, Op. 22/1.* SAINT-SAËNS: *Caprice, Op. 52.*

(B) *** Pickwick Dig. PCD 966; *IMPC 966* [id.].

This is a generous collection (64 minutes) of mostly sugar-plum works for violin and orchestra, played with uninhibited romanticism by the rich-toned Udagawa. With the violin balanced forward, the Glazunov receives a heartfelt performance which rivals almost any, even if the finale does not offer quite such bravura fireworks as Itzhak Perlman (at full price). It is valuable to have all three of the haunting pieces which Tchaikovsky called *Souvenirs d'un lieu cher* – the *Méditation* and *Mélodie*, much better known than the central *Scherzo*. They are here done in Glazunov's orchestral arrangements. The Chausson *Poème* is warmly convincing if a little heavy-handed, the Sarasate Andalusian *Romanze* dances delightfully, and only in the final Saint-Saëns *Caprice* does Udagawa's playing sound a little effortful in its virtuosity. Warm, full recording to match.

Ulster Orchestra, Vernon Handley or Bryden Thomson

'An Irish rhapsody': HARTY: *The Londonderry air. Irish Symphony: The fair day (scherzo). In the Antrim Hills.* STANFORD: *Irish rhapsody No. 4 (The Fisherman of Loch Neagh and what he saw), Op. 141; Symphony No. 3 (Irish): Scherzo.* MOERAN: *In the mountain country (symphonic impressions).* BAX: *In the faery hills; Roscatha.*

(M) *** Chan. Dig. CHAN 6525; *MBTD 6525* [id.].

It was a happy idea for Chandos to create this Irish anthology from a catalogue rich in music influenced by that country. It is especially good to have the *Scherzo* from Harty's *Irish Symphony* (a real lollipop), together with the skippity jig from the similar work by Stanford. His *Irish rhapsody No. 4* is also very colourful, and the two Bax pieces offer a strong contrast: one atmospheric, the other more dramatic and lively. Excellent performances throughout; all the recordings except the obligatory (and analogue) *Londonderry air* are of Chandos's best digital quality.

Vienna Philharmonic Orchestra, Claudio Abbado

'New Year Concert 1988' (with Vienna Boys' Ch.): REZNIČEK: *Donna Diana: overture.* Josef STRAUSS: *Brennende Liebe; Auf Ferienreisen; Im Fluge* (polkas). Johann STRAUSS, Jnr: *Die Fledermaus overture; Neue pizzicato polka; Freut euch des Lebens* (waltz); *Chit-chat polka; Un Ballo in maschera: Quadrille on themes from Verdi's opera. Liechtes Blut polka; Seid unschlungen Millionen* (waltz); *Perpetuum mobile; Banditen-Galopp; An der schönen blauen Donau.* Johann STRAUSS, Snr: *Radetzky march.*

*** DG Dig. 423 662-2; *423 662-4*.

If this record, which also includes the Vienna Boys' Choir, does not quite match Karajan's, it still has a real sense of occasion and offers some delectable performances. Obvious favourites like *The Blue Danube*, *Die Fledermaus overture* and, of course, the *Radetzky march* are duplicated, but most of the programme is new. With Rezniček's *Donna Diana* opening the proceedings vivaciously, the mixture is nicely varied to include the familiar and the unfamiliar, and both playing and recording are excellent. Audience participation is taken for granted and is seldom too intrusive but adds to the feeling of enjoyment and spontaneity.

Vienna Philharmonic Orchestra, (i) Sir Georg Solti or (ii) Willi Boskovsky

'Light Cavalry': Overtures: (i) SUPPÉ: *Light Cavalry; Poet and peasant; Morning, noon and night; Pique dame;* (ii) *Beautiful Galatea.* NICOLAI: *The merry wives of Windsor.* REZNIČEK: *Donna Diana.* STRAUSS, Johann Jnr: *Die Fledermaus.*
(B) **(*) Decca 421 170-2; *421 170-4.*

Suppé overtures represented some of the first repertoire recorded by Solti for Decca in the days of mono LP (when he wanted to record Wagner!). These are his later, stereo versions, first issued in 1960. They generate characteristic intensity and excitement, and the recording has a spectacularly wide dynamic range – too wide for the cello solos in *Morning, noon and night* and *Poet and peasant*, where the instrument is backwardly balanced and sounds more like a viola. Boskovsky's performances are altogether more mellow, yet in *Donna Diana* the exhilarating but relaxed forward impulse is nicely judged. The sound is appropriately bright and vivid, especially brilliant in the four favourite Suppé overtures conducted by Solti.

Wallace, John (trumpet)

'Man – the measure of all things' (with Philh. O, Warren-Green): MONTEVERDI: *Orfeo: Toccata.* TORELLI: *Sinfonia a 4 in C.* ALBINONI: *2 Concerti a 6 in C; Sonata di concerto a 7 in D.* VIVALDI: *Double concerto in C.* FRANCHESCINI: *Sonata in D.* PURCELL: *Sonata in D.* BONONCINE: *Sinfonia decima a 7.* ALBERTI: *Sinfonia teatrale a 4.*
**(*) Nimbus Dig. NI 5017 [id.].

The title of this collection aims to epitomize the spirit of the Italian Renaissance, which produced a great flowering of the arts. The collection, covering a period of nearly two centuries of trumpet music, almost defeats its own object of showing the diversity of baroque style since, during this period, trumpet devices did not change very much. The music explores all the possibilities of one, two and four trumpets, and the ear finds welcome relief in Albinoni's *Concerto a 6* for trumpet, oboes and bassoon. John Wallace is a splendid soloist; in the multiple works he is joined by John Miller, David Mason and William Stokes, who play with comparable bravura. The recording was made in the resonant acoustics of All Saints', Tooting, which tend to blur the opening Monteverdi *Toccata* and the following Torelli *Sinfonia*, which features all four soloists. But for the most part the reverberation colours the music attractively.

Wickens, Derek (oboe)

'The classical oboe' (with RPO, Howarth): VIVALDI: *Oboe concerto in A min., RV 461.* ALESSANDRO MARCELLO: *Oboe concerto in D min.* HAYDN: *Oboe concerto in C.*
*** ASV CDDCA 1003; *ZCDCA 1003* [id.].

During his years with the RPO, Wickens repeatedly demonstrated in yearningly beautiful solos that he was one of the most characterful of London's orchestral players. Though at times he seems to be looking for his back desk rather than his solo spot, his artistry comes out vividly on this well-recorded disc, with the CD providing believable projection for the oboe against Howarth's sympathetic accompaniments.

Williams, John (guitar)

Guitar concertos (with ECO, (i) Sir Charles Groves; (ii) Daniel Barenboim): (i) GIULIANI: *Concerto No. 1 in A, Op. 30.* VIVALDI: *Concertos in A and D.* RODRIGO: *Fantasia para un gentilhombre;* (ii) *Concierto de Aranjuez.* VILLA-LOBOS: *Concerto.* (i) CASTELNUOVO-TEDESCO: *Concerto No. 1 in D, Op. 99.*

(M) *** Sony M2YK 45610 (2) [id.].

This bouquet of seven concertante works for guitar from John Williams could hardly be better chosen, and the performances are most appealing. Moreover the transfers are very well managed. Only the Vivaldi concertos (unidentified but attractive, especially the *D major* with its striking central *Largo*) bring quality which sounds in the least dated. Elsewhere the orchestral texture is full and pleasing and, if the guitar is very forward and larger than life, the playing is so expert and spontaneous that one hardly objects. All these performances are among the finest ever recorded, and Groves and Barenboim provide admirably polished accompaniments, matching the eager spontaneity of their soloist.

Williams, John (guitar), (i) London Symphony Orchestra, Paul Daniel

ALBÉNIZ: (i) *Iberia suite* (arr. for guitar & orchestra by Steve Gray): *El Albaicín; Triana; Rondeña.* GRANADOS: *Valses poéticos* (trans. Williams). LLOBET: 9 *Catalan folksongs.* RODRIGO: *Invocation et danse; En los Trigales.*
*** Sony Dig. SK 48480 [id.].

The arrangement for guitar and orchestra of three substantial movements from Albéniz's piano suite, *Iberia*, makes an unusual but attractive concerto. In the last of the three, *Rondeña*, the solo guitar enters only after the first (fast) section, but Williams's artistry readily justifies the translation to the new and bigger medium, with the suggestions of guitar music in the original piano-writing providing ample justification. Williams's own transcription of the charming little waltz suite of Granados is a delight too, a piano work which he was drawn to by hearing Alicia de Larrocha playing it. The unpretentious *Catalan folksongs* of Llobet and the two Rodrigo pieces are original guitar music, masterfully played by Williams. Warm, immediate recording.

(The) Wallace Collection, Simon Wright

20th-century brass music (with John Wallace (trumpet), Michael Thompson Horn Qt): BRITTEN: *Fanfare for St Edmundsbury for 3 trumpets; Russian funeral for brass and percussion. Simple symphony* (arr. Matthews/Wright). TIPPETT: *Fanfare for the four corners. Sonata for 4 horns; Festal brass with blues.* LUTOSLAWSKI: *Mini overture for brass quintet.*
**(*) Collins Dig. 1229-2; *1229-4* [id.].

The available repertory of authentic brass music is really opening up now and this is something of an avant-garde banquet, if not quite as diversely entertaining as either of the two collections by the London Gabrieli Brass. Britten's remarkably ingenious *Fanfare for St Edmundsbury* gives the participants three different melodic lines in turn, each with a different tonality; then they are fitted together with ear-tickling results. The *Russian funeral march* uses folk material in a characteristically offbeat Britten manner. These are the two highlights. Tippett's *Sonata for four horns* is very prolix, especially the second movement *Allegro giocoso*, but is ingeniously contrived; the *Festal brass with blues* (quoting from the *Third Symphony*) is even more approachable. Elliot Carter's *Quintet* is altogether thornier and fragmented, but Lutoslawski's short overture is succinct and witty. But why include an arrangement of Britten's *Simple symphony*? It resounds sonorously enough here, but is so much more effective on strings. As it happens the fast movements come off best, notably the famous *Playful pizzicato*, but the *Sentimental sarabande* is coarsened. The playing is expert (Michael Thomson's horn group produces phenomenal bravura) and the well balanced Abbey Road recording cannot be faulted.

Yepes, Narciso (guitar)

'Guitarra española' (with Spanish R. & TV O, Odón Alonso; LSO, Rafael Frübeck de Burgos): SANZ: *Suite española.* MUDARRA: *Fantasia que contrahaza la harpa en la manera de Ludovico.* NARVÁEZ: *Diferencias sobre 'Guárdame las vacas'.* SOLER: *Sonata in E.* SOR: *10 Études; Theme and variations, Op. 9.* ALBÉNIZ: *Suite española: Asturias (Leyenda). Recuerdos de viaje: Rumores de la caleta. Malagueña. Piezas caracteristicas: Torre bermeja (Serenata). Malaguena, Op. 165.* GRANADOS: *Danza española No. 4 (Villanesca).* TÁRREGA: *Alborada (Capriccio); Danza mora; Sueño; Recuerdos de la Alhambra; Marieta (Mazurka); Capricho árabe (Serenata); Tango.*

FALLA: *El amor brujo: El círculo mágico; Canción del fuego fatuo. Three-cornered hat: Danza del molinaro (Farruca). Homenaje: Le tombeau de Claude Debussy.* TURINA: *Sonata, Op. 61. Fandaguillo, Op. 36; Garrotín y soleares; Ráfaga.* BACARISSE: *Passapie; Concertino in A min. for guitar and orchestra Op. 72.* YEPES: *Catarina d'Alió.* RODRIGO: *En los trigales; Concierto de Aranjuez; Fantasia para un gentilhombre; Concierto madrigal for 2 guitars and orchestra* (with Godelieve Monden, Phil. O, Garcia Navarro). PUJOL: *El abejorro; Estudios.* TORROBA: *Madroños.* MONTSALVATGE: *Habañera.* OHANA: *Tiento; Concierto tres gráficos for guitar and orchestra.* RUIZ-PIPÓ: *Canción y danza No. 1; Tablas para guitarra y orquestra.* ANON:. *Jeux interdits (Romance); Canciones populares catalanes: La filla del marxant; La filadora; El mestre; La cançó del lladre.*
(M) *** DG 435 841-2 (5).

This collection is based on a pair of early stereo LPs called 'Spanish guitar music of five centuries' (Alonso Mudarra was born around 1510), to which much other repertory has been added from Yepes' later records. So the set also celebrates his long-lived and distinguished recording achievement in music from his own country. It was inevitable that the three most famous concertante works of Rodrigo would be included, which will involve duplication for many collectors, but the other concertante works, by Barcarisse, Ruiz-Pipó and Ohana are less familiar and very welcome. Among the more ambitious solo pieces are the *Suite* of Sanz and Soler *Sonatas*, plus the *Studies* of Sor. But many of the miniatures are equally memorable in their atmospheric potency (not least the Falla transcriptions), when Yepes's performances – with their vivid palette and high level of concentration – constantly remind us of Beethoven's assertion that a guitar is an orchestra all by itself. Generally excellent sound.

Instrumental Recitals

Amato, Donna (piano)

'A piano portrait': LISZT: *Hungarian rhapsody No. 2* (cadenza by Rachmaninov); *Consolation No. 3; Liebestraum No. 3.* DEBUSSY: *Arabesque No. 1; Suite bergamasque: Clair de lune. Préludes: La fille aux cheveux de lin; La cathédrale engloutie.* RAVEL: *Pavane pour une infante défunte.* GERSHWIN: *3 Preludes; Rhapsody in blue* (solo piano version). Song transcriptions: *The man I love; Swanee; Oh, lady be good; I'll build a stairway to paradise; 'S wonderful; I got rhythm.*
*** Olympia OCD 352; Altarus *AIR-TC 9007* [id.].

The young American pianist Donna Amato here proves her mettle in standard repertoire and, more importantly, confirms her ability to create 'live' performances in the recording studio. None of the readings is routine or conventional: the Liszt *Consolation* has an attractive simplicity and the famous *Liebestraum*, while not lacking romantic impulse, has an agreeable lack of gush. Her Debussy is particularly impressive: the *Arabesque* has a lightly chimerical variety of touch and colour and the two most famous pieces are made to seem refreshingly unhackneyed. The highlight, however, is *La cathédrale engloutie*, an unforgettably powerful evocation, played quite superbly. She is, not surprisingly, completely at home with Gershwin. The song transcriptions are splendidly stylish and sparkling and her solo account of the *Rhapsody in blue* is highly idiomatic. In its strong, natural impulse and rhythmic freedom it can be spoken of in the same breath as Bernstein's version, although it has completely its own character. Donna Amato's style is not that of a Horowitz, and so it was perhaps a pity she chose to open with the Liszt *Hungarian rhapsody*, which would have been better placed later on in the programme, while the Ravel *Pavane* is a little too sober; but as a whole this 76-minute recital, recorded very realistically indeed in Salen Church Hall, Ski, Norway, is most enjoyable.

Barere, Simon (piano)

'The complete HMV recordings, 1934–6': LISZT: *Étude de concert, G.144/2. Années de pèlerinage, 2nd Year (Italy): Sonnetto 104 del Petrarca, G.161/5. Gnomenreigen, G.145/2; Réminiscences de Don Juan, G.418* (2 versions); *Rapsodie espagnole, G.254; Valse oubliée No. 1, G.215.* CHOPIN: *Scherzo No. 3 in C sharp min., Op. 39; Mazurka No. 38 in F sharp min., Op. 59/3; Waltz No. 5 in A flat, Op. 42.* BALAKIREV: *Islamey* (2 versions). BLUMENFELD: *Étude for the left hand.* GLAZUNOV: *Étude in C, Op. 31/1.* SCRIABIN: *Études: in C sharp min., Op. 2/1; in D sharp min., Op. 8/12* (2 versions). LULLY/GODOWSKI: *Gigue in E.* RAMEAU/GODOWSKI: *Tambourin in E min.* SCHUMANN: *Toccata in C, Op. 7* (2 versions).
❀ (***) Appian mono CDAPR 7001 (2) [id.].

We have had to wait nearly a decade for the new medium to get round to Simon Barere, but now at last he is adequately represented by Carnegie Hall recitals of the music of Chopin, Liszt and Rachmaninov. This two-CD set offers all of Barere's HMV recordings, made in the mid-1930s, including the alternative takes he made in the studio. In several cases, including Balakirev's *Islamey* and Liszt's *Réminiscences de Don Juan*, Barere became dissatisfied with the performances after publication and re-recorded them, and this set includes a generous appendix of alternative published takes, and two rejected takes that were not included in the original LP compilation, the Chopin *Mazurka* and the Schumann *Toccata*. What can one say of his playing without exhausting one's stock of superlatives? His fingerwork is quite astonishing and his virtuosity almost in a class on its own. The set contains an absolutely stunning account of the *Réminiscences de Don Juan*, and his *Islamey* knocks spots off any successor in sheer virtuosity and excitement; it is altogether breathtaking, and much the same might be said of his *Rapsodie espagnole*. Nor is there any want of poetry – witness the delicacy of the Scriabin *C sharp minor Étude* or Liszt's *La leggierezza*. Bryan Crimp's excellent booklet is not only full of interesting discographical material but also details Barere's extraordinary childhood development and subsequent career. Readers wanting to investigate this legendary artist should start here, for this is the most desirable of all the Barere sets listed in this volume. One of the most important functions of the gramophone is to chart performance traditions that would otherwise disappear from view, and this set is one to celebrate.

'Simon Barere at the Carnegie Hall, Vol. 3': BEETHOVEN: *Piano sonata No. 27 in E min., Op. 90.* LISZT: *Études de concert Nos. 2, La leggierezza; 3, Un sospiro, S.144.* WEBER: *Piano sonata No. 1 in C: Presto, J.138.* SCHUMANN: *Carnaval, Op. 9.* CHOPIN: *Andante spianato and Grande polonaise brillante in E flat, Op. 22; Ballade No. 1 in G min., Op. 23; Études: in C sharp min.; in G flat; in F; Op. 10/4, 5 & 8; Fantaisie in F min., Op. 49; Impromptu No. 1 in A flat, Op. 29; Nocturne No. 8 in D flat, Op. 27/2; Scherzo No. 3 in C sharp min., Op. 39; Waltz No. 5 in A flat, Op. 42.*
(*(**)) APR mono CDAPR 7009 (2) [id.].

All these recordings were made at Carnegie Hall recitals at various times between 1946 and 1949 and are of varying quality. The Beethoven *Sonata*, Op. 90, is splendidly played but is disfigured by heavy surfaces and some distortion. The Liszt items, which were made two years earlier, are better. The playing of *La leggierezza* is pretty breathtaking and, for that matter, so is his hair-raising account of the Weber *Perpetuum mobile*. Schumann's *Carnaval* is artistically more controversial, with some scrambled passages (the end of the *Préamble* is a case in point), and it suffers from particularly shallow recording quality. Barere must have been an impressive Chopin interpreter if some of the performances on the second CD are anything to go by. The variety and quality of touch in the *D flat Nocturne*, Op. 27/2, are to be marvelled at, and one is reminded of Harold Schonberg's phrase, 'miracles of light-fingered dexterity' quoted on the sleeve. Some of the performances suffer from rough – not to say execrable – recording quality (the *F minor Fantasy* has obtrusive surfaces) but they all serve as evidence of Barere's stature. All the same, this set is for the converted; collectors are better advised to set out on their investigation of this extraordinary artist with the 1934–6 HMV recordings.

Bate, Jennifer (organ)

Organ of Beauvais Cathedral: *'Virtuoso French organ music':* BOËLLMANN: *Suite gothique.* GUILMANT: *Cantilène pastorale; March on 'Lift up your heads'.* SAINT-SAËNS: *Improvisation No. 7.* GIGOUT: *Toccata in B min.; Scherzo; Grand choeur dialogué.*
**(*) Unicorn Dig. DKPCD 9041; *DKPC 9041* [id.].

The playing here has enormous flair and thrilling bravura. Jennifer Bate's imaginative touch makes Boëllmann's *Suite gothique* sound far better music than it is. In the closing *Toccata*, as in the spectacular Guilmant march based on Handel's famous chorus, the panache and excitement of the playing grip the listener firmly, and the clouding of the St Beauvais acoustic is forgotten. But in the swirling Saint-Saëns *Improvisation* and the Gigout *Scherzo*, detail is masked. In the massive *Grand choeur dialogué*, the clever timing makes the firm articulation register, but although the Unicorn engineers achieve a splendidly sumptuous sound-image, elsewhere there is blurring caused by the wide reverberation of the empty cathedral.

Bergen Wind Quintet

BARBER: *Summer music, Op. 31.* SAEVERUD: *Tunes and dances from Siljustøl, Op. 21a.* JOLIVET: *Serenade for wind quintet with principal oboe.* HINDEMITH: *Kleine Kammermusik, Op. 24/2.*
*** BIS CD 291 [id.].

Barber's *Summer music* is a glorious piece dating from the mid-1950s; it is in a single movement. Saeverud's *Tunes and dances from Siljustøl* derive from piano pieces of great charm and sound refreshing in their transcribed format. Jolivet's *Serenade* is hardly less engaging, while Hindemith's *Kleine Kammermusik*, when played with such character and finesse, is no less welcome. Throughout, the fine blend and vivacious ensemble give consistent pleasure, and the recording seems ideally balanced within an ambience that brings bloom and atmosphere without being too reverberant. On CD, the illusion of realism is very striking. Highly recommended.

Bream, Julian (guitar)

'Homage to Segovia': TURINA: *Fandanguillo, Op. 36; Sevillana, Op. 20.* MOMPOU: *Suite compostelana.* TÓRROBA: *Sonatina.* GERHARD: *Fantasia.* FALLA: *Homenaje pour le tombeau de Claude Debussy; Three-cornered hat: Miller's dance.* OHANA: *Tiento.*

*** BMG/RCA Dig. RD 85306 [RCD1 5306].

Readers who have already acquired Bream's earlier digital recital concentrating on the music of Albéniz and Granados (see the Composer section, above) will find this hardly less impressive, both musically and technically. The programme here is even more diverse, with the Gerhard *Fantasia* adding a twentieth-century dimension while Ohana's *Tiento* has a comparable imaginative approach to texture. Throughout, Bream plays with his usual flair and spontaneity, constantly imaginative in his use of a wide dynamic range and every possible colouristic effect. The recording has the most tangible realism and presence.

'Guitarra': MUDARRA: *Fantasias Nos. 10 and 14.* MILAN: *Fantasia No. 22.* NARVAEZ: *La canción del Emperador; Conde Claros.* SANZ: *Galliardas; Pasacalles; Canarios.* GUERAU: *Villano; Canario.* MURCIA: *Prelude and allegro.* SOR: *Variations on a theme by Mozart, Op. 9.* AQUADO: *Rondo in A, Op. 2/3.* TARREGA: *Prelude in A min; Recuerdos de la Alhambra.* GRANADOS: *La Maja de Goya. Danza española No. 5.* ALBÉNIZ: *Suite española: Cádiz.* TÓRROBA: *Sonata in A.* TURINA: *Fandanguillo.* FALLA: *Homenaje pour le tombeau de Claude Debussy. Three-cornered hat: Miller's dance.*
*** BMG/RCA Dig. RD 86206.

A wholly admirable survey of Spanish guitar music covering four hundred years and featuring four different instruments, all especially built by José Ramanillos: a Renaissance guitar, vihuela, baroque guitar and a modern classical guitar. Bream's natural dexterity is matched by his remarkable control of colour and unerring sense of style. Many of the early pieces are quite simple but have considerable magnetism. Three of the items included in the latter part of the recital come from his Albéniz/Granados coupling, reviewed in the Composer section, others from the shorter collection above, dedicated to Segovia, notably the exciting Turina *Fandanguillo*, a real highlight. The presence of the recordings is remarkable, the focus sharp and believable.

'Romantic guitar': PAGANINI: *Grand sonata in A.* MENDELSSOHN: *Song without words: Venetian boat song, Op. 19/6; String quartet No. 1: Canzonetta.* SCHUBERT: *Piano sonata No. 18 in G, D.894: Minuet.* TARREGA: *Prelude (Lagrima); 3 Mazurkas.*
(M) ** BMG/RCA GD 86798; *GK 86798.*

A pleasant but not distinctive recital, well recorded. The Paganini *Grand sonata* is a shade inflated for a work conceived in terms of an intimate instrument like the guitar. Of the other items the Tarrega pieces have the greatest memorability in this form.

Bream, Julian and John Williams (guitars)

'Together': LAWES: *Suite for 2 guitars.* CARULLI: *Duo in G, Op. 34.* SOR: *L'Encouragement, Op. 34.* ALBÉNIZ: *Córdoba.* GRANADOS: *Goyescas: Intermezzo.* FALLA: *La vida breve: Spanish dance No. 1.* RAVEL: *Pavane pour une infante défunte.*
*** BMG/RCA RD 83257.

'Together again': CARULLI: *Serenade, Op. 96.* GRANADOS: *Danzas españolas Nos. 6 and 11.* ALBÉNIZ: *Bajo la Palmera, Op. 32. Iberia: Evocación.* GIULIANI: *Variazioni concertanti, Op. 130.*
*** BMG/RCA RD 80456.

In this case two guitars are better than one; these two fine artists clearly strike sparks off each other. In the first recital, Albéniz's *Córdoba* is hauntingly memorable and the concert closes with a slow, stately version of Ravel's *Pavane* which is unforgettable. Here Bream justifies a tempo which he did not bring off so effectively in his solo version (now deleted). On the second disc, it is again music of Albéniz that one remembers for the haunting atmosphere the two artists create together. The sound of these reissues is truthful and atmospheric, although the digital remastering for CD does not succeed in removing all the background hiss. This is distinctly noticeable in the first collection but in the second is only very slight, and the effect is not intrusive.

Brendel, Alfred (piano)

'For Amnesty International': BACH: *Italian concerto in F, BWV 971.* HAYDN: *Andante with variations in F min., Hob XVII/6.* BEETHOVEN: *Piano sonata No. 14 in C sharp min. (Moonlight).* LISZT: *Harmonies poétiques et religieuses: Funérailles.* BERG: *Sonata, Op. 1.* BUSONI: *Preludio – Fantasia – Ciaccona.*
*** Ph. Analogue/Dig. 426 814-2 [id.].

This compilation derives both from studio recordings and from recitals given in the Vienna Grosser Konserthaussaal in 1972 and 1981, and thus the recordings included have come from both analogue and digital sources, and the latter are not always superior. Among the finest is the Bach *Italian concerto*, meticulously articulated in a warm but clean acoustic and in excellent analogue sound, recorded in 1976, and the marvellous Busoni *Toccata*, recorded live in 1972 and superbly played and thoroughly exhilarating (in spite of one or two tired notes inevitable on a live occasion). The Haydn, also included in the four-CD set of the *Sonatas*, is digital but made in a slightly drier studio than the 1972 Beethoven *Moonlight sonata*, which it immediately precedes. The Alban Berg *Sonata*, a studio recording from 1982, is also commanding and powerful, and Liszt's *Funérailles*, a 1981 Viennese occasion, is very distinguished indeed. Some of Brendel's best performances and designed to make a contribution to one of the world's best causes. Strongly recommended on both counts.

Britton, Harold (organ)

Organ of Royal Albert Hall: *'Organ spectacular':* SUPPÉ: *Light Cavalry overture.* LEMARE: *Andantino in D flat.* VERDI: *Aida: Grand march.* ALBINONI: *Adagio* (arr. Giazotto). WAGNER: *Ride of the Valkyries.* BACH: *Toccata and fugue in D min., BWV 565.* TCHAIKOVSKY: *None but the lonely heart.* ELGAR: *Pomp and circumstance march No. 1.* SOUSA: *Liberty Bell.* WIDOR: *Symphony No. 5: Toccata.*
(BB) *** ASV CDQS 6028; *ZCQS 6028.*

If one is to have a collection mainly of arrangements of orchestral lollipops on an organ, the instrument at the Royal Albert Hall is surely an ideal choice: it offers the widest dynamic range, including an effective recession of quieter passages readily at the player's command – used to good purpose in *Light Cavalry* – but can also produce truly spectacular fortissimos, with a wide amplitude and a blaze of colour from its multitude of stops. Harold Britton is obviously fully at home on the instrument and plays in an aptly extrovert style for such a recital, obviously enjoying himself. The CD is in the demonstration class – there are few problems of muddying from reverberation.

Chung, Kyung Wha (violin), Phillip Moll (piano)

'Con amore': KREISLER: *La Gitana; Liebeslied; Praeludium and allegro in the style of Pugnani. Liebesfreud.* POLDINI: *Dancing doll.* WIENIAWSKI: *Scherzo-Tarantelle; Caprice in A min.* ELGAR: *Salut d'amor, Op. 12; La Capricieuse, Op. 17.* TCHAIKOVSKY: *Valse sentimentale.* NOVAČEK: *Moto perpetuo.* DEBUSSY: *Beau soir.* CHOPIN: *Nocturne in C sharp min.* GOSSEC: *Gavotte.* CHAMINADE: *Sérénade espagnole.* SAINT-SAËNS: *Caprice (after a study in the form of a waltz), Op. 52/6.* BRAHMS: *Hungarian dance No. 1.*
*** Decca Dig. 417 289-2 [id.].

Kyung Wha Chung's collection, '*Con amore*', reflects that title in a delightfully varied choice of items, sweet as well as brilliant. When she claims in all seriousness that she does not think of herself as a virtuoso violinist, she really means that technical brilliance is only an incidental for her; and the poise and flair of all these items show her at her most winningly characterful, helped by Phillip Moll's very sympathetic accompaniment and well-balanced recording, which has fine presence on CD.

Clarion Ensemble

'Trumpet collection': FANTINI: *Sonata; Brando; Balletteo; Corrente.* MONTEVERDI: *Et e pur dunque vero.* FRESCOBALDI: *Canzona a canto solo.* PURCELL: *To arms, heroic prince.* A. SCARLATTI: *Si suoni la tromba.* BISHOP: *Arietta and Waltz; Thine forever.* DONIZETTI: *Lo L'udia.* KOENIG: *Post horn galop.* ARBAN: *Fantasia on Verdi's Rigoletto.* CLARKE: *Cousins.* ENESCU: *Legende.*
❀ *** Amon Ra CD-SAR 30 [id.].

The simple title '*Trumpet collection*' covers a fascinating recital of music for trumpet written over three centuries and played with great skill and musicianship by Jonathan Impett, using a variety of original instruments, from a keyed bugle and clapper shake-key cornopean to an English slide trumpet and a posthorn. Impett is a complete master of all these instruments, never producing a throttled tone; indeed in the Purcell and Scarlatti arias he matches the soaring soprano line of Deborah Roberts with uncanny mirror-image precision. Accompaniments are provided by other members of the Clarion Ensemble, including Paul Nicholson who plays a fortepiano with great flair and with the slightly dry timbre particularly suited to act as a foil to the brass sounds. The Frescobaldi *Canzona* brings a duet for trumpet and trombone, with a background harpsichord filigree, which is most effective. With demonstration-worthy recording – one could readily believe the instrumentalists to be at the other end of one's room – this is as enjoyable as it is interesting, with the *Post horn galop* and Arban's *Rigoletto variations* producing exhilarating bravura.

Van Cliburn (piano)

'The world's favourite piano music': LISZT: *Liebestraume No. 3; Consolation No. 5.* RACHMANINOV: *Preludes: in C sharp min., Op. 3/2; in G min., E flat, C min., Op. 23/5–7; in G, Op. 32/5.* BEETHOVEN: *Für Elise.* MOZART: *Piano sonata in A, K.330: Rondo alla turca.* DEBUSSY: *Rêverie.* BRAHMS: *Intermezzi: in C sharp min., Op. 117/3; in E flat min., Op. 118/6; Waltz in A flat, Op. 32/5.* SCHUBERT: *Moment musical in F min., D.780/3.* SCHUMANN: *Kinderszenen: Träumerei.* TCHAIKOVSKY: *The Seasons: Barcarolle, Op. 37b/6.* CHOPIN: *Fantaisie-Impromptu, Op. 66.*
(M) *** BMG/RCA 9026 60973-2.

The title may be hype but there are quite a few favourites here, and the playing is very distinguished. Indeed the quality of the five Rachmaninov *Preludes* makes one wish Van Cliburn had recorded a complete set; the famous *C sharp minor* is very arresting indeed. Both Liszt's *Liebestraume* (plus the poetic account of the little-known *Fifth Consolation*) and Chopin's *Fantaisie-Impromptu* show him on his very finest form. The recordings, made between 1970 and 1975, give absolutely no cause for complaint: the piano timbre is firm and full.

Curley, Carlo (organ)

'The Emperor's Fanfare' (Organ of Girard College Chapel, Philadelphia): SOLER: *Emperor's fanfare* (arr. Biggs). WAGNER: *Tristan und Isolde: Liebestod.* JONGEN: *Choral.* BACH: *Toccata and fugue in D min., BWV 565.* ALBINONI: *Adagio* (arr. Giazotto). ALAIN: *Litanies.* SCHUBERT: *Ave Maria.* KARG-ELERT: *Nun danket alle Gott, Op. 65/9.* GRIEG: *Sigurd Jorsalfar: Homage march.* GUILMANT: *March upon Handel's 'Lift up your heads', Op. 15.*
*** Argo Dig. 430 200-2; *430 200-4* [id.].

The flamboyant Carlo Curley describes with engaging enthusiasm the organ he plays here: 'Nearly one hundred feet from the [Girard] Chapel's marble floor and above the vast, coffered ceiling, entirely covered incidentally with real gold leaf, the organ, all thirty-five metric tonnes, and with 6,587 hand-made pipes, is miraculously suspended. In a chapel so cavernous, and with such remarkable reverberation, it is well nigh impossible to identify the source of the sound.' Yet the Argo engineers manage to provide an excellent focus and capture the extremely wide dynamic range of Curley's playing with precision at both ends of the spectrum. The performances are full of drama and temperament, unashamedly romantic yet very compelling. The title-piece by Soler is an anachronistic but irresistible arrangement by E. Power Biggs which provides an opportunity for great splashes of throaty timbre and uses – as does the Alain *Litanies* – the powerful *Tuba mirabilis* stop. 'Its pipes', Curley tells us, 'lie horizontally or *en chamade*, and this stop speaks with an unrivalled speed and clarity on twenty-five inches of wind pressure, a veritable hurricane when compared to the two to four inches common to modern instruments.' The sheer verve and panache of Curley's playing, matching the eloquence of his prose and the depth and spectacle of the reproduced sound – the pedals are stunningly caught – cannot fail to entertain any organ fancier.

'Brightly shining' (Organ of Girard College Chapel, Philadelphia): REGER: *Fantasia on 'Wie schön leucht't uns der Morgenstern', Op. 40/1.* VIERNE: *Pièce en style libre: Berceuse in A.* FRANCK: *Cantabile, Op. 2.* DUPRÉ: *Prelude and fugue in G min., Op. 7/3.* BARBER (arr. Curley): *Adagio, Op. 11.* LANGLAIS: *Chant du paix.* BOËLLMAN: *Suite gothique, Op. 25.*
** Argo Dig. 430 837-2 [id.].

This second Curley recital on the huge Girard College Chapel organ brings a degree of disappointment. The Reger *Fantasia* – a set of variations some 18 minutes in length – brings characteristic bravura and flair, the Boëllman *Suite gothique*, too, is played with charisma, while the registration in the Franck *Cantabile* piquantly tickles the ear. But the transcription of Barber's *Adagio for strings* is a self-defeating proposition. The recording on this occasion is somewhat more plangent at fortissmo levels, which perhaps suits the French repertory, but is a little wearing.

'Organ imperial' (Organ of Church of St Mary Redcliffe, Bristol): ELGAR: *Imperial march, Op. 32* (arr. Martin); *Enigma variations: Nimrod* (arr. Harris). *Chanson de matin; Chanson de nuit, Op. 15/1–2* (both arr. Brewer); *Organ sonata No. 1 in G, Op. 28.* PARRY: *Choral prelude on 'Eventide'.* S. S. WESLEY: *Choral song and fugue.* S. WESLEY: *Short pieces Nos. 8, Air; 9, Gavotte in F.* COCKER: *Tuba tune.* WHITLOCK: *Organ piece No. 2, Folk tune.* LEMARE: *Rondo capriccio – a study in accents, Op. 54.* VAUGHAN WILLIAMS: *Prelude on a Welsh hymn tune: Rhosymedre.*
*** Argo Dig. 433 450-2; *433 450-4* [id.].

If anything this collection is even finer than Carlo Curley's first recital in this Argo series, made in Phiadelphia. The recording is amazingly spectacular and real: the dynamic range in *Nimrod* from a serene and gentle opening to a blazing climax followed by a beautiful decrescendo is quite breathtaking. Elgar's *Sonata* was written in 1895 not long before *Enigma*, and it responds equally well to Curley's flamboyant treatment and is gripping from beginning to end, yet with the central movements appropriately mellow. The other shorter pieces including, Whitlock's simple but engaging *Folk tune*, Norman Cocker's jaunty *Tuba tune* (a real hit) are hardly less telling, while the syncopations of Edwin Lemare's *Rondo capriccio* are precisely handled, without any transatlantic jazziness. This is a wholly rewarding programme, the playing is that of a master, and the recording is magificent.

Davies, Philippa (flute), Thelma Owen (harp)

'The Romance of the flute and harp': HASSELMANS: *La Source, Op. 44; Feuilles d'automne.* GODARD: *Suite, Op. 16: Allegretto.* GODEFROID: *Étude de concert.* FAURÉ: *Berceuse, Op. 16; Impromptu, Op. 86.* DÖPPLER: *Mazurka.* MENDELSSOHN: *Spring song, Op. 62/3.* THOMAS: *Watching the wheat.* SAINT-SAËNS: *Le Cygne.* BIZET: *Fair maid of Perth: Intermezzo.* PARISH-ALVARS: *Serenade.* DEBUSSY: *Syrinx; Suite bergamasque: Clair de lune.*
(B) *** Pickwick Dig. PCD 835; *CIMPC 835.*

An unexpectedly successful recital which effectively intersperses harp solos with music in which the flute takes the leading role. The playing is most sensitive and the recording is very realistic indeed. The programme, too, is well chosen and attractively laid out. Highly recommended for playing on a pleasant summer evening.

Drake, Susan (harp)

'Echoes of a waterfall': HASSELMANS: *La Source, Op. 44; Prelude, Op. 52; Chanson de mai, Op. 40.* ALVARS: *Divertissement, Op. 38.* GODEFROID: *Bois solitaire; Étude de concert in E flat min., Op. 193.* GLINKA: *Variations on a theme of Mozart.* THOMAS: *Echoes of a waterfall: Watching the wheat; Megan's daughter.* SPOHR: *Variations on Je suis encore, Op. 36.*
*** Hyp. CDA 66038; *KA 66038* [id.].

The music is lightweight and sometimes facile, but the young Welsh harpist, Susan Drake, is a beguiling exponent, and her technique is as impressive as her feeling for atmosphere. Those intrigued by the title of the collection will not be disappointed by the sounds here (the recording is excellent) which balance evocation with a suitable degree of flamboyance when the music calls for it. The Thomas evocation of watery effects is certainly picturesque, as is Hasselmans' charming *La Source*, and both the Spohr and (especially) the Glinka *Variations* have considerable appeal.

Du Pré, Jacqueline (cello)

Early BBC recordings, Vol. 1 (with Stephen Kovacevich, Ernest Lush): BACH: (Unaccompanied) *Cello suites Nos. 1 in G; 2 in D min., BWV 1007/8.* BRITTEN: *Cello sonata in C, Op. 65; Scherzo; Marcia.* FALLA: *Suite populaire espagnole* (arr. Maréchal).
(M) (***) EMI mono CDM7 63165-2.

Early BBC recordings, Vol. 2 (with Ernest Lush, (i) William Pleeth): BRAHMS: *Cello sonata No. 2 in F, Op. 99.* F. COUPERIN: (i) *13th Concert a 2 instrumens* (*Les Goûts-réunis*). HANDEL: *Cello sonata in G min.* (arr. Slatter).
(M) (***) EMI mono CDM7 63166-2.

These two discs gather together some of the radio performances which Jacqueline du Pré gave in her inspired teens. Her 1962 recordings of the first two Bach *Cello suites* may not be immaculate, but her impulsive vitality makes phrase after phrase at once totally individual and seemingly inevitable. In two movements from Britten's *Cello sonata in C*, with Stephen Kovacevich as her partner, the sheer wit is deliciously infectious, fruit of youthful exuberance in both players. The first of the two discs is completed by Falla's *Suite populaire espagnole*, with the cello matching any singer in expressive range and rhythmic flair. The second has fascinating Couperin duets played with her teacher, William Pleeth; the Handel *Sonata* is equally warm and giving. Best of all is the Brahms *Cello sonata No. 2*, recorded at the 1962 Edinburgh Festival. Though there are incidental flaws, the broad sweep of this magnificent work is conveyed masterfully. Few of Du Pré's later records give a more vivid portrait of her than these. The quality of the mono sound varies but, with clean transfers, the vitality of the performances is unimpaired.

Eden, Bracha and Alexander Tamir (piano duet)

'Dances around the world': RACHMANINOV: *Polka italienne.* MOSZKOWSKI: *Spanish dances, Op. 65/1–2.* GRIEG: *Norwegian dances Nos. 2–3.* BRAHMS: *Hungarian dances and Waltzes.* DVOŘÁK: *Slavonic dances, Op. 46/6–7; Op. 72/8.* SCHUBERT: *Waltzes.* BARBER: *Souvenirs: Pas de deux.* DEBUSSY: *Petite suite: Menuet and ballet.*
(BB) *** Pickwick Dig. PWK 1134.

Eden and Tamir travel the world as a piano duo, and this record is exactly like going to one of their concerts: it is both exhilarating and beguiling, full of variety and spontaneity. They sound as if they are enjoying everything they play, and so do we. Very good sound too.

Fábián, Márta (cimbalom)

Baroque music for cimbalom (with Ágnes Szakály, cimbalom, Imre Kovács, flute, Béla Sztankovits, guitar): BACH: *French suites Nos. 2 in C min., BWV 813; 3 in B min., BWV 814; 5 in G, BWV 816.* PACHELBEL: *Partita in C min.* TELEMANN: *Trio sonata.*
(B) *** Hung. White Label HRC 097.

In order to play Bach's *French suites* on the cimbalom, two instruments and four hands are needed, and here Hungary's most famous virtuoso on the national instrument is joined by her colleague to do just that. The effect is piquantly effective. To make the recital even more rewarding, the solo cimbalom is also joined by flute and guitar to play a winningly tuneful six-movement *Partita* by Pachelbel and a no less engaging *Trio sonata* by Telemann. With excellent recording this is a disc that is as rewarding as it is unusual.

Fergus-Thompson, Gordon (piano)

'Reverie': DEBUSSY: *Rêverie; Arabesque No. 1; Suite bergamasque: Clair de lune.* SCRIABIN: *Étude, Op. 42/4.* BACH: *Chorales: Wachet auf* (trans. Busoni); *Jesu, joy of man's desiring* (trans. Hess). GLINKA: *The Lark* (trans. Balakirev). GODOWSKY: *Alt Wien.* SAINT-SAËNS: *The Swan* (arr. Godowsky). SCHUMANN: *Arabeske in C, Op. 18; Kinderszenen: Träumerei.* BRAHMS: *Intermezzo in A, Op. 118.* GRIEG: *Lyric pieces: Butterfly, Op. 43/1; Nocturne, Op. 54/4.* RAVEL: *Le tombeau de Couperin: Forlane. Pavane pour une infante défunte.*
(M) *** ASV Dig. CDWHL 2066; *ZCWHL 2066.*

This 76-minute recital fills a real need for a high-quality recital of piano music for the late evening, where the mood of reverie is sustained without blandness. Gordon Fergus-Thomson's performances are of high sensibility throughout, from the atmospheric opening Debussy items to the closing Ravel *Pavane*. Perhaps his Bach is a little studied but the rest is admirably paced, and the two favourite Grieg *Lyric pieces* are particularly fresh. Excellent recording.

Fernández, Eduardo (guitar)

'The World of the Spanish guitar': ALBÉNIZ: *Sevilla; Tango; Asturias.* LLOBET: *6 Catalan folksongs.* GRANADOS: *Andaluza; Danza triste.* TÁRREGA: *Estudio brillante; 5 Preludes; Minuetto; 3 Mazurkas; Recuerdos de la Alhambra.* SEGOVIA: *Estudio sin luz; Neblina; Estudio.* TURINA: *Fandagillo; Ráfaga.*
(B) *** Decca Dig 433 820-2; *433 820-4* [id.].

Fernández is most naturally recorded in the Henry Wood Hall. His programme is essentially an intimate one and centres on the highly rewarding music of Tárrega, although opening colourfully with items from Albéniz's *Suite española*. The Llobet group of *Folksongs*, and Segovia's hauntingly atmospheric *Neblina* ('Mist') make further highlights. Later there is bravura from Turina, notably the spectacular *Ráfaga* ('Gust of wind') but even here, though the playing is vibrant, there is no flashiness. With an hour of music and digital sound, this well-chosen programme is excellent value.

Fowke, Philip (piano)

'Virtuoso transcriptions': BACH/RACHMANINOV: *Suite from the Solo violin partita in E min., BWV 1006.* SCHUBERT/RACHMANINOV: *Wohin.* KREISLER/RACHMANINOV: *Liebeslied; Liebesfreud.* BUSONI: *Sonatina No. 6 (Fantasy on 'Carmen').* WEBER/TAUSIG: *Invitation to the dance.* GLINKA/BALAKIREV: *The Lark.* Johann STRAUSS Jnr/SCHULZELVER: *Arabesque on themes from 'The Blue Danube'.*
*** CRD CRD 3396; *CRDC 4096* [id.].

Philip Fowke plays with prodigious bravura but treats these display pieces with obvious seriousness of purpose. The presentation, while perhaps a little lacking in fun, still brings freshness to everything included here. It is amazing how pianistic Bach's violin music becomes in Rachmaninov's hands. It is a sparkling collection, bringing out of the cupboard music which still has the power to delight and amaze. The recording is excellent.

'French Impressions'

'French impressions' (played by: Er'ella Talmi, flute; Avigail Amheim, clarinet; Gad Levertov, viola; Alice Giles, harpsichord; Kaminkovsky Quartet): RAVEL: *Introduction and allegro.* DEBUSSY: *Sonata for flute, viola & harp.* ROUSSEL: *Trio, Op. 58.* CAPLET: *Conte fantastique.*
(BB) *** Pickwick/CDI Dig. PWK 1141.

Excellent, highly sensitive playing throughout an interesting and rewarding programme. This is one of the finest modern versions of Ravel's magically atmospheric *Introduction and allegro*, and the improvisatory nature of the lovely Debussy *Sonata* is captured equally well. The Roussel is of a drier vintage, but the programme ends in high drama with André Caplet's imaginative story in music based on Edgar Allan Poe's *Masque of the Red Death*. As always in this fine series, the recording has a remarkable illusion of presence and realism, and the ambience is perfectly judged.

Fretwork

'In nomine': 16th-century English music for viols: TALLIS: *In nomine a 4, Nos. 1 & 2; Solfaing song a 5; Fantasia a 5; In nomine a 4, No. 2; Libera nos, salva nos a 5.* TYE: *In nomine a 5 (Crye); In nomine a 5 (Trust).* CORNYSH: *Fa la sol a 3.* BALDWIN: *In nomine a 4.* BULL: *In nomine a 5.* BYRD: *In nomine a 4, No. 2. Fantasia a 3, No. 3.* TAVERNER: *In nomine; In nomine a 4.* PRESTON: *O lux beata Trinitas a 3.* JOHNSON: *In nomine a 4.* PARSONS: *In nomine a 5; Ut re mi fa sol la a 4.* FERRABOSCO: *In nomine a 5; Lute fantasia No. 5; Fantasia a 4.*
*** Amon Ra CD-SAR 29 [id.].

This was Fretwork's début CD; it immediately demonstrates their special combination of musical understanding, warmth and refinement in this repertoire. They play with polish and elegance and there is a certain aristocratic melancholy here that gives this music great character. The collection is not so obviously of strong popular appeal as the later collection for Virgin but is nevertheless very rewarding and distinguished, and it includes the complete consort music of Thomas Tallis. The sound is naturally pleasing in a fairly rich acoustic and readers can be assured that there is no vinegar in the string-timbre here; indeed, the sound itself is quite lovely in its gentle, austere atmosphere.

'Heart's ease': HOLBORNE: *The Honiesuckle; Countess of Pembroke's paradise; The Fairie round.* BYRD: *Fantasia a 5 (Two in one); Fancy in C.* DOWLAND: *Mr Bucton, his galliard; Captaine Digorie Piper, his galliard; Lachrimae antiquae pavan; Mr Nicholas Gryffith, his galliard.* BULL: *Fantasia a 4.* FERRABOSCO: *In nomine a 5.* GIBBONS: *In nomine a 5; Fantasia a 4 for the great dooble base.* LAWES: *Airs for 2 division viols in C: Pavan of Alfonso; Almain of Alfonso. Consort sett a 5 in C: Fantasia; Pavan; Almain.*
*** Virgin Dig. VC7 90706-2; *VC 790706-4* [id.].

An outstanding collection of viol consort music from the late Tudor and early Stuart periods; the playing is both stylish and vivacious, with a fine sense of the most suitable tempo for each piece. The more lyrical music is equally sensitive. This is a tuneful entertainment, not just for the specialist collector, and Fretwork convey their pleasure in all this music. The William Byrd *Fancy* (from *My Ladye Nevells Booke*) is played exuberantly on the organ by Paul Nicholson, to bring some contrast before the closing Lawes *Consort set.* The recording is agreeably warm, yet transparent too.

Gilbert, Kenneth (harpsichord)

Pièces de clavecin: CLÉRAMBAULT: *Suites Nos. 1 in C; 2 in C min.* D'ANGELBERT: *Gailliarde et Double; Chaconne du vieux gautier.* L. COUPERIN: *Pavane in F sharp min.* GASPARD LE ROUX: *Suite No. 5 in F.* MARAIS: *Polonaise in D min.* LEBÈGUE: *Les cloches in F.*
(M) *** DG Dig. 431 709-2; *431 709-4* [id.].

The two Clérambault suites recorded here are all that survive. They have splendid improvisatory preludes, rather in the style of Louis Couperin; they also have a genuine vein of lyricism, not inappropriate in a composer of so much vocal music. Gaspard Le Roux's *Suite* also dates from the same period (1705) and is attractively inventive, especially its impressive fifth movement, *Chaconne.* There is also much of appeal in the rest of the progamme here, not least the engaging piece by Lebègue, *Les cloches*, which is something of a find. Kenneth Gilbert plays persuasively and authoritatively; most appropriately he uses a modern copy, by David Rubio, of the 1680 Vaudry harpsichord from the Victoria and Albert Museum. The 1981 recording, made in the Henry Wood Hall in London, is vividly real.

Hall, Nicola (guitar)

'Virtuoso guitar transcriptions': RACHMANINOV: *Prelude in G min., Op. 23/5.* FALLA: *La vida breve: Dance.* ALBÉNIZ: *Suite española: Granada.* SARASATE: *Zapateado, Op. 23/2.* PAGANINI: *Caprice No. 24, Op. 1.* PARADIS: *Sicilienne.* BACH: *Partita in D min., BWV 1004.*
*** Decca Dig. 430 839-2 [id.].

Nicola Hall is a pupil of John Williams and even he has expressed amazement at her easy virtuosity in the Rachmaninov *Prelude*. All the transcriptions here are her own, and like the playing itself pay tribute to her musicianship as well as her absolute command of the instrument. Whether in the easy lilt and colour of Granados or the gentle melancholy of Paradis's *Sicilienne*, she communicates readily and her performance of the Bach *Partita* is remarkably strong and articulate, with the great *Chaconne* particularly impressive in its commanding closing section. The recording has striking realism and presence.

Hardenberger, Håkan (trumpet)

'The virtuoso trumpet' (with Roland Pöntinen): ARBAN: *Variations on themes from Bellini's 'Norma'*. FRANÇAIX: *Sonatine*. TISNÉ: *Héraldiques*. HONEGGER: *Intrada*. MAXWELL DAVIES: *Sonata*. RABE: *Shazam!*. HARTMANN: *Fantasia brillante on the air Rule Britannia*.
*** BIS CD 287 [id.].

This collection includes much rare and adventurous repertoire, not otherwise available and very unlikely to offer frequent access in live performance. Moreover, Hardenberger plays with electrifying bravura in the Maxwell Davies *Sonata* and the virtuoso miniatures. Antoine Tisné's five *Héraldiques* are eclectic but highly effective on the lips of such an assured player; *Scandé* and the following *Élégiaque* are notably characterful. But easily the most memorable item is the Françaix *Sonatine* (originally for violin and piano) in which two delicious brief outer movements frame a pleasing central *Sarabande*. Honegger's improvisatory *Intrada* is an effective encore piece. The recording is eminently realistic, with the CD giving superb presence.

HANSEN: *Cornet sonata in E flat, Op. 18*. ENESCU: *Legend*. HINDEMITH: *Trumpet sonata*. SCHMITT: *Trumpet suite, Op. 133*. LIGETI: *Mysteries of the macabre* (arr. Howarth).
*** Ph. Dig. 426 144-2 [id.].

A mixed bag. Hansen's piece is amiable, and Hindemith's otherwise unmemorable *Sonata* has a fine, elegiac slow movement, while the Schmitt *Suite* has great variety and is very demanding technically. Enescu's *Legend* has an engaging melancholy, while Ligeti's *Mysteries of the macabre* inhabits the world of the outrageous avant-garde and comes complete with rhythmic vocal noises. The reason for its composition remains as mysterious as its title. The three stars are for the playing and the very real recording, but there is not much music here that one would wish to return to very urgently.

Horowitz, Vladimir (piano)

'At the Met.': D. SCARLATTI: *Sonatas: in A flat, Kk. 127; in F min., Kk. 184 & 466; in A, Kk. 101; in B min., Kk. 87; in E, Kk. 135*. CHOPIN: *Ballade No. 4 in F min., Op. 52; Waltz No. 9 in A flat, Op. 69/1*. LISZT: *Ballade No. 2 in B min., G. 171*. RACHMANINOV: *Prelude No. 6 in G min., Op. 23/5*.
*** BMG/RCA Dig. RCD 14585 [RCD1 4585].

The playing is in a class of its own, and all one needs to know is that this recording reproduces the highly distinctive tone-quality Horowitz commanded. This recital, given at the Metropolitan Opera House and issued here at the time of his London Festival Hall appearance in 1982, comes closer to the real thing than anything else on record, except his DG recitals – see below. The quality of the playing is quite extraordinary.

'In London': *God save the Queen* (arr. Horowitz). CHOPIN: *Ballade No. 1 in G min., Op. 23; Polonaise No. 7 in A flat (Polonaise-Fantasie), Op. 61*. SCHUMANN: *Kinderszenen, Op. 15*. SCRIABIN: *Étude in D sharp min., Op. 8/12*.
*** BMG/RCA Dig. RD 84572.

Highlights from the memorable London recital Horowitz gave in 1982, though omitting the elegant Scarlatti sonatas he played on that occasion, doubtless because it would duplicate '*Horowitz at the Met.*' – see above. However, room could surely have been found for the Rachmaninov *Sonata*, or his encores, as the CD is not generously filled. As those who attended this electrifying recital will know, there were idiosyncratic touches, particularly in the *Kinderszenen* (and also in the Chopin *Ballade*), but this is remarkable testimony to his wide dynamic range and his refined *pianopianissimo*. There are many fascinating points of detail in both works (but notably the Chopin) which give one the feeling of hearing the music for the first time.

Recital: BACH/BUSONI: *Chorale prelude: Nun komm der Heiden Heiland.* MOZART: *Piano sonata No. 10 in C, K. 330.* CHOPIN: *Mazurka in A min., Op. 17/4; Scherzo No. 1 in B min., Op. 20; Polonaise No. 6 in A flat, Op. 53.* LISZT: *Consolation No. 3 in D flat.* SCHUBERT: *Impromptu in A flat, D. 899/4.* SCHUMANN: *Novellette in F, Op. 21/1.* RACHMANINOV: *Prelude in G sharp min., Op. 32/12.* SCRIABIN: *Étude in C sharp min., Op. 2/1.* MOSZKOWSKI: *Étude in F, Op. 72/6* (recording of performances featured in the film *Vladimir Horowitz – The Last Romantic*).
*** DG Dig. 419 045-2; *419 045-4* [id.].

Possibly the best recording Horowitz ever received, though his RCA compact discs have also given a splendid sense of his *pp* tone. Recorded when he was over eighty, this playing betrays remarkably little sign of frailty. The Mozart is beautifully elegant and the Chopin *A minor Mazurka*, Op. 17, No. 4, could hardly be more delicate. The only sign of age comes in the *B minor Scherzo*, which does not have the leonine fire and tremendous body of his famous 1950 recording. However, it is pretty astonishing for all that.

'The studio recordings': SCHUMANN: *Kreisleriana, Op. 16.* D. SCARLATTI: *Sonatas: in B min., Kk. 87; in E, Kk. 135.* LISZT: *Impromptu (Nocturne) in F sharp; Valse oubliée No. 1.* SCRIABIN: *Étude in D sharp min., Op. 812.* SCHUBERT: *Impromptu in B flat, D. 935/3.* SCHUBERT/TAUSIG: *Marche militaire, D. 733/1.*
❀ *** DG 419 217-2 [id.].

Horowitz plays in the studio just as if he were in front of an audience, and the freshness and accuracy would be astonishing if we had not already heard him repeating the trick. The subtle range of colour and articulation in the Schumann is matched in his Schubert *Impromptu*, and the Liszt *Valse oubliée* offers the most delicious, twinkling rubato. Hearing Scarlatti's *E major Sonata* played with such crispness, delicacy and grace must surely convert even the most dedicated authenticist to the view that this repertoire can be totally valid in terms of the modern instrument. The Schubert–Tausig *Marche militaire* makes a superb encore, played with the kind of panache that would be remarkable in a pianist half Horowitz's age. With the passionate Scriabin *Étude* as the central romantic pivot, this recital is uncommonly well balanced to show Horowitz's special range of sympathies. Only Mozart is missing, and he is featured elsewhere. The recording is extremely realistic and present in its CD format.

'In Moscow': D. SCARLATTI: *Sonata in E, Kk. 380.* MOZART: *Sonata No. 10 in C, K. 330.* RACHMANINOV: *Preludes: in G, Op. 32/5; in G sharp min. Op. 32/12.* SCRIABIN: *Études: in C sharp min., Op. 2/1; in D sharp min., Op. 8/12.* LISZT/SCHUBERT: *Soirées de Vienne; Petrarch Sonnet 104.* CHOPIN: *Mazurkas, Op. 30/4; Op. 7/3.* SCHUMANN: *Kinderszenen: Träumerei.*
*** DG Dig. 419 499-2; *419 499-4* [id.].

This is familiar Horowitz repertoire, played with characteristic musical discernment and spontaneity. Technically the pianism may not quite match his finest records of the analogue era, but it is still both melting and dazzling. The sound too is really excellent, much better than he ever received from his American engineers in earlier days.

'A Tribute': SCARLATTI: *Sonatas, Kk.55; Kk.380.* CHOPIN: *Ballade No. 1 in G min., Op. 23; Mazurkas: in C sharp min., Op. 30/4; B min., Op. 33/4; Étude in F, Op. 10/8.* SCRIABIN: *Sonata No. 9 (Black mass), Op. 68; Étude in D sharp min., Op. 8/12.* LISZT: *Années de pèlerinages, 1st Year: Vallée d'Obermann.* SCHUMANN: *Arabeske in C, Op. 18; Kinderszenen: Träumerei.* DEBUSSY: *L'isle joyeuse.* MOSZKOWSKI: *Étude in A flat, Op. 72/11.* HOROWITZ: *Variations on a theme from Bizet's Carmen.*
**(*) Sony MK 45829 [id.]; *40-45829.*

These celebrated performances come from the 1960s, last appearing as part of a three-CD compilation, *'Horowitz Live at Carnegie Hall'*, containing concert performances from 1965, 1966 and 1968; they have been discussed at length in past issues of the Penguin *Guide*. Suffice it to say that few of these performances have lost their magic and some, such as the Scriabin *Ninth Sonata* (*The Black Mass*) have never been surpassed. The recordings are not quite of the very highest quality but serve to convey much of the electricity of the occasion.

'The last recording': HAYDN: *Piano sonata in E flat, Hob XVI/20.* CHOPIN: *Mazurka in C min., Op. 56/3. Nocturnes: in E flat, Op. 55/2; in B, Op. 62/1. Fantaisie impromptu, Op. 66; Études: in*

A flat; E min., Op. 25/1 & 5. LISZT: *Prelude: Weinen, Klagen, Sorgen, Zagen; Concert paraphrase on Isoldens Liebestod.*
*** Sony Dig. SK 45818 [id.].

Rarely did Horowitz betray his advanced years, and the Haydn for the most part has great delicacy and elegance: it is far less tense and taut than either of his previous accounts of this big, late *E flat Sonata*. Only once (the fortissimo left-hand octaves in the slow movement) does one feel a lapse in his concentration and perspective. The Chopin pieces offer some fresh insights and display a command of tone gradation that is still pretty remarkable, except perhaps for an unexceptionable account of the *Fantaisie-impromptu*. Ah, if only the piano sound the CBS engineers produce here could have been lavished on his earlier recitals from the 1960s! There is a fine written tribute to Horowitz from Murray Perahia.

Recital: SCHUMANN: *Kinderszenen, Op. 15; Toccata in C, Op. 7.* D. SCARLATTI: *Sonatas: in G, Kk. 455; in E, Kk. 531; in A, Kk. 322.* SCHUBERT: *Impromptu No. 3 in G flat, D. 889.* SCRIABIN: *Poème, Op. 32/1; Études: in C sharp min., Op. 2/1; in D sharp min, Op. 8/12.*
(B) **(*) Sony MYK 42534.

Horowitz's 1968 recital offers marvellous playing of repertoire he knew and loved, recorded when he was still at his technical peak. The recording is dry (there is a hint of wow, but it appears only once or twice); even so, this is magical playing: the Schumann and Scarlatti are superb – but then so is the Scriabin, and Schubert's *G flat Impromptu* is infinitely subtle in its gradations of dynamic and colour.

'Encores': BIZET/HOROWITZ: *Variations on a theme from Carmen.* SAINT-SAËNS/LISZT/HOROWITZ: *Danse macabre.* MOZART: *Sonata No. 11, K.331: Rondo alla turca.* MENDELSSOHN/LISZT/HOROWITZ: *Wedding march and variations.* MENDELSSOHN: *Élégie, Op. 85/4; Spring song, Op. 62/6; The shepherd's complaint, Op. 67/5; Scherzo a capriccio: Presto.* DEBUSSY: *Children's corner: Serenade of a doll.* MOSZKOWSKI: *Études, Op. 72/6 & 11; Étincelles, Op. 36/6.* CHOPIN: *Polonaise in A flat, Op. 53.* SCHUMANN: *Kinderszenen: Träumerei.* LISZT: *Hungarian rhapsody No. 15; Valse oubliée No. 1.* RACHMANINOV: *Prelude in G min., Op. 23/5.* SOUSA/HOROWITZ: *The Stars and stripes forever.*
(M) (***) BMG/RCA mono GD 87755; *GK 87755* [7755-2-RG; *7755-4-RG*].

These encore pieces have been around for some time and, apart from the Rachmaninov *Prelude* and the Mendelssohn, derive from the days of the 78-r.p.m. record and the mono LP. Allowances have to be made for the quality which, as one would expect in this kind of compilation, is variable. So in its different way is the playing, which varies from dazzling to stunning!

Hough, Stephen (piano)

'The Piano Album': MACDOWELL: *Hexentanz, Op. 12.* CHOPIN: *Chant polonaise No. 1.* QUILTER: *The crimson petal; The fuchsia tree.* DOHNÁNYI: *Capriccio in F min., Op. 28/8.* PADEREWSKI: *Minuet in G, Op. 14/1. Nocturne in B flat, Op. 16/4.* SCHLOZER: *Étude in A flat, Op. 1/2.* GABRILOWITSCH: *Mélodie in E; Caprice-burlesque.* RODGERS: *My favourite things.* WOODFORDE-FINDEN: *Kashmiri song.* FRIEDMAN: *Music box.* SAINT-SAËNS: *Carnival: The Swan.* ROSENTHAL: *Papillons.* GODOWSKI: *The gardens of Buitenzorg.* LEVITZKI: *Waltz in A, Op. 2.* PALMGREN: *En route, Op. 9.* MOSZKOWSKI: *Siciliano, Op. 42/2; Caprice espagnole, Op. 3.*
❀ *** Virgin Dig. VC7 90732-2; *VC 790732-4* [id.].

There are few young pianists who can match Stephen Hough in communicating on record with the immediacy and vividness of live performance; this dazzling recital of frothy showpieces presents the perfect illustration. This Virgin Classics collection captures more nearly than almost any other recent record – even those of Horowitz – the charm, sparkle and flair of legendary piano virtuosos from the golden age of Rosenthal, Godowski and Lhévinne. So many of the twenty items are frivolous that it may be surprising that any serious pianist can stomach them; yet the very first item, MacDowell's *Hexentanz* (*Witches' dance*), launches the listener into pure pianistic magic, with playing totally uninhibited and with articulation and timing that are the musical equivalent of being tickled up and down the spine. One would hardly expect Hough's own arrangements of sentimental little songs by Roger Quilter or Amy Woodforde-Finden to be worth hearing at all – yet, in their tender expressiveness, they are most affecting. In the grand tradition, Hough does a Valse-caprice arrangement he himself has made of *My favourite things* from *The Sound of Music*, as well as firework pieces by Rosenthal and Moszkowski, among others, along with old-fashioned favourites like Paderewski's *Minuet in G* and Godowski's arrangement of the Saint-Saëns *Swan*. It is a feast for piano-lovers, very well recorded in venues in both London and New York.

Hurford, Peter (organ)

Ratzeburg Cathedral organ: *'Romantic organ music'*: WIDOR: *Symphony No. 5, Op. 42: Toccata.* VIERNE: *Pièces en style libre: Berceuse.* ALAIN: *Litanies.* FRANCK: *Chorale No. 3.* KARG-ELERT: *Marche triomphale; Nun danket alle Gotte, Op. 65.* BRAHMS: *Chorale preludes: O wie selig, seid, ihr doch; Schmücke dich; Es ist ein' Ros' entsprungen, Op. 122.* MENDELSSOHN: *Organ sonata in A, Op. 65/3.* REGER: *Introduction and passacaglia in D min.*
*** Argo Dig. 410 165-2 [id.].

There are not many records of Romantic organ music to match this in colour, breadth of repertory and brilliance of performance, superbly recorded. The ever-popular Widor item leads to pieces just as efficient at bringing out the variety of organ sound, such as the Karg-Elert or the Alain. These are performances which defy all thought of Victorian heaviness, and the Ratzeburg organ produces piquant and beautiful sounds. On CD the presence and range are breathtaking.

Sydney Opera House organ: *'Great organ works'*: BACH: *Toccata and fugue in D min., BWV 565; Jesu, joy of man's desiring.* ALBINONI: *Adagio* (arr. Giazotto). PURCELL: *Trumpet tune in D.* MENDELSSOHN: *A Midsummer Night's Dream: Wedding march.* FRANCK: *Chorale No. 2 in B min.* MURRILL: *Carillon.* WALFORD DAVIES: *Solemn melody.* WIDOR: *Organ symphony No. 5: Toccata.*
(M) **(*) Decca Dig. 425 013-2; *425 013-4* [id.].

Superb sound here, wonderfully free and never oppressive, even in the most spectacular moments. The Widor is spiritedly genial when played within the somewhat mellower registration of the magnificent Sydney instrument (as contrasted with the Ratzeburg Cathedral organ – see above), and the pedals have great sonority and power. The Murrill *Carillon* is equally engaging alongside the Purcell *Trumpet tune*, while Mendelssohn's wedding music has never sounded more resplendent. The Bach is less memorable, and the Albinoni *Adagio*, without the strings, is not an asset to the collection either.

'Organ spectacular': WIDOR: *Symphony No. 5: Toccata. Symphony No. 6: Allegro.* KARG-ELERT: *Marche triomphale: Nun danket alle Gott.* FRANCK: *Choral No. 3.* BACH: *Toccata and fugue in D min., BWV 565.* MENDELSSOHN: *Midsummer Night's Dream: Wedding march.* BOËLLMAN: *Suite gothique, Op. 25.* LISZT: *Fantasia and fugue on B-A-C-H.*
(M) *** Decca Dig. 430 710-2; *430 710-4* [id.].

This Ovation collection centres on the Ratzeburg Cathedral organ, but Hurford uses the instrument in St Sermin, Toulouse, for the Franck *Choral*, while the Bach and Mendelssohn items feature the magnificent Sydney organ, which has striking sonority and power. The ever-popular Widor *Toccata* leads to other pieces that are just as efficient at bringing out the variety of organ sound possible at Ratzeburg, such as the Karg-Elert or the spectacle of Liszt's venture into Bach polyphony. The digital recording is in the demonstration class and the recital offers 69 minutes of music.

Israeli Flute Ensemble

'Flute Serenade': BEETHOVEN: *Serenade in D, Op. 25*❀. MOZART: *Flute quartet No. 1 in D, K.285.* SCHUBERT: *String trio in B flat, D.471.* HOFFMEISTER: *Flute quartet in A.*
(BB) *** Pickwick/CDI Dig. PWK 1139.

We have already praised this delightful account of Beethoven's *D major Serenade* in our composer index. The rest of the concert is hardly less winning, including not only one of the more memorable of Mozart's *Flute quartets* but also Hoffmeister's ingenious transcription of a favourite Mozart piano sonata, with its *Rondo Alla turca* finale sounding very sprightly in the arrangement for flute, violin and piano. The Schubert *String trio* makes a graceful interlude and an attractive change of texture; and the recording adds to the listener's pleasure by its complete naturalness of timbre and balance: one can readily imagine the players sitting at the end of one's room.

Johnson, Emma (clarinet)

'A Clarinet celebration' (with Gordon Back): WEBER: *Grand duo concertante; Variations concertantes.* BURGMÜLLER: *Duo.* GIAMPIERI: *Carnival of Venice.* SCHUMANN: *Fantasy pieces, Op. 73.* LOVREGLIO: *Fantasia de concerto, La Traviata.*
*** ASV Dig. CDDCA 732; *ZCDCA 732* [id.].

These are party pieces rather than encores, all of them drawing electric sparks of inspiration from this winning young soloist. Even in such virtuoso nonsense as the Giampieri *Carnival of Venice* and the Lovreglio *Fantasia*, Johnson draws out musical magic, while the expressiveness of Weber and Schumann brings heartfelt playing, with phrasing creatively individual. Gordon Back accompanies brilliantly, and the sound is first rate.

Kang, Dong-Suk (violin), Pascal Devoyon (piano)

French violin sonatas: DEBUSSY: *Sonata in G min.* RAVEL: *Sonata in G.* POULENC: *Violin sonata.* SAINT-SAËNS: *Sonata No. 1 in D min.*
(BB) *** Naxos Dig. 8.550276; *4550276* [id.].

One of the jewels of the Naxos catalogue, this collection of four of the finest violin sonatas in the French repertoire is self-recommending. The stylistic range of this partnership is evident throughout: they seem equally attuned to all four composers. This is warm, freshly spontaneous playing, given vivid and realistic digital recording in a spacious acoustic. A very real bargain.

Kayath, Marcelo (guitar)

'Guitar classics from Latin America': PONCE: *Valse.* PIAZZOLA: *La muerte del angel.* BARRIOS: *Vals, Op. 8/3; Choro de saudade; Julia florida.* LAURO: *Vals venezolanos No. 2; El negrito; El marabino.* BROUWER: *Canción de cuna; Ojos brujos.* PERNAMBUCO: *Sons de carrilhões; Interrogando; Sono de maghia.* REIS: *Si ela perguntar.* VILLA-LOBOS: *5 Preludes.*
(B) *** Pickwick Dig. PCD 853; *CIMPC 853* [id.].

Marcelo Kayath's inspirational accounts of the Villa-Lobos *Preludes* can stand comparison with the finest performances on record. He has the rare gift of playing in the studio as at a live recital; obviously he soon becomes unaware of his surroundings, for he plays everything here with consummate technical ease and the most appealing spontaneity. His rubato in the Barrios *Vals* is particularly effective, and he is a fine advocate too of the engaging Lauro pieces and the picaresque writing of João Pernambuco, a friend of Villa-Lobos. The recording, made in a warm but not too resonant acoustic, is first class, and there is a fine illusion of presence. Even though this is a budget-priced issue, it carries excellent notes.

'Guitar classics from Spain': TARREGA: *Prelude in A min.; Capricho arabe; Recuerdos de la Alhambra.* GRANADOS: *La Maja de Goya.* ALBÉNIZ: *Granada; Zambra; Grandina; Sevilla; Mallorca.* TORROBA: *Prelude in E; Sonatina; Nocturno.* RODRIGO: *Zapateado.* TRAD.: *El Noy de la mare.*
(B) *** Pickwick Dig. PCD 876; *CIMPC 876* [id.].

Following the success of his first, Latin-American recital, Marcelo Kayath gives us an equally enjoyable Spanish collection, full of colour and spontaneity. By grouping music by several major composers, he provides a particularly revealing mix. The two opening Tarrega pieces are predominantly lyrical, to bring an effective contrast with the famous fluttering *Recuerdos de la Alhambra*, played strongly. Then after the Granados come five of Albéniz's most colourful and tuneful geographical evocations, while the Torroba group includes the *Sonatina*, a splendid piece. After Rodrigo he closes with the hauntingly memorable *El Noy de la mare.* There is over an hour of music and the recording has a most realistic presence; but take care not to set the volume level too high.

King, Thea (clarinet), Britten Quartet

Clarinet music: HOWELLS: *Rhapsodic quintet*. COOKE: *Clarinet quintet*. MACONCHY: *Clarinet quintet*. FRANKEL: *Clarinet quintet, Op. 28*. HOLBROOKE: *Eilean shona*.
*** Hyp. Dig. CDA 66428 [id.].

Five strongly characterized works for clarinet quintet by British composers make up a most attractive disc, beautifully played by Thea King and the outstanding Britten Quartet. The masterpiece which sets the pattern for the sequence is the beautiful *Rhapsodic quintet* of Howells, one of the finest of his early works, dating from 1917. The Frankel, Maconchy and Cooke works all come from the post-war period, all written between 1956 and 1962, strong pieces that make their points tautly and crisply. The Frankel ends with a moving elegy. The Holbrooke rounds the group off, a brief, song-like soliloquy for clarinet and strings inspired by a Celtic story. The recording is clear and forward with a fine bloom on all the instruments.

Kissin, Yevgeni (piano)

'Carnegie Hall Début' (30 September 1990) *Highlights*: LISZT: *Étude d'exécution transcendante No. 10; Liebestraum No. 3; Rhapsodie espagnole*. SCHUMANN: *Abegg Variations, Op. 1; Études symphoniques, Op. 13; Widmung* (arr. Liszt).
*** BMG/RCA Dig. 09026 61202-2 [61202-2].

Yevgeni Kissin caused something of a sensation in 1984 when he played both the Chopin *Concertos* in the Great Hall of the Moscow Conservatoire while still only twelve years of age. The present recording of highlights from his Carnegie Hall début was made a few days before his nineteenth birthday. He has phenomenal pianistic powers; not only is this a *tour de force* in terms of technical prowess but also in sheer artistry. Both sets of Schumann *Variations* are remarkable: Op. 13 is infinitely more impressive and natural than Pogorelich's rendition, and is full of poetic insights. The Liszt *Rhapsodie espagnole* is played with superb bravura. Kissin's range of colour and keyboard command throughout is dazzling. The Carnegie Hall was packed and the recording balance, while a bit close, is perfectly acceptable. The excitement of the occasion is conveyed vividly. The Prokofiev *Sonata No. 6* has been omitted to get the recital on to a single CD (66 minutes); but surely there would also have been room for the same composer's *Étude*, Op. 2/3, which brought the house down – and rightly so.

'In Tokyo' (12 May 1987): CHOPIN: *Nocturne in A flat, Op. 32/2; Polonaise in F sharp min., Op. 44*. LISZT: *Concert studies Nos. 1 in D flat (Waldesrauschen); 2 in F min. (La Leggierezza)*. PROKOFIEV: *Sonata No. 6 in A, Op. 82*. RACHMANINOV: *Études tableaux, Op. 39/1 & 5; Lilacs*. SCRIABIN: *Étude in C sharp min., Op. 42/5; Mazurka in E min., Op. 25/3*.
*** Sony Dig. SK 45931 [id.].

Kissin was only fifteen at the time of his Tokyo début, but he sounds fully mature throughout this recital. He plays Prokofiev's *Sixth Sonata* for all it is worth with no holds barred, and the effect is altogether electrifying. Moreover, this is not merely an exhibition of brilliant technique but a display of remarkable artistic understanding – one finds oneself on the edge of one's chair. He is no less at home in the Rachmaninov *Études tableaux* and the Liszt *La Leggierezza*, which he delivers with marvellous assurance and poetic feeling. His Scriabin, too, is pretty impressive, and the only unremarkable part of his concert is the group of Japanese encores. The microphone placing is too close – but no matter, this is breathtaking piano playing.

Kremer, Gidon (violin), Elena Bashkirova (piano)

SCHUBERT: *Fantasia in C, D.934*. STRAVINSKY: *Duo concertante*. PROKOFIEV: (Solo) *Violin sonata, Op. 115*. RAVEL: *Sonate posthume*. SATIE: *Choses vues droite et à gauche (sans lunettes)*.
(M) *** Ph. 426 387-2; *426 387-4*.

This disc is worth having just for Ravel's posthumously published *Sonata*, a youthful work in a single movement that is surprisingly mature and with many magical anticipations of the future. It is a delightful piece, played marvellously. So too are the Prokofiev and Stravinsky works, full of bravura, yet with the latter displaying an agreeably cool lyrical element; while the Satie miniatures combine wit and sparkle with an attractive finesse. The Schubert *Fantasia* is full of spontaneous romantic flair, and the recital ends with another surprise, Milhaud's delicious *Printemps*, a real lollipop, yet not in the least trivial. Excellent recording.

Lack, Fredell (violin)

Sonatas (with Albert Hirsh or Barry Snyder (piano)): CORIGLIANO: *Sonata for violin and piano.* DIAMOND: *Sonata No. 2 for violin and piano.* LEES: *Sonata No. 2 for violin and piano.* MENNIN: *Sonata concertante for violin and piano.*
** Bay Cities Dig. BCD 1018 [id.].

Fredell Lack was a frequent broadcaster in the UK in the days of the Third Programme, playing mostly enterprising repertoire. She now teaches in the United States and is Professor of Music and Artist-in-Residence in Houston, Texas. John Corigliano's *Sonata* (1963) is spiky, very Stravinskyish but lively and inventive; it is not as spiky or rebarbative though as the *Sonata No. 2* of Benjamin Lees, composed in 1973. David Diamond's *Sonata No. 2* (1981) is a thoughtful, well-wrought piece and, along with Peter Mennin's *Sonata concertante* (1956), forms the strongest part of the recital. These artists are decently recorded.

Larrocha, Alicia de (piano)

'Spanish fireworks': FALLA: *3 Dances.* M. ALBÉNIZ: *Sonata.* I. ALBÉNIZ: *Iberia: Trianna. Navarra; Sevilla; Asturias.* MOMPOU: *Secreto.* GRANADOS: *Zapateado; Allegro de concierto; Danzas españolas No. 5 (Andaluza); Quejas o la majas el Ruisenor; El Pele.* TURINA: *Sacromonte; Zapateado.*
(M) *** Decca Dig./Analogue 417 795-2.

Alicia de Larrocha can certainly provide bravura when called for, as in the glittering Granados *Allegro de concierto*. But this is a recital that relies for its appeal on evocation and colour – as in the same composer's haunting *Quejas o la majas el Ruisenor*, the excerpts from the Isaac Albéniz *Suite española*, or the atmospheric Mompou *Secreto* – and the sheer distinction and character of its pianism, coolly shown in the delectable *Sonata* of Mateo Albéniz. At 71 minutes the programme is very generous, and the recording, partly digital and partly analogue, is consistently realistic.

'Musica española': FALLA: *Three-cornered hat: 3 dances. El amor brujo: suite.* TURINA: *Sacromonte, Op. 55/5. Zapateado, Op. 8/3.* HALFFTER: *Danza de la pastora; Danza de la gitana.* MONSALVATGE: *Sonatina para Yvette. Divertimento No. 2 (Habanera).* NIN-CULMELL: *6 Tonadas, Vol.2.* SURIÑACH: *3 Canciones y danzas españolas.* ❀ MOMPOU: *Impresiones íntimas; Preludio a Alicia de Larrocha. Música callada, IV; 7 cançons i dansas.*
(M) *** Decca 433 929-2 (2) [id.].

Alicia de Larrocha is ideally cast here. She opens vibrantly with the Falla ballet music, and so vivid is her colouring that one hardly misses the orchestra. Elsewhere her phrasing is always musical, articulation remarkably clean and rhythms firm. Much of the music is delightful. Joaquín Nin-Culmell's *6 Tonadas* are flashingly characterful in their folk feeling: the closing *Muñeira* (*Galicia*) has spectacular flamenco fireworks in Miss de Larrocha's hands. Xavier Monsalvatge's *Sonata* was written for his daughter's tenth birthday; however, even though its finale quotes 'Twinkle twinkle, little star', its audaciously quirky satire has more in common with Poulenc and Satie than Debussy's *Children's corner*. Miss de Larrocha plays the whole sonata with breathtaking virtuosity. The Mompou pieces have much charm and an atmosphere all their own – they are discussed in more detail under their composer entry. They are digitally recorded; the rest of the recital is analogue but hardly less real. The piano timbre is firm, the acoustic unconfined, and there is a fine sense of presence.

LaSalle Quartet

Chamber music of the Second Viennese School: BERG: *Lyric suite; String quartet, Op. 3.* SCHOENBERG: *String quartets: in D; No. 1 in D min., Op. 7; No. 2 in F sharp min., Op. 10/3* (with Margaret Price); *No. 3, Op. 30; No. 4, Op. 37.* WEBERN: *5 Movements, Op. 5; String quartet* (1905); *6 Bagatelles, Op. 9; String quartet, Op. 28.*
(M) *** DG 419 994-2 (4) [id.].

DG have compressed their 1971 five-LP set on to four CDs, offering them at a reduced and competitive price. They have also retained the invaluable and excellent documentary study edited by Ursula Rauchhaupt – which runs to 340 pages! It is almost worth having this set for the documentation alone. The LaSalle Quartet give splendidly expert performances, even if at times their playing seems a little cool; and they are very well recorded. An invaluable issue for all who care about twentieth-century music.

Lawson, Peter (piano)

'The American piano sonata, Vol. 1': COPLAND: *Piano sonata.* IVES: *Three page sonata.* CARTER: *Piano sonata.* BARBER: *Piano sonata, Op. 26.*
*** Virgin Dig. VC7 91163-2 [id.].

An indispensable collection for anyone interested in American piano music. Considering its excellence, the Copland *Sonata* (1939–41) has been uncommonly neglected since Andor Foldes's mono LP of the 1950s. Peter Lawson plays it with an understanding that is persuasive and an enthusiasm that is refreshing. Elliott Carter's *Sonata* (1946, revised 1982) owes much to the Copland. Its idiom is thoroughly accessible (far more so than some of Carter's more impenetrable later music) as well as convincing. Lawson can hold his own with such earlier recordings as the Charles Rosen, and he certainly has the advantage of fresher recording quality. In the 1950s and 1960s, the Barber *Sonata*, Op. 26, like that of Ginastera, had a far stronger profile than any other American sonata, and the catalogue has recently been enriched by the return of Horowitz's and Van Cliburn's recordings. Lawson comfortably takes its various hurdles in his stride, and he also gives us the Charles Ives *Three page Sonata.* A generous and valuable recital.

Leonhardt, Gustav (clavichord)

'Clavichord recital': C. P. E. BACH: *Sonatas: in D min.; G min., Wq. 51/4 & 6; in B min./F sharp min., Wq. 63/4.* RITTER: *Suite in F sharp min.* J. S. BACH: *Fantasia & fugue in A min., BWV 904; French suite No. 2 in C min., BWV 813.* W. F. BACH: *3 Polonaises (in E flat min., E min. & F min.).*
*** Ph. Dig. 422 349-2.

A fine recital from the distinguished Dutch scholar-musician. The actual clavichord used is not specified, but it reproduces well on this disc, which must be played at a very low level indeed if it is to give anything like a truthful impression of the instrument. Leonhardt plays with the authority of the scholar and the imagination of the artist. Apart from the two J. S. Bach pieces, probably the most interesting things on the disc are the three *Polonaises* of Wilhelm Friedemann. Leonhardt opens with a *Suite in F sharp minor* by Christian Ritter (*c.* 1645–*c.* 1717) who was, like Wilhelm Friedemann, an organist at Halle, but a composer of moderate interest. The C. P. E. Bach *Sonata*, Wq. 63/4, is tonally unusual for its period: its three movements are all in different keys: B minor, D major and F sharp minor. First-rate sound.

Lin, Cho-Liang (violin), Sandra Rivers (piano)

'Bravura': FALLA: *Suite populaire espagnole.* KREISLER: *Liebeslied; Liebesfreud. Tambourin chinois.* MOZART: *Serenade, K. 250: Rondo.* RACHMANINOV: *Vocalise.* WIENIAWSKI: *Capriccio-valse in E, Op. 7.* SARASATE: *Introduction and Tarantella, Op. 43.*
*** Sony Dig. MK 39133 [id.].

Some first-rate playing here from this remarkable young virtuoso. He tosses off these pieces with great aplomb and brilliance. But besides his pyrotechnics, he is also able to find poetry in these miniatures and is well supported by Sandra Rivers. A most attractive recital, as well recorded as it is played.

Lipatti, Dinu (piano)

CHOPIN: *Sonata No. 3 in B min., Op. 58.* LISZT: *Années de pèlerinage: Sonetto del Petrarca, No. 104.* RAVEL: *Miroirs: Alborada del gracioso.* BRAHMS: *Waltzes, Op. 39/1, 2, 5, 6, 10, 14 & 15* (with Nadia Boulanger). ENESCU: *Sonata No. 3 in D, Op. 25.*
(M) (***) EMI mono CDH7 63038-2.

The Chopin *Sonata*, the Liszt and the Ravel were recorded in 1947–8, the Brahms *Waltzes*, with Nadia Boulanger, as long ago as 1937; while the Enescu *Sonata* comes from a 1943 wartime broadcast from Swiss Radio. The Chopin is one of the classics of the gramophone, and it is good to have it on CD in this excellent-sounding transfer. The Brahms *Waltzes* are played deliciously with tremendous sparkle and tenderness; they sound every bit as realistic as the post-war records. The Enescu *Sonata* is an accessible piece, with an exuberant first movement and a rather atmospheric *Andantino*, but the sound is not as fresh as the rest of the music on this valuable CD. A must for all with an interest in the piano.

Lloyd Webber, Julian (cello)

'British cello music' (with (i) John McCabe, piano): (i) RAWSTHORNE: *Sonata for cello and piano.* ARNOLD: *Fantasy for cello.* (i) IRELAND: *The Holy Boy.* WALTON: *Passacaglia.* BRITTEN: *Teme (Sacher); Cello suite No. 3.*
*** ASV Dig. CDDCA 592; *ZCDCA 592* [id.].

A splendid recital and a most valuable one. Julian Lloyd Webber has championed such rarities as the Bridge *Oration* at a time when it was unrecorded and now devotes this present issue to English music that needs strong advocacy; there is no alternative version of the Rawsthorne *Sonata*, in which he is most ably partnered by John McCabe. He gives this piece – and, for that matter, the remainder of the programme – with full-blooded commitment. Good recording.

'The romantic cello' (with Yitkin Seow, piano): POPPER: *Elfentanz, Op. 39.* SAINT-SAËNS: *Carnival of the animals: The Swan. Allegro appassionato, Op. 43.* FAURÉ: *Après un rêve.* MENDELSSOHN: *Song without words, Op. 109.* RACHMANINOV: *Cello sonata, Op. 19:* slow movt. DELIUS: *Romance.* CHOPIN: *Introduction and polonaise brillante, Op. 3.* ELGAR: *Salut d'amour, Op. 12.*
(BB) **(*) ASV CDQS 6014; *ZCQS 6014.*

Julian Lloyd Webber has gathered together a most attractive collection of showpieces for the cello, romantic as well as brilliant. Such dazzling pieces as the Popper – always a favourite with virtuoso cellists – is on record a welcome rarity. The recording, a little edgy, if with undoubted presence, favours the cello and is vivid, with good body and range.

Lympany, Moura (piano)

'Best-loved piano classics', Volume 1: CHOPIN: *Fantaisie-impromptu, Op. 66; Études, Op. 10/4 & 5.* BRAHMS: *Waltz, Op. 39/15.* MOZART: *Sonata No. 11, 'Alla Turca', K.331.* BEETHOVEN: *Minuet in G; Für Elise.* SCHUMANN: *Kinderszenen: Träumerei.* LISZT: *Concert study: Un sospiro.* DVOŘÁK: *Humoresque. Op. 101/7.* MACDOWELL: *To a wild rose.* CHAMINADE: *Autumn.* DEBUSSY: *Suite bergamasque: Clair de lune. Children's corner: Golliwog's cakewalk.* RACHMANINOV: *Prelude in C sharp min., Op. 3/2.* RUBINSTEIN: *Melody in F, Op. 3/1.* GRANADOS: *Goyescas: The Maiden and the nightingale.* FALLA: *El amor brujo: Ritual fire dance.* ALBÉNIZ: *Tango, Op. 165/2.*
(M) *** EMI Dig. CDZ7 62523-2; *LZ 762523-4.*

The popularity and generosity of the programme here speak for themselves. Miss Lympany has lost none of the flair and technical skill which earned her her reputation: the whole programme has the spontaneity of a live recital. At times the playing has a masculine strength, and pieces like *Träumerei* and *Clair de lune* emerge the more freshly through a total absence of sentimentality. Liszt's *Concert study: Un sospiro* is played with commanding passion, and even the more trivial items sound newly minted. At medium price this is very good value, with the

Spanish pieces ending the collection memorably, the bold Falla *Fire dance* contrasting with the more lyrical Granados and Albéniz items. The piano timbre is faithful and realistic, if a little dry.

'Best-loved piano classics, Volume 2': BACH, arr. Hess: *Jesu, joy of man's desiring.* DAQUIN: *Le Coucou.* HANDEL: *Suite No. 5: Air and variations (The harmonious blacksmith).* BEETHOVEN: *Rondo a capriccio, Op. 129; Piano sonata No. 14 (Moonlight)*: lst movt. DEBUSSY: *Images: Reflets dans l'eau. Préludes*, Book 1: *La fille aux cheveux de lin; La cathédrale engloutie.* CHOPIN: *Waltzes: in C sharp min., Op. 64/2; in G flat, Op. 70/1; Mazurka in A min., Op. 17/4.* ALBÉNIZ: *Malagueña, Op. 165/3.* RAVEL: *Jeux d'eau.* PADEREWSKI: *Minuet in G, Op. 14/1.* SCHUMANN: *Waldszenen: Der Vogel als Prophet.* SATIE: *Gymnopédie No. 1.* SCRIABIN: *Étude in D sharp min., Op. 8/12.*
(M) *** EMI Dig. CDZ7 67204-2; *LZ 767204-4.*

Moura Lympany begins here with Myra Hess's famous arrangement of Bach's *Jesu, joy of man's desiring*, presented with an innocent simplicity of line which is immediately appealing. She is equally good in Handel's famous set of variations and in the French impressionism. There is sparkle in the Chopin and Albéniz, and she is equally captivating in Daquin and Satie. As in her first recital, the piano image is clear and vivid with plenty of presence, and at 71 minutes the programme is certainly generous.

McLachlan, Murray (piano)

Piano music from Scotland: SCOTT: *8 Songs* (trans. Stevenson): *Since all thy vows, false maid; Wha is that at my bower-door?; O were my love yon lilac fare; Wee Willie Gray; Milkwort and bog-cotton; Crowdieknowe; Ay waukin, O; There's news, lasses, news.* CENTER: *Piano sonata; 6 Bagatelles, Op. 3.; Children at play.* STEVENSON: *Beltane bonfire. 2 Scottish ballads: The Dowie Dens O Yarrow; Newhaven fishwife's cry.*
❀ *** Olympia Dig. OCD 264 [id.].

An important, fascinating and rewarding recital. For most collectors, Scottish music comprises dozens of wonderful folk-songs and a single orchestral piece, Hamish MacCunn's overture *The Land of the mountain and the flood.* Francis George Scott (1880–1958) was a prolific and striking composer of songs and we obviously need a major Scottish artist to record a representative selection of his work. Meanwhile Ronald Stevenson's very free transcriptions, somewhat after the fashion of Liszt's concert paraphrases, are imaginatively creative in their own right, with the witty, scherzando grotesquerie of *Wee Willie Gray* surpassed by the even more complex *Crowdieknowe*, with its quotations from the *Requiems* of Verdi and Berlioz included in the endpiece. Ronald Center's *Piano sonata* is restless and mercurial, lacking much in the way of repose, but the joyous syncopations of the first movement are infectious and the work is a major contribution to the repertory and not in the least difficult to approach. The *Six Bagatelles* are even more strikingly diverse in mood. The second introduces an engaging wooden-legged waltz, the third, *Mesto*, has a whiff of Satie and the fifth, *Andantino*, a flavour of Poulenc, yet both retain their Scottish individuality. *Children at play* is an enchanting piece, with a musical-box miniaturism of texture at times, yet the writing is by no means inconsequential. All this music is played with commitment and considerable bravura by Murray McLachlan, who is clearly a sympathetic exponent, and the recording is extremely vivid and real. Our Rosette is awarded not just for enterprise, but equally from admiration and pleasure.

Meyer, Marcelle (piano)

'The Indispensable Marcelle Meyer': CHABRIER: *10 Pièces pittoresques; Ballabille; Habanera; Feuillet; Aubade; Impromptu; Ronde champêtre; Air de ballet; Joyeuse marche; Bourrée fantasque; 3 Valses romantiques pour 2 pianos* (with Poulenc); *Idylle.* RAVEL: *Pavane pour une infante défunte; Menuet antique; Menuet sur le nom d'Haydn; Jeux d'eau; Miroirs; Alborada del gracioso; Sonatine; Le Tombeau de Couperin; Valses nobles et sentimentales; Gaspard de la nuit.* DEBUSSY: *Images I & II; Masques; L'Isle joyeuse; Poissons d'or.* POULENC: *3 Mouvements perpétuels.* FALLA: *Danse du meunier.* ALBÉNIZ: *Sous le palmier; Navarra.* MILHAUD: *Scaramouche* (with Milhaud). STRAVINSKY: *3 mouvements de Petroushka; Ragtime* (2 versions); *Serenade; Sonate.* R. STRAUSS: *Burlesque pour piano et orchestre* (with O de la Société des Concerts du Conservatoire, Cluytens).
(M) (***) EMI mono CZS7 67405-2 (6) [id.].

Marcelle Meyer enjoyed a great reputation in France between the wars and no one who has ever heard her Scarlatti sonatas could understand why she was not more widely celebrated. These were issued on an EMI Référence LP in the 1980s and should be transferred to CD without delay. They have a pianistic finesse, delicacy and a refinement of keyboard colour that remind one of Lipatti. She was said to be Ravel's favourite pianist, though it must be said that the performances she recorded here come from the very end of her life and show her at less than her impressive best. However there is much impeccable pianism, and this box at last does belated justice to a much neglected and refined artist.

Moiseiwitsch, Benno (piano)

1938–1950 recordings: MUSSORGSKY: *Pictures at an exhibition.* BEETHOVEN: *Andanti favori, WoO 57; Rondo in C, Op. 51/1.* WEBER: *Sonata No. 1: Presto; Invitation to the dance* (arr. Tausig). MENDELSSOHN: *Scherzo in E min., Op. 16.* SCHUMANN: *Romanzen: No. 2, Op. 28/2.* CHOPIN: *Nocturne in E flat, Op. 9/2; Polonaise in B flat, Op. 71/2; Barcarolle, Op. 60.* LISZT: *Liebestraume No. 3; Étude de concert: La leggierezza. Hungarian rhapsody No. 2 in C sharp min. Concert paraphrase of Wagner's Tannhäuser overture.* DEBUSSY: *Pour le piano: Toccata. Suite bergamasque: Clair de lune. Estampes: Jardins sous la pluie.* RAVEL: *Le tombeau de Couperin: Toccata.*
(**(*)) APR mono CDAPR 7005 (2) [id.].

Moiseiwitsch never enjoyed quite the exposure on records to which his gifts entitled him, though in the earlier part of his career he made a great many. Later, in the electrical era he was a 'plum-label' artist and was not issued on the more prestigious and expensive 'red-label'. In this he was in pretty good company, for Solomon and Myra Hess were similarly relegated. This anthology gives a good picture of the great pianist in a wide variety of repertory: his *Pictures at an exhibition*, made in 1945, was for some time the only piano version; and those who identify him solely with the Russians will find his Chopin *Barcarolle* and Debussy *Jardins sous la pluie* totally idiomatic. The transfers are variable – all are made from commercial copies, some in better condition than others.

Organ Toccatas

'Grand Toccatas for organ' (played on various organs): BACH: *Toccata and fugue in D min., BWV 565.* CORETTE: *Carillon en F.* ALAIN: *Litanies* (Jean-Louis Gill). BUXTEHUDE: *Toccata and fugue in F, BuxWV 157.* KERLL: *Capriccio sopra 'Coucou'.* MOZART: *Fantasia in F min., K.608.* LISZT: *Prelude & fugue on the name, B-A-C-H* (Lionel Rogg). PACHELBEL: *Toccata in C.* MUFFAT: *Toccata No. 11 & Fugues Nos. 2, 4 & 6.* DANDRIEU: *Magnificat* (Werner Jacob). CLÉRAMBAULT: *Caprice sur les grands jeux* (Marie-Madeleine Duruflé). COUPERIN: *Offertoire sur les grands jeux* (Maurice Duruflé). BOËLY: *Toccata in B min.* SAINT-SAËNS: *Fantaisie in E flat* (Daniel Roth). MENDELSSOHN: *Prelude & fugue in C min., Op. 37/1.* BRAHMS: *Prelude and fugue in G min.* (Viktor Lukas). REGER: *Toccata in D min., Op. 59/5.* MULET: *Carillon-sortie.* DURUFLÉ: *Suite No. 5: Toccata* (Noel Rawsthorne). MURRILL: *Carillon* (Simon Preston). FRANCK: *Pièce héroïque.* GIGOUT: *Toccata in B min.* BOËLLMANN: *Suite gothique, Op. 25: Toccata.* WIDOR: *Symphony No. 5: Toccata* (Guy Morançon). VIERNE: *Toccata in B flat, Op. 53* (Gaston Littaize). TOURNEMIRE: *Fantaisie de l'Épiphanie* (André Marchal). GRISON: *Toccata in F* (Jane Parker-Smith). DUPRÉ: *Le tombeau de Titelouze: Toccata (Placare Christe servulis)* (Philip Ledger). JONGEN: *Toccata* (Jan Valach). MESSIAEN: *L'Ascension: Transports de joie d'une âme devant la gloire du Christ qui est la sienne* (Olivier Messiaen).
(B) *** EMI CZS7 67291-2 (2) [id.].

An extraordinarily diverse anthology – using a wide geographical range of organs – assembled with dedication and perception. Many of the players use more than one instrument and, after the famous Bach introduction, the music is arranged in approximate chronological order. Not surprisingly, as the source is French EMI, there is a strong bias towards French repertoire and organs but, when so much of the programme has a strong appeal, there is no reason to grumble. The choice includes several engaging examples of *Carillons*, notably those by Corette (which has a throaty exuberance) and our own Herbert Murrill. Overall, the variety of mood is remarkable: Pachelbel is sombre, Johann Kaspar Kerll spring-like with his cuckoo imitations, and Dandrieu grandiloquent. Towards the end of the first disc, the German repertoire brings a more massive style, capped at the beginning of the second disc by Noel Rawsthorne's powerful Liszt *Prelude and fugue*, recorded in Liverpool. Then after Saint-Saëns has charmed the ear, the second half produces a whole series of first-class French pieces, ending with ear-catching items like Mulet's *Carillon-sortie*, Jongen's *Toccata* and Alain's rhythmically quirky *Litanies*. Messiaen then provides an appropriately mystical end-piece. Vibrant transfers throughout; sometimes, as in the four pieces played by Guy Morançon on the Rouen Cavaillé-Coll instrument, the sound is a shade harsh, but almost never muddy – except, perhaps, in the 1956 Messiaen excerpt.

Paik, Kun Woo (piano)

POULENC: *Nocturnes Nos. 1, 5 & 6; Presto; Improvisations Nos. 10, 12 & 15. Intermezzo; Mouvements perpétuelles Nos. 1–3.* DEBUSSY: *Pour le piano; Suite bergamasque: Clair de lune.* SATIE: *Gnossiennes Nos. 4 & 5; Ogives Nos. 1–2: Vaisseaux; Casque. Celui qui parle trop; Espaňaña; Embryons desséchés; Gymnopédies Nos. 1–3.*
(BB) *** Virgo Dig. VJ7 91465-2; *VJ 791465-4* [id.].

The distinguished Korean pianist Kun Woo Paik has already given us a splendid Liszt recital on Virgo; if his collection of French music is slightly more idiosyncratic, there is still much to relish, notably Poulenc's *Mouvements perpétuelles* – and indeed the other pieces by this composer. His withdrawn performance of *Clair de lune* is a little indulgent and the *Gnossiennes* also find him a shade mannered, while the *Gymnopédies* are very languorous. But the outer movements of Debussy's *Pour le piano* bring some electrifying bravura, and his imagination is given full rein in the quirkier Satie miniatures. There is 75 minutes of music here and, even though the back-up documentation is disappointingly sparse, this is undoubtedly a bargain.

Parkening, Christopher (guitar)

'*A tribute to Segovia*': TORROBA: *Castles of Spain.* SOR: *Variations on a theme of Mozart.* GRANADOS: *Tonadilla.* SANZ: *Suite española.* ALBÉNIZ: *Torre bermeja.* SEGOVIA: *Estudio sin luz; Remembranza.* SANTIAGO DE MURCIA: *Suite in D min.* LLOBET: *Suite catalán.*
*** EMI Dig. CDC7 49404-2 [id.].

Christopher Parkening here makes his own highly individual contribution to the Spanish celebrations with a tribute, not only to Segovia, but to others, notably with the early *Suite in D minor* by Santiago de Murcia, a composer of the late 17th and early 18th centuries, whose music is very appealing. Parkening's style has a lower profile than that of Julian Bream and John Williams. His playing is very intimate and seductive, rhythmically free (witness the presentation of the theme in the Sor *Variations*), but beguilingly spontaneous. The digital recording allows him to often play very gently, and this makes a delightful hour of music for the late evening. The Granados and Sanz pieces are quite memorable.

Parker-Smith, Jane (organ)

Organ of Coventry Cathedral: *'Popular French Romantics'*: WIDOR: *Symphony No. 1: March pontifical. Symphony No 9 (Gothique), Op. 70: Andante sostenuto.* GUILMANT: *Sonata No. 5 in C min., Op. 80; Scherzo.* GIGOUT: *Toccata in B min.* BONNET: *Elfes, Op. 7.* LEFÉBURE-WÉLY: *Sortie in B flat.* VIERNE: *Pièces de fantaisie: Clair de lune, Op. 53/5; Carillon de Westminster, Op. 54/6.*
*** ASV Dig. CDDCA 539; *ZCDCA 539* [id.].

The modern organ in Coventry Cathedral (built by Harrison and Harrison of Durham) is surprisingly well suited to French repertoire. Its bright, full-bodied tutti, with just a touch of harshness, adds a nice bite to Jane Parker-Smith's very pontifical performance of the opening Widor *March* and creates a blaze of splendour at the close of the famous Vierne *Carillon de Westminster*, the finest performance on record. The detail of the fast, nimble articulation in the engagingly Mendelssohnian *Elfes* of Joseph Bonnet is not clouded; yet here, as in the splendid Guilmant *Scherzo* with its wider dynamic range, there is also a nice atmospheric effect. Hardly less enjoyable is the robustly jocular *Sortie* of Lefébure-Wély, which is delivered with fine geniality and panache. Overall, a most entertaining recital.

Organ of Beauvais Cathedral: *'Popular French Romantics' Vol. 2:* FRANCK: *Prélude, fugue et variation, Op. 18.* GUILMANT: *Grand choeur in D* (after Handel). MULET: *Carillon-sortie.* RENAUD: *Toccata in D min.* SAINT-SAËNS: *Prelude and fugue.* VIERNE: *Symphony No. 1: Finale. Stèle pour un enfant défunt.* WIDOR: *Symphony No. 4: Andante and Scherzo.*
*** ASV Dig. CDDCA 610; *ZCDCA 610* [id.].

The organ at Beauvais is even more suitable for this repertoire and the programme is admirably laid out. With his *Prélude and fugue*, Saint-Saëns is in more serious mood than usual but showing characteristic facility in fugal construction; Widor is first mellow and then quixotic – his *Scherzo* demands the lightest articulation and receives it. High drama and great bravura are provided by the Vierne *Finale* and later by Albert Renaud's *Toccata* and Henri Mulet's *Carillon-sortie*, while Franck's *Prélude, fugue et variation* and the poignant Vierne *Stèle pour un enfant défunt* (written after the death of a child of close friends, to whom the composer was greatly attached) bring attractive lyrical contrast: here Jane Parker-Smith's registration shows particular subtlety. The organ is splendidly recorded, its hint of harshness in tutti giving a proper French tang; and detail is not muddied.

Perahia, Murray (piano)

'Aldeburgh Recital': BEETHOVEN: *32 Variations in C min., WoO 80.* SCHUMANN: *Carnival jest from Vienna, Op. 26.* LISZT: *Hungarian rhapsody No. 12.* RACHMANINOV: *Études-tableaux in C, Op. 33/2; in E flat min., A min., D, Op. 39/5, 6 & 9.*
*** Sony Dig. SK 46437; *40-46437* [id.].

This concert is misleadingly called 'The Aldeburgh Recital', giving the impression that it is a recording of a public event, rather than the repertoire which he actually played during the festival. Not that this matters too much, for Murray Perahia plays with all the spontaneity and freshness that distinguish his concert appearances. Listening to his Rachmaninov serves as a reminder that the Russians have no monopoly on this repertoire; there is a depth and sense of pain that eludes even such artists as Ovchinnikov and Kissin. Perahia produces an extraordinary range of colour and tone; though one knows him to be a great Schumann interpreter, it is good to hear him in such barnstorming repertoire as the *Hungarian rhapsody No. 12* and the *Études-tableaux*, with which we do not normally associate him. This is one of the finest recitals to have appeared in a year not exactly lacking in remarkable piano CDs.

Perkins, Laurence (bassoon), Michael Hancock (piano)

'L'après-midi d'un dinosaur': HURLSTONE: *Sonata in F.* ELGAR: *Romance, Op. 62.* JACOB: *4 Sketches.* GOUNOD (arr. Perkins): *Funeral march of a marionette.* IBERT: *Carignane.* PIERNÉ: *Solo de concert, Op. 35.* SENAILLE: *Allegro spirituoso.* SAINT-SAËNS: *Sonata in G, Op. 108.*
*** Hyp. CDH 66054; *KH 88027* [id.].

An ingenious title for a highly enjoyable recital, very well recorded (although the acoustic is a trifle over-resonant). The sonatas of Hurlstone and Saint-Saëns are agreeably fluent but, among the miniatures, that Hitchcock tune, Gounod's *Funeral march of a marionette*, and Senaille's *Allegro spirituoso* (made famous by the veteran bassoonist, Archie Camden, as a filler in the days of 78-r.p.m. discs for the last side of Mozart's *Bassoon concerto*) stand out. All the playing is characterful, bringing out the instrument's elegance as well as its humour. The recording balance is very well managed.

Petri, Michala (recorder or flute)

'Greensleeves' (with Hanne Petri, harpsichord, David Petri, cello): ANON.: *Greensleeves to a grounde; Divisions on an Italian ground.* EYCK, Jacob van: *Prins Robberts Masco; Philis Schoon Herderinne; Wat Zal Men op den Avond Doen; Engels Nachtegaeltje.* CORELLI: *Sonata, Op. 15/5: La Folia.* HANDEL: *Andante.* LECLAIR: *Tambourin.* F. COUPERIN: *Le rossignol vainqueur; Le rossignol en amour.* J. S. BACH: *Siciliano.* TELEMANN: *Rondino.* GOSSEC: *Tambourin.* PAGANINI: *Moto perpetuo, Op. 11.* BRUGGEN: *2 Studies.* CHRISTIANSEN: *Satie auf hoher See.* HENRIQUES: *Dance of the midges.* SCHUBERT: *The Bee.* MONTI: *Czárdás.* HERBERLE: *Rondo presto.* RIMSKY-KORSAKOV: *Flight of the bumble-bee.*

(M) *** Ph. Dig. 420 897-2.

Marvellously nimble playing from Michala Petri, and 71 minutes, digitally recorded at mid-price, so one can afford to pick and choose. Some of the music opening the recital is less than distinctive, but the Couperin transcriptions are a delight and Paganini's *Moto perpetuo* vies with Henriques' *Dance of the midges* for sparkling bravura. There are some attractively familiar melodies by Bach and Handel, among others, to provide contrast, and Henning Christiansen's *Satie auf hoher See* is an unexpected treat. Monti's *Czárdás* ends the programme infectiously.

Petri, Michala (recorder), George Malcolm (harpsichord)

Recorder sonatas: VIVALDI: *Il Pastor fido: Sonata No. 6 in G min., RV 58.* CORELLI: *Sonata in C, Op. 5/9.* D. BIGAGLIA: *Sonata in A min.* BONONCINI: *Divertimento da camera No. 6 in C min.* SAMMARTINI: *Sonata in G, Op. 13/4.* B. MARCELLO: *Sonata in F, Op. 2/1.*
❀ *** Ph. Dig. 412 632-2 [id.].

Six recorder sonatas in a row might seem too much of a good thing, but the playing is so felicitous and the music has such charm that the collection is immensely enjoyable, even taken complete, and if sensibly dipped into is a source of much delight. There are many individual highlights. The Corelli *Sonata* has a memorable *Tempo di gavotta* as its finale which reminds one a little of Handel's *Harmonious blacksmith*; the work in A minor by the composer with the unlikely name of Diogenio Bigaglia (*c.* 1676–*c.* 1745) is a winner, with a nimble minuet and sparkling finale. Bononcini's *Divertimento da camera* alternates slow and fast sections, and in the third-movement *Largo* George Malcolm makes the delicate accompaniment sound like a harp. Sammartini's *Sonata* is enchanting, with its opening *Andante* in siciliano form and three more delectable movements to follow. Throughout, Michala Petri's playing is wonderfully fresh: she has made many records for Philips, but none more enticing than this. George Malcolm proves an equally imaginative partner, and both artists embellish with admirable flair and taste, never overdoing it. The Philips recording is quite perfectly balanced and wonderfully tangible.

Petrov, Nikolai (piano)

French music: RAMEAU: *Cyclope; La poule.* BIZET: *Nocturne No. 1 in D; Variations chromatiques in C min.* SAINT-SAËNS: *Toccata (Étude No. 6 in F, Op. 111); Étude en forme d'une valse. Piano concerto No. 2: Scherzo* (arr. Bizet). DUKAS: *Variations, interlude et final.* DEBUSSY: *Images oubliées.* RAVEL: *L'enfant et les sortilèges: Foxtrot (5 o'clock).*
**(*) Olympia OCD 122 [id.].

Nikolai Petrov is a big player and (to judge from the present compilation) an enterprising one. This recital includes some rarities, including the splendid Dukas *Variations, interlude et final*, and is probably worth getting for that alone. There are also the Bizet *Variations* and his remarkable transcription of the *Scherzo* of the Saint-Saëns *Second Piano concerto.* Although Petrov has formidable technical equipment and does produce too big a tone, he is far from insensitive to dynamic nuance. All the same, his *Images oubliées* do not match those of Kocsis (Philips) for sheer beauty and refinement of sound. His companion recital of *Fantaisies* by C. P. E. Bach, Brahms, Liszt, Mendelssohn and Mozart (Olympia OCD 198) is less beguiling, for all its easy virtuosity (most impressive in Liszt's *Don Juan* paraphrase).

Peyer, Gervase de (clarinet), Gwenneth Pryor (piano)

French music for clarinet and piano: SAINT-SAËNS: *Sonata, Op. 167.* DEBUSSY: *Première rhapsodie; Arabesque No. 2; Prélude: La fille aux cheveux de lin.* POULENC: *Sonata.* SCHMIDT: *Andantino, Op. 30/1.* RAVEL: *Pièce en forme de habañera.* PIERNÉ: *Canzonetta, Op. 19.*
❀ *** Chan. Dig. CHAN 8526; *ABTD 1236.*

A gorgeous record. Gervase de Peyer has already made some thirty or so records, but none more attractive than this, and he is accompanied by Gwenneth Pryor with wonderful sympathy. In Debussy's *Rhapsodie* she provides a subtle background tapestry for his languorous opening cantilena (marked *Rêveusement lente*); she then opens up for the work's climax yet lets the clarinet dominate as it must. The Saint-Saëns *Sonata* is an attractively crafted piece, full of engaging invention, with the opening melody returning neatly to close the work at the end of the fourth movement. Poulenc's *Sonata* is characteristically witty, with contrast in its lovely central *Romanza* (*très calme*); and the other short pieces wind down the closing mood of the recital, with De Peyer's luscious timbre drawing a charming portrait of *The girl with the flaxen hair* before the nimbly tripping closing encore of Pierné. This is a quite perfect record of its kind, the programme like that of a live recital and played with comparable spontaneity. The recording is absolutely realistic; the balance could hardly be improved on.

Piano Circus

FITKIN: *Sextet.* NYMAN: *1–100.* SEDDON: *16.* RACKHAM: *Which ever way your nose bends.*
*(**) Decca Dig. 433 690-2 [id.].

The Chris Fitkin *Sextet* makes a delightful *apéritif* for a fun collection of mainly minimalist works. Its gamelan-like jingling lasts just long enough – seven minutes of not-very-much. Tim Seddon's *16* has similar attractions, only with Cuban rhythms dominating and an exciting close, where the other two works are both far too long for their own good. The undoubted flair of these six talented and inventive performers is not nearly enough to sustain interest through Nyman's slow interplay of ideas or Simon Rackham's 31 minutes of even more tenuous, over-stretched material. Excellent sound.

'Piano pops'

'Piano Pops' (played by: (i) Garrick Ohlsson; (ii) Ronald Smith; (iii) Moura Lympany; (iv) Cyril Smith and Phyllis Sellick; (v) Daniel Adni; (vi) John Ogdon): (i) CHOPIN: *Polonaise No. 5 in F sharp min., Op. 55;* (ii) *Mazurkas Nos. 1 in F sharp min.; 2 in C sharp min.; 4 in E flat min., Op. 6/1, 2 & 4; 34 in C, Op. 56/2; 47 in A min., Op. 67/4;* (iii) *Nocturnes Nos. 2 in E flat, Op. 9/2; 5 in F sharp, Op. 15/2.* (iv) DEBUSSY: *Petite suite:* 4th movement. RACHMANINOV: *Lilacs.* BENJAMIN: *Mattie rag; Jamaican rumba.* SCOTT: *Water wagtail.* BIZET: *Jeux d'enfants: La bal.* FAURÉ: *Dolly: Berceuse.* WALTON: *Façade: Popular song.* MILHAUD: *Scaramouche: Brazileira.* (v) MENDELSSOHN: *Songs without words: Venetian gondola song, Op. 19/6;* (i) *Midsummer night's dream: Scherzo* (trans. Rachmaninov). (vi) BEETHOVEN: *5 Variations on Rule Brittania.* (i) TCHAIKOVSKY: *Lullaby.* RIMSKY-KORSAKOV: *Flight of the bumble-bee* (both trans. Rachmaninov). (v) GRIEG: *Lyric pieces: Melody; Norwegian dance (Halling), Op. 47/3–4; Nocturne; Scherzo, Op. 54/4–5.* GRAINGER: *Irish tune from County Derry; Molly on the shore; Shepherd's hey.*
(B) *** EMI *TC2-MOM 130.*

It is difficult to imagine a more attractively varied collection of piano genre pieces than this. Moreover, with a fine roster of artists to draw on, the performances are consistently distinguished. Highlights include Moura Lympany's Chopin *Nocturnes*, meltingly played; Daniel Adni sympathetic in Grieg and sprightly in Percy Grainger; Garrick Ohlsson bringing prodigious bravura to the Rachmaninov transcriptions, and John Ogdon showing Beethoven in a spontaneously light-hearted mood. But the undoubted pearl of the collection is the set of nine pieces played with consistent charm and sparkle by Cyril Smith and Phyllis Sellick (piano duo, three hands). Excellent, fresh transfers: this sounds splendid in the car.

Pinnock, Trevor (harpsichord)

'The harmonious blacksmith': HANDEL: *Suite 5: The Harmonious blacksmith.* FISCHER: *Urania: Passacaglia in D min.* COUPERIN: *Les baricades mystérieuses.* BACH: *Italian concerto in F, BWV 971.* RAMEAU: *Gavotte in A min.* D. SCARLATTI: *2 Sonatas Kk.380/1.* FIOCCO: *Suite 1: Adagio in F.* DAQUIN: *Le Coucou.* BALBASTHE: *La Suzanne in E min.*
**(*) DG 413 591-2 [id.].

A delightful collection of harpsichord lollipops, superbly and stylishly played and brilliantly – if aggressively – recorded. If one samples the famous title-piece, being careful to set the volume control at a realistic level, in the CD format the presence and tangibility of the instrument are spectacular. However, the bright sharpness of focus can become just a little tiring if the recital is taken all at once.

Pollini, Maurizio (piano)

PROKOFIEV: *Piano sonata No. 7 in B flat, Op. 83.* STRAVINSKY: *Three movements from Petrushka.* BOULEZ: *Piano sonata No. 2.* WEBERN: *Variations for piano, Op. 27.*
*** DG 419 202-2.

The Prokofiev is a great performance, one of the finest ever committed to disc; and the Stravinsky *Petrushka* is electrifying. Not all those responding to this music will do so quite so readily to the Boulez, fine though the playing is; but the Webern also makes a very strong impression. This is the equivalent of two LPs and is outstanding value.

Pöntinen, Roland (piano)

Russian piano music: STRAVINSKY: *3 Movements from Petrushka.* SCRIABIN: *Sonata No. 7 in F sharp (White Mass), Op. 64.* SHOSTAKOVICH: *3 Fantastic dances.* RACHMANINOV: *Études-tableaux, Opp. 33 & 39.* PROKOFIEV: *Toccata.* KHACHATURIAN: *Toccata.*
*** BIS Dig. CD 276 [id.].

Roland Pöntinen gives a suitably ardent and inflammable account of the *Seventh Sonata*, the so-called '*White Mass*', and is fully attuned to the Scriabin sensibility, conveying its wild, excitable character to good effect. His playing has real temperament and sense of colour, and this well-recorded recital shows his very considerable technique and prowess to advantage. A very enjoyable programme.

Preston, Simon (organ)

'Variations on America' (Organ of Methuen Memorial Music Hall): SOUSA: *Stars and Stripes.* SAINT-SAËNS: *Danse macabre.* IVES: *Variations on 'America'.* BUCK: *Variations on 'The last rose of summer'.* BOSSI: *Étude symphonique, Op. 78.* LEMARE: *Andantino in D flat.* GUILMANT: *Sonata No. 1 in D min., Op. 42.*
*** Argo Dig. 421 731-2; *421 731-4* [id.].

Here we are introduced to another fascinating American organ. The instrument in question originated in Boston Music Hall. After a delayed Atlantic crossing it was installed in 1863, and for two decades it anteceded the Boston Symphony Orchestra as the prime focus of Boston music-making. When the orchestra was inaugurated, the organ was moved to the Methuen Memorial Hall, which was built specially to house it, and the instrument we now hear was rebuilt to modern specifications in the 1940s. Simon Preston is perhaps not as flamboyant a musical personality as Carlo Curley, but he gives a dazzling display of the instrument's capabilities, from the flashily registered opening Sousa march through to the dashing passage-work of Guilmant's finale. On the way we encounter Charles Ives's gleefully disrespectful treatment of a solemn national tune, equally famous on both sides of the Atlantic, more variations by Donald Buck, who was resident organist in Boston in the 1970s, a sentimental *Andantino* by Lemare, which is perhaps better known as a setting of the words, *Moonlight and roses*, plus more rhetorical bravura from Bossi and transcribed orchestral spectacle from Saint-Saëns. One can appreciate here not only the skill of the Argo engineers but also that of the architect, Henry Vaughan, who designed the hall in Methuen, Massachusetts, which so effectively displays the colour and range of this remarkable instrument.

'The world of the organ' (organ of Westminster Abbey): WIDOR: *Symphony No. 5: Toccata.* BACH: *Chorale prelude, Wachet auf, BWV 645.* MOZART: *Fantasia in F min., K.608.* WALTON: *Crown imperial* (arr. Murrill). CLARKE: *Prince of Denmark's march* (arr. Preston). HANDEL: *Saul: Dead march.* PURCELL: *Trumpet tune* (arr. Trevor). ELGAR: *Imperial march* (arr. Martin). VIERNE: *Symphony No. 1: Finale.* WAGNER: *Tannhäuser: Pilgrims' chorus.* GUILMANT: *March on a theme of Handel.* SCHUMANN: *Study No. 5* (arr. West). KARG-ELERT: *Marche triomphale (Now thank we all our God).*
(B) *** Decca 430 091-2; *430 091-4.*

A splendid bargain compilation from the Argo catalogue of the early to mid-1960s, spectacularly recorded, which offers 69 minutes of music and is in every sense a resounding success. Simon Preston's account of the Widor *Toccata* is second to none, and both the Vierne

Finale and the Karg-Elert *March triomphale* lend themselves admirably to Preston's unashamed flamboyance and the tonal splendour afforded by the Westminster acoustics. Walton's *Crown imperial*, too, brings a panoply of sound which compares very favourably with an orchestral recording. The organ has a splendid trumpet stop which makes both the Purcell piece and Clarke's *Prince of Denmark's march*, better known as the '*Trumpet voluntary*', sound crisply regal.

Prometheus Ensemble

'French impressions': RAVEL: *Introduction & allegro for harp, flute, clarinet and string quartet.* DEBUSSY: *Danses sacrée et profane; Sonata for flute, viola and harp.* ROUSSEL: *Serenade.*
*** ASV Dig. CDDCA 664; *ZCDCA 664* [id.].

This young group gives eminently well-prepared and thoughtful accounts of all these pieces. Although these performances do not displace earlier versions, no one investing in them will be disappointed. The *Danses sacrée et profane* sound particularly atmospheric and the Debussy *Sonata* is played with great feeling and sounds appropriately ethereal. The Roussel, too, is done with great style and, even if the *Introduction and allegro* does not supersede the celebrated Melos account, the Prometheus do it well.

Rév, Lívia (piano)

'For children': BACH: *Preludes in E, BWV 939; in G min., BWV 930.* DAQUIN: *Le coucou.* MOZART: *Variations on Ah vous dirai-je maman, K.265.* BEETHOVEN: *Für Elise.* SCHUMANN: *Album for the young Op. 63:* excerpts. CHOPIN: *Nocturne in C min., Op. posth.* LISZT: *Etudes G. 136/1 & 2.* BIZET: *Jeux d'enfants: La Toupie.* FAURÉ: *Dolly: Berceuse.* TCHAIKOVSKY: *Album for the young, Op. 39: Maman; Waltz.* VILLA-LOBOS: *Prole do bebê:* excerpts. JOLIVET: *Chansons naïve 1 & 2.* PROKOFIEV: *Waltz, Op. 65.* BARTÓK: *Evening in the country; For Children:* excerpts. DEBUSSY: *Children's corner:* excerpts. MAGIN: *3 Pieces.* MATAČIĆ: *Miniature variations.*
*** Hyp. CDA 66185; *KA 66185.*

A wholly delectable recital, and not just for children either. The whole is more than the sum of its many parts, and the layout provides excellent variety, with the programme stimulating in mixing familiar with unfamiliar. The recording is first class. Highly recommended for late evening listening.

Richter, Sviatoslav (piano)

CHOPIN: *Préludes, Op. 28/2; 4–11; 13; 19; 21 & 23.* TCHAIKOVSKY: *Nocturne in F, Op. 10/1; Valse-scherzo in A, Op. 7.* RACHMANINOV: *Études-tableaux, Op. 33/3, 5 & 6; Op. 39 1–4; 7 & 9.*
*** Olympia OCD 112 [id.].

Some marvellous playing here from Richter. He plays an odd assortment of Chopin *Preludes*, Nos. 4 through to 10 in the published sequence, then 23, 19, 11, 2, 23 and 21! These obviously derive from a public concert, as there is applause. He is distinctly ruminative and wayward at times. The two Tchaikovsky pieces are done with extraordinary finesse and the Rachmaninov is masterly. The piano does not sound fresh, either in the *C sharp minor Étude-tableau* of Op. 33 or (not surprisingly) in the last of Op. 39, where one or two octaves sound 'tired', but it is all right elsewhere in the set. There is some magical playing in the *A minor* piece and some dazzling virtuosity elsewhere. The recordings are not top drawer and the disc gives no details of their provenance; but the sound is perfectly acceptable.

DEBUSSY: *Estampes; Préludes, Book I: Voiles; Le vent dans la plaine; Les collines d'Anacapri.* PROKOFIEV: *Visions fugitives, Op. 22, Nos. 3, 6 & 9; Sonata No. 8 in B flat, Op. 84.* SCRIABIN: *Sonata No. 5 in F sharp, Op. 53.*
❀ (M) *** DG 423 573-2.

The Debussy *Préludes* and the Prokofiev *Sonata* were recorded at concerts during an Italian tour in 1962, while the remainder were made the previous year in Wembley Town Hall. The former sound more open than the rather confined studio acoustic – but what playing! The

Scriabin is demonic and the Debussy could not be more atmospheric. The performance of the Prokofiev *Sonata* is, like the legendary Gilels account, a classic of the gramophone.

Rifkin, Joshua (piano)

Rags and tangos: SCOTT: *Evergreen rag; Modesty rag; Peace and plenty rag; Troubadour rag.* NAZARETH: *Apanhei-te Cavaquinho; Vitorioso; Odeon; Nove de Julho; Labirinto; Guerreiro; Plangente; Cubanos; Fon-Fon!.* LAMB: *Ragtime nightingale; American beauty rag; Bohemia rag; Topliner rag.*
(M) *** Decca Dig. 425 225-2 [id.].

James Scott was born in southwestern Missouri but supposedly met Joplin in St Louis in 1906. He shows a similar spirited, yet easy-going melodic personality: the indelible yet attractively relaxed *Modesty rag* could become as popular as Joplin's *Entertainer*, given the proper exposure. *Peace and plenty* shows him at his most rhythmically glittering, and *Troubadour* has an insinuating charm. Ernesto Nazareth lived in Rio de Janeiro and his style is more romantic, often intimate. But a number like *Plangente* gets under the skin just the same, and the glittering upper tessitura of *Apanhei-te* is very engaging, while *Cavaquinho* is prettily pert. Joseph Lamb was a New Yorker (he met Joplin in 1909): his music has a certain city sophistication and is ripe with outside influences. Joshua Rifkin is a master of this repertoire: his playing is full of rhythmic vitality, yet he understands the harmonic and melodic nuances of this special musical style, witness his subtle account of Nazareth's *Vitorioso*. Excellent recording, and well over an hour of music.

Rogé, Pascal (piano) and **Wind Ensemble**

French chamber music: SAINT-SAËNS: *Caprice sur des airs danois et russes.* D'INDY: *Sarabande et menuet.* ROUSSEL: *Divertissement.* TANSMAN: *Danse de la sorcière.* FRANÇAIX: *L'heure du berger.* POULENC: *Élégie.* MILHAUD: *Sonata, Op. 47.*
❀ *** Decca Dig. 425 861-2 [id.].

A well-chosen and varied recital of French chamber music, performed with elegance and charm by these fine wind players and by Pascal Rogé at the piano. The Saint-Saëns *Caprice sur des airs danois et russes* was written for a visit the composer made to Russia in 1887 with three wind players. It is great fun, as is most of the music on the disc, notably the delightful minuet of Vincent d'Indy's *Sarabande et menuet*, the early Roussel *Divertissement* and Alexandre Tansman's *Danse de la sorcière*. Perhaps the humour of Françaix's *L'heure du berger* may strike some as a bit arch but, played with such flair, such thoughts are instantly banished. Poulenc's *Élégie* for horn and piano, composed on the death of Dennis Brain, is eloquently played by André Cazalet. It is invidious to mention him alone, as the flautist, Catherine Cantin, and those stalwarts of French wind music, Maurice Bourgue, Michel Portal, and Amaury Wallez, are equally splendid. Milhaud's *Sonata*, Op. 47, for flute, oboe, clarinet and piano (from 1918) has the fresh, easy-going zest of this composer at his best. The recording is very well balanced and should give unqualified delight to all who are sensible enough to buy it.

Rubinstein, Artur (piano)

'A French programme': RAVEL: *Valses nobles et sentimentales Nos. 1–8; La vallée des cloches. Le tombeau: Forlane.* POULENC: *Mouvements perpetuels (Assez modéré; Très modéré; Alerte); Intermezzo in A flat; Intermezzo No. 2 in D flat.* FAURÉ: *Nocturne in A flat, Op. 33/3.* CHABRIER: *10 Pièces pittoresques: Scherzo-Valse.*
*** BMG/RCA RD 85665 [5665-2-RC].

This recital dates from the mid-1960s. The playing is eminently aristocratic and the Ravel pieces and the Poulenc could hardly be bettered. The recording, like the rest of Rubinstein's analogue records, has been enhanced in its new format and is fully acceptable; admirers of this artist need have no qualms about investigating this disc.

Schiller, Allan (piano)

'Für Elise': Popular piano pieces: BEETHOVEN: *Für Elise.* FIELD: *Nocturne in E (Noontide).* CHOPIN: *Mazurka in B flat, Op. 7/1; Waltz in A, Op. 34/2. 3 Écossaises, Op. 72/3; Fantaisie-impromptu, Op. 66.* MENDELSSOHN: *Songs without words: Venetian gondola song, Op. 19; Bees' wedding, Op. 67.* LISZT: *Consolation No. 3 in D flat.* DE SEVERAC: *The music box.* DEBUSSY: *Suite bergamasque: Clair de lune. Arabesques Nos. 1 and 2. Prélude: The girl with the flaxen hair.* GRIEG: *Wedding day at Trodhaugen; March of the dwarfs.* ALBÉNIZ: *Granada; Tango; Asturias.*
(BB) *** ASV CDQS 6032; *ZCQS 6032.*

A particularly attractive recital, diverse in mood, spontaneous in feeling and very well recorded. The acoustic is resonant, but the effect is highly realistic. There are many favourites here, with Allan Schiller at his most personable in the engaging Field *Nocturne*, De Severac's piquant *Music box* and the closing *Asturias* of Albéniz, played with fine bravura. The Chopin group, too, is particularly successful, with the Scottish rhythmic snap of the *Écossaises* neatly articulated and the famous *B flat Mazurka* presented most persuasively.

Scott Whiteley, John (organ)

Organ of York Minster: *'Great Romantic organ music':* TOURNEMIRE: *Improvisation on the Te Deum.* JONGEN: *Minuet-Scherzo, Op. 53.* MULET: *Tu es Petra.* DUPRÉ: *Prelude and fugue in G min., Op. 3/7.* R. STRAUSS: *Wedding prelude.* KARG-ELERT: *Pastel in B, Op. 92/1.* BRAHMS: *Chorale prelude: O Gott, du frommer Gott, Op. 122/7.* LISZT: *Prelude and fugue on BACH, G.260.*
*** York CD 101.

A superb organ recital, with the huge dynamic range of the York Minster organ spectacularly captured on CD and pianissimo detail registering naturally. John Scott Whiteley's playing is full of flair: the attractively complex and sparklingly florid *Prelude and fugue* of Marcel Dupré is exhilarating and reaches a high climax, while the grand Liszt piece is hardly less overwhelming. The shorter lyrical pieces add serenity and proper contrast at the centre of a recital that is as well planned as it is played and recorded. The opening Tournemire *Improvisation* is very arresting indeed, while Jongen's *Minuet-Scherzo* displays Scott Whiteley's splendidly clear articulation.

Snowden, Jonathan (flute), Andrew Litton (piano)

'Danse de la chèvre' (music for flute and piano): WIDOR: *Suite.* FAURÉ: *Fantaisie, Morceau de concours.* DEBUSSY: *Syrinx.* HONEGGER: *Danse de la chèvre.* ROUSSEL: *Joueurs de flûte.* MESSIAEN: *Le merle noir.* POULENC: *Flute sonata.*
*** Virgin Dig. VC7 90846-2; *VC7 90846-4* [id.].

The brilliant first flute of the LPO, deftly accompanied by the conductor, Andrew Litton, a formidable pianist, here gathers a vintage collection of French works for flute. The Poulenc *Sonata* is dazzlingly done, and so are the other virtuoso pieces, all strongly characterized. The surprise is the opening item by Widor, delicate and pointed, charmingly lyrical, a *Suite* by a composer now remembered only for his heavyweight organ works. Good, though slightly recessed recording.

Söllscher, Göran (guitar)

'Cavatina': MYERS: *Cavatina; Portrait.* ALBÉNIZ: *Granada.* TÁRREGA: *Maria; Rosita.* BARRIOS: *Villancico de Navidad.* YOCOH: *Sakura.* LLOBET: arr. of Catalan folksongs: *La filla del marxant; La canço del lladre; El noi de la mare.* LAURO: *El Marabino.* CRESPO: *Norteña.* PATIÑO: *Nevando está.* NEUMANN: *Karleksvals.* CARMICHAEL: *Georgia on my mind.* ANON.: *Romance d'amour.*
*** DG Dig. 413 720-2 [id.].

Göran Söllscher is at his finest here. The programme is essentially Romantic and very tuneful and atmospheric. The indelible opening Myers *Cavatina* is of course the justly famous *Deerhunter* theme, while even the anonymous *Romance* will be familiar. Whether in the attractive Llobet arrangements of Catalan folksongs, the two evocative portraits from Tárrega, or Yocoh's colourful *Sakura* (from Japan), this is the kind of music-making that remains in the memory, for even while the playing is relaxed there is no doubt about Söllscher's magnetism. Hoagy Carmichael's *Georgia on my mind* gives the feeling of a final lollipop as the stylish closing encore. The sound is most naturally balanced, and the immediacy and realism are apparent.

Tan, Melvyn (fortepiano)

'Salonkonzert': BEETHOVEN: *Horn sonata in F, Op. 17* (with M. Garcin-Marrou). MENDELSSOHN: *6 Songs without words; Rondo capriccioso, Op. 14*. SCHUBERT: *Introduction and variations on 'Trockne Blumen' for flute & piano, D.802* (with K. Hünteler). WEBER: *Grand duo concertante for clarinet & piano, Op. 48* (with E. Hoeprich).
*** EMI Dig. CDC7 54021-2 [id.].

This so-called '*Salonkonzert*' is a thoroughly enjoyable affair. The Beethoven *Horn sonata*, played on period instruments, is a very different musical experience from the familiar modern performance; the uneven horn-tone with its strong bottom notes makes a striking contrast with the fortepiano. It is played with great expertise and musicianship by Michel Garcin-Marrou. He is partnered with style and fluency by Melvyn Tan, who also captures the spirit of the six Mendelssohn *Songs without words*, Op. 14, as well as the familiar *Rondo capriccioso*, to perfection. Listening to Schubert's *Introduction and variations on 'Trockne Blumen'*, even in such a sympathetic account as that of Konrad Hünteler, makes one understand Mozart's aversion to the early flute, with its pale, watery tone and occasional flatness. The Weber *Grand duo concertante* is much more enjoyable and finds expert advocacy from Eric Hoeprich. The balance is thoroughly natural and realistic, with the fortepiano observed at just the right distance.

Thibaud, Jacques (violin), Pablo Casals (cello), Alfred Cortot (piano)

BEETHOVEN: *Piano trios Nos. 7 in B flat (Archduke), Op. 97; 11 (Variations on 'Ich bin der Schneider Kakadu'); 7 Variations in E flat on 'Bei Männern'* (from Mozart's *Die Zauberflöte*) *for cello and piano; Violin sonata No. 9 in A (Kreutzer), Op. 47*. SCHUBERT: *Piano trio No. 1 in B flat, D.898*. MENDELSSOHN: *Piano trio No. 1 in D min., Op. 63*. HAYDN: *Piano trio in G, Op. 73/2*. BRAHMS: *Double concerto in A min. for violin, cello and orchestra, Op. 102* (with Barcelona Orchestra).
(M) (**(*)) EMI mono CHS7 640572 (3) [id.].

The Brahms *Double concerto*, recorded in 1929 and the first recording of the work, has tremendous intensity which shines through the less than sumptuous sound. Cortot appears as conductor and draws playing of a radiant vitality from the Barcelona Orchestra. The Mendelssohn *D minor Trio* was also long a classic and shows what real chamber-music playing is about. Nothing is done to impress the public; this performance conveys the sense of music-making among friends. The 1927 sound calls for tolerance, though one suspects that the originals, reproduced on appropriate equipment, would yield more natural results. There have been better performances than the 1929 Thibaud–Cortot *Kreutzer* (Cortot was always more intent on the spirit than the letter) but few finer of the Schubert *B flat Trio*, made in 1926, among the best-sounding of the lot. A valuable document, for the most part adequately transferred.

Turovsky, Eleonora (violin), Yuli Turovsky (cello)

French music for violin and cello: RAVEL: *Sonata*. J. RIVIER: *Sonatine*. HONEGGER: *Sonatine*. MARTINŮ: *Duo*.
*** Chan. Dig. CHAN 8358; *ABTD 1121* [id.].

The most substantial piece here is the Ravel *Sonata*, which opens magically and is beautifully played by these two artists. Jean Rivier's *Sonatine* is slight but charming, while the Honegger and Martinů works are more challenging. There is over an hour's music here, repertoire that one seldom encounters in the concert hall. A very well-recorded programme, designed rather for the connoisseur of French music than for the wider record-collecting public, but well worth investigating.

Vaidman, Vera (violin), Emanuel Krasovsky (piano)

'Romantic strings': TCHAIKOVSKY: *Méditation; Mélodie, Op. 42/1 & 2; Valse-Scherzo, Op. 34.* DVOŘÁK: *Violin sonatina in G.* SCHUBERT: *Violin sonatina in A min., D.835.* KREISLER: *Schön Rosmarin; Liebeslied; Liebesfreud.*
(BB) *** Pickwick/CDI Dig. PWK 1137.

Misguidedly mistitled, this collection is a recital of the highest calibre. Though the three memorable Tchaikovsky pieces are played superbly, the highlight is the wonderfully spontaneous account of the Dvořák *Sonatina*, written during the composer's American period and with a melodic inspiration to match the *New World Symphony*. It is played here with all the freshness of new discovery. The charm of the Schubert work is equally well caught, and the three Kreisler lollipops make splendid bonnes-bouches at the end. This is an outstanding partnership in every way, and the recording is absolutely real and natural.

Wild, Earl (piano)

'The virtuoso piano': HERZ: *Variations on 'Non più mesta' from Rossini's La Cenerentola.* THALBERG: *Don Pasquale fantasy, Op. 67.* GODOWSKY: *Symphonic metamorphosis on themes from Johann Strauss's Kunsterleben (Artist's life).* RUBINSTEIN: *Étude (Staccato), Op. 23/2.* HUMMEL: *Rondo in E flat, Op. 11.* PADEREWSKI: *Theme and variations, Op. 16/3.*
(M) *** Van. 08.4033.71 [OVC 4033].

Earl Wild's famous performances from the late 1960s re-emerge on CD with their scintillating brilliance given even greater projection by the digital remastering. The piano sound is slightly dry but not lacking in depth of sonority, especially in the two Liszt operatic paraphrases, which are splendidly authoritative here. Wild's technique is prodigious and his glittering bravura in the engaging Herz *Rossini variations* and Thalberg's equally entertaining *Don Pasquale fantasy* is among the finest modern examples of the grand tradition of virtuoso pianism. Godowsky's piece may have a heavy title, but in Earl Wild's hands, for all the decorative complexities, the lilting waltz-rhythms are still paramount.

Williams, John (guitar)

'Spanish guitar music': I. ALBÉNIZ: *Asturias; Tango; Cordoba; Sevilla.* SANZ: *Canarios.* TORROBA: *Nocturno; Madroños.* SAGRERAS: *El Colibri.* M. ALBÉNIZ: *Sonata in D.* FALLA: *Homenaje; Three-cornered hat: Corregidor's dance; Miller's dance. El amor brujo: Fisherman's song.* CATALAN FOLKSONGS: *La Nit de Nadal; El noy de la mare; El testamen de Amelia.* GRANADOS: *La maja de Goya. Spanish dance No. 5.* TARREGA: *Recuerdos de la Alhambra.* VILLA-LOBOS: *Prelude No. 4 in E min.* MUDARRA: *Fantasia.* TURINA: *Fandanguillo, Op. 36.*
(M) *** Sony SBK 46347 [id.].

John Williams has the full measure of this repertoire. He can show strong Latin feeling, as in the vibrant *Farruca* of the *Miller's dance* from Falla's *Three-cornered hat*, or create a magically atmospheric mood, as in the hauntingly registered transcription of the *Fisherman's song* from *El amor brujo*. He can play with thoughtful improvisatory freedom, as in the Villa-Lobos *Prelude*, with its pianissimo evocation, or be dramatically spontaneous, as in the memorable performance of Turina's *Fandanguillo*, which ends the recital magnetically. The instinctive control of atmosphere and dynamic is constantly rewarding throughout a varied programme, and the technique is phenomenal, yet never flashy, always at the service of the music. The remastering brings a clean and truthful, if very immediate, image. Background is minimal and never intrusive.

Yamash'ta, Stomu (percusssion)

20th-Century music: HENZE: *Prison song.* TAKEMITSU: *Seasons.* MAXWELL DAVIES: *Turis campanarum sonantium.*

(M) *** Decca 430 005-2 [id.].

Henze's remarkable *Prison song* was written especially for Yamash'ta. The words of the poem (from the *Prison Diary of Ho Chi Minh*) are mixed in with a prerecorded *musique concrète* tape, and to this the percussionist adds his own rhythmic commentary. Yamash'ta both recites and plays, and the result is an artistic *tour de force*. Toru Takemitsu's *Seasons* is strong in atmosphere but does not quite match the imaginative quality of Peter Maxwell Davies's *Turis campanarum sonantium*. In this work, perhaps the most ambitious of the three here recorded, Yamash'ta creates and holds the strongest possible tension and builds a climax of tremendous power. The Decca recording is truly spectacular, and this is a reissue not to be missed by those interested in twentieth-century avant-garde writing.

Yepes, Narciso (guitar)

Spanish guitar music: TÁRREGA: *Recuerdos de la Alhambra; Capricho arabe; Serenata; Tango; Alborada; Marieta mazurka.* SOR: *Theme and variations, Op. 9; Minuet in G, Op. 11/1. Variations on Marlborough, Op. 28.* SANZ: *Spanish suite.* RODRIGO: *En los trigales.* GRANADOS: *Spanish Dance No. 4.* ALBÉNIZ: *Rumores de la Caleta; Malagueña, Op. 165. Suite española: Asturias (Leyenda).* Arr. LLOBET: *La canço del lladre; La filla del marxant* (Catalan folksongs). SEGOVIA: *El noi de la mare.* YEPES: *Forbidden games* (film score): *Romance.* VILLA-LOBOS: *Prelude No. 1.* RUIZ PIPÓ: *Canción and Danza No. 1* (CD only: ALBÉNIZ: *Piezas caracteristicas No. 12.* MOMPOU: *Canco i danca.* ASENCIO: *Collectici itim*).
❀ (B) *** DG Compact Classics 413 434-2 (2); *413 434-4.*

This cassette can be recommended with the utmost enthusiasm to anyone wanting an inexpensive, generous (88 minutes) and representative programme of Spanish guitar music. Narciso Yepes is not only an outstanding exponent of this repertoire, he also has the rare gift of consistently creating electricity in the recording studio, and all this music springs vividly to life. In popular favourites like the famous opening *Recuerdos de la Alhambra* of Tárrega, the exciting transcription of Falla's *Miller's dance*, the earlier Baroque repertoire (the *Suite* of Sanz is particularly appealing), and in the communicative twentieth-century items by Rodrigo and Ruiz Pipó, Yepes' assured and always stylish advocacy brings consistent pleasure. The tape transfer level is quite high and the attendant hiss is not a problem. There are three extra items, all valuable, on the pair of CDs, which sound first class – but this is surely a case where the tape is the best buy: it costs much less and can be used both domestically and in the car.

Zabaleta, Nicanor (harp)

'Arpa española': ALBÉNIZ: *Managueña, Op. 165/3; Suite española: Granada (Serenata); Zaragoza (Capricho); Asturias (Leyenda). Mallorca, Op. 202; Tango español.* FALLA: *Serenata andaluza.* TURINA: *Ciclo pianistico No. 1: Tocata y fuga.* GOMBAU: *Apunte bético.* GRANADOS: *Danza española No. 5.* HALFFTER: *Sonatina* (ballet): *Danza de la pastora.* LÓPEZ-CHAVARRI: *El viejo castillo moro.*
❀ (M) *** DG 435 847-2 [id.].

A good deal of the music here belongs to the guitar (or piano) rather than the harp, but Nicanor Zabaleta, with his superb artistry and sense of atmosphere makes it all his own, The harp provides a fuller, bigger sound than the guitar (in spite of the frequent efforts of recording engineers to make the guitar sound larger than life) but this is tempered by Zabaleta's feeling for the music's intimacy and his impeccable taste. With the presence and magnetism of this playing, the opening pieces from Albéniz's *Suite española* show distinction as well as charm: who could resist the swirling cascades of the *Zaragoza*? Throughout this delightful programme, Zabaleta gives each piece strong individuality of character. In the Granados *Spanish dance No. 5* he matches the magnetism of Julian Bream's famous recording, and Manuel de Falla's *Serenata andaluza* is hardly less captivating. DG's sound balance is near perfection, as is the choice of acoustic, and the magic distilled by Zabaleta's concentration, often at the gentlest levels of dynamic, is unforgettable.

Vocal Recitals and Choral Collections

Academy of Ancient Music, Christopher Hogwood

'Music from the time of Elizabeth I' (with Judith Nelson, Mary Beverley, David James, Paul Elliott, David Thomas, Sneak's Noyse, Roderick Skeaping): (Viols) HOLBORNE: *Heres Paternus; Mylinda.* (Keyboard) FARNABY: *The old spagnoletta.* BULL: *Regina galliard; Spanish pavane; Corantos: Alarm & Battle.* (Lute) JOHNSON: Duo: *Flat pavane and galliard. Greensleeves with variations.* HOLBORNE: *Tinternell.* (Sackbuts & cornetts) *Galliard. The night watch; Last will and testament.* (Vocal) BYRD: *Though Amaryllis dance in green; I joy not in no earthly bliss.* MARENZIO: *I must depart all hapless.* WEELKES: *On the plains fairy trains: Sweet heart arise; Welcome sweet pleasure.* ANON.: Rustic ballads: *Tomorrow the fox will come to town; Martyn said to his man; The baffled knight.*
*** O-L 433 193-2 [id.].

This admirable concert seeks to show the difference between couth and uncouth, the contrast between the elegant madrigals, viol consorts, lute and keyboard music, heard in the household of the Elizabethan *compleat gentleman*, and the broadsheet songs and the waits' band music from the taverns. It is all rather more sophisticated in its finesse and polish than would have been likely with the real thing, but makes an entertaining and beguiling concert. The programme is well laid out to alternate the vocal pieces, most beautifully sung, with instrumental interludes, and ends with the more robust items including a deliciously bawdy song about a too-courteous knight who meets a resourceful maid in the fields and is persuaded to ride the day long with her beside him 'as though they had been brother and sister' in the hopes of her promised later submission to his will. But when she reaches her 'father's hall' she speeds inside and shuts the wicket gate in his face. With first class performances, naturally balanced, very realistic recording, and striking presence this is one of the very best collections of its kind.

Albanese, Licia (soprano)

Arias from: PUCCINI: *Madama Butterfly; La Bohème; Manon Lescaut; Tosca; Turandot; La Rondine; Suor Angelica.* VERDI: *La Traviata.* MOZART: *Le nozze di Figaro.* CILEA: *Adriana Lecouvreur.* CHARPENTIER: *Louise.* TCHAIKOVSKY: *Eugene Onegin.*
(M) (***) BMG/RCA mono GD 60384 [60394-2-RG].

As the range of these recordings indicates, Licia Albanese was not limited to the Puccini repertory, though that was always at the centre, above all *Butterfly*. Her bright, clear voice might have seemed ideal for recording, but sadly a trick of vibrato often marred the sweetness and purity and made it sound older than it was, particularly under pressure. These recordings, mostly made between 1945 and 1950, present her at her peak, and consistently the charm and power of characterization make each item compelling. Fascinatingly, the last and longest of the items, Tatiana's letter scene from Tchaikovsky's *Eugene Onegin*, was from a role she never sang on stage. Here Stokowski conducting his own orchestra adds to the natural warmth and expressiveness. Good bright transfers.

Ambrosian Singers, RPO, Elmer Bernstein

'Musical spectacular' (Songs and production numbers from MGM Musicals, with Nick Curtis and Mary Carewe): Excerpts from: *Kismet; Band Wagon; Meet me in St Louis; Gigi; Singin' in the rain; The Pirate; Brigadoon; Ziegfeld Follies.*
*** Chan. Dig. CHAN 8781 [id.].

An indispensable wallow for MGM film-buffs, given Chandos's most spectacular recording, sumptuous yet brilliant in the most exciting way without being too fierce. If Judy Garland's voice seems inseparable from *The Trolley song*, Mary Carewe provides a pretty impressive cover version here, showing plenty of spirit and warm vocal colour in her own right; Nick Curtis makes an equally personable stand-in for Gene Kelly in *Singin' in the rain*. They have the right voices and peppy style for this repertoire, and the Ambrosian Singers follow them across the

Atlantic with a convincing twang to their diction. Elmer Bernstein conducts with great zest and, in the *Gigi* sequence, a voluptuous feeling for the lyrical tunes. Of its kind, this is hard to beat.

Amis, John

'My Music' (with Jeffrey Tate, Ian Wallace, Steve Race, Donald Swann): POULENC: *Babar the Elephant* (with Leslie Howard, piano); *Tell me where is fancy bred; Hotel.* RIDOUT: *Ferdinand the Bull* (with Levon Chilingirian). *3 Poems from Façade.* GRAINGER: *The old woman at the Christening.* TRAD.: *Ye banks and braes.* RACE: *On a sleeping friend; Oh mistress mine.* SWANN: *Joseph wonders; Bilbo's last song.* Whistling items: ARNOLD: *Thème pour mon Ami(s).* ELGAR: *Salut d'amour.* SCHUBERT: *Piano trio No. 2:* excerpt.
*** Nimbus Dig. NI 5342; *NC 5342* [id.].

This is a delightfully idiosyncratic collection issued to celebrate the seventieth birthday of John Amis in June 1992. Those who have enjoyed his contributions to 'My Music' on both radio and television will relish the range of his contributions: singing, reciting and – not least – whistling, with various friends accompanying. Particularly delightful are the Shakespeare and Belloc settings by Steve Race and a Coward-like cabaret song by Penelope Thwaites, both accompanied by their respective composers. Malcolm Arnold shows his melodic magic in a charming *Thème pour mon Ami(s)*, a number for whistling, and only Amis would ever dare to turn Elgar's *Salut d'amour* or the theme from the slow movement of Schubert's *E flat Piano trio* into whistling numbers. The major items are welcome too, both with Amis narrations: Poulenc's well-known *Babar the Elephant* and Alan Ridout's *Ferdinand* (*the Bull*), with accompaniment for solo violin alone, played by Levon Chilingirian. Idiosyncratically, Amis's recitations of three poems from Edith Sitwell's *Façade* are done to the rhythms of Walton but without Walton's music.

Angeles, Victoria de los (soprano)

Opera arias from: VERDI: *Ernani; Otello.* PUCCINI: *La Bohème.* BOITO: *Mefistofele.* ROSSINI: *La Cenerentola.* MASCAGNI: *Cavalleria Rusticana.* CATALANI: *La Wally.* MOZART: *Le nozze di Figaro.* WAGNER: *Tannhäuser; Lohengrin.* MASSENET: *Manon.* GOUNOD: *Faust.*
(M) (***) EMI mono CDH7 63495-2 [id.].

Most of the items here are taken from an early LP recital by de los Angeles that has rarely been matched in its glowing beauty and range of expression. The *Willow song* and *Ave Maria* from *Otello* have never been sung with more aching intensity than here, and the same goes for the Mascagni and Catalani arias. The final cabaletta from *Cenerentola* sparkles deliciously with de los Angeles, as so often, conveying the purest of smiles in the voice. The CD reissue is augmented by the valuable Mozart, Massenet, Gounod and Wagner items, all recorded in the days of 78s.

Spanish song recital: FALLA: excerpts from: *La vida breve; 7 Canciones populares españolas.* GRANADOS: *Goyescas: La maja y el ruiseñor.* TURINA: *Canto a Sevilla; Saeta en forma de Salve; Poema en forma de canciones: No. 3 Cantares.*
(M) (**(*)) EMI mono CDH7 64028-2 [id.].

This Spanish collection brings together many of the most ravishing of Victoria de los Angeles's very earliest recordings, made between 1948 and 1951. Though the CD transfer adds an unwanted brightness to the voice in some of the fortissimos, and the opening items from *La vida breve* betray their origin on 78-r.p.m. discs with a surface swish, the golden freshness of this most naturally beautiful of voices remains magical. Though recorded in London, the performances – thanks to the inspiration of the singer – are very idiomatic, not least the rare Turina suite, with the then recently founded Philharmonia Orchestra, conducted by Stanford Robinson, Anatole Fistoulari and Walter Susskind. Gerald Moore accompanies in the Falla folksongs, with Victoria de los Angeles at her most sparkling. The transfer adds an edge to high violin lines, as it does to the voice.

'On wings of song': MENDELSSOHN: *Auf Flügeln des Gesanges.* GRIEG: *Ich liebe dich.* BRAHMS: *Wiegenlied.* DVOŘÁK: *Als die alte Mutter (Songs my mother taught me).* MARTINI: *Plaisir d'amour.* HAHN: *L'enamourée.* DELIBES: *Les filles de Cadiz.* MONTSALVATGE: *5 Cançiones negras.* SADERO: *Irish lullaby.* YRADIER: *Era la vo.* OVALLE: *La paloma.* LUNA: *Azulao.* CHAPI:

De españa vengo. RODRIGO: *Carceleras; Madrigales amatorios: Econ qué la lavaré?; Vos me metasteis; De donde vénis, amores?; De los alamos vengo, madre.*
(M) *** EMI CDM7 69502-2 [id.].

Opening with a glorious performance of Mendelssohn's *On wings of song*, followed by a delightfully lyrical *Ich liebe dich*, both of which immediately take wing, Victoria de los Angeles goes on to cover a wide range of repertoire, not all of which suits her quite so well: *Les filles de Cadiz*, for instance, needs a frothier approach than she manages. But later in the recital there are some delicious moments, especially in the Spanish repertoire in which she is so naturally idiomatic. The good things here easily outweigh the lesser and everything is sung with ravishing tone and fine musicianship, the voice vividly projected by the CD remastering.

Atlanta Chorus and Symphony Orchestra, Robert Shaw

'The many moods of Christmas' (arr. R. Russell Bennett): *Good Christian men, rejoice; Patapan; O come all ye faithful; O Sanctissima; Away in a manger; Fum fum fum; March of the Kings; What Child is this?; Bring a torch, Jeanette, Isabella; Angels we have heard on high; The first nowell; I saw three ships; Deck the halls.* GRÜBER: *Silent night.* MENDELSSOHN: *Hark! the herald angels sing.* BACH: *Break forth, O beauteous heav'nly light.* REDNER-BROOKS: *O little town of Bethlehem.*
*** Telarc CD 80087 [id.].

The carols here are arranged into four groups, each lasting about 12 minutes, and the scoring and use of both chorus and orchestra is as flamboyantly imaginative as one would expect from a musician of the calibre of Robert Russell Bennett. Moreover the dynamic range of the recording is dramatically wide and the expansion of sound for the climaxes of *O come all ye faithful* and *Hark the herald angels sing*, with thrillingly realistic brass, is almost overwhelming. The chorus is backwardly balanced and with some choral pianissimos the words are barely audible, but the musical effect remains impressive. Technically, this is vintage Telarc, with the hall's ambience seen as of primary importance in its warm colouring of the rich-hued sounds from voices and instrumentalists alike. Highly recommended on all counts.

Augér, Arleen (soprano)

'Love songs' (with Dalton Baldwin, piano): COPLAND: *Pastorale; Heart, we will forget him.* OBRADORS: *Del Cabello más sutil.* OVALLE: *Azulao.* R.STRAUSS: *Ständchen; Das Rosenband.* MARX: *Selige Nacht.* POULENC: *Fleurs.* CIMARA: *Stornello.* QUILTER: *Music, when soft voices die; Love's philosophy.* O.STRAUS: *Je t'aime.* SCHUMANN: *Widmung; Du bist wie eine Blume.* MAHLER: *Liebst du um Schönheit.* TURINA: *Cantares.* LIPPE: *How do I love thee?* COWARD: *Conversation Piece: I'll follow my secret heart.* GOUNOD: *Serenade.* SCHUBERT: *Liebe schwärmt auf allen Wegen.* BRIDGE: *Love went a-riding.* FOSTER: *Why, no one to love.* DONAUDY: *O del mio amato ben.* BRITTEN (arr.): *The Salley Gardens.* LOEWE: *Camelot: Before I gaze at you again.*
❀ *** Delos Dig. D/CD 3029 [id.].

This extraordinarily wide-ranging recital is a delight from the first song to the last. Arleen Augér opens with Copland and closes with *Camelot*, and she is equally at home in the music by Roger Quilter (*Love's philosophy* is superbly done), Noël Coward and the *Rückert* song of Mahler. Britten's arrangement of *The Salley Gardens*, ravishingly slow, is another highlight. The layout of the recital could hardly have been managed better: each song creates its new atmosphere readily, but seems to be enhanced by coming after the previous choice. Dalton Baldwin's accompaniments are very much a partnership with the singing, while the playing itself is spontaneously perceptive throughout. With a good balance and a very realistic recording, this projects vividly like a live recital.

'Ave Maria'

'Ave Maria': Sacred arias (sung by Leontyne Price, Sutherland, Pavarotti, Horne, Te Kanawa): SCHUBERT: *Ave Maria.* MOZART: *Exsultate jubilate.* GOUNOD: *O divine redeemer.* Arias from:

HANDEL: *Samson; Messiah.* VERDI: *Requiem.* BERLIOZ: *Requiem.* BRAHMS: *German requiem.* ROSSINI: *Stabat Mater.* BACH: *Christmas oratorio.*
(M) *** Decca 425 016-2; *425 016-4.*

Decca are very good at creating anthologies of this kind and this 70-minute collection, superbly sung and splendidly recorded, makes a most enjoyable recital, with plenty of contrast between items. The programme is framed by Leontyne Price in rich voice in Schubert and admirably flexible in Mozartian coloratura; while Joan Sutherland's *Let the bright seraphim* also shows her in outstanding form. Pavarotti's golden tones bring distinction to the *Ingemisco* and *Sanctus* from the *Requiems* of Verdi and Berlioz respectively; and he is equally impressive in the livelier *Cujus animam* from Rossini's *Stabat Mater.* Kiri Te Kanawa contributes a memorable *I know that my Redeemer liveth*, taken from Solti's complete *Messiah*, and is in ravishing voice in Brahms's *Ihr habt nur Traurigkeit.*

Bach Choir, Sir David Willcocks

'Family carols' (with Philip Jones Brass Ens.): *O come, all ye faithful; Gabriel's message; Angelus ad Virginem; Ding dong merrily on high; A virgin most pure; God rest ye merry, gentlemen; In dulci jubilo; Unto us a son is born; Once in Royal David's city; Hush, my dear, lie still and slumber.* WILLCOCKS: *Fanfare.* RUTTER: *Shepherd's pipe carol; Star carol.* KIRKPATRICK: *Away in a manger.* GRUBER: *Stille Nacht.* arr. VAUGHAN WILLIAMS: *Sussex carol.* MENDELSSOHN: *Hark! the herald angels sing.*
(M) *** Decca Dig. 417 898-2; *417 898-4* [id.].

An admirably chosen and beautifully recorded collection of traditional carols. Fresh simplicity is the keynote here; the brass fanfares bring a touch of splendour but the music is not over-scored. *Silent night* has seldom sounded more serene, and Rutter's infectiously rhythmic *Shepherd's pipe carol* makes a refreshing contrast. The digital sound is in no way clinical; indeed the resonance is perfectly judged.

Baker, Dame Janet (mezzo-soprano)

Lieder (with Martin Isepp, piano): SCHUMANN: *Frauenliebe und Leben* (song-cycle), *Op. 42* *** ❀. SCHUBERT: *Heimliches Lieben; Minnelied; Die Abgeblühte Linde. Der Musensohn.* BRAHMS: *Die Mainacht; Das Mädchen spricht; Nachtigall; Von ewiger Liebe.*
(M) *** Saga SCD 9001 [id.].

Janet Baker's inspirational account of *Frauenliebe und Leben*, part of this early Lieder recital for Saga, has never been surpassed. The Schubert songs are not quite on this level (*Der Musensohn* a little jerky), but the Brahms are beyond praise. This is singing of a quality that you find only once or twice in a generation and – whatever the price – this CD is a collector's piece. The stereo on the original LP was curiously balanced, with voice and piano unnaturally separated, but the CD transfer transforms the sound, with oddities ironed out. Set in a dryish acoustic, the quality is now full-bodied, with a vivid sense of presence to make the transcendental performances even more involving.

'An Anthology of English song': VAUGHAN WILLIAMS: *The call; Youth and love.* IRELAND: *A thanksgiving; Her song.* HEAD: *A piper.* ARMSTRONG GIBBS: *This is a sacred city (by a bierside); Love is a sickness.* DUNHILL: *The cloths of heaven; To the Queen of Heaven.* WARLOCK: *Balulalow; Youth.* HOWELLS: *King David; Come sing and dance.* GURNEY: *Sleep; I will go with my father a-ploughing.* FINZI: *Come away, come away Death; It was a lover and his lass.*
(M) *** Saga SCD 9012 [id.].

Like the companion collection of Lieder, this Saga recital served as the (then) Miss Janet Baker's gramophone début, and the recording's quality is considerably improved in the CD transfer. Although the recital is only 44 minutes long, it makes a charming collection, superbly sung. The singer's artistry reveals moments of pure enchantment in these unpretentious settings of English lyrics. Janet Baker chose them herself and, though the majority have not immediate popular appeal, they grow more and more attractive on repetition – the melismatic 'Alleluias' in Howell's *Come sing and dance*, the golden simplicity of Gurney's *I will go with my father a-ploughing*, the warm, flowing line of Warlock's *Balulalow.* Martin Isepp is an outstanding accompanist, always sympathetic. The balance is close; yet, although the acoustic is confined, the voice glows with presence, even if there are hints at times of too high a modulation on the analogue master tape, with the sound not absolutely stable. However, the artistry of the singing triumphs over any inadequacies in the sound-balance.

French song recital (with the Melos Ensemble): RAVEL: *3 Poèmes de Stéphane Mallarmé; Chansons madécasses.* CHAUSSON: *Chanson perpétuelle, Op. 37.* DELAGE: *4 Poèmes hindous.*
❀ (M) *** Decca 425 948-2 [id.].

This is a very beautiful record. Chausson's extended cantilena about a deserted lover has a direct communication which Janet Baker contrasts with the subtler beauties of the Ravel songs. She shows great depth of feeling for the poetry here and an equally evocative sensitivity to the songs about India, written in 1912 by Ravel's pupil, Maurice Delage, which are by no means inferior to the mélodies by his more famous contemporaries. With superbly atmospheric playing from the Melos group and an outstanding 1966 (originally Oiseau-Lyre) recording, this is a ravishing collection which must be placed among Dame Janet's most outstanding records.

Bär, Olaf (baritone), Geoffrey Parsons (piano)

Lieder: BEETHOVEN: *Ich liebe dich.* SCHUBERT: *Schwanengesang: Ständchen; Der Doppelgänger; Die Taubenpost. Die schöne Müllerin: Das Wandern; Frühlingstraum; Die Post; Der Leiermann.* SCHUMANN: *Dichterliebe: In wunderschönen Monat Mai; Ich grolle nicht; Das ist ein Flöten und Geigen; Ein Jüngling liebt ein Mädchen; Aus alten Märchen winkt es.* BRAHMS: *Wie bist du meine Königen; Wir wandelten.* WOLF: *Verborgenheit; Der Gärtner; Auftrag; Storchenbotschaft.*
(M) *** EMI Dig. CDD7 64292-2 [id.]. *ET 764292-4.*

Outstanding among today's newer generation of Lieder-singers, Olaf Bär, admirably accompanied by Geoffrey Parsons, here produces a generous and consistently rewarding 70-minute Lieder recital, let down only by the non-provision of translations. There is no more civilized, thoughtful or mellifluous Lieder-singer among baritones today, with each of the 24 songs poised and beautifully crafted. At times strong and passionate, at others light and lilting, but always sensitive to word-meanings, this well chosen collection, mostly of excerpts from complete song-cycles, should surely tempt the listener to explore their sources more fully. The words make all the difference in winning converts to a genre still widely regarded as difficult. Opening with Beethoven's *Ich liebe dich*, sung with much charm, highlights include the disturbingly dark power of Schubert's *Der Doppelgänger*, the contrasting innocence of *Das Wandern* and the beautiful Schumanesque evocation of *Mondnacht* after the boldly vigorous *Ich grolle nicht* ('I bear no grudge'). No less memorable is the engaging lyrical flow of Brahms's *Wir wandalten*, and the sharply diverse character of the four favourite Wolf Mörike settings which end the programme. The recording is well balanced and projects realistically, and although the documentation is limited, this is still highly recommendable, especially to newcomers to this repertoire.

Battle, Kathleen (soprano)

'Salzburg recital' (with James Levine, piano): PURCELL: *Come all ye songsters; Music for a while; Sweeter than roses.* HANDEL: *O had I Jubal's lyre.* MENDELSSOHN: *Bei der Wiege; Neue Liebe.* R. STRAUSS: *Schlagende Herzen; Ich wollt'ein Sträusslein binden; Säusle, liebe Myrte.* MOZART: *Ridente la calma; Das Veilchen; Un moto di gioia.* FAURÉ: *Mandoline; Les roses d'Ispahan; En prière; Notre amour.* Spirituals: *Honour, honour; His name so sweet; Witness; He's got the whole world in his hands.*
*** DG Dig. 415 361-2 [id.].

Kathleen Battle is at her most characterful and provocative in this recital with Levine, recorded live in the Mozarteum in Salzburg as part of the 1984 Festival. Her singing of Susanna's little alternative aria from *Figaro, Un moto di gioia*, is a particular delight, and Levine – from Ohio, like Battle herself – proves a splendidly pointed and provocative accompanist. Helpfully atmospheric recording.

Battle, Kathleen (soprano), Jessye Norman (soprano)

'Spirituals in concert' (with Ch. and O, James Levine): *Ride on, King Jesus; Swing low, sweet chariot; Gospel train; He's got the whole world in his hand; Great day;* etc.
*** DG Dig. 429 790-2; *429 790-4* [id.].

The American critic, Will Crutchfield, writes of the recital recorded here: 'In the hands of artists like these, the Spiritual is not only alive and flourishing but enjoying a kind of Golden Age'. Also seen on television, this was a larger-than-life event, with some items made too glossy. But with two such dynamic, characterful artists giving heartfelt performances, the result is consistently compelling, the more so when most items are relative rarities. There is fun in the mixture too, typified by the most surprising and memorable of the items, *Scandalize my name*, an overtly comic duet on a serious theme, with piano accompaniment alone, very like a cabaret number. The singers' timing in it is delicious, pointing their witty attempts to upstage each other. The live recording, not ideally balanced, has plenty of presence.

Battle, Kathleen (soprano), Wynton Marsalis (trumpet)

'Baroque duet' (with O of St Luke's, John Nelson): HANDEL: *Samson: Let the bright seraphim. Ode for the Birthday of Queen Anne: Eternal source of light devine. O! come chiare e belle* (cantata): *Alle voci del bronzo guerriero.* A. SCARLATTI: *Arie con tromba sola: Si suoni la tromba; Con voce festiva; Rompe sprezza; Mio tesoro per te moro* (aria in the form of a French minuet). *Su le sponde del Tebro* (cantata). PREDIERI: *Zenobia: Pace una volta.* STRADELLA: *Il Barcheggio: Sinfonia.* BACH: *Cantatas Nos. 21: Seufzer, Tränen, Kummer, Not; 51: Jauchzet Gott in allen Landen; Sei Lob und Preis mit Ehren Allejujah.*
*** Sony Dig. SK 46672 [id.].

This is a natural successor to Wynton Marsalis's earlier recital with Edita Gruberová yet its content is even more enterprising and generous. The playing and singing is peerless, and Kathleen Battle together with her justly famous colleague consistently thrill and delight the ear by their ability to sustain their melodic lines with amazing ease in the musical upper stratosphere. If anything Handel's *Let the bright Seraphim* comes off better than before, while the same composer's *Alle voci del bronzo guerriero* is even more spectacular, and the first of the four 'arias with trumpet solo' by Scarlattti is yet another exciting martial number. The other three are remarkably varied in musical style (though not a whit less less demanding) and the last, *Mio tesoro per te moro* is plaintively expressive as well as brilliant. Scarlatti's fine cantata, *Su le sponde del Tebro* has even greater variety and includes another touching lament, this time for the soprano alone. To right the balance, Stradella's *Sinfonia* is a four-movement dance suite for trumpet and strings. But there are countless opportunities for voice and trumpet to echo each other to delectable effect, never more so than in *Pace una volta* from Luca Predieri's opera seria, *Zenobia*, where the breathtakingly florid intrumental and vocal interchanges anticipate Donizetti's dueting for voice and flute of a century later. Accompaniments are first class, the stereo clearly separates voice and trumpet to left and right and they are very realistically recorded and given fine presence against a pleasing ambience. Very highly recommended though not to be taken all at once.

Berganza, Teresa (mezzo-soprano)

Venetian concert (with Yasunori Imamura, lute, theorbo, chitarra; Joerg Ewald, harpsichord or organ; and continuo): STROZZI: *Non ti doler mio cor; Rissolvetevi pensieri.* SANCES: *Misera, hor si ch'il pianto; O perduti diletti.* MONTEVERDI: *Confitebor tibi Domine.* MILANUZZI: *Ut re mi.* FONTEI: *Auree stelle.* MINISCALCHI: *Fuggir pur mi convien; Fuggir voglio.* LAMORETTI: *Bell'il vana tua beltade.* (Instrumental): MOLINARO: *Fantasia nono.* PALESTRINA: *Vestiva i colli.* RORE: *Anchor che col partire.*
*** Claves CD-50 8206 [id.].

Teresa Berganza is the star of this attractive concert of Venetian music, with little of the included repertoire at all familiar. The vocal contributions are characteristically intelligent and stylish – but expressively telling, too. The instrumental numbers provide suitable contrast and are very well done; the recording has fine presence. The collection is well documented.

Operatic arias (with ROHCG O or LSO, Gibson) from: GLUCK: *Orfeo ed Euridice; Alceste; Elena e Paride.* PERGOLESI: *La serva padrona.* CHERUBINI: *Medea.* PAISIELLO: *Nina pazza per amore.* ROSSINI: *Il Barbiere di Siviglia; L'Italiana in Algeri; Semiramide; La Cenerentola; Stabat Mater.*
(M) *** Decca 421 327-2 [id.].

This wide selection from Berganza's repertory comes mainly from recordings of the 1960s, when the voice was at its most beautiful, although the *Cenerentola* excerpt is from 1959. The musical intensity combines formidably with an amazing technique (shown throughout the Rossini excerpts), and only occasionally in the classical arias does one sense a lack of warmth. First-rate recording, vividly transferred.

Spanish and Italian songs (with Felix Lavilla, piano): CHERUBINI: *Ahi! che forse ai miei di.* CESTI: *Intorno all'idol mio.* PERGOLESI: *Confusa, smarrita.* A. SCARLATTI: *Qual mia colpa . . . Se delitto è l'adorati; Chi vuol innamorarsi; La Rosaura (Un cor da voi ferito); Elitropio d'amor.* GURIDI: *Canzones castellanas: Cómo quieres que adivine; Mañanita de San Juan.* LAVILLA: *4 canciones vascas.* TURINA: *Saeta en forma de Salve a la Virgen de la Esperanza, Op. 60.* GRANADOS: *El tra la la y el Punteado; El majo timido; La maja dolorosa.* TURINA: *Está tu imagen, que admiro (Farruca).*
(M) *** Decca 425 947-2 [id.].

If anyone in the world could approach Victoria de los Angeles in Spanish song at that time it was Berganza, and her singing here is very nearly as spontaneous-sounding and imaginative. The second of the two Guridi songs included is especially beautiful with a movingly tender melody. The arias by Cherubini, Scarlatti and others would have gained from having more than just a piano accompaniment, but the classical quality of the singing is most beguiling. The 1962 recording was made in Decca's West Hampstead studio and is vivid and well balanced.

Bergonzi, Carlo (tenor)

Operatic arias from: VERDI: *Aida; Luisa Miller; La forza del destino; Il Trovatore; Un ballo in maschera; Don Carlo.* MEYERBEER: *L'Africaine.* GIORDANO: *Andrea Chénier.* CILEA: *Adriana Lecouvreur.* PUCCINI: *Tosca; Manon Lescaut; La Bohème.*
(M) *** Decca 421 318-2 [id.].

This recital of his early stereo recordings shows Bergonzi on peak form. He does not attempt the rare pianissimo at the end of *Celeste Aida*; but here among Italian tenors is a thinking musical artist who never resorts to vulgarity. The recording (of whatever vintage) has transferred well and retains the bloom on the voice. This is essentially a programme of favourites, but everything sounds fresh.

Berlin German Opera Chorus and Orchestra, Sinopoli

Opera choruses: MOZART: *Die Zauberflöte.* BEETHOVEN: *Fidelio.* WEBER: *Der Freischütz.* WAGNER: *Tannhäuser.* VERDI: *Nabucco; I Lombardi; Macbeth; Il Trovatore; Aida.*
*** DG Dig. 415 283-2 [id.].

A splendid collection of choruses, full of character, the atmosphere of each opera distinctive. The pianissimo at the beginning of the famous *Fidelio Prisoners' chorus* has striking intensity, while the exuberant *Hunting chorus* from *Freischütz* is irresistible in its buoyancy. On the other hand, Sinopoli's broadening of the sustained tune in the short *Aida* excerpt may for some seem too deliberate. Needless to say, the orchestral playing is first class; the balance, with the orchestra placed vividly forward and the chorus set back within a warmly resonant acoustic, is most convincing, although words are not always sharply clear.

Bernac, Pierre (baritone), **Francis Poulenc** (piano)

Mélodies: POULENC: *Banalités; Calligrammes (Guillaume Apollinaire); Chansons villageoises; Main dominée par le coeur; 4 Poèmes de Guillaume Apollinaire; Tu vois le feu du soir.* DEBUSSY:

Beau soir; L'échelonnement des haies; Le promenoir de deux amants. RAVEL: *Histoires naturelles; Mélodies hébraïques.* SATIE: *Le Chapelier; Daphénéo; La statue de bronze.*
(M) (***) Sony mono MPK 46731 [id.].

In 1950 Bernac's voice was fresher than ever and his powers of characterization remarkable. In addition to the two-dozen Poulenc songs, there are another fourteen by Ravel and a handful by Debussy and Satie. They sound very well indeed and should not be missed. Thirty-eight songs by a great interpreter in very acceptable recorded sound at mid-price is a real bargain.

Bjoerling, Jussi (tenor)

Operatic recital: Arias from: PONCHIELLI: *La Gioconda.* PUCCINI: *La Fanciulla del West; Manon Lescaut.* GIORDANO: *Fedora.* CILEA: *L'Arlesiana.* VERDI: *Un Ballo in maschera; Requiem.* MASCAGNI: *Cavalleria Rusticana* (with Tebaldi). LEHÁR: *Das Land des Lächelns.*
(M) *** Decca 421 316-2; *421 316-4.*

Jussi Bjoerling provides here a flow of headily beautiful, finely focused tenor tone. These may not be the most characterful renderings of each aria, but they are all among the most compellingly musical. The recordings are excellent for their period (1959–60). The Lehár was the last solo recording he made before he died in 1960. The transfers to CD are admirably lively and present.

Live recital (with Frederick Schauwecker, piano): VERDI: *Requiem: Ingemisco.* SCHUBERT: *Die Allmacht; An die Leier; An Sylvia; Was ist Silvia?; Die Forelle; Frühlingsglaube.* BEETHOVEN: *Adelaïde.* BRAHMS: *Ständchen.* RACHMANINOV: *Lilacs; In the silence of the night.* GRIEG: *Ein Traum.* TOSTI: *Ideale.* R. STRAUSS: *Zueignung.* Songs by SJÖGREN; PETERSON-BERGER. Arias from: TCHAIKOVSKY: *Eugene Onegin.* PUCCINI: *Turandot; Tosca.* VERDI: *Rigoletto.*
(M) (***) BMG/RCA mono GD 60520 [id.].

On record Bjoerling has generally been remembered for his fine interpretations of central operatic roles. He gave this 1958 recital in New York largely as a counter-thrust to his much-publicized rupture with the Metropolitan Opera (over pay). His immaculate legato is the glory of his Lieder-singing here, as it always was of his operatic singing. It is thrilling to hear even Schubert songs treated to big, heroic tone, as in *Die Allmacht* or even *An die Leier*, though rhythmically Bjoerling is often erratic and he is not helped by the scrappy playing of his accompanist. The encores bring the biggest excitement, with the audience welcoming each of the Italian items with applause as they recognize them. The mono recording of the voice is splendidly forward and vivid.

Bott, Catherine (soprano), New London Consort, Philip Pickett

'Music from the time of Columbus': VERARDI: *Viva El Gran Re Don Fernando.* ANON.: *A los Maytines era; Propinan de Melyor; Como no le andare yo; Nina y viña; Calabaza, no sé, buen amor; Perdí la mi rueca; Al alva venid buen amigo; Dale si la das.* URREDA: *Muy triste.* J. PONCE: *Como esta sola mi vida.* ANCHIETA: *Con amores mi madre.* ENCINA: *Triste españa; Mortal tristura; Mas vale trocar; Ay triste que vengo; Quedate carillo.* MEDINA: *No ay plazer en esta vida.* DE LA TORRE: *Danza alta.* DE MONDEJAR: *Un solo fin des mis males.*
*** Linn Dig. CKD 007 [id.].

Among the records specially issued to celebrate the quincentenary, this collection stands high for thoughtful and imaginative realization. Philip Pickett has drawn on the impressively extensive 'Palace Songbook' of Ferdinand and Isabella, held at the Biblioteca Real in Madrid, and the even earlier 'Cancionero Musical della Biblioteca Columbino', found in the Library of Columbus's illegitimate son, Fernando Colon. The songs offered here are broadly divided into two groups, the romantic ballads, usually of a melancholy disposition (the word 'triste' occurs frequently), and the usually jollier *villancio* form, which brings a repeated refrain. The programme – opening with a tribute to the King and Queen whose patronage of the arts was so tangible at the time – is admirably chosen to counterbalance the two opposing moods, with instrumental interludes bringing further variety. Catherine Bott is the most delightful soloist, singing freshly and simply, often with ravishing tone, and there is much to give pleasure. In the anonymous songs it is fascinating to discover just how international medieval folk music was, for more than once the listener is reminded of the Auvergne songs collected later in France by Canteloube. The two most delightful items are saved until the end, first a truly beautiful love song, *Al alva venid buen Amigo* ('Come at dawn my friend') in which a young woman reflects on her lover's visits, and then lets her thoughts change to consider the birth of 'him who made the world' from the Virgin Mary. In complete contrast is the robust and charmingly naughty villancio, *Dale si la das* ('Come on, wench of Carasa'). The recording is first class, naturally balanced in a pleasing acoustic, and full documentation is provided.

Bowman, James (alto), **King's Consort, Robert King**

VIVALDI: *Salve regina in C min., RV 616.* TELEMANN: *Weg mit Sodoms gift'gen Fruchter.* PERGOLESI: *Salve regina in F min.* BACH: *Cantata No. 54; Widerstehe doch der Sunde.*
*** Mer. Dig. CDE 84138; *KE 77138.*

James Bowman's collection of four varied items suited to the counter-tenor voice makes for an unusual and attractive mixture, beautifully performed by singer and instrumentalists alike. Maybe beauty is brought out too much in the Bach *Cantata* with its severe text, but the singer's artistry is consistent throughout, helped by full, well-balanced recording.

Burrows, Stuart (tenor), **John Constable** (piano)

'The world of favourite ballads': TOURS: *Mother o' mine.* RAY: *The sunshine of your smile.* FOSTER: *I dream of Jeannie.* HAYDN-WOOD: *Roses of Picardy.* MARSHALL: *I hear you calling me.* BALFE: *Come into the garden, Maud.* ADAMS: *The star of Bethlehem; Thora.* SANDERSON: *As I sit here.* JOHNSON: *When you and I were young, Maggie.* DANKS: *Silver threads among the gold.* LINTON: *I give thanks for you.* WEATHERBY: *Danny Boy.* HANDEL: *Silent worship.* AITKEN: *Maire my girl.* E. PURCELL: *Passing by.* DE KOVEN: *Oh, promise me.* GREEN: *Gortnamona.* COATES: *I hear you singing.* MOLLOY: *The Kerry dance.* DEL RIEGO: *O dry those tears.*
(B) *** Decca 430 090-2; *430 090-4.*

With his headily beautiful voice at its freshest – the recordings were made in 1978 – and much simple charm, Burrows makes an excellent interpreter of popular ballads like these. The engineers, recording in a London chapel, placed the microphones rather close, but the effect on CD is to give a most vivid presence. John Constable accompanies strongly.

(i) **Burrows, Stuart** (tenor), (ii) **Joan Sutherland** (soprano)

'The world of operetta' (with Ambrosian Light Opera Ch., New Philh. O, Bonynge; Nat. PO, Robin Stapleton or Bonynge): LEHÁR: *Land of Smiles:* (i) *You are my heart's delight. Paganini: Girls were made to love and kiss;* (ii) *Love live forever. The Merry Widow*: (ii) *Vilja;* (ii) *Love unspoken* (Waltz duet; with Werner Krenn). *Frasquita:* (i) *Farewell my love. Fredericka: Maiden, o maiden.* ROMBERG: *The Student Prince:* (ii) *Students' chorus; Deep in my heart, dear;* (i) *Serenade. The Desert Song:* (ii) *Desert song.* FRIML: *Rose Marie: Indian love call.* GERMAN: *Tom Jones: Waltz song.* SIECZYNSKI: (i) *Vienna, city of my dreams.* O. STRAUS: *The Chocolate Soldier*: (ii) *My hero.* MILLÖCKER: *The Dubarry: The Dubarry.*
(B) *** Decca 433 233-2; *433 233-4* [id.].

It was a brilliant idea for Decca to centre a bargain collection of operetta excerpts in English on Stuart Burrows and Joan Sutherland. These recordings come from two quite different sources, but they match up admirably. Stuart Burrows is stirring in *You are my heart's delight*, charmingly vivacious in *Girls were made to love and kiss* and wonderfully heady in the *Serenade* from *Frasquita*, while Joan Sutherland is at her most ravishing in the *Indian love call* from *Rose Marie* and in *Vilja*. Sutherland combines with Werner Krenn in the most delightful operetta number of all, the Waltz duet, *Love unspoken*, from *The Merry Widow*. The whole programme is vivacious and vividly recorded, and it makes a perfect counterpart to Decca's bargain Viennese anthology, sung in German, '*Golden operetta*' – see below.

Callas, Maria (soprano)

Arias from: ROSSINI: *Il barbiere di Siviglia.* VERDI: *Macbeth; Don Carlos.* PUCCINI: *Tosca.* GLUCK: *Alceste.* BIZET: *Carmen* (with Nicolai Gedda). SAINT-SAËNS: *Samson et Dalila.* MASSENET: *Manon.* CHARPENTIER: *Louise.*
(M) *** EMI CD-EMX 2123; *TC-EMX 2123.*

This compilation on the EMI Eminence label brings together at budget price some of Callas's most cherishable performances, mostly taken from recital material. An excellent sampler, well recorded and satisfactorily transferred on to a mid-priced CD.

'The incomparable Callas' (Arias from): BELLINI: *Norma.* DONIZETTI: *Lucia.* VERDI: *Ernani; Aida.* PONCHIELLI: *La Gioconda.* PUCCINI: *Tosca.* GLUCK: *Orphée et Eurydice.* GLUCK: *Roméo et Juliette.* THOMAS: *Mignon.* MASSENET: *Le Cid.* BIZET: *Carmen.* SAINT-SAËNS: *Samson et Dalila.*
(M) *** EMI CDM7 63182-2 [id.].

Callas's later sets of *Lucia* and *Norma* are both well represented here, but even finer is the *Suicidio!* from her second version of Ponchielli's *La Gioconda*, among her finest achievements. The *Carmen* items taken from the complete set are more questionable in their fierceness but are totally individual – as indeed, flawed or not, is the last-recorded item here, Aida's *Ritorna vincitor*, made in 1972. The transfers capture the voice well.

'Mad scenes and Bel canto arias' (with Philh. O, Rescigno) from: DONIZETTI: *Anna Bolena; La figlia del reggimento; Lucrezia Borgia; L'Elisir d'amore.* THOMAS: *Hamlet.* BELLINI: *Il Pirata.*
*** EMI CDC7 47283-2 [id.].

If, as ever, the rawness of exposed top-notes mars the sheer beauty of Callas's singing, few recital records ever made can match, let alone outshine, her collection of mad scenes in vocal and dramatic imagination. This is Callas at her very peak; Desmond Shawe-Taylor suggested this as the collection which, more than any other, summed up the essence of Callas's genius. For the CD reissue further arias have been added, notably excerpts from Donizetti's *La figlia del reggimento, L'Elisir d'amore* and *Lucrezia Borgia* (from the mid-1960s), a fair example of the latterday Callas, never very sweet-toned, yet displaying the usual Callas fire. Nevertheless, the main part of the recital is indispensable; the digital remastering has enhanced the originally excellent recordings and given the voice striking presence.

'Callas à Paris' (with French Nat. R. O, Prêtre): Arias from: GLUCK: *Orphée et Eurydice; Alceste.* BIZET: *Carmen.* SAINT-SAËNS: *Samson et Dalila.* MASSENET: *Manon; Le Cid.* GOUNOD: *Roméo et Juliette.* THOMAS: *Mignon.* CHARPENTIER: *Louise.*
*** EMI CDC7 49059-2.

The original LP collection, '*Callas à Paris*', dating from 1961 with the singer at her most commanding and characterful, is here augmented with five items from the sequel disc of two years later, when the voice was in decline. The vocal contrast is clear enough, and the need at the time to patch and re-patch the takes in the later sessions makes the results sound less spontaneous and natural. But the earlier portraits of Carmen, Alceste, Dalila and Juliette find Callas still supreme. Her mastery of the French repertory provides a fascinating slant on her artistry.

'The unknown recordings': WAGNER: *Tristan: Liebestod.* Arias from: VERDI: *Don Carlos; I Lombardi; I vespri siciliani; Attila.* BELLINI: *Il Pirata.* ROSSINI: *La Cenerentola; Guglielmo Tell; Semiramide.*
*** EMI CDC7 49428-2 [id.].

The collection brings together unpublished material from several sources, mainly alternative recordings of arias which appeared earlier in other versions, but also live recordings made in Athens and Amsterdam. The alternative readings all bring fresh illumination of a supreme artist who was both deeply thoughtful and spontaneous in that she never merely repeated herself. These items of early Verdi, Rossini and Bellini are all most cherishable, but just as fascinating is her very early Athens account of Isolde's *Liebestod* in Italian and her 1959 Holland Festival performances of passages from Bellini's *Il Pirata* and Verdi's *Don Carlos.* Variable recording, helped by skilled and refined EMI transfers.

Cambridge Singers, John Rutter

'Portrait': BYRD: *Sing joyfully; Non vos relinquam.* FAURÉ: *Cantique de Jean Racine; Requiem: Sanctus.* RUTTER: *O be joyful in the Lord; All things bright and beautiful; Shepherd's pipe carol; Open thou mine eyes; Requiem: Out of the deep.* PURCELL: *Hear my prayer, O Lord.* STANFORD: *Beati quorum via; The Bluebird.* TRAD.: *This joyful Eastertide; In dulci jubilo.* HANDEL: *Messiah: For unto us a child is born.* FARMER: *A pretty bonny lass.* MORLEY: *Now is the month of maying.* DELIUS: *To be sung of a summer night on the water.* VICTORIA: *O magnum mysterium.* TERRY: *Myn lyking.*
(M) *** Coll. Dig./Analogue CSCD 500; *CSCC 500* [id.].

This splendid mid-priced sampler makes a wonderfully rewarding concert. John Rutter has arranged the items here with great skill so that serene music always makes a contrast with the many exuberant expressions of joy, his own engaging hymn-settings among them. Thus the bright-eyed hey-nonny songs of John Farmer and Thomas Morley are aptly followed by the lovely wordless *To be sung of a summer night on the water* of Delius, and Stanford's beautiful evocation of *The Bluebird* (one of Rutter's own special favourites). The sound, vivid and atmospheric, suits the colour and mood of the music quite admirably. Not to be missed!

'There is sweet music' (English choral songs): STANFORD: *The blue bird.* DELIUS: *To be sung of a summer night on the water I & II.* ELGAR: *There is sweet music; My love dwelt in a Northern land.* VAUGHAN WILLIAMS: *3 Shakespearean songs: Full fathom five; The cloud-capp'd towers; Over hill, over dale.* BRITTEN: *5 Flower songs, Op. 47.* Folksongs: arr. MOERAN: *The sailor and young Nancy.* Arr. GRAINGER: *Brigg Fair: Londonderry air.* Arr. CHAPMAN: *Three ravens.* Arr. HOLST: *My sweetheart's like Venus.* Arr. BAIRSTOW: *The oak and the ash.* Arr. STANFORD: *Quick! We have but a second.*
❀ *** Coll. Dig. COLCD 104 [id.].

Opening with an enchanting performance of Stanford's *The blue bird* and followed by equally expressive accounts of Delius's two wordless summer evocations, this most attractive recital ranges from Elgar and Vaughan Williams, both offering splendid performances, to various arrangements of folksongs, less fashionable today than they once were, but giving much pleasure here. The recording, made in the Great Hall of University College, London, has an almost ideal ambience: words are clear, yet the vocal timbre is full and natural. A highly recommendable anthology.

'Flora gave me fairest flowers' (English madrigals): MORLEY: *My bonny lass she smileth; Fyer, fyer! Now is the month of Maying.* EAST: *Quick, quick, away dispatch!* GIBBONS: *Dainty fine bird; Silver swan.* BYRD: *Though Amaryllis dance in green; This sweet and merry month of May; Lullaby.* WEELKES: *Hark, all ye lovely saints.* WILBYE: *Weep, weep, mine eyes; Flora gave me; Draw on sweet night; Adieu sweet Amaryllis.* TOMKINS: *Too much I once lamented; Adieu ye city-prisoning towers.* FARMER: *Little pretty bonny lass.* BENNETT: *Round about.* WEELKES: *Ha ha! this world doth pass; Death hath deprived me.* RAMSEY: *Sleep, fleshly birth.*
*** Coll. Dig. COLCD 105 [id.].

John Rutter's Cambridge Singers bring consistent unanimity of ensemble and a natural expressive feeling to this very attractive programme of madrigals. Perhaps the first group, devoted to love and marriage, may be thought rather consistently mellifluous; but the second, '*Madrigals of times and season*', is nicely contrasted, with the clean articulation of Morley's *Now is the month of Maying* made the more telling by the lightness of the vocal production. John Wilbye's lovely *Draw on sweet night*, which follows, makes a perfect contrast. After two items about '*Fairies, spirits and conceits*', the concert closes in a mood of moving Elizabethan melancholy with a group devoted to mourning and farewell. Superb recording in a most flattering acoustic makes this collection the more enjoyable, though one to be dipped into rather than heard all at once.

'Faire is the Heaven' (Music of the English Church): PARSONS: *Ave Maria.* TALLIS: *Loquebantur variis linguis; If ye love me.* BYRD: *Misere mei; Haec dies; Ave verum corpus; Bow thine ear.* FARRANT: *Hide not thou thy face; Lord, for thy tender mercy's sake.* GIBBONS: *O clap your hands; Hosanna to the Son of David.* PURCELL: *Lord, how long wilt thou be angry; Thou knowest, Lord; Hear my prayer, O Lord.* STANFORD: *Beati quorum via.* Arr. WOOD: *This joyful Eastertide.* HOWELLS: *Sing lullaby; A spotless rose.* WALTON: *What cheer?* VAUGHAN WILLIAMS: *O taste*

and see. BRITTEN: *Hymn to the Virgin.* POSTON: *Jesus Christ the apple tree.* HARRIS: *Faire is the Heaven.*
*** Coll. COLCD 107 [id.].

These recordings were made in the Lady Chapel of Ely Cathedral, and the ambience adds beauty to the sound without in any way impairing clarity of focus. The music ranges from examples of the Roman Catholic Rite as set by Tallis, Byrd and Robert Parsons (with a touch of almost Latin eloquence in the presentation), through widely varied Reformation music, to the Restoration, represented by three Purcell anthems, and on to the Anglican revival and the twentieth century. The Reformation group is particularly successful, with the opening Tallis and closing Gibbons works rich in polyphony and Byrd's *Bow thine ear* wonderfully serene. Of the modern items, the Howells pieces are quite lovely and Walton's *What cheer?*, with its engaging imitation, is attractively genial. The Britten and Poston items, both well known, are hardly less engaging; and the concert ends with the ambitious title-number, William Harris's *Faire is the Heaven*, sung with great feeling and considerable power. There is no more successful survey of English church music in the current catalogue and certainly not one presented with more conviction.

'Christmas with the Cambridge Singers': MASON: *Joy to the world.* SWEELINCK: *Hodie Christus natus est.* RUTTER: *Shepherd's carol; What sweeter music.* Arr. WOOD: *Ding dong! merrily on high.* TRAD., arr. RUTTER: *'Twas in the moon of winter time; Personent hodie; Somerset wassail; Still, still; Coventry carol; What child is this?; Quem pastores laudavere.* TRAD., arr. WILLCOCKS: *Sussex carol; The Infant King.* SCHEIDT: *In dulci jubilo.* HANDEL: *Messiah: For unto us a child is born.* ADAM: *O holy night.* VICTORIA: *O magnum mysterium.* BERLIOZ: *L'enfance du Christ: Shepherds' farewell.* BRITTEN: *New year carol.* GRUBER: *Silent night.*
**(*) Collegium Dig./Analogue COLCD 111; *COLC 111* [id.].

Another atmospheric Christmas collection from Rutter. Although *Joy to the World* and Scheidt's setting of *In dulci jubilo* effectively feature trumpets, most of the programme is serene. Indeed the famous *Messiah* chorus could do with a shade more exuberance. The Berlioz excerpt is pleasing, yet it would have had more character sung in French, and Adam's *O holy night* is unashamedly romantic. But there are the usual felicitous arrangements here, and this is a pleasing record for late evening: Rutter's own carols are always enticing. The recording, made in the glowing ambience of the Great Hall of University College School, London, is very naturally balanced.

'Hail gladdening light' (Music of the English church): Anthems and Introits: ANON.: *Rejoice in the Lord.* PURCELL: *Remember not, Lord, our offences.* AMNER: *Come, let's rejoice.* TOMKINS: *When David heard.* BAIRSTOW: *I sat down under his shadow.* GROSS: *These are they that follow the Lamb.* Latin motets: TAVERNER: *Christe Jesu, pastor bone.* PHILIPS: *O beatum et sacrosanctum diem.* HOWELLS: *Nunc dimittis.* VAUGHAN WILLIAMS: *O vos omnes.* DERING: *Factum et silentium.* STANFORD: *Justorum animae.* Hymns & other poetry settings: WOOD: *Hail gladdening light.* TAVERNER: *A hymn to the Mother of God; Hymn for the dormition of the Mother of God.* ELGAR: *They are at rest.* WALTON: *A Litany.* MORLEY: *Nolo mortem peccatoris.* TALLIS: *O nata lux.* RUTTER: *Loving shepherd of thy sheep.* STONE: *The Lord's prayer.* SHEPPARD: *In manus tuas.* HARRIS: *Bring us, O Lord God.*
*** Coll. Dig. COLCD 113; *COLC 113* [id.].

The opening anthems and introits of this generous 72-minute concert are appealingly diverse, with the Purcell and Amner settings enhanced by being placed together. But then Edward Bairstow's individual and beautiful *I sat down under his shadow* really catches the attention, and Howells's *Nunc dimittis* for double choir is glorious in its richness of texture and harmony. The Vaughan Williams *O vos omnes* is delightfully characteristic, using the alto soloist almost like a viola, and later the title hymn by Charles Wood is refreshingly buoyant. The two Marian hymns of John Taverner are the highlight of the concert, the first with its extraordinarily powerful dissonances, the second gentle and tender: they are most memorably sung. Elgar's *They are at rest also* brings a continuing sense of haunting elegiac simplicity, and the rest of the programme has striking variety. Rutter's own contribution was composed especially for this record. Excellent recording as usual with this label, and beautifully blended choral tone. This is one of Rutter's most rewarding programmes.

'Ave gracis plena' (Music in honour of the Virgin Mary): GREGORIAN CHANT: *Alma redemptoris mater; Ave redemptoris caelorum; Regina caeli laetare; Salve regina.* ANON.: *There is no rose of*

such virtue. GUERRERO: *Ave Virgo sanctissima.* VICTORIA: *Ave Maria* (for 4 voices); *Vidi speciosam; Ave Maria for double choir.* DERING: *Ave Virgo gloriosa.* PALESTRINA: *Stabat Mater.* BRUCKNER: *Ave Maria.* VERDI: *Laudi alla Vergine Maria.* STRAVINSKY: *Ave Maria.* TCHAIKOVSKY: *Dostoino Yest.* HOWELLS: *Regina caeli.* arr. WOOD: *Hail! Blessed Mary.* VILLETTE: *Hymne à la Vierge.* SWAYNE: *Magnificat.* BYRD: *Alleluia. Ave Maria.* HOLST: *Ave Maria.*
**(*) Coll. COLCD 116; *COLC 116* [id.].

John Rutter's concerts are always well planned and this one is no exception. The music is divided into four groups, to match the four periods of the Christian calendar: Advent to Candlemass, Candlemass to Holy Week, Easter to the Sunday after Pentecost, and Trinity to Advent. As it happens, the pieces for the two central periods are the most stimulating. They are framed by early settings (with the exception of Holst's *Ave Maria* – one of the highlights), and the choir's style in the sixteenth-century Latin music is rather too smooth, almost bland, although the *Ave Maria* for double choir by Victoria which concludes the programme is richly serene. But it is the beautiful *Ave Maria* of Bruckner, and the surprisingly limpid setting of Stravinsky, which alongside the more vibrant Tchaikovsky *Dostoino Yest* most readily catch the ear, though most memorable of all is Howells's *Regina caeli* for double choir which rises up gloriously to the heavens. The most unusual items are Pierre Villette's *Hymne à la Vierge*, with its creamily soft-centred harmonies, and what must be the most individual *Magnificat* ever!. Giles Swayne's kaleidoscopic piece with its fragmented rhythms is based on a Jola ploughing song from Senegal, and is quite stunningly effective. Beautifully blended choral tone throughout and fine recording ensure a welcome for this 71-minute programme which is admirably documented.

Canciones (Spanish songs)

Canciones (sung by (i) Pilar Lorengar with (ii) LPO or SRO, López Cobos; (iii) Alicia de Larrocha (piano); (iv) Kiri te Kanawa, Roger Vignoles (piano); (v) Marilyn Horne, Martin Katz (piano); (vi) Tereza Berganza, Félix Lavilla (piano)): (i; ii) GRANADOS: *Goyescas: La maja y el reuiseñor.* (i; iii) TONADILLAS: *La maja de Goya; Amor y odio; El tra-la-lá y el punteado; El majo olvidado; El majo tímido; Callejo; El mirar de la maja; Las currutacas modestas; El majo discreto. 3 majas dolorosa (Nos. 1–3); 6 Canciones amatorias: Mir que soy niña; Iban al pinar; Mañanica era; No lloréis, ojuelos; Llorad, corazon; Gracia mía.* (iv) OBRADORS: *5 Canciones clásicas españolas: Al amor; Corazón, por qué pasáis . . .; Con amores, la mi madre; 2 Cantares populares; Coplas de Curro Dulce.* (i; ii) FALLA: *La vida breve: Vivan los que rien; Allí está, riyendo.* (v) *7 Canciones populares españolas.* NIN: *4 Villancicos españoles.* (vi) GURIDI: *Canciones castellanas: Cómo quieres que adivine; Mañanita de San Juan.* LAVILLA: *4 Canciones vascas.* (i; ii) TURINA: *Saeta en forma de salve; Farruca; Canto a Sevilla.*
(M) ** Decca Analogue/Dig. 433 917-2 (2) [id.].

This is valuable repertoire, most of it not otherwise available, but unfortunately the performances are uneven. At the very opening the LPO under Jesús López-Cobos provides an evocative introduction to Granados's most famous melody from *Goyescas* but, when Pilar Lorengar enters, the sensuous feeling is less evident. In the following *Tonadillas, Majas dolorosas* and *Canciones amatorias* there is further disappointment. With a celebrated Spanish soprano accompanied by the most vividly characterful of Spanish pianists, the casting of these colourful, finely wrought songs might seem ideal. But Lorengar's tone, never perfectly steady, grew slacker with the years (this recital dates from 1978), and the singing is not even vibrant in an aptly Spanish way. Thanks to the pianist, however, Spanish fire is rarely lacking for long, even if the partnership is unequal, and the same applies when López Cobos returns to direct the two numbers from *La vida breve.* With the *Canciones clásicas espanolas* of Fernando Obradors, Kiri te Kanawa takes over and with the advantage of modern digital sound projects these songs most appealingly. Then Marilyn Horne at her most vibrantly sensitive sings the *Spanish popular songs* of Falla and four others of Nin, admirably accompanied by Roger Vignoles, followed by Teresa Berganza, with her husband at the piano. The freshness of her singing consistently charms the ear and not least attractive here are Lavilla's own *4 Canciones vascas*, for which Berganza obviously has a special affection. Finally Pilar Lorengar returns to provide somewhat squally versions of three fine concert songs of Turina, with lavish orchestral accompaniments. Excellent recording, but no translations are provided.

Carreras, José (tenor)

'The essential José Carreras': Arias from: PUCCINI: *La Bohème; Manon Lescaut; Turandot; Tosca.* LEONCAVALLO: *I Pagliacci.* DONIZETTI: *L'elisir d'amore; Lucia di Lammermoor.* VERDI: *Il Trovatore; Luisa Miller.* BERNSTEIN: *West Side story.* Neapolitan songs. FRANCK: *Panis angelicus.*
*** Ph. 432 692-2; *432 692-4* [id.].

José Carreras has a less flamboyant personality than Pavarotti and less vocal presence than Domingo – but he is a very pleasing singer in his own right and his style is entirely without vulgarity. In the famous Puccini warhorses some might prefer more robust fervour, but one can believe in Mimi being attracted to a Rodolfo who sings as winningly as this, and the Donizetti arias also suit the voice well. If *Di quella pira* from *Trovatore* was a less suitable choice, Carreras makes up for it in the Neapolitan songs, which are sung with a refined lyrical fervour that is refreshing, even if sometimes listeners may seek a more gutsy, peasant style. Accompaniments are always sympathetic, the sound is first class, and the recital plays for 70 minutes; even so, this should have been offered at mid-price.

Neapolitan songs (with ECO, Muller): DENZA: *Funiculi, funicula; I'te vurria vasà.* CARDILLO: *Core 'ngrato.* D'ANNIBALE: *'O paese d'o sole.* FALVO: *Dicitencello vuie.* LAMA: *Silenzio cantatore.* MARIO: *Santa Lucia luntana.* DI CURTIS: *Tu, ca nun chiagne! Torna a Surriento.* DI CAPUA: *'O sole mio.* BOVIO/TAGLIAFERRI: *Passione.* CIOFFI: *'Na sera 'e maggio.* CANNIO: *'O surdato 'nnamurato.*
**(*) Ph. Dig. 400 015-2 [id.].

José Carreras produces refined tone here. The performances have plenty of lyrical fervour and are entirely lacking in vulgarity. The opening *Funiculi, funicula* is attractively lilting, but elsewhere some listeners will wish for a more gutsy style. The recording is first class. The compact disc combines naturalness with added presence, yet the sound remains warmly atmospheric.

'Canciones españolas' (with (i) ECO, Stapleton, Benzi or Ros Marba; (ii) Martin Katz): PADILLA: *Valencia.* GREVER: *Júrame.* ALONSO: *Maitechu mia.* LARA: *Granada.* VIVES: *Doña Francisquita: Por el humo.* SOUTULLO/VERT: *El último romántico: Noche de amor, noche misteriosa.* SERRANO: *Alma de Dios.* (ii) FALLA: *7 Canciones populares españolas.* MOMPOU: *Combat del somni.* OBRADORS: *2 Canciones clásicas españolas.* TURINA: *Poema en forma de canciones.*
(M) *** Ph. Analogue/Dig. 432 825-2 [id.].

An admirably chosen 65-minute recital showing Carreras's artistry and versatility and offering much that is as rare as it is attractive. The popular songs like *Valencia* and *Granada* have a great deal in common with Neapolitan repertoire. They are vigorously and stylishly sung and Carreras is equally at home drawing out the rather more flimsy melodies of the zarzuela arias, notably the charming *Noche de amor, noche misteriosa.* The second half of the programme is recorded digitally and the pianist Martin Katz makes a considerable contribution, for the mood of many of these songs is created by the piano. This applies not only to the Falla group (which is very welcome sung by a male voice) but also to the engaging Mompou triptych (the title means *Fight against sleep*) and the equally imaginative Turina *Poema*, a miniature cycle of five sharply contrasted vocal vignettes. With excellent recording throughout, this is highly recommendable.

(i) Carreras, José, (ii) Plácido Domingo and (iii) Luciano Pavarotti (tenors)

'In concert at the Baths of Caracalla, Rome, 7 July 1990' (with Maggio Musicale Fiorentino O & Rome Opera O, Mehta): Arias from: (i) CILEA: *L'Arlesiana.* (ii) MEYERBEER: *L'Africaine.* (iii; ii) PUCCINI: *Tosca;* (ii) *Turandot.* (iii) LEHÁR: *Das Land des Lächelns.* (i) GIORDANO: *Andrea Chénier.* (i–iii) Songs by DE CRESCENDO; CARDILLO; DE CURTIS; LARA; SOROZÁBAL. Medley including excerpts from BERNSTEIN: *West Side story.* LLOYD WEBBER: *Memory. La vie en rose; Mattinata; 'O sole mio; Amapola.* Encores.
*** Decca 430 433-2; *430 433-4* [id.].

Planned years in advance to coincide with the football World Cup in Rome in 1990, this unmatchable extravaganza relied on the devotion of all three great tenors to that game. The success of the resulting record with the wider musical public (it temporarily ousted Nigel Kennedy's *Four Seasons* from the top place in the 'Charts') means that our comments are of no real consequence. A series of purple patches – even the orchestra goes over the top – vividly recorded and with the voices close-miked inevitably brings a feeling of coarseness, although there are undoubted physical thrills if you enjoy loud, straining, tenor *fortissimos*. There are a few, rarer moments of quiet singing. José Carreras was not in his best voice, yet he is still impressive in *L'Improvviso* from *Andrea Chénier*, as is Domingo in the Lehár and the excerpt from the Spanish zarzuela. Pavarotti's Puccini makes the usual strong impact but can be heard with more finesse on his studio recordings. However, there is certainly a sense of occasion here, with the rivalry between the three superstars in the culminating trio a special delight: a far cry from the animosity that comparable tenors of the past often showed towards one another.

Caruso, Enrico (tenor)

'Opera arias and songs': Arias from: VERDI: *Rigoletto; Aida.* MASSENET: *Manon.* DONIZETTI: *L'Elisir d'amore.* BOITO: *Mefistofele.* PUCCINI: *Tosca.* MASCAGNI: *Iris; Cavalleria Rusticana.* GIORDANO: *Fedora.* PONCHIELLI: *La Gioconda.* LEONCAVALLO: *I Pagliacci.* CILEA: *Adriana Lecouvreur.* BIZET: *Les pêcheurs de perles.* MEYERBEER: *Les Huguenots.* Songs.
(M) (***) EMI mono CDH7 61046-2 [id.].

The EMI collection on the Références label brings together Caruso's earliest recordings, made in 1902 and 1904 in Milan with misty piano accompaniment. The very first were done impromptu in Caruso's hotel, and the roughness of presentation reflects that; but the voice is glorious in its youth, amazingly well caught for that period. It was the sound of these very recordings which, more than anything else, first convinced a wide public that the gramophone was more than a toy.

'Prima voce': Arias from: DONIZETTI: *L'Elisir d'amore; Don Sebastiano; Il duca d'Alba.* GOLDMARK: *La regina di Saba.* GOMEZ: *Lo schiavo.* HALÉVY: *La juive.* LEONCAVALLO: *Pagliacci.* MASSENET: *Manon.* MEYERBEER: *L'Africana.* PUCCINI: *Tosca; Manon Lescaut.* VERDI: *Aida; Un ballo in maschera; La forza del destino; Rigoletto; Il Trovatore.*
(M) (***) Nimbus mono NI 7803 [id.].

The Nimbus method of transfer to CD, reproducing ancient 78s on a big acoustic horn gramophone of the 1930s, tends to work best with acoustic recordings, when the accompaniments then emerge as more consistent with the voice. There is an inevitable loss of part of the recording range at both ends of the spectrum, but the ear can often be convinced. This Caruso collection, very well chosen to show the development of his voice, ranges from early (1904) recordings of Massenet, Puccini and Donizetti with piano accompaniment to the recording that the great tenor made in 1920, not long before he died, of his very last role, as Eleazar in Halévy's *La juive*, wonderfully characterized.

'Caruso in song': Popular songs & ballads; Neapolitan songs. Arias by HANDEL and ROSSINI.
(M) (***) Nimbus mono NI 7809 [id.].

A whole collection of drawing-room ballads – *For you alone* in English, *Because* in French – as well as Neapolitan songs like *Santa Lucia* and *O sole mio*, are sung here with transparent, heartfelt sincerity, and the voice even on these pre-electric recordings seems to ring out with extra amplification, not least in the riotous account of the American wartime song, *Over there* – one verse English, one verse French. The recordings of the two arias, Handel's *Ombra mai fu* and Rossini's *Domine Deus*, date from 1920, only months before the great tenor's death, and there the weighty, baritonal quality comes over impressively.

'21 Favourite arias': from LEONCAVALLO: *I Pagliacci.* PUCCINI: *Tosca; La Bohème.* VERDI: *Rigoletto; Aida; La Forza del destino; Otello; Il Trovatore.* MEYERBEER: *L'Africana.* HALÉVY: *La Juive.* GIORDANO: *Andrea Chénier.* DONIZETTI: *La Favorita; L'Elisir d'amore.* BIZET: *Les Pêcheurs de perles; Carmen.* PONCHIELLI: *La Gioconda.* GOUNOD: *Faust.* FLOTOW: *Martha.* HANDEL: *Serse.*
(***) BMG/RCA RD 85911 [RCA 5911-2-RC].

Taken from RCA's earlier Caruso reissue series using the digital Soundstream system (which sought to eliminate the unnatural resonances of the acoustic recording horn, well before the age of general digital recording), these transfers are often surprisingly real and convincing. The selection, unlike EMI's Références disc of Caruso, ranges widely over the great tenor's career, with some fine examples of his work in the French repertory as well as in popular Italian items. An outstanding disc, with the voice remarkably fresh; few technical apologies need to be made here.

Chaliapin, Feodor (bass)

Russian opera arias: MUSSORGSKY: *Boris Godunov: Coronation scene; Clock scene; Farewell and Death of Boris.* Excerpts from: GLINKA: *Life for the Tsar; Russlan and Ludmilla.* DARGOMINSKY: *Russalka.* RUBINSTEIN: *The Demon.* BORODIN: *Prince Igor.* RIMSKY-KORSAKOV: *Sadko.* RACHMANINOV: *Aleko.*
❀ (M) (***) EMI mono CDH7 61009-2 [id.].

Not only the glory of the voice, amazingly rich and consistent as recorded here between 1908 (aged 35) and 1931, but also the electrifying personality is vividly caught in this superb Références CD. The range of expression is astonishing. If posterity tends to think of this megastar among basses in the role of Mussorgsky's *Boris* (represented here in versions previously unissued), he is just as memorable in such an astonishing item as *Farlaf's Rondo* from *Russlan and Ludmilla*, with its tongue-twisting chatter made thrilling at such speed and with such power. The presence of the singer is unwaveringly vivid in model transfers, whether the original recording was acoustic or electric.

Clare College, Cambridge, Choir and Orchestra, John Rutter

'Carols from Clare': RUTTER: *Shepherd's pipe carol; Nativity carol.* TRAD., arr. Rutter: *Infant holy, infant lowly; Angel tidings; Quelle est cette odeur agréable; Once in Royal David's city; Il est né le divin enfant; I saw three ships; In dulci jubilo; Quem pastores Laudavere; Rocking; The twelve days of Christmas; Here we come a-wassailing; The coming of our King; O come, O come, Immanuel; The infant king; Noël nouvelet; O little town of Bethlehem; Gabriel's message; Sans day carol; Flemish carol; Past three o'clock.* CANTELOUBE: *Shepherd's noël.* GRÜBER: *Silent night.*
(M) *** EMI CDM7 69950-2; *EG 769950-4.*

Rutter's own *Shepherd's pipe carol* is delightful and here, as throughout, the discreet yet colourful use of the orchestral palette frames each set of words most tastefully. Rutter's own arrangements are very effective. The charming French carol *Il est né le divin enfant*, has a rustic dance flavour, and the presentation of *I saw three ships, In dulci jubilo, Rocking, Past three o'clock* and Grüber's *Silent night* is equally colourful. The recorded sound, while lacking a little in sharpness of focus, remains warmly atmospheric. An ideal collection for Christmas Eve: it plays for nearly 75 minutes.

'The Holly and the ivy' (Carols): RUTTER: *Donkey carol; Mary's lullaby.* TRAD., arr. RUTTER: *King Jesus hath a garden; Wexford carol;* (Flemish) *Cradle song; Child in a manger; In dulci jubilo; I saw three ships; The holly and the ivy.* TRAD., arr. WOODWARD: *Up! Good Christian folk.* TRAD., arr. WILLCOCKS: *Gabriel's message; Ding! dong! merrily on high; Quelle est cette odeur agréable.* TRAD., arr. PETTMAN: *I saw a maiden.* DARKE: *In the bleak mid-winter.* PRAETORIUS: *The noble stem of Jesse; Omnis mundus jocundetur.* TCHAIKOVSKY: *The crown of roses.* POSTON: *Jesus Christ the apple tree.* TRAD., arr. VAUGHAN WILLIAMS: *Wassail song.*
❀ (M) *** Decca 425 500-2; *425 500-4.*

This outstanding collection, recorded by Argo in the Lady Chapel at Ely Cathedral in 1979, is a model of its kind and the effect is far more transparent and real than Rutter's companion EMI carol record (although that offers 15 minutes' more music). There is surprisingly little duplication and Rutter's admirers, among whom we can be counted, will surely want both discs for the Christmas season. If only one is needed, then this Decca reissue is first choice. The opening arrangement of *King Jesus hath a garden*, using a traditional Dutch melody, immediately sets the mood with its pretty flute decorations. Moreover Rutter's own gentle syncopated *Donkey carol*, which comes fourth, is indispensable to any Christmas celebration.

The whole programme is a delight – not always especially ecclesiastical in feeling, but permeated throughout by the spirit of Christmas joy.

Collegium Aureum or Collegium Terpsichore

'Dances from Terpsichore' (with Siegfried Behrend; Siegfried Fink).
(B) *** Pickwick IMPX 9026.

An unexpectedly successful and rewarding collection of early dance music, some of it sounding quite primitive, but with the later items, collected by Praetorius, more sophisticated; yet all full of vitality and presented here with the most piquant instrumental effects. The performances by the Collegium Terpsichore are especially spontaneous, but the whole programme of 36 items encourages dipping into.

Crespin, Régine (soprano)

French songs: BERLIOZ: *Nuits d'été.* RAVEL: *Shéhérazade* (with SRO, Ansermet). DEBUSSY: *3 Chansons de Bilitis.* POULENC: *Banalities: Chansons D'Orkenise; Hôtel. La courte paille: Le carafon; La reine de coeur. Chansons villageoises: Les gars qui vont à la fête. 2 Poèmes de Louis Aragon.* (with J. Wustman).
*** Decca 417 813-2 [id.].

Régine Crespin's outstanding performances of the Berlioz and Ravel song-cycles with Ansermet are discussed under their composer entries. The Debussy and Poulenc *mélodies* come from a recital made four years earlier with John Wustman. The Poulenc songs are particularly vivid, robust in feeling and with an attractive bravura in *Le carafon* (*The water jug*). The Debussy *Chansons de Bilitis* are also strongly characterized by a singer at her peak at the time of making these recordings. John Wustman accompanies sympathetically and is given striking presence in the piano-accompanied section of the programme.

Deller, Alfred (counter-tenor)

'The three ravens' (with Desmond Dupré, guitar & lute): *The three ravens; Cuckoo; How should I your true love know; Sweet nightingale; I will give my love an apple; The oak and the ash;* (Lute): *Go from my window. King Henry; Coventry carol. Barbara Allen; Heigh ho, the wind and the rain; Waly, waly; Down in yon forest; Matthew, Mark, Luke and John.* (Lute): *A Toye. The tailor and the mouse; Greensleeves; The Wraggle Taggle gipsies; Lord Rendall; Sweet Jane; The frog and the mouse; The seeds of love; Near London town; Who's going to shoe your pretty little foot?; Blow away the morning dew; Searching for lambs; Sweet England; Dabbling in the dew; Just as the tide was a-flowing.*
(M) *** Vanguard 08.8026 71 [OVC 8026].

This CD represents the content of two LPs, and the recordings date from 1956 when Alfred Deller's voice was at its freshest and most winning. In songs which demand a simple line his sweet, pure timbre is ravishing and the performances of the title-song, *How should I your true love know, I will give my love an apple,* the *Coventry carol* and *The seeds of love* are all glorious examples. In one or two of the livelier numbers, *Heigh ho, the wind and the rain* for instance, some might wish for a more robust effect, but *The tailor and the mouse, The frog and the mouse* and the dainty *Who's going to shoe your pretty little foot?* have great charm. Deller is given intimate accompaniments by Desmond Dupré, who also provides two solo interludes. With a 73-minute programme this is not a disc to play all at once; but with the songs played in groups, Deller's lovely tone and natural artistry will give great pleasure. The recording is impeccable.

Divas

'Prima voce': Divas 1906–35 (Tetrazzini; Melba; Patti; Hempel; Galli-Curci; Ponselle; Lehmann; Turner; Koshetz; Norena; Nemeth; Muzio): Arias from: VERDI: *Un ballo in maschera; Rigoletto; Aida; Il Trovatore.* THOMAS: *Mignon.* MOZART: *Die Zauberflöte.* ROSSINI: *Il Barbiere di Siviglia.* MASSENET: *Manon.* PUCCINI: *Madama Butterfly.* BEETHOVEN: *Fidelio.*

RIMSKY-KORSAKOV: *Sadko.* BORODIN: *Prince Igor.* GOUNOD: *Roméo et Juliette.* BOITO: *Mefistofele.* Songs: YRADIER: *La Calesera.* DENAUDY: *O del mio amato ben.*
(M) (***) Nimbus mono NI 7802 [id.].

The six supreme prima donnas on this compilation are all very well represented. The soprano voice benefits more than most from the Nimbus process, so that with extra bloom Tetrazzini's vocal 'gear-change' down to the chest register is no longer obtrusive. She is represented by three recordings of 1911, including Gilda's *Caro nome* from *Rigoletto*; and Galli-Curci has three items too, including Rosina's *Una voce poco fa* from *Il Barbiere di Siviglia.* The tragically short-lived Claudia Muzio and the Russian, Nina Koshetz, have two each, while the others are each represented by a single, well-chosen item. They include Melba in *Mimi's farewell*, the 60-year-old Patti irresistibly vivacious in a Spanish folksong, *La calesera*, and Frieda Hempel in what is probably the most dazzling of all recordings of the Queen of the Night's second aria from *Zauberflöte.*

'Prima Voce': Divas Volume 2, 1909–40 (Hempel, Galli-Curci, Farrar, Kurz, Garrison, Gluck, Ivogün, Onegin, Schoene, Norena, Ponselle, Leider, Vallin, Teyte, Koshetz, Flagstad, Favero): Arias from: BELLINI: *I Puritani.* MOZART: *Le nozze di Figaro; Die Entführung aus dem Serail.* PUCCINI: *Tosca.* VERDI: *Rigoletto; La forza del destino.* OFFENBACH: *Les contes d'Hoffmann; La Périchole.* GODARD: *Jocelyn.* BIZET: *Carmen.* J. STRAUSS, Jnr: *Die Fledermaus.* THOMAS: *Hamlet.* WAGNER: *Tristan und Isolde; Die Walküre.* MASSENET: *Werther.* PONCE: *Estrellita.* MASCAGNI: *Lodoletta.*
(M) (***) Nimbus mono NI 7818 [id.].

As in the first *Divas* volume, the choice of items will delight any lover of fine singing, a most discriminating choice. Maria Ivogün, Schwarzkopf's teacher, contributes a wonderfully pure and incisive *Martern aller Arten* (*Entführung*) dating from 1923, and Lotte Schoene is unusually and characterfully represented by Adele's *Mein Herr Marquis* from *Fledermaus.* Frida Leider's *Liebestod* is nobly sung but is surprisingly fast by latterday standards. Maggie Teyte sings delectably in an aria from *La Périchole*; and though some of the pre-electric items in Nimbus's resonant transfers suggest an echo-chamber, the voices are warm and full.

Domingo, Plácido (tenor)

'Vienna, city of my dreams' (with Amb. S., ECO, Rudel): Arias from: LEHÁR: *Paganini; Merry Widow; Land of smiles.* ZELLER: *Vogelhändler.* KÁLMÁN: *Gräfin Mariza.* FALL: *Rose von Stambul.* O. STRAUSS: *Walzerträume.* J. STRAUSS: *Nacht in Venedig.* SIECZYNSKI: *Wien, du Stadt.*
*** EMI Dig. CDC7 47398-2 [id.].

Having such a golden tenor sound in Viennese operetta makes a winning combination, and Domingo, always the stylist, rebuts the idea that only a German tenor can be really idiomatic. A delightful selection including one or two rarities, very well recorded.

Operatic recital (1970–80 recordings): Arias from: VERDI: *Aida; Giovanna d'Arco; Un ballo in maschera; Don Carlos.* GOUNOD: *Faust.* BOITO: *Mefistofele.* PUCCINI: *Manon Lescaut; Tosca.*
(M) *** EMI CDM7 63103-2; *EG 763103-4.*

Compiled from Domingo's contributions to EMI opera sets in the 1970s, this mid-price CD includes some 71 minutes of music. The remastering brings the advantage of negligible background noise, but otherwise there is no great gain in presence; however, the sound is admirably clear and well balanced. If Domingo has recorded such items as the *Manon Lescaut* excerpt more perceptively, and if his singing of *Faust* is less stylish here than it usually is in French music, the range of achievement is formidable and the beauties great. The Puccini arias sound especially real, combining a fresh clarity with a pleasing atmosphere.

'Great love scenes' (with Renata Scotto, Kiri Te Kanawa, Ileana Cotrubas) from: PUCCINI: *Madama Butterfly; La rondine.* CILEA: *Adriana Lecouvreur.* MASSENET: *Manon.* GOUNOD: *Roméo et Juliette.* CHARPENTIER: *Louise.*
*** Sony MK 39030 [id.].

This compilation from various CBS opera sets brings an attractively varied group of love duets, with Domingo matched against three splendid heroines. Scotto is the principal partner, better as Adriana than as Butterfly, Juliette or Manon, but still warmly individual, responding to the glory of Domingo's singing which is unfailingly beautiful and warmly committed. The wonder is that his exceptional consistency never falls into routine; these are all performances to entice one back to the complete operas. Good recording.

'Ave Maria' (with Vienna Boys' Choir, VSO, Froschauer): HERBECK: *Pueri concinite.* TRAD.: *Adeste fidelis.* FRANCK: *Panis angelicus.* SCHUBERT: *Ave Maria.* KIENZL: *Der Evangelimann: Selig sind, die Verfolgung leiden.* HANDEL: *Xerxes: Ombra mai fù.* EYBLER: *Omnes de Saba venient.* BACH/GOUNOD: *Ave Maria.* FAURÉ: *Crucifix.* BIZET: *Agnus Dei.* LUTHER: *A mighty fortress is our God (Ein feste Burg).*
*** BMG/RCA RD 70760 [RCD1 3835].

This collection dates from 1979 and can be recommended unreservedly. Domingo is in freshest voice and these famous religious 'pops' are sung with golden tone and a simple eloquence that is most engaging. Nothing sounds routine and the Vienna Boys make a considerable contribution, notably in the dialogue of the excerpt from Kienzl's *Evangelimann.* In the closing chorale (*Ein feste Burg*) the Chorus Viennensis join the group to excellent effect. Attractively atmospheric recording, with Domingo's voice given fine presence and bloom.

'Bravissimo, Domingo': Arias from: VERDI: *Il Trovatore; Un ballo in maschera* (with Leontyne Price). *Rigoletto; Otello; Don Carlos* (with Sherrill Milnes). *Aida; La Traviata.* PUCCINI: *Tosca; Manon Lescaut* (with Leontyne Price). *Turandot.* LEONCAVALLO: *Pagliacci.* CILEA: *Adriana Lecouvreur.* GOUNOD: *Roméo et Juliette; Faust.* GIORDANO: *Andrea Chénier.* MASCAGNI: *Cavalleria Rusticana.* BIZET: *Carmen.*
*** BMG/RCA RD 87020 [RCD1 7020].

This selection of recordings ranges wide over Domingo's recording career. The opening items come from complete sets and *Di quella pira* immediately establishes the ringing vocal authority. The excerpts from *Cav.* and *Pag.* are equally memorable, as are the duets with Sherrill Milnes. With over 72 minutes offered, this is generous enough; although the remastered recordings sometimes show their age in the orchestra, the voice always remains fresh.

'Bravissimo Domingo!', Vol. 2: Arias from: VERDI: *Rigoletto; I vespri siciliani; Il Trovatore; Luisa Miller; La Forza del destino.* PUCCINI: *Tosca; La Bohème.* BELLINI: *Norma* (with Amb. Op. Ch.). MASCAGNI: *Cavalleria Rusticana* (with John Alldis Ch.). WAGNER: *Lohengrin.* MASSENET: *Werther.* DONIZETTI: *L'Elisir d'amore.* TCHAIKOVSKY: *Eugene Onegin.* FLOTOW: *Martha.* GIORDANO: *Andrea Chénier.*
*** BMG/RCA RD 86211 [RCA-6211-2-RC].

Opening stylishly with *Questa o quella*, and always establishing his sense of Verdian line, this second RCA collection is if anything even more attractive than the first. There is not a single below-par performance, and Domingo seems as at home in Tchaikovsky's and Wagner's lyricism as he is in the Italian repertoire. *Che gelida manina* (after an engaging little gasp from Mimi) is noble as well as eloquent, and the Donizetti and Flotow arias show the warm timbre of this remarkably consistent artist. Excellent remastering throughout the 72 minutes of music offered.

'The Plácido Domingo album': Arias from: MOZART: *Don Giovanni.* FLOTOW: *Martha.* GOUNOD: *Faust; Roméo et Juliette.* BIZET: *Carmen.* WAGNER: *Lohengrin.* DONIZETTI: *L'elisir d'amore.* PUCCINI: *La Bohème; Tosca* (with Paul Plishka); *Turandot.* LEONCAVALLO: *Pagliacci.* GIORDANO: *Andrea Chénier.* MASCAGNI: *Cavalleria rusticana.* TCHAIKOVSKY: *Eugene Onegin.* VERDI: *Il Trovatore* (with Leontyne Price); *La Traviata; Rigoletto; Luisa Miller; Simon Boccanegra; Un ballo in maschera; I vespri siciliani; Aida; Don Carlo* (with Sherrill Milnes); *Otello* (with Katia Ricciarelli & Milnes); *La forza del destino.*
(M) *** BMG/RCA GD 60866 (2) [60866-2].

With 31 items included, on a pair of mid-priced CDs playing for some 137 minutes, this is as attractive a Domingo collection as the current catalogue offers, particularly as the selection, while ranging widely over popular repertoire, devotes the second CD entirely to Verdi, roles which suit the strength of his personality and show the voice at its most vibrant, especially the thrilling *Di quella pira* from *Il Trovatore.* The selection ranges over Domingo's RCA recording career, covering a decade of excellence from 1969 to 1978. Most of the items come from his complete sets, but the opening *Il mio tesoro* derives from an early recital and very fine it is, quite different from John McCormack's famous version, but showing almost comparable breath control. Domingo is equally at home in Tchaikovsky's and Wagner's lyricism and brings an extra dimension to Italian repertoire. *Che gelida manina* (after an engaging little gasp from

Mimi – Caballé, though she is uncredited) is noble as well as eloquent. The Donizetti and Flotow arias show the warm timbre of this remarkably consistent artist, just as Bizet's *Flower song* shows his eloquence and ardour, and Verdi's *Quest o quella* his crisp rhythmic style. Excellent remastering throughout: the voice is brightly and cleanly caught: the RCA engineers were not afraid to have him sing directly into their microphones.

'Gala opera concert' (with LAPO, Giulini): Arias from: DONIZETTI: *L'Elisir d'amore; Lucia di Lammermoor.* VERDI: *Ernani; Il Trovatore; Aida.* HALÉVY: *La Juive.* MEYERBEER: *L'Africaine.* BIZET: *Les Pêcheurs de perles; Carmen* (with R. Wagner Chorale).
*** DG Dig. 400 030-2 [id.].

Recorded in 1980 in connection with a gala in San Francisco, this is as noble and resplendent a tenor recital as you will find. Domingo improves in detail even on the fine versions of some of these arias he had recorded earlier, and the finesse of the whole gains greatly from the sensitive direction of Giulini, though the orchestra is a little backward. Otherwise excellent recording, with tingling digital brass in the *Aida* excerpt.

'The best of Domingo': Arias from: VERDI: *Aida; Rigoletto; Luisa Miller; Un ballo in maschera; La Traviata.* BIZET: *Carmen.* FLOTOW: *Martha.* DONIZETTI: *L'Elisir d'amore.* OFFENBACH: *Contes d'Hoffmann.*
*** DG 415 366-2 [id.].

A popular recital showing Domingo in consistent form, the voice and style vibrant and telling, as the opening *Celeste Aida* readily shows, followed by an agreeably relaxed *La donna è mobile.* In the lyric arias, the *Flower song* and the excerpts from *Martha* and *L'Elisir d'amore* there is not the honeyed sweetness of a Gigli, but in the closing *Hoffmann* scena the sheer style of the singing gives special pleasure. The sound is vivid throughout.

Arias from: VERDI: *Rigoletto; Aida; Il Trovatore; La Traviata; Ernani; Macbeth.* DONIZETTI: *L'Elisir d'amore; Lucia di Lammermoor.* BIZET: *Carmen; Les Pêcheurs de perles.* MEYERBEER: *L'Africaine.* PUCCINI: *La Fanciulla del West.* LEHÁR: *Land des Lächelns.* Songs: LEONCAVALLO: *Mattinata.* LARA: *Granada.* CURTIS: *Nonti scorda.* GREVER: *Mucho.* CARDILLO: *Catari, catari.*
(B) *** DG Compact Classics *419 091-4* [id.].

A self-recommending Compact Classcs tape, offering nearly an hour and a half of Domingo in excellent operatic form. The programme includes obvious favourites but some less-expected items too, and the songs are welcome in showing the great tenor in lighter mood. A bargain, very useful for a long journey if you like to turn your car into La Scala Motorway.

'The Domingo Edition': Highlights from: BIZET: *Carmen* (435 401-2; *435 401-4*). PUCCINI: *La Fanciulla del West* (435 407-2; *435 407-4*); *Manon Lescaut* (435 408-2; *435 408-4*); *Turandot* (435 409-2; *435 409-4*). VERDI: *Aida* (435 410-2; *435 410-4*); *Un ballo in maschera* (435 411-2; *435 411-4*); *Don Carlos* (453 412-2; *435 412-4*); *Luisa Miller* (435 413-2; *435 413-4*); *Macbeth* (435 414-2; *435 414-4*); *Nabucco* (435 415-2; *435 415-4*); *Rigoletto* (435 426-2; *435 416-4*); *La Traviata* (435 417-2; *435 417-4*); *Il Trovatore* (435 418-2; *435 418-4*); WAGNER: *Tannhäuser* (435 405-2; *435 405-4*); *Die Meistersinger*; WEBER: *Oberon* (435 406-2; *435 406-4*). *French opera*: excerpts from: MEYERBEER: *L'Africaine.* GOUNOD: *Roméo et Juliette.* BERLIOZ: *Requiem; Damnation de Faust.* HALÉVY: *La Juive.* DE LISLE: *La Marseillaise* (arr. Berlioz) (with Ch. & O de Paris, Barenboim: 435 403-2; *435 403-4*). *French opera*, Vol. 2, excerpts from: BERLIOZ: *Béatrice et Bénédict.* MASSENET: *Werther.* BIZET: *Les pêcheurs de perles.* SAINT-SAENS: *Samson et Dalila* (435 404-2; *435 404-4*). Arias and excerpts from: DONIZETTI: *Lucia di Lammermoor; L'elisir d'amore.* MASCAGNI: *Cavalleria rusticana.* MOZART: *Don Giovanni.* VERDI: *Ernani.* PUCCINI: *Tosca* (435 419-2; *435 419-4*). Songs & tangos: *Amapola; Volver; Mañequita linda; Maria; Ay, ay, ay; Non ti scordar di me; Uno; Alma de bohemio; Granada; Mi buenos aires querido; Siboney; Júrame.* LEONCAVALLO: *Mattinata.* LEHÁR: *Dein ist mein ganzes Herz* (435 420-2; *435 4204-4*).
(M) **(*) DG Analogue/Dig. 435 400-2; *435 400-4* (20).

DG's *'Domingo Edition'*, 20 discs at mid-price, aims to be a comprehensive tribute to a unique tenor, concentrating on representing him in his complete opera recordings. Domingo himself in his note on the series promises that 'it contains many of the recordings I count among my best', and he is 'especially pleased that this Edition is not just a collection of tenor arias', but instead a mixture of long and short items that give an impression of each opera. No fewer than

16 of the 20 discs are operatic highlights issues, all of which have separate listings in the composer index, with three more devoted to what are broadly described as arias, but which range far wider than that in their selection from the Domingo discography on DG. The last disc is devoted to middle-of-the road material, *Songs and Tangos* collecting items from 1976 and 1981, rather disappointing, when the arrangements are so souped-up and the voice aggressively over-amplified. Only one of the recordings here was made before 1976, but then they followed thick and fast, representing him in a wide range of his finest roles, yet this collection tends to underline the problems the DG engineers often seem to have had over recording so large a voice. Instead of having it firmly focused, it has regularly been given a halo of reverberation at a slight distance. Nonetheless, no one could miss its glorious bloom.

The highlights discs generally offer between 65 and 70 minutes of music, with none lasting under an hour (and several are the only available selections of excerpts from that particular opera), but the discs of separate arias and ensembles are much less generous at around 50 minutes. They are partly drawn from complete sets of various kinds – including Daniel Barenboim's Paris recordings of Berlioz's *Requiem, Damnation of Faust* and *Béatrice et Bénédict* – and partly from two 'Gala' recordings, made live, the 1984 recital from Los Angeles conducted by Giulini and Domingo's visit to the Met. in New York in 1988, conducted by James Levine with Kathleen Battle as his partner in duets. It is a charming rarity to have Domingo here in a baritone role, singing Don Giovanni to Battle's Zerlina in *La ci darem la mano.* That comes from the third of the discs of separate items, devoted to the Italian repertory and ranging from Mozart to Mascagni and Puccini by way of Donizetti (items from *Lucia* and *L'elisir d'amore*) and Verdi. All these CDs and tape equivalents are available separately, and it is sensible to pick and choose according to taste. Overall this represents a formidable achievement.

Domingo, Plácido (tenor), Itzhak Perlman (violin)

'Together' (with New York Studio Orchestra, Jonathan Tunick): TOSELLI: *Serenata.* PONCE: *Estrellita.* MASSENET: *Élégie.* KALMAN: *Die Czardasfurstin: Weiss du es noch?* KREISLER: *The old refrain.* RACHMANINOV: *When night descends; O cease thy singing, maiden fair.* OFFENBACH: *Contes d'Hoffmann: Barcarolle.* TOSTI: *Ideale.* TRAD.: *Danny Boy.* HANDEL: *Serse: Ombra mai fu.* ROMBERG: *Student Prince: Serenade.* GODARD: *Jocelyn: Berceuse.* TCHAIKOVSKY: *None but the lonely heart.* R. STRAUSS: *Morgen.*
*(*) EMI Dig. CDC7 54266-2; *EL 754266-4* [id.].

If the example of McCormack and Kreisler in duet in pre-electric days is what inspired this issue, this disc of crossover material provides poor competition, even with full-ranging digital sound. Domingo's voice is made to sound unnatural, as though recorded in a separate echo-chamber. Perlman's tone is ungraciously caught too, and having his loud solo starting Toselli's *Serenade* right at the start brings that home abrasively. Sadly, the essential element of charm is undermined, when the impression is of Domingo singing consistently loud. It comes as some relief at the end having Strauss's *Morgen* and Rachmaninov's *O cease thy singing*, rather gentler than the rest.

Domingo, Plácido, José Carreras (tenors), Montserrat Caballé (soprano)

'Barcelona Olympic Games ceremony' (with Juan Pons, Teresa Berganza, Giacomo Aragall, Barcelona SO, Garcia Navarro): *Barcelona Games medley* (arr. Parera). Arias from: MASSENET: *Le Cid.* DONIZETTI: *La Favorita* (Domingo). BELLINI: *Norma.* MASSENET: *Hérodiade* (Caballé). VERDI: *Macbeth; Un ballo in maschera* (Pons). LEONCAVALLO: *Pagliacci.* VERDI: *Otello* (Carreras). ROSSINI: *L'Italiana in Algeri.* THOMAS: *Mignon* (Berganza). PONCHIELLI: *La Gioconda* (Aragall). OFFENBACH: *Contes d'Hoffmann: Barcarolle* (Caballé & Berganza).
**(*) BMG/RCA Dig. 09026 61204-2 [61204-2; *61204-4*].

This CD arrived on our table the very morning of the Barcelona Olympics opening ceremony. It was, very sensibly, recorded six months before the event, in the studio. The opening 13-minute 51-second pot-pourri, cleverly arranged by Tony Parera, uses snippets from a dozen favourite operas, ingeniously assembled into what used to be called a 'musical switch'. The singers enter into the spirit of the thing, and the result is a teeming cascade of memorable ideas. Then each of the six singers has a chance to shine in at least one complete aria. Not surprisingly,

Domingo steals the show. Caballé's *Casta diva* is finely conceived but squally on top. Berganza is good in Rossini but at her most charming in the tuneful *Connais-tu le pays?* from *Mignon*. Carreras is better in Leoncavallo than in Verdi's *Otello*, but at this stage in his career perhaps not really suited to either role; but Caballé and Berganza join together for a seductive *Barcarolle*, which is an undoubted highlight. Most of the other items are less distinctive.

Early Music Consort of London, David Munrow

'Music of the Gothic era': Notre Dame period: LEONIN: *Organum Viderunt omnes*. PEROTIN: *Organum Viderunt omnes*. Ars Antiqua: *Motets from the Bamberg and Montpellier Codices* by Petrus de Cruce, Adam de la Halle and Anon. Ars Nova: *Motets from the Roman de Fauvel. Chantilly/Ivrea Codices* by Machaut; De Vitry.
*** DG 415 292-2.

This issue draws on the fine three-LP set, '*Music of the Gothic Era*', made by the late lamented David Munrow just before his death in 1976. It offers two items from the first LP, one each by Leonin and Perotin, and gives us more from the other two, from the so-called *Ars antiqua* (1250–1320) and includes two motets of Adam de la Halle, and the *Ars nova* (1320–80), representing such figures as Philippe de Vitry and Machaut. David Munrow had exceptional powers both as a scholar-performer and as a communicator, and it is good that his work is remembered on compact disc. The performances are wonderfully alive and vital, and the digital remastering as expert as one would expect. A strong recommendation.

'Music of the Crusades': Anonymous thirteenth-century French music, and music by: MARCABRU; CUIOT DE DIJON; WALTER VON DER VOGEL-WEIDE; FAIDIT; CONON DE BETHUNE; RICHARD COEUR-DE-LION; THIBAUT DE CHAMPAGNE.
(M) *** Decca 430 264-2; *430 264-4*.

Of all the Early Music groups, the Early Music Consort under the late David Munrow can be relied on best to entertain and titillate the ear without ever descending into vulgarity. The characteristic combination of familiarity with their repertoire and imaginative flair which characterizes the work of this group informs the whole programme. Most of the accompaniments are purely speculative (only the melodic line survives in some cases) but the performances, like the realizations, are brilliantly effective and the presentation deserves the highest praise for its blend of scholarship and inventiveness. The 1970 (Argo) recording sounds as fresh here as the day it was made.

Ferrier, Kathleen (contralto)

Lieder, arias and songs: MAHLER: *Kindertotenlieder* (with VPO, Walter). GLUCK: *Orfeo ed Euridice*: excerpts including *Che faro*. PURCELL: *Ode for Queen Mary: Sound the trumpet. Indian Queen: Let us not wander* (with I. Baillie). HANDEL: *Ottone: Spring is coming; Come to me*. GREEN: *O praise the Lord; I will lay me down in peace*. MENDELSSOHN: *I would that my love* (with I. Baillie, G. Moore).
(M) (***) EMI mono CDH7 61003-2 [id.].

It was especially tragic that Kathleen Ferrier made so few recordings in which the technical quality matched her magical artistry. This disc includes many of her EMI mono records, which generally sound much better than the Decca repertoire listed below. The Gluck *Orfeo* excerpts (deriving from a broadcast) have undoubtedly been enhanced and the 1949 *Kindertotenlieder* also comes over very well. Particularly worth having are the duets with Isobel Baillie, as these artists obviously worked especially well together. Generally, the new transfers are vivid and show a considerable enhancement of their previous LP incarnations.

'The world of Kathleen Ferrier': TRAD.: *Blow the wind southerly; The Keel Row; Ma bonny lad; Kitty my love*. arr. BRITTEN: *Come you not from Newcastle*. HANDEL: *Rodelinda: Art thou troubled? Serse: Ombra mai fu*. GLUCK: *Orfeo: What is life?* MENDELSSOHN: *Elijah: Woe unto them; O rest in the Lord*. BACH: *St Matthew Passion: Have mercy, Lord, on me*. SCHUBERT: *An die Musik; Gretchen am Spinnrade; Die junge Nonne; Der Musensohn*. BRAHMS: *Sapphische Ode; Botschaft*. MAHLER: *Rückert Lieder: Um Mitternacht*.
❀ (B) (***) Decca mono 430 096-2; *430 096-4*.

This selection, revised and expanded from the original LP issue, admirably displays Kathleen

Ferrier's range, from the delightfully fresh folksongs to Mahler's *Um Mitternacht* in her celebrated recording with Bruno Walter and the VPO. The noble account of *O rest in the Lord* is one of the essential items now added, together with an expansion of the Schubert items (*Die junge Nonne* and *An die Musik* are especially moving). The CD transfers are remarkably trouble-free and the opening unaccompanied *Blow the wind southerly* has uncanny presence. The recital plays for 65 minutes and fortunately there are few if any technical reservations to be made here about the sound quality.

'Kathleen Ferrier Edition' (complete, as detailed on the 10 separate CDs listed below).
(M) (**(*)) Decca mono 433 802-2 (10) [id.].

Volume 1: GLUCK: *Orfeo ed Euridice* (abridged) (with Soloists, Glyndebourne Festival Ch., Southern PO, Stiedry).
(M) (**) Decca mono 433 468-2.

Volume 2: BACH: *St Matthew Passion*: Arias & choruses (with soloists, Bach Ch., Jacques O, Jacques).
(M) (**) Decca mono 433 469-2.

Volume 3: PERGOLESI: *Stabat Mater* (orch. Scott) (with Joan Taylor, Nottingham Oriana Ch., Boyd Neel String O, Roy Henderson). Arias: GLUCK: *Orpheus and Euridice: What is life?* HANDEL: *Rodelinda: Art thou troubled? Serse: Ombra mai fu.* BACH: *St Matthew Passion: Have mercy, Lord, on me* (all with LSO or Nat. SO, Sargent). *Cantata No. 11: Ah, tarry yet, my dearest Saviour.* MENDELSSOHN: *Elijah: O woe unto them; O rest in the Lord.*
(M) (**(*)) Decca mono 433 470-2; *430 470-4.*

Volume 4: Lieder: SCHUMANN: *Frauenliebe und Leben* (song-cycle); *Volksliedchen; Widmung* (with John Newmark (piano)). BRAHMS: *Sapphische Ode; Botschaft.* SCHUBERT: *Gretchen am Spinnrade; Die junge Nonne; An die Musik; Der Musensohn* (with Phyllis Spurr (piano)); *Ganymed; Du liebst mich nicht; Lachen und Weinen* (with Benjamin Britten (piano)). GRÜBER: *Silent night.* TRAD.: *O come all ye faithful* (with Boyd Neel String O, Neel).
(M) (***) Decca mono 433 471-2.

Volume 5: BBC Broadcasts (1949–53): BRAHMS: *4 Serious Songs, Op. 121* (with BBC SO, Sargent). CHAUSSON: *Poème de l'amour et de la mer, Op. 19* (with Hallé O, Barbirolli). Recital (with Ernest Lush (piano)): FERGUSON: *Discovery* (song-cycle). WORDSWORTH: *Red skies; The wind; Clouds.* RUBBRA: *3 Psalms: Nos. 6, O Lord rebuke me not; 23, The Lord is my shepherd; 150, Praise ye the Lord.*
(M) (**) Decca mono 433 472-2.

Volume 6: Broadcast recitals: English and German songs: STANFORD: *The fairy lough; A soft day.* PARRY: *Love is a bable.* VAUGHAN WILLIAMS: *Silent noon.* BRIDGE: *Go not, happy day.* WARLOCK: *Sleep; Pretty ring-time.* Folksongs, arr. BRITTEN: *O, Waly, Waly; Come you not from Newcastle?* arr. HUGHES: *Kitty, my love* (with Frederick Stone (piano)). PURCELL: *From silent shades: Mad Bess of Bedlam. The Fairy Queen: Hark! the echoing air.* HANDEL: *Atalanta: Like as the love-lorn turtle. Admeto: How changed the vision.* Lieder: WOLF: *Verborgenheit; Der Gärtner; Auf ein altes Bild; Auf einer Wanderung.* JENSEN: *Altar* (with Phyllis Spurr (piano)). BACH: *Vergiss mein nicht; Ach dass nicht die letzte Stunde* (with Millicent Silver (harpsichord)). *Bist du bei mir* (with John Newmark (piano)).
(M) (***) Decca mono 433 473-2.

Volume 7: Bach and Handel arias (with LPO, Boult): Arias from BACH: *Mass in B min.; St Matthew Passion; St John Passion.* HANDEL: *Samson; Messiah; Judas Maccabaeus.*
❀ (M) Decca mono 433 474-2; *433 474-4.*

Volume 8: '*Blow the wind southerly*' British songs & Folksongs (with Phyllis Spurr or (i) John Newmark (piano)): TRAD., arr. WHITTAKER: *Ma bonny lad; The keel row; Blow the wind southerly.* arr. HUGHES: *I have a bonnet trimmed with blue; I know where I'm going; I will walk with my love; The stuttering lovers; Down by the Sally Gardens; The lover's curse.* arr. SHARP: *My boy Willie.* arr. ROBERTON: (i) *The fidgety bairn.* arr. JACOBSON: (i) *Ca' the yowes.* arr. BRITTEN: *O Waly, Waly.* arr. WARLOCK: *Willow, willow.* arr. GREW: *Have you seen buy a whyte lillie grow?.* arr. QUILTER: *Ye banks and braes; Drink to me only; Now sleeps the crimson petal; The fair house of joy; To daisies; Over the mountains.*
❀ (M) *** Decca mono 433 475-2; *433 475-4.*

Volume 9: Broadcast Edinburgh Festival recital, 1949. Lieder (with Bruno Walter, piano): SCHUBERT: *Die junge Nonne. Rosamunde: Romance. Du bist mich nicht; Der Tod und das Mädchen; Suleika; Du bist die Ruh'.* BRAHMS: *Immer leiser wird mein Schlummer; Der Tod das ist die kuhle Nacht; Botschaft; Von ewiger Liebe.* SCHUMANN: *Frauenliebe und Leben* (song-cycle), *Op. 42.*
(M) (***) Decca mono 433 476-2.

Volume 10: MAHLER: *3 Rückert Lieder* (with VPO, Bruno Walter). BRAHMS: *Alto rhapsody, Op. 53* (with LPO Ch., LPO, Clemens Kraus); *2 Songs with viola, Op. 91* (with Phyllis Spurr (piano), Max Gilbert (viola)). *Vier ernste Gešange, Op. 121* (with John Newmark (piano)).
(M) (***) Decca mono 433 477-2.

The previous Decca Ferrier anthology appeared on seven LPs, and later a shorter survey appeared on four cassettes. The CD coverage is much more comprehensive, but even so omits Mahler's *Das Lied von der Erde*, which is still available separately at full price, with a transfer very unflattering to the VPO violins. Moreover Decca seemed not always to be able to preserve their 78-r.p.m. masters without deterioration, which the CD transfers can sometimes emphasize. Yet even so there is much treasure here and these records readily demonstrate not only Ferrier's star quality and amazing range, but also the consistency with which the radiant vocal quality lit up almost everything she recorded. Even so, the single disc selections from Bach's *St Matthew Passion* and Gluck's *Orfeo ed Euridice* are a mixed blessing – they are discussed separately under their composer entries. So is the Brahms/Mahler collection, including the *Alto rhapsody* and three *Rückert Lieder*, and her superb 1952 recording swan-song combining Bach and Handel arias, lovingly accompanied by Boult and the LPO. John Culshaw produced this disc, and ensured that at least one Decca CD is technically fully worthy of Kathleen's art. The other collection which is unmissable (and which is generally well engineered) is her recital of British songs and folksongs. It is given the title of the unaccompanied lyric by which she is most fondly remembered by the greater musical public, '*Blow the wind southerly*'. Even that transfer is not completely free from distortion, but the sense of the singer's presence is unforgettable. That recital contains much that is utterly magical – Ferrier's way with folksongs brought a simple innocence that few other singers have approached – but it earns its Rosette with a very special, wonderfully tender performance of *I will walk with my love*, where the gloriously gently vocal halo she places gently round the climactic word, 'boy' is achingly beautiful.

The 1946 Pergolesi *Stabat Mater*, comes off remarkably well, mainly because of Roy Henderson's excellence as a choral trainer, and the recording was good for its period and still sounds lively. This is included on Volume three, with more Ferrier favourites, reasonably well transferred, including Gluck's *What is life (Che farò)*, Handel's *Art thou troubled* and Mendelssohn's *O rest in the Lord* (from *Elijah*), all showing the glorious voice at its most nobly resonant.

As Volume 4 demonstrates, Ferrier was a deeply impressive Lieder singer. Had she lived, her art would undoubtedly have deepened considerably beyond what is displayed here. There are more tender, more loving emotions in Schumann' *Frauenliebe und Leben* than Ferrier was able to convey in 1950, and she is not helped by the limited accompaniment of John Newmark. Yet she is never less than compelling, and her Schubert and Wolf bring a natural warmth and dedication and a lightness of touch that are disarming; any shortcomings are here outweighed by the beauty of the voice. She identifies readily with *Die junge Nonne* and there is a special glow for *An die Musik*, while the Brahms songs are beautifully sung. Generally the sound here is very good and background noises not too distracting. The three items accompanied by Benjamin Britten come from a BBC broadcast of 1952: the sound here is more opaque, and in *Du liebst mich nicht* the recording fades out before the end. Kathleen Ferrier had a marvellously robust Lancashire sense of fun and she would have surely found a natural riposte to suit such a minor calamity. The recital ends with two very touching carols, recorded with Boyd Neel for the Christmas market in 1948.

Volume 5 is very much a curate's egg. The performance of the *Four serious songs* in English with Sargent comes from a BBC broadcast of 1949 while the Barbirolli/Hallé performance of Chausson has a similar 1951 source. The quality is poor, the surfaces are noisy; indeed the general effect in the Chausson is little short of execrable. But the rest of the CD offers a broadcast recital of 12th January 1952 with results that are more than acceptable. The rare Howard Ferguson cycle, the even rarer Wordsworth songs, of which *Clouds* is totally memorable, and the very characteristic Rubbra Psalm settings show the singer at her most searching and imaginative, and they are well accompanied by Ernest Lush. Here the voice has excellent presence, and there are only occasional clicks from the acetate original.

Volume 6 is also strongly recommendable. Again one discovers that the magic of Ferrier's voice was never so potent as when she was singing English songs, and the opening group, with the highly sympathetic Frederick Stone – taken from a broadcast recital given just over a year before the singer's untimely death – brings a natural spontaneity and projection of warm feeling that are irresistible, especially when the transfers are generally of such vivid immediacy. The second recital on this disc derives from a Norwegian broadcast made three years earlier, with a rather noisier background, but this group is famous for Jensen's *Altar*, which Ferrier introduces herself with apologetic charm. The bonuses include private recordings of two rare Bach items with harpsichord, where the surface noise is very distracting, and then the programme end with a glorious *Bist du bei mir*, where the background miraculously abates. (This comes, remarkably, from a 1950 Voice of America recording held in the Library of Congress.)

The 1949 Edinburgh Festival recital is less than technically perfect but still makes enjoyable listening. The piano sound may be a bit hazy, but this historic occasion gives a wonderful idea of the intensity of a live Ferrier recital. Here account here of *Frauenliebe und Leben* is freer and even more compelling than the performance she recorded earlier. Walter's accompaniments may not be flawless, but they are comparably inspirational. The recital is introduced by a brief talk on Walter and the Edinburgh Festival given by Ferrier, so welcome when the *Altar* introduction is so brief. The CD transfer does not seek to 'enhance' the sound, but most of the background has been cleaned up; there are moments when the vocal focus slips, but the ear readily adjusts. Throughout the series backup documentation is adequate rather than generous, with the same biographical note common to each disc.

Galli-Curci, Amelita (soprano)

'Prima voce': Arias from: AUBER: *Manon Lescaut.* BELLINI: *I Puritani; La Sonnambula.* DONIZETTI: *Don Pasquale; Linda di Chamounix; Lucia di Lammermoor.* GOUNOD: *Roméo et Juliette.* MEYERBEER: *Dinorah.* ROSSINI: *Il Barbiere di Siviglia.* THOMAS: *Mignon.* VERDI: *Rigoletto; La Traviata.*
(M) (***) Nimbus mono NI 7806 [id.].

More than in most of these transfers made via an acoustic horn gramophone, the resonance of the horn itself can be detected, and the results are full and forward. Galli-Curci's perfection in these pre-electric recordings, made between 1917 and 1924, is a thing of wonder, almost too accurate for comfort, but tenderness is there too, as in the Act II duet from *La Traviata* (with Giuseppe de Luca) and the *Addio del passato*, complete with introductory recitative, but with only a single stanza. Yet brilliant coloratura is what lies at the root of Galli-Curci's magic, and that comes in abundance.

Galway, James (flute), BBC Singers, King's School, Canterbury, Choristers, Galway

'James Galway's Christmas carol': GRÜBER: *Silent night.* RUTTER: *Shepherd's pipe carol.* BACH: *Suite No. 3: Air. Christmas oratorio: Sinfonia and Chorale. Sheep may safely graze.* OVERTON: *Fantasia on I saw three ships.* TRAD.: *Greensleeves; Zither carol; Patapan; Past three o'clock; I wonder as I wander.* IRELAND: *The holy boy.* BACH/GOUNOD: *Ave Maria.* POSTON: *Jesus Christ the apple tree.* RYAN: *We wish you a merry Christmas.*
(M) *** BMG/RCA Dig. 09026 61233 [61233-2].

James Galway's silvery timbre introduces Grüber's *Silent night* unaccompanied before the choir joins in and he later adds an obbligato descant. These are all effectively simple arrangements, in which Galway both directs chorus and orchestra and makes regular and attractive solo contributions. John Rutter's engaging *Shepherd's pipe carol* was an obvious choice in a programme that has a happy freshness about its presentation throughout. The interspersed orchestral numbers bring an effective degree of contrast. With clear yet full recorded sound, the ambience mellow but not too ecclesiastical, this is a Christmas compilation that will give a great deal of pleasure.

Gigli, Beniamino (tenor)

Opera arias from: GOUNOD: *Faust.* BIZET: *Carmen; Les Pêcheurs de perles.* MASSENET: *Manon.* HANDEL: *Serse.* DONIZETTI: *Lucia di Lammermoor; L'Elisir d'amore.* VERDI: *Rigoletto; Aida.* LEONCAVALLO: *I Pagliacci.* MASCAGNI: *Cavalleria Rusticana.* PUCCINI: *La Bohème; Tosca.* GIORDANO: *Andrea Chénier.* PIETRI: *Maristella.*
❀ (M) (***) EMI mono CDH7 61051-2 [id.].

No Italian tenor has sung with more glowing beauty than Beniamino Gigli. His status in the inter-war period as a singing superstar is vividly reflected in this Références collection of 18 items, the cream of his recordings made between 1927 and 1937. It is specially welcome to have two historic ensemble recordings, made in New York in 1927: the *Quartet* from *Rigoletto* and the *Sextet* from *Lucia di Lammermoor.* In an astonishing line-up Gigli is joined by Galli-Curci, Pinza, De Luca and Louise Homer. Excellent transfers.

Arias and excerpts from: GIORDANO: *Andrea Chénier.* DONIZETTI: *La Favorita; L'elisir d'amore; Lucia di Lammermoor.* GOUNOD: *Faust; Roméo et Juliette.* LALO: *Le roi d'Ys.* PUCCINI: *Tosca.* PONCHIELLI: *La Gioconda.* BIZET: *Les pêcheurs de perles.* VERDI: *Attila; I Lombardi.* GOMES: *Lo schiavo; Il Guarany.*
(M) (***) BMG/RCA mono GD 87811 [7811-2-RG].

This RCA compilation with its bright, forward CD transfers of the original 78s ranges wide, from pre-electrics like Chénier's big aria, always a favourite with him, to ten items from the early electric period – 1925–30 – and with two little songs by Gomes from 1951 as a postscript. Specially notable from these American recordings are the duets and trios with his great contemporaries at the Met. in New York, Ezio Pinza, Titta Ruffo and Elisabeth Rethberg. The voice is consistently close and immediate, with an astonishing sense of presence, yet with none of the histrionic harshness one can expect from other tenors.

'Prima voce': Volume 1 (1918–24): Arias from: BOITO: *Mefistofele.* CATALANI: *Loreley.* DONIZETTI: *La Favorita.* FLOTOW: *Martha.* GIORDANO: *Andrea Chénier.* GOUNOD: *Faust.* LALO: *Le roi d'Ys.* LEONCAVALLO: *Pagliacci.* MASCAGNI: *Iris.* MEYERBEER: *L'Africana.* PONCHIELLI: *La Gioconda.* PUCCINI: *Tosca.* Songs.
(M) (***) Nimbus mono NI 7807 [id.].

This collection of 22 items recorded between 1918 and 1924 shows the voice at its most honeyed, even lighter and more lyrical than it became later, with the singer indulging in fewer of the mannerisms that came to decorate his ever-mellifluous singing. Few tenor voices have ever matched Gigli's in rounded, golden beauty, and the Nimbus transfers capture its bloom in a way that makes one forget pre-electric limitations. In the one item sung in French, by Lalo, he sounds less at home, a little too heavy; but the ease of manner in even the most taxing arias elsewhere is remarkable, and such a number as the *Serenade* from Mascagni's *Iris* is irresistible in its sparkle, as are the Neapolitan songs, notably the galloping *Povero Pulcinella* by Buzzi-Peccia. One oddity is a tenor arrangement of Saint-Saëns's *The Swan.*

'Prima Voce': Volume 2 (1925–40). Arias from: DONIZETTI: *L'elisir d'amore; Lucia di Lammermoor.* PUCCINI: *Manon Lescaut; La Bohème; Tosca.* VERDI: *La forza del destino; La Traviata; Rigoletto.* THOMAS: *Mignon.* BIZET: *I pescatori di perle.* PONCIELLI: *La Gioconda.* MASSENET: *Manon.* GOUNOD: *Faust.* RIMSKY-KORSAKOV: *Sadko.* GLUCK: *Paride ed Elena.* CILEA: *L'Arlesiana.* CACCINI: Song: *Amarilli.*
(M) (***) Nimbus mono NI 7817 [id.].

Issued to celebrate the Gigli centenary in 1990, the Nimbus selection concentrates on recordings he made in the very early years of electrical recording up to 1931, when his voice was at its very peak, the most golden instrument, ideally suited to recording. The items are very well chosen and are by no means the obvious choices, though it is good to have such favourites as the *Pearlfishers duet* with de Luca and the 1931 version of Rodolfo's *Che gelida manina.* The Nimbus transfers are at their best, with relatively little reverberation.

Gomez, Jill (soprano), John Constable (piano)

'Cabaret classics': WEILL: *Marie Galante: 4 Songs. Lady in the Dark: My ship. Street scene: Lonely house. Knickerbocker holiday: It never was you.* ZEMLINSKY: *3 Songs from Op. 27.* SCHOENBERG: *4 Brettl Lieder.* SATIE: *3 Café-concert songs: La Diva de l'Empire; Allons-y, Chochotte; Je te veux.*
❀ *** Unicorn Dig. DKPCD 9055; *DKPC 9055* [id.].

Jill Gomez here assembles a delectable collection of 'cabaret classics', with Arnold Schoenberg providing the surprise in four songs in popular Viennese style which he wrote at the turn of the century when he was making ends meet as music director of the Uberbrettl Cabaret in Berlin. Jill Gomez's delicious performances make clear that writing these innocently diatonic numbers can have been no chore to the future ogre of the avant-garde. This is the music of love in every sense, delicately provocative, both first-class Schoenberg and excellent light music. The same is true of the two Kurt Weill groups, strikingly contrasted at the beginning and end of the recital. The French-text songs from *Marie Galante* use material adapted from *Happy End*. They are charming in their own right, with his characteristic tanginess given extra subtlety. Weill's mastery is even more strikingly illustrated in the three Broadway songs, ravishing numbers all three: *My ship, Lonely house* and *It never was you.* It is worth getting the record just for Gomez's ecstatic pianissimo top A at the end of that last item. The other groups, as delightful as they are revealing, are from Alexander von Zemlinsky (not quite so light-handed), and the Parisian joker, Satie, in three café-concert songs, including the famous celebration of English music-hall, *La Diva de l'Empire.* John Constable is the idiomatic accompanist. Gomez's sensuously lovely soprano is caught beautifully.

'Recital of French songs': BIZET: *Chanson d'avril; Adieux de l'hôtesse arabe; Vous ne priez pas; La chanson de la rose.* BERLIOZ: *Le coucher du soleil; L'Origine de la harpe; La belle voyageuse.* DEBUSSY: *Proses lyriques: De rêves; De grêve; De fleurs; De soir. Noël des enfants qui n'ont plus de maisons.*
(M) *** Saga SCD 9034 [id.].

Jill Gomez's collection, recorded early in her career, brings a whole series of delectable songs, many of them little known. The charming Bizet songs are little more than simple ballads, but Gomez, sensitively accompanied by John Constable, transforms them magically, singing with her most golden tone. The Berlioz items are weightier, and bring some immaculate legato singing, while even the Debussy *Proses lyriques*, written in the early 1890s are among the composer's least known songs, again with Gomez at her most poised. The brisk little song, *Noël des enfants qui n'ont plus de maisons*, the last that Debussy ever wrote, a wartime inspiration of 1915, provides a crisp conclusion. The voice is very well caught, despite the age of the recording.

'Spanish songs': GRANADOS: *Tonadillas al estilo antiguo, Nos. 1–6.* TURINA: *Poema en forma de canciones, Op. 19.* FALLA: *Trois Mélodies. Siete canciones populares españolas.*
(M) *** Saga SCD 9007 [id.].

Jill Gomez's memorably delectable recital of Spanish songs (including Falla's *Seven Spanish popular songs*) is one of the highlights of the Saga catalogue. In its original, LP format, this issue was spoilt by noisy surfaces, but now one can hear the recording in its pristine glory, wonderfully fresh and naturally balanced. The performances are in every way outstanding and the repertoire a delight.

Gothic Voices, Christopher Page

'The Guardian of Zephirus' (Courtly songs of the 15th century, with Imogen Barford, medieval harp): DUFAY: *J'atendray tant qu'il vous playra; Adieu ces bons vins de Lannoys; Mon cuer me fait tous dis penser.* BRIQUET: *Ma seul amour et ma belle maistresse.* DE CASERTA: *Amour ma' le cuer mis.* LANDINI: *Nessun ponga speranza; Giunta vaga bilta.* REYNEAU: *Va t'en mon cuer, avent mes yeux.* MATHEUS DE SACTO JOHANNE: *Fortune, faulce, parverse.* DE INSULA: *Amours n'ont cure le tristesse.* BROLLO: *Qui le sien vuelt bien maintenir.* ANON.: *N'a pas long temps que trouvay Zephirus; Je la remire, la belle.*
*** Hyp. CDA 66144; *KA 66144* [id.].

Most of this repertoire is unfamiliar, with Dufay the only famous name; but everything here is of interest, and the listener inexperienced in medieval music will be surprised at the strength of its character. The performances are naturally eloquent and, although the range of colour is limited compared with later writing, it still has immediacy of appeal, especially if taken in short bursts. The recording balance is faultless and the sound first rate. With complete security of intonation and a chamber-music vocal blend, the presentation is wholly admirable. There is full back-up documentation.

'The Service of Venus and Mars': DE VITRY: *Gratissima virginis; Vos quie admiramini; Gaude gloriosa; Contratenor.* DES MOLINS: *De ce que fol pense.* PYCARD: *Gloria.* POWER: *Sanctus.* LEBERTOUL: *Las, que me demanderoye.* PYRAMOUR: *Quam pulchra es.* DUNSTABLE: *Speciosa facta es.* SOURSBY: *Sanctus.* LOQUEVILLE: *Je vous pri que j'aye un baysier.* ANON.: *Singularis laudis digna; De ce fol, pense. Lullay, lullay; There is no rose; Le gay playsir; Le grant pleyser; Agincourt carol.*
*** Hyp. Dig. CDA 66283; *KA 66283* [id.].

The subtitle of this collection is '*Music for the Knights of the Garter, 1340–1440*'; few readers will recognize many of the names in the list of composers above. But the music itself is fascinating and the performances bring it to life with extraordinary projection and vitality. The recording too is first class, and this imaginatively chosen programme deservedly won the 1988 *Gramophone* award for Early Music. Readers interested in trying medieval repertoire could hardly do better than to start here.

'A song for Francesca': ANDREAS DE FLORENTINA: *Astio non mori mai. Per la ver'onesta.* JOHANNES DE FLORENTINA: *Quando la stella.* LANDINI: *Ochi dolenti mie. Per seguir la speranca.* ANON.: *Quando i oselli canta; Constantia; Amor mi fa cantar a la Francesca; Non na el so amante.* DUFAY: *Quel fronte signorille in paradiso.* RICHARD DE LOQUEVILLE: *Puisquie je suy amoureux; Pour mesdisans ne pour leur faulx parler; Qui ne veroit que vos deulx yeulx.* HUGO DE LATINS: *Plaindre m'estuet.* HAUCOURT: *Je demande ma bienvenue.* GROSSIN: *Va t'ent souspir.* ANON.: *O regina seculi; Reparatrix Maria; Confort d'amours.*
*** Hyp. Dig. CDA 66286; *KA 66286* [id.].

No group is more persuasive in presenting medieval music than Gothic Voices under Christopher Page. The title, '*A Song for Francesca*', refers not only to the fourteenth-century French items here, but to the fact that the Italians too tended to be influenced by French style. More specifically, the collection is a well-deserved tribute to Francesca MacManus, selfless worker on behalf of many musicians, not least as manager of Gothic Voices. The variety of expression and mood in these songs, ballatas and madrigals is astonishing, some of them amazingly complex. The Hyperion recording is a model of its kind, presenting this long-neglected music most seductively in a warm but clear setting.

Great Singers

'Prima voce': Great singers 1909–38 (Tetrazzini; Caruso; Schumann-Heink; McCormack; Galli-Curci; Stracciari; Ponselle; Lauri-Volpi; Turner; Tibbett; Supervia; Gigli; Anderson; Schipa; Muzio; Tauber): Arias from: BELLINI: *La Sonnambula; I Puritani; Norma.* LEONCAVALLO: *Pagliacci.* MOZART: *Don Giovanni; Die Zauberflöte.* ROSSINI: *Il Barbiere di Siviglia.* PUCCINI: *Turandot.* VERDI: *Un ballo in maschera.* BIZET: *Carmen.* PUCCINI: *La Bohème.* SAINT-SAËNS: *Samson et Dalila.* MASCAGNI: *L'amico Fritz.* Song: REFICE: *Ombra di Nube.*
(M) (***) Nimbus mono NI 7801 [id.].

Those who have resisted the bottled or tinny sound of many historic recordings will find the Nimbus transfers more friendly and sympathetic, even if technically there is an inevitable loss of recorded information at both ends of the spectrum because of the absolute limitations of the possible frequency range on this kind of reproducer.

This compilation makes a good starting point, even if the method still does not provide the ideal answer. The Tetrazzini item with which the selection opens, *Ah non giunge* from Bellini's *La Sonnambula*, is one of the supreme demonstrations of coloratura on record, and the programme goes on to a magnificent Caruso of 1910 and an unforgettable performance of the coloratura drinking-song from Donizetti's *Lucrezia Borgia* by the most formidable of contraltos, Ernestine Schumann-Heink. Then follows John McCormack's famous account of *Il mio tesoro* from Mozart's *Don Giovanni*, with the central passage-work amazingly done in a single breath. Other vintage items include Galli-Curci's dazzling account of *Son vergin vezzosa* from Bellini's *I*

Puritani, Eva Turner in her incomparable 1928 account of Turandot's aria, Gigli amiably golden-toned in *Che gelida manina* from *La Bohème*, and a delectable performance of the *Cherry duet* from Mascagni's *L'amico Fritz* by Tito Schipa and Mafalda Favero, riches indeed!

Hendricks, Barbara (soprano), Dmitri Alexeev (piano)

Spirituals: *Deep river; Ev'ry time I feel the spirit; Fix me, Jesus; Git on boa'd little child'n; His name is so sweet; Hold on!; Joshua fit de battle of Jericho; Nobody knows de trouble I've seen; Oh what a beautiful city!; Plenty good room; Roun' about de mountain; Sometimes I feel like a motherless child; Swing low, sweet chariot; Talk about a child that do love Jesus; Were you there?; When I lay my burden down.*
*** EMI Dig. CDC7 47026-2 [id.].

So often spirituals can be made to seem too ingenuous, their deep reserve of feeling degraded into sentimentality. Not so here: Barbara Hendricks' vibrant identification with the words is thrilling, the jazz inflexions adding natural sophistication, yet not robbing the music of its directness of communication. Her lyrical singing is radiant, operatic in its eloquence of line, yet retaining the ecstasy of spirit, while the extrovert numbers – *Joshua fit de battle of Jericho* a superb example – are full of joy in their gutsy exuberance. Dmitri Alexeev accompanies superbly and the very well-balanced recording has remarkable presence.

Hilliard Ensemble, Paul Hillier

'The Singing Club': RAVENSCROFT: *A round of three country dances; There were three ravens.* HILTON: *Call George again, boys.* W. LAWES: *Drink to the knight of the moonshine bright; She weepeth sore in the night; Dainty, fine aniseed water; Gather ye rosebuds.* WILSON: *Where the bee sucks.* PURCELL: *'Tis woman makes us love; Sir Walter enjoying his damsel.* BATTISHILL: *Epitaph.* ARNE: *The singing club; To soften care; Elegy on the death of Mr Shenstone; Sigh no more, ladies.* BISHOP: *Foresters sound the cheerful horn.* J. S. SMITH: *The Ancreontick song.* PEARSALL: *There is a paradise on earth; O who will o'er the downs so free.* BARNBY: *Sweet and low.*
**(*) HM Dig HMC 901153 [id.].

The Hilliard Ensemble are particularly at home in the earlier songs here: their blending and intonation cannot be faulted and they show a nice feeling for the gentle melancholy of the period. They manage the more robust glees with panache, notably the *Wedding night song* of Inigo Jones, whose lyrics make a ribald pun on the writer's name, and Purcell's risqué narrative based on a true story of Sir Walter Raleigh's first conquest in the woods. Words are admirably clear throughout and the recording, made in London's Henry Wood Hall, gives a very real impression of the group standing back just behind the speakers. In some of the later nineteenth-century items the style, though not insensitive, is just a little pale.

'Summer is icumen in': ST GODRIC: *Sainte Marie viergene, Crist and Sainte Marie; Saint Nicholas.* Medieval anonymous English songs, including: *Summer is icumen in; Fuweles in the Frifth; Edi be thu; Worldes blisse; Gabriel fram heven-king; Mater ora filium; Gaude virgo mater Christi.* Motets; Mass: excerpts.
*** HM HMC 901154 [id.].

Sumer is icumen in is given twice, in Latin as well as in the Early English version, as is *Campanis cum cymbalis.* Even more valuable are the motets and movements from the Mass, among the earliest transcribed polyphonic works from this country, sung here with persuasive intensity. Paul Hillier gives a helpful, highly informed commentary in the booklet, which also provides full texts. Excellent, well-balanced recording.

'Draw on sweet night' (English madrigals): MORLEY: *O griefe even on the bud; When loe, by breake of morning; Aprill is in my mistris face; Sweet nimphe, come to thy lover; Miraculous love's wounding; Fyer and lightning in nets of goulden wyers.* WEELKES: *Thule, the period of cosmographie; O care thou wilt dispatch mee; Since Robin Hood; Strike it up tabor.* WILBYE: *Sweet hony sucking bees; Adew sweet Amarillis; Draw on sweet night.* J. BENNET: *Weepe O mine eyes.* GIBBONS: *The silver swanne.* TOMKINS: *See, see the shepherd's queene.* WARD: *Come sable night.* VAUTOR: *Sweet Suffolk owle.*
*** EMI Dig. CDC7 49197-2 [id.].

This is an entirely enchanting concert. As might be guessed from the spelling above, Tudor pronunciation is used, which seems to add extra bite to the vocal timbre. Perhaps at times the singing might be a shade more flamboyant, but it does not lack spontaneity, even when its style is a little lacking in geniality. Intonation and ensemble are flawless, and some of the songs are in five or six parts. The music itself is admirably chosen to cover a wide range of moods; perhaps the singers do not always reflect the lighter moments with enough sparkle; but there is so much here to ravish the ear that few will mind. The balance is slightly recessed in an attractive acoustic: the recording is very real and present.

Horne, Marilyn (mezzo-soprano)

'Beautiful dreamer' (The Great American Songbook, with ECO, Carl Davis): FOSTER: *Jeannie with the light brown hair; Beautiful dreamer; If you've only got a moustache; Camptown Races.* COPLAND: *5 Old American Songs.* TRAD.: *Sometimes I feel like a motherless child; I've just come from the fountain; Shenandoah,* etc.
*** Decca Dig. 417 242-2 [id.].

Marilyn Horne is tangily characterful in this American repertory which draws from her a glorious range of tone, and she bridges the stylistic gaps between popular and concert repertory with supreme confidence. The Copland songs are particularly delightful, and the Decca recording is outstandingly vivid.

Jenkins, Florence Foster (soprano)

'The glory of the human voice???' (with Cosme McMoon, piano; also (i) Jenny Williams (soprano); Thomas Burns (baritone)): MOZART: *Die Zauberflöte: Der Hölle Rache.* LIADOV: *Musical snuff box.* MCMOON: *Like a bird; Serenata Mexicano.* DELIBES: *Lakmé: Bell song.* DAVID: *La Perle du Brésil: Charmant oiseau.* BACH/PAVLOVICH: *Biassy.* J. STRAUSS: *Die Fledermaus: Mein Herr Marquiss.* (i) GOUNOD: *A Faust travesty: Valentine's aria; Jewel song; Faust's cavatina: Emotion's strange; Final trio: My heart is overcome* (all in English).
(M) (***) BMG/RCA GD 61175; *GK 61175* [61175-2-RG].

Glory? Well, not quite. The phenomenon of Madame Florence Foster Jenkins in New York was a wonder for many years, and the accompanying note of this compendium reissue of her recorded oeuvre describes how it all worked. Once and for all she did not die of a broken heart after her last Carnegie Hall concert, if only because her box-office receipts were so substantial. What was never ascertained is whether she took herself entirely seriously, but it seems rather likely that she did. Certainly her performances of the staccato upper tessitura of the Queen of the Night's aria from *Die Zauberflöte* or Liadov's *Musical snuff-box* has a special kind of accuracy that would be very difficult to imitate. Getting the other example of vocal glory included here involved keen initiative on the part of RCA officials who spotted the talent of Jenny Williams and Thomas Burns when they paid to make their own record of selections from *Faust.* They were reluctant to reveal their achievement to the world, but their royalties, too, must in the end have convinced them that they should not hide their lights under a bushel. A unique, joyful record, an encouragement to us all, however awful our voices.

Jurinac, Sena (soprano)

R. STRAUSS: *Four Last songs (Vier letzte Lieder).* Opera arias from: MOZART: *Così fan tutte; Idomeneo.* SMETANA: *The Bartered bride; The Kiss.* TCHAIKOVSKY: *Joan of Arc; Queen of Spades.*
(M) (***) EMI mono CDH7 63199-2.

This EMI Références issue, very well transferred, celebrates a magical, under-recorded singer. It brings together all of Jurinac's recordings for EMI outside the complete operas, and adds a live radio recording from Sweden – with Fritz Busch conducting the Stockholm Philharmonic Orchestra – of Strauss's *Four Last songs*, most beautifully done, if with rather generalized expression. Busch was also the conductor for the Glyndebourne recordings of excerpts from *Così fan tutte* and *Idomeneo.*

Kanawa, Dame Kiri Te (soprano)

'Come to the fair' (with Medici Qt; Nat. PO, Gamley): EASTHOPE MARTIN: *Come to the fair.* LAMBERT: *She is far from the land.* TRAD.: *Early one morning; The last rose of summer; Island spinning song; The ash grove; The Keel Row; Comin' thro' the rye; Annie Laurie; O can ye sew cushions; The Salley gardens; Greensleeves; The gentle maiden; I have a bonnet trimmed with blue; Danny Boy.*
*** EMI Dig. CDC7 47080-2 [id.].

Following very much in the Kathleen Ferrier tradition, Dame Kiri Te Kanawa sings this repertoire with infectious charm. She can be exhilaratingly robust, as in the title-piece and *The Keel Row*, yet at the next moment provide a ravishing lyricism, as in *The last rose of summer* or *The Salley gardens*. The orchestral accompaniments are decorative but simple (*Greensleeves*, a highlight, is especially felicitous). The recording has splendid presence. A captivating recital in every way.

'Portrait': Arias from: PUCCINI: *Tosca; Gianni Schicchi* VERDI: *La Traviata.* HUMPERDINCK: *Hänsel und Gretel.* MOZART: *Don Giovanni.* R. STRAUSS: *Morgen; Ruhe, meine Seele.* SCHUBERT: *Gretchen am Spinnrade.* SCHUMANN: *Du bist wie eine Blume.* FAURÉ: *Après un rêve.* WALTON: *Façade: Old Sir Faulk; Daphne; Through gilded trellises.*
**(*) Sony MK 39208 [id.].

CBS's sampler portrait of Dame Kiri may not be as representative of her usual repertory as the rival Decca disc (417 645-2), but the rarities – such as the Walton songs – are just as winning as the more predictable items. Recordings are not all of the most vivid, but made reasonably compatible.

'Ave Maria' (with St Paul's Cathedral Choir, ECO, Rose): GOUNOD: *Messe solennelle à Sainte Cécile: Sanctus. O divine Redeemer.* MOZART: *Ave verum, K. 618; Solemn Vespers: Laudate Dominum.* FRANCK: *Panis angelicus.* HANDEL: *Solomon: Let the bright Seraphim; Let their celestial concert.* MENDELSSOHN: *On wings of song.* BACH: *Jesu, joy of man's desiring.* SCHUBERT: *Ave Maria.*
**(*) Ph. Dig. 412 629-2; *412 629-4* [id.].

Countless music-lovers who heard Dame Kiri sing *Let the bright Seraphim* at the wedding of the Prince and Princess of Wales will be pleased to have this record available, and they will not be disappointed, for the trumpet playing, too, is suitably resplendent. This comes at the end, and the rest of the programme lacks something in variety, although the voice always sounds beautiful and the naturally expressive singing gives much pleasure. The chorus, backwardly balanced, might have been more clearly focused.

'Kiri – A Portrait': CANTELOUBE: *Chants d'Auvergne: Baïlèro.* GAY: *Beggar's opera: Virgins are like the fair flow'r; Cease your funning.* HANDEL: *Messiah: Rejoice greatly; I know that my Redeemer liveth.* BRAHMS: *German Requiem: Ihr habt nun Traurigkeit.* MOZART: *Concert aria: Vado, ma dove? oh Dei!, K.583. Le nozze di Figaro: Dove sono.* BIZET: *Je dis que rien ne m'épouvante.* PUCCINI: *Tosca: Vissi d'arte.* VILLA-LOBOS: *Bachianas brasileiras No. 5.*
*** Decca 417 645-2; *417 645-4* [id.].

Decca's portrait of Dame Kiri gathers together many of her most delectable recordings of recent years, a winning compendium of her art, whether seductive in Canteloube and Villa-Lobos, dazzling in Handel, or sparkling in *The Beggar's opera*. The recordings capture the voice at its fullest and most golden.

King's College, Cambridge, Choir, Cleobury

ALLEGRI: *Miserere mei, Deus.* FRESCOBALDI: *Messa sopra l'aria della Monica.* MARENZIO: *Magnificat.* NANINO: *Adoramus te, Christe.* UGOLINI: *Beata es Virgo Maria.*
**(*) EMI CDC7 47065-2 [id.].

An attractively planned concert of Renaissance choral music. Marenzio's fine *Magnificat* and the stirring *Beata es Virgo Maria* of Ugolini (a contemporary of Allegri) make a strong impression – the latter reminding the listener of Andrea Gabrieli. The performances are generally excellent and the King's acoustic provides its usual beautiful aura. The account of

Allegri's *Miserere*, although effective, lacks the ethereal memorability of the finest versions; its treble soloist, Timothy Beasley-Murray, is made to sound almost over-confident, with his upward leap commandingly extrovert. The CD gains much from the background silence, but the choral focus is mistier than one might have expected.

King's College, Cambridge, Choir, Philip Ledger

'Festival of lessons and carols' (1979) includes: TRAD.: *Once in Royal David's city; Sussex carol; Joseph and Mary; A maiden most gentle; Chester carol; Angels, from the realms of glory.* HANDEL: *Resonet in laudibus.* ORD: *Adam lay ybounden.* GRÜBER: *Stille Nacht.* MATHIAS: *A babe is born.* WADE: *O come all ye faithful.* MENDELSSOHN: *Hark! the herald angels sing.*
(M) *** EMI CDM7 63180-2 [id.]; *EG 763180-4.*

This most recent version on record of the annual King's College ceremony has the benefit of modern recording, even more atmospheric than before. Under Philip Ledger the famous choir keeps its beauty of tone and incisive attack. The opening processional, *Once in Royal David's city*, is even more effective heard against the background quiet of CD, and this remains a unique blend of liturgy and music.

'Procession with carols on Advent Sunday' includes: PALESTRINA (arr. from): *I look from afar; Judah and Jerusalem, fear not.* PRAETORIUS: *Come, thou Redeemer of the earth.* TRAD.: *O come, o come, Emmanuel!; Up, awake and away!; 'Twas in the year; Cherry tree carol; King Jesus hath a garden; On Jordan's bank the Baptist's cry; Gabriel's message; I wonder as I wander; My dancing day; Lo! he comes with clouds descending.* BYRT: *All and some.* P. NICOLAI, arr. BACH: *Wake, o wake! with tidings thrilling.* BACH: *Nun komm' der Heiden Heiland.*
(M) *** EMI CDM7 63181-2 [id.]; *EG 763181-4.*

This makes an attractive variant to the specifically Christmas-based service, though the carols themselves are not quite so memorable. Beautiful singing and richly atmospheric recording; the wide dynamic range is demonstrated equally effectively by the atmospheric opening and processional and the sumptuous closing hymn.

King's College, Cambridge, Choir, Sir David Willcocks

'Carols from King's': TRAD., arr. WILLCOCKS: *On Christmas night; Tomorrow shall be my dancing day; Cherry tree carol; The Lord at first; A Child is born in Bethlehem; While shepherds watched.* TRAD., arr. VAUGHAN WILLIAMS: *And all in the morning.* CORNELIUS: *Three Kings.* EBERLING: *All my heart this night rejoices.* GRÜBER: *Silent night* (arr. Willcocks). Trad. Italian, arr. WOOD: *Hail, blessed Mary.* TRAD., arr. SULLIVAN: *It came upon the midnight clear.* Trad. French, arr. WILLCOCKS: *Ding dong! merrily.* Trad. Basque, arr. PETTMAN: *I saw a maiden.* DARKE: *In the bleak midwinter.* Trad. German: *Mary walked through a wood of thorn.* BAINTON: *A Babe is born I wys.* PRAETORIUS: *Psallite unigenito.*
(B) *** CfP CD-CFP 4586; *TC-CFP 4586* [CDB 67356].

This recital was planned and recorded as a whole in 1969. The programme has an attractive lyrical flavour, with plenty of delightful, unfamiliar carols to add spice to favourites like *Tomorrow shall be my dancing day* and *In the bleak midwinter*, which sound memorably fresh. The arrangements are for the most part straightforward, with added imaginative touches to charm the ear, like the decorative organ 'descant' which embroiders *Ding dong! merrily on high.* The King's intimacy gives much pleasure here, yet the disc ends with a fine, robust version of *While shepherds watched.* Most rewarding and a real bargain.

'Christmas music from King's' (with Andrew Davis, organ, D. Whittaker, flute, Christopher van Kampen, cello, & Robert Spencer, lute): SWEELINCK: *Hodie Christus natus est.* PALESTRINA: *Hodie Christus natus est.* VICTORIA: *O magnum mysterium; Senex puerum portabat.* BYRD: *Senex puerum portabat; Hodie beata virgo.* GIBBONS: *Hosanna to the Son of David.* WEELKES: *Hosanna to the Son of David; Gloria in excelsis Deo.* ECCARD: *When to the temple Mary went.* MACONCHY: *Nowell! Nowell!* arr. BRITTEN: *The holly and the ivy.* PHILIP (The Chancellor): *Angelus ad virginem.* arr. POSTON: *Angelus ad virginem; My dancing day.* POSTON: *Jesus Christ the apple tree.* BERKELEY: *I sing of a maiden.* TAYLOR: *Watts's cradle song.* CAMPION: *Sing a song of joy.* PEERSON: *Most glorious Lord of life.* Imogen HOLST: *That Lord that lay in Assë stall.* WARLOCK: *Where riches is everlastingly.*

(M) **(*) EMI CDM7 64130-2 [id.]; *EG 764130-4.*

A happily chosen survey of music (63 minutes) inspired by the Nativity from the fifteenth century to the present day. As might be expected, the King's choir confidently encompasses the wide variety of styles from the spiritual serenity of the music of Victoria to the attractive arrangements of traditional carols by modern composers, in which an instrumental accompaniment is added. These items are quite delightful and they are beautifully recorded (in 1965). The motets, from a year earlier, were among the first recording sessions made by the EMI engineers in King's College Chapel, and at the time they had not solved all the problems associated with the long reverberation period, so the focus is less than sharp. Even so, this group demonstrates the unique virtuosity of the Cambridge choir, exploiting its subtlety of tone and flexibility of phrase.

'The world of King's': HANDEL: *Coronation anthem: Zadok the Priest* (with ECO). ALLEGRI: *Miserere.* PALESTRINA: *Hodie Beata Virgo.* TALLIS: *Sancte Deus.* VIVALDI: *Gloria in D, RV 589: Gloria; Et in terra pax* (with ASMF). BYRD: *Ave verum corpus.* CROFT: *Burial service.* GIBBONS: *This is the record of John* (with Jacobean Consort of Viols). BACH: *O Jesu so meek.* HANDEL: *Chandos anthem No. 9: O Praise the Lord with one consent* (with ASMF).
(B) *** Decca 430 092-2; *430 092-4.*

A fine demonstration of the creative excellence of Sir David Willcocks's regime at King's, recorded for Argo between 1958 and 1966 and including the famous performance of Allegri's *Miserere* with the ethereal treble solo of the young Roy Goodman, now better known – nearly thirty years later – for his music-making with the Hanover Band. The soaring lines of Tallis and the serenity of Byrd are to be heard alongside the most famous of Gibbons's verse-anthems (with accompanying viols) and William Croft's nobly austere *Funeral service* (given complete). The excellence of the sound throughout, bright and fresh, with the King's acoustics always an atmospheric asset, is a tribute to the original Argo engineering.

King's College, Cambridge, Choir, Willcocks or Philip Ledger

'Christmas carols from King's College': GAUNTLETT: *Once in Royal David's city.* TRAD., arr. VAUGHAN WILLIAMS: *O little town of Bethlehem.* TRAD., arr. STAINER: *The first nowell.* TRAD., arr. LEDGER: *I saw three ships.* TRAD. German, arr. HOLST: *Personent hodie.* TERRY: *Myn Lyking.* HOWELLS: *A spotless rose.* KIRKPATRICK: *Away in a manger.* HADLEY: *I sing of a maiden.* TRAD. French, arr. WILLCOCKS: *O come, o come Emmanuel.* TRAD. arr. WILLCOCKS: *While shepherds watched; On Christmas night.* arr. WOODWARD: *Up! Good Christian folk and listen.* DARKE: *In the bleak midwinter.* GRÜBER: *Silent night.* TRAD. arr. WALFORD DAVIES: *The holly and the ivy.* TRAD., arr. SULLIVAN: *It came upon the midnight clear.* CORNELIUS: *Three kings.* SCHEIDT: *A Child is born in Bethlehem.* TRAD. German, arr. PEARSALL: *In dulci jubilo.* WADE: *O come, all ye faithful.* MENDELSSOHN: *Hark! the herald angels sing.*
(M) *** EMI CDM7 63179-2 [id.]; *EG 763179-4.*

With 71 minutes of music and 22 carols included, this collection, covering the regimes of both Sir David Willcocks and Philip Ledger, could hardly be bettered as a representative sampler of the King's tradition. Opening with the famous processional of *Once in Royal David's city*, to which Willcocks contributes a descant (as he also does in *While shepherds watched*), the programme is wide-ranging in its historical sources, from the fourteenth century to the present day, while the arrangements feature many famous musicians. The recordings were made between 1969 and 1976, and the CD transfers are first class. The two closing carols, featuring the Philip Jones Brass Ensemble, are made particularly resplendent.

Kirkby, Emma (soprano), Consort of Musicke, Rooley

'Madrigals and wedding songs for Diana' (with David Thomas, bass): BENNET: *All creatures now are merry-minded.* CAMPION: *Now hath Flora robbed her bowers; Move now measured sound; Woo her and win her.* LUPO: *Shows and nightly revels; Time that leads the fatal round.* GILES: *Triumph now with joy and mirth.* CAVENDISH: *Come, gentle swains.* DOWLAND: *Welcome, black night . . . Cease these false sports.* WEELKES: *Hark! all ye lovely saints; As Vesta was.* WILBYE: *Lady Oriana.* EAST: *Hence stars! too dim of light; You meaner beauties.* LANIER: *Bring*

away this sacred tree; The Marigold; Mark how the blushful morn. COPERARIO: *Go, happy man; While dancing rests; Come ashore, merry mates.* E. GIBBONS: *Long live fair Oriana.*
*** Hyp. CDA 66019 [id.].

This wholly delightful anthology celebrates early royal occasions, aristocratic weddings, and in its choice of Elizabethan madrigals skilfully balances praise of the Virgin Queen with a less ambivalent attitude to nuptial delights. Emma Kirkby is at her freshest and most captivating, and David Thomas, if not quite her match, makes an admirable contribution. Accompaniments are stylish and well balanced, and the recording is altogether first rate.

Lehmann, Lotte (soprano)

Song recital: CIMARA: *Canto di primavera.* SADERO: *Fà la nana.* GOUNOD: *Vierge d'Athènes.* PALADILHE: *Psyché.* DUPARC: *La vie antérieure.* HAHN: *Infidélité; L'enamourée; D'une prison.* GRECHANINOV: *My native land (Heimat).* WORTH: *Midsummer.* SJÖBERG: *Visions (Tonerna).* TRAD.: *Drink to me only; Schlafe, mein süsses Kind.* BALOCH: *Do not chide me.* WOLF: *Nun lass uns Frieden schliessen; Und willst du deinen Liebsten sterben sehen?; Der Knabe und das Immlein.* R. STRAUSS: *Wozu noch, Mädchen; Du meines Herzens Krönelein.* BRAHMS: *Das Mädchen spricht; Mein Mädel hat einen Rosenmund.* SCHUMANN: *Waldesgespräch; Du bist wie eine Blume; Frühlingsnacht.* SCHUBERT: *Im Abendrot; Der Jüngling an der Quelle; An die Nachtigall; Nacht und Träume; An Die Musik.*
(M) (**(*)) BMG/RCA mono GD 87809 [7809-2-RG].

Bringing together Lehmann's 78-r.p.m. recordings, made for RCA between 1935 and 1947, this is a fascinating, often unexpected collection, with Italian, French and English songs as well as German Lieder. The transfers bring the singer vividly face to face with the listener, but this is not as full a portrait as the Références collection of her singing opera arias, recorded in the 1920s and early '30s (see above).

London Symphony Chorus and Orchestra, Richard Hickox

Opera choruses: BIZET: *Carmen: Toreador chorus.* VERDI: *Il Trovatore: Anvil chorus. Nabucco: Gli arredi festivi; Va pensiero. Macbeth: Che faceste?. Aida: Grand march.* GOUNOD: *Faust: Soldiers' chorus.* BORODIN: *Prince Igor: Polovtsian dances.*
(B) *** Pickwick Dig. PCD 908; *CIMPC 908.*

The opening *Toreador chorus* from *Carmen* is zestfully infectious and the *Soldiers' chorus* from *Faust* is equally buoyant. The noble line of Verdi's *Va pensiero* is shaped beautifully by Hickox, with the balance between voices and orchestra particularly good. In *Gli arredi festivi* from *Nabucco* and the famous Triumphal scene from *Aida* the orchestral brass sound resonantly sonorous, even if the fanfare trumpets could have been more widely separated in the latter piece. The concert ends with Borodin's *Polovtsian dances* most excitingly done. The digital recording, made at the EMI Abbey Road studio, has the atmosphere of an idealized opera house, and the result is in the demonstration bracket, with a projection and presence fully worthy of this polished but uninhibited singing.

Lott, Felicity (soprano), Graham Johnson (piano)

Mélodies on Victor Hugo poems: GOUNOD: *Sérénade.* BIZET: *Feuilles d'album: Guitare. Adieux de l'hôtesse arabe.* LALO: *Guitare.* DELIBES: *Eclogue.* FRANCK: *S'il est un charmant gazon.* FAURÉ: *L'absent; Le papillon et la fleur; Puisqu'ici bas.* WAGNER: *L'attente.* LISZT: *O quand je dors; Comment, disaint-ils.* SAINT-SAËNS: *Soirée en mer; La fiancée du timbalier.* M. V. WHITE: *Chantez, chantez jeune inspirée.* HAHN: *Si mes vers avaient des ailes; Rêverie.*
(B) *** HM HMA 901138 [id.].

Felicity Lott's collection of Hugo settings relies mainly on sweet and charming songs, freshly and unsentimentally done, with Graham Johnson an ideally sympathetic accompanist. The recital is then given welcome stiffening with fine songs by Wagner and Liszt, as well as two by Saint-Saëns that have a bite worthy of Berlioz. It makes a headily enjoyable cocktail. Now reissued in the Musique d'Abord series, this is a bargain not to be missed.

Luca, Giuseppe de (baritone)

'Prima voce': Arias from: VERDI: *Don Carlos, Ernani, Il Trovatore, La Traviata, Rigoletto.* ROSSINI: *Il Barbiere di Siviglia.* DONIZETTI: *L'elisir d'amore.* BELLINI: *I Puritani.* DIAZ: *Benvenuto Cellini.* PUCCINI: *La Bohème.* PONCHIELLI: *La Gioconda.* WOLF-FERRARI: *I gioielli della madonna.* Songs: DE LEVA: *Pastorale.* ROMILLI: *Marietta.*
(M) (***) Nimbus mono NI 7815 [id.].

There has never been a more involving account on record of the Act IV Marcello–Rodolfo duet than the one here with de Luca and Gigli, a model of characterization and vocal art. The baritone's mastery emerges vividly in item after item, whether in the power and wit of his pre-electric version of *Largo al factotum* (1917) or the five superb items (including the *Bohème* duet and the *Rigoletto* numbers, flawlessly controlled) which were recorded in the vintage year of 1927. Warm Nimbus transfers.

McCormack, John (tenor)

'The art of John McCormack' (with Gerald Moore; O, cond. Walter Goehr; Fritz Kreisler): MARTINI: *Plaisir d'amour.* HANDEL: *Semele: Where'er you walk. Il pastor fido: Caro amor. Atalanta: Come, my beloved.* MOZART: *Oh what bitter grief is mine; Ridente la calma.* SCHUBERT: *Who is Sylvia?.* BRAHMS: *Die Mainacht; Feldeinsamkeit.* R. STRAUSS: *Allerseelen; Morgen; Du meines Herzen Krönelein.* WOLF: *Auch kleine Dinge; Herr was trägt der Boden hier; Schlafendes Jesuskind; Wo find ich Trost; Anakreons Grab.* RACHMANINOV: *Before my window; How fair this spot; To the children.* FRANCK: *La procession.* FAURÉ: *L'Automne.* DONAUDY: *O del mio amato ben; Luoghi sereni.* ELGAR: *Is she not passing fair?.* QUILTER: *Now sleeps the crimson petal.*
(M) (***) EMI mono CDH7 63306-2.

Even though it opens – winningly – with Martini's *Plaisir d'amour*, this McCormack anthology centres on his classical 78-r.p.m. discs, from finely spun Handelian lyricism through German Lieder and songs by Rachmaninov (with Fritz Kreisler ready at hand to provide violin obbligatos) to French mélodie and songs of Elgar and Quilter. His French pronunciation was hardly colloquial, nor was he ever entirely at home in German, yet his contributions to the Wolf Society recordings celebrated a unique feeling for this composer, readily shown here. Overall, the recordings span a long time-period and include a batch of pre-electrics from 1924. But transfers are exemplary. Desmond Shaw Taylor's notes are indispensable too.

Popular songs and Irish ballads. TRAD.: *The garden where the praties grow; Terence's farewell to Kathleen; Believe me if all those endearing young charms; The star of the County Down; Oft in the stilly night; The meeting of the waters; The Bard of Armagh; Down by the Salley Gardens; She moved thro' the fair; The green bushes.* BALFE: *The harp that once through Tara's halls.* ROECKEL: *The green isle of Erin.* SCHNEIDER: *O Mary dear.* LAMBERT: *She is far from the land.* HAYNES: *Off to Philadelphia.* MOLLOY: *The Kerry dance; Bantry Bay.* MARSHALL: *I hear you calling me.* E. PURCELL: *Passing by.* WOODFORD-FINDEN: *Kashmiri song.* CLUTSAM: *I know of two bright eyes.* FOSTER: *Jeannie with the light brown hair; Sweetly she sleeps, my Alice fair.*
(M) (***) EMI mono CDH7 69788-2.

In Irish repertoire like *The star of the County Down* McCormack is irresistible, but in lighter concert songs he could also spin the utmost magic. *Down by the Salley Gardens* and Stephen Foster's *Jeannie with the light brown hair* are superb examples, while in a ballad like *I hear you calling me* (an early pre-electric recording from 1908) the golden bloom of the vocal timbre combining with an artless line brings a ravishing frisson on the closing pianissimo. Many of the accompaniments are by Gerald Moore, who proves a splendid partner. Occasionally there is a hint of unsteadiness in the sustained *piano* tone, but otherwise no apology need be made for the recorded sound which is first class, while the lack of 78-r.p.m. background noise is remarkable.

'Prima voce': Arias and excerpts from: DONIZETTI: *Lucia di Lammermoor; L'elisir d'amore; La figlia del reggimento.* VERDI: *La Traviata; Rigoletto.* PUCCINI: *La Bohème.* BIZET. *Carmen; I pescatore di perle.* DELIBES: *Lakmé.* GOUNOD: *Faust.* PONCHIELLI: *La gioconda.* BOITO: *Mefistofele.* MASSENET: *Manon.* MOZART: *Don Giovanni.* WAGNER: *Die Meistersinger.* HERBERT: *Natomah.* HANDEL: *Semele; Atalanta.*

(M) (***) Nimbus mono NI 7820 [id.].

With the operas represented ranging from Handel's *Atalanta* and *Semele* to *Natomah*, by Victor Herbert, the heady beauty of McCormack's voice, his ease of production and perfect control are amply illustrated in these 21 items. His now legendary 1916 account of *Il mio tesoro* from *Don Giovanni*, with its astonishing breath control, is an essential item; but there are many others less celebrated which help to explain his special niche, even in a generation that included Caruso and Schipa. Characteristic Nimbus transfers.

Martinelli, Giovanni (tenor)

'Prima voce': Arias from: GIORDANO: *Andrea Chénier; Fedora.* LEONCAVALLO: *Pagliacci.* MASCAGNI: *Cavalleria Rusticana; Iris.* TCHAIKOVSKY: *Eugene Onegin.* VERDI: *Aida; Ernani; La forza del destino; La Traviata.*
(M) (***) Nimbus mono NI 7804 [id.].

This collection of 17 fine examples of Martinelli's very distinctive and characterful singing covers his vintage period from 1915 to 1928, with one 1927 recording from Verdi's *La forza del destino* so clear that you can hear a dog barking outside the studio. The other two items from *Forza* are just as memorable, with Martinelli joined by Giuseppe de Luca in the Act IV duet, and by Rosa Ponselle and the bass, Ezio Pinza, for the final duet, with the voices astonishingly vivid and immediate.

Melchior, Lauritz (tenor)

'Prima voce': Arias from: WAGNER: *Siegfried; Tannhäuser; Tristan und Isolde; Die Walküre; Die Meistersinger; Götterdämmerung.* LEONCAVALLO: *Pagliacci.* MEYERBEER: *L'Africana.* VERDI: *Otello.*
(M) (***) Nimbus mono NI 7816 [id.].

The Nimbus disc of Melchior, issued to celebrate his centenary in 1990, demonstrates above all the total consistency of the voice between the pre-electric recordings of *Siegfried* and *Tannhäuser*, made for Polydor in 1924, and the *Meistersinger* and *Götterdämmerung* extracts, recorded in 1939. Of those, the Siegfried–Brünnhilde duet from the *Prologue* of *Götterdämmerung* is particularly valuable. It is fascinating too to hear the four recordings that Melchior made with Barbirolli and the LSO in 1930–31: arias by Verdi, Leoncavallo and Meyerbeer translated into German. As a character, Otello is made to sound far more prickly. Characteristic Nimbus transfers.

Monteverdi Choir, English Baroque Soloists, Gardiner

'Sacred choral music': D. SCARLATTI: *Stabat Mater.* CAVALLI: *Salve regina.* GESUALDO: *Ave, dulcissima Maria.* CLÉMENT: *O Maria vernana rosa.*
*** Erato/Warner Dig. 2292 45219-2 [id.].

This collection is centred round Domenico Scarlatti's *Stabat Mater*, which is praised in the Composer section. The shorter works which fill out this collection are no less worthwhile, notably the rewarding Gesualdo motet from the *Sacrae cantiones*, whose remarkably expressive opening has few precedents in its harmonic eloquence, and another Marian motet by Jacques Clément, better known as Clemens non Papa. The recording is very good indeed without being in the demonstration bracket.

Musica Reservata, John Beckett

'Music at the time of Christopher Columbus' by DE CABEZON; JUAN FERNANDES DE MADRID; DEL ENCINA; MUDARRA; DE LA TORRE; DE CEBALLOS; GARÇIMUÑOZ; MILLAN; ANON.
(M) ** Ph. 432 821-2 [id.].

Aptly reissued to celebrate the quincentennial celebrations, this 1968 collection will not appeal to all tastes. The Musica Reservata under John Beckett resist the delicacy of nuance and preciosity of much madrigal singing, drawing their analogy (with less than scrupulous logic) from the kind of vocal production one encounters in folk singing. Unfortunately, they push this to an extreme that is not always comfortable here: too much rough tone and absence of phrasing and these singers would have been banished (quite properly) to the local hostelry rather than tolerated at court. The repertoire is exploratory, and many of these pieces are well worth getting to know, but the wilful cultivation of coarse tone becomes wearing and the concert, which is very well recorded, must be approached with considerable caution.

Muzio, Claudia (soprano)

'Prima voce': Arias from: MASCAGNI: *Cavalleria Rusticana.* VERDI: *La forza del destino; Otello; Il Trovatore; La Traviata.* PUCCINI: *Tosca; La Bohème.* GIORDANO: *Andrea Chénier.* BOITO: *Mefistofele.* CILEA: *Adriana Lecouvreur; L'Arlesiana.* BELLINI: *La Sonnambula.* Songs by BUZZI-PECCIA; PERGOLESI; REGER; DELIBES; REFICE.
(M) (***) Nimbus mono NI 7814 [id.].

This Nimbus collection of recordings by the sadly short-lived Claudia Muzio duplicates much that is contained on the EMI Références CD of her. The main addition here is the Act III duet from *Otello* with Francesco Merli, but some cherishable items are omitted. The Nimbus acoustic transfer process sets the voice more distantly as well as more reverberantly than the EMI, with its distinctive tang less sharply conveyed.

New College, Oxford, Choir, Higginbottom

'Carols from New College': O come all ye faithful; The angel Gabriel; Ding dong merrily on high; The holly and the ivy; I wonder as I wander; Sussex carol; This is the truth; A Virgin most pure; Rocking carol; Once in Royal David's city. ORD: *Adam lay y-bounden.* BENNETT: *Out of your sleep.* HOWELLS: *A spotless rose; Here is the litle door.* DARKE: *In the bleak midwinter.* MATHIAS: *A babe is born; Wassail carol.* WISHART: *Alleluya, a new work is come on hand.* LEIGHTON: *Lully, lulla, thou little tiny child.* JOUBERT: *There is no rose of such virtue.*
*** CRD CRD 3443; *CRDC 4443* [id.].

A beautiful Christmas record, the mood essentially serene and reflective. Apart from the lovely traditional arrangements, from the Czech *Rocking carol* to the Appalachian *I wonder as I wander*, many of the highlights are more recently composed. Both the Mathias settings are memorable and spark a lively response from the choir; Howells' *Here is the little door* is matched by Wishart's *Alleluya* and Kenneth Leighton's *Lully, lulla, thou little tiny child* in memorability. In some of these and in the opening *O come all ye faithful* and the closing *Once in Royal David's city*, Howard Moody adds weight with excellent organ accompaniments, but fifteen of the twenty-one items here are sung unaccompanied, to maximum effect. The recording acoustic seems ideal and the balance is first class. The documentation, however, consists of just a list of titles and sources – and the CD (using the unedited artwork from the LP) lists them as being divided on to side one and side two!

'O Sing unto the Lord' (with Instrumental Ens. led by Roy Goodman): VAUGHAN WILLIAMS: *O Clap your hands* (motet). STANFORD: *Magnificat and Nunc dimittis in G.* TAVERNER: *Mater Christi* (motet). PURCELL: *O Sing unto the Lord* (Verse anthem). BAINTON: *And I saw a new heaven.* BRITTEN: *Missa brevis.* MONTEVERDI: *Beatus vir.* HARVEY: *I love the Lord.*
❀ *** Proudsound PROUCD 114 02; *PROU 114* [id.].

It is difficult to conceive of a better or more rewarding collection of (mainly British) church music than this, marvellously sung by this fine choir of 16 trebles and 12 men. The recording, made in New College Chapel, is ideally balanced, very real indeed, and offers the most beautiful choral textures, used over the widest range of dynamic. The programme opens quite spectacularly with Vaughan Williams's brief but ambitious setting of Psalm 47 for double chorus, brass, percussion and organ (a demonstration item if ever there was one) and continues with Stanford's inspired *Magnificat and Nunc dimittis in G*, with a memorable treble solo in the former from Daniel Johnson, and with Michael Morton (bass) almost equally impressive in the latter. Then the programme ranges from Taverner's fine motet, *Mater Christi*, written some 400 years earlier, to Harvey's rich modern setting of Psalm 16, with its satisfyingly pungent dissonances. In between come one of Purcell's finest verse-anthems (with a convincing authentic accompaniment led by Roy Goodman), Bainton's glorious *And I saw a new heaven*, Britten's

Missa brevis (which anyone who enjoys the *Ceremony of carols* will equally relish) and Monteverdi's madrigal-styled *Beatus vir* with its florid polyphony dramatically broadening at the end for the closing *Amen*.

New London Consort, Philip Pickett

'The Pilgrimage to Santiago' (21 cantigas from the collection of King Alfonso el Sabio).
*** O-L Dig. 433 148-2 (2) [id.].

This two-disc set offers one of the most exciting collections of medieval music ever recorded. Philip Pickett and his brilliant team of singers and players present what is described as 'a musical journey along the medieval pilgrim road to the shrine of St James at Santiago de Compostela'. The 21 pieces, lasting over two hours, together provide a mosaic of astonishing richness and vigour, directly related to the four main pilgrim routes to the shrine, via Navarre, Castille, Leon and Galicia. Though each item has a direct religious inspiration, this is secular music with an earthy vigour and rhythmic complexity that in many of the pieces with their catchy syncopations relates directly to Spanish dance or 20th century pop music. Scholarly as the approach is, the results are anything but esoteric or pale. Pickett argues the importance of the Islamic influence in Spain, with bells and percussion often added to the fiddles, lutes, tabors and other early instruments. So the long opening cantiga, *Quen a virgen ben servira*, begins with an instrumental introduction, where (echoing Islamic examples) the players attract attention with tuning-up and flourishes, before the singing begins. The main cantiga then punctuates the 12 narrative stanzas sung by the solo soprano with a catchy refrain, *Those who serve the virgin well will go to paradise*. The principal cantigas have been recorded before, but never previously with their full complement of verses, hypnotic in their repetitions. The texts are mostly Galician, though Latin is used too, with the simpler songs often sounding like carols. Standing out among the singers is the soprano, Catherine Bott, the soloist in most of the big cantigas, warm as well as pure-toned, negotiating the weird sliding portamentos that, following Islamic examples, decorate some of the vocal lines. Vivid sound, though the stereo spread of the chorus is limited.

Norman, Jessye (soprano)

'Sacred songs' (with Amb. S., RPO, Gibson): GOUNOD: *Messe solennelle à Sainte Cécile: Sanctus. O Divine Redeemer.* FRANCK: *Panis angelicus.* ADA: *The Holy City.* ANON.: *Amazing grace. Greensleeves. Let us break bread. I wonder.* MAGGIMSEY: *Sweet little Jesus Boy.* YON: *Gesù Bambino.*
*** Ph. Dig. 400 019-2 [id.].

Miss Norman's restraint is very telling here; she sings with great eloquence, but her simplicity and sincerity shine through repertoire that can easily sound sentimental. The Gounod *Sanctus* is especially fine, but the simpler traditional songs are also very affecting. The compact disc is very much in the demonstration class, strikingly natural and giving the soloist remarkable presence, especially when she is singing unaccompanied.

'Live' (with Geoffrey Parsons, piano): HAYDN: *Arianna a Naxos.* HANDEL: *Rinaldo: Lascia ch'io pianga. Dank sei dir Herr.* MAHLER: *Des Knaben Wunderhorn: Wer hat dies Liedlein erdacht? Das irdische Leben; Rheinlegendchen. Scheiden und Meiden.* BERG: *Liebe; Mignon; Die Nachtigall; Schliesse mir die Augen beid* (2 versions). R. STRAUSS: *Ich trage meine Minne; Seitdem dein Aug'; Kling!; Wir beide wollen springen.* RAVEL: *Étude en forme de habañera.* Spirituals: *Great day; He's got the whole world in his hands.*
*** Ph. Dig. 422 235-2 [id.].

Recorded live at various venues during Jessye Norman's appearances in eleven different cities on her European tour in 1987, this recital record follows up her earlier one from Hohenems (422 048-2), even sharing the same Baroque works and spirituals, though in different performances. Here more than in Hohenems the applause tends to be intrusive, but the glory of the unique voice is more compelling than ever. As before, her free-ranging expressiveness may worry purists, but the intensity of communication is what matters. By far the biggest item is the Haydn at the start, given a highly dramatic performance of extremes. It was a charming idea to interlace an extended sequence of Mahler and Berg songs, all lyrical and accessible. Ravel's *Habañera* setting, an extended wordless *vocalise*, makes an unexpected but satisfying conclusion. The disc comes in a slip-case with a separate booklet of words and translations, plus a note by the singer about her first, seminal visit to Europe in 1968.

'Classics': Arias from: VERDI: *Il Corsaro*. MOZART: *Le nozze di Figaro*. BIZET: *Carmen*. R. STRAUSS: *Ariadne auf Naxos*. PURCELL: *Dido and Aeneas*. GOUNOD: *Messe solennelle de Sainte Cécile*. Songs: POULENC: *Les chemins de l'amour*. SCHUBERT: *Auf dem See; Ave Maria*. BERLIOZ: *Nuits dété: L'île inconnue*. BRAHMS: *Von ewiger Liebe*. MAHLER: *Kindertotenlieder: Oft denk' ich, sie sind nur ausgegangen*. R. STRAUSS: *Frühling*. GERSHWIN: *Our love is here to stay*.
(M) **(*) Ph. 434 161-2; *434 161-4* [id.].

A well-chosen recital to show the range of Jessye Norman's repertoire. She opens splendidly in Medora's aria from *Il Corsaro*, and while the Mozart and Richard Strauss excerpts both show her at her finest, her *Lament* from *Dido and Aeneas* is most moving of all. All are drawn from the complete sets of these operas, as is the *Carmen* excerpt, which is the more valuable as her contribution is the most memorable thing about an otherwise disappointing set. She is less naturally as home in the French Mélodies than in German Lieder, although Poulenc's waltz song, *Les Chemins d'amour* is quite charming. The record ends with her fine account of Gounod's *Sanctus*, but it is a pity that the introductory orchestral chord here is so bold and loud, coming immediately after the gently sustained close of Schubert's *Ave Maria*. This was simply bad planning, but even worse is the total absence of translations or any information whatsover about the music. Instead there is a quite superfluous eulogy about the singer.

Opera choruses

'Great opera choruses' from: VERDI: *Nabucco* (Mormon Tabernacle Ch., Rudel); *Macbeth* (Teatro Comunale di Bologna, Chailly); *Aida* (La Scala, Milan, Maazel). BELLINI: *Norma* (Welsh Nat. Op., Bonynge). BEETHOVEN: *Fidelio* (Chicago Symphony Ch., Solti). WAGNER: *Lohengrin* (VPO, Solti). BOITO: *Mefistofele: Prologue* (London Op. Ch., Trinity Boys' Ch., Fabritiis).
(M) **(*) Decca 430 742-2; *430 742-4* [id.].

The highlight of this digital collection of choruses is the complete *Prologue* from Chailly's vibrant recording of Boito's *Mefistofele*, where the Devil (Nicolai Ghiaurov at his most commandingly resonant) sets up a wager with heaven, promising to tempt Faust away from his philosophizing, to enjoy more hedonistic pleasures. The many layered texture of choral and brass sounds is splendidly captured by the Decca engineers, and the result is both dramatic and highly atmospheric. The disc, however, opens with the Mormon Tabernacle Choir, without the benefit of the flattering Tabernacle resonance, giving an eloquent but not very histrionic account of Verdi's *Va pensiero*, which ends with a self-conscious sustaining of the final choral note in a long diminuendo. This ensures that the drama of Chailly's *Patria opressa* is the more striking, followed by a comparably vividly recorded, but not especially excitingly sung *March scene* from *Aida*. The Welsh National Opera Chorus then come on stage to demonstrate lustily just how it should be done, in a Bellini purple patch, heralded by some engulfingly spectacular crashes on the tam tam. Solti takes over for a movingly contoured account of the *Prisoners' chorus* from *Fidelio*, then his brilliant Act III *Lohengrin Prelude* really wakes things up and the *Bridal chorus* – again given sophisticated choral sound – makes a telling contrast.

Operatic Duets: 'Great love duets'

'Great love duets' (sung by Sutherland, Freni, Pavarotti, Tebaldi, Corelli, M. Price, Cossutta): PUCCINI: *Madama Butterfly; La Bohème; Tosca; Manon Lescaut*. VERDI: *Otello; La Traviata*.
(M) *** Decca 421 308-2.

This collection in Decca's mid-price Opera Gala series is very well chosen, starting and ending with duets from two of Karajan's outstanding Puccini recordings for Decca, *Madama Butterfly* and *La Bohème*, both with Freni and Pavarotti. The *Bohème* item includes not only the duet *O soave fanciulla* but the two favourite arias which precede it, *Che gelida manina* and *Sì, mi chiamano Mimì*. Sutherland is represented by *La Traviata*, Tebaldi by *Manon Lescaut* and Margaret Price by *Otello*, all very well transferred.

Operatic Duets: 'Great operatic duets'

'Great operatic duets' (sung by Sutherland, Pavarotti, Freni, Ludwig, Horne, Bergonzi, Fischer-Dieskau, Del Monaco, Bastianini): from DELIBES: *Lakmé.* PUCCINI: *Madama Butterfly.* BELLINI: *Norma.* VERDI: *La forza del destino; Don Carlo.* OFFENBACH: *Contes d'Hoffmann.*
(M) *** Decca 421 314-2.

Again at mid-price, Decca provides a further excellent collection of duets, ranging rather more widely, from some of the company's finest recordings of the 1960s and '70s. The choice is imaginative and the transfers excellent, to bring out the fine quality of the original analogue sound.

'Great operatic duets' (sung by: (i) Sutherland/Pavarotti; (ii) M. Price/Pavarotti; (iii) Te Kanawa/Aragall; (iv) Te Kanawa/Carreras; (v) Caballé/Baltsa/Pavarotti/Milnes; (vi) Sutherland/Caballé) from VERDI: (i) *La Traviata; Otello;* (ii) *Un ballo in maschera.* PUCCINI: (iii) *Tosca;* (iv) *Manon Lescaut.* PONCHIELLI: (v) *La Gioconda.* BELLINI: (vi) *Norma.*
(M) *** Decca 430 724-2; *430 724-4* [id.].

A splendid collection, with every item full of vibrant star-quality and offered in typically vivid Decca sound. Pavarotti and Sutherland are well matched in *La Traviata*, and later he makes an equally charismatic partnership with Margaret Price in *Teco io sto* from Verdi's *Un ballo in maschera*, while Sutherland duets equally impressively with Caballé in the *Norma* excerpt. Kiri te Kanawa, in glorious voice, and Carreras pair thrillingly in *Manon Lescaut*, and the 67-minute recital ends with a foretaste of Pavarotti's Love duet from *Otello*, but with Sutherland sounding not quite at her best, in a 1988 version recorded in New York with Bonynge.

Operetta: 'Golden operetta'

'Golden operetta': J. STRAUSS, Jnr: *Die Fledermaus: Mein Herr Marquis* (Gueden); *Csardas* (Janowitz). *Eine Nacht in Venedig: Lagunen waltz* (Krenn). *Wiener Blut: Wiener Blut* (Gueden). *Der Zigeunerbaron: O habet Acht* (Lorengar). *Casanova: Nuns' chorus* (Sutherland, Amb. S.). ZELLER: *Der Obersteiger: Sei nicht bös* (Gueden). LEHÁR: *Das Land des Lächelns: Dein ist mein ganzes Herz* (Bjoerling). *Die lustige Witwe: Vilja-Lied* (Sutherland); *Lippen schweigen* (Holm, Krenn). *Schön ist die Welt* (Krenn). *Der Graf von Luxemburg: Lieber Freund . . . Bist du's, Lachendes Gluck* (Holm, Krenn). *Giuditta: Du bist meine Sonne* (Kmentt). LECOCQ: *Le Coeur et la main: Bonsoir Perez le capitaine* (Sutherland). OFFENBACH: *La Périchole: Letter song. La Grande Duchesse de Gérolstein: J'aime les militaires* (Crespin).
(M) *** Decca 421 319-2.

A valuable and generous anthology, not just for the obvious highlights: Joan Sutherland's *Vilja* and the delightful contributions from Hilde Gueden – notably a delicious *Sei nicht bös* – recorded in 1961 when the voice was at its freshest; but also Régine Crespin at her finest in Offenbach (the duchess reviewing her troops) and the charming *Letter song* from *La Périchole.* In their winningly nostalgic account of the *Merry Widow waltz* Renate Holm and Werner Krenn hum the melody, having sung the words, giving the impression of dancing together. The recording throughout is atmospheric, with plenty of bloom and with the voices given a natural presence.

Partridge, Ian (tenor), Stephen Roberts (baritone)

'Songs by Finzi and his friends' (with Benson, piano): FINZI: *To a poet; Oh fair to see, Op. 13/a–b* (song collections). GURNEY: *Sleep; Down by the Salley Gardens; Hawk and buckle.* MILFORD: *If it's ever spring again; The colour; So sweet love seemed.* GILL: *In memoriam.* FERRAR: *O mistress mine.*
**(*) Hyp. CDA 66015 [id.].

Finzi's sensitive response to word-meanings inspires a style of setting that is often not unlike an operatic recitative. His individuality and poetic originality are not always matched by memorability, but the songs of his contemporaries and friends – even where the names are unknown – make immediate communication even on a first hearing. An imaginative collection, well sung, worth exploring by those interested in the repertoire. The recording is somewhat over-resonant.

Pavarotti, Luciano (tenor)

Neapolitan songs (with Ch. and O of Teatro Comunale, Bologna, Guadagno, or Nat. PO, Chiaramello): DI CAPUA: *O sole mio; Maria, Mari.* TOSTI: *A vuchella. Marechiare.* CANNIO: *O surdato 'nnamurato.* GAMBARDELLA: *O Marenariello.* ANON.: *Fenesta vascia.* DE CURTIS: *Torna a Surriento. Tu, ca nun chiagne.* PENNINO: *Pecchè . . .* D'ANNIBALE: *O paese d'o sole.* TAGLIAFERRI: *Piscatore 'e pusilleco.* DENZA: *Funiculi, funicula.*
*** Decca 410 015-2 [id.].

Neapolitan songs given grand treatment in passionate Italian performances, missing some of the charm but none of the red-blooded fervour. The recording is both vivid and atmospheric and is digitally remastered most successfully.

'Mamma' (Italian and Neapolitan popular songs with O and Ch., Henry Mancini): BIXIO: *Mamma; Vivere; Mia canzone al vento; Parlami d'amore.* DE CURTIS: *Non ti scordar di me.* BUZZI-PECCIA: *Lolita:* excerpts. GASTALDON: *Musica proibita.* CESARINI: *Firenze sogna.* KRAMER: *In un palco della scala.* RIVI: *Addio, sogni di gloria!* D'ANZI: *Voglio vivere così.* DI LAZZARO: *Chitarra romana.* DE CRESCENZO: *Rondine al nido.* TRAD.: *Ghirlandeina.* CALIFONA: *Vieni sul mar'.* ARONA: *Campana di San Giusto.*
**(*) Decca Dig. 411 959-2 [id.].

Larger-than-life arrangements by Henry Mancini of popular Italian and Neapolitan songs with larger-than-life singing to match. Vulgarity is welcomed rather than skirted, which is fair enough in this music. Larger-than-life recording, too.

'Pavarotti's greatest hits': from PUCCINI: *Turandot; Tosca; La Bohème.* DONIZETTI: *La fille du régiment; La Favorita; L'Elisir d'amore.* R. STRAUSS: *Der Rosenkavalier.* BIZET: *Carmen.* BELLINI: *I Puritani.* VERDI: *Il Trovatore; Rigoletto; Aida; Requiem.* GOUNOD: *Faust.* PONCHIELLI: *La Gioconda.* LEONCAVALLO: *I Pagliacci* and *Mattinata.* ROSSINI: *La danza.* DE CURTIS: *Torna a Surriento.* FRANCK: *Panis angelicus.* SCHUBERT: *Ave Maria.* DENZA: *Funiculi, funicula.*
*** Decca 417 011-2; *417 011-4* (2) [id.].

This collection of 'greatest hits' can safely be recommended to all who have admired the golden beauty of Pavarotti's voice. Including as it does a fair proportion of earlier recordings, the compilation demonstrates the splendid consistency of his singing. Songs are included, as well as many well-chosen excerpts from opera. The sound is certainly vibrant on CD, but this remains at full price; Decca have since issued an even more generous collection on a pair of mid-priced discs, appropriately called '*Tutto Pavarotti*', see below.

'Passione' (with Bologna Teatro Comunale O, Chiaramello): TAGLIAFERRI: *Passione.* COSTA: *Era de maggio.* ANON.: *Fenesta che lucive; La Palummella; Te voglio bene assaje.* NARDELIA: *Chiove.* FALVO: *Dicitencello vuie.* DE CURTIS: *Voce 'e notte.* DI PAPUA: *I 'te vurria vasa.* MARIO: *Santa Lucia luntana.* LAMA: *Silenzio cantatore.* CARDILLO: *Core 'ngrato.*
*** Decca Dig. 417 117-2 [id.].

With the advantage of first-class recording, this perhaps is the most attractive of Pavarotti's Neapolitan collections. The voice sounds fresh, the singing is ardent and the programme is chosen imaginatively. The great tenor obviously identifies with this repertoire and sings everything with the kind of natural response that skirts vulgarity. The orchestrations by Giancarlo Chiaramello show a feeling for the right kind of orchestral colour: they may be sophisticated, but they undoubtedly enhance the melodic lines. If the title of the collection suggests hyperbole, there is in fact a well-judged balance here between passionate romanticism and concern for phrasing and detail.

'Anniversary': Arias from: PUCCINI: *La Bohème; Tosca.* GIORDANO: *Andrea Chénier.* BELLINI: *La Sonnambula.* PONCHIELLI: *La Gioconda.* VERDI: *La Traviata; Un ballo in maschera.* LEONCAVALLO: *Pagliacci.* BOITO: *Mefistofele.* ROSSINI: *Gugliemo Tell.* MASCAGNI: *Cavalleria Rusticana.*
**(*) Decca 417 362-2; *417 362-4* [id.].

Pavarotti's recital celebrated the 25th anniversary of his operatic début. It is a good compilation of mixed items from complete opera sets, some of them relatively rare and mostly imaginatively done, though the *Andrea Chénier* items could be subtler. Good, bright recording of various vintages.

'Mattinata': Songs by BELLINI; GIORDANI; ROSSINI; GLUCK; TOSTI; DONIZETTI; LEONCAVALLO; BEETHOVEN and others.
(M) **(*) Decca 417 796-2; *417 796-4*.

Pavarotti is at home here in the lightweight items. Giordani's *Caro mio ben* is very nicely done and the romantic songs have a well-judged ardour. Gluck's *Che farò*, the one operatic aria included, is rather less impressive. The tone is not always golden, but most of the bloom remains. Vivid transfers.

'Volare' (popular Italian songs, with Ch. & O of Teatro Comunale di Bologna, Mancini): MODUGNO: *Volare.* DENZA: *Occhi di fata.* BIXIO: *La strada nel bosco; Chi è più felice di me; La canzone dell' amore; Cantate con me; Bimmi tu primavera.* SIBELLA: *La girometta.* D'ANZI: *Malinconia d'amore.* BONAGURA: *Luna marinara.* CASSARINI: *Fra tanta gente.* MASCHERONI: *Fiorin fiorello.* DE CURTIS: *Ti voglio tanto bene.* RUCCIONE: *Una chitarra nella notte.* MASCAGNI: *Serenata.* FERILLI: *Un amore così grande.*
**(*) Decca Dig. 421 052-2; *421 052-4* [id.].

Supported by Henry Mancini in characteristically colourful arrangements, Pavarotti throws his considerable weight into these popular Neapolitan songs, not the most tasteful renderings but very satisfying for aficionados, helped by aptly ripe recording.

Donizetti and Verdi arias (with Vienna Op. O, Downes) from: DONIZETTI: *Dom Sébastien, roi de Portugal; Il Duca d'Alba; La Favorita; Lucia di Lammermoor.* VERDI: *Un ballo in maschera; I due Foscari; Luisa Miller; Macbeth.*
(M) *** Decca 421 304-2.

Pavarotti's 'Opera Gala' issue of Verdi and Donizetti presents the tenor in impressive performances of mainly rare arias, recorded in 1968, early in his career, with the voice fresh and golden. Good, full recording.

'King of the high Cs': Arias from: DONIZETTI: *La fille du régiment; La Favorita.* VERDI: *Il Trovatore.* R. STRAUSS: *Der Rosenkavalier.* ROSSINI: *Guglielmo Tell.* BELLINI: *I Puritani.* PUCCINI: *La Bohème.*
(M) *** Decca 421 326-2; *421 326-4*.

A superb display of Pavarotti's vocal command as well as his projection of personality. Though the selections come from various sources, the recording quality is remarkably consistent, the voice vibrant and clear; the accompanying detail and the contributions of the chorus are also well managed. The Donizetti and Puccini items are particularly attractive.

'Pavarotti in concert' (with Teatro Comunale, Bologna, O, Bonynge): BONONCINI: *Griselda: Per la gloria d'adorarvi.* HANDEL: *Atalanta: Care selve.* A. SCARLATTI: *Già il sol dal Gange.* BELLINI: Songs: *Ma rendi pur contento; Dolente immagine di fille mia; Malinconia, ninfa gentile; Bella nice, che d'amore; Vanne, o rosa fortunata.* TOSTI: Songs: *La serenata; Luna d'estate; Malia; Non t'amo più!* RESPIGHI: *Nevicata; Poggia; Nebbie.* ROSSINI: *La danza.*
(M) **(*) Decca 425 037-2; *425 037-4* [id.].

In the classical items Pavarotti is more subdued than usual. He is in his element in Tosti and, with evocative accompaniments from Bonynge, he makes the three Respighi songs the highlight of a recital which is nicely rounded off with a spirited but never coarse version of Rossini's *La danza*. The 1974 Decca sound is both atmospheric and vivid in its CD format.

'Tutto Pavarotti': Arias from: VERDI: *Aida; Luisa Miller; La Traviata; Il Trovatore; Rigoletto; Un ballo in maschera.* DONIZETTI: *L'Elisir d'amore; Don Pasquale.* PONCHIELLI: *La Gioconda.* FLOTOW: *Martha.* BIZET: *Carmen.* MASSENET: *Werther.* MEYERBEER: *L'Africana.* BOITO: *Mefistofele.* LEONCAVALLO: *Pagliacci.* MASCAGNI: *Cavalleria Rusticana.* GIORDANO: *Fedora.* PUCCINI: *La Fanciulla del West; Tosca; Manon Lescaut; La Bohème; Turandot.* ROSSINI: *Stabat Mater.* BIZET: *Agnus Dei.* ADAM: *O holy night.* DI PAPUA: *O sole mio.* TOSTI: *A vucchella.* CARDILLO: *Core 'ngrato.* TAGLIAFERRI: *Passione.* CHERUBINI: *Mamma.* DALLA: *Caruso.*
(M) *** Decca 425 681-2; *425 681-4* (2) [id.].

Opening with Dalla's *Caruso*, a popular song in the Neapolitan tradition, this selection goes on through favourites like *O sole mio* and *Core 'ngrato* and one or two religious items, notably

Adam's *Cantique de Noël*, to the hard core of operatic repertoire. Beginning with *Celeste Aida*, recorded in 1972, the selection of some 22 arias from complete sets covers Pavarotti's distinguished recording career with Decca from 1969 (*Cielo e mar* and the *Il Trovatore* excerpts) to 1985, although the opening song was, of course, recorded digitally in 1988. The rest is a mixture of brilliantly transferred analogue originals and a smaller number of digital masters, all or nearly all showing the great tenor in sparkling form. The records and tapes are at mid-price, but there are no translations or musical notes.

'Gala concert at the Royal Albert Hall' (with RPO, Kurt Adler): Arias from: PUCCINI: *Tosca; Turandot.* VERDI: *Macbeth; I Lombardi; Luisa Miller. Un giorno di regno: Overture.* DONIZETTI: *Lucia di Lammermoor.* CILEA: *L'Arlesiana.* DE CURTIS: Song: *Torna a Surriento.* BERLIOZ: *Les Troyens: Royal hunt and storm.*
(M) **(*) Decca 430 716-2; *430 716-4*.

This disc celebrates a much-hyped appearance by Pavarotti at the Royal Albert Hall in 1982. It would be unfair to expect much subtlety before such an eager audience, but the live recording conveys the fever well. There are bold accounts of the two most famous arias from *Tosca*, and the celebrated *Nessun dorma* from *Turandot*, and even simple recitatives as intimate as Macduff's in *Macbeth* are proclaimed grandly. The bright digital recording shows up some unevenness in the voice, but no one will miss the genuine excitement, with the electricity of the occasion conveyed equally effectively on disc or tape.

'O Holy night' (with Wandsworth School Boys' Ch., Nat. PO, Adler): ADAM: *Cantique de noël (O holy night).* STRADELLA: *Pieta Signore.* FRANCK: *Panis angelicus.* MERCADANTE: *Parola quinta.* SCHUBERT: *Ave Maria.* BACH/GOUNOD: *Ave Maria.* BIZET: *Agnus Dei.* BERLIOZ: *Requiem: Sanctus.* TRAD.: *Adeste fideles.* YON: *Jesù bambino.* SCHUBERT, arr. Melichar: *Mille cherubini in coro.* GLUCK: *Orfeo ed Euridice: Che farò senza Euridice.* ROSSINI: *Stabat mater: Cuius animam.* VERDI: *Requiem: Ingemisco.*
(M) **(*) Decca 433 710-2; *433 710-4* [id.].

Pavarotti is hardly a model of taste but he avoids the worst pitfalls; and if this sort of recital is what you are looking for, then Pavarotti is a good choice, with his beautiful vocalizing helped by full, bright recording. Note too that one or two of these items are less hackneyed than the rest, for instance the title setting by Adam, Mercadante's *Parola quinta* and the *Sanctus* from Berlioz's *Requiem Mass*. The Gluck and Rossini excerpts (using other orchestras and conductors) like the fine account of Verdi's *Ingemisco*, have been added to fill out the reissue.

Pavarotti, Luciano (tenor) and Mirella Freni (soprano)

Arias and duets from: PUCCINI: *Tosca; La Bohème.* ROSSINI: *Guglielmo Tell.* BOITO: *Mefistofele.*
(M) *** Decca 421 878-2; *421 878-4*.

Both artists come from the same small town in Italy, Modena, where they were born in 1935. Their great introductory love-duet as Mimi and Rodolfo, perhaps the most ravishing in all opera (from *Che gelida manina*, through *Sì, mi chiamano Mimì* to the soaring *O soave fanciulla*) is an obvious highlight here, but the much less familiar *Lontano, lontano* from *Mefistofele* shows no less memorably that the voices were made for each other. It was a very good idea to include a substantial selection from their 1978–9 *Tosca*, with some marvellous singing in Act III. The only slight disappointment is Freni's *Vissi d'arte*; otherwise this is 70 minutes of vintage material, given Decca's top drawer sound.

Ponselle, Rosa (soprano)

Arias from: VERDI: *Ernani; Otello; La forza del destino; Aida.* MEYERBEER: *L'Africana.* SPONTINI: *La Vestale.* PONCHIELLI: *La Gioconda.* BELLINI: *Norma.* BACH-GOUNOD: *Ave Maria.* RIMSKY-KORSAKOV: *The nightingale and the rose* & Songs.
(M) (***) BMG/RCA mono GD 87810 [7810-2-RG].

The clarity and immediacy of the RCA transfers make a complete contrast with the warmly atmospheric Nimbus transfers of the same singer. Though the voice is exposed more, with less bloom on it, the character and technical command are, if anything, even more impressively presented. To sample the greatness of Ponselle, try her dazzling 1928 account of *Ernani involami* or her poised *Casta diva*. Notable too is the final trio from *La forza del destino* with Martinelli and Pinza, even more immediate than on Nimbus's Martinelli disc.

'Prima voce': Arias from: BELLINI: *Norma*. PONCHIELLI: *La Gioconda*. SPONTINI: *La vestale*. VERDI: *Aida; Ernani; La forza del destino; Otello*. Songs by: ARENSKY; RIMSKY-KORSAKOV; DE CURTIS; DI CAPUA; JACOBS-BOND.
(M) (***) Nimbus mono NI 7805.

One of the most exciting American sopranos ever, Rosa Ponselle tantalizingly cut short her career when she was still at her peak. Only the Arensky and Rimsky songs represent her after her official retirement, and the rest make a superb collection, including her classic accounts of *Casta diva* from Bellini's *Norma* and the duet, *Mira o Norma*, with Marion Telva. The six Verdi items include her earlier version of *Ernani involami*, not quite so commanding as her classic 1928 recording, but fascinating for its rarity. Equally cherishable is her duet from *La forza del destino* with Ezio Pinza.

Ricciarelli, Katia (soprano), José Carreras (tenor)

'Duetti d'amore' from PUCCINI: *Madama Butterfly*. VERDI: *I Lombardi*. DONIZETTI: *Poliuto; Roberto Devereux*.
(M) *** Ph. 426 644-2; *426 644-4*.

The two Donizetti duets are among the finest he ever wrote, especially the one from *Poliuto*, in which the hero persuades his wife to join him in martyrdom. This has a depth unexpected in Donizetti. Both these items receive beautiful performances here; the Puccini love-duet is made to sound fresh and unhackneyed, and the *Lombardi* excerpt is given with equal tenderness. Stylish conducting and refined recording.

Rogers, Nigel (tenor), Anthony Bailes (lute)

'Airs de cour' (songs from the reign of Louis XIII): MAUDUIT: *Eau vive, source d'amour*. DE COURVILLE: *Si je languis d'un martire incogneu*. ANON.: *C'est un amant, ouvrez la porte*. BATAILLE: *Un jour que ma rebelle; Ma bergère non légère; Qui veut chasser une migraine*. GUÉDRON: *Si jamais mon âme blessée; Césses mortels de soupir; Quel espoir de guarir*. LE FÉGUEUX: *Petit sein où l'amour a bâti son séjour*. MOULINIÉ: *Paisible et ténébreuse nuit; Quelque merveilleuse chose; Je suis ravi de mon Uranie; Enfin la beauté que j'adore*. BOËSSET: *Plaignez la rigueur de mon sort; N'espérez plus, mes yeux; Ennuis, désespoirs et douleurs*. GRAND RUE: *Lors que tes beaux yeux, mignonne*.
(M) *** EMI CDM7 63070-2.

A beautifully sung and most naturally recorded recital of *airs de cour* (Court songs) which will give much pleasure to the non-specialist listener who might not normally venture into this repertoire. There is sentiment, melancholy (though usually not so overt as in Elizabethan lute songs), gaiety and (cultivated) high spirits. The love-songs are nicely expressive, and the recital attractively intersperses the gay settings with the more dolorous expressions of feeling like the lovely *Quel espoir de guarir* or the two closing songs by Étienne Moulinié. The CD has great presence and realism; the balance between voice and the sympathetic lute accompaniments of Anthony Bailes is ideal. It is a great pity that translations are not provided; even so, the French words are easy to follow.

Royal Opera House, Covent Garden

Royal Opera House Covent Garden (An early history on record). Singers included are: Melba, Caruso, Tetrazzini, McCormack, Destin, Gadski, Schorr, Turner, Zanelli, Lehmann, Schumann, Olczewska, Chaliapin, Gigli, Supervia, Tibbett, Tauber, Flagstad, Melchior. Arias from: GOUNOD: *Faust*. VERDI: *Rigoletto, Otello*. DONIZETTI: *Lucia di Lammermoor*. VERDI: *La Traviata*. PUCCINI: *Madama Butterfly; Tosca*. WAGNER: *Götterdämmerung; Die Meistersinger; Tristan und Isolde*. R. STRAUSS: *Der Rosenkavalier*. MUSSORGSKY: *Boris Godunov*. GIORDANO: *Andrea Chénier*. BIZET: *Carmen*. MOZART: *Don Giovanni*.
(M) (**(*)) Nimbus mono NI 7819 [id.].

Nimbus's survey of great singers at Covent Garden ranges from Caruso's 1904 recording of

Questa o quella from *Rigoletto* to the recording of the second half of the *Tristan* love duet, which Kirsten Flagstad and Lauritz Melchior made in San Francisco in November 1939, a magnificent recording, never issued in Britain. The Vienna recording of the *Rosenkavalier* Trio with Lehmann, Schumann and Olczewska similarly reproduces a classic partnership at Covent Garden, while Chaliapin's 1928 recording of the *Prayer* and *Death of Boris* was actually recorded live at Covent Garden, with the transfer giving an amazingly vivid sense of presence. Those who like Nimbus's acoustic method of transfer will enjoy the whole disc, though the reverberation round some of the early offerings – like the very first, Melba's *Jewel song* from *Faust* – is cavernous. Particularly interesting is the 1909 recording of part of Brünnhilde's Immolation scene, with Johanna Gadski commandingly strong.

St George's Canzona, John Sothcott

Medieval songs and dances: *Lamento di Tristano; L'autrier m'iere levaz. 4 Estampies real; Edi beo thu hevene quene; Eyns ne soy ke plente fu; Tre fontane.* PERRIN D'AGINCOURT: *Quant voi en la fin d'este.* Cantigas de Santa Maria: *Se ome fezer; Nas mentes semper teer; Como poden per sas culpas; Maravillosos et piadosos.*
*** CRD CRD 3421; *CRDC 4121* [id.].

As so often when early music is imaginatively re-created, one is astonished at the individuality of many of the ideas. This applies particularly to the second item in this collection, *Quant voi en la fin d'este*, attributed to the mid-thirteenth-century trouvère, Perrin d'Agincourt, but no less to the four Cantigas de Santa Maria. The fruity presentation of *Como poden per sas culpas* ('As men may be crippled by their sins, so they may afterwards be made sound by the Virgin') is admirably contrasted with the strong lyrical appeal of the following *Maravillosos et piadosos*, directly extolling the virtues and compassion of Saint Mary. Among the four *Estampies real* the one presented last (band 11 on the CD) is haunting in its lilting melancholy. The instrumentation is at times suitably robust but does not eschew good intonation and subtle effects. The group is recorded vividly and the acoustics of St James, Clerkenwell, are never allowed to cloud detail. The sound is admirably firm and real in its CD format.

St John's College, Cambridge, Choir, George Guest

'Christmas weekend': GRÜBER: *Silent night.* RUTTER: *Shepherd's pipe carol.* MENDELSSOHN: *Hark the herald angels.* TRAD.: *O little town of Bethlehem; Born on earth; The twelve days of Christmas; Up! good Christian folk; Good King Wenceslas; While shepherds watched; God rest you merry, gentlemen; The holly and the ivy; Away in a manger; The first nowell; I saw three ships; Suo Gan.*
(B) *** Decca 421 022-2; *421 022-4*.

This is first rate in every way, a wholly successful concert of mostly traditional carols, in sensitive arrangements without frills. The singing is straightforwardly eloquent, its fervour a little restrained in the Anglican tradition, yet with considerable underlying depth of feeling. The full character of every carol is well brought out; the expressive simplicity of *I saw three ships* and Rutter's *Shepherd's pipe carol* is most engaging.

Schipa, Tito (tenor)

Opera arias from: GLUCK: *Orfeo ed Eurydice.* A. SCARLATTI: *La Donna ancora e fedele; Pirro e Demetrio* (& Song: *Sento nel core*). BELLINI: *La Sonnambula.* DONIZETTI: *Don Pasquale; L'Elisir d'amore; Lucia di Lammermoor.* VERDI: *Rigoletto; Falstaff.* PONCHIELLI: *La Gioconda.* PUCCINI: *La Bohème; Tosca.* MASCAGNI: *Cavalleria Rusticana; L'amico Fritz.* MASSENET: *Werther; Manon.*
(M) (**(*)) EMI mono CDH7 63200-2 [id.].

This EMI collection is particularly valuable for containing Schipa's first recordings, made in 1913. Whether in *Lucia*, *Rigoletto* or *Cavalleria*, the voice and the interpretations are even fresher than they were later. The disc is also indispensable for containing one of the most delectable of all Schipa records, his delicious account of the *Cherry duet* from *L'amico Fritz* with Mafalda Favero. But his RCA account of the aria for which he was most famous, *Una furtiva lagrima* from *L'Elisir d'amore*, is preferable to this (see below), and the transfers are not as immaculate as one expects of this EMI series.

Arias from: MASSENET: *Werther; Manon.* CILEA: *L'Arlesiana.* ROSSINI: *Il Barbiere di Siviglia.* DONIZETTI: *L'Elisir d'amore; Lucia di Lammermoor.* LEONCAVALLO: *Pagliacci.* VERDI: *Rigoletto; La Traviata.* MOZART: *Don Giovanni.* HANDEL: *Xerxes.* BELLINI: *La Sonnambula.* Songs by TOSTI and others.
(M) (***) BMG/RCA mono GD 87969 [7969-2-RG].

RCA provides vivid, very immediate transfers of a sparkling collection of Neapolitan songs as well as arias. Few tenors have matched Schipa for the point and personality of his singing within his carefully chosen limits. It is like being face to face with the singer.

'Prima voce': Arias from: MASCAGNI: *Cavalleria Rusticana. L'amico Fritz.* VERDI: *Rigoletto; Luisa Miller.* DONIZETTI: *Lucia di Lammermoor; Don Pasquale; L'elisir d'amore.* LEONCAVALLO: *Pagliacci.* MASSENET: *Manon; Werther.* ROSSINI: *Il barbiere di Siviglia.* THOMAS: *Mignon.* FLOTOW: *Martha.* CILEA: *L'Arlesiana.*
(M) (***) Nimbus mono NI 7813 [id.].

The first nine items on this well-chosen selection of Schipa's recordings date from the pre-electric era. The voice is totally consistent, heady and light and perfectly controlled, between the *Siciliana* from Mascagni's *Cavalleria*, recorded with piano in 1913, to the incomparable account of more Mascagni, the *Cherry duet* from *L'amico Fritz*, made with Mafalda Favero in 1937. It says much for his art that Schipa's career continued at full strength for decades after that. The Nimbus transfers put the voice at a slight distance, with the electrical recordings made to sound the more natural.

Schumann-Heink, Ernestine (contralto)

'Prima voce': Arias from: DONIZETTI: *Lucrezia Borgia.* MEYERBEER: *Le Prophète.* WAGNER: *Das Rheingold; Rienzi; Götterdämmerung.* HANDEL: *Rinaldo.* Songs by: ARDITTI; BECKER; SCHUBERT; WAGNER; REIMANN; MOLLOY; BRAHMS; BOEHM & TRAD.
(M) (***) Nimbus mono NI 7811 [id.].

Schumann-Heink combines to an astonishing degree a full contralto weight and richness with the most delicate flexibility, as in the *Brindisi* from Donizetti's *Lucrezia Borgia.* This wide-ranging collection, resonantly transferred by the Nimbus acoustic method, presents a vivid portrait of a very great singer.

(Heinrich) Schütz Choir, Roger Norrington

'A Baroque Christmas' (with London String Players, Philip Jones Brass Ensemble; Camden Wind Ensemble; Charles Spinks): SCHÜTZ: *Hodie Christus natus est; Ach Herr, du Schöpfer aller Ding.* PURCELL: *Behold I bring you glad tidings.* ANON.: *Soberana Maria.* HAMMERTSCHMIDT: *Alleluja! Freuet euch, ihr Christen alle.* BOUZIGNAC: *Noé! Pastores, cantate Dominum.* G. GABRIELI: *O magnum mysterium.* MONTEVERDI: *Christe Redemptor.* PRAETORIUS: *Singt, ihr lieben Christen all.* HASSLER: *Angeles ad pastores ait.*
❀ (M) *** Decca 430 065-2; *430 065-4* [id.].

A superlative collection which celebrates the joyful Renaissance approach to Christmas. The glorious opening number is matched in memorability by the engaging lullaby, *Soberana Maria*, and *Noé! Pastores* has a delightful interplay between Gabriel (Hazel Holt) and the Shepherds. Giovanni Gabrieli's *O magnum mysterium* is justly famous and sounds superbly sonorous here, while the Michael Praetorius carol has a tune most will readily recognize. The performances are splendid and the 1968 analogue recording remains in the demonstration bracket. There are few more unusual or more rewarding Christmas celebrations than this.

Schwarzkopf, Dame Elisabeth (soprano)

'Elisabeth Schwarzkopf sings operetta' (with Philharmonia Ch. and O, Ackermann): Excerpts from: HEUBERGER: *Der Opernball.* ZELLER: *Der Vogelhändler.* LEHÁR: *Der Zarewitsch; Der*

Graf von Luxembourg; Giuditta. J. STRAUSS, J: *Casanova.* MILLÖCKER: *Die Dubarry.* SUPPÉ: *Boccaccio.* SIECZYŃSKY: *Wien, du Stadt meiner Träume.*
❀ *** EMI CDC7 47284-2 [id.].

This is one of the most delectable recordings of operetta arias ever made, and it is here presented with excellent sound. Schwarzkopf's 'whoopsing' manner (as Philip Hope-Wallace called it) is irresistible, authentically catching the Viennese style, languor and sparkle combined. Try for sample the exquisite *Im chambre séparée* or *Sei nicht bös*; but the whole programme is performed with supreme artistic command and ravishing tonal beauty. This outstanding example of the art of Elisabeth Schwarzkopf at its most enchanting is a disc which ought to be in every collection. The compact disc transfer enhances the superbly balanced recording even further, manages to cut out nearly all the background, give the voice a natural presence, and retain the orchestral bloom.

75th Birthday Edition: WOLF: 24 Lieder and Lieder by: SCHUBERT; SCHUMANN; R. STRAUSS. Arias from: MOZART: *Le nozze di Figaro; Così fan tutte; Don Giovanni.* HUMPERDINCK: *Hänsel und Gretel.* LEHÁR: *Die lustige Witwe.* J. STRAUSS, Jnr: *Die Fledermaus.* PUCCINI: *Turandot.* R. STRAUSS: *Ariadne auf Naxos; Der Rosenkavalier; Capriccio.* VERDI: *Requiem.* Various encores by BACH; BEETHOVEN; MARTINI; TCHAIKOVSKY; DEBUSSY; ARNE etc.
(M) *** EMI stereo/mono CMS7 63790-2 (5).

The five discs of the Birthday Edition, available in a box, provide a comprehensive survey of Schwarzkopf's astonishing achievement on record, not least in the early years of her career in the days before stereo was universally adopted. The individual discs – the Wolf Lieder collection as well as the four recitals listed below – are available separately. With excellent transfers, all can be warmly recommended.

'Encores' (with Gerald Moore or Geoffrey Parsons): BACH: *Bist du bei mir.* GLUCK: *Einem Bach der fliesst.* BEETHOVEN: *Wonne der Wehmut.* LOEWE: *Kleiner Haushalt.* WAGNER: *Träume.* BRAHMS: *Ständchen; 3 Deutsche Volkslieder.* MAHLER: *Um schlimme Kinder artig zu machen; Ich atmet' einen linden Duft; Des Antonius von Padua Fischpredigt.* TCHAIKOVSKY: *Pimpernella.* arr. WOLF-FERRARI: *7 Italian songs.* MARTINI: *Plaisir d'amour.* HAHN: *Si mes vers avaient des ailes.* DEBUSSY: *Mandoline.* arr. QUILTER: *Drink to me only with thine eyes.* ARNE: *When daisies pied; Where the bee sucks.* arr. GUND: *3 Swiss folk songs.* arr. WEATHERLY: *Danny Boy.* J. STRAUSS, Jnr: *Frühlingsstimmen* (with VPO, Joseph Krips).
(M) *** EMI stereo/mono CDM7 63654-2.

Schwarzkopf herself has on occasion nominated this charming account of *Danny Boy* as her own favourite recording of her singing, but it is only one of a whole sequence of lightweight songs which vividly capture the charm and intensity that made her recitals so memorable, particularly in the extra items at the end. As a rule she would announce and explain each beforehand, adding to the magic. The range here is wide, from Bach's heavenly *Bist du bei mir* to the innocent lilt of the Swiss folksong, *Gsätzli*, and Strauss's *Voices of spring.*

'Unpublished recordings' (with (i) Philh. O, Thurston Dart; (ii) Kathleen Ferrier, VPO, Karajan; (iii) Philh. O, Galliera; (iv) Walter Gieseking, Philh. O, Karajan): J. S. BACH: (i) *Cantata No. 199: Mein Herze schwimmt im Blut: Auf diese Schmerzens Reu; Doch Gott muss mir genädig sein; Mein Herze schwimmt im Blut.* (ii) *Mass in B min.: Christe eleison; Et in unum Dominum; Laudamus te.* (iii) MOZART: *Nehmt meinen Dank, K.383.* (iv) GIESEKING: *Kinderlieder.* R. STRAUSS: *4 Last songs.*
(M) (**(*)) EMI CDM7 63655-2.

Long-buried treasure here includes Bach duets with Kathleen Ferrier conducted by Karajan, a collection of charming children's songs by Gieseking, recorded almost impromptu, and, best of all, a live performance of Strauss's *Four Last songs* given under Karajan at the Festival Hall in 1956, a vintage year for Schwarzkopf. Sound quality varies, but the voice is gloriously caught.

Lieder (with Gerald Moore or Geoffrey Parsons): SCHUBERT: *Die Vögel;* Liebhaber in allen Gestalten; Heidenröslein; Die Forelle; Der Einsame; Der Jüngling an der Quelle; An mein Klavier; Erlkönig; Was bedeutet die Bewegung & Ach, um deine feuchten Schwingen (Suleika I & II); Hänflings Liebeswerbung; Meeres Stille; Gretchen am Spinnrade. SCHUMANN: *Der Nussbaum; Aufträge; 2 Venetian Lieder; Die Kartenlegerin; Wie mit innigstem Behagen (Suleika).* R. STRAUSS: *Hat gesagt, bleibt's nicht dabei; SchlechtesWetter; Wiegenliedchen; Meinem Kinde; Wiegenlied; 3 Ophelia Lieder; Die Nacht.*

(M) (***) EMI stereo/mono CDM7 63656-2.

With the Schubert selection including a high proportion of favourites, this compilation provides a fine survey of Schwarzkopf's unique achievement as a Lieder-singer outside the specialist area of Hugo Wolf. The earliest recordings, made in 1948, are of two Schubert songs, *Die Vögel* and a Goethe setting, *Liebhaber in allen Gestalten*, and the latest, Schumann's *Der Nussbaum*, from 25 years on in her career, all beautifully transferred.

Opera arias: MOZART: *Le nozze di Figaro; Così fan tuti; Don Giovanni.* HUMPERDINCK: *Hänsel und Gretel.* LEHÁR: *Die lustige Witwe;* J. STRAUSS, Jnr: *Die Fledermaus.* PUCCINI: *Turandot.* R. STRAUSS: *Ariadne auf Naxos; Der Rosenkavalier; Capriccio.* VERDI: *Messa da requiem.*
(M) (***) EMI stereo/mono CDM7 63657-2.

This fine collection of arias is taken from various sets Schwarzkopf contributed to in the 1950s. They range from Mozart operas, conducted by Karajan and Furtwängler, to the glories of her supreme recordings of Strauss operas, Ariadne's lament, the Marschallin's final solo in Act I of *Rosenkavalier* and the Countess's final aria in *Capriccio.* Also featured is the *Recordare* from de Sabata's early recording of the Verdi *Requiem.*

'To my friends' (with Parsons, piano): WOLF: *Mörike Lieder: Storchenbotschaft; Fussreise; Elfenlied; Bei einer Trauung; Jägerlied; Selbstgeständnis; Heimweh; Nixe Binsefuss; Mausfallen Sprüchlein; Nimmersatte Liebe; Lebe Wohl; Das verlassene Mägdlein; Auf eines altes Bild.* LOEWE: *Die wandelnde Glocke.* GRIEG: *Ein Schwan.* BRAHMS: *Mädchenlied; Am jüngsten Tag; Therese; Blinde Kuh.*
(M) *** Decca 430 000-2 [id.].

This glowing collection of Lieder was Schwarzkopf's last record and also the last recording supervised by her husband, Walter Legge. With excellent Decca sound, the charm and presence of Schwarzkopf, which in a recital conveyed extraordinary intensity right to the very end of her career, comes over vividly. Most cherishable of all are the lighter, quicker songs like *Mausfallen Sprüchlein* ('My St Trinians reading', as she herself says) and *Blinde Kuh* ('Blind man's bluff'). Superbly balanced, bringing the artists right into one's room.

4 Last Songs & Orchistral Lieder.
❀ *** EMI CDC7 47276-2 [id.]. Elisabeth Schwarzkopf, Berlin RSO or LSO, Szell.

As we go to press, EMI have restored Schwarzkopf's raptly beautiful recording of Strauss's *Four Last Songs* to the catalogue, plus the dozen orchestral songs – equally inspired performances – which she recorded with George Szell.

Sequentia, Benjamin Bagby and Barbara Thornton

'Sons of Thunder' (Music for Santiago de Compostela from the Codex Calixtinus, 12th century): *Vox Iberica I.*
*** HM/BMG Dig. RD 77199.

'Codex las Huelgas' (Music from the Royal Convent of Las Huelgas de Burgos, 13th/14th century): *Vox Iberica II.*
*** BMG/RCA Dig. 05472 77238-2.

Directed by Benjamin Bagby and Barbara Thornton, the singers of the German-based group, Sequentia, give incisive, sharply focused performances of these two collections of early Spanish church music. The twelfth-century disc is the more austere but still offers amazingly complex and imaginative music. The second disc of thirteenth- and fourteenth-century music is more varied, with many of the items for women's voices, designed for the convent of Las Huelgas, where the manuscripts were preserved. Like the secular pieces contained in the outstanding Oiseau-Lyre set of the New London Consort, *'Pilgrimage to Santiago'*, they are drawn from the collection assembled by Alfonso el Sabio (the Wise) between 1250 and 1280, an amazingly fruitful source. Performances are consistently sharp and compelling, recorded in fresh, forward sound.

The Sixteen, Harry Christophers

Music from The Eton Choirbook: BROWNE: *Salve Regina; Stabat Mater.* LAMBE: *Nesciens mater* (with Plainsong); *Stella caeli.* CORNYSHE: *Ave Maria.* WYLKYNSON: *Salve Regina.* DAVY: *Stabat Mater.*
**(*) Mer. CDE 84175; *KE 77175* [id.].

The current catalogue is not exactly overflowing with this repertoire, and these performances usefully fill a gap. They are more than a stop-gap, however, for the singing has plenty of character and a fine sense of line. Those unfamiliar with this repertoire will find these performances, which come from the early 1980s, eminently persuasive, though the sound-quality is not of consistent excellence.

Sopranos

'Famous soprano arias' (sung by: (i) Régine Crespin; (ii) Tebaldi; (iii) Maria Chiara; (iv) Sutherland; (v) G. Jones; (vi) Felicia Weathers; (vii) Suliotis) from: PUCCINI: (i) *Madama Butterfly;* (ii) *Gianni Schicchi;* (iii) *La Bohème;* (ii) *Tosca.* CATALANI: (iii) *La Wally.* VERDI: (iv) *Rigoletto;* (iii) *I vespri siciliani;* (v) *Aida;* (i) *Otello.* GOUNOD: (iv) *Faust.* PONCHIELLI: (viii) *La Gioconda.*
❀ (B) *** Decca 433 624-2; *433 624-4.*

It would be difficult to conceive a more winning recital of miscellaneous popular arias derived from this source, opening with the most famous soprano aria of all, *Un bel dì*, excitingly and tenderly sung by Régine Crespin. It is gratifying to see the art of Maria Chiara acknowledged: she is enchanting in the *Boléro* from Verdi's *I vespri siciliani* and makes a ravishing Mimi. Felicia Weathers is both captivating and individual in her long scena from *Otello*, while Tebaldi's *O mio babbino caro* has great vocal charm. She ends the recital with a characteristically melting account of *Vissi d'arte*, made in 1960. Sutherland's two contributions were also recorded in that same year: her lyrical coloratura in *Caro nome* is quite delicious. Dame Gwyneth Jones is in glorious voice in the two major arias from *Aida* (1968), while Eleana Suliotis, sometimes an uneven singer, is at her strongest and most commanding in her searingly powerful *Suicido* from *La Gioconda*, vocally as well as dramatically thrilling.

'Great sopranos of our time' ((i) Scotto; (ii) Schwarzkopf; (iii) Sutherland; (iv) Nilsson; (v) De los Angeles; (vi) Freni; (vii) Callas; (viii) Cotrubas; (ix) Caballé): (i) PUCCINI: *Madama Butterfly: Un bel dì.* (vi) *La Bohème: Sì, mi chiamano Mimì.* (ii) MOZART: *Così fan tutte: Come scoglio.* (iii) *Don Giovanni: Troppo mi spiace . . . Non mi dir.* (iv) WEBER: *Oberon: Ozean du Ungeheuer.* (v) ROSSINI: *Il Barbiere di Siviglia: Una voce poco fa.* (vii) DONIZETTI: *Lucia di Lammermoor: Sparsa è di rose . . . Il dolce suono . . . Spargi d'amaro.* (viii) BIZET: *Les Pêcheurs de perles: Comme autrefois.* (ix) VERDI: *Aida: Qui Radames . . . O patria mia.*
(M) *** EMI CD-EMX 9519; *TC-EMX 2099.*

An impressive collection, drawn from a wide variety of sources. It is good to have Schwarzkopf's commanding account of *Come scoglio* and Nilsson's early recording of the Weber, not to mention the formidable contributions of Callas and the early Sutherland reading of *Non mi dir*, taken from Giulini's complete set of *Giovanni*. The CD transfers are bright and vivid, and this makes a fascinating mid-priced anthology.

Souzay, Gérard (baritone)

Mélodies (with Jacqueline Bonneau): FAURÉ: *Tristesse; Au bord de l'eau; Après un rêve; Clair de lune; Arpège; En sourdine; L'Horizon chimérique; Spleen; C'est l'extase; Prison; Mandoline.* CHAUSSON: *Nanny; Le charme; Sérénade italienne; Le Colibri; Cantique à l'épouse; Les papillons; Le temps de lilas.* Airs: BOESSET: *Me veux-tu voir mourir?.* ANON.: *Tambourin.* BATAILLE: *Cachez, beaux yeux; Ma bergère non légère.* CANTELOUBE: *Brezairola; Malurous qu'o uno fenno.*
❀ (M) (***) Decca mono 425 975-2.

The great French baritone made these recordings for Decca when he was at the very peak of his form. The Fauré were recorded in 1950 and the glorious Chausson songs in 1953. Souzay was endowed with the intelligence of Bernac as well as his powers of characterization, the vocal purity of Panzera and a wonderful feeling for line. The Decca transfer does complete justice to the original sound, and it is good to have these performances without the surface distractions of LP. Full texts and translations are provided. A marvellous record worth as many rosettes as stars!

Stade, Frederica von (mezzo-soprano)

Opera arias from: ROSSINI: *Otello*. HAYDN: *La fedelta premiata; Il mondo della luna*. MOZART: *La clemenza di Tito*.
*** Ph. 420 084-2 [id.].

Von Stade's Philips recital is a splendid compilation of some of her finest performances from complete sets of rare operas. It is sad that the Philips Haydn series did not achieve wider circulation, when it included such delectable items as those here; it is also valuable to have reminders of her contribution to the Rossini *Otello* set and to Colin Davis's recording of Mozart's *Clemenza di Tito*. Good original sound, well transferred.

Stefano, Giuseppe Di (tenor)

Neapolitan songs (with New SO, Pattacini or Olivieri): DE CURTIS: *Torna a Surriento; Tu ca'nun chiagne; Sona chitarra! A canzone 'e Napule; Ti voglio tanto bene*. BONGIOVANNI: *Lacreme napulitane*. TAGLIAFERRI: *Napule canta; Pusilleco*. CALIFANO: *'O surdato 'nnammurato*. CARDILLO: *Catari, catari*. COSTA: *Era di maggio matenata; Scetate*. NICOLAVALENTE: *Addio, mia bella Napoli*. CESANNI: *Firenze sogna*. DI LAZZARO: *Chitarra romana*. NEN: *Parlami d'amore Mariu*. BARBENS: *Munasterio 'e Santa-Chiara*.
(M) *** Decca 417 794-2.

Di Stefano was still in magnificent voice in the mid-1960s when he recorded these popular Neapolitan songs – including many comparative rarities as well as obvious choices like *Torna a Surriento*, *Catari, catari*, and *Addio, mia bella Napoli*. Despite the inevitable touches of vulgarity, the singing is both rich-toned and charming. The recording is admirably clear and vivid.

Streich, Rita (soprano)

'Arias and waltzes' (with Berlin RIAS Ch. & O, Kurt Gaebel or Richard Kraus; German Opera, Berlin, Ch. & O, Reinhard Peters): Arias from: MOZART: *Le nozze di Figaro*. RIMSKY-KORSAKOV: *Le coq d'or; Sadko*. DONIZETTI: *Lucia di Lammermoor; Linda di Chamounix*. DVOŘÁK: *Rusalka*. NICOLAI: *Die lustigen Weiber von Windsor*. PUCCINI: *Gianni Schicchi; Turandot*. SUPPÉ: *Boccaccio*. J. STRAUSS Jnr: *Die Fledermaus* (also Waltzes: *Geschichten aus dem Wienerwald; Frülingsstimmen*). BELLINI: *I Capuleti ed i Montecchi*. MEYERBEER: *Dinorah*. VERDI: *Falstaff* (also *Lo spazzacamino* '*The chimney sweep*'). BIZET: *Les pêcheurs de perles*. MASSENET: *Manon*. OFFENBACH: *Contes d'Hoffmann*. DELIBES: *Lakmé*. Songs: SAINT-SAËNS: *Le rossignol et la rose*. ARDITI: *Parla waltz*. GODARD: *Berceuse de Jocelyn*.
❀ (M) *** DG mono 435 748-2 (2) [id.].

It was high time that DG created a CD anthology from their archive of recordings of Rita Streich, whose exquisite art is unknown to many of the younger generation. The prettiest coloratura soprano voice of the second half of the twentieth century (and she was hardly less attractive to look at!), she measured up well to all the competition from the 'Golden Age'. It was a small voice but perfectly formed, and it recorded marvellously well. Her upper tessitura glittered like a diamond necklace in famous display arias like Delibes's *Bell song* from *Lakmé*, and she was the perfect temperamental Doll in Offenbach's *Tales of Hoffmann*). She was also a delighful Mozartian. Her Queen of the Night's arias from *Die Zauberflöte* – see our main composer index – have never been surpassed, and she opens this programme with a quite lovely account of Susanna's *Deh vieni* from *Le nozze di Figaro*. But, alongside the flute-like coloratura she brought to Bellini and Donizetti, she could also ravish the ear with gentle lyricism in the simplest way. She scintillated in the waltzes of Johann Strauss (especially *Voices of spring* and the *Waltz song (Mein Herr Marquiss)* from *Die Fledermaus*) and was at her most winning in slighter lollipops. Many of the most memorable pieces included here come from a recital she recorded in 1958 with the Berlin RIAS Choir and Radio Orchestra under Kurt Gaebel, in the Jesus Christus Kirche. Included were the Strauss Waltzes and *Die Fledermaus* excerpts, Dvořák's *Invocation to the moon*, the charming *Hab'ich nur deine Liebe* from *Boccacio* and the equally delightful *Shadow song* from *Dinorah*. Godard's highly romantic *Berceuse* is the most famous item, but it is in the deliciously fragile Saint-Saëns vocalise, *Le rossignol et la rose*, and in Verdi's captivating song of the chimney sweep (*Lo spazzacamino*) that her magic sends a shiver of special pleasure to the nape of the neck. One of these she chose to represent her art on the BBC's 'Desert Island Discs' programme, and we cannot remember which.

Sutherland, Dame Joan (soprano)

'Greatest hits': Excerpts from: HANDEL: *Samson*. LEHÁR: *Merry widow*. J. STRAUSS Jnr: *Casanova*. DONIZETTI: *Fille du régiment*. DELIBES: *Lakmé*. BELLINI: *Norma*. GOUNOD: *Faust*. DONIZETTI: *Lucia di Lammermoor: Mad scene*. Song: ARDITI: *Il bacio*.
(M) *** Decca 417 780-2; *417 780-4* [id.].

These recordings all come from the period when the voice was at its freshest: *Let the bright seraphim*, the *Bell song* from *Lakmé*, and the vivacious *Jewel song* from *Faust* in 1961; while the luscious version of *Vilja* (with chorus) was made in 1963. The lively excerpt from *La fille du régiment* comes from the complete set, as does the Mad scene from *Lucia di Lammermoor* – the 1961 first recording, under Pritchard. The sound is consistently vivid.

'Opera gala': Excerpts from: BELLINI: *Norma*. DONIZETTI: *Lucia di Lammermoor: Mad scene; Linda di Chamounix*. VERDI: *Ernani; I vespri siciliani*.
❀ (M) *** Decca 421 305-2.

Sutherland's 'Opera Gala' disc is one of the most cherishable of all operatic recital records, bringing together the glorious, exuberant items from her very first recital disc, made within weeks of her first Covent Garden success in 1959 and – as a valuable supplement – the poised account of *Casta diva* she recorded the following year as part of the '*Art of the Prima Donna*'. It was this 1959 recital which at once put Sutherland firmly on the map among the great recording artists of all time. Even she has never surpassed the freshness of these versions of the two big arias from *Lucia di Lammermoor*, sparkling in immaculate coloratura, while the lightness and point of the jaunty *Linda di Chamounix* aria and the *Boléro* from *I vespri siciliani* are just as winning. The sound is exceptionally vivid and immediate, though the accompaniments under Nello Santi are sometimes rough in ensemble.

'Romantic French arias' (with SRO, Bonynge) from: OFFENBACH: *Robinson Crusoé; La Grande-Duchesse de Gérolstein*. MEYERBEER: *Dinorah; Robert le Diable*. CHARPENTIER: *Louise*. AUBER: *Manon Lescaut; Fra Diavolo*. BIZET: *Les pêcheurs de perles; Vasco de Gama*. MASSENET: *Cendrillon*. MASSÉ: *Les noces de Jeannette*. GOUNOD: *Mireille; Le Tribut de Zamora; Faust*. LECOCQ: *Le coeur et la main*.
(M) *** Decca 421 879-2; *421 879-4* [id.].

This 73-minute recital encompasses much of the cream of a two-LP album, recorded in September 1969; for those new to the selection it will come as a delightful surprise to discover that Offenbach's *Robinson Crusoé* includes an irresistible waltz-song for the heroine as she steps ashore on Crusoe's island and is met by cannibals (*Take me to the man I adore*). Sutherland opens with that and sings here and in all the other brilliant numbers with great flair and abandon, relishing her virtuosity. The romantic side is represented by such enchanting items as Massenet's sad little Cinderella aria, Dinorah's sweet lullaby for her pet goat, a nightingale aria from Victor Massé's *Les noces de Jeannette* and a ravishing account of *Depuis le jour* from *Louise* to make most modern rivals sound pale and thin. Bizet's rare *Chanson bohème* from *Vasco da Gama* is most engaging, and the aria from his *Pearlfishers* is the only relative disappointment. The sound-balance in the Victoria Hall, Geneva, is quite well managed, but the CD transfer makes the voice sound brighter than usual.

'Operetta gala' (with New Philh. O, Bonynge): Arias from: OFFENBACH: *La Grande-Duchesse; La Périchole*. ZELLER: *Der Vogelhändler*. MILLOCKER: *Die Dubarry*. FALL: Medley. LEHÁR: *Eva; Die lustige Witwe (The merry widow); Paganini*. O. STRAUS: *Ein Walzertraum; The Chocolate soldier*. HEUBERGER: *Der Opernball*. J. STRAUSS, Jnr: *Casanova*. KREISLER: *The King steps out*. POSFORD: *Balalaika*.
(M) *** Decca 421 880-2; *421 880-4* [id.].

Opening with the vivacious military song from *La Grande-Duchesse de Gérolstein* (which derives from her French compilation), Sutherland goes on to charm us with the *Letter song* from *La Périchole* and then offers a substantial selection from her 1966 (two-disc) lilting, whoopsing operetta compilation, originally entitled rather cosily *'Love, live forever'*. In *Im chambre séparée* her sensuous charm is disarming; and she is splendid in a fizzing number like *The Dubarry*, with the Ambrosians providing enthusiastic support. What is immediately obvious is Sutherland's own delight in singing this music, and the accompaniments have matching infectious qualities, with Bonynge obviously entirely at home, providing the necessary light touch and idiomatic feeling for rubato. The sumptuous recording catches the glory of Sutherland's voice to perfection against a sparklingly rich orchestral and vocal backing. The chorus are splendid throughout.

'The age of Bel canto' (with Marilyn Horne, Richard Conrad, LSO or LPO, Bonynge): Arias & excerpts from: PICCINI: *La buonna figliuola.* HANDEL: *Samson.* BONONCINI: *Astarto; Griselda.* SHIELD: *Rosina.* MOZART: *Die Zauberflöte.* BOIELDIEU: *Angela.* ROSSINI: *Semiramide.* WEBER: *Der Freischütz.* DONIZETTI: *Don Pasquale.* VERDI: *Attila.* BELLINI: *La straniera.* GRAUN: *Montezuma.*
(M) *** Decca 421 881-2; *421 881-4* [id.].

It is good to be reminded what a fine Mozartian Sutherland is, in the Queen of the Night's *O zittre nicht*, and the delightful point of Shield's *Light as thistledown* is irresistible. As for her duet, *Serbami ognor* from *Semiramide*, it brings a performance of equal mastery. Added to the items from the original, 1963 recital, to make up a total timing of nearly 72 minutes, comes a generous addition – two charming arias from the Sutherland/Bonynge 1966 records of *Griselda* and *Montezuma.* Here the balance is brighter, the voice more forward: in the main recital there is a more natural, concert-hall effect, very realistically transferred to CD.

'Command performance' (with LSO or New Philh. O, Bonynge): Arias from: WEBER: *Oberon.* MASSENET: *Le Cid.* MEYERBEER: *Dinorah; Les Huguenots.* LEONCAVALLO: *Pagliacci.* VERDI: *I Masnadieri; Luisa Miller.* ROSSINI: *La cambiale di matrimonio.* BELLINI: *Beatrice di Tenda.*
(M) *** Decca 421 882-2; *421 882-4* [id.].

The idea behind this 1963 'Command performance' recital was that Queen Victoria would have asked for just such a concert, had she been able to invite Joan Sutherland to Windsor. The reissue omits the frothier items and, to make the concert more generous, her scena *O beau pays de la Touraine* from *Les Huguenots* is added as an appendix, ravishingly sung, taken from her (1969) complete set. As to Sutherland's singing, there was still too much of the 'mooning' style which had overtaken her in the early 1960s, words disappearing in the quest for ever more cooingly beautiful tone; but the coloratura is ecstatically beautiful, enlivening what would otherwise be too consistently languid an experience. The rare Verdi and Bellini arias are especially welcome. The recording is of Decca's best vintage, especially rich in the *Les Huguenots* excerpt.

'Tribute to Jenny Lind' (with various orchestras, Pritchard or Bonynge): Arias from BELLINI: *Beatrice di Tenda; I Puritani; La sonnambula.* DONIZETTI: *Rosamonda d'Inghilterra; La fille du régiment.* MOZART: *Le nozze di Figaro.* MEYERBEER: *L'étoile du nord.* ROSSINI: *Semiramide.* VERDI: *I Masnadieri.* Songs: ARDITI: *Il bacio.* BENEDICT: *The gypsy and the bird.* BISHOP: *Lo! here the gentle lark.*
(M) *** Decca 421 883-2; *421 883-4* [id.].

This recorded tribute from one great singer to another encompasses virtually the whole of Joan Sutherland's career onwards from her delectably fresh (1961) recording of Rosamonda's aria (Donizetti), complete with flute obbligato, and three frothier items from the original second LP of *'Command performance'* (1962) with Benedict's *The gypsy and the bird*, a piece of Victorian nonsense of course, but providing with its trills and roulades a glorious opportunity for display – one of her most inspired pieces of singing on record. The 1968 *Fille du régiment* is justly celebrated, while the Meyerbeer excerpts come from her (1969) two-LP set of French repertoire, the bulk of which is available on the CD listed above. The careers of the two sopranos linked in the title were comparably successful, and their remarkable coloratura, impressive breath control and felicitous ornamentation had a good deal in common, but Sutherland almost certainly had the greater emotional range. Excellent sound throughout: all in all, a fascinating 74-minute collection.

'The art of the prima donna': Arias from: ARNE: *Artaxerxes*. HANDEL: *Samson*. BELLINI: *Norma; I Puritani; La Sonnambula*. ROSSINI: *Semiramide*. GOUNOD: *Faust; Roméo et Juliette*. VERDI: *Otello; Rigoletto; La Traviata*. MOZART: *Die Entführung aus dem Serail*. THOMAS: *Hamlet*. DELIBES: *Lakmé*. MEYERBEER: *Les Huguenots*.
❀ (M) *** Decca 425 493-2 (2) [id.].

This ambitious early two-disc recital (from 1960) remains one of Joan Sutherland's outstanding gramophone achievements. By electing to sing each one of the fabulously difficult arias in tribute to a particular soprano of the past – from Mrs Billington in the eighteenth century, through Grisi, Malibran, Pasta and Jenny Lind in the nineteenth century, to Lilli Lehmann, Melba, Tetrazzini and Galli-Curci in this – Sutherland is herself asking to be judged by the standards of the Golden Age. On the basis of recorded reminders, she comes out with flying colours, showing a greater consistency and certainly a wider range of sympathy than even the greatest Golden Agers possessed. The sparkle and delicacy of the *Puritani Polonaise*, the freshness and lightness of the Mad scene from Thomas's *Hamlet*, the commanding power of the *Entführung* aria and the breathtaking brilliance of the Queen's aria from *Les Huguenots* are all among the high spots here, while the arias which Sutherland later recorded in her complete opera sets regularly bring performances just as fine as – and often finer than – the later versions. The freshness of the voice is caught superbly in the recording, which on CD is amazingly full, firm and realistic.

'Prima donna assoluta': Arias from OFFENBACH: *Contes d'Hoffmann*. DONIZETTI: *Fille du régiment; Lucia di Lammermoor*. GOUNOD: *Faust*. BELLINI: *I Puritani*. VERDI: *La Traviata*.
(B) *** Decca 425 605-2.

Issued on Decca's cheapest label, this captivating recital concentrates on excerpts from Sutherland's complete sets. However, the closing *Lucia di Lammermoor* Mad scene derives from her famous 1959 Decca début record, conducted by Nello Santi, representing one of the most magical and thrilling displays of coloratura ever recorded: the luminous freshness of the voice is unforgettable. The other recordings come from between 1960 and 1972, and this disc is in every way a bargain. The documentation, however, is entirely biographical.

Russian music (with LSO, Richard Bonynge, (i) Osian Ellis; or (ii) Josef Sivo, SRO, Horst Stein): GLIÈRE: *Coloratura concerto;* (i) *Harp concerto*. STRAVINSKY: *Pastorale*. CUI: *Ici-bas*. GRETCHANINOV: *Lullaby*. (ii) GLAZUNOV: *Violin concerto*.
(M) **(*) Decca 430 006-2 [id.].

The two highly engaging concertos are discussed in the composer index. Dreamy beauty perhaps goes a little far in Sutherland's account of Stravinsky's early *Pastorale* (there is too much vocal sliding), while the Cui and Gretchaninov songs are accompanied by Richard Bonynge at the piano. The addition of Sivo's account of the Glazunov *Violin concerto* for the CD reissue is no great advantage. There is some less than ideal intonation, and the performance, though well recorded, is not distinctive.

Sutherland, Dame Joan (soprano), **Marilyn Horne** (mezzo-soprano) and **Luciano Pavarotti** (tenor)

'Duets and trios from the Lincoln Center' (with NY City Op. O, Bonynge): excerpts from VERDI: *Ernani; Otello; Il Trovatore*. BELLINI: *Norma*. PONCHIELLI: *La Giaconda*.
**(*) Decca Dig. 417 587-2 [id.].

Not all gala concerts make good records, but this is an exception; almost every item here puts an important gloss on the achievements of the three principal stars in the concerted numbers. It is good to have a sample not only of Sutherland's Desdemona but of Pavarotti's Otello in their account of the Act I duet. The final scene from *Il Trovatore* is more compelling here than in the complete set made by the same soloists five years earlier. The microphone catches a beat in the voices of both Sutherland and Horne, but not as obtrusively as on some studio discs. Lively accompaniment under Bonynge; bright, vivid digital recording, but over-loud applause.

Sutherland, Dame Joan and Luciano Pavarotti (tenor)

Operatic duets (with Nat. PO, Bonynge) from: VERDI: *La Traviata; Otello; Aida* (with chorus). BELLINI: *La Sonnambula.* DONIZETTI: *Linda di Chamounix.*
*** Decca 400 058-2; *400 058-4* [id.].

This collection offers a rare sample of Sutherland as Aida (*La fatale pietra . . . O terra, addio* from Act IV), a role she sang only once on stage, well before her international career began; and with this and her sensitive impersonations of Desdemona, Violetta and the Bellini and Donizetti heroines, Sutherland might have been expected to steal first honours here. In fact these are mainly duets to show off the tenor, and it is Pavarotti who runs away with the main glory, though both artists were plainly challenged to their finest and the result, with excellent accompaniment, is among the most attractive and characterful duet recitals. The recording is admirably clear and well focused.

Operatic duets from: DONIZETTI: *Lucia di Lammermoor; L'elisir d'amore; Maria Stuarda; La fille du régiment.* VERDI: *Rigoletto.* BELLINI: *I Puritani.*
*** Decca 417 815-2 [id.].

Taken from the complete opera recordings they made together from the late 1960s onwards, this collection of operatic duets finds both superstars in glowing form, with Decca recordings of the finest vintage for the period, beautifully transferred to CD.

Tallis Scholars, Peter Phillips

'Christmas carols and motets': Ave Maria settings by JOSQUIN DES PRES; VERDELOT; VICTORIA. *Coventry carol* (2 settings). BYRD: *Lullaby.* PRAETORIUS: *Es ist ein Ros'entsprungen; Joseph lieber, Joseph mein; In dulci jubilo; Wachet auf.* BACH: *Wachet auf.* Medieval carols: *Angelus ad virginem; There is no rose; Nowell sing we.*
*** Gimell Dig. CDGIM 010; *1585T-10* [id.].

Wonderfully serene singing from the Tallis Scholars, recorded with superb naturalness and presence, makes this a very special Christmas record. There is something unique about a carol, and even the very early music here has that special intensity of inspiration which brings memorability. There are some familiar melodies too, notably those set by Praetorius; but much of this repertoire will come as refreshingly new to most ears. The singing has a purity of spirit. The CD is very much in the demonstration class for the clear choral image, heard against the ideal acoustics of St Pierre et St Paul, Salle, Norfolk.

Tebaldi, Renata (soprano)

'The Early Recordings': VERDI: *Aida: Act I, Ritorna vincitor!; Act III* (complete; with Stignani, Caselli, Protti, del Monaco, Ac. di Santa Cecilia Ch. & O, Erede); *Il Trovatore: Tacea la notte placida.* Arias from: GOUNOD: *Faust.* PUCCINI: *Madama Butterfly; Manon Lescaut; Tosca; La Bohéme.*
(M) (***) Decca mono 425 989-2 [id.].

This fascinating collection includes the very first records Tebaldi made for Decca in November 1949, in effect the start of a new era in operatic recording. More recital recordings were made in 1951. This led to her early version of *Aida* of 1952, here represented by Act III, opposite two of her regular partners, neither showing anything like her finesse: the coarse Mario del Monaco and the colourless Aldo Protti, firmer here than he was to become. Though her later recordings are more refined in expressive detail, the freshness of these performances is a delight and, with the reservations noted concerning the mixed blessings of the *Aida* cast, our Rosette for her two-disc set, below, could be extended to cover many of the earlier items included here. Good transfers.

'La Tebaldi': (arias recorded between 1955 & 1968): PUCCINI: *Madama Butterfly; La Bohème; Tosca; Gianni Schicchi; Suor Angelica; Turandot; La rondine.* BOITO: *Mefistofele.* VERDI: *Aida; Otello; Il Trovatore; La forza del destino; Don Carlo; Un ballo in maschera; Giovanna d'Arco.* ROSSINI: *Guglielmo Tell.* CILEA: *Adriana Lecouvreur; L'arlesiana.* GIORDANO: *Andrea Chénier.*

CATALANI: *La Wally.* PONCHIELLI: *La Gioconda.* MASCAGNI: *Cavalleria rusticana.* REFICE: *Cecilia.*
❀ (B) *** Decca 430 481-2 (2) [id.].

This two-disc collection superbly celebrates one of the sopranos with a special place in the history of recording, the prima donna who in the early days of LP most clearly reflected a great period of operatic expansion. Unlike her great rival, Callas, thrilling, dynamic, unpredictable, often edgy and uneven on record, Tebaldi was above all reliable, with her creamy-toned voice, exceptionally even from top to bottom, and with its natural warmth ideally suited to recording. The 24 items here, entirely devoted to the Italian opera, cover the full range of her repertory, from her justly famous assumption of the role of Butterfly to her personification of Leonora in *La forza del destino*, while she was an unforgettably moving Mimì in *La Bohème*. Many of the items are taken from the complete sets she recorded for Decca, generally more freely expressive than those originally issued on recital discs. The actual interpretations are totally consistent, though over the years the detail grew ever more refined. Excellent transfers. An indispensable set for all those who respond to this lovely voice, bringing a magical feeling of vulnerability to her personifications, when she creates a gentle, glowing pianissimo.

Tetrazzini, Luisa (soprano)

'Prima voce': Arias from: BELLINI: *La Sonnambula.* DONIZETTI: *Lucia di Lammermoor.* ROSSINI: *Il Barbiere di Siviglia.* THOMAS: *Mignon.* VERACINI: *Rosalinda.* VERDI: *Un ballo in maschera; Rigoletto; La Traviata; Il Trovatore; I vespri siciliani.* Songs.
(M) (***) Nimbus mono NI 7808 [id.].

Tetrazzini was astonishing among coloratura sopranos not just for her phenomenal agility but for the golden warmth that went with tonal purity. The Nimbus transfers add a bloom to the sound, with the singer slightly distanced. Though some EMI transfers make her voice more vividly immediate, one quickly adjusts. Such display arias as *Ah non giunge* from *La Sonnambula* or the *Boléro* from *I vespri siciliani* are incomparably dazzling, but it is worth noting too what tenderness is conveyed through Tetrazzini's simple phrasing and pure tone in such a tragic aria as Violetta's *Addio del passato*, with both verses included. Lieder devotees may gasp in horror, but one of the delightful oddities here is Tetrazzini's bright-eyed performance, with ragged orchestral accompaniment, of what is described as *La serenata inutile* by Brahms – in fact *Vergebliches Ständchen*, sung with a triumphant if highly inauthentic top A at the end, implying no closure of the lady's window!

Tibbett, Lawrence (baritone)

Arias from: LEONCAVALLO: *Pagliacci.* ROSSINI: *Il Barbiere di Siviglia.* VERDI: *Un ballo in maschera; Simon Boccanegra; Falstaff.* PUCCINI: *Tosca.* BIZET: *Carmen.* GOUNOD: *Faust.* WAGNER: *Die Walküre.* GRUENBERG: *Emperor Jones.* HANSON: *Merry Mount.* GERSHWIN: *Porgy and Bess.*
(M) (***) BMG/RCA mono GD 87808 [7808-2-RG].

The glorious, characterful timbre of Tibbett's baritone is superbly caught in RCA's clear, immediate transfers, with the vibrato never obtrusive as it can be on some records. It is sad that so commanding a singer was heard relatively little outside America; but this is a superb memorial, not just for the classic arias but for such an item as the excerpt from Louis Gruenberg's *Emperor Jones*, a role he created.

'Tibbett in opera': excerpts from: LEONCAVALLO: *Pagliacci.* BIZET: *Carmen.* PUCCINI: *Tosca.* VERDI: *Un ballo in maschera; Simon Boccanegra; Rigoletto; Otello.* ROSSINI: *Il barbiere di Siviglia.* GOUNOD: *Faust.* WAGNER: *Tannhäuser, Die Walküre.*
(M) (***) Nimbus mono NI 7825 [id.].

The scale and resonance of Lawrence Tibbett's voice come over vividly in this fine selection of his recordings made between 1926 and 1939. Particularly interesting is the whole of *Wotan's farewell*, with Stokowski conducting the Philadelphia Orchestra in 1934. It is an over-the-top performance that carries total conviction, even if the sheer volume produces some clangorous resonances in the Nimbus transfer. Also memorable is the celebrated *Boccanegra* Council chamber sequence, recorded in 1939 with Martinelli and Rose Bampton in the ensemble.

Turner, Dame Eva (soprano)

Opera arias and songs: Arias from VERDI: *Il Trovatore; Aida.* PONCHIELLI: *La Gioconda.* PUCCINI: *Tosca; Madama Butterfly; Turandot.* MASCAGNI: *Cavalleria Rusticana.* WAGNER: *Lohengrin; Tannhäuser.* Songs: GRIEG: *I love thee.* TOSTI: *Goodbye.* RONALD: *O lovely night.* DEL RIEGO: *Homing.* D'HARDELOT: *Because; Sometime in my dreams.*
(M) (***) EMI mono CDH7 69791-2.

The art of Eva Turner is superbly celebrated in this generous selection of recordings made between 1928 and 1933. They include not only her celebrated 1928 recording of Turandot's *In questa reggia* but also magnificent samples of her portrayals of Aida, Leonora in *Trovatore* and La Gioconda, as well as half a dozen songs and ballads. Most fascinating of all are her two Wagner recordings, of *Elsa's dream* from *Lohengrin* and *Elisabeth's greeting* from *Tannhäuser*, sung in English. The result is among the most thrilling of all the recordings ever made by Dame Eva, rich and intense. It is a delight also to have Dame Eva's spoken introduction, recorded in June 1988 when she was in her ninety-eighth year. Keith Hardwick's transfers, quite apart from the help from CEDAR, are models of their kind, with the voice astonishingly vivid.

Walker, Sarah (mezzo-soprano)

'Blah, blah, blah' (with Roger Vignoles, piano, in cabaret at the Wigmore Hall): GERSHWIN: *Blah, blah, blah; They all laughed; Three times a day; Boy, what love has done to me.* PORTER: *Tale of the oyster; Where O where?.* BERNSTEIN: *Who am I?.* NICHOLAS: *Place settings; Usherette's blues.* DRING: *Song of a nightclub proprietress.* BOLCOM: *Lime jello, marshmallow, cottage-cheese surprise.* FLANDERS and SWANN: *A word on my ear.* LEHMANN: *There are fairies at the bottom of my garden.* WRIGHT: *Transatlantic lullaby.* BAKER: *Someone is sending me flowers.* SCHOENBERG: *3 Brettl Lieder.*
*** Hyp. Dig. CDA 66289; *KA 66289* [id.].

Recorded live at the Wigmore Hall in London, Sarah Walker's recital of trifles is one of the happiest records you could wish to find, as well as one of the funniest. Her comic timing is masterly in such delectable revue numbers as Cole Porter's *Tale of the oyster* or William Bolcom's culinary patter-song, *Lime jello, marshmallow, cottage-cheese surprise.* Perhaps surprisingly, she does such a song as *There are fairies at the bottom of my garden* straight, restoring its touching quality in defiance of Beatrice Lillie's classic send-up. Also, by treating a popular number such as *Transatlantic lullaby* as a serious song, she not only underlines purely musical qualities but touches a deeper vein than one might expect in a cabaret sequence. Three of Schoenberg's *Brettl Lieder*, in deft English translations by Michael Irwin, are sung just as delightfully – and more provocatively than the German versions which were recorded by Jill Gomez in her delectable '*Cabaret classics*' recital. The title, *Blah, blah, blah*, comes from the opening number, a witty concoction by George Gershwin with words by his brother, Ira, which reduces the popular love-song lyrics to the necessary – and predictable – rhymes. Roger Vignoles, always an understanding accompanist, here excels himself with playing of flair and brilliance, exuberantly encompassing every popular idiom in turn. The recording, unlike most made at the Wigmore Hall, captures some of the bloom of its acoustic; but that means that the voice is set slightly at a distance. Texts are provided but, with such clear diction from the singer, they are needed only occasionally.

Walker, Sarah (mezzo-soprano), Thomas Allen (baritone)

'The Sea' (with Roger Vignoles, piano): IRELAND: *Sea fever.* HAYDN: *Mermaid's song; Sailor's song.* DIBDIN: *Tom Bowling.* WALTON: *Song for the Lord Mayor's table; Wapping Old Stairs.* WOLF: *Seemanns Abschied.* FAURÉ: *Les Berceaux; Au cimetière; L'horizon chimerique.* SCHUBERT: *Lied eines Schiffers an die Dioskuren.* BORODIN: *The Sea; The Sea Princess.* DEBUSSY: *Proses lyriques: De grêve.* IVES: *Swimmers.* SCHUMANN: *Die Meerfee.* BERLIOZ: *Nuits d'été: L'ile inconnue.* MENDELSSOHN: *Wasserfahrt.* BRAHMS: *Die Meere.* TRAD.: *The Mermaid.* Arr. BRITTEN: *Sail on, sail on.*
❀ *** Hyp. CDA 66165 [id.].

With Roger Vignoles as master of ceremonies in a brilliantly devised programme, ranging wide, this twin-headed recital celebrating 'The Sea' is a delight from beginning to end. Two outstandingly characterful singers are mutually challenged to their very finest form, whether in solo songs or duets. As sample, try the setting of the sea-song, *The Mermaid*, brilliantly arranged by Vignoles, with hilarious key-switches on the comic quotations from *Rule Britannia*. Excellent recording.

Welitsch, Ljuba (soprano)

Arias from: TCHAIKOVSKY: *Eugene Onegin*. VERDI: *Aida*. PUCCINI: *Tosca; La Bohème*. WEBER: *Der Freischütz*. R. STRAUSS: *Salome: Closing scene*.
(M) (***) EMI mono CDH7 61007-2.

This immaculately transferred collection gathers together the handful of studio recordings Welitsch made for EMI after the Second World War (notably *Tatiana's letter song* from 1948, done in German). As a splendid bonus comes the radio recording, made in Vienna in 1944, of the closing scene from Strauss's *Salome*, where the extra vibrancy of live performance is caught vividly, despite the fuzziness of sound, here reasonably clarified in the digital transfer.

Westminster Abbey Choir, Preston

Christmas carols: TRAD.: *Up! awake; There stood in heaven a linden tree; The holly and the ivy; Ding dong merrily on high; Up! good Christian folk; In dulci jubilo; Rocking; Illuminare Jerusalem; Good King Wenceslas*. OLDHAM: *Remember O thou man*. WISHART: *Alleluya, a new work*. CHARPENTIER: *Salve puerule*. POSTON: *Jesus Christ the apple tree*. PRAETORIUS: *Resonet in laudibus*. MAXWELL DAVIES: *Nowell (Out of your sleep arise)*. HAMMERSCHMIDT: *Alleluja! Freuet euch*. MENDELSSOHN: *Hark! the herald angels sing*. SCHEIDT: *Puer natus*. GARDNER: *Tomorrow shall be my dancing day*. BRITTEN: *Shepherd's carol*.
*** DG Dig. 413 590-2.

An excellent concert in every way. The programme is nicely balanced between old favourites and rewarding novelty, the traditional material spiced with modern writing, which readily captures the special essence that makes a carol instantly recognizable as a Christmas celebration. Fresh singing of fine vigour, expressively responsive, is combined with first-class sound, the ambience nicely judged.

Westminster Cathedral Choir, Hill

'Treasures of the Spanish Renaissance': GUERRERO: *Surge propera amica mea; O altitudo divitiarum; O Domine Jesu Christe; O sacrum convivium; Ave, Virgo sanctissima; Regina coeli laetare*. LOBO: *Versa est in luctum; Ave Maria; O quam suavis es, Domine*. VIVANCO: *Magnificat octavi toni*.
*** Hyp. CDA 66168; *KA 66168* [id.].

This immensely valuable collection reminds us vividly that Tomas Luis de Victoria was not the only master of church music in Renaissance Spain. Francisco Guerrero is generously represented here, and the spacious serenity of his polyphonic writing (for four, six and, in *Regina coeli laetare*, eight parts) creates the most beautiful sounds. A criticism might be made that tempi throughout this collection, which also includes fine music by Alonso Lobo and a superb eight-part *Magnificat* by Sebastian de Vivanco, are too measured, but the tension is held well, and David Hill is obviously concerned to convey the breadth of the writing. The singing is gloriously firm, with the long melismatic lines admirably controlled. Discreet accompaniments (using Renaissance double harp, bass dulcian and organ) do not affect the essentially a cappella nature of the performances. The Westminster Cathedral acoustic means the choral tone is richly upholstered, but the focus is always firm and clear.

White, Robert (tenor)

'Favourite Irish songs of Princess Grace' (with Monte Carlo PO, Stapleton): *Danny Boy; Pretty Kitty Kelly; Galway Bay; MacNamara's Band; Oft in the stilly night; Molly Malone; The last rose*

of summer; The foggy dew; Mother Machree; Off to Philadelphia; I hear you calling me; My wild Irish rose; The Salley gardens; She is far from the land; The star of County Down; Macushla; Mistress Biddy was a giddy little witch; The Rose of Tralee; I'll take you home again, Kathleen.
*** Virgin VC7 90705-2; *VC 790705-4* [id.].

Princess Grace of Monaco was the sponsor for a Foundation to support a comprehensive archive of Irish music in Monte Carlo, from which these songs are taken; the colourful orchestral arrangements are by Peter Hope and Robert Docker. Among contemporary singers, Robert White is unsurpassed in this repertoire. His golden tenor and wonderfully free upper range make the lyrical numbers, like *I hear you calling me* and *The Salley gardens*, sound quite ravishing, while the light-hearted *MacNamara's Band* and *The star of County Down* sparkle splendidly. The total lack of artifice in the singing, combined with an obvious emotional response, brings consistent pleasure. A superb voice, naturally caught by the engineers and very well balanced with the warmly recorded orchestral accompaniments, sympathetically directed by Robin Stapleton. This is outstanding of its kind.

White, Willard (bass), Graeme McNaught (piano)

COPLAND: *Old American songs, Sets 1–2.* American spirituals: *Go down, Moses; I couldn' hear nobody pray; Were you there when they crucified my Lord?; When I lay my burden down; Steal away; 1; Gospel train; Swing low, sweet chariot; Deep river; Ev'ry time I feel de spirit.* IVES: *In the mornin'.* Folksongs from Barbados and Jamaica: *Linstead Market; Cordelia Brown; Murder in the market.*
*** Chan. Dig. CHAN 8960; *ABTD 1552.* [id.].

Willard White with his darkly opulent voice, exceptionally well caught in the Chandos recording, provides this apt and attractive recital to go with his earthy accounts of the Copland songs. The spirituals come in relatively simple arrangements, mainly by Melanie Marshall and Hall Johnson but with one, *In the Mornin'*, by Ives. *Swing low, sweet chariot* is left unaccompanied. These are heartfelt performances that will delight all admirers of this singer. What makes the disc special are the three songs from Barbados and Williard White's native Jamaica. He and his Scottish accompanist, Graeme McNaught, point the Caribbean rhythms delectably. *Linstead Market* celebrates the very place where Willard White was born, while the concluding song, *Murder in the Market*, brings a hilarious stanza sung falsetto when the murderess gives her defiant answer. But the gem of the whole disc is *Cordelia Brown*, haunting as only a song in Caribbean rhythm can be, a sort of fast tango, which White sings with real love.

Winchester Cathedral Choir, Martin Neary

'A solemn musick' (with Baroque Brass of London): PURCELL: *Funeral music for Queen Mary and Motets; Jehova, quam multi sunt hostes.* CROFT: *Burial service.* BACH: *O Jesu Christ, mein Lebens Licht, BWV 118.* BLOW: *Salvator mundi.* HUMFREY: *Hymne to God the Father.* GREENE: *Lord, let me know mine end.* BATTISHILL: *O Lord, look down from heaven.*
*** EMI Dig. CDC7 47772-2 [id.].

Martin Neary's splendid new version of Purcell's *Funeral music* is discussed under its composer entry. The rest of the programme, music with similar associations by other composers, is also very rewarding, usually elegiac in mood but sometimes with dramatic contrasts, as in Croft's *Burial service.* Particularly fine are Greene's *Let me know mine end* and Pelham Humfrey's *Hymne to God the Father*, with the solo beautifully sung by the counter-tenor, David Hurley. The recording is diffuse but pleasingly atmospheric.

York Minster Choir, Francis Jackson (organ)

'On Christmas night': TRAD.: *The first nowell; While shepherds watched; Coventry carol; Good King Wenceslas; The holly and the ivy; O come, all ye faithful; In dulci jubilo; God rest you merry, gentlemen; On Christmas night (Sussex carol).* WAINWRIGHT: *Christians awake!* GAUNTLETT: *Once in Royal David's city.* HOPKINS: *We three kings.* GRÜBER: *Silent night.* WOODWARD: *Ding dong! merrily on high.* MENDELSSOHN: *Hark! the herald angels sing.*
(M) **(*) Chan. CHAN 6520; *MBTD 6520* [id.].

Because Francis Jackson is an imaginative player (and not because of the balance or any intrusive accompaniments) one is often more aware of the organ than usual; but the singing itself has an affecting, simple beauty and the words are clear. The York Minster acoustics are beautifully controlled by the Chandos engineers so that there is no overhang or blurring, yet the music-making is pleasingly coloured by the ambience. The effect is perhaps less individual than the King's or Clare records but is refreshing in its absence of the imposed personalities of arrangers.